# Great Britain

David Else,
David Atkinson, James Bainbridge, Oliver Berry,
Fionn Davenport, Belinda Dixon, Peter Dragicevich,
Nana Luckham, Etain O'Carroll, Andy Symington, Neil Wilson

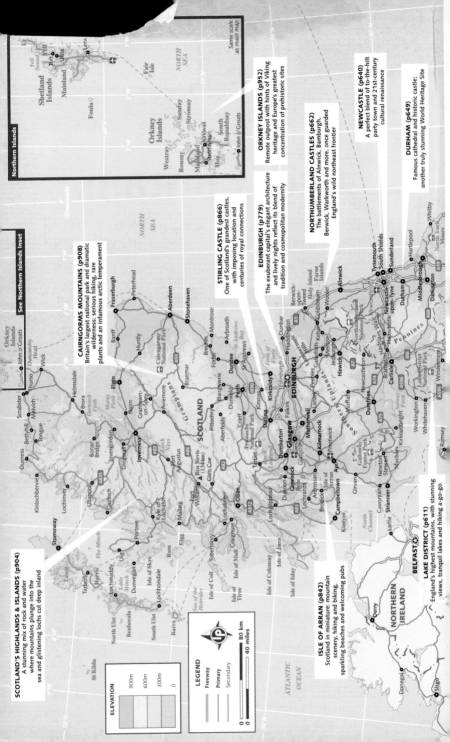

**Northern Islands**

See Northern Islands inset

Same scale as main map

NORTH SEA

**ORKNEY ISLANDS (p952)**
Remote outpost with hints of Viking heritage and Europe's greatest concentration of prehistoric sites

**NEWCASTLE (p640)**
A perfect blend of to-the-hilt party town and 21st-century cultural renaissance

**DURHAM (p649)**
Famous cathedral and historic castle; another truly stunning World Heritage Site

**NORTHUMBERLAND CASTLES (p662)**
The battlements of Alnwick, Bamburgh, Berwick, Warkworth and more, once guarded England's wild northeast frontier

**EDINBURGH (p779)**
The exuberant capital's elegant architecture and lively nights reflect its blend of tradition and cosmopolitan modernity

**STIRLING CASTLE (p866)**
One of Scotland's grandest castles, with imposing location and centuries of royal connections

**CAIRNGORMS MOUNTAINS (p908)**
Britain's largest national park and dramatic wilderness: serious hiking, rare plants and an infamous arctic temperament

**SCOTLAND'S HIGHLANDS & ISLANDS (p904)**
A stunning mix of rock and water where mountains plunge into the sea and glistening lochs cut deep inland

**ISLE OF ARRAN (p842)**
Scotland in miniature: mountain scenery, hiking and biking, sparkling beaches and welcoming pubs

**LAKE DISTRICT (p611)**
England's highest mountains, with stunning views, tranquil lakes and hiking a-go-go

NORTH SEA

NORTH SEA

ATLANTIC OCEAN

NORTHERN IRELAND

BELFAST

**LEGEND**
Freeway
Primary
Secondary

ELEVATION
900m
600m
300m
0

0   80 km
0   40 miles

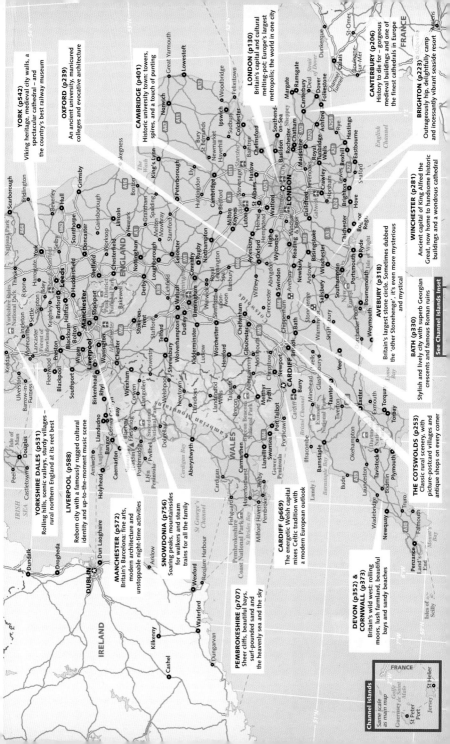

**YORK (p542)**
Viking heritage, medieval city walls, a spectacular cathedral – and the country's best railway museum

**OXFORD (p239)**
An ancient university, manicured colleges and evocative architecture

**CAMBRIDGE (p401)**
Historic university town: towers, spires, and a touch of punting

**LONDON (p130)**
Britain's capital and cultural melting-pot; Europe's largest metropolis; the world in one city

**CANTERBURY (p223)**
History to die for – gorgeous medieval buildings and one of the finest cathedrals in Europe

**BRIGHTON (p206)**
Outrageously hip, delightfully camp and incessantly vibrant seaside resort

**WINCHESTER (p281)**
Ancient capital of King Alfred the Great, now home to handsome historic buildings and a wondrous cathedral

**AVEBURY (p318)**
Britain's largest stone circle. Sometimes dubbed the 'other Stonehenge', it's even more mysterious and mystical

**BATH (p330)**
Stylish and lively city with superb Georgian crescents and famous Roman ruins

See Channel Islands Inset

**THE COTSWOLDS (p253)**
Classic rural scenery, with picture-postcard villages and antique shops on every corner

**DEVON (p352) & CORNWALL (p373)**
Britain's wild west: rolling moors, lush farmland, beautiful bays and sandy beaches

**CARDIFF (p669)**
The energetic Welsh capital mixes Celtic tradition with a modern European outlook

**PEMBROKESHIRE (p707)**
Sheer cliffs, beautiful bays, surf-pounded sand and the heavenly sea and the sky

**SNOWDONIA (p756)**
Soaring peaks, mountainsides for walkers and steam trains for all the family

**MANCHESTER (p572)**
Britain's Barcelona: fine arts, modern architecture and unstoppable night-time activities

**LIVERPOOL (p588)**
Reborn city with a famously rugged cultural identity and up-to-the-moment music scene

**YORKSHIRE DALES (p531)**
Rolling hills, scenic valleys, sturdy villages – rural northern England at its reet best

**Channel Islands**
Same scale as main map

FRANCE

Guernsey St Peter Port
Jersey St Helier

# On the Road

**DAVID ELSE**
**Coordinating Author**
Working on this and several previous editions of Lonely Planet's *Great Britain* guide, I've travelled the length and breadth of my own homeland. This picture was taken during a road trip around England and Scotland, at the iconic – and gigantic – Angel of the North (p648). I'm the one on the right.

**DAVID ATKINSON** My last day of research. After three months, thousands of miles and my own body weight in Welsh cheese, I am in Llandudno (p747) checking those last few details. As I finished, my wife and two-year-old little girl arrived to meet me. It was time for a large drink. And to go home.

**JAMES BAINBRIDGE** On a ramble out of Guernsey's capital St Peter Port (p977), I leant on a fence and felt very far from the cares of everyday life. Soon afterwards I popped out to Vazon Bay (p978), where the beach is overlooked by the Fort Hommet gun casement and Crabby Jack's (p978) restaurant.

**FIONN DAVENPORT** This picture was taken in the Liverpool Superstore…which I visited purely for research purposes. It was just before I got 'Liverpool FC 4Ever' tattooed on my heart. Not the skin above my heart. My actual heart.

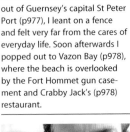

**OLIVER BERRY** I've hiked all over the world from Corsica to Canada, but for me there's still nowhere that quite compares with the Lakeland fells. Helvellyn and Scaféll Pike get all the plaudits (and most of the visitors) – here I'm standing on top of one of the less-visited fells, Sergeant Man, after a long slog up from Easedale Tarn. You can just see the shimmer of Lake Windermere (p614) in the far background over my left shoulder.

**BELINDA DIXON** I'm drinking in my favourite view. From Plymouth's Smeaton's Tower (p362) you see a historic harbour, a lively city and the wildernesses of Dartmoor. Which sums up what the south-west has: a rich past, a vibrant present and a future full of exciting possibilities. It's a whole lot of fun way out west.

**PETER DRAGICEVICH** Alternative music, Camden and booze go together, but alternative music, Camden, drinking wine and lazing in the sun is a rarer combination. This photo was taken on a particularly blissful Sunday afternoon at Proud (p191) in the Stables Market at Camden. There was a band playing inside, but the sun won out.

**NANA LUCKHAM** The cycleway around Rutland Water (p445) is the best place in the country to rediscover cycling, so I took the opportunity to get back in the saddle after a 15-year break. It was a perfect English summer's day until, shortly after this picture was taken, it poured with rain and I got a puncture.

**ETAIN O'CARROLL** It's a privilege living in Oxford (p239) and being surrounded by such a wealth of history and architecture, but there's a whole other world behind those college walls. The divide between town and gown is very much alive and I always feel a bit like I'm on the outside looking in.

**ANDY SYMINGTON** For all the doubters, Vatersay (p951) proves that there are some very fine beaches in Scotland. White sand, turquoise seas, and the coconut smell of suntan lotion. Ok, the last bit's a lie, but they're beautiful for a stroll even if you don't dare freeze your toes off.

**NEIL WILSON** Think Scarborough (p557) and you think sandcastles on the beach, donkey rides, and fish and chips. But there's much more to the place than traditional seaside resort stuff – like an impressive medieval castle, a Roman look-out station (that's it I'm sitting on), and superb coastal hiking. Yorkshire's like that – there's a lot more to discover beyond the main attractions.

*For full author biographies see p1012.*

# Great Britain Highlights

Modern Britain is a tale of three countries. A visitor looking for castles and cathedrals, 'olde' pubs, rolling hills and a sense of history permeating the whole country won't be disappointed. But there are also contemporary attractions to be enjoyed, from regenerated provincial cities with cutting-edge architecture to the best in global cuisine. Sample a little of both traditional and modern worlds and you'll get a real taste of Britain in the 21st century.

ROCCO FASANO

**1**

## FISH & CHIPS

England's contributions to the culinary world may be limited, but for a simple and incredibly tasty meal nothing beats fresh fish and chips, doused with salt and vinegar, and preferably eaten at the seaside after a ride on the rollercoaster.

**Caroline Sieg, Lonely Planet staff**

## PINT DOWN THE PUB

Whether it's a quick after-work drink or a celebration of whatever kind, the traditional pub (p96) is still the centre of socialising in Britain. And as well as making new friends over a pint, these days you can also often get decent pub grub to go with your drink.

**Sally Schafer,
Lonely Planet staff**

**3**

ORIEN HARVEY

SIMON GREENWOOD

**2**

## CLEANING UP IN BATH

After a day shopping and discovering Bath's Georgian architecture, enjoy a session at Thermae Bath Spa (p334) – Britain's only natural thermal spa. The tourist board claims that it uses the same warm, mineral-rich water that the Romans used 2000 years ago. Hopefully they've changed it since then.

**Judith Holford, traveller**

RICHARD I'ANSON

**4**

## LOSING YOUR HEAD IN HISTORY AT THE TOWER OF LONDON

Europe's best-preserved medieval fortress (p161) lives up to all expectations. You can wander around on your own to discover quieter corners or join one of the Beefeater tours for insights into the Tower's 1000-year history. But whatever you do, don't miss the Crown Jewels, the Bloody Tower and the scaffold site with a list of the unfortunates to have died here.

**Peter Dragicevich, author**

DAVID TOMLINSON

It might be one of England's oldest seaside resorts, but Brighton (p223) still has plenty of life left in it. The pier and the beach are good fun during the day but it's in the evening, when the bars, restaurants and clubs start filling up, that the city truly recalls its Regency decadence.

**Nana Luckham, author**

### 5 OXFORD & CAMBRIDGE

Oxford and Cambridge may have a long-standing rivalry but they both offer a highly educational look at student life over the last 800 years. In Oxford (p239) you're following in the footsteps of Tolkien, Lyra, CS Lewis and Inspector Morse, while in Cambridge (pictured above; p401) the top attractions are the beautiful colleges and the chance to punt on the river.

**Etain O'Carroll, author**

### 6

LAWRENCE WORCESTER

GARETH McCORMAC

### 7 MAGICAL MYSTERY STONES

Survivors from Britain's ancient past are scattered around the country. Stonehenge (p315) and Avebury (p318) in England are easily accessible; while Skara Brae (pictured above; p959), Maes Howe (p958) and Callanish (p947) in Scotland might be more difficult to get to, but they make up for their isolation with amazing insights into prehistoric life.

**Clifton Wilkinson, author**

## YORK & ITS AWE-INSPIRING CATHEDRAL

'Too much history' was how a friend once described York (p542), but if the past is your thing then York will press all the right buttons. And there's plenty to do still, even if you're more interested in great shopping, old pubs and cool restaurants than in old stones and tales of yore.

**Clifton Wilkinson, Lonely Planet staff**

MICAH WRIGHT

## VISITING THE LAKE DISTRICT

The world-famous Lake District (p611) is pretty much a year-round destination, but a few periods have their own special attractions – autumn for the colours, spring for the daffodils and rhododendrons, and winter for real peace and quiet.

**robynsj123 (online name), traveller**

DAVID TOMLINSON

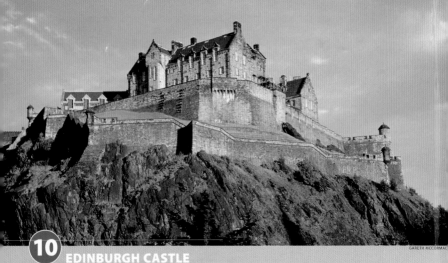

GARETH MCCORMAC

## 10 EDINBURGH CASTLE

Edinburgh Castle (p781) is an astonishing architectural monument, its towers, walls and damp underground spaces arranged with a complexity demanded by its dramatic volcanic site. The views across town are stunning and provide an excellent introduction to the general layout of the city.

**Leighg (online name), traveller**

BROWNSTOCK INC./PHOTOLIBRARY

## 11 KELVINGROVE ART GALLERY & MUSEUM, GLASGOW

Glasgow's *numero uno* educational haven (p815) has a multitude of weird and wonderful artefacts, from the majestic stuffed elephant which greets you upon arrival, to Salvador Dalí's *Christ of St John of the Cross*. You'll be hard-pressed not to find something which piques your interest.

**Zaineb Al-Hassani, traveller**

## HAY-ON-WYE

Bookworms beware! The secondhand bookshops in this Welsh border town (p732) are so numerous that you may find yourself spending more time and money here than you'd planned.

**David Atkinson, author**

**12**

JEFF MORGAN HAY ON WYE/PHOTOLIBRARY

HARDBACKS 50ᴾ
PAPERBACKS 30ᴾ

## ISLE OF SKYE

Extremely popular – and with every right to be – Skye (p937) packs in just about every Scottish experience you could want, from whisky tasting and gourmet dining to mountain climbing and sea kayaking.

**Andy Symington, author**

**13**

GARETH MCCORMACK

GARETH MCCORMACK

**14**  **SNOWDONIA**

Climb mountains, ride rapids and hike trails in what is arguably Wales's most beautiful area (p756), before falling into your luxury hotel for some well-deserved R&R.

**David Atkinson, author**

# LONDON TUBE MAP

# Contents

# Regional Map Contents

Highlands & Northern Islands pp906–7

Central Scotland pp848–9

Edinburgh

Glasgow & Southern Scotland pp808–9   pp782–3

Cumbria & the Lake District p609

Northeast England p639

Yorkshire pp516–17

Northwest England p571

North Wales p746

The Midlands & the Marches pp438–9

Mid Wales p723

Oxford, the Cotswolds & Around p238

East Anglia p400

South Wales p694

Cardiff p672

London p134–5

Southwest England p278–9

Southeast England p205

The Channel Islands p975

# Destination Great Britain

What is it that makes this damp little island moored off the northwest coast of Europe such a fascinating place to explore? For starters, Britain is a land for all seasons. Summer or winter, spring or autumn, there's always something to engage your imagination, be it the summer solstice at Stonehenge or the New Year street parties in Edinburgh.

There are over 5000 years of history to engage with, from the Stone Age village of Skara Brae to the space-age domes of the Eden Project, and from the stark simplicity of a Welsh chapel to the pomp and circumstance of Buckingham Palace. There are castles and cathedrals by the score, medieval monasteries and aristocratic mansions, and a roll-call of picturesque places with endearingly odd names, such as Lydiard Tregoze and Llanfairpwllgwyngyllgogerychwyrndrobwllllantysiliogogogoch.

Britain has given the world Shakespeare and soccer, the Beatles, James Bond, Monty Python and the programmable computer, not forgetting traffic lights, milky tea and the world's least scary police. These cultural contributions are celebrated in a collection of fascinating museums and art galleries that range from world-class institutions like the Tate Britain and the Victoria & Albert Museum, to delightfully dotty local curiosities – where else but Britain would you find the Pencil Museum and a dog-collar museum?

Then there's a geography textbook's worth of scenic landscapes, such as the rolling hop fields of Kent with their conical oast houses; the honeyed stone cottages and hedgerow-lined country lanes of the Cotswold hills; the soaring, silver-grey sea cliffs of Pembrokeshire, scabbed with yellow lichen; and the jagged, rock-girt peaks of the Isle of Skye.

Whatever the weather, there's a diverse menu of adventure activities to choose from, including some of Europe's best surfing, scuba-diving, sailing and hiking; plus less-strenuous pastimes such as trainspotting at York's National Railway Museum and whale-watching off Scotland's west coast.

As you travel around the region, what are the issues of the day that you'll hear Britons chatting about in the pub, at the bus stop and on the train? The national obsession with the weather has always seemed baffling to outsiders, who have often found it difficult to discern any difference between the mild winters and soggy summers. But in recent years the normally benign British weather has turned savage. Is it climate change in action? People are talking about an increase in summer storms and torrential downpours, and how 2007 saw the wettest summer, and 2008 the dullest August, since records began. There have been tornadoes in London and Birmingham, and many parts of the country, notably Yorkshire, Lincolnshire, Gloucestershire and south Wales, have suffered devastating flooding. Instead of looking forward to the summer sun, many now fear the summer floods.

Napoleon famously described Britain as a nation of shopkeepers, but today it has become a nation of homeowners. In the 1950s less than 40% of Britons owned their own homes; today the figure is more than 70%, and it's the ambition of many to get a foot on the property ladder as soon as they can afford it. Wherever two or more Brits are gathered together, the conversation will soon turn to the subject of house prices. Encouraged by the belief that prices can only go up, by banks offering loans for 125%

of a house's value, and by TV channels clogged with 'property porn', thousands of Britons have sunk their savings into bricks and mortar.

But at the time of going to press, Britain was under a cloud in more ways than one, with recession looming on the horizon. The global credit crunch that began in late 2007 has seen interest rates rise, mortgages dry up and house prices tumble – possibly by as much as 30% by 2010. Those who bought into the get-rich-quick, property-owning dream in the last few years are feeling the clammy grip of negative equity, and tens of thousands of homes are being repossessed.

The economic crisis has seen a backlash against the investment bankers, chief executives and hedge fund managers whose actions are seen by many as the cause of the credit crunch – ordinary people suffer while the 'fat cats' walk away with millions in their pockets. Financially speaking, Britain today is one of the most unequal societies in the developed world. Back in 1970 the average chief executive of a FTSE 100 company was paid around 10 times the earnings of the average employee; today that multiple is well over 100 times, and the wealthiest 10% of the population get 40% of the income. The popular mood is now in favour of increased regulation of the financial sector.

Britain's unexpected success in the 2008 Olympics – taking fourth place in the medal table with 19 gold (the Paralympic team came in second place overall, with 42 gold) – prompted a surge of interest in cycling, rowing and sailing, and increased expectations for the London Olympics in 2012. The London Games will ensure the arrival of large numbers of overseas visitors (and their money), a raised profile for British tourism, new housing and sports facilities for the capital, plus increased fitness and improved health for the entire nation. Or so say supporters. Detractors claim that the billions of pounds being spent are unlikely to be recouped, and local groups protest that a nature reserve, garden allotments and even popular sports venues are being bulldozed to make way for the Olympic Park.

But before the Olympics take place, one of the government's most controversial policies will grind into action. In 2009 the government will begin issuing biometric ID cards to British citizens. Supporters claim the cards will help combat crime and illegal immigration, and will make it easier to prove your identity to banks, the police and government agencies. Anti–ID card campaigners say the policy is an infringement of personal privacy and civil liberties, and that the unified database underlying the scheme is an IT disaster waiting to happen. Whatever the outcome, Britain is already one of the most spied-upon societies in the world, with 4.2 million CCTV surveillance cameras – about one for every 15 people. Something to think about as you travel around the country – Big Brother is watching you!

**FAST FACTS**

Population: 59 million

Area: 88,500 sq miles (230,000 sq km)

Inflation: 5.2% (October 2008)

Unemployment: 5.7% (August 2008)

Head of State: Queen Elizabeth II

Per capita GNP: approximately £23,500 (US$41,000)

Average annual rainfall in southeast England: 550mm

Average annual rainfall in northwest Highlands: 3000mm

Male life expectancy (posh part of Glasgow): 82

Male life expectancy (poor part of Glasgow): 54

# Getting Started

Here's a handy slogan to remember while you're planning your trip: travel in Britain is a breeze. Granted, it may not be totally effortless, but it's easy compared with many parts of the world. In this compact landscape you're never far from the next town, the next pub, the next national park or the next impressive castle on your hit list of highlights.

## WHEN TO GO

Any visitor to Britain will soon understand the locals' obsession with the weather. Extremes of hot or cold are rare, but variability is a given. The key word is *changeable:* the weather can be bad one minute, great the next. It wouldn't be unusual in April, for example, for the morning to be warm enough for T-shirts, lunchtime to be cloudy, the afternoon see a downpour and drop in temperature, and the day polished off by an overnight dump of snow.

Despite apparent randomness, there is a seasonal pattern. Temperatures are higher in summer (June to August), and there's normally more sunshine, though July and August, along with the winter months, are often the rainiest months of the year. Conversely, winter (November to February) may enjoy fantastic clear spells between bouts of rain or snow, while spring (March to May) or autumn (September to October) can often produce the finest weather of the year. There are also north–south variations: southern England might be chilly, while northern Scotland enjoys a heatwave. Or vice versa. Be prepared for anything and you won't get a surprise.

With all that in mind, May to September is undoubtedly the best period to travel in Britain. July and August are busiest (it's school holiday time), especially in coastal towns, national parks, and historic cities like Oxford, Edinburgh and York. In April and October you take a chance on the weather but avoid the crowds, although some hotels and attractions close from mid-October to Easter, and tourist offices have limited hours.

Overall, the least hospitable months for visitors are November to February. It's cold in the south, very cold in the north, and daylight is short. In Scotland, north Wales and the hills of northern England, roads can sometimes be closed by snow. Reaching the islands off the Scottish mainland (and occasionally other parts of Britain) can also be a problem as high winds disrupt ferry services.

For winter visits, London and the big cities are an exception – they're busy all the time, with such a lot to see that the weather is immaterial. Besides, you're almost as likely to have a damp day in June as you are in January…

For more weather facts and figures, see Climate Charts, p987.

## COSTS & MONEY

If you're a global traveller, whatever your budget you'll know that Britain is expensive compared with many other countries. But don't let that put you off. If funds are tight you'll still have a great trip with some forward planning, a bit of shopping around and a modicum of common sense. A lot of stuff is cheap or good value, and some is completely free. The following gives some guidelines; for more details see the Directory (p982) and Transport (p996) chapters.

For midrange travellers, basic hotels cost around £50 to £120 for a double room, except in London, where doubles in midrange hotels start at around £80, and around £150 in London gets you something pretty decent for the night, although you could easily spend more. When it comes to eating, a decent three-course meal with wine in a smart restaurant will set you back about £25 to £35 per person. In London this jumps to about £60, although if you choose carefully you can still get a great meal (with a glass or two of wine) for around £30. Of course, you can go wild at somewhere outrageously posh or trendy, and not get much change from £150.

Backpackers on a tight budget need £36 a day for bare survival in London, with dorm beds from £18, basic sustenance £12, and transport around £6 unless you prefer to hoof it.

Whatever your bracket, extras in London might include clubbing (£6 to £12, up to £25 at weekends), a pint in a pub (£2.80 to £3.50) or admission to museums and galleries (£10 to £20 a day, though many places don't charge).

Out of London, costs drop; shoestringers need around £30 per day for hostels and food. Midrangers will be fine on £60 to £85 per day, allowing £25 to £35 per person for B&B accommodation, £12 to £18 for lunch, snacks and drinks, £15 to £25 for an evening meal. Admission fees are the same for everyone – work on around £10 per day for general admission costs.

Travel costs depend on transport choice. Trains can cost anything from £10 to £50 per 100 miles, depending when you buy your ticket. Long-distance buses (called coaches in Britain) cost about half the train fare for an equivalent journey. Car drivers should allow £12 per 100 miles for fuel, plus around £5 per day for parking. Rental costs £25 to £60 per day, depending on model and duration.

## TRAVELLING RESPONSIBLY

Britons share their compact and increasingly crowded island with around 33 million cars, vans, buses and lorries – that's more than one vehicle for every two people. Traffic congestion and carbon emissions are serious problems that are only now beginning to be tackled head-on.

In the past, the government's response to overcrowded roads has been to build more of them; today, politicians have been forced to look at other approaches. While London has its congestion charge, Sustrans (www.sustrans.org.uk) – a group focused on sustainable transport – is busy creating a national network of cycle routes; and Worcester (p494), Peterborough (p413) and Darlington (p653) have been chosen as showcase sustainable transport towns, with government-funded projects to promote cycling, walking and public transport as realistic alternatives to car use.

Although a car can be useful in some parts of the country, notably the Scottish Highlands, if you don't want to contribute to – or get caught up in – British gridlock, then think about using public transport rather than hiring a car. And think twice before taking a domestic flight within Britain – remember it's a relatively small geographical area. Taking the London to Edinburgh route as an example, if you add on travel time from the city

**HOW MUCH?**

See also the Lonely Planet Index, inside front cover.

B&B £25 per person

CD £12

The *Guardian* (newspaper) 80p

Restaurant meal £25 per person

Large latte £2.30

---

**COSTS FOR KIDS**

Taking your children into museums and historic sites can be absolutely free, half-price, or just a bit cheaper than the adult cost, so we've detailed kids' rates (as well as adult prices) throughout this book. At camp sites and self-catering hostels, children usually pay about 50% to 75% of the adult rate. At hotels, children aged between two and 12 years old usually get 50% to 75% discount. Kids under two usually stay free of charge, while over-12s (or over-16s at some places) attract the full rate, on the assumption that growing children need a bed and will probably eat as much as their parents.

---

**DON'T LEAVE HOME WITHOUT...**

Travel in Britain is not like crossing the Sahara or exploring the Amazon. Anything can be bought as you go. Our advice is to take only what you absolutely need, which may include the following:

- rain jacket
- comfortable shoes
- small day-pack (for carrying that rain jacket when the sun shines)
- a taste for beer that isn't icy cold
- listening skills and a sense of humour

---

centre to the airport (one hour in London, 15 minutes in Edinburgh), and check-in time (say one hour, minimum) to the flight time (one hour), then the 4½-hour train journey actually looks pretty good (and you don't have to queue for check-in and security, either).

## READING UP

There's nothing like a good book to set the mood for your own trip. The choice of books about Britain can be daunting, so here's a list of our favourites to add an extra dimension to your planning or help you penetrate that famous British reserve a little while you're on the road.

- *Notes from a Small Island* by Bill Bryson, although based on travels in the 1970s, is still incisive. This American author really captures the spirit of Britain three-and-a-half decades ago. When he pokes fun he's spot on, so the locals don't mind.
- *The English: A Portrait of a People* by Jeremy Paxman examines the evolution of English national identity in recent years, through the sharp and often cynical eyes of Britain's favourite blunt Yorkshireman and TV news presenter.
- *Coasting* by Jonathan Raban records a journey around Britain in an old sailing yacht, and is a brilliant and very readable meditation on the people and culture of this island nation.
- *London: The Biography* by Peter Ackroyd is the definitive description of Britain's biggest city as a living, breathing organism.
- *The Thistle and the Rose: Six Centuries of Love and Hate Between the Scots and the English,* by Allan Massie, takes a historical perspective on the often stormy relationship between Britain's two largest countries.
- *Adrift in Caledonia* by Nick Thorpe is an entertaining and insightful tale of travelling around Scotland by hitching rides on a variety of vessels, from canal barge and rowing boat to steam puffer and square-rigged sailing ship.
- *On Borrow's Trail* by Hugh Oliff retraces the journeys through Wales made by 19th-century writer George Borrow, combining a rich synopsis of the original observations with modern photos and colour illustrations.
- *Two Degrees West* by Nicholas Crane describes a walk in a perfectly straight line (two degrees west of the Greenwich meridian) across Britain, wading rivers, cutting through towns, sleeping in fields and meeting an astounding selection of people along the way.
- *Great British Bus Journeys* by David McKie is a wry and witty travelogue showing that 'unknown' towns and villages can be just as fascinating as tourist hot spots.

# TOP 10

GREAT BRITAIN

## MUST-SEE MOVIES

Predeparture planning is no chore if it includes a trip to the cinema or a night on the sofa with a DVD. Our parameters for a 'British' film? Anything about Britain. Anything that gives a taste of history, scenery or peculiar cultural traits. For more info on some of these and other titles, see p76.

1 *Brief Encounter* (1945) Director: David Lean

2 *Whisky Galore* (1949) Director: Alexander Mackendrick

3 *Under Milk Wood* (1972) Director: Andrew Sinclair

4 *Educating Rita* (1983) Director: Lewis Gilbert

5 *My Beautiful Laundrette* (1985) Director: Stephen Frears

6 *Four Weddings and a Funeral* (1994) Director: Mike Newell

7 *Trainspotting* (1996) Director: Danny Boyle

8 *Bend It Like Beckham* (2002) Director: Gurinder Chadha

9 *Atonement* (2007) Director: Joe Wright

10 *Hot Fuzz* (2007) Director: Edgar Wright

## RAVE READS

Travel broadens the mind. Especially if you read before you go. For a taste of life in Britain through the ages, try a few of these novels – from past classics to contemporary milestones. For more details on some of these (and other great books), see p73.

1 *Oliver Twist* (1837) Charles Dickens

2 *Wuthering Heights* (1847) Emily Brontë

3 *Tess of the D'Urbervilles* (1891) Thomas Hardy

4 *The Rainbow* (1915) DH Lawrence

5 *How Green Was My Valley* (1939) Richard Llewellyn

6 *Greenvoe* (1972) George Mackay Brown

7 *Behind the Scenes at the Museum* (1995) Kate Atkinson

8 *Last Orders* (1996) Graham Swift

9 *White Teeth* (2000) Zadie Smith

10 *The Falls* (2003) Ian Rankin

## TOP OF THE POPS

British popular music is probably the most popular in the world. Britain has produced hundreds of internationally famous bands and artists from the Beatles and the Rolling Stones to the Kaiser Chiefs and the Arctic Monkeys. Here's a lucky dip of typically British chart-topping pop and rock from 1960 onward.

1 *You Don't Have to Say You Love Me* by Dusty Springfield (1966)

2 *Honky Tonk Women* by the Rolling Stones (1969)

3 *Won't Get Fooled Again* by The Who (1971)

4 *Anarchy in the UK* by the Sex Pistols (1976)

5 *Love Will Tear Us Apart* by Joy Division (1980)

6 *House of Fun* by Madness (1982)

7 *Wonderwall* by Oasis (1995)

8 *Wannabe* by the Spice Girls (1996)

9 *If You Tolerate This Your Children Will Be Next* by the Manic Street Preachers (2000)

10 *The Dark of the Matinee* by Franz Ferdinand (2004)

## INTERNET RESOURCES

The internet is a wonderful planning tool for travellers, and there are millions of sites about Britain. Before plunging into the cybermaze, try these for starters:

**A Nice Cup of Tea...** (www.nicecupofteaandasitdown.com) Light-hearted look at a quintessentially British pastime.

**Backpax Magazine** (www.backpaxmag.com) Cheerful info on cheap travel, visas, activities and work.

**BAFA** (British Arts Festivals Association; www.artsfestivals.co.uk) Listing over 100 festivals around Britain: opera, theatre, literature, comedy, classical, folk, jazz and more.

**BBC** (www.bbc.co.uk) Immense and invaluable site from the world's best broadcaster.

**DirectGov** (www.direct.gov.uk/en/DisabledPeople) Information and advice for travellers with disabilities, including interactive map showing wheelchair-accessible toilets, parking etc in 100 towns around Britain.

**eFestivals** (www.efestivals.co.uk) News, confirmed (and rumoured) artists, tickets and updates from the lively world of rock, pop, dance and world music gatherings.

**Lonely Planet** (www.lonelyplanet.com) Loads of travel news, features, accommodation reviews, and the legendary Thorn Tree bulletin board.

**UK Student Life** (www.ukstudentlife.com) Language courses, and where to go outside study time.

**Visit Britain** (www.visitbritain.com) The nation's official tourism website; accommodation, attractions, events and much more.

# Events Calendar

Countless festivals and events are held around the country throughout the year. Below is a selection of biggies that are worth tying in with your travels, and some of the smaller – and, frankly, more bizarre – events that are also worth catching. In addition, many towns have annual fairs or fêtes; many of these are listed in the regional chapters.

## JANUARY

**UP HELLY AA**                              last Tue of Jan
Shetland Islanders (p969) honour their Nordic heritage by dressing up as Vikings and burning a longship.

## FEBRUARY

**JORVIK VIKING FESTIVAL**              mid-Feb
Horned helmets galore, plus mock invaders and Viking longship races in York (p549).

**SHROVETIDE FOOTBALL**              Shrove Tue
It's football, Jim, but not as we know it: day-long match, 3-mile pitch, hundreds of players, very few rules. See p462 for details.

## MARCH

**CRUFTS DOG SHOW**              early/mid-Mar
Highlight of the canine year. Top dogs abound in Birmingham. See p480 for details.

**UNIVERSITY BOAT RACE**
late Mar/early Apr
Traditional rowing contest (p174) on the River Thames, between the teams of Oxford and Cambridge Universities.

## APRIL

**GRAND NATIONAL**              1st Sat in Apr
The most famous horse race (p598) of them all, with notoriously high jumps in Aintree, Liverpool.

**CHELTENHAM JAZZ FESTIVAL**
late Apr/early May
One of the largest jazz gatherings in the country; big names, up-and-comings, concerts and funky club-dance evenings. See p264.

## MAY

**FA CUP FINAL**              early May
Gripping end to venerable football tournament, held in Wembley Stadium, London. For more, see (p68).

**BRIGHTON FESTIVAL**              May
If it's art, you'll find it at Brighton's lively and innovative three-week feast (p226), which covers everything from music, theatre, literature and the visual arts to a children's parade, pyrotechnics and performance poetry.

**CHELSEA FLOWER SHOW**              late May
Blooming marvellous. See p174 for more.

**BATH INTERNATIONAL
MUSIC FESTIVAL**              mid-May–early Jun
Top-class classical music and opera in Bath, plus jazz and world music, with art-full Fringe attached. See p335.

**COOPER'S HILL CHEESE-ROLLING
COMPETITION**              late May
Simple concept, centuries old: a big lump of cheese is rolled down a very steep hill, chased by hundreds of locals. The winner keeps the cheese. Losers may have broken legs. See p262 for more.

**GLYNDEBOURNE**              late May-Aug
Mozart is the mainstay of this world-famous opera festival, held annually since 1934 in country-house gardens near Lewes, Sussex. See p223 for details.

## JUNE

**DERBY WEEK**              early Jun
Horse racing and people-watching abound at the Epsom racetrack in Surrey (see www.epsomderby .co.uk for more details).

**COTSWOLDS OLIMPICKS**              early Jun
Since 1612 the locals of Chipping Camden have competed in events such as shin-kicking, sack-racing and climbing the slippery pole. See p257.

**ALDEBURGH FESTIVAL** Jun
Classical music held in Aldeburgh, the spiritual home of Benjamin Britten (1913–76) – one of Britain's best 20th-century composers – see p422.

**TROOPING THE COLOUR** mid-Jun
Bearskins and pageantry in London's Whitehall for the Queen's birthday parade (p175).

**ROYAL ASCOT** mid-Jun
More horse racing, more people-watching, plus outrageous hats; find out more at www.ascot.co.uk.

**ISLE OF WIGHT FESTIVAL** mid-Jun
Successful revival of the 1960s rip-roaring hippie happening; see p296.

**WIMBLEDON LAWN TENNIS CHAMPIONSHIPS** late Jun
Two weeks of rapid-fire returns; see p175.

**GLASTONBURY FESTIVAL** late Jun
The village of Glastonbury is practically synonymous with the Glastonbury Festival (www.glastonburyfestivals.co.uk), an often mud-soaked extravaganza of music, street theatre, dance, cabaret, carnival, ecology, spirituality and general all-round weirdness that's been held on and off on Piltdown Farm, near Glastonbury.

**PRIDE** Jun/Jul
Formerly Mardi Gras and Pride in the Park, and occasionally EuroPride – Britain's major gay and lesbian festival, held in London.

## JULY

**HENLEY ROYAL REGATTA** early Jul
Premier rowing and social event. No hippies here. See p252.

**T IN THE PARK** early Jul
Open-air pop, rock and dance music. Scotland's answer to Glastonbury; see p823 for details.

**WORLD MOUNTAIN BIKE BOG SNORKELLING CHAMPIONSHIPS** early Jul
Bogs, bikes and snorkels; the name says it all. Henley it ain't. See p737. There's another leg to the event in August, see p28.

**INTERNATIONAL EISTEDDFOD** mid-Jul
Lively mix of cultures from Wales and far beyond; see p755.

**LATITUDE FESTIVAL** mid-Jul
More than just a music festival, this relative newcomer to Britain's festival calendar (www.latitudefestival.co.uk) packs in poetry, literature, comedy and drama, too. Held in Henham Park, Southwold (p423).

**BUXTON FESTIVAL** mid-late Jul
Relaxed and eclectic mix of opera, music and literature, this renowned festival (www.buxtonfestival.co.uk) is one of the largest of its kind in the country.

**SESIWN FAWR** late Jul
Three-day rock, folk and beer bash in Dolgellau. Fast-growing and free. See p759.

**ROYAL WELSH AGRICULTURAL SHOW** late Jul
National agricultural and cultural gathering; see p736.

**FARNBOROUGH AIRSHOW** late Jul
Established in 1948 as a showcase for the best of British aviation, the world's largest air show is held in Farnborough, Surrey. The air show ranges from traditional WWII aircraft to cutting-edge technology, with thrilling aerobatic displays, fly-pasts and simulated aerial dogfights. See www.farnborough.com for details.

**COWES WEEK** late Jul/early Aug
The world's longest-running yachting regatta – dating from 1827 – is a spectacular display of world-class yacht racing and a highlight of the society calendar; see p295.

**EDEN SESSIONS** Jul/Aug
The famous biomes of the Eden Project (p382) are transformed into Cornwall's most spectacular live-music venue, where a 6000-strong crowd bops along to a line-up of the best of British rock and pop.

## AUGUST

**NATIONAL EISTEDDFOD** early Aug
The ancient bardic tradition continues; a festival of Welsh language, music and literature at its most powerful. See p755.

**THREE CHOIRS FESTIVAL** early Aug
Britain's premier, and the world's oldest, choral festival (www.3choirs.org), held once every three years at the cathedrals of Gloucester (p267), Hereford (p499) or Worcester (p494).

**EDINBURGH MILITARY TATTOO**    Aug
Three weeks of pageantry and soldierly displays. For details, see p795.

**EDINBURGH INTERNATIONAL
FESTIVAL**    Aug/Sep
World-class arts gathering, overshadowed only by its own Fringe. See p795.

**GREEN MAN FESTIVAL**    mid-Aug
Set near Crickhowell, this festival is an old-school gathering of campfires and late-night guitar strumming, featuring the best of the UK modern folk scene plus international acts from the alternative world. See p731.

**NOTTING HILL CARNIVAL**    late Aug
London's most colourful festival is a multicultural feast of music, dancing and costumed street parades that celebrates the city's African-Caribbean community. See also p175.

**READING FESTIVAL**    late Aug
This three-day rock and pop extravaganza is a true original, from the glory days of 1970s prog rock and heavy metal to the 1990s appearances of Kurt Cobain and the Stone Roses. Recent years have seen the festival turn more mainstream, but unpopular bands can still expect to be sent packing amid a hail of hurled plastic bottles.

**LEEDS FESTIVAL**    late Aug
Dubbed the 'Reading of the North', and pretty much the same type of thing; a rock-music extravaganza (see p522).

**WORLD BOG SNORKELLING
CHAMPIONSHIPS**    late Aug
Following July's filthy cycling event (for more information, see p27), now it's the swimmers' turn

to snorkel through the mire. Crazy, but the crowds love it.

**BIG CHILL**    late Aug
Most head here to recover from summer's excesses; an eclectic and relaxed mix of live music, club events, DJs, multimedia and visual art. Held on the deer-park grounds of Eastnor Castle in Herefordshire; see p502 for more information.

## SEPTEMBER

**BRAEMAR GATHERING**    1st Sat in Sep
With more than 20,000 people (including the royals), 'gathering' is an understatement for this famous Highland knees-up. See p899 for more information.

## OCTOBER

**HORSE OF THE YEAR SHOW**    early Oct
Birmingham's top show-jumping event. No long faces here. See also p480.

## NOVEMBER

**BONFIRE NIGHT**    5 Nov
Bonfires and fireworks across Britain fill the skies in commemoration of Guy Fawke's failed Gunpowder Plot of 1605 (a terrorist attempt to blow up Parliament). See also Frenzied Pyromania (p223).

## DECEMBER

**NEW YEAR CELEBRATIONS**    31 Dec
Get drunk and kiss strangers as the bells chime midnight. The biggest crowds are in London's Trafalgar Sq and Edinburgh's Princes St.

# Itineraries
## CLASSIC ROUTES

### HOORAY FOR HIGHLIGHTS    One to Two Weeks / London to Cambridge

This is an unashamed tour of Britain's top tourist attractions. Yes, some can get crowded, but it's for a reason – they're stunningly scenic or rich in history.

Start with spectacular, irrepressible **London** (p130), then visit ancient cathedral cities **Winchester** (p281) and **Salisbury** (p311). Next is classic, pre-historic **Stonehenge** (p315); and onwards to **Bath** (p330) for Roman remains and grand Georgian architecture.

Loop over to **Cardiff** (p669) for fantastical castles and nautical heritage, and cruise through the rural **Cotswolds** (p253) to reach the university town of **Oxford** (p239) and Shakespeare's birthplace, **Stratford-upon-Avon** (p487).

Then strike out north to the **Lake District** (p611) and over the border to **Edinburgh** (p779) for its historic castles, new parliament and more tartan than you can shake a kilt at, before heading to the **Isle of Skye** (p937) for Scotland's most stunning scenery.

Heading south again, stop in at **York** (p542) for its glorious cathedral and first-class train museum before finishing at **Cambridge** (p401), another ancient university town, for more sightseeing and maybe a gentle punt on the river.

Without stopping much you could do this 1300-mile journey in a week and a half. But pause to drink in the culture and history, not to mention the occasional beer in a country pub, and three weeks becomes a much better option.

## THE GRAND TOUR

One to Two Months /
London to Cambridge (The Long Way)

This is a trip for those with time, or an urge to see everything. So brace yourself, and let's be off. From **London** (p130) aim for **Canterbury Cathedral** (p206), then head down the coast to hip and happening **Brighton** (p223), and across to historic cities **Winchester** (p281) and **Salisbury** p311) and the delightful **New Forest** (p291). Travel via prehistoric **Stonehenge** (p315) to Westcountry gems **Bath** (p330) and **Bristol** (p320).

Next to Wales, via stunning **Chepstow Castle** (p697) and energetic **Cardiff** (p669), to the coastal paradise of **Pembrokeshire** (p707). Retrace to the **Brecon Beacons** (p724) and through book-mad **Hay-on-Wye** (p732) to reach the cosy **Cotswolds** (p253), charming **Oxford** (p239), spectacular **Warwick Castle** (p485), and Shakespeare's birthplace **Stratford-upon-Avon** (p487). Continue north to **Chester** (p584), then divert into north Wales for the grand **Conwy Castle** (p751) and **Caernarfon Castle** (p770); and equally stunning mountains of **Snowdonia National Park** (p756). Then ferry across the Mersey to **Liverpool** (p588) and to **Manchester** (p572) for a taste of city life, followed by a change of scenery in the **Lake District** (p611) and a journey back in time along **Hadrian's Wall** (p655).

Hop across the border to Scotland, via the tranquil southern Uplands countryside and **border towns** (p827), to good-time **Glasgow** (p809). Then trek to **Ben Nevis** (p914), from where it's easy to reach for the **Isle of Skye** (p937).

Time to head south again, via **Loch Ness** (p918) and **Stirling Castle** (p866) to **Edinburgh** (p779), through the abbey border-towns of **Kelso** (p831) and **Jedburgh** (p833), to reach World Heritage Site **Durham** (p649) and the ancient Viking capital of **York** (p542), ending with a final flourish in beautiful **Cambridge** (p401).

This energetic pack-it-in loop is over 2000 miles. If you don't want to hurry, just leave out a few places. With even more time, you could expand the trip to include Devon and Cornwall, Norfolk and Suffolk, Mid Wales or the east coast of Scotland.

## PASTORAL PLEASURES

**Three to Four Weeks /
New Forest to Outer Hebrides**

Britain may be small, and crowded in places, but there are some beautiful national parks and rural areas to enjoy.

First stop, the **New Forest** (p291) for a spot of walking, cycling or horse riding, or simply relaxing, then to **Devon** (p352) and **Cornwall** (p373), which tempt with wild moors, grassy hills, and a beautiful coast of cliffs and sandy beaches.

The **Cotswolds** (p253) promise quintessential English countryside, with neat fields, clear rivers and endless pretty villages of honey-coloured stone – all glowing contentedly when the sun is out.

Head west again, to Wales, through the rolling hills of the **Brecon Beacons** (p724), and down to the heavenly sea and sky of **Pembrokeshire** (p707). Then go north to scale the stunning peaks of **Snowdonia National Park** (p756), with mountains for walkers and steam trains for all the family.

Then it's back to England, through the valleys of the **Yorkshire Dales National Park** (p531) and over the mountains of the **Lake District** (p611), to Scotland where two new national parks await: the glorious combination of **Loch Lomond** (p851) and **Trossachs National Park** (p869), and the mountain wilderness of the **Cairngorms** (p908).

That may be wondrous enough, but Britain's pastoral pleasures are crowned by Scotland's famous Highlands and islands, where jewels include peaks, such as **Ben Nevis** (p914) and **Torridon** (p934), while out to sea the lovely islands – **Isle of Arran** (p842), **Isle of Islay** (p855), **Isle of Jura** (p857), **Isle of Mull** (p861), **Isle of Skye** (p937), **Lewis** (p945), **North Uist** (p949), **South Uist** (p950) and others – bask in the afternoon sun.

**This is a tour to recharge your batteries and fill your lungs with fresh air. The main route is around 1300 miles, plus another 300 miles if you visit all the islands. Allow three weeks, or a month if you don't rush.**

# ROADS LESS TRAVELLED

## URBAN ODYSSEY                          One to Two Weeks / Bristol to Manchester

If you want to dig under Britain's skin a little, take this ride through some of the country's less well-known and revitalised cities.

Kick off in **Bristol** (p320), once a poor cousin to neighbour Bath, today with fierce pride, a rich historic legacy and a music scene that rivals cool northern outposts. Next stop **Birmingham** (p474), a city that oozes transformation, with an attractive waterside, energised museums and a space-age shopping centre. Continue north to dynamic **Leeds** (p521), the 'Knightsbridge of the North', a mecca for shoppers, clubbers and drinkers. But don't dawdle. Down your pint. We're off again – to culturally restyled and famously to-the-hilt party town **Newcastle-upon-Tyne** (p640).

Still want more? It's got to be **Glasgow** (p809). Sign up here for pubs and clubs, some truly electric venues, fabulous galleries and – only in Scotland – slick but unpretentious bars.

Pausing for coffee and toast, head next for **Liverpool** (p588). The Beatles are done to death, but there are lively *current* music venues and rich trade-port heritage – plus a rather famous football team.

Finish in **Manchester** (p572), self-styled 'Barcelona of Britain', a long-time hotbed of musical endeavour, with thriving arts and club scenes, galleries a go-go, dramatic new architecture and – oh yes – another well-known football team.

**In theory you could do this 725-mile street trip in a week, but Britain's cities may tempt you to linger longer. Better to allow at least 10 days. Two weeks would be even better. Don't say we didn't warn you…**

## RURAL RETREATS                         Two to Three Weeks / Norfolk to Fife

For some of Britain's best-known national parks and natural beauties, see p31; this fabulous jaunt takes you through less-frequented (but no less scenic) countryside.

Surprisingly close to London sit the tranquil counties of **Norfolk** (p424) and **Suffolk** (p416), their coastlines dotted with picturesque harbours, shingle beaches, salt marshes, bird reserves and the occasional old-fashioned seaside resort. Inland lie rivers and lakes, pretty villages and endless miles of flat countryside perfect for gentle cycling.

Next is **Wiltshire** (p311), best known for Stonehenge and Salisbury but also a rural delight of quiet country lanes and tranquil villages, plus the hills of the southern Cotswolds – low-key and less frequented than their northern counterparts in Gloucestershire.

Between England and Wales lie the farmlands and cider orchards of the **Marches** (p436), while over the border loom the Cambrian Mountains of Mid Wales (p722) – big, wild and rarely on tourist itineraries. Then it's back to England and the **North York Moors National Park** (p561), with heather-covered hills and delightful dales. Not far away, the **Northumberland coast** (p662) is famous for empty beaches, dramatic castles and delicious crab sandwiches.

Inland sit the wild and empty big-sky landscapes of the hills atop the **Cheviot** (p661) and **Northumberland National Park** (p660), blending into the undulating hills, green valleys, stately homes, ruined abbeys and ancient **border towns** (p827) of Scotland's southern Uplands.

For a final fling, cross the Firth of Forth to reach the 'kingdom' of **Fife** (p873), with lush rolling farmland ideal for cycling and a delightful coastline peppered with quaint harbours, perfect for an after-lunch stroll.

You could see these 'hidden' parts of Britain in two weeks if you don't stop much, covering about 1000 miles. Allow three weeks if you plan to wear your hiking boots, or want to relax over tea and cake, and catch a little local flavour off the beaten track.

# TAILORED TRIPS

## BRITAIN ON LOCATION

Love the movies? Here are a few places where you can visit the set.

Britain's best-loved film hero Harry Potter gets around – locations in the films include **Gloucester Cathedral** (p267), **Oxford University** (p241), **Alnwick Castle** (p663), **North York Moors Railway** (p565) and **Glenfinnan** (p936).

In Scotland, landmark Hitchcock thriller *The 39 Steps* features the **Forth Bridge** (p805); the comedy *Whisky Galore* was set in the **Outer Hebrides** (p944); **Edinburgh** (p779) is the scene for tartan-noir masterpiece *Trainspotting;* while **Dunnottar Castle** (p898) was the backdrop for Zeffirelli's *Hamlet.*

In Wales, the Dylan Thomas classic *Under Milk Wood* was filmed in **Fishguard** (p718) in Pembrokeshire, while some of Lara Croft's unfeasibly epic *Tomb Raider* adventures were shot in **Snowdonia National Park** (p756).

In northern England, quirky *Little Voice* was filmed in **Scarborough** (p557); *Calendar Girls* in the scenic valleys of the **Yorkshire Dales** (p531); and late-'90s hit *The Full Monty* in former steel-city **Sheffield** (p519).

For the latest film version of *Pride and Prejudice*, Austen power comes to Derbyshire; the stately home of **Chatsworth** (p473) plays Darcy's family abode, while dramatic Peak District outcrops provide a perfect spot for the heroine's love-lost contemplation. For *The Da Vinci Code* **Lincoln Cathedral** (p448) stood in for Westminster, and visitor numbers doubled overnight.

## BRITAIN'S WORLD HERITAGE

Unesco's World Heritage Sites have great environmental or cultural significance. There are around 700 sites globally, and around 20 in Britain – together making up a great itinerary of highlights and unexpected treasures.

Obvious contenders include the **Tower of London** (p161), the historical maritime sites of **Greenwich** (p170), the ancient megaliths of **Stonehenge** (p315) and **Avebury** (p318), and the Roman-Georgian city of **Bath** (p330). Less obvious, but just as valid, sites include the industrial heritage of **Blaenavon** (p697) and **Ironbridge Gorge** (p506), the mills of **Saltaire** (p527) and the waterfront of **Liverpool** (p588), while

the coast of **Dorset** (p297) and **East Devon** (p357) is one of the few natural sites on this list.

In the south of England there's **Blenheim Palace** (p251) and **Canterbury Cathedral** (p206), while the north boasts **Fountains Abbey** (p554). In Wales, the castles of **Caernarfon** (p770), **Conwy** (p751), **Beaumaris** (p773) and **Harlech** (p765) together form one site, as do **Durham Castle** (p651) and **Durham Cathedral** (p650). In Scotland, sites include **Edinburgh's Old Town** (p781) and **New Town** (p790), **New Lanark** (p825), and the neolithic sites of the **Orkney Islands** (p952).

Recent additions to the list include **Hadrian's Wall** (p655) and the landscape and industrial heritage of the coast of **Cornwall** (p373). For more details see www.ukworldheritage.org.uk.

## BRITAIN FOR KIDS

'Are we nearly there yet?' Travel through England with offspring in tow needn't be arduous. Certainly not if you visit some of these places.

**London** (p174) justifiably tops nearly every list – with a mesmerising choice of kid-friendly attractions. Bristol has **Explore @ Bristol** (p321), an interactive science museum bursting with hands-on exhibits, while Cardiff has a fairy-tale **castle** (p671) and up-to-the-moment **Techniquest** (p674).

For more battlements, there's **Warwick Castle** (p485) in Warwick. Knights in armour? You bet. And children of a ghoulish disposition can creep around the dungeons. It's a short distance, but a leap across centuries, to the **National Space Centre** (p443). Highlights include zero-gravity toilets and germ-devouring underpants. Kids love it. And it *is* rocket science.

Hungry after crossing the galaxy? **Cadbury World** (p477) in Birmingham is a lip-smacking exploration of chocolate production and consumption. Just make sure those samples settle in tiny tummies before you reach **Alton Towers** (p493), Britain's finest theme park, with a stomach-churning selection of roller coasters and other thrills.

The ultramodern **Glasgow Science Centre** (p814) is a bounty of discovery, complete with interactive science mall, and Dundee offers **Sensation** (p889) for more hands-on, and heads-in, activity.

Finish at **Our Dynamic Earth** (p789) in Edinburgh, a special-effects marvel recreating the planet's history from the Big Bang to teatime.

## GREAT BRITISH GRUB

Eat and drink your way from Land's End to John o'Groats with this selection of the best of traditional British foodstuffs.

**Cornwall** (p373) is home to the Cornish pasty – any local bakery will sell them – while the dairy farms of **Devon** (p352) are famous for their clotted cream; you can enjoy a Devonshire cream tea at pretty much any tearoom in the county.

**Kent** (p204) grows the hops that give English beer its flavour – sample a pint of real ale at the **Thomas Becket** (p210) in Canterbury before heading to **London** (p130) to track down that classic delicacy, jellied eels.

Moving up through the **Midlands** (p436), you might fancy a nibble at a Melton Mowbray pork pie (p92) on your way to Wales, whose national cuisine is famed for tasty saltmarsh lamb, raised on the **Gower Peninsula** (p704) and laver bread (p89).

Heading north, you soon reach the home of **Lancashire** (p600) hotpot and **Yorkshire** (p515) pudding.

Classic British fish and chips are best enjoyed at the seaside – the **Magpie Cafe** (p568) in Whitby claims to serve the best in Britain.

Scotland's most famous dish is, of course haggis (p92), but there are plenty of other Scottish specialities, such as Cullen skink (p92). And no visit north of the border would be complete without sampling a single malt whisky – **Dufftown** (p903) is at the heart of the Speyside distillery region.

# History

It may be a small island on the edge of Europe, but Britain has never been on the sidelines of history. For thousands of years, invaders and incomers have arrived, settled and made their mark here. The result is Britain's fascinating mix of landscape, culture and language – a dynamic pattern that shaped the nation and continues to evolve today.

For many visitors, this rich historic legacy is Britain's main attraction – everything from Stonehenge to Glen Coe, via Hadrian's Wall, Canterbury Cathedral, Caernarfon Castle and the Tower of London. Even if you're no fan of dates and dynasties, we hope the overview this chapter provides will help you get the most from your trip.

## FIRST ARRIVALS

Stone tools discovered near the town of Lowestoft in Suffolk show that human habitation in Britain stretches back at least 700,000 years, although exact dates depend on your definition of 'human'. As the centuries rolled on, Ice Ages came and went, sea levels rose and fell, and the island now called Britain was frequently joined to the European mainland. Hunter-gatherers crossed the land bridge, moving north as the ice melted and retreating to warmer climes when the glaciers advanced once again.

Around 4000 BC a new group of migrants arrived and settled, most notably in open chalky hill areas such as the South Downs and Salisbury Plain in southern England. Alongside their fields these early settlers used rocks and turf to build massive burial mounds, and many of these can still be seen

Built around 3000 BC, Stonehenge is older than the famous Great Pyramid of Giza.

---

**THREE IN ONE**

The countries of England, Wales and Scotland make up the state of Great Britain. Three countries in one might seem a strange set-up, and visitors are sometimes confused about the difference between England and Britain – as are a lot of English people (although the Welsh and Scots are clear on the distinction). But getting a grip on this basic principle will ease your understanding of British history and culture, and make your travel more enjoyable, too.

Just for the record, the United Kingdom (UK) consists of Great Britain and Northern Ireland. The island of Ireland consists of Northern Ireland and the Republic of Ireland (also called Eire). 'British Isles' is a geographical term for the whole group of islands that make up the UK, the Republic of Ireland and some autonomous or semiautonomous islands, such as the Channel Islands and the Isle of Man.

Got all that? Good. Now read on…

---

## TIMELINE

| 4000 BC | c 500 BC | c 55 BC |
|---|---|---|
| Neolithic peoples migrate from continental Europe. They differ significantly from previous arrivals: instead of hunting and moving on, they settle in one place and start farming. | The Celts, a group of people originally from central Europe, arrive in Britain and by the middle of the 1st millennium BC have settled across much of the island, absorbing the indigenous people. | Relatively small groups of Roman invaders under the command of Emperor Julius Caesar make forays into southern England from the northern coast of continental Europe (today's France). |

today, including the West Kennet Long Barrow (p320) in Wiltshire, and the great passage grave at Maes Howe (p958), Orkney.

But perhaps the most enduring, and certainly the most impressive, legacy left by these nascent Britons are the great stone circles such as Callanish (p947) on Lewis in Scotland, and – most famous of all – the elaborate and enigmatic sites of Avebury (p318) and Stonehenge (p315) in southern England.

## IRON & CELTS

Move on a millennium or two, and it's the Iron Age. The population expanded and began to divide into specific groups or tribes. Across the whole island of Britain the forests were cleared with increasing efficiency as more land was turned to farming. This led to a patchwork pattern of fields, woods and small villages that still exists in many parts of rural lowland Britain.

As landscapes altered, this was also a time of cultural change. By around 500 BC, the Celts had settled across much of the island of Britain, absorbing the indigenous people. A Celtic-British population – sometimes known as the 'ancient Britons' – developed, divided into about 20 different tribes, including the Cantiaci (in today's county of Kent), the Iceni (today's Norfolk), the Brigantes (northwest England), the Picts and Caledonii (Scotland), and the Ordovices (parts of Wales). You noticed the Latin-sounding names? That's because the tribal tags were first handed out by the next arrivals on Britain's shores…

## ENTER THE ROMANS

Although there had been some earlier expeditionary campaigns, the main Roman invasion of the region they called Britannia was in AD 43. Within a decade most of the land was under Roman control, and most of the occupation was straightforward: several Celtic-British tribal kings realised collaboration was more profitable than battle. For example, King Togidubnus of the Regnenses tribe changed his name to Tiberius Cogidumnus and built a Roman-style villa, which can still be seen today at Fishbourne (p233) near the town of Chichester; and a historian called Nennius suggests in his *Historia Britonum* (written around the year 800) that the people of Wales revered their Roman rulers so much that one governor, Magnus Maximus, was transformed into a mythical hero called Maxen Wledig.

By around AD 80 Britannia comprised much of today's England and Wales. And although it's tempting to imagine noble natives battling courageously against occupying forces, Roman control and stability was probably welcomed by the general population, tired of feuding chiefs and insecure tribal territories, allowing Roman settlement to continue for almost four centuries.

Intermarriage was common between locals and incomers (many from other parts of the Empire – including today's Belgium, Spain and Syria – rather than Rome itself) so that a Romano-British population evolved,

*Walks Through Britain's History* (published by AA) guides you to castles, battlefields and hundreds of other sites with a link to the past.

| **AD 43** | **60** | **122** |
|---|---|---|
| Emperor Claudius orders the first major Roman invasion of England. His army wages a ruthless campaign, and the Romans control pretty much everywhere in southern England by AD 50. | The warrior-queen Boudica (also known as Boadicea) leads a rebel army against the Romans, destroys the Roman town of Colchester and gets as far as Londinium, the Roman port on the present site of London. | Rather than conquer wild north British tribes, Emperor Hadrian settles for building a coast-to-coast barricade. For nearly 300 years, Hadrian's Wall marks the northernmost limit of the Roman Empire. |

---

**LEGACY OF THE LEGIONS**

To control their new territory, the Romans built garrisons across England. Many developed into towns, later called 'chesters', today remembered by names like Winchester, Manchester, and of course Chester. ('Cester' was a variation – hence Cirencester, Bicester, Leicester etc.) The Romans are also well known for their roads, initially built so soldiers could march quickly from place to place, and later so that trade could develop. Wherever possible the roads were straight lines (because it was efficient, not – as the old joke goes – to stop ancient Britons hiding round corners), and included Ermine Street between London and York, Watling Street between Kent and Wales, and the Fosse Way between Exeter and Lincoln. As you travel around England today, you'll notice that many modern highways still follow Roman roads. In a country better known for old lanes and turnpike routes winding through the landscape, these ruler-straight highways clearly stand out on the map.

---

particularly in the towns, while indigenous Celtic-British culture remained in rural areas.

Along with stability and wealth, the Romans introduced another cultural facet – a new religion called Christianity, after it was recognised by Emperor Constantine in the 4th century. But by this time, although Romano-British culture was thriving in Britannia, back in its Mediterranean heartland the Empire was already in decline.

It was an untidy finale. The Romans were not driven out by the ancient Britons (after more than 300 years, Romano-British culture was so established there was nowhere for many to go 'home' to). In reality, Britannia was simply dumped by the rulers in Rome, and the colony slowly fizzled out of existence. But historians are neat folk, and the end of Roman power in Britain is generally dated at 410.

## THE EMERGENCE OF ENGLAND

When Roman power faded, the province of Britannia went into decline, and entered a period known by some historians as the Dark Ages. Romano-British towns were abandoned and rural areas became no-go zones as local warlords fought over fiefdoms. The vacuum didn't go unnoticed and once again invaders crossed from the European mainland – this time Germanic tribes called Angles and Saxons.

Historians disagree on what happened next; either the Anglo-Saxons largely overcame or absorbed the Romano-British and Celts, or the indigenous tribes simply adopted Anglo-Saxon language and culture. Either way, by the late 6th century much of England was predominantly Anglo-Saxon, divided into separate kingdoms dominated by Wessex (in today's southern England), Mercia (today's Midlands) and Northumbria (today's northern England and southern Scotland).

| 200 | c 410 | 5th century |
|---|---|---|
| The Romans build a defensive wall around the city of London with four main entrance gates, still remembered today by the districts of Aldgate, Ludgate, Newgate and Bishopsgate. | The end of Roman imperial control in the province of Britannia, as the Empire enters a period of decline leading to its final termination – marked by the abdication of the last emperor in 476. | Teutonic tribes from the area now called Germany – known today as the Anglo-Saxons – migrate to England, and quickly spread across much of the country. |

Some areas remained unaffected by the incomers (the Celtic language was still being spoken in parts of southern England when the Normans invaded 500 years later) but the overall impact was immense. Today, the core of the English language is Anglo-Saxon, many placenames have Anglo-Saxon roots, and the very term 'Anglo-Saxon' has become a (much abused and factually incorrect) byword for 'pure English'.

Northumbria was initially the dominant Anglo-Saxon kingdom, however, in the 8th century the kingdom of Mercia became stronger and its ruler, King Offa, marked a clear border between England and Wales – a defensive ditch called Offa's Dyke that can still be seen today. A century later, at the top of the league was the kingdom of Wessex, ruled by King Egbert, grandfather of the future King Alfred.

## THE WAKING OF WALES

Meanwhile, away from the emerging kingdoms of England, the Celts on the outer fringes of the British Isles (particularly in Ireland) had kept alive their own distinct yet Roman-influenced culture, along with the ideals of Christianity. And while the Anglo-Saxons took advantage of the post-Roman void in eastern Britain, towards the end of the 5th century others played the same game on the west side of the island: the Scotti people (from today's Ireland) invaded the land of the Picts (today's Scotland).

In response to the invasion, people from the kingdom of Gododdin (in today's Scotland) came to northwest Wales. Their initial plan was to drive out the Scotti invaders, but they stayed and settled in the area, which became the kingdom of Gwynedd. (The modern county in northern Wales still proudly bears this name.)

The struggle between Welsh settlers and Irish raiders along the coast carried on for the rest of the Dark Ages. At the same time, more settlers came to

---

### BRITAIN'S MYTHICAL MONARCH

It was during the Dark Ages that a particularly powerful leader, whose name just may have been Arthur, came to prominence. He may have been a Romano-Briton, he may have been a Celt. He may have come from southern England, or was maybe born in Wales. Or maybe Scotland. He might have fought against the Anglo-Saxons, or against pagan Celts. In truth, virtually nothing is known about this mythical figure from the mists of time, but King Arthur has nevertheless become the focus of many legends. Along with Merlin the magician and the Knights of the Round Table, Arthur inspired a huge body of literature, not least by the Welsh in the epic tale the *Mabinogion* (see also the boxed text, Myths & Legends, p742) and by Thomas Malory in his masterpiece *Le Morte d'Arthur*. Numerous sites in Britain, from Tintagel in Cornwall to Arthur's Seat in Edinburgh, via Snowdonia, Glastonbury and Pembrokeshire, claim Arthurian links that you'll undoubtedly come across as you travel around Britain today.

---

| late 5th century | 597 | 7th century |
| --- | --- | --- |
| The Scotti people (from today's Ireland) invade the territory of the Picts (most notably in today's Scotland) and establish the kingdom of Dalriada (covering much of the area of the modern-day region of Argyll). | Pope Gregory sends missionary Augustine to England to revive interest in Christianity among the southern Anglo-Saxons. His colleague Aidan similarly converts many people in the north. They later become St Augustine and St Aidan. | Anglo-Saxons from the expanding English kingdom of Northumbria attempt to colonise southeast Alba (today's southern Scotland). The (by now) indigenous Scotti people are forced to defend their territory. |

---

**MISSIONARY ENDEAVOURS**

The invasion of the 'pagan' Anglo-Saxons forced the Christian religion (introduced by the Romans) out of England to the edges of the British Isles – Wales, Scotland and Ireland. The pope of the time, Gregory, decided this was a poor show, and sent missionaries to revive interest in the faith in the late 6th century. One holy pioneer was the theologian Augustine (later venerated as St Augustine), who successfully converted Angles in Kent, and some good-looking specimens were sent to Rome as proof – giving rise to Pope Gregory's famous quip about Angles looking like angels. Meanwhile in northern England another missionary called Aidan (later beatified as St Aidan) was even more successful. With admirable energy and fervour, he converted the entire populations of Mercia and Northumbria, and still had time to establish a monastery in 635 at Lindisfarne (see p665), a beautiful site on the coast at Holy Island that can still be visited today.

---

Wales from today's Cornwall and western France, and Christian missionaries arrived from Ireland in the 6th and 7th centuries.

While these newcomers arrived from the west and south, the people of Wales were also under pressure to the east – harassed by the Anglo-Saxons of England pretty much constantly for hundreds of years. In response, by the 8th century the disparate tribes of Wales had started to band together and sow the seeds of nationhood. They called themselves *cymry* (fellow countrymen), and today *Cymru* is the Welsh word for Wales.

## THE STIRRING OF SCOTLAND

While Wales was becoming established in the west of the island of Britain, similar events were taking place to the north, in the land the Romans had called Caledonia. The Picts were the region's dominant tribe, and called their kingdom Alba.

In the power vacuum that followed the fizzle-out of Roman rule in Britannia, Alba was invaded from two sides: first, towards the end of the 5th century, the Scotti crossed the sea from today's Ireland and established the kingdom of Dalriada (in today's Argyll); then in the 7th century Anglo-Saxons from the expanding English kingdom of Northumbria had moved in to colonise southeast Alba. But by this time the Scotti were well dug in, foreshadowing the time when yet another name – Scotland – would be applied to northern Britain.

## THE VIKING ERA

Just as the new territories of England, Wales and Scotland were becoming established, Britain was yet again invaded by a bunch of pesky Continentals. This time, Vikings appeared on the scene.

It's a classic historical image: blonde Scandinavians, horned helmets, big swords and rampant pillaging. Tradition has it that Vikings turned up,

| 8th century | 8th century | 843 |
|---|---|---|
| King Offa of Mercia orders the construction of a clear border between his kingdom and Wales – a defensive ditch called Offa's Dyke that is still visible today. | Faced by enemies on both sides (English to the east, Vikings to the west) the disparate tribes of Wales start to band together and sow the seeds of nationhood, calling themselves *cymry*, or 'fellow countrymen'. | Kenneth MacAilpin, the king of the Scotti, takes advantage of having a Pictish mother, and declares himself ruler of both the Scots and the Picts, and therefore king of all Alba. |

---

**WHOSE PATRON SAINT IS THIS?**

Along the coast of Wales, the struggle between settlers and raiding Irish pirates was a major feature of life during the Dark Ages. Even St Patrick, the patron saint of Ireland, is reputed to have been a Welshman, captured by brigands and taken to Ireland as a slave.

At around the same time, other visitors from Ireland to Wales were Christian missionaries. Among them was a monk named Dewi, who became known as David and later became patron saint of Wales.

So in a fair swap, the patron saint of Wales was an Irishman, while the patron saint of Ireland could well have been Welsh. It seems odd, but then the patron saint of England, St George, was born in what is now Turkey, and the patron saint of Scotland, St Andrew, was a Palestinian, so maybe in the British Isles it's all par for the course.

---

killed everyone, took everything, and left. There's *some* truth in that, but many Vikings settled for good, and their legacy remains throughout much of northern England – in the form of local dialect (geographical terms such as 'fell' and 'dale' come from Norse *fjell* and *dalr*), and even in traces of Nordic DNA in some of today's inhabitants.

The main wave of Vikings came from today's Denmark, and conquered east and northeast England. By the middle of the 9th century, they started to expand southwards into central England, but blocking their route were the Anglo-Saxon armies led by the king of Wessex, Alfred the Great – and one of English history's best-known characters. The conflict that followed was seminal to the foundation of the nation state of England, but it didn't all go Alfred's way. For a few months he was on the run, wading through swamps, hiding in peasant hovels, and famously burning cakes. It was the stuff of legend, which is just what you need when the chips are down. By 886, Alfred had garnered his forces and pushed the Vikings back to the north.

Thus England was divided in two: north and east was Viking 'Danelaw', while south and west was Anglo-Saxon territory. Alfred was hailed as king of the English – the first time the Anglo-Saxons regarded themselves as a truly united people.

Alfred's son and successor was Edward the Elder. After more battles, he gained control of the Danelaw, and thus – for the first time – the whole of England. But it was hardly cause for celebration: the Vikings were still around, and later in the 10th century more raids from Scandinavia threatened the fledgling English unity. Over the following decades, control swung from Saxon (King Edgar), to Dane (King Knut), and back to Saxon again (King Edward the Confessor). As England came to the end of the first millennium AD, the future was anything but certain.

| 850 | 9th century | 927 |
|---|---|---|
| Vikings from today's Denmark invade the eastern and north-eastern regions of England and occupy much of the territory, establishing their capital at Yorvik – today's city of York. | King Rhodri Mawr of Wales defeats a Viking force and begins Welsh unification process. His grandson, King Hywel, draws up a set of laws, remarkable for the time, noted for a sense of 'human rights'. | Athelstan, grandson of Alfred the Great, son of Edward the Elder, is the first monarch to be specifically crowned King of England, building on his ancestors' success in regaining Viking territory. |

**DOMINATING THE LANDSCAPE**

If you're travelling through Wales, it won't take you long to notice the country's most striking architectural asset: the castle. There are around 600 in all, giving Wales the dubious honour of being Europe's most densely fortified country. Most were built in medieval times, first by William the Conqueror, then by other Anglo-Norman kings, to keep a lid on the Welsh. In the late 13th century, Edward I built the spectacular castles at Caernarfon (p770), Harlech (p765), Conwy (p751) and Beaumaris (p773) – now jointly listed as a Unesco World Heritage Site. Other castles to see include Criccieth (p768), Raglan (p696), Pembroke (p712), Chepstow (p697) and Caerphilly (p683). Great for visitors, of course, but a sore point for patriotic Welsh; the writer Thomas Pennant called them 'the magnificent badge of our subjection'.

## HIGHS & LOWS IN WALES

Meanwhile, as England fought off the Viking threat, Wales was also dealing with the Nordic intruders. Building on the initial cooperation forced upon them by Anglo-Saxon oppression, in the 9th and 10th centuries the small kingdoms of Wales began cooperating, through necessity, to repel the Vikings.

King Rhodri Mawr (who died in 878) defeated a Viking force off Anglesey and began the unification process. His grandson Hywel the Good is thought to have been responsible for drawing up a set of laws to bind the disparate Welsh tribes. Things were going well, but just as Wales was becoming a recognisable entity, the young country was faced with more destructive onslaughts than it could handle, and in 927 the Welsh kings recognised the Anglo-Saxon King Athelstan as their overlord in exchange for an anti-Viking alliance.

## SCOTLAND BECOMES A KINGDOM

While the Welsh were forming their own nation, similar events were being played out in Alba. In the 9th century, the king of the Scotti of Dalriada was one Kenneth MacAilpin (usually Anglicised to MacAlpin). His father was a Scotti, but his mother was a Pict princess, so MacAlpin took advantage of the Pictish custom of matrilineal succession to declare himself ruler of both the Scots *and* the Picts, and therefore king of all Alba.

In a surprisingly short time, the Scots gained cultural and political ascendancy. The Picts were absorbed, and Pictish culture simply – and quite suddenly – came to an end. As part of this process, Alba became known as Scotia.

In the 11th century, Scottish nation-building was further consolidated by King Malcolm III (whose most famous act was the 1057 murder of Macbeth – as immortalised by William Shakespeare). With his English queen, Margaret, he founded the Canmore dynasty that would rule Scotland for the next two centuries.

| **1066** | **1085–86** | **1095** |
|---|---|---|
| The Battle of Hastings – a crucial date in English history. Incumbent King Harold is defeated by an invading Norman army, and England has a new monarch: William the Conqueror. | King William orders a census of England's current stock and future potential: called the Domesday Book (from the old word *dom*, meaning accounting or reckoning), it's still a highly significant historical document today. | The start of the First Crusade – a campaign of Christian European armies against Muslim occupation of Jerusalem and the Holy Land. A series of crusades continue until 1272. |

## 1066 & ALL THAT

While Wales and Scotland laid the foundations of nationhood, back in England things were unsettled, as the royal pendulum was still swinging between Saxon and Danish-Viking monarchs. When King Edward the Confessor died, the crown passed to Harold, his brother-in-law. That should've settled things, but Edward had a cousin in Normandy (the northern part of today's France) called William, who thought *he* should have succeeded to the throne of England.

The end result was the Battle of Hastings in 1066, the most memorable of dates for anyone who has studied English history – or for anyone who hasn't. William sailed from Normandy with an army of Norman soldiers, and landed near the town of Hastings, on England's southern coast. The Saxons were defeated, and King Harold was killed – according to tradition by an arrow in the eye.

William became king of England, earning himself the prestigious epithet Conqueror. His successor William II had a less auspicious reign; he was mysteriously assassinated during a hunting trip and succeeded by Henry I – the first of a long line of kings called Henry.

In the years after the invasion, the French-speaking Normans and the English-speaking Anglo-Saxon inhabitants kept pretty much to themselves. A strict hierarchy of class developed, known as the feudal system. At the top was the monarch, below that the nobles (barons, bishops, dukes and earls), then knights and lords, and at the bottom were peasants or 'serfs', effectively slaves.

The feudal system may have established the basis of a class system which to a certain extent still exists in England today, but intermarriage was not completely unknown. Henry himself married a Saxon princess. Nonetheless, such unifying moves stood for nothing after Henry's death: a bitter struggle for succession followed, finally won by Henry II, who took the throne as the first king of the House of Plantagenet.

*Myths and Legends of the British Isles* by Richard Barber is ideal if you want a break from historical facts. Gen up on King Arthur and the Knights of the Round Table, plus much more from the mists of time.

## NORMAN IMPACT ON WALES & SCOTLAND

By the time the Normans arrived in England, the Welsh no longer needed anti-Viking protection and had returned to their independent ways. Not if William the Conqueror had anything to do with it. To secure his new kingdom, and keep the Welsh in theirs, William built castles and appointed feudal barons along the border. The Lords Marcher, as they were known, became massively rich and powerful, and the parts of western England along the Welsh border are still called the Marches today.

In Scotland, King Malcolm III and Queen Margaret were more accommodating to Norman ways – or, at least, they liked the way the Normans ran a country. Malcolm's successor, David I (r 1124–53), was impressed, too, and adopted the Norman feudal system, as well as granting land to great

| **12th century** | **1124–53** | **1215** |
|---|---|---|
| Oxford University is founded. There's evidence of teaching in the area since 1096, but King Henry II's 1167 ban on students attending the University of Paris solidified Oxford's importance. | The rule of David I of Scotland. The Scottish aristocracy adopt the Norman feudal system, and the king grants land to great Norman families. | King John signs the Magna Carta (the 'great charter'), determining distribution of power and a fledgling bill of human rights, limiting the monarch's absolute rule and eventually leading to the creation of Parliament. |

**LOOKING SOUTH**

The arrival of William the Conqueror was a seminal event, as it marked the end of Britain's century-old ties to the Nordic countries (only in Orkney and Shetland did the Viking presence continue, until the 15th century). The mainland's perspective turned to France, Western Europe and the Mediterranean, giving rise to massive cultural implications that were to last into our own time. In addition, the Norman landing capped an era of armed invasion. Since 1066, in the near-on thousand years to the present day, Britain has never again been seriously invaded by a foreign power.

Norman families. By 1212, a courtier called Walter of Coventry remarked that the Scottish court was 'French in race and manner of life, in speech and in culture'.

But while the French-Norman effect changed England and lowland Scotland over the following centuries, further north the Highland clans remained inaccessible in their glens – a law unto themselves for another 600 years.

## ROYAL & HOLY SQUABBLING

Meanwhile, back in England, the rule of Henry I had come to an end, and the fight to take his place continued the enduring English habit of competition for the throne, and introduced an equally enduring tendency of bickering between royalty and the church. Things came to a head in 1170 when Henry II had 'turbulent priest' Thomas Becket murdered in Canterbury Cathedral – still an important shrine today (see p206).

Perhaps the next king, Richard I, wanted to make amends for his forebear's unholy actions by leading a crusade – a Christian 'Holy War' – to liberate Jerusalem and the Holy Land (today's Levant) from occupation by Muslim 'heathens' under their leader Saladin. This campaign became known as the Third Crusade, and although the Christian armies under Richard captured the cities of Acre and Jaffa, they did not take Jerusalem.

Unfortunately, Richard's overseas activities meant he was too busy to bother about governing England – although his bravery, and ruthlessness, earned him the sobriquet Richard the Lionheart – and in his absence the country fell into disarray.

*A Brief History of British Kings & Queens by Mike Ashley provides a concise and comprehensive overview, with timelines, biographies and family trees. Good for pub-quiz training, too.*

Richard was succeeded as king by his brother John, but under his harsh rule things got even worse for the general population. According to legend, it was during this time that a nobleman called Robert of Loxley, better known as Robin Hood, hid in Sherwood Forest and engaged in a spot of wealth redistribution. (For a medieval re-enactment of this merry tale, see p458.)

## EXPANSIONIST EDWARD

The next king was Henry III, followed in 1272 by Edward I, a skilled ruler and ambitious general. During a busy 35-year reign, he expounded English

| 1240 | 1272 | 1286 |
|---|---|---|
| King Llywelyn of Wales (Llywelyn the Great) dies; his grandson, also called Llywelyn, succeeds the throne, but is recognised by Henry III of England only as the Prince (not King) of Wales. | Edward I invades Wales, and the former kingdom becomes a dependent principality. Edward makes his own son Prince of Wales. | The death of King Alexander III of Scotland, and then his granddaughter Margaret, leads to a dispute over the Scottish throne. Edward I of England gets involved… |

nationalism and was unashamedly expansionist in his outlook, leading campaigns into Wales and Scotland.

Some decades earlier, the Welsh king Llywelyn the Great (who died in 1240) had attempted to set up a state in Wales along the lines of the new feudal system in England, and his grandson Llywelyn ('Llewellyn the Last') was recognised by Henry III as the first Prince (but not King) of Wales. But Edward I had no time for such niceties, and descended on Wales in a bloody invasion that lasted much of the 1270s. In the end, Wales became a dependent principality, owing allegiance to England. There were no more Welsh kings, and just to make it clear who was boss, Edward made his own son the Prince of Wales. Ever since, the British sovereign's eldest son has been automatically given the title. (Most recently, Prince Charles was formally proclaimed Prince of Wales at Caernarfon Castle in 1969, much to the displeasure of Welsh nationalists.)

Edward I then looked north. For the past 200 years, Scotland had been ruled by the Canmores, but the dynasty effectively ended in 1286 with the death of Alexander III. He was succeeded by his four-year-old granddaughter, Margaret (the 'Maid of Norway'), who was engaged to the son of Edward I, but she died in 1290 before the wedding could take place.

There followed a dispute for the Scottish throne for which there were 13 *tanists* (contestants), but in the end it came down to two: John Balliol and Robert Bruce of Annandale. Arbitration was needed and Edward I was called in; he chose Balliol. But having finished the job, Edward then sought to formalise his feudal overlordship and travelled through Scotland forcing clan leaders to swear allegiance. In a final blow to Scottish pride, Edward removed the Stone of Scone (also known as the Stone of Destiny or Fatal Stone), on which the kings of Scotland had been crowned for centuries, from an abbey at Scone, and sent it to London (see Stone of Destiny, p785).

That was just too much. In response, Balliol got in touch with Edward's old enemy, France, and arranged a treaty of cooperation, the start of an anti-English partnership – the 'Auld Alliance' – that was to last for many centuries (and to the present day when it comes to rugby and football).

Edward wasn't the sort of bloke to brook opposition, though. In 1296 the English army defeated Balliol, forcing the Scottish barons to accept Edward's rule, and his ruthless retaliation earned him the title 'Hammer of the Scots'. But still the Scottish people refused to lie down: in 1297, at the Battle of Stirling Bridge, the English were defeated by a Scots army under the leadership of William Wallace. More than 700 years later, Wallace is still remembered as the epitome of Scottish patriots (see National Wallace Monument, p867).

## HARD TIMES

Back in England, Edward I was succeeded by Edward II, but the new model lacked the military success of his forebear, and his favouring of personal

The story of William Wallace is told in the Mel Gibson epic film *Braveheart*. In devolution debates of the 1990s, the patriotic pride engendered by this movie did more for Scottish nationalism than any politician's speech.

| 1296–97 | 1314 | 1337–1453 |
|---|---|---|
| The Scottish army is defeated by the English under Edward I ('Hammer of the Scots'). The English army is defeated by the Scots at the Battle of Stirling Bridge, under the leadership of William Wallace. | Wars between England and Scotland continue. Edward II and the English army are defeated by the Scots under Robert the Bruce at the Battle of Bannockburn. | England battles against France in a long conflict known as the Hundred Years' War. (Actually a series of mini-wars, which lasted more than a century, too…) |

friends over barons didn't help. Edward failed in the marriage department, too, and his rule came to a grisly end when his wife, Isabella, and her lover, Roger Mortimer, had him murdered in Berkeley Castle.

By this time, Robert the Bruce (grandson of Robert Bruce of Annandale) had crowned himself King of Scotland (1306), been beaten in battle, gone on the run, and while hiding in a cave been famously inspired to renew his efforts by a spider persistently spinning its web. Bruce's army went on to defeat Edward II and the English at the Battle of Bannockburn in 1314, another milestone in Scotland's long fight to remain independent.

Next in line was Edward III. Highlights of his reign – actually lowlights – include the start of the Hundred Years' War with France in 1337 and the arrival of a plague called the Black Death about a decade later, which eventually wiped out 1.5 million people, more than a third of the country's population.

Another change of king didn't improve things either. Richard II had barely taken the throne when the Peasants' Revolt erupted in 1381. This attempt by commoners to overthrow the feudal system was brutally suppressed, further injuring an already deeply divided country.

*What the Tudors & Stuarts Did For Us,* by TV presenter and historian Adam Hart-Davis, covers great achievements and innovations in this key period of history.

## STEWARTS ENTER THE SCENE

While the Hundred Years' War raged (or rather, rumbled) between England and France, things weren't much better in Scotland. After the death of Robert the Bruce in 1329, the country was ravaged by endless internal conflicts and plague epidemics.

Bruce's son became David II of Scotland, but he was soon caught up in battles against fellow Scots disaffected by his father and aided by England's Edward III. So when David died in 1371, the Scots quickly crowned Robert Stewart (Robert the Bruce's grandson) as king, marking the start of the House of Stewart, which was to crop up again in England a bit later down the line.

## HOUSES OF YORK & LANCASTER

In 1399, the ineffectual Richard II, the last of the House of Plantagenet, was ousted by a powerful baron called Henry Bolingbroke, who became Henry IV – the first monarch of the House of Lancaster.

Less than a year later, his rule was disrupted by a final cry of resistance from the downtrodden Welsh, led by royal-descendant Owain Glyndŵr (Owen Glendower to the English). It wasn't a good result for Wales: the rebellion was crushed; vast areas of farmland were destroyed; Glyndŵr died an outlaw; and the Welsh elite were barred from public life for many years.

Henry IV was followed, neatly, by Henry V, who decided it was time to stir up the dormant Hundred Years' War. His defeat of France at the Battle of Agincourt and the patriotic tear-jerker speech he was given by Shakespeare

| 1348 | 1381 | 1399 |
|---|---|---|
| The Black Death – a highly contagious bubonic plague – arrives in Britain, having swept across Europe, killing over 1.5 million people (more than a third of the country's population at the time). | Richard II is confronted by the Peasants' Revolt. This attempt by commoners to overthrow the feudal system is brutally suppressed, further injuring an already deeply divided country. | Richard II, the last of the Plantagenet dynasty, is ousted by a powerful baron called Henry Bolingbroke, who becomes Henry IV – the first monarch of the House of Lancaster. |

('cry God for Harry, England and St George') ensured his pole position among the most famous English kings of all time.

Still keeping things neat, Henry V was followed by Henry VI, whose main claim to fame was overseeing the building of great places of worship (King's College Chapel, p404, in Cambridge; Eton Chapel, p275, near Windsor – both architectural wonders can still be admired today), interspersed with great bouts of insanity.

When the Hundred Years' War finally ground to a halt in 1453, you'd have thought things would be calm for a while. But no. The English forces returning from France threw their energies into another battle – a civil conflict dubbed the Wars of the Roses.

Briefly it went like this: Henry VI of the House of Lancaster (whose emblem was a red rose) was challenged by Richard, Duke of York (proud holder of a white-rose flag). Henry was weak and it was almost a walkover for Richard, but Henry's wife, Margaret of Anjou, was made of sterner mettle and her forces defeated the challenger. But it didn't rest there: Richard's son Edward entered with an army, turned the tables, drove out Henry, and became King Edward IV – the first monarch of the House of York.

> Shakespeare's *Henry V* was filmed most recently in 1989 – a superb modern epic, starring English cinema darling Kenneth Branagh as the eponymous king.

## DARK DEEDS IN THE TOWER

Life was never easy for the guy at the top. Edward IV hardly had time to catch his breath before facing a challenger to his own throne. Enter scheming Richard Neville, Earl of Warwick, who liked to be billed as 'the kingmaker'. In 1470 he teamed up with the energetic Margaret of Anjou to shuttle Edward into exile and bring Henry VI to the throne. But a year later Edward IV came bouncing back, and this time there was no messing about; he killed Warwick, captured Margaret, and had Henry snuffed out in the Tower of London.

Although Edward IV's position seemed secure, he ruled for only a decade before being succeeded by his 12-year-old son, now Edward V. But the boy-king's reign was even shorter than his dad's. In 1483 he was mysteriously murdered, along with his brother, and once again the Tower of London was the scene of the crime.

With the 'little princes' dispatched, this left the throne open for their dear old Uncle Richard. Whether he was the princes' killer is still the subject of debate, but his rule as Richard III was short-lived. Despite being rewarded with another famous Shakespearean sound bite ('A horse, a horse, my kingdom for a horse'), few tears were shed in 1485 when he was tumbled from the top job by a nobleman from Wales called Henry Tudor, who became King Henry VII.

## MOVES TOWARDS UNITY

There hadn't been a Henry on the throne for a while, and this new incumbent harked back to the days of his namesakes with a skilful reign. After the

| 1400 | 1415 | 1459–87 |
|---|---|---|
| Freedom-fighter of royal descent, Owain Glyndŵr (Owen Glendower) leads Welsh rebels against the English army, but the revolt is crushed and Glyndŵr dies an outlaw. | The invading English army under Henry V defeats the French army at the Battle of Agincourt – a crucial battle in the Hundred Years' War, although the war itself continues for almost another 40 years. | The Wars of the Roses – an English civil war between two competing dynasties: the House of Lancaster and the House of York. The Yorkists are eventually successful, enabling King Edward IV to gain the throne. |

---

**HELL OF A JOB**

A glance at the story of Britain's ruling dynasties clearly shows that life was never dull for the guy at the top. Despite immense power and privilege, the position of monarch (or, perhaps worse, *potential* monarch) probably ranks as one of history's least safe occupations. Kings and queens to meet an untimely end include Harold (killed in battle), William II (assassinated), Llywelyn 'the Last' of Wales (overthrown by Edward, King of England), Charles I (beheaded by Republicans), Edward V (murdered by a wicked uncle), Richard II (probably starved to death), John (too much eating and drinking), Mary Queen of Scots (executed), James II (deposed), Edward II (dispatched by his queen and her lover), Macbeth (murdered by a rival for the throne) and William III (died after his horse tripped over a molehill). As you visit the castles and battlefields of Britain, you may feel a touch of sympathy – but only a touch – for those all-powerful figures continually looking over their shoulder.

---

*Medieval Women by Henrietta Leyser looks through a female lens at the period from AD 500 to 1500: a life of work, marriage, sex and children (not necessarily in that order).*

York-vs-Lancaster Wars of the Roses, Henry VII's Tudor neutrality was important. He also diligently mended fences with his northern neighbours by marrying off his daughter to James IV of Scotland, thereby linking the Tudor and Stewart lines.

On top of his family links with Scotland, Henry VII was also half Welsh. He withdrew many of the anti-Welsh restrictions imposed after the Glyndŵr uprising, and his countrymen were only too grateful to enjoy new-found preferential treatment at the English court and career opportunities in English public life.

Matrimony may have been more useful than warfare for Henry VII, but the multiple marriages of his successor, Henry VIII, were a very different story. Fathering a male heir was his problem – hence the famous six wives – but the Pope's disapproval of divorce and remarriage led to Henry's split with the Roman Catholic Church. Parliament made Henry the head of the Protestant Church of England – marking the start of a period known as the English Reformation – and the beginning of a pivotal division between Catholics and Protestants that still exists in some areas of Britain.

In 1536 Henry followed this up by 'dissolving' many monasteries in Britain and Ireland, a blatant takeover of their land and wealth rather than a symptom of the struggle between church and state. Nonetheless, the general populace felt little sympathy for the wealthy and often corrupt abbeys, and in 1539–40 another monastic land grab swallowed the larger ones as well.

*Six Wives: the Queens of Henry VIII by David Starky is an accessible, modern study of the multiply marrying monarch.*

At the same time, Henry signed the Acts of Union (1536 and 1543), formally uniting England and Wales for the first time. This was welcomed by the aspiring Welsh gentry, as it meant English law and parliamentary representation for Wales, plus plenty of trade opportunities. The Welsh language, however, ceased to be recognised in the law courts.

| 1485 | 1509–47 | 1536–43 |
|---|---|---|
| Henry Tudor defeats Richard III at the seminal Battle of Bosworth to become King Henry VII, establishing the Tudor dynasty and finally ending the York–Lancaster rivalry for the throne. | Rule of King Henry VIII. The Pope's disapproval of Henry's numerous divorces results in the Reformation. | Henry VIII signs the Acts of Union, a series of parliamentary acts, formally uniting England and Wales – a move welcomed by the Welsh elite, banned from court since the failed Glyndŵr uprising over a century earlier. |

In Scotland, James IV had been succeeded by James V, who died in 1542, broken-hearted, it is said, after yet another defeat at the hands of the English. His baby daughter Mary became queen and Scotland was ruled by regents.

From his throne in England Henry VIII sent a proposal that Mary should marry his son. But the regents rejected his offer and – not forgetting the Auld Alliance – Mary was sent to France instead. Henry was furious and sent his armies to ravage southern Scotland and sack Edinburgh in an (unsuccessful) attempt to force agreement to the wedding – the Rough Wooing, as it was called with typical Scottish irony and understatement.

## THE ELIZABETHAN AGE

When Henry VIII died, he was succeeded by his son Edward VI, then by daughter Mary I, but their reigns were short. So, unexpectedly, Henry's third child, Elizabeth, came to the throne.

As Elizabeth I, she inherited a nasty mess of religious strife and divided loyalties, but after an uncertain start she gained confidence and turned the country around. Refusing marriage, she borrowed biblical imagery and became known as the Virgin Queen – perhaps the first English monarch to create a cult image.

Highlights of her 45-year reign included the naval defeat of the Spanish Armada, the far-flung explorations of English seafarers Walter Raleigh and Francis Drake, the expansion of England's increasingly global trading network, not to mention a cultural flourishing thanks to writers such as William Shakespeare and Christopher Marlowe.

*Elizabeth* (1998), directed by Shekhar Kapur and starring Cate Blanchett, covers the early years of the Virgin Queen's rule – a time of forbidden love, unwanted suitors, intrigue and death.

## MARY QUEEN OF SCOTS

Meanwhile, Elizabeth's cousin Mary (daughter of Scottish King James V, and a Catholic) had become Queen of Scotland. She had spent her childhood in France and had married the French dauphin (crown prince), thereby becoming queen of France as well. Why stop at two? After her husband's death, Mary returned to Scotland, and from there ambitiously claimed the English throne as well – on the grounds that Elizabeth was illegitimate.

Mary's plans failed; she was imprisoned and forced to abdicate, but then escaped to England and appealed to Elizabeth for help. This could have been a rookie error, or she might have been advised by courtiers with their own agenda. Either way, it was a bad move. Mary was – not surprisingly – seen as a security risk and imprisoned once again. In an uncharacteristic display of indecision, Elizabeth held Mary under arrest for 19 years before finally ordering her execution, moving her frequently from house to house, so that today England has many stately homes (and even a few pubs) claiming 'Mary Queen of Scots slept here'.

| 1542 | 1558–1603 | 1603 |
| --- | --- | --- |
| King James V of Scotland dies, and is succeeded by his daughter Mary. To evade marriage proposals from Henry VIII she is sent to France – later to return as Mary Stuart, Queen of Scots. | Queen Elizabeth I rules over a period of creativity, expansion and boundless optimism, characterised by the work of playwrights William Shakespeare and Christopher Marlowe, and the explorations of Walter Raleigh and Francis Drake. | King James of Scotland inherits the throne of England and becomes James I of England and VI of Scotland, the first English monarch of the House of Stuart. |

# RULING BRITANNIA

Below is a brief overview of Britain's rulers over the past 1200 years, divided into the three main kingdoms of England, Wales and Scotland until the time they're united (England and Wales in 1536; then Scotland joining England and Wales in 1707). As you travel around the country, having this basic grasp of when their reigns started and ended (thanks to natural or unplanned events) should make your visit much more rewarding.

## ENGLAND

### Saxons & Danes

Alfred the Great 871–99
Edward the Elder 899–924
Athelstan 924–39
Edmund I 939–46
Eadred 946–55
Eadwig 955–59
Edgar 959–75

Edward the Martyr 975–79
Ethelred II (the Unready) 979–1016
Knut 1016–35
Harold I 1035–40
Harthacanute 1040–42
Edward the Confessor 1042–66
Harold II 1066

### Normans

William I (the Conqueror) 1066–87
William II 1087–1100

Henry I 1100–35
Stephen 1135–54

### House of Plantagenet

Henry II 1154–89
Richard I (Lionheart) 1189–99
John 1199–1216
Henry III 1216–72

Edward I 1272–1307
Edward II 1307–27
Edward III 1327–77
Richard II 1377–99

### House of Lancaster

Henry IV (Bolingbroke) 1399–1413
Henry V 1413–22

Henry VI 1422–61 & 1470–71

### House of York

Edward IV 1461–70 & 1471–83
Edward V 1483

Richard III 1483–85

### House of Tudor

Henry VII 1485–1509
Henry VIII 1509–47
Edward VI 1547–53

Mary I 1553–58
Elizabeth I 1558–1603

### House of Stuart

James I 1603–25

Charles I 1625–49

### Protectorate (Republic)

Oliver Cromwell 1649–58

Richard Cromwell 1658–59

| 1605 | 1642–49 | 1665–66 |
|---|---|---|
| King James' attempts to smooth religious relations are set back by an anti-Catholic outcry following the infamous Gunpowder Plot, a terrorist attempt to blow up Parliament led by Guy Fawkes. | English Civil War between the monarchist 'Cavaliers' and Oliver Cromwell's army, known as the 'Roundheads', results in the execution of Charles I, the exile of Charles II, and (briefly) a parliamentary republic. | 'The Great Plague' kills 100,000 people, including 20% of London's population. The following year sees the Great Fire of London, when the capital is virtually burnt to the ground. |

### Restoration
Charles II 1660–85
James II 1685–88
Mary II 1688–94

William III (of Orange) 1688–1702
Anne 1702–14

### House of Hanover
George I 1714–27
George II 1727–60
George III 1760–1820

George IV 1820–30
William IV 1830–37
Victoria 1837–1901

### Houses of Saxe-Coburg & Windsor
Edward VII 1901–10
George V 1910–36
Edward VIII 1936

George VI 1936–52
Elizabeth II 1952–

### WALES
### Rulers of Gwynedd (main Welsh kingdom)
Rhodri ap Merfyn (Rhodri Mawr, the Great) 844–78
Gruffydd ap Llywelyn (first king of all Wales) 1039–63
Owain Gwynedd 1137–70
Dafydd ap Owain 1170–95

Llywelyn (the Great) 1195–1240
Dafydd ap Llywelyn 1240–46
Llywelyn (the Last) 1246–82

### SCOTLAND
### House of MacAilpin
Kenneth (king of Alba – Picts and Scots) 840–58
Donald II (first king of Scotland) 889–900
Malcolm I 943–54

Malcolm II 1005–34
Duncan 1034–1040
Macbeth 1040–57

### House of Canmore
Malcolm III 1058–93
Donald III 1093–97
Alexander I 1107–24
David I 1124–53
Malcolm IV 1153–65

William 1165–1214
Alexander II 1214–49
Alexander III 1249–86
Margaret (Maid of Norway) 1286–90

### Interregnum (period between monarchs)
John Balliol 1292–96

William Wallace 1297–98

### House of Bruce
Robert (the Bruce) I 1306–29

David II 1329–71

### House of Stewart/Stuart
Robert II 1371–90
Robert III 1390–1406
James I 1406–37
James II 1437–60
James III 1460–88

James IV 1488–1513
James V 1513–42
Mary (Queen of Scots) 1542–67
James VI of Scotland (& I England)
1567–1625

| 1688 | 1692 | 1707 |
| --- | --- | --- |
| King James II is overthrown, and Dutch ruler William of Orange and his wife Mary (daughter of James) jointly ascend the throne – a largely bloodless coup known as the Glorious Revolution. | Glen Coe Massacre; members of the MacDonald clan refuse to swear allegiance to King William of England; as punishment they are murdered by members of the Campbell clan. | The Act of Union finally links the countries of England, Wales and Scotland under one parliament (based in London) for the first time in history. |

## UNITED & DISUNITED BRITAIN

When Elizabeth died in 1603, despite a bountiful reign one thing the Virgin Queen failed to provide was an heir. She was succeeded by her closest relative, the Scottish King James, the safely Protestant son of the murdered Mary. He became James I of England and VI of Scotland, the first English monarch of the House of Stuart (Mary's time in France had Gallicised the Stewart name). Most importantly, James united England, Wales and Scotland into one kingdom for the first time in history – another step towards British unity, at least on paper – although the terms 'Britain' and 'British' were still not yet widely used in this context.

But the divide between king and Parliament continued to smoulder, and the power struggle worsened during the reign of Charles I, eventually degenerating into the English Civil War. The antiroyalist forces were led by Oliver Cromwell, a Puritan who preached against the excesses of the monarch and established church, and his parliamentarian (or Roundhead) army was pitched against the king's forces (the Cavaliers) in a war that tore England apart – although fortunately for the last time in history. It ended with victory for the Roundheads, the king executed, and England declared a republic – with Cromwell hailed as 'Protector'.

The Civil War had been a bitter conflict, but it failed to exhaust Cromwell's appetite for mayhem; a devastating rampage to gain control of Ireland followed quickly in its wake. Meanwhile, the Scots suffered their own parallel civil war between the royalists and radical 'Covenanters' who sought freedom from state interference in church government.

## THE RETURN OF THE KING

By 1653 Cromwell was finding Parliament too restricting and assumed dictatorial powers, much to his supporters' dismay. On his death in 1658, he was followed half-heartedly by his son, but in 1660 Parliament decided to re-establish the monarchy – as republican alternatives were proving far worse.

Charles II (the exiled son of Charles I) came to the throne, and his rule – known as 'the Restoration' – saw scientific and cultural activity bursting forth after the straight-laced ethics of Cromwell's time. Exploration and expansion were also on the agenda. Backed by the army and navy (which had been modernised by Cromwell), colonies stretched down the American coast, while the East India Company set up headquarters in Bombay (now Mumbai), laying foundations for what was to become the British Empire.

The next king, James II, had a harder time. Attempts to ease restrictive laws on Catholics ended with his defeat at the Battle of the Boyne by William III, the Protestant ruler of Holland, better known as William of Orange. Ironically, William was married to James' own daughter Mary, but it didn't stop him doing the dirty on his father-in-law.

Charles I wore two shirts on the day of his execution, reputedly to avoid shivering and being thought a coward.

| 1714 | 1721–42 | 1746 |
|---|---|---|
| The British throne passes to the House of Hanover. Violent struggles for the throne are a thing of the past, so the Hanoverian kings increasingly rely on Parliament to govern the country. | Leading member of Parliament Robert Walpole becomes Britain's first prime minister. | Battle of Culloden; the end of the Jacobite Rebellions – the attempts by supporters of the ousted King James II to regain the throne. |

---

**THE JACOBITE REBELLIONS**

Despite, or perhaps because of, the 1707 Act of Union, anti-English feeling in Scotland refused to disappear. The Jacobite rebellions, most notably those of 1715 and 1745, were attempts to overthrow the Hanoverian monarchy and bring back the Stuarts. Although these are iconic events in Scottish history, in reality there was never much support for the Jacobite cause outside the Highlands: the people of the Lowlands were mainly Protestant and feared a return to Catholicism, which the Stuarts represented.

The 1715 rebellion was led by James Edward Stuart (the Old Pretender), the son of the exiled James II of England and VII of Scotland. When the attempt failed, he fled to France, and to impose control on the Highlands the English military (under the notorious General Wade) constructed roads into previously inaccessible glens.

In 1745 James' son Charles Edward Stuart (Bonnie Prince Charlie, the Young Pretender) landed in Scotland to claim the crown for his father. He was successful initially, moving south into England as far as Derby, but the prince and his Highland supporters suffered a catastrophic defeat at the Battle of Culloden in 1746. For more details see p923. His legendary escape to the Western Isles is eternally remembered in the *Skye Boat Song*. And in a different way, General Wade is remembered, too – many of the roads his troops built are still in use today.

---

William and Mary both had equal rights to the throne and their joint accession in 1688 was known as the Glorious Revolution. Lucky they were married or there might have been another civil war.

## KILLIECRANKIE & GLEN COE

In Scotland, things weren't quite so glorious. Anti-English (essentially anti-William and anti-Protestant) feelings ran high, as did pro-James ('Jacobite') support. In 1689 Jacobite leader Graham of Claverhouse, better known as 'Bonnie Dundee', raised a Highlander army and routed English troops at Killiecrankie.

Then in 1692 came the infamous Glen Coe Massacre. On English government orders members of the Campbell clan killed most of the MacDonald clan for failing to swear allegiance to William (see A Betrayal of Hospitality, p917).

The atrocity further fuelled Catholic–Protestant divisions, and further tightened English domination of the island of Britain, although Jacobite sentiment later surfaced in two rebellions (see above) before finally succumbing to history.

For full details on Britain's rulers through history, see the regal website www.royal.gov.uk.

## FULL FINAL UNITY

In 1694 Mary died, leaving just William as monarch. He died a few years later and was followed by his sister-in-law Anne (the second daughter of James II). In 1707, during Anne's reign, the Act of Union was passed, bringing an end to the independent Scottish Parliament, and finally linking the countries of

| 1749 | 1776–83 | 1799–1815 |
|---|---|---|
| Author and magistrate Henry Fielding founds the Bow Street Runners, cited as London's first professional police force. A 1792 Act of Parliament allowed the Bow Street model to spread across England. | The American War of Independence is the British Empire's first major reverse, forcing England to withdraw – for a while, at least – from the world stage, a fact not missed by French ruler Napoleon. | The era of the Napoleonic Wars. A weakened Britain inspires Napoleon to threaten invasion, but his ambitions are curtailed by heroes Nelson and Wellington at the famous Battles of Trafalgar (1805) and Waterloo (1815), respectively. |

England, Wales and Scotland under one parliament (based in London) for the first time in history. The nation of Britain was now established as a single state, with a bigger, better and more powerful parliament, and a constitutional monarchy with clear limits on the power of the king or queen.

The new-look Parliament didn't wait long to flex its muscles. On the side, the Act of Union banned any Catholic (or anyone married to a Catholic) from ascending the throne, a rule still in force today. And although the Glorious Revolution was relatively painless in Britain, the impact on Ireland (where the Protestant ascendancy dates from William's victory) sowed the seeds for division that continued into our own time.

In 1714 Anne died without leaving an heir, marking the end of the Stuart line. The throne was then passed to distant (but still safely Protestant) German relatives, the House of Hanover.

By the mid-18th century, struggles for the British throne seemed a thing of the past, and the Hanoverian kings increasingly relied on Parliament to govern the country. As part of the process, from 1721 to 1742 a senior parliamentarian called Sir Robert Walpole effectively became Britain's first prime minister.

> James Cook's voyage to the southern hemisphere was primarily a scientific expedition. His objectives included monitoring the transit of Venus, an astronomical event that happens only twice every 180 years or so (most recently in 2004).

## THE EMPIRE STRIKES OUT

Stronger control over the British Isles was mirrored by even greater expansion abroad. The British Empire – which, despite its official title, was predominantly an *English* entity – continued to grow in America, Canada and India. The first claims were made to Australia after Captain James Cook's epic voyage in 1768.

The Empire's first major reverse came when the American colonies won the War of Independence (1776–83). This setback forced Britain to withdraw from the world stage for a while, a gap not missed by French ruler Napoleon. He threatened to invade Britain and hinder the power of the British overseas, before his ambitions were curtailed by navy hero Viscount Horatio Nelson and military hero the Duke of Wellington at the famous Battles of Trafalgar (1805) and Waterloo (1815).

## THE INDUSTRIAL AGE

While the Empire expanded abroad, at home Britain had become the crucible of the Industrial Revolution. Steam power (patented by James Watt in 1781) and steam trains (launched by George Stephenson in 1825) transformed methods of production and transport, and the towns of the English Midlands became the first industrial cities.

This population shift in England was mirrored in Scotland. From about 1750 onwards, much of the Highlands region had been emptied of people, as landowners casually expelled entire farms and villages to make way for more-profitable sheep farming, a seminal event in Scotland's history known

| 1820–70s | 1837–1901 | 1884 |
|---|---|---|
| Industrial development across Britain, notably in the English Midlands, the Scottish Lowlands and the valleys of south Wales. | Under the reign of Queen Victoria, the British Empire expands from Canada through Africa and India to Australia and New Zealand – billed as 'the Empire where the sun never sets'. | Greenwich Mean Time (named for the Royal Observatory, in the village of Greenwich outside London, where the primary meridian was first established) is adopted internationally. |

as the Clearances (see p927). Industrialisation just about finished off the job. Although many of the dispossessed left for the New World, others came from the glens to the burgeoning factories of the Lowlands. The tobacco trade with America boomed and then gave way to textile and engineering industries, as the cotton mills of Lanarkshire and the Clyde shipyards around Glasgow expanded rapidly.

The same happened in Wales. By the early 19th century copper, iron and slate were being extracted in the Merthyr Tydfil and Monmouth areas. The 1860s saw the Rhondda valleys opened up for coal mining, and Wales soon became a major exporter of coal, as well as the world's leading producer of tin plate.

Across Britain, industrialisation meant people were on the move as never before. People left the land and villages their families had occupied for generations. Often they went to the nearest factory, but not always. People from rural Dorset migrated to the Midlands, for example, while farmers from Scotland and England settled in south Wales and became miners. The rapid change from rural to urban society caused great dislocation, and although knowledge of science and medicine also improved alongside industrial advances, it also meant a rapid rise in population, so for many people the side effects of Britain's economic blossoming were poverty and deprivation.

Nevertheless, by the time Queen Victoria took the throne in 1837, Britain's factories dominated world trade and Britain's fleets dominated the oceans. The rest of the 19th century was seen as Britain's Golden Age (for some people, it still is) – a period of confidence not seen since the days of the last great queen, Elizabeth I.

In a final move of PR genius, Benjamin Disraeli, the queen's prime minister and highly skilled spin doctor, had Victoria crowned Empress of India. She'd never even been to the subcontinent, but the British people simply loved the idea.

The times were optimistic, but it wasn't all tub-thumping jingoism. Disraeli and his successor William Gladstone also introduced social reforms to address the worst excesses of the Industrial Revolution. Education became universal, trade unions were legalised and the right to vote was extended to commoners. Well, to male commoners. Women didn't get the vote for another few decades. Disraeli and Gladstone may have been enlightened gentlemen, but there *were* limits.

## WWI

When Queen Victoria died in 1901, it seemed that Britain's energy fizzled out, too, and the country entered a period of decline. Meanwhile, in continental Europe, other states were more active: the military powers of Russia, Austro-Hungary, Turkey and Germany were sabre-rattling in the Balkan states, a dispute that eventually culminated in WWI. When German forces entered Belgium, on

At its height the British Empire covered 20% of the land area of the Earth and contained a quarter of the world's population.

*Birdsong* by Sebastian Faulks is a novel partly set in the trenches of WWI. Understated and severely moving, it tells of love, passion, fear, waste, incompetent generals and the poor bloody infantry.

| 1914 | 1916 | 1918 |
|---|---|---|
| Archduke Franz Ferdinand of Austria is assassinated in the Balkan city of Sarajevo – the final spark in a decade-long crisis that starts the Great War, now called WWI. | Welsh politician David Lloyd George becomes prime minister of Britain. He remains Britain's only Welsh (and Welsh-speaking) prime minister. | WWI ends; the same year sees the emergence of the Labour Party, led by Keir Hardie, a Scottish politician representing a Welsh constituency (the coal-mining town of Merthyr Tydfil) in the London-based Parliament. |

their way to invade France, Britain and the Allied countries were drawn in, too, and the 'Great War' became a vicious conflict of stalemate and slaughter – most infamously on the fields of Flanders and the beaches of Gallipoli.

By the war's weary end in 1918 over a million Britons had died (not to mention millions more from many other countries) and there was hardly a street or village untouched by death, as the sobering lists of names on war memorials all over Britain still show. The conflict added 'trench warfare' to the dictionary, and further deepened the huge gulf that had existed between ruling and working classes since the days of the Norman feudal system.

## DISILLUSION & DEPRESSION

For soldiers who did return from WWI, disillusion led to questioning of the social order. Many supported the ideals of a new political force – the Labour Party, to represent the working class – upsetting the balance long enjoyed by the Liberal and Conservative parties since the days of Walpole; as the right to vote was extended to all men aged over 21 and women over 30. The first Labour leader was Keir Hardie, a Scottish politician representing a Welsh constituency (the coal-mining town of Merthyr Tydfil) in the London-based Parliament.

The Labour Party was elected to government for the first time in 1923, in coalition with the Liberals, with James Ramsay MacDonald as prime minister. A year later, the Conservatives were back in power, but by this time the world economy was in decline and industrial unrest was a common feature of the 1920s. When 500,000 workers marched in protest through the streets, the government's response included sending in the army – setting the stage for the style of industrial conflict that was to plague Britain for the next 50 years.

Unrest at home was mirrored by unrest in Ireland, Britain's oldest colony. WWI was no sooner over than Britain was involved in the bitter Anglo-Irish War, which ended in mid-1921 with most of Ireland achieving full independence (although six counties in the north remained British). The new political entity may have been billed as the United Kingdom of Great Britain and Northern Ireland, but the decision to divide the island of Ireland in two was to have long-term repercussions that still dominate political agendas in both the UK and the Republic of Ireland today.

The unrest of the 1920s worsened in the '30s as the world economy slumped and the Great Depression took hold – a decade of misery and political upheaval. Even the royal family took a knock when Edward VIII abdicated in 1936 so he could marry a woman who was twice divorced and – horror of horrors – American. The ensuing scandal was good for newspaper sales and hinted at the prolonged 'trial by media' suffered by royals in more recent times.

The throne was taken by Edward's less-than-charismatic brother George VI and Britain dithered through the rest of the decade, with

'the decision to divide the island of Ireland in two was to have long-term repercussions'

| 1926 | 1939–45 | 1945 |
|---|---|---|
| Increasing mistrust of the government, fuelled by soaring unemployment, leads to the General Strike. Millions of workers – train-drivers, miners, ship-builders – down tools and bring the country virtually to a halt. | WWII rages across Europe and much of Africa and Asia. Britain and its Allies, including America, Russia, Australia, India and New Zealand, eventually defeat the armies of Germany, Turkey, Japan and Italy. | WWII ends, and in the immediate postwar election the Labour Party under Clement Attlee defeats the Conservatives under Winston Churchill – despite the latter's pivotal role in Britain's WWII victory. |

mediocre government failing to confront the country's deep-set social and economic problems.

## WWII

Meanwhile, on mainland Europe, Germany saw the rise of Adolf Hitler, leader of the Nazi party. Many feared another Great War, but Prime Minister Neville Chamberlain met the German leader in 1938 and promised Britain 'peace for our time' (a phrase still remembered, although usually misquoted as 'peace in our time'). He was wrong. The following year Hitler invaded Poland. Two days later Britain was once again at war with Germany.

The German army moved with astonishing speed, swept west through France, and pushed back British forces to the beaches of Dunkirk in northern France in June 1940. An extraordinary flotilla of rescue vessels turned total disaster into a brave defeat – and Dunkirk Day is still remembered with pride and sadness in Britain every year.

By mid-1940 most of Europe was controlled by Germany. In Russia, Stalin had negotiated a peace agreement. The USA was neutral, leaving Britain virtually isolated. Neville Chamberlain, reviled for his earlier 'appeasement', stood aside to let a new prime minister – Winston Churchill – lead a coalition government. (See the boxed text, p58, for more Churchillian details.)

In 1941 the tide began to turn as the USA entered the war to support Britain, and Germany became bogged down on the eastern front fighting Russia. The following year, British forces were revitalised thanks to Churchill's focus on arms manufacturing, and the Germans were defeated in North Africa.

By 1944 Germany was in retreat. Britain and the USA controlled the skies, Russia's Red Army pushed back from the east, and the Allies were again on the beaches of France as the Normandy landings (D-Day, as it's better remembered) marked the start of the liberation of Europe from the west, and according to Churchill the beginning of the end of the war. By 1945 Hitler was dead, and his country ruined. Two atomic bombs forced the surrender of Germany's ally Japan, and finally brought WWII to a dramatic and terrible close.

> The Normandy landings was the largest military armada in history; more than 5000 ships were involved, with hundreds of thousands of troops landed in the space of about four days.

## SWINGING & SLIDING

In Britain, despite the victory, there was an unexpected swing on the political front. An electorate tired of war and hungry for change tumbled Churchill's Conservatives and voted in the Labour Party, led by Clement Attlee. This was the dawn of the 'welfare state'; key industries (such as steel, coal and railways) were nationalised, and the National Health Service was founded. But rebuilding Britain was a slow process, and the postwar 'baby boomers' experienced food rationing well into the 1950s.

The impact of depleted reserves were felt overseas, too, as parts of the British Empire became independent, including India and Pakistan in 1947

| 1946–48 | 1948 | 1948 |
| --- | --- | --- |
| The Labour Party nationalises key industries such as shipyards, coalmines and steel foundries. Britain's 'big four' train companies are combined into British Railways. | The Olympics are held in London, the first Games since Berlin in 1936; venues around Britain include Wembley Stadium, Windsor Great Park and Henley-on-Thames. | Aneurin Bevan, the health minister in the Labour government, launches the National Health Service – the core of Britain as a 'welfare state'. Since then, life expectancy in Britain has increased by 10 years. |

## CHURCHILL

Ask any British person to name a 'great hero of British history' and Winston Churchill will be high on the list, along with King Arthur, Owain Glyndŵr, William Wallace, Admiral Nelson and the Duke of Wellington – and quite possibly Margaret Thatcher and David Beckham. More than 60 years after the end of WWII, Churchill's legacy is undeniable.

Although he was from an aristocratic family, Churchill's early years were not auspicious; he was famously a 'dunce' at school – an image he actively cultivated in later life. As a young man he joined the British Army, serving mainly in India, Sudan and South Africa, also acting as a war correspondent for various newspapers, and writing several books about his exploits.

In 1901 Churchill was elected to Parliament as a Conservative MP, but in 1904 he defected to the Liberals, then the main opposition party. A year later, after a Liberal election victory, he became a government minister, then worked his way up through the ranks, including Minister of Munitions in WWI, before rejoining the Conservatives in 1922. Through the rest of the 1920s, Churchill held various ministerial positions. High points of this period included alleged plans in 1926 to combat striking coalminers with machine gun–wielding troops and calling Benito Mussolini a 'genius', a sobriquet trumped in 1929 by his reference to Mohandas Gandhi as 'a half-naked fakir'.

The 1930s were quiet on the political front for Churchill – apart from his criticism of Prime Minister Neville Chamberlain's 'appeasement' of Hitler and his call for British rearmament to face a growing German threat – so he concentrated on writing. His multivolume *History of the English-Speaking Peoples* was drafted during this period; although biased and flawed by modern standards, it remains his best-known work.

In 1939 Britain entered WWII and by 1940 Churchill was prime minister, taking additional responsibility as Minister of Defence. Hitler had expected an easy victory, but Churchill's extraordinary dedication (not to mention his radio speeches – most famously offering 'nothing but blood, toil, tears and sweat' and promising to 'fight on the beaches') inspired the British people to resist. Between July and October 1940 the Royal Air Force withstood Germany's aerial raids to win what became known as the Battle of Britain – a major turning point in the war, and a chance for land forces to rebuild their strength. It was an audacious strategy, but it paid off and Churchill was lauded as a national hero – praise that continued to the end of the war and until his death in 1965, and an honour bestowed upon him still today.

and Malaya in 1957, followed by much of Africa and the Caribbean. Through the next decade, people from these ex-colonies were drawn to the mother country. In many cases they were specifically invited; postwar Britain was still rebuilding and needed the additional labour.

But while the Empire's sun may have been setting, Britain's royal family was still going strong. In 1952 George VI was succeeded by his daughter Elizabeth II, and following the trend set by earlier queens Elizabeth I and Victoria, she has remained on the throne for more than five decades, overseeing a period of massive social and economic change.

| 1952 | 1960s | 1960s |
|---|---|---|
| Princess Elizabeth becomes Queen Elizabeth II, when her father, George VI, dies. (She is on safari in Kenya when she hears the news.) Her coronation takes place in Westminster Abbey, London, in June 1953. | Overseas, it's the era of African and Caribbean independence from Britain, including Nigeria (1960), Tanzania (1961), Jamaica and Trinidad & Tobago (1962), Kenya (1963), Malawi (1964), The Gambia (1965) and Barbados (1966). | At home, it's the era of Beatlemania. Successful songs like 'Please, Please Me' and 'I Want to Hold Your Hand' ensure that pop band The Beatles becomes a household name in Britain, then America – then the world. |

By the late 1950s, recovery was strong enough for Prime Minister Harold Macmillan to famously remind the British people they'd 'never had it so good'. Some saw this as a boast for a confident future, others as a warning about difficult times ahead. But many people didn't care either way, as by this time the 1960s had arrived, and grey old Britain was suddenly more fun and lively than it had been for generations – especially if you were over 10 and under 30. There was the music of the Beatles, the Rolling Stones, Cliff Richard and the Shadows, while cinema audiences flocked to see Michael Caine, Peter Sellers and Glenda Jackson.

Alongside the glamour, 1960s business seemed swinging, too. But by the 1970s economic decline had set in once again. A deadly combination of inflation, the oil crisis and international competition revealed the weakness of Britain's economy, and a lot that was rotten in British society, too. The ongoing struggle between disgruntled working classes and ruling classes was brought to the boil once again; the rest of the decade was marked by strikes, disputes and general all-round gloom – especially when the electricity was cut, as power stations went short of fuel or workers walked out.

Neither the Conservatives – also known as the Tories – under Edward Heath, nor Labour under Harold Wilson and Jim Callaghan, proved capable of controlling the strife. The British public had had enough, and the elections of May 1979 returned the Conservatives, led by a little-known politician named Margaret Thatcher.

## THE THATCHER YEARS

Soon everyone had heard of Mrs Thatcher. Love her or hate her, no one could argue that her methods weren't direct and dramatic. The industries nationalised in the late 1940s were now seen as inefficient and a drain on resources, and were sold off with a sense of purpose that made Henry VIII's dissolution of the monasteries seem like a Sunday-school picnic.

Naturally, these moves were opposed by those working in the nationalised industries (and by many other sections of society) via strikes, marches and organised industrial disputes. But Mrs Thatcher's government waged a relentless assault on the power of trade unions, fronted by the closure of coalmines throughout Britain – most notably in the English Midlands, Yorkshire, south Wales and parts of Scotland. In response, the nationwide strike by miners in the early 1980s was one of the most bitter labour disputes in British history, but the pit closures went ahead. (Since 1984 around 140 coal pits have closed across Britain, with a quarter of a million jobs lost.)

Looking back from a 21st-century vantage point, most commentators agree that by economic measures Mrs Thatcher's policies were largely successful, but by social measures they were a failure. The newly competitive Britain created by the Thatcher government's monetarist policies was now also a greatly polarised Britain. On one side were the people who gained from

*Windrush - The Irresistible Rise of Multi-Racial Britain*, by Mike and Trevor Phillips, traces the history of Britain's West Indian immigrants – from 1949's first arrivals (on the ship *Empire Windrush*) to their descendants living in our own time.

*One of Us: A Biography of Mrs Thatcher*, by respected journalist and commentator Hugo Young, covers the early life of the 'iron lady' and her time in power, showing that her grip on events, and on her own party, wasn't as steely as it seemed.

*Things Can Only Get Better* by John O'Farrell is a witty, self-deprecating tale of 1980s politics – the era of Conservative domination – from a struggling Labour viewpoint.

| 1970s | 1971 | 1978–79 |
|---|---|---|
| Many immigrants of Asian origin arrive and settle in Britain, after being evicted by dictator Idi Amin from Uganda in East Africa – where they'd lived for generations since British colonial times. | Britain adopts 'decimal' currency (1 pound equals 100 pence) and drops the ancient system of 1 pound equals 20 shillings or 240 pennies, the centuries-old bane of school maths lessons. | The 'Winter of Discontent', the final nail in the coffin of a decade, is characterised by inflation, inept governments (on the left and right), trade union disputes, power blackouts, strikes and shortages. |

the prosperous wave of jobs and opportunities in the 'new' industries – the financial, IT and services sectors; on the other side were those left drowning in its wake – the unemployed and dispossessed – as the 'old' industries, such as mining and manufacturing, played an increasingly smaller role in the country's economic picture. Even Thatcher fans were occasionally unhappy about the uncompromising methods favoured by the 'iron lady', but any dissent had little impact and by 1988 she was the longest-serving British prime minister of the 20th century, although her repeated electoral victories were helped considerably by the Labour Party's weak campaigns and destructive internal struggles.

The pendulum started to swing in early 1990s: Mrs Thatcher was ousted when her introduction of the hugely unpopular 'poll tax' breached even the Conservatives' limits of tolerance. The voters regarded Labour with even more suspicion, however, allowing new Conservative leader John Major to unexpectedly win the 1992 election.

Britain enjoyed another half-decade of political stalemate, as the Conservatives stagnated and Labour was rebuilt on the sidelines, but business continued to boom. In line with a global upswing, by the late 1990s the British economy was in better shape than it had been for years. In two decades the economic base had shifted almost completely from heavy industry to the services industry. (A situation still existing today, with many Britons employed in less labour-intensive light engineering, high-tech and electronic fields, including computers and telecommunications, and the finance and retail sectors.)

## NEW LABOUR, NEW MILLENNIUM

In the general election of 1997, 'New' Labour swept to power under a fresh-faced leader called Tony Blair. After nearly 18 years of Conservative rule, to the majority of Brits it really seemed that Labour's rallying call ('things can only get better') was true – and some people literally danced in the street when the results were announced.

Under Prime Minister Blair, the government disappointed old socialist stalwarts who'd expected a swing back to the left. New Labour was a more centrist force, adopting many market reforms favoured by moderate Conservatives. Ministers kept a tight rein on public spending, much to the pleasure of financial institutions. In turn, this sometimes blurred the distinction between Labour and the Liberal Democrats, and prompted the Conservatives to take a sizeable jump to the right.

As well as fiscal prudence, the new Labour government introduced major constitutional reforms in other areas. Devolution, at least in part, was granted to Scotland and Wales, with a Scottish Parliament established in Edinburgh, and Cardiff seeing the arrival of the Welsh Assembly, reversing some of the

*A History of Britain by historian and TV star Simon Schama is a highly accessible three-volume set, putting events from 3000 BC to AD 2000 into a modern context.*

| 1979 | 1982 | 1990 |
|---|---|---|
| The Conservative Party, led by Margaret Thatcher, wins the general election, a major milestone in Britain's 20th-century history, ushering in a decade of dramatic political and social change. | Britain is victorious in its war against Argentina over the invasion of the Falkland Islands, boosting patriotism and leading to a bout of public flag-waving not seen since WWII, or probably since Agincourt. | Mrs Thatcher is ousted as leader, and the Conservative Party enters a period of decline, thanks partly to the introduction of the hugely unpopular 'poll tax', but remains in power thanks to weak Labour opposition. |

centuries-old unification laws introduced by rulers as far back as Edward I and Henry VII. (See p780 and p676 for more devolution details.)

Tony Blair and New Labour enjoyed an extended honeymoon period, and the next election (in 2001) was another walkover, although the main opposition parties – the Conservatives and Liberal Democrats, plus the Scottish Nationalists and Plaid Cymru (the Welsh nationalists) in Wales and Scotland – regained some seats. But overall the Conservative Party continued to struggle, allowing Labour to win a historic third term in 2005, and a year later Mr Blair became the longest-serving Labour Party prime minister in British history.

*The Unfulfilled Prime Minister: Tony Blair's Quest for a Legacy* covers the period from 1997 to 2005, one of 'huge disappointment' according to author Peter Riddell.

However, as the decade wore on, the honeymoon became a distant memory, and the Labour government was forced to deal with a seemingly unending string of problems, controversies and crises. Most evident were the invasions of Iraq and Afghanistan, and the threat of terrorism at home, brought so shockingly to the surface in London on 7 July 2005, when bombers attacked underground trains and a bus, killing 52 people.

Other international issues that dominated the headlines and dogged the government included the expansion of the EU to include the former Eastern-bloc countries, reflecting wide-ranging discussion on the benefits and disadvantages of accepting economic migrants and asylum seekers into Britain.

## THE FUTURE'S BROWN?

In June 2007 Tony Blair resigned as leader of the Labour Party and prime minister of the country, allowing Gordon Brown, the Chancellor of the Exchequer (the British term for Minister of Finance) and for so long the prime-minister-in-waiting, to finally get the top job.

Mr Brown's first three months in office were promising; the new leader seemed calm and in control, and Labour enjoyed a post-Blair renewal of public support. But then it all went wrong. Much-publicised (though never officially announced) plans for a 'snap' general election were suddenly shelved, thanks to weakening opinion polls, making the new leader seem suddenly indecisive and cynical. A photo-opportunity trip to Iraq timed to deflect attention from the Tory party annual conference did little to alleviate the cynicism.

Economic policy seemed to go awry, too. Budgetary measures established when Mr Brown was Chancellor came into force, penalising some of the country's lowest earners with higher taxes. This was especially bizarre, given the previous decade of social policy, largely driven by Mr Brown, that focused on alleviating poverty. A government attempt to reverse the debacle, involving tax refunds costing £2.7 billion, was criticised by opposition parties of either missing all the intended targets, or – in light of impending

| 1997 | 1999 | 2003–04 |
|---|---|---|
| After many years of Conservative government, the Labour party (now branded 'New Labour') under the leadership of Tony Blair wins the general election with a record-breaking parliamentary majority. Mr Blair becomes prime minister. | Devolution of political power from the British Parliament in England to the separate Scottish Parliament and Welsh Assembly – reversing the trend towards the three countries' unity dating back to the days of Edward I. | Britain joins the US-led invasion of Iraq, with strong reactions for and against from the public and Conservative opposition. General public sentiment sours when Mr Blair concedes that weapons of mass destruction may never be found. |

by-elections – of being a cynical move by a prime minister once lauded for his polices of prudence and long-term fiscal planning.

Then came the by-elections. In May 2008, in the industrial town of Crewe, formerly a Labour stronghold, voters swung decisively to the Conservatives. A month later attention switched to Henley, a Tory stronghold; Labour was never going to win here, but the end result – fifth place with around 1000 votes, compared to the winning 20,000 – was simply embarrassing. They say bad things come in threes, and Labour's third sorry tale was the Glasgow East by-election, where the former Labour stronghold was captured by the Scottish National Party. The winning margin was minute (just 365 votes) but represented a massive swing of 24%. In the previous election Labour received over 13,000 votes; this time it was around 10,000.

Alongside these local disappointments for Labour, the global economic downturn and accompanying rise in fuel and food costs, and the fall in house values, were all blamed on the government, such that in late June 2008, a poll showed 74% of people thought the new prime minister 'a disappointment' after Mr Blair. In addition, the Labour party's coffers were reported to be over £20 million in the red. Not the best way for Gordon Brown to celebrate his first anniversary in the top job.

Outside of government, in December 2005 the Conservatives elected David Cameron as their party leader; a charismatic figure from the beginning, his confidence and standing continued to grow thanks partly to policies based on tax cuts, capped immigration and measures to reduce crime, and partly to Labour's stream of public relations disasters under Gordon Brown. Meanwhile, Nick Clegg became leader of the Liberal Democrats in December 2007, meaning all three major parties will enter the next election (expected in 2009, and due by 2010 at the latest) with new leaders. Towards the end of 2008, Mr Brown's handling of the global financial crisis earned the Labour government many plaudits and a rise in the opinion polls, but it remains to be seen if the voters will award Labour yet another term in office, or if the combination of events overseas, economic gloom at home and in-fighting at the heart of government will mean the political pendulum finally swings back the other way.

| 2005 | 2007 | 2008 |
| --- | --- | --- |
| Labour re-elected for third term, with Tony Blair still at the helm, although some commentators report his increasing frustration as the quest for a 'lasting legacy' to mark his time as leader goes unfulfilled. | After more than a decade in the top job, and several months of uncertainty as he prepared to step down, Tony Blair resigns and Gordon Brown takes over as Labour leader and Britain's prime minister. | Gordon Brown's first year in office is marked by some apparently ill-conceived policies and falls in Labour's poll-ratings, but public opinion turns again following his response to the global credit crisis. |

# The Culture

## THE NATIONAL PSYCHE

In the 1958 film *A Night To Remember* – about the sinking of the *Titanic* – we see tux-clad card players dealing hands of bridge as the ship goes down, the band playing *Abide With Me* as water laps along the deck, and toffs dressed in their Sunday best 'prepared to go down as gentlemen'. How very, very British.

Calmness in the face of adversity, a laconic sense of humour, a sense of decency and fair play, and mastery of understatement (just look at the title of that film) are all fundamental facets of the British character – at least, as seen by the British themselves. Ask the French, for example, and you might get a rather different list of attributes that includes stand-offishness, anti-intellectualism, public drunkenness and being crap at cooking.

But in as much as there exists such a thing as 'British identity', it's a relatively recent creation, and one that was forged in adversity – in the empire-building of the 19th century, and in the two world wars of the 20th. This idealised British character – the plucky, stiff-upper-lipped, source-of-the-Nile-discovering, Everest-conquering, all-round hero and decent chap (or chapess) – is celebrated in countless films released in the decade or two following WWII, from *Brief Encounter* to *633 Squadron*.

From the 1960s on, it has also been mercilessly satirised in hundreds of films and TV shows, from the classic *Carry On...* comedies (Brits in colonial India calmly taking afternoon tea as a battle rages around them), to the Black Knight in *Monty Python and the Holy Grail* (reduced to a limbless torso but still exhorting his opponent to come back and fight like a man).

You might think that much of this mythical Britishness is a thing of the past, but a lot of it lives on. *The British Character* by 'Pont' (one of *Punch* magazine's finest cartoonists) was first published in the late 1930s, but pretty much all the national idiosyncrasies that are gently mocked in this collection of cartoons are still recognisable today, including the importance of forming an orderly queue, an unflinching belief in the miraculous cure-all properties of a nice cup of tea, and a love of animals that borders on clinically insane.

But today, just as the prime minister is promoting the idea of 'citizenship ceremonies' for new immigrants and 'celebrations of Britishness' for the rest of the nation, British identity seems to be disintegrating.

Scotland and Wales have always had a strong sense of themselves, nurturing their differences in the face of centuries of English cultural dominance. Since the creation of separate parliaments in Edinburgh and Cardiff in the late 1990s, this process has accelerated, forcing the English to rediscover their own national identity. For them, English and British have meant pretty much the same thing for as long as they can remember. Today, there is more celebration of individual Scots, English and Welsh identity than there is of a British one – even the supposedly all-encompassing 'Team GB' brand used in the 2008 Olympics caused a controversy because it left out Northern Ireland.

## LIFESTYLE

When it comes to family life, many British people regard the 'Victorian values' of the late 19th century as an idyllic benchmark – a time of perfect morals and harmonious nuclear families, a high point from which the country has been sliding ever since. As recently as the 1960s, only 2% of couples would 'live in sin' before getting married; today 'cohabiting' (there's still not

For a deeper understanding of peculiar British sensibilities as you travel around, *Eccentric Britain* by Benedict le Vay is invaluable. In the same series are *Eccentric London*, *Eccentric Edinburgh* and *Eccentric Oxford*.

For an amusing insight into what it means to be a Brit, search www.amazon.com for *The British Character* by Pont, or check out the cartoons online at www.punchcartoons.com.

**QUEUING FOR BRITAIN**

The British are famously addicted to forming orderly queues, be it for buses, train tickets, or to pay at the supermarket. The order is sacrosanct and woe betide any foreigner who gets this wrong. Few things are more calculated to spark an outburst of tutting – about as publicly cross as most Brits get – than 'pushing in' at a queue.

A similar etiquette applies to escalators – especially in London. If you want to stand still, then keep to the right, so that people can pass on the left. There's a definite convention here and offenders have been hung, drawn and quartered (well, they've at least provoked another outburst of tutting) for blocking the path of folk in a hurry.

a proper word for it) is perfectly acceptable in most circles – around 60% of couples who marry are already living together, and at any given time about a third of all couples living together are unmarried.

In line with this, the number of unmarried couples having children has also increased in the last 40 years; whereas 'illegitimate' children were comparatively rare in the 1960s and were socially stigmatised, today about 40% of births in the UK are to unmarried couples. The 'pro-family' lobby argues that married couples provide more stability and a better environment for children. But marriage apparently provides no guarantees: currently about one in three British marriages ends in divorce.

All the above applies to heterosexual marriage of course. It's been legal for gay or lesbian couples to get hitched only since the 2005 Civil Partnership Act came into force. This was a landmark step, but there's still a way to go before full tolerance and equality is reached.

It's a similar situation when it comes to race. General tolerance prevails in most parts of Britain, with commercial organisations and official bodies such as the police trying hard to stamp out discrimination. But bigotry can still lurk close to the surface: far-right political parties won several seats in the local council elections of 2006, and it's not unusual to hear people openly discuss other races in quite unpleasant terms – in smart country pubs as much as rough city bars. And while it's no longer OK for comedians to tell racist jokes on prime-time TV (as it was until the 1980s), this type of humour still goes down well in some quarters.

Along with race, another major issue in Britain is health – with the words 'obesity epidemic' appearing regularly in newspaper headlines. Currently over 60% of the adult population is overweight, and almost 25% is clinically obese (in France and Italy, the rate is below 10%). The Scots are the worst, with child obesity levels at twice the UK average, and a proportion of overweight adults that is second only to the USA.

So while the Brits are pigging out on junk food, at least they're not smoking as much. Tobacco has moved down to second on the health-risk charts, and although it's still a major cause of disease, about 75% of the population does not smoke – the lowest figures since records began. And perhaps that's why there's been mostly support (albeit sometimes grudging) for the smoking ban that was introduced in restaurants and many pubs in England and Wales in mid-2007, bringing them into line with Scotland where a ban on smoking in all enclosed public spaces has been in force since 2006.

Time to celebrate? Oh yes – with a big drink. Across the country, alcohol consumption is on the rise, with the relatively new phenomenon of 'binge drinking' among young people a major concern for doctors, police and politicians. And it's not just the boys on the booze; thanks largely to a change in social attitudes (there's no more stigma attached to a woman getting drunk than there is to a man), around 70% of women

Some truly fascinating interviews with everyday people from around Britain have been compiled onto CD as radio-program-style 'audio books', available from www.rovingear.co.uk. It's like listening to an interesting local in the pub...

are drinking more than the recommended amount – up from just 10% in the mid-1990s.

And alcohol isn't the only drug. A major survey in 2006 showed that about 10% of British adults had used a recreational drug in the last year. That figure included 24% of 16- to 24-year-olds, of whom around 6% use cocaine and 5% use ecstasy, while at any given time around 8% of the population regularly or occasionally uses cannabis. Since cannabis was downgraded to a Class C drug in 2005 its use, particularly among young people, has fallen significantly. But whether this is due to the downgrading, or simply because weed has gone out of fashion, is impossible to say. Cocaine use, on the other hand, has doubled in the last decade.

## ECONOMY

Britain once led the world in coal mining, steel-making and engineering, but its days as a centre of heavy industry are long gone. The old order has been replaced by the service sector, finance, energy, life sciences, and high-tech engineering and electronics. The service sector now accounts for 73% of British GDP, industry 26%, and agriculture a mere 1%.

The financial sector accounts for only half as much GDP as manufacturing, but it has been responsible for most of the growth in the British economy in the last decade. London is the world's leading financial centre, and Edinburgh is the fifth-largest in Europe. Tourism is another important contributor to the British economy, injecting £4 billion annually and employing one in 15 of the workforce. The biggest single employer in Britain, however, is the government – one in five employees works in the public sector.

'London is the world's leading financial centre'

On the face of things, the British economy looks successful, having grown continuously from 1982 to 2008; it's the fifth-largest economy in the world, and the second-largest in Europe after Germany. Unemployment is fairly low (5.7% in August 2008) and wages are high – at around £25,100 (US$46,300) a year in 2008, average income in Britain has overtaken that in the USA for the first time since the 19th century.

However, critics claim that this success has been built on the insecure foundations of an irrational housing market and a mountain of consumer debt. The ratio of household debt to national income in 2008 was 1.62, the highest of any major economy, and the total stock of consumer debt has trebled over the last 10 years – at £1,325 billion it is now greater than Britain's GDP.

The global credit crunch that began in late 2007 hit Britain hard. The nationalisation of Northern Rock and Bradford & Bingley – two major British banks – was followed by a massive taxpayer bailout of the financial sector, including the merger of HBOS with Lloyds TSB to create a megabank that holds one third of the country's savings and current accounts. House prices tumbled, unemployment increased and, at the time of writing in late 2008, Britain's economy was in a recession.

## POPULATION

Britain's population is around 59 million. The highest concentration is in England, which has a population of 51 million, with London the largest city in the country. The other main centres in England are Birmingham (Britain's second-largest city), Manchester and Sheffield (ranking third and fourth in size), with Liverpool and Leeds not far away – in distance and size.

Wales has around three million people, with the population concentrated along the coast between Cardiff (the Welsh capital) and Swansea and in the former mining valleys running north from there. Scotland has around five million people, with the population concentrated in and around the cities of Glasgow and Edinburgh. Scotland's Highland region is Britain's most

---

**POPULATION FIGURES**

Throughout this book we give the population figures for towns and cities drawn from the 2001 national census. In some cases the numbers may have changed by the time you read this, but you'll still know if a place is a tiny village or a major metropolis.

---

sparsely populated area, with an average of just 20 people per sq mile, a legacy of the notorious Clearances (see p927).

A European Commission report in 2008 predicted that Britain's relatively high birth rate – at 1.91 children per woman, it is the highest it has been for a generation – and young average age will see it become the most populous country in Europe by 2060, with a population of 77 million, overtaking Germany as its headcount shrinks from 82 million to 70 million. The average age of the population is also predicted to increase, creating a potential crisis in funding for health care and pensions.

A major characteristic of Britain's population is the so-called 'north–south divide', the split between wealthy and densely populated southeast England and the rest of the UK. For example, around London there are towns where high-tech jobs are on the rise and there's less than 1% unemployment. In sharp contrast, economic depression is a major issue in parts of the Midlands, northern England, south and north Wales and parts of Scotland – an 'archipelago of deprivation' according to one report.

Despite government efforts to relocate public- and private-sector jobs to 'the regions' (the BBC, for example, is moving 1500 London-based staff to new offices in Manchester by 2011) people – and the work opportunities that attract them – still seem relentlessly drawn to the capital and its environs.

'A major characteristic of Britain's population is the so-called "north–south divide"'

Meanwhile, and contrary to expectations, an even more significant migration is under way. In the last decade, over one million people in Britain have moved from urban to rural areas. The new country-dwellers seek a better life–work balance, with many working from home via phone and the internet. Others use their skills to set up small businesses, providing new employment opportunities for the locals – especially valuable in rural areas where traditional jobs such as farming are on the wane. But there are downsides, too, most notably the rise in rural house prices. This is pushing property beyond the reach of local inhabitants and forcing *them* to move to the towns that the incomers have just vacated.

## MULTICULTURALISM

More than four million Britons belong to ethnic minorities. Strictly speaking, Britain has been multicultural for millennia, made up as it is of three different countries with distinct languages, histories and cultures, colonised centuries ago by a melting pot of Romans, Celts, Saxons, Vikings and Normans. However, this 'native' multiculturalism has been greatly influenced by peoples from all over the world – French Huguenots, Russian Jews, West Indians, Poles and Somalis, to name but a few – who have immigrated here over the centuries.

In the 20th century, mass immigration to Britain began with the arrival of many thousands of Afro-Caribbeans and Asians in the 1950s and '60s, which saw the country's non-white population increase from a few thousand in 1945 to 1.4 million in 1970. Today, British Asians (of Indian, Pakistani, Bangladeshi and Sri Lankan descent) account for 5.3% of the population, Black British (Caribbean and African descent) 2.7%, and British Chinese 0.7%.

More recently, the opening up of the European Union to eastern European countries in 2004 has seen the influx of up to 800,000 Poles, Lithuanians, Slovenes, Czechs and others, joining an established British Polish community that settled here after WWII.

Britain's approach to this melting pot of languages and cultures has been to tolerate the emergence of ethnic communities that continue to use their native languages and customs, in contrast to the French model of assimilation, which demands that immigrants speak French and adopt French cultural norms.

However, in recent years this policy has come under attack. The climate of fear that followed 9/11 in the USA and the London bombings in July 2005 has seen many people claim that Muslim communities are breeding grounds for terrorists. The government has reacted by proposing 'citizenship ceremonies' for immigrants along the lines of those in the USA, and the creation of a new public holiday to 'celebrate Britishness'.

## SPORT

If you want to take a short cut into the heart of British culture, watch the British at play. They're fierce and passionate about their sport, whether participating or watching. The mood of the nation is more closely aligned to the success of its international teams in major competition than to budget announcements from the Chancellor of the Exchequer, or even the weather.

The British invented – or at least laid down the modern rules for – many of the world's most popular spectator sports, including cricket, tennis, golf, rugby and football. Trouble is, the national teams aren't always so good at playing them (as the newspapers continually like to remind us), although recent years have seen some notable success stories. But a mixed result doesn't dull the fans' enthusiasm. Every weekend, thousands of people turn out to cheer their favourite team, and sporting highlights such as Wimbledon or the Derby keep the entire nation enthralled, while the biggest sporting event of all – the Olympic Games – is coming to London in 2012.

Perhaps surprisingly, unlike many countries Britain has no dedicated large-circulation sports newspaper (apart from perhaps the *Sportsman*, concentrating mainly on the betting angle). But read the excellent coverage in the back pages of the *Daily Telegraph*, the *Times* and the *Guardian* and you'll see there's no need for one. The tabloid newspapers also cover sport, especially if a star has been caught with their pants down. Talking of which, despite the name, the *Daily Sport* is not a sports paper, unless photos of glamour models wearing only a pair of Arsenal socks counts as 'sport'.

This section gives an overview of spectator sports you might see as part of your travels around Britain; the regional chapters have more details. For information on participation sports, see p108.

For dates and details of football, cricket, horse racing and other events in Britain tomorrow, next week or next month, start with http://news .bbc.co.uk/sport and click on Scores & Fixtures, then Calendar.

### Football (Soccer)

Despite what the fans may say in Madrid or São Paulo, the English football league has some of the finest teams and players in the world. It's the richest too, with multimillion-pound sponsorship deals regularly clinched by powerful agents.

At the top of the tree is the **Premier League** (www.premierleague.com) for the country's top 20 clubs, although the hegemony enjoyed by superclubs Arsenal, Liverpool and globally renowned (and part US-owned) Manchester United has been challenged in recent years by former underdogs Chelsea, thanks to the seemingly bottomless budget of Russian owner Roman Abramovich.

Down from the premiership, 72 other teams play in the three divisions called the Championship, League One and League Two. The Scottish Premier

---

**THE SWEET FA CUP**

The (English) Football Association (www.fa.com) held its first interclub knockout tournament in 1871. Fifteen clubs took part, playing for a nice piece of silverware called the FA Cup – then worth about £20.

Nowadays, around 600 clubs compete for this legendary and priceless trophy. It differs from many other competitions in that every team – from the lowest-ranking part-timers to the stars of the Premier League – is in with a chance. The preliminary rounds begin in August, and the world-famous Cup Final is held in May. It's been staged at Wembley for decades, with a few years out at Cardiff's Millennium Stadium while the national ground was rebuilt.

The team with the most FA Cup victories is Manchester United (a total of 11), but public attention and affection is invariably focused on the 'giant-killers' – minor clubs that claw their way up through the rounds, unexpectedly beating higher-ranking competitors. The best-known giant-killing event occurred in 1992, when Wrexham, then ranked 24th in Division 3, famously beat league champions Arsenal. Other shocks include non-league Kidderminster Harriers' 1994 defeats of big boys Birmingham City and Preston North End, and Oldham Athletic beating premier leaguers Manchester City in 2005.

The Scottish Football Association (www.scottishfa.co.uk) has its own Scottish Cup competition, first held in 1874. The cup itself is the original, making it the oldest football trophy in the world. One of the most famous giant-killings north of the border was when mighty Celtic was humbled in 2000 by lowly Inverness Caledonian Thistle, inspiring the immortal tabloid headline 'Super Caley go ballistic; Celtic are atrocious'.

In recent years, competitions such as the Premier League and Champions League (against European teams) have a higher profile, greater kudos, and simply more money to play with. But nothing raises community spirit more than a town team doing better than expected. Gates (attendances) are down, and perhaps the FA Cup will one day be consigned to history – but what a sweet and glorious history it's been!

---

League is dominated by Glasgow Rangers and Glasgow Celtic (p823). In Wales, football is less popular (rugby is the Welsh passion), although some of the bigger teams such as Wrexham, Cardiff City and Swansea City play in the lower English leagues.

The football season lasts from August to May, so seeing a match can easily be included in most visitors' itineraries – but tickets for the big games in the upper division are like gold dust, and cost £20 to £50 even if you're lucky enough to find one. Your best chance might be websites like www.sportstoursinternational.co.uk – offering tickets along with travel and accommodation.

If you can't get in to see the big names, tickets for lower-division games are cheaper and more easily available – either on the spot, ordered through a club website, or through a specialist such as www.ticketmaster.co.uk or www.myticketmarket.com.

## Rugby

A wit once said that football was a gentlemen's game played by hooligans, while rugby was the other way around. That may be true, and rugby is very popular, especially since England became world champions in 2004; it's worth catching a game for the display of skill (OK, and brawn), and the fun atmosphere on the terraces. Tickets cost around £15 to £40 depending on the club's status and fortunes.

There are two variants of the game: rugby union (www.rfu.com) is played in southern England, Wales and Scotland, while rugby league (www.therfl.co.uk) is the main sport in northern England, although there is a lot of crossover. Many rules and tactics of both 'codes' are similar, although in

---

**RUGBY ROOTS**

Rugby traces its origins to a football match in 1823 at Rugby School, in Warwickshire in the English Midlands. A player called William Webb Ellis, frustrated at the limitations of mere kicking, reputedly picked up the ball and ran with it towards the opponents' goal. True to the British sense of fair play, rather than Ellis being dismissed from the game, a whole new sport was developed around his tactic, and the Rugby Football Union was formally inaugurated in 1871.

---

league there are 13 players in each team (ostensibly making the game faster), while rugby union sides have 15 players each.

The main season for club matches is roughly September to Easter, while the international rugby union calendar is dominated by the annual Six Nations Championship (England, Scotland, Wales, Ireland, France and Italy) between January and April. It's usual for the Scots to support Wales, or vice versa, when either team is playing the 'old enemy' England. Scots will enthusiastically support France too – keeping alive memories of the Auld Alliance (see Expansionist Edward, p44), but it's all very good-natured, really.

## Cricket

Cricket has its origins in southeast England, with the earliest written record dating to 1598. It became an international game during Britain's colonial era, when it was exported to the countries of the Commonwealth, particularly the Indian subcontinent, the West Indies and Australasia.

To outsiders (and many locals) the rules and terminology may appear ridiculously arcane and confusing, and progress seems so *slow*. Surely, say the nonbelievers, this is the game for which TV highlights were invented. But for aficionados the game provides 'resolute and graceful confrontations within an intricate and psychologically thrilling framework'. OK, the quote is from a cricket fan. Nonetheless, at least one cricket match should feature in your travels around Britain. If you're patient and learn the intricacies, you could find cricket as enriching and enticing as the many thousands of Brits (especially the English) who remain glued to their radio or TV all summer.

'Cricket has its origins in southeast England'

County cricket (www.ecb.co.uk) is the mainstay of the domestic game, while international one-day games and five-day test matches are played against sides such as Australia and the West Indies at landmark grounds like Lords in London, Edgbaston in Birmingham and Headingley in Leeds. Test match tickets cost £25 to £100 and tend to sell fast. County championships usually charge £10 to £15, and rarely sell out. Watching a local game on the village green is free of charge.

Twenty20 cricket is a short form of the game, introduced in Britain in 2003. Matches last only 2½ hours, encouraging batsmen to go all out for big scores. Purists look down on it as an inferior sport, but it makes a good introduction for anyone who lacks the inclination to sit through five days of test-match stalemate.

## Golf

If you want to watch men with sticks hit little white balls (and it is mostly men's golf that draws the crowds), the main event is the British Open (www.opengolf.com), known to all as simply 'the Open'. It's played every July in rotation on nine courses around the country: 2009 Turnberry; 2010 St Andrews ('the birthplace of golf' – see p873); 2011 Royal St George's (Sandwich, Kent); and 2012 Royal Lytham & St Annes (Lancashire). Other important competitions include the British Amateur Championship and the Welsh Open at Celtic Manor Hotel near Newport, south Wales – the course for 2010's Ryder Cup. Spectator tickets start at about £10, going up to £75 for a good position at the major events.

## Horse Racing

There's a horse race somewhere in Britain pretty much every day, but the top event in the calendar is Royal Ascot in mid-June, when even the Queen turns up to put a fiver each way on Lucky Boy in the 3.15. For details see www.ascot.co.uk.

Other highlights include the Grand National steeplechase at Aintree (www.aintree.co.uk) in early April, and the Derby (www.epsomderby.co.uk), run at Epsom on the first Saturday in June. The latter is especially popular with the masses so, unlike Ascot, you won't see morning suits and outrageous hats anywhere.

Queen Elizabeth II is a great horse-racing fan, with 19 Ascot winners to date from the royal stables. The 2005 Grand National clashed with Prince Charles' marriage; rumours abound that the start was delayed so the Queen could attend the nuptials *and* see the race.

## Tennis

Tennis is widely played at club and regional levels, but the best-known tournament is the All England Lawn Tennis Championships at Wimbledon (www.wimbledon.org), when tennis fever sweeps through the country for the last week of June and the first week of July. In between matches, the crowds traditionally feast on strawberries and cream; that's 28 tonnes of strawberries and 7000L of cream annually, to be precise.

Current British tennis darlings are Andy Murray (ranked number six in the world at time of research) and 14-year-old Laura Robson (who won the girls' junior championship 2008). Demand for seats at Wimbledon always outstrips supply, but to give everyone an equal chance the tickets are sold (unusually) through a public ballot. You can also take your chance on the spot: about 6000 tickets are sold each day (but not the last four days) and queuing at dawn should get you into the ground.

# MEDIA
## Newspapers & Magazines

Breakfast need never be boring in Britain. For such a small country, there's a huge range of newspapers to read over your cornflakes.

The bottom end of the market is occupied by easy-to-read tabloids, full of sensational 'exclusives' and simplistic political coverage. The *Sun* is a national institution with mean-spirited content and headlines based on outrageous puns – a good combination apparently, as it's Britain's biggest-selling paper, with a circulation of around three million and a readership of around nine million. The *Daily Mirror,* once the 'paper of the workers', tried to compete head-on with the *Sun* for a while, then rediscovered its left-of-centre, pro-Labour heritage. The *Daily Sport* takes bad taste to the extreme, with stories of sex, celebrities and aliens (sometimes of celebrities having sex *with* aliens), and pictures of seminaked women of improbable proportions.

The *Daily Mail* and *Daily Express* bill themselves as middle-market, but are little different to the tabloids, both thunderously right-of-centre with a steady stream of crime, scandal and the-country's-going-to-the-dogs scare stories about threatening immigrants and rampant homosexuals. Some may find this diet distasteful, but about eight million readers don't.

At the upper end of the market are the broadsheets: the *Daily Telegraph* is right-of-centre and easily outsells its rivals; the *Times* is conservative, Murdoch-owned, thorough and influential; the *Guardian* is left-of-centre and innovative; and the *Independent* lives up to its title. 'Tabloid' and 'broadsheet' have always referred more to substance than actual dimensions, but the distinction is now totally content-based as several serious papers have adopted smaller, handy-to-carry sizes.

Most dailies have Sunday stablemates (the *Sunday Mirror, Sunday Express, Sunday Telegraph* and so on) and there's also the long-standing liberal-slanted *Observer*. The weekend broadsheets are filled more with comment and analysis than hot news, and on their day of rest the British settle in armchairs to plough through endless supplements; the *Sunday Times* alone comes in 12 different parts.

Most of the papers mentioned here are available all over Britain, but can have an English bias, so Scotland maintains a flock of home-grown dailies. These include the Edinburgh-based *Scotsman,* the Glasgow-based *Herald* (founded in 1783, the oldest daily in the English-speaking world), and the popular tabloid *Daily Record.* The old-fashioned, family-oriented *Sunday Post* has been a bestseller since 1914. In Wales, the *Western Mail* is the national daily, with *Wales on Sunday* taking over at weekends.

There are also local and regional papers throughout Britain. These range from the *Evening Standard,* London's commuter favourite, and city dailies like the *Manchester News* or *Swansea Evening Post* – the latter famous as the paper where Dylan Thomas cut his journalistic teeth – to obscure but much-loved small-town newspapers such as the *Oban Times* where we have seen the immortal headline 'Remarks Lead To Incidents'.

Weekly news magazines include the right-wing *Spectator,* established in 1828 and until recently edited by Boris Johnson, now the mayor of London; the left-wing *New Statesman;* and that champion of free trade and globalisation, *The Economist.* And then there's the fortnightly *Private Eye,* child of the sixties and scourge of the establishment, peddling a very British brand of satire.

> Want to read the papers online? Find them at *Daily Express* (www.express .co.uk), *Daily Telegraph* (www.telegraph.co.uk), *Guardian* (www.guardian .co.uk), *Independent* (www.independent .co.uk), *Mirror* (www .mirror.co.uk), *Sun* (www .thesun.co.uk) and *Times* (www.timesonline.co.uk).

## TV & Radio

Alongside the wide range of newsprint stands an equally wide range of TV and radio. The BBC – funded by an annual licence fee (currently £139.50) payable by everyone who owns a TV set – is the country's leading broadcaster and a national institution, with several channels of the world's best programming dominating national radio and TV. Foreigners are frequently amazed that public service broadcasting can produce such a range of professional, innovative, up-to-date and stimulating programs (and without adverts too!). Ever-increasing competition from cable and satellite channels, though, means some shows tend to be dumbed down as ratings are chased, especially as the majority of households now have digital receivers, in preparation for the analogue switch-off scheduled for 2012.

The main BBC TV stations are BBC One and BBC Two; others include BBC Three, BBC Four, BBC News and children's channel CBBC. Major commercial broadcasters include ITV and Channel 4 – both with several channels. Satellite broadcasting is heavily dominated by Sky, part of the gargantuan News International Corporation.

In the face of criticism that it is too London-centric, the BBC has announced plans to increase the number of programs made by divisions such as BBC Scotland and BBC Wales; a new channel, BBC Alba, was launched in 2008, broadcasting seven hours a day in Scottish Gaelic. In addition to producing locally focused news, drama, current affairs and Gaelic- and Welsh-language programs, these subsidiaries also create content for mainstream broadcasting throughout Britain – Cardiff famously produces the *Doctor Who* series and its spin-off *Torchwood.*

Turning to radio, the main BBC stations include Radio 1, playing everything from syrupy pop to underground garage, with a predominantly young audience. When you get too old for this, tune into Radio 2, playing favourites from the 1960s to today, plus country, jazz and world music, with presenters who also got too old for Radio 1. Predominantly classical music is played on Radio 3, but this station also goes into roots and world music, while media gem Radio 4 offers a mix of news, comment, current affairs, drama and comedy. Other BBC stations include Radio 5 Live (a mix of sport and talk) and Radio 7 (drama and comedy).

Alongside the BBC are many commercial radio broadcasters. Every city has at least one music station, while national stations include pop-orientated Absolute Radio and pleasantly nonhighbrow classical specialist Classic FM. To find the right spot on the dial, see p983.

## RELIGION

The Church of England (or Anglican Church) was founded in the 16th century at the behest of Henry VIII, and today remains wealthy and influential – even in these increasingly secular times. It's traditionally conservative, and predominantly Conservative (sometimes called 'the Tory Party at prayer'); only since 1994 have women been ordained as priests. The debate has now moved on to the rights and wrongs of gay clergy, an issue which threatens to split the worldwide Anglican Communion.

In what many feel to be an anachronistic arrangement, the Church of England remains the officially established church of the British state, though its writ extends only to England. The British monarch is the Supreme Governor of the Church of England, and its leader, the Archbishop of Canterbury, is appointed by the prime minister; 26 bishops and archbishops have the automatic right to speak and vote in parliament's House of Lords.

Scotland's national church is the presbyterian Church of Scotland, a true child of the Reformation that has no bishops. It has had a great influence on Scotland's history, not least in spearheading the provision of universal education in the 17th and 18th centuries, and has split and re-formed many times, creating numerous spin-off minorities, notably the Scottish Episcopal Church (a member of the Anglican Communion) and the notoriously conservative, Sabbath-observing Free Church of Scotland (known as the Wee Frees).

Other Christian faiths include Roman Catholic (about 10% of the population, bolstered by the recent influx of Catholics from Poland), plus sizeable groups of Methodists, Baptists and other nonconformists – most notably in Wales, where the Anglican Church ceased to be the established church way back in the 1920s, and the Church–Chapel divide between the Protestant and nonconformist faiths is still clearly evident.

In the 2001 national census, around 35 million people stated their religion as Christian, and although many write 'C of E' or 'Church of Scotland' when filling in the forms, only about a million regularly attend Sunday services. Generally, attendances are down every year at mainstream churches across Britain, with evangelical and charismatic churches the only ones attracting growing congregations.

The 2001 census also recorded around 1.5 million Muslims in Britain (about 3% of the population). Other faiths include Hindu (1%), Sikh (0.7%), Jewish (0.5%) and Buddhist (0.3%). Nowadays more non-Christians regularly visit their places of worship than do all the Anglicans, Catholics, Methodists and Baptists combined – especially if you include those Druids at Stonehenge, and all those wags who amusingly wrote 'Jedi Knight' in the 'Other' category on the census form.

The increasing numbers of practising Muslims in Britain has led to public debate over how some aspects of devout Islamic practice – notably compliance with sharia law and women wearing the hijab – can fit into the everyday life of a liberal Western society. Some solutions have been found, with major British banks introducing sharia-compliant mortgages (sharia law forbids

'the Church of England remains the officially established church of the British state'

charging interest on a loan), but controversy rages in other areas, with some schools banning the hijab (along with the wearing of any 'symbols of religious affiliation', no matter what the religion).

# ARTS
## Literature
Modern English literature – that is, poetry and prose in the English language – starts around 1387 (yes, that's modern in history-soaked Britain) with *The Canterbury Tales,* Geoffrey Chaucer's classic collection of fables, stories and morality tales using travelling pilgrims – the Knight, the Wife of Bath, the Nun's Priest and so on – as a narrative hook. For more background see the boxed text, p211.

Two centuries later, enter William Shakespeare. Still Britain's best-known playwright, he was pretty good at poetry too. The famous line 'Shall I compare thee to a summer's day?' comes from sonnet No 18; in all he penned more than 150.

Then came the metaphysical poets of the early 17th century. Their vivid imagery and far-fetched conceits or comparisons daringly pushed the boundaries. In *A Valediction: Forbidding Mourning,* for instance, John Donne compares two lovers with the points of a compass. Racy stuff in its day.

Perhaps you're more familiar with *Auld Lang Syne,* traditionally sung at New Year throughout Britain and, indeed, most of the world. The words were penned by prolific 18th-century Scots poet and lyricist Robert Burns, whose works are the third most-translated in the world (after the Bible and Shakespeare). His light-hearted *Address to a Haggis* plays an important part in 'Burns Night', a Scottish celebration held on 25 January. For more on Robert Burns, see p841.

### FROM DAFFODILS TO DETECTIVES
The stars of the 19th century were the Romantics. John Keats, Percy Bysshe Shelley and Lord Byron wrote with emotion and were passionate about nature, exalting the senses and the power of the imagination. The best-known Romantic poet, William Wordsworth, lived in the Lake District, and his famous lines from *Daffodils,* 'I wandered lonely as a cloud', were inspired by a walk along the shore of Ullswater lake.

The Romantic movement produced a genre called 'literary Gothic', exemplified by Mary Shelley's *Frankenstein* and satirised in *Northanger Abbey* by Jane Austen, still one of Britain's best-known and best-loved novelists; intrigues and passions boiling under the stilted reserve of provincial middle-class social convention are beautifully portrayed in Austen's *Emma* and *Pride & Prejudice.*

Next came the reign of Queen Victoria and the era of industrial expansion, when key novels of the time explored social and political issues. In *Oliver Twist,* Charles Dickens captures the lives of young thieves in the London slums, and in *Hard Times* he paints a brutal picture of capitalism's excesses. Meanwhile, Thomas Hardy's classic *Tess of the D'Urbervilles* deals with the peasantry's decline, and *The Trumpet Major* paints a picture of idyllic English country life interrupted by war and encroaching modernity. North of the border, Sir Walter Scott produced the classic Scottish novel *Waverley,* set in the time of the 1745 Jacobite rebellion. (For more on Scott, see p828.)

Other major figures from this era include the Brontë sisters. Charlotte Brontë's *Jane Eyre* and Anne Brontë's *The Tenant of Wildfell Hall* are classics of passion, mystery and love. Fans still flock to Haworth (p529), the sisters' former home, perched on the edge of the wild Pennine moors that inspired so many of their books.

Of the Brontë family's prodigious output, *Wuthering Heights* by Emily Brontë is the best known – an epic tale of obsession and revenge, where the dark and moody landscape plays as great a role as any human character.

Also popular at this time were two important Scottish novelists – Robert Louis Stevenson, best known for his children's books *Treasure Island* and *Kidnapped*; and Sir Arthur Conan Doyle, inventor of detective Sherlock Holmes – and that 'prophet of British imperialism', Nobel Prize winner Rudyard Kipling, author of *The Jungle Book, Kim,* and Margaret Thatcher's favourite poem, *If-*.

## WAR & PEACE

In the 20th century, the pace of writing increased. A landmark was the 1908 success of Welsh poet WH Davies, whose *The Autobiography of a Super-Tramp* contained the immortal words 'What is this life if, full of care/We have no time to stand and stare?'.

A few years later, inspired by the tragedy of WWI, poet Rupert Brooke's *The Soldier* is romantic and idealistic, while Wilfred Owen's *Dulce et Decorum Est* is harshly cynical about the 'glory' of war. DH Lawrence, their contemporary, picked up the theme of change and produced *Sons and Lovers* and *The Rainbow,* novels set in the English Midlands that follow the lives and loves of generations as the country changes from 19th-century idyll to the modern world we recognise today. In 1928 Lawrence further pushed his explorations of sexuality in *Lady Chatterley's Lover,* initially banned as pornographic. Torrid affairs are no big deal today, but the quality of the writing still shines.

Other highlights of the interwar years included EM Forster's *A Passage to India,* about the hopelessness of British colonial rule, and Daphne du Maurier's romantic suspense novel *Rebecca,* set on the Cornish coast. Evelyn Waugh gave us *Brideshead Revisited* and Richard Llewellyn wrote the Welsh classic *How Green Was My Valley*. In a different world entirely, JRR Tolkien published *The Hobbit,* trumping it some 20 years later with his awesome trilogy *The Lord of the Rings*.

After WWII, Compton Mackenzie lifted postwar spirits with *Whisky Galore* (adapted for film in 1949), a comic novel about a cargo of booze washed up from a sinking ship onto a Scottish island. Elsewhere, a less whimsical breed of writer emerged. George Orwell wrote *Animal Farm* and *Nineteen Eighty-Four,* his closely observed studies of totalitarian rule, while the Cold War inspired Graham Greene's *Our Man in Havana,* in which a secret agent studies the workings of a vacuum cleaner to inspire fictitious spying reports.

Another spook of that period was Ian Fleming's red-blooded hero James Bond – better known today as a movie franchise. He first appeared in 1953 in the book *Casino Royale,* then swashbuckled his way through numerous thrillers for another decade. Meanwhile, TH White's *The Once and Future King* covers battles of a different time – the magical world of King Arthur and the Knights of the Round Table.

An entire postwar generation of children was turned on to reading by the books of Enid Blyton, whose tales of adventure in the *Famous Five* and *Secret Seven* series of novels were enormously popular in the 1950s and '60s, and still are today – the *Famous Five* books still sell a million copies a year worldwide. Often criticised for being racist and sexist, the author famously replied that she was not interested in the views of critics aged over 12.

The 20th century was also a great time for poets. Landmarks include WH Auden's *Funeral Blues* (still his most popular work thanks to a reading in the film *Four Weddings and a Funeral*) and TS Eliot's epic *The Wasteland,* although he is better known for *Old Possum's Book of Practical Cats* – turned into the musical *Cats* by Andrew Lloyd Webber. In the 1960s writer Roger McGough and friends were determined to make art relevant to daily life and produced *The Mersey Sound* – landmark pop poetry for the streets.

For extra insight while travelling, the *Oxford Literary Guide to Great Britain and Ireland* gives details of towns, villages and countryside immortalised by writers.

Different again was the harsh, gritty verse of Ted Hughes, sometimes renowned as much for the stormy relationship with his wife (American poet Sylvia Plath) as for his works, although he became poet laureate of England from 1984 until his death in 1998. Meanwhile, Dylan Thomas, also known for his energetic boozing, came to the fore with *Portrait of The Artist As A Young Dog*, although his most celebrated work is a radio play, *Under Milk Wood* (1954), exposing the tensions of small-town Wales (for more on the setting for *Under Milk Wood*, see p706).

## SWINGING SIXTIES TO NEW MILLENNIUM

New writers during the swinging '60s and '70s included Muriel Spark, who introduced the world to a highly unusual Edinburgh schoolmistress in *The Prime of Miss Jean Brodie*, and Martin Amis, who was just 24 in 1973 when he wrote *The Rachel Papers*, a witty, minutely observed story of sexual obsession in puberty. Since then Amis has published many books, including *London Fields* and *The Information*, all greeted with critical acclaim and high sales. Similarly, Ian McEwan was one of Britain's angriest young novelists, earning the nickname Ian Macabre for his early work like *The Cement Garden* and *The Comfort of Strangers*, but in 1998 he cracked the establishment and became a Booker Prize winner with *Amsterdam*.

In contrast, authors Sebastian Faulks and Louis de Bernières struggled for recognition, then hit the jackpot with later works. Their respective novels *Birdsong*, a perfect study of passion and the horrors of WWI, and *Captain Corelli's Mandolin*, a tale of love, war and life on a Greek island, were massive sellers in the 1990s. Though born in Japan, adopted Brit Kazuo Ishiguro produced a brilliant dissection of the death of the English aristocracy in the Booker Prize–winning *The Remains of the Day*, made into an acclaimed movie by Merchant and Ivory.

Contemporary novels in a different vein include 1993's *Trainspotting* by Irvine Welsh, a deep, dark look at Edinburgh's drug culture and the start of a new genre coined 'Tartan Noir'. Other successful modern Scottish novelists include Iain Banks (who also writes sci-fi under the cunning pseudonym of Iain M Banks) and Ian Rankin, whose Detective Inspector Rebus novels are always eagerly awaited.

Another notable work of the same era was *The Buddha of Suburbia* by Hanif Kureishi, about the hopes and fears of a group of suburban Anglo-Asians in London, and a forerunner of the many multicultural tales that dominate bestseller lists today.

As English literature entered the new millennium, two of the biggest-selling British authors were JK Rowling and Phillip Pulman; Rowling's *Harry Potter* and Pulman's *His Dark Materials* series took children's literature to a level where they could be enjoyed by adults too.

Back in the real world, Zadie Smith was only 25 when *White Teeth* became a major hit of 2000. She followed it with the equally hyped, and almost as good, *The Autograph Man* and *On Beauty*, the latter winning the prestigious Orange Prize for Fiction in 2006.

Other star novelists covering (loosely defined) 'multicultural Britain' themes include Monica Ali, whose *Brick Lane* was shortlisted for the 2003 Man Booker Prize, and Hari Kunzru, who received one of the largest advances in publishing history for his debut *The Impressionist*. His second novel *Transmission* was published in 2004. The same year Andrea Levy won the Orange Prize for her novel, *Small Island*, about a Jamaican couple settled in 1950s London. The author is of Jamaican origin and draws on rich family memories of the time. Two years later, the book won the best-in-10-years 'Orange of Orange' award.

As the Pennine moors haunt Brontë novels, so the marshy Cambridgeshire Fens dominate *Waterland* by Graham Swift – a tale of personal and national history, betrayal and compassion, and a landmark work of the 1980s.

Also set in London are Alan Hollinghurst's 2004 Booker Prize winner *The Line of Beauty,* about high-society gays in the 1980s Thatcher era; and *The Book of Dave* by prolific novelist, journalist, broadcaster and social commentator Will Self, published in 2006. Although ostensibly fanciful (a new religion based on the rantings of a grumpy taxi driver), like many of Self's works it's a wonderfully incisive satire on urban lifestyles in 21st-century Britain. Meanwhile, Martin Amis produced the stylised and frankly confusing *Yellow Dog* in 2002 and Nick Hornby left lad-lit behind and displayed a deeper maturity in 2006's darkly comic *A Long Way Down.*

The big event of 2007 was the award of the Nobel Prize for literature to Doris Lessing, in recognition of a long career of ground-breaking, politically aware novels that include *The Golden Notebook,* widely acclaimed as a classic of feminism (though the author denies it is any such thing). In the same year, Ian McEwan's latest novel *On Chesil Beach* hit the shelves, harkening back to the sexual awakening of the 1960s.

Nick Hornby is easily lumped in the lad-lit bracket, but *Fever Pitch* (about football and relationships) and *High Fidelity* (about music and relationships) are spot-on studies of young British blokeishness.

## Cinema

In the early years of the 20th century, silent movies from Britain gave the Americans a run for their money, and *Blackmail* by Alfred Hitchcock – still one of Britain's best-known film directors – launched the British film industry's era of sound production in 1929.

*How Green Was My Valley,* a tale of everyday life in the coal-mining villages of Wales, was made in 1941. Still perhaps the best-known Welsh film of all time, it also annoys more Welsh people than any other, as it features stereotypical characters and no Welsh actors, and was shot in a Hollywood studio. It is worth a watch, though, for a taste of the period.

The website of the British Film Institute – www.screenonline.org.uk – has complete coverage of Britain's film and TV industry.

After a decline in film output during WWII, the British film recovery in the 1940s and '50s was led by Ealing Studios with a series of eccentric comedies, such as *Kind Hearts and Coronets* and *The Ladykillers,* both starring Alec Guinness.

More-serious box-office hits of the time included *Hamlet,* starring Laurence Olivier (the first British film to win an Oscar in the Best Picture category) and Carol Reed's *The Third Man.* An absolute classic of the era is *Brief Encounter,* directed by David Lean, who went on to make *Lawrence of Arabia* and *Doctor Zhivago.* The 1960s saw a glut of gritty dramas tinged with black humour, exploring a British society that was undergoing a social and sexual revolution, including *Saturday Night and Sunday Morning, A Taste of Honey* and *Billy Liar.* The decade was also the heyday of the *Carry On…* films, a series of saucy comedies that were as British as roast beef.

Super-spy James Bond exploded onto the big screen in 1962, with *Dr No* starring Scotland's very own Sean Connery. Since then about 20 Bond movies have been made, and Bond has been played by other British actors including Roger Moore, Timothy Dalton and, since 2006, Daniel Craig. More-recent producers have brought a somewhat chauvinistic Bond into the modern age, with the enlightened casting of Dame Judi Dench as Bond's boss, 'M'.

*Passport to Pimlico* is an Ealing Studios film classic, the story of a London suburb declaring independence from the rest of the country.

By the end of the 1960s, British film production had declined again and didn't pick up until David Puttnam's *Chariots of Fire* won four Oscars in 1981.

Perhaps inspired by this success, TV company Channel 4 began financing films for the large and small screen, one of the first being *My Beautiful Laundrette* – a story of multicultural life and love in the Thatcher era. The following year, Richard Attenborough's big-budget epic *Gandhi* carried off eight Oscars including Best Director and Best Picture, while another classic of the 1980s was *Withnail and I,* staring Richard E Grant and Paul McGann. The '80s and early '90s were also the pinnacle of the Merchant-Ivory production company, which turned out meticulously detailed period pieces, often set in Edwardian England or colonial India, including *Heat and Dust, The Remains of the Day,* and Oscar-winners *Howards End* and *Room with a View.*

The 1990s saw another minor renaissance in British film-making, ushered in by *Four Weddings and a Funeral,* featuring US star Andie MacDowell and introducing Hugh Grant as a likeable and self-deprecating Englishman. This spearheaded a genre of 'Brit-flicks', including Mike Leigh's *Secrets and Lies,* a Palme d'Or winner at Cannes, *Bhaji on the Beach,* a quirky East-meets-West-meets-Blackpool road movie, *The Full Monty,* which in 1997 became Britain's most successful film ever, and *Trainspotting,* a hard-hitting film about Edinburgh's drugged-out underbelly that launched the careers of Scottish actors Ewan McGregor and Robert Carlyle. Other British stars more frequently seen in Hollywood these days include Welsh thespians Anthony Hopkins and Catherine Zeta Jones.

More great films of the 1990s include: *Lock, Stock and Two Smoking Barrels,* going on to spawn a host of gangster copycats; *East is East,* a beautifully understated study of the clash between first- and second-generation immigrant Pakistanis in Britain; and the Oscar-winning series of *Wallace and Gromit* animations. *Breaking the Waves* is a perfect study of culture clash in 1970s Scotland, and *Human Traffic* is an edgy romp through Cardiff's clubland. Also released was *Notting Hill,* starring Julia Roberts with Hugh Grant as, yes, a likeable and self-deprecating Englishman. Much more enjoyable was *Sense and Sensibility,* with English doyennes Emma Thompson and Kate Winslet as the Dashwood sisters, and Hugh Grant as, you guessed it, a likeable and self-deprecating Englishman.

Award-winning Welsh-language films of the 1990s include *Hedd Wynn,* a heartbreaking story of a poet killed in WWI, and *Soloman and Gaenor,* a passionate tale of forbidden love at the turn of the 20th century.

The great success of 2000, and a classic of the Brit-flick genre, was *Billy Elliot,* yet another film with Britain's declining industry as backdrop, but also about people rising above it, particularly the son of a hardened coalminer who strives to becomes a ballet dancer. In contrast, *About a Boy* was a feel-good movie about a dating ploy leading unexpectedly to fatherly responsibilities, starring the ever-popular Hugh Grant as (surprise, surprise) a likeable and self-deprecating Englishman. Meanwhile, *Bend It Like Beckham* addressed more fundamental themes: growing up, first love, sex, class, race – and football.

Despite the success stories of the 1990s, as we go through the first decade of the 21st century the UK film industry has returned to its customary precarious financial state. Advocates call for more government funding, as in reality most UK-made and UK-set films are paid for with US money – epitomised perhaps by the globally renowned series of Harry Potter adventures, starting with *Harry Potter and the Philosopher's Stone* in 2001, with roughly a movie per year as we follow the schoolboy wizard through at least six years of education. (To visit parts of Britain where Harry Potter and many other films have been made, see www.visitbritain.com/moviemap or the Britain on Location itinerary, p34.)

Other notable British films of this decade (so far) include: *Shaun of the Dead,* a great low-budget horror spoof where the hero fails to notice walking corpses because most of his neighbours are zombies at the best of times; *24 Hour Party People,* about the iconic Hacienda Club and all-round pop excess in 1980s Manchester; *Hitchhikers Guide to the Galaxy,* already a cult book and radio series; and *Wallace & Gromit: The Curse Of The Were-Rabbit,* another handcrafted marvel from director Nick Park.

*Brief Encounter* is frequently cited as a milestone in British cinema – a film where the drama comes from the acting (Trevor Howard and Celia Johnstone) rather than the set (uninspiring suburbs and railway-station buffets). It's a story of unexpected love and smouldering sexual attraction that can never be fulfilled.

*Chariots of Fire* is an inspiring dramatisation of a true story: the progress of two athletes from university to the 1924 Olympics, their friendship and rivalry, and – for one of them – the conflict of sport with faith. When receiving his Oscars, the director boasted: 'the British are coming'.

A highlight of 2006 was *Pride and Prejudice,* another Jane Austen masterpiece skilfully adapted for the silver screen, filmed in Derbyshire and Lincolnshire and starring Keira Knightley (a long way from *Bend it like Beckham*), along with fellow British stars Matthew MacFadyen, Brenda Blethyn and the perennial Judi Dench.

Big British hits of recent years include *Hot Fuzz,* an offbeat cop comedy starring Simon Pegg (from *Shaun of the Dead*); *Atonement,* a masterly adaptation of Ian McEwan's novel that saw actors James McAvoy and Keira Knightley prove that they are much more than just pretty faces; and *Casino Royale* and *Quantum of Solace,* in which Daniel Craig made James Bond cool once more.

*Seachd: The Inaccessible Pinnacle* (2007), recorded in Gaelic, caused a controversy when Bafta refused to enter it in the Best Foreign Language Film category in the 2008 Academy Awards. It's a magical tale of Gaelic myth and mystery in which the biggest star is probably the stunning scenery of the Isle of Skye.

## Music

### POP & ROCK

Since the dawn of the swinging '60s, Britain has been firmly on the main stage – with access all areas – of pop and rock music's colourful history. Major early exports were the Beatles, the Rolling Stones, The Who, the Kinks, and Welsh soul man Tom Jones, followed in the 1970s by stardust-speckled heroes like the Bay City Rollers, Marc Bolan and David Bowie. Other big-name artists of the time – in some cases even still performing – include Cream (featuring Eric Clapton), the Faces (starring Rod Stewart), Genesis (initially fronted by Peter Gabriel and later by Phil Collins) and Roxy Music (featuring for a while the highly influential Brian Eno), plus Pink Floyd, Deep Purple, Led Zeppelin, Queen and Elton John – all very different but all globally renowned, and with some, such as Bowie, still producing decent material today.

In the late '70s and early '80s, the self-indulgent 'prog rock' of the 'dinosaur bands' was replaced by punk music. It was energetic, anarchic ('here's three chords, now form a band' ran a famous fanzine quote) and frequently tuneless, but punk was great fun and returned pop to grass-roots level – at least for a while. The infamous Sex Pistols produced one album and a clutch of (mostly banned) singles, while more prolific bands included the Clash, the Damned, the Buzzcocks, the Stranglers and the UK Subs.

Punk begat 'New Wave' (ie everything that was a bit punky), with leading exponents including the Jam, the Tourists and Elvis Costello. This merged briefly with the ska revival of the 1980s led by the Specials, influencing bands such as Madness and the Beat. Meanwhile, a punk-and-reggae-influenced trio called the Police – fronted by bassist Sting – became one of the biggest names of the decade, and Gothic lost boys the Cure carved their own existential post-punk path.

Around the same time, heavy metal enjoyed an upsurge, with bands like Black Sabbath (featuring once-again-famous Ozzy Osbourne) and Judas Priest exporting soulful melodies and intriguing interpretations of established religion to concert halls worldwide.

The ever-changing 1980s also saw a surge of electronica with the likes of Depeche Mode and Cabaret Voltaire, and the rise of New Romantic bands such as Spandau Ballet, Duran Duran and Culture Club – all frills and fringes, and a definite swing of pop's pendulum away from untidy punks. More hits and highlights were supplied by the Eurythmics, Texas,

---

**WAIT, THERE'S MORE**

This section concentrates on pop and rock. Of course, Britain enjoys many other rich and diverse musical genres – jazz, roots, fusion, banghra, R&B, drum'n'bass, dance, techno, chill-out, dub, gospel, urban, hip hop and so on – but we simply haven't got the space to cover them here.

and Wham! – a two-piece boy band headed by a bright young fellow called George Michael.

Meanwhile, a whole new sound was emerging in northwest England. Fusing elements of punk, rock and dance music, the pioneering Joy Division (later evolving into New Order), the Stone Roses and Happy Mondays epitomised the late-'80s/early-'90s Madchester Sound (p581).

Concurrently, the painfully morose but curiously engaging Smiths, fronted by Morrissey (also enjoying a comeback), enjoyed world fame, while on the other side of the Pennines, Leeds-based the Wedding Present championed guitar- and frustration-driven melodies that still influence many bands today.

Dance music and superclubs did their best to dominate the scene but the '90s also saw the renaissance of British indie bands, with the likes of Blur, Elastica, Suede, Supergrass, Ocean Colour Scene, the Manic Street Preachers, the Verve, Pulp, Travis, Feeder, Super Furry Animals, Stereophonics, Catatonia, Radiohead and, above all, Oasis reviving the guitar-based format. Heralded as the 'Britpop' revolution, part of the even bigger Cool Britannia phenomenon that combined new music, new art, new fashion and New Labour politics, it is largely thanks to these bands that the indie guitar sound remains such a major feature of British pop music today

By the cusp of the millennium, Cool Britannia's shine had predictably faded, but a host of bands such as Coldplay, Franz Ferdinand, Badly Drawn Boy, Snow Patrol and Razorlight played on, and spawned a wave of imitators. Perhaps one of the more successful Britpop survivors was Damon Albarn of Blur, now conquering the charts again with Gorillaz. The Libertines similarly influenced music and fashion, although ex-frontman Pete Doherty is now more famous for drug-and-supermodel scandals than his subsequent band Babyshambles.

As the first decade of the 21st century draws to a close, British pop and rock have divided into a host of genres mixing a wide range of influences including glam, punk, electronica and folk (while British folk itself, thanks largely to the rise of world music, enjoys its biggest revival since the 1960s). Worth a listen are atmospheric and eclectic British Sea Power; the energetic and nostalgic Go! Team; the rousing mix of rock, country, psychedelia and folk that is The Coral; hugely popular Yorkshire rockers the Arctic Monkeys; Dundee's indie darlings The View; and Britain's jazz-soul diva Amy Winehouse.

If you get the chance to enjoy Britain's live-music scene (see p80, as well as the boxed texts on music in the city sections throughout this book), you'll not only enjoy a good night out, with a bit of luck you'll also get the chance to feel smug about seeing unknown bands before they achieve world domination.

'British folk itself, thanks largely to the rise of world music, enjoys its biggest revival since the 1960s'

## CLASSICAL MUSIC & OPERA

The country that gave you the Beatles, Rod Stewart and the Manic Street Preachers is also a powerhouse of classical music, with several professional symphony orchestras, dozens of amateur orchestras, and an active National Association of Youth Orchestras. England, Wales and Scotland each has a national opera company, and the multimillion-pound renovation at the Royal Opera House in London's Covent Garden is bringing in big crowds. Such enthusiasm is all the more remarkable given Britain's small number of well-known classical composers, especially compared with countries like Austria, Germany and Italy.

Key figures include: Henry Purcell, who flourished in the Restoration period but is still regarded as one of the finest English composers; Thomas Arne, best known for the patriotic anthem 'Rule Britannia'; Edward Elgar, famous for his 'Enigma Variations'; Gustav Holst, from Cheltenham, who

---

**LIVE & KICKING**

In Britain you're never short of live music. London and several other cities have stadiums and world-class concert halls for major pop, rock, jazz and classical events, and across the country there's a massive choice of smaller venues where the less-well-known do their thing. Bands large and small are pretty much guaranteed to play in London, but often tour extensively, so a weekend break in Blackpool, Sheffield or Glasgow could include seeing a band at the Tower Ballroom, the legendary Leadmill or King Tut's. Down the scale again, you can hear great sounds (and some really dire stuff) in pubs and small clubs everywhere. As well as local listings, country-wide agencies like **See** (www.seetickets.com) are useful for planning, while the **Indie Travel Guide** (www.howdoesitfeel.co.uk/indieindex.html) features local bands, venues and clubs across Britain (and beyond). North of the border, **Gigs in Scotland** (www.gigsinscotland.com) is the absolute authority. Options for live music are of course more restricted in the countryside – but then you're in the wrong place for bright lights and decibels anyway…

---

wrote 'The Planets' (everyone knows the 'Mars, Bringer of War' bit); Ralph Vaughan-Williams, whose London Symphony ends with chimes from Big Ben; and Benjamin Britten, perhaps the finest British composer of the last century, best known for the 'Young Person's Guide to the Orchestra' and the opera *Peter Grimes*. Also of note are Welsh composers William Mathias, Alun Hoddinott and Karl Jenkins; and Scotland's Alexander Campbell Mackenzie and Oliver Knussen.

More recently, the works of Sir Michael Tippett, Peter Maxwell Davies, John Tavener and Harrison Birtwhistle have found international fame, while the music of composer William Lloyd Webber has been brought to public attention by his sons Julian and Andrew.

Best known of all British classical music concert programs is The Proms (short for 'promenade' – because people used to walk about, or stand, while they listened) – one of the world's greatest music festivals, held from mid-July to mid-September each year at the Royal Albert Hall in London, and widely broadcast on radio and TV.

**FOLK MUSIC**

See www.bbc.co.uk/proms for full details of dates, tickets and when to sing 'Land of Hope and Glory'.

Scotland, England and Wales all have long histories of folk music, each with its own distinctive traditions, melodies and native instruments. Scotland has its bagpipes and bodhrán (a hand-held drum), England the Northumbrian pipes and brass bands, Wales the harp and male voice choirs. These days, though, folk music generally refers to a single musician or small group singing traditional songs live in a pub (or on stage), usually accompanied by instruments such as guitar, fiddle and penny whistle.

British folk music mines a rich seam of regional culture, from the rhythmic 'waulking songs' of the tweed weavers of the Outer Hebrides to the jaunty melodies of England's morris dancers. Local history plays its part too – many Welsh folk songs recall Owain Glyndŵr's battles against English domination, while English folk lyrics range from memories of the Tolpuddle Martyrs to sea shanties sung by Liverpool sailors. In Scotland, the Jacobite rebellion of 1745 was a rich source of traditional songs, while *Flower of Scotland* – written in 1967 by popular folk duo The Corries, and today the unofficial Scottish national anthem – harks back to the Battle of Bannockburn in 1314.

Scottish Gaelic and Welsh traditional music are celebrated annually in the **Mod** (www.the-mod.co.uk) and the **Eisteddfod** (www.eisteddfod.org.uk) respectively.

Probably the most famous English folk singer of the 20th century is Lancashire-born Ewan MacColl (1915–89), a politically active musician who was banned from entering the USA because of his membership of

**BUILDING ON SUCCESS**

Two men have dominated modern British architecture for the last 30 years: Sir Norman Foster and Lord Richard Rogers. Both have designed numerous landmark buildings in Britain, and around the globe – they will each be designing towers to replace the World Trade Center in New York – although their styles are quite distinct.

Foster favours clean designs with flowing lines. Key works in London include the conical Swiss Re Tower (known universally as the Gherkin), winner of the prestigious Stirling prize; the sensuous Great Court glass roof at the British Museum (p159); and the sinuous Millennium Bridge between St Paul's and the Tate Modern. Other splendid recent examples of his work include the Imperial War Museum North (p577) in Manchester, and the Sage concert hall (p647) in Newcastle-Gateshead.

In contrast, the work of Rogers is technical and intricate. Perhaps his best-known work was the Millennium Dome (p171), now renamed The 02, a tent-like structure with a vast curving white roof held aloft by cables and spindly yellow towers. A more recent work is the massive Paddington Basin complex, near the London train station of the same name. Rogers has also worked for the mayor of London on 20,000 new homes.

Meanwhile, Foster's project for London was City Hall (p165; properly known as the Greater London Authority Building), which opened in July 2002. It looks like a tilted beehive, and the glass walls mean you can see everyone inside, hard at work – a deliberate symbol of local-government transparency – while at the top there's the spectacular Londoner's Lounge where you can admire the panoramic views and buy a traditional British cappuccino.

the Communist Party. He wrote two classics that were huge hits for other people – *The First Time Ever I Saw Your Face* (written for his lover, Peggy Seeger; a No 1 hit for Roberta Flack in 1972), and *Dirty Old Town* (about his home town of Salford, a hit for The Dubliners in the 1960s and again for The Pogues in the 1980s).

In Wales, Daffyd Iwan is the highest-profile folk musician, having been prominent in the fight for Welsh language rights since the 1970s. Other Welsh performers worth listening to include harpists Robin Huw Bowen and Sian James, and contemporary folk bands Bob Delyn a'r Ebillion and Mabsant.

In Scotland, the Battlefield Band – famous for mixing bagpipes with electronic keyboards – has been reinventing traditional Scottish music (and its members) since the 1970s, and is still performing today. Anyone with an interest in Scottish folk songs should also check out Eddi Reader – as well as releasing a haunting album of songs by Scottish national poet Robert Burns, she has revived many old folk tunes and, along with songwriter Boo Hewerdine, created many contemporary classics.

## Architecture
One of the many good reasons to visit Britain is to savour its rich architectural heritage – everything from 5000-year-old Bronze Age burial mounds to the stunning steel-and-glass constructions of the 21st century.

Perhaps the best-known construction of prehistoric times is the mysterious stone circle of Stonehenge (p315) – top of the highlight hit list for many visitors – although the Callanish Standing Stones on Scotland's Isle of Lewis are even older. The Scottish islands also hold many of Europe's best surviving remains from the Bronze Age and Iron Age, such as the stone villages of Skara Brae (p959) in Orkney and Jarlshof (p971) in Shetland.

Other highlights are the Roman ramparts of Hadrian's Wall (p655) and the well-preserved Roman swimming pools and steam rooms that gave the city of Bath its name. Bath is also top of the hit lists for most visitors thanks to architecture from a later time – the 18th- and early 19th-century Georgian period that produced grand houses, squares, parades and the famous Royal Crescent. But if we turn the clock back, it's clear that for much of the past millennium architecture has been dominated by two aspects: worship and defence. This gives Britain its incredibly diverse and truly magnificent collection of cathedrals, minsters, abbeys and monasteries dotted across the country. Not to mention an equally diverse collection of forts and castles – from evocative ruins such as Helmsley Castle (p562) and Richmond Castle (p537) via the dramatic battlements of castles such as Stirling (p866) in Scotland and Conwy (p751) in Wales, and the finely maintained 'modern' classics like Leeds Castle (p218) and Windsor Castle (p272), to the iconic Tower of London (p161) itself, with walls and moats, battlements and ramparts from every century since the Norman Conquest.

Castles were good for keeping out the enemy, but there were few other benefits of living in a large damp pile of stones, and as times grew more peaceful from around the 16th century, the landed gentry started to build fine residences – known simply as 'country houses'. There was a particular boom in England, Wales and parts of Scotland in the 18th century, and one of the most distinctive features of the British countryside today is the sheer number (not to mention size) of these grand and beautiful structures.

As well as the grand cathedrals, England has over 12,000 parish churches – many packed with historical or architectural significance. Wales and Scotland have many more.

But it's not all about big houses. Alongside the stately homes, ordinary domestic architecture from the 16th century onwards can also still be seen in rural areas: black-and-white 'half-timbered' houses still characterise counties such as Worcestershire, brick-and-flint cottages pepper Suffolk and Sussex, and hardy, centuries-old structures built with slate or local gritstone are a feature of areas such as Derbyshire, north Wales and the Lake District.

In our own era, the rebuilding that followed WWII showed scant regard for the aesthetics of cities, or for the lives of the people who lived in them, as 'back-to-back' terraces of slum houses were demolished and replaced by tower-blocks (simply shifting horizontal rows of deprivation to the vertical, according to some critics). Public buildings of the 1960s were often little better; heavy concrete 'brutalism' was much beloved by architects of the time – a style epitomised by London's South Bank Centre, although even this monstrosity has its fans today.

Perhaps the insensitivity of the 1960s and '70s is why, on the whole, the British are conservative in their architectural tastes and often resent ambitious or experimental designs, especially when they're applied to public buildings, or when form appears more important than function. But a familiar pattern often unfolds: after a few years of resentment, first comes a nickname (in London, the bulging cone of the Swiss Re building was dubbed 'the Gherkin', and the near-spherical City Hall was called 'Livingstone's Ball' by some, a reference to London's then high-profile mayor), then comes grudging acceptance, and finally comes pride and affection for the new building. The Brits just don't like to be rushed, that's all.

With this attitude in mind, over the last 15 years or so British architecture has started to redeem itself, and many big cities now have contemporary buildings their residents can enjoy and admire. Highlights include Manchester's theatrical Imperial War Museum North (p577); the soaring wood and glass arcs of Sheffield's Winter Gardens (p519); Birmingham's chic new Bullring (p483); The Deep aquarium in Hull (p539); the Welsh National Assembly building, the Senedd (p676), and the Wales Millennium Centre (p674), both on the Cardiff waterfront; the mysterious, symbolic flourishes of the Scottish Parliament Building (p789) in Edinburgh; the interlocking arches of Glasgow's Scottish Exhibition & Conference Centre (p822; already affectionately called 'the Armadillo'); and the Sage concert hall (p647) in Newcastle-Gateshead.

---

**LISTED BUILDINGS**

As you travel around Britain you'll often see churches, castles, great houses, tiny cottages and even 20th-century apartment blocks referred to as 'listed', because they're included on the list of buildings of historic or cultural importance, and therefore protected from development, demolition and so on. There are three main types of listed building: Grade I for the most important, down to Grade III for those of less significance.

---

In recent years a rash of new skyscrapers has been on the drawing board, but the 2008 economic downturn resulted in several flagship projects – including the Lumiere Tower in Leeds and the V Building in Birmingham – being put on hold.

## Painting & Sculpture

For centuries, artists in Britain were influenced by the great European movements, and in the days before cameras, portrait-painting was a reliable if unadventurous source of income for many 18th-century artists. William Hogarth was a breakaway figure from the comfortable world of portraiture, producing a series of paintings that satirised social abuses. His most celebrated work is *A Rake's Progress,* displayed today at Sir John Soane's Museum (p160), London.

Top names among the 18th-century portrait artists include Sir Joshua Reynolds, whose paintings in the 'grand style' include *Lady Anstruther* (on view today in London's Tate Britain gallery, p156), and his rival, Thomas Gainsborough, who produced informal works with subjects at ease in a landscape, such as *Mr & Mrs Andrews* (at the National Gallery, p154).

Two other key figures of the 18th-century British art scene were Joseph Wright, whose interest in science inspired the oddly titled but beautifully executed *An Experiment on a Bird in the Air Pump,* and George Stubbs, whose passion for animal anatomy, particularly horses, is evident in many works at the Tate Britain, and in countless prints on countless country pub walls.

Gainsborough's landscape tradition was continued by John Constable, who painted mainly in Suffolk (still billed as 'Constable Country' by the local tourist board). His most famous work is *The Haywain* (National Gallery, p154) – an idyllic rural scene.

Constable's contemporaries include poet, painter and visionary William Blake, and JMW Turner, whose works increasingly subordinated picture details to the effects of light and colour. By the 1840s, Turner's compositions became almost entirely abstract and were widely vilified, though today they are celebrated as works of genius. Both artists have rooms dedicated to their work at the Tate Britain, and Edinburgh's National Gallery of Scotland (p791) has an annual exhibition of Turner watercolours (in January).

In 1848 Sir John Everett Millais, William Holman Hunt and Dante Gabriel Rossetti formed the Pre-Raphaelite Brotherhood, which combined the simplicity of early Italian art with a closely observed realism. Millais' *Ophelia,* showing the damsel picturesquely drowned in a pool, is an excellent example of their style, and can be seen at the Tate Britain gallery. However, one of the best collections of Pre-Raphaelite art is in the Birmingham Museum & Art Gallery (p475). A good friend of the Pre-Raphaelites was William Morris; he saw late-19th-century furniture and interior design as increasingly vulgar, and with Rossetti and Edward Burne-Jones founded the Arts and Crafts Movement. This movement encouraged the revival of a decorative approach to features such as wallpaper, tapestries and windows. Many of his designs are still used today.

'the Arts and Crafts Movement... encouraged the revival of a decorative approach to features such as wallpaper, tapestries and windows'

North of the border, Charles Rennie Mackintosh, fresh from the Glasgow School of Art, fast became a renowned artist, designer and architect. He is still Scotland's greatest exponent of art nouveau, and much of his work remains in his home city (see p814). Mackintosh influenced a group of artists from the 1890s called the Glasgow Boys, among them James Guthrie and EA Walton, who were also much taken with French Impressionism. Perhaps inevitably, another group of decorative artists and designers emerged called the Glasgow Girls.

In the 20th century, the place of British art in the international arena was ensured by Henry Moore's and Barbara Hepworth's monumental sculptures, Francis Bacon's contorted paintings, David Hockney's highly representational images of – among other things – dachshunds and swimming pools, and the works of a group known as the Scottish Colourists – Francis Cadell, SJ Peploe, Leslie Hunter and JD Ferguson. Much of Hockney's work can be seen at Salt's Mill gallery (p527) in Bradford (his home town); some of Moore's work can be seen at the Yorkshire Sculpture Park (p528), between Sheffield and Leeds; Hepworth is forever associated with St Ives in Cornwall (p390); while the colourist seascapes of Peploe and Cadell have been turned into the type of prints and postcards eternally favoured by Scottish souvenir shops.

The *Angel of the North* is one of the most viewed works of art in the world. It stands beside the busy A1 highway and millions of drivers each year can't help but see this huge sculpture. See www .gateshead.gov.uk/angel.

Paul Nash, an official war artist in WWI and WWII, and Graham Sutherland, Nash's counterpart in WWII, followed in the Romantic and visionary tradition of Blake and Turner. Between the wars, Welsh sister-and-brother artists Gwen and Augustus John flourished; Gwen John painted gentle, introspective portraits of women friends, cats and nuns – and famously became the model and lover of French artist Auguste Rodin. Augustus was Britain's leading portrait painter of the time, with such famous sitters as Thomas Hardy and George Bernard Shaw. One place to admire works by the Johns is the Glynn Vivian Art Gallery (p701) in Swansea.

The Scottish Colourists were followed in the interwar years by a group known as the Edinburgh School. This group included William MacTaggart, who was much influenced by the French expressionists and went on to become one of Scotland's best-known painters. His rich and colourful landscapes can be seen in the National Gallery of Scotland, and in the Hunterian Art Gallery (p815) in Glasgow.

After WWII, Howard Hodgkin and Patrick Heron developed a British version of American abstract expressionism. At the same time, but in great contrast, Manchester artist LS Lowry was painting his much-loved 'matchstick men' figures set in an urban landscape of narrow streets and smoky factories. A good place to see his work is in the Lowry centre (p577), Manchester.

In 1956 a young artist called Richard Hamilton created a photomontage called *Just what is it that makes today's homes so different, so appealing?* as a poster for the Whitechapel Art Gallery in London. It launched the pop-art movement in Britain, and the style was loved by millions when Peter Blake designed the record cover for the Beatles' seminal album *Sergeant Pepper's Lonely Hearts Club Band*. This influenced Scottish artists Alan Davie and Sir Eduardo Paolozzi, who became leading figures in the world of pop art and abstract expressionism. Their works can be seen in Edinburgh's Dean Gallery (p792).

The Whitechapel Art Gallery helped launch the career of sculptor Anthony Caro, with a ground-breaking exhibition in 1963. Creating large abstract works primarily in steel and bronze, Caro has become a highly influential figure, considered by many to be Britain's greatest living sculptor. For more heavy metal see www.anthonycaro.org.

Moving towards our own era, the British art scene of the 1990s was dominated by a group of young artists championed by advertising tycoon Charles

Saatchi, and displayed at his eponymous gallery (www.saatchi-gallery.co.uk). As 'Britpop' developed in the music industry, so the paintings, sculptures and installations of these artists became known as 'Britart'. As notorious as they were talented – some would say more of the former, less of the latter – the group included Damien Hirst, infamous for his use of animals, alive and dead; Tracey Emin, most famous for *My Bed*, a combination of soiled sheets and 'sluttish detritus' (according to one review); and Rachel Whiteread, initially best known for *House*, her resin cast of the interior of an entire house.

The early years of the 21st century have, inevitably, been dubbed the 'post-Britart' era. A body of less obviously shocking artists is emerging, although none has become a household name yet. Of the previous generation, Whiteread is still a major figure on the art scene today: in 2006 she created a massive labyrinthine installation called *Embankment* for the equally gigantic Turbine Hall at the Tate Modern (p164) in London, and in 2008 was shortlisted for the prestigious Angel of the South project (but did not win the commission).

Other key artists of today include the sculptor Antony Gormley, whose *Angel of the North* overlooks the city of Gateshead near Newcastle. A massive steel construction of a human figure with outstretched wings, more fitting for a 747 than a heavenly being, it was initially derided by the locals, but it is now an instantly recognised symbol of northeast England.

'The early years of the 21st century have…been dubbed the "post-Britart" era'

## Theatre

However you budget your time and money, make sure that you see some British theatre as part of your travels. It easily lives up to its reputation as the finest in the world. The Edinburgh Festival is globally renowned (even though Glasgow is the heart of Scottish theatre), Cardiff has a top-class venue, and London's West End is the international centre for theatrical arts – whatever New Yorkers say.

But first, let's set the stage with some history. Britain's best-known theatrical name is of course William Shakespeare, whose plays were first performed in the 16th century at the Globe Theatre. His brilliant plots and sharp prose, and the sheer size of his canon of work (including classics such as *Hamlet* and *Romeo and Juliet*), have turned him into a national icon (see p487). The Globe has been rebuilt (see p165), so you can see the Bard's plays performed in Elizabethan style, in the round (with part of the audience standing around the semicircular stage).

---

**SOUNDS OF SUMMER**

If you're a fan of the performing arts, some fine productions are staged outdoors from May to September, in castle grounds (where plays like *Macbeth* at dusk are pure magic) or purpose-built venues such as Regent's Park Theatre (p169) in London and cliff-edge Minack Theatre (p389) in Cornwall. The best-known open-air music event is Glyndebourne (p223) – a program of world-class opera in the spectacular setting of a country-house garden.

Summertime also inspires villages, towns and cities across the country to stage arts and music festivals – everything from small-scale weekend shows to massive spectaculars like the Bath International Music Festival, via specialist events like Buxton Opera Festival, Whitby Folk Festival, Cheltenham Jazz Festival and the Three Choirs Festival (held once every three years at the cathedrals of Gloucester, Hereford or Worcester).

And finally there's the open-air long-weekend pop and rock extravaganzas, such as the Big Chill (in the genteel grounds of Eastnor Castle), the endearing and increasingly popular Truck (near Abingdon), the colourful Womad global music gathering in Reading, and of course the daddy of them all, Glastonbury (p342). For more information see www.efestivals.co.uk.

England's first theatre was built in 1576 on the northern outskirts of London and was called – rather unimaginatively – 'The Theatre'. Shakespeare's famous Globe Theatre came a little later.

Britain's theatres were firmly closed as dens of iniquity in Oliver Cromwell's day, but when Charles II returned from exile in 1660 he opened the doors again, and encouraged radical practices such as employing actresses (female roles had previously been played by boys) – an innovation loved by London audiences – and Britain's first female playwright, Aphra Behn, who had worked as a political spy for the king. This was also the era of humorous plays known as Restoration comedies, delighting in bawdy wordplay and mockery of the upper classes. The leading lady of the day was Nell Gwyn, who became Charles II's mistress.

In the 18th century, theatres were built in most of the larger British cities. The Bristol Old Vic and The Grand in Lancaster date from this time, along with plays such as Oliver Goldsmith's uproarious *She Stoops to Conquer*. Top of the bill was actor David Garrick, who later gave his name to one of London's leading theatres.

The innovation of gas lighting at London's Drury Lane and Covent Garden theatres set the 19th-century stage for some wonderful shows, including the brilliant comedies of Oscar Wilde (everyone's heard of *The Importance of Being Earnest*, even if they haven't seen it). The second half of the 19th century saw the founding of the Royal Shakespeare Company with a performance of *Much Ado About Nothing* in Stratford-upon-Avon's Memorial Theatre, and the rise of the music hall, peddling popular music and comedy to the working-class masses.

The Edwardian era was the heyday of the music hall, but two world wars and the advent of the movies saw the British stage take a back seat for a few decades. The 1950s marked the emergence of new playwrights with new freedoms, such as John Osborne, whose best-known work is *Look Back in Anger*. A contemporary was Harold Pinter, who developed a new dramatic style and perfectly captured the stuttering illogical diction of real-life conversation. On the boards, actors Laurence Olivier, John Gielgud and Peggy Ashcroft were at their professional peak.

In the 1960s and 1970s, plays by Tom Stoppard *(Rosencrantz and Guildenstern Are Dead)*, Peter Shaffer *(Amadeus)*, Michael Frayn *(Noises Off)* and Alan Ayckbourn *(The Norman Conquests)* took the country by storm – and famous British actors such as Helen Mirren, Glenda Jackson, Judi Dench and Tom Courtenay did justice to them on stage.

In the 1990s and the first decade of the 21st century, big names in British theatre include Brenda Blethyn, Charles Dance, Judi Dench (still!), Ian McKellen, Anthony Sher, Simon Callow, Toby Stephens, Jane Horrocks, Ewan McGregor, Rhys Ifans and Ralph Fiennes – although most perform in stage productions only once or twice a year, combining this with more lucrative appearances on the small or silver screen.

In London, other stars of the stage these days are the directors, especially Nicholas Hytner at the National Theatre, whose successes include *The History Boys* by the perennially dour playwright Alan Bennett. After winning numerous accolades in Britain, the play transferred to Broadway – where it charmed the notoriously tough New York critics and eventually scooped six Tony awards (the most for any production since Arthur Miller's *Death of a Salesman* in 1949).

It's thanks to the quality and success of British drama that native actors are frequently joined by colleagues from across the pond, as the likes of Kathleen Turner, Gwyneth Paltrow, Matthew Perry, Macaulay Culkin, Christian Slater, Kim Cattrall, Gael Garcia Bernal, David Schwimmer and Kevin Spacey have performed in London productions in recent years, exchanging Hollywood glamour for pay cuts and the genuine cred that only

Harold Pinter wrote numerous plays but will probably still best be known for his landmark work *The Birthday Party*, a study of sinister figures and shady untold pasts.

*Look Back in Anger* launched the career of playwright John Osborne and actor Alan Bates, with rebellious lead character Jimmy Porter perfectly capturing the spirit of an unhappy and frustrated postwar generation.

---

### IT'S ALL A BIT OF A PANTOMIME

If any British tradition seems specially designed to bemuse outsiders, it has to be pantomime, performed in theatres all over the country, usually to family audiences over the Christmas and New Year season. Essentially a pantomime is a comedy play or review, with dialogue, routines, songs, dances and lots of custard-pie humour (and – despite the name – no mime) loosely based on stories such as *Cinderella* or *Jack and the Beanstalk*.

Pantomime's roots go back to Celtic legends, medieval morality plays and the art of mumming, but the modern version is a post-Christmas ritual, with people packing out theatres to see old favourite 'pantos' updated to touch on recent political scandals or celebrity gossip, and always featuring a star from a TV soap or game show, or from the world of pop or sport. Pantos also feature routines that everyone knows and joins in ('Where's that dragon/wizard/pirate/lion?' – 'He's behind you!') and tradition dictates that the leading 'boy' is played by a woman, and the leading lady, or 'dame', played by a man. It may be bizarre, but for kids and families it's a great evening out. Oh no, it isn't! Oh yes, it is! Oh no, it isn't…

---

treading West End boards can bestow. (For more cues on London's current drama scene, see p192.)

And while there's often an urge among producers to stick with the big names and safe (and profitable) productions, the risk and innovation normally more associated with fringe events does sometimes filter through too, making London's theatre arguably more innovative and exciting than it's been since the Restoration, and certainly – according to some critics – since the angry postwar era of Osborne and company. Only London could produce an entirely new genre by turning a TV talk show for losers, misfits, weirdos and gender-benders into the wonderfully perverse, and highly controversial, *Jerry Springer – the Opera*.

Alongside the frivolity, perhaps the most notable, and possibly most predictable, trend in recent times has been the upsurge in political theatre in the wake of the Iraq War. The satire and analysis spread all the way from the fringe – where plays such as *Justifying War*, *The Madness of George Dubya* and *A Weapons Inspector Calls* were on show – to the West End, where political drama *Guantanamo* deeply moved and impressed audiences. The National Theatre of Scotland's *Black Watch,* based on interviews with soldiers in Iraq, was the runaway hit of the 2006 Edinburgh Festival and later transferred not only to London's Barbican Theatre, but across the Atlantic to New York.

Despite the vital message of *Guantanamo* and *Jerry*'s much-deserved success, for many visitors to London the theatres of the West End mean one thing: musicals, from *Jesus Christ Superstar* in the 1970s, to *Bollywood Dreams* and *The Woman in White* in 2006, via *Cats, Les Mis, Chicago, Phantom, The Lion King* and all the rest. Many of today's shows are based on the pop lexicon, with singalongs from *Mamma Mia* to *Fame*, proving that – just like in Shakespeare's day – all we really want to do is join in.

A London tradition is the 'long run' – plays that are performed season after season. The record holder is *The Mousetrap* by Agatha Christie; the play has been running at London's St Martin's Theatre for more than 50 years.

# Food & Drink

Once upon a time, in the later medieval period and the 17th century, many people in Britain – especially the wealthy – ate a varied diet, although Queen Elizabeth I did reputedly have the kitchen at Hampton Court Palace moved because the smell of cooking food drifted into her bedroom and spoilt her clothes. Then along came the Industrial Revolution, with mass migration from the country to the city, and food quality took a nosedive – a legacy that means there's still no English equivalent for the phrase *bon appétit*.

A post-industrial culinary heritage of ready-sliced white bread, fatty meats and vegetables boiled to death, all washed down by tea with four sugars, remains firmly in place in many parts of the country. And that's before we get on to treats like pork scratchings and deep-fried Mars Bars.

But today the tide has turned once again. In 2005 food bible *Gourmet* magazine famously singled out London as having the best collection of restaurants in the world, and in the years since then the choice for food-lovers – whatever their budget – has continued to improve so it's now easy to find decent food in other cities, as well as in country areas across Britain. Wherever you travel, for each greasy spoon (cheap cafe) or fast-food joint, there's a local pub or fine restaurant serving up enticing home-grown specialities.

Why the improvement? Reasons include the infamous outbreaks of foot-and-mouth and 'mad cow' disease. They're history now, and British beef is once again exported to the world, but an upside of the bad press was a massive surge in demand for better-quality food, so there's now a plethora of natural, unadulterated, chemical-free products available in shops, markets and restaurants across the country.

For locals and visitors, better food often means organic food, but there are some anomalies: those organic tomatoes taste good, but is it environmentally friendly to fly them in from Spain? Same goes for organic avocados from Thailand, or organic peas from Kenya (where, incidentally, local people watch their crops and cattle die as large-scale market gardens dam rivers and take all the water). Meanwhile, it seems impossible to buy British apples in supermarkets during the autumn cropping season, although you can always choose between 10 different varieties flown in from New Zealand, Chile or South Africa.

But despite 'food miles' and other dilemmas, British food continues to change for the better, due partly to outside influence. For decades most towns have boasted Chinese and Indian restaurants, so chow mein or vindaloo is no longer considered exotic, while curry is the most popular takeaway food in Britain, outstripping even fish and chips. As well as the food in 'Indian' restaurants (in many cases actually Pakistani- or Bangladeshi-owned and staffed), dishes from Japan, Korea, Thailand and other countries east of Suez have become readily available too. From the other side of the world have come restaurants specialising in South American, African or Caribbean cuisine. Closer to home, pastas and a wide range of Mediterranean specialities – from countries as diverse as Morocco and Greece – are commonplace not only in decent restaurants, but also in everyday cafes and pubs.

Good food in pubs? Yes indeed. Not so many years ago if you felt peckish in your average British boozer, your choice would be a ham or cheese roll, with pickled onions if you were lucky. These days, pubs are a good-value option whether you're looking for a toasted sandwich or a three-course meal.

Then there are 'gastropubs', serving truly excellent food, but still in a relaxed informal atmosphere. You'll find mismatched cutlery, no tablecloths,

Queen Elizabeth I decreed that mutton could only be served with bitter herbs – intended to stop consumption and help the wool trade – but her subjects discovered that mint sauce *improved* the taste. It's been roast lamb's favourite condiment ever since.

According to campaign group the Soil Association (www.soilassociation .org), three out of four households in Britain buy organic, and over 85% want pesticide-free food. For more, see www .whyorganic.org.

and waiters in T-shirts, and you pay at the bar along with your drinks, but nothing beats the luxury of a wholesome shepherd's pie washed down by a decent real ale without the worry of guessing which fork to use. This in turn is part of a growing trend in Britain to order good beer to accompany food, rather than automatically turning to the wine list.

Of course, there's more to eating than restaurants and gastropubs. Lavishly illustrated food sections in weekend newspapers indicate that cooking at home is now officially fashionable. Feeding on this is the current phenomenon of 'celebrity chefs', including Hugh Fernley-Whittingstall, who famously scored a £2-million deal with his publishers in early 2006, and Gordon Ramsay, who featured in a list of Britain's richest self-made entrepreneurs a few months later. They are not alone. Every night, on a TV channel near you, a star of the kitchen demonstrates imaginative and simple techniques for producing stylish, tasty and healthy food.

But behind the scenes the Brits still have an odd attitude to eating at home. They love to sit on the sofa and *watch* TV food shows. Inspired, they rush out and buy all the glossy cookery books. Then on the way back home, they pop into the supermarket and buy a stack of ready-made meals. Freshly created food sounds great in theory, but in reality the recipe for dinner is more likely to be something like this: open freezer, take out package, bung in microwave, ping, eat.

In fact, more junk food and ready-made meals are consumed in the UK than in the rest of Europe put together. So it's no surprise that the British are getting increasingly heavy, with over 60% of the adult population overweight, and almost 25% clinically obese. But despite the vast intakes, average nutrition rates are lower now than they were in the 1950s when postwar rationing was still in force.

So yes, without doubt, as a local or a visitor, you can find great food in Britain. It's just that not all the Brits seem to like eating it.

Rick Stein is a TV chef, energetic restaurateur and good-food evangelist. His books, *Food Heroes* and *Food Heroes – Another Helping*, extol small-scale producers and top-notch local food, from organic veg to wild-boar sausages.

## FOOD

Although grazing on a steady supply of snacks is increasingly commonplace, the British culinary day is still punctuated by the three main meals of breakfast, lunch and dinner, also called – depending on social class and location – breakfast, dinner and tea.

### Breakfast

Most working people make do with toast or a bowl of cereal before dashing to the office or factory, but a weekend treat for many is the 'fry-up breakfast': bacon, sausage, egg, mushrooms, baked beans and fried bread. Other additions may include tomatoes (also fried, of course) and black pudding – slices of a large sausage made from ground meat, offal, fat and blood. It's known in other countries as 'blood sausage', but the British version has a high content of oatmeal so doesn't fall apart in the pan when fried.

The same dish will inevitably be encountered at hotels and B&Bs, preceded by cereal and followed by toast and marmalade, where it's known as 'Full English Breakfast' (in England), and just 'Full Breakfast' in Wales and Scotland – although north of the border you might get oatcakes instead of fried bread. In Wales you may be offered laver bread – not a bread at all, but seaweed, a tasty speciality often served with oatmeal and bacon on toast.

If you don't feel like eating half a farmyard it's quite OK to ask for just the egg and tomatoes, for example, while some B&Bs offer other alternatives, such as kippers (smoked fish) – especially in Scotland – or a 'continental breakfast', which completely omits the cooked stuff and may even add something exotic like croissants.

## Lunch

One of the many great inventions that Britain gave the world is the sandwich. The word originates from Sandwich, a town in southeast England, and slapping a slice of cheese or ham between two bits of bread may seem a simple concept, but no one apparently thought of it until the 18th century when the Earl of Sandwich ordered his servants to bring cold meat between bread so he could keep working at his desk or, as some historians claim, keep playing cards late at night. Of course, he didn't really invent the idea – various cultures around the world had been doing it for millennia – but the name stuck and sandwiches became fashionable food for the aristocracy. Their popularity grew among the lower classes in the early days of the Industrial Revolution; labourers heading for mines and factories needed a handy way to carry their midday meal to work.

A favourite sandwich ingredient is Marmite, a dark and pungent yeast extract that generations of British kids have loved or hated. Either way, it's a passion that continues through adulthood. In 2006, when the manufacturer of Marmite moved from selling the stuff in a near-spherical glass jar to a (much more practical) plastic tube, much was the consternation across the land. Similar to the Australian icon, Vegemite (but not the same – oh no, sir!), it's also popular on toast at breakfast and especially great for late-night munchies.

Another speciality – especially in pubs – is the ploughman's lunch. Basically it's bread and cheese and, although hearty yokels probably did carry such food to the fields (just as probably wrapped in a red spotted handkerchief) over many centuries, the meal is actually a modern phenomenon. It was invented in the 1960s by the marketing chief of the national cheesemakers' organisation as a way to boost consumption, neatly cashing in on public nostalgia and fondness for tradition – even if it was fake.

A basic ploughman's lunch is still offered in some pubs – and it undeniably goes well with a pint or two of local ale at lunchtime – but these days the meal has usually been smartened up to include butter, salad, pickle (a thick, vinegary vegetable-based condiment), pickled onion and dressings. At some pubs you get a selection of cheeses. You'll also find other variations, such as farmer's lunch (bread and chicken), stockman's lunch (bread and ham), Frenchman's lunch (brie and baguette) and fisherman's lunch (you guessed it, with fish).

For cheese and bread in a different combination, try Welsh rarebit – a sophisticated variation of cheese on toast, seasoned and flavoured with butter, milk and sometimes a little beer. *Cawl* (a thick broth) is another traditional Welsh dish; for a takeaway lunch in Scotland look out for *stovies* (tasty pies of meat, mashed onion and fried potato) and Scotch pies (hard-cased pies of minced meat, sometimes eaten cold). In restaurants and cafes, sample

---

### NAME THAT PASTY

A favourite in southwest England is the Cornish pasty – originally a mix of cooked vegetables wrapped in pastry – now available in many parts of Britain and often including meat varieties (much to the chagrin of the Cornish people). Invented long before Tupperware, the pasty was an all-in-one-lunch pack that tin miners carried underground and left on a ledge ready for mealtime. So pasties weren't mixed up, they were marked with owners' initials – always at one end, so the miner could eat half and safely leave the rest to snack on later without it mistakenly disappearing into the mouth of a workmate. And before going back to the surface, the miners traditionally left the last corner of the pasty as a gift for the spirits of the mine known as 'knockers', to ensure a safe shift the next day.

**SNACK BOX**

Despite promotion, and general awareness, of the need for a healthy diet, items such as biscuits, chocolate and crisps still form a large part of the average British person's daily intake – as a stroll down the aisles in any supermarket will immediately show.

Among biscuits, 'international' favourites include bourbons and garibaldis, while home-grown iconic styles and brands include chocolate 'digestives' (a name originating from early advertising campaigns that claimed the biscuits had antacid properties) and HobNobs (famously lauded by comedian Peter Kay as 'the Marines of the biscuit world' because they don't fall apart when immersed – that is, when you dip them in a cup of tea).

Moving onto chocolate bars, long-standing favourites include the well-known global brands such as the Mars Bar, KitKat, Twix and Snickers (in the UK still remembered fondly as the Marathon by anyone over 40). A firm favourite of the 1980s and '90s, the Wispa bar, was discontinued in 2003 but made a comeback in 2007 after a surprisingly well-supported 'Bring Back Wispa' internet campaign.

And then there are crisps – the thin fried slices of potato eaten cold from a packet, known to most other parts of the world as 'chips' (but not in Britain, where chips are chunks of potato deep fried and eaten hot – often with fish – known elsewhere as 'fries'). The main brands of crisp are Walkers, Golden Wonder and McCoy's, and the main flavours are ready-salted, smoky bacon, cheese and onion, and salt and vinegar. Others include prawn cocktail and roast chicken. Kettle Chips are marketed as a more upmarket brand, with flavours such as sea salt and balsamic vinegar, and sour cream and chives.

Until the 1980s most British crisp manufacturers used the same colour packing for the same flavours. So ready salted was in a blue packet, cheese and onion in green, and so on. Then Walkers took the revolutionary step of packaging cheese and onion in blue, salt & vinegar in green, and ready-salted in red. The confusion was great, and the public controversy even greater, but the end result – bizarrely – was a massive gain in market share for Walkers, and the near disappearance of Golden Wonder. A concurrent series of clever – and occasionally controversial – TV adverts featuring footballer Gary Linekar helped a lot, too.

Naturally, Walkers kept its colour scheme but many years later so-called 'instinctive' crisp buyers still get home from the shop with a flavour they weren't expecting.

Scotch broth (a thick soup of barley, lentils and mutton stock), sometimes offered as a starter, but filling enough as a meal in itself.

## Dinner

In the view of many outsiders, a typical British dinner is a plate of roast beef. It's more of an English tradition than a British one (and is also why the French call English people *'les rosbifs'*), but good-quality roasts from well-reared cattle grace menus everywhere from Cornwall to the Highlands. Perhaps the most famous beef comes from Scotland's Aberdeen Angus cattle, while the best-known food from Wales is lamb (although a lowly vegetable, the leek, is a national emblem). Venison – usually from red deer – is readily available in Scotland, as well as in parts of Wales and England, most notably in the New Forest.

The traditional accompaniment for British beef is Yorkshire pudding. It's simply roasted batter, but very tasty when properly cooked. Bring sausages and Yorkshire pud together and you have another favourite dish: toad-in-the-hole. Another variant, often served in pubs and cafes, especially in northern England, is 'filled Yorkshire puddings', which, as the name suggests, is a big bowl-shaped Yorkshire pudding filled with meat stew, beans, vegetables or – in these multicultural days – curry.

But perhaps the best-known classic British staple is fish and chips, often bought from the 'chippie' as a takeaway wrapped in paper to enjoy at home,

Like the taste of meat, but not battery pens? Go to the Royal Society for the Prevention of Cruelty to Animals (www.rspca.org.uk) and follow links to Freedom Food, for cruelty-free lamb, beef, chicken and salmon producers and suppliers.

or 'open' to eat immediately as you walk back from a late night at the pub. Sometimes the fish can be greasy and tasteless (especially once you get far from the sea), but in towns with salt in the air this deep-fried delight is always worth trying.

Of course, the Scottish food that everyone knows is haggis, essentially a large sausage made from a sheep's stomach filled with minced meat and oatmeal. Some restaurants in Scotland serve haggis and it's also available deep-fried at takeaways. If you're wary of a full helping of the Scottish national dish, search the menu for Highland chicken, a meal that stuffs portions of haggis mix into baked chicken – that way you can sample a small serving.

Scottish salmon is also well known, and available everywhere in Britain smoked or poached, but there's a big difference between bland fatty salmon from fish farms and the lean, tasty, wild version. The latter is more expensive but, as well as the taste, there are sound environmental reasons for preferring the nonfarmed variety. For example, some reports indicate that farmed fish may be contaminated with toxins transmitted via food pellets, while other reports claim that farmed fish are more prone to diseases which are then transmitted to wild fish, and other aquatic species, and their numbers decline because they have no immunity. Other British seafood includes herring, trout and haddock; in Scotland the latter is best enjoyed with potato and cream in the old-style soup called Cullen skink.

In Yorkshire the eponymous pudding is traditionally eaten *before* the main meal, a reminder of days when food was scarce. The pudding was a stomach-filler, so diners didn't worry so much about a tiny main course.

## Regional Specialities

If fish is your thing, Yorkshire's coastal resorts are particularly famous for huge servings of cod – despite it becoming an endangered species, thanks to overfishing – while restaurants in Devon and Cornwall regularly conjure up prawns, lobster, oysters, mussels and scallops. Elsewhere on your travels, seafood specialities include Norfolk crab, Northumberland kippers, and jellied eels in London, while restaurants in Scotland, west Wales and southwest England regularly conjure up seafood such as oysters, scallops, prawns, lobster and mussels.

Meat-based treats in northern and central England include Cumberland sausage – a tasty mix of minced pork and herbs so large it has to be spiralled to fit on your plate. For a snack, try Melton Mowbray pork pies (motto: 'gracious goodness for over 100 years') – cooked ham compressed in a casing of pastry and always eaten cold, ideally with pickle. A legal victory in 2005 ensured that only pies made in the eponymous Midlands town could carry the Melton Mowbray moniker – in the same way that fizzy wine from other regions can't be called champagne.

Another British speciality that enjoys the same protection is Stilton – a strong white cheese, either plain or in a blue-vein variety. Only five dairies in the whole country – four in the Vale of Belvoir, and one in Derbyshire in

### THE PIG, THE WHOLE SHEEP & NOTHING BUT THE COW

One of the many trends enjoyed by modern British cuisine is the revival of 'nose to tail' cooking – that is, using the whole animal, not just the more obvious cuts such as chops and fillet steaks. This does not mean boiling or grilling a pig or sheep all in one go – although spit-roasts are popular. It means utilising the parts that may at first seem unappetising or, frankly, inedible. So as well as dishes involving liver, heart, chitterlines (intestines) and other offal, traditional delights like bone marrow on toast or tripe (stomach) and onions once again grace the menus of fashionable restaurants. The movement is particularly spearheaded by chef Fergus Henderson at his St John's restaurant in London, and via his influential recipe book, *Nose to Tail Eating: A Kind of British Cooking*, and 2007's follow-up, *Beyond Nose to Tail*.

central England – are allowed to produce cheese with this name. Bizarrely, the cheese *cannot* be made in the village of Stilton in Cambridgeshire, although this is where it was first sold – hence the name.

## Puddings

After the main course comes dessert or 'pudding'. Best known perhaps is Bakewell pudding, an English speciality that blundered into the recipe books around 1860 when a cook at the Rutland Arms Hotel in the Derbyshire town of Bakewell was making a strawberry tart, but mistakenly (some stories say drunkenly) spread the egg mixture on top of the jam instead of stirring it into the pastry. Especially in northern England, the Bakewell pudding (pudding, mark you, not 'Bakewell tart' as it's sometimes erroneously called) features regularly on local dessert menus and is certainly worth sampling.

Other favourites include sherry trifle (a classic from the same 1970s era that gave us cheese cubes and tinned pineapple chunks on cocktail sticks) and treacle sponge. While key ingredients of most puddings are self-explanatory, they're perhaps not so for spotted dick, a suet pudding with currants. Plus sugar, of course. Most puddings have loads of butter or sugar, preferably both. Light, subtle and healthy? Not on your life.

More of a cake than a pudding, Welsh speciality *bara brith* (spicy fruit loaf) is a delight, while Scottish bakeries usually offer milk scones and griddle scones as well as plain varieties. Other sweet temptations include *bannocks* (half scone, half pancake), shortbread (a sweet biscuit) and Dundee cake (a rich fruit mix topped with almonds).

Then there's the dome-shaped plum pudding, full of fruit, nuts and brandy or rum, traditionally eaten at Christmas, when it's called – surprise, surprise – Christmas pudding. It is steamed (rather than baked), cut into slices, and served with brandy butter after the traditional Christmas lunch of turkey and Brussels sprouts, and shortly before the traditional sleep on the sofa when the annual Queen's speech airs on TV. Watch out for coins inserted in the pudding by superstitious cooks – if you bite one it means good luck for the next year, but it may play havoc with your fillings.

'the international favourite banoffee pie...is a British invention'

Rhubarb crumble is made from the stewed stem of a large-leafed garden plant, topped with a baked mix of flour, butter and sugar – and best served with custard or ice cream. For much of the 20th century rhubarb was a very popular food, with overnight trains dubbed the 'rhubarb express' bringing tons of the stuff to London and other cities from the main growing area in Yorkshire, between the towns of Leeds, Wakefield and Morely, known – inevitably – as the 'rhubarb triangle'. Rhubarb fell out of fashion around the 1980s but is currently enjoying a renaissance in gourmet restaurants as well as humble kitchens.

And to polish of our *tour de table,* a reminder that the international favourite banoffee pie (a delightfully sticky dessert made from bananas and toffee) is a British invention, first developed in a restaurant in Sussex in southern England in the early 1970s. A plaque on the wall of the restaurant proudly commemorates this landmark culinary event.

## DRINKS
### Alcoholic

Among alcoholic drinks, Britain is best known for its beer. Typically ranging from dark brown to bright orange in colour, and generally served at room temperature, technically it's called 'ale' and is more commonly called 'bitter' in England and Wales. This is to distinguish it from lager – the drink that most of the rest of the word calls 'beer' – which is generally yellow and served cold. In Scotland, ales are designated by strength –

light, heavy, export and strong – or by a notional 'shilling' scale; so you'd order a 'pint of heavy' or a 'pint of 80-shilling' rather than simply a 'pint of bitter'.

International lager brands like Foster's, Carling and Budweiser are available in Britain, but as you travel around the country you should definitely try some traditional beer, also known as real ale. But be ready! If you're used to the 'amber nectar' or 'king of beers' a local British brew may come as a shock. A warm, flat and expensive shock. This is partly to do with Britain's climate and partly to do with the beer being served by hand pump rather than gas pressure. Most important, though, is the integral flavour: traditional British beer doesn't *need* to be chilled or fizzed to make it palatable. (In contrast, sample a cheap lager that's sat in its glass for an hour and you'll see it has very little actual taste.)

Another key feature is that real ale must be looked after, meaning a willingness on the part of pub landlords to put in extra effort – usually on food and atmosphere, as well as beer. But the extra effort is why many pubs don't serve real ale, so beware of places where bar staff give the barrels as much care and attention as they give the condom machine in the toilets. There's nothing worse than a bad pint of real ale.

If beer doesn't tickle your palate, try cider – available in sweet and dry varieties. In western parts of England, notably Herefordshire and the counties of the Southwest Peninsula, you could try 'scrumpy', a very strong dry cider traditionally made from local apples. Many pubs serve it straight from the barrel.

On hot summer days, you could go for a shandy – beer (lager or bitter) and lemonade mixed in equal quantities – an astonishing combination for some visitors, but very refreshing and, of course, not very strong. Another hybrid is 'snakebite', an equal mix of cider and lager, favoured especially by students, as it reputedly gets you drunk quickly – thanks to the lager's bubbles and the cider's strength – the very reason some pubs refuse to serve it.

Back to more-sensible tipples, many visitors are surprised to learn that wine is produced in Britain, and has been since the time of the Romans. Today, more than 450 vineyards and wineries produce around two million bottles a year – many highly regarded and frequently winning major awards. English white sparkling wines have been a particular success story recently, many produced in the southeast of the country where the chalky soil and climatic conditions are similar to those of the Champagne region in France. At the 2005 International Wine and Spirit Competition, a wine called Ridgeview Marret Bloomsbury from the Ditchling Vineyard in East Sussex beat entrants from 55 other countries to win the accolade 'best sparkling wine in the world'. For more on English wine, see p217.

Moving on to something stronger, the usual arrays of gin, vodka, rum and so on are served in pubs and bars, but the spirit most visitors associate with Britain – and especially Scotland – is whisky (note the spelling – it's *Irish* whiskey that has an 'e'). More than 2000 brands are produced, but the two main kinds are single malt, made from malted barley, and blended whisky, made from unmalted grain blended with malts. Single malts are rarer (there are only about 100 brands) and more expensive.

When ordering a dram in Scotland remember to ask for whisky – only the English and other foreigners say 'Scotch' (what else would you be served in Scotland?). And if you're bemused by the wide choice, ask to try a local whisky – although if your budget is low, you might want to check the price first. A measure of blended whisky costs around £2, a straightforward single malt around £3, while a rare classic could be £10 or more.

CAMRA, the Campaign for Real Ale (www.camra.org.uk), promotes the understanding of traditional British beer – and recommends good pubs that serve it. Look for endorsement stickers on pub windows.

---

**VEGETARIANS**

It's official – vegetarians are no longer weird. Many restaurants and pubs in England have at least a token vegetarian dish (another meat-free lasagne, anyone?), but better places offer much more imaginative choices. Vegans will find the going more tricky, except of course at dedicated vegetarian/vegan restaurants – and where possible we recommend good options throughout this book. For more ideas see www.happycow.net.

---

## Nonalcoholic

In England a drink means any ingestible liquid, so if you're from overseas and a local asks, 'would you like a drink?', don't automatically expect a gin and tonic. They may well mean a 'cuppa' – a cup of tea – England's best-known beverage. Tea is sometimes billed as the national drink, although coffee is equally popular these days; the Brits consume 165 million cups a day (compared with about 180 million cups of tea per day) and the British coffee market is worth almost £700 million a year – but with the prices some coffee shops charge, maybe that's not surprising. And a final word of warning – when you're ordering a coffee and the server says 'white or black', don't panic. It simply means, 'do you want milk in it?'.

## WHERE TO EAT & DRINK

There's a huge choice of places to eat in Britain, and this section outlines just some of your options. For details on opening times, see p986. For the tricky issue of tipping see p992, and for some pointers on restaurants' attitudes to kids see p986.

## Picnics & Self-catering

When shopping for food, as well as the more obvious chain stores and corner shops, markets can be a great place for bargains – everything from dented tins of tomatoes for 1p to home-baked cakes and organic goat's cheese. Farmers markets are always worth a browse; they're a great way for producers to sell good food direct to consumers, with both sides avoiding the grip of the supermarkets.

For tasty details on the whereabouts of farmers markets see www .farmersmarkets.net.

## Cafes & Teashops

The traditional British cafe is nothing like its continental namesake. For a start, asking for a brandy with your coffee may cause confusion, as few cafes in Britain serve alcohol. Often pronounced 'caffy', or shortened to 'caff', most are basic places serving basic food. Meals like meat pie or omelette with chips cost around £3 to £4. Sandwiches, cakes and other snacks are £1 to £2. Quality varies enormously: some cafes definitely earn their 'greasy spoon' handle, while others are neat and clean.

Smarter cafes are called teashops, and you might pay a bit more for extras like twee decor and table service. Teashops are your best bet for sampling a 'cream tea' – a plate of scones, clotted cream and jam, served with a pot of tea. This is known as a Devonshire tea in some other English-speaking countries, but not in Britain (except of course in the county of Devon, where Devonshire cream tea is a well-known – and much-hyped – local speciality).

In country areas, many market towns and villages have cafes catering for tourists, walkers, cyclists and other outdoor types, and in summer they're open every day. Good cafes are a wonderful institution and always worth a stop during your travels.

**EATING INTO THE FINANCES**

Most of the Eating sections throughout this book are divided into three price bands: budget (main course and drink for under £8); midrange (£8–16) and top end (over £16). For more guidance, see Costs, p21.

As well as the traditional establishments, in most cities and towns you'll also find American-flavoured coffee shops – there seems to be a Starbucks on every corner – and Euro-style cafe-bars, serving decent lattes and espressos, and offering bagels or ciabattas rather than beans on toast (and you'll probably be able to get that brandy, too). Some of these modern places even have outside chairs and tables – rather brave considering the narrow pavements and inclement weather much of Britain enjoys.

## Restaurants

London has scores of excellent eateries that could hold their own in major cities worldwide, while places in Bath, Cardiff, Leeds, Edinburgh and Manchester give London a run for its money (actually, often for rather less money). We've taken great pleasure in seeking out some of the best and best-value restaurants in Britain, and recommending a small selection throughout this book.

## Pubs & Bars

The difference between pubs and bars is sometimes vague, but generally bars are smarter, larger and louder than pubs, with a younger crowd. Drinks are more expensive too, unless there's a gallon-of-vodka-and-Red-Bull-for-a-fiver promotion – which there often is. Another key difference between pubs and bars these days is that many pubs serve food, and are family-friendly – a great option if you want beer with your steak pie, and the kids want fish and chips. Look out for signs that say 'children welcome', or similar, but families eating in pubs is so common now that sometimes signs aren't even necessary. If in doubt, ask the bar staff when you go in.

As well as beer, cider, wine and the other alcoholic drinks mentioned earlier in this chapter, pubs and bars offer the usual choice of spirits, often served with a 'mixer', producing British favourites such as gin and tonic, rum and coke, or vodka and lime. These drinks are served in measures called singles and doubles. A single is 35mL – just over 1 fluid oz (US). A double is of course 70mL – still disappointingly small when compared to measures in other countries. To add further to your disappointment, the vast array of cocktail options, as found in America, is generally restricted to more-upmarket city bars in Britain.

And while we're serving out warnings, here are three more. First, if you see a pub calling itself a 'free house' it's simply a place that doesn't belong to a brewery or pub company, and thus is free to sell any brewer's beer. Unfortunately, it doesn't mean the beer is free of charge. Second, note that smoking is banned in pubs (and restaurants) – so smokers often loiter on the pavement outside. Third, please remember that drinks in British pubs are ordered and paid for at the bar. If the pub serves food, that's usually ordered and paid for at the bar as well. You can always spot the out-of-towners – they're the ones sitting forlornly at a bare table wondering why a waiter hasn't arrived.

When it comes to gratuities, it's not usual to tip bar staff. However, if you're ordering a large round, or the service has been good, you can say to the person behind the bar, 'and one for yourself'. They may not actually have a drink, but they'll add the monetary equivalent to the total you pay and keep it as a tip.

Since the major coffee-shop chains arrived in Britain in the 1990s, around 80% of local cafes have closed. *Eggs, Bacon, Chips & Beans* by Russell Davies celebrates this dying breed. The conversation continues at http://russelldavies.typepad.com.

Apart from good service, what makes a good pub? It's often surprisingly hard to pin down but, in our opinion, the best pubs follow a remarkably simple formula: a welcoming atmosphere, pleasant surroundings and, in villages where pubs have been the centre of the community for centuries, often a sense of history too (see Drinking in History, p98). The best pubs also offer a good range of hand-pulled beer, and a menu of snacks and meals that are cooked on the premises, not shipped in by the truck-full and defrosted in the microwave. After months of painstaking research, this is the type of pub that we recommend throughout this book. Of course there are many more pubs in Britain than even we could sample, and nothing beats the fun

## BRITAIN'S TOP PICKS

Looking for something special? Here's our highly subjective selection of favourite eateries, ranging from temples of gastronomy to humble-but-excellent pubs, with other parameters – such as the finest food (obviously), the friendliest staff or simply the best view – thrown in for good measure.

| Restaurant | Location | Go for... | Page |
| --- | --- | --- | --- |
| 5 North St | Winchcombe | friendly service, good atmosphere, great food | p258 |
| Al Frash | Birmingham | no-frills decor and hearty balti | p481 |
| Al Fresco | Brighton | the sea-view is the star, and the food is excellent, too | p227 |
| Blake's Coffee House | Newcastle-upon-Tyne | Sunday-morning cures all week long | p646 |
| Bordeaux Quay | Bristol | high-quality dishes, low food miles | p328 |
| Cap'n Jaspers | Plymouth | funky outdoor cafe favoured by bikers, fisherfolk, locals and tourists | p364 |
| Chelsea Cafe | Swansea | fish, fish and more fresh fish | p703 |
| Cross | Kingussie | marvellous restaurant-with-rooms tucked away in a former tweed mill | p912 |
| Daffodil | Cheltenham | modern food in a converted art-deco cinema | p265 |
| Drunken Duck | Hawkshead | first-class Cumbrian cooking | p622 |
| Engineer | London | gastropub eating with a hip vibe | p188 |
| Fifteen | London | a touch of fame and a wide range of price options | p185 |
| Hungry Man | Jersey | long-standing favourite seaside kiosk serving cream teas and snacks | p977 |
| Kitchin | Edinburgh | local Scottish produce in an elegant but unpretentious restaurant | p799 |
| Le Gallois | Cardiff | haute cuisine and hippie chic, first-class French-Welsh dishes | p679 |
| Lighthouse | Aldeburgh | welcoming atmosphere and top-notch international dining | p423 |
| Lighthouse Tearoom | Isle of Arran | much more than a tearoom, excellent fish dishes and snacks | p845 |
| Loch Fyne Oyster Bar | Inveraray | now a chain throughout Britain, but the original is still the best | p853 |
| Magpie Cafe | Whitby | fantastic fish and chips (but crowds to match) | p568 |
| Mawddach | Dolgellau | another gem in Wales' crown of foodie gems | p760 |
| Midsummer House | Cambridge | excellent French Mediterranean cuisine in a Victorian setting | p410 |
| Modern | Manchester | amazing city views with food to match | p580 |
| Monster Mash | Edinburgh | the very best in comfort-food dining | p798 |
| Plas Bodegroes | Pwllheli | one of Wales' few Michelin star–rated eateries | p769 |
| Teza Indian Canteen | Carlisle | 21st-century Indian cuisine | p635 |
| Three Chimneys | Isle of Skye | wonderful rural location, some of the best Scottish specialities in the country | p942 |
| Two Fat Ladies at the Buttery | Glasgow | ancient oak-panelled rooms, modern Scottish cuisine | p820 |
| Ultracomida Deli | Aberystwyth | superb eatery with tapas and Welsh-Spanish fusion | p744 |
| Walnut Tree Inn | Abergavenny | quite simply, one of the best places to eat in Wales | p734 |

**DRINKING IN HISTORY**

As you travel around Britain, in between visits to castles and cathedrals you'll probably visit a few pubs, where you can't fail to notice the splendid selection of names, often illustrated with attractive signboards. In days gone by, these signs were vital because most of the ale-swilling populace couldn't read. Today pub signs are still a feature of the landscape, and remain as much a part of British history as medieval churches or fine stately homes.

Many pub names have connections to royalty. The most popular is the Red Lion, with more than 500 pubs in Britain bearing this title. It dates from the early 17th century, when King James VI of Scotland became King James I of England. Lest the populace forget his origin, he ordered that the lion, his heraldic symbol, be displayed in public places.

The second most popular pub name is the Crown, which has more obvious royal connections, while the third most popular, the Royal Oak, recalls the days when King Charles II escaped Cromwell's republican army by hiding in a tree. (Look hard at most Royal Oak pub signs and you'll see his face peeping out from between the leaves.)

Other names with clear royal connections include the King's Arms, the Queen's Head, the Prince of Wales and so on. Less obviously royal is the White Hart, the heraldic symbol of Richard II, who in 1393 decreed that every pub should display a sign to distinguish it from other buildings. The decree rounded off by saying anyone failing in this duty 'shall forfeit his ale', so many landlords chose the white hart as a sign of allegiance, and an insurance against stock loss.

Look carefully at the colour of the rose painted on signs for the Rose and Crown, especially if you're in the north of England. West of the Pennine Hills it should be the red rose of the House of Lancaster; east of the Pennines it's the white rose depicting the House of York. Woe betide any pub sign that is sporting the wrong colour!

While some pub names crop up in their hundreds, others are far from common, although many still have links to history. Nottingham's most famous pub, Ye Olde Trip to Jerusalem, commemorates knights and soldiers departing for crusades in the Holy Land in the 12th century. Pub names such as the George and Dragon may date from the same era – as a story brought back from the East by returning crusaders. Move on several centuries and pub names such as the Spitfire, the Lancaster or the Churchill recall the days of WWII.

For a more local perspective, the Nobody Inn near Exeter in Devon is said to derive from a mix-up over a coffin, a pub called the Hit or Miss near Chippenham in Wiltshire recalls a close-run game of village cricket, while the Quiet Woman near Buxton in Derbyshire, with a sign of a headless female, is a reminder of more-chauvinistic times.

of doing your own investigation, so, armed with the advice in this book, we urge you to get out there and tipple your tastebuds.

## FOOD GLOSSARY

**aubergine** – large purple-skinned vegetable; 'eggplant' in the USA and Australia
**bangers** – sausages (colloquial)
**bap** – a large, wide, flat, soft bread roll
**bill** – the total you need to pay after eating in a restaurant ('check' to Americans)
**bitter** – ale; a type of beer
**black pudding** – type of sausage made from dried blood and other ingredients
**bun** – bread roll, usually sweet eg currant bun, cream bun
**BYO** – bring your own (usually in the context of bringing your own drink to a restaurant)
**caff** – abbreviated form of cafe
**candyfloss** – light sugar-based confectionary; called 'cotton candy' in the USA, 'fairy floss' in Australia
**chips** – sliced, deep-fried potatoes, eaten hot (what Americans call 'fries')
**cider** – beer made from apples
**clotted cream** – cream so heavy or rich that it's become almost solid (but not sour)
**corkage** – a small charge levied by the restaurant when you BYO (bring your own)

**courgette** – green vegetable ('zucchini' to Americans)

**cream tea** – cup of tea and a scone loaded with jam and cream

**crisps** – thin slices of fried potato bought in a packet, eaten cold; called 'chips' or 'potato chips' in the USA and Australia

**crumpet** – circular piece of doughy bread, toasted before eating, usually covered with butter

**cuppa** – a cup of tea

**dram** – whisky measure

**greasy spoon** – cheap cafe

**icing** – thick, sweet and solid covering on a cake; called 'frosting' in the USA

**jam** – fruit conserve often spread on bread

**jelly** – sweet dessert of flavoured gelatine

**joint** – cut of meat used for roasting

**kippers** – salted and smoked fish, traditionally herring

**pickle** – a thick, vinegary vegetable-based condiment.

**Pimms** – popular English spirit mixed with lemonade, mint and fresh fruit

**pint** – beer (as in 'let me buy you a pint')

**sarnie** – sandwich

**scrumpy** – a type of strong dry *cider* originally made in England's West Country; many pubs serve it straight from the barrel

**shandy** – beer and lemonade mixed together in equal quantities; when ordering, specify a bitter shandy or a lager shandy

**shepherd's pie** – two-layered oven dish with a ground beef and onion mixture on the bottom and mashed potato on the top – no pastry

**snakebite** – equal mix of cider and lager; favoured by students as it reputedly gets you drunk quickly thanks to the lager's bubbles and the cider's strength

**squash** – fruit drink-concentrate mixed with water

**stout** – dark, full-bodied beer made from malt; Guinness is the most famous variety

**sweets** – what Americans call 'candy' and Australians call 'lollies'

**tattie** – Scottish term for 'potato'

**tipple** – an old-fashioned word for drink, often used ironically eg 'Do you fancy a tipple?'; a tippler is a drinker

**treacle** – molasses or dark syrup

# Environment

The island of Britain sits at the eastern edge of the North Atlantic and consists of three nations: England in the south and centre, Scotland to the north and Wales to the west – together making up the state of Great Britain (see p36 for more definitions). Further west lies the island of Ireland; this, together with the island of Britain and several smaller islands, comprises the archipelago of the British Isles. Looking southeast, France is just 20 miles away, while to the northeast lie the countries of Scandinavia.

## THE LAND

Geologically at least, Britain is part of Europe. It's on the edge of the Eurasian land mass, separated from the mother continent by the shallow English Channel. (The French are not so proprietorial, and call it La Manche – the sleeve.) About 10,000 years ago, Britain was *physically* part of Europe, but then sea levels rose and created the island we know today. Only in more recent times has there been a reconnection, in the form of the Channel Tunnel.

When it comes to topology, Britain is not a place of extremes – there are no Himalayas or Lake Baikals – but even a short journey can take you through a surprising mix of landscapes.

Southern England's countryside is gently undulating, with a few hilly areas like the Cotswolds and a mix of cities, towns and farmland. East Anglia is mainly low and flat, while the Southwest Peninsula has wild moors and rich pastures – hence Devon's world-famous cream – plus a rugged coast with sheltered beaches, making it a favourite holiday destination.

In the north of England, farmland remains interspersed with towns and cities, but the landscape is noticeably more bumpy. A line of large hills called the Pennines (fondly tagged 'the backbone of England') runs from Derbyshire to the Scottish border, and includes the peaty plateaus of the Peak District, the wild moors around Haworth (immortalised in Brontë novels), the delightful valleys of the Yorkshire Dales and the frequently windswept but ruggedly beautiful hills of Northumberland.

Perhaps England's best-known landscape is the Lake District, a small but spectacular cluster of mountains in the northwest, where Scaféll Pike (a towering 978m) is England's highest peak.

The landscape of Wales is also defined by hills and mountains: notably the rounded Black Mountains and Brecon Beacons in the south, and the spiky peaks of Snowdonia in the north, with Snowdon (1085m) the highest peak

The Environment Agency is responsible for everything from clean air and flood warnings to boat permits and fishing licences. Find lots more at www.environment -agency.gov.uk.

---

**COMPARING COVERAGE**

Statistics can be boring, but these essential measurements may be handy for planning or perspective as you travel around.

**Wales**: 8000 sq miles
**Scotland**: 30,500 sq miles
**England**: 50,000 sq miles
**Great Britain**: 88,500 sq miles
**UK**: 95,000 sq miles
**British Isles**: 123,000 sq miles

For comparison: France is about 210,000 sq miles, Texas 260,000 sq miles, Australia nearly 3 million sq miles and the USA over 3.5 million sq miles. When Britain is compared with these giants, it's amazing that such a small island can make so much noise.

---

**WILD READING**

Is it a rabbit or a hare? A gull or a tern? Buttercup or cowslip? If you need to know a bit more about Britain's plant and animal kingdoms, the following guidebooks are ideal for entry-level naturalists:

- *Complete Guide to British Wildlife* by Paul Sterry is portable and highly recommended, covering mammals, birds, fish, plants, snakes, insects and fungi, with brief descriptions and excellent photos.

- If feathered friends are enough, the *Complete Guide to British Birds* by Paul Sterry combines clear photos and descriptions, plus when and where each species may be seen.

- *Wildlife of the North Atlantic* by world-famous film-maker Tony Soper beautifully covers the animals seen from beach, boat and cliff-top, in the British Isles and beyond.

- The Gem series includes handy little books on wildlife topics, such as *Birds*, *Trees*, *Fish* and *Wild Flowers*.

---

in Wales. In between lie the wild Cambrian Mountains of Mid Wales, rolling to the west coast of spectacular cliffs and shimmering river estuaries.

For real mountains, though, you've got to go to Scotland, especially the wild, remote and thinly populated northwest Highlands – separated from the rest of the country by a diagonal gash in the earth's crust called the Boundary Fault. Ben Nevis (1344m) is Scotland's – and Britain's – highest mountain, but there are many more to choose from. The Highlands are further enhanced by the vast cluster of beautiful islands that lie off the loch-indented west coast.

South of the Scottish Highlands is a relatively flat area called the central Lowlands, home to the bulk of Scotland's population. Further south, down to the border with England, things get hillier again; this is the southern Uplands, a fertile farming area.

## WILDLIFE

For a small country, Britain has a diverse range of plants and animals. Some native species are hidden away, but there are undoubted gems, from woods carpeted in shimmering bluebells to a stately herd of deer in the mountains. This wildlife is part of the fabric of Britain, and having a closer look will enhance your trip enormously.

### Animals

In farmland areas rabbits are everywhere, but if you're hiking through the countryside look out for brown hares, an increasingly rare species, related to rabbits but much larger, with longer legs and ears. Males battle for territory by boxing on their hind legs in early spring and are, of course, as 'mad as a March hare'.

Although hare numbers are on the decline, down on the riverbank the once-rare otter is making a comeback. In southern Britain otters inhabit the banks of rivers and lakes, and in Scotland they frequently live on the coast. Although their numbers are growing, they are mainly nocturnal and hard to spot, but keep your eyes peeled and you might be lucky.

Meanwhile, the black-and-white striped badger is under threat from farmers who believe they transmit bovine tuberculosis to cattle. Conservationists say the case is far from proven, and seem to have won the argument; mooted badger culls were abandoned by the government in July 2008.

Common birds of farmland and similar countryside include: the robin, with its instantly recognisable red breast and cheerful whistle; the wren, whose loud trilling song belies its tiny size; and the yellowhammer, with a

*Wildlife of Britain* by George McGavin et al is subtitled 'the definitive visual guide'. Although too heavy to carry around, this beautiful photographic book is great for pre-trip inspiration or post-trip memories.

song that sounds like (if you use your imagination) 'a-little-bit-of-bread-and-no-cheese'. You might also hear the warbling cry of a skylark as it flutters high over the fields – a classic, but now threatened, sound of the British countryside.

Between the fields, hedges provide cover for flocks of finches, but these seed-eaters must watch out for sparrowhawks – birds of prey that come from nowhere at tremendous speed. Another predator, the barn owl, makes a wonderful sight flying silently along hedgerows, listening for the faint rustle of a vole or shrew. In rural Wales or Scotland you might see a buzzard, Britain's most common large raptor.

A classic British mammal is the red fox. These wily beasts adapt well to any situation, so you're just as likely to see them scavenging in towns, and even in city suburbs, as in the countryside. A controversial law banning the hunting of foxes with dogs was introduced in 2005, but as this activity (a traditional country pursuit or savage bloodsport, depending on who you talk to) killed only a small proportion of the total fox population, opinion is still divided on whether the ban has had any impact on numbers.

In woodland areas, mammals include the small white-spotted fallow deer and the even smaller roe deer. If you hear rustling among the fallen leaves it might be a hedgehog – a cute-looking, spiny-backed insect-eater – but it's an increasingly rare sound these days; conservationists say that hedgehogs will be extinct in Britain by 2025, possibly thanks to increased building in rural areas, the use of insecticides in farming, and the changing nature of both the countryside and the city parks and gardens that once made up the hedgehog's traditional habitat. You're much more likely to see grey squirrels; this species was introduced from North America and has proved so adaptable that native British red squirrels are severely endangered. Pine martens, which are seen in some forested regions, especially in Scotland, are much larger than squirrels. With beautiful brown coats, they were once hunted for their fur, but are now fully protected.

*Britain's Best Wildlife* by Mike Dilger is a 'Top 40' countdown of favourites compiled by experts and the public, with details on when and where to see the country's finest wildlife spectaculars.

Out of the trees and up in the moors, birds include the red grouse, and the curlew with its elegant curved bill. Golden plovers are beautifully camouflaged so you have to look hard, but you can't miss the show-off lapwings with their spectacular aerial displays.

The most visible moorland mammal is the red deer. Herds survive on Exmoor and Dartmoor, in the Lake District, and in larger numbers in Scotland. The males are most spectacular after June, when their antlers have

---

**SEEING RED**

The red squirrel used to be commonplace in many parts of woodland Britain, but it's now one of the country's most endangered mammal species. Once numbering in the millions, populations have declined significantly over the last 50 years to about 150,000 – confined mainly to Scotland, with isolated groups in the Lake District, Norfolk and the Isle of Wight. The simple reason for this is the arrival of larger grey squirrels from America.

The problem isn't that grey squirrels attack their red cousins. The problem is food. Greys can eat hazelnuts and acorns when they are still tough, whereas reds can only eat these nuts when they're soft and ripe. So the greys get their fill first, and there's not much left for the reds. So thorough are the greys in cleaning up, that once they arrive in an area the reds are usually gone within about 15 years.

One place where reds can do well is pine plantations, as they are more adept than greys at getting the seeds out of pine cones. However, even this advantage is threatened, as in recent years the indomitable and adaptable greys have started learning the cone seed–popping technique.

---

**ACTING THE GOAT**

Britain is not known as a place to see wild goats, but one small herd has been gamboling merrily on the moorland near Lynmouth in Devon for almost 1000 years, although they narrowly escaped a cull in 2005. Wild goats can also be seen on the Great Orme peninsula in north Wales, but these are new kids on the block, having been introduced only a century ago.

---

grown, ready for the rutting season. The stags keep their antlers through the winter and then shed them again in February.

Mountain birds include red kites (in Wales there has been a successful project to reintroduce these spectacular fork-tailed raptors – see Go Fly a Kite, p739) and, on the high peaks of Scotland, the grouse's northern cousin, the ptarmigan, dappled brown in the summer but white in the winter. Also in the Scottish mountains, keep an eye peeled for golden eagles, Britain's largest birds of prey, as they glide and soar along ridges.

If there's water nearby you have a chance of spotting an osprey; the best places in Britain to see this magnificent bird include Rutland Water (p445) and the Cairngorms (p908). You could also look along the riverbanks for signs of water voles, endearing rodents that were once very common but are now all but wiped out by wild mink, another American immigrant (first introduced to stock fur farms).

Perhaps unexpectedly, Britain is home to herds of 'wild' ponies, notably in the New Forest, Exmoor, Dartmoor and parts of Wales, but although these animals roam free they are privately owned and regularly managed.

On the coasts of Britain, particularly in Cornwall, Pembrokeshire and northwest Scotland, the dramatic cliffs are a marvellous sight in early summer (around May), when they are home to hundreds of thousands of breeding seabirds. Guillemots, razorbills and kittiwakes, among others, fight for space on impossibly crowded rock ledges. The sheer numbers of birds makes this one of Britain's finest wildlife spectacles, as the cliffs become white with droppings and the air is filled with their shrill calls.

Also in coastal areas, look out for the comical puffin (especially common in Shetland), with its distinctive rainbow beak and 'nests' burrowed in sandy soil. In total contrast, gannets are one of the largest seabirds and make dramatic dives for fish, often from a great height.

And finally, the sea mammals. There are two species of seal that frequent British coasts; the larger grey seal is more often seen than the (misnamed) common seal. Dolphins, porpoises, minke whales and basking sharks can all be seen off the west coast, particularly off Scotland, and especially from May to September when viewing conditions are better. Whale-watching trips (which are also good for seeing other marine wildlife) are available from several Scottish harbour towns, and we give details throughout this book.

For more in-depth information on the nation's flora and fauna, www .wildaboutbritain.co.uk is an award-winning site that's comprehensive, accessible and interactive.

## Plants

In any part of Britain, the best places to see wildflowers are in areas that evade large-scale farming. For example, in the chalky hill country of southern England and in limestone areas such as the Peak District and Yorkshire Dales, many fields erupt with great profusions of cowslips and primroses in April and May.

Some flowers prefer woodland, and again the best time to visit is April and May. This is because the leaf canopy of the woods is not yet fully developed, allowing sunlight to break through to encourage plants such as bluebells (a beautiful and internationally rare species).

You can't miss the swaths of gorse, a spiky bush found in heath areas, most notably in the New Forest in southern England. Legend says that it's the season for kissing when gorse blooms. Luckily, its vivid yellow flowers show year-round.

In contrast, the blooming season for heather is quite short. On the Scottish mountains, the Pennine moors of northern England, and Dartmoor in the south, the wild hill-country is covered in a riot of purple in August and September.

Britain's natural deciduous trees include oak, ash, hazel and rowan, with seeds and leaves supporting a vast range of insects and birds. The New Forest in southern England and the Forest of Dean on the Wales–England border are good examples of this type of habitat. In some parts of Scotland stands of indigenous Caledonian pine can still be seen. As you travel through Britain you're also likely to see non-native pines, standing in plantations empty of wildlife – although an increasing number of deciduous trees are also planted these days.

> If you want to know more about those pretty plants you see while strolling through the countryside, you need *The Wildflowers of Britain and Ireland* by Charles Coates – a neat, portable and well-ordered book, ideal for nonbotanists.

## NATIONAL PARKS

Way back in 1810, poet and outdoors-lover William Wordsworth suggested that the Lake District should be 'a sort of national property, in which every man has a right'. More than a century later, the Lake District became a national park (although quite different from Wordsworth's vision), along with the Brecon Beacons, Cairngorms, Dartmoor, Exmoor, Loch Lomond and the Trossachs, the New Forest, the Broads (in Norfolk and Suffolk – often known as the Norfolk Broads), Northumberland, the North York Moors, the Peak District, the Pembrokeshire Coast, Snowdonia and the Yorkshire Dales. A new park, the South Downs in southern England, is in the process of being created.

Combined, Britain's national parks now cover over 10% of the country. It's an impressive total, but the term 'national park' can cause confusion. First, these areas are not state owned: nearly all land is private, belonging to farmers, companies, estates and conservation organisations. Second, they are not total wilderness areas, as in many other countries. In Britain's national parks you will often find roads, railways, villages and even towns. Development is strictly controlled, but about 250,000 people live and work inside national-park boundaries. Some work in industries such as quarrying, which ironically does great damage to these supposedly protected landscapes. On the flip side, these industries provide vital jobs (although sometimes for people outside the park), and several wildlife reserves have been established on former quarry sites.

> The latest edition of the ever-popular *Wildlife Walks* book, published by the Wildlife Trusts, suggests great days out on foot in 500 wildlife reserves across the country.

Despite these apparent anomalies, national parks still contain vast tracts of wild mountains and moorland, rolling downs and river valleys, and other areas of quiet countryside, all ideal for long walks, cycle rides, easy rambles, sightseeing or just lounging around. To help you get the best from the parks, they all have information centres and facilities (trails, car parks, camp sites etc) for visitors. For more details see www.nationalparks.gov.uk.

It's worth noting also that there are many beautiful parts of Britain that are *not* national parks (such as Mid Wales, the North Pennines in England, and many parts of Scotland). These can be just as good for outdoor activities or simply exploring by car or foot, and are often less crowded than the popular national parks.

## ENVIRONMENTAL ISSUES

With Britain's long history of human occupation, it's not surprising that the land's appearance is almost totally the result of people's interactions with the environment. Ever since neolithic farmers learnt how to make axes, trees have been cleared so that crops could be planted – a trend that has continued into our own time. In Scotland particularly, the Clearances of the 18th century (see p927) meant that people were moved off the land

**NATIONAL PARKS**

| National Park | Features | Activities | Best Time to Visit | Page |
|---|---|---|---|---|
| Brecon Beacons | great green ridgelines, waterfalls; Welsh mountain ponies, red kites, buzzards, peregrine falcons, otters, kingfishers, dinosaurs | horse riding, cycling, caving, canoeing, hang-gliding | Mar & Apr: spring lambs shaking their tails | p724 |
| Cairngorms | soaring snowy peaks, pine forests; ospreys, pine martens, wildcats, grouse, capercaillies | skiing, bird-watching, walking | Feb: for the snow | p908 |
| Dartmoor | rolling hills, rocky tors and serene valleys; wild ponies, deer, peregrine falcons | walking, off-road cycling, horse riding | May-Jun: wildflowers in bloom | p365 |
| Exmoor | sweeping moors, craggy sea cliffs; red deer, wild ponies, horned sheep | horse riding, walking | Sep: heather in bloom | p345 |
| Lake District | majestic fells, rugged mountains, shimmering lakes; ospreys, red squirrels, golden eagles | water sports, walking, cycling, mountaineering, rock climbing | Sep-Oct: summer crowds gone, autumn colours abound | p611 |
| Loch Lomond & Trossachs | sparkling lochs, brooding mountains; deer, squirrels, badgers, foxes, buzzards, otters | climbing, walking, cycling | Sep & Oct: after the summer rush | p851 & p869 |
| New Forest | woodlands & heath; wild ponies, otters, Dartford warbler, southern damselfly | walking, cycling, horse riding | Apr-Sep: lush vegetation, wild ponies grazing | p291 |
| Norfolk Broads | expansive shallow lakes, rivers & marshlands; water lilies, wildfowl, otters | walking, cycling, boating | Apr-May: birds most active | p430 |
| Northumberland | wild rolling moors, heather & gorse; black grouse, red squirrels, Hadrian's Wall | walking, cycling, climbing | Sep: heather flowering | p660 |
| North York Moors | heather-clad hills, deep-green valleys, lonely farms, isolated villages; merlins, curlews, golden plovers | on- & off-road cycling | Aug-Sep: heather flowering | p561 |
| Peak District | high moors, tranquil dales, limestone caves; kestrels, badgers, grouse | walking, cycling, hang-gliding, rock climbing | Apr-May: lambs | p463 |
| Pembrokeshire Coast | wave-ravaged shoreline of cliffs & beaches; puffins, fulmars, shearwaters, grey seals, dolphins, porpoises | walking, kayaking, coasteering, mountain biking, horse riding | Apr-May: spring flowers clinging to cliff-tops | p707 |
| Snowdonia | major mountain ranges, lakes & estuaries; curlews, choughs, red kites, wild goats, Snowdon lilies, buzzards, polecats | walking, cycling, canoeing, sailing, horse riding | May-Sep: summit temperatures mellow out | p756 |
| Yorkshire Dales | rugged hills & lush valleys crossed by stone walls & dotted with monastic ruins | walking, cycling, climbing | Apr-May: lambs | p531 |

to make room for sheep, who nibbled to death any saplings brave enough to try growing on the mountainsides. Today, the Highlands is undoubtedly a wilderness, a place of stunning and rugged beauty, but don't be under any impression that it is 'natural' or 'unspoilt'.

Even more dramatic environmental changes hit rural areas after WWII in the late 1940s, continuing into the '50s and '60s, especially in England, when a drive to be self-reliant in food meant new – intensive and large-scale – farming methods. This changed the landscape from a patchwork of small fields to a scene of vast prairies as walls were demolished, trees felled, ponds filled, wetlands drained and, most notably, hedgerows ripped out.

*The Great Food Gamble*, by well-known hard-hitting writer and broadcaster John Humphrys, studies the past 50 years of British agriculture, decrying factory farming, international subsidies, pollution and poor-quality food – among many other ills.

For many centuries these hedgerows had formed a network of dense bushes, shrubs and trees that stretched across the countryside, protecting fields from erosion, supporting a varied range of flowers and providing shelter for numerous insects, birds and small mammals. But in the postwar rush to improve farm yields, thousands of miles of hedgerow were destroyed. And from 1984 to 2002 another 25% disappeared. However, the tide might be turning – albeit very slowly.

Hedgerows have come to symbolise many other environmental issues in rural areas, and in recent years the destruction has abated, partly because farmers recognise the anti-erosion qualities, partly because they don't need to remove any more, and partly because they're encouraged to 'set aside' such areas as wildlife havens – although in 2008 set-aside land was under threat as farmers sought to take advantage of soaring grain prices. Nonetheless, subsidies from government or European agencies are now available to replant hedgerows. Ironic, when only 20 years ago there were subsidies to pull them out.

Of course, environmental issues are not exclusive to rural areas. In Britain's towns and cities, topics such as air pollution, light pollution, levels of car use, road building, airport construction, public-transport provision and household-waste recycling are never far from the political agenda, although some might say they're not near enough to the top of the list. Over the past decade the main political parties have lacked engagement, although the opposition Conservatives have made sustainability a major tenet – even changing their logo in 2006 to include a tree. Their party leader David Cameron famously made a big deal about cycling to work, which looked good (and would have been fine if they'd emphasised the health benefits) until the press discovered his chauffer still drove his official car to Parliament, carrying a huge stack of paperwork and a change of clothes. On the other side of the political fence, the Labour government has also come in for criticism; for example, an independent scientific study released in 2007 reported that the UK's carbon dioxide emissions in 2020 may be a 17% reduction on current levels, significantly lower than the 30% target. The government has also been lampooned in some quarters for the promotion of 'headline-grabbing' environmental initiatives (such as the Green Homes Project information portal, which critics say does little more than tell you how to insulate your roof) on one hand, while approving multimillion-pound motorway widening and airport expansion schemes on the other.

Britain's new 'hedgerows' are the long strips of grass and bushes alongside motorways and major roads. Rarely trod by humans, they support rare flowers, thousands of insect species plus mice, shrews and other small mammals – so kestrels are often seen hovering nearby.

But perhaps the politicians are only representing public opinion. While numerous surveys show high proportions of respondents *saying* they care, a poll in mid-2008 revealed that only 1% of holidaymakers considered the environmental impact of flying as a priority when booking their trip.

Meanwhile, back in rural Britain, in addition to hedgerow clearance, hot environmental issues include farming methods such as irrigation, monocropping and pesticide use. The results of such unsustainable methods, say environmentalists, are rivers running dry, fish poisoned by run-off, and fields with one type of grass and not another plant to be seen. These 'green deserts'

---

### ENVIRONMENTAL VOLUNTEERING  *Fayette Fox*

Britain boasts many excellent, affordable volunteering opportunities for folks who enjoy working outdoors with their hands, learning new skills and meeting people. Here are a few ideas.

#### WWOOF (World Wide Opportunities on Organic Farms)

The premise is simple: WWOOFers offer their services to help on a farm, and in return get free accommodation and meals. There are thousands of WWOOF farms globally, but the organisation's roots are British, founded by Londoner Sue Coppard in 1971, as a way to get into the countryside and support the organic movement. Today, underneath the agricultural exterior, **WWOOF** (www.wwoof.org/wwoof_uk) is also a cultural exchange, attracting international volunteers of all ages. WWOOFers usually help for a week or two, but they can stay for more or less time by arrangement.

#### BTCV (British Trust of Conservation Volunteers)

BTCV volunteers work in the countryside on tasks such as removing invasive bracken, maintaining paths and repairing bridges. And it's not *all* donkey work; **BTCV** (www.btcv.org.uk) teaches traditional land-management methods such as dry-stone walling and coppicing. No experience is necessary, just a willingness to muck in. Groups stay in basic accommodation and cook meals together. It's a great way to meet people from all over the UK. Weekend and week-long projects across Britain are offered year-round, and volunteers pay a fee to take part. If time or money is short, day-long conservation activities (free) are also available.

#### Other Options

The **National Trust** (www.nationaltrust.org.uk) offers a range of volunteering trips catering to different ages and interests. For something wilder, in Scotland the **John Muir Trust** (www.jmt.org) runs activities and conservation projects from April to October, typically at the weekend. Volunteering is free, but you have to arrange your own food and accommodation. There are sometimes opportunities for camping.

---

support virtually no insects, which in turn caused populations of some wild bird species to drop by an incredible 70% from 1970 to 1990. This is not a case of old wizened peasants recalling the idyllic days of their forebears; you only have to be more than 30 years old in Britain to remember a countryside where birds such as skylarks or lapwings were visibly much more numerous.

But all is not lost. In the face of apparently overwhelming odds, Britain still boasts a great biodiversity, and some of the best wildlife habitats are protected to a greater or lesser extent, thanks to the creation of national parks and similar conservation zones – often within areas privately owned by conservation campaign groups such as the **Wildlife Trusts** (www.wildlifetrusts .org), **Woodland Trust** (www.woodland-trust.org), **National Trust** (NT; www.nationaltrust.org.uk) and **Royal Society for the Protection of Birds** (RSPB; www.rspb.org.uk). Many of these areas are open to the public – ideal spots for walking, bird-watching or simply enjoying the peace and beauty of the countryside.

Also on the plus side, and especially important for an island nation such as Britain, sea protection is better than it's ever been. Major efforts been made to stem the flow of sewage into the sea. Oil spills still occur, but the clean-up process is quick and efficient. While some coastal areas may still be dirty and polluted, there are many other areas (around southwest England, and much of Wales and Scotland, for example) where the water is clear and many popular holiday beaches are proud holders of 'blue flag' awards. These awards show they meet international standards of cleanliness – on the sand and in the waves. The birds and whales like clean water too; the tourists are happy, the locals make some money and the scenery is stunning. Everybody wins!

Britain buries most of its rubbish in 'landfill sites' such as disused quarries and gravel pits. By 2015, say environmental campaigners, these will all be full. Options will then be more recycling, or more controversial methods such as incineration.

# Outdoor Activities

What's the best way to get off the beaten track as you travel around Britain? Simple: enjoy some outdoor activity. Fresh air is good for your body and soul, of course, and becoming *actively* involved in the country's way of life is much more rewarding than staring at it through a camera lens or car window.

This chapter focuses on walking and cycling, as these are the most popular and accessible outdoor activities – things you can do virtually on a whim – and the perfect way to open up some beautiful corners of the country. You can enjoy short rambles or long tours, conquer mountains or cruise across plains. There's something for young and old, and these activities are often perfect for families.

Britain supplies the goods for thrill-seekers, too. The coast has excellent spots for surfing and sailing, while rock climbers can test their skills on sheer sea-cliffs or inland crags, and that's before we get onto cutting-edge activities like mountain boarding and kitesurfing.

So pack your bags and your sense of adventure. Whatever your budget, a walk or ride through the English countryside – and possibly something involving more adrenalin – could be a highlight of your trip.

First stop for outdoor fans should be www .visitbritain.com – follow links to Holiday Ideas and Outdoor Activities for details about walking and cycling routes, maps and tours, plus walking and cycling festivals around the country.

## WALKING

Britain is a crowded island so open areas are highly valued, and every weekend millions of British people put on their boots and take to the countryside. It might be a short riverside stroll or a major hike over mountain ranges – or anything in between.

Every village and town is surrounded by a web of footpaths, while most patches of open country are crossed by paths and tracks, so the options are limitless. You can walk from place to place in true backpacking style, or base yourself in one spot for a week or so and go out on day-walks to explore the surrounding countryside.

### Access & Rules

The joy of walking in Britain comes from freedom provided by the 'right of way' network – public paths and tracks across private property. If you come from a country where private land is jealously guarded with barbed wire, this British feature can be a major revelation: nearly all land in Britain (including national parks) is privately owned, but if there's a right of way, you can follow it through fields, woods, even farmhouse yards, as long as you keep to the route and do no damage.

The main types of rights of way for walkers are footpaths and bridleways (the latter open to horse riders and mountain-bikers, too). You'll also see 'byways', which due to a quirk of history are open to *all* traffic, so don't be surprised if you're disturbed by the antics of off-road driving fanatics or have to wade through mud churned up by chunky tyres.

---

**FIRST STEPS**

So you've arrived in a new area, and want to know more about local options for walking, cycling or other outdoor activities. Step 1: Flip to the start of each regional chapter throughout this book for an overview of the best opportunities in that area. Step 2: Find the local tourist office, where you can pick up leaflets, maps and guidebooks, find out about bike hire or guided walks, and get information on other activities in that region, such as surf schools and riding stables. Step 3: Head out, and enjoy!

Rights of way offer endless options, but thanks to a major new law in 2004, walkers in England and Wales can now move freely *beyond* rights of way in some mountain and moorland areas. This doesn't apply to bikes nor in enclosed fields or cultivated areas, and where permitted it's clearly shown on maps and by 'Access Land' or 'Open Access' notices on gates and signposts. The land is still privately owned (and is occasionally closed, for example if wild birds are nesting, or when farmers round up sheep), but the so-called 'right to roam' or 'freedom to roam' legislation opens thousands of square miles of landscape previously off limits to walkers. It's a milestone ruling resulting from more than 70 years of campaigning by the Ramblers Association and other groups. For more see www.countrysideaccess.gov.uk.

Scotland has a different legal system to England and Wales, with fewer rights of way, but has a tradition of relatively free access in mountain and moorland areas (although there are restrictions during the grouse- and deer-hunting seasons).

## Where to Walk
Here's a quick rundown of some great British walking areas, with everything to tempt you, from gentle hills to high summits, whether you're a casual rambler or an energetic peak-bagger.

### SOUTHERN ENGLAND
Within striking distance of London lie the chalky hills of the South Downs (p204) and the tranquil coast of Norfolk (p425), but the emptiest, highest and wildest area in southern England is Dartmoor National Park (p366), where the rounded hills are dotted with Bronze Age remains and granite tors (rocky outcrops) – looking for all the world like abstract sculptures. Also in the southwest, Exmoor National Park (p347) has heather-covered hills cut by deep valleys and edged by spectacular cliffs, great beaches, quiet villages and busy seaside resorts.

In the deep south lies the New Forest (p291). Visitors to Britain love this name, as the area is more than 1000 years old and there aren't *that* many trees – but there are great open areas of gorse and heath, and it's a wonderful place for easy strolls.

Just over the water, the Isle of Wight (p294) is a good first choice if you're new to walking in Britain, or simply not looking for high peaks and wilderness. Many routes are signposted, and you can always get back to your starting point using the island's excellent bus service.

### CENTRAL ENGLAND
The gem of central England are the Cotswold Hills (p237). This is classic English countryside, with gentle paths through neat fields, mature woodland, and pretty villages with churches, farms and cottages of honey-coloured stone. The Marches (p437), where England borders Wales, has more good options.

Further north, the pride of the Midlands is the Peak District (p465), divided into two distinct areas: the White Peak, characterised by farmland, limestone and verdant dales; and the Dark Peak, with high peaty moorlands, heather and gritstone outcrops.

### NORTHERN ENGLAND
In the northwest of the country, the Lake District (p610) is the heart and soul of walking in England – a wonderful area of soaring peaks, endless views, deep valleys and, of course, beautiful lakes.

Britain's 'right of way' network has existed for centuries (some paths literally for millennia), so single trails slicing through the wilderness, as found in Australia or the USA, simply don't exist here. Even famous long-distance routes simply link many shorter paths.

The Ramblers Association's *Walk Britain* is an invaluable annual publication, outlining routes and walking areas, with handy lists of walker-friendly B&Bs and hostels all over Britain.

---

**THERE'S COLD IN THEM THERE HILLS**

The British countryside appears gentle and welcoming, and often is, but sometimes the weather can turn nasty. If you're walking on the high hills or open moors, it's vital to be well equipped. You should carry warm and waterproof clothing (even in summer), good map and compass, some drink, food and high-energy stuff like chocolate. If you're really going off the beaten track, leave details of your route with someone. Sounds a bit extreme, but carrying a whistle and torch (flashlight) – in case of an emergency – is no bad thing either.

---

Further north, keen walkers love the starkly beautiful hills of Northumberland National Park (p660), while the nearby coast is less daunting but just as dramatic – perfect for wild seaside strolls.

For something a little gentler, the valleys and rolling hills of the Yorkshire Dales (p533) makes it one of the most popular walking areas in England.

### SOUTH & MID WALES

The Brecon Beacons National Park (p726) includes a large group of mountains, forming a natural border between the central and southern parts of Wales – a range of gigantic rolling whalebacks, with broad ridges and table-top summits, cut by deep valleys.

Out in the wild west is Pembrokeshire Coast National Park (p710), a wonderful array of beaches, cliffs, rock arches, stacks, buttresses, islands, coves and harbours, with a hinterland of tranquil farmland and secret waterways, and a relatively mild climate year-round. You have to go to Cornwall to get anything else like this, and to northwest Scotland for anything better.

### NORTH WALES

For walkers, north Wales *is* Snowdonia (p758), where the remains of ancient, eroded volcanoes bequeath a striking landscape of jagged peaks, sharp ridges and steep cliffs. There are challenging walks on Mt Snowdon itself – at 1085m, the highest peak in England and Wales – and many more on the surrounding Glyders or Carneddau ranges, or further south around Cader Idris.

### SOUTHERN & CENTRAL SCOTLAND

This extensive region embraces several areas just perfect for keen walkers, including Ben Lomond (p851), the best-known peak in the area, and the nearby Trossachs range, now within the new Loch Lomond & Trossachs National Park (p852). Also here is the splendid Isle of Arran (p843) – 'Scotland in miniature' – with a great choice of coastal rambles and high-mountain hikes.

The website www .walkingworld.com offers downloadable maps and descriptions of thousands of routes around Britain, plus other services for walkers.

### NORTH & WEST SCOTLAND

For serious walkers, this is heaven, where complex geology and the forces of nature have created a landscape of utter grandeur. Here you'll find two of Scotland's most famous place names, Glen Coe (p917) and Ben Nevis (p914), Britain's highest mountain at 1344m, while off the west coast lie the dramatic mountains of the Isle of Skye (p937).

Keep going north and west, and things just keep getting better: a remote and beautiful area, sparsely populated, with scenic glens and lochs, and some of the largest, wildest and finest mountains in Britain.

## Long-distance Walks

Many walkers savour the chance of completing one of Britain's famous long-distance routes. There are over 500, including around 20 official National

Trails (in England and Wales) or Long Distance Routes (in Scotland) with better signposting and maintenance, making them ideal for beginners or visitors. Other long walks such as the Dales Way are not national trails, but just as popular.

You don't have to follow these routes end-to-end; you can walk just a section for a day or two, or use the route as a basis for loops exploring the surrounding area. Here's a short list of our favourites to get you started.

**Coast to Coast Walk** The number-one favourite. A top-quality hike across northern England, through three national parks and spectacular scenery of valleys, plains, mountains, dales and moors; 190 miles. See p518.

**Cotswold Way** A fascinating walk through classic picture-postcard countryside with smatterings of English history; 102 miles. See p254.

**Dales Way** A great walk through the farmland and valleys of the Yorkshire Dales, leading into the Lake District; 84 miles. See p533.

**Glyndŵr's Way** A long loop through the beautiful and remote rolling hills of Mid Wales, the land of 15th-century Welsh freedom fighter Owain Glyndŵr; 135 miles. See p738.

**Great Glen Way** A nonarduous route along the geological fault that splits Scotland, including a section beside famous Loch Ness; 73 miles. See p913.

**Hadrian's Wall Path** In the footsteps of the legions, an epic stride across northern England; 84 miles. See p656.

**Offa's Dyke Path** A historical hike along the ancient defensive ditch following the border between England and Wales through a tremendous range of scenery; 177 miles. See p695.

**Pembrokeshire Coast Path** An awe-inspiring walk along one of the finest coastlines in Britain, and best-loved long route in Wales; 186 miles. See p710.

**Pennine Way** The granddaddy of them all, along the mountainous spine of northern England and into Scotland; 256 miles. See p640.

**South West Coast Path** A roller-coaster romp round the southwest tip of England, past beaches, bays, shipwrecks, seaside resorts, fishing villages and cliff-top castles; 630 miles. See p280.

**Southern Upland Way** Striding through the heart of Scotland's southern Uplands, an extremely remote and challenging route; 212 miles. See p808.

**Speyside Way** Billed as a walk that 'captures the spirit of Scotland', this scenic riverside route links the Cairngorm foothills to the sea – and passes several whisky distilleries; 65 miles. See p850.

**Thames Path** A journey of contrasts beside England's best-known river, from rural Gloucestershire to the heart of London; 184 miles. See p237.

**West Highland Way** Scotland's – and Britain's – most popular long-distance path, leading walkers from the outskirts of Glasgow to Fort William in the highlands, past mountains, lochs and fast-flowing rivers; 95 miles. See p850.

For details on national trail options in England and Wales stroll over to www.nationaltrail.co.uk. For long-distance routes in Scotland see www.snh.org.uk. Some of the best guidebooks to individual national trails are produced by Trailblazer (www.trailblazer-guides.com) and Cicerone (www.cicerone.co.uk). For more information on other long walks in Britain see www.ramblers.org.uk.

> Many long-distance routes are served by baggage-carrying services, ideal to avoid lugging heavy gear as you stroll effortlessly between B&Bs. These include www.carrylite.com, www.cumbria.com/packhorse, www.walk-free.co.uk, www.southernuplandway.com and www.sherpavan.com.

## CYCLING

A bike is the perfect transport for exploring back-road Britain; it's a cheap and enjoyable way of getting around, with a tiny carbon footprint. And thanks to the success of Britain's cyclists at the 2008 Beijing Olympics, cycling is enjoying a surge in popularity – even if it means pottering along country lanes rather than hammering round a velodrome.

If you prefer cycle-touring, Britain boats a vast network of quiet roads leading through farmland, moorland and peaceful villages, while off-road riders can go further into the wilds on the many tracks and bridleways that cross the country.

---

**ROUTE OF ALL KNOWLEDGE**

For comprehensive coverage of a selection of long and short walking routes, we (naturally) recommend Lonely Planet's very own *Walking in Britain*, which also covers getting there, and places to stay and eat along the way. If you're on two wheels, there's Lonely Planet's *Cycling Britain*.

---

The Cyclists Touring Club is the oldest cycling organisation in Britain. It was founded in 1878, when the bike of choice was the penny farthing, and the national scandal of the day was 'lady bicyclists' wearing trousers.

And whether on-road or off-road is your thing, the options are endless. You can cruise through flat or rolling landscapes, taking it easy and stopping for cream teas, or thrash all day through hilly areas, revelling in steep ascents and swooping downhill sections. You can cycle from place to place, camping or staying in B&Bs (many of which are cyclist-friendly), or you can base yourself in one place for a few days and go out on rides in different directions. All you need is a map and a sense of adventure, and the roads of Britain are yours for the taking.

## Access & Rules

Bikes aren't allowed on motorways, but you can cycle on all other public roads, although main roads (A-roads) tend to be busy with traffic and should be avoided. Many B-roads suffer heavy traffic, too, so best for cycling are the small C-roads and unclassified roads ('lanes') that cover rural Britain, meandering through quiet countryside and linking picturesque villages.

Cycling is *not* allowed on footpaths, but mountain bikers can ride on unmade roads or bridleways that are a public right of way. For more off-road riding it's often worth seeking out forestry areas; among the vast plantations, signposted routes of varying difficulty have been opened up, ranging from delightful dirt roads ideal for families to precipitous drops and technical stretches for hardcore single-track fans.

For transporting bikes on trains, see p1004.

## Where to Cycle

While you can cycle in any part of Britain, some places are better than others. This section gives a brief overview.

### SOUTHERN ENGLAND

Down at the southwest tip of the country, Cornwall (p373) and Devon (p352) are beautiful, and enjoy a good climate, but the rugged landscape can mean tough days in the saddle if you overdo the mileage. Somerset (p339), Dorset (p297) and Wiltshire (p311) have more-gentle hills (plus a few steep valleys to keep you on your toes) and a beautiful network of quiet lanes, making them perfect for leisurely cycle touring. In Hampshire, the ancient woodland and open heath of the New Forest (p291) is especially good for on-road and off-road rides, while in Sussex the South Downs (p204) have numerous mountain-bike options.

---

**BOOTS & BIKES – HANDY WEBSITES**

Before you set off, the website of the **Ramblers Association** ( ☎ 020-7339 8500; www.ramblers .org.uk), the country's leading organisation for walkers, is a mine of background information. For two-wheeled travel, the website of the **Cyclists' Touring Club** ( ☎ 0870 873 0060; www.ctc .org.uk), the UK's recreational cycling and campaigning body, includes a cycle-hire directory and mail-order service for maps and books. See also **Everyday Cycling** (www.everydaycycling.com) for comprehensive information, tips and advice for noncompetitive on-road and off-road cyclists, leisure riders and bike-commuters.

**RAILWAYS RIDE AGAIN**

Wherever you go in Britain, look out for the leisurely options offered by the network of excellent cycle routes along the route of abandoned railway lines. The tracks and trains are long gone, but these flat routes remain an excellent way to trundle through the landscape – often dramatic and effortless at the same time.

## EASTERN ENGLAND

The counties of Norfolk and Suffolk (see p399) are generally low-lying and flat, with quiet lanes winding through farmland and picturesque villages, past rivers, lakes and welcoming country pubs – which all make for great for easy pedalling.

## CENTRAL ENGLAND

The Cotswolds (p254) offer good cycling options, with lanes through farmland and quaint villages. From the western side of the hills you get fantastic views over the Severn Valley, but you wouldn't want to go up this escarpment too often!

The Marches (p437), where England borders Wales, are another rural delight, with good quiet lanes and some off-road options for cyclists in the hills.

The Peak District (p465) is a very popular area for mountain biking and road cycling, although the hills are steep in places.

## NORTHERN ENGLAND

It's no accident that many of Britain's top racing cyclists come from northern England – the mountain roads make an excellent training ground. The North York Moors National Park (p561) offers exhilarating off-road rides, while the Yorkshire Dales (p532) are great for cycle touring. These areas are hilly and some routes can be strenuous, but the scenery is superb and it's all well worth the effort.

## WALES

The varied Welsh landscape, crossed by a wonderful network of lanes and tracks, makes an excellent place to cycle, although much of it is hilly so low gears will often be the order of the day.

In the north, the rugged peaks of Snowdonia National Park (p757) provide a dramatic backdrop to any cycling trip. An easier option is the nearby Isle of Anglesey (p772).

Mid Wales offers quiet cycling in a scenic and surprisingly little-visited region, while the area around the Brecon Beacons (p725) is popular for cycletourists and off-roaders. Finally, the lovely Pembrokeshire region (p708) is also excellent on a bike – although the hills go all the way to the sea!

## SCOTLAND

The Scottish Borders (p827) is an excellent area for touring, with a combination of rolling farmland, lochs, glens, hills and a peaceful, intimate charm. For off-road fans, there's a fantastic range of specially constructed routes in the Galloway Forest Park (p838), and several other sites across the southern part of the country. See www.7stanes.gov.uk.

Cyclists in search of the wild and remote will love the Highlands (p905). There aren't many roads, but traffic is usually light. As you pass majestic mountains, beautiful lochs and coasts with views of mystical islands, it won't just be the pedalling that takes your breath away.

For off-road cycling, the best book is *Where to Mountain Bike in Britain*, with a great range of routes across the country. Or see www.wheretomtb .com.

---

**THE NATIONAL CYCLE NETWORK**

Anyone riding a bike through Britain will almost certainly come across the National Cycle Network (NCN), a 10,000-mile web of roads and traffic-free tracks. Strands of the network in busy cities are aimed at commuters or schoolkids (where the network follows city streets, cyclists normally have their own lane, separate from motor traffic), while other sections follow the most remote roads in the country – perfect for touring.

The whole scheme is the brainchild of Sustrans (derived from 'sustainable transport'), a campaign group barely taken seriously way back in 1978 when the network idea was first announced. But the growth of cycling, coupled with near-terminal car congestion, has earned the scheme lots of attention – not to mention many millions of pounds from national government and regional authorities.

Several long-distance touring routes use the most scenic sections of the NCN and, it has to be said, a few less-than-scenic urban sections. Other features include a great selection of artworks to admire along the way. In fact, the network is billed as the country's largest outdoor sculpture gallery. The whole scheme is a resounding success and a credit to the visionaries who persevered against inertia all those years ago.

For more details on the NCN, see www.sustrans.org.uk – as well as providing general information, cycling tips and useful contacts, you can order maps and route guides or a copy of *Cycling in the UK*, covering more than 40 day-rides and longer 'holiday routes'.

---

If you really want to get away from traffic, head for the islands. Ferries (which carry bikes) go from the mainland to the Western Isles (p850) – wonderful getaway options for two-wheeled travel.

## OTHER ACTIVITIES

While walking and cycling can be done at the drop of a hat, many other activities need a bit more organisation – and often specialist gear, guides or instructors. Ask at tourist offices about local operators and adventure centres.

### Coasteering

If a simple walk along the cliff tops admiring the view just doesn't cut the mustard, and you'd like to combine elements of rock climbing with the element of water, then the wacky activity of coasteering might appeal. It's like mountaineering, although instead of going up a mountain, you go along the coast – a steep rocky coast, often with waves breaking around your feet. And if the rock gets too steep, you jump in and start swimming. The birthplace (and best place) for coasteering is Pembrokeshire Coast National Park (see the boxed text, p709), although Anglesea, Cornwall (p373) and Devon (p352) are gaining popularity. It's not the thing to do on your own, but joining an organised group for a half-day or full-day outing is easy enough. The outdoor centres provide wetsuits, helmets and buoyancy aids. You provide an old pair of training shoes and a sense of adventure. For more information see www.coasteering.org.

### Fishing

Fishing is enormously popular in Britain, but in many areas it's highly regulated, with prime stretches of river privately owned and angling rights fiercely protected. There's a fishing club on the idyllic trout-filled River Itchen in Hampshire, where it's rumoured even Prince Charles had to join the waiting list.

Fly fishers in Britain mainly catch salmon, brown trout and rainbow trout, while coarse fishing is principally for perch, carp, bream and the occasional

---

**CANAL & WATERWAY TRAVEL**

Britain's inland waterways consist of rivers and lakes plus a surprisingly extensive canal network. Built in the early Industrial Revolution, canals were the country's main form of transport until the 19th century coming of the railways. Today, canals are alive again, part of a booming leisure-boat industry, dubbed the 'New Canal Age'. Mile-for-mile, canals are being restored and reopened at the same rate they were built in their 1790s heyday.

Travel by boat reveals a hidden side of Britain, as canals lead through idyllic villages, pretty countryside and colourful waterside pubs. It also offers an unexpected view of cities such as London and Birmingham. With 2000 miles of navigable canals and rivers, there's plenty to explore. Across the waterway network, boats are easily hired (for a few hours, a day or a week, or longer – no special skills are needed), and exploring Britain this way can be immensely rewarding. For families or groups it's a fascinating, fun and economical combination of transport and accommodation.

For more information see www.britishwaterways.co.uk and www.waterscape.com.

---

oversized pike. There are plenty of well-stocked rivers and reservoirs, as well as stretches of wild waterways, but wherever you fish in England and Wales, you'll need to obtain a licence – available from post offices (from £3 per day to £60 for the season) or from the website of the **Environment Agency** (www.environment-agency.gov.uk).

The fishing-licence situation in Scotland is more complicated, as you may need separate permits for different rivers. They can be very costly. For more details, check the website of the **Scottish Federation for Coarse Angling** (www.sfca.co.uk).

If you want to try your luck, tourist-office staff can direct you to local clubs or places offering a day or two's fishing, such as stocked reservoirs that allow public access or smart hotels with private lakes or stretches of river.

On the sea, it's a different story. At resort-towns around the coast of Britain, you can easily find skippered boats offering angling trips, usually with tackle, bait (and lunch) included in the fee. Details are given in the individual town sections.

## Golf

Britain, and particularly Scotland, is the original home of golf, with around 2000 golf courses around the country – and more golf courses per capita in Scotland than any other country in the world.

Golf courses fall into two main categories: private and public. Some exclusive private clubs admit only golfers who have a handicap certificate from their own club, but most welcome visitors. Public courses run by town or city councils are open to anyone.

A round on a public course will cost from around £10 (more at weekends). Private courses average £40 to £50. Top-end hotels may have arrangements with nearby courses, which get you reduced fees or guaranteed tee-off times.

A very good starting point for golfers from overseas is the **Golf Club of Great Britain** ( ☎ 020-8390 3113; www.golfclubgb.co.uk); this friendly organisation can advise on where to play and arranges regular tournaments. Other handy websites include the **English Golf Union** (www.englishgolfunion.org) and **Scottish Golf Union** (www.scottishgolf.com), the latter with lots of detail aimed specifically at visitors.

## Horse Riding & Pony Trekking

There's a theory that humans are genetically programmed to absorb the world at a horse's walking pace. It's all to do with our nomadic ancestors,

---

**SCRAMBLING**

Scrambling covers the twilight zone between serious hiking and rock climbing, and seems to have been invented in Britain. This activity definitely involves using your hands, as well as your feet – and often involves a little rush of adrenalin, too. While experienced climbers may cruise effortlessly up a scramble route, someone new to the game may need a rope and a lot of encouragement. Classic scrambles in Britain include Bristly Ridge and Crib Coch in Snowdonia National Park (p756), Jack's Rake and Striding Edge (p632) in the Lake District (p611), and the Aonach Eagach ridge (p917) in Glen Coe. Local guidebooks can suggest many more. Scrambling is great fun, as long as you know what you're doing.

---

apparently. Add the extra height, and seeing Britain from horseback is highly recommended.

In rural areas and national parks such as Dartmoor and Northumberland in England, the Cambrian Mountains of Mid Wales, and the Galloway Hills in Scotland, riding centres cater to all levels of proficiency – with ponies for kids and beginners, and horses for the more experienced.

Many riding centres advertise in national-park newspapers (available free from tourist offices). A half-day pony trek costs around £15, a full day £35. The website of the **British Horse Society** (www.bhs.org.uk) lists approved riding centres and – if you fancy a few days in the saddle – outfits offering riding holidays.

## Kitebuggying

Bring together a wing-shaped parachute, three wheels, a flat beach and good breeze, and – whoosh – you're picking up serious speed; welcome to the world of kitebuggying. Often available wherever there's a big stretch of sand, good places to start include Pembrey in Carmarthenshire and Burnham Deepdale in Norfolk, a great backpacker-friendly base for other activities, too.

## Mountain boarding & Kiteboarding

Imagine hurtling down a grassy hillside on a gigantic skateboard, and you've pretty much got mountain boarding. If that's not enough, add a wing-shaped parachute, and it's a kiteboard – so you can get the wind to pull you around whenever gravity gives up. There are mountain-boarding centres in Yorkshire, Derbyshire, Shropshire, Cornwall and the Brecon Beacons and near Helensburgh in Scotland (among other places), but you can do it practically anywhere there's a grassy slope – as long as you've got the landowner's permission, of course. For more information see www.atbauk.org.

## Rock Climbing & Mountaineering

Britain is the birthplace of modern rock climbing, and few places in the world offer such a wide range of mountains, cliffs and crags in such a compact area – not to mention an ever-growing number of indoor climbing walls.

Areas for mountaineering in Britain include, naturally enough, the high mountains of Scotland (especially the northwest), with favourite spots including Glen Coe (p917), the area around Ben Nevis (p914), and the Cuillin Ridge (p937) on the Isle of Skye. In Wales, Snowdonia National Park (p757) offers long and short routes, while England's main centre for long routes is the Lake District (p610), and there are some fine short routes here as well.

*(Continued on page 125)*

# BRITISH EXPERIENCES

For such a small island Britain punches way above its weight when it comes to world famous cultural, architectural and scenic highlights. Over five thousand years of history have left each of the three nations – England, Wales and Scotland – with a wealth of unique attractions providing tangible evidence of fascinating and interconnected pasts. Instantly associated with Britain, many of these sights are the highlights of any trip to the country, while the culinary renaissance of recent years has seen the once-disparaged food of Britain added to the visitor's must-do list.

# Architecture

With a long and complex history it's not surprising that Britain has plenty of amazing architecture reflecting the island's past. A journey around the country can take you from neolithic wonders to the best in 21st-century design, and is the perfect way to get to grips with a complicated subject.

### ❶ Stone Age

Stonehenge (pictured below; p315) and Avebury (p318) are Britain's best-known prehistoric sites, but at the other end of the country Orkney (p952) has incredible stone circles, burial mounds and a preserved Stone Age village that will also have your jaw dropping.

### ❷ What the Romans did for us

For the best examples of cultured Roman life in Britain head for Chester (p584), St Albans (p270) and Bath (p330), or that final frontier of Roman expansion, Hadrian's Wall (pictured p117; p655).

### ❸ Conquest, castles & cathedrals

The Norman conquest brought European architecture to Britain, leaving a legacy of castles – the Tower of London (p161), Caernarfon (pictured opposite; p770), Stirling (p866) – and cathedrals – Salisbury (p312), Durham (p650), York (p542) – that are top of many a visitor's hit-list.

### ❹ Gorgeous Georgian

The 18th century saw grandiose stately homes for the aristocracy – Blenheim Palace (p251), Castle Howard (p553), Chatsworth House (image above; p473), Culzean Castle (p842) – and beautiful, symmetrical squares decorating the major cities, most notably in London (p153) and Edinburgh's New Town (p790).

### ❺ 21st century

After some architectural horrors in the postwar period, British buildings are now at the cutting edge of international design. Check out London's 'Gherkin' (p174), Manchester's Imperial War Museum North (p577), Glasgow's 'Armadillo' (pictured above; p822) and many more.

# Brit Lit

The authors, poets and playwrights of Britain have enduring appeal that stretches way beyond 'this sceptred isle'. The opportunity to inspect their homes, see where they drew their inspiration from, or watch their work performed live, is a memorable way for visitors to appreciate their literary achievements.

### ❶ Shakespeare

Visit Shakespeare's grave and the buildings associated with his life (p487), or catch one of his plays at London's Globe (p165) or in Stratford-upon-Avon (pictured opposite; p487) and see why he's the world's most popular playwright.

### ❷ Charles Dickens

The 19th-century England of Dickens can be glimpsed in his only surviving London home, Dickens House Museum (pictured opposite; p160), or down in Kent (p204) where several towns provided backdrops to some of his most famous scenes.

### ❸ The Brontës

Who would have thought that three sisters tucked away in a quiet Yorkshire parsonage could write novels as passionate as *Wuthering Heights* and *Jane Eyre*? Discover where they got their inspiration with a trip to Haworth (p529) and the nearby Pennine moors.

### ❹ Robert Burns

Scottish hero, poet and sometime customs officer, Robert Burns (p841) was a prolific writer whose poems became so popular that he's celebrated by all good Scots on January 25 each year.

### ❺ Jane Austen

Skilfully written with a deceptively light touch masking cutting satire, Austen's enduringly popular novels – *Pride and Prejudice*, *Sense and Sensibility* – feature many quintessentially English locations, with the most attractive undoubtedly being Bath (p330).

# Great British Landscapes

Britain still preserves some stunning, away-from-it-all landscapes where you can exercise your body and invigorate your mind. There might not be record-breaking peaks or vast deserts, but from bleakly beautiful Scottish uplands to neatly manicured gardens, there are ample opportunities to enjoy this 'green and pleasant land'.

### 1 Snowdonia National Park

Home to Wales's tallest peak, this national park (p756) is also one of Britain's most popular areas for outdoor activities, offering everything from kayaking to climbing – and spectacular views to admire while catching your breath.

### 2 Parks & Gardens

The British are a nation of gardeners and like nothing more than having a look around other people's gardens, too. From subtropical wonders like Inverewe Garden (p934), in western Scotland, to formal grounds of stately homes such as Stourhead (pictured opposite; p317) in Wiltshire, everyone here has green fingers.

### 3 Lake District

Moderate in scale, big on atmosphere, the lakes, villages and mountains of this region (p611) make it the most celebrated area in England. Made famous by Romantic poets such as Wordsworth, it's still possible to enjoy some peace and tranquillity.

### 4 Southwest coast

The smugglers may have gone but the beaches, coves and cliffs where they carried out their illicit trade now draw in the tourists. Join the surfers at Croyde (p371) and Newquay (pictured below; p376) or pretend you're in the Caribbean on the Isles of Scilly (p393).

### 5 Highlands

Wonderful, wild (for Britain) and forever associated with the Scottish clans – tartan, bagpipes and all – the Highlands of Scotland (p904) offer some stunning scenery, including Ben Nevis, the country's highest mountain.

# Food

The last decade or so has seen a food revolution in Britain with aficionados rediscovering the delights of traditional British cuisine. Top chefs have been praised for innovative takes on old favourites, but the multicultural nature of 21st-century Britain means that you can also expand your culinary horizons with dishes from around the world.

### ❶ Farmers Markets

The boom in farmers markets is one of the best indications that the British now see their food as more than just a functional necessity, with shoppers paying extra for fresh produce and something made locally and with a little more attention to detail.

### ❷ World on a plate

Traditional favourites – roast beef, fish and chips, haggis (pictured right) – are still easily found, but to experience modern Britain through its food try a curry in Glasgow, Chinese in Manchester and dishes from just about everywhere in London.

### ❸ Gastropubs

A new generation of pubs has been at the forefront of the changes in eating out, adding 'gastro' to their names and providing gourmet selections comprising top-quality ingredients.

*(Continued from page 116)*

Other popular areas for short or single-pitch climbing are the Peak District (p463) and the Yorkshire Dales National Park (p531). In southern England, good climbing areas include Cheddar Gorge (p342) and the tors of Dartmoor (p366). Britain also offers the exhilaration of sea-cliff climbing, most notably in Pembrokeshire (p708) and Cornwall (p373); nothing makes you concentrate more on finding the next hold than waves crashing 30m below!

The website of the **British Mountaineering Council** (www.thebmc.co.uk) covers indoor climbing walls, access rules (don't forget, all mountains and outcrops are privately owned), competitions and so on. In Scotland, the main bodies are the **Scottish Mountaineering Club** (www.smc.org.uk) and the **Mountaineering Council of Scotland** (www.mcofs.org.uk).

UK climbing grades are different to those in the USA and continental Europe; there's a handy conversion table at www.rockfax.com.

## Sailing & Windsurfing

Britain has a nautical heritage and sailing is a very popular pastime, in everything from tiny dinghies to ocean-going yachts. In recent years there's been a massive surge in windsurfing, too. Places to sail include the coasts of Norfolk (p424) and Suffolk (p416), southeast England (eg Brighton, Eastbourne and Dover), Devon (p352), Cornwall (p373), and the Solent (between the Isle of Wight and the south coast – and one of the most popular sailing areas in Britain). In Wales, places include the Gower Peninsula (p704) and Pembrokeshire Coast National Park (p709). In Scotland, head for the Firth of Forth near Edinburgh (p779), the area north of Largs (west of Glasgow; p840), or Inverness (p920). There are also many inland lakes and reservoirs, ideal for training, racing or just pottering.

Your first port of call for any sailing or windsurfing matter should be the **Royal Yachting Association** ( ☎ 0845 345 0400; www.rya.org.uk). This organisation can provide all the details you need about training centres where you can learn the ropes, improve your skills or simply charter a boat for pleasure.

## Surfing & Kitesurfing

If you've come from the other side of the world, you'll be delighted to learn that summer water temperatures in Britain are roughly equivalent to winter temperatures in southern Australia (approximately 13°C). But as long as you've got a wetsuit, there are many excellent surfing opportunities. Britain's huge tidal range means there's often a completely different set of breaks at low and high tides. Look for beaches that have been awarded 'blue flags', which means the local town authority is taking sea (and sand) cleanliness seriously.

The best places to start are Cornwall and Devon, where the west coast is exposed to the Atlantic; from Land's End to Ilfracombe there's a string of surf spots. Newquay (p376) is the British surf capital, with all the trappings from Kombi vans to bleached hair. In 2006 a national newspaper carried a story about two guys from Hawaii who spent a year in Cornwall because the surf was more intriguing and challenging.

Southwest Wales has many good surfing spots, including Manorbier, Newgale and Whitesands near St Davids (p715). It's easy to hire boards and gear, or arrange lessons. In the south, conditions at Porthcawl are also very good and the Gower Peninsula has a lively scene, especially at Rhossili Bay (p704).

Away from the west coast hot spots, there are smaller surf scenes in Norfolk (p424) and in Yorkshire (p515), on England's east coast.

Surfers Against Sewage (www.sas.org.uk) is an active campaign group whose name says it all. Although the situation is improving, some British towns still discharge a fair amount of crap into the sea.

Scotland's west coast is mainly sheltered by islands, and on the east coast the swells are unreliable, so it's the north, particularly around Thurso (p929), which has outstanding world-class possibilities, and a surprisingly large and lively surf scene.

The main national organisation is the **British Surfing Association** ( ☎ 01637-876474; www.britsurf.co.uk); its website has news on approved instruction centres, courses, competitions and so on. Another good site is www.a1surf.com, with comprehensive links and weather forecasts. Combine these sites with *Surf UK* by Wayne Alderson, a comprehensive guidebook covering almost 400 breaks, and you're sorted.

If regular surfing doesn't offer enough airtime, strap on a wing-shaped parachute, and let the wind do the work. Kitesurfing is one of the fastest-growing water sports in the world. Brisk winds, decent waves and great beaches make Cornwall (p373) and Pembrokeshire (p709) favourite spots, but it's possible on other beaches along the British coastline. There are several schools that can show you the ropes. Contact the **British Kite Surfing Association** (www.kitesurfing.org) for more information.

# England

TONY WHEELER

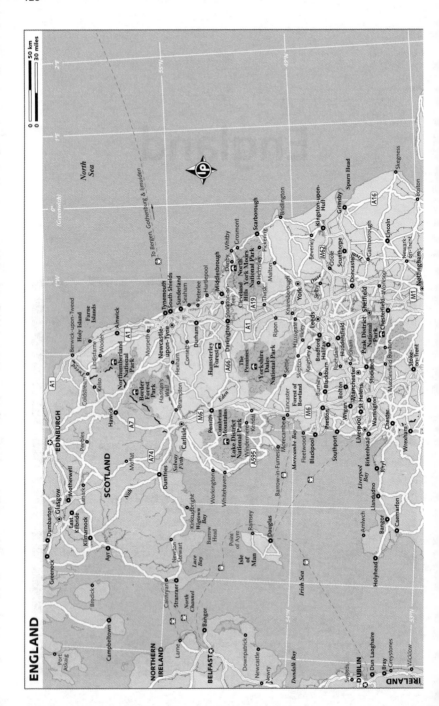

# ENGLAND

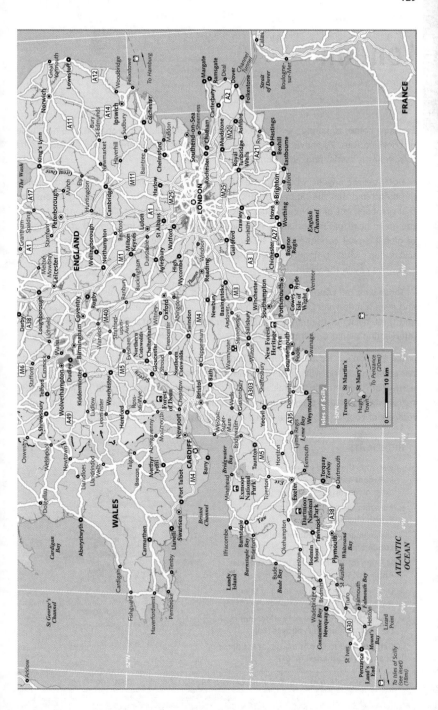

# London

Everyone comes to London with a preconception of the metropolis shaped by a multitude of books, movies, TV shows and songs. Whatever yours is, prepare to have it shattered by this endlessly fascinating, amorphous city.

Don't believe anyone who claims to know London – you could spend a lifetime exploring it and find that the slippery thing's gone and changed on you. One thing is constant: that great serpent of a river enfolding the city in its sinuous loops, linking London both to the green heart of England and the world. The Empire may be long gone but the engines of global capital continue to be stoked by the side of the River Thames. This only adds to London's vibrant, finger-on-the-pulse persona. It's also what makes it the third-most expensive city in the world.

Those who call London grey are only telling part of the story. It's also surprisingly green and even a little wild. Deer still wander some of its parks, foxes roam the streets at night and the tenacity of the foliage leaves you in little doubt that a few years without human intervention would transform the whole place into Sleeping Beauty's castle.

But London's in no danger of slumbering anytime soon. Since Roman times the world has come to London, put down roots and whinged about the weather. There is no place on earth that is more multicultural; any given street yields a rich harvest of languages. Those narrow streets are also steeped in history, art, architecture and popular culture. With endless reserves of cool, London is one of the world's great cities, if not the greatest.

---

## HIGHLIGHTS

- Watching the world pass by on a sunny day in **Regent's Park** (p168) or any of London's other green oases
- Admiring the booty of an empire at the **British Museum** (p159)
- Losing your head in history at the **Tower of London** (p161)
- Meeting the dead famous in **Westminster Abbey** (p154)
- Discovering the next cool thing in skinny jeans in the city's **live-music venues** (p194)
- Seeing the locals through beer goggles in the capital's numerous **pubs** (p189)
- Getting closer to God at the top of the dome of **St Paul's Cathedral** (p161)

---

| ■ TELEPHONE CODE: 020 | ■ POPULATION: 7.51 MILLION | ■ AREA: 609 SQ MILES |

## HISTORY

London first came into being as a Celtic village near a ford across the River Thames, but it wasn't until after the Roman invasion, in the year AD 43, that the city really began to take off. The Romans enclosed their Londinium in walls that are still echoed in the shape of the City of London (the big 'C' City) today.

By the end of the 3rd century, Londinium was almost as multicultural as it is now, with 30,000 people of various ethnic groups, and temples dedicated to a large number of cults. Internal strife and relentless barbarian attacks took their toll on the Romans who abandoned Britain in the 5th century, reducing the conurbation to a sparsely populated backwater.

The Saxons then moved into the area, establishing farmsteads and villages. Their 'Lundenwic' prospered, becoming a large, well-organised town divided into 20 different wards. As the city grew in importance, it caught the eye of Danish Vikings who launched many invasions and razed the city in the 9th century. The Saxons held on until, finally beaten down in 1016, they were forced to accept the Danish leader Knut (Canute) as king of England, after which London replaced Winchester as its capital. In 1042 the throne reverted to the Saxon Edward the Confessor, whose main contribution to the city was the building of Westminster Abbey.

A dispute over his successor led to what's known as the Norman Conquest (Normans broadly being Vikings with shorter beards). When William the Conqueror won the watershed Battle of Hastings in 1066, he and his forces marched into London where he was crowned king. He built the White Tower (the core of the Tower of London), negotiated taxes with the merchants, and affirmed the city's independence and right to self-government.

The throne has passed through various houses since (the House of Windsor has warmed its cushion since 1910), with royal power concentrated in London from the 12th century. From then to the late 15th century, London politics were largely taken up by a three-way power struggle between the monarchy, the Church and city guilds.

The greatest threat to the burgeoning city was that of disease caused by unsanitary living conditions and impure drinking water. In 1348 rats on ships from Europe brought the bubonic plague, which wiped out a third of London's population of 100,000 over the following year.

Violence became commonplace in the hard times that followed. In 1381, miscalculating or just disregarding the mood of the nation, the king tried to impose a poll tax on everyone in the realm. Tens of thousands of peasants marched on London. Several ministers were murdered and many buildings razed before the so-called Peasants' Revolt ran its course. The ringleaders were executed, but there was no more mention of a poll tax (until Margaret Thatcher, not heeding the lessons of history, tried to introduce it in the 1980s).

Despite these setbacks, London was consolidated as the seat of law and government in the kingdom during the 14th century. An uneasy political compromise was reached between the factions, and the city expanded rapidly in the 16th century under the House of Tudor.

The Great Plague struck in 1665 and 100,000 Londoners perished by the time the winter cold arrested the epidemic. Just as the population considered a sigh of relief, another disaster struck.

The mother of all blazes, the Great Fire of 1666, virtually razed the place, destroying most of its medieval, Tudor and Jacobean architecture. One plus was that it created a blank canvas upon which master architect Sir Christopher Wren could build his magnificent churches.

London's growth continued unabated and by 1700 it was Europe's largest city with 600,000 people. An influx of foreign workers brought expansion to the east and south, while those who could afford it headed to the more salubrious environs of the north and west, divisions that still largely shape London today.

Georgian London saw a surge in artistic creativity with the likes of Dr Johnson, Handel, Gainsborough and Reynolds enriching the city's culture while its architects fashioned an elegant new metropolis. At the same time the gap between the rich and poor grew ever wider, and lawlessness was rife.

In 1837 the 18-year-old Victoria ascended the throne. During her long reign (1837–1901), London became the fulcrum of the expanding British Empire, which covered a quarter of the earth's surface. The Industrial Revolution saw the building of new docks and railways (including the first underground line in 1863), while the Great

Exhibition of 1851 showcased London to the world. The city's population mushroomed from just over two million to 6.6 million during Victoria's reign.

Road transport was revolutionised in the early 20th century when the first motor buses were introduced, replacing the horse-drawn versions that had trotted their trade since 1829.

Although London suffered relatively minor damage during WWI, it was devastated by the Luftwaffe in WWII when huge swathes of the centre and East End were flattened and 32,000 people were killed. Ugly housing and low-cost developments were hastily erected in postwar London, and immigrants from around the world flocked to the city and changed its character forever.

The last major disaster to beset the capital was the Great Smog on 6 December 1952, when a lethal combination of fog, smoke and pollution descended on the city and killed some 4000 people.

Prosperity gradually returned, and the creative energy that had been bottled up in the postwar years was suddenly unleashed. London became the capital of cool in fashion and music in the 'Swinging Sixties'.

The party didn't last long, however, and London returned to the doldrums in the harsh economic climate of the 1970s. Recovery began – for the business community at least – under the iron fist of Margaret Thatcher, elected Britain's first woman prime minister in 1979. Her monetarist policy and determination to crush socialism sent unemployment skyrocketing and her term was marked by civil unrest.

In 2000 the modern metropolis got its first Mayor of London (as opposed to the Lord Mayor of the City of London), an elected role covering the City and all 32 urban boroughs. The position was taken in 2008 by Boris Johnson, a Conservative known for his unruly shock of blond hair, appearances on TV game shows and controversial editorials in *Spectator* magazine. One thing the bicycle-riding mayor will have to contend with is the city's traffic snarls. A congestion charge on cars entering the central city had initial success when introduced by his predecessor, but rush-hour congestion has now increased to pre-charge levels.

July 2005 was a roller-coaster month for London. Snatching victory from the jaws of Paris (the favourites), the city won its bid to host the 2012 Olympics and celebrated with a frenzy of flag-waving. The following day, the party abruptly ended as suicide bombers struck on three tube trains and a bus, killing 52 people. Only two weeks later a second terrorist attack was foiled. But Londoners are not easily beaten and they immediately returned to the tube, out of defiance and pragmatism.

Work is continuing in earnest in the East End to transform a 200-hectare site into the Olympic Park, complete with new legacy venues and an athletes' village that will be turned into housing post-Olympics. It's expected that the project will rejuvenate this economically depressed area – and with a price tag of £9 billion, you'd certainly hope so. The improved transport connections will certainly help. An expanded East London line will link the East End to Highbury & Islington in the north and Clapham and Crystal Palace in the south.

It won't be ready for the Olympics, but the Crossrail project will add a new east–west route to the colourful spaghetti of the tube map.

## ORIENTATION

The M25 ring road encompasses the 609 sq miles that is broadly regarded as Greater London. The city's main geographical feature is the murky Thames, which snakes around but roughly divides the city into north and south.

The old City of London (note the big 'C') is the capital's financial district, covering roughly a square mile bordered by the river and the many gates of the ancient (long-gone) city walls: Newgate, Moorgate etc. The areas to the east of the City are collectively known as the East End. The West End, on the City's other flank, is effectively the centre of London nowadays. It actually falls within the City of Westminster, which is one of London's 32 boroughs and has long been the centre of government and royalty. Surrounding these central areas are dozens of former villages (Camden, Islington, Clapham etc), each with its own High Street, which were long ago swallowed by London's sprawl.

Londoners commonly refer to areas by their postcode. The letters correspond to compass directions from the centre of London, approximately St Paul's Cathedral. EC means East Central, W means West and so on.

## Maps

No Londoner would be without a pocket-sized *London A-Z*, which lists nearly 30,000 streets and still doesn't cover London in its entirety. Lonely Planet also publishes an excellent *London City Map*.

# INFORMATION
## Bookshops

**Daunt Books** (Map pp142-3; ☎ 7224 2295; 83 Marylebone High St W1; ✚ Baker St) An exquisitely beautiful store, with guidebooks, travel literature, fiction and reference books all sorted by country.

**Forbidden Planet** (Map pp146-7; ☎ 7420 3666; 179 Shaftesbury Ave WC2; ✚ Tottenham Court Rd) On a different planet from our lonely one, populated by comicbook heroes, sci-fi figurines, horror and fantasy literature.

**Foyle's** (Map pp146-7; ☎ 7437 5660; 113-119 Charing Cross Rd WC2; ✚ Tottenham Court Rd) Venerable independent store with an excellent collection of poetry and women's literature.

**Grant & Cutler** (Map pp146-7; ☎ 7734 2012; 55-57 Great Marlborough St W1; ✚ Oxford Circus) Foreign-language titles.

**Judd Books** (Map pp136-7; ☎ 7387 5333; 82 Marchmont St WC1; ✚ Russell Sq) Delightfully musty second-hand and bargain-books store.

**Stanfords** (Map pp146-7; ☎ 7836 1321; 12-14 Long Acre WC2; ✚ Covent Garden) The granddaddy of travel bookstores.

**Travel Bookshop** (Map pp138-9; ☎ 7229 5260; 13 Blenheim Cres W11; ✚ Ladbroke Grove) Hugh Grant's haunt in *Notting Hill* and a wealth of guidebooks and travel literature.

**Waterstone's** Piccadilly (Map pp146-7; ☎ 7851 2400; 203-206 Piccadilly W1; ✚ Piccadilly Circus); Bloomsbury (Map pp136-7; ☎ 7636 1577; 82 Gower St WC1; ✚ Goodge St) Both beautiful branches of the chain. Check out the 5th View bar in the Piccadilly store.

## Emergency

**Police/Fire/Ambulance** ( ☎ 999)
**Rape & Sexual Abuse Support Centre** ( ☎ 8683 3300)
**Samaritans** ( ☎ 0845-790 9090)

## Internet Access

You'll find free wireless access at many bars, cafes and hotels, and large tracts of London, notably Canary Wharf and the City, are covered by pay-as-you-go wireless services that you can sign up to in situ (about £10/5 per day/hour). You'll usually pay less at an internet cafe (about £1 to £2 per hour). Although it's unlikely you'll be caught, piggybacking off someone's unsecured connection is illegal and people have been prosecuted for it. Some reliable internet cafes:

**BTR** (Map pp142-3; ☎ 7209 0984; 39 Whitfield St W1; ✚ Goodge St)

**easyInternetcafe** (www.easy.com) Oxford St (Map pp142-3; 358 Oxford St W1; ✚ Bond St); Trafalgar Sq (Map pp146-7; 456 The Strand WC2; ✚ Charing Cross); Kensington (Map pp138-9; 160 Kensington High St W8; ✚ High St Kensington) Attached to Subway outlets.

**Internet Lounge** (Map pp140-1; ☎ 7370 1734; 24 Earl's Court Gardens SW5; ✚ Earl's Court)

## Internet Resources

The Lonely Planet website (www.lonelyplanet.com) has lots of London information. You can also try the following:

**BBC London** (www.bbc.co.uk/london)
**Evening Standard** (www.thisislondon.co.uk)
**Londonist** (www.londonist.com)
**Time Out** (www.timeout.com/london)
**Urban Path** (www.urbanpath.com)
**View London** (www.viewlondon.co.uk)
**Walk It** (www.walkit.com) Enter your destination and get a walking map, time estimate and information on calories burnt and carbon-dioxide saved.

## Media

It's hard to avoid London's free press, with vendors pushing freebies in your face outside every central tube stop on weekdays. The best is the reasonably weighty morning *Metro*, while come mid-afternoon the trashier *London Lite* and *London Paper* are available.

All the national dailies have plenty of London coverage, but the city's only real paper is the tabloid *Evening Standard* which comes out in early and late editions. *Time Out* (£2.95) is the local listing guide *par excellence*, published every Tuesday.

## Medical Services

To find a local doctor or hospital, consult the local telephone directory or call ☎ 100 (toll free). There is always one local chemist that is open 24 hours (see local newspapers or notices in chemist windows).

Hospitals with 24-hour accident and emergency units:

**Royal Free Hospital** (Map pp134-5; ☎ 7794 0500; Pond St NW3; ✚ Belsize Park)

**St Thomas' Hospital** (Map pp142-3; ☎ 7188 7188; Lambeth Palace Rd SE1; ✚ Waterloo)

**University College Hospital** (Map pp136-7; ☎ 0845-155 5000; 235 Euston Rd WC1; ✚ Euston Sq)

*(Continued on page 152)*

# GREATER LONDON

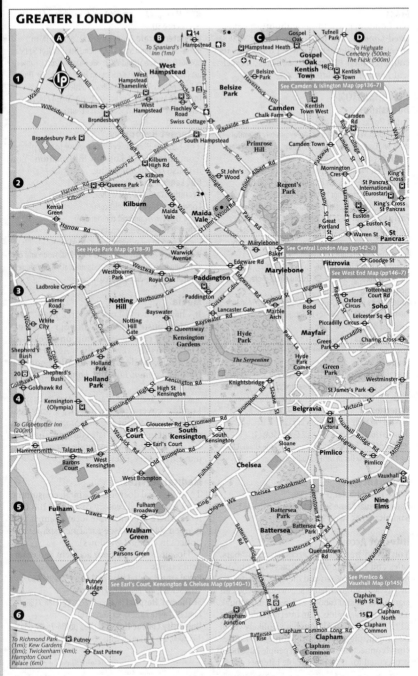

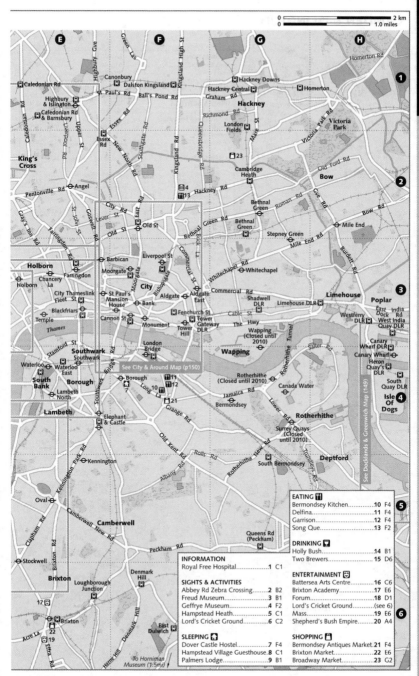

# CAMDEN & ISLINGTON

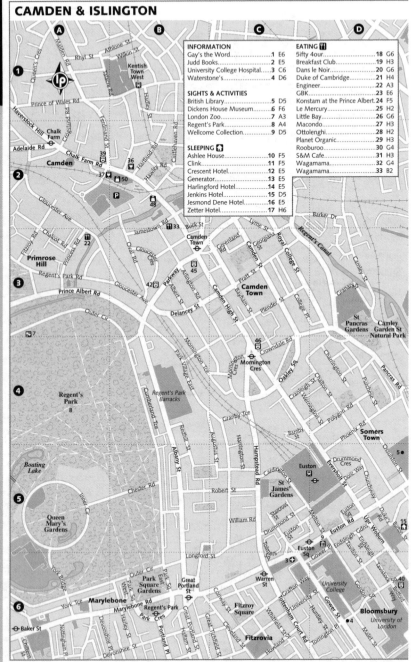

**INFORMATION**
| | |
|---|---|
| Gay's the Word | **1** E6 |
| Judd Books | **2** E5 |
| University College Hospital | **3** C6 |
| Waterstone's | **4** D6 |

**SIGHTS & ACTIVITIES**
| | |
|---|---|
| British Library | **5** D5 |
| Dickens House Museum | **6** F6 |
| London Zoo | **7** A3 |
| Regent's Park | **8** A4 |
| Wellcome Collection | **9** D5 |

**SLEEPING**
| | |
|---|---|
| Ashlee House | **10** F5 |
| Clink | **11** F5 |
| Crescent Hotel | **12** E5 |
| Generator | **13** E5 |
| Harlingford Hotel | **14** E5 |
| Jenkins Hotel | **15** D5 |
| Jesmond Dene Hotel | **16** E5 |
| Zetter Hotel | **17** H6 |

**EATING**
| | |
|---|---|
| 5ifty 4our | **18** G6 |
| Breakfast Club | **19** H3 |
| Dans le Noir | **20** G6 |
| Duke of Cambridge | **21** H4 |
| Engineer | **22** A3 |
| GBK | **23** E6 |
| Konstam at the Prince Albert | **24** F5 |
| Le Mercury | **25** H2 |
| Little Bay | **26** G6 |
| Macondo | **27** H3 |
| Ottolenghi | **28** H2 |
| Planet Organic | **29** H3 |
| Rooburoo | **30** G4 |
| S&M Cafe | **31** H3 |
| Wagamama | **32** G4 |
| Wagamama | **33** B2 |

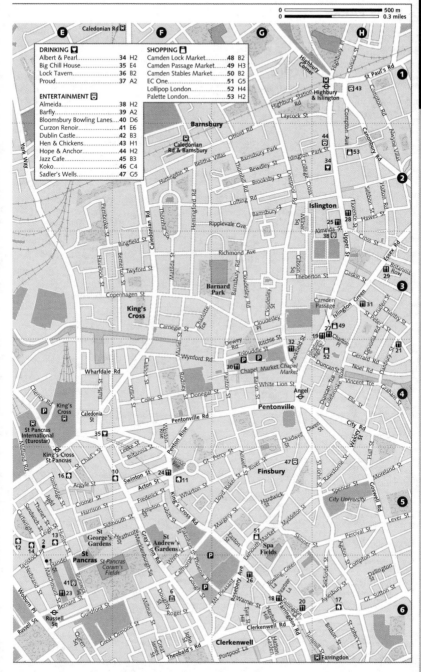

**DRINKING** 🍸
Albert & Pearl...........................34 H2
Big Chill House........................35 E4
Lock Tavern.............................36 B2
Proud......................................37 A2

**ENTERTAINMENT** 🎭
Almeida...................................38 H2
Barfly......................................39 A2
Bloomsbury Bowling Lanes....40 D6
Curzon Renoir.........................41 E6
Dublin Castle...........................42 B3
Hen & Chickens......................43 H1
Hope & Anchor.......................44 H2
Jazz Cafe................................45 B3
Koko.......................................46 C4
Sadler's Wells.........................47 G5

**SHOPPING** 🛍️
Camden Lock Market...............48 B2
Camden Passage Market........49 H3
Camden Stables Market..........50 B2
EC One...................................51 G5
Lollipop London.......................52 H4
Palette London........................53 H2

# HYDE PARK

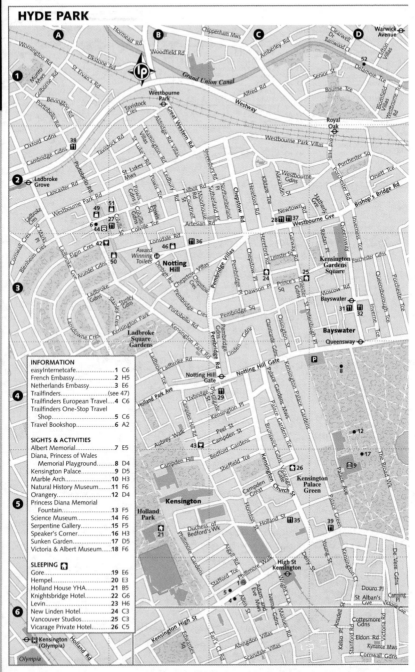

**INFORMATION**

Olympia

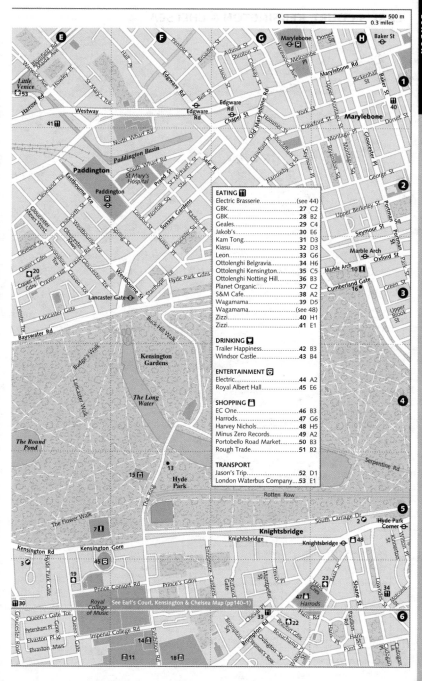

EATING 🍴
Electric Brasserie.....................(see 44)
GBK......................................**27** C2
GBK......................................**28** B2
Geales..................................**29** C4
Jakob's.................................**30** E6
Kam Tong..............................**31** D3
Kiasu...................................**32** D3
Leon....................................**33** G6
Ottolenghi Belgravia................**34** H6
Ottolenghi Kensington..............**35** C5
Ottolenghi Notting Hill.............**36** B3
Planet Organic........................**37** C2
S&M Cafe..............................**38** A2
Wagamama.............................**39** D5
Wagamama.............................(see 48)
Zizzi...................................**40** H1
Zizzi...................................**41** E1

DRINKING 🍷
Trailer Happiness.....................**42** B3
Windsor Castle........................**43** B4

ENTERTAINMENT 🎭
Electric.................................**44** A2
Royal Albert Hall.....................**45** E6

SHOPPING 🛍
EC One.................................**46** B3
Harrods................................**47** G6
Harvey Nichols.......................**48** H5
Minus Zero Records..................**49** A2
Portobello Road Market.............**50** B3
Rough Trade...........................**51** B2

TRANSPORT
Jason's Trip............................**52** D1
London Waterbus Company........**53** E1

# EARL'S COURT, KENSINGTON & CHELSEA

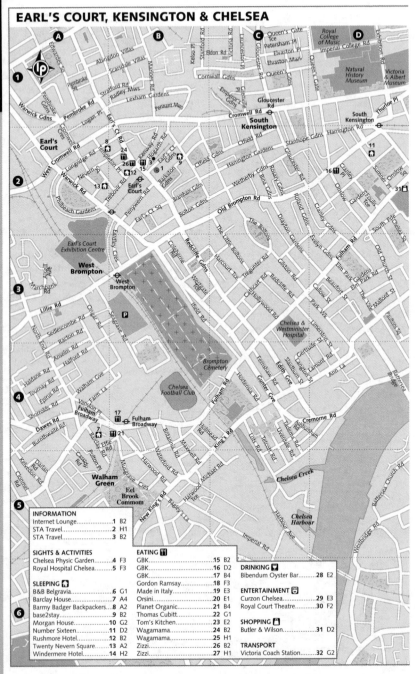

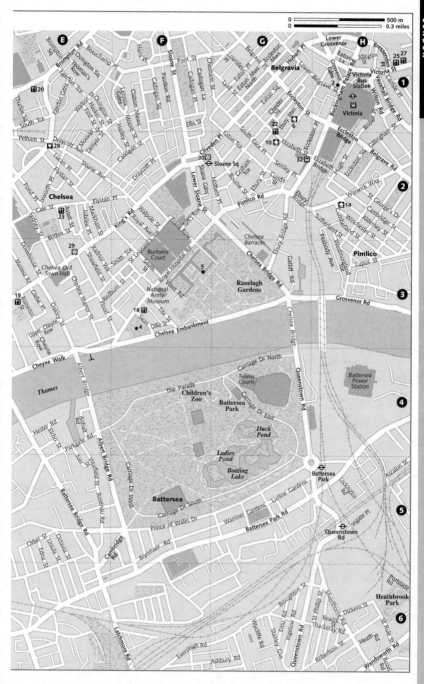

LONDON

# CENTRAL LONDON

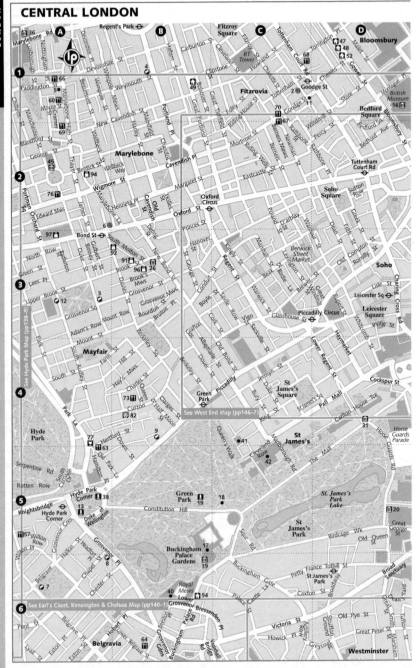

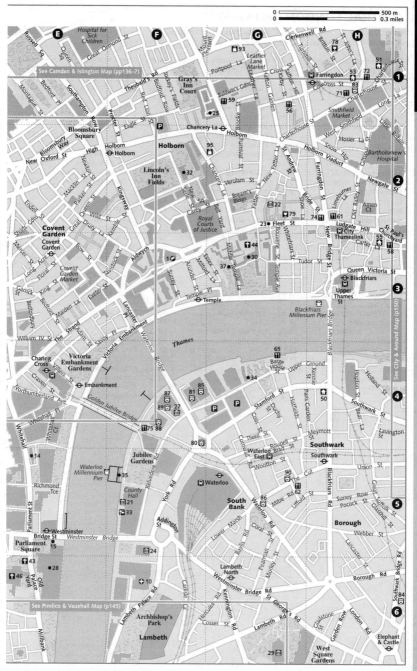

# CENTRAL LONDON (pp142–3)

## INFORMATION
Australian High Commission.......**1** F3
BTR.............................................**2** C1
Canadian High Commission........**3** A3
Chinese Embassy.........................**4** B1
Daunt Books................................**5** A1
easyInternetcafe.........................**6** A2
German Embassy..........................**7** A6
Irish Embassy...............................**8** A6
Japanese Embassy.......................**9** B4
St Thomas's Hospital..................**10** F6
STA Travel...................................**11** C1
Trailfinders............................(see 97)
US Embassy................................**12** A3

## SIGHTS & ACTIVITIES
Australian War Memorial..........**13** A5
Banqueting House......................**14** E5
Big Ben.......................................**15** E5
British Museum...........................**16** D1
Buckingham Palace....................**17** B5
Canada Gate..............................**18** C5
Canada Memorial.......................**19** B5
Churchill Museum & Cabinet War
   Rooms.....................................**20** D5
Dalí Universe..............................**21** F5
Dr Johnson's House....................**22** G2
Fleet St......................................**23** G2
Florence Nightingale Museum...**24** F5
Gray's Inn..................................**25** G1
Handel House Museum..............**26** B3
Hayward Gallery.......................**27** F4
Houses of Parliament................**28** E6
Imperial War Museum..............**29** G6
Inner Temple.............................**30** G3
Institute of Contemporary Arts..**31** D4
Lincoln's Inn..............................**32** F2
London Aquarium......................**33** F5
London Bicycle Tour Company..**34** G4

London Duck Tours Departure
   Point.................................(see 33)
London Eye................................**35** F5
Madame Tussauds.....................**36** A1
Middle Temple...........................**37** G3
New Zealand War Memorial...**38** A5
Queen's Gallery........................**39** B6
Royal Mews...............................**40** B6
Spencer House...........................**41** C4
St James's Palace......................**42** C5
St Margaret's Church...............**43** E6
Temple Church...........................**44** G3
Wallace Collection....................**45** A2
Westminister Abbey..................**46** E6

## SLEEPING 🏠
Arosfa Hotel..............................**47** D1
Arran House Hotel...............(see 47)
Hotel Cavendish........................**48** D1
London Central YHA.................**49** B1
Mad Hatter Hotel.....................**50** H4
Malmaison.................................**51** H1
Ridgemount Private Hotel........**52** D1
Rookery.....................................**53** H1
Rubens at the Palace.................**54** B6
St Paul's YHA.............................**55** H3

## EATING 🍴
Bleeding Heart Restaurant &
   Bistro......................................**56** G1
Boxwood Cafe..........................**57** A5
GBK...........................................**58** H3
Konditor & Cook......................**59** G1
La Fromagerie..........................**60** A1
Leon..........................................**61** H2
Mesón Don Felipe....................**62** G5
Nobu.........................................**63** A5
Olivomare.................................**64** B6
Ooze.....................................(see 70)
Oxo Tower Brasserie...............**65** G4

Ping Pong.................................**66** A1
Ping Pong.................................**67** C1
Ping Pong.............................(see 88)
Planet Organic..........................**68** C1
Providores & Tapa Room.........**69** A2
Salt Yard...................................**70** C1
Smiths of Smithfield.................**71** H1
St John......................................**72** H1
Tamarind..................................**73** B4
Wagamama...............................**74** H2
Wagamama...............................**75** F4
Zizzi.........................................**76** A2

## DRINKING 🍷 🍸
Galvin @ Windows...................**77** A4
Jerusalem Tavern......................**78** H1
Ye Olde Cheshire Cheese.........**79** G2

## ENTERTAINMENT 🎭
BFI IMAX..................................**80** F4
BFI Southbank..........................**81** F4
Curzon Mayfair........................**82** B4
Fabric.......................................**83** H1
Ministry of Sound....................**84** H6
National Theatre.......................**85** F4
Old Vic.....................................**86** G5
Purcell Room.......................(see 87)
Queen Elizabeth Hall...............**87** F4
Royal Festival Hall...................**88** F4
Southbank Centre.....................**89** F4
Young Vic................................**90** G5

## SHOPPING 🛍
Butler & Wilson........................**91** B3
Gray's Antique Market.............**92** B3
International Magic...................**93** G1
KJ's Laundry.............................**94** A2
London Silver Vaults.................**95** G2
Paul Smith Sale Shop...............**96** B3
Selfridges.................................**97** A3

# PIMLICO & VAUXHALL

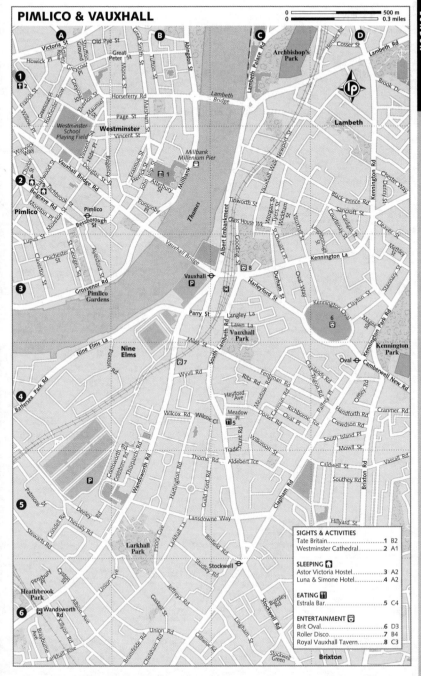

| SIGHTS & ACTIVITIES | |
| --- | --- |
| Tate Britain | 1 B2 |
| Westminster Cathedral | 2 A1 |

| SLEEPING | |
| --- | --- |
| Astor Victoria Hostel | 3 A2 |
| Luna & Simone Hotel | 4 A2 |

| EATING | |
| --- | --- |
| Estrala Bar | 5 C4 |

| ENTERTAINMENT | |
| --- | --- |
| Brit Oval | 6 D3 |
| Roller Disco | 7 B4 |
| Royal Vauxhall Tavern | 8 C3 |

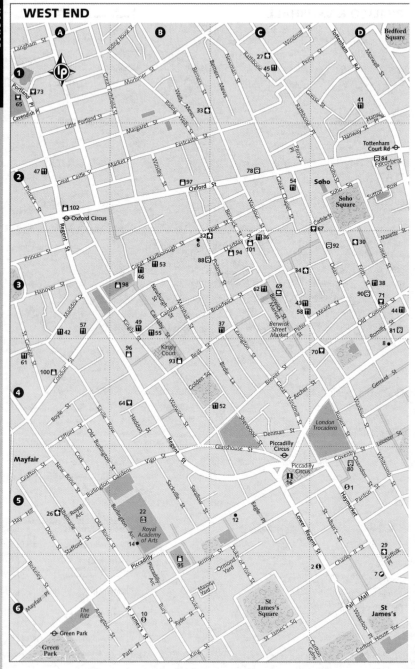

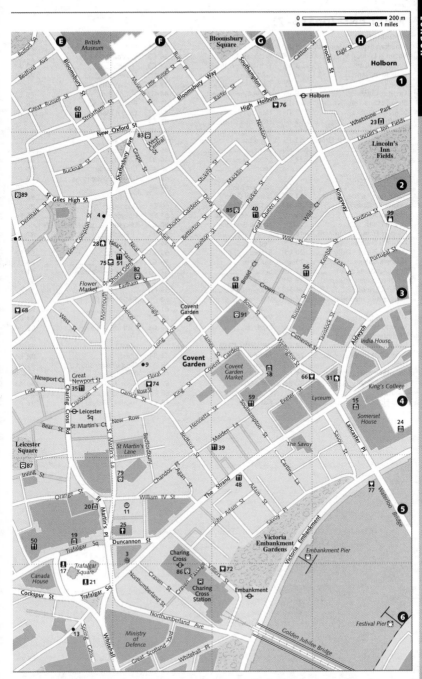

LONDON

# WEST END (pp146–7)

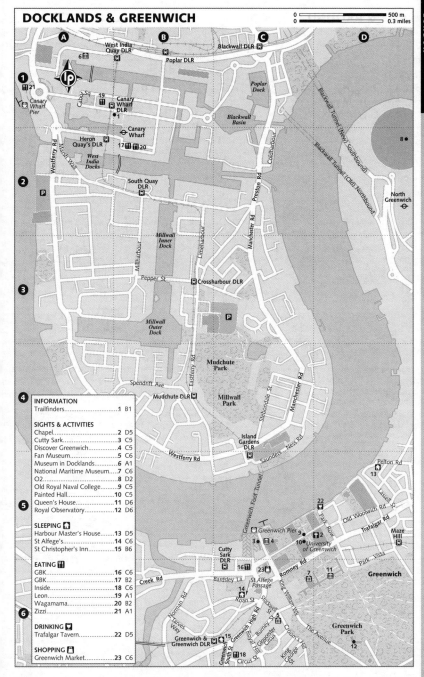

# DOCKLANDS & GREENWICH

0                500 m
0                0.3 miles

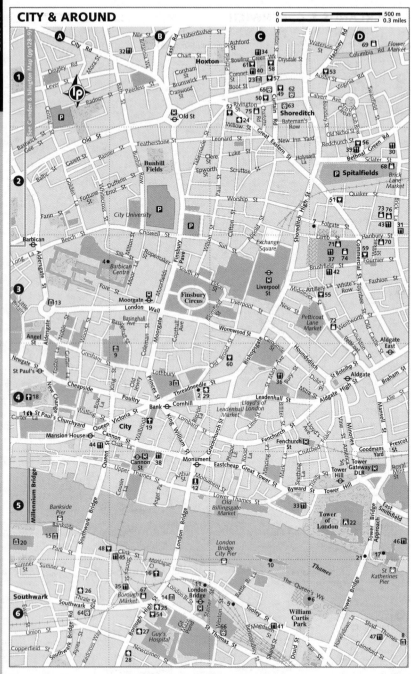

# CITY & AROUND

# CITY & AROUND (p150)

**INFORMATION**
City of London Information
Centre...................................**1** A4
Trailfinders.............................**2** B4

**SIGHTS & ACTIVITIES**
Bank of England Museum.........**3** B4
Barbican................................**4** A3
Britain at War Experience.........**5** C6
City Hall................................**6** D6
Dennis Severs' House...............**7** D2
Design Museum.......................**8** D6
Guildhall................................**9** B4
HMS Belfast..........................**10** C6
London Dungeon....................**11** B6
Monument............................**12** B5
Museum of London.................**13** A3
Old Operating Theatre Museum &
Herb Garret........................**14** B6
Shakespeare's Globe...............**15** A5
Southwark Cathedral..............**16** B6
St Katharine Docks.................**17** D5
St Paul's Cathedral.................**18** A4
St Stephen's Walbrook.............**19** B4
Tate Modern.........................**20** A5
Tower Bridge Exhibition..........**21** D5
Tower of London....................**22** D5
White Cube............................**23** C1

**SLEEPING**
Hoxton.................................**24** C1
Orient..................................**25** B6

Southwark Rose Hotel............**26** A6
St Christopher's Inn................**27** B6
St Christopher's Village...........**28** B6
Threadneedles.......................**29** B4

**EATING**
Brick Lane Beigel Bake............**30** D2
Cafe Bangla...........................**31** D2
Fifteen.................................**32** B1
GBK.....................................**33** C5
Hoxton Apprentice.................**34** C1
Konditor & Cook....................**35** B6
Konditor & Cook....................**36** C4
Leon....................................**37** B5
Leon....................................**38** D3
Les Trois Garçons...................**39** D2
Macondo..............................**40** C1
Magdalen..............................**41** C6
S&M Cafe.............................**42** D3
Story Deli..............................**43** D2
Wagamama............................**44** B6
Wagamama............................**45** A4
Zizzi....................................**46** D5
Zizzi....................................**47** D6

**DRINKING**
Anchor.................................**48** A5
Bar Music Hall.......................**49** C1
Bricklayer's Arms...................**50** C1
Commercial Tavern.................**51** D2
Favela Chic...........................**52** C1
George & Dragon...................**53** D1

George Inn............................**54** B6
Grapeshots............................**55** D3
Loungelover...........................**56** D2
Mother.................................**57** C1
Red Lion...............................**58** C1
Ten Bells...............................**59** D3
Vertigo 42.............................**60** C4
Zigfrid Von Underbelly............**61** C1

**ENTERTAINMENT**
Barbican Centre.....................(see 4)
Cargo...................................**62** C1
Comedy Cafe.........................**63** C1
Menier Chocolate Factory........**64** A6
Plastic People.........................**65** C1
SeOne..................................**66** C6

**SHOPPING**
Borough Market.....................**67** B6
Brick Lane Market...................**68** D2
Columbia Road Flower Market..**69** D1
Duke of Uke..........................**70** D3
FairyGothMother....................**71** D3
Petticoat Lane Market.............**72** D3
Rough Trade..........................**73** D2
Spitalfields Market..................**74** D3
Start....................................**75** C1
Sunday (Up)Market................**76** D2

**LONDON**

*(Continued from page 133)*

## Money

Banks and ATMs (called cash machines or cash points) are two a penny in central London. You can change cash easily at banks, bureaux de change, travel agents and post offices, where rates are usually fair. If you use bureaux de change, check commission rates *and* exchange rates; some can be extortionate.

There are decent bureaux in all London's airports, some charging a £3 flat fee. The following are also reliable (both have many branches):

**American Express** (Amex; Map pp146-7; ☎ 7484 9610; 30-31 Haymarket SW1; ☒ 9am-6pm Mon-Sat, 10am-4pm Sun; ⊖ Piccadilly Circus)

**Thomas Cook** (Map pp146-7; ☎ 0845-308 9570; 30 St James's St SW1; ☒ 9am-5.30pm Mon, Tue, Thu & Fri, 10am-5.30pm Wed; ⊖ Green Park)

## Post

Most High Streets have a post office, where you'll get to join in the national pastime: queuing. The **Trafalgar Square post office** (Map pp146-7; 24 William IV St WC2; ☒ 8.30am-6.30pm Mon-Fri, 9am-5.30pm Sat; ⊖ Charing Cross) has the main poste-restante service for London. London post offices usually open from around 9am to 5pm, Monday to Friday. Some also open 9am to noon on Saturdays.

## Telephone

The only businesses to rival food outlets for sheer number of shopfronts on London's High Streets are mobile-phone stores. It's a good idea to pick up a local SIM card if you're staying for any length of time; not only will you avoid international roaming charges on your home mobile account, some also offer cheap international call rates (eg 6p per minute to Australia). Then there's the added advantage of being able to dish out a local number to hotties you meet at bars! **Carphone Warehouse** ( ☎ 0870-087 0870; www.carphone-warehouse.com) has branches all over the city and a bewildering array of pre-pay plans available. SIMs are often free.

Many internet cafes have booths where you can dial internationally for less than the standard British Telecom (BT) rate. Another handy alternative is to buy a calling card from a corner store which allows you to connect via a local number to an internet-based international service, with charges as low as 2p per minute.

## Toilets

If you're caught short in London, public toilets can be hard to find. Only a handful of tube stations have them but the bigger National Rail stations usually do (although they're often coin operated). If you can face five floors on an escalator, department stores are a good bet. In a busy pub, no-one's going to notice you sneaking in to use the loo, but if you're spotted it would be polite to order a drink afterwards.

## Tourist Information

For a list of all tourist offices in London and around Britain, see www.visitmap.info/tic.

**Britain & London Visitor Centre** (Map pp146-7; www.visitbritain.com; 1 Regent St SW1; ☒ 9.30am-6.30pm Mon, 9am-6.30pm Tue-Fri, 10am-4pm Sat & Sun; ⊖ Piccadilly Circus) Books accommodation, theatre and transport tickets, and offers a bureau de change, international telephones and terminals for accessing tourist information on the web. It's open longer hours in summer.

**City of London Information Centre** (Map p150; ☎ 7332 1456; www.cityoflondon.gov.uk; St Paul's Churchyard EC4; ☒ 9.30am-5.30pm Mon-Sat; ⊖ St Paul's) Tourist information, fast-track tickets to attractions and guided walks (£6, daily in summer). Open Sunday during summer.

## Travel Agencies

**STA Travel** ( ☎ 0871-230 0040; www.statravel.co.uk) Victoria (Map pp140-1; ☎ 0871-468 0649; 52 Grosvenor Gardens SW1; ⊖ Victoria); Soho (Map pp146-7; ☎ 7432 7474; 85 Shaftesbury Ave W1; ⊖ Leicester Sq); Tottenham Court Rd (Map pp142-3; ☎ 0871-468 0623; 11 Goodge St W1; ⊖ Goodge St); Earl's Court (Map pp140-1; ☎ 7341 3693; 2 Hogarth Rd SW5; ⊖ Earl's Court) Long-standing and reliable with several branches in London.

**Trailfinders** (www.trailfinders.com) One Stop Travel Shop (Map pp138-9; ☎ worldwide travel 7938 3939, visa & passport service 0845-050 5905, immunisation centre 7938 3999; 194 Kensington High St W8; ⊖ High St Kensington); European Travel (Map pp138-9; 215 Kensington High St W8; ⊖ High St Kensington); City (Map p150; 1 Threadneedle St EC2; ⊖ Bank); Canary Wharf (Map p149; 30A The South Colonnade; ⊖ Canary Wharf) Also has branches in Waterstones, Piccadilly (p133), Harrods (p197) and Selfridges (p197).

## DANGERS & ANNOYANCES

Considering its size and disparities in wealth, London is generally safe. That said, keep your wits about you and don't flash your cash unnecessarily. A contagion of youth-on-youth knife crime is cause for concern, so walk away

**LONDON IN...**

**Two Days**
Only two days? Start in **Trafalgar Square** (below) and see at least the outside of all the big-ticket sights: (**London Eye** (p166), **Houses of Parliament** (p155), **Westminster Abbey** (p154), **St James's Park and Palace** (p157), **Buckingham Palace** (p156), **Green Park** (p157), **Hyde Park** (p168) and **Kensington Gardens & Palace** (p168) and then motor around the **Tate Modern** (p164) until you get booted out. In the evening, explore **Soho** (p158). On day two race around the **British Museum** (p159) then head to the City. Start with our **walking tour** (p172) and finish in the **Tower of London** (p161). Head to the East End for an evening of **ethnic food** (p185) and **hip bars** (p190).

**Four Days**
Take the two-day itinerary but stretch it to a comfortable pace. Stop at the **National Gallery** (p154) while you're at Trafalgar Sq, explore inside Westminster Abbey and **St Paul's Cathedral** (p161) and allow half a day for each of the Tate Modern, British Museum and Tower of London. On your extra evenings, check out **Camden** and **Islington** (p191) or splurge on a slap-up dinner in **Chelsea** (p187).

**One Week**
As above, but add in a day each for **Greenwich** (p170), **Kew Gardens** (p171) and **Hampton Court Palace** (p172).

if you sense trouble brewing and take care at night. When travelling by tube, choose a carriage with other people in it and avoid deserted suburban stations. Following reports of sexual attacks and robberies, shun unlicensed minicabs.

Nearly every Londoner has a story about a wallet/phone/bag being nicked from under their noses – or arses, in the case of bags on floors in bars. Watch out for pickpockets on crowded tubes, night buses and streets. That friendly drunk who bumped into you may now be wandering off with your wallet.

### Scams

When using ATMs, guard your PIN details carefully. Don't use one that looks like it's been tampered with as there have been incidents of card cloning.

It should come as no surprise that some Soho strip clubs and hostess bars are dodgy, and people should be especially wary of those that tout for business on the street.

## SIGHTS

With so much to see and do, it can be hard to know where to start. Weather will be a determining factor: the museums and galleries are great for a rainy day, but when the sun shines make like a Londoner and head to the parks – you never know whether this fine day will be your last. Otherwise, attack the sights by area using the ordering of this section as your guide.

### Trafalgar Square

Trafalgar Sq is the public heart of London, hosting rallies, marches and feverish New Year festivities. Londoners congregate here to celebrate anything from football victories to the ousting of political leaders. Formerly ringed by gnarling traffic, the square's been tidied up and is now one of the world's grandest public places. At the heart of it, Nelson surveys his fleet from the 43.5m-high **Nelson's Column** (Map pp146–7), erected in 1843 to commemorate Nelson's 1805 victory over Napoleon off Cape Trafalgar in Spain. At the edges of the square are four plinths, three of which have permanent statues, while the **fourth plinth** (Map pp146–7) is given over to temporary modern installations.

The square is flanked by splendid buildings: **Canada House** to the west, the National Gallery and National Portrait Gallery to the north, and **South Africa House** and the church of **St Martin-in-the-Fields** (Map pp146–7) to the east. Further south stands **Admiralty Arch** (Map pp146–7), built in honour of Queen Victoria in 1910, beyond which the Mall (rhymes with 'shall', not 'shawl') is the ceremonial route leading to Buckingham Palace.

## NATIONAL GALLERY

Gazing grandly over Trafalgar Sq through its Corinthian columns, the **National Gallery** (Map pp146-7; ☎ 7747 2885; www.nationalgallery.org .uk; Trafalgar Sq WC2; admission free; ☷ 10am-6pm Sat-Thu, to 9pm Fri; ⊖ Charing Cross) is the nation's most important repository of art. Four million visitors descend annually to admire its 2300-plus Western European paintings, spanning the years 1250 to 1900.

Highlights include Turner's *The Fighting Temeraire* (voted Britain's greatest painting), Botticelli's *Venus and Mars* and Van Gogh's *Sunflowers*. *Da Vinci Code* fans will make a beeline for Leonardo's *The Virgin of the Rocks*, the sister of the one hanging in the Louvre. The medieval religious paintings in the Sainsbury Wing are fascinating, but for a short, sharp blast of brilliance you can't beat the truckloads of Monets, Manets, Cézannes, Degas and Renoirs in rooms 43 to 46.

It's all a bit overwhelming for one visit, but as admission's free it's possible to dip into it again and again. Free one-hour guided tours leave at 11.30am and 2.30pm daily. If you prefer, you can devise and print off your own tour from the flashy computer screens of Art Start, the gallery's interactive multimedia system. Visit on Friday evenings for live music and free talks.

## NATIONAL PORTRAIT GALLERY

The fascinating **National Portrait Gallery** (Map pp146-7; ☎ 7312 2463; www.npg.org.uk; St Martin's Pl WC2; admission free; ☷ 10am-6pm Sat-Wed, to 9pm Thu & Fri; ⊖ Charing Cross) is like stepping into a picture book of English history or, if you're trashy, an *OK* magazine spread on history's celebrities ('What's *she* wearing?').

Founded in 1856, the permanent collection (around 10,000 works) starts with the Tudors on the 2nd floor and descends to contemporary figures. Among the modern mob, look out for a full-length painting of Dame Judi Dench, a 3D depiction of JK Rowling and a photographic study of David Bowie, seated in a seedy toilet with a dead-looking Natasha Vojnovic across his lap.

An audio guide (£2) will lead you through the gallery's most famous pictures. Look out for the temporary exhibitions, especially the prestigious National Portrait Award (June to

> ### LONDON FOR FREE
>
> London may be an expensive city to eat, drink and sleep in, but when it comes to sights, most of the very best things are free. Apparent from all the breathtaking parks and buildings, you won't pay a penny to visit the following: National Gallery, National Portrait Gallery, Tate Britain, Tate Modern, British Museum, Museum of London, Bank of England Museum, Imperial War Museum, Victoria & Albert Museum, Natural History Museum, Science Museum, Geffrye Museum, British Library, Guildhall, Wellcome Collection and the Wallace Collection.

September). There's also an interesting view over the rooftops to Trafalgar Sq and Nelson's backside from the top-floor restaurant.

## Westminster & Pimlico

Purposefully positioned outside the old City (London's fiercely independent burghers preferred to keep the monarch and Parliament at arm's length), Westminster has been the centre of the nation's political power for a millennium. The area's many landmarks combine to form an awesome display of power, gravitas and historical import. Neighbouring Pimlico can't compete but it does boast some decent B&Bs and the wonderful Tate Britain gallery.

### WESTMINSTER ABBEY

If you're one of those boring sods who boast about spending months in Europe without ever setting foot in a church, get over yourself and make this the exception. Not merely a beautiful place of worship, **Westminster Abbey** (Map pp142-3; ☎ 7222 5152; www.Westminster Abbey .org; 20 Dean's Yard SW1; adult/child £12/9, tours/audio guides £5/4; ☷ 9.15am-4.30pm Mon, Tue, Thu & Fri, to 6pm Wed, to 2.30pm Sat; ⊖ Westminster) serves England's history cold on slabs of stone. For centuries the country's greatest have been interred here, including most of the monarchs from Henry III (died 1272) to George II (1760).

Unlike St Paul's, Westminster Abbey has never been a cathedral (the seat of a bishop). It's what is called a 'royal peculiar' and is administered directly by the Crown. Every monarch since William the Conqueror has been crowned here, with the exception of a couple of unlucky Eds who were murdered (Edward V) or abdicated (Edward VIII) before the magic moment. Look out for the incongruously ordinary-looking **Coronation Chair**.

The building itself is an arresting sight. Though a mixture of architectural styles, it is considered the finest example of Early English Gothic in existence. The original church was built in the 11th century by King (later Saint) Edward the Confessor, who is buried in the chapel behind the main altar. Henry III began work on the new building in 1245 but didn't complete it; the French Gothic nave was finished in 1388. Henry VII's magnificent Late Perpendicular–style **Lady Chapel** was consecrated in 1519 after 16 years of construction.

Apart from the royal graves, keep an eye out for the many famous commoners interred here, especially in **Poet's Corner** where you'll find the resting places of Chaucer, Dickens, Hardy, Tennyson, Dr Johnson and Kipling as well as memorials to the other greats (Shakespeare, Jane Austen, Emily Bronte etc). Elsewhere you'll find the graves of Handel and Sir Isaac Newton.

The octagonal **Chapter House** (☺ 10.30am-4pm) dates from the 1250s and was where the monks would meet for daily prayer before Henry VIII's dissolution of the monasteries. Used as a treasury and 'Royal Wardrobe', the cryptlike **Pyx Chamber** (☺ 10.30am-4pm) dates from about 1070. The neighbouring **Abbey Museum** (☺ 10.30am-4pm) has as its centrepiece death masks of generations of royalty.

Parts of the Abbey complex are free to visitors. This includes the **Cloister** (☺ 8am-6pm), which featured prominently in *The Da Vinci Code*, and the 900-year-old **College Garden** (☺ 10am-6pm Tue-Thu Apr-Sep, to 4pm Oct-Mar). Free concerts are held here from 12.30pm to 2pm on Wednesdays from mid-July through August. Adjacent to the abbey is **St Margaret's Church** (Map pp142-3; ☺ 9.30am-3.30pm Mon-Fri, to 1.30pm Sat, 2-5pm Sun), the House of Commons' place of worship since 1614. There are windows commemorating churchgoers Caxton and Milton, and Sir Walter Raleigh is buried by the altar.

Of course, admission to the Abbey is free if you wish to attend a service. On weekdays, Matins is at 7.30am, Holy Communion at 8am and 12.30pm, and Choral Evensong at 5pm. There are services throughout the day on Sundays. You can sit and soak in the atmosphere, even if you're not religious.

## HOUSES OF PARLIAMENT

Coming face-to-face with one of the world's most recognisable landmarks is always a surreal moment, but in the case of the **Houses of Parliament** (Map pp142-3; ☎ 0870-906 3773; www .parliament.uk; Parliament Sq SW1; ✛ Westminster) it's a revelation. The BBC's standard title shot just doesn't do justice to the ornate stonework and golden filigree of Charles Barry and Augustus Pugin's neo-Gothic masterpiece (1840).

Officially called the Palace of Westminster, the oldest part is **Westminster Hall** (1097), which is one of only a few parts that survived a catastrophic fire in 1834. Its roof, added between 1394 and 1401, is the earliest known example of a hammer-beam roof and has been described as the greatest surviving achievement of medieval English carpentry.

However, the palace's most famous feature is its clock tower, aka **Big Ben** (Map pp142–3). Ben is actually the 13-ton bell, named after Benjamin Hall, who was commissioner of works when the tower was completed in 1858.

At the business end, Parliament is divided into two houses. The green-hued **House of Commons** is the lower house where the 646 elected Members of Parliament sit. Traditionally the home of hereditary bluebloods, the scarlet-decorated **House of Lords** now has peers appointed through various means. Both houses debate and vote on legislation, which must then be approved by the Queen. At the annual State Opening of Parliament (usually in November), the Queen takes her throne in the House of Lords, having processed in the gold-trimmed Irish State Coach from Buckingham Palace. It's well worth lining the route for a gawk at the Crown Jewels sparkling in the sun.

When Parliament is in session, visitors are admitted to the **House of Commons Visitors' Gallery** (admission free; ☺ 2.30-10.30pm Mon & Tue, 11.30am-7.30pm Wed, 10.30am-6.30pm Thu, 9.30am-3pm some Fri). Expect to queue for at least an hour and possibly longer during Question Time (at the beginning of each day). The **House of Lords Visitors' Gallery** (admission free; ☺ 2.30-10pm Mon & Tue, 3-10pm Wed, 11am-7.30pm Thu, from 10am some Fri) is also open.

Note that parliamentary recesses (ie holidays) last for three months over the summer, and a couple of weeks over Easter and Christmas. When parliament is in recess there are guided **tours** (75-min tours adult/child £12/5) of both chambers and other historic areas. UK residents can approach their MPs to arrange a free tour and to climb the clock tower.

### WESTMINSTER CATHEDRAL

Begun in 1895, the neo-Byzantine **Westminster Cathedral** (Map p145; ☎ 7798 9055; www.westminster cathedral.org.uk; Victoria St SW1; admission free; ⏱ 7am-7pm; ✪ Victoria) is the headquarters of Britain's once suppressed Roman Catholic Church. It's still a work in progress, the vast interior part dazzling marble and mosaic and part bare brick; new sections are completed as funds allow. Look out for Eric Gill's highly regarded stone **Stations of the Cross** (1918).

The **Chapel of St George and the English Martyrs** displays the body of St John Southwark, a priest who was hanged, drawn and quartered in 1654 for refusing to reject the supremacy of the pope.

The distinctive 83m red-brick and white-stone **tower** (adult/child £5/2.50) offers splendid views of London and, unlike St Paul's dome, you can take the lift. Call ahead to book a Cathedral tour (£5).

### TATE BRITAIN

Unlike the National Gallery, it's Britannia that rules the walls of **Tate Britain** (Map p145; ☎ 7887 8008; www.tate.org.uk; Millbank SW1; admission free; ⏱ 10am-5.50pm; ✪ Pimlico). Reaching from 1500 to the present, it's crammed with local heavy-weights like Blake, Hogarth, Gainsborough, Whistler, Spencer and, especially, Turner, whose work dominates the **Clore Gallery**. His 'interrupted visions' – unfinished canvases of moody skies – wouldn't look out of place in the contemporary section, alongside the work of David Hockney, Francis Bacon, Tracey Emin and Damien Hirst. The always-controversial (and often painfully conceptual) annual Turner Prize is exhibited in the gallery from October to January.

There are free hour-long guided tours, taking in different sections of the gallery, held daily at midday and 3pm, as well as additional tours at 11am and 2pm on weekdays. The popular **Rex Whistler Restaurant** ( ☎ 7887 8825; mains £16), featuring an impressive mural from the artist, is open for breakfast, lunch and snacks.

### BANQUETING HOUSE

The beautiful, classical design of the **Banqueting House** (Map pp142-3; ☎ 3166 6154; www.hrp.org.uk/ BanquetingHouse; cnr Horse Guards Ave & Whitehall SW1; adult/child £4.50/2.25; ⏱ 10am-5pm Mon-Sat; ✪ Westminster) was conceived by Inigo Jones for James I in 1622. It's the only surviving part of Whitehall Palace after the Tudor bit burnt down in 1698. The key attraction is the ceiling, painted by Rubens in 1635 at the behest of Charles I. Sadly he didn't get to enjoy it for long as in 1649 he was frogmarched out of the 1st-floor balcony to lose his head for treason. A bust outside commemorates the king. An audio guide is included in the price.

### CHURCHILL MUSEUM & CABINET WAR ROOMS

The **Cabinet War Rooms** (Map pp142-3; ☎ 7930 6961; www.iwm.org.uk; Clive Steps, King Charles St SW1; adult/child £12/free; ⏱ 9.30am-6pm, last entry 5pm; ✪ Westminster) were Prime Minister Winston Churchill's underground military HQ during WWII. Now a wonderfully evocative and atmospheric museum, the restored and preserved rooms (including Churchill's bedroom) capture the drama of the time. The **Churchill Museum** offers an intriguing exposé of the public and private faces of the man.

## St James's & Mayfair

Put on your best rah-rah voice to wander this aristocratic enclave of palaces, exclusive gentlemen's clubs, famous hotels, historic shops and elegant buildings; indeed, there are some 150 historically noteworthy buildings within St James's 36 hectares alone.

### BUCKINGHAM PALACE

With so many imposing buildings in the capital, the Queen's well-proportioned but relatively plain city pad is an anticlimax for some. Built in 1803 for the Duke of Buckingham, **Buckingham Palace** (Map pp142-3; ☎ 7766 7302; www .royalcollection.org.uk; The Mall SW1; adult/child £16/8.75; ⏱ 9.45am-6pm late Jul–late Sep; ✪ St James's Park) replaced St James's Palace as the monarch's London home in 1837. When she's not off giving her one-handed wave in far-flung parts of the Commonwealth, Queen Elizabeth II divides her time between here, Windsor and Balmoral. If you've got the urge to drop in for a cup of tea, a handy way of telling whether she's home is to check whether the yellow, red and blue royal standard is flying.

Nineteen lavishly furnished staterooms are opened up to visitors when Her Majesty the Queen takes her holidays. The tour includes

**Queen Victoria's Picture Gallery** (76.5m long, with works by Rembrandt, Van Dyck, Canaletto, Poussin and Vermeer) and the **Throne Room**, with his-and-hers pink chairs initialled 'ER' and 'P'.

### Changing of the Guard

If you're a fan of bright uniforms, bearskin hats, straight lines, marching and shouting, join the throngs outside the palace at 11.30am (daily from May to July and on alternate days for the rest of the year, weather permitting), when the regiment of guards outside the palace changes over in one of the world's most famous displays of pageantry. It does have a certain freak-show value, but gets dull very quickly. If you're here in November, the procession leaving the palace for the State Opening of Parliament is much more impressive (p155).

### Queen's Gallery

Originally designed by John Nash as a conservatory, it was smashed up by the Luftwaffe in 1940 before being converted to a **gallery** (Map pp142–3; ☎ 7766 7301; Buckingham Palace Rd SW1; adult/child £8.50/4.25; ☼ 10am-5.30pm; ☻ Victoria) in 1962, housing works from the extensive Royal Collection.

### Royal Mews

Indulge your Cinderella fantasies while inspecting the exquisite state coaches and immaculately groomed royal horses housed in the **Royal Mews** (Map pp142–3; ☎ 7766 7302; Buckingham Palace Rd SW1; adult/child £7.50/4.80; ☼ 10am-5pm Aug & Sep, 11am-4pm mid-Mar–Jul & Oct; ☻ Victoria). Highlights include the stunning gold coach (1762) that has been used for every coronation since George IV, and the royal weddings' 1910 Glass Coach. We're pretty sure these aren't about to change back into pumpkins anytime soon.

### ST JAMES'S PARK & ST JAMES'S PALACE

With its manicured flowerbeds and ornamental lake, **St James's Park** is a wonderful place to stroll and take in the views of Westminster, Buckingham Palace and St James's Palace.

The striking Tudor gatehouse of **St James's Palace** (Map pp142–3; Cleveland Row SW1; ☻ Green Park), initiated by the palace-mad Henry VIII in 1530, is best approached from St James's St to the north of the park. This was the residence of Prince Charles and his sons before

they shifted next door to **Clarence House** (1828), following the death of its previous occupant, the Queen Mother, in 2002. It's a great place to pose for a photograph beside one of the resolutely unsmiling royal guards.

### GREEN PARK

Green Park's 47-acre expanse of meadows and mature trees links St James's Park to Hyde Park and Kensington Gardens, creating a green corridor from Westminster all the way to Kensington. It was once a duelling ground and served as a vegetable garden during WWII. Although it doesn't have lakes, fountains or formal gardens, it's blanketed with daffodils in spring and semi-naked bodies whenever the sun shines.

The only concession to formality is the **Canada Memorial** (Map pp142–3) near **Canada Gate** (Map pp142–3), which links the park to Buckingham Palace. At its western end is **Hyde Park Corner**, where you'll find the **Australian** and **New Zealand War Memorials** (Map pp142–3).

### INSTITUTE OF CONTEMPORARY ARTS

A one-stop contemporary-art bonanza, the exciting program at the **ICA** (Map pp142–3; ☎ 7930 3647; www.ica.org.uk; The Mall SW1; Mon-Fri £2, Sat & Sun £3; ☼ noon-11pm Mon, to 1am Tue-Sat, to 10.30pm Sun; ☻ Charing Cross), as it's commonly known, includes film, photography, theatre, installations, talks, performance art, DJs, digital art and book readings. Stroll around the galleries, watch a film, browse the bookshop, then head to the bar for a beer.

### SPENCER HOUSE

The ancestral home of Princess Diana's family, **Spencer House** (Map pp142–3; ☎ 7499 8620; www .spencerhouse.co.uk; 27 St James's Pl SW1; adult/child £9/7; ☼ 10.30am-5.45pm Sun Feb-Jul & Sep-Dec; ☻ Green Park) was built in the Palladian style between 1756 and 1766. It was converted into offices after the Spencers moved out in 1927, but an £18 million restoration 60 years later returned it to its former glory. Visits are by guided tour (last tour 4.45pm). Check the website for the few summer dates when the gardens (£3.50) are opened.

### HANDEL HOUSE MUSEUM

George Frideric Handel's pad from 1723 to his death in 1759 is now a moderately interesting **museum** (Map pp142–3; ☎ 7399 1953; www.handel house.org; 25 Brook St W1K; adult/child £5/2; ☼ 10am-6pm

Tue, Wed, Fri & Sat, to 8pm Thu, noon-6pm Sun; ⊖ Bond St) dedicated to his life. He wrote some of his greatest works here, including *Messiah*, and music still fills the house during live recitals (see the website for details).

From songs of praise to *Purple Haze*, Jimi Hendrix lived next door at number 23 many years (and genres) later.

## West End

Synonymous with big-budget musicals and frenzied flocks of shoppers, the West End is a strident mix of culture and consumerism. More a concept than a fixed geographical area, it nonetheless takes in Piccadilly Circus and Trafalgar Sq to the south, Regent St to the west, Oxford St to the north and Covent Garden and the Strand to the east.

Elegant **Regent St** and frantic **Oxford St** are the city's main shopping strips. They're beautifully lit at Christmas to coax the masses away from the home fires and into the frying-pan sections of the many department stores (see p197).

At the heart of the West End lies **Soho**, a grid of narrow streets and squares hiding gay bars, strip clubs, cafes and advertising agencies. **Carnaby St** was the epicentre of the Swinging London of the 1960s, but is now largely given over to chain fashion stores, although some interesting independent boutiques still lurk in the surrounding streets.

Lisle and Gerrard Sts form the heart of **Chinatown**, which is full of reasonably priced Asian restaurants and unfairly hip youngsters. Its neighbour, pedestrianised **Leicester** (*les*-ter) **Sq** heaves with tourists – and buskers, inevitably. Dominated by large cinemas, it sometimes hosts star-studded premieres.

### PICCADILLY

Named after the elaborate collars (picadils) that were the sartorial staple of a 17th-century tailor who lived nearby, Piccadilly became the fashionable haunt of the well-heeled (and collared), and still boasts establishment icons such as the Ritz hotel and Fortnum & Mason department store (p197). It meets Regent St, Shaftesbury Ave and Haymarket at neon-lit, turbo-charged **Piccadilly Circus**, home to the popular but unremarkable **Eros statue** (Map pp146-7; ⊖ Piccadilly Circus). Ironically the love god looks over an area long linked to prostitution, both male and female, although it's less conspicuous these days.

### Royal Academy of Arts

Set back from Piccadilly, the grandiose **Royal Academy of Arts** (Map pp146-7; ☎ 7300 8000; www.royalacademy.org.uk; Burlington House, Piccadilly W1; admission varies; ♥ 10am-6pm Sat-Thu, to 10pm Fri; ⊖ Green Park) hosts high-profile exhibitions and a small display from its permanent collection. The crafty Academy has made it a condition of joining its exclusive club of 80 artists that new members donate one of their artworks. Past luminaries have included Constable, Gainsborough and Turner, while Sir Norman Foster, David Hockney and Tracey Emin are among the current crop.

### Burlington Arcade

The well-to-do **Burlington Arcade** (Map pp146-7; 51 Piccadilly W1; ⊖ Green Park), built in 1819, is most famous for the Burlington Berties, uniformed guards who patrol the area keeping an eye out for offences such as running, chewing gum or whatever else might lower the arcade's tone.

### COVENT GARDEN

A hallowed name for opera fans due to the presence of the esteemed Royal Opera House (p195), Covent Garden is one of London's biggest tourist traps, where chain restaurants, souvenir shops, balconied bars and street entertainers vie for the punters' pound.

In the 7th century the Saxons built Lundenwic here, a satellite town to the City of London. It reverted back into fields until the 1630s, when the Duke of Bedford commissioned Inigo Jones to build London's first planned square. Covent Garden's famous fruit, vegetable and flower market, immortalised in the film *My Fair Lady*, eventually took over the whole piazza, before being shifted in 1974.

In the 18th and 19th centuries, the area immediately north of Covent Garden was the site of one of London's most notorious slums, the 'rookery' of St Giles. Much of it was knocked down in the 1840s to create New Oxford St, but the narrow lanes and yards around Monmouth St still carry an echo of the crammed conditions of the past.

### London Transport Museum

Newly refurbished and reopened, this **museum** (Map pp146-7; ☎ 7379 6344; www.ltmuseum.co.uk; Covent Garden Piazza WC2; adult/child £10/free; ♥ 10am-6pm Sat-Thu, 11am-9pm Fri; ⊖ Covent Garden) houses vintage vehicles ranging from sedan chairs to train carriages, along with fascinating posters and photos. You can get your tube-map boxer shorts at the museum shop.

### THE STRAND

Described by Benjamin Disraeli in the 19th century as Europe's finest street, this 'beach' of the River Thames – built to connect Westminster (the seat of political power) and the City (the commercial centre) – still boasts a few classy hotels but has lost much of its lustre. Look for the two Chinese merchants above the door at number 216; Twinings have been selling tea here continuously since 1787, making it London's oldest store.

### Somerset House

The first **Somerset House** (Map pp146–7; ☎ 7845 4600; www.somersethouse.org.uk; Strand WC2; 7.30am–11pm; Temple) was built for the Duke of Somerset, brother of Jane Seymour, in 1551. For two centuries it played host to royals (Elizabeth I once lived here), foreign diplomats, wild masked balls, peace treaties, the Parliamentary army during the Civil War and Oliver Cromwell's wake. Having fallen into disrepair, it was pulled down in 1775 and rebuilt in 1801 to designs by William Chambers. Among other weighty organisations, it went on to house, the Royal Academy of the Arts, the Society of Antiquaries, the Navy Board and, that most popular of institutions, the Inland Revenue.

The tax collectors are still here, but that doesn't dissuade Londoners from attending open-air events in the grand central courtyard, such as live performances in summer and ice-skating in winter. The riverside terrace is a popular spot to get caffeinated with views of the River Thames.

Near the Strand entrance, the **Courtauld Gallery** (Map pp146–7; ☎ 7848 2733; adult/child £5/free, 10am–2pm Mon free; to 6pm) displays a wealth of 14th- to 20th-century works, including a roomful of Rubens and works by Van Gogh, Renoir and Cézanne. Downstairs, the **Embankment Galleries** are devoted to temporary exhibitions; prices and hours vary.

## Bloomsbury & Fitzrovia

With the University of London and British Museum within its genteel environs, it's little wonder that Bloomsbury has attracted a lot of very clever, bookish people over the years. Between the world wars, these pleasant streets were colonised by a group of artists and intellectuals known collectively as the **Bloomsbury Group**, which included novelists Virginia Woolf and EM Forster and the economist John Maynard Keynes. **Russell Square**, its very heart, was laid out in 1800 and is one of London's largest and loveliest.

Neighbouring Fitzrovia is only marginally less exalted, although media types outnumber intellectuals in the ever-expanding strip of restaurants and bars around Charlotte St and Goodge St.

### BRITISH MUSEUM

The largest museum in the country and one the oldest and finest in the world, this famous **museum** (Map pp142–3; ☎ 7323 8000; www.thebritishmuseum.org; Great Russell St WC1; admission free; 10am–5.30pm Sat–Wed, to 8.30pm Thu & Fri; Tottenham Court Rd or Russell Sq) boasts vast Egyptian, Etruscan, Greek, Oriental and Roman galleries among many others.

Before you get to the galleries, you'll be blown away by the **Great Court**, which was restored and augmented by Norman Foster in 2000. The courtyard now boasts a spectacular glass-and-steel roof, making it one of the most impressive architectural spaces in the capital. In the centre is the **Reading Room**, with its stunning blue-and-gold domed ceiling, where Karl Marx wrote the *Manifesto of the Communist Party*. Off to the right is the **Enlightenment Gallery**, the oldest and grandest gallery in the museum, and the first section of the redesigned museum to be built (in 1823).

---

### BRITAIN & GREECE SQUABBLE OVER MARBLES

Wonderful though it is, the British Museum can sometimes feel like one vast repository for stolen booty. Much of what's on display wasn't just 'picked up' along the way by Victorian travellers and explorers, but taken or purchased under 'dubious circumstances.

Restive foreign governments occasionally pop their heads over the parapet to demand the return of their property. The British Museum says 'no' and the problem goes away until the next time. Not the Greeks, however. They've been kicking up a stink demanding the return of the so-called Elgin Marbles, the ancient marble sculptures that once adorned the Parthenon. The British Museum, and successive British governments, steadfastly refuse to hand over the priceless works that were removed and shipped to England by the British ambassador to the Ottoman Empire, Lord Elgin, between 1801 and 1805. (When Elgin blew all his dough, he sold the marbles to the government.) The diplomatic spat continues. Only time will tell who blinks first.

---

The enthralling exhibits began in 1753 with a 'cabinet of curiosities' bequeathed by Sir Hans Sloane to the nation on his death; this has mushroomed over the years partly through the plundering of the empire.

Among the must-sees are the **Rosetta Stone**, discovered in 1799 and the key to deciphering Egyptian hieroglyphics; the controversial **Parthenon Sculptures**, which once adorned the walls of the Parthenon in Athens (see boxed text, above); the stunning **Oxus Treasure** of 7th- to 4th-century BC Persian gold; and the Anglo-Saxon **Sutton Hoo** burial relics.

You'll need multiple visits to savour even the highlights here; happily there are 14 30-minute free 'eye opener' tours between 11am and 3.45pm daily, focusing on different parts of the collection. Other tours include the 90-minute highlights tour at 10.30am, 1pm and 3pm daily (adult/child £8/5), and there is a range of audio guides (£3.50). Given the museum's mind-boggling size and scope, an initial tour is highly recommended.

## Holborn & Clerkenwell

In these now fashionable streets, it's hard to find an echo of the notorious 'rookeries' of the 19th century, where families were squeezed into damp, fetid basements, living in possibly the worst conditions in the city's long history. This is the London documented so vividly by Dickens. It was also the traditional stopping point for a last drink on the way to the gallows at Tyburn Hill, which is fitting as many of the condemned hailed from here, as did many of those who were transported to Australia.

### SIR JOHN SOANE'S MUSEUM

Not all of this area's inhabitants were poor, as is aptly demonstrated by the remarkable home of celebrated architect and collector extraordinaire Sir John Soane (1753–1837). Now a fascinating **museum** (Map pp146-5; ☎ 7405 2107; www.soane.org; 13 Lincoln's Inn Fields WC2; admission free, tour 11am Sat £5; ✆ 10am-5pm Tue-Sat, 6-9pm 1st Tue of month; ✆ Holborn), the house has been left largely as it was when Sir John was taken out in a box. Among his eclectic acquisitions are an Egyptian sarcophagus, dozens of Greek and Roman antiquities and the original *Rake's Progress*, William Hogarth's set of caricatures telling the story of a late, 18th-century London cad. Soane was clearly a very clever chap – check out the ingenious folding walls in the picture gallery.

### DICKENS HOUSE MUSEUM

Dickens' sole surviving **London residence** (Map pp136-7; ☎ 7405 2127; www.dickensmuseum.com; 48 Doughty St WC1; adults/under 16yr/concession £5/3/4; ✆ 10am-5pm Mon-Sat, 11am-5pm Sun; ✆ Russell Sq) is where his work really flourished – *The Pickwick Papers*, *Nicholas Nickleby* and *Oliver Twist* were all written here. The handsome four-storey house opened as a museum in 1925, and visitors can stroll through rooms chock-a-block with fascinating memorabilia.

## The City

For most of its history, the City of London *was* London. Its boundaries have changed little since the Romans first founded their gated community here two millennia ago. You can always tell when you're within it, as the Corporation of London's coat of arms appears on the street signs.

It's only in the last 250 years that the City has gone from being the very essence of London and it's main population centre to just its central business district. But what a business district it is – you could easily argue that the 'square mile' is the very heart of world capitalism.

Currently fewer than 10,000 people actually live here, although some 300,000 descend on it each weekday where they generate almost three-quarters of Britain's entire GDP before squeezing back onto the tube. On Sundays it becomes a virtual ghost town, which is a good time to poke around, even if you won't be able to smell the fear of the planet's leading bankers coping with the 'credit crunch'.

Apart from the big-ticket sights, visitors tend to avoid the City, which is a shame as it's got enough interesting churches, intriguing architecture, hidden gardens and atmospheric lanes to spend weeks exploring.

### ST PAUL'S CATHEDRAL

Dominating the City with a dome second in size only to St Peter's in Rome, **St Paul's Cathedral** (Map p150; ☎ 7236 4128; www.stpauls.co.uk; adult/child £10/3.50; ☒ 8.30am-4pm Mon-Sat; ⊖ St Paul's) was designed by Wren after the Great Fire and built between 1675 and 1710. Four other cathedrals preceded it on this site, the first dating from 604.

The dome is renowned for somehow dodging the bombs during the Blitz, and became an icon of the resilience shown in the capital during WWII. Outside the cathedral, to the north, is a **monument to the people of London**, a simple and elegant memorial to the 32,000 Londoners who weren't so lucky.

Inside, some 30m above the main paved area, is the first of three domes (actually a dome inside a cone inside a dome) supported by eight huge columns. The walkway round its base is called the **Whispering Gallery**, because if you talk close to the wall, your words will carry to the opposite side 32m away. It can be reached by a staircase on the western side of the southern transept (9.30am to 3.30pm only). It is 530 lung-busting steps to the **Golden Gallery** at the very top, and an unforgettable view of London.

The **Crypt** has memorials to up to 300 military demigods including Wellington, Kitchener and Nelson, whose body lies below the dome. But the most poignant memorial is to Wren himself. On a simple slab bearing his name, a Latin inscription translates as 'If you seek his memorial, look about you'.

Audio tours lasting 45 minutes are available for £4. Guided tours (adult/child £3/1)

leave the tour desk at 11am, 11.30am, 1.30pm and 2pm (90 minutes). Evensong takes place at 5pm most weekdays and at 3.15pm on Sunday.

### TOWER OF LONDON

If you pay only one admission fee while you're in London, make it the **Tower of London** (Map p150; ☎ 0844-482 7777; www.hrp.org.uk; Tower Hill EC3; adult/child £17/9.50; ☒ 10am-5.30pm Sun & Mon, 9am-5.30pm Tue-Sat Mar-Oct, 10am-4.30pm Sun & Mon, 9am-4.30pm Tue-Sat Nov-Feb; ⊖ Tower Hill). One of the city's three World Heritage Sites (joining Westminster Abbey and Maritime Greenwich), it's a window onto a gruesome and fascinating history.

In the 1070s, William the Conqueror started work on the White Tower to replace the timber-and-earth castle he'd already built here. By 1285, two walls with towers and a moat were built around it and the defences have barely been altered since. A former royal residence, treasury, mint and arsenal, it became most famous as a prison when Henry VIII moved to Whitehall Palace in 1529 and started dishing out his preferred brand of punishment.

The most striking building is the huge **White Tower**, with its solid Romanesque architecture and four turrets, which today houses a collection from the Royal Armouries. On the 2nd floor is the **Chapel of St John the Evangelist**, dating from 1080 and therefore the oldest church in London.

On the small green in front of the church stood Henry VIII's **scaffold**, where seven people were beheaded, including Anne Boleyn and her cousin Catherine Howard (his second and fifth wives).

To the north is the **Waterloo Barracks**, which now contains the spectacular **Crown Jewels**. On the far side of the White Tower is the **Bloody Tower**, where the 12-year-old Edward V and his little brother were held 'for their own safety' and later murdered, probably by their uncle, the future Richard III. Sir Walter Raleigh did a 13-year stretch here, when he wrote his *History of the World*, a copy of which is on display.

On the patch of green between the Wakefield and White Towers you'll find the latest in the tower's long line of famous ravens, which legend says could cause the White Tower to collapse should they leave. Their wings are clipped in case they get any ideas.

To help get your bearings, take the hugely entertaining free guided tour with any of the Tudor-garbed Beefeaters. Hour-long tours leave every 30 minutes from the Middle Tower; the last tour's an hour before closing.

## TOWER BRIDGE

London was still a thriving port in 1894 when elegant Tower Bridge was built. Designed to be raised to allow ships to pass, electricity has now taken over from the original steam engines. A lift leads up from the modern visitors' centre in the northern tower to the **Tower Bridge Exhibition** (Map p150; ☎ 7403 3761; www.towerbridge.org .uk; adult/child £6/3; ☽ 10am-6.30pm Apr-Sep, 9.30am-6pm Oct-Mar; ⊖ Tower Hill), where the story of its building is recounted with videos and animatronics. If you're coming from the Tower, you'll pass by Dead Man's Hole, where corpses that had ended up in the River Thames (through suicide, murder or accident) were regularly retrieved.

## MUSEUM OF LONDON

Visiting the fascinating **Museum of London** (Map p150; ☎ 0870 444 3851; www.museumoflondon.org.uk; 150 London Wall EC2; admission free; ☽ 10am-5.50pm Mon-Sat, noon-5.50pm Sun; ⊖ Barbican) early in your stay helps to make sense of the layers of history that make up this place. The Roman section, in particular, illustrates how the modern is grafted on to the ancient; several of the city's main thoroughfares were once Roman roads, for instance.

At the time of writing, the section encompassing 1666 (the Great Fire) to the present day was being redesigned. It should re-open in late 2009, featuring the Lord Mayor's ceremonial coach as its centrepiece.

## GUILDHALL

Plum in the middle of the 'square mile', the **Guildhall** (Map p150; ☎ 7606 3030; www.cityoflondon.gov .uk; Gresham St EC2; admission free; ☽ 10am-5pm Mon-Sun May-Sep, to 5pm Mon-Sat Oct-Apr; ⊖ Bank) has been the seat of the City's local government for eight centuries. The present building dates from the early 15th century.

Visitors can see the **Great Hall** where the mayor is sworn in and where important chaps like the Tsar of Russia and the Prince Regent celebrated beating Napoleon. It's an impressive space decorated with the shields and banners of London's 12 principal livery companies, carved galleries (the west of which is protected by disturbing statues of giants Gog and Magog) and a beautiful oak-panelled

roof. There's also a lovely bronze statue of Churchill sitting in a comfy chair.

Beneath it is London's largest **medieval crypt** ( ☎ 7606 3030, ext 1463; visit by free guided tour only, bookings essential) with 19 stained-glass windows showing the livery companies' coats of arms.

The **Clockmakers' Museum** (admission free; ☽ 9.30am-4.45pm Mon-Fri) charts 500 years of timekeeping with over 700 ticking exhibits, and the **Guildhall Art Gallery** ( ☎ 7332 3708; adult/child £2.50/1; ☽ 10am-5pm Mon-Sat, noon-4pm Sun) displays around 250 artworks. Included in admission is entry to the remains of an ancient **Roman amphitheatre**, which lay forgotten beneath this site until 1988.

## ST STEPHEN'S WALBROOK

In the 3rd century, a Roman temple stood here, and in the 7th century a Saxon church. Rebuilt after the Great Fire, the current **St Stephen's** (Map p150; ☎ 7626 9000; www.ststephenwalbrook.net; 29 Walbrook EC2; ⊖ Bank) is one of Wren's greatest masterpieces, with elegant Corinthian columns supporting a beautifully proportioned dome. Henry Moore sculpted the round central altar from travertine marble in 1972.

## INNS OF COURT

All London barristers work from within one of the four atmospheric Inns of Court, positioned between the walls of the old City and Westminster. It would take a lifetime working here to grasp all the intricacies of their arcane protocols – they're similar to the Freemasons, and both are 13th-century creations. It's best just to soak up the dreamy ambience of the alleys and open spaces and thank your lucky stars you're not one of the bewigged barristers scurrying about. A roll call of former members would include the likes of Oliver Cromwell, Charles Dickens, Mahatma Gandhi and Margaret Thatcher.

**Lincoln's Inn** (Map pp142-3; ☎ 7405 1393; www .lincolnsinn.org.uk; Lincoln's Inn Fields WC2; ☽ grounds 9am-6pm Mon-Fri, chapel 12.30-2.30pm Mon-Fri; ⊖ Holborn) is largely intact and has several original 15th-century buildings. It's the oldest and most attractive of the bunch, boasting a 17th-century chapel and pretty landscaped gardens.

**Gray's Inn** (Map pp142-3; ☎ 7458 7800; www.grays inn.org.uk; Gray's Inn Rd WC1; ☽ grounds 10am-4pm Mon-Fri, chapel to 6pm Mon-Fri; ⊖ Chancery Lane) was largely rebuilt after the Luftwaffe levelled it.

**Middle Temple** (Map pp142-3; ☎ 7427 4800; www. middletemple.org.uk; Middle Temple Lane EC4; ☽ 10-11.30am

& 3-4pm Mon-Fri; ✆ Temple) and **Inner Temple** (Map pp142-3; ☎ 7797 8247; King's Bench Walk EC4; ⏲ 10am-4pm Mon-Fri; ✆ Temple) both sit between Fleet St and Victoria Embankment – the former is the best preserved while the latter is home to the intriguing **Temple Church** (Map p142-3; ☎ 7353 8559; www.templechurch.com; ⏲ varies, check website or call ahead), another landmark to feature prominently in *The Da Vinci Code*.

## BARBICAN

Like Marmite, you either love or hate the concrete **Barbican** (Map p150; ☎ 7638 4141; www .barbican.org.uk; Silk St EC2; ✆ Barbican). It's true that parts of it are extraordinarily ugly, particularly the forbidding high-rise tower blocks (romantically named Shakespeare, Cromwell and Lauderdale). But at the time of its construction, this vast complex of offices and residences with an arts centre at its heart was revolutionary.

It was designed by Chamberlain, Powell and Bon, disciples of Le Corbusier, to fill a WWII bomb-pummelled space with democratic modern housing. Sadly this dream never really materialised, and today around 80% of the flats are privately owned. It's been fashionable to loath the Barbican in the past, but in 2001 the complex became listed, and more people are finding beauty in its curved roofs, brightly planted window boxes and large central 'lake'.

The Barbican Centre (p195) is at its heart. It also houses the **Barbican Art Gallery** ( ☎ 7638 4141; Level 3; adult/child £8/6; ⏲ 11am-8pm Thu-Mon, 11am-6pm Tue & Wed), home to temporary exhibitions of contemporary art, and the smaller **Curve Gallery** ( ☎ 7638 4141; Level 0; admission free; ⏲ 11am-8pm).

## BANK OF ENGLAND MUSEUM

Guardian of the country's financial system, the Bank of England was established in 1694 when the government needed to raise cash to support a war with France. It was moved here in 1734 and largely renovated by Sir John Soane. Its **museum** (Map p150; ☎ 7601 5545; www .bankofengland.co.uk; Bartholomew Lane EC2; admission free; ⏲ 10am-5pm Mon-Fri; ✆ Bank) traces the history of the bank and banking system, and is surprisingly interesting.

## THE MONUMENT

Designed by Wren to commemorate the Great Fire, the **Monument** (Map p150; ☎ 7626 2717; www. themonument.info; Monument St; ✆ Monument) is 60.6m

high, the exact distance from its base to the bakery on Pudding Lane where the blaze began. Climb the 311 tight spiral steps (not advised for claustrophobes) for an eye-watering view from beneath the symbolic vase of flames. It was closed for repairs at the time of writing but scheduled to reopen in 2009; check the website for prices and opening hours.

## DR JOHNSON'S HOUSE

The Georgian **house** (Map pp142-3; ☎ 7353 3745; www.drjohnsonshouse.org; 17 Gough Sq EC4; adult/child £4.50/1.50; ⏲ 11am-5.30pm Mon-Sat May-Sep, to 5pm Mon-Sat Oct-Apr; ✆ Chancery Lane) where Samuel Johnson and his assistants compiled the first English dictionary (between 1748 and 1759) is full of prints and portraits of friends and intimates, including the good doctor's Jamaican servant to whom he bequeathed this grand residence.

## FLEET ST

As 20th-century London's 'Street of Shame', **Fleet St** (Map pp142-3; ✆ Temple) was synonymous with the UK's scurrilous tabloids until the mid-1980s when the press barons embraced computer technology, ditched a load of staff and largely relocated to the Docklands.

## ST KATHARINE DOCKS

A centre of trade and commerce for 1000 years, **St Katharine Docks** (Map p150) is now a buzzing waterside area of pleasure boats and eateries. It was badly damaged during the war but survivors include the popular **Dickins Inn**, with its original 18th-century timber framework, and **Ivory House** (built 1854) which used to store ivory, perfume and other precious goods.

## East End

Traditionally the most economically depressed part of the metropolis, a fair bit of cash is being splashed around at present in the lead up to the 2012 Olympic Games. Dockland's Canary Wharf and Isle of Dogs are now an island of tower blocks, rivalling those of the City itself.

## HOXTON, SHOREDITCH & SPITALFIELDS

Fans of the long-running TV soap *Eastenders* may find it hard to recognise its setting in traditionally working class but increasingly trendy enclaves like these. The fact is you're more likely to hear a proper Cockney accent in

Essex these days than you are in much of the East End. Over the centuries waves of immigrants have left their mark here and it's a great place to come for diverse ethnic cuisine and vibrant but largely attitude-free nightlife.

### Geffrye Museum

If you like nosing around other people's homes, the **Geffrye Museum** (Map pp134-5; ☎ 7739 9893; www.geffrye-museum.org.uk; 136 Kingsland Rd E2; admission free; ☺ 10am-5pm Tue-Sat, noon-5pm Sun; ✪ Old St, then ☒ 243) will be a positively orgasmic experience. Devoted to middle-class domestic interiors, these former almshouses (1714) have been converted into a series of living rooms dating from 1630 to the current Ikea generation. On top of the interiors porn, the back garden has been transformed into period garden 'rooms' and a lovely walled herb garden (April to October only).

### Dennis Severs' House

This extraordinary **Georgian House** (Map p150; ☎ 7247 4013; www.dennissevershouse.co.uk; 18 Folgate St E1; ✪ Liverpool St) is set up as if its occupants had just walked out the door. There are half-drunk cups of tea, lit candles and, in a perhaps unnecessary attention to detail, a full chamber pot by the bed. More than a museum, it's an opportunity to meditate on the minutiae of everyday Georgian life through silent exploration.

Bookings are required for the Monday evening candlelit sessions (£12; call for times), but you can just show up on the first and third Sundays of the month (£8; midday to 4pm) or the following Mondays (£5; midday to 2pm).

### White Cube

Set in an industrial building with an impressive glazed-roof extension **White Cube** (Map p150; ☎ 7930 5373; www.whitecube.com; 48 Hoxton Sq N1; admission free; ☺ 10am-6pm Tue-Sat; ✪ Old St) has an interesting program of contemporary-art exhibitions from sculptures to video, installations and painting.

### DOCKLANDS

The Port of London was once the world's greatest, the hub of the enormous global trade of the British Empire. Since being pummelled by the Luftwaffe in WWII its fortunes have been topsy-turvy, but the massive development of Canary Wharf into a second busi-

ness district has replaced its crusty seadogs with hordes of dark-suited office workers. It's now an interesting if slightly sterile environment, best viewed while hurtling around on the DLR (p201).

The **Museum in Docklands** (Map p149; ☎ 0870 444 3856; www.museumindocklands.org.uk; Hertsmere Rd, West India Quay E17; annual admission adult/child £5/free; ☺ 10am-6pm Mon-Sat; DLR West India Quay), housed in a heritage-listed warehouse, uses artefacts and multimedia to chart the history of the Docklands from Roman trading to its renewal in the twilight of the 20th century.

## South of the River Thames

Londoners once crossed the river to the area controlled by the licentious Bishops of Southwark for all kinds of raunchy diversions frowned upon in the City. It's a much more seemly area now, but the theatre and entertainment tradition remains.

### SOUTHWARK
### Tate Modern

It's hard to miss this surprisingly elegant former power station on the side of the river, which is fortunate as the tremendous **Tate Modern** (Map p150; ☎ 7887 8888; www.tate.org.uk; Queen's Walk SE1; admission free; ☺ 10am-6pm Sun-Thu, to 10pm Fri & Sat; ☒ ; ✪ Southwark) really shouldn't be missed. Focusing on modern art in all its wacky and wonderful permutations, it's been extraordinarily successful in bringing challenging work to the masses, becoming one of London's most popular attractions.

Outstanding temporary exhibitions (on the 4th floor; prices vary) continue to spark excitement, as does the periodically changing large-scale installation in the vast Turbine Hall. The permanent collection is organised into four main sections. On floor three you'll find *Material Gestures* (postwar painting and sculpture, including Mark Rothko's affecting *Seagram Murals*) and *Poetry and Dream* (Pablo Picasso, Francis Bacon and surrealism). On the 5th floor, *Idea and Object* showcases minimalism and conceptual art, while in *States of Flux* cubism and futurism rub shoulders with pop art (Roy Lichtenstein, Andy Warhol) and Soviet imagery.

The multimedia guides (£2) are worthwhile for their descriptions of selected works, and there are free daily guided tours of the collection's highlights (Level 3 at 11am and midday; Level 5 at 2pm and 3pm). Make sure you

**TATE-A-TATE**

To get between London's Tate galleries in style, the **Tate Boat** – which sports a Damien Hirst dot painting – will whisk you between the two, stopping en route at the London Eye. Services run 10am to 6pm daily at 40-minute intervals. A River Roamer hop-on hop-off ticket (purchased on board) costs £8, single tickets £4.

cop the view from the top floor's restaurant and bar.

### Shakespeare's Globe

While today's Londoners might nab a budget flight to Amsterdam to behave badly, in Shakespeare's time they'd cross London Bridge to Southwark. Free from the city's constraints, you could hook up with a prostitute, watch a bear being tortured for your amusement and then head to the theatre, the most famous of which was the **Globe** (Map p150; ☎ 7401 9919; www.shakespeares-globe.org; 21 New Globe Walk SE1; adult/child £9/6.50; ☺ 10am-6pm May-Sep, last entry 5pm, to 5pm Oct-Apr; ⊖ London Bridge), where a clever fellow was producing box-office smashes like *Macbeth* and *Hamlet*.

Originally built in 1599, the Globe burned down in 1613 and was immediately rebuilt. The Puritans, who regarded theatres as dreadful dens of iniquity, eventually closed it in 1642. Its present incarnation was the vision of American actor and director Sam Wanamaker, who sadly died before the opening night in 1997.

Admission includes a guided tour of the open-roofed theatre, faithfully reconstructed from oak beams, handmade bricks, lime plaster and thatch. There's also an extensive exhibition about Shakespeare and his times.

Plays are still performed here, and while Shakespeare and his contemporaries dominate, modern plays are also staged (see the website for upcoming performances). As in Elizabethan times, 'groundlings' can watch proceedings for a modest price (£5; seats are £15 to £35), but there's no protection from the elements and you'll have to stand.

### Southwark Cathedral

Although the central tower dates from 1520 and the choir from the 13th century, **Southwark Cathedral** (Map p150; ☎ 7367 6700; Montague Close SE1;

suggested donation £4-6.50; ☺ 8am-6pm Mon-Fri, 9am-6pm Sat & Sun; ⊖ London Bridge) is largely Victorian. Inside are monuments galore, including a Shakespeare Memorial; it's worth picking up one of the small guides. Catch Evensong at 5.30pm on Tuesday, Thursday and Friday, 4pm on Saturday and 3pm on Sunday.

### Old Operating Theatre Museum & Herb Garret

One of London's most genuinely gruesome attractions, the **Old Operating Theatre Museum** (Map p150; ☎ 7188 2679; www.thegarret.org.uk; 9A St Thomas St SE1; adult/child £5.45/3; ☺ 10.30am-4.45pm; ⊖ London Bridge) is Britain's only surviving 19th-century operating theatre, rediscovered in 1956 within the garret of a church. The display of primitive surgical tools is suitably terrifying, while the pickled bits of humans are just unpleasant.

It's a hands-on kind of place, with signs saying 'please touch', although obviously the pointy things are locked away. For a more intense experience, check the website for their regular 20-minute 'special events'.

### City Hall

The Norman Foster–designed, wonky-egg-shaped **City Hall** (Map p150; ☎ 7983 4000; www.london.gov.uk; Queen's Walk SE1; admission free; ☺ 8am-8pm Mon-Fri) is an architectural feast of glass, and home to the mayor's office, the London Assembly and the Greater London Assembly (GLA). Visitors can see the mayor's meeting chamber and attend debates. On some weekends the top-floor reception hall, known as **London's Living Room**, is opened for the public to enjoy its panoramic views. Its accessed via a glass winding ramp similar to the one in Berlin's Reichstag (see website for dates).

### Design Museum

The whiter-than-white **Design Museum** (Map p150; ☎ 7403 6933; www.designmuseum.org; 28 Shad Thames SE1; adult £8.50; ☺ 10am-5.45pm; ⊖ Tower Hill) is a must for anyone interested in beautiful, practical things. The permanent collection has displays of modern British design and there are also regular temporary exhibitions including the annual *Designs of the Year* competition.

### HMS Belfast

Launched in 1938, the **HMS Belfast** (Map p150; ☎ 7407 6328; www.iwm.org.uk/hmsbelfast; Morgan's Lane, Tooley St SE1; adult/child £10.30/free; ☺ 10am-6pm

Mar-Oct, to 5pm Nov-Feb; ⊖ London Bridge) took part in the D-Day landings and saw action in Korea. Explore the nine decks and see the engine room, gun decks, galley, chapel, punishment cells, canteen and dental surgery.

### London Dungeon

Older kids love the **London Dungeon** (Map p150; ☎ 0871-423 2240; www.thedungeons.com; 28-34 Tooley St SE1; adult/child £19.95/14.95; ☑ 10.30am-5pm, longer hrs some weeks, check website; ⊖ London Bridge) as the terrifying queues during school holidays and weekends testify. It's all spooky music, ghostly boat rides, macabre hangman's drop-rides, fake blood and actors dressed up as torturers and gory criminals (including Jack the Ripper and Sweeney Todd). Beware the interactive bits.

### Britain at War Experience

You can pop down to the London Underground air-raid shelter, look at gas masks and ration books, stroll around Southwark during the Blitz and learn about the battle on the Home Front at the **Britain at War Experience** (Map p150; ☎ 7403 3171; www.britainatwar.co.uk; 64-66 Tooley St SE1; adult/child £11/4.95; ☑ 10am-5.30pm Apr-Sep, to 4.30pm Oct-Mar). It's crammed with fascinating WWII memorabilia.

### SOUTH BANK
### London Eye

It may seem a bit Mordor-ish to have a giant eye overlooking the city, but the **London Eye** (Map pp142-3; ☎ 0870 5000 600; www.londoneye.com; adult/child £15.50/7.75; ☑ 10am-8pm Jan-May & Oct-Dec, to 9pm Jun & Sep, to 9.30pm Jul & Aug; ⊖ Waterloo) doesn't actually resemble an eye at all, and, in a city where there's a CCTV camera on every other corner, it's probably only fitting. Originally designed as a temporary structure to celebrate the year 2000, the Eye is now a permanent addition to the cityscape, joining Big Ben as one of London's most distinctive landmarks.

This 135m-tall, slow-moving Ferris wheel (although we're not supposed to call it that for all kinds of technical reasons) is the largest of its kind in the world. Passengers ride in an enclosed egg-shaped pod that takes 30 minutes to rotate completely and offers a 25-mile view on a clear day. It's so popular that it's advisable to book your ticket online to speed up your wait (you also get a 10% discount), or you can pay an additional £10 to jump the queue.

Joint tickets for the London Eye and Madame Tussauds can be purchased (adult/child £35/25), as well as a 40-minute, sightseeing **River Cruise** (adult/child £12/6) with a multilingual commentary.

### London Aquarium

One of the largest in Europe, the **London Aquarium** (Map pp142-3; ☎ 7967 8000; www.london aquarium.co.uk; County Hall SE1; adult/child £14/9.75; ☑ 10am-6pm, last entry 5pm; ⊖ Waterloo) has three levels of fish organised by geographical origin, but you'll be peering over children's excited heads during holidays. Check the website for shark-feeding times.

### Dalí Universe

The brochure invites you to 'enter the mind of a genius' – a daunting prospect seeing as it's a place where clocks melt and telephones morph into lobsters. **Dalí Universe** (Map pp142-3; ☎ 0870 744 7485; www.daliuniverse.com; County Hall SE1; adult/child £12/8; ☑ 9.30am-7pm Sat-Thu, to 8pm Fri; ⊖ Waterloo) is a large collection that focuses on the surrealist master's rare etchings, movies, furniture and sculptures rather than his famous canvases. Included in the price, **Picasso: Art of a Genius** also concentrates on rare work, such as tapestry and ceramic design. You can download a two-for-one entry voucher from the website; last entry is an hour prior to closing.

### Hayward Gallery

Part of the Southbank Centre (p195), the **Hayward** (Map pp142-3; ☎ 0871 663 2587; www.south bankcentre.co.uk/visual-arts; Belvedere Rd SE1; admission prices vary; ☑ 10am-6pm Sat-Thu, to 10pm Fri; ⊖ Waterloo) hosts a changing roster of modern art (video, installations, photography, collage, painting etc).

### LAMBETH
### Imperial War Museum

You don't have to be a lad to appreciate the **Imperial War Museum** (Map pp142-3; ☎ 7416 5000; www.iwm.org.uk; Lambeth Rd SE1; admission free; ☑ 10am-6pm; ⊖ Lambeth North) and its spectacular atrium with spitfires hanging from the ceiling, rockets (including the massive German V2), field-guns, missiles, submarines, tanks, torpedoes and other military hardware. Providing a telling lesson in modern history, highlights include a re-created WWI trench and WWII bomb shelter as well as a **Holocaust Exhibition**.

### Florence Nightingale Museum

The thought-provoking **Florence Nightingale Museum** (Map pp142-3; ☎ 7620 0374; www.florence -nightingale.co.uk; 2 Lambeth Palace Rd SE1; adult/child £5.80/4.80; ⏰ 10am-5pm Mon-Fri, to 4.30pm Sat & Sun, last admission 1hr before closing; ➌ Waterloo) recounts the story of 'the lady with the lamp' who led a team of nurses during the Crimean War. She established a training school for nurses here at St Thomas' hospital in 1859.

## Chelsea, Kensington & Knightsbridge

Known as the royal borough, residents of Kensington and Chelsea are certainly paid royally, earning the highest incomes in the UK (shops and restaurants will presume you do too). Knightsbridge is where you'll find some of London's best-known department stores, including Harrods (p197) and Harvey Nicks (p197), while Kensington High St has a lively mix of chains and boutiques. Thanks to the surplus generated by the 1851 Great Exhibition, which allowed the purchase of a great chunk of land, South Kensington boasts some of London's most beautiful and interesting museums all on one road.

### VICTORIA & ALBERT MUSEUM

A vast, rambling and wonderful museum of decorative art and design, the **Victoria & Albert** (V&A; Map pp138-9; ☎ 7942 2000; www.vam .ac.uk; Cromwell Rd SW7; admission free; ⏰ 10am-5.45pm Sat-Thu, to 10pm Fri; ➌ South Kensington) is part of Prince Albert's legacy to Londoners in the wake of the Great Exhibition.

It's a bit like the nation's attic, comprising four million objects collected from Britain and around the globe. Spread over nearly 150 galleries, it houses the world's greatest collection of decorative arts, including ancient Chinese ceramics, modernist architectural drawings, Korean bronze, Japanese swords, cartoons by Raphael, spellbinding Asian and Islamic art, Rodin sculptures, actual-size reproductions of famous European architecture and sculpture (including Michelangelo's *David*), Elizabethan gowns, ancient jewellery, an all-wooden Frank Lloyd Wright study and a pair of Doc Martens. Yes, you'll need to plan.

The British Galleries (1500 to 1900) take up the entire western wing, while the eastern wing will hold the revamped Mediterranean and Renaissance Galleries (due to be completed in late 2009).

To top it all off, it's a fabulous building, with an attractive garden cafe as well as the original, lavishly decorated V&A cafe.

### NATURAL HISTORY MUSEUM

Let's start with the building itself: stripes of pale blue and honey-coloured stone are broken by Venetian arches decorated with all manner of carved critters. Quite simply, it's one of London's finest.

A sure-fire hit with kids of all ages, the **Natural History Museum** (Map pp138-9; ☎ 7942 5725; www.nhm.ac.uk; Cromwell Rd SW7; admission free; ⏰ 10am-5.50pm; ➌ South Kensington) is crammed full of interesting stuff, starting with the giant dinosaur skeleton that greats you in the main hall. In the main dinosaur section, the fleshless fossils are bought to robotic life with a very realistic 4m-high animatronic Tyrannosaurus Rex and his smaller, but no less sinister-looking, cousins.

The Earth Galleries are equally impressive. An escalator slithers up and into a hollowed-out globe where two main exhibits – *The Power Within* and the *Restless Surface* – explain how wind, water, ice, gravity and life itself impact on the earth. For parents not sure on how to broach the facts of life, a quick whiz around the Human Biology section should do the trick – rather graphically.

The **Darwin Centre** (☎ 7942 5011) houses some 22 million zoological exhibits, which can be visited by prearranging a free tour.

### SCIENCE MUSEUM

With seven floors of interactive and educational exhibits, the **Science Museum** (Map pp138-9; ☎ 0870-870 4868; www.sciencemuseum.org .uk; Exhibition Rd SW7; admission free; ⏰ 10am-6pm; ➌ South Kensington) covers everything from the Industrial Revolution to the exploration of space. There is something for all ages, from vintage cars, trains and aeroplanes to labour-saving devices for the home, a wind tunnel and flight simulator. Kids particularly love the interactive sections. There's also a 450-seat **IMAX cinema**.

### KENSINGTON PALACE

Dating from 1605, **Kensington Palace** (Map pp138-9; ☎ 0870 751 5170; www.hrp.org.uk; Kensington Gardens W8; adult/child £13/6.15; ⏰ 10am-6pm Mar-Oct, to 5pm Nov-Feb; ➌ High St Kensington) was the birthplace of Queen Victoria in 1819 but is best known today as the last home of Princess Diana. Hour-long tours

LONDON

take you around the surprisingly small **state-rooms**. A collection of Princess Di's dresses is on permanent display, along with frocks and ceremonial gowns from Queen Elizabeth and her predecessors. There's an audio tour included in the entry fee.

### KENSINGTON GARDENS
Blending in with Hyde Park, these **royal gardens** (Map pp138-9; admission free; ☿ dawn-dusk; ✆ Queensway) are part of Kensington Palace and hence popularly associated with Princess Diana. Diana devotees can visit the **Diana, Princess of Wales Memorial Playground** (Map pp138–9) in its northwest corner, a much more restrained royal remembrance than the over-the-top **Albert Memorial** (Map pp138–9), a lavish marble, mosaic and gold affair opposite the Royal Albert Hall, built to honour Queen Victoria's purportedly humble husband, Albert (1819–61).

The gardens also house the **Serpentine Gallery** (Map pp138-9; ☎ 7402 6075; www.serpentinegallery.org; admission free; ☿ 10am-6pm), one of London's edgiest contemporary-art spaces. The **Sunken Garden** (Map pp138–9), near the palace, is at its prettiest in summer, while tea in the **Orangery** (Map pp138–9) is a treat any time of the year.

### HYDE PARK
At 145 hectares, **Hyde Park** (Map pp138-9; ☿ 5.30am-midnight; ✆ Marble Arch, Hyde Park Corner or Queensway) is central London's largest open space. Henry VIII expropriated it from the Church in 1536, when it became a hunting ground and later a venue for duels, executions and horse racing. The 1851 Great Exhibition was held here and during WWII the park became an enormous potato field. These days, it serves as an occasional concert venue and a full-time green space for fun and frolics. There's boating on the Serpentine for the energetic or, near Marble Arch, **Speaker's Corner** (Map pp138–9) for oratorical acrobats. These days, it's largely total nutters and religious fanatics who maintain the tradition begun in 1872 as a response to rioting.

A more soothing structure, the **Princess Diana Memorial Fountain** (Map pp138–9) is a meandering stream that splits at the top, flows gently downhill and reassembles in a pool at the bottom. It was unveiled here in mid-2004 with inevitable debate over matters of taste and gravitas.

### ROYAL HOSPITAL CHELSEA
Designed by Wren, the **Royal Hospital Chelsea** (Map pp140-1; ☎ 7881 5246; Royal Hospital Rd SW3; admission free; ☿ 10am-noon & 2-4pm Mon-Sun; ✆ Sloane Sq) was built in 1692 to provide shelter for ex-servicemen. Today it houses hundreds of war veterans known as Chelsea Pensioners, charming old chaps who are generally regarded as national treasures. As you wander around the grounds or inspect the elegant chapel and interesting museum, you'll see them pottering about in their winter blue coats or summer reds. The Chelsea Flower Show takes place in the hospital grounds in May.

### CHELSEA PHYSIC GARDEN
One for the garden obsessives (the less hardcore should head to the many free parks or Kew), this historic **botanical garden** (Map pp140-1; ☎ 7352 5646; www.chelseaphysicgarden.co.uk; 66 Royal Hospital Rd SW3; adult/child £7/4; ☿ noon-5pm Wed-Fri, to 6pm Sat & Sun; ✆ Sloane Sq) is one of the oldest in Europe, established in 1673 for apprentice apothecaries to study medicinal plants. An audio guide is included in the price and tours leave at 3pm on Sunday.

### MARBLE ARCH
London's grandest bedsit – with a one-room flat inside – **Marble Arch** (Map pp138-9; ✆ Marble Arch) was designed by John Nash in 1828 as the entrance to Buckingham Palace. It was moved here in 1851.

The infamous Tyburn Tree, a three-legged gallows, once stood nearby. It is estimated that up to 50,000 people were executed here between 1196 and 1783.

## Marylebone
With one of London's nicest high streets and Regent's Park on its doorstep, increasingly hip Marylebone is an interesting area to wander.

### REGENT'S PARK
A former royal hunting ground, **Regent's Park** (Map pp136-7; ✆ Regent's Park) was designed by John Nash early in the 19th century, although what was actually laid out is only a fraction of the celebrated architect's grand plan. Nevertheless, it's one of London's loveliest open spaces – at once lively and serene, cosmopolitan and local – with football pitches, tennis courts and a boating lake. **Queen Mary's Gardens**, towards the south of the park, is particularly pretty, with spectacular roses in summer.

**Open Air Theatre** ( ☎ 7935 5756; www.openairtheatre.
org) hosts performances of Shakespeare here
on summer evenings, along with comedy
and concerts.

## LONDON ZOO

A huge amount of money has been spent to
bring **London Zoo** (Map pp136-7; ☎ 7722 3333; www
.londonzoo.co.uk; Regent's Park NW1; adult/child £15.40/11.90;
⏰ 10am-5.30pm Mar-Oct, to 4pm Nov-Feb; ⊖ Camden
Town), established in 1828, into the modern
world. It now has a swanky new £5.3-million
gorilla enclosure and is involved in gorilla
conservation in Gabon. Feeding times, reptile
handling and the petting zoo are guaranteed
winners with the kids.

## WALLACE COLLECTION

Housed in a beautiful, opulent Italianate
mansion, the **Wallace Collection** (Map pp142-
3; ☎ 7563 9500; www.wallacecollection.org; Hertford
House, Manchester Sq W1; admission free, audio guide £3;
⏰ 10am-5pm; ⊖ Bond St) is a treasure trove of
exquisite 18th-century French furniture,
Sèvres porcelain, arms, armour and art by
masters such as Rubens, Titian, Rembrandt
and Gainsborough. Oliver Peyton's Wallace
Restaurant occupies a lovely glassed-in courtyard at its centre.

## MADAME TUSSAUDS

With so much fabulous free stuff to do in
London, it's a wonder that people still join
lengthy queues to visit pricey **Madame Tussauds**
(Map pp142-3; ☎ 0870 400 3000; www.madame-tussauds
.co.uk; Marylebone Rd NW1; adult/child £25/21; ⏰ 9.30am-
5.30pm Mon-Fri, 9am-6pm Sat & Sun; ⊖ Baker St), but in
a celebrity-obsessed, camera-happy world, the
opportunity to pose beside Posh and Becks is
not short on appeal.

The life-sized wax figures are remarkably
lifelike and are as close to the real thing as
most of us will get. It's interesting to see which
are the most popular; nobody wants to be
photographed with Richard Branson, but
Prince Charles and Camilla do a brisk trade.

Honing her craft by making effigies of
victims of the French Revolution, Tussaud
brought her wares to England in 1802. Her
Chamber of Horrors still survives (complete with the actual blade that took Marie
Antoinette's head) but it's now joined by
Chamber Live, where actors lunge at terrified
punters in the dark. The Spirit of London ride
is wonderfully cheesy but the conversion of

the old planetarium into the Stardome show
is just lame.

Tickets are cheaper when ordered online
and for entries after 5pm. Combined tickets
with London Eye and London Dungeon are
also available (adult/child £50/35).

## North London

Once well outside the city limits, the former
hamlets of North London have long been
gobbled up by the metropolis, and yet still
maintain a semblance of a village atmosphere
and distinct local identity. Not as resolutely
wealthy as the west or as gritty as the east,
the Norf is a strange mix of genteel terrace
houses and council estates, containing some
of London's hippest neighbourhoods.

### EUSTON & KING'S CROSS

Most people are content to experience King's
Cross subterraneously, as it's a major interchange on the tube network, but the conversion of spectacular **St Pancras station** (Map
pp136-7) into the new Eurostar terminal and
a ritzy apartment complex seems to be reviving its fortunes. The streets are still grey and
car-choked, but some decent accommodation
options and interesting bars have sprung up.

### British Library

You need to be a 'reader' (ie member) to use
the vast collection of the **library** (Map pp136-7;
☎ 7412 7332; www.bl.uk; 96 Euston Rd NW1; admission free;
⏰ to 6pm Mon & Wed-Fri, to 8pm Tue, to 5pm Sat, 11am-5pm
Sun; ⊖ King's Cross St Pancras), but the Treasures
gallery is open to everyone. Here you'll find
Shakespeare's first folio, Leonardo da Vinci's
notebooks, the lyrics to *A Hard Day's Night*
scribbled on the back of Julian Lennon's
birthday card, St Thomas More's last letter
to Henry VIII, Jane Austen's correspondence,
religious texts from around the world, and,
most importantly, the 8th-century Lindisfarne
Gospels and 1215 Magna Carta.

### Wellcome Collection

Say what you like about pharmaceutical companies, but when one of their charitable trusts
spends £30 million opening a new, free, gallery,
it's very welcome indeed. The **Wellcome Collection**
(Map pp136-7; ☎ 7611 2222; www.wellcomecollection.org;
183 Euston Rd NW1; admission free; ⏰ 10am-6pm Tue, Wed,
Fri & Sat, to 10pm Thu, 11am-6pm Sun; ⊖ Euston Sq) focuses
on the interface of art, science and medicine.
There are interactive displays where you can

scan your face and watch it stretched into the statistical average, wacky modern sculptures inspired by medical conditions and creepy things like an actual cross-section of a body.

## CAMDEN

Technicolour hairstyles, facial furniture, intricate tattoos and ambitious platform shoes are the look of Bohemian Camden, a lively neighbourhood of pubs, live-music venues, interesting boutiques and, most famously, Camden Market (see p198). There are usually a few cartoon punks hanging around earning a few bucks for being photographed by tourists, as well as none-too-discreet dope dealers.

## ST JOHN'S WOOD

Posh St John's Wood is famous for two things: cricket and Abbey Road Studios. Local traffic is by now pretty used to groups of tourists lining up on the **zebra crossing** (Map pp134–5) outside 3 Abbey Rd to recreate the cover of the Beatles' 1969 album *Abbey Road*.

### Lord's Cricket Ground

The next best thing to watching a test at **Lord's** (Map pp134-5; ☎ 7616 8595; www.lords.org; St John's Wood Rd NW8; tours adult/child £12/6; ☉ tours 10am, noon & 2pm when there's no play; ⊖ St John's Wood) is the absorbingly anecdotal 100-minute tour of the ground and facilities. It takes in the famous (members only) Long Room and the **MCC Museum** featuring evocative memorabilia including the tiny Ashes trophy. For more information on attending test matches, see p196.

## HAMPSTEAD & HIGHGATE

These quaint and well-heeled villages, perched on hills above London, are home to an inordinate number of celebrities.

### Hampstead Heath

With its 320-hectares of rolling meadows and wild woodlands, **Hampstead Heath** (Map pp134-5; ☒ Gospel Oak or Hampstead Heath) is a million miles away – well, approximately four – from central London. A walk up **Parliament Hill** affords one of the most spectacular views of the city and on summer days it's popular with picnickers. Also bewilderingly popular are the murky brown waters of the separate single-sex or mixed bathing ponds (basically duck ponds with people splashing about in them), although most folk are content just to sun themselves around London's 'beach'.

**Kenwood House** ( ☎ 8348 1286; www.english-heritage.org.uk/server/show/nav.12783; Hampstead Ln NW3; admission free; ☉ 11.30am-4pm; ⊖ Archway or Golders Green, then ☒ 210) is a magnificent neoclassical mansion on the northern side of the heath, and houses a small collection of paintings by European masters.

### Highgate Cemetery

The **cemetery** ( ☎ 8340 1834; www.highgate-cemetery.org; Swain's Lane N6; ⊖ Archway) weaves a creepy kind of magic, with its Victorian symbols – shrouded urns, obelisks, upturned torches (life extinguished) and broken columns (life cut short) – eerily overgrown graves and the twisting paths on the western side.

Admission to the western side is by tour only (adult/child £5/1; 2pm weekdays, on the hour 11am to 4pm weekends). On the other, less atmospheric **eastern side** (admission £3; ☉ 10am-5pm Mon-Fri, 11am-5pm Sat & Sun Apr-Oct, to 4pm Nov-Mar) you can pay your respects to Karl Marx and George Eliot.

From Archway station, walk up Highgate Hill until you reach Waterlow Park on the left. Go through the park; the cemetery gates are opposite the exit.

### Freud Museum

After fleeing Nazi-occupied Vienna in 1938, Sigmund Freud lived the last year of his life here. The fascinating **Freud Museum** (Map pp134-5; ☎ 7435 2002; www.freud.org.uk; 20 Maresfield Gardens NW3; adult £5; ☉ noon-5pm Wed-Sun) has maintained his study and library much as he left it, with his famous couch, his books and his collection of small Egyptian figures and other antiquities. Excerpts of dream analysis are scattered around the house and there's a video presentation upstairs.

## Greenwich

Simultaneously the first and last place on earth, Greenwich (*gren*-itch) straddles the hemispheres as well as the ages. More than any of the villages swamped by London, it has retained its own sense of identity based on splendid architecture and strong connections with the sea and science. All the great architects of the Enlightenment made their mark here, leaving an extraordinary cluster of buildings that have earned 'Maritime Greenwich' its place on Unesco's World Heritage list.

Greenwich is easily reached on the DLR or via train from London Bridge. The operator

**Thames River Services** ( ☎ 7930 4097; www.westminster pier.co.uk) has boats departing half-hourly from Westminster Pier (single/return £7.50/9.80, one hour), or alternatively take the cheaper Thames Clippers ferry (p201).

## OLD ROYAL NAVAL COLLEGE

Also designed by Wren, the **Old Royal Naval College** (Map p149; ☎ 8269 4747; www.oldroyalnaval college.org; 2 Cutty Sark Gardens SE10; admission free; ☺ 10am-5pm Mon-Sat; DLR Cutty Sark) is a magnificent example of monumental classical architecture. Parts are now used by the University of Greenwich and Trinity College of Music, but you can visit the **chapel** and the extraordinary **Painted Hall**, which took artist Sir James Thornhill 19 years of hard graft to complete.

The complex was built on the site of the 15th-century Palace of Placentia, the birthplace of Henry VIII and Elizabeth I. This Tudor connection will be explored in **Discover Greenwich**, a new centre due to open in late 2009. The **tourist office** ( ☎ 0870 608 2000; www.green-wich.gov.uk) will be housed here, but until then look for it in temporary buildings nearby.

## NATIONAL MARITIME MUSEUM

Directly behind the old college, the **National Maritime Museum** (Map p149; ☎ 8858 4422; www.nmm .ac.uk; Romney Rd SE10; admission free; ☺ 10am-5pm, last entry 4.30pm; DLR Cutty Sark) completes Greenwich's trump hand of historic buildings. The **museum** itself houses a massive collection of paraphernalia recounting Britain's seafaring history. Exhibits range from interactive displays to humdingers like Nelson's uniform complete with a hole from the bullet that killed him.

At the centre of the site, the elegant Palladian **Queen's House** has been restored to something like Inigo Jones' intention when he designed it in 1616 for the wife of Charles I. It's a stunning setting for a gallery focusing on illustrious seafarers and historic Greenwich.

Behind Queen's House, idyllic **Greenwich Park** climbs up the hill, affording great views of London. It's capped by the **Royal Observatory**, which Charles II had built in 1675 to help solve the riddle of longitude. Success was confirmed in 1884 when Greenwich was designated as the prime meridian of the world, and Greenwich Mean Time (GMT) became the universal measurement of standard time. On this spot you can stand with your feet straddling the western and eastern hemispheres.

If you arrive just before lunchtime, you will see a bright-red ball climb the observatory's northeast turret at 12.58pm and drop at 1pm – as it has every day since 1833 when it was introduced for ships on the River Thames to set their clocks by.

The observatory's newly revamped galleries are split into those devoted to astronomy and those devoted to time. There's also a 120-seat **planetarium** (adult/child £6/4) screening a roster of digital presentations; check the website for details.

## CUTTY SARK

A famous Greenwich landmark, this **clipper** (Map p149; ☎ 8858 3445; www.cuttysark.org.uk; King William Walk) was the fastest ship in the world when it was launched in 1869. Despite a fire in 2007, only a fraction of the ship was destroyed as much of its fabric had already been removed for conservation. By early 2010 it should have re-opened and be better displayed than ever – you'll even be able to walk under her. Watch the website for details.

## FAN MUSEUM

Housed in an 18th-century Georgian house, the engaging **Fan Museum** (Map p149; ☎ 8305 1441; www.fan-museum.org; 12 Croom's Hill SE10; admission £4; ☺ 11am-5pm Tue-Sat, noon-5pm Sun; DLR Cutty Sark) is one of a kind. Only a fraction of its collection of hand-held fans from around the world, dating back to the 17th century, are on display at any one time.

## THE O2

The world's largest dome (365m in diameter) opened on 1 January 2000 at a cost of £789 million as the Millennium Dome, but closed on 31 December, only hours before the third millennium began. Renamed **The O2** (Map p149; ☎ 8463 2000; www.theo2.co.uk; Peninsula Sq SE10; ⊖ North Greenwich), it's now a 20,000-seater sports and entertainment arena surrounded by shops and restaurants. It has hosted some massive concerts, including the one-off Led Zeppelin reunion and a 21-night purple reign by Prince. On concert nights, there are shuttle-boat services from central London.

# Outside Central London

## KEW GARDENS

In 1759 botanists began rummaging around the world for specimens they could plant in the 3-hectare plot known as the **Royal Botanic**

**Gardens, Kew** (Map pp134-5; ☎ 8332 5655; www.kew .org.uk; Kew Rd; adult/child £13/free; 🕑 9.30am-6.30pm Mon-Fri, to 7.30pm Sat & Sun, earlier closing in winter; ⊖ Kew Gardens). They never stopped collecting, and the gardens, which have bloomed to 120 hectares, provide the most comprehensive botanical collection on earth (including the world's largest collection of orchids) as well as a delightful pleasure garden. It's now recognised as a Unesco World Heritage Site.

You can easily spend a whole day wandering around, but if you're pressed for time, the **Kew Explorer** (adult/child £4/1) is a hop-on hop-off road train that leaves from Victoria Gate, taking in the gardens' main sights.

Highlights include the enormous **Palm House**, a hothouse of metal and curved sheets of glass; the stunning **Princess of Wales Conservatory**; the red-brick, 1631 **Kew Palace** (adult/child £5/2.50; 🕑 10am-5pm Easter–30 Sep), formerly King George III's country retreat; the celebrated **Great Pagoda** designed by William Chambers in 1762, due to reopen in 2009 following restoration; and the **Temperate House**, which is the world's largest ornamental glasshouse and home to its biggest indoor plant, the 18m Chilean Wine Palmand.

The gardens are easily reached by tube, but you might prefer to take a cruise on a riverboat from the **Westminster Passenger Services Association** ( ☎ 7930 2062; www.wpsa.co.uk), which runs several daily boats from April to October, departing from Westminster Pier (return adult/child £16.50/8.25, 90 minutes).

### HAMPTON COURT PALACE
Built by Cardinal Thomas Wolsey in 1514 but coaxed out of him by Henry VIII just before the chancellor fell from favour, **Hampton Court Palace** (Map pp134-5; ☎ 0844-482 7777; www.hrp.org .uk/HamptonCourtPalace; adult/child £13.50/6.65; 🕑 10am-6pm Apr-Oct, to 4.30pm Nov-Mar; 🚉 Hampton Court) is England's largest and grandest Tudor structure. It was already one of the most sophisticated palaces in Europe when, in the 17th century, Wren was commissioned to build an extension. The result is a beautiful blend of Tudor and 'restrained baroque' architecture.

Take a themed tour led by costumed historians or, if you're in a rush, visit the highlights: **Henry VIII's State Apartments**, including the Great Hall with its spectacular hammer-beamed roof; the **Tudor Kitchens**, staffed by 'servants'; and the **Wolsey Rooms**. You could easily spend a day exploring the palace and its 60 acres of

riverside gardens, especially if you get lost in the 300-year-old **maze**.

Hampton Court is 13 miles southwest of central London and is easily reached by train from Waterloo. Alternatively, the riverboats that head from Westminster to Kew (p171) continue here (return adult/child £19.50/9.75, 3½ hours).

### RICHMOND PARK
London's wildest **park** (Map pp134-5) spans more than 1000 hectares and is home to all sorts of wildlife, most notably herds of red and fallow deer. It's a terrific place for bird-watching, rambling and cycling.

To get there from the Richmond tube station, turn left along George St then left at the fork that leads up Richmond Hill.

### HORNIMAN MUSEUM
Set in an art-nouveau building amid gorgeous gardens, **Horniman Museum** (Map pp134-5; ☎ 8699 1872; www.horniman.ac.uk; 100 London Rd SE23; admission free; 🕑 10.30am-5.30pm; 🚉 Forest Hill) has three main themes: Anthropology (Britain's third-most important collection of ethnographical objects), Natural History (250,000 specimens) and a fab assortment of Musical Instruments.

Trains to Forest Hill leave from London Bridge. The museum is a well-signposted five-minute walk from the station, uphill along London Rd.

## CITY WALKING TOUR
The City of London has as much history and interesting architecture in its square mile as the rest of London put together. This tour focuses on the City's hidden delights (secluded parks, charming churches) in a journey from the ancient to the ultra-modern.

It's fitting to start at **St Bartholomew-the-Great (1)**, as this fascinating 12th-century church was once a site of pilgrimage for travellers to London. In more recent times, it's been used for scenes in *Four Weddings & A Funeral* and *Shakespeare In Love*.

Head out through the Tudor gatehouse, where in the distance you'll see the Victorian arches of Smithfield's meat market, which has occupied this site just north of the old city walls for 800 years. Executions were held here, most famously the burning of Protestants under Mary I and the grisly killing of Scottish hero William Wallace (portayed by

# CITY WALK

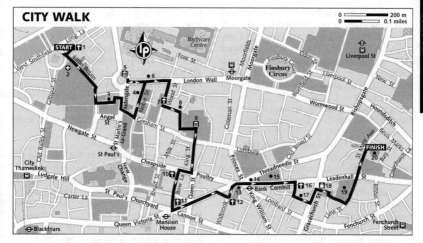

0 ——— 200 m
0 ——— 0.1 miles

## WALK FACTS

**Start** St Bartholomew-the-Great
**Finish** 30 St Mary Axe
**Distance** 2 miles
**Duration** two hours

Mel Gibson in *Braveheart*) in 1305; a plaque on the front of **St Batholemew's Hospital (2)** commemorates him. Also note the shrapnel damage to the wall, the legacy of an attack in 1916 by a German Zeppelin.

Head back towards the gate and turn right into Little Britain. Follow it as it curves to the right and look out for the large oak marking the entrance to **Postman's Park (3)**. This lovely space includes a touching legacy of Victorian socialism: a tiled wall celebrating everyday heroes.

Turn right at the end of the park, then left and left again into Noble St. You're now inside the City's **walls (4)**, remnants of which you'll pass on your left. Take the stairs up to the footbridge and cross towards the **Museum of London (5**, p162). Its Roman section will give you a feel for the layout of the City.

Turn left when leaving the museum and follow the Highwalk. On your left you'll see **ruins (6)** of the barbicans (defensive towers) that once guarded the northwestern corner of the walls, with the Barbican centre (p163) behind them.

Take the escalator (by Pizza Express) down to Wood St and head towards the remaining tower of **St Alban's (7)**, a Wren-designed

church destroyed in WWII. Turn left and you'll find a sweet garden on the site of **St Mary Aldermansbury (8)**, capped by a bust of Shakespeare. The 12th-century church was ruined in the war then shipped to Missouri where it was re-erected.

Turn right onto Aldermansbury and head to the **Guildhall (9**, p162). Take King St down to Cheapside, cross the road and head right to elegant **St Mary-le-Bow (10)**. The church was rebuilt by Wren after the Great Fire, and then rebuilt again after WWII. The term 'Cockney' traditionally refers to someone born within the sound of this church's bell.

Backtrack to Bow Lane and follow this narrow path to beautiful **St Mary Aldermary (11)**, rebuilt in the Perpendicular Gothic style in 1682 following the Great Fire. Turn left onto Queen Victoria St and then right into Bucklersbury, where you'll see **St Stephen's Walbrook (12**, p162) directly in front of you.

Leaving the church, you'll pass **Mansion House (13)**, built in 1752 as the official residence of the Lord Mayor. As you approach the busy Bank intersection, lined with neo-classical temples to commerce, you might think you've stumbled into the ancient Roman forum (the actual forum was a couple of blocks east). Head for the **equestrian statue of the Iron Duke (14)**, behind which a metal pyramid details the many significant buildings here. Directly behind you is the **Royal Exchange (15)**; walk through it and exit through the door on the right, then turn left onto Cornhill.

If you're not churched out, cross the road to **St Michael's (16)**, a 1672 Wren design that still has its box pews. Hidden in the warren of tiny passages behind the church is its **churchyard (17)**. Head through to Gracechurch St, turn left and cross the road to wonderful **Leadenhall Market (18)**. This is roughly where the ancient forum once stood.

As you wander out the far end, the famous **Lloyd's building (19)** displays its innards for all to see.

Once you turn left onto Lime St, you'll see ahead of you Norman Foster's 180m **30 St Mary Axe building (20)**. Its dramatic curved shape has given birth to many nicknames (the Crystal Phallus, the Towering Innuendo), but it's the Gherkin by which it's fondly referred. Built nearly 900 years after St Bartholomew-the-Great, it's testimony to the City's ability to constantly reinvent itself for the times.

## LONDON FOR CHILDREN

London has plenty of sights that parents and kids can enjoy together, and many of them are free, including the Natural History Museum (p167), Science Museum (p167) and all of the city's parks, many of which have excellent playgrounds. Pricier but popular attractions include London Dungeon (p166), London Zoo (p169), Madame Tussauds (p169), Tower of London (p161), London Aquarium (p166) and the London Eye (p166).

On top of that, there are a number of city farms (see www.london-footprints.co.uk/visit farms.htm) and the big galleries have activities for children. However, don't expect a warm welcome in swanky restaurants or pubs.

All top-range hotels offer in-house babysitting services. Prices vary enormously from hotel to hotel, so ask the concierge about hourly rates. Alternatively try www.sitters .co.uk: membership costs £12.75 for three months, then sitters cost around £8 per hour plus a £4 booking fee.

## TOURS

One of the best ways to get yourself orientated when you first arrive in London is with a 24-hour hop-on/hop-off pass for the double-decker bus tours operated by the **Original London Sightseeing Tour** ( ☎ 8877 1722; www.the originaltour.com; adult/child £22/12) or the **Big Bus Company** ( ☎ 7233 9533; www.bigbustours.com; adult/child £24/10). The buses loop around interconnecting routes throughout the day, providing a com-

mentary as they go, and the price includes a river cruise and three walking tours. You'll save a couple of pounds by booking online.

There are loads of walking tour operators, including **Citisights** ( ☎ 8806 3742; www.chr.org .uk/cswalks.htm), focusing on the academic and the literary; **London Walks** ( ☎ 7624 3978; www.walks .com), including Harry Potter tours, ghost walks and the ever-popular Jack The Ripper tours; and **Mystery Tours** ( ☎ 07957-388280; mysterywalks@ hotmail.com).

Other unusual options:

**Black Taxi Tours of London** ( ☎ 7935 9363; www .blacktaxitours.co.uk; 8am-6pm £95, 6pm-midnight £100, plus £5 on weekends) Takes up to five people on a two-hour spin past the major sights with a chatty cabbie as your guide.

**City Cruises** ( ☎ 7740 0400; www.citycruises.com; single/ return trips from £6.40/7.80, day pass £10.50; ☉ 10am-6pm Sep-May, later Jun-Aug) Operates a ferry service between Westminster, Waterloo, Tower and Greenwich piers.

**London Bicycle Tour Company** (Map pp142-3; ☎ 7928 6838; www.londonbicycle.com; 1A Gabriel's Wharf, 56 Upper Ground SE1; tour incl bike £14.95-17.95; ⊖ Waterloo) Offers themed 2½- to 3½-hour tours of the 'East', 'Central' or 'Royal West'.

**London Duck Tours** (Map pp142-3; ☎ 7928 3132; www.londonducktours.co.uk; County Hall; adult/child £21.50/15.50; ⊖ Waterloo) Cruise the streets in the same sort of amphibious landing craft used on D-Day, before making a dramatic plunge into the River Thames.

## FESTIVALS & EVENTS

Although not renowned as a festival city, London has a few events that might sway your plans.

**Chinese New Year** Late January or early February sees Chinatown (p158) snap, crackle and pop with fireworks, a colourful street parade and eating aplenty.

**University Boat Race** (www.theboatrace.org) A posh-boy grudge match held annually since 1829 between the rowing crews of Oxford and Cambridge Universities (late March).

**Chelsea Flower Show** (www.rhs.org.uk/chelsea; Royal Hospital Chelsea; admission £18-41) Held in May, the world's most renowned horticultural show attracts green fingers from near and far.

**Camden Crawl** (www.thecamdencrawl.com; 1/2-day pass £30/50) Your chance to spot the next big thing in the music scene or witness a secret gig by an established act, with 28 of Camden's intimate venues given over to live music for two full days in April.

**London Marathon** (www.london-marathon.co.uk) Up to half-a-million spectators watch the whippet-thin champions and often bizarrely clad amateurs take to the streets in late April.

**Trooping the Colour** Celebrating the Queen's official birthday (in June), this ceremonial procession of troops, marching along the Mall for their monarch's inspection, is a pageantry overload.

**Royal Academy Summer Exhibition** (www.royal academy.org.uk; Royal Academy of Arts; adult/child £8/3) Running from mid-June to mid-August, this is an annual showcase of works submitted by artists from all over Britain, mercifully distilled to 1200 or so pieces.

**Meltdown Festival** (www.southbankcentre.co.uk/ festivals-series/meltdown) Held late June, when the South- bank Centre hands over the curatorial reigns to a legend of contemporary music (such as David Bowie, Morrissey or Patti Smith) to pull together a full program of concerts, talks and films.

**Wimbledon Lawn Tennis Championships** (www .wimbledon.org; tickets by public ballot) Held at the end of June, the world's most splendid tennis event is as much about strawberries, cream and tradition as smashing balls.

**Pride** (www.pridelondon.org) The big event on the gay and lesbian calendar, a technicolour street parade heads through the West End in late June or early July, culminat- ing in a concert in Trafalgar Sq.

**Notting Hill Carnival** (www.nottinghillcarnival.biz) Held over two days in August, this is Europe's largest and London's most vibrant outdoor carnival, where London's Caribbean community shows the city how to party. Unmissable and truly crazy.

# SLEEPING

Take a deep breath and sit down before read- ing this section because no matter what your budget, London is a horribly pricey city to sleep in – one of the most expensive in the world, in fact. Anything below £80 per night for a double is pretty much 'budget', and at the top end, how does a £3500 penthouse sound? For this book we've defined the price categories for London differently than for the other chapters. Double rooms ranging between £80 to £150 per night are considered midrange; cheaper or more expensive options fall into the budget or the top-end categories respectively.

Ignoring the scary money stuff for a minute, London has a wonderful selection of interesting hotels, whether they be brim- ming with history or zany modern decor. Most of the ritzier places offer substantial discounts on the weekends, for advance bookings and at quiet times (if there is such a thing in London).

Public transport is exceptionally good, so you don't need to be sleeping at Buckingham Palace to be at the heart of things. However,

if you're planning some late nights and don't fancy enduring the night buses (a consum- mate London experience, but one you'll want only once) it'll make sense not to wander too far from the action (see p192).

London's a noisy city, so expect a bit of the din to seep into your room. If you're a light sleeper, earplugs are a sensible precaution, as is requesting a room back from the street and higher up.

It's now becoming the norm for budget and midrange places to offer free wireless internet. The expensive places will offer it too, but often charge. Hostels tend to serve up free breakfast (of the toast and cereal variety). If your hotel charges for breakfast, check the prices; any- thing over £8 just isn't worth it when there are so many eateries to explore.

Budget accommodation is scattered about, with some good options in West London, Southwark, Victoria and King's Cross. For something a little nicer, check out Victoria, Bloomsbury, Fitzrovia, Bayswater and Earl's Court. If you've the cash to splash, con- sider Mayfair, the West End, Clerkenwell and Kensington.

## St James's & Mayfair

Home to some of London's most famous 'establishment' hotels (such as the Ritz and Claridges), you'll need to be seriously cashed up to consider staying here.

**Brown's Hotel** (Map pp146-7; ☎ 7493 6020; www .brownshotel.com; 30 Albemarle St W1; d £325-615, ste £840- 3000; ☐ wi-fi; ⊖ Green Park) Stay here and you're in good company – Rudyard Kipling penned many of his works here, Kate Moss has fre- quented the spa and both Queen Victoria and Winston Churchill dropped in for tea. There's a lovely old world feel to Brown's, but without the snootiness of some others in the neighbourhood. The rooms have every modern comfort.

## Westminster & Pimlico

Handy to the big sights but lacking a strong sense of neighbourhood, the streets get prettier the further you stray from bustling Victoria station. Despite being the queen's own hood, there are some surprisingly affordable options.

### BUDGET

**Astor Victoria Hostel** (Map p145; ☎ 7834 3077; www .astorhostels.com; 71 Belgrave Rd SW1; dm £16-19, d & tw £60;

wi-fi; Pimlico) This cheap and cheerful hostel has plenty of mixed or women-only dorms but only a scattering of private rooms, so book early. There are two comfortable lounges with PCs, a fully equipped kitchen and weekly dinners for bonding over grub.

**Morgan House** (Map pp140-1; 7730 2384; www .morganhouse.co.uk; 120 Ebury St SW1; s/d & tw/tr without bathroom £52/72/92, with bathroom £86/92/112; Victoria) More homely than swanky, this pleasant Georgian house offers romantic iron beds (some a little saggy), chandeliers, period fireplaces, sparkling bathrooms and a full English breakfast.

### MIDRANGE

**Luna & Simone Hotel** (Map p145; 7834 5897; www .lunasimonehotel.com; 47-49 Belgrave Rd SW1; s £45-65, d & tw/tr/q £95/115/140; wi-fi; Pimlico) The ensign of Luna (the moon) and Simone (the owner) is etched into the glass porch and this personal touch continues inside with the friendly service. The blue-and-yellow rooms aren't huge but they're clean and calming; the ones at the back are quieter. A full English breakfast is included.

**Windermere Hotel** (Map pp140-1; 7834 5163; www.windermere-hotel.co.uk; 142-144 Warwick Way SW1; s £95-134, d £119-144, tw £126-144, f £159; wi-fi; Victoria) Chintzy but homely, this early-Victorian town house has 22 rooms, all traditionally British in decor. Lively floral curtains correspond with matching bedspreads, tartan headboards complement armchairs, and tables are draped in lace. Most have lacklustre but perfectly adequate en suites.

**B&B Belgravia** (Map pp140-1; 7259 8570; www.bb-belgravia.com; 64-66 Ebury St SW1; s/d/tw/tr/q £99/115/125/145/155; wi-fi; Victoria) This small hotel's unassuming facade belies a chic, contemporary interior comprising stylish bathrooms and floor-to-ceiling dark-wood cupboards. The only design blip is the easyJet-style, orange staff uniform. Outside, the pretty courtyard garden is a suntrap.

**Rubens at the Palace** (Map pp142-3; 7834 6600; www.rubenshotel.com; 39 Buckingham Palace Rd SW1; s £129, d £139-279, ste £329-579; wi-fi; Victoria) Opposite Buckingham Palace, it's perhaps not surprising to find that Rubens is a firm favourite with Americans looking for that quintessential British experience. With decor and service as traditional as high tea, it doesn't disappoint. The rooms are octogenarian chic, full of heavy patterned fabrics, dark wood, thick drapes and crowns above the beds.

## West End

This is the heart of the action, so naturally accommodation comes at a price, and a hefty one at that. A couple of hostels cater for would-be Soho hipsters of more modest means.

### BUDGET

**Oxford St YHA** (Map pp146-7; 7734 1618; www.yha .org.uk; 14 Noel St W1; dm/tw £25/64; wi-fi; Oxford Circus) In most respects, this is a bog-standard YHA hostel with tidy rooms and all the usual facilities (kitchen, TV room, laundry). What it's got going for it are a terrific (albeit noisy) location and decent views over London's rooftops from some of the rooms.

### TOP END

**Hazlitt's** (Map pp146-7; 7434 1771; www.hazlittshotel .com; 6 Frith St W1; d/ste from £205/300; ; Tottenham Court Rd) Staying in this charming Georgian house (1718) is a trip back into a time when four-poster beds and claw-footed baths were the norm for gentlefolk. Each of the individually decorated 23 rooms is packed with antiques and named after a personage connected with the house.

**Haymarket Hotel** (Map pp146-7; 7470 4000; www.haymarkethotel.com; 1 Suffolk Pl SW1; d £250-325, ste £395-3000; wi-fi; Piccadilly Circus) The building was designed by John Nash (Buckingham Palace's main man) but the rest is Kit Kemp all the way (see boxed text, p178). We love the gold loungers around the sunset-lit indoor swimming pool.

**Soho Hotel** (Map pp146-7; 7559 3000; www.soho hotel.com; 4 Richmond Mews W1; d £280-350, ste £385-2750; wi-fi; Oxford Circus) Hello Kitty! This Kit Kemp–designed hotel (see boxed text, p178) has a giant cat sculpture in a reception that looks like a psychedelic candy store; try to refrain from licking the walls.

Also recommended:

**Covent Garden Hotel** (Map pp146-7; 7806 1000; www.coventgardenhotel.co.uk; 10 Monmouth St WC2; d £235-330, ste £385-1150; wi-fi; Covent Garden) First-time guests get a complimentary massage in this well-positioned Firmdale hotel.

**One Aldwych** (Map pp146-7; 7300 1000; www .onealdwych.com; 1 Aldwych WC2; d £380-460, ste £625-1160; wi-fi; Covent Garden) Granite bathrooms, long swimming pool with underwater music, majestic bar and restaurant, modern art, and a lift that changes colour to literally lift your mood.

## Bloomsbury & Fitzrovia

Only one step removed from the West End and crammed with Georgian town-house conversions, these neighbourhoods are much more affordable. You'll find a stretch of lower-priced hotels along Gower St and on the pretty Cartwright Gardens crescent.

### BUDGET

**London Central YHA** (Map pp142-3; ☎ 0870-770 6144; www.yha.org.uk; 104-108 Bolsover St W1; dm £19-32; ☐ wi-fi; ⊕ Great Portland St) The newest and best of London's YHA hostels, everything's got that just-out-of-the-wrapper look and most of the four- to six-bed rooms have en suites. Communal space is lacking but there's a flash cafe-bar attached to reception.

**Generator** (Map pp136-7; ☎ 7388 7666; www.generator hostels.com/London; Compton Pl, 37 Tavistock Pl WC1; dm £20-25, s & tw/tr/q £70/75/100; ☐ wi-fi; ⊕ Russell Sq) Lashings of primary colours and shiny metal are the hallmarks of this futuristic but fun hostel. This former police barracks has 850 beds; a bar that stays open until 2am and hosts quizzes, pool competitions, karaoke and DJs; safe-deposit boxes; and a large eating area but no kitchen. Come to party.

**Ridgemount Private Hotel** (Map pp142-3; ☎ 7636 1141; www.ridgemounthotel.co.uk; 65-67 Gower St WC1; s/d/tr/q without bathroom £42/58/78/92, with bathroom £54/75/93/104; ☐ wi-fi; ⊕ Goodge St) There's a comfortable, welcoming feel at this old-fashioned, slightly chintzy place that's been in the same family for 40 years.

**Arran House Hotel** (Map pp142-3; ☎ 7636 2186; www.arranhotel-london.com; 77-79 Gower St WC1; s/d/tr/q without bathroom £50/77/95/101, with bathroom £60/100/118/122; ☐ wi-fi; ⊕ Goodge St) Period features such as cornicing and fireplaces, a pretty pergola-decked back garden and a comfy lounge with PCs and TV lift this hotel from the average to the attractive. Squashed en suites or shared bathrooms are the trade-off for these reasonable rates.

### MIDRANGE

**Jenkins Hotel** (Map pp136-7; ☎ 7387 2067; www.jenkinshotel.demon.co.uk; 45 Cartwright Gardens WC1; s £52, s/d/tr with bathroom from £72/89/105; ⊕ Russell Sq) This modest hotel has featured in the TV series of Agatha Christie's *Poirot*. Rooms are small but the hotel has charm.

**Crescent Hotel** (Map pp136-7; ☎ 7387 1515; www.crescenthoteloflondon.com; 49-50 Cartwright Gardens WC1; s £49-81, d & tw/tr/q £97/110/120; ☐ ; ⊕ Russell Sq) One of the cheaper options on the crescent overlooking Cartwright Gardens, there's a homely feel to this humble hotel, despite the odd saggy bed.

**Arosfa Hotel** (Map pp142-3; ☎ 7636 2115; www.arosfa london.com; 83 Gower St WC1E; s £60-65, d/tr/q £90/102/110; ☐ wi-fi; ⊕ Goodge St) While the decor of the immaculately presented rooms is unremarkable, Arosfa's guest lounge has been blinged up with chandeliers, clear plastic chairs and a free internet terminal. Recent refurbishments have added en suites to all 15 bedrooms, but they're tiny (putting the 'closet' back into water closet).

**Hotel Cavendish** (Map pp142-3; ☎ 7636 9079; www.hotelcavendish.com; 75 Gower St WC1E; s £85, d £105-130, tr/q £120/140; ☐ wi-fi; ⊕ Goodge St) Following a complete refurbishment a few years back, bedrooms have a contemporary look, with flat-screen TVs, and all are equipped with compact en-suite shower rooms (some have pretty tiles and bumper mirrors). The two gardens at the back are a good place to catch some rays.

### BOOKING SERVICES

It's possible to make same-day accommodation bookings for free at most tourist offices, and **Visit London** ( ☎ 08456 443 010; www.visitlondonoffers.com) also has good deals.

**At Home in London** ( ☎ 8748 1943; www.athomeinlondon.co.uk) Can arrange B&B accommodation and charges percentage booking fees.

**British Hotel Reservation Centre** ( ☎ 7592 3055; www.bhrconline.com) Free online booking.

**Lastminute** (www.lastminute.com) Has kiosks at the Britain & London Visitor Centre (p152) and Victoria station.

**London Homestead Services** ( ☎ 7286 5115; www.lhslondon.com) Charges a 5% booking fee.

**LondonTown** ( ☎ 7437 4370; www.londontown.com) Hotel, hostels and B&B bookings.

**Uptown Reservations** ( ☎ 7937 2001; www.uptownres.co.uk) Books upmarket B&Bs, mainly around Chelsea and the West End.

**YHA** ( ☎ 01629-592 700; reservations@yha.org.uk) Operates its own central reservations service, provided you give at least two weeks' notice.

LONDON

---

**THE KIT KEMP CLUB**

Kit Kemp's interiors purr loudly rather than whisper. She's waved her magically deranged wand over all the hotels of London's boutique Firmdale chain – including Covent Garden (p176), Haymarket (p176), Soho (p176), Charlotte St (below), Knightsbridge (opposite) and Number Sixteen (opposite) – creating bold, playful spaces full of zany fabrics, crazy sculpture and sheer luxury. Yet somehow she manages to create an old-fashioned feel from a thoroughly modern sensibility. While nonconformity is the norm, key values are shared throughout the chain: the staff are welcoming, guest lounges are inviting spaces with honesty bars, each bedroom features a dressmaker's dummy (some in miniature) and each bathroom is crafted from beautiful grey-flecked granite.

---

**Harlingford Hotel** (Map pp136-7; ☎ 7387 1551; www .harlingfordhotel.com; 61-63 Cartwright Gardens WC1; s/d & tw/tr/q £85/110/125/135; 🖳 wi-fi; ✦ Russell Sq) This family-run hotel sports refreshing, upbeat decor such as bright-green mosaic-tiled bathrooms (with trendy sinks), fuchsia bedspreads and colourful paintings. With lots of stairs and no lift, consider requesting a 1st-floor room.

**TOP END**

**Charlotte Street Hotel** (Map pp146-7; ☎ 7806 2000; www.charlottestreethotel.com; 15 Charlotte St W1; d £210-295, ste £350-950; 🖳 wi-fi; ✦ Goodge St) Another of the Firmdale clan (see boxed text, above), this one's a favourite with media types, with a small gym and a screening room.

**Sanderson** (Map pp146-7; ☎ 7300 1400; www .sandersonlondon.com; 50 Berners St W1; d £305-875, ste £611-925, apt £2500-3500; 🕃 🖳 wi-fi; ✦ Goodge St) Liberace meets Philippe Starck in an 18th-century French bordello – and that's just the reception. A 3-D space scene in the lift shuttles you into darkened corridors leading to blindingly white rooms complete with sleigh beds, oil paintings hung on the ceiling, en suites behind glass walls and pink silk curtains. Très chic.

## Holborn & Clerkenwell

The availability of accommodation hasn't kept pace with Clerkenwell's revival, but it's still a great area to stay. The best pickings aren't exactly cheap.

**Rookery** (Map pp142-3; ☎ 7336 0931; www.rookery hotel.com; Peter's Lane, Cowcross St EC1; s £175, d £210-495; 🖳 wi-fi; ✦ Farringdon) Taking its name from London's notorious slums (Fagin's house in *Oliver Twist* was set a few streets west), this antique-strewn luxury hotel recreates an early-19th-century ambience with none of the attendant grime or crime. For a bird's-eye view of St Paul's, book the Rook's Nest but be warned: Fagin never had a lift.

**Zetter Hotel** (Map pp136-7; ☎ 7324 4444; www .thezetter.com; 86-88 Clerkenwell Rd EC1M; d £188-400; 🖳 wi-fi; ✦ Farringdon) A slickly beautiful 21st-century conversion of a Victorian warehouse. The furnishings are an enticing blend of old and new, and the facilities cutting edge. You can even choose the colour of your room's lighting.

**Malmaison** (Map pp142-3; ☎ 7012 3700; www.mal maison.com; 18-21 Charterhouse Sq EC1; s from £205, d £225-250, ste £295-475; 🖳 wi-fi; ✦ Farringdon) Given Malmaison's grand frontage onto a hidden-away square, the *Alice in Wonderland* lobby of chessboard carpet, black seats that look like pawns and supersized chairs are a quirky surprise. Once in the rooms, the look is more classic with contemporary fittings in neutral shades.

## The City

Bristling with bankers during the week, you can often pick up a considerable bargain in the City on weekends.

**St Paul's YHA** (Map pp142-3; ☎ 0870 770 5764; www .yha.org.uk; 36 Carter Lane EC4; dm £27; 🖳 wi-fi; ✦ St Paul's) This former St Paul's Cathedral Choir Boys School is located in a lovely building just notes away from the cathedral itself. After the facade, the interiors are a bit of let down, but the dorms are small and have their own TVs and lockers. There's a licensed cafeteria but no kitchen.

**Threadneedles** (Map p150; ☎ 7657 8080; www .theetoncollection.com; 5 Threadneedle St EC2; d £370-499, ste £582-617; 🕃 🖳 wi-fi; ✦ Bank) The incredible stained-glass dome in the lobby points to its former status as a bank HQ. Today the bar and restaurant are still popular with suits, but the atmosphere is chic. At weekends this top-end spot is an absolute bargain.

## Hoxton, Shoreditch & Spitalfields

It's always had a rough-edged reputation, but London's East End is being gentrified faster than you can say 'awrigh' guv'. Staying here, you'll be handy to some of London's best bars.

**our pick** **Hoxton** (Map p150; ☎ 7550 1000; www.hoxtonhotels.com; 81 Great Eastern St; d & tw £59-189; ✗ ⬚ wi-fi; ⊖ Old St) A novel approach to pricing means that while all the rooms are identical, the first ones on any given day are offered at £59, an absolute steal for a hotel of this calibre. Rooms are a decent size, scrupulously clean, have comfy beds with quality linen and a well designed desk space where you can access the internet through the TV.

## South of the River Thames

Just south of the river is good if you want to immerse yourself in workaday London and still be central.

### BUDGET

**Dover Castle Hostel** (Map pp134-5; ☎ 7403 7773; www.dovercastlehostel.com; 6a Great Dover St; dm £10-16; ⬚ wi-fi; ⊖ Borough) If living in a pub is your fantasy, this is your chance. It's a modest affair (what do you expect for a tenner?), but the dorms are tidy, freshly painted and get loads of natural light. If you fancy a sound sleep, bring earplugs or drink yourself into oblivion downstairs.

**St Christopher's Village** (Map p150; ☎ 7407 1856; www.st-christophers.co.uk; 163 Borough High St SE1; dm £16-24, d & tw £52; ⬚ ; ⊖ London Bridge) With three locations on the same street sharing a main reception, there's quite a range of experiences on offer here. The main hub is the Village, a huge, up-for-it party hostel, with a club that opens until 4am on the weekends and a spa pool on the roof terrace. It's either heaven or hell, depending on what side of 30 you're on. The others are much smaller, quieter and, frankly, more pleasant. St Christopher's Inn (121 Borough High St) is situated above a very nice pub, while the Orient (59 Borough High St), above a cafe, has a separate women's floor. For these last two, you still need to book and check in at the Village.

### MIDRANGE

**Mad Hatter Hotel** (Map pp142-3; ☎ 7401 9222; www.fullershotels.com/frames/1044; 3-7 Stamford St SE1; r £145-165; ⊖ Southwark) There's nothing particularly mad (or even unusual) about it, but this is a good basic hotel with decent-sized rooms and unassuming decor hiding behind a lovely Victorian frontage. Prices fall below £100 on weekends.

Also recommended:
**Southwark Rose Hotel** (Map p150; ☎ 7015 1480; www.southwarkrosehotel.co.uk; 47 Southwark Bridge

Rd SE1; d weekdays/weekends £180/105, ste £245; ✗ ⬚ wi-fi; ⊖ Borough) It's pricey during the week, but this business hotel drops its rates considerably for weekenders.

## Chelsea, Kensington & Knightsbridge

Classy Chelsea and Kensington offer easy access to the museums and fashion retailers. It's all a bit sweetie-darling, along with the prices.

### BUDGET

**Holland House YHA** (Map pp138-9; ☎ 7937 0748; www.yha.org.uk; Holland Walk W8; dm £15-25; ⬚ wi-fi; ⊖ High St Kensington) Built out of the bombed-out remains of a 1607 mansion in the heart of Holland Park, there's an unfortunate school-camp vibe to the large dorm rooms. However, it's well looked after and the cheapest option for miles around, and the setting is unforgettable.

### MIDRANGE

**Vicarage Private Hotel** (Map pp138-9; ☎ 7229 4030; www.londonvicaragehotel.com; 10 Vicarage Gate W8; s/d/tr/q without bathroom £52/88/109/116, with bathroom £88/114/145/160; ⬚ wi-fi; ⊖ High St Kensington) If you were staying here 15 years ago, Princess Di would have been your neighbour – you can see Kensington Palace from the doorstep. This grand Victorian town house looks onto a cul-de-sac, so you shouldn't have a problem with noise in the simply furnished rooms. The cheaper ones (without bathrooms) are on floors three and four, so you may get a view as well as a workout.

### TOP END

**Number Sixteen** (Map pp140-1; ☎ 7589 5232; www.numbersixteenhotel.co.uk; 16 Sumner Pl SW7; s £120-165, d £200-270; ⬚ wi-fi; ⊖ South Kensington) The least pricey of the Firmdale hotels (see boxed text, opposite), with a lovely garden tucked away.

**Knightsbridge Hotel** (Map pp138-9; ☎ 7584 6300; www.knightsbridgehotel.com; 10 Beaufort Gdn SW3; s £170-185, d £210-295, ste £345-595; ⬚ wi-fi; ⊖ Knightsbridge) Another Firmdale (see boxed text, opposite), this one's on a quiet, tree-lined cul-de-sac very close to Harrods. It's the most restrained of the chain.

**Gore** (Map pp138-9; ☎ 7584 6601; www.gorehotel.com; 190 Queen's Gate SW7; r £187-390; ⬚ wi-fi; ⊖ Gloucester Rd) A short stroll from the Royal Albert Hall, the Gore serves up British grandiosity (antiques, carved four-posters, a secret bathroom in the Tudor room) with a large slice of camp.

LONDON

How else could you describe the Judy Garland room (complete with ruby slippers) and the Nellie room (Dame Nellie Melba, dahling), named after famous former occupants?

**Levin** (Map pp138-9; ☎ 7589 6286; www.thelevinhotel .co.uk; 28 Basil St SW3; d £235-445; ⊖ Knightsbridge) As close as you can get to sleeping in Harrods, the Levin knows its market. Despite the baby-blue colour scheme, there's a subtle femininity to the decor, although it's far too elegant to be flouncey.

## Notting Hill, Bayswater & Paddington

Don't be fooled by Julia Roberts' and Hugh Grant's shenanigans, Notting Hill and the areas immediately north of Hyde Park are as shabby as they are chic. There are some nice gated squares surrounded by Georgian town houses, but the area is better exemplified by the Notting Hill Carnival (p175), where the West Indian community who made the area their home from the 1950s party up big time.

Scruffy Paddington has lots of cheap hotels, with a major strip of unremarkable ones along Sussex Gardens, worth checking if you're short on options.

### MIDRANGE

**Vancouver Studios** (Map pp138-9; ☎ 7243 1270; www .vancouverstudios.co.uk; 30 Prince's Sq W2; apt £85-170; 🖳 wi-fi; ⊖ Bayswater) Technically apartments, it's only the addition of kitchenettes and a self-service laundry that differentiate these smart but reasonably priced studios (sleeping from one to three people) from a regular Victorian town-house hotel. In spring, the garden is filled with colour and fragrance.

**New Linden Hotel** (Map pp138-9; ☎ 7221 4321; www .newlinden.co.uk; 58-60 Leinster Sq W2; s £95, d £129-179, tr/ f/ste £210/150/189; 🖳 wi-fi; ⊖ Bayswater) Cramming in a fair whack of style for the price, this terrace-house hotel has interesting modern art in the rooms and carved wooden fixtures from India combined with elegant wallpaper in the guest lounge. The quiet location, helpful staff and monsoon shower heads in the deluxe rooms make this an excellent proposition.

### TOP END

**Hempel** (Map pp138-9; ☎ 7298 9000; www.the-hempel .co.uk; 31-35 Craven Hill Gardens; d £239-315, ste £319-1345; 🖳 wi-fi; ⊖ Bayswater) As soon as you enter the expansive all-white lobby with sunken seating areas, supermodern fireplaces and dramatic ceiling-grazing flower arrangement, you know you're in for something special. Created by Anouska Hempel, every detail is a feat of superb design, from the Zen garden to the minimalist but luxurious rooms.

## North London
### EUSTON & KING'S CROSS

While hardly a salubrious location, King's Cross is handy to absolutely everything and has some excellent budget options.

**Ashlee House** (Map pp136-7; ☎ 7833 9400; www .ashleehouse.co.uk; 261-265 Grays Inn Rd; dm £21-24, s/tw & tr £57/76; 🖳 ; ⊖ King's Cross) This hostel is a cheery surprise in a gritty but central location. There's a large tube map and London scenes on the walls, green dice tables in the small lounge, bright paintwork in the compact rooms and stripy duvets on the blue bunk beds.

**Jesmond Dene Hotel** (Map pp136-7; ☎ 7837 4654; www.jesmonddenehostel.co.uk; 27 Argyle St; s/d & tw/tr/q from £50/60/85/120; 🖳 wi-fi; ⊖ King's Cross) A surprisingly pleasant option for a place so close to busy King's Cross station, this modest hotel has clean but small rooms, some of which share bathrooms. A full English breakfast is included in the price.

**Clink** (Map pp136-7; ☎ 7183 9400; www.clinkhostel .com; 78 King's Cross Rd; dm £21-28, tw with/without bathroom £70/60, d/tr 70/78; 🖳 wi-fi; ⊖ King's Cross) If anyone can think of a more right-on London place to stay than the courthouse where the Clash went on trial, please let us know. You can watch TV from the witness box or sleep in the cells, but the majority of the rooms are custom-built and quite comfortable.

### HAMPSTEAD & HIGHGATE

A little further out but still in transport Zone 2, the following are both excellent options within walking distance of Hampstead Heath.

**Palmers Lodge** (Map pp134-5; ☎ 7483 8470; www.palmerslodge.co.uk; 40 College Cres NW3; dm £15-22, tw £46-50, d £52; 🅿 wi-fi; ⊖ Swiss Cottage) Reminiscent of a period murder mystery (in a good way), this former children's hospital has bags of character. Listed by English Heritage, it's stuffed with cornicing, moulded ceilings, original fireplaces and imposing wooden panelling. Ceilings are high, rooms are spacious, there's a chapel bar with pews, a grand stairway and a roomy lounge. Privacy curtains make the 28-bed men's dorm bearable (imagine you're in the hold of a pirate ship), but they don't shut out the amorous noises in the couples dorm.

**Hampstead Village Guesthouse** (Map pp134–5; ☎ 7435 8679; www.hampsteadguesthouse.com; 2 Kemplay Rd NW3; s £55–75, d £80–95, apt £100–175; 🖳 wi-fi; ✛ Hampstead) Eclectic, cluttered and thoroughly charming, this grand Victorian house has an easygoing hostess, comfy beds and a delightful back garden. There's also a studio flat, which can accommodate up to five people.

## Greenwich

If you'd rather keep the bustle of central London at arm's length and nightclubbing is your idea of hell, Greenwich offers a villagey ambience and some great old pubs to explore.

### BUDGET

**St Christopher's Inn** (Map p149; ☎ 8858 3591; www.st-christophers.co.uk; 189 Greenwich High Rd SE10; dm £18–22, tw £44–50; 🖳 wi-fi; 🚇 /DLR Greenwich) The nicest of the St Christopher's chain, this lovely old Georgian block is right by the station, with bright six- to eight-bed dorms and bunk-style twins. The downstairs pub is a nicer place to hang out in than the claustrophobic basement lounge.

### MIDRANGE

**St Alfege's** (Map p149; ☎ 8853 4337; www.st-alfeges.co.uk; 16 St Alfege Passage SE10; s/d £60/90; 🖳 wi-fi; DLR Cutty Sark) Both the house and the host have personality plus, so much so that they were featured on TV's *Hotel Inspector* series. The two double rooms are elegant and comfortable, but the single would suit the vertically challenged and going to the toilet in the wardrobe might take some getting used to.

**Harbour Master's House** (Map p149; ☎ 8293 9597; http://website.lineone.net/~harbourmaster; 20 Ballast Quay SE10; d £85; 🚇 Maze Hill) The 1855 building, Harbour Master's House, is Grade II–listed and perfectly positioned by the River Thames,

but don't expect views from this self-contained flat in the vaulted cellar. However, the windows let in natural light and it's great value for its size, with a large lounge and separate kitchen/dining area.

## West London

Earl's Court is lively, cosmopolitan and so popular with travelling Antipodeans it's been nicknamed Kangaroo Valley. There are no real sights, but it does have inexpensive digs and an infectious holiday atmosphere.

### BUDGET

**Barmy Badger Backpackers** (Map pp140–1; ☎ 7370 5213; www.barmybadger.com; 17 Longridge Rd SW5; dm £16–18, d/tw £38; 🖳 wi-fi; ✛ Earl's Court) A humble but friendly hostel in a big old house, most of the rooms (including the dorms) have their own toilet. There's a big kitchen and a small garden out the back.

**our pick Globetrotter Inn** (Map pp134–5; ☎ 8746 3112; www.globetrotterinn.com; Ashlar Ct, Ravenscourt Gardens W6; dm £20–24, d & tw £60; 🖳 ; ✛ Stamford Brook) At the far reaches of Zone 2 (so still relatively central), this former nurses' home inhabits an attractive art-deco building in a leafy part of West London. It's certainly not boutique (there are 390 beds), but high ceilings and an attractive central lawn with a fountain give a sense of space, and personal reading lights and curtains in the dorms allow extra privacy.

### MIDRANGE

**Barclay House** (Map pp140–1; ☎ 7384 3390; www.barclayhouselondon.com; 21 Barclay Rd SW6; s/d £68/88, apt £135–200; 🖳 wi-fi; ✛ Fulham Broadway) A proper homestay B&B, the two comfy bedrooms in this charming Victorian town house share a bathroom and an exceptionally welcoming hostess. You'll be well set up to conquer London with helpful tips, maps, umbrellas and a full stomach. There's also a self-contained, two-bedroom apartment downstairs.

**Rushmore Hotel** (Map pp140–1; ☎ 7370 3839; www.rushmore-hotel.co.uk; 11 Trebovir Rd SW5; s £69–79, d & tw £89–99, tr/q £115/139; 🖳 wi-fi; ✛ Earl's Court) The soft pastel colours, draped fabrics and simple designs of this modest hotel create a cheery, welcoming atmosphere, heightened by the friendly family that run the joint. There's no lift, so a complimentary workout is provided for those on the upper floors. The double rooms can be tight but the twins have a bit more space.

**Twenty Nevern Square** (Map pp140-1; ☎ 7565 9555; www.twentynevernsquare.co.uk; 20 Nevern Sq SW5; s £79-140, d £85-189; ☐ wi-fi; ✆ Earl's Court) An Ottoman theme runs through this contemporary town-house hotel, where a mix of wooden furniture, luxurious fabrics and natural light helps maximise space even though the cheaper bedrooms are not particularly large.

**base2stay** (Map pp140-1; ☎ 0845 262 8000; www.base2stay.com; 25 Courtfield Gardens SW5; s £93, d £107-127, tw £127; ☐ wi-fi; ✆ Earl's Court) With smart decor, power showers, flat-screen TVs with internet access and artfully concealed kitchenettes, this boutique establishment feels like a four-star hotel without the hefty price tag.

## Airports
**Yotel** ( ☎ 7100 1100; www.yotel.com; r per 4/5/6 hr £38/45/53, 7-24 hr £59; ☐ wi-fi) Heathrow (Terminal 4); Gatwick (South Terminal) The best news for early-morning flyers since coffee-vending machines, Yotel's smart 'cabins' offer pint-sized luxury: comfy beds, soft lights, internet-connected TVs, monsoon showers and fluffy towels. Swinging cats isn't recommended, but when is it ever?

# EATING
Dining out in London has become so fashionable that you can hardly open a menu without banging into some celebrity chef or restaurateur. Unfortunately, this doesn't automatically guarantee quality – food and service can be hit-and-miss regardless of price tag. In this section, we steer you towards restaurants and cafes distinguished by their location, value for money, unique features, original settings and, of course, good food. Vegetarians needn't worry. London has a host of dedicated meat-free joints, while most others offer at least a token dish.

## Westminster & Pimlico
There's very little action around these parts at night and those restaurants that are worth the detour will set you back a few quid.

**our pick Olivomare** (Map pp142-3; ☎ 7730 9022; 10 Lower Belgrave St SW1; mains £14-19; ☽ lunch & dinner Mon-Sat; ✆ Victoria) The Sardinian seaside comes to Belgravia in a dazzling white dining room with flavoursome seafood dishes and authentic wines. The grilled sea bass with olives and tomato is a treat and the service impeccable.

**Thomas Cubitt** (Map pp140-1; ☎ 7730 6060; 44 Elizabeth St SW1; mains £16-21; ✆ Victoria) The bar below gets rammed into the impressively high rafters with the swanky Belgravia set, but don't let that put you off this excellent, elegant dining room. The culinary focus is thoroughly British and deftly executed. The downstairs menu is cheaper (£9 to £14).

## St James's & Mayfair
Like on the Monopoly board, if you land on Mayfair you may have to sell a house (to afford to eat here).

**Sketch** (Map pp146-7; ☎ 0870 777 4488; 9 Conduit St W1; Parlour mains £4-14, Gallery mains £11-27, Lecture Room 2-course lunch £30, 8-course dinner £90; ✆ Oxford Circus) A design enthusiast's wet dream, with shimmering white rooms, video projections, designer Louis XIV chairs and toilet cubicles shaped like eggs. And that's just the Gallery, which becomes a buzzy restaurant and bar at night. The ground-floor Parlour has decadent cakes and decor, but is surprisingly affordable; perfect for breakfast, or afternoon tea served on fine bone china. The swanky Lecture Room upstairs is the realm of three-Michelin-starred chef Pierre Gagnaire, whose book *Reinventing French Cuisine* gives a hint of what to expect.

**Nobu** (Map pp142-3; ☎ 7447 4747; Metropolitan Hotel, 19 Old Park Ln W1; dishes £10-26; ✆ Hyde Park Corner) One of London's most famous eateries, Nobu's dining room is surprisingly unremarkable but it does have nice views over Hyde Park. It's nonetheless out of this world when it comes to exquisitely prepared and presented Japanese dishes. Ordering the sublime lunchtime *bento* box (£28) is a sensible way of limiting the financial pain, especially compared to the £50 to £90 chef's choices.

**Wild Honey** (Map pp146-7; ☎ 7758 9160; 12 St George St W1; mains £16-22; ✆ Oxford Circus) If you fancy a swanky evening at a top Mayfair restaurant without breaking the bank, Wild Honey offers an excellent-value pre-theatre menu (£19 for three courses). Of course, the danger is that once you're ensconced in this elegant dining room, you won't be able to resist the delights of the full Modern European menu.

**Tamarind** (Map pp142-3; ☎ 7629 3561; 20 Queen St W1; mains £16-28; ✆ Green Park) London's only Michelin-starred Indian restaurant serves up mouth-watering spicy classics. The set lunches are a good deal (two/three courses £17/19).

**Hibiscus** (Map pp146-7; ☎ 7629 2999; 29 Maddox St W1; 3-course lunch/dinner £25/60; ✆ Oxford Circus) Claude and Claire Bosi have generated an avalanche of praise from London critics since moving their Michelin-starred restaurant from Shropshire to Mayfair. Expect adventurous French and English cuisine in an elegant dining room.

## West End

Soho and Covent Garden are the gastronomic heart of London, with stacks of restaurants and cuisines to choose from at budgets to suit both booze hounds and theatre-goers. If you're craving a decent coffee, this is the place to come.

### BUDGET

**Nordic Bakery** (Map pp146-7; ☎ 3230 1077; 14a Golden Sq W1; snacks £3-5; ☺ 8am-8pm Mon-Fri, 11am-7pm Sat, 11am-6pm Sun; ⊖ Piccadilly Circus) As simple and stylish as you'd expect from the Scandinavians, this small cafe has bare wooden walls and uncomplicated Danish snacks such as sticky cinnamon buns and salmon served on dark-rye bread.

**Neal's Yard Salad Bar** (Map pp146-7; ☎ 7836 3233; Neal's Yard WC2; mains £3-12; ⊖ Covent Garden) Occupying both sides of the courtyard, this bright-orange salad bar has waiters in black bow ties serving fresh, leafy meals and moist Brazilian cakes.

**Yauatcha** (Map pp146-7; ☎ 7494 8888; 15 Broadwick St W1; dishes £3-18; ⊖ Piccadilly Circus) Dim-sum restaurants don't come much cooler than this, and the menu is fantastic and Michelin-starred. Upstairs, the chilled-out teahouse serves pretty cakes.

**Fernandez & Wells** (Map pp146-7; ☎ 7287 2814; 73 Beak St W1; mains £4-5; ☺ 8am-7pm Mon-Fri, 9am-7pm Sat & Sun; ⊖ Piccadilly Circus) With its sister deli around the corner, there's no shortage of delicious charcuterie and cheese to fill the fresh baguettes on the counter of this teensy cafe. The coffee's superb.

**Sacred** (Map pp146-7; ☎ 7734 1415; 13 Ganton St W1; ☺ 7.30am-8.30pm Mon-Fri, 9.30am-8pm Sat, 10am-7pm Sun; ⊖ Oxford Circus) The spiritual paraphernalia and blatant Kiwiana don't seem to deter the smart Carnaby St set from lounging around this eclectic cafe. It must be something to do with the excellent coffee, appealing counter food and deliciously filling cooked breakfasts (try the scrambled eggs with salmon and goats' cheese).

**Hummus Bros** (Map pp146-7; ☎ 7734 1311; 88 Wardour St W1; meals £4-7; ⊖ Piccadilly Circus) Don't come here if you're chickpea challenged, be-cause this informal place is hummus heaven. It comes in small or regular bowls with a choice of meat or vegie toppings and a side of pitta bread.

**Mother Mash** (Map pp146-7; ☎ 7494 9644; 26 Ganton St W1; mains £7; ⊖ Oxford Circus) If you've lived through a London winter, you'll know the importance of good comfort food. This Mother certainly does, offering choices of four types of mashed potato, eight varieties of sausage (including a vegetarian version), six choices of pie and five types of gravy (including the traditional, parsley-based East End 'liquor').

Also recommended:

**Breakfast Club** (Map pp146-7; ☎ 7434 2571; 33 D'Arblay St W1; 🖳 ; ⊖ Oxford Circus) See p188.

**Konditor & Cook** (Map pp146-7; ☎ 7292 1684; Curzon, 99 Shaftesbury Ave W1; ⊖ Leicester Sq) See p186.

**Red Veg** (Map pp146-7; ☎ 7437 3109; 95 Dean St W1; ⊖ Tottenham Court Rd) Everyone's favourite communist vegetarian burger bar.

### MIDRANGE

**Abeno Too** (Map pp146-7; ☎ 7379 1160; 17-18 Great Newport St WC2; mains £8-15; ⊖ Leicester Sq) Specialists in *okonomi-yaki* (Japanese-style pancakes), which are cooked in front of you on a hotplate. Sit at the bar or by the window and feast. Japanese noodle dishes are also available.

**Sarastro** (Map pp146-7; ☎ 7836 0101; 126 Drury Ln WC2; mains £8-16; ⊖ Covent Garden) This Turkish-influenced restaurant is gaudy, kitsch and loads of fun. The opera theme – with balcony tables, gold everywhere (even the ceiling), crushed velvet and myriad lamps – is totally over the top. Good for pre- and post-theatre meals.

**Spiga** (Map pp146-7; ☎ 7734 3444; 84-86 Wardour St W1; mains £9-18; ⊖ Piccadilly Circus) With Italian movie posters on the walls, warm, colourful decor and a tasty menu of pastas, pizzas, fish and meat dishes, this popular restaurant is a winner.

**Kettners** (Map pp146-7; ☎ 7734 6112; 29 Romilly St W1; mains £9-20; ⊖ Leicester Sq) Founded in 1867 (no, that's not a typo), Kettners has served the likes of Oscar Wilde and Edward VIII. Nowadays it dishes up pizza and burgers, which you can wash down with champagne while soaking in the gently fading grandeur and tinkling piano.

### TOP END

**National Gallery Dining Rooms** (Map pp146-7; ☎ 7747 2525; Sainsbury Wing, National Gallery, Trafalgar Sq WC2; 2

**TOP FIVE BLOW THE INHERITANCE**

- **Gordon Ramsay** (p187)
- **Lecture Room at Sketch** (p182)
- **Hibiscus** (p182)
- **Hakkasan** (below)
- **Nobu** (p182)

courses £25; ☾ lunch daily, dinner Fri; ⊖ Charing Cross) It's fitting that Oliver Peyton's acclaimed restaurant should celebrate British food (such as smoked haddock, traditional Suffolk cob chicken and 'Farmer Shep's aged sirloin'), being in the National Gallery and overlooking Trafalgar Sq. For a much cheaper option with the same views, ambience, quality produce and excellent service, try a salad, pie or tart at the adjoining bakery (mains £4.50 to 9.50).

## Bloomsbury & Fitzrovia
Tucked away behind busy Tottenham Court Rd, Fitzrovia's Charlotte and Goodge Sts form one of central London's most vibrant eating precincts.

**Salt Yard** (Map pp142-3; ☎ 7637 0657; 54 Goodge St W1; tapas £5-8; ⊖ Goodge St) Named after the place where cold meats are cured, this softly lit joint serves delicious Spanish and Italian tapas. Try the roasted chicken leg with gnocchi, wild garlic and sorrel, or flex your palate with courgette flowers stuffed with cheese and drizzled with honey.

**Ooze** (Map pp142-3; ☎ 7436 9444; 62 Goodge St W1; mains £7-15; ⊖ Goodge St) The humble risotto gets its moment on the catwalk in this breezy Italian restaurant. There are a handful of grills on the menu, but it's the 16 varieties of oozy, but still slightly crunchy, risotto that take centre stage.

**La Perla** (Map pp146-7; ☎ 7436 1744; 11 Charlotte St W1; mains £9-17; ☾ closed Sun lunch; ⊖ Goodge St) The service is lovely, but it's the street tacos that have us infatuated: mini tacos loaded up with tomato, coriander, onion, chilli and your choice of pork, prawns or chicken.

**Hakkasan** (Map pp146-7; ☎ 7907 1888; 8 Hanway Pl W1; mains £10-60; ⊖ Tottenham Court Rd) Hidden down a lane like all fashionable haunts need to be, the first Chinese restaurant to get a Michelin star combines celebrity status, a stunning design, persuasive cocktails and incredibly sophisticated Chinese food.

## Holborn & Clerkenwell
Similarly hidden away, Clerkenwell's gems are well worth digging for. Pedestrianised Exmouth Market is a good place to start.

### BUDGET
**Little Bay** (Map pp136-7; ☎ 7278 1234; 171 Farringdon Rd EC1; mains before/after 7pm £6/8; ⊖ Farringdon) The crushed-velvet ceiling, handmade twisted lamps that improve around the room (as the artist got better) and elaborately painted bar and tables showing nymphs frolicking is bonkers but fun. The hearty food is very good value.

Also recommended is:

**Konditor & Cook** (Map pp142-3; ☎ 7404 6300; Gray's Inn Rd, WC1; ⊖ Chancery Ln) See p186.

### MIDRANGE
**Bleeding Heart Restaurant & Bistro** (Map pp142-3; ☎ 7242 8238; Bleeding Heart Yard EC1; bistro £8-16, restaurant £13-25; ⊖ Farringdon) Locals have taken this place, tucked in the corner of Bleeding Heart Yard, to their hearts. Choose from formal dining in the downstairs restaurant or more relaxed meals in the buzzy bistro – wherever, the French food is divine.

**5ifty 4our** (Map pp136-7; ☎ 7336 0603; 54 Farringdon Rd; mains £9-13.50; ⊖ Farringdon) Britain and Malaysia go back a long way and this smart-looking restaurant celebrates that fact with tasty fusion dishes like lamb shanks with redang sauce.

**Great Queen Street** (Map pp146-7; ☎ 7242 0622; 32 Great Queen St WC2; mains £10-14; ☾ lunch Tue-Sat, dinner Mon-Sat; ⊖ Holborn) There's no tiara on this Great Queen, her claret-coloured walls and mismatched wooden chairs suggesting cosiness and informality. But the food's still the best of British, including brawn, lamb that melts in the mouth and Arbroath smokie (a whole smoked fish with creamy sauce).

**Smiths of Smithfield** (Map pp142-3; ☎ 7251 7950; 67-77 Charterhouse St EC1; mains 1st fl £11-17, top fl £17-29; ⊖ Farringdon) This converted meat-packing warehouse endeavours to be all things to all people and succeeds. Hit the ground-floor bar for a beer, follow the silver-clad ducts and wooden beams upstairs to a relaxed dining space, or continue up for two more floors of feasting, each slightly smarter and pricier than the last.

**St John** (Map pp142-3; ☎ 7251 0848; 26 St John St EC1; mains £14-23; ⊖ Farringdon) Bright whitewashed brick walls, high ceilings and simple wooden furniture keep diners free to concentrate on its world-famous nose-to-tail offerings. Expect offal, ox tongue and tripe.

### TOP END
**Dans le Noir** (Map p136-7; ☎ 7253 1100; 30-31 Clerkenwell Green EC1; 2/3 courses £29/37; ❸ Farringdon) If you've ever felt in the dark about food, eating in the pitch black might suit you. A visually impaired waiter guides you to your table, plate and cutlery. Then it's up to you to guess what you're eating and enjoy the anonymous conviviality of the dark…

## The City
You'll be sorely dismayed if you've got an empty belly on a Sunday morning in the City. Even during the busy weekdays, your best bets are the chains (p186) or the **Konditor & Cook** (Map p150; ☎ 0845-262 3030; 30 St Mary Axe EC3; ❸ Liverpool St) bakery in the Gherkin.

## Hoxton, Shoreditch & Spitalfields
From the hit-and-miss Bangladeshi restaurants of Brick Lane to the Vietnamese strip on Kingsland Rd, and the Jewish, Spanish, French, Italian and Greek eateries in between, the East End's cuisine is as multicultural as its residents.

### BUDGET
**Brick Lane Beigel Bake** (Map p150; ☎ 7729 0616; 159 Brick Lane E2; most bagels less than £2; ⏰ 24hr; ❸ Liverpool St) A relic of London's Jewish East End, it's more a takeaway than a cafe and sells dirt-cheap bagels. They're a good snack on a bellyful of booze.

**Cafe Bangla** (Map p150; ☎ 7247 7885; 128 Brick Ln E1; mains £4-13; ❸ Liverpoool St) Dining in the famous curry houses of Brick Lane is inevitably more about the experience than the food. Among the hordes of practically interchangeable restaurants, this one stands out for its murals of scantily-clad women riding dragons, alongside a tribute to Princess Di.

**Song Que** (Map pp134-5; ☎ 7613 3222; 134 Kingsland Rd E2; mains £5-7; ❸ Old St) If you arrive after 7.30pm, expect to queue as this humble eatery has already had its cover blown as one of the best Vietnamese in London. There's never much time to admire the institutional-green walls, fake lobsters and bizarre horse portrait, as you'll be shunted out shortly after your last bite.

**Macondo** (Map p150; ☎ 7729 1119; 8-9 Hoxton Sq N1; mains £5-8; ⏰ 9.30am-11pm Sun-Thu, to midnight Fri & Sat; ❸ Old St) A welcome respite from the full English breakfast, Macondo brings some Latin loving to eggs on toast, transforming it into eggs on tortilla with spicy *tomatillo* or bitter *anchilo* pepper sauce. Beverages range from excellent coffee to cocktails, best enjoyed on a sunny day on the outdoor tables facing the square.

We also recommend the **S&M Cafe** (Map p150; ☎ 7247 2252; 48 Brushfield St E1; ❸ Liverpool St) – turn to p188.

### MIDRANGE
**Story Deli** (Map p150; ☎ 7247 3137; 3 Dray Walk; pizzas £9-10; ❸ Liverpool St) This organic cafe with mismatched cutlery poking out of jam jars, vintage mirrors leaning haphazardly against walls, high ceilings and solid wooden furniture (mismatched of course) is justifiably popular. The pizzas are thin and crispy, and you can rest assured that anything fishy has been sustainably caught.

**Hoxton Apprentice** (Map p150; ☎ 7749 2828; 16 Hoxton Sq N1; mains £9-17; ❸ Old St) Similar in concept to Fifteen (below), both professionals and apprentices work the kitchen in this restaurant, housed appropriately enough in a former Victorian primary school. The music selection's awful (hotel-lobby piano when we visited), but the prices are reasonable and it's under the auspices of the Training For Life charity.

**ourpick** **Fifteen** (Map p150; ☎ 0871-330 1515; www .fifteen.net; 15 Westland Pl N1; breakfast £2-8.50, trattoria £9-18, restaurant £22-24; ❸ Old St) It can only be a matter of time before Jamie Oliver becomes Sir Jamie. His culinary philanthropy started at Fifteen, set up to give unemployed young people a shot at a career. The Italian food is beyond excellent and, surprisingly, even those on limited budgets can afford a visit. In the trattoria, a croissant and coffee will only set you back £3.50, while a £9 pasta makes for a delicious lunch.

### TOP END
**Les Trois Garçons** (Map p150; ☎ 7613 1924; 1 Club Row E1; mains £18-32; ❸ Liverpool St) The name may prepare you for the French menu, but nothing on earth could prepare you for the camp decor. A virtual menagerie of stuffed and bronze animals fills every surface, while chandeliers dangle between a set of suspended handbags. The food is good, if overpriced, and the small army of bow-tie-wearing waiters unobtrusively

---

**CHAIN-CHAIN-CHAIN, CHAIN OF FOODS**

It's an unnerving, but not uncommon, experience to discover the idiosyncratic cafe or pub you were so proud of finding on your first day in London popping up on every other high street. But among the endless Caffe Neros, Pizza Expresses and All-Bar-Ones are some gems, or, at least, great fallback options.

Some of the best:

**GBK** (Map pp142-3, pp138-9 pp136-7, pp140-1, p149 p150pp146-7 www.gbkinfo.com) Producing creative burger constructions in 19 Gourmet Burger Kitchens.

**Leon** (Map pp142-3, p149000, pp146-7; www.leonrestaurants.co.uk) Focusing on fresh, seasonal food (salads, wraps and the like).

**Ping Pong** (Map pp142-3, pp146-7 www.pingpongdimsum.com) Stylish Chinese dumpling joints.

**Wagamama** (Map pp142-3,pp138-9 pp136-7pp140-1p149 p150pp146-7 www.wagamama.com) Japanese noodles taking over the world from their London base.

**Zizzi** (Map pp142-3,pp138-9pp140-1p149 p150pp146-7www.zizzi.co.uk) Wood-fired pizza.

---

deliver complimentary bread and tasty gifts from the kitchen.

## South of the River Thames

You'll find plenty of touristy eateries on the riverside between Westminster and Tower Bridges, making the most of the constant foot traffic and iconic London views. For a feed with a local feel, head to Borough Market, Bermondsey St or the Cut in Waterloo.

### BUDGET

**Konditor & Cook** (Map p150; ☎ 7407 5100; 10 Stoney St SE1; snacks £2-5; ◉ London Bridge) The original location of arguably the best bakery in London, it serves excellent muffins, sweets, bread and coffee. There's only one table but everything is yours to take away.

**Estrala Bar** (Map p145; ☎ 7793 1051; 111-115 South Lambeth Rd SW8; tapas £2-8, mains £8-12; ◉ breakfast, lunch & dinner; ◉ Oval) In a Portuguese pocket of South London, Estrala's waistcoated waiters deliver the national dish, *bacalhau* (salt cod), in several different guises, along with excellent tapas.

**Mesón Don Felipe** (Map pp142-3; ☎ 7928 3237; 53 The Cut SE1; tapas £3-6; ◉ Waterloo) The Don is tops for tapas and an authentic Spanish atmosphere, helped along by bright orange walls and theatrical but friendly staff. Serves are a decent size for the price, which explains why this place is always rammed with satisfied customers.

### MIDRANGE

**Bermondsey Kitchen** (Map pp134-5; ☎ 7407 5719; 194 Bermondsey St SE1; mains £10-15; ◉ London Bridge) Smart but informal, this place sits somewhere between a restaurant and a gastropub,

serving cocktails and tapas all day. They do an outrageously tasty bouillabaisse, lunch specials under £10 and excellent brunch on the weekends.

**Garrison** (Map pp134-5; ☎ 7089 9355; 99-101 Bermondsey St SE1; mains £12-15; ◉ breakfast, lunch & dinner; ◉ London Bridge) It may be a gastropub but the ambience is more French country kitchen than London boozer, with soft colours and baskets of fresh vegetables proudly displayed. Vegetarians will find they're almost as well served by interesting, beautifully presented options as carnivores.

**Delfina** (Map pp134-5; ☎ 7357 0244; 50 Bermondsey St SE1; mains £13-16; ◉ lunch Mon-Fri, dinner Fri; ◉ London Bridge) This restaurant-cum-art-gallery, in a converted Victorian chocolate factory, serves delicious modern cuisine with an Asian twist to a backdrop of contemporary canvases. Studios upstairs house artists, and there's an exhibition space downstairs showing more works.

**Magdalen** (Map p150; ☎ 7403 1342; 152 Tooley St SE1; mains £15-20; ◉ lunch Mon-Fri, dinner Mon-Sat; ◉ London Bridge) Roasting up the best of the critters that walk, hop, flap and splash around these fair isles, Magdalen isn't the place to bring a vegetarian or a weight-conscious waif on a date. Carnivorous couplings, however, will appreciate the elegant room and traditional treats presented in interesting ways. Love that pork crackling!

### TOP END

**Oxo Tower Brasserie** (Map pp142-3; ☎ 7803 3888; Barge House St SE1; 2 courses £20; ◉ Waterloo) The spectacular views are the big drawcard, so skip the restaurant and head for the slightly less extravagantly priced brasserie, or if you're not hungry, the bar. Italian with a twist is the focus of the very proficient kitchen.

## Chelsea, Kensington & Knightsbridge

These highbrow neighbourhoods harbour some of London's very best (and priciest) restaurants. Perhaps the Chelsea toffs are secretly titillated by the foul-mouthed tele-chefs in their midst.

### BUDGET

**Jakob's** (Map pp138-9; ☎ 7581 9292; 20 Gloucester Rd SW7; mains £4-10; ⊖ Gloucester Rd) A charismatic cafe-delicatessen serving a mixture of Armenian, Persian and Mediterranean dishes including salads, falafel and quiches.

**Orsini** (Map pp140-1; ☎ 7581 5553; 8a Thurloe Pl SW3; snacks £2-6, mains £7-12; ⊖ South Kensington) Marinated in authentic Italian charm, this tiny family-run eatery serves excellent espresso and deliciously fresh baguettes stuffed with Parma ham and mozzarella.

**Made in Italy** (Map pp140-1; ☎ 7352 1880; 249 King's Rd SW3; pizza £5-13, mains £15-19; ⊖ Sloane Sq) Pizza is served by the tasty quarter-metre at this traditional trattoria. Sit on the Chelsea roof terrace and dream of Napoli.

**Ottolenghi** Kensington (Map pp138-9; ☎ 7937 0003; 1 Holland St W8; ⊖ High St Kensington); Belgravia (Map pp138-9; ☎ 7823 2707; 13 Motcomb St SW1; ⊖ Knightsbridge) is another decent option. See p188.

### MIDRANGE

**Tom's Kitchen** (Map pp140-1; ☎ 7349 0202; 27 Cale St SW3; breakfast £2-11, lunch 2-courses £14, mains £17-22; ☽ breakfast Mon-Fri, lunch & dinner daily; ⊖ South Kensington) Tom Aikens is the notorious kitchen firebrand who's gradually taking over Chelsea; around the corner you'll find his Michelin-starred, mortgage-your-mother eponymous restaurant and his blinged-up fish diner. This excellent, informal British-French restaurant sits between the two: dinners can be pricey but a delicious breakfast or lunch needn't break the bank.

### TOP END

**Boxwood Cafe** (Map pp142-3; ☎ 7235 1010; Berkeley Hotel, Wilton Pl SW1; mains £16-31; ⊖ Knightsbridge) A New York–style cafe set up by superchef Gordon Ramsay, in a valiant attempt to kick back with young folk and make fine dining in London 'a little bit more relaxed'.

**Gordon Ramsay** (Map pp140-1; ☎ 7352 4441; www .gordonramsay.com; 68 Royal Hospital Rd SW3; set lunch/dinner

£40/90; ⊖ Sloane Sq) One of Britain's finest restaurants and the only one in the capital with three Michelin stars. The food is, of course, blissful and perfect for a luxurious treat. The only quibble is that you don't get time to linger. Bookings are made in specific eat-it-and-beat-it time slots and, if you've seen the chef on TV, you won't argue.

## Notting Hill, Bayswater & Paddington

Notting Hill teems with good places to eat, from cheap takeaways to atmospheric pubs and restaurants worthy of the fine-dining tag. Queensway has the best strip of Asian restaurants this side of Soho.

### BUDGET

**Kam Tong** (Map pp138-9; ☎ 7229 6065; 59-63 Queensway W2; yum cha £2-3, mains £7-14; ⊖ Bayswater) When most of the clientele are actually Chinese, you know you're on to a good thing, which can't be said for the trendy dumpling chains that have sprung up around London recently. Kam Tong serves genuine Cantonese dishes and wonderful yum cha, but we can't help wondering where the pushy trolley-pushers are (you order from a menu instead).

**Kiasu** (Map pp138-9; ☎ 7727 8810; 48 Queensway W2; mains £6-8; ⊖ Bayswater) Highly rated by local Malaysians and Singaporeans, as well as those who know a tasty cheap thing when they see it, Kiasu serves 'Food from the Straits of Malacca'. You'll also find Thai and Vietnamese food on the menu, but it's hard to go past the delicious and filling *laksa*.

Also recommended:

**Ottolenghi** (Map pp138-9; ☎ 7727 1121; 63 Ledbury Rd W11; ⊖ Notting Hill Gate) See p188.

**S&M Cafe** (Map pp138-9; ☎ 8968 8898; 268 Portobello Rd W10; ⊖ Ladbroke Grove) See p188.

### MIDRANGE

**Geales** (Map pp138-9; ☎ 7727 7528; 2 Farmer St W8; mains £8-17; ☽ closed lunch Mon; ⊖ Notting Hill Gate) It may have opened in 1939 as a humble chippery, but now it's so much more. Fresh fish from sustainable fisheries in Devon and Cornwall star in a variety of guises – either battered and British or with an Italian sensibility. Tables spill out onto the pleasant side street.

**Electric Brasserie** (Map pp138-9; ☎ 7908 9696; 191 Portobello Rd W11; breakfast £2-8, mains £9-28; ⊖ Ladbroke Grove) The leather-and-cream look is suitably cool for the brasserie that's attached to the Electric Cinema. And the food's very good, too; head to the back area for a darker, moodier dinner.

## Marylebone

You won't go too far wrong planting yourself on a table anywhere along Marylebone's charming High Street.

### TOP END

**Providores & Tapa Room** (Map pp142-3; ☎ 7935 6175; 109 Marylebone High St W1; mains £18-25; ☻ Baker St) New Zealand's greatest culinary export since kiwifruit, chef Peter Gordon works his fusion magic here, matching his creations with exclusively NZ wine. Downstairs, in a cute play on words, the Tapa Room (as in the Polynesian bark-cloth) serves sophisticated tapas, along with excellent brunch on the weekends.

## North London

Allow at least an evening to explore Islington's Upper St, along with the lanes leading off it. Camden's great for cheap eats, while neighbouring Chalk Farm and Primrose Hill are salted with gastropubs and upmarket restaurants.

### BUDGET

**Breakfast Club** (Map pp136-7; ☎ 7226 5454; 31 Camden Passage N1; mains £5-9; ☻ 8am-10pm Mon-Fri, 9.30am-10pm Sat & Sun; ☻ Angel) Eighties survivors will immediately clock this place and, with dishes like *Hungry Like The Wolf* (the big breakfast) and *When Haloumi Met Salad*, they'll feel right at home.

**Rooburoo** (Map pp136-7; ☎ 7278 8100; 21 Chapel Market N1; mains £5-10; ☻ Angel) Waltzing Matilda isn't in this Roo's repertoire, but a hell of a lot to down a breath mint first.

**Ottolenghi** (Map pp136-7; ☎ 7226 5454; 287 Upper St N1; mains £5-10; ☻ 8am-10pm Mon-Sat, 9am-7pm Sun; ☻ Angel) Mountains of meringues tempt you through the door, where a sumptuous array of sweet and savoury bakery treats greet you. The big communal table is great for conversation surfing (aka eavesdropping). Dinners are as light and tasty as the oh-so-white interior design.

**S&M Cafe** (Map pp136-7; ☎ 7359 5361; 4/6 Essex Rd N1; mains £6-10; ☻ breakfast, lunch & dinner daily; ☻ An-

gel) The S&M refers to sausages and mash in this cool diner (featured in the movie *Quadrophenia*) that won't give your wallet a spanking. There's a range of sausages, mashes and gravies.

**Le Mercury** (Map pp136-7; ☎ 7354 4088; 140A Upper St N1; mains £6-10; ☻ Highbury & Islington) A cosy Gaelic haunt ideal for a romantic dalliance, given that it appears much more expensive than it is. Sunday lunch by the open fire upstairs is a treat, although you'll have to book.

Another option is **Macondo** (Map pp136-7; ☎ 7226 7275; 20 Camden Passage N1; ☻ Angel); for details see p185.

### MIDRANGE

**Konstam at the Prince Albert** (Map pp136-7; ☎ 7833 5040; 2 Acton St WC1; mains £11-17; ☻ closed Sun; ☻ King's Cross) As London a restaurant as you can get, since Chef Oliver Rowe sources all but a few of his ingredients from within the tube map. Sit below the bizarrely elegant draped metal beads and watch your often adventurous London-centric dish take shape in the open kitchen.

**Duke of Cambridge** (Map pp136-7; ☎ 7359 3066; 30 St Peter's St N1; mains £12-17; ☻ Angel) Pioneers in bringing sustainability to the table, this tucked-away gastropub serves only organic food, wine and beer, fish from sustainable sources and locally sourced fruit, vegetables and meat.

**our pick Engineer** (Map pp136-7; ☎ 7722 0950; 65 Gloucester Ave NW1; mains £13-17; ☻ Chalk Farm) One of London's original gastropubs, serving up consistently good international cuisine to hip north Londoners. The courtyard garden is a real treat on balmy summer nights.

## Greenwich
### MIDRANGE

**Inside** (Map p149; ☎ 8265 5060; 19 Greenwich South St SE10; mains £13-17; ☻ /DLR Greenwich) Cap off your genteel Greenwich visit with white linen and smart food (British with a dash of Turkish) in this elegant dining room. The lunch special (two courses for £12) is a steal.

## Self-Catering

There are supermarkets absolutely everywhere in central London. Look out for the big names: Waitrose, Tesco, Sainsbury's, Marks & Spencer, Morrisons and Asda.

**Planet Organic** Fitzrovia (Map pp142-3; ☎ 7436 1929; 22 Torrington Pl WC1; ☻ Goodge St); Islington (Map pp136-

7; 64 Essex Rd, N1; ✆ Angel); Bayswater (Map pp138-9; ☎ 7727 2227; 42 Westbourne Grove W2; ✆ Bayswater); Fulham (Map pp140-1; ☎ 7731 7222; 25 Effie Rd; ✆ Fulham Broadway) As the name suggests, everything in this cafe-supermarket is organic. Fresh vegies are sourced (where possible) directly from British farms.

**La Fromagerie Cafe** (Map pp142-3; ☎ 7935 0341; 2-6 Moxon St W1; mains £8-13; ✆ Baker St) This cafe-providore has bowls of delectable salads, antipasto, peppers and beans scattered about the long communal table. Huge slabs of bread invite you to tuck in, and all the while the heavenly waft from the cheese room beckons.

# DRINKING

As long as there's been a city, Londoners have loved to drink – and, as history shows, often immoderately. The pub is the focus of social life and there's always one near at hand. When the sun shines, drinkers spill out into the streets, parks and squares as well. It was only in 2008 that drinking was banned on the tube!

Soho is undoubtedly the heart of bar culture, with enough variety to cater to all tastes. Camden's great for grungy boozers and rock kids, although it's facing stiff competition on the Bohemian-cool front from the venues around Hoxton and Shoreditch.

Now that Princes William and Harry have hit their stride, the Sloane Ranger scene has been reborn in exclusive venues in South Ken(sington), although the 'Turbo Sloanes' now count mega-rich commoners among their numbers.

The rest of us mere mortals will find plenty of pub-crawl potential in places like Islington, Clerkenwell, Southwark, Notting Hill, Earl's Court…hell, it's just not that difficult. The reviews below are simply to make sure you don't miss out on some of the most historic, unusual, best-positioned or excellent examples of the genre.

## St James's & Mayfair

**Absolut Ice Bar** (Map pp146-7; ☎ 7478 8910; 31-33 Heddon St W1; ☯ midday-midnight; admission Thu-Sat £15, Sun-Wed £12; ✆ Piccadilly Circus) At -6°C, this bar made entirely of ice is literally the coolest in London. Entry is limited to 40 minutes and your ticket includes a vodka cocktail served in an ice glass. The compulsory futuristic silver polyester cape is to protect the bar from your body heat, not the other way around, so wear warm togs. It's a gimmick, sure, but a good one, and there are plenty of places nearby that charge the same for a cocktail alone.

**Galvin at Windows** (Map pp142-3; ☎ 7208 4021; The Hilton, 22 Park Ln W1; ✆ Hyde Park Corner) Drinks are, well, pricey, but the view's astounding from this 28th-floor eyrie.

## West End
### CAFES

**Flat White** (Map pp146-7; ☎ 7734 0370; 17 Berwick St W1; ☯ 8am-7pm Mon-Fri, 9am-6pm Sat & Sun; ✆ Piccadilly Circus) Trailblazers of the unexpected and thoroughly welcome Kiwi invasion of Soho cafes, Flat White is both named after and delivers the holy grail of Antipodean coffee. The beach scenes on the walls are a comfort on a cold day.

**Monmouth Coffee Company** (Map pp146-7; ☎ 7379 3516; 27 Monmouth St WC2; snacks £1-2; ✆ Covent Garden) While the array of treats displayed on the counter is alluring, it's the coffee that's the star, nay god, here. Chat to a caffeinated stranger on one of the tight tables at the back, or grab a takeaway and slink off to a nearby lane for your fix.

### BARS & PUBS

**Be At One** (Map pp146-7; ☎ 7240 9889; 23 Wellington St WC2; ☯ happy hours 5-8pm Mon & Tue, to 7pm Wed-Sat, 6pm-close Sun; ✆ Covent Garden) Forgive the silly name and make the most of the generous happy hours (two cocktails for £6.50).

**Coach & Horses** (Map pp146-7; ☎ 7437 5920; 29 Greek St W1; ✆ Leicester Sq) This Soho institution has been patronised by Sigmund Freud, Francis Bacon, Dylan Thomas, Peter Cooke and Peter O'Toole. The Wednesday night East End singalong is tops.

**Gordon's Wine Bar** (Map pp146-7; ☎ 7930 1408; 47 Villiers St WC2; ⊖ Charing Cross) What's not to love about this cavernous wine cellar lit by candles and practically unchanged over the last 100 years? Choose between wines, sherries, ports and Madeiras accompanied by warming home-cooked grub. In summer, the crowd spills out into Embankment Gardens.

**Lamb & Flag** (Map pp146-7; ☎ 7497 9504; 33 Rose St WC2; ⊖ Covent Garden) Everyone's Covent Garden 'find', this popular historic pub is often jammed. It was built in 1623 and formerly called the 'Bucket of Blood'.

**Queen Mary** (Map pp146-7; ☎ 7240 9404; Waterloo Pier WC2; ⊖ Embankment) Climb aboard this steamer for a welcoming publike atmosphere with great views of the London Eye and the South Bank.

## Holborn & Clerkenwell

**Jerusalem Tavern** (Map pp142-3; ☎ 7490 4281; 55 Britton St; ⊖ Farringdon) Pick a wood-panelled cubbyhole to park yourself in at this gorgeous former 18th-century coffee shop–turned-inn, and choose from a selection of St Peter's beers such as cinnamon and apple, grapefruit or, if you're not feeling fruity, creamy ale or bitter.

**Princess Louise** (Map pp146-7; ☎ 7405 8816; 208 High Holborn WC1; ⊖ Holborn) This late-19th-century Victorian boozer is arguably London's most beautiful pub. Spectacularly decorated with fine tiles, etched mirrors, plasterwork and a gorgeous central horseshoe bar, it gets packed with the after-work crowd.

## The City

**Vertigo 42** (Map p150; Tower 42, Old Broad St, EC2; ⊖ Liverpool St) Book a two-hour slot in this 42nd-floor bar with vertiginous views across London.

**Ye Olde Cheshire Cheese** (Map pp142-3; Wine Office Ct, 145 Fleet St EC4; ⊖ Holborn) Rebuilt six years after the Great Fire, it was popular with Dr Johnson, Thackeray, Dickens and the visiting Mark Twain. Touristy but always atmospheric and enjoyable for a pub meal.

## Hoxton, Shoreditch & Spitalfields

**Bar Music Hall** (Map p150; ☎ 7729 7216; 134 Curtain Rd EC2; ⊖ Old St) Keeping the East End music-hall tradition alive but with a modern twist, this roomy space with a central bar amuses the friendly punters with DJs and live bands. Music runs the gamut from punk to jazz to rock and disco.

**Commercial Tavern** (Map p150; ☎ 7247 1888; 142 Commercial St E1; ⊖ Liverpool St) The zany decor's a thing of wonder in this reformed East End boozer. Check out the walls coated in buttons and jigsaw-puzzle pieces. The little boys' room has been wallpapered like, well, a little boy's room: Popeye, astronauts and cyclists all make an appearance.

**Grapeshots** (Map p150; ☎ 7247 8215; 2/3 Artillery Passage E1; ⊖ Liverpool St) Half the fun of this wine bar is walking down the Dickensian passage, complete with old street lamps, that leads to it. Once inside, there's a decent wine list and the old-world ambience continues.

**Loungelover** (Map p150; ☎ 7012 1234; 1 Whitby St E1; ☽ 6pm-midnight Sun-Thu, to 1am Fri & Sat; ⊖ Liverpool St) Book a table, sip a cocktail and admire the Louis XIV chairs, the huge hippo head, the cage-turned–living room, the jewel-encrusted stag's head and the loopy chandeliers. Utterly fabulous.

**Ten Bells** (Map p150; ☎ 7366 1721; cnr Commercial & Fournier Sts E1; ⊖ Liverpool St) The most famous Jack the Ripper pub, Ten Bells was patronised by his last victim before her grisly end, and possibly by the slayer himself. Admire the wonderful 18th-century tiles and ponder the past over a pint.

The following are all good stops on a Hoxton hop:

**Bricklayer's Arms** (Map p150; ☎ 7613 0469; 63 Charlotte Rd EC2; ⊖ Old St) Back-street pub with an interesting crowd.

**Favela Chic** (Map p150; ☎ 7613 4228; 91-93 Great Eastern St EC2; entry after 9pm £5-10; ☽ 5pm-1am Tue-Thu, to 2am Fri, 6pm-2am Sat; ⊖ Old St) Ticks the following boxes: hip young things; crazy theme nights; lumberyard-meets-jungle decor; fun and funky music.

**Mother** (Map p150; ☎ 7613 0469; 333 Old St EC1; entry Fri & Sat £5; ⊖ Old St) Red-and-gold flocked wallpaper, chequer-board floors and live alternative music and DJs on weekends. Downstairs, 333 is a part nightclub/part live venue.

**Red Lion** (Map p150; ☎ 7729 7920; 41 Hoxton St N1; ⊖ Old St) Old corner pub with eclectic furniture and cheap drinks.

**Zigfrid Von Underbelly** (Map p150; ☎ 7613 1988; 11 Hoxton Sq N1; ⊖ Old St) Furnished like an oversized lounge room (check out the disturbing family portrait over the fireplace), it's simultaneously the coolest and the most fun of the Hoxton Sq venues.

## South of the River Thames

**Anchor** (Map p150; ☎ 7407 1577; 34 Park St SE1; ⊖ London Bridge) A 17th-century boozer just east of the

Globe Theatre, it has a terrace offering superb views over the River Thames. Dr Johnson was once a regular.

**George Inn** (Map p150; ☎ 7407 2056; Talbot Yard, 77 Borough High St SE1; ✆ London Bridge or Borough) Tucked away in a cobbled courtyard is London's last surviving galleried coaching inn, dating from 1677 and now belonging to the National Trust. Charles Dickens and Shakespeare used to prop up the bar here (but not together, obviously). There are outdoor tables for sunny days.

## Chelsea, Kensington & Knightsbridge

**Bibendum Oyster Bar** (Map pp140-1; ☎ 7581 5817; 81 Fulham Rd SW3; ✆ South Kensington) If chubby, rubber-clad men are your thing, slurp up a bi-valve and knock back a champers in the foyer of the wonderful art-nouveau Michelin House (1911). The Michelin Man is everywhere: in mosaics, stained glass, crockery and echoed in the architecture itself.

## Notting Hill, Bayswater & Paddington

**Trailer Happiness** (Map pp138-9; ☎ 7727 2700; 177 Portobello Rd W11; ✆ Ladbroke Grove) Think shag-pile carpets, 1960s California kitsch and trashy trailer-park glamour. Try the Tiki cocktails and share a flaming volcano bowl of Zombie with a friend to ensure your evening goes off with a bang.

**Windsor Castle** (Map pp138-9; ☎ 7243 9551; 114 Campden Hill Rd W11; ✆ Notting Hill Gate) A memorable pub with oak partitions separating the original bars. The panels have tiny doors so big drinkers will have trouble getting past the front bar. It also has one of the loveliest walled gardens of any pub in London. Thomas Paine (*The Rights of Man* writer) is rumoured to be buried in the cellar.

## Marylebone

**Artesian** (Map pp146-7; Langham Hotel, 1C Portland Pl W1; ✆ Oxford Circus) For a dose of colonial glamour with a touch of the orient, the sumptuous bar at the Langham Hotel hits the mark. Rum is its speciality, concocting award-winning cocktails (£15) from the 60 varieties that are on offer.

**Heights** (Map pp146-7; 7580 0111; St George's Hotel, 14 Langham Pl W1; ✆ Oxford Circus) Take the lift up to this understated bar with huge windows to showcase the panorama. It's an unusual view, managing to miss most of the big sights, but impressive nonetheless.

## North London
### EUSTON & KING'S CROSS

**Big Chill House** (Map pp136-7; 257-259 Pentonville Rd N1; entry after 10pm Fri & Sat £5; ✆ King's Cross) Come the weekend, the only remotely chilled-out space in this busy bar, split over two levels, is its first-rate and generously proportioned rooftop terrace.

### CAMDEN & ISLINGTON

**Albert & Pearl** (Map pp136-7; ☎ 7354 9993; 181 Upper St; entry after midnight £3; ✆ High-bury & Islington) The chap behind Fabric (p193) has a finger in this chic cocktail-filled pie (pie with cocktails – now there's an idea). DJs play until the small hours on Friday and Saturday nights.

**Lock Tavern** (Map pp136-7; 35 Chalk Farm Rd NW1; ✆ Camden Town) The archetypal Camden pub, the Lock has both a rooftop terrace and a beer garden and attracts an interesting crowd with its mix of ready conviviality, pleasant sur-rounds and regular live music.

**Proud** (Map pp136-7; Stables Market NW1; entry after 7.30pm Mon-Sat £10; ✆ Camden Town) No, despite the name it's not a gay bar. Proud occupies a former horse hospital within Stables Market, with booths in the stalls, ice-cool rock pho-tography on the walls and deckchairs printed with images of Marilyn Manson and Pete Doherty. Spin around the gallery during the day or enjoy bands at night.

### HAMPSTEAD & HIGHGATE

**Holly Bush** (Map pp134-5; ☎ 7435 2892; 22 Holly Mount NW3; ✆ Hampstead) Dating from the early 19th century, this beautiful pub has a secluded hill-top location, open fires in winter and a knack for making you stay a bit longer than you had intended. It's above Heath St, reached via the Holly Bush Steps.

**Flask** (Map pp134-5; ☎ 8340 7260; 77 Highgate West Hill N6; ✆ Highgate) Charming candlelit nooks and crannies, an old circular bar complete with pumps (don't knock yourself when you sit down) and a lovely beer garden make this the perfect place for a pint after visiting Highgate Cemetery (p170).

**Spaniard's Inn** (Map pp134-5; ☎ 8731 6571; Spaniard's Rd NW3; ✆ Hampstead, then 🚌 21) A marvellous tavern that dates from 1585, complete with dubious claims that Dick Turpin, the dandy highwayman, was born here and used it as a hideout. More savoury sorts like Dickens, Shelley, Keats and Byron also availed themselves of its charms. There's a big, blissful garden and good food.

## Greenwich

**Trafalgar Tavern** (Map p149; ☎ 8858 2909; Park Row SE10; DLR Cutty Sark) An 1837 Regency-style pub that stands above the site of the Placentia Palace where Henry VIII was born. Dickens, Gladstone and Disraeli have all darkened its doors, although they wouldn't have had the wonderful views of the O2 and Canary Wharf high-rises to admire.

## ENTERTAINMENT

From West End luvvies to End End geezers, Londoners have always loved a spectacle. With bear baiting and public executions no longer an option, they've learnt to make do with having the world's best theatres, nightclubs and live-music scene to divert them. Yet the gladiatorial contests that the Romans brought to these shores still survive on the football fields, especially when Chelsea goes head to head with Arsenal.

For a comprehensive list of what to do on any given night, check out *Time Out*. The listings in the free tube papers are also good.

## Theatre

London is a world capital for theatre and there's a lot more than mammoth musicals to tempt you into the West End. The term 'West End' – as with Broadway – generally refers to the big-money productions like musicals, but also includes such heavyweights as the **Royal Court Theatre** (Map pp140-1; ☎ 7565 5000; www.royalcourttheatre.com; Sloane Sq SW1; ⊖ Sloane Sq), the patron of new British writing; the **National Theatre** (Map pp142-3; ☎ 7452 3000; www.national theatre.org.uk; South Bank SE1; ⊖ Waterloo), which has cheaper tickets for both classics and new plays from some of the world's best companies; and the **Royal Shakespeare Company** (RSC; ☎ 0870 609 1110; www.rsc.org.uk), with productions of the Bard's classics and other quality stuff. Kevin Spacey continues his run as artistic director (and occasional performer) at the **Old Vic** (Map pp142-3; ☎ 0870-060 6628; www.oldvictheatre.com; The Cut SE1; ⊖ Waterloo).

On performance days, you can buy half-price tickets for West End productions (cash only) from the official **Leicester Square Half-Price Ticket Booth** (Map pp146-7; ✆ 10am-7pm Mon-Sat, noon-3pm Sun; Leicester Sq; ⊖ Leicester Sq), on the south side of Leicester Sq. The booth is the one

with the clock tower; beware of touts selling dodgy tickets.

Off West End – where you'll generally find the most original works – includes venues such as the **Almeida** (Map pp136-7; ☎ 7359 4404; www.almeida.co.uk; Almeida St N1; ⊖ Highbury & Islington), **Battersea Arts Centre** (Map pp134-5; ☎ 7223 2223; www .bac.org.uk; Lavender Hill SW11; ⊖ Clapham Junction) and the **Young Vic** (Map pp142-3; ☎ 7922 2920; www .youngvic.org; 66 The Cut SE1; ⊖ Waterloo). The next rung down is known as the Fringe and these shows take place anywhere there's a stage (and can be very good).

Other interesting companies, such as the not-for-profit **Donmar Warehouse** (Map pp146-7; ☎ 0870-060 6624; www.donmarwarehouse.com; 41 Earlham St WC2; ⊖ Covent Garden) and the **Menier Chocolate Factory** (Map p150; ☎ 7907 7060; www.menierchocolate factory.com; 55 Southwark St SE1; ⊖ London Bridge), have started Off West End and ended up with West End reputations.

As far as the blockbuster musicals go, you can be fairly confident that *Les Miserables* and *Phantom of the Opera* will still be chugging along, as well as the new revival of *Oliver!* For a comprehensive look at what's being staged where, visit www.officiallondon theatre.co.uk, www.theatremonkey.com or http://london.broadway.com.

## Nightclubs

London's had a lot of practice perfecting the art of clubbing – Samuel Pepys used the term in 1660! – and the volume and variety of venues in today's city is staggering. Clubland's no longer confined to the West End, with megaclubs scattered throughout the city wherever there's a venue big enough, cheap enough or quirky enough to hold them. Some run their own regular weekly schedule, while others host promoters on an ad-hoc basis. The big nights are Friday and Saturday, although you'll find some of the most cutting-edge sessions midweek. Admission prices vary widely; it's often cheaper to arrive early or pre-book tickets.

**Cargo** (Map p150; ☎ 7739 3440; www.cargo-london .com; 83 Rivington St EC2; admission free-£16; ⊖ Old St) A hugely popular club with local and international DJs and a courtyard where you can simultaneously enjoy big sounds and the great outdoors.

**our pick** **End** (Map pp146-7; ☎ 7419 9199; www.end-club.com; 18 West Central St WC1; admission £6-16; ✆ from around 10.30pm Mon-Sat, 5.30am-midday Sun; ⊖ Totten-

## GAY & LESBIAN LONDON

London's had a thriving scene since at least the 18th century, when the West End's 'Mollie houses' were the forerunners of today's gay bars. The West End, particularly Soho, remains the visible centre of gay and lesbian London, with numerous venues clustered around Old Compton St and its surrounds. However, Soho doesn't hold a monopoly on gay life. One of the nice things about the city is that there are local gay bars in many neighbourhoods.

Despite, or perhaps because of, its grimness and griminess, Vauxhall's taken off as a hub for the hirsute, hefty and generally harder-edged sections of the community. The railway arches are now filled with dance clubs, leather bars and a sauna.

Also in southwest London, Clapham's got some of the friendliest gay bars in the city, while Earl's Court (West London), Islington (North London) and Limehouse (East End) have their own miniscenes.

Generally, London's a safe place for lesbians and gays. It's rare to encounter any problem with sharing rooms or holding hands in the inner city, although it would pay to keep your wits about you at night and be conscious of your surroundings.

The easiest way to find out what's going on is to pick up the free press (*Pink Paper, Boyz, QX*) from a venue, but be warned: the mags can be somewhat… confronting. The gay section of *Time Out* is useful, as are www.gaydarnation.com (for men) and www.gingerbeer.co.uk (for women).

Here are some places to get you started:

**Candy Bar** (Map pp146-7; ☎ 7494 4041; 4 Carlisle St W1; ✪ Tottenham Court Rd) Long-running lesbian hang-out.

**Friendly Society** (Map pp146-7; ☎ 7434 3805; 79 Wardour St W1; ✪ Piccadilly Circus) Soho's quirkiest gay bar, this Bohemian basement is bedecked in kids'-room wallpaper and Barbie dolls.

**G-A-Y Bar** (Map pp146-7; ☎ 7494 2756; 30 Old Compton St W1; ✪ Leicester Sq) At the time of research the famous club night of the same name was planning to move. Find out where to from this, its little boozy sister.

**Gay's the Word** (Map pp136-7; ☎ 7278 7654; 66 Marchmont St WC1; ✪ Russell Sq) Books and mags of all descriptions.

**George & Dragon** (Map p150; ☎ 7012 1100; 2 Hackney Rd E2; ✪ Old St) Appealing corner pub where the crowd is often as eclectically furnished as the venue.

**Ghetto** (Map pp146-7; ☎ 7287 3726; 5-6 Falconberg Ct W1; admission £3-7; ✪ Tottenham Court Rd) Home to a roster of crazy nights such as the Cock, with inexpensive drinks and alternative music.

**Heaven** (Map pp146-7; ☎ 7930 2020; The Arches, Villiers St WC2; ✪ Charing Cross) One of the world's best-known gay clubs, Saturday night's the big one (£15) but Monday's Popcorn is lots of frothy fun (free before midnight, £5 after).

**Popstarz** (Map pp146-7; www.popstarz.org/popzmini; Sin, Andrew Borde St WC1; admission free-£7; ⏲ 10pm-4am Fri; ✪ Tottenham Court Rd) London's legendary indie club night. The online flyer gets you in cheaper.

**Royal Vauxhall Tavern** (RVT; Map p145; ☎ 7820 1222; 372 Kennington Ln SE11; admission free-£7; ✪ Vauxhall) A much-loved pub with crazy cabaret and drag acts.

**Two Brewers** (Map pp134-5; ☎ 7498 4971; 114 Clapham High St SW4; admission free-£5; ✪ Clapham Common) Friendly gay bar with regular acts and a nightclub out the back.

---

ham Court Rd) The End offers an eclectic range of cutting-edge nights starting with Durrr on Monday, devoted to underground music, live acts and kids in skinny jeans. If you've got a Wednesday drum-'n'-bass itch, Swerve's where you can scratch it, while the aptly named Jaded kicks off at 5.30am Sunday.

**Fabric** (Map pp142-3; ☎ 7336 8898; www.fabriclondon .com; 77A Charterhouse St EC1; admission £13-16; ⏲ 10pm-6am Fri, 11pm-8am Sat; ✪ Farringdon) In 2008 Fabric was once again voted the world's best club by *DJ* magazine. Fabric's not a meat market but its three dance floors are based in a converted meat cold-store opposite the actual Smithfield meat market. Friday's *FabricLive* offers an 'urban music soundclash' (drum 'n' bass, breakbeats, hip hop and live acts), while Saturday sees house, techno and electro.

**Guanabara** (Map pp146-7; ☎ 7242 8600; www. guanabara.co.uk; cnr Parker St & Drury Lane WC2; admission £5-10; ✪ Covent Garden) Brazil comes to London with live music seven nights a week. On Wednesday enjoy an authentic *Roda de Samba*, tuck into Brazilian snacks, sip on a

---

**NOVEL NIGHTS OUT**

It seems that some of the cool kids are bored with simply going clubbing, listening to a band or propping up a bar with a pint. To plant your finger on the party pulse, check out some of these activity-based haunts.

**Bloomsbury Bowling Lanes** (Map pp136-7; ☎ 7183 1979; cnr Bedford Way & Tavistock Sq WC1; ☒ noon-2am Mon-Thu, to 3am Fri & Sat, 1-10pm Sun; ✷ Russell Sq) With eight 10-pin bowling lanes, a diner and details down to the carpet all dating from the 1950s and shipped in from America, this place is the real deal. And the fun doesn't stop with dubious footwear and a burger; there are also private karaoke rooms, a cinema screening independent movies, DJs and up-and-coming live bands.

**Lucky Voice** (Map pp146-7; ☎ 7439 3660; 52 Poland St W1F; ☒ 5.30pm-1am Mon-Thu, 3pm-1am Fri & Sat, 3-10.30pm Sun; 4-person booth per hr £20-40; ✷ Oxford Circus) Moulded on the private karaoke bars of Tokyo, superstylish Lucky Voice is a low-lit maze of dark walls with hidden doors revealing snug leather-clad soundproofed booths for your secret singalong. Select one of 50,000 songs from a touch screen, pick up a microphone and you're away. In the Super Lucky rooms, there are wigs and blow-up guitars to enhance your performance. Drinks and bento boxes are ordered by the touch of a button; expect to spend a fortune in Dutch courage.

**Roller Disco** (Map p145; ☎ 0844-736 5375; www.rollerdisco.info; Renaissance Rooms, off Wandsworth Rd SW8; ☒ 8pm-midnight Thu, to 2am Fri & Sat; admission incl skate hire £10-13; ✷ Vauxhall) Remember those adolescent roller discos you used to go to? Well, this is your chance to dust off your skating skills and roll to a changing soundtrack of disco, funk, house, garage and R&B. Dressing up like a twat is encouraged.

---

Caipirinha and shake your booty. Admission is free before 9pm.

**Mass** (Map pp134-5; ☎ 7738 7875; www.mass-club .com; St Matthew's Church, Brixton Hill SW2; admission £5-10; ☒ 10pm-6am Fri & Sat; ✷ Brixton) The congregation's swollen at this Brixton church under its new high priests, with regular services of live music and club nights.

**Ministry of Sound** (Map pp142-3; ☎ 0870-060 0010; http://club.ministryofsound.com/club; 103 Gaunt St SE1; admission £12-20; ☒ 10pm-6am Fri, 11pm-7am Sat; ✷ Elephant & Castle) Where the global brand started, it's London's most famous club and still packs in a diverse crew with big local and international names.

**Plastic People** (Map p150; 147-149 Curtain Rd EC2; admission £5-13; ✷ Old St) Taking the directive 'underground club' literally, Plastic People provides a low-ceilinged subterranean den of dubstep, techno, electro and no-frills fun times.

**SeOne** (Map p150; ☎ 0870-246 2050; www.seone -london.com; 41-43 Saint Thomas St SE1; ✷ London Bridge) Under the railway arches of London Bridge, this mammoth venue can (and frequently does) cram in 3000 up-for-it ravers.

## Live Music
### ROCK & JAZZ
While London may have stopped swinging in the 1960s, every subsequent generation has given birth to a new set of bands in the city's thriving live venues: Punk in the 1970s, New Romantics in the 1980s, Brit Pop in the 1990s and the current crop of skinny-jeaned rockers and electro acts thrilling the scenesters today. You'll find interesting young bands gigging around venues all over the city. Big-name gigs sell out quickly, so check www.seetickets.com before you travel.

**100 Club** (Map pp146-7; ☎ 7636 0933; www.the 100club.co.uk; 100 Oxford St W1; ✷ Oxford Circus) This legendary London venue once showcased the Stones and was at the centre of the punk revolution. It now divides its time between jazz, rock and even a little swing.

**Barfly** (Map pp136-7; ☎ 0844-847 2424; www .barflyclub.com; 49 Chalk Farm Rd NW1; ✷ Chalk Farm) Pleasantly grungy, and the place to see the best new bands. The same crew run a couple of other joints around town.

**Brixton Academy** (Map pp134-5; ☎ 0844-477 2000; www.brixton-academy.co.uk; 211 Stockwell Rd SW9; ✷ Brixton) This Grade-II listed art-deco venue is always winning awards for 'best live venue' (something to do with the artfully sloped floor, perhaps) and hosts big-name acts in a relatively intimate setting (5000 capacity).

**Dublin Castle** (Map pp136-7; ☎ 7485 1773; www .thedublincastle.com; 94 Parkway NW1; ✷ Camden Town) There's live punk or alternative music most nights in this pub's back room.

**Forum** (Map pp134-5; ☎ 0844-847 2405; www.kentish townforum.com; 9-17 Highgate Rd NW5; ✆ Kentish Town) A grand old theatre and one of London's best large venues.

**Hope & Anchor** (Map pp136-7; ☎ 7700 0550; 207 Upper St; admission free-£6; ✆ Angel) Live music's still the focus of the pub that hosted the first London gigs of Joy Division and U2 (only nine people showed up).

**Jazz Cafe** (Map pp136-7; ☎ 7485 6834; 5 Parkway NW1; ✆ Camden Town) Jazz is just one part of the picture at this intimate club that stages a full roster of rock, pop, hip hop and dance, including famous names.

**Koko** (Map pp136-7; ☎ 0870-432 5527; www.koko .uk.com; 1A Camden High St NW1; ✆ Mornington Cres) Occupying the grand Camden Palace theatre, Koko hosts live bands most nights and the regular Club NME (£5) on Friday.

**Ronnie Scott's** (Map pp146-7; ☎ 7439 0747; www .ronniescotts.co.uk; 47 Frith St W1; ✆ Leicester Sq) London's legendary jazz club has been pulling in the hep cats since 1959.

**Shepherd's Bush Empire** (Map pp134-5; ☎ 8354 3300; www.shepherds-bush-empire.co.uk; Shepherd's Bush Green W12; ✆ Shepherd's Bush) A slightly dishevelled, mid-size theatre that hosts some terrific bands.

See also Bar Music Hall (p190) and Proud (p191).

### CLASSICAL
With four world-class symphony orchestras, two opera companies, various smaller ensembles, brilliant venues, reasonable prices and high standards of performance, London is a classical capital. Keep an eye out for the free (or nearly so) lunchtime concerts held in many of the city's churches.

**Barbican Centre** (Map p150; ☎ 0845 120 7500; www .barbican.org.uk; Silk St EC2; ✆ Barbican) This hulking complex has a full program of film, music, theatre, art and dance including loads of concerts from the London Symphony Orchestra, which is based here.

**Southbank Centre** (Map pp142-3; ☎ 0871-663 2509; www.southbankcentre.co.uk; South Bank; ✆ Waterloo) Home to the London Philharmonic Orchestra, London Sinfonietta and the Philharmonia Orchestra, among others, this centre has three premier venues: the **Royal Festival Hall** (Map pp142-3) and the smaller **Queen Elizabeth Hall** (Map pp142-3) and **Purcell Room** (Map pp142-3), which host classical, opera, jazz and choral music. The precinct is a riverside people-watching mecca of glassed-in shops and restaurants. Look out for free recitals in the foyer.

**Royal Albert Hall** (Map pp138-9; ☎ 7589 8212; www.royalalberthall.com; Kensington Gore SW7; ✆ South Kensington) A splendid circular Victorian arena that hosts classical concerts and the occasional contemporary act, but is best known as the venue for the Proms.

## Opera & Dance
**Coliseum** (Map pp146-7; ☎ 0871-911 0200; www.eno .org; St Martin's Lane WC2; tickets £10-85; ✆ Leicester Sq) The glamorous home of the progressive English National Opera; all performances are in English.

**Royal Opera House** (Map pp146-7; ☎ 7304 4000; www. royaloperahouse.org; Royal Opera House, Bow St WC2; tickets £5-190; ✆ Covent Garden) The gleaming Royal Opera House has been attracting a younger audience since its £213-million millennium redevelopment, which also seems to have breathed new life into its programming. The Royal Ballet,

---

**BURLESQUE IS BACK**

Basques, suspenders, cinched waists, circle skirts, tweed, top hats, trilbies, spats, feathers, fox-trot, lindy hop, divas, mime artists and of course cabaret – burlesque's retro sexy sophistication sizzles. Revived by Immodesty Blaize in the UK and Dita von Teese stateside, there's no hotter trend for night owls. Here are the most decadently divine nights: don't forget to dress up and adopt an air of languid panache.

**Agent Lynch** (www.agentlynch.com)
**Immodesty Blaize** (www.immodestyblaize.com)
**Jitterbugs** (www.jitterbugs.co.uk)
**Lady Luck** (www.ladyluckclub.co.uk)
**Madame Jo Jo's** (www.madamejojos.com)
**Velvet London** (www.myspace.com/velvetlondon)
**Viva Cake** (www.myspace.com/vivacakebitches)
**Volupté** (www.volupte-lounge.com)

Britain's premier classical ballet company, is also based here.

**Sadler's Wells** (Map pp136-7; ☎ 0844-412 4300; www .sadlers-wells.com; Rosebery Ave EC1; tickets £10-49; ⊖ Angel) A glittering modern venue that was in fact first established in the 17th century, Sadler's Wells has been given much credit for bringing modern dance to the mainstream.

## Comedy

When London's comics aren't being terribly clever on TV, you might find them doing stand-up somewhere in your neighbourhood. There are numerous venues to choose from, and many pubs getting in on the act.

**99 Club** ( ☎ 7739 5706; www.the99club.co.uk; admission £10-25) Not quite the famous 100 Club, this virtual venue takes over various bars around town from Tuesday to Sunday night, with four rival clones on Saturday.

**Comedy Cafe** (Map p150; ☎ 7739 5706; www.com edycafe.co.uk; 66-68 Rivington St EC2; admission free-£15; ⊖ Old St) Have dinner and watch some comedy; take to the stage on Wednesday if you're brave/foolhardy/drunk.

**Comedy Store** (Map pp146-7; ☎ 7839 6642; www .thecomedystore.co.uk; 1A Oxendon St SW1; admission £13-18; ⊖ Piccadilly Circus) One of London's first comedy clubs, featuring the capital's most famous improvisers, the Comedy Store Players, on Wednesday and Sunday.

**Hen & Chickens** (Map pp136-7; ☎ 7704 2001; www .henandchickens.com; 109 St Paul's Rd N1; admission £10-18; ⊖ Highbury & Islington) Catch a chuckle in the theatre above this Islington boozer.

**Soho Theatre** (Map pp146-7; ☎ 7478 0100; www .sohotheatre.com; 21 Dean St W1; ⊖ Tottenham Court Rd) Where grown-up comedians graduate to once they start pulling the crowds.

## Cinemas

Glitzy premieres usually take place in one of the mega multiplexes in Leicester Sq.

For less mainstream movies try **Curzon Cinemas** ( ☎ 0870 756 4621; www.curzoncinemas.com; tickets £8-12) Mayfair (Map pp142-3; 38 Curzon St W1; ⊖ Green Park); Soho (Map pp146-7; 99 Shaftesbury Ave W1; ⊖ Leicester Sq); Renoir (Map pp136-7; Brunswick Sq WC1; ⊖ Russell Sq); Chelsea (Map pp140-1; 206 Kings Rd SW3; ⊖ Sloane Sq). They're some of a clutch of independent cinemas spread throughout the capital.

**BFI Southbank** (Map pp142-3; ☎ 7928 3232; Belvedere Rd SE1; tickets £9; ⊖ Waterloo) A film-lover's fantasy, it screens some 2000 flicks a year, ranging from classics to foreign art house. There's

also the *Mediatheque* viewing stations, where you can explore the British Film Institute's extensive archive of movies and watch whatever you like for free.

**BFI IMAX** (Map pp142-3; ☎ 0870-787 2525; www .bfi.org.uk/imax; Waterloo Rd SE1; tickets £13; ⊖ Waterloo) Watch 3-D movies and cinema releases on the UK's biggest screen: 20m high (nearly five double-decker buses) and 26m wide.

**Electric** (Map pp138-9; ☎ 7908 9696; www.electric cinema.co.uk; 191 Portobello Rd W11; tickets £13-15; ⊖ Ladbroke Grove) Grab a glass of wine from the bar, head to your leather sofa (£30) and snuggle down to watch a flick. All cinemas should be like this. Tickets are cheapest on Monday.

## Sport

As the capital of a football-mad nation, London is brimming over with sporting spectacles during the cooler months. The Wimbledon Lawn Tennis Championships (p175) is one of the biggest events on the city's summer calendar.

### FOOTBALL

Tickets for Premier League football matches are ridiculously hard to come by for casual fans these days, but if you want to try your luck, the contacts for London's Premiership clubs are listed here:

**Arsenal** ( ☎ 7704 4040; www.arsenal.com)

**Chelsea** ( ☎ 0870 300 2322; www.chelseafc.com)

**Fulham** ( ☎ 0870 442 1234; www.fulhamfc.com)

**Tottenham Hotspur** ( ☎ 0870 420 5000; www .tottenhamhotspur.com)

**West Ham United** ( ☎ 0870 112 2700; www.whufc.com)

### RUGBY

**Twickenham** ( ☎ 0870 405 2000; www.rfu.com; Rugby Rd, Twickenham; tickets £10-45, more for internationals; ⊠ Twickenham) is the home of English rugby union, but as with football, tickets for tests are difficult to get unless you have contacts. The ground also boasts the **World Rugby Museum** ( ☎ 0870 405 2001; ⏰ 10am-5pm Tue-Sat, 11am-5pm Sun) which can be combined with a tour of the stadium (adult/child £10/7; bookings recommended).

### CRICKET

Cricket is as popular as ever in the land of its origin. Test matches take place at two venerable grounds: **Lord's Cricket Ground** (Map pp134-5; ☎ 7616 8500; www.lords.org; St John's Wood Rd NW8; ⊖ St John's Wood) and the **Brit Oval** (Map pp134-5; ☎ 0871-246 1100; www.surreycricket.com; Kennington SE11; ⊖ Oval).

Tickets are from £24 to £80, but if you're a fan it's worth it. If not, it's an expensive and protracted form of torture.

## SHOPPING

Napoleon famously described Britain as a nation of shopkeepers, which doesn't sound at all bad to us! From world-famous department stores to quirky backstreet retail revelations, London is a mecca for shoppers with an eye for style and a card to exercise. If you're looking for something distinctly British, eschew the Union Jack–emblazoned kitsch of the tourist thoroughfares and fill your bags with Twinings tea, Paul Smith shirts, Royal Doulton china and Marmite. For bookshops, see p133.

### Antiques & Crafts

Curios, baubles and period pieces abound along Camden Passage in Islington, Bermondsey Antiques Market and the Saturday market at Portobello (see p198).

**Grays Antiques Market** (Map pp142-3; ☎ 7629 7034; 58 Davies St W1; ⊖ Bond St) Top-hatted doormen welcome you to this wonderful building full of specialist stallholders. Make sure you head to the basement where the Tyburn River still runs through a channel in the floor.

**London Silver Vaults** (Map pp142-3; ☎ 7242 3844; 53-63 Chancery Lane WC2; ⊖ Chancery Lane) Has 72 subterranean shops forming the world's largest collection of silver under one roof.

### Department Stores

London's famous department stores are a tourist attraction in themselves, even if you don't intend to contribute to the orgy of consumption.

**Harrods** (Map pp138-9; ☎ 7730 1234; 87 Brompton Rd SW1; ⊖ Knightsbridge) An overpriced theme park for fans of Britannia, Harrods is always crowded with slow tourists.

**Harvey Nichols** (Map pp138-9; ☎ 7235 5000; 109-125 Knightsbridge SW1; ⊖ Knightsbridge) London's temple of high fashion, jewellery and perfume.

**Fortnum & Mason** (Map pp146-7; ☎ 7734 8040; 181 Piccadilly W1; ⊖ Piccadilly Circus) The byword for quality and service from a bygone era, steeped in 300 years of tradition. It is especially noted for its old-world, ground-floor food hall, where Britain's elite come for their cornflakes and bananas.

**Liberty** (Map pp146-7; ☎ 7734 1234; 214-220 Regent St W1; ⊖ Oxford Circus) An irresistible blend of contemporary styles and indulgent pampering in a mock-Tudor fantasyland of carved dark wood. Access from Great Marlborough St.

**Selfridges** (Map pp142-3; ☎ 0870 837 7377; 400 Oxford St W1; ⊖ Bond St) The funkiest and most vital of London's one-stop shops, where fashion runs the gamut from street to formal. The food hall is unparalleled and the cosmetics hall the largest in Europe.

### Fashion

If there's a label worth having, you'll find it in central London. Oxford St is the place for high-street fashion, while Regent St cranks it up a notch. Carnaby St is no longer the hip hub that it was in the 1960s, but the lanes around still have some interesting boutiques. These days, stylists are more likely to seek out attention-grabbing new looks on Portobello Rd. For something different, head to Camden, Exmouth Market or Islington's Upper and Cross Sts.

Kensington High St has a nice mix of chains and boutiques, Bond St has designers galore, while Knightsbridge draws the hordes with quintessentially English department stores. Savile Row is famous for bespoke tailoring, and Jermyn St is the place for Sir to buy his smart clobber (particularly shirts).

Look out for dress agencies that sell second-hand designer clothes, bags and shoes – there are particularly rich pickings in the wealthier parts of town.

**Albam** (Map pp146-7; ☎ 3157 7000; 23 Beak St W1; ⊖ Oxford Circus) UK-produced classic duds for stylish dudes.

**Butler & Wilson** Chelsea (Map pp140-1; ☎ 7352 3045; 189 Fulham Rd SW3; ⊖ South Kensington); Mayfair (Map pp142-3; ☎ 7409 2955; 20 South Moulton St W1; ⊖ Bond St) Camp costume jewellery, antique baubles and vintage clothing.

**EC One** Clerkenwell (Map pp136-7; ☎ 7713 6185; 41 Exmouth Market EC1; ⊖ Farringdon); Notting Hill (Map pp138-9; ☎ 7243 8811; 184 Westbourne Grove W11; ⊖ Notting Hill Gate) Husband-and-wife team Jos and Alison Skeates sell beautiful contemporary collections by British and international jewellery designers.

**KJ's Laundry** (Map pp142-3; ☎ 7486 7855; 74 Marylebone Ln W1; ⊖ Bond St) Break out of the high-street uniform in this women's boutique, which sources ranges from up-and-coming designers.

**Lollipop London** (Map pp136-7; ☎ 7226 4005; 114 Islington High St N1; ⊖ Angel) A girlie boutique stocking shoes and accessories from independent designers.

**Palette London** (Map pp136-7; ☎ 7288 7428; 21 Canonbury Ln N1; ⊖ Highbury & Islington) Fancy an original 1970s Halston dress or 1980s Chanel? Vintage meets modern and fashion meets collectables in this interesting store.

**Paul Smith Sale Shop** (Map pp142-3; ☎ 7493 1287; 23 Avery Row W1; ⊖ Bond St) Classic Paul Smith shirts and other delights by London's most commercially successful designer, at a discounted price.

**Rigby & Peller** (Map pp146-7; ☎ 7491 2200; 22A Conduit St W1S 2XT; ⊖ Oxford Circus) Get into some right royal knickers with a trip to the Queen's corsetière.

**Start** (Map p150; ☎ 7729 3334; 42-44 Rivington St EC2; ⊖ Old St) Spilling over three stores on the same lane (womenswear, menswear and men's formal), your quest for designer jeans starts here.

**Topshop Oxford Circus** (Map pp146-7; ☎ 7636 7700; 216 Oxford St W1; ⊖ Oxford Circus) Billed as the

---

### ROLL OUT THE BARROW

London has more than 350 markets selling everything from antiques and curios to flowers and fish. Some, such as Camden and Portobello Rd, are full of tourists, while others exist just for the locals and sell everything from lunch to underwear. Here's a sample:

**Bermondsey Antiques Market** (Map p134-5; Bermondsey Sq SE1; ⊙ 4am-1pm Fri; ⊖ Borough) The place to come for opera glasses, bowling balls, hatpins, costume jewellery, porcelain or other curios.

**Borough Market** (Map p150; cnr Borough High & Stoney Sts SE1; ⊙ 11am-5pm Thu, noon-6pm Fri, 9am-4pm Sat; ⊖ London Bridge) A farmers market sometimes called London's Larder, it has been here in some form since the 13th century. It's wonderfully atmospheric; you'll find everything from organic falafel to boars' heads.

**Brick Lane Market** (Map p150; Brick Lane E1; ⊙ early-2pm Sun; ⊖ Liverpool St) This is an East End pearler, a sprawling bazaar featuring everything from fruit and vegies to paintings and bric-a-brac.

**Brixton Market** (Map pp134-5; Electric Ave & Granville Arcade; ⊙ 10am-dusk Mon, Tue & Thu-Sat, to 1pm Wed; ⊖ Brixton) Immortalised in the Eddie Grant song, Electric Ave is a cosmopolitan treat that mixes everything from reggae music to exotic foods and spices.

**Broadway Market** (Map pp134-5; Broadway Mkt E8; ⊙ 9am-5pm Sat; ⊖ Bethnal Green) Graze from the organic food stalls, choose a cooked meal and then sample one of the 200 beers on offer at the neighbouring Dove Freehouse.

**Camden Market** (⊙ 10am-5.30pm; ⊖ Camden Town) London's most famous market is actually a series of markets spread along Camden High St and Chalk Farm Rd. It's been quieter since the major fire in 2008, but the **Lock** (Map pp136-7) and **Stables** (Map pp136-7) markets are still the place for punk fashion, cheap food, hippy shit and a whole lotta craziness.

**Camden Passage Market** (Map pp136-7; Camden Passage N1; ⊙ 10am-2pm Wed, to 5pm Sat; ⊖ Angel) Get your fill of antiques and trinkets galore. Not in Camden (despite the name).

**Columbia Road Flower Market** (Map p150; Columbia Rd; ⊙ 8am-2pm Sun; ⊖ Old St) The best place for East End barrow-boy banter ('We got flowers cheap enough for ya mother-in-law's grave'). Unmissable.

**Greenwich Market** (Map p149; College Approach SE10; ⊙ 11am-7pm Wed, 10am-5pm Thu & Fri, 10am-5.30pm Sat & Sun; DLR Cutty Sark) Rummage through antiques, vintage clothing and collectibles on weekdays, arts and crafts on weekends, or just chow down in the food section.

**Petticoat Lane Market** (Map p150; Wentworth St & Middlesex St E1; ⊙ 9am-2pm Mon-Fri & Sun; ⊖ Aldgate) A cherished East End institution overflowing with cheap consumer durables and jumble sale ware.

**Portobello Road Market** (Map pp138-9; Portobello Rd W10; ⊙ 8am-6.30pm Mon-Wed , Fri & Sat, to 1pm Thu; ⊖ Ladbroke Grove) One of London's most famous (and crowded) street markets. New and vintage clothes are its main attraction, with antiques at its south end and food at the north.

**Spitalfields Market** (Map p150; 105a Commercial St E1; ⊙ 10am-4pm Mon-Fri, 9am-5pm Sun; ⊖ Liverpool St) It's housed in a Victorian warehouse but the market's been here since 1638. Thursdays are devoted to antiques and Fridays to fashion and art, but Sunday's the big day.

**Sunday (Up)market** (Map p150; The Old Truman Brewery, Brick Lane E1; ⊙ 10am-5pm Sun; ⊖ Liverpool St) Handmade handbags, jewellery, new and vintage clothes and shoes, plus food if you need refuelling.

**TOP FIVE ECCENTRIC STORES**

- **Duke of Uke** (Map p150; ☎ 7247 7924; 22 Hanbury St E1; ✪ Liverpool St) Devoted entirely to ukuleles and banjos.
- **FairyGothMother** (Map p150; ☎ 7247 7924; 15 Lamb St E1; ✪ Liverpool St) Purveyors of custom-made corsets and vampy evening wear, not all in black.
- **Hamleys** (Map pp146-7; ☎ 0844-855 2424; 188-196 Regent St W1; ✪ Oxford Circus) A seemingly endless wonderland of toys.
- **International Magic** (Map pp142-3; ☎ 7405 7324; 89 Clerkenwell Rd EC1; ✪ Chancery Ln) If you've ever fancied pulling a rabbit out of hat, here's where you'll find the hat.
- **Old Curiosity Shop** (Map pp146-7; ☎ 7405 9891; 13-14 Portsmouth St WC2; ✪ Holborn) Having been constructed from recycled ship timber in 1567, this is London's oldest shop building. It now sells out-there handmade, high-fashion shoes.

'world's largest fashion store', the Topshop branch on Oxford Circus is a constant frenzy of shoppers searching for the latest look at reasonable prices. It's been given a shot of cool by being home to a range by London's favourite local supermodel rock chick, Kate Moss. Topman is next door.

### Music

Nick Hornby's book *High Fidelity* may have done for London music-store workers what *Sweeney Todd* did for barbers, but those obsessive types still lurk in wonderful independent stores all over London. For personality, visit the following:

**BM Soho** (Map pp146-7; ☎ 7437 0478; 25 D'Arblay St W1; ✪ Oxford Circus) Your best bet for dance – if they haven't got what you're after, they'll know who has.

**Minus Zero Records** (Map pp138-9; ☎ 7229 5424; 2 Blenheim Cres W11; ✪ Ladbrooke Grove) The place for collectables, like Bowie 7in singles.

**Ray's Jazz** (Map pp146-7; ☎ 7437 5660; Foyle's, 113-119 Charing Cross Rd WC2; ✪ Tottenham Court Rd) Where aficionados will find those elusive back catalogues from their favourite jazz and blues artists.

**Rough Trade** East (Map p150; ☎ 7392 7788; Dray Walk, 91 Brick Ln E1; ✪ Liverpool St); West (Map pp138-9; ☎ 7229 8541; 130 Talbot Rd W11; ✪ Ladbroke Grove) At the forefront of the punk explosion of the 1970s, it's the best place to come for pretty much anything of an indie or alternative bent.

**Sister Ray** (Map pp146-7; ☎ 7734 3297; 34-35 Berwick St W1; ✪ Oxford Circus) If you need to be told that this store is named after a 17-minute distorted Velvet Underground classic about a trannie smack dealer, then this shop's not for you.

If you'd like to purchase schmaltz without attitude, try the giant Oxford St **HMV** (Map pp146-7;

☎ 7631 3423; 150 Oxford St W1; ⏰ 9am-9pm; ✪ Oxford Circus), which has many central branches.

## GETTING THERE & AWAY

London is the major gateway to England, so further transport information can be found in the main Transport chapter.

### Air

For information on flying to/from London see p996.

### Bus

Most long-distance coaches leave London from **Victoria Coach Station** (Map p140-1; ☎ 7824 0000; 164 Buckingham Palace Rd SW1; ✪ Victoria), a lovely art-deco building. The arrivals terminal is in a separate building across Elizabeth St from the main coach station.

### Car

See p1000 for reservation numbers of the main car-hire firms, all of which have airport and various city locations.

### Train

The reopening of beautiful St Pancras station makes London only 2¼ hours by train from Paris on the Eurostar (see p998). The vast vaulted concourse has all the services found in an airport terminal, and a giant statue of embracing lovers that Londoners love to hate.

London's main-line terminals are all linked by the tube and each serves a different destination. Most stations now have left-luggage facilities (around £4) and lockers, toilets (a 20p coin) with showers (around £3), newsstands and bookshops, and a range of eating and drinking outlets. St Pancras, Victoria and Liverpool St stations have shopping centres attached.

If you can't find your destination below, see the journey planner at www.nationalrail .co.uk.

**Charing Cross** (Map pp146-7) Canterbury.

**Euston** (Map pp136-7) Manchester, Liverpool, Carlisle, Glasgow.

**King's Cross** (Map pp136-7) Cambridge, Hull, York, Newcastle, Scotland.

**Liverpool Street** (Map p150) Stansted airport, Cambridge.

**London Bridge** (Map p150) Gatwick airport, Brighton.

**Marylebone** (Map pp138-9) Birmingham.

**Paddington** (Map pp138-9) Heathrow airport, Oxford, Bath, Bristol, Exeter, Plymouth, Cardiff.

**St Pancras** (Map pp136-7) Gatwick and Luton airports, Brighton, Nottingham, Sheffield, Leicester, Leeds, Paris.

**Victoria** (Map pp140-1) Gatwick airport, Brighton, Canterbury.

**Waterloo** (Map pp142-3) Windsor, Winchester, Exeter, Plymouth.

## GETTING AROUND
### To/From the Airports
#### HEATHROW

Transport connections to Heathrow are excellent and the journey to and from the city is painless. The cheapest option is the Underground (opposite). The Piccadilly line is accessible from every terminal (£4, one hour to central London, departing from Heathrow every five minutes from around 5am to 11.30pm). If it's your first time in London, it's a good chance to practise using the tube as it's at the beginning of the line and therefore not too crowded when you get on. Although for first timers, buying a ticket can still be confusing, with little signage and the sometimes impenetrable accents. If there are vast queues at the airport ticket office, use the automatic machines instead; some accept credit cards as well as cash. Keep your bags near you and expect a scramble to get off if you're hitting the city at rush hour (7am to 9am and 5pm to 7pm weekdays).

The fastest and easiest way to central London is the **Heathrow Express** ( ☎ 0845 600 1515; www.heathrowexpress.co.uk), an ultramodern train to Paddington station (one way/return £14.50/28, 15 minutes, every 15 minutes 5.10am to 11.25pm). You can purchase tickets on board (£2 extra), online or from self-service machines (cash and credit cards accepted) at both stations.

There are taxi ranks for black cabs outside every terminal. A black cab to the centre of

London will cost you between £40 and £70, a minicab around £35.

#### GATWICK

There are **National Rail** (www.nationalrail.co.uk) services from Gatwick's South Terminal to Victoria (£9.50, 37 minutes), running every 15 minutes during the day and hourly through the night. Other trains head to St Pancras (£8.90, 63 minutes), stopping at London Bridge, City Thameslink, Blackfriars and Farringdon. If you're racing to make a flight, the **Gatwick Express** ( ☎ 0845 850 1530; www.gatwickexpress.co.uk) departs Victoria every 15 minutes from 5.50am to 12.35am (one way/return £18/31, 30 minutes, first/last train 4.35am/1.35am).

Prices start very low, depending on when you book, for the **EasyBus** (www.easybus.co.uk) minibus service between Gatwick and Victoria (return from £11, allow 1½ hours, every 30 minutes from 3am to 1am). You'll be charged extra if you have more than one carry-on and one check-in bag.

Gatwick's taxi partner, **Checker Cars** (www.checker cars.co.uk), has a counter in each terminal. Fares are quoted and paid in advance (about £83 for the 65-minute ride to Central London). A black cab costs similar, a minicab around £55.

#### STANSTED

The **Stansted Express** ( ☎ 0845 600 7245; www.stansted express.com) connects with Liverpool St station (one way/return £17/26, 46 minutes, departing every 15 minutes 5.10am to 10.55pm, first/last train 4.40am/11.25pm).

As with Gatwick, **EasyBus** (www.easybus.co.uk) has services between Stansted, Baker St and Victoria (return from £13, allow 1¾ hours, every 30 minutes from 3am to 1.05am). The **Airbus A6** ( ☎ 0870 580 8080; www.nationalexpress.com) links with Victoria coach station (one way/return £10/16, allow 1¾ hours, departing at least every 30 minutes).

A black cab to/from central London costs about £100, a minicab around £55.

#### LONDON CITY

The Docklands Light Railway (DLR) connects London City Airport to the tube, taking 22 minutes to reach Bank station (£4). A black taxi costs around £25 to/from central London.

#### LUTON

There are regular **National Rail** (www.nationalrail.co.uk) services from St Pancras (£14, 28 to 48 minutes) to Luton Airport Parkway station, where a shuttle bus (£1) will get you to the airport within 10 minutes. **EasyBus** (www.easybus.co.uk) minibuses head from Victoria and Baker St to Luton (return from £12, allow 1¼ hours, departing every 30 minutes). A black taxi costs around £95 to/from central London, minicabs around £55.

## Car

Don't even think about it. Driving in London is a nightmare: traffic is heavy, parking is either impossible or expensive and wheel-clampers keep busy. If you drive into central London from 7am to 6pm on a weekday, you'll need to pay an £8 per day congestion charge (visit www.tfl.gov.uk/roadusers/congestioncharging/ to register) or face a hefty fine. If you're hiring a car to continue your trip, take the tube to Heathrow and pick it up from there.

## Public Transport

Although locals love to complain about it, London's public transport is excellent, with tubes, trains, buses and boats conspiring to get you anywhere you need to go. **Transport for London** (TFL; www.tfl.gov.uk) is the glue that hinges the network together. Its website has a handy journey planner and information on all services, including cabs. As a creature of leisure, you'll be able to avoid those bits that Londoners hate (especially the sardine squash of rush-hour tubes), so get yourself an Oyster Card (p202) and make the most of it.

### LONDON UNDERGROUND, DLR & OVERGROUND

'The tube', as it's universally known, extends its subterranean tentacles throughout London and into the surrounding counties, with services running every few minutes from 5.30am to roughly 12.30am (from 7am on Sunday).

It's incredibly easy to use. Tickets (or Oyster card top-ups) can be purchased from counters or machines at the entrance to each station using either cash or credit card. They're then inserted into the slot on the turnstiles (or you touch your Oyster card on the yellow reader) and the barrier opens. Once you're through you can jump on and off different lines as often as you need to get to your desired destination. See the boxed text (p202) for information about fares, zones and Oyster cards.

Also included within the network are the driverless Docklands Light Railway (DLR),

and the train lines shown on tube maps as 'Overground'. The DLR links the City to Docklands, Greenwich and London City Airport. It's very Jetsons-like, especially when it hurtles between the Canary Wharf skyscrapers; try to get the front-row seat.

The tube map itself is an acclaimed piece of graphic design using coloured lines to demonstrate how the 14 different routes intersect. However, it's not remotely to scale. The distance between stations is much greater the further from central London you travel, while Leicester Sq and Covent Garden stations are only 250m apart.

### BOAT

The myriad boats that ply the River Thames are a great way to travel, avoiding traffic jams while affording great views. Passengers with daily, weekly or monthly travelcards (Oyster or otherwise) get one-third off all fares.

**Thames Clippers** ( ☎ 0871-781 5049; www.thamesclippers.com) runs regular commuter services between Embankment, Waterloo, Bankside, London Bridge, Tower, Canary Wharf, Greenwich and Woolwich piers (adult £2.50 to £6.50, child £1.25 to £3.25), from 7am to 12.30pm (from 9am weekends). Another service runs from Putney to Blackfriars during the morning and evening rush hours.

Leisure services include the Tate-to-Tate boat (see boxed text, p165), Westminster-to-Greenwich services (p170) and a loop route taking in Westminster, Embankment, Festival, Bankside, London Bridge and St Katherine's piers (day pass adult/child £7.80/3.70, May to September). For boats to Kew Gardens and Hampton Court Palace, see p172.

**London Waterbus Company** (Map pp138-9; ☎ 7482 2660; www.londonwaterbus.com; single/return £6.50/5) and **Jason's Trip** (Map pp138-9; ☎ 7286 3428; www.jasons.co.uk; opposite 60 Blomfield Rd W9; single/return £7.50/8.50) both run canal boat journeys between Camden Lock and Little Venice; see websites for times. London has some 40 miles of inner-city canals, mostly built in the 19th century.

### BUS

Travelling round London by double-decker bus is an enjoyable way to get a feel for the city, but it's usually more difficult and slower than the tube. A recommended scenic route is number 24, which runs from Victoria to Hampstead Heath through the West End. Heritage 'Routemaster' buses with conduc-

### LONDON'S OYSTER DIET

To get the most out of London, you need to be able to jump on and off public transport like a local, not scramble to buy a ticket each time at hefty rates. The best and cheapest way to do this is with an Oyster card, a reusable smartcard on which you can load either a season ticket (weekly/monthly £24.20/93) or pre-paid credit. The card itself is free with a season ticket, otherwise it's £3.

London is divided into six concentric transport zones, although almost all of the places covered in this book are in Zones 1 and 2. The season tickets quoted above will give you unlimited transport on tubes, buses and most National Rail services within these zones. All you need to do is touch your card to the sensors on the station turnstiles or at the front of the bus.

If you opt for pay as you go, the fare will be deducted from the credit on your card at a much lower rate than if you were buying a one-off paper ticket. An Oyster bus trip costs 90p as opposed to £2, while a Zone 1 tube journey is £1.50 as opposed to £4. Even better, in any single day your fares will be capped at the equivalent of the Oyster day-pass rate for the zones you've travelled in (Zones 1 and 2 peak/off-peak £6.30/4.80).

Assuming you'll avoid the tube during peak hours (before 9.30am), this ready reckoner gives the cheapest options for your length of stay:

- one–four days: non-Oyster off-peak daily (£5.30 per day)
- five–25 days: Oyster weeklies topped up with pre-pay for any remaining days
- 26–31 days: monthly

tors operate on route 9 (from Aldwych to Royal Albert Hall) and 15 (between Trafalgar Sq and Tower Hill); these are the only buses without wheelchair access.

Buses run regularly during the day, while less-frequent night buses (prefixed with the letter 'N') wheel into action when the tube stops. Single-journey bus tickets (valid for two hours) cost £2 (90p on Oyster, capped at £3 per day); cash day passes are £3.50 and books of six tickets are £6. Children ride for free. At stops with yellow signs, you have to buy your ticket from the automatic machine *before* boarding. Buses stop on request, so clearly signal the driver with an outstretched arm.

### TAXI

London's famous black cabs are available for hire when the yellow light above the windscreen is lit. To get an all-London licence, cabbies must do 'The Knowledge', which tests them on up to 25,000 streets within a 6-mile radius of Charing Cross and all the points of interest from hotels to churches. Fares are metered, with flag fall at £2.20 and the additional rate dependent on time of day, distance travelled and taxi speed. A 1-mile trip will

cost between £4.40 and £8. To order a black cab by phone, try **Dial-a-Cab** ( ☎ 7253 5000); you must pay by credit card and will be charged a premium.

Licensed minicabs operate out of agencies (most busy areas have a walk-in office with drivers waiting); they are a cheaper alternative to black cabs and quote a fare for the trip in advance. The cars are recognisable by the ⊖ symbol displayed in the window. To find a local minicab firm, visit www.tfl.gov .uk/tfl/gettingaround/findaride.

There have been many reports of sexual assault and theft by unlicensed minicab drivers. Only use drivers from proper agencies; licensed minicabs aren't allowed to tout for business, so avoid the shady characters hanging around outside nightclubs or bars.

### TRAIN

Particularly south of the river, where tube lines are in short supply, the various rail companies are an important part of the public transport picture. More stations are being fitted with Oyster readers, but you should check before travelling as to whether you need to purchase a separate ticket.

# Southeast England

This corner of England is both blessed and cursed by its proximity to London. The well-off counties of Kent, East and West Sussex and Surrey are among the most popular parts of Britain to live and visit, home to commuter hubs and business communities as well as huge crowds of visitors when the weather gets sunny. Yet the region is also peppered with picturesque villages, meandering country lanes and out-of-the way country pubs, enveloped in manicured farmland and rolling chalk downs. A string of alternately tacky, old-fashioned and hedonistic seaside towns line the shore, exploiting the mild climate and fast links from London. And all along the coast you can soak up maritime history, dine out on seafood and charge around beaches and cliff tops.

Here too you'll find England's spiritual heart at Canterbury, with its magnificent cathedral and ancient winding streets; the surrounding landscape is littered with royal residences, stately homes and castles, which serve as a reminder of the region's long ties with the monarchy.

The closest stretch of land to Continental Europe, the southeast coast is rich with remnants of its critical role as the nation's front line of defence, from the site of the Battle of Hastings, to the secret war tunnels at Dover Castle, to the scattered ruins of Roman palaces. The formidable cliffs, castles and fortified ports still remain, but these days they're raided by sightseers armed with cameras and picnics rather than belligerent Normans.

**SOUTHEAST ENGLAND**

## HIGHLIGHTS

- Shopping, dining and partying in boisterous **Brighton & Hove** (p223)
- Following in the footsteps of pilgrims to ancient **Canterbury Cathedral** (p206)
- Lapping up tales of ghosts and smugglers in the cobbled backstreets of romantic **Rye** (p218)
- Strolling past candy-coloured beach huts and feasting on oysters at **Whitstable** (p211)
- Conjuring up knights and dragons at romantic moated marvel **Leeds Castle** (p218)
- Exploring the atmospheric WWII tunnels under sprawling **Dover Castle** (p214)
- Bringing on the vertigo as you walk the 150m-high chalk cliffs of **Beachy Head** (p222)

| ■ POPULATION: 8 MILLION | ■ AREA: 3560 SQ MILES | ■ THIS REGION HAS THE GREATEST CONCENTRATION OF VINEYARDS IN GREAT BRITAIN |
|---|---|---|

## Information

**Tourism South East** (www.visitsoutheastengland.com) is the official website for south and south-east England. Other helpful websites include the following:

**Kent Attractions** (www.kentattractions.co.uk)
**Visit Kent** (www.visitkent.co.uk)
**Visit Surrey** (www.visitsurrey.com)
**Visit Sussex** (www.visitsussex.org)

## Activities

The southeast of England may be Britain's most densely populated corner, but there are still plenty of off-the-beaten-track walking and cycling routes to enjoy here. We concentrate on the highlights here, but you'll find more information throughout the chapter and in the Outdoor Activities chapter (p108). Regional tourist offices are also well stocked with leaflets, maps and guides to start you off walking, cycling, paragliding, sailing and more.

### CYCLING

Finding quiet roads for cycle touring takes a little extra perseverance in southeast England, but the effort is richly rewarded. Long-distance routes that form part of the **National Cycle Network** (NCN; www.sustrans.org.uk) include the following:

**Downs & Weald Cycle Route** (150 miles; NCN routes 2, 21) London to Brighton and on to Hastings.
**Garden of England Cycle Route** (165 miles; NCN routes 1, 2) London to Dover and then Hastings.

You'll also find less-demanding routes on the NCN website. Meanwhile there are plenty of uppers and downers to challenge mountain-bikers on the South Downs Way National Trail (100 miles), which takes hard nuts two days but mere mortals around four. There are also a number of excellent trails at Devil's Punchbowl in the Surrey Hills.

### WALKING

Two long-distance trails meander steadily westward through the region, but there are plenty of shorter ambles to suit your schedule, stamina and scenery wish list.

**South Downs Way National Trail** (100 miles) At the time of writing the rolling chalk South Downs were hotly tipped to become England's newest national park, and this trail is a beautiful roller-coaster walk along prehistoric drove ways between the ancient capital of Winchester and the seaside resort Eastbourne.

**North Downs Way** (153 miles) This popular walk begins near Farnham in Surrey but one of its most beautiful sections runs from near Ashford to Dover in Kent, and there's also a loop that takes in Canterbury near its end.

Both long-distance routes have sections ideal for shorter walks. History buffs will revel in the 1066 Country Walk, which connects with the South Downs Way. Devil's Punchbowl offers breathtaking views, sloping grasslands and romantic wooded areas.

## Getting There & Around

The southeast is easily explored by train or bus, and many attractions can be visited in a day trip from London. Contact the **National Traveline** ( ☎ 0871 200 2233; www.travelinesoutheast.org.uk) for comprehensive information on public transport in the region.

### BUS

Explorer tickets (adult/child £6.40/4.50) provide day-long unlimited travel on most buses throughout the region; buy them at bus stations or on your first bus.

**Stagecoach Coastline** (www.stagecoachbus.com) serves the coastline, East Kent and East Sussex areas. Travellers can buy an unlimited day (£7) or week (£18) ticket.

### TRAIN

If you're based in London but day-tripping around the southeast, the BritRail London Plus Pass allows unlimited regional rail travel for two days in eight (£102), four days in eight (£164), or seven days in fifteen (£197) and must be purchased outside the UK; see p1004 for more details.

You can secure 33% discounts on most rail fares over £10 in the southeast by purchasing a **Network Railcard** ( ☎ 08457 225 225; www.railcard.co.uk/network/network.htm; per yr £20). Children under 15 can save 60%, but a minimum £1 fare applies.

# KENT

Kent isn't described as the garden of England for nothing. Inside its sea-lined borders you'll find a clipped landscape of gentle hills, lush farmland, cultivated country estates and fruitful orchards. It's also the booze garden of England, producing the world-renowned Kent hops, some of the country's

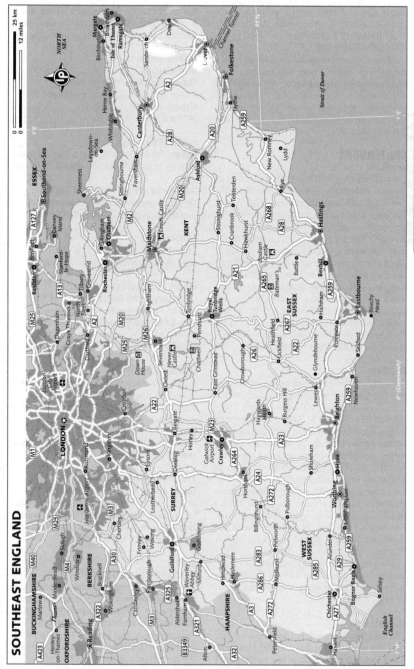

finest ales and even award-winning wines from its numerous vineyards. At it's heart is spellbinding Canterbury crowned by its fascinating cathedral.

Here too are beautiful coastal stretches dotted with beach towns and villages, from old-fashioned Broadstairs, to gentrified Whitstable, to the aesthetically challenged port town of Dover, which is close enough to France to smell the garlic or hop over on a day trip to taste it.

## CANTERBURY
pop 43,552

Canterbury tops the charts when it comes to English cathedral cities and is one of southern England's top attractions. The World Heritage–listed cathedral that dominates its centre is considered by many to be one of Europe's finest, and the town's narrow medieval alleyways, riverside gardens and ancient city walls are a joy to explore. But Canterbury isn't just a showpiece to times past; it's a spirited place with an energetic student population and a wide choice of contemporary bars, restaurants and arts. But book ahead for the best hotels and eateries: pilgrims may no longer flock here in their thousands but there's a year-round flood of tourists to replace them.

### History

Canterbury's past is as rich as it comes. From AD 200 there was a Roman town here, which later became the capital of the Saxon kingdom of Kent. When St Augustine arrived in England in 597 to carry the Christian message to the pagan hordes, he chose Canterbury as his *cathedra* (primary see) and set about building an abbey on the outskirts of town. Following the martyrdom of Thomas Becket (see boxed text, p208), Canterbury became northern Europe's most important centre of pilgrimage, which in turn led to Geoffrey Chaucer's *The Canterbury Tales*, one of the most outstanding poetic works in English literature (see boxed text, p211).

Blasphemous murders and rampant tourism thrown aside, the city of Canterbury still remains the primary see for the Church of England.

### Orientation

The Old Town is enclosed by a bulky medieval city wall that makes a wonderful walk. The Unesco World Heritage Site encompasses the cathedral, St Augustine's Abbey and St Martin's Church. Much of the centre is pedestrianised, but there is parking inside the wall.

## Information
### BOOKSHOPS
**Chaucer Bookshop** ( ☎ 01227-453912; 6-7 Beer Cart Lane) Antiquarian and used books.
**Waterstone's** ( ☎ 01227-456343; 20-21 St Margaret's St)

### INTERNET ACCESS
**Dotcafe** ( ☎ 01227-478778; 19-21 St Dunstan's St; per hr £3; ☼ 10am-7pm) Large cyber cafe near the railway station.
**Main library** ( ☎ 01227-463608; 18 High St; ☼ 9.30am-6pm Mon-Sat) Free internet access in the same building as the Royal Museum & Art Gallery.

### LAUNDRY
**Canterbury Laundrette** ( ☎ 01227-452211; Nunnery Fields; ☼ 9am-6pm Mon-Fri, to 4pm Sat, to 3pm Sun)

### MEDICAL SERVICES
**Canterbury Health Centre** ( ☎ 01227-452444; 26 Old Dover Rd) For general medical consultations.
**Kent & Canterbury Hospital** ( ☎ 01227-766877; Etherbert Rd) Has an emergency room and is a mile from the centre.

### MONEY
ATMs and other major banks are on High St, near the corner of St Margaret's St.
**Lloyd's TSB** (28 St Margaret's St) Has a bureau de change.

### POST
**Post office** (19 St George's St; ☼ 9am-5.30pm Mon-Sat) Inside WH Smith's.

### TOURIST INFORMATION
**Tourist office** ( ☎ 01227-378100; www.canterbury .co.uk; 12 Sun St; ☼ 9.30am-5pm Mon-Sat, 10am-4pm Sun Easter-Oct, 10am-4pm Mon-Sat Nov-Easter) Situated opposite the cathedral gate; the staff can help book accommodation, excursions and theatre tickets.

## Sights
### CANTERBURY CATHEDRAL

The Church of England could not have a more imposing mother church than this extraordinary early Gothic **cathedral** ( ☎ 01227-762862; www.canterbury-cathedral.org; adult/concession £7/5.50; ☼ 9am-6.30pm Mon-Sat Easter-Sep, 9am-4.30pm Mon-Sat Oct-Easter, plus 12.30-2.30pm & 4.30-5.30pm Sun year-round), the centrepiece of the city's World Heritage

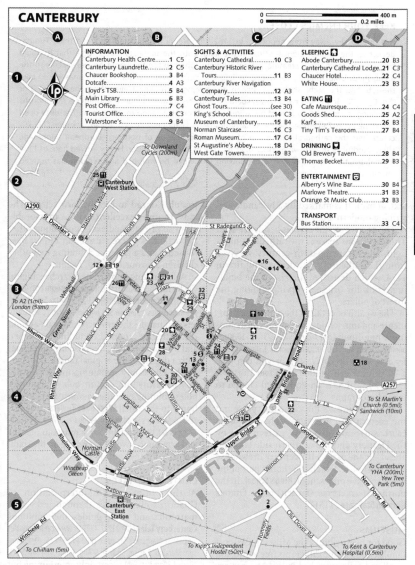

# CANTERBURY

0 — 400 m
0 — 0.2 miles

**INFORMATION**

| | |
|---|---|
| Canterbury Health Centre | **1** C5 |
| Canterbury Laundrette | **2** C5 |
| Chaucer Bookshop | **3** B4 |
| Dotcafe | **4** A3 |
| Lloyd's TSB | **5** B4 |
| Main Library | **6** B3 |
| Post Office | **7** C4 |
| Tourist Office | **8** C3 |
| Waterstone's | **9** B4 |

**SIGHTS & ACTIVITIES**

| | |
|---|---|
| Canterbury Cathedral | **10** C3 |
| Canterbury Historic River Tours | **11** B3 |
| Canterbury River Navigation Company | **12** A3 |
| Canterbury Tales | **13** B4 |
| Ghost Tours | (see 30) |
| King's School | **14** C3 |
| Museum of Canterbury | **15** B4 |
| Norman Staircase | **16** C3 |
| Roman Museum | **17** C4 |
| St Augustine's Abbey | **18** D4 |
| West Gate Towers | **19** B3 |

**SLEEPING**

| | |
|---|---|
| Abode Canterbury | **20** B3 |
| Canterbury Cathedral Lodge | **21** C3 |
| Chaucer Hotel | **22** C4 |
| White House | **23** B3 |

**EATING**

| | |
|---|---|
| Cafe Mauresque | **24** C4 |
| Goods Shed | **25** A2 |
| Karl's | **26** B3 |
| Tiny Tim's Tearoom | **27** B4 |

**DRINKING**

| | |
|---|---|
| Old Brewery Tavern | **28** B4 |
| Thomas Becket | **29** B3 |

**ENTERTAINMENT**

| | |
|---|---|
| Alberry's Wine Bar | **30** B4 |
| Marlowe Theatre | **31** B3 |
| Orange St Music Club | **32** B3 |

**TRANSPORT**

| | |
|---|---|
| Bus Station | **33** C4 |

**SOUTHEAST ENGLAND**

---

Site and repository of over 1400 years of Christian history.

It's an overwhelming edifice filled with enthralling stories, striking architecture and a very real and enduring sense of spirituality, although visitors can't help but pick up on the ominous undertones of violence and bloodshed that whisper from its walls.

This ancient structure is packed with monuments commemorating the nation's battles. Also here is the grave and heraldic tunic of one of the nation's most famous warmongers, Edward the Black Prince (1330–76). The spot in the northwest transept where Archbishop Thomas Becket met his grisly end has been drawing pilgrims for over 800 years (see boxed

**KEEP YOUR ENEMIES CLOSE...**

Not one to shy away from nepotism, in 1162 King Henry II appointed his good mate Thomas Becket to the highest clerical office in the land, with the understandable logic that it would be easier to force the increasingly vocal religious lobby to toe the line if he was pally with the archbishop. Unfortunately for Henry, he had underestimated how seriously Thomas would take the job, and the archbishop soon began disagreeing with almost everything the king said or did. By 1170 Henry had become exasperated with his former favourite and after a few months of sulking 'suggested' to four of his knights that Thomas was too much to bear. The dirty deed was done on 29 December. Becket's martyrdom – and canonisation in double-quick time (1173) – catapulted the cathedral to the top of the premier league of northern European pilgrimage sites. Mindful of the growing criticism at his role in Becket's murder, Henry arrived here in 1174 for a dramatic mea culpa, and after allowing himself to be whipped and scolded was granted absolution.

text, above). It is marked by a lit candle and striking modern altar.

The doorway to the crypt is beside the altar. This cavernous space is the cathedral's highlight, an entrancing 11th-century survivor from the cathedral's last devastating fire in 1174, which destroyed the rest of the building. Look for original carvings among the forest of pillars.

The wealth of detail in the cathedral is immense and unrelenting, so it's well worth joining a one-hour **tour** (adult/child £5/3; 10.30am, noon & 2.30pm Mon-Fri, 10.30am, noon & 1.30pm Sat Apr-Sep, noon & 2pm Mon-Sat Oct-Mar), or you can take a 30-minute self-guided **audio tour** (adult/child £3.95/1.95). There is an additional charge to take photographs.

When you leave the cathedral, go round the eastern end and turn right into **Green Court**, surrounded on the eastern side by the Deanery and the northern side (straight ahead) by the early-14th-century Brewhouse and Bakehouse, which now house part of the very exclusive prep school, **King's School**. In the northwestern corner (far left) is the famous **Norman Staircase** (1151).

### MUSEUMS

Good for history buffs, the Museum Passport (adult/child £6.20/3.70) grants free admission to all the following. Individual charges are given with each listing.

A fine 14th-century building, once the Poor Priests' Hospital, now houses the absorbing **Museum of Canterbury** ( ☎ 01227-475202; www .canterbury-museums.co.uk; Stour St; adult/child £3.50/2.25; 10.30am-5pm Mon-Sat year-round, plus 1.30-5pm Sun Jun-Sep), which has varied exhibits from pre-Roman times to the assassination of Becket,

Joseph Conrad to locally born celebs. The kids' room is excellent, with a memorable glimpse of real medieval poo among other fun activities. There's also a fun Rupert Bear Museum and a gallery celebrating that other children's favourite of old, Bagpuss.

A fascinating subterranean archaeological site forms the basis of the **Roman Museum** ( ☎ 01227-785575; Butchery Lane; adult/child £3/2; 10am-5pm Mon-Sat year-round, plus 1.30-5pm Sun Jun-Oct), which actually lets you handle the artefacts and walk around reconstructed rooms, including a kitchen and a market place. The museum culminates with a display of the original mosaic floors.

The city's only remaining medieval gateway, a brawny 14th-century bulk with murder holes pointing over the passing cars below, is home to the small **West Gate Towers** ( ☎ 01227-789576; St Peter's St; adult/concession £1.25/75p; 11am-12.30pm & 1.30-3.30pm Mon-Sat), a museum of arms and armour. It's worth squeezing up the spiral staircase for the rooftop views.

### CANTERBURY TALES

A three dimensional interpretation of Chaucer's classic tales through jerky animatronics and audio guides, the ambitious **Canterbury Tales** ( ☎ 01227-479227; www.canterburytales .org.uk; St Margaret's St; adult/child £7.25/5.25; 10am-5pm Mar-Jun, 9.30am-5pm Jul & Aug, 10am-5pm Sep & Oct, 10am-4.30pm Nov-Feb) is certainly entertaining but could never do full justice to Chaucer's tales. It's a lively and fun introduction for the young or uninitiated, however. See also p211.

### ST AUGUSTINE'S ABBEY

An integral but often overlooked part of the Canterbury World Heritage Site, **St Augustine's Abbey** (EH; ☎ 01227-767345; adult/child £4.20/2.10;

10am-6pm daily Jul & Aug, 11am-5pm Sat & Sun Sep-Mar, 10am-5pm Wed-Sun Apr-Jun) was founded in AD 597, marking the rebirth of Christianity in southern England. Later requisitioned as a royal palace, it was to fall into disrepair and now only stumpy foundations remain. A small museum and a worthwhile audio tour do their best to underline the site's importance and put flesh back on its now humble bones.

### ST MARTIN'S CHURCH

This stumpy little **church** ( ☎ 01227-768072; North Holmes Rd; admission free; 11am-4pm Tue, Thu & Sat Apr-Sep, to 3pm Oct-Mar) is thought to be England's oldest parish in continuous use, and where Queen Bertha (wife of the Saxon King Ethelbert) welcomed Augustine upon his arrival in the 6th century. The original Saxon church has been swallowed by a medieval refurbishment, but it's still worth the 900m walk east of the abbey.

## Tours

**Canterbury Historic River Tours** ( ☎ 07790-534 744; www.canterburyrivertours.co.uk; adult/child £6.50/5; 10am-5pm Apr-Sep) Will take you on a rowing-boat tour including (prebooked) candlelit tours, from behind the Old Weaver's House on St Peter's St.

**Canterbury River Navigation Company** ( ☎ 07816-760869; www.crnc.co.uk; Westgate Gardens; adult/child £7/4; Apr-Sep) Relaxing punt trips.

**Canterbury Walks** ( ☎ 01227-459779; www .canterbury-walks.co.uk; adult/under 12yr/senior & student £4.70/3.20/4.20; 2pm daily Apr-Oct, plus 11.30am Mon-Sat Jul–mid-Sep) Chaperoned walking tours; leave from the tourist office.

**Ghost Tours** ( ☎ 07779-575831; adult/child £7/5.50) Depart from outside Alberry's wine bar in St Margaret's St at 8pm year-round every Friday and Saturday. Only groups need book.

## Festivals & Events

Myriad musicians, comedians, theatre groups and other artists from around the world come to the party for two weeks in mid-October, during the **Canterbury Festival** ( ☎ 01227-452853; www .canterburyfestival.co.uk).

## Sleeping

### BUDGET

**Yew Tree Park** ( ☎ 01227-700306; www.yewtreepark .com; Stone St, Petham; tent & 2 adults £12-17; Mar-Sep; P wi-fi) Set in gentle rolling countryside 5 miles southeast of the city, this lovely family-run camp site has plenty of soft grass to pitch a

tent on and a heated swimming pool. Call for directions and transportation information.

**Kipp's Independent Hostel** ( ☎ 01227-786121; www .kipps-hostel.com; 40 Nunnery Fields; dm/s/d £15/20/35; ) This red-brick town house is popular for its laid-back, homely atmosphere with friendly hosts and long-term residents, lots of communal areas, clean though cramped dorms, bike hire and garden. It's just south of the centre.

**Canterbury YHA** ( ☎ 01227-462911; www.yha.org .uk; 54 New Dover Rd; dm £20.95; P ) This grand Victorian Gothic-style villa is a little way out of town, but it's spacious and organised, with a garden and cheaper, prepared-tent accommodation. It's a great deal, and also has single rooms. It's 1.25 miles southeast of the centre, and open year-round by advanced booking. Wheelchair access available.

### MIDRANGE

**White House** ( ☎ 01227-761836; www.canterburybreaks .co.uk; 6 St Peter's Lane; s/d £55/70; ) This elegant white Regency town house, supposedly once home to Queen Victoria's head coachman, has a friendly welcome, seven spick-and-span rooms with crisp white linen and country touches, and a grand guest lounge complete with fireplace and beaten leather sofas.

**Canterbury Cathedral Lodge** ( ☎ 01227-865350; www.canterburycathedrallodge.org; Canterbury Cathedral precincts; r from £79; wi-fi) The position of this modern, circular lodge is unbeatable. It's right opposite the cathedral within the precinct itself. The clean, modern rooms – done out in white and blond wood – have excellent facilities but what really makes this place are the views. Call in good time, as it's often booked up with large groups.

### TOP END

**Chaucer Hotel** ( ☎ 01227-464427; www.swallowhotels .com; 63 Ivy Lane; s/d from £105/130; P ) Just outside the old city walls, this once-elegant red-brick Georgian house now has the aura of a chain hotel: plush but more than a little bland. The position makes up for its lack of personality, however.

**Abode Canterbury** ( ☎ 01227-766266; www.abode hotels.co.uk; 30-33 High St; s/d from £89/109) The only boutique hotel in town, rooms here are graded from 'comfortable' to 'fabulous' and for the most part they live up to their names, and they come with little features such as handmade beds, cashmere throws, velour bathrobes, beautiful modern bathrooms and little tuck boxes of locally produced snacks. There's a splendid champagne bar, restaurant and tavern here too.

## Eating

**Karl's** ( ☎ 01227-764380; 43 St Peter's St; snacks £3-7; ☺ 9am-6pm Mon-Sat) The walls of this bright little deli are crammed with fine cheeses, artisan breads and pastries, coffee beans and food-friendly wines. You can sample their delicious wares (including fantastic deli sandwiches and cheeseboards) in a comfy dining space at the back of the shop or in their small garden.

**Tiny Tim's Tearoom** ( ☎ 01227-450793; 34 St Margaret's St; mains £7-13; ☺ 9.30-5pm Tue-Sat, 10.30am-4pm Sun) Not a hint of chintz in this English tearoom, it's pure 1930s elegance. Come in to enjoy big breakfasts full of Kent ingredients, or tiers of cakes, crumpets and sandwiches for high tea. There's a sunny courtyard garden outside and they sell chutneys, breads and local Kent wines to take away.

**Cafe Mauresque** ( ☎ 01227-464300; www.cafemauresque.com; 8 Butchery Lane; mains £7-17; ☺ noon-10pm Sun-Thu, to 10.30pm Fri & Sat) Fun little North African and Spanish spot with a plain cafe upstairs as well as a romantic basement swathed in exotic fabric, serving up rich tagines, couscous and tapas. There are hubbly bubbly hookah pipes to finish off your meal.

**ourpick Goods Shed** ( ☎ 01227-459153; Station Rd West; lunch £8-12, dinner £10-16; ☺ market 10am-7pm Tue-Sat, to 4pm Sun, restaurant lunch & dinner Tue-Sun) Farmers market, food hall and fabulous restaurant all rolled into one, this converted station warehouse by the railway is a hit with everyone from self-caterers to sit-down gourmets. The chunky wooden tables sit slightly above the market hubbub but in full view of its appetite-whetting stalls, and country-style daily specials exploit the freshest farm goodies available.

## Drinking

**Old Brewery Tavern** ( ☎ 01227-826682; Abode Canterbury, 30-33 High St) Trendy boozer in a large open space adorned with black-and-white prints of brewery workers of old and a white-brick courtyard with a huge curved wood and soft leather sofa. The choice of beers is plentiful, and there's a good wine list as well as a solid menu of English pub classics like fish pie and gammon, egg and chips – albeit a swanky version. Enter from White Horse Lane.

**Thomas Becket** ( ☎ 01227-464384; 21 Best Lane) A classic English pub with a garden's worth of hops hanging from its timber frame, several quality ales to sample and a traditional decor of copper pots, comfy seating and a fireplace to cosy up to on winter nights. It also serves decent pub grub (mains £6 to £9).

## Entertainment

**Alberry's Wine Bar** ( ☎ 01227-452378; St Margaret's St) Every night is different at this after-hours music bar that puts on everything from smooth live jazz to DJ-led drum and bass to commercial pop. It's a two-level place where you can relax over a French Kiss (cocktail or otherwise) above, before partying in the basement bar below.

**Orange St Music Club** ( ☎ 01227-760801; www.orangestreetmusic.com; 15 Orange St; ☺ Tue-Sat) This Bohemian music and cultural venue in a 19th-century hall puts on a medley of jazz, salsa, folk, DJ competitions, comedy and even poetry.

**Marlowe Theatre** ( ☎ 01227-787787; www.marlowetheatre.com; The Friars) Canterbury's central venue for performing arts brings in touring plays, dances, concerts and musicals year-round.

## Getting There & Away

Canterbury is 58 miles from London and 15 miles from Margate and Dover.

### BUS

The bus station is just within the city walls on St George's Lane. There are frequent buses to London Victoria (£12.70, two hours, hourly) and services to Dover (£5.20, 35 minutes, hourly). There are also buses to Margate (53 minutes, three per hour), Broadstairs (one hour, twice hourly), Ramsgate (80 minutes, twice hourly) and Whitstable (30 minutes, every 15 minutes).

### TRAIN

There are two train stations: Canterbury East (for the YHA hostel), accessible from London Victoria; and Canterbury West, accessible from London's Charing Cross and Waterloo East stations.

London-bound trains leave frequently (£20.90, 1½ hours, two to three hourly), as do Canterbury East to Dover Priory trains (£6.70, 16 to 28 minutes, every 30 minutes).

Canterbury will be a stop on the UK's first high-speed rail line, with trains pulling in at London St Pancras from late 2009. It is expected to reduce journey times significantly.

**THE CANTERBURY TALES**

If English literature has a father figure, then it is Geoffrey Chaucer (1342/3–1400). Chaucer was the first English writer to introduce characters – rather than 'types' – into fiction, and he did so to greatest effect in his most popular work, *The Canterbury Tales.*

Written between 1387 and his death, the *Tales* is an unfinished series of 24 vivid stories as told by a party of pilgrims on their journey from London to Canterbury and back. Chaucer successfully created the illusion that the pilgrims, not Chaucer (though he appears in the tales as himself), are telling the stories, which allowed him unprecedented freedom as an author.

Chaucer's achievement remains a high point of European literature, but it was also the first time that English came to match Latin (the language of the Church) and French (spoken by the Norman court) as a language of high literature. *The Canterbury Tales* remains one of the pillars of the literary canon, but more than that it's a collection of rollicking good yarns of adultery, debauchery, crime and edgy romance, and filled with Chaucer's witty observances of human nature. That said, contemporary modern readers tend to make more sense of modern translations than the often obscure original Middle English version.

SOUTHEAST ENGLAND

### Getting Around

Canterbury's centre is mostly pedestrianised. Car parks are dotted along and just within the walls, otherwise parking is by pay and display. Day trippers may prefer to use one of the city's three Park & Ride sites, which cost £2.50 per day and are connected to the centre by buses every 10 minutes from 7am to 7.30pm Monday to Saturday, and 10am to 6pm Sunday.

Taxi companies include **Cathedral Cars** (☎ 01227-451000) and **Cabwise** (☎ 01227-712929). **Downland Cycles** (☎ 01227-479643; www.downlandcycles.co.uk; 9.30am-5pm Mon-Sat, 10am-4.30pm Sun) rents bikes from the Malthouse on St Stephen's Rd. Bikes cost £12 per day with helmet.

## WHITSTABLE

**pop 30,159**

Best known for its succulent oysters, which have been harvested here since Roman times, pretty little Whitstable has transformed into a popular destination for weekending metropolitans, attracted by the clapboard houses, pretty shingle beach and candy-coloured beach huts that line the shoreline. The town has nevertheless managed to retain the character of a working fishing town – its thriving harbour and fish market (Whitstable's famous oysters are harvested between September and April) coexist with boutiques, organic delis and swanky restaurants.

### Information

The **tourist office** (☎ 01227-275482; www.visitwhitstable.co.uk; 7 Oxford St; 10am-5pm Mon-Sat Jul & Aug, to 4pm Mon-Sat Sep-Jun) can help you find and book accommodation, though at the time of writing there were plans to shut the office down, in which case Canterbury would become the nearest tourist office. The nearby **library** (☎ 01227-273309; 31-33 Oxford St; 9am-6pm Mon-Fri, to 5pm Sat, 10am-4pm Sun) can make you a temporary member to use its internet terminals.

### Sights & Activities

The modest **Whitstable Museum & Gallery** (☎ 01227-276998; www.whitstable-museum.co.uk; 8 Oxford St; admission free; 10am-4pm Mon-Sat year-round, 1-4pm Sun Jul & Aug) has good exhibits on Whitstable's oyster and fishing industry as well as a corner dedicated to the actor Peter Cushing, the town's most famous resident, who died in 1994.

For a week at the end of July, the town hosts seafood, arts and music extravaganza, the **Whitstable Oyster Festival** (www.whitstableoysterfestival.co.uk), offering a packed schedule of events, from history walks, crab-catching and oyster-eating competitions to a beer festival and traditional 'blessing of the waters'.

### Sleeping & Eating

**Hotel Continental** (☎ 01227-280280; www.hotelcontinental.co.uk; 29 Beach Walk; s/d/huts from £60/70/100, d with sea view & balcony £100; P) The rooms in this elegant seaside art-deco building are nothing special – come for the quirky converted fishermen's huts right on the beach. Room rates increase by £15 to £100 a night during high season.

**Crab & Winkle** (☎ 0845-257 1587; South Quay, the Harbour; mains £12-18; noon-9pm) Sitting above the fish market in a black clapboard house, this bright restaurant has large windows overlooking the harbour, a buzzing vibe and excellent seafood with a few options for meat-lovers thrown in.

## Getting There & Away

Buses 4 and 6 go to Canterbury (30 minutes) every 15 minutes.

# ISLE OF THANET

You won't need a ferry or a wetsuit to reach this island, which was swallowed by the mainland during the first millennium as the Watsun Channel dried up. It now forms a perky peninsula jutting out to sea at the far eastern tip of the country. But in its island days, Thanet was the springboard to several epoch-making episodes of English history. It was here that the Romans kicked off their invasion in the first century AD, and where Augustine landed in AD 597 to begin his conversion of the pagans. These days, Thanet's pretty coastline is home to a string of Victorian resorts that are only invaded by the summer bathing-suit brigade. Walkers can also look to conquer the **Thanet Coastal Path**, a 20-mile trail that hugs the shore from Margate to Pegwell Bay via Broadstairs and Ramsgate.

## Margate

pop 57,000

A popular seaside resort for over 250 years thanks to its fine-sand beaches, Margate's tatty seafront and amusement arcades seem somewhat removed from the candy-striped beach huts and crowd-pleasing Punch and Judy puppet shows of its Victorian heyday. Major cultural regeneration projects – including a spectacular new Turner Contemporary art gallery – should reverse the town's fortunes.

Visit the **tourist office** ( ☎ 01843-292019; www.tourism.thanet.gov.uk; 12-13 The Parade; ✆ 9.15am-4.15pm Mon-Fri, 10am-4pm Sat) for maps and information.

### SIGHTS

Margate's unique attraction is the mysterious, subterranean **Shell Grotto** ( ☎ 01843-220008; www.shellgrotto.co.uk; Grotto Hill; adult/child £2.50/1.50; ✆ 10am-5pm daily Easter-Oct, 11am-4pm Sat & Sun Nov-Easter) Discovered in 1835, it's a claustrophobic collection of rooms and passageways embedded with millions of shells arranged in symbol-rich mosaics. It has inspired feverish speculation over the years but presents few answers; some think it a 2000-year-old pagan temple, others

an elaborate 19th-century hoax. Either way, it's an exquisite place worth seeing.

A new **Turner Contemporary** ( ☎ 01843-294208; www.turnercontemporary.org) gallery – to highlight the town's links with the artist JMW Turner – is due to open in 2010.

In the meantime, Turner Contemporary exhibitions take place at the **Turner Contemporary Project Space** (53-57 High St) and **Droit House** (Stone Pier).

### GETTING THERE & AWAY

Buses to Margate leave from London Victoria (£12.10, 2½ hours, five daily). From Canterbury, take bus 8 (55 minutes, three hourly).

Trains run twice hourly from London Victoria and less frequently from Charing Cross (£23.90, one hour 50 minutes). Margate is due to be joined to London St Pancras from December 2009 when the UK's first high-speed rail line opens.

## Broadstairs

pop 24,370

Unlike its bigger, brasher neighbours, the charming resort village of Broadstairs revels in its quaintness, plays the Victorian nostalgia card at every opportunity, and names every second business after the works of its most famous holidaymaker, Charles Dickens. The town's elegant cliff-top buildings, neatly manicured gardens, wide saffron-sand bay and wistful Punch and Judy shows, however, hide a far grittier history of smuggling and shipbuilding.

The **tourist office** ( ☎ 01843-861232; 2 Victoria Pde, Dickens House Museum; ✆ 10am-5pm daily Jun-Sep, 10am-5pm Wed-Sat Sep-Apr, 10am-5pm Tue-Sat Apr-Jun) has details of the annual, weeklong **Dickens Festival** in mid-June which culminates in a banquet-cum-ball in Victorian dress (£18). It's located in the quaint **Dickens House Museum** ( ☎ 01843-861232; www.dickenshouse.co.uk; 2 Victoria Pde; adult/child £2.50/1.30; ✆ 10am-5pm Apr-Oct), which was actually the home of Mary Pearson Strong, inspiration for the character of Betsey Trotwood in *David Copperfield*. Diverse Dickensiana on display includes letters from the author.

### SLEEPING & EATING

**East Horndon Hotel** ( ☎ 01843-868306; www.easthorndonhotel.com; 4 Eastern Esplanade; s/d £35/66; ☐ wi-fi) This elegant hotel sits on manicured lawns a few yards from the beach. The comfortable rooms are slightly bland but have sea views to make up for it, several with little balconies where you can sit out to enjoy the sun set over the bay.

**Tartar Frigate** ( ☎ 01843-862013; 42 Harbour St; mains £14-16.50) Dating back to the 18th century, this seafront pub is a great place to be in summer when tourists and locals alike spill out onto the beach. The seafood restaurant upstairs has excellent food and great views of the bay and the pub has regular live folk music.

### GETTING THERE & AWAY

The Thanet Loop bus runs every 10 minutes through the day to Ramsgate (£2, 20 minutes) and Margate (£2, 20 minutes).

Bus 8 runs to Canterbury (1½ hours, three per hour) via Margate and bus 9 via Ramsgate (hourly). National Express buses leave High St for London Victoria (£12.10, three hours, five daily).

Trains run to London Victoria (£25.80, 110 minutes, twice hourly) and there are less frequent services to London Bridge and Charing Cross. You may have to change at Ramsgate.

## Ramsgate
pop 38,200

The most diverse of Kent's coastal towns, Ramsgate has a friendlier feel than rival Margate and is more vibrant than quaint little neighbour Broadstairs. A forest of sails whistle serenely in the breeze below the town's handsome curved harbour walls, surrounded by laid-back seafront bars and cosmopolitan street cafes that give the town a tang of nearby France. History buffs are kept busy by the town's neo-Gothic architecture and rich maritime heritage, while the town's wide Blue Flag beaches appeal to families, sun worshippers and surfers.

You'll find the **tourist office** ( ☎ 01843-583333; www.tourism.thanet.gov.uk; 17 Albert Ct; ☻ 9am-5pm daily Jun-Sep, Tue-Sat Apr & May, to 12.15pm Wed-Sat Sep-Mar) in a small alleyway off Leopold St.

When the sun's out, rollerbladers, surfers and sunbathers all head to the east of the main harbour where Ramsgate's reddish-sand-and-shingle beach and elegant promenade sit under an imposing cliff.

The **Ramsgate Maritime Museum** ( ☎ 01843-290399; www.ekmt.fogonline.co.uk; The Clock House, Royal Harbour; adult/child £1.50/75p; ☻ 10am-5pm Tue-Sun Easter-Sep, 11am-4.30pm Thu-Sun Oct-Easter) is inside the town's 19th-century clock tower near the harbour. Here, too, is a line marking Ramsgate's own meridian (the town has its own Ramsgate Mean Time).

### SLEEPING

**Glendevon Guesthouse** ( ☎ 01843-570909; www.glen devonguesthouse.co.uk; 8 Truro Rd; s/d from £55/55) This ecofriendly guesthouse run by energetic and outgoing young hosts is a 10-minute stroll from the action down at the harbour. The hallways of this grand Victorian house are decorated with watercolours by local artists, and there are bookshelves full of games, books and videos to borrow. All the rooms have very comfy beds and small kitchens, and breakfast is a convivial affair taken around one large table.

**our pick Royal Harbour Hotel** ( ☎ 01843-591514; www.royalharbourhotel.co.uk; Nelson Crescent; s/d from £65/85, superior £100-215; ☐ wi-fi) Occupying two regency town houses on a glorious seafront crescent, this boutique hotel feels enveloped in warmth and quirkiness – an eclectic collection of books, magazines, games and artwork line the hotel, and there's a gramophone with old LPs and an honesty bar in the lounge, complimentary cheese and biscuits in the evening and hot water bottles when it's chilly. Rooms range from tiny nauticalesque 'cabins' to country-house style, four-poster doubles, most with postcard views over the forest of masts below.

### GETTING THERE & AWAY

National Express bus 22 runs to London Victoria (£12.70, three hours, five daily) via Margate and Broadstairs. There are also local buses to Canterbury, Broadstairs and Ramsgate. Trains run to London Victoria and Charing Cross (£25.80, 1¾ to two hours, twice hourly).

There's also a ferry service to Ostend in Belgium run by **Transeuropa Ferries** ( ☎ 01843-595522; www.transeuropaferries.com; 4 per day) from Ramsgate New Port just west of the centre (from £36 per passenger with car, five hours).

When the UK's first high-speed rail line opens (due for late 2009 at the time of writing), there will be a direct link between Ramsgate and London St Pancras, which should significantly reduce journey times.

## Deal

Julius Caesar and his armies set foot on Deal's peaceful shingle beach in 55 BC, for their first exploratory dip into Britain. Today there's a gorgeous little 16th-century **castle** (EH; ☎ 01304-372762; Victoria Rd; adult/5-15yr/under 5yr £4.20/2.10/free; ☼ 10am-6pm Apr-Sep) with curvaceous bastions that form petals in a Tudor-rose shape. Far from delicate, however, it's the largest and most complete link of Henry VIII's chain of defence on the south coast.

And hardly a mile south is another link in the 16th-century coastal defences, **Walmer Castle** (EH; ☎ 01304-364288; Kingsdown Rd; adult/5-15yr/under 5yr £6.50/3.30/free; ☼ 10am-6pm Apr-Sep, to 4pm Wed-Sun Mar & Oct), the much-altered and really rather lavish official residence of the warden of the Cinque Ports. English hero, the Duke of Wellington, died here.

## DOVER

### pop 39,078

As a town itself, depressing Dover's air of decay and run-down, post-war architecture has little to offer to travellers, most of whom pass quickly through on their way to, and from, the Continent. Lucky, then, that the town has a couple of stellar attractions to redeem it. The port's vital strategic position so close to mainland Europe gave rise to a sprawling hilltop castle, with some 2000 years of history to its credit. Also here are the spectacular white cliffs that are as much a symbol of English wartime resilience as Winston Churchill or the Battle of Britain.

### Orientation

Dover Castle dominates the town from a high promontory east of town, above the white cliffs. Ferry departures are from the Eastern Docks southeast of the castle. Dover Priory train station is a short walk west of the centre. The bus station is on Pencester Rd.

### Information

Banks and ATMs are located on Market Sq.
**Mangle laundrette** (21 Worthington St; per load £4; ☼ 8am-8pm)
**Post office** (Pencester Rd; ☼ 9am-5.30pm Mon-Sat)

**Tourist office** ( ☎ 01304-205108; www.whitecliffs country.org.uk; Biggin St; ☼ 9am-5.30pm daily Jun-Aug, 9am-5.30pm Mon-Fri, 10am-4pm Sat & Sun Sep-May) Located in the Old Town Gaol on Biggin St and has accommodation and ferry-booking services (both free).
**White Cliffs Medical Centre** ( ☎ 01304-201705; 143 Folkestone Rd)

## Sights & Activities

### DOVER CASTLE

The almost impenetrable **Dover Castle** (EH; ☎ 01304-211067; adult/5-15yr/under 5yr £10.30/5.20/free; ☼ 10am-6pm daily Apr-Sep, to 5pm daily Oct, to 4pm Thu-Mon Nov-Mar; Ⓟ ), one of the most impressive in England, was built to bolster the country's weakest point at this, the shortest sea-crossing to mainland Europe. It sprawls across the city's hilltop, commanding a tremendous view of the English Channel as far as the French coastline.

The site has been in use for as many as 2000 years. On the vast grounds are the remains of a **Roman lighthouse** that dates from AD 50 and may be the oldest standing building in Britain. Beside it lies a restored **Saxon church**.

The robust 12th-century **keep**, with walls up to 7m thick, is filled with reconstructed scenes of Henry VIII's visit, and its base shelters a sound-and-light re-creation of a brutal 13th-century siege. But it's the warren of claustrophobic **secret wartime tunnels** under the castle that are the biggest draw. Excellent 50-minute tours delve into the hillside passageways, which were first excavated during the Napoleonic Wars and then expanded to house a command post and hospital in WWII. They now house reconstructed scenes of their wartime use, complete with sounds, smells and erratic lighting. One of Britain's most famous wartime operations, code-named Dynamo, was directed from here in 1940. It saw the evacuation of hundreds of thousands of troops from the French beaches of Dunkirk.

Buses 90C and 111 run from Dover Priory station to the castle.

### ROMAN PAINTED HOUSE

Some of the most extensive, if stunted, Roman wall paintings north of the Alps are on show at the **Roman Painted House** ( ☎ 01304-203279; New St; adult/child £2/80p; ☼ 10am-5pm Tue-Sun Apr-Sep), although they're housed in an amateurish museum. Several scenes depict Bacchus (the god of wine and revelry), which makes perfect sense as this large villa was built around

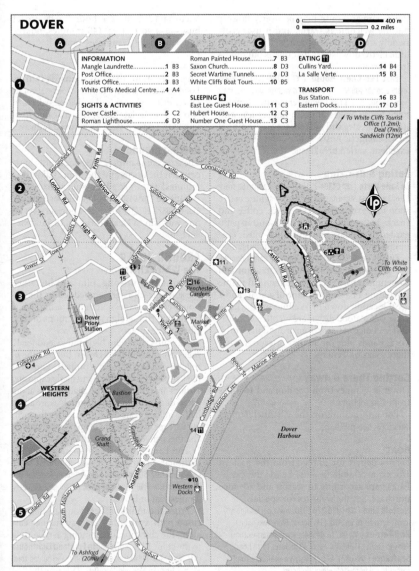

## DOVER

0 — 400 m
0 — 0.2 miles

**INFORMATION**
Mangle Laundrette.................**1** B3
Post Office.................**2** B3
Tourist Office.................**3** B3
White Cliffs Medical Centre.....**4** A4

**SIGHTS & ACTIVITIES**
Dover Castle.................**5** C2
Roman Lighthouse.................**6** D3

Roman Painted House.............**7** B3
Saxon Church.................**8** D3
Secret Wartime Tunnels.........**9** D3
White Cliffs Boat Tours.........**10** B5

**SLEEPING**
East Lee Guest House.............**11** C3
Hubert House.................**12** C3
Number One Guest House.....**13** C3

**EATING**
Cullins Yard.................**14** B4
La Salle Verte.................**15** B3

**TRANSPORT**
Bus Station.................**16** B3
Eastern Docks.................**17** D3

To White Cliffs Tourist Office (1.2mi); Deal (7mi); Sandwich (12mi)

To White Cliffs (50m)

**SOUTHEAST ENGLAND**

AD 200 as a *mansio* (hotel) for travellers in need of a little lubrication to unwind.

## Sleeping

B&Bs are clustered along Castle St, Maison Dieu Rd and Folkestone Rd.

**Number One Guest House** ( ☎ 01304-202007; www .number1guesthouse.co.uk; 1 Castle Street; d from £45; **P** )

Set in a grand Georgian town house at the foot of Dover Castle, with rooms decorated in traditional Victorian style. There's also a pretty walled garden with lovely views, and breakfast is served in bed.

**Hubert House** ( ☎ 01304-202253; www.hubert house.co.uk; 9 Castle Hill Rd; s/d incl breakfast from £40/55; **P** **☐** wi-fi) The comfortable bedrooms in this Georgian house may be overly flowery but the welcome is warm, and it uses eco-friendly and fair-trade products. It has its own little bistro downstairs that opens out onto a front terrace.

**East Lee Guest House** ( ☎ 01304-210176; www .eastlee.co.uk; 108 Maison Dieu Rd; d with/without breakfast from £55/50; **P** ) This lovely terracotta-shingled town house makes quite an impression with its grand, elegantly decorated communal areas, energetic hosts, super-comfy beds and excellent, varied breakfasts.

## Eating & Drinking

**La Salle Verte** ( ☎ 01304-201547; 14-15 Cannon St; snack £2-6; ⏲ 9am-4.30pm daily) The funkiest little coffee shop in Dover serves great cakes, coffee and snacks both inside and in a little suntrap patio garden. It also lays on regular live-music evenings showcasing local Kent musicians.

**Cullins Yard** ( ☎ 01304-211666; 11 Cambridge Rd; ⏲ 10am-midnight daily) This bar, restaurant and sometime music venue has a nautical theme (including a bar in the shape of a boat) and a great location down by Wellington Docks. A variety of seafood dishes are on offer as well as a wide choice of beers from around the world. Local bands play on Sunday afternoons and there's jazz on Fridays.

## Getting There & Away

Dover is 75 miles from London and 15 miles from Canterbury.

For information on the Channel Tunnel services, see p998.

### BOAT

Ferries depart for France from the Eastern Docks (accessible by bus) below the castle. Fares vary according to season and advance purchase. See the websites for specials.

**Norfolk Line** ( ☎ 0870-870 1020; www.norfolkline .com) Services to Dunkirk (1¾ hours, every two hours).

**P&O Ferries** ( ☎ 08716-645645; www.poferries.com) Runs to Calais (1½ hours, every 40 minutes to an hour).

**Seafrance** ( ☎ 0871-423 7119; www.seafrance.com) Ferries to Calais roughly every 1½ hours.

**SpeedFerries** ( ☎ 0871-222 7456; www.speedferries .com) Services to Boulogne (50 minutes, up to five daily).

### BUS

Dover's **bus station** (Pencester Rd) is in the heart of town. Stagecoach East Kent has a Canterbury to Dover service (35 minutes, hourly). National Express run 20 daily coaches from London

Victoria (£12.10, 2¾ hours). Stagecoach buses also go to Deal (40 minutes, hourly) and Sandwich (55 minutes, hourly).

### TRAIN

There are more than 40 trains daily from London Victoria and Charing Cross stations to Dover Priory via Ashford and Sevenoaks (£26, two hours). In late 2009, Dover is due to be linked to London via a high-speed railway.

## Getting Around

The ferry companies run regular shuttle buses between the docks and the train station (five minutes) as they're a long walk apart.

**Heritage** ( ☎ 01304-204420) and **Star Taxis** ( ☎ 01304-228822, 201010) have 24-hour services. A one-way trip to Deal costs £15; to Sandwich it's £20.

# AROUND DOVER
## The White Cliffs

Immortalised in song, film and literature, these iconic cliffs are embedded in the national consciousness, acting as a big, white 'Welcome Home' sign to generations of travellers and soldiers.

The cliffs rise 100m high and extend for 10 miles on either side of Dover, but it is the 6-mile stretch east of town – properly known as the Langdon Cliffs – that particularly captivates visitors' imaginations. The chalk here is about 250m deep, and the cliffs themselves are about half-a-million years old, formed when the melting ice caps of northern Europe were gouging a channel between France and England.

The Langdon Cliffs are managed by the National Trust, which has a **tourist office** ( ☎ 01304-202756; admission free; ⏲ 10am-5pm Mar-Oct, 11am-4pm Nov-Feb) and **car park** (£3 for non-members) 2 miles east of Dover.

From the tourist office, you can follow a stony path as it winds its way further east along the cliff tops for a bracing 2-mile walk to the stout Victorian **South Foreland Lighthouse** (NT; ☎ 01304-215484; adult/child £4/2; ⏲ guided tours 11am-5.30pm Fri-Mon mid-Mar–Oct). This was the first lighthouse to be powered by electricity, and site of the first international radio transmissions in 1898.

The cliffs are 2 miles east of Dover along Castle Hill Rd and the A258 road to Deal or off the A2 past the Eastern Docks. Buses 113 and 90/1 from Dover stop near the main entrance.

**ENGLISH WINE**

Mention English wine not too long ago and you'd likely hear a snort of derision. Not any more. Thanks to warmer temperatures and determined winemakers, English wine, particularly of the sparkling variety, is developing a fan base all of its own.

Legend has it that the Romans first brought over grapevine cuttings 2000 years ago, and that vineyards blossomed in English soil. But by the time the 20th century rolled around, there wasn't a wine producer in sight – until some bright spark started planting vines again in the 1950s.

These days, there are more than 400 English vineyards, and interest (and sales) in domestic wine has grown dramatically, with the likes of Nyetimber, Chapel Down and Ridgeview enjoying award-winning success around the world.

The best vineyards are in the south, particularly Sussex, Essex and Kent, whose chalky soil is likened to the Champagne region in France. Many vineyards now offer tours and wine tastings. Two of the most popular are **Chapel Down Vinery** ( ☎ 01580-763 033; www.englishwinesgroup.com; adult/child £6.50/2; ☽ tours Jun-Sep) and **Denbies Wine Estate** ( ☎ 01306-876 616; www.denbiesvineyard. co.uk; adult/child £7.25/3; ☽ tours year-round).

To see the cliffs in all their full-frontal glory, **White Cliffs Boat Tours** ( ☎ 01303-271388; www .whitecliffsboattours.co.uk; adult/child £6/3; ☽ daily Jul & Aug, Sat & Sun Apr-Jun, Sep & Oct) runs 40-minute water tours at 10am, noon, 2pm and 4pm from the Western Docks.

## THE KENT WEALD

Taking its name from an old German world *wald*, meaning 'forest', the Weald, as it's known by locals, is all out of woodland these days, but you'll find postcard villages, manicured lawns and ripe fields. The region also has more than its fair share of country estates, castles and gardens.

### Down House

Charles Darwin's home from 1842 until his death in 1882, **Down House** (EH; ☎ 01689-869119; adult/5-14yr £7.20/3.60; ☽ 11am-5pm daily Jul & Aug, 11am-5pm Wed-Sun Mar-Jun, Sep & Oct, closed Nov-Feb) witnessed the development of Darwin's theory of evolution by natural selection. The house and gardens have been restored to look much as they would have in Darwin's time, including Darwin's study, where he undertook much of his reading and writing; the drawing room, where he tried out some of his indoor experiments; and the gardens and greenhouse, where some of his outdoor experiments are recreated. There are three self-guided trails in the area, where you can follow in the great man's footsteps. You can pick up trail booklets at the house. At the time of writing, the UK was putting forward Down House, Downe village and the surrounding area as its World Heritage Site Nomination bid for

2009, the year that sees the 200th anniversary of Darwin's birth and the 150th anniversary of the publication of the *Origin of the Species*, his seminal work.

Down House is in Luxted Rd, Downe, off the A21. Take bus 146 from Bromley North or Bromley South railway station, or service R8 from Orpington.

### Chartwell

The home of Sir Winston Churchill from 1924 until his death in 1965, **Chartwell** ( ☎ 01732-868 381; Westerham; adult/child £11.20/5.60, garden & studio only £5.60/2.80; ☽ 11am-5pm Wed-Sun Apr-Jun, Sep & Oct, Tue-Sun Jul & Aug), 6 miles east of Sevenoaks, offers a breathtakingly intimate insight into the life of England's famous cigar-chomping bombast.

This 19th-century house and its rambling grounds have been preserved much as Winnie left them, full of books, pictures, maps and personal mementos. Churchill was also a prolific painter and his daubings are scattered throughout the house and fill the garden studio.

Transport options are limited without a car. Kent Passenger Services bus 238 runs from Sevenoaks train station (30 minutes, every two hours) on Wednesdays from May to mid-September. Arriva 401 runs on Sundays and bank holiday Mondays only.

### Hever Castle

This idyllic little **castle** ( ☎ 01732-865224; www .hevercastle.co.uk; adult/5-14yr £11.50/6.30, gardens only £9.30/6; ☽ noon-5pm Mar-Oct, to 4pm Nov) seems to have leapt right out of a film set. It's encircled by a narrow moat and surrounded by family-friendly gardens, complete with cute topiary of woodland creatures and wandering ducks and swans.

The castle is famous for being the child-hood home of Anne Boleyn, mistress to Henry VIII and then his doomed queen. It dates from 1270, with a Tudor house added in 1505 by the Bullen (Boleyn) family. The castle later fell into disrepair until 1903, when American multimillionaire William Waldorf Astor bought it, pouring obscene amounts of money into a massive refurbishment. The exterior is unchanged from Tudor times, but the interior is thick with Edwardian panelling.

From London Bridge trains go direct to Hever (£8.50, 40 minutes, hourly), a poorly signposted 1-mile walk from the castle; and to Edenbridge (£8.50, 50 minutes), from where it's a 4-mile taxi or bike ride. If you're driving, Hever Castle is 3 miles off the B2026 near Edenbridge.

## Leeds Castle

This immense moated pile is, for many, the world's most romantic **castle** ( ☎ 01622-765 400; www.leeds-castle.com; adult/4-15yr/senior & student £15/9.50/12.50; ☻ 10.30am-6pm Apr-Oct, to 4pm Nov-Mar), and it's certainly one of the most visited in Britain. While it looks formidable enough from the outside – a hefty structure balancing on two islands amid a large lake and sprawling estate – it's actually known as something of a 'ladies castle'. This stems from the fact that in its over 1000 years of history, it has been home to a who's who of medieval queens, most famously Henry VIII's first wife, Catherine of Aragon.

The castle was transformed from fortress to lavish palace over the centuries, and its last owner, the high-society hostess Lady Baillie, used it as a princely family home and party pad to entertain the likes of Errol Flynn, Douglas Fairbanks and JFK.

The castle's vast estate offers enough attractions of its own to justify a day trip: peaceful walks, a duckery, aviary and falconry demonstrations. You'll also find a quirky dog-collar museum and a hedge maze, overseen by a grassy bank where fellow travellers can shout encouragement or misdirections.

Since Lady Baillie's death in 1974, a private trust has managed the property. This means that some parts of the castle are periodically closed for private events.

Leeds Castle is just east of Maidstone. National Express runs one direct bus daily from London Victoria coach station, leaving at 9am and returning at 3pm (£12.30, 1½ hours). It must be prebooked. There is a combined entrance and bus-fare ticket that costs £22.

You can also get a train from London Bridge, London Victoria or London Cannon St to Bearstead (£15, 50 minutes) from where you can catch a connecting coach to the castle (£5 return).

# EAST SUSSEX

Home to lush countryside, medieval villages and gorgeous coastline, this lovely corner of the country is besieged by weekending Londoners whenever the weather is fine. Here you'll find an air of romance amid the cobbled medieval streets of Rye, historic Battle, where William the Conqueror first engaged the Saxons in 1066, and the breathtaking white cliffs of Beachy Head, near the civilised seaside town of Eastbourne. Brighton, a highlight of a visit here, offers vibrant nightlife, offbeat shopping and shingly shores. But you needn't follow the crowds to enjoy East Sussex. It's just as rewarding to get off the beaten track, linger along its winding country lanes and stretch your legs across the rolling South Downs.

## RYE
pop 4195

If you're searching for a perfect example of a medieval village, look no further than Rye. Once a Cinque Port, this exquisitely pretty place looks as if it's been pickled, put on a shelf and promptly forgotten about by old Father Time. Even the most hardened cynic can't fail to be bewitched by Rye's cobbled lanes, mysterious passageways and crooked half-timbered Tudor buildings. Romantics can lap up the townsfolk's tales of resident smugglers, ghosts, writers and artists, and hole up in one of a slew of gorgeous accommodation in its heart.

The town sits prettily atop a rocky outcrop, and sheep graze where the waters once lapped. If you do visit – and you absolutely should – try to avoid summer weekends when hoards of day-trippers dilute the town's time-warp effect.

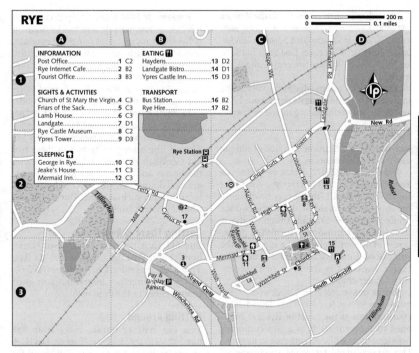

**RYE**

0 — 200 m
0 — 0.1 miles

SOUTHEAST ENGLAND

## Information

The **tourist office** ( ☎ 01797-226696; www.visitrye.co.uk; Strand Quay; ⏰ 10am-5pm Apr-Oct, to 4pm Nov, Dec & Mar, to 3pm Jan & Feb) runs a town-model audiovisual history for £3. More fun is the freaky collection of penny-in-the-slot novelty machines upstairs. It also sells a *Rye Town Walk* map (£1), and rents out multilingual audio tours (adult/child £3/1).

You can get online at **Rye Internet Cafe** ( ☎ 01797-224276; 46 Ferry Rd; per min 5p; ⏰ 8am-10pm Mon-Sat, 10am-9pm Sun). The **post office** ( ⏰ 8.30am-5.30pm Mon-Fri, to 1pm Sat) is on Cinque Ports St.

## Sights

From the tourist office, turn your back to the water, go through Strand Quay and wobble up the cobblestones of famous **Mermaid St**, bristling with 15th-century timber-framed houses with quirky house names such as 'The House with Two Front Doors' and 'The House Opposite'.

Turn right at the T-junction for the striking Georgian **Lamb House** (NT; ☎ 01797-229542; West St; adult/child £3.50/1.80; ⏰ 2-6pm Thu & Sat late Mar–Oct), a favourite stomping ground for local apparitions, but not that of its most famous resident,

American writer Henry James, who lived here from 1898 to 1916, during which he wrote *The Wings of the Dove*.

Continue around the dog-leg into cobbled Church Sq, ringed by historic houses, including the **Friars of the Sack**, which was once part of a 13th-century Augustinian friary but is now a private home. The pretty **Church of St Mary the Virgin** ( ⏰ 9am-6pm Apr-Sep, to 4pm Oct-Mar) is a hotchpotch of medieval and later styles and its turret clock is the oldest in England (1561) still working with its original pendulum mechanism. You can climb the Church tower (adult/child £2/free) for great views of the town and surrounding countryside.

Turn right at the square's east corner for the sandcastle archetype **Ypres Tower** (tower & museum adult/child £3/1.80; ⏰ 10.30am-5pm Thu-Mon Apr-Oct, 10.30am-3.30pm Sat & Sun Nov-Mar), pronounced 'wipers'. This 13th-century building has great views over Romney Marsh and Rye Bay, and houses one part of Rye Castle Museum. It's overseen by a friendly warden, who's full of colourful tales from the tower's long history as fort, prison, mortuary and museum (the last two at overlapping times).

The other branch of the **Rye Castle Museum** ( ☎ 01797-226728; www.ryemuseum.co.uk; 3 East St; adult/child £2.50/1.80; ☺ 10.30am-1pm & 2-5pm Thu-Mon Apr-Oct), a short stroll away on East St, is home to an 18th-century leather fire engine and other intriguing loot.

At the northeastern edge of the village, the thickset pale-stone **Landgate** dates from 1329, and is the only remaining gate out of four.

## Sleeping

Rye boasts an exceptional choice of unique historic accommodation.

**Jeake's House** ( ☎ 01797-222828; www.jeakeshouse .com; Mermaid St; s/d from £55/110; P ) An inviting, ivy-drenched 17th-century town house on cobbled Mermaid St, Jeake's was once home to US poet Conrad Aitken. Today it lives life as a handsomely furnished guesthouse. You can literally take a pew in the snug book-lined bar, and, continuing the theme, breakfast is served in an 18th-century former chapel.

**George in Rye** ( ☎ 01797-224065; www.thegeorgeinrye.com; 98 High St; d from £125; ☐ wi-fi) This coaching inn at the heart of Rye has managed to reinvent itself as a contemporary boutique hotel while staying true to its roots. Downstairs, an old-fashioned wood-panelled lounge is warmed by roaring log fires, while the bedrooms are chic and understated with the odd splash of psychedelic colour. The George's restaurant – dealing in contemporary Sussex-sourced food and good English wines – can compete with the best Rye has to offer.

**Mermaid Inn** ( ☎ 01797-223065; www.mermaidinn .com; Mermaid St; d £150-240; P ) Few inns can claim to be as atmospheric as this ancient hostelry, dating from 1420. Every room is different – but each is thick with dark beams, lit by leaded windows and some graced by secret passageways that now act as fire escapes. Small wonder it's such a popular spot – these days you're as likely to spot a celeb or a royal as the resident ghost.

## Eating & Drinking

**Ypres Castle Inn** ( ☎ 01797-223248; www.yprescastleinn .co.uk; Gun Gardens; meals £7-15; ☺ noon-3pm & 6-9pm) You can have a match on a boules pitch, enjoy some live bands or chow down on scrumptious seasonal food like Rye bay scallops at this warm, country-style pub. The beer's not bad either.

**Haydens** ( ☎ 01797-224501; 108 High St; snacks/meals from £3/9; ☺ 10am-5pm daily, dinner Fri & Sat) Staunch believers in organic and fair-trade produce, these guys dish up delicious omelettes, ploughman's lunches, salads and pancakes in their light, breezy cafe. There's a wonderful elevated terrace at the back with great views over the town and surrounding countryside.

**Landgate Bistro** ( ☎ 01797-222829; www.landgate bistro.co.uk; 5/6 Landgate; mains £13-15.50; ☺ dinner Tue-Sat & Sun before bank holiday, lunch Sat & Sun) There's fine dining to be had in these two old Georgian cottages. Take a seat among the beams and exposed brickwork of their graceful dining room for a top-notch feast of local delights such as game, Dover sole and Romney Marsh lamb.

## Getting There & Away

Bus 711 runs between Dover (two hours, hourly) and Hastings (30 minutes) via Rye. Trains run to London Charing Cross (£22.60, two hours, three per hour), but you must change either in Hastings or Ashford.

## Getting Around

You can rent all-terrain bikes from **Rye Hire** ( ☎ 01797-223033; 1 Cyprus Pl; per day/4 hrs £12/8; ☺ 8am-5pm Mon-Fri, 8am-noon Sat). Call ahead for Sunday hire.

# BATTLE

pop 5190

This little, unassuming village has a monumental place in British history. Battle grew up around the point where invading French duke William of Normandy, aka William the Conqueror, scored a decisive victory over local King Harold in 1066, so beginning Norman rule and changing the face of the country forever.

The train station is a short walk from High St, and is well signposted. The **tourist office** ( ☎ 01424-773721; Gatehouse; ☺ 10am-6pm Apr-Sep, to 4pm Oct-Mar) is next to Battle Abbey. The post office, banks and ATMs are also on High St.

Another day, another photogenic ruin? Hardly. On this spot raged *the* pivotal battle in the last successful invasion of England in 1066, an event with unparalleled impact on the country's subsequent social structure, architecture and well…pretty much everything. Only four years later, the conquering Normans began constructing **Battle Abbey** (EH; ☎ 01424-773792; adult/child £6.50/3.30; ☺ 10am-6pm

Apr-Sep, to 4pm Oct-Mar) right in the middle of the battlefield, a penance ordered by the Pope for the loss of life incurred here.

Only the foundations of the original church remain, the altar's position marked by a plaque – also supposedly the spot England's King Harold famously took an arrow in his eye. But other impressive monastic buildings survive and make for atmospheric explorations.

The battlefield's innocently rolling lush hillsides do little to evoke the ferocity of the event, but high-tech interactive presentations and blow-by-blow audio tours do their utmost to bring the battle to life.

National Express bus 023 from London (£11.60, 2¼ hours, daily) to Hastings passes through Battle. Bus 4/5 runs to Hastings (26 minutes, hourly). Trains also run to London Charing Cross (£18, one hour 20 minutes, twice hourly).

## AROUND BATTLE
### Bodiam Castle

Surrounded by a square moat teeming with oversized goldfish, this archetypal four-towered **castle** (NT; ☎ 01580-830436; adult/child £5.20/2.60; ☻ 10am-6pm mid-Feb–Oct, to 4pm Sat & Sun Nov–early Feb) makes you half expect to see a fire-breathing dragon appear or a golden-haired princess lean over its walls. It is the legacy of 14th-century soldier of fortune (the polite term for knights that slaughtered and pillaged their way around France) Sir Edward Dalyngrigge, who married the local heiress and set about building a castle to make everybody knew who was boss.

Parliamentarian forces left the castle in ruins during the English Civil War, but in 1917 Lord Curzon, former viceroy of India, bought it and restored the exterior. Much of the interior remains unrestored, but it's possible to climb to the battlements for some sweeping views.

The castle is 9 miles northeast of Battle off the B2244. Stagecoach bus 349 stops at Bodiam from Hastings (38 minutes) once every two hours during the day Monday to Saturday.

### Bateman's

It was love at first sight when Rudyard Kipling, author of *The Jungle Book*, set eyes on **Bateman's** (NT; ☎ 01435-882302; adult/child £7.20/3.60; ☻ 11am-5pm Sat-Wed mid-Mar–Oct), the glorious little 1634 Jacobean mansion he would call home for the last 34 years of his life, and where he would draw inspiration for the *Just So Stories* and other vivid tales.

Even today, the house is pervaded with a sense of Kipling's cosy contentment here. Everything is pretty much just as the writer left it after his death in 1936, down to the blotting paper on his study desk. Furnishings often reflect his fascination with the East, with many oriental rugs and Indian artefacts adding colour.

The house is surrounded by lovely gardens and a small path leads down to a water mill that grinds corn on Wednesday and Saturday at 2pm.

Bateman's is about half a mile south of the town of Burwash along the A259.

## EASTBOURNE
pop 106,562

This classic, old-fashioned seaside resort has long brought to mind images of octogenarians dozing in deck chairs, but while many of Eastbourne's seafront hotels still have that retirement-home feel, there's a concerted effort to promote its many charms to sprightlier generations. You certainly can't doubt the appeal of its pebbly beaches, scrupulously snipped seaside gardens and picturesque arcade-free promenade, but if you're looking for cosmopolitan buzz, grab your ice cream and head for Brighton.

The **tourist office** ( ☎ 0871-663 0031; www.visiteastbourne.com; Cornfield Rd; ☻ 9.30am-5.30pm Mon-Fri, to 5pm Sat Apr-Sep, to 4.30pm Sat Mar & Oct, to 1pm Sat Nov-Feb) can fix you up with accommodation for £3.

Nearby, email can be found at **Coffee Republic** ( ☎ 01323-438576; 69 Terminus Rd; per 20/60 min £1/3; ☻ 7am-6pm).

### Sights & Activities

Eastbourne's pretty filigree-trimmed pier, a lovely place to watch the sunset, also has a curious Victorian **Camera Obscura** (adult/child £2/1; ☻ noon-5pm Apr-Sep) that projects images of the outside world into a dish within a darkened room. In July, daredevils in feathery frocks hurl themselves from the pier in the annual birdman competition.

Eastbourne's two museums are entirely given up to nostalgia. The **Museum of Shops** ( ☎ 01323-737143; 20 Cornfield Tce; adult/child £4.50/3.50; ☻ 10am-5pm) is swamped by an obsessive collection of how-we-once-lived memorabilia, while **Eastbourne Heritage Centre** ( ☎ 01323-411189;

---

**THE LAST INVASION OF ENGLAND**

The most famous battle in the history of England took place in 1066, a date seared into every English schoolchild's brain. The Battle of Hastings began when Harold's army arrived on the scene on 14 October and created a three-ring defence consisting of archers, then cavalry, with massed infantry at the rear. William marched north from Hastings and took up a position about 400m south of Harold and his troops. He tried repeatedly to break the English cordon, but Harold's men held fast. William's knights then feigned retreat, drawing some of Harold's troops after them. It was a fatal mistake. Seeing the gap in the English wall, William ordered his remaining troops to charge through, and the battle was as good as won. Among the English casualties was King Harold who, as tradition has it, was hit in the eye by an arrow, and struck down by Norman knights as he tried to pull it out. At news of his death the last English resistance collapsed.

In their wonderfully irreverent *1066 And All That* (1930), WC Sellar and RJ Yeatman suggest that 'the Norman conquest was a Good Thing, as from this time onward England stopped being conquered and thus was able to become top nation…'. When you consider that England hasn't been successfully invaded since, it's hard to disagree.

---

www.eastbourneheritagecentre.co.uk; 2 Carlisle Rd; adult/child £1/free; ☼ 2-5pm mid-Mar–early Oct) livens up exhibits on the town's history with eccentric asides, such as Donald McGill, the pioneer of the 'naughty postcard'.

## Tours

**City Sightseeing** ( ☎ 0170-886 6000; www.city-sightseeing. co.uk; adult/child £7/3.50; ☼ tours every 30 min 10am-4.30pm May-Sep, every 60 min till 4pm Oct & mid-Mar–end Apr) runs buses around local sights, including Beachy Head cliffs.

## Sleeping

At the time of writing, a new YHA hostel was due to open in Eastbourne in 2009. For further details, contact the **YHA** ( ☎ 01629-592 700; www.yha.org.uk)

**Da Vinci Hotel** ( ☎ 01323-727173; www.davinci .uk.com; 10 Howard Square; d from £69; ☐ ) Pegged as an 'art hotel', each room in this boutique B&B is named after a famous artist and prints are hung accordingly, with bold, bright colours to match. There's a space in the reception dedicated to displaying the work of local artists.

**Albert & Victoria** ( ☎ 01323-730948; www.albert andvictoria.com; 19 St Aubyns Rd; s/d £45/70) Book ahead to stay at this delightful Victorian terrace house with opulent rooms, canopied beds, crystal chandeliers and wall frescoes in the breakfast room, mere paces from the seafront promenade.

## Eating

Eastbourne's 'restaurant row' can be found on the seafront end of Terminus Rd.

**Beach House** ( ☎ 01323-738228; www.thegreenhouse bar.com; light meals £5-10; ☼ 10am-5pm Mon-Sat) The nicest of Eastbourne's beachfront cafes is a laid-back space with a large wooden deck on the beach. It serves great big breakfasts and homemade burgers, as well as wines and beer on tap.

**Meze Restaurant** ( ☎ 01323-731893; 15 Pevensey Rd; www.meze-restaurant.com; mains £11-18.50; ☼ lunch & dinner) Great Turkish food is prepared before your eyes over a large open grill at this popular local restaurant. The decor is part bistro, part Turkish bazaar, the large portions are great value and the ebullient proprietor offers a warm welcome.

## Getting There & Around

National Express operates buses to London Victoria (£12, 2¾ hours, daily) and to Brighton (£3.20, 55 to 75 minutes, daily). Bus 12 runs to Brighton (one hour 15 minutes, three per hour, twice hourly on Sunday).

Trains for London Victoria (£21.60, 1½ hours) leave every half-hour. There's also a thrice-hourly service to Brighton (£7.80, 30 to 40 minutes).

**Wheely Good Fun** ( ☎ 01323-479077) hires out bicycles and inline skates. It's located at Fisherman's Green on Royal Pde.

## AROUND EASTBOURNE
### Beachy Head

The famous cliffs of Beachy Head are the highest point of a string of chalky rock faces that slices across this rugged stretch of coast at the southern end of the South Downs. It's a spot of thrilling beauty, at least until you remember that this is also one of England's top suicide spots.

From Beachy Head, the famous Seven Sisters Cliffs roller-coaster their way west. Along the way, you'll stumble upon tiny seaside hamlet Birling Gap, where you can stop for a drink, snack or ice cream at the **Birling Gap Hotel** ( ☎ 01323-423197; Seven Sisters Cliffs, Birling Gap, East Dene).

Beachy Head is off the B2103, from the A259 between Eastbourne and Newhaven. Eastbourne's City Sightseeing tour bus (opposite) stops at the cliff top.

## GLYNDEBOURNE

In 1934 science teacher John Christie and his opera-singer wife decided to build a 1200-seat opera house in the middle of nowhere. It seemed a magnificent folly at the time. But now, **Glyndebourne** ( ☎ 01273-812321; www.glyndebourne.com) is one of England's best places to enjoy the lyric arts, with a season that runs from late May to the end of August. Tickets can be gold dust so book well ahead. And bring your glad rags: dress code is strictly black tie and evening dress. Glyndebourne is 4 miles east of Lewes off the B2192.

## BRIGHTON & HOVE
pop 247, 817

Brighton and Hove is the most vibrant seaside resort in England and a high point of any visit to the region. It's a thriving, cosmopolitan city with a Bohemian spirit; home to an exuberant gay community, a dynamic student population and a healthy number of ageing and new-age hippies, as well as traditional candyfloss

fun. Brighton rocks all year round, but really comes to life during the summer months, when tourists, language students and revellers from London, keen to explore the city's legendary nightlife, summer festivals, and multitude of trendy restaurants, slick boutique hotels and shops, pour into the city.

Brighton has embraced the outlandish ever since the Prince Regent built his party palace here in the 19th century, and these days anyone can join in the fun. Celebrities rub shoulders with dreadlocked hippies, drag queens party next to designer-clad urbanites, and kids toddle around the tables of coffee-quaffing media types.

The town's increase in popularity over the past few years isn't all good, however. Chain bars are slowly sneaking into once staunchly alternative areas, and some long-term residents grumble that the city's trendy status and the influx of moneyed Londoners are prompting a sharp rise in prices and pretension, detracting from the very alternative spirit that makes the city unique in the first place.

### Orientation

Brighton Town and its western neighbour Hove were jointly made a city in 2000. The train station is half a mile north of the beach, while the tiny bus station is tucked away in Poole Valley close to Brighton Pier. Old Steine (pronounced steen) is the major thoroughfare linking pier and centre.

To the west lies a tangle of pedestrian alleyways known as the Lanes, packed with pubs, restaurants and shops. A short walk north is the North Laine, full of quirky stores and

---

**FRENZIED PYROMANIA**

The English enjoy an evening of frenzied pyromania nationwide on **Bonfire Night** (5 November) in memory of Guy Fawkes' 1605 plot to blow up the Houses of Parliament. But unassuming little Lewes has double the reason to host one of the craziest fireworks celebrations you're ever likely to see.

In 1555, at the height of Mary Tudor's Catholic revival, 17 Protestant martyrs were burned at the stake in the town's High St. Lewes has not forgotten, and every 5 November tens of thousands of people gather for the famous fireworks display, in which effigies of the pope are burnt in memory of the martyrs. These days he's often joined by modern-day figures, prime ministers, presidents and terrorists among them. Locals parade the streets in outlandish medieval garb with flaming crosses, and send barrels filled with bangers to crack and fizzle their way down to the river, chased by local youth.

Though not shy of controversy, there's no sectarian fervour these days and it's one of the most enjoyable nights on the southeastern calendar.

Bohemian cafes. The city's effervescent gay scene flourishes in Kemptown, east of Old Steine along St James' St.

Brighton's burgeoning marina, east of town, is also a vibrant waterside shopping, dining, drinking and water-sports centre.

## Information

### BOOKSHOPS

**Borders Books** ( ☎ 01273-731122; Churchill Square Shopping Centre; ☽ 9am-10pm Mon-Sat, 11am-5pm Sun)
**Brighton Books** ( ☎ 01273-693845; 18 Kensington Gardens; ☽ 10am-6pm Mon-Sat) Second-hand bookshop.

### INTERNET ACCESS

**Internet Junction** ( ☎ 01273-607650; 109 Western Rd; per hr £2.50)
**Jubilee Library** ( ☎ 01273-296961; Jubilee St; ☽ 10am-7pm Mon & Tue, to 5pm Wed & Fri, to 8pm Thu, to 5pm Sat, 11am-4pm Sun) Bring ID and sign up to use machines for free.
**Netpama** ( ☎ 01273-227188; 37 Preston St; per hr £2)

### INTERNET RESOURCES

**Brighton City Guide** (www.brighton.co.uk)
**visitbrighton.com** (www.visitbrighton.com)

### LAUNDRY

**Preston St Laundrette** ( ☎ 01273-738556; 75 Preston St; ☽ 8am-7.30pm Mon-Sat, 9am-7pm Sun)

### MEDICAL SERVICES

**Royal Sussex County Hospital** ( ☎ 01273-696955; Eastern Rd) Has an accident and emergency department; 2 miles east of the centre.
**Wistons Clinic** ( ☎ 01273-506263; 138 Dyke Rd) For general medical consultations; less than a mile from the centre.

### MONEY

**American Express** ( ☎ 01273-712906; 82 North St) Has bureau de change.
**NatWest** (Castle Sq) Bank with ATM.

### POST

**Post office** (2-3 Churchill Square Shopping Centre; ☽ 9am-5.30pm Mon-Fri, 9am-3pm Sat)

### TOURIST INFORMATION

**Tourist office** ( ☎ 0906-711 2255; www.visitbrighton .com; Royal Pavilion Shop, Royal Pavilion; ☽ 9.30am-5.30pm daily) Overworked staff and a 50p-per-minute telephone line provide local information. You may find the website and on-site 24-hour-accessible computer more helpful.

## Sights

### ROYAL PAVILION

An absolute must of a visit to Brighton is the **Royal Pavilion** ( ☎ 01273-290900; www.royalpavilion.org .uk; adult/under 15yr £8.50/5.10; ☽ 10am-4.30pm Oct-Mar, 9.30am-5pm Apr-Sep), the glittering, exotic party-pad-cum-palace of Prince George, later Prince Regent then King George IV. It's easily one of the most self-indulgently decadent buildings in England and an apt symbol of Brighton's reputation for hedonism. The flamboyant Indian-style domes and Moorish minarets outside are only a prelude to the palace's lavish oriental-themed interior, where no colour is deemed too strong, dragons swoop and snarl from gilt-smothered ceilings, gem-encrusted snakes slither down pillars, and crystal chandeliers seem ordered by the ton. While gawping is the main activity, you can pick up an audio tour (included in the admission price) to learn more about the palace, room by room.

### BRIGHTON MUSEUM & ART GALLERY

Set in the Royal Pavilion's renovated stable block, this **museum and art gallery** ( ☎ 01273-290 900; Royal Pavilion Gardens; admission free; ☽ 10am-7pm Tue, to 5pm Wed-Sat, 2-5pm Sun) has a glittering collection of 20th-century art and design, including a crimson Salvador Dali sofa modelled on Mae West's lips. There's also an enthralling gallery of world art, and an 'images of Brighton' multimedia exhibit containing a series of oral histories of the city.

### BRIGHTON PIER

This grand old centenarian **pier** (Palace Pier; www.brightonpier.co.uk; admission free), full of glorious gaudiness, is the place to come to experience the tackier side of Brighton. There are plenty of stomach-churning fairground rides and dingy amusement arcades to keep you amused, and candyfloss and Brighton rock to chomp on while you're doing so.

Look west and you'll see the sad remains of the **West Pier** (www.westpier.co.uk), a skeletal iron hulk that attracts flocks of birds at sunset. It's a sad end for a Victorian marvel upon which the likes of Charlie Chaplin and Stan Laurel once performed. Construction on a *Jetsons*-esque Brighton i-360 observation tower on this site is imminent, and the planners hope to open to the public in 2010. Much of the West Pier wreckage will be left intact, however, in the hope that it can one day be restored.

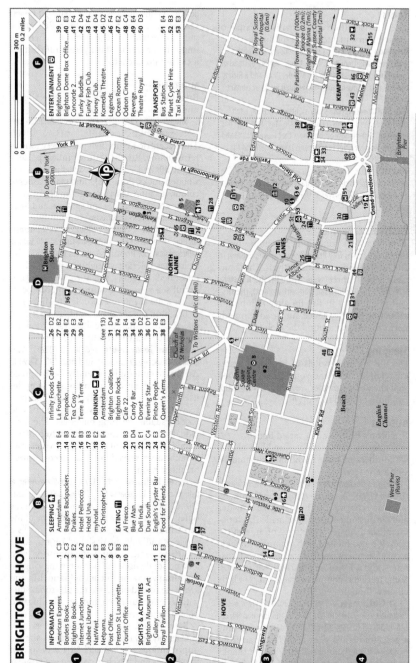

# BRIGHTON & HOVE

**INFORMATION**
American Express..............1 C3
Borders Books..................2 C3
Brighton Books.................3 C2
Internet Junction..............4 A2
Jubilee Library.................5 E2
NatWest..........................6 B3
Netpama...........................7 B3
Post Office........................8 C3
Preston St Laundrette........9 B3
Tourist Office...................10 E3

**SIGHTS & ACTIVITIES**
Brighton Museum & Art
Gallery...........................11 E3
Royal Pavilion..................12 E3

**SLEEPING**
Amsterdam......................13 E4
Baggies Backpackers.........14 B3
Drakes............................15 F4
Hotel Pelirocco.................16 B3
Hotel Una.......................17 B3
myhotel...........................18 E2
St Christopher's................19 E4

**EATING**
Al Fresco.........................20 B3
Blue Man........................21 D4
Deli India........................22 E1
Due South.......................23 C4
English's Oyster Bar..........24 E3
Food for Friends...............25 D3
Infinity Foods Cafe............26 D2
La Fourchette...................27 B2
Pompoko........................28 E2
Tea Cosy.........................29 E3
Terre à Terre....................30 E4

**DRINKING**
Amsterdam...............(see 13)
Brighton Coalition.............31 D4
Brighton Rocks................32 F4
Cafe 22..........................33 E4
Candy Bar......................34 E4
Dorset............................35 D2
Evening Star....................36 D1
Pintxo People...................37 C4
Queen's Arms.................38 E3

**ENTERTAINMENT**
Brighton Dome.................39 E3
Brighton Dome Box Office..40 E3
Concorde 2......................41 F4
Funky Buddha..................42 D4
Funky Fish Club................43 F4
Honey Club......................44 D4
Komedia Theatre..............45 D2
Legends...........................46 F4
Ocean Rooms..................47 E2
Odeon Cinema................48 C4
Revenge..........................49 E4
Theatre Royal...................50 D3

**TRANSPORT**
Bus Station......................51 E4
Planet Cycle Hire..............52 B3
Taxi Rank........................53 E3

## Tours

The tourist office can organise a range of guided tours, including the following:

**Brighton Walks** ( ☎ 01273-888596; www.brighton walks.com; adult/child £6/3.50) A huge variety of standard and offbeat themes including a Murder Walk and a Rich & Famous tour. Show up for prescheduled walks or contact to book.

**City Sightseeing** (www.city-sightseeing.co.uk; adult/child £7/3; ☉ tours every 30 min late May–late Sep) Has open-top, hop-on hop-off bus tours that leave from Grand Junction Rd near Brighton Pier and take you around the main sights.

**Tourist Tracks** (www.tourist-tracks.com) Has MP3 audio guides downloadable from their website (£5) or available on a preloaded MP3 player at the tourist office (£6 per half-day).

## Festivals & Events

There's always something fun going on in Brighton, from **Gay Pride** (www.brightonpride.org) in late July to food and drink festivals. The showpiece is May's three-week-long **Brighton Festival** ( ☎ 01273-709709; www.brighton-festival.org.uk), the biggest arts festival in Britain after Edinburgh, attracting theatre, dance, music and comedy performers from around the globe.

## Sleeping

Despite a glut of hotels in Brighton, prices are relatively high and you'd be wise to book well ahead for summer weekends and for the Brighton Festival in May.

### BUDGET

Brighton's hostels are a varied bunch – several catering to raucous stag and hen nights, while others are more traditional and homely. Choose wisely!

**Baggies Backpackers** ( ☎ 01273-733740; 33 Oriental Pl; dm/d £13/35) A warm familial atmosphere, worn-in charm, motherly on-site owner and clean, snug dorms have made this long-established hostel something of an institution. It's also blessed with a homely kitchen, a cosy basement music room thick with cassettes, and a TV room piled high with videos. Some travellers complain that it can get a little cliquey, though.

**St Christopher's** ( ☎ 01273-202035; www.palace brighton.co.uk; Palace Hotel, 10/12 Grand Junction Rd; dm £16-19.50, s/d £25/50; ☐ ) Don't count on getting a peaceful night's sleep at this basic seafront hostel – it's a magnet for party people thanks to its location in the heart of the Brighton

action. While quiet is a rare luxury, it boasts sea views, a spot near Brighton Pier and a pub downstairs for cheap meals. There are under-bed cages to stash your stuff (bring a lock) but no kitchen.

### MIDRANGE

Brighton is blessed with a wide selection of midrange accommodation.

**Snooze** ( ☎ 01273-605797; www.snoozebrighton.com; 25 St George's Terrace; s/d incl breakfast from £35/65; ☐ wi-fi) This eccentric Kemptown pad is very fond of retro styling. Rooms feature vintage posters, bright '60s and '70s patterned wallpaper, flying wooden ducks, floral sinks and mad clashes of colour. It's more than just a gimmick though – rooms are comfortable and spotless, and there are great vegie breakfasts.

**Amsterdam** ( ☎ 01273-688825; www.amsterdam .uk.com; 11-12 Marine Pde; d with bathroom £60-140, without bathroom from £50) Popular gay-run hotel that also welcomes tolerant straights, with tastefully decorated, spacious, bright rooms and wonderful sea views, including a fabulous penthouse suite (£160 to £200). It sits above one of Brighton's best gay bars and saunas, which guests can use half price. Request a room on higher floors if you're a light sleeper.

**Paskins Town House** ( ☎ 01273-601203; www .paskins.co.uk; 18/19 Charlotte St; d from £90; ☐ wi-fi) An environmentally friendly B&B spread between two elegant town houses. It prides itself on using ecofriendly products such as recycled toilet paper, low-energy bulbs and biodegradable cleaning materials. The individually designed rooms are beautifully maintained, and excellent organic and vegetarian breakfasts are served in the art-deco-inspired breakfast room.

**Hotel Pelirocco** ( ☎ 01273-327055; www.hotel pelirocco.co.uk; 10 Regency Sq; s £50-65, d £90-140, suite £300; ☐ wi-fi) One of Brighton's first theme hotels, this is still the nuttiest (and one of the most fun) places to stay in town. There's a range of individually designed rooms, some by artists, some by big-name sponsors, from a basic single done up like a boxing ring, to the Motown room, full of gold satin, LPs and a vintage record player, to the playroom suite with a 3m circular bed, mirrored ceiling and pole-dancing area.

**Hotel Una** ( ☎ 01273-820464; www.hotel-una.co.uk; 55/56 Regency Sq; s/d from £70/110; ☐ wi-fi) A simple, unpretentious place, Hotel Una is devoid of the themes and kitsch decor that are popular in so many of the city's hotels. Instead you'll find caramel-coloured floorboards and rooms in soothing shades of brown and cream, with the odd miniature sauna or whirlpool bath thrown in.

### TOP END

**Drakes** ( ☎ 01273-696934; www.drakesofbrighton.com; 43-44 Marine Pde; r £100-325; 🖳 wi-fi) Drakes oozes understated class: a stylish, minimalist boutique hotel that eschews the need to shout its existence from the rooftops. Feature rooms have giant free-standing tubs set in front of full-length bay windows with stunning views out to sea. It also has one of Brighton's best restaurants, Gingerman.

**myhotel** ( ☎ 01273-224300; www.myhotels.co.uk; 17 Jubilee St; r incl breakfast £140-600; 🅿 🖳 wi-fi) The rooms in this trendy new hotel look like space-age pods, full of curved white walls, floor-to-ceiling observation TVs and suspended flat-screen TVs, with the odd splash of neon orange or pink. You can even hook up your iPod and play music through speakers in the ceiling. There's a cocoon-like cocktail bar downstairs, and if you've money to burn, a suite with a steam room and harpooned vintage carousel horse.

## Eating

Brighton easily has the best choice of eateries on the south coast, with cafes, diners and restaurants to fulfil every whim.

### BUDGET

Brighton is one of the UK's best destinations for vegetarians, and its innovative meat-free menus are also terrific value for anyone on a tight budget.

**Pompoko** ( ☎ 01273-703072; 110 Church St; mains £4-5; 🕑 11am-10pm Tue-Thu, to 11pm Fri & Sat, to 9pm Sun) Simple Japanese food in a small but perfectly formed little cafe. It's quick, cheap and delicious, with an emphasis on home-style curries, soups and noodle dishes.

**Deli India** ( ☎ 01273-699985; 81 Trafalgar St; curries £5; 🕑 10am-7pm Tue-Fri, to 6pm Sat, 11am-3pm Sun) Light and healthy Indian food made without artificial flavours, cream or heavy oil is on offer in this delicatessen and teashop. The deli's shelves are packed with lentils, chapatti flours, chutneys, spices and cookbooks to take home.

**Infinity Foods Cafe** ( ☎ 01273-670743; 50 Gardner St; mains £5-8; 🕑 9.30am-5pm Mon-Sat) The sister establishment of Infinity Foods wholefoods shop, a Brighton institution, serves a wide variety of vegetarian and organic food, with many vegan and wheat- or gluten-free options including tofu burgers, meze plates and falafel.

**Food for Friends** ( ☎ 01273-202310; www.foodfor friends.com; 17a Prince Albert St; mains £8-13; 🕑 lunch & dinner) This airy, glass-sided restaurant attracts the attention of passers-by as much as it does the loyalty of its customers, with an ever-inventive choice of vegetarian and vegan food. Children are also catered for.

Another worthy contender is **Tea Cosy** ( ☎ 01273-677055; 3 George St; Diana Spencer memorial tea £8; 🕑 noon-5pm Wed, 11am-6pm Thu-Sat, noon-6pm Sun), a barmy tearoom full of strict etiquette rules and royal-family memorabilia.

### MIDRANGE

**Al Fresco** ( ☎ 01273-206532; The Milkmaid Pavilion, Kings Rd Arches; mains £9-20; 🕑 noon-midnight) The star here is the view. Al Fresco sits a mere 100m from the West Pier, a curved-glass structure with a huge, staggered outdoor terrace and amazing views up and down the seafront and out to sea. The pizzas, pastas and Italian meat dishes make a tasty accompaniment to the views.

**our pick** **Terre à Terre** ( ☎ 01273-729051; 71 East St; mains £10-15; 🕑 noon-10.30pm Tue-Fri, to 11pm Sat, to 10pm Sun) Even staunch meat-eaters will come out raving about this legendary vegetarian restaurant. Terre à Terre offers a sublime dining experience, from the vibrant, modern space, to the entertaining menus, to the delicious, inventive dishes full of rich robust flavours.

**La Fourchette** ( ☎ 01273-722556; www.lafourchette .co.uk; 105 Western Rd; set lunch/dinner from £10/26.50; 🕑 lunch & dinner Mon-Thu, 11am-11pm Fri-Sun) Grown up, romantic dining, sleek decor and fine French bistro food are the name of the game at this charming Gallic bistro. There are particularly good, locally caught fish dishes and the service is excellent if a little over-attentive.

**English's Oyster Bar** ( ☎ 01273-327980; www .englishs.co.uk; 29-31 East St; mains £10-29; 🕑 lunch & dinner) A 60-year institution, this Brightonian seafood paradise dishes up everything from oysters to lobster to Dover sole. It's converted from fishermen's cottages, with echoes of the elegant Edwardian era inside and buzzing alfresco dining on the pedestrian square outside.

**Blue Man** ( ☎ 01273-325529; 11 Little East St; mains £11-16; 🕑 3-6pm) Tiny dining room tucked away near the seafront serving excellent, large portions of North African food, in a spicy, cosy atmosphere, full of ambient lighting, mosaic tables and scatter cushions. After you're full, you can sit back and suck on an apple hubble bubble.

**Due South** ( ☎ 01273-821218; www.duesouth.co.uk; 139 Kings Rd Arches; mains £14-20; ⊗ lunch & dinner Mon-Sat, lunch Sun) Sheltered under a cavernous Victorian arch on the seafront, with a curvaceous front window and small bamboo-screened terrace on the promenade, this refined, yet relaxed, restaurant specialises in dishes cooked with the best environmentally sustainable and seasonal Sussex produce.

## Drinking

Outside London, Brighton's nightlife is the best in the south, with its unique mix of seafront clubs and bars. Drunken stag and hen parties and charmless, tacky nightclubs rule on West Street, which is best avoided. For more ideas, visit www.drinkinbrighton.co.uk.

**Evening Star** ( ☎ 01273-328931; www.eveningstar brighton.co.uk; 55 Surrey St) This cosy, unpretentious pub is a beer-drinker's nirvana, with a wonderful selection of award-winning real ales, Belgian beers, organic lagers and real ciders. It's a short stagger away from the station

**Brighton Coalition** ( ☎ 01273-772842; 171-181 Kings Rd Arches) On a summer's day, there's nowhere better to sit and watch the world go by than this popular beach bar, diner and club. It's a cavernous place with a funky brick-vaulted interior and a wide terrace spilling onto the promenade. All sorts of fun things happen here, from comedy and live music to club nights.

**Pintxo People** ( ☎ 01273-732323; www.pintxopeople .co.uk; 95 Western Rd; ⊗ to midnight Mon-Fri, to 1am Sat) This place is principally a Spanish restaurant, but go upstairs and you'll find a sultry bar with huge squishy sofas, red-leather stools, a martini station and a staggering cocktail list. Or sit on one of the rustic wooden tables downstairs, sink a few sangrias and nibble on tapas.

**Dorset** ( ☎ 01273-605423; www.thedorset.co.uk; 28 North Rd) This laid-back Brighton institution throws open its doors and windows in fine weather and spills tables onto the pavement. You'll be just as welcome for a morning coffee as for an evening pint here, and if you decide not to leave between the two, there's always the decent gastropub menu.

**Brighton Rocks** ( ☎ 01273-601139; 6 Rock Pl; ⊗ 4pm-late) This cocktail bar is firmly on the Kemptown gay scene, but welcomes all comers. The cocktails are tasty, there's a damn fine 'grazing' menu and the bar plays regular host to theme parties and art launches.

## Entertainment

Brighton offers the best entertainment line up on the south coast, with clubs to rival London and Manchester for cool. Keep tabs on what's hot and what's not by searching out publications such as the *List*, the *Source* and *What's On*.

### NIGHTCLUBS

When Britain's top DJs aren't plying their trade in London, Ibiza or Aya Napia, chances are you'll spy them here. All Brighton's clubs open until at least 2am, and many as late as 5am.

**Funky Buddha** ( ☎ 01273-725541; www.funky buddha.co.uk; Kings Rd Arches; admission £2-8) Twin giant, brick, subterranean tunnels, with bars at the front and back, playing funky house, '70s, R&B and disco to a stylish and attitude-free crowd.

**Ocean Rooms** ( ☎ 01273-699069; www.oceanrooms .co.uk; 1 Morley St; admission £3-10) This enduring favourite crams in three floors of dance variety, from an all-white bar to a dance floor where you can lap up the efforts of top DJs, from hip hop to drum and bass, to breakbeat.

**Funky Fish Club** ( ☎ 01273-699069; www.funkyfish club.co.uk; 19-23 Marine Parade; admission £3-10) Fun, friendly and unpretentious little club playing soul, funk jazz, Motown and old-skool breaks. There are no big-name DJs or stringent door policies, just cheap drinks and a rocking party atmosphere.

**Honey Club** ( ☎ 01273-202807; www.thehoneyclub .co.uk; 214 Kings Rd Arches; admission £5-12) A cavernous seafront club that jumps from strength to strength, almost as popular with DJs as it is with the weekly queues of clubbers that pile into its glittering depths. Dress up, party hard, then cool off on the balcony chillout area or dip your aching feet in the sea.

**Concorde 2** ( ☎ 01273-673311; www.concorde2 .co.uk; Madeira Dr, Kemptown; admission £8-20) Brighton's best-known and best-loved club is a disarmingly unpretentious den, where DJ Fatboy Slim pioneered the Big Beat Boutique and still occasionally graces the decks. There is a huge variety of club nights here and live bands each month, ranging from world music to rock.

---

### GAY & LESBIAN BRIGHTON

Perhaps it's Brighton's long-time association with the theatre, but for more than 100 years the city has been a gay haven. Gay icons Noel Coward and Ivor Novello were regular visitors, but in those days the scene was furtive and separate. From the 1960s onwards, the scene really began to open up, especially in the Kemptown area and around Old Steine. Today, with more than 25,000 gay men and 10,000 to 15,000 lesbians living in the city, it is the most vibrant queer community in the country outside London.

Kemptown (aka Camptown), on and off St James' St, is where it's all at. In recent years the old Brunswick Town area of Hove has emerged as a quieter alternative to the traditionally cruisy (and sometimes seedy) Kemptown, but the community here has responded by branching out from the usual pubs that served as nightly pick-up joints. Now you will find a rank of gay-owned businesses, from cafes and hotels to bookshops, as well as the more obvious bars, clubs and saunas.

For up-to-date information on what's going on in gay Brighton, check out the websites www .gay.brighton.co.uk and www.realbrighton.com, or pick up the free monthly magazine **Gscene** (www.gscene.com) from various venues or the tourist office.

#### For drinking...

**Cafe 22** ( ☎ 01273-626 682; 129 St James' St; snacks £2-3; ☽ 8am-6pm Mon-Fri, 10am-6pm Sat & Sun) This cool coffee-shop hang-out and internet cafe is *the* place to get word on everything going on in town.

**Amsterdam** ( ☎ 01273-688 825; www.amsterdam.uk.com; 11-12 Marine Pde; ☽ noon-2am) Hotel, sauna, restaurant and extremely hip bar above the pier; its sun terrace is a particular hit.

**Candy Bar** ( ☎ 01273-622 424; www.thecandybar.co.uk; 129 St James' St; ☽ 9pm-2am) Slick cafe-bar-club for the girls, with pink-lit arches, curvaceous bar, pool table and dance floor.

**Queen's Arms** ( ☎ 01273-696 873; www.queensarmsbrighton.com; 7 George St; ☽ 3pm-late) Plenty of camp in the cabaret and karaoke acts at this pub make it a definite stop on the Brighton gay trail.

#### For dancing...

Bars and pubs may be fun, but the real action takes place on and off the dance floor.

**Revenge** ( ☎ 01273-608 133; www.revenge.co.uk; 7 Marine Pde; ☽ 10.30pm-3am) Nightly disco with occasional cabaret.

**Legends** ( ☎ 01273-624 462; 31-34 Marine Pde; ☽ 9am-2am) Club and basement bar underneath the Amsterdam, playing 1990s music and club anthems with the odd touch of drag.

---

### CINEMAS

**Odeon Cinema** ( ☎ 0871-224 4007; cnr King's Rd & West St) Check out this seafront cinema for mainstream movies.

**Duke of York** ( ☎ 01273-602503; Preston Circus) About a mile north of North Rd, showing art-house films and old classics.

### THEATRE

**Brighton Dome** ( ☎ 01273-709709; www.brighton-dome .org.uk; 29 New Rd) Once the stables and exercise yard of King George IV, this art-deco complex houses three theatre venues within the Royal Pavilion estate. The box office is on New Rd.

**Theatre Royal** ( ☎ 01273-328488; New Rd) Built by decree of the Prince of Wales in 1806, this venue hosts plays, musicals and operas.

**Komedia Theatre** ( ☎ 01273-647100; www.komedia .co.uk; Gardner St) This former billiards hall and supermarket is now a stylish comedy, theatre and cabaret venue.

## Shopping

A busy maze of narrow lanes and tiny alleyways that was once a fishing village, the **Lanes** is Brighton's most popular shopping district. Its every twist and turn is jam-packed with jewellers and gift shops, coffee shops and boutiques selling everything from antique firearms to hard-to-find vinyls. There's another, lessclaustrophobic shopping district in **North Laine**, a series of streets north of the Lanes, including Bond, Gardner, Kensington and Sydney Sts, that are full of retro-cool boutiques and Bohemian cafes. Head west from the Lanes and you'll hit Churchill Square Shopping Centre and Western Rd, where you'll find all the mainstream high-street stores.

---

**TOP FIVE BEACH TOWNS**

- Brighton & Hove (p223)
- Whitstable (p211)
- Ramsgate (p213)
- Broadstairs (p212)
- Eastbourne (p221)

---

## Getting There & Away
Brighton is 53 miles from London and transport is fast and frequent.

### BUS
**National Express** ( ☎ 08705-808080; www.national express.com) coaches leave for London Victoria (£10.90, 80 minutes, hourly), and there are regular coach links to all London airports.

Buses 28, 29 and 29A go to Lewes (£2.80, 35 minutes), bus 12 to Eastbourne (£3, 80 minutes), and bus 700 to Chichester (£3, 80 minutes) and Arundel (two hours).

### TRAIN
There are two hourly services to London Victoria (£19, 50 to 70 minutes) and two to London Bridge (50 minutes to 1¼ hours). For £2 on top of the rail fare, you can get a PlusBus ticket that gives unlimited travel on Brighton & Hove buses for the day. There's one direct service to Portsmouth (£14.50, 1½ hours, hourly), twice-hourly services to Chichester, Eastbourne and Hastings, and links to Canterbury and Dover.

## Getting Around
Brighton is a sizable place, but you'll be able to cover most of it on foot. Alternatively, you can buy a day ticket (£3) from the driver to scoot back and forth on Brighton & Hove buses.

Parking can be expensive. Brighton and Hove operates a pay-and-display parking scheme. In the town centre, it's usually £1.50 per half-hour with a maximum stay of two hours. Alternatively, there's a Park & Ride on the outskirts of town at Withdean.

Cab companies include **Brighton Streamline Taxis** ( ☎ 01273-747474) and **City Cabs** ( ☎ 01273-205 205), and there's a taxi rank at the junction of East St and Market St.

You can rent bikes from **Planet Cycle Hire** ( ☎ 01273-748881; West Pier Promenade; half-/full day £8/12; ☺ 10am-6pm Thu-Tue May-Sep, to 4pm Fri-Mon Oct-Apr), next to West Pier. Deposit and ID required.

# WEST SUSSEX

After the fast-paced adventures of Brighton and East Sussex, West Sussex comes as welcome respite. The serene hills and valleys of the South Downs ripple across the county, which is fringed by sheltered coastline. Beautiful Arundel and cultured Chichester make a good base from where to explore the county's winding country lanes and remarkable Roman ruins.

## ARUNDEL
pop 3297
Arundel is perhaps the prettiest town in West Sussex. Clustered around a vast fairytale castle, its hillside streets burst with antique stores, teashops, excellent restaurants and the odd boutique hotel – it makes a great weekend break or stopover. While much of the town appears medieval – especially the whimsical castle that has been home to the dukes of Norfolk for centuries – most of it dates from Victorian times.

### Information
The **tourist office** ( ☎ 01903-882268; www.sussex bythesea.com; 61 High St; ☺ 10.30am-4pm Mon-Sat, 2-4pm Sun Easter-Oct, 10am-3pm daily Nov-Easter) has maps, an accommodation-booking service (£1.50), and a small **museum** ( ☎ 01903-883890; www.arun delmuseum.org.uk; admission free; ☺ 10am-3pm Easter-Aug, 11am-1pm Sep-Easter) on Arundel's history, temporarily located in the Mill Rd car park while it looks for a new home.

### Sights & Activities
Originally built in the 11th century, all that's left of the first **Arundel Castle** ( ☎ 01903-882173; www.arundelcastle.org; adult/under 16yr/student & senior £13/7.50/10.50; ☺ 11am-5pm Tue-Sun Easter-Oct), are the modest remains of its keep at its core. Thoroughly ruined during the English Civil War, most of what you see today is the result of passionate reconstruction by the eighth, 11th and 15th dukes of Norfolk between 1718 and 1900. The current duke still lives in part of the castle. Highlights include

the atmospheric keep, the massive Great Hall and the library, which has paintings by Gainsborough and Holbein.

The other architectural landmark in town is Arundel's ostentatious 19th-century **cathedral** ( ☎ 01903-882297; www.arundelcathedral.org; ⏰ 9am-6pm summer, to dusk winter), built in the French Gothic style by the 15th duke. Inside are the remains of his ancestor, St Philip Howard, now a canonised Catholic martyr who was caught praying for a Spanish victory against the English in 1588.

## Sleeping

**Arundel YHA** ( ☎ 0870 770 5676; www.yha.org.uk; Warningcamp; dm £17.95; P 🖳 ) Catering to South Downs walkers and families, this large Georgian hostel has excellent facilities and is set in sprawling grassy grounds on a charming country lane, 20- to 30-minutes' walk from town off the A27 (call for directions).

**Arundel House** ( ☎ 01903-882136; www.arundel houseonline.com; 11 High St; d from £100; 🖳 wi-fi) The modern rooms in this lovely restaurant-with-rooms may be small but they're beautifully styled and very comfortable, with showers big enough for two. The restaurant down-stairs serves some of the best food in Arundel (three-course dinner £28), which happily extends to breakfast.

Also worth a look is **April Cottage** ( ☎ 01903-885401; www.april-cottage.co.uk; London Rd; d from £70; P 🖳 wi-fi), a charming, friendly B&B with countryside views that's a 20-minute walk from town.

## Eating

**Zigs** ( ☎ 01903-884 500; www.zigsrestaurant.co.uk; 51 High St; mains £6-18; ⏰ 9.30am-3.30pm Mon & Tue, to 9.30pm Wed-Sat, to 6pm Sun) The slick, modern furnishings of this Parisian-style bistro fit in perfectly with the low ceilings and oak beams of its old town-house setting. It specialises in *tartines* (*pain Poîlane* – an unusual French bread with a slightly sour flavour – topped with assorted hot and cold toppings) and *piérrades* (hot volcano stones on which you cook your own food at the table).

**Town House** ( ☎ 01903-883847; 65 High St; set lunch £14-18, set dinner £22-27.50; ⏰ Tue-Sat) The only thing that rivals the stunning 16th-century Florentine gilded-walnut ceiling at this elegant eatery is the acclaimed Mediterranean-influenced cuisine and sparkling atmosphere. Book ahead.

## Getting There & Away

Trains are the way to go here. They run to London Victoria (£20.50, 1½ hours, twice hourly), and to Chichester (20 minutes, twice hourly); change at Ford or Barnham. There are also links to Brighton (£7.80, one hour 20 minutes, twice hourly); change at Ford or Barnham.

# AROUND ARUNDEL
## Bignor Roman Villa

Discovered in 1811 by a farmer ploughing his fields, **Bignor** ( ☎ 01903-869259; www.bignorromanvilla .co.uk; adult/child £4.35/1.85; ⏰ 10am-6pm Jun-Sep, to 5pm May & Oct, Tue-Sun Mar & Apr) was built around AD 190 and is home to an astonishingly fine collection of mosaics preserved within an at-mospheric thatched complex that's historic in its own right. The wonderful mosaic floors include vivid scenes of chunky-thighed gladi-ators, a beautiful Venus whose eyes seem to follow you about the room and an impressive 24m-long gallery design.

While Bignor is well worth the trip, it's a devil of a place to reach without your own wheels. It's located 6 miles north of Arundel off the A29.

# CHICHESTER
pop 27,477

Sitting on flat plains between the South Downs and the sea, this prosperous Georgian mar-ket town has plenty of countryside charm. It's home to an array of traditional tea-and-crumpet shops, well-mannered townsfolk, a fine cathedral and streets of handsome 18th-century town houses. It doesn't stint on cosmopolitan culture either. A famous theatre-and-arts festival takes place every year, and there's a superb modern-art gallery. The ad-ministrative capital of West Sussex, the town is within easy reach of some fascinating Roman remains that recall its days as a sprawling port garrison shortly after the invasion of AD 43.

## Orientation & Information

Striking crown-shaped Market Cross, built in 1501, marks the centre of town. The streets around it are pedestrianised and everything you'd want to see is within walking distance.

There is a **tourist office** ( ☎ 01243-775888; www .visitchichester.org; 29a South St; ⏰ 9.15am-5.15pm Mon-Sat year-round, plus 11am-3.30pm Sun Apr-Sep) and a **post office** (cnr Chapel & West Sts), and **Internet Junction**

SOUTHEAST ENGLAND

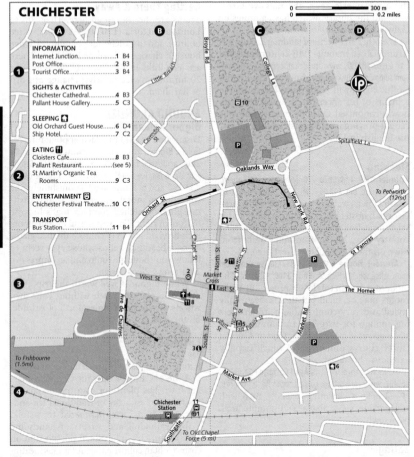

# CHICHESTER

0        300 m
0        0.2 miles

**INFORMATION**
Internet Junction.................**1** B4
Post Office..........................**2** B3
Tourist Office......................**3** B4

**SIGHTS & ACTIVITIES**
Chichester Cathedral...........**4** B3
Pallant House Gallery...........**5** C3

**SLEEPING**
Old Orchard Guest House......**6** D4
Ship Hotel..........................**7** C2

**EATING**
Cloisters Cafe......................**8** B3
Pallant Restaurant.................(see 5)
St Martin's Organic Tea
Rooms.............................**9** C3

**ENTERTAINMENT**
Chichester Festival Theatre.....**10** C1

**TRANSPORT**
Bus Station..........................**11** B4

( ☎ 01243-776644; 2 Southdown Bldg, Southgate; per hr £1; ☯ 9am-8pm Mon-Fri, 11am-8pm Sat & Sun) has double-quick net access.

## Sights

### CHICHESTER CATHEDRAL

This elegant **cathedral** ( ☎ 01243-782595; www.chichestercathedral.org.uk; West St; requested donation £5; ☯ 7.15am-7pm Jun-Aug, to 6pm Sep-May) was begun in 1075 and largely rebuilt in the 13th century. Three storeys of beautiful arches sweep upwards, and Romanesque carvings are dotted around. The free-standing church tower was built in the 15th century and the spire is from the 19th century. There are also a few bold, modern flourishes, including an entrancing stained-glass window by Marc Chagall and

the not-so-pretty disembodied likenesses of the Queen and Prince Phillip outside the main entrance.

Guided tours operate at 11.15am and 2.30pm Monday to Saturday, Easter to October, and the excellent cathedral choir is guaranteed to give you goose bumps during the daily **Evensong** ( ☯ 5.30pm Mon-Sat, 3.30pm Sun).

### PALLANT HOUSE GALLERY

One of many handsome Georgian houses in town, **Pallant House** ( ☎ 01243-774557; www.pallant.org.uk; 9 North Pallant; adult/child/student £6.50/2/3.50; ☯ 10am-5pm Tue-Sat, 12.30-5pm Sun), once owned by a wealthy wine merchant, now houses a superb collection of 20th-century, mostly British, art, with names such as Caulfield,

Freud, Sutherland and Moore represented, as well as international artists including Picasso, Cézanne, and Rembrandt.

## Festivals & Events

For three weeks in June and July, the annual **Chichester Festivities** ( ☎ 01243-785718; www.chifest .org.uk) puts on an abundance of terrific theatre, art, guest lectures, fireworks and performances of every musical genre.

## Sleeping

Most accommodation in Chichester is midrange, with little for budget travellers.

**Old Orchard Guest House** ( ☎ 01243-536547; www .oldorchardguesthouse.co.uk; 8 Lyndhurst Rd; s/d from £45/60) Freshly baked bread and jams are served up for breakfast in the garden or conservatory at this disarming central Georgian town house, which has three spacious and gracious old-style rooms.

**Old Chapel Forge** ( ☎ 01243-264380; www.oldchapel forge.co.uk; Lagness; d from £60; P 🖳 wi-fi) For those with their own wheels, this gorgeous, eco-friendly B&B, set in a 17th-century house and a converted stone chapel, is a good bet. The chapel rooms, with their high-vaulted ceilings and open views across the countryside, are particularly special.

**Ship Hotel** ( ☎ 01243-778000; North St; s/d £95/120; 🖳 wi-fi) The grand central staircase in this former Georgian town house leads to 36 polished blond wood, suede and leather rooms; they're the nicest option in the city centre. There's an excellent all-day brasserie, too.

## Eating

**Pallant Restaurant** ( ☎ 01243-784701; 9 North Pallant; snacks £2-6.50; ✌ 10am-5pm Tue-Sat, noon-5pm Sun) In the Pallant House gallery, this sophisticated cafe has paintings and display cases, and a sunny courtyard that's a good spot for sandwiches, cakes and heartier main meals.

**Cloisters Cafe** ( ☎ 01243-783718; Cathedral Cloisters; snacks £2.50-5; ✌ 9am-5pm Mon-Sat, 10am-4pm Sun) Sparkling marble-floored cafe in the cathedral grounds with sunny walled garden and airy atmosphere. It's a good spot for simple sandwiches, cakes and fair-trade drinks.

**St Martin's Organic Tea Rooms** ( ☎ 01243-786 715; www.organictearooms.co.uk; 3 St Martins St; mains £4-10; ✌ 10am-6pm Mon-Sat) A little cocoon of nooks and crannies tucked away in a part 18th-century, part medieval town house, this passionately organic cafe serves freshly

ground coffee and wholesome, mostly vegetarian, food from Welsh rarebits to risottos. There's also a sinful selection of desserts.

## Entertainment

**Chichester Festival Theatre** ( ☎ 01243-781312; www .cft.org.uk; Oakland's Park) This modern playhouse was built in 1962 and has a long and distinguished history. Sir Laurence Olivier was the theatre's first director and Ingrid Bergman, Sir John Gielgud and Sir Anthony Hopkins are a few of the other famous names to have played here.

## Getting There & Away

Chichester is 60 miles from London and 18 miles from Portsmouth.

### BUS

Chichester is served by Coastliner bus 700, which runs between Brighton (2¼ hours, hourly) and Portsmouth (one hour, hourly). National Express has a rather protracted service from London Victoria (£12.60, four hours, twice daily).

### TRAIN

Chichester can be reached easily from London Victoria (£20.60, 1¾ hours, half-hourly) via Gatwick airport and Arundel. It's also on the coastline between Brighton (£10.50, 50 minutes, twice hourly) and Portsmouth (£6.20, 30 to 40 minutes, twice hourly).

## AROUND CHICHESTER

### Chichester Harbour

Spreading its watery tentacles to the south of town, Chichester Harbour is designated an Area of Outstanding Natural Beauty (AONB) and has a lovely, sandy beach west of the harbour, ideal for a spot of sea air and strolling.

At West Itchenor, 1½-hour harbour cruises are run by **Chichester Harbour Water Tours** ( ☎ 01243-670504; www.chichesterharbourwatertours.co.uk; adult/child £6.50/3).

### Fishbourne Roman Palace & Museum

Anyone mad about mosaics should head straight for **Fishbourne Palace** ( ☎ 01243-785 859; www.sussexpast.co.uk; Salthill Rd; adult/child £7/3.70; ✌ 10am-5pm Mar-Jul, Sep & Oct, to 6pm Aug, to 4pm Nov-Feb), the largest known Roman residence in Britain. Happened upon by labourers in the 1960s, it's thought that this once-luxurious mansion was built around AD 75 for a

Romanised local king. Housed in a modern pavilion are its foundations, hypocaust and painstakingly relaid mosaics. The centre-piece is a spectacular floor depicting Cupid riding a dolphin flanked by sea horses and panthers. There's a fascinating little museum and replanted Roman gardens.

Fishbourne Palace is 1.5 miles west of Chichester, just off the A259. Buses 56 and 700 leave from Monday to Saturday from outside Chichester Cathedral and stop at the bottom of Salthill Rd (five minutes' walk away, roughly hourly). The museum is a 10-minute stroll from Fishbourne train station.

## Petworth

On the outskirts of its namesake village, the imposing 17th-century stately home, **Petworth House** (NT; ☎ 01798-342207; adult/child £9.50/4.80; ⊙ 11am-5pm Sat-Wed Apr-Oct), has an extraordinary art collection, the National Trust's finest. JMW Turner was a regular visitor and the house is still home to the largest collection of his paintings outside London's Tate Gallery. There are also many paintings by Van Dyck, Reynolds, Gainsborough, Titian, Bosch and William Blake. Other highlights are the fabulously theatrical grand staircase and the exquisite Carved Room, which ripples with wooden reliefs by master chiseller Grinling Gibbons.

The surrounding **Petworth Park** (adult/child £3.80/1.90; ⊙ 8am-sunset), is the highlight – the fulfilment of Lancelot 'Capability' Brown's romantic natural-landscape theory. It's home to herds of deer and is the site of open-air concerts in summer.

Petworth is 5 miles from the train station at Pulborough, from where bus 1 runs to Petworth Sq (15 minutes, hourly Monday to Saturday). If driving, it's 12 miles northeast of Chichester off the A285.

# SURREY

Surrey is the heart of commuterville, chosen by well-off Londoners when they spawn, move out of the city and buy a country pad. For the most part, though, it's made up of uninspiring towns and dull, sprawling suburbs. Further away from the roaring motorways and packed rush-hour trains, the county reveals some inspiring landscapes made famous by authors Sir Arthur Conan Doyle, Sir Walter Scott and Jane Austen.

# FARNHAM
pop 36,298

Farnham is Surrey's nicest market town. Practically empty during the week, it's a relaxing place to visit, and the town's main enticements include exquisite Georgian homes, independent boutiques (some of which are on the pricey side), walking and cycling in the surrounding countryside and popping into one of Surrey's only intact castles.

## Orientation & Information

The easiest way to explore Farnham is on foot. The most interesting part of town is its historical centre, where East, West, South and Castle Sts meet.

The Borough (the eastern end of West St) is the town's main shopping street. The train station is at the southern end of South St (Station Hill).

The **Waverley Locality Office** ( ☎ 01252-712667; tourism@farnham.gov.uk; South St; ⊙ 9am-noon Mon & Sat, 9.30am-5pm Tue-Fri) has free maps of the town and surrounding countryside, the free *Farnham Heritage Trail* pamphlet and an updated list of accommodation in the area. It also offers free internet access.

You'll find a couple of banks with ATMs on the Borough. The main post office and a bureau de change are on West St, which is the continuation of the Borough.

## Sights

Constructed in 1138 by Henry de Blois, the grandson of William the Conqueror, there is not much left of the **Farnham Castle keep** ( ☎ 01252-713393; admission incl audio tour £3; ⊙ noon-5pm Fri-Sun & public holidays 21 Mar–30 Sep) today except the beautiful old ramparts. Even if the keep is closed, it is worth walking around the outside (everyone seems to ignore the private signs) to drink in the lovely view.

A residential palace house, Farnham Castle was built in the 13th century for the bishops of Winchester as a stopover on journeys to/from London. From 1926 to the 1950s, it was taken over by the bishops of Guildford. It is now owned by the Farnham Castle International Briefing & Conference Centre, but you can visit it on a **guided tour** ( ☎ 01252-721194; adult/child £2.50/1.50; ⊙ 2-4pm Wed 2.30pm Fri Apr-Aug).

Farnham Castle is located up the old steps at the top of Castle St.

## Sleeping & Eating

Accommodation in Farnham tends towards the midrange to top end, and there is a good choice of tempting eateries.

**Hotel de Vie** ( ☎ 01252-823030; 22 Firgrove Hill; s/d from £90) This plush, sexy boutique hotel has a naughty edge – around the lounge, bar and lobby are prints from the Moulin Rouge and pictures of ladies in corsets and killer heels. Rooms (with names like 'Oriental Pleasures' and 'Gothic Nights') come stocked with erotic DVDs and literature; two of them even have a love swing. If you do choose to emerge from your room, there's a pretty good restaurant.

**Bush Hotel** ( ☎ 01252-715237; www.mercure-uk.com; The Borough; s/d £120/150; 🖳 ) This 17th-century inn is right in the heart of the action and benefits from a cosy beamed bar, a pretty garden at the back and recently renovated rooms.

**Nelson Arms** ( ☎ 01252-716078; 50 Castle St; 2-course lunch £7.95, dinner £9.95-18.95) A rustic, low-ceilinged, cosy bar with a few modern touches, a small terrace at the back and good-value, locally sourced food.

## Entertainment

**Farnham Maltings** ( ☎ 01252-745444; Bridge Sq; www .farnhammaltings.com) is a creative, multipurpose spot with a riverside bar, live music, amateur theatre, exhibitions, workshops and comedy.

## Getting There & Away

Train services run from London Waterloo (one hour, half-hourly). From Winchester, there are trains to Woking (30 minutes, two per hour). Change there for trains to Farnham (25 minutes, half-hourly). The train station is at the end of South St, on the other side of the A31 from the old town centre.

**Stagecoach** ( ☎ 0845-121 0190) bus X64 runs from Winchester to Farnham (one hour 10 minutes) at 10 minutes past the hour. The stop is on the Borough.

# AROUND FARNHAM
## Waverley Abbey

Said to be the inspiration for Sir Walter Scott's eponymous novel, Waverley Abbey sits ruined and forlorn on the banks of the River Wey about 2 miles southeast of Farnham. This was the first Cistercian abbey built in England (construction began in 1128) and was based on a parent abbey at Cîteaux in France.

Across the Wey is the impressive **Waverley Abbey House** (which is closed to the public), built in 1783 using bricks from the demolished abbey. In the 19th century it was owned by Florence Nightingale's brother-in-law, and the famous nurse was a regular visitor. Fittingly, the house was used as a military hospital in WWI. Since 1973, it has been the headquarters of the Crusade for World Revival (CWR), a Christian charity.

The abbey and house are located off the B3001.

## Hindhead

The tiny hamlet of Hindhead, 8 miles south of Farnham off the A287, lies in the middle of the largest area of open heath in Surrey. During the 19th century, a number of prominent Victorians bought up property in the area, including Sir Arthur Conan Doyle (1859–1930), the creator of Sherlock Holmes. One of the three founders of the National Trust, Sir Robert Hunter, lived in nearby Haslemere, and today much of the area is administered by the foundation.

The most beautiful part of the area is to the northeast, where you'll find a natural depression known as the **Devil's Punchbowl**. There are a number of excellent trails and bridle paths here. To get the best view, head for **Gibbet Hill** (280m), which was once an execution ground.

The **Hindhead YHA Hostel** ( ☎ 0870-770 5864; www.yha.org.uk; Devil's Punchbowl, Thursley; dm £12.95) is a completely secluded cottage run by the National Trust on the northern edge of the Punchbowl. It's perfect if you like walking – the nearest bus stop and car park are a half-mile away.

Bus 18 and 19 run hourly to Hindhead from Farnham.

**SOUTHEAST ENGLAND**

# Oxford, the Cotswolds & Around

A haven of lush rolling hills, rose-clad cottages, bucolic views and graceful stone churches, Oxford and the Cotswolds are as close to chocolate-box Britain as you're likely to get. This whole region reeks with charm and is riddled with implausibly pretty villages, thatched cottages, fire-lit inns and grandiose manors. In places there's a fine line between delightfully quaint and cloyingly twee, but it's easy to avoid the peddling of nostalgia and the crowds that flock here and discover your very own slice of old-world England.

Beyond the bucolic views and romantic rural retreats, you'll find a stunning array of grand cities and elegant towns to visit. Top of the bill is Oxford, home to the world-renowned university and the academic elite. Its wonderful college buildings, superb museums and dreamy atmosphere make it a great base for exploring the area.

Just north of here is Churchill's extraordinary pile, Blenheim Palace, and to the west you'll find the Regency grandeur of Cheltenham and the glorious cathedral in Gloucester. To the south the Queen herself has a weekend pad, the majestic Windsor Castle, and nearby are the sedate and intellectual charms of the scholarly town of Eton.

You can see most of these attractions on a day trip from London but to really do them justice you should plan at least an overnight stay in Oxford and the Cotswolds. Public transport here is good but a car or bike will help you get off the beaten track and away from the crowds. Be prepared for busy roads in the summer months though, especially around the Cotswolds.

---

## HIGHLIGHTS

- Following in the footsteps of Lyra, Tolkien, CS Lewis and Inspector Morse as you tour the **Oxford colleges** (p241)

- Discovering deserted **Cotswold villages** (p253) straight out of medieval England

- Soaking up the atmosphere in the Queen's very own hideaway, **Windsor Castle** (p272)

- Feeling the hairs on the back of your neck rise as you revel in the reverberations at a concert in **Gloucester Cathedral** (p267)

- Wandering the quiet medieval streets of **Painswick** (p261) at sunset and wallowing in their unspoilt splendour

---

- POPULATION: 3.8 MILLION  ■ AREA: 4239 SQ MILES  ■ UFO HOT SPOT: UFFINGTON

# History

The Bronze Age chalk horse at Uffington and the Iron Age hill fort close by are some of the earliest evidence of settlement in this part of England. In Roman times the region was traversed by a network of roads, some of which still exist today, and as word of the good hunting and fertile valleys spread, the region became heavily populated.

By the 11th century the wool and grain trades had made the locals rich, William the Conqueror had built his first motte and bailey in Windsor, and the Augustinian abbey in Oxford had begun training clerics. In the 12th century Henry II fortified the royal residence at Windsor, and in the 13th century Oxford's first colleges were established.

Meanwhile, local farmers continued to supply London with corn, wool and clothing. The Cotswolds in particular flourished and amassed great wealth. By the 14th century the wool merchants were rolling in money and building the beautiful villages and graceful wool churches that still litter the area today.

The region's proximity to London also meant that it became a popular retreat for wealthy city dwellers. The nobility and aristocracy flocked to Hertfordshire and Buckinghamshire, building country piles as retreats from the city, while the farm labourers made redundant by mechanisation moved back to the towns and cities. Today the area remains affluent and is home to busy commuters and a popular choice for wealthy Londoners looking for second homes.

# Information

The popularity of the Cotswolds as a holiday destination means that you'll find helpful tourist offices in all towns and a wealth of information on the area. Outside the Cotswolds, the region is far less visited and information points can be rather thin on the ground. St Albans and Windsor are your best bets for assistance, or visit www.visitsoutheastengland.com and www.enjoyengland.com for the local low-down.

# Activities

Walking or cycling through the Cotswolds is an ideal way to get away from the crowds and discover some of the lesser-known vistas and villages of the region. You'll also find great walking and cycling opportunities in Buckinghamshire's leafy Chiltern Hills and along the meandering River Thames. For more information, see Outdoor Activities (p108) or specific suggestions for walks and rides throughout this chapter.

## CYCLING

Gentle gradients and scenic vistas make the Cotswolds ideal for cycling, with only the steep western escarpment offering a challenge to the legs. Plenty of quiet country lanes and gated roads criss-cross the region, or follow the waymarked **Thames Valley Cycle Way** (NCN routes 4, 5).

Mountain bikers can use a variety of bridleways in the **Cotswolds** and **Chilterns**, and in the west of the region the **Forest of Dean** has many dirt-track options, and some dedicated mountain-bike trails.

## WALKING

The **Cotswold Hills** offer endless opportunities for day hikes, but if you're looking for something more ambitious, the **Cotswold Way** (www.nationaltrail.co.uk/Cotswold) is an absolute classic. The route covers 102 miles from Bath to Chipping Campden and takes about a week to walk.

Alternatively, the **Thames Path** (www.nationaltrail.co.uk/thamespath) follows the river downstream from its source near Cirencester to London. It takes about two weeks to complete the 184-mile route, but there's a very enjoyable five-day section from near Cirencester to Oxford.

Finally the 87-mile **Ridgeway National Trail** (www.nationaltrail.co.uk/ridgeway) meanders along the chalky grassland of the Wiltshire downs near Avebury, down into the Thames Valley and then along the spine of the Chilterns to Ivinghoe Beacon near Aylesbury in Buckinghamshire offering wonderful views of the surrounding area.

# Getting There & Around

Thanks to the region's proximity to the capital, there are frequent trains and buses rumbling in and out of London. Getting across the region can be more frustrating and time consuming though. Renting a car gives you the most freedom, but be prepared for busy roads in the Cotswolds during the summer months and daily rush-hour traffic closer to London.

**Traveline** ( ☎ 0871 2002233; www.traveline.org.uk) provides timetable information on all public transport.

# OXFORD, THE COTSWOLDS & AROUND

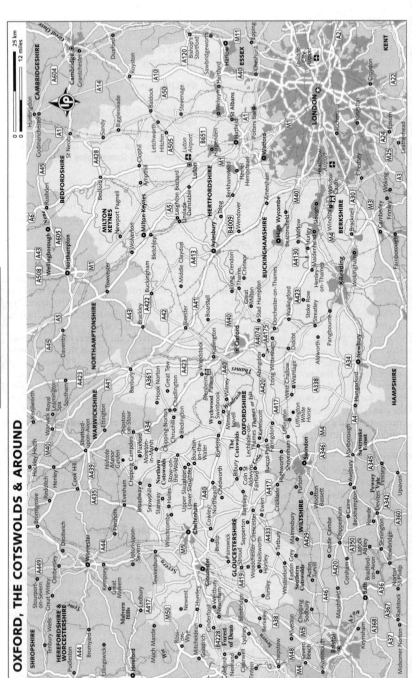

## BUS

Major bus routes are run by **Stagecoach** (www .stagecoachbus.com) and **Arriva** (www.arrivabus.co.uk) with a host of smaller companies offering services to local towns and villages. See the destination information for specific details of routes.

If you plan to do a lot of travelling by bus, there are a variety of bus passes available that allow unlimited travel across the region. Check routes before buying, however, as bad connections can rot up your best-laid plans.

Arriva offers the Go Anywhere (£7) ticket that allows you unlimited use of its services across the UK (excluding London) for a day. The better-value Stagecoach Explorer and Megarider tickets allow one-/seven-/28-day travel across Southern England (excluding London) for £8/20/75.

## TRAIN

For general rail information, call **National Rail** ( ☎ 08457-48 49 50; www.nationalrail.co.uk).

If you're planning a lot of rail travel in southern England, it may be worth investing in a **Network Railcard** (www.railcard.co.uk; per yr £20), which allows you and three other adults a 33% discount on rail tickets and up to four children (five to 15 years) a 60% discount. There are some restrictions on travel (such as discounts being only available after 10am on weekdays), but if you're travelling with family or friends it can make for great savings.

# OXFORDSHIRE

A well-bred, well-preened kind of place, Oxfordshire is a region of old money, academic achievement and genteel living. Dominated by its world-famous university, and renowned for its brilliant minds, the county town is a major highlight with over 1500 listed buildings, a choice of excellent museums and an air of refined sophistication. Yet there is a lot more to the county, and rustic charm, good manners and grand attractions are in abundant supply. Don't miss Blenheim Palace, an extravagant baroque pile that was birthplace of Sir Winston Churchill, or the elegant riverside town of Henley, famous for its ever-so-posh Royal Regatta.

## Activities

As well as the long-distance national trails, walkers may be interested in the **Oxfordshire Way**, a scenic, 65-mile waymarked trail running from Bourton-on-the-Water to Henley-on-Thames, and the **Wychwood Way**, a historic, 37-mile route from Woodstock, which runs through an ancient royal forest. The routes are divided up into manageable sections, described in leaflets available from most local tourist offices and libraries.

The quiet roads and gentle gradients also make Oxfordshire good cycling territory. The main waymarked route through the county is the **Oxfordshire Cycleway**, which takes in Woodstock, Burford and Henley. If you don't have your own wheels, you can hire bikes in Oxford (p250).

You'll find more information at www .oxfordshire.gov.uk/countryside.

## Getting Around

You can pick up bus and train timetables for most routes at local tourist offices. The main train stations are in Oxford and Banbury and have frequent connections to London Paddington and Euston, Hereford, Birmingham, Bristol and Scotland.

The main bus operators are the **Oxford Bus Company** ( ☎ 01865-785400; www.oxfordbus.co.uk) and **Stagecoach** ( ☎ 01865-772250; www.stagecoachbus .com/oxfordshire).

# OXFORD

pop 134,248

An air of genteel sophistication and long-held privilege hits you as soon as you arrive in Oxford. The august buildings, hushed college quads, grand libraries and gowned cyclists mark it out as a place unlike most others. Although traffic and shoppers rush along the streets, inside the hallowed walls of the city's 39 colleges a reverent hush and studious calm descends. Here the weight of centuries of academic achievement and the university's world-class reputation are all too obvious.

Oxford is a conservative, bookish kind of place where intellectual ideals are the common currency and pursuit of excellence the holy grail. It's a wonderful place to ramble; the oldest colleges date back almost 750 years and little has changed since then. Yet, the university is only part of Oxford's story – long before Mensa was ever born the Morris motor car was rolling off the production lines in Cowley. The new Mini has now replaced the Morris, but the real-world majority still outnumber the academic elite, and along with all that fine architecture is a working city home to disadvantaged council estates, the usual glut of high-street chain shops and plenty of chichi restaurants, trendy bars and expensive boutiques.

## History
Strategically placed at the confluence of the River Cherwell and the River Thames (called the River Isis here, from the Latin *Tamesis*), Oxford was a key Saxon town that grew dramatically in importance when Henry II banned Anglo-Norman students from attending the Sorbonne in 1167. Students soon flocked to Oxford's Augustinian abbey in droves.

Whether bored by the lack of distractions or revolted by the ignorance of the country folk we'll never know, but the new students managed to create a lasting enmity with the local townspeople, culminating in the St Scholastica's Day Massacre in 1355 (see p244). Thereafter, the king ordered that the university be broken up into colleges, each of which then developed its own traditions.

The first colleges, Balliol, Merton and University, were built in the 13th century, with at least three more being added in each of the following three centuries. Newer colleges, such as Keble, were added in the 19th and 20th centuries and today, there are 39 colleges catering for about 20,000 students.

Meanwhile, the arrival of the canal system in 1790 created a link with the industrial Midlands and work and trade suddenly expanded beyond the academic core. However, the city's real industrial boom came when William Morris began producing cars here in 1913. The Bullnose Morris and the Morris Minor were both produced in the Cowley factories to the east of the city, where BMW's new Mini runs off the production line today.

## Orientation
Oxford is fairly compact and can easily be covered on foot. Carfax Tower makes a good central landmark and is a short walk from the bus and train stations, which are conveniently located close to the centre of town.

The university buildings are scattered throughout the city, with the most important and architecturally significant in the centre. Jericho, in the northwest, is the trendy, artsy

end of town, with slick bars and restaurants and an art-house cinema, while Cowley Rd, southeast of Carfax, is the edgy student and immigrant area packed with cheap places to eat and drink. Further out, in the salubrious northern suburb of Summertown, you'll find more upmarket restaurants and bars.

## Information
### BOOKSHOPS
**Blackwell** ( ☎ 01865-333000; www.blackwell.co.uk; 48-51 Broad St) 'The Knowledge Retailer' stocks any book you could ever need.
**Waterfields** ( ☎ 01865-721809; www.waterfields books.co.uk; 52 High St) Collection of rare, second-hand and antiquarian books.

### EMERGENCY
**Police** ( ☎ 0845 8 505 505; St Aldate's)

### INTERNET ACCESS
**C-Works** ( ☎ 01865-722044; 1st fl, New Bailey Hse, New Inn Hall St; per 50min £1; ☯ 9am-9pm Mon-Sat, to 7pm Sun)
**Links** ( ☎ 01865-204207; 33 High St; per 45min £1; ☯ 10am-9pm Mon-Sat, to 8pm Sun)

### INTERNET RESOURCES
**Daily Info** (www.dailyinfo.co.uk) Daily listings for events, gigs, performances, accommodation and jobs.
**Oxford City** (www.oxfordcity.co.uk) Accommodation and restaurant listings as well as entertainment, activities and shopping.
**Oxford Online** (www.visitoxford.org) Oxford's official tourism website.

### LAUNDRY
**Coin Wash** (127 Cowley Rd; per load £3.50; ☯ 8am-10pm)

### MEDICAL SERVICES
**John Radcliffe Hospital** ( ☎ 01865-741166; Headley Way, Headington) Three miles east of the city centre.

### MONEY
Every major bank and ATM is represented on or near Cornmarket St.

### POST
**Post office** ( ☎ 0845 722 3344; 102 St Aldate's; ☯ 8.30am-5.30pm Mon, 9.30am-5.30pm Tue, 9am-5.30pm Wed-Sat)

### TOURIST INFORMATION
**Tourist office** ( ☎ 01865-252200; www.visitoxford.org; 15-16 Broad St; ☯ 9.30am-5pm Mon-Sat, to 6pm Thu-Sat

Jul & Aug, 10am-4pm Sun) Stocks a *Welcome to Oxford* brochure (£1), which features a walking tour and college opening times, as well as the *University of Oxford* leaflet and *Oxford Accessible Guide* for travellers with disabilities. It can book accommodation for a £4 fee plus a 10% deposit.

## UNIVERSITIES
**Oxford Brookes** ( ☎ 01865-484848; www.brookes.ac .uk; Gipsy Lane) Oxford's lesser-known university.
**Oxford University** ( ☎ 01865-270000; www.ox.ac.uk)

## Sights
### UNIVERSITY BUILDINGS & COLLEGES
### Christ Church College
The largest and grandest of all of Oxford's colleges, **Christ Church** ( ☎ 01865-276492; www.chch .ox.ac.uk; St Aldate's; adult/under 16yr £4.90/3.90; ⊗ 9am-5pm Mon-Sat, 1-5pm Sun) is also its most popular. The magnificent buildings, illustrious history and latter-day fame as a location for the Harry Potter films have tourists coming in droves.

The college was founded in 1525 by Cardinal Thomas Wolsey, who suppressed 22 monasteries to acquire the funds for his lavish building project. Over the years numerous luminaries have been educated here including Albert Einstein, philosopher John Locke, poet WH Auden, Charles Dodgson (Lewis Carroll) and 13 British prime ministers.

The main entrance is below imposing **Tom Tower**, the upper part of which was designed by former student Sir Christopher Wren. Great Tom, the 7-ton tower bell, still chimes 101 times each evening at 9.05pm (Oxford is five minutes west of Greenwich), to sound the curfew imposed on the original 101 students.

Mere visitors, however, are not allowed to enter the college this way and must go further down St Aldate's to the side entrance. Immediately on entering is the 15th-century cloister, a relic of the ancient Priory of St Frideswide, whose shrine was once a focus of pilgrimage. From here, you go up to the **Great Hall**, the college's magnificent dining room, with its hammer-beam roof and imposing portraits of past scholars.

Coming down the grand staircase, you'll enter **Tom Quad**, Oxford's largest quadrangle, and from here, **Christ Church Cathedral**, the smallest cathedral in the country. Inside, brawny Norman columns are topped by elegant vaulting, and beautiful, stained-glass windows adorn the walls. Look out for a rare depiction of the murder of Thomas Becket.

You can also explore another two quads and the **Picture Gallery**, with its modest collection of Renaissance art. To the south of the college is **Christ Church Meadow**, a leafy expanse bordered by the Rivers Isis and Cherwell rivers and ideal for leisurely walking.

### Magdalen College
Set amid 40 hectares of lawns, woodlands, river walks and deer park, **Magdalen** (mawd-len; ☎ 01865-276000; www.magd.ox.ac.uk; High St; adult/under 16yr £4/3; ⊗ noon-6pm Jul-Sep, 1pm-6pm/dusk Oct-Jun) is one of the wealthiest and most beautiful of Oxford's colleges.

An elegant Victorian gateway leads into a medieval chapel, with its glorious 15th-century tower, and on to the remarkable cloisters, some of the finest in Oxford. The strange gargoyles and carved figures here are said to have inspired CS Lewis' stone statues in *The Chronicles of Narnia*. Behind the cloisters, the lovely Addison's Walk leads through the grounds and along the banks of the River Cherwell for just under a mile.

Magdalen has a reputation as an artistic college, and some of its most famous students and fellows have included Oscar Wilde, Poet Laureate Sir John Betjeman and Nobel Laureate Seamus Heaney.

The college also boasts a fine choir that sings *Hymnus Eucharisticus* at 6am on May Day (1 May) from the top of the 42m bell tower. The event now marks the culmination of a solid night of drinking for most students as they gather in their glad rags on Magdalen Bridge to listen to the dawn chorus.

Opposite the college and sweeping along the banks of the River Cherwell are the beautiful **Botanic Gardens** ( ☎ 01865-286690; www.botanic -garden.ox.ac.uk; adult/under 16yr £3/free; ⊗ 9am-6pm May-Aug, to 4.30pm Oct-Apr). The gardens are the oldest in Britain and were founded in 1621 for the study of medicinal plants.

### Sheldonian Theatre
The monumental **Sheldonian Theatre** ( ☎ 01865-277299; www.sheldon.ox.ac.uk; Broad St; adult/under 16yr £2/1; ⊗ 10am-12.30pm & 2-4.30pm Mon-Sat Mar-Oct, 10am-12.30pm & 2-3.30pm Mon-Sat Nov-Feb) was the first major work of Christopher Wren, at that time a university Professor of Astronomy. Inspired by the classical Theatre of Marcellus in Rome, it has a rectangular front end and a semicircular back, while inside, the ceiling of the main hall is blanketed by a fine

OXFORD, THE COTSWOLDS & AROUND

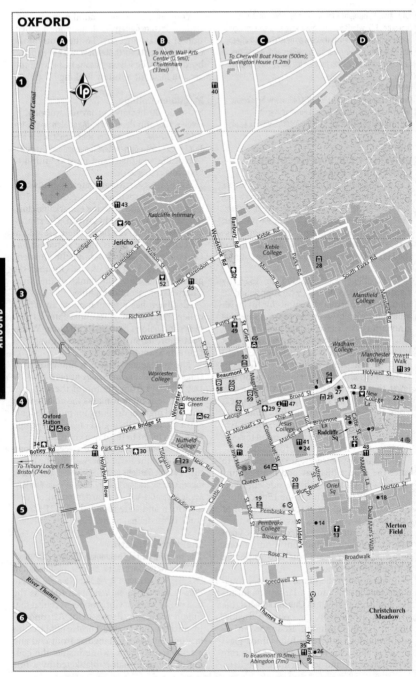

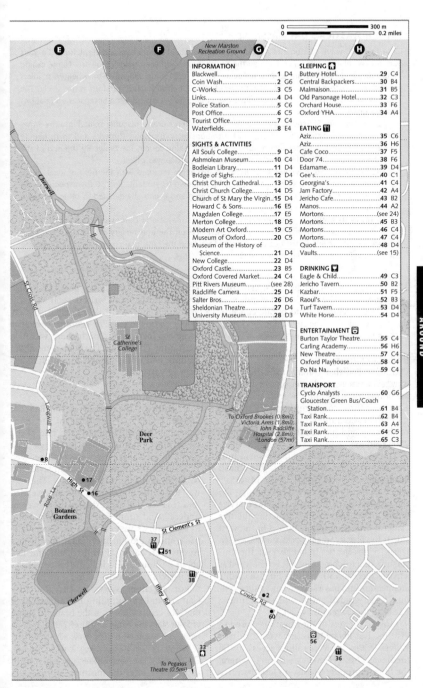

**INFORMATION**
Blackwell.....................................**1** D4
Coin Wash..................................**2** G6
C-Works.....................................**3** C5
Links.........................................**4** D4
Police Station.............................**5** C6
Post Office..................................**6** C5
Tourist Office..............................**7** C4
Waterfields................................**8** E4

**SIGHTS & ACTIVITIES**
All Souls College.........................**9** D4
Ashmolean Museum...................**10** C4
Bodleian Library.........................**11** D4
Bridge of Sighs...........................**12** D4
Christ Church Cathedral..............**13** D5
Christ Church College.................**14** D5
Church of St Mary the Virgin......**15** D4
Howard C & Sons......................**16** E5
Magdalen College.....................**17** E5
Merton College.........................**18** D5
Modern Art Oxford....................**19** C5
Museum of Oxford.....................**20** C5
Museum of the History of
   Science..................................**21** D4
New College...............................**22** D4
Oxford Castle.............................**23** B5
Oxford Covered Market..............**24** C4
Pitt Rivers Museum.............(see 28)
Radcliffe Camera........................**25** D4
Salter Bros.................................**26** D6
Sheldonian Theatre....................**27** D4
University Museum......................**28** D3

**SLEEPING**
Buttery Hotel.............................**29** C4
Central Backpackers....................**30** B4
Malmaison.................................**31** B5
Old Parsonage Hotel..................**32** C3
Orchard House...........................**33** F6
Oxford YHA...............................**34** A4

**EATING**
Aziz...........................................**35** C6
Aziz...........................................**36** H6
Cafe Coco..................................**37** F5
Door 74.....................................**38** F6
Edamame...................................**39** D4
Gee's.........................................**40** C1
Georgina's.................................**41** C4
Jam Factory...............................**42** A4
Jericho Cafe...............................**43** B2
Manos........................................**44** A2
Mortons...............................(see 24)
Mortons.....................................**45** B3
Mortons.....................................**46** C4
Mortons.....................................**47** C4
Quod..........................................**48** D4
Vaults..................................(see 15)

**DRINKING**
Eagle & Child.............................**49** C3
Jericho Tavern............................**50** B2
Kazbar.......................................**51** F5
Raoul's......................................**52** B3
Turf Tavern................................**53** D4
White Horse...............................**54** D4

**ENTERTAINMENT**
Burton Taylor Theatre.................**55** C4
Carling Academy........................**56** H6
New Theatre...............................**57** C4
Oxford Playhouse.......................**58** C4
Po Na Na...................................**59** C4

**TRANSPORT**
Cyclo Analysts ...........................**60** G6
Gloucester Green Bus/Coach
   Station..................................**61** B4
Taxi Rank..................................**62** B4
Taxi Rank..................................**63** A4
Taxi Rank..................................**64** C5
Taxi Rank..................................**65** C3

OXFORD, THE COTSWOLDS & AROUND

## ST SCHOLASTICA'S DAY MASSACRE

The first real wave of students arrived in Oxford in the 12th century and right from the start an uneasy relationship grew between the townspeople and the bookish blow-ins. Name calling and drunken brawls escalated into full-scale riots in 1209 and 1330 when browbeaten scholars abandoned Oxford to establish new universities in Cambridge and Stamford respectively. The riots of 10 and 11 February 1355 changed everything, however, and left a bitter scar on relations for hundreds of years.

Celebrations for St Scholastica's Day grew nasty when a drunken scuffle spilled into the street and years of simmering discontent and frustrations let loose. Soon students and townspeople were at each other's throats, with hundreds more rushing to join the brawl. By the end of the day the students had claimed victory and an uneasy truce was called.

The next morning, however, the furious townspeople returned with the help of local villagers armed with pickaxes, shovels and pikes. By sundown 63 students and 30 townspeople were dead. King Edward III sent troops to quell the rioting and eventually decided to bring the town under the control of the university.

To prove its authority, the university ordered the mayor and burgesses (citizens) to attend a service and pay a penny for every student killed on the anniversary of the riot each year. Incredibly, it took 600 years for the university to extend the olive branch and award a Doctorate of Civil Law to Mayor William Richard Gowers, MA, Oriel.

17th-century painting of the triumph of truth over ignorance. The Sheldonian is now used for college ceremonies and public concerts, but you can climb to the cupola for good views of the surrounding buildings.

### Bodleian Library

Oxford's **Bodleian Library** ( ☎ 01865-277224; www.bodley.ox.ac.uk; Broad St) is one of the oldest public libraries in the world, and one of England's three copyright libraries. It holds more than seven million items on 118 miles of shelving and has seating space for up to 2500 readers.

The oldest part of the library surrounds the stunning Jacobean-Gothic **Old Schools Quadrangle** ( ☑ 9am-5.15pm Mon-Fri, to 4.45pm Sat), which dates from the early 17th century. On the eastern side of the quad is the **Tower of Five Orders**, an ornate building depicting the five classical orders of architecture. On the west side is the **Divinity School** (admission adult/under 14yr £2/free; ☑ 9am-5pm Mon-Fri, to 4.30pm Sat), the university's first teaching room. It is renowned as a masterpiece of 15th-century English Gothic architecture and has a superb fan-vaulted ceiling. A self-guided audio tour (40 minutes; £2.50) to these areas is available.

Most of the rest of the library is closed to visitors, but **library tours** (admission £6; ☑ tours 10.30am, 11.30am, 2pm & 3pm) allow access to the medieval Duke Humfrey's library, where the library proudly boasts, no less than five

kings, 40 Nobel Prize winners, 25 British prime ministers and writers such as Oscar Wilde, CS Lewis and JRR Tolkien studied. You'll also get to see 17th-century **Convocation House and Court**, where parliament was held during the Civil War. The tour takes about an hour and is not suitable for children less than 11 years old.

### Radcliffe Camera

Just south of the library is the **Radcliffe Camera** (Radcliffe Sq; ☑ no public access), the quintessential Oxford landmark and one of the city's most photographed buildings. The spectacular circular library was built between 1737 and 1749 in grand Palladian style, and boasts Britain's third-largest dome. The only way to see the library is to join an extended tour (£12), which also explores the warren of underground tunnels and passages leading to the library's vast book stacks. Tours take place once a month (more often in July and August) on Saturday at 10.30am and last about an hour and a half. Advanced booking is recommended.

For excellent views of the Radcliffe Camera and surrounding buildings, climb the 14th-century tower in the beautiful **Church of Saint Mary the Virgin** ( ☎ 01865-279111; www.university-church.ox.ac.uk; High St; tower adult/under-16yr £2.50/1.50; ☑ 9am-6pm Jul & Aug, 9am-5pm Sep-Jun). On Sunday the tower does not open until about noon, after the morning service.

## New College

From the Bodleian, stroll under the **Bridge of Sighs**, a 1914 copy of the famous bridge in Venice, to **New College** ( ☎ 01865-279555; www .new.ox.ac.uk; Holywell St; admission Easter-Sep £2, Oct-Easter free; ⏰ 11am-5pm Easter-Sep, 2-4pm Oct-Easter). This 14th-century college was the first in Oxford to accept undergraduates and is a fine example of the glorious Perpendicular style. The chapel here is full of treasures including superb stained glass, much of it original, and Sir Jacob Epstein's disturbing statue of Lazarus.

During term time, visitors may attend the beautiful Evensong, a choral church service held nightly at 6pm. Access for visitors is through the New College Lane gate from Easter to early October, and through the Holywell St entrance the rest of the year.

William Spooner was once a college warden here, and his habit of transposing the first consonants of words gave rise to the term 'spoonerism'. Local lore suggests that he once reprimanded a student by saying, 'You have deliberately tasted two worms and can leave Oxford by the town drain'.

## Merton College

From the High St follow the wonderfully named Logic Lane to **Merton College** ( ☎ 01865-276310; www.merton.ox.ac.uk; Merton St; admission free; ⏰ 2-4pm Mon-Fri, 10am-4pm Sat & Sun), one of Oxford's original three colleges. Founded in 1264, Merton was the first to adopt collegiate planning, bringing scholars and tutors together into a formal community and providing a planned residence for them. The charming 14th-century **Mob Quad** here was the first of the college quads.

Just off the quad is a 13th-century **chapel** and the **Old Library** (admission on guided tour only), the oldest medieval library in use. It is said that Professor JRR Tolkien spent many hours here while writing *The Lord of the Rings*. Other literary giants associated with the college include TS Eliot and Louis MacNeice.

## All Souls College

One of the wealthiest of Oxford's colleges and unique in not accepting undergraduate students, **All Souls** ( ☎ 01865-279379; www.all-souls .ox.ac.uk; High St; admission free; ⏰ 2-4pm Mon-Fri) is primarily an academic research institution. It was founded in 1438 as a centre of prayer and learning, and today fellowship of the college is one of the highest academic honours

in the country. Each year, the university's top finalists are invited to sit a fellowship exam, with an average of only two making the grade annually.

Much of the college facade dates from the 1440s, and, unlike other older colleges, the front quad is largely unchanged in five centuries. It also contains a beautiful 17th-century sundial designed by Christopher Wren. Most obvious, though, are the twin mock-Gothic towers on the north quad. Designed by Nicholas Hawksmoor in 1710, they were lambasted for ruining the Oxford skyline when first erected.

### ASHMOLEAN MUSEUM

A vast, rambling collection of art and antiquities is on display at the mammoth **Ashmolean** ( ☎ 01865-278000; www.ashmolean.org; Beaumont St; admission free; ⏰ 10am-5pm Tue-Sat, noon-5pm Sun), Britain's oldest public museum. Established in 1683, it is based on the extensive collection of the remarkably well-travelled John Tradescant, gardener to Charles I, and it is housed in one of Britain's best examples of neo-Grecian architecture.

Bursting with Egyptian, Islamic and Chinese art; rare porcelain, tapestries and silverware; priceless musical instruments; and extensive displays of European art (including works by Raphael and Michelangelo), it's impossible to take it all in at once. At the time of writing, the Ashmolean was undergoing a £61-million redevelopment with 39 new galleries due to open in a state-of-the-art building in late 2009. The 'Treasures of the Ashmolean Museum' exhibition offers a cross-section of highlights from the vast collection. As part of the redevelopment, the entire museum was closed temporarily from January 2009, so check the website for up-to-date details.

### UNIVERSITY & PITT RIVERS MUSEUMS

Housed in a glorious Victorian Gothic building with slender, cast-iron columns, ornate capitals and a soaring glass roof, the **University Museum** ( ☎ 01865-272950; www.oum.ox.ac.uk; Parks Rd; admission free; ⏰ 10am-5pm) is worth a visit for its architecture alone. However, the real draw is the mammoth natural-history collection of more than five million exhibits ranging from exotic insects and fossils to a towering T-Rex skeleton.

**Pitt Rivers Museum** ( ☎ 01865-270927; www .prm.ox.ac.uk; admission free; ⏰ 10am-4.30pm Tue-Sun, noon-4.30pm Mon), hidden away through a door at the back of the main exhibition hall, is a treasure trove of weird and wonderful displays to satisfy every armchair adventurer's wildest dreams. In the half-light inside are glass cases and mysterious drawers stuffed with Victorian explorers' prized booty. Feathered cloaks, necklaces of teeth, blowpipes, magic charms, Noh masks, totem poles, fur parkas, musical instruments and shrunken heads lurk here, making it a fascinating place for adults and children. At the time of writing the museum was closed for renovations, due to reopen in spring 2009.

Both museums run workshops for children almost every weekend and are known for their child-friendly attitude.

### OXFORD CASTLE

**Oxford Castle Unlocked** ( ☎ 01865-260666; www .oxfordcastleunlocked.co.uk; 44-46 Oxford Castle; adult/under 15yr £7.50/5.35; ☑ 10am-5pm, last tour 4pm) explores the 1000-year history of Oxford's castle and prison. Tours begin in the 11th-century Crypt of St George's Chapel, possibly the first formal teaching venue in Oxford, and continue on into the Victorian prison cells and the 18th-century Debtors' Tower where you can learn about the inmates' grisly lives, daring escapes and cruel punishments. You can also climb the Saxon St George's Tower, which has excellent views of the city, and clamber up the original medieval motte.

### OTHER ATTRACTIONS

Far removed from Oxford's musty hallways of history, **Modern Art Oxford** ( ☎ 01865-722733; www.modernartoxford.org.uk; 30 Pembroke St; admission free; ☑ 10am-5pm Tue-Sat, noon-5pm Sun) is one of the best contemporary-art museums outside London, with a wonderful gallery space and plenty of activities for children.

Nearby, the **Museum of Oxford** ( ☎ 01865-252761; www.museumofoxford.org.uk; St Aldate's; admission free; ☑ 10am-5pm Tue-Fri, noon-5pm Sat & Sun) is dedicated to the history of the city and its university, and explores everything from Oxford's prehistoric mammoths to its history of car manufacturing.

Science, art, celebrity and nostalgia come together at the **Museum of the History of Science** ( ☎ 01865-277280; www.mhs.ox.ac.uk; Broad St; admission free; ☑ noon-5pm Tue-Fri, 10am-5pm Sat, 2-5pm Sun), where the exhibits include everything from a blackboard used by Einstein to the

world's finest collection of historic scientific instruments, all housed in a beautiful 17th-century building.

A haven of traditional butchers, fishmongers, cobblers and barbers, the **Oxford Covered Market** (www.oxford-covered-market.co.uk; ☑ 8.30am-5.30pm Mon-Sat) is the place to go for Sicilian sausage, handmade chocolates, traditional pies, funky T-shirts and expensive brogues. It's a fascinating place to explore and, if you're in Oxford at Christmas, a must for its traditional displays of freshly hung deer, wild boar, ostrich and turkey.

## Activities

A quintessential Oxford experience, **punting** is all about sitting back and quaffing Pimms as you watch the dreaming spires float by. Which, of course, requires someone else to do the hard work – punting is far more difficult than it appears. Be prepared to spend much of your time struggling to get out of a tangle of low branches or avoiding the path of an oncoming eight. For tips on how to punt, see p408.

Punts are available from mid-March to mid-October, 10am to dusk, and hold five people including the punter (£12/14 per hour weekdays/weekends).

The most central location to rent punts is at Magdalen Bridge, from **Howard C & Sons** ( ☎ 01865-202643; High St; deposit £30). From here, you can punt downstream around the Botanic Gardens and Christ Church Meadow or upstream around Magdalen Deer Park. Alternatively, head for the **Cherwell Boat House** ( ☎ 01865-515978; www.cherwellboathouse.co.uk; Bardwell Rd; deposit £60) for a countryside amble, where the destination of choice is the busy boozer, the **Victoria Arms** ( ☎ 01865-241382; Mill Lane). To get to the boathouse, take bus 2 or 7 from Magdalen St to Bardwell Rd and follow the signposts.

## Tours

**Blackwell** ( ☎ 01865-333606; oxford@blackwell.co.uk; 48-51 Broad St; adult/child £6.50/4; ☑ late May–Oct) Oxford's most famous bookshop runs 1½ -hour tours, including a literary tour (2pm Tuesdays and 11.30am Thursdays), an 'Inklings' tour (11.45am Wednesdays) – the Inklings was an informal literary group whose membership included CS Lewis and JRR Tolkien – and a town-and-gown tour (2pm Fridays).

**City Sightseeing** ( ☎ 01865-790522; www.citysight seeingoxford.com; adult/under 16yr £11.50/6; ☑ every 10-15min 9.30am-6pm Apr-Oct) Runs hop-on hop-off bus tours from the bus and train stations or any of the 20 dedicated stops around town.

**Tourist office** ( ☎ 01865-252200; www.visitoxford .org; 15-16 Broad St; ☽ 9.30am-5pm Mon-Sat, 10am-4pm Sun) Runs two-hour tours of Oxford city and colleges (adult/under 16yr £7/3.50; at 11am and 2pm year-round, also at 10.30am and 1pm during July and August), Inspector Morse tours (£7.50/4; 1.30pm Saturday), family walking tours (£5.50/3.50; 1.30pm school holidays) and a selection of themed tours (adult/child £7.50/4) that run on various dates throughout the year.

**Oxford River Cruises** ( ☎ 08452-269396; www.ox fordrivercruises.com) Choose from a range of River Thames tours including river sightseeing trips (adult/child £15/7.50; 50 minutes, Thursday and Sunday from March to October), lunchtime picnics trips (adult/child under 12yr £42/29, Thursday and Sunday from March to October) and sunset dinner cruises (£42, Wednesday and Saturday from May to September).

**Oxon Carts** ( ☎ 07747-024600; www.oxoncarts.com; 15min taster tour £10, 1hr tour £30) Runs a fleet of five pedicabs around Oxford's narrow lanes where the buses simply can't go. Passengers receive a copy of a 1904 map of the city and a personal guide to its buildings and history.

**Salter Bros** ( ☎ 01865-243421; www.salterssteamers .co.uk; Folly Bridge; boat trips adult/child £8.50/4.80; ☽ mid-May–mid-Sep) Offers boat trips along the River Isis to Abingdon.

## Sleeping

Oxford accommodation is generally over-priced and underwhelming, with suffocating floral patterns the B&B norm. The following places stand out for their value for money and good taste. Book ahead between May and September, and if you're stuck you'll find a string of B&Bs along the Iffley, Abingdon, Banbury and Headington roads.

### BUDGET

**Central Backpackers** ( ☎ 01865-242288; www.central backpackers.co.uk; 13 Park End St; dm £16-19; ☐ ) A good budget option right in the centre of town, this small hostel has basic, bright and simple rooms that sleep four to 12 people. There's a small but decent lounge with satellite TV, a rooftop terrace and free internet and luggage storage.

**Oxford YHA** ( ☎ 01865-727275; www.yha.org.uk; 2A Botley Rd; dm/d £22/56; ☐ ) Bright, well-kept, clean and tidy, this is Oxford's best budget option with simple but comfortable dorm accommo-dation, private rooms and loads of facilities in-cluding a restaurant, library, garden, laundry and a choice of lounges. All rooms are en suite

and are bright and cheery, a far better option than some of the city's cheapest B&Bs.

### MIDRANGE

**Oxford Rooms** (www.oxfordrooms.co.uk; r £40-120) Didn't quite make the cut for a place at Oxford? Well at least you can experience life inside the hallowed college grounds and breakfast in a grand college hall by staying overnight in one of their student rooms. Most rooms are singles and pretty functional with basic furnishings, shared bathrooms and internet access, though there are some en-suite, twin and family rooms available. Some rooms have old-world character and views over the college quad, while others are more modern but in a nearby annexe. There's limited availability during term time, but a good choice of rooms during university holidays, and you'll get a full description before you book.

**Beaumont** ( ☎ 01865-241767; www.oxfordcity.co.uk/ accom/beaumont; 234 Walton St; s £45-55, d £60-78) A class above most B&Bs at this price, this place is all crisp, white linen, pale and trendy flock wallpaper, mosaic bathrooms and beautiful, hand-picked furniture. The simple but elegant decor gives it a really tranquil atmosphere, despite being close to the city centre.

**Tilbury Lodge** ( ☎ 01865-862138; www.tilburylodge .com; 5 Tilbury Lane; s £70, d £80-90; P ☐ ) Spacious, top-of-the-line rooms with plush, modern decor and excellent bathrooms make this styl-ish B&B worth the trip outside the centre of town. Giant pillows in funky fabrics adorn the big beds, light streams through the large windows and, downstairs, there's a conserva-tory for guest use.

**our pick** **Orchard House** ( ☎ 01865-249200; www .theorchardhouseoxford.co.uk; 225 Iffley Rd; s £75-85, d £85-95; P ) Set in beautiful secluded gardens just a short walk from the city centre, this lovely arts-and-crafts-style house is a wonderful retreat from the city. The two bedrooms are sleek and stylish and very spacious, each with its own sofa and breakfast table, and the lime-stone bathrooms are luxuriously modern.

**Burlington House** ( ☎ 01865-513513; www.burling ton-house.co.uk; 374 Banbury Rd; s £65, d £85-95; P ☐ ) Simple, elegant rooms decked out in re-strained, classical style are available at this Victorian merchant house. The rooms are big, bright and uncluttered, with plenty of period character and immaculately kept bathrooms. It's not central, but it has good public trans-port to town and is well worth the trip.

**Buttery Hotel** ( ☎ 01865-811950; www.thebuttery hotel.co.uk; 11-12 Broad St; s/d from £60/95; 💻 ) Right in the heart of the city with views over the college grounds, the Buttery is Oxford's newest hotel. Considering its location, it's a great deal, with spacious, modern rooms, decent bathrooms and the pick of the city's attractions on your doorstep.

### TOP END

**Malmaison** ( ☎ 01865-268400; www.malmaison-oxford .com; 3 Oxford Castle; d/ste from £160/245; 💻 ) Lock yourself up for the night in one of Oxford's most spectacular settings. This former Victorian prison has been converted into a sleek and slinky hotel with plush interiors, sultry lighting, dark woods and giant beds. If you're planning a real bender, go for the Governor's Suite, complete with four-poster bed and mini cinema. Look out for online promotions when you can bag a room for as little as £99.

**our pick Old Parsonage Hotel** ( ☎ 01865-310210; www.oldparsonage-hotel.co.uk; 1 Banbury Rd; r £170-250; 🅿 💻 ) Wonderfully quirky and instantly memorable, the Old Parsonage is a small boutique hotel with just the right blend of old-world character, period charm and modern luxury. The 17th-century building oozes style with a contemporary-art collection, artfully mismatched furniture and chic bedrooms with handmade beds and marble bathrooms.

## Eating

Oxford has plenty of choice when it comes to eating out, but unfortunately ubiquitous chain restaurants dominate the scene, especially along George St and around the pedestrianised square at the castle. Head to Walton St in Jericho, to St Clements, Summertown or up the Cowley Rd for a more quirky selection of restaurants.

### BUDGET

**Vaults** ( ☎ 01865-279112; Church of St Mary the Virgin; mains £3.25-5; 🕙 10am-5pm) Does a great selection of wholesome soups, salads, pastas and paellas with plenty of choice for vegetarians. Set in a vaulted 14th-century Congregation House with lovely gardens, overlooking Radcliffe Sq, it's one of the most beautiful lunch venues in Oxford.

**Georgina's** ( ☎ 01865-249527; Ave 3, Oxford Covered Market; mains £5-8; 🕙 8.30am-5pm Mon-Sat) Hidden up a scruffy staircase in the covered market and plastered with old cinema posters, this is a funky little cafe serving a bumper crop of bulging salads, hearty soups and such goodies as goats' cheese quesadillas and scrumptious cakes.

**our pick Edamame** ( ☎ 01865-246916; 15 Holywell St; sushi £2.50-3.50, mains £6-7; 🕙 lunch Wed-Sun, dinner Thu-Sat) You'll find this tiny Japanese place by looking for the queue out the door as you head down Holywell St, but it's well worth the wait. The food here is simply divine with the best rice and noodle dishes in town and sushi (Thursday night only) to die for.

**Manos** ( ☎ 01865-311782; 105 Walton St; mains £6-9; 🕙 closed Sun dinner) For delicious home-cooked tastes of the Med, head for this Greek deli and restaurant where you'll find a great selection of dishes bursting with flavour. The ground floor has a cafe and deli, while downstairs has more style and comfort, with giant cushions surrounding low tables.

**Jericho Cafe** ( ☎ 01865-310840; 112 Walton St; mains £7-9) Chill out and relax with the paper over a coffee and a doorstep of cake, or go for some of the wholesome lunch and dinner specials, which encompass everything from sausages and mash to Lebanese lamb kibbeh. There are plenty of hearty salads, lots of choice for vegies and bulging platters of meze.

**Cafe Coco** ( ☎ 01865-200232; 23 Cowley Rd; mains £7-14) Chilled out but always buzzing, this Cowley Rd institution is a sort of hip hang-out, with classic posters on the walls and a bald clown in an ice bath. The food is vaguely Mediterranean, with everything from pizzas to merguez thrown in, and can be a bit hit-and-miss but most people come for the atmosphere.

A chain worth keeping your eye out for is **Mortons** (baguettes £2.40-2.80) Oxford Covered Market ( ☎ 01865-200867; 103 Covered Market); Broad St (22 Broad St); Little Clarendon St (36 Little Clarendon St); New Inn Hall St (22 New Inn Hall St). Good for a quick bite en route between colleges, the ever-popular Mortons has a fine selection of baguettes.

### MIDRANGE

**Aziz** ( ☎ 01865-794945; 228 Cowley Rd; mains £8-10) Thought by many to be Oxford's best curry house, this award-winning restaurant attracts vegans, vegetarians and curry lovers in hoards. There's an extensive menu, chilled surroundings and portions generous enough to ensure you'll be rolling out the door. There's a second branch on Folly Bridge ( ☎ 01865-247775).

**Jam Factory** ( ☎ 01865-244613; www.thejamfacto ryoxford.com; 27 Park End St; mains £8-12) Arts centre, bar and restaurant rolled into one, the Jam Factory is a laid-back, boho kind of place, with changing exhibitions and hearty breakfasts, an excellent-value, £10 two-course lunch and an understated menu of modern British dishes.

**Door 74** ( ☎ 01865-203374; 74 Cowley Rd; mains £8-13; ☾ closed Mon & Sun dinner) This cosy little place woos its fans with a rich mix of largely Mediterranean flavours, friendly service and a quirky interior. The menu is limited, but each dish is cooked to perfection and combines classic ingredients with a modern twist.

**Quod** ( ☎ 01865-202505; www.quod.co.uk; 92 High St; mains £10.50-15.50) Bright, buzzing and decked out with modern art and beautiful people, this designer joint dishes up Mediterranean brasserie-style food to the masses. It doesn't take reservations, is always heaving and, at worst, will tempt you to chill by the bar with a cocktail while you wait.

### TOP END
**Gee's** ( ☎ 01865-553540; www.gees-restaurant.co.uk; 61 Banbury Rd; mains £15-21.50) Set in a Victorian conservatory, this top-notch place is a sibling of Quod's but much more conservative. Popular with the visiting parents of university students, the food is modern British and European and the setting stunning, but it's all a little stiff.

## Drinking
### PUBS
**Turf Tavern** ( ☎ 01865-243235; 4 Bath Pl) Hidden away down narrow alleyways, this tiny medieval pub is one of the town's best-loved and bills itself as 'an education in intoxication'. It's always heaving with a mix of students, professionals and the lucky tourists who manage to find it, and has plenty for outdoor seating for sunny days.

**Eagle & Child** ( ☎ 01865-302925; 49 St Giles) Affectionately known as the 'Bird & Baby', this atmospheric place has been a pub since 1650 and is still a hotchpotch of nooks and crannies. It was once the favourite haunt of Tolkien, CS Lewis and their literary friends and still attracts a mellow crowd.

**White Horse** ( ☎ 01865-728318; 52 Broad St) This tiny olde-worlde place was a favourite retreat for TV detective Inspector Morse, and it can get pretty crowded in the evening. It's got buckets of character and makes a great place for a quiet afternoon pint and intellectual conversation.

### BARS
**Raoul's** ( ☎ 01865-553732; 32 Walton St) This trendy retro-look bar is one of Jericho's finest and is always busy. Famous for its perfectly mixed cocktails and funky music, it's populated by effortlessly cool punters trying hard not to spill their drinks as people squeeze by.

**Kazbar** ( ☎ 01865-202920; 25-27 Cowley Rd) This funky Moroccan-themed bar has giant windows, low lighting, warm colours and a cool vibe. It's buzzing most nights with hip young things sipping cocktails and filling up on the Spanish and North African tapas (£3 to £5).

**Jericho Tavern** ( ☎ 01865-311775; 56 Walton St) Chilled out and super cool with big leather sofas, tasselled standard lamps and boldly patterned wallpaper, this hip bar also has a live-music venue upstairs. Adorned with giant portraits of John Peel, Supergrass and Radiohead, it's supposedly where Radiohead (who hail from nearby Abingdon) played their first gig.

## Entertainment
### NIGHTCLUBS
Despite its large student population, Oxford's club scene is fairly limited, with several cattle-mart clubs in the centre of town and a lot of crowd-pleasing music. Try the following for something a little more adventurous.

**Carling Academy** ( ☎ 01865-813500; www.carling -academy.co.uk; 190 Cowley Rd; club admission up to £6; ☾ box office noon-5.30pm Mon-Fri, to 4pm Sat) Oxford's best club and live-music venue had a recent makeover and now hosts everything from big-name DJs to indie sounds, hard rock, funk nights and chart-busting bands.

**Po Na Na** ( ☎ 01865-249171; 13-15 Magdalen St; admission up to £6; ☾ Thu-Sat) Looking a little rough around the edges now, this small cave-like place is hung with Moroccan lanterns and drapes and, in between the regular club nights, attracts some big-name DJs and live events. Expect funk, soul, electro, drum 'n' bass, house and indie rock.

### THEATRE
The city's main stage for quality drama is the **Oxford Playhouse** ( ☎ 01865-305305; www.oxfordplay house.com; Beaumont St). Just around the corner, the **Burton Taylor Theatre** ( ☎ 01865-305305; www .burtontaylor.co.uk; Gloucester St) hosts quirky student shows, while the **Pegasus Theatre** ( ☎ 01865- 722851; www.pegasustheatre.org.uk; Magdalen Rd) hosts alternative independent productions.

For ageing pop stars try the **New Theatre** ( ☎ 0870 606 3500; www.newtheatreoxford.org.uk; George St), and for drama, dance, live music and art, the **North Wall Arts Centre** ( ☎ 01865-319452; www.thenorthwall.com).

Also look out for the highly original, mostly Shakespearean performances by **Creation Theatre** ( ☎ 01865-761393; www.creationtheatre .co.uk) in a variety of non-traditional venues, including city parks, the BMW plant and Oxford Castle.

### CLASSICAL MUSIC

With a host of spectacular buildings with great acoustics and two orchestras, Oxford is an excellent place to attend a classical concert. You'll find the widest range of events at www .musicatoxford.com. Alternatively, watch out for posters around town or contact one of these groups:

**City of Oxford Orchestra** ( ☎ 01865-744457; www .cityofoxfordorchestra.co.uk)
**Oxford Contemporary Music** ( ☎ 01865-488369; www.ocmevents.org)
**Oxford Philomusica** ( ☎ 01865-736202; www .oxfordphil.com)

## Getting There & Away

### BUS

Oxford's main bus/coach station is at **Gloucester Green**, in the heart of the city. Competition on the Oxford–London route is fierce, with two companies running buses (£15 return, four per hour) at peak times. Services run all through the night and take about 90 minutes to reach central London:

**Oxford Espress** ( ☎ 01865-785400; www.oxfordbus .co.uk)
**Oxford Tube** ( ☎ 01865-772250; www.oxfordtube.com)

The Heathrow Express (£18, 70 minutes) runs half-hourly 4am to 10pm and at midnight and 2am, while the Gatwick Express (£22, two hours) runs hourly 5.15am to 8.15pm and every two hours 10pm to 4am.

National Express has five direct buses to Birmingham (£11, two hours), and one service to Bath (£9.50, two hours) and Bristol (£13.80, 2¾ hours). All these destinations are easier to reach by train.

Stagecoach serves most of the small towns in Oxfordshire and runs the X5 service to Cambridge (£9, 3½ hours) roughly every half-hour. If you're planning a lot of bus journeys it's worth buying a Goldrider pass

(£20), which allows unlimited bus travel in Oxfordshire for seven days.

### CAR & MOTORCYCLE

Thanks to a complicated one-way system and a shortage of parking spaces, driving and parking in Oxford is a nightmare. Drivers are strongly advised to use the five Park & Ride car parks on major routes leading in to town. Three car parks are free to use, the others cost £1. The return bus journey to town (10 to 15 minutes, every 10 minutes) costs £2.50.

### TRAIN

There are half-hourly services to London Paddington (£22.50, one hour) and roughly hourly trains to Birmingham (£22, 1¼ hours), Worcester (£29, 1½ hours) and Hereford (£17.40, two hours). Hourly services also run to Bath (£19.60, 1¼ hours) and Bristol (£21.40, 1½ hours), but require a change at Didcot Parkway.

## Getting Around

### BICYCLE

The *Cycle into Oxford* map available from the tourist office shows all local cycle routes. You can hire bikes from **Cyclo Analysts** ( ☎ 01865-424444; 150 Cowley Rd; per day/week £14/40).

### BUS

If sightseeing has worn you out, buses 1 and 5 go to Cowley Rd from Carfax, 2 and 7 go along Banbury Rd from Magdalen St, and 16 and 35 run along Abingdon Rd from St Aldate's.

A multi-operator Plus Pass (per day/week/ month £5/17/46) allows unlimited travel on Oxford's bus system.

### TAXI

There are taxi ranks at the train station and bus station, as well as on St Giles and at Carfax. Be prepared to join a long queue after closing time. For a green alternative, call **Oxon Carts** ( ☎ 07747 024600; info@oxoncarts.com), a pedicab service.

## WOODSTOCK
### pop 2389

The charming village of Woodstock is full of picturesque creeper-clad cottages, elegant town houses, buckled roofs, art galleries and antique shops. It's an understandably popular spot, conveniently close to Oxford, yet a quintessential rural retreat. The big draw here is Blenheim Palace, the opulent country pile of the Churchill family, but the village itself is a gracious and tranquil spot even on busy summer days.

The hub of the village is the imposing **town hall**, built at the Duke of Marlborough's expense in 1766. Nearby, the **Church of St Mary Magdalene** had a 19th-century makeover but retains its Norman doorway, Early English windows and a musical clock.

Opposite the church, the **Oxfordshire Museum** ( ☎ 01993-811456; Park St; admission free; ⏰ 10am-5pm Tue-Sat, 2-5pm Sun) has displays on local history, art, archaeology and wildlife. It also houses the **tourist office** ( ☎ 01993-813276).

## Blenheim Palace

One of England's greatest stately homes, **Blenheim Palace** ( ☎ 08700 602080; www.blenheim-palace.com; adult/under 16yr £16.50/10, park & garden only £9.50/4.80; ⏰ palace 10.30am-5.30pm daily mid-Feb–Oct, Wed-Sun Nov–mid-Dec, park open year-round) is a monumental baroque fantasy designed by Sir John Vanbrugh and Nicholas Hawksmoor between 1705 and 1722. The land and funds to build the house were granted to John Churchill, Duke of Marlborough, by a grateful Queen Anne after his decisive victory at the Battle of Blenheim. Now a Unesco World Heritage Site, Blenheim (*blen*-num) is home to the 11th duke and duchess.

Inside, the house is stuffed with statues, tapestries, ostentatious furniture and giant oil paintings in elaborate gilt frames. Highlights include the **Great Hall**, a vast space topped by 20m-high ceilings adorned with images of the first duke in battle; the opulent **Saloon**, the grandest and most important public room; the three **state rooms** with their plush decor and priceless **china cabinets**; and the magnificent 55m **Long Library**.

From the library, you can access the **Churchill Exhibition**, which is dedicated to the life, work and writings of Sir Winston, who was born at Blenheim in 1874 (see the boxed text, p58). For an insight into life below stairs, the **Untold Story** exhibition explores the family's history through the eyes of the household staff.

If the crowds in the house become too oppressive, retire to the lavish gardens and vast parklands, parts of which were landscaped by Lancelot 'Capability' Brown. To the front, an artificial lake sports a beautiful bridge by Vanbrugh, and a mini train is needed to take visitors to a maze, adventure playground and butterfly house. For a quieter and longer stroll, glorious walks lead to an arboretum, cascade and temple.

## Sleeping & Eating

Woodstock has a good choice of accommodation, but it's not cheap. Luxurious, old-world hotels are the thing here so plan a day trip from Oxford if you're travelling on a budget.

**Laurel's Guesthouse** ( ☎ 01993-812583; www.laurelsguesthouse.co.uk; 40 Hensington Rd; s/d £75/80; ⏰ closed Dec & Jan P ) Packed with Victorian charm and character, this comfortable B&B has rooms featuring cast-iron or ornate wood beds, antique furniture and open fireplaces. The rooms are small and the bathrooms are tiny, but it's the period charm you'll remember.

**Bear Hotel** ( ☎ 01993-811124; www.macdonaldhotels.co.uk/bear; Park St; d from £92; P 💻 ) One of England's oldest hotels, the lavish Bear has long been a hideaway for romantic couples. The 13th-century coaching inn has recently been refurbished and, along with the open fireplaces, stone walls and exposed beams, you'll get the height of modern luxury. Book in advance and you could be in for a great deal.

**Brotherton's Brasserie** ( ☎ 01993-811114; 1 High St; mains £9-14; ⏰ closed Tue in winter) Set in an atmospheric 17th-century house clad in Virginia creeper and lit with the warm glow of gaslight, this popular brasserie is one of the best spots in town. Deep-red walls, scrubbed wooden floors and bare tables give it a rustic but homely feel, and the menu features everything from light pastas to hearty wild-boar casserole.

## Getting There & Away

Stagecoach bus 20 runs every half-hour (hourly on Sunday) from Oxford bus station (20 minutes). **Cotswold Roaming** ( ☎ 01865-308300; www.cotswold-roaming.co.uk) offers a Cotswolds/Blenheim combination tour (adult/under 15 years £40/27.50), with a morning at Blenheim and a half-day Cotswolds tour in the afternoon. The price includes admission to the palace.

## HENLEY-ON-THAMES
pop 10,513

A conservative but well-heeled kind of place, Henley is an attractive town set on the banks of the river, studded with elegant stone houses, a few Tudor relics and a host of chichi shops. The town bursts into action in July when it becomes the location for the Henley

Royal Regatta, a world-famous boat race and weeklong posh picnic hosted by high-end corporate entertainers.

The **tourist office** ( ☎ 01491-578034; www.vis ithenley-on-thames.com; The Barn, King's Rd; ☑ 10am-5pm Mon-Sat Jun-Sep, to 4pm Mar-May & Oct, to 3pm Nov-Feb) is next to the handsome town hall.

## Sights

Life in Henley has always focused on the river, and the impressive **River & Rowing Museum** ( ☎ 01491-415600; www.rrm.co.uk; Mill Meadows; museum only adult/child £3.50/2.50, museum & Wind in the Willows adult/under 18yr £7/5; ☑ 10am-5.30pm May-Aug, 10am-5pm Sep-Apr) takes a look at the town's relationship with the River Thames, the history of rowing and the wildlife and commerce the river supports. Hands-on activities and interactive displays make it a good spot for children, and the 'Wind in the Willows' exhibition brings Kenneth Grahame's stories of Ratty, Mole, Badger and Toad to life.

Walking around Henley, you'll come across a wealth of historic buildings, with many Georgian gems lining Hart St, the main drag. You'll also find the imposing **town hall** here, and the 13th-century **St Mary's Church** with its 16th-century tower topped by four octagonal turrets.

## Festivals & Events

### HENLEY ROYAL REGATTA

The first ever Oxford and Cambridge boat race was held in Henley in 1839, and ever since the cream of English society has descended on this small town each year for a celebration of boating, back slapping and the beau monde.

The five-day **Henley Royal Regatta** ( ☎ 01491-572153; www.hrr.co.uk) has grown into a major fixture in the social calendar of the upwardly mobile, and is a massive corporate entertainment opportunity. These days, hanging out on the lawn swilling champagne and looking rich and beautiful is the main event, and although rowers of the highest calibre compete, most spectators appear to take little interest in what's happening on the water.

The regatta is held in the first week of July, but you'll need contacts in the rowing or corporate worlds to get tickets in the stewards' enclosure. Mere mortals should head for the public enclosure (tickets £11 to £14), where you can lay out your gourmet picnic and hobnob with the best of them.

### HENLEY FESTIVAL

In the week following the regatta, the town continues its celebrations with the **Henley Festival** ( ☎ 01491-843404; www.henley-festival.co.uk), a vibrant black-tie affair that features everything from big-name international stars to quirky, alternative acts – anything from opera to rock, jazz, comedy and swing. The main events take place on a floating stage on the River Thames, and tickets vary in price from £35 for a space on the promenade to £59 for a seat in the grandstand.

## Sleeping & Eating

Henley has a good choice of accommodation, especially at the top end, but if you're planning to visit during either festival, book well in advance.

**Old School House** ( ☎ 01491-573929; www. oldschool househenley.co.uk; 42 Hart St; d £75-85; ℗ ) This small, quiet guesthouse in the town centre is a 19th-century school house in a walled garden, with a choice of two pretty guest rooms decked out in simple but comfortable style. Exposed timber beams and rustic furniture give it plenty of character, and the central location can't be beaten at this price.

**ourpick Hotel du Vin** ( ☎ 01491-848400; www.hoteldu vin.com; New St; d £145-295; ℗ 🖳 ) Set in the former Brakspears Brewery, this upmarket hotel chain scores highly for its blend of industrial chic and top-of-the-line designer sophistication. The spacious rooms and opulent suites are slick and stylish and are matched by a walk-in humidor, incredible billiards rooms, huge wine cellar and a popular bistro (mains £15 to £21).

**Green Olive** ( ☎ 01491-412220; 28 Market Pl; meze £4-10) A popular Henley haunt, Green Olive dishes up piled plates of traditional Greek meze in a bright and airy building with a lovely garden to the rear. Choose from over 50 dishes including spanakopitta, souvlaki, mussels with feta, stifado and moussaka.

**Chez Gerard Brasserie** ( ☎ 01491-411099; 40 Hart Street; mains £9-15) A welcome addition to the Henley restaurant scene, this stalwart chain of French brasseries has a chilled atmosphere, wooden floors, modern art on the walls and a selection of mismatched furniture. The menu features French classics as well as Moroccan tagines, pastas and grills.

## Getting There & Around

There are no direct train or bus services between Henley and Oxford. Trains to

London Paddington take about one hour (£12.50, hourly).

If you fancy seeing the local area from the river, **Hobbs & Son** ( ☎ 01491-572035; www.hobbs -of-henley.com) runs hour-long afternoon river trips from April to September (adult/under 16 years £7/5) and hires five-seater rowing boats (£13 per hour) and four-seater motorboats (£25 per hour).

## UFFINGTON WHITE HORSE

One of England's oldest chalk carvings, the **Uffington White Horse** is a stylised image cut into a hillside almost 3000 years ago. No-one is sure why the people of the time went to so much trouble to create the image or what exactly it is supposed to represent, but the mystery only adds to the sense of awe. This huge figure measures 114m long and 49m wide but is best seen from a distance, or, if you're lucky enough, from the air, because of the stylised lines of perspective.

Just below the figure is **Dragon Hill** – so called because it is believed that St George slew the dragon here – and above it the grass-covered earthworks of **Uffington Castle**. From

the Courthill Centre, near Wantage, a wonderful 5-mile walk leads along the Ridgeway to the White Horse.

In the nearby village of Uffington, you can visit the lovely 13th-century **St Mary's Church**, known locally as the 'Cathedral of the Vale', and the **Uffington Museum** ( ☎ 01367-820259; Broad St; admission free; ⊠ 2-5pm Sat & Sun Easter-Oct). The museum is set in the old school room featured in Thomas Hughes' *Tom Brown's Schooldays* and features displays on the author, local history and archaeology.

# THE COTSWOLDS

Glorious honey-coloured villages riddled with beautiful old mansions, thatched cottages, atmospheric churches and rickety almshouses draw crowds of tourists to the Cotswolds, a region of lush rolling hills that grew wealthy during a boom in the medieval wool trade. Prosperous merchants secured the region's place in history by building the stunning homes and villages that still litter the area today. If you've ever craved exposed beams, dreamed

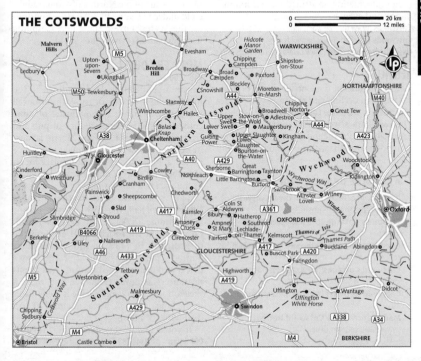

THE COTSWOLDS

of falling asleep under English-rose wallpaper or lusted after a cream tea in mid-afternoon, there's no finer place to fulfil your fantasies.

This is prime tourist territory, however, and the most popular villages can be besieged in summer. Plan to visit the main centres early in the morning or late in the evening, focus your attention on the south or take to the hills on foot or by bike to avoid the worst of the crowds. One of the greatest joys of the Cotswolds is just wandering off down quiet country roads to a deserted picture-postcard village seemingly undisturbed since medieval times.

## Orientation & Information

The limestone hills of the Cotswolds extend across a narrow band of land east of the M5, stretching almost as far as Oxford at their widest point, north to Chipping Campden and almost as far south as Bath. Most of the region lies within Gloucestershire, but parts leak out into Oxfordshire, Wiltshire, Somerset, Warwickshire and Worcestershire. The Cotswolds are protected as an Area of Outstanding Natural Beauty (AONB).

For information on attractions, accommodation and events:

**Cotswolds** (www.the-cotswolds.org)
**Cotswolds Tourism** (www.cotswolds.com)
**Oxfordshire Cotswolds** (www.oxfordshirecotswolds.org)

## Activities

The gentle hills of the Cotswolds are perfect for walking, cycling and riding.

The long-distance **Cotswold Way** (102 miles) gives walkers a wonderful overview of the area. The route meanders from Chipping Campden to Bath, with no major climbs or

---

### A COTTAGE OF YOUR OWN

If you'd like to rent your own Cotswold cottage, try these websites:

**Campden Cottages** (www.campdencottages.co.uk)

**Cotswold Cottage Company** (www.cotswoldcottage.co.uk)

**Cotswold Cottages** (www.cotswold-cottages.org.uk)

**Cotswold Retreats** (www.cotswoldretreats.co.uk)

**Manor Cottages & Cotswold Retreats** (www.manorcottages.co.uk)

---

difficult stretches, and is easily accessible from many points en route if you fancy tackling a shorter section. Ask at local tourist offices for details of day hikes or pick up a copy of one of the many walking guides to the region.

Away from the main roads, the winding lanes of the Cotswolds make fantastic cycling territory, with little traffic, glorious views and gentle gradients. Again, the local tourist offices are invaluable in helping to plot a route.

## Getting Around

Public transport through the Cotswolds is fairly limited, with bus services running to and from major hubs only, and train services just skimming the northern and southern borders. For help planning an itinerary pick up the *Explore the Cotswolds* brochures at local tourist offices. If you want to rent a car for greater flexibility you'll find car hire in most major towns.

Alternatively, **Cotswold Roaming** ( ☎ 01865-308300; www.cotswold-roaming.co.uk) runs guided bus tours from Oxford between April and October. Half-day tours of the Cotswolds (adult/child under 15 years £20/12) include Minster Lovell, Burford and Bibury while full-day tours of the North Cotswolds (adult/child under 15 years £30/20) feature Bourton-on-the-Water, Lower Slaughter, Chipping Campden and Stow-on-the-Wold.

## MINSTER LOVELL
### pop 1200

Set on a gentle slope leading down to the meandering River Windrush, Minster Lovell is a gorgeous village with a cluster of stone cottages nestled beside an ancient pub and riverside mill. One of William Morris' favourite spots, the village has changed little since medieval times and is a glorious place for an afternoon pit stop, a quiet overnight retreat or the start to a valley walk.

The main sight here is the ruins of **Minster Lovell Hall**, the 15th-century manor house home to Viscount Francis Lovell. Lovell fought with Richard III at the Battle of Bosworth in 1485, and joined Lambert Simnel's failed rebellion after the king's defeat and death. Lovell's mysterious disappearance was never explained and when a skeleton was discovered inside a secret vault in the house in 1708, it was assumed he had died while in hiding.

If you'd like to stay overnight, the **Mill & Old Swan** ( ☎ 0844 980 2313; www.deverevenues.co.uk;

---

**A STEP BACK IN TIME**

Squirreled away in the gorgeous village of Great Tew, is a pub little changed since medieval times, its flagstone floors, open fireplaces, low beams and outside loo all part of its 16th-century charm. The **Falkland Arms** ( ☎ 01608-683653; www.falklandarms.org.uk; Great Tew; r £80-110) sits right on the village green and plays host to a fine collection of local ales, ciders and wines. Traditional clay pipes and snuff are on sale behind the bar, and the clientele are a mix of lucky locals and those willing to make a special trip to enjoy its mellow atmosphere and beautiful surroundings. The food (mains £5 to £9) ranges from homemade soups and crusty baguettes to traditional Sunday roasts with all the trimmings; upstairs, the six guest rooms offer four-poster or cast-iron beds and period style. It doesn't get much more authentic than this.

Great Tew is about 4 miles east of Chipping Norton.

---

d £70-170; P 💻 ) offers charming period-style rooms in the 17th-century Old Swan or sleek, contemporary design in the 19th-century converted mill. The Old Swan serves decent pub food (£9 to £14).

**Swanbrook** (www.swanbrook.co.uk) runs three buses Monday to Saturday (one on Sunday) between Cheltenham (£7, one hour) and Oxford (30 minutes) via Minster Lovell. Stagecoach bus 233 between Witney and Burford stops here 10 times a day, Monday to Saturday (10 minutes each way).

## BURFORD
pop 1877

Slithering down a steep hill to a medieval crossing point on the River Windrush, the remarkable village of Burford is little changed since its glory days at the height of the wool trade. It's a stunningly picturesque place littered with higgledy-piggledy stone cottages, fine Cotswold town houses and the odd Elizabethan or Georgian gem. In between, a glut of antique shops, tearooms and specialist boutiques peddle nostalgia to the hoards of visitors who make here in summer, but despite the crowds it's easy to get off the main drag and wander along quiet side streets seemingly lost in time.

The helpful **tourist office** ( ☎ 01993-823558; Sheep St; 9.30am-5.30pm Mon-Sat Mar-Oct, to 4pm Mon-Sat Nov-Feb) provides the *Burford Trail* leaflet (10p) with information on walking in the local area.

### Sights & Activities

Burford's main attraction lies in its incredible collection of buildings, including the 16th-century **Tolsey House** (Toll House; High St; admission free; 2-5pm Tue-Fri & Sun, 11am-5pm Sat Mar-Oct), where the wealthy wool merchants held their meet-

ings. This quaint building perches on sturdy pillars and now houses a small museum on Burford's history.

Just off the High St, you'll find the town's 14th-century **almshouses** and the gorgeous **Church of St John the Baptist**. The Norman tower here is topped by a 15th-century steeple, and inside you'll find a fine fan-vaulted ceiling and medieval screens dividing the chapels.

Younger visitors will enjoy a visit to the excellent **Cotswold Wildlife Park** ( ☎ 01993-823006; www.cotswoldwildlifepark.co.uk; adult/under 16yr £10/7.50; 10am-4.30pm Mar-Sep, to 3.30pm Oct-Feb), set around a Victorian manor house. The park is home to everything from penguins to white rhinos and giant cats.

If you have the time and fancy getting away from the crowds, it's worth the effort to walk east along the picturesque river path to the untouched and rarely visited village of **Swinbrook** (3 miles), where the beautiful church has some remarkable tombs.

### Sleeping & Eating

**Cotland House** ( ☎ 01993-822382; www.cotlandhouse .com; Fulbrook Hill; s/d £40/70) A five-minute walk from town, this delightful B&B effortlessly mixes contemporary style with period charm. Although the rooms aren't spacious, they are gloriously comfortable with cast-iron beds, crinkly white linen and soft throws.

**our pick** **Lamb Inn** ( ☎ 01993-823155; www.cotswold -inns-hotels.co.uk/lamb; Sheep St; r £145-255; P 💻 wi-fi) Step back in time with a stay at the Lamb, a 15th-century inn just dripping with character. Expect flagstone floors, beamed ceilings, creaking stairs and a charming, laid-back atmosphere downstairs, and luxurious period-style rooms with antique furniture and cosy comfort upstairs. You'll get top-notch modern British food in the restaurant (three-course dinner

£27 to £33) or less formal dining (mains £9 to £13) in the bar.

**Angel** ( ☎ 01993-822714; www.theangelatburford. co.uk; 14 Witney St; mains £15-16) Set in a lovely 16th-century coaching inn, this atmospheric brasserie serves up an innovative menu of modern British and European food. Dine in by roaring fires in winter, or eat alfresco in the lovely walled garden in warmer weather.

### Getting There & Away

From Oxford, Swanbrook runs three buses a day (one on Sunday) to Burford (45 minutes). Stagecoach bus 233 runs between Witney and Burford 10 times a day, Monday to Saturday (20 minutes). Bus 853 goes to Cheltenham three times daily Monday to Saturday and once on Sunday.

## CHIPPING NORTON

pop 5688

The sleepy but attractive town of Chipping Norton is somewhat spoiled by constant traffic but has plenty of quiet side streets to wander and none of the Cotswold crowds. Handsome Georgian buildings, stone cottages and old coaching inns cluster around the market square, and on Church St you'll find a row of beautiful honey-coloured **almshouses** built in the 17th century. Further on is the secluded **Church of St Mary**, a classic example of the Cotswold wool churches, with a magnificent 15th-century Perpendicular nave and clerestory. The town's most enduring landmark, however, is the arresting **Bliss Mill** (now converted to apartments) on the outskirts of town. This monument to the industrial architecture of the 19th century is more like a stately home than a factory and is topped by a domed tower and chimney stack of the Tuscan order.

For overnight accommodation, **Norten's B&B** ( ☎ 01608-645060; www.nortens.co.uk; 10 New St; s £35-50, d £50-65) offers a range of contemporary rooms with simple, stylish design. The downstairs **cafe** (mains £4-7; ☯ 10am-10pm) serves a good range of Mediterranean food.

Alternatively, make your way 4 miles southwest of town to the pretty village of Kingham where the **Plough** ( ☎ 01608-658327; www.kinghamplough.co.uk; The Green, Kingham; s £65-75, d £75-95; P ☐ wi-fi) offers stylish rooms and sublime food.

Stagecoach bus 20 runs between Chippy and Oxford roughly every half-hour.

## MORETON-IN-MARSH

pop 3198

Home to some beautiful buildings but utterly ruined by the through traffic, Moreton-in-Marsh is useful for its transport links. **Pulhams Coaches** ( ☎ 01451-820369; www.pulhamscoaches.com) runs seven services daily between Moreton and Cheltenham (one hour, Monday to Saturday) via Stow-on-the-Wold (15 minutes) and Bourton-on-the-Water (20 minutes). Two Sunday services run from May to September only.

There are trains roughly every 90 minutes to Moreton from London Paddington (£29, 1½ hours) via Oxford (£9.70, 35 minutes) and on to Worcester (£10.60, 45 minutes) and Hereford (£14.30, 1½ hours).

## CHIPPING CAMPDEN

pop 1943

A truly unspoiled gem in an area full of achingly pretty villages, Chipping Campden is a glorious reminder of life in the Cotswolds in medieval times. The graceful curving main street is flanked by a wonderful array of wayward stone cottages, fine terraced houses, ancient inns and historic homes, liberally sprinkled with chichi boutiques and upmarket shops. Despite its obvious allure, the town remains relatively unspoiled by tourist crowds and is a wonderful place to visit.

Pop into the helpful **tourist office** ( ☎ 01386-841206; www.visitchippingcampden.com; High St; ☯ 10am-5pm Mon-Fri) to pick up a town trail guide to give you some information on the town's most historic buildings and get you off the main drag and down some of the gorgeous back streets.

The town's most obvious sight is the wonderful 17th-century **Market Hall** with its multiple gables and elaborate timber roof. Further on, at the western end of the High St, is the 15th-century **St James'**, one of the great wool churches of the Cotswolds. Built in the Perpendicular style, it has a magnificent tower and some graceful 17th-century monuments. Nearby on Church St is a remarkable row of **almshouses** dating from the 17th century, and the Jacobean lodges and gateways of the now-ruined Campden House. The surviving **Court Barn** ( ☎ 01386-841951; www.courtbarn.org.uk; Church St; adult/child under 16yr £3.75/free; ☯ 10.30am-5.30pm Tue-Sat, 11.30am-5.30pm Sun Apr-Sep, 11am-4pm Tue-Sat, 11.30am-4pm Sun Oct-Mar) is now a museum of craft and design featuring work from the Arts and Crafts Movement (see p83).

### THE COTSWOLDS OLIMPICKS

The medieval sport of shin-kicking lives on in Chipping Campden, where each year the townspeople gather to compete at the **Cotswolds Olimpicks**, a traditional country sports day first celebrated in 1612. It is one of the most entertaining and bizarre sporting competitions in England, and many of the original events such as welly wanging (throwing), the sack race and climbing a slippery pole are still held. The competition was mentioned in Shakespeare's *Merry Wives of Windsor* and has even been officially sanctioned by the British Olympic Association. It is held annually at the beginning of June.

About 4 miles northeast of Chipping Campden, **Hidcote Manor Garden** (NT; ☎ 01386-438333; Hidcote Bartrim; adult/under 18yr £8.50/4.25; ☼ 10am-5pm Sat-Wed mid-Mar–Oct, plus 10am-5pm Fri Jul & Aug) is one of the finest examples of arts and crafts landscaping in Britain.

### Sleeping & Eating

**Manor Farm** ( ☎ 01386-840390; www.manorfarmbnb .demon.co.uk; s/d £55/65) Set in a beautiful 17th-century farmhouse, this lovely B&B has all the period charm of a Cotswold home but with contemporary style and modern facilities. Along with the exposed oak beams and creaking stairs, you'll find king-size beds, power showers and neutral colour schemes.

**Eight Bells** ( ☎ 01386-840371; www.eightbellsinn .co.uk; Church St; s £55-85, d £85-125) Dripping with old-world character and charm, but also decidedly modern, this 14th-century inn has a range of sleek, comfortable rooms and a well-respected restaurant serving a British and Continental menu (mains £11 to £12) in rustic settings.

**our pick** **Cotswold House Hotel** ( ☎ 01386-840330; www.cotswoldhouse.com; The Square; r £150-650; P 🖵 ) If you're after a spot of luxury, look no further than this chic Regency town house turned boutique hotel. Bespoke furniture, massive beds, Frette linens, cashmere throws, private gardens and hot tubs are the norm here. You can dine in style at Juliana's (two-/three-course set dinner £39.50/49.50) or take a more informal approach at Hick's Brasserie (mains £9 to £18), a slick operation with an ambitious menu.

### Getting There & Around

Between them, buses 21 and 22 run almost hourly to Stratford-upon-Avon or Moreton-in-Marsh. Bus 21 also stops in Broadway. There are no Sunday services.

To catch a real glimpse of the countryside, try hiring a bike from **Cotswold Country Cycles** ( ☎ 01386-438706; www.cotswoldcountrycycles. com; Longlands Farm Cottage; per day £15) and discovering the quiet lanes and gorgeous villages around town.

## BROADWAY

pop 2496

The crooked stone cottages, town houses and lanes of Broadway have inspired writers, artists and composers in times past with graceful, golden-hued cottages set at the foot of a steep escarpment. It's a quintessentially English place pitted with antique shops, tearooms and art galleries, and is justifiably popular in the summer months, but take the time to wander away from the main street and you'll be rewarded with quiet back roads lined with stunning cottages, flower-filled gardens and picturesque churches.

The **tourist office** ( ☎ 01386-852937; www.beautiful broadway.com; Russell Sq; ☼ 10am-5pm Mon-Sat, 2-5pm Sun) is just off the High St.

Beyond the charm of the village itself, there are few specific attractions. If you're feeling energetic, the lovely, 12th-century **Church of St Eadburgha** is a signposted 1-mile walk from town. Near here, a more challenging path leads uphill for 2 miles to **Broadway Tower** ( ☎ 01386-852390; www.broadwaytower.co.uk; adult/under 14yr £3.80/2.30; ☼ 10.30am-5pm Apr-Oct, 11am-3pm Sat & Sun Nov-Mar), a crenulated, 18th-century Gothic folly on the crest of the escarpment. It has a small William Morris exhibition on one floor and stunning views from the top.

Broadway is littered with chintzy B&Bs, but for something more atmospheric, try **Hadley House** ( ☎ 01386-853486; www.cotswolds.info/webpage/hadley -house.htms; Leamington Rd; s/d £60/70; P 🖵 wi-fi), a cosy B&B with beautiful rooms in soothing pale colours with a splash of deep red.

Alternatively, **Windrush** ( ☎ 01386-853 577; www.broadway-windrush.co.uk; Station Rd; d £80-100; P ) is a friendly B&B with newly refurbished rooms decked out in simple neutral colours, with flat-screen TVs, bathrobes and complementary toiletries.

For food, the **Swan** ( ☎ 01386-852278; www .theswanbroadway.co.uk; 2 The Green; mains £8-15) is an informal place with stylish, contemporary decor, wooden floors, leather seats and a mouth-watering, modern menu.

Sleek and stylish **Russells** ( ☎ 01386-853555; www.russellsofbroadway.com; 20 High St; mains £10-21) has upmarket modern British fare. It also has a selection of slick, modern rooms (£120 to £325) with simple design, flat-screen TVs and lots of little luxuries.

Bus 22 goes to Moreton-in-Marsh, Chipping Campden and Stratford (20 minutes, four daily Monday to Saturday) and bus 606 goes to Cheltenham (50 minutes, four Monday to Saturday).

## WINCHCOMBE
pop 3682

Winchcombe is a sleepy Cotswold town, very much a working, living place with butchers, bakers and small independent shops giving it a very lived-in, authentic feel. It was capital of the Saxon kingdom of Mercia and one of the most important towns in the Cotswolds until the Middle Ages, and today the remnants of its illustrious past can be seen in the beautiful houses lining the streets, and the picturesque cottages on Vineyard St and Dents Tce and in majestic Sudeley Castle. Winchcombe is also blessed with good accommodation and fine-dining choices, making it a great base for exploring the area.

The helpful **tourist office** ( ☎ 01242-602925; www.winchcombe.co.uk; High St; ☼ 10am-1pm & 2-5pm Mon-Sat, 10am-4pm Sun Apr-Oct, to 4pm Sat & Sun Nov-Mar) can help plan an itinerary.

When wandering around town, look out for the fine gargoyles that adorn the lovely St Peter's Church. Just outside the town are the evocative ruins of Cistercian **Hailes Abbey** (EH; ☎ 01242-602398; adult/under 15yr £3.50/1.80; ☼ 10am-5pm Easter-Oct), once one of the country's main pilgrimage centres.

The town's main attraction is magnificent **Sudeley Castle** ( ☎ 01242-602308; www.sudeleycastle.co.uk; adult/under 15yr £7.20/4.20; ☼ 10.30am-5pm Sun-Thu mid-Mar–Oct), once a favoured retreat of Tudor and Stuart monarchs. The house is still used as a family home, and much of the interior is off limits to visitors, but you can get a glimpse of its grand proportions while visiting the exhibitions of costumes, memorabilia and paintings and the surrounding gardens. If you want an insight into real life in the castle, join one of the 'Connoisseur Tours' (£15, Tuesday, Wednesday and Thursday 11am, 1pm and 3pm, mid-March to October).

## Sleeping & Eating

**White Hart Inn** ( ☎ 01242-602359; www.the-white-hart-inn.com; r £40-115) An excellent option in the centre of town. Choose the cheaper 'rambler' rooms with shared bathrooms or go for more luxury in a superior room. You'll also get a good choice of food in the bar (mains £7 to £8) and modern British fare in the main restaurant (mains £10.50 to £19.50).

**Parks Farm** ( ☎ 01242-603874; www.parksfarm.co.uk; Sudeley; d £50-60; P ) Stay on a 17th-century Cotswold hill farm just outside the town for an insight into local life. This friendly B&B has two cosy rooms with views over the rolling hills, and guests are served breakfast in a beamed kitchen with one large table and a roaring Aga.

our pick **5 North St** ( ☎ 01242-604566; 5 North St; 2/3-course lunch £20.50/24.50, 3-course dinner £33-43; ☼ lunch Wed-Sat, dinner Tue-Sun) The top spot to eat for miles around, this Michelin-starred restaurant has no airs and graces, just beautifully prepared food in down-to-earth surroundings. Deep-red walls, wooden tables and friendly service make it a very unpretentious place, but the food is thoroughly ambitious with a keen mix of British ingredients and French flair.

## Getting There & Away

Bus 606 runs from Broadway (65 minutes, four daily Monday to Saturday) to Cheltenham via Winchcombe.

## STOW-ON-THE-WOLD
pop 2074

A popular stop on a tour of the Cotswolds, Stow is anchored by a large market square surrounded by handsome buildings and steep-walled alleyways originally used to funnel sheep into the fair. The town has long held a strategic place in Cotswold history, standing as it does on the Roman Fosse Way and at the junction of six roads. Today it's littered with antique shops, boutiques, tearooms and delis thronged with passengers from passing coach tours. On a quiet day it's a wonderful place but all a little artificial if you're looking for true Cotswold charm.

The **tourist office** ( ☎ 01451-831082; Hollis House; ☼ 9.30-5.30pm Mon-Sat) on Market Sq sells discounted tickets to local attractions. Staying overnight is a good way to see Stow at its best. The comfortable but basic **Stow-on-the-Wold YHA** ( ☎ 0870 770 6050; www.yha.org.uk; The Square; dm £15.95; P ) is in a wonderful 16th-century town house and has a warm welcome for families. For something more upmarket try atmospheric **Number 9** ( ☎ 01451-870333; www.number-nine.info; 9 Park St; s £45-50, d £65-75) with its contemporary-styled rooms.

The best bet for food is the **Old Butchers** ( ☎ 01451-831700; www.theoldbutchers.com; 7 Park St; mains £12-17) a smart and sophisticated place serving robust, local ingredients whipped up into sublime dishes. Alternatively you'll find more traditional English favourites at the old-world **Eagle & Child** ( ☎ 01451-830670; Digbeth St; mains £10-16).

Bus 55 links Stow with Moreton, Bourton and Cirencester eight times daily Monday to Saturday. Bus 801 runs to Cheltenham, Moreton and Bourton four times daily Monday to Friday and nine times on Saturday.

The nearest train stations are 4 miles away at Kingham and Moreton-in-Marsh.

## BOURTON-ON-THE-WATER
pop 3093

An undeniably picturesque town, Bourton has sold its soul to tourism, becoming a Cotswolds theme park with its handsome houses and pretty bridges overshadowed by a series of crass, commercial attractions. Take your pick from the model railway and village, bird-conservation project, perfume factory, maze and motor museum, or visit in the winter when the village's understated charm is free to reveal itself.

One occasion worth battling the crowds for is the annual **water football match**, held in the river on the August Bank Holiday Monday. The tradition dates back to the 1800s.

If you'd like to stay chic and stylish, **Dial House** ( ☎ 01451-822244; www.dialhousehotel.com; The Chestnuts; r £110-230) is unpretentious but seriously luxurious, with hand-painted wallpaper, giant beds, silky throws and a wonderful mix of period charm and designer style. The restaurant (mains £10 to £23) serves up excellent modern British cuisine.

Bus 801 operates to Cheltenham, Moreton and Stow (up to four daily Monday to Friday, nine Saturday).

## THE SLAUGHTERS
pop 400

An antidote to the commercialism of Bourton, the picture-postcard villages of Upper and Lower Slaughter still attract the crowds of tourists, yet manage to maintain their unhurried medieval charm. The village names are derived from the Old English 'sloughtre', meaning slough or muddy place, but today the River Eye is contained within limestone banks and meanders peacefully through the village past the 17th-century Lower Slaughter Manor (now a top-notch hotel) to the **old mill** ( ☎ 01451-820052; www.oldmill-lowerslaughter.com; admission £2; 10am-6pm Mar-Oct) which houses a small museum and teashop.

To see the Slaughters at their best, arrive on foot from Bourton (a 1-mile walk) across the fields. From here you can continue for another mile across the fields to Upper Slaughter, with its own fine manor house and glorious cottages.

Swanbrook runs six buses Monday to Saturday between Cheltenham (30 minutes) and Northleach, and three to Oxford (one hour).

## CIRENCESTER
pop 15,861

Refreshingly unpretentious, with narrow, winding streets and graceful town houses, charming Cirencester is an affluent, elegant kind of place. The lovely market square is surrounded by wonderful 18th-century and Victorian architecture, and the nearby streets showcase a harmonious medley of buildings from various eras.

Under the Romans, Cirencester was second only to London in terms of size and importance and, although little of this period remains, you can still see the grassed-over ruins of one of the largest amphitheatres in the country. The medieval wool trade was also good to the town, with wealthy merchants funding the building of a superb church.

Today, Cirencester is the most important town in the southern Cotswolds and retains an authentic, unaffected air, with the lively Monday and Friday markets as important as the expensive boutiques and trendy delis that line its narrow streets.

The **tourist office** ( ☎ 01285-654180; Park St; 10am-5pm Mon-Sat, 2-5pm Sun) is located in the museum and has a leaflet detailing a guided walk around the town and its historic buildings.

## Sights

### CHURCH OF ST JOHN THE BAPTIST

Standing elegantly on the Market Sq, cathedral-like **St John's** (suggested donation £3; ☺ 10am-5pm) is one of England's largest parish churches. An outstanding Perpendicular-style tower with wild flying buttresses dominates the exterior, but it is the majestic three-storey south porch that is the real highlight. Built as an office by late-15th-century abbots, it subsequently became the medieval town hall.

Soaring arches, magnificent fan vaulting and a Tudor nave adorn the light-filled interior, where you'll also find a 15th-century, painted stone pulpit and memorial brasses recording the matrimonial histories of important wool merchants. The east window contains fine medieval stained glass, and a wall safe displays the **Boleyn Cup**, made for Anne Boleyn, second wife of Henry VIII, in 1535.

### CORINIUM MUSEUM

Modern design, innovative displays and computer reconstructions bring one of Britain's largest collections of Roman artefacts to life at the **Corinium Museum** ( ☎ 01285-655611; www .cotswolds.gov.uk/museum; Park St; adult/under 16yr £3.95/2; ☺ 10am-5pm Mon-Sat, 2-5pm Sun). You can dress as a Roman soldier, meet an Anglo-Saxon princess and discover what Cirencester was like during its heyday as a wealthy medieval wool town. Highlights of the Roman collection include the beautiful Hunting Dogs and Four Seasons floor mosaics, and a reconstructed Roman kitchen and butcher's shop.

## Sleeping & Eating

**Old Brewhouse** ( ☎ 01285-656099; www.theoldbrew house.com; 7 London Rd; s £50-55, d £65-70; **P** ) Set in a charming 17th-century town house, this lovely B&B has bright, pretty rooms with cast-iron beds and subtle, country-style florals or patchwork quilts. The beautiful garden room even has its own patio.

**No 12** ( ☎ 01285-640232; ww.no12cirencester.co.uk; 12 Park St; d £85) This Georgian town house right in the centre of town has gloriously unfussy rooms kitted out with a tasteful mix of antiques and modern furnishings. Think feather pillows, merino blankets, extra-long beds, slick modern bathrooms and a host of little extras to make you smile.

**Piazza Fontana** ( ☎ 01285-643133; 30A Castle St; mains £9-17; ☺ closed Sun) An authentic family-run Italian joint hidden away in a courtyard, serving up a great selection of traditional pastas, meat and fish dishes just done to perfection. It's well worth seeking out for its informal atmosphere and top-notch service.

**Jesse's Bistro** ( ☎ 01285-641497; Blackjack St; mains £12.50-21.50; ☺ lunch Mon-Sat, dinner Tue-Sat) Hidden away in a cobbled stable yard with its own fishmonger and cheese shop, Jesse's is a great little place with flagstone floors, wrought-iron chairs and mosaic tables. The modern menu features a selection of great dishes, but the real treat is the fresh fish and meat cooked in the wood-burning oven.

## Getting There & Away

National Express buses run roughly hourly from Cirencester to London (£17, 2½ hours) and to Cheltenham Spa (30 minutes) and Gloucester (one hour). Stagecoach bus 51 also runs to Cheltenham Monday to Saturday (40 minutes, hourly). Bus 852 goes to Gloucester (four daily Monday to Saturday).

# BIBURY
## pop 623

Once described by William Morris as 'the most beautiful village in England', Bibury is another Cotswold gem with a cluster of gorgeous riverside cottages and tangle of narrow streets flanked by wayward stone buildings. It's an impossibly quaint place whose main attraction is **Arlington Row**, a stunning sweep of cottages now thought to be the most photographed street in Britain. Originally built as a sheep house in the 14th century, the building was converted into weavers' cottages in the 17th century. Also worth a look is the 17th-century **Arlington Mill**, just a short stroll away across Rack Isle, a wildlife refuge once used to dry cloth.

Few visitors make it past these two sights, but for a glimpse of the real Bibury, venture into the village proper behind Arlington Row, where you'll find a cluster of stunning cottages and the Saxon **Church of St Mary**. Although much altered since its original construction, many 8th-century features are still visible among the 12th- and 13th-century additions.

Despite its popularity Bibury, is seriously lacking in decent accommodation. The best place to stay is in the nearby village of Coln, where the jasmine-clad **New Inn** ( ☎ 01285-750651; www.new-inn.co.uk; Coln-St-Aldwyns; d £120-180) offers contemporary rooms in 16th-century surroundings. It's also the best bet in the area for food with its modern British menu (mains £9 to £15) served in the main restaurant, bar and gorgeous garden.

Buses 860, 863, 865, 866 and 869 pass through Bibury en route to Cirencester at least once daily from Monday to Saturday (20 minutes).

## TETBURY
pop 5250

Once a prosperous wool-trading centre, Tetbury has managed to preserve most of its architectural heritage – its busy streets are lined with medieval cottages, sturdy old town houses and Georgian Gothic gems. It's an unspoilt place with a rather regal character: even HRH Prince Charles has a shop here – Highgrove – though it's unlikely you'll find him serving behind the counter.

Along with goodies from the Highgrove Estate, Tetbury is a great place for antique fans with a shop of old curios on almost every corner. You'll also find plenty of chichi boutiques and interior-design shops, but they're tempered by the bakers, butchers and delis that ground the town and give it a sense of real identity.

As you wander round, look out for the row of gorgeous medieval weavers' cottages that line the steep hill at **Chipping Steps**, leading up to the **Chipping** (market), which is surrounded by graceful 17th- and 18th-century town houses. From here, it's a short stroll to Market Sq, where the 17th-century **Market House** stands as if on stilts. Close by, the Georgian Gothic **Church of St Mary the Virgin** has a towering spire and wonderful interior.

Just south of Tetbury is the **National Arboretum** ( ☎ 01666-880220; www.forestry.gov.uk/westonbirt; adult £5-8, under 18yr £2; ☷ 9am-dusk) at Westonbirt. The park boasts a magnificent selection of temperate trees, with some wonderful walks and great colour throughout the year, especially in autumn.

The friendly **tourist office** ( ☎ 01666-503552; www.visittetbury.co.uk; 33 Church St; ☷ 9.30am-4.30pm Mon-Sat Mar-Oct, to 2.30pm Nov-Feb) has plenty of information on the town and its history and stocks a trail guide to the arboretum.

### Sleeping & Eating

**Ormond's Head** ( ☎ 01666-505690; www.theormond.co.uk; 23 Long St; s £59-99, d £69-140; ℗ ) This modern hotel has a range of individually styled rooms with subtle, but striking, fabrics and funky wall-

papers. It's an unassuming place that offers excellent value for money. Expect duck-down duvets, flat-screen TVs, a DVD library and warm welcome for families. The modern bar and grill downstairs serve excellent-value food (mains £9 to £15).

**Talboys House** ( ☎ 01666-503597; www.talboyshouse .com; 17 Church Street; s £45 d £95-120) Grab a slice of India in this quirky joint with exotic rooms decked out in Bollywood style. This 19th-century wool merchant's house is now a haven of sultry colour schemes, embroidered fabrics, carved woods and Indian toiletries.

**Chef's Table** ( ☎ 01666-504466; 49 Long St; bistro mains £8-13; ☷ 9.30am-3.30pm) This fantastic deli and bistro is the place to go to stock up for a picnic in the National Arboretum or a mouth-watering lunch of local organic ingredients. Go for rabbit and tarragon pie or shellfish and saffron chowder, and if you're feeling inspired you can join the cookery school (runs on selected days during the summer months; day course £120) to learn how to do it at home.

**Blue Zucchini** ( ☎ 01666-505852; 7-9 Church St; dinner mains £10-14; ☷ lunch & dinner Tue-Sat, lunch Sun & Mon) This popular cafe and bistro is a bright, cheery place that's usually buzzing. It's great for a coffee and a look at the papers and serves a good selection of contemporary classics for lunch and dinner.

### Getting There & Away

Bus 29 runs between Tetbury and Stroud (30 minutes, six daily Monday to Saturday). Bus 620 goes to Bath (1¼ hours, six daily Monday to Friday, four on Saturday), stopping at Westonbirt's Arboretum en route.

## PAINSWICK
pop 1666

One of the most beautiful and unspoilt towns in the Cotswolds, hilltop Painswick is an absolute gem. Largely untouched since medieval times, totally unassuming and gloriously uncommercial, it's like gaining access to an outdoor museum that is strangely lost in time. Despite its obvious charms, Painswick sees only a trickle of visitors, so you can wander the narrow winding streets and admire the picture-perfect cottages, handsome stone town houses and medieval inns in your own good time.

### Sights & Activities

The village centres on **St Mary's Church**, a fine, Perpendicular wool church surrounded by table-top tombs and 99 clipped yew trees. Legend has it that, should the 100th yew tree be allowed to grow, the devil would appear and shrivel it. They planted it anyway – to celebrate the millennium – but there's been no sign of the Wicked One.

Sliding downhill beside and behind the church is a series of gorgeous streetscapes. Look out for **Bisley St**, the original main drag, which was superseded by the now ancient-looking New St in medieval times. Just south of the church, rare **iron stocks** stand in the street.

Just a mile north of town, the ostentatious **Painswick Rococo Garden** ( ☎ 01452-813204; www .rococogarden.co.uk; adult/under 16yr £5.50/2.75; ☯ 11am-5pm Jan-Oct) is the area's biggest attraction. These flamboyant pleasure gardens were designed by Benjamin Hyett in the 1740s and have now been restored to their former glory. Winding paths soften the otherwise strict geometrical precision, bringing visitors around the central vegetable garden to the many Gothic follies dotted in the grounds. There's also a children's nature trail and maze.

If you're visiting in late May, enquire about the **Coopers Hill cheese-rolling competition** (www .cheese-rolling.co.uk), held in the nearby village of Cranham. A 200-year-old tradition sees locals running, tumbling and sliding down a local hill in pursuit of a 7lb block of Double Gloucester cheese. For the truly committed, there is also an uphill competition.

### Sleeping & Eating

**St Michaels** ( ☎ 01452-814555; www.stmichaelsrestaurant .co.uk; Victoria St; d £80; 2/3-course dinner £28/32.50; ☯ lunch & dinner Wed-Sat, dinner Sun; ☐ ) The three rooms at St Michaels are a handsome mix of luxurious fabrics, exposed stone work, rustic furniture and carved woods. Each is individual in style and features flat-screen TVs, fresh-cut flowers and a sense of tranquil calm. The restaurant downstairs serves modern British and European cuisine with a touch of Asian and Czech influence.

**Cardynham House** ( ☎ 01452-814006; www.cardyn ham.co.uk; The Cross; s £65-85 d £80-185) The individually decorated rooms at 15th-century Cardynham House offer four-poster beds, heavy-patterned fabrics and buckets of character. Choose the Shaker-style New England room, the opulent Arabian Nights room, the chintzy Old Tuscany room, or for your own private pool and garden, the Pool Room. Downstairs, the

**Bistro** (mains £11.50-16.50; ☯ lunch Tue-Sun, dinner Tue-Sat) serves modern British cuisine.

### Getting There & Around

Bus 46 connects Cheltenham (30 minutes) with Painswick hourly Monday to Saturday. Bus 256 connects Painswick to Gloucester twice daily on Wednesday and Saturday.

# GLOUCESTERSHIRE

Gloucestershire has a languid charm that makes a welcome break from the crowds of the Cotswolds, and its sleepy thatched villages and rustic allure are relatively undiscovered by the tour buses. The county's headline attraction is the elegant Regency town of Cheltenham where graceful period houses, tree-lined streets and upmarket boutiques and restaurants vie for attention. Gloucester, by comparison is a dowdy cousin, but its magnificent Gothic cathedral makes it well worth a visit. To the north, Tudor Tewkesbury has a superb Norman abbey and streets lined with crooked, half-timbered houses; while to the west, the tranquil and picturesque Forest of Dean is a leafy backwater perfect for cycling and walking.

## Information

Much of Gloucestershire falls into the Cotswold district. Information on sights, activities, accommodation and transport can be found on www.glos-cotswolds.com.

## Activities

Gloucestershire's quiet roads, gentle gradients and numerous footpaths are ideal for walking and cycling. Tourist offices can help with route planning and they stock numerous guides to the trails.

**Compass Holidays** ( ☎ 01242-250642; www.compass -holidays.com; bikes per day/week from £12/52) hires bikes and also offers a bag-drop service along the Cotswold Way (£8 per bag per day, minimum two bags) as well as guided cycling tours of the area.

## Getting Around

A host of companies operate bus services in Gloucestershire. Most tourist offices stock local bus timetables or can help with finding connecting services. As always, **Traveline** ( ☎ 0871 200 22 33; www.traveline.org.uk) has details of all routes.

# CHELTENHAM
pop 98,875

The shining star of the region, Cheltenham is a historic but cosmopolitan hub at the western edge of the rustic Cotswolds. The city oozes an air of gracious refinement, its streetscapes largely left intact since its heyday as a spa resort in the 18th century. At the time, it rivalled Bath as *the* place for the sick, hypochondriac and merely moneyed to go, and today it is still riddled with historic buildings, beautifully proportioned terraces and manicured squares.

Cheltenham is an affluent kind of place, its well-heeled residents attracted by the genteel architecture, leafy crescents, wrought-iron balconies and expansive parks – all of which are kept in pristine condition. Bolt on a slew of festivals of all persuasions and a host of fine hotels, restaurants and shops, and it's easy to come to the conclusion that it's the perfect base to explore the region.

## History

Cheltenham languished in relative obscurity until pigeons began eating and thriving on salt crystals from a local spring in the early 18th century. It wasn't long before a pump was bored and Cheltenham began to establish itself as a spa town. Along with the sick, property speculators arrived in droves and the town started to grow dramatically. Graceful terraced housing was thrown up, parks were laid out and the rich and famous followed. By the time George III visited in 1788 the town's fate had been sealed and Cheltenham became the most fashionable holiday destination for England's upper crust. The town has retained its period glamour and allure and today remains the most complete Regency town in England.

## Orientation

Central Cheltenham is fairly compact and easy to get around on foot. The rather tatty High St runs roughly east–west; south from it is the Promenade, a more elegant shopping area, which extends into Montpellier, the most exclusive area of town. Pittville Park and the old Pump Room are about a mile north of High St.

The bus station is behind the Promenade in the town centre, but the train station is out on a limb to the west; bus D runs to the town centre every 10 minutes.

## Information

You'll find all the major banks and the main **post office** ( ☎ 0845 722 3344; 225-227 High St) on High St.

The **tourist office** ( ☎ 01242-522878; www.visit cheltenham.info; 77 The Promenade; ⏰ 9.30am-5.15pm Mon-Sat, from 10am Wed) runs a free accommodation-booking service, sells event tickets and stocks copies of walking, cycling and driving guides to the Cotswolds.

For internet access, try the **Loft** ( ☎ 01242-539573; 8-9 Henrietta St; per hr £4; ⏰ 10am-7pm Mon-Thu, to 6pm Fri & Sat, noon-5pm Sun).

## Sights
### THE PROMENADE & MONTPELLIER

Famed as one of England's most beautiful streetscapes, **The Promenade** is a wide, tree-lined boulevard flanked by imposing period buildings. The **Municipal Offices**, built as private residences in 1825, are among the most striking on this street and they face a **statue of Edward Wilson** (1872–1912), a local man who joined Captain Scott's ill-fated second expedition to the South Pole.

Continuing on from here, you'll pass the grandiose **Imperial Gardens**, built to service the Imperial Spa (now the Queens Hotel), en route to **Montpellier**, Cheltenham's most fashionable district. Along with the handsome architecture of the area, there's a buzzing collection of bars, restaurants and boutiques. Along Montpellier Walk, **caryatids** (draped female figures based on those on the Acropolis in Athens) act as structural supports between the shops, each balancing an elaborately carved cornice on its head.

### PITTVILLE PUMP ROOM

Built in 1830 as a centrepiece to a vast estate, the **Pittville Pump Room** ( ☎ 01242-227979; www .pittvillepumproom.org.uk; Pittville Park; admission free; ⏰ 10am-4pm Wed-Mon) is Cheltenham's finest Regency building. Originally used as a spa and social centre, it is now used as a concert hall. You can wander into the main auditorium and sample the pungent spa waters, or just explore the vast parklands and lake it overlooks.

### ART GALLERY & MUSEUM

Cheltenham's excellent **Art Gallery & Museum** ( ☎ 01242-237431; www.cheltenham.artgallery.museum; Clarence St; admission free; ⏰ 10am-5.20pm Mon-Sat) is well worth a visit for its depiction of Cheltenham life through the ages. It also has wonderful displays on William Morris and the Arts and Crafts Movement (p83), as well as Dutch and British art, rare Chinese and English ceramics and a section on Edward Wilson's expedition to Antarctica.

### HOLST BIRTHPLACE MUSEUM

The composer Gustav Holst was born in Cheltenham in 1874, and his childhood home has been turned into the **Holst Birthplace Museum** ( ☎ 01242-524846; www.holstmuseum.org.uk; 4 Clarence Rd; adult/under 16yr £3.50/3; ⏰ 10am-4pm Tue-Sat mid-Feb–mid-Dec). The rooms are laid out in typical period fashion and feature much Holst memorabilia, including the piano on which most of *The Planets* was composed.

## Tours

Guided 1¼-hour **walking tours** (£4; ⏰ 11am Mon-Fri & 11.30am Sat late Jun–mid-Sep) of Regency Cheltenham depart from the tourist office. You can also book tickets for a rolling program of day-long **coach tours** (adult/under 12yr £29/14) to various locations in the Cotswolds here.

## Festivals & Events

Cheltenham is renowned as a city of festivals, and throughout the year you'll find major events going on in the city. For more information or to book tickets, visit www.cheltenham festivals.com.

**Folk Festival** A showcase of traditional and new-age folk talent in February.

**National Hunt Festival** The hottest week in the racing calendar on both sides of the Irish Sea; in March.

**Jazz Festival** An imaginative program hailed as the UK's finest jazz fest, held in April.

**Science Festival** Exploring the delights and intrigues of the world of science in June.

**Music Festival** A celebration of traditional and contemporary sounds with a geographical theme, in July.

**Literature Festival** A 10-day celebration of writers and the written word in October.

## Sleeping

**YMCA** ( ☎ 01242-524024; www.cheltenhamymca.com; 6 Victoria Walk; dm/s £18.50/27.50) This elegant building right in the city centre now houses the cheapest beds in town. The four-bed dorms are fairly basic and well worn, but it's a great location and you'll find nothing else at this rate.

**Big Sleep** ( ☎ 01242-696999; www.thebigsleephotel .com; Wellington St; r £65-90; [P] [🖥]) A luxury budget hotel, the Big Sleep chain offers stylish minimalism with thoroughly modern rooms fea-

turing flat-screen TVs. At this price, it's an absolute steal, and if you're travelling with friends or family, the large family or group rooms make it an even better deal. You can also bring your own food and eat it in the bar.

**Cheltenham Townhouse** ( ☎ 01242-221922; www .cheltenhamtownhouse.co.uk; 12 Pittville Lawn; s £55-95, d £70-120; [P] [🖥]) Modern decor with pale, neutral colours, stylish accessories, DVD players and broadband make this central option a good bet for a midrange budget. The Townhouse is set on a quiet street just out of the centre, but the spacious rooms, simple, sleek decor and sparkling bathrooms make it worth the trip.

**Hotel Kandinsky** ( ☎ 01242-527788; www.alias hotels.com; Bayshill Rd; s £95, d £125-155; [P]) Gloriously quirky, keenly priced and extravagantly decked out, this is a 'funkier than average' hotel, with lots of eclectic modern art, exotic furniture, designer style and an extremely efficient but laid-back attitude. The slick, modern Cafe Paradiso (mains £14 to £19) serves an ambitious modern British menu.

**ourpick Thirty Two** ( ☎ 01242-771110; www.thirty twoltd.com; 32 Imperial Square; s/d from £139/154; [P] [🖥] wifi) In a league of its own, this slick, boutique B&B is a rare find. It may charge hotel prices, but it's well worth it. You get the personal service of a B&B but the luxury, style and comfort of a top-notch hotel. Expect views over the Imperial Gardens, muted colours, contemporary artwork, luxurious fabrics and rooms that could easily feature in a glossy style magazine.

## Eating

**Gusto** ( ☎ 01242-239111; 12 Montpellier Walk; mains £6-8; ⏰ 9.30am-6pm Mon-Thu, to 6.30pm Fri, to 5.30pm Sat) This Italian-style deli and cafe is a great place for lunchtime treats made with authentic Italian ingredients. Choose from pizzas, salads, meats and gorgeous pastas (try the gorgonzola and walnut for a real taste sensation).

**Storyteller** ( ☎ 01242-250343; 11 North Pl; mains £8-15) Feel-good comfort food draws the crowds to this enduringly popular restaurant that dishes up generous portions of barbecue ribs, seafood platters and vegetarian burritos on a menu fusing tastes from as far afield as Mexico and Asia.

**Laze Daze** ( ☎ 01242-257878; 81 The Promenade; mains £9-17) Overlooking the Promenade and just a stone's throw from the tourist office, this relaxed place serves a good range of

OXFORD, THE COTSWOLDS & AROUND

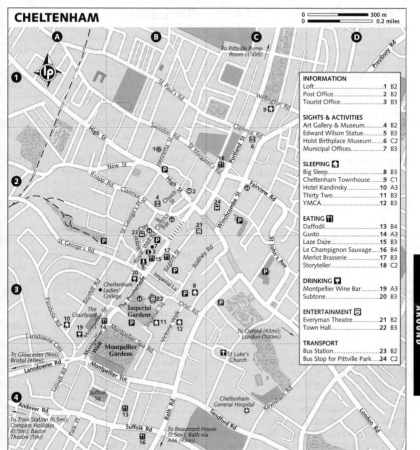

CHELTENHAM

| INFORMATION | | |
| --- | --- | --- |
| Loft | 1 | B2 |
| Post Office | 2 | B2 |
| Tourist Office | 3 | B3 |

| SIGHTS & ACTIVITIES | | |
| --- | --- | --- |
| Art Gallery & Museum | 4 | B2 |
| Edward Wilson Statue | 5 | B3 |
| Holst Birthplace Museum | 6 | C2 |
| Municipal Offices | 7 | B3 |

| SLEEPING | | |
| --- | --- | --- |
| Big Sleep | 8 | B3 |
| Cheltenham Townhouse | 9 | C1 |
| Hotel Kandinsky | 10 | A3 |
| Thirty Two | 11 | B3 |
| YMCA | 12 | B3 |

| EATING | | |
| --- | --- | --- |
| Daffodil | 13 | B4 |
| Gusto | 14 | A3 |
| Laze Daze | 15 | B3 |
| Le Champignon Sauvage | 16 | B4 |
| Merlot Brasserie | 17 | B3 |
| Storyteller | 18 | C2 |

| DRINKING | | |
| --- | --- | --- |
| Montpellier Wine Bar | 19 | A3 |
| Subtone | 20 | B3 |

| ENTERTAINMENT | | |
| --- | --- | --- |
| Everyman Theatre | 21 | B2 |
| Town Hall | 22 | B3 |

| TRANSPORT | | |
| --- | --- | --- |
| Bus Station | 23 | B2 |
| Bus Stop for Pittville Park | 24 | C2 |

**OXFORD, THE COTSWOLDS & AROUND**

contemporary brasserie-style food ranging from Barbary duck and venison steak to stuffed peppers and steamed mussels. The lunch and early-evening set menus are a great deal (two/three courses £10/13).

**Merlot Brasserie** ( ☎ 01242-574008; 2a Ormond Terrace, Regent St; mains £11-16) A popular option right in the centre of town, the Merlot offers a menu of modern Mediterranean flavours. It's a stylish place with contemporary design, subtle lighting and leather seats, and is a good option for lunch (mains £8 to £9).

**Daffodil** ( ☎ 01242-700055; 18-20 Suffolk Pde; mains £14-19) A perennial favourite, the Daffodil is as loved for its top-notch modern British brasserie-style food as for its flamboyant surroundings. Set in a converted art deco cinema, it harks back to the Roaring Twenties and features live jazz and blues every Monday night.

## Drinking

**Subtone** ( ☎ 01242-575925; 117 The Promenade; admission £2-6; ☼ 8pm-late Thu-Sat) One of the city's most popular venues, Subtone has three floors of DJs and live music at its basement club and piano bar. Expect everything from jazz and house to funk and rock.

**Montpellier Wine Bar** ( ☎ 01242-527774; Bayshill Lodge, Montpellier St; ☼ 10am-11pm) Slick, sophisticated and self-consciously cool, this is where Cheltenham's beautiful people come to hang out, sip wine and dine on modern British food (mains £12 to £17). There's an extensive wine list, cask ales and plenty of people-watching.

## Entertainment

The **Everyman Theatre** ( ☎ 01242-572573; www .everymantheatre.org.uk; Regent St) is Cheltenham's main stage and hosts everything from Elvis impersonators to comedy and panto, while the modern **Bacon Theatre** ( ☎ 01242-258002; www .bacontheatre.co.uk; Hatherly Rd) showcases touring shows, jazz and ballet. Classical-music lovers should look out for concerts at the **Pittville Pump Room** ( ☎ 01242-227979; www.pittvillepumproom .org.uk; Pittville Park). The **town hall** ( ☎ 01242-227979; www.cheltenhamtownhall.org.uk; Imperial Sq) offers more mainstream talent as well as hosting many festival events.

## Getting There & Away

For information on public transport to and from Cheltenham, pick up a free copy of the handy *Getting There by Public Transport* guide from the tourist office.

### BUS

National Express runs buses to London roughly hourly (£18, 3½ hours) and Swanbrook bus 853 goes to Oxford three times daily Monday to Saturday (£7, 1½ hours, one on Sunday).

Bus 94 (30 minutes) runs to Gloucester every 10 minutes Monday to Saturday and every 20 minutes on Sunday. Bus 51 goes to Cirencester (40 minutes, hourly).

Pulhams bus 801 runs to Moreton (one hour) via Bourton (35 minutes) and Stow (50 minutes) seven times daily Monday to Saturday. Castleways Coaches 606 runs four times daily Monday to Saturday to Broadway (50 minutes) via Winchcombe (20 minutes).

### TRAIN

Cheltenham has trains to London (£50, 2¼ hours), Bristol (£9.20, 50 minutes), Gloucester (£3.10, nine minutes) and Bath (£14.30, 1¼ hours) roughly every half-hour.

## Getting Around

**Compass Holidays** ( ☎ 01242-250642; www.compass-holidays.com; bikes per day/week from £12/52) has bicycles for hire at the train station. Bus D runs to Pittville Park from Portland St every 10 minutes.

# TEWKESBURY
pop 9978

Higgledy-piggledy Tewkesbury remains stuck in medieval glory with crooked half-timbered houses, buckled roof lines and narrow alleyways giving it a charming, old-world atmosphere. Take time to wander the ancient passageways that lead up to the town from the rivers Avon and Severn and then wander along Church St to Tewkesbury's most glorious building, the magnificent medieval abbey church.

The **tourist office** ( ☎ 01684-855040; www.visit cotswoldsandsevernvale.gov.uk; 100 Church St; ⏰ 9.30am-5pm Mon-Sat year-round, 10am-4pm Sun Easter-Oct) is housed in a 17th-century hat shop also home to the heritage centre.

## Sights & Activities
### HERITAGE CENTRE & MUSEUM

The **Out of the Hat** ( ☎ 01684-855040; www.outofthehat .org.uk; 100 Church St; adult/child £4.70/2.50; ⏰ 9.30am-5pm Mon-Sat year-round, 10am-4pm Sun Easter-Oct) heritage centre explores the history of the town and has plenty of interactive games for young visitors.

There's also a second small **museum** ( ☎ 01684-292901; www.tewkesburymuseum.org; 64 Barton St; admission adult/child £1.50/75p; ⏰ 1-4.30pm Tue-Fri, 11am-4pm Sat Mar-Aug, noon-3pm Tue-Fri, 11am-3pm Sat Sep-Oct, 11am-3pm Sat Nov-Mar) housed in a timber-framed building, which displays finds from Roman and medieval times as well as hosting an exhibition on Antarctic exploration.

### TEWKESBURY ABBEY

This magnificent **abbey** ( ☎ 01684-850959; www .tewkesburyabbey.org.uk; guided tours £3; ⏰ 7.30am-6pm May-Sep, to 5pm Oct-Apr) is one of Britain's largest churches, far bigger than many of the country's cathedrals. The Norman abbey, built for the Benedictine monks, was consecrated in 1121 and was one of the last monasteries to be dissolved by Henry VIII. Although many of the monastery buildings were destroyed, the abbey church survived after being bought by the townspeople for the princely sum of £453 in 1542.

The church has a massive 40m-high tower and some spectacular Norman piers and arches in the nave. The Decorated-style chancel dates from the 14th century, however, and still retains much of its original stained glass. The church also features an organ dating from 1631, originally made for Magdalen

College, Oxford, and an extensive collection of medieval tombs. The most interesting is that of John Wakeman, the last abbot, who is shown as a vermin-ridden skeleton.

The church makes a wonderfully atmospheric venue for a range of summer concerts. You can find information on the website or at the **visitor centre** ( 10am-5.30pm Mon-Sat Apr-Sep) by the gate, which also houses an exhibition on the abbey's history.

## Sleeping & Eating

**Ivydene House** ( ☎ 01684-592453; www.ivydenehouse .net; Uckinghall; s/d £45/70; P ) This gorgeous B&B is well out of town but such a gem you'll be delighted you made the effort to get here. The rooms are luxuriously styled with a mix of contemporary fashion, classic furniture, soft colour schemes and gorgeous fabrics. Uckinghall is 7 miles north of Tewkesbury off the A38.

**Aubergine** ( ☎ 01684-292703; 73 Church St; mains £10-17;  Tue-Sat) Set in a 15th-century building that's decidedly modern inside, this place is a welcome change from Tewkesbury's tearooms. The menu ranges from standard fare to more adventurous dishes such as venison casserole with honey and roast cardamom vegetables.

**My Great Grandfathers** ( ☎ 01684-292687; www .mygreatgrandfathers.com; 84-85 Church St; mains £9-15;  Wed-Sun) Exposed oak beams and half-timbered walls set the tone in this otherwise modern place serving excellent afternoon teas and an interesting menu of classic and modern British cuisine.

## Getting There & Away

Bus 41 (25 minutes) runs to Cheltenham every 15 minutes and hourly on Sunday, and bus 71 (30 minutes, hourly) goes to Gloucester. The nearest train station is 1.5 miles away at Ashchurch.

## GLOUCESTER
pop 123,205

Gloucester (*glos*-ter) began life as a settlement for retired Roman soldiers, but really came into its own in medieval times when the pious public brought wealth and prosperity to what was then a prime pilgrimage city. The faithful flocked to see the grave of Edward II and soon financed the building of what remains one of England's most beautiful cathedrals.

In more recent years Gloucester has fallen into serious decline and despite investment

the centre remains a rather dowdy, workaday place. Only a glimmer of its medieval character remains but the city's historic docks have been redeveloped and are worth a visit.

## Orientation & Information

The city centre is based on a medieval cruciform pattern, with Northgate, Southgate, Eastgate and Westgate Sts converging on The Cross.

The **tourist office** ( ☎ 01452-396572; www.visit gloucester.info; 28 Southgate St;  10am-5pm Mon-Sat Sep-Jun , plus 11am-3pm Sun Jul & Aug) is conveniently located in the centre of town.

## Sights
### GLOUCESTER CATHEDRAL

The main reason to visit Gloucester is to see its magnificent **Gothic cathedral** ( ☎ 01452-528095; www .gloucestercathedral.org.uk; College Green; suggested donation £3;  8am-6pm), a stunning example of English Perpendicular style. Originally the site of a Saxon abbey, a Norman church was built here by a group of Benedictine monks in the 12th century, and when Edward II was murdered in 1327, the church was chosen as his burial place. Edward's tomb proved so popular, however, that Gloucester became a centre of pilgrimage and the income generated from the pious pilgrims financed the church's conversion into the magnificent building seen today.

Inside, the cathedral skilfully combines the best of Norman and Gothic design with sturdy columns, creating a sense of gracious solidity and wonderful Norman arcading draped with beautiful mouldings. From the elaborate 14th-century wooden choir stalls, you'll get a good view of the imposing **Great East Window**, one of the largest in England.

To see the window in more detail, head for the **Tribune Gallery**, where you can also see an **exhibition** (admission £2;  10.30am-4pm Mon-Fri, to 3pm Sat) on its making. As you walk around the **Whispering Gallery**, you'll notice that even the quietest of murmurs reverberates across the wonderfully elaborate lierne vaulting. Beneath the window in the northern ambulatory is Edward II's magnificent tomb, and nearby is the late-15th-century **Lady Chapel**, a glorious patchwork of stained glass.

One of the cathedral's greatest treasures, however, is the exquisite **Great Cloister**. Completed in 1367, it is the first example of fan vaulting in England and is only matched in beauty by Henry VIII's Chapel at Westminster

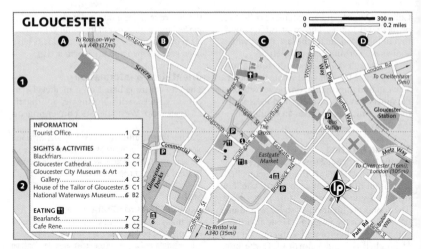

**GLOUCESTER**

0 ——— 300 m
0 ——— 0.2 miles

| INFORMATION | |
| --- | --- |
| Tourist Office............................1 C2 | |

| SIGHTS & ACTIVITIES | |
| --- | --- |
| Blackfriars.................................2 C2 | |
| Gloucester Cathedral................3 C1 | |
| Gloucester City Museum & Art | |
| Gallery...............................4 C2 | |
| House of the Tailor of Gloucester.5 C1 | |
| National Waterways Museum.....6 B2 | |

| EATING | |
| --- | --- |
| Bearlands................................7 C2 | |
| Cafe Rene...............................8 C2 | |

Abbey. You (or your children) might recognise the cloister from the first two Harry Potter films: it was used in the corridor scenes at Hogwart's School.

A wonderful way to take in the glory of the cathedral is to attend one of the many musical recitals and concerts held here. The stunning acoustics and breathtaking surroundings are pretty much guaranteed to make your hair stand on end.

For more cathedral insights and a fantastic view of the town, climb the 69m **tower** on an hour-long guided **tour** (adult/under 16yr £3/1; tours 2.30pm Wed-Fri, 1.30pm & 2.30pm Sat & bank holidays). Because of the steep steps it's not recommended for children under 10. Civic Trust volunteers also provide guided tours of the **cathedral** ( 10.45am-3.15pm Mon-Sat, noon-2.30pm Sun).

### OTHER SIGHTS & ACTIVITIES

A major part of the city's regeneration is taking place at **Gloucester Docks**, once Britain's largest inland port. Fifteen beautiful Victorian warehouses, many now restored, surround the canal basins and house a series of museums, shops and cafes.

The largest warehouse, Llanthony, is home to the newly revamped **National Waterways Museum** ( 01452-318200; www.nwm.org.uk; adult/under 16yr £3.95/2.75; 10am-5pm), a hands-on kind of place where you can discover the history of inland waterways. Included in the admission price is a 45-minute **boat trip** (non–museum visitors adult/child under 16yr £4.75/3.50; tours noon, 1.30pm & 2.30pm Apr-Oct) along the canal.

Back in the centre of town the 13th-century **Blackfriars** (Ladybellgate St; admission free), one of Britain's best-preserved Dominican friaries, is also worth visiting, as is the **Gloucester City Museum & Art Gallery** ( 01452-396131; www.gloucester.gov.uk/citymuseum; Brunswick Rd; admission free; 10am-5pm Tue-Sat), which houses everything from dinosaur fossils to paintings by Turner and Gainsborough.

### Sleeping & Eating

Gloucester's accommodation options are pretty grim. You'd be far better off staying in Cheltenham (10 minutes by train) instead.

**Cafe Rene** ( 01452-309340; www.caferene.co.uk; 31 Southgate St; mains £7-10; noon-11.30pm) For a decent but predictable choice of pub grub head to this cheery joint through the archway on Southgate. There's live music on Wednesday nights and a pleasant beer garden outside. Food is served until 9.30pm and includes everything from wraps and sandwiches (£4.50) at lunch to burgers, chilli, pasta and curry by night.

**Bearlands** ( 01452-419966; Longsmith St; 2-/3-course dinner £23/25; closed Mon & Sun) Crisp white linen, a large airy conservatory and an atmospheric vaulted wine cellar make Bearlands an interesting and popular venue. It's a stylish place serving a competent modern British menu in relaxing surroundings.

### Getting There & Away

National Express has buses roughly every two hours to London (£18, 3½ hours). Bus 94 runs

---

**THE TAILOR OF GLOUCESTER**

Beatrix Potter's magical tale of good-hearted mice saving a feverish Gloucester tailor from ruin was inspired by a local legend about real-life tailor John Prichard. As in Potter's tale, he left a coat for the mayor at cutting stage on a Friday night and returned to his workshop on Monday to find it finished, save for a single button hole.

Commercially minded Mr Prichard was soon encouraging people to come in and see his workshop where 'waistcoats are made at night by the fairies'. In reality, his two assistants had slept off a Saturday-night bender at the workshop and hoped to make amends by finishing the coat.

The **House of the Tailor of Gloucester** ( ☎ 01452-422856; 9 College Ct; ☺ 10am-4pm Mon-Sat, noon-4pm Sun), the house that Potter used in her illustrations, is now a museum and souvenir shop dedicated to the author.

---

to Cheltenham (30 minutes, six hourly), with an express bus X94 cutting the journey to 15 minutes during rush hour. The quickest journey between the two cities is by train (10 minutes, every 20 minutes). Trains also run to Chepstow in Wales (£6.40, 28 minutes, at least every two hours).

## FOREST OF DEAN
pop 79,982

An ancient woodland with a unique, almost magical character, the Forest of Dean is the oldest oak forest in England and a wonderfully scenic place to walk, cycle or paddle. Its steep, wooded hills, winding, tree-lined roads, and glimmering lakes and rivers make it prime territory for fans of outdoor pursuits.

The forest was formerly a royal hunting ground and a centre of iron and coal mining, and its mysterious depths were supposedly the inspiration for JRR Tolkien's setting for *The Lord of the Rings*. Numerous other writers, poets, artists and craftspeople have been inspired by the stunning scenery. The forest was designated England's first National Forest Park in 1938.

Covering 42 sq miles between Gloucester, Ross-on-Wye and Chepstow, the forest is in an isolated position, but Coleford, the main population centre, has good transport connections. The **tourist office** ( ☎ 01594-812388; www.visitforestofdean.co.uk; High St, Coleford; ☺ 10am-5pm Mon-Sat Apr-Sep, plus 10am-2pm Sun Jul & Aug, 10am-4pm Mon-Fri Oct-Mar, plus 10am-2pm Sat Oct, Feb & Mar) stocks walking and cycling guides and also offers a free accommodation booking service.

## Sights & Activities
Your first stop should be the **Dean Heritage Centre** ( ☎ 01594-822170; www.deanheritagemuseum.com; Camp Mill, Soudley; adult/under 16yr £5/3; ☺ 10am-5pm

Mar-Oct, to 4pm Sat & Sun Nov-Feb), which explains the history of the forest and its free miners from medieval times to the industrial age. There's also a reconstructed forest home, adventure playground and art gallery on site.

If you're travelling with children, **Puzzle Wood** ( ☎ 01594-833187; www.puzzlewood.net; adult/under 12yr £4/3; ☺ 10am-5.30pm Apr-Sep, 11am-4pm Oct) is a must. This overgrown pre-Roman, open-cast ore mine has a maze of paths, weird rock formations, tangled vines and eerie passageways and offers a real sense of discovery. Puzzle Wood is 1 mile south of Coleford on the B4228.

Mined for iron ore for more than 4000 years, the **Clearwell Caves** ( ☎ 01594-832535; www.clearwellcaves.com; adult/under 16yr £5.50/3.0; ☺ 10am-5pm Feb-Oct) are a warren of passageways, caverns and pools that help explain the forest's history of mining. The caves are signposted off the B4228 a mile south of Coleford.

In contrast to the caves, **Hopewell Colliery** ( ☎ 01594-810706; www.hopewellcoalmine.co.uk; adult/under 14yr £4/3; ☺ 10am-4pm Easter-Oct) offers underground tours of the mine workings, with miners as guides. The colliery is on the B4226 between Coleford and Cinderford.

## Sleeping & Eating

**our pick** **St Briavels Castle YHA** ( ☎ 0870 770 6040; www.yha.org.uk; Lydney; dm from £15.95; **P** ) Live like a king for a night at this unique hostel set in an imposing moated castle once used as King John's hunting lodge. Loaded with character and a snip at this price, the hostel also hosts lively medieval banquets on Monday, Wednesday and Saturday in August.

**Tudor Farmhouse Hotel** ( ☎ 01594-833046; www.tudorfarmhousehotel.co.uk; High St, Clearwell; s £60, d £90-140) You'll find oak beams, exposed stonework and old-world charm at this rustic 13th-century hotel and former farmhouse. There's a wide variety of rooms, from comfortable singles to luxurious four-posters and a popular restaurant (dinner mains £15 to £20) serving modern British fare.

**Garden Cafe** ( ☎ 01594-860075; www.gardencafe.co.uk; Lwr Lydbrook; mains £8-13; ☀ lunch Fri-Sun, dinner Fri, Sat & Mon) An award-winning organic cafe on the banks of the River Wye, this place is set in a converted malt house and surrounded by a beautiful walled garden. The food ranges from classic dishes such as pork schnitzel to the more exotic Imam Byaldi: stuffed aubergine with pine nuts, tomato and raisins.

### Getting There & Around
From Gloucester, bus 31 (one hour, half-hourly) runs to Coleford and there are trains to Lydney (20 minutes, hourly). The **Dean Forest Railway** ( ☎ 01594-845840; www.deanforestrail way.co.uk) runs steam trains from Lydney to Parkend (day ticket adult/under 16 years £9/5) on selected days from March to December.

You can hire road/mountain/premium bikes (£14/18/22 per day), buy maps and get advice on cycling routes at **Pedalabikeaway** ( ☎ 01594-860065; www.pedalabikeaway.com; Cannop Valley; ☀ Tue-Sun) near Coleford.

# HERTFORDSHIRE

The sleepy county of Hertfordshire is a pastoral place home to swathes of London commuters and little visited by tourists. The historic town of St Albans with its elegant Georgian streetscapes and Roman remains is well worth a visit, as is Hatfield House, a spectacular stately home and the county's premier attraction.

## ST ALBANS
pop 114,710

A bustling market town with a host of crooked Tudor buildings and elegant Georgian town houses, St Albans was founded after the Roman invasion of AD 43. Then known as Verulamium, it was renamed St Albans in the 3rd century after a Roman soldier, Alban, was beheaded for sheltering a Christian priest. He became England's first Christian martyr and the pilgrims that soon flocked here helped build a magnificent cathedral in his honour. The town is also home to an excellent Roman museum, an array of chichi shops and some wonderful pubs.

### Orientation & Information
Modern St Peter's St, 10 minutes' walk west of the train station on Victoria St, is the focus of the town, but it's worth exploring the quiet back streets lined with elegant buildings or following George St into Fishpool St, a charming lane that winds its way past old-world pubs to leafy Verulamium Park.

The **tourist office** ( ☎ 01727-864511; www.stal bans.gov.uk; Market Pl; ☀ 10am-5pm Mon-Sat, 10am-4pm every 2nd Sun of the month & mid-Jul–mid-Sep) is in the grand town hall in the marketplace. It stocks the *St Albans City Trail*, a free guide to the town's most historic buildings, and has information on guided walks (adult/child £3/1.50).

### Sights
#### ST ALBANS CATHEDRAL
Set in beautiful tranquil grounds away from the din of the main streets, St Albans' magnificent **cathedral** ( ☎ 01727-890200; www.stalbans thedral.org.uk; admission by donation; ☀ 8am-5.45pm) is a lesson in architectural history. The church began life as a Benedictine monastery in 793, built by King Offa of Mercia around the tomb of St Alban. In Norman times, it was completely rebuilt using material from the old Roman town of Verulamium, and then, in the 12th and 13th centuries, Gothic extensions and decorations were added.

The deceptively simple nave gives way to stunningly ornate ceilings, semi-lost wall paintings, an elaborate nave screen and, of course, the shrine of St Alban. There's also a luminescent rose window from the 20th century. The best way to appreciate the wealth of history contained in the building is to join a **free guided tour** ( ☀ 11.30am & 2.30pm Mon-Fri, 11.30am & 2pm Sat, 2.30pm Sun). If you miss the tour you can pick up a very helpful free plan and guide at the entrance.

#### VERULAMIUM MUSEUM & ROMAN RUINS
A fantastic exposé of everyday life under the Romans, the **Verulamium Museum** ( ☎ 01727-751810; www.stalbansmuseums.org.uk; St Michael's St; adult/child £3.30/2; ☀ 10am-5.30pm Mon-Sat, 2-5.30pm Sun) is home to a large collection of arrowheads, glassware and grave goods. Its centrepiece however, is the **Mosaic Room**, where five superb mosaic floors, uncovered between 1930 and 1955, are laid out. You can also see re-creations of Roman rooms, and learn about life in the settlement through interactive and audiovisual displays.

Every second weekend, the museum is invaded by Roman soldiers who demonstrate the tactics and tools of the Roman army.

Adjacent **Verulamium Park** has remains of a basilica, bathhouse and parts of the city wall. You can pick up a map of the area with information on the site from the museum or tourist office.

Across the busy A4147 are the grassy foundations of a **Roman theatre** ( ☎ 01727-835035; www.romantheatre.co.uk; adult/child £2/1; ☽ 10am-5pm Mar-Oct, to 4pm Nov-Feb), which once seated 2000 spectators.

## Sleeping & Eating

**Park House** ( ☎ 01727-811910; www.parkhouseonline.co.uk; 30 The Park; s/d £35/55; P ☐ wi-fi) Bright rooms with crisp, white linens, white wicker chairs and subtle floral patterns give this small B&B a fresh and airy feel. It's set in a quiet residential area within walking distance of town, and is a good deal for the price.

**St Michael's Manor** ( ☎ 01727-864444; www.stmichaelsmanor.com; Fishpool St; r from £145; P ☐ ) Set in beautiful grounds complete with a glistening lake, this elegant, classically styled hotel has a range of comfortable rooms with views over the gracious gardens. An air of restrained luxury permeates the place, with tip-top service in the modern British restaurant (mains £14 to £20).

**Lussmanns Eatery** ( ☎ 01727-851941; Waxhouse Gate; mains £7-16; ☽ 11.30am-10pm Mon-Thu, to 10.30pm Fri & Sat, to 9pm Sun) This bright, modern restaurant just off the High St is enduringly popular with locals despite ample competition around town. It serves a menu of mainly Mediterranean dishes in a bright, modern space with oak, leather and metal decor.

**Darcy's** ( ☎ 01727-730777; 2 Hatfield Rd; mains £11-18) This stylish, contemporary restaurant has a menu of modern European dishes with the odd Aussie influence thrown in. Go for barbecue kangaroo with aubergine relish or play it safe with sea bass on a bed of Catalan stew.

## Drinking

**our pick** **Ye Olde Fighting Cocks** ( ☎ 01727-869152; 16 Abbey Mill Lane) Reputedly the oldest pub in England, this unusual, octagonal-shaped inn has oodles of charm. Oliver Cromwell spent a night here, stabling his horses in what's now the bar, and underground tunnels lead to the cathedral. Drink in this historic atmosphere while you nurse your pint.

**Rose & Crown** ( ☎ 01727-851903; 10 St Michael's St) Another St Albans favourite, this 16th-century pub with beautiful beer garden features live music during the week.

## Getting There & Away

Trains depart London St Pancreas to St Albans station (£8.90, 23 minutes, every 10 minutes), which is on Victoria St, a 10-minute walk east of St Peter's St.

# AROUND ST ALBANS
## Hatfield House

For over 400 years, **Hatfield House** ( ☎ 01707-287010; house & garden adult/child £10/4.50, park only £2.50/1.50; ☽ noon-4pm Wed-Sun & public holidays, gardens 11am-5.30pm Easter-Sep) has been home to the Cecils, one of England's most influential political families. This magnificent Jacobean mansion was built between 1607 and 1611 for Robert Cecil, first earl of Salisbury and secretary of state to both Elizabeth I and James I, and is awash with grandiose portraits, tapestries, furnishings and armour. Look out for the grand marble hall, the stunning carved-oak staircase and the stained glass in the chapel.

Outside, the vast grounds were landscaped by 17th-century botanist John Tradescant, and you can see an old oak tree that marks the spot where Elizabeth I, who spent much of her childhood here, first heard of her accession to the throne.

If you'd really like to get into the character of the house, you can attend a four-course Elizabethan banquet, complete with minstrels and court jesters, in the atmospheric Great Hall on Friday nights (£47.50). Book on ☎ 01707-262055.

The house is opposite Hatfield train station, and there are trains from London King's Cross station (£7.40, 20 minutes, half-hourly). Between them, buses 300, 301 and 724 run every 10 minutes between St Albans and Hatfield (32 minutes).

## Shaw's Corner

Preserved in time and much as he left it, **Shaw's Corner** (NT; ☎ 01438-820307; www.nationaltrust.org.uk/shawscorner; Ayot St Lawrence; adult/child £4.95/2.50; ☽ 1-5pm Wed-Sun mid-Mar–Nov) is a tranquil Arts and Crafts–influenced building that was home to George Bernard Shaw (1856–1950) for the last 44 years of his life. His study contains his typewriter, pens, inkwell and dictionaries, and in the garden you can see his writing hut (which revolves to catch the sun) where he penned several works including *Pygmalion,* the play on which the film *My Fair Lady* was based. The Oscar he received for the screenplay is also on display.

Ayot St Lawrence is 6 miles north of St Albans, off the B651. Bus 304 from St Albans will drop you off at Gustardwood, 1.5 miles from Ayot St Lawrence.

# BERKSHIRE

Posh and prosperous Berkshire is littered with handsome villages, historic houses and exquisitely maintained villages, and acts as a country retreat for some of London's most influential figures. The Queen's favourite weekend getaway, Windsor Castle, is here, as is one of the world's most prestigious schools, Eton. Few visitors make it past these top attractions, but kids of all ages will enjoy the thrills and spills of Legoland while the gentle rolling countryside hides plenty of pretty villages worth exploring.

## WINDSOR & ETON
pop 30,568

Dominated by the massive bulk and heavy influence of Windsor Castle, these twin towns have a rather surreal atmosphere, with the pomp and ceremony of the changing of the guards in Windsor each morning and the sight of school boys dressed in formal tail coats wandering the streets of Eton.

Windsor Castle, with its romantic architecture and superb state rooms, is an absolute must-see, while across the bridge over the River Thames, England's most famous public school has an altogether different flavour. To cater for the droves of tourists that visit these star attractions, Windsor town centre is full of expensive boutiques, grand cafes and trendy restaurants. Eton, by comparison, is far quieter, its pedestrianised centre lined with antique shops and art galleries. Both towns exude an air of affluence, and if you're travelling on a tight budget, a day trip from London is probably your best bet.

### Orientation

Windsor and Eton are separated by the River Thames, with a pedestrianised bridge linking the two towns. The massive castle marks the centre of Windsor, with the town's main drag, Peascod St, leading away from its soaring stone walls. Castle Hill and Thames St skirt the edge of the castle, the latter leading down to the bridge to Eton.

### Information

The **Royal Windsor Information Centre** ( ☎ 01753-743900; www.windsor.gov.uk; Old Booking Hall, Windsor Royal Shopping Arcade; ✆ 10am-5pm Mon-Sat, to 4pm Sun) sells bus and local-attraction tickets, and has an **accommodation booking service** ( ☎ 01753-743907; £5).

There are plenty of banks with ATMs along the High and Thames Sts. The **post office** is in Peascod St and you'll get free internet access at the **Windsor library** ( ☎ 01753-743940; Bachelors Acre).

### Sights
#### WINDSOR CASTLE

The largest and oldest occupied fortress in the world, **Windsor Castle** ( ☎ 020-7766 7304; www .royalcollection.org.uk; adult/child £15/8.50; ✆ 9.45am-4pm Mar-Oct, to 3pm Nov-Feb) is a majestic vision of battlements and towers used for state occasions and as the Queen's weekend retreat.

William the Conqueror first established a royal residence in Windsor in 1070 when he built a motte and bailey here, the only naturally defendable spot in the Thames valley. Since then successive monarchs have rebuilt, remodelled and refurbished the castle complex to create the massive and sumptuous palace that stands here today. Henry II replaced the wooden stockade in 1165 with a stone round tower and built the outer walls to the north, east and south; Charles II gave the state apartments a baroque makeover; George IV swept in with his preference for Gothic style; and Queen Victoria refurbished a beautiful chapel in memory of her beloved Albert.

The castle largely escaped the bombings of WWII, but in 1992 a devastating fire tore through the building destroying or damaging more than 100 rooms. By chance, the most important treasures were in storage at the time, and with skilled craftsmanship and painstaking restoration, the rooms were returned to their former glory.

Join a free guided tour (every half-hour) or take a multilingual audio tour of the lavish state rooms and beautiful chapels. The State Apartments and St George's Chapel are closed at times during the year; check the website for details. If the Queen is in residence, you'll see the Royal Standard flying from the Round Tower.

Windsor Castle is one of England's most popular attractions. Come early and be prepared to queue.

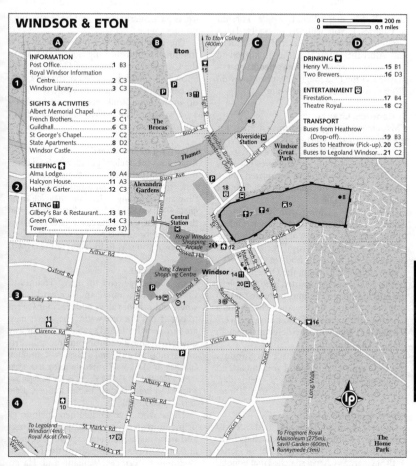

# WINDSOR & ETON

| INFORMATION | |
| --- | --- |
| Post Office | 1 B3 |
| Royal Windsor Information | |
| Centre | 2 C3 |
| Windsor Library | 3 C3 |

| SIGHTS & ACTIVITIES | |
| --- | --- |
| Albert Memorial Chapel | 4 C2 |
| French Brothers | 5 C1 |
| Guildhall | 6 C3 |
| St George's Chapel | 7 C2 |
| State Apartments | 8 D2 |
| Windsor Castle | 9 C2 |

| SLEEPING | |
| --- | --- |
| Alma Lodge | 10 A4 |
| Halcyon House | 11 A3 |
| Harte & Garter | 12 C3 |

| EATING | |
| --- | --- |
| Gilbey's Bar & Restaurant | 13 B1 |
| Green Olive | 14 C3 |
| Tower | (see 12) |

| DRINKING | |
| --- | --- |
| Henry VI | 15 B1 |
| Two Brewers | 16 D3 |

| ENTERTAINMENT | |
| --- | --- |
| Firestation | 17 B4 |
| Theatre Royal | 18 C2 |

| TRANSPORT | |
| --- | --- |
| Buses from Heathrow | |
| (Drop-off) | 19 B3 |
| Buses to Heathrow (Pick-up) | 20 C3 |
| Buses to Legoland Windsor | 21 C2 |

OXFORD, THE COTSWOLDS & AROUND

## Queen Mary's Dolls' House

Your first sight will be an incredible dolls' house, designed by Sir Edwin Lutyens for Queen Mary in 1924. The attention to detail is spellbinding – there's running water, electricity and lighting and vintage wine in the cellar! The house was intended to accurately depict households of the day, albeit on a scale of 1:12.

## State Apartments

After the dolls' house, a **gallery** with drawings by Leonardo da Vinci and a **China Museum**, visitors enter the stunning State Apartments, home to some exquisite paintings and architecture and still used by the Queen.

The **Grand Staircase** sets the tone for the rooms, all of which are elaborate, opulent and

suitably regal. Highlights include **St George's Hall**, which incurred the most damage during the fire of 1992. The dining chairs here, dwarfed by the scale of the room, are standard size. On the ceiling, the shields of the Knights of the Garter (originally from George IV's time here) were recreated after the fire.

For intimate gatherings (just 60 people), the Queen entertains in the **Waterloo Chamber** – the super-shiny table is French-polished and then dusted by someone walking over it with dusters on their feet. During large parties, this room is used for dancing and the table is tripled in size and set up in St George's Hall.

The **King's Dressing Room** has some of the most important Renaissance paintings in the royal collection. Alongside Sir Anthony

OXFORD, THE COTSWOLDS & AROUND

Van Dyck's magnificent *Triple Portrait* of Charles I, you will see works by Hans Holbein, Rembrandt, Peter Paul Rubens and Albrecht Dürer. Charles II kipped in here instead of in the **King's Bedchamber** – maybe George IV's magnificent bed (now on display) would have tempted him.

### St George's Chapel

This elegant chapel, commissioned for the Order of the Garter by Edward IV in 1475, is one of Britain's finest examples of Perpendicular Gothic architecture. The nave and fan-vaulted roof were completed under Henry VII but the final nail was struck under Henry VIII in 1528.

The chapel – along with Westminster Abbey – serves as a **royal mausoleum**, and its tombs read like a history of the British monarchy. The most recent royal burial occurred in April 2002, when the body of George VI's widow, Queen Elizabeth, the Queen Mother (1900–2002), was transported here in a splendid and sombre procession and buried alongside her husband. And in April 2005, Prince Charles and Camilla Parker-Bowles were blessed here following their civil marriage in the town's Guildhall.

St George's Chapel closes on Sunday, but time your visit well and you can attend Evensong at 5.15pm daily except Wednesday, or services at 10.45am, 11.45am and 5.15pm.

### Albert Memorial Chapel

Originally built in 1240 and dedicated to Edward the Confessor, this small chapel was the place of worship for the Order of the Garter until St George's Chapel snatched that honour. After the death of Prince Albert at Windsor Castle in 1861, Queen Victoria ordered its elaborate redecoration as a tribute to her husband. A major feature of the restoration is the magnificent vaulted roof, whose gold mosaic pieces were crafted in Venice. There's a monument to the prince, although he's actually buried with Queen Victoria in the Frogmore Royal Mausoleum in the castle grounds.

### Windsor Great Park

Stretching behind Windsor Castle almost all the way to Ascot, Windsor Great Park covers about 40 sq miles and features a lake, walking tracks, a bridleway and gardens. The **Savill Garden** ( ☎ 01753-860222; www.theroyallandscape.co.uk; adult/child £7/3.50; 🕙 10am-6pm Mar-Oct, to 4pm Nov-Feb) is particularly lovely and has a stunning visitors centre.

The **Long Walk** is a 3-mile walk along a tree-lined path from King George IV Gate to the Copper Horse statue (of George III) on Snow Hill, the highest point of the park. The Queen can occasionally be spotted driving down the Long Walk, accompanied only by a bodyguard. The walk is signposted from the town centre.

### Changing of the Guard

A fabulous spectacle of pomp, with loud commands, whispered conversations, triumphant tunes from a military band and plenty of shuffling and stamping of feet, the **changing of the guard** ( 🕙 11am Mon-Sat Apr-Jun, alternate days Jul-Mar) draws the crowds to the castle gates each day. It's a must for any visitor, but you'll get a better view if you stay to the right of the crowd.

### ETON COLLEGE

Cross the bridge over the River Thames to Eton and you'll enter another world, one where old-school values and traditions seem to ooze from the very walls. The streets here are surprisingly hushed as you make your way down to the most enduring and most illustrious symbol of England's class system, **Eton College** ( ☎ 01753-671177; www.etoncollege.com; adult/child £4.20/3.45, tours £5.50/4.50; 🕙 10.30am-4.30pm Mar & Apr, Jul-Sep [school holidays], 2-4.30pm term time, guided tours 2.15pm & 3.15pm).

Those who have studied here include 19 prime ministers, countless princes, kings and maharajahs, famous explorers, authors and economists, among them the Duke of Wellington, Princes William and Harry, George Orwell, Ian Fleming, Aldous Huxley, Sir Ranulph Fiennes and John Maynard Keynes.

Eton is the largest and most famous public (meaning very private) school in England. It was founded by Henry VI in 1440 with a view towards educating 70 highly qualified boys awarded a scholarship from a fund endowed by the king. Every year since then, 70 King's Scholars (aged 12 to 14) have been chosen based on the results of a highly competitive exam; these pupils are housed in separate quarters from the rest of the 1300 or so other students who are known as Oppidans.

While the King's Scholars are chosen exclusively on the basis of exam results, Oppidans must be able to foot the bill for £26,000 per-annum fees as well as passing entrance exams.

**A WORLD FIRST**

In June 1215, King John met his barons and bishops in a large field 3 miles southeast of Windsor, and over the next few days they hammered out an agreement on a basic charter of rights guaranteeing the liberties of the king's subjects and restricting the monarch's absolute power. The document they signed was the Magna Carta, the world's first constitution. It formed the basis for statutes and charters throughout the world's democracies. (Both the national and state constitutions of the United States, drawn up more than 500 years later, paraphrase directly from this document.)

Runnymede – from the Anglo-Saxon words *ruinige* (take council) and *moed* (meadow) – was chosen because it was the largest piece of open land between the king's residence at Windsor and the bishop's palace at Staines. Today, the field remains pretty much as it was, except now it features two **lodges** (1930) designed by Sir Edward Lutyens. In the woods behind the field are two **memorials**, the first to the Magna Carta designed by Sir Edward Maufe (1957). The second is to John F Kennedy, and was built by Geoffrey Jellicoe in 1965 on an acre of land granted in perpetuity to the US government following Kennedy's assassination.

Runnymede is on the A308 3 miles south east of Windsor. Bus 41 stops near here on the Windsor to Egham route.

All the boys are boarders and must comply with the strong traditions at Eton. The boys still wear formal tail coats, waistcoats and white collars to lessons, the school language is full of in-house jargon, and fencing, shooting, polo and beagling are on the list of school sporting activities.

Luckily for the rest of us, the college is open to visitors and a guided tour can go a long way to giving you an insight into how this most elite of schools functions. Tours take in the **chapel** (which you can see from Windsor Castle), the **cloisters**, the **Museum of Eton Life**, the **lower school** and the **school yard**. As you wander round, you may recognise some of the buildings, as the college is often used as a film set. *Chariots of Fire*, *The Madness of King George*, *Mrs Brown* and *Shakespeare in Love* are just some of the classics that have been filmed here.

**LEGOLAND WINDSOR**

A fun-filled theme park of white-knuckle rides, **Legoland** ( ☎ 08705 040404; www.legoland.co.uk; adult/child 3-15yr £34/26; ☯ hours vary) is more about the thrills of scaring yourself silly than the joys of building your own make-believe castle from the eponymous bricks. The professionals have already done this for you, with almost 40-million Lego bricks transformed into some of the world's greatest landmarks. You'll also get live shows, 3-D cinema and slightly tamer activities for the less adventurous. If you prebook online, you save about £3 off the whopping ticket prices.

The Legoland shuttle bus departs from High St and Thames St from 10am, with the last bus returning 30 minutes after the park has closed.

If you're planning to take the first bus of the morning, use the High St stop as it often fills up here and consequently does not stop in Thames St.

**Tours**

Open-top double-decker bus tours of the town are run by **City Sightseeing Tours** ( ☎ 0871-666 0000; www.city-sightseeing.com; adult/child £7/4; ☯ every ½-hr daily mid-Mar–mid-Nov, Sat & Sun mid-Nov–Dec) and leave from Castle Hill opposite the Harte & Garter Hotel. From Easter to October, **French Brothers** ( ☎ 01753-851900; www.frenchbrothers.co.uk; Clewer Court Rd; ☯ 11am-5pm) runs a variety of boat trips to Runnymede, Maidenhead and around Windsor and Eton. The 45-minute round trip to Runnymede costs £4.90 for adults and £2.45 for children. Boats leave from just next to Windsor Bridge. If you fancy doing the hop-on hop-off bus plus a 35-minute boat trip, a combined boat and bus ticket costs £11.50/6.25 per adult/child.

**Sleeping**

Windsor has a good selection of quality hotels and B&Bs, but few budget options.

**Alma Lodge** ( ☎ 01753-855620; www.almalodge.co.uk; 58 Alma Rd; s £45-60 d £60-75; P ☐ wi-fi) This elegant Victorian house, within walking distance of the centre of town, has large ensuite rooms with plenty of period features. A sweeping staircase greets you on arrival and ferries you up to rooms with ornate ceilings, original fireplaces and period style.

**Halcyon House** ( ☎ 01753-863262; www.halcyon-house .co.uk; 21 Clarence Rd; s/d £70/80; P ☐ wi-fi) Another fine Victorian house, this place offers an entirely different experience with simple stylish rooms that feature muted colour schemes and sparkling new bathrooms. The period features, such as the old fireplaces, remain but the overall effect is far more modern.

**Harte & Garter** ( ☎ 01753-863426; www.harteandgarter .com; High St; r £105-145; 🖵 ) Right opposite the castle and newly renovated, this Victorian hotel blends period style with modern furnishings. High ceilings, giant fireplaces, decorative cornices and dark woods seamlessly combine with contemporary fabrics, plasma-screen TVs and roll-top baths. Some rooms enjoy wonderful views over the castle and all guests can enjoy the luxurious spa in the converted stable block.

## Eating

**Green Olive** ( ☎ 01753-866655; 10 High St; meze £4-10) A great spot for a light lunch or tantalising evening meal, this place dishes up generous portions of traditional Greek meze in bright, simple surroundings. You can choose from over 50 different dishes and combine a riot of flavours before rolling out the door.

**Tower** ( ☎ 01753-863426; High St; mains £9.50-17.50; 🕒 7-10pm) Giant windows with views over the castle give this place an immediate allure, as do the grand chandeliers and high ceilings. The menu is brasserie style with a choice of classic British cuisine featuring grills, fish and steaks simply and perfectly done. It's also a good spot to sample the finest of English institutions: afternoon tea.

**Gilbey's Bar & Restaurant** ( ☎ 01753-854921; 82-83 High St, Eton; mains £12.50-21.50, set 2-/3-courses menu £13.75/18.75) This small restaurant in Eton has the feel of a continental cafe, with terracotta tiling and a sunny courtyard garden and conservatory. The superb modern British menu is almost surpassed by the wide and interesting choice of wines, making it one of the top spots to eat in town.

## Drinking

Windsor and Eton are packed with pubs, with a cluster under the railway arches of the central station.

**our pick Two Brewers** ( ☎ 01753-855426; 34 Park St) This 17th-century inn perched on the edge of Windsor Great Park is close to the castle's tradesmen's entrance and supposedly frequented by staff from the castle. It's a quaint and cosy place with dim lighting, obituaries

---

**READING FESTIVAL**

Each August Bank Holiday weekend about 240,000 revellers descend on the rather industrial town of Reading for one of the country's biggest music events. The **Reading Festival** (www.readingfestival.com) is a three-day extravaganza that features top acts in pop, rock and dance music. Tickets will set you back about £65 per day or £155 for a three-day pass.

---

to castle footmen, and royal photographs with irreverent captions on the wall.

**Henry VI** ( ☎ 01753-866051; 37 High St, Eton) Another old pub, but this time the low ceilings and subtle lighting are mixed with leather sofas and modern design. It's the kind of place where you can sit back with an afternoon pint and read the paper. There's a nice garden for alfresco dining and live music at weekends.

## Entertainment

**The Firestation** ( ☎ 01753-866865; www.windsorarts centre.org; cnr St Leonard's & St Mark's Rds) hosts a range of comedy, film, theatre, music and dance events with plenty of interest for kids.

The **Theatre Royal** ( ☎ 01753-853888; www.theatre royalwindsor.co.uk; 32-34 Thames St) features a wide repertoire of theatre productions from pantomime to first runs.

## Getting There & Away

Windsor is 21 miles west of central London and only about 15 minutes by car from Heathrow airport.

### BUS

Green Line bus 702 departs for Windsor and Legoland from London Victoria coach station (£2 to £8 depending on time of travel, 1½ hours, hourly, about every two hours Sunday). Bus 77 connects Windsor with Heathrow airport (one hour). Buses depart from the High St, Windsor, opposite the Parish Church.

### TRAIN

There are two Windsor and Eton train stations – trains from Central station on Thames St go to London Paddington (27 to 43 minutes) and trains from Riverside station near the bridge to Eton, go to London Waterloo (56 minutes). Services run half-hourly from both stations and tickets cost £7.70.

# Southwest England

Southwest England offers up, on one verdant, sea-fringed platter, the pick of Britain's cities, coast and countryside. Stretching west from Hampshire to the soaring cliffs and golden sands of Cornwall, the region takes in Dorset's chocolate box–pretty villages, Wiltshire's prehistoric sites, Bath's exquisite Georgian cityscape, Bristol's buzzing nightlife, hippie-chic Somerset and Devon's beguiling blend of moors and shores. Here you can surf surging waves off Cornwall and Devon or find your very own fossil on Dorset's Jurassic Coast; party hard at the resorts of Bournemouth, Torquay and Newquay, or revel in family-holiday nostalgia on the Isle of Wight. Skim around Weymouth's Olympic sailing venues or slip off your shoes, jump on a ferry and island-hop around the chilled-out Isles of Scilly.

Inland lie three tempting national parks: the rugged wildernesses of Dartmoor and Exmoor and the gentler woods of the New Forest. Stonehenge, Avebury, Tintagel and Glastonbury wade in with blockbuster ancient sites, Stourhead and Longleat bring stately-home grandeur, Bath bags the Roman relics, while Portsmouth, Plymouth and Falmouth drip with a nautical past. For years snooty urbanities have ridiculed England's southwest as a sleepy backwater, full of straw-chewing yokels, out of step with modern life. The thatched cottages, cream teas and fudge shops can (thankfully) still be found. But the region also has some of the country's best restaurants at Newquay, Padstow, Bristol and Dartmouth; cutting-edge art and culture scenes at St Ives and Bristol; inspiring eco-initiatives at the Eden Project and Totnes; and enough ultramodern boutique hotels to keep you pretty and pampered for years. Rejuvenated, reinvented and really rather fabulous, England's southwest is gently, politely, having the last laugh.

## HIGHLIGHTS

- Being swept away by kitesurfing (p377) and gourmet grub (p377), near **Newquay**
- Finding your very own fossil on Dorset's **Jurassic Coast** (p303)
- Hiking exhilarating wilderness trails on **Dartmoor National Park** (p365)
- Steaming through the giant tropical greenhouses of the **Eden Project** (p381)
- Soaking in a thermally heated, roof-top pool in gorgeously Georgian **Bath** (p334)
- Tracking down Banksy's guerrilla graffiti on the hip streets of **Bristol** (p326)
- Becoming a barefoot beachcomber on Cornwall's bewitching **Isles of Scilly** (p393)
- Clambering aboard Nelson's warship in salty seadog **Portsmouth** (p286)
- Connecting with your inner love-child in crystal-crammed **Glastonbury** (p342)
- Circling stone circles at **Avebury** (p318) and **Stonehenge** (p315)

| POPULATION: 4.06 MILLION | AREA: 8973 SQ MILES | NUMBER OF ICE-CREAMS SOLD ON A SUNNY DAY IN BOURNEMOUTH: 90,000 |
|---|---|---|

# SOUTHWEST ENGLAND

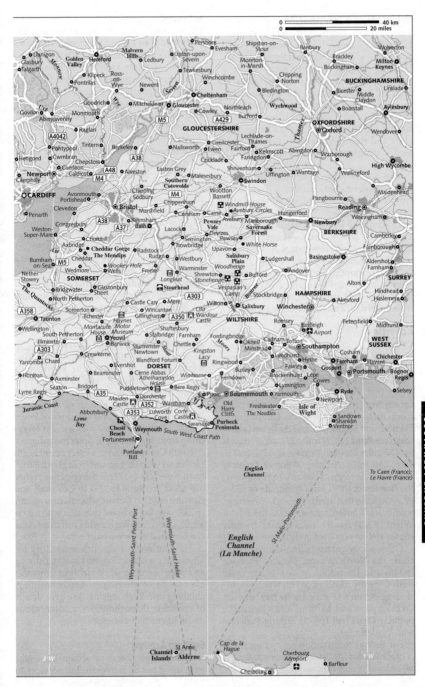

## Orientation & Information

The Southwest Peninsula stretches west from Hampshire's gentle hills via the Isle of Wight and the New Forest National Park to Dorset. Heading north it draws in rural Wiltshire and Somerset, and the vibrant cities of Bath and Bristol. Further south and west come the wildernesses of Exmoor and Dartmoor, Devon's coastal resorts, the cities of Exeter and Plymouth, Cornwall's beaches, cliffs and fishing villages, and then Land's End – mainland England's most westerly point.

The South West Tourist Board (www.visitsouthwest.com) covers a huge area from Gloucester and Dorset all the way to the west of Cornwall. The main website has links to themed subsites exploring nature, adventure, family and heritage holidays around the region. Hampshire is covered by www.visit-hampshire.co.uk.

The free monthly listings magazine **twenty 4-seven** (www.twenty4-seven.co.uk) covers all the latest bars, gigs and clubs, and is available from tourist offices, bars and restaurants.

## Activities

### CYCLING

Cycling the southwest is a superb, if sometimes taxing, way to experience England's great outdoors. National Cycle Network (NCN) routes that cross the region include the **West Country Way** (NCN route 3), a 250-mile jaunt from Bristol to Padstow via Glastonbury, Taunton and Barnstaple; and the **Devon Coast to Coast Cycle Route** (NCN route 27), which travels for 102 miles between Exmoor and Dartmoor. The 160-mile circular **Wiltshire Cycleway** runs along the county's borders. In Hampshire, the **New Forest** (p291) has hundreds of miles of cyclepaths that snake through a historic, wildlife-rich environment, while the Isle of Wight (p294) has 62-miles of bike-friendly routes and its very own cycling festival.

Off-road mountain-biking highlights include the North Wessex Downs, Exmoor (p346) and Dartmoor (p366). Many cycle trails trace the routes of old railway lines, including Devon's 11-mile **Granite Way** between Okehampton and Lydford and Cornwall's popular **Camel Trail** (p375) linking Padstow with Wadebridge.

For further information on cycling trails, contact **Sustrans** ( ☎ 0845 113 00 65; www.sustrans.org.uk) or local tourist offices.

### WALKING

Often called the 630-mile adventure, the **South West Coast Path** (www.southwestcoastpath.com) is Britain's longest national walking trail, and stretches west from Minehead on Exmoor, via Land's End to Poole in Dorset. You can pick it up at many points along the coast for a short (and spectacular) day's stroll, or tackle longer stretches. The **South West Coast Path Association** (www.swcp.org.uk) publishes an annual guide.

For wilderness hikes the National Parks of Dartmoor (p366) and Exmoor (p347) are hard to beat – Dartmoor is bigger and more remote – Exmoor's ace in the pack is a cracking 34 miles of precipitous coast. The region's third national park, the New Forest, is an altogether gentler affair, but still offers hundreds of miles of trails. Other hiking highlights are Exmoor's **Coleridge Way** (p347), the Isle of Wight (p294) and Bodmin Moor (p379).

In northeast Wiltshire, the **Ridgeway National Trail** starts near Avebury and winds 44 miles through chalk hills to meet the River Thames at Goring. The trail then continues another 41 miles (another three days) through the Chiltern Hills.

### WATER SPORTS & OTHER ACTIVITIES

Testing your mettle in washing-machine waves may draw you to the southwest's coasts. Top spots are Britain's 2012 Olympic sailing venues at Weymouth and Portland (p307), the yachting havens of the Isle of Wight, and the watery playgrounds of Poole (p301), where you can try your hand at everything from kitesurfing to powerboating.

North Cornwall, and to a lesser extent north Devon, serve up the best surf in England. Partytown Newquay (p377) is the epicentre, other top spots are Bude (p373) in Cornwall and Croyde (p371) in Devon, while Bournemouth (p298) is trying to boost its waves with a new artificial surf reef. Regionwide surf conditions can be found at www.a1surf.com.

The southwest is also prime territory for kitesurfing, windsurfing, sea kayaking, diving and wake boarding; while plenty of firms also offer caving, coasteering, mountain boarding, climbing and kitebuggying. We give details of providers throughout; www.adventuresw.co.uk has further options.

## Getting Around

It is perfectly possible to get around the southwest using public transport, but services to some of the more remote areas are limited; using your own wheels gives you more flexibility. **Traveline South West** ( ☎ 0871 200 22 33; www.travelinesw.com) can answer regionwide questions about bus and train routes (calls cost 10p per minute). Timetables and public transport maps are available from stations and tourist offices.

## BUS
The region's bus network is fairly comprehensive, but becomes increasingly patchy the further you move away from the main towns; Dartmoor and west Cornwall can be particularly tricky to negotiate. National Express coaches usually provide the quickest routes between cities and larger towns.

**First Travel** ( ☎ timetables 0871 200 22 33, customer service 0870 010 6022; www.firstgroup.com) The region's largest bus company. The FirstDay Southwest ticket (adult/child £7/5.20) is valid for one day on most First buses in Devon, Cornwall, Bristol, Somerset and Dorset.

**PlusBus** (www.plusbus.info) Allows you to add local bus travel to your train ticket. Participating cities include Bath, Bristol, Taunton and Weymouth. Tickets cost from £2 to £3 per day and can be bought at railway stations.

**Stagecoach** ( ☎ timetables 0871 200 22 33, customer service 0845 121 0190) A key provider in Hampshire. A one-day Explorer Ticket costs £7/4 per adult/child.

**Wilts & Dorset** ( ☎ 01202-673555; www.wdbus.co.uk) One-day Explorer tickets (adult/child £7/4) cover transport on most Wilts & Dorset buses and some other companies.

## CAR & MOTORCYCLE
The major car-hire firms have offices at the region's airports and main-line train stations; rates are similar to elsewhere in the UK, starting at around £35 per day for a small hatchback (see p1000). The M5 runs past Bath and Bristol, becomes the A38 at Exeter and continues on into Cornwall. The M3 and M27 head into Hampshire from the southeast, linking Winchester, Portsmouth and Southampton, before becoming the A31 and heading into Dorset.

Another main route is the A303, which cuts west across Salisbury Plain past Stonehenge on its way towards Exeter and Plymouth, before joining the A38 into Cornwall.

## TRAIN
A key train line to the southwest follows the historic Great Western Railway route to Bristol, from where there are regular links to London Paddington, as well as services north to Scotland via Birmingham. Bristol also has connections to many other towns and cities across the region including Bath, Swindon, Chippenham, Weymouth, Southampton and Portsmouth. Trains from London Waterloo also travel to Salisbury, Southampton, Portsmouth and Weymouth.

Beyond Exeter, the main line heads west via Liskeard, St Austell, Truro and Penzance, with spur lines to Barnstaple, Paignton, Gunnislake, Looe, Falmouth, St Ives and Newquay.

The **Freedom of the SouthWest Rover pass** (adult/child £95/45) allows eight days' unlimited travel over 15 days in an area that includes Salisbury, Bath, Bristol and Weymouth.

# HAMPSHIRE
Hampshire is the historic heart of the ancient kingdom of Wessex, a Dark Age territory that at its height stretched from Kent through Dorset, Wiltshire, Somerset, Bath and Devon to Cornwall. Kings Alfred the Great, Knut and William the Conqueror all based their reigns in Hampshire's ancient cathedral city of Winchester. Its jumble of historic buildings sits in an undulating landscape of chalk downs and fertile valleys. The county's coast is awash with heritage – in rejuvenated Portsmouth you can clamber aboard the pride of Nelson's navy, HMS *Victory*, wonder at the *Mary Rose* (Henry VIII's flagship), and wander wharfs buzzing with restaurants, shops and bars. Hampshire's southwestern corner claims the lovely open heath and woodlands of the New Forest and is the perfect springboard for happy holidays on the Isle of Wight – both areas are covered in separate sections in this chapter.

## WINCHESTER
pop 41,420
Calm, collegiate Winchester is a mellow must-see for all visitors to the region. The past still echoes strongly around the flint-flecked walls of this ancient cathedral city and capital of Saxon kings. Winchester's architecture is exquisite, from the handsome Elizabethan and Regency buildings in the narrow winding streets, to the wondrous cathedral at its core. Thanks to a lush riverside location the city also has charming waterside trails to explore.

### History
Winchester really took off when the powerful West Saxon bishops moved their Episcopal

SOUTHWEST ENGLAND

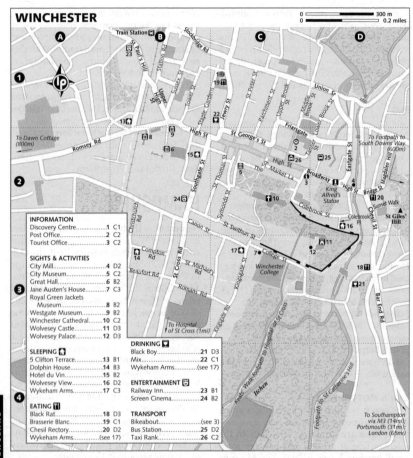

## WINCHESTER

0 ............ 300 m
0 ............ 0.2 miles

**INFORMATION**
Discovery Centre..................1 C1
Post Office.............................2 C2
Tourist Office........................3 C2

**SIGHTS & ACTIVITIES**
City Mill..................................4 D2
City Museum...........................5 C2
Great Hall...............................6 B2
Jane Austen's House.............7 C3
Royal Green Jackets
  Museum...............................8 B2
Westgate Museum.................9 B2
Winchester Cathedral.........10 C2
Wolvesey Castle..................11 D3
Wolvesey Palace..................12 D3

**SLEEPING**
5 Clifton Terrace..................13 B1
Dolphin House.....................14 B3
Hotel du Vin........................15 B2
Wolvesey View.....................16 D2
Wykeham Arms.....................17 C3

**EATING**
Black Rat..............................18 D3
Brasserie Blanc.....................19 C1
Chesil Rectory......................20 D2
Wykeham Arms...............(see 17)

**DRINKING**
Black Boy..............................21 D3
Mix.......................................22 C1
Wykeham Arms............(see 17)

**ENTERTAINMENT**
Railway Inn...........................23 B1
Screen Cinema.....................24 B2

**TRANSPORT**
Bikeabout.......................(see 3)
Bus Station...........................25 D2
Taxi Rank.............................26 C2

see here in AD 670, making Winchester the most important town in the powerful kingdom of Wessex. King Alfred the Great (r 871–99) made it his capital, and it remained so under Knut (r 1016–35) and the Danish kings. After the Norman invasion of 1066, William the Conqueror arrived here to claim the throne of England, and in 1086 he commissioned local monks to write the all-important Domesday Book, an administrative survey of the entire country and the most significant clerical accomplishment of the Middle Ages. Winchester thrived up until the 12th century, when a fire gutted most of the city, after which London took its crown. A long slump lasted until the 18th century, when the town revived as a trading centre.

## Orientation

The city centre is compact and easily managed on foot. The partly pedestrianised High St runs from west to east. The bus station is in the middle of town opposite the Guildhall and tourist office; the train station is five minutes' walk northwest.

## Information

The **tourist office** ( ☎ 01962-840500; www.visitwinchester.co.uk; High St; ⏰ 9.30am-5.30pm Mon-Sat & 11am-4pm Sun May-Sep, 10am-5pm Mon-Sat Oct-Apr), in the Gothic Revival Guildhall, has information and an accommodation booking service. The new **Discovery Centre** ( ☎ 0845 603 5631; Jewry St; admission free; ⏰ 9am-7pm Mon-Fri, 9am-5pm Sat, 10am-4pm Sun), a library-cum-entertainment space, has free internet access. There's a **post office** (🕙 9.30am-6pm Mon-Sat) on Middle Brook St, and there are plenty of banks and ATMs on High St.

## Sights

### WINCHESTER CATHEDRAL

Almost 1000 years of history are crammed into Winchester's superb **cathedral** (☎ 01962-857200; www.winchester-cathedral.org.uk; adult/child £5/free, combined admission & tower tour £8; 🕙 8.30am-6pm Mon-Sat, to 5.30pm Sun), which is not only the city's star attraction but one of southern England's most awe-inspiring buildings. The exterior, with a squat tower and a slightly sunken rear, isn't at first glance appealing, despite a fine Gothic facade. But the interior contains one of the longest medieval naves (164m) in Europe, and a fascinating jumble of features from all eras.

The cathedral sits beside foundations that mark the town's original 7th-century minster church. The cathedral was begun in 1070 and completed in 1093, and subsequently entrusted with the bones of its patron saint, St Swithin (bishop of Winchester from 852 to 862). The latter is best known for the proverb that states that if it rains on St Swithin's Day (15 July), it will rain for a further 40 days and 40 nights.

Soggy ground and poor workmanship spelled disaster for the early church; the original tower collapsed in 1107 and major restructuring continued until the mid-15th century. Look out for the monument at the rear to diver William Walker, who saved the cathedral from collapse by delving repeatedly into its waterlogged underbelly from 1906 to 1912 to bolster rotting wooden foundations with vast quantities of concrete and brick.

On the south side of the nave, the **Cathedral Library & Triforium Gallery** (adult/child £1/50p; 🕙 11am-4pm Tue-Sat, 1.30-4pm Mon Apr-Oct) provides a fine elevated view of the cathedral body, and contains the dazzlingly illuminated pages of the 12th-century *Winchester Bible* – its colours as bright as if they were painted yesterday.

You can also see the grave of one of England's best-loved authors, Jane Austen. It's near the entrance in the northern aisle. Austen died a stone's throw from the cathedral in 1817 at **Jane Austen's House** (8 College St), where she spent her last six weeks. It's now a private residence and is marked by a slate plaque.

The transepts are the most original parts of the cathedral, and the intricately carved medieval choir stalls are another must-see, sporting everything from mythical beasts to a mischievous green man.

Flooding often prevents tours of the **crypt** (tours free; 🕙 10.30am, 12.30pm & 2.30pm Mon-Sat) from going ahead; if it is open, look out for the poignant solitary sculpture by Anthony Gormley called *Sound 2*.

Cathedral body **tours** (free; 🕙 hourly 10am-3pm Mon-Sat) last one hour. There are also **tower and roof tours** (£5; 🕙 2.15pm Mon-Fri, 11.30am & 2.15pm Sat Jun-Sep, 2.15pm Wed, 11.30am & 2.15pm Sat Oct-May) up narrow stairwells and with views as far as the Isle of Wight. Sunday services take place at 8am, 10am and 11.15am, with evensong at 3.30pm. Evensong is also held at 5.30pm Monday to Saturday.

### THE GREAT HALL

Winchester's other showpiece is the cavernous **Great Hall** (☎ 01962-846476; Castle Ave; suggested donation adult/child £1/50p; 🕙 10am-5pm), the only part of 11th-century Winchester Castle that Oliver Cromwell spared from destruction. Crowning the wall like a giant-sized dartboard of green and cream spokes is what centuries of mythology have called **King Arthur's Round Table**. It's actually a 700-year-old fake, but a fascinating one nonetheless. It's thought to have been constructed in the late 13th century and later painted in the reign of Henry VIII (King Arthur's image is unsurprisingly reminiscent of Henry's youthful face).

This hall was also the stage for several dramatic English courtroom dramas, including the trial in 1603 of adventurer Sir Walter Raleigh, who was sentenced to death but received a reprieve at the last minute.

### MUSEUMS

**City Museum** (☎ 01962-863064; The Square; admission free; 🕙 10am-5pm Mon-Sat & noon-5pm Sun Apr-Oct, 10am-4pm Tue-Sat & noon-4pm Sun Nov-Mar) whizzes through Winchester's fascinating Roman and Saxon history, lingers on its Anglo-Norman golden age, pays homage to Jane Austen, and reconstructs several early-20th-century Winchester shops.

Fitting snugly into one of Winchester's two surviving medieval gateways, **Westgate Museum** (☎ 01962-869864; High St; admission free; 🕙 10am-5pm Mon-Sat & noon-5pm Sun Apr-Oct, 10am-4pm Tue-Sat & noon-4pm Sun Feb & Mar) was once a debtors' prison with a macabre set of gibbeting irons last used to display an executed criminal's body in 1777.

Scrawled crudely all over the interior walls is the 17th-century graffiti of prisoners.

There's a clutch of army museums dotted around the Peninsula Barracks on Romsey Rd. The highlight is the **Royal Green Jackets Museum** ( ☎ 01962-828549; www.winchestermilitarymuseums.co.uk; adult/child £2/1; ☽ 10am-5pm Mon-Sat, noon-4pm Sun Mar–mid-Nov), which has a mini rifle-shooting range, a room of 6000 medals and an impressive blow-by-blow diorama of Napoleon's downfall, the Battle of Waterloo.

### WOLVESEY CASTLE & PALACE

The fantastical, crumbling remains of early-12th-century **Wolvesey Castle** (EH; ☎ 023-9237 8291; admission free; ☽ 10am-5pm Apr-Sep) still huddle in the protective embrace of the city's walls, despite the building having been largely demolished in the 1680s. According to legend, its odd name comes from a Saxon king's demand for an annual payment of 300 wolves' heads. It was completed by Henry de Blois, and it served as the Bishop of Winchester's residence throughout the medieval era. Queen Mary I and Philip II of Spain celebrated their wedding feast here in 1554. Access is via College St. Today the bishop lives in the adjacent **Wolvesey Palace**.

### CITY MILL

The city's 18th-century water-powered **mill** (NT; ☎ 01962-870057; Bridge St; adult/child £3.40/1.70; ☽ 11am-5pm March-Dec) is now working again; you can see the process in action and buy stone-ground flour in the shop.

### HOSPITAL OF ST CROSS

Monk, bishop, knight, politician and grandson of William the Conqueror, Henry de Blois was a busy man. But he still found time to establish this still-impressive **hospital** ( ☎ 01962-851375; www.stcrosshospital.co.uk; St Cross Rd; adult/child/senior £2.50/50p/£2; ☽ 9.30am-5pm daily Apr-Oct, 10.30am-3.30pm Mon-Sat Nov-Mar) in 1132. As well as healing the sick and housing the needy, the hospital was built to feed and bed pilgrims and crusaders en route to the Holy Land. It's the oldest charitable institution in the country, and is still roamed by 25 elderly black- or red-gowned brothers in pie-shaped trencher hats, who continue to hand out alms. Take a peek into the stumpy church, the brethren hall, the kitchen and the peaceful gardens. The best way to arrive is via the 1-mile Keats' Walk (right). Upon entering, claim the

centuries-old traditional Wayfarer's Dole – a crust of bread and horn of ale (now a small swig of beer) from the Porter's Gate.

## Activities
### WALKING

Winchester has a tempting range of rambles. The 1-mile **Keats' Walk** meanders through the water meadows to Hospital of St Cross (left). Its beauty is said to have prompted the poet to pen the ode *To Autumn* – pick up the trail near Wolvesey Castle. Alternatively, head down Wharf Hill, through the water meadows to **St Catherine's Hill** (1 mile). The tranquil **Riverside Walk**, meanwhile, trails a short distance from the castle along the bank of the River Itchen to High St. The stiffer **Sunset Walk** up St Giles' Hill rewards with fine city views, especially at dusk – to get here head up East or Magdalen Hills. St Giles' Hill is also the beginning (or end) of the **South Downs Way** (p204).

## Sleeping

**5 Clifton Terrace** ( ☎ 01962-890053; chrissiejohnston@ hotmail.com; 5 Clifton Tce; s/d/f £55/65/89; P ⊒ ) Blending old and new, this tall Georgian town house sees plush furnishings rub shoulders with antiques, and modern comforts coexist alongside claw-foot baths. The owners are utterly charming.

**Wolvesey View** ( ☎ 01962-852082; www.wintonian .com; 10 Colebrook Pl; s/d £40/68; P ⊒ ) Book the Yellow Room here and you'll open the curtains to grandstand views of Wolvesey Castle's fairytale tumblings. It's a simply furnished, family-run affair, with shared bathrooms – all hidden away in a quiet cul-de-sac.

**Dawn Cottage** ( ☎ 01962-869956; dawncottage@ hotmail.com; 99 Romsey Rd; s/d £55/68; P ) Expect lovely views, a sun deck and pretty gardens at this tranquil, vine-covered house a mile from the middle of town.

**Dolphin House** ( ☎ 01962-853284; www.dolphin housestudios.co.uk; 3 Compton Rd; s/d £55/70; P ) A kind of B&B-plus, the two rooms (with attached bathroom) in this charming town house share a compact kitchen to which your Continental breakfast is delivered – allowing for lazy lie-ins. The terrace, complete with cast-iron tables and chairs, overlooks a gently sloping lawn.

**ourpick Wykeham Arms** ( ☎ 01962-853834; www .accommodating-inns.co.uk; 75 Kingsgate St; s £90-100, d £105-150) At 250-odd years old, the Wykeham is bursting with history – it used to be a brothel and also put up Nelson for a night (some say the two events coincided). Creaking, winding stairs lead to the cosy, traditionally styled bedrooms above the pub, while the posher rooms (over the converted post office, opposite) look out onto a pocked-sized courtyard garden.

**Hotel du Vin** ( ☎ 01962-841414; www.hotelduvin .com; Southgate St; r £135-205; **P** 🖵 wi-fi) Tucked in behind a red-brick facade and gleaming white porticoes, this oh-so-chic hotel boasts ultracool minimalist furniture, ornate chaises lounges and opulent stand-alone baths. The bistro delivers Georgian elegance and modern versions of English and French classics (mains £16).

## Eating

**Wykeham Arms** ( ☎ 01962-853834; 75 Kingsgate St; mains £9-14; 🕒 lunch & dinner Mon-Sat, lunch Sun) Somehow reminiscent of an endearingly eccentric old uncle, this charming pub-restaurant has 1400 tankards hanging from the ceilings, as well as an impressive array of school canes. The food is legendary – try the pan-fried salmon, or sausages flavoured with local bitter, then finish off with some seriously addictive sticky toffee pudding.

**Brasserie Blanc** ( ☎ 01962-810870; 19 Jewry St; mains £13; 🕒 lunch & dinner) Get a taste of French home cooking, Raymond (Blanc) style, at this super-sleek chain. The celebrity chef may not necessarily sauté your starter himself, but the chicken stuffed with morel mushrooms and the Toulouse sausage with onion gravy are full of Gallic charm.

**Black Rat** ( ☎ 01962-844465; 88 Chesil St; mains £17; 🕒 dinner Mon-Fri, lunch & dinner Sat & Sun) Worn wooden floorboards and warm red-brick walls give this relaxed restaurant a cosy feel. Duck with brioche, mushrooms with truffle-oil and woodpigeon with pine nuts all find their way onto the sanded-down tables.

**Chesil Rectory** ( ☎ 01962-851555; 1 Chesil St; 1-/2-/3-course lunch £15/19/23, 2-/3-/6-course dinner £39/49/65; 🕒 dinner Tue, lunch & dinner Wed-Sat) Duck through the hobbit-sized door, settle down amid the 15th-century beams and prepare to enjoy some fine modern Continental cuisine. Confit of duck, Solent sea bass with oyster sauce, and ravioli of lobster with diver-caught scallops all feature on the assured menu.

## Drinking

Winchester isn't big on late-night revelry, though the students head for cheap pubs along Jewry St.

**Black Boy** ( ☎ 01962-861754; 1 Wharf Hill; 🕒 noon-11pm) This adorable old pub is filled with obsessive and sometimes freaky collections, from pocket watches to wax facial features, bear traps and sawn paperbacks.

**Mix** ( ☎ 01962-860900; 10 Jewry St; 🕒 4pm-midnight Mon-Thu, Fri & Sat 4pm-1am, Sun 4-11pm) A poseur's paradise: perch elegantly on a velvet dressing-table chair in this black, pink and aquamarine champagne and cocktail bar.

The Wykeham Arms (see left) is full of character and a wonderful place for a pint.

## Entertainment

For listings, pick up the free *What's On in Winchester* from the tourist office.

**Railway Inn** ( ☎ 01962-867795; www.liveattherailway .co.uk; 3 St Paul's Hill; 🕒 5pm-midnight Sun-Thu, to 2am Fri, to 1am Sat) Catch live bands from 8pm at this grungy place behind the station.

**Screen Cinema** ( ☎ 01962-877007; www.screencinemas .co.uk; Southgate St) Watch movies in a converted 19th-century military chapel.

## Getting There & Away

Winchester is 65 miles west of London and 14 miles north of Southampton.

### BUS

National Express has several direct buses to London Victoria bus station (£13, 2¼ hours). Buses also run to Southampton (40 minutes).

### TRAIN

Trains leave every 20 minutes from London Waterloo (£24, one hour) and Southampton (15 to 23 minutes) and hourly from Portsmouth (£8.60, one hour). There are also fast links to the Midlands.

## Getting Around

There's plenty of day parking within five minutes' walk of the centre or you can use the Park & Ride for £2.70 per day. For a taxi try the rank outside Sainsbury's on Middle Brook St or phone **Wintax Taxis** ( ☎ 01962-878727).

## PORTSMOUTH

pop 187,056

Prepare to splice the main brace, hoist the halyard and potter around the poop deck – Portsmouth is the principal port of Britain's Royal Navy, and its historic dockyard ranks alongside Greenwich as one of England's most fascinating centres of maritime history. Here you can jump aboard

Lord Nelson's glorious warship *HMS Victory*, which led the charge at Trafalgar, and glimpse the atmospheric remains of Henry VIII's 16th-century flagship, the *Mary Rose*.

Regeneration at the nearby Gunwharf Quays has added new glitz to the city's waterfront. A spectacular millennium-inspired structure, the Spinnaker Tower – keelhauled by the British media for delays and spiralling costs – finally opened here in 2005, with views to knock the wind from the critics' sails.

However, Portsmouth is by no means a city noted for its beauty; it was heavily bombed during WWII and a combination of sometimes soulless postwar architecture and surprisingly deserted waterfront promenades can leave a melancholy impression. But the city's fine array of naval museums justifies an overnight stay, while the suburb of Southsea boasts some fair beaches, bars and good restaurants.

## Orientation

It's easy to find Portsmouth's key sights – the futuristic Spinnaker Tower (p288) soars into the sky to point the way. The central quay area alongside, known as The Hard, also has the Historic Dockyard, tourist office, train station and the passenger-ferry terminal for the Isle of Wight. Just southeast lies Old Portsmouth, where more ancient buildings feature amid the postwar rebuild. Next door sits The Point, a cluster of sea-worn, atmospheric buildings around the old harbour. Southsea is about 2 miles south.

## Information

**Laundry Care** ( ☎ 023-9282 6245; 59 Osborne Rd; ☻ 8am-6pm)

**Online Cafe** ( ☎ 023-9283 1106; 163 Elm Grove, Southsea; internet access per 10min/1hr 50p/£2.60; ☻ 9am-9pm Mon-Fri, 10am-9pm Sat & Sun)

**Post office** (Palmerston Rd, Southsea)

**Tourist office** ( ☎ 023-9282 6722; www.visitportsmouth.co.uk; The Hard; ☻ 9.30am-5.45pm Apr-Sep, to 5.15pm Oct-Mar) Can arrange walking tours (£2), and has an accommodation service.

**Tourist office branch** ( ☎ 023-9282 6722; Clarence Esplanade, Southsea; ☻ 9.30am-5.45pm Jul & Aug, to 5.15pm Mar-Jun, to 4pm Sep-Feb) Next to the Blue Reef Aquarium, this branch gives discounts to several attractions (if you buy tickets in advance).

## Sights & Activities

### PORTSMOUTH HISTORIC DOCKYARD

Portsmouth's blockbuster attraction is the **Historic Dockyard** ( ☎ 023-9283 9766; www.historicdock-

yard.co.uk; adult/child single-attraction ticket £10/8, all-inclusive ticket £18.50/14; ☻ 10am-6pm Apr-Oct, 10am-5.30pm Nov-Mar, last admission 1½hr before closing). Set in the heart of the country's most important naval port, it comprises three stunning ships and a clutch of museums that pay homage to the historical might of the Royal Navy. Together they make for a full day's outing, though you may spend much of your time swimming through a tide of schoolchildren. The all-inclusive ticket provides access for one year to all the ships and museums, and it includes a harbour tour (see p288) – the single ticket limits you to just one of the attractions.

### The Ships

As resplendent as she is venerable, the dockyard's star sight is **HMS Victory** (www.hms-victory.com), Lord Nelson's flagship at the 1805 Battle of Trafalgar and the site of his infamous 'Kiss me, Hardy…' dying words when victory over the French had been secured. This remarkable ship is topped by a forest of ropes and masts, and weighted by a swollen belly filled with cannonS and paraphernalia for an 850-strong crew. Clambering through the low-beamed decks is a stirring experience and there's huge demand for the excellent 40-minute tours – arrive early to bag a place (you can't book in advance).

Equally thrilling are the remains of 16th-century warship and darling of Henry VIII, the **Mary Rose** (www.maryrose.org). This 700-ton floating fortress sank off Portsmouth after a mysterious incident of 'human folly and bad luck' in 1545. In an astoundingly ambitious piece of marine archaeology, the ship was raised from its watery grave in 1982. It now presents a ghostly image that could teach Hollywood a few tricks, its vast flank preserved in dim lighting, dripping and glistening in a constant mist of sea water. (At the time this book went to press, we were advised that the ship hall would be closed due to capital works, and wouldn't re-open until 2011 or 2012, but information and displays on the ship will be available in the Mary Rose Museum; see opposite.)

Anywhere else, the magnificent warship **HMS Warrior**, built in 1860, would grab centre stage. This stately dame was at the cutting edge of technology in her day, riding the transition from wood to iron and sail to steam. Visitors can wander freely around the four decks to imagine life in the Victorian navy.

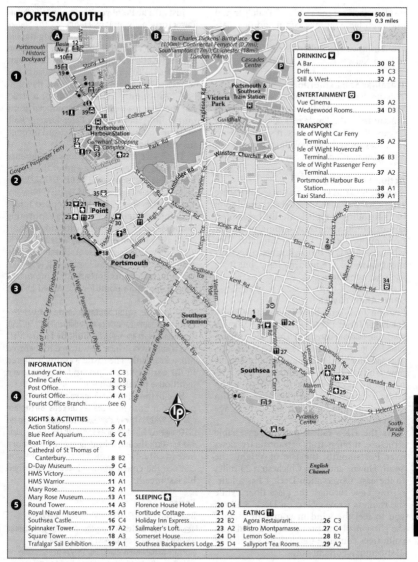

## PORTSMOUTH

**DRINKING**
A Bar.............................................**30** B2
Drift..............................................**31** C3
Still & West..................................**32** A2

**ENTERTAINMENT**
Vue Cinema.................................**33** A2
Wedgewood Rooms....................**34** D3

**TRANSPORT**
Isle of Wight Car Ferry
    Terminal..................................**35** A2
Isle of Wight Hovercraft
    Terminal..................................**36** B3
Isle of Wight Passenger Ferry
    Terminal..................................**37** A2
Portsmouth Harbour Bus
    Station.....................................**38** A1
Taxi Stand...................................**39** A1

**INFORMATION**
Laundry Care.................................**1** C3
Online Café....................................**2** D3
Post Office......................................**3** C3
Tourist Office.................................**4** A1
Tourist Office Branch..........(see 6)

**SIGHTS & ACTIVITIES**
Action Stations!.............................**5** A1
Blue Reef Aquarium.......................**6** C4
Boat Trips.......................................**7** A1
Cathedral of St Thomas of
    Canterbury................................**8** B2
D-Day Museum..............................**9** C4
HMS Victory.................................**10** A1
HMS Warrior................................**11** A1
Mary Rose.....................................**12** A1
Mary Rose Museum......................**13** A1
Round Tower................................**14** A3
Royal Naval Museum....................**15** A1
Southsea Castle............................**16** C4
Spinnaker Tower..........................**17** A2
Square Tower................................**18** A3
Trafalgar Sail Exhibition...............**19** A1

**SLEEPING**
Florence House Hotel...................**20** D4
Fortitude Cottage.........................**21** A2
Holiday Inn Express.....................**22** B2
Sailmaker's Loft...........................**23** A2
Somerset House............................**24** D4
Southsea Backpackers Lodge..**25** D4

**EATING**
Agora Restaurant.........................**26** C3
Bistro Montparnasse....................**27** C4
Lemon Sole...................................**28** B2
Sallyport Tea Rooms....................**29** A2

## Mary Rose Museum

At this museum, which is set away from
the ship herself, you can bear witness to the
Herculean salvage operation to raise the
*Mary Rose* from the seabed. Crammed full
of recovered treasures and fascinating facts,
displays also feature a 15-minute film showing
just how they managed to extract her from

Portsmouth Harbour. A single-attraction
ticket to this museum also includes admission to the ship (see opposite).

## Royal Naval Museum

This huge museum has five galleries of naval
history, model ships, battle dioramas, medals, paintings and much more. Audiovisual

displays recreate the Battle of Trafalgar and one even lets you take command of a battleship – see if you can cure the scurvy and avoid mutiny. One gallery is entirely devoted to Lord Nelson.

### Trafalgar Sail Exhibition
This small **exhibition** ( 10am-5pm Apr-Oct, to 4pm Nov-Mar) showcases HMS *Victory*'s only remaining sail from the Battle of Trafalgar. Clearly bearing the scars of conflict, it's riddled with the holes made by Napoleonic cannons – a telling illustration of the battle's ferocity.

### Action Stations!
Stumble into this warehouse-based **interactive experience** (www.actionstations.org) and you'll soon be controlling a replica Merlin helicopter, commanding a warship, upping periscope or jumping aboard a jerky simulator. The whole set-up is a thinly disguised recruitment drive for the modern navy, but it's a fun one, nonetheless.

### SPINNAKER TOWER
Soaring to 170m above Gunwharf Quays, **Spinnaker Tower** ( 023-92857520; www.spinnaker tower.co.uk; Gunwharf Quays; adult/child £7/5.50; 10am-10pm Aug, 10am-6pm Sun-Fri & 10am-10pm Sat Sep & Oct, 10am-6pm Nov-Jul) is Portsmouth's unmistakable new landmark, and a symbol of the city's newfound razzle-dazzle. Its two sweeping white arcs resemble a billowing sail from some angles, and a sharp skeletal ribcage from others.

As the UK's tallest publicly accessible structure, it offers truly extraordinary views over Portsmouth, the Isle of Wight, the South Downs and even Chichester, 23 miles to the east. Observation Deck 1 has a hair-raising view through the glass floor, while the roofless Crow's Nest on Deck 3 allows you to feel the wind in your hair. Below, the glitzy mall and promenades dotted with palm trees complete the designers' vision of 21st-century Portsmouth.

### OTHER SIGHTS & ACTIVITIES
A short waterside walk from Gunwharf Quays, but a world apart in atmosphere, **The Point** is home to cobbled streets full of character and dotted with salty seadog pubs. It's a top spot from which to gaze at the Spinnaker Tower and the passing parade of ferries and navy ships.

Just off The Point you can mount the **Round Tower** (originally built by Henry V), the **Square Tower** of 1494, and take a stroll along the old fort walls. A short walk back from the water, the airy **Cathedral of St Thomas of Canterbury** ( 023-9282 3300; www.portsmouthcathedral.org.uk; High St; 9am-5pm) retains fragments of its 12th- and 17th-century incarnations, but a striking modern makeover has introduced some quirky little statuettes by Peter Eugene Ball; look for Thomas Becket with a sword through his mitred head.

There's a cluster of attractions on Clarence Esplanade at the Southsea end of the waterfront. **Blue Reef Aquarium** ( 023-9287 5222; www.bluereefaquarium.co.uk; adult/child £9/7; 10am-5pm Mar-Oct, to 4pm Nov-Feb) has open-topped tanks, huge underwater walkways and a captivating 'seahorse ranch' – a sure hit with kids. A short stroll away is bunkerlike **D-Day Museum** ( 023-9282 7261; www.ddaymuseum.co.uk; Clarence Esplanade; adult/child £6/4.20; 10am-5.30pm Apr-Sep, to 5pm Oct-Mar), which recounts Portsmouth's important role as departure point for the Allied D-Day forces in 1944.

Alongside, squat **Southsea Castle** ( 023-9282 7261; www.southseacastle.co.uk; adult/child £3.50/2.50; 10am-5.30pm Apr-Sep) was built by Henry VIII and is said to be where he watched his beloved *Mary Rose* sink. The castle was much altered in the early 19th century and there's now a lighthouse plonked on top.

East of the Historic Dockyard you can also poke your nose into **Charles Dickens' Birthplace** ( 023-9282 7261; www.charlesdickensbirthplace.co.uk; 393 Old Commercial Rd; adult/child £3.50/2.50; 10am-5.30pm mid-Apr–Oct); the hard-hitting author was born here in 1812. He also died here in 1870 – you can see the couch upon which he breathed his last breath.

## Tours
**Boat trips** ( 023-9272 8060; Historic Dockyard; 11am-3pm Easter-Oct) Weather permitting, 40-minute harbour tours leave on the hour from just inside the entrance to the Historic Dockyard. They're free with the all-inclusive Dockyard ticket or can be bought separately (adult/child £5/3).

**Walking tours** (adult/child £3/free; 2.30pm Sun) The tourist office runs a program of guided tours; check with the office for details and departure points.

## Sleeping
Most B&Bs are in Southsea. Centrally located spots fill up quickly, so book ahead.

**Southsea Backpackers Lodge** ( ☎ 023-9283 2495; www.portsmouthbackpackers.co.uk; 4 Florence Rd, Southsea; dm £15, d £33-38; **P** 🖳 ) This old-fashioned backpackers hostel is a warren of four- to eight-bed dorms. The shower-to-people ratio isn't that high, but there are other extras like a pool table, patio and BBQ.

**Fortitude Cottage** ( ☎ 023-9282 3748; www .fortitudecottage.co.uk; 51 Broad St, The Point; s from £45, d £70-80) The ferry-port views from this fresh and airy B&B are interesting, if industrial. The lovely bay-windowed breakfast area is ideal for munching a sausage as the ships come in.

**Florence House Hotel** ( ☎ 023-9275 1666; www .florencehousehotel.co.uk; 2 Malvern Rd, Southsea; d £70-140; **P** 🖳 wi-fi) Edwardian elegance combines beautifully with modern flourishes at this superstylish oasis of boutique bliss. It's a winning combination of plush furnishings, sleek bathrooms, open fireplaces and the odd chaise lounge – the suite, complete with spa bath, is top-notch.

**ourpick** **Somerset House** ( ☎ 023-9275 3555; www.somersethousehotel.co.uk; 10 Florence Rd, Southsea; d £110-190) At this late-Victorian sister to Florence House (above), opposite, the same team has created another achingly tasteful haven of designer calm. Here, stained glass, dark woods and polished floors cosy up to Balinese figurines and the very latest word in luxury bathrooms.

Also recommended:

**Sailmaker's Loft** ( ☎ 023-9282 3045; sailmakersloft@ aol.com; 5 Bath Sq, The Point; s/d £28/55) Unbeatable views across the water towards Gosport.

**Holiday Inn Express** ( ☎ 0870 417 6161; www.hiex press.com; The Plaza; r £105; **P** 🖳 ) Spotlessly bland, but set right amid Gunwharf Quays' restaurants and bars.

## Eating

**Sallyport Tea Rooms** ( ☎ 023-9281 6265; 35 Broad St, The Point; breakfast £3.75-5.25, lunch £3-5; ⏱ 10am-5pm Tue-Sun) Just as a traditional teashop should be: civilised, filled with fussy collectibles and serving up loose-leaf speciality teas and other old-fashioned delights to the strains of 1940s jazz.

**Agora Restaurant** ( ☎ 023-9282 2617; 9 Clarendon Rd, Southsea; mains £8.50-10.50; ⏱ dinner) Festooned with fake beams, this familial little Turkish hookah bar serves up tasty Mediterranean food, washed down with ouzo and raki. Watch out for its occasional belly-dancing nights.

**ourpick** **Lemon Sole** ( ☎ 023-9281 1303; 123 High St, Old Portsmouth; mains £9.50-18; ⏱ lunch & dinner) A colourful little pick-your-own seafood restaurant, Lemon Sole lets you size up freshly netted critters at a counter, then choose how you want them cooked. Try the seafood and shellfish chowder, the devilled mackerel or the stunning fish platters (£39 for two). The menu includes vegie and meat options, too. It's all tucked away in a lemon-yellow, gold and blue interior with a whole wall full of wine bottles at the end.

**Bistro Montparnasse** ( ☎ 023-9281 6754; 103 Palmerston Rd, Southsea; lunch mains £11-22, 2-/3-course dinner £27/32; ⏱ lunch & dinner Tue-Sat) Along with polished wooden floors and chic decor, this classy, cosy bistro serves up French classics with an English twist. Wild mushroom and spinach Wellington, and local sea bass with crab ravioli are among the treats.

## Drinking

For a taste of modern Portsmouth, pick your way through the rows of bars and trendy terraced and balconied eateries that line Gunwharf Quays.

**A Bar** ( ☎ 023-9281 15585; 58 White Hart Rd, Old Portsmouth; ⏱ 11am-11pm) There's actually been a pub here since 1784 – these days it's home to worn floorboards, squishy leather sofas, a soundtrack of groovy tunes and a chilled, gently trendy vibe.

**Still & West** ( ☎ 023-9282 1567; 2 Bath Sq, The Point) This relaxed salty-seadog pub has served many a sailor and smuggler in the last 300 years. The waterside terrace is a great spot to down a beer to a backdrop of passing yachts and ferries.

**Drift** ( ☎ 023-9277 9839; www.driftbar.com; 78 Palmerston Rd, Southsea; ⏱ 10pm-3am) All slick chrome and smooth wood, this hip London-style bar languishes behind a frosted glass and pebble-dashed front. The lounge showcases DJs at the weekends and acoustic sets on Sundays.

## Entertainment

Southsea is thick with nightclubs and live-music venues.

**Wedgewood Rooms** ( ☎ 023-9286 3911; www .wedgewoodrooms.co.uk; Albert Rd, Southsea) One of Portsmouth's best live-music venues; also hosting DJs and comedians.

For cinema, head to **Vue** (www.myvue.com; Gunwharf Quays).

**SOUTHWEST ENGLAND**

## Getting There & Away

Portsmouth is 100 miles southwest of London.

### BOAT

**P&O Ferries** ( ☎ 08716 645 645; www.poferries.com) sails twice a week to Bilbao in Spain (10 hours). **Brittany Ferries** ( ☎ 0870 366 5333; www.brittanyferries.co.uk) has overnight services to St Malo (10¾ hours), Caen (5½ hours) and Cherbourg (3 hours) in France. **LD Lines** ( ☎ 0844 576 8836; www.ldlines.co.uk) has overnight ferries to Le Havre (8½ hours) in France. **Condor Ferries** ( ☎ 0845 609 1024; www.condorferries.co.uk) runs a weekly car-and-passenger service to Cherbourg (5½ hours).

Prices for all routes vary wildly depending on times and dates of travel – an example fare is £152 return for a car and two adults on the Portsmouth-Cherbourg route. Book in advance, be prepared to travel off-peak and look out for special deals.

The Continental Ferryport is north of the Historic Dockyard.

For details on how to reach the Isle of Wight from Portsmouth, see p294.

### BUS

There are 15 National Express buses from London (£14.30, 2½ hours) daily; some go via Heathrow airport (£14.30, 2¾ hours) and continue to Southampton (50 minutes). Bus 700 runs to Chichester (one hour) and Brighton (3½ hours) half-hourly Monday to Saturday, and hourly on Sunday.

### TRAIN

Trains run every 15 minutes from London Victoria (£24.40, two hours 20 minutes) and Waterloo Stations (£24.40, one hour and 40 minutes). Trains also go to Southampton (£7.80, 40 to 55 minutes, four hourly), Brighton (£12.80, one hour and 40 minutes, hourly), Winchester (£7.90, one hour, hourly) and Chichester (£5.60, 30 to 46 minutes, twice an hour).

For the Historic Dockyard get off at the final stop, Portsmouth Harbour.

## Getting Around

Bus 6 operates between the Portsmouth Harbour bus station and South Parade Pier in Southsea, via Old Portsmouth.

For a taxi try **Aquacars** ( ☎ 023-9266 6666, 9265 4321) in Southsea, or the rank near the bus station.

## SOUTHAMPTON

pop 234,224

A no-nonsense port city and gateway to the Isle of Wight, Southampton lies deep in the folds of the Solent, an 8-mile inlet fed by the rivers Itchen and Test. The city was once a flourishing medieval port but its centre was gutted by merciless bombing in WWII and consequently there's little left of its early heritage. Southampton today is more a transport hub than an appealing place to stay. Its gritty waterfront waved the *Titanic* off on its ill-fated voyage in 1912, while larger-than-life ocean liners such as the *QEII* still dock here.

The **tourist office** ( ☎ 023-8083 3333; www.visit-southampton.co.uk; 9 Civic Centre Rd; ☉ 9.30am-5pm Mon-Sat, 10.30am-3.30pm Sun) has details of free 90-minute **guided walks** ( ☉ 10.30am Jul & Sep, 10.30am & 2.30pm Aug, 10.30am Sun Oct-Jun), which meet at the Bargate on High St.

## Sights & Activities

Set in a 14th-century waterfront warehouse, the **Maritime Museum** ( ☎ 023-8063 5904; The Wool House, Town Quay; adult/child £2/1; ☉ 10am-4pm Tue-Sat, 1-4pm Sun) tells the tragic story of the *Titanic* and outlines Southampton's history. The building was once a prison – look out for the inmates' names carved in the impressive timber roof.

For a glimpse of Southampton's medieval heyday, visit the nearby **Medieval Merchant's House** (EH; ☎ 023-8022 1503; French St; adult/child £3.70/2; ☉ noon-5pm Sun late-Mar–Sep), which dates back to 1290.

The **Southampton Art Gallery** ( ☎ 023-8083 2277; www.southampton.gov.uk/art; admission free; Commercial Rd; ☉ 10am-5pm Tue-Sat, 1-4pm Sun) features some of the best names in 20th-century British art, including work by Spencer, Turner and Gainsborough.

## Getting There & Away

### AIR

**Southampton International Airport** ( ☎ 0870 040 0009; www.southamptonairport.com) has links to 40 UK and European destinations, including Amsterdam, Paris and Dublin. There are five trains an hour between the airport and the main train station (seven minutes).

### BOAT

**Red Funnel** ( ☎ 0844 844 9988; www.redfunnel.co.uk) runs regular passenger and car ferries to the Isle of Wight (see p294). There's a half-hourly **ferry service** ( ☎ 023-8084 0722; one-way adult/child

£3.20/2.40) from the Town Quay to Hythe in the New Forest.

### BUS
National Express runs to London and Heathrow 16 times a day (£13.80, 2½ hours). It also runs a 7.20pm bus to Lymington (40 minutes) via Lyndhurst (20 minutes) in the New Forest.

Bus M27 runs to Portsmouth six times daily (40 minutes). Buses 31 and 32 run to Winchester (one hour) every two hours Monday to Saturday, and half-hourly on Sunday. Buses 56 and 56A go to all the main towns in the New Forest hourly (every two hours on Sunday). Ask about the good-value Explorer tickets that are valid on these routes.

### TRAIN
Trains to Portsmouth run every 15 minutes (£7.80, 40 to 55 minutes) and to Winchester (20 minutes) every 20 minutes.

# NEW FOREST

With typical, accidental, English irony, the New Forest is anything but new. This ancient swathe of wild heath and woodland has a unique history and archaic traditions that date to 1079, when William the Conqueror designated it a royal hunting preserve. Verderers, or commoners, still have ancient grazing rights on 130 sq km of the forest; its incarnation as a national park is much more modern – it was only awarded that protective status in 2005. The forest's combined charms make it a joy to explore. Wild ponies mooch around its picturesque scrubland, deer flicker in the distance and rare birds flit among the foliage. A scattering of genteel villages dot the landscape connected by a web of walking and cycling routes.

The park is also a hugely popular destination for campers; Lyndhurst's tourist office has a free brochure detailing designated areas. For more information, go to www.thenewforest.co.uk.

## Activities
### CYCLING
With all that picturesque scenery, the New Forest makes for superb cycling country, and hundreds of miles of trails link the main villages and the key railway station at Brockenhurst

*New Forest Cycle Map* (£2) shows the approved off-road and quieter 'on-road' routes. *New Forest Cycle Experience Route Pack* (£4) features seven trips, ranging from a 4-mile jaunt through the forest to a 24-mile leg test round the cliffs of the Isle of Wight. David Hancock's *Mountain Bike Guide to Hampshire and the New Forest* (£5) outlines routes of 13 to 20 miles. Maps and guides can be bought from Lyndhurst tourist office (p292) or via its website (www.thenewforest.co.uk).

There are several rental shops. You'll need to pay a deposit (usually £20) and provide identification.

**AA Bike Hire** ( ☎ 023-8028 3349; www.aabikehire newforest.co.uk; Fern Glen, Gosport Lane, Lyndhurst; adult/child per day £10/5)

**Country Lanes** ( ☎ 01590-622627; www.countrylanes .co.uk; Railway Station, Brockenhurst; bike/tandem per day £14/25; ☺ Easter-Oct)

**Cyclexperience** ( ☎ 01590-624204; www.newforest-cyclehire.co.uk; Brookley Rd, Brockenhurst; adult/child per day £11/6)

**Forest Leisure Cycling** ( ☎ 01425-403584; www .forestleisurecycling.co.uk; The Cross, Village Centre, Burley; adult/child per day from £11/6)

### HORSE RIDING
No, we're *not* talking about saddling up one of the wild ponies. But riding *is* a wonderful way to roam the New Forest. These stables can arrange rides, and they welcome beginners:

**Arniss Equestrian Centre** ( ☎ 01425-654114; Godshill, Fordingbridge; per hr £20)

**Burley-Villa** (Western Riding; ☎ 01425-610278; per 1-/2hr hack £28/48) It's off the B3058, just south of New Milton.

### OTHER ACTIVITIES
There are regular guided walks with Forestry Commission staff called **Rambles with a Ranger** ( ☎ 023-8028 3141; walks per person £4). **New Forest Activities** ( ☎ 01590-612377; www.newforestactivities .co.uk), near Beaulieu, offers canoeing (per hour adult/child £15/12, per two hours adult/child £25/20), kayaking (per two hour £25) and archery (per 1½ hour adult/child £20/15).

## Getting There & Around
There are regular bus services from Southampton and Bournemouth. Trains run every hour to Brockenhurst from London Waterloo (£29.50, two hours) via Winchester (£8, 31 minutes) and on to Bournemouth (£5, 25 minutes). Local trains also link Brockenhurst with Lymington (see p294).

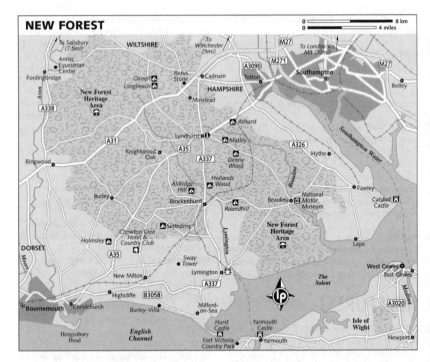

## NEW FOREST

The **New Forest Tour Bus** ( ☎ 023-8061 8233; www.thenewforesttour.info; adult/child £9/4.50; ☀ tours hourly 10am-4pm late-May–Aug) is a two-hour hop-on hop-off bus service that passes through Lyndhurst's main car park, Brockenhurst Station, Lymington and Beaulieu; buses also have cycle trailers.

A **Wilts & Dorset** (www.wdbus.co.uk) Network Ticket offers unlimited travel on main bus lines in the region (one/seven days £7.50/20); the tourist office in Lyndhurst also sells them.

## LYNDHURST
### pop 2281

A good base from which to explore the national park or simply stop off for a pint, a cuppa or a map, the quaint country village of Lyndhurst is one of the New Forest's larger settlements. It has an excellent **tourist office** ( ☎ 023-8028 2269; www.thenewforest.co.uk; High St; ☀ 10am-5pm), as well as several cosy pubs and restaurants.

### Sleeping & Eating

**Acorns** ( ☎ 023-8028 4559; www.acornsoflyndhurst.co.uk; 31 Romsey Rd; d £50-70; **P** ) One of many B&Bs

along the A337 into the village from the south, Acorns gains from being set back from the road. Simple rooms, decked out in cream and pine, sit behind a flower-filled front garden.

**Crown Hotel** ( ☎ 023-8028 2922; www.crownhotel -lyndhurst.co.uk; 9 High St; s/d £88/145; **P** 🖳 ) There's such a deeply established feel to this oak-panelled, old-English coaching inn that you half expect to see a well-trained butler gliding up the grand stairs. The mullioned windows and ancient beams frame bedroom furnishings that are sometimes a little staid, and sometimes surprisingly snazzy.

**Waterloo Arms** ( ☎ 023-8028 2113; Pikes Hill; mains £7-15; ☀ lunch & dinner) This cosy 17th-century thatched pub serves good-value meals in a snug wood-beamed interior. On the town's northern edge, it's signposted off the A337 to Cadnam.

**our pick** **Whitley Ridge** ( ☎ 01590-622354; www.whit leyridge.com; Beaulieu Rd; Brockenhurst; r £95) If you hanker after a country-house atmosphere, head here. Set in 14 acres of dappled grounds, this ivy-clad Georgian pile pampers guests amid elegant period-style rooms finished with contemporary twists (think flat-screen TVs and gilt mirrors). The classy restaurant conjures up organic, seasonal, locally sourced creations finished with dashes of Anglo-French flair, and it's all tucked away four miles south of Lyndhurst at Brockenhurst.

### Getting There & Away
Buses 56 and 56A run twice hourly to Southampton (30 minutes) Monday to Saturday, with five buses on Sunday. Lyndhurst has no train station, and the nearest stop is at Brockenhurst, 8 miles south (see p291).

**White Horse Ferries** ( ☎ 023-8084 0722; www.hythe ferry.co.uk) operates a service from Southampton to Hythe, 13 miles east of Lyndhurst, every half-hour (£4 off-peak return, 12 minutes).

## AROUND LYNDHURST
Petrol-heads, historians and ghost-hunters all gravitate to **Beaulieu** ( ☎ 01590-612345; www .beaulieu.co.uk; adult/child/family £16/8/44; ☻ 10am-6pm Jun-Sep, to 5pm Oct-May) – pronounced *bew*-lee – a tourist complex based on the site of what was once England's most important 13th-century Cistercian monastery. Following Henry VIII's monastic land-grab of 1536, the abbey fell to the ancestors of current proprietors, the Montague family.

Moto-maniacs will be in raptures at Lord Montague's **National Motor Museum**, a splendid collection of vehicles that will sometimes leave you wondering if they are really are cars, or strange hybrid planes, boats or metal bubbles with wheels. It's hard to resist the romance of the early classics, or the oomph of winning F1 cars. Here, too, are several jet-powered land-speed record-breakers including *Bluebird*, which famously broke the record (403mph, or 649km/h) in 1964. There are even celebrity bangers – look out for Mr Bean's Austin Mini and James Bond's whizz-bang speed machines.

Beaulieu's grand but indefinably homely **palace** began life as a 14th-century Gothic abbey gatehouse, but received a 19th-century Scottish Baronial makeover from Baron Montague in the 1860s. Don't be surprised if you hear eerie Gregorian chanting or feel the hairs on the back of your neck quiver – the abbey is supposedly one of England's most haunted buildings.

The New Forest Tour Bus stops directly outside the complex on its circular route via Lyndhurst, Brockenhurst and Lymington. You can also get here from Lymington (35 minutes) by catching bus 112, which continues to Hythe and the ferry to Southampton.

## LYMINGTON
pop 14,227
Yachting haven, New Forest base and jumping-off point to the Isle of Wight – the bustling harbour town of Lymington has several strings to its tourism bow. This pleasing Georgian town also boasts a range of inns, nautical stores and quirky bookshops, as well as a few stretches of utterly quaint cobbled streets.

### Information
Lymington's main **library** ( ☎ 01590-673050; North Close; ☻ 9.30am-7pm Mon, Tue, Thu & Fri, 9.30am-1pm Wed, 9.30am-5pm Sat) has free internet access.

**Lymington Laundrette** ( ☎ 01590-672898; 11 New St; ☻ 8am-6pm Mon-Fri, to 1pm Sat) can make hiking gear smell sweet again; it's next door to the tourist office.

The **tourist office** ( ☎ 01590-689000; www.the newforest.co.uk; New St; ☻ 10am-5pm Mon-Sat Jul-Sep, to 4pm Mon-Sat Oct-Jun), a block off the High St next to the museum, sells walking tours of town and can help with accommodation.

### Sights
Lymington was once known as a contrabandist port, and tales of local smugglers, salt-makers

SOUTHWEST ENGLAND

---

**DETOUR: CHEWTON GLEN**

This is your chance to play at being lord of the manor. The five-star **Chewton Glen Hotel & Country Club** ( ☎ 01425-275341; www.chewtonglen.com; r £300-540, ste £485-1280; ℗ ☒ ▢ ) has the kind of effortless elegance that sees staff anticipating your needs before you've even realised them yourself. The sprawling grounds are framed by a croquet lawn that seems to have been snipped with nail scissors; the sophisticated rooms are chock-full of character and antiques; the superb Marryat restaurant has won many a plaudit; and the spa is sublime – you may not have known you wanted an aromatherapy sauna, but the staff did. Chewton is a mile or so north of New Milton village, in the south of the New Forest.

and yachties pack the **St Barbe Museum** ( ☎ 01590-676969; www.stbarbe-museum.org.uk; New St; adult/child £3/2; ⓨ 10am-4pm Mon-Sat).

## Sleeping & Eating

**Angel Inn** ( ☎ 01590-672050; www.roomattheinn.co.uk; 108 High St; s £50, d £80-100; Ⓟ ) There's a snug feel to this swish hotel, which is set in a renovated Georgian coaching inn. The rooms are warmly decorated and full of wood, while the cosy pub-bistro dishes up seared tuna, blue-cheese and chive tart, and Aberdeen Angus burgers (mains £7 to £18).

**ourpick Stanwell House** ( ☎ 01590-677123; www .stanwellhouse.com; 14 High St; s £99-135, d £135-165, ste £195; 🖵 ) The epitome of discreet luxury, this beautiful boutique hotel is the place to wait for your ship to come in. Cane chairs dot the elegant conservatory, flowers frame a long, walled garden, and the rooms are an eclectic mix of stand-alone baths, rococo mirrors, gently distressed furniture and plush throws. The seafood restaurant (open noon to 10pm daily; tapas £6, mains £13 to £35) rustles up bouillabaisse and seafood platters, and the chic bistro tempts you with fine dining (two/three courses from £20/24). There's even a vaguely decadent satin-cushion-strewn bar.

## Getting There & Away

The bus station is just off High St. Lymington has two train stations: Lymington Town and Lymington Pier. The latter is where the Isle of Wight ferry drops off and picks up. Trains to Southampton (£7.80, 45 minutes) via Brockenhurst leave every half-hour.

**Wightlink Ferries** ( ☎ 0870 582 7744; www.wightlink .co.uk) cross to Yarmouth on the Isle of Wight (see right).

# ISLE OF WIGHT

This lovely island, just a few miles off the Hampshire coast, does its utmost to bottle and sell traditional childhood-holiday nostalgia. A popular escape for yachties, cyclists, walkers and the bucket-and-spade brigade since Victorian times, it alternates between chocolate-box quaint and crazy-golf kitsch, and between rosy-cheeked activity and rural respite. But the 21st century has also seen a youthful buzz inject life into the island's southern resort towns, attracting a new generation of urbanites

and romantic weekenders with gastropubs, slick hotels and big music festivals. Still, the island's principal appeal remains: a surprisingly mild climate, myriad outdoorsy activities and lush green hills that roll down to 25 miles of clean, unspoilt beaches.

For good online information, check out www.islandbreaks.co.uk.

## Activities

### CYCLING

The Isle of Wight will make pedal-pushers smile – there is a 62-mile cycleway, and the island has its very own **Cycling Festival** ( ☎ 01983-203891; www.sunseaandcycling.com) every September. The tourist office has exhaustive information and sells trail guides.

Bike rentals are available all over the island for around £14 per day or £45 per week. Recommended companies:

**Tavcycles** ( ☎ 01983-812989; www.tavcycles.co.uk; 140 High St, Ryde)

**Wight Cycle Hire** ( ☎ 01983-731800; www.wightcycle-hire.co.uk) Yarmouth (Station Rd, Yarmouth); Brading (Station Rd, Brading) Offers delivery and collection across the island.

**Wight Off Road** ( ☎ 01983-408587; 105 High St, Sandown)

### WALKING

This is one of the best spots in southern England for gentle rambling; the island has a network of 500 miles of well-marked walking paths, including 67 miles of coastal routes. The island's **Walking Festival** ( ☎ 01983-813813; www.isleofwightwalk-ingfestival.co.uk), held over two weeks in May, is fêted as the largest in the UK. Tourist offices sell trail pamphlets (from £3).

### OTHER ACTIVITIES

**Water sports** are a serious business on Wight's northern shores – especially sailing but also windsurfing, sea kayaking and surfing. Powerboat trips also run out to the Needles (p297). Wight also offers **gliding** lessons, **para-gliding**, and even **llama trekking**. Tourist offices can help fix you up with all of these.

## Getting There & Away

The cost of car fares to the Isle of Wight can vary enormously – make savings by booking ahead, asking about special offers and travelling in off-peak periods.

**Wightlink** ( ☎ 08705 82 77 44; www.wightlink.co.uk) operates a passenger ferry from The Hard in Portsmouth to Ryde pier (day return adult/child £13.50/6.50, 20 minutes) and a car-and-

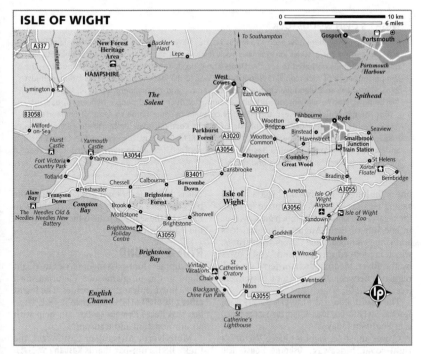

ISLE OF WIGHT

passenger ferry to Fishbourne (day return adult/child £11/5.40, 40 minutes). Both run every half-hour. Car fares start at £47 for a short-break return.

The Wightlink car ferry between Lymington and Yarmouth costs £10.80/5.40 per adult/child (day return), and from £40 for cars (30 minutes, every half-hour).

**Hovertravel** ( ☎ 01983-811000; www.hovertravel.co.uk) hovercrafts shuttle foot passengers between Southsea (near Portsmouth) and Ryde (day return adult/child £12.50/6.25, 10 minutes, every half-hour).

**Red Funnel** ( ☎ 08448 44 99 88; www.redfunnel.co.uk) operates car ferries between Southampton and East Cowes (day return adult/child £12/6, from £40 with car, 55 minutes) and high-speed passenger ferries between Southampton and West Cowes (day return adult/child £16.60/8.30, 25 minutes). Check for deals that include admission to island attractions.

## Getting Around

**1st Call** ( ☎ 01983-400055; 15 College Close, Sandown) provides car hire (from £23 per day), collecting and delivering vehicles island wide.

**Southern Vectis** ( ☎ 01983-827000; www.island buses.info) operates buses between the eastern towns about every 30 minutes; regular services are less frequent to the remoter southwest side between Blackgang Chine Fun Park and Brook. Twice daily between Easter and September the Island Coaster compensates by shuttling (each way) from Ryde, in the northeast, all the way around the southern shore to Alum Bay in the far southwest.

**Stagecoach Island Line** (www.island-line.com) runs trains twice-hourly from Ryde to Shanklin (25 minutes). The **Isle of Wight Steam Railway** ( ☎ 01983-885923; www.iwsteamrailway.co.uk; ☼ May-Sep) branches off Smallbrook Junction and goes to Wootton Common (adult/child £9/4.50, first class £13/8.50).

Rover Tickets provide unlimited use of buses and trains for a day (adult/child £10/5), two days (£15/7.50) or a week (adult/child/family £20/10/40).

## COWES

Pack your yachting cap – this hilly Georgian harbour town on the island's northern tip is famous for **Cowes Week** (www.skandiacowesweek.co.uk),

**WIGHT'S OWN WOODSTOCK**

Bizarrely for somewhere now seen as a family holiday haven, from the late 1960s the Isle of Wight was the setting for a series of infamous rock festivals. At the final one an incredible 600,000 doped-up hippies gathered to see the Doors, the Who, Joni Mitchell and – most famously – the last performance of rock icon Jimi Hendrix, who was to die less than three weeks later, aged just 27. Some of the so-called love children later ran amok, and the incident led to an Isle of Wight Act being passed in parliament, with all gatherings of over 10,000 people henceforth banned.

But the noughties have seen the island once again become home to some of England's top music events. The new generation of **Isle of Wight Festival** (www.isleofwightfestival.org), held in mid-June, has already been headlined by the likes of REM, Coldplay, The Feeling, the Kaiser Chiefs and Keane, while dance-oriented **Bestival** (www.bestival.net), in early to mid-September, has seen the Pet Shop Boys, Scissor Sisters and more.

one of the longest-running and biggest annual sailing regattas in the world. Started in 1826, the regatta still sails with as much gusto as ever in late July or early August. Fibreglass toys and vintage sailboats line Cowes' waterfronts, which are lopped into East and West Cowes by the River Medina; a chain ferry shuttles regularly between the two (foot passengers free, cars £1.50).

The **tourist office** ( ☎ 01983-813813; 9.30am-5pm Mon-Sat Easter-Oct, 10am-3.30pm Tue-Sat Nov-Easter) is at Fountain Quay.

Cowes' must-see sight is Queen Victoria's right-royal hideaway, **Osborne House** (EH; ☎ 01983-200022, 281784; East Cowes; adult/child £10/5; 10am-6pm Apr-Sep, 10am-4pm Oct, pre-booked tours only Nov-Mar), which is the kind of lemon-frosted confection of pomp that only the Victorian era knew how to execute. It was built between 1845 and 1851, and Queen Victoria grieved here for many years after the death of her husband, and died here herself in 1901. The obscenely extravagant rooms include the stunning Durbar Room, while the gardens have a delightful Swiss Cottage where the royal ankle-biters would play.

### Sleeping & Eating
**Anchorage** ( ☎ 01983-247975; www.anchoragecowes .co.uk; 23 Mill Hill Rd, West Cowes; s £40, d £60-80; P ) A five-minute walk from town leads to this B&B of unfussy cream and blue rooms. There's also a green theme, with ecofriendly water and heating systems, and breakfasts full of fair-trade and island foods.

**Fountain** ( ☎ 01983-292397; www.fountaininn-cowes .com; High St, West Cowes; s £75, d £95-120) It may be a classic old pub, but the bedrooms are all airy drapes, white linen and leather headboards – the best have views across the Solent. The cool

cafe is the venue for espressos and pastries; the bar's the place for hearty pub grub (mains £7 to £12); and the seafront patio is the spot to watch the world drift by.

## RYDE & AROUND
The nippiest foot-passenger ferries to Wight alight in this un-glamorous Victorian town that's lined with seafront arcades. The **tourist office** ( ☎ 01983-813813; 81-83 Union St; 9.30-5pm Mon-Sat & 10am-3.30pm Sun Apr-Oct) can help with accommodation and transport.

More North Africa than East Wight, the funky B&B-cum-bar that is **Kasbah** ( ☎ 01983-810088; www.kas-bah.co.uk; 76 Union St; s/d £50/80; lunch & dinner; wi-fi) brings a hot blast of the Mediterranean to Ryde. Intricate lanterns, stripy throws and furniture fresh from Marrakesh dot the smoothly comfy rooms. Falafel, tapas and paella (mains £7) are on offer in the chilled bar downstairs.

About 7 miles east of Brading you can go to sleep in a gunboat – the **Xoron Floatel** ( ☎ 01983-874596; www.xoronfloatel.co.uk; Bembridge Harbour; s/d £35/56) was a warship in WWII, but is now a cheery, bunting-draped houseboat B&B, with cosy cabins (and attached bathrooms).

## VENTNOR & AROUND
The Victorian town of Ventnor slaloms so steeply down the island's southern coast that you'd be forgiven for mistaking it for the south of France. The winding streets are also home to a scattering of quirky boutiques, musicians and artists.

Six miles north, in the bucket 'n' spade resort of Sandown, the sprawling **Isle of Wight Zoo** ( ☎ 01983-403883; Sandown; adult/child £5.95/4.95; 10am-6pm Apr-Sep, 10am-4pm Oct) has Britain's largest collection of tigers.

Back in Ventnor, the busy bar at the beachside **Spy Glass Inn** ( ☎ 01983-855338; www.thespyglass .com; The Esplanade; flats £70) is festooned with nautical knick-knacks and serves up crowd-pleasing grub (mains £8).

Up the hill at the boutique hotel **Hambrough** ( ☎ 01983-856333; www.thehambrough.com; Hambrough Rd; d £150-187, ste £210; P ), it's hard to say which are the better views: the 180-degree vistas out to sea, or the rooms themselves, full of subtle colours, clean lines and satiny furnishings. Espresso machines, dressing gowns and heated floors keep the luxury gauge set to high; one room overlooks the hills behind.

## SOUTH WIGHT

The southernmost point of the island is marked by the stocky mid-19th-century **St Catherine's Lighthouse**. Far more exciting, however, is the nearby stone rocket-ship lookalike, **St Catherine's Oratory**. This odd construction is a lighthouse dating from 1314 and marks the highest point on the island.

The kids will love **Blackgang Chine Fun Park** ( ☎ 01983-730052; www.blackgangchine.com; admission £9.50; ☽ 10am-10pm mid-Jul–Aug, 10am-5pm Apr-early Jul, Sep & Oct), a couple of miles northwest of St Catherine's Lighthouse. This Victorian land-scaped garden-turned-themepark has water gardens, animated shows and a hedge maze.

Slightly further west, you'll find a dose of pure hippie-chic: **Vintage Vacations** ( ☎ 07802-758113; www.vintagevacations.co.uk; Chale; 4-person caravans per weekend £150-220, per week £360-495; ☽ Apr-Oct; P ) is a dairy farm that rents out 10 1960s aluminium Airstream trailers from California. All are lovingly refitted with retro furnishings – camping has never been so cool.

## WEST WIGHT

Rural and remote, the Isle of Wight's westerly corner is where the island really comes into its own. Sheer white cliffs rear from a surging sea and the stunning coastline peels away to Alum Bay in the far west and the most famous chunks of chalk in the region: the **Needles**. These jagged rocks rise shardlike out of the sea, forming a line like the backbone of a prehistoric sea monster.

Established in 1862, the **Needles Old Battery** (NT; ☎ 01983-754772; adult/child £4.65/2.35; ☽ 10.30am-5pm daily Jul & Aug, 10.30am-5pm Tue-Sun mid-Mar–Jun, Sep & Oct, 11am-3pm Sat & Sun Feb–mid-March) was used as an observation post during WWII – trek down the 60m tunnel through the cliff to a search-light lookout. The same site also houses the **New Battery** ( ☎ 01983-754772; admission free; ☽ 11am-4pm Tue & Sat mid-Mar–Oct), with its exhibitions on the clandestine space-rocket testing carried out here in the 1950s.

Twenty-minute **boat trips** ( ☎ 01983-761587; www.needlespleasurecruises.co.uk; adult/child £4/3; ☽ 10.30am-4.30pm Apr-Oct) head out from Alum Bay to the Needles, providing close-up views of those jagged white cliffs.

Four miles east along the north coast is the port of Yarmouth, an appealing tangle of cafes, pubs and restaurants. It's also home to Henry VIII's last great fortress, **Yarmouth Castle** (EH; ☎ 01983-760678; Quay St; adult/child £3.50/1.80; ☽ 11am-4pm Sun-Thu Apr-Oct). The facade, which is all that's left of it now, dates from 1547.

## Sleeping

**Totland Bay YHA** ( ☎ 0845 371 9348; www.yha.org.uk; Hirst Hill, Totland; dm £15.95; P ) This large, marvellous Victorian house overlooking the water has mostly family-oriented dorms and a maximum of eight beds per room.

**Brighstone Holiday Centre** ( ☎ 01983-740244; www. brighstone-holidays.co.uk; 1-/2-person tents £7/9, caravans from £16, B&B per adult/child £28/14, 2-person cabins per week from £300; P ) What a view to wake up to – this B&B, camp site and cabin park perches atop cliffs looking towards the spectacular bluffs at Alum Bay. It's located on the A3055, 6 miles east of Freshwater.

# DORSET

For many, Dorset conjures up the kind of halcyon holiday memories you find in flickering 1970s home movies. But this county's image deserves a dramatic revamp. In party-town Bournemouth the snapshots are as likely to be of stag and hen party frenzies as buckets and spades on the sand; Poole provides images of the super-rich; and Dorset's Jurassic Coast would catch the eye of even the most jaded cinematographer. This stunning shoreline is studded with exquisite sea-carved bays and creamy-white rock arches around Lulworth Cove, while beaches at Lyme Regis are littered with fossils ripe for the picking. Dorchester provides a biopic of Thomas Hardy; the massive Iron Age hill fort at Maiden Castle is a battle-ground epic; and the really rather rude chalk figure at Cerne Abbas will linger long in the memory. Then comes the regenerated resort of Weymouth, preparing to be catapulted onto TV screens worldwide as the sailing venue for Britain's 2012 Olympics.

## Orientation & Information

Dorset stretches along the south coast from Lyme Regis on the western (Devon) border, to Christchurch, which abuts Hampshire on the east. Dorchester, the county town, sits in between providing a central base for exploring, but Lyme Regis or Weymouth will suit those who prefer the coast.

Dorset has several useful websites:
**Dorset County Council** (www.dorset-cc.gov.uk)
**Rural Dorset** (www.ruraldorset.com)
**West Dorset** (www.westdorset.com)

## Getting Around

Dorset has two slow railway lines – one running from Bristol and Bath through Dorchester West to Weymouth, the other chugging from London and Southampton to Bournemouth and Poole.

The main bus company in east and central Dorset is **Wilts & Dorset** ( ☎ 01202-673555; www.wdbus.co.uk). For western Dorset and on to Devon and southern Somerset, **First** ( ☎ 0870 010 6022; www.firstgroup.com) is the main operator.

## BOURNEMOUTH

pop 163,600

In Bournemouth, four worlds collide: old folks, families and corporate delegates meet club-loads of boozers out on a bender. Sometimes the edges rub – painfully. On weekend evenings parts of town transform into a massive frenzy of stag and hen parties, full of angels with L plates and blokes in frocks, blond wigs and slingbacks. But there's also a much sunnier side to the town. In 2007 a survey revealed Bournemouth had the happiest residents in the UK – thanks partly to its glorious 7-mile sandy beach. The town sprang to life as a resort in the Victorian era but these days it's busy adding a much more modern attraction: Europe's first artificial surf reef is set to bring even bigger barrels and more amped-up board riders to the town.

## Orientation & Information

Bournemouth sprawls along the coast towards Poole to the west and Christchurch to the east. The main pier marks the central seafront area; the town centre and train station are northeast from here.

**Bournemouth Library** ( ☎ 01202-454848; 22 The Triangle; ✛ 10am-7pm Mon, 9.30am-7pm Tue, Thu & Fri, 9.30am-5pm Wed) Internet access.
**Cyber Place** ( ☎ 01202-290099; 25 St Peter's Rd; per hr £2; ✛ 9.30am-midnight)
**Tourist office** ( ☎ 0845 051 1700; www.bournemouth .co.uk; Westover Rd; ✛ 10am-5.30pm Mon-Fri Sep-Jun, to 6pm Jul & Aug, 10.30am-5pm Sun)

## Sights & Activities

Backed by 3000 deckchairs, Bournemouth's expansive, sandy **beach** regularly clocks up seaside awards for its immense promenade backed by ornamental gardens, cafe and toilets. The resort also prides itself on two piers (Bournemouth and Boscombe). Around Bournemouth Pier you can hire beach **chalets** ( ☎ 01202-451781; per day/week from £11/52; ✛ 9am-6pm April-Oct), deckchairs (per day £2), windbreaks (£2) and parasols (£4), as well as sit-on-board **kayaks** ( ☎ 07970-971867; per 30mins £5).

In a bid to produce barrelling 8ft waves, the **Boscombe Artificial Reef** is being built just east of Boscombe Pier. The tourist office can advise on surfboard hire and tuition. **Surf Steps Bournemouth Surf School** ( ☎ 0800 0437873; www.bournemouthsurfschool.co.uk; ✛ Feb-Nov), near Boscombe Pier, run surfing lessons (adult/child per three hours £35/30) and half-day body-boarding sessions (£25).

Bournemouth's **Pleasure Gardens** are a Grade II–listed belt of greenery, shrubs and herbaceous perennials that stretches 1.5 miles northwest from the seafront. The area is still noted for its chines (sharp-sided valleys), many of which are lined with holiday villas. **Alum Chine**, a mile west of the centre is a good example.

An ostentatious mix of Italianate holiday home and Scottish baronial pile, the **Russell-Cotes Art Gallery & Museum** ( ☎ 01202-451858; www .russell-cotes.bournemouth.gov.uk; Russell-Cotes Rd; admission free; ✛ 10am-5pm Tue-Sun) is set in landscaped grounds, which include a formal Japanese garden, with views across Poole Bay. It's renowned for Victorian art and sculpture, and a fine Japanese collection gathered by the museum's benefactors, Sir Merton and Lady Russell-Cotes, during a visit to Japan in 1885.

The marine habitats of the **Oceanarium** ( ☎ 01202-311933; www.oceanarium.co.uk; West Promenade; adult/child £8.50/6; ✛ 10am-5pm) include the Great Barrier Reef, the Amazon River and the inky realms of the deep sea. Highlights are the

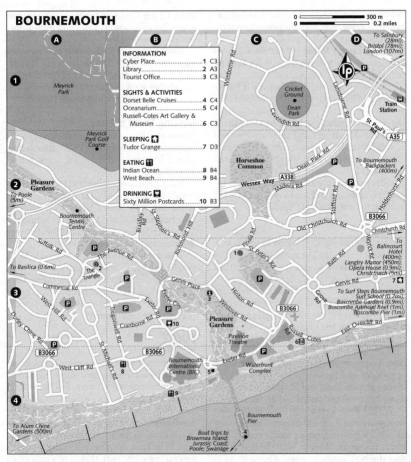

## BOURNEMOUTH

**INFORMATION**
Cyber Place.........................1 C3
Library................................2 A3
Tourist Office.....................3 C3

**SIGHTS & ACTIVITIES**
Dorset Belle Cruises...........4 C4
Oceanarium.......................5 C4
Russell-Cotes Art Gallery &
   Museum...........................6 C3

**SLEEPING**
Tudor Grange....................7 D3

**EATING**
Indian Ocean.....................8 B4
West Beach........................9 B4

**DRINKING**
Sixty Million Postcards........10 B3

guitarfish, flesh-eating piranhas and giant sea turtles.

**Dorset Belle Cruises** (☎ 01202-558550; www.dorset belles.co.uk) runs trips to the sheer white chalk cliffs at Old Harry – the start of the Jurassic Coast (p303; adult/child £13/6, 2½ hours, trips 10.30am Thursday to Tuesday), as well as ferries to Swanage, Poole and Brownsea Island (p300).

## Sleeping

Bournemouth has huge concentrations of budget B&Bs, especially around the central St Michael's Rd and to the east of the train station.

**Bournemouth Backpackers** (☎ 01202-299491; www .bournemouthbackpackers.co.uk; 3 Frances Rd; dm £13-15)

Containing aluminium bunk beds and set in a suburban house, the dorms in this hostel may be plain but the place is cheap and friendly. Reservations can only be made by email or by phoning between 5pm and 7pm on Sundays.

**Tudor Grange** (☎ 01202-291472; www.tudorgrange hotel.co.uk; 31 Gervis Rd; s £60-90, d £80-120, f £100-140) Five hundred years of history positively waft from the panelled walls and grand staircase of this pint-sized baronial pile. Rooms are either antique and flowery or historic with a twist – old oak meets buff throws.

**Balincourt Hotel** (☎ 01202-552962; www.balincourt .co.uk; 58 Christchurch Rd; s/d from £50/80) This Victorian B&B is a labour of love – even the china on the tea tray is hand painted to match each room's colour scheme. The decor is bright and deeply tasteful – respecting both the house's heritage and modern anti-frill sensibilities.

**our pick** **Langtry Manor** ( ☎ 0800 988 5720; www .langtrymanor.com; Derby Rd; s £79-148, d £98-236) Prepare for a delicious whiff of royal indiscretion – this minimansion was built by Edward VII for his mistress Lillie Langtry. It instantly immerses you in a world of opulent grandeur – from the red carpet rolled out in the entrance to the immense chandeliers and intricately carved woods inside. The rooms combine Edwardian elegance with modern touches – recessed lights and Jacuzzis. The King's Suite is a real jaw-dropper: a monumental, climb-up-to-get-in four-poster bed, and a tile fireplace big enough to have two seats inside.

## Eating

**Basilica** ( ☎ 01202-757722; 73 Seamoor Rd; tapas from £3, mains £6-10; ☺ Mon-Sat) The menu at this groovy bistro visits more Mediterranean countries than your average InterRailer – expect mezze, Parma ham parcels, grilled halloumi and pasta with chorizo. The brick-lined interior is dotted with tables hacked out of single chunks of wood, and with jars of olives.

**Indian Ocean** ( ☎ 01202-311222; 4 West Cliff Rd; mains £8-11; ☺ lunch & dinner) Don't be fooled by this place's unimpressive glass frontage – the interior is modern and funkily lit and the menu includes unusual karai and Bangladeshi specials as well as tried and tested Indian favourites.

**our pick** **West Beach** ( ☎ 01202-587785; West Promenade; mains £21; ☺ lunch & dinner) The venue of choice for Bournemouth's foodie crowd, this buzzy restaurant delivers both the best views and the best meals in town. The seafood is exemplary: rock oysters with shallot vinegar, monkfish medallions with Parma ham and a seafood platter crammed with crab claws, lobster, razor clams and crevettes (£30 per person). The view is of the seafront – it's so close to the beach that sand drifts right up to the door.

## Drinking & Entertainment

Most of the main venues are clustered around Firvale Rd, St Peter's Rd and Old Christchurch Rd.

**Sixty Million Postcards** ( ☎ 01202-292697; 19 Exeter Rd; ☺ noon-midnight Sun-Wed, to 1am Thu, to 2am Fri & Sat) A hip crowd inhabits this quirky drinking den. The worn wooden floors, battered sofas and fringed lampshades are home to everything

from DJ sets (including indie, synth-pop and space disco) to board games and impromptu Sunday jumble sales.

**Opera House** ( ☎ 01202-399922; www.operahouse .co.uk; Boscombe Arcade, 570 Christchurch Rd) This restored Victorian theatre lines up gigs (from jazz to rude-boy punk), DJ sets (from Northern soul to drum 'n' bass), gay nights and comedy.

## Getting There & Away

National Express shuttles to London (£18, 2½ hours, hourly), Bristol (£15.40, four hours, one daily) and Oxford (£19, three hours, three daily).

Bus X3 runs from Salisbury (1¼ hours, half-hourly Monday to Saturday, nine on Sunday), while the X35 comes from Southampton (1¾ hours, two daily Monday to Saturday). There's a multitude of M1/M21 buses between Bournemouth and Poole (15 minutes).

Trains run from London Waterloo (£26.10, two hours, half-hourly Monday to Saturday, hourly Sunday). There are regular connections to Poole (10 minutes, half hourly), Dorchester South (£9, 45 minutes, hourly) and Weymouth (£11.40, one hour, hourly).

## POOLE

pop 144,800

A few miles west of Bournemouth, Poole was once the preserve of hard-drinking sailors and sunburned daytrippers. But these days you're as likely to encounter super-yachts and Porsches, because the town borders Sandbanks, one of the most expensive chunks of real estate in the world. However, you don't have to be knee-deep in cash to enjoy Poole's agreeable ancient port, thanks to a quaint old harbour dotted with restaurants and nautical pubs, some irresistible boat trips and a wide variety of tempting water sports.

## Sights & Activities
### BROWNSEA ISLAND

This small wooded **island** (NT; ☎ 01202-707744; adult/child £4.90/2.40; ☺ 10am-6pm mid-Jul–Aug, 10am-5pm mid-Mar–Jul & Sep, 10am-4pm Oct) in Poole Bay is now a nature reserve and wildlife haven run by the National Trust (NT). There are several tranquil walks around the island, which is home to a population of deer, peacocks and rare red squirrels, as well as terns, gulls and wading birds.

To get to the island, catch a ferry from Poole Quay. Try **Brownsea Island Ferries** ( ☎ 01929-462383;

www.brownseaislandferries.com; adult/child £8/5.50), which also offers **cruises** to Sandbanks (adult/child £8/5.50) and the other bay islands, as well as a daily trip to Wareham (£5). It also runs occasional cruises along the Jurassic Coast (see boxed text, p303; adult/child £13/5) to the Old Harry rocks – a set of limestone stacks that have been separated from each other by sea erosion.

#### POOLE OLD TOWN & HARBOUR

Poole Old Town has rows of attractive 18th-century buildings, including a wonderful Customs House and Guildhall. The town's rightly proud of the new-look **Poole Museum** (☎ 01202-262600; 4 High St; admission free; 10am-5pm Mon-Sat & noon-5pm Sun Apr-Oct). Housed in a sensitively restored 18th-century harbour warehouse, it cracks through Poole's history both ashore and afloat – the star attraction is the 30ft-long Iron Age log boat, carved from a single tree 2300 years ago, which was recovered from the depths of Poole Harbour.

#### WATER SPORTS

Poole's beaches sit 3 miles southeast of the old town at **Sandbanks**, a 2-mile, wafer-thin peninsula of land that curls around the expanse of Poole Harbour. The houses in this super-rich suburb are some of the most exclusive in the world, but the beaches that border them are free, and have some of the best water-quality standards in the country.

A clutch of water-sport operators base themselves at Sandbanks – **H2O Sports** (☎ 01202-733744; www.h2o-sports.co.uk; 91 Salterns Rd) offers courses in windsurfing and power-kiting (£49 per three hours). **FC Watersports Academy** (☎ 01202-708283; www.fcwatersports.co.uk) hires out kayaks (£10 per hour) and sailing dinghies (£20 per hour) and runs windsurfing tuition (from £25 per hour), kitesurfing classes (£100 per day) and a two-day start-sailing course (£165). Or try to wakeboard with **Surface2Air** (☎ 01202-738448; www.s2as.com; 14 Station Rd), at £60 per hour.

Towards Hamworthy, west of Poole, you can learn to sail at **Moonfleet** (☎ 0800 019 1369; www.moonfleet.net; Cobbs Quay Marina), with two/five days costing £185/425, or cling to a jet ski with **Absolute Aqua** (☎ 01202-666118; www.absoluteaqua.co.uk; Parkstone Marina) from £135 a day.

#### POOLE LIGHTHOUSE

This cutting-edge **arts centre** (☎ 0844 406 8666; www.lighthousepoole.co.uk; 21 Kingland Rd) hosts a vibrant events calendar, including live music, theatre, film and exhibitions.

### Sleeping & Eating

**our pick** **Saltings** (☎ 01202-707349; www.the-saltings.com; 5 Salterns Way; d £70-85) You can almost hear the languid drawl of Noël Coward in this utterly delightful 1930s B&B, where charming art-deco flourishes include curved windows, arched doorways and decorative up-lighters. Immaculate rooms feature dazzling white, spearmint and pastel blue as well as mini-fridges, digital radios and Lush toiletries. One room is more like a little suite, with its own seating area and pocket-sized balcony. Saltings is halfway between Poole and Sandbanks.

**Milsoms Hotel** (☎ 01202-609000; www.milsomshotel.co.uk; 47 Haven Rd; d £75; P) Supersleek and semi-boutique, this mini-hotel sits above Poole's branch of the Loch Fyne seafood restaurant chain. Bedrooms are decked out in achingly tasteful tones of mauve and cream, and finished with thoughtful extras such as cafetières and Molton Brown bath products.

**our pick** **Guildhall Tavern** (☎ 01202-671717; 15 Market St; mains £15-20; lunch & dinner Tue-Sun) More Provence than Poole, the grub at this French-run brassiere is Gallic gourmet charm at its best: unpretentious and top-notch. Expect char-grilled sea bass flambéed with Pernod, or beef with Roquefort sauce. Exquisite aromas fill the dining room, along with the quiet murmur of people enjoying very good food.

Other options:

**Quayside** (☎ 01202-683733; www.poolequayside.co.uk; 9 High St; s £35-50, d £55-75, f £60-80) Snug rooms, pine, and jazzy prints in the heart of the old harbour.

**Custom House** (☎ 01202-676767; Poole Quay; mains from £12; lunch & dinner) Harbourside terrace, funky bar-bistro and fine-dining venue all rolled into one.

**Storm** (☎ 01202-674970; 16 High St; mains £13-18; dinner) Superb fish restaurant – the robust, eclectic menu depends on what the owner's caught.

### Getting There & Away

Countless buses cover the 20-minute trip to Bournemouth. National Express runs hourly to London (£18, three hours). Train connections are as for Bournemouth (opposite); just add 13 minutes to times to London Waterloo (£26).

**Sandbanks Ferry** (☎ 01929-450203; www.sandbanksferry.co.uk; pedestrian/car 90p/£3) shuttles to Studland every 20 minutes. This is a shortcut from Poole to Swanage, Wareham and the West

Dorset coast, but summer queues can be horrendous. **Brittany Ferries** ( ☎ 0870 907 6103; www.brittany-ferries.com) sails between Poole and Cherbourg in France (2¼ to 6½ hours, one to three daily); expect to pay around £90 per foot passenger, or £335 for a car and two passengers.

To hire a bike call ☎ 01202-855383 and they'll be dropped off at your hotel or B&B (per day £8).

Bus 152 goes from Poole to Sandbanks (15 minutes, three-hourly Easter to September, hourly October to Easter). For a taxi try **Dial-a-Cab** ( ☎ 01202-666822).

## SOUTHEAST DORSET

With its string of glittering bays and towering rock formations, the southeast Dorset shoreline is the most beautiful in the county. Also known as the 'Isle' of Purbeck (although its actually a peninsula), it's also the start of the Jurassic Coast (see boxed text, opposite) and the scenery and geology, especially around Lulworth Cove, make swimming irresistible and hiking memorable. The hinterland harbours the immense, fairytale ruins of Corfe Castle and some intriguing sights linked to Lawrence of Arabia.

### Wareham & Around
**pop 2568**

Saxons established the sturdy settlement of Wareham on the banks of the River Frome in the 10th century, and their legacy lingers in the remains of their defensive walls and one of Dorset's last remaining Saxon churches. Wareham is also famous for its connections to the enigmatic figure of TE Lawrence, immortalised in David Lean's epic *Lawrence of Arabia*.

The **Purbeck tourist office** ( ☎ 01929-552740; www .purbeck.gov.uk; Holy Trinity Church, South St; ⊗ 9.30am-5pm Mon-Sat & 10am-4pm Sun Easter-Oct, 9.30am-4pm Mon-Sat Nov-Easter) is opposite the library.

#### SIGHTS

TE Lawrence was the British scholar, military strategist and writer made legendary for his role in helping unite Arab tribes against Turkish forces in WWI. The tiny cottage of **Clouds Hill** (NT; ☎ 01929-405616; adult/child £4/2; ⊗ noon-5pm Thu-Sun Apr-Oct) was Lawrence's rural retreat and remains largely unchanged since his death in 1935. There's a small exhibition exploring his incredible life and

wartime achievements, and a few relics that hint at his enduring fascination with the art and culture of the Middle East. Clouds Hill is 8 miles northeast of Wareham on an unclassified road.

The bijou **Wareham Museum** ( ☎ 01929-553448; East St, Wareham; admission free; ⊗ 10am-4pm Mon-Sat Easter-Oct) provides a good potted history of Lawrence's life, along with press cuttings on the speculation surrounding his death.

Wareham's delightful Saxon **St Martin's Church** in North St dates from about 1020. Inside there's a 12th-century fresco on the northern wall, and a marble effigy of Lawrence of Arabia.

Lawrence was stationed at Bovington Camp, now a **Tank Museum** ( ☎ 01929-405096; www.tankmuseum.org; adult/child £11/7; ⊗ 10am-5pm), 6 miles east of Wareham. He died at Bovington Military Hospital six days after a motorcycle accident nearby. The museum has a collection of more than 300 armoured vehicles, from the earliest WWI prototypes to remnants from the first Gulf War.

Nearby is **Monkey World** ( ☎ 01929-462537; www .monkeyworld.co.uk; Longthorns; adult/child £10.50/7.25; ⊗ 10am-5pm Sep-Jun, to 6pm Jul & Aug), a sanctuary for rescued chimpanzees, orang-utans, gibbons, marmosets and some ridiculously cute ring-tailed lemurs.

#### SLEEPING & EATING

**our pick Trinity** ( ☎ 01929-556689; www.trinitybnb.co.uk; 32 South St; d £60, f £80) You wouldn't be surprised to meet a bloke in doublet and hose here – this 15th-century B&B oozes so much character. Bedrooms are framed by fantastic brickwork and inglenook fireplaces; the staircase is a swirl of ancient timber; floors creak under stately rugs; and rooms are alive with nooks and crannies.

**Anglebury** ( ☎ 01929-552988; www.angleburyhouse. co.uk; 15 North St; mains £9-13; ⊗ lunch daily, dinner Tue-Sat) Lawrence of Arabia and Thomas Hardy have, apparently, both had cuppas in the coffee shop attached to this 16th-century inn. Simple rooms (singles/doubles £35/70) are done out in creams, floral fabrics and pine while the restaurant dishes up hearty fare such as trout wrapped in bacon, and lamb in Pernod.

#### GETTING THERE & AWAY

Wareham is on the main railway line from London Waterloo to Weymouth (2½ hours); trains run hourly.

---

**A BOX-OFFICE COAST**

The kind of massive, hands-on geology lesson you wish you had at school, the Jurassic Coast is England's first natural World Heritage Site (England's other World Heritage Sites are cultural). This puts it on a par with the Great Barrier Reef and the Grand Canyon. This exquisite shoreline, stretching from Exmouth in East Devon to just beyond Swanage in Dorset, encompasses 185 million years of the earth's history in just 95 miles – so in a few hours' walk you can cover millions of years of geology.

The area was formed when massive earth movements tilted the rocks from west to east. Gradually, erosion exposed the different strata – leaving the oldest formations in the west and the youngest in the east. It's a tangible timeline: Devon's rusty-red Triassic rocks are some 200 to 250 million years old; the dark clay Jurassic cliffs around Lyme Regis (see boxed text, p309) ensure superb fossil hunting; and the bulk of the coast from Lyme Regis to the Isle of Purbeck is around 140 to 200 million years old. Pockets of much younger creamy-coloured Cretaceous rocks (a mere 65 to 140 million years old) also pop up, notably around Lulworth Cove (below), where erosion has sculpted a stunning display of cliffs, coves and arches – particularly at Durdle Door (below).

The website www.jurassiccoast.com has more information, and local tourist offices sell the *Official Guide to the Jurassic Coast* (£4.95). Responsible fossil hunting is encouraged – these nuggets of prehistory would otherwise be destroyed by the sea. Be aware, though, that the coast is highly unstable in places – official advice is to keep well away from the cliffs, stay on public paths, check tides times, only pick up from the beach (never dig out from cliffs), always leave some behind for others, and tell the experts if you find a stunner.

---

Buses 142 and 143 run hourly between Poole (35 minutes) and Swanage via Wareham (every two hours on Sunday).

## Corfe Castle

The massive, shattered ruins of Corfe Castle loom so dramatically from the landscape it's like blundering into a film set. The defensive fragments tower over an equally photogenic village, which bears the castle's name, and makes for a romantic spot for a meal or an overnight stay.

**Corfe Castle** (NT; ☎ 01929-481294; adult/child £5.10/2.50; ⏰ 10am-6pm Apr-Sep, 10am-5pm Feb, Mar & Oct, 10am-4pm Nov-Jan) was the ancestral home of Sir John Bankes, right-hand man and attorney general to Charles I, and was besieged by Cromwellian forces during the Civil War. Following a six-week defence directed by the plucky Lady Bankes, the castle was eventually betrayed from within and gunpowdered to pieces by the Roundheads. The Bankes family established its new family seat at Kingston Lacy.

The 450-year-old **Bankes Hotel** (☎ 01929-481288; www.dorset-hotel.co.uk; East St; mains £8-14; ⏰ lunch & dinner) is an atmospheric place for a pint and quality pub grub. The bedrooms (singles £50 to £75, doubles £60 to £90) are a mass of mullioned windows, creaking floors and slightly worn bathrooms.

Buses 142 and 143 run to Corfe Castle hourly from Poole (50 minutes) via Wareham (15 minutes), before going on to Swanage (20 minutes).

The **Swanage Steam Railway** ( ☎ 01929-425800; www.swanagerailway.co.uk; Day Rover adult/child £12/10; hourly Apr-Oct plus many weekends Nov, Dec, Feb & Mar) runs between Swanage and Norden (20 minutes) and stops at Corfe Castle.

## Lulworth Cove & the Coast

South of Corfe Castle the coast steals the show. For millions of years the elements have been creating an intricate shoreline of curved bays, caves, stacks and weirdly wonderful rock formations.

The coast's iconic feature is **Durdle Door**, an immense, 150-million-year-old Portland natural stone arch that plunges into the sea 3 miles west of Lulworth Cove. Part of the Jurassic Coast (see boxed text, above), it was created by a combination of massive earth movements and then erosion. Today it's framed by shimmering bays – bring a swimsuit and head down the hundreds of steps for an unforgettable dip.

A mile hike east along the coast from the Durdle Door leads to **Lulworth Cove**, where a pleasing jumble of thatched cottages and fishing gear leads down to a perfect circle of white

**SOUTHWEST ENGLAND**

**SOUTHWEST ENGLAND**

---

### ELIZABETHAN EXTRAVAGANCE

The exquisite **Morton's House Hotel** ( ☎ 01929-480988; www.mortonshouse.co.uk; Corfe Castle, East St; r £149-249; P ) was built in the 16th century in the shape of an 'E' in honour of Queen Elizabeth I. A fitting tribute, it's crammed with Tudor and Jacobean character: stone fireplaces, wood-panelled friezes and Elizabethan-themed suites (avoid the modern annex). It's a place to languish in front of a crackling fire or stuff yourself silly with a rich Sunday roast – traditional, classy and very, very English.

---

cliffs broken only by a distant segment of sea. It's a charismatic place to stay and inevitably draws summertime coach-party crowds.

The creamy, dreamy-white **Lulworth Castle** (EH; ☎ 01929-400352; www.lulworth.com; admission £7; ⏱ 10.30am-6pm Sun-Fri Apr-Oct, to 4pm Nov-Mar), at the neighbouring village of East Lulworth, looks more like a French chateau than a traditional English castle. Built in 1608 as a hunting lodge, it's been sumptuously restored after a 1929 fire. Check out the massive four-poster bed, and the suits of armour in the basement.

**Jurassic Kayak Tours** ( ☎ 01305-835301; www.jurassic-kayaking.com; Lulworth Cove Visitor Centre, Main St) offers a seal's-eye view of the cliffs on a paddle from Lulworth Cove to Durdle Door, on sit-aboard kayaks (£40, three hours). Weather dependent, they run most weekends in summer.

The bedrooms at the cool **Bishops Bistro** ( ☎ 01929-400880; www.bishopscottage.co.uk; Main St, Lulworth Cove; s £35-45, d £60-100, f £160; ⏱ 9am-5pm May-Sep) throw together antique furniture and slinky modern fabrics – and make it work. The funky cafe (mains £3 to £8) serves up spicy seafood or ploughman's with cider.

**Rose Cottage** ( ☎ 01929-400150; www.rosecottage.fsworld.co.uk; Main St, Lulworth Cove; s £35-50, d £70-80) is an archetypal thatched cottage with flowers winding around the door, thick walls, low lintels and rooms full of rustic charm.

**Lulworth Beach** ( ☎ 01929-400404; www.lulworthbeachhotel.com; Lulworth Cove; d £80-95) is an oh-so-stylish hotel 180m from the beach with rooms finished in blondwood, coconut matting and flashes of leather and lime – the best room has its own private sea-view deck.

There's a basic single-storey **YHA** ( ☎ 0870 770 5940; www.yha.org.uk; School Lane; dm £14; ⏱ Mar-Oct) in West Lulworth, and a great cliff-top camp site

at **Durdle Door Holiday Park** ( ☎ 01929-400200; www.lulworth.com; sites per tent £10-20; ⏱ Mar-Oct).

## DORCHESTER
**pop 16,171**

With Dorchester, you get two towns in one: a real-life, bustling county town, and Thomas Hardy's fictional Casterbridge. The writer was born just outside Dorchester and clearly used it to add authenticity to his writing – so much so that his literary locations can still be found amid the town's white Georgian terraces and red-brick buildings. You can also visit his former homes here and see his original manuscripts. Incredibly varied museums (teddy bears, terracotta warriors and Tutankhamen) and some attractive places to sleep and eat combine to make an appealing base for a night or two.

### Orientation & Information

Most of Dorchester's action takes place along South St, which runs north into pedestrianised Cornhill and then emerges at High St.

The **tourist office** ( ☎ 01305-267992; www.westdorset.com; Antelope Walk; ⏱ 9am-5pm Mon-Sat Apr-Oct, to 4pm Nov-Mar) brims over with Hardy information, and sells 'location' guides to the places in his novels.

### Sights
#### THOMAS HARDY SITES

The Hardy collection in the **Dorset County Museum** ( ☎ 01305-262735; www.dorsetcountymuseum.org; High West St; adult/child £6/5; ⏱ 10am-5pm daily Jul-Sep, closed Sun Oct-Jun) is the biggest in the world and offers extraordinary insight into his creative process – reading his cramped handwriting, it's often possible to spot where he's crossed out one word and substituted another. There's also a wonderful reconstruction of his study at Max Gate (see below), and a letter from Siegfried Sassoon, asking Hardy if Sassoon can dedicate his first book of poems to him.

A trained architect, Hardy designed **Max Gate** (NT; ☎ 01305-262538; Alington Ave; adult/child £3/1.50; ⏱ 2-5pm Mon, Wed & Sun Apr-Sep), where he lived from 1885 until his death in 1928. *Tess of the D'Urbervilles* and *Jude the Obscure* were both written here, and the house contains several pieces of original furniture, but otherwise it's a little slim on sights. The house is a mile east of Dorchester on the A352.

The small cob-and-thatch **Hardy's Cottage** (NT; ☎ 01305-262366; admission £3.50; ⏱ 11am-5pm

Sun-Thu Apr-Oct), where the author was born, is again short on attractions, but it makes an evocative stop for Hardy completists. It's in Higher Bockhampton, 3 miles northeast of Dorchester.

### OTHER SIGHTS

Dorchester was once a thriving Roman settlement: you can see evidence of this in the remains of a 1st-century **Roman villa** – look out for the foundations and remarkable mosaic floors behind the town hall.

As well as its superb Hardy exhibits, the **Dorset County Museum** (opposite) has some impressive fossils from the Jurassic Coast, including a huge ichthyosaur on one wall, and a 1m dinosaur skull hanging over the stairs. Reflecting the area's rich Bronze and Iron Age past, there are also archaeological finds from Maiden Castle (p306) and a treasure trove of gold neck rings and bronze coins cashes.

The **Tutankhamen Exhibition** ( ☎ 01305-269571; www.tutankhamun-exhibition.co.uk; High West St; adult/child £7/5.50; ☼ 9.30am-5.30pm) re-creates the sights, sounds and smells of ancient Egypt in a fake-gold mock-up of the pharaoh's tomb. The **Terracotta Warriors Museum** ( ☎ 01305-266040; www.terracottawarriors.co.uk; East Gate, East High St; adult/child £5.75/4; ☼ 10am-5pm Apr-Oct, to 4.30pm Nov-Mar) whisks you off to 8th-century China for a reconstruction of the famous figures. The **Teddy Bear Museum** ( ☎ 01305-266040; East Gate, East High St; adult/child £5.75/4; ☼ 10am-5pm Apr-Oct, to 4.30pm Nov-Mar) rounds off this surreal exhibition combo – it's populated by historical and famous bears, as well as a rather disturbing family of human-sized teddies.

On the northern side of town is **Poundbury**, a cod-Georgian town dreamt up by Prince Charles as a model housing development for the 21st century.

### Sleeping

**our pick** **Beggar's Knap** ( ☎ 01305-268191; beggarsknap@hotmail.co.uk; 2 Weymouth Ave; s £45, d £65-75) Fabulous and far from impoverished, this vaguely decadent guesthouse spins the clock back to the Victorian era. Opulent, raspberry-red rooms drip with chandeliers and gold brocade, while beds (ranging from four-poster to French sleigh) are draped in fine cottons. The breakfast room, with its towering plants and a huge harp, is gorgeous.

**Slades Farm** ( ☎ 01305-264032; www.bandbdorset .org.uk; Charminster; s £45, d £70-90) Barn conversions

don't come much more stylish than this – oatmeal and cream walls meeting ceilings in gentle curves. The riverside paddock is perfect to laze in after a breakfast full of local delicacies. You'll find this place 2 miles north of Dorchester on the Cerne Abbas road (it's on the latter bus route).

**Casterbridge Hotel** ( ☎ 01305-264043; www.caster bridgehotel.co.uk; 49 High East St; s £60-65, d £70-125, f £110-155) In the 1780s this hotel was the town jail. Now marble fireplaces, ruched furnishings and Thomas Hardy books in the rooms make it worth spending a night in an old prison. Six bedrooms are in a 1980s annexe.

Also recommended:

**Aquila Heights B&B** ( ☎ 01305-267145; www .aquilaheights.co.uk; 44 Maiden Castle Rd; s £34, d £66-75, f £90-110) Pine and photo-placemat style B&B with fabulous breakfast choices.

**Westwood House** ( ☎ 01305-268018; www.west woodhouse.co.uk; 29 High West St; s £45-50, d £60-85, f £120) Elegant Georgian B&B with prettily painted wicker chairs.

### Eating

**Prezzo** ( ☎ 01305-259678; 6 High West St; mains £8-11; ☼ lunch & dinner) A reliable outpost of this Italian chain. The baroque interior is filled with black-leather sofas and twisted willow – top-notch pizzas and pastas are on the menu.

**Sienna** ( ☎ 01305-250022; 36 High West St; 2-course set lunch/dinner £19.50/30.50; ☼ lunch & dinner Tue-Sat) This smart little bistro is home to some fine pan-European flavour combos. Roast pollack with crab gnocchi, asparagus risotto with parmesan ice cream and Dorset lamb with shepherd's pie all sit cosily on the same menu.

### Getting There & Around

There's a direct daily National Express coach to London (£19.80, four hours).

Bus 31 travels from Dorchester to Weymouth (30 minutes, hourly), and to Lyme Regis (1¾ hours). Bus 10 travels to Weymouth (35 minutes, three per hour Monday to Saturday, six on Sunday). Bus 387 goes to Poole (1¼ hours, three daily Monday to Saturday).

There are two train stations – Dorchester South and Dorchester West. Trains run at least hourly from Weymouth (11 minutes) to London Waterloo (£41.30, 2½ hours) via Dorchester South, Bournemouth (£9, 45 minutes) and Southampton (£18.60, 1¼ hours).

**SOUTHWEST ENGLAND**

Dorchester West has connections to Bath (£13, 1¾ hours) and Bristol (£13, two hours); trains run every two hours.

**Dorchester Cycles** ( ☎ 01305-268787; 31 Great Western Rd) hires out bikes for £15 per day.

## AROUND DORCHESTER
### Maiden Castle

The huge steep-sided ramparts of **Maiden Castle** (EH; admission free; ⏲ 24hr) encircle 120 acres – the equivalent of 50 football pitches, making it the largest Iron Age hill fort in Britain. Started around 500 BC, the remains of clusters or roundhouses and a road network suggest the fort was once densely populated. The Romans besieged then captured it in 43 AD – an ancient Briton skeleton with a Roman crossbow bolt in the spine was found at the site. The sheer scale of the ramparts is awe-inspiring and the winding complexity of the west entrance reveals just how hard it would be to storm. Finds from the site are displayed at Dorset County Museum (p304). Maiden Castle is 1.5 miles southwest of Dorchester.

### Cerne Abbas & the Cerne Giant

If you had to describe an archetypal sleepy Dorset village, you'd come up with something a lot like Cerne Abbas: its houses run the gamut of England's historical architectural styles, roses climb countless doorways, and half-timbered houses frame a honey-coloured, 12th-century church.

But this village also packs one heck of a surprise – a real nudge-nudge, wink-wink tourist attraction in the form of the **Cerne Giant**. Nude, full frontal and notoriously well endowed, this chalk figure is revealed in all his glory on a hill on the edge of town. Some claim he's Roman but the first historical reference comes in 1694, when three shillings were set aside for his repair. The Victorians found it all deeply embarrassing and allowed grass to grow over his most outstanding feature.

The village has the not-so-new **New Inn** ( ☎ 01300-341274; www.newinncerneabbas.co.uk; 14 Long St; d from £90; ℗ ), a 13th-century pub with rustic, comfy rooms (avoid the newer extension) and an excellent menu of bar food. For top-notch dining head for the ivy-smothered, thatched **Royal Oak** ( ☎ 01300-341797; Long St; mains from £7; ⏲ lunch & dinner) and its menu of whole crab or lobster salad, Dartmouth smokehouse eels and Lyme Bay scallops in lemon butter.

Dorchester, 8 miles to the south, is reached on bus D12 (20 minutes, three daily Monday to Saturday).

## WEYMOUTH & AROUND

As the venues for the sailing events in Britain's 2012 Olympics, Weymouth and neighbouring Portland are in the middle of a multimillion-pound building spree. But despite the bustle and the waterfront spruce-up, evidence of their core characters remains. Weymouth's billowing deckchairs, candy-striped beach kiosks and Punch-and-Judy stands are the epitome of a faded Georgian resort, while Portland's pock-marked central plateau and remote cliffs still proudly proclaim a rugged, quarrying past.

### Weymouth
**pop 48,279**

Weymouth has been a popular seaside spot since King George III (the one who suffered from a nervous disorder) took an impromptu dip here in 1789. Some two-and-a-half centuries later, it's still popular with beachgoers.

#### ORIENTATION & INFORMATION

Weymouth is strung out along its seafront. To the west the rejuvenated old harbour is a vibrant jumble of brightly painted Georgian town houses, restaurants and pubs. The Isle of Portland, really a 4-mile-long peninsula, lies a few miles south.

The **tourist office** ( ☎ 01305-785747; www.visit weymouth.co.uk; The Esplanade; ⏲ 9.30am-5pm Apr-Oct, 10am-4pm Nov-Mar) sells discounted tickets to many local attractions and can, for a fee, help arrange local accommodation.

#### SIGHTS & ACTIVITIES

The fine sandy **beach** is a place to surrender to your inner kitsch and rent a deckchair, sun-lounger or pedalo (each £5 per hour). Or, go all Californian and join a volleyball game. For sailing, kitesurfing, diving and windsurfing lessons, see the boxed text, opposite.

The 19th-century **Nothe Fort** ( ☎ 01305-766626; www.fortressweymouth.co.uk; Barrack Rd; adult/child £4.50/1; ⏲ 10.30am-5.30pm daily May-Sep, 2.30-4.30pm Sun Oct-Apr) is full of cannons, rifles, searchlights and 12-inch coastal guns. It also details the Roman invasion of Dorset, a Victorian soldier's drill, and Weymouth in WWII. Commanding an armoured car and clambering around the magazine prove popular with regiments of children.

---

**WATER SPORTS IN WEYMOUTH & PORTLAND**

Stunning to look at, the seas round Weymouth and Portland are also a massive watery playground that's so good, they're to host the sailing events for the 2012 Olympics. In part it's due to Portland Harbour – 890 hectares of sheltered water created by breakwaters begun by convict labour in the mid-1800s.

You can beat the Olympians to it by learning to sail at the new **Weymouth & Portland National Sailing Academy** ( ☎ 0845 337 3214; www.sail-laser.com; Portland Harbour; per 2/4 days £175/315). **Windtek** ( ☎ 01305-787900; www.windtek.co.uk; 109 Portland Rd, Wyke Regis) offers windsurfing lessons (£90/150 per one/two days), and hires out gear (£15 per hour) if you have a Royal Yachting Association card. Staff can teach you to kitesurf, too (£95 per day).

There's a huge variety of depths, seascapes and wrecks for divers – sunken ships range from paddle steamers and East Indiamen to WWII vessels. For experienced divers **Scimitar Diving** ( ☎ 07765 326728; www.scimitardiving.co.uk) sets off from Weymouth Harbour for off-shore dives (from £40 per diver, per day). It also rents out a range of gear, from £25. **Fathom and Blues** ( ☎ 01305-826789; www.fathomandblues.co.uk; Boscawen Centre, Castletown, Portland) runs training courses for divers, from £95 per day.

---

Beside the old harbour, Brewer's Quay has a shopping centre and plentiful attractions, including **Timewalk** ( ☎ 01305-777622; Hope Sq; adult/child £4.50/3.25; � 10am-5.30pm Mar-Oct), which explores various key events in Weymouth's history. These include the Black Death, the Spanish Armada and the town's transition from fishing harbour to tourist resort. **Weymouth Museum** ( ☎ 01305-777622; admission free; ☉ 10am-4.30pm), alongside, has displays on smuggling, paddle steamers and shipwrecks.

Seals, otters and seahorses entertain you at the 3-hectare aquatic park at **Sea Life** ( ☎ 01305-761070; www.sealife.co.uk; Lodmoor Country Park; adult/child £15/10.50; ☉ 10am-4pm).

**White Motor Boats** ( ☎ 01305-785000; www.white motorboat.freeuk.com; return adult/child £7/5; ☉ Apr-Oct) runs a cracking 35-minute jaunt across to Portland Castle (p308) from Cove Row on the harbour (three to four daily).

**SLEEPING**

There are also plenty of camp sites near Chesil Beach and Weymouth Bay.

**Old Harbour View** ( ☎ 01305-774633; fax 750828; 12 Trinity Rd; d £75-85) A few doors down from Harbourside, fresh, suitably nautical bedrooms are tucked away in a pretty Georgian terrace.

**Chatsworth** ( ☎ 01305-785012; www.thechatsworth .co.uk; 14 The Esplanade; s £35-45, d £80-108) Watery views are everywhere at this super-trendy B&B – the terrace is just a yardarm from yacht berths, while bedrooms overlook the seafront or the harbour. Inside, the views are of purple satins, vanilla candles and worn wood.

**EATING & DRINKING**

**King Edward's** ( ☎ 01305-786924; 100 The Esplanade; mains £6; ☉ lunch & dinner) It has to be done: sitting on Weymouth seafront and scoffing fish 'n' chips. King Edward's is a classic chippy – all burgundy tiles and wrought iron. You can eat inside or out, and then chase it down with an ice cream from the kiosks dotting the prom. For a waterside drink, head off to the pubs and bars lining the old harbour.

**La Baroque** ( ☎ 01305-750666; 19 Trinity Rd; tapas £4, mains £13; ☉ lunch & dinner) Baroque by name, baroque by nature: munch tapas surrounded by raspberry walls and heavy gilt pictures in the wine bar, or pop upstairs to Toulouse Lautrec prints and classy dining.

**our pick Perry's** ( ☎ 01305-785799; 4 Trinity Rd; mains £12-18; ☉ lunch Tue-Fri, dinner Tue-Sat) Effortlessly stylish, but also relaxed, this Georgian town house is a study of snowy white tablecloths and flashes of pink. You won't be able to resist the Lyme Bay scallops, twice-baked Dorset Blue Vinny cheese soufflé or crab soup. Weymouth's cognoscenti book the window table on the 1st floor (it has a fabulous harbour view) for a two-course lunch – a bargain at £15.

**GETTING THERE & AWAY**

**Bus**

There's one direct National Express coach to London (£19.80, 4¼ hours) each day.

Bus 10 is the quickest to Dorchester (30 minutes, three per hour Monday to Saturday, six buses on Sunday). The hourly bus 31 also stops in Dorchester en route to Lyme Regis

**SOUTHWEST ENGLAND**

(two hours) and Axminster. The X53 travels from Weymouth to Wareham (50 minutes, six daily) and Poole (1¼ hours), and to Abbotsbury (35 minutes), Lyme Regis (1½ hours) and Exeter (three hours) in the opposite direction. Bus 1 travels regularly over to Portland (30 minutes).

### Train
Trains run hourly to London (£43, 2¾ hours) via Dorchester South (11 minutes) and Bournemouth (£11.40, one hour), and every two hours to Dorchester West, Bath (£13.20, two hours) and Bristol (£13.80, 2¼ hours).

## Portland
The Isle of Portland is in the midst of a multi-million-pound pre-Olympic building boom. Waterside waste ground is being transformed into a shiny new sailing centre, restaurants, glitzy apartment blocks and a hotel. But inland the peninsula's quarrying past still holds sway – evidenced by the huge craters and large slabs of limestone littering the landscape. Proud and at times bleak, Portland is also curiously compelling, and its water sports and wind-whipped coasts make it worth visiting.

Portland is essentially a craggy chunk of rock joined to the mainland by the long sweep of Chesil Beach (right). Its unique white limestone has been quarried for centuries, and has been used in some of the world's finest buildings – including the British Museum, St Paul's Cathedral and the United Nations headquarters in New York. One abandoned quarry, **Tout Quarry**, has been transformed into a sculpture park where snaking footpaths lead past 50 works of art which have been carved into the rock in situ. The *Philosopher's Stone*, *Fallen Fossil* and *Green Man* are particularly worth hunting out.

The 41ft tower of the red-and-white striped **lighthouse** ( ☎ 01305-820495; adult/child £2.50/1.50; 🕙 11am-5pm Apr-Sep) at Portland Bill offers views of The Race, a surging vortex of conflicting tides. A summer-only **tourist office** ( ☎ 01305-861233; 🕙 11am-5pm Apr-Sep) sits alongside.

Sturdy **Portland Castle** (EH; ☎ 01305-820539; adult/child £4/2; 🕙 10am-6pm Jul-Aug, to 5pm Apr-Jun & Sep, to 4pm Oct) is one of the finest examples of the defensive forts constructed during Henry VIII's castle-building spree. You can try on period armour while enjoying great views over Portland harbour.

For diving, sailing and windsurfing lessons, see p307.

Bus 1 runs to Portland from Weymouth every half-hour; between June and September it goes on to Portland Bill. For the White Motor Boat ferry from Weymouth, see p307.

### Chesil Beach
One of the most breathtaking beaches in Britain, Chesil is 17 miles long, 15m high and moving inland at the rate of 5m a year. This mind-boggling, 100-million-ton pebble ridge is the baby of the Jurassic Coast (see p303); a mere 6000 years old, its stones range from pea-sized in the west to hand-sized in the east. More recently it became famous as the setting for Ian McEwan's acclaimed novel about sexual awakening, *On Chesil Beach*.

**Chesil Beach Centre** ( ☎ 01305-760579; Ferrybridge; 🕙 10am-5pm Apr-Sep, 11am-4pm Oct-Mar) organises talks and guided walks. Around 600 free-flying swans chose to nest at the 600-year-old **Abbotsbury Swannery** ( ☎ 01305-871858; New Barn Rd, Abbotsbury; adult/child £8.50/5.50; 🕙 10am-5pm mid-Mar–Oct), which shelters beside the massive lagoon that backs the beach. Wandering the network of trails that snakes between the swans' nests is an awe-inspiring experience.

## LYME REGIS
**pop 4406**
The genteel resort of Lyme Regis is prime fossil hunting territory. A combination of erosion and frequent landslides means dinosaur-era finds can often be picked up along the shores, so everyone – from proper palaeontologists to those out for a bit of fun – can engage in a spot of coastal rummaging. Lyme was also the setting for the film version of *The French Lieutenant's Woman*, starring Meryl Streep, which immortalised the iconic Cobb harbour defences in movie history.

### Information
Lyme Regis' **tourist office** ( ☎ 01297-442138; lyme .tic@westdorset-dc.gov.uk; Guildhall Cottage, Church St; 🕙 10am-5pm Mon-Sat & 10am-4pm Sun Apr-Oct, 10am-3pm Mon-Sat Nov-Mar) is on the corner of Church and Bridge Sts.

### Sights & Activities
Mary Anning found the first full ichthyosaurus skeleton near Lyme in 1814, and the site of her former home is now the excellent **Lyme Regis Philpot Museum** ( ☎ 01297-443370; www.lymereg ismuseum.co.uk; Bridge St; adult/child £3/free; 🕙 10am-5pm Mon-Sat & 11am-5pm Sun Easter-Oct, 11am-4pm Wed-Sun

---

**FOSSIL FEVER**

In Lyme, fossil fever is catching. The town sits in one of the most unstable sections of Britain's coast and regular landslips mean nuggets of prehistory are constantly popping out of the cliffs. If you are bitten by the bug, the best cure is one of the regular **fossil walks** run by the Dinosaurland Fossil Museum (see below). Alternatively, meet **Dr Colin Dawes** ( ☎ 01297-443758; ⊙ tours 1pm Sun year round, plus Wed & Fri May-Sep) at the Old Forge Fossil Shop in Broad St. Walks cost from £8 for adults, £5 for children. For the best chances of a find, time your trip to Lyme to within two hours of low tide.

---

Nov-Easter). An incredibly famous fossilist in her day, Miss Anning did much to pioneer the science of modern-day palaeontology; the museum exhibits her story along with spectacular fossils and other prehistoric finds.

**Dinosaurland Fossil Museum** ( ☎ 01297-443541; www.dinosaurland.co.uk; Coombe St; adult/child £4.50/3.50; ⊙ 10am-5pm, closed some weekdays Nov-Feb) is a mini, indoor Jurassic Park – packed with the remains of belemnites and the graceful plesiosaurus. Lifelike dinosaur models will thrill youngsters – the fossilised tyrannosaurus eggs and 73kg dinosaur dung will have them in raptures.

The **Cobb**, a curling harbour wall–cum–sea defence, was first built in the 13th century. It's been strengthened and extended over the years so it doesn't present the elegant line it once did, but it's still hard to resist wandering its length for a wistful, sea-gazing Meryl moment at the tip.

## Sleeping & Eating

**Old Lyme Guest House** ( ☎ 01297-442929; www.old lymeguesthouse.co.uk; 29 Coombe St; s from £40, d £70; (P)) Once home to Lyme's old post office, this stone-fronted house is now an award-winning B&B. It has several frilly rooms finished in pale creams and soft hues, topped off by patterned curtains and china trinkets.

**ourpick Coombe House** ( ☎ 01297-443849; www .coombe-house.co.uk; 41 Coombe St; d £52-58) Easygoing and stylish, this is a fabulous-value B&B of airy rooms, bay windows, wicker and white wood. There's also a self-contained, ground-floor studio flat, complete with minikitchen. Breakfast is delivered to your door on a trol-

ley, complete with toaster – perfect for a lazy lie-in in Lyme.

**Alexandra** ( ☎ 01297-442010; www.hotelalexandra .co.uk; Pound St; s £65, d £105-165; ⊙ lunch & dinner) This grand 18th-century hotel was once home to a countess; today, it's all dignified calm and murmured chatter. Rooms are scattered with antique chairs and fine drapes and most have captivating views of the Cobb and the sea. The glorious terrace prompts urges to peruse the *Telegraph* in a panama hat.

**Harbour Inn** ( ☎ 01297-442299; Marine Pde; mains £5-10; ⊙ lunch & dinner) One of a trio of harbourside pubs, this one pips its neighbours for atmosphere and sheer range of pub grub.

**ourpick Broad Street** ( ☎ 01297-445792; 57 Broad St; 3 courses £27; ⊙ dinner Thu-Sat, plus Tue, Wed & Sun Jun-Sep & school holidays). Whitewashed walls, crisp white linen and old chapel chairs dot the interior of this innovative restaurant. The food has flair too: confit of duck, roast tomato and beetroot purée sit alongside pot-roast pollack with spinach and leeks. The ingredients' local credentials are outlined on the menu, and include wild garlic gathered from the woods. Bookings are essential.

## Getting There & Away

Bus 31 runs to Dorchester (1¼ hours, hourly) and Weymouth (1¾ hours). Bus X53 goes west to Exeter (1¾ hours, six daily) and east to Weymouth (1½ hours).

# SHERBORNE

pop 9350

Sherborne gleams with a mellow, orangey-yellow stone – it's been used to build a central cluster of 15th-century buildings and the impressive abbey church at their core. This serene town exudes wealth. The five local fee-paying schools include the famous Sherborne School, and its pupils are a frequent sight as they head off to lessons from boarding houses scattered around the town. The number of boutique shops and convertibles in the car parks reinforces the well-heeled feel. Evidence of splashing the cash 16th- and 18th-century style lies on the edge of town: two castles, one a crumbling ruin, the other a marvellous manor house, complete with a Capability Brown lake.

Sherborne's **tourist office** ( ☎ 01935-815341; sherborne.tic@westdorset-dc.gov.uk; Digby Rd; ⊙ 9am-5pm Mon-Sat Apr-Oct) stocks the free *All About Sherborne* leaflet, which has a map and town trail. **Walking tours** (£3; ⏰ 11am Fri May-Sep) depart from the tourist office and last 1½ hours.

## Sights

### SHERBORNE ABBEY

At the height of its influence, the magnificent **Abbey Church of St Mary the Virgin** ( ☎ 01935-812452; suggested donation £2; ⏰ 8.30am-6pm late Mar-late Oct, to 4pm Nov–mid-Mar) was the central cathedral of the 26 Saxon bishops of Wessex. Established early in the 8th century, it became a Benedictine abbey in 998 and functioned as a cathedral until 1075. Highlights include the oldest fan vaulting in the country and the elaborate marble effigies marking the tomb of John Lord Digby, Earl of Bristol.

On the edge of the abbey lie the beautiful 15th-century **St Johns' Almshouses** (admission £1.50; ⏰ 2-4pm Tue & Thu-Sat May-Sep).

### OLD CASTLE

These days the epitome of a picturesque ruin, Sherborne's **Old Castle** (EH; ☎ 01935-812730; adult/child £2.50/1.30; ⏰ 10am-6pm Jul & Aug, to 5pm Apr-Jun & Sep, to 4pm Oct) was built by Roger, Bishop of Salisbury in around 1120. Queen Elizabeth gave it to her one-time favourite Sir Walter Raleigh in the late 16th century. He spent large sums of money modernising it before opting for a new-build instead – moving across the River Yeo to start work on the next Sherborne Castle. The old one became a Royalist stronghold during the English Civil War, but Cromwell reduced the 'malicious and mischievous castle' to rubble after a 16-day siege in 1645.

### SHERBORNE CASTLE

Having had enough of the then 400-year-old Old Castle, Sir Walter Raleigh began building **New Castle** ( ☎ 01935-813182; www.sherbornecastle.com; castle & gardens adult/child £9/free, gardens only £4.50/free; ⏰ 11am-4.30pm Tue-Thu & Sun & 2-4.30pm Sat Apr-Oct) in 1594; it's really a splendid manor house. He got as far as the central block before falling out of favour with the royals and ending up back in prison – this time at the hands of James I. In 1617 James sold the castle to Sir John Digby, the Earl of Bristol, who added the wings we see today. In 1753, the grounds received a mega-makeover at the hands of landscape gardener extraordinaire Capability Brown – visit today and marvel at the massive lake he added, along with a remarkable 12 hectares of waterside gardens.

### SHERBORNE MUSEUM

This **museum** ( ☎ 01935-812252; www.sherborne museum.co.uk; Church Lane; adult/child £2/free; ⏰ 10.30am-4.30pm Tue-Sat & 2.30-4.30pm Sun Apr-Oct) has a digital version of the *Sherborne Missal*, the most exquisite illuminated manuscript to survive from the Middle Ages. With this high-tech copy you can turn the virtual pages and zoom in on sections of text.

## Sleeping

**Cumberland House** ( ☎ 01935-817554; sandie@ba ndbdorset.co.uk; Green Hill; s £45, d £64-74) There are few straight lines in this 17th-century B&B; instead, walls undulate towards each other in charming rooms finished in white, beige and tiny bursts of vivid pink. Breakfast is either Continental (complete with chocolate croissants) or full English – either way, there's freshly squeezed orange juice.

**Eastbury Hotel** ( ☎ 01935-813131; www.theeastbury hotel.co.uk; Long St; s £68, d £120-160) The best rooms here have real 'wow' factor – black and gold lacquer screens frame minimalist free-standing baths, and shimmering fabrics swathe French sleigh beds. The standard rooms are much more standard, but are still elegant with stripy furnishings and pared-down wicker chairs.

Also recommended:

**Antelope** ( ☎ 01935-812077; www.theantelopehotel .co.uk; Green Hill; s £54-60, d £60-85) A creaking old coaching inn with simple rooms at the top of town.

**Stoneleigh Barn** ( ☎ 01935-815964; www.stoneleigh barn.com; North Wootton; s/d/f £56/80/95) A flower-smothered, tastefully converted 18th-century barn, two miles southeast of town.

## Eating

**Pear Tree Deli** ( ☎ 01935-812828; Half Moon St; mains £4-8; ⏰ 9am-5pm Mon-Sat, 10am-4pm Sun) Full of mouth-watering aromas, this delectable deli is packed with gourmet picnic supplies. Spinach and feta pie, homemade soups and a wealth of local cheeses are coupled with irresistible cakes and puds.

**Paprika** ( ☎ 01935-816429; Half Moon St; mains £7-12; ⏰ lunch & dinner) Expect excellent, well-spiced food in this Indian restaurant. The menu is a mix of the usual fare and some surprises: honey and cashew chicken, garlic masala and Thai prawn risotto.

**Green** ( ☎ 01935-813821; 3 The Green; 2/3 courses £25/30; ⏰ lunch & dinner Tue-Sat) Local food features strongly at this intimate, cream and green restaurant at the top of Cheap St. Tempting flavour combos include Dorset venison with butternut squash, or local crab with tarragon and avocado.

## Getting There & Away

Bus 57 runs from Yeovil (30 minutes, half-hourly Monday to Saturday), as does bus 58 (15 minutes, every two hours Monday to Saturday, six buses on Sunday), which sometimes continues to Shaftesbury (1½ hours, four daily Monday to Saturday). Buses D12 and D13 run to Dorchester (one hour, three to six daily Monday to Saturday).

Hourly trains go to Exeter (£14.50, 1¼ hours), London (£38.40, 2½ hours) and Salisbury (£10.10, 45 minutes).

# WILTSHIRE

In Wiltshire you get the very best of ancient England. This verdant landscape is rich with the reminders of ritual and is littered with more ancient barrows, processional avenues and mysterious stone rings than anywhere else in Britain. These prehistoric sites tease and tantalise the imagination – there's the prehistoric majesty of Stonehenge, intensely atmospheric Avebury, and in soaring Silbury Hill, the largest constructed earth mound in Europe. Then there's the serene 800-year-old cathedral at Salisbury, the supremely stately homes at Stourhead and Longleat, and the impossibly pretty village of Lacock – the county is crammed full of English charm waiting to be explored.

## Information

The **Visit Wiltshire** (www.visitwiltshire.co.uk) website is a good source of information.

## Getting Around

### BUS

The bus coverage in Wiltshire can be patchy, especially in the northwest of the county. The two main operators:

**First** ( ☎ 0871 200 22 33; www.firstgroup.com) Serves the far west of the county.
**Wilts & Dorset Buses** ( ☎ 01722-336855; www.wdbus .co.uk) Covers most destinations; its Explorer ticket is valid for a day (adult/child £7.50/4.50).

### TRAIN

Rail lines run from London to Salisbury and beyond to Exeter and Plymouth, branching off north to Bradford-on-Avon, Bath and Bristol,

---

> **TOP FIVE ANCIENT SITES**
>
> ■ **Avebury** (p318) Bigger than Stonehenge in atmosphere and acreage, this huge stone ring encases an entire village.
>
> ■ **Stonehenge** (p315) The world's most famous collection of megaliths – shame no-one has a clue what it was for.
>
> ■ **Maiden Castle** (p306) Massive and rampart-ringed, this is the biggest Iron Age hill fort in Britain.
>
> ■ **Glastonbury Tor** (p343) Myth-rich and mighty hard to climb, this iconic mound looks down onto the Vale of Avalon.
>
> ■ **Old Sarum** (p315) A stunning Iron Age stronghold on Salisbury Plain.

but most of the smaller towns and villages aren't served by trains.

## SALISBURY
pop 43,335

Centred on a majestic cathedral that's topped by the tallest spire in England, the gracious city of Salisbury makes a charming base from which to explore the rest of Wiltshire. It's been an important provincial city for more than 1000 years, and its streets form an architectural timeline ranging from medieval walls and half-timbered Tudor town houses to Georgian mansions and Victorian villas. Salisbury is also a lively, modern place, boasting plenty of bars, restaurants and terraced cafes, as well as a concentrated cluster of excellent museums.

## Orientation

From miles around, Salisbury Cathedral's soaring spire points you towards the centre of town, which stretches north to Market Sq, an expanse dominated by its impressive Guildhall. The train station is a 10-minute walk to the west of the market, while the bus station is 90m north up Endless St.

## Information

**Library** ( ☎ 01722-324145; Market Pl; ☺ 10am-7pm Mon, 9am-7pm Tue, Wed & Fri, 9am-5pm Thu & Sat) Provides 30 minutes of internet access for free.
**Post office** (cnr Castle St & Chipper Lane)
**Tourist office** ( ☎ 01722-334956; www.visitwiltshire .co.uk/salisbury; Fish Row, Market Sq; ☺ 9.30am-6pm Mon-Sat & 10.30am-4.30pm Sun Jun-Sep, 9.30am-5pm Mon-Sat & 10.30am-4pm Sun May, 9.30am-5pm Mon-Sat Oct-Apr)

**Washing Well Laundrette** ( ☎ 01722-421874; 28 Chipper Lane; ⏲ 8am-9pm)

## Sights

### SALISBURY CATHEDRAL

Britain is a nation endowed with countless stunning churches, but few can match the grandeur and sheer spectacle of **Salisbury Cathedral** ( ☎ 01722-555120; www.salisburycathedral.org.uk; requested donation adult/child £5/3; ⏲ 7.15am-6.15pm Sep-May, to 7.15pm Jun-Aug). Built between 1220 and 1258, the cathedral bears all the hallmarks of the early English Gothic style, with an elaborate exterior decorated with pointed arches and flying buttresses, and a sombre, austere interior designed to keep its congregation suitably pious.

Beyond the highly decorative **West Front**, a small passageway leads into the 70m-long nave, lined with handsome pillars of Purbeck stone. In the north aisle look out for a fascinating **clock** dating from 1386, probably the oldest working timepiece in the world. At the eastern end of the ambulatory the glorious **Prisoners of Conscience** stained-glass window (1980) hovers above the ornate tomb of Edward Seymour (1539–1621) and Lady Catherine Grey.

The splendid **spire**, the tallest in Britain, was added in the mid-14th century. At 123m and 6500 tons it represented an enormous technical challenge for its medieval builders, requiring cross-bracing, scissor arches and supporting buttresses to keep it upright. Look closely and you'll see that the additional weight has buckled the four central piers of the nave. Sir Christopher Wren surveyed the cathedral in 1668 and detected a 75cm lean; reinforcement continues to this day.

There are 1½-hour tower **tours** (adult/child £5.50/4.50; ⏲ 2.15pm year-round, plus 11.15am Mar-Oct & Dec, plus 3.15pm Apr-Sep, plus 5pm mid-Jun–mid-Aug), which climb up 332 vertigo-inducing steps to the base of the spire. From here there are jaw-dropping views across the city and the surrounding countryside.

One of the four surviving copies of the **Magna Carta**, the historic agreement made between King John and his barons in 1215, is kept in the cathedral's **Chapter House** ( ⏲ 9.30am-5.30pm Mar–mid-Jun & mid-Aug–Oct, to 6.45pm mid-Jun–mid-Aug, 10am-4.30pm Nov-Feb).

### CATHEDRAL CLOSE

The medieval cathedral close, a tranquil enclave surrounded by beautiful houses, has an otherworldly feel. Many of the buildings date from the same period as the cathedral, although the area was heavily restored during an 18th-century clean-up by James Wyatt. The close is encircled by a sturdy outer wall, constructed in 1333; the stout gates leading into the complex are still locked every night.

The highlight of the **Salisbury & South Wiltshire Museum** ( ☎ 01722-332151; www.salisburymuseum.org.uk; 65 The Close; adult/child £5/2; ⏲ 10am-5pm Mon-Sat Sep-Jun, 10am-5pm Mon-Sat & 2-5pm Sun Jul & Aug) is the interactive Stonehenge gallery. There are also archaeological finds recovered from Old Sarum (p315) and lots of ceramics, historical artefacts and paintings, including a dreamy watercolour of Stonehenge by JMW Turner.

You can have a nose around **Arundells** ( ☎ 01722-326546; www.arundells.org.uk; 59 The Close; admission £8; ⏲ tours 1-4pm Sat-Tue late Mar-Sep), the fine, grey-stone home of late British prime minister Edward Heath (1916–2005). Look out for the paintings by Winston Churchill that nestle amid sailing memorabilia and political cartoons. The house is open for guided tours only, which have to be prebooked.

Built in 1701, **Mompesson House** (NT; ☎ 01722-335659; The Close; adult/child £4.50/2.20; ⏲ 11am-5pm Sat-Wed Mar-Oct) is a fine Queen Anne building with magnificent plasterwork ceilings, exceptional period furnishings and a wonderful carved staircase. All that made it the perfect location for the 1995 film *Sense and Sensibility*.

Military buffs will revel in the **Rifles** ( ☎ 01722-419419; www.thewardrobe.org.uk; 58 The Close; adult/child £3.25/1; ⏲ 10am-5pm daily Apr-Oct, 10am-5pm Tue-Sun Nov-Mar). Also referred to as the Wardrobe, this museum is home to detailed displays about the Royal Berkshire, Wiltshire and Duke of Edinburgh regiments.

### ST THOMAS'S CHURCH

This elegant **church** (Minster St) was built for cathedral workmen in 1219 and named after St Thomas Becket. Modified in the 15th century, its most famous feature is the amazing **doom painting** above the chancel arch, painted in 1475. This depicts Christ on the day of judgment, sitting astride a rainbow flanked by visions of heaven and hell; on the hell side, look out for two naked kings and a nude bishop, a miser with his moneybags, and a female alehouse owner, the only person allowed to hang on to her clothes.

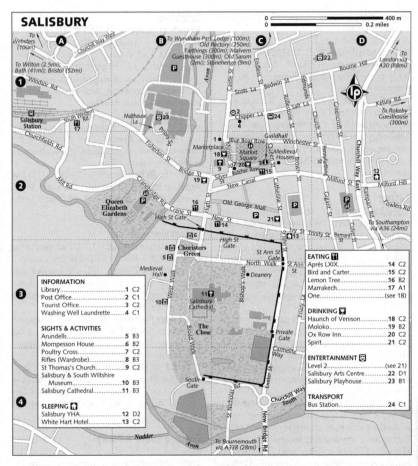

**SALISBURY**

| | |
|---|---|
| 0 | 400 m |
| 0 | 0.2 miles |

To Websters (100m)

Churchill Way West

To Wyndham Park Lodge (100m); Old Rectory (250m); Farthings (300m); Malvern Guesthouse (300m); Old Sarum (2mi); Stonehenge (9mi)

To London via A30 (88mi)

To Wilton (2.5mi); Bath (41mi); Bristol (52mi)

Windsor Rd

Salisbury Station

South Western Rd

Churchfields Rd

Mill Rd

Queen Elizabeth Gardens

Malthouse La

Priory St

Fisherton St

Crane Bridge Rd

Crane St

High St Gate

Bridge St

New Canal

Silver

Butcher Row

St Thomas's Church

Marketplace

Market Square

Guildhall

Medieval Houses

Blue Boar Row

Winchester St

Scots La

Bedwin St

Endless St

Castle St

Chipper La

Salt La

Rollestone St

Edmunds St

Church St

Greencroft St

Bourne Hill

Kelsey Rd

To Rokeby Guesthouse (300m)

Milford Hill

Fowlers Rd

To Southampton via A36 (24mi)

Old George Mall

New St

Ivy St

Trinity St

Barnard St

Friary La

Choristers Green

Chorisers Green

Medieval Hall

West Walk

Salisbury Cathedral

The Close

Broad Walk

Bishop's Walk

Deanery

North Walk

St Ann St Gate

St Ann St

Private Gate

Carmelite Way

Exeter St

South Gate

St Nicholas Rd

Nadder

Avon

Nadder

To Bournemouth via A338 (28mi)

Churchill Way South

Churchill Way East

Churchill Way

Rampart Rd

Milford Hill

Milford St

New Bridge Rd

**INFORMATION**

| | | |
|---|---|---|
| Library | **1** | C2 |
| Post Office | **2** | C1 |
| Tourist Office | **3** | C2 |
| Washing Well Laundrette | **4** | C1 |

**SIGHTS & ACTIVITIES**

| | | |
|---|---|---|
| Arundells | **5** | B3 |
| Mompesson House | **6** | B2 |
| Poultry Cross | **7** | C2 |
| Rifles (Wardrobe) | **8** | B3 |
| St Thomas's Church | **9** | C2 |
| Salisbury & South Wiltshire Museum | **10** | B3 |
| Salisbury Cathedral | **11** | B3 |

**SLEEPING** 🏠

| | | |
|---|---|---|
| Salisbury YHA | **12** | D2 |
| White Hart Hotel | **13** | C2 |

**EATING** 🍴

| | | |
|---|---|---|
| Aprés LXIX | **14** | C2 |
| Bird and Carter | **15** | C2 |
| Lemon Tree | **16** | B2 |
| Marrakech | **17** | A1 |
| One | (see 18) | |

**DRINKING** 🍸

| | | |
|---|---|---|
| Haunch of Venison | **18** | C2 |
| Moloko | **19** | C2 |
| Ox Row Inn | **20** | C2 |
| Spirit | **21** | C2 |

**ENTERTAINMENT** 🎭

| | | |
|---|---|---|
| Level 2 | (see 21) | |
| Salisbury Arts Centre | **22** | D1 |
| Salisbury Playhouse | **23** | B1 |

**TRANSPORT**

| | | |
|---|---|---|
| Bus Station | **24** | C1 |

**SOUTHWEST ENGLAND**

## Tours

**Salisbury City Guides** ( ☎ 01722-320349; www .salisburycityguides.co.uk; adult/child £4/2; ❧ 11am daily Apr-Oct, Sat & Sun only Nov-Mar) leads 1½-hour tours from the tourist office. There is also an 8pm ghost walk on Fridays from May to September.

## Sleeping

**Salisbury YHA** ( ☎ 0845 371 9537; www.yha.org.uk; Milford Hill; dm £17.50; ℗ ) A real gem: a rambling, welcoming hostel in a listed 19th-century building. Rooms range from doubles to dorms, while a cafe-bar, laundry and dappled gardens add to the appeal.

**Rokeby Guesthouse** ( ☎ 01722-329800; www.roke byguesthouse.co.uk; 3 Wain-a-long Rd; s/d from £45/55; ℗ 🖳 wi-fi) Fancy furnishings, freestanding baths and lovely bay windows make this cheerful B&B stand out from the crowd. The decking overlooking the lawn and the mini-gym help, too.

**Old Rectory** ( ☎ 01722-502702; www.theoldrectory -bb.co.uk; 75 Belle Vue Rd; s £35-50, d £55-80; ℗ ) This serene, airy B&B is full of spick-and-span rooms decked out in cream and shades of blue. The delightful enclosed garden has views of St Edmund's Church – you can even cook up a storm on the B&B's BBQ.

**Websters** ( ☎ 01722-339779; www.websters-bed -breakfast.com; 11 Hartington Rd; s £40-45, d £55-58; ℗ 🖳 ) Websters' exterior charms include quaint blue shutters and dinky arched windows. Inside it's all flowery wallpaper, patterned duvets, extra tea-tray treats and a genuinely warm welcome.

Also recommended:

**Malvern Guesthouse** ( ☎ 01722-327995; www .malvernguesthouse.com; 31 Hulse Rd; d from £55; **P** ) Family-run guesthouse with floral-themed rooms and homemade marmalade.

**White Hart Hotel** ( ☎ 01722-327476; St John St; www. mercure-uk.com; s from £90, d £120; **P** **⌨** ) For a bit of pomp and pampering, duck under the porticos of this 17th-century hotel standing right opposite the cathedral close. The service is appropriately attentive and rooms are suitably swish – the wood-rich four-poster bedrooms are positively opulent.

## Eating

**ourpick** **Bird and Carter** ( ☎ 01722-417908; 3 Fish Row, Market Sq; snacks from £4; ◷ 8.30am-6pm Mon-Sat, 10am-4pm Sun) Nestling amid 15th-century beams, this deli-cum-cafe blends old-world charm with a tempting array of antipasti, charcuterie and local goodies. Grab a goats' cheese and aubergine panini to go, or duck upstairs to eat alongside weathered wood, stained glass and old church pews.

**Lemon Tree** ( ☎ 01722-333471; 92 Crane St; mains £8-13; ◷ lunch & dinner Mon-Sat) The menu at this tiny bistro is packed with character – how about crispy duck with cherry sauce, pear and brie toast or roasted mozzarella wrapped in Parma ham? The patio-garden makes warm-weather dining a delight.

**One** ( ☎ 01722-411313; 1-5 Minster St; mains £8-15; ◷ lunch & dinner) Sloping floors, slanting beams and fake pony-hide chairs surround you in this quirky restaurant, located above the Haunch of Venison pub (right). The menu is equally eclectic, featuring hot smoked mackerel salad, grilled sausage bratwurst and good old English cottage pie.

**Marrakech** ( ☎ 01722-411112; 129-133 South Western Rd; mains £9; ◷ lunch Tue-Sat, dinner daily) For a taste of Casablanca, without leaving Wiltshire, dive into this funky little restaurant's terracotta-coloured dining room, where five-vegetable couscous, marinated chicken tagine, falafel and mezze all end up on tiled Moroccan tables.

**Après LXIX** ( ☎ 01722-340000; 69 New St; mains £10-18; ◷ lunch & dinner Mon-Sat) With artfully soft lighting and whitewashed walls, this Soho-style bistro is ideal for a romantic meal. Dishes reflect Italian, French and British influences – try the wild boar sausages with red wine jus or the seared tuna salad.

## Drinking

**Haunch of Venison** ( ☎ 01722-322024; 1-5 Minster St) Featuring wood-panelled snugs, spiral staircases and wonky ceilings, this 14th-century pub is packed with atmosphere – and ghosts. One is a cheating whist player whose hand was severed in a game (track down his mummified bones inside).

**Spirit** ( ☎ 01722-330053; 46 Catherine St; ◷ 4pm-midnight Tue-Sat) This hip hang-out is packed with the young and beautiful, who enjoying the banging tunes on the decks and a choice of multicoloured cocktails.

Try the **Ox Row Inn** ( ☎ 01722-424921; 11 Ox Row, Market Sq) for local ales, and the Cold War–themed **Moloko** ( ☎ 01722-507050; 5 Bridge St) is the bar for flavoured vodkas.

## Entertainment

**Salisbury Arts Centre** ( ☎ 01722-321744; www.salisbur yartscentre.co.uk; Bedwin St) Housed in the converted St Edmund's church, this innovative arts centre showcases cutting-edge theatre, dance and live gigs; photography and arts exhibitions are held in the foyer.

**Salisbury Playhouse** ( ☎ 01722-320333; www.salis-buryplayhouse.com; Malthouse Lane) is the town's big arts venue, hosting top touring shows, musicals and new plays.

**Level 2** ( ☎ 01722-330053; 48 Catherine St; ◷ 10.30pm-2am Thu-Sat) The club above Spirit (see Drinking, above), Level 2 pumps out dance-floor fillers and drum 'n' bass, and has guest DJs on Friday.

## Getting There & Away

### BUS

Three National Express coaches run direct to London via Heathrow each day (£14.40, 3½ hours). There's a daily coach to Bath (£8.80, 1½ hours) and Bristol (£8.80, two hours).

Buses X4 and X5 travel direct to Bath (two hours, hourly Monday to Saturday). Regular buses run to Avebury. Tour buses leave Salisbury for Stonehenge regularly; see p316.

### TRAIN

Trains run half-hourly from London Waterloo (£27.60, 1½ hours) and hourly on to Exeter (£25.70, two hours) and the southwest. Another line runs from Portsmouth (£14.40, 1½ hours, hourly) via Southampton (£7.20, 30 minutes), with connections to Bath (£8, one hour, hourly) and Bristol (£9.50, 1¼ hours, hourly).

## AROUND SALISBURY
### Old Sarum
The huge ramparts of **Old Sarum** (EH; ☎ 01722-335398; adult/child £3/1.50; ☼ 9am-6pm Jul & Aug, 10am-5pm Apr-Jun & Sep, 10am-4pm Oct & Mar, 11am-3pm Nov-Feb) sit on a grassy rise about 2 miles from Salisbury. It began life as a huge hill fort during the Iron Age, and was later occupied by both the Romans and the Saxons. By the mid-11th century it was a town – one of the most important in the west of England. William the Conqueror convened one of his earliest councils here, with the first cathedral being built in 1092, snatching the bishopric from nearby Sherborne Abbey. But Old Sarum always had problems: it was short on water and exposed to the elements, and in 1219 the bishop was given permission to move the cathedral to a new location beside the River Avon, founding the modern-day city of Salisbury. By 1331 the cathedral had been demolished for building material and Old Sarum was practically abandoned; a scale model in Salisbury Cathedral (p312) illustrates how the site once looked.

There are free guided tours at 3pm in June, July and August, and medieval tournaments, open-air plays and mock battles are held on selected days.

Between them, buses 5, 6 and 9 run four times an hour from Salisbury to Old Sarum (hourly on Sundays).

## STONEHENGE
**Stonehenge** (EH/NT; ☎ 01980-624715; adult/child £6.50/3.30; ☼ 9am-7pm Jun & Aug, 9.30am-6pm mid-Mar–May & Sep–mid-Oct, 9.30am-4pm mid-Oct–mid-Mar) is Britain's most iconic archaeological site. This compelling ring of monolithic stones has been attracting a steady stream of pilgrims, poets and philosophers for the last 5000 years.

Despite the constant flow of traffic from the main road beside the monument, and the huge numbers of visitors who traipse around the perimeter on a daily basis, Stonehenge still manages to be a mystical, ethereal place – a haunting echo from Britain's forgotten past, and a reminder of the people who once walked the many ceremonial avenues across Salisbury Plain. Even more intriguingly, it's still one of Britain's great archaeological mysteries: despite countless theories about what the site was used for, ranging from a sacrificial centre to a celestial timepiece, in truth, no one really knows what drove prehistoric Britons to expend so much time and effort on its construction.

You can't stroll around the centre of the site during normal opening hours, but unforgettable evening and early-morning **Stone Circle Access Visits** (☎ 01722-343834; adult/child £13/6) can be arranged. Each visit only takes up to 26 people, so you'll need to book well in advance.

### The Site
The first phase of construction at Stonehenge started around 3000 BC, when the outer circular bank and ditch were erected. A thousand years later, an inner circle of granite stones, known as bluestones, was added. It's thought that these mammoth 4-ton blocks were hauled from the Preseli Mountains in South Wales, some 250 miles away – an almost inexplicable feat for Stone Age builders equipped with only the simplest of tools. Although no-one is entirely sure how the builders transported the stones so far, it's thought they probably used a system of ropes, sledges and rollers fashioned from tree trunks – Salisbury Plain was still covered by forest during Stonehenge's construction.

Around 1500 BC, Stonehenge's main stones were dragged to the site, erected in a circle and crowned by massive lintels to make the trilithons (two vertical stones topped by a horizontal one). The sarsen (sandstone) stones were cut from an extremely hard rock found on the Marlborough Downs 20 miles from the site. It's estimated dragging one of these 50-ton stones across the countryside would require about 600 people.

Also around this time, the bluestones from 500 years earlier were rearranged as an inner **bluestone horseshoe** with an **altar stone** at the centre. Outside this lies the **trilithon horseshoe** of five massive sets of stones was erected. Three of these are intact; the other two have just a single upright. Then came the major **sarsen circle** of 30 massive vertical stones, of which 17 uprights and six lintels remain.

Much further out, another circle was delineated by the 58 **Aubrey Holes**, named after John Aubrey, who discovered them in the 1600s. Just inside this circle are the **South and North Barrows**, each originally topped by a stone. Like many stone circles in Britain (including Avebury, p318), the inner horseshoes are aligned to coincide with sunrise at the midsummer solstice, which some claim supports the theory that the site was some kind of astronomical calendar.

Prehistoric pilgrims would have entered the site via the **Avenue**, whose entrance to the circle

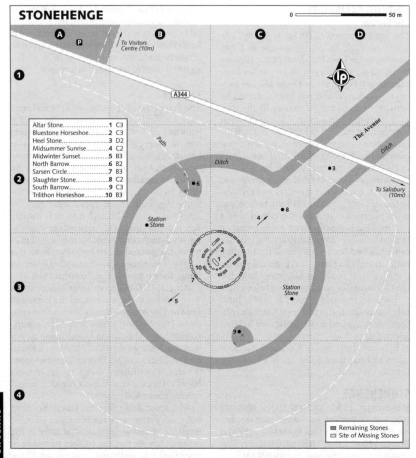

**STONEHENGE**

0 — 50 m

To Visitors Centre (10m)

A344

The Avenue

Ditch

To Salisbury (10m)

| | | |
|---|---|---|
| Altar Stone..........................**1** C3 | | |
| Bluestone Horseshoe...........**2** C3 | | |
| Heel Stone..........................**3** D2 | | |
| Midsummer Sunrise...............**4** C2 | | |
| Midwinter Sunset.................**5** B3 | | |
| North Barrow......................**6** B2 | | |
| Sarsen Circle.......................**7** B3 | | |
| Slaughter Stone...................**8** C2 | | |
| South Barrow......................**9** C3 | | |
| Trilithon Horseshoe.............**10** B3 | | |

Path

Ditch

Station Stone

Station Stone

Remaining Stones
Site of Missing Stones

is marked by the **Slaughter Stone** and the **Heel Stone**, located slightly further out on one side.

A marked pathway leads around the site, and although you can't walk freely in the circle itself, it's possible to see the stones fairly close up. An audio guide is included in the admission price.

### Getting There & Away

The **Stonehenge Tour** ( ☎ 01722-336855; return adult/child £11/5) leaves Salisbury's railway and bus stations half-hourly in June and August, and hourly between September and May. Tickets last all day, so you can hop off at Old Sarum (p315) on the way back.

Taxis charge £35 to go to the site – they wait for an hour and then come back.

Several companies offer organised tours:
**Salisbury Guided Tours** ( ☎ 01722-337960; www .salisburyguidedtours.com)
**Wessex Tourist Guides** ( ☎ 01980-623463)

## AROUND STONEHENGE

Stonehenge actually forms part of a huge complex of ancient monuments. North of Stonehenge and running roughly east–west is the **Cursus**, an elongated embanked oval; the slightly smaller **Lesser Cursus** is nearby. Theories abound as to what these sites were used for, ranging from ancient sporting arenas to processional avenues for the dead.

Other prehistoric sites around Stonehenge include the burial mounds, the **New King Barrows**, and **Vespasian's Camp**, an Iron Age hill fort.

Just north of Amesbury and 1.5 miles east of Stonehenge is **Woodhenge**, a series of concentric rings that would once have been marked by wooden posts. Excavations revealed the skeleton of a child buried near the centre with a cloven skull.

Leaflets available from the Stonehenge visitor centre detail walking routes.

## STOURHEAD

Overflowing with vistas, temples and follies, **Stourhead** (NT; ☎ 01747-841152; Stourton; house or garden adult/child £6.30/3.80, house & garden £10.50/5.80; ☺ house 11.30am-4.30pm Fri-Tue mid-Mar–Oct, garden 9am-7pm or sunset year round) is landscape gardening at its finest. The Palladian house has some fine Chippendale furniture and paintings by Claude and Gaspard Poussin, but it's a sideshow to the magnificent 18th-century gardens, which spread out across the valley. A lovely 2-mile circuit takes you past the most ornate follies, around the lake and to the **Temple of Apollo**; a 3½-mile side trip can be made from near the **Pantheon** to **King Alfred's Tower** (adult/child £2.20/1.20; ☺ 11.30am-4.30pm mid-Mar–Oct), a 50m-high folly with wonderful views.

Stourhead is off the B3092, 8 miles south of Frome (in Somerset).

## LONGLEAT

Half ancestral mansion, half safari park, **Longleat** ( ☎ 01985-844400; www.longleat.co.uk; house & grounds adult/child £10/6, safari park £11/8, all-inclusive passport £22/16; ☺ house 10am-5pm year round, safari park 10am-4pm Apr-Nov, other attractions 11am-5pm Apr-Nov) became the first stately home in England to open its doors to the public, in 1946. It was prompted by finance: heavy taxes and mounting bills after WWII meant the house had to earn its keep. Britain's first safari park opened on the estate in 1966, and soon Capability Brown's landscaped grounds had been transformed into an amazing drive-through zoo, populated by a menagerie of animals more at home in an African wilderness than the fields of Wiltshire. These days the zoo is backed up by a throng of touristy attractions, including a narrow-gauge railway, 'Doctor Who 'exhibit, Postman Pat village, pets' corner and butterfly garden. Under all these tourist trimmings it's easy to forget the house itself, which contains fine tapestries, furniture and decorated ceilings, as well as seven libraries containing around 40,000 tomes. The highlight, though, is an extraordinary series of paintings and psychedelic murals by the present-day marquess, who trained as an art student in the '60s and upholds the long-standing tradition of eccentricity among the English aristocracy – check out his website at www.lordbath.co.uk.

Longleat is just off the A362, 3 miles from both Frome and Warminster.

## LACOCK

With its geranium-covered cottages, higgledy-piggledy rooftops and idyllic location next to a rushing brook, pockets of the medieval village of Lacock seem to have been preserved in aspic since the mid-19th century. The village has been in the hands of the National Trust since 1944, and in many places is remarkably free of modern development – there are no telephone poles or electric streetlights, and although villagers drive around the streets, the main car park on the outskirts keeps it largely traffic-free. Unsurprisingly, it's also a popular location for costume dramas and feature films – the village and its abbey pop up in the Harry Potter films, *The Other Boleyn Girl* and BBC adaptations of *Moll Flanders* and *Pride and Prejudice*.

### Sights

#### LACOCK ABBEY

**Lacock Abbey** (NT; ☎ 01249-730459; abbey, museum, cloisters & grounds adult/child £9/4.50, abbey, cloisters & grounds £7.20/3.60; ☺ abbey 1-5.30pm Wed-Mon mid-Mar–Oct, cloisters & grounds 11am-5.30pm Mar-Oct, museum 11am-5.30pm late Feb-Oct plus Sat & Sun Nov-Jan) was founded as an Augustinian nunnery in 1232 by Ela, Countess of Salisbury. After the Dissolution the abbey was sold in 1539 to Sir William Sharington, who converted the nunnery into a home, demolished the church, tacked a tower onto the corner of the abbey and added a brewery. The wonderful Gothic entrance hall is lined with bizarre terracotta figures; spot the scapegoat with a lump of sugar on its nose. Some of the original 13th-century structure is evident in the cloisters and there are traces of medieval wall paintings. The recently restored botanic garden is also worth a visit.

In the early 19th century, William Henry Fox Talbot (1800–77), a prolific inventor, developed the photographic negative while working at the abbey: the **Fox Talbot Museum of Photography** (NT; ☎ 01249-730459; museum, cloisters &

grounds adult/child £5.50/2.70; ⊙ 11am-5.30pm Mar-Oct, 11am-4pm Sat & Sun Nov-Feb) details his ground-breaking work and displays a fine collection of his snapshots.

## Sleeping & Eating

**King John's Hunting Lodge** ( ☎ 01249-730313; king johns@amserve.com; 21 Church St; s/d £60/90, f £115-140; ⊙ tearooms 11am-5.30pm) Housed in Lacock's old-est building, this tearoom-cum-B&B is run by an ex-shepherdess, who's now a celebrity chef. Tearoom (snacks £3 to £8) specialities include 'priddy oggies' (a pastry with pork and Stilton), cheese muffins and homemade elder-flower cordial. Upstairs, snug, resolutely old-fashioned rooms are crammed with creaky furniture and Tudor touches.

**ourpick Sign of the Angel** ( ☎ 01249-730230; www .lacock.co.uk; 6 Church St; s £82, d £120-145; ℗ ) If you want to slumber amid a slice of history, check into this 15th-century beamed bolt-hole. Crammed with antique beds, tapestries and burnished chests, its comfort levels are brought up to date with free-standing sinks and slipper baths. The restaurant (mains from £14) revels in English classics – try the 'angel plate' of cold meats and bubble and squeak, then squeeze in treacle tart with clotted cream.

Other options:

**George Inn** ( ☎ 01249-730263; 4 West St; mains from £8; ⊙ lunch & dinner) A horse brass–hung pub dispensing grub and local ales.

**Lacock Pottery B&B** ( ☎ 01249-730266; www .lacockbedandbreakfast.com; s £49-59, d £76-96; ℗ ) An oatmeal colour scheme and antiques grace this airy former workhouse, which is overlooked by the church.

## Getting There & Away

Bus 234 runs hourly, Monday to Saturday, from Chippenham (15 minutes).

# AVEBURY

☎ 01672

While tour buses usually head for Stonehenge, prehistoric purists make for the massive ring of stones at **Avebury**. Though it lacks the huge slabs of rock and dramatic trilithons of its sister site across the plain, Avebury is argu-ably a much more rewarding place to visit. Much of the village is actually inside the stone circle; you get much closer to the action than you do at Stonehenge; and it's bigger, older and much quieter. It may also have been a more important ceremonial site, judging by its massive scale and location at the centre of

a complex of barrows, burial chambers and processional avenues.

## Orientation & Information

Two main roads bisect the village, but it's much easier to use the National Trust car park on the A4361, just a short walk from the village. The **tourist office** ( ☎ 01380-734669; www.visitwiltshire.co.uk; Chapel Centre, Green St; ⊙ 9.30am-5pm Wed-Sun Apr-Oct, 9.30am-4.30pm Thu-Sun Nov-Mar) is housed in a con-verted chapel near the centre of the village.

## Sights

### STONE CIRCLE

With a diameter of about 348m, Avebury is the largest stone circle in the world. It's also one of the oldest, dating from around 2500 to 2200 BC, between the first and second phase of construction at Stonehenge. The site origi-nally consisted of an outer circle of 98 standing stones from 3m to 6m in length, many weigh-ing up to 20 tons, carefully selected for their size and shape. The stones were surrounded by another circle delineated by a 5.5m-high earth bank and a 6m- to 9m-deep ditch. Inside were smaller stone circles to the north (27 stones) and south (29 stones).

The present-day site represents just a frac-tion of the circle's original size; tragically, many of the stones were buried, removed or broken up during the Middle Ages, when Britain's pagan past became something of an embarrassment to the church. In 1934, wealthy businessman and archaeologist Alexander Keiller supervised the re-erection of the buried stones, and planted markers to indicate those that had disappeared; he later bought the site for posterity using funds from his family's marmalade fortune.

Modern roads into Avebury neatly dissect the circle into four sectors. Start at High St, near the Henge Shop, and walk round the circle in an anticlockwise direction. There are 11 standing stones in the southwest sec-tor, including the **Barber Surgeon Stone**, named after the skeleton of a man found under it. The equipment buried with him suggested he was a medieval travelling barber-surgeon, possibly killed when a stone accidentally fell on him.

The southeast sector starts with the huge **portal stones** marking the entry to the circle from West Kennet Ave. The **southern inner circle** stood in this sector and within this circle was the **Obelisk** and a group of stones known as the

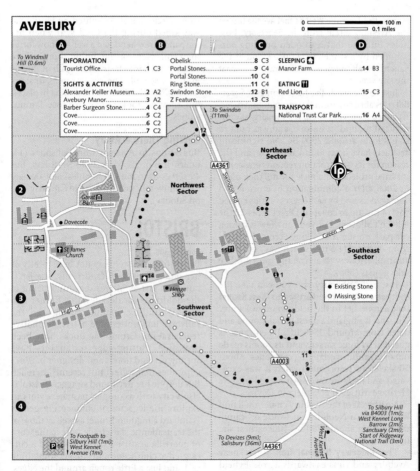

**AVEBURY**

| | | |
|---|---|---|
| **INFORMATION** | | |
| Tourist Office...........................**1** C3 | | |
| | | |
| **SIGHTS & ACTIVITIES** | | |
| Alexander Keiller Museum......**2** A2 | | |
| Avebury Manor.......................**3** A2 | | |
| Barber Surgeon Stone.............**4** C4 | | |
| Cove.......................................**5** C2 | | |
| Cove.......................................**6** C2 | | |
| Cove.......................................**7** C2 | | |
| Obelisk...................................**8** C3 | **SLEEPING** | |
| Portal Stones..........................**9** C4 | Manor Farm..........................**14** B3 | |
| Portal Stones........................**10** C4 | | |
| Ring Stone.............................**11** C4 | **EATING** | |
| Swindon Stone.......................**12** B1 | Red Lion................................**15** C3 | |
| Z Feature...............................**13** C3 | | |
| | **TRANSPORT** | |
| | National Trust Car Park...........**16** A4 | |

• Existing Stone
○ Missing Stone

**Z Feature**. Just outside this smaller circle, only the base of the **Ring Stone** remains.

The northwest sector has the most complete collection of standing stones, including the massive 65-ton **Swindon Stone**, the first stone encountered and one of the few never to have been toppled. In the northern inner circle in the northeast sector, three sarsens remain of what would have been a rectangular **cove**.

### AVEBURY MANOR

Although it dates back to the 16th century, **Avebury Manor** (NT; ☎ 01672-539250; manor & garden adult/child £4/2, garden only £3/1.50; ☒ manor 2-4.40pm Mon, Tue & Sun, gardens 11am-5pm Fri-Tue) was modified during the Edwardian era. Keiller bought the

manor in 1939 and spent much of his later life here; now owned by the National Trust, the house is still used as a private residence, but it's a little scant on attractions. Entry is by timed ticket. The manor is on the western fringe of the village.

Housed in the old stables of Avebury Manor, the **Alexander Keiller Museum** (NT; ☎ 01672-539250; adult/child £4.20/2.10; ☒ 10am-6pm Apr-Oct, to 4pm Nov-Mar) explores the archaeological history of the circle and traces the story of the man who dedicated his life to unlocking the secret of the stones.

### OTHER SITES

Avebury is surrounded by a network of ancient monuments. Lined by 100 pairs of

SOUTHWEST ENGLAND

stones, the 1.5-mile **West Kennet Avenue** linked the Avebury circle with the **Sanctuary**. Post holes indicate that a wooden building surrounded by a stone circle once stood at the Sanctuary, although no one knows quite what the site was for.

Just to the west, the huge dome of **Silbury Hill** rises abruptly from the surrounding fields. At more than 40m high, it's the largest constructed mound in Europe, and was built in stages from around 2500 BC. No significant artefacts have been found at the site, and the reason for its construction remains unclear. A massive project to stabilise the hill took place in 2008 after a combination of erosion and damaged caused by earlier excavations caused part of the top to collapse. Direct access to the hill isn't allowed, but you can view it from a car park on the A4. Hiking across the fields from Avebury (1.5 miles each way) is a more atmospheric way to arrive; the tourist office sells guides (50p).

Just east of Silbury Hill you can take the footpath half a mile further to **West Kennet Long Barrow**. Set in the fields south of Silbury Hill, this is England's finest burial mound and dates from around 3500 BC. Its entrance is guarded by huge sarsens and its roof is made out of gigantic overlapping capstones. About 50 skeletons were found when it was excavated, and finds are on display at the Wiltshire Heritage Museum & Gallery in Devizes.

Northwest of the Avebury circle you'll find **Windmill Hill**, a Neolithic enclosure or 'camp' dating from about 3700 BC (the earliest site in the area).

The **Ridgeway National Trail** starts near Avebury and runs eastwards across Fyfield Down, where many of the sarsen stones at Avebury (and Stonehenge) were collected.

### Sleeping & Eating

**our pick** **Manor Farm** ( ☎ 01672-539294; fax 01672-539294; High St; s/d £60/80) Your chance to sleep in style inside a stone circle – this red-brick farmhouse snuggles just inside the henge. The quietly comfy rooms blend old woods with bright furnishings; there's a splendid freestanding claw-foot bath; and the views out onto the 4000-year-old standing stones ratchet up the atmosphere.

**Red Lion** ( ☎ 01672-539266; redlion.avebury@whitbread.com; Swindon Rd; mains from £10; ⚅ lunch & dinner; Ⓟ) Having a pint here means downing a drink at the only pub in the world inside a

stone circle. It's also haunted by Flori, who was killed during the Civil War when her husband threw her down a well – it now forms the centrepiece of the dining room, where you can tuck into hearty pub grub of the pie 'n' mash school. The rustic rooms upstairs (singles/doubles £50/80) are peeling in places, but they do look out onto those famous stones.

### Getting There & Away

Bus 5 runs to Avebury from Salisbury (1¾ hours, five or six Monday to Saturday). Bus 49 serves Swindon (30 minutes) and Devizes (25 minutes, hourly Monday to Saturday, five on Sunday).

# BRISTOL

**pop 393,300**

Boom-town Bristol may not be as pretty as her older sister Bath (and really, she isn't) but she's just as interesting. After being in the doldrums for decades, this former hub of shipbuilding, manufacturing and the railways has undergone a transformative regeneration. Crumbling docks have been prettified, cutting-edge restaurants have sprung up, and hotels and designer bars occupy sites that were, until recently, derelict. But despite her newfound swagger, Bristol is also a city with a complex past; here you can explore the legacies of engineering genius Isambard Kingdom Brunel as well as those of the transatlantic slave trade. Mix in the work of guerrilla graffiti artist Banksy and a cutting-edge club scene and you get something real, and just a little rough around the edges. But there's also a sense that this little sister's time has come.

## HISTORY

A small Saxon village at the confluence of the Rivers Frome and Avon became the thriving medieval Brigstow (later Bristol) as the city began to develop its trade in cloth and wine with mainland Europe. Over the following centuries Bristol became one of Britain's major ports, and grew wealthy on the proceeds of the transatlantic slave 'trade'. By the time these shipments of human cargo were finally abolished in the British Empire in 1807, it's thought 500,000 Africans had been enslaved by Bristol merchants – one fifth of all people kidnapped and sold into slavery by British vessels.

During the 18th and 19th centuries Bristol became first an important hub for shipbuilding, then of the Great Western Railway – you can still see that legacy in the creations of Victorian engineering genius, Isambard Kingdom Brunel (look out for his ships, bridges and train lines). During WWII, Bristol became a target for German bombing; much of the city centre had been levelled by the time peace was declared in 1945. The postwar rush for reconstruction left the city with plenty of concrete carbuncles, but over the last decade the city has undergone extensive redevelopment, especially around the dockside.

## ORIENTATION

The city centre, north of the river, is easy to get around on foot, but it's hilly. The central area centres on the narrow streets by the markets and Corn Exchange and the newly developed docklands. Park St is lined with trendy shops and cafes, while a strip of Whiteladies Rd (northwest of Park St), is the hub of bar and restaurant life. The genteel suburb of Clifton, with its Georgian terraces and boutique shops, is on the hilltop west of the centre.

As in any big city, it pays to keep your wits about you after dark, especially around the suburb of St Paul's, just northeast of the centre. It's a rundown area with a heavy drug scene, and is best not visited alone at night.

The main train station is Temple Meads, a mile southeast of the centre. Some trains use Bristol Parkway, 5 miles to the north. The bus station is on Marlborough St, northeast of the city centre.

## INFORMATION
### Bookshops

**Blackwell's/George's** ( ☎ 0117-927 6602; 89 Park St) This vast bookshop sells both secondhand and new titles.
**Stanfords** ( ☎ 0117-929 9966; 29 Corn St) You'll find a superb collection of maps and books at this travel specialist.

### Emergency
**Police station** ( ☎ 0845 456 7000; Nelson St)

### Internet Access
**Bristol Central Library** ( ☎ 0117-903 7200; College Green; access free; ⏱ 9.30am-7.30pm Mon, Tue & Thu, 10am-5pm Wed, 9am-5pm Fri & Sat, 1-5pm Sun)

### Internet Resources
**This is Bristol** (www.thisisbristol.com) Web edition of the *Bristol Evening Post*.

**Venue** (www.venue.co.uk) Online version of Bristol's listings guide, with reviews of clubs, bars and restaurants.
**Visit Bristol** (www.visitbristol.co.uk) Official tourism website with info on events, accommodation, transport and exploring the city.
**What's on Bristol** (www.whatsonbristol.co.uk) Useful online city guide with comprehensive listings.

### Laundry
**Alma Laundrette** ( ☎ 0117-973 4121; 78 Alma Rd; ⏱ 7am-9pm)

### Medical Services
**Bristol Royal Infirmary** ( ☎ 0117-923 0000; 2 Marlborough St)

### Money
You'll find all the main banks along Corn St, including Barclays at number 40, Lloyds at 55, and NatWest at 32.

### Post
**Post office** ( ☎ 0845 722 3344) Baldwin St (**Baldwin St**); Upper Maudlin St (**Upper Maudlin St**); The Galleries (**The Galleries, Broadmead**)

### Tourist Information
**Tourist office** ( ☎ enquiries 0906 711 2191 per min 50p, accommodation 0845 408 0474; www.visitbristol .co.uk; Explore @ Bristol, Anchor Rd; ⏱ 10am-6pm Mar-Oct, 10am-5pm Mon-Sat & 11am-4pm Sun Nov-Feb) Well stocked with leaflets, transport maps and local info; books accommodation for £3.

### Travel Agencies
**STA Travel** ( ☎ 0871 230 8569; 43 Queen's Rd)
**Trailfinders** ( ☎ 0117-929 9000; 48 Corn St; ⏱ 9am-6pm)

## SIGHTS

**Explore @ Bristol** ( ☎ 0117-9155000; www.at-bristol.org. uk; Anchor Rd; adult/child £9/7; ⏱ 10am-5pm Mon-Fri, to 6pm Sat, Sun & school holidays) is Bristol's impressive science museum, with several zones spanning space, technology and the human brain. In the Curiosity Zone you get to walk through a tornado, spin on a human gyroscope and strum the strings of a virtual harp. It's fun, imaginative and highly interactive, and should keep kids of all ages enthralled for a few hours. A £4 million aquarium is due to open at the same site in 2009.

One of Bristol's most famous sons was Cary Grant (aka Archibald Leach), who was born

# BRISTOL

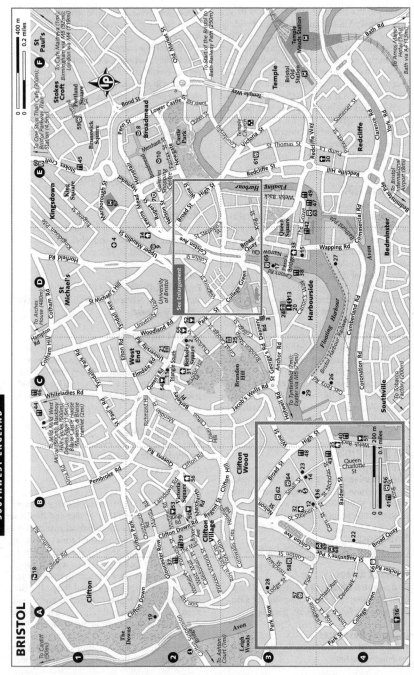

here in 1904; look out for his **statue** in neighbouring Millennium Sq.

## Museums & Galleries

Housed in a stunning Edwardian baroque building, the **City Museum & Art Gallery** ( ☎ 0117-922 3571; Queen's Rd; admission free; ⦿ 10am-5pm) has an excellent collection of British and French art; galleries dedicated to ceramics and decorative arts; and archaeological, geological and natural history wings. Look out for the museum's best-known resident, Alfred the Gorilla.

The 18th-century **Georgian House** ( ☎ 0117-921 1362; 7 Great George St; admission free; ⦿ 10am-5pm Wed-Sat) provides an atmospheric illustration of aristocratic life in Bristol during the Georgian era – and the city's links to the slave trade. The six-storeyed house was home to West India merchant John Pinney, along with his slave Pero – after whom Pero's Bridge across the harbour is named. It's still decorated throughout in period style, typified by the huge kitchen (complete with cast-iron roasting spit) and the grand drawing rooms.

The Elizabethan **Red Lodge** ( ☎ 0117-921 1360; Park Row; admission free; ⦿ 10am-5pm Wed-Sat) was built in 1590 but was much remodelled in 1730, and its architecture reflects both periods. The highlight is the Elizabethan Oak Room, which still features its original oak panelling, plasterwork ceiling and carved chimneypiece.

In the northern suburb of Henbury lies **Blaise Castle House Museum** ( ☎ 0117-903 9818; Henbury Rd; admission free; ⦿ 10am-5pm Wed-Sat), a late-18th-century house and social history museum. Displays include vintage toys, costumes and other Victorian ephemera. Across the road is **Blaise Hamlet**, a cluster of picturesque thatched cottages designed for estate servants by John Nash in 1811. Bus 43 (45 minutes, every 15 minutes) passes the castle from Colston Ave; bus 1 (20 minutes, every 10 minutes) from St Augustine's Pde doesn't stop quite as close, but is quicker and more frequent.

The massive avant-garde **Arnolfini Arts Centre** ( ☎ 0117-917 2300; www.arnolfini.org.uk; 16 Narrow Quay; admission free; ⦿ 10am-6pm Tue-Sun) has had an impressive facelift, and remains the top venue in town for exhibitions of dance, photography and art.

A £25 million scheme to turn the city's old Industrial Museum into a flagship **Museum of Bristol** is due to be completed by 2011. Sited on the Harbourside inside huge 1950s transit sheds, displays will include historic working cranes, boats and trains. A steam railway

**SOUTHWEST ENGLAND**

runs from the site along to Brunel's SS *Great Britain*, below.

The British Empire & Commonwealth Museum closed in autumn 2008 ahead of a planned relocation to London.

## SS Great Britain

In 1843 the pioneering engineer Isambard Kingdom Brunel designed the mighty **SS Great Britain** ( ☎ 0117-926 0680; www.ssgreatbritain.org; Great Western Dockyard; adult/child £11/5.65; ✆ 10am-5.30pm Apr-Oct, to 4.30pm Nov-Mar), the first transatlantic steamship to be driven by a screw propeller. For 43 years the ship served as a luxury ocean-going liner and cargo vessel, before being damaged in 1886 near the Falkland Islands. The cost of repairs proved uneconomic and the ship's owners sold her off as a coal hulk, an ignominious fate for such a grand vessel. By 1937 she was no longer watertight and was abandoned near Port Stanley in the Falklands. There she remained, forgotten and rusted, before finally being towed back to Bristol in 1970.

Since then a massive 30-year program of restoration costing £11.3 million has allowed the ship to rediscover her former splendour. The ship's rooms have been refurbished in impeccable detail, including the ship's galley, surgeon's quarters, mess hall and the great engine room; but the highlight is the amazing 'glass sea' on which the ship sits, enclosing an airtight dry dock that preserves the delicate hull and allows visitors to see the groundbreaking screw propeller up close. Moored nearby is a replica of John Cabot's ship **Matthew**, which sailed from Bristol to Newfoundland in 1497.

Tickets to the SS *Great Britain* also allow access to the neighbouring **Maritime Heritage Centre** ( ☎ 0117-927 9856; Great Western Dockyard, Gas Ferry Rd; ✆ 10am-5.30pm Apr-Oct, to 4.30pm Nov-Mar), which has various exhibits relating to the ship's illustrious past, and the city's boat-building heritage.

The steam-powered **Bristol Harbour Railway** (single/return £2/3; ✆ Sat & Sun late May-early Sep) runs along the dock from the site of the new Museum of Bristol to the SS *Great Britain* and the maritime centre.

## Clifton & the Suspension Bridge

The most famous landmark in the trendy, leafy suburb of Clifton is another Brunel masterpiece, the 76m-high **Clifton Suspension Bridge** (www.clifton-suspension-bridge.org.uk), which spans the Avon Gorge from Clifton over to Leigh Woods in northern Somerset. It's undoubtedly one of Britain's most elegant bridges; initial construction work began in 1836, but sadly Brunel died before the bridge's completion in 1864. It was mainly designed to carry light horse-drawn traffic and foot passengers, but these days around 12,000 cars cross it every day – testament to the quality of the construction and the vision of Brunel's design.

It's free to walk or cycle across the bridge; car drivers pay a 30p toll. There's a **visitor information point** ( ☎ 0117-974 4665; visitinfo@clifton-suspension-bridge.org; ✆ 10am-5pm) near the tower on the Leigh Woods side. Free guided tours of the bridge take place at 3pm on Sunday between Easter and mid-September.

The grassy parks of **Clifton Down** and **Durdham Down** (often referred to as just The Downs) beside the bridge make a fine spot for a picnic. Nearby, a well-worn observatory houses a **camera obscura** ( ☎ 0117-974 1242; adult/child £2/1; ✆ from 10.30am daily Easter-Oct, Sat & Sun Nov-Easter) which offers incredible views of the suspension bridge. Opening hours vary depending on the weather.

**Bristol Zoo** ( ☎ 0117-974 7399; www.bristolzoo.org.uk; Clifton; adult/child £12/7.40; ✆ 9am-5.30pm summer, to 5pm winter) is renowned as much for its conservation work as for its exotic residents. Attractions include a group of West African gorillas, underwater walkways for viewing seals and penguins, and a Brazilian rainforest where you can get up close and personal with agouti, capybara and golden lion tamarins.

See p330 for details of buses to Clifton and the zoo.

## Bristol Cathedral

Originally founded as the church of an Augustinian monastery in 1140, **Bristol Cathedral** ( ☎ 0117-926 4879; www.bristol-cathedral.co.uk; College Green; donations requested; ✆ 8am-6pm) has a remarkably fine Norman chapter house and gate, while the attractive chapels have eccentric carvings and beautiful heraldic glass. Although much of the nave and the west towers date from the 19th century, the 14th-century choir has fascinating misericords depicting apes in hell, quarrelling couples and dancing bears. The south transept shelters a rare Saxon carving of the *Harrowing of Hell*, discovered under the chapter-house floor after a 19th-century fire.

## St Mary Redcliffe

**St Mary Redcliffe** ( ☎ 0117-929 1487; www.stmaryred cliffe.co.uk; Redcliffe Way; ☯ 9am-5pm Mon-Sat, 8am-7.30pm Sun) boasts a soaring 89m-high spire, a grand hexagonal porch and a vaulted ceiling decorated with gilt bosses. At the entrance to the America Chapel is a whale rib presented to the church by John Cabot as a souvenir of his trip to Newfoundland in 1497.

## BRISTOL FOR CHILDREN

There's no shortage of things to keep kids happy in Bristol, with loads of hands-on activities and interesting events. Most hotels and some B&Bs can rustle up a baby cot or heat up a bottle; confirm that when you book. Baby-changing facilities are available in most supermarkets, department stores, shopping centres and major attractions.

The brilliant **Bristol Zoo Gardens** (opposite) has enough hairy apes and even hairier spiders to keep whippersnappers entertained for hours, and there are plenty of hands-on exhibits at the **Explore @ Bristol** (p321) science museum on the old Harbourside. Chug along the dockside on the steam **Bristol Harbour Railway** (opposite) to the **SS Great Britain** (opposite), where kids can join a detective trail in search of the missing ship's cat, Sinbad.

At the **City Museum & Art Gallery** (p323), Alfred the Gorilla guides youngsters through a world of dinosaurs, Egyptology and archaeology; there are also self-led trails, an activity program and a touch-the-artefact zone for children aged zero to five. Seadogs, meanwhile, can trawl for treasure on a **Pirate Walk** (right). In August, look to the skies for Bristol's **balloon and kite festivals** (right).

**Bristol Babysitting Agency** ( ☎ 07791-478028; www. bristolbabysitting.co.uk) can recommend accredited local childminders.

## TOURS

The **Bristol Highlights Walk** ( ☎ 0870 444 0654; www .bristolvisitor.co.uk; adult/under 12yr £3.50/free; ☯ 11am Sat Apr-Sep) tours the old town, city centre and Harbourside. It's run every Saturday; just turn up outside the tourist office. Themed tours exploring Clifton, Brunel and the history of Bristol traders are run on request.

**MP3 Tours** (www.visitbristol.co.uk/site/sightsee ing-and-tours; free), which can be downloaded from the Visit Bristol website, cover Brunel, the slave trade, pirates, churches and general heritage.

**City Sightseeing** ( ☎ 0870 444 0654; www.city-sight seeing.com; 24hr ticket adult/child £10/5, single trips £1/50p; ☯ 10am-4pm Easter-Sep) has an open-topped hop-on, hop-off bus visiting all the major attractions. Buses leave Broad Quay hourly (every 30 minutes from July to September).

**Bristol Packet Boat Trips** ( ☎ 0117-927 3416; www. bristolpacket.co.uk; 24hr ticket adult/child £4.75/2.75; ☯ Mar-Oct) offers cruises around the harbour area, as well as weekend day trips to Avon Gorge (return adult/child £12/8.75, May to October) and Bath (single adult/child £22.50/15, Sunday late May to September).

**Pirate Walk** ( ☎ 07950 566483; adult/child/family £5/3.50/12.50; ☯ tours 6.15pm daily Apr-Sep, 2pm Sat & Sun Oct-Mar) is a child-friendly, swashbuckling two-hour trail of pirates, smugglers and other ne'er-do-wells, which leaves from the tourist office.

## FESTIVALS & EVENTS

Bristol has an ever-expanding program of annual events; the tourist office can advise on dates and details.

**Bristol Shakespeare Festival** (www.bristolshakes peare.org.uk) Between May and September, venues across the city host this festival, the largest open-air event of its type in Britain.

**St Paul's Carnival** ( ☎ 0117-944 1478) This giant street party takes place on the first Saturday of July.

**Bristol Harbour Festival** ( ☎ 0117-922 3719) The city's biggest waterside event is held in early August – expect bands, theatre and circus entertainment to a backdrop of tall ships and maritime displays.

**International Balloon Fiesta** ( ☎ 0117-953 5884; www.bristolfiesta.co.uk) Held in August at Ashton Court, over the Clifton Suspension Bridge.

**International Kite Festival** ( ☎ 0117-977 2002; www.kite-festival.org.uk) Held in September, also at Ashton Court.

**Encounters** ( ☎ 0117-929 9188; www.encounters-festival.org.uk) This film festival is held at the Watershed every November.

**Christmas market** Held in evenings in late November and December, at St Nicholas Market.

## SLEEPING
### Budget

**Bristol Backpackers** ( ☎ 0117-925 7900; www.bristolback packers.co.uk; 17 St Stephen's St; dm/tw £15/36; 🖳 ) This longstanding traveller's friend is a decent budget option, although the dorms and doubles are cramped, and crowded in summer. There's no curfew, so prepare to join in the noise at weekends.

---

**AEROSOL ANTIHERO**

Bristol brings you close to a man who specialises in stencils, subverted art and stunts: the guerrilla graffiti artist Banksy (www.banksy.co.uk). Banksy's true identity is a closely guarded secret, but it's rumoured he was born in 1974 in Yate (near Chipping Sodbury), 12 miles from Bristol, and cut his teeth in a city graffiti outfit. Headline-grabbing works include issuing spoof British £10 notes (with Princess Diana's head on them instead of the Queen's); replacing 500 copies of Paris Hilton's debut album in record shops with remixes (featuring tracks titled *Why Am I Famous?* and *What Have I Done?*); painting an image of a ladder going up and over the Israeli West Bank Barrier; and covertly inserting his own version of a primitive cave painting (with a human hunter-gatherer pushing a shopping trolley) into the British Museum in London.

His works feature in the streets of Bristol, too. Look out for his notorious **love triangle** stencil (featuring an angry husband, a two-timing wife, and a naked man dangling from a window) at the bottom of Park St. Banksy's ghostly take on **Charion**, the River Styx boatman, graces the side of the Thekla Social (p328), and there's a large mural called **Mild Mild West** featuring a Molotov cocktail–wielding teddy bear on Cheltenham Rd, opposite the junction with Jamaica St.

For more, check out www.banksy.co.uk; the tourist office has produced a free miniguide.

---

**Bristol YHA** ( ☎ 0870 770 5726; www.yha.org.uk; 14 Narrow Quay; dm £18-20, s £25-35, d £40-45; 🖳 ) You can pay through the nose for a location like this, in the heart of the Harbourside action, just steps away from the water. Facilities are superb: modern four-bed dorms and doubles, a cycle store, games room and the excellent Grainshed coffee lounge.

## Midrange

**Arches House** ( ☎ 0117-924 7398; www.arches-hotel.co.uk; 132 Cotham Brow; s £29-45, d £52-63) Vegetarians will love this Victorian guesthouse – breakfasts are meat-free and packed with organic, fairtrade treats. The rooms are traditional but the thinking is very modern: electricity comes from renewable sources; cleaning products are eco-friendly; and the owners could run classes in recycling and composting.

**Downs Edge** ( ☎ 0117-968 3264; www.downsedge.com; Saville Rd; s £55-59, d £75-80; 🅿 🖳 wi-fi) A few miles from the centre of town and surrounded by botanical gardens, this double-gabled B&B provides a soothing slice of rural life. Elegant, antique-filled rooms create a country house atmosphere, reinforced by breakfasts full of compotes, overnight porridge and softly poached eggs.

**Victoria Square Hotel** ( ☎ 0117-973 9058; www.vicsquare.com; Victoria Sq; s £59-95, d £75-115, f £85-125; 🅿 🖳 wi-fi) Split across two Victorian town houses overlooking a tree-shrouded Clifton square, this hotel is owned by Best Western, so function takes precedence over flair, but most rooms have traces of Victorian character and soft beds.

## Top End

**Berkeley Square Hotel** ( ☎ 0117-925 4000; www.cliftonhotels.com; 15 Berkeley Sq; s £79-137, d £115-180; 🅿 🖳 wi-fi) In the middle of the kind of leafy square in which a nightingale would sing, this hip hotel brings baroque imagination to a Georgian town house. Painted gazelle heads, Day-Glo settees and rococo mirrors dot the lobby, while the bedrooms mix DVD players and gratis sherry with classic finishes.

**Arnos Manor Hotel** ( ☎ 0117-971 1461; www.arnosmanorhotel.co.uk; 470 Bath Rd; s/d from £105/125; 🅿 🖳 wi-fi) Built for the Bristol magnate William Reeve in 1760, this smart hotel has an original crenellated chateau plus an extension tacked on the side. The poshest rooms are in the old building, and boast half-tester beds, spa baths and bags of space; the annexe rooms are more corporate, but still have rubber ducks in the bath.

**Mercure Brigstow Hotel** ( ☎ 0117-929 1030; www.mercure.com; Welsh Back; r midweek £149-250, weekend £99-250; 🖳 wi-fi) Despite an ugly concrete-and-glass facade, this is one of Bristol's funkiest, freshest places to stay. Bedrooms boast trendy floating beds, curved wood-panel walls and tiny TVs set into bathroom tiles. Make sure you bag a room with a river view.

**ourpick Hotel du Vin** ( ☎ 0117-925 5577; www.hotelduvin.com; Narrow Lewins Mead; d £145-160, ste £195-215; 🅿 🖳 wi-fi) This enclave of stylish, sexy luxury is housed in converted sugar warehouses, neatly signalling the sweet indulgence found within. To be found are fabulous futon beds, claw-foot baths, frying-pan showerheads and a mix of chic furniture, industrial beams and iron pillars that grace sumptuous rooms. The stunning double-height loft suites may make you weep when you have to leave.

## EATING

Eating out in Bristol is a real highlight – the city is jammed with restaurants of every description, ranging from classic British 'caffs' to designer dining emporiums.

### Budget

#### RESTAURANTS

**Obento** ( ☎ 0117-929 7392; 69 Baldwin St; mains £4-9; ☼ lunch & dinner Tue-Sun) Somewhere to satisfy those wasabi cravings, this minimalist Japanese restaurant finds diners tucking into teriyaki chicken, fresh sushi and hot noodles at sleek bench tables. Its neatly packaged, three-course bento lunchboxes are practically works of art.

**One Stop Thali Cafe** ( ☎ 0117-942 6687; 12A York Rd; set meal £6.95; ☼ lunch) The bustle and buzz of an Indian street market comes to this cute Montpelier diner, which serves traditional thalis (multicourse Indian dishes) that change depending on what the chef's picked up. It's fresh, spicy and authentic, and the six-course £6.95 menu is ridiculously cheap.

#### CAFES & QUICK EATS

**Bar Chocolat** ( ☎ 0117-974 7000; 19 The Mall; ☼ 9am-6pm Mon-Sat, 11am-5pm Sun) Don't even try to resist this holy temple to the cocoa bean – it'll get you anyway, so succumb with a smile. Hot chocolates, chocolate-flavoured coffees and chocolate with a fair-trade conscience are all on offer at this cosy cafe – just remember to leave room for some handmade chocolates before you leave.

**Pieminister** ( ☎ 0117-942 9500; 24 Stokes Croft; pies £3; ☼ 10am-7pm Sat, 11am-4pm Sun) Offering so much more than just steak 'n' kidney, Pieminister drags the good old British pie into the 21st century. Try the wittily named Poussin Boots (red wine, chicken and pancetta) or the vegie Bush pie (cheddar cheese, cabbage, mushroom and onion).

#### SELF-CATERING

**Papadeli** ( ☎ 0117-973 6569; 84 Alma Rd) This Italian deli is stocked with the kind of zesty flavours and sweet treats you'd normally only find in a Tuscan street market. Fresh pasta salads, salami sandwiches and goats' cheese tarts are served in the main cafe, or you can load up with picnic supplies and Italian cakes at the counter.

**St Nicholas Market** (Corn St; ☼ 9.30am-5pm Mon-Sat) The city's lively street market has a bevy of food stalls selling everything from artisan bread to cheese toasties. Look out for local farmers markets on Wednesdays, and a slow food market on the first Sunday of each month.

### Midrange

**riverstation** ( ☎ 0117-914 4434; The Grove; mains £8-19; ☼ lunch & dinner) Yet another riverside restaurant that satisfies Bristol's style-conscious gourmands – this one is a split-level eatery with a fabulous barrelled roof. The downstairs cafe rustles up light lunches, coffee and featherlight pastries, while up on the 1st floor it's all effortless elegance and European cuisine.

**Clifton Sausage** ( ☎ 0117-973 1192; 7-9 Portland St; mains £10-18; ☼ lunch & dinner) Hog heaven for sausage lovers, this groovy Clifton gastropub serves up no fewer than eight types of bangers 'n' mash, including Gloucester Old Spot and a vegie-friendly cheddar, leek and mustard. Worn wooden floorboards and tables complement the comfort eating – while the rhubarb crumble and sorbet round things off nicely.

**Quartier Vert** ( ☎ 0117-973 4482; 84 Whiteladies Rd; mains £11.50-18.50; ☼ lunch & dinner) The QV has been a Whiteladies staple for two decades, and after several revamps has settled on Spanish and southern Med flavours, supplemented with designer cheeses, sausages, tapas and home-baked bread. Wine-tasting and slow food courses will knock that philistinic palate into shape.

**Severnshed** ( ☎ 0117-925 1212; The Grove; mains from £12; ☼ lunch & dinner) Typifying 'new-Bristol', this former boathouse was built by Brunel – now it's home to a designer bar, bistro and waterside cafe. The renovation is a beautiful blend of industrial trappings and contemporary chrome, while the food is a winning fusion of flavours – try the beef with oyster mushrooms, spicy Thai monkfish or the bouillabaisse. The 977 menu (served before 7pm) features two courses for £9.77.

Other recommendations:

**Mud Dock** ( ☎ 0117-934 9734; 40 The Grove; mains £9-16; ☼ lunch & dinner Mon-Sat, 10am-4.30pm Sun)

Ultratrendy combo of bar, bistro and bike shop, in a brick warehouse by the harbour.

**La Taverna Dell'Artista** ( ☎ 0117-929 7712; 33 King St; mains £13-25; ☺ dinner Tue-Sat) This chaotic, cramped Italian is an old fave with the post-theatre crowd.

## Top End

**Cafe Maitreya** ( ☎ 0117-951 0100; 89 St Marks Rd; 3 courses £20.95; ☺ dinner Tue-Sat) Regularly notching up awards and rave reviews, the Maitreya has firmly established itself as one of the city's most inventive eateries. The seasonal menu is renowned for its culinary creativity, and dabbles in everything from red onion *tartelette* to cashew-nut roulade.

**Glassboat** ( ☎ 0117-929 0704; Welsh Back; lunch mains £7-8, dinner mains £16; ☺ closed Sun) With its floor-to-ceiling glass windows, this double-decked barge has some of the most romantic tables in the city. The fine wood-panelled interior is lit by soft globe lanterns, the menu is a happy marriage of British and French country dishes, and the views across the water are dreamy.

**our pick Bordeaux Quay** ( ☎ 0117-943 1200; Canons Way; brasserie mains £10, restaurant mains £17-21; ☺ lunch & dinner) Funky, friendly, Bordeaux Quay neatly fulfils all your food needs in one: it's a restaurant, brasserie, bar, deli, bakery and cookery school. Its efforts to shrink the food-miles map have produced a menu bursting with organic, seasonal, regionally sourced ingredients, and proves 'sustainable' can equal 'delectable'. Settle down at a sanded wooden table in the cool, calm interior and tuck into the squash and rocket linguini or the roast sea bass with *beurre rouge* (a butter and red-wine sauce). Great, green, guilt-free food.

## DRINKING

The fortnightly listings magazine *Venue* (www.venue.co.uk, £1.50) contains the latest info on what's hot and what's not. The freebie mag *Folio* is published monthly.

**Elbow Room** ( ☎ 0117-930 0242; 64 Park St; ☺ noon-2am Sun-Thu, to 4am Fri & Sat) Part dimly lit bar, part hustler's pool hall, this is a favourite hangout for Bristol's style-conscious crowd. Rack up the balls and knock back the bourbons to a soundtrack of jazz and funk – for budding Fast Eddies, there's a pool competition every Monday.

**Woods** ( ☎ 0117-925 0890; 1 Park St Ave; ☺ 4pm-2am Sun-Thu, to 4am Fri, to 6am Sat) Cultured and cool, this is another haunt for Bristol's beautiful

people, crammed with glitter balls, refectory benches and Victoriana sofas, plus 50 whiskies behind the bar.

**Apple** ( ☎ 0117-925 3500; Welsh Back; ☺ noon-midnight Mon-Sat, to 10.30pm Sun) Bristol's legendary cider boat stocks an impressive 40 varieties of the golden elixir and specialises in organic and craft-produced varieties – staff even offer taster samples (try a tipple of the raspberry and strawberry varieties). You can sip your scrumpy on the covered deck, or at tables that spill over onto the quayside.

**MBargo** ( ☎ 0117-925 3256; 30 Triangle St West; ☺ noon-2am) Marble and leather set the scene for a swanky bar with a huge cocktail list – the soundtrack ranges from 1970s and '80s crowd-pleasers to uberhip hip-hop.

**Hophouse** ( ☎ 0117-923 7390; 16 King's Rd) Lime and chocolate candy stripes, (presumably) ironic flock wallpaper and oh-so-polished wood make this Clifton bar a trendy spot to sip a designer beer and watch the neighbourhood's media types stroll on by.

**Albion** ( ☎ 0117-975 3522; Boyce's Ave) Another venerable pub packed with evening drinkers from Clifton's well-heeled streets.

## ENTERTAINMENT
### Cinemas

**Watershed** ( ☎ 0117-927 5100; www.watershed.co.uk; 1 Canon's Rd) This is the city's leading art-house cinema and digital media centre, specialising in new indie releases and the occasional silver-screen classic.

### Nightclubs

The Bristol club scene moves fast, so check the latest listings to see where the big nights are happening.

**Timbuk2** ( ☎ 0117-945 8459; 22 Small St; admission £5-10; ☺ 9am-2pm) A scruffy-chic club-venue, crammed underneath the arches off Corn St. It hosts a mixed bag of breaks, house, drum 'n' bass and jungle.

**Native** ( ☎ 0117-930 4217; www.nativebristol.co.uk; 15 Small St; admission £5-8; ☺ 10pm-4am) Bristol's top ticket, this tiny 200-cover club is right on the cutting edge, with drum 'n' bass, Latin, jungle, dubstep, hip-hop and jazz all making the playlist, along with a revolving line-up of guest DJs.

**Thekla Social** ( ☎ 0117-929 3301; www.thekla.co.uk; The Grove; admission £5-7; ☺ 9pm-2am) After a hefty refit, Bristol's venerable club-boat is back with nights to cater for all tastes: electro-punk, indie, disco and new wave, plus live gigs and legendary leftfield night Blowpop once a month.

**Carling Academy** (☎ 0117-927 9227; Frogmore St; admission £6-10; ⏱ 10pm-3am Fri & Mon, 7-11pm gig nights) Bristol's original superclub can hold a 2000-strong crowd on its biggest nights, but it's practically never that busy. There's indie and R & B during the week, and big house nights on weekends.

**Cosies** (☎ 0117-942 4110; www.cosies.co.uk; 34 Portland Sq; admission after 9pm £2; ⏱ 10am-2am Thu & Fri, 8pm-2am Sat & Sun, 10am-10pm Mon-Wed) This diminutive club is a real gem, especially if you're sick of the big beats and designer attitude of some of Bristol's larger venues. Upstairs there's a bistro and wine bar, but it's the weekend reggae nights that draw in the crowds.

## Theatre

**Tobacco Factory** (☎ 0117-902 0344; www.tobaccofactory.com; Raleigh Rd) This small-scale theatre venue stages cutting-edge drama and dance. Catch bus 24 or 25 from Broadmead to the Raleigh Rd stop.

The **Bristol Old Vic** (King St) pulled down the curtain and launched a £9 million refurbishment appeal in 2007, to save it from permanent closure. For the latest see www.bristol-old-vic.co.uk.

## Live Music

Big names play at the Carling Academy (see above), while a host of smaller venues feature emerging acts.

**Fleece & Firkin** (☎ 0117-945 0996; www.fleecegigs.co.uk; St Thomas St) A small, intimate venue, much favoured by indie artists and breaking names on the local scene.

**Colston Hall** (☎ 0117-922 3686; www.colstonhall.org; Colston St) Bristol's biggest concert hall hosts everything from big-name comedy to touring bands. A £20 million refit will see a swanky glass and recycled-copper foyer tacked onto the old red-brick building.

**Croft** (☎ 0117-987 4144; www.the-croft.com; 117-119 Stokes Croft) Chilled venue with a policy of supporting new names and Bristol-based artists. There's usually no cover charge if you arrive by 10pm Sunday to Thursday.

## GETTING THERE & AWAY
### Air

**Bristol International Airport** (☎ 0871 334 4344; www.bristolairport.co.uk) is 8 miles southwest of the city. Many flights are holiday charters but there are also scheduled flights to European destinations.

**Air Southwest** (☎ 0870 043 4553; www.airsouthwest.com) Several UK destinations including Jersey, Leeds, Manchester, Newquay and Plymouth.

**easyJet** (☎ 0871 244 2366, per min 10p; www.easyjet.com) Budget flights to UK destinations including Belfast, Edinburgh, Glasgow, Newcastle and Inverness, as well as numerous European cities.

**Ryanair** (☎ 0871 246 0000, per min 10p; www.ryanair.com) Flights to Irish airports including Derry, Dublin and Shannon, as well as European destinations.

### Bus

National Express coaches go to Birmingham (£17, two hours, nine daily), London (£18, 2½ hours, at least hourly), Cardiff (£7, 1¼ hours, nine daily) and Exeter (£12.40, two hours, four daily). There's also a direct daily bus to Nottingham (£26, five hours) and Oxford (£13.80, three hours).

Bus X39 (one hour, several per hour) runs to Bath. Buses 375 and 376 go to Wells (one hour) and Glastonbury (1¼ hours) every half-hour (hourly on Sunday). There are buses to most destinations around Somerset and Wiltshire from Bath and Wells.

### Train

Bristol is an important rail hub, with regular connections to London (£62, 1¾ hours) and the southwest, including Exeter (£19, 1¼ hours), Plymouth (£44, 2½ hours) and Penzance (£60, four hours). **Cross Country** (www.crosscountrytrains.co.uk) trains travel north to Glasgow (£101, 5¾ hours, five direct daily) via Birmingham (£31, 1½ hours, eight direct daily). Most main-line trains arrive at Temple Meads.

Bath makes for an easy day trip (single £5.50, 11 minutes, four per hour).

## GETTING AROUND
### To/From the Airport

Bristol International Flyer runs buses (single/return adult £7/8, child £6/7, 30 minutes, half-hourly 5am to 11pm) to the airport from Marlborough St bus station and Temple Meads train station. A taxi to the airport costs around £25.

### Bicycle

To hire a bike, try the **Ferry Station** (☎ 0117-376 3942; Narrow Quay; half-/full day £7/12; ⏱ 8am-6pm Mon-Fri,

10am-6pm Sat & Sun) on the waterfront or **Blackboy Hill Cycles** ( ☎ 0117-973 1420; 180 Whiteladies Rd; per day £10; ⏰ 9am-5.30pm Mon-Sat). The 13-mile off-road **Bristol to Bath Railway Path** (www.bristolbathrailway path.org.uk) follows the course of an old train track between the two cities. In Bristol pick it up around half a mile northeast of Temple Meads Train Station.

## Boat

The most scenic way to travel around the city is with the **Bristol Ferry Boat Co** ( ☎ 0117-927 3416; www.bristolferry.com), which runs two routes. One is from the city centre to Temple Meads (40 minutes, six to 10 daily April to September, weekends only October to March), stopping at Welsh Back, Bristol Bridge and Castle Park (for Broadmead shopping centre). The other route goes from the city centre to Hotwells (40 minutes, 12 to 16 daily year-round), stopping at the SS *Great Britain* and Mardyke. An adult single fare is £1.60 (child £1.30), or you can pay £7 for a day's unlimited travel (child/family £5/20).

## Bus

Every 15 minutes, bus 73 runs from Parkway Station to the centre (30 minutes). Buses 8 and 9 run every 15 minutes from St Augustine's Pde to Clifton (10 minutes), the foot of Whiteladies Rd and Bristol Zoo Gardens; add another 10 minutes from Temple Meads.

**FirstDay tickets** (adult/child £4/2.80) are valid on all buses for one day in zones one and two, which contain all the key sites. The **FirstFamily ticket** (£7.30) buys one days' travel for two adults and three children, but is only valid after 9am Monday to Friday.

## Car & Motorcycle

Bristol has a seriously confusing one-way system and very heavy traffic – it's best to avoid driving altogether and instead use public transport or the **Park & Ride** ( ☎ 0117-922 2910; before 10am return Mon-Fri £3, after 10am Mon-Fri £2.50, Sat £2), which runs every 10 minutes (Monday to Saturday) from Portway, Bath Rd and Long Ashton. Park & Ride car parks are well signed on routes into the city.

## Taxi

The taxi rank on St Augustine's Pde is a central but rowdy place on weekend nights. There are plenty of companies; try **Streamline Taxis** ( ☎ 0117-926 4001).

# BATH

**pop 90,144**

If you only explore one English city outside London, make it Bath. Tucked into the folds of seven grassy hills and blessed by healing thermal springs, this romantic city of honey-coloured stone blends past and present with imagination and ease. Here you'll find one of the finest Roman bathhouses in the world, extensive, exquisite Regency architecture and a chic new spa that lets you swim alfresco in a heated rooftop pool after a mud wrap and full body massage. With its grand Georgian terraces, Palladian parades and lofty town houses, Bath boasts so many listed buildings that the whole city has been named a World Heritage Site by Unesco. Yes, it can be expensive and too busy for its own good, but add hip hotels, excellent eateries and an absorbing collection of museums and you have one of Britain's most appealing cities. The Romans never had it so good.

## HISTORY

Bath is blessed with natural hot springs; prehistoric peoples probably knew about them – legend has it King Bladud, a Trojan refugee and father of King Lear, founded Bath some 2800 years ago and was cured of leprosy by a dip in the muddy swamps. The Romans established the town of Aquae Sulis in AD 44 and built the extensive thermal baths complex, and a temple to the goddess Sulis-Minerva.

Long after the Romans decamped, the Anglo-Saxons arrived and in 944 a monastery was founded on the site of the present abbey. Throughout the Middle Ages, Bath was an ecclesiastical centre and a wool-trading town and it wasn't until the early 18th century that Richard 'Beau' Nash (an influential socialite and dandy) and Ralph Allen made Bath's bathing complexes the centre of fashionable society. Allen developed the quarries at Coombe Down, constructed Prior Park and employed the two John Woods (father and son) to create the glorious buildings you see today.

As the 18th century wore on, Beau Nash lost his influence and sea bathing started to draw visitors away from Bath, and in 1970 what was then the last spa closed. But the 21st century has brought a revival: Thermae Bath Spa (see boxed text, p334) means you can once again soak in style in those soothing waters, while the £360 million mock-Georgian SouthGate development will add 60 new shops and 100 apartments to the mix.

## ORIENTATION

Like Rome, Bath is famed for its seven hills, and although the city centre is compact it will test your legs. Most street signs are carved into the golden stone of the buildings.

The most obvious landmark is the abbey, across from the Roman Baths and Pump Room. Just under £20 million is being spent on jazzing up Bath's public transport stations – after two years in a temporary home on Avon St, by mid-2009 the bus station will be alongside the train station.

## INFORMATION

Scattered around the city you'll find i-plus points, free touch-screen kiosks providing tourist information.

**Bath Quarterly** (www.bathquarterly.com) Guide to sights, accommodation, restaurants and events.

**Laundrette** (4 Margarets Bldgs; per load £2; ☒ 6am-9pm)

**Main post office** (☎ 0845 722 3344; 27 Northgate St)

**Police station** (☎ 0845-456700; Manvers St; ☒ 7am-midnight)

**Retailer Internet** (☎ 01225-443181; 13 Manvers St; per 20min £1; ☒ 9am-9pm Mon-Sat, 3-9pm Sun)

**Royal United Hospital** (☎ 01225-428331; Combe Park)

**Tourist office** (☎ 0906 711 2000, per min 50p; www.visitbath.co.uk; Abbey Churchyard; ☒ 9.30am-5pm Mon-Sat, 10am-4pm Sun)

**What's On** (www.whatsonbath.co.uk) Up-to-date listing of the city's events and nightlife.

## SIGHTS
### Baths

Ever since the Romans arrived in Bath, life in the city has revolved around the three natural springs that bubble up near the abbey. In typically ostentatious style, the Romans constructed a glorious complex of bathhouses above these thermal waters, to take advantage of their natural temperature – a constant 46°C. The buildings were left to decay after the Romans departed and, apart from a few leprous souls who came looking for a cure in the Middle Ages, it wasn't until the end of the 17th century that Bath's restorative waters again became fashionable. It's no longer possible to take a dip in the Roman Baths themselves; for modern-day dunks head for the sparkling new Thermae Bath Spa (see boxed text, p334).

The 2000-year-old baths now form one of the best-preserved ancient Roman spas in the world. The **Roman Baths Museum** (☎ 01225-477785; www.romanbaths.co.uk; Abbey Churchyard; adult/child £11/6.80, incl Fashion Museum £14/8.30; ☒ 9am-6pm Mar-Jun, Sep & Oct, 9am-10pm Jul & Aug, 9.30am-5.30pm Nov-Feb) gets very, very busy in summer; you can usually dodge the worst crowds by visiting early on a midweek morning, or by avoiding July and August. An audio guide (read by the bestselling author Bill Bryson) is included in the admission price.

The first sight inside the complex is the **Great Bath**. Head down to water level and along the raised walkway to see the Roman paving and lead base. A series of excavated passages and chambers beneath street level leads off in several directions and lets you inspect the remains of other smaller baths and hypocaust (heating) systems.

One of the most picturesque corners of the complex is the 12th-century **King's Bath**, built around the original sacred spring; 1.5 million litres of hot water still pour into the pool every day. You can see the ruins of the vast **Temple of Sulis-Minerva** under the **Pump Room**, and recent excavations of the **East Baths** give an insight into its 4th-century form.

### Bath Abbey

Edgar, the first king of united England, was crowned in a church in Abbey Courtyard in 973, but the present **Bath Abbey** (☎ 01225-422462; www.bathabbey.org; requested donation £2.50; ☒ 9am-6pm Mon-Sat Easter-Oct, to 4.30pm Nov-Easter, plus 1-2.30pm & 4.30-5.30pm Sun year-round) was built between 1499 and 1616, making it the last great medieval church raised in England. The nave's wonderful fan vaulting was erected in the 19th century.

Outside, the most striking feature is the west facade, where angels climb up and down stone ladders, commemorating a dream of the founder, Bishop Oliver King. The abbey boasts the second-largest collection of wall monuments after Westminster Abbey. Among those buried here are Sir Isaac Pitman, who devised the Pitman method of shorthand, and Beau Nash.

On the abbey's southern side, steps lead down to the small **Heritage Vaults Museum** (admission free; ☒ 10am-3.30pm Mon-Sat), which explores the abbey's history and its links with the nearby baths. It also contains fine stone bosses, archaeological artefacts and a weird model of the 10th-century monk Aelfric, dressed in his traditional black Benedictine habit.

**SOUTHWEST ENGLAND**

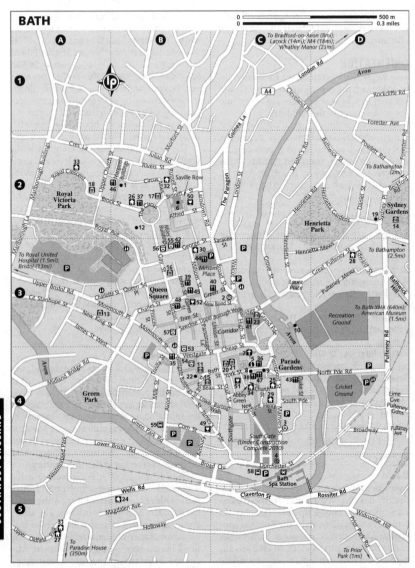

**BATH**

SOUTHWEST ENGLAND

## Royal Crescent & The Circus

The crowning glory of Georgian Bath and the city's most prestigious address is Royal Crescent, a semicircular terrace of majestic houses overlooking a private lawn and the green sweep of Royal Victoria Park. Designed by John Wood the Younger (1728–82) and built between 1767 and 1775, the houses

would have originally been rented for the season by wealthy socialites. These days flats on the crescent are still keenly sought after, and entire houses almost never come up for sale.

For a glimpse into the splendour and razzle-dazzle of Georgian life, head for **No 1 Royal Crescent** ( ☎ 01225-428126; www.bath-preservation-trust.org.uk; adult/child £5/2.50; ☒ 10.30am-5pm

Tue-Sun Feb-Oct, to 4pm Nov), which contains an astonishing amount of period furniture. Only materials available during the 18th century were used in its refurbishment, so it's about as authentically Georgian as you can get; the same can't be said for the endearingly hammy staff dressed in period costume.

A walk east along Brock St from the Royal Crescent leads to the **Circus**, a magnificent circle of 30 houses. Plaques on the houses commemorate famous residents such as Thomas Gainsborough, Clive of India and David Livingstone. To the south is the restored 18th-century **Georgian Garden**, where gravel replaces grass (to protect women's long dresses from unsightly stains).

## Assembly Rooms & Fashion Museum

Opened in 1771, the city's glorious **Assembly Rooms** ( ☎ 01225-477789; Bennett St; admission free; ⏰ 11am-6pm Mar-Oct, to 5pm Nov-Feb) were where fashionable Bath socialites once gathered to waltz, play cards and listen to the latest chamber music. You're free to wander around the rooms, as long as they haven't been reserved for a special function. Highlights include the card room, tearoom and the truly splendid ballroom, all of which are lit by their original 18th-century chandeliers.

In the basement, the **Fashion Museum** ( ☎ 01225-477173; www.fashionmuseum.co.uk; adult/child £7/5, incl Roman Baths Museum £14/8.30; ⏰ 10.30am-5pm

Mar-Oct, to 4pm Nov-Feb) displays costumes worn from the 16th to late-20th centuries, including some alarming crinolines that would have forced women to approach doorways side on.

## Jane Austen Centre

Bath is known to many as a location in Jane Austen's novels. *Persuasion* and *Northanger Abbey* were both largely set in the city; the writer visited it many times and lived here from 1801 to 1806 (a plaque marks one of her former houses at **No 4 Sydney Pl**, opposite the Holburne Museum). The author's connections with the city are explored at the **Jane Austen Centre** ( ☎ 01225-443000; www.janeausten.co.uk; 40 Gay St; adult/child £6.50/3.50; ⏰ hours vary), where displays also include period costume and contemporary prints of Bath.

## Other Museums

Housed in an 18th-century Gothic chapel, the **Building of Bath Museum** ( ☎ 01225-333895; www .bath-preservation-trust.org.uk; The Vineyards, The Paragon; admission £4; ⏰ 10.30am-5pm Tue-Sun mid-Feb–Nov) details how Bath's Georgian splendour came into being, tracing the city's evolution from a sleepy spa town to one of the centres of Georgian society. There are some intriguing displays on contemporary construction methods, and the museum also explores the way in which social class and interior decor

**BATH'S REBIRTH**

Larking about in the Roman Baths might be off the agenda, but thankfully you can still sample the city's curative waters at **Thermae Bath Spa** ( ☎ 0844 888 0844; www.thermaebathspa.com; Hot Bath St; New Royal Bath spa session per 2hr/4hr/day £22/32/52, spa packages from £65; ☿ New Royal Bath 9am-10pm). Here the old **Cross Bath**, incorporated into an ultramodern shell of local stone and plate glass, is now the setting for a variety of spa packages. The New Royal Bath ticket includes steam rooms, waterfall shower and a choice of bathing venues – including the jaw-dropping open-air rooftop pool, where you can swim in the thermal waters in front of a backdrop of Bath's stunning cityscape. Other exotic treatments include peat baths, body cocoons, Vichy showers and the ominous-sounding 'Kraxen stove' (an Alpine hay chamber, apparently).

Across the street are treatment rooms above the old **Hot Bath**, while the Hetling Pump Room, opposite, houses a **visitor centre** ( ☿ 10am-5pm Mon-Sat, to 4pm Sun) that explores the history of bathing in Bath.

were intimately linked during the Georgian era; heaven forbid should you use a wallpaper that outstripped your station…

The 18th-century **Holburne Museum** ( ☎ 01225-466669; Great Pulteney St; adult/child £4.50/3.50; ☿ 10am-5pm Tue-Sat, 11am-5pm Sun) houses the booty of Sir William Holburne, a 19th-century Bath resident who brought together an outstanding collection of porcelain, antiques and paintings by great 18th-century artists such as Gainsborough, Turner and Guardi.

In 1781 astronomer William Herschel discovered Uranus from the garden of his home, which now houses the **Herschel Museum of Astronomy** ( ☎ 01225-446865; 19 New King St; adult/child £4/2.50; ☿ 1-5pm Mon, Tue, Thu & Fri, 11am-5pm Sat & Sun Feb-Dec). The house is decorated as it would have been in the 18th century; an astrolabe in the garden marks where Herschel would probably have placed his telescope.

The **Victoria Art Gallery** ( ☎ 01225-477233; www.victoriagal.org.uk; Pulteney Bridge; admission free; ☿ 10am-5pm Tue-Sat, 1.30-5pm Sun) houses the city's main arts collection, with most items dating from the 15th to 20th centuries. There are some particularly fine canvases by Gainsborough, Turner and Sickert, as well as a wonderful series of Georgian caricatures from the wicked pens of artists such as James Gillray and Thomas Rowlandson.

The **American Museum** ( ☎ 01225-460503; www.americanmuseum.org; Claverton Manor; adult/child £7.50/4; ☿ noon-5pm Tue-Sun mid-Mar–Oct) houses a collection of stateside artefacts, memorabilia and furniture dating from the 17th century. There are 15 individually decorated rooms scattered around the manor house, including a suitably sparse Shaker Room and a New Orleans room, decked out in the lavish style of a plantation

villa. Even the trees and plants in the surrounding grounds have a Yankee provenance. The museum is 2 miles southeast of the city centre; bus 18 and several other buses to the university stop nearby.

The **Museum of East Asian Art** ( ☎ 01225-464640; www.meaa.org.uk; 12 Bennett St; adult/child £4/1.50; ☿ 10am-5pm Tue-Sat, noon-5pm Sun) contains more than 500 jade, bamboo, porcelain and bronze objects from Cambodia, Korea and Thailand, and substantial Chinese and Japanese carvings, ceramics and lacquerware.

## TOURS
### Guided Tours

The most popular, and daftest, guided stroll around the city is the **Bizarre Bath Comedy Walk** ( ☎ 01225-335124; www.bizarrebath.co.uk; adult/student £8/5; ☿ 8pm Mar-Sep), a chaotic and frequently hilarious blend of street theatre, live performance and guided tour. Wallflowers be warned – you'll probably find yourself being roped into the act whether you like it or not. Tours leave from outside the Huntsman Inn on North Parade Passage (south of York St) and last about 1½ hours.

**Jane Austen's Bath** ( ☎ 01225-443000; adult/child £5/4) focuses on the Georgian city and sites associated with the author. Tours leave from the Abbey Churchyard at 11am on Saturday, Sunday and bank holidays.

The free, two-hour **Mayor's Guide walking tour** ( ☎ 01225-477411; www.thecityofbath.co.uk), a good all-round introduction to Bath, sets off from outside the Pump Room at 10.30am and 2pm Sunday to Friday, and at 10.30am Saturday. From May to September there are additional tours at 7pm on Tuesday, Friday and Saturday.

**Bath City Sightseeing** ( ☎ 01225-330444; www .city-sightseeing.com) provides a hop-on hop-off **city tour** (adult/child £10/6; ⏰ 9.30am-5pm Mar-May, Oct & Nov, to 6.30pm Jun-Sep) on an open-topped bus. Commentary is in seven languages. Buses stop every 20 minutes or so at various points around town. There's also a second route, the **Skyline tour**, that runs year round and travels out to Prior Park; the same tickets are valid on both routes.

There are also minibus tours to some of the surrounding attractions around Bath:

**Mad Max Tours** ( ☎ 07990 505970; www.madmax tours.co.uk) One-day tours to Stonehenge, Avebury, Lacock and Castle Combe (£27.50), and half-day tours to Stonehenge and Lacock (£15).

**Scarper Tours** ( ☎ 07739 644155; www.scarpertours .com) Twice-daily tour to Stonehenge (adult/child £14/8).

## Boat Trips

Various cruise operators offer boat trips up and down the River Avon; try **Bath City Boat Trips** ( ☎ 07974 560197; www.bathcityboattrips.com; adult/ child £7/5; ⏰ 11am-5pm) or the **Pulteney Princess** ( ☎ 07791 910650; www.pulteneyprincess.co.uk; adult/child £7/3; ⏰ 11.30am-5pm). Trips for both companies leave from the landing stage just to the east of Pulteney Bridge.

For cruises to Bristol, see p325.

## FESTIVALS & EVENTS

The annual events calendar in Bath would keep even the most demanding Georgian socialite busy, with a varied program of music, arts and theatre throughout the year. **Bath Festivals** ( ☎ 01225-463362; www.bathfestivals.org.uk; 2 Church St; ⏰ 9.30am-5.30pm Mon-Sat) has an overview and handles all bookings.

**Bath Literature Festival** (www.bathlitfest.org.uk) This annual festival takes place in late February or early March, and attracts bookworms and big-name authors alike.

**Bath International Music Festival** (www.bathmusicfest .org.uk) From mid-May to early June this festival takes over the city, with a main program of classical music and opera, as well as jazz, world and folk gigs in the city's smaller venues.

**Bath Fringe Festival** (www.bathfringe.co.uk) Hits town around mid-May to early June; it's the biggest fringe festival in Britain after Edinburgh, with all kinds of theatre shows and street acts dotted around town.

**Jane Austen Festival** (www.janeausten.co.uk/festival/) Held in September, the highlight of this festival is a grand Georgian costumed parade through the city's streets, all the way to the Royal Crescent.

**Mozartfest** (www.bathmozartfest.org.uk) Takes place annually in mid-October.

**Bath Film Festival** (www.bathfilmfestival.org.uk) Held in early November.

## SLEEPING

Bath gets incredibly busy; the tourist office books rooms for a £3 fee, and sells the brochure *Bath & Beyond* (£1; free through the website). If you can, avoid weekends, when room prices can rise dramatically.

### Budget

**Bath Backpackers' Hostel** ( ☎ 01225-446787; bath@ hostels.co.uk; 13 Pierrepont St; dm £12-13; 🖳 ) It may be grungy (expect peeling paint, worn carpets and saggy beds), but Bath's indie hostel is a friendly affair and slap-bang in the middle of town. There's a party 'dungeon' in the cellar, no curfew and a fair bit of noise at night.

**Bath YHA** ( ☎ 0845 371 9303; www.yha.org.uk; dm £14, d from £35; 🅿 🖳 ) Hostels don't come much grander than this Italianate mansion, a steep climb (or a short hop on bus 18) from the city centre. The refurbished rooms are surprisingly modern and many look out across the private tree-lined gardens; book early if you're after a double.

### Midrange

There's a wide range of midrange options; generally you'll get better value for money the further you head from the city centre.

**Oldfields** ( ☎ 01225-317984; www.oldfields.co.uk; 102 Wells Rd; s £49-99, d £65-135, f from £85; 🅿 ) This has to be one of the best deals in Bath: spacious rooms and soft beds for comfort; brass bedsteads and antique chairs for character; and Laura Ashley fabrics and Molton Brown bathstuffs for luxury. It's all wrapped up in a lemon-coloured stone house with views over Bath's rooftops.

**Paradise House** ( ☎ 01225-317723; www.paradise -house.co.uk; 88 Holloway; s £60-115, d £65-170; 🅿 ) If the tourist crowds become too much for you, beat a retreat to this chimney-crowned villa and its charming walled garden. It's an old-world treat, with half-tester beds, gilded mirrors and oil paintings in the drawing room, and a lighter palette in the bedrooms (plus Jacuzzis and four-posters for the high-rollers).

**Henry Guest House** ( ☎ 01225-424052; www.thehenry .com; 6 Henry St; s £35-65, d £70-130, f from £105) Some of the best-value rooms in town are just five minutes' walk from the centre of Bath, at this stylish Georgian terrace. Crisp linens and a judicious scattering of cushions give the rooms a light, airy feel; the odd ornate fire-place and mock-Georgian chair help with the heritage mood.

**Dorian House** ( ☎ 01225-426336; www.dorianhouse .co.uk; 1 Upper Oldfield Park; s £65-78, d £80-155; P ⬜ wi-fi) Owned by a cellist with the London Symphony Orchestra, this chic B&B is a symphony of sumptuous style. The marble bathrooms, scattered antiques, elaborate floor tiles and plush throws all chime together perfectly, with never a duff note.

**Three Abbey Green** ( ☎ 01225-428558; www.three abbeygreen.com; 3 Abbey Green; d £85-125, f £125-175) Built when 'Beau' Nash was a teenager, this great-value B&B sits near the abbey in the kind of secluded square around which he would have strolled. It's not quite as stylish as the dandy inside, where simplicity and smartness see plain whites offset by tartan checks or colour tints.

**Brocks** ( ☎ 01225-338374; www.brocksguesthouse.com; 32 Brock St; d £87-125) Part of the Georgian terrace linking the Circus and the Royal Crescent, Brocks nestles in the heart of elegant Bath. Teddy bears sit in lemon, cream and blue rooms – the ones to the rear have views of yet more classy architecture and the leafy hills beyond.

Also recommended:

**Abbey Rise** ( ☎ 01225-316177; www.abbeyrise.co.uk; 97 Wells Rd; s £48-58, d £68-78, f £75-90; P ) Attractively refurbished, contemporary B&B whose owner trained as a housekeeper at Buckingham Palace.

**Milsoms** ( ☎ 01225-750128; www.milsomshotel.co.uk; 24 Milsom St; d from £85) Smooth city-chic and cocoabean colours above Loch Fyne Restaurant.

## Top End

**ourpick Queensberry Hotel** ( ☎ 01225-447928; www .thequeensberry.co.uk; 4 Russell St; s £95-300, d £105-425; P ) One to save your pennies for – this boutique barnstormer is sexy, swanky and super. It's hidden away in four town houses, where modern fabrics, muted colour schemes and funky throws meet polished wardrobes, feature fireplaces and Zen-tinged furniture. Gleaming bathrooms house his 'n' hers sinks and posh smellies, while designer-print cushions pepper sofas and oversized beds. The walled garden is a chilled refuge from the city fizz. Prepare to be pampered.

**Dukes** ( ☎ 01225-787960; www.dukesbath.co.uk; Great Pulteney St; s £115, d £135-175, ste £170-215; P ) The rooms at this Grade I–listed Palladian pile are some of the most regal you'll find in Bath. Themes include Asian finery, Italianate splendour, English

botanica or French baroque – either way, you get original cornicing and carved plasterwork.

**Royal Crescent Hotel** ( ☎ 01225-823333; www.royal-crescent.co.uk; 16 Royal Cres; d £290-850; P ⬜ wi-fi) Set right in the middle of the poshest postcode in town, this opulent hotel's ornaments and antiques would have welcomed guests in the 18th century. Expect paintings by Gainsborough, a sweeping secret garden and more chaises longues, chandeliers and sash windows than your average royal palace.

# EATING

As befits a historic watering hole, Bath has some top-notch restaurants. Look out for TV chef Jamie Oliver's new Milsom Pl eatery, **Jamie's Italian** (www.jamieoliver.com/Italian) – it wasn't yet open at the time of writing, but we expect that its quality will match that of Jamie's other restaurants.

## Budget

### RESTAURANTS

**Sally Lunn's** ( ☎ 01225-461634; 4 North Parade Passage; lunch mains £5-6, dinner mains from £8; ☽ lunch & dinner) People have been taking afternoon tea here since the 1680s, and it's still high on many a tourist to-do list. The atmosphere – quintessential English chintz – makes it a genteel spot to devour the trademark Sally Lunn's bun.

**Walrus & the Carpenter** ( ☎ 01225-314864; 28 Barton St; mains £7-15; ☽ lunch & dinner) Another Bath classic, this bistro eschews snootiness in favour of a homelier mix of mismatched furniture, chummy service and down-home food. The menu's divided into 'befores' and 'afters' – the kebabs, moussakas and huge burgers are old faves.

### CAFES & QUICK EATS

**Boston Tea Party** ( ☎ 01225-313901; 19 Kingsmead Sq; mains from £4; ☽ 7.30am-7pm Mon-Sat, from 8.30am Sun) With a lovely outside terrace spilling onto Kingsmead Sq, the Bath outpost of this small southwest franchise is always full to bursting at lunchtime – thanks to its prodigious selection of sandwiches, homemade soups and sweet treats.

**Cafe Retro** ( ☎ 01225-339347; 18 York St; mains £5-11; ☽ breakfast, lunch & dinner Tue-Sat, breakfast & lunch Mon) A place to make a stand (well, actually a laid-back 'sit') against bland, insidious global coffee-shop chains, Cafe Retro is a quirky gem. Settle down alongside Bath's boho trendies and munch a burger, linger over brunch or sink a salad – smashing.

**SELF-CATERING**

**Deli Shush** ( ☎ 01225-443563; 8A Guildhall Market; ⏲ 8am-5.30pm Mon-Sat) Serrano ham, antipasti, samosas and 20 types of olives fill the shelves of this designer deli that's set inside the Guildhall Market. You'll also find delicious crêpes, tangy cheeses and a wealth of other takeaway goodies at the nearby stalls.

**our pick Paxton & Whitfield** ( ☎ 01225-466403; 1 John St; ⏲ Mon-Sat) Cheese lovers be warned – you will simply never want to leave. This upmarket fromagerie overflows with utterly oozing brie, whiffy Stilton and the kind of extra-mature cheddar that makes your tongue stick to the roof of your mouth. If they could bottle the smell they could sell that, too.

## Midrange

**Circus** ( ☎ 01225-318918; 34 Brock St; lunch mains £7, dinner mains £11; ⏲ lunch & dinner Mon-Sat) As elegant as the architectural edifices that surround it, this bistro near the Royal Crescent plays on its superchic surrounds. The ladies who lunch like the fresh, fashionable food, too.

**Firehouse Rotisserie** ( ☎ 01225-482070; 2 John St; mains £11-15; ⏲ lunch & dinner Mon-Sat) Stateside flavours and a Californian vibe characterise this excellent American restaurant, run by a couple of ex-LA chefs. The menu evokes Mexico and the deep South, with signature dishes including rotisserie chicken, Louisiana catfish and Texan steak.

**Demuth's** ( ☎ 01225-446059; 2 North Parade Passage; mains £11.50-16; ⏲ lunch & dinner) Having made Bath's vegetarians smile for more than 20 years, Demuth's still delights. Imaginative, superbly flavoured seasonal fare includes asparagus tart, spinach and chickpea curry, and a 'vitality salad'. If that sounds too healthy, finish off with the devilish apricot and calvados tart.

**Onefishtwofish** ( ☎ 01225-330236; 10A North Pde; mains £13-18; ⏲ dinner Tue-Sun) Tables are crammed in under a barrel-brick roof, full of twinkly light in this cosy cellar restaurant. Seafood is shipped in from Devon ports, and chefs cook up everything from wonton salmon to Marseillaise bouillabaisse.

**our pick Pinch** ( ☎ 01225-421251; 11 Margarets Bldgs; 2-course lunch £10, dinner mains £14-20; ⏲ lunch & dinner Wed-Sat) Pinch brings the flavours of Bordeaux, Burgundy and the Left Bank to Bath, many Brits will dearly wish there were

more snug eateries like this over here. The menu is packed with duck, rabbit, langoustine and beef and is suffused with classic French flavours: garlic and thyme; cinnamon and saffron; Champagne and brandy.

Also recommended:

**FishWorks** ( ☎ 01225-448707; 6 Green St; mains from £13; ⏲ lunch & dinner) 'Pick your own' dinner at this fab fishmonger-cum-seafood restaurant.

**Parisienne** ( ☎ 01225-447147; Milsom Place; mains £7-13; ⏲ breakfast & lunch) Croissants and *moules marinières* (mussels cooked in a wine and onion sauce) bring a soupçon of Left Bank cafe-culture to Bath.

## Top End

**Olive Tree Restaurant** ( ☎ 01225-447928; 4 Russell St; lunch/dinner mains £14/18; ⏲ lunch Tue-Sun, dinner daily) Break out the glad-rags – the Queensberry Hotel's (opposite) restaurant is a posh, pricey extravaganza of boutique British cuisine. You'll need a gastronomic glossary – expect galantine of wood pigeon and dark chocolate *panna cotta* with griottine cherries.

**Hole in the Wall** ( ☎ 01225-425242; 16 George St; mains £15-20; ⏲ lunch & dinner Mon-Sat) This long-standing favourite with Bath's gourmands takes you on a cook's tour through Anglo-French flavours – braised pork with Puy lentils, or Chew Magna lamb with potato fondant. The cellar dining room is half country restaurant, half urbane elegance.

## DRINKING

**Common Room** ( ☎ 01225-425550; 2 Saville Row; ⏲ 6pm-2am Mon-Sar) Next door to an anarchic antiques shop, this tiny little bar is a favourite with Bath's beautiful people. It's got all the designer credentials – exposed brickwork, blondwood floors, black leather sofas – and a more chilled atmosphere than at the drinking dens on George St.

**Raven** ( ☎ 01225-425045; Queen St) Highly respected by real-ale aficionados, this fine city drinking den commands a devoted following for its well-kept beer, traditional atmosphere and blues and jazz nights.

**Porter** ( ☎ 01225-424104; George St) It's somehow typical of Bath that it has a vegetarian pub; this spit-and-sawdust affair is run by the folk behind Moles nightclub and it's usually jammed to the rafters on Friday and Saturday nights.

**Bath Tap** ( ☎ 01225-404344; 19-20 St James Pde; ⏲ to 2am Thu-Sat) The classic pub hang-out for Bath's gay community, with a late weekend licence and a fun range of theme nights ranging from drag to cabaret.

**Crystal Palace** ( ☎ 01225-482666; Abbey Green) You couldn't ask for a nicer location for this popular pub, tucked away in the shadow of the abbey on a tree-shaded green. Local beers and a gorgeous patio garden make this a top spot for a quiet pint.

## ENTERTAINMENT

*Venue* magazine (www.venue.co.uk; £1.50) has comprehensive listings of Bath's theatre, music and gig scenes. Pick up a copy at any newsagency.

### Nightclubs

**Moles** ( ☎ 01225-404445; www.moles.co.uk; 14 George St; admission £5-7; ⦿ 9pm-2am Mon-Thu, to 4am Fri & Sat, 8pm-12.30am Sun) The best venue in town continues to go from strength to strength, hosting a regular line-up of cutting-edge new acts and breaking bands, as well as occasional club nights.

**Porter Cellar Bar** ( ☎ 01225-424104; George St; ⦿ 11.30am-midnight Mon-Thu, to 1am Fri & Sat, noon-11.30pm Sun) Just across the street and also run by the folk at Moles, this crowded, rustic venue hosts the bands who aren't yet big enough to play at the larger venue.

**Delfter Krug** ☎ 01225-443352; Sawclose; ⦿ noon-late Mon-Sat) A massive, rambling pub opposite the theatre, equipped for all eventualities – upstairs club for housey tunes and DJs, downstairs bar for dedicated drinkers, and a street terrace for when the weather's fine.

### Theatre & Cinemas

**Theatre Royal** ( ☎ 01225-448844; www.theatreroyal. org.uk; Sawclose) This high-class theatre features drama, opera and ballet in the main auditorium, experimental productions in the Ustinov Studio, and young people's theatre at 'the egg'.

**Little Theatre** ( ☎ 0871 704 2061; St Michael's Pl) Bath's art-house cinema, screening fringe and foreign-language flicks.

## GETTING THERE & AWAY

Bath's bus and train stations are having a multimillion-pound revamp. By mid-2009 the bus station should have left its temporary home of Avon St and be back alongside the train station on Dorchester St.

### Bus

National Express coaches run to London (£21.25, 3½ hours, 10 daily) via Heathrow

(£17.50, 2¾ hours), and to Bristol (45 minutes, every 30 minutes) for buses to the north. Services to most other cities require a change at Bristol or Heathrow.

Buses X39 and 339 (55 minutes, several per hour) and 332 (50 minutes, hourly, seven on Sunday) run to Bristol. Other useful services include X71 and X72 to Devizes (one hour, hourly Monday to Saturday, six on Sunday) and 173 and 773 to Wells (1¼ hours, hourly Monday to Saturday, seven on Sunday).

### Train

There are trains to London Paddington (£60.50, 1½ hours, half-hourly) and Cardiff (£14.90, 1¼ hours, four hourly), and several each hour to Bristol (£5.50, 11 minutes), from where you can connect with the mainline trains to northern England and the southwest.

Trains travel approximately hourly to Oxford (£17.20, 1½ hours, change at Didcot Parkway), Weymouth (£12.60, two hours) and Dorchester West (£12.30, 1¾ hours); and Portsmouth (£29, 2½ hours) hourly via Salisbury (£13, one hour).

## GETTING AROUND
### Bicycle

The 13-mile **Bristol & Bath Railway Path** (www .bristolbathrailwaypath.org.uk) runs along the disused track of the old Midland Railway, which was decommissioned in the late 1960s. At the time of going to press there weren't any bike-hire companies operating in Bath, so you could bring your own bike, or hire a bike in Bristol and start the ride there (for bike hire in Bristol, see p329).

### Bus

Bus 18 runs from the bus station, High St and Great Pulteney St up Bathwick Hill past the YHA to the university every 10 minutes. Bus 4 runs every 20 minutes to Bathampton from the same places. A FirstDay pass for unlimited bus travel in the city costs £4/2.70 per adult/child.

### Car & Motorcycle

Bath has serious traffic problems (especially at rush hour). **Park & Ride** ( ☎ 01225-394041; ⦿ 6.15am-7.30pm) services operate at Lansdown to the north, Newbridge to the west and Odd Down to the south (tickets return £2.50, 10 minutes to the centre, every 10 to 15 minutes).

# SOMERSET

Sleepy Somerset provides the type of pleasing pastoral wanderings that are reminiscent of a simpler, calmer, kinder world. Its landscape of knotted hedgerows, hummocked hills and russet-coloured fields is steeped in ancient rites and scattered with ancient sites. The cloistered calm of the cathedral city of Wells acts as a springboard for the spectacular limestone caves and gorges around Cheddar, while hippie haven Glastonbury adds an ancient abbey, mud-drenched festival and masses of Arthurian myth. Whether you're into 'Olde Worlde' or New Age, this is a place to wander, ponder and drink in the sights at your own laid-back pace.

## Orientation & Information

Somerset hugs the coast of the Bristol Channel. The Mendip Hills (the Mendips) follow a line below Bristol, just north of Wells and Cheddar, while the Quantock Hills (the Quantocks) sit just east of Exmoor National Park (p345). Most places of interest are in northern Somerset. Bath makes a good base in the east; Glastonbury and Wells are more central options.

Individual towns have tourist offices; the **Somerset Visitor Centre** ( ☎ 01934-750833; www .visitsomerset.co.uk; Sedgemoor Services M5 South, Axbridge; ☼ 9.15am-5pm daily Easter-Oct, Mon-Fri Nov-Easter) provides general information.

## Getting Around

Most buses in Somerset are operated by **First** ( ☎ 0845 606 4446; www.firstgroup.com), supplemented by a few smaller operators. For timetables and general travel information contact **Traveline South West** ( ☎ 0871 200 22 33; www.travelinesw.com). Area timetables are available at bus stations and tourist offices.

Key train services link Bath, Bristol, Bridgwater, Taunton and Weston-Super-Mare. The M5 heads south past Bristol, to Bridgwater and Taunton, with the A39 leading west across the Quantocks to Exmoor.

## WELLS
### pop 10,406

With Wells, small is beautiful. This tiny, picturesque metropolis is England's smallest city, and only qualifies for the 'city' title thanks to a magnificent medieval cathedral, which sits in the centre beside the grand Bishop's Palace.

Wells has been the main seat of ecclesiastical power in this part of Britain since the 12th century, and is still the official residence of the Bishop of Bath and Wells. Medieval buildings and cobbled streets radiate out from the cathedral green to a marketplace that has been the bustling heart of Wells for some nine centuries (Wednesday and Saturday are market days). Wells' excellent restaurants and busy shops help make it a good launching pad for exploring northern Somerset.

## Information

**Tourist office** ( ☎ 01749-672552; www.wellstourism .com; Market Pl; ☼ 9.30am-5.30pm Mon-Sat & 10am-4pm Sun Easter-Oct, 10am-4pm Mon-Sat Nov-Easter) Stocks the *Wells City Trail* leaflet (30p) and sells discount tickets to the nearby attractions of Wookey Hole and Cheddar Gorge.
**Wells Laundrette** ( ☎ 01458-830409; 39 St Cuthbert St; ☼ 8am-8pm) Opposite St Cuthbert's Church.

## Sights
### WELLS CATHEDRAL

Set in a marvellous medieval close, the **Cathedral Church of St Andrew** ( ☎ 01749-674483; www.wellsca thedral.org.uk; Chain Gate, Cathedral Green; requested donation adult/child £5.50/2.50; ☼ 7am-7pm Apr-Sep, 7am-dusk Oct-Mar) was built in stages between 1180 and 1508. The building incorporates several Gothic styles, but its most famous asset is the wonderful **west front**, an immense sculpture gallery decorated with more than 300 figures, built in the 13th century and restored to its original splendour in 1986. The facade would once have been painted in vivid colours, but has long since reverted to its original sandy hue. Apart from the figure of Christ, installed in 1985 in the uppermost niche, all the figures are original.

Inside, the most striking feature is the pair of **scissor arches** separating the nave from the choir, designed to counter the subsidence of the central tower. High up in the north transept is a wonderful **mechanical clock** dating from 1392 – the second-oldest surviving in England after the one at Salisbury Cathedral (p312). The clock shows the position of the planets and the phases of the moon.

Other highlights are the elegant **lady chapel** (1326) at the eastern end and the seven **effigies** of Anglo-Saxon bishops ringing the choir. The 15th-century **chained library** houses books and manuscripts dating back to 1472. It's only open at certain times during the year or by prior arrangement.

From the north transept follow the worn steps to the glorious **Chapter House** (1306), with its delicate ceiling ribs sprouting like a palm from a central column. Externally, look out for the **Chain Bridge** built from the northern side of the cathedral to Vicars' Close to enable clerics to reach the cathedral without getting their robes wet. The **cloisters** on the southern side surround a pretty courtyard.

**Guided tours** (⌣ Mon-Sat) of the cathedral are free, and usually take place every hour. As you wander, keep an eye out for the cathedral cat, a ginger tabby called Louis.

### CATHEDRAL CLOSE

Wells Cathedral forms the centrepiece of a cluster of ecclesiastical buildings dating back to (and even earlier than) the Middle Ages. Facing the west front, on the left are the 15th-century **Old Deanery** and the **Wells & Mendip Museum** (☎ 01749-673477; 8 Cathedral Green; www.wellsmuseum.org.uk; adult/child £3/1; ⌣ 10am-5.30pm daily Easter-Oct, 11am-4pm Wed-Mon Nov-Easter), with exhibits on local life, cathedral architecture and the infamous Witch of Wookey Hole.

Further along, **Vicars' Close** is a stunning cobbled street of uniform houses dating back to the 14th century, with a chapel at the end; members of the cathedral choir still live here. It is thought to be the oldest complete medieval street in Europe. Passing under the Chain Bridge, inspect the outside of the Lady chapel and a lovely medieval house called the Rib, before emerging at a main road called the Liberty.

**Penniless Porch**, a corner gate leading onto Market Sq and built by Bishop Bekynton around 1450, is so-called because beggars asked for alms here.

### BISHOP'S PALACE

Beyond the cathedral, the moated 13th-century **Bishop's Palace** (☎ 01749-678691; www.bishopspalacewells.co.uk; adult/child £5.50/1.10; ⌣ 10.30am-6pm Sun-Fri & 10.30am-2pm Sat Jan-Oct, 10.30am-3.30pm Wed-Sun Nov & Dec) is a real delight. Purportedly the oldest inhabited building in England, ringed by water and surrounded by a huge fortified wall, the palace complex contains several fine Italian Gothic state rooms, an imposing Great Hall and beautiful tree-shaded gardens. The natural wells that gave the city its name bubble up in the palace's grounds, feeding the moat and the fountain in the market square. The swans in the moat have been trained to ring a bell outside one of the windows when they want to be fed.

## Sleeping

**Islington Farm** (☎ 01749-673445; www.islingtonfarmatwells.co.uk; Silver St; s/d £50/65; P ) Set beside a rushing stream, this ivy-clad farmhouse is two minutes' walk south of the city centre and yet still has idyllic rural views. Snug rooms have all the beams, fireplaces and old-world charm you could want. A self-catering cottage in the old stables sleeps four (£650 per week).

**our pick** **Beryl** (☎ 01749-678738; www.beryl-wells.co.uk; Hawkers Lane; s £65-75, d £85-120; P ) A mile from the city centre, this tree-shaded, gabled Victorian mansion is set in 13 acres of private parkland and boasts the kind of luxurious accommodation you'd normally find at double (or triple) the price. The richly furnished rooms have bags of country character, with swags, frills and elegant drapes and a smattering of veneered antiques. Wake up to views of rolling countryside, elegant lawns or Wells Cathedral, then take a dip in the heated outdoor swimming pool.

**Ancient Gate House Hotel** (☎ 01749-672029; www.ancientgatehouse.co.uk; Sadler St; s £76, d £91-105; P ) Wildly wonky walls, a stone spiral staircase and plenty of beams make this 15th-century inn a character-filled place to rest your head. Firmly traditional furnishings add to the atmosphere, while a handful of rooms look out directly onto the cathedral.

Also recommended:

**Canon Grange** (☎ 01749-671800; www.canongrange.co.uk; Cathedral Green; d £70; P ) Old-fashioned B&B in a 15th-century house overlooking Cathedral Green.

**Swan Hotel** (☎ 01749-836300; www.swanhotelwells.co.uk; Sadler St; s £82-112, d £104-180; P ) Elegant 15th-century coaching inn with large period-themed rooms.

## Eating

**Cloister Restaurant** (☎ 01749-676543; Wells Cathedral, Cathedral Green; mains £6; ⌣ 10am-5pm Mon-Sat & 1-5pm Sun Mar-Oct, 10am-5pm Mon-Sat Nov-Feb) Tucked away under ancient stone arches inside the cathedral's west cloister, this atmospheric bistro dishes up hearty, homemade soul food: rich risottos, exquisite quiches and wicked cakes.

**Goodfellows** (☎ 01749-673866; 5 Sadler St; cafe mains £7, restaurant mains £13-17; ⌣ cafe lunch Mon & Tue, lunch & dinner Wed-Sat, restaurant lunch Mon, lunch & dinner Tue-Sat) This sophisticated eatery can satisfy pretty much any hunger pang you have: the cafe rustles up treats like warm goats' cheese bruschetta; the in-store bakery proves there is an

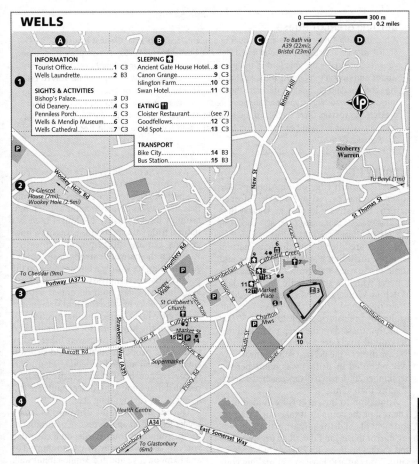

## WELLS

0 ——————— 300 m
0 ——————— 0.2 miles

**INFORMATION**
Tourist Office.........................**1** C3
Wells Laundrette.................**2** B3

**SIGHTS & ACTIVITIES**
Bishop's Palace.....................**3** D3
Old Deanery..........................**4** C3
Penniless Porch.....................**5** C3
Wells & Mendip Museum.....**6** C3
Wells Cathedral......................**7** C3

**SLEEPING**
Ancient Gate House Hotel...**8** C3
Canon Grange......................**9** C3
Islington Farm......................**10** C3
Swan Hotel...........................**11** C3

**EATING**
Cloister Restaurant............(see 7)
Goodfellows.........................**12** C3
Old Spot...............................**13** C3

**TRANSPORT**
Bike City..............................**14** B3
Bus Station..........................**15** B3

art to piling fresh fruit and custard onto pastry cases; and the formal dining room serves up a classy blend of Somerset produce and French-inspired cuisine.

**Old Spot** ( ☎ 01749-689099; 12 Sadler St; 2/3 courses £18.50/21.50; ☽ lunch Wed-Sun, dinner Tue-Sat) Worn floorboards, a tiled and mirrored bar and very comfy chairs set the scene at this superstylish restaurant. The menu is imaginative, too: flavour favourites include black pudding salad, cod with garlic purée, and warm apple and almond pud.

### Getting There & Around

The bus station is south of Cuthbert St, on Princes Rd. National Express runs direct to London once a day (£19, 4½ hours), al-

though it's usually more convenient to travel to Bristol by local bus, and from there catch a more frequent coach to London.

Bus 173 runs from Bath to Wells (1¼ hours, hourly, seven on Sunday). Bus 376 travels to Wells from Bristol (one hour, hourly) before continuing on to Glastonbury (15 minutes) and Street (25 minutes). Bus 29 travels to Taunton (1¼ hours, seven daily Monday to Friday, five or six on weekends) via Glastonbury. Bus 126 runs to Cheddar (25 minutes) hourly Monday to Saturday and every two hours on Sunday. There's no train station in Wells.

**Bike City** ( ☎ 01749-671711; 31 Market St; ☽ 9am-5.30pm Mon-Thu, to 5pm Fri & Sat) charges £15 per day for bike hire.

**SOUTHWEST ENGLAND**

---

**DETOUR: GLENCOT HOUSE**

A breathtaking 19th-century mansion built in opulent Jacobean style, **Glencot House** ( ☎ 01749-677160; www.glencothouse.co.uk; Wookey Hole; d £165-230, 4-poster-bed r £245-260; **P** ) is a place to indulge your senses and live out your lord-of-the-manor fantasies. It's surrounded by 7 hectares of private woods and riverside grounds, and even has its own cricket pitch. Walnut panelling, carved ceilings and dazzling chandeliers decorate the public rooms, while the bedrooms drip with flowing furnishings, swags and drapes and are peppered with chaises longues, country prints and antique dressers. Downstairs there's a billiard room, fire-lit drawing room, minicinema, sauna and plunge pool, as well as a wood-beamed dining hall that could have fallen straight from the pages of *The Remains of the Day*.

---

## WOOKEY HOLE

On the southern edge of the Mendips, the River Axe has carved out a series of deep caverns collectively known as **Wookey Hole** ( ☎ 01749-672243; www.wookey.co.uk; adult/child/family £15/10/45; ☉ 10am-5pm Apr-Oct, 10.30am-4pm Nov-Mar). The caves are littered with dramatic natural features, including a subterranean lake and some fascinating stalagmites and stalactites (one of which is supposedly the legendary Witch of Wookey Hole, who was turned to stone by a local priest). The caves were inhabited by prehistoric people for some 50,000 years, but these days the deep pools and underground rivers are more often frequented by cave divers – the deepest subterranean dive ever recorded in Britain was made here in September 2004, when divers reached a depth of more than 45m.

Admission to the caves is by guided tour. The rest of the complex is taken up by an assortment of child-friendly attractions including mirror mazes, an Edwardian penny arcade and a valley stuffed with 20 giant plastic dinosaurs. You can also have a go at making your own sheet of paper in the Victorian papermill. Some prehistoric finds are on show at the on-site museum, but many are on display at the Wells & Mendip Museum (p340).

Bus 670 runs from Wells (10 minutes, nine daily, four on Sunday).

## CHEDDAR GORGE
☎ 01934

If Wookey Hole is a little too touristy for your tastes, then you'd better brace yourself for **Cheddar Gorge Caves** ( ☎ 01934-742343; www.cheddarcaves.co.uk; Explorer Ticket adult/child £15/9.50; ☉ 10am-5.30pm Jul & Aug, 10.30am-5pm Sep-Jun), a spectacular series of limestone caverns that are always jammed with visitors throughout the summer months.

As early as the 12th century the caves' constant temperature of around 7°C made them the perfect place to store cheese, and the tunnels and caverns gave their name to this tangy, crumbly local speciality. No longer used as a natural fridge, these days the caves draw huge crowds, but are still genuinely impressive. Although the network extends deep into the surrounding rock, only a few are open to the public; the most impressive are Cox's Cave and Gough's Cave, both decorated with an amazing gallery of stalactites and stalagmites, and subtly lit to bring out the spectrum of colours in the limestone rock. After the end of the last Ice Age, the caves were inhabited by prehistoric people; a 9000-year-old skeleton (imaginatively named 'Cheddar Man') was discovered here in 1903, and genetic tests have revealed that some of his descendants are still living in the surrounding area.

Outside the caves, the 274 steps of **Jacob's Ladder** lead up to an impressive panorama of the surrounding countryside; on a clear day you can see all the way to Glastonbury Tor and Exmoor. A signposted 3-mile-circuit walk follows the cliffs along the most spectacular parts of **Cheddar Gorge**.

The **tourist office** ( ☎ 01934-744071; cheddar.tic@sedgemoor.gov.uk; ☉ 10am-5pm daily Easter-Sep, 10.30am-4.30pm Oct, 11am-4pm Sun only Nov-Easter) is at the southern end of the gorge.

**Rocksport** ( ☎ 01934-742343; caves@visitcheddar.co.uk) offers abseiling and climbing (£16) and trips into the more remote caverns (from £20).

Bus 126 runs to Wells (25 minutes) hourly Monday to Saturday and every two hours on Sunday.

## GLASTONBURY
pop 8429

Realign those chakras and open that third eye – you've just touched down in England's hippie-central. A bohemian haven and centre for New Age culture since the days of the Summer of Love, Glastonbury is still a favourite hang-out for mystics and counterculture types of all descriptions. Crammed with goddess temples, trance workshops and Beltane ceremonies, this is the place to answer the call of the shaman, hear the healing drum and possibly even take part in a mystical singing bowl experience. For many the town is synonymous with the world-famous Glastonbury Festival, an often mud-soaked musical extravaganza which has been held nearby for more than 30 years. But look past the tie-dye and through the crystals, and you'll find the town itself is much more – it claims to be the birthplace of Christianity in England and boasts absorbing museums, a few fabulous places to stay and a lovely old pub where there isn't a joss stick in sight.

## Information

The **tourist office** ( ☎ 01458-832954; www.glastonbury tic.co.uk; The Tribunal, 9 High St; ⊗ 10am-5pm Apr-Sep, to 4pm Oct-Mar) stocks free maps and accommodation lists, and sells leaflets describing local walks and the *Glastonbury Millennium Trail* (60p).

## Sights

### GLASTONBURY ABBEY

Legend has it that Joseph of Arimathea, great-uncle of Jesus, owned mines in this area and returned here with the Holy Grail (the chalice from the Last Supper) after the death of Christ. Joseph supposedly founded England's first church on the site, now occupied by the ruined **abbey** ( ☎ 01458-832267; www.glastonburyab bey.com; Magdalene St; adult/child £5/3; ⊗ 9.30am-6pm or dusk Sep-May, from 9am Jun-Aug), but the earliest proven Christian connection dates from the 7th century, when King Ine gave a charter to a monastery in Glastonbury. In 1184 the church was destroyed by fire and reconstruction began in the reign of Henry II.

In 1191, monks claimed to have had visions confirming hints in old manuscripts that the 6th-century warrior-king Arthur and his wife Guinevere were buried in the abbey grounds. Excavations uncovered a tomb containing a skeletal couple, who were reinterred in front of the high altar of the new church in 1278. The tomb survived until 1539, when Henry VIII dissolved the monasteries and had the last abbot hung, drawn and quartered on the tor.

The remaining ruins at Glastonbury mainly date from the church that was built after the 1184 fire. It's still possible to make out some of the nave walls, the ruins of the St Mary's chapel, and the remains of the crossing arches, which may have been scissor-shaped, like those in Wells Cathedral (p339). The site of the supposed tomb of Arthur and Guinevere is marked in the grass. The grounds also contain a small museum, cider orchard and herb garden, as well as the **Holy Thorn** tree, which supposedly sprung from Joseph's staff and mysteriously blooms twice a year, at Christmas and Easter.

### GLASTONBURY TOR

The iconic hump of Glastonbury Tor is crowned by a ruined tower and rears steeply from the Somerset flatlands. This 160m-high grassy mound on the edge of town provides both glorious views over the surrounding countryside, and a focal point for a bewildering array of myths. According to some it's the home of a faery king, while an old Celtic legend identifies it as the stronghold of Gwyn ap Nudd (ruler of Annwyn, the Underworld) – but the most famous legend identifies the tor as the mythic Isle of Avalon, where King Arthur was taken after being mortally wounded in battle by his nephew Mordred, and where Britain's 'once and future king' sleeps until his country calls again.

Whatever the truth of the legends, the tor has been a site of pilgrimage for many years, and was once topped by the medieval church of **St Michael**, although today only the tower remains. On the way up to the tor look out for **Gog** and **Magog**, two gnarled oak trees believed to be the last remains of an ancient processional avenue.

It takes 45 minutes to walk up and down the tor. Parking is not permitted nearby, but the **Tor Bus** (adult/child £2.50/1.50) leaves from Dunstan's car park near the abbey. The bus runs every 30 minutes from 10am to 7.30pm from April to September, and from 10am to 3.30pm from October to March. It also stops at Chalice Well and the Rural Life Museum.

### CHALICE WELL & GARDENS

Shaded by knotted yew trees and surrounded by peaceful paths, the **Chalice Well & Gardens** ( ☎ 01458-831154; www.chalicewell.org.uk; Chilkwell St; adult/child £3.25/2.70; ⊗ 10am-5.30pm Apr-Oct, to 4pm Nov-Mar) have been sites of pilgrimage since

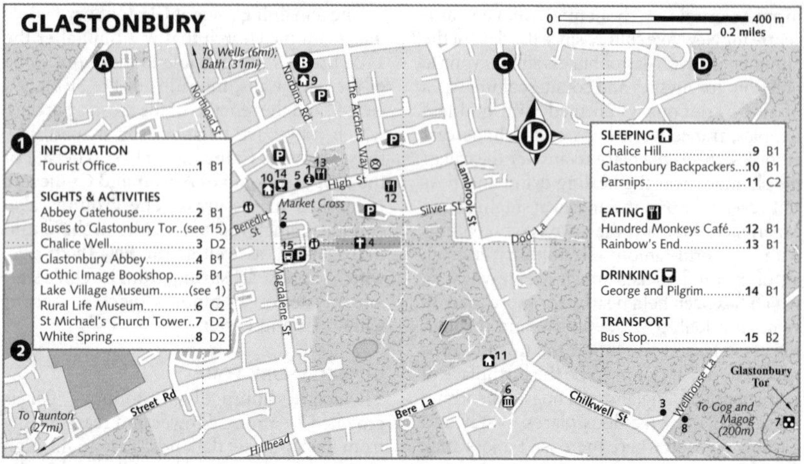


the days of the Celts. The iron-red waters from the 800-year-old well are rumoured to have healing properties, good for everything from eczema to smelly feet; some legends also identify the well as the hiding place of the Holy Grail. You can drink the water from a lion's-head spout, or rest your feet in basins surrounded by flowers.

The Chalice Well is also known as the 'Red Spring' or 'Blood Spring'; its sister, **White Spring**, surfaces across Wellhouse Lane. Spigots from both springs empty into the street, where there's often a queue to fill containers.



### RURAL LIFE MUSEUM

Somerset's agricultural heritage is explored at the **Rural Life Museum** (☎ 01458-831197; Abbey Farm, Chilkwell St; admission free; ⏰ 10am-5pm Tue-Fri & 2-6pm Sat & Sun Apr-Oct, 10am-5pm Tue-Sat Nov-Mar), which contains a varied collection of artefacts relating to traditional trades such as willow growing, peat digging, cider making and cheese making. There are often live displays of local skills, so if you fancy trying your hand at beekeeping, lace making and spinning, this is the place to do it. The late-14th-century tithe barn has fine carvings on the gables and porch, and an impressive timber roof; it now houses a collection of vintage agricultural machinery.

### LAKE VILLAGE MUSEUM

Upstairs from Glastonbury's tourist office, in the medieval courthouse, the **Lake Village Museum** (EH; ☎ 01458-832954; The Tribunal, 9 High St; adult/child £2/1.50; ⏰ 10am-5pm Apr-Sep, to 4pm Oct-Mar) displays finds from a prehistoric bog village discovered in nearby Godney. The houses in the village were clustered in about six groups and were built from reeds, hazel and willow. It's thought they were occupied by summer traders who lived the rest of the year at Glastonbury Tor.

## Tours

There are lots of companies offering guided tours of Glastonbury's main sights.

**Mystical Tours of Glastonbury** (☎ 01458-831453; www.gothicimagetours.co.uk; 7 High St), based at the Gothic Image bookshop, offers a range of tours including three-hour guided trips to Wearyall Hill, Gog and Magog and Glastonbury Tor itself. Prices per person depend on group sizes and range from £12 (if there are more than four people) to £70. It also runs day tours to Stonehenge and Avebury (£140 per person).

## Sleeping

If you're a fan of wind chimes, organic brekkies and homemade muesli, then Glastonbury's B&Bs won't disappoint.

**Glastonbury Backpackers** (☎ 01458-833353; www.glastonburybackpackers.com; 4 Market Pl; dm/tw/d £14/35/40; Ⓟ 💻) A happy, hippie hang-out, Glastonbury's hostel is a friendly, welcoming affair, with doubles and dorms decked out in jazzy colours. There's a TV lounge, kitchen and cafe-bar downstairs.

**Parsnips** (☎ 01458-835599; www.parsnips-glastonbury.co.uk; 99 Bere Lane; s/d £50/65; Ⓟ 💻) Swimming against the tie-dye and crystal tide, this stylish B&B has opted instead for a fresh design topped with gingham flourishes and plumped-up quilts. There's a comfy guest lounge, a bright conservatory and a refreshing lack of spiritual guidance.

**our pick Chalice Hill** ( ☎ 01458-830828; www.chalicehill.co.uk; Dod Lane; s/d £70/90; **P** ) This grandly luxurious, utterly delightful B&B is the place to stay in Glastonbury. Set in a rambling Georgian house, it's dripping with quirky charm – stripped wooden floors combine with a sweeping staircase, ornate mirrors and stylish modern art. The effect is deeply elegant, but also wonderfully easygoing. The fact that it's a five-minute walk into town, and is surrounded by soothing, tree-shaded grounds, adds to the appeal.

### Eating & Drinking

**Rainbow's End** ( ☎ 01458-833896; 17A High St; mains £4-7; ☺ 10am-4pm) The classic Glastonbury wholefood cafe, with ranks of potted plants and wooden tables and a rotating menu of organic offerings such as vegie moussaka, sweet potato flan and fiery chilli. Needless to say, the carrot cake is divine.

**Hundred Monkeys Cafe** ( ☎ 01458-833386; 52 High St; mains £5-10; ☺ 10am-6pm Mon-Wed, to 9pm Thu-Sat, to 3.30pm Sun) A refreshingly nonalternative option with leather sofas, pine tables and a huge blackboard listing fresh pastas, salads and mains. If you've a spare half-hour ask about the origin of the name – the original 100th monkey.

**George and Pilgrim** ( ☎ 01458-831146; 1 High St; mains £7-10; ☺ lunch daily, dinner Mon-Sat) The creaking timbers and stone arches in this 15th-century inn are evidence that Glastonbury's New Age incarnation is a mere blip on a very ancient timeline. The snug interior is home to a warm welcome, an excellent pint and some above-average pub grub – try the homemade beef and onion burger.

### Getting There & Away

There's one early-morning National Express service to Bath (£6.10, 1¼ hours), which goes on to London (£19, 4¼ hours).

Bus 29 travels to Glastonbury from Taunton (50 minutes, five to seven daily). Bus 376 travels to Wells (30 minutes, hourly) and Bristol (1¼ hours), and also to Street (15 minutes). Bus 377 goes to Yeovil, while bus 375 heads to Bridgwater (both one hour, hourly Monday to Saturday, every two hours Sunday).

There is no train station in Glastonbury.

# EXMOOR NATIONAL PARK

Exmoor is an adventure, from dawn deer-spotting safaris to test-your-mettle hikes, from moorland gallops to cracking cycle rides, from clambering the coast path to a summertime dip in a cold, cold sea. This compact national park is a bit like England's version of the Wild West, except here cliffs replace cowboys, red deer replace cattle, and gumboots replace gun-slingers. Part wilderness expanse, part rolling fields, these days Exmoor isn't all rustic B&Bs and hugger-mugger pubs. Instead, it's scattered with pockets of boutique bliss, from refined restaurants to sumptuous country-house hotels where the service is sublime, the beds are soft and a fire crackles in the grate.

The amiable market town of Dulverton shelters south of the swathes of bracken-smothered higher moorland that encircle the picturesque village of Exford. This un-fenced wilderness plunges down to a coast dotted with charming stop-off points, from the twin villages of Lynton and Lynmouth in the west, via the pretty harbour at Porlock to the medieval town of Dunster, complete with a brooding red-brick castle. Expansive and exciting – Exmoor awaits.

## Orientation

The park is only about 21 miles wide from west to east and stretches just 12 miles from north to south. Waymarked paths criss-cross the moor, and a dramatic section of the South West Coast Path runs from Minehead (a family-fun resort just outside the park) to Padstow in Cornwall.

## Information

There are several tourist offices within the park:

**Dulverton** ( ☎ 01398-323841; NPCDulverton@exmoor-nationalpark.gov.uk; 7-9 Fore St; ☺ 10am-5pm Apr-Oct, 10.30am-3pm Nov-Mar)

**Dunster** ( ☎ 01643-821835; NPCDunster@exmoor-nationalpark.gov.uk; Dunster Steep; ☺ 10am-5pm Easter-Oct, limited hrs Nov-Easter)

**Lynmouth** ( ☎ 01598-752509; Lyndale Car Park; ☺ 10.30am-3pm Easter-Oct)

**Lynton** ( ☎ 01598-752225; info@lyntourism.co.uk; Lynton Town Hall, Lee Rd; ☺ 10am-4pm Mon-Sat, to 2pm Sun)

**Porlock** ( ☎ 01643-863150; www.porlock.co.uk; West End, High St; ◷ 10am-5pm Mon-Sat & 10am-1pm Sun Mar-Oct, 10.30am-1pm Tue-Fri & 10am-2pm Sat Nov-Mar)

All information outlets stock the free *Exmoor Visitor* newspaper, an excellent source of information about accommodation, guided walks, activities, attractions, transport and the moor's fragile environment.

There are four comprehensive websites covering Exmoor:

**Exmoor National Park** (www.exmoor-nationalpark.gov .uk) The official National Park Authority site.

**Exmoor Tourist Association** (www.exmoor.com) Lists details on accommodation and activities.

**Visit Exmoor** (www.visit-exmoor.info) Excellent information site with advice on activities, events, accommodation and eating out.

**What's On Exmoor** (www.whatsonexmoor.com) Local listings and information.

## Activities

**Active Exmoor** ( ☎ 01398-324599; www.activeexmoor .com) is a central contact point for all the national park's outdoor activity providers, ranging from riding to rowing and sailing to surfing. It also has information for more-experienced white-water kayakers and rock climbers.

**Wimbleball Lake Watersports Centre** ( ☎ 01398-371460) runs a range of courses from sailing, windsurfing and kayaking taster sessions (£18 for one hour), to two-day windsurfing (£145 per person) and sailing (£145 per person) courses.

### CYCLING

A network of bridleways and quiet lanes makes Exmoor great cycling country, but you're not going to get away without tackling a few hills. Popular trails travel through the Brendon Hills, the Crown Estate woodland and along the old Barnstaple railway line. NPA (National Park Authority) centres sell the map *Exmoor for Off-Road Cyclists* (£10), and the *Bike It Dunster* and *Bike It Wimbleball* leaflets (75p) – the leaflets feature a family, beginner and explorer route. All are also available at the NPA's online shop.

Several sections of the **National Cycle Network** (NCN; www.sustrans.org.uk) cross the park, including the **West Country Way** (NCN route 3) from Bristol to Padstow, and the **Devon Coast to Coast Cycle Route** (NCN route 27) between Exmoor and Dartmoor.

**Exmoor Mtb Experiences** ( ☎ 01643-705079; www .exmoormtbexperiences.co.uk), near Minehead, runs guided off-road days from £25 and all-inclusive weekends from £150. For bike hire, see p348.

### MOORLAND SAFARIS

Several companies offer 4WD 'safari' trips across the moor, which stop at all the main beauty spots and provide lots of useful background. If you're a nature-lover or a keen photographer, bird- and deer-watching safaris can be arranged. Half-day trips start at around £20.

**Barle Valley Safaris** ( ☎ 01643-851386; www.exmoor -barlevalley-safaris.co.uk) Located at Dulverton, Dunster and Minehead.

**Discovery Safaris** ( ☎ 01643-863444; Porlock)

**Exmoor Safari** ( ☎ 01643-831229; www.exmoorsafari .co.uk; Exford)

### PONY TREKKING & HORSE RIDING

Exmoor is popular riding country and lots of stables offer pony and horse treks from around £25 per hour – see the *Exmoor Visitor* for full details.

**Brendon Manor Riding Stables** ( ☎ 01598-741246) Near Lynton.

**Burrowhayes Farm** ( ☎ 01643-862463; www.bur rowhayes.co.uk; Porlock)

**Outovercott Stables** ( ☎ 01598-753341; www .outovercott.co.uk; Lynton)

---

### BEER & BREAKFAST?

You'll want to raise a toast to this one – **Old Cider House** ( ☎ 01278-732228; www.oldciderhouse .co.uk; 25 Castle St, Nether Stowey; d £60-80; Ⓟ ) is quite possibly the only B&B in Britain where guests design and brew their own beer. The process involves as much formulation, mashing, boiling and fermenting as ale addicts could possibly want. Once your top tipple is ready, it's bottled up, labelled and shipped to your door. All-inclusive, two-night beer-brewing breaks start at £225 per person; nonparticipants pay £99. Bedrooms are unfussy in plain colours and pine. But then, take part in enough 'tutored tasting sessions' and you probably won't notice the bedspread. If you're not staying, ask for a pint of the B&B's Stowey Brewery Ale in the local Rose and Crown.

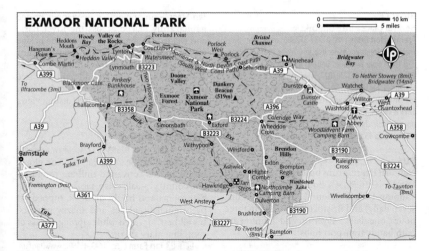

## WALKING

The open moors and profusion of marked bridleways make Exmoor an excellent area for hiking. The best-known routes are the **Somerset & North Devon Coast Path**, which is part of the **South West Coast Path** (www.southwestcoastpath.com), and the Exmoor section of the **Two Moors Way**, which starts in Lynmouth and travels south to Dartmoor and beyond.

The **Coleridge Way** (www.coleridgeway.co.uk) winds for 36 miles through Exmoor, the Brendon Hills and the Quantocks, taking in Coleridge's home at Nether Stowey and the village of Porlock, where he's said to have written *Kubla Khan*.

Part of the 180-mile **Tarka Trail** falls within the park. A combination of cycling and walking paths, road routes and even a train journey, it is based on the countryside that inspired Henry Williamson's *Tarka the Otter*. Join it at Combe Martin, hike along the cliffs to Lynton/Lynmouth, then head across the moor towards Barnstaple.

Organised **walks** run by the NPA are held throughout the year – visit www.exmoornationalpark.gov.uk or see the listings in the *Exmoor Visitor* for details. Its autumn dawn safaris to see rutting stags are superb, as are its summertime evening deer-watching hikes. Short walks cost £3; longer walks are £5.

For hard-core hikers, **Mountains+Moor** ( ☎ 01643-841610;  www.mountainsandmoor.co.uk; Minehead) offers navigation lessons (from £80 per two days) and summer mountain-craft courses (£110/270 per two/five days), which

include camp-craft, rope work and river crossings, and take the form of mini-expeditions.

Dulverton (p348) and Lynton (p349) make good bases.

## Sleeping & Eating

There are **YHA hostels** ( ☎ 01629-592700; www.yha.org.uk) in Minehead and Ilfracombe (outside the park), and Exford within the park.

The YHA also runs camping barns (from £7.50 per person) at Woodadvent Farm near Roadwater and at Northcombe Farm, near Dulverton (p348). There are a number of official camp sites along the coast.

For more-comfy sleeping options, Exmoor's accommodation ranges from rustic rooms above pubs to cosy B&Bs to spoil-yourself-silly country-house hotels. We outline many; however, for an overview, see www.exmoor.com. If you'd like to hire a cottage, contact **Exmoor Holiday Group** (www.exmoor-holidays.co.uk).

## Getting There & Around

Once outside the key towns, getting around Exmoor by bus can be tricky, as regular services are very limited. Bus 300 shuttles regularly along the coast between Minehead and Lynmouth, while bus 400, the **Exmoor Explorer** (round trip adult/child £6/3) offers a handy circular route that takes in Minehead, Dunster, Wheddon Cross, Exford and Porlock. It operates only on Saturday and Sunday between June and September (two daily); from late July to the end of August it also runs on Tuesday and Thursday.

SOUTHWEST ENGLAND

### BICYCLE

Several places hire out bikes:

**Fremington Quay** ( ☎ 01271-372586; www.bike trail.co.uk; Fremington; per day adult/child £10/7.50; ✆ 10am-5pm Wed-Sun) Delivers bikes to your door.

**Pompys** ( ☎ 01643-704077; www.pompyscycles.co.uk; Minehead; per day £12.50; ✆ 9am-5pm Mon-Sat) Offers full-suspension mountain bikes from £25.

**Tarka Trail** ( ☎ 01271-324202; Train Station, Barnstaple; per day adult/child £10/7; ✆ 9.15am-5pm Apr-Oct) Can be picked up 15 miles west of the park boundary.

### BUS

National Express runs buses to Tiverton from London (£16.50, 4¾ hours, three daily) and Taunton from London (£16.70, four hours, seven daily) and Bristol (£14.80, two to three hours, one daily). Tiverton and Taunton are both handy transport hubs.

### TRAIN

Regular main-line trains serve Tiverton and Taunton. Once there, local buses link to Dulverton (right), Dunster (p352) and beyond.

The **West Somerset Steam Railway** ( ☎ 01643-704996; www.west-somerset-railway.co.uk) chugs from Bishops Lydeard to Minehead, 20 miles away (adult/child return £13.40/6.70, 1¼ hours). There are stops at Dunster and other stations, depending on the time of year. Trains run pretty much daily from mid-March to October, otherwise occasional days only. Bus 28 runs to Bishops Lydeard from Taunton (15 minutes, 11 daily Monday to Saturday, nine on Sunday).

The *Taunton & West Somerset Public Transport Guide*, free from tourist offices, contains timetables for all the main bus routes.

## DULVERTON

Dulverton is the southern gateway to Exmoor, and sits at the base of the Barle Valley near the confluence of two key rivers, the Exe and Barle. It's a solid, no-nonsense sort of country town, home to a collection of gun sellers, fishing-tackle stores and gift shops, as well as the **NPA Visitor Centre** ( ☎ 01398-323841; www .exmoor-nationalpark.gov.uk; 7-9 Fore St; ✆ 10am-5pm Apr-Oct, 10.30am-3pm Nov-Mar).

### Activities

#### WALKING

There's a lovely 12-mile (including hills) circular walk along the river from Dulverton to Tarr Steps – an ancient stone clapper bridge haphazardly placed across the River Barle and shaded by gnarled old trees. The bridge was supposedly built by the devil for sunbathing. It's a four- to five-hour trek for the average walker. You can add another three or four hours to the walk by continuing from Tarr Steps up Winsford Hill for distant views over Devon.

### Sleeping & Eating

**Town Mills** ( ☎ 01398-323124; www.townmills dulverton.co.uk; High St; s/d £50/75; **P** ) The glossy rooms in this converted mill are resolutely 'un-country' – all crisp fabrics, sparkling bathrooms and bright artwork, topped off by original fireplaces and snazzy mirrors. It's all best surveyed while sipping a glass of complimentary sherry.

**our pick** **Tarr Farm** ( ☎ 01643-851507; www.tarrfarm .co.uk; s/d £90/150, mains £13-18; ✆ lunch & dinner; **P** ) One of Exmoor's best bolt-holes. Snuggled in a beguiling wooded valley next to the tourist honey-pot of Tarr Steps (left), this old Somerset farmhouse has been transformed into a superstylish retreat. The beds are draped in fine cottons and sprinkled with satin cushions; luxury touches include fluffy bathrobes, power-showers and organic bath products. The restaurant plates up new-country treats – expect Exmoor beef with wild mushrooms, and local lamb with red onion confit.

**Woods** ( ☎ 01398-324007; 4 Bank Sq; mains £11-18; ✆ lunch & dinner) This deservedly popular gastropub has built up a devoted following by giving excellent local ingredients imaginative treatments, all helped along by a rustic atmosphere and excellent service. Tummy treats include local lobster, pork-belly with samphire, and Ruby Red sirloin steak.

Other recommendations:

**Northcombe Camping Barn** ( ☎ 0870 770 8868; www.yha.org.uk; per person £7.50) A converted watermill about 1 mile from town.

**Ashwick House** ( ☎ 01398-323868; www.ashwick house.com; s £84-94, d £138-158) A grand, gorgeous minibaronial pile crammed full of Edwardian features. Near Ashwick, 4 miles from Dulverton.

### Getting There & Away

Bus 398 (six daily, Monday to Saturday) stops at Dulverton on its way from Minehead (50 minutes) and Dunster (40 minutes) to Tiverton (55 minutes). Bus 25B shuttles to Taunton (1½ hours, seven daily Monday to Saturday).

## LYNTON & LYNMOUTH

The attractive harbour of Lynmouth is rooted at the base of a steep, tree-lined valley, where the River West Lyn empties into the sea along Exmoor's northern coastline. Its similarity to the harbour at Boscastle (p374) is striking, and, in fact, the two harbours share more than just a common geography: like Boscastle, Lynmouth is famous for a devastating flash flood. A huge wave of water swept through Lynmouth in 1952 and the town paid a much heavier price than its Cornish cousin; 34 people lost their lives, and memory of the disaster remains strong in the village today.

Today Lynmouth is a busy tourist harbour town lined with pubs, souvenir sellers and fudge shops. At the top of the rocky cliffs is the more genteel Victorian resort of Lynton, which can be reached via an amazing water-operated railway, or a stiff climb up the cliff path.

The **tourist office** ( ☎ 01598-752225; info@lyntourism.co.uk; Lynton Town Hall, Lee Rd; ☺ 10am-4pm Mon-Sat, to 2pm Sun) provides a free newspaper called *Lynton & Lynmouth Scene* (www.lyntonandlynmouthscene.co.uk), which has accommodation, eating and activities listings.

There's a small **NPA visitor centre** ( ☎ 01598-752509; Lyndale Car Park; ☺ 10am-3pm Easter-Oct) near Lynmouth harbour.

## Sights & Activities

The history of Lynmouth's flood is explored at the **Lyn & Exmoor Museum** ( ☎ 01598-752317; St Vincent's Cottage, Market St, Lynton; adult/child £1/20p; ☺ 10am-12.30pm & 2-5pm Mon-Fri & 2-5pm Sun Apr-Oct), which also houses some interesting archaeological finds and a collection of tools, paintings and period photos.

The **Cliff Railway** ( ☎ 01598-753486; www.clif-frailwaylynton.co.uk; single/return adult £1.95/2.85, child £1.10/1.85; ☺ 10am-6pm Easter-Oct, later at peak times) is an extraordinary piece of Victorian engineering that was designed by George Marks, believed to be a pupil of Brunel. Two cars linked by a steel cable descend or ascend the slope according to the amount of water in the cars' tanks. It's been running like clockwork since 1890, and it's still the best way to commute between the two villages. The views aren't bad, either.

From the Lynmouth crossroads follow the signs 200m to **Glen Lyn Gorge** ( ☎ 01598-753207; adult/child £4/3; ☺ Easter-Oct), the steepest of the two valleys into Lynmouth. There are several lovely gorge walks and a small **exhibition centre** devoted to hydroelectric power.

### WALKING

The villages are in superb walking country. The South West Coast Path, the Coleridge Way and the Tarka Trail all pass through Lynmouth, and it is the official starting point of the Two Moors Way.

The most popular hike is to the stunning **Valley of the Rocks** just over a mile west of Lynton. Many of the tortuous rock formations have names – look out for the Devil's Cheesewring and Ragged Jack – and the valley is also home to a population of feral goats.

Other popular trails wind to the lighthouse at **Foreland Point** east of Lynmouth, and **Watersmeet**, 2 miles upriver from Lynmouth, where a National Trust teashop is housed in a Victorian fishing lodge.

## Sleeping

There are plenty of mid-price B&Bs dotted along Lee Rd in Lynton.

**Victoria Lodge** ( ☎ 01598-753203; www.victorialodge.co.uk; Lee Rd, Lynton; s £60-120, d £70-140) The rooms here positively drip with swags, pelmets and padded cushions, often in hard-to-ignore patterns – that they're named after princesses provides a clue to opulence levels. You'll also tuck into a right royal breakfast of homemade kedgeree, Victoria omelette or the enormous Exmoor Works.

**ourpick St Vincent House** ( ☎ 01598-752244; www.st-vincent-hotel.co.uk; Castle Hill, Lynton; d £74; P ) Run by an Anglo-Belgian couple and named Hotel of the Year by Les Routiers, no less, this elegant establishment brings a dollop of class to the quiet streets of Lynton. The house once belonged to a comrade of Nelson's, and all the delightful, pared-back rooms are named after battleships from Horatio's fleet. There's a relaxed, old-world atmosphere and a spiral staircase so sweeping that you'll feel like a film star.

**Hunters' Inn** ( ☎ 01598-763230; www.thehuntersinn.net; s £55-80, d £80-130) Tucked away in the heart of the heavily wooded Heddon Valley, west of Lynton, this 19th-century coaching inn is an Exmoor institution. Cosy, creaky rooms add to the atmosphere, as do views over tumbling hills and the sense of sleeping snugly somewhere in the middle of nowhere. Local ales and excellent pub grub are on offer in the welcoming, well-worn bar.

SOUTHWEST ENGLAND

**Sea View Villa** ( ☎ 01598-753460; www.seaviewvilla
.co.uk; 6 Summer House Path, Lynmouth; s £40, d £90-120)
Adding a dash of Georgian grandeur to sea-side Lynmouth, this 1721 villa makes for a supremely elegant night's kip. Egyptian cotton, Indian silk and suede fabrics grace rooms done out in 'Champagne', 'ginger' and 'vanilla'. Eggs Benedict, smoked salmon and cafetière coffee ensure the breakfast is classy, too.

## Eating

**Greenhouse** ( ☎ 01598-753358; 6 Lee Rd; mains £9; ☻ 9am-9.30pm) Cole Porter tunes, a log-burning stove and conservatory-style dining create a cafe-cum-restaurant with gently eccentric charm. Evenings see a smooth segue from gourmet baguettes, cinnamon-scented toast and superb cream teas to suppertime comfort food like pan-fried salmon with hollandaise, and crab with new potatoes.

**St Vincent Restaurant** ( ☎ 01598-752244; Castle Hill, Lynton; 2/3 courses £24/27; ☻ dinner Wed-Sun Easter-Oct) Part of the St Vincent House hotel (p349), this cracking little eatery is the top table in town. Subdued lighting, polished wooden floors and intimate tables set the scene for dishes that fuse Mediterranean flavours with Exmoor fish and game. The Westcountry lamb with olives, tomatoes, capers and garlic is hard to resist, but leave room for the crème Catalane brûlée.

## Entertainment

**Lynton Cinema** ( ☎ 01598-753397; www.lyntoncinema .co.uk; Lee Rd; adult/child £4.25/2.75), This 68-seater cinema, set in a converted Methodist church, is a superbly atmospheric spot to catch the latest movies.

## Getting There & Away

Bus 300 runs from Lynmouth to Minehead (55 minutes), via Porlock (30 minutes), three to four times daily.

If you're driving, the most scenic route to Porlock is the steep, twisting road that hugs the coast all the way from Lynmouth. The scenery is worth the £2 toll, and you get to avoid the notoriously steep descent via Porlock Hill.

## PORLOCK & AROUND

The small village of **Porlock** is one of the prettiest on the north Exmoor coast; the huddle of thatched cottages lining its main street is framed on one side by the sea, and on the other by a jumble of houses that cling to the steeply sloping hills behind. Winding lanes lead to the picturesque breakwater of Porlock Weir, a compact collection of pubs, shops and hotels, 2 miles to the west. Coleridge's famous poem *Kubla Khan* was written during a brief sojourn in Porlock (helped along by a healthy slug of laudanum and a vicious head cold), and the villages are popular with summertime tourists, as well as walkers on the Coleridge Way and the South West Coast Path.

The village of **Selworthy**, 2.5 miles southeast of Porlock, forms part of the 5060-hectare Holnicote Estate, the largest NT-owned area of land on Exmoor. Though its cob-and-thatch cottages look ancient, the village was almost entirely rebuilt in the 19th century by local philanthropist and landowner Thomas Acland, to provide accommodation for elderly workers on his estate.

Porlock's **tourist office** ( ☎ 01643-863150; www .porlock.co.uk; West End, High St; ☻ 10am-5pm Mon-Sat & 10am-1pm Sun Mar-Oct, 10.30am-1pm Tue-Fri & 10am-2pm Sat Nov-Mar) is a mine of local knowledge, and is also the point of contact for information on the Coleridge Way.

For interesting artefacts and photos of the village, check to see if the tiny **Dovery Manor Museum**, housed in a pretty, 15th-century building in High St, has reopened after refurbishments.

## Sleeping & Eating

**Reines House** ( ☎ 01643-862913; www.reineshouse.co.uk; Parson St; s £25, d £50-54) Simplicity and bargain prices define this snug, central B&B. Expect shades of subtle cream and buttercup-yellow, tasteful scatter cushions and views of the church from the front rooms. Two rooms share bathrooms.

**our pick** **SeaView** ( ☎ 01643-863456; www.seaview porlock.co.uk; High Bank; s £27, d £50-55) You can lie in bed and gaze across Porlock Bay to the cliffs of Wales (they're only 12 miles away) in this delightful, village-centre B&B. It's crammed full of quirky charm, from art-deco bedroom furniture and distressed cabinets to a dining room dripping with oil paintings and antiques. The compact single is more like a minisuite, while the attic room looks out onto the tree-covered Porlock Hill behind. Smoked haddock, local organic eggs and dry-cured bacon make breakfast a treat.

SOUTHWEST ENGLAND

---

**MOOR ELEGANCE**

**Andrews on the Weir** ( ☎ 01643-863300; www.andrewsontheweir.co.uk; Porlock Weir; mains £14-20, 2-course lunch £10; ☒ lunch & dinner Wed-Sun) Every meal becomes an 'experience' at this outlandishly fine restaurant-with-rooms, hovering beside the lapping waves on Porlock Weir. Local contacts (including Porlock fishermen and Exmoor farmers) help the chefs source the very best produce, from farm-reared meat to sea-fresh fish. The cuisine is classic British with a dash of Gallic panache, the atmosphere is all effortless elegance, and the tablecloths are sharp enough to cut your finger on. Classy with a capital 'C'. Doubles rooms cost £100 to £180

---

**Ship Inn** ( ☎ 01643-862507; www.shipinnporlock.co.uk; High St, Porlock; mains £7-14, s/d £40/60; ☒ lunch & dinner; **P** ) Once a favoured haunt of smugglers and the poet Coleridge, this 13th-century thatched inn is still a snug spot for a pint and some great grub. Try the 'Chef's Pie of the Day' – the beef and horseradish is a triumph. The pine and faintly floral bedrooms feature all the home comforts you need after a day on the moors.

## Getting There & Away

Bus 300 runs from Lynmouth to Porlock (30 minutes, three to four times daily) and on to Minehead (20 minutes). Bus 39 (six daily Monday to Saturday) links Porlock to Porlock Weir (seven minutes) and Minehead (20 minutes).

# DUNSTER

Dominated by a striking russet-red castle and centred on a chaotically cobbled market square, the pretty village of Dunster can claim not only to be easy on the eye, but also architecturally interesting. Its unusual features include a medieval packhorse bridge, a 16th-century stone dovecote and a curious octagonal yarn market. In high summer it's a favourite on the coach-tour trail, but make a visit outside that time and the village is still a joy to explore.

The beautiful **St George's Church** dates mostly from the 15th century and boasts a wonderfully carved fan-vaulted rood screen. Further down the road is the **watermill** ( ☎ 01643-821759; Mill Lane; adult/child £3.20/1.95; ☒ 11am-4.45pm daily Jun-Sep, 11am-4.45pm Sat-Thu Apr, May & Oct), a working 18th-century mill.

The **NPA visitor centre** ( ☎ 01643-821835; Dunster Steep; ☒ 10am-5pm Easter-Oct, limited hrs Nov-Easter) is in the main car park.

## Dunster Castle

Although it served as a fortress for around 1000 years, present-day **Dunster Castle** (NT; ☎ 01643-821314; adult/child £8.60/4.20, castle & garden £8.60/4.20, garden only £4.80/2.20; ☒ castle 11am-4.30pm mid-Mar–late Jul, Sep & Oct, to 5pm late Jul-Aug, gardens 11am-4pm Feb–mid-Mar & Nov-Jan, 10am-5pm mid-Mar–Oct) bears little resemblance to the original Norman stronghold. The 13th-century gateway is probably the only original part of the castle; the turrets, battlements and towers were all added later during a romantic remodelling at the hands of Victorian architects. Despite its 19th-century makeover, the castle is still an impressive sight, and is decorated with Tudor furnishings, gorgeous 17th-century plasterwork and ancestral portraits of the Luttrell family. The terraced gardens are also worth exploring, with fine views across Exmoor and the coastline, and an important national collection of strawberry trees.

## Sleeping & Eating

**our pick** **Spears Cross** ( ☎ 01643-821439; www.spears cross.co.uk; 1 West St; s £48, d £75-85) Beam enthusiasts will be in hog-heaven in this 15th-century gem of a B&B – the bedrooms are a mass of burnished old-English planking and latticeworks of ancient wood and painted plaster. Posh new bathrooms and fluffy bathrobes ensure you're steeped in luxury as well as history, and breakfast is a smorgasbord of locally sourced delights – don't miss out on the sausages made from local free-range, rare-breed pork.

**Yarn Market Hotel** ( ☎ 01643-821425; www.yarn markethotel.co.uk; High St; s £60-65, d £90-100, f £120-160; **P** ) Despite a historic exterior, the rooms in this small hotel are all modern identikit furniture and floral fabrics. But the suites may suit families, and wet walkers and unlucky cyclists will find the drying rooms and emergency puncture-repair kits very handy.

**Luttrell Arms** ( ☎ 01643-821555; www.luttrellarms.co.uk; High St; B&B d £116-150; **P** ) In medieval times this glorious old coaching inn was the guesthouse of the Abbots of Cleeve – lucky abbots. Huge flagstones, heavy armchairs and faded tapestries dot the lounge and bar, and the lavish four-poster-bed bedrooms put some royal retreats to shame. Weekends require a two-night dinner, bed and breakfast booking (doubles £160 to £190).

Reeve's Restaurant ( ☎ 01643-821414; High St; mains £15-25; ☒ lunch & dinner Tue-Sat) Reeve's is all rustic-chic – slim leather chairs and boxy wooden tables accompany some extremely stylish food. The menu's full of the flavours of the local moors and shores; escallop of venison sits alongside pan-seared red mullet and slow-cooked honey-glazed belly pork.

### Getting There & Away
Bus 28 runs from Minehead to Taunton via Dunster hourly Monday to Saturday, and nine times on Sunday. Bus 398 travels from Dunster to Dulverton (40 minutes, six daily except Sunday), and to Minehead (10 minutes, six daily except Sunday) in the opposite direction.

The West Somerset Steam Railway (p348) stops at Dunster during the summer.

# DEVON

If counties were capable of emotions, those in the rest of England would envy Devon. It's all to do with a rippling landscape studded with prehistoric sites, historic homes, vibrant cities, ancient villages, intimate coves and wild, wild moors. If exhilaration is your thing, you'll be right at home: here you can get churned around by crashing surf, ride white-water rapids or hike hundreds of miles along precipitous cliffs. Landscape and lifestyle ensure food is fresh from furrow or sea: eat a Michelin-starred meal at a swanky restaurant or a fresh crab sandwich sitting on the beach – it's up to you. In Devon a day's drive can take you from Exeter's serene cathedral, via Torbay's coast, to the yachting haven of Dartmouth, where Agatha Christie's mysterious gardens wait in the wings. Totnes provides the eco-awareness, Plymouth provides the party and wild Dartmoor provides the great escape, while the north coast – rugged, remote and surf-dashed – tempts you into the waves. Whether you see them as envy-inducing, green-tinged or green-fringed, the delights of Devon are tempting indeed.

### Orientation & Information
To the east Devon is bordered by Somerset and Dorset – the county boundary stretches from north coast Exmoor to south coast Lyme Regis. To the west the border with Cornwall follows the River Tamar from its source in north Devon to the estuary at Plymouth. Dartmoor occupies much of the centre of the county.

Discover Devon ( ☎ 0870 608 5531; www.discover devon.com) has plenty of useful information.

### Getting Around
Traveline South West ( ☎ 0871 200 2233; www.tra velinesw.com) can answer timetable questions. Tourist offices stock timetables, the Devon Bus Map and the Discovery Guide to Dartmoor.

First ( ☎ timetables 0871 200 2233, customer services 0845 600 1420; www.firstgroup.com) is the key bus operator in north, south and east Devon, and Dartmoor; Stagecoach Devon ( ☎ 01392-427711; www.stagecoachbus.com) operates mostly local buses, especially in Exeter and Torbay.

The Day Explorer (£2.20 to £4.50) allows one day's travel on Stagecoach Devon buses (prices vary depending on the area), while the Goldrider pass (£6 to £12) is valid for one week.

Devon's rail network skirts the south coast through Exeter and Plymouth to Cornwall. Key lines branching off include the 39-mile Tarka Line from Exeter to Barnstaple, the 15-mile Tamar Valley Line from Plymouth to Gunnislake and the scenic Exeter to Paignton line, which runs via Torquay. The Devon Day Ranger (£10) allows a day's unlimited travel on the county's trains.

## EXETER
pop 116,393
Well-heeled and comfortable, Exeter exudes evidence of its centuries-old role as the spiritual and administrative heart of Devon. The city's gloriously Gothic cathedral presides over stretches of cobbled streets, fragments of the terracotta Roman city wall and a tumbling of medieval and Georgian buildings. A snazzy new shopping centre brings bursts of the modern, thousands of university students ensure a buzzing nightlife and the vibrant quayside acts as a launch pad for cycling or kayaking trips. Throw in some super-stylish places to stay and eat and you have a relaxed but lively base for further explorations.

### History
Exeter's past can be read in its buildings. The Romans marched in around AD 55 – their 42-acre fortress included a 2-mile defensive wall, crumbling sections of which remain, especially in Rougemont and Northernhay Gardens. Saxon and Norman times saw growth: a cas-

tle went up in 1068, the cathedral 40 years later. The Tudor wool boom brought Exeter an export trade, riches and half-timbered houses; prosperity continued into the Georgian era when hundreds of merchants built genteel homes. The Blitz of WWII brought devastation. In just one night in 1942, 156 people died and 30 acres of the city were flattened. Fast forward to 2007 and the £220 million Princesshay shopping centre has added shimmering glass and steel lines to the architectural mix.

## Orientation

South of the ruined castle, the city centre radiates out from the grassy square around the cathedral; the redeveloped quay is 500m south. There are two main train stations, Central and St David's; most long-distance trains use St David's, a mile northwest of the centre.

## Information

### BOOKSHOPS

**Waterstone's** ( ☎ 01392-218392; 48-49 High St; 🕙 9am-5.30pm Mon-Fri, 9am-6pm Sat, 10.30am-4.30pm Sun)

### EMERGENCY

**Police station** ( ☎ 08452 777444; Heavitree Rd; 🕙 24hr)
**Royal Devon & Exeter Hospital** ( ☎ 01392-411611; Barrack Rd)

### INTERNET ACCESS

**Exeter Library** ( ☎ 01392-384200; Castle St; 🕙 9.30am-7pm Mon, Tue, Thu & Fri, 10am-5pm Wed,

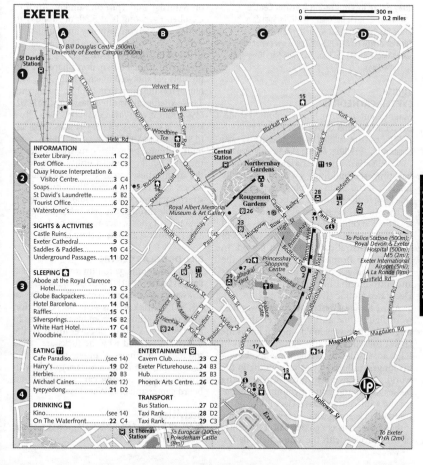

**EXETER**

| INFORMATION | | |
| --- | --- | --- |
| Exeter Library | 1 | C2 |
| Post Office | 2 | C3 |
| Quay House Interpretation & Visitor Centre | 3 | C4 |
| Soaps | 4 | A1 |
| St David's Laundrette | 5 | B2 |
| Tourist Office | 6 | D2 |
| Waterstone's | 7 | C3 |

| SIGHTS & ACTIVITIES | | |
| --- | --- | --- |
| Castle Ruins | 8 | C2 |
| Exeter Cathedral | 9 | C3 |
| Saddles & Paddles | 10 | C4 |
| Underground Passages | 11 | D2 |

| SLEEPING | | |
| --- | --- | --- |
| Abode at the Royal Clarence Hotel | 12 | C3 |
| Globe Backpackers | 13 | C4 |
| Hotel Barcelona | 14 | D4 |
| Raffles | 15 | C1 |
| Silversprings | 16 | B2 |
| White Hart Hotel | 17 | C4 |
| Woodbine | 18 | B2 |

| EATING | | |
| --- | --- | --- |
| Cafe Paradiso | (see 14) | |
| Harry's | 19 | D2 |
| Herbies | 20 | B3 |
| Michael Caines | (see 12) | |
| tyepyedong | 21 | D2 |

| DRINKING | | |
| --- | --- | --- |
| Kino | (see 14) | |
| On The Waterfront | 22 | C4 |

| ENTERTAINMENT | | |
| --- | --- | --- |
| Cavern Club | 23 | C2 |
| Exeter Picturehouse | 24 | B3 |
| Hub | 25 | B3 |
| Phoenix Arts Centre | 26 | C2 |

| TRANSPORT | | |
| --- | --- | --- |
| Bus Station | 27 | D2 |
| Taxi Rank | 28 | D2 |
| Taxi Rank | 29 | C3 |

**SOUTHWEST ENGLAND**

9.30am-4pm Sat, 11am-2.30pm Sun) First 30 minutes free, then per hr £3.

## LAUNDRY
**Soaps** ( ☎ 01392-491930; Isambard Pde; ☺ 8.15am-7.45pm Mon-Sat, 9.15am-5.45pm Sun; per load £1.70
**St David's Laundrette** (St David's Hill; per load £2.20; ☺ 8am-9pm)

## MEDIA
*The List* magazine (50p) details events, listings, bars and restaurants in the Exeter area.

## POST
**Post office main branch** ( ☎ 01392-223344; Bedford St; ☺ 9am-5.30pm Mon-Sat)

## TOURIST INFORMATION
**Quay House Interpretation & Visitor Centre** ( ☎ 01392-271611; The Quay; ☺ 10am-5pm daily Easter-Oct, 11am-4pm Sat & Sun Nov-Easter)
**Tourist office** ( ☎ 01392-265700; www.exeter.gov .uk/visiting; Paris St; ☺ 9am-5pm Mon-Sat, 10am-4pm Sun Jul & Aug)

## Sights
### EXETER CATHEDRAL
Magnificent in warm, honey-coloured stone, Exeter's **Cathedral Church of St Peter** ( ☎ 01392-255573; www.exeter-cathedral.org.uk; Cathedral Cl; suggested donation £4; ☺ 9.30am-6.30pm Mon-Fri, 9am-5pm Sat, 7.30am-6.30pm Sun) is framed by lawns and wonky half-timbered buildings – a quintessentially English scene often peopled by picnickers snacking to the sound of the bells.

The site has been a religious one since at least the 5th century but the Normans started the current building in 1114; the towers of today's cathedral date from that period. In 1270 Bishop Bronescombe remodelled the whole building, a process that took 90 years and introduced a mix of Early English and Decorated Gothic styles.

Above the **Great West Front** scores of weather-worn figures line an image screen that was originally brightly painted – now it forms the largest collection of 14th-century sculpture in England. Inside, the ceiling is mesmerising – the longest unbroken Gothic vaulting in the world, it sweeps up to meet ornate ceiling bosses in gilt and vibrant colours. Look out for the 15th-century **Exeter Clock** in the north transept: in keeping with medieval astronomy it shows the earth as a golden ball at the centre of the universe with the sun, a fleur-de-lys,

travelling round. Still ticking and whirring, it chimes on the hour.

The huge oak canopy over the **Bishop's Throne** was carved in 1312, while the 1350 **minstrels' gallery** is decorated with 12 angels playing musical instruments. Cathedral staff will point out the famous sculpture of the **lady with two left feet** and the tiny **St James Chapel**, built to repair the one destroyed in the Blitz in 1942. Look out for its unusual carvings: a cat, a mouse and, oddly, a rugby player.

In the **Refectory** ( ☎ 01392-285988; ☺ 10am-4.45pm Mon-Sat) you can tuck into cakes, quiches and soups at trestle tables surrounded by vaulted ceilings, stained glass and busts of the great, the good and the dead.

Free 45-minute guided tours run at 11am and 2.30pm Monday to Friday, 11am on Saturday and 4pm on Sunday, April to October. Evensong is at 5.30pm Monday to Friday and 3pm on Saturday and Sunday.

### UNDERGROUND PASSAGES
Prepare to crouch down, don a hard hat and possibly get spooked in what is the only system of its kind open to the public in England. These medieval, vaulted **passages** ( ☎ 01392-665887; Paris St; adult/child £5/3.50; ☺ 9.30am-5.30pm Mon-Sat, 10.30am-4pm Sun Jun-Sep, 11.30am-5.30pm Tue-Fri, 9.30am-5.30pm Sat & 11.30am-4pm Sun Oct-May) were built to house pipes bringing fresh water to the city. Unlike modern utility companies, the authorities opted to have permanent access for repairs, rather than dig up the streets each time – genius. Guides lead you on a scramble through the network regaling you with tales of ghosts, escape routes and cholera. The last tour is an hour before closing.

### BILL DOUGLAS CENTRE
A delightful homage to film and fun, the **Bill Douglas Centre** ( ☎ 01392-264321; www.billdouglas.org; University of Exeter, Old Library, Prince of Wales Rd; admission free; ☺ 10am-4pm Mon-Fri) is a compact collection of all things celluloid, from magic lanterns to Mickey Mouse. Inside discover just what the butler did see and why the flicks are called the flicks. In a mass of movie memorabilia Charlie Chaplin bottle stoppers mingle with Ginger Rogers playing cards, James Bond board games and Star Wars toys.

## Activities
**Saddles & Paddles** ( ☎ 01392-424241; www.sadpad.com; 4 Kings Wharf, The Quay; ☺ 9.30am-5.30pm) on Exeter

quayside rents out bikes (adult/child per hour £5/4, per hour £14/10) and Canadian canoes (per one/six hours £10/35) allowing you to explore Exeter's canal and the footpaths that wind toward the sea.

## Tours

**Redcoat Guided Tours** ( ☎ 01392-265203; www.exeter .gov.uk/visiting; 2 to 5 daily Apr-Oct, 2 to 3 daily Nov-Mar) are free and hugely varied. Themes range from ghosts and murder to Romans and religion – there's even a torch-lit prowl through the catacombs. Tours leave from Cathedral Yard or the quay, pick up a program from the tourist office.

## Sleeping

### BUDGET

**Globe Backpackers** ( ☎ 01392-215521; www.exeterback packers.co.uk; 71 Holloway St; dm £15, 7th night free, d £40; 💻 ) This relaxed hostel is housed inside a rambling house near the quay. It's spotlessly clean and run by a friendly husband-and-wife team. There's only one double room so plan ahead.

**Exeter YHA** ( ☎ 0845 371 9516; www.yha.org.uk; 47 Countess Wear Rd; dm £15.95; P 💻 ) Exeter's official hostel is in a spacious 17th-century house overlooking the River Exe. The facilities are good and the dorms are reasonably sized, but being 2 miles out of town is a drawback. Catch bus K or T from High St, or 57 or 85 from the bus station to School Lane and follow the signs.

### MIDRANGE

**Woodbine** ( ☎ 01392-203302; www.woodbineguest house.co.uk; 1 Woodbine Tce; s/d £38/65) A bit of a surprise sits behind this archetypal flower-framed B&B facade: fresh, contemporary rooms with low beds and flashes of burgundy – there is even underfloor heating in the showers.

**ourpick Raffles** ( ☎ 01392-270200; www.raffles-exeter.co.uk; 11 Blackall Rd; s/d/f £38/68/78; P ) Creaking with antiques and oozing atmosphere, this late-Victorian B&B is a lovely blend of old woods and tasteful modern fabrics. Plant stands and dado rails add to the turn-of-the-century feel, while the largely organic breakfasts, walled garden and much coveted parking make it a great value choice.

**White Hart Hotel** ( ☎ 01392-279897; www.roomat theinn.info; 66 South St; s £60, d £70-75; P ) They've been putting people up here since the Plantagenets were on the throne (1300s). The courtyard is a wisteria-fringed bobble of cobbles and the bar is book-lined and beamed. Rooms are either traditional (dark woods and rich drapes) or contemporary (laminate floors and light fabrics).

**Silversprings** ( ☎ 01392-494040; www.silversprings .co.uk; 12 Richmond Rd; s £55, d £80-90, f £95, ste £100) This oh-so-chi-chi Georgian town house will either leave you longing to recline and varnish your nails or slightly overwhelmed. Rooms are all gilt mirrors and silky, vibrant fabrics – the best have real coffee, a free half-bottle of wine and fluffy bathrobes.

### TOP END

**ourpick Hotel Barcelona** ( ☎ 01392-281000; www.ali ashotels.com; Magdalen St; s £105, d £125-145; P 💻 ) The fabulous revamp of this former eye hospital has more wit than a festival full of comedians. The building's medical past features alongside ultra-arty twists: plush deep-green carpets slice across the original hospital flooring, while the hospital lift still ferries guests up and down. But with rich woods, vivid furnishings and deeply luxurious bathrooms, it's unlike any institution you've ever seen. You can even sleep in the old operating theatre – room 220 – without a trolley bed (or a surgeon) in sight.

**Abode at the Royal Clarence Hotel** ( ☎ 01392-319955; www.abodehotels.co.uk/exeter; Cathedral Yard; r £125-250) Georgian grandeur meets minimalist chic in these, the poshest rooms in town, where wonky floors and stained glass blend with pared-down furniture and neutral tones. The top-end suite is bigger than most people's apartments; its slanted ceilings and beams frame a grandstand cathedral view.

## Eating

**Herbies** ( ☎ 01392-258473; 15 North St; mains £5-9; 🕒 lunch Mon-Sat, dinner Tue-Sat) Cosy and gently groovy, Herbies has been cheerfully feeding Exeter's vegetarians for 20 years. It's *the* place in town to tuck into delicious butterbean and vegetable pie, Moroccan tagine or cashew-nut loaf. It's strong on vegan dishes, too.

**tyepyedong** ( ☎ 01392-251888; 175 Sidwell St; mains £7-9; 🕒 lunch & dinner Mon-Sat) Tucked away in an unlikely terrace of modern shops, this fusion food and noodle bar has a pristine, modern feel and rustles up great-value *ramen* and *udon* noodles – the lunchtime dish-and-a-drink deal costs £5.

SOUTHWEST ENGLAND

**Harry's** ( ☎ 01392-202234; 86 Longbrook St; mains £7-19; ☺ lunch & dinner) Harry's is the kind of welcoming neighbourhood bistro you wish was on your own doorstep, but rarely is. The decor is all wooden chairs, blackboards and gilt mirrors; the food includes goats' cheese and walnut burgers, chargrilled chicken and classic pizzas.

**Cafe Paradiso** ( ☎ 01392-281000; Magdalen St; mains lunch £4-9, dinner £11-28; ☺ lunch & dinner) Set in a futuristic glass-sided circus top, Hotel Barcelona's funky restaurant is dotted with Rothko-esque artwork and (intriguingly) painted white bicycles. Lunch is chic (silver mullet with herb gnocchi), while there's stylish dining at night – try the wood-fired trout.

**Michael Caines** ( ☎ 01392-223638; www.michaelcaines .com; Cathedral Yard; mains £24; ☺ breakfast, lunch & dinner) Housed in the Royal Clarence and run by a locally-famous Michelin-starred chef, the food here is a complex fusion of Westcountry ingredients and full-bodied French flavours. Top tips are the monkfish with red wine butter or the Devon lamb with ratatouille. There's a bargain two-course lunch (£14.50) and a seven-course tasting menu (£58).

## Drinking

**On The Waterfront** ( ☎ 01392-210590; The Quay; ☺ lunch & dinner) In 1835 this was a warehouse; now its red-brick, barrel-vaulted ceilings stretch back from a minimalist bar. The tables that stretch along the quayside are perfect for a riverside pint.

**Kino** ( ☎ 01392-281000; Hotel Barcelona; Magdalen St; ☺ 6pm-1.30am Mon-Sat) More like a film set than a cocktail lounge, Kino's centrepiece is a stunning 1930s-style bar. Original film posters line the walls, while all around wannabe movie stars sip the seriously good cocktails and ponder their profiles.

## Entertainment

**Phoenix Arts Centre** ( ☎ 01392-667080; www. exeterphoenix.org.uk; Gandy St) The city's art and soul; Phoenix is a vibrant hub of exhibitions, performance, music, dance, film, classes and workshops. There's a buzzing cafe-bar too.

**Exeter Picturehouse** ( ☎ 01392-435522; www.picture-houses.co.uk; 51 Bartholomew St West) This intimate, independent cinema screens mainstream and art-house movies.

**Hub** ( ☎ 01392-424628; 1 Mary Arches St; ☺ 8pm-midnight, 9pm-2am when bands play) A showcase for

everything from thrash metal to alternative rock and DJs.

**Cavern Club** ( ☎ 01392-495370; www.cavernclub.co.uk; 83-84 Queen St; ☺ 11am-5pm Mon-Sat & 8pm-1am Sun-Thu, to 2am Fri & Sat) A longstanding venue for big-name DJs and breaking acts from the indie scene.

## Getting There & Away
### AIR

Scheduled services connect **Exeter International Airport** ( ☎ 01392-367433; www.exeter-airport.co.uk) with cities in Europe and the UK, including Glasgow, Manchester and Newcastle, as well as the Channel Islands and the Isles of Scilly. A key operator is **FlyBe** ( ☎ 0871 700 2000; www.flybe.com).

### BUS

Bus X38 goes to Plymouth (£6, 1¼ hours, hourly). Bus X9 runs to Bude (£5.50, three hours, five daily, two on Sunday) via Okehampton.

On Sundays throughout the year, bus 82 runs two to five times daily across Dartmoor from Exeter to Plymouth (£6, 2¼ hours), taking in Moretonhampstead (45 minutes), Postbridge (1¼ hours) and Princetown (1 hour 20 minutes). It also runs twice on Saturdays between May and September. Between late July and late August it also runs twice a day, Monday to Friday, but only between Moretonhampstead and Plymouth – bus 359 from Exeter to Moretonhampstead connects with the service. Bus X64 runs to Totnes (one hour, six daily Monday to Saturday, two on Sunday).

### TRAIN

Trains link Exeter St David's to London Paddington (£58, 2¾ hours, hourly), Bristol (£20, 1¼ hours, half-hourly) and Penzance (£15, three hours, hourly). Main-line trains run to Plymouth (£6.90, one hour, two or three per hour); a branch line also shuttles to Torquay (£6, 45 minutes, hourly) and Paignton (£6.30, 50 minutes). Frequent trains go to Totnes (£8.50, 45 minutes).

The picturesque Tarka Line connects Exeter Central with Barnstaple (£7, 1¼ hours, every two hours Monday to Saturday, four to six on Sunday).

## Getting Around
### TO/FROM THE AIRPORT

Buses 56 and 379 run from the bus station and Exeter St David's train station to Exeter

International Airport (20 to 30 minutes, hourly), 5 miles east of the city. The service stops at 6pm.

### BUS
The one-day Explorer pass (adult/child £6/4) gives unlimited transport on Stagecoach's Exeter buses. Bus H links St David's and Central train stations and passes near the bus station.

### CAR
The tourist office has a list of car-hire offices; try **Europcar** ( ☎ 01392-275398; Water Lane; ☯ 8.30am-5.30pm Mon-Fri, to 1pm Sat).

Park & Ride buses run from Matford (bus PR5) and Honiton Rd (PR2), every 10 minutes.

### TAXI
There are taxi ranks at St David's train station and on High St, or call **Capital Taxis** ( ☎ 01392-433433), **Club Cars** ( ☎ 01392-213030) or **Gemini** ( ☎ 01392-666666).

For bike hire see (p354).

## AROUND EXETER
### Powderham Castle
The historic home of the Earl of Devon, **Powderham** ( ☎ 01626-890243; www.powderham.co.uk; adult/child £8.50/6.50; ☯ 10am-5.30pm Easter-Oct, closed Sat) is a stately but still friendly place, built in 1391, damaged in the Civil War and remodelled in the Victorian era. A visit takes in a fine wood-panelled Great Hall, park land with 650 deer and a glimpse of life 'below stairs' in the kitchen. The earl and family are still resident and, despite its grandeur, for charming, fleeting moments it feels like you're actually wandering through someone's sitting room.

Powderham is on the River Exe near Kenton, 8 miles south of Exeter. Bus 2 runs from Exeter (20 minutes, every 15 minutes Monday to Saturday, every 30 minutes Sunday).

### A La Ronde
**A La Ronde** (NT; ☎ 01395-265514; Summer Lane, Exmouth; adult/child £5.40/2.70; ☯ 11am-5pm Sat-Wed late Mar-Oct) is a DIY job with a difference. This delightfully quirky 16-sided cottage was built in 1796 for two spinster cousins to display a mass of curiosities acquired on a 10-year European grand tour. Its glass alcoves, low lintels and tiny doorways mean it's like clambering through a doll's house – highlights are a delicate feather frieze

in the drawing room and a gallery smothered with a thousand seashells. In a fabulous collision of old and new, this can only be seen via remote control CCTV from the butler's pantry. The house is 10 miles south of Exeter, near Exmouth; bus 57 runs close by.

## SOUTH DEVON COAST
### Torquay & Paignton
pop 110,370

For decades the bright 'n' breezy seaside resort of Torquay pitched itself as an exotic 'English Riviera' – playing on a mild microclimate, palm trees and promenades. But these days Torquay's nightclubs and bars attract a much younger crowd and the result is a sometimes bizarre clash of cultures: coach parties meet stag parties on streets lined with fudge shops and slightly saucy postcards. Chuck in some truly top-notch restaurants, a batch of good beaches and an Agatha Christie connection, and it all makes for some grand days out beside the sea. Just to the south of Torquay is Paignton with its seafront prom, multicoloured beach huts and faded 19th-century pier.

The **tourist office** ( ☎ 0870 707 0010; www.theenglishriviera.co.uk; Vaughan Pde; ☯ 9.30am-5pm Mon-Sat & 10am-4.30pm Sun May-Sep, 9.30am-5pm Mon-Sat Oct-Apr) sells discounted tickets to local attractions.

### SIGHTS & ACTIVITIES
Torquay has two famous former residents: Agatha Christie, who was born in Torquay in 1890 and lived at the manor house of Greenway (p359), near Dartmouth; and Basil Fawlty, the deranged Torquay hotelier played memorably by John Cleese in the classic British comedy *Fawlty Towers*.

**Torquay Museum** ( ☎ 01803-293975; 529 Babbacombe Rd; adult/child £4/2.50; ☯ 10am-5pm Mon-Sat & 1.30-5pm Sun Jul-Sep) has an intriguing selection of Agatha Christie memorabilia including family photos, first edition novels and a couple of display cases devoted to her famous detectives Hercule Poirot and Miss Marple.

**Torbay Belle** ( ☎ 01803-528555) runs boat trips to Brixham (p358; adult/child return £6/3) from North Quay in the harbour, and to Dartmouth (p359; adult/child return £14/7) from Haldon Pier. The trips to Agatha Christie's garden at Greenway leave from Princess Pier.

Torquay is surrounded by 20 beaches, the best of which is family-friendly **Babbacombe**, about 2 miles north of the centre, which still has a working 1920s **funicular** ( ☎ 01803-328750; adult/child return £1.75/1.20; ☺ 9.30am-5.25pm Easter-Sep) connecting the beach to the cliff-top.

### SLEEPING

Torquay is practically wall-to-wall B&Bs and hotels, with a concentrated cluster around Avenue and Bridge Rds.

**Torquay International Backpackers** ( ☎ 01803-299924; www.torquaybackpackers.co.uk; 119 Abbey Rd; dm/d £14/30) Relics of happy travels (world maps, board games and homemade wind chimes) are everywhere in this funky, friendly, laid-back hostel. The owners hand out guitars and organise barbecues, beach trips and local pub tours.

**Headland View** ( ☎ 01803-312612; www.headland view.com; Babbacombe Downs; s/d £45/64) Set high on the cliffs at Babbacombe, this B&B is awash with nauticalia: from boat motifs on the curtains to 'welcome' lifebelts on the walls. Four rooms have tiny flower-filled balconies over-looking a cracking stretch of sea.

**ourpick** **Lanscombe House** ( ☎ 01803-606938; www.lanscombehouse.co.uk; Cockington Lane; s £50-60, d £75-110) Laura Ashley herself would love the lashings of tasteful fabrics, four-poster beds and free-standing slipper baths on show here. Set amid the calm of Cockington Country Park between Torquay and Paignton, it has a lovely English cottage garden where you can hear owls hoot at night.

**Hillcroft** ( ☎ 01803-297247; www.thehillcroft.co.uk; 9 St Lukes Rd; d £75-85, ste £130-180) Full of boutique flourishes, the themed rooms in this mini hotel veer from French antique to Asian chic. The sumptuous bathrooms range from grotto-esque to sleekly styled, and the top-floor suite is gorgeous.

### EATING & DRINKING

Torbay sizzles with some seriously good restaurants, including one with a Michelin star, as well the full complement of chippies.

**Number 7** ( ☎ 01803-295055; Beacon Tce; mains £15; ☺ dinner & lunch Wed-Sat) Fabulous smells fill the air at this buzzing harbourside fish bistro, where the menu is packed with super-fresh crab, lobster and monkfish, often with un-expected twists. Try the king scallops with vermouth or fish and prawn tempura.

**Elephant** ( ☎ 01803-200044; www.elephantrestaurant .co.uk; 3 Beacon Tce; 2/3 courses £33/40, brasserie mains £14; ☺ dinner Tue-Sat, brasserie lunch & dinner Tue-Sat & lunch Sun) One to remember. Torbay's Michelin-starred restaurant is full of imaginative flavour fusions; try venison with vanilla and beet-root or sea bass with hog's pudding gnocchi. If that's a bit much, they'll do you a steak. There's fine dining in The Room or brasserie fare downstairs.

Other recommendations:

**Hole In The Wall** ( ☎ 01803-200755; 6 Park Lane) Heavily beamed, tardis-like boozer – an atmospheric spot for a pint.

### GETTING THERE & AWAY

Bus 12 runs to Paignton from Torquay (20 minutes, every 10 minutes) and on to Brixham (40 minutes). Bus X80 goes to Totnes (one hour, every two hours) and on to Plymouth (£5.20, 1¾ hours). Bus 111 goes to Dartmouth (1¾ hours, hourly Monday to Saturday, three on Sunday).

A branch train line runs from Exeter via Torquay (£6, 45 minutes, hourly) to Paignton (£6.30, 50 minutes). The **Paignton & Dartmouth Steam Railway** ( ☎ 01803-555872; www.paignton-steam-railway.co.uk; adult/child return £8/5.50) puffs from Paignton on the charming 7-mile trip (30 minutes) to Kingswear on the River Dart, linked by ferry to Dartmouth (car/pedestrian £3.30/1, six minutes). Generally four to nine trains run daily between April and October, but there are exceptions – check with the operator.

## Brixham
pop 17,460

An appealing, pastel-painted tumbling of fishermen's cottages leads down to Brixham's horseshoe harbour, signalling a very different place from Torquay. Here gently tacky arcades coexist with winding streets, brightly coloured boats and one of England's busiest working fishing ports. Although picturesque, Brixham is far from a neatly packaged resort and its brand of gritty charm offers a more accurate glimpse of life along Devon's coast.

The **tourist office** ( ☎ 0870 707 0010; www.the englishriviera.co.uk; Old Market House, The Quay; ☺ 9.30am-5pm Mon-Sat, 10am-4pm Sun Apr-Oct) is right beside the harbour.

A full-sized replica of Devon seafarer Sir Francis Drake's ship, the **Golden Hind** ( ☎ 01803-856223; adult/child £3/2; ☺ 10am-4pm Mar-Sep), is tied up in Brixham harbour. It's remarkably small; the Elizabethan original had a crew of 60. Today you get to cross the gangplank, peer in the tiny captain's cabin and prowl around the poop deck.

SOUTHWEST ENGLAND

The displays at **Brixham Heritage Museum** ( ☎ 01803-856267; www.brixhamheritage.org.uk; Bolton Cross; adult/child £2/1.50; ☒ 10am-5pm Mon-Fri, 10am-1pm Sat, closed Nov-Jan) explore the town's salty history with exhibits on smuggling and the curious items dragged up by local trawlers.

There are plenty of chippies scattered around the quay but for a real taste of the British seaside, try a pot of prawns or fresh crab from **Browse Seafoods** ( ☎ 01803-882484), next to the tourist office.

Bus 22 runs along the coast to Kingswear (30 minutes, half-hourly Monday to Saturday, hourly Sunday) from where you can catch the river ferry over to Dartmouth. Bus 12 connects Torquay and Bixham via Paignton (see opposite).

## Dartmouth
pop 5693

A bewitching blend of primary-coloured boats and delicately shaded houses, Dartmouth is hard to resist. Buildings cascade down steep, wooded slopes towards the River Dart while 17th-century shops with splendidly carved and gilded fronts line narrow lanes. Its popularity with a trendy sailing set means there's a risk of too many boutiques and upmarket restaurants, but Dartmouth is also a busy port and the constant traffic of working boats ensures an authentic tang of the sea. Agatha Christie's summer home and a captivating art deco house are both nearby, adding to the town's appeal.

Dartmouth hugs the quay on the west side of Dart estuary; the village of Kingswear on the east bank provides a key transport link to Torbay and is connected by an array of car and foot ferries. Dartmouth's **tourist office** ( ☎ 01803-834224; www.discoverdartmouth.com; Mayor's Ave; ☒ 9.30am-5.30pm Mon-Sat year round, plus 10am-2pm Sun Apr-Oct) houses the Newcomen Engine, an early (1712) steam engine.

**Greenway** (NT; ☎ 01803-842382; Greenway Rd, Galmpton; adult/child £6/3; ☒ 10.30am-5pm Wed-Sun Mar-Sep), the enchanting summer home of crime writer Agatha Christie, sits beside the River Dart near Dartmouth. Woods speckled with splashes of magnolias, daffodils and hydrangeas hug the water, while the planting creates intimate, secret spaces – the boathouse and views over the river are delightful. After extensive renovation the house was due to open in 2009. Driving to Greenway is discouraged; you can hike along the Dart Valley Trail from Kingswear (4 miles)

or sail upriver from Dartmouth on the **Greenway Ferry** ( ☎ 01803-844010; adult/child £6/4). Boats run only when the property is open; times vary and it's best to book.

**Coleton Fishacre** (NT; ☎ 01803-752466; Brownstone Rd, Kingswear; adult/child £6.40/3.20; ☒ garden 10.30am-5pm, house 11am-4.30pm Wed-Sun mid-Mar–Oct) was built in the 1920s for the D'Oyly Carte family of theatre impresarios – they also owned London's Savoy Hotel. Its gorgeous art deco embellishments include original Lalique tulip uplighters, comic bathroom tiles and a stunning saloon – complete with tinkling piano. The croquet terrace leads to deeply shelving subtropical gardens and suddenly revealed vistas of the sea. Hike the 4 miles along the cliffs from Kingswear, or drive.

**Dartmouth Castle** (EH; ☎ 01803-833588; adult/child £4/2; ☒ 10am-6pm daily Jul & Aug, 10am-5pm Apr-Jun & Sep, 10am-4pm Oct, 10am-4pm Sat & Sun only Nov-Mar), at the mouth of the estuary, is great for some battlement scrambling. In the centre of town the row of wonky timber-framed houses that looks near to collapse is the **Butterwalk** – it's actually managed to remain standing since the late 17th century.

### SLEEPING

**Hill View House** ( ☎ 01803-839372; www.hillviewdartmouth.co.uk; 76 Victoria Rd; s £39-47, d £57-70) This eco-conscious place to kip features environmentally-friendly toiletries, natural cotton, long-life lightbulbs and organic breakfasts. Rooms are tastefully decked out in cream and brown and there's a 5% discount for non-car users.

**Brown's Hotel** ( ☎ 01803-832572; www.brownshoteldartmouth.co.uk; 29 Victoria Rd; s £65, d £85-170) How do you combine leather curtains, pheasant feather–covered lampshades and animal-print chairs and still make it look classy? The owners of this smoothly sumptuous hotel have worked it out. Look out for the lobster and frites evenings in their tapas bar too.

**Orleans** ( ☎ 01803-835450; www.orleans-guesthouse-dartmouth.co.uk; 24 South Town; d £85-95, ste £165) Purple and gold fabrics, marble fireplaces and bare floorboards grace this oh-so-chic guesthouse. There's a bay window in which to enjoy a game of chess – if you can tear your eyes away from the boats on the water below.

### EATING & DRINKING

**our pick Crab Shell** ( ☎ 01803-839036; 1 Raleigh St; sandwiches £4; ☒ lunch, closed Jan-Mar) The shellfish gracing the sarnies here has been landed on the quay a few steps away, and much of the fish has been smoked locally. Opt to fill your bread with mackerel with horseradish mayo, kiln-roast salmon with dill, or classic, delicious Dartmouth crab.

**Taylor's** ( ☎ 01803-832748; 8 The Quay; mains £15; ⏰ lunch Tue-Sat, dinner Fri & Sat, nightly Jul & Aug) The huge bay windows here mean you can watch boats bobbing about, while the menu ensures a tastebud treat too. There's everything from grilled lobster or Devon lamb to asparagus and goats-cheese tart.

**New Angel** ( ☎ 01803-839425; 2 South Embankment; mains £18-23; ⏰ breakfast, lunch & dinner Tue-Sat, breakfast & lunch Sun & Mon) The fanciest, most famous joint in town. Awarded a Michelin star and run by celebrity chef John Burton Race (of *French Leave* fame), it serves up pheasant, Devon duck and local fish with more than a soupçon of continental flair.

### GETTING THERE & AWAY

Bus 93 runs to Plymouth (£5.30, two hours, hourly, four on Sunday) via Kingsbridge (one hour). Bus 111 goes to Torquay (1¾ hours, hourly Monday to Saturday, three on Sunday) via Totnes. Ferries shuttle across the river to Kingswear (car/pedestrian £3.30/1) every six minutes; they run from 6.30am to 10.45pm.

**River Link** ( ☎ 01803-834488; www.riverlink.co.uk; adult/child return £9/6; ⏰ Apr-Oct) runs cruises along the River Dart to Totnes (1¼ hours, two to four daily).

For details of the Paignton & Dartmouth Steam Railway, see p358.

## Totnes
pop 8194

Totnes has such a reputation for being alternative that local jokers wrote 'twinned with Narnia' under the town sign. For decades famous as Devon's hippie haven, eco-conscious Totnes also became Britain's first 'transition town' in 2005, when it began trying to wean itself off a dependence on oil. Sustainability aside, Totnes boasts a gracious Norman castle, a mass of fine Tudor buildings, an unusual Jazz Age house and a tempting vineyard.

The **tourist office** ( ☎ 01803-863168; www.totnes information.co.uk; Coronation Rd; ⏰ 9.30am-5pm Mon-Sat) is in the town's old mill.

### SIGHTS & ACTIVITIES

The white and vivid blue Modern Movement **High Cross House** ( ☎ 01803-864114; Dartington Hall Estate; adult/child £3.50/2.50; ⏰ Tue-Fri: 10.30am-12.30pm & 2-4.30pm late Jul–Aug, 2-4.30pm May–mid-Jul & Sep-Oct) was built in 1932, making its rectilinear and curved design one of the first examples of its kind in the country. The interior is gorgeous: all pared-down shapes, smooth woods and understated elegance. High Cross sits alongside the main road inside the Dartington Hall Estate, 1.5 miles west of Totnes.

**Sharpham Vineyard** ( ☎ 01803-732203; www .sharpham.com; Ashprington; tours & tastings £5-50; ⏰ 10am-5pm Mon-Sat Mar-Dec plus Sun Jun-Aug) shelters in a tranquil riverside setting. It provides the chance to wander among the vines, learn about vinification and indulge in tutored tastings – they also make cheese on the estate so you can nibble that, too. The vineyard is 3 miles south of Totnes, signed off the A381 – or walk from town along the Dart Valley Trail.

**Totnes Castle** (EH; ☎ 01803-864406; adult/child £2.50/1.30; ⏰ 10am-6pm Jul & Aug, to 5pm Easter-Sep, to 4pm Oct) occupies a commanding position on a grassy hilltop above town. Little remains of the original Norman motte-and-bailey fortress but the outer keep is still standing, and the views of the town and surrounding fields are fantastic.

**Canoe Adventures** ( ☎ 01803-865301; www.canoe adventures.co.uk; per 5hr £17) organises trips on the Dart in 12-seater Canadian canoes. They often work in a campfire or a pub visit, and their monthly moonlit paddles are a treat.

### SLEEPING

**Old Forge** ( ☎ 01803-862174; www.oldforgetotnes.com; Seymour Pl; s £52, d £62-82, f £107) This 600-year-old B&B used to be a smithy and the town jail – thankfully comfort has replaced incarceration: deep-red and sky-blue furnishings cosy up to bright throws and spa baths. The delightful family room even has its own decked sun terrace.

**Maltsters Arms** ( ☎ 01803-732350; www.tuckenhay .com; d from £75-110) The rooms in this old creekside pub are anything but ordinary, ranging from silky and eastern to authentically nautical – one even sports painted oil drums and real anchors. It's hidden away in the hamlet of Tuckenhay, 4 miles south of Totnes.

**Steam Packet Inn** ( ☎ 01803-863880; www.steam packetinn.co.uk; St Peters Quay; d/f £80/110) Plucked from the pages of a design magazine, the minimalist bedrooms of this wharfside former warehouse are full of painted wood panels, willow arrangements and neutral tones. Ask for a river view room then watch the world float by.

### EATING

**Willow Vegetarian Restaurant** ( ☎ 01803-862605; 87 High St; mains £5.50; ✆ lunch Mon-Sat, dinner Wed, Fri & Sat) The hang-out of choice for Totnes' New Agers, this rustic wholefood cafe does a nice line in couscous, quiches, hotpots and home-made cakes. Look out for the curry nights.

**Rumour** ( ☎ 01803-864682; 30 Fore St; mains £10.50-14; ✆ 10am-11pm Mon-Sat, 6-10.30pm Sun) It's so friendly here it's almost like dining in a friend's front room. The menu is packed with pizzas, pan-fried sea trout and Salcombe ice cream; its pioneering eco-policy includes using heat from the kitchen to warm the water.

**our pick** **Riverford Field Kitchen** ( ☎ 01803-762074; www.riverford.co.uk; Wash Barn, near Buckfastleigh; 2 courses adult/child £14/7; ✆ lunch, plus some Fri & Sat dinner) For a taste of ecofriendly Totnes head for this futuristic farm bistro. Vegetables are plucked to order from the fields in front of you to ensure minimal food miles, the meats are organic and locally sourced, and the dining area is a huge, hip hangar-like canteen. The food treatments are imaginative, too – try the marinated grilled Moroccan lamb and cumin and saffron veg. Planning laws require you to book and take a tour of the fields. The farm is three miles west of Totnes.

### GETTING THERE & AWAY

Bus X64 runs to Exeter (one hour, six daily Monday to Saturday, two on Sunday). Bus X80 comes from Plymouth (1¼ hours, hourly) and goes on to Paignton (20 minutes) and Torquay (30 minutes).

Frequent trains go to Exeter (£8.50, 45 minutes) and Plymouth (£5, 30 minutes, hourly). The privately run **South Devon Railway** ( ☎ 0845 345 1420; www.southdevonrailway.org) is beside the main-line station. Its steam trains chuff to Buckfastleigh (adult/child return £9.30/5.60, four or five daily Easter to October) on the edge of Dartmoor.

You can also cruise down the river to Dartmouth (opposite).

## PLYMOUTH

pop 256,633

If parts of Devon are costume dramas or nature programs, Plymouth is a healthy dose of reality TV. Gritty, and certainly not always pretty, its centre has been subjected to buildings even the architect's mother might question. But despite often being dismissed for its partying, poverty and urban problems, this is a city of huge spirit and great assets. Its setting on the fringes of an impressive natural harbour and just a few miles from the wilderness expanse of Dartmoor makes it an ideal base for activities. Add a rich maritime history, a Barbican area creaking with half-timbered houses, some unusual attractions and a decidedly lively nightlife, and you have a place to reconnect with the real before another foray into the delights of Devon's chocolate-box-pretty moors and shores.

### History

Plymouth's history is dominated by the sea. The first recorded cargo left the city in 1211 and by the late 16th century it was the port of choice for explorers and adventurers. It's waved off Sir Francis Drake, Sir Walter Raleigh, the fleet that defeated the Spanish Armada, the pilgrims who founded America, Charles Darwin, Captain Cook and countless boats carrying emigrants to Australia and New Zealand.

During WWII Plymouth suffered horrendously at the hands of the Luftwaffe – more than 1000 civilians died in the Blitz, which reduced the city centre to rubble. The 21st century has brought largescale regeneration of the city's waterfront areas and the architectural mishmash of the £200 million Drake Circus shopping centre.

### Orientation

Plymouth's pedestrianised centre is south of the train station. Further south again the headland Hoe area is packed with guesthouses and B&Bs; to the east of the Hoe the regenerated Barbican is packed with good places to eat and drink.

### Information

**Hoegate Laundrette** ( ☎ 01752-223031; 55 Notte St; ✆ 8am-6pm Mon-Fri, 9am-1pm Sat)
**Plymouth Library** ( ☎ 01752-305923; Drake Circus; ✆ 9am-7pm Mon-Fri, 9am-5pm Sat) Free internet access.
**Police station** (Charles Cross; ✆ 24hr)
**Post office** (5 St Andrew's Cross; ✆ 9am-5.30pm Mon-Sat)
**Tourist office** ( ☎ 01752-306330; www.visitplymouth .co.uk; 3-5 The Barbican; ✆ 9am-5pm Mon-Sat & 10am-4pm Sun Apr-Oct, 9am-5pm Mon-Fri & 10am-4pm Sat Nov-Mar) Housed inside the Plymouth Mayflower building.

**University Bookseller** ( ☎ 01752-660428; 42 Drake Circus; ⏱ 10am-4pm Mon-Sat)

## Sights & Activities
### PLYMOUTH HOE

Francis Drake supposedly spied the Spanish fleet from this grassy headland overlooking Plymouth Sound; the fabled bowling green on which he finished his game was probably where his **statue** now stands. Later the Hoe became a favoured holiday spot for the Victorian aristocracy, and the headland is backed by an impressive array of multistoreyed villas and once-grand hotels.

The red-and-white-striped former lighthouse, **Smeaton's Tower** ( ☎ 01752-603300; The Hoe; adult/child £2/1; ⏱ 10am-4pm Tue-Sat Apr-Oct, to 3pm Nov-Mar), was built 14 miles offshore on the Eddystone Rocks in 1759, then moved to the Hoe in 1882. Climbing its 93 steps provides an illuminating insight into lighthouse-keepers' lives and a stunning view of the city, Dartmoor and the sea.

### BARBICAN

To get an idea of what old Plymouth was like before the Blitz, head for the Barbican, with its many Tudor and Jacobean buildings (now converted into galleries, craft shops and restaurants).

The Pilgrim Fathers' *Mayflower* set sail for America from the Barbican on 16 September 1620. The **Mayflower Steps** mark the point of departure (track down the passenger list displayed on the side of a shop nearby); scores of other famous voyages are also marked by plaques at the steps, including one led by Captain James Cook, who set out from the Barbican in 1768 in search of a southern continent.

**Plymouth Mayflower** ( ☎ 01752-306330; 3-5 The Barbican; ⏱ 9am-5pm Mon-Sat & 10am-4pm Sun Apr-Oct, 9am-5pm Mon-Fri & 10am-4pm Sat Nov-Mar) is a hi-tech rundown through Plymouth's nautical heritage, providing the background to the Pilgrim Fathers' trip with plenty of interactive gizmos and multisensory displays.

The **Plymouth Gin Distillery** ( ☎ 01752-665292; www.plymouthgin.com; 60 Southside St; tours £6; ⏱ 10.30am-4.30pm Mon-Sat, 11.30am-3.30pm Sun) is the oldest producer of this kind of spirit in the world – they've been making gin here since 1793. The Royal Navy ferried it round the world in countless officers' messes and the brand was specified in the first recorded recipe for a dry martini in the 1930s. Tours wind past the stills and take in a tutored tasting before depositing you in the heavily beamed medieval bar for a free tipple.

A footbridge leads from the Barbican across the harbour to the **National Marine Aquarium** ( ☎ 01752-220084; The Barbican; www.national-aquarium.co.uk; adult/child £9.50/5.75; ⏱ 10am-6pm Apr-Oct, 10am-5pm Nov-Mar). Here sharks swim in coral seas teeming with moray eels, turtles and vividly coloured fish, while other displays highlight successful breeding programs of cardinal fish, coral and incredibly cute seahorses.

### MERCHANT'S HOUSE

The 17th-century **Merchant's House** ( ☎ 01752-304774; 33 St Andrews St; adult/child £1.50/1; ⏱ 10am-5pm Tue-Sat Apr-Sep) is packed with curiosities from manacles, truncheons and a ducking stool to a replica 19th-century schoolroom and an entire Victorian pharmacy where you get to try old-fashioned pill rolling.

### BOAT TRIPS & WATER SPORTS

**Sound Cruising** ( ☎ 01752-671166; www.soundcruising.com; Phoenix Warf) offers regular boat trips from Phoenix Warf out to the warships at Plymouth's naval base (1½-hour trips adult/child £6/2.75) and up the River Tamar to the Cornish village of Calstock (4½-hour trips adult/child £9.50/6.50).

The little yellow **Mount Batten Ferry** (adult/child return £3/2) shuttles (half-hourly) from beside the Mayflower Steps across to the Mount Batten Peninsula (10 minutes), where the **Mount Batten Centre** ( ☎ 01752-404567; www.mount-batten-centre.com; 70 Lawrence Rd, Mount Batten) does lessons in kayaking (two days £75) and sailing (two days £145).

## Sleeping

Fertile B&B hunting grounds are just back from Hoe, especially around Citadel Rd.

### BUDGET & MIDRANGE

**Jewell's** ( ☎ 01752-254760; 220 Citadel Rd; s £25, d £45-55, f £60-65) Traces of the Victorian era linger in the high ceilings and ornate plasterwork of this friendly B&B. Rooms are bright and modern with lilac armchairs and filmy blue curtains; top-quality bathrooms add another layer of class.

**Four Seasons** ☎ 01752-223591; www.fourseasonsguesthouse.co.uk; 207 Citadel Rd East; s £31-46, d £50-62, f £60) This place is crammed full of treats, from the big bowls of free sweets to the mounds of

SOUTHWEST ENGLAND

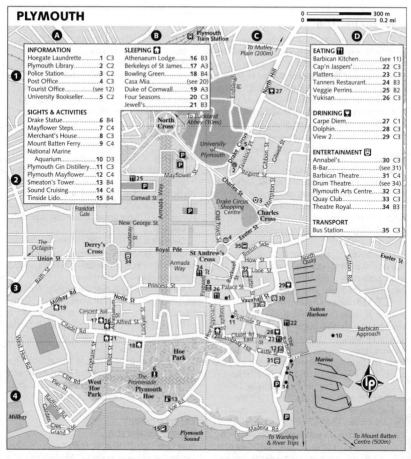

# PLYMOUTH

| | | 0 | 300 m |
| | | 0 | 0.2 mi |

**INFORMATION**
Hoegate Laundrette..........**1** C3
Plymouth Library...............**2** C2
Police Station....................**3** C2
Post Office........................**4** C3
Tourist Office...............(see 12)
University Bookseller.........**5** C2

**SIGHTS & ACTIVITIES**
Drake Statue.....................**6** B4
Mayflower Steps................**7** C4
Merchant's House..............**8** C4
Mount Batten Ferry...........**9** C4
National Marine
    Aquarium....................**10** D3
Plymouth Gin Distillery.....**11** C3
Plymouth Mayflower..........**12** C3
Smeaton's Tower..............**13** B4
Sound Cruising.................**14** C4
Tinside Lido......................**15** B4

**SLEEPING**
Athenaeum Lodge..........**16** B3
Berkeleys of St James.....**17** A3
Bowling Green.................**18** B4
Casa Mia......................(see 20)
Duke of Cornwall.............**19** A3
Four Seasons..................**20** C3
Jewell's.........................**21** B3

**EATING**
Barbican Kitchen...........(see 11)
Cap'n Jaspers'................**22** C3
Platters...........................**23** C3
Tanners Restaurant..........**24** B3
Veggie Perrins.................**25** B2
Yukisan............................**26** C3

**DRINKING**
Carpe Diem......................**27** C1
Dolphin............................**28** C3
View 2.............................**29** C3

**ENTERTAINMENT**
Annabel's.........................**30** C3
B-Bar.............................(see 31)
Barbican Theatre..............**31** C4
Drum Theatre................(see 34)
Plymouth Arts Centre........**32** C3
Quay Club........................**33** C3
Theatre Royal...................**34** B3

**TRANSPORT**
Bus Station......................**35** C3

---

Devon bacon for breakfast. They've got the basics right too: tasteful rooms decorated in gold and cream.

**Casa Mia** ( ☎ 01752-265742; www.casa-mia-onthehoe .com; 201 Citadel Rd East; s/d/f £30/60/60) A flower-filled patio and a highly polished brass step hint at what to expect here: a cheerful, traditional and spotlessly clean B&B. Tucked away from main roads, it's still only a few minutes' walk from the Barbican.

**Bowling Green** ( ☎ 01752-209090; www.bowlinggreen hotel.co.uk; 10 Osborne Pl; s £46-56; d £66, f £76) Some of the airy cream-and-white rooms in this family-run hotel look out onto the modern in-carnation of Drake's famous bowling green. If you tire of watching people throw woods after jacks you can play chess in the conservatory.

Other recommendations:
**Athenaeum Lodge** ( ☎ 01752-665005; www .athenaeumlodge.com; 4 Athenaeum St; s £32, d £46-60; 🖳 ) Grade II Georgian B&B with a few frills and flounces.
**Berkeleys of St James** ( ☎ 01752-221654; www .onthehoe.co.uk; 4 St James Pl East; s/d/f £40/57/75) Cosy B&B dishing up breakfasts full of local, organic goodies.

**TOP END**
**Duke of Cornwall** ( ☎ 01752-275850; www.thedukeofcorn wallhotel.co.uk; Millbay Rd; s £94, d £87-160) With one of the most striking edifices in Plymouth, this grand turret-topped, gable-studded pile is the most luxurious place to stay in town. The rooms are massive, if a touch old fashioned; the four-poster suite, complete with champagne and compli-mentary fruit basket, is the pick of the bunch.

**SOUTHWEST ENGLAND**

---

**AN ART DECO DIP**

Tucked between the Hoe and the shore, **Tinside Lido** ( ☎ 01752-261915; Hoe Rd; adult/child £3.65/2.40; ⏰ noon-6pm Mon-Fri, 10am-6pm Sat & Sun late May-late Jul, from 10am daily late Jul-early Sep) is an outdoor, saltwater art deco pool first opened to the public in 1935. During its heyday in the '40s and '50s, thousands of Plymouthians flocked to the pool on summer days (backed by the soothing strains of a string orchestra). In the '70s and '80s the pool fell into disrepair before closing in 1992. It's since been restored to its former glory thanks to a hefty £3.4 million refurbishment and now it's packed throughout summer with schoolkids and sun-worshippers; sadly, though, there's no sign of the string orchestra returning just yet.

---

## Eating

**ourpick** **Cap'n Jaspers** ( ☎ 01752-262444; www .capn-jaspers.co.uk; Whitehouse Pier, Quay Rd; snacks £3-5; ⏰ 7.45am-11.45pm) Unique, quirky and slightly insane, this outdoor cafe has been delighting bikers, tourists and locals for decades with its motorised gadgets and teaspoons attached by chains. The menu is of the burger and bacon-butty school – trying to eat the 'half a yard of hot dog' is a Plymouth rite of passage. Try the local crab rolls – the filling could have been caught by the bloke sitting next to you.

**ourpick** **Barbican Kitchen** ( ☎ 01752-604448; 60 Southside St; snacks £5, mains £11-16; ⏰ lunch & dinner, closed dinner Sun) In this bistro-style baby sister of Tanners Restaurant (below), the wood and stone interior fizzes with bursts of shocking pink and lime. The food is attention grabbing too – try the calves' liver with horseradish mash or the honey, goats' cheese and apple crostini. The Devon beefburger, with a slab of stilton, is divine.

**Platters** ( ☎ 01752-227262; 12 The Barbican; mains £13; ⏰ lunch & dinner) The fish in this down-to-earth eatery is so fresh it's just stopped flapping – try the skate in butter or the locally caught sea bass. You could pay twice as much nearby and end up with something half as good.

**Tanners Restaurant** ( ☎ 01752-252001; www.tan nersrestaurant.com; Finewell St; 2-/3-course dinner £26/32; ⏰ lunch & dinner Tue-Sat) Plymouth's top table is run by the (locally famous) Tanner brothers. Renowned for reinventing British and French classics, they dish up lamb with gnocchi, char-grilled asparagus with soft poached egg, and roasted quail with pancetta. Gourmands should try to book the five-course meal (£37).

Also recommended:

**Yukisan** ( ☎ 01752-250240; 51 Notte St; mains £14; ⏰ lunch & dinner) Super-fresh sushi, light tempura and noodles worth mastering chopsticks for.

**Veggie Perrin's** ( ☎ 01752-252888; 97 Mayflower St; mains £8; ⏰ lunch & dinner Mon-Sat) Excellent, authentic, vegetarian Indian food.

## Drinking

Like any navy city, Plymouth has a more than lively nightlife. Union St is clubland, Mutley Plain and North Hill have a studenty vibe, while the Barbican has more restaurants amid the bars. All three areas get rowdy, especially at weekends.

**Carpe Diem** ( ☎ 01752-252942; 50 North Hill; ⏰ 11am-midnight) A beautifully lit, funky bar done out in a kaleidoscope of colours – there's a heated, open-air chill-out room too.

**View 2** ( ☎ 01752-252564; Vauxhall Quay; ⏰ to 2am, later at weekends) Just round from the heart of the Barbican, this cool venue's waterside terrace is perfect for a lunchtime pizza or drink. In the evening enjoy comedy, salsa, easy listening, soul, funk and R&B.

**Dolphin** ( ☎ 01752-660876; 14 The Barbican) This wonderfully unreconstructed Barbican boozer is all scuffed tables, padded bench seats and an authentic, no-nonsense atmosphere.

## Entertainment

### BARS & NIGHTCLUBS

**Quay Club** ( ☎ 01752-224144; 11 The Parade; ⏰ 10am-2am Sun-Thu, to 3am Fri, to 4am Sat) Next to the Jazz Cafe, this cavernous club is a favourite with Plymouth's night owls, with rock and indie on Thursday; funk, soul and Latin on Friday; and chart and dance on Saturday.

**Annabel's** ( ☎ 01752-260555; 88 Vauxhall St; ⏰ to 2am Fri & Sat) The stage spots in this quirky cabaret-cum-dance venue are filled by an eclectic collection of acts; crowd-pleasing tunes fill the dance floor while classy cocktails fill your glass.

### THEATRE & CINEMA

**Theatre Royal** ( ☎ 01752-267222; www.theatreroyal.com; Royal Pde) Plymouth's main theatre stages large-scale touring and home-grown productions; its studio Drum Theatre is renowned for featuring new writing.

**Barbican Theatre** ( ☎ 01752-267131; www.barbicanthe atre.co.uk; Castle St) A tiny theatre with regular dance and drama, and a buzzing bar – the B-Bar.

**Plymouth Arts Centre** ( ☎ 01752-206114; www .plymouthac.org.uk; 38 Looe Street; ✆ 10am-8.30pm Mon-Sat, 5.30-8.30pm Sun) A place to feed body and mind – this centre combines an independent cinema, modern art exhibitions, and a licensed vegie-friendly cafe (lunch Monday to Saturday, dinner Tuesday to Saturday).

## Getting There & Away

### BUS

National Express runs regular coaches to Birmingham (£43.50, 5½ hours, four daily), Bristol (£26, three hours, four daily), London (£29, five to six hours, eight daily) and Penzance (£6.90, 3¼ hours, seven daily).

Bus X38 runs to Exeter (£6, 1¼ hours, hourly); bus X80 runs every half hour to Torquay (1¾ hours) via Totnes (one hour 10 minutes) from Monday to Saturday, and hourly on Sunday.

Bus 82 (the Transmoor link) runs across Dartmoor between Plymouth and Exeter via Princetown, Postbridge and Moretonhampstead. On Sundays year round there are two to five buses; between May and September it also runs twice on Saturdays; and between late July and late August it also runs twice on weekdays, with one bus connection on to Exeter.

### TRAIN

Services run to London (£63, 3½ hours, half-hourly), Bristol (£40, two hours, two or three per hour), Exeter (£6.90, one hour, two or three per hour) and Penzance (£9, two hours, half-hourly).

## AROUND PLYMOUTH
### Buckland Abbey

Stately **Buckland Abbey** (NT; ☎ 01822-853607; Yelverton; adult/child £7/3.50; ✆ 10.30am-5.30pm Fri-Wed mid-Mar–Oct, 2-5pm Sat & Sun Nov–mid-Mar) was origin ally a Cistercian monastery and 13th-century abbey church, but was transformed into a family residence by Sir Richard Grenville before being purchased in 1581 by his cousin and nautical rival Sir Francis Drake. Its displays include Drake's Drum, said to beat by itself when Britain is in danger of being invaded. There's also a very fine Elizabethan garden.

Buckland Abbey is 11 miles north of Plymouth. You'll need your own transport to get here.

# DARTMOOR NATIONAL PARK

Dartmoor is an ancient, compelling landscape, so different from the rest of Devon that a visit can feel like falling straight into the third book of *The Lord of the Rings*. Exposed granite hills (called tors) crest on the horizon, linked by swathes of honey-tinged moors. On the fringes, streams tumble over moss-smothered boulders in woods alive with twisted trees. The centre of this 368-sq-mile wilderness is the higher moor; a vast, treeless expanse. It's moody and utterly empty; you'll either find its desolate beauty exhilarating or chilling, or quite possibly a bit of both.

Dotted with free-grazing ponies and sheep, in places Dartmoor National Park is picture-postcard pretty. But peel back the picturesque and there's a core of hard reality – stock prices mean many farming this harsh environment struggle to make a profit. It's a mercurial place where the urban illusion of control over our surroundings is stripped away and the elements are in charge. Dartmoor inspired Sir Arthur Conan Doyle to write *The Hound of the Baskervilles* and in sleeting rain and swirling mists you suddenly see why; the moor morphs into a bleak, wilderness where tales of a phantom hound can seem very real indeed.

Dartmoor offers superb walking, cycling, riding, climbing and white-water kayaking. But it's not all adventure and endurance; there are also rustic pubs, fancy restaurants and posh country house hotels – the perfect bolt-holes when the mists roll in.

## Orientation

Dartmoor occupies a massive chunk of central Devon – its fringes stretch to within 7 miles of Plymouth and 6 miles of Exeter. The A38 dual carriageway borders its southeast edge while the A30 skirts the north en route from Exeter to Cornwall via Okehampton. The B3212 carves a path across the centre, linking the villages of Moretonhampstead, Postbridge and Princetown. From there the B3357 leads into Tavistock.

The northwest moor is the highest and most remote, peaking at 621m at High Willhays. The lower, southwest moor (400m to 500m) is particularly rich in prehistoric sites. About 40% of Dartmoor is common land but 15% is leased to the Ministry of Defence for live firing practice and access can be restricted; see p366.

## Information

The main **High Moorland Visitors Centre** ( ☎ 01822-890414; www.dartmoor-npa.gov.uk; 10am-5pm Apr-Oct, 10am-4pm Nov-Mar) is located in Princetown (p368); there are smaller centres at **Haytor** ( ☎ 01364-661520; 10am-5pm Easter-Oct, 10am-4pm Sat & Sun Nov & Dec) and **Postbridge** ( ☎ 01822-880272; 10am-5pm daily Easter-Oct, 10am-4pm Sat & Sun Nov & Dec), p368.

The free *Dartmoor Visitor* newspaper is packed with useful info, including details of guided walks. The larger centres also stock walking guides, Ordnance Survey (OS) maps and books; all have leaflets on hiking, horse riding, cycling and other activities.

The **Dartmoor Tourist Association** (www.discov erdartmoor.co.uk) is another useful information source.

Don't feed the Dartmoor ponies as this encourages them to move dangerously near to the roads.

## Activities

### CLIMBING

Experienced climbers will have to book at some popular sites – the park information centres can provide a free leaflet and further advice. For lessons, try the **Rock Centre** ( ☎ 01626-852717; www.rockcentre.co.uk; Rock House, Chudleigh; per half/full day £15/25).

### CYCLING

There are a couple of marked cycling routes around the moor including the 7-mile, traffic-free **Plym Valley Cycle Way** along the disused Great Western Railway between Plymouth and Yelverton, and the **Dartmoor Way**, a 90-mile circular cycling and walking route through Okehampton, Chagford, Buckfastleigh, Princetown and Tavistock.

A good option for bike hire is **Devon Cycle Hire** ( ☎ 01837-861141; www.devoncyclehire .co.uk; Sourton Down, near Okehampton; bikes per day £12), which is handily situated along the 11-mile Okehampton to Lydford **Granite Way**. Alternatively try **Okehampton Cycles** ( ☎ 01837-53248; North Rd, Okehampton).

### HORSE RIDING

There are lots of places to saddle up on Dartmoor. *Dartmoor Visitor* has full details. A half-day ride costs around £30.

**Babeny Farm Riding Stables** ( ☎ 01364-631296; Poundsgate)

**Shilstone Rocks** ( ☎ 01364-621281; Widecombe-in-the-Moor).

**Skaigh Stables** ( ☎ 01837-840917; www.skaighstables .co.uk; Belstone)

### WALKING

Every year thousands of people explore Dartmoor's open heaths and rocky tors. There are some 730 miles of public footpaths and bridleways to discover; Jarrold's *Dartmoor, Short Walks* (£5.99) is a good introduction for family day strolls, and the national park information centres can advise on all types of self-guided trails and run a range of **guided walks** (£3-8, free if you show your bus ticket). Themes include Sherlock Holmes, myths, geology, industry and archaeology. They also organise magical, moonlit rambles amid stone rows.

The **West Devon Way** (part of the Dartmoor Way) is a 14-mile hike between Tavistock and Okehampton, while the 18-mile **Templer Way** is a two- to three-day leg-stretch from Haytor on Dartmoor to coastal Teignmouth. Other highlights are the circular 90-mile **Dartmoor Way** and the 117-mile **Two Moors Way**, which runs from Wembury on the south coast near Plymouth, across Dartmoor and Exmoor to Lynmouth on the north Devon coast.

Be prepared for Dartmoor's notoriously fickle weather and carry a map and compass as many trails are not way marked. Be aware that the military uses three separate areas of Dartmoor as training ranges where live ammunition is used – check to see if your intended route crosses them; if it does find out firing times via the **Firing Information Service** ( ☎ 0800 4584868; www.dartmoor-ranges.co.uk). The OS Explorer Map No 28 (1:50,000; £7.99) is the most comprehensive and shows park boundaries and MOD firing-range areas.

### WHITE WATER ACTIVITIES

The raging River Dart makes Dartmoor a top spot for thrillseekers. Experienced kayakers can get permits from www.dartaccess.co.uk or the **British Canoe Union** (BCU; ☎ 0845 370 9500; www.bcu.org.uk). **CRS Adventures** ( ☎ 07891 635964; www.crsadventures.co.uk) in Ashburton runs a range of white-water activities (from £70 for a half day). Rivers are only open in the winter.

## Sleeping

From spoil-yourself-silly luxury (try Gidleigh Park, p370, or Holne Chase, p371) to snoozing under the stars with some lovely thatched

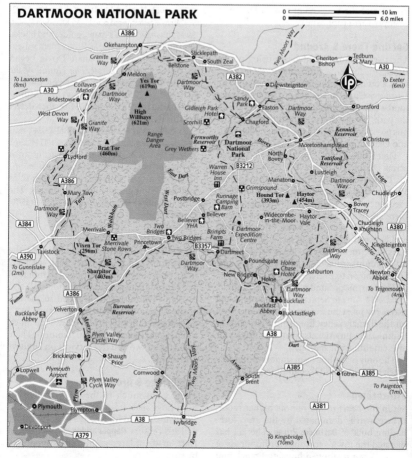

# DARTMOOR NATIONAL PARK

cottages in between, Dartmoor has the widest range of sleeping options around. We detail them throughout this section.

There are YHA hostels at Postbridge (p368) and Okehampton (p370); and the association also has bare-bones camping barns, such as the one near Postbridge (p368). For YHA bookings call ☎ 01629-592700. You'll find are independent hostels and camping barns at Moretonhampstead (p370), Widecombe-in-the-Moor (p369) and Princetown (p368).

Dartmoor is also a top venue for a spot of 'wild camping' – so called by devotees to distinguish it from the 'mild camping' of official sites. Pitching a tent on some sections of the open moor is allowed provided you stick to some simple but strict rules – pick up a free leaflet from the park information centres then pack your pack.

The **Dartmoor Tourist Association** ( ☎ 01822-890567; www.discoverdartmoor.com; High Moor Visitors Centre, Princetown) produces an annual *Dartmoor Guide* with full accommodation listings.

## Eating & Drinking

Dartmoor can cater for all tastes and budgets. There's the double-Michelin-starred Gidleigh Park (p370) near Chagford and classy Holne Chase (p371) near Widecombe-in-the-Moor. Or try the stylish bar food at the Rugglestone Inn at Widecombe (p369), the hiker-friendly grub and authentic pub atmosphere at the Warren House Inn in Postbridge (p368), or some of the best cream teas in Devon at Brimpts Farm (opposite).

## Getting There & Around

The park authorities advocate using public transport for environmental reasons and, with a bit of planning, it is a real option. The *Discovery Guide to Dartmoor,* free from most tourist offices, details bus and train services in the park. Buses travel into the moor from various points including Totnes, Exeter, Plymouth and Okehampton.

First's bus 82 (the Transmoor link) runs across Dartmoor between Plymouth and Exeter via Princetown, Two Bridges, Postbridge, the Warren House Inn and Moretonhampstead. Frequencies vary wildly: on Sundays year round there are two to five buses, between May and September it also runs twice on Saturdays, and between late July and late August it also runs twice on weekdays – these services stop at Moretonhampstead, with only one bus connection on to Exeter.

The Dartmoor Sunday Rover ticket (adult/child £6/4, June to September) buys unlimited travel on most bus routes, and train travel on the Tamar Valley line from Plymouth to Gunnislake. Buy tickets from bus drivers or at Plymouth train station.

The only main-line train station within easy reach of the park is Okehampton (p370).

## Princetown

Set in the heart of the remote higher moor, Princetown is dominated by the grey, foreboding bulk of **Dartmoor Prison**. The jail has dictated the town's fortunes for hundreds of years. When it stopped housing French and American prisoners of war in the early 1800s, Princetown fell into decline and parts of the town still have a bleak, neglected feel. But the settlement is also a useful insight into the harsh realities of moorland life and makes an atmospheric base for some excellent walks.

The prison reopened as a convict jail in 1850 and just up from its looming gates the **Dartmoor Prison Heritage Centre** ( ☎ 01822-892130; adult/child £2/1; ⓨ 9.30am-12.30pm & 1.30-4.30pm Mon-Thu & Sat, to 4pm Fri & Sun) provides a chilling glimpse of life (past and present) inside – look out for the straitjackets, manacles and mock-up cells, and the escape tale of Frankie 'the mad axeman' Mitchell, supposedly sprung by '60s gangster twins the Krays. The centre also sells the bizarrely cheery garden ornaments made by the inmates.

The **High Moorland Visitors Centre** ( ☎ 01822-890414; www.dartmoor-npa.gov.uk; ⓨ 10am-5pm Apr-Oct, 10am-4pm Nov-Mar) stocks maps, guides and books. The building started life as Princetown's main hotel, where Arthur Conan Doyle began his classic Dartmoor tale *The Hound of the Baskervilles*. Ask staff to point you towards Foxtor Mires (2 to 3 miles away), the inspiration for the book's Grimpen Mire, then detect the story's other locations.

The **Plume of Feathers** ( ☎ 01822-890240; www.theplumeoffeathers.co.uk; Plymouth Hill; dm/s/d £13/35/70, sites £13; ⓨ 11.30am-8.30pm) in the heart of town serves up typical bar food. It also offers no-nonsense rooms with shared bathrooms, as well as camping and bunk-bed dorms. The similar **Railway Inn** ( ☎ 01822-890240; s/d £35/70) is next door.

### GETTING THERE & AWAY

Between late July and late August bus 82 (the Transmoor Link) runs twice each weekday from Princetown to Postbridge (10 minutes) and Moretonhampstead (30 minutes). It also runs to Plymouth (50 minutes) in the opposite direction. The service also runs twice on Saturdays between May and September, when it goes on to Exeter (40 minutes). There are between two and five services on Sundays year round.

## Postbridge & Around

There's not much to the quaint village of Postbridge apart from a couple of shops, pubs and whitewashed houses. It's best known for its 13th-century **clapper bridge** across the East Dart, made of large granite slabs supported by stone pillars.

There's a **park information centre** ( ☎ 01822-880272; ⓨ 10am-4pm Apr-Oct) in the car park, and a post office and shop in the village.

### SLEEPING & EATING

our pick **Two Bridges** ( ☎ 01822-890581; www.twobridges.co.uk; Two Bridges; s £95-120, d £140-190) There's a real feel of a classy country house to this classic moorland hotel. That's no doubt down to the gently elegant rooms, huge inglenook fireplaces and squishy leather sofas; former guests Wallis Simpson, Winston Churchill and Vivien Leigh probably liked it too. It's 3 miles southwest of Postbridge.

our pick **Warren House Inn** ( ☎ 01822-880208; mains £4-9; ⓨ 11am-11pm, food served noon-8.30/9pm, to 4pm Mon & Tue Nov-Mar) Plonked amid miles of open

---

**PREHISTORIC DARTMOOR**

The first settlers arrived on Dartmoor somewhere around 12,000 years ago, after the end of the last ice age. The moor looked very different then; it was almost entirely covered by trees, which provided a rich source of food, fuel and natural shelter. Evidence of prehistoric people is dotted all over Dartmoor; over 1500 cairns and burial chambers have been discovered, and the area has more ceremonial rows and stone circles than anywhere else in Britain. The **Grey Wethers** stone circles stand side by side on a stretch of open moor halfway between Chagford and Postbridge, about quarter of a mile from another stone circle near **Fernworthy**. **Scorhill** stone circle, near Gidleigh, is sometimes called the Stonehenge of Dartmoor, although only half of the original stones remain. Another intriguing site is at **Merrivale**, on the main road from Princetown to Tavistock, where you'll find several stone rows and standing stones, as well as a small ceremonial circle and the remains of several stone huts. But the most impressive site is the Bronze Age village of **Grimspound**, just off the B3212, where you can wander around the circular stone wall that once surrounded the village, and the ruins of several granite round houses.

---

moor, this former tin miners' haunt exudes the kind of hospitality you only get in a pub in the middle of nowhere. A Dartmoor institution, its stone floors, trestle tables and hearty food are warmed by a fire that's reputedly been crackling since 1845. It's on the B3212, 2 miles northeast of Postbridge.

**Brimpts Farm** ( ☎ 01364-631450; Dartmeet; cream teas £3; ⏰ 11.30am-5.30pm Sat-Sun & school holidays, 2-5.30pm Mon-Fri) It's been serving cream teas since 1913, and it's still one of the best places to tuck in on the moor. Expect freshly baked scones, homemade jams and utterly, utterly gooey clotted cream. It's signed off the B3357, Two Bridges to Dartmeet road.

Also recommended:

**Bellever YHA Hostel** ( ☎ 0870 770 5692; bellever@yha.org.uk; dm £14; ⏰ Mar-Oct) Rustic, cosy, well-equipped hostel a mile south of Postbridge.

**Runnage Camping Barn** ( ☎ 01822-880222; www.runnagecampingbarns.com; camping from £5, dm £7) Snuggle down in the converted hayloft of this working farm near Postbridge.

### GETTING THERE & AWAY

Bus 82 (the Transmoor Link) runs from Plymouth via Princetown, Two Bridges, Postbridge and Warren House Inn to Moretonhampstead. Between late July and late August it runs twice each weekday. It also goes twice on Saturdays between May and September – there are between two and five services on Sundays year round.

## Widecombe-in-the-Moor

pop 652

This is archetypal Dartmoor, down to the ponies grazing on the village green. Widecombe's honey-grey, 15th-century buildings circle a church, the 40m tower of which has seen it dubbed the Cathedral of the Moor. Inside search out the boards telling the fire-and-brimstone tale of the violent storm of 1638 – it knocked a pinnacle from the roof, killing several parishioners. As ever on Dartmoor the devil was blamed, said to be in search of souls.

The village is commemorated in the traditional English folksong 'Widecombe Fair'; the event of the same name takes place on the second Tuesday of September.

### SLEEPING & EATING

**Dartmoor Expedition Centre** ( ☎ 01364-621249; www.dartmoorbase.co.uk; dm £12, loft r £14; **P** ) The real fires, hot showers and dorm beds at this 300-year-old converted barn are all best enjoyed after the climbing, orienteering and caving the centre organises. It's 2 miles west of Widecombe.

**Higher Venton Farm** ( ☎ 01364-621235; www.ventonfarm.com; Widecombe; d £50-60; **P** ) This 16th-century farmhouse could be used to define the architectural style 'picture-postcard thatch'. With low lintels and winding stone stairs, there's not a straight line in the place.

**Rugglestone Inn** ( ☎ 01364-621327; mains £5-10; Widecombe; ⏰ lunch & dinner) You'll find plenty of locals in front of this intimate old pub's wood-burning stove. Its stone floor and low beams also set the scene for hearty helpings of handmade sausages and mash or fisherman's pie.

**Old Inn** ( ☎ 01364-621207; The Green; mains £9; ⏰ lunch & dinner) Right beside the village green, this 14th-century hostelry has been carefully, if incongruously, renovated in blond beams, light panelling and quirky quotes. Somewhere to sip a cappuccino and dine on steak-and-ale pie or smoked-fish crumble.

### GETTING THERE & AWAY

Bus 272 goes to Tavistock (1¼ hours, three buses, late May to early September) via Two Bridges (50 minutes) and Princetown (55 minutes), but only on Sundays in the summer.

Bus 274 runs to Okehampton (1¾ hours, three on summer Sundays only) via Moretonhampstead. Several other buses also stop at Widecombe on Sunday only as part of the Sunday Rover scheme: check with the park information centres.

## Chagford & Around
pop 1470

With its wonky thatches and cream- and white-fronted buildings, Chagford gathers round a busy square – at first glance every inch a timeless moorland town. But the purveyors of waxed jackets and hip flasks have also been joined by health-food shops and contemporary pottery galleries. A former Stannary town (where local tin was weighed and checked), Chagford was also the first town west of London to get electric street lights.

### SLEEPING & EATING

**Sparrowhawk Backpackers** ( ☎ 01647-440318; www .sparrowhawkbackpackers.co.uk; 45 Ford St; dm/d £15/35) Set in the village of Moretonhampstead, 5 miles away, the bright, light dorms in this ecofriendly hostel are housed in converted stables. The central courtyard, ringed by rickety outbuildings, is a great spot to swap traveller's tales.

**Easton Court** ( ☎ 01647-433469; www.easton.co.uk; Easton Cross, Easton; s/d £60/75) It's worth staying here just for breakfast – choices include fresh fish or soufflé omelette. The rooms are lovely too with their cast-iron beds, soft sofas and views of wooded hills.

**Sandy Park** ( ☎ 01647-433267; www.sandyparkinn .co.uk; Sandy Park; s/d £50/90; mains £8-12; ☯ lunch & dinner, closed Sun dinner) Part pub, part chic place to stay, at this 17th-century thatch you can sip a pint of real ale in a cosy, exposed-beam bar, sample classy Dartmoor fare in the restaurant, then totter upstairs to sleep amid plump pillows and classic furnishings.

### GETTING THERE & AWAY

Bus 179 runs to Okehampton (one hour, two to three daily). Bus 173 travels from Moretonhampstead to Exeter via Chagford twice daily.

## Okehampton
pop 7029

Okehampton has a staging-post feel, huddling as it does on the edge of the mind-expanding sweep of the higher moor, an uninhabited tract of bracken-covered slopes and granite tors. With its clusters of traditional shops and pubs, it's an agreeable place to stock up before a foray into the wilderness. The **tourist office** ( ☎ 01837-53020; oketic@visit.org .uk; Museum Courtyard, 3 West St; ☯ 10am-5pm Mon-Sat Easter-Oct) can help with local accommodation and walks.

### SIGHTS & ACTIVITIES

A Norman motte and ruined keep are all that remain of Devon's largest **castle** (EH; ☎ 01837-52844; adult/child £3/1; ☯ 10am-5pm Apr-Jun & Sep, 10am-6pm Jul & Aug). This towering, crumbling ruin teeters on top of a wooded spur and provides picturesque rampart clambering; a free audio guide fills in the missing parts.

The **Finch Foundry** (NT; ☎ 01837-840046; adult/child £4/2; ☯ 11am-5.30pm Wed-Mon Apr-Oct), with its three working water wheels, is a charming 3½-hour walk along the Tarka Trail in Sticklepath.

### SLEEPING & EATING

**Okehampton YHA** ( ☎ 0845 371 9651; www.yha.org.uk; Klondyke Rd; dm £14; ℗ ) This former railway shed has had a bright revamp and is now a hugely popular hostel. No doubt something to do

---

**DETOUR: GIDLEIGH PARK HOTEL**

**Gidleigh Park Hotel** ( ☎ 01647-432367; www.gidleigh.com; s £360, d £480-1325) Brace yourself (and your bank balance) – staying somewhere this prestigious doesn't come cheap. This sumptuous oasis of supreme luxury teams crests, crenellations and roaring fires with shimmering sanctuaries of blue marble, waterproof TVs and private saunas. Rates include dinner at the double-Michelin-starred restaurant, where three courses would normally set you back a hefty £85 – crafty local gourmands opt for the £33 two-course lunch instead. This dollop of utter extravagance is two miles from Chagford.

with the sailing, rock climbing and kayaking courses it runs.

**Collaven Manor** ( ☎ 01837-861522; www.collaven manor.co.uk; Sourton; s £65, d £106-146) The bedrooms in this delightful, clematis-clad mini manor house are framed by tapestries and window seats; dinner includes venison stroganoff and guinea fowl in Madeira sauce (three courses £25.50) – nonresidents need to book.

**Tors** ( ☎ 01837-840689; Belstone; s/d £30/60; mains £8-15; ⓨ lunch & dinner) Tucked away in the picturesque village of Belstone this welcoming country pub offers simple, traditional rooms, hearty food and views onto the moor. It's 2 miles east of Okehampton.

**GETTING THERE & AWAY**
Bus X9 runs from Exeter (50 minutes, hourly Monday to Saturday, two on Sunday) via Okehampton to Bude (one hour). Bus 179 goes two or three times daily to Chagford (30 minutes) and Moretonhampstead (50 minutes).

## NORTH DEVON
Intensely rugged and, in places, utterly remote, the north Devon coast is a coast to inspire. It's also hugely varied: drastically concertinaed cliffs, excellent surf breaks and ancient fishing villages rub shoulders with classic, slightly faded British seaside resorts.

### Braunton & Croyde
pop 8319
The cheerful, chilled village of Croyde is Devon's surf central. Here olde-worlde meets new wave: thatched roofs peep out over racks of wetsuits; crowds of cool guys in board shorts sip beer outside 17th-century inns. Inland, Braunton also has surf shops and board hire. The **tourist office** ( ☎ 01271-816400; www.brauntontic .co.uk; The Bakehouse Centre, Braunton; ⓨ 10am-4pm Mon-Sat Easter-Oct, plus Sun Jul & Aug) provides information and also houses a small local museum.

The water's hard to resist. **Le Sport** ( ☎ 01271-890147; Hobbs Hill, Croyde; ⓨ 9am-5.30pm, to 9pm peak times) is among those hiring wetsuits and boards (half/full day £12/18). The British Surfing Association (BSA) approved **Surf South West** ( ☎ 01271-890400; www.surfsouthwest.com; Croyde Burrows Beach; ⓨ late Mar-Oct) and **Surfing Croyde Bay** ( ☎ 01271-891200; www .surfingcroydebay.co.uk; 8 Hobbs Hill, Croyde) provide lessons from around £33 per half day.

**SLEEPING & EATING**
Croyde gets very busy in the summer – book ahead, even for camp sites.

**Bay View Farm** ( ☎ 01271-890501; www.bayviewfarm .co.uk; sites from £20) On the road from Braunton, this is one of the area's best camp sites, with laundry and showers.

**Mitchum's Campsites** ( ☎ 07875 406473; www .croydebay.co.uk; sites £24-30) There are two locations, one in Croyde village and one by the beach, but they're only open on certain weekends in summer, so phone ahead.

**Thatch** ( ☎ 01271-890349; www.thethatch-croyde.co.uk; 14 Hobbs Hill, Croyde; d £60-80) Set above a legendary surfer's hang-out, the bedrooms in this cavernous ancient pub are smart and modern, featuring delicate creams, browns and subtle checks. Some share bathrooms.

**Chapel Farm** ( ☎ 01271-890429; www.chapelfarm croyde.co.uk; Hobbs Hill, Croyde; s/d £44/68; **P** ) This lovely old thatched farmhouse has beamed rooms, rustic furniture and an inglenook fireplace; there's also self-catering in the old smithy behind the house.

**GETTING THERE & AWAY**
Bus 308 runs from Barnstaple (40 minutes, hourly Monday to Saturday, five on Sunday).

### Ilfracombe
pop 12,430
Like a matinee idol past his prime, for years Ilfracombe had a sagging, crumpled feel. The

steeply sloping streets of this Victorian watering hole are lined with town houses with cast-iron balconies; formal gardens, crazy golf and ropes of twinkling lights line the promenade. But these days there's more to Ilfracombe, as evidenced by a string of smart eateries and places to sleep, a Damien Hirst connection and the chance to go surfing or take a 'dip' in the past.

The best local beach is 5 miles west at Woolacombe – try the **Nick Thorn Hunter Surf Academy** ( ☎ 01271-871337; www.nickthornhuntersurfacademy.com; ☼ 9am-5pm Apr-Sep; wetsuit & board hire half/full day £14/18) where lessons cost from £30 for 2½ hours. Ilfracombe's **tourist office** ( ☎ 01271-863001; www.visitilfracombe.co.uk; ☼ 10am-5pm Mon-Sat, plus Sun Apr-Oct) is inside the Landmark Theatre.

**Tunnelsbeaches** ( ☎ 01271-879882; www.tunnelsbeaches.co.uk; Granville Rd; adult/child £1.95/1.50; ☼ 10am-5/6pm Easter-Oct, 9am-9pm Jul & Aug) is a beautifully evocative series of Victorian tidal swimming pools. Passageways hacked out of solid rock in the 1800s lead to a pocket-sized beach where you can still plunge into the sea water. Displays show the same spot in the 19th century, conveying a world of woollen bathing suits, segregated swimming and boating etiquette ('gentlemen who cannot swim should never take ladies upon the water').

### SLEEPING & EATING

**Ocean Backpackers** ( ☎ 01271-867835; www.oceanbackpackers.co.uk; 29 St James Pl; dm £10-14, d £35) The dorms aren't that big but this indie hostel favourite is well run and the owners can help organise surfing, kayaking and archery.

**Norbury House Hotel** ( ☎ 01271-863888; www.norburyhouse.co.uk; Torrs Park; d £70-80; f & ste £100; **P** ) This former gentleman's residence is now dotted with low-level beds, cool lamps and artfully placed cushions. Set on the hill overlooking Ilfracombe, there are impressive views from its terraced gardens.

**Westwood** ( ☎ 01271-867443; www.west-wood.co.uk; Torrs Park Rd; d £90-105; **P** ) Modern, minimal and marvellous, this ultrachic B&B is a study in neutral tones and dashes of vivid colour. It's graced by ponyskin chaises longues and stand-alone baths; some rooms have sea glimpses.

ourpick **11, The Quay** ( ☎ 01271-868090; www.11thequay.com; 11 The Quay; cafe mains from £5, restaurant £10-20; ☼ lunch & dinner) Full of Chelsea chic, this supremely distinctive eatery is owned by the artist Damien Hirst (famous for

preserving dead cows and sharks). Chose from tasty cafe fare in the Bakery or chi-chi dining with superb views upstairs. Seared skate or Lundy lobster and chips feature on the menu; Mr Hirst's artwork features on the walls – including chunks of his *Pharmacy* installation and, with delicious irony, fish in formaldehyde.

### GETTING THERE & AWAY

Bus 3 (40 minutes, every half hour Monday to Saturday, hourly Sunday) runs to Barnstaple. Bus 300 heads to Lynton (one hour) and Minehead (two hours) three times daily.

## Clovelly

**pop 452**

Clovelly is picture-postcard pretty. Its white cottages cascade down cliffs to meet a curving crab claw of a harbour, which is lined with lobster pots and set against a deep blue sea. Clovelly's cobbled streets are so steep cars can't negotiate them, so supplies are still brought in by sledge – you'll see these big bread baskets on runners leaning outside people's homes. Clovelly's tenants enjoy enviably low rents (around £400 a year) and although the village is often branded artificial, 98% of the houses are occupied – in some Westcountry villages half the properties are second homes.

Entry to the privately owned village is via the **visitor centre** ( ☎ 01237-431781; adult/child £5.50/3.50). Land Rovers ferry visitors up and down the slope for £2 from Easter to October.

Charles Kingsley, author of the children's classic *The Water Babies,* spent much of his early life in Clovelly. You can visit his former house, as well as an old fisherman's cottage and the village's twin chapels.

Bus 319 runs five times daily to Bideford (40 minutes) and Barnstaple (one hour).

## Hartland Abbey

This 12th-century **monastery-turned-stately-home** ( ☎ 01237-441264; www.hartlandabbey.com; adult/child £8/2; ☼ house 2-5pm Sun-Thu, grounds noon-5pm Sun-Fri late May-Sep) was another post-dissolution handout, given to the sergeant of Henry VIII's wine cellar in 1539. It boasts some fascinating murals, ancient documents, paintings by English masters and Victorian photos, as well as marvellous gardens.

Hartland Abbey is 15 miles west of Bideford, off the A39 between Hartland and Hartland Quay.

# CORNWALL

If you were creating a perfect holiday haven from scratch, you'd probably come up with Cornwall. This rugged wedge of rock offers impossibly pretty beaches, improbably quaint villages and impressively craggy cliffs. Beloved by the bucket-and-spade brigade for generations, these days the entire county is in the midst of a renaissance that ranges from cooking to culture. You can sample Rick Stein's foodie empire at Padstow or Jamie Oliver's cooking-cum-community program just along the coast. Indulge in an adrenalin sports frenzy at party-town Newquay or explore global habitats at the Eden Project. Go all mystical at Arthurian Tintagel, all arty at St Ives, or all funky at a festival. Or kick off your shoes, grab a knapsack and go island-hopping around the enchanting Isles of Scilly. Better still, do it all – and in one trip. In Cornwall you can. It really is rather wonderful way out west.

## Orientation & Information
Cornwall is shaped like a giant door wedge. Around 88 miles end to end, it's 50 miles wide in the east but tapers to only eight miles wide in the west. A new unitary authority is due to take over from Cornwall's district councils in April 2009. **Visit Cornwall** ( ☎ 01872-322900; www.visitcornwall.co.uk) has information on everything from Cornish cuisine to events, accommodation and adventure sports.

## Getting Around
Most of Cornwall's main bus, train and ferry timetables are collected into one handy brochure (available free from bus stations and tourist offices). **Traveline South West** ( ☎ 0871 200 2233; www.travelinesw.com) can also answer timetable queries.

### BUS
The main bus operator in Cornwall is **First** ( ☎ timetables 0871 200 2233, customer services 0845 600 1420; www.firstgroup.com). A FirstDay ticket (adult/child £7/5.20) offers unlimited travel on the network for 24 hours.

Smaller, countywide operator **Western Greyhound** ( ☎ 01637-871871; www.westerngreyhound.com) also does Day Rover tickets (adult/child £7/4.50). Many tourist attractions (including the Eden Project) offer discounts if you arrive by bus.

### TRAIN
Key routes from London, Bristol and the north pass through Exeter, Plymouth, Liskeard, Truro and Camborne en route to Penzance; there are also branch lines to St Ives, Falmouth, Newquay and Looe.

The **Devon and Cornwall Rover** allows unlimited travel across the counties. Three days' travel in one week costs £40; eight days' travel in 15 costs £60. You can buy it at most main train stations.

The **Freedom of the South West Rover pass** (adult £95) allows eight days' travel in 15 days in an area west of (and including) Salisbury, Bath, Bristol and Weymouth.

## NORTH CORNWALL
The north Cornish coast is where Atlantic rollers smack hard into the county's granite cliffs and, for many, it's the quintessential Cornish landscape – a wild mix of grassy headlands, craggy bluffs and pounding surf. It's also where you'll find the county's best beaches and biggest waves, so in summer the winding cliff-top roads can be jammed with tourists. But visit in the off-season when the weather's cooler and the holidaymakers have left for home, and you might have some of Cornwall's finest sand all to yourself.

### Bude
pop 9242
Tucked in at the end of the River Neet and a 19th-century canal, Bude is both a popular family getaway and surfing hangout, thanks to its fantastic nearby beaches. Closest to town is Summerleaze, a classic bucket-and-spade affair with bags of space at low tide; just to the north is Crooklets, which often has decent surf, as does Widemouth Bay (pronounced widmouth), 3 miles south of town.

**Bude Visitor Centre** ( ☎ 01288-354240; www.visitbude.info; The Crescent; ⊙ 10am-5pm Mon-Sat, plus 10am-4pm Sun summer) is in a car park at the end of town. The **Castle Heritage Centre** ( ☎ 01288-357301; The Castle; adult/child £3.50/2.50; ⊙ 10am-6pm Easter-Oct, 10am-4pm Nov-Easter) evokes Bude's maritime, geological and social history with great imagination – look out for exhibits on local inventor Sir Goldsworth Gurney, whose pioneering creations included theatrical limelight and steam carriages. **Outdoor Adventure** ( ☎ 01288-362900; www.oasurfschool.co.uk) runs surf lessons at Widemouth Bay from £25 for a half day.

The nine fresh, uncluttered rooms at **Dylan's Guesthouse** ( ☎ 01288-354705; www.dylansguesthouse inbude.co.uk; Downs View; s/d £45/60) are decked out in white linen, chocolate throws and pleasant pine.

**Life's a Beach** ( ☎ 01288-355222; Summerleaze Beach; mains £11-16; ☿ Mon-Sat) transforms from a lunchtime bistro to a snazzy candlelit restaurant by night and specialises in seafood. Or check out **Scrummies** ( ☎ 01288- 359522; Lansdown Rd; mains from £7; ☿ 8am-10pm), a fab fish cafe where the skate and monkfish are caught by the owner – try the crab pasta or lobster (half/whole £12/24) and chips.

Bus 595 runs between Bude and Boscastle (30 minutes, six daily Monday to Saturday, four on summer Sundays), where you can pick up connections to Tintagel, Wadebridge, St Columb Major and on to Truro. Bus 581 links Bude with Widemouth Bay (10 minutes, hourly Monday to Saturday, four on summer Sundays).

## Boscastle

On 16 August 2004 the pretty, sleepy harbour-side village of Boscastle was catapulted onto TV screens worldwide. The most devastating flash flood to hit Britain for 50 years forced 440 million gallons of water through the heart of the village in just a few hours. It swept away a hundred cars and caused devastating damage to many of the village's oldest buildings; 58 properties were flooded and much of the village was evacuated by helicopter. Miraculously not a single person lost their life.

Residents have spent years piecing Boscastle back together, with many properties now completely refurbished. The new **visitor centre** ( ☎ 01840-250010; www.visitboscastle andtintagel.com; ☿ 10am-5pm Mar-Oct) sits by the harbour.

The quirky **Museum of Witchcraft** ( ☎ 01840-250111; The Harbour; adult/child £3/2.50; ☿ 10.30am-6pm Mon-Sat, 11.30am-6pm Sun) has the world's largest collection (apparently) of witch-related memorabilia. Among its artefacts are spooky poppets (a kind of voodoo doll), wooden witch mirrors, enchanted skulls and a hideous cast-iron 'witch's bridle' designed to extract confessions from suspected hags.

### SLEEPING & EATING

**Riverside Hotel** ( ☎ 01840-250216; www.hotelriverside .co.uk; s/d £35/65) Housed in one of the village's oldest buildings, this lovely B&B has fresh, modern rooms (think pink, peach or raspberry red) and a delightful riverside terrace for sandwiches and cream teas.

**Old Rectory** ( ☎ 01840-250225; www.stjuliot.com; St Juliot; s/d £58/86; ☿ Mar-Nov; P ) Formerly the home of the vicar of St Juliot, the Old Rectory is famous as the house where Thomas Hardy fell in love with his future wife, Emma Lavinia Gifford (the rector's sister-in-law). Period antiques, Victorian knick-knacks and heavy drapes recreate the Hardy-era atmosphere; bookworms can stroll through the woods to St Juliot Church, which features in the pages of Hardy's novel *A Pair Of Blue Eyes*.

**Wellington Hotel** ( ☎ 01840-250202; www.boscastle -wellington.com; The Harbour; d £80-184; P ) Closer to a fortified castle than a hotel, this traditional coaching inn has welcomed weary travellers for more than 500 years (previous guests include Edward VII and Thomas Hardy). Bag a turret room for an antique atmosphere, chunky rugs, gentlemen's armchairs and unbeatable views.

### GETTING THERE & AWAY

For buses see the Getting There & Away section for Tintagel, opposite.

## Tintagel
### pop 1822

The spectre of King Arthur looms large over the village of Tintagel and its spectacular cliff-top **castle** (EH; ☎ 01840-770328; adult/child £4.70/2.40; ☿ 10am-6pm Apr-Sep, 10am-5pm Oct, 10am-4pm Nov-Mar). Though the present-day ruins mostly date from the 13th century, archaeological digs have revealed the foundations of a much earlier fortress, fuelling speculation that the legendary king may indeed have been born at the castle as local fable claims. Part of the crumbling stronghold stands on a rock tower cut off from the mainland, accessed via a bridge and steep steps, and it's still possible to make out several sturdy walls and much of the castle's interior layout.

The village is awash with touristy shops and tearooms making the most of the King Arthur connection, but there's not much to keep you for long. The **Old Post Office** (NT; ☎ 01840-770024; Fore St; adult/child £2.80/1.40; ☿ 11am-5.30pm mid-Mar-Sep, 11am-4pm Oct) is a beautiful example of a traditional Cornish longhouse and mostly dates from the 1500s; it was still used as the village's post office during the 19th century.

The **tourist office** ( ☎ 01840-779084; www.visit-boscastleandtintagel.com; Bossiney Rd; ⓨ 10am-5pm Mar-Oct, 10.30am-4pm Nov-Feb) has a few exhibits exploring local history and the Arthur legend.

### GETTING THERE & AWAY

Bus 597 runs from Truro to St Columb Major where the connecting 594 goes via Wadebridge to Tintagel (two hours, seven daily Monday to Saturday) and on to Boscastle (10 minutes).

## Padstow
### pop 3162

If anywhere symbolises Cornwall's culinary renaissance it's Padstow. Decades ago this was an industrious fishing village where the day's catch was battered and served up in newspaper. Today it's seared, braised or char-grilled, garnished with wasabi and dished up in some of the poshest restaurants this side of the Tamar. The transformation is largely due to one man, celebrity chef Rick Stein (see p686), whose property portfolio now includes three eateries, three shops, six places to stay and even (with glorious irony) a fish-and-chip outlet. Some locals wryly refer to the town as 'Pad-stein' while others warmly welcome the jobs. Either way it's hard not to be charmed by Padstow's seaside setting, with a cluster of cafes and fishermen's cottages nestled around its old harbour.

The **tourist office** ( ☎ 01841-533449; www.padstowlive.com; North Quay; ⓨ 10am-5pm Mon-Sat) charges £3 to book accommodation.

Much favoured by directors of costume dramas, the stately manor house of **Prideaux Place** ( ☎ 01841-532411; admission £7, grounds only £2; ⓨ 12.30-4pm Sun-Thu Easter–mid-Apr & mid-May–Sep) above the village was built by the Prideaux-Brune family (who still reside here), purportedly descendants of William the Conqueror.

The disused Padstow-to-Bodmin railway line now forms the **Camel Trail**, one of Cornwall's most popular cycling tracks. The trail starts in Padstow and runs east through Wadebridge (5.75 miles), Bodmin (11 miles) and beyond. Bikes can be hired from **Padstow Cycle Hire** ( ☎ 01841-533533; www.padstowcyclehire.com; South Quay; ⓨ 9am-5pm) and **Brinhams** ( ☎ 01841-532594; South Quay; ⓨ 9am-5pm) for £9 to £12 per day.

The **Jubilee Queen** ( ☎ 07836 798457) offers one-hour boat trips (adult/child £8/4) around

the bay and offshore islands, leaving from the harbourside.

Padstow is surrounded by some excellent beaches, including the ones at **Treyarnon Bay** and **Polzeath**, where the beachside **Animal Surf Academy** ( ☎ 01208-880617; www.animalsurfacademy.co.uk; Polzeath) does tuition (from £20 per 2½ hours) and **Ann's Cottage** ( ☎ 01208-863317; www.annscottagesurf.co.uk; Polzeath) rents boards and wetsuits (£3 per hour each).

### SLEEPING

**Treyarnon Bay YHA** ( ☎ 0845 371 9664; www.yha.org.uk; Tregonnan; dm £14; P 🖳 ) This 1930s beach house is arguably Cornwall's best hostel. Its unbeatable setting above Treyarnon Bay is topped off by a home-cooking cafe, designer lounge and comfy dorms with top-drawer sea views. Bus 556 from Padstow stops at nearby Constantine several times daily.

**Treverbyn House** ( ☎ 01841-532855; www.treverbynhouse.com; Station Rd; d from £75) Harry Potter would feel at home at this charming villa of five colour-coded rooms – it's even got a turret hideaway. Pine beds, pocket-sprung mattresses, stunning views and a choice of three breakfasts make this a top Padstow choice.

**Althea Library** ( ☎ 01841-532717; www.althealibrary.co.uk; 27 High St; d £76-120; P ) One of the nicest B&Bs in central Padstow, Althea has a couple of cosy, tasteful rooms tucked away on the first floor of this listed cottage, as well as a more expensive 'nook suite'. The pretty lounge has a CD player and board games, and the range-cooked breakfasts will keep you going for hours.

**Ballaminers House** ( ☎ 01841-540933; www.ballaminershouse.co.uk; Little Petherick; tw/d £70/85; P ) Two miles south of Padstow, this smart stone farmhouse blends old-world atmosphere and modern elegance. Calming rooms are dotted with Balinese furniture and antique chests, and boast sweeping views of the surrounding fields.

### EATING

**Rojano's** ( ☎ 01841-532796; 9 Mill Sq; pizzas £7, pasta £8; ⓨ lunch & dinner Tue-Sun) This bright, buzzy Italian joint turns out excellent pizza and pasta, served either in the snug, sunlit dining room or the tiny front terrace.

**Rick Stein's Cafe** ( ☎ 01841-532700; Middle St; mains £8.50-15; ⓨ closed Sun) Stripped-down versions of Stein's Seafood Restaurant fare are on offer at this continental backstreet cafe-bistro. It's buzzy and busy, with a faint seaside feel; everything from homemade carrot cake to grilled mackerel fillets occupy the specials blackboard.

**Pescadou** ( ☎ 01841-532359; South Quay; mains £14-18; ☯ lunch & dinner) Mr Stein isn't the only one around town who can turn out top-notch seafood, as this brightly toned brasserie next to the Old Custom House pub proves. Our tip? Try the rosemary-roasted turbot.

**our pick** **Seafood Restaurant** ( ☎ 01841-532700; www.rickstein.com; Riverside; mains £18-45; ☯ lunch & dinner) The place that kick-started the Stein empire, and still the best of the bunch. Unsurprisingly, superb seafood is the menu's cornerstone, and huge swathes of the ingredients are certified Cornish. You'll need friends in high places to get a table, but this is one eatery that lives up to the hype.

### GETTING THERE & AWAY
Bus 555 goes to Bodmin Parkway (50 minutes, hourly, six on summer Sundays) via Wadebridge. Bus 554 travels to St Columb Major, with connecting buses to Truro (1¼ hours, five daily Monday to Saturday), while bus 556 serves Newquay (1¼ hours, seven daily Monday to Saturday, five on summer Sundays).

## Newquay
pop 19,423

Hoards of hard-core surfers, party animals and wannabe-boardriders all make a beeline for bright, breezy, brash Newquay. Perched on the cliffs above a cluster of white-sand beaches and packed with enough pubs, bars and dodgy clubs to give Ibiza a run for its money, it's the capital of Cornish surfing, and if you're looking to learn how to brave the waves, this is the place to do it.

### INFORMATION
**Laundrette** ( ☎ 01637-874487; 90 Tower Rd; ☯ 8am-8pm)

**Tad & Nick's Talk'n'Surf** ( ☎ 01637-874868; 72 Fore St; per min/hr 5p/£3; ☯ 10am-6pm)

**Tourist office** ( ☎ 01637-854020; www.newquay .co.uk; Marcus Hill; ☯ 9.30am-5.30pm Mon-Sat, 9.30am-12.30pm Sun)

### SIGHTS & ACTIVITIES
Newquay is set amid some of the finest beaches on the north coast. **Fistral**, west of

---

**TOP FIVE BEACHES**

- For superb swimming: Perran Sands, **Perranporth** (p379)

- For scenic views: **Bedruthan Steps** (below), near Newquay

- For peaceful strolling: Gwithian and Godrevy Towans, near **St Ives** (p391)

- For family fun: **Holywell Bay** (below), near Newquay

- For learning to surf: Fistral or Watergate Bay, both near **Newquay** (opposite)

---

Towan Head, is England's best-known surfing beach and the venue for the annual Boardmasters surfing festival. Below town are **Great Western** and **Towan**; a little further up the coast you'll find Tolcarne, Lusty Glaze and Porth. All the beaches are good for swimming and supervised by lifeguards in summer.

Just east of Newquay is **Watergate Bay**, home to the latest branch of Jamie Oliver's Fifteen Cornwall restaurant, a swish new hotel and some superb adventure sports (see boxed text, opposite). The stately rock towers of **Bedruthan Steps** are a few miles further east towards Padstow; **Crantock** beach lies 3 miles to the southwest; a little further west again is family-friendly **Holywell Bay**.

Back in Newquay, the **Blue Reef Aquarium** ( ☎ 01637-878134; www.bluereefaquarium.co.uk; Towan Promenade; adult/child £8.50/6; ☯ 10am-5pm) displays a selection of weird and wonderful aquatic characters, including jellyfish, seahorses, octopi and rays.

Most of Newquay is relentlessly modern, but on the cliff above Towan Beach stands the 14th-century **Huer's House**, a lookout for approaching pilchard shoals. Until they were fished out early in the 20th century, these shoals were enormous: one catch of 1868 netted a record 16.5 million fish.

### SLEEPING
Although Newquay has stacks of sleeping options, in high season prices rocket, the best get booked up, and some require a weeks' booking.

#### Budget
There are plenty of surf lodges in Newquay – the best ones have secure board storage and links with local surf schools.

**Base Surf Lodge** ( ☎ 01637-874852; www.basesur flodge.com; 20 Tower Rd; dm £15-20) A superior surf lodge; slatted blinds, tiled floors and big sunset murals brighten up the lounge-bar, while pine bunk beds and off-white walls characterise the upstairs dorms.

**Goofys** ( ☎ 01637-872684; www.goofys.co.uk; 5 Headland Rd; dm £15-25, d £30-60; P 💻 ) Friendly, funky Goofys bridges the gap between surf lodge and B&B. Rooms range from simple, airy doubles to quads with bunk beds; all are en suite and the price includes bedding, towels and a hearty buffet breakfast.

**Reef Surf Lodge** ( ☎ 01637-879058; www.reefsur flodge.info; 10-12 Berry Rd; dm £15-30; d £35-70; 💻 ) An oh-so-fancy foyer and bar (think stripped pine, brushed aluminium and a sign-cum-water feature) give this place a super-slick feel. And it is cleaner, smarter and better organised than many – but it *is* still a surf lodge, so expect dorms, shared facilities and chronic overcrowding in the summer.

### Midrange & Top End

**Carlton Hotel** ( ☎ 01637-872658; www.carltonhotel newquay.co.uk; 6 Dane Rd; s £45, d £68-94; P ) Swanky rooms, frilly edged beds, DVD players and country-cream furnishings run throughout this upmarket B&B on a quiet terrace just off Headland Rd.

**ourpick The Hotel** ( ☎ 01637-860543; www.water gatebay.co.uk; Watergate Bay; d £95-295, ste £205-400; P ) This chic surf-side hotel is a kind of upmarket beachcombers paradise. Set plumb on the headland at Watergate Bay, its bedrooms are all pared-down simplicity, with crinkly linen, creaky wicker chairs and gauzy drapes; the best have mini seaview balconies. The decked terrace, complete with bar and outdoor pool, overlooks the bay, and the whole little holiday haven is just steps from the beach.

**Headland Hotel** ( ☎ 01637-872211; www.headland hotel.co.uk; Fistral Beach; d £95-350; P 💻 ) Clinging to cliffs above Fistral beach, this red-brick pile is all about old-style pampering. Ritzy rooms range from budget singles to ornate sea-view suites, and there are even pools, tennis courts and nine holes of golf.

### EATING

**Fistral Chef** ( ☎ 01637-850718; 2 Beacon Rd; breakfasts £2-6, mains £6-10; ☽ breakfast & lunch) Fantastic all-day breakfasts and chunky sandwiches are the mainstays of this popular all-day cafe, which also opens for Thai meals several nights a week.

**New Harbour Restaurant** ( ☎ 01637-874062; South Quay Hill; mains £10-15; ☽ lunch & dinner) In a lovely spot beside the old harbour, this relaxed restaurant is a fine place to escape the crowds along Newquay's main drag. Fish and seafood are the menu's staple – think crab claws, homemade fishcakes and skate wing.

**ourpick Beach Hut** ( ☎ 01637-860877; Watergate Bay; mains £13-17; ☽ breakfast, lunch & dinner) Surfboards on the walls, panoramic views of the waves and floorboards patterned by sandy footprints help make this beachside bistro the perfect hang-out. The menu redefines 'surf 'n' turf': miso-blackened mackerel, Fowey mussels with Cornish cider and homemade burgers with smoked Tintagel cheese. In the winter they tend to close at dusk.

**ourpick Fifteen Cornwall** ( ☎ 01637-861000; www. fifteencornwall.com; Watergate Bay; lunch mains £18, 6-course

---

**SURF'S UP**

Dig out the board shorts, slip on the shades and prepare to dangle your toes off the nose – Newquay is one of England's best places to learn to surf and is awash with schools, offering everything from half-day taster lessons (£25 to £30) to full-blown, multiday 'surfaris' (from £130). Reputable operators include the British Surfing Association's **National Surfing Centre** (BSA; www .nationalsurfingcentre.com Fistral Beach ☎ 01637-850737; Lusty Glaze ☎ 01637-851487), **Animal Surf Academy** (www.animalsurfacademy.co.uk Tolcarne Beach, Newquay ☎ 01637-850808; Polzeath ☎ 01208-880617) and the **Extreme Academy** ( ☎ 01637-860840; www.extremeacademy.co.uk; Watergate Bay). If you choose another school, make sure it's BSA approved.

For surf hire try **Overhead** ( ☎ 01637-850808; Beacon Rd & 19 Cliff Rd) or **Fistral Beach Surf Hire** ( ☎ 01637-850584; Fistral Beach). Average costs are: boards £10/25/45 for one/three/seven days; wetsuits £5/12/25 for one/three/seven days.

Extreme Academy (above) also offers lessons in kitebuggying, waveskiing and the new craze: stand-up paddle-surf. It also does kitesurfing, as does **Mobius Kite School** ( ☎ 08456 430 630; Cubert; www.mobiusonline.co.uk).

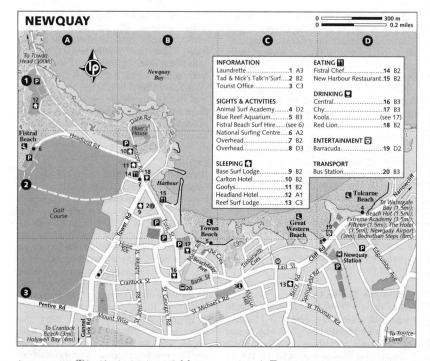

## NEWQUAY

0                    300 m
0                    0.2 miles

**INFORMATION**
Laundrette..........................1 A3
Tad & Nick's Talk'n'Surf.....2 B2
Tourist Office....................3 C3

**SIGHTS & ACTIVITIES**
Animal Surf Academy........4 D2
Blue Reef Aquarium..........5 B3
Fistral Beach Surf Hire.....(see 6)
National Surfing Centre....6 A2
Overhead..........................7 B2
Overhead..........................8 D3

**SLEEPING**
Base Surf Lodge.................9 B2
Carlton Hotel...................10 B2
Goofys.............................11 B2
Headland Hotel................12 A1
Reef Surf Lodge................13 C3

**EATING**
Fistral Chef.....................14 B2
New Harbour Restaurant.15 B2

**DRINKING**
Central............................16 B3
Chy................................17 B3
Koola...........................(see 17)
Red Lion.........................18 B2

**ENTERTAINMENT**
Barracuda........................19 D2

**TRANSPORT**
Bus Station......................20 B3

dinner menu £50; ⊗ breakfast, lunch & dinner) Celebrity chef Jamie Oliver opened the second UK branch of his Fifteen restaurant in 2006 in a stunning location on Watergate Bay. Designed to give underprivileged Cornish youngsters an opportunity to train and work in a professional restaurant environment, Fifteen is one of the hottest tickets in the county. If you manage to bag a table, the beach views, electric atmosphere and contemporary cooking won't disappoint.

## DRINKING & ENTERTAINMENT

**Chy** ( ☎ 01637-873415; www.the-chy.co.uk; 12 Beach Rd; ⊗ 10am-3am Fri, Sat & Mon, to 6pm Tue-Thu & Sun) Chrome, wood and leather dominate this stylish cafe-bar overlooking Towan Beach. The patio is perfect for a gourmet breakfast or lunchtime salad, or pitch up late when the DJs take to the decks, the beers flow and the beautiful people arrive en masse.

**Koola** ( ☎ 01637-873415; www.thekoola.com; 12 Beach Rd; ⊗ 10pm-3am daily summer, Mon & Sat winter) Underneath the Chy, the Koola is the venue of choice for connoisseur clubbers, with house, latin, and drum-'n'-bass nights, and a regular slot for local DJs Jelly Jazz.

**Central** ( ☎ 01637-878310; 11 Central Sq) As its name suggests, this rowdy pre-club pub is right in the heart of town, and the outside patio is always overflowing on warm summer nights.

Other options:

**Red Lion** ( ☎ 01637-871195; North Quay Hill) Established surfers' pub with regular live music and plenty of ales on tap.

**Barracuda** ( ☎ 01637-875800; 27-29 Cliff Rd; ⊗ 9pm-3am) One of the largest clubs in town with big-name DJs on weekends.

## GETTING THERE & AWAY

**Newquay Airport** ( ☎ 01637-860600; www.newquaycornwallairport.com) has regular flights to UK airports, including London, Belfast, Birmingham, Cardiff, Edinburgh and the Isles of Scilly. Bus 556 travels hourly to the airport from town.

National Express has direct buses to London (£38.50, seven hours, four to five daily), Plymouth (£6.40, 1½ hours, five daily) and Penzance (£7.20, 1¾ hours, two to seven daily).

There are trains every couple of hours between Newquay and Par (£5.20, 45 minutes) on the main London–Penzance line.

## St Agnes & Perranporth

The secluded beaches and reliable swells around the coastal towns of St Agnes and Porthtowan are popular with surfers and holidaymakers alike. The tiny National Trust cove of **Chapel Porth**, tucked away at the bottom of a beautiful river valley, is a particularly fine spot; a dramatic coast path snakes along the clifftops to the abandoned mine at **Wheal Coates** and breathtaking views at **Tubby's Head**.

North of St Agnes is the beach town of Perranporth, packed with scarlet-faced holidaymakers in summer and all but deserted in the winter months. The beach at Perranporth (sometimes referred to as **Perran Sands**) is one of the north coast's finest and is popular with surfers, kiteboarders and swimmers alike.

**Driftwood Spars** ( ☎ 01872-552428; www.driftwood spars.com; d £86-102; **P** ), a lively beachside pub at Trevaunance Cove near St Agnes, has 15 delightful rooms upstairs, many of which have sea views and attractive nautical touches.

The **Rose-in-Vale Hotel** ( ☎ 01872-552202; www .rose-in-vale-hotel.co.uk; Mithian; dinner, B&B £164; **P** ) is a grand country-house hotel set in flower-filled grounds 2 miles from St Agnes. It has 18 tasteful rooms and a smart country restaurant.

Over at Porthtowan, one of the favourite hang-outs for Cornwall's beach crowd, the **Blue Bar** ( ☎ 01209-890329; www.blue-bar.co.uk; Porthtowan; mains £9; ☽ lunch & dinner) has a bright surf-style interior and a seaview patio overlooking Porthtowan beach. Burgers, sandwiches and salads are on the menu, and there's live music and DJs at weekends.

**Watering Hole** ( ☎ 01872-572888; Perranporth Beach) is another lively beach bar with outdoor tables on the sand, regular bands and a buzzy surf-shack vibe.

### GETTING THERE & AWAY

Bus 501 travels along the north coast from Newquay to St Ives, Sunday to Friday, between late May and October (three to four buses daily), stopping at St Agnes and Perranporth en route. Bus T1 travels from Truro to St Agnes (40 minutes, hourly), but only a few daily buses travel on to Perranporth (15 minutes, five daily Monday to Saturday).

## Bodmin Moor

Cornwall's 'roof' is a high heath pockmarked with bogs and granite hills, including Rough Tor (pronounced *row-tor*, 400m) and Brown Willy (419m), Cornwall's highest points. It's a

desolate place that works on the imagination; for years there have been reported sightings of the Beast of Bodmin, a large, black cat-like creature, although no-one's ever managed to snap a decent picture.

**Bodmin tourist office** ( ☎ 01208-76616; www.bod minlive.com; Mount Folly; ☽ 10am-5pm Mon-Sat) is in the Shire Hall. It also houses the **Charlotte Dymond Courtroom Experience** (adult/child £3.75/2.25; ☽ 11am-4pm Mon-Sat Easter-Oct, Mon-Fri Nov-Easter), which re-creates one of Cornwall's most notorious Victorian court cases – you get to cast your own verdict at the end.

The A30 cuts across the centre of the moor from **Launceston**, which has a medieval **castle** (EH; ☎ 01566-772365; adult/child £2.50/1.30; ☽ 10am-6pm Jul-Aug, 10am-5pm Apr-Jun & Sep, 10am-4pm Oct) and an interesting granite **church**.

**Jamaica Inn** ( ☎ 01566-86250; www.jamaicainn .co.uk; s £65, d £80-110; **P** ), out on the desolate moor near Bolventor, was made famous by Daphne du Maurier's novel of the same name. Modernised and inevitably touristy, on a misty winter's night the inn can still feel hugely atmospheric; it also has a small smuggling museum and a room devoted to du Maurier.

About a mile south is **Dozmary Pool**, said to have been where Arthur's sword, Excalibur, was thrown after his death. It's a 4-mile walk northwest of Jamaica Inn to Brown Willy.

The **Bodmin & Wenford Railway** ( ☎ 0845 125 9678; www.bodminandwenfordrailway.co.uk; adult/child return £7.50/4; ☽ Mar-Oct) is the last standard-gauge railway in Cornwall plied by steam locomotives. Trains are still decked out in original 1950s livery and chug from Bodmin Parkway and Bodmin General station to Boscarne Junction, where you can join up with the Camel Trail cycle route (p375). There are two to four return trips daily depending on the season.

### GETTING THERE & AWAY

Bodmin has bus connections with St Austell (bus 529, one hour, hourly Monday to Saturday, five on Sunday) as well as Bodmin Parkway (bus 555, 15 minutes, hourly Monday to Saturday, six on summer Sundays) on the London–Penzance train line.

## SOUTHEAST CORNWALL

Dotted with picturesque fishing villages and traced by a patchwork of fields, southeast Cornwall offers a much gentler side of the county than the stark, sea-pounded granite cliffs of the north. Carpeted with wildflowers and criss-crossed by hedgerows, this is still working dairy country, where much of Cornwall's famously rich milk and clotted cream is produced.

## Looe

pop 5280

Looe is a pleasing mixture of bucket-and-spade resort and historic fishing port. Although the industry has declined, Looe has the second-biggest fish market in Cornwall (after Newlyn), and high tide still brings the bustle of landing and ice-packing the catch. The port has been a holiday hot-spot since Victorian times when bathing machines rolled up to the water's edge off **Banjo Pier**. Split into East and West Looe and divided by a broad estuary, inter-village rivalry is intense, with locals referring to living on the 'sunny' or the 'money' side of town.

The **tourist office** ( ☎ 01503-262072; www.visit -southeastcornwall.co.uk; Fore St; ◔ 10am-5pm Easter-Oct, plus occasional days Nov-Easter) is in the Guildhall.

Half a mile west, the **Monkey Sanctuary** ( ☎ 01503-262532; www.monkeysanctuary.org; St Martins; adult/child £6/3.50; ◔ 11am-4.30pm Sun-Thu Easter-Sep) is guaranteed to raise a few 'aaahhhhs' over its unfeasibly cute (and disturbingly human) woolly and capuchin monkeys. The sanctuary is also strong on rehabilitation, conservation and anti-cruelty campaigns.

The tiny St George's Island (often called Looe Island) sits just offshore. This 22-acre nature reserve is run by the Cornwall Wildlife Trust. The boat **Islander** ( ☎ 07814 139223; adult/ child return £7.50/4) will drop you off and collect you; trips run three hours either side of high tide. Other boat trips set out from **Buller Quay** for destinations including Polperro (£19) and Fowey (£12). Check the signs on the quay for sailings, then leave your contact details in one of the books alongside.

### SLEEPING

**Beach House** ( ☎ 01503-262598; www.thebeachhouse looe.com; Hannafore Point; d £80-120; ℗ ) The guesthouse goes grandiose at this double-gabled pile overlooking Hannafore Point. The compact rooms are named after Cornish beaches and the balconies, puffy beds and breakfast pancakes make for a luxurious night's stay.

**Barclay House** ( ☎ 01503-262929; www.barclayhouse .co.uk; St Martins Rd, East Looe; d from £110; ℗ ▯ ) A

swimming pool, sauna and gym may well tempt you to this grand mini hotel in East Looe. That, or the classy modern fixtures, bold colours (think aquamarine, gold and pistachio) and river views.

Also recommended:

**Schooner Point** ( ☎ 01503-262670; www.schoon-erpoint.co.uk; 1 Trelawney Tce; d £50-60; ℗ ) Pastel-shaded, chintz-free B&B with great vegie breakfasts and great views.

**Trehaven Manor** ( ☎ 01503-262028; www.tre havenhotel.co.uk; Station Rd; d £68-122; ℗ ) Antique wardrobes, original fireplaces and deep armchairs fill this old-world B&B.

### GETTING THERE & AWAY

Trains travel the scenic Looe Valley Line from Liskeard (£2.90, 30 minutes, 11 daily Monday to Saturday, eight on Sunday) on the London–Penzance line.

Bus 572 travels to Plymouth (1¼ hours, six daily Monday to Saturday); bus 573 goes to Polperro (30 minutes, hourly Monday to Saturday, five on Sunday).

## Fowey

pop 2273

Nestled on the steep tree-covered hillside overlooking the River Fowey, opposite the old fishing harbour of Polruan, Fowey (pronounced Foy) is a pretty tangle of pale-shaded houses and snaking lanes. Its long maritime history includes being the base for 14th-century raids on France and Spain; to guard against reprisals Henry VIII constructed **St Catherine's Castle** (EH; admission free) above Readymoney Cove, south of town. The town later prospered by shipping china clay extracted from pits at St Austell, but the industrial trade has long declined and Fowey has now reinvented itself for summertime tourists and second-home owners.

The **tourist office** ( ☎ 01726-833616; www.fowey .co.uk; 5 South St; ◔ 9am-5.30pm Mon-Sat, 10am-5pm Sun) is also home (and shares opening hours with) the compact **Daphne du Maurier Literary Centre**, which is devoted to the author of *Rebecca*, *Frenchman's Creek* and the short story that inspired Hitchcock's film *The Birds*. Du Maurier (1907–89) lived at houses in nearby Polridmouth Cove, Readymoney Cove and Ferryside, overlooking the Bodinnick ferry (none of these are open to the public). Every May Fowey hosts the **Daphne du Maurier Literary Festival** (www.dumaurier.org) in her honour.

Fowey is at the southern end of the Saints' Way, a 26-mile waymarked trail running to Padstow on the north coast. **Ferries** ( ☎ 01726-870232; car/pedestrian £2.30/90p; ☒ schedule varies) cross the river to Bodinnick. A **passenger ferry** (foot passengers & bikes only; £1) shuttles over the estuary to the village of **Polruan**, which provides a quaint starting point for some cracking coastal walks.

### SLEEPING & EATING

**Golant YHA** ( ☎ 0845 371 9019; www.yha.org.uk; Penquite House; dm £15.50; **P** ☐ ) Sheltering amid 14 acres of tree-shaded grounds, this whitewashed Georgian manor house makes a fantastic base. It has a cafe-bar, games room and views of the estuary. You can even rent a tepee.

**Globe Posting House Hotel** ( ☎ 01726-833322; www.globeposinghouse.co.uk; 19 Fore St; s/d £50/70) This tiny cob-walled cottage in the middle of Fore St has a clutch of snug, low-ceilinged rooms arranged around its rabbit-warren corridors.

**Old Quay House** ( ☎ 01726-833302; 28 Fore St; www.theoldquayhouse.com; d £160-300) Set in a blissful waterside location, this boutique beauty proves that the British seaside can be sexy. Rooms are all natural fabrics, rattan chairs and achingly tasteful tones – the best have stunning estuary-view balconies.

**Marina Villa Hotel** ( ☎ 01726-833315; www.the marinahotel.co.uk; The Esplanade; d £172-264) Accolades aplenty ensure the beautiful crowd flocks to this collection of nautical-chic rooms (think deluge showers, ornate mirrors and sleigh beds). The pricier rooms have riverside balconies too.

**Sam's** ( ☎ 01726-832273; 20 Fore St; mains £4-10) Forget razor-sharp napkins and snooty service – this great little local's favourite is a cross between *Cheers* and a backstreet French bistro. Squeeze into one of the booths, sink a beer and tuck into mussels, calamari rings or stacked-up Samburgers.

**Food For Thought** ( ☎ 01726-832221; 4 Town Quay; menu £19.95; ☒ lunch & dinner) There's a touch of the French Riviera to this smart restaurant on the corner of Town Quay, which has an excellent fixed-price menu and a pleasant awning-shaded terrace.

### GETTING THERE & AWAY

Bus 25 from St Austell (55 minutes, hourly) runs to Fowey via Par, the closest train station.

## Lanhydrock House

**Lanhydrock** (NT; ☎ 01208-265950; adult/child £9/4.50, gardens only £5/2.50; ☒ house 11am-5.30pm Tue-Sun mid-Mar–Sep, to 5pm Oct, gardens 10am-6pm year round) is reminiscent of the classic 'upstairs-downstairs' film *Gosford Park*. Set in 900 acres of sweeping grounds above the River Fowey, parts date from the 17th century but the property was extensively rebuilt after a fire in 1881, creating the quintessential Victorian county house. Highlights include the gentlemen's smoking room (complete with old Etonian photos, moose heads and tigerskin rugs), the children's toy-strewn nursery, and the huge original kitchens.

Lanhydrock is 2.5 miles southeast of Bodmin; you'll need your own transport to get here.

## Restormel Castle

A glorious, fairytale crumbling ruin, the 13th-century **Restormel Castle** ( ☎ 01208-872687; adult/child £2.50/1; ☒ 10am-6pm Jul & Aug, 10am-5pm mid-Mar–Jun & Sep, 10am-4pm Oct) has one of the best-preserved circular keeps in England. A series of wooden steps snakes past the remains of the first-floor rooms and onto the second-floor crenellated battlements. One of the past owners, Edward, the Black Prince, is thought to have stayed here at least twice – perhaps drawn to hunt the 300 deer in his surrounding land. The castle is 1.5 miles north of Lostwithiel, on the main London–Penzance rail line.

## The Eden Project

If any one thing is emblematic of Cornwall's regeneration, it is the **Eden Project** ( ☎ 01726-811911; www.edenproject.com; Bodelva; adult/child £15/5; ☒ 10am-6pm Apr-Oct, 10am-4.30pm Nov-Mar). Ten years ago the site was a dusty, exhausted clay pit, a symbol of the county's industrial decline. Now it's home to the largest plant-filled greenhouses in the world and is effectively a superb, monumental education project about how much people depend on the natural world. Tropical, temperate and desert environments have been recreated inside the massive biomes, so a single visit carries you from the steaming rainforests of South America to the dry deserts of North Africa.

The Core, a newly-built education centre (constructed according to the Fibonacci sequence, one of nature's most fundamental building blocks) was opened in 2006. In summer the biomes become a spectacular backdrop to a series of gigs known as the **Eden Sessions** (recent artists include The Verve, Goldfrapp and The Kaiser Chiefs), and from November to February Eden transforms itself into a winter wonderland for the **Time of Gifts** festival, complete with a full-size ice rink.

It's impressive and immensely popular: crowds (and queues) can be large, so avoid peak times. Eden is about 3 miles northeast of St Austell. Shuttle buses run from St Austell, Newquay and Truro: check times with **Traveline South West** ( ☎ 0871 200 22 33; www .travelinesw.com). Combined bus and admission tickets are available onboard. Alternatively, if you arrive by bike or on foot, you'll get £3 off the admission price. Last entry is 90 minutes before the site closes.

### The Lost Gardens of Heligan

Before he dreamt up the Eden Project, ex-record producer Tim Smit was best known for rediscovering the lost gardens of **Heligan** ( ☎ 01726-845100; www.heligan.com; Pentewan; adult/child £8.50/5; ☼ 10am-6pm Mar-Oct, 10am-5pm Nov- Feb). Heligan was the former home of the Tremayne family, and during the 19th century was renowned as one of Britain's finest landscaped gardens. The grounds fell into disrepair following WWI (when many staff were killed) and are only now being restored to their former glory. Formal terraces, flower gardens, a working kitchen garden and a spectacular jungle walk through the 'Lost Valley' are just some of Heligan's secrets.

The Lost Gardens of Heligan are 1.5 miles from Mevagissey and 7 miles from St Austell. Bus 526 (30 minutes, six daily, three on Sunday) links Heligan with Mevagissey and St Austell train station.

### Roseland Peninsula

Stretching into the sea south of Truro, this beautiful rural peninsula gets its name not from flowers but from the Cornish word *ros*, meaning promontory. Highlights include the coastal villages of **Portloe**, a wreckers' hangout on the South West Coast Path, and **Veryan**, awash with daffodils in spring and framed by two thatched roundhouses. Nearby are the beaches of **Carne** and **Pendower**, which join at low tide to form one of the best stretches of sand on Cornwall's south coast.

**St Mawes** has a rare, beautifully preserved clover-leaf **castle** (EH; ☎ 01326-270526; admission £3.60; ☼ 10am-6pm daily Jul & Aug, 10am-5pm Sun-Fri Apr-

---

**TOP FIVE GARDENS**

- **Glendurgan Gardens** (p386) – The Helford
- **Heligan** (left) – near Mevagissey
- **Trebah** (p386) – The Helford
- **Trelissick** (opposite) – near Falmouth
- **Tresco Abbey Garden** (p395) – Isles of Scilly

Check out www.gardensofcornwall.com for further tips.

---

Jun & Sep, 10am-4pm daily Oct, 10am-4pm Fri-Mon Nov-Mar), commissioned by Henry VIII and designed as the sister fortress to Pendennis (p384) across the estuary.

**St Just-in-Roseland** boasts one of the most beautiful churchyards in the country, full of flowers it tumbles down to a creek filled with boats and wading birds.

## TRURO
pop 17,431

Cornwall's capital city has been at the centre of the county's fortunes for over eight centuries. Truro first grew up around a now vanished hilltop castle, built by Richard Lucy, a minister of Henry II's. Throughout the Middle Ages it was one of Cornwall's five Stannary towns, where tin and copper was assayed and stamped. Truro was granted its own bishop in 1877, with the city's three-spired cathedral following soon after. Today, the city makes an appealing base, with a good selection of shops and restaurants and Cornwall's main museum.

### Information

**Library** ( ☎ 01872-279205; Union Pl; ☼ 9am-6pm Mon-Fri, 9am-4pm Sat) Net access costs £3 per hour.

**Post office** (High Cross; ☼ 9am-5.30pm Mon-Sat)

**Tourist office** ( ☎ 01872-274555; www.acornishriver .co.uk; Boscawen St; ☼ 9am-5pm Mon-Fri, plus Sat Apr-Oct).

### Sights

The **Royal Cornwall Museum** ( ☎ 01872-272205; www.royalcornwallmuseum.org.uk; River St; admission free; ☼ 10am-4.45pm Mon-Sat) has excellent displays exploring the county's industrial and archaeological past. There are also temporary exhibitions of art, photography and local craft.

Built on the site of a 16th-century parish church in soaring Gothic Revival style, **Truro Cathedral** ( ☎ 01872-276782; www.trurocathedral.org.uk;

High Cross; suggested donation £4; 7.30am-6pm Mon-Sat, 9am-7pm Sun) was finally completed in 1910, making it the first new cathedral in England since London's St Paul's. It contains a soaring high-vaulted nave, some fine Victorian stained glass and the impressive Father Willis Organ.

The **Lemon St Market** (Lemon St) houses craft shops, cafes, delicatessens and an upstairs art gallery. There are several excellent galleries around town, including the upmarket **Lemon St Gallery** ( 01872-275757; 13 Lemon St; 10.30am-5.30pm Mon-Sat).

## Sleeping

**Carlton Hotel** ( 01872-272450; www.carltonhotel.co.uk; 49 Falmouth Rd; s £47-57, d £67-77; P ) The furnishings may be standard B&B (pastel colours, easy-clean carpets, ancient kettles) but extras such as Sky TV and a guest sauna and Jacuzzi seal the deal.

**Bissick Old Mill** ( 01726-882557; www.bissickoldmill .co.uk; Ladock; d £75-95; P ) There's not a corn sack in sight at this beautifully converted 17th-century mill. Instead it's all Egyptian cotton sheets, handmade soap and in-room fridges, topped off by plenty of beams and old mill wheels. Ladock is 7 miles northeast of Truro.

**Royal Hotel** ( 01872-270345; www.royalhotelcorn wall.co.uk; Lemon St; s £80, d £100-110; P ) The bedrooms at this Georgian-fronted hotel are zingy affairs thanks to bold, bright designs and citrus tints. There are super-sleek 'aparthotels' just behind the main building too (£140 a night).

Other recommendations:

**Fieldings** ( 01872-262783; www.fieldingsintruro.com; 35 Treyew Rd; s/d £23/46) Homely Edwardian house with great city views.

**Alverton Manor** ( 01872-276633; www.alver tonmanor.co.uk; Tregolls Rd; s £80, d £95-180; P ) A convent-turned-hotel crammed with antiques, sleigh beds and flowery drapes.

## Eating

**Xen Noodle Bar** ( 01872-222998; 47-49 Calenick St; mains £4-8; lunch & dinner Mon-Sat) Minimalistic and moreish, this inventive noodle bar keeps the crowds happy with Szechuan, Hong Kong and Canton flavours as well as Chinese classics.

**Saffron** ( 01872-263771; Quay St; mains £8-16; lunch & dinner Mon-Sat) Asparagus, Cornish meats, seafood and strawberries: Saffron is all about local, seasonal food dished up with flair. Daily changing mains include Cornish lamb, spider-crab chowder, Cajun monkfish, and falafel with crème fraiche.

**Indaba Fish** ( 01872-274700; Tabernacle St; mains £14-18; dinner) The chef here used to work for Rick Stein, and this swish fish emporium has a similar emphasis on classic, straightforward seafood, ranging from Falmouth oysters and Newlyn lobster to sea bream with garlic mash. Vegetarians and fish phobics are catered for too.

## Drinking

**Old Ale House** ( 01872-271122; Quay St) What a relief – a city-centre pub that eschews chrome 'n' cocktails and sticks with burnished wood 'n' beer mats. The daily ales are chalked up behind the bar and there's often live jazz at weekends.

**Heron** ( 01872-272773; Malpas; 11am-3pm & 6-11pm Mon-Sat, 7-10.30pm Sun) Two miles along the river estuary from Truro, this creekside pub in the tiny village of Malpas serves good beer and excellent pub grub.

**Ml Bar** ( 01872-277214; Lemon Quay; 10am-1am Fri & Sat, 10am-midnight Sun-Thu) A sleek city-slicker style bar where guest DJs have a fondness for hip hop, jazz, funk and soul.

## Entertainment

**Hall for Cornwall** ( 01872-262466; www.hallforcornwall .co.uk; Lemon Quay) The county's main venue for touring theatre and music, housed in Truro's former town hall on Lemon Quay.

**SOUTHWEST ENGLAND**

---

### DETOUR: TRELISSICK

At the head of the Fal estuary, 4 miles south of Truro, **Trelissick** (NT; 01872-862090; Feock; adult/child £6.60/3.30; 10.30am-5.30pm Feb-Oct, 11am-4pm Nov-Jan) is one of Cornwall's most beautiful landscaped gardens, with several tiered terraces covered in magnolias, rhododendrons and hydrangeas. A lovely walk runs all the way from the main garden along the river to the estate's private beach.

**Enterprise Boats** ( 01326-374241; www.enterprise-boats.co.uk; adult/child one way £4.50/3) operates boats from Falmouth and Truro that call in at Trelissick Gardens, otherwise you'll need your own transport.

---

### DETOUR: LUGGER HOTEL

**Lugger Hotel** ( ☎ 01872-501322; www.lug gerhotel.co.uk; Portloe; r £160-350) Teetering over the harbour's edge in the beautiful old fishing town of Portloe, this supremely indulgent boutique hotel is the ultimate romantic getaway. A range of higgledy-piggledy rooms are dotted around the old smugglers' inn and a couple of adjoining fishermen's cottages, creating a charming mix of rough oak beams; clean, contemporary furnishings and huge, decadent beds. Downstairs the elegant restaurant serves fish fresh from the boats and the panoramic portside terrace makes the ideal place for watching the sun go down. You may find it very hard to leave.

---

**L2** ( ☎ 01872-261199; Calenick St; cover charge £3-5; ☺ 9pm-1.30am Mon, 9.30pm-1am Wed & Thu, 9.30pm-3am Fri & Sat) Truro's biggest nightclub features a wide variety of themed nights – it can get rowdy at kicking-out time.

## Getting There & Away

### BUS

There are direct National Express coaches to London Victoria (£38.50, eight hours, four daily). Bus X18 (one hour, hourly Monday to Saturday, six on Sunday) travels to Penzance via Redruth and Camborne, and bus 14B (1½ hours, hourly Monday to Saturday) travels to St Ives; lots of services travel to Falmouth and Newquay. The bus station is beside Lemon Quay.

### TRAIN

Truro is on the main line between London Paddington (£70, 4½ to five hours, hourly) and Penzance (£7, 45 minutes, hourly). There's a branch line to Falmouth (£3.50, 20 minutes, every two hours).

## WEST CORNWALL

For exhilarating swathes of wind-blasted, spray-dashed coast, it's hard to top west Cornwall, especially around St Just-in-Penwith. Sleepy fishing villages, such as Mousehole, provide the picturesque; the Tate St Ives adds art history; the Lizard Peninsula supplies stunning gardens; while Penzance provides an authentic maritime atmosphere and bursts of seaside chic.

## Falmouth

pop 20775

Falmouth is a pleasing blend of bustling port, holiday resort and mildly alternative student town. Flanked by the third deepest natural harbour in the world, its fortunes were made in the 18th and 19th centuries when clippers, trading vessels and mail packets from across the world stopped off to unload their cargoes. Today Falmouth still has an important shipyard as well as an absorbing National Maritime Museum. Thousands of students from the nearby Combined Universities in Cornwall campus lend the town a laid-back vibe, as does the batch of sandy beaches just around the headland to the south of town.

The **tourist office** ( ☎ 01326-312300; www.acor nishriver.co.uk; 11 Market Strand; ☺ 9.30am-5.15pm Mon-Sat Mar-Oct, Mon-Fri Nov-Feb, plus 10.15am-1.45pm Sun Jul & Aug) is beside the Prince of Wales Pier.

### SIGHTS & ACTIVITIES

#### National Maritime Museum

The **National Maritime Museum** ( ☎ 01326-313388; www.nmmc.co.uk; Discovery Quay; adult/child £7.95/5.25; ☺ 10am-5pm) houses one of the largest maritime collections in the UK, second only to its sister museum in Greenwich in London. At the heart of the complex is the huge Flotilla Gallery, where boats dangle from the ceiling on slender steel wires, while suspended walkways wind their way around the collection of yachts, schooners, punts and canoes. Other highlights include the Set Sail exhibit, which tells the story of nine groundbreaking boats, and the Lookout, with a 360-degree panorama of Falmouth Bay.

#### Pendennis Castle

Perched on a promontory overlooking Falmouth harbour, **Pendennis Castle** (EH; ☎ 01326-316594; adult/child £5.50/2.80; ☺ 10am-6pm Jul-Aug, 10am-5pm Apr-Jun & Sep, 10am-4pm Oct-Mar, closes 4pm Sat year round) provides an evocative taste of its 460-year-old history. Henry VIII first constructed Cornwall's largest fortress here to defend the entrance to the Fal estuary in tandem with its sister fortress at St Mawes (p382), on the opposite side. Highlights include a superbly atmospheric Tudor gun deck (complete with cannon flashes, smoke and shouted commands), a WWI guard house and a remarkable re-creation of a WWII-observation post.

## Boat Trips

Boat trips set out from the Prince of Wales Pier to the River Helford (p386) and Frenchman's Creek (£8 return), the 500-year-old Smuggler's Cottage pub (£6.50 return) and Truro (£8 return, one hour). The pier is lined with boat companies' booths; try **Enterprise Boats** ( ☎ 01326-374241) or **Newman's Cruises** ( ☎ 01872-580309).

Passenger ferries make the harbour mouth dash across to St Mawes and Flushing from the pier every hour in summer.

## Beaches

The nearest beach to town is busy **Gyllyngvase**, a short walk from the town centre, where you'll find plenty of flat sand and a decent beach cafe. Further around the headland, **Swanpool** and **Maenporth** are usually quieter.

## SLEEPING

Falmouth is crammed with B&Bs and hotels, especially along Melvill Rd and Avenue Rd.

**Dolvean Hotel** ( ☎ 01326-313658; www.dolvean .co.uk; 50 Melvill Rd; s £41, d £70-92; P ☐ wi-fi) There's hardly a piece of fabric in this plush five-star B&B that isn't ruched, swagged and draped. The bigger rooms sport brass bedsteads and antique mirrors, while the lounge is a shrine to Victoriana.

**Hawthorne Dene Hotel** ( ☎ 01326-311427; www .hawthornedenehotel.co.uk; 12 Pennance Rd; s/d £40/80; P ) Edwardian elegance rules the roost at this family-run hotel with its ranks of old photos and booklined gentleman's lounge. The antique-themed bedrooms feature springy beds, polished woods and teddy bears – most also have a sea view.

**St Michael's Hotel** ( ☎ 01326-312707; www. stmichaelshotel.co.uk; s £90-150, d £120-200; P ) Bedrooms with gingham checks, light candy stripes and painted, slatted wood make this luxurious hotel reminiscent of a Long Island beach retreat. The cracking sea views, spa, swimming pool and sauna also help the holiday mood.

Other recommendations:

**Trelawney** ( ☎ 01326-316607; 6 Melvill Rd; s £30-40, d £48-90) Modern cream-and-pine rooms and brekkies full of organic goodies.

**Greenbank** ( ☎ 01326-312440; www.greenbank-hotel .co.uk; Harbourside; d 120-215, ste £260; P ) Upmarket

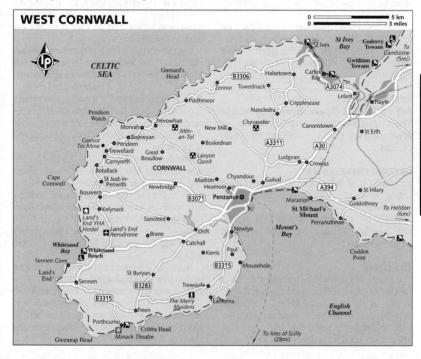

**WEST CORNWALL**

hotel where fabrics veer from traditional quilted to bursts of animal print.

### EATING & DRINKING

**Boathouse** ( ☎ 01326-315425; Trevethan Hill; mains £6-10; ☻ lunch & dinner) This fantastic gastropub is so laid-back it's almost horizontal. It's especially popular with Falmouth's creative crowd, who come for the generous plates of food, cold beer and chilled-out vibe.

**Harbour View** ( ☎ 01326-315315; 24 Arwenack St; mains £7-15; ☻ lunch & dinner Wed-Mon, lunch only Sun-Tue winter) On a fine summer evening settle into a candy-coloured chair on this bistro's funky deck and enjoy a captivating view of the water. Then choose between Cornish sardines, Fal estuary scallops or the delicate, delicious seafood linguini.

**our pick Hunky Dory** ( ☎ 01326-212997; 46 Arwenack St; mains £12-25; ☻ dinner) Fishers often ferry their just-caught catch past diners at this stylish restaurant – the seafood is that fresh. The design blends pale wood and rough whitewashed walls, while the menu mixes European and Asian flavours with classic Cornish produce – try the crispy-skinned sea bass or the Newlyn cod wrapped in prosciutto.

Top spots for a pint include the **Quayside** ( ☎ 01326-312113; Arwenack St), with outside seating on the harbour, and the nearby **Chain Locker** ( ☎ 01326-311685; Quay St), which is nautical but nice.

### ENTERTAINMENT

**Poly** ( ☎ 01326-212300; www.thepoly.org; 24 Church St) The former Falmouth Arts Centre has re-invented itself into an excellent art-house cinema.

### GETTING THERE & AWAY

Falmouth is at the end of the branch train line from Truro (£3.50, 20 minutes, every two hours).

Buses 89/90 run to Truro (1¼ hours, half-hourly Monday to Saturday) and on to Newquay.

## The Lizard

For a taste of Cornwall's stormier side, head for the ink-black cliffs, rugged coves and open heaths of the mercurial Lizard Peninsula. Wind-lashed in winter, in summer it bristles with wildflowers, butterflies and coves that are perfect for a secluded swim. The Lizard used to be at the centre of Cornwall's smuggling industry and is still alive with tales of Cornish 'free-traders', contraband liquor and the government's preventive boats. The most notorious excise dodger was John Carter, the so-called King of Prussia – Prussia Cove near Marazion is named after him.

For more information visit www.lizard-peninsula.co.uk.

### GOONHILLY EARTH STATION

The last thing you'd expect to find in the middle of the Lizard are the vast dishes of the **Goonhilly Earth Station** ( ☎ 0800 679593; www.goonhilly.bt.com; adult/child £7.95/5.50; ☻ 10am-6pm Jul & Aug, 10am-5pm mid-Mar–Jun & Sep-Oct, 11am-4pm Nov–mid-Mar) which make up the largest satellite station on earth. The multimedia visitor centre has lots of interactive exhibits and romps through the last 200 years of telecommunications.

### RIVER HELFORD

The **River Helford** flows across the north of the Lizard. Lined with overhanging oaks and hidden inlets, it is the perfect smugglers' hideaway. **Frenchman's Creek**, the inspiration for Daphne du Maurier's novel of the same name, can be reached on foot from the car park in **Helford** village.

On the northern bank of the river is **Trebah** ( ☎ 01326-252200; www.trebahgarden.co.uk; adult/child Mar-Oct £7/2, Nov-Feb £3/1; ☻ 10.30am-6.30pm, last entry 5pm), billed as Cornwall's 'Garden of Dreams'. First planted in 1840, it's one of Cornwall's finest subtropical gardens, dramatically situated in a steep ravine filled with giant rhododendrons, huge Brazilian rhubarb plants and jungle ferns.

**Glendurgan Gardens** (NT; ☎ 01326-250906; adult/child £6/3; ☻ 10.30am-5.30pm Tue-Sat Feb-Oct, plus Mon Aug) are just east of Trebah. They were established in the 18th century by the wealthy Fox family, who imported exotic plants from the New World. Look out for the stunning views of the River Helford, the 19th-century maze and the secluded beach near Durgan village.

Six miles from Helston at the western end of the river, the **National Seal Sanctuary** ( ☎ 01326-221361; www.sealsanctuary.co.uk; Gweek; adult/child £11.50/8.50; ☻ 10am-5pm May-Sep, 9am-4pm Oct-Apr) cares for sick and orphaned seals washed up along the Cornish coastline before returning them to the wild.

## LIZARD POINT & AROUND

Three miles west of Helston is **Porthleven**, another quaint fishing port with excellent beaches nearby. **Cadgwith** is the quintessential Cornish fishing village, with thatched, white-washed cottages and a small harbour.

**Lizard Point** is a 3½-mile walk along the South West Coast Path. At the peninsula's tip is the **Lizard Lighthouse** ( ☎ 01326-290065; adult/child £3.50/2.50; ☺ 11am-6pm daily Jul & Aug, 11am-5pm Sun-Thu May & Jun, noon-5pm Sun-Wed Mar & Apr), built in 1751 and now entirely automated. Lizard Point is one of the most dangerous bits of coast in Cornwall: hundreds of ships have foundered on its rocky shores. The views from the surrounding cliff tops are some of the most dramatic in all of Cornwall.

A mile west is beautiful **Kynance Cove**, overlooked by towering cliffs and flower-covered headland; much of the red-green serpentine rock fashionable during the Victorian era was mined here.

### SLEEPING

**Lizard YHA** ( ☎ 0845 371 9550; www.yha.org.uk; dm £16; ☺ Apr-Oct) Few top-end hotels can boast the kind of spectacular sea view enjoyed by this gloriously situated hostel, in a renovated Victorian hotel right below the lighthouse on Lizard Point.

**Housel Bay Hotel** ( ☎ 01326-290417; www .houselbay.com; The Lizard; d £90-140; **P** ) By far the most impressive hotel on Lizard Point, this grand gabled manor was built by a group of luxury-loving Victorian entrepreneurs. It's still a gorgeous place to stay, with plenty of antiques, period rugs and a charming old-world atmosphere.

### GETTING THERE & AWAY

Bus T2 runs from Truro to Helston (50 minutes, eight daily Monday to Saturday, five on Sunday) and on to Goonhilly (20 minutes), Coverack (30 minutes) and St Keverne (40 minutes).

To reach Lizard village, near Lizard Point, catch bus T34 from Helston (45 minutes, hourly Monday to Saturday, five on Sunday).

## St Michael's Mount

Looming up from the waters of Mount's Bay, the island abbey of **St Michael's Mount** (NT; ☎ 01736-710507; adult/child £6.60/3; ☺ 10.30am-5pm Sun-Fri Mar-Oct) is one of Cornwall's iconic landmarks. Set on a collection of craggy cliffs and connected to the mainland by a cobbled causeway that's submerged by the rising tide, there's been a monastery here since at least the 5th century. After the Norman conquest the island was given to the Benedictine monks of Mont St Michel in Normandy, who raised a new chapel on the site in 1135. The mount later served as a fortified stronghold and is now the family home of the St Aubyns, and under the stewardship of the National Trust.

Highlights include the rococo Gothic drawing room, the original armoury, the 14th-century priory church and its subtropical **gardens** (adult/child £3/1) which teeter dramatically above the sea. You can walk across the causeway at low tide, or catch a ferry at high tide in the summer.

Bus 2 passes Marazion as it travels from Penzance to Falmouth (half hourly Monday to Saturday, six on Sunday).

## Penzance

pop 21,168

Stretching along the glittering sweep of Mount's Bay, Penzance has been the last stop on the main railway line from London since the days of the Great Western Railway. With its hotchpotch of winding streets, old shopping arcades and grand seafront promenade, it's much more authentic than the polished-up, prettified towns of Padstow and St Ives, and makes an excellent base for exploring the rest of west Cornwall and Land's End.

### INFORMATION

**Library** ( ☎ 01736-363954; Morrab Rd; internet access per hr £3; ☺ 9.30am-6pm Mon-Fri, to 4pm Sat)

**Polyclean Laundrette** ( ☎ 01736-364815; 4 East Tce; ☺ 9am-7.30pm) Opposite the railway station.

**Tourist office** ( ☎ 01736-362207; www.visit-west cornwall.com; Station Approach; ☺ 9am-5pm Mon-Fri, plus 10am-4pm Sat Easter-Sep & 10am-2pm Sun Jul & Aug) Next to the bus station.

**www.penzance.co.uk** Useful local guide to Penzance and the surrounding area.

### SIGHTS & ACTIVITIES

**Penlee House Gallery & Museum** ( ☎ 01736-363625; www.penleehouse.org.uk; Morrab Rd; admission £2, free Sat; ☺ 10am-5pm Mon-Sat May-Sep, 10.30am-4.30pm Mon-Sat Oct-Apr) displays a fine range of paintings by artists of the Newlyn School (including Stanhope Forbes) and hosts regular exhibitions on Cornwall's art history.

**PENZANCE**

| INFORMATION | |
|---|---|
| Library..................1 C2 | |
| Polyclean Laundrette.........2 D1 | |
| Tourist Office..................3 D1 | |

| SIGHTS & ACTIVITIES | |
|---|---|
| Jubilee Pool......................4 D3 | |
| Penlee House Gallery & Museum..................5 B2 | |

| SLEEPING | |
|---|---|
| Abbey Hotel..................6 C2 | |
| Camilla House..................7 C3 | |
| Glencree House..................8 B3 | |
| Summer House..................9 C3 | |

| EATING | |
|---|---|
| Abbey Restaurant........(see 6) | |
| Archie Brown's..................10 C2 | |
| Bar Coco's..................11 C2 | |
| Blue Snappa..................12 C2 | |

| DRINKING | |
|---|---|
| Turk's Head..................13 C2 | |

| TRANSPORT | |
|---|---|
| Bus Station..................14 D1 | |
| Scillonian Ferry Departures..................15 D2 | |

At the eastern end of Penzance's 19th-century promenade the glorious 1930s **Jubilee Pool** ( ☎ 01736-334832; www.jubileepool.co.uk; adult/child/family £3.85/2.75/12.20; ☼ 10.30am-6pm May-Sep) offers you the chance to take a dip in a classic art deco lido. Since falling into disrepair in the 1980s, it's been thoroughly spruced-up and is now open to alfresco bathers throughout the summer – just don't expect the water to be warm.

The busy fishing harbour of **Newlyn**, on the western edge of Penzance, was the centre of the Newlyn School of artists in the late 19th century; the **Newlyn Art Gallery** ( ☎ 01736-363715; www.newlynartgallery.co.uk; ☼ 10am-5pm Mon-Sat Easter-Sep, Wed-Sat Oct-Easter) showcases their modern counterparts.

## SLEEPING
### Budget
Penzance has lots of low-price B&Bs, especially along Alexandra Rd and Morrab Rd.

**Penzance YHA** ( ☎ 0845 371 9653; www.yha.org.uk; Castle Horneck, Alverton; dm £15.50; P 🖳 ) Housed inside an 18th-century Georgian manor on the outskirts of town, this official hostel has an onsite cafe, laundry and four- to 10-bed dorms. Buses 5 and 6 run from the bus station to Alverton; it's a 500m walk from the bus stop.

**Glencree House** ( ☎ 01736-362026; www.glencree house.co.uk; 2 Mennaye Rd; d £40-62; P ) Modest sea views, a budget bill and a slap-up breakfast make this old fashioned B&B worth booking; the smoked kippers, proper coffee and croissants will leave you crying off lunch.

### Midrange & Top End
**Camilla House** ( ☎ 01736-363771; www.camillahouse .co.uk; 12 Regent Tce; s £35, d £74-85; P 🖳 ) Set in a Georgian Master Mariner's house, this five-star B&B stands out for its classy rooms, period features and environmentally conscious stance. Fluffy bathrobes, pillow treats and views over the prom will tempt you too.

**Summer House** ( ☎ 01736-363744; www.sum merhouse-cornwall.com; Cornwall Tce; s £85, d £95-125; ☼ closed Nov-Mar; P ) For a touch of Chelsea-on-Sea chic, check into this elegant Regency house. Checks, pinstripes and cheery colours characterise the five bedrooms, and downstairs there's a Mediterranean restaurant with alfresco terrace.

**Abbey Hotel** ( ☎ 01736-366906; www.theabbey online.co.uk; Abbey St; d £130-200) Bucking the pared-down trend, this flower-filled, period town house offers a taste of Penzance's 17th-century heyday. All the cosy rooms have their own offbeat style and higgledy-piggledy layout, topped off with floral fabrics and canopied beds.

### EATING & DRINKING

**Bar Coco's** ( ☎ 01736-350222; 13 Chapel St; tapas £2-6; ⏱ lunch & dinner Mon-Sat) More Cádiz than Cornwall, this funky little tapas bar is an ideal spot to sample mini platters of *cerveza, patatas* and chorizo. You can say '*buenas tardes*' to Mediterranean-style sardines, tuna and monkfish too.

**Archie Brown's** ( ☎ 01736-362828; Bread St; mains £4-6; ⏱ 9.30am-5pm Mon-Sat) This much-loved vegie/vegan cafe serves up hearty portions of old faves including homity pie, hot chilli and crumbly carrot cake.

**Blue Snappa** ( ☎ 01736-363352; 35 Market Pl; mains £6-15; ⏱ breakfast, lunch & dinner, closed Sun eve) They do a good line in hip surfer chic at this buzzing bar-brasserie; the menu meanwhile will leave you torn between slow-roast belly pork, smoked pollack with garlic or a flavoursome vegie risotto.

**Abbey Restaurant** ( ☎ 01736-330680; Abbey St; mains £16-20, 2/3 courses £19/23; ⏱ lunch & dinner Tue-Sat) Underpinned by top-quality produce, the Abbey turns out consistently fabulous food in a light-filled dining room. It's not cheap, but tucking into your roast monkfish or hot chocolate soufflé, you'll feel it's money well spent.

**Turk's Head** ( ☎ 01736-363093; Chapel St) They pull a fine pint of real ale at this, the oldest boozer in Penzance. It's said a smugglers' tunnel used to link the pub with the harbour – handy for sneaking in that liquid contraband.

### GETTING THERE & AWAY

The *Scillonian* ferry regularly sails from Penzance to the Isles of Scilly; see p396. Helicopters to the Isles of Scilly leave from just outside town; see p396.

### Bus

National Express coaches travel to London (£38.50, nine hours, five daily), Exeter (£24, five hours, two daily) and Plymouth (£7.20, 3½ hours, seven daily). For buses to Land's End see p390.

### Train

Regular services journey to London Paddington (£90, six hours, eight daily) via Truro. There are frequent trains to St Ives (£4.80, 20 minutes, hourly) via St Erth.

## Mousehole

The compact harbour town Mousehole (pronounced 'mow-zel') was once at the heart of Cornwall's thriving pilchard industry, but these days it's better known for its colourful Christmas lights. Despite hideously high numbers of second homes, it's still one of Cornwall's most appealing villages, with a tight-packed knot of slate-roofed cottages gathered around the harbour.

The designer decor at the **Old Coastguard Hotel** ( ☎ 01736-731222; www.oldcoastguardhotel. co.uk; d £140-210) would have bemused ancient mariners, but guests love the arty lighting, smooth leather chairs and balconies with jaw-dropping sea views. The sunlit restaurant also looks out over the glittering bay and specialises, unsurprisingly, in fantastic seafood.

Bus 6 makes the 20-minute journey to Penzance half-hourly.

## Minack Theatre

At the **Minack** ( ☎ 01736-810181; www.minack.com; tickets from £8.50) the actors are constantly upstaged by the setting. Carved directly into the steep cliffs overlooking Porthcurno Bay, this alfresco amphitheatre is the legacy of Rowena Cade, an indomitable local woman who came up with the idea in the 1930s, helped with the construction for 20 years and oversaw the theatre until her death in 1983. From the original production of *The Tempest* in 1932, the Minack has grown into a full-blown theatrical venue, with 750 seats and a 17-week season running from mid-May to mid-September. The cliffs provide the scenery, the sea provides the backdrop, while basking sharks and the moon rising over the waves provide charming distractions. Regulars bring a bottle of wine, umbrellas and lots of blankets.

The **visitor centre** (adult/child £3.50/1.40; ⏱ 9.30am-5.30pm Apr-Sep, 10am-4pm Oct-Mar) recounts the story of the making of the theatre; it's closed when there's a matinee.

The Minack is above beautiful Porthcurno beach, 3 miles from Land's End and 9 miles from Penzance. Bus 1A from Penzance to Land's End stops at Porthcurno, Monday to Saturday.

SOUTHWEST ENGLAND

## Land's End

At the most westerly point of mainland England, the coal-black cliffs, heather-covered headlands and booming Atlantic surf at Land's End should steal the show. Unfortunately the tawdry **Legendary Land's End** ( ☎ 0870 458 0099; www.landsend-landmark.co.uk; adult/child £11/7; ☻ 10am-5pm summer, 10am-3pm winter) theme park does rather get in the way. But you can bypass the kitsch models and multimedia shows and opt for an exhilarating cliff-top stroll instead. On a clear day the Isles of Scilly are visible, 28 miles out to sea.

Land's End is 9 miles from Penzance (and 886 miles from John O'Groats). Buses 1 and 1A travel from Penzance (one hour, seven to 10 daily Monday to Saturday). Bus 300 heads to St Ives (one hour 20 minutes, four daily May to October).

## St Just-in-Penwith

pop 1890

It's hard to imagine today, but a century ago the grey-granite settlement of St Just was at the heart of a vibrant tin- and copper-mining industry. The old **Geevor Tin Mine** ( ☎ 01736-788662; www.geevor.com; adult/child £7.50/4.50; ☻ 9am-5pm Sun-Fri Easter-Oct, to 3pm Nov-Mar) at Pendeen, north of St Just, finally closed in 1990, and now offers hourly tours of the underground shafts (three daily in winter), providing an amazing insight into the dark and dangerous conditions in which Cornwall's miners worked.

Clinging to the cliffs nearby is **Botallack Mine**, one of Cornwall's most dramatic engine houses, which have abandoned mine shafts extending right out beneath the raging Atlantic waves. The mine is not open to the public.

**Land's End YHA** ( ☎ 0845 371 9643; www.yha.org .uk; Letcha Vean; dm £10; ☻ Easter-Oct; Ⓟ ) is in an isolated spot half a mile south of the village. This no-frills affair has smallish dorms and a basic kitchen, but is ideal if you're hiking the coast path.

St Just is 6 miles north of Land's End. Buses 17/17A/17B travel from St Ives (1¼ hours) via Penzance (half hourly Monday to Saturday, five on Sunday).

## St Ives

pop 9870

Sitting on the fringes of a glittering arc-shaped bay, St Ives was once one of Cornwall's busiest pilchard-fishing harbours, but it's better known now as the centre of the county's arts scene. From the old harbour, cobbled alleyways and switchback lanes lead up into the jumble of buzzy galleries, cafes and brassieres that cater for thousands of summer visitors. It makes for an intriguing mix of boutique chic and traditional seaside, and while the high-season traffic can take the shine off things, St Ives is still an essential stop on any Cornish grand tour.

### INFORMATION

**Library** ( ☎ 01736-795377; 1 Gabriel St; internet access per hr £3; ☻ 9.30am-9.30pm Tue, to 6pm Wed-Fri, to 12.30pm Sat)

**Post office** ( ☎ 01736-795004; Tregenna Pl; ☻ 9am-5.30pm Mon-Fri, 9am-12.30pm Sat)

**Tourist office** ( ☎ 01736-796297; ivtic@penwith.gov .uk; Street-an-Pol; ☻ 9am-5.30pm Mon-Fri, 9am-5pm Sat, 10am-4pm Sun) Inside the Guildhall.

**www.stives-cornwall.co.uk** Official town website with accommodation and activity guides.

### SIGHTS & ACTIVITIES

#### Tate St Ives

St Ives has been a focal point for artists for generations. Turner sketched the town in 1811 and by the 1930s the sculptor Barbara Hepworth and the abstract painters Peter Lanyon and Ben Nicholson had set up camp. In the 1960s and '70s St Ives' artistic avant-garde included Terry Frost, Patrick Heron and Roger Hilton.

The work of many of these local artists features at the stunning **Tate St Ives** ( ☎ 01736-796226; www.tate.org.uk/stives; Porthmeor Beach; adult/18yr & under £5.75/free, joint ticket with Barbara Hepworth museum £8.75/free; ☻ 10am-5pm Mar-Oct, 10am-4pm Tue-Sun Nov-Feb) gallery, which hovers like a white concrete curl above Porthmeor Beach. On the top floor there's a stylish cafe-bar with imaginative bistro food and some of the best sea views in St Ives.

There are plenty more galleries around town; at the **Sloop Craft Centre** you'll find a treasure trove of tiny artists' studios selling everything from handmade jewellery to driftwood furniture.

### Barbara Hepworth Museum & Sculpture Garden

Barbara Hepworth (1903–75) was one of the leading abstract sculptors of the 20th century, and a key figure in the St Ives art scene; fittingly her former studio has been transformed into a moving archive and **museum** ( ☎ 01736-796226; www.tate.org.uk/stives; Barnoon Hill; adult/18yr & under £4.75/free, joint ticket with Tate St Ives £8.75/free; ☉ 10am-5pm daily Mar-Oct, 10am-4pm Tue-Sun Nov-Feb). The studio itself has remained almost untouched since her death in a fire, and the adjoining garden contains some of her most famous sculptures. Hepworth's work is scattered throughout St Ives; look for her sculptures outside the Guildhall and inside the 15th-century parish church of St Ia.

### St Ives Museum
Housed in a pier-side building variously used as a pilchard-packing factory, sailor's mission and copper mine, **St Ives Museum** ( ☎ 01736-796005; Wheal Dream; adult/child £1.50/50p; ☉ 10am-5pm Mon-Fri, to 4pm Sat, mid-Mar–Oct) contains local artefacts relating to blacksmithery, fishing and shipwrecks.

### Beaches
The largest town beaches are **Porthmeor** and **Porthminster**, but the tiny cove of **Porthgwidden** is also popular. Nearby, on a tiny peninsula of land known locally as The Island, the pre-14th-century **Chapel of St Nicholas**, patron saint of children and sailors, is the oldest (and smallest) church in St Ives. **Carbis Bay**, to the southeast, is popular with families and sunseekers.

On the opposite side of the bay from St Ives, the receding tide reveals over 3 miles of golden beach at **Gwithian** and **Godrevy Towans**, both popular spots for kiteboarders and surfers. The lighthouse just offshore at Godrevy was the inspiration for Virginia Woolf's classic stream-of-consciousness novel *To The Lighthouse*.

Several places on Porthmeor Beach and Fore St rent wetsuits and surfboards; try **Windansea** ( ☎ 01736-794830; 25 Fore St; per 24hr £5). The BSA-approved **Shore Surf School** ( ☎ 01736-755556; per half-day £25) is based at Hayle, 6 miles away; lessons are held where the conditions are best on the day.

### Boat Trips
Boats heading out on sea-fishing trips and cruises to the grey-seal colony on Seal Island (adult/child £9/6) include those run by the **St Ives Pleasure Boat Association** ( ☎ 07821 774178).

---

> **SEARCHING FOR STONES**
>
> The area between St Just and St Ives is remarkably rich in ancient sites and dotted with dolmens, menhirs and mysterious stone circles. Track down **Lanyon Quoit** (a table-shaped dolmen between Madron and Morvah), the **Mên-an-Tol stone** (a ring-shaped stone near Madron), the **Merry Maidens** (Cornwall's most complete stone circle, near Trewoofe) and **Chysauster Iron Age Village** ( ☎ 07831 757934; adult/child £2.50/1.30; ☉ 10am-6pm Jul-Aug, 10am-5pm Apr-Jun & Sep, 10am-4pm Oct), the most complete prehistoric settlement in Cornwall. Bodmin Moor (p379) also has plenty of ancient monuments.

## SLEEPING
### Budget
**St Ives International Backpackers** ( ☎ 01736-799444; www.backpackers.co.uk/st-ives; The Stennack; dm £12-18; ☐ ) Not one of the smartest backpackers around, this shabby indie hostel is pretty battered with cramped dorms and threadbare carpets, but it is handy for town.

**Chy Lelan** ( ☎ 01736-797560; www.chylelan.co.uk; Bunkers Hill; d £50-60) Set in the heart of St Ives' winding cobbled streets, these two 17th-century cottages have been converted into vaguely floral rooms. They're on the small side, but some provide glimpses of the sea.

**Cornerways** ( ☎ 01736-796706; www.cornerwaysstives .com; 1 Bethesda Pl; d £50-80) The bedroom size at this former fisherman's cottage suggests past seafarers weren't big blokes. But the pastel decor is fresh, you get free tickets to the Tate and you're just steps away from the harbour and the beach.

### Midrange
**Pebble Private Hotel** ( ☎ 01736-794168; www.pebble -hotel.co.uk; 4 Park Ave; s £35-45, d £84-110) Swirly retro fabrics, gorgeous glossy satins and mock-flock wallpaper set this groovy B&B a world away from its chintz-and-pine cousins. It also makes it a favourite sleep for hip young things.

**Treliska** ( ☎ 01736-797678; www.treliska.com; 3 Bedford Rd; s £40-60, d £64-80) Another beautifully finished B&B that's far beyond lace doilies and photo placemats – here it's all clean lines, chrome bath taps and elegantly understated wooden furniture.

**Organic Panda** ( ☎ 01736-793890; www.organicpanda .co.uk; 1 Pednolver Tce; d £80-120; ☐ ☐ wi-fi) Sleep with

SOUTHWEST ENGLAND

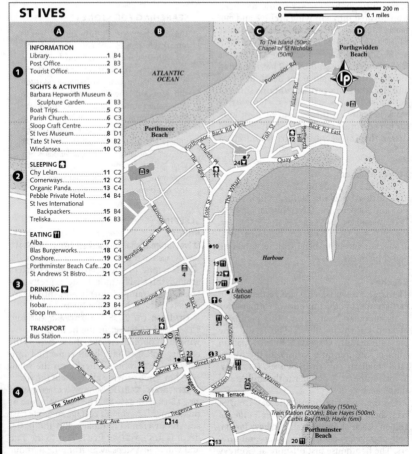

**ST IVES**

a clear conscience (and in style) at this super-sleek B&B, which is run along all-organic lines. Spotty cushions, technicolour artwork and timber-salvage beds keep the funk factor high; the sea views steal the show outside.

**our pick Primrose Valley** ( ☎ 01736-794939; www .primroseonline.co.uk; Porthminster Beach; d £105-155, ste £175-225; **P** ) One of St Ives' secret gems, this swish guesthouse-cum-boutique hotel has ecofriendly credentials and a real eye for interior design. All the rooms have characteristic quirks – some boast blonde wood, leather armchairs and exposed brick, while others delight with sea blues, Philippe Starck lights and mosaic-lined bathrooms. Throw in a locally sourced breakfast, Manhattan-style lounge-bar and fab location near Porthminster Beach,

and you have one of the best little boltholes in Cornwall.

**Top End**
**Blue Hayes** ( ☎ 01736-797129; www.blue-hayes.co.uk; Trelyon Ave; r £160-190; **P** ) Another boutique beauty, Blue Hayes boasts five luxurious cream-coloured suites (including one with its own private roof patio), body-jet showers and a balustraded breakfast terrace overlooking the bay.

**EATING**
St Ives' harbourside is awash with brasseries, but the back lanes house top options too.

**Blas Burgerworks** ( ☎ 01736-797272; The Warren; burgers £5-9; ☻ dinner Tue-Sun) The humble burger becomes a work of art at this fab diner where creations range from beetburgers in sunflower baps to black-bean burgers laced with lashings of chilli sauce.

**Onshore** ( ☎ 01736-796000; The Wharf; pizzas £8-16; ☯ lunch & dinner) Sometimes you just want a pizza – and this bright and breezy outlet delivers gourmet versions baked to perfection in a wood-fired oven.

**St Andrews St Bistro** ( ☎ 01736-797074; 16 Andrews St; mains £9-15; ☯ dinner) A hectic heap of North African rugs and oddball furniture covers this eatery where modern-British fare meets African and Middle Eastern cuisine. Artisan bread, lentil curries, grilled fish and spicy casseroles all feature on the menu.

**Porthminster Beach Cafe** ( ☎ 01736-795352; Porthminster Beach; lunch £9-17, dinner £17-22) More bistro than beach cafe, this buzzy eatery directly overlooks Porthminster Beach. Balconies and picture windows make the most of an azure view, while the monkfish curry and Cornish scallops make the most of the fruits of the sea.

**our pick Alba** ( ☎ 01736-797222; Old Lifeboat House; mains £15-20; ☯ lunch & dinner) The award-winning Alba is a byword for sophisticated seafood in a stylish, open-plan setting. Try the Provençale fish soup, whisky-cured salmon or lobster pasta – but do leave room for the chocolate and rum mousse. In-the-know locals bag tables five, six or seven for their gorgeous harbour views.

### DRINKING
**Hub** ( ☎ 01736-799099; The Wharf; ☯ 10am-late) This funky open-plan cafe-bar cranks up DJs and live music by night, and serves up lattes and hot chocolate by day.

**Isobar** ( ☎ 01736-796042; Tregenna Pl; ☯ to 2am) St Ives' main nightspot boasts a pared-back bar on the ground floor and a hot-and-sweaty club upstairs, with regular funk, house and techno nights, and the odd crowd-pleasing burst of cheese.

**Sloop Inn** ( ☎ 01736-796584; The Wharf) The Sloop Inn is a classic old fishermen's boozer, complete with low ceilings, tankards behind the bar and a comprehensive selection of Cornish ales.

### GETTING THERE & AWAY
National Express coaches go to London (£38.50, 8½ hours, two daily) and Plymouth (£7.20, three hours, four daily).

Buses 17/17A/17B travel to Penzance (30 minutes) regularly; the circular bus 300 stops at Land's End en route.

St Ives is on a scenic branch train line from St Erth (£2.50, 20 minutes, hourly), which is on the main London–Penzance line.

## ISLES OF SCILLY
Flung far into the sea off the end of England, the captivating Isles of Scilly have something of the Mediterranean about them. The archipelago is scattered 28 miles west of Land's End where, washed by the Gulf Stream, they enjoy a comparatively balmy climate. Only five of the 140 islands are inhabited; St Mary's is the largest and busiest, closely followed by Tresco, while only a few hardy souls live on Bryher, St Martin's and St Agnes. Traditionally farming, fishing and flower-growing were the key industries, but these days tourism is by far the biggest money spinner. Whether enjoying the laid-back lifestyle, island hopping, or some of the best beaches in England, many visitors find themselves Scilly addicts – drawn back again and again by the subtropical gardens, barefoot beachcombing and castaway vibe.

### Information
The **Isles of Scilly Tourist Board** ( ☎ 01720-422536; tic@scilly.gov.uk; Hugh Town, St Mary's; ☯ 8.30am-6pm Mon-Fri, 9am-5pm Sat & 9am-2pm Sun May-Sep, shorter hr in winter) is on St Mary's.

Useful websites include www.scillyonline.co.uk and the tourist office's site (www.simplyscilly.co.uk), which has full accommodation listings.

The islands get extremely busy in summer, while many businesses shut down completely in winter. All of the islands, except Tresco, have a simple camp site, but many visitors choose to stay in self-catering accommodation – check out **Island Properties** ( ☎ 01720-422082; www.scillyhols.com; St Mary's).

### St Mary's
The largest and busiest island in the Scillys is St Mary's, which contains many of the islands' big hotels, B&Bs, restaurants and shops. The Scillonian ferry and most flights from the mainland arrive on St Mary's, but the other main islands (known as the 'off-islands') are easily reached via the inter-island launches that leave regularly from the harbour.

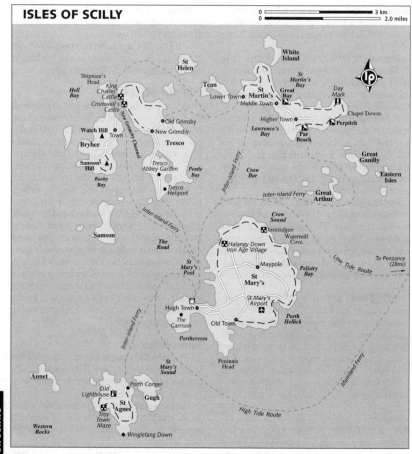

## ISLES OF SCILLY

0 — 3 km
0 — 2.0 miles

White Island
St Helen
Shipman's Head
Hell Bay
King Charles Castle
Cromwell's Castle
Tean
Lower Town
St Martin's Bay
St Martin's
Great Bay
Day Mark
Middle Town
Higher Town
Chapel Downs
Perpitch
Old Grimsby
Watch Hill
New Grimsby
Town
Bryher
Tresco
Lawrence's Bay
Par Beach
New Grimsby Channel
Samson Hill
Tresco Abbey Garden
Pentle Bay
Crow Bar
Great Ganilly
Eastern Isles
Rushy Bay
Tresco Heliport
Inter-island Ferry
Inter-island Ferry
Great Arthur
Crow Sound
Samson
The Road
Innisidgen
Watermill Cove
Inter-island Ferry
Halangy Down Iron Age Village
Maypole
Pelistry Bay
Low Tide Route
To Penzance (28mi)
St Mary's Pool
St Mary's
St Mary's Airport
Hugh Town
The Garrison
Old Town
Porth Hellick
Porthcressa
Mainland Ferry
Annet
St Mary's Sound
Peninnis Head
Old Lighthouse
Porth Conger
Gugh
St Agnes
Troy Town Maze
Wingletang Down
High Tide Route
Western Rocks

About a mile west of the airport is the main settlement of **Hugh Town**, where you'll find the bulk of the island's hotels and guesthouses. The islands have an absorbing, unique history, which is explored to the full in the **Isles of Scilly Museum** ( ☎ 01720-422337; Church St; adult/child £2/50p; ☷ 10am-4.30pm daily summer, 10am-noon Mon-Sat winter, or by arrangement) where exhibits include artefacts recovered from shipwrecks (including muskets, a cannon and a ship's bell), Romano-British finds and a fully rigged 1877 pilot gig.

A little way east of Hugh Town is **Old Town**, once the island's main harbour but now home to a few small cafes, a village pub and a curve of beach. Look out for the minuscule Old Town Church where evocative services are still conducted by candlelight – the graveyard contains a memorial to Augustus Smith, founder of the Abbey Garden, as well as the grave of former British prime minister Harold Wilson.

The small inlets scattered around the island's coastline are best reached on foot or by bike: Porth Hellick, Watermill Cove and the remote Pelistry Bay are worth seeking out. The pick of St Mary's prehistoric sites are the Iron Age village at Halangy Down, a mile north of Hugh Town, and the barrows at Bant's Carn and Innisidgen.

**Scilly Walks** ( ☎ 01720-423326; www.scillywalks .co.uk) leads excellent three-hour archaeological and historical tours, costing £5/2.50 per adult/child, as well as visits to the off-islands. **Will Wagstaff** ( ☎ 01720-422212) runs regular bird-watching tours.

For diving on St Mary's contact **Island Sea Safaris** ( ☎ 01720-422732); it also offers white-knuckle speedboat rides around the islands (£20 to £30) and snorkelling trips to the local seal colonies (£40).

The traditional sport of pilot gig racing is still hugely popular in the Scillys. These six-oared wooden boats were originally used to race out to secure valuable pilotage of sailing ships. The modern season runs between May and September – look out for the races on Wednesday and Friday evenings, when boats from the different islands battle it out amid heaving seas. Island Sea Safaris (above) will take you alongside (£10). Every May St Mary's hosts the World Pilot Gig Championships, which attracts teams from as far away as Holland and the USA.

### SLEEPING

**Camp site** ( ☎ 01720-422670; tedmoulson@aol.com; Tower Cottage, Garrison; sites per person £6-8) A nine-acre site tucked away on the garrison above Hugh Town. The facilities are fairly basic but still a cut above many other sites on Scilly.

**Crebinick Guest House** ( ☎ 01720-422968; www.cre binick.co.uk; Church St, Hugh Town; d £70-84) They've been putting up guests in this sturdy granite house since before WWII. The traditional rooms are a little small but are homely affairs and the owners are full of helpful holiday tips.

**Blue Carn Cottage** ( ☎ 01720-422214; Old Town; d £74) Removed from the relative bustle of Hugh Town, this whitewashed B&B near Old Town is a truly welcoming affair, run by a family of Scilly flower farmers. DVD players and cosy surroundings distinguish the rooms, while there's a game-stocked guest lounge and huge breakfasts with Fairtrade ingredients.

**Star Castle Hotel** ( ☎ 01720-422317; www.star-cas tle.co.uk; The Garrison; d £160-288, ste £220-328) Shaped like an eight-pointed star, this former fort on Garrison Point is one of the fanciest places to stay on Scilly, with higgledy-piggledy, heritage-themed rooms filled with plush sofas and vast beds.

**St Mary's Hall Hotel** ( ☎ 01720-422316; www.st maryshallhotel.co.uk; Church St, Hugh Town; d £180-250, ste £260-280) Say *ciao* to this Italianate mansion which is full of grand wooden staircases, bits of art and panelled walls. Rooms are either flowery and chintzy or candy-striped, while the superplush designer suites have LCD TVs and a galley kitchen.

## Tresco

Once owned by Tavistock Abbey, Tresco is the second-largest island, and the second most visited after St Mary's. The main attraction is the magical **Tresco Abbey Garden** ( ☎ 01720-424105; www.tresco.co.uk; adult/child £9/free; ✹ 9.30am-4pm), first laid out in 1834 on the site of a 10th-century Benedictine abbey. The terraced gardens feature more than 5000 subtropical plants, including species from Brazil, New Zealand and South Africa, and the intriguing Valhalla collection made up of figureheads and nameplates salvaged from the many ships that have foundered off Tresco's shores.

There are only two places to stay on the island, apart from self-catering cottages.

**New Inn** ( ☎ 01720-422844; www.tresco.co.uk; d £140-230) They've been whetting Scillonian whistles here for several centuries. Smart bedrooms are done out in subtle colours, with some boasting views over the channel to Bryher. The dining (mains £5 to £18) has made Michelin's *Eating Out in Pubs.*

**Island Hotel** ( ☎ 01720-422883; www.tresco.co.uk; d £260-550, ste £360-720; ✹ ) The bedrooms here will make you smile, even if the bill makes you wince. Chose to sleep amid gingham checks or in luxurious gold and navy blue suites, then plump for a private garden patio or seaview balcony. Thankfully, the price includes dinner.

## Bryher & Samson

Only around 70 people live on Bryher, making it Scilly's smallest and wildest inhabited island. Covered by rough bracken and heather, this chunk of rock takes the full force of Atlantic storms; Hell Bay in a winter gale is a powerful sight. Watch Hill provides cracking view over the islands, and Rushy Bay is one of the finest beaches in the Scillys. From the quay, occasional boats visit local seal and bird colonies and deserted Samson Island, where abandoned settlers' cottages tell a story of hard subsistence living.

The bare-bones **camp site** ( ☎ 01720-422886; www.bryhercampsite.co.uk; sites from £8.50) is near the quay.

**Hell Bay Hotel** ( ☎ 01720-422947; www.tresco.co.uk; d £260-600) is a real pamper pad. This oasis of luxury consists entirely of upmarket, impeccably finished suites, most of which boast sleek, contemporary decor, sitting rooms and private balconies. Prices include dinner.

**SOUTHWEST ENGLAND**

## St Martin's

The most northerly of the main islands, St Martin's is renowned for its beautiful beaches. The largest settlement is **Higher Town** where you'll find a small village shop and **Scilly Diving** ( ☎ 01720-422848; www.scillydiving.com; Higher Town), which offers two-hour snorkelling safaris (£22), subaqua trips for experienced divers (from £35) and lessons and taster sessions (from £33). A short way to the west is **Lower Town**, home to a cluster of tightly huddled cottages and the island's only hotel.

There are several small art galleries scattered across the island, as well as a tiny vineyard and a flower farm.

Worth hunting out are Lawrence's Bay on the south coast, which becomes a broad sweep of sand at low tide; Great Bay on the north, arguably Scilly's finest beach; White Island in the northwest, which you can cross to (with care) at low tide; the red-and-white candy-striped Day Mark in the east, a navigational aid built back in 1687; and the secluded cove of Perpitch in the southeast.

The **camp site** ( ☎ 01720-422888; chris@stmartinscampsite.freeserve.co.uk; Middle Town; sites £6.50-8.50) is towards the western end of Lawrence's Bay.

**Polreath** ( ☎ 01720-422046; Higher Town; d £80-100) is a traditional cottage and one of the few B&Bs on the island. Rooms are snug and cosy, and it's handy for the island bakery and post office.

**St Martin's on the Isle** ( ☎ 01720-422090; www.stmartinshotel.co.uk; d £300-560) is the only hotel on St Martin's, and arguably one of the best in the Scillys, with landscaped grounds, an indoor swimming pool and a private quay. The 30 lavish, elegant bedrooms have sea or garden views, and rates include a supremely classy dinner.

## St Agnes

England's most southerly community somehow transcends even the tranquillity of the other islands in the Isles of Scilly; with its cloistered coves, coastal walks and a scattering of prehistoric sites, it's an ideal spot to stroll, unwind and reflect. Visitors disembark at **Porth Conger**, near the decommissioned **Old Lighthouse** – one of the oldest lighthouses in the country. Other points of interest include the 200-year-old stone **Troy Town Maze**, and the inlets of Periglis Cove and St Warna's Cove (dedicated to the patron saint of shipwrecks). At low tide you can cross over to the island of **Gugh**, where you'll find intriguing standing stones and Bronze Age remains.

The **camp site** ( ☎ 01720-422360; www.troytownscilly.co.uk; Troy Town Farm; sites £6.50-10.50) is at the southwestern corner of the island.

The little stone-walled **Covean Cottage** ( ☎ 01720-422620; d £58-70) is the perfect location for getting away from the crowds; it offers four pleasant, good-value rooms and serves excellent cream teas, light meals and sticky treats during the day.

The most southwesterly pub in all of England, the **Turk's Head** ( ☎ 01720-422434; mains £6.50-10) is a real treat, with fine views, excellent beers, good pub grub and a hearty island atmosphere.

## Getting There & Away

There's no transport to or from the islands on Sundays.

### AIR

The **Isles of Scilly Skybus** ( ☎ 0845 710 5555; www.ios-travel.co.uk) flies between St Mary's and Land's End (adult/child £125/76, 15 minutes) and Newquay (£145/88, 30 minutes) several times daily year round. Cheaper saver fares are available for flights leaving Land's End after 2pm, or leaving St Mary's before noon. There's also at least one daily flight to Exeter (£232/138, 50 minutes) and Bristol (£278/162, 70 minutes). All prices are return fares.

**British International** ( ☎ 01736-363871; www.islesofscillyhelicopter.com) helicopters fly to St Mary's (20 minutes, 11 daily Monday to Friday, 17 on Saturday late June to late September, seven to 10 daily late September to late June) and Tresco (20 minutes, four to six daily Monday to Saturday April to October, four daily November to March) from Penzance heliport.

Standard return fares are £152/90 for an adult/child; a cheap day returns cost £102/65. Parking at the heliport costs £6 per day.

### BOAT

The ferry *Scillonian* ( ☎ 0845 710 5555; www.ios-travel.co.uk) sails between Penzance and St Mary's (adult/child £92/46 return, two hours 40 minutes, daily Monday to Saturday). The crossing can be notoriously rough – landlubbers might be better off taking the chopper.

## Getting Around

Inter-island launches sail regularly from St Mary's harbour in summer to the other main islands. The boats usually leave in the morning and return late afternoon, although there are several boats daily to Tresco. A return trip to most off-islands costs £7 – ask around at the harbour to see what's on offer.

If you're travelling between the islands, make sure you label luggage clearly with your name and the island you're going to.

The airport bus service (single £3) leaves from the Strand in Hugh Town around 40 minutes before each flight. A circular bus shuttles around St Mary's several times daily in summer (£1 to all destinations).

There's a twice-daily trip (£6 ) around St Mary's on **Island Rover** ( ☎ 01720-422131; www.islandrover.co.uk), a vintage open-top bus. It leaves at 10.15am and 1.30pm from the park. Ferry passengers can buy bus tickets on board the boat.

Bikes are available from **Buccaboo Hire** ( ☎ 01720-422289; Porthcressa, Hugh Town) from around £8 per day.

For taxis, try **Island Taxis** ( ☎ 01720-422126) or **Scilly Cabs** ( ☎ 01720-422901).

# East Anglia

Perched on the back end of Britain, East Anglia is characterised by its flat, sprawling land-scape where vast fenlands sweep gently out to the sea. This is a country of big skies, mysterious marshes and stunning sunsets, but the counties of Cambridgeshire, Suffolk, Norfolk and Essex feature far more than lush farmland and sparking waters. Hidden between the meandering rivers and gentle hills are magnificent cities, achingly pretty villages and mile upon mile of sweeping, sandy beach.

During the Middle Ages East Anglia flourished thanks to the thriving wool trade, and rich merchants built ostentatious mansions, impressive trading halls and comfortable cottages. The rich, royal, noble and good flocked here and soon majestic cathedrals and abbeys adorned the region's towns and cities. The elaborate half-timbered houses and the superb cathedrals in Ely, Peterborough, Norwich and Bury stand testament to the enormous wealth amassed during this time. While business boomed in rural areas, the country's academic elite were gathering at Cambridge, building colleges and chapels and establishing a reputation for one of the finest institutions in the country. The city remains East Anglia's most visited attraction and its otherworldly atmosphere, gowned cyclists, ancient pubs and earnest attitude are set against a backdrop of some of England's most stunning classical architecture.

Surrounding all the medieval finery is a coastline that rivals any in the country and of-fers everything from traditional bucket-and-spade resorts to wildlife reserves, broad, sandy beaches, pretty seaside villages, and access to one of the region's most tranquil charms, the inland waterways of the Norfolk Broads.

## HIGHLIGHTS

- Dreaming of your student days as you **punt** (p407) past Cambridge's historic colleges
- Wandering aimlessly along the pristine sands of **Holkham Beach** (p432)
- Soaking up the medieval atmosphere in topsy-turvy **Lavenham** (p418)
- Walking the prom, dining on sublime food and just chilling out in understated **Aldeburgh** (p422)
- Relaxing on a slow boat through the tranquil waterways of the **Norfolk Broads** (p430)

★ Holkham Beach

Norfolk Broads ★

Cambridge ★

Aldeburgh ★

★ Lavenham

**EAST ANGLIA**

| ■ POPULATION: 3.3 MILLION | ■ AREA: 6055 SQ MILES | ■ LENGTH OF SOUTHEND PIER (WORLD'S LONGEST PLEASURE PIER: 1.33 MILES |

## History

East Anglia was a major Saxon kingdom and the treasures unearthed in the *Sutton Hoo* burial ship (see p417) proved that they enjoyed something of the good life here.

The region's heyday, however, was in the Middle Ages, during the wool and weaving boom when Flemish weavers settled in the area and the grand churches and world-famous university began to be established.

By the 17th century much of the region's marshland and bog had been drained and converted into arable land and the good times rolled. The emergence of a work-happy urban bourgeoisie coupled with a strong sense of religious duty resulted in the parliamentarianism and Puritanism that would climax in the Civil War. Oliver Cromwell, the uncrowned king of the parliamentarians, was a small-time merchant residing in Ely when he answered God's call to take up arms against the fattened and corrupt monarchy of Charles I.

East Anglia's fortunes waned in the 18th century, however, when the Industrial Revolution got under way up north. The cottage industries of East Anglia dwindled and today crops have replaced sheep as the rural mainstay. During WWII East Anglia became central to the fight against Nazi Germany. With plenty of flat open land and its proximity to mainland Europe, it was an ideal base for the RAF and the United States Air Force. The remains of these bases can still be seen today.

## Information

You can get tourist information for the region from the **East of England Tourist Board** (☎ 01284-727470; www.visiteastofengland.com).

## Activities

East Anglia is a great destination for walking and cycling enthusiasts with miles of coastline to discover, vast expanses of flat land for leisurely touring and plenty of inland waterways for quiet boating. We concentrate on the highlights here, but you'll find more information throughout the chapter. Regional tourist websites are packed with walking, cycling and sailing information, and tourist offices are stacked high with leaflets, maps and guides covering outdoor activities.

### CYCLING

East Anglia is famously flat and riddled with quiet roads; even the unfit can find vast swaths

for a gentle potter on two wheels. All four counties boast networks of quiet country lanes, where the biggest natural hazard is the wind sweeping in unimpeded from the coast. When it's behind you though, you can freewheel for miles. There's gorgeous riding to be had along the Suffolk and Norfolk coastlines and in the Fens. Finding quiet roads in Essex is a little more of a challenge but not impossible. Mountain bikers should head for Thetford Forest, near Thetford, while much of the popular on- and off-road Peddars Way (below) walking route is also open to cyclists.

### WALKING

East Anglia is not everybody's idea of classic walking country; you won't find any challenging peaks here, but gentle rambles through farmland, beside rivers and lakes and along the wildlife-rich coastline are in ample supply.

The **Peddars Way and Norfolk Coast Path** (www .nationaltrail.co.uk/peddarsway) is a six-day, 88-mile national trail from Knettishall Heath near Thetford to Cromer on the coast. The first half trails along an ancient Roman road, then finishes by meandering along the beaches, sea walls, salt marshes and fishing villages of the coast. Day trippers and weekend walkers tend to dip into its coastal stretches, which also cover some of the best birdwatching country in England.

Curving round further south, the 50-mile **Suffolk Coast Path** (www.suffolkcoastand heaths.org) wanders between Felixstowe and Lowestoft, via Snape Maltings, Aldeburgh, Dunwich and Southwold, but is also good for shorter rambles.

### OTHER ACTIVITIES

With wind and water so abundant here, it's a popular destination for **sailing**, both along the coast and in the Norfolk Broads, where you can easily hire boats and arrange lessons. It's also possible to just put-put your way around the Broads in **motorboats**. Alternatively, the wide and frequently empty beaches of the Norfolk coast make great spots for **land yachting** and **kitesurfing**.

## Getting There & Around

Getting about East Anglia on public transport, both rail and coach, is straightforward. Consult **Traveline** (☎ 0871 200 2233; www.travelineeastanglia.org.uk) for all public transport information.

**EAST ANGLIA**

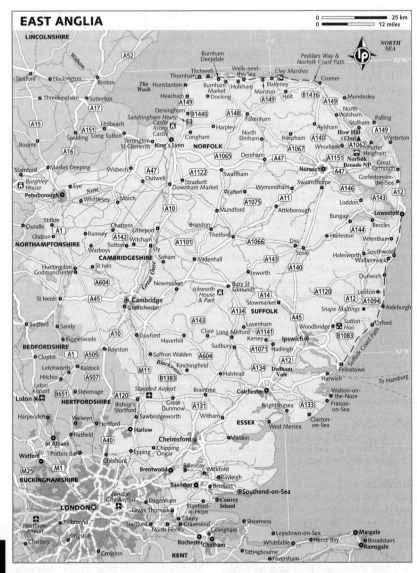

# EAST ANGLIA

## BUS

**First Group** (www.firstgroup.com) offer a FirstDay pass for a day's unlimited bus travel on its regional services. It costs £10/6.50 per adult/child. There's also a FirstWeek pass costing £25 and £17 respectively

**Stagecoach** (www.stagecoachbus.com) Explorer and Megarider tickets allow one-/seven-/28-day travel across Southern England (excluding London) for £8/20/75.

## TRAIN

**National Express East Anglia** ( ☎ 0845 600 7245; www .nationalexpresseastanglia.com) offers some handy regional rail passes to explore Norfolk, Suffolk and parts of Cambridgeshire. The Anglia Plus

Pass is a great option for families and gives unlimited regional travel after 8.45am on weekdays and any time at weekends. It costs £13 for one day (plus £2 each for up to four accompanied children) or £26 for any three separate days over a period of seven days (plus £2 each for up to four children).

You can also get discounts of up to 33% on most rail fares over £10 in the southeast by purchasing a **Network Railcard** ( ☎ 08457 225 225; www .railcard.co.uk/network; per yr £20). Children under 15 can save 60%, but a minimum £1 fare applies.

# CAMBRIDGESHIRE

The beautiful university town of Cambridge is famous for its august old buildings, gowned cyclists, wobbly punters and glorious chapels, but beyond the breathtaking city and its brilliant minds, lies a county of vast open landscapes, epic sunsets and unsullied horizons. The flat reclaimed fen, lush farmland and myriad waterways make perfect walking and cycling territory while the extraordinary cathedrals at Peterborough and Ely, and the rip-roaring Imperial War Museum at Duxford, would be headline attractions anywhere else.

## Getting Around

The region's public transport radiates from Cambridge, which is a mere 55-minute train ride from London. This line continues north through Ely to King's Lynn in Norfolk. From Ely, branch lines run east through Norwich, southeast into Suffolk and northwest to Peterborough. The useful *Cambridgeshire and Peterborough Passenger Transport Map* is available in tourist offices.

## CAMBRIDGE

pop 108,863

Renowned worldwide for its academic prowess, Cambridge is a grand old dame of a city, dripping with ancient architecture, soaked in history and tradition and in many ways oblivious to the passing of time. Many of its cobbled laneways, leafy paths and glorious colleges remain firmly stuck in the past leaving you to experience the city in much the same way as Newton, Darwin and Wordsworth would once have done.

Everywhere you go the sheer weight of academic achievement seems to seep from the very walls. Whether strolling along the picturesque college 'Backs', sitting in a time-less pub or just rambling the streets you'll get glimpses of college life, the bookish, gowned students, perfectly manicured but unused lawns, bowler-hatted porters and snippets of overheard debate creating a very strong sense of 'us' and 'them'. Beyond the academic core, Cambridge is a small but fashionable city with breathtaking views, designer boutiques and plenty of upmarket hotels and restaurants to help you part with your cash.

## History

First a Roman fort and then a Saxon settlement, Cambridge was little more than a rural backwater until 1209, when the university town of Oxford exploded in a riot between town and gown. Fed up with the constant brawling between locals and students, a group of scholars upped and left to found a new university in Cambridge.

Initially students lived in halls and religious houses, but gradually a collegiate system, where tutors and students lived together in a formal community, developed. The first Cambridge college, Peterhouse, was founded in 1284. The collegiate system is still intact today and unique to Oxford and Cambridge.

By the 14th century the royalty, nobility, church, trade guilds and anyone rich enough to court the prestige that their own institution offered, began to found their own colleges. It was 500 years before female students were allowed into the hallowed grounds though.

The honour roll of famous Cambridge graduates reads like an international who's who of high achievers: 81 Nobel Prize winners (more than any other institution in the world), 13 British prime ministers, nine archbishops of Canterbury, an immense number of scientists, and a healthy host of poets and authors. Crick and Watson discovered DNA here, Isaac Newton used Cambridge to work on his theory of gravity, Stephen Hawking is a professor of mathematics here, and Charles Darwin, William Wordsworth, Vladimir Nabokov, David Attenborough and John Cleese all studied here.

The university celebrates its 800th birthday in 2009; look out for special events, lectures and concerts to mark its intriguing eight centuries.

## Orientation

The colleges and university buildings comprise the centre of the city. The central area,

EAST ANGLIA

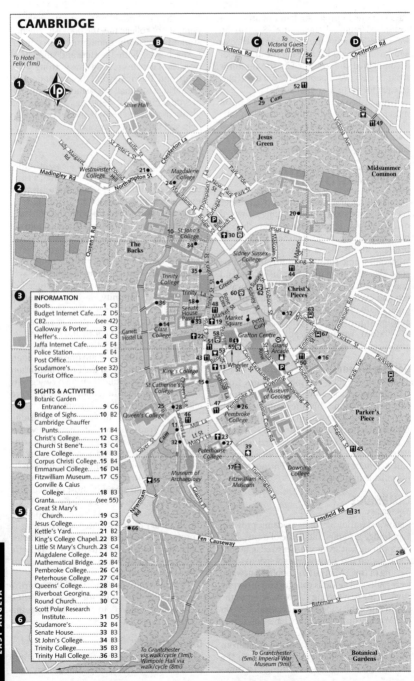

# CAMBRIDGE

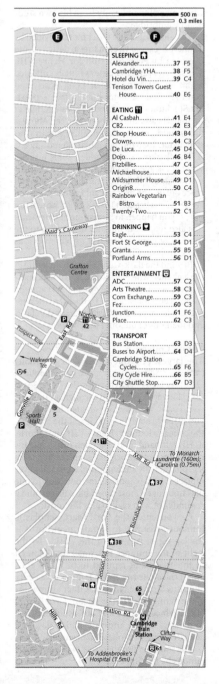

0            500 m
0            0.3 miles

**SLEEPING**
| | | |
|---|---|---|
| Alexander | 37 | F5 |
| Cambridge YHA | 38 | F5 |
| Hotel du Vin | 39 | C4 |
| Tenison Towers Guest House | 40 | E6 |

**EATING**
| | | |
|---|---|---|
| Al Casbah | 41 | E4 |
| CB2 | 42 | E3 |
| Chop House | 43 | B4 |
| Clowns | 44 | C3 |
| De Luca | 45 | D4 |
| Dojo | 46 | B4 |
| Fitzbillies | 47 | C4 |
| Michaelhouse | 48 | C3 |
| Midsummer House | 49 | D1 |
| Origin8 | 50 | C4 |
| Rainbow Vegetarian Bistro | 51 | B3 |
| Twenty-Two | 52 | C1 |

**DRINKING**
| | | |
|---|---|---|
| Eagle | 53 | C4 |
| Fort St George | 54 | D1 |
| Granta | 55 | B5 |
| Portland Arms | 56 | D1 |

**ENTERTAINMENT**
| | | |
|---|---|---|
| ADC | 57 | C2 |
| Arts Theatre | 58 | C3 |
| Corn Exchange | 59 | C3 |
| Fez | 60 | C3 |
| Junction | 61 | F6 |
| Place | 62 | C3 |

**TRANSPORT**
| | | |
|---|---|---|
| Bus Station | 63 | D3 |
| Buses to Airport | 64 | D4 |
| Cambridge Station Cycles | 65 | F6 |
| City Cycle Hire | 66 | B5 |
| City Shuttle Stop | 67 | D3 |

lying in a wide bend of the River Cam, is easy to get around on foot or by bike. The best-known section of the Cam is the Backs, which combines lush river scenery with superb views of six colleges, and King's College Chapel. The other 25 colleges are scattered throughout the city. The bus station is on Drummer St, but the train station is a 20-minute walk to the south. For cheap and cheerful restaurants, internet cafes, launderettes and late-night shops try Mill Rd.

## Information
### BOOKSHOPS
**Galloway & Porter** ( ☎ 01223-367876; 30 Sidney St) Remaindered and damaged stock.
**Heffers** ( ☎ 01223-568568; 20 Trinity St) Vast temple of academic tomes and lighter reads.

### EMERGENCY
**Police station** ( ☎ 01223-358966; Parkside)

### INTERNET ACCESS
The going rate for internet access is about £1 per hour.
**Budget Internet Cafe** ( ☎ 01223-313875; 30 Hills Rd; ⏰ 9am-11pm)
**CB2** ( ☎ 01223-508503; 5-7 Norfolk St; ⏰ noon-midnight)
**Jaffa Internet Cafe** ( ☎ 01223-308380; 22 Mill Rd; ⏰ 10am-10pm)

### INTERNET RESOURCES
**Visit Cambridge** (www.visitcambridge.org) The official tourism site for the city.
**What's On** (www.cam.ac.uk/whatson) Listing of all public events at the University.

### LAUNDRY
**Monarch Laundrette** ( ☎ 01223-247599; 161 Mill Rd; per wash £3.50; ⏰ 8.30am-8pm) Near the train station.

### LEFT LUGGAGE
**Scudamore's** ( ☎ 01223-359750; www.scudamores .com; Granta Pl; per piece £5)

### MEDICAL SERVICES
**Addenbrooke's Hospital** ( ☎ 01223-245151; Hills Rd) Southeast of the centre.
**Boots** ( ☎ 01223-350213; 28 Petty Cury)

### MONEY
You'll find all the major banks and a host of ATMs around St Andrew's St and Sidney St.

**EAST ANGLIA**

**POST**
**Post office** ( ☎ 01223-323325; 9-11 St Andrew's St)

**TOURIST INFORMATION**
**Tourist office** ( ☎ 0871 266 8006; www.visitcambridge.org; Wheeler St; ☼ 10am-5.30pm Mon-Fri, 10am-5pm Sat year-round, plus 11am-3pm Sun Apr-Sep) This large, busy office helps with maps, accommodation, tours and tickets. You can pick up a guide to the Cambridge colleges (£3.99) here or a leaflet (£1.20) outlining a city walk.

## Sights

### CAMBRIDGE UNIVERSITY
Cambridge University comprises 31 colleges; five of these – King's, Queen's, Clare, Trinity and St John's – charge tourists admission. Some other colleges deem visitors too disruptive and simply deny them entry. Most colleges close to visitors for the Easter term and all are closed for exams from mid-May to mid-June. Opening hours vary year to year, so contact the colleges or the tourist office for up-to-date information.

### King's College Chapel
In a city crammed with show-stopping architecture, this is the show-stealer. Chances are you will already have seen it on a thousand postcards, tea towels and choral CDs before you catch your first glimpse of the grandiose **King's College Chapel** ( ☎ 01223-331212; www.kings.cam.ac.uk/chapel; King's Pde; adult/concession £5/3.50; ☼ during term 9.30am-3.30pm Mon-Fri, 9.30am-3.15pm Sat, 1.15pm-2.30pm Sun, outside academic terms 9.30am-4.30pm Mon-Sat, 10am-5pm Sun), but still it awes. It's one of the most extraordinary examples of Gothic architecture in England, and was begun in 1446 as an act of piety by Henry VI and finished by Henry VIII around 1516.

While you can enjoy stunning front and back views of the chapel from King's Pde and the river, the real drama is within. Mouths drop open upon first glimpse of the inspirational **fan-vaulted ceiling**, its intricate tracery soaring upwards before exploding into a series of stone fireworks. This vast 80m-long canopy is the work of John Wastell and is the largest expanse of fan vaulting in the world.

The chapel's length is also remarkably light, its sides flanked by lofty **stained-glass windows** that retain their original glass, rare survivors of the excesses of the Civil War in this region. It's said that these windows were ordered to be spared by Cromwell himself, who knew of their beauty from his own studies in Cambridge.

The antechapel and the choir are divided by a superbly carved **wooden screen**, designed and executed by Peter Stockton for Henry VIII. The screen bears his master's initials entwined with those of Anne Boleyn. Look closely and you may find an angry human face – possibly Stockton's – amid the elaborate jungle of mythical beasts and symbolic flowers. Above is the magnificent bat-wing organ, originally constructed in 1686 though much altered since.

The thickly carved wooden stalls just beyond the screen are a stage for the chapel's world-famous **choir**. You can hear them in full voice during the magnificent **Evensong** (admission free; ☼ 5.30pm Mon-Sat, 10.30am & 3.30pm Sun term time only). If you happen to be visiting at Christmas it is also worth queuing for admission to the incredibly popular Festival of Nine Lessons and Carols on Christmas Eve.

Beyond the dark-wood choir, light suffuses the **high altar**, which is framed by Rubens' masterpiece *Adoration of the Magi* (1634) and the magnificent east window. To the left of the altar in the side chapels an **exhibition** charts the stages and methods of building the chapel.

### Trinity College
The largest of Cambridge's colleges, **Trinity** ( ☎ 01223-338400; www.trin.cam.ac.uk; Trinity St; adult/child £2.50/1 Mar-Oct; ☼ Library noon-2pm Mon-Fri, Hall 3-5pm, Chapel 10am-5pm), is entered through an impressive Tudor gateway first created in 1546. As you walk through have a look at the statue of the college's founder, Henry VIII, that adorns it. His left hand holds a golden orb, while his right grips not the original sceptre but a table leg, put there by student pranksters and never replaced. It's a wonderful introduction to one of Cambridge's most venerable colleges, and a reminder of who really rules the roost.

As you enter the **Great Court**, scholastic humour gives way to wonderment, for it is the largest of its kind in the world. To the right of the entrance is a small tree, planted in the 1950s and reputed to be a descendant of the apple tree made famous by Trinity alumnus Sir Isaac Newton. Other alumni include Tennyson, Francis Bacon, Lord Byron, HRH Prince Charles and at least nine prime ministers, British and international, and a jaw-dropping 31 Nobel Prize winners.

The square is also the scene of the run made famous by the film *Chariots of Fire* – 350m in

43 seconds (the time it takes the clock to strike 12). Although many students attempt it, Harold Abrahams (the hero of the film) never actually did, and the run wasn't even filmed here. If you fancy your chances remember that you'll need Olympian speed to even come close.

The college's vast hall has a dramatic hammer-beam roof and lantern, and beyond this are the dignified cloisters of Nevile's Court and the renowned **Wren Library** ( noon-2pm Mon-Fri, plus 10.30am-12.30pm Sat during term). It contains 55,000 books dated before 1820 and more than 2500 manuscripts, including AA Milne's original *Winnie the Pooh*. Both Milne and his son, Christopher Robin, were graduates.

Henry VIII would have been proud to note, too, that his college would eventually come to throw the best party in town, the lavish May Ball in June.

### Gonville & Caius College

Known locally as Caius (pronounced keys), **Gonville and Caius** ( 01223-332400; www.cai.cam.ac.uk; Trinity St) was founded twice, first by a priest called Gonville, in 1348, and then again in 1557 by Dr Caius (Keys – it was common for academics to use the Latin form of their names), a brilliant physician who supposedly spoilt his legacy by insisting the college admit no 'deaf, dumb, deformed, lame, chronic invalids, or Welshmen'! Fortunately for the college his policy didn't last long, and the wheelchair-using megastar of astrophysics, Stephen Hawking, is now a fellow here.

The college is of particular interest thanks to its three fascinating gates: Virtue, Humility and Honour. They symbolise the progress of the good student, since the third gate (the *Porta Honoris*, a fabulous domed and sundial-sided confection) leads to the Senate House and thus graduation.

### Trinity Hall College

Henry James once wrote of the delightfully diminutive **Trinity Hall** ( 01223-332500; www.trinhall.cam.ac.uk; Trinity Lane), 'If I were called upon to mention the prettiest corner of the world, I should draw a thoughtful sigh and point the way to the gardens of Trinity Hall.' Wedged cosily among the great and the famous, but unconnected to better-known Trinity, it was founded in 1350 as a refuge for lawyers and clerics escaping the ravages of the Black Death, thus earning it the nickname of the 'Lawyers' College'. The college's 16th-century library has original Jacobean reading desks and chained books (an early antitheft device) on the shelves. Writer JB Priestley, astrophysicist Stephen Hawking and actresss Rachel Weisz are among Trinity Hall's graduates.

### St John's College

After King's College, **St John's** ( 01223-338600; www.joh.cam.ac.uk; St John's St; adult/child £2.80/1.70;  10am-5pm Mon-Fri, 9.30am-5pm Sat & Sun Mar-Oct, Sat & Sun only Nov-Feb) is one of the city's most photogenic colleges, and is also the second-biggest after Trinity. Founded in 1511, it sprawls along both banks of the river, joined by the Bridge of Sighs, a masterpiece of stone tracery. Over the bridge is the 19th-century New Court, an extravagant neo-Gothic creation, and out to the left stunning views of the Backs.

### Christ's College

Over 500 years old and a grand old institution, **Christ's** ( 01223-334900; www.christs.cam.ac.uk; St Andrew's St;  9am-dusk) is worth visiting if only for its gleaming Great Gate emblazoned with heraldic carvings of spotted Beaufort yale (antelope-like creatures), Tudor roses and portcullis. Its founder, Lady Margaret Beaufort, hovers above like a guiding spirit. A stout oak door leads into First Court, which has an unusual circular lawn, magnolias and wisteria creepers. Pressing on through the Second Court there is a gate to the Fellows' Garden, which contains a mulberry tree under which 17th-century poet John Milton reputedly wrote *Lycidas*. In 2009 the college celebrates the 200th anniversary of the birth of naturalist Charles Darwin, who studied here, with a special exhibition in his college rooms.

### Corpus Christi College

Entry to this illustrious **college** ( 01223-338000; www.corpus.cam.ac.uk; Trumpington St) is via the so-called New Court that dates back a mere 200 years. To your right is the door to the Parker Library, which holds the finest collection of Anglo-Saxon manuscripts in the world. As you enter take a look at the statue on the right, that of the eponymous Matthew Parker, who was college master in 1544 and Archbishop of Canterbury to Elizabeth I. Mr Parker was known for his curiosity, and his endless questioning gave rise to the term 'nosy parker'. Meanwhile monastic atmosphere still oozes from the inner Old Court, which retains its medieval form. Look out for the fascinating

EAST ANGLIA

sundial and plaque to playwright and past student Christopher Marlowe (1564–93), author of *Dr Faustus* and *Tamburlaine*.

## Other Colleges

Tranquil 15th-century **Jesus College** ( ☎ 01223-339339; www.jesus.cam.ac.uk; Jesus Lane), was once a nunnery before its founder, Bishop Alcock, expelled the nuns for misbehaving. Highlights include a Norman arched gallery, a 13th-century chancel and art-nouveau features by Pugin, William Morris (ceilings), Burne-Jones (stained glass) and Madox Brown.

Originally a Benedictine hostel, riverside **Magdalene College** ( ☎ 01223-332100; www.magd .cam.ac.uk; Magdalene St) has the dubious honour of being the last college to allow women students; when they were finally admitted in 1988, male students wore black armbands and flew the college flag at half-mast. Its greatest asset is the Pepys Library, housing the magnificent collection of books the famous mid-17th-century diarist bequeathed to his old college.

The oldest and smallest college, **Peterhouse** ( ☎ 01223-338200; www.pet.cam.ac.uk; Trumpington St), is a charming place founded in 1284. Much of the college was rebuilt or added over the years, including the exceptional little chapel built in 1632, but the main hall is bona fide 13th century and beautifully restored. Just to the north is **Little St Mary's Church**, inside which is a memorial to Peterhouse student Godfrey Washington, great-uncle of George. His family coat of arms was the stars and stripes, the inspiration for the US flag.

The gorgeous 15th-century **Queen's College** ( ☎ 01223-335511; www.queens.cam.ac.uk; Silver St; adult £2) sits elegantly astride the river and has two enchanting medieval courtyards: Old Court and Cloister Court. Here too is the beautiful half-timbered President's Lodge and the tower in which famous Dutch scholar and reformer Desiderius Erasmus lodged from 1510 to 1514. He had plenty to say about Cambridge: the wine tasted like vinegar, the beer was slop and the place was too expensive, but he did note that the local women were good kissers.

The 16th-century **Emmanuel College** ( ☎ 01223-334200; www.emma.cam.ac.uk; St Andrew's St) is famous for its exquisite chapel designed by Sir Christopher Wren. Here too is a plaque commemorating John Harvard (BA 1632) a scholar here who later settled in New England and left his money to found his namesake university in the Massachusetts town of Cambridge.

## THE BACKS

Behind the grandiose facades, stately courts and manicured lawns of the city's central colleges lies a series of gardens and parklands butting up against the river. Collectively known as the Backs, these tranquil green spaces and shimmering waters offer unparalleled views of college life. The graceful bridges and weeping willows can be seen from the pathways that cross the Backs, from the comfort of a chauffeur-driven punt or from the lovely pedestrian bridges that meander across the river.

The oldest crossing is at **Clare College**, built in 1639 and ornamented with decorative balls. Its architect was paid a grand total of 15p for his design and, feeling aggrieved at such a measly fee, it's said he cut a chunk out of one of the balls adorning the balustrade so the bridge would never be complete. The fanciful **Bridge of Sighs** (built in 1831) at St John's is best observed from the stylish bridge designed by Wren just to the south. Most curious of all though is the flimsy looking wooden construction joining the two halves of Queen's College. Known as the **Mathematical Bridge**, it was first built in 1749 and – despite what unscrupulous guides may tell you – it isn't the handiwork of Sir Isaac Newton (he died in 1727), originally built without nails, or taken apart by students who then couldn't figure out how to put it back together.

## GREAT ST MARY'S CHURCH

Cambridge's staunch university **church** ( ☎ 01223-741716; www.gsm.cam.ac.uk; Senate House Hill; tower admission adult/child £2.50/1.25; ◷ 9am-5pm Mon-Sat, 12.30-5pm Sun, to 4pm Sep-Apr) was built between 1478 and 1519 in the late-Gothic Perpendicular style. If you're fit and fond of a view, climb the 123 steps of the tower for superb vistas of the dreamy spires, albeit marred by wire fencing.

The beautiful classical building directly across King's Pde is the **Senate House**, designed in 1730 by James Gibbs; graduations are held here in summer, when gowned and mortarboarded students parade the streets to pick up those all-important scraps of paper.

## ROUND CHURCH

The beautiful **Round Church** ( ☎ 01223-311602; www.christianheritageuk.org.uk; Bridge St; adult/child £2/ free; ◷ 10am-5pm Tue-Sat, 1-5pm Sun) is another of Cambridge's gems and one of only four such structures in England. It was built by the mysterious Knights Templar in 1130 and shelters an unusual circular nave ringed by chunky Norman pillars. It now houses an exhibition on Cambridge's Christian heritage.

### CHURCH OF ST BENE'T

The oldest structure in the county, the **Saxon tower** of this Franciscan **church** (www.stbenets.org .uk; Bene't St) was built around 1025. The round holes above the belfry windows were designed to offer owls nesting privileges; they were valued as mouse killers.

### FITZWILLIAM MUSEUM

Fondly dubbed 'the Fitz' by locals, this colossal neoclassical pile was one of the first public **art museums** ( ☎ 01223-332900; www.fitzmuseum.cam .ac.uk; Trumpington St; admission free; ✆ 10am-5pm Tue-Sat, noon-5pm Sun) in Britain, built to house the fabulous treasures that the seventh Viscount Fitzwilliam had bequeathed to his old university. An unabashedly over-the-top building, it sets out to mirror its contents in an ostentatious jumble of styles that mixes mosaic with marble, Greek with Egyptian and more. It was begun by George Basevi in 1837, but he did not live to see its completion: while working on Ely Cathedral he stepped back to admire his handiwork, slipped and fell to his death.

The lower galleries are filled with priceless treasures from ancient Egyptian sarcophagi to Greek and Roman art, Chinese ceramics to English glass, and some dazzling illuminated manuscripts. The upper galleries showcase works by Leonardo da Vinci, Titian, Rubens, the Impressionists, Gainsborough and Constable, right through to Rembrandt and Picasso.

### SCOTT POLAR RESEARCH INSTITUTE

For anyone interested in polar exploration or history the **Scott Polar Research Institute** ( ☎ 01223-336540; www.spri.cam.ac.uk/museum; Lensfield Rd; admission free; ✆ 11am-1pm & 2-4pm Tue-Fri, noon-4pm Sat) has a fantastic collection of artefacts, journals, paintings, photographs, clothing, equipment and maps in its museum. You can learn about the great polar explorers and their harrowing expeditions and read the last messages left to wives, mothers and friends by Scott and his polar crew. You can also examine Inuit carvings and scrimshaw (etched bones), sledges and snow scooters and see the scientific and domestic equipment used by various expeditions.

### CAMBRIDGE UNIVERSITY BOTANIC GARDEN

Founded by Charles Darwin's mentor, Prof John Henslow, the beautiful **Botanic Garden** ( ☎ 01223-336265; www.botanic.cam.ac.uk; entrance on Bateman St; adult/under 16yr £4/free; ✆ 10am-6pm Apr-Sep, to 5pm Feb, Mar & Oct, to 4pm Nov-Jan) is home to 8000 plant species, a wonderful arboretum, tropical houses, a winter garden and flamboyant herbaceous borders.

### KETTLE'S YARD

Neither gallery nor museum, this **house** ( ☎ 01223-352124; www.kettlesyard.co.uk; cnr Northampton & Castle Sts; admission free; ✆ house 2-4pm Tue-Sun, gallery 11.30am-5pm Tue-Sun) nonetheless oozes artistic excellence, with a collection of 20th-century art, furniture, ceramics and glass that would be the envy of many an institution. It is the former home of HS 'Jim' Ede, a former assistant keeper at the Tate Gallery in London, who opened his home to young artists, resulting in a beautiful collection by the likes of Miro, Henry Moore and others. There are also exhibits of contemporary art in the modern **gallery** next door.

## Activities

### PUNTING

Gliding a self-propelled punt along the Backs is a blissful experience once you've got the knack, though it can also be a manic challenge to begin. If you wimp out you can always opt for a relaxing chauffeured punt.

**Cambridge Chauffer Punts** ( ☎ 01223-354164; www .punting-in-cambridge.co.uk; Silver St; per hr £16, chauffeured per punt £60 or per person £11)

**Granta** ( ☎ 01223-301845; www.puntingincambridge .com; Newnham Rd; per hr £14, chauffeured per person £10)

**Scudamore's** ( ☎ 01223-359750; www.scudamores .com; Silver St; per hr £18, chauffeured per person £12-14)

## Tours

**City Sightseeing** ( ☎ 01223-423578; www.city -sightseeing.com; adult/child £10/5; ✆ 10am-4pm) Hop-on hop-off tour buses running every 20 to 30 minutes with 21 stops around town.

**Green Wheels Pedicabs** ( ☎ 01223-858485) Trishaw tours around the city on 20-minute (£6 per person) or 45-minute (£10 per person) loops. Minimum two people.

**Riverboat Georgina** ( ☎ 01223-307694; www.georgina .co.uk; per person £16-24) Two-hour cruises from the river at Jesus Lock including a cream tea or boatman's lunch.

**Walking tours** ( ☎ 01223-457574; tours@cambridge .gov.uk; tickets incl entry to King's/St John's Colleges adult/ under 12yr £10/5; ✆ tours 11.30pm & 1.30pm, with extra

---

**HOW TO PUNT**

Punting looks pretty straightforward but, believe us, it's not. As soon as we dried off and hung our clothes on the line, we thought it was a good idea to offer a couple of tips on how to move the boat and stay dry.

■ Standing at the end of the punt, lift the pole out of the water at the side of the punt.

■ Let the pole slide through your hands to touch the bottom of the river.

■ Tilt the pole forward (that is, in the direction of travel of the punt) and push down to propel the punt forward.

■ Twist the pole to free the end from the mud at the bottom of the river, and let it float up and trail behind the punt. You can then use it as a rudder to steer with.

■ If you haven't fallen in yet, raise the pole out of the water and into the vertical position to begin the cycle again.

---

tours at 10.30am & 2.30pm Jul-Aug) The tourist office also arranges colourful 'Ghost Tours' (adult/child under 12yr £5/3; 6pm Friday) and 'Punt and Ghost Tours' (adult/child under 12yr £15/7.50; 7pm Saturday). The tourist office has more details; book in advance.

## Sleeping

### BUDGET

**Cambridge YHA** ( ☎ 0870 770 5742; www.yha.org.uk; 97 Tenison Rd; dm incl breakfast £19.95; 🖳 ) Within walking distance of the city centre and cheap and cheerful; it's hard to knock this well-worn hostel close to the train station. The dorms are small and pretty basic and with lots of groups using the hostel it can be noisy, but it's got a great atmosphere and a surprisingly good breakfast.

**Cambridge Rooms** (www.cambridgerooms.co.uk; r £40-120) If you fancy experiencing a night inside the hallowed college grounds you can rent one of the student rooms and see how life is on the inside. Accommodation varies from functional singles (with shared bathroom) overlooking the college quad to more modern, en suite rooms in a nearby annexe. Although some twin and family rooms do exist, most rooms are singles but the website will give a clear indication of what you can expect before you make a booking. If you do decide to stay you can wander the grounds, see the chapel and have breakfast in the ancient college hall. There's limited availability during term time but a good choice of rooms during university holidays.

### MIDRANGE

Some of Cambridge's most central B&Bs use their convenient location as an excuse not to upgrade. Some of the better places are a bit of a hike from town but well worth the effort.

**Carolina** ( ☎ 01223-247015; www.carolinaguesthouse .co.uk; 138 Perne Rd; s/d from £30/55; 🅿 🖳 wi-fi) This lovely, bright B&B is a homely place with cosy rooms decked out in pale blue colour schemes, crisp linens and rustic wooden furniture. Almost all rooms are en suite and there's a spacious garden as well as free wi-fi. It's a 30-minute walk from the city centre but right on a regular bus route.

**Victoria Guest House** ( ☎ 01223-350086; www.cam bridge-accommodation.com; 55-57 Arbury Rd; s £35-60, d £50-75, all incl breakfast; 🅿 🖳 wi-fi) A fairly central option worth seeking out, the Victoria has a range of tasteful rooms with contemporary decor and a hint of period character. Rooms vary in size and not all have en suite facilities but the friendly owners and incredible breakfasts are a real bonus.

**Tenison Towers Guest House** ( ☎ 01223-363924; www.cambridgecitytenisontowers.com; 148 Tenison Rd; s/d £35/60) This exceptionally friendly and homely B&B is really handy if you're arriving by train, but well worth seeking out whatever way you arrive in town. The rooms are bright and simple with pale colours and fresh flowers and the aroma of freshly baked muffins greets you on arrival.

**Alexander** ( ☎ 01223-525725; www.beesley-schuster .co.uk; 56 St Barnabas Rd; d & tw incl breakfast £60-75) Set in a Victorian house in quiet residential area, the Alexander has two homely rooms with period fireplaces, big windows and lots of light. There's a two-night minimum stay but with a convenient location and friendly atmosphere it's worth booking in advance. Continental breakfast only.

## TOP END

**our pick** **Hotel du Vin** ( ☎ 01223-227330; www.hotel
duvin.com; Trumpington St; d from £140; ☐ wi-fi) This
boutique hotel chain really knows how to
do things right. Its Cambridge offering has
all the usual trademarks from quirky but incredibly stylish rooms with monsoon showers and luxurious Egyptian-cotton sheets to
the atmospheric vaulted cellar bar and the
French-style bistro (mains £12.75 to £22.75).
The central location, character-laden building
and top-notch service make it a great deal at
this price.

**Hotel Felix** ( ☎ 01223-277977; www.hotelfelix.co.uk;
Whitehouse Lane, Huntingdon Rd; s/d incl breakfast from
£145/180; ☐ ☐ ) This luxurious boutique hotel
occupies a lovely grey-brick Victorian villa
in landscaped grounds a mile from the city
centre. Its 52 rooms embody designer chic
with minimalist style but lots of comfort. The
slick restaurant serves Mediterranean cuisine
with a modern twist (mains £14.50 to £19).

## Eating

You won't go hungry in Cambridge, it's
packed with chain restaurants, particularly
around the city centre and on Bridge St. If
you're looking for something more authentic
though you'll have to search a little harder.

### BUDGET

**our pick** **Michaelhouse** ( ☎ 01223-309167; Trinity St;
mains £3.55-6.35; ⏱ 9.30am-5pm Mon-Sat) You can
sup fair-trade coffee and nibble focaccia
among soaring medieval arches or else take
a pew within reach of the altar at this stylishly
converted church, which still has a working
chancel. The simple lunch menu is mostly
vegetarian but also offers wine and beer.

**CB2** ( ☎ 01223-508503; 5-7 Norfolk St; mains £4-13;
⏱ noon-midnight) Internet cafe, bistro, music
venue and cinema all rolled into one, this
lively place dishes up a great range of rustic global cuisine in a relaxed and friendly
atmosphere. The menu features everything
from salads, pastas and wraps to heartier
bistro specials. There's live music on the
top floor on Wednesday nights and every
other Thursday.

**Clowns** ( ☎ 01223-355711; 54 King St; mains £5-9; ⏱ 8am-
midnight) A cheap and cheerful Cambridge institution frequented by students and dons,
town and gown, this thoroughly laid-back
place dishes up some of the best Italian dishes
in town. It also does a range of great sand-

wiches and gelato, best consumed on the
roof terrace.

Bright and airy **Origin8** ( ☎ 01223-354434; 62 St
Andrew's Street; mains £3-6.50; ⏱ 8am-6pm Mon-Sat, 11am-
5pm Sun) is a cafe-cum-deli and butcher's shop
and prides itself on its local organic ingredients. It's a great place to stop for lunch or pick
up some goodies for a picnic. Alternatively
try **Fitzbillies** ( ☎ 01223-352500; www.fitzbillies.co.uk;
52 Trumpington St; ⏱ shop 9am-5.30pm, restaurant 9am-
9.30pm), Cambridge's oldest bakery, beloved
by generations of students for its ultrasticky
buns. For a heartier meal **Dojo** ( ☎ 01223-363471;
1-2 Miller's Yard, Mill Lane; mains £6-7; ⏱ lunch & dinner) is
a popular student haunt offering a great range
of noodle and rice dishes.

### MIDRANGE

**Al Casbah** ( ☎ 01223-579500; www.al-casbah.co.uk; 62
Mill Rd; mains £7.50-9) Decked out like a Bedouin
tent, this Algerian restaurant dishes up steaming plates of classic North African favourites.
Expect tabouleh, falafel, brochettes, *merguez*
(spicy lamb sausage) and wonderful grills
from the indoor charcoal barbecue.

**De Luca** ( ☎ 01223-356666; www.delucacucina
.co.uk; 83 Regent St; mains £8-19.50; ⏱ 11am-late)
Contemporary-style and classic Italian food
collide in this light-filled restaurant in the
centre of town. The open kitchen, glass ceiling
and exposed brickwork make it a bright and
lively place to dine and with a great wine list
and plenty of cocktails it's as popular for long
lunches as it is for boozy nights out.

**our pick** **Rainbow Vegetarian Bistro** ( ☎ 01223-
321551; www.rainbowcafe.co.uk; 9a King's Pde; mains £8.50-
9.50; ⏱ 10am-10pm Tue-Sat) First-rate vegetarian
food and a pious glow emanate from this snug
subterranean gem, accessed down a narrow
passageway off King's Pde. It's decorated in
funky colours and serves up organic dishes
with a hint of the exotic, such as scrumptious
Indonesian gado gado and Moroccan tagine.

**Chop House** ( ☎ 01223-359506; 1 King's Pde; mains £9-15;
⏱ 11am-10.30pm Mon-Fri, to 11pm Sat, 10am-10.30pm Sun)
Set on the busy corner of Kings Pde and Bene't
St, this place has giant windows overlooking the
street, scrubbed wooden floors and a menu of
classic English cuisine. If you're craving sausage
and mash, a sizzling steak, suet pudding, fish
pie or potted ham look no further.

### TOP END

**Twenty-Two** ( ☎ 01223-351880; www.restaurant22.co.uk;
22 Chesterton Rd; set dinner £27.50; ⏱ 7-9.45pm Tue-Sat)

Discretely disguised amid a row of Victorian terraced housing is this outstanding restaurant, blessed by both its romantic candlelit ambience and its wonderful gourmet English and European menu with a commitment to local produce.

**Midsummer House** ( ☎ 01223-369299; www.midsum merhouse.co.uk; Midsommer Common; set lunch £30, 3-course dinner £60; ◷ lunch Wed-Sun, dinner Tue-Sat) For sheer gastronomic delight this sophisticated place serves up what is possibly the best food in East Anglia. With two Michelin stars and a host of rave reviews from famous foodies it's *the* place to go for a special occasion. The menu is French Mediterranean and the setting a wonderful Victorian villa backing onto the river.

## Drinking

Cambridge is awash with historic pubs that echo with the same equal mix of intellectual banter and rowdy merrymaking that they have done for centuries past.

**Eagle** ( ☎ 01223-505020; Bene't St) Cambridge's most famous pub has loosened the tongues and pickled the grey cells of many an illustrious academic in its day; among them Nobel Prize–winning scientists Crick and Watson, who discussed their research into DNA here. It's a traditional 16th-century pub with five cluttered cosy rooms, the back one popular with WWII airmen, who left their signatures on the ceiling.

**Fort St George** ( ☎ 01223-354327; Midsummer Common) The ideal English summertime pub sandwiched between the grassy expanse of Midsummer Common and the punt-littered River Cam, this place has lots of outdoor seating and great views of the river. The 16th-century interior with its crooked beams and sloping floors makes a fine alternative when the sun goes in.

**Portland Arms** ( ☎ 01223-357268; 129 Chesterton Rd) The best spot in town to catch a gig and see the pick of up-and-coming bands, the Portland is a popular student haunt and music venue. Its wood-panelled interior, unpretentious attitude and spacious terrace make a good bet any day of the week.

**Granta** ( ☎ 01223-505016; Newnham Rd) If the exterior of this picturesque waterside pub, overhanging a pretty mill pond, looks strangely familiar it could be because it's the darling of many a TV director. Its terrace sits directly beside the water and when your Dutch courage has been sufficiently fuelled, there are punts for hire alongside.

## Entertainment

Thanks to a steady stream of students and tourists there's always something on in Cambridge. Look out for the noticeboards around town laden down with posters advertising classical concerts, theatre shows, academic lectures and live music. It's also worth picking up a *What's On* events guide from the tourist office or logging on to www.cam.ac.uk/whatson for details of university events.

### NIGHTCLUBS

Despite the huge student population, Cambridge isn't blessed with the best clubs in the country. Many students stick to the college bars late at night and swear that they are the best venues in town. Pity they're not open to the rest of us.

**Fez** ( ☎ 01223-519224; www.cambridgefez.com; 15 Market Passage; admission £5-10; ◷ 8pm-3am) Hip hop, dance, R&B, techno, funk – whatever you're into you'll find it at Cambridge's most popular club, the Moroccan-themed Fez. Famous for booking top-name DJs, hosting great club nights and its sought-after VIP lounges, it's well worth arriving early to avoid the massive queues.

**The Place** ( ☎ 01223-324600; www.placenightclub .co.uk; 22 Sidney St; admission £5; ◷ 10pm-2am) This sleek club aims to be *the* place to see and be seen in the city, with designer decor and VIP booths with moody blue lighting and white leather sofas. In reality it's pretty mainstream with club classics, crowd-pleasing tunes and the usual suspects on the dance floor.

### THEATRE

**Corn Exchange** ( ☎ 01223-357851; www.cornex.co.uk; Wheeler St) The city's main centre for arts and entertainment, this place attracts top names in pop and rock.

**Arts Theatre** ( ☎ 01223-503333; www.cambridgeart sttheatre.com; 6 St Edward's Passage) For everything from pantomime to West End drama try the Arts Theatre.

**Junction** ( ☎ 01223-511511; www.junction.co.uk; Cambridge Leisure Park, Clifton Way) For dance, comedy, live music and club nights try the Junction.

**ADC** ( ☎ 01223-300085; www.adctheatre.com; Park St) Current home to the university's Footlights comedy troupe, which jump-started the careers of scores of England's comedy legends, ADC is the leading student theatre.

EAST ANGLIA

## Getting There & Away

Cambridge is well served by trains, though not so well by bus. Trains run at least every 30 minutes from London's King's Cross and Liverpool St stations (£17.90, 45 minutes to 1¼ hours). There are also three trains per hour to Ely (£3.30, 15 minutes) and hourly connections to Bury St Edmunds (£7.60, 44 minutes) and King's Lynn (£8.30, 48 minutes).

From Parkside, Parker's Piece there are regular buses to Stansted airport (£10.50, 55 minutes), Heathrow (£26, 2½ to three hours) and Gatwick (£30.50, 3¾ hours) airports while a Luton (£13, 1½ hours) service runs every two hours.

Buses to Oxford (£9, 3¼ hours) are regular but take a very convoluted route.

## Getting Around

### BICYCLE

There are few more bike-friendly cities than Cambridge, and joining the ranks of students on their mad dashes to lectures or leisurely rides around town is an experience in itself.

**Cambridge Station Cycles** ( ☎ 01223-307125; www .stationcycles.co.uk; Station Bldg, Station Rd; per half-day/ day/week £8/10/20)

**City Cycle Hire** ( ☎ 01223-365629; www.citycyclehire .com; 61 Newnham Rd; per half-day/day/week from £5/10/15)

### BUS

A free gas-powered City Shuttle runs around the centre stopping at Emmanuel St every 15 minutes from 9am to 5pm. City bus lines run around town from Drummer St bus station; C1, C3 and C7 stop at the train station. Dayrider passes (£3) offer unlimited travel on all buses within Cambridge for one day; Megarider passes (£10) are valid for one week. Buy them on-board.

### CAR

Cambridge's centre is largely pedestrianised. It's best to use one of the five free Park & Ride car parks on the outskirts of town. Shuttle buses (£2.20) run to the centre every 10 minutes between 7am and 7pm daily, then every 20 minutes until 10pm.

### TAXI

For a taxi, phone **Camtax** ( ☎ 01223-242424) or **Panther** ( ☎ 01223-715715).

## AROUND CAMBRIDGE

### Grantchester

Old thatched cottages with gardens dripping in flowers, breezy meadows and some classic cream teas aren't the only reason to make the pilgrimage along the river to the picture-postcard village of Grantchester. You'll also be following in the footsteps of some of the world's greatest minds on a 3-mile walk, cycle or punt that has changed little since Edwardian times.

The journey here is idyllic on a sunny day and once you arrive you can flop into a deckchair under a leafy apple tree and wolf down calorific cakes at the quintessentially English **Orchard tea garden** ( ☎ 01223-845788; www .orchard-grantchester.com; Mill Way; ☺ approximately 9.30am-5.30pm). This was the favourite haunt of the Bloomsbury Group (a group of writers, painters and intellectuals, including authors EM Forster and Virginia Woolf and economist John Maynard Keynes, who became friends at Cambridge in the early 1900s) and other cultural icons who came to camp, picnic, swim and discuss their work. If you're after something stronger to whet your thirst the riverside **Red Lion** ( ☎ 01223-840121; 33 High St, Grantchester) makes a good stop.

### Imperial War Museum

The romance of the winged war machine is alive and well at Europe's biggest **aviation museum** ( ☎ 01223-835000; www.iwm.org.uk; adult/under 16yr £16/free; ☺ 10am-6pm mid-Mar–Sep, to 4pm Oct–mid-Mar) in Duxford, 9 miles south of Cambridge at Junction 10 of the M11. Almost 200 lovingly waxed aircraft from dive bombers to biplanes, Spitfire to Concorde are housed on this vast airfield, which was a frontline fighter station in WWII. Once home to the Dambuster squadron of Lancasters, it is now home to the Red Arrows.

Also included is the stunning **American Air Museum** hangar, designed by Norman Foster, which has the largest collection of American civil and military aircraft outside the USA, and the slick **AirSpace hangar** which houses an exhibition on British and Commonwealth aviation. WWII tanks and artillery can be seen in the **land-warfare hall**, and the regular **airshows** of modern and vintage planes are legendary.

Monday to Saturday, Stagecoach bus Citi7 runs to Duxford (45 minutes, every half-hour) from Emmanuel St in Cambridge. The last bus back from the museum is at 5.30pm. The service runs hourly on Sundays.

**EAST ANGLIA**

# ELY

pop 15,102

A small but charming city steeped in history and dominated by a jaw-dropping cathedral, Ely (ee-lee) makes an excellent day trip from Cambridge. Beyond the dizzying heights of the cathedral towers lie medieval streets, pretty Georgian houses and riverside walks reaching out into the eerie fens that surround the town. The abundance of eels that once inhabited the undrained fens gave the town its unusual name and if you're brave you can still sample eel stew or eel pie in local restaurants. Ely is a sleepy kind of place where traditional tearooms and antique shops vie for attention, but it also ranks as one of the fastest-growing cities in Europe, meaning change is surely on the way.

## Information

The helpful **tourist office** ( ☎ 01353-662062; http://visitely.eastcambs.gov.uk; 29 St Mary's St; ⏰ 10am-5pm Apr-Oct, 11am-4pm Mon-Fri & Sun, 10am-5pm Sat Nov-Mar) has leaflets on the town's 'Eel Trail' walking tour. The tourist office also organises a guided walking tour of the city at 2.30pm on Sunday (£3.50).

## Sights

### ELY CATHEDRAL

Dominating the town and visible across the flat fenland for vast distances, the stunning silhouette of **Ely Cathedral** ( ☎ 01353-667735; www.cathedral.ely.anglican.org; adult/child under 16yr/concession £5.50/free/4.70; ⏰ 7am-7pm Easter-Aug, 7.30am-6pm Mon-Sat, 7.30am-5pm Sun Sep-Easter) is locally dubbed the 'Ship of the Fens'.

Walking into the early-12th-century Romanesque nave, you're immediately struck by its clean, uncluttered lines and lofty sense of space. The cathedral is renowned for its entrancing ceilings and the masterly 14th-century octagon and lantern towers, which soar upwards in shimmering colours.

The vast 14th-century Lady Chapel is the biggest in England; it's filled with eerily empty niches that once held statues of saints and martyrs. They were hacked out unceremoniously by iconoclasts during the English Civil War. However, the astonishingly delicate tracery and carving remain.

The cathedral is a breathtaking place, its incredible architecture and light making it a popular film location. You may recognise some of its fine details from scenes in *Elizabeth: the Golden Age* or *The Other Boleyn Girl* but wandering back to the streets it can be difficult to imagine how such a small and tranquil city ended up with such a fine monument.

Although a sleepy place today, Ely has been a place of worship and pilgrimage since at least AD 673 when Etheldreda, daughter of the king of East Anglia, founded a nunnery here. A colourful character, Ethel shrugged off the fact that she had been twice married in her determination to become a nun and was canonised shortly after her death. The nunnery was later sacked by the Danes, rebuilt as a monastery, demolished and then resurrected as a church after the Norman Conquest. In 1109 Ely became a cathedral, built to impress

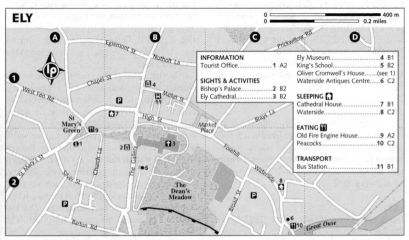

**ELY**

0 — 400 m
0 — 0.2 miles

| INFORMATION | |
| --- | --- |
| Tourist Office | 1 A2 |

| SIGHTS & ACTIVITIES | |
| --- | --- |
| Bishop's Palace | 2 B2 |
| Ely Cathedral | 3 B2 |

| Ely Museum | 4 B1 |
| --- | --- |
| King's School | 5 B2 |
| Oliver Cromwell's House | (see 1) |
| Waterside Antiques Centre | 6 C2 |

| SLEEPING 🛏 | |
| --- | --- |
| Cathedral House | 7 B1 |
| Waterside | 8 C2 |

| EATING 🍴 | |
| --- | --- |
| Old Fire Engine House | 9 A2 |
| Peacocks | 10 C2 |

| TRANSPORT | |
| --- | --- |
| Bus Station | 11 B1 |

mere mortals and leave them in no doubt about the power of the church.

For more insight into the fascinating history of the cathedral join a free **guided tour** (☷ 10.45am, 1pm, 2pm & 3pm May-Sep, 10.45am, 2pm & 3pm Oct-Apr). You can also explore the **Octagon Tower** (£3.50; ☷ 10.45am, 1pm, 2.15pm, 3pm May-Sep) on a tour or attend the spine-tingling **Evensong** (☷ 5.30pm Mon-Sat, 4pm Sun) or Sunday **choral service** (☷ 10.30am).

Near the entrance a **stained-glass museum** (☎ 01353-660347; www.stainedglassmuseum.com; adult/child £3.50/2.50; ☷ 10.30am-5pm Mon-Fri, to 5.30pm Sat, to 6pm Sun Easter-Oct, to 5pm Nov-Easter) tells the history of decorated glasswork from the 14th century onwards. Joint admission to the cathedral and museum is £8 for adults and £6.50 for children.

### OTHER SIGHTS

Just beside the cathedral are the former **Bishop's Palace** (now a nursing home) and **King's School**, which keeps the cathedral supplied with fresh-faced choristers. Across St Mary's Green is the attractive half-timbered **Oliver Cromwell's House** (☎ 01353-662062; 29 St Mary's St; adult/child under 16yr £4.85/3; ☷ 10am-4pm Apr-Oct, 11am-4pm Nov-Mar), where England's warty warmonger lived with his family from 1636 to 1646, when he was the local tithe collector. The house now has Civil War exhibits, portraits and waxworks, and echoes with canned commentaries of – among other things – the great man's grisly death, exhumation and posthumous decapitation.

In the town's Old Gaol House you'll find **Ely Museum** (☎ 01353-666655; www.elymuseum.org.uk; Market St; adult/child £3/free; ☷ 10.30am-5pm Tue-Sat, 1-5pm Sun May-Oct, 10.30am-4pm Wed-Mon Nov-Apr), which charts the history of the town and the surrounding fens.

Ely is also a great place for rummaging through antiques, and signs lead down to the river and bargain-hunting team **Waterside Antiques Centre** (☎ 01353-667066; The Wharf; ☷ 9.30am-5.30pm Mon-Sat, 11.30am-5.30pm Sun). From here, charming riverside ambles flank the **Great Ouse**.

### Sleeping & Eating

Accommodation is mostly one- or two-room B&Bs so book ahead for your first choice.

**Cathedral House** (☎ 01353-662124; www.cathedralhouse.co.uk; 17 St Mary's St; s £50, d £75-90; ℗) Set in a lovely Georgian house bursting with antiques and curios, this elegant B&B offers three individually decorated rooms all with

period features and cast-iron baths. Outside there's a beautiful walled garden and views of the cathedral.

**Waterside** (☎ 01353-614329; www.29waterside.org.uk; 29 Waterside; d £60) This pocket-sized B&B is in a wonderfully character-rich 18th-century oak-beamed and wooden-floored building near the waterfront. It's furnished with reclaimed pine and has a pretty walled garden.

**Peacocks** (☎ 01353-661100; www.peacockstearoom.co.uk; 65 Waterside; cream tea £5.50; ☷ 10.30am-5pm Wed-Sun) Voted one of Britain's top teashops by the ladies who know at the Tea Guild, this wisteria-clad place serves a vast selection of leaf teas, as well as luscious homemade cakes, and soups, salads and sambos.

**Old Fire Engine House** (☎ 01353-662582; www.theoldfireenginehouse.co.uk; 25 St Mary's St; mains £14-17; ☷ closed Sun dinner) Backed by beautiful gardens and showcasing a variety of artwork, this delightfully homely place serves classic English food and top-notch afternoon teas. Expect the likes of steak-and-kidney pie or roast pheasant with bread sauce and redcurrant jelly, washed down with a carefully chosen wine.

### Getting There & Away

Ely is on the A10, 15 miles northeast of Cambridge. Following the Fen Rivers Way (map available from tourist offices), it's a lovely 17-mile towpath walk.

The easiest way to get to Ely from Cambridge is by train (15 minutes, every 20 minutes). There are also twice-hourly trains to Peterborough (£8.10, 35 minutes) and Norwich (£13.50, one hour), and hourly services to King's Lynn (£5.40, 30 minutes).

## PETERBOROUGH

pop 156,061

A lively city that's shopping mad, Peterborough is riddled with shopping malls but the real reason to visit is the glorious cathedral, which alone makes it worthy of a day trip from Cambridge or London.

Peterborough's bus and train stations are an easy walk west of the city centre. The **tourist office** (☎ 01733-452336; www.visitpeterborough.com; 3-5 Minster Precincts; ☷ 9am-5pm Mon & Wed-Fri, 10am-5pm Tue, 10am-4pm Sat) is in front of the cathedral's western face.

### Peterborough Cathedral

England may be filled with fine cathedrals boasting ostentatious facades, but few can rival the instant 'wow' factor of Peterborough's unique early-13th-century western front, with its three cavernous Gothic arches.

Visitors enter the **cathedral** ( ☎ 01733-355300; www.peterborough-cathedral.org.uk; requested donation £3; ☺ 9am-5.15pm Mon-Fri, to 5pm Sat, noon-5pm Sun), which was founded in 1118, through an odd 14th-century porch that peeks out between the arches. Inside, you'll be immediately struck by the height of the magnificent three-storeyed Norman nave and by its lightness, created by the mellow local stone and fine clerestory windows. The nave is topped by a breathtaking early-13th-century painted-timber ceiling that is one of the earliest and most important of its kind in Europe, and still sports much of its original diamond-patterned paintwork.

Press on below the Gothic tower, which was painstakingly reconstructed in the 19th century, to the northern choir aisle and you'll find the rather plain tombstone of Henry VIII's first wife, the tragic Catherine of Aragon, buried here in 1536. Her divorce, engineered by the king because she could not produce a male heir, led to the Reformation in England. Her only child (a daughter) was not even allowed to attend her funeral. Just beyond this is the cathedral's wonderful 15th-century eastern tip, which has superb fan vaulting thought to be the work of master mason John Wastell, who worked on King's College Chapel in Cambridge.

Loop around into the southern aisle, and you'll find gold lettering marking the spot where the ill-fated Mary, Queen of Scots was once buried. On the accession of her son, James, to the throne, her body was moved to Westminster Abbey.

### Getting There & Away
There are regular trains to London (£24.50, 55 minutes to 1½ hours), Cambridge (£13, 50 minutes) and Ely (£8.90, 35 minutes).

# ESSEX

The butt of some of England's cruellest jokes and greatest snobbery for years, Essex is a land full of chavs (think Vicky Pollard's character from *Little Britain*), bottle blondes, boy racers and brash seaside resorts – or so the stereotype goes. But beyond the fake Burberry bags and slots 'n' dodgems resorts there's a rural idyll

of sleepy medieval villages and rolling countryside. One of England's best-loved painters, Constable, found inspiration here, and the rural Essex of his time remains hidden down winding lanes little changed for centuries. Here too is the historic town of Colchester, Britain's oldest, with a sturdy castle and vibrant arts scene, and even Southend-on-Sea, the area's most popular resort, has a softer side in the traditional cockle sellers and cobbled lanes of sleepy suburb Leigh.

## COLCHESTER
**pop 104,390**
Dominated by its sturdy castle and ancient walls, Colchester claims the title as Britain's oldest recorded city, with settlement noted here as early as the 5th century BC. Centuries later in AD 43, the Romans came, saw, conquered and constructed their northern capital Camulodunum here. So too, the invading Normans, who saw Colchester's potential and built the monstrous war machine that is the castle.

Today the city is a maze of narrow streets but despite its historic setting and the odd half-timbered gem, the city has a rather dowdy atmosphere. But at the time of writing this was set to change, with a series of major redevelopments planned for the city, including a spectacular new cultural centre, Firstsite.

### Orientation & Information
There are two train stations, but most services stop at North station, about half a mile north of the centre. The current bus station is off Queen St near the tourist office, but by 2010 will move to a new location on Vineyard St.

The **tourist office** ( ☎ 01206-282920; www.visitcolchester.com; 1 Queen St; ☺ 9.30am-6pm Mon-Sat, 11am-4pm Sun Apr-Sep, 10am-5pm Mon-Sat Oct-Mar) is opposite the castle.

### Sights & Activities
England's largest surviving Norman keep, bigger even than that of the Tower of London and once a hair-raising symbol of foreign invasion, now slumbers innocently amid a lush park. **Colchester Castle** ( ☎ 01206-282939; www.colchestermuseums.org.uk; adult/child £5.20/3.40; ☺ 10am-5pm Mon-Sat, 11am-5pm Sun) was begun in 1076, building upon the foundations of a Roman fort. The interactive castle museum is exceptional, with plenty of try-on togas and sound effects to

keep young curiosity alive. There are also illuminating guided tours (adult/child £2.10/1.10) of the Roman vaults, Norman rooftop chapel and castle walls.

Beside the castle, a solid Georgian town house hosts the **Hollytrees Museum** ( ☎ 01206-282940; High St; admission free; ☽ 10am-5pm Mon-Sat, 11am-5pm Sun), which trawls through 300 years of domestic life with quirky surprises that include a shipwright's boat-cum-pram and a make-your-own Victorian silhouette feature.

Tymperleys, a magnificent timber-framed 15th-century building 100m east of the castle just off the High St, also houses the hypnotic **Clock Museum** ( ☎ 01206-282939; admission free; ☽ 10am-1pm & 2-5pm Tue-Sat Apr-Oct), which echoes to the steady tick-tocking of one of the largest clock collections in Britain.

A short stroll north of High St will bring you to the Tudor **Dutch Quarter**, where the half-timbered houses and rickety roof lines remain as a testament to the 16th-century Protestant weavers who fled here from Holland.

Already being promoted as a future star attraction at the time of writing, **firstsite:newsite** ( ☎ 01206-577067; www.firstsite.uk.net) will be a massive purpose-built arts and education centre in St Botolph's. The stunning curved glass and copper building will contain gallery space, a library, auditorium and conference facilities and will play host to exhibitions, events and performances. Although construction has been much delayed, it is hoped the centre will open in late 2009. Check the website or tourist office for the latest information.

## Tours

The tourist office has a variety of themed, guided **walking tours** (adult/child £3/2; ☽ 11.30am Mon-Sat, 2pm Sun Jul & Aug, 11.30am Sat Mar-Jun, Sep & Oct) of the town and sells tickets for **City Sightseeing** (www.city-sightseeing.com; adult/child £7.50/3; ☽ Apr-Sep) open-top bus tours.

## Sleeping & Eating

Colchester has some excellent, lovingly cared for and reasonably priced B&Bs that give the town's ancient hotels a real run for their money. Independent restaurants are in short supply but you'll find all the usual chains along North Hill.

**ourpick Charlie Browns** ( ☎ 01206-517451; www .charliebrownsbedandbreakfast.co.uk; 60 East St; s £30-45, d £45-60; P ☐ wi-fi) A former hardware shop turned boutique B&B, this place offers incredible value with a couple of stunning rooms blending 14th-century character with 21st-century style. Antique and modern furniture mix seamlessly with the half-timbered walls, limestone bathrooms and rich fabrics to create an intimate, luxurious feel. It's an absolute steal at these rates and should be your first port of call.

**Rutland House** ( ☎ 01206-573437; www.rutlandhouse bandb.co.uk; 121 Lexden Rd; s £40-55, d £60-75; P ) This is another great B&B with three gorgeous individually furnished rooms in a 1920s house. Choose from Victorian character, 1930s style or contemporary design. Each room has TV and DVD, soft colour schemes and plenty of little extras.

**Life Cafe** ( ☎ 01206-574777; 3 Culver St; mains £5-5.50; ☽ 8am-7pm Mon-Fri, to 5pm Sat) This cafe-cum-gallery is bathed in light from the giant floor-to-ceiling windows that look out over the busy street. The menu features a good selection of interesting panini, pastas and salads, as well as plenty of cakes and speciality brews.

**Lemon Tree** ( ☎ 01206-767337; www.the-lemon-tree .com; 48 St John's St; mains £11-15; ☽ 10.30am-9.30pm Mon-Sat) This zesty little eatery is graced by a knobbly Roman wall and serves creative English and Continental cuisine. Decor strikes a nice chic-to-rustic balance and there are tasty blackboard specials, frequent gourmet nights and occasional live jazz.

## Getting There & Around

Colchester is 62 miles from London. There are three daily National Express buses from London Victoria (£10.30, 2¼ hours) and rail services every 15 to 20 minutes from London Liverpool St (£18.70, 55 minutes). For a cab, call **A1 Taxis** ( ☎ 01206-544744).

## SOUTHEND-ON-SEA

pop 160,257

Crass, commercialised and full of flashing lights, Southend is London's lurid weekend playground, full of gaudy amusements and seedy nightclubs. But beyond the tourist tat, roller-coasters and slot machines there's a glorious stretch of sandy beach, an absurdly long pier and in the suburb of Old Leigh, a traditional fishing village of cobbled streets, cockle sheds and thriving art galleries. Southend is also becoming increasingly well known for its live-music scene and is a good place to catch a gig.

EAST ANGLIA

## Information

The **tourist office** ( ☎ 01702-215120; www.visitsouthend .co.uk; Southend Pier, Western Esplanade; �ువ 8.15am-6pm Mon-Fri, 8.15am-8pm Sat & Sun Apr-May & Oct, 8.15am-8pm daily Jun-Sep, 8.15am-4pm Mon-Fri, 8.15am-6pm Sat & Sun Nov-Mar) is at the entrance to the pier. Banks and shops crowd along the High St.

## Sights & Activities

Other than mile upon mile of tawny imported-sand and shingle **beaches**, Southend's main attraction is the world's longest **pier** ( ☎ 01702-215620; pier train adult/child £3/1.50, pier walk & ride £2.50/1.50; �ువ 8.15am-8pm Easter-Oct, 8.15am-4pm Mon-Fri, 8.15am-6pm Sat & Sun Nov-Easter), built in 1830. At a staggering 1.34 miles long it's an impressive edifice and a magnet for boat crashes, storms and fires, the last of which ravaged its tip in 2005. It's a surprisingly peaceful stroll to the lifeboat station at its head and you can hop on the Pier Railway to save the long slog back.

Afterwards, dip beneath the pier's entrance to see the antique slot machines at the **museum** ( ☎ 01702-611214; www.southendpiermuseum.co.uk; adult/ child under 12yr £1/free; �ువ 11am-5pm Tue, Wed, Sat & Sun May-Oct) and embrace Southend's tacky seaside soul on the head-spinning rides at **Adventure Island** ( ☎ 01702-443400; www.adventureisland.co.uk; Western Esplanade; �ువ roughly 11am-8pm daily Apr-Aug, Sat & Sun Sep-Mar).

If the seaside tat is not your thing, swap the candyfloss for steaming cockles wrapped in newspaper in the traditional fishing village of **Old Leigh**, just west along the seafront. Wander the cobbled streets, cockle sheds, art galleries and craft shops for a taste of life before the amusement arcades took over. The **Leigh Heritage Centre** ( ☎ 01702-470834; High St, Old Town, Leigh-on-Sea; �ువ 10.30am-3pm) offers an insight into the history and heritage of the village and its buildings.

## Sleeping & Eating

**Beaches** ( ☎ 01702-586124; www.beachesguesthouse.co.uk; 192 Eastern Esplanade; s £40, d £65-85; 🖳 wi-fi) A welcome respite from violent florals and heavy swag curtains, rooms at Beaches are bright, simple and tasteful with white Egyptian-cotton bed linen, feather duvets and subtle colour schemes. The uncluttered rooms, continental breakfast and quiet location make it one of the best deals around.

**Pebbles** ( ☎ 01702-582329; www.mypebbles.co.uk; 190 Eastern Esplanade; s from £45, d £60-85; 🖳 ) Almost

next door is the stylish Pebbles with its subtle contemporary style. The rooms here still retain their Victorian features but the decor is modern with funky wallpapers, plenty of cushions and big, comfy beds.

**Pipe of Port** ( ☎ 01702-614606; www.pipeofport.com; 84 High St; mains £9-16) A Southend institution, this subterranean wine bar–cum-bistro is an atmospheric place with old-world character, candlelit tables, sawdust-covered floor and its own unique charm. It's famous for its pies, casseroles and fish dishes as well as the lengthy wine list.

**Fleur de Provence** ( ☎ 01702-352987; www.fleurde provence.co.uk; 52 Alexandra St; mains £16-18, 3-course set meal £15; �ువ lunch & dinner Mon-Fri, dinner Sat) Chic, sleek and sophisticated, this is probably Southend's top dining establishment, serving modern French cuisine with a flourish. It's away from the centre of town but well worth the trip for its romantic ambience and fine food.

## Entertainment

Southend has a lively music scene with a powerful new wave of bands collectively known as the 'Southend sound' putting the town on the map and forcing the national music press to sit up and take notice. Along with local hopefuls you'll also get regular gigs by big-name bands at **Chinnerys** ( ☎ 01702-467305; www.chinnerys .co.uk; 21 Marine Pde) and the **Riga Music Bar** ( ☎ 01702-348020; www.rigamusicbar.co.uk; 228 London Rd).

## Getting There & Around

The easiest way to arrive is by train. There are trains roughly every 15 minutes from London Liverpool St to Southend Victoria and from London Fenchurch St to Southend Central (£8.90, 55 minutes). The seafront is a 10- to 15-minute walk from either train station. Trains leave Southend Central for Leigh-on-Sea (10 minutes) every 10 to 15 minutes.

# SUFFOLK

Littered with picturesque villages seemingly lost in time, and quaint seaside resorts that have doggedly refused to sell their souls to tourism, this charming county makes a delightfully tranquil destination. Suffolk built its wealth and reputation on the back of the medieval wool trade and although the once-busy coastal ports little resemble their time in the limelight, the inland villages remain largely untouched, with magnificent wool churches and lavish medieval homes attesting to the once great might of the area. To the west are the picture-postcard villages of Lavenham and Long Melford; further north the languid charm and historic buildings attract visitors to Bury St Edmunds; and along the coast the genteel seaside resorts of Aldeburgh and Southwold seem miles away from their more brash neighbours to the north and south.

## Information
You can whet your appetite for the region further through the websites www.visitsuffolkattractions.co.uk and www.visit-suffolk.org.uk.

## Getting Around
Consult **Suffolk County Tourism** (www.suffolkonboard.com) or **Traveline** ( ☎ 0871 200 2233; www.travelineastanglia.co.uk) for local transport information. The two main bus operators in rural areas are **Beestons** (www.beestons.co.uk) and **Chambers** (www.chamberscoaches.co.uk).

## IPSWICH
pop 117,069
Suffolk's county capital was one of the very first Saxon towns in England and a thriving medieval centre, but today its handful of medieval churches and beautiful timber-framed buildings are lost in the sea of plastic shopfronts. Change is nigh though with waterfront warehouses filling up with trendy bars and restaurants. Ipswich doesn't merit a detour or an overnight stay, but it's the main transport hub of the region and has a few gems worth seeking out if you're passing through.

The **tourist office** ( ☎ 01473-258070; www.visit-ipswich.com; 9am-5pm Mon-Sat) is in 15th-century St Stephen's Church, off St Stephen's Lane. It's a 15-minute walk northeast of the train station, across the roundabout and along Princes St.

Just north of the tourist office is the glorious wedding-cake facade of decorative pargeting on the 17th-century **Ancient House** (40 Buttermarket; 9am-5.30pm Mon-Sat), its four panels each representing the continents discovered at the time. It's one of the finest examples of the craft you'll see anywhere and crawls with mythological creatures and characters.

Set in a lovely rolling park 300m north of town, the multigabled 16th-century **Christchurch Mansion** ( ☎ 01473-433554; Soane St; admission free; mansion & gallery 10am-5pm Mon-Sat, noon-4.30pm

Sun Apr-Oct, 10am-dusk Tue-Sat, 2.30pm-dusk Sun Nov-Mar) is filled with period furniture and works by the likes of Constable and Gainsborough.

**our pick** **Samford Restaurant** ( ☎ 01473-786616; Suffolk Food Hall, Orwell Bridge; mains £8-12; 10am-6pm Mon-Sat, 10.30am-4.30pm Sun) in the Suffolk Food Hall looks down over the river and the busy deli, butcher, cheesemonger, baker and vegetable stalls below. The menu features a bumper crop of seasonal dishes using local ingredients.

There are trains every 20 minutes to London's Liverpool St station (£34.50, 1¼ hours), and twice hourly to Norwich (£11.50, 40 minutes) and Bury St Edmunds (£6.40, 30 to 40 minutes). There are bus services roughly every half-hour to Sudbury (one hour) Monday to Saturday and less frequently on Sunday.

## AROUND IPSWICH
### Sutton Hoo
Somehow missed by plundering grave robbers and left undisturbed for 1300 years, the hull of an enormous Anglo-Saxon ship was discovered here in 1939, buried under a mound of earth. The ship was the final resting place of Raedwald, King of East Anglia until AD 625, and was stuffed with a fabulous wealth of Saxon riches. The massive effort that went into his burial gives some idea of just how important an individual he must have been.

Many of the original finds and a full-scale reconstruction of his ship and burial chamber can be seen in the **visitors centre** (NT; ☎ 01394-389700; www.nationaltrust.org.uk/suttonhoo; Woodbridge; adult/child £6.20/3.20; 10.30am-5pm daily Jul & Aug, Wed-Sun mid-Mar–Jun, Sep & Oct, Sat & Sun 11am-4pm Nov–mid-Mar). The finest treasures, including the king's exquisitely crafted helmet, shields, gold ornaments and Byzantine silver, are displayed in London's British Museum (p159) but replicas are on show here.

Access to the original burial mounds is restricted but you can join a one-hour **guided tour** (adult/child £2.50/1.25) that explores the area and does much to bring this fascinating site back to life.

*Sutton Hoo* is 2 miles east of Woodbridge and 6 miles northeast of Ipswich off the B1083. Buses 71 and 73 visit *Sutton Hoo* 10 times per day Monday to Saturday, passing through Woodbridge (10 minutes) en route to Ipswich (40 minutes).

## STOUR VALLEY

The soft, pastoral landscape and impossibly pretty villages of the Stour Valley have provided inspiration for some of England's best-loved painters. Constable and Gainsborough grew up or worked here, and the topsy-turvy timber-framed houses and elegant churches that date to the region's 15th-century weaving boom are still very much as they were. This now-quiet backwater once produced more cloth than anywhere else in England, but in the 16th century, production gradually shifted elsewhere and the valley reverted to a tranquil, pastoral landscape.

## Long Melford

pop 3675

Strung out along a winding road, the village of Long Melford is home to a clutch of historic buildings and two impressive country piles. The 2-mile High St is supposedly the longest in England and is flanked by some stunning timber-framed houses, Georgian gems and Victorian terraces, and at one end has a sprawling village green lorded over by the magnificently pompous **Great Church of the Holy Trinity** ( ☎ 01787-310845; ⌚ 10am-5pm Apr-Sep, to 4pm Mar & Oct, to 3pm Nov-Feb). A spectacular example of a 15th-century wool church, it has wonderful stained-glass windows and a tower dating from 1903.

From outside, the romantic Elizabethan mansion of **Melford Hall** (NT; ☎ 01787-376395; www.nationaltrust.org.uk/melfordhall; adult/child £5.80/2.90; ⌚ 1.30-5pm Wed-Sun May-Sep, 1.30-5pm Sat & Sun Apr & Oct) little seems changed since it entertained the queen in 1578. Inside, there's a panelled banqueting hall, much Regency and Victorian finery and a display on Beatrix Potter, who was related to the Parker family who owned the house from 1786 to 1960.

There's a noticeably different atmosphere at Long Melford's other red-brick Elizabethan mansion, **Kentwell Hall** ( ☎ 01787-310207; www.kentwell.co.uk; adult/child £8.50/5.50; ⌚ 11am-5pm Apr-Sep). Despite being full of Tudor pomp and centuries-old ghost stories, it is still used as a private home and has a wonderfully lived-in feel. It's surrounded by a rectangular moat and there's a Tudor-rose maze and a rare-breeds farm that'll keep the kids happy. Kentwell hosts special events throughout the year, including several full Tudor re-creations when the whole estate bristles with bodices and hose. Check the website for details.

Long Melford is also famed for its **antique shops**, thanks in part to a hit '80s TV series called *Lovejoy* that was shot here. Viewing appointments are required in some.

### SLEEPING & EATING

**High Street Farmhouse** ( ☎ 01787-375765; www.highstreetfarmhouse.co.uk; High St; s/d incl breakfast £35/60; P ) This 16th-century farmhouse offers a choice of big, bright rooms full of rustic charm. Expect patchwork quilts, pretty florals, knotty pine and cast-iron or four-poster beds. There's a lovely mature garden outside and hearty breakfasts on offer.

**Black Lion Hotel & Restaurant** ( ☎ 01787-312356; www.blacklionhotel.net; the Green; s £97.50-110, d £150-195; P ) Flamboyant rooms with serious swag curtains, four-poster and half-tester beds, rich fabrics and a creative combination of contemporary style and traditional elegance are on offer at this small hotel on the village green. Go for the deep-red Yquem for pure, sultry passion or try the Sancerre for something a little more restful. The hotel has two restaurants (mains £12 to £17) and a lovely walled Victorian garden.

**Scutcher's Bistro** ( ☎ 01787-310200; www.scutchers.com; Westgate St; mains £12-19; ⌚ lunch & dinner Tue-Sat) Despite the rather mismatched decor, this unpretentious place is renowned throughout the Stour Valley for its exquisite food. The menu features classic and modern English dishes that leave locals coming back regularly for more.

### GETTING THERE & AWAY

Buses leave from the High St outside the post office with hourly services Monday to Saturday to Bury St Edmunds (50 minutes).

## Lavenham

pop 1738

One of East Anglia's most beautiful and rewarding towns, topsy-turvy Lavenham is home to a wonderful collection of exquisitely preserved medieval buildings that lean and lurch to dramatic effect. Lavenham's 300 half-timbered and pargeted houses and thatched cottages have been left virtually untouched since its heyday in the 15th century when it made its fortunes on the back of the wool trade. Curiosity shops, art galleries, quaint tearooms and ancient inns line the streets, where the predominant colour is 'Suffolk pink', a traditional finish of whitewash mixed with red ochre. On top of the medieval atmosphere and beautiful streetscapes, Lavenham has an excellent choice of accommodation making it one of the most popular spots in the area with visitors.

### SIGHTS

Many of Lavenham's most enchanting buildings cluster along High St, Water St and around Market Pl, which is dominated by the early-16th-century **guildhall** (NT; ☎ 01787-247646; www .nationaltrust.org.uk/lavenham; adult/child £4/1.65; ⊙ 11am-5pm Apr-Oct, 11am-4pm Sat & Sun Nov, 11am-4pm Wed-Sun Mar), a superb example of a close-studded, timber-framed building. It is now a local-history museum with displays on the wool trade, and in its tranquil garden you can see dye plants that produced the typical medieval colours.

Also on the Market Pl, the atmospheric 14th-century **Little Hall** ( ☎ 01787-247019; www .littlehall.org.uk; adult/child £2.50/free; ⊙ 2-5.30pm Wed, Thu, Sat & Sun Easter-Oct) is another gem, with soft ochre plastering, timber frame and crown-post roof. Once home to a successful wool merchant, it's now a private residence open to the public.

At the village's high southern end rises the stunning **Church of St Peter & St Paul** ( ⊙ 8.30am-5.30pm Apr-Sep, to 3.30pm Oct-Mar), a late-Perpendicular church that seems to lift into the sky with its beautifully proportioned windows and soaring steeple. Built between 1485 and 1530, it was one of Suffolk's last great wool churches, completed on the eve of the Reformation and now a lofty testament to Lavenham's past prosperity.

### SLEEPING & EATING

**De Vere House** ( ☎ 01787-249505; www.deverehouse .co.uk; Water St; s £75, d £80-95; **P** ) This stunning medieval house is just dripping with character and the two guest rooms are decked out in classical style. One features a carved four-poster bed, chaise longue and roll-top bath while the other is all exposed beams and Edwardian style. There's a private reading room for guests and a courtyard garden for breakfast.

**ourpick Lavenham Priory** ( ☎ 01787-247404; www.lavenhampriory.co.uk; Water St; s/d from £75/100; **P** ) A rare treat, this sumptuously restored 15th-century B&B steals your heart as soon as you walk in the door. Every room oozes Elizabethan charm with cavernous fireplaces, leaded windows and exquisite period features.

Now an upmarket six-room B&B, it must be booked well in advance.

**Swan Hotel** ( ☎ 01787-247477; www.theswanatlaven ham.co.uk; High St; s £75-85, d £115-280; **P** ) A warren of stunning timber-framed 15th-century buildings now shelters one of the region's best-known hotels. Rooms are suitably spectacular, some with immense fireplaces, colossal beams and magnificent four-posters. Elsewhere the hotel cultures a gentlefolk's country-club feel. The stunning beamed Great Hall is an atmospheric place to try the modern English cuisine (three-course set dinner £31.95).

**Great House** ( ☎ 01787-247431; www.greathouse.co.uk; Market Pl; s £85-120, d £85-180; ⬜ wi-fi) Chic design blends effortlessly with 15th-century character at this much-loved restaurant with rooms in the centre of town. The guest accommodation is decidedly contemporary with funky wallpaper, sleek furniture and plasma-screen TVs but there are plenty of period features and a decanter of sherry on the side. The acclaimed French restaurant (three-course lunch/dinner £16.95/26.95) serves classic French dishes with a modern flourish.

### GETTING THERE & AWAY

Chambers Buses connects Lavenham with Bury St Edmunds (30 minutes) hourly until 6pm Monday to Saturday (no service on Sunday). The nearest train station is Sudbury.

## Hadleigh
pop 7239

Though it's hard to envisage now, the quiet country town of Hadleigh was once one of the biggest and busiest wool towns in East Anglia, and hidden just off the High St is a lovely cluster of buildings to prove it.

The town's principal jewel is its handsome three-storeyed 15th-century **guildhall** ( ☎ 01473-827752; Church St; www.fohg.co.uk; admission free; ⊙ 2-5pm Sun-Fri late Jun–late Sep), timber framed and topped by a splendid crown-post roof. Next door, there are some fabulous original features (including a very stiff oaken door) to appreciate in 12th-century **St Mary's Church**, with its lanky spire and lofty ceiling.

Also beside the church is the high-and-mighty **Deanery Tower**, built in 1495 as a gatehouse to an archbishop's mansion that never actually got built. It's a very fanciful affair embellished with decorous battlements and oriel windows.

Hadleigh is 2 miles southeast of Kersey. There are hourly buses from Ipswich (28 minutes) and Sudbury (28 minutes).

## BURY ST EDMUNDS
### pop 36,218

Once home to one of the most powerful monasteries of medieval Europe, Bury has long attracted travellers for its powerful history, atmospheric ruins, handsome Georgian architecture and bustling agricultural markets. It's a genteel kind of place with tranquil gardens, a newly completed cathedral and a lively buzz. Bury is also home to Greene King, the famous Suffolk brewer.

### History

Bury's slogan 'Shrine of a King, Cradle of the Law' recalls two defining events in the town's history. St Edmund, last Saxon king of East Anglia, was decapitated by the Danes in 869, and in 903 the martyr's body was reburied here. Soon a series of ghostly miracles emanated from his grave and the shrine became a centre of pilgrimage and the core of a new Benedictine monastery. In the 11th century,

King Knut built a new abbey which soon became one of the most famous and wealthy in the country.

In 1214 the English barons chose the abbey to draw up a petition that would form the basis of the Magna Carta, making it a 'Cradle of the Law' and setting the country on the road to a constitutional government.

In medieval times the town grew rich on the wool trade and prospered until Henry VIII got his grubby hands on the abbey in 1539 and closed it down as part of the dissolution.

### Orientation & Information

Bury is easily navigated thanks to the original 11th-century grid layout. The train station is 900m north of the tourist office, with frequent buses to the centre. The bus station is in the town's heart.

Bury's **tourist office** ( ☎ 01284-764667; tic@stedsbc .gov.uk; 6 Angel Hill; ☉ 9.30am-5pm Mon-Sat Easter-Oct, 10am-3pm Sun May-Sep, 10am-4pm Mon-Fri, 10am-1pm Sat Nov-Easter) has maps and advice and is also the starting point for guided walking tours (£3, 2.30pm Easter to September). Audio tours

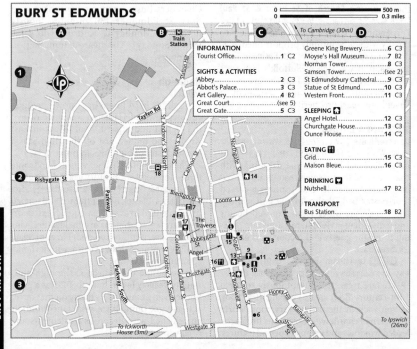

**BURY ST EDMUNDS**

| INFORMATION | |
|---|---|
| Tourist Office | 1 C2 |

| SIGHTS & ACTIVITIES | |
|---|---|
| Abbey | 2 C3 |
| Abbot's Palace | 3 C3 |
| Art Gallery | 4 B2 |
| Great Court | (see 5) |
| Great Gate | 5 C3 |

| | |
|---|---|
| Greene King Brewery | 6 C3 |
| Moyse's Hall Museum | 7 B2 |
| Norman Tower | 8 C3 |
| Samson Tower | (see 2) |
| St Edmundsbury Cathedral | 9 C3 |
| Statue of St Edmund | 10 C3 |
| Western Front | 11 C3 |

| SLEEPING | |
|---|---|
| Angel Hotel | 12 C3 |
| Churchgate House | 13 C3 |
| Ounce House | 14 C2 |

| EATING | |
|---|---|
| Grid | 15 C3 |
| Maison Bleue | 16 C3 |

| DRINKING | |
|---|---|
| Nutshell | 17 B2 |

| TRANSPORT | |
|---|---|
| Bus Station | 18 B2 |

(adult/child £2.50/1.50) of the abbey ruins are also available.

## Sights

### ABBEY & PARK

Now a picturesque ruin residing in beautiful gardens behind the cathedral, the once all-powerful **abbey** (admission free; ☺ dawn-dusk) still impresses despite the townspeople having made off with much of the stone after the dissolution. The Reformation also meant an end to the veneration of relics, and St Edmund's grave and bones have long since disappeared.

You enter the park via one of two well-preserved old gates: opposite the tourist office, the staunch mid-14th-century **Great Gate** is intricately decorated and ominously defensive, complete with battlements, portcullis and arrow slits. The other entrance sits further up Angel Hill, where a gargoyle-studded early-12th-century **Norman Tower** looms.

Just beyond the Great Gate is a peaceful garden where the **Great Court** was once a hive of activity, and further on a dovecote marks the only remains of the **Abbot's Palace**. Most impressive, however, are the remains of the **western front**, where the original abbey walls were burrowed into in the 18th century to make way for houses. The houses are still in use and look as if they have been carved out of the stone like caves. Nearby is **Samson Tower** and in front of it a beautiful **statue of St Edmund** by Dame Elisabeth Frink (1976). The rest of the abbey spreads eastward like a ragged skeleton, with various lumps and pillars hinting at its immense size.

### ST EDMUNDSBURY CATHEDRAL

Completed in 2005, the 45m-high Millennium Tower of **St Edmundsbury Cathedral** (St James; ☎ 01284-748720; www.stedscathedral.co.uk; Angel Hill; requested donation £3; ☺ 8am-6pm) is a vision in Lincolnshire limestone, and its traditional Gothic-style construction gives a good idea of how the towers of many other English cathedrals must once have looked fresh from the stonemason's chisel.

Most of the rest of the building dates from the early 16th century, though the eastern end is postwar 20th century, and the northern side was completed in 1990. The overall effect is light and lofty, with a gorgeous hammer-beam roof and a striking sculpture of the crucified Christ by Dame Elisabeth Frink in the north transept. The impressive entrance porch has a

tangible Spanish influence, a tribute to Abbot Anselm (1121–48), who opted against pilgrimage to Santiago de Compostela in favour of building a church dedicated to St James (Santiago in Spanish) right here.

For a proper insight into the church's history and heritage join one of the guided tours of the cathedral at 11.30am from May to September.

### GREENE KING BREWERY

Churning out some of England's favourite booze since Victorian times, this famous **brewery** ( ☎ 01284-714297; www.greeneking.co.uk; Crown St; day/evening tours £8/10; ☺ museum 10.30am-4.30pm Mon-Sat, tours 11am Mon, 2pm Tue, 11am & 2pm Wed-Fri, 10.30am, 12.30pm & 2.30pm Sat, 11.30am Sun, evening tour 7pm Mon-Fri) has a museum (admission free) and runs tours, after which you can appreciate what all the fuss is about in its brewery bar. Tours are popular so book ahead.

### ART GALLERY & MOYSE'S HALL MUSEUM

Bury's grand **art gallery** ( ☎ 01284-762081; www .burystedmundsartgallery.org; Cornhill; adult/child £1/50p; ☺ 10.30am-5pm Tue-Sat) is housed in a beautiful 18th-century former theatre and hosts a top-notch selection of temporary exhibitions of contemporary art.

Just across the square, **Moyse's Hall Museum** ( ☎ 01284-706183; Cornhill; adult/child £3/2; ☺ 10am-5pm) wows with its impressive 12th-century undercroft and tells some particularly gruesome stories in a room dedicated to death, burial and witchcraft. Among other curiosities, you'll discover a mummified cat that was purposefully buried alive in a building's walls, and a book bound in the tanned skin of an infamous murderer.

## Sleeping

**Churchgate House** ( ☎ 01284-750233; www.churchgate house.co.uk; 35 Churchgate St; s/d from £55/90; P ⬜ wi-fi) This beautiful Georgian house in the centre of town has spacious rooms decked out in glorious period style. From the antique beds and dressers to the gilt-framed prints and cosy armchairs this place just oozes tradition.

**Ounce House** ( ☎ 01284-761779; www.ouncehouse.co.uk; Northgate St; s/d from £75/110; P ) Heavy swag curtains, plenty of gilt, antique furniture and tasteful florals abound at this dignified Victorian merchant's house in the centre of town. There are only a few rooms up for grabs here so if classical elegance is your thing, book in advance.

**Angel Hotel** ( ☎ 01284-714000; www.theangel.co.uk; 3 Angel Hill; s/d from £75/137; **P** ⌨ ) Peeking from behind a shaggy mane of vines, this famous old coaching inn has hosted many a dignitary in its long history, including fictional celebrity Mr Pickwick whom Dickens wrote enjoyed an 'excellent roast dinner' here. Rooms are split between a slick contemporary wing and a traditional Georgian building.

## Eating

**Grid** ( ☎ 01284-706004; www.thegridrestaurant.co.uk; 34 Abbeygate St; mains £9-15, set 2-course lunch/dinner £10.50/14.95) Set in a 16th-century building but all slick, modern style, this relaxed restaurant serves a good selection of sandwiches (£6) and light bites (£5) as well as full meals during the day and a menu of modern English dishes by night.

**Maison Bleue** ( ☎ 01284-760623; www.maisonbleue .co.uk; 31 Churchgate St; mains £13.50-19.95; ⌚ lunch & dinner Tue-Sat) Muted colours, pale leather banquettes, white linens and contemporary style merge with a menu of imaginative dishes in this seafood restaurant. Although the menu is heavy on fish and seafood there are some vegetarian and meat dishes available.

## Drinking

**Nutshell** ( ☎ 01284-764867; The Traverse) Recognised by the *Guinness Book of Records* as Britain's smallest, this midget-sized timber-framed pub is an absolute gem and a tourist attraction in its own right. Mind how you knock back a pint here as in the crush you never know who you're going to elbow.

## Getting There & Away

Centrally placed, Bury is a convenient point from which to explore western Suffolk. There are three daily National Express buses to London (£12.80, 2½ hours). From Cambridge, Stagecoach bus 11 runs to Bury (65 minutes) hourly from Monday to Saturday; the last bus back to Cambridge leaves at 7.45pm.

Trains go to Ipswich (£6.40, 30 to 40 minutes, two per hour), Ely (£7.60, 30 minutes, six daily) and hourly to Cambridge (£7.60, 44 minutes), all of which have links to London.

## AROUND BURY ST EDMUNDS

### Ickworth House & Park

The puffed-up pomposity of stately home **Ickworth House** (NT; ☎ 01284-735270; www.nationaltrust .org/ickworth; adult/child house & park £8.30/3.30, park only

£4.20/1.10; ⌚ house 1-5pm Fri-Tue mid-Mar–Sep, to 4.30pm Oct, park 8am-8pm year-round) is palpable from the minute you catch sight of its immense oval rotunda and wide outspread wings. The building is the whimsical creation of fourth Earl of Bristol and Bishop of Derry, Frederick Hervey (1730–1803; see opposite), and contains fine paintings by Titian, Gainsborough and Velasquez. There's also a lovely Italian garden, parkland bearing the landscaping eye of Capability Brown, a deer enclosure and a hide to explore.

The east wing of the house now functions as the slick **Ickworth Hotel** ( ☎ 01284-735350; www .ickworthhotel.com; d from £290; **P** ⌨ ), where the traditional surroundings mix with designer furniture and contemporary style to create a luxurious country hideout. Despite its glam design, families are very welcome with a play group and games room laid on.

Ickworth is 3 miles southwest of Bury on the A143. Burtons bus service 344/5 from Bury train station (15 minutes) to Haverhill can drop you nearby.

## ALDEBURGH

pop 2790

One of the region's most charming coastal towns, the small fishing and boat-building village of Aldeburgh has an understated appeal that attracts visitors back year after year. Ramshackle fishing huts sell fresh-from-the-nets catch, handsome pastel-coloured houses, independent shops and art galleries line the High St, and a sweeping shingle beach stretches along the shore offering tranquil big-sky views. Although it's a popular place, the town remains defiantly unchanged with a low-key atmosphere and a great choice of food and accommodation.

Information can be found at the **tourist office** ( ☎ 01728-453637; atic@suffolkcoastal.gov.uk; 152 High St; ⌚ 9am-5.30pm Apr-Oct, 9am-5.30pm Mon-Sat, 9am-5pm Sun Nov-Mar) which also has maps of the Suffolk Coast and Heaths Path, which passes around half a mile north of town.

Aldeburgh also has a lively cultural scene. Composer Benjamin Britten and lesser known poet George Crabbe both lived and worked here; Britten founded East Anglia's primary arts and music festival, the **Aldeburgh Festival** ( ☎ 01728-687110; www.aldeburgh.co.uk), which takes place in June and has been going for over 60 years. Britten's legacy is commemorated by Maggi Hambling's wonderful *Scallop* sculpture, a short stroll left along the seashore.

---

**THE ECCENTRIC EARL**

The Hervey family had a long reputation for eccentricity but perhaps the biggest weirdo of them all was the creator of Ickworth House, Frederick. As Bishop of Derry (Ireland) he was renowned for his agnosticism, vanity and oddity, and known for forcing his clergymen to race each other through peat bogs in the middle of the night, sprinkling flour on the floor of his house to catch night-time adulterers and championing the cause of Catholic emancipation (he was, after all, a Protestant bishop).

Not content with his life in Ireland, in later years Frederick took to travelling around Europe, where he indulged each and every one of his passions: women, wine, art and intrigue. He tried to pass himself off as a spy in France, horrified visiting English aristocrats with his dress sense and manners in Italy; and once chucked a bowl of pasta onto a religious procession because he hated the sound of tinkling bells.

---

Aldeburgh's other photogenic gem is the intricately carved and timber-framed **Moot Hall** ( ☎ 01728-454666; www.aldeburghmuseum.ork.uk; adult/child £1/free; 2.30-5pm Sat & Sun Apr, 2.30-5pm daily May, Sep & Oct, noon-5pm Jun-Aug), which now houses a local-history museum.

## Sleeping & Eating

**our pick** **Ocean House** ( ☎ 01728-452094; www.ocean housealdeburgh.co.uk; 25 Crag Path; s/d £70/90) Right on seafront and with only the sound of the waves to lull you to sleep at night, this beautiful Victorian guesthouse has wonderfully cosy, period-styled rooms. Expect pale pastels, subtle florals and tasteful furniture and the sound of classical music wafting from the rooms occupied by visiting music students. There's a grand piano on the top floor, a gaily painted rocking horse, bikes to borrow and table tennis in the cellar.

**Dunan House** ( ☎ 01728-452486; www.dunanhouse .co.uk; 41 Park Rd; r incl breakfast £75-85) Set well back off the street in lovely gardens, this charming B&B has a range of individually styled rooms mixing contemporary and traditional elements to surprisingly good effect. With friendly hosts and breakfast assembled from local, wild and home-grown produce it's a real treat.

**Regatta Restaurant** ( ☎ 01728-452011; www .regattaaldeburgh.com; 171 High St; mains £8.50-13.50; noon-2pm & 6-10pm) Good ol' English seaside food is given star treatment at this sleek, contemporary restaurant where local fish is the main attraction. The celebrated owner-chef supplements his wonderful seafood with meat and vegetarian options and regular gourmet nights.

**Lighthouse** ( ☎ 01728-453377; www.lighthouserestaurant .co.uk; 77 High St; mains £9-17; 10am-2pm & 6.30-late) This unassuming bistro-style restaurant is a fantastic place to dine, with wooden tables and floors, a menu of simple but sensational international dishes and a relaxed and friendly atmosphere. Despite the top-notch food and accolades piled upon it, children are very welcome.

## Getting There & Away

Aldeburgh is not well connected in terms of transport and your best bet is to take one of the frequent bus services to Ipswich (1½ hours) and to continue on from there.

## AROUND ALDEBURGH

Strung along the coastline north of Aldeburgh is a poignant trail of serene and little-visited coastal heritage towns that are gradually succumbing to the sea. Most dramatically, the once-thriving port town of Dunwich is now a quiet village, with 12 churches and chapels and hundreds of houses washed away by the sea.

The region is a favourite haunt of the binocular-wielding birdwatcher brigade, and **RSPB Minsmere** ( ☎ 01728-648281; Westleton; adult/child £5/1.50; 9am-dusk) flickers with airborne activity year-round. Another step south towards Aldeburgh is the odd early-20th-century 'Tudorbethan' holiday village of **Thorpeness**, which sports idiosyncratic follies, a windmill and a boating lake. Looming just north of Thorpeness is **Sizewell**, a notorious nuclear-power plant topped by a golf-ball-shaped tumour.

With public transport lacking you'll need your own wheels, or the will to walk or bike this stretch of peaceful and varied coastline.

## SOUTHWOLD

pop 3858
Southwold is the kind of genteel seaside resort where beach huts cost an arm and a leg (one

reputedly changed hands recently for a whopping £48,000) and the visitors are ever so posh. Its reputation as a well-heeled holiday getaway has earned it the nickname 'Kensington-on-Sea' after the upmarket London borough, and its lovely sandy beach, pebble-walled cottages, cannon-dotted cliff-top and rows of beachfront bathing huts are all undeniably picturesque.

However, this down-to-earth town also has a traditional pier, boat rides, fish and chips and its very own brewery, **Adnams** ( ☎ 01502-727200; www.adnams.co.uk; Adnams Pl, Sole Bay Brewery). The **tourist office** ( ☎ 01502-724729; www.visit-southwold.co.uk; 69 High St; ⏰ 10am-5pm Mon-Sat, 11am-4pm Sun Easter-Oct, 10.30am-3.30pm Mon-Fri, to 4.30pm Sat Nov-Mar) can help with accommodation and information.

Starting inland, the **Church of St Edmund** (Church St; admission free; ⏰ 9am-6pm Jun-Aug, to 4pm Sep-May) is worth a quick peek for its fabulous medieval screen and 15th-century bloodshot-eyed Jack-o-the-clock, which grumpily overlooks the church's rear. A mere stone's throw away is an old weavers' cottage that now houses the **Southwold Museum** ( ☎ 01502-726097; www.southwoldmuseum.org; 9-11 Victoria St; admission free; ⏰ 10.30am-noon & 2-4pm Aug, 2-4pm Apr-Oct), where you can gen up on the explosive 132-ship and 50,000-men Battle of Solebay (1672), fought just off the coast.

But Southwold's shorefront is really the place to be. Take time to amble along its promenade and admire the squat 19th-century **lighthouse** before ending up at the cute little **pier** ( ☎ 01502-722105; www.southwoldpier.co.uk). In the 'under the pier' show you'll find a quirky collection of handmade slot machines, a mobility masterclass for zimmerframe-users and a dog's-eye view of Southwold.

If you fancy getting out on the water, the **Coastal Voyager** ( ☎ 07887-525082; www.coastalvoyager.co.uk) offers a range of boat trips, including a 30-minute high-speed Sea Blast (adult/child £18/9), a leisurely river cruise (£22/11) to nearby Blythburgh and a three-hour trip to Scroby Sands (£27/13) to see a seal colony and wind farm.

### Sleeping & Eating

Despite Southwold's charm and popularity, decent accommodation is thin on the ground.

**Gorse House** ( ☎ 01502-725468; www.gorsehouse.com; 19B Halesworth Rd; Reydon; d from £55; **P** ) A 10-minute walk from the seafront but well worth the effort, this lovely B&B is one of the best in the area. The

two rooms here are newly decorated in simple, contemporary style with subtle-patterned wallpapers, silky throws and flat-screen TVs.

**Sutherland House** ( ☎ 01502-724544; www.sutherlandhouse.co.uk; 56 High St; d £140-200; **P** 🖥 wi-fi) Set in a beautiful 15th-century house dripping with character and period features, this small hotel has just three rooms featuring pargetted ceilings, exposed beams and elm floorboards, but is decked out in sleek, modern style. The top-notch restaurant (mains £10 to £20) specialises in local food with the menu showing how many miles the principal ingredient in each dish has travelled.

**Crown** ( ☎ 01502-722275; www.adnams.co.uk; 90 High St; mains £12-17; ⏰ lunch & dinner) This special old posting inn has a superb restaurant that changes its meaty seasonal menu daily. It also has a wine bar and wood-panelled snugs, and serves real ales. Crown also has a few plush rooms (doubles from £132).

### Getting There & Away

Bus connections are surprisingly limited: your best bet is to catch one of the hourly services to Lowestoft (45 minutes) or Halesworth train station (30 minutes) and continue from there.

# NORFOLK

Big skies, sweeping beaches, windswept marshes, meandering inland waterways and pretty flint houses make up the county of Norfolk, a handsome rural getaway with a thriving regional capital. You're never far from water here, whether it's the tranquil setting of rivers and windmills in the Norfolk Broads or the wide sandy beaches, fishing boats and nature reserves along the coast. They say the locals have 'one foot on the land, and one in the sea' and beach and boating holidays are certainly a highlight of the area, but twitchers flock here too for some of the country's best birdwatching, and in Norwich, the county's bustling capital, you'll find a stunning cathedral and castle, medieval churches, a lively market and an excellent choice of pubs, clubs and restaurants.

### Information

Some handy websites:
**Independent Traveller's Norfolk** (www.itnorfolk.co.uk)
**Norfolk Coast** (www.norfolkcoast.co.uk)

**Norfolk Tourist Attractions** (www.norfolktouristat tractions.co.uk)
**Visit Norfolk** (www.visitnorfolk.co.uk)
**Visit West Norfolk** (www.visitwestnorfolk.com)

## Activities

Waymarked walking trails include the well-known Peddars Way and Norfolk Coast Path (p399). Other long-distance paths include the **Weavers Way**, a 57-mile trail from Cromer to Great Yarmouth, and the **Angles Way** (www.east suffolklinewalks.co.uk/anglesway), which negotiates the valleys of the Rivers Waveney and Little Ouse for 70 miles. Meanwhile the **Wherryman's Way** (www.wherrymansway.net) is a 35-mile walking and cycling route through the Broads, following the River Yare from Norwich to Great Yarmouth.

For a real challenge, the **Around Norfolk Walk** is a 220-mile circuit that combines most of the above.

If you're planning to do the Norfolk Coast Path and don't fancy carrying your bags, **Walk Free** ( ☎ 01328-711902; www.walk-free.co.uk; per bag £5) provides a bag courier service.

## Getting Around

For comprehensive travel advice and timetable information contact **Traveline East Anglia** ( ☎ 0871 200 22 33; www.travelineeastanglia.co.uk).

## NORWICH

pop 121,550

Norwich (pronounced norritch) had its heyday in the Middle Ages when the boom in the wool trade saw the city prosper beyond its wildest dreams. Today meandering laneways, leafy greens, grand squares, crooked half-timbered buildings and a host of medieval churches help it retain its charm. Although there's a truly magnificent cathedral and a sturdy Norman castle to visit, it's the easygoing, artsy atmosphere of this compact and affluent city that gives it its real character. The bustling markets, contemporary-art galleries and young, student population create an affable, breezy attitude that makes it an excellent base for touring the area. Add to this the easy access to the long, sweeping beaches of the coast and the shimmering waters of the Norfolk Broads and you couldn't get much finer.

## History

Though Norwich's history stretches back well over a thousand years, the city's golden age was during the Middle Ages, when it was England's most important city after London. Its relative isolation meant that it traditionally had stronger ties to the Low Countries than to London and when Edward III encouraged Flemish weavers to settle here in the 14th century this connection was sealed. The arrival of the immigrants helped establish the wool industry that fattened the city and sustained it right through to the 18th century.

Mass immigration from the Low Countries peaked in the troubled 16th century. In 1579 more than a third of the town's citizens were foreigners of a staunch Protestant stock, which proved beneficial during the Civil War when the Protestant parliamentarians caused Norwich little strife.

Today the spoils of this rich period in the city's history are still evident, with 36 medieval churches (see www.norwichchurches .co.uk) adorning the streets whose layout is largely unchanged since this time.

## Orientation

The castle crowns central Norwich, surrounded by a compact medieval street plan. Within the circle of river and city walls, there are scattered medieval churches and the Anglican cathedral. At the city's heart is its candy-stripe canopied **market** (Market Sq; ☺ approximately 8am-4.30pm), one of the biggest and oldest markets in England, running since 1025. The enormous modern Forum building houses Norfolk's main library and the tourist office.

## Information

Banks and ATMs can be found around the Market Square.

**Battlenet** ( ☎ 01603-765595; 2a Queens Rd; per hr £2; ☺ 11am-6pm Mon & Tue, 11am-9pm Wed, 11am-10pm Thu & Fri, 10am-7pm Sat, 10am-6pm Sun) Internet cafe popular with gamers.
**Boots** ( ☎ 01603-767970; 19 Castle Mall) Well-stocked pharmacy.
**Library** ( ☎ 01603-774774; The Forum; ☺ 9am-9.30pm Mon-Fri, 9am-8.30pm Sat, 10.30am-4.30pm Sun) Free internet for those with ID and the patience to fill out a few forms.
**Norfolk & Norwich University Hospital** ( ☎ 01603-286286; Colney Lane) Four miles west of the centre.
**Post office** ( ☎ 01603-761635; 84-85 Castle Mall)
**Tourist office** ( ☎ 01603-727927; www.visitnorwich .co.uk; The Forum; ☺ 9.30am-6pm Mon-Sat, 10.30am-4.30pm

# NORWICH

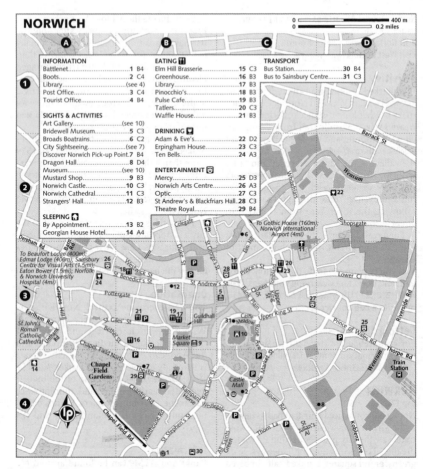

0 | 400 m
0 | 0.2 miles

**INFORMATION**
Battlenet..............................1 B4
Boots..................................2 C4
Library.............................(see 4)
Post Office..........................3 C4
Tourist Office.......................4 B4

**SIGHTS & ACTIVITIES**
Art Gallery........................(see 10)
Bridewell Museum..................5 C3
Broads Boatrains...................6 C2
City Sightseeing..................(see 7)
Discover Norwich Pick-up Point.7 B4
Dragon Hall..........................8 D4
Museum............................(see 10)
Mustard Shop.......................9 B3
Norwich Castle.....................10 C3
Norwich Cathedral.................11 C3
Strangers' Hall.....................12 B3

**SLEEPING**
By Appointment....................13 B2
Georgian House Hotel............14 A4

**EATING**
Elm Hill Brasserie.................15 C3
Greenhouse........................16 B3
Library..............................17 B3
Pinocchio's.........................18 B3
Pulse Cafe..........................19 B3
Tatlers..............................20 C3
Waffle House.......................21 B3

**DRINKING**
Adam & Eve's......................22 D2
Erpingham House..................23 C3
Ten Bells...........................24 A3

**ENTERTAINMENT**
Mercy...............................25 D3
Norwich Arts Centre...............26 A3
Optic...............................27 C3
St Andrew's & Blackfriars Hall..28 C3
Theatre Royal......................29 B4

**TRANSPORT**
Bus Station........................30 B4
Bus to Sainsbury Centre..........31 C3

Sun Apr-Oct, 9.30am-5.30pm Mon-Sat Nov-Mar) Just inside the Forum on Millennium Plain.

## Sights

### NORWICH CASTLE, MUSEUM & ART GALLERY

Perched on a hilltop overlooking central Norwich, this massive Norman **castle keep** ( ☎ 01603-493636; www.museums.norfolk.gov.uk; castle & exhibitions adult/child £5.80/4.25, exhibitions £3/2.20; ⏲ 10am-4.30pm Mon-Fri, 10am-5pm Sat, 10am-5.30pm Mon-Sat in school hols, 1-5pm Sun) is a sturdy example of 12th-century aristocratic living. The castle is one of the best-preserved examples of Anglo-Norman military architecture in the country, despite a 19th-century facelift and a gigantic shopping centre grafted to one side.

It's now home to an art gallery and superb interactive museum. The **museum** crams in a wealth of history, including lively exhibits on Boudicca and the Iceni, the Anglo-Saxons and Vikings, natural history displays and even an Egyptian gallery complete with mummies. Every room is enlivened with plenty of fun for kids, but best of all is the atmospheric keep itself, which sends shivers down the spine with graphic displays on grisly punishments meted out in its days as a medieval prison. Guided tours (£2) also run around the battlements (minimum age eight) and dungeons (minimum age five).

Meanwhile the **art gallery** houses paintings of the acclaimed 19th-century Norwich School of landscape painting founded by John

Crome and – trust the English – the world's largest collection of ceramic teapots.

## NORWICH CATHEDRAL

Norwich's most stunning landmark is the magnificent Anglican **cathedral** ( ☎ 01603-218300; www.cathedral.org.uk; suggested donation £5; ⏰ 7am-7pm mid-May–mid-Sep, to 6pm mid-Sep–mid-May), its barbed spire soaring higher than any in England except Salisbury, while the size of its cloisters is second to none.

Begun in 1096, the cathedral is one of the finest Anglo-Norman abbey churches in the country, rivalled only perhaps by Durham. The sheer size of its nave is impressive but its most renowned feature is the superb Gothic rib-vaulting added in 1463. Among the spidery stonework are 1200 sculpted roof bosses depicting bible stories. Together they represent one of the finest achievements of English medieval masonry.

Similar bosses can be seen in closer detail in the cathedral's remarkable cloisters. Built between 1297 and 1430, the two-storey cloisters are unique in England today and were originally built to house a community of about 100 monks.

Outside the cathedral's eastern end is the grave of WWI heroine Edith Cavell, a Norfolk nurse who was shot by the Germans for helping POWs to escape. The cathedral close also contains handsome houses and the old chapel of King Edward VI School (where English hero Admiral Nelson was educated). Its current students make up the choir, which performs in at least one of the three services held daily.

Fascinating guided tours of the cathedral (minimum donation £1.50) take place daily at 10.45am, 12.30pm and 2.15pm.

## ELM HILL

Head west from the cathedral up Wensum St to reach Elm Hill, an utterly charming medieval cobbled street of crooked timber beams and doors, intriguing shops and snug cafes. It's one of the oldest intact streets in the city and now centre of the local antique business. At the far end of Wensum St is Tombland, where the market was originally located. Despite its ominous overtones, 'tomb' is an old Norse word for empty, hence space for a market.

## OTHER MUSEUMS

Though it's more shop than museum, the **Mustard Shop** ( ☎ 01603-627889; www.colmansmustard shop.com; 15 Royal Arcade; admission free; ⏰ 9.30am-5pm Mon-Sat) tells the 200-year story of Colman's Mustard, a famous local product. It's in the lavish art nouveau Royal Arcade.

Nearby is **Bridewell Museum** ( ☎ 01603-629127; Bridewell Alley; adult/child £3.20/1.75; ⏰ 10am-4.30pm Tue-Fri, 10am-5pm Sat Easter-Oct), housed in a former merchant's house and 14th-century bridewell or 'prison for women, beggars and tramps', and filled with fascinating paraphernalia and reconstructions of Norwich's principal shops and industries.

About 250m west of here, along St Andrew's St and Charing Cross is the mazelike early-14th-century town house **Strangers' Hall** ( ☎ 01603-667229; adult/child £3.20/1.75; ⏰ 10.30am-4.30pm Wed & Sat), with atmospheric rooms furnished in period styles from Tudor to Victorian. Another remarkable medieval building, originally used as a trading hall, **Dragon Hall** ( ☎ 01603-663922; www.dragonhall.org; 115-123 King St; adult/child £5/3; ⏰ 10am-5pm Mon-Fri, 11am-4pm Sun) has a stunning crown-post roof and timber-framed great hall from 1430.

## SAINSBURY CENTRE FOR VISUAL ARTS

Housed in the first major building by Norman Foster, now the darling of Britain's architectural set, the **Sainsbury Centre** ( ☎ 01603-593199; www.scva.org.uk; admission free; ⏰ 10am-5pm Tue & Thu-Sun, to 8pm Wed) is the most important centre for the arts in East Anglia. Filled with an eclectic collection of works by Picasso, Moore, Degas and Bacon, displayed beside art from Africa, the Pacific and the Americas, it also houses changing exhibitions that cover everything from local heritage to international art movements.

To get here take bus 25/26/27 from Castle Meadow (20 minutes).

## Tours

The tourist office organises a dizzying array of guided **city walks** (adult/child £4/1.50) between March and October, with daily walks from June to September. Walks depart at 11.30am or 2pm from the office. Check for up-to-date details on www.visitnorwich.co.uk/blue -badge.aspx. **City Sightseeing** ( ☎ 0871 666 000; www.city-sightseeing.com; adult/child £8/4; ⏰ hourly 10.15am-4.15pm Apr-Oct) runs a hop-on hop-off bus service stopping at nine destinations around the city centre including city hall. You can take a similar tour by road train with **Discover Norwich** ( ☎ 01603-440015; www.discovernorwich.com;

adult/child £4/2) from Easter to October, while **Broads Boatrains** ( ☎ 01603-701701; www.cityboats.co.uk; 1hr city cruise adult/child £8.50/6.50) runs a variety of cruises from Griffin Lane, Station Quay, and Elm Hill Quay.

## Sleeping

### BUDGET

Norwich has a dearth of budget accommodation, and floral-patterned B&Bs that have seen better days are your only choice in this price category. You'll find most of them around the train station or outside the ring road.

**Edmar Lodge** ( ☎ 01603-615599; www.edmarlodge .co.uk; 64 Earlham Rd; s/d from £38/43; P 🖥 wi-fi) Although the rooms here are somewhat dated, the facilities are modern with en suite bathrooms, flat-screen TVs, DVD players and free wi-fi. It's a 10-minute walk from town but worth the trip.

**Eaton Bower** ( ☎ 01603-462204; www.eatonbower .co.uk; 20 Mile End Rd; s/d from £40/50; P 🖥 wi-fi) A little out of town but worth the effort, this small B&B has a choice of cosy rooms with subtle patterns and traditional styling. En suite bathrooms, free wi-fi, private parking and a touch of period character make it one of the best bets in this price range.

### MIDRANGE & TOP END

**Beaufort Lodge** ( ☎ 01603-667402; www.beaufortlodge .com; 60-62 Earlham Rd; s/d £45/60; P 🖥 ) Giant windows wash the rooms in this Victorian house with light, and the spacious bedrooms feature pretty fabrics and wallpapers in period style. The effect is bright and airy, with tasteful traditional touches, en suite bathrooms and plenty of space. It's a great deal and just a 10-minute walk from town.

**Gothic House** ( ☎ 01603-631879; www.gothic -house-norwich.com; King's Head Yard, Magdalen St; s/d £55/90; P 🖥 wi-fi) Set in a quiet courtyard in the heart of the city, this Grade II Regency house has two immaculate rooms with faithful period decor. Each has a private bathroom, great character and buckets of charm.

**ourpick By Appointment** ( ☎ 01603-630730; www .byappointmentnorwich.co.uk; 25-29 St George's St; s/d incl breakfast from £70/110; 🖥 ) This fabulously theatrical and delightfully eccentric B&B occupies three heavy-beamed 15th-century merchants' houses, also home to a labyrinthine restaurant well known for its classic English fare.

Its antique furniture, creaky charm and superb breakfasts make this well worth booking in advance.

**Georgian House Hotel** ( ☎ 01603-615655; www .georgian-hotel.co.uk; 32-34 Unthank Rd; s/d from £90/115; P 🖥 wi-fi) A rambling, elegant Victorian house turned hotel, this place has a choice of spacious, modern rooms decked out in contemporary style. There's a large tree-filled garden and a popular restaurant (mains £12 to £18).

## Eating

Norwich has a great choice of places to eat with plenty of options for vegetarians.

### BUDGET

**Greenhouse** ( ☎ 01603-631007; www.greenhousetrust .co.uk; 42-48 Bethel St; snacks & mains £3.50-6; 🕙 10am-5pm Tue-Sat) This organic, free-trade, vegetarian/vegan cafe is bound to leave you feeling wholesome with a menu of simple dishes, noticeboards crammed with posters for community events, and a lovely vine-covered, herb-planted terrace.

**ourpick Pulse Cafe** ( ☎ 01603-765562; Labour in Vain Yard, Guildhall Hill; mains £4.50-7.50; 🕙 10am-6.30pm Mon, 10am-10pm Tue & Wed, 10am-11pm Thu-Sat, 11.30am-4pm Sun) This funky lounge bar in the old firestation stables serves a bumper crop of hearty vegetarian dishes from Thai curries to smoked tofu and mushroom stroganoff, and leek and potato pie. There's also a great choice of sambos, organic ciders and beers and scrummy deserts. Eat in the tranquil courtyard or in the stylish upstairs lounge.

**Waffle House** ( ☎ 01603-612790; www.wafflehouse .co.uk; 39 St Giles St; waffles £5-9; 🕙 10am-10pm Mon-Sat, 11am-10pm Sun) Pop in for a crisp and light Belgian waffle with sweet or savoury toppings at this down-to-earth and friendly cafe beloved by Norwich families, students and professionals. Organic and free-range ingredients are used to concoct such delicacies as vegetable and cashew stir-fry and a stunning chocolate mousse.

**Library** ( ☎ 01603-616606; 4a Guildhall Hill; 1/2/3 courses £6/8/10.50; 🕙 closed Sun dinner) Set in a 19th-century library complete with original shelving, this chilled brassiere is a great spot for a good-value lunch. The menu is heavy on meat and fish with dishes cooked in a nifty wood-fired grill, while the interior is sleek and stylish with exhibitions of work by contemporary local artists.

## MIDRANGE

**Pinocchio's** ( ☎ 01603-613318; 11 St Benedict's St; mains £7-8; ✆ noon-2pm Tue-Sat, 5-11pm Mon-Sat) This bubbly Italian brasserie has a cheerful modern interior with plenty of quirky features including a giant modern mural. The menu features the usual array of pizzas and pastas as well as some top-notch specials including slow-cooked wild boar with juniper, orange and thyme. There's live music on Monday and Thursday evenings when it's best to book ahead.

**Elm Hill Brasserie** ( ☎ 01603-624847; www.elmhill brasserie.co.uk; 2 Elm Hill; mains £11-16; ✆ closed Sun) On the corner of the city's most famous street, this simple and elegant restaurant is bathed with light from its giant windows. Scrubbed wooden floors, contemporary style, a relaxed atmosphere and a menu of unfussy, classic French dishes made from seasonal, local ingredients has the punters coming in droves.

**Tatlers** ( ☎ 01603-766670; www.tatlers.com; 21 Tombland; set lunch £14-18, dinner mains £12-17; ✆ closed Sun) This converted Victorian town house is home to one of the city's best eateries, where local suppliers and ingredients are as important as the final menu. The truly divine dishes are modern English with a strong French influence and are served in a series of unpretentious dining rooms. The set lunch is an excellent-value choice but book in advance.

## Drinking

It was once said that Norwich had a pub for every day of the year and although that may not be completely true, there's certainly plenty of choice. You'll find hip and trendy or quaint and traditional pubs all across the city centre, but start your quest in Tombland or St Benedict's St for a taste of what's on offer.

**Adam & Eve's** ( ☎ 01603-667423; www.adamand evenorwich.co.uk; Bishopsgate) A 13th-century brewhouse built to quench the thirst of cathedral builders, this is now Norwich's oldest-surviving pub, and an adorable little sunken-floored gem. It's a tiny place just loaded with character and has a pleasant outdoor courtyard.

**Ten Bells** ( ☎ 01603-667833; 76 St Benedict's St) This is the kind of faded 18th-century pub where people feel instantly at ease, calmed by the real ales, mellow red velvet and quirky memorabilia, and amused by the red phone booth in the corner. It also fancies itself as an intellectuals' hang-out, with poetry readings and arts-school regulars.

**Erpingham House** ( ☎ 01603-630090; www.kitch enandbar.co.uk; 22 Tombland; ✆ noon-midnight Mon-Thu, noon-2am Fri & Sat) If you're looking for something more modern, this stylish bar and brasserie is set in a grand old house by the cathedral. There's a sleek interior and plenty of wine and cocktail-drinking luvvies to mingle with.

## Entertainment

Norwich has a flourishing arts scene and pulsating weekend nightlife. For information on what's on, from ballet to boozing try www.norwichtonight.com or for live music, www.norfolkgigs.co.uk.

### NIGHTCLUBS

Nightclubs seem to cluster around the Prince of Wales Rd and run from 9pm or 10pm to at least 2am.

**Mercy** ( ☎ 01603-627666; www.mercynightclub.com; 86 Prince of Wales Rd; admission free-£8; ✆ Thu-Sat) A former cinema complete with mock-marble entrance and Renaissance-inspired decor, Mercy is a massive club with three dance floors, huge projection screens and DJs that favour R&B and club classics.

**Optic** ( ☎ 01603-617977; www.optic-club.co.uk; 50 Prince of Wales Rd; admission free-£8.50; ✆ Mon & Wed-Sat) This place markets itself as Norwich's upmarket club, with a strict dress code and a dislike for Burberry, facial piercings and excessive tattoos. Club nights feature everything from '70s funk to chart-topping anthems.

### THEATRE

**St Andrew's and Blackfriars Hall** ( ☎ 01603-628477; www.standrewshall.co.uk; St Andrew's Plain) Once home to Dominican Blackfriars, this spookily Gothic-looking place now serves as an impressive civic centre where concerts, markets and festivals are held.

**Theatre Royal** ( ☎ 01603-630000; www.theatreroyal norwich.co.uk; Theatre St) Features programs by touring drama, opera and ballet companies.

**Norwich Arts Centre** ( ☎ 01603-660352; www.norwi chartscentre.co.uk; St Benedict's St) Also in a medieval church; has a wide-ranging program of alternative drama, concerts, dance and jazz.

## Getting There & Away

**Norwich International Airport** ( ☎ 0844 748 0112; www .norwichinternational.com) is just 4 miles north of town, and has cheap flights to Europe and several British destinations. Bus 11 runs from the airport to the bus and rail stations hourly.

**EAST ANGLIA**

National Express runs buses to London (£14.90, three hours, five daily). First Eastern Counties runs hourly buses to King's Lynn (1½ hours) and Cromer (one hour). There are twice-hourly services to Great Yarmouth (40 minutes).

There are twice-hourly train services to Ely (£13.50, one hour), hourly services to Cambridge (£12.40, 1¼ hours), as well as regular links to Peterborough (£15, 1½ hours). Twice-hourly trains also go to London Liverpool St (£40, two hours). For city cabs, call **Loyal Taxis** ( ☎ 01603-619619).

If you're driving, the city has six Park & Ride locations (£3.30 per vehicle).

## NORFOLK BROADS

A mesh of navigable slow-moving rivers, freshwater lakes, wild water meadows, fens, bogs and saltwater marshes make up the Norfolk Broads, a 125-mile stretch of lock-free waterways and the county's most beautiful attraction. The Broads are home to some of the UK's rarest plants and animals and are protected as a national park, with flourishing nature reserves and bird sanctuaries attracting gangs of birdwatchers. But the area's appeal reaches far further, with boaters, families and those in search of scenic tranquillity arriving in droves.

Despite the area's popularity, it's easy to lose yourself in the hypnotic peace of the waterways. A boat is by far the best vantage point and anyone fond of the water will undoubtedly want to linger here. Apart from the waterways and the wildlife there are restored wind mills, medieval churches and glorious gardens to explore. Walkers and cyclists will also find a web of trails crossing the region, and with the Broads highest point, How Hill, just 12m above sea level, they're accessible for all.

Around How Hill you'll find many of the picturesque wind pumps first built by 12th-century peat-cutters to drain the marshland. As the peat was dug out the holes created filled with water and created a landscape of interconnected lakes and rivers. The pumps returned water to the rivers and helped manage drainage in the area. In no other area of England has human effort changed the natural landscape so dramatically.

### Orientation

The Broads forms a triangle, with the Norwich–Cromer road, the Norwich–Lowestoft road and the coastline as the three sides.

Wroxham, on the A1151 from Norwich, and Potter Heigham, on the A1062 from Wroxham, are the main centres. Along the way there are plenty of waterside pubs, villages and market towns where you can stock up on provisions, and stretches of river where you can feel you are the only person around.

### Information

Details on scores of conservation centres and birdwatching hides can be found through the **Broads Authority** ( ☎ 01603-610734; www.broads -authority.gov.uk). There's more information on Norfolk Broads at www.norfolkbroads.com and the RSPB at www.rspb.org.uk.

### Getting Around

You can hire a variety of launches, from large cabin cruisers to little craft with outboards, for a couple of hours messing about on the water. No previous experience is necessary, but remember to stay on the right-hand side of the river, that the rivers are tidal and to stick to the speed limit – you can be prosecuted for speeding.

You can hire boats from **Blakes** ( ☎ 0870 2202 498; www.blakes.co.uk) and **Hoseasons** ( ☎ 01502-502588; www.hoseasons.co.uk) among others. Depending on boat size, facilities and season, a boat for two to four people costs around £450 to £850 for a week including fuel and insurance.

For shorter trips, boat yards around Wroxham and Potter Heigham hire out boats by the hour or day. Peak-season prices start from £30 for two hours, £55 for four hours and £80 for one day. Alternatively, **Broads Tours** (www.broads.co.uk) Wroxham ( ☎ 01603-782207; The Bridge); Potter Heigham ( ☎ 01692-670711; Broads Haven) runs 1½-hour pleasure trips (adult/child £6.50/5) from April to October.

Bike and canoe hire are available from the **Broads Authority** ( ☎ 01603-782281; www.broads-author ity.gov.uk) at a variety of locations from Easter to October. Bikes cost £11 per day (you can also hire child seats and tandems) while Canadian canoes cost £25 per day or £15 per half-day.

## GREAT YARMOUTH
### pop 90,810

On first glance Great Yarmouth is little more than a tatty, traditional seaside resort complete with neon-lit esplanade, jingling amusement arcades, grim greasy spoons, crazy golf and cheek-by-jowl hotels. But scratch under the surface and you'll find the old town rich in history and heritage.

The **tourist office** ( ☎ 01493-846345; www.great -yarmouth.co.uk; 25 Marine Pde; ❂ 9.30am-5.30pm Easter-Oct, 9.30am-4.30pm Sat & Sun Nov-Easter) is on the seafront and can point you towards the lovely Weavers Way (p425) walking trail, which cuts into the Broads from here.

Most absorbing of Yarmouth's museums is **Time & Tide** ( ☎ 01493-743930; www.museums.norfolk .gov.uk; Blackfriars Rd; adult/child £5/4.15; ❂ 10am-5pm Easter-Oct, 10am-4pm Mon-Fri, noon-4pm Sat & Sun Nov-Mar), in a Victorian herring-curing works. It tackles everything from prehistory to penny arcades and maritime heritage, and reconstructs typical 17th-century row houses. There are plenty of activities for children.

You can see how life was in Great Yarmouth's **Row Houses** (EH; ☎ 01493-857900; South Quay; adult/child £3.70/1.90; ❂ noon-5pm Apr-Sep) in these preserved houses reconstructed as they would have been in 1870 and 1942. Displays show how life was for tenants over the centuries, from wealthy merchants to tenement families.

A cluster of other museums surround historic South Quay. The 16th-century **Elizabethan House Museum** (NT; ☎ 01493-855746; 4 South Quay; adult/child £3.20/1.75; ❂ 10am-5pm Mon-Fri, 1.15-5pm Sat & Sun Easter-Oct) is a fine merchant's house faithfully reconstructed, while around the corner, the **Tolhouse Museum** ( ☎ 01493-745526; Tolhouse St; adult/child £3.20/1.75; ❂ 10am-5pm Mon-Fri, 1.15-5pm Sat & Sun Easter-Oct) is a medieval gaol. The **Norfolk Nelson Museum** ( ☎ 01493-850698; www .nelson-museum.co.uk; 26 South Quay; adult/child £3.20/1.90; ❂ 10am-5pm Mon-Fri, 1-4pm Sun Apr-Oct, to 4pm Nov & Jan-Mar, closed Sat) celebrates the life, times, romances and death of the one-eyed hero of Trafalgar, who was a regular visitor to Great Yarmouth.

B&Bs are everywhere, especially chock-a-block Trafalgar St, and cost from £20 to £40 per person. One of the best is **No 78** ( ☎ 01493-850001; www.no78.co.uk; 78 Marine Pde; s £35, d £45-80; 🖵 ), a chic, modern place that bucks the chintzy local trends and offers really beautiful, bright, contemporary rooms with an eco-conscience.

There are hourly buses (40 minutes) and trains (£5.20, 33 minutes) to Norwich.

# NORTH COAST NORFOLK

The north coast of Norfolk has something of a split personality, with a string of busy seaside towns with brash attractions and hoards of people clustering along the eastern end ,and a collection of small villages with trendy

gastropubs and boutique hotels littering the western end. In between sit stunning beaches, and the marshy coast that attracts hoards of visiting seabirds.

## Cromer
**pop 3800**
Once a fashionable Victorian coastal resort, Cromer is now firmly part of the bucket-and-spade brigade with a wonderful stretch of safe, sandy beachfront, family entertainment on the pier, a glut of fish 'n' chip shops and plenty of trashy amusement arcades. The town has recently seen some major investment though and may yet return to its former glory.

Stay long enough to wander off the beach and you'll find the quaint **Cromer Museum** ( ☎ 01263-513543; www.museums.norfolk.gov.uk; East Cottages, Tucker St; adult/under 16yr £2.90/1.75; ❂ 10am-5pm Mon-Sat, 2-5pm Sun Mar-Oct, 10am-4pm Mon-Sat Nov-Feb). Set in a Victorian fisherman's cottage, the museum depicts life in the town in the 19th century.

If you wish to stay overnight the superb **Captain's House** ( ☎ 01263-515434; www.captains-house .co.uk; 5 The Crescent; d £70-140; 🅿 🖵 ) is a bright and airy Georgian house with lovingly decorated rooms.

Cromer has direct trains to Norwich hourly Monday to Saturday and services every two hours on Sunday (£5.20, 44 minutes).

## Cley Marshes
One of England's premier birdwatching sites, Cley (pronounced Cly) Marshes is a mecca for twitchers with over 300 species of bird recorded here. There's a **visitors centre** ( ☎ 01263-740008; www.norfolkwildlifetrust.org.uk; adult/child £3.75/ free; ❂ 10am-5pm Apr-Oct, to 4pm Nov-Mar) built on high ground and a series of hides hidden amid the golden reedbeds.

If you wish to stay in the area, the stunning 17th-century **Cley Windmill** ( ☎ 01263-740209; www .cleymill.co.uk; d £78-145) is a wonderfully quirky place with nine bedrooms, a circular living room and great views across the marshes.

## Blakeney Point
The pretty village of **Blakeney** was once a busy fishing and trading port before its harbour silted up. These days it's a good place to jump aboard boat trips out to a 500-strong colony of common and grey seals that live, bask and breed on nearby Blakeney Point. The hour-long trips (adult/child £8/4) run

daily from April to October, but the best time to come is between June and August when the common seals pup. Trips run either from Blakeney Harbour or nearby Morston.

**Beans Boat Trips** ( ☎ 01263-740505; www.beansboattrips.co.uk; Morston)

**Bishop's Boats** ( ☎ 01263-740753; www.norfolkseal trips.co.uk; Blakeney Harbour)

**Temples Seal Trips** ( ☎ 01263-740791; www.sealtrips .co.uk; Morston)

## Wells-next-the-Sea
pop 2451

Thronged with crowds on holiday weekends, this harbour town has plenty of seaside tat on the waterfront but a surprisingly tranquil old town set back from the sea. Attractive Georgian houses and flint cottages surround a large green, while kids bounce between toy shops and ice-cream parlours, and pensioners check out the curios.

The small **tourist office** ( ☎ 0871 200 3071; www .visitnorthnorfolk.com; Staithe St; ☑ 10am-5pm Mon-Sat, 10am-4pm Sun Mar–mid-Jul, Sep & Oct) can help with all inquiries and information on the **narrow-gauge steam train** ( ☎ 01328-711630; www.wellswalsingham railway.co.uk; adult/child return £7.50/6) that chuffs 5 miles to **Little Walsingham**, where there are shrines and a ruined abbey that have drawn pilgrims since medieval times. The train trip takes 30 minutes and there are three to five departures from daily April to October.

If you fancy staying overnight, the **Wells YHA** ( ☎ 0870 770 6084; www.yha.org.uk; Church Plains; dm £15.95; ☑ ) has simple rooms in an or-nately gabled early-20th-century church hall. Alternatively try the tranquil **Fern Cottage** ( ☎ 01328-710306; www.ferncottage.co.uk; Standard Rd; s/d £60/80; ☑ ). Set in a beautiful Georgian house, the rooms here retain some period character with open fireplaces and cast-iron beds.

For food the **Globe Inn** ( ☎ 01328-710206; www .globeatwells.co.uk; mains 8-14; ☑ noon-2.30pm & 6-9pm) is a good bet. It's on the green and also has a selection of bright, spacious rooms with contemporary style (£65 to £110).

The Coast Hopper bus goes through Wells roughly hourly in summer on its way between Hunstanton (50 minutes) and Sheringham (45 minutes).

## Wells-next-the-Sea to King's Lynn

Once past Wells the atmosphere changes: gone are the tacky seaside resorts and the crowds of weekenders and back come the beautiful Norfolk villages, their flint cottages and narrow streets awash with coloured render and beautiful flowering gardens. Along this stretch of the Norfolk coast are a string of small, quiet villages that seem largely untouched by the tourist crowds, save for the wonderful choice of gastropubs, trendy B&Bs and boutique hotels.

### HOLKHAM

The pretty village of Holkham is well worth a stop for its imposing stately home, incredible stretch of beach and for the pleasure of walking its picturesque streets lined with elegant buildings.

The main draw here is **Holkham Hall** ( ☎ 01328-710227; www.holkham.co.uk; hall & museum adult/child £10/5; ☑ noon-5pm Sun-Thu Easter & Jun-Sep), a grand Palladian mansion set in a vast deer park designed by Capability Brown. The slightly industrial-looking brick mansion is the ancestral seat of the Earls of Leicester and has a sumptuous interior, dripping with gilt, tapestries, fine furniture and family history. The Marble Hall (it's actually alabaster), magnificent state rooms and giant kitchen shouldn't be missed. You can also visit the **Bygones Museum** (museum only adult/child £5/2.50) in the stable block. It showcases everything from mechanical toys to agricultural equipment and vintage cars.

For many, Holkham's true delight is not the stately home but the pristine 3-mile **beach** that meanders along the shore. Regularly voted one of England's best, it's a popular spot with walkers but the vast expanse of sand swallows people up and gives a real sense of isolation with giant skies stretching overhead. The only place to park for access to the beach is Lady Anne's Drive (parking £3.50).

Recover after a jaunt on the beach with tea or a snack at the **Marsh Larder** ( ☎ 01328-711285; Main Rd; ☑ 10am-5pm) in the stunning Ancient House, or have a more substantial meal at the much-lauded **Victoria Arms** ( ☎ 01328-711008; www .victoriaatholkham.co.uk; Park Rd; mains £12-17; ☑ noon-2.30pm daily, 7-9pm Mon-Fri, 7-9.30pm Sat & Sun). The menu here is modern British with an emphasis on local ingredients. The Victoria also has a choice of individually decorated rooms (£120 to £170) with a relaxed, colonial feel. You'd be well advised to book ahead.

The Coast Hopper bus goes through Holkham roughly hourly in summer on its way between Hunstanton (40 minutes) and Sheringham (55 minutes).

## BURNHAM DEEPDALE & AROUND

Littered with pretty little villages and a host of ancient watering holes, trendy gastropubs and boutique hotels, this part of the Norfolk coast is one of the most appealing.

In-the-know backpackers and walkers flock to Burnham Deepdale, a tiny village flanked by the Norfolk Coastal Path, surrounded by beaches, reedy marshes and gentle cycling routes. It's also home to one of the country's best backpacker hostels. **Deepdale Farm** ( ☎ 01485-210256; www.deepdalefarm.co.uk; camping per adult/child £8/4, dm £9.50-12.50, tw £28-42, tepees for 2/6 £60/90; **P** **Q**) is an ecofriendly backpackers' haven with small and stylish en suite dorms in converted 17th-century stables, camping space with Native American-style tepees, a coffee shop, laundry, barbecue and **tourist office** ( ☎ 01485-210256; ☼ 10am-4pm Apr-Sep, closed Tue-Wed Oct-Mar).

Just west of the hostel is the **White Horse** ( ☎ 01485-210262; www.whitehorsebrancaster.co.uk; mains £10-14; ☼ lunch & dinner; **P** **Q**), an award-winning gastropub with a menu strong on fish and seafood.

Just inland at the lovely Georgian town of Burnham Market you'll find plenty of elegant old buildings, flint cottages, delis and independent retailers. It's another excellent base with a trio of accommodation options to suit any taste. The **Hoste Arms** ( ☎ 01328-738777; www.hostearms.co.uk; The Green; d £95-305; **P** ) and its sister properties the **Vine House** (d £125-280) and the **Railway Inn** (d £74-140) offer everything from over-the-top classical rooms to trendy, contemporary suites.

Continuing west along the coast is the quiet village of Thornham, home to the **Orange Tree** ( ☎ 01485-512213; www.theorangetreethornham .co.uk; High St; mains £10-15; ☼ bar 11am-11pm Mon-Sat, to 10.30pm Sun, food noon-2pm & 6.30-9pm Mon-Thu, noon-2.30pm & 6.30-9.30pm Sat, noon-4pm & 6.30-8.30pm Sun), an old world pub with a modern interior and excellent food, and the **Lifeboat Inn** ( ☎ 01485-512236; www.lifeboatinn.co.uk; Ship Lane; 3-course dinner £29; ☼ bar 11am-midnight, food available noon-2.30pm & 6.30-9.30pm), a 16th-century inn laden with character and famous for its locally sourced dishes.

The Coast Hopper bus stops outside Deepdale Farm roughly hourly in summer on its run between Sheringham (65 minutes) and Hunstanton (25 minutes); it also goes less frequently to King's Lynn (one hour). Ask at the tourist office for timetables.

# KING'S LYNN

pop 34,565

Once one of England's most important ports, the area around King's Lynn's medieval harbour is awash with cobbled lanes and narrow streets flanked by old merchants' houses. Unfortunately, the rest of the town is not so pretty, with modern architectural blunders and high-street chain stores blighting the landscape. Stick to the waterfront though and you'll get some sense of just how important the town once was.

Long labelled 'the Warehouse on the Wash', the port was once so busy that it was said you could cross from one side of the River Great Ouse to the other by simply stepping from boat to boat. Something of the salty port-town tang can still be felt in old King's Lynn, though the petite modern-day port barely passes as a shadow of its former self.

## Orientation

Old King's Lynn huddles along the eastern bank of the river. The train station is on its eastern side, while unexciting modern King's Lynn and the bus station are between them. Three markets still take place weekly on Tuesday, Friday and Saturday. The biggest is the Tuesday market, held in er, Tuesday Market Pl, while the others are conducted in front of St Margaret's Church.

## Information

Banks and ATMs can be found around Tuesday Market Pl.

**Post office** ( ☎ 01553-692185; Baxter's Plain)

**Tourist office** ( ☎ 01553-763044; www.visitwest norfolk.com; ☼ 10am-5pm Mon-Sat, noon-5pm Sun Apr-Sep, 10.30am-4pm Mon-Sat, noon-4pm Sun Oct-Mar) In the Custom House (Purfleet Quay). Guided walks ( ☎ 01553-774297; adult/child £3/1) of historic Lynn start from here between May and October. The walks take 1½ to two hours.

## Sights

Start your tour of Old Lynn at grand **St Margaret's Church** which bears flood-level marks by the west door. Inside are two extraordinarily elaborate Flemish brasses and a remarkable 17th-century moon dial, which tells the tide, not the time.

Wander across Margaret Plain to take a look at 15th-century **St Margaret's House**, once the warehouse of the Hanseatic League (the

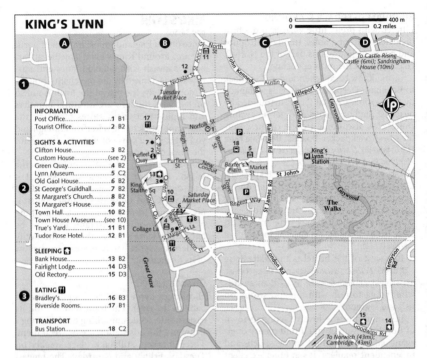

**KING'S LYNN**

0 ——— 400 m
0 ——— 0.2 miles

**INFORMATION**
Post Office..........................1 B1
Tourist Office......................2 B2

**SIGHTS & ACTIVITIES**
Clifton House......................3 B2
Custom House...................(see 2)
Green Quay........................4 B2
Lynn Museum......................5 C2
Old Gaol House..................6 B2
St George's Guildhall..........7 B2
St Margaret's Church...........8 B2
St Margaret's House............9 B2
Town Hall..........................10 B2
Town House Museum.....(see 10)
True's Yard.......................11 B1
Tudor Rose Hotel..............12 B1

**SLEEPING**
Bank House.......................13 B2
Fairlight Lodge..................14 D3
Old Rectory......................15 D3

**EATING**
Bradley's..........................16 B3
Riverside Rooms................17 B1

**TRANSPORT**
Bus Station.......................18 C2

Northern European merchants' group), then loop around the corner to **Green Quay** ( ☎ 01553-818500; www.thegreenquay.co.uk; South Quay; admission free; ☒ 9am-5pm), a museum charting life in the Wash. Exhibitions look at the wildlife, flora and fauna of the area and the effects of climate change.

Turn right on College Lane to explore the old cells and gawp at the town's priceless civic treasures in the **Old Gaol House** ( ☎ 01553-774297; Saturday Market Pl; adult/child £2.90/2.10; ☒ 10am-5pm Mon-Sat Easter-Oct, 10am-4pm Tue-Sat Nov-Easter); its pride and joy is the breathtaking 650-year-old King John Cup, exquisitely decorated with scenes of hunting and hawking.

Next door is the flint-and-brick **town hall**, dating back to 1421, and the petite **Town House Museum** ( ☎ 01553-773450; 46 Queen St; adult/under 10yr £3/1.65; ☒ 10am-5pm Mon-Sat May-Sep) which deals with the history of the town.

Continue along Queen St past **Clifton House**, with its barley-sugar columns and strange merchants' watchtower, to **Purfleet Quay**, in its heyday the principal harbour. The odd boxy building with the lantern tower is the 17th-century **Custom House**, which houses the tourist office. Inside are displays on the merchants and smugglers of the Lynn in times past.

A short hop north again is the biggest 15th-century guildhall in England. **St George's Guildhall** has been variously incarnated as a warehouse, courthouse and armoury and now contains art galleries, a theatre and eateries. Then topping King St is the roomy **Tuesday Market Place** flanked by handsome old buildings.

Turn right into St Nicholas St to see the **Tudor Rose Hotel**, a late-15th-century house with its original main door. North of here, on the corner of St Ann's St, is **True's Yard** ( ☎ 01553-770479; www.truesyard.co.uk; North St; adult/child £3/1.50; ☒ 10am-4pm Tue-Sat). Housed in two restored fishermen's cottages, the museum explores Lynn's maritime past and the lives fishermen endured.

From here head back towards the centre of town to visit the newly revamped **Lynn Museum** ( ☎ 01553-775001; www.museums.norfolk.gov .uk; Market St; adult/child £3/1.65 Apr-Sep, free Oct-Mar; ☒ 10am-5pm Tue-Sat), home to the Seahenge gallery, which displays a 4000-year-old timber circle and explores the lives of the people who created it.

## Festivals

July's **King's Lynn Festival** ( ☎ 01553-767557; www
.kingslynnfestival.org.uk) is East Anglia's most important cultural gathering. It offers a diverse
program of concerts and recitals of all kinds
from medieval ballads to opera. The main
festival is preceded by a free rock-and-pop
bash, **Festival Too** (www.festivaltoo.co.uk), now one
of Europe's biggest free festivals.

## Sleeping

**Fairlight Lodge** ( ☎ 01553-762234; www.fairlightlodge
.co.uk; 79 Goodwins Rd; s/d incl breakfast £35/52; Ⓟ )
Simple, fresh rooms with subtle florals and
plenty of little extras such as homemade biscuits make this B&B excellent value. Not all
rooms are en suite but there's a pretty garden,
great breakfasts and friendly hosts.

**Old Rectory** ( ☎ 01553-768544; www.theoldrectory
-kinslynn.com; 33 Goodwins Rd; s/d incl breakfast £38/52; Ⓟ )
Set in an elegant former rectory, this B&B offers tastefully decorated rooms with en suite
bathrooms. Just a short walk from town via
parkland, this place also offers free pick-up
from the bus and rail stations.

**Bank House** ( ☎ 01553-660492; www.thebankhouse
.co.uk; Kings Staithe Sq; s £80-90, d £100-120, all incl breakfast;
Ⓟ ▣ ) This outstanding B&B has ticks in all
the right boxes: history, location, atmosphere,
comfort and welcome. On the waterfront near
the tourist office, this 18th-century former
bank is now an elegantly furnished town
house with five hotel-standard rooms, mixing
original features and modern furnishings.

## Eating

**Riverside Rooms** ( ☎ 01553-773134; 27 King St; mains
£12-19; Ⓥ lunch & dinner Mon-Sat) Overlooking the
water from a converted 15th-century warehouse, with criss-crossing beams overhead
and elegant white-linen tables below, this
place serves a confident but uninspired menu
of classic dishes.

**Bradley's** ( ☎ 01553-819888; www.bradleysbytheriver
.co.uk; 10 South Quay; mains £13-19; Ⓥ lunch & dinner
Mon-Sat, lunch Sun) Eat in the elegant Georgian
dining room at this riverside restaurant, or
relax at the bar with some lighter snacks
(£8); either way you're bound to be pleased
as this is probably the finest food the city
has to offer.

## Getting There & Away

King's Lynn is 43 miles north of Cambridge
on the A10. There are hourly trains from
Cambridge (£8.30, 48 minutes) and London
King's Cross (£25.90, two hours). First Eastern
Counties runs hourly buses to Norwich. Bus
29 goes to Hunstanton from where you can
catch the Coast Hopper service along the
north Norfolk coast.

## AROUND KING'S LYNN
### Castle Rising Castle

There's something bordering on ecclesiastical about the beautifully embellished keep
of this **castle** (EH; ☎ 01553-631330; www.castlerising
.co.uk; adult/child £4/2.50; Ⓥ 10am-6pm Apr-Oct, 10am-
4pm Wed-Sun Nov-Mar), built in 1138 and set in
the middle of a massive earthwork upon
which pheasants scurry about like guards.
So extravagant is the stonework that it's no
surprise to learn that it shares stonemasons
with some of East Anglia's finest cathedrals.
It was once the home of Queen Isabella, who
(allegedly) arranged the gruesome murder of
her husband, Edward II.

It's well worth the trip 4 miles northeast
of King's Lynn off the A149. Bus 41 runs
here (13 minutes) hourly from King's Lynn
bus station.

### Sandringham House

Royalists and those bemused by the English
sovereigns will have plenty to mull over at
this, the Queen's country **estate** ( ☎ 01553-
612908; www.sandringhamestate.co.uk; adult/child 5-15yr
£9/5, gardens & museum only £6/3.50; Ⓥ 11am-4.45pm
late-Mar–Oct unless royal family is in residence) set in 25
hectares of landscaped gardens and lakes,
and open to the hoi polloi when the court is
not at home.

Queen Victoria bought the estate in 1862
for her son, the Prince of Wales (later Edward
VII), but he promptly had it overhauled in
the style later named Edwardian. Visitors
can shuffle around the house's ground-floor
rooms, regularly used by the royal family,
then head out to the old stables, which house
a **museum** filled with diverse royal memorabilia including the superb vintage royal car
collection. Look out for the pet cemetery just
outside the museum. There are guided tours
of the gardens on Friday and Saturday at 11am
and 2pm.

Sandringham is 6 miles northeast of King's
Lynn off the B1440. First Eastern Counties
bus 411 or Coastliner run here from the
King's Lynn bus station (24 minutes, every
15 minutes.).

EAST ANGLIA

# The Midlands & the Marches

Those who aren't in the know may write off the Midlands as an industrial and cultural wasteland. But while the region does have more than its fair share of bleak industrial settlements, it also has important castles at Kenilworth and Warwick; dazzling cathedrals at Lichfield and Lincoln; Stratford-upon-Avon, a pilgrimage site for Shakespeare-lovers from around the world; and some of Britain's most beautiful countryside.

The landscape, from the wild open moorland of the Peak District to the rich farmland, rivers and long sandy coastline of Lincolnshire, is peppered with charming villages, country lanes and stately homes. Though many of the Midlands' cities aren't that attractive, they're full of infectious, cosmopolitan energy, and bubble over with influences from a hundred different nations.

A tranquil slice of England hugging the Welsh borders, the Marches are rich territory for hill-walkers, cyclists, history buffs and those in search of authentic rural life. Fairy-tale black-and-white villages hide down country lanes, venerable cathedrals grace Worcester and Hereford, the River Wye snakes through Herefordshire, attracting canoeists from across the county, and the excellent locally produced foods, ales and ciders attract numerous fans of their own. The Marches' peaceful landscapes and warm inhabitants belie a far more exciting past, however, and its rippling hills and farmland are strewn with battle-scarred castles and time-worn ruins – testimony to centuries of turbulent fighting.

## HIGHLIGHTS

- Walking or cycling the many footpaths and trails in the **Peak District National Park** (p465)

- Enjoying first-rate shopping then taking in a balti in the vibrant city of **Birmingham** (p474)

- Visiting exquisite **Hardwick Hall** (p463), one of the country's finest Elizabethan mansions

- Marvelling at the vast facade of Lincoln's **cathedral** (p448) in the historic hilltop town

- Watching Shakespeare's stories come to life at **Stratford-upon-Avon** (p487)

- Exploring the enormous **Rutland Water** (p445) area by bicycle

- POPULATION: 9.7 MILLION
- AREA: 10,960 SQ MILES
- GALLONS OF CIDER PRODUCED YEARLY IN HEREFORDSHIRE: 63 MILLION

## History

This region has seen its share of action over the centuries. In the Marches, territorial scuffles and all-out battles took place between feuding kingdoms along what is today the border separating England and Wales. In the 8th century the Anglo-Saxon King Offa of Mercia built an earthwork barricade along the border to attempt to quell the ongoing tension. It became known as Offa's Dyke, and much of it is still traceable as a very popular walking route today.

In an effort to subdue the Welsh and secure his new kingdom, William the Conqueror set up powerful, feudal barons – called Lords Marcher after the Anglo-Saxon word *mearc*, meaning 'boundary' – along the border, from where they repeatedly raided Wales, taking as much territory as possible under their control.

Meanwhile Birmingham, Staffordshire and Shropshire were making a name for themselves as centres of industry, from the wool trade to the metal, iron and coal industries. The region gradually became the most intensely industrialised in the country, giving birth to the Industrial Revolution at Shropshire in the 18th century.

## Orientation

It is perhaps easiest to orientate yourself here by motorways. The M1 winds north from London, demarcating the eastern half of the region and running parallel with a line of the East Midlands' major towns: Bedford, Northampton, Leicester, Derby and Nottingham, in that order. Heading north from London, the M40 passes Stratford-upon-Avon and Warwick on its way to the M42 and Birmingham in the centre of the Midlands. Routes spider out from Birmingham: the M6 runs east towards Coventry and the M1, and northwest up towards Wolverhampton, Stafford and Stoke-on-Trent; the M5 splits off at West Bromwich and heads down towards Worcester and Hereford; the M54 splits off at Wolverhampton to head over to Telford and Shrewsbury.

## Information

The **Heart of England Tourist Board** ( ☎ 01905-761100; www.visitheartofengland.com) has centralised tourist information for the region and is a good place to start your planning. **East Midlands Tourism** (www.enjoyenglandeastmidlands.com) is the official website for the East Midlands. Other helpful websites:

**Go Leicestershire** (www.goleicestershire.com)
**Peak District & Derbyshire** (www.visitpeakdistrict.com)
**Visit Nottinghamshire** (www.visitnottingham.com)
**Visit Lincolnshire** (www.visitlincolnshire.com)

## Activities

Regional tourist websites are packed with walking, cycling and sailing information, and tourist offices are stacked high with leaflets, maps and guides covering activities offered in the area.

### CYCLING

Derbyshire and the Peak District (p465) are full of country lanes for touring cyclists, and tracks and bridleways for mountain bikers – with something for every level of ability. Bikes can be hired at various points around the Peak District, especially in the areas where old railway lines have been converted into delightful walking and cycling tracks.

There are quiet country roads and purpose-built cycle ways in the National Forest in Leicestershire and you can hire bikes at Rutland Water in Oakham. Shropshire in particular is ideal for touring, and you can rent bicycles in Shrewsbury, Church Stretton, Ludlow, Ironbridge and Ledbury.

Areas apt for off-road biking include the woods of Hopton near Ludlow, as well as Eastridge near Shrewsbury. High-level riding on the Long Mynd above Church Stretton is also rewarding.

In Herefordshire, you'll find the **Ledbury Loop** – a 17-mile rural circuit based around the town of Ledbury (p501).

Tourist offices stock many free route leaflets, and you can also find them through the **National Cycle Network** (www.sustrans.org).

### WALKING

The Peak District National Park is one of the finest areas in England for walking (see p465). It's also home to the start of the **Pennine Way National Trail**, which leads keen walkers for 268 miles through Yorkshire and Northumberland into Scotland. Mammoth walking trails aside, the Peak District is criss-crossed with a vast network of paths for walkers. Ideal bases include the villages and towns of Buxton, Matlock Bath, Edale and Castleton, or the national-park centre at Fairholmes on the Derwent Reservoir.

## THE MIDLANDS & THE MARCHES

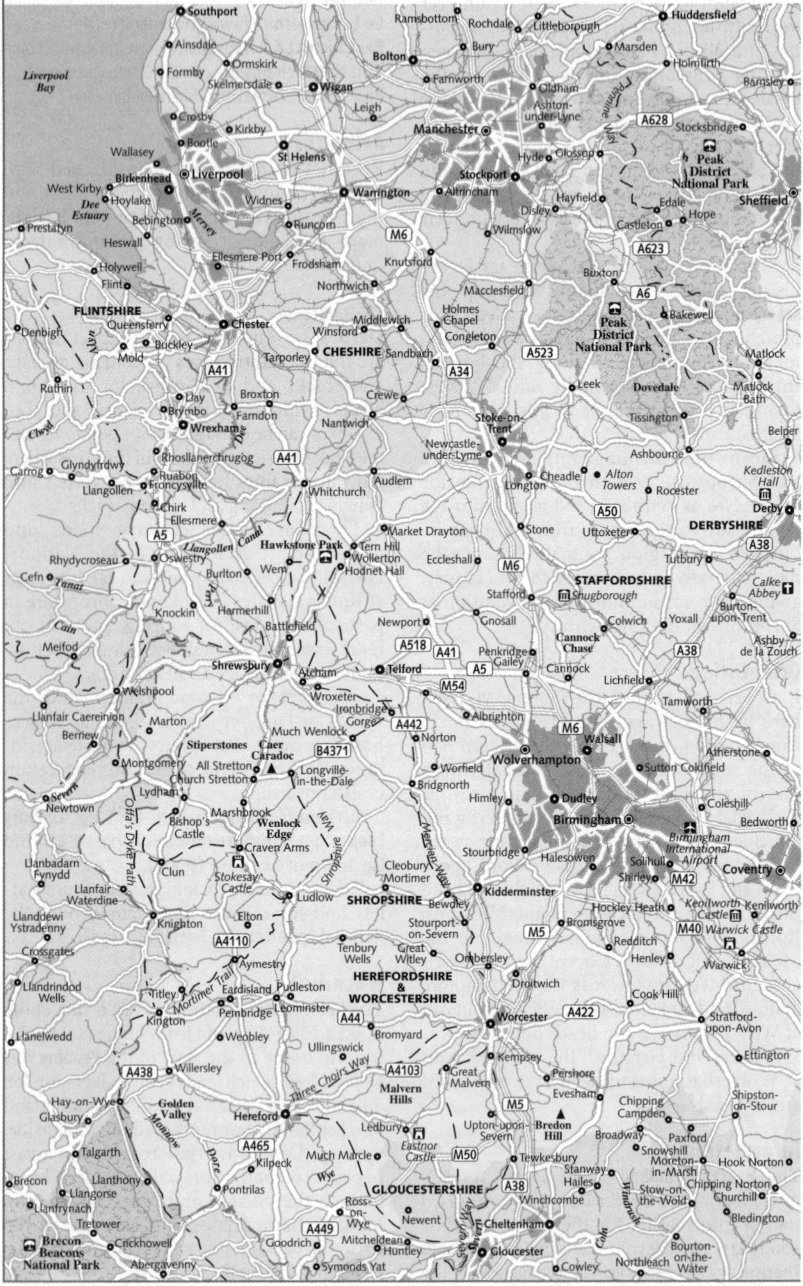

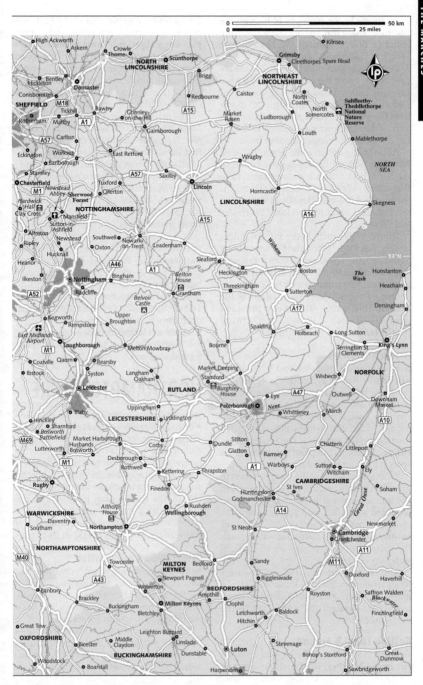

To follow in the footsteps of history, the 140-mile **Viking Way** (p446) trails from the Humber Bridge through the Lincolnshire Wolds to Oakham in Leicestershire.

One of many great routes on which to muddy your hiking boots, the glorious **Offa's Dyke** is a 177-mile national trail following an ancient earthen border defence. Running south–north from Chepstow to Prestatyn, it passes through some of the most spectacular scenery in Britain, but it's not for the inexperienced or unfit.

A less taxing option is the gentle 107-mile **Wye Valley Walk**, which follows the course of the River Wye from Chepstow upstream to Rhayader in Wales. Another firm favourite is the beautiful 100-mile **Three Choirs Way** linking the cathedral cities of Hereford, Worcester and Gloucester.

Shorter walks include the famous ridges of Wenlock Edge (p509) and the lovely Long Mynd (p510). These are in turn swallowed by the circular 136-mile **Shropshire Way**, which loops from Shrewsbury south to Ludlow.

One of the loveliest spots of all is the Malvern Hills (p496), offering easy paths and breathtaking views on the boundary between Worcestershire and Herefordshire.

### OTHER ACTIVITIES

Both easy-grade canoeing and white-water fun can be had at Symonds Yat (p501) on the River Wye, while the river gorge's rocky buttresses are also a popular rock-climbing spot. The Long Mynd is renowned for its gliding and paragliding, with facilities in Church Stretton. Or for something completely different, tourist offices can point you towards hot spots for mountain boarding.

A canal boat is one of the most fun ways to get active, with the metropolis of Birmingham the unlikely epicentre. Get a group of you on board with bikes, and you can enjoy the canal-side paths by wheel or by foot at your leisure, as you gently chug your way through the country's massive network of artificial waterways (see p480).

Sailors, windsurfers and water-lovers of all levels also flock to Rutland Water, a giant reservoir. You could also try steering a boat through the waterways of the Lincolnshire fens.

### Getting There & Around

Public transport can be a hit-and-miss affair in the Marches, Northamptonshire and Lincolnshire. Without your own wheels, getting to countryside attractions takes time, planning and patience. **National Express** ( ☎ 08718 818181; www.nationalexpress.com) is the main coach service in the region and throughout the country, and Birmingham is a major hub. For general route information you can consult **Traveline** ( ☎ 0871 200 2233; www.travelinemidlands.co.uk).

The main bus operators:

**Arriva** ( ☎ 0844 800 4411; www.arrivabus.co.uk) An Arriva Go Anywhere ticket gives one day of unlimited travel.

**First Travel** ( ☎ 0800 587 7381; www.firstgroup.com) A FirstDay Wyvern ticket (adult/child £5.50/3.80) offers the same deal on the First network in Worcestershire, Herefordshire and adjoining counties.

**Stagecoach** ( ☎ 01788-535555; Dayrider Gold tickets adult/child £6.50/4.50)

**Travel West Midlands** (www.travelwm.co.uk)

Rail networks are extensive in the Midlands, but less so in the rural Marches, where they're only good for major towns. Useful train operators:

**London Midland** (www.londonmidland.com) Operates a train service throughout the Midlands and has excellent connections with London.

**Wrexham and Shropshire** (www.wrexhamandshrop shire.co.uk) Operates a direct train service from Shropshire to London Marylebone.

# NORTHAMPTONSHIRE

While it lacks a major 'must-see' attraction, Northamptonshire is a great place to explore. Winding country lanes punctuate the gentle countryside, which is studded with fetching, honey-coloured limestone towns, storybook thatched cottages, historic Saxon Churches and grand country estates including Althorp House, the final resting place of Princess Diana. What's more, Northamptonshire is refreshingly free from the tourist hordes, so you won't have to fight to take in its charms.

## Orientation & Information

Northamptonshire is roughly 50 miles long and 20 miles wide, running southwest to northeast. The M1 cuts diagonally across the county just below Northampton, which lies in the middle. Attractions are scattered.

For general information about the county, check the website www.explorenorthampton shire.co.uk. Otherwise, visit Northampton's tourist office (opposite).

## Getting Around

A car can be a convenient way of getting around Northamptonshire. Turning a corner on a winding country lane to discover a sleepy village is one of the joys of a visit here. All the major car-hire companies have branches in Northampton.

Buses do run to most places of interest from Northampton and other nearby towns, but services can be sporadic; some run only a few times daily, so it's best to check times with the operator:

**Stagecoach** (www.stagecoachbus.com/northants)
**Traveline** ( ☎ 0871 200 2233)

## NORTHAMPTON
pop 194,458

Hugging the banks of the River Nene, this unassuming market town played a surprisingly significant role in English history. In the Middle Ages, it was one of the largest towns in the country, a thriving commercial centre with strong links to royalty. Today the city's rich past is blighted by some nasty examples of postwar town planning, although there are a few remaining buildings of architectural note. The town is also famous for footwear and was once the heart of the boot and shoe industry.

## Orientation

The town is centred on Market Sq, with the main pedestrianised shopping route, Abington St, running east from it, where it becomes the Kettering Rd, with its hotels and bars. To the south of Market Sq are the guildhall and the tourist office. The town's infamously ugly bus station is to the north.

## Information

The helpful **tourist office** ( ☎ 01604-838800; www .explorenorthamptonshire.co.uk; The Guildhall, St Giles Sq; ☼ 10am-5pm Mon-Sat) was in a temporary home next to the Derngate Royal Theatre at the time of writing but will move to Sessions House on George Row during 2009.

## Sights & Activities

Even those without a shoe fetish can get a kick out of the impressive displays at **Northampton Museum & Art Gallery** ( ☎ 01604-838111; Guildhall Rd; admission free; ☼ 10am-5pm Mon-Sat, 2-5pm Sun), where you can learn about the history of shoemaking through interactive exhibits and follow the height of footwear fashion throughout the ages. There are also some fine paintings and an exhibition on Northampton's history from the Stone Age onwards.

The **Church of the Holy Sepulchre** ( ☎ 01604-754782; ☼ noon-4pm Wed, 2-4pm Sat May-Sep) is Northampton's oldest building at nine centuries and counting. It is also one of the few surviving round churches in the country. Founded after the first earl of Northampton returned from the Crusades in 1100, it is modelled on its Jerusalem namesake.

## Getting There & Away

Northampton has good rail links with Birmingham (£10.70, one hour, hourly) and London Euston (£21.20, one hour, three hourly). The train station is about half a mile west of town along Gold St.

National Express coaches run services to London (£11.50, 2¼ hours, five daily), to Nottingham (£11.60, 2½ hours, daily) and to Birmingham (£6.40, one hour and 40 minutes, twice daily). Greyfriars bus station is on Lady's Lane, just north of the Grosvenor shopping centre.

## AROUND NORTHAMPTON
### Althorp

**Althorp House** ( ☎ 01604-770107; www.althorp.com; adult/ child £12.50/6, plus access to upstairs of house £2.50; ☼ 11am-5pm Jul & Aug, last entry 4pm) is most famous as the resting place of Diana, Princess of Wales, who is commemorated in a memorial and museum in the grounds of her ancestral home.

The stern looking 16th-century mansion was already well known for its outstanding collection of art and books, and you'll see works by Rubens, Gainsborough and Van Dyck. Profits from ticket sales go to the Princess Diana Memorial Fund. The limited number of tickets available must be booked by phone or on the web. Althorp should be pronounced *altrup*.

Althorp is off the A428, 5.5 miles northwest of Northampton. Bus 207 (five daily, not Sundays) links Northampton with Althorp, leaving from Greyfriars bus station.

# LEICESTERSHIRE & RUTLAND

Leicestershire isn't at the forefront of most people's minds when it comes to the country's tourist destinations, but this compact county shouldn't be overlooked. At its heart, Leicester is a vital mix of different cultures and faiths, and the surrounding countryside is home to rolling hills and woodland as well as some major historical sites including magnificent Belvoir Castle.

Tiny Rutland merged with Leicestershire in 1974, but in April 1997 regained 'independence' as a county. With magnificent Rutland Water and charming settlements, it's a hit with lovers of water sports and picturesque villages.

## Orientation & Information

Leicestershire and Rutland together look like an upside-down map of Australia. Leicester is virtually bang in the centre of its county, with the M1 motorway running north–south just to the west, dividing the largely industrial towns and National Forest of the west from the more rural

east including Belvoir Castle. To the east of Leicester, Rutland, wedged between four counties, revolves around central Rutland Water.

For general countywide information, contact **Leicestershire Tourism** ( ☎ 0844 8885181; www .goleicestershire.com).

## Getting There & Around

**Arriva Midlands** (www.arrivabus.co.uk) operates Leicestershire bus services. For the latest timetables, bus routes and numbers contact **Traveline** ( ☎ 0871 200 2233).

## LEICESTER
### pop 279,923

Filled with the sense of excitement that comes from a mix of cultures and ethnicities,

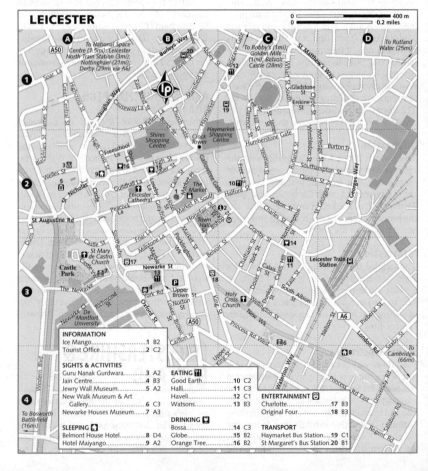

### LEICESTER

| INFORMATION | |
|---|---|
| Ice Mango | 1 B2 |
| Tourist Office | 2 C2 |

| SIGHTS & ACTIVITIES | |
|---|---|
| Guru Nanak Gurdwara | 3 A2 |
| Jain Centre | 4 B3 |
| Jewry Wall Museum | 5 A2 |
| New Walk Museum & Art Gallery | 6 C3 |
| Newarke Houses Museum | 7 A3 |

| SLEEPING | |
|---|---|
| Belmont House Hotel | 8 D4 |
| Hotel Maiyango | 9 A2 |

| EATING | |
|---|---|
| Good Earth | 10 C2 |
| Halli | 11 C3 |
| Haveli | 12 C1 |
| Watsons | 13 B3 |

| DRINKING | |
|---|---|
| Bossa | 14 C3 |
| Globe | 15 B2 |
| Orange Tree | 16 B2 |

| ENTERTAINMENT | |
|---|---|
| Charlotte | 17 B3 |
| Original Four | 18 B3 |

| TRANSPORT | |
|---|---|
| Haymarket Bus Station | 19 C1 |
| St Margaret's Bus Station | 20 B1 |

Leicester (*les*-ter) may not be beautiful but it has a lot going on. Around since the Roman times, it had an unwelcome refurbishment at the hands of the Luftwaffe, while industrial decline hollowed it out and poor urban planning capped off the aesthetic crimes against the city. But Leicester, home to a large, dynamic Asian community, has reinvented itself as a socially and environmentally progressive melting pot, and many of the city's most interesting events are staged around festivals such as Diwali and Eid-ul-Fitr. Current regeneration projects including a new 'cultural quarter' topped with a bold, curved-glass performing-arts centre, are set to broaden its appeal further.

## Orientation

For drivers, Leicester is plagued by a maze of one-way streets and forbidden turns. Although there isn't a ring road as such, the A594 does almost a whole circuit and most attractions flank it or are contained within it.

The centre of the Asian community, Belgrave Rd (the 'Golden Mile'), is about a mile northeast of the centre. Castle Park, with many historic attractions, lies immediately west of the centre.

## Information

**Ice Mango** ( ☎ 0116-262 6255; www.icemango.co.uk; 4 Market Pl; per hr £2; ☺ 9.30am-6.30pm Mon-Fri, to 7pm Sat, noon-5.30pm Sun) Relaxed coffee house with computers for internet access.

**Tourist office** ( ☎ 0844 888 5181; www.goleicestershire .com; 7-9 Every St; ☺ 10am-5.30pm Mon-Fri, to 5pm Sat)

## Sights

### JEWRY WALL & MUSEUMS

All Leicester's **museums** (www.leicester.gov.uk/museums) are free.

Despite its name, **Jewry Wall** is one of England's largest surviving Roman civil structures and has nothing to do with Judaism. You can wander the excavated remains of the Roman public baths, which date back almost two millennia.

Notwithstanding its grim external appearance, the **Jewry Wall Museum** ( ☎ 0116-225 4971; St Nicholas Circle; ☺ 11am-4.30pm Feb-Oct & some school holidays) contains wonderful Roman mosaics and frescoes, and an interactive exhibition, 'the Making of Leicester', which explains the history of the city from the Iron age to the year 2000 with archaeological reconstructions and paintings.

Leicester's oldest museum, the **New Walk Museum & Art Gallery** ( ☎ 0116-225 4900; New Walk; ☺ 10am-5pm Mon-Sat, from 11am Sun) has a huge range of exhibits on offer, from child-friendly interactive explorations of the natural world, to a quirky mummy-filled gallery set up like an Egyptian tomb, to a collection of 20th-century German art.

**Newarke Houses Museum** ( ☎ 0116-225 4980; The Newarke; ☺ 10am-5pm Mon-Sat, from 11am Sun) is made up of two 16th-century buildings. Revolving around the theme 'ordinary people, extraordinary lives', it shows how Leicester residents would have lived during different time periods. Features include reconstructed living rooms, a toy gallery and a gallery telling the story of the Royal Leicestershire Regiment.

### NATIONAL SPACE CENTRE

This **centre** ( ☎ 0116-261 0261; www.spacecentre.co.uk; adult/child £12/10; ☺ 10am-5pm Tue-Sun, plus Mon during school holidays, last entry 3.30pm) does an excellent job of helping us ordinary mortals understand space science. Interactive displays cover cosmic myths, the history of astronomy and the development of space travel, while in the Space Now! area you can check on the status of all current space missions. Films in the domed Space Theatre (included in the admission price) launch you to the far reaches of the galaxy, and in the Human Spaceflight exhibition you can test out your astronaut capabilities and take a space-shuttle flight simulator to an ice moon.

The centre is off the A6 about 1.5 miles north of the city centre. Take bus 54 from Charles St in the centre.

### TEMPLES

Materials were shipped in all the way from India to convert a disused church into a **Jain Centre** ( ☎ 0116-254 1150; www.jaincentre.com; 32 Oxford St; ☺ 8.30am-8.30pm Mon-Fri, to 6.30pm Sun), the first Jain temple outside the subcontinent and the only one in Europe. The building is faced with marble, and the temple boasts a forest of beautifully carved pillars inside.

Close to the Jewry Wall is the Sikh **Guru Nanak Gurdwara** ( ☎ 0116-262 8606; 9 Holy Bones; ☺ 1-4pm Thu, 7-8.30pm Sat). There is a small museum, which contains an impressive model of the Golden Temple in Amritsar, India, and a Sikh/Panjabi heritage exhibition.

## Festivals & Events

Leicester hosts numerous cultural and religious festivals throughout the year. Contact the tourist office for details.

**Comedy festival** ( ☎ 0116-261 6812; www.comedy festival.co.uk) In February; is the country's longest running comedy festival, drawing big names as well as fresh comic talent.

**Caribbean carnival** (www.lccarnival.org.uk) In August the city hosts the biggest UK Caribbean carnival outside London's Notting Hill Carnival.

**Diwali** The Hindu community celebrates this during autumn, and the celebration, the largest of its kind outside India, draws visitors from around the world.

## Sleeping

**Belmont House Hotel** ( ☎ 0116-254 4773; www.belmonthotel.co.uk; De Montfort St; s/d £115/120; **P** **□**) In an elongated Georgian building, this hotel has spotless rooms, although it looks a little old-fashioned. There are normally great deals to be had if you book ahead.

**our pick Hotel Maiyango** ( ☎ 0116-251 8898; www.maiyango.com; 13-21 St Nicholas Pl; d from £135; **□**) The nicest place to stay in Leicester has spacious, sexy rooms, decorated with handmade Asian furniture, bright contemporary art and massive plasma TVs. There are complimentary snacks and magazines in all rooms and the hotel lobby doubles up as a large, airy bar complete with wraparound terrace and views over the city. There's another bar and a restaurant downstairs.

## Eating

The Golden Mile on Belgrave Rd is located a mile to the north of the centre (take bus 22 or 26 from Haymarket bus station). It's well known for its excellent Indian restaurants and has some of the best Indian vegetarian food in the country. It's also a good place to buy saris and jewellery and is the epicentre of Leicester's Diwali festival.

**Halli** ( ☎ 0116-255 4667; www.hallirestaurant.com; 153 Granby St; dishes £3-6; ⏱ noon-3pm Mon-Fri, to 11pm Sat, to 8pm Sun) Great-value, tasty South Indian vegetarian cooking including excellent *dosas*, served in simple surroundings.

**Good Earth** ( ☎ 0116-262 6260; 19 Free Lane; mains £3.25-6.25; ⏱ noon-3pm Mon-Fri, 10am-4pm Sat) Tucked away on a side street, this wholesome vegetarian restaurant is justifiably popular for its vegie bakes, huge, fresh salads and homemade cakes.

**Bobby's** ( ☎ 0116-251 0555; 154 Belgrave Rd; mains £5-12; ⏱ noon-10pm Tue-Sun) A Belgrave Rd institution, this Indian restaurant serves up tongue-tingling vegetarian curries cooked without onions or garlic. There's a counter downstairs selling Indian sweets, and samosas and the like.

**Haveli** ( ☎ 0116-251 0555; 61 Belgrave Gate; mains £5-12; ⏱ 6pm-midnight Tue-Sun) Delicious and varied Indian

menu served up by extremely friendly staff in a large, lively dining room with some interesting decor, including life-sized fake humans.

**Watsons** ( ☎ 0116-222 7770; www.watsons-restaurant.com; 5-9 Upper Brown St; mains £12-17; ⏱ lunch & dinner Mon-Sat) Set in a converted cotton mill opposite the Phoenix Theatre, this is one of Leicester's finest places to eat out. Mediterranean-inspired food is served in a bright dining room to a soundtrack of mellow jazz. There's also a courtyard bar.

## Drinking

Amid the rash of chain pubs in the centre, there are a few places for more discerning drinkers.

**Bossa** ( ☎ 0116-255 9551; 110 Granby St; ⏱ 11am-10.30pm Mon-Thu, to 1am Fri & Sat) Latin rhythms, cheap, tasty snacks and a relaxed, Bohemian crowd populate this pint-sized, gay-friendly bar-cafe.

**Globe** ( ☎ 0116-262 9819; 43 Silver St; ⏱ 11am-11pm Sun-Thu, to 1am Fri & Sat) At last, that rare beast: a traditional old pub (built in 1720) in a city centre overrun with chains and style bars – just fine draught ales, a warm atmosphere and little alcoves to lose yourself in.

**Orange Tree** ( ☎ 0116-223 5256; 99 High St) This unpretentious, relaxed bar is a relief among the neighbouring chain pubs. It's kitted out with colourful modern art and there's a beer garden that packs out in the summer. Meals are £4.50 to £7.45.

## Entertainment

**Charlotte** ( ☎ 0116-255 3956; www.thecharlotte.co.uk; 8 Oxford St; ⏱ doors open 8pm) Leicester's legendary venue has staged Oasis and the Stone Roses, among others, before they became megastars. It's a small, grungy, lively place with a late licence and club nights catering for all sorts of musical tastes.

**Original Four** ( ☎ 0116-254 1638; 2 King St; admission Sat £12) Behind a mock-Tudor facade, this place cooks up four floors of diverse beats: a bar, cocktail lounge, dance floor and dedicated space for live music. It has seen more popular days but is still one of the best clubbing options in town.

## Getting There & Away

National Express operates from St Margaret's bus station on Gravel St, north of the centre. Buses run to Nottingham (£3.50, one hour, 20 daily), and Coventry (£5.70, 45 minutes, four daily). Other options for Coventry include the X67 (one hour, hourly).

Trains run to London St Pancras (£21, one hour and 20 minutes, four hourly) and Birmingham (£8.40, one hour, twice hourly).

A tourist jaunt rather than a serious transport option, the classic **Great Central Railway** ( ☎ 01509-230726; www.gcrailway.co.uk; return tickets adult/child £12/8) operates steam locomotives between Leicester North station on Redhill Circle and Loughborough Central. This dual-track railway runs the 8-mile route along which Thomas Cook ran his original package tour in 1841. The trains run regularly from June to August and some weekends the rest of the year. Take bus 70 from Haymarket bus station.

### Getting Around

Central Leicester is easy to get around on foot. As an alternative to local buses, the open-top bus run by **Discover Leicester** ( ☎ 0844 888 5151; adult/child under 15yr £7/5; ☼ 10am-4pm Jul-Sep) runs a jump-on jump-off bus around the city and up to Belgrave Rd, the Great Central Railway and the National Space Centre, with on-board commentary from a local expert. It starts by the Thomas Cook statue outside Leicester train station, around 10 minutes past the hour.

## AROUND LEICESTER
### Bosworth Battlefield

The **Battlefield Heritage Centre** ( ☎ 01455-290429; bosworthbattlefield.com; admission £3.25; ☼ 11am-5pm Apr-Oct) features an interactive exhibition about the Wars of the Roses and the battle that ended it – the Battle of Bosworth. This is one of the most important battle sites in England, where Richard III was defeated by the future Henry VII in 1485. 'A horse, a horse, my kingdom for a horse' was Richard's famous death cry (at least according to William Shakespeare). He may be known as a villain for his supposed role in the murder of the 'princes in the tower', but Leicester has adopted him as something of a folk hero, not the hunchback of Shakespearean spin. The battle is re-enacted annually in August.

The battlefield is 16 miles southwest of Leicester at Sutton Cheny, off the A447. Bus 153 runs hourly from Leicester to Market Bosworth, 3 miles to the north. The **Bosworth Gold Cars** ( ☎ 01455-291999) taxi firm can also take you there.

### Belvoir Castle

Deep in the countryside, **Belvoir Castle** ( ☎ 01476-871000; www.belvoircastle.com; adult/child £12/6; ☼ 11am-5pm Sat-Thu May-Aug, 11am-5pm Sat & Sun Sep, sporadically Oct, Mar & Apr) is a magnificent baroque and Gothic fantasy rebuilt in the 19th century after suffering serious damage during the English Civil War. It is also home to the duke and duchess of Rutland. Much of the sumptuous interior is open to the public, and collections of weaponry, medals and art (including pieces by Reynolds, Gainsborough and Holbein) are highlights. There are marvellous views across the countryside, and peacocks roam the gardens.

Belvoir (*bee*-ver) is 6 miles west of Grantham, off the A1; Grantham is about 25 miles east of Nottingham along the A52.

## RUTLAND

Rutland's motto 'Multum in Parvo' (so much in so little) refers to its status as England's smallest county. Rutland Water, one of the largest reservoirs in Europe, makes it a haven for water-sport lovers, as well as climbers and birdwatchers. The **Oakham tourist office** ( ☎ 01572-758441; Catmose St, Oakham; ☼ 10.30am-5pm Mon-Sat, 2-4pm Sun) is housed in the Rutland County Museum, and there's also a **Rutland Water tourist office** ( ☎ 01572-653026; Sykes Lane, Empingham; ☼ 10am-5pm Easter-Sep, to 4pm Tue-Sat Oct-Mar, shorter hr in winter).

In Rutland Water, the **Rutland Belle** ( ☎ 01572-787630; www.rutlandwatercruises.com; the Harbour, Whitwell Park; adult/child £7/4.50) offers pleasure cruises every afternoon, April to September. The **Watersports Centre** ( ☎ 01780-460154; Whitwell) organises windsurfing, canoeing and sailing and offers tuition, and the **Rutland Sailing School** ( ☎ 01780-721999; www.rutlandsailingschool.co.uk; Edith Weston) offers tuition to sailors of all abilities, from catamarans to dinghies.

For bike hire, contact **Rutland Water Cycling** ( ☎ 01780-460705; www.rutlandcycling.co.uk; Whitwell Car Park).

The sleepy county town of **Oakham** has a famous school and **Oakham Castle** (admission free; ☼ 10.30am-1pm & 1.30-5pm Mon-Sat, 2-4pm Sun Mar-Oct, shorter hr Nov-Feb), where an impressive Great Hall from a 12th-century Norman structure still stands.

South of Oakham is the village of **Lyddington**, home to the **Bede House** (EH; ☎ 01572-822438; adult/child £3.70/1.90; ☼ 10am-5pm Thu-Mon Apr-Sep). Originally a wing of the medieval rural palace of the bishops of Lincoln, it was converted into almshouses in 1600. Look out for the beautifully carved cornice in the Great Chamber.

**ourpick Hambleton Hall** ( ☎ 01572-756991; Hambleton, Oakham; mains £32-36; ✆ lunch & dinner) surveys the countryside from a regal peninsula in Rutland Water. The elegant Victorian is one of England's finest country retreats. Its Michelin-starred restaurant attracts food and wine lovers from miles around, who come to dine on passionate cooking featuring wonderfully fresh ingredients such as fresh herbs and vegetables from its own garden and wild mushrooms picked in local woods. After the main event, relax in one of the countrified luxury rooms, stroll the glorious grounds, or work it off in the pool or on the tennis courts.

Bus 19 runs from Nottingham's Broadmarsh bus station to Oakham (1¼ hours, hourly). Trains run hourly from Leicester, Peterborough and Birmingham.

# LINCOLNSHIRE

This sparsely populated corner of eastern England has a reputation for being flat, plain and proper, although on closer look it's uncommonly friendly and remarkably varied: the stunning stately homes and time-capsule towns of rural Lincolnshire are ready fodder for a steady stream of moviemakers searching for ready-made period sets.

County capital, Lincoln, is the perfect place to start, with a stunning Gothic cathedral, Tudor streetscapes and a dramatic hilltop location. The gently rippling hills of the Lincolnshire Wolds smooth down to eastern marshlands and sandy coast, and the dyke-scored Lincolnshire Fens flat-iron the southeast. While flamboyant medieval churches, red-roofed stone houses and windmills grace many towns, here too you'll find brash beach resort Skegness and rich wildlife reserves where the loudest din is birdsong.

## Information

**South West Lincs** (www.southwestlincs.com)
**Visit Lincolnshire** (www.visitlincolnshire.com)
**Visit the Fens** (www.visitthefens.co.uk)

## Activities

The 140-mile **Viking Way** trails from the Humber Bridge through the Lincolnshire Wolds to Oakham in Leicestershire. It can be more rewarding to explore the area by bike; leaflets on county cycle trails are available at tourist offices.

To mess around on boats, the **Lincolnshire Fens** offers a rich and varied choice of navigable waterways.

## Getting There & Away

Other than a speedy rail link between Grantham and London, Lincolnshire isn't the easiest county to get to and around. You're better off on the buses to reach Stamford and Lincoln, and don't be surprised if you have to change services en route.

## Getting Around

For regional travel information, contact **Traveline** ( ☎ 0871 200 2233; www.travelineeastmidlands.org .uk) or consult the travel pages of the **Lincolnshire County Council** (www.lincolnshire.gov.uk) website. Useful bus operators include **Lincs Interconnect** ( ☎ 0845 234 3344; www.lincsinterconnect.com) and **Stagecoach** (www.stagecoachbus.com/lincolnshire).

## LINCOLN
pop 85,595

An undervisited delight, Lincoln's tightly knotted core of cobbled streets and majestic medieval architecture is enough to leave visitors breathless, albeit as much for its punishing slopes as for the superb stonework and timber-framed treasures to be found there. An extraordinary cathedral, an unusual Norman castle and compact Tudor streets crown Lincoln's hilltop; the town then tumbles down the hillside losing charm and picking up modern pace as it goes.

At the hill's base, the university breathes life into a waterfront quarter where bars are positioned to watch boats come and go. While there's little to keep you for a longer stay, Lincoln has a welcoming aura and enough cultural clout in its centre to keep you very happy for a day or two at a stretch.

## History

With a hill that affords views for miles around and a river for swift sea access, it's hardly surprising that Lincoln's defensive location has been exploited by invading forces for the last 2000 years. The Romans set up camp soon after arriving in Britain and in the 11th century the Normans speedily constructed a castle after their invasion. The city yo-yoed between Royalist and Parliamentarian forces during the Civil War, and the warfare theme continued into the 20th century, when Lincoln's heavy-engineering industry spawned the world's first tank, which saw action in WWI.

## Orientation

The cathedral stands imperiously on top of the hill in the old city, with the castle and other attractions clustered nearby. Three-quarters of a mile downhill is the new town, and the bus and train stations. Joining the two is the appositely named Steep Hill, and believe us, they're not kidding – even locals stop to catch their breath.

## Information

Several banks and ATMs sit on the High St. Check www.lincolntoday.co.uk and www.lincoln.gov.uk for events listings.

**County hospital** ( ☎ 01522-512512; off Greetwell Rd)
**Launderette** ( ☎ 01522-543498; 8 Burton Rd; per load £3; ◷ 8.30am-8pm Mon-Fri, to 5pm Sat & Sun) Self-service.

**Post office** ( ☎ 01522-526031; 90 Bailgate)
**Systems Health Check Internet Cafe** ( ☎ 01522-522635; 61 Steep Hill; per hr £2; ◷ 10am-7pm)
**Tourist office** (www.visitlincolnshire.com) Main branch ( ☎ 01522-873213; 9 Castle Hill; ◷ 9.30am-6pm Mon-Sat & 10.30am-4.30pm Sun Jul-Sep, 9.30am-5pm Mon-Fri & 10am-5pm Sat & Sun Oct-Jun); Cornhill branch ( ☎ 873256; 21 Cornhill; ◷ 9.30am-5.30pm Mon-Sat, 11am-3pm Sun Jul-Sep, 9.30am-5pm Mon-Fri & 10am-5pm Sat Oct-Jun)

## Sights

The tourist office sells the Lincoln Time Travel Pass, which gives access to several heritage sites including the castle, cathedral and Bishop's Palace (single/family £10/20) and lasts three days.

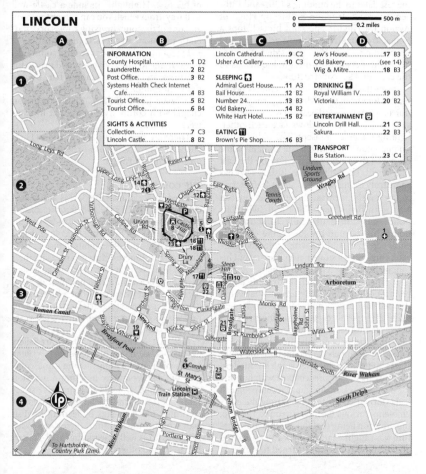

**LINCOLN**

| | | 0   500 m |
| | | 0   0.2 miles |

**INFORMATION**
County Hospital................1 D2
Launderette....................2 B2
Post Office.....................3 B2
Systems Health Check Internet
  Cafe..........................4 B3
Tourist Office..................5 B2
Tourist Office..................6 B4

**SIGHTS & ACTIVITIES**
Collection.......................7 C3
Lincoln Castle..................8 B2

Lincoln Cathedral..............9 C2
Usher Art Gallery.............10 C3

**SLEEPING** 🛏
Admiral Guest House.......11 A3
Bail House.....................12 B2
Number 24.....................13 B3
Old Bakery.....................14 B2
White Hart Hotel.............15 B2

**EATING** 🍴
Brown's Pie Shop............16 B3

Jew's House...................17 B3
Old Bakery.................(see 14)
Wig & Mitre..................18 B3

**DRINKING** 🍷
Royal William IV.............19 B3
Victoria.........................20 B2

**ENTERTAINMENT** 🎭
Lincoln Drill Hall.............21 C3
Sakura.........................22 B3

**TRANSPORT**
Bus Station...................23 C4

## LINCOLN CATHEDRAL

All kinds of marvels and mischief can be found in the county's top attraction, **Lincoln cathedral** ( ☎ 01522-544545; www.lincolncathedral.com; adult/under 16yr £4/1; ⓨ 7.15am-8pm Mon-Fri, to 6pm Sat & Sun Jun-Aug, 7.15am-6pm Mon-Sat, to 5pm Sun Sep-May). This soaring edifice has three great towers that dominate the city, one of which is the third-highest in England at 81m, but it's claimed that until a storm in 1547 its spire was a jaw-dropping 160m high, topping even the great pyramids of Giza.

A vast, imposing facade carved with gargoyles, kings, dragons and hunters leers over the Great West Door. On closer inspection, you'll spot that the facade is divided into two eras, the lower of which is from the Norman cathedral toppled in an earthquake in 1185; the rest dates to the building's 12th- and 13th-century reconstruction by Bishop Hugh of Avalon (St Hugh). The saint himself tops a pinnacle on one side of the West Front, and his counterpart on the other side is a swineherd who devoted his meagre lifesavings to the cathedral's reconstruction.

Inside the lofty nave, there's a chunky black-marble font from the 11th century, ringed with fearsome mythological beasts. Two magnificent stained-glass rose windows face each other, lighting the great transept. The oldest is the unique Dean's Eye, which still contains some original 13th-century glass picturing the Last Judgement. The 14th-century Bishop's Eye has some truly exquisite carved stone-leaf tracery.

Up in the central tower, the veteran Victorian bell, Great Tom, still swings its ponderous 2m, 270kg bulk to sound the hours. Just beyond the tower, the elaborate choir screen is studded with grotesque characters including a stonemason sticking out his tongue just to the left of the door.

St Hugh's Choir, which is currently under restoration, is topped by an unusual vault, dubbed the 'crazy vault' for its odd angles, while the superbly carved and canopied stalls below are a classic example of medieval craftsmanship. Just beyond this, the Angel Choir is graced by 28 angels carved high up the walls. It was built as a shrine to St Hugh but modern pilgrims are mostly preoccupied with hunting for the famous Lincoln Imp, a lovably roguish little horned character that is now the city's emblem. Various legends surround the imp, the most fun being that the mischievous creature was caught chatting up one of the carved angels and was promptly turned to stone.

For one last stop before leaving, take a peek at the cathedral's round Chapterhouse, where the climax of The Da Vinci Code film was shot in 2005.

There are one-hour tours at least twice a day plus less-frequent tours of the roof and the tower. Evensong takes place daily at 5.30pm (3.45pm on Sunday) and Eucharist is sung at 9.30am on Sunday.

## LINCOLN CASTLE

After installing himself as king in 1066, William the Conqueror speedily set about building castles to keep his new kingdom in line, and **Lincoln Castle** ( ☎ 01522-511068; www.lincolnshire.gov.uk/lincolncastle; adult/child £4/2.65; ⓨ 10am-6pm daily May-Aug, to 5pm Apr & Sep, to 4pm Oct-Mar) was one of his first. Highlights include a castle-wall walkway, from which you can survey the town, and one of the four surviving copies of democratic milestone **Magna Carta** (dated 1215).

Lincoln Castle also has its gruesome side. It was home to the city's court and prison for centuries, and public executions here used to draw thousands of bloodthirsty spectators. The castle has a chilling Victorian prison chapel with coffin-style pews that inmates were locked into.

There are free tours of the castle at 11am and 2pm daily from April to September and on weekends in winter.

## THE COLLECTION

Opened to acclaim in 2005, this **archaeology museum** ( ☎ 01522-550990; www.thecollection.lincoln.museum; Danes Tce; admission free; ⓨ 10am-4pm) details the archaeological history of Lincolnshire and is full of child-friendly exhibits to inspire budding Indiana Joneses. Kids can measure their height against a woolly mammoth, design their own beast on a touch screen or deck themselves out like a knight or a Roman soldier. Other interesting artefacts include an impressive 7m log dugout and a 4000-year-old local skull.

Just east is the historic **Usher Art Gallery** ( ☎ 01522-527980; Lindum Rd; admission free; ⓨ 10am-4pm), which now belongs to the same complex but sits separately in a grand mansion amid parkland. It holds an impressive selection of portraits, and the largest collection of paintings and drawings by leading English watercolour practitioner, Peter de Wint (1784–1849) as well as works by JMW Turner, LS Lowry and others.

## Sleeping

**Hartsholme Country Park** ( ☎ 01522-873578; hartshol
mecp@lincoln.gov.uk; Skellingthorpe Rd; tent sites £7-15;
☺ Mar-Oct) Decent camping ground with OK
facilities. The main draw is that it's next to
a sprawling nature reserve filled with lovely
lakes, woods and meadows. It's 3 miles southwest of the train station. Take the regular
daytime SB6 or evening 66A bus towards
Birchwood Estate from Lincoln bus station;
alight at Swanpool (15 minutes).

**Admiral Guest House** ( ☎ 01522-544467; nicola
.major1@ntlworld.com; 16-18 Nelson St; s/d/f £30/50/55; ☐ )
This place suffers from a mismatched, chintzy
interior, but is good value, well located and
run by friendly, knowledgeable hosts.

**Old Bakery** ( ☎ 01522-576057; www.theold-bakery
.co.uk; 26-28 Burton Rd; r from £53; ☐ wi-fi) This wonderful guesthouse, set above an excellent restaurant (right), has four sweet, characterful
rooms. The welcome is warm but unobtrusive
and the delicious breakfasts feature goodies
such as homemade muffins.

**our pick Number 24** ( ☎ 01522-514650; www
.number24.biz; 24 Drury Lane; s/d from £50/90; ☐ ) Make
sure you get in here early – there's only one
room and it's a corker. A short stroll away
from the cathedral, it's decked out in unfussy
country style with marvellous views of castle
and cathedral, a private sitting room and roof
terrace, and lots of thoughtful touches like a
selection of books and magazines, fresh fruit,
flowers and chocolates.

**Bail House** ( ☎ 01522-520883; www.bailhouse.co.uk; 34
Bailgate; s/d from £65/79, d superior £139-165; ☐ ☐ wi-fi)
Stone walls, worn flagstones, Mediterranean-
style gardens and one room with an extraordinary medieval, timber-vaulted ceiling are
only a few of the charms of this lovingly
restored town house in central Lincoln.
There's even a heated outdoor swimming
pool for fair-weather days.

**White Hart Hotel** ( ☎ 01522-526222; www.whitehart
-lincoln.co.uk; Bailgate; s/d £75/100; ☐ ☐ wi-fi) You
can't get more central or venerable than
Lincoln's grand dame of hotels, neatly sandwiched between castle and cathedral, and
with a history of hostelry dating back 600
years. It has four-dozen luxurious country-
casual rooms, a few with partial views of the
cathedral facade.

## Eating

**our pick Brown's Pie Shop** ( ☎ 01522-527330; 33 Steep
Hill; pies £7-11; ☺ lunch & dinner) Not strictly a pie
shop, this restaurant dishes up large servings
of speciality pies, steaks and other hearty fare.
Eat in the bustling, bright, white dining room,
or in a lovely brick-vaulted basement area for
candlelit evenings. The local wild-rabbit and
beef-and-stout pies are particularly tasty and
there are regularly changing guest-star pies.

**Wig & Mitre** ( ☎ 01522-535190; www.wigandmitre
.com; 30 Steep Hill; mains £11-20; ☺ 8am-midnight)
Civilised pub-restaurant the Wig & Mitre
has an excellent, upscale menu but manages to retain the mellow cosiness of a local
pub. No music will disturb your meal here,
and the candlelit evening meals are good for
romantic liaisons.

**Jew's House** ( ☎ 01522-524851; Steep Hill; set lunch/
dinner £12/27; ☺ lunch & dinner Tue-Sun) Pass through
the ancient round-arched doorway of this
12th-century stone house and you'll immediately know you're in for a treat. This ancient
house, an attraction in its own right, is flush
with antiques and oil paintings, and its award-
winning Anglo-French cuisine will not disappoint. Dress smart and book ahead.

**Old Bakery** ( ☎ 01522-576057; www.theold-bakery
.co.uk; 26-28 Burton Rd; mains £15-21; ☺ lunch & dinner Tue-Sun)
This old bakery conversion in the shadow of
Lincoln Castle's walls is one of the town's most
popular restaurants. The pretty dining room,
which opens up into an airy, slate-floored conservatory, serves award-winning, local produce,
impeccably presented – including very addictive
bread, baked fresh on the premises, of course.

## Drinking

**Victoria** ( ☎ 01522-536048; 6 Union Rd) A serious
beer-drinkers' pub with a pleasant patio looking up at the castle's western walls, Victoria
has a huge selection of guest brews, cask ales,
thick stouts and superb ciders, and preserves
a mellow historic ambience undisturbed by
sports or flashy lights. The pub runs two beer
festivals a year.

**Royal William IV** ( ☎ 01522-528159; Brayford Wharf;
☺ 10am-11pm Sun-Thu, to midnight Fri & Sat) This
friendly pub provides some respite from the
brash chain bars, pubs and restaurants that
line the regenerated Brayford Wharf beside
the university. There's plenty of outdoor seating, though, if you want to watch the action.

## Entertainment

**Lincoln Drill Hall** ( ☎ 01522-873894; www.lincolndrillhall
.com; Free School Lane) The city's premier venue for
music, theatre and comedy.

**Sakura** ( ☎ 01522-525828; 280-281 High St; ☺ 10pm-3am Mon-Sat) Every night is different at this Japanese-themed chain club, which alternately rocks to old-school funk, garage, R&B, '80s and '90s nights and house music, with some high-profile guest DJs to get the party started. It has some kaleidoscopic cocktails, and sake-based drinks.

### Getting There & Away
Lincoln is 142 miles from London, 94 miles from Cambridge and 81 miles from York.

National Express runs a direct service between Lincoln and London (£21, 4¾ hours, daily). Buses also run from Lincoln to Birmingham (£14.50, three hours, daily).

Getting to and from Lincoln usually involves changing trains. There are links to Boston (£9.20, 1¼ hours, hourly) and Skegness (£12.60, two hours, hourly); change at Sleaford. There are also trains to Cambridge (£21.90, 2½ hours, hourly), change at Peterborough or Ely; and links to Grantham (£8.20, 1½ hours, twice hourly).

### Getting Around
Regular buses link the lower town bus and train stations with the uptown cathedral area. To avoid the climb up Steep Hill, a 'Walk and Ride' electric bus also runs every 20 minutes during the day from outside the House of Fraser store on High St to Castle Sq (adult/child £1/50p, five minutes).

## GRANTHAM
### pop 34,592
This sedate red-brick town is notable for its famous former inhabitants. Sir Isaac Newton was born and brought up in the area and is celebrated with a proud statue in front of the town's guildhall. More famously, Britain's first female prime minister, Margaret Thatcher, started life above her father's grocery shop at 2 North Pde, now a chiropractor's clinic; there's a small plaque on the house to honour its former resident, although the Iron Lady is yet to be granted her own plinth.

The **tourist office** ( ☎ 01476-406166; granthamtic@southkesteven.gov.uk; St Peter's Hill; ☺ 9.30am-4.30pm Mon-Fri, to 1pm Sat) is in the guildhall complex.

Until a commemorative statue is erected, Maggie must content herself with her latex puppet from the hit 1980s political satire *Spitting Image*, in the town's **museum** ( ☎ 01476-568783; St Peter's Hill; admission free; ☺ 10am-4pm Mon-

Sat). Here too is one of her sparkly evening gowns and famous handbags, as well as displays on Sir Isaac Newton.

You can easily spot the part 13th-, part 16th-century parish church of **St Wulfram's** ( ☺ 9am-4pm Mon-Sat Apr-Sep, to 12.30pm Mon-Fri, 10am-1pm Sat Oct-Mar) thanks to its pin-sharp 85m spire. It has an interesting crypt chapel, and hidden up a steep stairwell is a rare 16th-century chained library where a young Newton once pored over his studies.

A dream location for English period dramas (several have been filmed here), serene Restoration country mansion, **Belton House** (NT; ☎ 01476-566116; A607; adult/child under 16yr £9.50/5.50, grounds only £7.50/4.50; ☺ 12.30-5pm Wed-Sun Apr-Oct), stands in a 400-hectare park, 3 miles northeast of Grantham. Built in 1688 for Sir John Brownlow, it shelters some astonishingly ornate woodcarvings attributed to the master Dutch carver Grinling Gibbons. In the beautiful gardens is a sundial made famous in Helen Cresswell's children's classic *Moondial*. Bus 609 (15 minutes) runs here from near Grantham's train station.

### Sleeping & Eating
**Red House** ( ☎ 01476-579869; www.red-house.com; 74 North Pde; s/d from £30/48; P ☐ wi-fi) This handsome Georgian town house near Maggie's birthplace has large, spick-and-span rooms. The welcome is very friendly, beauty treatments are available and rooms have mini fridges and microwaves.

**Angel & Royal Hotel** ( ☎ 01476-565816; www.angelandroyal.co.uk; High St; s/d from £68/100; P ☐ wi-fi) This veteran coaching inn claims to be England's oldest, with no fewer than seven kings of England purportedly having stayed here since 1200. Its 29 rooms are each individually decorated, with beds occupied by a teddy bear, quaint floral patterns and copious olde-English charm. There's a grand restaurant in a baronial hall for fine dining and Sunday lunches.

### Getting There & Away
Grantham is 25 miles south of Lincoln, and Stagecoach bus 1 runs between the two (one hour and 20 minutes, twice hourly Monday to Saturday, five times on Sunday). Bus 4 run by Kimes Coaches runs to Stamford (1½ hours, four daily Monday to Saturday), as does National Express (£6.40, 30 minutes).

You'll need to change at Newark to get to Lincoln by train (£8.20, 1½ hours, two hourly).

Direct trains run from London King's Cross to Grantham (£28.20, 1¼ hours, twice hourly).

## STAMFORD
**pop 19,525**

This handsome town has a sunny disposition all year round thanks to the warm honey-coloured Lincolnshire limestone of its buildings. Nestling against the River Welland and a lush waterside park, handsome Stamford's tangle of streets is bursting with fine medieval and Georgian constructions. And if you feel as though you're walking through a period drama, there's a reason: Stamford has been used as a set for more drama productions than you can shake a clapperboard at.

The **tourist office** ( ☎ 01780-755611; stamfordtic@ southkesteven.gov.uk; 27 St Mary's St; ☺ 9.30am-5pm Mon-Sat & 10am-3.30pm Sun Apr-Oct) is in the Stamford Arts Centre, and helps with accommodation. They can also arrange guided town walks and chauffeured punt trips.

The **Stamford Museum** ( ☎ 01780-766317; Broad St; admission free; ☺ 10am-4pm Mon-Sat) has a muddle of displays on the town's history including models of circus-performing midget Charles Stratton (aka Tom Thumb) and local heavyweight Daniel Lambert.

### Sleeping & Eating

**Rock Lodge** ( ☎ 01780-481758; www.rock-lodge.co.uk; 1 Epingham Rd; s/d £70/90; P ) This imposing Edwardian town house sits haughtily above clipped green lawns, but the welcome is all smiles. The country casual rooms are well looked after and breakfasts (complete with homemade jams) are excellent.

**ourpick** **George** ( ☎ 01780-750750; www.george hotelofstamford.com; 71 St Martin's St; s/d from £90/130, 4-poster d £205; P ☐ wi-fi) Recognised by a gallows sign across the road, welcoming travellers but warning off highwaymen, this wonderful riverside hotel likes to call itself 'England's greatest coaching inn', and with some justification. Parts of it date back a thousand years and its long history is reflected in its 47 luxurious rooms, each of which has its own unique character and flair, decor and price tag. The oak-panelled restaurant serves classy British and international cuisine

**Finnans** ( ☎ 01780-752505; www.finnansbrasserie.co.uk; 8-9 Paul's St; mains £8-14; ☺ lunch & dinner Tue-Thu, 9am-close Fri & Sat) Seasonal, local food from a delicious, unpretentious and regularly changing menu is served up at this friendly brasserie.

### Getting There & Away

Stamford is 46 miles south of Lincoln and 21 miles south of Grantham.

National Express serves Stamford from London (£13.10, 2¾ hours, daily). Kimes operates between Stamford and Grantham (1½ hours, four daily Monday to Saturday), as does National Express (£6.40, 30 minutes, two daily). Delaine Buses run to Peterborough (one hour, hourly).

There are trains to Cambridge (£16, 1¼ hours, hourly) and Ely (£10.80, 55 minutes, hourly). Trains to Norwich (£22, 2¼ hours) usually involve changing at Ely or Peterborough.

## AROUND STAMFORD
### Burghley House

Built to impress back in the 16th century, this dizzyingly flamboyant **Elizabethan palace** ( ☎ 01780-752451; www.burghley.co.uk; adult/child incl sculpture garden £10.90/5.40; ☺ 11am-5pm Sat-Thu Easter-Oct) still does a damn fine job of it today. Lying just a mile south of Stamford, Burghley (bur-lee) is the home of the Cecil family and was built by Queen Elizabeth's adviser William Cecil. These days it's a regular star of the silver screen, with hit films like *The Da Vinci Code* and *Elizabeth: The Golden Age* just some of the productions utilising its flashy interior as a dramatic stage.

Its roof bristles with cupolas, pavilions, belvederes and chimneys, and every inch of its 18 magnificent staterooms seems drenched with lavish finery. Hundreds of masterpieces from Gainsborough to Brueghel hang from the walls, while other rooms skip the frames and are splashed with wonderful 17th-century Italian murals overflowing with muscles, mammaries and mythology. Most impressive is the Heaven Room, which writhes with floor-to-ceiling gods and goddesses; on the flip side, there's the nearby stairway to Hell, which depicts Satan as a giant cat-eyed uterus devouring the world. Other highlights include cavernous Tudor kitchens decorated with turtle skulls left over from the master's soup and an exhibit detailing the career of David Cecil, the Lord Burghley who was an Olympic athlete and part inspiration for the film *Chariots of Fire*.

Meanwhile, the landscaped deer park outside is now home to a splendid **sculpture garden** with organic-looking contemporary works sprinkled sympathetically and often humorously throughout the grounds.

The house is a pleasant 15-minute walk through the park from Stamford train station. The internationally famous **Burghley Horse Trials** take place here in early September.

# BOSTON
### pop 35,124

During the Middle Ages, Boston was a major port and wool-trading centre, but the town's true claim to fame came in the 1607, when pilgrims from Nottinghamshire tried to get from Boston to the Netherlands. These religious separatists suffered persecution and imprisonment but were able to make it to the Netherlands the year after, and later to the New World. When word of their success made it back here, a crowd of locals followed them across the Atlantic to found a namesake town in the new colony of Massachusetts.

Lying near the mouth of the River Witham, in the bay known as The Wash, the town has been well and truly eclipsed by its US namesake and is a shadow of its former self. Although there isn't much to keep you here for long, the labyrinthine streets are pleasant enough to wander around and much of the Tudor heritage is still in evidence.

The **tourist office** ( ☎ 01205-356656; South St; ticboston@boston.gov.uk; Market Pl; ⏰ 9.30am-5pm Mon-Sat) is in the Haven Gallery, just down from the guildhall.

## Sights & Activities

Appropriate to the town's big-shot status in medieval times, the early-14th-century **St Botolph's Church** ( ☎ 01205-362864; church free, tower adult/under 18yr £2.50/1; ⏰ 9am-4.30pm Mon-Sat, btwn services Sun) has a showy 88m-high tower, fondly dubbed the Boston Stump for its square tip, as its fenland base was not firm enough to support a thin spire. Puff your way up the 365 steps on a clear day and you'll see to Lincoln, 32 miles away.

Downstairs, there's a 17th-century **pulpit** from which John Cotton, the fiery vicar of St Botolph, delivered lengthy sermons in the 1630s, apparently convincing his parishioners to follow in the footsteps of the Pilgrim Fathers.

You can see the very cells in which the Pilgrim Fathers were imprisoned in the 14th-century **guildhall** ( ☎ 01205-365954; South St; adult/child £3/2; ⏰ 10am-4.30pm Mon-Sat & 1.30-4.30pm Sun May-Sep), one of Lincolnshire's oldest brick buildings and testament to Boston's great wealth at

the time. The guildhall has recently emerged from renovations and there are fun, interactive exhibits (for example, you can sit in the famous cells and close the bars behind you), as well as a restored 16th-century courtroom, and a mock-up of a Georgian kitchen.

## Sleeping

A delightful vine-covered Victorian villa 10 minutes' walk from Boston's centre, **Palethorpe House** ( ☎ 01205-59000; 138 Spilsby Rd; s/d £50/70; ℗ ⌨ ) has just two beautifully refurbished en-suite rooms complete with living rooms. Continental breakfasts are served only during the week.

## Getting There & Away

Brylaine Travel bus 5 runs between Lincoln and Boston (1½ hours, hourly), or you can take the train from Lincoln, changing at Sleaford (£9.20, 1¼ hours).

# SKEGNESS
### pop 16,806

If candyfloss, gaudy funfairs and a seafront parade drowning in amusement arcades and greasy fish-and-chip shops are your bag, then 'Skeggy' is the place to come. Thousands of classic seaside fun-seekers head here every year to do brave impressions of sunbathing on vast bucket-and-spade beaches, and live it up at cabaret shows, bingo halls and cheesy discos. But the resort also works to keep fresh generations of punters rolling in, and its more recent attractions include an orphaned seal-pup sanctuary, facilities for windsurfing and kitesurfing and a fancy skate park.

Cheap and cheerful B&Bs are just about everywhere and start at just £18 per person, but the **tourist office** ( ☎ 01754-899887; www.fun coast.co.uk; Grand Pde; ⏰ 9.30am-5pm daily Easter-Oct, to 4.30pm Mon-Fri Nov-Easter) will also help you find digs. It's opposite the **Embassy Centre** ( ☎ 0845 6740505; www.embassytheatre.co.uk), the mothership of Skeggy's cabaret scene, which puts on anything from comedy to Elvis tributes. From July to September, this stretch of beach saturates the night sky with light pollution as 25,000 glowing light bulbs ignite the town's famous light display, the **Skegness Illuminations**.

Skegness is simple to reach by public transport, with Stagecoach 7 buses departing from Boston (1¼ hours, hourly Monday to Saturday), and Stagecoach 6 buses from Lincoln (1¾ hours, hourly Monday to Saturday, five on Sunday).

There are trains between Skegness and Boston (40 minutes, at least hourly Monday to Saturday, nine on Sunday).

## LOUTH
### pop 15,930

Louth sits on the River Lud, sandwiched between the Wolds and the marches of the Lincolnshire coast. This largely Georgian market town is cleaved into two hemispheres – east and west – as the zero longitude line splits the town; it is marked by a plaque in Eastgate and sculptures dot the line as part of the Louth Art Trail. Louth was also once the scene of a dramatic, if short-lived, revolt against Henry VIII in 1536.

The **tourist office** ( ☎ 01507-609289; louthinfo@e-lindsey.gov.uk; New Market Hall, off Cornmarket; ☑ 9am-5pm Mon-Sat Easter-Sep, to 4.30pm Oct-Easter) has maps and can help find accommodation.

While mustering the strength to climb Louth's main attraction – the tallest parish-church spire in England – pop into **Louth Museum** ( ☎ 01507-601211; www.louthmuseum.co.uk; 4 Broadbank; adult/child £2/1.20; ☑ 10am-4pm Tue-Sat Apr-Oct) to see its reproduction of an enormous panorama of Louth, which was painted from the top of the church's tower in the 19th century.

To make the comparison with today's views, head for the spire itself. The part medieval, part Tudor **St James' Church** ( ☑ 10.30am-4pm Easter-Christmas) was described by Sir John Betjeman as 'one of the last great medieval Gothic masterpieces' and is propped up by dramatic buttresses and fortified by battlements.

Inside, take a good look down the nave and you'll see that the left row of pillars – which are older than their opposite twins – are lurching off balance. Strange to think that the famous New World adventurer Captain John Smith, of Pocahontas fame, once worshiped here. A long elbow-scraping climb up to the tower (£1.50) is rewarded by views better still than you'd hoped.

Louth's most elegant street is Georgian Westgate, which runs from beside the church. Opposite the mid-17th-century **church precincts** at No 47 is Westgate Pl. Sneak through its archway and you'll find an impossibly cute row of terraced houses, one of which bears a plaque commemorating Tennyson's four-year residence here.

Louth is 23 miles northeast of Lincoln, from where bus 10 runs (one hour, two hourly).

# NOTTINGHAMSHIRE

Nottinghamshire is awash with myth and storytelling. Home to outlaw Robin Hood and his band of thieves, it's is also the birthplace of provocative writer DH Lawrence and played host to hedonist poet Lord Byron. The city of Nottingham is the vibrant hub, drawing business people, shoppers and clubbers from around the region. Delve into the surrounding countryside and you'll come across the occasional gem of a stately home.

## Orientation & Information

Nottinghamshire is tall and thin, spreading a surprising distance north of Nottingham to finish level with Sheffield. Most of the county's attractions are in the southern half including Nottingham, with Newstead and Eastwood just north, Sherwood Forest in the centre and Newark-on-Trent and Southwell to the east.

See www.visitnottingham.co.uk for county-wide information.

## Getting Around

A journey planner and comprehensive bus, rail, tram and plane information can be found at www.itsnottingham.info. **Sherwood Forester buses** ( ☎ 0845 9 808080; Ranger ticket adult/child £6/3; ☑ Sun & bank holidays Jun-Aug) go to tourist attractions all over Nottinghamshire; some offer admission discounts if you show the ticket.

## NOTTINGHAM
### pop 266,988

Forever associated with merry men in tights and a cranky sheriff, Nottingham today is a dynamic mix of medieval and modern. Multistorey car parks and postwar architectural eyesores live alongside centuries-old landmarks and an old town formed from a warren of former lace shops and factories, on which the city's wealth was built in the 19th century. The city's industrial heyday is long gone, but its nightlife, culture and shopping are booming. Fashion designer Paul Smith is a local lad, while the clubs and bars are some of the liveliest in the country.

## Orientation

Like other Midlands cities, Nottingham is enclosed by an inner ring road within which lie most of the attractions, bars and restaurants. The train station is on the southern edge of the centre. There are two bus stations: Victoria

# THE MIDLANDS & THE MARCHES

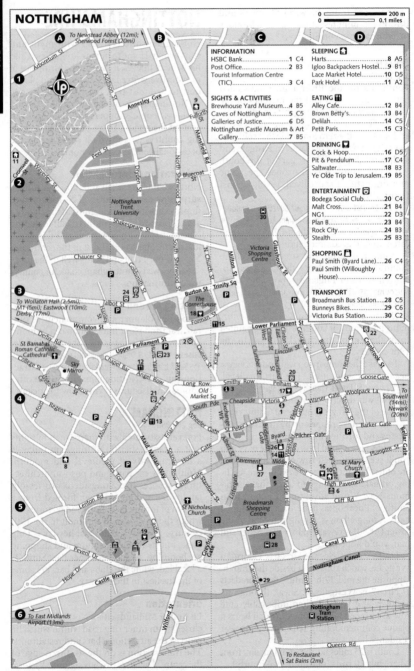

## NOTTINGHAM

**INFORMATION**
HSBC Bank.............................1 C4
Post Office............................2 B3
Tourist Information Centre
(TIC)..................................3 C4

**SIGHTS & ACTIVITIES**
Brewhouse Yard Museum....4 B5
Caves of Nottingham...........5 C5
Galleries of Justice..............6 D5
Nottingham Castle Museum & Art
Gallery..............................7 B5

**SLEEPING**
Harts....................................8 A5
Igloo Backpackers Hostel....9 B1
Lace Market Hotel.............10 D5
Park Hotel..........................11 A2

**EATING**
Alley Cafe..........................12 B4
Brown Betty's....................13 B4
Delilah...............................14 C5
Petit Paris..........................15 C3

**DRINKING**
Cock & Hoop.....................16 D5
Pit & Pendulum..................17 C4
Saltwater............................18 B3
Ye Olde Trip to Jerusalem..19 B5

**ENTERTAINMENT**
Bodega Social Club.............20 C4
Malt Cross..........................21 B4
NG1...................................22 D3
Plan B................................23 B4
Rock City...........................24 B3
Stealth...............................25 B3

**SHOPPING**
Paul Smith (Byard Lane).....26 C4
Paul Smith (Willoughby
House)..............................27 C5

**TRANSPORT**
Broadmarsh Bus Station.....28 C5
Bunneys Bikes....................29 C6
Victoria Bus Station...........30 C2

bus station is hidden away behind the Victoria shopping centre, just north of the centre, while Broadmarsh bus station is beneath Broadmarsh shopping centre to the south.

## Information

**HSBC Bank** ( ☎ 08457 404 404; 12 Victoria St; ☯ 9am-5pm Mon-Fri)

**Post office** ( ☎ 0845 722 3344; Queen St; ☯ 9am-5.30pm Mon-Fri, 9am-4.30pm Sat)

**Tourist office** ( ☎ 0115-915 5330; www.visitnotting ham.com; 1-4 Smithy Row; ☯ 9am-5.30pm Mon-Fri, to 5pm Sat, 10am-4pm Sun) The staff here are very helpful. Ask them about discount combination tickets for major attractions. There are a few terminals to access the internet here.

## Sights & Activities
### NOTTINGHAM CASTLE MUSEUM & ART GALLERY

William the Conqueror erected Nottingham's original castle, but the stately building that stands there now – more of a mansion than a castle – has been around since the 1670s; the last Nottingham Castle was demolished after the English Civil War.

The **castle museum** ( ☎ 0115-915 3700; joint ticket with the Brewhouse Yard Museum adult/child £3.50/2; ☯ 10am-5pm Mar-Oct, to 4pm Nov-Feb) opened in 1878. It vividly sets out Nottingham's history and displays some of the medieval alabaster carvings for which Nottingham was noted. Textiles and costumes peculiar to the city are also on show. Upstairs, there's an **art gallery** with changing exhibitions and some fine permanent pieces including works by Dante Gabriel Rossetti. There's also a stylish cafe and an excellent shop.

An underground passageway, **Mortimer's Hole** (45min tours £2; ☯ tours 11am, 2pm & 3pm Mon-Sat, noon, 1pm, 2pm, 3pm Sun May-Aug), leads from the castle to Brewhouse Yard. Roger Mortimer, who arranged Edward II's murder, is said to have been captured by supporters of Edward III who entered via this passage. Ask to see the Sheriff Room (there is still a Sheriff of Nottingham today, a purely symbolic role).

### CAVES OF NOTTINGHAM

Nottingham stands on Sherwood sandstone that's riddled with artificial caves dating back to medieval times. Bizarrely, the entrance to the most fascinating, readily accessible **caves** ( ☎ 0115-988 1955; www.cityofcaves.com; adult/child £5.50/4.25; ☯ 10.30am-4pm Mon-Sun) is inside Broadmarsh shopping centre, on the upper level. These contain an air-raid shelter, a medieval underground tannery, several pub cellars and a mock-up of a Victorian slum dwelling.

### WOLLATON HALL

Built in 1588 by land and coal-mine owner, Sir Francis Willoughby, **Wollaton Hall** ( ☎ 0115-915 3900; Wollaton Park, Derby Rd; admission free, tours £2.50/1.50; ☯ 11am-5pm Apr-Oct, to 4pm Nov-Mar) is a magnificent example of Elizabethan architecture at its most extravagant. Architect Robert Smythson was also responsible for the equally avant-garde Longleat in Wessex (p317). The Hall reopened in 2008 after a major restoration project.

The **Industrial Museum**, in the 18th-century stable block, displays lace-making equipment, Raleigh bicycles, a gigantic 1858 beam engine and oddities such as a locally invented, 1963 video recorder that never got off the ground.

Wollaton Hall is on the western edge of the city, 2.5 miles from the centre; get there on bus 30, which stops right in front (15 minutes). Wollaton Park, surrounding the hall, is a popular picnic spot.

### BREWHOUSE YARD MUSEUM

Housed in five 17th-century cottages carved into the cliff below the castle, this engaging **museum** ( ☎ 0115-915 3600; Castle Blvd; joint admission with Nottingham Castle adult/child £3.50/2; ☯ 10am-4.30pm) re-creates everyday life in Nottingham over the past 300 years with particularly fine reconstructions of traditional shops.

### GALLERIES OF JUSTICE

In the impressive Shire Hall building, the well-presented **Galleries of Justice** ( ☎ 0115-952 0555; www.galleriesofjustice.org.uk; High Pavement; adult/child £8.95/6.95; ☯ 10am-4pm Tue-Sun Apr-Sep, 10am-3pm Tue-Fri & 11am-4pm Sat & Sun Nov-Mar) takes you through an interactive history of the judicial system. From medieval ordeals by water or hot iron to modern crime detection, 'gaolers' and 'prisoners' guide you through – you could even end up being 'sent down' yourself.

## Tours

**Nottingham Tours** ( ☎ 0115-925 9388; www.notting hamtours.com) Offers a well-respected walking tour of the city, as well as tours of Sherwood Forest and boat trips.

**Original Nottingham Ghost Walk** ( ☎ 01773-769300; www.ghost-walks.co.uk; adult/child £4/3; ☯ 7pm Sat Jan-Nov) Departs from Ye Olde Salutation Inn, Maid Marian Way, to delve into the city's supernatural past – descend into the medieval caves if you dare...

## Sleeping

**Igloo Backpackers Hostel** ( ☎ 0115-947 5250; www.ig loohostel.co.uk; 110 Mansfield Rd; dm £13.50) A favourite of backpackers, this basic 36-bed independent hostel is a short walk north of Victoria bus station (entrance on Fulforth St). It's always full at weekends so book ahead. Breakfast is extra.

**Park Hotel** ( ☎ 0115-978 6299; www.parkhotelnottingham .co.uk; 5-7 Waverley St; s/d from £60/85; ☐ wi-fi) This rather sinister-looking, turn-of-the-century mansion has recently been transformed into a slick, modern hotel with comfortable rooms decked out in warm reds and browns. Breakfast is extra.

**Lace Market Hotel** ( ☎ 0115-852 3232; www.lace markethotel.co.uk; 29-31 High Pavement; s/d £90/115; Ⓟ ) This is a lovely boutique hotel in a beautifully historic, well-heeled pocket of the city centre. It's in an old town house with a slick contemporary interior and young, attentive staff. Check the website for weekend discounts.

**Harts** ( ☎ 0115-988 1900; www.hartsnottingham .co.uk; Standard Hill, Park Row; s/d from 120; Ⓟ ☐ wi-fi) A swish boutique hotel in a striking modern building, it's a short walk away from the castle. Rooms are the pinnacle of understated chic and there's an outstanding, buzzy restaurant as well as a lovely garden with sweeping views out over the countryside. Regular discounts are available through the website.

## Eating

**Brown Betty's** ( ☎ 0115-941 3464; 17B St James St; sandwiches & salads £3-7; ☺ 9am-6pm Mon-Sat) Cheap and delicious sandwiches, pastas and salads. The huge 'hungry man' breakfast ciabattas are particularly mouth-watering.

**Delilah** ( ☎ 0115-948 4461; delilahfinefoods.co.uk; 15 Middle Pavement; dishes £4-10; ☺ 9am-6pm Mon-Sat) This fine food and wine shop is brimming with fantastic cheese, meats, olives, breads and other gourmet favourites. At their food bar, you can take a seat to enjoy a tapas-style grazing menu, or grab an outstanding sandwich or deli platter to take away.

**ourpick Alley Cafe** ( ☎ 0115-955 1013; www.alleycafe .co.uk; Cannon Court; mains £5-6; ☺ 11am-6pm Mon & Tue, till late Wed-Sat) This pint-sized cafe-bar has created quite a buzz with its excellent, globally inspired vegetarian and vegan dishes, not to mention its funky DJs and tunes. It's hidden down an ancient back alley – seek it out.

**Petit Paris** ( ☎ 0115-947 3767; petitparisrestaurant.co.uk; 2 King's Walk; 2-/3-course menu from £15/18; ☺ lunch & dinner Mon-Sat) Great value two- and three-course menus are to be had at this informal and lively French bistro hidden up a little alleyway in the town centre. There are plenty of traditional favourites like coq au vin and frogs' legs, and there's a daily changing specials board.

**Restaurant Sat Bains** ( ☎ 0115-986 6566; Lenton Lane; www.restaurantsatbains.com; set dinner £49; ☺ lunch & dinner) Tucked away on the outskirts of town, Nottingham's only Michelin-starred restaurant delivers outstanding, inventive modern European cooking. There are also a few beautiful rooms on offer for that full-on luxury experience. Book well in advance.

## Drinking

**Pit & Pendulum** ( ☎ 0115-950 6383; 17 Victoria St) Cavernous Gothic-style pub with rough stone walls and plenty of nooks and crannies to lose yourself in. The dull orange lighting and horror-themed decorations, including flaming torch brackets at the entrance, thrones, chains, stocks and toilets accessed through a fake bookcase, make it look like Dracula's local.

**Saltwater** ( ☎ 0115-954 2664; www.saltwater-restaurant .com; The Cornerhouse, Forman St; ☺ noon-midnight Sun-Wed, to 1am Thu, to 2am Fri & Sat) The entrance – through the chain restaurants of the Cornerhouse shopping centre – is less than salubrious, but inside you'll find a stylish, buzzing bar with a well-turned out clientele and great cocktails. Best is the expansive plant-filled rooftop terrace with awesome views over the city's rooftops. There's also a restaurant serving top-notch modern British and European food.

**ourpick Ye Olde Trip to Jerusalem** ( ☎ 0115-947 3171; Brewhouse Yard, Castle Rd) Tucked into the cliff below the castle, this fantastically atmospheric alehouse claims to be England's oldest pub – it supposedly slaked the thirst of departing crusaders. The phrase 'nooks and crannies' could have been invented for here. Just when you think there are no more, you'll find another – and there are usually more than enough to accommodate the many tourists who come to sample the brews.

**Cock & Hoop** ( ☎ 0115-852 3231; 25 High Pavement) This atmospheric town-house pub has an almost genteel atmosphere that is far removed from some of the gaudy, loud nightspots that surround it. There are real ales, great Sunday lunches and it's dog-friendly.

## Entertainment

Nightclub fads come and go at breakneck speed in Nottingham. Check the local guides for info.

**ourpick Bodega Social Club** ( ☎ 0115-950 5078; www.thebodegasocialclub.co.uk; 23 Pelham St) The sister club of the Social in London plays everything from house to electro to classic rock to hip hop. DJs rock the upstairs dance floor and they put on hugely popular live shows from up-and-coming indie bands to burlesque.

**NG1** ( ☎ 0115-958 8440; www.ng1club.co.uk; 76-80 Lower Parliament St; admission £3-10) Nottingham's very own gay superclub, NG1 is pure, unpretentious, hedonistic fun, with two dance floors belting out classic funky house, pop, cheese or indie depending on the night.

**Plan B** (15-16 Hurts Yard; admission free) Stashed away up an alley, this sexy little club plays house, electro and indie and has regular acoustic jams. It also does a nice line in cheap cocktails.

**Stealth** ( ☎ 0115-958 0672; www.stealthattack .co.uk; Masonic Pl, Goldsmith St; admission £2-10) One of the city's best clubs, Stealth has an eclectic music mix, from electro to drum and bass, to highly charged all-nighters that lure an up-for-it crowd from miles around. Next door, a music venue called the Rescue Rooms hosts regular live bands.

**Malt Cross** ( ☎ 0115-941 1048; www.maltcross.com; 16 St James's St; ☯ 11am-11pm Mon-Thu, to 12.30am Fri & Sat) In an old Victorian music hall with a colourful history (it was a brothel in a previous incarnation), this place has a friendly, laid-back vibe. Good live music and decent food are all dished up under the glass arched roof, an architectural treasure in itself.

**Rock City** ( ☎ 0115-941 2544; www.rock-city.co.uk; 8 Talbot St) The dance floor packs out here on the popular 'Tuned' student night on Thursday, and on '90s night every Friday. Big-name pop acts usually head here.

## Shopping

**Paul Smith** is the local boy who conquered London's heady fashion scene. He's done so well, he has not one, but two upmarket exclusive shops in the city centre: one on **Byard Lane** ( ☎ 0115-9506 712; 10 Byard Lane) and one in **Willoughby House** ( ☎ 0115-968 5990; Willoughby House, 20 Low Pavement).

## Getting There & Away

Nottingham is well situated for both trains and buses. The train station just to the south of the town centre has frequent – but not fast – services that go to Birmingham (£13,

1½ hours), Manchester (£17, two hours) and London (£21, two hours).

Coaches are the cheaper option, mostly operating from the dingy confines of Broadmarsh bus station. There are five direct services to Birmingham and around 10 to London. Bus services to outlying villages are regular and reliable too. Services to Southwell, Eastwood and Newark mostly depart from Broadmarsh bus station. If you're going further, the nearby airport might be your best bet.

There are several train companies serving Nottingham. Useful services include the following:

**Cross Country Trains**( ☎ 0870 010 0084; www.cross countrytrains.co.uk) Goes to Birmingham and as far as Cardiff.

**East Midlands Airport** ( ☎ 0871 919 9000; www .nottinghamema.com)

**East Midlands Trains** ( ☎ 08457 125678; www .eastmidlandstrains.co.uk) Serves East Midlands, London and up north.

**London Midland** ( ☎ 0844 811 0133; www.london midland.com) Links up to Liverpool to the northwest, and as far south as London St Pancras.

**Trent Barton** ( ☎ 01773-712265; www.trentbuses. co.uk) Buses depart from Broadmarsh and Victoria bus stations.

## Getting Around

For information on buses within Nottingham, call **Nottingham City Transport** ( ☎ 0115-950 6070; www.nctx.co.uk). The Kangaroo ticket gives you unlimited travel on buses and trams within the city for £3.40.

The city tram system (www.thetram.net; single/all day from £1.50/£2.70) runs to the centre from Hucknall, 7 miles to the north of central Nottingham, through to the town centre and the train station.

Full details on Nottingham transport can be found at the **Nottingham Travelwise Service** (www.itsnottingham.info). You can also pick up a free transport planner and map from the tourist office.

**Bunneys Bikes** ( ☎ 0115-947 2713; 97 Carrington St; bike hire per day £9; ☯ 9am-5.30pm Mon-Fri, to 5pm Sat, 11am-3pm Sun) is near the train station.

## AROUND NOTTINGHAM
### Newstead Abbey

With its attractive gardens, evocative lakeside ruins and notable connections with Romantic poet Lord Byron (1788–1824), whose country pile it was, **Newstead Abbey** ( ☎ 01623-455900;

www.newsteadabbey.org.uk; adult/child £7/4, gardens only £3/2; ☺ house noon-5pm Apr-Sep, garden 9am-dusk) is a popular weekend destination for tourists and local families alike. Founded as an Augustinian priory around 1170, it was converted into a home after the dissolution of the monasteries in 1539. Beside the still-imposing facade of the priory church are the remains of the manor. It now houses some interesting Byron memorabilia, from pistols to manuscripts, and you can have a peek at his old living quarters. Many of the rooms are re-created in convincing period styles.

The house is 12 miles north of Nottingham, off the A60. Pronto buses run from Victoria bus station, stopping at Newstead Abbey gates (30 minutes, three hourly Monday to Saturday, hourly on Sunday), from where you will have to walk a mile to the house and gardens. The Sherwood Forester bus runs right there on summer Sundays and bank holiday Mondays.

### DH Lawrence Sites

The **DH Lawrence Birthplace Museum** ( ☎ 01773-717353; 8A Victoria St, Eastwood; admission Mon-Fri free, Sat & Sun £2; ☺ 10am-5pm Apr-Oct, to 4pm Nov-Mar), former home of the controversial Nottingham author (1885–1930), has been reconstructed as it would have been in his childhood, with period furnishings.

Down the road, the **Durban House Heritage Centre** ( ☎ 01773-717353; Mansfield Rd; admission Mon-Fri free, Sat & Sun £2; ☺ 10am-5pm Apr-Oct, to 4pm Nov-Mar) sheds light on the background to Lawrence's books by re-creating the life of the mining community at the turn of the 20th century. A combined ticket for Durben House and the DH Lawrence Birthplace Museum costs £3.50.

Eastwood is about 10 miles northwest of the city. Take Trent Barton service 1 or follow the A610.

### Sherwood Forest Country Park

You'll have to put in some effort to lose yourself like an outlaw: today's Sherwood Forest can be incredibly crowded, especially in summer. Stray off the main circuit, though, and you can still find peaceful (and beautiful) spots. The **Sherwood Forest Visitor Centre** ( ☎ 01623-824490; www.sherwood-forest.org.uk; admission free, parking £3; ☺ 10am-5.30pm Apr-Oct, to 4.30pm Nov-Mar) houses 'Robyn Hode's Sherwode', a deeply naff exhibition of wooden cut-outs, murals and life-size figures describing

the lifestyles of bandits, kings, peasants and friars. One of the most popular attractions is the **Major Oak**, a 1-mile walk from the visitors centre and supposedly once a hiding place for Mr Hood; these days it seems to be on its last legs. The **Robin Hood Festival** is a massive medieval re-enactment that takes place here every August.

**Sherwood Forest YHA** ( ☎ 0845 371 9139; www.yha.org.uk; Forest Corner, Edwinstowe; dm member/nonmember £18/21) is a modern hostel with comfortable dorms just a bugle-horn cry away from the visitor centre.

Sherwood Forester buses run the 20 miles to the park from Nottingham on Sunday and bank holiday Mondays (May to September). Catch bus 33 from Nottingham Monday to Saturday.

## SOUTHWELL
pop 6285

Southwell is a sleepy market town straight out of a Jane Austen novel. **Southwell Minster** ( ☎ 01636-812649; suggested donation £3; ☺ 8am-7pm May-Sep, to dusk Oct-Apr) is a grand Gothic cathedral, its two heavy, square front towers belying the treats within. The nave dates from the 12th century, although there is evidence of an earlier Saxon church floor, itself made with mosaics from a Roman villa. A highlight of the building is the chapterhouse, filled with 13th-century carvings of leaves, pigs, dogs and rabbits. The library is fascinating, with illuminated manuscripts and heavy tomes from the 16th century and earlier.

A visit to **Southwell Workhouse** (NT; ☎ 01636-817250; Upton Rd; adult/child £5.80/3; ☺ noon-5pm Wed-Sun Apr-Sep, 11am-4pm Sat & Sun Oct–Mar) is a sobering but fascinating experience. An audio guide, narrated by 'inmates' and 'officials', describes the life of paupers in the mid-19th century to good (if grim) effect.

Bus 100 runs from Nottingham (50 minutes, every 20 minutes, hourly on Sunday), and Stagecoach bus 29 runs to Newark-on-Trent (25 minutes, every 30 minutes, every two hours on Sunday).

# DERBYSHIRE

Derbyshire is one of the most beguiling parts of the country, home to romantic bronze and purple moors, remote windswept farms, stark villages and rolling green hills lined with stone fences and speckled with sheep.

Part of the county lies within the Peak District National Park, and for many visitors the two areas are synonymous – although the park overlaps several other counties, and Derbyshire has a great deal to offer outside the confines of the park. There's the incongruous seaside jollity of Matlock Bath, the twisted spire of Chesterfield cathedral, and some wonderful stately homes including magical, ramshackle Calke Abbey and majestic Chatsworth.

Derbyshire is one of the most visited counties in England, and justifiably so.

## Orientation

Derbyshire's main city, Derby, lies toward the south of this very pretty county, which stretches much taller than it does wide. The north contains some of the prettiest stretches of the Peak District, but the south is also blessed with some fine scenery, perhaps most instantly accessible from the pretty market town of Ashbourne. Matlock Bath is almost plumb in the county's centre.

## Activities

Outdoor activities in Derbyshire include walking, cycling, rock climbing, caving and paragliding, to name but a few. Many take place inside the Peak District National Park (see p463).

## Getting There & Around

**Derbyshire Wayfarer** (Traveline, ☎ 0871 200 2233; day pass adult/child/family £8/4/13) Covers buses and trains throughout the county and beyond (eg to Manchester and Sheffield).

**Trent Barton Buses** ( ☎ 01773-712265; www.trent barton.co.uk; day ticket £4) Operates the TransPeak bus service.

## DERBY
pop 229,407

Once a relaxed market town, the Industrial Revolution created a major manufacturing centre out of Derby, which made its fortune churning out silk, china, railways and Rolls-Royce aircraft engines. It's not the most attractive of towns but it is a useful stepping stone to some lovely Derbyshire countryside. History buffs can learn about the development of English engineering, and bone-china fans can take a tour of the Royal Crown Derby Factory.

## Information

The helpful **tourist office** ( ☎ 01332-255802; www.visit derby.co.uk; Market Pl; ☻ 9.30am-5.30pm Mon-Fri, to 5pm Sat, 10.30am-2.30pm Sun) is in the main square.

## Sights

Derby's grand 18th-century **cathedral** (Queen St; ☻ 9.30am-4.30pm Mon-Sat) boasts a 64m-high tower and impressive wrought-iron screens. Large windows enhance the magnificent light interior. Tours run at 10.30am on the second Monday in the month. Don't miss the huge tomb of Bess of Hardwick, one of Derbyshire's most formidable residents in days gone by. For more about her, see Hardwick Hall (p463). Bird-lovers should watch out for peregrines, regularly spotted around the tower.

Next to the River Derwent in a former silk mill (Britain's first 'modern' factory), the **Derby Museum of Industry & History** ( ☎ 01332-255308; Silk Mill Lane; admission free; ☻ 11am-5pm Mon, 10am-5pm Tue-Sat, 1-4pm Sun & bank holidays) tells the city's manufacturing history; trainspotters will have a field day, while plane buffs should get a buzz out of displays on the development of the Rolls-Royce aero-engine.

The factory of **Royal Crown Derby** ( ☎ 01332-712841; www.royalcrownderby.co.uk; Osmaston Rd; tours £4.95, 4 daily Mon-Fri, demonstration studio only £2.95/2.75; ☻ 9am-5pm Mon-Sat, 10am-4pm Sun) turns out some of the finest bone china in England. In the demonstration studio, you'll see workers skilfully making delicate china flowers, using little more than a hat pin, a spoon handle and even a head-lice comb.

## Sleeping

**Crompton Coach House** ( ☎ 01332-365735; www.coach housederby.co.uk; 45 Crompton St; s/d incl breakfast £30/60) Bright, sunny rooms along with cheery hosts make this colourful B&B the best option in a city short on choices for the cash-conscious traveller. It lies just south of the central shopping area.

**Cathedral Quarter Hotel** ( ☎ 01332-8523207; www .cathedralquarterhotel.com; 16 St Mary's Gate; s/d from £100/120; ☐ wi-fi) A taste of boutique comes to Derby in this new luxury hotel in a characterful late-19th-century building, complete with grand, sweeping staircase. Rooms are suitably plush and there's an on-site spa as well as a wood-panelled, fine-dining restaurant.

## Eating & Drinking

**our pick** **Soul Restaurant and Deli** ( ☎ 01332-346989; 26-28 Green Lane; sandwiches £5-8; ☻ 11.30am-4pm & 5.30-11.30pm Tue-Sat) This outstanding, bright, bustling deli and restaurant is dedicated to using local ingredients in its sandwiches, meze platters, cheeses, cakes and salads. It also serves heavier, but no less delicious, two- and three-course lunch and dinner menus and has regular live jazz.

**Brunswick Inn** ( ☎ 01332-290677; www.brunswickinn .co.uk; 1 Railway Tce) This award-winning inn has a warm ambience and a warren of rooms done out in maroon leather upholstery and wood panels, but the real reason to come here is the beers (some made on-site), which are a dream for real-ale lovers.

### Getting There & Away

At the time of writing, a brand-new bus station is scheduled to open in 2009. In the meantime, buses are running from temporary stands on Full St, Derwent St, Corporation St, Morledge St and Albert St. TransPeak buses run between Nottingham and Manchester via Derby, Matlock, Bakewell and Buxton (Derby to Nottingham 30 minutes, Derby to Bakewell one hour, hourly). Outgoing services currently leave from Derwent St just north of the tourist office. From London, there are trains to Derby (two hours, hourly), continuing to Chesterfield, Sheffield and Leeds. There is also a direct service from Birmingham (45 minutes, three per hour).

## AROUND DERBY
### Kedleston Hall

Sitting proudly in vast landscaped parkland, the superb neoclassical mansion of **Kedleston Hall** (NT; ☎ 01332-842191; adult/child £7/3; ⏰ noon-4pm Sat-Wed Easter-Oct) is a must for fans of stately homes. The Curzon family has lived here since the 12th century; Sir Nathaniel Curzon tore down an earlier house in 1758 so this stunning masterpiece could be built. Meanwhile, the poor old peasants in Kedleston village had their humble dwellings moved a mile down the road, as they interfered with the view. Ah, the good old days…

Entering the house through a grand portico, you reach the breathtaking **Marble Hall** with its massive alabaster columns and statues of Greek deities. Curved corridors on either side offer splendid views of the park – don't miss the arc of floorboards, specially cut from bending oak boughs. Other highlights include richly decorated bedrooms and a circular saloon with a domed roof, modelled on the Pantheon in Rome.

Another great building, Government House in Calcutta (now Raj Bhavan), was modelled on Kedleston Hall, as a later Lord Curzon was viceroy of India around 1900. His collection of oriental artefacts is on show, as is his wife's 'peacock' dress – made of gold and silver thread and weighing 5kg.

If the sun is out, take a walk around the lovingly restored 18th-century-style **pleasure gardens**.

Kedleston Hall is 5 miles northwest of Derby, off the A52. By bus, service 109 between Derby and Ashbourne goes within about 1.5 miles of Kedleston Hall (25 minutes, every two hours Saturday only).

### Calke Abbey

Like an enormous, long-neglected cabinet of wonders, **Calke Abbey** (NT; ☎ 01332-863822; adult/child £9/4; ⏰ 12.30-5pm Sat-Wed Apr-Oct) is not your usual opulent stately home. Built around 1703, it's passed through a dynasty of eccentric and reclusive baronets and has been left much as it was in the late 1800s – a mesmerising example of a country house in decline. The result is a ramshackle maze of secret corridors, underground tunnels and rooms crammed with ancient furniture, mounted animal heads, dusty books, stuffed birds and endless piles of bric-a-brac from the last three centuries. Some rooms are in fabulous condition, while others are deliberately untouched, complete with crumbling plaster and mouldy wallpaper. (You exit the house via a long, dark tunnel – a bit more thrilling than one might like, given the state of the buildings.) A stroll round the gardens is a similar time-warp experience – in the potting sheds nothing has changed since about 1930, but it looks like the gardener left only yesterday.

Admission to Calke Abbey house is by timed ticket at busy times. On summer weekends it's wise to phone ahead and check there'll be space. You can enter the gardens and grounds at any time. Calke is 10 miles south of Derby off the A514. Visitors coming by car must enter via the village of Ticknall. The Arriva bus 68A from Derby to Swadlincote stops at Ticknall (40 minutes, hourly) and from there it's a 2-mile walk through the park.

### Ashbourne
**pop 7600**

Standing at the very southern edge of the Peak District National Park, pretty little Ashbourne throngs during the holidays and weekends with hikers and other visitors, who come to this stone town to recharge in the flurry of cafes, pubs and antique shops on the precariously slanted main street.

The **tourist office** ( ☎ 01335-343666; Market Pl; ☽ 9.30am-5pm Apr-Oct, 10am-4pm Mon-Sat Nov-Feb) can provide leaflets or advice on B&Bs in the area.

Ashbourne is of particular interest to walkers and cyclists because it's the southern terminus of the **Tissington Trail**, a former railway line and now a wonderful easy-gradient path cutting through fine west-Derbyshire countryside. The Tissington Trail takes you north towards Buxton and connects with the High Peak Trail running south towards Matlock Bath.

About a mile outside town along Mapleton Lane, **Ashbourne Cycle Hire** ( ☎ 01335-343156; day hire £14) is on the Tissington Trail, with a huge stock of bikes and trailers for all ages, and free leaflets showing the route with pubs and teashops along the way.

Ivy-covered **Bramhall's** ( ☎ 01335-346158; www.bramhalls.co.uk; 6 Buxton Rd; s/d £40/70) lies just up the road from the main market square. Its has a fine restaurant and some lovely B&B rooms.

**Patrick & Brooksbank** ( ☎ 01335-346753; 22 Market Pl) is a great little deli and cafe with excellent homemade cookies, handmade chocolates, cheeses, breads and meats – just right for a takeaway to eat out on the hills.

Down-to-earth **Smith's Tavern** ( ☎ 01335-342264; 36 St John's St) is a cosy, cluttered and popular pub with great cask ales and a regularly changing menu of tasty grub.

Without your own transport, bus is the only way to get to Ashbourne and the trip takes from 40 minutes to just under an hour. Direct buses include the Arriva 109 (five services daily Monday to Saturday), and the One, operated by Trent Barton (hourly Monday to Saturday). On Sunday, TM Travel's 108 has four services to Ashbourne.

## MATLOCK BATH
pop 2202

Unashamedly tacky, Matlock Bath is like a seaside resort that lost its way and ended up at the foot of the Peak District National Park. Wander down the gaudy promenade and you'll find amusement arcades, Victorian cafes, pubs and souvenir shops, while the rest of the town stretches up the hillside behind. Bisected by the smooth, twisty A6, the town's buzz becomes a roar of engines at the weekend, as hundreds of motorcyclists flock here and the crowds of leather-clad bike enthusiasts only add to the town's fun atmosphere.

It sits next to the pleasant town of Matlock, which has little in the way of sights but is a handy gateway to the scenic dales.

### Orientation & Information

Matlock Bath is 2 miles south of Matlock. Everything revolves around North Pde and South Pde, a line of seaside-style shops, attractions, pubs and places to eat along one side of the main road (the A6) through town, with the murmuring River Derwent and a plush gorge on the other side.

Matlock Bath's **tourist office** ( ☎ 01629-55082; www.derbyshire.gov.uk; the Pavilion; ☽ 9.30am-5pm daily Mar-Oct, 10.30am-4pm Nov-Feb) is run by helpful staff armed with reams of leaflets and guidebooks.

### Sights & Activities

You can amuse yourself quite nicely simply strolling along the promenade, chomping on chips or candyfloss. For a scenic detour, you can walk across the river to the park on the other side where steep paths lead to some great cliff-top viewpoints.

At the enthusiast-run **Mining Museum** ( ☎ 01629-583834; www.peakmines.co.uk; the Pavilion; adult/child £3/2; ☽ 10am-5pm May-Sep, 11am-3pm Nov-Apr) you can clamber through the shafts and tunnels where Derbyshire lead miners once eked out a risky living. Bizarrely, part of the museum was once a dancehall. For £2/1 extra per adult/child, you can go down **Temple Mine** and pan for 'gold'.

For a different view, go to the **Heights of Abraham** ( ☎ 01629-582365; adult/child £11/8; ☽ 10am-5pm daily Mar-Oct, to 4.30pm Nov-Feb), which claims to be the Peak District's 'oldest attraction'. It's a great family day out, with cavern tours, woodland walks and an adventure playground. The price includes a spectacular cable-car ride up from the valley floor.

From the cable-car base, walking trails lead up to viewpoints on top of **High Tor**. You can see down to Matlock Bath and over to **Riber Castle**, a Victorian folly.

A mile south of Matlock Bath is **Masson Mills Working Textile Museum** ( ☎ 01629-581001; adult/child £2.50/1.50; ☽ 10am-4pm Mon-Fri, 11am-5pm Sat, 11am-4pm Sun). Built in 1783 for pioneering industrialist Sir Richard Arkwright it was seen as a masterpiece in its time. Today it's a working museum, and one of the **Derwent Valley Mills** (www.derwentvalleymills.org) that make up

---

**SHROVE TUESDAY FOOTBALL**

Shrove Tuesday comes before Ash Wednesday, the first day of Lent – the Christian time of fasting – so Shrove Tuesday is the day to use up all your rich and fattening food. This led to the quaint tradition of Pancake Day in England and the flamboyant Mardi Gras festival in other parts of the world.

On Shrove Tuesday, various English towns celebrate with pancake races, but in Ashbourne they go for something much more energetic. Here they play Shrovetide Football, but it's nothing like the football most people are used to. For a start, the goals are 3 miles apart, the 'pitch' is a huge patch of countryside, and the game lasts all afternoon and evening (then starts again the day after). There are two teams, but hundreds of participants, and very few rules indeed. A large leather ball is fought over voraciously as players maul their way through fields and gardens, along the river, and up the main street – where shop windows are specially boarded over for the occasion. Visitors come from far and wide to watch, but only the brave should take part!

---

this Unesco World Heritage Site, with renovated looms and weaving machines, and the world's largest collection of bobbins bringing over 200 years of textile history to life. It has the added attraction of a 'shopping village' including three floors of High St textile and clothing names.

From the beginning of September to October, don't miss the **Matlock Illuminations** (Derwent Gardens; adult/under 16yr £4/free; ☽ from dusk Fri-Sun), with streams of pretty lights, outrageously decorated Venetian boats on the river and fireworks.

### Sleeping

Matlock Bath has several B&Bs in the heart of things on North Pde and South Pde, and a few places just out of the centre. There are also more choices in nearby Matlock.

**Sunnybank Guesthouse** ( ☎ 01629-584621; sunnybankmatlock@aol.com; Clifton Rd; s/d £40/64) This lovely, well-kept guesthouse is blessed with bright bedrooms, most with fine views over the surrounding countryside. The comfortable, wooden-floored breakfast room has a reassuring and lingering scent of marmalade and toast.

**Temple Hotel** ( ☎ 01629-583911; www.templehotel .co.uk; Temple Wk; s/d £65/92; **P** ) The views from this hillside hotel are fantastic – so lovely that Lord Byron once felt inspired to etch a poem on the restaurant window. The hotel itself feels slightly old fashioned and the rooms don't seem to have been updated for years. Bar meals are available.

### Eating & Drinking

North Pde and South Pde are lined end to end with cafes, teashops and takeaways serving artery-clogging fish and chips, fried chicken, pies and burgers.

**Fishpond** ( ☎ 01629-581000; 204 South Pde) This pub gets a lively, spirited crowd and is surprisingly boisterous for a pub in rural Derbyshire. It has a mixed bag of live music.

**Victorian Tea Shop** ( ☎ 01629-583325; 118 North Pde; ☽ 10am-5.30pm Mon-Fri) For the pick of the teahouses, this place is all lace curtains, cream cakes and delicate crockery.

### Getting There & Away

The Peak District is extremely well served by public transport, and Matlock is a hub. Buses 213 and 214 go to and from Sheffield (one hour 10 minutes) several times a day. There are buses to and from Derby (1¼ hours, hourly) and Chesterfield (35 minutes, hourly). Several trains a day serve Derby (30 minutes).

## CHESTERFIELD
### pop 100,879

This town has nothing much to recommend it except for one famous landmark: the startling crooked spire of **St Mary & All Saints Church** ( ☎ 01246-206506; admission free, tours adult/child £4/2; ☽ 9am-5pm). Dating from 1360, the giant spire corkscrews 68m high and leans almost 3m southwest. There are various theories why: it probably was due to green-timber warping, although some still prefer to believe that when a virgin got married in the church the spire was so shocked that it twisted to see the sight for itself. Tour times vary; call to arrange.

The **tourist office** ( ☎ 01246-345777; Rykneld Sq; ☽ 9am-5.30pm Mon-Sat Apr-Oct, to 5pm Nov-Mar) is right opposite the crooked spire in a sleek black building. It's very useful for planning a trip to the Peak District.

THE MIDLANDS &
THE MARCHES

The easiest way to get here is by train. Chesterfield is between Nottingham/Derby (20 minutes) and Sheffield (10 minutes), with services about hourly. The station is just east of the centre.

## HARDWICK

Elizabethan **Hardwick Hall** (NT; ☎ 01246-850430; adult/child £9.50/4.75; ☒ noon-4.30pm Wed, Thu, Sat & Sun Mar-Oct, 11am-3pm Sat & Sun Dec) should rank high on your list of must-see stately homes. It was home to the 16th century's second-most-powerful woman, Elizabeth, countess of Shrewsbury – known to all as Bess of Hardwick. Bess gained power and wealth by marrying upwards four times and she unashamedly modelled herself on the era's most famous woman – Queen Elizabeth I.

Bess's fourth husband died in 1590, leaving her with a huge pile of cash to play with, and she had Hardwick Hall built using the designs of eminent architect Robert Smythson. Glass was a status symbol, so she went all out on the windows; as a contemporary ditty quipped, 'Hardwick Hall – more glass than wall'. Also magnificent are the High Great Chamber and Long Gallery. These and many other rooms and broad stairways are decorated with tremendous tapestries.

Next door is Bess's first house, **Hardwick Old Hall** (EH; adult/child £4/2, joint ticket £11/5; ☒ 11am-6pm Mon & Wed-Sun Apr-Sep, to 5pm Oct), now a romantic ruin.

Also fascinating are the formal gardens, and the hall sits in the great expanse of **Hardwick Park** with short and long walking trails leading across fields and through woods. Ask at the ticket office for details. Just near the south gate is the sandstone **Hardwick Inn** (☎ 01246-850 245; Hardwick Park, Doe Lea), a historic pub with a sunny little patio and a surprisingly sophisticated menu.

Hardwick Hall is 10 miles southeast of Chesterfield, just off the M1. The Pronto bus from Chesterfield to Nottingham stops at Glapwell, from where it's a 2-mile walk to Hardwick Hall.

# PEAK DISTRICT

One of the most beautiful parts of the country, the Peak District National Park crams in pretty villages, wild moorland, grand houses, deep, dark limestone caves and the southernmost hills of the Pennines. No one knows for certain how the Peak District got its name – certainly not from the landscape, which has hills, moors and valleys, but no peaks. It's rumoured to be named after an Anglo-Saxon tribe, the Peacsaetna, who once lived here.

This is one of England's best-loved national parks (it's the busiest in Europe, and the world's second busiest after Mt Fuji), but don't be put off by its popularity. Escaping the crowds is no problem if you avoid summer weekends, and even then, with a bit of imagination, it's easy to find your own peaceful spot to take it all in.

## Orientation & Information

The Peak District is principally in Derbyshire but spills into five adjoining counties including Yorkshire, Staffordshire and Cheshire; it's one of the largest national parks in England. This 555-sq-mile protected area is divided into two distinct zones: the harsher, higher, untamed Dark Peak to the north, characterised by peaty moors and dramatic gritstone cliffs called 'edges'; and the lower, prettier, more pastoral White Peak to the south, with green fields marked by dry-stone walls, divided by deep dales.

There are tourist offices (those run by the national park are called visitor centres) in Buxton, Bakewell, Castleton, Edale and other locations, all overflowing with maps, guidebooks and leaflets detailing walks, cycle rides and other activities. For general information, the free *Peak District* newspaper and the official park website at www.peakdistrict.org cover transport, activities, local events, guided walks and so on.

## Activities

### CAVING & CLIMBING

The Peak District limestone is riddled with caves and caverns including 'showcaves' open to the public in Castleton, Buxton and Matlock Bath (described in each of those sections). For serious caving (or potholing) trips, tourist offices can provide a list of accredited outdoor centres, and if you know what you're doing, Castleton makes a great base.

For guidebooks, gear (to buy or hire) and a mine of local information, contact **Hitch n Hike** (☎ 01433-651013; www.hitchnhike.co.uk; Mytham Bridge, Bamford, Hope Valley, Derbyshire), a specialist caving and outdoor activity shop in Bamford, near Castleton. The website also has more info about caving in the area.

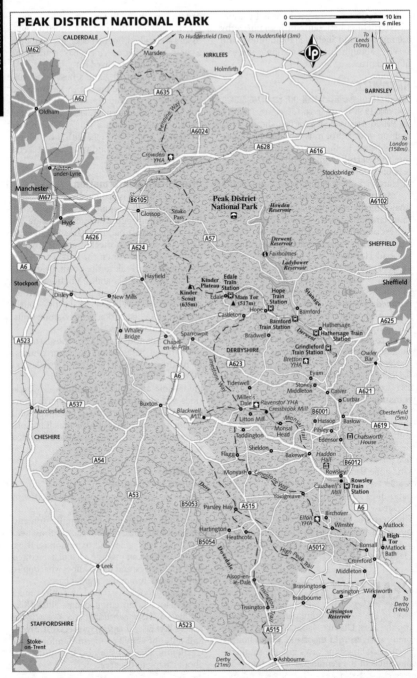

# PEAK DISTRICT NATIONAL PARK

If you're keen on climbing, the Peak District is a great place to indulge and has long been a training ground for England's top mountaineers. There are multipitch routes on limestone faces such as High Tor, overlooking Matlock Bath, and there's a great range of short climbing routes on the famous gritstone 'edges' of Froggatt, Curbar and Stanage.

### CYCLING

The Peak District is a very popular cycling area, especially the White Peak and the parts of Derbyshire south of here around Matlock and Ashbourne, which have a network of quiet lanes and tracks for mountain bikers. In the Dark Peak there are fewer roads, and they are quite busy with traffic, although there are some good off-road routes. A good place to start any ride is a tourist office, which can supply maps, books and leaflets for cyclists and mountain bikers.

In the Dark Peak, Edale is a popular starting point for mountain bikers, and near the Derwent Reservoir is also good. In the White Peak, all the villages mentioned in this section make good bases for cycle tours.

For easy traffic-free riding, head for the 17.5-mile **High Peak Trail**, a route for cyclists and walkers on the mostly flat track of an old railway. You can join the trail at Cromford, near Matlock Bath, but it starts with a very steep incline, so if you seek easy gradients, a better start is Middleton Top, a mile or so southwest. The trail winds through beautiful hills and farmland to a village called Parsley Hay, and continues on for a few more miles towards Buxton.

At Parsley Hay another former railway turned walking-and-cycling route, the **Tissington Trail**, heads south for 13 miles to Ashbourne. You can go out and back as far as you like, or make it a triangular circuit, following the busy B5053 or (a better choice) the quiet lanes through Bradbourne and Brassington.

The **Pennine Bridleway** is another good option, suitable for horse riders, cyclists and walkers.

There are several bike-hire centres in the Peak District including **Derwent Cycle Hire** ( ☎ 01433-651261) in the Derwent Valley, and **Parsley Hay** ( ☎ 01298-84493) and **Middleton Top** ( ☎ 01629-823204) for the Tissington and High Peak Trails. Tourist offices have a leaflet detailing all other hire centres. Charges hover around £12 to £17 per day for adults' bikes (deposit and ID required), and kids' bikes and trailers are also available.

### WALKING

The Peak District is one of the most popular walking areas in England, crossed by a vast network of footpaths and tracks – especially in the White Peak – and you can easily find a walk of a few miles or longer, depending on your energy and interests. If you want to explore the higher realms of the Dark Peak, which often involves the local art of 'bog trotting', make sure your boots are waterproof and be prepared for wind and rain – even if the sun is shining when you set off.

The Peak's most famous walking trail is the **Pennine Way**, with its southern end at Edale and its northern end over 250 miles away in Scotland. If you don't have a spare three weeks, from Edale you can follow the trail north across wild hills and moors for just a day or two, or even less. An excellent three-day option is to Hebden Bridge, a delightful little town in Yorkshire.

The 46-mile **Limestone Way** winds through the Derbyshire countryside from Castleton to Rocester in Staffordshire on a mix of footpaths, tracks and quiet lanes. The northern section of this route, through the White Peak between Castleton and Matlock, is 26 miles and hardy folk can do it over a long summer day, but two days is better. The route goes via Miller's Dale, Monyash, Youlgreave and Bonsall, with Youth Hostel Association (YHA) hostels and B&Bs along the way and ample pubs and cafes. Tourist offices have a detailed leaflet.

## Sleeping

Tourist offices have lists of accommodation for every budget. Perhaps the best budget options are the various camping barns (beds per person from £6.50) dotted around the Peak. Usually owned by farmers, they can be booked centrally through the **YHA** ( ☎ 0870 770 8868; www.yha.org.uk).

## Getting There & Around

The Peak District authorities are trying hard to wean visitors off their cars, and tourist offices stock all kinds of timetables covering local buses and trains. For more details, see (p459).

## BUXTON

### pop 24,112

With its grand Georgian architecture, central crescent, flourishing parks and thermal waters, Buxton invites comparisons to Bath. It's smaller in scale, however, and lodged a little less up its own backside. It was the Romans who discovered the area's natural warm-water springs, but the town's glory days came in the 18th century when 'taking the waters' was highly fashionable. After years of relative obscurity, ambitious restoration projects recovered the town's sparkle, especially the resurrection of the Opera House, which had fallen into disuse in the 1970s.

Every Tuesday and Saturday, colourful stalls light up Market Pl. The town itself is full of book, antique and craft shops and quirky cafes, and is perfect for idle browsing.

Situated just outside the border of the Peak District National Park, Buxton is an excellent, picturesque base to get to the northern and western areas.

## Orientation & Information

Buxton effectively has two centres: the historical area, with the Crescent, Opera House and Pavilion; and Market Pl, surrounded by pubs and restaurants. There are several banks with ATMs on the Quadrant.

**Cyber@Emporium** ( ☎ 01298-214455; 28 High St; ⊙ noon-9pm Tue-Fri, 11am-9pm Sat, 11am-7pm Sun; per hr £3)

**Post office** (Spring Gardens; ⊙ 8.30am-6pm Mon-Fri, to 3pm Sat) Inside the Co-operative.

**Tourist office** ( ☎ 01298-25106; www.peakdistrict -tourism.gov.uk; Pavilion Gardens; ⊙ 9.30-5pm daily Oct-Mar, 10am-4pm Apr-Sep)

## Sights & Activities

Buxton's gorgeously restored **Opera House** ( ☎ 0845 127 2190; www.buxtonoperahouse.org.uk; Water St) enjoys a full program of drama, dance, concerts and comedy as well as staging some renowned festivals and events. Tours (£2.50) of the auditorium and backstage areas are available at 11am most Saturday mornings.

Next to the Opera House is the **Pavilion**, an impressive palace of glass and cast iron built in 1871 and overlooking the impeccably manicured **Pavilion Gardens**. Skirting the gardens, the grand, pedestrian **Broad Walk** is the perfect place for a gentle evening stroll.

Another impressive Buxton construction, the graceful curved terrace of the **Crescent**, is reminiscent of the Royal Crescent in Bath and is being transformed into a luxury hotel, due for completion in 2010. Just east of here is **Cavendish Arcade**, formerly a thermal bathhouse (you can still see the chair used for lowering the infirm into the restorative waters) with

several craft and book shops and a striking coloured-glass ceiling.

Opposite the Crescent, the **Pump Room**, which dispensed Buxton's spring water for nearly a century, now hosts temporary art exhibitions. Just outside is **St Ann's Well**, a fountain from which Buxton's famous thermal waters still flow – and where a regular procession of tourists queue to fill plastic bottles and slake their thirst with the liquid's 'curative' power.

**Poole's Cavern** ( ☎ 01298-26978; www.poolescavern .co.uk; adult/child £7/4; ⊙ 10am-5pm Mar-Nov) is a magnificent natural limestone cavern, about a mile from central Buxton. Guides take you deep underground to see an impressive formation of stalactites (the ones that hang down), including one of England's longest, and distinctive 'poached egg' formation stalagmites.

**Parsley Cycle Hire** ( ☎ 01298-84493), at the junction of the High Peak and Tissington Trails, is the nearest place to rent bicycles (half-/full day £11/14).

## Sleeping

Buxton is awash with good-value, elegant guesthouses – many dating from Victorian times – that are steeped in atmosphere. You'll find the pick of the bunch located on Broad Walk.

**ourpick Roseleigh Hotel** ( ☎ 01298-24904; www .roseleighhotel.co.uk; 19 Broad Walk; s/d incl breakfast from £33/70; P ▣ wi-fi) This gorgeous family-run B&B in a spacious old terraced house has lovingly decorated rooms, many with fine views out onto the ducks paddling in the picturesque Pavilion Gardens lake. The owners are a welcoming couple, both seasoned travellers, with plenty of interesting tales to tell. There's a large guest lounge full of travel guides and maps for browsing, and a large Paddington bear if you get lonely.

**Stoneridge Guest House** ( ☎ 01298-26120; www .stoneridge.co.uk; 9 Park Rd; s/d incl. breakfast from £40/63; P ▣ wi-fi) Bright B&B in an elegant Victorian stone house a short walk from the Opera House with a pretty patio and garden and large, crisp white bedrooms with a few tartan touches. The breakfasts are delicious and they can make packed lunches.

**Old Hall Hotel** ( ☎ 01298-22841; www.oldhallhotel buxton.co.uk; the Square; s/d incl breakfast £65/100 ▣ wi-fi) There is a tale to go with every creak of the floorboards at this genial, history-soaked establishment, supposedly the oldest hotel in England. Mary, Queen of Scots, was held here

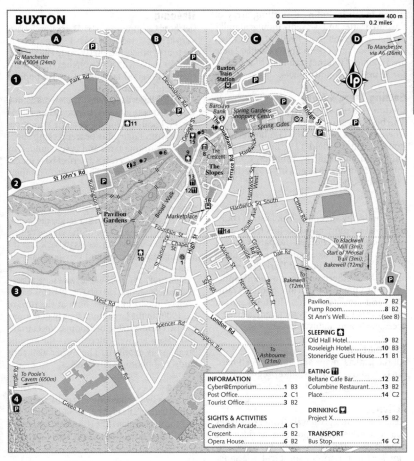

**BUXTON**

0              400 m
0          0.2 miles

from 1576 to 1578, and the wood-panelled corridors and rooms are as well appointed and as elegant as they must have been in her day.

## Eating & Drinking

**Columbine Restaurant** ( ☎ 01298-78752; Hall Bank; mains £11-13; ✆ 7-10pm Mon & Wed-Sat) Perched on the slope leading down to the Crescent, this excellent understated restaurant is top choice among Buxtonites in the know. It delivers large portions of excellent local produce including some good vegetarian choices.

**Place** ( ☎ 01298-214565; www.theplacebuxton.co.uk; 9-11 Market St; mains £11-14; ✆ dinner Tue & Wed, lunch & dinner Thu-Sat, lunch Sun) Lively, trendy modern restaurant serving light lunches and sandwiches as well as more expensive modern European

cooking. There's a good choice for vegetarians and they also have some smart accommodation upstairs (doubles from £60).

**Beltane Cafe Bar** ( ☎ 01298-26010; 8A Hall Bank; ✆ 10am-11pm Sun-Fri, to 1am Sat) The laid-back atmosphere, good selection of real ales and hard-to-find lagers, and evenings of live jazz, blues, soul and folk make this funky cafe-bar a popular spot. The food's not bad either and it's particularly known for its delectable crepes.

**our pick Project X** ( ☎ 01298-77079; The Old Court House, George St; ✆ 8am-midnight) The lavender walls, bright artwork, fairy lights, stacks of cookbooks and separate Moroccan-style nook make for an eclectic, cosy space that attracts local Buxton hipsters as well as tea-sipping grannies. It's a sociable place with a delicious, varied menu including a startling array of flavoured lattes and wickedly indulgent milkshakes. Things get more hectic at night when people flood in for beers and cocktails. There are a couple of internet terminals that are free for 30 minutes for customers.

## Getting There & Away

Buxton is well served by public transport. The best place to get the bus is Market Sq, where services go to Derby (1½ hours, twice hourly), Chesterfield (1¼ hours, several daily) and Sheffield (65 minutes, every 30 minutes). Trains run to and from Manchester (50 minutes, hourly).

# EDALE

Surrounded by sweeping Peak District countryside at its most majestic, this tiny cluster of imposing stone houses and parish church is an enchanting place to pass the time. Edale lies between the White and Dark Peak areas, and is the southern terminus of the Pennine Way and a popular departure point for ramblers and mountain bikers. Its train station makes this seemingly remote enclave very accessible – and highly popular.

## Information

All the leaflets, maps and guides you'll need can be found at the **tourist office** ( ☎ 01433-670207; www.edale-valley.co.uk; Grindsbrook; ☯ 10am-5pm).

## Activities

Heading south, a great walk from Edale takes you up to **Hollins Cross**, a point on the ridge that runs south of the valley. From here, you can aim west to the top of spectacular **Mam Tor** and watch the hang-gliders swoop around above. Or go east along the ridge, with great views on both sides, past the cliffs of **Back Tor** to reach Lose Hill (which, naturally, faces Win Hill). Or you can continue south, down to the village of Castleton (right).

From Edale you can also walk north onto the **Kinder Plateau**, which is dark and brooding in the mist, and gloriously high and open when the sun is out. Weather permitting, a fine circular walk starts by following the Pennine Way through fields to **Upper Booth**, then up a path called Jacobs Ladder and along the southern edge of Kinder, before dropping down to Edale via the steep rocky valley of Grindsbrook Clough, or the ridge of Ringing Roger.

## Sleeping

**Fieldhead Campsite** ( ☎ 01433-670386; www.fieldhead-campsite.co.uk; sites per person £4.50; **P** ) Right next to the tourist office, this pretty camp site spreads over six fields with some pitches right by the river. With good facilities, it is also popular with youth groups.

our pick **Upper Booth Farm** ( ☎ 01433-670250; www.upperboothcamping.co.uk; sites per person/car £4/2; ☯ Feb–Nov; **P** ) Located along the Pennine Way about a mile from Edale, this peaceful camp site is set on a working farm and is surrounded by spectacular scenery. It's a perfect base for exploring the High Peak. There's also a camping barn and a small shop here.

**Edale YHA** ( ☎ 0845 371 9515; www.yha.org.uk; dm members/nonmembers incl. breakfast from £12/15; **P** 🖳 ) This Spartan hostel is in a large, old country house 1.5 miles east of the village centre, with spectacular views across to Back Tor. It's also an activity centre and very popular with youth groups.

**Stonecroft** ( ☎ 01433-670262; www.stonecroftguesthouse.co.uk; Grindsbrook; B&B from £70; **P** ) This handsomely fitted-out home, built at the turn of the 1900s in the large stone typical of the area has two comfortable bedrooms. Vegetarians and vegans are well catered for – the organic breakfast is excellent. The owner also runs landscape-photography courses.

## Eating

Edale has two walker-friendly pubs, the refurbished **Old Nag's Head** ( ☎ 01433-670291; Grindsbrook) and the **Rambler Inn** ( ☎ 01433-670268; Grindsbrook), which also does B&B. Both serve OK pub grub (£5 to £10).

## Getting There & Away

Edale is on the train line between Sheffield and Manchester (about eight daily Monday to Friday, five at weekends). Trains also stop at several other Peak villages. At the weekends and on bank holidays, the bus 260 connects Edale to Castleton (25 minutes, seven daily) with the final bus going on to Buxton.

# CASTLETON

**pop 1200**

Sitting by the foot of 517m-high Mam Tor and topped by the ruins of Peveril Castle, tidy little Castleton has a couple of narrow lanes with sturdy gritstone houses and colourful gardens, and a good collection of cosy country pubs. Oh yes – and about a million tourists on summer

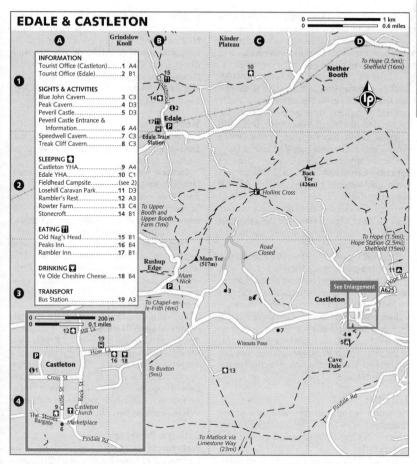

## EDALE & CASTLETON

**INFORMATION**
Tourist Office (Castleton)........1 A4
Tourist Office (Edale)..............2 B1

**SIGHTS & ACTIVITIES**
Blue John Cavern...................3 C3
Peak Cavern...........................4 D3
Peveril Castle.........................5 D3
Peveril Castle Entrance &
  Information........................6 A4
Speedwell Cavern..................7 C3
Treak Cliff Cavern..................8 C3

**SLEEPING**
Castleton YHA.......................9 A4
Edale YHA.............................10 C1
Fieldhead Campsite............(see 2)
Losehill Caravan Park............11 D3
Rambler's Rest......................12 A3
Rowter Farm..........................13 C4
Stonecroft............................14 B1

**EATING**
Old Nag's Head.....................15 B1
Peaks Inn.............................16 B4
Rambler Inn..........................17 B1

**DRINKING**
Ye Olde Cheshire Cheese.......18 B4

**TRANSPORT**
Bus Station...........................19 A3

weekends. But don't let that put you off. Come here when it's quieter to take in beautiful walks in the surrounding area and visit the famous 'showcaves', where a semiprecious stone called Blue John has been mined for centuries.

### Orientation & Information

Castleton stands at the western end of the Hope Valley. The main road from the village goes up the narrow, spectacular gorge of Winnats Pass towards Edale (the A625 route used to cut across Mam Tor, but the peak's brittle shale led to a landslip in 1977 that destroyed the road).

Cross St is the main street, and most of the pubs, shops, cafes, B&Bs, the YHA hostel and the modern **tourist office** ( ☎ 01433-620679; ⏰ 9.30am-5.30pm Mar-Oct, 10am-5pm Nov-Feb) are

here or just nearby. There's also an interesting museum covering local Peak District information from Blue John geology to hang-gliding history.

### Sights

Perched high on a hill to the south of Castleton is ruined **Peveril Castle** (EH; ☎ 01433-620613; adult/child £4/2; ⏰ 10am-6pm May-Aug, to 5pm Sep & Oct & Apr, to 4pm Thu-Mon Nov-Mar), well worth the steep walk up from the village. William Peveril, son of William the Conqueror, built it originally, and Henry II added the central keep in 1176. The ruins are full of atmosphere, made even more special by stunning views over the Hope Valley, straight down to Castleton's medieval street grid and north to Mam Tor and beyond.

The area around Castleton is riddled with underground limestone caves, and four are open to the public. Although mostly natural, they have expanded from extensive lead, silver and Blue John mining over the centuries.

The most convenient, **Peak Cavern** ( ☎ 01433-620285; www.devilsarse.com; adult/child £7/5; ☺ 10am-5pm daily April-Oct, Sat & Sun Nov-Mar, last tour 4pm) is easily reached by a pretty streamside walk from the village. It has the largest natural cave entrance in England, known (not so prettily) as the Devil's Arse. Visits are by hourly guided tour only.

Claustrophobics should steer clear of **Speedwell Cavern** ( ☎ 01433-620512; www.speedwell cavern.co.uk; adult/child £8/6; ☺ 10am-5pm daily, last tour 4pm), which includes a unique boat trip through a flooded mineshaft, where visitors glide in eerie silence (save for the garrulous guides) to reach a huge subterranean lake called the Bottomless Pit.

**Treak Cliff Cavern** ( ☎ 01433-620571; adult/child £7/4; ☺ 10am-5pm daily, last tour 4.15pm) is a short walk from Castleton, with colourful exposed seams of Blue John and great limestone stalactites including the much-photographed 'stork'.

**Blue John Cavern** ( ☎ 01433-620638; adult/child £8/4; ☺ 9.30am-5.30pm summer, to dusk winter) is an impressive set of natural caverns, where the rich veins of the Blue John mineral are dazzling. You can get here on foot up the closed section of the Mam Tor road.

## Activities

Castleton is the northern terminus of the Limestone Way (p465), which includes narrow, rocky Cave Dale, far below the east wall of the castle.

If you feel like a shorter walk, you can follow the Limestone Way up Cave Dale for a few miles, then loop round on paths and tracks to the west of Rowter Farm (right) to meet the Buxton Rd. Go straight (north) on a path crossing fields and another road to eventually reach Mam Nick, where the road to Edale passes through a gap in the ridge. Go up steps here to reach the summit of Mam Tor for spectacular views along the Hope Valley. (You can also see the fractured remains of the old main road.) The path then aims northwest along the ridge to another gap called Hollins Cross, from where paths and tracks lead back down to Castleton. This 6-mile circuit takes three to four hours.

A shorter option from Castleton is to take the path direct to Hollins Cross, then go to Mam Tor, and return by the same route (about 4 miles, two to three hours). From Hollins Cross, you can extend any walk by dropping down to Edale, or you can walk direct from Castleton to Edale via Hollins Cross. Maps are available at the tourist office, and its *Walks Around Castleton* leaflet (30p) has plenty of alternative routes.

## Sleeping

Prices listed are peak weekend rates, but almost all Castleton options have good weekday deals.

**Castleton YHA** ( ☎ 0845 371 9628; www.yha.org.uk; Castle St; dm members/non-members from £14/17; ℗ ☐ ) Rambling, old building with an abundance of rooms, this hostel is a great pit stop with knowledgeable staff who also conduct guided walks. There's a licensed bar too.

**Rambler's Rest** ( ☎ 01433-620125; www.ramblersrest -castleton.co.uk; Mill Bridge; s/d from £25/40; ℗ ) This well-appointed, attractively restored 17th-century stone cottage has five comfortable rooms, three of them en suite, and one big enough to accommodate a family or small group.

For campers, the nearest place is well-organised **Losehill Caravan Park** ( ☎ 01433-620636; Hope Rd; per site £8, plus per person £6). **Rowter Farm** ( ☎ 01433-620271; site per person £4, ☺ Easter-Sep) is a simple camp site about 1 mile west of Castleton in a stunning location up in the hills. Drivers should approach via Winnats Pass; if you're on foot you can follow paths from Castleton village centre as described earlier.

## Eating & Drinking

**Peaks Inn** ( ☎ 01433-620247; www.peaks-inn.co.uk; How Lane; mains £5-10) Large buzzing pub with gleaming wooden floors, leather sofas, fires in winter and a selection of hearty meals including good Sunday roasts and a number of daily specials.

**Ye Olde Cheshire Cheese Inn** ( ☎ 01433-620330; How Lane; mains £7-9) Tradition is everything at this well-known alehouse. The home cooking needs a little attention but go for the peaceful, snug atmosphere.

## Getting There & Away

You can get to Castleton from Bakewell on bus 173 (45 minutes, five daily Monday to Friday, three daily at weekends) via Hope and Tideswell. The 68 goes to Buxton every afternoon from Monday to Saturday.

The nearest train station is Hope, about 1 mile east of Hope village (a total of 3 miles east of Castleton) on the line between Sheffield and Manchester. On summer weekends, a bus runs between Hope station and Castleton tying in with the trains, although it's not a bad walk in good weather.

## EYAM
### pop 900

Quaint little Eyam (*ee*-em), a former lead-mining village, has a morbid and touching history. In 1665 a consignment of cloth from London delivered to a local tailor carried the dreaded Black Death. Thanks to the noble village inhabitants, what could have become a widespread disaster remained a localised tragedy: as the plague spread, the rector, William Mompesson, and his predecessor Thomas Stanley, convinced villagers to quarantine themselves rather than transmit the disease further. Selflessly, they did so; by the time the plague ended in late 1666, it had wiped out whole families, killing around 270 of the village's 800 inhabitants. People in surrounding villages remained relatively unscathed. Even independently of this poignant story, Eyam, with its sloping streets of old cottages backed by rolling green hills, forms a classic postcard view of the Peak District and is well worth a visit.

### Sights

**Eyam Parish Church** ( ☎ 01433-630930; ⊙ 9am-6pm Apr-Sep, to 4pm Oct-Mar) dates from Saxon times and carries a moving display on the plague and its devastating effect on the village. Look out for the plague register, recording those who died, name by name, day by day, and the stained-glass window telling the story of the plague, installed in 1985. Perhaps most touching is the extract from a letter the rector wrote to his children about his wife, Catherine Mompesson, who succumbed to the disease. Her headstone lies in the churchyard. In the same grounds is an 8th-century **Celtic cross**, one of the finest in England. Before leaving, you could also check your watch against the **sundial** on the church wall.

Around the village, many buildings have information plaques attached including the **plague cottages**, where the tailor lived, next to the church.

**Eyam Museum** ( ☎ 01433-631371; www.eyam.org .uk; Hawkhill Rd; adult/child £2/1; ⊙ 10am-4.30pm Tue-Sun Easter-Oct) has some vivid displays on the tragic effect of the plague on Eyam's popu-lation, but also has exhibits on the village's Saxon past and its time as a lead-mining and silk-weaving centre.

Look out for the **stocks** on the village green – somewhere handy to leave the kids, perhaps, while you look at the church.

### Activities

Eyam makes a great base for **walking** and **cy-cling** in the surrounding White Peak area. A short walk for starters leads up Water Lane from the village square, then up through fields and a patch of woodland to meet another lane running between Eyam and Grindleford; turn right here and keep going uphill, past another junction to **Mompesson's Well**, where food and other supplies were left during the plague time for Eyam folk by friends from other villages. The Eyam people paid for the goods using coins sterilised in vinegar. You can retrace your steps back down the lane, then take a path that leads directly to the church. This 2-mile circuit takes about 1½ hours at a gentle pace.

### Sleeping

**Bretton YHA** ( ☎ 0845 371 9626; www.yha.org.uk; Bretton, Hope Valley; dm members/nonmembers £14/15) If the Eyam YHA is full, this basic place, the smallest hostel in the Peaks, is only 1.5 miles away.

**Eyam YHA** ( ☎ 0845 371 9738; www.yha.org.uk; Hawkhill Rd; dm members/nonmembers from £15/18) Simple place in a fine, old Victorian house with a folly, perched up a hill overlooking the village.

**Crown Cottage** ( ☎ 01433-630858; www.crown-cot tage.co.uk; Main Rd; d £60) is bright and walker- and cyclist-friendly – plus it's full to the rafters most weekends. Book ahead to be sure of a spot.

### Getting There & Away

Eyam is 7 miles north of Bakewell and 12 miles east of Buxton. Bus 175 from Bakewell goes to Eyam (three daily Monday to Saturday, no Sunday service). From Buxton, buses 65 and 66 run to and from Chesterfield, stopping at Eyam (40 minutes, about six daily).

## BAKEWELL
### pop 3979

The largest town in the Peak District after Buxton (though it's hardly a metropolis), Bakewell isn't as pretty or atmospheric as its graceful spa-town neighbour, but it's a useful base for cyclists and walkers. It has

THE MIDLANDS &
THE MARCHES

a famous pudding (the Bakewell Pudding – it's not a tart you know), a couple of fine country houses within ambling distance and a reputation as a notorious traffic bottleneck during the summer months.

## Orientation & Information

The centre of town is Rutland Sq, from where roads radiate to Matlock, Buxton and Sheffield. The helpful **tourist office** ( ☎ 01629-813227; Bridge St; ☺ 10am-5pm) in the old Market Hall has racks of leaflets and books about Bakewell and the national park.

## Sights & Activities

Bakewell's weekly market is on Monday, when the square behind the tourist office is very lively. Up on the hill above Rutland Sq, **All Saints Church** has some ancient Norman features, and even older Saxon stonework remains including a tall cross in the churchyard, which sadly has suffered at the hands of time.

Near the church, the **Old House Museum** ( ☎ 01629-813642, Cunningham Pl; adult/child £3/1.50; ☺ 11am-4pm Apr-Oct) displays a Tudor loo and, also on a scatological theme, shows how early Peakland houses used to be made with materials including cow dung.

A stroll from Rutland Sq down Bridge St brings you – not surprisingly – to the pretty **medieval bridge** over the River Wye, from where riverside walks lead in both directions. Go upstream through the water meadows, and then along Holme Lane to reach **Holme Bridge**, an ancient stone structure used by Peak District packhorses for centuries.

On the northern edge of Bakewell, a former railway line has been converted to a walking and cycling track called the **Monsal Trail**. From Bakewell you can cycle about 3 miles north and 1 mile south on the old railway itself, and there are numerous other tracks and country lanes nearby. The nearest bike hire is near Buxton (see p466). Walkers on the Monsal Trail follow alternate sections of the old railway and pretty footpaths through fields and beside rivers. From Bakewell, an excellent out-and-back walk (3 miles each way) goes to the dramatic viewpoint at Monsal Head, where a good pub, Stables Bar at the Monsal Head Hotel, provides welcome refreshment. Allow three hours for the round trip.

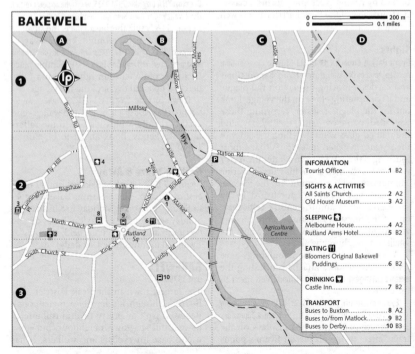

**BAKEWELL**

| INFORMATION | |
|---|---|
| Tourist Office | 1 B2 |

| SIGHTS & ACTIVITIES | |
|---|---|
| All Saints Church | 2 A2 |
| Old House Museum | 3 A2 |

| SLEEPING | |
|---|---|
| Melbourne House | 4 A2 |
| Rutland Arms Hotel | 5 B2 |

| EATING | |
|---|---|
| Bloomers Original Bakewell Puddings | 6 B2 |

| DRINKING | |
|---|---|
| Castle Inn | 7 B2 |

| TRANSPORT | |
|---|---|
| Buses to Buxton | 8 A2 |
| Buses to/from Matlock | 9 B2 |
| Buses to Derby | 10 B3 |

Other walking routes go to the stately homes of Haddon Hall (below) and Chatsworth House (right). You could take a bus or taxi there and walk back, so you don't muddy the duke's carpet.

## Sleeping

**Melbourne House** ( ☎ 01629-815357; Buxton Rd; s/d £35/50; P ) Located in a picturesque, listed building dating back more than three centuries, this is an inviting B&B in the very best Peak District tradition. It is situated on the main road leading to Buxton.

**Rutland Arms Hotel** ( ☎ 01629-812812; www .rutlandarmsbakewell.com; The Square; s/d £65/120; P ) Aristocratic but slightly careworn, this hotel is the most refined of Bakewell's accommodation. Get a higher room if traffic noise keeps you up at night.

## Eating & Drinking

Bakewell's streets are lined with cute teashops and bakeries, most with 'pudding' in the name, selling the town's eponymous cake. It would be bad manners not to try the local speciality when in town.

**Bloomers Original Bakewell Puddings** ( ☎ 01629-814844; Water St) Piled high with local cheeses, pies, meats and breads, this is the place to come to stock up for some alfresco dining. The eponymous puddings are among the best in town and come in three different sizes.

**Castle Inn** ( ☎ 01629-812103; Bridge St) The ivy-draped Castle Inn is one of the better pubs in Bakewell, with four centuries' practice in warming the cockles of hamstrung hikers.

## Getting There & Away

Buses serve Bakewell from Derby via Matlock (most 90 minutes but there are some faster buses, twice hourly) and Chesterfield (45 minutes, hourly). The TransPeak service goes on to Nottingham (one hour 50 minutes, hourly).

# AROUND BAKEWELL
## Haddon Hall

One of the finest medieval houses you'll find anywhere, exquisite **Haddon Hall** ( ☎ 01629-812855; www.haddonhall.co.uk; adult/child £9/5; ☑ last admission 4pm Sat-Mon Apr & Oct, daily May-Sep), is quick to weave its spell. The hall dates back to the 12th century, and what you see today dates mainly from the 14th to 16th centuries. Haddon Hall was abandoned in the 18th and 19th centuries, so it escaped the 'moderni-

sation' experienced by many other country houses. Highlights include the **Chapel**; the **Long Gallery**, stunningly bathed by natural light; and the vast **Banqueting Hall**, virtually unchanged since the days of Henry VIII.

The house is 2 miles south of Bakewell on the A6. You can get there on any bus heading for Matlock (every 30 minutes) or walk along the footpath through the fields, mostly on the east side of the river.

## Chatsworth

The great stately home, manicured gardens and perfectly landscaped park of Chatsworth together form a major highlight for many visitors to England.

The main draw is sumptuous **Chatsworth House** ( ☎ 01246-582204; www.chatsworth.org; adult/child £11/6; ☑ 11am-5.30pm Mar-Dec). Known as the 'Palace of the Peak', this vast edifice has been occupied by the dukes of Devonshire for centuries. The original house was started in 1551 by the inimitable Bess of Hardwick; a little later came Chatsworth's most famous guest, Mary, Queen of Scots. She was imprisoned here on and off between 1570 and 1581 at the behest of Elizabeth I, under the guard of Bess's fourth husband, the earl of Shrewsbury. The **Scots bedrooms** (adult/child incl the house £12/5), nine Regency rooms named after the imprisoned queen, are sometimes open to the public.

The house was extensively altered between 1686 and 1707, and again enlarged and improved in the 1820s; much of what you see dates from these periods. Among the prime attractions are the painted and decorated ceilings, although the 30 or so rooms are all treasure troves of splendid furniture and magnificent artworks.

The house sits in 25 sq miles of **gardens** (adult/child £7/4), home to a fountain so high it can be seen from miles away in the hills of the Dark Peak, and several bold, modern sculptures, of which the Duke and Duchess of Devonshire are keen collectors. For the kids, an **adventure playground** (admission £5.25) provides hours of fun.

Beyond that is another 400 hectares of parkland, originally landscaped by Lancelot 'Capability' Brown, open to the public for walking and picnicking.

Chatsworth is 3 miles northeast of Bakewell. If you're driving, it's £2 to park. Buses 170 and 218 go direct from Bakewell to Chatsworth

(15 minutes, several daily). On Sunday, bus 215 also runs to Chatsworth.

Another option is to walk or cycle from Bakewell. Start out on the quiet lane that leads uphill from the old train station; walkers can take footpaths through Chatsworth park via the mock-Venetian village of Edensor (*ensor*), and cyclists can pedal via Pilsley.

# BIRMINGHAM

**pop 977,087**

Once the butt of many a joke, England's second-largest city – nicknamed 'Brum' – has spectacularly redefined its image from aesthetically challenged urban basket case to vibrant, cultural hot spot. Huge regeneration projects have revitalised the industrial landscapes and canals that criss-cross the city; now there are more glamorous shops, swanky bars and hectic nightclubs than you can shake a bargepole at.

Lookswise, though, it's still not a pretty picture. The unfortunate combination of WWII bombs and woeful town planning left a legacy of concrete and ring roads that may never be completely disguised. But, no matter: Birmingham is making the most of what it's got. Established cultural and architectural gems dot the city centre and planners keep coming up with ever more innovative makeovers, such as the striking postindustrial Bullring shopping centre. Although the manufacturing industry that defined the city as the 'workhorse of the world' is declining, Birmingham will no doubt adapt. More self-assured than it has been in ages, it is hampered by only one thing – its inhabitants' accent, which is consistently voted England's least attractive.

## HISTORY

Birmingham's first mention of any note was in the Domesday Book of 1086, where it was described as a small village. Over the next few centuries Birmingham established itself in the field of industry, starting off with the wool trade in the 13th century, and becoming an important centre for the metal and iron industries from the 16th century onwards.

It was also here that, in the mid-18th century, the pioneers of the Industrial Revolution formed the Lunar Society, which brought together geologists, chemists, scientists, engineers and theorists, including Erasmus Darwin, Matthew Boulton, James Watt, Joseph Priestly

and Josiah Wedgwood, all of whom contributed to the ideas and vision of the times.

By this time, Birmingham had become the largest town in Warwickshire, and the world's first true industrial town, its population tripling by the end of the century. It had also become polluted, dirty and unsanitary.

In the mid-1800s, under enlightened mayors such as Joseph Chamberlain (1836–1914), Birmingham became a trendsetter in civic regeneration, but WWII air raids and postwar town planning were later to give the city an unattractive face.

## ORIENTATION

The one aspect of Birmingham that's still indisputably a nightmare is driving in it. The endless ring roads, roundabouts and underpasses make it particularly confusing for motorists to navigate. It's wise to park somewhere and explore the city on foot until you get your bearings.

Taking the huge Council House as the centre, to the west is Centenary Sq, the International Convention Centre and Symphony Hall, and the development at Gas St Basin and Brindleyplace. Southeast of the Council House, most of Birmingham's shops can be found along pedestrianised New St and in the modern City Plaza, Pallasades and Pavilions shopping centres. The Arcadian Centre is further south but still in the centre, and marks the beginning of Chinatown. Between New St station and Digbeth coach station is the Bullring, a sleek, architecturally striking shopping complex (see www.bullring.co.uk).

## INFORMATION
### Bookshops

**Bonds Books** ( ☎ 0121-427 9343; www.bondsbooks .co.uk; 97A High St, Harborne) Well-known independent bookshop, about 10 minutes' bus journey from the centre.
**Waterstone's** High St ( ☎ 0121-633 4353; 24 High St); New St ( ☎ 0121-631 4333; 128 New St)

### Emergency
**Police station** ( ☎ 0845 113 5000; Steelhouse Lane)

### Internet Access
**Central Library** ( ☎ 0121-303 4511; Chamberlain Sq; 🕙 9am-8pm Mon-Fri, to 5pm Sat) Internet access is free by reservation.
**Unis Internet Lounge** ( ☎ 0121-632 6172; loft level, Pavilions Shopping Centre; per hr £2; 🕙 9.30am-6pm Mon-Wed, Fri & Sat, to 7pm Thu, 11am-5pm Sun) Internet lounge and coffee bar.

## Internet Resources

**BBC Birmingham home page** (www.bbc.co.uk/bir mingham)

**Birmingham Council** (www.birmingham.gov.uk)

**Birmingham Museums & Art Gallery** (www.bmag .org.uk) Information on most of the city's museums and galleries, including opening hours, admission costs and forthcoming exhibitions.

**Birmingham UK** (www.birminghamuk.com)

**icBirmingham** (http://icbirmingham.icnetwork.co.uk) The local newspaper's website.

**Gay Birmingham** (www.gaybrum.com) Information for gay visitors.

**Travel West Midlands** (www.travelwm.co.uk) Travel planning from the main bus company.

## Laundry

**Laundry & Dry Cleaning Centre** ( ☎ 0121-771 3659; 236 Warwick Rd, Sparkhill)

## Left Luggage

**New Street Station** ( ☎ 0121-632 6884; station forecourt; locker hire per day £6; ⊙ 7am-11pm Mon-Sat, 8am-10pm Sun)

## Media

The numerous free magazines available in hotel lobbies, bars and restaurants will let you know what's hot on the Birmingham scene. The pick of the bunch is the fortnightly *What's On* magazine, available for free at some bars and the tourist office.

## Medical Services

**Birmingham Children's Hospital** ( ☎ 0121-333 9999; Steelhouse Lane)

**Heartlands Hospital** ( ☎ 0121-424 2000; Bordesley Green E) Catch bus 15, 17, 97 or 97A.

## Money

**American Express** ( ☎ 0121-644 5555; Bank House, 8 Cherry St)

**HSBC Bank** (Cherry St)

**Lloyds TSB** (2 Brindleyplace)

**NatWest Bank** (Arcadian Centre)

**Thomas Cook Exchange** ( ☎ 0121-643 5057; 130 New St)

## Post

**Central post office** (1 Pinfold St, Victoria Sq; ⊙ 9am-5.30pm Mon-Fri, to 6pm Sat)

## Tourist Information

**Tourist office** (www.visitbirmingham.com) Main branch ( ☎ 0121-202 5099; The Rotunda, 150 New St;

⊙ 9.30am-5.30pm Mon & Wed-Sat, 10am-5.30pm Tue, 10.30am-4.30pm Sun); Welcome Centre (cnr New & Corporation Sts; ⊙ 9am-5pm Mon-Sat, 10am-4pm Sun) The smaller, brochure-stuffed branch has a wide range of maps and themed leaflets.

## DANGERS & ANNOYANCES

As in most large cities, it's wise to avoid walking alone late at night in unlit areas, particularly if you're a woman. The area around Digbeth bus station is not very well lit, is quiet and appears run down.

## SIGHTS & ACTIVITIES
### Town Centre

The central pedestrianised Victoria Sq features a giant **fountain** of a bathing woman (nicknamed 'the floozy in the jacuzzi' by locals), and a drab **statue of Queen Victoria**. It adjoins Chamberlain Sq, with its **memorial to Joseph Chamberlain**, one of Birmingham's more enlightened mayors. These squares share some eye-catching architecture. The imposing **Council House** forms the northeastern face of the precinct. Its northwestern corner is formed by the modernist **Central Library**, whose brutal design looks like an upturned ziggurat, with the Paradise Forum shop and cafe complex underneath it.

To the south stands the **Town Hall**, opened in 1834. Designed to look like the Temple of Castor and Pollux in Rome and featuring a 70ft-high organ, recent refurbishment has restored it to its former glory and reinvented it as a performing-arts venue. For those who won't make it to Gateshead to see Antony Gormley's *Angel of the North* statue (p648), his wingless **Iron Man** (1993), on Victoria Sq, is a step in the same direction.

West of the precinct, Centenary Sq is another pedestrian square closed off at the western end by the **International Convention Centre** and the Symphony Hall (p482), and overlooked by the Repertory Theatre (p482). Inside Centenary Sq is the **Hall of Memory War Memorial**, and there are often temporary exhibitions in the square.

The striking **Birmingham Museum & Art Gallery** ( ☎ 0121-303 2834; www.bmag.org.uk; Chamberlain Sq; admission free; ⊙ 10am-5pm Mon-Thu & Sat, 10.30am-5pm Fri, 12.30-5pm Sun) houses an impressive collection of Victorian art including a selection of major Pre-Raphaelite works. There are also fascinating displays on local and natural history, archaeology, world cultures, and a number of

THE MIDLANDS & THE MARCHES

# BIRMINGHAM

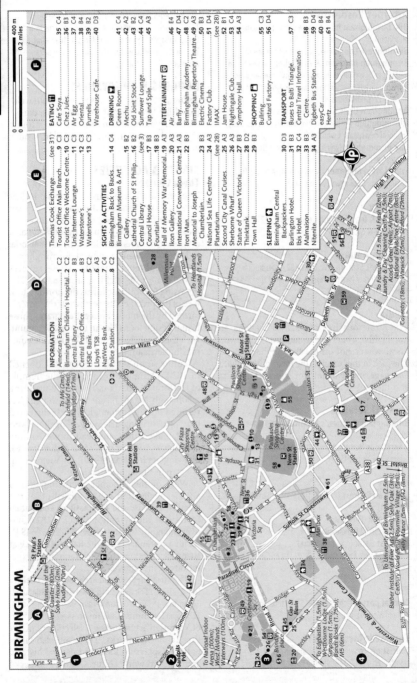

**INFORMATION**

| | |
|---|---|
| American Express | 1 C2 |
| Birmingham Children's Hospital | 2 B3 |
| Central Library | 3 B3 |
| Central Post Office | 4 B3 |
| HSBC Bank | 5 C2 |
| Lloyds TSB | 6 A3 |
| NatWest Bank | 7 C4 |
| Police Station | 8 C2 |
| Thomas Cook Exchange | (see 31) |
| Tourist Office Main Branch | 9 C2 |
| Tourist Office Welcome Centre | 10 C3 |
| Unis Internet Lounge | 11 C3 |
| Waterstone's | 12 C3 |
| Waterstone's | 13 C3 |

**SIGHTS & ACTIVITIES**

| | |
|---|---|
| Birmingham Back to Backs | 14 C4 |
| Birmingham Museum & Art Gallery | 15 B2 |
| Cathedral Church of St Philip | 16 B2 |
| Central Library | (see 3) |
| Council House | 17 B3 |
| Fountain | 18 B3 |
| Hall of Memory War Memorial | 19 A3 |
| Ikon Gallery | 20 A3 |
| Iron Man | 21 A3 |
| International Convention Centre | 22 B3 |
| Memorial to Joseph Chamberlain | 23 B3 |
| National Sea Life Centre | 24 A3 |
| Planetarium | (see 28) |
| Second City Canal Cruises | 25 A3 |
| Sherborne Wharf | 26 A3 |
| Statue of Queen Victoria | 27 B3 |
| Thinktank | 28 D2 |
| Town Hall | 29 B3 |

**SLEEPING**

| | |
|---|---|
| Birmingham Central Backpackers | 30 D3 |
| Burlington Hotel | 31 C3 |
| Ibis Hotel | 32 C4 |
| Malmaison | 33 B3 |
| Nitenite | 34 A3 |

**EATING**

| | |
|---|---|
| Cafe Soya | 35 C4 |
| Chez Jules | 36 B3 |
| Mr Egg | 37 C4 |
| Oriental | 38 B4 |
| Purnells | 39 B2 |
| Warehouse Cafe | 40 D3 |

**DRINKING**

| | |
|---|---|
| Green Room | 41 C4 |
| Mechu | 42 A2 |
| Old Joint Stock | 43 B2 |
| Sunflower Lounge | 44 C4 |
| Tap and Spile | 45 A3 |

**ENTERTAINMENT**

| | |
|---|---|
| Air | 46 E4 |
| Barfly | 47 D4 |
| Birmingham Academy | 48 C2 |
| Birmingham Repertory Theatre | 49 A3 |
| Electric Cinema | 50 B3 |
| Factory Club | 51 D4 |
| IMAX | (see 28) |
| Jam House | 52 B1 |
| Nightingale Club | 53 C4 |
| Symphony Hall | 54 A3 |

**SHOPPING**

| | |
|---|---|
| Bullring | 55 C3 |
| Custard Factory | 56 D4 |

**TRANSPORT**

| | |
|---|---|
| Buses to Balti Triangle | 57 C3 |
| Central Travel Information Centre | 58 B3 |
| Digbeth Bus Station | 59 D4 |
| easyCar | 60 B4 |
| Hertz | 61 B4 |

interactive exhibits for kids. Other highlights include a fine porcelain collection, and works by Degas, Braque, Renoir and Canaletto. You can indulge in a cream tea in the elegant Edwardian tearoom.

One of England's smallest cathedrals, the impressive **Cathedral Church of St Philip** ( ☎ 0121-262 1840; Colmore Row; donations requested; ☻ 7.30am-6.30pm Mon-Fri, 8.30am-5pm Sat & Sun) was constructed in a neoclassical style between 1709 and 1715. The Pre-Raphaelite artist Edward Burne-Jones was responsible for the magnificent stained-glass windows: the *Last Judgement,* which can be seen at the western end, and *Nativity, Crucifixion* and *Ascension* at the eastern end.

The **Birmingham Back to Backs** (NT; ☎ 0121-666 7671; 55-63 Hurst St; adult/child £5.40/2.70; ☻ 10am-5pm Tue-Sun, guided tour only) is a cluster of restored working people's houses: the only survivor of some 20,000 courts of back-to-back houses built during the 19th century for the city's expanding working-class population. The tour takes you through four homes, where you learn the stories of the people who lived here during different periods, from the 1840s to the 1970s.

Should you wish to stay longer, the National Trust has even turned part of the court into self-catering accommodation.

### Gas St, Brindleyplace & the Mailbox

Birmingham sits on the hub of England's canal network (the city actually has more miles of canals than Venice), and visiting narrowboats can moor in the Gas St Basin right in the heart of the city. Nearby Brindleyplace, a waterfront development of trendy shops, restaurants and bars created during the 1990s, has transformed the area west of Centenary Sq into a lively night-time destination. A similar development to the southeast, the buzzing **Mailbox** has a mixture of designer boutiques, smart restaurants, chain bars and upmarket fast-food joints.

The **Ikon Gallery** ( ☎ 0121-248 0708; www.ikon-gallery.co.uk; 1 Oozells Sq, Brindleyplace; admission free; ☻ 11am-6pm Tue-Sun) is a stylishly converted Gothic schoolhouse divided into smallish rooms. It has changing exhibitions of contemporary visual art. The adjoining cafe serves great tapas and sandwiches to refuel between cultural hot spots.

The **National Sea Life Centre** ( ☎ 0121-643 6777; www.sealifeeurope.com; 3A Brindleyplace; adult/child £12.50/8.50; ☻ 10am-4pm Mon-Fri, to 5pm Sat & Sun), a state-of-the-art facility designed by Sir Norman Foster, is the largest inland aquarium in England and is flooded with exotic marine life. There's a sea-horse breeding facility, and the otter and turtle sanctuaries are a hit with kids. Arrive early in the school holidays – the queues can be enormous.

### Jewellery Quarter

Birmingham has been a major player on the jewellery-production scene for some 200 years, and the Jewellery Quarter is the place to go for a piece of the action. The tourist office provides a free booklet *Jewellery Quarter: The Essential Guide,* which includes background information about the industry and details of walking trails around the district's manufacturers and showrooms.

In the **Museum of the Jewellery Quarter** ( ☎ 0121-554 3598; 75-79 Vyse St; admission free; ☻ 11.30am-4pm Tue-Sun), the Smith & Pepper jewellery factory is preserved as it was on the day it closed in 1981 after 80 years of operation. You can explore the long history of the trade in Birmingham and watch jewellery-making demonstrations.

The Jewellery Quarter is about three-quarters of a mile northwest of the centre; catch one of a host of buses (101 is the easiest), or take the metro from Snow Hill or the train from Moor St to Jewellery Quarter station.

About 1.5 miles from the Jewellery Quarter is **Soho House** ( ☎ 0121-554 9122; Soho Ave, Handsworth; admission free; ☻ 11.30am-4pm Tue-Sun Apr-Oct), where the industrialist Matthew Boulton lived from 1766 to 1809. It successfully recreates the styles of the 1700s, and includes the dining room where Boulton and the members of the Lunar Society would meet to discuss their world-changing ideas (see p474). Buses 74 and 79 pass nearby, or take the metro to Benson Rd station from Snow Hill.

### Outlying Areas

Chocoholic magnet **Cadbury World** ( ☎ 0845 450 3599; www.cadburyworld.co.uk; Linden Rd; adult/child £13/9.95) takes you on a mouth-watering journey through the origins, manufacture and consumption of the ever popular cocoa-based confectionery, seen through the eyes of one of the world's largest chocolate-makers. Kids – and sweet-toothed grown-ups – will love it. Ride a beanmobile, take a wander down Cocoa Rd, paved with 'talking chocolate splodges', or try your hand at chocolate-making. Book ahead – it's very popular in July

## BIRMINGHAM IN...

### Two Days

Shopping is one of Birmingham's major attractions these days. Work out your credit cards as you browse the series of exceptional commercial redevelopments that have rejuvenated the city. Take in the quirkily original **Custard Factory** (p483) before heading up to the more mainstream **Bullring** (p483) with its space-age Selfridges building and hundreds of outlets. Dip south to the chic designer stores of the **Mailbox** (p477) and then take the trek up to the historical **Jewellery Quarter** (p477). Even if you're all out of cash, it's well worth a look. Worshipping at the altar of consumerism can work up an appetite; head back towards the Custard Factory and soothe your conscience with some wholesome vegie nourishment at the **Warehouse Cafe** (p481). Then head to the nearby **Factory Club** (p482) for a rocking night out. Gently does it on day two. Nourish the soul with the free, Pre-Raphaelite-studded **Birmingham Museum & Art Gallery** (p475). Then, to get up close and personal with the city's history, check out the restored courtyard of 19th-century working people's houses at the **Birmingham Back to Backs** (p477). Culture fix satisfied, catch a bus or taxi to the famous **Balti Triangle** (p481) to sample the curry dish that was born in Birmingham.

### Four Days

Follow the two-day itinerary, but add a **cruise** (p480) along Birmingham's extraordinary canal network. A show at the world-class **Birmingham Repertory Theatre** (p482) should be next on the cards. Next morning, make a pilgrimage to the **Barber Institute of Fine Art** (below) to see one of the region's most outstanding art collections.. For a sweet interlude, make your way down to the chocolate paradise of **Cadbury World** (p477) for a seriously sugary experience. In the evening, take in an art-house film at the **Electric Cinema** (p482), the oldest working cinema in the country.

and August. Opening hours vary: it's closed for some of December and most of January, but open from 10am to 3pm or 10am to 4pm for most of the rest of the year (phone or check the website for details).

Cadbury World is part of pretty **Bournville Village**, designed for early-20th-century factory workers by the Cadbury family. Large houses, each unique, are set around a green. **Selly Manor** ( ☎ 0121-472 0199; Maple Rd; adult/child £3.50/1.50; ☑ 10am-5pm Tue-Fri year-round, plus 2-5pm Sat & Sun Apr-Sep), dating from 1327 or earlier, was carefully taken apart and reconstructed by George Cadbury in order to save it from destruction. It has 18th-century furnishings and a Tudor garden.

The easiest way to get to Bournville is by train from Birmingham New St (11 minutes).

East of the centre, the Millennium Point development is designed to help people understand science and technology. The focal point is **Thinktank** ( ☎ 0121-202 2222; www.thinktank.ac; Curzon St; adult/child £9.25/7.25; ☑ 10am-5pm, last admission 4pm), an ambitious attempt to make science accessible (primarily to kids). Interactive

displays cover topics such as the body and medicine, science in everyday life, nature, future technology, and industrial history. There's also an IMAX cinema (see p483) and a **Planetarium** (admission £2, advance booking required). A visit to the **Barber Institute of Fine Art** ( ☎ 0121-414 7333; www.barber.org.uk; admission free; ☑ 10am-5pm Mon-Sat, noon-5pm Sun) is, for art-lovers, a highlight of a trip to Birmingham. The collection takes in Renaissance masterpieces, paintings by Old Masters such as Rubens and Van Dyck, British greats including Gainsborough, Reynolds and Turner, an array of Impressionist pieces and modern classics by the likes of Picasso and Schiele.

The Barber Institute is at the University of Birmingham, 2.5 miles south of the city centre. Take the train from New St to University station, or catch bus 61, 62 or 63 from Corporation St.

## BRUM NIGHTLIFE WALKING TOUR

Birmingham by night is one of the liveliest city centres in the UK. This tour, about 2 miles long, will take you through some of the town's most memorable nightspots. Put aside two to three hours if you're pressed for time, otherwise just go with the flow…

Start off at the magnificent **Old Joint Stock** (**1**; p482) pub where you can share the suits' relief as they spill out of the nearby offices. Skirt by the old cathedral, ease your way through Victoria and Chamberlain Squares and on to the cluster of bars at Summer Row for a swift cocktail at trendy **Mechu** (**2**; p482). Next, wander through Centenary Sq, mingling with the theatre fans and concertgoers. Hungry yet? Just a little bit further and Brindleyplace has several swanky options – take in some tapas and fine sherry at the airy, arty Spanish cafe at the **Ikon Gallery** (**3**; p477). Appetite sated? Now creep out to Broad St. Dodge the screeching hen and lairy stag parties and duck into the one oasis of sanity in this part of town, the **Tap and Spile** (**4**; p481). Fine ales on tap in a nooks-and-crannies pub are your reward. Now take the downstairs exit by the canal and stroll south by the water to join Birmingham's bright young things in the stylish bars of the flashy **Mailbox** development (**5**; p477). There are plenty of other sleek places to be seen in this well-heeled part of town, which could

easily distract you from the final leg of our tour, the Arcadian Centre, chock-a-block with night-time options. After all that activity, finish off the evening with a few drinks at the laid-back **Green Room** (**6**; p482), perhaps stopping for a late-night grease fest at the legendary **Mr Egg** (**7**; p481). You've got this far, the rest of the night is up to you…

## BIRMINGHAM FOR CHILDREN

The most obvious place to keep the kids entertained is Cadbury World (p477), where kids will learn about the history of chocolate as well as gorge themselves on it. Ease away the sugar high with a family cruise (p480) down one of Birmingham's many narrow canals; a crucial part of the kids' education on why the city really mattered in the UK's development.

---

**WALK FACTS**

**Start** Old Joint Stock
**Finish** Mr Egg
**Distance** 2 miles
**Duration** two hours or more

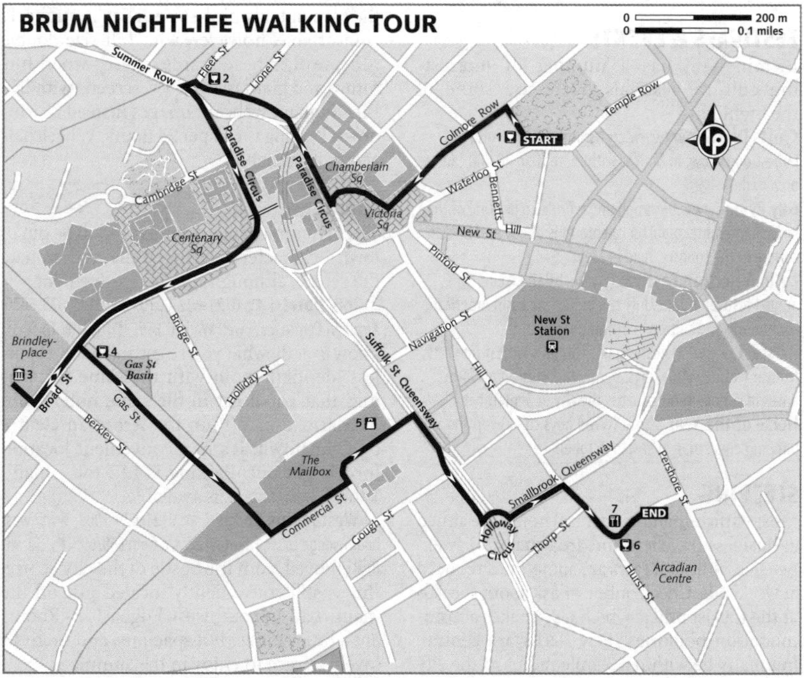

---

BRUM NIGHTLIFE WALKING TOUR

Just away from the Brindleyplace section of the canal, the National Sea Life Centre (p477) has water creatures aplenty. Playful otters will appeal to everyone, but especially to the little ones. There's also plenty to explore at the Thinktank (p478), a gigantic attraction where the goal is to make science exciting and accessible, in particular for children. And you can keep them quiet under the vast domed ceiling of the Planetarium (p478) in the same complex.

## TOURS

**Second City Canal Cruises** ( ☎ 0121-236 9811; www .secondcityboats.co.uk; adult/child £5/3) Hour-long tours leave by arrangement from the Canalside Souvenir Shop in Gas St Basin.

**Sherborne Wharf** ( ☎ 0121-455 6163; www.sher-bornewharf.co.uk; Sherborne St; adult/child £6.50/5; ◔ 11.30am, 1pm, 2.30pm & 4pm daily mid-Apr–Oct, Sat & Sun all year) Canal cruises leave from the International Convention Centre quayside.

**West Midlands Waterways** ( ☎ 0121-200 7400; www.waterscape.com; Cambrian House, 2 Canalside; ◔ 9am-5pm Mon-Fri, 10am-5pm Sat & Sun Apr-Oct) Has leaflets, advice on days out by the water and details on how and where to hire canal boats. It's off King Edward Rd.

## FESTIVALS & EVENTS

Birmingham has a number of interesting cultural festivals. Here are some of the highlights.

**Crufts Dog Show** (www.crufts.org.uk) The world's largest dog show, in March, with more than 20,000 canines on parade.

**Gay Pride** (www.birminghamgaypride.co.uk) One of the largest and most colourful celebrations of gay and lesbian culture in the country, held in May.

**Latin American Festival** (www.abslatin.co.uk) This annual festival in June/July celebrates the Latin American community and culture in Birmingham.

**Artsfest** (www.artsfest.org.uk) The UK's largest free arts festival features visual arts, dance and musical performances in various venues across the city in September.

**Horse of the Year Show** (www.hoys.co.uk) Top show-jumping equestrian event, in October.

## SLEEPING

Most of Birmingham's central hotels are aimed at business travellers and are usually fairly expensive, although rates are sometimes reduced at weekends. Check online or ask about specials at the tourist office, which also makes accommodation bookings. Few B&Bs are central, but many lie within a 3-mile radius of the city

centre, especially in Acocks Green (to the south-east) and the area that stretches from Edgbaston to Selly Oak (southwest).

### Budget

**ourpick Birmingham Central Backpackers** ( ☎ 0121-643 0033; www.birminghamcentralbackpackers.com; 58 Coventry St; dm from £16; ◻ wi-fi) Fun, friendly laid-back backpackers spread across two buildings a short walk from Digbeth bus station. Staff go to a lot of effort to make guests feel welcome, and there's a comfortable lounge with huge projector screen and collection of DVDs (free popcorn on movie nights), a little plant-filled garden, and a bar. There are some manically bright four- to eight-bed dorms, including a pod room – with enclosed beds based on Japanese capsule hotels.

**Formule 1** ( ☎ 0121-773 9583; www.hotelformule1 .com; 3 Bordesley Park Rd, Small Heath Highway; r £25; Ⓟ ) Cheap, soulless, modern and clean: this place uses the same formula here as it does elsewhere. Rooms fit up to three people and it's about 1.5 miles from the centre.

**Nitenite** ( ☎ 0121-236 9000; www.nitenite.com; 18 Holliday St; r £45; Ⓟ ◻ wi-fi) The rooms, they say, are inspired by luxury yacht cabins, and they are suitably pint-sized. They're strangely comfortable, however, with full-size double beds, leather headboards, cherry-wood furniture and giant plasma TV screens with live Birmingham webcam images instead of windows. Parking is £14 per 24 hours. Wheelchair access is available.

### Midrange

The better midrange options tend to be out of town – character-challenged chains dominate the centre, although they are convenient.

**Ibis Hotel** ( ☎ 0121-622 6010; fax 0121-622 6020; Arcadian Centre, Ladywell Walk; d £65; Ⓟ ◻ wi-fi) You know exactly what you're getting here: a spotless identikit room with the same furnishings that you'll get in the same hotel chain in Marrakesh. Within the Arcadian Centre by Chinatown, it's in a convenient location for a night out. Parking is £12 for a night. Wheelchair access is available.

**Westbourne Lodge** ( ☎ 0121-429 1003; www.west-bournelodge.co.uk; Fountain Rd; s/d from £49/69; Ⓟ ◻ wi-fi) Removed from the bustle of the city centre, this is still conveniently located just off the main road in southwest Edgbaston. Rooms are a little chintzy but spacious, and there's a lovely terrace to enjoy in the summer.

## Top End

**Burlington Hotel** ( ☎ 08448799019; www.burlingtonhotel .com; Burlington Arcade, 126 New St; s/d Sun-Thu £175/195, Fri & Sat £83/107; P 🖳 wi-fi) The venerable old gentleman of Birmingham hotels, the Burlington is lavishly and conservatively furnished with wood panelling, marble, classical columns and expensive glass lampshades. Rooms range from classic Victorian in style to the bland and modern. The restaurant is a fine option for sophisticated continental cuisine.

**Malmaison** ( ☎ 0121-246 5000; www.malmaison -birmingham.com; 1 Wharfside St; d from £160; P 🖳 ) This boutique hotel in the Mailbox shopping centre is certainly style-conscious. Trendy music plays in the black-wood, minimalist lobby and the rooms, done out in crisp white and green, have floor-to-ceiling windows looking out onto the street. There's an equally smart bistro specialising in French classics as well as home-grown, local food, a great wine and champagne bar, and a spa. Wheelchair access is available.

## EATING

Birmingham's most famous contribution to cuisine is the balti, a Pakistani dish that has been adopted by curry houses across the country. The heartland is the Birmingham Balti Triangle in Sparkbrook, 2 miles south of the centre. Pick up a complete listings leaflet in the tourist office (or see the website www .thebaltiguide.com) and head out on bus 4, 5, 6, 12, 31 or 37 from Corporation St.

**Mr Egg** ( ☎ 0121-622 4344; 22 Hurst St; chips £1.50) A Birmingham institution, this greasy spoon is the place to go for a 3am lard fest when you're feeling a bit worse for wear. Look out for the picture of a dapper egg with breeches and a walking stick.

**Al Frash** ( ☎ 0121-753 3120; www.alfrash.com; 186 Ladypool Rd, Sparkbrook; mains £5.20-7.90; 🕑 5pm-1am Sun-Thu, to 2am Fri & Sat) This is the best place in Birmingham to experience the legendary balti. Don't go expecting flourishes or fancy decor – you won't find it here; just huge, tasty, great-value portions, and warm service. If you're getting the bus ask the driver to stop by Ladypool Rd.

**Oriental** ( ☎ 0121-633 9988; 4 The Mailbox; mains £6.20-19; 🕑 noon-11pm) Supersleek pan-Asian place that is easily the Mailbox's most stylish restaurant. Eat Malaysian, Thai and Chinese food while sitting on quirky silver chairs adorned with silk-screen faces in a moody red, brown and black space, topped off with the odd chandelier and bursts of gilt wallpaper.

**Cafe Soya** ( ☎ 0121-622 3888; Upper Dean St; mains £6.50-8.90; 🕑 noon-11pm) Excellent cafe dishing up rich, flavoursome plates of Chinese and Vietnamese food – try the huge bowls of noodle soup, or fragrant spicy rice dishes. There's a great selection of vegetarian dishes and it also does a nice line in soya-based desserts and soya bean shakes.

**Warehouse Cafe** ( ☎ 0121-633 0261; 54-57 Allison St; mains £10-14; 🕑 11am-10pm, to 6pm Sun) Low-key little vegie and vegan cafe serving a good selection of vegie snacks, curries, meze and salad, as well as tasty homemade cakes. It also has a small shop selling organic products.

**Chez Jules** ( ☎ 0121-633 4664; www.chezjules.co.uk; 5A Ethel St; mains £10.50-15.50, 2-course lunch £8; 🕑 noon-4pm & 5-11pm Mon-Sat, noon-4pm Sun) French finesse defines the hearty, classic dishes served up at this excellent bistro. Burgundy walls, a spacious dining area, long benches – perfect for group dining – and reasonable house-wine prices add a certain *je ne sais quoi*.

**ourpick Purnells** ( ☎ 0121-212 9799; www.pur nellsrestaurant.com; 55 Cornwall St; 3-course lunch/dinner £19/39; 🕑 noon-4.30pm & 7pm-1am Tue-Fri, 7pm-1am Sat) Run by celebrated chef Glynn Purnell. Exquisite, inventive dishes (such as monkfish with liquorice charcoal) are served in an airy Victorian red-brick building with striking modern interior.

**Simpsons** ( ☎ 0121-454 3434; www.simpsonsrestaurant .co.uk; 20 Highfield Rd, Edgbaston; 3-course set lunch/dinner £25/30; 🕑 lunch & dinner Mon-Sat, lunch Sun) Far out of the centre in a glorious Victorian house, it's worth making the journey for the top-quality modern cooking, served in an elegant dining room or conservatory overlooking the gardens. Reservations are recommended. If you fancy staying the night, there are four luxurious, themed bedrooms upstairs.

## DRINKING

Chain pubs litter the city centre, especially on the deeply unappealing main Broad St drag. There are, however, more than a few gems if you know where to look.

**Tap and Spile** ( ☎ 0121-632 5602; Gas St; 🕑 11am-11pm Sun-Thu, 11am-4am Fri & Sat) Overlooking the canal, this traditional pub is full of hidden alcoves and corners, especially once you move away from the minuscule top bar. There's a good selection of ales on tap here too.

**Old Joint Stock** ( ☎ 0121-200 1892; 4 Temple Row West; ☽ closed Sun) This vast, high-ceilinged temple of beer, a former bank, serves good ales to a cheerful crowd. There's also an 80-seat theatre upstairs that puts on plays and regular comedy shows.

**Sunflower Lounge** ( ☎ 0121-472 0138; 76 Smallbrook Queensway; ☽ noon–11pm Mon-Wed, noon–1am Thu & Fri, 1pm–2am Sat, 5-10.30pm Sun) A quirky little mod bar in an unlikely setting by a dual carriageway near the New St rail station, this is a relatively undiscovered gem favoured by the indie crowd, and with a great alternative soundtrack. Live gigs occur regularly in the tiny underground basement venue.

**Green Room** ( ☎ 0121-605 4343; www.greenroomcafe bar.co.uk; Arcadian Centre, Hurst St; ☽ 11am–11pm Mon-Wed, to midnight Thu, to 2am Fri & Sat, to 10.30pm Sun) This place has a mellow vibe. Sink into a leather sofa and drink a coffee or a beer, or head for the outside tables to watch the street action. There's good food here too.

**Mechu** ( ☎ 0121-710 4222; 47-59 Summer Row; ☽ noon–1am Mon-Wed, noon–3am Fri, 5pm–3am Sat) The natty grey suede interior, streetside tables and strong cocktails attract an after-work crowd to drink, eat and dance in the late-night bar.

## ENTERTAINMENT

Tickets for most Birmingham events can be purchased through the national **TicketWeb** ( ☎ 08700 600 100; www.ticketweb.co.uk). It is cheaper to book online than on the phone. Also check the listings (see p475) for what's going on.

### Nightclubs

Birmingham's nightlife is fast-paced and exuberant. Discover how fun the city's after-hours life can be at any of the following venues.

**Factory Club** ( ☎ 0121-224 7502; www.factoryclub .co.uk; Custard Factory, Gibb St; ☽ from 10pm) The crew working this joint know only too well they are mixing it in the coolest club in town with a truly eclectic range of nights, from Asian dub to breakbeat to electro pop. A blast.

**Air** ( ☎ 0845 009 8888; www.airbirmingham.com; Heath Mill Lane; ☽ from 10pm) This supersleek superclub is home to the renowned Godskitchen night (www.godskitchen.com), where some of the country's top DJs whip the crowd into a frenzy with trance mixes.

**Nightingale Club** ( ☎ 0121-622 1718; www.nightin galeclub.co.uk; Kent St; ☽ from 9pm) Birmingham's most established gay nightclub, the Nightingale rocks on three levels, with pop on the bottom

floor and techno upstairs. Even after some 30 years of action it's still the region's top gay club and is known as a starting place for top-name DJs, with regular live acts.

### Live Music

**Jam House** ( ☎ 0121-200 3030; www.thejamhouse.com; 1 St Paul's Sq; ☽ noon–midnight Mon & Tue, noon–2am Wed-Fri, 6pm–2am Sat) This legendary live-music bar is all class. Presided over by pianist Jools Holland, it features live swing, jazz, R&B and rock and roll, mixed in with the occasional reggae and ska. Drinks are pricey, but the vibe is worth it. The global cuisine of the top-floor restaurant isn't bad either.

**Birmingham Academy** ( ☎ 0121-262 3000; www.bir mingham-academy.co.uk; 52-54 Dale End) The best rock and pop venue in town, regularly attracting big-name acts such as Macy Gray and the Strokes. It also has regular nights showcasing local bands.

**Barfly** ( ☎ 0121-633 8311; www.barflyclub.com; 78 Digbeth High St) This place is a grooming stable for up-and-coming indie bands, spawned by the success of a London-based night. The entrance is on Milk St.

**Symphony Hall** ( ☎ 0121-780 3333; www.sympho nyhall.co.uk; Broad St; tickets from £8) For classical music, including performances by the City of Birmingham Symphony Orchestra, seek out the ultramodern Symphony Hall, which is known for its superb acoustics. World-music and jazz acts also feature. The recently renovated Town Hall (same contact as Symphony Hall) also serves as a concert venue.

The giant **National Exhibition Centre** ( ☎ 0121-767 2937), near Birmingham International Airport, hosts major rock and pop acts, as does its sister venue, the **National Indoor Arena** ( ☎ 0121-767 2937; King Edwards Rd) behind Brindleyplace.

### Theatre & Cinemas

**Birmingham Repertory Theatre** ( ☎ 0121-236 4455; www.birmingham-rep.co.uk; Centenary Sq, Broad St) In two venues, the Main House and the more experimental Door, 'the Rep' presents top-notch drama and musicals, with an emphasis on contemporary work.

**Electric Cinema** ( ☎ 0121-643 7879; www.theelec tric.co.uk; 47-49 Station St; adult/child £6/4, per sofa £12) Projectors have been rolling here for nigh 100 years, making it the oldest working cinema in the UK. It has an interesting art-house line-up as well as two-seater sofas from where you can text in an order and have food and drink (including champagne) brought to your seat.

**IMAX** ( ☎ 0121-202 2222; www.imax.ac; Curzon St; adult/child £8.25/6.25) Birmingham's first IMAX cinema, with a five-storey screen, is housed in the same building as the Thinktank (p478).

## SHOPPING

**Custard Factory** ( ☎ 0121-224 7777; www.custardfactory .com; Gibb St, Digbeth) One of the quirkiest places to shop in Birmingham, full of original, independent shops. So named because the building was constructed a century ago by custard magnate Sir Alfred Bird, this eye-catching development is a memorable place to buy things you never knew you wanted. Funky niche shops are dotted between an arts and media centre.

**Jewellery Quarter** (www.the-quarter.com) The obvious place for unique local shopping in Birmingham. Much of the jewellery manufactured in England comes from this region and there are more than a hundred shops selling traditionally handcrafted gold and silver jewellery, watches and more. The Museum of the Jewellery Quarter (p477) has leaflets detailing notable retail outlets and artisans.

**Bullring** ( ☎ 0121-632 1500) This hellhole-turned-gleaming mall boasts '26 football pitches worth of shops, boutiques and restaurants'. The curved, silver Selfridges department store is worth a visit for the architecture alone.

## GETTING THERE & AWAY
### Air

Birmingham has a busy **international airport** ( ☎ 0870 733 5511; www.bhx.co.uk) with flights mainly to European destinations and New York. It's about 8 miles east of the centre of Birmingham.

### Bus

Most intercity buses are running from a temporary bus station in Digbeth while the old coach station is being rebuilt. **National Express** ( ☎ 08717 818181, www.nationalexpress.com) runs coaches between Birmingham and destinations around England including London (£15.70 single, 2¾ hours, every 30 minutes), Oxford (£11.60 single, 1½ to two hours, five daily) and Manchester (£12.60 single, 2½ hours, 12 daily). Bus X20 runs to Stratford-upon-Avon hourly on weekdays and every two hours on weekends (1¼ hours) from Birmingham Moor St.

### Train

Most of the longer-distance trains are operated by Virgin Trains from New St station, beneath the Pallasades shopping centre, including those to/from London Euston (value advance single £10.50, 1½ hours, every 30 minutes) and Manchester (value advance single £9, 1¾ hours, every 15 minutes). Trains to London Marylebone run from Birmingham Snow Hill (two hours and 20 minutes, two hourly). Other services, such as those to Stratford-upon-Avon (£5.90 single, 50 minutes, hourly), run from Snow Hill and Moor St stations.

In July and August, the **Shakespeare Express steam train** ( ☎ 0121-708 4960; www.vintagetrains.co.uk; standard return £20) operates between Birmingham Snow Hill and Stratford-upon-Avon twice each Sunday. Journeys take one hour.

## GETTING AROUND
### To/From the Airport

Trains are the easiest option for getting to the airport. They run frequently between New St and Birmingham International station (20 minutes, every 10 minutes). Buses 58 and 900 run to the airport (45 minutes, every 20 minutes) from Moor St Queensway. A **taxi** ( ☎ 0121-427 8888) from the airport to the centre costs about £20.

### Car

**easyCar** ( ☎ 0906 333 3333; www.easycar.co.uk; 17 Horse Fair, Birmingham)
**Hertz** ( ☎ 0121-782 5158; 7 Suffolk St Queensway)

### Public Transport

**Network West Midlands** ( ☎ 0121-214 7214; www .networkwestmidlands.com) provides general travel advice for getting around the West Midlands, including for those with mobility difficulties. The Daytripper ticket (adult/child £4.90/3.10) gives all-day travel on buses and trains after 9.30am; if you need to start earlier, buy the network one-day ticket (£6.10). Tickets are available from the **Central Travel Information Centre** (New St Station). **Traveline** ( ☎ 0871 200 22 33) has comprehensive travel information.

Local trains operate from Moor St station, which is only a few minutes' walk from New St; follow the red line on the pavement.

Birmingham's tram system, the **Metro** (www.travelmetro.co.uk), runs from Snow Hill to Wolverhampton via the Jewellery Quarter, West Bromwich and Dudley. Fares start at £1.10 and rise to £2.50 for the full length. A day pass covering both Metro and bus costs adult/child £4.60/3.05.

**TOA black cabs taxis** ( ☎ 0121-427 8888) is a good, reliable taxi firm.

# WARWICKSHIRE

Warwickshire could have been just another picturesque English county of rolling hills and market towns were it not for the birth of a rather well-known wordsmith. Stratford-upon-Avon is one of the country's most visited areas outside London, attracting Shakespeare-hungry tourists from around the world. Also popular is magnificent Warwick Castle, rich in history and theme-park atmosphere.

Other, lesser-known attractions can be just as rewarding, however: try the russet ruins of Kenilworth Castle or visit the cathedrals (yes, plural) that shaped Coventry's past.

## Orientation & Information

Coventry sits to the north of the county. Kenilworth, Warwick and Stratford-upon-Avon run in a line southwest from Coventry along the A46.

The Shakespeare Country tourism website (www.shakespeare-country.co.uk) has information on the whole region.

## Getting Around

The Warwickshire transport site (www.warwickshire.gov.uk/transport) has details of local bus and train services, as well as news on roads. Coventry is a major transport hub, with rail connections to London Euston and Birmingham New St.

A good ticket option is the Chiltern Rover (adult £39), which allows return train travel from London Marylebone or Paddington to Stratford-upon-Avon, Warwick or Leamington Spa on three chosen days within a seven-day period. It also includes unlimited travel in areas between, including Oxfordshire and Buckinghamshire, and free travel on Warwickshire's Stagecoach bus network. You can only buy the ticket from London's Marylebone Station.

## COVENTRY

pop 300,848

The city was blitzed so badly in WWII that the Nazis coined a new verb 'Coventrieren', meaning 'to flatten'; postwar planning then capped off the aesthetic crimes. Today,

Coventry's city centre is, for the most part, an unattractive mass of concrete, but is worth visiting for its striking modern cathedral, which was built alongside the haunting bombed-out ruins of the old one. The city also has an interesting industrial history as a prolific car-maker, the products of which can be seen in an absorbing transport museum.

## Orientation & Information

Central Coventry is surrounded by a stark concrete ring road; most of the city's sights lie within. The main Pool Meadow bus station is central, while the train station is just outside of the ring road to the south. The **tourist office** ( ☎ 024-7623 4297; www.visitcoventry.co.uk; Millennium Pl; ⏰ 9.30am-5.30pm Mon-Fri, 9am-5pm Sat, 10am-3pm Sun) is in the Coventry Transport Museum. In St Michael's Tower in the Coventry Cathedral, there's another **tourist office** ( ☎ 024-7622 5616).

## Sights

The pretty **cathedral quarter** is historically the richest part of the city. The wonderfully evocative **cathedral ruins** of St Michael's Cathedral, destroyed by Nazi incendiary bombs in the blitz of 14 November 1940, still stand as a permanent memorial. You can climb the 180 steps of its **Gothic spire** for some panoramic views (£2.50). Symbolically adjoining the old cathedral's sandstone walls is the Sir Basil Spence–designed **cathedral** ( ☎ 024-7622 7597; www.coventrycathedral.org.uk; Priory Row; suggested donation £3; ⏰ 9am-5pm), a modern, almost Gothic, architectural masterpiece. It includes a giant Graham Sutherland tapestry of Christ, glorious stained-glass nave windows (best seen from the altar), and a towering etched-glass front. Look out for the Jacob Epstein statue of St Michael's conquest over the devil outside the main entrance. The story of Coventry's original cathedral, the Benedictine priory of **St Mary's** which was dismantled following the Reformation, is told through interactive computer displays and archaeological finds at the small but excellent **Priory Visitor Centre** ( ☎ 024-7655 2242; Priory Row; admission free; ⏰ 10am-5pm Mon-Sat, noon-4pm Sun).

Further north, the extensive **Coventry Transport Museum** ( ☎ 024-7623 4270; www.transport-museum.com; Hales St; admission free; ⏰ 10am-5pm) boasts the biggest collection of British-built vehicles in the world, most of them assembled in Coventry, ranging from early bicycles to vintage fire engines. There's interactive fun in the shape of the 'Coventry Blitz Experience' and the Thrust SSC land speed record simulator.

## Getting There & Away

Coventry is a convenient transport hub. Trains go south to London Euston (one hour and 10 minutes, every 20 minutes) and Bournemouth (three hours, hourly), and you will rarely have to wait more than 10 minutes for a train to Birmingham. From the main bus station, there is a constant flow of National Express buses to most parts of the country. Bus X17 goes to Kenilworth, Leamington Spa and Warwick (every 20 minutes).

# WARWICK

**pop 25,434**

Most visitors come to this quiet county town drawn by its magnificent turreted castle. It's an overwhelming sight – as are the queues in summer. Several other sights are less over-run, but also well worth stopping for. A quick stroll round the centre reveals well-preserved historic buildings – survivors of a fire in 1694 that destroyed much of the town – as well as absorbing museums and fine riverside views.

## Orientation & Information

Warwick is simple to navigate; the A429 runs right through the centre with Westgate at one end and Eastgate at the other. The town centre lies just north of this axis. The castle, which looms over the River Avon, is just south.

The **tourist office** ( ☎ 01926-492212; www.warwick -uk.co.uk; Court House, Jury St; ☥ 9.30am-4.30pm), near the junction with Castle St, sells the informative *Warwick Town Trail* leaflet (50p).

## Sights & Activities
### WARWICK CASTLE

Incredibly well-preserved medieval **Warwick Castle** ( ☎ 0870 442 2000; www.warwick-castle.co.uk; adult/ child £18/11; ☥ 10am-6pm Apr-Sep, to 5pm Oct-Mar; P ) is an absolute stunner. Part of the Tussauds Group, it is prone to commercialism, crowds and cheesiness, of which the deeply naff Warwick Ghosts 'Alive' experience (entry £2.75) is a prime example. However, its grandeur and a palpable sense of history, including displays on influential historical figures such as 'kingmaker' Earl of Warwick Richard Neville, make it a must-see.

Plan on spending a full day if time permits. With eerily lifelike waxwork-populated private apartments, sumptuous interiors, ramparts, armour displays, dungeons (with torture chamber), gorgeous landscaped gardens and a 19th-century power-generating mill house, there's more than enough to see.

### COLLEGIATE CHURCH OF ST MARY

Originally built in 1123, the magnificent **Collegiate Church of St Mary** ( ☎ 01926-492909; Old Sq; suggested donation £2; ☥ 10am-6pm Apr-Oct, to 4.30pm Nov-Mar) has a soaring tower, visible for miles around. Climb it for a spectacular panorama (adult/child £2/50p). It was completed in 1704 after the 1694 Great Fire of Warwick gutted the original along with much of the church. The remarkable Beauchamp Chapel (built 1442–64) survived and the bronze tomb of Richard Beauchamp, earl of Warwick, still graces its centre. Ask one of the knowledge-able guides to point out 'the angel', a ghostly outline barely visible on the wall that was only recently spotted. Don't miss the 12th-century crypt with remnants of a medieval dunking stool, used to drench scolding wives.

### LORD LEYCESTER HOSPITAL

At the Westgate end of the town, the road cuts through a sandstone cliff, above which perches the improbably leaning, timber-framed **Lord Leycester Hospital** ( ☎ 01926-491422; High St; adult/child £4.90/3.90, garden only £2; ☥ 10am-5pm Tue-Sun Apr-Sep, 10am-4.30pm Tue-Sun Oct-Mar). Despite its name, it was never a hospital. Robert Dudley, earl of Leicester and favourite of Queen Elizabeth I, made it a retirement home for soldiers and their wives in 1571 – and it still is today. It has a beautiful courtyard, a fine chapel and a guildhall. There is also a small regimental museum and a cafe.

## Sleeping

The nearest hostel is in Stratford-upon-Avon (see p490). Midrange B&Bs line Emscote Rd, the eastern end of the main road through Warwick towards Leamington Spa.

**Park Cottage Guest House** ( ☎ 01926-410319; www .parkcottagewarwick.co.uk; 113 West St; s/d £50/65; P ) This 16th-century listed building has a pretty garden and six spacious rooms, each with a teddy bear for company. The hosts make a real effort to make guests feel welcome and are full of advice about the area.

**Charter House** ( ☎ 01926-496965; sheila@penon .gotadsl.co.uk; 87-91 West St; s/d incl breakfast from £56/85;

**THE MIDLANDS & THE MARCHES**

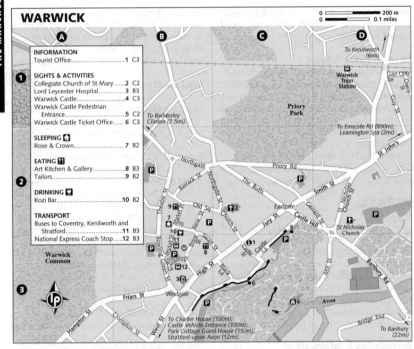

P ▣ ) This cute little timbered cottage has three rooms convincingly decorated in medieval period styles, and a long list of choices on the breakfast menu. Book early.

**Rose & Crown** ( ☎ 01926-411117; www.roseandcrownwar wick.co.uk; 30 Market Pl; r incl breakfast from £70; P ▣ wi-fi) Most of the smart modern rooms look out onto Warwick's main square. They lie above a chic gastropub, which serves excellent food. There are only five rooms, so call in advance.

### Eating & Drinking

**Art Kitchen & Gallery** ( ☎ 01926-494303; 7 Swan St; mains £7-13; ☽ lunch & dinner daily) This place serves fresh, tasty Thai food with an emphasis on local produce and is very popular. All of the art on display, from bold prints on the walls to photos of celebs in the loos, is for sale.

**Tailors** ( ☎ 01926-410590; 22 Market Pl; 3-course dinner £27.50; ☽ 6-10pm Mon-Sat) Warwick's newest restaurant, set in a former gentlemen's tailor shop, serves fine modern English cuisine such as roasted wood pigeon and braised pork belly, in a small, simple dining room.

**Kozi Bar** ( ☎ 01926-493318; 62 Market Pl; ☽ 10am-11pm Mon-Thu, till 2am Fri & Sat) The dark orange

walls, leather sofas and deep rattan armchairs create a warm ambience at this coffee shop, restaurant and cocktail bar. There's a sunny garden at the back for the summer, and on the weekend it turns into Warwick's only late-night bar playing mainstream house and club classics.

### Getting There & Away

National Express coaches operate from Puckerings Lane. Stagecoach X17 runs to Coventry (55 minutes). Stagecoach bus 16 goes to Stratford-upon-Avon (40 minutes, hourly) in one direction, and Leamington Spa (15 minutes) the other. The main bus stops are on Market St.

Trains run to Birmingham (30 minutes, every half-hour), Stratford-upon-Avon (30 minutes, hourly) and London (1½ hours, every 20 minutes).

## KENILWORTH
**pop 23,219**

The only thing that makes a visit to this unremarkable middle-England town truly worthwhile are the hauntingly atmospheric ruins of its castle. With crumbling walls and vivid history, it inspired Walter Scott to use it as a setting for his novel, called...*Kenilworth*.

## Information

Contact the **tourist office** ( ☎ 01926-852595; Library, 11 Smalley Pl; 🕙 9am-7pm Mon & Thu, 9am-5.30pm Tue & Fri, 10.30am-5.30pm Wed, 9.30am-4pm Sat) for local tourist information.

## Sights & Activities

Red-sandstone **Kenilworth Castle** (EH; ☎ 01926-852078; adult/child £6.20/3.10; 🕙 10am-5pm Mar-Oct, 10am-4pm Nov-Feb) isn't as popular as its commercial neighbour in Warwick, but is arguably more rewarding, and the dramatic ruins are brought to life through an excellent audio tour. It was founded around 1120 and enlarged in the 14th and 16th centuries. A number of powerful men, including John of Gaunt, Simon de Montfort and Robert Dudley (favourite of Elizabeth I), held sway here. Following the Civil War siege, the castle's vast lake was drained in 1644, and it fell into disrepair.

You can learn about the relationship between Dudley and the 'Virgin Queen', who visited the castle to tremendous fanfare, in an exhibition in the recently restored Leicester's Gatehouse. At the time of writing work was underway to recreate the magnificent gardens Dudley had built for Elizabeth in 1575, and they were due to open in late spring 2009.

## Sleeping & Eating

**Loweridge Guest House** ( ☎ 01926-859522; www.lower idgeguesthouse.co.uk; Hawkesworth Dr; s/d incl breakfast £70/95; P 🖥 ) This handsome Victorian house has a grand staircase and elegant guest lounge straight out of *Country Life*. There are four huge rooms with swish, modern bathrooms, and three have their own private sun-trap patio. It's a 10-minute walk from the town centre, off Coventry road.

**Clarendon Arms** ( ☎ 01926-852017; 44 Castle Hill; mains £6-12.95) Right opposite the castle, this atmospheric pub provides visitors with home-cooked food, a warm ambience and a cosy little beer garden.

**Virgins & Castle** ( ☎ 01926-853737; 7 High St; pub food £4-6, mains £9-11) This worn, homely old pub is a real local favourite, full of nooks and crannies to lose yourself in. It has a decent menu of Filipino specialities.

## Getting There & Away

Bus X17 runs to and from Warwick (20 minutes), Coventry (25 minutes) and Leamington Spa (15 minutes).

## STRATFORD-UPON-AVON

**pop 22,187**

Few towns are so dominated by one man's legacy as Stratford is by William Shakespeare, who was born here in 1564. Be prepared to fight the tourist masses for breathing space in the historic buildings associated with England's most famous wordsmith – especially during summer and on most weekends. But if you choose your time, this pretty, historic market town should definitely be on your 'to visit' list: be sure to take in a play if you're hitting the Shakespeare trail. It is also a handy base for exploring the mighty Warwick and Kenilworth Castles and the northern part of the picturesque Cotswold Hills.

## Orientation

Arriving by coach or train, you'll find yourself within walking distance of the town centre, which is easy to explore on foot. Transport is only really essential for visiting Mary Arden's House.

## Information

**Cyber Junction** ( ☎ 01789-263400; www.cyberjunction .co.uk; 28 Greenhill St; per hr £4; 🕙 10am-6pm Mon-Fri, 10.30am-5.30pm Sat) Internet access and game play.

**Sparklean Laundrette** ( ☎ 01789-269075; 74 Bull St; 🕙 8am-9pm)

**Tourist office** ( ☎ 0870 160 7930; www.shakespeare -country.co.uk; Bridgefoot; 🕙 9am-5.30pm Mon-Sat, 10am-4pm Sun Apr-Oct, 9am-5pm Mon-Sat, 10am-3pm Sun Nov-Mar) Helpful, but frantically busy in summer.

## Sights

### THE SHAKESPEARE HOUSES

The **Shakespeare Birthplace Trust** ( ☎ 01789-204016; www.shakespeare.org.uk; adult/child all 5 properties £15/7.50, 3 in-town houses £9/4.50; 🕙 generally 9am-5pm Mon-Sat, 10am-5pm Sun Jun-Aug, hr vary rest of year) manages five buildings associated with Shakespeare. Three of the houses are central, one is an easy walk away, and the fifth a drive or bike ride out; a combination ticket costs about half as much as the individual admission fees combined. Opening times are complicated and vary during the low season (check the website for details). In summer, enormous crowds pack the small Tudor houses; a visit out of season is much more enjoyable. Note that wheelchair access to the properties is restricted.

The number-one Shakespeare attraction, **Shakespeare's Birthplace** (Henley St), has olde-worlde charm hidden behind a modern exterior. It's been a tourist hot spot for three centuries (though there's no conclusive evidence Will was born here). Famous 19th-century visitor-vandals have scratched their names on a window, and the guest book bears the signatures of some literary luminaries. Family rooms have been recreated in the style of Shakespeare's time, and in short performances throughout the day some of Shakespeare's most famous characters come to life. There's also a virtual reality display downstairs for visitors unable to access the upper areas. Tickets include admission to the adjacent **Shakespeare Exhibition**, where well-devised displays chart the life of Stratford's most famous son.

When Shakespeare retired, he bought a handsome home at New Pl on the corner of Chapel St and Chapel Lane. He died there in April 1616 and the house was demolished in 1759. An attractive Elizabethan **knot garden** now occupies part of the grounds. Displays in the adjacent **Nash's House**, where Shakespeare's granddaughter Elizabeth lived, describe the town's history and contain a collection of 17th-century oak furniture and tapestries.

Shakespeare's daughter Susanna married respected doctor John Hall, and their fine Elizabethan town house, **Hall's Croft** (☎ 01789-292107), stands near Holy Trinity Church. The main exhibition offers a fascinating insight into medicine back in the 16th century.

Before marrying Shakespeare, Anne Hathaway lived in Shottery, a mile west of the centre, in a pretty thatched farmhouse now known as **Anne Hathaway's Cottage** (☎ 01789-292100). As well as contemporary furniture, there's an orchard and **Shakespeare Tree Garden**, with examples of all the trees mentioned in Shakespeare's plays. A footpath (no bikes allowed) leads to Shottery from Evesham Pl.

Mary Arden was Shakespeare's mother, and a **house** (☎ 01789-293455) at Wilmcote, 3 miles west of Stratford, was her childhood home. If you cycle there via Anne Hathaway's Cottage, follow the Stratford-upon-Avon Canal towpath to Wilmcote rather than retracing your route or riding back along the busy A3400. The easiest way to get there otherwise is on a bus tour (see right). Mary Arden's house

is now home to the **Shakespeare Countryside Museum**, with exhibits tracing local country life over the past four centuries. There's a collection of rare-breed farm animals here, as well as regular falconry displays.

### OTHER SIGHTS

**Holy Trinity Church** (☎ 01789-266316; Old Town; admission to church free, Shakespeare's grave adult/child £1.50/50p; ☺ 8.30am-6pm Mon-Sat & 12.30-5pm Sun Apr-Oct, 9am-4pm Mon-Sat & 12.30-5pm Sun Nov-Mar), where Shakespeare is buried, is thought to be the most visited parish church in England. It's a lovely building in its own right, situated on the banks of the River Avon. The transepts from the mid-13th century are the oldest part. In the chancel are photocopies of Shakespeare's baptism and burial records, the graves of Will and his wife, and a bust created seven years after Shakespeare's death but before his wife's and therefore assumed to be a good likeness.

The exuberantly carved **Harvard House** (☎ 01789-204507; High St; adult/child £3.50/free, incl with Shakespeare Houses ticket; ☺ noon-5pm Wed-Sun Jul & Aug, Fri-Sun May, Jun, Sep & Oct) was home to the mother of John Harvard, after whom Harvard University in the USA was named in the 17th century. It now houses a **Museum of British Pewter**.

The **Guild Chapel** (cnr Chapel Lane & Church St) dates from 1269, though it was rebuilt in the 15th century. It's not open to the public except for services (10am Wednesday and noon Saturday April to September). Next door is **King Edward VI School**, which Shakespeare probably attended; it was originally the guildhall.

## Tours

Two-hour **guided walks** (☎ 01789-292478; adult/child £5/2; ☺ 11am Mon-Wed, 2pm Thu-Sun) depart from Waterside, opposite Sheep St. Chill-seekers can go to the same starting point for the **Stratford Town Ghost Walk** (adult/child £5/3; ☺ 7.30pm Mon, Thu & Fri).

Open-top buses of **City Sightseeing** (☎ 01789-299123; www.city-sightseeing.com; adult/child £11/5.50; ☺ every 20min Apr-Sep, fewer in winter) leave from the tourist office and go to each of the Shakespeare properties. They operate on a hop-on, hop-off basis, and are a convenient way of getting to the out-of-town houses.

**Avon Boating** (☎ 01789-267073; www.avon-boating.co.uk) runs river cruises (adult/child £4/2.50 per hour), which depart from either side of the tramway bridge. **Bancroft Cruisers** (☎ 01789-

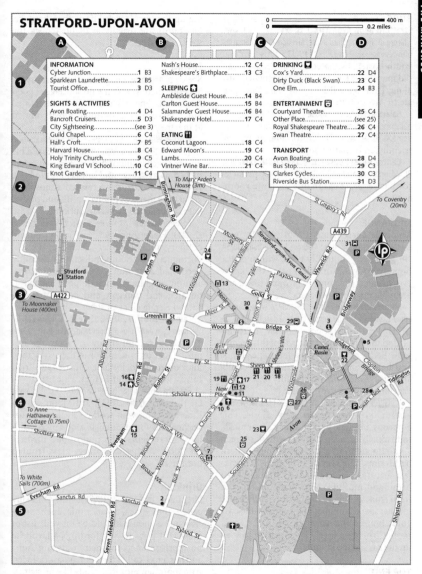

# STRATFORD-UPON-AVON

| INFORMATION | | |
|---|---|---|
| Cyber Junction | .1 | B3 |
| Sparklean Laundrette | .2 | B5 |
| Tourist Office | .3 | D3 |

| SIGHTS & ACTIVITIES | | |
|---|---|---|
| Avon Boating | .4 | D4 |
| Bancroft Cruisers | .5 | D3 |
| City Sightseeing | (see 3) | |
| Guild Chapel | .6 | C4 |
| Hall's Croft | .7 | B5 |
| Harvard House | .8 | C4 |
| Holy Trinity Church | .9 | C5 |
| King Edward VI School | .10 | C4 |
| Knot Garden | .11 | C4 |

| | | |
|---|---|---|
| Nash's House | .12 | C4 |
| Shakespeare's Birthplace | .13 | C3 |

| SLEEPING | | |
|---|---|---|
| Ambleside Guest House | .14 | B4 |
| Carlton Guest House | .15 | B4 |
| Salamander Guest House | .16 | B4 |
| Shakespeare Hotel | .17 | C4 |

| EATING | | |
|---|---|---|
| Coconut Lagoon | .18 | C4 |
| Edward Moon's | .19 | C4 |
| Lambs | .20 | C4 |
| Vintner Wine Bar | .21 | C4 |

| DRINKING | | |
|---|---|---|
| Cox's Yard | .22 | D4 |
| Dirty Duck (Black Swan) | .23 | C4 |
| One Elm | .24 | B3 |

| ENTERTAINMENT | | |
|---|---|---|
| Courtyard Theatre | .25 | C4 |
| Other Place | (see 25) | |
| Royal Shakespeare Theatre | .26 | C4 |
| Swan Theatre | .27 | C4 |

| TRANSPORT | | |
|---|---|---|
| Avon Boating | .28 | D4 |
| Bus Stop | .29 | C3 |
| Clarkes Cycles | .30 | C3 |
| Riverside Bus Station | .31 | D3 |

269669; www.bancroftcruisers.co.uk) runs 45-minute trips (adult/child £4.50/3, daily April to October) leaving from Clopton Bridge, opposite Cox's Yard.

## Sleeping

Stratford's big hotels tend to be geared towards group travel, so they're often out of the price range of many independent travellers, and they fill up fast. B&Bs are plentiful though, and offer good-quality rooms in attractive Victorian houses. Vacancies can be hard to find, especially during summer. If there's no room at any of the following, the tourist office charges £3 plus 10% deposit to find something.

## BUDGET

**Stratford-upon-Avon YHA** ( ☎ 0845 371 9661; www
.yha.org.uk; Hemmingford House, Alveston; dm incl breakfast
members/nonmembers £20/23; P 💻 ) This four-star
youth hostel is situated in a large, 200-year-
old mansion 1.5 miles east of the town centre
along Tiddington Rd. Buses 18 and 18A operate to Alveston from Bridge St.

**Salamander Guest House** ( ☎ 01789-205728; www
.salamanderguesthouse.co.uk; 40 Grove Rd; s/d incl breakfast
from £20/40; P 💻 wi-fi) Comfortable rooms and
friendly, informative hosts.

**Carlton Guest House** ( ☎ 01789-293548; 22 Evesham
Pl; s/d incl breakfast £20/52; P ) The jolly proprietor has several reasonable en-suite rooms
available.

## MIDRANGE

**Ambleside Guest House** ( ☎ 01789-297239; www
.amblesideguesthouse.co.uk; 41 Grove Rd; s/d from £30/50;
P 💻 ) Lovely, nonfrilly B&B, with spotless,
homely rooms, amiable hosts who know
everything that's going on around town, and
great big organic breakfasts.

**Moonraker House** ( ☎ 01789-268774; www.moonrak
erhouse.com; 40 Alcester Rd; s/d incl breakfast from £47/70;
P 💻 ) Pristine to the point of fussy, the rooms
behind the whitewashed facade of this memorable B&B are frilly, almost feminine affairs,
and have a Shakespeare theme. Impeccably
attentive owners provide healthy organic and
vegetarian options for breakfast.

**our pick White Sails** ( ☎ 01789-264326; www.white
-sails.co.uk; 85 Evesham Rd; r from £95; P 💻 wi-fi) This
gorgeous, intimate guesthouse has four plush,
individually furnished rooms with flat-screen
TVs, climate control and glamorous modern
bathrooms. The service is fantastic – breakfast features goodies such as freshly baked
bread and muffins, homemade muesli and
fresh fruit, and there are plenty of other nice
touches like complimentary sherry in the cosy
guest lounge and teddy bears in the bathrooms. There's a lovely large garden to soak
up the rays in the summer.

## TOP END

**Shakespeare Hotel** ( ☎ 0870 400 8182; www.mercure
.com; Chapel St; s/d £135/150; P 💻 ) A labyrinth of
rooms enchants guests at this classic Tudor
hotel. The pick of the rooms are those named
after Shakespeare's plays. Some you have
to stoop to get into, but with their wood-
panelled headboards complemented by luxury
bathrooms, they are a great base for soak-

ing up the town's rich Elizabethan heritage.
Discounts are usually available; check the
website for deals.

## Eating

Shakespeare pilgrimages clearly work up an
appetite: there's certainly no shortage of good
restaurants. Sheep St is clustered with refined
but relaxed eating options, mostly aimed
at theatregoers.

**Vintner Wine Bar** ( ☎ 01789-297259; 5 Sheep St; mains
£7-13; 🕘 9.30am-10pm Mon-Fri, to 9.30pm Sun) This
quirky space is full of beams, exposed brick,
tucked-away spaces and low ceilings to bang
your head on. There's a relaxed atmosphere
and a tasty menu of burgers, grills and pastas,
with some good vegetarian options.

**Coconut Lagoon** ( ☎ 01789-293546; 21 Sheep St; mains
£7.50-13; 🕘 noon-2.30pm & 5-11pm Tue-Sun) Fusing
culinary influences as diverse as Dutch,
Portuguese and South Indian, this elegantly
decorated restaurant has the tastiest curry
around. Highlights include pork cooked in
nutmeg and vinegar, and coconut milk–
bathed Kerala chicken stew.

**Lambs** ( ☎ 01789-292554; 12 Sheep St; mains £11-18;
🕘 noon-2pm daily, plus 5-10pm Mon-Sat, 6-9.30pm Sun)
The classiest joint in town – from the imposing manor-house door to the aristocratic
interior, to the delectable cuisine (pan-fried
calves' liver £16) and a fancy wine list.

**Edward Moon's** ( ☎ 01789-267069; 9 Chapel St; mains
£11-17; 🕘 lunch & dinner) Edward Moon was an
itinerant cook who worked in the colonial
service and loved English food spiced with
local ingredients. His philosophy inspires
the food at this charming, glass-fronted
brasserie.

## Drinking

**Dirty Duck** ( ☎ 01789-297312; Waterside) Officially
called the 'Black Swan', this enchanting
riverside alehouse should be on your list of
must-visit pubs in Stratford. It's a favourite
postperformance thespian watering hole,
and has a roll-call of former regulars (Olivier,
Attenborough etc) that reads like an actors'
*Who's Who*. The adjoining restaurant (11am
to 10pm) is good value.

**One Elm** ( ☎ 01789-404919; 1 Guild St) This modern
gastropub, smart with leather chairs, trendy
wallpaper and a courtyard garden, makes
a change from all the 'olde worlde' charm.
There's a tempting menu of free-range,
sustainable goodies.

**Cox's Yard** ( ☎ 01789-404600; Bridgefoot) Large riverside complex with a pub, cafe and music venue. It's a lovely place to enjoy a coffee, drink or a full-blown meal while watching the swans glide past.

## Entertainment

**Royal Shakespeare Company** (RSC; ☎ 0844 800 1110; www.rsc.org.uk; tickets £8-38; ⏰ 9.30am-8pm Mon-Sat) Seeing a RSC production is a must. Major stars have trod the boards here and productions are of very high standard. At the time of writing, the main Royal Shakespeare Theatre was closed for extensive renovations and was due to reopen in 2010. The adjoining Swan Theatre is also closed during this time. In the meantime, performances take place in the striking temporary Courtyard Theatre by the Other Place. The box office is in the foyer of the Courtyard Theatre until the main theatre reopens. Ticket prices depend on the performance and venue, but there are offers for under-25-year-olds, students, seniors and other groups, plus discounts for previews. Call or check the website for details – and book ahead for good seats. There are usually a few tickets sold on the day of performance.

## Getting There & Away

The train station is a few minutes' walk west of the centre. Chiltern Railways offers direct services to London Marylebone (2¼ hours). Cheap returns (£16.90) are often available after 11am.

National Express destinations from Stratford's Riverside bus station include Birmingham (£7.20, one hour, twice daily), Oxford (£9.20, one hour, daily) and London Victoria (£16, 3½ hours, five daily).

In July and August, the **Shakespeare Express steam train** ( ☎ 0121-708 4960; www.vintagetrains.co.uk) operates between Birmingham Snow Hill and Stratford stations (adult/child £10/5, return £20/10, one hour, twice Sunday only).

## Getting Around

### BICYCLE

Stratford is small enough to explore on foot, but a bicycle is good for getting out to the surrounding countryside or the rural Shakespeare properties. The canal towpath offers a fine route to Wilmcote.

**Clarkes Cycles** ( ☎ 01789-205057; Guild St; per half-/full day from £6/10; ⏰ 9.15am-5pm Tue-Sat) rents out bikes. It's most easily reached down a little alley off Henley St.

### BOAT

Punts, canoes and rowing boats are available for hire from Avon Boating (p488) by Clopton Bridge – it's under the Thai Boathouse restaurant.

# STAFFORDSHIRE

Stoke-born novelist Arnold Bennett once wrote that Staffordshire was 'unsung by searchers after the extreme', but that doesn't mean that it's boring. Wedged between the urban sprawls of Birmingham and Manchester, the county is surprisingly beautiful, from rolling Cannock Chase, a magnet for walkers and cyclists, to the jagged backbone of the Peak District known as the Roaches. The stern might of Lichfield's cathedral, the wild rides at Alton Towers, and the neoclassical mansion of Shugborough are among the county's other charms.

## Orientation

Staffordshire's attractions are spread fairly evenly around the county: Stoke to the northwest; the Peak District and Leek northeast, with Alton Towers just south; Lichfield to the southeast; and Stafford just southwest of the centre.

## Information

**Staffordshire Tourism** ( ☎ 01889-880151; www.staffordshire.gov.uk/tourism) has general information on where to stay and what to do in the county.

## Getting There & Around

**London Midland** ( ☎ 0844 811 0133; www.londonmidland.com) Offers a range of train services across the region.
**Travel Line** ( ☎ 0871 200 2233; www.travelinemidlands.co.uk) Can help you find the best local and long-distance transport options throughout the region.
**Virgin Trains** ( ☎ 0845 722 2333; www.virgintrains.co.uk) Offers train services to and from London and in the region.

# LICHFIELD

### pop 27,900

This pretty market town, full of cobbled streets and courtyard gardens, is home to one of the country's most beautiful cathedrals, a monumental three-spired Gothic master-piece that is visible from miles away. It's also been something of a thinktank in its time: famed wit and lexicographer Samuel Johnson was born here, and Erasmus Darwin, Charles' grandfather and an important man in his own right, lived and studied here for years.

## Information

The **tourist office** ( ☎ 01543-412121; www.visitlichfield .com; Lichfield Garrick, Castle Dyke; ◷ 9am-5pm Mon-Sat) doubles as the box office for the Lichfield Garrick theatre.

## Sights & Activities

### LICHFIELD CATHEDRAL

The magnificent **Lichfield Cathedral** ( ☎ 01543-306120; admission free, but donation requested; ◷ 7.30am-6.15pm) boasts a fine Gothic west front adorned with exquisitely carved statues of the kings of England from Edgar to Henry I, and the major saints. Approach the blackened facade from town by Minster Pond and you won't be the first to get goosebumps as you look up to the cathedral's hallmark three spires – especially when they are floodlit by night. Most of what you see dates from the various rebuildings of the Norman cathedral between 1200 and 1350.

A superb illuminated manuscript from 730, the *Lichfield Gospels*, is displayed in the beautifully vaulted mid-13th-century chapter-house, while the Lady Chapel to the east boasts 16th-century Flemish stained glass. Following archaeological work in 2003, a Saxon statue of the Archangel Gabriel was uncovered beneath the nave, and was on display for a month in 2006. At the time of writing it was expected to be on permanent display from around 2009, if the restoration work was successful.

A stroll round the tranquil **Cathedral Close**, which is ringed with imposing 17th- and 18th-century houses, is also rewarding.

### OTHER SIGHTS & ACTIVITIES

The amateurish but absorbing **Samuel Johnson Birthplace Museum** ( ☎ 01543-264972; www.samu eljohnsonbirthplace.org; Breadmarket St; admission free; ◷ 10.30am-4.30pm Apr-Sep, 11am-3.30pm Oct-Mar) charts the life of one of the most remarkable figures in the history of the English language. Samuel Johnson, the pioneering lexicographer, was born here in 1709 and spent his formative years in this ramshackle, five-storey property that belonged to his bookseller

father. Credited with inventing the dictionary, Samuel Johnson was immortalised in the famous biography *The Life of Samuel Johnson*, written by his close friend James Boswell. On the ground floor is a bookshop containing several of Johnson's works.

Grandfather of the more famous Charles, Erasmus Darwin was himself a remarkable autodidact, doctor, inventor, philosopher and poet, influencing the Romantics. The **Erasmus Darwin House** ( ☎ 01543-306260; Beacon St; adult/child £3/2; ◷ noon-5pm Tue-Sun, last admission 4.15pm), where he lived from 1758 to 1781, commemorates his life with a video, pictures and personal items. Exhibits and displays illustrate his varied work and association with luminaries such as Wedgwood, Boulton and Watt.

## Sleeping

**No 8 The Close** ( ☎ 01543-418483; www.ldb.co.uk/accom modation.htm; 8 The Close; s/d incl breakfast from £28/48) Sitting in the shadow of the cathedral, No 8 The Close is a listed 19th-century town house that's also a family home. There are three comfortable B&B rooms here but there's no sign outside the house; you should call in advance to make arrangements.

**George Hotel** ( ☎ 01543-414822; www.thegeorgeli chfield.co.uk; 12-14 Bird St; s/d Fri-Sun £50/63, Mon-Thu from £80; P ⌨ ) A maze of rooms winds through this 18th-century coaching inn in the heart of the city. It's well located and comfortable but some of the rooms could do with a revamp.

## Eating & Drinking

**Tudor of Lichfield** ( ☎ 01543-263951; Bore St; sandwiches £3-5; ◷ 9am-5.30pm Mon-Sat, 11am-4.30pm Sun) This cafe scores points over its local rivals in terms of age – the half-timbered building it is housed in was built in 1510. The signs are still there, with a suit of armour glowering over punters as they sip their morning coffee. It also sella a tempting array of handmade chocolates.

**King's Head** ( ☎ 01543-256822; 4 Queen St) Samuel Johnson described Lichfield folk as 'the most sober, decent people in England' – but that was 250 years ago, and there are plenty of pubs to go round these days. The King's Head has a welcoming vibe, is a great place to sample real ales and it puts on regular live music.

## Getting There & Away

Buses 112 and 7 run to Birmingham, while the 825 serves Stafford (1¼ hours, hourly). The bus station is opposite the central Lichfield City train station, which runs trains to Birmingham New St station (30 minutes, every 15 minutes). Direct trains to London Euston (from one hour and 15 minutes, around eight daily) depart from Lichfield Trent Valley station, about 1.5 miles from town.

## STOKE-ON-TRENT
pop 240,636

Stoke-on-Trent is Staffordshire's industrial heart, and is famed for its pottery production. There's not too much of interest here for the visitor, however, unless you happen to be a fan of porcelain. For a preview of Stoke, check out Arnold Bennett's memorable descriptions of the area in its industrial heyday in his novel *Anna of the Five Towns* (something of a misnomer as Stoke actually consists of six suburbs).

### Orientation

Stoke-on-Trent is made up of Tunstall, Burslem, Hanley, Stoke, Fenton and Longton, together often called 'the Potteries'. Hanley is the official 'city centre'. Stoke-on-Trent train station is south of Hanley, but buses from outside the main entrance run there in minutes. The bus station is in the centre of Hanley.

### Information

Ask at the helpful **tourist office** ( ☎ 01782-236000; www.visitstoke.co.uk; Victoria Hall, Bagnall St, Hanley; ☯ 9.15am-5.15pm Mon-Sat), adjacent to the bus station, for a map with the locations of the various showrooms, factory shops and visitors centres.

### Sights & Activities

The recently expanded **Wedgwood Visitor Centre** ( ☎ 0870 606 1759; www.thewedgwoodvisitorcentre.com; Barlaston; Mon-Fri £8.25, Sat & Sun £6.25; ☯ 9am-5pm Mon-Fri, 10am-5pm Sat & Sun), set in 81 hectares of attractive parkland, offers an absorbing look at the bone-china production process. Tours take in an extensive collection of historic pieces, and you can watch artisans calmly painting their designs onto china. Best of all, a troupe of Star Wars–esque anthropomorphic robots churn out perfect plates and mugs. Equally interesting are the film and displays on the life of founder Josiah Wedgwood (1730–95). An innovative potter, he was also a driving force behind the construction of England's canal system and the abolition of slavery.

Wedgewood celebrates its 250th anniversary in 2009.

The **Potteries Museum & Art Gallery** ( ☎ 01782-232323; Bethesda St, Hanley; admission free; ☯ 10am-5pm Mon-Sat & 2-5pm Sun Mar-Oct, 10am-4pm Mon-Sat & 1-4pm Sun Nov-Feb) covers the history of the Potteries and houses an impressively extensive ceramics display as well as a fine-art collection (Picasso, Degas).

Constructed around Stoke's last remaining bottle kiln, the **Gladstone Pottery Museum** ( ☎ 01782-319232; Uttoxeter Rd, Longton; adult/child £6/4.50; ☯ 10am-5pm) presents a taste of what life was like for people working in the Victorian potteries. Those of a scatological bent will enjoy the 'Flushed with Pride' exhibition, which charts the story of the toilet from chamber pots and shared privy holes (with smell effects!) to modern hi-tech conveniences. Buses 6 and 6A go to the museum from Hanley.

### Getting There & Away

National Express coaches run to/from London (four hours, five daily) and Manchester (1½ hours, eight daily). Trains run to Stafford (20 minutes, every 30 minutes) and London (1¾ hours, hourly).

## AROUND STOKE-ON-TRENT
### Little Moreton Hall

Spectacular black-and-white, timber-framed moated manor house, **Little Moreton Hall** (NT; ☎ 01260-272018; adult/child £6.40/3.20; ☯ 11.30am-5pm Wed-Sun late Mar–Oct, 11.30am-4pm Sat & Sun Nov–late Dec) dates back to the 16th century; within its over-the-top exterior there are a series of important wall paintings and an indefinable sense of romance. Little Moreton is off the A34 south of Congleton.

### Alton Towers

The most popular theme park in England, **Alton Towers** ( ☎ 0870 444 4455; www.altontowers .com; adult/under 12yr £35/26; ☯ 9.30am-5pm Oct–mid-Mar, longer hr mid-Mar–Sep) is a great option for thrill-seekers. There are more than 100 rides, including upside-down roller coasters and log flumes, and new thrills are introduced with relative frequency. Entry prices are almost as steep as the rides and are highest during school holidays.

There's a hotel within the park, but most visitors opt to stay in nearby villages. Alton itself is an attractive village with several B&Bs. The **Dimmingsdale YHA** ( ☎ 0845 371 9513; www.yha

.org.uk; Oakamoor; dm members/nonmembers £14/17) is 2 miles northwest of the park. There are plenty of good rambles around the hostel too.

Alton Towers is east of Cheadle off the B5032. Public transport is sketchy, but various train companies offer all-in-one packages from London and other cities; check the website for current details.

# WORCESTERSHIRE

Serene Worcestershire's southern and western fringes burst with lush countryside, stunning walking trails and attractive riverside market towns, though the northern and eastern plains blend into the West Midlands, and have little to offer to visitors. Plump at the county's core is the capital Worcester, with its magnificent cathedral and world-renowned Royal Worcester Porcelain Works. Just south, the hillside Victorian resort of Great Malvern sits regally at the heart of the rolling Malvern Hills (the Malverns).

## Information

For online information check out www.visit worcestershire.org, and for news try www .worcesternews.co.uk.

## Activities

The longest riverside walk in the UK, the **Severn Way** winds its way through Worcestershire via Worcester and Upton-upon-Severn, while the **Three Choirs Way** links Worcester to Hereford and Gloucester.

Cyclists can pick up the handy *Elgar Ride Variations* leaflet from tourist offices detailing routes around the Malverns.

## Getting Around

There are a few regular rail links from Worcester, and Kidderminster is the southern railhead of the popular Severn Valley Railway. Buses to rural areas can be frustratingly infrequent.

## WORCESTER

pop 94,029

An ancient cathedral city on the banks of the River Severn, Worcester's (*woos*-ter) postwar architectural clangers and soulless shopping centre tend to eclipse the architectural gems that sprinkle the city. Scratch beneath the surface, however, and you'll be rewarded with a magnificent cathedral, pockets of

timber-framed Tudor and elegant Georgian architecture, riverside walks, and tales of the Civil War, which finished here.

## Information

The **tourist office** ( ☎ 01905-726311; www.visitworces ter.com; Guildhall, High St; ☷ 9.30am-5pm Mon-Sat) will organise 1½-hour **walking tours** ( ☎ 01905-222117; www.worcesterwalks.co.uk; adult £4; ☷ 11am Mon-Fri). Internet access is available at **Coffee Republic** ( ☎ 01905-25069; 31 High St; per 20/60min £1/3; ☷ 7am-6pm), opposite the Guildhall.

## Sights

### WORCESTER CATHEDRAL

Dominating the centre of the city, the majestic edifice of **Worcester Cathedral** ( ☎ 01905-732900; www.worcestercathedral.org.uk; suggested donation £3; ☷ 7.30am-6pm) encapsulates an assortment of styles and eras, and is full of the stories and symbols of England's violent past.

The atmospheric Norman crypt is the largest in England and dates back to when St Wulfstan, the only Saxon bishop to hang on to his see under the Normans, started building the cathedral in 1084. Other highlights include a striking 13th-century Lady Chapel and a lovely 12th-century circular chapterhouse.

You'll find the cathedral's most notorious inhabitant, King John, buried in the choir. Famous for his treachery towards older brother Richard Lionheart, and squabbles with the barons that forced him to sign the Magna Carta, John left England in chaos. In a somewhat fitting break from tradition, the stone lion under his feet is biting back. To boost his slim chances of passing the pearly gates, the dying king asked to be buried disguised as a monk.

The strong-legged can tackle the 249 steps up the **tower** (adult/child £3/1; ☷ 11am-5pm Sat & school holidays Easter-Sep); once up top, spare a thought for the unhappy Charles II, who surveyed his troops from here during the Battle of Worcester.

One-hour-long **cathedral tours** (adult/child £3/ free; ☷ 11am & 2.30pm daily Mon-Sat Apr-Sep, Sat only rest of year) run from the gift shop. Evensong is a splendid affair; it's held at 5.30pm Monday to Wednesday, Friday and Saturday, and at 4pm Sunday.

### COMMANDERY

Recently reopened after a major refurbishment, the town's history museum, the **Commandery** ( ☎ 01905-361821; www.worcestercitymuseums.org.uk;

College St; adult/child £5.25/2.25; ☉ 10am-5pm Mon-Sat, 1.30-5pm Sun) is housed in a splendid Tudor building that has been used, among other things, as a monastic hospital, a family home, and King Charles II's Civil War Headquarters during the Battle of Worcester in 1651. Engaging audio guides and interactive exhibits tell the story of the Commandery and of Worcester during key periods in its history. A highlight is the fascinating 'painted chamber', covered with intriguing 15th-century religious frescos.

### ROYAL WORCESTER PORCELAIN WORKS

The king of British porcelain manufacture has come a long way since founder Dr John Wall started making ornate bone china as a hobby in 1751. Granted a royal warrant in 1789, the factory still supplies Her Royal Highness (HRH) with some of her preferred crockery, and now runs an entire visitor complex to promote its wares.

Worth visiting even for those that aren't ceramic-crazy, the **Worcester Porcelain Museum** ( ☎ 01905-746000; www.worcesterporcelainmuseum.org.uk; Severn St; adult/concession £5/4.25; ☉ 9am-5.30pm Mon-Sat, 11am-5pm Sun) enlivens its exhaustive collection of works with quirky asides detailing everything from the china's use by British Royals to the factory's sidelines in porcelain dentures and 'portable fonts' designed for cholera outbreaks. Entry includes an audio tour.

The enjoyable **Visitor Experience Tour** (adult/concession £5/4.25; ☉ 10am-5.30pm Mon-Sat, 11am-5pm Sun) walks visitors through the porcelain's design and manufacture. Combined tickets for the museum and tour cost £9/8 per adult/child.

You can browse the bewildering array of porcelain goodies in the on-site **shops**, from the daintiest traditional dinnerware to bonnet-shaped candle snuffers.

## Sleeping

**ourpick** **Burgage House** ( ☎ 01905-25396; www.burgagehouse.co.uk; 4 College Precincts; s/d £36/65) A well-camouflaged little gem, hidden on a narrow cobbled street overlooking the cathedral. The four huge rooms (three of which are accessed up a beautiful curved stone staircase) are decked out with paintings and tapestries and are elegant yet incredibly homely; those at the

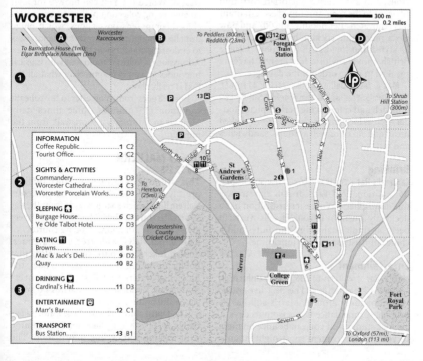

### WORCESTER

front have stunning views. It's run in a warm, unobtrusive manner and is family-friendly.

**Ye Olde Talbot Hotel** ( ☎ 01905-23573; www.oldeng lish.co.uk; Friar St; s/d £70/90) Attached to a popular bar and bistro right in the centre of town, this pleasantly decorated inn dates back to the 13th century and is pretty good value. Rooms sport rich fabrics, deep colours, modern gadgets and an occasional smattering of antique features. Discounted parking is available nearby.

**Barrington House** ( ☎ 01905-422965; www.bar ringtonhouse.eu; 204 Henwick Rd; r £85; P 🖵 wi-fi) Lovely Georgian house by the river with wonderful views, pretty walled garden, three plush bedrooms and hearty breakfasts served with eggs from the owners' hens.

## Eating

**Quay** ( ☎ 01905-745792; The Quay; mains £7-14; 🕑 lunch & dinner) This place has an informal setting right next to the river with plenty of outside tables to soak up the atmosphere. Come for light lunches, afternoon tea or more substantial dinners served in a candlelit dining room.

**Browns** ( ☎ 01905-26263; The Old Cornmill, South Quay; mains £14-24; 🕑 lunch & dinner Mon-Sat, lunch Sun) Housed in a converted Victorian corn mill adjacent to the river, this top-class restaurant was renovated after flooding in 2007 and now has a mezzanine cocktail bar in addition to its stylish but low-key dining room. Classic British cooking with a few French flavours sneaked in is the order of the day here.

**Mac & Jack's Deli** ( ☎ 01905-731331; 44 Friar St; 🕑 9.30am-5.30pm Tue-Thu, 9am-6pm Fri & Sat) Bright little deli and cafe serving perfect picnic fodder such as local meats, cheeses, freshly baked bread and cakes, as well as soups, sandwiches and tarts to eat-in.

## Drinking

**Cardinal's Hat** ( ☎ 01905-22066; 31 Friar St) Despite its traditional old-English pub appearance, this atmospheric Worcester institution has a decidedly Austrian flavour. It sells Austrian beers in traditional steins and flutes and a choice of Austrian food at lunchtime.

## Entertainment

**Marr's Bar** ( ☎ 01905-613336; www.marrsbar.co.uk; 12 Pierpoint St; 🕑 from 8pm) The best live-music venue for miles around, Marr's still has its original sprung dance floors from its days as a dance studio, and you can bounce on them to your heart's content most nights thanks

to packed listings. Gigs range from acoustic sessions to comedy.

## Getting There & Around

Worcester has two stations but most trains run to Worcester Foregate (the other is Worcester Shrub Hill). Trains run hourly to London Paddington (£32.30, 2¼ to three hours) and Hereford (£6.80, 43 to 50 minutes).

National Express has two direct daily services to London Victoria (£21.10, four hours). Bus 44 runs to Great Malvern (30 minutes, twice-hourly), bus 363 goes to Upton-upon-Severn (30 minutes, hourly), and bus 417 goes to Ledbury (50 minutes, five daily Monday to Saturday).

Bikes can be hired from **Peddlers** ( ☎ 01905-24238; 46 Barbourne Rd; per day from £8).

## AROUND WORCESTER
### Elgar Birthplace Museum

England's greatest classical composer, Edward Elgar, receives due pomp and circumstance at the **Elgar Birthplace Museum** ( ☎ 01905-333224; www.elgarmuseum.org; Lower Broadheath; adult/child £6/2; 🕑 11am-5pm), partly housed in the humble cottage in which he was born in 1857, 3 miles west of Worcester. You can browse through an engrossing collection of the walrus-mustachioed composer's possessions, which range from his gramophone and musical manuscripts to endearing doodlings in the morning paper. Admission includes an audio tour with musical interludes so you can appreciate what all the fuss is really about.

Bus 308 goes from Worcester to Broadheath Common (15 minutes, three times daily Monday to Saturday), a short walk from the museum.

## GREAT MALVERN
pop 35,558

This well-to-do Victorian spa town tumbles prettily down the slopes of the gorgeous **Malvern Hills**, which soar upwards from the flat Worcestershire plains. The place positively glows with health and well being courtesy of its lush hill views, wide tree-lined avenues, booted hikers and pure spring waters that bubble up in unexpected places. Today the medicinal waters that first attracted over-findulgent Victorians are harnessed for a successful bottled-water business.

The **tourist office** ( ☎ 01684-892289; www.malvern hills.gov.uk; 21 Church St; 🕑 10am-5pm) is brimming with walking and cycling information. The

**library** ( ☎ 01684-566553; Graham Rd; ⏰ 9.30am-5.30pm Mon, Fri & Sat, 9.30am-8pm Tue-Thu) has free internet access; bring ID.

In June the town goes music-mad in the biannual **Elgar Festival** ( ☎ 01684-892277; www.elgar-festival.com) to celebrate the life and works of the composer who lived nearby at Malvern Link.

## Sights & Activities

### GREAT MALVERN PRIORY

The 11th-century **Great Malvern Priory** ( ☎ 01684-561020; www.greatmalvernpriory.org.uk; Church St; suggested donation £3; ⏰ 9am-6.30pm Apr-Oct, 9am-4.30pm Nov-Mar) is packed with remarkable features: it's lined with clumsy Norman pillars and hides a delightfully bizarre collection of 14th-century misericords under the tip-up seats of the monks' stalls. Every one a delight, they depict everything from three rats hanging a cat to the mythological basilisk, and run through domestic labours of the months from the 15th century.

### MALVERN MUSEUM OF LOCAL HISTORY

Straddling the pathway in the grand Priory Gatehouse (1470), the **Malvern Museum of Local History** ( ☎ 01684-567811; Abbey Rd; adult/child £2/50p; ⏰ 10.30am-5pm Easter-Oct, closed Wed during school term) offers a small but thorough exploration of the things for which Great Malvern is renowned, from hills geology to Victorian water cures.

### MALVERN THEATRES

One of the country's best provincial theatres, **Malvern Theatre** ( ☎ 01684-892277; www.malvern -theatres.co.uk; Grange Rd) packs in a lively program of classical music, dance, comedy, drama and cinema.

The quirky little **Theatre of Small Convenience** ( ☎ 01684-568933; www.wctheatre.co.uk; Edith Walk) is set in a converted Victorian men's lavatory decked out in theatrical Italianate flourishes. It's one of the world's smallest theatres, seating just 12 people for acts that range from puppetry to opera.

### WALKING

The jack-in-the-box Malvern Hills, which pop up dramatically out of the innocently low Severn plains on the boundary between Worcestershire and Herefordshire, are made up of 18 named peaks; highest of the bunch being Worcester Beacon at 419m. The hills are criss-crossed by more than 100 miles of paths;

trail guides (£1.75) are available at the tourist office. More than 70 springs and fountains pouring out the famous medicinal waters are dotted around the hills, and the tourist office has a map guide (£3.95) to all of them.

## Sleeping

**Como House** ( ☎ 01684-561486; www.comohouse.co.uk; Como Rd; s/d £40/60; P ⌨ wi-fi) This handsome Malvern-stone converted schoolhouse has three tastefully furnished, south-facing rooms, a self-catering apartment and a large garden, complete with a bridged pond and numerous statues. The owner picks guests up from the station and drops them off at walking points.

**Bredon House Hotel** ( ☎ 01684-566990; www.bredon house.co.uk; 34 Worcester Rd; s/d from £45/70; P ⌨ ) A short saunter from the centre, this genteel family- and pet-friendly Victorian hotel has superb views and courteous service. Rooms are decorated in a quirky but tasteful mix of new and old, and the books, magazines and family photographs dotted around the communal areas give it a homely feel.

**Treherne House** ( ☎ 01684-572445; www.tre hernehouse.co.uk; 53 Guarlford Rd; r from £90; P ) This fine old gentleman's residence-turned-boutique B&B has sumptuous bedrooms with a hint of French reproduction styling and to-die-for food. It's on the outskirts of town.

## Eating

**St Ann's Well Cafe** ( ☎ 01684-560285; St Ann's Well; piece of cake £2; ⏰ lunch daily Apr-Sep, Sat & Sun only Oct-Mar) The best of Malvern's many cafes is in a handsome early-19th-century villa, a steep 99-step ascent from town. It rewards the climb with great vegetarian and vegan food, wholesome salads and sinful cakes, which you can wash down with fresh spring water that bubbles into a carved basin by the door.

**Pepper and Oz** ( ☎ 01684-562676; 23 Abbey Rd; mains £7-18.50; ⏰ lunch & dinner Tue-Sat) Right by the museum, this brasserie has a lovely alfresco terrace and photography gallery, and serves solid classics such as butch Herefordshire steaks. There's a decent wine list and it also does good-value pretheatre menus.

**Leaf Coffee and Food House** ( ☎ 01684-574989; 1 Edith Walk; mains £9-13; ⏰ 8am-3pm Mon-Fri, 9am-4pm Sun) Big wooden tables and fresh flowers welcome visitors to this wholesome cafe. They use locally sourced and fair-trade produce to make great salads, sandwiches, burgers and cakes.

## Getting There & Around

There are twice-hourly trains to Worcester (12 to 18 minutes) and every half-hour to Hereford (£6.50, 30 minutes). Trains also go regularly to Ledbury (13 minutes).

National Express runs one bus daily to London (£21.10, 3½ hours) via Worcester (20 minutes). Bus 44 connects Worcester (30 minutes, hourly) with Great Malvern.

Handy for walkers, bus 244 – otherwise known as the 'Malvern Hills Hopper' – runs a hop-on, hop-off service (five daily weekends and bank holidays mid-April to October) through the hills to Upton-upon-Severn and Eastnor Castle.

# HEREFORDSHIRE

Sleepy, rural Herefordshire is well off the mainstream tourist track. It can be difficult to negotiate, especially without a car, but your efforts will be rewarded by a tapestry of lush fields, black-and-white timbered villages, twisting lanes and more then enough leafy orchards to give you a taste for the county's famous ciders. The scenic River Wye ambles through the county, tempting canoeists and other water babies. County capital Hereford is home to a small cathedral, where you'll find the superb medieval Mappa Mundi; and perched on the border with Wales is renowned bookshop mecca, Hay-on-Wye (p732).

## Information

For online county-wide information on attractions, accommodation and events:

**Visit Heart of England** (www.visitheartofengland.com)
**Visit Herefordshire** (www.visitherefordshire.co.uk)

## Activities

Herefordshire is a haven for walkers, with several established long-distance paths meandering through it. **Offa's Dyke Path** hugs the Welsh border, while the 107-mile **Wye Valley Walk** begins in Chepstow (Wales) and follows the river upstream into Herefordshire and then on to Rhayader in Wales. The **Three Choirs Way** is a 100-mile route connecting the cathedrals of Hereford, Worcester and Gloucester, where the music festival of the same name has been celebrated for more than three centuries.

The **Herefordshire Trail** (www.herefordshiretrail.com) is a 150-mile circular loop linking Leominster, Ledbury, Ross-on-Wye and Kington.

## Getting Around

Busy railway stations with nationwide links can be found at Hereford, Leominster and Ledbury. To plan your way about, pick up a free *Public Transport Map & Guide* from tourist offices and bus stations, or go online through **Hereford Bus** (www.herefordbus.info) and **National Traveline** ( ☎ 0870 200 2233; www.traveline midlands.co.uk).

# HEREFORD

**pop 56,353**

Straddling the River Wye at the heart of the county, agricultural capital Hereford is known for its cattle, cider and relationship with the composer Elgar. Even though it's the county capital it has a sluggish, provincial feel, although there are some youthful pockets in the centre and along its riverside. Hereford's most cherished possession is the extraordinary medieval map, the Mappa Mundi, housed in its dignified cathedral.

## Orientation & Information

The triangular, pedestrianised High Town is the city's heart, just north of the River Wye. The cathedral is close to the river, while the bus and train stations lie to the northeast, on Commercial Rd.

The **tourist office** ( ☎ 01432-268430; www.visitherefordshire.co.uk; 1 King St; 🕑 9am-5pm Mon-Sat) is opposite the cathedral. **Guided walks** (£3; 🕑 11am Mon-Sat, 2.30pm Sun May-Sep) start from here. There's free internet access at the **library** (Broad St; 🕑 9.30am-7.30pm Tue, Wed & Fri, 9.30am-5.30pm Thu, 9.30am-4pm Sat), in the same building as the Hereford Museum & Art Gallery.

## Sights

### HEREFORD CATHEDRAL

After the Welsh torched the town's original cathedral, the new **Hereford Cathedral** ( ☎ 01432-374200; www.herefordcathedral.org; 5 College Cloisters; suggested donation £4; 🕑 7.30am-Evensong) began life on the same site in the 11th century. The building has evolved into a well-packaged lesson on the entire history of English architecture: the sturdy south transept is Norman but holds a 16th-century triptych; the exquisite north transept with its soaring windows dates from the 13th century; the choir and the tower date from the

14th century; and the Victorian influence is visible almost everywhere.

But the cathedral is best known for two ancient treasures housed here. The magnificent 13th-century **Mappa Mundi** (adult/child £4.50/3.50; 10am-5pm Mon-Sat & 11am-3pm Sun May-Sep, 10am-4pm Mon-Sat Oct-Apr) is a large calfskin vellum map intricately painted with the vivid world vision of the era's scholars, and an enthralling pictorial encyclopedia of the times. It is the largest and best-preserved example of this type of cartography anywhere, but more than that it's a bewitching journey through the world as then envisioned, roamed by basilisks and mythological monsters. Navigate your way through the barely recognisable mash of continents and you can even find Hereford itself.

The same wing contains the world's largest surviving **chained library**, hooked to its shelves by a cascade of long thin shackles. The unique collection of rare books and manuscripts includes a 1217 copy of the revised Magna Carta and the 8th-century *Hereford Gospels*, although the gospels' fragility means they aren't always on display.

The cathedral comes alive with Evensong at 5.30pm Monday to Saturday and 3.30pm on Sunday, and every three years in August it holds the famous **Three Choirs Festival** (www.3choirs.org), shared with Gloucester and Worcester Cathedrals.

### OTHER SIGHTS

Marooned in a sea of bustling shops, the **Old House** ( 01432-260694; admission free; 10am-5pm Tue-Sat year-round, plus 10am-4pm Sun Apr-Sep) is a wonderfully creaky black-and-white, three-storey wooden house, built in 1621, panelled and furnished in exquisitely carved wood.

The quirky collection at **Hereford Museum & Art Gallery** ( 01432-260692; Broad St; admission free; 10am-5pm Tue-Sat year-round, plus 10am-4pm Sun Apr-Sep) includes everything from 19th-century witches' curses to Roman antiquities. There's also some dressing-up gear to keep kids entertained.

Don't forget to claim your free samples in the **Cider Museum & King Offa Distillery** ( 01432-354207; www.cidermuseum.co.uk; Pomona Pl; adult/child £3.50/2; 10am-5pm Tue-Sat Apr-Oct, 11am-3pm Tue-Sat Nov-Mar), which explores cider-making history.

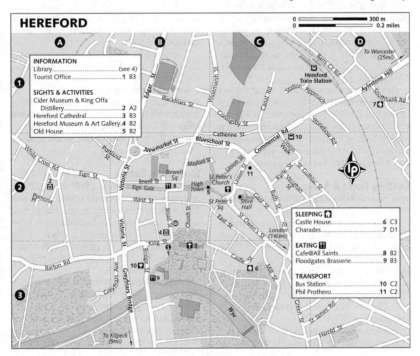

| HEREFORD | | | |
|---|---|---|---|

INFORMATION
Library......................................(see 4)
Tourist Office................................1 B3

SIGHTS & ACTIVITIES
Cider Museum & King Offa
  Distillery.................................2 A2
Hereford Cathedral.........................3 B3
Hereford Museum & Art Gallery..4 B2
Old House...................................5 B2

SLEEPING
Castle House...............................6 C3
Charades....................................7 D1

EATING
Cafe@All Saints.............................8 B2
Floodgates Brasserie.....................9 B3

TRANSPORT
Bus Station................................10 C2
Phil Prothero..............................11 C2

Look for the fine costrels (minibarrels) and horn mugs used by agricultural workers to carry and quaff their wages, which were partially paid in cider.

## Sleeping

**Charades** ( ☎ 01432-269444; www.charadeshereford.co.uk; 34 Southbank Rd; s/d £45/65; **P** ) This imposing Georgian house built around 1870 has five recently revamped, comfortable rooms, some with soul-restoring views over the countryside. The house itself has character in spades – look for old service bells in the hall. It's handy for the bus station, but a 1km walk from the cathedral.

**Castle House** ( ☎ 01432-356321; www.castlehse.co.uk; Castle St; s £120, d £175-220; **P** ) This refined multi-award-winning Georgian town house, once the bishop's residence, is Hereford's best boutique hotel. Rooms have rich fabrics and classic decor with full modern conveniences. There's a lovely garden and riverside seating, as well as a seriously sophisticated restaurant with an inventive menu. Wheelchair access is available.

## Eating

**Cafe@All Saints** ( ☎ 01432-370414; www.cafeatallsaints.co.uk; High St; mains £3.60-8.75; ☽ 9am-5pm Mon-Sat) Sit underneath great stone arches as you sip fair-trade coffee or chow down on wholesome (mostly vegetarian) lunches in this natty two-level cafe in a working church. You can even enjoy a glass of wine – just remember, God's watching.

**Floodgates Brasserie** ( ☎ 01432-349000; Left Bank Village, Bridge St; mains £12.50-18; ☽ lunch & dinner) Part of the Left Bank Village complex, in a prime riverside spot, this sleek modern restaurant is slightly lacking in character but it has a lovely terrace overlooking the river, a sunny interior and a fine modern European menu.

## Getting There & Around

Hire bikes at **Phil Prothero** ( ☎ 01432-359478; Bastion Mews) for £12 per day.

There are hourly trains to London Paddington (£37.20, 3¼ hours) via Newport, South Wales; and to Birmingham (£12.90, 1½ hours). National Express goes to London (£20.40, 4¼ hours, four daily), Heathrow (£21.10, 4¼ hours, two daily), Gloucester (£5.90, 1¼ hours, five daily) and Ross-on-Wye (30 minutes, four daily) or Ledbury (25 minutes, two daily).

Bus 420 runs every two hours to Worcester (1¼ hours). Bus 38 runs hourly to Ross-on-

Wye (40 minutes, six on Sunday), and bus 476 goes hourly to Ledbury (30 minutes, five on Sunday) – both from the bus station on Commercial Rd.

# AROUND HEREFORD

## Kilpeck Church

Deep in the Herefordshire countryside is the tiny hamlet of Kilpeck, home to a beguiling little Norman **church** that has barely changed since the 12th century. Original carvings encircle the building, from cartoon like pigs and bunnies, mythical monsters, grimacing heads, to a famous spread-legged *sheila-na-gig* (Celtic fertility figure). It's an extraordinary sight, well worth the 1-mile trip south of the main A465 road that comes from Hereford. Kilpeck is 9 miles south of Hereford, off the A465.

## ROSS-ON-WYE

### pop 10,085

Snoozy little Ross-on-Wye, which perches prettily on a red sandstone bluff over a kink in the River Wye, is a gentle place to rest before or after exertions in the beautiful countryside that surrounds it. The town sparks to life in mid-August, when the **International Festival** brings fireworks, raft races, music and street theatre.

The salmon-pink 17th-century Market House sits atop its weathered sandstone columns in the Market Place. It contains a **Heritage Centre** ( ☎ 01989-260675; ☽ 10am-5pm Mon-Sat, 10.30am-4pm Sun Apr-Oct, 10.30am-4pm Mon-Sat Nov-Mar) with local-history displays. The **tourist office** ( ☎ 01989-562768; tic-ross@herefordshire.gov.uk; Edde Cross St; ☽ 9am-5pm Mon-Sat) has information on activities and walks.

## Sleeping & Eating

**White House Guest House** ( ☎ 01989-763572; www.whitehouseross.com; Wye St; s/d £45/65; **P** ☐ wi-fi) This 18th-century stone house has a great location across the road from the River Wye. Vivid window boxes give it a splash of colour and the rooms, decorated in rich shades of burgundy and crisp white, are peaceful and comfortable.

**Bridge at Wilton** ( ☎ 01989-562655; www.bridge-house-hotel.com; Wilton; s/d from £80/98; **P** ) A distinguished Georgian country house, a riverside setting a short tumble down from town, and a highly praised modern British restaurant dedicated to local produce make this a wonderful spot to linger. Eight classically styled rooms overlook the gardens and river.

The closest hostel is 6 miles south at Welsh Bicknor (below).

## Drinking

**Hope & Anchor** ( ☎ 01989-563003; Wye St) This friendly riverside pub is a great place to while away the time, especially in the summer, when tables spread right down the grassy bank to the water's edge and overflow with happy customers.

## Getting There & Around

Buses 38 and 33 run hourly Monday to Saturday to and from Hereford and Gloucester respectively (40 minutes each way).

You can hire bikes from **Revolutions** ( ☎ 01989-562639; 48 Broad St; per day from £10).

# AROUND ROSS-ON-WYE
## Goodrich

Seemingly part of its craggy bedrock, **Goodrich Castle** (EH; ☎ 01600-890538; adult/child £5/2.50; ⏱ 10am-6pm daily Jun-Aug, 10am-5pm daily Mar-May, Sep & Oct, 10am-4pm Wed-Sun Nov-Feb) is an exceptionally complete medieval castle, topped by a superb 12th-century keep that rewards the trek up tight winding staircases with spectacular views. A small exhibition tells the story of the castle from its 11th-century origins to its demise in the 1600s.

**Welsh Bicknor YHA** ( ☎ 0845 371 9666; www.yha .org.uk; dm £18; ⏱ Apr-Oct; ⓟ ) is well worth the thigh-pumping 1½-mile climb to reach it from Goodrich village. This austere-looking former Victorian rectory surveys the glorious countryside from 10 hectares of lovely riverside grounds. The Wye Valley Walk passes the hostel.

Goodrich is 5 miles south of Ross off the A40. Bus 34 stops here every two hours on its way between Ross (15 minutes) and Monmouth (20 minutes).

## Symonds Yat

A remote little nook, huddled against the River Wye, Symonds Yat is well worth a visit for water babies, bird enthusiasts and those fond of a relaxed riverside pint. An ancient hand-hauled ferry (adult/child 80/40p) joins two separate hill-backed villages on either bank, usually with a few ducks hitching a ride on the back. There's an abrupt change of mood in upper Symonds Yat West, where you'll find

a big tacky fairground jingling to the sound of pocket change, slot machines and carousels.

### ACTIVITIES

This area is renowned for canoeing and rock climbing and there's also good hiking in the nearby Forest of Dean. The **Wyedean Canoe Centre** ( ☎ 01594-833238; www.wyedean.co.uk) hires out canoes/kayaks from £20/16 per half-day, and also organises multiday kayaking trips, white-water trips, caving and climbing. Note that the river has a strong current and is not suitable for swimming.

From Symonds Yat East, it's a steep but easy walk (at least on a dry day) up 504m to the crown of the region, **Symonds Yat Rock**, from where you'll get a fabulous view of the river and valley. You can catch a rare glimpse of the world's fastest creature doing aerial acrobatics here, as peregrine falcons nest in the cliffs opposite.

If that all sounds like too much hard work, **Kingfisher Cruises** ( ☎ 01600-891063) runs sedate 35-minute gorge cruises from beside the ferry crossing.

### SLEEPING & EATING

**Garth Cottage** ( ☎ 01600-890364; www.garthcottage -symondsyat.com; Symonds Yat East; d £72; ⏱ Apr-Oct; ⓟ ) The pick of accommodation on the east side, this friendly, family-run B&B sits demurely by the riverside near the ferry crossing, and has spotless, bright rooms with river views. Breakfast is served in the conservatory or on the terrace, both overlooking the water.

**Saracen's Head** ( ☎ 01600-890435; www.saracenshead inn.co.uk; Symonds Yat East; mains £10-20; ⓟ ) This black-and-white traditional inn is Symonds Yat's focal point, next to the ferry crossing. It has some river-view rooms (doubles from £74) sporting pine furniture and polished wood floors, and two luxury suites in the boathouse. It's a popular spot to enjoy a meal while waiting for the moment when the ferryman topples into the river.

### GETTING THERE & AWAY

Bus 34 can drop you off on the main road 1.5 miles from the village. Bikes are available for hire from the Royal Hotel (Symonds Yat East) for £13 per day.

# LEDBURY
## pop 8491

An atmospheric little town abundant with history and antique shops, Ledbury is a fa-

THE MIDLANDS &
THE MARCHES

vourite destination for day trippers. The best way to pass the time is to simply wander its dense core of crooked black-and-white streets, which zero in on a delightfully leggy market house.

The helpful **tourist office** ( ☎ 01531-636147; ticledbury@herefordshire.gov.uk; 3 The Homend; ☼ 10am-5pm Mon-Sat Apr-Oct, to 4pm Nov-Mar) has details about a lovely 17-mile cycle route called the Ledbury Loop (50p). To get online visit part ice-cream parlour, part internet cafe **Ice Bytes** ( ☎ 01531-634700; 38 The Homend; per 15min £1).

## Sights

Ledbury's centrepiece is the delicate black-and-white **Market House**, a 17th-century timber-framed structure precariously balanced atop 16 narrow wooden posts supposedly gleaned from the defeated Spanish Armada. From here, wander up the narrow cobbled **Church Lane**, crowded with tilted timber-framed buildings, including the **Painted Room** (admission free; ☼ 11am-1pm & 2-4pm Mon-Fri Easter-Sep), with jigsaw-puzzle 16th-century floral frescos.

Here too are several small museums, including **Butcher's Row House** ( ☎ 01531-632942; Church Lane; admission free; ☼ 11am-5pm Easter-Sep), a pocket-sized folk museum stuffed with curios, from 19th-century school clothing to an 18th-century communal 'boot' bath that used to be carted from door to door for the poor to scrub in. The **Heritage Centre** ( ☎ 01531-260692; admission free; ☼ 10.30am-4.30pm Easter-Oct) sits in another half-timbered treasure opposite and has more displays on the town.

At the top of the lane lies the 12th-century church of **St Michael and All Angels**, with a splendid 18th-century spire and tower separate from the church.

## Sleeping & Eating

Budget travellers may struggle to find accommodation in Ledbury.

**Talbot Hotel** ( ☎ 01531-632963; www.visitledbury.co.uk/talbot; New St; s/d £55/80; **P** ) A black-and-white, late-16th-century coaching inn with a lively little bar and dark oak–panelled restaurant, the Talbot also has a handful of simple, compact rooms in what used to be the hay loft. It can get a little noisy on weekends and breakfast costs extra.

**Feathers Hotel** ( ☎ 01531-635266; www.feathers-ledbury.co.uk; High St; s/d from £85/125; **P** ) This charming black-and-white Tudor hotel

looms over the main road. It has a mixture of rooms – ask for one in the oldest part of the building, which come with slanting floorboards and painted beams. Most of the modern rooms lack character. There's also a swimming pool.

**Cameron & Swan** ( ☎ 01531-636 791; www.cameronandswan.co.uk; 15 The Homend; mains £6-7; ☼ lunch) New, bustling deli-cafe serving tasty deli platters, homemade tarts, cakes and bakes in a bright, airy dining room.

## Getting There & Around

There are roughly hourly trains to Hereford (15 minutes), less often to Great Malvern (11 minutes), Worcester (23 to 27 minutes) and Birmingham (£11.50, 1¼ hours).

Bus 476 runs to Hereford hourly (30 minutes, every two hours on Sunday); bus 132 runs hourly to Gloucester (one hour).

You can hire mountain bikes at **Saddle Bound Cycles** ( ☎ 01531-633433; 3 The Southend; per day £12).

## AROUND LEDBURY
### Eastnor Castle

Built more for fancy than fortification, the extravagant 19th-century medieval-revival folly of **Eastnor Castle** ( ☎ 01531-633160; www.eastnorcastle.com; adult/child £8/5, grounds only £4/2) seems to have leapt out of the pages of a bedtime story. The opulent interior continues the romantic veneer, decorated in Gothic and Italianate features, tapestries and antiques. Even when the castle is closed – call or check the website, as the opening days are quite complicated – its maze, adventure playground and lakeside walks are worth a look. Its beautiful deer park is also stage to the **Big Chill** ( ☎ 020-7684 2020; www.bigchill.net; ☼ Aug), when campers, musicians, performers and artists round off the summer festival season in relaxed fashion.

The castle is just over 2 miles east of Ledbury on the A438. The Malvern Hills Hopper bus runs here from Upton-upon-Severn and Great Malvern on summer weekends and bank holidays.

# SHROPSHIRE

Dreamily beautiful and sparsely populated, Shropshire ripples over the River Severn from the Welsh border to Birmingham. The surroundings are most beautiful to the south, where the land is ripe with stunning moorland, gurgling rivers and pretty villages; and its undulating, heather-tickled hills make for wonderful walking territory. The lovely Tudor town of Shrewsbury is the county capital, and nestled nearby is the remarkable World Heritage Site of Ironbridge Gorge. At the county's base you'll find foodie-magnet Ludlow, with its handsome castle and epicurean ways.

## Information

For online county information:

**North Shropshire** (www.northshropshire.co.uk)
**Secret Shropshire** (www.secretshropshire.org.uk)
**Shropshire Tourism** (www.shropshiretourism.info)
**Virtual Shropshire** (www.virtual-shropshire.co.uk)
**Visit South Shropshire** (www.visitsouthshropshire.co.uk)

## Getting Around

You can hop on handy rail services from Shrewsbury to Church Stretton, Craven Arms and Ludlow. The invaluable *Shropshire Bus & Train Map,* available free from tourist offices, shows public-transport routes. **Shropshire Hills Shuttle Buses** (www.shropshire hillsshuttles.co.uk) also drops off walkers along popular hiking routes on weekends and bank holidays. Call **Traveline** ( ☎ 0870 200 2233; www.traveline.org.uk) with any queries.

## SHREWSBURY

pop 67,126

The higgledy-piggledy mass of medieval streets in the heart of Shropshire's most picturesque town doesn't take long to work its magic. Ancient passageways wind their way between crooked Tudor buildings; dusky-red sandstone warms an ancient abbey and castle, and elegant parks tumble down to the River Severn.

Nudging a horseshoe loop in the river, Shrewsbury's defensive potential was crucial to keeping the Welsh in line for many centuries. Then in medieval times the town grew fat on the wool trade. It is also the birthplace of Charles Darwin (1809–82), who rocked the world with his theory of evolution.

## Orientation

Shrewsbury's near-island status helps preserve the Tudor and Jacobean streetscapes of its centre and protects it from unattractive urban sprawl. The train station is a five-minute walk northeast of the centre and is as far as you'll need to venture.

## Information

**Library** ( ☎ 01743-255300; Castle Gates; 🕑 9.30am-5pm Mon, Wed, Fri & Sat, 9.30am-8pm Tue & Thu, 1-4pm Sun) Free internet access.
**Royal Shrewsbury Hospital** ( ☎ 01743-261000; Mytton Oak Rd)
**Tourist office** ( ☎ 01743-281200; www.visitshrews bury.com; Music Hall, The Square; 🕑 9.30am-5.30pm Mon-Sat, 10am-4pm Sun May-Sep, 10am-5pm Mon-Sat Oct-Apr) Guided 1½-hour walking tours (adult/child £3.50/1.50) leave the tourist office at 2.30pm Monday to Saturday, and 11am Sunday from May to September and at 2.30pm Saturday only from November to April.

## Sights
### SHREWSBURY ABBEY

Most famous as a setting for the monastic whodunits the *Chronicles of Brother Cadfael* by Ellis Peters, the lovely red-sandstone **Shrewsbury Abbey** ( ☎ 01743-232723; www.shrewsburyabbey.com; Abbey Foregate; donation adult/child £2/1; 🕑 10am-4.30pm Mon-Sat, 11.30am-2.30pm Sun) is what remains of a large Benedictine monastery founded in 1083, its outbuildings mostly lost and its flanks unceremoniously chopped. It's graced by a mix of Norman, Early English and Victorian features and there's an exceptional 14th-century west window of heraldic glass. The abbey is renowned for its fine acoustics and a noticeboard provides information on up-coming recitals.

### SHREWSBURY MUSEUM & ART GALLERY

Rowley's House, the stunning timber-framed Tudor merchant's mansion and warehouse in which **Shrewsbury Museum & Art Gallery** ( ☎ 01743-361196; www.shrewsburymuseums.com; Barker St; admission free; 🕑 10am-5pm Mon-Sat, to 4pm Sun Jun-Sep, 10am-4pm Oct-May) is housed, is as much of an attraction as its exhibits, which range from Roman finds to Darwin's times. At the time of writing, the museum was due to move to the Music Hall in 2011, forming a part of a new museum and tourist office. It will be closed for several months each year until then.

## Other Sights

Shrewsbury's main sights are easily negotiated on foot so it's a great place for a self-guided tour.

Start at the tourist office. The mellow-stone building balancing on chunky legs opposite you is Shrewsbury's 16th-century **Market Hall**, hub of the historic wool trade. Look out for the holes in the pillars, which were used to count how many fleeces were sold.

The most impressive of Shrewsbury's black-and-white beauties, the stern timber-framed **Ireland's Mansion** grabs attention to your left as you step up to High St. Turn right and cross over into charmingly named, narrow little **Grope Lane** with its overhanging buildings, and you'll emerge into atmospheric **Fish Street** and see some steps leading to the 14th-century **Bear Steps Hall** (☾ 10am-4pm), now home to a small exhibition space. On the hall's other side is **Butcher Row**, home to more atmospheric black-and-white lovelies.

Head another street north to check out the magnificent spire of medieval **St Mary's Church** (St Mary's St; ☾ 11am-4pm Fri-Sun May-Sep), one of the highest in England. Duck inside for a peek at the astonishingly vivid Jesse window made from rare mid-14th-century glass.

Turn left into Windsor Place, before taking the second right into Castle St. You can't miss the entrance on the right to russet **Shrewsbury Castle**, which houses the stiff-upper-lip **Shropshire Regimental Museum** (☎ 01743-358516; adult/child £2.50/1.50; ☾ 10am-5pm Mon-Sat, to 4pm Sun May-Sep, 10am-4pm Tue-Sat Feb-Apr) and has wonderful views.

Back near the entrance is Jacobean-style **Council House Gatehouse**, dating from 1620, and **Old Council House**, where the Council of the Welsh Marches used to meet.

Opposite the castle is an unusually grand **library**, with a severe-looking **statue** of Shrewsbury's most famous son, Charles Darwin. Returning to St Mary's St, follow it into Dogpole and turn right into Wyle Cop, Welsh for 'hilltop'. Henry VII stayed in the seriously overhanging **Henry Tudor House** before the Battle of Bosworth. At the bottom of Wyle Cop is the graceful 18th-century **English Bridge**, which takes you across to **Shrewsbury Abbey**.

If your feet aren't yet aching, double back over the bridge and stroll left along the riverside to enjoy an ice cream in the sweeping gardens of **Quarry Park**, and listen to the cacophonous bells of odd 18th-century round church **St Chad's**, which surveys the park and the river.

## Sleeping

**164 B&B** (☎ 01743-367750; www.164bedandbreakfast .co.uk; 164 Abbey Foregate; s/d £35/54, with bathroom £45/58; P ☐ wi-fi) Despite the age of the building you won't find any chintz or faux-Tudor interiors here. This B&B celebrates its lovely 16th-cen-

tury timber frame with bright colours, contemporary fabrics and a quirky mix of artwork. As an extra treat, breakfast is served in bed.

**Mad Jack's** (☎ 01743-358870; www.madjacksuk.com; 15 St Mary's St; s/d from £65/75) The foot-sinking cream carpets, leather furniture and soft fur throws of this guesthouse's four smart rooms blend in perfectly with the quirks of the old building. There's a good restaurant downstairs.

**Tudor House** (☎ 01743-351735; www.tudorhouse shrewsbury.com; 2 Fish St; s/d from £69/79; ☐ wi-fi) If you're feeling nostalgic, this creaky medieval house has old-world charm by the bucket-load. The building is festooned with floral window boxes and its handful of traditional oak-beamed rooms are turned out in high-shine fabrics, some with spindly metal-framed headboards entwined with flowers. Not all rooms have an en suite.

**Lion Hotel** (☎ 01753 353 107; www.thelionhotelshrews bury.co.uk; Wyle Cop; s/d from £76/92; P ) A cowardly lion presides over the doorway of this grand old coaching inn. The most famous hotel in town, it has hosted many a luminary through its 400-year history. At the time of writing the hotel was undergoing a major refurbishment.

There are plenty more B&Bs huddled around Abbey Foregate.

## Eating

**Good Life Wholefood Restaurant** (☎ 01743-350455; Barracks Passage; mains £3.50-7; ☾ lunch Mon-Sat) Healthy, freshly prepared vegetarian food is the name of the game in this cute little refuge off Wyle Cop. Favourites include quiches, nut loaf and slightly less health-conscious cakes and desserts.

**Cornhouse** (☎ 01743-231991; www.cornhouse.co.uk; 59A Wyle Cop; mains £8-14; ☾ lunch & dinner) This cosy corner holds a relaxed wine bar and restaurant, successfully mixing contemporary style with period features from its working corn-house days. Its consistently good British food is served up in the shadow of a superb cast-iron spiral staircase.

**Mad Jack's** (☎ 01743-358870; www.madjacksuk .com; 15 St Mary's St; mains £11-16; ☾ 10am-10pm) Posh cafe, restaurant and bar that's passionate about local produce. Breakfasts, light lunches, afternoon tea and dinners are served in a bright, elegant dining room or a lovely plant-filled courtyard. Highlights include pistachio-crusted local lamb and chocolate torte with fennel ice cream.

**Drapers Hall** (☎ 01743-344679; St Mary's Pl; mains £12-17.50; ☾ lunch & dinner) The sense of his-

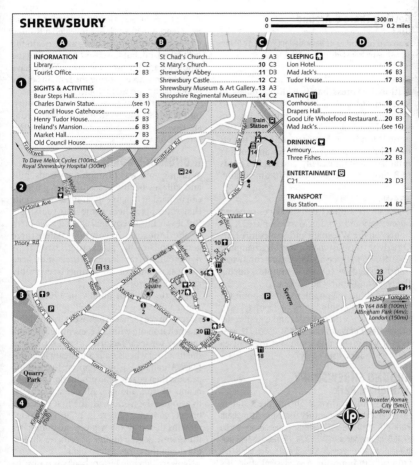

# SHREWSBURY

| INFORMATION | |
|---|---|
| Library | 1 C2 |
| Tourist Office | 2 B3 |
| **SIGHTS & ACTIVITIES** | |
| Bear Steps Hall | 3 B3 |
| Charles Darwin Statue | (see 1) |
| Council House Gatehouse | 4 C2 |
| Henry Tudor House | 5 B3 |
| Ireland's Mansion | 6 B3 |
| Market Hall | 7 B3 |
| Old Council House | 8 C2 |
| St Chad's Church | 9 A3 |
| St Mary's Church | 10 C3 |
| Shrewsbury Abbey | 11 D3 |
| Shrewsbury Castle | 12 C2 |
| Shrewsbury Museum & Art Gallery | 13 A3 |
| Shropshire Regimental Museum | 14 C2 |
| **SLEEPING** | |
| Lion Hotel | 15 C3 |
| Mad Jack's | 16 B3 |
| Tudor House | 17 B3 |
| **EATING** | |
| Cornhouse | 18 C4 |
| Drapers Hall | 19 C3 |
| Good Life Wholefood Restaurant | 20 B3 |
| Mad Jack's | (see 16) |
| **DRINKING** | |
| Armoury | 21 A2 |
| Three Fishes | 22 B3 |
| **ENTERTAINMENT** | |
| C21 | 23 D3 |
| **TRANSPORT** | |
| Bus Station | 24 B2 |

tory is palpable in this well-fossilised 16th-century hall, fronted by an elegant Elizabethan facade. Award-wining, Anglo-French haute cuisine is divided between dark oak-panelled rooms decked out in sumptuous fabrics and antique screens. The connoisseur's wine list is also well worthy of a special occasion.

## Drinking

**Armoury** ( ☎ 01743-340525; www.armoury-shrewsbury .co.uk; Victoria Ave) There's a great warmth and conviviality to this converted riverside warehouse. Towering bookshelves, old pictures and curios help straddle the divide between posh restaurant (mains £9 to £17) and informal pub; large, curved windows invite in plenty of light, while a plethora of blackboard

menus invite you to sample wines, guest ales and hearty British dishes.

**Three Fishes** ( ☎ 01743-344793; 4 Fish St) The quintessential creaky Tudor alehouse, with a jolly owner, mellow regulars and hops hanging from the 15th-century beamed ceiling. No music here, just plenty of good-value real ales on tap and solid bar food.

## Entertainment

**C21** ( ☎ 01743-271821; 21 Abbey Foregate; admission after 10pm £3-7; ☽ 8.30pm-3am) A polished city-chic club for over-25-year-olds to indulge in late-night cocktails and dance-floor acrobatics. On Mondays it's home to Shrewsbury's main gay and lesbian night.

## Getting There & Around

### BIKE

You can hire bikes at **Dave Mellor Cycles** ( ☎ 01743-366662; www.thecycleshop.co.uk; 9 New St).

### BUS

National Express has two direct buses to London (£17.80, 4½ hours) and two to Birmingham (£5.70, 1½ hours). Bus 96 serves Ironbridge (30 minutes) every two hours Monday to Saturday. Bus 435 travels to Ludlow (1¼ hours) via Church Stretton (45 minutes) eight times daily, and bus 553 heads to Bishop's Castle (one hour) 10 times daily.

### TRAIN

There are five direct daily services between Shrewsbury and London Marylebone (£33, 3½ hours) on the Wrexham and Shropshire line. Otherwise you must change at Wolverhampton (£42.40, 2½ to three hours). Trains run twice-hourly to Ludlow (£8.40, 30 minutes) during the week and hourly at weekends.

Shrewsbury is a popular starting point for two scenic routes into Wales: one loop takes in Shrewsbury, northern Wales and Chester; the other, **Heart of Wales Line** ( ☎ 0870 9000 772; www.heart-of-wales.co.uk), runs southwest to Swansea (£19, 3¾ hours, four daily).

## AROUND SHREWSBURY
### Attingham Park

The most impressive of Shropshire's stately homes is late-18th-century mansion **Attingham Park** (NT; ☎ 01743-708123; house & grounds adult/child £7.40/3.70, grounds only £4.20/2.20; ⏰ house 1-5pm Thu-Tue mid-Mar–Oct, grounds 10am-dusk Thu-Tue mid-Mar–Oct). Built in imposing neoclassical style, it's reminiscent of many a bodice-ripping drama. Behind the high-and-mighty facade, you'll find a picture gallery by John Nash, and two wings respectively decorated into staunch masculine and delicate feminine Regency interiors. A herd of deer roam the landscaped grounds and there are pleasant walks along the River Tern.

Attingham Park is 4 miles southeast of Shrewsbury at Atcham. Buses 81 and 96 (18 minutes) run six times a day Monday to Friday, less frequently on weekends.

## Wroxeter Roman City

The crumbled foundations of one of Roman Britain's largest cities, Viroconium, can be seen at **Wroxeter** (EH; ☎ 01743-761330; adult/child £4.20/2.10; ⏰ 10am-5pm Mar-Oct, to 4pm Wed-Sun Nov-Feb). Geophysical work has revealed a Roman city as large as Pompeii lying underneath the lush farmland, but the costs of excavating the whole lot are, for now, too great. You'll have to make do with exploring the remains of the public baths and marketplace.

Wroxeter is 6 miles southeast of Shrewsbury, off the B4380. Bus 96 stops nearby, and runs six times a day Monday to Friday, less frequently on weekends.

## IRONBRIDGE GORGE

Winding your way through the woods, hills and villages of this peaceful river gorge, it can be hard to imagine the trailblazing events that took place here some 300 years ago. But it was this sleepy enclave that gave birth to the Industrial Revolution, when three generations of the pioneering Darby family set about transforming their industrial processes and in so doing irreversibly changed the world.

The story began quietly in 1709, when Abraham Darby determinedly set about restoring an old furnace to prove it was possible to smelt iron ore with coke, eventually paving the way for local factories to mass-produce the first iron wheels, rails and steam locomotives. Abraham Darby II's innovative forging process then enabled the production of single beams of iron, allowing Abraham Darby III to astound the world with the first ever iron bridge, constructed here in 1779. The bridge remains the valley's showpiece and dominates the main village, a jumble of cottages slithering down the gorge's steep bank.

Now written into history books as the birthplace of the Industrial Revolution, Ironbridge is a World Heritage Site and the Marches' top attraction. Ten very different museums now tell the story in the very buildings where it took place.

## Orientation & Information

Driving or cycling can make life easier, as the museums are peppered throughout the long gorge. See p509 for public-transport options.

The **tourist office** ( ☎ 01952-884391; www.visitironbridge.co.uk; Tollhouse; ⏰ 10am-5pm) is by the bridge.

## Sights & Activities

The great-value **passport ticket** (adult/child £15/10) that allows year-round entry to all of the sites can be bought at any of the museums or the tourist office. The museums open from 10am to 5pm unless stated otherwise.

### MUSEUM OF THE GORGE

A good way to begin your visit is the **Museum of the Gorge** (The Wharfage; adult/child £3/2.50), which offers an overview of the site. Housed in a Gothic warehouse by the river, it's filled with touch screens, fun exhibits and details of the horrific consequences of pollution and environmental hazards at the cutting edge of industry (Abraham I and III both died at 39). An absorbing video sets the museum in its historical context.

### COALBROOKDALE MUSEUM OF IRON & DARBY HOUSES

What was once the Coalbrookdale iron foundry, where pioneering Abraham Darby first smelted iron ore with coke, now houses the **Coalbrookdale Museum of Iron** (adult/child £5.95/4.25). An army of men and boys once churned out heavy-duty iron equipment here, and later, ever more fancy ironwork castings. The excellent interactive exhibits

chart the company's history and showcase some extraordinary creations.

The early industrial settlement that surrounds the site has also happily survived, with workers' cottages, chapels, church and graveyard undisturbed. Just up the hill are the beautifully restored 18th-century **Darby Houses** ( ☎ 01952-433522; adult/child £4/2.50; ☻ Apr-Oct), which housed generations of the industrial bigwigs in gracious but modest Quaker comfort. Rosehill House is furnished with much original furniture, and next door Dale House includes the wood-panelled office in which Abraham Darby III pored over his bridge designs.

### IRON BRIDGE & TOLLHOUSE

The flamboyant arching **Iron Bridge** that gives the area its name was a symbol of the iron industry's success; a triumph of engineering that left contemporaries flabbergasted by its apparent flimsiness. As well as providing a crossing the river, it ensured that Abraham Darby III and his village would be given a prominent place in the history books. The **tollhouse** (admission free; ☻ 10am-5pm) houses a small exhibition on the bridge's history.

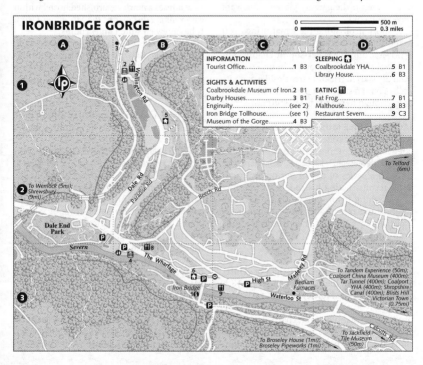

**IRONBRIDGE GORGE**

0 ——————— 500 m
0 ——————— 0.3 miles

| INFORMATION | |
|---|---|
| Tourist Office | 1 B3 |

| SIGHTS & ACTIVITIES | |
|---|---|
| Coalbrookdale Museum of Iron | 2 B1 |
| Darby Houses | 3 B1 |
| Enginuity | (see 2) |
| Iron Bridge Tollhouse | (see 1) |
| Museum of the Gorge | 4 B3 |

| SLEEPING | |
|---|---|
| Coalbrookdale YHA | 5 B1 |
| Library House | 6 B3 |

| EATING | |
|---|---|
| Fat Frog | 7 B1 |
| Malthouse | 8 B3 |
| Restaurant Severn | 9 C3 |

To Telford (6mi)

To Wenlock (5mi); Shrewsbury (9mi)

Dale End Park

To Tandem Experience (50m); Coalport China Museum (400m); Tar Tunnel (400m); Coalport YHA (400m); Shropshire Canal (400m); Blists Hill Victorian Town (0.75mi)

Bedlam Furnaces

To Broseley House (1mi); Broseley Pipeworks (1mi)

To Jackfield Tile Museum (50m)

### BLISTS HILL VICTORIAN TOWN

To travel back to 19th-century Britain, hear the pounding of steam hammers and the clip-clop of horse hooves, or tip your hat to a cycling bobby, head to the vast open-air Victorian theme park, **Blists Hill** ( ☎ 01952-433522; Legges Way, Madeley; adult/child £10.50/7.50; ☻ 10am-5pm). This ambitious project does a remarkably good job of reconstructing an entire village, encompassing everything from a working foundry to a chemist to a bank, where you can exchange your cash for shillings to use on-site. Costumed staff explain displays, craftspeople demonstrate skills, and you can even join in an old-fashioned knees-up round the piano at the Victorian pub.

### COALPORT CHINA MUSEUM & TAR TUNNEL

When iron-making moved elsewhere, Coalport china slowed the region's decline and the restored works now house an absorbing **Coalport China Museum** (adult/child £6/4.25) tracing the region's glory days as a manufacturer of elaborate pottery and crockery. Craftspeople demonstrate china-making techniques, and two enormous bottle kilns are guaranteed to awe even if the gaudily glazed chinaware leaves you cold.

A short stroll along the canal brings you to the 200-year-old **Tar Tunnel** (adult/child £2/1.50; ☻ Apr-Sep), dug as a water-supply channel but halted abruptly when natural bitumen unexpectedly started trickling treacle-like from its walls. You can still don a hard hat and stoop in deep enough to see the black stuff ooze.

### JACKFIELD TILE MUSEUM

A kaleidoscopic collection of Victorian tiles, faience and ceramics can be found at the **Jackfield Tile Museum** (adult/child £6/4.25), displayed through a series of gas-lit period-style galleries reconstructing lustrous tiled interiors of everything from pubs to churches, tube stations and remarkably fancy toilets. Kids especially love the fairy-tale friezes for children's hospital wards.

### BROSELEY PIPEWORKS

Sucking on tobacco was the height of gentlemanly fashion in the late 17th and early 18th centuries, and the **Broseley Pipeworks** (adult/child £4/2.50; ☻ 1-5pm mid-May–Sep), once Britain's most prolific pipe manufacturer, charts the history of the industry. A vast range of clay pipes from short-stemmed 'pipsqueaks' to arm-length

'church wardens' were produced here, until the factory finally closed in 1957; now visitors can explore its time-capsule contents, which are largely unchanged since the last worker turned out the lights. It's a mile-long walk to get here, signposted from the bridge.

### ENGINUITY

Championing Ironbridge's spirit of brains before brawn, the fabulous interactive design and technology centre **Enginuity** (adult/child £6.25/5.25) invites you to move a steam engine with the flick of a wrist, X-ray everyday objects, power up a vacuum cleaner with self-generated electricity and basically dive head first into a vast range of hands-on, brains-on challenges, games and gadgets that explore design and engineering in modern life. If you have kids with you, allow at least two hours.

## Sleeping

**Coalbrookdale YHA** ( ☎ 0845 371 9325; www.yha.org .uk; 1 Paradise Rd, Coalbrookdale; dm £17; ℗ ) The austere former Literary and Scientific Institute, a grand blue-grey building from 1859 sitting high on the hillside behind sturdy iron gates, now houses a newly refurbished hostel within easy walking distance of the Museum of Iron. It has a few en suite family rooms.

**Coalport YHA** ( ☎ 0845 371 9325; www.yha.org.uk; High St, Coalport; dm £17; ℗ ) This historic former china factory, a big bluff industrial-looking building mere paces from the China Museum and the canal, and close to pleasant countryside walks, now houses an 83-bed hostel. The plain, modern rooms betray little of their long history, however. It has family-friendly rooms.

**our pick** **Library House** ( ☎ 01952-432299; www.library house.com; 11 Severn Bank; s/d from £65/75; ℗ ☐ wi-fi) This lovingly restored Georgian library building is hugged by vines, backed by a beautiful garden and elegantly decorated with light colours, deep cream sofas, rows of vintage books, and the odd African artefact. There are three charming, individually decorated rooms, with seriously comfortable beds, each named after a famous writer, and the welcome from hosts and family dog is exceedingly friendly.

## Eating

**Malthouse** ( ☎ 01952-433712; www.themalthouseiron bridge.com; The Wharfage; mains £8-17; ☻ lunch & dinner) This former malting house would be worth visiting for the enormous plates of good British cooking alone, but the vibrant atmosphere, regular live jazz and riverfront terrace are an added bonus. Stylish contemporary rooms (£63) are also available.

**Fat Frog** ( ☎ 01952-432240; www.fat-frog.co.uk; Coalbrookdale; mains £10-16; ☼ lunch & dinner Mon-Sat, lunch Sun) This quirky French bar-bistro is cluttered with toy frogs and showbiz memorabilia, has a rustic candlelit basement and plays nostalgic music from the ebullient Gallic proprietor's prime. The food is excellent and, as you'd expect, there's a great wine list with plenty of half-bottles.

**Restaurant Severn** ( ☎ 01952-432233; 33 High St; 2-/3-course dinner £25/27; ☼ dinner Wed-Sat, lunch Sun) The highly praised food is a hybrid of British and French at this exciting fine-dining waterfront restaurant. The simple decor and laid-back service attests to the fact that the real star here is the food – a delectable, locally sourced menu that changes weekly.

### Getting There & Away
The nearest train station is 6 miles away at Telford. Bus 96 runs every two hours (Monday to Saturday) between Shrewsbury (40 minutes) and Telford (15 to 20 minutes) via Ironbridge, stopping near the Museum of the Gorge. Bus 9 runs from Bridgnorth (30 minutes, four daily).

### Getting Around
The Gorge Connect bus connects nine of the museums every half-hour on weekends and bank holidays only. It costs 50p per journey, or there's a Day Rover pass (£2.50/1.50 per adult/child). The service is free to museum-passport holders.

Midweek your only options are to walk or hire a bike from **Broseley House** ( ☎ 01952-882043; www.broseleyhouse.co.uk; 1 The Square, Broseley; per day £15), a mile and a half south of the bridge; booking is advised. You may also like to look into **Tandem Experience** ( ☎ 0845 60 66 456; www.tandeming.co.uk; tandem per day £50), located next to the Tile Museum; the price includes tuition for tandem riding.

## MUCH WENLOCK
pop 1959

A tangle of narrow winding streets and historical buildings from the Tudor, Jacobean and Georgian eras, an arresting timbered guildhall and the enchanting remains of a 12th-century priory make this little town a real gem. It also claims to have jump-started the modern Olympics.

The **tourist office** ( ☎ 01952-727679; muchwenlock.tourism@shropshire-cc.gov.uk; The Square; ☼ 10.30am-1pm & 2-5pm Mon-Sat Apr-Oct, plus Sun Jun-Aug) shares a 19th-century building and opening hours with the local **museum** (admission free).

### Sights & Activities
The tourist office provides a map to the town's sights of historical interest, as well as copies of *The Olympian Trail*, a leaflet for a pleasant 1½-mile walking tour of the town exploring the link between the village and the modern Olympics.

Otherwise, you can skip straight to the atmospheric 12th-century ruins of **Wenlock Priory** (EH; ☎ 01952-727466; adult/child £3.50/1.80; ☼ 10am-5pm daily May-Aug, 10am-5pm Wed-Sun Apr, Sep & Oct, 10am-4pm Thu-Sun Nov-Feb) which rise up from vivid green lawns sprinkled with quirky topiaries of bears, cats and rabbits. The remains include part of a finely decorated chapterhouse and an unusual carved lavabo, and there's a particularly entertaining audio tour.

### Sleeping & Eating
The closest hostel is Wilderhope Manor YHA (p510).

**Talbot Inn** ( ☎ 01952-727077; www.the-talbot-inn.com; High St; s/d £40/80; P ) An atmospheric old place with colossal beams, cavernous fireplaces and good home-style fare (mains £10 to £15). There are some simple rooms in a converted 18th-century malthouse, with whitewashed walls, exposed beams and pine furniture.

**Raven Hotel** ( ☎ 01952-727251; www.ravenhotel.com; Barrow St; s/d £85/120; P ) Much Wenlock's finest, this 17th-century coaching inn and converted stables has thick oak beams, open fires and rich country-chic styling throughout. The excellent restaurant (two-/three-course meal £25/30) overlooks a flowery courtyard and serves up classic British and Mediterranean fare.

### Getting There & Away
Bus 436 runs from Shrewsbury (35 minutes) to Bridgnorth (20 minutes) hourly (five on Sunday).

## AROUND MUCH WENLOCK
The spectacular limestone escarpment of **Wenlock Edge** swells up like an immense

petrified wave, its ancient oceanic rock rich in fossils and its flanks frothy with woodland. It stretches for 15 miles from Much Wenlock to Craven Arms and makes for wonderful walking and dramatic views. The National Trust (NT) owns much of the ridge, and there are many waymarked trails starting from car parks dotted along the B4371. There are no convenient buses along this route.

For a bite, a beer or a bed, the 17th-century **Wenlock Edge Inn** ( ☎ 01746-785678; B4371, Hilltop; s/d £50/70; P ) is a good choice for hikers en route. It's a down-to-earth place with a recently revamped lively restaurant and bar with a fine choice of ales and Belgian beers. The food is a notch up from standard pub grub and provides hearty sustenance for the road ahead (mains £9 to £15). There are also some country-style rooms available. The pub is about 4.5 miles southwest of Much Wenlock on the B4371.

For top-value budget accommodation, ramble out to the remote **Wilderhope Manor YHA** ( ☎ 0845 371 9149; www.yha.org.uk; Longville-in-the-Dale; dm £17; ☯ Fri, Sat & school holidays; P ), a gloriously atmospheric gabled Elizabethan manor, with oak spiral staircases, heavy beams, wood-panelled walls, an impressive stone-floored dining hall and surprisingly spacious rooms. The hostel is set deep in lush countryside and adjoins a picturesque if stinky farmyard.

You can catch buses from Ludlow and Bridgnorth to Shipton, a half-mile walk from Wilderhope.

## CHURCH STRETTON & AROUND
pop 3841

Set deep in a valley formed by the Long Mynd and the Caradoc Hills, this scenic if restrained little town is the ideal base from which to venture into the glorious surroundings. It also shelters some interesting old buildings, including a 12th-century Norman church most famous for its weather-beaten but still undauntedly exhibitionist *sheila-na-gig* over its north door.

The **tourist office** ( ☎ 01694-723133; www.church stretton.co.uk; Church St; ☯ 9.30am-1pm & 2-5pm Mon-Sat), adjoining the library, has abundant walking information as well as free internet access.

### Sleeping
**Bridges Long Mynd YHA** ( ☎ 01588-650656; www .yha.org.uk; Ratlinghope; dm £16; P ) Once the village school, this old stone pile is one of the country's longest-running YHA hostels, with

a handful of basic but comfortable dorms. Hidden away in the Shropshire hills, it's a perfect base for exploring the county's walking trails – it's right on the doorstep of the Shropshire Way and walks to Long Mynd and Stiperstones. Boulton's bus 551 comes here from Shrewsbury on Tuesday only. On weekends and bank holidays from April to October, the Long Mynd shuttle runs hourly to Church Stretton.

**Mynd House** ( ☎ 01694-722212; www.myndhouse.com; Ludlow Rd, Little Stretton; s/d/f from £37/70/120; P ☐ wi-fi). Set right at the foot of the Long Mynd, this welcoming, family-friendly guesthouse has splendid views out over the hills and makes an excellent base for cycling, hiking or strolling. Rooms are clean and airy, and there's a small bar and cosy lounge stocked with local books. There are maps for guests to borrow, and lots of advice on where to go hiking in the surrounding area.

**Jinlye Guest House** ( ☎ 01694-723243; www.jin lye.co.uk; Castle Hill, All Stretton; s/d £50/80; P ) The Long Mynd is literally your back garden, so you'll have sheep as your neighbours at this beautifully restored crofter's cottage perched on the hilltop, and graced by old beams, log fires and leaded windows. Bedrooms are bright and elegantly furnished with antiques and the odd floral frill. Expect a good old-fashioned welcome. Wheelchair access is available.

### Eating
**Berry's Coffee House** ( ☎ 01694-724452; www.berrys coffeehouse.co.uk; 17 High St; meals £6-8; ☯ 10am-5pm daily) A sociable cafe in an 18th-century building with little conservatory just off the main street. Berry's is proud of its organic, free-range, fair-trade, wholesome offerings, but makes up for all that goodness with wicked desserts.

**Studio** ( ☎ 01694-722672; 59 High St; set menus £22.50-27.50; ☯ dinner Wed-Sat) A former artist's studio, still littered with interesting works, sets the scene for the town's best and most intimate restaurant. The award-winning menu jumps confidently between modern British and traditional French food, and uses plenty of local game and fish.

### Getting There & Around
There are hourly trains to Shrewsbury (20 minutes), and bus 435, which runs between Shrewsbury (45 minutes) and Ludlow (40 minutes) six times daily, stops here.

---

**SHROPSHIRE'S MOST ECCENTRIC HOTEL**

**Hundred House Hotel** ( ☎ 01746-730353; www.hundredhouse.co.uk; A442, Norton; s/d £90/105; Ⓟ ▯ ) offers a taste of escapism at its barmiest and best. Unashamedly romantic bedrooms are crammed with flamboyant decor, heart-shaped cushions and mirrors and antique beds, and seven out of 10 rooms sport suggestive velvet-covered swings entwined with ribbons. Shampoo comes in carafes and pillows are sprinkled with lavender water. The quirky herb gardens are another adventure, full of hidden corners and pathways, including a trail to a teddy bears' picnic sculpture. The owners devote just as much passion to their food; the excellent menu (mains £15 to £19) uses local produce to perfection. Hundred House is 6 miles north of Bridgnorth.

---

You can hire 24-speed mountain bikes with front or full suspension and cheaper, simpler bikes from **Shropshire Hills Bike Hire** ( ☎ 723302; 6 Castle Hill, All Stretton; per day from £10).

## BISHOP'S CASTLE
pop 1630

Home to a bewitching mixture of breweries, half-timbered buildings, second-hand bookshops and eclectic boutiques, this languid little border town makes stress seem like an alien concept. At the top of High St sits the adorable Georgian **town hall** and delightfully crooked 16th-century **House on Crutches** ( ☎ 630007; admission free; ☽ 1-5pm Sat & Sun), which also houses the town **museum**.

The pleasingly potty **Old Time** ( ☎ 01588-638467; www.bishopscastle.co.uk; 29 High St; ☽ 10am-6pm Mon-Sat, 10am-2pm Sun) offers limited tourist information.

### Activities
Walk along the **Shropshire Way**, which runs through the town and joins up with **Offa's Dyke Path** to the south; the **Kerry Ridgeway** to the south; or head north and risk the forbidding ridges of the **Stiperstones**, where Satan is said to hold court.

### Sleeping & Eating
**Poppy House** ( ☎ 01588-638443; www.poppyhouse.co.uk; 20 Market Sq; s/d £40/70) Sweet little beamed rooms with dark burgundy bedspreads and lots of little extras, like books and magazines and a complimentary breakfast-in-bed service win this B&B much praise. The downstairs restaurant (mains £9 to £18; open 10am to 5pm and 6.30pm to 11pm) has an interesting menu, featuring the likes of eel wrapped in prosciutto and sea bass on caramelised pineapple.

**Castle Hotel** ( ☎ 01588-638403; www.thecastlehotelbishopscastle.co.uk; The Square; s/d £45/90; Ⓟ ) Occupying a regal position in an elevated square, this hand-some 18th-century coaching inn has lovely terraced gardens and seven relaxing beamed rooms, many with soul-restoring views over the town and the valley. The oak-panelled restaurant dishes up classic British food and the bar serves a good choice of local brews.

### Drinking
**Three Tuns** ( ☎ 01588-638797; Salop St) One of Shropshire's most famous alehouses is a surprisingly ordinary place but for the fact that it is next door to a Victorian brewery, close enough to smell the roasting malt. Though they're no longer run by the same folk, you can still sample the brewery's best at the Three Tuns bar.

**Six Bells Inn** ( ☎ 01588-630144; Church St; mains £7.50-13; ☽ lunch & dinner Tue-Sat, lunch Sun) This historic 17th-century coaching inn is alive with loyal locals and ramblers who come to sample ales from its adjoining brewery. The pub also has a reputation for traditional English comfort food like homemade pies and Big Nev's bangers made with local ale.

### Getting There & Away
Buses 435 runs to and from Shrewsbury (one hour) seven times daily.

## LUDLOW
pop 9548

Fanning out from the rambling ruins of a fine Norman castle, beautiful Ludlow's muddle of narrow streets, flanked by half-timbered Jacobean and elegant Georgian buildings, is a magnet for foodies from miles around. This picturesque town is a temple to gastronomy, hosting independent butchers, bakers, grocers, cheesemongers and a handful of exceptional restaurants. Our advice: book ahead and punch a few extra holes in your belt – you can always work it all off in the nearby Shropshire hills afterwards.

Ludlow's helpful **tourist office** ( ☎ 01584-875053; www.ludlow.org.uk; Castle Sq; ☺ 10am-5pm) is in the 19th-century assembly rooms. There's also a small back-to-front **museum** ( ☎ 01584-813666; admission free; ☺ 10.30am-1pm & 2-5pm Easter-Oct) on the town and surrounding area here.

Internet can be tracked down at the **library** ( ☎ 01584-813600; 7-9 Parkway; ☺ 9.30am-5pm Mon-Wed & Sat, 9.30am-7.30pm Fri) and clothes can be washed, dried and pressed at **Ludlow Laundry** (Tower St; per bag £5; ☺ 9am-6pm Mon-Sat).

## Sights & Activities

With seductive delicatessens and distracting antique dealers around every corner, the best way to explore Ludlow is to simply surrender to getting pleasurably lost on foot.

The town's finest attraction is **Ludlow Castle** ( ☎ 01584-873355; www.ludlowcastle.com; Castle Sq; adult/child/senior & student £4.50/2.50/4; ☺ 10am-7pm Aug, to 5pm Apr-Jul & Sep, 10am-4pm Oct-Mar, weekends only Dec & Jan), which sits in an ideal defensive location atop a cliff above a crook in the river. One of a line of fortifications built along the Marches to ward off the marauding Welsh, it is full of secret passageways, ruined rooms, tucked-away nooks and mysterious stairwells. The sturdy Norman keep was built around 1090 and has wonderful views over the surrounding hills and the river below.

The castle was transformed into a 14th-century palace by the notorious Roger Mortimer, who was instrumental in the grisly death of Edward II, but its chequered history is reflected in different architectural styles. The round chapel in the inner bailey was built in 1120 and is one of few surviving in England.

The waymarked 30-mile **Mortimer Trail** to Kington starts just outside the castle entrance. The tourist office can provide a free leaflet on en-route services, or a more thorough booklet for £1.50. Also see www.mortimercountry.co.uk.

Some delightfully cheeky medieval misericords lurk in the choir of the **Church of St Laurence** ( ☎ 01584-872073; www.stlaurences.org.uk; King St; requested donation £2; ☺ 10am-5.30pm Apr-Sep, 11am-4pm Oct-Mar), one of the largest parish churches in Britain. These painstakingly carved 'mercy seats' show scenes of domestic 15th-century life both pious and profane, including a beer-swilling chap raiding his barrel.

Guided walks (£2) run from April to October, leaving the Cannon in Castle Sq at 2.30pm on Saturday and Sunday. You can also take the **ghost walk** (www.shropshireghostwalks.co.uk; adult/child £4/3; ☺ 8pm Fri) from outside the Church Inn on the Buttercross.

## Festivals & Events

Markets are held in Castle Sq every Monday, Wednesday, Friday and Saturday. The town's busy calendar peaks with the **Ludlow Festival** ( ☎ 01584-872150; www.ludlowfestival.co.uk), a fortnight of theatre and music in June and July that uses the castle as its dramatic backdrop. No surprise that most of the other events are foodie affairs. The renowned **Ludlow Marches Food & Drink Festival** ( ☎ 01584-873957; www.foodfestival.co.uk) is one of Britain's best, and takes place over a long weekend in September.

## Sleeping

**Mount** ( ☎ 01584-874084; www.themountludlow.co.uk; 61 Gravel Hill; s/d from £30/55; Ⓟ ) The glorious sunset views from this good-looking Victorian house are worth the modest price tag alone. Walkers and cyclists are well catered for, despite unforgivingly crisp white bed linen and cream carpets, and the welcoming hostess offers lifts from the railway station.

**Feathers Hotel** ( ☎ 01584-875261; www.feathersatludlow.co.uk; Bull Ring; s/d from £75/95; Ⓟ ) Three storeys of stunning black-and-white timber-framed facade serve to introduce this famous Jacobean inn. Not all rooms are in the wonderfully atmospheric original building, so make sure you're getting the real deal when booking. Newer rooms follow the usual bland template with antique-styled trimmings. The deeply atmospheric restaurant (set lunch/dinner £15/25) is recommended.

**Degreys** ( ☎ 01584-872764; www.degreys.co.uk; 73 Lower Broad St; r £75-140) Set in an Elizabethan town house at Ludlow's heart, this classy B&B has nine luxurious rooms with low ceilings, beams, leaded windows and solid oak beds. The balance of period features and modern luxury is spot on and there's a fantastic traditional English tearoom downstairs.

Other options include the following:

**Dinham Hall Hotel** ( ☎ 01584-876464; www.dinhamhall.co.uk; s £95, d £140-240; Ⓟ ) Resplendent 18th-century country manor with superb traditional restaurant, opposite the castle.

**Castle House Lodgings** ( ☎ 01584-874465; www.castle-accomodation.com; Ludlow Castle; apt sleeping 4 people for 3 nights £545-825; Ⓟ ) Glorious self-catering apartments in Castle House, within Ludlow Castle grounds.

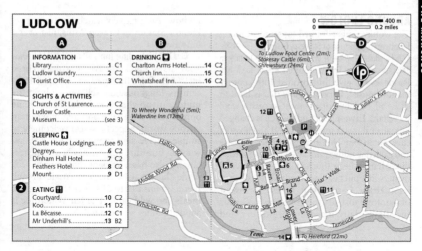

## LUDLOW

## Eating

If you can afford to splurge on food, this is unquestionably the place to do it. While we've picked our favourites, you needn't go far for more epicurean delights.

**Ludlow Food Centre** ( ☎ 01584-856000; Bromfield; mains £5-8; ☼ 9.30am-5.30pm Mon-Sat, 10.30am-4.30pm Sun) Wonderful food shop selling fresh baked bread and cakes, cheese, local meats, ciders, fresh pies and quiches ripe for a picnic. There's also a bright cafe selling similarly scrumptious produce in a converted barn next door. Two miles north west of Ludlow, just off the A49.

**Courtyard** ( ☎ 01584-878080; www.thecourtyard -ludlow.co.uk; 2 Quality Sq; mains £5.50-10; ☼ lunch Mon-Sat, dinner Thu-Sat) Light relief from too much gastronomic extravagance, this simple cafe, tucked away in a tranquil courtyard, has a faithful local following for its lightning service and tasty seasonal food.

**La Bécasse** ( ☎ 01584-872325; www.labecasse.co.uk; 17 Corve St; 2-course lunch £20, 6-course gourmand menu £55; ☼ dinner Tue-Sat, lunch Wed-Sun) Artfully presented modern French cuisine bursting with inventive flavour fusions – the spectacular tasting menu is enough to make you weak at the knees. The serious business of eating is conducted within the oak-panelled and exposed brick walls of a 17th-century coach house.

**Koo** ( ☎ 01584-878462; 127 Old St; 3-course set menu £22-26; ☼ dinner Tue-Sat) Three- and four-course Japanese menus are served up in this bright green cubby hole, overseen by its friendly Japanese owner who's always eager to chat with diners about Japanese culture and etiquette. During the festival, takeaway bento boxes are available for impromptu picnics.

**Mr Underhill's** ( ☎ 01584-874431; www.mr-underhills. co.uk; Dinham Weir; 6-course set menu £45-55; ☼ dinner Wed-Sun) Ludlow's only Michelin-starred restaurant is set in a converted corn mill that dips its toes in the river. Expect exquisite modern British food, though there's little choice before dessert, so make any dietary requests beforehand. It also offers stylish rooms (singles £120, doubles £140 to £190, suites £235 to £290). Reserve well in advance.

## Drinking

For an atmospheric pint, traditional hop-strewn pub the **Church Inn** ( ☎ 01584-872174) is tucked away on narrow Buttercross, and the quiet little **Wheatsheaf Inn** ( ☎ 01584-872980; Lower Broad St) has a good choice of local ales. For a more contemporary atmosphere head for the **Charlton Arms Hotel** ( ☎ 01584-872813), a rambling place on the other side of the river with a couple of terraces and sublime views.

## Getting There & Around

Trains go twice-hourly to Shrewsbury (£8.40, 30 minutes) and Hereford (£6.40, 25 minutes), and hourly to Church Stretton (16 minutes). Slower buses go to Shrewsbury (bus 435, 1½ hours, five daily) and to nearby towns.

You can hire bikes from **Wheely Wonderful** ( ☎ 01568-770755; www.wheelywonderfulcycling.co.uk; Petchfield Farm, Elton; bike/tandem per day £18/36), 5 miles west of Ludlow.

## AROUND LUDLOW

The wonky timber-framed tops and stunning Jacobean gatehouse of **Stokesay Castle** (EH; ☎ 01588-672544; adult/5-15yr/under 5yr £5/2.50/free; ☼ 10am-5pm daily Apr-Sep, 10am-5pm Wed-Sun Oct & Mar, 10am-4pm Thu-Sun Nov-Feb) give this fortified 13th-century manor house a fairy-tale glow that is hard to shake off. Built by Britain's most successful wool merchant, Lawrence of Ludlow, it has changed little since it was completed in 1291 and boasts a cavernous Great Hall, original timber staircase and gabled windows, and an enchanting garden that's hardly been touched since the original owners first pitched their medieval forks.

Stokesay Castle is 6 miles northwest of Ludlow, just off the A49. Bus 435 runs five times daily between Shrewsbury and Ludlow. Alternatively, catch the train from Ludlow Station to Craven Arms, just over a mile away.

**our pick** **Waterdine Inn** ( ☎ 01547-528214; www .waterdine.com; Llanfair Waterdine; s/d incl dinner & breakfast £80/160; **P** ), a timbered and ivy-clad 16th-century longhouse, is well and truly in the middle of nowhere, with the River Teme border with Wales the only reminder of an outside world. Expect a warm welcome and simple cottage-style rooms with low ceilings, wooden furniture and springy beds. The restaurant also has a homely, dinner-party feel, while the fantastic modern Anglo-French menu (mains £12 to £18) focuses on organic meats and wild game. Llanfair Waterdine is about 12 miles west of Ludlow.

# Yorkshire

With a population as big as Scotland's, and an area half the size of Belgium, Yorkshire is almost a country in itself. It even has its own flag (a white rose on a blue ground), its own distinctive dialect (known as 'Tyke'), and its own official celebration (Yorkshire Day, 1 August). Needless to say, while Yorkshire folk are proud to be English, they're even prouder to be natives of 'God's Own Country', as they (only half-jokingly) refer to their home patch.

The region has its roots in the 9th-century Danelaw, a Viking-governed area that roughly coincides with the boundaries of present-day Yorkshire. It was originally divided into three parts – the North, West and East Ridings (from the Old English 'thriding', derived from a Norse word meaning 'one-third'). Today it's split into four separate counties: South Yorkshire, West Yorkshire, North Yorkshire and the East Riding of Yorkshire.

So what is it that makes Yorkshire so special? First there's the landscape – from the dark, brooding moors to the lush, green dales that roll their way to the dramatic cliffs of the coast, Yorkshire has some of Britain's most beautiful scenery. Second, there's the sheer breadth of history – here you can explore virtually every facet of the British experience, from the Middle Ages to the 20th century. But ultimately, Yorkshire's greatest appeal lies in its people. Proud, industrious and opinionated, they have a warmth and friendliness that soon breaks through any initial gruffness. Stay here for any length of time and you'll come away believing, like the locals, that God is indeed a Yorkshirewoman.

---

### HIGHLIGHTS

- Exploring the medieval streets of **York** (p542) and its awe-inspiring cathedral
- Pulling on your hiking boots and striding out across the moors of the **Yorkshire Dales National Park** (p531)
- Chilling out in **Leeds** (p521): shopping, eating, drinking, dancing
- Being beside the seaside at **Scarborough** (p557) with its traditional bucket-and-spade atmosphere
- Riding a steam train on the **North Yorkshire Moors Railway** (p565), one of England's most scenic railway lines
- Going underground: discovering the dark side of mining at the **National Coal Mining Museum for England** (p528)

---

- POPULATION: 4.96 MILLION
- AREA: 5958 SQ MILES
- CALORIES IN A YORKSHIRE 'FAT RASCAL': 350

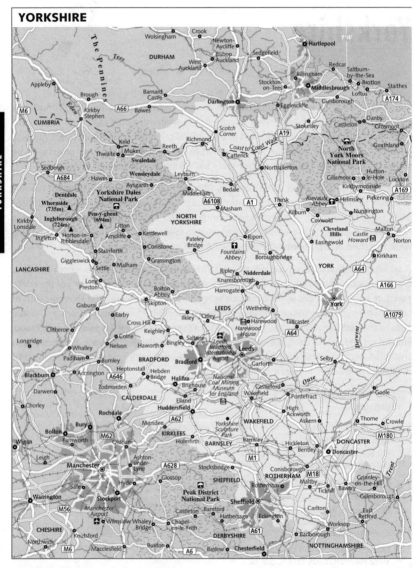

# History

As you drive through Yorkshire on the main A1 road, you're following in the footsteps of the Roman legions who conquered northern Britain in the 1st century AD. In fact, many Yorkshire towns – including York, Catterick and Malton – were founded by the Romans, and many modern roads (eg the A1, A59, A166 and A1079) follow the lines of Roman roads.

When the Romans departed in the 5th century, native Britons battled for supremacy with invading Angles and, for a while, Yorkshire was part of the kingdom of Northumbria. In the 9th century the Vikings arrived and conquered most of northern Britain. They

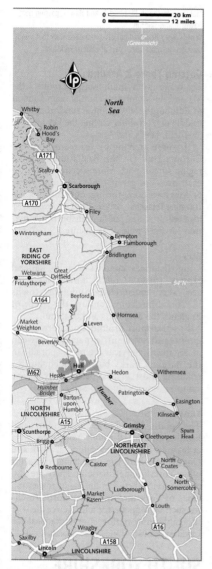

Battle of Stamford Bridge, before returning south to meet his appointment with William the Conqueror – and a fatal arrow – at the Battle of Hastings.

The inhabitants of northern England did not take the subsequent Norman invasion lying down. The Norman nobles built a chain of formidable castles throughout Yorkshire, including those at York, Richmond, Scarborough, Pickering and Helmsley. They also oversaw the establishment of the great abbeys of Rievaulx, Fountains and Whitby.

The Norman land grab formed the basis of the great estates that supported England's medieval aristocrats. By the 15th century, the duchies of York and Lancaster had become so wealthy and powerful that they ended up battling for the English throne – the Wars of the Roses (1455–87) were conflict abetween the supporters of King Henry VI of the House of Lancaster (the red rose) and Richard, Duke of York (the white rose). They ended with the defeat of the Yorkist king Richard III by the Earl of Richmond, Henry Tudor, at the Battle of Bosworth Field.

Yorkshire prospered quietly, with fertile farms in the north and the cutlery business of Sheffield in the south, until the big bang of the Industrial Revolution transformed the landscape – South Yorkshire became a centre of coal mining and steel works, while West Yorkshire was home to a massive textile industry, and the cities of Leeds, Bradford, Sheffield and Rotherham flourished. By the late 20th century another revolution was taking place. The heavy industries had died out, and the cities of Yorkshire were reinventing themselves as shiny, hi-tech centres of finance, higher education and tourism.

## Information

The **Yorkshire Tourist Board** (www.yorkshire.com; 312 Tadcaster Rd, York, YO24 1GS) has plenty of general leaflets and brochures – postal and email enquiries only. For more detailed information contact the local tourist offices listed throughout this chapter.

## Activities

Yorkshire's varied landscape of wild hills, tranquil valleys, high moors and spectacular coastline offers plenty of opportunities for outdoor activities. See www.outdoor yorkshire.com for more details.

divided the territory that is now Yorkshire into *thridings* (thirds), which all met at Jorvik (York), the thriving commercial capital.

In 1066 Yorkshire was the scene of a pivotal showdown in the struggle for the English crown, when the Anglo-Saxon king Harold II rode north to defeat the forces of the Norwegian king Harold Hardrada at the

### CYCLING

Yorkshire has a vast network of country lanes, although the most scenic areas also attract lots of motorists so even minor roads can be busy at weekends.

Options include the following:

**North York Moors** Off-road bikers can avail themselves of the networks of bridle paths, former railways and disused mining tracks now converted to two-wheel use.

**Whitby to Scarborough** A 20-mile traffic-free route that follows a disused railway line, providing an effortless way to tour this rugged coast.

**White Rose Cycle Route** (NCN route 65) A 120-mile cruise from Hull to York and on to Middlesbrough, via the rolling Yorkshire Wolds and the dramatic western scarp of the North York Moors, with a traffic-free section on the old railway between Selby and York. It is part of the National Cycle Network (p114).

**Yorkshire Dales** Great cycling in the quieter areas in the north around Swaledale and Wensleydale, and the west around Dentdale. There's an excellent network of old drove roads (formerly used for driving cattle to market) which wind across lonely hillsides and tie in neatly with the country lanes in the valleys.

### WALKING

For shorter walks and rambles the best area is the **Yorkshire Dales** (p531), with a great selection of walks through scenic valleys or over wild hilltops, with a few higher summits thrown in for good measure. The **Yorkshire Wolds** (p539) hold hidden delights, while the quiet valleys and dramatic coast of the **North York Moors** (p561) also have many good opportunities.

All tourist offices stock a mountain of leaflets on local walks (free or up to £1.50), and sell more detailed guidebooks and maps. At train stations and tourist offices, it's worth looking out for leaflets detailing walks from train stations. Some tie in with train times, so you can walk one way and ride back.

Long-distance possibilities include the following:

**Cleveland Way** A venerable moor-and-coast classic (see p561).

**Coast to Coast Walk** England's No 1 walk, 190 miles across northern England from the Lake District across the Yorkshire Dales and North York Moors. The Yorkshire section takes a week to 10 days and offers some of the finest walking of its kind in England.

**Dales Way** Charming and not-too-strenuous amble from the Yorkshire Dales to the Lake District (see p533).

**Pennine Way** The Yorkshire section of England's most famous walk runs for over 100 miles via Hebden Bridge,

Malham, Horton-in-Ribblesdale and Hawes, passing near Haworth and Skipton.

**Wolds Way** Beautiful but oft-overlooked walk that winds through the most scenic part of eastern Yorkshire.

## Getting There & Around

The major north–south transport routes – the M1 and A1 motorways and the main London to Edinburgh railway line – run through the middle of Yorkshire, serving the key cities of Sheffield, Leeds and York.

If you're arriving by sea from northern Europe, Hull (in the East Riding) is the region's main port. More specific details for each area are given under Getting There & Away sections throughout this chapter. **Traveline Yorkshire** ( ☎ 0871 200 2233; www.yorkshire travel.net) provides public-transport information for the whole of Yorkshire.

### BUS

Long-distances coaches run by **National Express** ( ☎ 08717 818181; www.nationalexpress .com) serve most cities and large towns in Yorkshire from London, the south of England, the Midlands and Scotland.

Bus transport around Yorkshire is frequent and efficient, especially between major towns. Services are more sporadic in the national parks but still adequate for reaching most places, particularly in the summer months (June to September).

### TRAIN

The main line between London and Edinburgh runs through Yorkshire, with at least 10 trains a day calling at York and Doncaster, where you can change trains for other Yorkshire destinations. There are also direct services between the major towns and cities of Yorkshire and other northern cities such as Manchester and Newcastle. For timetable information contact **National Rail Enquiries** ( ☎ 08457 484950; www.nationalrail.co.uk).

# SOUTH YORKSHIRE

As in the valleys of South Wales, it was a confluence of natural resources – coal, iron ore and ample water – that made South Yorkshire a crucible of the British iron, steel and mining industries. From the 18th century to the 20th, the region was the industrial powerhouse of northern England.

The blast furnaces of Sheffield and Rotherham and the coal pits of Barnsley and Doncaster may have closed long ago, but the hulking reminders of that irrepressible Victorian dynamism remain, not only in the old steel works and pit-heads – some of which have been converted into enthralling museums and exhibition spaces – but also in the grand civic buildings that grace Sheffield's city centre, fitting testaments to the untrammelled ambitions of their 19th-century patrons.

## SHEFFIELD
**pop 525,800**

Steel is everywhere in Sheffield. Today, however, it's not the steel of the foundries, mills and forges that made the city's fortune, or the canteens of cutlery that made 'Sheffield steel' a household name, but the steel of scaffolding and cranes, of modern sculptures and supertrams, and of new steel-framed buildings rising against the skyline.

The steel industry that made the city famous is long since gone, but after many years of decline Sheffield is on the up again – like many of northern England's cities it has grabbed the opportunities presented by urban renewal with both hands and is working hard to reinvent itself. The new economy is based on services, shopping and the 'knowledge industry' that flows from the city's universities.

## Orientation

The most interesting parts of Sheffield are clustered in the 'Heart of the City' district about 300m northwest of the train station (and immediately west of the bus station), a compact area outlined by Arundel Gate, Furnival St, Carver St, West St, Church St and High St. Stretching west from here, Division St and Devonshire St have hip clothes and record shops, popular restaurants and trendy bars.

## Information

**Central Library** ( ☎ 0114-273 4711; Surrey St; ☽ 10am-8pm Mon, 9.30am-5.30pm Tue & Thu-Sat, 9.30am-5pm Wed) Internet access.
**Post office** (Norfolk Row; ☽ 8.30am-5.30pm Mon-Fri, 8.30am-3pm Sat)
**Tourist office** ( ☎ 0114-221 1900; www.sheffieldcitycentre.com; 14 Norfolk Row; ☽ 10am-5pm Mon-Sat)
**Waterstone's** ( ☎ 0114-272 8971; 24-26 Orchard Sq; ☽ 9am-6pm Mon-Sat, 10.30am-5pm Sun) Books and maps.

## Sights & Activities

Since 2000 the city centre has been in the throes of a massive redevelopment that will continue into 2020 and beyond, so expect building sites and roadworks for several years to come.

Of the parts that are already complete, pride of place goes to the **Winter Gardens** (admission free; ☽ 8am-6pm), a wonderfully ambitious public space with a soaring glass roof supported by graceful arches of laminated timber. The 21st-century architecture contrasts sharply with the Victorian **town hall** nearby, and is further enhanced by the **Peace Gardens** – complete with fountains, sculptures and lawns full of lunching office workers whenever there's a bit of sun.

Sheffield's cultural revival is spearheaded by the **Millennium Gallery** ( ☎ 0114-278 2600; www.museums-sheffield.org.uk; Arundel Gate; admission free, special exhibitions £6; ☽ 10am-5pm Mon-Sat, 11am-5pm Sun), a collection of four galleries under one roof. The **Ruskin Gallery** houses an eclectic collection of paintings, drawings and manuscripts established and inspired by Victorian artist, writer, critic and philosopher John Ruskin, while the **Metalwork Gallery** charts the transformation of Sheffield's steel industry into craft and design – the 'Sheffield steel' stamp on locally made cutlery and tableware now has the cachet of designer chic.

The nearby **Graves Gallery** ( ☎ 0114-278 2600; Surrey St; admission free; ☽ 10am-5pm Mon-Sat) has a neat and accessible display of British and European modern art; the big names represented include Cézanne, Gaugin, Miró, Klee and Picasso.

## Festivals & Events

Each year around April, Sheffield plays host to the immensely popular **World Snooker Championship** (www.worldsnooker.com), staged at the Crucible Theatre.

## Sleeping & Eating

Tourism has not quite taken off yet in Sheffield, and most of the city-centre hotels cater primarily to business travellers. New restaurants are springing up – there are several in the Leopold Sq development on Leopold St – but the main restaurant areas are outside the centre.

There's a mile-long strip of bars, restaurants, cafes and takeaways on Ecclesall Rd, a mile to the southwest of the city centre,

YORKSHIRE

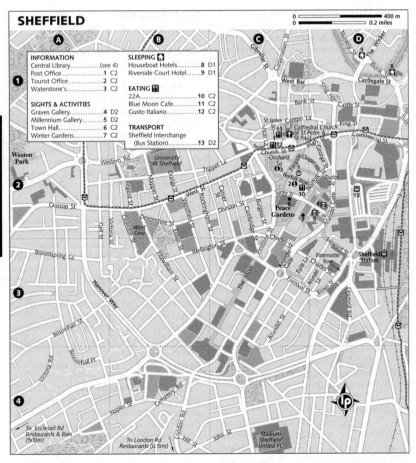

### SHEFFIELD

| | |
|---|---|
| **INFORMATION** | |
| Central Library..............(see 4) | |
| Post Office.....................**1** C2 | |
| Tourist Office..................**2** C2 | |
| Waterstone's....................**3** C2 | |
| **SIGHTS & ACTIVITIES** | |
| Graves Gallery................**4** D2 | |
| Millennium Gallery..........**5** D2 | |
| Town Hall......................**6** C2 | |
| Winter Gardens..............**7** C2 | |

| | |
|---|---|
| **SLEEPING** | |
| Houseboat Hotels.............**8** D1 | |
| Riverside Court Hotel........**9** D1 | |
| **EATING** | |
| 22A...............................**10** C2 | |
| Blue Moon Cafe..............**11** C2 | |
| Gusto Italiano................**12** C2 | |
| **TRANSPORT** | |
| Sheffield Interchange | |
| (Bus Station)................**13** D2 | |

while London Rd, a mile south of the city centre, has a concentration of good-value ethnic restaurants ranging from Turkish to Thai. To find student bars and eateries head along Division St and Devonshire St just west of the city centre.

**Riverside Court Hotel** ( ☎ 0114-273 1962; www.riversidecourt.co.uk; 4 Nursery St; s/d/tr from £37/47/65) The riverside location and relative proximity to the city centre make this hotel a pretty good choice if you don't want to get stung for a midweek business rate; the rooms were undergoing a facelift at the time of research.

**Houseboat Hotels** ( ☎ 0114-232 6556; www.houseboathotels.com; Victoria Quays, Wharfe St; d/q from £75/95) Here's something a bit different – kick off your shoes and relax on board your very own permanently moored houseboat, complete with self-catering kitchen and patio area. Guests are entitled to use the gym facilities at the Hilton across the road.

**our pick Gusto Italiano** ( ☎ 0114-275 1117; 18 Church St; mains £3-6; 7am-6.30pm Mon-Fri, 8am-6pm Sat) A *real* Italian cafe, from the Italian owners serving homemade Italian food to the genuine Italian coffee being enjoyed by Italian customers reading the Italian newspapers...you get the idea – Gusto Italiano is a great place for a hot lunch, or just cake and coffee.

**22A** ( ☎ 0114-276 7462; 22A Norfolk Row; mains £5-8; 8am-5pm Mon-Sat) Nice music, nice people, nice place. This homely cafe serves hearty breakfasts and offers a mean wrap at lunchtime – hummus and roasted vegie is our favourite – and serves it with a decent cup of java.

**Blue Moon Cafe** ( ☎ 0114-276 3443; 2 St James St; mains £5-7; ☽ 8am-8pm Mon-Sat) Tasty vegie and vegan creations, soups and other good-for-you dishes, all served with the ubiquitous salad, in a very pleasant atmosphere – perfect for a spot of Saturday-afternoon lounging.

### Getting There & Away
For all travel-related info in Sheffield and South Yorkshire, call ☎ 01709-515151 or consult www.travelsouthyorkshire.com.

#### BUS
The bus station – called the Interchange – is just east of the centre, about 250m north of the train station. National Express services link Sheffield with most major centres in the north; there are frequent buses linking Sheffield with Leeds (£5.20, 50 to 75 minutes, hourly), Manchester (£7.60, 1½ hours, three daily) and London (£16.50, 4½ hours, eight daily).

#### TRAIN
Sheffield is served by trains from all directions: Leeds (£8.20, 40 to 75 minutes, twice hourly); London St Pancras (£81, two to three hours, hourly) via Derby or Nottingham; Manchester Piccadilly (£13.80, one hour, twice hourly); and York (£14.50, 1¼ hours, twice hourly).

### Getting Around
Buses run every 10 minutes during the day (Monday to Saturday, less frequently on Sundays). Sheffield also boasts a modern **Supertram** (www.supertram.com; tickets £1.20-2.70) that links the train station to the city centre and outer suburbs.

# WEST YORKSHIRE

What steel was to South Yorkshire, so wool was to West Yorkshire. It was the tough and unforgiving textile industry that drove the county's economy from the 18th century on, and the woollen mills and factories – and the canals that were built to transport raw materials and finished products – that defined much of its landscape. But that's all in the past, and recent years have seen the transformation of a once hard-bitten area into quite a picture postcard.

Leeds and Bradford, two adjoining cities so big that they've virtually become one, are the perfect case in point. Though both were founded amid the dark, satanic mills of the Industrial Revolution, both are undergoing radical redevelopment and reinvention, prettifying their town centres and trying to tempt the more adventurous tourist with a slew of new museums, galleries, restaurants and bars.

Beyond the cities, West Yorkshire is a landscape of bleak moorland dissected by deep valleys dotted with old mill towns and villages. The relics of the wool and cloth industries are still visible in the rows of weavers' cottages and workers' houses built along ridges overlooking the towering chimneys of the mills in the valleys – landscapes that were so vividly described by the Brontë sisters, West Yorkshire's most renowned literary export and biggest tourist draw.

### Getting Around
The Metro is West Yorkshire's highly efficient train and bus network, centred on Leeds and Bradford – which are also the main gateways to the county. For transport information call **Metroline** ( ☎ 0113-245 7676; www.wymetro.com). The excellent Day Rover (£5 for train or bus, £6 train and bus) tickets are good for travel on buses and trains after 9.30am on weekdays and all day at weekends. There's a range of additional Rovers covering buses and/or trains, plus heaps of useful Metro maps and timetables, available from bus and train stations and most tourist offices in West Yorkshire.

## LEEDS
pop 750,200

One of the fastest growing cities in the UK, Leeds is the glitzy, glamorous embodiment of newly rediscovered northern self-confidence. More than a decade of redevelopment has seen the city centre transform from near-derelict mill town into a vision of 21st-century urban chic, with skyscraping office blocks, glass-and-steel waterfront apartment complexes and renovated Victorian shopping arcades.

Known as the 'Knightsbridge of the North', Leeds has made itself into a shopping mecca, its streets lined with bustling malls sporting the top names in fashion. And when you've shopped till you drop there's a plethora of pubs, clubs and excellent restaurants to relax in. From cutting-edge couture to contemporary cuisine, Leeds will serve it to you on a plate…or more likely in a stylishly designed bag. Amid all this cutting-edge style, it seems fitting that the network of city bus routes includes peach, mauve and magenta lines as well as the more humdrum red, orange and blue.

## Orientation

Easily managed on foot, most of the action in Leeds' city centre is concentrated between Boar Lane to the south and the Headrow – the main drag – to the north, all within 10 to 15 minutes' walk from the train station. Briggate, which runs north–south between the two, is the focus of most of the shopping, while the best nightlife is concentrated in the warren of small streets at the eastern end of Boar Lane. In recent years there has been substantial waterfront development along the River Aire at the Calls and around Brewery Wharf.

## Information

**Central Library** ( ☎ 0113-247 6016; Calverley St; ⊙ 9am-8pm Mon-Wed, 9am-5pm Thu & Fri, 10am-5pm Sat, 1-5pm Sun) Internet access.

**Gateway to Yorkshire/Leeds Visitor Centre** ( ☎ 0113-242 5242; www.visitleeds.co.uk; The Arcade, Leeds City Train Station; ⊙ 9am-5.30pm Mon-Sat, 10am-4pm Sun)

**Leeds General Infirmary** ( ☎ 0113-243 2799; Great George St)

**Post office** (St John's Centre, 116 Albion St; ⊙ 9am-5.30pm Mon-Sat)

**Waterstone's** ( ☎ 0113-244 4588; 93-97 Albion St; ⊙ 9am-6.30pm Mon-Sat, 10.30am-4.30pm Sun) Maps and books.

## Sights & Activities

Leeds' most interesting museum is undoubtedly the **Royal Armouries** ( ☎ 0113-220 1940; www .armouries.org.uk; Armouries Dr; admission free; ⊙ 10am-5pm), beside the snazzy Clarence Dock residential development. It was originally built to house the armour and weapons from the Tower of London but was subsequently expanded to cover 3000 years' worth of fighting and self-defence. It all sounds a bit macho, but the exhibits are as varied as they are fascinating: films, live-action demonstrations and hands-on technology can awaken interests you never thought you had, from jousting to Indian elephant armour – we dare you not to learn something. Catch bus 95, or take the Waterbus (adult/child £2/1, 15 minutes, two to four daily) along the river from the Embankment at the Neville St bridge.

One of the world's largest textile mills has been transformed into the **Leeds Industrial Museum** ( ☎ 0113-263 7861; www.leeds.gov.uk/ armleymills; Canal Rd; adult/child £3/1; ⊙ 10am-5pm Tue-Sat, 1-5pm Sun), telling the story of Leeds' industrial past, both glorious and ignominious. The city became rich off the sheep's back but at some cost in human terms – working conditions were, well, Dickensian. As well as a selection of working machinery, there's a particularly informative display on how cloth is actually made. Take bus 5 from the train station.

If all this industrial stuff makes you feel starved of a bit of high culture, get yourself to the **Leeds Art Gallery** ( ☎ 0113-247 8256; www.leeds .gov.uk/artgallery; The Headrow; admission free; ⊙ 10am-8pm Mon & Tue, noon-8pm Wed, 10am-5pm Thu-Sat, 1-5pm Sun). It's packed with 19th- and 20th-century British heavyweights – Turner, Constable, Stanley Spencer, Wyndham Lewis et al – along with contemporary pieces by more recent arrivals like Antony Gormley, sculptor of the *Angel of the North* (p648). Pride of place, however, goes to the outstanding genius of Henry Moore (1898–1986), who graduated from the Leeds School of Art. The adjoining **Henry Moore Institute** ( ☎ 0113-246 7467; www.henry-moore-fdn.co.uk; The Headrow; admission free; ⊙ 10am-5.30pm Thu-Mon, 10am-9pm Wed), in a converted Victorian warehouse, showcases the work of 20th-century sculptors but not, despite the name, anything by Moore; for more of Moore, head to the Yorkshire Sculpture Park (p528).

## Festivals & Events

The August Bank Holiday (the weekend preceding the last Monday in August) sees 50,000-plus music fans converge on Bramham Park, 10 miles outside the city centre, for the **Leeds Festival** ( ☎ 0871 231 0821; www.leedsfestival.com), one of England's biggest rock music extravaganzas, spread across four separate stages.

## Sleeping

There are no budget options in the city centre and the midrange choices are between absolute fleapits and chain hotels. If you want somewhere cheapish you're forced to head for the 'burbs, where there are plenty of decent B&Bs and smallish hotels.

### MIDRANGE

**Golden Lion Hotel** ( ☎ 0113-243 6454; www.thegold enlion-leeds.co.uk; 2 Lower Briggate; s/d from £85/99; **P** ) They don't come much more central than

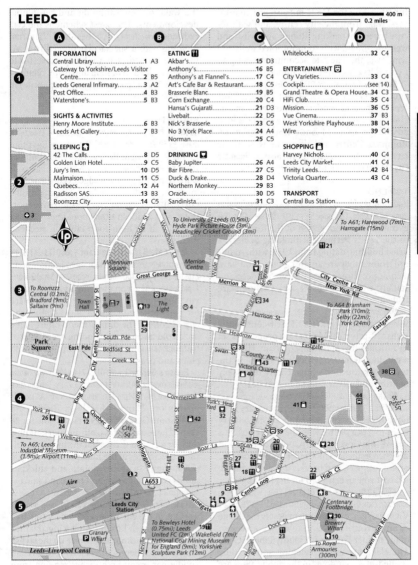

**LEEDS**

Leeds' oldest hotel which, after a much-needed makeover, can now compete with the rest. The rooms are tidy and modern, if a little small, while the public areas retain a comfortably old-fashioned atmosphere.

**Jury's Inn** ( ☎ 0113-283 8800; www.jurysinns.com; Kendell St, Brewery Pl; r £60-103; P 😃 ) The successful Irish hotel chain has another hit with its

Leeds hotel; large, functional rooms, plenty of personal charm and few complaints. If you're walking, it's just across the Centenary footbridge from the city centre, in the heart of the fashionable Brewery Wharf district.

**Bewleys Hotel** ( ☎ 0113-234 2340; www.bewleys hotels.com; City Walk, Sweet St; r £69; P 😃 ) Bewleys is super-convenient for motorists, just off

Junction 3 on the M621 but also just 10 minutes' walk from the city centre, and with secure basement parking. Rooms are stylish and well appointed, with soundproofed walls and windows; the flat rate accommodates up to two adults plus three kids under 16.

**Roomzzz Central** ( ☎ 0113-233 0400; www.roomzzz .co.uk; 2 Burley Rd; r from £79; P ᄆ ) This outfit offers bright and modern luxury apartments complete with fitted kitchen, with the added advantage of a 24-hour hotel reception. Roomzzz Central is half a mile west of the city centre; by 2009 there will also be **Roomzzz City** (12 Swinegate), right in the city centre.

### TOP END

**Radisson SAS** ( ☎ 0113-236 6000; www.leeds.radissonsas .com; 1 The Light, Cookridge St; r £100-130; P ᄆ ) An extraordinary conversion of the former HQ of the Leeds Permanent Building Society, a listed building dating from 1930, with 'standard' rooms that are anything but – you have a choice of three styles: hi-tech, art deco and Italian, while the business-class rooms are truly luxurious.

**Malmaison** ( ☎ 0113-398 1000; www.malmaison.com; 1 Swinegate; s/d/ste from £130/160/275) Self-consciously stylish, this typical Malmaison property is set in a former bus and tram company HQ with a fabulous waterfront location and all of the trademark touches – huge comfy beds, sexy lighting and all the latest designer gear.

**42 The Calls** ( ☎ 0113-244 0099; www.42thecalls.co.uk; 42 The Calls; r/ste from £150/199; ᄆ ) This snazzy boutique hotel in what was once a 19th-century grain mill is a big hit with the trendy business crowd, who love its sharp, polished lines and designer aesthetic. The smaller studio rooms are pretty compact, and breakfast is not included; it'll cost you an extra £15 for the full English.

**our pick** **Quebecs** ( ☎ 0113-244 8989; www.theeton collection.com; 9 Quebec St; s/d/ste from £160/170/280; ᄆ ) Victorian grace at its opulent best is the theme of our favourite hotel in town, a conversion of the former Leeds and County Liberal Club. The elaborate wood panelling and heraldic stained-glass windows in the public areas are matched by the contemporary design of the bedrooms. Two of the deluxe split-level suites – the cutely named Sherbert and Liquorice suites – have dramatic spiral staircases.

## Eating

The Leeds restaurant scene is constantly evolving, with new places springing up in the wake of new shopping and residential developments. The latest scheme is the **Corn Exchange** (www.cornx.net), a beautiful Victorian building with a spectacular domed roof. At the time of research it was being converted to house a collection of food and drink retailers, with a new branch of Anthony's (opposite) in the central piazza.

### BUDGET

**Akbar's** ( ☎ 0113-245 6566; www.akbars.co.uk; 15 Eastgate; mains £5.50-7; ◷ dinner only) Bit of an Egyptian theme going on at this exceptionally popular Indian restaurant – sarcophagi and cat-gods watch over the cutting-edge decor beneath a 'night in the desert' ceiling. The traditional curry dishes come in pyramid-size portions, and it doesn't take bookings – expect to wait half an hour for a table on weekend nights.

**Art's Cafe Bar & Restaurant** ( ☎ 0113-243 8243; www.artscafebar.co.uk; 42 Call Lane; mains lunch £5-7, dinner £10-14; ◷ noon-11pm Mon-Fri, noon-2am Sat, 10.30am-11pm Sun) Local art on the walls and a bohemian vibe throughout make this a popular place for quiet reflection, a chat and a really good cup of coffee. The dinner menu offers half a dozen old favourites, including beer-battered haddock (sustainably sourced, of course) with chips and peas.

**Hansa's Gujarati** ( ☎ 0113-244 4408; www.hansas restaurant.com; 72-74 North St; mains £5-7; ◷ 5-10pm Mon-Thu, 5-11pm Fri, 6-11pm Sat, noon-2pm Sun) A Leeds institution, Hansa's has been dishing up wholesome Gujarati vegetarian cuisine for 20 years. The restaurant is plain and unassuming, save for a Hindu shrine, but the food is exquisite – specialities of the house include *samosa chaat*, a mix of spiced potato and chickpea samosas with a yogurt and tamarind sauce.

**Norman** ( ☎ 0872 080 8000; www.normanbar.co.uk; 36 Call Lane; mains £7-9; ◷ noon-2am Mon-Sat, noon-midnight Sun) One of the city's hippest bars – a touch of tongue-in-cheek kitsch (think fringed lampshades and a cuckoo clock) spice up the stylish modern lines here – offers a tempting Asian noodle-bar menu with dishes ranging from squid tempura and edamame beans to seafood ramen and Vietnamese beef salad.

### MIDRANGE

**Nick's Brasserie** ( ☎ 0113-246 9444; www.nicksbrasserie .com; 20 Dock St; mains £10-14; ◷ noon-10pm Tue-Sat, noon-3pm Sun) Housed in a converted red-brick warehouse on up-and-coming Dock St,

Nick's offers an intriguing menu that sees crab linguini with chilli and lime, and leek and ricotta canneloni, alongside stalwarts such as devilled whitebait and steak-frites with pepper sauce. Weekend brunch (served noon to 4pm) ranges from a trad fry-up or bacon sandwich to eggs Benedict or scrambled egg with smoked salmon.

**Livebait** ( ☎ 0113-244 4144; 11-15 Wharf St, High Court; mains £10-17; ⏲ noon-3pm & 5-10.30pm) Quality seafood – from Whitby crab and Canadian lobster to fresh oysters and langoustines – is the order of the day in this friendly and welcoming restaurant. Classic fish and chips is done with a light and crispy batter and served with homemade tartare sauce and deliciously minty mushy peas.

**Brasserie Blanc** ( ☎ 0113-220 6060; www.brasserie blanc.com; Victoria Mill, Sovereign St; mains £11-17; ⏲ noon-2.45pm & 5.30-10.30pm Mon-Fri, noon-11pm Sat, noon-10pm Sun) The latest offering from Raymond Blanc manages to create a surprisingly intimate and romantic space amid the cast-iron pillars and red brick of an old Victorian warehouse. The menu is unerringly French, from escargots to Toulouse sausage, and there's a lovely outdoor terrace overlooking the river.

**No 3 York Place** ( ☎ 0113-245 9922; www.no3yorkplace .co.uk; 3 York Pl; mains £12-17; ⏲ lunch & dinner Mon-Fri, dinner Sat) Any debate over which is the best restaurant in town will include this superb French eatery, with its designer dining area and regularly changing menu of Gallic delicacies – how about roast duck with endive tarte tatin, or wood pigeon with caramelised apple and thyme jus?

**Anthony's at Flannel's** ( ☎ 0113-242 8732; www .anthonysatflannels.co.uk; 3rd fl, Flannel's Fashion Centre, 68-78 Vicar Lane; 2-/3-course lunch £15/18; ⏲ 9am-6pm Tue-Thu, 9am-11pm Fri & Sat, 11am-5pm Sun) The brasserie-style brother of the award-winning Anthony's (below), this bright and cheerful modern restaurant set amid white walls and timber beams features much of Anthony's style stuffed into its excellent sandwiches, salads, lunches and luxurious afternoon teas (£12). If you want to see and be seen, there's also Anthony's Patisserie in the classy setting of the Victoria Quarter arcade across the street.

**TOP END**

**Anthony's** ( ☎ 0113-245 5922; www.anthonysrestaurant .co.uk; 19 Boar Lane; 2-/3-course dinner £34/42; ⏲ noon-2pm Tue-Sat, 7-9pm Tue-Thu, 7-10pm Fri & Sat) Probably the most talked-about restaurant in town,

Anthony's serves superb British cuisine to a clientele so eager that they'll think nothing of booking a month in advance. If you go at any time except Saturday evening, you'll get away with making your reservations a day or so earlier.

## Drinking

Leeds is justifiably renowned for its selection of pubs and bars. Glammed-up hordes of party animals crawl the cluster of venues around Boar Lane and Call Lane, where bars are opening (and closing) all the time. Most bars open till 2am; many turn into clubs after 11pm or midnight, with an admission charge.

**Baby Jupiter** ( ☎ 0113-242 1202; 11 York Pl) A retro gem with lots of purple velvet, hanging fishbowls and images from old sci-fi films, the basement bar sports a cool soundtrack that ranges from indie, funk and soul to punk, new wave and electro.

**Bar Fibre** ( ☎ 08701 200888; 168 Lower Briggate) Leeds' most popular gay bar, which spills out onto the cleverly named Queen's Court, is where the beautiful congregate to congratulate themselves on being so lucky. There's another cluster of gay bars downhill at the junction of Lower Briggate and the Calls.

**Duck & Drake** ( ☎ 0113-246 5806; 43 Kirkgate) A down-to-earth traditional boozer with a well-worn atmosphere, a cast of regular pub characters, and no fewer than 16, hand-pulled real ales to choose from.

**Northern Monkey** ( ☎ 0113-242 6630; 115 The Headrow) An attractive bare-floorboards-and-leather-sofas kind of bar catering to a youngish crowd – Becks and vodkas behind the bar, and an indie soundtrack with guest DJs on Friday and Saturday nights.

**Oracle** ( ☎ 0113-246 9912; 3 Brewery Pl) *The* place to be seen on a summer afternoon, Oracle has a huge outdoor terrace overlooking the River Aire. It serves gourmet burgers and a great selection of international beers just made to be served cold, from Guinness to Grolsch to Tsingtao. Upstairs there's a very chic cocktail and champagne bar that also sells spirits by the bottle, including Remy Martin at £300 a pop.

**Sandinista** ( ☎ 0113-305 0372; 5/5A Cross Belgrave St) This laid-back bar has a Latin look but a unifying theme, attracting an eclectic clientele with its mixed bag of music and unpretentious atmosphere. If you're not too fussed about looking glam, this is the spot for you.

**Whitelocks** ( ☎ 0113-245 3950; Turk's Head Yard) There's lots of polished wood, gleaming brass and colourful stained glass in this popular traditional pub dating from 1715. Theakstons, Deuchars IPA and several other real ales are on tap, and in summer the crowds spill out into the courtyard.

## Entertainment

In order to make sense of the ever-evolving scene, get your hands on the fortnightly *Leeds Guide* (£1.90; www.leedsguide.co.uk) or *Absolute Leeds* (£1.50; www.absolute leeds.co.uk).

### NIGHTCLUBS

The tremendous Leeds club scene attracts people from miles around. In true northern tradition people brave the cold wearing next to nothing, even in winter, which is a spectacle in itself. Clubs charge a variety of admission prices, ranging from as little as £1 on a slow weeknight to £10 or more on Saturday.

**HiFi Club** ( ☎ 0113-242 7353; www.thehificlub.co.uk; 2 Central Rd) This intimate club is a good break from the hardcore sound of four to the floor: if it's Tamla Motown or the percussive beats of dance-floor jazz that shake your booty, this is the spot for you.

**Cockpit** ( ☎ 0113-244 1573; www.thecockpit.co.uk; Swinegate) Snugly ensconced in a series of railway arches, the legendary Cockpit is the antidote to dance clubs. A live music venue of note – Coldplay, White Stripes, Flaming Lips and Amy Winehouse have all cut their teeth here – it also hosts The Session on Friday nights, a superb indie/electro/guitar club night.

**Mission** ( ☎ 0870 122 0114; www.clubmission.com; 8-13 Heaton's Ct) A massive club that redefines the term 'up for it'. Thursday night is gay go-go dancers bopping to commercial pop, while Saturdays are for the signature Glasshouse house session.

**Wire** ( ☎ 0113-234 0980; www.wireclub.co.uk; 2-8 Call Lane) This small, atmospheric basement club, set in a forest of Victorian cast-iron pillars, throbs to a different beat every night, from rock 'n' roll to drum 'n' bass. Popular with local students.

### THEATRE & OPERA

**City Varieties** ( ☎ 0113-243 0808; www.cityvarieties.co.uk; Swan St) This old-fashioned music hall features anything from clairvoyants to comedy acts to country music.

**Grand Theatre & Opera House** ( ☎ 0113-222 6222; www.leedsgrandtheatre.com; 46 New Briggate) Hosts musicals, plays and opera, including performances by the acclaimed **Opera North** ( ☎ 0113-244 5326; www.operanorth.co.uk).

**West Yorkshire Playhouse** ( ☎ 0113-213 7700; www.wyplayhouse.com; Quarry Hill Mount) The Playhouse has a reputation for excellent live drama, from the classics to cutting-edge new writing.

### CINEMA

**Hyde Park Picture House** ( ☎ 0113-275 2045; www.hyde parkpicturehouse.co.uk; Brudenell Rd) This Edwardian cinema shows a meaty range of art-house and mainstream choices. Take bus 56 from the city centre.

**Vue Cinema** ( ☎ 08712 240240; www.myvue.com; 22 The Light, The Headrow) For mainstream first-run films, head for the Vue on the second floor of The Light entertainment complex.

### SPORT

**Leeds United Football Club** ( ☎ 0113-226 1000; www.leedsunited.com; Elland Rd) Leeds supporters know all about pain: relegation from the Premiership in 2004 to the relative wilderness of the Championship was bad enough, but in 2007 they dropped another rung down the ladder to League One. All the same, loyal fans continue to pack the Elland Rd stadium in their masses. Take bus 93 or 96 from City Sq.

Headingley has been hosting cricket matches since 1890. It is still used for test matches and is the home ground of the **Yorkshire County Cricket Club** ( ☎ tickets 0113-278 7394; www.yorkshireccc.org.uk). Take bus 18 or 56 from the city centre.

## Shopping

Leeds' city centre has so many shopping arcades that they all seem to blend into one giant mall. The latest development – **Trinity Leeds**, between Commercial St and Boar Lane, scheduled to open in 2010 – will be the city's biggest.

The mosaic-paved, stained-glass-roofed Victorian arcades of **Victoria Quarter** ( ☎ 0113-245 5333; www.v-q.co.uk), between Briggate and Vicar Lane, are well worth visiting for aesthetic reasons alone; dedicated shoppers can join the footballers' wives browsing boutiques by Louis Vuitton, Vivienne Westwood and Swarovski. The flagship store here, of course, is **Harvey Nichols** ( ☎ 0113-204 8000; 107-111 Briggate).

Just across the street to the east you'll find the opposite end of the retail spectrum in **Leeds City Market** ( ☎ 0113-214 5162; www.leedsmarket .com; Kirkgate; 9am-5pm Mon-Sat, 9am-1pm Wed, open-air market Thu-Tue). Once the home of Michael Marks, who later joined Spencer, this is Britain's largest covered market, selling fresh meat, fish, fruit and vegetables, as well as household goods.

## Getting There & Away

### AIR
Eleven miles northwest of the city via the A65, **Leeds Bradford International Airport** ( ☎ 0113-250 9696; www.lbia.co.uk) offers flights to a range of domestic and international destinations. The Metroconnect 757 bus (£2, 40 minutes, every 30 minutes, hourly on Sunday) runs between Leeds bus station and the airport. A taxi costs about £18.

### BUS
**National Express** ( ☎ 08717 818181; www.nationalexpress .com) serves most major cities, including hourly services from London (£20, 4½ hours) and half-hourly services from Manchester (£8.40, 1¼ hours).

**Yorkshire Coastliner** ( ☎ 01653-692556; www .yorkshirecoastliner.co.uk) offers a range of useful services from Leeds to York, Castle Howard, Goathland and Whitby (840 and 842), and to York, Scarborough (843), Filey and Bridlington (845 and X45). A Freedom Ticket (£12) gives passengers unlimited bus travel for a day.

### TRAIN
Leeds City Station has hourly services from London King's Cross (£103, 2½ hours), Sheffield (£11, 45 minutes), Manchester (£15, one hour) and York (£10, 30 minutes).

Leeds is also the starting point for services on the famous Settle–Carlisle Line. For more details see p535.

## Getting Around
Metro's FreeCityBus service runs every few minutes from 6.30am to 7.30pm Monday to Saturday, linking the bus and train stations to all the main shopping areas in the city centre.

The various Day Rover passes (see p521) covering trains and/or buses are good for reaching Bradford, Haworth and Hebden Bridge.

# AROUND LEEDS
## Saltaire
A Victorian-era landmark, Saltaire was a model industrial village built in 1851 by philanthropic wool-baron and teetotaller Titus Salt. The rows of neat honey-coloured cottages – now a Unesco World Heritage Site – overlook what was once the largest factory in the world.

The factory is now **Salt's Mill** ( ☎ 01274-531163; www.saltsmill.org.uk; admission free; 10am-5.30pm Mon-Fri, 10am-6pm Sat & Sun), a splendidly bright and airy building where the main draw is a permanent exhibition of art by local boy David Hockney (b 1937). In a fitting metaphor for the shift in the British economy from making things to selling them, this former engine of industry is now a shrine to retail therapy, housing shops selling books, crafts and outdoor equipment, and a cafe.

Saltaire's **tourist office** ( ☎ 01274-774993; www .visitsaltaire.com; 2 Victoria Rd; 10am-5pm) has maps of the village and runs hour-long guided walks (adult/child £3.50/2.50) through the town throughout the year.

Saltaire is 9 miles west of Leeds centre, and 3 miles north of Bradford centre. It's easily reached by Metro rail from either.

## Harewood
The great park, sumptuous gardens and mighty edifice of **Harewood House** ( ☎ 0113-218 1010; www.harewood.org; adult/child £13.50/8.50; grounds 10am-6pm, house 11am-4.30pm mid-Mar–Oct, house & grounds 10am-4pm Sat & Sun Nov–mid-Mar) could easily fill an entire day trip from Leeds, and also makes a good port of call on the way to Harrogate.

A classic example of a stately English pile, the house was built between 1759 and 1772 by the era's superstar designers – John Carr designed the exterior, Lancelot 'Capability' Brown laid out the grounds, Thomas Chippendale supplied the furniture (the largest commission he ever received, costing the unheard-of amount of £10,000), Robert Adams designed the interior, and Italy was raided to create an appropriate art collection. The superb terrace was added 100 years later by yet another top name, Sir Charles Barry – he of the Houses of Parliament.

Many locals come to Harewood just to relax or saunter through the grounds, without even thinking of going inside the house. Hours of entertainment can be had in the **Bird Garden**, with many exotic species including penguins (feeding time at 2pm is a highlight), and there's also a boating lake, cafe and adventure playground. For more activity, there's a network of walking trails around the lake or through the parkland.

Harewood is about 7 miles north of Leeds on the A61. Take bus 36 (20 minutes; at least half-hourly Monday to Saturday, hourly on Sunday) which continues to Harrogate. Visitors coming by bus get half-price admission, so hang on to your ticket. From the main gate, it's a 2-mile walk through the grounds to the house and gardens, or you can use the free shuttle service.

## National Coal Mining Museum for England

For close to three centuries, West and South Yorkshire was synonymous with coal production; the collieries shaped and scarred the landscape, while entire villages grew up around the pits, each male inhabitant and their descendants destined to spend their working lives underground. The industry came to a shuddering halt in the 1980s, but the imprint of coal is still very much in evidence, even if there's only a handful of collieries left. One of these, at Claphouse, is now the **National Coal Mining Museum for England** ( ☎ 01924-848806; www.ncm.org.uk; Overton, near Wakefield; admission free; ⏲ 10am-5pm, last tour 3.15pm), a superb testament to the inner workings of a coal mine.

The highlight of a visit is the underground tour – equipped with helmet and head-torch you descend almost 150m in the 'cage' then follow subterranean passages to the coal seam where massive drilling machines now stand idle. Former miners work as guides, and explain the details – sometimes with a suitably authentic and almost impenetrable mix of local dialect (known in Yorkshire as Tyke) and technical terminology.

Up on top, there are audiovisual displays, some fascinating memorabilia (including sketches by Henry Moore) and exhibits about trade unions, strikes and the wider mining communities – only slightly over-romanticised in parts. You can also stroll round the pit-pony stables (their equine inhabitants also now retired) or the slightly eerie bathhouse, unchanged since the miners scrubbed off the coal dust and emptied their lockers for the last time. There are also nature trails in the surrounding fields and woods.

The museum is about 10 miles south of Leeds on the A642 between Wakefield and Huddersfield, which drivers can reach via Junction 40 on the M1. By public transport, take a train from Leeds to Wakefield (15 minutes, at least hourly), and then bus 232 towards Huddersfield (25 minutes, hourly).

## Yorkshire Sculpture Park

One of England's most impressive collections of sculpture is scattered across the formidable 18th-century estate of Bretton Park, 500-odd acres of lawns, fields and trees. A bit like the art world's equivalent of a safari park, the **Yorkshire Sculpture Park** ( ☎ 01924-830302; www .ysp.co.uk; Bretton, near Wakefield; admission free, parking £4; ⏲ 10am-6pm Apr-Sep, 10am-5pm Oct-Mar) showcases the work of dozens of sculptors both national and international, but the main focus of this outdoor gallery is the work of local kids Barbara Hepworth (1903–75), who was born in nearby Wakefield, and Henry Moore.

The rural setting is especially fitting for Moore's work: the artist was hugely influenced by the outdoors and preferred his art to be sited in the landscape rather than indoors. Other highlights include pieces by Andy Goldsworthy and Eduardo Paolozzi. There's also a program of temporary exhibitions and installations by visiting artists, plus a bookshop and cafe.

The park is 12 miles south of Leeds and 18 miles north of Sheffield, just off Junction 38 on the M1 motorway. If you're on public transport, take a train from Leeds to Wakefield (15 minutes, at least hourly), or from Sheffield to Barnsley (20 minutes, at least hourly); then take bus 444 which runs between Wakefield and Barnsley via Bretton Park (30 minutes, hourly Monday to Saturday).

## HEBDEN BRIDGE
pop 4086

Tucked tightly into the fold of a steep-sided valley, Yorkshire's funkiest little town is a former mill town that refused to go gently into that good night with the dying of industry's light; it raged a bit and then morphed into an attractive little tourist trap with a distinctly bohemian atmosphere. Besides the honest-to-God Yorkshire folk who have lived here for years, the town is home to university academics, artists, die-hard hippies and a substantial gay community – all of which explains the abundance of craft shops, organic cafes and secondhand bookstores.

The **Hebden Bridge Visitor & Canal Centre** ( ☎ 01422-843831; www.calderdale.gov.uk; Butlers Wharf, New Rd; ۞ 9.30am-5.30pm Mon-Fri, 10.30am-5pm Sat & Sun mid-Mar–mid-Oct, 10am-5pm Mon-Fri, 10.30am-4.15pm Sat & Sun rest of year) has a good stock of maps and leaflets on local walks, including a saunter to **Hardcastle Crags**, the local beauty spot, and nearby **Gibson Mill** (NT; ☎ 01422-844518; adult/child £3.60/1.80; ۞ 11am-4pm Wed, Sat & Sun Mar-Oct, 11am-3pm Sat & Sun Nov-Feb), a renovated 19th-century cotton mill.

From the centre, a short stroll along the attractive waterfront of the Rochdale Canal leads to the **Alternative Technology Centre** ( ☎ 01422-842121; www.alternativetechnology.org.uk; Hebble End Mill; admission free; ۞ 10am-5pm Mon-Fri, noon-5pm Sat, noon-4pm Sun), which promotes renewable energy, recycling and sustainable lifestyles through a series of intriguing exhibits and workshops.

Above the town is the much older village of **Heptonstall**, its narrow cobbled street lined with 500-year-old cottages and the ruins of a beautiful 13th-century church. But it is the churchyard of the newer St Thomas' Church that draws literary pilgrims, for here is buried the poet Sylvia Plath (1932–63), wife of another famous poet, Ted Hughes (1930–98), who was born in nearby Mytholmroyd.

## Sleeping & Eating

**Pennine Camp & Caravan Site** ( ☎ 01422-842287; High Greenwood House, Heptonstall; sites per person £4; ۞ Apr-Oct) A large, sloping field with a block of facilities in a converted barn, this camp site is about 3 miles northwest of town, on the minor road beyond Heptonstall that leads towards Widdop Reservoir.

**Mankinholes YHA** ( ☎ 0845 371 9751; www.yha.org.uk; Todmorden; dm £16) A converted 17th-century manor house 4 miles southwest of Hebden Bridge, this hostel has limited facilities (no TV room) but it is very popular with walkers; the Pennine Way passes only half a mile away.

**White Lion Hotel** ( ☎ 01422-842197; www.white lionhotel.net; Bridge Gate; s/d from £50/70) The choicest accommodation in town is this large 400-year-old coaching inn smack in the middle of it; the rooms in the converted coach house are that little bit more comfortable than the ones in the main house. Downstairs is an excellent real-ale pub and a restaurant (mains £7 to £10) with a standard pub grub menu.

**Crown Fisheries** ( ☎ 01422-842599; 8 Crown St; mains £4-5; ۞ 10am-6.30pm) A terrific chip shop that serves up a great fish supper (fish,

chips, bread and butter, and tea), and also does takeaways.

There are several appealing cafes along pedestrianised Bridge Gate in a peaceful setting beside the river and the old packhorse bridge that gave the town its name.

## Getting There & Away

Hebden Bridge is on the Leeds–Manchester train line (£3.75, 50 minutes, every 20 minutes Monday to Saturday, hourly on Sunday). Get off at Todmorden for the Mankinholes YHA.

## HAWORTH
pop 6100

It seems that only Shakespeare himself is held in higher esteem than the beloved Brontë sisters – Emily, Anne and Charlotte; at least, judging by the 8 million visitors a year who trudge up the hill from the train station to pay their respects at the handsome parsonage where the literary classics *Jane Eyre* and *Wuthering Heights* were born.

Not surprisingly, the whole village is given over to Brontë-linked tourism, but even without the literary associations Haworth is still worth a visit, though you'll be hard pushed not to be overwhelmed by the cottage industry that has grown up around the Brontës and their wonderful creations.

## Information

The **tourist office** ( ☎ 01535-642329; www.haworth-vil lage.org.uk; 2-4 West Lane; ۞ 9am-5.30pm Apr-Sep, to 5pm Oct-Mar) has an excellent supply of information on the village, the surrounding area and, of course, the Brontës.

Main St is lined with cafes, tearooms, pubs and shops selling everything imaginable bearing the Brontë name. Handy stops might include: the **post office** (98 Main St; ۞ 9am-5.30pm Mon-Fri, to 12.30pm Sat); **Venables & Bainbridge** ( ☎ 01535-640300; 111 Main St; ۞ 11am-5pm), selling used books including many vintage Brontë volumes; and **Rose & Co Apothecary** ( ☎ 01535-646830; 84 Main St; ۞ 10.30am-5.30pm), the beautifully restored chemist shop so favoured by Branwell Brontë.

## Sights

Your first stop should be **Haworth Parish Church** (admission free), a lovely old place of worship built in the late 19th century on the site of the 'old' church that the Brontë sisters knew, which

YORKSHIRE

**BAD LUCK BRONTËS**

The Rev Patrick Brontë, his wife Maria and six children moved to Haworth Parsonage in 1820. Within four years Maria and the two eldest daughters had died from cancer and tuberculosis. The treble tragedy led the good reverend to keep his remaining family close to him, and for the next few years the children were home-schooled in a highly creative environment.

The children conjured up mythical heroes and fantasy lands, and produced miniature home-made books. It was an auspicious start, at least for the three girls, Charlotte, Emily and Anne; the lone boy, Branwell, was more of a painter but lacked his sisters' drive and discipline. After a short stint as a professional artist, he ended up spending most of his days in the Black Bull pub, drunk and stoned on laudanum obtained across the street at Rose & Co Apothecary.

While the three sisters were setting the London literary world alight with the publication of three superb novels – *Jane Eyre, Wuthering Heights* and *Agnes Grey* – in one extraordinary year (1847), Branwell was fading quickly and died of tuberculosis in 1848. The family was devastated, but things quickly got worse. Emily fell ill with tuberculosis soon after her brother's funeral; she never left the house again and died on 19 December. Anne, who had also been sick, was next; Charlotte took her to Scarborough to seek a sea cure but she died on 28 May 1849.

The remaining family never recovered. Despite her growing fame, Charlotte struggled with depression and never quite adapted to her high position in literary society. Despite her misgivings she eventually married, but she too died, in the early stages of pregnancy, on 31 March 1855. All things considered, it's hardly surprising that poor old Patrick Brontë spent the remaining years of his life going increasingly insane.

was demolished in 1879. In the surrounding churchyard, gravestones are covered in moss or thrust to one side by gnarled tree roots, giving the place a tremendous feeling of age.

Set in a pretty garden overlooking the church and graveyard, the **Brontë Parsonage Museum** ( ☎ 01535-642323; www.bronte.info; admission £6; ☷ 10am-5.30pm Apr-Sep, 11am-5pm Oct-Mar) is where the Brontë family lived from 1820 till 1861. The rooms are meticulously furnished and decorated exactly as they were in the Brontë era, with many personal possessions on display. There's also a neat and informative exhibition, which includes the fascinating miniature books the Brontës wrote as children.

### Activities

Above Haworth stretch the bleak moors of the South Pennines – immediately familiar to Brontë fans – and the tourist office has leaflets on local **walks** to endless Brontë-related places. A 6.5-mile favourite leads to Top Withins, a ruined farm thought to have inspired *Wuthering Heights,* even though a plaque clearly states that the farmhouse bore no resemblance to the one Emily wrote about.

Other walks can be worked around the **Brontë Way,** a longer route linking Bradford and Colne via Haworth. Alternatively, you can walk or cycle the 8 miles south to Hebden Bridge via the scenic valley of Hardcastle Crags.

### Sleeping & Eating

Virtually every second house on Main St offers B&B; they're mostly indistinguishable from each other but some are just that little bit cuter. There are a couple of good restaurants in town and many of the B&Bs also have small cafes that are good for a spot of lunch – mediocre servings of local dishes and nice safe bets like sandwiches.

**Haworth House** ( ☎ 01535-643374; 6 Church St; s/d from £25/50) Tucked along the alley beside the church, this place has mostly spacious rooms with a New Age vibe, though the smaller, cheaper rooms are pretty cramped. Breakfast (£3 to £4 extra) is served in your bedroom.

**Aitches** ( ☎ 01535-642501; www.aitches.co.uk; 11 West Lane; s/d from £37/52) A very classy, stone-built Victorian house with four en suite rooms, each differently decorated with a pleasantly olde-worlde atmosphere. There's a residents' dining room where a three-course meal will cost £16 (prebooked, minimum four persons).

**Old Registry** ( ☎ 01535-646503; www.theoldregistry haworth.co.uk; 2-4 Main St; r £75-100) This place is a bit special, an elegantly rustic hotel where each of the carefully themed rooms has a four-poster bed, whirlpool bath or valley view: the Blue Heaven room is just that, at least for fans of Laura Ashley's delphinium blue.

**Weaver's Restaurant with Rooms** ( ☎ 01535-643822; www.weaverssmallhotel.co.uk; 15 West Lane; s/d £60/100, mains £12-18; ⏰ lunch Wed-Fri & Sun, dinner Tue-Sat) A stylish and atmospheric restaurant, Weaver's offers a menu featuring local specialities such as black pudding with corned beef hash, and sausage and mash with caramelised onion. Upstairs are three comfy bedrooms, two with views towards the moors.

Other options:

**Haworth YHA** ( ☎ 0845 371 9520; www.yha.org.uk; Longlands Dr; dm £14; P 🖳 ) A big old house with a games room, lounge, cycle store and laundry. It's on the northeastern edge of town, off Lees Lane.

**Apothecary Guest House** ( ☎ 01535-643642; www .theapothecaryguesthouse.co.uk; 86 Main St; s/d £35/55) Oak beams and narrow, slanted passageways lead to smallish rooms with cheerful decor.

**Old White Lion Hotel** ( ☎ 01535-642313; www .oldwhitelionhotel.com; West Lane; s/d from £57/80) Pub-style accommodation – comfortable if not spectacular – above an oak-panelled bar and highly rated restaurant (mains £10 to £16).

**Cobbles and Clay** ( ☎ 01535-644218; 60 Main St; mains £3-7; ⏰ 9am-5pm) Attractive, child-friendly cafe offering fair-trade coffee and healthy salads and snacks.

**Haworth Old Hall** ( ☎ 01535-642709; www.haworth oldhall.co.uk; Sun; mains £8-12) Sixteenth-century pub serving real ale and decent food. If you want to linger longer, two comfortable doubles cost £65.

## Getting There & Away

From Leeds, the easiest approach to Haworth is via Keighley, which is on the Metro rail network. Bus 500 runs from Keighley bus station to Haworth (15 minutes, hourly) and continues to Todmorden and Hebden Bridge. However, the most interesting way to get from Keighley to Haworth is via the Keighley & Worth Valley Railway (see boxed text, right).

# YORKSHIRE DALES NATIONAL PARK

The Yorkshire Dales – named from the old Norse word *dalr*, meaning 'valleys' – is the central jewel in the necklace of three national parks strung across the neck of northern England, with the dramatic fells of the Lake District to the west and the brooding heaths of the North York Moors to the east.

From well-known names like Wensleydale and Ribblesdale, to obscure and evocative Langstrothdale and Arkengarthdale, these glacial valleys are characterised by a distinctive landscape of high heather moorland, stepped skylines and flat-topped hills rising above green valley floors patchworked with drystone dykes and dotted with picture-postcard towns and hamlets, where sheep and cattle still graze on village greens. And in the limestone country in the southern Dales you'll find England's best examples of karst scenery.

The Dales have been protected as a national park since the 1950s, assuring their status as a walker's and cyclist's paradise. But there's plenty for non-walkers as well, from exploring the legacy of fictional vet James Herriot of *All Creatures Great and Small* fame, to sampling Wallace and Gromit's favourite teatime snack at the Wensleydale Creamery.

## Orientation & Information

The Yorkshire Dales National Park divides into two parts: in the north, two main valleys run west to east – broad expansive Wensleydale (home of the famous cheese) and narrow secretive Swaledale. In the busier, southern part, the main valleys – Ribblesdale, Malhamdale, Littondale and Wharfedale – run north to south.

The main Dales gateways are Skipton in the south and Richmond in the northeast. Good bases in the park itself include Settle, Grassington and Hawes. All have excellent tourist offices, stocking a mountain of local guidebooks and maps, and providing accommodation details.

To the northwest and west, the towns of Kirkby Stephen and Kirkby Lonsdale also make handy jumping-off points, although both are actually in the county of Cumbria (despite definite Dales affiliations).

---

**STEAM ENGINES & RAILWAY CHILDREN**

Haworth is on the **Keighley & Worth Valley Railway** (KWVR; ☎ 01535-645214; www.kwvr .co.uk; adult/child return £9/4.50, adult/child Day Rover £14/7), which runs steam and classic diesel engines between Keighley and Oxenhope. It was here, in 1969, that the classic movie *The Railway Children* was shot; Mr Perks was stationmaster at Oakworth, where the Edwardian look has been meticulously maintained. Trains operate about hourly at weekends all year; in holiday periods they run hourly every day.

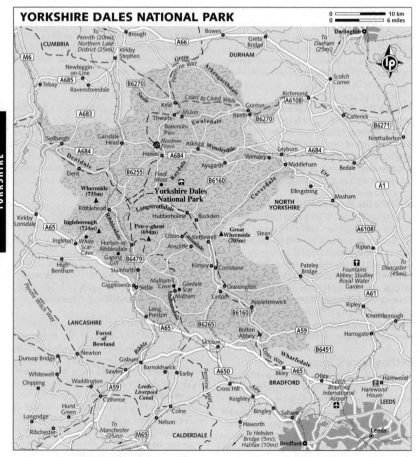

The *Visitor* newspaper, available from tourist offices, lists local events and walks guided by park rangers, as well as many places to stay and eat. The official park website at www .yorkshiredales.org.uk is also useful.

## Activities
### CYCLING

Other than on busy summer weekends, this is excellent cycling country. Most roads follow the rivers along the bottom of the Dales so, although there are some steep climbs, there's also plenty on the flat. Tourist offices stock maps and leaflets with suggested routes (on-road and off-road) for a day or longer.

One example is the **Yorkshire Dales Cycle Way**, an exhilarating 130-mile loop, taking in the best of the park. Skipton is a convenient starting point, from where you ride up Wharfedale, then steeply over Fleet Moss to Hawes. From here turn east along Wensleydale to Aysgarth, then north over the wild hills to Reeth. The roads are steep but the scenery is breathtaking. Follow Swaledale westwards, through remote Keld and down to the market town of Kirkby Stephen. Then it's south to Sedbergh, and up beautiful Dentdale to pop out at Ribblehead. It's plain sailing now, through Horton-in-Ribblesdale to Stainforth, one more climb over to Malham, and finally back to Skipton for tea and medals.

There's also lots of scope for off-road riding, with around 500 miles of bridleways and trails – check out www.mtbthedales.org.uk for inspiration.

### WALKING

The Yorkshire Dales has a vast footpath network, offering everything from easy strolls to challenging hikes; we suggest a few options throughout this section. Look out at tourist offices for leaflets describing walks from train stations, notably on the Settle–Carlisle Line. Serious walkers should equip themselves with 1:25,000 OS Explorer Maps Nos 2 and 30.

Two of England's most famous long-distance routes cross the Dales. The **Pennine Way** goes through the rugged western half of the park. If you haven't got three weeks to cover all 259 miles, a few days hiking between Malham and Hawes, for example, is well worth the effort. The **Coast to Coast Walk** (p518) passes through Swaledale in the northern Dales. Following the route for a day or two is highly recommended; see p538.

Another long-distance possibility is the **Dales Way** (www.dalesway.org.uk), which begins in Ilkley, follows the River Wharfe through the heart of the Dales, and finishes at Bowness-on-Windermere in the Lake District. If you start at Grassington, it's an easy five-day journey (60 miles). A handy companion is *Dales Way Route Guide* by Arthur Gemmell and Colin Speakman (£5.99), available at most bookshops.

## Getting There & Around

The main gateway towns of Skipton and Richmond are well served by public transport, and local bus services radiate from there. Pick up the useful *Dales Explorer Travel Guide*, a free map available from tourist offices that covers bus and train services in the region, or consult the comprehensive **Traveldales website** (www.traveldales.org.uk).

Going by train, the best and most interesting access to the Dales is via the famous **Settle–Carlisle Line** (p535). From the south, trains start in Leeds and pass through Skipton, Settle and numerous small villages, offering unrivalled access to the hills straight from the station platform. Of course, if you're coming from the north, Carlisle is the place to get on board.

Around 90% of visitors to the park arrive by car, and the narrow roads can be extremely crowded in summer; parking can also be a serious problem. If you can, try to use public transport as much as possible.

## SKIPTON
pop 14,300

This busy market town on the southern edge of the Dales takes its name from the Anglo-Saxon *scaepe ton* (sheep town) – no prizes for guessing how it made its money. Monday, Wednesday, Friday and Saturday are market days on High St, bringing crowds from all over and giving the town something of a festive atmosphere. The **tourist office** ( ☎ 01756-792809; www.skiptononline.co.uk; 35 Coach St; ☼ 10am-5pm Mon-Fri, 9am-5pm Sat) is on the northern edge of the town centre.

## Sights & Activities

A pleasant stroll from the tourist office along the canal path leads to **Skipton Castle** ( ☎ 01756-792442; www.skiptoncastle.co.uk; High St; admission £5.80; ☼ 10am-6pm Mon-Sat, noon-6pm Sun Mar-Sep, to 4pm Oct-Feb), one of the best-preserved medieval castles in England – a fascinating contrast to the ruins you'll see elsewhere.

From the castle, wander along Skipton's pride and joy – the broad and bustling **High St**, one of the most attractive shopping streets in Yorkshire. On the first Sunday of the month it hosts the Northern Dales farmers market.

No trip to Skipton is complete without a cruise along the Leeds–Liverpool Canal that runs through the middle of town. **Pennine Boat Trips** ( ☎ 01756-790829; www.canaltrips.co.uk; The Wharf, Coach St; adult/child £6/3) runs hour-long trips daily from April to October; call for departure times.

## Sleeping & Eating

There's a strip of B&Bs just outside the centre on Keighley Rd. All those between Nos 46 and 57 are worth trying.

**Carlton House** ( ☎ 01756-700921; www.carltonhouse.rapidial.co.uk; 46 Keighley Rd; s/d from £28/55) A handsome house with five pretty, comfortable rooms – no frills but lots of floral prints. The house is deservedly popular on account of the friendly welcome.

**Bizzie Lizzies** ( ☎ 01756-793189; 36 Swadford St; mains £5-8; ☼ 11.30am-9pm, takeaway till 11.30pm) This sit-down fish-and-chip restaurant overlooking the canal has won several awards for quality, a rare thing for what is essentially deep-fried fast food. There's also a takeaway counter.

**Canalside** ( ☎ 01756-795678; www.canalsideskipton.co.uk; Waterside Ct, Coach St; mains lunch £7-9, dinner £13-17; ☼ noon-9.30pm Wed-Mon) Set in a converted warehouse overlooking the canal basin, this brisk modern restaurant enjoys the best location in town. The menu runs from game pie and confit duck to Dales beef and pan-fried sea bass.

Also recommended:

**Bojangles** ( ☎ 01756-709333; 20 Newmarket St; mains £3-4) Best coffee in town, American-style breakfasts and burgers.

**Narrow Boat** ( ☎ 01756-797922; 38 Victoria St) Traditionally styled pub with a great selection of local ales and foreign beers, friendly service and bar food.

### Getting There & Away

Skipton is the last stop on the Metro rail network from Leeds and Bradford (£7.10, 40 minutes, half-hourly, hourly on Sunday). For heading into the Dales, see the boxed text opposite.

For Grassington, take bus 72 (30 minutes, hourly Monday to Saturday, no Sunday service) from Skipton train station, or 66A (hourly, Sunday) from the Market Pl.

## MALHAM
**pop 120**

Stretching west from Grassington to Ingleton is the largest area of limestone country in England, which has created a distinctive landscape dotted with dry valleys, potholes, limestone pavements and gorges. Two of the most spectacular features – Malham Cove and Gordale Scar – lie near the pretty village of Malham.

The **national park centre** ( ☎ 01969-652380; malham@yorkshiredales.org.uk; ◷ 10am-5pm daily Apr-Oct, 10am-4pm Sat & Sun Nov-Mar) at the southern edge of the village has the usual wealth of information. Note that Malham can only be reached via narrow roads that can be very congested in summer; leave your car at the national park centre and walk into the village.

### Sights & Activities

A half-mile walk north from Malham village leads to **Malham Cove**, a huge rock amphitheatre lined with 80m-high vertical cliffs. You can hike steeply up the left-hand end of the cove (on the Pennine Way footpath) to see the extensive limestone pavement above the cliffs. Another 1.5 miles further north is **Malham Tarn**, a glacial lake and nature reserve.

A mile east of Malham along a narrow road (very limited parking) is spectacular **Gordale Scar**, a deep limestone canyon with scenic cascades and the remains of an Iron Age set-

tlement. The national park centre has a leaflet describing the **Malham Landscape Trail**, a 5-mile circular walk that takes in Malham Cove, Gordale Scar and the Janet's Foss waterfall.

The **Pennine Way** passes right through Malham; Horton-in-Ribblesdale (opposite) lies a day's hike away to the northwest.

### Sleeping & Eating

**Malham YHA** ( ☎ 0845 371 9529; www.yha.org.uk; dm £14; P ) In the village centre you'll find this purpose-built hostel; the facilities are top-notch and young children are well catered for.

**Beck Hall** ( ☎ 01729-830332; www.beckhallmalham .com; s/d from £25/50; P 🖳 ) This rambling 17th-century country house on the edge of the village has 15 individually decorated rooms – we recommend the Green Room, with its old-style furnishings and four-poster bed. There's a rustling stream flowing through the garden and a nice tearoom (snacks about £4).

## RIBBLESDALE & THE THREE PEAKS

Scenic Ribblesdale cuts through the southwestern corner of the Yorkshire Dales National Park, where the skyline is dominated by a trio of distinctive hills known as the **Three Peaks** – Whernside (735m), Ingleborough (724m) and Pen-y-ghent (694m). Easily accessible via the Settle–Carlisle railway line, this is one of England's most popular areas for outdoor activities, attracting thousands of hikers, cyclists and cavers each weekend.

### Settle
**pop 3621**

The busy market town of Settle, dominated by its grand neo-Gothic town hall, is the gateway to Ribblesdale. Narrow cobbled streets lined with shops and pubs lead out from the central market square (Tuesday is market day), and the town offers plenty of accommodation options.

The **tourist office** ( ☎ 01729-825192; settle@ytbtic .co.uk; Town Hall, Cheapside; ◷ 9.30am-4.30pm Apr-Oct, 9.30am-4pm Nov-Mar) has maps and guidebooks, and an excellent range of local walks leaflets.

#### SLEEPING & EATING

**Golden Lion Hotel** ( ☎ 01729-822203; info@goldenlion .yorks.net; Duke St; s/d £43/75; lunch mains £8, dinner £9-14) This handsome 17th-century coaching inn has 12 warm and comfortable rooms, a traditional pub and a pleasant restaurant that is one of the most popular in town.

---

### THE SETTLE–CARLISLE LINE

The Settle–Carlisle Line (SCL), built between 1869 and 1875, offers one of England's most scenic railway journeys. The 72-mile line's construction was one of the great engineering achievements of the Victorian era: – 5000 navvies armed with picks and shovels built 325 bridges, 21 viaducts and blasted 14 tunnels in horrific conditions – nearly 200 of them died in the process.

Trains run between Leeds and Carlisle via Settle about eight times a day. The first section of the journey from Leeds is along the Aire Valley, stopping at **Keighley**, where the Keighley & Worth Valley Railway branches off to **Haworth** (p529); **Skipton** – gateway to the southern Dales; and **Settle**. The train then labours up the valley beside the River Ribble, through **Horton-in-Ribblesdale**, across the spectacular **Ribblehead Viaduct** and then through Blea Moor Tunnel to reach remote **Dent** station, at 350m the highest main-line station in the country.

The line reaches its highest point (356m) at Ais Gill where it leaves the Dales behind before easing down to **Kirkby Stephen**. The last halts are **Appleby** and **Langwathby**, just northwest of Penrith (a jumping-off point for the Lake District), before the train finally pulls into **Carlisle**.

The entire journey from Leeds to Carlisle takes two hours and 40 minutes and costs £22/27 for a single/day return; from Settle to Carlisle is 1¾ hours and £16/18. Various hop-on-hop-off passes for one or three days are also available. You can pick up a free SCL timetable – which includes a colour map of the line and brief details about places of interest – from most Yorkshire stations; for more information contact **National Rail Enquiries** ( ☎ 08457 484950) or click on to www.settle-carlisle.co.uk.

**Ye Olde Naked Man** ( ☎ 01729-823230; Market Pl; mains £3-7) Formerly an undertakers – look for the 'naked man' on the outside wall, dated 1663 – and now a bakery and cafe selling coffee, tea and scones with clotted cream.

Around Market Pl there are several other cafes, including the excellent **Shambles** ( ☎ 01729-822652; Market Pl; fish & chips £5-7).

### GETTING THERE & AWAY

The easiest access is by train. Trains from Leeds or Skipton heading to Carlisle stop at the station near the town centre; those heading for Morecambe (on the west coast) stop at Giggleswick, about 1.5 miles outside town.

## Horton-in-Ribblesdale
pop 560

A favourite with outdoor enthusiasts, the little village of Horton and its railway station is 5 miles north of Settle. Everything centres on the Pen-y-ghent Cafe which acts as the village **tourist office** ( ☎ 01729-860333; horton@ytbtic.co.uk), wet-weather retreat and hikers' information centre.

Horton is the starting point for climbing Pen-y-ghent and for doing the **Three Peaks Walk** (see boxed text, p536); it's also a stop on the Pennine Way. At the head of the valley, 5 miles north of Horton, is the spectacular **Ribblehead Viaduct**, built in 1874 and the longest on the Settle–Carlisle line – more than 30m high and 400m long. You can hike there along the Pennine Way and travel back by train from Ribblehead station.

### SLEEPING & EATING

Horton is popular, so it's wise to book accommodation in advance.

**Dub-Cote Farm Camping Barn** ( ☎ 01729-860238; www.threepeaksbarn.co.uk; per person £10) This 17th-century stone barn enjoys a lovely hillside setting a mile southeast of the village, and is equipped with self-catering facilities (BYO sleeping bag and pillow case).

**Golden Lion** ( ☎ 01729-860206; www.goldenlionhotel.co.uk; s/d from £40/60; bunkhouse per person £10) The Golden Lion is a lively pub that offers comfortable B&B rooms and a basic, 15-bed bunkroom upstairs, and three public bars downstairs where you can tuck into a bit of grub washed down with a pint of hand-pulled ale.

**Crown Hotel** ( ☎ 01729-860209; www.crown-hotel.co.uk; s/d from £30/60; **P** ) Another popular rest stop with walkers, the Crown has a variety of basic rooms (with slightly over-the-top floral decoration) and a cosy bar that serves a range of meals.

**Pen-y-ghent Cafe** ( ☎ 01729-860333; mains £3-7; 🕑 9am-6pm Mon & Wed-Fri, 8am-6pm Sat & Sun) A traditional caff run by the same family since 1965, the Pen-y-ghent fills walkers' fuel tanks with fried eggs and chips, homemade scones

YORKSHIRE

and pint-sized mugs of tea. It also sells maps, guidebooks and walking gear.

## Ingleton
pop 2000

The village of Ingleton, perched precariously above a river gorge, is the caving capital of England. It sits at the foot of one of the country's most extensive areas of limestone upland, crowned by the dominating peak of Ingleborough and riddled with countless potholes and cave systems.

The **tourist office** ( ☎ 01524-241049; www.visitingle ton.co.uk; 🕑 10am-4pm Apr-Sep) is beside the main car park, while **Bernie's Cafe** ( ☎ 01524-241802; 4 Main St) is the centre of the local caving scene.

Ingleton is the starting point for two famous Dales hikes. The shorter and easier of the two is the circular, 4.5-mile **Waterfalls Walk** (www .ingletonwaterfallswalk.co.uk), which passes through native oak woodland on its way past a series of spectacular waterfalls on the Rivers Twiss and Doe. Around 120,000 people climb **Ingleborough** (724m) every year, but that doesn't make the 6-mile round trip any less of an effort; this is a proper hill walk, so pack waterproofs, food, water, and a map and compass.

Although most of the local caves are accessible only to experienced potholers, some are open to the general public. **White Scar Cave** ( ☎ 01524-241244; www.whitescarcave.co.uk; adult/child £7.50/4.50; 🕑 10am-4.30pm daily Feb-Oct, Sat & Sun only Nov-Jan) is the longest show cave in England, with a series of underground waterfalls and impressive dripstone formations leading to the 100m-long Battlefield Cavern, one of the largest cave chambers in the country. The cave is 1.5 miles northeast of the village on the B6255 road.

**Gaping Gill**, on the southeastern flank of Ingleborough, is one of the most famous caves in England. A huge vertical pothole 105m deep, it was the largest known cave shaft in the UK until the discovery of Titan in Derbyshire in 1999. Gaping Gill is normally off-limits to non-cavers, but twice a year, on the May and August Bank Holiday weekends, local caving clubs set up a winch so that members of the public can descend into the depths in a special chair (£10 per person). For details see www .bpc-cave.org.uk and www.cravenpotholeclub .org, and click on the Gaping Gill link.

Ingleton is 10 miles northwest of Settle; take bus 581 from Settle train station (25 minutes, two daily).

## HAWES
pop 700

Hawes is the beating heart of Wensleydale, a thriving and picturesque market town (market day is Tuesday) with the added attraction of its own waterfall in the village centre. On busy summer weekends, however, Hawes' narrow arteries can get seriously clogged with traffic – leave the car in the parking area beside the **national park centre** ( ☎ 01969-666210; hawes@york shiredales.org.uk; Station Yard; 🕑 10am-5pm year-round) at the eastern entrance to the village.

### Sights & Activities

Sharing a building with the park centre is the **Dales Countryside Museum** (adult/child £3/free), a beautifully presented social history of the area that explains the forces that shaped the landscape, from geology to lead mining to land enclosure.

At the other end of the village lies the **Wensleydale Creamery Visitor Centre** ( ☎ 01969-

667664; www.wensleydale.co.uk; admission £2; ☺ 9.30am-5pm Mon-Sat, 10am-4.30pm Sun), devoted to the production of Wallace and Gromit's favourite crumbly, white cheese. You can visit the cheese museum and then try before you buy in the shop, which is free to enter. There are one-hour tours of the creamery between 10am and 3pm.

About 1.5 miles north of Hawes is 30m-high **Hardraw Force**, the highest unbroken waterfall in England. By international standards it's not that impressive (except after heavy rain); access is through the Green Dragon pub, which levies a £2 admission fee.

## Sleeping & Eating

**Bainbridge Ings Caravan & Camp Site** ( ☎ 01969-667354; www.bainbridge-ings.co.uk; tent, car & 2 adults £10.50, hikers & cyclists per person £4) An attractive site set in stone-walled fields around a spacious farmhouse about half a mile east of town. Gas, milk and eggs are sold on site.

**Hawes YHA** ( ☎ 0845 371 9120; www.yha.org.uk; Lancaster Tce; dm £16; **P** ) A modern place on the western edge of town, at the junction of the main A684 (Aysgarth Rd) and B6255, this is a family-friendly hostel with great views of Wensleydale.

**Green Dragon Inn** ( ☎ 01969-667392; www.green dragonhardraw.co.uk; Hardraw; s/d from £24/45) A fine old pub with flagstone floors, low timber beams, ancient oak furniture and Theakstons on draught, the Dragon serves up a tasty steak and ale pie and offers B&B accommodation in plain but adequate rooms.

**Herriot's Guest House** ( ☎ 01969-667536; www.herri otsinhawes.co.uk; Main St; r per person from £36) A delightful guesthouse set in an old stone building close to the bridge by the waterfall, Herriot's has seven comfy, en suite bedrooms set above an art gallery and coffee shop.

**Cart House** ( ☎ 01969-667691; www.hardrawforce .co.uk; Hardraw; mains £6; ☺ 10am-5.30pm Mar-Nov) Across the bridge from the Green Dragon, this craft shop and tearoom offers a healthier diet of homemade soup, organic bread, and a 'Fellman's Lunch' of Wensleydale cheese, pickle and salad. There's a basic camp site at the back (£10 for two adults, tent and car).

**Chaste** ( ☎ 01969-667145; Market Pl; mains £13) An unusual name for a bistro, but this place is far from coy when it comes to promoting Yorkshire produce – almost everything on the menu, from the all-day breakfast to the vegetable hotpot to the black pudding

and mashed potato is either homemade or locally sourced.

## Getting There & Away

Dales & District buses 156 and 157 run from Bedale to Hawes (1¼ hours, eight daily Monday to Saturday, four on Sunday) via Leyburn, where you can connect with transport to/from Richmond. To get to Bedale from Northallerton train station on the main York–Newcastle line, take bus 73 (25 minutes, half-hourly Monday to Saturday, every two hours Sunday).

From Garsdale station on the Settle–Carlisle line, bus 113 runs to Hawes (20 minutes, three daily Monday to Saturday); on Sundays and bank holidays bus 808 goes to Hawes from Ribblehead station (50 minutes, two daily). Check the bus times at www.york shiretravel.net or a tourist office before using these routes.

## RICHMOND
pop 8200

The handsome market town of Richmond is one of England's best-kept secrets, perched on a rocky outcrop overlooking the River Swale and guarded by the ruins of a massive castle. A maze of cobbled streets radiates from the broad, sloping market square, lined with elegant Georgian buildings and photogenic stone cottages, with glimpses of the surrounding hills and dales peeking through the gaps.

## Orientation & Information

Richmond lies east of the Yorkshire Dales National Park but makes a good gateway for the northern part. The centre of everything is Market Pl (market day is Saturday). The **tourist office** ( ☎ 01748-828742; www.richmond.org; Friary Gardens, Victoria Rd; ☺ 9.30am-5.30pm Apr-Oct, 9.30am-4.30pm Nov-Mar) has the usual maps and guides, plus several leaflets showing walks in town and the surrounding countryside.

## Sights

Top of the pile is the impressive heap that is **Richmond Castle** (EH; ☎ 01748-822493; admission £4; ☺ 10am-6pm Apr-Sep, 10am-4pm Oct-Mar), founded in 1070 and one of the first castles in England since Roman times to be built of stone. It's had many uses through the years, including a stint as a prison for conscientious objectors during WWI (there's a small and sobering exhibition about their part in the castle's history).

The best part is the view from the top of the remarkably well-preserved 30m-high keep which towers over the River Swale.

Military buffs will enjoy the **Green Howards Museum** ( ☎ 01748-822133; www.greenhowards.org.uk; Trinity Church Sq; adult/child £3.50/free; ☿ 10am-4.30pm Mon-Sat, closed 24 Dec–31 Jan), which pays tribute to the famous Yorkshire regiment. In a different vein, the **Richmondshire Museum** ( ☎ 01748-825611; Ryder's Wynd; adult/child £2.50/1.50; ☿ 10.30am-4.30pm Apr-Oct) is a delight, with local history exhibits including an early Yorkshire cave-dweller and displays on lead mining, which forever altered the Swaledale landscape a century ago; you can also see the original set that served as James Herriot's surgery in the TV series *All Creatures Great and Small*.

Built in 1788, the **Georgian Theatre Royal** ( ☎ 01748-823710; www.georgiantheatreroyal.co.uk; Victoria Rd; tours per person £3.50; ☿ tours hourly 10am-4pm Mon-Sat mid-Feb–mid-Dec) is the most complete Georgian playhouse in Britain. Tours include a look at the country's oldest surviving stage scenery, painted between 1818 and 1836.

## Activities

Walkers can follow paths along the River Swale, both upstream and downstream from the town. A longer option is to follow part of the famous long-distance **Coast to Coast Walk** (p518) all the way to Reeth (11 miles) and take the bus back (see www.dalesbus.info/richmond).

In September/October the town hosts the **Richmond Walking & Book Festival** (www.richmond walking.com), 10 days of guided walks, talks, films and other events.

Cyclists can also follow Swaledale – as far as Reeth may be enough, while a trip to Keld and then over the high wild moors to Kirkby Stephen is a more serious but very rewarding 33-mile undertaking.

## Sleeping

**Willance House** ( ☎ 01748-824467; www.willance house.com; 24 Frenchgate; s/d £40/65) This is an oak-beamed house, built in 1600, with three immaculate rooms (one with a four-poster bed) that combine old-fashioned charm and all mod cons.

**Frenchgate Hotel** ( ☎ 01748-822087; www.thefrench gate.co.uk; 59-61 Frenchgate; s/d from £58/98; **P** ) Eight elegant bedrooms occupy the upper floors of this converted Georgian town house, now a boutique guesthouse decorated with local art. The rooms have cool designer fittings that

set off a period fireplace here, a Victorian roll-top bath there; downstairs there's an excellent restaurant (three-course dinner £29) and a hospitable lounge with oak beams and an open fire.

**our pick Millgate House** ( ☎ 01748-823571; www .millgatehouse.com; Market Pl; r £95-125; **P** 🖳 ) Behind an unassuming green door lies the unexpected pleasure of one of the most attractive guesthouses in England. While the house itself is a Georgian gem crammed with period details, it is overshadowed by the multi-award-winning garden at the back, which has superb views over the River Swale and the Cleveland Hills – if possible, book the Garden Suite.

There's a batch of pleasant places along Frenchgate, and several more on Maison Dieu and Pottergate (the road into town from the east). These include **66 Frenchgate** ( ☎ 01748-823421; www.66frenchgate.co.uk; 66 Frenchgate; s/d from £40/60; 🖳 ), where one of the three rooms has a superb river view, **Pottergate Guesthouse** ( ☎ 01748-823826; 4 Pottergate; d from £44) and **Emmanuel House** ( ☎ 01748-823584; 41 Maison Dieu; d from £40).

## Eating & Drinking

**Butler's Cafe-Bar** ( ☎ 01748-825252; Victoria Rd; mains £2-5; ☿ 10am-2pm Mon & Tue, 10am-3pm Wed-Sat) Tucked away at the top of the Georgian Theatre Royal building, this little place serves fair-trade coffee, speciality teas and delicious hot, buttered muffins – try to get the one table with a view over Friary Gardens.

**A Taste of Thailand** ( ☎ 01748-829696; 15 King St; mains £6-8; ☿ 5-11pm) Does exactly what it says on the tin – an extensive menu of Thai favourites and a convenient BYO policy (corkage £2).

**Seasons Restaurant & Cafe** ( ☎ 01748-825340; Richmond Station, Station Rd; mains restaurant £14-17, cafe £6-10; ☿ restaurant 5.30-10pm, cafe 9am-11pm) Housed in the newly restored Victorian station building, this attractive, open-plan eatery shares space with a boutique brewery, artisan bakery, ice-cream factory and cheesemonger – and yes, all this local produce is on the menu.

Surprisingly, despite a vast choice, few of the pubs in Richmond are up to much. After extensive research, the best we found were the **Black Lion Hotel** ( ☎ 01748-823121; Finkle St), with cosy bars, low beams and good beer and food, and the determinedly old-fashioned **Unicorn Inn** ( ☎ 01748-823719; 2 Newbiggin), a free house serving Theakstons and Old Speckled Hen.

### Getting There & Away

From Darlington (on the railway between London and Edinburgh) it's easy to reach Richmond on bus X26 or X27 (35 minutes, every 15 minutes, every 30 minutes on Sunday). All buses stop in Market Pl.

On Sundays and bank holiday Mondays only, from late May to late September, the Fountains Flyer bus 802 runs from Leeds to Richmond (3½ hours, one daily) via Fountains Abbey, Ripon, Masham and Middleham.

# EAST RIDING OF YORKSHIRE

In command of the East Riding of Yorkshire is the tough old sea dog of Hull, a no-nonsense port that looks to the North Sea an d the broad horizons of the Humber estuary for its livelihood. Just to its north, and in complete contrast to Hull's salt and grit, is East Riding's most attractive town, Beverley, with lots of Georgian character and one of England's finest churches.

### Getting There & Around

Hull is easily reached by rail from Leeds, York, Beverley, Filey and Scarborough, and is also the hub for regional bus services. The website at www.gettingaround.eastriding.gov.uk lists local transport operators.

## HULL

**pop 256,200**

Tough and uncompromising, Hull is a curmudgeonly English seaport with a proud seafaring tradition. It has long been the principal cargo port of England's east coast, with an economy that grew up around carrying wool out and bringing wine in. It was also a major whaling and fishing port until the trawling industry died out, and it remains a busy cargo terminal and departure point for ferries to the Continent.

### Orientation

The train and bus stations – collectively known as Hull Paragon Interchange – sit on the western edge of the city centre; all the main sights are within 20 minutes' walk from here. Arriving by car, head for the multistorey car park at Princes Quay Shopping Centre, or the car park at The Deep.

### Information

**Central Library** ( ☎ 01482-223344; Albion St; ☯ 9.30am-8pm Mon-Thu, 9.30am-5.30pm Fri, 9am-4.30pm Sun) Internet access.

**Post office** (63 Market Pl; ☯ 9am-5.30pm Mon-Sat)

**Tourist office** ( ☎ 01482-223559; www.hullcc.gov.uk; 1 Paragon St; ☯ 10am-5pm Mon-Sat, 11am-3pm Sun)

**Waterstone's** ( ☎ 01482-580234; 19-21 Jameson St; ☯ 9am-6pm Mon-Sat, 10.30am-4.30pm Sun) Books and maps.

### Sights

#### THE DEEP

Hull's biggest tourist attraction is **The Deep** ( ☎ 01482-381000; www.thedeep.co.uk; Tower St; adult/child £8.75/6.75; ☯ 10am-6pm, last entry 5pm), a vast aquarium housed in a colossal, angular building that appears to lunge above the muddy waters of the Humber like a giant shark's head. Inside it's just as dramatic, with echoing commentaries and computer-generated interactive displays that guide you through the formation of the oceans and the evolution of sea life. The largest aquarium is 10m deep, filled with sharks, stingrays and colourful coral fishes, with moray eels draped over rocks like scarves of iridescent slime. A glass elevator plies up and down inside the tank, though you'll get a better view by taking the stairs. Don't miss the cafe on the very top floor, which has a great view of the Humber estuary.

#### MUSEUM QUARTER

Hull has several city-run **museums** ( ☎ 01482-300300; 36 High St; www.hullcc.gov.uk/museums; admission free; ☯ 10am-5pm Mon-Sat, 1.30-4.30pm Sun) concentrated in an area promoted as the Museum Quarter. All share the same contact details, admission and opening hours.

The fascinating **Streetlife Museum** contains re-created street scenes from Georgian and Victorian times and from the 1930s, with all sorts of historic vehicles to explore, from stagecoaches to bicycles to buses and trams. Behind the museum, marooned in the mud of the River Hull, is the **Arctic Corsair** ( ☯ tours 10am-4.30pm Wed & Sat, 1.30-4.30pm Sun). Tours of this Atlantic trawler, a veteran of the 1970s 'Cod Wars', demonstrate the hardships of fishing north of the Arctic Circle.

### Festivals & Events

**Hull Literature Festival** (www.humbermouth.org.uk) Last two weeks of June. A celebration of Hull's rich literary heritage: besides the connection with the English poet Philip Larkin

(1922–85), poets Andrew Marvell and Stevie Smith and playwrights Alan Plater and John Godber all hail from here.

**Hull Jazz Festival** (www.hulljazzfestival.co.uk) July. Week-long festival brings an impressive line-up of great jazz musicians to the city.

**Hull Fair** ( ☎ 01482-300300; www.hullcc.gov.uk) Second week in October. Europe's largest travelling funfair, with 250 different attractions including all kinds of stalls selling everything from palm reading to candy floss and all manner of rides, from the gentle, traditional kind to more modern white-knucklers.

## Sleeping & Eating

Good accommodation in the city centre is pretty thin on the ground – mostly business-oriented chain hotels and a few mediocre guesthouses. The tourist office will help book accommodation for free.

**Clyde House Hotel** ( ☎ 01482-214981; www.clyde househotel.co.uk; 13 John St; s/d £30/50) Overlooking leafy Kingston Sq, and close to the New Theatre, this is one of the best B&B options in the city centre; the rooms are nothing fancy, but are tidy and comfortable, and the owners are friendly and helpful.

**Kingston Theatre Hotel** ( ☎ 01482-225828; www .kingstontheatrehotel.com; 1-2 Kingston Sq; s/d/ste from £45/65/80) A slightly more formal hotel sharing the same central location as the Clyde, this place offers charming if not quite memorable rooms; upgrade to a suite if you're looking for a little leg room.

**McCoy's** ( ☎ 01482-327757; Colonial Chambers, Princes Dock St; mains £3-5; ☽ 8am-6pm Mon-Sat) This home-grown alternative to Starbucks serves excellent coffee, and a breakfast menu that ranges from porridge to a vegetarian fry-up to scrambled egg with smoked salmon. There are freshly baked cakes and pastries through the day, with salads and sarnies at lunch.

**Hitchcock's Vegetarian Restaurant** ( ☎ 01482-320233; 1 Bishop Lane, High St; per person £15; ☽ 8-9pm Tue-Sat) The word 'quirky' could have been invented to describe this place – an atmospheric maze of small rooms, an all-you-can-eat vegetarian buffet whose theme (Thai, Indian, Spanish, whatever) is chosen by the first person to book that evening, BYO alcohol, and no credit cards. But hey – the food is excellent and the welcome is warm. Bookings necessary.

**Cook's Endeavour** ( ☎ 01482-213844; 5 Scale Lane; 2-/3-course dinner £25/30; ☽ dinner Mon-Sat) Set in a quaint 15th-century building – the oldest surviving house in Hull – this wittily named place specialises in local produce, including Yorkshire beef and Whitby crab, prepared in traditional English style.

## Drinking & Entertainment

Come nightfall – especially at weekends – Hull can be raucous and often rowdy, especially in the streets around Trinity Sq in the Old Town, and on the strip of pubs along Beverley Rd to the north of the city centre.

**Hull Truck Theatre** ( ☎ 01482-323638; www.hulltruck .co.uk; Spring St) Home to acclaimed playwright John Godber, who made his name with gritty comedies *Bouncers* and *Up'n'Under* – he is one of the most-performed playwrights in the English-speaking world – Hull Truck presents a lively program of drama, comedy and Sunday jazz. It's just northwest of the Old Town.

**Hull New Theatre** ( ☎ 01482-226655; www .hullcc.gov.uk; Kingston Sq) A traditional regional theatre hosting popular drama, concerts and musicals.

**Welly Club** ( ☎ 01482-326131, 01482-221676; www .giveitsomewelly.com; 105-107 Beverley Rd; admission free-£5; ☽ to 2am, closed Wed & Sun) The Welly is best known these days for the regular Saturday house night Déjà Vu (www.clubdejavu .co.uk), which was voted the best club night in Yorkshire in 2007. Choose Thursdays if indie rock appeals more than house and trance.

**Minerva** ( ☎ 01482-326909; Nelson St) If you're more into pubbing than clubbing, try a pint of Timothy Taylors at this lovely, 200-year-old pub down by the waterfront; on a sunny day you can sit outdoors and watch the ships go by.

## Getting There & Away

National Express operates coaches direct from London (£24, 6½ hours, two daily) and Manchester (£15, 3¼ hours, one daily). Both National Express and bus X46 run to/from York (£7.60, 1¾ hours, one daily).

Hull has good rail links north and south to Newcastle (£43, 1½ hours, hourly, change at York) and London King's Cross (£61, 2½ hours, every two hours), and west to York (£17, 1¼ hours, every two hours) and Leeds (£16, one hour, hourly).

The ferry port is 3 miles east of the centre at King George Dock; a bus connects the train station with the ferries. For details of ferry services to Zeebrugge and Rotterdam see p998.

# BEVERLEY
pop 29,110

Handsome, unspoilt Beverley is one of the most attractive of Yorkshire towns largely on account of its magnificent minster – a rival to any cathedral in England – and the tangle of streets that lie beneath it, each brimming with exquisite Georgian and Victorian buildings.

## Orientation & Information

All the sights are a short walk from either the train or the bus station. There's a large market in the main square on Saturdays, and a smaller one on Wednesday on the square called – Wednesday Market.

**Library** ( ☎ 01482-885355; Champney Rd; ⏰ 9.30am-5pm Mon & Wed, 9.30am-7pm Tue, Thu & Fri, 9am-1pm Sat) Internet access and a small art gallery with changing exhibitions.

**Post office** (Register Sq; ⏰ 9am-5.30pm Mon-Fri, 9am-12.30pm Sat)

**Tourist office** ( ☎ 01482-391672; www.beverley.gov.uk; 34 Butcher Row; ⏰ 9.30am-5.15pm Mon-Fri & 10am-4.45pm Sat year-round, 11am-3pm Sun Jul & Aug)

**WH Smith** ( ☎ 01482-870494; 39-41 Toll Gavel; ⏰ 8.45am-5.30pm Mon-Sat, 10am-4pm Sun) Books and maps.

## Sights

One of the great glories of English religious architecture, **Beverley Minster** ( ☎ 01482-868540; www.beverleyminster.org; admission by donation; ⏰ 9am-5.30pm Mon-Sat May-Aug, 9am-5pm Sep-Oct & Mar-Apr, 9am-4pm Nov-Feb, also noon-4pm Sun year-round) is the most impressive church in the country that is not a cathedral. Construction began in 1220 – it was the third church to be built on this site, with the first dating from the 7th century – and continued for two centuries, spanning the Early English, Decorated and Perpendicular periods of the Gothic style.

The soaring lines of the exterior are imposing, but it is inside that the charm and beauty lie. The 14th-century **north aisle** is lined with original stone carvings, mostly of musicians – indeed, much of our knowledge of early musical instruments comes from these images – but also of goblins, devils and grotesque figures. Look out for the bagpipe player.

Close to the altar, the elaborate and intricate **Percy Canopy** (1340), a decorative frill above the tomb of local aristocrat Lady Eleanor Percy, is a testament to the skill of the sculptor, and the finest example of Gothic stone carving in England. In complete contrast, in the nearby

chancel, is the 10th-century Saxon **frith stool**, a plain and polished stone chair that once gave sanctuary to anyone escaping the law.

In the roof of the tower is a restored **treadwheel crane** (guided tours £4; ⏰ 11.15am & 2.15pm Mon-Sat), where workers ground around like hapless hamsters to lift the huge loads necessary to build a medieval church; access is by guided tour only.

Doomed to play second fiddle, **St Mary's Church** ( ☎ 01482-865709; admission free; ⏰ 9.30am-4.30pm Mon-Fri, 10am-4pm Sat & 2-4pm Sun Apr-Sep, 9.30am-noon & 1-4pm Mon-Fri Oct-Mar) at the other end of town was built between 1120 and 1530; the west front (early 15th century) is considered one of the finest of any parish church in England. In the north choir aisle there is a **carving** (c 1330) of a rabbit dressed as a pilgrim that is said to have inspired Lewis Carroll's White Rabbit.

## Sleeping & Eating

**Friary YHA** ( ☎ 0845 371 9004; www.yha.org.uk; Friar's Lane; dm from £14; ℗ ) In Beverley, it's the cheapest accommodation that has the best setting and location – this hostel is housed in a beautifully restored 14th-century Dominican friary mentioned in Chaucer's *The Canterbury Tales*, and is only 100m from the minster and a short walk from the train station.

**Eastgate Guest House** ( ☎ 01482-868464; 7 Eastgate; s/d £45/60) This red-brick Victorian town house offers 15 very comfortable rooms in a central location, and the sort of hearty breakfast that will see you passing up lunch in favour of a snack.

**Kings Head** ( ☎ 01482-868103; 38 Saturday Market; s/d £50/65; 🖳 ) A Georgian coaching inn that has been given a modern makeover, the Kings Head is a lively, family-friendly pub with 12 bright and cheerful rooms above the bar – the pub opens late on weekend nights, but earplugs are supplied for those who don't want to join the revelry!

**Lempicka Continental Cafe** ( ☎ 01482-866960; 13 Wednesday Market; mains £5-7) Named and themed after Polish artist Tamara de Lempicka, this stylish and sepia-toned little cafe has a 1930s deco atmosphere and serves good fair-trade coffee and tea, wicked hot chocolate, homemade cakes and daily lunch specials.

**Grant's Bistro 22** ( ☎ 01482-887624; 22 North Bar Within; 2-course lunch/dinner £13/25; ⏰ lunch Tue-Sat, dinner Mon-Sat) The top place in town is a great place for a romantic dinner *à deux*, with dark wood tables, fresh flowers and candlelight. The menu makes the most of fresh local beef, game and especially seafood.

### Getting There & Away

There are frequent bus services from Hull including numbers 121, 122, 246 and X46/X47 (30 minutes, every 20 minutes). Bus X46/X47 links Beverley with York (1¼ hours, hourly).

There are regular trains to Scarborough via Filey (£11, 1½ hours, every two hours); trains to/from Hull (£4.90, 15 minutes) run twice an hour.

# NORTH YORKSHIRE

The largest of Yorkshire's four counties – and the largest county in England – is also the most beautiful; unlike the rest of northern England, it has survived almost unscarred by the Industrial Revolution. On the contrary, North Yorkshire has always, since the Middle Ages, been about sheep and the woolly wealth that they produce.

Instead of closed-down factories, mills and mines, the man-made monuments that dot the landscape round these parts are of the magnificent variety – the great houses and wealthy abbeys that sit ruined or restored, a reminder that there was plenty of money to be made off the sheep's back.

All the same, North Yorkshire's biggest attraction is an urban one. Sure, the genteel spa town of Harrogate and the bright and breezy seaside resorts of Scarborough and Whitby have many fans, but nothing compares to the unparalleled splendour of York, England's most visited city outside London.

### Getting There & Around

The main gateway town is York, which has excellent road and rail links to the rest of the country (see p552). For countywide public-transport information, call **Traveline Yorkshire** ( ☎ 0871 200 2233; www.yorkshiretravel.net). There are various Explorer passes, and individual bus and train companies also offer their own saver schemes, so it's worth asking for advice on the best deal when you buy your ticket.

## YORK

**pop 181,100**

Nowhere in northern England says 'medieval' quite like York, a city of extraordinary cultural and historical wealth that has lost little of its preindustrial lustre. Its medieval spider's web of narrow streets is enclosed by a magnificent circuit of 13th-century walls. At its heart lies the immense, awe-inspiring minster, one of the most beautiful Gothic cathedrals in the world. The city's long history and rich heritage is woven into virtually every brick and beam, and modern, tourist-oriented York – with its myriad museums, restaurants, cafes and traditional pubs – is a carefully maintained heir to that heritage.

### Orientation

Compact and eminently walkable, York has five major landmarks to take note of: the wall enclosing the old city centre; the minster at the northern corner; Clifford's Tower at the southern end; the River Ouse that cuts the centre in two; and the train station to the west. Just to avoid the inevitable confusion, remember that round these parts *gate* means street and *bar* means gate.

### Information

**American Express** (Amex; ☎ 01904-676501; 6 Stonegate; ☺ 9am-5.30pm Mon-Fri, 9am-5pm Sat) With foreign exchange service.

**Borders** ( ☎ 01904-653300; 1-5 Davygate; ☺ 9am-9pm Mon-Sat, 11am-5pm Sun) Well-stocked bookshop.

**City Library** ( ☎ 01904-552815; Museum St; ☺ 9am-8pm Mon-Wed & Fri, 9am-5.30pm Thu, 9am-4pm Sat; per 30min £1) Internet access.

**Post office** (22 Lendal; ☺ 8.30am-5.30pm Mon & Tue, 9am-5.30pm Wed-Sat)

**Thomas Cook** ( ☎ 01904-653626; 4 Nessgate) Full-service travel agent and currency exchange.

**York District Hospital** ( ☎ 01904-631313; Wiggington Rd) A mile north of the centre.

**York Visitor Centre** ( ☎ 01904-550099; www.visityork .org; De Grey Rooms, Exhibition Sq; ☺ 9am-6pm Mon-Sat & 10am-5pm Sun Apr-Sep, 9am-5pm Mon-Sat & 10am-4pm Sun Oct-Mar) There's another branch at the train station (same hours).

### Sights

#### YORK MINSTER

Not content with being Yorkshire's most important historic building, the awe-inspiring **York Minster** ( ☎ 01904-557200; www.yorkminster.org; adult/child minster only £5.50/free, all areas £9.50/3; ☺ minster 9am-5pm Mon-Sat & noon-3.45pm Sun Apr-Oct, 9.30am-5pm Mon-Sat & noon-3.45pm Sun Nov-Mar) is also the largest medieval cathedral in all of Northern Europe. Seat of the archbishop of York, primate of England, it is second in importance only to Canterbury, home of the primate of *all* England – the separate titles were created to settle a debate over whether York or Canterbury was the true centre of the English church. But that's where Canterbury's superiority ends, for this is without doubt one of the world's most beautiful Gothic buildings. If this is the only cathedral you visit in England, you'll still walk away satisfied – so long as you have the patience to deal with the constant flow of school groups and organised tours that will invariably clog up your camera's viewfinder.

The first church on this spot was a wooden chapel built for the baptism of King Edwin of Northumbria on Easter Day 627; its location is marked in the crypt. It was replaced with a stone church that was built on the site of a Roman basilica, parts of which can be seen in the foundations. The first Norman minster was built in the 11th century; again, you can see surviving fragments in the foundations and crypt.

The present minster, built mainly between 1220 and 1480, manages to encompass all the major stages of Gothic architectural development. The transepts (1220 to 1255) were built in Early English style; the octagonal chapter house (1260 to 1290) and the nave (1291 to 1340) in the Decorated style; and the west towers, west front and central, or lantern, tower (1470 to 1472) in Perpendicular style.

You enter via the south transept, which was badly damaged by fire in 1984 but has now been fully restored. To your right is the 15th-century **choir screen** depicting the 15 kings from William I to Henry VI. Facing this is the magnificent **Five Sisters Window**, with five lancets over 15m high. This is the minster's oldest complete window; most of its tangle of coloured glass dates from around 1250. Just beyond it to the right is the 13th-century **chapter house**, a fine example of the Decorated style. Sinuous and intricately carved stonework – there are more than 200 expressive carved heads and figures – surrounds an airy, uninterrupted space.

Back in the main church, take note of the unusually tall and wide **nave**, whose aisles (to the sides) are roofed in stone in contrast to the central roof, which is wood painted to look like stone. On both sides of the nave are painted stone shields of the nobles who met with Edward II at a parliament in York. Also note the **dragon's head** projecting from the gallery – it's a crane believed to have been used to lift a font cover. There are several fine windows dating from the early 14th century, but the most impressive is the **Great West Window** (1338), with its beautiful stone tracery.

Beyond the screen and the choir is the **lady chapel** and, behind it, the **high altar**, which is dominated by the huge **Great East Window** (1405). At 23.7m by 9.4m – roughly the size of a tennis court – it is the world's largest medieval stained-glass window and the cathedral's single most important treasure. Needless to say, its epic size matches the epic theme depicted within: the beginning and end of the world as described in Genesis and the Book of Revelations.

At the heart of the minster is the massive **tower** (adult/child £4/2; ⏰ 9.30am-5pm Mon-Sat & 12.30-5pm Sun Apr-Oct, from 10am Nov-Mar), which is well worth climbing for the unparalleled views of York. You'll have to tackle a fairly claustrophobic climb of 275 steps and, most probably, a queue of people with cameras in hand. Access to the tower is near the entrance in the south transept, which is dominated by the exquisite **Rose Window** commemorating the union of the royal houses of Lancaster and York, through the marriage of Henry VII and Elizabeth of York, which ended the Wars of the Roses and began the Tudor dynasty (see p47).

Another set of stairs in the south transept leads down to the **undercroft** (adult/child £4/2; ⏰ 9.30am-5pm Mon-Sat, 12.30-5pm Sun), where you'll also find the **treasury** and the **crypt** – these should on no account be missed. In 1967 the foundations were shored up when the central tower threatened to collapse; while engineers worked frantically to save the building, archaeologists uncovered Roman and Norman remains that attest to the site's ancient history – one of the most extraordinary finds is a Roman culvert, still carrying water to the Ouse. The treasury houses 11th-century artefacts including relics from the graves of medieval archbishops. The crypt contains fragments from the Norman cathedral, including the font showing King Edwin's baptism that also marks the site of the original wooden chapel.

### AROUND THE MINSTER

Owned by the minster since the 15th century, **St William's College** ( ☎ 01904-637134; College St) is an attractive half-timbered Tudor building with elegant oriel windows built for the minster's chantry priests.

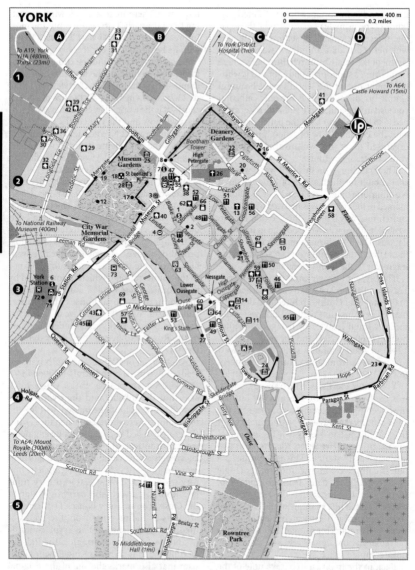

The **Treasurer's House** (NT; ☎ 01904-624247; Minster Yard; admission £5.80, house & basement £8; ⏰ 11am-4.30pm Sat-Thu Apr-Oct, 11am-3pm Sat-Thu Nov) was home to the minster's medieval treasurers. Substantially rebuilt in the 17th and 18th centuries, the 13 rooms house a fine collection of furniture and provide a good insight into 18th-century life. The house is also the setting for one of the city's most enduring ghost stories: during the 1950s a plumber working in the basement swore he saw a band of Roman soldiers walking *through* the walls; his story remains popular if unproven – but you can explore the cellar to find out.

Tucked away behind an inconspicuous gate and seemingly cut off from the

**YORKSHIRE**

rest of the town, the **Church of the Holy Trinity** (☎ 01904-613451; Goodramgate; ☻ 10am-5pm Tue-Sat May-Sep, 10am-4pm Oct-Apr) is a fantastically atmospheric old building, having survived almost unchanged for the last 200 years, with rare 17th- to 18th-century box pews, 15th-century stained glass, and wonky walls that seem to have been built without plumb line or spirit level.

**CITY WALLS**
If the weather's good, don't miss the chance to walk the **City Walls** (admission free; ☻ 8am-dusk), which follow the line of the original Roman walls – it gives a whole new perspective on the city. The full circuit is 4.5 miles (allow 1½ to two hours); if you're pushed for time, the short stretch from Bootham Bar to Monk Bar is worth doing for the views of the minster.

Start and finish in the Museum Gardens or at **Bootham Bar** (on the site of a Roman gate), where a multimedia exhibit provides some historical context, and go clockwise. Highlights include **Monk Bar**, the best-preserved medieval gate, which still has a working portcullis, and **Walmgate Bar**, England's only city gate with an intact barbican (an extended gateway to ward off uninvited guests).

At Monk Bar you'll find the **Richard III Museum** (☎ 01904-634191; www.richardiiimuseum.co.uk; admission £2.50; ☻ 9am-5pm Mar-Oct, 9.30am-4pm Nov-Feb). The museum sets out the case of the murdered 'Princes in the Tower' and invites visitors to judge whether their uncle, Richard III, killed them (see p47).

You can download a free guide to the wall walk at www.visityork.org/explore.

**SHAMBLES**
The narrow, cobbled lane known as the **Shambles** (www.yorkshambles.com), lined with 15th-century Tudor buildings that overhang so much they seem to meet above your head, is the most visited street in Europe. Quaint and picturesque it most certainly is, and it hints at what a medieval street may have looked like – if it was overrun with people told they had to buy a tacky souvenir and be back on the tour bus in 15 minutes. It takes its name from the Saxon word *shamel,* meaning 'slaughterhouse' – in 1862 there were 26 butcher shops on this one street.

**JORVIK**
Interactive multimedia exhibits aimed at 'bringing history to life' often achieve just the

---

### YORK: FROM THE BEGINNING

York – or the marshy area that preceded the first settlement – has been coveted by pretty much everyone that has ever set foot on this island. In the beginning there were the Brigantes, a local tribe that minded their own business. In AD 71 the Romans – who were spectacularly successful at minding everyone else's business – built their first garrison here for the troops fighting the poor old Brigantes. They called it Eboracum, and in time a civilian settlement prospered around what became a large fort. Hadrian used it as the base for his northern campaign, while Constantine the Great was proclaimed emperor here in AD 306 after the death of his father. After the collapse of the Roman Empire, the town was taken by the Anglo-Saxons who renamed it Eoforwic and made it the capital of the independent kingdom of Northumbria.

Enter the Christians. In 625 a Roman priest, Paulinus, arrived and managed to convert King Edwin and all his nobles. Two years later, they built the first wooden church; for most of the next century the city was a major centre of learning, attracting students from all over Europe.

The student party lasted until 866, when the next wave of invaders arrived. This time it was those marauding Vikings, who chucked everybody out and gave the town a more tongue-friendly name, Jorvik. It was to be their capital for the next 100 years, and during that time they put a rest to their pillaging ways and turned the city into an important trading port.

The next arrival was King Eadred of Wessex, who drove out the last Viking ruler in 954 and reunited Danelaw with the south, but trouble quickly followed. In 1066 King Harold II managed to fend off a Norwegian invasion-rebellion at Stamford Bridge, east of York, but his turn came at the hands of William the Conqueror a few months later at the Battle of Hastings. Willie exercised his own brand of tough love in York. After his two wooden castles were captured by an Anglo-

---

opposite, but the much-hyped **Jorvik** ( ☎ 01904-543403; www.vikingjorvik.com; Coppergate; adult/child £8.50/6, Jorvik & Dig combined £11.25/8.50; 🕙 10am-5pm Apr-Oct, 10am-4pm Nov-Mar) – the most visited attraction in town after the minster – manages to pull it off with admirable aplomb. It's a smells-and-all reconstruction of the Viking settlement that was unearthed here during excavations in the late 1970s, brought to you courtesy of a 'time-car' monorail that transports you through 9th-century Jorvik (the Viking name for York). While some of the 'you will now travel back in time' malarkey is a bit naff, it's all done with a sense of humour tied to a historical authenticity that will leave you with a pretty good idea of what life must have been like in Viking-era York. In the exhibition at the end of the monorail, look out for the **Lloyds Bank Turd** – a fossilised human stool that measures an eye-watering nine inches long and half a pound in weight, and must be the only jobbie in the world to have its own Wikipedia entry.

You can cut time spent waiting in the queue by booking your tickets online and choosing the time you want to visit – it only costs £1 extra.

### DIG

Under the same management as Jorvik, **Dig** ( ☎ 01904-543403; www.digyork.co.uk; St Saviour's Church, St Saviourgate; adult/child £5.50/5, Dig & Jorvik £11.25/8.50; 🕙 10am-5pm) cashes in on the popularity of archaeology programs on TV by giving you the chance to be an 'archaeological detective', unearthing the 'secrets' of York's distant past as well as learning something of the archaeologist's world – what they do, how they do it and so on. Aimed mainly at kids, it's much more hands-on than Jorvik, and a lot depends on how good – and entertaining – your guide is.

### CLIFFORD'S TOWER

There's precious little left of York Castle except for this evocative stone **tower** (EH; ☎ 01904-646940; admission £3; 🕙 10am-6pm Apr-Sep, 10am-5pm Oct, 10am-4pm Nov-Mar), a highly unusual figure-of-eight design built into the castle's keep after the original one was destroyed in 1190 during anti-Jewish riots. An angry mob forced 150 Jews to be locked inside the tower and the hapless victims took their own lives rather than be killed. There's not much to see inside but the views over the city are excellent.

### YORK CASTLE MUSEUM

Opposite Clifford's Tower, this excellent **museum** ( ☎ 01904-653611; www.yorkcastlemuseum .org.uk; adult/child £7.50/4, with Yorkshire Museum £9.50/6; 🕙 9.30am-5pm) contains displays of everyday

Scandinavian army, he torched the whole city (and Durham) and the surrounding countryside so that the rebels knew who was boss – this was the 'harrying of the north'. The Normans then set about rebuilding the city, including a new minster. From that moment, everything in York was rosy – except for a blip in 1137 when the whole city caught fire – and over the next 300 years it prospered through royal patronage, textiles, trade and the church.

No sooner did the church finally get built, though, than the city went into full recession. In the 15th century Hull took over as the region's main port and the textile industry moved elsewhere. Henry VIII's inability to keep a wife and the ensuing brouhaha with the church that resulted in the Reformation also hit York pretty hard. Henry did establish a branch of the King's Council here to help govern the north, and this contributed to the city's recovery under Elizabeth I and James I.

The council was abolished during Charles I's reign, but the king established his court here during the Civil War, which drew the devastating attentions of the Parliamentarians. They besieged the rabidly promonarchist York for three months in 1644, but by a fortunate accident of history their leader was a local chap called Sir Thomas Fairfax, who prevented his troops from setting York alight, thereby preserving the city and the minster.

Not much happened after that. Throughout the 18th century the city was a fashionable social centre dominated by the aristocracy, who were drawn by its culture and new racecourse. When the railway was built in 1839 thousands of people were employed in the new industries that sprung up around it, such as confectionery. These industries went into decline in the latter half of the 20th century, but by then a new invader was asking for directions at the city gates, armed only with a guidebook.

life through the centuries, with reconstructed domestic interiors and a less-than-homely prison cell where you can try out the condemned man's bed – in this case the highwayman Dick Turpin's (he was imprisoned here before being hanged in 1739). There's a bewildering array of evocative objects from the past 400 years, gathered together by a certain Dr Kirk from the 1920s onwards for fear that the items would become obsolete and disappear completely. He wasn't far wrong, which makes this place all the more interesting.

### NATIONAL RAILWAY MUSEUM

Many railway museums are the sole preserve of lone men in anoraks comparing dog-eared notebooks and getting high on the smell of machine oil, coal smoke and nostalgia. But this place is different. York's **National Railway Museum** ( ☎ 0844 815 3139; www.nrm.org.uk; Leeman Rd; admission free; 🕙 10am-6pm daily, closed 24-26 Dec) – the biggest in the world, with more than 100 locomotives – is so well presented and full of fascinating stuff that it's interesting even to folk whose eyes don't mist over at the thought of a 4-6-2 A1 Pacific class chuffing into a tunnel.

Highlights for the trainspotters among us include a replica of George Stephenson's *Rocket* of 1829, the world's first 'modern' steam locomotive; the sleek and streamlined

*Mallard,* which set the world speed record for a steam locomotive in 1938 (126 mph); a 1960s Japanese *Shinkansen* bullet train; and the world-famous *Flying Scotsman,* the first steam engine to break the 100 mph barrier (still in bits in the workshop at time of research – it should be on display by early 2009). There's also a massive 4-6-2 loco from 1949 that's been cut in half so you can see how it works.

But even if you're not a rail nerd you'll enjoy looking around the gleaming, silk-lined carriages of the royal trains used by Queen Victoria and Edward VII, or having a *Brief Encounter* moment over tea and scones at the museum's station platform cafe called, erm, Brief Encounter. Allow at least two hours to do the museum justice.

The museum is about 400m west of the train station; if you don't fancy walking you can ride the road train (adult/child £2/1) that runs every 30 minutes from 11am to 4pm between the minster and the museum.

### OTHER SIGHTS

Most of York's Roman archaeology is hidden beneath the medieval city, so the displays in the **Yorkshire Museum** ( ☎ 01904-629745; www.yorkshiremuseum.org.uk; adult/child £5/3.50, with York Castle Museum £9.50/6; 🕙 10am-5pm) are invaluable if you

---

**THE YORK PASS**

If you plan on visiting a lot of sights, you can save some money by using a **York Pass** (www.yorkpass.com; 1/2/3 days adult £24/32/36, child £14/18/22); it grants you free access to most pay-to-visit sights in town, as well as free passage on a handful of tours and discounts at a range of eateries. It's available at the tourist offices, or you can buy online.

---

want to get an idea of what Eboracum was like. There are excellent exhibits on Viking and medieval York too, including priceless artefacts such as the 8th-century Coppergate helmet, a 9th-century Anglian sword decorated with silver, and the 15th-century Middleham Jewel, an engraved gold pendant adorned with a giant sapphire.

In the peaceful **Museum Gardens** ( dawn-dusk) you can see the **Multangular Tower**, a part of the city walls that was once the western tower of the Roman garrison's defensive ramparts; the Roman stonework at the base has been built over with 13th-century additions.

On the other side of the Museum Gardens are the ruins of **St Mary's Abbey** (founded 1089), dating from 1270 to 1294. The ruined **Gatehall** was its main entrance, providing access from the abbey to the river. The adjacent **Hospitium** dates from the 14th century, although the timber-framed upper storey is a much-restored survivor from the 15th century; it was used as the abbey guesthouse. **St Mary's Lodge** was built around 1470 to provide VIP accommodation.

Adjacent to Museum Gardens on Exhibition Sq is the 19th-century **York City Art Gallery** ( 01904-551861; www.yorkartgallery.org .uk; Exhibition Sq; admission free; 10am-5pm), which includes works by Reynolds, Nash, Boudin. LS Lowry and controversial York artist William Etty, the first major British artist to specialise in painting nudes back in the 1820s.

Built between 1357 and 1361, the **Merchant Adventurers' Hall** ( 01904-654818; www.theyorkcom pany.co.uk; Fossgate; admission £2.50; 9am-5pm Mon-Thu, 9am-3.30pm Fri & Sat, noon-4pm Sun Apr-Sep, 9.30am-3.30pm Mon-Sat Oct-Mar) is one of the most handsome timber-framed buildings in Europe, and testifies to the power of the medieval guilds that controlled all foreign trade into and out of York until 1830 – a handy little monopoly.

There are displays of oil paintings and antique silver, but the building itself is the star.

If you're a fan of the Georgian style, then a visit to **Fairfax House** ( 01904-655543; www.fairfax house.co.uk; Castlegate; adult/child £5/free; 11am-4.30pm Mon-Thu & Sat, 1.30-5pm Sun, guided tours 11am & 2pm Fri) should be on your itinerary. Built in 1762 by John Carr (of Harewood House fame; see p527), this exquisitely restored town house features the best example of rococo stucco work to be found in the north of England, and houses a superb collection of Georgian furniture.

## Tours

There's a bewildering range of tours on offer, from historic walking tours to a host of ever more competitive night-time ghost tours – York is reputed to be England's most haunted city. For starters, check the tourist office's own suggestions for walking itineraries at www.visityork.org/explore.

### BOAT
**YorkBoat** ( 01904-628324; www.yorkboat.co.uk; 1hr daytime cruises adult/child £7/3.30, evening cruises £9/5.50) runs one-hour cruises on the River Ouse departing from King's Staith at 10.30am, noon, 1.30pm and 3pm (and Lendal Bridge 10 minutes later) February to November. The evening 'ghost cruise' departs from King's Staith at 6.30pm April to October.

### BUS
**York Citysightseeing** ( 01904-655585; www.city-sight seeing.com; day tickets adult/child £9/4; 9am-5pm) operates two hop-on hop-off routes calling at all the main sights; buses leave every 15 minutes from Exhibition Sq outside the main tourist office.

### WALKING
**Association of Voluntary Guides** ( 01904-640780; www.york.touristguides.btinternet.co.uk; tours 10.15am, also 2.15pm Apr-Sep & 6.45pm Jun-Aug) Free two-hour walking tours of the city starting from Exhibition Sq in front of York City Art Gallery.

**Breadcrumbs Trail** ( 01904-610676; www.end papers.co.uk; Collage Corner, 2 Norman Ct) Explore York by following the Hansel-and-Gretel-type trails laid out in the book – a novel and excellent way to keep the kids entertained. The book (£9.95) is available from bookshops and El Piano restaurant (see p550).

**Ghost Hunt of York** ( 01904-608700; www.ghost hunt.co.uk; adult/child £5/3; tours 7.30pm) Award-winning and highly entertaining 75-minute tour laced with authentic ghost stories; the kids just love this one. Begins at the Shambles, no need to book.

**Original Ghost Walk of York** ( ☎ 01904-764222; www.theoriginalghostwalkofyork.co.uk; adult/child £4/2.50; ⏱ tours 8pm) An evening of ghouls, ghosts, mystery and history courtesy of a well-established group departing from the King's Arms pub by Ouse Bridge.

**Roam'in Tours of York** ( ☎ 07931 668935; www .roamintours.co.uk) Two-hour history and specialist tours (adult/child £4/2) with a guide, or you can take a DIY audio tour (£4.50).

**Yorkwalk** ( ☎ 01904-622303; www.yorkwalk.co.uk; adult/ child £5.50/2.50) Offers a series of two-hour themed walks on an ever-growing list of themes, from the classics – Roman York, the snickelways (alleys) and City Walls – to specialised walks on chocolates and sweets, women in York, secret York and the inevitable graveyard, coffin and plague tour. Walks depart from Museum Gardens Gate on Museum St.

## Festivals & Events

For a week in mid-February, York is invaded by Vikings once again as part of the **Jorvik Viking Festival** ( ☎ 01904-643211; www.vikingjorvik .com; Coppergate), which features battle re-enactments, themed walks, markets and other bits of Viking-themed fun.

## Sleeping

Beds are tough to find midsummer, even with the inflated prices of the high season. The tourist office's accommodation booking service charges £4, which might be the best four quid you spend if you arrive without a booking.

Needless to say, prices get higher the closer to the city centre you are. However, there are plenty of decent B&Bs on the streets north and south of Bootham. Southwest of the town centre, there are B&Bs clustered around Scarcroft Rd, Southlands Rd and Bishopthorpe Rd.

It's also worth looking at serviced apartments if you're planning to stay two or three nights. **City Lets** ( ☎ 01904-652729; www.cityletsyork .co.uk) offers a good selection of places from around £90 a night for a two-person apartment – we particularly like the stylish, modern flats in the peaceful courtyard at Talbot Court on Low Petergate.

### BUDGET

**York Backpackers** ( ☎ 01904-627720; www.yorkback packers.co.uk; 88-90 Micklegate; dm/d from £14/35; 🖥 ) Housed in a Grade I Georgian building that was once home to the High Sheriff of Yorkshire, this large and well-equipped hostel

was closed for refurbishment at the time of research, but should be open for 2009.

**York YHA** ( ☎ 0845 371 9051; www.yha.org.uk; 42 Water End, Clifton; dm £18.50; 🅿 🖥 ) Originally the Rowntree (Quaker confectioners) mansion, this handsome Victorian house makes a spacious and child-friendly youth hostel, with most of the rooms being four-bed dorms. It's about a mile northwest of the city centre; there's a riverside footpath from Lendal Bridge (poorly lit so avoid after dark). Alternatively, take bus 2 from Station Ave or Museum St.

**Golden Fleece** ( ☎ 01904-625171; www.goldenfleece .yorkwebsites.co.uk; 16 Pavement; per person from £45) Four distinctive, Gothic-themed rooms (including the Shambles Room, with views over York's most famous street) above the bar in what claims to be York's most haunted pub – we've yet to see a ghost, but we liked what we did see: nice furnishings, comfortable beds and great hospitality.

### MIDRANGE

**Elliotts B&B** ( ☎ 01904-623333; www.elliottshotel.co.uk; 2 Sycamore Pl; s/d from £38/75; 🅿 🖥 ) A beautifully converted 'gentleman's residence', Elliotts leans towards the boutique end of the guesthouse market with stylish and elegant rooms, and hi-tech touches such as flat-screen TVs and free wi-fi. Excellent location, both quiet and central.

**23 St Mary's** ( ☎ 01904-622738; www.23stmarys .co.uk; 23 St Mary's; s £45-55, d £70-90; 🅿 🖥 ) A smart and stately town house with nine chintzy, country house–style rooms, some with hand-painted furniture for that rustic look, while others are decorated with antiques, lace and polished mahogany.

**Brontë House** ( ☎ 01904-621066; http://bronteguest house.yorkwebsites.co.uk; 22 Grosvenor Tce; s/d from £40/76; 🖥 ) The Brontë offers five homely en-suite rooms, each decorated differently; our favourite is the double with a carved, 19th-century sleigh bed, William Morris wallpaper and assorted bits and bobs from another era.

**Dairy Guesthouse** ( ☎ 01904-639367; www.dairyguest house.co.uk; 3 Scarcroft Rd; s/d from £55/75; 🅿 ) A lovely Victorian home that has retained many of its original features, including pine doors, stained glass and cast-iron fireplaces, but the real treat is the flower- and plant-filled courtyard that leads to the cottage-style rooms. Minimum two-night stay at weekends.

**Hedley House Hotel** ( ☎ 01904-637404; www.hed leyhouse.com; 3 Bootham Tce; s/d/f from £50/80/90; 🅿 🖥 )

Run by a couple with young children, this smart red-brick terrace-house hotel could hardly be more family-friendly – plus it has private parking at the back, and is barely five minutes' walk from the city centre through the Museum Gardens.

**Guy Fawkes** ( ☎ 0845 460 2020; www.theguyfaw keshotel.com; 25 High Petergate; s/d/ste from £65/90/200; ▣ ) Directly opposite the minster is this comfortable hotel whose premises include a cottage that is reputed to be the birthplace of Guy Fawkes himself. We're not convinced, but the cottage is still the handsomest room in the building, complete with a four-poster and lots of red velvet.

**Arnot House** ( ☎ 01904-641966; www.arnothouse york.co.uk; 17 Grosvenor Tce; r £75-80; ℗ ) With three beautifully decorated rooms (provided you're a fan of Victorian floral patterns), including one with an impressive four-poster bed and curtain-draped bath, Arnot House sports an authentically old-fashioned look that appeals to a more mature clientele – and there are no children allowed.

**Judges Lodging Hotel** ( ☎ 01904-638733; www .judgeslodgings.com; 9 Lendal; s/d from £85/100) Despite being housed in an elegant Georgian mansion that was built for a wealthy physician, this is really a place for the party crowd to crash – it's within easy reach of city-centre pubs, and the hotel's own lively courtyard bar rocks late into the night.

Also recommended:

**Alcuin Lodge** ( ☎ 01904-632222; www.alcuinlodge .com; 15 Sycamore Pl; s/d from £35/60; ▣ ) Elegant rooms in a beautiful Edwardian house, with fair-trade coffee and healthy breakfasts.

**Briar Lea Guest House** ( ☎ 01904-635061; www.briar lea.co.uk; 8 Longfield Tce; s/d from £35/60) Clean, simple rooms and a friendly welcome in a central location.

**St Raphael** ( ☎ 01904-645028; www.straphaelguest house.co.uk; 44 Queen Annes Rd; s/d from £59/68; ▣ ) Historic house with that half-timbered look, great central location and home-baked bread at breakfast.

**Monkgate Guesthouse** ( ☎ 01904-655947; www .monkgateguesthouse.com; 65 Monkgate; s/d from £40/76; ℗ ) Attractive and very child-friendly guesthouse with special family 'suite' with separate bedroom for two kids.

**TOP END**

**Mount Royale** ( ☎ 01904-628856; www.mountroyale .co.uk; The Mount; r £100-210; ℗ ) A grand, early-19th-century listed building that has been converted into a superb luxury hotel, complete with a solarium, beauty spa and outdoor heated tub and swimming pool. The rooms in the main house are gorgeous, but the best of the lot are the open-plan garden suites, reached via a corridor of tropical fruit trees and bougainvillea.

**Dean Court Hotel** ( ☎ 01904-625082; www.dean court-york.co.uk; Duncombe Pl; s/d from £104/135; ℗ ▣ ) Do not be put off by the Best Western sign – this is no charmless chain hotel, but a gracious Victorian building that once housed the York Minster clergy. You won't find a better location – right across the street from the minster (though you only get a church view from the superior rooms).

**Middlethorpe Hall** ( ☎ 01904-641241; www.mid dlethorpe.com; Bishopsthorpe Rd; s/d from £130/190; ℗ ▣ ) York's top spot is this breathtaking 17th-century country house set in 20 acres of parkland that was once the home of diarist Lady Mary Wortley Montagu. The rooms are spread between the main house, the restored courtyard buildings and three cottage suites. Although we preferred the grandeur of the rooms in the main house, every room is beautifully decorated with original antiques and oil paintings carefully collected so as to best reflect the period.

## Eating

Eating well in York is not a problem – there are plenty of fine options throughout the city centre; most pubs also serve food.

**BUDGET**

**Blake Head Vegetarian Cafe** ( ☎ 01904-623767; 104 Micklegate; mains £4-6; ◷ 9.30am-5pm Mon-Sat, 10am-5pm Sun) A bright and airy space at the back of a bookshop, filled with modern oak furniture and funky art, the Blake Head offers a tempting menu of daily lunch specials such as crispy bean burger with corn relish or hummus and roast red pepper open sandwich; great ginger and lemon cake too.

**El Piano** ( ☎ 01904-610676; www.elpiano.co.uk; 15 Grape Lane; mains £7; ◷ 11am-11pm Mon-Sat) With a menu that is 100% vegan, nut-free and gluten-free, this colourful, Hispanic-style spot is a vegetarian haven with a lovely cafe downstairs and three themed rooms upstairs: check out the Moroccan room, complete with floor cushions. Takeaways available too.

**Cafe Concerto** ( ☎ 01904-610478; 21 High Petergate; snacks £2-6, mains £9-14; ◷ 10am-10pm) Walls papered with sheet music, chilled jazz on the stereo and battered, mismatched tables and chairs set the Bohemian tone in this comforting coffee shop that serves breakfasts, bagels and cappuccinos big enough to float a boat in during the day, and a sophisticated bistro menu in the evening.

### MIDRANGE

**Betty's** ( ☎ 01904-659142; www.bettys.co.uk; St Helen's Sq; mains £6-11, afternoon tea £15; ⊙ 9am-9pm) Afternoon tea, old-school style, with white-aproned waitresses, linen tablecloths and a teapot collection ranged along the walls. House speciality is the Yorkshire Fat Rascal – a huge fruit scone smothered in melted butter.

**Little Betty's** ( ☎ 01904-622865; 46 Stonegate; mains £8-10; ⊙ 10am-5.30pm) Betty's younger sister is more demure and less frequented, but just as good; you head upstairs and back in time to what feels like the interwar years – on any given day you are bound to spot a couple of Agatha Christie lookalikes nibbling crumpets in a corner.

**Siam House** ( ☎ 01904-624677; 63a Goodramgate; mains £8-14; ⊙ dinner Mon-Sat) Delicious, authentic Thai food in about as authentic an atmosphere as you could muster up 6000km from Bangkok. The early bird, three-course special (£12, order before 6.30pm) is an absolute steal.

**La Vecchia Scuola** ( ☎ 01904-644600; 62 Low Petergate; mains £8-15; ⊙ lunch & dinner) Housed in the former York College for Girls, the faux elegant dining room – complete with self-playing grand piano – is straight out of *Growing Up Gotti*, but there's nothing fake about the food: authentic Italian cuisine served in suitably snooty style by proper Italian waiters.

**Fiesta Mexicana** ( ☎ 01904-610243; 14 Clifford St; mains £9-12; ⊙ dinner) Chimichangas, tostadas and burritos served in a relentlessly cheerful atmosphere, while students and party groups on the rip add to the fiesta; it's neither subtle nor subdued, but when is Mexican food ever so?

**Melton's Too** ( ☎ 01904-629222; 25 Walmgate; mains £9-13; ⊙ 10.30am-10.30pm Mon-Sat, 10.30am-9.30pm Sun) A comfortable, chilled out, booth-lined cafe-bar and bistro, Melton's younger brother serves everything from cake and cappuccino to tapas-style snacks to a three-course dinner of Whitby crab, braised beef with Yorkshire pudding, and local strawberries with clotted cream.

**Living Room** ( ☎ 01904-461000; www.thelivingroom .co.uk; 1 Bridge St; mains £9-15; ⊙ 10am-midnight Sun-Wed, 10am-1am Thu-Sat) The Living Room snapped up a hot location when it opened back in 2004, and has been making the most of its balcony tables overlooking the river ever since. The menu fo-

cuses on quality versions of classic dishes from around the world, from fish and chips and steak-and-ale pie to Thai fish cakes and Peking duck. Sunday brunch served noon to 6pm.

### TOP END

**Melton's** ( ☎ 01904-634341; www.meltonsrestaurant.co.uk; 7 Scarcroft Rd; mains £15-18; ⊙ lunch Tue-Sat, dinner Mon-Sat) Foodies come from far and wide to dine in one of Yorkshire's best restaurants. It tends to specialise in fish dishes but doesn't go far wrong with practically everything else, from sea trout with sorrel to marinaded wild boar. There's a good value lunch and early dinner set menu (£18.50 for two courses).

**Blue Bicycle** ( ☎ 01904-673990; www.theblue bicycle.com; 34 Fossgate; mains £15-22; ⊙ lunch & dinner) Once upon a time, this building was a well-frequented brothel; these days it serves up a different kind of fare to an equally enthusiastic crowd. French food at its finest – the occasional anti-*foie gras* protester outside the door gives a clue as to the menu – served in a romantic candlelit room makes for a top-notch dining experience.

**ourpick J Baker's** ( ☎ 01904-622688; www.jbakers .co.uk; 7 Fossgate; 2-/3-course dinner £23/27.50; ⊙ lunch & dinner) Superstar chef Jeff Baker left Leeds' Pool Court and his Michelin star to pursue his own vision of Modern British cuisine here. The ironic 70s-style colour scheme (think chocolate/oatmeal/tango) with moo-cow paintings is echoed in the unusual menu, which offers witty, gourmet interpretations of retro classics, from macaroni cheese to Bakewell tart – the 'sausage roll and beans' is actually more like French *cassoulet*, and the Crunchie bar dessert is superb.

## Drinking

With only a couple of exceptions, the best drinking holes in town are the older, traditional pubs. In recent years, the area around Ousegate and Micklegate has gone from moribund to mental, especially at weekends.

**Ackhorne** ( ☎ 01904-671421; 9 St Martin's Lane) Tucked away from beery, sloppy Micklegate, this locals' inn is as comfortable as old slippers; some of the old guys here look like they've merged with the bar. There's a pleasant beer garden at the back.

**Black Swan** ( ☎ 01904-686911; Peasholme Green) A classic black-and-white Tudor building where you'll find decent beer, friendly people and live jazz on Sundays.

**our pick Blue Bell** ( ☎ 01904-654904; 53 Fossgate)
This what a real English pub looks like – a
tiny, wood-panelled room with a smouldering
fireplace, decor (and beer and smoke stains)
dating from c 1798, a pile of ancient board
games in the corner, friendly and efficient
bar staff, and Timothy Taylor and Black Sheep
ales on tap. Bliss, with froth on top.

**Little John** ( ☎ 01904-658242; 5 Castlegate) This
historic pub – the third oldest in York – is
the city's top gay venue, with regular club
nights and other events. In 1739 the corpse
of executed highwayman Dick Turpin was
laid out in the cellar here for the public to
view at a penny a head; the pub is said to be
haunted by his ghost. Not sure what's scarier
though – the ghost story, or the Thursday-
night karaoke session…

**King's Arms** ( ☎ 01904-659435; King's Staith; lunch
about £6) York's best-known pub is a creaky
old place with a fabulous riverside location,
with tables spilling out onto the quayside – a
perfect spot for a summer's evening.

**Ye Olde Starre** ( ☎ 01904-623063; 40 Stonegate)
Licensed since 1644, this is York's oldest
pub – a warren of small rooms and a small
beer garden, with half a dozen real ales on tap.
It was used as a morgue by the Roundheads
during the Civil War, but the atmosphere's
improved a lot since then.

## Entertainment

There are a couple of good theatres in York,
and an interesting art-house cinema, but as far
as clubs are concerned, forget it: historic York
is best enjoyed without them anyway.

**York Theatre Royal** ( ☎ 01904-623568; www.yorktheatre
royal.co.uk; St Leonard's Pl) Stages well-regarded
productions of theatre, opera and dance.

**Grand Opera House** ( ☎ 01904-671818; www.grand
operahouseyork.org.uk; Clifford St) Despite the
name there's no opera here, but a wide
range of productions from live bands and
popular musicals to stand-up comics and
pantomime.

**City Screen** ( ☎ 0871 704 2054; www.picturehouses
.co.uk; 13-17 Coney St) Appealing modern building
in a converted printing works, screening both
mainstream and art-house films; nice cafe-bar
on the terrace overlooking the river.

## Shopping

Coney St, Davygate and the adjoining streets
are the hub of York's high-street shopping
scene, but the real treat for visitors are the

antique, bric-a-brac and secondhand book
shops, which are concentrated in Micklegate
and Fossgate.

**Antiques Centre** ( ☎ 01904-635888; www.antiques
centreyorkeshop.co.uk; 41 Stonegate) A Georgian town
house with a veritable maze of rooms and corridors, showcasing the wares of around 120
dealers; everything from lapel pins and snuff
boxes to oil paintings and longcase clocks.
And the house is haunted, too…

**Azendi** ( ☎ 01904-672822; www.azendi.com; 20
Colliergate) This jewellery boutique sells a range
of beautiful contemporary designs in silver,
white gold and platinum.

**Barbican Books** ( ☎ 01904-652643; www.barbican
bookshop.co.uk; 24 Fossgate) Wide range of secondhand titles, with special subjects that
include railways, aviation, and walking
and mountaineering.

**Ken Spelman Booksellers** ( ☎ 01904-624414;
www.kenspelman.com; 70 Micklegate) This fascinating shop has been selling rare, antiquarian
and secondhand books since 1910; with an
open fire crackling in the grate in winter, it's
a browser's paradise.

## Getting There & Away
### BUS

For timetable information call **Traveline
Yorkshire** ( ☎ 0871 200 2233; www.yorkshiretravel.net),
or check the computerised 24-hour information points at the train station and Rougier St.
All local and regional buses stop on Rougier
St, about 200m northeast of the train
station.

There are National Express coaches
to London (£24, 5¼ hours, four daily),
Birmingham (£25, 3¼ hours, one daily) and
Newcastle (£14, 2¾ hours, four daily).

### CAR

A car is more of a hindrance than a help in
the city centre; use one of the Park & Ride car
parks on the edge of the city. If you want to
explore the surrounding area, rental options
include **Europcar** ( ☎ 01904-656161), by platform
1 in the train station (which also rents bicycles and stores luggage for £4 per bag); and
**Hertz** ( ☎ 01904-612586) near platform 3 in the
train station.

### TRAIN

York is a major railway hub with frequent direct services to Birmingham (£40, 2¼ hours),
Newcastle (£25, one hour), Leeds (£10, 25

minutes), London's King's Cross (£103, two hours), Manchester (£20, 1½ hours) and Scarborough (£12, 50 minutes).

There are also trains to Cambridge (£67, 2¾ hours), changing at Peterborough.

## Getting Around

York is easy to get around on foot – you're never really more than 20 minutes from any of the major sights.

### BICYCLE

The tourist offices have a useful free map showing York's cycle routes. If you're energetic you could pedal out to Castle Howard (15 miles), Helmsley and Rievaulx Abbey (12 miles) and Thirsk (a further 12 miles), and then catch a train back to York. There's also a section of the Trans-Pennine Trail cycle path from Bishopthorpe in York to Selby (15 miles) along the old railway line.

You can rent bikes from **Bob Trotter** ( ☎ 01904-622868; 13 Lord Mayor's Walk; ☺ 9am-5.30pm Mon-Sat, 10am-4pm Sun), outside Monk Bar; and **Europcar** ( ☎ 01904-656161; ☺ 8am-8.30pm Mon-Sat, 9am-8.30pm Sun), by platform 1 in the train station; both charge around £10 a day.

### BUS

Local bus services are operated by **First York** ( ☎ 01904-622992; www.firstgroup.com); single fares range from £1 to £2.50, and a day pass valid on all local buses is £3.50 (available at Park & Ride car parks).

### TAXI

**Station Taxis** ( ☎ 01904-623332) has a kiosk outside the train station.

## AROUND YORK
## Castle Howard

Stately homes may be two a penny in England, but you'll have to try pretty damn hard to find one as breathtakingly stately as **Castle Howard** ( ☎ 01653-648333; www.castlehoward .co.uk; adult/child house & grounds £10.50/6.50, grounds only £8/5; ☺ house 11am-4.30pm, grounds 10am-4.30pm Mar-Oct & 1st three weeks of Dec), a work of theatrical grandeur and audacity set in the rolling Howardian Hills. This is one of the world's most beautiful buildings, instantly recognisable from its starring role in *Brideshead Revisited* – which has done its popularity no end of good since the TV series first aired in the early 1980s.

When the earl of Carlisle hired his pal Sir John Vanbrugh to design his new home in 1699, he was hiring a bloke who had no formal training and was best known as a playwright; luckily Vanbrugh hired Nicholas Hawksmoor, who had worked for Christopher Wren, as his clerk of works – not only would Hawksmoor have a big part to play in the house's design but the two would later work wonders with Blenheim Palace (p251).

If you can, try to visit on a weekday, when it's easier to find the space to appreciate this hedonistic marriage of art, architecture, landscaping and natural beauty. As you wander about the peacock-haunted grounds, views open up over the hills, Vanbrugh's playful Temple of the Four Winds and Hawksmoor's stately mausoleum, but the great baroque house with its magnificent central cupola is an irresistible visual magnet. Inside, it is full of treasures, such as the chapel's Pre-Raphaelite stained glass.

Castle Howard is 15 miles northeast of York, off the A64. There are several organised tours from York – check with the tourist office for up-to-date schedules. Yorkshire Coastliner bus 840 (40 minutes from York, one daily) links Leeds, York, Castle Howard, Pickering and Whitby.

## THIRSK
### pop 9100

Monday and Saturday are market days in handsome Thirsk, which has been trading on its tidy, attractive streets and cobbled square since the Middle Ages. Thirsk's brisk business was always helped by its key position on two medieval trading routes: the old drove road between Scotland and York, and the route linking the Yorkshire Dales with the coast. That's all in the past, though: today, the town is all about the legacy of James Herriot, the wry Yorkshire vet adored by millions of fans of *All Creatures Great and Small*.

Thirsk does a good job as the real-life Darrowby of the books and TV series, and it should, as the real-life Herriot was in fact local vet Alf Wight, whose house and surgery has been dipped in 1940s aspic and turned into the incredibly popular **World of James Herriot** ( ☎ 01845-524234; www.worldofjamesherriot .org; 23 Kirkgate; adult/child £5.50/3.90; ☺ 10am-5pm Easter-Oct, 11am-4pm Nov-Easter), an excellent museum full of Wight-related artefacts, a video documentary of his life and a re-creation of the TV-show sets.

Thirsk's **tourist office** ( ☎ 01845-522755; thirsk@ytbtic.co.uk; 49 Market Pl; ☿ 10am-5pm Easter-Oct, 11am-4pm Nov-Easter) is on the main square.

Thirsk is well served by trains on the line between York and Middlesbrough; however, the train station is a mile west of town and the only way to cover that distance is on foot or by taxi ( ☎ 01845-522473). There are also frequent daily buses from York (45 minutes).

## AROUND THIRSK

Nestled in the secluded valley of the River Skell lie two of Yorkshire's most beautiful attractions – an absolute must on any northern itinerary. The beautiful and strangely obsessive water gardens of the **Studley Royal** estate were built in the 19th century to enhance the picturesque ruins of 12th-century **Fountains Abbey** (NT; ☎ 01765-608888; www.fountainsabbey.org.uk; adult/child £7.90/4.20; ☿ 10am-5pm Mar-Oct, 10am-4pm Nov-Feb). Together they present a breathtaking picture of pastoral elegance and tranquillity that have made them a Unesco World Heritage Site, and the most visited of all the National Trust's pay-in properties.

After falling out with the Benedictines of York in 1132, a band of rebel monks came here to what was then a desolate and unyielding patch of land to establish their own monastery. Struggling to make it on their own, they were formally adopted by the Cistercians in 1135; by the middle of the 13th century the new abbey had become the most successful Cistercian venture in the country. It was during this time that most of the abbey was built, including the church's nave, transepts and eastern end, and the outlying buildings (the church tower was added in the late 15th century).

After the Dissolution (p47) the abbey's estate was sold into private hands and between 1598 and 1611 Fountains Hall was built using stone from the abbey ruins. The hall and ruins were united with the Studley Royal estate in 1768.

Studley Royal was owned by John Aislabie (once Chancellor of the Exchequer), who dedicated his life to creating the park after a financial scandal saw him expelled from parliament. The main house of Studley Royal burnt down in 1946 but the superb landscaping, with its serene artificial lakes, survives almost unchanged from the 18th century.

Fountains Abbey is 4 miles west of Ripon off the B6265. Public transport is limited to shuttle bus 139 from Ripon on Sundays and bank holidays only (10 minutes, hourly), from mid-May to October.

---

### BLACK SHEEP OF THE BREWING FAMILY

The village of Masham is a place of pilgrimage for connoisseurs of real ale – it's the frothing fountainhead of Theakston's beers, which have been brewed here since 1827. The company's most famous brew, Old Peculier, takes its name from the Peculier of Masham, a parish court established in medieval times to deal with religious offences, including drunkenness, brawling, and 'taking a skull from the churchyard and placing it under a person's head to charm them to sleep'. The court seal is used as the emblem of Theakston Ales.

To the horror of real ale fans, and after much falling out among members of the Theakston family, the Theakston Brewery was taken over by much-hated megabrewer Scottish and Newcastle in 1987. Five years later, Paul Theakston – who had refused to go and work for S&N, and was determined to keep small-scale, artisan brewing alive – bought an old maltings building in Masham and set up his own brewery, which he called Black Sheep. He managed to salvage all kinds of traditional brewing equipment, including six Yorkshire 'stone square' brewing vessels, and was soon running a successful enterprise.

History came full circle in 2004 when Paul's four brothers took the Theakston brewery back into family ownership. Both breweries now have visitor centres – the **Black Sheep Brewery** ( ☎ 01765-680100; ☿ 10.30am-4.30pm Sun-Thu, 10.30am-11pm Fri & Sat) and the **Theakston Brewery** ( ☎ 01765-680000; www.theakstons.co.uk; ☿ 10.30am-5.30pm Jul & Aug, 10.30am-4.30pm May, Jun, Sep & Oct); both offer guided tours (best booked in advance).

Masham (pronounced 'massam') is 9 miles northwest of Ripon on the A6108 to Leyburn. Bus 159 from Ripon (25 minutes, every two hours Monday to Saturday) and the Fountains Flyer bus 802 from Leeds (2¾ hours, one daily, Sundays and bank holidays only, late May to late September) stop at Masham.

# HARROGATE

**pop 85,128**

The quintessential Victorian spa town, prim, pretty Harrogate has long been associated with a certain kind of old-fashioned Englishness, the kind that seems to be the preserve of retired army chaps and formidable dowagers who, inevitably, will always vote Tory. They come to Harrogate to enjoy the formidable flower shows and gardens that fill the town with magnificent displays of colour, especially in spring and autumn. It is fitting that the town's most famous visitor was Agatha Christie, who fled here incognito in 1926 to escape her broken marriage.

Yet this picture of Victoriana redux is not quite complete. While it's undoubtedly true that Harrogate remains a firm favourite of visitors in their golden years, the New Britain makeover has left its mark in the shape of smart new hotels and trendy eateries catering to the boom in Harrogate's newest trade – conferences. All those dynamic young sales and marketing guns have to eat and sleep somewhere…

## Orientation & Information

Harrogate is almost surrounded by parks and gardens, notably the 80-hectare **Stray** in the south. The train and bus stations are right in the centre of town, a few minutes' walk from the main sights.

The **tourist office** ( ☎ 0845 389 3223; www.harrogate .gov.uk/tourism; Crescent Rd; ☉ 9am-6pm Mon-Sat & 10am-1pm Sun Apr-Sep, 9am-5pm Mon-Fri & 9am-4pm Sat Oct-Mar) is in the Royal Baths Assembly Rooms; staff can tell you about free historical walking tours offered daily from Easter to October.

## Sights & Activities

### THE WATERS

The ritual of 'taking the waters' as a health cure became fashionable in the 19th century and peaked during the Edwardian era in the years before WWI. Charles Dickens visited Harrogate in 1858 and described it as 'the queerest place, with the strangest people in it, leading the oddest lives of dancing, newspaper reading and dining'; sounds quite pleasant, really.

You can learn all about the history of Harrogate as a spa town in the ornate **Royal Pump Room Museum** ( ☎ 01423-556188; Crown Pl; admission £3; ☉ 10am-5pm Mon-Sat, 2-5pm Sun Apr-Oct, to 4pm Nov-Mar), built in 1842 over the most famous of the sulphur springs. It gives an insight into how the phenomenon shaped the town and records the illustrious visitors that it attracted; at the end you get the chance to sample the spa water, if you dare.

If drinking the water isn't enough, you can immerse yourself in it at the fabulously tiled **Turkish Baths** ( ☎ 01423-556746; www.harrogate .co.uk/turkishbaths; Parliament St; admission £11.50-17.20; ☉ 9am-9pm) nearby. This mock Moorish facility is gloriously Victorian and offers a range of watery delights – hot rooms, steam rooms, plunge pools and so on; a visit should last around an hour and a half. There's a complicated schedule of opening hours that are by turns single sex and mixed pairs – call or check online for details.

### GARDENS

A huge green thumbs-up to Harrogate's gardeners; the town has some of the most beautiful public gardens in England. The **Valley Gardens** are overlooked by the vast, glass-domed **Sun Pavilion**, built in 1933. The nearby bandstand houses concerts on Sunday afternoons from June to August. Flower-fanatics should make for the **Harlow Carr Botanical Gardens** ( ☎ 01423-565418; www.rhs.org.uk; Crag Lane, Beckwithshaw; adult/child £6.50/2.20; ☉ 9.30am-6pm Mar-Oct, 9.30am-4pm Nov-Feb), the northern showpiece of the Royal Horticultural Society. The gardens are 1.5 miles southwest of town; to get here, take the B6162 Otley Rd or walk through the Pine Woods southwest of the Valley Gardens.

## Festivals & Events

The year's main event is the immense **Spring Flower Show** ( ☎ 0870 758 3333; www.flowershow.org.uk), held in late April, followed in late September by the **Autumn Flower Show**. Both take place at the Great Yorkshire Showground; admission prices range from £10 to £14.

If prize delphiniums aren't your thing, there's a lot more fun to be had at the **Great Yorkshire Show** ( ☎ 01423-541000; www.greatyork shireshow.org; adult/child £18/8), a three-day exhibition staged in mid-July by the Yorkshire Agricultural Society (also held at the showground). It's a real treat, with all manner of primped and prettified farm animals competing for prizes, and entertainment ranging from show-jumping and falconry to cookery demonstrations and hot-air balloon rides.

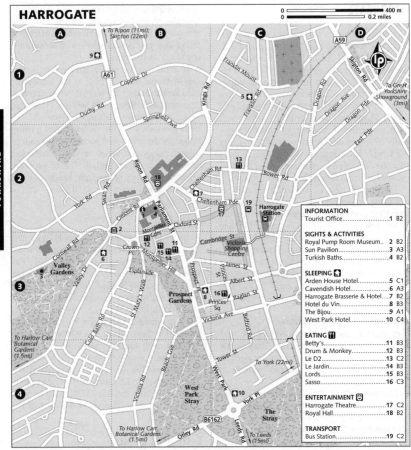

**HARROGATE**

## Sleeping

**Cavendish Hotel** ( ☎ 01423-509637; cavendishhotel@
gmail.com; 3 Valley Dr; s/d from £55/65, 4-poster £90) There
are several guesthouses ranged along tree-
lined Valley Dr, a quiet and peaceful corner of
town that is only a short walk from the centre.
The Cavendish is one of the best – the rooms
are homely but show a touch of style, and
many have a view over Valley Gardens.

**Arden House Hotel** ( ☎ 01423-509224; www
.ardenhousehotel.co.uk; 69-71 Franklin Rd; s/d from £45/75;
P 🖳 ) This grand old Edwardian house has
been given a modern makeover with stylish
contemporary furniture, Egyptian cotton
bed linen and posh toiletries, but still retains
some lovely period details including tiled,
cast-iron fireplaces. Attentive service, good

breakfasts and a central location are the icing
on the cake.

**West Park Hotel** ( ☎ 01423-524471; www.westpark
hotel.co.uk; 19 West Park; d from £75; P ) Not quite sure
what's going on with the decor here – old-
style Harrogate having a go at contemporary
but not quite pulling it off; a bit like your
dad trying to dance to house music. Still, the
location is lovely – the best rooms have views
over the park – and the staff are really friendly
and helpful.

**The Bijou** ( ☎ 01423-567974; www.thebijou.co.uk; 17
Ripon Rd; s/d from £75/85; P 🖳 ) Bijou by name
and bijou by nature, this Victorian villa sits
firmly at the boutique end of the B&B spectrum – you can tell that a lot of thought and
care has gone into the design of the place.

The husband-and-wife team who own the place make fantastic hosts, warm and helpful but unobtrusive.

**Harrogate Brasserie & Hotel** ( ☎ 01423-505041; www.harrogatebrasserie.co.uk; 28-30 Cheltenham Pde; s/d from £60/90) Stripped pine, leather armchairs and subtle colour combinations make this one of Harrogate's most appealing places to stay. The cheerful cosy accommodation is complemented by an excellent restaurant and bar, with live jazz Wednesday to Sunday evenings.

**Hotel Du Vin** ( ☎ 01423-856800; www.hotelduvin.com; Prospect Pl; r/ste from £125/165; P ⬚ ) An extremely stylish boutique hotel that has made the other lodgings in town sit up and take notice. The loft suites with their exposed oak beams, hardwood floors and designer bathrooms are the nicest rooms we've seen in town, but even the standard rooms are spacious and very comfortable, each with a trademark huge bed draped in soft Egyptian cotton.

## Eating

**Le Jardin** ( ☎ 01423-507323; www.lejardin-harrogate.com; 7 Montpellier Parade; mains £8; ☽ lunch & dinner Tue-Fri, 10am-8pm Sat, noon-3pm Sun) This cool little bistro has a snug, intimate atmosphere, especially in the evening when candlelight adds a romantic glow. During the day locals throng the tables to enjoy great salads, sandwiches and homemade ice cream.

**Betty's** ( ☎ 01423-502746; www.bettys.co.uk; 1 Parliament St; mains £8-10, afternoon tea £15; ☽ 9am-9pm) A classic tearoom in a classic location with views across the park, Betty's is a local institution. It was established in 1919 by a Swiss immigrant confectioner who took the wrong train, ended up in Yorkshire and decided to stay. Exquisite home-baked breads, scones and cakes, quality tea and coffee, and a downstairs gallery lined with art nouveau marquetry designs of Yorkshire scenes commissioned by the founder in the 1930s.

**Drum & Monkey** ( ☎ 01423-502650; 5 Montpellier Gardens; mains £8-12; ☽ lunch & dinner Mon-Sat) This is a classic seafood restaurant of the old school, with traditional decor of mahogany and polished brass buffed up like the medals on a retired major's blazer, and a menu that would not have looked out of place in the 1930s, ranging from lobster bisque and asparagus with hollandaise, to Dover sole *bonne femme* and hearty seafood pie.

**Le D2** ( ☎ 01423-502700; 7 Bower Rd; 2-course lunch/dinner £9/15; ☽ lunch & dinner Tue-Sat) This bright and airy bistro is always busy, with diners drawn back again and again by the relaxed atmosphere, warm and friendly service, and a menu that takes fresh local produce and adds a twist of French sophistication.

**Lords** ( ☎ 01423-508762; 8 Montpellier St; mains lunch £10, dinner £15-18; ☽ lunch & dinner Tue-Sat, noon-8.30pm Sun) An elegant little place with a cosy, clubbish atmosphere enhanced by prints of cricket scenes and a collection of autographed cricket bats. The menu runs to Harrogate versions of classic comfort food – this is not just any burger, this is a Yorkshire venison and Ribblesdale cheese burger…

**Sasso** ( ☎ 01423-508838; 8-10 Princes Sq; mains £14-21; ☽ lunch & dinner Tue-Sat, dinner Mon) A top-class basement trattoria where homemade pasta is served in a variety of traditional and authentic ways, along with a host of other Italian specialities.

## Entertainment

The town has two main entertainment venues – **Harrogate Theatre** ( ☎ 01423-502116; www.harrogatetheatre.com; Oxford St), a historic Victorian building dating from 1900, and the **Royal Hall** ( ☎ 0845 130 8840; www.royalhall.co.uk; Ripon Rd), a gorgeous Edwardian theatre that is now part of the Harrogate International conference centre. Both stage a varied program of drama, comedy and popular musicals.

## Getting There & Away

Trains run to Harrogate from Leeds (£6.20, 40 minutes, about half-hourly) and York (£6.20, 45 minutes, hourly).

National Express coaches 561 and 381 run from Leeds (£3.40, 40 minutes, five daily). Bus 36 comes from Ripon (30 minutes, every 20 minutes), continuing to Leeds.

## SCARBOROUGH
pop 57,649

Scarborough is where the whole tradition of English seaside holidays began. And it began earlier than you might think – it was in the 1660s that a book promoting the medicinal properties of a local spring (now the site of Scarborough Spa) pulled in the first flood of visitors. A belief in the health-giving effects of sea-bathing saw wheeled bathing carriages appear on the beach in the 1730s, and with the arrival of the railway in 1845 Scarborough's fate was sealed. By the time the 20th century rolled in it was all donkey rides, fish and chips, seaside rock and boat trips round the bay, with saucy postcards, kiss-me-quick hats and blokes from Leeds with knotted hankies on their heads just a decade or two away.

Like all British seaside towns, Scarborough has suffered a downturn in recent decades as people jetted off to the Costa Blanca on newly affordable foreign holidays, but things are looking up again. The town retains all the trappings of the classic seaside resort, but is in the process of reinventing itself as a centre for the creative arts and digital industries – the Victorian spa is being redeveloped as a conference and entertainment centre, a former museum has been converted into studio space

for artists, and there's free, open-access wi-fi along the promenade beside the harbour – an area being developed as the town's bar, cafe and restaurant quarter.

As well as the usual seaside attractions, Scarborough offers excellent coastal walking, a new geology museum, one of Yorkshire's most impressively sited castles, and a renowned theatre that is the home base of popular playwright Alan Ayckbourn, whose plays always premier here.

## Orientation

Scarborough is built around a high headland with the castle perched on top, and beaches to its north and south. The train station and town centre are on a plateau above the

### SCARBOROUGH

| | | |
|---|---|---|
| 0 | | 500 m |
| 0 | | 0.3 miles |

**INFORMATION**
Laundrette..........................1 B2
Post Office..........................2 B3
Scarborough Library............3 B3
Tourist Office.......................4 B3
Waterstone's........................5 B3

**SIGHTS & ACTIVITIES**
Grave of Anne Brontë..........6 C2
Roman Signal Station...........7 D2
Rotunda Museum................8 B3
St Mary's Church.................9 C2
Scarborough Castle............10 D2
Secretspot Surf Shop..........11 B3

**SLEEPING**
Beiderbecke's Hotel...........12 B3
Crown Spa Hotel...............13 B4
Hotel Helaina....................14 B2
Interludes.........................15 C2
Windmill Hotel..................16 A3

**EATING**
Bonnet's...........................17 B3
Golden Grid.......................18 C2
Lanterna...........................19 C2
Marmalade's.................(see 12)
Roasters...........................20 B3

**ENTERTAINMENT**
Scarborough Spa................21 C4
Stephen Joseph Theatre....22 B3

South Beach, which has the harbour at its north end.

Most of the resort activity – bars, restaurants, amusements, funfair – are concentrated on Sandside, beside the harbour; the North Beach is less frantic. The walk from train station to harbour is about 15 minutes.

## Information

**Laundrette** ( ☎ 01723-375763; 48 North Marine Rd)

**Post office** (11-15 Aberdeen Walk; 9am-5.30pm Mon-Fri, 9am-12.30pm Sat)

**Scarborough Library** ( ☎ 01723-383400; Vernon Rd; 9.30am-5.30pm Mon-Fri, 9.30am-noon Sat; per 30min £1) Internet access.

**Tourist office** ( ☎ 01723-383637; www.discoveryork shirecoast.com; Brunswick Shopping Centre, Westborough; 9.30am-5.30pm daily Easter-Oct, 10am-4.30pm Mon-Sat Nov-Easter)

**Waterstone's** ( ☎ 01723-500414; 97-98 Westborough; 9am-5.30pm Mon-Sat, 10am-4pm Sun) Books and maps.

## Sights & Activities

Scarborough is not exclusively about sandcastles, seaside rock and walks along the prom. The massive medieval keep of **Scarborough Castle** (EH; ☎ 01723-372451; admission £4; 10am-6pm Apr-Sep, 10am-5pm Thu-Mon Oct, 10am-4pm Thu-Mon Nov-Mar) occupies a commanding position atop its headland – legend has it that Richard I loved the views so much his ghost just keeps coming back. Take a walk out to the edge of the cliffs where you can see the 2000-year-old remains of a **Roman signal station** – the Romans appreciated this viewpoint too.

Below the castle is **St Mary's Church** ( ☎ 01723-500541; Castle Rd; 10am-4pm Mon-Fri, 1-4pm Sun May-Sep), dating from 1180; in the little cemetery across the lane from the church is the grave of Anne Brontë.

The newly restored **Rotunda Museum** ( ☎ 01723-374839; www.rotundamuseum.co.uk; Vernon Rd; adult/child £4.50/free; 10am-5pm Tue-Sun) is dedicated to seaside rock of a different kind – the coastal geology of northeast Yorkshire, which has yielded many of Britain's most important dinosaur fossils. There's also a gallery illustrating how geology has shaped Scarborough's history and landscape.

Of all the family-oriented attractions on the waterfront, the best of the lot is the **Sea Life Centre & Marine Sanctuary** ( ☎ 01723-373414; www.sealife.co.uk; Scalby Mills; adult/child £12.95/9.50; 10am-6pm) overlooking North Bay. You can see coral reefs, turtles, octopuses, sea horses and many other fascinating sea creatures, though the biggest draw is the seal rescue centre. It's at the far north end of North Beach; a **miniature railway** ( ☎ 01723-260004; www.nbr.org.uk; 10.30am-4.45pm Apr-Sep) runs the 0.75-mile route (return fare £2.80).

There are some decent waves on England's northeast coast, which support a growing surfing scene. **Scarborough Surf School** ( ☎ 01723-585585; www.scarboroughsurfschool.co.uk; Cayton Bay) is based 4 miles south of town, but you can get information and advice from the **Secretspot Surf Shop** ( ☎ 01723-500467; 4 Pavilion Tce) near the train station.

## Sleeping

In Scarborough, if a house has four walls and a roof it'll offer B&B; competition is intense and in such a tough market multinight-stay special offers are two a penny, which means that single-night rates are the highest of all.

### BUDGET

**Scalby Close Caravan Park** ( ☎ 01723-366212; www.scalbyclosepark.co.uk; Burniston Rd; sites £18; Easter-Oct) A small park about 2 miles north of town with plenty of pitches for vans and tents (rate includes car and up to four people) as well as fixed holiday caravans for rent (£160 to £350 per week). Take bus 12 or 21.

**Scarborough YHA** ( ☎ 0845 371 9657; www.yha.org.uk; Burniston Rd; dm £18; P ) This idyllic hostel set in a converted 17th-century water mill has comfortable four- and six-bed dorms and family-friendly facilities. It's 2 miles north of town along the A166 to Whitby; take bus 3, 12 or 21.

**Brambles Lodge Guest House** ( ☎ 01723-374613; www.brambleslodgeguesthouse.co.uk; 156-158 Filey Rd; s/d from £30/50; P ) Set in a modern house on the A165 to Filey about 1.5 miles south of the town centre, this B&B offers bright and cheerful rooms, a warm welcome and excellent value. You can take a bus into town or walk there in 20 minutes or so.

### MIDRANGE

**Interludes** ( ☎ 01723-360513; www.interludeshotel.co.uk; 32 Princess St; s/d from £30/54; ) Owners Ian and Bob have a flair for the theatrical and have brought it to bear with visible success on this lovely, gay-friendly Georgian home plastered with old theatre posters, prints and other thespian mementos. The individually decorated rooms are given to colourful flights of fancy that can't but put a smile on your face. Children, alas, are not welcome.

**Windmill Hotel** ( ☎ 01723-372735; www.windmill-hotel.co.uk; Mill St; s/d from £32/64; **P** ) Quirky doesn't begin to describe this place – a beautifully converted 18th-century windmill in the middle of town. There are tight-fitting but comfortable doubles around a cobbled courtyard, but try to get the balcony flat (£85 to £100 a night) in the upper floors of the windmill itself, with great views from the wraparound balcony.

**Hotel Helaina** ( ☎ 01723-375191; www.hotelhelaina.co.uk; 14 Blenheim Tce; r £54-84; **▣** ) Location, location, location – you'd be hard pushed to find a place with a better sea view than this elegant guesthouse perched on the cliff top overlooking North Beach. And the view inside the rooms is pretty good too, with sharply styled contemporary furniture and cool colours. The standard rooms are a touch on the small side – it's well worth splashing out on the deluxe room with the bay window.

**ourpick** **Beiderbecke's Hotel** ( ☎ 01723-365766; www.beiderbeckes.com; 1-3 The Crescent; s/d from £65/105; **P** **▣** ) Set in an elegant Georgian terrace in the middle of town, on a quiet street overlooking gardens, this hotel combines stylish and spacious rooms with attentive but friendly and informal service. It's not quite boutique, but with its intriguing modern art on the walls and snazzily coloured toilet seats it's heading in that direction.

### TOP END

**Crown Spa Hotel** ( ☎ 0800 072 6134; www.crownspahotel.com; Esplanade; s/d from £75/130; **P** **▣** ) This grand old hotel opened its doors in 1845 and has been going strong ever since, changing constantly with the times. After a recent refurbishment it's more opulent than ever, offering superb sea views and a luxurious spa.

**Wrea Head Country House Hotel** ( ☎ 01723-378211; www.englishrosehotels.co.uk; Barmoor La, Scalby; s/d £80/135; **P** ) This fabulous country house about 2 miles north of the centre is straight out of *Remains of the Day*. The 20 individually styled bedrooms have canopied, four-poster beds, plush fabrics and delicate furnishings, while the leather couches in the bookcased, wood-heavy lounges are tailor-made for important discussions over cigars and expensive brandy.

## Eating

**Bonnet's** ( ☎ 01723-361033; 38-40 Huntriss Row; mains £4-7; ☒ 9am-5pm Mon-Sat, 11am-4pm Sun) One of the oldest cafes in town, open since 1880, Bonnet's serves delicious cakes and light meals in a quiet courtyard, and sells handmade chocolates in the adjoining shop.

**Roasters** ( ☎ 07971 808549; 8 Aberdeen Walk; mains £5; ☒ 9am-5pm) A funky coffee shop with chunky pine tables, brown leather chairs and an excellent range of freshly ground coffees. There's a juice and smoothie bar too, and the lunch menu includes ciabatta sandwiches, salads and jacket potatoes.

**Golden Grid** ( ☎ 01723-360922; 4 Sandside; mains £7-12; ☒ 11am-11pm) Whoever said fish and chips can't be eaten with dignity hasn't tried the Golden Grid, a sit-down fish restaurant that has been serving the best cod in Scarborough since 1883. The setting is staunchly traditional, with starched white tablecloths and starched white aprons, as is the menu – as well as fish and chips there's steak pie, mushy peas and Yorkshire pud with onion gravy.

**Marmalade's** ( ☎ 01723-365766; 1-3 The Crescent; mains £12-16; ☒ noon-9.30pm) The stylish brasserie in Beiderbecke's Hotel – cream and chocolate colours, art with a musical theme, and cool jazz in the background – has a menu that adds a gourmet twist to traditional dishes: steak and ale pie with pease pudding, roast rack of lamb with forest berries, sea bass stuffed with lemon and herbs.

**Lanterna** ( ☎ 01723-363616; 33 Queen St; mains £13-19; ☒ dinner Mon-Sat) A snug, old-fashioned Italian trattoria that specialises in fresh local seafood and classic dishes from the old country – as well as sourcing Yorkshire produce, the chef imports delicacies direct from Italy, including truffles, olive oil, prosciutto and a range of cheeses.

## Entertainment

**Stephen Joseph Theatre** ( ☎ 01723-370541; www.sjt.uk.com; Westborough) Stages a good range of drama – renowned chronicler of middle-class mores Alan Ayckbourn premieres his plays here.

**Scarborough Spa** ( ☎ 01723-376774; www.scarboroughspa.co.uk; South Bay) The revitalised spa complex stages a wide range of entertainment, especially in the summer months – orchestral performances, variety shows, popular musicals and old-fashioned afternoon tea dances.

## Getting There & Away

Bus 128 goes along the A170 from Helmsley to Scarborough (1½ hours, hourly) via Pickering, while buses 93 and X93 come from Whitby (one hour, every 30 minutes) via Robin Hood's Bay (hourly). Bus 843 arrives from Leeds (£16, 2¾ hours, hourly) via York.

There are regular trains from Hull (£12, 1½ hours, hourly), Leeds (£20, one hour 20 minutes, hourly) and York (£15, 50 minutes, hourly).

## Getting Around

Tiny, Victorian-era funicular railways rattle up and down Scarborough's steep cliffs between town and beach daily from February till the end of October (60p). Local buses leave from the western end of Westborough and outside the train station.

For a taxi call ☎ 361009; £5 should get you to most places in town.

# NORTH YORK MOORS NATIONAL PARK

Inland from the North Yorkshire coast, the wild and windswept North York Moors rise in isolated splendour. Three-quarters of all the world's heather moorland is to be found in Britain, and this is the largest expanse in all of England. Ridge-top roads climb up from lush green valleys to the bleak open moors where weatherbeaten stone crosses mark the line of ancient drove roads, and where in summer the heather blooms in billowing drifts of purple haze.

This is classic walking country, and the moors are criss-crossed with footpaths old and new, and dotted with pretty, flower-bedecked villages. The national park is also home to one of Britain's most picturesque steam railways.

## Orientation & Information

The main gateway towns are Helmsley and Pickering in the south, and Whitby in the northeast – all have good tourist offices. The national park also has visitor centres at Sutton Bank, Danby and Robin Hood's Bay; see also www.visithemoors.co.uk.

The park produces the very useful *Moors & Coast* visitor guide, available at tourist offices, hotels etc, with information on things to see and do. The OS Landranger 1:50,000 map, sheet 94, covers most of the national park.

## Activities

Tourist offices stock an excellent range of walking leaflets (around 60p to 75p), as well as more comprehensive walking and cycling guidebooks.

### CYCLING

Once you've climbed up onto the escarpment, the North York Moors make fine cycling country, with quiet lanes through the valleys and scenic roads over the hills. There's also a great selection of off-road tracks for mountain bikes (see www.mtb-routes.co.uk/northyorkmoors).

### WALKING

There are more than 1400 miles of footpaths criss-crossing the moors. The most scenic walking areas are along the western escarpment and the cliff tops on the coast, while the green and tranquil valleys offer relaxed rambling.

The famous **Coast to Coast walk** (p518) passes through the park, and the **Cleveland Way** covers three sides of the moors' outer rim on its 109-mile, nine-day route from Helmsley to Filey.

The **Cook Country Walk**, named after explorer Captain Cook who was born and raised in this area, links several monuments commemorating his life. This 40-mile, three-day route follows the flanks of the Cleveland Hills from Marton (near Middlesbrough) to Staithes, then south along the coast to Whitby.

## Getting There & Around

From the south, there are regular buses from York (17 miles outside the park) to Helmsley, Pickering, Scarborough and Whitby. From the north, head for Middlesbrough then take the Esk Valley railway line, which stops at Danby, Grosmont and several other villages in the park. The **North Yorkshire Moors Railway** (NYMR; see p565) runs north–south across the park from Pickering to Grosmont. Using these two railway lines, much of the moors area is easily accessible for those without wheels. Call **Traveline Yorkshire** ( ☎ 0871 200 2233; www.yorkshiretravel.net) for all public bus and train information.

The **Moorsbus** ( ☎ 01845-597000) operates on Sundays from May to October, daily from mid-July to early September, and is ideal for reaching out-of-the-way spots. Pick up a timetable and route map from tourist offices, or go to www.visitthemoors.co.uk and click on

YORKSHIRE

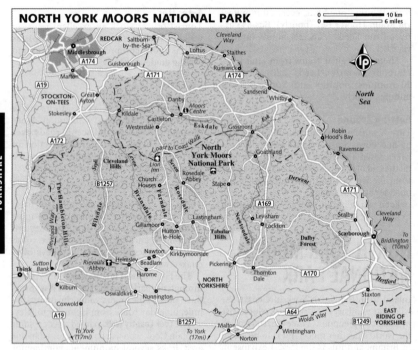

'Discover the Place' then 'Public Transport'. A standard day pass costs £4, and for £12 the pass is valid on the Esk Valley railway too. Family tickets and one-off fares for short journeys are also available.

There's also a free public-transport map, the *Moors Explorer Travel Guide,* available from tourist offices.

If you're planning to drive on the minor roads over the moors, beware of wandering sheep and lambs – hundreds are killed by careless drivers every year.

## HELMSLEY
### pop 1620

Helmsley is a classic North Yorkshire market town, a handsome place full of old houses, historic coaching inns and – inevitably – a cobbled market square, all basking under the watchful gaze of a sturdy Norman castle. Nearby are the romantic ruins of Rievaulx Abbey and a fistful of country walks.

### Orientation & Information

The centre of everything is Market Pl (market day is Friday); all four sides are lined with spe-ciality shops, cosy pubs and cafes. The **tourist office** ( ☎ 01439-770173; 9.30am-5.30pm daily Mar-Oct, 10am-4pm Fri-Sun Nov-Feb) sells maps and books, and helps with accommodation.

### Sights & Activities

The impressive ruins of 12th-century **Helmsley Castle** (EH; ☎ 01439-770442; admission £4; 10am-6pm Apr-Sep, 10am-5pm Mar & Oct, 10am-4pm Thu-Mon Nov-Mar) are defended by a striking series of deep ditches and banks to which later rulers added the thick stone walls and defensive towers – only one tooth-shaped tower survives today following the dismantling of the fortress by Sir Thomas Fairfax after the Civil War. The castle's tumultuous history is well explained in the visitor centre.

Just outside the castle, **Helmsley Walled Garden** ( ☎ 01439-771427; admission £4; 10.30am-5pm daily Easter-Oct, Mon-Fri Nov-Easter) would be just another plant and produce centre were it not for its dramatic position and fabulous selection of flowers, fruits and vegetables – some of which are quite rare – not to mention the herbs, including 40 varieties of mint. If you're into horticulture with a historical twist, this is Eden.

South of the castle stretches the superb landscape of **Duncombe Park** estate with the stately home of **Duncombe Park House** ( ☎ 01439-770213; www.duncombepark.com; house & gardens £7.25, gardens only £4; ☺ house by guided tour only, hourly 12.30-3.30pm, gardens 11am-5.30pm Sun-Thu Easter-Oct) at its heart. From the house and formal gardens, wide grassy walkways and terraces lead through woodland to mock-classical temples, while longer walking trails are set out in the parkland – now protected as a nature reserve. The house, ticket office and information centre are 1.5 miles south of town, an easy walk through the park.

You could easily spend a day here, especially if you take in one of the many walks in Duncombe Park. Cream of the crop is the 3.5-mile route to **Rievaulx Abbey** (right) – the tourist office can provide route leaflets and advise on buses if you don't want to walk both ways. This route is also the opening section of the **Cleveland Way** (p518).

## Sleeping

**Wrens of Rydale** ( ☎ 01439-771260; www.wrensofryedale .co.uk; Gale Lane, Nawton; tent & 2 adults £8, with car £14; ☺ Apr-Oct) This excellent, sheltered camp site with three acres of pristine parkland is 3 miles east of Helmsley, just south of Beadlam.

**Helmsley YHA** ( ☎ 0845 371 9638; www.yha.org.uk; Carlton Lane; dm £16; P ) This family-friendly hostel a quarter mile east of the market square looks a bit like an ordinary suburban home; its location at the start of the Cleveland Way means that it's almost always full, so book in advance.

There are a number of old coaching inns on Market Pl that offer B&B, half-decent grub and a pint of hand-pumped real ale. The **Feathers Hotel** ( ☎ 01439-770275; www.feathershotelhelmsley .co.uk; Market Pl; s/d from £44/80) has four-poster beds in some rooms and historical trimmings throughout. For something plusher head for the **Feversham Arms** ( ☎ 01439-770766; www.fever shamarms.com; s/d from £130/140; P ), where country charm meets boutique chic.

## Eating

**Star Inn** ( ☎ 01439-770397; www.thestaratharome.co.uk; Harome; mains £15-20; ☺ dinner Mon-Sat, lunch Tue-Sat, noon-6pm Sun) This thatch-roofed country pub is home to one of Yorkshire's best restaurants, with a Michelin-starred menu that revels in top-quality produce from the surrounding farms – slow roast belly pork with black pudding and apple salad, or wood pigeon with roast hazelnut pesto. It's the sort of place you won't want to leave, and the good news is you don't have to: the adjacent lodge has eight magnificent bedrooms (£130 to £150), each decorated in classic but luxurious country style. It's about 2 miles south of Helmsley just off the A170.

Helmsley is a bit of a foodie town, sporting a couple of quality delicatessens on the main square. There's **Perns** ( ☎ 01439-770249; 18 Market Pl), a butcher, deli and wine merchant under the same ownership as the Star at Harome; and flower-bedecked **Hunters of Helmsley** ( ☎ 01439-771307; www.huntersofhelmsley.com; 13 Market Pl), a cornucopia of locally made chutneys, jams, beers, cheeses, bacon, humbugs and ice cream – a great place to stock up for a gourmet picnic.

## Getting There & Away

All buses stop in the main square. Bus 31X runs from York to Helmsley (1¼ hours, two daily Monday to Saturday). From Scarborough take bus 128 (£7, 1½ hours, hourly Monday to Saturday, four on Sunday) via Pickering.

# AROUND HELMSLEY
## Rievaulx

In the secluded valley of the River Rye, amid fields and woods loud with birdsong, stand the magnificent ruins of **Rievaulx Abbey** (EH; ☎ 01439-798228; admission £5; ☺ 10am-6pm daily Apr-Sep, 10am-5pm Thu-Mon Oct, 10am-4pm Thu-Mon Nov-Mar). This idyllic spot was chosen by Cistercian monks in 1132 as a base for missionary activity in northern Britain. St Aelred, the third abbot, famously described the abbey's setting as 'everywhere peace, everywhere serenity, and a marvellous freedom from the tumult of the world'. But the monks of Rievaulx (pronounced ree-voh) were far from unworldly, and soon created a network of commercial interests, ranging from sheep farms to lead mines, that formed the backbone of the local economy. The extensive ruins give a wonderful feel for the size and complexity of the community that once lived here – their story is fleshed out in a series of fascinating exhibits in the neighbouring visitor centre.

In the 1750s landscape-gardening fashion favoured a Gothic look, and many aristocrats had mock ruins built in their parks. The Duncombe family (left) went one better, as their lands contained a real medieval ruin – Rievaulx Abbey. They built **Rievaulx Terrace & Temples** (NT; ☎ 01439-798340; admission £4.80; ☺ 11am-6pm Apr-Sep, 11am-5pm Oct & Nov) so that lords and ladies could stroll effortlessly in the 'wilderness' and admire the abbey in the valley below. Today, you can do the same, with views over Ryedale and the Hambleton Hills forming a perfect backdrop.

Rievaulx is about 3 miles west of Helmsley. Note that there's no direct access between the abbey and the terrace – their entrance gates are about a mile apart, though easily reached along a lane (steeply uphill if you're going from abbey to terrace).

## Coxwold
pop 190

Coxwold is a neatly symmetrical village of golden stone – just two rows of cottages perched atop grassy banks on either side of the single street – that nestles in beautiful countryside about 7 miles southwest of Helmsley.

Apart from the picture-postcard beauty of the place, the main attraction is 15th-century **Shandy Hall** ( ☎ 01347-868465; www.shandean.org; admission gardens/house £4.50/2.50; ☺ house 2-4.30pm Wed, 2.30-4.30pm Sun May-Sep, gardens 11am-4.30pm May-Sep), the former home of ebullient eccentric Laurence Sterne (1713–68), author of *Tristram Shandy*. The house is full of 'Sterneana', with lots of information on this entertaining character who was seemingly the first to use the expression 'sick as a horse'.

Nearby is **Byland Abbey** (EH; ☎ 01347-868614; admission £3.50; ☺ 11am-6pm daily Jul & Aug, Wed-Sun Apr-Jun & Sep), the elegant remains of a fine Cistercian creation, now a series of lofty arches surrounded by open green slopes.

A decent option for a good night's sleep is **Fauconberg Arms** ( ☎ 01347-868214; www.fauconbergarms.com; Main St; s/d £75/85, mains £11-16; (P) ), a cosy local in the heart of the village that also offers a fine continental-style menu in its elegant restaurant.

## HUTTON-LE-HOLE
pop 210

With a scatter of gorgeous stone cottages, a gurgling brook and a flock of sheep grazing contentedly on the village green, Hutton-le-Hole must be a contender for the best-looking village in Yorkshire. The dips and hollows on the green may have given the place its name – it was once called simply Hutton Hole but wannabe posh Victorians added the Frenchified 'le', which the locals defiantly pronounce 'lee'.

The **tourist office** ( ☎ 01751-417367; ☺ 10am-5.30pm mid-Mar–early Nov) has leaflets on walks

in the area, including a 5-mile circuit to the nearby village of Lastingham.

Attached to the tourist office is the largely open-air **Ryedale Folk Museum** ( ☎ 01751-417367; www.ryedalefolkmuseum.co.uk; adult/child £5/3.50; ☺ 10am-5.30pm mid-Mar–Oct, 10am-dusk Nov–mid-Mar, closed 21 Dec–20 Jan), a constantly expanding collection of North York Moors buildings from different eras, including a medieval manor house, simple farmers' houses, a blacksmith's forge and a row of 1930s village shops. Demonstrations and displays throughout the season give a pretty fascinating insight into local life as it was in the past.

The **Daffodil Walk** is a 2.5-mile circular walk following the banks of the River Dove. As the name suggests, the main draws are the daffs, usually at their best in the last couple of weeks in April.

## Sleeping & Eating

**Lion Inn** ( ☎ 01751-417320; www.lionblakey.co.uk; Blakey Ridge; s/d from £35/54; mains £9-16; (P) ) From Hutton, the Blakey Ridge road climbs over the moors to Danby and, after 6 miles passes one of the highest and most remote pubs in England (altitude 404m). With its low-beamed ceilings and cosy fireplaces, hearty grub and range of real ales, the Lion is a firm favourite with hikers and bikers.

**Burnley House** ( ☎ 01751-417548; www.burnleyhouse.co.uk; d £70-90; (P) ) This elegant Georgian home offers comfortable bedrooms and a hearty breakfast, but the best features are the lovely sitting room and garden where you can relax with a cup of tea and a book.

## Getting There & Away

Hutton-le-Hole is 2.5 miles north of the main A170 road, about halfway between Helmsley and Pickering. Moorsbus services (p561) through Hutton-le-Hole include the M3 between Helmsley and Danby (seven per day) and the M1 and M2 between Pickering and Danby (eight per day) via the Lion Inn. Outside times when the Moorsbus runs, you'll need your own transport to get here.

## PICKERING
pop 6600

Pickering is a lively market town with an imposing Norman castle that advertises itself as 'the gateway to the North York Moors'. That gateway is the terminus of the wonderful North Yorkshire Moors Railway (NYMR), a picturesque survivor from the great days of steam.

The **tourist office** ( ☎ 01751-473791; www.ryedale .gov.uk; The Ropery; ☻ 9.30am-5.30pm Mon-Sat, to 4pm Sun Mar-Oct, 10am-4pm Mon-Sat Nov-Feb) has the usual details as well as plenty of NYMR-related info.

## Sights & Activities

The privately owned **North Yorkshire Moors Railway** (NYMR; ☎ Pickering Station 01751-472508, recorded timetable 01751-473535; www.nymr.co.uk; Pickering–Grosmont Day Rover ticket adult/child £14.50/7.30, Pickering–Whitby £20/12) runs for 18 miles through beautiful countryside to the village of Grosmont. Lovingly restored steam locos pull period carriages, resplendent in polished brass and bright paintwork, appealing to railway buffs and daytrippers alike. For visitors without wheels, it's ideal for reaching out-of-the-way villages in the middle of the moors. Grosmont is also on the main railway line between Middlesbrough and Whitby, which opens up yet more possibilities for walking and sightseeing.

Dating mostly from the 13th and 14th centuries, **Pickering Castle** (EH; ☎ 01751-474989; admission £3.50; ☻ 10am-6pm Apr-Sep, 10am-4pm Thu-Mon Oct) is a lot like the castles we drew as kids: thick stone walls around a central keep, perched atop a high motte (mound) with great views of the surrounding countryside.

## Sleeping & Eating

**White Swan Hotel** ( ☎ 01751-472288; www.white-swan .co.uk; Market Pl; s/d from £110/145, mains £9-15; P ▣ ) The top spot in town successfully combines a smart pub, a superb restaurant serving local dishes with a continental twist, and a luxurious boutique hotel all in one. Nine modern rooms in the converted coach house up the ante with flat-screen TVs and other stylish paraphernalia that add to the luxury found throughout the hotel.

There's a strip of B&Bs on tree-lined Eastgate (the A170 to Scarborough), and a few more on Westgate (heading towards Helmsley). Decent options include the flower-clad **Rose Folly** ( ☎ 01751-475057; www.rosefolly .freeserve.co.uk; 112 Eastgate; s/d £30/55; P ), with lovely rooms and a beautiful breakfast conservatory; and **Eleven Westgate** ( ☎ 01751-475111; www.eleven westgate.co.uk; 11 Westgate; d £60-68), a pretty house with patio and garden.

There are several cafes and teashops on Market Pl, but don't overlook the **tearoom** (mains £2-6) at Pickering station, which serves

excellent home-baked goodies and does a tasty roast-pork roll with apple sauce, crackling and stuffing.

## Getting There & Away

In addition to the NYMR trains, bus 128 between Helmsley (40 minutes) and Scarborough (50 minutes) runs hourly via Pickering. Yorkshire Coastliner services 840 and 842 between Leeds and Whitby link Pickering with York (£11, 70 minutes, hourly).

## DANBY
pop 290

The Blakey Ridge road from Hutton-le-Hole swoops steeply down to Danby, a compact, stone-built village set deep amid the moors at the head of Eskdale. It's home to the **Moors Centre** ( ☎ 01439-772737; www.visitthemoors .co.uk; ☻ 10am-5pm Apr-Oct, 10.30am-3.30pm Nov, Dec & Mar, 10.30am-3.30pm Sat & Sun Jan-Feb), the national park's HQ, which has interesting exhibits on the natural history of the moors as well as a cafe, an accommodation booking service and a huge range of local guidebooks, maps and leaflets.

There are several short circular walks from the centre, but a more challenging objective is **Danby Beacon**, a stiff 2 miles uphill to a stunning 360-degree panorama across the moors. Or you can cheat, and just drive up.

The **Duke of Wellington** ( ☎ 01287-660351; www .danby-dukeofwellington.co.uk) is a fine traditional pub that was used as a recruitment centre during the Napoleonic Wars; it serves good beer and food (mains £7 to £8) and has nine well-appointed bedrooms (singles/doubles from £45/70).

You can reach Danby on the delightful **Esk Valley Railway** ( ☎ 08457 484950; www.eskva lleyrailway.co.uk) – Whitby is 20 minutes east, Middlesbrough 45 minutes west. There are four departures daily Monday to Saturday, and two on Sunday.

## WHITBY
pop 13,600

Whitby is a town of two halves, split down the middle by the mouth of the River Esk. It's also a town with two personalities – on the one hand a busy commercial and fishing port, with a bustling quayside fishmarket; on the other a traditional seaside resort, complete with sandy beach, amusement arcades and promenading holidaymakers slurping ice-cream cones in the sun.

It's the combination of these two facets that makes Whitby more interesting than your average resort. The town has managed to retain much of its 18th-century character, recalling the time when James Cook – Whitby's most famous adopted son – was making his first forays at sea on his way towards becoming one of the best-known explorers in history. The narrow streets and alleys of the old town hug the riverside, now lined with restaurants, pubs and cute little shops, all with views across the handsome harbour where colourful fishing boats ply to and fro. Keeping a watchful eye over the whole scene is the atmospheric ruined abbey atop the East Cliff.

But Whitby also has a darker side. Most famously, it was the inspiration and setting for part of Bram Stoker's Gothic horror story *Dracula* (see boxed text, opposite). Less well known is the fact that Whitby is famous for the jet (fossilised wood) that has been mined from the local sea cliffs for centuries; this smooth, black substance was popularised in the 19th century when Queen Victoria took to wearing mourning jewellery made from Whitby jet. In recent years these morbid associations have seen the rise of a series of hugely popular Goth festivals (opposite).

## Orientation

Whitby is cut in half by the River Esk, with only one very busy bridge linking the two sides. The east side (East Cliff) is the older part of town; the newer (19th-century) town grew up on the West Cliff. The bus and train stations are in the town centre on the west side of the river.

Note that many streets have two names – for example, Abbey Tce and Hudson St are opposite sides of the same street, as are West Tce and the Esplanade.

## Information

**Java Cafe-Bar** ( ☎ 01947-820832; 2 Flowergate; per 10 min £1) Internet access.

**Laundrette** (72 Church St)

**Post office** ( ☒ 8.30am-5.30pm Mon-Sat) Inside the Co-op supermarket.

**Tourist office** ( ☎ 01947-602674; www.visitwhitby .com; Langborne Rd; ☒ 9.30am-6pm May-Sep, 10am-4.30pm Oct-Apr)

**Whitby Bookshop** ( ☎ 01947-606202; 88 Church St; ☒ 9.30am-5pm) Local history and secondhand books.

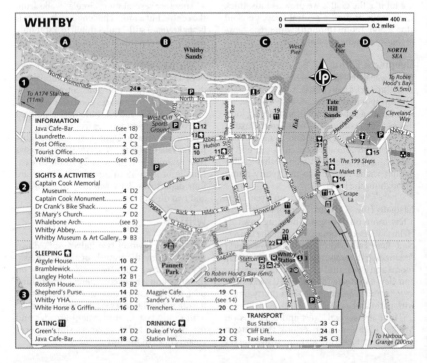

**WHITBY**

0 — 400 m
0 — 0.2 miles

**INFORMATION**
Java Cafe-Bar.........................(see 18)
Laundrette...............................1 D2
Post Office..............................2 C3
Tourist Office.........................3 C3
Whitby Bookshop....................(see 16)

**SIGHTS & ACTIVITIES**
Captain Cook Memorial
 Museum................................4 D2
Captain Cook Monument..........5 C1
Dr Crank's Bike Shack..............6 C2
St Mary's Church......................7 D2
Whalebone Arch.....................(see 5)
Whitby Abbey..........................8 D2
Whitby Museum & Art Gallery..9 B3

**SLEEPING**
Argyle House..........................10 B2
Bramblewick...........................11 C2
Langley Hotel..........................12 B1
Rosslyn House.........................13 B2
Shepherd's Purse.....................14 D2
Whitby YHA............................15 D2
White Horse & Griffin..............16 D2

**EATING**
Green's...................................17 D2
Java Cafe-Bar..........................18 C2

Magpie Cafe............................19 C1
Sander's Yard.........................(see 14)
Trenchers...............................20 C2

**DRINKING**
Duke of York..........................21 D2
Station Inn.............................22 C3

**TRANSPORT**
Bus Station.............................23 C3
Cliff Lift.................................24 B1
Taxi Rank..............................25 C3

## Sights

There are ruined abbeys and there are picturesque ruined abbeys, and then there's **Whitby Abbey** (EH; ☎ 01947-603568; admission £5; ⌚ 10am-6pm daily Apr-Sep, 10am-4pm Thu-Mon Oct-Mar), dominating the skyline above the East Cliff like a great Gothic tombstone silhouetted against the sky. It looks more like it was built as an atmospheric film set than as a monastic establishment, it is hardly surprising that this medieval hulk inspired the Victorian novelist Bram Stoker – who holidayed in Whitby – to make it the setting for Count Dracula's dramatic landfall.

The 199 steps of **Church Stairs** lead steeply up to the abbey from the end of Church St, passing the equally atmospheric **St Mary's Church** ( ⌚ 10am-5pm Apr-Oct, 10am-4pm Nov-Mar) and its spooky graveyard, a favourite haunt of Goth courting couples.

The fascinating **Captain Cook Memorial Museum** ( ☎ 01947-601900; www.cookmuseumwhitby .co.uk; Grape Lane; adult/child £4/3; ⌚ 9.45am-5pm Apr-Oct, 11am-3pm Sat & Sun Mar) occupies the house of the ship owner with whom Cook began his seafaring career. Highlights include the attic where Cook lodged as a young apprentice, Cook's own maps and letters, etchings from the South Seas and a wonderful model of the *Endeavour*, with all the crew and stores laid out for inspection.

At the top of the cliff on the west side of the harbour, the **Captain Cook Monument** shows the great man looking out to sea, often with a seagull perched on his head. Nearby is the **Whalebone Arch**, which recalls Whitby's days as a whaling port. Down below, Whitby's days as a seaside resort continue with donkey rides, ice cream and bucket-and-spade escapades on **Whitby Sands**.

Set in a park to the west of the town centre is the wonderfully eclectic **Whitby Museum & Art Gallery** ( ☎ 01947-602908; www.whitbymuseum.org .uk; Pannett Park; adult/child £3/1; ⌚ 9.30am-4.30pm Tue-Sun), with displays of fossil plesiosaurs and dinosaur footprints, Cook memorabilia, ships in bottles, jet jewellery and the 'Hand of Glory' – a preserved human hand reputedly cut from the corpse of an executed criminal.

## Activities

For a cracking day out, take a bus to Robin Hood's Bay, explore the village, have lunch, then hike the 6-mile **cliff-top footpath** back to Whitby (allow three hours).

---

### WHITBY'S DARK SIDE

The famous story of *Dracula*, inspiration for a thousand lurid movies, was written by Bram Stoker while staying at a B&B in Whitby in 1897. Although most Hollywood versions of the tale concentrate on deepest, darkest Transylvania, much of the original book was set in Whitby, and many sites can still be seen today. The tourist office sells an excellent *Dracula Trail* leaflet (80p).

---

First choice for a bike ride is the excellent 20-mile Whitby to Scarborough **Coastal Cycle Trail**, which starts a mile south of the town centre and follows the route of an old railway line via Robin Hood's Bay. Bikes can be hired from **Dr Crank's Bike Shack** ( ☎ 01947-606661; 20 Skinner St; ⌚ 10am-5pm, closed Wed & Sun).

## Festivals & Events

**Whitby Gothic Weekends** (www.wgw.topmum.co.uk; tickets £45) Twice yearly, last weekend of April and October. Goth heaven, with gigs, events and the Bizarre Bazaar – dozens of traders selling Goth gear, jewellery, art and music.
**Moor & Coast Festival** (www.moorandcoast.co.uk; tickets £35) May Bank Holiday weekend. Beards, sandals and real ale galore at this traditional festival of folk music, dance and dubious Celtic art.
**Musicport Festival** (www.whitbymusicport.com; tickets £75) Mid-October. A weekend-long festival of world music.

## Sleeping

B&Bs are concentrated in West Cliff in the streets to the south and east of Royal Crescent; if a house here ain't offering B&B, chances are it's derelict. Accommodation can be tough to find at festival times; it's wise to book ahead.

### BUDGET

**Harbour Grange** ( ☎ 01947-600817; www.whitbybackpack ers.co.uk; Spital Bridge; dm £15) Overlooking the harbour and less than 10 minutes' walk from the train station, this tidy hostel is conveniently located but has an 11.30pm curfew – good thing we're all teetotal early-to-bedders, right?

**Whitby YHA** ( ☎ 0845 371 9049; www.yha.org.uk; Church Lane; dm £22; P 🖳 ) With an unbeatable position next to the abbey, this hostel doesn't have to try too hard, and it doesn't. You'll have to book well in advance to get your body into one of the basic bunks. Hike up from the station, or take bus 97 (hourly Monday to Saturday).

**MIDRANGE**

**White Horse & Griffin** ( ☎ 01947-604857; www.white horseandgriffin.co.uk; 87 Church St; s/d/f from £35/60/85) Walk through the appropriately olde-worlde frontage of this handsome 18th-century coaching inn and discover a boutique hotel with individually designed, superstylish rooms that manage to mix the best of tradition (antique panelling, restored period furniture, real flame fires) with the kind of sleek, contemporary lines and modern comforts you'd expect from a top-class guesthouse.

**Shepherd's Purse** ( ☎ 01947-820228; www.theshepherds purse.com; 95 Church St; r £45-60) This place combines a beads-and-baubles boutique with a wholefood shop and guesthouse accommodation in the courtyard at the back. The plainer rooms that share a bathroom are perfectly adequate, but we recommend the rustic en-suite bedrooms situated around the courtyard; the four-poster beds feel a bit like they've been shoehorned in, but the atmosphere is cute rather than cramped.

**Langley Hotel** ( ☎ 01947-604250; www.langleyhotel .com; 16 Royal Cres; s/d from £70/90; **P** ) With a cream and crimson colour scheme, and a gilt four-poster bed in one room, this grand old hotel exudes a whiff of Victorian splendour. Go for room 1 or 2, if possible, to make the most of the panoramic views from West Cliff.

Other recommendations:

**Rosslyn House** ( ☎ 01947-604086; rosslynhouse@ googlemail.com; 11 Abbey Tce; s/d from £29/50) Bright and cheerful with a friendly welcome.

**Bramblewick** ( ☎ 01947-604504; www.bramblewick .co.uk; 3 Havelock Pl; s/d from £27/60; **P** ) Friendly owners, hearty breakfasts and abbey views from top-floor room.

**Argyle House** ( ☎ 01947-602733; www.argyle-house .co.uk; 18 Hudson St; s/d £32/60) Comfortable as old slippers, and kippers for breakfast.

## Eating & Drinking

**Java Cafe-Bar** ( ☎ 01947-820832; 2 Flowergate; mains £4-6) A cool little diner with stainless-steel counters and retro decor, with internet access, music vids on the flat screen and a menu of healthy salads, sandwiches and wraps washed down with excellent coffee.

**Sander's Yard** ( ☎ 01947-820228; 95 Church St; mains £6-8) A vegie place in a pleasant courtyard behind the Shepherd's Purse wholefood shop, Sander's serves a great range of healthy, interesting snacks, sandwiches and home-baked cakes.

**Magpie Cafe** ( ☎ 01947-602058; 14 Pier Rd; mains £8-15; ☽ lunch & dinner) Flaunts its reputation for serving the 'world's best fish and chips'; damn fine they are too, but the world and his dog knows about it, and summertime queues can stretch along the street.

**Trenchers** ( ☎ 01947-603212; New Quay Rd; mains £9-15; ☽ lunch & dinner) Top-notch fish and chips minus the 'world's best' tagline – this place is your best bet if you want to avoid the queues at the Magpie (don't be put off by the modern look).

**Green's** ( ☎ 01947-600284; www.greensofwhitby.com; 13 Bridge St; bistro mains £10-18, restaurant 2-/3-course dinner £34/40; ☽ lunch & dinner Fri-Sun, dinner Mon-Thu) The classiest eatery in town is ideally situated to take its pick of the fish and shellfish freshly landed at the harbour, which makes its way onto the menu as crab with linguini, scallops with parmesan, pesto and prosciutto, and langoustine tempura.

Most of Whitby's pubs serve food, including the popular **Duke of York** (Church St) at the bottom of the Church Stairs, which has great views over the harbour and serves Timothy Taylor ales. But the best place in town for atmosphere and real ale is the **Station Inn** (New Quay Rd), which offers an impressive range of cask-conditioned beers including Theakston's Black Bull and Black Dog Abbey Ale.

## Getting There & Away

Buses 93 and X93 run south to Scarborough (one hour, every 30 minutes) via Robin Hood's Bay (15 minutes, hourly), and north

---

**CAPTAIN COOK – WHITBY'S ADOPTED SON**

Although he was born in Marton (now a suburb of Middlesbrough), Whitby has adopted the famous explorer Captain James Cook, and ever since the first tourists got off the train in Victorian times local entrepreneurs have mercilessly cashed in on his memory, as endless 'Endeavour Cafes' and 'Captain Cook Chip Shops' testify.

Still, Whitby played a key role in James Cook's eventual success as a world-famous explorer. It was here that he first went to sea, serving his apprenticeship with local ship owners, and the design of the ships used for his voyages of discovery – including the famous *Endeavour* – were based on the design of Whitby 'cats', flat-bottomed ships that carried coal from Newcastle to London.

to Middlesbrough (hourly), with fewer services on Sunday. See p527 for details of the Yorkshire Coastliner service from Leeds to Whitby.

Coming from the north, you can get to Whitby by train along the Esk Valley Railway from Middlesbrough (£4.40, 1½ hours, four per day), with connections from Durham and Newcastle. From the south, it's easier to get a train from York to Scarborough, then a bus from Scarborough to Whitby.

## Getting Around

Whitby is a compact place and hiking up and down the steep hills helps to burn off the fish and chips. But if you need one, there's a **taxi rank** outside the train station. Whitby Sands can be reached from West Cliff via the **cliff lift** (75p; ☼ May-Sep), an elevator that has been running since 1931.

## AROUND WHITBY
### Robin Hood's Bay

Robin Hood's Bay (www.robin-hoods-bay .co.uk) has nothing to do with the hero of Sherwood Forest – the origin of the name is a mystery, and the locals call it Bay Town, or just Bay. But there's no denying that this picturesque fishing village is one of the prettiest spots on the Yorkshire coast.

Leave your car at the parking area in the upper village, where 19th-century ship's captains built comfortable Victorian villas, and walk downhill to **Old Bay**, the oldest part of the village (don't even think about driving down). This maze of narrow lanes and passages is dotted with tearooms, pubs, craft shops and artists' studios – there's even a tiny cinema – and at low tide you can go down onto the beach and fossick around in the rock pools.

There are several pubs and cafes – best pub for ambience and real ale is **Ye Dolphin** ( ☎ 01947-880337; King St), while the **Swell Cafe** ( ☎ 01947-880180; Chapel St) does great coffee and has a terrace with a view over the beach.

Bay is 6 miles south of Whitby; you can walk here along the coastal path in two or three hours, or bike it along the cycle trail in 40 minutes. Also, bus 93 runs hourly between Whitby and Scarborough via Robin Hood's Bay – the bus stop is at the top of the hill, in the new part of town.

**YORKSHIRE**

# Northwest England

Modern Britain – that place defined by throbbing urban conurbations fuelled by industry and innovation, separated, however thinly in parts, by often stunning bits of greenery – was in large part defined and determined by the Northwest. It was here that the modern world took its first tentative steps in the wake of the Industrial Revolution, which was born round these parts.

Why bother with the heaving relics of an industrial past that can surely only be sexy to history buffs and gadget freaks? Because, not content with setting the pace for one world-changing revolution, the Northwest is all about leading the charge into the unknown landscapes of the new millennium and you absolutely don't want to miss this particular ride.

At its heart is Manchester, a city that has laid down numerous markers of cool, from the musical revolution known as Madchester to a collection of museums so diverse and interesting as to make your head spin. Just down the road is Liverpool, which has known some tough times but just refuses to play second fiddle to anyone. And, if you need a change of pace, there's marvellous Chester, where rich layers of history are revealed in its multi-tiered architecture.

To the north there's the Queen of the Resorts in Blackpool, home to a futuristic pleasure park full of rides that will make your stomach turn and your eyes pop; and just as you begin to wonder if there's any respite to humankind's concrete pawprint, the landscape reveals itself in all its gorgeous wonder, not least on the Isle of Man.

**NORTHWEST ENGLAND**

## HIGHLIGHTS

- Seeing exactly what kind of hell war is in the **Imperial War Museum** (p577) in Manchester

- Getting to the root of the game at Preston's **National Football Museum** (p603)

- Having your insides churned and twisted at Blackpool's **Pleasure Beach** (p601)

- Getting to grips with the **Isle of Man** (p603) – about as exotic as England gets

- Walking down the tunnel from the dressing rooms on a tour of **Old Trafford** (p577) – no-one but the most ardent Liverpool or Manchester City fan could fail to be impressed!

- Learning a valuable history lesson at the outstanding **International Slavery Museum** (p593) in Liverpool

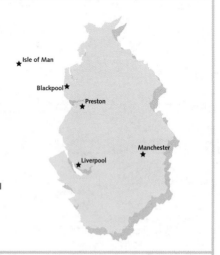

| ■ POPULATION: 6.7 MILLION | ■ AREA: 5473 SQ MILES | ■ ENGLAND'S LAST TEMPERANCE (NO ALCOHOL) BAR IS FITZPATRICK'S (RAWTENSTALL, LANCASHIRE) |

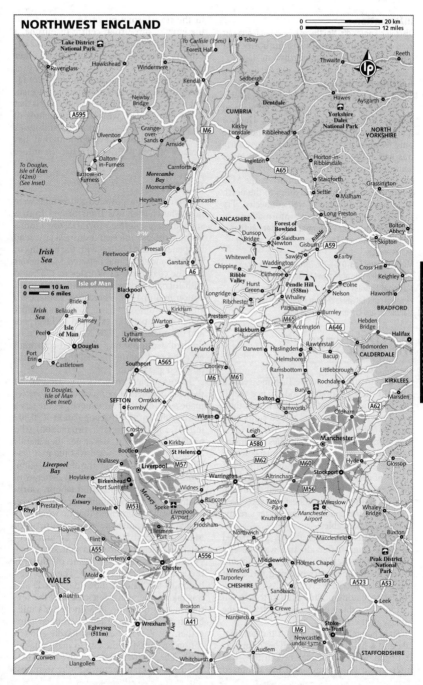

# NORTHWEST ENGLAND

0 — 20 km
0 — 12 miles

To Carlisle (35mi) Tebay
Lake District National Park
Forest Hall
Thwaite Reeth

Ravenglass Hawkshead Windermere
Kendal Sedbergh Hawes Aysgarth

A595 CUMBRIA Dentdale
Newby Bridge Kirkby Lonsdale Ribblehead Yorkshire Dales National Park NORTH YORKSHIRE

Ulverston Grange-over-Sands Arnside Ingleton A65 Horton-in-Ribblesdale

Dalton-in-Furness Carnforth Stainforth Grassington

To Douglas, Isle of Man (42mi) (See Inset) Barrow-in-Furness Morecambe Bay Morecambe Settle Malham

Heysham Lancaster LANCASHIRE Long Preston

54°N 3°W Forest of Bowland Bolton Abbey

Fleetwood Dunsop Bridge Slaidburn Newton Gisburn A59 Skipton

**Irish Sea** Preesall Whitewell Sawley Earby Cross Hill

Cleveleys Garstang A6 Chipping Waddington Clitheroe Keighley

0 — 10 km
0 — 6 miles Isle of Man Ribble Valley Pendle Hill (558m) Whalley Colne Haworth

Blackpool Longridge Hurst Green Nelson BRADFORD

Irish Sea Bride Bellaugh Ramsey Ribchester Padiham Burnley Hebden Bridge

Peel Isle of Man KirkHam Preston M65 Accrington A646 Halifax

Port Erin Douglas Warton Blackburn CALDERDALE

Castletown Lytham St Anne's Leyland Darwen Haslingden Rawtenstall Todmorden

54°N To Douglas, Isle of Man (See Inset) Southport A565 Chorley Helmshore Bacup KIRKLEES

Ainsdale M6 M61 Ramsbottom Littleborough Marsden

SEFTON Ormskirk Bury Rochdale A62

Formby Bolton

Wigan Leigh Farnworth Oldham

Crosby A580 Manchester

**Liverpool Bay** Kirkby M62 M60 Hyde

Bootle St Helens Stockport Glossop

Wallasey Liverpool M57 Warrington Altrincham M56

Hoylake Birkenhead Port Sunlight Widnes Runcorn Tatton Park Wilmslow Whaley Bridge

Rhyl Prestatyn Dee Estuary Heswall Speke Liverpool Airport Knutsford Manchester Airport Macclesfield Buxton

Holywell Ellesmere Port Frodsham Northwich

Flint A55 Queensferry A556 Middlewich Holmes Chapel Peak District National Park

Denbigh Mold Chester Winsford Congleton A523 A53

WALES Tarporley CHESHIRE Sandbach Leek

Ruthin Broxton Nantwich Crewe

Eglwyseg (511m) Wrexham A41 Stoke-on-Trent

Corwen Audlem Newcastle-under-Lyme

Llangollen Whitchurch STAFFORDSHIRE

NORTHWEST ENGLAND

## Information
**Discover England's Northwest** (www.visitnorthwest
.com) is the centralised tourist authority that
covers the whole of the northwest.

## Getting Around
The towns and cities covered in this chapter
are all within easy reach of each other, and
are well linked by public transport. The two
main cities, Manchester and Liverpool, are
only 34 miles apart and are linked by hourly
bus and train services. Chester is 18 miles
south of Liverpool, but is also easily accessible from Manchester by train or via the M56
motorway. Blackpool is 50 miles to the north
of both cities, and is also well connected. Try
the following for transport information:
**Greater Manchester Passenger Transport Author-
ity** (www.gmpte.com) For extensive info on Manchester
and its environs.

**Merseytravel** ( ☎ 0161-236 7676; www.merseytravel
.gov.uk) Taking care of all travel in Merseyside.

**National Express** ( ☎ 08717 81 81 81; www.nation
alexpress.com) Extensive coach services in the northwest;
Manchester and Liverpool are major hubs.

# MANCHESTER
**pop 394,270**
Ask a Mancunian to name Britain's second
city and there's a pretty good chance they'll
say 'London,' such is the confidence in their
native town. It's pretty well-placed confidence
too, as Manchester's resume makes for a
pretty impressive read. Few cities in Europe
have embraced change so enthusiastically;
it's where much of the best music of the last
couple of decades came from; and it has both
the world's best-supported football team and,
as of 2008, the world's richest one too. Need
a substitute for London? Manchester's ready,
willing and very able.

But Manchester has always performed
on a big stage. After all, this was the city
that adopted the Shropshire suckling and
raised it into the overwhelming force that
was the Industrial Revolution, so what's a
little self-inflating urban redesign to a burgh
that knows a thing or two about altering the
history of the world?

The change and influence of the last decade and a half has been nearly as dramatic.
It began with a musical revolution, was
interrupted by a bomb and has climaxed

in the transformation of Manchester into
the envy of any urban centre in Europe, a
modern metropolis that has embraced 21st-
century style and technology like no other
in Britain.

There are museums and enough heritage
to satisfy even the most demanding historian,
but what makes Manchester so inviting is that
it has managed to weave the mementos of
its past with a forward-looking, ambitious
program of urban development that has
already offered a vision of what the future
might hold.

## HISTORY
Canals and steam-powered cotton mills were
how Manchester was transformed from a
small disease-infested provincial town into a
very big disease-infested industrial city. It all
happened in the 1760s – with the opening of
the Bridgewater Canal between Manchester
and the coal mines at Worsley in 1763, and
with Richard Arkwright patenting his super
cotton mill in 1769. Thereafter, Manchester
and the world would never be the same again.
When the canal was extended to Liverpool
and the open sea in 1776, Manchester – now
dubbed 'Cottonopolis' – kicked into high
gear and took off on the coal-fuelled, steam-
powered gravy train.

There was plenty of gravy to go around, but
the good burghers of 19th-century Manchester
made sure that the vast majority of the city's
swollen citizenry (with a population of 90,000
in 1801, and 100 years later, two million), who
produced most of it, never got their hands
on any of it. Their reward was life in a new
kind of urban settlement: the industrial slum.
Working conditions were scarcely better, with
impossibly long hours, child labour, work-
related accidents and fatalities commonplace.
Mark Twain commented that he would like
to live here because the 'transition between
Manchester and Death would be unnotice-
able'. So much for Victorian values.

The wheels started to come off towards
the end of the 19th century. The USA had
begun to flex its own industrial muscle and
was taking over a sizeable chunk of the textile trade; production in Manchester's mills
began to slow, and then it stopped altogether. By WWII there was hardly enough
cotton produced in the city to make a table-
cloth. The postwar years weren't much better: 150,000 manufacturing jobs were lost

between 1961 and 1983 and the port – still the UK's third largest in 1963 – finally closed in 1982 due to declining traffic.

The nadir came on 15 June 1996, when an IRA bomb wrecked a chunk of the city centre, but the subsequent reconstruction proved to be the beginning of the glass-and-chrome revolution so much in evidence today.

## ORIENTATION

Shoe power and the excellent Metrolink tram are the only things you'll need to get around the compact city centre. All public transport converges at Piccadilly Gardens, a few blocks southeast of the cathedral. Directly north is the on-the-up boho Northern Quarter, with its offbeat boutiques, hip cafes and fabulous record shops. A few blocks south is the Gay Village, centred on Canal St and, just next to it, Chinatown, basically a bunch of restaurants clustered around Portland St.

Southwest of the city centre is Castlefield and Deansgate Locks, a development that has successfully converted the 19th-century canalside industrial infrastructure into a groovy weekend playground for the city's fine young things. Further west again – and accessible via Metrolink – are the recently developed Salford Quays, home to the fab Lowry complex and the Imperial War Museum North. Not far away is Old Trafford football stadium, where Manchester United's global stars earn their fabulous keep.

For information on getting around, see p583.

## INFORMATION
### Bookshops

**Cornerhouse** ( ☎ 0161-200 1514; www.cornerhouse .org; 70 Oxford St) Art and film books, specialist magazines and kitschy cards.
**Waterstone's** Deansgate ( ☎ 0161-832 1992); St Anne's Sq ( ☎ 0161-837 3000)

### Emergency

**Ambulance** ( ☎ 0161-436 3999)
**Police station** ( ☎ 0161-872 5050; Bootle St)

### Internet Access

**Central Library** ( ☎ 0161-234 1982; St Peter's Sq; per 30min £1; ⏱ internet access 1-6pm Mon-Sat)
**L2K Internet Gaming Cafe** ( ☎ 0161-244 5566; 32 Princess St; per 30min £2; ⏱ 9am-10pm Mon-Fri, 9am-9pm Sat & Sun)

### Internet Resources

**City Life** (www.manchestereveningnews.co.uk) The city's evening paper in electronic form.
**Manchester After Dark** (www.manchesterad.com) Reviews and descriptions of the best places to be when the sun goes down.
**Real Manchester** (www.realmanchester.com) Online guide to nightlife.
**Virtual Manchester** (www.manchester.com) Restaurants, pubs, clubs and where to sleep.
**Visit Manchester** (www.visitmanchester.com) The official website for Greater Manchester.

### Medical Services

**Cameolord Chemist** ( ☎ 0161-236 1445; St Peter's Sq; ⏱ 10am-10pm)
**Manchester Royal Infirmary** ( ☎ 0161-276 1234; Oxford Rd)

### Post

**Post office** (Brazennose St; ⏱ 9am-5.30pm Mon-Fri)

### Tourist Information

**Tourist office** ( ☎ 0871 222 8223; www.visitmanch ester.com; Town Hall Extension, St Peter's Sq; ⏱ 10am-5.15pm Mon-Sat, 10am-4.30pm Sun)

## SIGHTS & ACTIVITIES
### City Centre

The city's main administrative centre is the superb Victorian Gothic **town hall** (admission free, tours adult/child £5/4; ⏱ tours 2pm Sat Mar-Sep) that dominates Albert Sq. The interior is rich in sculpture and ornate decoration, while the exterior is crowned by an impressive 85m-high tower. You can visit the building on your own, but because it's the city's main administrative centre you won't get the same access as you would by taking an organised tour, which departs from the tourist office.

Just behind the town hall, the elegant Roman Pantheon lookalike **Central Library** ( ☎ 0161-234 1900; St Peter's Sq; admission free; ⏱ 10am-8pm Mon-Thu, 10am-6pm Fri & Sat) was built in 1934. It is the country's largest municipal library, with more than 20 miles of shelves.

#### MANCHESTER ART GALLERY

A superb collection of British art and a hefty number of European masters are on display at the city's top **gallery** ( ☎ 0161-235 8888; www.man chestergalleries.org; Mosley St; admission free; ⏱ 10am-5pm Tue-Sun). The older wing, designed by Charles Barry (of Houses of Parliament fame) in 1834, has an impressive collection that includes 37

**NORTHWEST ENGLAND**

# MANCHESTER

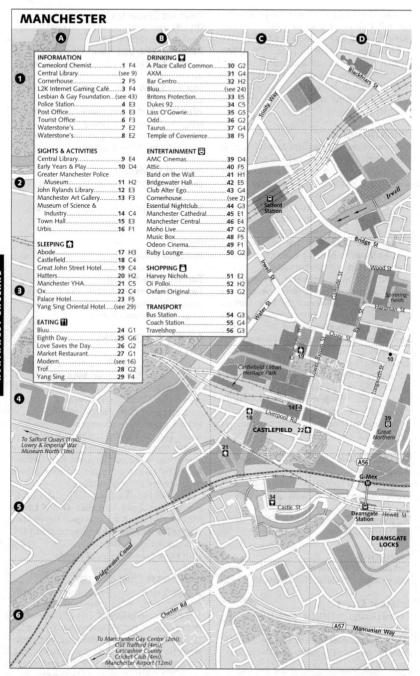

**INFORMATION**
Cameolord Chemist...............1 F4
Central Library.....................(see 9)
Cornerhouse.........................2 F5
L2K Internet Gaming Café......3 F4
Lesbian & Gay Foundation...(see 43)
Police Station.......................4 E3
Post Office...........................5 E3
Tourist Office.......................6 F3
Waterstone's........................7 E2
Waterstone's........................8 E2

**SIGHTS & ACTIVITIES**
Central Library.....................9 E4
Early Years & Play...............10 D4
Greater Manchester Police
   Museum...........................11 H2
John Rylands Library............12 E3
Manchester Art Gallery........13 F3
Museum of Science &
   Industry...........................14 C4
Town Hall...........................15 E3
Urbis.................................16 F1

**SLEEPING**
Abode................................17 H3
Castlefield..........................18 C4
Great John Street Hotel.......19 C4
Hatters..............................20 H2
Manchester YHA.................21 C5
Ox....................................22 C4
Palace Hotel.......................23 F5
Yang Sing Oriental Hotel.....(see 29)

**EATING**
Bluu.................................24 G1
Eighth Day.........................25 G6
Love Saves the Day.............26 G2
Market Restaurant..............27 G1
Modern.............................(see 16)
Trof.................................28 G2
Yang Sing..........................29 F4

**DRINKING**
A Place Called Common........30 G2
AXM.................................31 G4
Bar Centro.........................32 H2
Bluu.................................(see 24)
Britons Protection...............33 E5
Dukes 92...........................34 C5
Lass O'Gowrie....................35 G5
Odd.................................36 G2
Taurus..............................37 G4
Temple of Covenience.........38 F5

**ENTERTAINMENT**
AMC Cinemas......................39 D4
Attic.................................40 F5
Band on the Wall.................41 H1
Bridgewater Hall.................42 E5
Club Alter Ego....................43 G4
Cornerhouse.......................(see 2)
Essential Nightclub..............44 G3
Manchester Cathedral..........45 E1
Manchester Central.............46 E4
Moho Live..........................47 G2
Music Box...........................48 F5
Odeon Cinema....................49 F1
Ruby Lounge.......................50 G2

**SHOPPING**
Harvey Nichols....................51 E2
Oi Polloi.............................52 H2
Oxfam Original....................53 G2

**TRANSPORT**
Bus Station.........................54 G3
Coach Station.....................55 G4
Travelshop..........................56 G3

To Salford Quays (1mi);
Lowry & Imperial War
Museum North (1mi)

Castlefield Urban
Heritage Park

CASTLEFIELD

G-Mex

Deansgate
Station

DEANSGATE
LOCKS

Bridgewater Canal

Chester Rd

To Manchester Gay Centre (2mi);
Old Trafford (4mi);
Lancashire County
Cricket Club (4mi);
Manchester Airport (12mi)

Mancunian Way

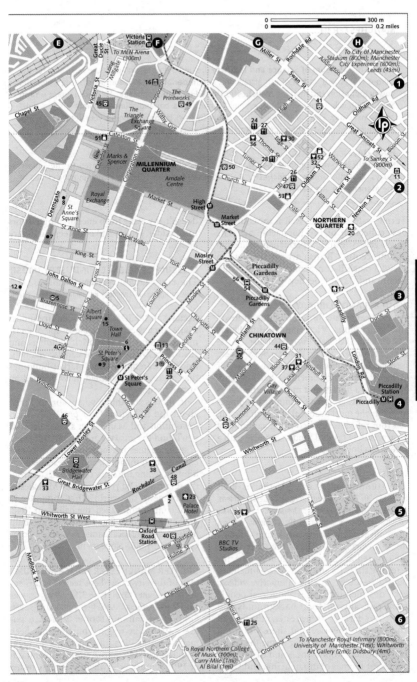

**MANCHESTER IN...**

**Two Days**
Explore the **Museum of Science and Industry** (below) before hopping on the Metrolink for the Salford Quays and its trio of top attractions: the **Imperial War Museum North** (opposite), the **Lowry** (opposite) and then the **Manchester United Museum** (opposite). Pick a restaurant – **Yang Sing** (p579) will do to kick off the evening – then find a bar and round the night off in a club.
The next day, kick off with a visit to **Urbis** (below) before indulging your retail chi in the boutiques and offbeat shops of the **Northern Quarter** (p583).

**Four Days**
Spread the two-day itinerary over three days, including a whole day devoted to the Salford Quays. Visit the **Greater Manchester Police Museum** (below) before examining the riches of the **Manchester Art Gallery** (p573).

Turner watercolours, as well as the country's best collection of Pre-Raphaelite art. The newer gallery features a permanent collection of 20th-century British art starring Lucien Freud, Francis Bacon, Stanley Spencer, Henry Moore and David Hockney.

### JOHN RYLANDS LIBRARY
An easy candidate for top building in town, this marvellous Victorian Gothic **library** ( ☎ 0161-834 5343; www.library.manchester.ac.uk; 35 Deansgate; admission free; ☽ 10am-5pm Mon & Wed-Sat, noon-5pm Tue & Sun) was one hell of a way for Rylands' widow to remember her husband, John. Less a library and more a cathedral to books, Basil Champneys' stunning building is arguably the most beautiful library in Britain. A £16m refit has resulted in the addition of a surprisingly tasteful modern annexe with a cafe and a bookshop.

### URBIS
The stunning glass triangle that is **Urbis** ( ☎ 0161-907 9099; www.urbis.org.uk; Cathedral Gardens, Corporation St; levels 2-4 admission free, charge for temporary exhibits; ☽ 10am-6pm Sun-Wed, 10am-8pm Thu-Sat) is a museum about how a city works and – often – doesn't work. The walls of the three floors are covered in compelling photographs, interesting statistics and informative timelines, but the best parts are the interactive videos, each of which tell stories about real people from radically different backgrounds and how they fare in Manchester. It's all well and good to theorise, but there's nothing like a real story to hammer home the truth. Homelessness, rootlessness and dislocation are major themes of urban living, and Urbis

doesn't shy away from encouraging visitors to consider what it's like to sleep on a park bench.

### MUSEUM OF SCIENCE & INDUSTRY (MOSI)
The city's largest **museum** ( ☎ 0161-832 1830; www.msim.org.uk; Liverpool Rd; admission free, charge for special exhibitions; ☽ 10am-5pm) comprises 2.8 hectares in the heart of 19th-century industrial Manchester. It's in a landscape of enormous, weather-stained brick buildings and rusting cast-iron relics of canals, viaducts, bridges, warehouses and market buildings that makes up Castlefield, now deemed an 'urban heritage park'.

If there's anything you want to know about the Industrial (and post-Industrial) Revolution and Manchester's key role in it, you'll find the answers among the collection of steam engines and locomotives, factory machinery from the mills, and the excellent exhibition telling the story of Manchester from the sewers up. Did you know that Manchester was home to the world's first computer (a giant contraption called 'the baby'), in 1948, or that the world's first submarine was built to the designs of local curate Reverend George Garrett, in 1880? Nope, neither did we.

### GREATER MANCHESTER POLICE MUSEUM
One of the city's best-kept secrets is this superb **museum** ( ☎ 0161-856 3287; www.gmp.police .uk; 57A Newton St; admission free; ☽ 10.30am-3.30pm Tue) housed within a former Victorian police station. The original building has been magnificently – if a little creepily – brought back to life, and you can wander in and out of 19th-century cells where prisoners rested

their heads on wooden (!!) pillows; visit a restored magistrates' court from 1895; and examine the case histories (complete with mugshots and photos of weapons) of some of the more notorious names to have passed through its doors.

## Salford Quays

West of the city centre along the Ship Canal, three major attractions draw in the punters, and a shopping centre makes sure they have outlets at which to spend their money. It's a cinch to get here from the city centre via Metrolink (£2); for the Imperial War Museum North and the Lowry, look for the Harbour City stop; get off at Old Trafford for the eponymous stadium.

### IMPERIAL WAR MUSEUM NORTH

War museums generally appeal to those with a fascination for military hardware and battle strategy (toy soldiers optional), but Daniel Libeskind's visually stunning **Imperial War Museum North** ( ☎ 0161-836 4000; www.iwm.org.uk /north; Trafford Wharf Rd; admission free; 10am-6pm Mar-Oct, 10am-5pm Nov-Feb) takes a radically different approach. War is hell, it tells us, but it's a hell we revisit with tragic regularity.

Although the audiovisuals and displays are quite compelling, the extraordinary aluminium-clad building itself is a huge part of the attraction, and the exhibition spaces are genuinely breathtaking. Libeskind designed three distinct structures (or shards) that represent the three main theatres of war: air, land and sea.

### LOWRY

Looking more like a shiny steel ship than an arts centre, the **Lowry** ( ☎ 0161-876 2020; www .thelowry.com; Pier 8, Salford Quays; 11am-8pm Tue-Fri, 10am-8pm Sat, 11am-6pm Sun & Mon) is the quays' most notable success. It attracts more than one million visitors a year to its myriad functions, which include everything from art exhibits and theatre to bars, restaurants and, inevitably, shops. You can even get married in the place.

The complex is home to more than 300 paintings and drawings by northern England's favourite artist, LS Lowry (1887–1976), who was born in nearby Stretford. He became famous for his humanistic depictions of industrial landscapes and northern towns, and gave his name to the complex.

### OLD TRAFFORD (MANCHESTER UNITED MUSEUM & TOUR)

Here's a paradox: the world's most famous and supported football club, beloved of fans from Bangkok to Buenos Aires, is the most hated club in England and has a smaller fan base in Manchester than its far less successful cross-town rival, Manchester City. United fans snigger and dismiss this as small-minded jealousy, while treating the **Old Trafford stadium** (www.manutd.com; Sir Matt Busby Way; 9.30am-5pm) like holy ground and the stars who play there like minor deities. Those stars return the compliment by winning everything – most recently a league and Champions' League double in 2008.

There's no denying that a visit to the stadium is one of the more memorable things you'll do here. We strongly recommend that you take the **tour** ( ☎ 0870 442 1994; adult/child £12/8; every 10min 9.40am-4.30pm except match days), which includes a seat in the stands, a stop in the changing rooms, a peek at the players' lounge (from which the manager is banned unless invited by the players) and a walk down the tunnel to the pitchside dugout, which is as close to ecstasy as many of the club's fans will ever get. It's pretty impressive stuff. The **museum** (adult/child £8.50/6.75; 9.30am-5pm), which is part of the tour but can be visited independently, has a comprehensive history of the club, and a state-of-the-art call-up system that means you can view your favourite goals – as well as having a holographic 'chat' with Sir Alex Ferguson.

## University of Manchester

About a mile south of the city, the University of Manchester is one of England's most extraordinary institutions, and is home to a superb art gallery.

### WHITWORTH ART GALLERY

Manchester's second most important **art gallery** ( ☎ 0161-275 7450; www.whitworth.manchester .ac.uk; University of Manchester, Oxford Rd; admission free; 10am-5pm Mon-Sat, noon-4pm Sun) has a wonderful collection of British watercolours. It also houses the best selection of historic textiles outside London, and has a number of galleries devoted to the work of artists from Dürer and Rembrandt to Lucien Freud and David Hockney.

All this high art aside, you may find that the most interesting part of the gallery is the group

**NORTHWEST ENGLAND**

of rooms dedicated to wallpaper – proof that bland pastels and horrible flowery patterns are not the final word in home decoration.

## MANCHESTER FOR CHILDREN

Urbis (p576) is always full of kids who find the interactive displays quite engaging, and the **Museum of Science and Industry** (p576) is the perfect all-day destination, offering a host of different activities and exhibits suited to younger visitors. Nearby, the canalside parks and walkways of Castlefield are pleasantly distracting. Manchester United's ground, **Old Trafford** (p577), is always popular with fans, who are getting younger and younger (kids seem to lose interest in Manchester City after they ask 'but what have they won?'). The **Imperial War Museum North** (p577) is designed to engage the interest of kids barely into double figures, despite its war-based themes not being a bunch of laughs.

If you're looking for some free time away from the kids, **Early Years & Play** ( ☎ 0161-234 7117; Overseas House, Quay St) is a city-centre crèche.

## QUIRKY MANCHESTER

You don't have to work too hard to find oddity in Manchester: spend enough time in Piccadilly Gardens and you'll know what we mean. As museums go, the **Greater Manchester Police Museum** (p576) is as memorable as it gets, especially if you spend any time in the Victorian police cells.

When you're done, you'll have to unwind with a pint in the **Temple of Convenience** (p580), a tiny basement pub with a terrific atmosphere located in…a former public toilet.

## TOURS

The tourist office (p573) sells tickets for all sorts of guided walks, which operate almost daily year round and cost £5/4 per adult/child.

## SLEEPING

The city's reputation as a capital of cool has seen the standards of style go up, and Manchester is now awash with all manner of designer digs. Remember that during the football season (August to May), rooms can be almost impossible to find if Manchester United is playing at home. If you are having difficulty finding a bed, the tourist office's accommodation service (£4) can help.

## City Centre

### BUDGET

**Manchester YHA** ( ☎ 0845 371 9647; www.yha.org .uk; Potato Wharf; dm incl breakfast from £14; **P** **Ⓛ** ) This purpose-built canalside hostel in the Castlefield area is one of the best in the country. It's a top-class option with four- and six-bed dorms, all with bathroom, as well as a host of good facilities.

**Hatters** ( ☎ 0161-236 9500; www.hattersgroup.com; 50 Newton St; dm/s/d/tr from £17/28/50/70; **P** **Ⓛ** ) The old-style lift and porcelain sinks are the only leftovers of this former milliner's factory, now one of the best hostels in town, with location to boot – smack in the heart of the Northern Quarter, you won't have to go far to get the best of alternative Manchester.

### MIDRANGE

**Ox** ( ☎ 0161-839 7740; www.theox.co.uk; 71 Liverpool Rd; d/tr from £55/75) Not quite your traditional B&B (breakfast is extra), but an excellent choice, nonetheless: nine ox-blood-red rooms with tidy amenities above a fine gastropub in the heart of Castlefield. It's the best deal in town for the location.

**Palace Hotel** ( ☎ 0161-288 1111; www.principal-hotels .com; Oxford St; r from £80) An elegant refurbishment of one of Manchester's most magnificent Victorian palaces has resulted in a pretty special boutique hotel, combining the grandeur of the public areas with the modern look of the bedrooms.

**Abode** ( ☎ 0161-247 7744; www.abodehotels.co.uk; 107 Piccadilly St; r from £80; **Ⓛ** ) Modern British style is the catchword at this converted textile factory, which has successfully combined the original fittings with 61 spanking-new bedrooms divided into four categories of ever-increasing luxury: Comfortable, Desirable, Enviable and Fabulous, the last being five seriously swanky top-floor suites.

**Castlefield** ( ☎ 0161-832 7073; www.castlefield-hotel .co.uk; 3 Liverpool Rd; s/d from £70/99; **P** ) This is another successful warehouse conversion that has resulted in a thoroughly modern business hotel. Overlooking the canal basin, it has spacious, comfortable rooms and excellent amenities, including a fitness centre and pool that are free to guests.

### TOP END

**ⓞⓤⓡ ⓟⓘⓒⓚ Yang Sing Oriental Hotel** ( ☎ 0161-920 9651; www.yangsingoriental.com; 36 Princess St; r/ste from £179/239; **Ⓛ** ) The city's most famous Chinese restaurant (see right) got into the hospitality business in 2008 with arguably the northwest's most luxurious small hotel. Japanese silk duvets and pillows; beautiful bespoke Asian furnishings; a complimentary minibar; and your choice of five separate room aromas (which you can select when booking) – just some of the extravagant offerings at this exquisitely elegant new hotel, which has already raised the hospitality bar by several notches.

**Great John Street Hotel** ( ☎ 0161-831 3211; www .greatjohnstreet.co.uk; Great John St; r £235-395; ▣ ) Elegant, designer luxury? Present. Fabulous rooms with all the usual delights (Egyptian cotton sheets, fabulous toiletries, freestanding baths and lots of high-tech electronics)? Present. A butler to run your bath in the Opus Grand Suite? Present. This former schoolhouse (ah, now you get it) is small and sumptuous – and just across the street from Granada TV studios.

## Salford Quays
**TOP END**

**Lowry** ( ☎ 0161-827 4000; www.rfhotels.com; 50 Dearman's Pl, Chapel Wharf; s/d from £350/385) Simply dripping with designer luxury and five-star comfort, Manchester's top hotel has fabulous rooms with enormous beds, ergonomically designed furniture, walk-in wardrobes, and bathrooms finished with Italian porcelain tiles and glass mosaic. You can soothe yourself with a skin-brightening treatment or an aromatherapy head-massage at the health spa.

# EATING

Only London can outdo Manchester for the choice of cafes and restaurants. There's something for every palate, from the ubiquitous-but-excellent selections in Chinatown to Wilmslow Rd (the extension of Oxford St/Rd), aka the Curry Mile, with its unsurpassed concentration of Indian and Pakistani eateries. Organic is the order of the day throughout the Northern Quarter (where you'll also find some excellent vegie spots), while the city's fanciest fare is to be found in the suburbs, especially West Didsbury. Following is but a small starter course.

## Budget

**Eighth Day** ( ☎ 0161-273 4878; 111 Oxford Rd; mains around £5; ☯ 9.30am-5pm Mon-Sat) New and most definitely improved after a major clean-up, this environmentally friendly hang-out is a

favourite with students. It sells everything to make you feel good about your place in the world, from fair-trade teas to homeopathic remedies. The vegetarian- and vegan-friendly menu is substantial.

**Trof** ( ☎ 0161-832 1870; 5-8 Thomas St; sandwiches £4, mains around £8; ☯ 9.30am-midnight) Great music, top staff and a fab selection of sandwiches, roasts and other dishes (the huge breakfast is a proper hangover cure), as well as a broad selection of beers and tunes (Tuesday night is acoustic night), have made this new opening a firm favourite with students.

**Love Saves the Day** ( ☎ 0161-832 0777; Tib St; lunch £6; ☯ 8am-7pm Mon-Wed, to 9pm Thu, to 8pm Fri, 10-6pm Sat, 10am-4pm Sun) The Northern Quarter's most popular cafe is a New York–style deli, small supermarket and sit-down eatery in one large, airy room. Everybody comes here – from crusties to corporate types – to sit around over a spot of lunch and discuss the day's goings-on. A wonderful spot. The house salad is £5.50.

## Midrange

**Al Bilal** ( ☎ 0161-257 0006; 87-89 Wilmslow Rd; mains £7-14; ☯ lunch & dinner Sun-Fri) It's a given that you cannot leave Manchester without tucking into a curry along Wilmslow Rd, which is as famous as Bradford or Birmingham for its Indian cuisine. There are so many great restaurants to pick from – and some pretty awful ones, too – but Al Bilal will treat you and your tummy just right with its excellent dishes.

**Yang Sing** ( ☎ 0161-236 2200; 34 Princess St; mains £9-16; ☯ lunch & dinner) A serious contender for best Chinese restaurant in England, Yang Sing attracts diners from all over with its exceptional Cantonese cuisine. From a dim-sum lunch to a full evening banquet, the food is superb, and the waiters will patiently explain the intricacies of each item to punters who can barely pronounce the names of the dishes.

**Bluu** ( ☎ 0161-839 7740; www.bluu.co.uk; Unit 1, Smithfield Market, Thomas St; 3-course lunch £15, dinner mains £10-15; ☯ lunch & dinner) It's a chain cafe-bar, but Manchester's version has retained its kudos thanks to its location, look and clientele – a steady stream of hipsters who appreciate its aforementioned strengths and menu, which offers an inventive choice of British and Continental dishes using only the freshest ingredients.

**Market Restaurant** ( ☎ 0161-834 3743; www.market-restaurant.com; 104 High St; mains £11-16; ☯ lunch

& dinner Wed-Fri, dinner Sat) It's a sorry-looking kind of place, but don't judge a restaurant by its shabby exterior: inside you'll find excellent British cuisine on a menu that changes monthly to take account of the season's best.

**our pick Modern** ( ☎ 0161-605 8282; Urbis, Cathedral Gardens, Corporation Street; 2-/3-course lunch £13/16, dinner mains £11-21; ☺ lunch & dinner) Top fare on top of the world, or an excellent meal atop Manchester's most distinctive landmark, Urbis, is one of the city's most enjoyable dining experiences. The food – mostly new British cuisine – will not disappoint, but it's being able to sit at a table close to the floor-to-ceiling windows that makes this place worthwhile.

## DRINKING

There's every kind of drinking hole in Manchester, from the really grungy ones that smell but have plenty of character to the ones that were designed by a team of architects but have the atmosphere of a freezer. Every neighbourhood in town has its favourites; here's a few to get you going.

### Bars

**A Place Called Common** ( ☎ 0161-832 9245; www.aplacecalledcommon.co.uk; 39-41 Edge St; ☺ noon-midnight Mon-Wed, to 1am Thu, to 2am Fri-Sat, 2pm-midnight Sun) Common by name but great by nature, this is a terrific boozer favoured by an unpretentious crowd who like the changing artwork on the walls and the DJs who play nightly.

**Bar Centro** ( ☎ 0161-835 2863; 72-74 Tib St; mains £6-9; ☺ noon-midnight Mon-Wed, to 1am Thu, to 2am Fri-Sat, 2pm-midnight Sun) A Northern Quarter stalwart, very popular with the bohemian crowd precisely because it doesn't try to be. Great beer, nice staff and a better-than-average bar

menu make this one of the choice spots in the area.

**Bluu** ( ☎ 0161-839 7740; www.bluu.co.uk; Unit 1, Smithfield Market, Thomas St; ☺ noon-midnight Sun-Mon, to 1am Tue-Thu, to 2am Fri-Sat) Our favourite of the Northern Quarter's collection of great bars. Bluu is cool, comfortable and comes with a great terrace on which to enjoy a pint and listen to music selected by folks with really good taste.

**Odd** ( ☎ 0161-833 0070; www.oddbar.co.uk; 30-32 Thomas St; ☺ 11am-11pm Mon-Sat, to 10.30pm Sun) This eclectic little bar – with its oddball furnishings, wacky tunes and antiestablishment crew of customers – is the perfect antidote to the increasingly samey look of so many modern bars. A slice of Mancuniana to be treasured.

**Temple of Convenience** ( ☎ 0161-288 9834; Great Bridgewater St; ☺ noon-midnight Mon-Thu, to 1am Fri-Sat, noon-11pm Sun) This tiny basement bar with a capacity of about 30 has a great jukebox and a fine selection of spirits, all crammed into a converted public toilet. Hardly your bog-standard pub.

### Pubs

**our pick Britons Protection** ( ☎ 0161-236 5895; 50 Great Bridgewater St; mains around £7) Whisky – 200 different kinds of it – is the beverage of choice at this liver-threatening, proper English pub that also does Tudor-style meals (boar, venison and the like). An old-fashioned boozer; no fancy stuff.

**Dukes 92** ( ☎ 0161-839 8646; 2 Castle St) Castlefield's best pub, housed in converted stables that once belonged to the duke of Bridgewater, has comfy, deep sofas inside and plenty of seating outside, overlooking lock 92 of the Rochdale Canal – hence the name. If it's sunny, there's no better spot to enjoy a pint of ale.

**Lass O'Gowrie** ( ☎ 0161-273 6932; 36 Charles St; mains around £6) A Victorian classic off Princess St that brews its own beer in the basement. It's a favourite with students, old-timers and a clique of BBC employees who work just across the street in the Beeb's Manchester HQ. It also does good-value bar meals.

## ENTERTAINMENT
### Nightclubs

A handy tip: if you want to thrive in Manchester's excellent nightlife, drop all mention of Madchester (see boxed text, opposite) and keep talk of being 'up for it' to strict irony.

---

**TOP FIVE PUBS FOR A PINT IN THE NORTHWEST**

- **Philharmonic** (p596); Liverpool
- **Temple of Convenience** (right); Manchester
- **Britons Protection** (right); Manchester
- **Albion** (p587); Chester
- **Baby Cream** (p597); Liverpool

---

NORTHWEST ENGLAND

## THE MADCHESTER SOUND

It is often claimed that Manchester is the engine room of British pop. If this is indeed the case, then the chief engineer was TV presenter and music impresario Tony Wilson (1950–2007), founder of Factory Records. This is the label that in 1983 released New Order's groundbreaking 'Blue Monday', to this day the best-selling 12" in British history, which successfully fused the guitar-driven sound of punk with a pulsating dance beat.

Wilson opened the now-legendary Haçienda, which really took off when the club embraced the new sound coming out of Chicago and Detroit: house. DJs Mike Pickering, Graeme Park and Jon Da Silva were the music's most important apostles, and when ecstasy hit the scene late in the late 1980s, it seemed that every kid in town was 'mad for it'.

Heavily influenced by these new arrivals, the city's guitar bands took notice and began shaping their sounds to suit the clubbers' needs. The most successful was the Stone Roses, who in 1989 released 'Fools Gold', a pulsating hit with the rapid shuffle of James Brown's 'Funky Drummer' and a druggie guitar sound that drove dancers wild. Around the same time, Happy Mondays hit the scene with the infectious 'Hallelujah'. The other big anthems of the day were 'The One I Love' by the Charlatans, 'Voodoo Ray' by A Guy Called Gerald, and 'Pacific' by 808 State – all local bands and producers. The party known as Madchester was officially opened.

The party ended in 1992. Overdanced and overdrugged, the city woke up with a terrible hangover. The Haçienda went bust, the Happy Mondays went nuts and the Stone Roses fell apart. The fertile crossover scene virtually disappeared and the two genres withdrew into a more familiar isolation. And then Oasis hit the scene.

They may have been Manchester's most successful ever band – and authors of a catchy tune or two – but Oasis' almost total debt to the Beatles' chord structures and melody lines, as well as the tiresome posturing of the Gallagher brothers, resulted in their inability to establish themselves as anything other than a super-successful flash in the pan. They may have their millions, but give us Morrissey, Marr and co any day of the week.

Today, there is no such thing as Madchester. Eager to transcend the clichés that their success engendered, most of the city's musical talents refuse to be labelled as having any particular sound: jazzy house giant Mr Scruff (whose excellent Keep It Unreal nights are yours for the dancing at Music Box; see below), for instance, doesn't sound anything like the folksy guitar style of Badly Drawn Boy or the funky hip-hop beats of Rae & Christian.

But fear not: there is still a terrific club scene and Manchester remains at the vanguard of dance-floor culture. There's a forever-changing mixture of club nights, so check the *Manchester Evening News* for details of what's on. Following are our favourite places.

**Music Box** ( ☎ 0161-236 9971; www.musicboxmanch ester.com; 65 Oxford St; admission £6-12; ♥ 8pm-midnight Wed & Thu, 10pm-3am Fri & Sat) Deep in Jilly's Rockworld complex you'll find our favourite club in town and – judging by the queues – almost everyone else's, too. The punters come for the superb monthly club nights, such as Mr Scruff's Keep It Unreal, as well a host of terrific one-offs.

**Attic** ( ☎ 0161-236 6071; www.thirstyscholar.co.uk; New Wakefield St; admission free; ♥ 11pm-2am Thu-Fri, to 3am Sat) This superb venue is at the top of a flight of stairs, in a building beneath a railway arch. Northern Soul nights share space with techno, alt grunge and live music nights. A student favourite and a great night out.

**Sankey's** ( ☎ 0161-950 4201; www.sankeys.info; Radium St, Ancoats; admission free-£12; ♥ 10pm-3am Thu & Fri, 10pm-4am Sat) With regulars like Danny Tenaglia, Sasha, and Layo & Bushwacka in the box, hard-core clubbers are in good hands when they trek out to the middle of Ancoats. Techno, breakbeats, tribal and progressive house.

## Cinemas

**Cornerhouse** ( ☎ 0161-228 2463; www.cornerhouse.org; 70 Oxford St) Your only destination for good arthouse releases; also has a gallery, bookshop and cafe.

**Odeon Cinema** ( ☎ 0870 224 4007; www.odeon .co.uk; The Printworks, Exchange Sq) An ultramodern 20-screen complex in the middle of the Printworks centre.

**AMC Cinemas** ( ☎ 0161-817 3000; www.amccinemas .co.uk; The Great Northern, 235 Deansgate) A new 16-screen multiplex in a retail centre that was formerly a goods warehouse for the Northern Railway Company.

## Live Music

### ROCK MUSIC

**Band on the Wall** ( ☎ 0161-834 1786; www.bandonthewall .org; 25 Swan St) A top-notch venue that hosts everything from rock to world music, with splashes of jazz, blues and folk thrown in for good measure.

**Manchester Central** ( ☎ 0161-834 2700; www .manchestercentral.co.uk; Windmill St) A midsized venue southwest of St Peter's Sq, hosting rock concerts by not-quite-super-successful bands as well as exhibitions and indoor sporting events.

**MEN Arena** ( ☎ 0161-950 5000; Great Ducie St) A giant arena north of the centre that hosts large-scale rock concerts (as well as being the home of the city's ice-hockey and basketball teams).

**Moho Live** ( ☎ 0161-834 8188; www.moholive.com; 21-31 Oldham St) A new 500-capacity live-music venue that has already proven incredibly popular with its line-up of live music and club nights.

**Ruby Lounge** ( ☎ 0161-834 1392; 26-28 High St) Terrific new live music venue in the Northern Quarter that features mostly rock bands.

### CLASSICAL MUSIC

**Bridgewater Hall** ( ☎ 0161-907 9000; www.bridgewa ter-hall.co.uk; Lower Mosley St) The world-renowned Hallé Orchestra has its home at this enormous and impressive concert hall, which hosts up to 250 concerts and events a year. It has a widespread program that includes opera, folk music, children's shows, comedy and contemporary music.

**Lowry** ( ☎ 0161-876 2000; www.thelowry.com; Pier 8, Salford Quays) Two theatres – the 1750-seat Lyric and 460-seat Quays – host a diverse range of performances, from dance to comedy.

**Manchester Cathedral** ( ☎ 0161-833 2220; Victoria St) Hosts a summer season of concerts by the Cantata Choir and ensemble groups.

---

**TOP FIVE MANCHESTER ALBUMS**

- *Some Friendly* Charlatans
- *Pills 'n' Thrills & Bellyaches* Happy Mondays
- *Stone Roses* The Stone Roses
- *Strangeways Here We Come* The Smiths
- *Permanent* Joy Division

---

**Royal Northern College of Music** ( ☎ 0161-907 5555; www.rncm.ac.uk; 124 Oxford Rd) Presents a full program of extremely high-quality classical music and other contemporary offerings.

## Sport

For most people, Manchester plus sport equals football, and football means Manchester United. That may be true for outsiders (which is why United is covered in the Sights & Activities section, p577), but not for most Mancunians. Like all good northerners, they're more comfortable supporting the scrappy underdog with the huge heart, rather than the well-oiled football machine.

### MANCHESTER CITY

Manchester's best-loved team is the perennial underachiever, Manchester City, who in 2008 turned the football world on its head by becoming the property of billionaire Sheikh Mansour bin Zayed Al Nahyan of Abu Dhabi who has promised to turn the Blues into the world's biggest club. Whatever happens, fans will continue to pack out the **City of Manchester Stadium** (Sportcity, Rowsley St), where you can also enjoy the **Manchester City Experience** ( ☎ 0870 062 1894; www.mcfc.co.uk; adult/child £9.50/6; ⊙ 10.30am, 2pm & 3.15pm Mon-Sat, 11.45am & 1.45pm Sun except match days): a tour of the ground, dressing rooms and museum before the inevitable steer into the kit shop. Tours must be booked in advance. Take bus 216, 217, 230, X36 or X37 from Piccadilly Gardens.

### LANCASHIRE COUNTY CRICKET CLUB

Cricket is a big deal here, and the **Lancashire club** ( ☎ 0161-282 4000; Warwick Rd), founded in 1816 as the Aurora before changing its name in 1864, is one of the most beloved of England's county teams. This is despite the fact that it hasn't won the county championship since 1930. The really big match in Lancashire's calendar is the Roses match against Yorkshire, but if you're not around for that, the other games in the county season (admission £11 to £17) are a great day out. The season runs throughout the summer.

International test matches, recently starring local hero Andrew 'Freddie' Flintoff, are also played here occasionally.

## SHOPPING

The huge selection of shops here will send a shopper's pulse into orbit; every taste and

The city's gay scene is unrivalled outside London, and caters to every taste. Its healthy heart beats loudest in the Gay Village, centred on handsome Canal St. Here you'll find bars, clubs, restaurants and – crucially – karaoke joints that cater almost exclusively to the pink pound.

The country's biggest gay and lesbian arts festival, **Queer Up North** ( ☎ 0161-833 2288; www .queerupnorth.com), takes place every two years – the next is in spring 2009. **Manchester Pride** ( ☎ 0161-236 7474; www.manchesterpride.com) is a 10-day festival in the middle of August each year and attracts over 500,000 people.

There are bars to suit every taste, but you won't go far wrong in **AXM** ( ☎ 0161-236 6005; www.axm-bar.co.uk; 10 Canal St), which is more of a cocktail lounge for the city's flash crowd; or **Taurus** ( ☎ 0161-236 4593; www.taurus-bar.co.uk; 1 Canal St), which is a little shabbier but equally good fun.

For your clubbing needs, look no further than **Club Alter Ego** ( ☎ 0161-236 9266; www.club alterego.co.uk; 105-107 Princess St; admission £5-9; ☻ 11pm-5am Thu-Sat), home to the fabulous Poptastic, and **Essential Nightclub** ( ☎ 0161-236 0077; www.essentialmanchester.com; 8 Minshull St; admission £5-9; ☻ 11pm-5am Thu-Sat), which is just as popular.

For more information, check with the **Manchester Gay Centre** ( ☎ 0161-274 3814; Sydney St, Salford) and the **Lesbian & Gay Foundation** ( ☎ 0161-235 8035; www.lgf.org.uk; 105-107 Princess St; ☻ 4-10pm). The city's best pink website is www.visitgaymanchester.co.uk.

budget is catered for. By the time you read this, the new Spinningfields retail centre on Deansgate will have opened, and the city will have yet *another* convenient, enclosed space for you to part with your money.

### Millennium Quarter
The area around New Cathedral St, Exchange Sq and the impressive Triangle shopping arcade is the hot new shopping district, full of chichi boutiques and the king of all department stores, **Harvey Nichols** ( ☎ 0161-828 8888; 21 New Cathedral St).

### Northern Quarter
Rag-trade wholesalers have given way to independent retailers stocking all manner of hip urban wear, retro fashions and other left-of-centre threads. Of the myriad shops, we like **Oi Polloi** ( ☎ 0161-831 7870; 70 Tib St), which specialises in trendy outdoor clothing and footwear; and the marvellous **Oxfam Original** ( ☎ 0161-839 3160; Unit 8, Smithfield Bldg, Oldham St), which has terrific retro gear from the 1960s and '70s.

### West End
Everything needs a catchy name, so the traditionally upmarket shopping area around St Anne's Sq, King St and Bridge St – full of attractive boutiques for designers, both home-grown and international – is now called the West End.

## GETTING THERE & AWAY
### Air
**Manchester Airport** ( ☎ 0161-489 3000; www.manch esterairport.co.uk), south of the city, is the largest airport outside London and is served by 17 locations throughout Britain.

### Bus
**National Express** ( ☎ 08717 81 81 81; www.nationalexpress .com) serves most major cities almost hourly from Chorlton St coach station in the city centre. Destinations include Liverpool (£5, 1¼ hours, hourly), Leeds (£7.60, one hour, hourly) and London (£23, 3¾ hours, hourly).

### Train
Manchester Piccadilly (east of the Gay Village) is the main station for trains to and from the rest of the country, although Victoria station (north of Urbis) serves Halifax and Bradford. The two stations are linked by Metrolink. Trains head to Blackpool (£12.20, 1¼ hours, half-hourly), Liverpool Lime St (£8.80, 45 minutes, half-hourly), Newcastle (£41.20, three hours, six daily) and London (£115, three hours, seven daily).

## GETTING AROUND
### To/From the Airport
The airport is 12 miles south of the city. A train to or from Victoria station costs £3.80, and a coach is £3.20. A taxi is nearly four times as much in light traffic.

## Public Transport

The excellent public-transport system can be used with a variety of **Day saver tickets** (bus £3, bus & train £3.80, bus & Metrolink £4.50, train & Metrolink £5, bus, train & Metrolink £6). For inquiries about local transport, including night buses, contact **Travelshop** ( ☎ 0161-228 7811; www.gmpte.com; 9 Portland St, Piccadilly Gardens; ☺ 8am-8pm).

### BUS

Centreline bus 4 provides a free service around the heart of Manchester every 10 minutes. Pick up a route map from the tourist office. Most local buses start from Piccadilly Gardens.

### METROLINK

There are frequent **Metrolink** ( ☎ 0161-205 2000; www.metrolink.co.uk) trams between Victoria and Piccadilly train stations and G-Mex (for Castlefield) as well as further afield to Salford Quays. Buy your tickets from the platform machine.

### TRAIN

Castlefield is served by Deansgate station with rail links to Piccadilly, Oxford Rd and Salford stations.

# CHESHIRE

Quiet and genteel, pastoral Cheshire is a very black-and-white kind of place, full of half-timbered Tudor farmhouses (surrounded by fields populated by Friesian cows) that are more than just a little reminiscent of ye olde England. Which is exactly why so many of the soccerati millionaires plying their overpaid trades in nearby Manchester and Liverpool choose to live here, usually in OTT mansions carefully guarded by tall security gates (nothing gives the illusion of good taste like a bit of bling and tradition). For the rest of us mere mortals, however, Cheshire is really just about Chester.

## CHESTER
pop 80,130

Marvellous Chester is one of English history's greatest gifts to the contemporary visitor. Its red-sandstone wall, which today gift-wraps a tidy collection of Tudor and Victorian buildings, was built during Roman times. The town was then called Castra

Devana, and was the largest Roman fortress in Britain.

It's hard to believe today, but throughout the Middle Ages Chester made its money as the most important port in the northwest. However, the River Dee silted up over time and Chester fell behind Liverpool in importance.

Besides its obvious elegance and grace, Chester ekes out a fairly substantial living as a major retail centre and tourist hot spot: visitors come, see and shop.

## Orientation

Most places of interest are inside the walls where the Roman street pattern is relatively intact. From the Cross (the stone pillar that marks the town centre), four roads fan out to the four principal gates.

## Information

**Cheshire Constabulary** ( ☎ 01244-350000; Town Hall, Northgate St)
**Chester Visitors' Centre** ( ☎ 01244-351609; www.visitchester.com; Vicar's Lane; ☺ 9.30am-5.30pm Mon-Sat & 10am-4pm Sun May-Oct, 10am-5pm Mon-Sat Nov-Apr)
**Countess of Chester Hospital** ( ☎ 01244-365000; Health Park, Liverpool Rd)
**Post office** (2 St John St; ☺ 9am-5.30pm Mon-Sat)
**Tourist office** ( ☎ 01244-402111; www.chester.gov.uk; Town Hall, Northgate St; ☺ 9am-5.30pm Mon-Sat & 10am-4pm Sun May-Oct, 10am-5pm Mon-Sat Nov-Apr)

## Sights & Activities
### CITY WALLS

A good way to get a sense of Chester's unique character is to walk the 2-mile circuit along the walls that surround the historic centre. Originally built by the Romans around AD 70, the walls were altered substantially over the following centuries but have retained their current position since around 1200.

Of the many features along the walls, the most eye-catching is the prominent **Eastgate**, where you can see the most famous **clock** in England after London's Big Ben, built for Queen Victoria's Diamond Jubilee in 1897.

At the southeastern corner of the walls are the **wishing steps**, added in 1785; local legend claims that if you can run up and down these uneven steps while holding your breath your wish will come true. We question the veracity of this claim because our wish was not to twist an ankle.

Just inside Southgate, known here as **Bridgegate** (as it's at the northern end of the

Old Dee Bridge), is the 1664 **Bear & Billet** pub, Chester's oldest timber-framed building and once a tollgate into the city.

### ROWS

Chester's other great draw is the **Rows**, a series of two-level galleried arcades along the four streets that fan out in each direction from the central Cross. The architecture is a handsome mix of Victorian and Tudor (original and mock) buildings that house a fantastic collection of individually owned shops. The origin of the Rows is a little unclear, but it is believed that as the Roman walls slowly crumbled, medieval traders built their shops against the resulting rubble banks, while later arrivals built theirs on top.

### OTHER SIGHTS & ACTIVITIES

The **cathedral** ( ☎ 01244-324756; www.chestercathedral .com; Northgate St; adult/child £4/1.50; ☺ 9am-5pm Mon-Sat, 12.30-5pm Sun) was a Benedictine abbey built on the remains of an earlier Saxon church dedicated to St Werburgh, patron saint of Chester. The abbey was closed in 1540 as part of Henry VIII's dissolution frenzy, but was reconsecrated as a cathedral the following year. Although the cathedral itself was given a substantial Victorian facelift, the 12th-century cloister and its surrounding buildings are essentially unaltered and retain much of the structure from the early monastic years. There are 1¼-hour **guided tours** (free; ☺ 9.30am-4pm Mon-Sat) to really get to grips with the building and its history.

The excellent **Grosvenor Museum** ( ☎ 01244-402008; www.grosvenormuseum.co.uk; Grosvenor St; admission free; ☺ 10.30am-5pm Mon-Sat, 2-5pm Sun) is the place to go if you want to study Chester's rich and varied history, beginning with a comprehensive collection of Roman tombstones, the largest display in the country. At the back of the museum is a preserved Georgian house, complete with kitchen, drawing room, bedroom and bathroom.

The **Dewa Roman Experience** ( ☎ 01244-343407; www.dewaromanexperience.co.uk; Pierpoint Lane; adult/child £4.75/3; ☺ 9am-5pm Mon-Sat, 10am-5pm Sun), just off Bridge St, takes you through a reconstructed Roman street to reveal what Roman life was like.

Chester's most complete set of genuine Roman remains is opposite the visitors centre, outside the city walls. Here you'll find what's left of the **Roman amphitheatre** (admission

free); once an arena that seated 7000 spectators (making it the country's largest), now it's little more than steps buried in grass.

Steps at the back of **St John the Baptist Church** (Vicar's Lane) lead down to the riverside promenade known as the **Groves**. Here you can hire different kinds of **boats** (per hr £7-9; ☺ 9am-6pm Apr-Sep) with pedals, oars or small engines. The Groves is also the departure point for river cruises (see below).

### Tours

The tourist office and Chester Visitors' Centre offer a broad range of walking tours departing from both centres. Each tour lasts between 1½ and two hours.

**Ghosthunter Trail** (adult/child £5/4; ☺ 7.30pm Thu-Sat Jun-Oct, 7.30pm Sat Nov-May) The ubiquitous ghost tour, looking for things that go bump in the night.

**History Hunter** (adult/child £4.50/3.50; ☺ 10.30am) Two thousand years of Chester history.

**Secret Chester** (adult/child £5/4; ☺ 2pm Tue, Thu, Sat & Sun May-Oct) Exactly what it says on the tin.

You can also take a cruise along the Dee; contact **Bithell Boats** ( ☎ 01244-325394; www.show boatsofchester.co.uk) for details of its 30-minute and hour-long cruises up and down the Dee, including a foray into the gorgeous Eaton Estate, home of the duke and duchess of Westminster. All departures are from the riverside along the Groves and cost from £6 to £12.

### Sleeping

If you're visiting between Easter and September, you'd better book early. Except for a handful of options – including the city's best – most of the accommodation is outside the city walls but within easy walking distance of the centre. Hoole Rd, just under a mile's walk from the centre and leading beyond the railway tracks to the M53/M56, is lined with budget to midrange B&Bs.

Brook St near the train station has a couple of good-value B&Bs from around £24 per person.

### BUDGET

**Chester YHA** ( ☎ 0845 371 9357; www.yha.org.uk; 40 Hough Green; dm £20) Located in an elegant Victorian home about a mile from the city centre, this hostel has a variety of dorms that sleep from two to 10 people; there's also a cafeteria, a kitchen and a shop on the premises.

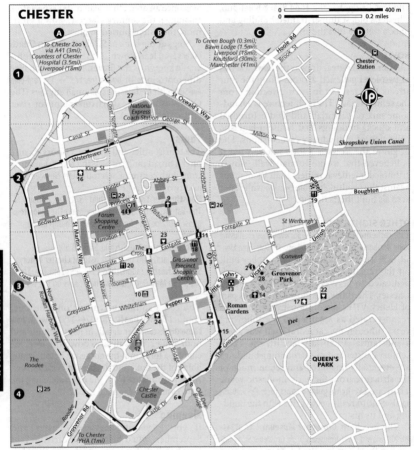

**CHESTER**

**NORTHWEST ENGLAND**

## MIDRANGE

**Grove Villa** ( ☎ 01244-349713; www.grovevillachester.com; 18 The Groves; r from £60) You won't find a more tranquil spot in town than this wonderfully positioned Victorian home overlooking the Dee. The rooms have antique beds and great river views.

**Bawn Lodge** ( ☎ 01244-324971; www.bawnlodge .co.uk; 10 Hoole Rd; r from £75) Spotless, colourful rooms make this charming guesthouse a very pleasant option. It's like staying with a favourite relative: no fuss but plenty of friendliness (and a delicious breakfast). Rates go up during the Chester Races (mainly in May and August).

**Chester Townhouse** ( ☎ 01244-350021; www.ches tertownhouse.co.uk; 23 King St; s/d £45/75; P ) Five beautifully decorated rooms in a handsome

17th-century house within the city walls make for a terrific option – you're close to the action and you'll sleep in relative luxury.

## TOP END

**our pick Green Bough** ( ☎ 01244-326241; www.green bough.co.uk; 60 Hoole Rd; r £175-345; P X Q ) The epitome of the boutique hotel, this exclusive, award-winning Victorian town house (winner of Small Hotel of the Year for 2006) has individually styled rooms dressed in the best Italian fabrics. The rooms come adorned with wall coverings, superb antique furniture and period cast-iron and wooden beds, including a handful of elegant four-posters. Modern touches include plasma-screen TVs, mini-stereos and a range of fancy toiletries.

## Eating

Chester has great food – it's just not in any of the tourist-oriented restaurants that line the Rows. Besides the better restaurants, you'll find the best grub in some of the pubs (see below).

**Old Harker's Arms** ( ☎ 01244-344525; www.hark ersarms-chester.co.uk; 1 Russell St; mains £9-14; ☿ 11am-late) An old-style boozer with a gourmet kitchen, this is the perfect place to tuck into Cumberland sausages or a Creole rice salad with sweet potatoes, and then rinse your palate with a pint of Waddies (as Wadworth Ale is know round here). It also serves bars snacks and sandwiches.

**Upstairs at the Grill** ( ☎ 01244-344883; www.upstair satthegrill.co.uk; 70 Watergate St; mains £15-25; ☿ dinner) A superb steakhouse almost hidden on the 2nd floor, this is the place to devour every cut of meat from American-style porterhouse to a sauce-sodden chateaubriand.

**Arkle** ( ☎ 01244-895618; www.chestergrosvenor.com; Chester Grosvenor Hotel & Spa, 58 Eastgate St; 3-course dinner £59; ☿ dinner Tue-Sat) Named after the famous Irish champion racehorse, Simon Radley's Arkle serves up a sumptuous feast of French-inspired classics such as tranche of monkfish with air-dried ham, and braised turbot with baby squid. It's elegant (gentlemen in jackets, please) and sophisticated and has a Michelin star to prove it.

## Drinking

**Falcon** ( ☎ 01244-314555; Lower Bridge St; mains from £5.50) This is an old-fashioned boozer with a lovely atmosphere; the surprisingly adventurous menu offers up dishes such as Jamaican peppered beef or spicy Italian sausage casserole. Great for both a pint and a bite.

**Albion** ( ☎ 01244-340345; 4 Albion St; mains £8-11) No children, no music, and no machines or big screens (but plenty of Union Jacks).

This 'family hostile' Edwardian classic pub is a throwback to a time when ale-drinking still had its own *rituals* – another word for ingrained prejudices. Still, this is one of the finest pubs in northwest England precisely because it doggedly refuses to modernise.

Other good pubs include the **Boat House** (The Groves), with great views overlooking the river, and the **Boot Inn** (Eastgate St), where 14 Roundheads were killed.

## Entertainment

### SPORT

### Horse Racing

Chester's ancient and very beautiful racetrack is the **Roodee** ( ☎ 01244-304600; www.chester-races .co.uk; ☿ May-Sep), on the western side of the walls, which has been hosting horse races since the 16th century. Highlights of the summer flat season include the two-day July Festival and the August equivalent.

## Getting There & Away

### BUS

**National Express** ( ☎ 08717 81 81 81; www.nationalexpress .com) coaches stop on Vicar's Lane, just opposite the tourist office by the Roman amphitheatre. Destinations include Birmingham (£10.70, 2½ hours, four daily), Liverpool (£6.90, one hour, three daily), London (£22.40, 5½ hours, three daily) and Manchester (£6.10, 1¼ hours, three daily).

For information on local bus services, ring the **Cheshire Bus Line** ( ☎ 01244-602666). Local buses leave from the Town Hall bus exchange on Princess St. On Sundays and bank holidays a **Sunday adventurer ticket** (adult/child £4/3) gives you unlimited travel in Cheshire.

### TRAIN

The train station is about a mile from the city centre via Foregate St and City Rd, or

NORTHWEST ENGLAND

### ROYAL MAY DAY

Since 1864 Knutsford has liked to go a bit wild on Royal May Day. The main festivities take place on the Heath, a large area of common land, and include Morris dancing, brass bands and a pageant of historical characters from fiction and fact. Perhaps the most interesting tradition is that of 'sanding', whereby the streets are covered in colourful messages written in sand. Legend has it that the Danish King Knut, while crossing the marsh between Over and Nether Knutsford, scrawled a message in the sand wishing happiness to a young couple who were on the way to their wedding. The custom is also practised on weddings and feast days.

Brook St. City-Rail Link buses are free for people with rail tickets, and operate between the station and Bus Stop A on Frodsham St. Trains travel to Liverpool (£4.45, 45 minutes, hourly), London Euston (£61.60, 2½ hours, hourly) and Manchester (£11.20, one hour, hourly).

### Getting Around

Much of the city centre is closed to traffic from 10.30am to 4.30pm, so a car is likely to be a hindrance. Anyway, the city is easy to walk around and most places of interest are close to the wall.

City buses depart from the **Town Hall Bus Exchange** ( ☎ 01244-602666).

**Davies Bros Cycles** ( ☎ 01244-371341; 5 Delamere St) has mountain bikes for hire at £14 per day.

## AROUND CHESTER

### Chester Zoo

The largest of its kind in the country, **Chester Zoo** ( ☎ 01244-380280; www.chesterzoo.org.uk; adult/child £15/11; ☑ 10am-dusk, last admission 4pm Mon-Fri, 5pm Sat & Sun Apr-Oct & 3pm Mon-Fri & 4pm Sat & Sun Nov-Mar) is about as pleasant a place as caged animals in artificial renditions of their natural habitats could ever expect to live. It's so big that there's even a **monorail** (adult/child £2/1.50) and a **waterbus** (adult/child £2/1.50) on which to get around. The zoo is on the A41, 3 miles north of Chester's city centre. Buses 11C and 12C (£2.50 return, every 15 minutes Monday to Saturday, half-hourly Sunday) run between Chester's Town Hall bus exchange and the zoo.

# LIVERPOOL

pop 469, 020

Desperate for the kind of recognition given its neighbour and perennial rival Manchester, Liverpool took to its role as European Capital of Culture for 2008 with admirable fervour. The title itself may not have amounted to much more than an appearance at the launch by Ringo Starr, and a year-long program of events that would have probably happened anyway, but the city grabbed the opportunity to remake and reshape itself with both hands…and still hasn't let go.

Frankly, the makeover was long overdue. Much of the city centre was something of a 1970s urban nightmare, a dodgy mix of shuttered buildings and ugly retail outlets; but a seemingly never-ending program of urban regeneration has seen the restoration of most of Liverpool's architectural treasures and the construction of some swanky new ones, including the mammoth, ultra-swish O1 Place, a retail centre that should generate the shekels the city desperately needs if it wants to reclaim some of its 19th-century greatness.

What's never been in question are Liverpool's cultural credentials. The city's store of superb museums and top-class art galleries – all free – have put paid to the scurrilous rumour that Liverpool peaked with the Beatles: in 2004 the whole of the waterfront and docks was declared a Unesco World Heritage Site because there are more listed buildings here than in any other city in England except London. And then, of course, there's the nightlife – as rich and varied as you'd expect from a good northern city.

## HISTORY

Liverpool grew wealthy on the back of the triangular trading of slaves, raw materials and finished goods. From 1700 ships carried cotton goods and hardware from Liverpool to West Africa, where they were exchanged for slaves, who in turn were carried to the West Indies and Virginia, where they were exchanged for sugar, rum, tobacco and raw cotton.

As a great port, the city drew thousands of Irish and Scottish immigrants, and its Celtic influences are still apparent. However, between 1830 and 1930 nine million emigrants – mainly English, Scots and Irish, but also Swedes, Norwegians and Russian Jews – sailed from here for the New World.

The start of WWII led to a resurgence of Liverpool's importance. More than one million American GIs disembarked here before D-Day and the port was, once again, hugely important as the western gateway for transatlantic supplies.

The GIs brought with them the latest American records, and Liverpool was thus the first European port of call for the new rhythm and blues that would eventually become rock 'n' roll. Within 20 years, the Mersey Beat was *the* sound of British pop, and four mop-topped Scousers had formed a skiffle band…

## ORIENTATION

Liverpool is a cinch to get around. The main attractions are Albert Dock (west of the city centre), and the trendy Ropewalks area (south of Hanover St and west of the two cathedrals). Lime St station, the Paradise St bus station, the 08 Place tourist office and the Cavern Quarter – a mecca for Beatles fans – lie just to the north.

The tourist office and many of the city's hotels have an excellent map with all of the city's attractions clearly outlined.

## INFORMATION
### Bookshops
**Waterstone's** ( ☎ 0151-708 6861; 14-16 Bold St)

### Emergency
**Merseyside police headquarters** ( ☎ 0151-709 6010; Canning Pl) Opposite Albert Dock.

### Internet Access
**CafeLatte.net** ( ☎ 0151-709 9683; 4 South Hunter St; per 30min £1.50; ☺ 9am-6pm)
**Planet Electra** ( ☎ 0151-708 0303; 36 London Rd; per 30min £1.50; ☺ 9am-5pm)

### Internet Resources
**Clubs in Liverpool** (www.clubsinliverpool.co.uk) Everything you need to know about what goes on when the sun goes down.
**Liverpool Magazine** (www.liverpool.com) Insiders' guide to the city, including lots of great recommendations for food and nights out.
**Mersey Guide** (www.merseyguide.co.uk) Guide to the Greater Mersey area.
**Merseyside Today** (www.merseysidetoday.co.uk) Guide to the city and surrounding area.
**Tourist office** (www.visitliverpool.com)

### Medical Services
**Mars Pharmacy** ( ☎ 0151-709 5271; 68 London Rd) Open until 10pm every night.
**Royal Liverpool University Hospital** ( ☎ 0151-706 2000; Prescot St)

### Post
**Post office** (Ranelagh St; ☺ 9am-5.30pm Mon-Sat)

---

**LIVERPOOL IN…**

**Two Days**
Head to the waterfront and explore the Albert Dock museums – the **Tate Liverpool** (p593), the **Merseyside Maritime Museum** (p592) and the unmissable **International Slavery Museum** (p593) – before paying tribute to the Fab Four at the **Beatles Story** (p593). Keep to the Beatles theme and head north towards the Cavern Quarter around Mathew St before surrendering to the retail giant that is **Liverpool ONE** (p598), with its hundreds of shops. Round off your evening with dinner at **London Carriage Works** (p596) and a pint at the marvellous **Philharmonic** (p596), and wrap yourself in the crisp linen sheets of the **Hope Street Hotel** (p595). Night hawks can tear it up in the bars (see City Centre, p596) and clubs (see Nightclubs, p597) of the hip **Ropewalks** area. The next day, explore the city's two **cathedrals** (p592) and check out the twin delights of the **World Museum Liverpool** (p591) and the **Walker Art Gallery** (p591).

**Four Days**
Follow the two-day itinerary but add in a **Yellow Duckmarine tour** (p594) to experience the docks from the water. Make a couple of pilgrimages to suit your interests: visit **Mendips** (see the boxed text, p592) and **20 Forthlin Rd** (see the boxed text, p592), the childhood homes of John Lennon and Paul McCartney, respectively; or walk on holy ground at Anfield, home of **Liverpool Football Club** (p598). Race junkies can head out to the visitor centre at **Aintree racecourse** (see the boxed text, p598), which hosts England's most beloved race, the Grand National.

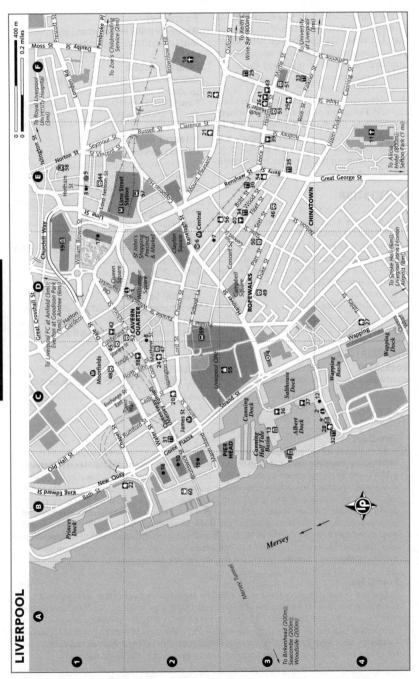

**NORTHWEST ENGLAND**

## Tourist Information

The tourist office has three branches in the city. It also has an **accommodation hotline** (☎ 0845 601 1125; 9am-5.30pm Mon-Fri, 10am-4pm Sat).

**08 Place tourist office** (☎ 0151-233 2008; Whitechapel; 9am-8pm Mon-Sat, 11am-4pm Sun Apr-Sep, 9am-6pm Mon-Sat, 11am-4pm Sun Oct-Mar) The main branch of the tourist office.

**Albert Dock tourist office** (☎ 0151-478 4599) Anchor Courtyard ( 10am-6pm); Merseyside Maritime Museum ( 10am-6pm)

## SIGHTS

The wonderful Albert Dock is the city's biggest tourist attraction, and the key to understanding the city's history, but the city centre is where you'll find most of Liverpool's real day-to-day life.

## City Centre
### ST GEORGE'S HALL

Arguably Liverpool's most impressive building, **St George's Hall** (☎ 0151-707 2391; William Brown St; admission free; 10am-5pm Tue-Sat, 1-5pm Sun) was built in 1854 and restored in recent years to the tune of £27 million – it finally reopened in 2007. Curiously, it was built as law courts *and* a concert hall – presumably a judge could pass sentence and then relax to a string quartet. Tours (£5) of the hall are run in conjunction with the tourist office; check for times.

### WALKER ART GALLERY

Touted as the 'National Gallery of the North', the city's foremost **gallery** (☎ 0151-478 4199; www.liverpoolmuseums.org.uk/walker; William Brown St; admission free; 10am-5pm) is the national gallery for northern England, housing an outstanding collection of art dating from the 14th century. Its strong suits are Pre-Raphaelite art, modern British art, and sculpture – not to mention the rotating exhibits of contemporary expression.

### WORLD MUSEUM LIVERPOOL

Natural history, science and technology are the themes of this sprawling **museum** (☎ 0151-478 4399; www.liverpoolmuseums.org.uk/wml; William Brown St; admission free; 10am-5pm), where exhibits range from birds of prey to space exploration. It also includes the country's only free planetarium. This vastly entertaining and educational museum is divided into four major sections: the Human World, one of the top anthropological collections in the country; the Natural World, which includes a new aquarium as well as live insect colonies; Earth, a geological treasure trove; and Space & Time, which includes the planetarium. Highly recommended.

**NORTHWEST ENGLAND**

## THE CATHEDRALS

The city's two cathedrals are separated by the length of Hope St.

### Metropolitan Cathedral of Christ the King

At the northern end of Hope St, off Mt Pleasant, you'll find the Roman Catholic **Metropolitan Cathedral of Christ the King** ( ☎ 0151-709 9222;  8am-6pm Mon-Sat, 8am-5pm Sun Oct-Mar). It was completed in 1967 according to the design of Sir Frederick Gibberd, and after the original plans by Sir Edwin Lutyens, whose crypt is inside. It's a mightily impressive modern building that looks like a soaring concrete tepee, hence its nickname – Paddy's Wigwam.

### Liverpool Cathedral

At Hope St's southern end stands the life work of Sir Giles Gilbert Scott (1880–1960), the neo-Gothic **Liverpool Cathedral** ( ☎ 0151-709 6271; www.liverpoolcathedral.org.uk; Hope St;  8am-6pm). Sir Giles' other contributions to the world were the red telephone box, and the power station in London that is now home to the Tate Modern. Size is a big deal here: this is the largest church in England and the largest Anglican cathedral in the world. The central bell is the world's third-largest (with the world's highest and heaviest peal), while the organ, with its 9765 pipes, is probably the world's largest operational model.

A new visitor centre features the **Great Space Film & Audio Tour** ( ☎ 0151-702 7255; adult/child £4.25/3.50;  9am-4pm Mon-Sat, noon-2.30pm Sun), a 10-minute, panoramic high-definition movie about the history of the cathedral. It's followed by your own audiovisual tour, courtesy of a snazzy headset.

There are terrific views of Liverpool from the top of the cathedral's 101m **tower** ( ☎ 0151-702 7217; adult/child £4.25/3, combined tower & Great Space tour adult/child £6.75/5;  10am-5pm Mon-Sat, noon-2.30pm Sun).

## Albert Dock

Liverpool's biggest tourist attraction is **Albert Dock** ( ☎ 0151-708 8854; www.albertdock.com; admission free), 2¾ hectares of water ringed by enormous cast-iron columns and impressive five-storey warehouses; these make up the country's largest collection of protected buildings and are a World Heritage Site.

### MERSEYSIDE MARITIME MUSEUM

The story of one of the world's great ports is the theme of this excellent **museum** ( ☎ 0151-478 4499; www.liverpoolmuseums.org.uk/maritime; Albert Dock; admission free;  10am-5pm) and, believe us, it's a graphic and compelling page-turner. One of the many great exhibits is Emigration to a New World, which tells the story of nine million emigrants and their efforts

---

### DOING THE BEATLES TO DEATH

Although it's kind of hard to stomach anyone banging on about the Beatles being the best band in the world – they broke up in 1970, that's nearly 40 years ago! – it is easy to understand how Liverpool is still making as much as it can out of the phenomenon that was the Fab Four.

It doesn't matter that two of them are dead, that the much-visited Cavern Club is a reconstruction of the original club that was the scene of their earliest gigs, or that, if he were alive, John Lennon would have devoted much of his cynical energy to mocking the 'Cavern Quarter' that has grown up around Mathew St. No, it doesn't matter at all, because the phenomenon lives on and a huge chunk of the city's visitors come to visit, see and touch anything – and we mean anything – even vaguely associated with the Beatles.

Which isn't to say that a wander around Mathew St isn't fun: from shucking oysters in the Rubber Soul Oyster Bar to buying a Ringo pillowcase in the From Me to You shop, virtually all of your Beatles needs can be taken care of. For decent memorabilia, check out the **Beatles Shop** ( ☎ 0151-236 8066; www.thebeatleshop.co.uk; 31 Mathew St).

True fans will undoubtedly want to visit the National Trust–owned **Mendips**, the home where John lived with his Aunt Mimi from 1945 to 1963, and **20 Forthlin Rd**, the plain terraced home where Paul grew up; you can only do so by prebooked **tour** ( ☎ 0151-427 7231; adult/child £15/3;  10.30am & 11.20am Wed-Sun Easter-Oct) from outside the National Conservation Centre. Visitors to Speke Hall (see p600) can also visit both from there.

If you'd rather do it yourself, the tourist offices stock the *Discover Lennon's Liverpool* guide and map, and *Robin Jones' Beatles Liverpool*.

to get to North America and Australia; the walk-through model of a typical ship shows just how tough conditions on board really were.

### INTERNATIONAL SLAVERY MUSEUM

Museums are, by their very nature, like a still of the past, but the extraordinary **International Slavery Museum** ( ☎ 0151-478 4499; www.liverpoolmu seums.org.uk/ism; Albert Dock; admission free; ☑ 10am-5pm) resonates very much in the present. It reveals slavery's unimaginable horrors – including Liverpool's own role in the triangular slave trade – in a clear and uncompromising manner. It does this through a remarkable series of multimedia and other displays, and it doesn't baulk at confronting racism, slavery's shadowy ideological justification for this inhumane practice.

The history of slavery is made real through a series of personal experiences, including a carefully kept ship's log and captain's diary. These tell the story of one slaver's experience on a typical trip, departing Liverpool for West Africa. The ship then purchased or captured as many slaves as it could carry before embarking on the gruesome 'middle passage' across the Atlantic to the West Indies. The slaves that survived the torturous journey were sold for sugar, rum and molasses, which were then brought back to England for profit. Exhibits include original shackles, chains and instruments used to punish rebellious slaves – each piece of metal is more horrendous than the next.

It's heady, disturbing stuff, but as well as providing an insightful history lesson, we are reminded of our own obligations to humanity and justice throughout the museum, not least by the displayed words of Gee Barton, whose son Anthony was murdered in a racially motivated attack in the Liverpool suburb of Huyton on 30 July 2005: 'Do not let my son's death be in vain'. A visit to this magnificent museum is a good place to start.

### TATE LIVERPOOL

Touted as the home of modern art in the north, this **gallery** ( ☎ 0151-702 7400; www.tate. org.uk/liverpool; Albert Dock; admission free, special exhibitions adult/child from £5/4; ☑ 10am-5.50pm daily Jun-Aug, 10am-5.50pm Tue-Sun Sep-May) features a substantial checklist of 20th-century artists across its four floors, as well as touring exhibitions from the mother ship on London's Bankside. But it's all

a little sparse, with none of the energy we'd expect from the world-famous Tate.

### BEATLES STORY

Liverpool's most popular **museum** ( ☎ 0151-709 1963; www.beatlesstory.com; Albert Dock; adult/child £12.50/6.50; ☑ 9am-7pm) won't illuminate any dark, juicy corners in the turbulent history of the world's most famous foursome – there's ne'er a mention of internal discord, drugs, Yoko Ono or the Frog Song – but there's plenty of genuine memorabilia to keep a Beatles fan happy. Particularly impressive is the full-size replica of the Cavern Club (which was actually tiny) and the Abbey Rd studio where the lads recorded their first singles, while George Harrison's crappy first guitar (now worth half a million quid) should inspire budding, penniless musicians to keep the faith. The museum is also the departure point for the Yellow Duckmarine tour (see p594).

## North of Albert Dock

The area to the north of Albert Dock is known as **Pier Head**, after a stone pier built in the 1760s. This is still the departure point for ferries across the River Mersey (see p599), and was, for millions of migrants, their final contact with European soil.

Their story – and that of the city in general – will be told in the enormous **Museum of Liverpool**, currently being built on an area known as Mann Island and not slated to open until 2010 or 2011. Until its opening, this part of the dock will continue to be dominated by a trio of Edwardian buildings known as the 'Three Graces', dating from the days when Liverpool's star was still ascending. The southernmost, with the dome mimicking St Paul's Cathedral, is the **Port of Liverpool Building**, completed in 1907. Next to it is the **Cunard Building**, in the style of an Italian palazzo, once HQ to the Cunard Steamship Line. Finally, the **Royal Liver Building** (pronounced *lie*-ver) was opened in 1911 as the head office of the Royal Liver Friendly Society. It's crowned by Liverpool's symbol, the famous 5.5m copper Liver Bird.

## LIVERPOOL FOR CHILDREN

The museums on Albert Dock are extremely popular with kids, especially the **Merseyside Maritime Museum** (opposite) – which has a couple of boats for kids to mess about on – and the **Beatles Story** (above). The **Yellow Duckmarine Tour** (p594) is a sure-fire winner. Slightly older (and

NORTHWEST ENGLAND

very old) kids – especially those into football – will enjoy the tour of Anfield Stadium, home to **Liverpool Football Club** (p598), as it means getting your feet on the sacred turf.

Need a break from the tots? Drop them off at **Zoe's Childminding Service** (☎ 0151-228 2685; 15 Woodbourne Rd), about 2 miles east of the city centre.

## QUIRKY LIVERPOOL

When a working public toilet is a tourist attraction, you know you have something special, and the men's loo at the **Philharmonic** (p596) is just that. The **Yellow Duckmarine Tour** (below), an amphibious exploration of Albert Dock, is a bit silly but the guides are hilarious, and the **ferry across the Mersey** (see below) is something special – the tired commuters will give you more than a stare if you sing the song too loudly. The **Grand National Experience** (see boxed text, p598) at Aintree is proof that the English really do love their horses, and the concerts at the **Philharmonic Hall** (p598) often throw up something avant-garde, instead of the Beethoven concerto you might expect.

## TOURS

**Liverpool Beatles Tour** (☎ 0151-281 7738; www .beatlestours.co.uk; tours £45-80) Your own personalised tour of every bit of minutiae associated with the Beatles, from cradle to grave. Tours range from the two-hour Helter Skelter excursion to There Are Places I Remember, by the end of which, presumably, you'll be convinced you were actually in the band. Pick-ups are arranged upon booking.

**Magical Mystery Tour** (☎ 0151-709 3285; www .cavernclub.org; per person £13; ⏰ 2.30pm year round, plus non Sat Jul & Aug) This two-hour tour takes in all Beatles-related landmarks – their birthplaces, childhood homes, schools and places such as Penny Lane and Strawberry Field – before finishing up in the Cavern Club (which isn't the original). Departs from outside the tourist office at the 08 Place.

**River Explorer Cruise** (☎ 0151-639 0609; www .merseyferries.co.uk; adult/child return £5.30/3; ⏰ hourly 10am-3pm Mon-Fri, 10am-5pm Sat & Sun) Do as Gerry & the Pacemakers wanted and take a ferry 'cross the Mersey, exploring the bay and all its attractions as you go. Departs from Pier Head.

**Yellow Duckmarine Tour** (☎ 0151-708 7799; www .theyellowduckmarine.co.uk; adult/child/family £12/10/34; ⏰ from 11am) Take to the dock waters in a WWII amphibious vehicle after a quickie tour of the city centre's main points of interest. It's not especially educational, but it is a bit of fun. Departs from Albert Dock, near the Beatles Story.

## FESTIVALS & EVENTS

**Aintree Festival** (☎ 0151-522 2929; www.aintree .co.uk) A three-day race meeting culminating in the world-famous Grand National steeplechase, held on the first Saturday in April.

**Merseyside International Street Festival** (www .brouhaha.uk.com) A three-week extravaganza of world culture beginning in mid-July and featuring indoor and outdoor performances by artists and musicians from pretty much everywhere.

**Creamfields** (☎ 0208-969 4477; www.cream.co.uk) An alfresco dance-fest that brings together some of the world's best DJs and dance acts during the last weekend in August. It takes place at the Daresbury Estate near Halton, Cheshire.

**Mathew St Festival** (☎ 0151-239 9091; www .mathewstreetfestival.com) The world's biggest tribute to the Beatles features six days of music, a convention and a memorabilia auction during the last week of August.

## SLEEPING

There have been some stylish new arrivals on the scene, but they lean towards the boutique and luxury end of the scale. For the rest, standardised business hotels and midrange chains dominate the city centre's hotel lists. Beds are extremely tough to find when Liverpool FC are playing at home (it's less of a problem with Everton) and during the Beatles convention in the last week of August.

### City Centre
#### BUDGET

**University of Liverpool** (☎ 0151-794 6440; www.liv .ac.uk; Greenbank Lane; r from £17.50) Accommodation in comfortable, modern rooms is provided out of term at the Roscoe and Gladstone Residence Hall, located at one end of Penny Lane. Besides its Beatles connections, this is a beautiful part of the city, with nice parks and a duck-filled lake nearby.

**International Inn** (☎ 0151-709 8135; www.inter nationalinn.co.uk; 4 South Hunter St; dm/d from £15/36) A superb converted warehouse in the middle of uni-land: heated rooms with tidy wooden beds and bunks, and attached bathrooms, accommodate from two to 10 people. Facilities include a lounge, baggage storage, laundry and 24-hour front desk. The staff is terrific and CafeLatte.net (see p589) internet cafe is next door.

#### MIDRANGE

**Aachen Hotel** (☎ 0151-709 3477; www.aachenhotel.co.uk; 89-91 Mt Pleasant; s/d from £50/70) This funky listed building is a perennial favourite, with a mix of rooms (some with attached bathroom, some shared). The decor is strictly late '70s to early '80s – lots of flower patterns and crazy colour schemes – but it's all part of the welcoming, offbeat atmosphere.

**Feathers Hotel** ( ☎ 0151-709 9655; www.feathers .uk.com; 119-125 Mt Pleasant; s/d from £55/80) A better choice than most of the similar-priced chain hotels, this rambling place spreads itself across a terrace of Georgian houses close to the Metropolitan Cathedral. The rooms are all comfortable (except for the wardrobe-sized singles at the top of the building) and all feature nice touches such as full-package satellite TV. The all-you-can-eat buffet breakfast is a welcome morning treat.

**Alicia Hotel** ( ☎ 0151-727 4411; www.feathers.uk.com; 3 Aigburth Dr, Sefton Park; r from £65) Once a wealthy cotton merchant's home, Alicia is a sister hotel to the more central Feathers (above), but it's a far more handsome place. Most of the rooms have extra luxuries, such as CD players and PlayStations. There's also a nice park on the grounds.

**TOP END**

**our pick** **Hope Street Hotel** ( ☎ 0151-709 3000; www .hopestreethotel.co.uk; 40 Hope St; r/ste from £115/180) Luxurious Liverpool's pre-eminent flagwaver is this stunning boutique hotel, on the city's most elegant street. The building's original features – heavy wooden beams, cast-iron columns and plenty of exposed brickwork – have been incorporated into a contemporary design inspired by the style of a 16th-century Venetian palazzo. King-sized beds draped in Egyptian cotton, oak floors with underfloor heating, LCD wide-screen TVs and sleek modern bathrooms (with REN bath and beauty products) are but the most obvious touches of class at this supremely cool address. Breakfast, taken in the marvellous London Carriage Works (p596), is not included.

**Hard Days Night Hotel** ( ☎ 0151-236 1964; www.hard daysnighthotel.com; Central Bldgs, North John St; r £120-160, ste from £180) You don't have to be a fan to stay here, but it helps: unquestionably luxurious, the 110 ultramodern, fully equipped rooms come with a specially commissioned piece of artwork by Shannon, who has made a career out of drawing John, Paul, George and Ringo. And if you opt for one of the suites, named after Lennon and McCartney (even the hotel acknowledges the band's pecking

order), you'll get a white baby grand piano in the style of 'Imagine'.

**62 Castle St** ( ☎ 0151-702 7898; www.62castlest.com; 62 Castle St; s/d from £150/180; **P** **☐** ) As exclusive a boutique hotel as you'll find anywhere, this wonderful new property successfully blends the traditional Victorian features of the building with a sexy, contemporary style. The 20 fabulously different suites come with plasmascreen TVs, drench showers and Elemis toiletries as standard.

### Albert Dock & Around
**BUDGET**

**Liverpool YHA** ( ☎ 0845 371 9527; www.yha.org.uk; 25 Tabley St; dm £16) It may look like an Eastern European apartment complex, but this awardwinning hostel, adorned with Beatles memorabilia, is one of the most comfortable you'll find anywhere in the country. The dorms with attached bathroom even have heated towel rails, and rates include breakfast.

**MIDRANGE**

**Premier Inn** ( ☎ 0870 990 6432; www.premierinn.co.uk; Albert Dock; r from £55; **P** ) As chain hotels go, this is perfectly fine; what makes us include it is its location, which is about two steps away from the Beatles Story museum on Albert Dock.

**Crowne Plaza Liverpool** ( ☎ 0151-243 8000; www .cpliverpool.com; St Nicholas Pl, Princes Dock, Pier Head; r from £82; **P** ) The paragon of the modern and luxurious business hotel, the Crowne Plaza has a marvellous waterfront location and plenty of facilities including a health club and swimming pool.

## EATING
Liverpool's dining scene is getting better all the time. There are plenty of choices in Ropewalks, along Hardman St and Hope St, along Nelson St in the heart of Chinatown or slightly further afield in Lark Lane, near Sefton Park, which is packed with restaurants.

### Budget
**Keith's Wine Bar** ( ☎ 0151-728 7688; 107 Lark Lane; mains around £5; ☽ 11am-11pm) This friendly, bohemian and mostly vegetarian hang-out (with a sensational wine cellar) is the favourite resting place of the city's alternative-lifestyle crowd.

**Everyman Bistro** ( ☎ 0151-708 9545; www.every man.co.uk; 13 Hope St; mains £5-8; ☽ noon-2am Mon-Fri, 11am-2am Sat, 7-10.30pm Sun) Out-of-work actors and other creative types on a budget make this great cafe-restaurant (located beneath the Everyman Theatre) their second home – with good reason. Great tucker and a terrific atmosphere.

**Italian Club** (☎ 0151-708 5508; 85 Bold St; mains £6-10; ☒ 9.30am-9pm) The Picinisco family must have been homesick for southern Italy, so they opened this fabulous spot, adorned it with family pictures and began serving the kind of food relatives visiting from the home country would be glad to tuck into.

### Midrange

**Tea Factory** (☎ 0151-708 7008; 79 Wood St; mains £7-12; ☒ 11am-late) Who knew that cod 'n' chips could be so…cool? The wide-ranging menu covers all bases from typical Brit to funky finger food such as international tapas, but it's the room, darling, that makes this place so popular. Rock stars and the impossibly beautiful have found a home here.

**Tokyou** (☎ 0151-445 1023; 7 Berry St; mains £8-13; ☒ 5-11.30pm) Cheap, healthy Asian cuisine from Japan, China, Taiwan and Korea reminds us of a larger chain like Wagamama, but this place is friendlier and more intimate. Whether takeaway or eat-in (at long picnic-style benches), the food is terrific.

**Quarter** (☎ 0151-707 1965; 7-11 Falkner St; mains £9-13; ☒ lunch & dinner) A gorgeous little wine bar and bistro with outdoor seating for that elusive summer's day. It's perfect for a lunchtime plate of pasta or just a coffee and a slice of mouthwatering cake.

### Top End

**Pan-American Club** (☎ 0151-709 7097; Britannia Pavilion, Albert Dock; mains £13-24; ☒ 11am-2am) A truly beautiful warehouse conversion has created this top-class restaurant and bar, easily one of the best dining addresses in town. Fancy steak dinners and other American classics can be washed down with drinks from the Champagne Lounge.

**Meet Argentinean** (☎ 0151-258 1816; 2 Brunswick St; mains lunch £9-26, dinner £15-21; ☒ noon-11pm) Liverpool's first Argentinean restaurant is really an elegant tribute to grilled beef – served the size of a small wheel, as any self-respecting gaucho would demand. Thankfully, some cuts are smaller but just as good; the 16oz grilled fillet steak was plenty for us.

**London Carriage Works** (☎ 0151-705 2222; www .tlcw.co.uk; 40 Hope St; 2-/3-course meals £35/45; ☒ 8am-10pm Mon-Sat, 8am-8pm Sun) Liverpool's dining

revolution is being led by Paul Askew's award-winning restaurant. Its followers are the fashionistas, socceristas and other members of the style brigade who share the large, open space that is the dining room – actually more of a bright glass box divided only by a series of sculpted glass shards. They indulge in the marvellous, eclectic ethnic menu, which reveals influences from every corner of the world.

## DRINKING

Put mildly, Scousers like a good night out. Health officials may despair, but Liverpool's wealth of pubs and bars of every hue only exist to satisfy a seemingly inexhaustible desire to get loaded, especially in the 'party zone' that is Ropewalks. Unless specified, all the bars included here open 11am until 2am Monday to Saturday, although most have a nominal entry charge after 11pm.

### City Centre

**Hannah's** (☎ 0151-708 5959; 2 Leece St) One of the top student bars in town. Try to land yourself a table on the outdoor patio, which is covered in the event of rain. It stays open late, has a friendly, easygoing crowd and some pretty decent music, making this one of the better places in which to have a drink.

**Magnet** (☎ 0151-709 6969; 39 Hardman St) Red leather booths, plenty of velvet and a suitably seedy New York–dive atmosphere where Iggy Pop or Tom Waits would feel right at home. The upstairs bar is very cool but totally chilled out, while downstairs the dancefloor shakes to the best music in town, spun by up-and-comers and supported with guest slots by some of England's most established DJs.

**Philharmonic** (☎ 0151-707 2837; 36 Hope St; ☒ to 11.30pm) This extraordinary bar, designed by the shipwrights who built the *Lusitania*, is one of the most beautiful in all of England. The interior is resplendent with etched and stained glass, wrought iron, mosaics and ceramic tiling – and if you think that's good, just wait until you see inside the marble men's toilets, the only heritage-listed lav in the country.

**Jacaranda** (☎ 0151-708 9424; 21-23 Slater St) The Beatles used to play in this cellar bar – the clue is in the pictures on the walls and the constant playing of their albums – but this is a great, no-nonsense boozer in its own right.

## GAY & LESBIAN LIVERPOOL

There's no discernible gay quarter in Liverpool, with most of the gay-friendly clubs and bars spread about Dale St and Victoria St in Ropewalks. **G-Bar** (☎ 0151-255 1148; 1-7 Eberle St), in a small lane off Dale St behind Metrolink, is the city's premier gay bar, even though it attracts a mixed crowd. **Curzon** (☎ 0151-236 5160; 8 Temple Lane) is what one might euphemistically term a man's bar, with lots of hairy, tough-looking guys getting to know each other. For something a little less provocative, **Masquerade Bar** (☎ 0151-236 7786; 10 Cumberland St) attracts a real mix of gays, lesbians and bis looking for a few laughs and a sing-song.

Many clubs host gay nights, but **Babystorm** (☎ 07845 298863; 12 Stanley St), a relatively new club and bar aimed primarily at the lesbian and bi community, has really taken off; it is a good rival to **Superstar Boudoir** (22-24 Stanley St) as the best gay club in town. For online listings, check out www.realliverpool.com.

## Albert Dock

**Blue Bar** (☎ 0151-709 7097; Edward Pavilion) You don't need a premiership contract to guarantee entry anymore, which means that mere mortals can finally enjoy the relaxed ambience of this elegant waterside lounge. So where have all the footballers gone? Downstairs, to the far more glam Baby Blue, a private members' bar.

**Baby Cream** (☎ 0151-702 5823; www.babycream.co.uk; Atlantic Pavilion) This super-trendy bar, run by the same crowd that created Liverpool's now-defunct-but-still-legendary Cream nightclub, is gorgeous and pretentious in almost equal measure.

## ENTERTAINMENT

The schedule is pretty full these days, whether it's excellent fringe theatre, a performance by the superb Philharmonic or an all-day rock concert. And then there's the constant backbeat provided by the city's club scene, which pulses and throbs to the wee hours, six nights out of seven. For all information, consult the *Liverpool Echo*.

## Nightclubs

Most of the city's clubs are concentrated in Ropewalks, where they compete for customers with a ton of late-night bars; considering the number of punters in the area on a Friday or Saturday night, we're guessing there's plenty of business for everyone. Most clubs open at 11pm and turf everyone out by 3am.

**Barfly** (☎ 0870 907 0999; 90 Seel St; admission £4-11; ☽ Mon-Sat) This converted theatre is home to our favourite club in town. The fortnightly Saturday Chibuku Shake Shake (www.chibuku.com) is one of the best club nights in all of England, led by a mix of superb DJs including Yousef (formerly of Cream) and superstars such as Dmitri from Paris and Gilles Peterson. The music ranges from hip-hop to deep house – if you're in town, get in line. Other nights feature a superb mixed bag of music, from trash to techno.

**Le Bateau** (☎ 0151-709 6508; 62 Duke St; admission £2-5; ☽ Thu-Sat) This oddly named club – there's nothing boatlike about this building – is home to a superb indie club, where 500 punters cram the dancefloor and shake it to sounds that have nothing to do with the charts – you'll hear everything from techno to hard rock.

**Nation** (☎ 0151-709 1693; 40 Slater St, Wolstenholme Sq; admission £4-13) It looks like an air-raid shelter, but it's the big-name DJs dropping the bombs at the city's premier dance club, formerly the home of Cream. These days, it also hosts live bands as well as pumping techno nights.

## Theatre

Most of Liverpool's theatres feature a mixed bag of revues, musicals and stage successes that are as easy on the eye as they are on the mind, but there is also more interesting work on offer.

**Everyman Theatre** (☎ 0151-709 4776; 13 Hope St) This is one of England's most famous repertory theatres, and it's an avid supporter of local talent, which has included the likes of Alan Bleasdale.

**Unity Theatre** (☎ 0151-709 4988; Hope Pl) Fringe theatre for those keen on the unusual and challenging. There's also a great bar on the premises.

## Live Music
### ROCK MUSIC

**Academy** (☎ 0151-794 6868; Liverpool University, 11-13 Hotham St) This is the best venue to see major touring bands.

NORTHWEST ENGLAND

NORTHWEST ENGLAND

**Cavern Club** ( ☎ 0151-236 1965; 8-10 Mathew St) The 'world's most famous club' is not the original basement venue where the Fab Four began their careers, but it's a fairly faithful reconstruction. There's usually a good selection of local bands, and look out for all-day gigs.

### CLASSICAL MUSIC
**Philharmonic Hall** ( ☎ 0151-709 3789; Hope St) One of Liverpool's most beautiful buildings, the art deco Phil is home to the city's main classical orchestra, but it also stages the work of avant-garde musicians such as John Cage and Nick Cave.

## Sport
Liverpool's two football teams – the reds of Liverpool FC and the blues of Everton – are pretty much the alpha and omega of sporting interest in the city. There is no other city in England where the fortunes of its football clubs are so inextricably linked with those of its inhabitants. Yet Liverpool is also home to the Grand National – the world's most famous steeplechase event – which is run on the first weekend in April at Aintree, north of the city (see boxed text, below).

### LIVERPOOL FC
Doff o' the cap to Evertonians and Beatlemaniacs, but no single institution represents the Mersey spirit and strong sense of identity more powerfully than **Liverpool FC** ( ☎ 0151-263 9199, ticket office 220 2345; www.liverpoolfc.tv; Anfield Rd), England's most successful football club. Virtually unbeatable for much of the 1970s and '80s, they haven't won the league championship since 1990, but their fortunes have improved dramatically under Spanish manager Rafa Benitez and a pair of billionaire

American owners. They pay local boy and legend Steve Gerrard the huge salary commensurate with his talent.

The club's home is the marvellous Anfield, but plans to relocate to a new 60,000-capacity stadium a stone's throw away in Stanley Park are still pending – construction on the new ground may well have begun by the time you read this. The experience of a live match is a memorable one, especially the sound of 40,000 fans singing 'You'll Never Walk Alone', but tickets are pretty tricky to come by. You may have to settle for a **tour** ( ☎ 0151-260 6677; combined ticket with museum adult/child £10/6; ⏲ every 2hrs except match days), which includes the home dressing room, a walk down the famous tunnel and a seat in the dugout, or you could just head to the **museum** (admission £5), which features plenty of memorabilia.

### EVERTON FC
Liverpool's 'other' team are the blues of **Everton FC** ( ☎ 0151-330 2400, ticket office 330 2300; www.evertonfc.com; Goodison Park), who may not have their rivals' winning pedigree but are just as popular locally.

**Tours** ( ☎ 0151-330 2277; adult/child £8.50/5; ⏲ 11am & 2pm Sun-Wed & Fri) of Goodison Park run throughout the year, except on the Friday before home matches.

## SHOPPING
Frankly, Liverpool's shopping scene was pretty paltry – the most interesting shops were along Bold St – but the opening of the simply ginormous Liverpool ONE shopping district ('centre' just feels too small) has changed all that. There are over 160 high-street stores and trendy boutiques under one huge roof: you need never go anywhere else again.

---

### THE GRAND NATIONAL

England loves the gee-gees, but never more so than on the first Saturday in April, when 40-odd veteran stalwarts of the jumps line up at Aintree to race across 4.5 miles and over the most difficult fences in world racing. Since the first running of the Grand National in 1839 – won by the aptly named Lottery – the country has taken the race to heart. There's hardly a household that doesn't tune in, with betting slips nervously in hand.

You can book **tickets** ( ☎ 0151-522 2929; www.aintree.co.uk) for the Grand National, or visit the **Grand National Experience** ( ☎ 0151-523 2600; adult/child with tour £8/5, without tour £4/3), a visitor centre that includes a race simulator – those jumps are very steep indeed. We recommend the racecourse tour, which takes in the stableyard and the grave of three-time winner Red Rum, the most loved of all Grand National winners.

---

**SOMETHING FOR THE WEEKEND**

Let's get a little greedy and do a two-for-one weekend, making the most of the fact that, despite their huge historic rivalries, Manchester and Liverpool are only 37 miles apart. Spend the first night in Liverpool – check in to the **Hope Street Hotel** (p595) to really do it in style. It's Friday night, so dinner downstairs in the **London Carriage Works** (p596) should be followed by a pint in the **Philharmonic** (p596) or a spot of dancing at one of the many clubs in and around Ropewalks. Saturday is all about the museums of the city centre and Albert Dock, which should leave you plenty of time to make your train to Manchester (a trip that's less than an hour).

Claim your room at Manchester's **Great John Street Hotel** (p579) – yup, we're still stylin', but if you're looking for something a little more demure, the **Ox** (p578) offers affordable cool. Then do a little window shopping before grabbing a bite. Pick a bar, any bar, and keep going: there's an unhealthy choice of clubs if you're not that keen on a Sunday-morning start.

You have your choice of things to visit, but we recommend **Urbis** (p576) and the **Imperial War Museum North** (p577) for a mere taste of the city's cool culture.

If dreams could come true, this would be our ideal way to spend the weekend: we'd have tickets to see Liverpool play (and beat) Chelsea on Saturday afternoon at **Anfield** (opposite), while Sunday afternoon would see us make the trek to **Old Trafford** (p577) to see United struggle to get a draw against Manchester City in the derby. Ah, to sleep, perchance to dream…

---

Alternative shoppers should still venture along Bold St, home to **Hairy Records** ( ☎ 0151-709 3121; 124 Bold St; ☺ 11am-5.30pm Mon-Sat), the best record shop in the city, and **Resurrection** ( ☎ 0151-709 2676; 25 Bold St; ☺ 10am-6pm Mon-Wed, Fri & Sat, to 8pm Thu, 11am-5pm Sun), where you can find individualistic styles far removed from the samey brands sold by high-street retailers.

## GETTING THERE & AWAY
### Air
**Liverpool John Lennon Airport** ( ☎ 0870 750 8484; www.liverpooljohnlennonairport.co.uk) serves a variety of international destinations including Amsterdam, Barcelona, Dublin and Paris, as well as destinations in the UK (Belfast, London and the Isle of Man).

### Bus
The **National Express Coach Station** ( ☎ 08705 808080; Norton St) is situated 300m north of Lime St station. There are services to/from most major towns, including Manchester (£5, 1¼ hours, hourly), London (£24, five to six hours, seven daily), Birmingham (£10.20, 2¾ hours, five daily) and Newcastle (£20.50, 6½ hours, three daily).

### Train
Liverpool's main station is Lime St. It has hourly services to almost everywhere, including Chester (£4.45, 45 minutes), London (£61.60, 3¼ hours), Manchester (£8.80, 45 minutes) and Wigan (£4.60, 50 minutes).

## GETTING AROUND
### To/From the Airport
The airport is 8 miles south of the centre. **Arriva Airlink** (per person £1.70; ☺ 6am-11pm) buses 80A and 180 depart from Paradise St station, and **Airportxpress 500** (per person £2.50; ☺ 5.15am-12.15am) buses leave from outside Lime St station. Buses from both stations take half an hour and run every 20 minutes. A taxi to the city centre should cost no more than £15.

### Boat
The famous cross-Mersey **ferry** (adult/child £1.35/1.05) for Woodside and Seacombe departs from Pier Head Ferry Terminal, next to the Royal Liver Building (to the north of Albert Dock).

### Car & Motorcycle
You won't have much use for a car in Liverpool, and it'll end up costing you plenty in car-parking fees. If you must drive, there are parking meters around the city and a number of open and sheltered car parks. Car break-ins are a major problem, so leave absolutely nothing of value in the car.

### Public Transport
Local public transport is coordinated by **Merseytravel** ( ☎ 0151-236 7676; www.merseytravel .gov.uk). Highly recommended is the **Saveaway ticket** (adult/child £3.70/1.90), which allows for one day's off-peak travel on all bus, train and ferry services throughout Merseyside.

NORTHWEST ENGLAND

Tickets are available at shops and post offices throughout the city. Paradise St bus station is in the city centre.

### MERSEYRAIL
**Merseyrail** (☎ 0151-702 2071; www.merseyrail.org) is an extensive suburban rail service linking Liverpool with the Greater Merseyside area. There are four stops in the city centre: Lime St, Central (handy for Ropewalks), James St (close to Albert Dock) and Moorfields.

### Taxi
**Mersey Cabs** (☎ 0151-298 2222) operates tourist taxi services and has some wheelchair-accessible cabs.

# AROUND LIVERPOOL

## PORT SUNLIGHT
Southwest of Liverpool across the River Mersey, on the Wirral Peninsula, Port Sunlight is a picturesque 19th-century village created by the philanthropic Lever family to house workers in its soap factory. The main reason to come here is the wonderful **Lady Lever Art Gallery** (☎ 0151-478 4136; www.liverpool museums.org.uk/ladylever; admission free; ☒ 10am-5pm), off Greendale Rd, where you can see some of the greatest works of the Pre-Raphaelite Brotherhood Movement (founded in 1848 by a group of English painters including John Everett Millais and William Holman Hunt in rejection of the strict rules developed by the Mannerist style of painting), as well as some fine Wedgwood pottery.

Take the Merseyrail to Bebington on the Wirral line; the gallery is a five-minute walk from the station. Alternatively, bus 51 from Woodside will get you here.

## SPEKE
A marvellous example of a black-and-white half-timbered hall can be visited at **Speke Hall** (NT; ☎ 0151-427 7231; www.nationaltrust.org.uk; house & gardens adult/child £7.50/3.80, gardens only adult/child £4.50/2.50; ☒ 1-5.30pm Wed-Sun Apr-Oct, 1-4.30pm Sat & Sun Nov-Mar), six miles south of Liverpool in the plain suburb of Speke. It contains several priest's holes where 16th-century Roman Catholic priests could hide when they were forbidden to hold Masses. Any airport bus from Paradise St will drop you within a half-mile of the entrance. Speke Hall can also be combined with a National Trust 1½-hour **tour** (☎ 0151-486 4006; with Speke Hall adult/child £15/3) to the childhood homes of both Lennon and McCartney (see boxed text, p592) – you can book at Speke Hall or at the tourist offices in Liverpool.

# LANCASHIRE

As industrious as it is isolated, Lancashire has a bit of everything. The southern half is just a teeny bit urban – indeed, there's no part of England so heavily urbanised – and it includes mighty Manchester, so big that it's administered separately (and given its own section in this chapter). But once you go north, past Blackpool – the empress of the traditional British seaside resort – you arrive at the undulating rolls of the Ribble Valley, a gentle and beautiful warm-up for the Lake District that lies just beyond Lancashire's northern border. Head north of the Ribble Valley and you'll come across the handsome Georgian county town of Lancaster.

## BLACKPOOL
pop 142,290
The queen bee of England's fun-by-the-sea-type resorts is unquestionably Blackpool. It's bold and brazen in its efforts to cement its position as the country's second-most-visited town after London. Tacky, trashy and, in recent years, a little bit tawdry, Blackpool doesn't care because 16 million annual visitors don't either.

Blackpool works so well because it has mastered the time-tested, traditional British holiday-by-the-sea formula with high-tech, 21st-century amusements that thrill even the most cynical observer. Basically, a holiday here is all about pure, unadulterated fun.

The town is famous for its tower, its three piers, its Pleasure Beach and its Illuminations, the latter being a successful ploy to extend the brief summer holiday season. From early September to early November, 5 miles of the Promenade are illuminated with thousands of electric and neon lights.

### Orientation & Information
Blackpool is surprisingly spread out, but can still be managed easily without a car; trams run the entire 7-mile length of the seafront Promenade.

**Tourist office** (www.visitblackpool.com) Central Promenade ( ☎ 01253-403223; ☉ 9am-5pm Mon-Sat, 10am-4pm Sun Apr-Sep) Clifton St ( ☎ 01253-478222; 1 Clifton St; ☉ 9am-5pm Mon-Sat);

## Sights

### PLEASURE BEACH

The main reason for Blackpool's immense popularity is the simply fantastic **Pleasure Beach** ( ☎ 0870 444 5566; www.blackpoolpleasurebeach.com; Freedom Pass £5; ☉ from 10.30am Apr-early Nov), a 16-hectare collection of more than 145 rides. It attracts some seven million visitors annually, and, as amusement parks go, this is the best you'll find anywhere in Europe.

The park's major rides include the Big One, the tallest and fastest roller coaster in Europe, reaching a top speed of 85mph before hitting a near-vertical descent of 75m; the Ice Blast, which delivers you up a 65m steel tower before returning to earth at 80mph; and the vertiginous Infusion, which features five loops, a double-line twist and a suspended looping coaster – which should help bring up that lunch just nicely.

The hi-tech, modern rides draw the biggest queues, but spare a moment to check out the marvellous collection of old-style wooden roller coasters, known as 'woodies'. You can see the world's first Big Dipper (1923), but be sure to have a go on the Grand National (1935), where carriages trundle along a 1½-mile track in an experience that is typically Blackpool – complete with riders waving their hands (despite the sombre-toned announcement not to).

Rides are divided into categories, and once you've gained entry to the park with your Freedom Ticket you can buy tickets for individual categories or for a mixture of them all. Alternatively, an Unlimited Ride **wristband** (1 day adult/child £26/17, 2 days £45) includes the £5 entrance fee; there are good discounts to be had if you book your tickets online.

There are no set times for closing; it depends on how busy it is.

### OTHER SIGHTS

Blackpool's most recognisable landmark is the 150m-high **Blackpool Tower** ( ☎ 01253-622242; www.theblackpooltower.co.uk; adult/child £17/13; ☉ 10am-6pm), built in 1894. Inside is a vast entertainment complex that should keep the kids happy, including a dinosaur ride, Europe's largest indoor jungle gym and a Moorish circus.

The highlight is the magnificent rococo **ballroom** ( ☉ 10am-6pm Mon-Fri & Sun, to 11pm Sat), with extraordinary sculptured and gilded plasterwork, murals, chandeliers and couples gliding across the beautifully polished wooden floor to the melodramatic tones of a huge Wurlitzer organ.

Across from Pleasure Beach is **Sandcastle Waterpark** ( ☎ 01253-343602; www.sandcastle-waterpark.co.uk; adult/child £12.60/11; ☉ from 10am daily May-Oct, Sat & Sun only Nov-Feb), an indoor water complex. It has 15 different slides and rides, including the Master Blaster, the world's largest indoor waterslide. Forget the beach – this is the most pleasant place to have a swim.

Of the three Victorian piers, the most famous – and the longest – is the **North Pier**, built in 1862 and opening a year later, charging a penny for admission. Today admission to its plethora of assorted rides and attractions is free.

Near the Central Pier is the state-of-the-art **Sealife Centre** ( ☎ 01253-622445; www.sealifeeurope.com; New Bonny St; adult/child £12.50/9.50; ☉ 10am-8pm), which features 2.5m-long sharks and a giant octopus.

## Sleeping

With more than 2500 hotels, B&Bs and self-catering units, Blackpool knows how to put visitors up for the night. Whatever you do, though, book ahead if you want a decent room during the Illuminations. If you want to stay close to the waterfront, prepare for a noisy, boisterous night; accommodation along Albert and Hornby Rds, 300m back from the sea, is that little bit quieter. The tourist offices will assist you in finding a bed.

**Big Blue Hotel** ( ☎ 0845 367 3333; www.bigbluehotel.com; Blackpool Pleasure Beach; s/d/ste from £75/90/160; Ⓟ 🖳 ) Cool, minimalist and very much a look into Blackpool's future, this hotel caters to 21st-century demands: smartly kitted-out rooms come with DVD players and computer

NORTHWEST ENGLAND

games, while its location at the southern entrance to Pleasure Beach should ensure that everyone has something to do.

**ourpick** **Number One** ( ☎ 01253-343901; www.num beroneblackpool.com; 1 St Lukes Rd; s/d from £70/120; **P** ) Far fancier than anything else around, this stunning boutique guesthouse is all luxury and contemporary style. Everything exudes a kind of discreet elegance, from the dark-wood furniture and high-end mod cons to the top-notch breakfast. It's on a quiet road just set back from the South Promenade near Pleasure Beach.

### Eating

Forget gourmet meals – the Blackpool experience is all about stuffing your face with burgers, doughnuts, and fish and chips. Most people eat at their hotels, where roast and three vegetables often costs just £5 a head.

There are a few restaurants around Talbot Sq (near the tourist office) on Queen St, Talbot Rd and Clifton St. Our favourite meal in town is at the Mediterranean **Kwizeen** ( ☎ 01253-290045; www.kwizeenrestaurant.co.uk; 49 King St; mains £13; ⏱ lunch & dinner), which serves a delicious suckling pig in a Sardinian style, topped with a bacon roulade.

### Getting There & Away

#### BUS

The central coach station is on Talbot Rd, near the town centre. Destinations include Liverpool (£8.60, 1½ hours, one daily), London (£27, 6½ hours, five daily) and Manchester (£6.90, 1¾ hours, five daily).

#### TRAIN

The main train station is Blackpool North, about five blocks east of the North Pier on Talbot Rd. There is a direct service from Manchester (£12.20, 1¼ hours, half-hourly) and Liverpool (£13.80, 1½ hours, seven daily), but most other arrivals change in Preston (£6.30, 30 minutes, half-hourly).

### Getting Around

A host of travel-card options for trams and buses ranging from one day to a week are available at the tourist offices and most newsagents. With more than 14,000 car-parking spaces in Blackpool, you'll have no problem parking. In 2008 a new **land train service** (one way/return £2/3; ⏱ from 10.30am Apr-Oct) began. It shuttles funsters between the central corridor car parks and the

main entrance to Pleasure Beach every five minutes or so throughout the day.

## LANCASTER

**pop 45,960**

Lancaster's county seat is handsome Lancaster, lined with Georgian buildings that lend the place an air of austere gentility. Folks have done business here since Roman times, but none more successfully than during the 18th century, when Lancaster was an important port in the slave trade (see International Slavery Museum, p593).

### Information

**Post office** (85 Market St; ⏱ 9am-5.30pm Mon-Fri, 9am-12.30pm Sat)

**Tourist office** ( ☎ 01524-841656; www.citycoastcou ntryside.co.uk; 29 Castle Hill; ⏱ 9am-5pm Mon-Sat)

### Sights

#### LANCASTER CASTLE & PRIORY

Lancaster's imposing **castle** ( ☎ 01524-64998; www .lancastercastle.com; adult/child £5/4; ⏱ 10am-5pm) was originally built in 1150. Later additions include the **Well Tower**, more commonly known as the Witches' Tower because it was used to incarcerate the accused of the famous Pendle Witches Trial of 1612, and the impressive twin-towered **gatehouse**, both of which were added in the 14th century. However, most of what you see today dates from the 18th and 19th centuries, when the castle was substantially altered to suit its new, and still current, role as a prison. Consequently, you can only visit the castle as part of a 45-minute **guided tour** ( ⏱ every 30min 10.30am-4pm), but you do get a chance to experience what it was like to be locked up in the dungeon.

Immediately next to the castle is the equally fine **priory church** ( ☎ 01524-65338; admission free; ⏱ 9.30am-5pm), founded in 1094 but extensively remodelled in the Middle Ages.

#### OTHER SIGHTS

The steps between the castle and the church lead down to the 17th-century **Judges' Lodgings** ( ☎ 01524-32808; adult/child £3/2; ⏱ 10.30am-1pm & 2-5pm Mon-Fri & 2-5pm Sat Jul-Sep, 2-5pm Mon-Sat Oct-Jun). Once the home of witch-hunter Thomas Covell (he who 'caught' the poor Pendle women), it is now home to a Museum of Furnishings by master builders Gillows of Lancaster, whose work graces the Houses of Parliament. It also houses a Museum of

---

**DETOUR: NATIONAL FOOTBALL MUSEUM**

It is fitting that this **museum** ( ☎ 01772-908442; Sir Tom Finney Way, Preston; admission free; ⏰ 10am-5pm Tue-Sat, 11am-5pm Sun), dedicated to the world's most popular game, should have its home in the stand of Preston North End FC. Although the game originated in the public schools of southern England, it was the Lancashire mill towns, led by Preston, that first began employing professionals in the 1870s and 1880s – basically because the working-class players couldn't afford to take the time off work to play. The towns helped launch the first professional league in 1888 (Preston North End were its first champions but they haven't won it since 1889). Besides outlining the history of the game, the museum is home to a number of fascinating (for football fans, anyway) exhibits, including a shirt worn in the world's first international match (30 November 1872: a thrilling 0-0 draw between England and Scotland); the oldest FA Cup trophy (from 1896); and jerseys worn by some of the game's true greats, including Sir Stanley Matthews and Diego Maradona. Oh, and just so you don't think that football is strictly a man's game, you'll find out that the world's first organised women's team were the Dick Kerrs Ladies from Preston. Preston is easily reached by train from Blackpool (£6.30, 30 minutes, half-hourly).

---

Childhood, which has memorabilia from the turn of the 20th century.

A trio of other museums complete the picture: the **Maritime Museum** ( ☎ 01524-64637; St George's Quay; adult/child £3/2; ⏰ 11am-5pm Easter-Oct, 12.30-4pm Nov-Easter), in the 18th-century Custom House, recalls the days when Lancaster was a flourishing port at the centre of the slave trade; the **Cottage Museum** ( ☎ 01524-64637; 15 Castle Hill; adult/child £1/free; ⏰ 2-5pm Easter-Sep) gives us a peep into life in early Victorian times; and the **City Museum** ( ☎ 01524-64637; Market Sq; admission free; ⏰ 10am-5pm Mon-Sat) has a mixed bag of local historical and archaeological exhibits.

Lancaster's highest point is the 22-hectare spread of **Williamson Park** (www.williamsonpark.com; admission free; ⏰ 10am-5pm Easter-Oct, 11am-4pm Nov-Easter), from which there are great views of the town, Morecambe Bay and the Cumbrian fells to the north. In the middle of the park is the **Ashton Memorial**, a 67m-high baroque folly built by Lord Ashton (the son of the park's founder, James Williamson) for his wife. More beautiful, however, is the Edwardian Palm House, now the **Tropical Butterfly House** (adult/child £4.50/3.50; ⏰ 10am-5pm Easter-Oct, 11am-4pm Nov-Easter), full of exotic and stunning species. Take bus 25 or 25A from the station, or else it's a steep short walk up Moor Lane.

### Sleeping & Eating

**Sun Hotel & Bar** ( ☎ 01524-66006; www.thesun hotelandbar.co.uk; 63 Church St; s/d from £45/65; P ) An excellent hotel in a 300-year-old building with a rustic, old-world look that stops at the bedroom door; a recent renovation has resulted in 16 pretty snazzy rooms. The pub downstairs is one of the best in town and a top spot for a bit of grub; there are three menus to choose from, with meals from £8 to £15.

**Royal King's Arms Hotel** ( ☎ 01524-32451; www .bestwestern.com; Market St; s/d from £50/70; P ) Lancaster's top hotel is a period house with modern, comfortable rooms and an all-round businesslike interior. Look out for the beautiful stained-glass windows, one of the only leftovers from the mid-19th century when Charles Dickens frequented the place. The hotel restaurant is an excellent dining choice, with mains around £11.

**Whale Tail Cafe** ( ☎ 01524-845133; www.whaletail cafe.co.uk; 78A Penny St; mains £6-7; ⏰ dinner Mon-Fri, lunch & dinner Sat & Sun) This gorgeous 1st-floor vegie restaurant has an elegant dining room and a more informal plant-filled yard for lunch on a sunny day. The spicy bean burger (£6) is particularly good.

### Getting There & Away

Lancaster is on the main west-coast railway line and on the Cumbrian coast line. Destinations include Carlisle (£23, one hour, hourly), Manchester (£12.60, one hour, hourly) and Morecambe (£1.80, 15 minutes, half-hourly).

# ISLE OF MAN

Beloved of tax dodgers and petrol-heads, the Isle of Man (Ellan Vannin in Manx, the Gaelic language of the island) has long had to endure notions about being populated by odd folk with even odder ways. This unfounded prejudice is hard to fathom, but a clue is perhaps in the islanders' dogged refusal to relinquish their quasi-independent status and become fully fledged Englanders, which invariably makes mainlanders suspicious.

But chances are that those same mainlanders have never actually seen the lush valleys, barren hills and rugged coastlines of what is a beautiful island. Perfect for walking, cycling, driving or just relaxing, this is a place that refuses to sell itself down the river of crass commercialism and mass tourism. Except, of course, for the world-famous summer season of Tourist Trophy (TT) motorbike racing, which attracts around 50,000 punters and bike freaks every May and June. Needless to say, if you want a slice of silence, be sure to avoid the high-rev bike fest.

## Orientation & Information

Situated in the Irish Sea, equidistant from Liverpool, Dublin and Belfast, the Isle of Man is about 33 miles long by 13 miles wide. Ferries arrive at Douglas, the port and main town on the southeast coast. Flights come in to Ronaldsway airport, 10 miles south of Douglas. Most of the island's historic sites are operated by Manx Heritage, which offers free admission for National Trust or English Heritage members. Unless otherwise indicated, **Manx Heritage** (MH; ☎ 01624-648000; www .gov.im/mnh) sites are open 10am to 5pm daily, from Easter to October. The Manx Heritage **4 Site Pass** (adult/child £11/5.50) grants you entry into four of the island's heritage attractions; pick it up at any of the tourist offices.

## Activities
### WALKING & CYCLING
With plenty of great marked trails, the Isle of Man is a firm favourite with walkers and is regularly voted one of the best walking destinations in Britain. Ordnance Survey (OS) Landranger Map 95 (£6.99) covers the whole island, while the free *Walks on the Isle of Man* is available from the tourist office in Douglas. The **Millennium Way** is a walking path that runs the length of the island amid some spectacular scenery. The most demanding of all the island's walks is the 95-mile **Raad ny Foillan** (Road of the Gull), a well-marked path that makes a complete circuit of the island and normally takes about five days to complete. The **Isle of Man Walking Festival** (www.isleofmanwalk ing.com) takes place over five days in June and

has proven such a success that a three-day **autumn festival** was added in 2007.

There are six designated off-road cycling trails on the island, each with varying ranges of difficulty. See www.gov.im/tourism/activi ties/events/mountainbiking.xml for details.

Besides having some great cycling trails, the Isle of Man is also the birthplace of the UK's top cyclist of the moment, Mark Cavendish, who won an unprecedented four stages in the 2008 Tour de France. He withdrew from the remainder of the tour in order to prepare for the Beijing Olympics, but failed to win a medal.

## Getting There & Away
### AIR
**Ronaldsway Airport** ( ☎ 01624-821600; www.iom-airport .com; Ballasalla) is 10 miles south of Douglas near Castletown.

Airline contacts:

**Aer Arann** ( ☎ 0800 587 2324; www.aerarann.com; one way £45) From Dublin.

**Blue Islands** ( ☎ 0845 620 2122; www.blueislands.com; one way £170) From Guernsey and Jersey.

**British Airways** ( ☎ 0870 850 9850; www.ba.com; one way £113) From Glasgow Prestwick and Edinburgh; linked with Loganair.

**Eastern Airways** ( ☎ 01652-681099; www.easternair ways.com; one way £90) From Newcastle and Birmingham.

**Flybe** ( ☎ 0871 700 0535; www.flybe.com) From Birmingham (£30), London Gatwick (£60), Luton (£50), Manchester (£27), Southampton (£35), Liverpool (£27) and Newquay (£61).

**Manx2** ( ☎ 0871 200 0440; www.manx2.com; from £49) From Belfast, Blackpool, Leeds-Bradford, Gloucester M5 and East Midlands.

**VLM Airlines** ( ☎ 0870 850 5400; www.flyvlm.com; from £120) From London, Amsterdam, Antwerp, Rotterdam, Brussels and Luxembourg.

### BOAT
**Isle of Man Steam Packet** ( ☎ 0870 552 3523; www .steam-packet.com; foot passenger single/return £30/32, car & 2 passengers single/return £122/94) is a car ferry and high-speed catamaran service from Liverpool and Heysham to Douglas. There is also a summer service (mid-April to mid-September) to Dublin (three hours) and Belfast (three hours). It's often cheaper to buy a return ticket than to pay the single fare.

## Getting Around
Buses link the airport with Douglas every 30 minutes between 7am and 11pm; a taxi should cost you no more than £18.

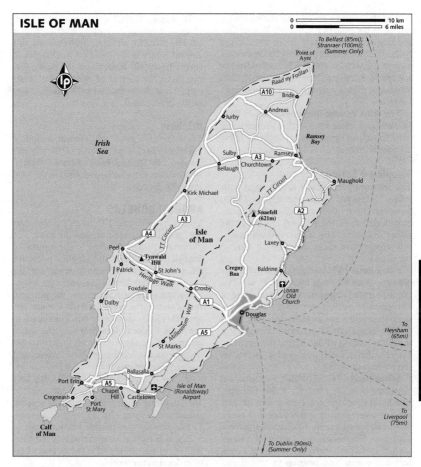

The island has a comprehensive **bus service** (www.iombusandrail.info); the tourist office in Douglas has timetables and sells tickets. It also sells the **Island Explorer** (1-day adult/child £13/6.50, 3-day £26/13), which gives you free rides on all public transport, including the tram to Snaefell and Douglas' horse-trams.

Bikes can be hired from **Eurocycles** ( ☎ 01624-624909; 8A Victoria Rd; per day £15-18;  Mon–Sat).

Petrol-heads will love the scenic, sweeping bends that make for some exciting driving – and the fact that outside of Douglas town there's no speed limit. Naturally, the most popular drive is along the TT route. Car-hire operators have desks at the airport, and charge from around £35 per day.

The 19th-century electric and steam **rail services** ( ☎ 01624-663366;  Easter–Sep) are a thoroughly satisfying way of getting from A to B:
**Douglas–Castletown–Port Erin Steam Train** (return £9.40)
**Douglas–Laxey–Ramsey Electric Tramway** (return £5.80)
**Laxey–Summit Snaefell Mountain Railway** (return £8)

## DOUGLAS
pop 26,218

All roads lead to Douglas, which is still recovering from the faded glories of its Victorian seaside past. Back then, the town was an exotic getaway for businessmen and their families during the 19th century. Still, it has the best of the island's hotels and restaurants – as well as the bulk of the finance houses that are frequented so regularly by tax-allergic Brits. The **tourist office** ( ☎ 01624-686766; www.visit isleofman.com; Sea Terminal Bldg; ⌚ 9.15am-7pm May-Sep, 9am-5pm Apr & Oct, 9am-5.30pm Mon-Fri & 9am-12.30pm Sat Nov-Mar) makes accommodation bookings for free.

The **Manx Museum** (MH; admission free; ⌚ 10am-5pm Mon-Sat) gives an introduction to everything from the island's prehistoric past to the latest TT race winners.

### Sleeping & Eating

The seafront promenade is crammed with B&Bs. Unless you booked back in the 1990s, however, there's little chance of finding ac- commodation during TT week and the weeks either side of it. The tourist office's camp- ing information sheet lists sites all around the island.

**Hilton Hotel** ( ☎ 01624-662662; www.hilton.co.uk /isleofman; Central Promenade; r from £70; P 🖳 ) The Hilton's brand of business hotel has come to Douglas and made a very good first impres- sion; the rooms are modern and functional (high-speed internet is standard throughout), if a little lacking in decorative imagination. There's also a small gym and a casino on the premises.

**Sefton Hotel** ( ☎ 01624-645500; www.seftonhotel .co.im; Harris Promenade; r from £95; P 🐾 ) Douglas' best hotel is an upmarket oasis with its own indoor water garden and rooms that range from plain and comfy to elegant and very luxurious. The rooms overlooking the water garden are superb, even better than the ones with sea views. You save up to 10% if you book online.

**Admiral House** ( ☎ 01624-629551; www.admiralhouse .com; Loch Promenade; s/d from £95/110; P ) This el- egant guesthouse overlooks the harbour near the ferry port. The 23 spotless and modern rooms are a cheerful alternative to the worn look of a lot of other seafront B&Bs. In the basement, the smart Ciapelli's is a top-notch Italian restaurant that is probably the best eatery in town, serving mains for around £9 to £12.

**Spill the Beans** ( ☎ 01624-614167; 1 Market Hill; snacks £3-5; ⌚ 9.30am-6pm Mon-Sat) The most pleasant coffee shop in Douglas delivers proper caf- feine kicks – who says you can't have coffee in a bowl? – as well as cakes, buns and other freshly made pastries.

**Tanroagan** ( ☎ 01624-472411; www.tanroagan.co.uk; 9 Ridgeway St; mains £9-18; ⌚ lunch & dinner Tue-Fri, dinner Sat) The place for all things from the sea, this elegant eatery is the trendiest in Douglas. It serves fresh fish straight off the boats, giv- ing them the merest of continental twists or just a spell on the hot grill. Reservations are recommended.

### Drinking

There are a few good pubs around, including the trendy **Bar George** ( ☎ 01624-617799; St George's Chambers, 3 Hill St), and **Rover's Return** ( ☎ 01624- 676459; 11 Church St), which specialises in the local brew, Bushy Ales.

## AROUND DOUGLAS

You can follow the TT circuit up and over the mountain or wind around the coast. The mountain route goes close to the summit of **Snaefell** (621m), the island's highest point. It's an easy walk up to the summit, or you can take the electric tram from Laxey, near the coast.

On the edge of Ramsey, on the north of the island, is the **Grove Rural Life Museum** (MH; admission £3.30; ⌚ 10am-5pm Apr-Oct). The church in the small village of **Maughold** is on the site of an ancient monastery; a small shelter houses quite a good selection of stone crosses and ancient inscriptions.

It's no exaggeration to describe the **Lady Isabella Laxey Wheel** (MH; admission £3.30), built in 1854 to pump water from a mine, as a 'great' wheel; it measures 22m across and can draw 1140L of water per minute from a depth of 550m. It is named after the wife of the then lieutenant-governor and is the largest wheel of its kind in the world.

The wheel-headed cross at **Lonan Old Church**, just north of Douglas, is the island's most impressive early Christian cross.

## CASTLETOWN & AROUND

At the southern end of the island is Castletown, a quiet harbour town that was originally the capital of the Isle of Man. The town is domi- nated by the impressive 13th-century **Castle Rushen** (MH; admission £4.80). The flag tower affords fine views of the town and coast. There's also a small **Nautical Museum** (MH; admission £3.30) dis- playing, among other things, its pride and joy, *Peggy*, a boat built in 1791 and still housed in its original boathouse. There is a school dating back to 1570 in **St Mary's church** (MH; admission free), behind the castle.

Between Castletown and Cregneash, the Iron Age hillfort at **Chapel Hill** encloses a Viking ship burial site.

On the southern tip of the island, the **Cregneash Village Folk Museum** (MH; admission £3) recalls traditional Manx rural life. The **Calf of Man**, the small island just off Cregneash, is a bird sanctuary. **Calf Island Cruises** ( ☎ 01624-832339; adult/child £10/5; ⏰ 10.15am, 11.30am & 1.30pm Apr-Oct, weather permitting) runs between Port Erin and the island.

For a decent bit of grub, the **Garrison Tapas Bar** ( ☎ 01624-824885; 5 Castle St; tapas £4-6; ⏰ lunch & dinner Mon-Sat, lunch Sun) brings Iberian flavour to a handsome 17th-century building in the centre of town. The paella (£20) is fantastic, and feeds four. A new terrace upstairs will keep smokers happy.

## Port Erin & Port St Mary

Port Erin, another Victorian seaside resort, plays host to the small **Railway Museum** (admission £1; ⏰ 9.30am-5.30pm Apr-Oct), which reveals the history of steam railway on the island.

Port Erin has a good range of accommodation, as does Port St Mary, across the headland and linked by steam train.

In Port Erin, our choice would be the Victorian classic **Falcon's Nest Hotel** ( ☎ 01624-834077; falconsnest@enterprise.net; Station Rd; s/d from £35/70), once supremely elegant, now just handsome in a nostalgic sort of way. The rooms are nothing special, but the views over the water are superb.

The slightly more splendid Victorian-style **Aaron House** ( ☎ 01624-835702; www.aaronhouse.co.uk; The Promenade, Port St Mary; s/d from £35/70) is a B&B that has fussed over every detail, from the gorgeous brass beds and claw-foot baths to the old-fashioned photographs on the walls; it's like stepping back in time, minus the inconvenience of cold and discomfort. The sea views are also sensational.

## PEEL & AROUND

The west coast's most appealing town, Peel has a fine sandy beach, but its real attraction is the 11th-century **Peel Castle** (MH; admission £3.30), stunningly positioned atop St Patrick's Island and joined to Peel by a causeway.

The excellent **House of Mananann** (MH; admission £5.50; ⏰ 10am-5pm) museum uses interactive displays to explain Manx history and its seafaring traditions. A combined ticket for both the castle and museum costs £7.70.

Three miles east of Peel is **Tynwald Hill** at St John's, where the annual parliamentary ceremony takes place on 5 July.

Peel has several B&Bs, including the **Fernleigh Hotel** ( ☎ 01624-842435; www.isleofman.com /accommodation/fernleigh; Marine Pde; r per person incl breakfast from £24; ⏰ Feb-Nov), which has 12 decent bedrooms. For a better-than-average bite, head for the **Creek Inn** ( ☎ 01624-842216; jeanmcaleer@manx .net; East Quay; mains around £8), opposite the House of Mananann, which serves Manx queenies (scallops with white cheese sauce) and has self-catering rooms from £38.

# Cumbria & the Lake District

Ever since William Wordsworth and his Romantic chums ventured into the hills in search of poetic inspiration in the late 18th century, this part of England has been a byword for natural grandeur, although in many ways the Cumbrian landscape, with its glacier-etched valleys, ridges and peaks, is closer to the rugged panoramas of the Scottish Highlands than the green and pleasant vistas of England. The region's distinctive jade-green hills (locally known as 'fells') have been a favoured haunt for generations of peak-baggers, trail trekkers and view junkies.

Unsurprisingly, the vast majority of Cumbria's 14 million annual visitors make a beeline for the landmark sights of the Lake District. Cruise boats putter across the silvery waterways of Windermere, Derwent Water and Coniston Water, while whitewashed inns and hugger-mugger pubs huddle beneath the lofty summits of England's three highest mountains, Scaféll, Scaféll Pike and Helvellyn. Literary connections are another major Lakeland draw: Wordsworth, Samuel Taylor Coleridge, Arthur Ransome and Beatrix Potter are all inextricably linked with this corner of England, and the Victorian critic John Ruskin created one of northern England's loveliest country estates at Brantwood, overlooking Coniston Water. But if you want to escape the inevitable crowds, it's worth taking the time to discover some of the region's lesser-known sights. Relatively few visitors investigate Cumbria's historic capitals, Penrith and Carlisle, while even fewer make the trek to explore Cumbria's bleakly beautiful coastline, where you'll find the spiritual home of sticky toffee pudding, the rosy-red ruins of Furness Abbey and the historic steam railway known as La'al Ratty.

**CUMBRIA & THE LAKE DISTRICT**

## HIGHLIGHTS

- Delving into the Lake District's literary heritage at **Dove Cottage** (p620) in Grasmere, **Rydal Mount** (p620) and **Hill Top** (p623)

- Playing lord of the manor at John Ruskin's country estate, **Brantwood** (p623), near Coniston

- Cruising in style around the idyllic islands of **Derwent Water** (p627)

- Admiring the outlandish artwork around **Grizedale Forest** (p622)

- Clambering aboard the pocket-sized choo-choos of the **Ravenglass & Eskdale Railway** (La'al Ratty; p632)

- Sampling contemporary Lakeland tucker at **Lucy's on a Plate** (p619) in Ambleside or the **Drunken Duck** (p622) in Hawkshead

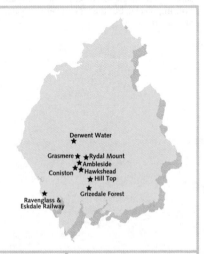

★ Derwent Water

Grasmere ★ ★ Rydal Mount
★ Ambleside
Coniston ★ ★ Hawkshead
★ Hill Top

Ravenglass &
Eskdale Railway
★ Grizedale Forest

| ■ POPULATION: 496,200 | ■ AREA: 2629 SQ MILES | ■ NUMBER OF LAKE DISTRICT PEAKS OVER 900M: 5 |

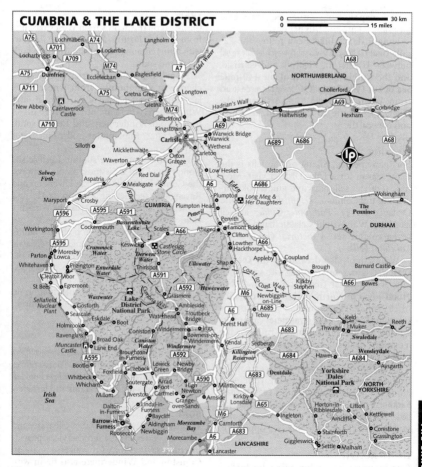

**CUMBRIA & THE LAKE DISTRICT**

## History

The earliest settlers arrived in the Lake District around 5000 years ago. The region was subsequently occupied by Celts, Angles, Vikings and Romans, and during the Dark Ages marked the centre of the kingdom of Rheged, which extended across much of modern Cumbria, Dumfries and Galloway, and was annexed by neighbouring Northumbria sometime in the 8th century.

During the Middle Ages Cumbria marked the start of 'The Debatable Lands', the wild frontier between England and Scotland. Bands of Scottish raiders known as Border Reivers regularly plundered the area, prompting the construction of distinctive *pele* towers, built to protect the inhabitants from border raiders,

and the stout fortresses at Carlisle, Penrith and Kendal.

The area was a centre for the Romantic movement during the 19th century, and writers including Coleridge, de Quincey and William Wordsworth were among the first to champion the area's natural beauty. The Lake District became one of the nation's first national parks in 1951, and the modern county of Cumbria was formed from the old districts of Cumberland and Westmorland in 1974.

## Activities

### CYCLING

Cycling is popular in Cumbria, especially mountain biking on the fells. Cycle-hire shops are widespread, and tourist offices stock a cycling map showing traffic-free routes; bike hire starts at around £15 per day.

Long-distance bikers can follow the 72-mile **Cumbria Way** (www.cumbriawaycycleroute.co.uk) between Ulverston, Keswick and Carlisle, and the Cumbrian section of the 140-mile **Sea to Sea Cycle Route** (C2C; www.c2c-guide.co.uk) from Whitehaven via the northern Lake District en route to the North Pennines and Newcastle.

### WALKING

For many people, hiking on the fells is the main reason for a Lake District visit. Most tourist offices sell maps and guidebooks, including the Collins *Lakeland Fellranger* and Ordance Survey's *Pathfinder Guides*, as well as Alfred Wainwright's classic hand-drawn, seven-volume set, *A Pictorial Guide to the Lakeland Fells*.

Wainwright also dreamt up the **Coast to Coast Walk** (www.golakes.co.uk/map/walks.asp), which cuts west to east from St Bees to Robin Hood's Bay in North Yorkshire, a distance of 191 miles. The Cumbrian section passes through Honister Pass, Grasmere, Patterdale, Kirkby Stephen and Shap en route to the Yorkshire Dales, a five- to seven-day hike of 82 miles.

Door-to-door baggage services can be useful if you don't want to lug your pack along the whole route. Contact **Coast to Coast Packhorse** ( ☎ 017683-71777; www.cumbria.com/pack-horse), **Sherpa Van** ( ☎ 020-8569 4101; www.sherpavan.com) or the YHA Shuttle Bus (see opposite).

### OTHER ACTIVITIES

Cumbria is a haven for adrenalin-fuelled activities ranging from rock climbing and orienteering to quad biking, fell running and ghyll scrambling (a cross between coasteering and river canyoning). Sailing, kayaking and windsurfing are obviously popular too, especially around Windermere, Derwent Water and Coniston.

Check out www.lakedistrictoutdoors.co.uk for the lowdown.

## Getting There & Away

### BUS

National Express coaches run direct from London and Glasgow to Windermere, Carlisle and Kendal; count on seven hours between London Victoria and Windermere.

### TRAIN

Carlisle is on the main Virgin West Coast line from London Euston–Manchester–Glasgow, with trains running roughly hourly from both north and south.

To get to the Lake District, you need to change at Oxenholme, from where regular trains travel west into Kendal and Windermere. There are at least three direct trains from Windermere and Kendal south to Lancaster, Manchester and Manchester Airport.

For something more soulful, Carlisle sits along two of the UK's most scenic railways: the Cumbrian Coast line via Ulverston and Ravenglass (see Getting Around, p631), and the Settle–Carlisle Railway across the Yorkshire Dales (see p535).

In the Lakes, you can hop aboard chuffing steam trains on the Ravenglass & Eskdale Railway (p632) or the Lakeside & Haverthwaite Steam Railway (p616) from Bowness/Ambleside to Windermere.

Call ☎ 08457 484950 for information on Day Ranger passes covering the Cumbrian rail network.

## Getting Around

**Traveline** ( ☎ 0871 200 22 33; www.travelinenortheast .info) provides travel information. Tourist offices stock the free *Getting Around Cumbria* booklet, with timetables for buses, trains and ferries.

### BOAT

Windermere, Coniston Water, Ullswater and Derwent Water all offer ferry services, providing time-saving links for walkers. Boats on Coniston and Windermere also tie in with the Cross-Lakes Shuttle (opposite).

### BUS

The main operator is **Stagecoach** (www.stagecoach bus.com). The North West Explorer ticket (one/four/seven days £9.50/21/30) gives unlimited travel on services in Cumbria and Lancashire. Twenty-four-hour Dayrider tickets can be purchased from the bus driver.

**Borrowdale Day Rider** (adult/child £5.25/4) Valid on bus 79 between Keswick and Seatoller.

**Carlisle Day Rider** (adult £3) Unlimited travel in Carlisle.

**Central Lakes Rider** (adult/child £6.30/4.70) Covers Bowness, Ambleside, Grasmere, Langdale and Coniston, includes the 599, 505 and 516.

**Honister Day Rider** (adult/child £6.25/4.50) Valid on bus 77 between Keswick and Borrowdale.

Useful buses include the 555 and 556 (Lakeslink) between Lancaster and Carlisle, which stop at all the main towns; bus 505 (Coniston Rambler), linking Kendal, Windermere, Ambleside and Coniston; and the X4/X5 from Penrith to Workington via Troutbeck, Keswick and Cockermouth.

We've given bus suggestions based on summer timetables; most routes run a reduced winter service. You can download timetables at http://www.stagecoachbus.com/northwest/timetables.php.

From Easter to October, the YHA Shuttle Bus connects eight Lake District hostels, and provides a baggage transport service for guests. Hostels on the route include Windermere, Hawkshead, Coniston Holly How, Elterwater, Langdale, Butharlyp How and Grasmere. Hostel-to-hostel transport costs £3, or £2.50 for bags; transport from Windermere Station costs £2 to Windermere YHA, and £2.50 to Ambleside YHA.

The **Cross-Lakes Shuttle** (9 or 10 possible returns daily; ☺ mid-Mar–Oct) allows you to cross from Windermere to Coniston using a combination of buses and boats; a return from Bowness to Coniston and back costs £16.60/9. For info and timetables, contact **Mountain Goat** ( ☎ 015394-45161) or do a search on www.lake-district.gov.uk.

### CAR

Driving in the Lake District can be a headache, especially on holiday weekends; you might find it easier to leave the car wherever you're staying and get around using local buses instead.

Many Cumbrian towns use a timed parking permit for on-street parking, which you can pick up for free from local shops and tourist offices.

# THE LAKE DISTRICT

If you're a lover of the great outdoors, the Lake District is one corner of England where you'll want to linger. This sweeping panorama of slate-capped fells, craggy hilltops, misty mountain tarns and glittering lakes has been pulling in the crowds ever since the Romantics pitched up in the early 19th century, and it remains one of the country's most popular beauty spots. Literary landmarks abound, from Wordsworth's boyhood school to the lavish country estate of John Ruskin at Brantwood, and there are enough hilltop trails, hidden pubs and historic country hotels to fill a lifetime of visits. Time to get inspired.

## Orientation

The Lake District is shaped in a rough star formation, with valleys, ridges and lakes radiating out from the high ground around Scafèll Pike. The busiest bases are Keswick, Ambleside, and Windermere and Bowness; Coniston and Ullswater make less hectic alternatives. Wasdale is the wildest and least accessible valley.

## Information

The Lake District's tourist offices are among the best in England, crammed with information on local hikes, activities and accommodation, and stocked with trail books, maps and hiking supplies. The main offices are in Windermere, Ambleside,

---

### CUMBRIA ON A SHOESTRING

The Lake District has plenty of lavish country-house hotels and boutique B&Bs, but you don't have to break the bank to visit. There are several fantastic hostels, housed in everything from shepherds' huts to converted mansions; the flagship YHA establishments in Ambleside, Windermere and Keswick are superb. Reservations can be made at www.yhabooking.org.uk or by calling ☎ 01629 592700.

Camping is also hugely popular in the Lakes, with lots of excellent sites dotted around the national park. The National Trust runs three sites at Low Wray, Wasdale and Great Langdale (the last two also offer funky wooden 'camping pods' for £20 to £35 per night); tourist offices publish an annual *Caravan and Camping Guide*, or you can visit www.lakedistrictcamping.co.uk.

The Lake District also has several camping barns (sometimes called 'stone tents'). Facilities are basic; you'll need the usual camping gear apart from a tent, although some places provide breakfast. Contact **Lakeland Camping Barns** ( ☎ 01946-758198; www.lakelandcampingbarns.co.uk).

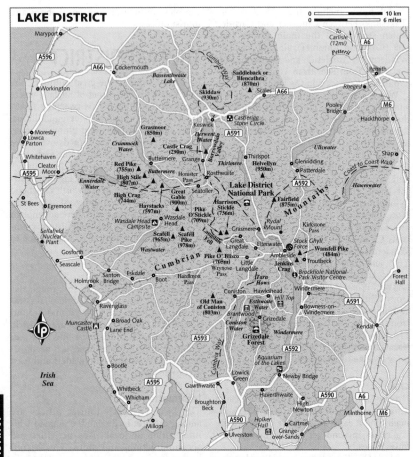

LAKE DISTRICT

Keswick and Carlisle, and there's a fantastic visitor centre at Brockhole (p614). It's worth noting that Ullswater, Coniston and Derwent Water lakes have a speed restriction of 10mph, and powerboats are banned on Grasmere, Crummock Water and Buttermere.

## KENDAL
### pop 28,398

Technically Kendal isn't in the Lake District, but it's a major gateway, so we've covered it here. Mention Kendal to any seasoned hillwalker and they'll mumble a single word – 'mintcake'. The town has been famous for its peppermint treat since the mid-19th century, and it's been a staple item in England's

backpacks ever since Edmund Hillary and Tensing Norgay munched it during their ascent of Everest in 1953. But Kendal is more than its mintcake: it's one of the largest and busiest towns in the South Lakes, with great restaurants, a funky arts centre and intriguing museums to explore.

## Information

**Kendal Laundrette** ( ☎ 01539-733754; Blackhall Rd; ⏱ 8am-6pm Mon-Fri, to 5pm Sat & Sun)
**Library** ( ☎ 01539-773520; 75 Stricklandgate; per hr £2; ⏱ 9.30am-5.30pm Mon & Tue, 9.30am-7pm Wed & Fri, 9.30am-1pm Thu, 9am-4pm Sat, noon-4pm Sun) Internet access.
**Post office** (75 Stricklandgate; ⏱ 9am-5.30pm Mon-Fri, to 12.30pm Sat)

---

**Tourist office** ( ☎ 01539-725758; kendaltic@southlakeland.gov.uk; Highgate; ☺ 9am-5pm Mon-Sat year-round, plus 10am-4pm Sun Easter-Oct) Inside the town hall.

## Sights

From 1945 to 1974, Alfred Wainwright, the accountant-cum-hillwalker who penned the classic handwritten *Pictorial Guides*, was honorary curator at the **Kendal Museum** ( ☎ 01539-721374; www.kendalmuseum.org.uk; Station Rd; adult/child £2.80/free; ☺ noon-5pm Thu-Sat). You can visit a reconstruction of his old office, complete with the great man's rucksack, spectacles and well-chewed pipe. Archaeological finds and spooky stuffed animals are dotted around the rest of the museum.

The **Abbot Hall Art Gallery** ( ☎ 01539-722464; www.abbothall.org.uk; admission £4.75; ☺ 10.30am-5pm Mon-Sat Apr-Oct, to 4pm Nov-Mar) is especially strong on portraiture and Lakeland landscapes. Look out for works by Constable, Varley and Turner, as well as portraits by John Ruskin and local boy George Romney, born in Dalton-in-Furness in 1734, and a key figure in the 'Kendal School'.

Opposite Abbot Hall is the **Museum of Lakeland Life** ( ☎ 01539-722464; www.lakelandmuseum.org.uk; adult/child £4.50/3.20; ☺ 10.30am-5pm Mon-Sat Apr-Oct, to 4pm Nov-Mar), which re-creates various scenes from Lakeland life, including spinning, mining, weaving and bobbin-making.

## Entertainment

**Brewery Arts Centre** ( ☎ 01539-725133; Highgate; www.breweryarts.co.uk) Kendal's old brewery is now an excellent arts complex with two cinemas, gallery space, cafe and a theatre hosting dance, performance and live music.

## Sleeping

**Kendal YHA** ( ☎ 0845 371 9641; www.yha.org.uk; 118 Highgate; dm from £18; ☺ Easter-Oct; 🖳 ) Next door to the Brewery Arts Centre, this Georgian hostel offers a choice of five doubles or bunks in four- to 10-bed dorms. There's a kitchen, lounge and cycle storage, plus evening grub on request.

**Balcony House** ( ☎ 01539-731402; www.balconyhouse.co.uk; 82 Shap Rd; s/d £45/60) A cut above Kendal's other guesthouses, it's traditional but comfy nonetheless. Despite the name, there's only one balcony room; all are finished in rosy tones or smart stripy wallpaper, and big comfy beds, DVD players and bathrobes are standard issue.

**Heaves Hotel** ( ☎ 01539-560396; www.heaveshotel.com; Heaves; s from £40, d £62-72; 🅿 ) Play lord of the manor at this mansion, surrounded by 4 hectares of grounds and woodland 4 miles south of Kendal along the A591. It's a true-blue country house, with old-fashioned rooms cluttered with antiques, old rugs and gilded mirrors, and most have bucolic views à la *Gosford Park*.

**Beech House** ( ☎ 01539-720385; www.beechhouse-kendal.co.uk; 40 Greenside; s £45-75, d £70-90; 🅿 ) Another spiffing B&B inside a creeper-clad house in central Kendal. Some rooms boast velour bedspreads and fluffy cushions, others LCD TVs, chequerboard bathrooms with rolltop tubs and drink-stocked minifridges; go for the larger Greenside or Penthouse rooms for maximum space.

## Eating
### RESTAURANTS

**Grain Store** (pizzas £6.50-8, mains £10-16.50; ☺ from 10am Mon-Sat) The Brewery Arts brasserie has recently had a decorative overhaul, but it's as buzzy and busy as ever. The gourmet pizzas are still in evidence, plus hefty club sandwiches and chargrilled wraps; things get more sophisticated by night, with enticing mains of Barbary duck and 'Cloonacool' char.

**New Moon** ( ☎ 01539-729254; 129 Highgate; mains £9.50-15; ☺ lunch & dinner Tue-Sat) Kendal's fooderati flock here for Med flavours mixed with the best of English ingredients. The decor's contemporary – think clean lines and funky cutlery – while the menu ranges from lamb meatballs with couscous to a stonking great

'Cumberland skillet'. The two-course pre-theatre menu, served before 7pm, is great value at £9.95.

## CAFES

**our pick** **1657 Chocolate House** ( ☎ 01539-740702; 54 Branthwaite Brow; lunches £2-6) Got a sweet tooth? Then dip into this chocaholic honeypot, brimming with handmade candies and umpteen varieties of mintcake. Upstairs, waitresses in bonnets serve up 18 types of hot chocolate, including almondy 'Old Noll's Potion' and the bitter-choc 'Dungeon'. Take that, Willy Wonka…

**Waterside Wholefoods** ( ☎ 01539-729743; Kent View, Waterside; lunches £4-10; ☺ 8.30am-4.30pm Mon-Sat) Organic bread, vegie chillis, piping-hot soups and Fairtrade coffee at a much-loved riverside cafe. Even committed carnivores won't be able to resist the wonderfully sticky homebaked cakes.

## Drinking & Entertainment

Kendal's arty crowd shoots the breeze over cappuccinos and real ales at the Vats Bar at the Brewery Arts Centre, while hipsters head for metro-chic **Mint** ( ☎ 01539-734473; 48/50 Highgate; ☺ to 2am Fri & Sat), with club nights and DJs at the weekend.

If all you're after is a pint and a pie, try the **Black Swan** ( ☎ 01539-724278; 8 Allhallows Lane), or the **Ring O' Bells** ( ☎ 01539-720326; Kirkland Ave), where even the beer is blessed – the pub stands on consecrated ground next to the parish church.

## Getting There & Around

### BUS

Kendal's handiest bus is the Lakeslink 555/556 (hourly Monday to Saturday, 10 on Sunday), which leaves Kendal en route to Windermere (30 minutes), Ambleside (40 minutes) and Grasmere (one hour), or Lancaster (one hour) in the opposite direction.

There are two daily buses from Kendal to Coniston (bus 505; one hour) via Windermere, Ambleside and Hawkshead, while the X35 travels south to Grange before returning via Haverthwaite Station, Ulverston and Barrow (hourly Monday to Saturday, four on Sunday).

### TRAIN

Kendal is on the Windermere (£3.40, 15 minutes, hourly) line from Oxenholme, 2

miles south of town, which has hourly trains from Carlisle (£16.50, 1¼ hours) and London Euston (£121, 3¾ hours).

## WINDERMERE & BOWNESS
pop 8432

Of all England's lakes, none carries the cachet of regal Windermere. Stretching for 10.5 silvery miles from Ambleside to Newby Bridge, it's been a centre for Lakeland tourism since the first steam trains chugged into town in 1847 (much to the chagrin of the local gentry, including William Wordsworth). The town itself is split into two: Windermere, 1.5 miles uphill from the lake, and bustling Bowness, where a bevy of boat trips, ice-cream booths and frilly teashops jostle for space around the shoreline.

## Orientation

The A592 travels into Bowness from southern Cumbria, tracking the lakeshore before joining the A591 northwest of town. The train and bus stations are in Windermere town. Most of the hotels and B&Bs are dotted around Lake Rd, which leads downhill to Bowness and the lakeshore.

## Information

**Brockhole National Park Visitor Centre** ( ☎ 015394-46601; www.lake-district.gov.uk; ☺ 10am-5pm Easter-Oct) The Lake District's flagship visitor centre is 3 miles north of Windermere on the A591, with a teashop, adventure playground and gardens.

**Library** ( ☎ 015394-62400; Broad St; ☺ 9am-7pm Mon, to 5pm Tue, Thu & Fri, to 1pm Sat, closed Wed & Sun) Internet access (£1 per half-hour).

**Post office** (21 Crescent Rd; ☺ 9am-5.30pm Mon-Fri, to 12.30pm Sat)

**Tourist office** Bowness ( ☎ 015394-42895; bowness tic@lake-district.gov.uk; Glebe Rd; ☺ 9.30am-5.30pm Easter-Oct, 10am-4pm Fri-Sun Nov-Mar) Windermere ( ☎ 015394-46499; windermeretic@southlakeland .gov.uk; Victoria St; ☺ 9am-5.30pm Mon-Sat, 9.30am-5.30pm Sun Apr-Oct, shorter hours in winter) The Windermere branch is located in a chalet opposite the Natwest bank.

## Sights

Most attractions are dotted around the Bowness lakeshore. Top draw for Tiggywinkle fans is the **World of Beatrix Potter** ( ☎ 015394-88444; www.hop-skip-jump.com; adult/child £6/3; ☺ 10am-5.30pm Apr-Sep, 10am-4.30pm Oct-Mar), which brings to life scenes from the author's books (in-

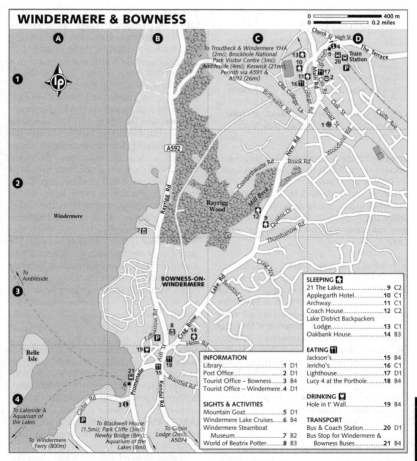

## WINDERMERE & BOWNESS

To Troubeck & Windermere YHA
(2mi); Brockhole National
Park Visitor Centre (3mi);
Ambleside (4mi); Keswick (21mi);
Penrith via A591 &
A592 (26mi)

Windermere

Rayrigg
Wood

BOWNESS-ON-
WINDERMERE

To
Ambleside

Belle
Isle

To Lakeside &
Aquarium of
the Lakes

To Windermere
Ferry (800m)

To Blackwell House
(1.5mi); Park Cliffe (3mi);
Newby Bridge (8mi);
Aquarium of the
Lakes (8mi)

To Gilpin
Lodge (2mi);
A5074

| INFORMATION | |
|---|---|
| Library | 1 D1 |
| Post Office | 2 D1 |
| Tourist Office – Bowness | 3 B4 |
| Tourist Office – Windermere | 4 D1 |

| SIGHTS & ACTIVITIES | |
|---|---|
| Mountain Goat | 5 D1 |
| Windermere Lake Cruises | 6 B4 |
| Windermere Steamboat Museum | 7 B2 |
| World of Beatrix Potter | 8 B3 |

| SLEEPING 🏠 | |
|---|---|
| 21 The Lakes | 9 C2 |
| Applegarth Hotel | 10 C1 |
| Archway | 11 C1 |
| Coach House | 12 C2 |
| Lake District Backpackers Lodge | 13 C1 |
| Oakbank House | 14 B3 |

| EATING 🍴 | |
|---|---|
| Jackson's | 15 B4 |
| Jericho's | 16 C1 |
| Lighthouse | 17 D1 |
| Lucy 4 at the Porthole | 18 B4 |

| DRINKING 🍷 | |
|---|---|
| Hole in t' Wall | 19 B4 |

| TRANSPORT | |
|---|---|
| Bus & Coach Station | 20 D1 |
| Bus Stop for Windermere & Bowness Buses | 21 B4 |

cluding Peter Rabbit's garden and Mr McGregor's greenhouse).

The **Aquarium of the Lakes** ( ☎ 015395-30153; www.aquariumofthelakes.co.uk; Lakeside, Newby Bridge; adult/3-15yr £8.50/5.50; ⏰ 9am-6pm Apr-Oct, to 5pm Nov-Mar), at the southern end of the lake near Newby Bridge, explores underwater habitats from tropical Africa through to Morecambe Bay. You could arrive by ferry from Bowness or Ambleside (for more information, see right), aboard the Lakeside & Haverthwaite Railway (p616), or via bus 618 from Windermere.

The **Windermere Steamboat Museum** is closed while plans for a revamped national boating museum gather steam. Check www.steamboat.co.uk for the latest news.

## Activities
### BOAT TRIPS

The first passenger ferry was launched back in 1845, and **Windermere Lake Cruises** ( ☎ 015395-31188; www.windermere-lakecruises.co.uk) keeps the tradition alive. Cruises allow you to jump off at one of the ferry landings (Waterhead/ Ambleside, Wray Castle, Brockhole, Bowness, Ferry Landing, Fell Foot Ferry and Lakeside) and catch a later boat back.

**Blue Cruise** (adult/5-15yr/family £6.20/3.10/17) Circular cruise around Windermere's shoreline and islands. Departs from Bowness with an optional stop at Ferry Landing.

**Bowness to Ferry House** (adult/5-15yr/family single £2.20/1.20/6.20) Ferry service which links up with the Cross-Lakes shuttle to Hill Top (p611) and Hawkshead (p622).

---

**THE LAKELESS LAKES**

This may come as something of a shock (except to pub-quiz enthusiasts), but the Lake District only has one lake – Bassenthwaite Lake, just northwest of Keswick. All the other lakes are actually **meres** (eg Buttermere, Thirlmere, Windermere), **waters** (Coniston Water, Derwent Water, Wastwater) or **tarns** (Sprinkling Tarn, Stickle Tarn, Blea Tarn).

---

**Green Cruise** (adult/5-15yr/family £6.20/3.10/17) A 45-minute cruise from Waterhead/Ambleside via Wray Castle and Brockhole Visitor Centre.

**Red Cruise** (adult/5-15yr/family £8.25/4.50/23) North lake cruise from Bowness to Ambleside.

**Yellow Cruise** (adult/5-15yr/family £8.50/4.70/24) South cruise from Bowness to Lakeside and the Aquarium of the Lakes.

A **Freedom of the Lake ticket** (adult/5-15yr/family £15/7.50/40) allows a day's unlimited travel. **Joint tickets** (return from Bowness adult/5-15yr/family £13.50/7.20/37.20, from Ambleside £18.70/9.35/52) are available with the Lakeside & Haverthwaite Steam Railway and the **Aquarium of the Lakes** (return ferry & aquarium from Bowness adult/5-15yr/family £15.25/8.70/45.50, from Ambleside £21.75/11.50/61.50).

If you'd rather explore under your own steam, from April to October rowing boats can be hired for £5/2.50 per adult/child. Open-top motorboats cost £15 per hour, or there's a closed-cabin version for £18. There's a 10mph speed limit on Windermere.

### LAKESIDE & HAVERTHWAITE RAILWAY

Classic standard-gauge steam trains puff their way along this vintage **railway** ( ☎ 015395-31594; www.lakesiderailway.co.uk; Haverthwaite Station; adult/5-15yr/family £5.40/2.70/14.80; ☷ mid-Mar–Oct) from Haverthwaite, near Ulverston, to Newby Bridge and Lakeside. There are five to seven daily trains in season, timed to correspond with the Windermere cruise boats. You can also opt to buy combo tickets with the Aquarium and Windermere Lake Cruises (p615).

## Sleeping

The main road from Windermere to Bowness is stacked with wall-to-wall guesthouses; you'll generally find better value uphill than down by the lakeshore.

**BUDGET**

**Lake District Backpackers Lodge** ( ☎ 015394-46374; www.lakedistrictbackpackers.co.uk; High St; dm £10-12.50; ▣ ) Rather underwhelming hostel with cramped bunk-bed dorms squeezed into a slate-roofed house down a little cul-de-sac near the station. Still, the beds are cheap, there's a cosy lounge (with Sky TV) and the managers organise biking and hiking trips.

**Windermere YHA** ( ☎ 0845 371 9352; www.yha.org.uk; Bridge Lane, Troutbeck; dm £12-14; ☷ mid-Feb–Nov; ℗ ▣ ) This YHA hostel occupies a white-washed house with panoramic lake views. The facilities are top-notch, with shipshape modern dorms, a well-stocked shop, a canteen and a gear-drying room. Buses stop at Troutbeck Bridge, a mile from the hostel; minibus pick-ups can be arranged between April and October.

**Park Cliffe** ( ☎ 015395-31344; www.parkcliffe.co.uk; Birks Rd; sites for 2 adults incl car & tent £19-25) Award-winning camp site midway between Windermere and Newby Bridge along the A592, with a choice of camping fields (fell-side or ghyll-side) and private bathrooms for an extra £12.50.

**MIDRANGE**

**Archway** ( ☎ 015394-45613; www.the-archway.com; 13 College Rd; d £46-60) Is this the best brekkie in Windermere? We think so – it's bursting with local produce from Lakeland tea to fresh eggs, homemade muesli, buttery pancakes and dry-cured bacon. The rooms are none too shabby, either – cool and uncluttered in white and pine, with hill views to the Langdale Pikes from the front.

**Applegarth Hotel** ( ☎ 015394-43206; www.lakesapplegarth.co.uk; College Rd; s £55-60, d £96-156; ℗ ) This Victorianate mansion is one of Windermere's most dashing guesthouses. Polished wood panels, antique lamps and stained glass conjure a staid Victorian vibe; cheaper rooms are bland, but the pricier ones feature four-posters and fell views.

**Coach House** ( ☎ 015394-44494; www.lakedistrictbandb.com; Lake Rd; d £60-80; ℗ ) Citrus yellows meet candy pinks and sky blues at this off-the-wall number, converted from a Victorian stables. The five rooms have cast-iron beds, bespoke decor and black-and-white en-suite showers, and there's a cosy sitting room for guests' use.

**21 The Lakes** ( ☎ 015394-45052; www.21thelakes.co.uk; Lake Rd; d £70-180; ℗ ) This place gives the English

B&B a well-deserved boot into the 21st century. There's a dazzling choice of camped-up rooms: suites range from the wood-beamed Grasmere (with flouncy four-poster and outdoor hot tub) to the chic Contemporary, with stripped pine, floating bed, sunken TV and 'aqua-air' bath. Glitzy, gaudy and great fun.

**Oakbank House** ( ☎ 015394-43386; www.oakbankhousehotel.co.uk; Helm Rd; d £82-88; P ) The pick of the Bowness B&Bs, inside a slate-topped house along Helm Rd. Rich reds, peaches and regal blues meet hefty wardrobes, wrought-iron bedsteads, plush sofas and rugs; the four superior rooms offer a smidgen more comfort. Lake views throughout, plus access to a nearby country club.

**TOP END**

**Gilpin Lodge** ( ☎ 015394-88818; www.gilpinlodge.co.uk; Crook Rd; r £135-155, ste £170-195; P ) This much-lauded country-house hotel reposes in 8 private hectares 2 miles from the lakeshore. Rooms are classic, all with moorland views, Molton Brown bath goodies and upmarket furniture; top of the heap are the spanking-new garden suites, with cedarwood hot tubs, adventurous wallpapers and glass-fronted lounges.

## Eating & Drinking

**Lighthouse** ( ☎ 015394-88260; Main Rd; mains £8-20; ☺ breakfast, lunch & dinner) Continental cafe-bar at the top of Windermere, ideal for pastries and coffee, or something more substantial at lunchtime. Plate-glass windows keep things light and bright; opt for a streetside table if the outlook's sunny.

**Lucy 4 at the Porthole** ( ☎ 015394-42793; 3 Ash St; mains £10-20; ☺ dinner Wed-Mon) The homely old Porthole has been overhauled courtesy of the Lake District's culinary trendsetter Lucy Nicholson (founder of Lucy's on a Plate and several other Ambleside eateries). It boasts the same laidback atmosphere, pick-and-mix menu and wine-bar feel as the original Lucy 4.

**Jackson's** ( ☎ 015394-46264; St Martin's Sq; mains £12-18) An old staple on the Bowness dining scene, Jackson's is small and unpretentious, with a dining room dotted with potted plants and wooden furniture. Straightforward bistro food – duck breast, pan-fried fish, hefty steaks – keep the local clientele well fed.

**Jericho's** ( ☎ 015394-42522; www.jerichos.co.uk; Waverley Hotel, College Rd; mains £14-18; ☺ dinner Tue-Sun) Windermere's top table excels at modern Brit cooking, which makes it a fave with the foodie guides. Tuck into sophisticated dishes – Gressingham duck, Scotch beef and baked portobello mushroom – in refined new surroundings on the ground floor of the Waverley Hotel.

**Hole in t' Wall** ( ☎ 015394-43488; Fallbarrow Rd) Polish off pub grub and ales at this venerable boozer, with the all-essential flagstones and fireplaces, plus a beer garden in case the Lakeland weather plays ball.

## Getting There & Away

**BUS**

There's a daily National Express coach from London (£32.50, 8½ hours) via Lancaster and Kendal. There's also a daily connection via Lancaster to Carlisle for Glasgow (£25, nine hours) and Edinburgh (£27.50, 10½ hours).

The Lakeslink Bus (No 555/556) runs hourly to Kendal (30 minutes) and on to Lancaster, and to Brockhole Visitor Centre (seven minutes), Ambleside (15 minutes) and Grasmere (30 minutes).

The Coniston Rambler (bus 505) travels from Windermere to Coniston (50 minutes, eight daily Monday to Saturday, six on Sunday) via Ambleside.

The open-topped Lakes Rider (bus 599) travels half-hourly (including Sundays) between Bowness, Windermere, Troutbeck, Brockhole, Rydal Church (for Rydal Mount, p620), Dove Cottage and Grasmere in summer.

**BOAT**

The **Windermere Ferry** ( ☺ 6.50am-9.50pm Mon-Sat & 9.10am-9.50pm Sun Mar-Oct; 6.50am-8.50pm Mon-Sat & 9.50am-8.50pm Sun Nov-Feb) runs roughly every twenty minutes (bicycles/motorbikes/cars cost £0.50/1/1.50/3.50) year-round from Ferry Nab, just south of Bowness, over to Ferry House on the lake's western side. Be prepared for long summer queues.

**TRAIN**

Windermere is the only town inside the national park accessible by train. It's on the branch line to Kendal and Oxenholme (£4, 30 minutes, 14 to 16 Monday to Saturday, 10 on Sunday), with regular connections to Manchester (£25.50, two hours, hourly) and London Euston (£123.50, four hours, eight to 10 daily Monday to Saturday, six on Sunday), and north to Glasgow (£35.50, hourly, two to 2½ hours) or Edinburgh (£35.50, 14 to 18 daily, two to three hours).

## AROUND BOWNESS
### Blackwell Arts & Crafts House

Two miles south of Bowness on the B5360, **Blackwell House** ( ☎ 015394-46139; www.blackwell.org .uk; adult/child £6.60/3.85; ☉ 10.30am-5pm Apr-Oct, to 4pm Feb-Mar & Nov-Dec) is one of the finest examples of the 19th-century Arts and Crafts Movement, a reaction against the machine-driven mentality of the Industrial Revolution. Designed by Mackay Hugh Baillie Scott, the house has all the hallmarks of classic Arts and Crafts: light, airy rooms, serene decor, and bespoke craftwork ranging from Delft tiles to handmade doorknobs and wood panelling.

## AMBLESIDE
### pop 3382

Sheltering at Windermere's northerly end among a dramatic cluster of fells, Ambleside is one of the Lake District's main walking bases. Hill trekkers throng to the town to stock up on hiking gear and supplies before tackling the classic trails nearby, and it can get uncomfortably crowded in the summer months. But despite its popularity, Ambleside feels a good deal less commercialised than neighbouring Windermere and Bowness, and with a selection of top-notch B&Bs and restaurants dotted around its slate-grey streets, it makes an ideal launch pad for exploring the central Lakes.

### Information

**Laundromat** ( ☎ 015394-32231; Kelsick Rd; ☉ 10am-6pm)

**Library** ( ☎ 015394-32507; Kelsick Rd; per hr £3; ☉ 10am-5pm Mon & Wed, to 7pm Tue & Fri, to 1pm Sat) Internet access.

**Post office** (Market Cross; ☉ 9am-5pm Mon-Sat)

**Tourist office** ( ☎ 015394-32582; tic@thehubofamble side.com; Central Buildings, Market Cross; ☉ 9am-5pm) Sells fishing permits, guidebooks and bus passes.

### Sights & Activities

Ambleside's best-known landmark is **Bridge House**, which spans the tumbling brook of **Stock Ghyll** downhill from Market Cross. Nearby at the **Armitt Museum** ( ☎ 015394-31212; www.armitt. com; Rydal Rd; adult £2.50; ☉ 10am-5pm), artefacts include a lock of John Ruskin's hair, a collection of botanical watercolours by Beatrix Potter, and prints by the pharmacist-turned-photographer Herbert Bell.

Football fans should check out **Homes of Football** ( ☎ 015394-34440; 100 Lake Rd; admission free; ☉ 10am-5pm Wed-Sun), displaying footy-themed photos amassed over two decades by the local photographer Stuart Clarke.

Down by the lakeshore, **cruise boats** set out from the Waterhead dock for Bowness (see p615). Self-powered vessels can be hired from **Low Wood Watersports & Activity Centre** ( ☎ 015394-39441; watersports@elhmail.co.uk), including row boats (one/four hours £10/25), kayaks (two/four hours £14/21), canoes (two/four hours £20/26), dinghies (two/four hours £35/53) and motor boats (one/four hours £18/45).

If you're feeling energetic, Ambleside marks the start of several well-known walks, including the wooded trail up to the 60ft waterfall of **Stock Ghyll Force**, or the three-hour round trip via **Wansfell** and **Jenkins Crag**, with views across to Coniston and the Langdale Pikes. Serious hikers can tackle the 10-mile **Fairfield Horseshoe** via Nab Scar, Heron Pike, Fairfield and Dove Crag.

### Sleeping
#### BUDGET

**Low Wray** ( ☎ 015394-32810; lowwraycampsite@national trust.org.uk; adult £4.50-5.50, 5-15yr £2-2.50, car £3-3.50; ☉ Easter-Oct) Quiet and spacious lakeside camp site run by the National Trust, with a supplies shop, bike rental and fab views. Advance bookings aren't taken, so pitch up early. It's 3 miles along the B5286; bus 505 stops nearby.

**Ambleside Backpackers** ( ☎ 015394-32340; www.engl-ishlakesbackpackers.co.uk; Old Lake Rd; dm £16; P 🖴 ) This indie hostel occupies a converted Lakeland cottage a short walk south from Ambleside's centre. It's clean, smart and tidy, with a spacious common room and kitchen, but the bunks are rammed in tight.

**Ambleside YHA** ( ☎ 0845 371 9620; www.yha.org .uk; Windermere Rd; dm from £18; P 🖴 wi-fi) Further along Lake Rd, this is another supremely well-organised YHA hostel, popular for its activity breaks (ranging from water sports to ghyll scrambling). Clean dorms, plenty of beds and top facilities (kitchen, bike rental, boat jetty and on-site bar) mean it's heavily subscribed in high season.

#### MIDRANGE

**Compston House Hotel** ( ☎ 015394-32305; www.com pstonhouse.co.uk; Compston Rd; d from £56) Take your pick of the Yankee-themed bedrooms at this entertaining B&B, run by an Anglicised New

York couple. Choices include sunny Florida, chic Manhattan, cowboy-style Texas and maritime Maine (complete with Cape Cod bedspread); there are blueberry muffins and maple pancakes for breakfast.

**Easedale Lodge** ( ☎ 015394-32112; www.easedaleam bleside.co.uk; Compston Rd; d £70-96) Twisted willow, zingy cushions and wrought-iron bed frames decorate this immaculate guesthouse. Some rooms boast cappuccino and creams, others have stripes, florals or cool greys; all have private bathrooms, although not necessarily en suite.

**Lakes Lodge** ( ☎ 015394-33240; www.lakeslodge.co.uk; Lake Rd; r from £90; 🖳 ) Don't be fooled by the stern slate exterior: inside this place is modern and minimal, all cool colours, funky furniture and razor-sharp lines. Slate-floored bathrooms mix with stark white walls in the rooms, all with flat screens and DVDs.

**Cote How Organic Guest House** ( ☎ 015394-32765; www.bedbreakfastlakedistrict.com; Rydal, near Ambleside; s £98-£108, d £110-120; 🅿 🖳 wi-fi) You won't find a greener place in the Lakes than this ecof-riendly cottage. Food is 100% local and or-ganic, power's sourced from a green supplier, and there's a 5% discount if you hang up your car keys, too. The three rooms are elegantly Edwardian, with cast-iron beds, roll-top baths and fireplaces. The house is 1.5 miles north of Ambleside.

### TOP END

**Waterhead Hotel** ( ☎ 08458-504503; waterhead@elhmail .co.uk; r £106-256; 🅿 🖳 ) This swish town house hotel has been revamped with all the boutique trappings: ice-white walls, wall-mounted TVs, mountain-sized beds, contemporary fabrics and oodles of leather, stripped wood and slate. The patio-bar is a beauty, nestled beside the lakeshore, and there's a similarly sophisticated vibe in the Bay Restaurant.

### Eating

**Lucy 4** ( ☎ 015394-34666; 2 St Mary's Lane; tapas £4-8; 🕑 5-11pm Mon-Sat, to 10.30pm Sun) Lucy's on a Plate is full you say? Don't fret – try this snazzy wine-bar offshoot, down the street. There's a massive list of wines and beers, plus an eclectic 'sharing' – Lucy's spin on traditional tapas.

**Pippins** ( ☎ 015394-31338; 10 Lake Rd; lunches £4-10) Another good spot for cheap eats, whether you're after a full English or a lunchtime burger or gourmet salad. The bar's open late, too.

**Apple Pie** ( ☎ 015394-33679; Rydal Rd; lunches £4-12; 🕑 breakfast & lunch) This sunny cafe on

Ambleside's main street is perennially popular for lunchtime sarnies, jacket spuds and after-noon cakes, not to mention its trademark pies (available in sweet and savoury concoctions).

**Zeffirelli's** ( ☎ 015394-33845; Compston Rd; pizza £5.50-7.45; 🕑 lunch & dinner) Zeff's is a buzzy pizza and pasta joint which doubles as Ambleside's jazz club after dark. The owners also run Ambleside's cinema; book ahead for the pop-ular £16.95 'Double Feature' menu, which in-cludes a main meal and a ticket to the flicks.

**Lucy's on a Plate** ( ☎ 015394-31191; www.lucys ofambleside.co.uk; Church St; lunch £6-12, dinner £15-25; 🕑 10am-9pm) Lucy's started life in 1989 as a specialist grocery, but over the last decade it's mushroomed into a full-blown gastronomic empire. This hugger-mugger bistro is Lucy's original outpost: laidback and informal, with a handwritten intro courtesy of the great lady and offbeat dishes veering from 'fruity porker' to 'fell-walker filler'. The secret's out, so plan ahead.

**Glass House** ( ☎ 015394-32137; Rydal Rd; lunch £8-14, dinner £13-19; 🕑 lunch & dinner) Housed in a con-verted watermill, this ritzy restaurant is the town's top table. Asian, Med and French fla-vours are underpinned by top-quality local in-gredients – Herdwick lamb, Lakeland chicken, and fish from the north-coast ports.

### Drinking & Entertainment

Ambleside has plenty of pubs: locals favour the **Golden Rule** ( ☎ 015394-33363; Smithy Brow) for its ale selection, while the **Royal Oak** ( ☎ 015394-33382; Market Pl) packs in the posthike punters.

Ambleside's two-screen **Zeffirelli's Cinema** ( ☎ 015394-33100; Compston Rd) is next to Zeff's, with extra screens in a converted church down the road.

### Shopping

Compston Rd has enough equipment shops to launch an assault on Everest, with branches of **Rohan** ( ☎ 015394-32946) and **Gaymer Sports** ( ☎ 015394-33305) on Market Cross. **Black's** ( ☎ 015394-33197; 42 Compston Rd) is a favourite with hikers, and the **Climber's Shop** ( ☎ 015394-32297; Compston Rd) specialises in rock-climbing gear.

### Getting There & Around

Lots of buses run through Ambleside, includ-ing the 555 to Grasmere and Windermere (hourly, 10 on Sunday), the 505 to Hawkshead and Coniston (10 Monday to Saturday, six on Sunday mid-March to October), and the

---

**CHAT LIKE A CUMBRIAN**

Like many corners of England, Cumbria has its own rich regional dialect. Celtic, Norse, Anglo-Saxon and the ancient Cumbric language have contributed to a wonderful repository of local words, many of which you're bound to hear on your travels. As well as the commonly used *beck* (river), *ghyll* (ravine) and *force* (waterfall), keep your ears peeled for *la'al* (little), *lowp* (jump), *gander* (look), *yat* (gate), *cowie* (thing), *yam* (home), *lewer* (money), *blether* (gossip) and our personal favourites, *jinnyspinner* (daddy-long-legs) and *snotter-geggin* (miserable person).

Cumbria even had its own system of counting, sometimes called 'sheep counting numerals' since they were once widely used by shepherds throughout northern England. The exact words vary according across the county, but nearly all start with *yan* (one), *tyan* (two) and *tethera* (three), and climb up to *dick* (ten), *bumfit* (fifteen) and *giggot* (twenty). Only in England…

---

516 (six daily, five on Sunday) to Elterwater and Langdale.

**Ghyllside Cycles** (☎ 015394-33592; www.ghyllside .co.uk; The Slack; per day £16) and **Bike Treks** (☎ 015394-31505; www.biketreks.net; Compston Rd; per half/full day £14/18) both rent mountain bikes, including maps, pump, helmet and lock.

## AROUND AMBLESIDE

While most people flock to poky Dove Cottage (right) in search of William Wordsworth, those in the know head for **Rydal Mount** (☎ 015394-33002; www.rydalmount.co.uk; adult/5-15yr £5.50/2, gardens only £3; ◷ 9.30am-5pm daily Mar-Oct, 10am-4pm Wed-Mon Nov & Feb), the Wordsworth family home from 1813 to his death in 1850.

Still owned by the poet's descendants, the house is a treasure trove of Wordsworth memorabilia. Downstairs, look out for William's pen, inkstand and picnic box, and a celebrated portrait of the poet by the American painter Henry Inman. Upstairs you can nose around the family bedrooms and Wordsworth's attic study, containing his encyclopedia and a sword belonging to his younger brother John, killed in a shipwreck in 1805.

Below the house is **Dora's Field**, which Wordsworth planted with daffodils in memory of his eldest daughter, who succumbed to tuberculosis in 1847.

The house is 1.5 miles northwest of Ambleside, off the A591. Bus 555 (and bus 599 from April to October), between Grasmere, Ambleside, Windermere and Kendal, stops at the end of the drive.

## GRASMERE
**pop 1458**

Even without its Romantic connections, gorgeous Grasmere would still be one of the Lakes' biggest draws. It's one of the prettiest of the Lakeland hamlets, huddled at the base of a sweeping valley dotted with woods, pastures and slate-coloured hills, but most of the thousands of trippers come in search of its famous former residents: opium-eating Thomas de Quincey, unruly Coleridge and grand old man William Wordsworth. With such a rich literary heritage, Grasmere unsurprisingly gets crammed; avoid high summer if you can.

### Sights

First stop is **Dove Cottage** (☎ 015394-35544; www .wordsworth.org.uk; adult/child £7.50/4.50; ◷ 9.30am-5.30pm), where Wordsworth penned some of his great early poems and kick-started the Romantic movement. The tiny cottage was a cramped but happy home for the growing family until 1808, when the cottage was leased by Wordsworth's opium-eating young friend Thomas de Quincey.

Covered with climbing roses, honeysuckle and latticed windows, the cottage contains some fascinating artefacts – keep your eyes peeled for a pair of William's ice skates and a set of scales used by de Quincey to weigh out his opium. Entry is by timed ticket to prevent overcrowding, and includes a half-hour tour.

Next door is the **Wordsworth Museum & Art Gallery**, which houses a fascinating collection of letters, portraits and manuscripts relating to the Romantic movement, and regularly hosts events and poetry readings.

You'll find several illustrious graves under the spreading yews of **St Oswald's churchyard** in the centre of Grasmere. William, Mary and Dorothy are all buried here, as well as the Wordsworth children Dora, Catherine and Thomas, and Coleridge's son Hartley.

Near the church, the village school where Wordsworth taught is now a famous gingerbread shop (opposite).

## Sleeping

**BUDGET**

**Thorney How YHA** ( ☎ 0845 371 9319; www.yha.org.uk; Easedale Rd; dm £13; ☯ Apr-Oct) Tucked away on a back lane 15 minutes from Grasmere, this rustic farmhouse is popular with families and walkers (the C2C route runs right outside the front door). The rooms are spartan, but you'll be staying in a historic spot – Thorney How was the first hostel purchased by the YHA, way back in 1931.

**Butharlyp How YHA** ( ☎ 0845 371 9319; www.yha .org.uk; Easedale Rd; dm £15.50; ☯ daily Feb-Nov, weekends Dec-Jan; P 🖵 ) You'll find more comfort at this Victorian house a mile nearer the village. Bright, modernish dorms (including plenty of doubles and quads), lovely grounds and a decent bar-restaurant (serving everything from puddings to Perry cider) make this another superior YHA.

**Grasmere Hostel** ( ☎ 015394-35055; www.grasme rehostel.co.uk; Broadrayne Farm; dm £17.50; P ) Quaint farmhouse turned excellent indie hostel, just off the A591 near the Traveller's Rest pub. It's brimming with backpacker spoils (en suite bathrooms for each dorm, two stainless-steel kitchens, even a Nordic sauna), although it feels cramped when it's full. Bus 555 stops nearby.

**MIDRANGE & TOP END**

**Beck Allans** ( ☎ 015394-35563; www.beckallans.com; College St; d £62-81; P ) Blending in seamlessly with the rest of the village, this grey-stone B&B is actually a modern build, so all the rooms are spacious, light and thoroughly up-to-date. Crisp whites and pine furniture predominate, all with gleaming bathrooms, some with power showers; self-catering apartments are available for longer stays.

**How Foot Lodge** ( ☎ 015394-35366; www.howfoot .co.uk; Town End; d £66-76; P ) Wordsworth groupies will adore this stone cottage just a stroll from William's digs at Dove Cottage. The six rooms are light and contemporary, finished in fawns and beiges; ask for the one with the private sun lounge for that indulgent edge.

**Raise View House** ( ☎ 015394-35215; www.raiseview house.co.uk; White Bridge; s/d £48/96; P 🖵 wi-fi) Look no further for fantastic fell views. Rolling hills and green fields unfurl from every window, especially from 'Helm Crag' and the double-aspect 'Stone Arthur'. The finish is elegantly English: Farrow and Ball paints, plumped-up cushions, puffy bedspreads and starchy linen.

**Lancrigg** ( ☎ 015394-35317; www.lancrigg.co.uk; Easedale; r £140-210; P ) Originally the home of Arctic adventurer John Richardson, Lancrigg now touts itself as the Lakes' only 100% vegetarian hotel. All the rooms have individual quirks: Whittington is lodged in the attic and reached via a private staircase, Franklin has Middle Eastern rugs and a four-poster, while Richardson has a plasterwork ceiling and claw-foot bath screened by lace curtains. It's half a mile along Easedale Rd.

**our pick Moss Grove Hotel · Organic** ( ☎ 015394-35251; www.mossgrove.com; r £225-325; P 🖵 wi-fi) If you're going to splash out in Grasmere, this ecofriendly beauty is the place to do it. Sheep-fleece insulation, natural-ink wallpapers and organic paints grace the walls, while the beds are made from reclaimed timber. Bedrooms are massive and minimal, with bespoke wallpapers, duckdown duvets, Bose hi-fis and fantastic underfloor-heated bathrooms; and the buffet breakfast overflows with organic and Fairtrade treats.

## Eating

**Sarah Nelson's Gingerbread Shop** ( ☎ 015394-35428; www.grasmeregingerbread.co.uk; Church Stile; 12 pieces of gingerbread £3.50; ☯ 9.15am-5.30pm Mon-Sat, 12.30-5pm Sun) Sarah Nelson's legendary gingerbread has been produced to the same secret recipe for the last 150 years, and is still served by ladies in frilly pinnies and starched bonnets.

**Rowan Tree** ( ☎ 015394-435528; Stocks Lane; mains £3-10, pizzas £6-9; ☯ lunch & dinner) Riverside cafe with an outside terrace above the brook. Lunch is mainly sandwiches, baguettes and pizzas, but supper also offers fishy dishes and vegie mains.

**Miller Howe Cafe** ( ☎ 015394-35234; Red Lion Sq; mains £5-12; ☯ breakfast & lunch) This chrome-tinged cafe-cum-art gallery serves up crusty sandwiches, baked spuds and handmade pies, plus the frothiest of cappuccinos and creamiest of cream teas.

**our pick Jumble Room** ( ☎ 015394-35188; Langdale Rd; mains £13-23; ☯ lunch & dinner Wed-Sun) You won't find a warmer welcome anywhere in Cumbria than at this boho bistro, run by an energetic husband-and-wife team with a dyed-in-the-wool dedication to Lakeland produce. It's a bit like having a gourmet feast in your front room: the informal atmosphere (colourful cushions, local artwork, jumble-sale furniture) is matched by the down-to-earth menu, stuffed with local fare, from haddock in beer batter to handmade game pie.

**CUMBRIA & THE LAKE DISTRICT**

## Getting There & Away

The hourly 555 runs from Windermere to Grasmere (15 minutes), via Ambleside, Rydal Church and Dove Cottage. The open-top 599 (two or three per hour March to August) runs from Grasmere south via Ambleside, Troutbeck Bridge, Windermere and Bowness.

# HAWKSHEAD

pop 1640

Wordsworth and Beatrix Potter both have connections to Hawkshead, an enticing muddle of rickety streets, whitewashed houses and country pubs halfway between Coniston and Ambleside. The village made its name as a medieval wool centre, overseen by the industrious monks from Furness Abbey (p632), but these days tourism is the main trade. Cars are banned in the village, so even on its busiest days it still feels fairly tranquil.

## Sights

Well-to-do young Lakeland gentleman from across the Lakes were sent for schoolin' at the **Hawkshead Grammar School** (admission £2; ☑ 10am-1pm & 2-5pm Mon-Sat & 1-5pm Sun Apr-Sep, 10am-1pm & 2-3.30pm Mon-Sat & 1-3.30pm Sun Oct), including a young William Wordsworth, who attended the school from 1779 to 1787. Pupils studied a punishing curriculum of Latin, Greek, mathematics, science and literature for up to 10 hours a day; no wonder naughty young Willie carved his name in one of the desks.

Beatrix Potter's husband, the solicitor William Heelis, was based in Hawkshead. His former office is now the **Beatrix Potter Gallery** (NT; ☎ 015394-36355; Red Lion Sq; adult/child £4/2; ☑ 10.30am-4.30pm Sat-Thu mid-Mar–Oct), displaying a selection of watercolours from the National Trust's Beatrix Potter collection.

The **Hawkshead Relish Company** ( ☎ 015394-36614; www.hawksheadrelish.com; The Square; ☑ 9.30am-5pm Mon-Fri, from 10am Sun) sells award-winning chutneys, relishes and mustards, from the superfruity Westmorland Chutney and classic piccalilli to beetroot-and-horseradish.

## Sleeping & Eating

**Hawkshead YHA** ( ☎ 0845 371 9321; www.yha.org.uk; dm from £16; ☑ ) Hawkshead's hostel is a wonder, set inside a Regency house a mile along the Newby Bridge road. Grand features – cornicing, panelled doors, a veranda – make this feel closer to a country hotel than a hostel.

Dorms are roomy, there's bike rental, and buses stop outside the door.

**Ann Tyson's Cottage** ( ☎ 015394-36405; www.anntysons.co.uk; Wordsworth St; s £29-55, d £58-78) In the middle of Hawkshead, this geranium-covered cottage once provided room and board for the Wordsworth boys, but it's now a pleasant olde-worlde B&B. Rooms are snug and chintzy; one has an antique bed once owned by John Ruskin.

**Yewfield** ( ☎ 015394-36765; www.yewfield.co.uk; Hawkshead Hill; d £78-120; Ⓟ ) Run by the owners of Zeff's in Ambleside, this swanky Victorian getaway features Oriental fabrics, wool-rich carpets, DVD players and oak panelling (although the Tower Room has a more classic feel). Breakfast is 100% vegie (sourced from the kitchen garden). It's 2 miles west of Hawkshead on the B5285.

**our pick** **Drunken Duck** ( ☎ 015394-36347; www.drunkenduckinn.co.uk; Barngates; mains £18 to £25; Ⓟ ) The deluxe Duck, 2 miles from Hawkshead on the B5285, blends the 400-year-old architecture of a Lakeland inn with the bespoke feel of a boutique hotel. Flagstones and fireplaces mix with leather and slate in the bar (stocked with home-brewed beers), and the restaurant is renowned for its inventive British flavours. The rooms (£120 to £250) are livened up by Roberts radios, enamel baths and antique chairs; some overlook a private tarn. Golly.

## Getting There & Away

Hawkshead is linked with Windermere, Ambleside and Coniston by bus 505 (10 Monday to Saturday, six on Sunday mid-March to October), and to Hill Top and Coniston by the Cross-Lakes Shuttle (p611).

# AROUND HAWKSHEAD

## Tarn Hows

This pretty artificial lake, backed by woods and mountains, was donated to the National Trust by Beatrix Potter in 1930, and is now a favourite hang-out for red squirrels. The lake is about two miles off the B5285 from Hawkshead along a narrow country lane; the small National Trust car park can get very busy at weekends.

## Grizedale Forest

Stretching across the hills between Coniston Water and Esthwaite Water is Grizedale, a dense woodland of oak, larch and pine, the name of which derives from the Old Norse for 'wild boar'. Some 40km of trails criss-cross the forest, but Grizedale is best known for its outlandish **sculptures**, which include a wooden xylophone, a wave of carved ferns and a huge Tolkienesque 'man of the forest'.

For information on the forest's trails, head for **Grizedale Visitors Centre** ( ☎ 01229-860010; www .forestry.gov.uk/grizedaleforestpark; ⊙ 10am-4pm Easter-Oct), where you'll also find **Grizedale Mountain Bike Hire** ( ☎ 01229-860369; www.grizedalemountainbikes .co.uk; per day adult £20-30, child £15; ⊙ 9am-5.30pm Mar-Oct, last hire 2pm).

Budding Tarzans can test their skills at nearby **Go Ape** ( ☎ 0870 458 9189; www.goape.co.uk; adult/ child £25/20; ⊙ 9am-5pm Mar-Oct, plus winter weekends), a gravity-defying assault course featuring rope ladders, bridges, platforms and zip-slides.

The X30 Grizedale Wanderer (four daily March to November) runs from Haverthwaite to Grizedale via Hawkshead and Moor Top, tying in with the Cross-Lakes Shuttle (p611).

## Hill Top

Ground zero for Potterites is the picture-postcard farmhouse of **Hill Top** (NT; ☎ 015394-36269; adult/child £5.80/2.90; ⊙ 10.30am-4.30pm Sat-Thu, garden 10.30am-5pm mid-Mar–Oct, 10am-4pm Nov-Feb, weekends only early Mar), where Beatrix wrote and illustrated many of her famous tales.

The house features in *Samuel Whiskers*, *Tom Kitten* and *Jemima Puddleduck*, while the garden appeared in *Peter Rabbit*, and the cast-iron kitchen range graced many of Potter's underground burrows.

Thanks to its worldwide fame (helped along by the 2006 biopic *Miss Potter*), Hill Top is one of the Lakes' most popular spots. Entry is by timed ticket, and the queues can be seriously daunting during the summer holidays.

Hill Top is 2 miles south of Hawkshead. Bus 505 travels through the village on its way between Coniston and Windermere, or you can catch the Cross-Lakes Shuttle (p611).

## CONISTON
**pop 1948**

Above the tranquil surface of Coniston Water, with its gliding steam yachts and quiet boats, looms the pockmarked peak known as the Old Man of Coniston (803m). The village grew up around the copper-mining industry; these days, Coniston makes a fine place for relaxing by the quiet lakeside.

The lake is famous for the world-record speed attempts made here by Sir Malcolm Campbell and his son, Donald, between the 1930s and 1960s. Tragically, after smashing the record several times, Donald was killed during an attempt in 1967, when his futuristic jet-boat *Bluebird* flipped at around 320mph. The boat and its pilot were recovered in 2001; Campbell was buried in the cemetery near St Andrew's church.

The lake also famously inspired Arthur Ransome's classic children's tale *Swallows & Amazons*. Peel Island, towards the southern end of Coniston Water, doubles in the book as 'Wild Cat Island', while the Gondola steam yacht (p624) apparently gave Ransome the idea for Captain Flint's houseboat.

## Information
**Coniston Tourist Office** ( ☎ 015394-41533; www .conistontic.org; Ruskin Ave; ⊙ 9.30am-5.30pm Easter-Oct, to 4pm Nov-Mar) The Coniston Loyalty Card (£2) offers local discounts, and there's wi-fi for a small donation.
**Hollands Cafe** ( ☎ 015394-41303; Tilberthwaite Ave; per hour £5) Internet access.
**Post office** (Yewdale Rd; ⊙ 9am-5.30pm Mon-Fri, to 12.30pm Sat)

## Sights
### RUSKIN MUSEUM
Coniston's **museum** ( ☎ 015394-41164; www.ruskin museum.com; adult/child £4.25/2; ⊙ 10am-5.30pm Easter–Nov, 10.30am-3.30pm Wed-Sun mid-Nov–Easter) explores Coniston's history, touching on copper mining, Arthur Ransome and the Campbell story – the museum's latest acquisitions are the tail fin and the air-intake from Donald Campbell's fated *Bluebird* boat. There's also an extensive section on John Ruskin, with displays of his writings, watercolours and sketchbooks.

### BRANTWOOD
John Ruskin (1819–1900), the Victorian polymath, philosopher and critic, purchased **Brantwood** ( ☎ 015394-41396; www.brantwood.org.uk; adult/5-15yr £6/1.20, gardens only £4/1.20; ⊙ 11am-5.30pm mid-Mar–mid-Nov, 11am-4.30pm Wed-Sun mid-Nov–mid-Mar) in 1871 and spent the next 20 years expanding and modifying the house and grounds, championing his concept of 'organic architecture' and the value of traditional 'Arts and Crafts' over soulless factory-made materials.

The result is a living monument to Ruskin's aesthetic principles (he even dreamt up some of the wallpaper designs). Upstairs you can view a collection of his watercolours, before stopping for tea at the nearby **Jumping Jenny** ( ☎ 015394-41715; lunches £4-8) cafe and catching a leisurely boat back to Coniston (see below).

## Activities
### BOAT TRIPS
For a dash of Victorian elegance, you can't top the puffing steam-yacht **Gondola** ( ☎ 015394-63850; adult/5-15yr £6.50/3.30), which switched from mucky coal to ecofriendly waste-wood logs, and still runs like clockwork between Brantwood and Coniston Pier.

Equally ecofriendly are the solar-powered **Coniston Launches** ( ☎ 015394-36216; www.coniston launch.co.uk). The Northern route (adult/three to 16 years return £6.20/3.10) calls at the Waterhead Hotel, Torver and Brantwood, while the Southern route (adult/three to 16 years return £8.60/4.80) sails to the jetties at Torver, Water Park, Lake Bank, Sunny Bank and Brantwood via Peel Island. You can break your journey and walk to the next jetty; trail leaflets are sold on board for £1.80. Extra cruise-tours are themed around the Campbells on Coniston (adult/five to 15 years £8/5; departing 1pm Tuesday mid-March to October) and Swallows and Amazons (adult/ five to 15 years £9/5.50; 12.35pm Wednesday mid-March to October).

**Coniston Boating Centre** ( ☎ 015394-41366; Coniston Jetty) hires out rowing boats, Canadian canoes and motorboats.

## Sleeping
**Coniston Hall Campsite** ( ☎ 015394-41223; sites from £12; ☽ Easter-Oct) Busy lakeside camp site a mile from town, with plenty of showers, a laundry room and a small shop – although it can be tough to find a peak-season pitch.

**Coppermines YHA** ( ☎ 0845 371 9630; www.yha .org.uk; dm £14; ☽ Easter-Oct) Hikers tackling the Old Man get a head start at this former mine-manager's house, huddled a couple of miles into the mountains along an unmetalled road. The small dorms, battered furniture and cosy kitchen are all part of the backcountry charm.

**Holly How YHA** ( ☎ 0845 371 9511; www.yha.org.uk; Far End; dm £16) Coniston's main hostel occupies a slate-fronted period house along the road towards Ambleside, and offers the usual YHA facilities: kitchens, evening meals and

bike hire, with a choice of four-, eight- or 10-bed dorms. It's a school-trip favourite, so book ahead.

**Wheelgate Country Guest House** ( ☎ 015394-41418; www.wheelgate.co.uk; Little Arrow; d £74-84) As long as you don't mind florals and frills, you'll be happy at this creeper-covered cottage in the centre of Coniston. The rooms are named after local lakes: try Derwent if you like oak-beamed character, Buttermere if you're a sucker for four-posters, and Coniston for countryside views.

**Crown Inn Coniston** ( ☎ 015394-41243; Tilberthwaite Ave; www.crowninnconiston.com; s £50, d £80-95; Ⓟ ) The bedrooms at this solid old inn have been given a spicy overhaul, and they're now spacious and comfortably equipped, with large beds and decent hot tubs for a posthike soak.

ourpick **Yew Tree Farm** ( ☎ 015394-41433; www .yewtree-farm.com; s £70, d £100-114) Farmhouses don't come finer than this whitewashed, slate-roofed beauty, which doubled for Hill Top in *Miss Potter* (fittingly, since Beatrix Potter owned Yew Tree in the 1930s). It's still a working farm, but these days offers luxurious lodgings alongside the cowsheds. Cream of the crop is 'Tarn Hows' with its wood-frame rafters, slate-floored bathroom and regal four-poster bed. If it's fully booked, console yourself with a nutty flapjack or a Hot Herdwick sandwich at the delightful Yew Tree Tea Room next door.

## Eating
**Bluebird Cafe** ( ☎ 015394-41649; Lake Rd; lunches £4-8; ☽ breakfast & lunch) Beside the Coniston jetty, the busy Bluebird is a fine spot for tea and cakes or a quick ice cream before hopping aboard the cross-lake launch.

**Black Bull** ( ☎ 015394-41335; www.conistonbrewery .com; Yewdale Rd; mains £6-14; ☽ lunch & dinner) Local punters and visiting hikers alike swing by the Old Bull for the best home-brewed ale in the Lakes, especially the trademark Bluebird Bitter and Old Man Ale. Pub grub is served in front of the log-fuelled fire: try the fantastic Cumberland Sausage platter, or tuck into locally hooked Esthwaite trout.

**Sun Hotel** ( ☎ 015394-41248; www.thesunconiston .com; mains £12-20; ☽ lunch & dinner) Squatting on the hillside, this old coaching inn has been whetting Coniston's whistles for centuries, but it's best known for its association with Donald Campbell, who was headquartered here during his fateful campaign. Campbell memorabilia litters the inn, and you'll find solid, uncomplicated fare in the bar (which still boasts its original range and 16th-century flagstoned floor).

## Getting There & Around

Bus 505 runs from Windermere (10 Monday to Saturday, six on Sunday mid-March to October), via Ambleside, with a couple of daily connections to Kendal (1¼ hours).

The Ruskin Explorer ticket (adult/child £14.95/6.50) includes the Windermere bus fare, a Coniston launch ticket and entrance to Brantwood; pick it up from the tourist office or the bus driver.

## LANGDALE

Travelling northwest from Coniston, the B5343 road passes into increasingly wild, empty countryside. Barren hilltops loom as you travel north past the old Viking settlement of Elterwater en route to Great Langdale, where the main road comes to an end and many of the Lakes' greatest trails begin – including the stomp up the Langdale Pikes past Harrison Stickle (736m) and Pike O' Stickle (709m), and the spectacular ascent of Crinkle Crags (819m). An ancient pack trail leads through Little Langdale over Wrynose and Hardknott Passes to the coast, passing a ruined Roman fort en route.

### GETTING THERE & AWAY

Bus 516 (the Langdale Rambler, six daily, five on Sunday) is the only scheduled bus service to the valley, with stops at Ambleside, Skelwith Bridge, Elterwater, and the Old Dungeon Ghyll hotel in Great Langdale.

### Elterwater

Ringed by trees and fields, the small, charming lake of Elterwater derives its name from the Old Norse for 'swan', after the colonies of whooper swans that winter here. With its maple-shaded village green and quiet country setting, it's a popular base for exploring the Langdale fells.

**Langdale YHA** ( ☎ 0845 371 9748; www.yha.org .uk; High Close, Loughrigg; dm £12; ☻ Mar-Oct; P ▣ ), halfway between Grasmere and Elterwater, has an impressive Victorian facade, but the rooms are standard YHA. Lots of dorm-size choice though, and good amenities including laundry, shop and games room.

**Elterwater YHA** ( ☎ 0845 371 9017; www.yha.org.uk; dm £14; ☻ Easter-Oct; ▣ ) is lodged inside an old barn

and farmhouse opposite the village pub. It's institutional – easy-clean fabrics, boarding-school bunk beds and a functional kitchen – but dead handy for local trails.

The smart **Eltermere Country House Hotel** ( ☎ 015394-37207; www.eltermere.co.uk; d from £90; P ) near the village YHA has 15 pleasant, modern rooms and lovely lakeside grounds, and a private jetty onto Elterwater.

The lovely old **Britannia Inn** ( ☎ 015394-37210; www.britinn.net; d £94-114; P ) is a longstanding walkers' favourite. All the rooms have been redone with fresh fabrics and shiny en suites, and hikers cram into the downstairs bar for hearty steaks, pints and pies (mains £8 to £16). The Sunday roast is rather fine, too.

### Great Langdale

Hemmed in by towering hills, this little hamlet is one of the Lake District's classic walking centres. Some of the most famous (and challenging) Lakeland fells are within reach, including Pike o' Blisco (705m), Crinkle Crags (859m) and the chain of peaks known as the 'Langdale Pikes': Pike O' Stickle (709m), Loft Crag (682m), Harrison Stickle (736m) and Pavey Ark (700m).

Many hikers choose to kip at the **Great Langdale Campsite** ( ☎ 015394-37668; langdalecamp@ nationaltrust.org.uk; adult £4.50-5.50, child £2-2.50, car £3-3.50), a typically well-run NT campground a mile up the valley of Great Langdale.

The classic stay in Great Langdale is the **Old Dungeon Ghyll** ( ☎ 015394-37272; www.odg.co.uk; d £100-110; P ), backed by soaring fells and built from sturdy Lakeland stone. It's been the getaway of choice for many well-known walkers and it's still endearingly old-fashioned: country chintz, battered armchairs and venerable furniture in the rooms; oak beams, wood tables and a crackling fire in the walker's bar; and more history per square inch than practically anywhere in the Lakes.

For more contemporary trappings, try the ivy-clad **New Dungeon Ghyll** ( ☎ 015394-37213; www .dungeon-ghyll.co.uk; d £108-120; P ) next door.

The **Stickle Barn** ( ☎ 015394-37356; Great Langdale; mains £4-12) is a popular choice for a posthike dinner, with curries, casseroles and stews to warm those weary bones. There's basic dorm accommodation in the bunkhouse out back.

### Little Langdale

Separated from Great Langdale by Lingmoor Fell (459m), Little Langdale is a quiet village on the road to Wrynose Pass. There are many little-known walks nearby, and at the head of the valley is the **Three Shire Stone**, marking the traditional meeting point of Cumberland, Westmoreland and Lancashire.

The only place to stay is the **Three Shires Inn** ( ☎ 015394-37215; www.threeshiresinn.co.uk; d £76-106; P ), ideally placed for walkers on the route to Lingmoor Fell via Blea Tarn. There are lunch mains for £7.25 to £8.75, and dinner mains from £14.

## WASDALE

The valley of Wasdale is as close as you'll get to true wilderness in the Lake District. Surrounded by a brooding circle of scree-scattered peaks, including the summits of Scaféll Pike and Great Gable, it's a world away from the bustling quays of Windermere: the only signs of human habitation are a couple of cottages and a sturdy inn, dwarfed by the green-grey arc of **Wastwater**, England's deepest lake. Little wonder that Wasdale recently topped a television poll to find Britain's favourite view: you won't find a grander spot this side of the Scottish highlands.

The only place for supplies is the **Barn Door Shop** ( ☎ 019467-26384; www.wasdaleweb.com) at Wasdale Head, right next to the Wasdale Head Inn.

### Sleeping & Eating

**Wasdale Head Campsite** ( ☎ 019467-26220; www .wasdalecampsite.org.uk; adult £4.50-5.50, child £2-2.50, car £3-3.50) This NT camp site is in a fantastically wild spot, nestled beneath the Scaféll range a mile from Wastwater. Facilities are basic (laundry room, showers and not much else), but the views are fine.

**Wastwater YHA** ( ☎ 0845 371 9350; www.yha.org.uk; Wasdale Hall, Nether Wasdale; dm £12; ☒ year-round by advance booking) Another stunning Lakeland hostel in a half-timbered 19th-century Gothic mansion in Nether Wasdale, at the lake's western end. There's a restaurant serving Cumbrian nosh and real ales, and many dorms have outlooks across the water.

**Lingmell House** ( ☎ 019467-26261; www.lingmell house.co.uk; Wasdale Head; d £60; P ) If you're really looking to escape, this stern granite house is the place, perched at the end of the valley's road. The rooms are sparse – don't expect creature comforts, or even much furniture – but at least traffic noise won't be a problem.

**ourpick Wasdale Head Inn** ( ☎ 019467-26229; www .wasdale.com; d £108-118; P ) This historic inn is mecca for British mountain climbing: one of the inn's early owners, Will Ritson, helped pioneer the techniques of early mountaineering in the late 19th century. Dog-eared photos and climbing memorabilia are dotted around the inn, and upstairs you'll find simple, snug rooms crammed with character: for more space, ask for one of the barn-conversion rooms across the way. Home-brewed ales, hearty food and a genuine slice of Lakeland history – what more could you ask for?

### Getting There & Away

The **Wasdale Taxibus** ( ☎ 019467-25308) runs between Gosforth and Wasdale twice daily on Thursday, Saturday and Sunday; ring to book a seat.

## KESWICK

pop 5257

Ask many people for their picture-perfect image of a Lakeland town, and chances are they'll come up with something close to Keswick. This sturdy slate town is nestled alongside one of the region's most idyllic lakes, Derwent Water, a silvery curve studded by wooded islands and criss-crossed by puttering cruise boats. Keswick makes a less frantic Lakeland base than Ambleside or Windermere, but there's plenty to keep you occupied: classic trails rove the surrounding hilltops, and the town is home to a clutch of oddball attractions including an original Batmobile and the world's largest pencil.

### Information

**Keswick Laundrette** ( ☎ 017687-75448; Main St; ☒ 7.30am-7pm)

**Keswick & the North Lakes** (www.keswick.org) Comprehensive guide to all things Keswick.

**Post office** ( ☎ 017687-72269; 48 Main St; ☒ 9am-5.30pm Mon-Fri, to 12.30pm Sat)

---

**WASDALE'S WHITE LIES**

Cumbrians are renowned for their tall tales, but Will Ritson, a popular 19th-century publican, took the propensity and finessed it into an art, telling porkies about giant turnips and a cross between a foxhound and a golden eagle (it could leap over drystone walls, see). In honour of Ritson, the Bridge Inn at Santon Bridge holds the **World's Biggest Liar Contest** (www.santonbridgeinn .com/liar) every November.

---

### THE BASSENTHWAITE OSPREYS

In 2001 the first wild ospreys to breed in England for 150 years set up home at Bassenthwaite Lake, near Keswick. There are two official viewpoints, both in **Dodd Wood**, about 3 miles north of Keswick on the A591 (follow signs for Dodd Wood and Cattle Inn). The **lower hide** ( 10am-5pm) is about 15 minutes' walk from the car park at Mirehouse, and the new **upper hide** ( 10.30am-4.30pm) is half an hour further. There's an informative osprey display and video feed at the **Whinlatter Forest Park visitor centre** ( 017687-78469; Braithwaite, near Keswick; 10am-5pm Apr-Aug).

A special Osprey Bus (six on weekends April to mid-July, daily mid-July to August) runs from Keswick; alternatively catch the X4 from Penrith or Cockermouth, or the X5 or 77 from Keswick. Disabled visitors can arrange for access to the lower hide by calling the Whinlatter visitor centre. Find out more at www.ospreywatch.co.uk.

---

**Tourist office** ( 017687-72645; keswicktic@lake -district.gov.uk; Moot Hall, Market Pl; 9.30am-5.30pm Apr-Oct, to 4.30pm Nov-Mar) Sells discounted launch tickets.

**U-Compute** ( 017687-72269; 48 Main St; 9am-5.30pm; per hr £3) Internet access above the post office.

## Sights & Activities

The heart of Keswick is the old Market Pl, overlooked by the town's former prison and meeting rooms at the **Moot Hall** (now occupied by the tourist office).

The River Greta runs parallel to Main St, overlooked by the green expanse of **Fitz Park**. Nearby is **Keswick Museum & Art Gallery** ( 017687-73263; Station Rd; admission free; 10am-4pm Tue-Sat Feb-Oct), hardly changed since its opening in 1898. Dusty cases fill the halls: exhibits include a Napoleonic teacup, a 664-year-old stuffed cat and a set of musical stones once played for Queen Victoria.

Back across the river, the equally odd **Cars of the Stars Motor Museum** ( 017687-73757; www .carsofthestars.com; Standish St; adult/child £5/3; 10am-5pm) houses a fleet of celebrity vehicles: Chitty Chitty Bang Bang, Mr Bean's Mini, a Batmobile, KITT from *Knightrider*, the A-Team van and the Delorean from *Back to the Future*, as well as lots of Bond cars.

At the southern end of Main St is the old Cumberland Pencil Factory, now the **Pencil Museum** ( 017687-73626; www.pencilmuseum.co.uk; Southy Works; adult/child £3/1.50; 9.30am-5pm). Keswick was once a centre for graphite mining; the museum's exhibits include a reconstruction of the old Borrowdale slate mine and the world's longest pencil (measuring 8m end to end).

A mile east of Keswick stands **Castlerigg Stone Circle**, a group of 48 stones between 3000 and 4000 years old, set on a hilltop surrounded by a brooding amphitheatre of mountains. The purpose of the circle is uncertain (current opinion is divided between a Bronze Age meeting place and a celestial timepiece), but one thing's for certain – those prehistoric builders knew a good site when they saw one.

### BOAT TRIPS

You can catch a cruise across Derwent Water with the **Keswick Launch Company** ( 017687-72263; www.keswick-launch.co.uk). Boats call at seven landing stages: Ashness Gate, Lodore Falls, High Brandlehow, Low Brandlehow, Hawse End, Nichol End and back to Keswick. Boats leave every hour (adult/child £8.50/4.25, 50 minutes). There are at least six daily boats from mid-March to mid-November, with extra sailings in summer, plus a twilight cruise at 7.30pm (adult/child £9/4.50, one hour, July and August). Only two boats run from mid-November to mid-March.

**Nichol End Marine** ( 017687-73082; Nichol End; 9am-5pm) hires out kayaks, rowboats and motorboats.

## Sleeping

### BUDGET

Tent-pitchers can try **Castlerigg Hall Camping Park** ( 017687-74499; www.castlerigg.co.uk; Rakefoot Lane, off A591; sites £14.50-16.50) and **Keswick Camping & Caravanning Club Site** ( 017687-72392; Crow Park Rd; adult £6.60-8.60, child £2.25-2.35, tent £2.90; Feb-Nov), down beside the lake.

**Keswick YHA** ( 0845 371 9746; www.yha.org.uk; Station Rd; dm £23; ) Fresh from a refit, this former woollen mill is now one of Lakeland's top YHAs. Some of the dorms, doubles and triples have balconies over the river and Fitz Park, and the hostel has all the facilities a discerning backpacker could wish for.

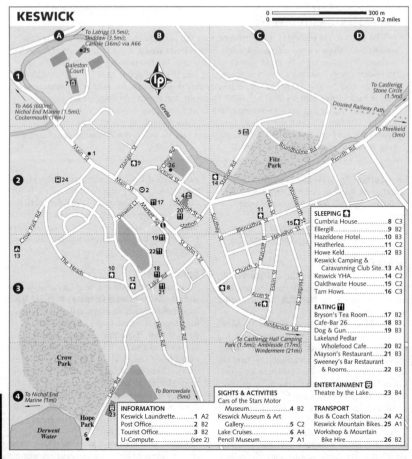

**KESWICK**

0 ————— 300 m
0 ————— 0.2 miles

To Latrigg (3.5mi);
Skiddaw (3.5mi);
Carlisle (36mi) via A66

To A66 (600m);
Nichol End Marine (1.5mi);
Cockermouth (14mi)

To Castlerigg
Stone Circle
(1.5mi)

Disused Railway Path

To Threlkeld
(3mi)

Fitz
Park

Crow
Park

Derwent
Water

Hope
Park

To Nichol End
Marine (1mi)

To Borrowdale
(5mi)

To Castlerigg Hall Camping
Park (1.5mi); Ambleside (17mi);
Windermere (21mi)

| SLEEPING | |
|---|---|
| Cumbria House | **8** C3 |
| Ellergill | **9** B2 |
| Hazeldene Hotel | **10** B3 |
| Heatherlea | **11** C2 |
| Howe Keld | **12** B3 |
| Keswick Camping & Caravanning Club Site | **13** A3 |
| Keswick YHA | **14** C2 |
| Oakthwaite House | **15** C2 |
| Tarn Hows | **16** C3 |

| EATING | |
|---|---|
| Bryson's Tea Room | **17** B2 |
| Cafe-Bar 26 | **18** B3 |
| Dog & Gun | **19** B3 |
| Lakeland Pedlar Wholefood Cafe | **20** B2 |
| Mayson's Restaurant | **21** B3 |
| Sweeney's Bar Restaurant & Rooms | **22** B3 |

| ENTERTAINMENT | |
|---|---|
| Theatre by the Lake | **23** B4 |

| INFORMATION | |
|---|---|
| Keswick Laundrette | **1** A2 |
| Post Office | **2** B2 |
| Tourist Office | **3** B2 |
| U-Compute | (see 2) |

| SIGHTS & ACTIVITIES | |
|---|---|
| Cars of the Stars Motor Museum | **4** B2 |
| Keswick Museum & Art Gallery | **5** C2 |
| Lake Cruises | **6** A4 |
| Pencil Museum | **7** A1 |

| TRANSPORT | |
|---|---|
| Bus & Coach Station | **24** A2 |
| Keswick Mountain Bikes | **25** A1 |
| Workshop & Mountain Bike Hire | **26** B2 |

## MIDRANGE

**Cumbria House** ( ☎ 017687-73171; www.cumb riahouse.co.uk; 1 Derwent Water Pl; r £52-64) Charming Georgian surroundings and an admirable eco-policy (Fairtrade coffee, local produce, and a 5% discount for car-free guests) make this another smart option. Families can rent the top three rooms as a single suite, with views all the way to Blencathra.

**Heatherlea** ( ☎ 017687-72430; www.heather lea-keswick.co.uk; 26 Blencathra St; d £54) One of the best choices in the B&B-heavy area around Blencathra St. Tasteful decor (pine beds, crimson-striped cushions, beige throws) distinguishes the rooms; it's worth bumping up to superior for the sparkling shower and gargantuan flat-screen TV.

**Ellergill** ( ☎ 017687-73347; www.ellergill.co.uk; 22 Stanger St; d £56-64) Velour bedspreads, plumped-up cushions and either regal purples or fiery reds give this B&B an opulent edge, marrying well with the house's Victorian features (including tiled hearths and a lovely hallway floor).

**Oakthwaite House** ( ☎ 017687-72398; www.oak thwaite-keswick.co.uk; 35 Helvellyn St; d £58-68) Just four rooms at this upper-crust guesthouse, but all scream achingly good taste. Digital TVs, power showers, white linen and cool shades throughout, with a cosy dormer room for that attic hideaway feel, or two swanky king-size rooms if you're a sucker for fell views.

**our pick Howe Keld** ( ☎ 017687-72417; www.howekeld .co.uk; 5-7 The Heads; s £45, d £80-90) On the edge of

Hope Park, this old workhorse has had a glamorous makeover. Gone are the chintzy wallpapers; in come luxury pocket-sprung beds, Egyptian cotton sheets and goosedown duvets, plus designer wall hangings and hand-made furniture courtesy of a local joiner.

Also recommended:

**Tarn Hows** ( ☎ 017687-73217; www.tarnhows.co.uk; 3-5 Eskin St; s £33, d £58-70) Cast-iron bedsteads and fancy quilts in a traditional Eskin St guesthouse.

**Hazeldene Hotel** ( ☎ 017687-72106; www.hazelde ne-hotel.co.uk; The Heads; d £75-95) Pick of the Victorian villas opposite Hope Park, with cheery doubles and a spacious suite with stone fireplace. Ask for park views.

## Eating

### CAFES

**Bryson's Tea Room** ( ☎ 017687-72257; 42 Main St; cakes £2-5) A historic Lakeland bakery turning out fruit cakes, Battenburgs, plum breads and florentines. Bag 'em up and take 'em home, or stop for afternoon tea at the upstairs caff.

**Lakeland Pedlar Wholefood Cafe** ( ☎ 017687-74492; www.lakelandpedlar.co.uk; Hendersons Yard; mains £3-10; ☺ 9am-5pm) Bikers and vegies are both well catered for at this homely cafe, noted for doorstep sandwiches, homemade soups, vegie chillis and ultracrumbly cakes. If you need to work off the calories, bikes are hired upstairs.

**Cafe-Bar 26** ( ☎ 017687-80863; 26 Lake Rd; mains £3.25-7.50) Big-city style in little-town Keswick. Bag a streetside table for authentic cappuccinos, wines and beers from across the globe, or bistro burgers, bruschetta and Cajun chicken tortillas.

### RESTAURANTS

**Mayson's Restaurant** ( ☎ 01768 774104; 33 Lake Rd; mains £6-10; ☺ lunch & dinner) If you're looking for a quick sit-down meal, this relaxed little buffet diner takes some beating. Choose your meal from the woks lined up on the bar (anything from Cajun chicken to chow mein), pick a drink and a table, and your meal will be dished up in double time. Potted plants and posters on the walls keep things cosy.

**Sweeney's Bar Restaurant & Rooms** ( ☎ 017687-772990; 18-20 Lake Rd; mains £7-12) Count on decent Brit cooking in comfortable surrounds at Sweeney's. It's half chic wine bar, half restaurant-with-rooms: leather sofas and polished tables spread over two floors, with a beer garden for soaking up the rays.

**Dog & Gun** ( ☎ 017687-73463; 2 Lake Rd; mains around £8) Russet-faced farmers rub shoulders with trail-weary hikers at Keswick's top pub, a wonderful place dotted with hunting prints, faded carpets and well-worn wood. The grub's honest and uncomplicated – mainly goulash, stews, steaks and pies – and there are Cumbrian ales to wash everything down.

## Entertainment

**Theatre by the Lake** ( ☎ 017687-74411; www.the atrebythelake.com; Lakeside) New and classic drama is performed here, on the shores of Derwent Water.

## Getting There & Away

The Lakeslink bus (555/556) runs hourly to Ambleside (40 minutes), Windermere (50 minutes) and Kendal (1½ hours), or the hourly X4/X5 travels from Penrith to Workington via Keswick (eight on Sunday). For buses to Borrowdale, see p630.

## Getting Around

Hire full-suspension bikes, hardtails and hybrids at **Keswick Mountain Bikes** ( ☎ 017687-75202; 1 Daleston Ct) for £15 to £20 per day. They have a second branch on Otley Rd.

# BORROWDALE & BUTTERMERE

Views don't get any more breathtaking than the one from the B5289 into Borrowdale. Historically, the valley was an important centre for farming and slate-mining – but these days Borrowdale is walkers' country, with countless paths crossing the surrounding fells, including landmark routes up to the summits of Great Gable and Scaféll Pike.

## Borrowdale

The B5289 tracks Derwent Water into the heart of Borrowdale Valley, overlooked by the impressive peaks of Scaféll and Scaféll Pike. Past the small village of **Grange-in-Borrowdale**, the valley winds into the jagged ravine of the **Jaws of Borrowdale**, a well-known hiking spot with wonderful views, notably from the summit of **Castle Crag** (290m).

From here, the road curls into the stout hamlet of **Rosthwaite**, which marks the starting point for the annual **Borrowdale Fell Race.** Held on the first Saturday in August, this muscle-shredding 17-mile slog makes the Iron Man Challenge look like child's play; you can see a list of previous winners in the bar at the Scaféll Hotel.

---

**THE ROOF OF ENGLAND**

In Scotland it's Ben Nevis (1344m), in Wales it's Snowdon (1085m), and in England it's **Scaféll Pike** (978m): collectively the three highest peaks of the British mainland, and the ultimate goal for British peak-baggers (especially for hardy souls attempting the Three Peaks Challenge, in which all three mountains are conquered in 24 hours).

The classic ascent up Scaféll Pike is from Wasdale Head (p626), but the more scenic route starts near Seathwaite Farm. The trail travels past Styhead Tarn before cutting along the Corridor Route towards the summit, descending via the neighbouring peaks of Broad Crag, Ill Crag and Great End, or the easier route past Esk Hause. It's a challenging 8-mile, six-hour round trip, and not for inexperienced hikers; don't even think about tackling it without proper supplies (rucksack, OS map, compass, food and water, and decent hiking boots) and a favourable weather forecast.

---

## SLEEPING & EATING

**Borrowdale YHA** ( ☎ 0845 371 9624; www.yha.org.uk; Longthwaite; dm £15.50; Ⓨ Feb-Dec) Purpose-built chalet-style hostel specialising in walking and activity trips. The facilities are great, but it's often booked out throughout the summer.

**Derwentwater YHA** ( ☎ 0845 371 9314; www.yha.org .uk; Barrow House; dm £16; Ⓨ Feb-Nov, weekends Nov-Jan; Ⓟ ▣ ) This lakeside mansion 2 miles south of Keswick boasts high-ceilinged dorms, a billiard room, playgrounds and an artificial waterfall that runs the hostel's hydrogenerator.

**Yew Tree Farm** ( ☎ 017687-77675; www.borrowdale herdwick.co.uk; Rosthwaite; d from £60; Ⓟ ) Floral mo-tifs run riot in the three rooms, all snuggled under low farmhouse ceilings; bathrooms are titchy, and there are no TVs, so you'll have to make do with the views. For brekkie, there's Cumbrian bacon and Herdwick bangers; stroll across the road for homebaked cakes at the Flock Inn tearoom.

**Scaféll Hotel** ( ☎ 017687-77208; www.scafell.co.uk; Rosthwaite; d £124-175; Ⓟ ) Rosthwaite's former coaching inn makes for a cosy stay. Period fur-niture and musty rugs conjure up an antique air (the newer annexe is more contemporary). En-suite bathrooms and country views are (nearly) universal.

**Hazel Bank** ( ☎ 017687-77248; www.hazelbankhotel .co.uk; Rosthwaite; r £170-190; Ⓟ ) Oozing English luxury from every corniced corner, this Lakeland mansion is another fancy getaway, reached via its own humpbacked bridge and ensconced in private gardens, with upmarket boudoirs stuffed with swags, drapes, ruffled curtains and half-tester beds.

## Honister Pass

This bleak, wind-battered mountain pass into Buttermere was once the most productive quarrying area in the Lake District, and still produces much of the region's grey-green Westmorland slate.

You can take tours of the old **Honister Slate Mine** ( ☎ 017687-77230; www.honister-slate-mine .co.uk; adult/child £9.75/4.75; Ⓨ tours 10.30am, 12.30pm & 3.30pm Mar-Oct), or test your mettle along the UK's first **Via Ferrata** (Iron Way; adult/under 16yr/16-18yr £19.50/9.50/15) – a vertiginous cliff trail once used by the Honister slate miners, using a system of fixed ropes and iron ladders. It's exhilarating, but unsurprisingly you'll need a head for heights.

## Buttermere

From the high point of Honister, the road drops sharply into the deep bowl of Buttermere, skirting the lakeshore to Buttermere village, 4 miles from Honister and 9 miles from Keswick. From here, the B5289 cuts past Crummock Water (once joined with its neighbour) before exiting the valley's northern edge.

Buttermere marks the start of Alfred Wainwright's all-time favourite circuit: up **Red Pike** (755m), and along **High Stile**, **High Crag** and **Haystacks** (597m). In fact, the great man liked it so much he decided to stay here for good: after his death in 1991, his ashes were scattered across the top of Haystacks as requested in his will.

Buttermere has limited accommodation. Walkers bunk down at the **Buttermere YHA** ( ☎ 0845 371 9508; www.yha.org.uk; dm £17.50), a slate-stone house above Buttermere Lake, while those looking for more luxury try the upmar-ket **Bridge Hotel** ( ☎ 017687-70252; www.bridge-hotel .com; r incl dinner £148-210; Ⓟ ).

## Getting There & Away

Bus 79 (the Borrowdale Rambler) runs hourly (eight times on Sunday) between Keswick and Seatoller, while the 77/77A (Honister Rambler) makes the round trip from Keswick to Buttermere via Borrowdale and Honister Pass four times daily March to November. For day tickets, see p610.

## ULLSWATER & AROUND

Second only to Windermere in terms of stature, stately Ullswater stretches for 7.5 miles between Pooley Bridge, and Glenridding and Patterdale in the south. Carved out by a long-extinct glacier, the deep valley in which the lake sits is flanked by an impressive string of fells, most notably the razor ridge of Helvellyn (p632), Cumbria's third-highest mountain.

The **Ullswater Information Centre** ( ☎ 017684-82414; ullswatertic@lake-district.gov.uk; Beckside car park; ☽ 9am-5.30pm Apr-Oct) details local hikes, hotels and events.

**Ullswater 'Steamers'** ( ☎ 017684-82229; www.ullswater-steamers.co.uk) set out from the Pooley Bridge jetty, stopping at Howtown and Glenridding. The company's two oldest vessels have worked on Ullswater for over a century: *Lady of the Lake* was launched in 1887, followed by *Raven* in 1889.

Up to 12 daily ferries run in summer, dropping to three in winter. Current returns from Pooley Bridge are £4.80 to Howtown, or £11.30 to Glenridding and back. Children travel half price.

### Sleeping & Eating

Campers are spoilt for choice. **Hillcroft Park** ( ☎ 017684-486363; Roe Head Lane, Pooley Bridge; sites £11-20) is closest to the village, while **Park Foot** ( ☎ 017684-86309; www.parkfootullswater.co.uk; Howtown Rd, Pooley Bridge; sites incl 2 adults, tent & car £12-24) has the best facilities (including tennis courts, bike hire and pony trekking).

**Helvellyn YHA** ( ☎ 0845 371 9742; www.yha.org.uk; Greenside; dm £12; ☽ Easter-Oct, phone ahead at other times) This high-altitude hostel is perched 274m above Glenridding, and is mainly used by Helvellyn hikers; guided walks can be arranged through the hostel staff.

**Pooley Bridge Inn** ( ☎ 017684-86215; www.pooleybridgeinn.co.uk; Pooley Bridge; d £75-100; P ) This weird inn looks like it's upped sticks from the Alsatian Alps. Hanging baskets, cartwheels and wooden balconies decorate the exterior, and inside you'll find dinky rooms heavy on the florals and oak beams.

**Inn on the Lake** ( ☎ 017684-82444; www.innonthelakeullswater.co.uk; Glenridding; d £128-184; P ▣ )

This hotel feels a little corporate, but you'll be treated to top-notch facilities: Jacuzzi baths, tennis courts, sauna and gym, plus a choice of mountain or lake views from the rooms.

**Traveller's Rest** ( ☎ 017684-82298; Glenridding; mains £5.50-15) This is a typically friendly Cumbrian pub with fire-lit lounges, a lovely fell-view patio and a hearty bar menu. Hungry hikers plump for the 'Traveller's Mixed Grill' (£14.70) of rump steak, lamb chop, gammon, black pudding and Cumberland sausage, all crowned with a fried egg.

The homely **Sun Inn** ( ☎ 486205; Pooley Bridge; mains £5-12) has the usual range of ales and a beautiful beer garden.

# CUMBRIAN COAST

While the central lakes and fells pull in a never-ending stream of visitors, surprisingly few ever make the trek west to explore Cumbria's coastline. And that's a shame: while it might not compare to the wild grandeur of Northumberland or the rugged splendour of Scotland's shores, Cumbria's coast is well worth exploring, with a cluster of sandy bays, seaside towns and the Roman harbour at Ravenglass, starting point for the La'al Ratty steam railway. Less attractive is the nuclear plant of Sellafield, still stirring up controversy some 50 years after its construction.

## Getting Around

The Cumbrian Coast railway line loops 120 miles from Lancaster to Carlisle, stopping at the coastal resorts of Grange, Ulverston, Ravenglass, Whitehaven and Workington.

## CARTMEL

**pop 1798**

Tiny Cartmel is known for three things: its 12th-century priory, its miniature racecourse and its world-famous sticky toffee pudding, on sale at the **Cartmel Village Shop** ( ☎ 015395-36201; www.stickytoffeepudding.co.uk; The Square; ☽ 9am-5pm Mon-Sat, 10am-4.30pm Sun).

A short walk from the central square, **Cartmel Priory** ( ☎ 015395-36261; ☽ 9am-5.30pm May-Oct, to 3.30pm Nov-Apr) was one of the few Cumbrian priories to escape demolition during the dissolution. Light pours in through the 15th-century east window, illuminating the tombs set into the flagstoned floor; note

---

**THE HIKE TO HELVELLYN**

Alongside Scaféll Pike, the hike up **Helvellyn** (950m) is the most famous (and challenging) Lake District trail. Wainwright adored it, and Helvellyn exercised a peculiarly powerful hold over William Wordsworth: the mountain crops up frequently in his work, and he continued to climb the peak well into his seventies.

The classic route up Helvellyn is the gravity-defying ridge scramble along **Striding Edge**, a challenging route for even experienced walkers, with dizzying drops to either side and a fair amount of hand-and-knee scrambling (don't consider it if you're even slightly wary of heights). Beyond the summit and its glorious 360-degree views, the usual descent is via **Swirral Edge** and **Red Tarn**. Count on at least 7 miles and six hours on the mountain, and, as usual, come suitably prepared unless you fancy coming down in the rescue chopper.

---

the memento mori of skulls and hourglasses, intended to remind the pious of their own inescapable mortality.

Bus 530/532 travels from Cartmel to Grange (40 minutes) 10 to 12 times from Monday to Saturday.

## HOLKER HALL & LAKELAND MOTOR MUSEUM

About 2 miles west of Cartmel is **Holker Hall** ( ☎ 015395-58328; www.holker-hall.co.uk; admission house & grounds £8.80, grounds only £5.70; ☯ house 10.30am-4.30pm Sun-Fri, grounds 10am-6pm Mar-Oct). Though parts of it date from the 16th century, the house was mostly rebuilt following a devastating fire in 1871. It's a typically ostentatious Victorian affair, covered with mullioned windows, gables and copper-topped turrets, and the wonderful grounds encompass a rose garden, woodland, ornamental fountains and a 22m lime tree.

Next to the ticket kiosk for the main house there's a fantastic **food hall** ( ☎ 015395-59084) stocking Lakeland produce.

A short stroll away is the **Lakeland Motor Museum** ( ☎ 015395-58509; adult/6-15yr £7/4.50; ☯ 10.30am-4.45pm), which houses a collection of classic cars (from Jaguars to Bentleys) and a replica of Donald Campbell's boat, *Bluebird* (p623).

## FURNESS ABBEY

Eight and a half miles southwest of Ulverston, the rosy ruins of **Furness Abbey** (EH; ☎ 01229-823420; admission £3.40; ☯ 10am-6pm daily Apr-Sep, to 5pm daily Oct, to 4pm Wed-Sun Nov-Mar) are all that remains of one of northern England's most powerful monasteries. You can still make out the abbey's basic footprint; various arches, windows and the north and south transept walls are still standing, alongside the remains of the abbey bell tower.

Several buses, including the hourly X35 from Ulverston, stop nearby.

## RAVENGLASS & AROUND

Originally a Roman harbour, Ravenglass is famous among steam enthusiasts as the start of the **Ravenglass & Eskdale Railway** ( ☎ 01229-717171; www.ravenglass-railway.co.uk), built in 1875 to ferry iron ore from the Eskdale mines to the coast. Affectionately known as La'al Ratty, the pocket-sized choo-choos chug for 7 miles into Eskdale and the Lake District foothills, terminating at Dalegarth Station, near Boot. There are up to 17 trips daily in summer, dropping to two in winter; single fares are adult/five to 15 years £6/3, or day tickets cost £10.20/5.10.

A mile south of Ravenglass is **Muncaster Castle** ( ☎ 01229-717614; www.muncaster.co.uk; adult/5-15yr incl owl centre, gardens & maze £7.50/5.50, castle extra £2.50/1.50; ☯ gardens 10.30am-6pm or dusk, castle noon-4.30pm Sun-Fri Feb-Nov), built around a 14th-century *pele* tower. Highlights include the dining room, great hall and an extraordinary octagonal library, but the house is most renowned for its spooks (you can arrange for your own overnight 'ghost sit' for £405 or £475). The castle's gardens contain an ornamental maze and an owl centre.

North of Ravenglass, the coast sweeps past the gloomy chimney stacks of **Sellafield**, Britain's largest nuclear reprocessing plant, towards **St Bees Head**, site of an RSPB bird reserve and official starting point for Wainwright's C2C route, which ends 190 miles east at Robin Hood's Bay (p569).

Ravenglass is on the Cumbrian Coast Line, with frequent links north and south. Bus 6 from Whitehaven stops at Ravenglass and terminates at Muncaster (70 minutes, five daily). Bus X6 travels the same route on Sunday (four daily).

# NORTH & EAST CUMBRIA

Many visitors speed through the northern and eastern reaches of Cumbria in a headlong dash for the Lake District, but this is an area that's worth exploring – a bleakly beautiful landscape of isolated farms, barren heaths and solid hilltop towns, cut through by the Roman barrier of Hadrian's Wall.

## CARLISLE

pop 69,527

Precariously perched on the tempestuous border between England and Scotland, in the area once ominously dubbed the 'Debatable Lands', Carlisle is a city with a notoriously stormy past. Sacked by the Vikings, pillaged by the Scots, and plundered by the Border Reivers, Carlisle has stood in the frontline of England's defences for the last 1000 years. The battlements and keeps of the stout medieval castle still stand watch, built from the same rosy red sandstone as the city's cathedral and terraced houses; but Cumbria's only city is a more peaceful place these days, with a buzzy student population that keeps this old city young at heart.

### History

A Celtic camp or *caer* provided an early military station for the Romans, and Carlisle became the northwest's main administrative centre following the construction of Hadrian's Wall. After centuries of intermittent conflict between Picts, Saxons and Viking raiders, the Normans seized Carlisle from the Scots in 1092.

The English developed Carlisle as a military stronghold throughout the Middle Ages, enlarging the walls, citadels and the great gates, and the city became an important strategic base for Royalist forces during the Civil War.

Peace came to the city with the Restoration, and the city developed as an industrial centre for cotton and textiles after the arrival of the railway in the mid 19th century.

### Orientation

From the M6, the main routes into town are London Rd and Warwick Rd. The train station is south of the city centre, a 10-minute walk from Town Hall Sq (also known as Greenmarket) and the tourist office. The bus station is on Lonsdale St, about 250m east.

Most of the town's B&Bs are dotted along Victoria Pl and Warwick Rd.

### Information

**@Cybercafe** ( ☎ 01228-512308; www.atcybercafe.co.uk; 8-10 Devonshire St; ۞ 10am-10pm Mon-Sat, 1-10pm Sun; per hr £3)

**Cumberland Infirmary** ( ☎ 01228-523444; Newtown Rd) Half a mile west of the city centre.

**Police station** ( ☎ 0845 33 00 247; English St; ۞ 8am-midnight)

**Post office** (20-34 Warwick Rd)

**Tourist office** ( ☎ 01228-625600; www.historic-carlisle .org.uk; Greenmarket; per 15min £1; ۞ 9.30am-5pm Mon-Sat, 10.30am-4pm Sun) Offers internet access.

**Waterstone's** ( ☎ 01228-542300; 66 Scotch St; ۞ 9am-5.30pm Mon-Sat, 10am-4pm Sun) Large chain bookshop stocking new titles and local books.

### Sights & Activities

#### CARLISLE CASTLE

Constructed in stages between the 10th and 15th centuries, the brooding, rust-red **Carlisle Castle** ( ☎ 01228-591922; adult/child £4.50/2.30; ۞ 9.30am-5pm Apr-Sep, 10am-4pm Oct-Mar) has witnessed some dramatic events over the centuries: Mary Queen of Scots was imprisoned here in 1568, and the castle was the site of a notorious eight-month siege during the English Civil War, when the Royalist garrison survived by eating rats, mice and the castle dogs before finally surrendering in 1645. Look out for the 'licking stones' in the dungeon, which Jacobite prisoners supposedly lapped for moisture.

Admission includes entry to the **Kings Own Royal Border Regiment Museum**, which explores the history of Cumbria's Infantry Regiment. There are guided tours from April to September.

#### CARLISLE CATHEDRAL

Carlisle's scarlet **cathedral** ( ☎ 01228-548151; www .carlislecathedral.org.uk; 7 The Abbey; donation £2; ۞ 7.30am-6.15pm Mon-Sat, to 5pm Sun) was founded as a priory church in 1122. During the 1644–45 siege by Parliamentarian troops, two-thirds of the nave was torn down to repair the city walls. Serious restoration didn't begin until 1853, but a surprising amount survives, including the 14th-century east window and part of the Norman nave. Other features include the 15th-century misericords, the lovely Brougham Triptych and some ornate choir carvings.

Surrounding the cathedral are other priory relics, including the 16th-century **Fratry** (see

CUMBRIA & THE LAKE DISTRICT

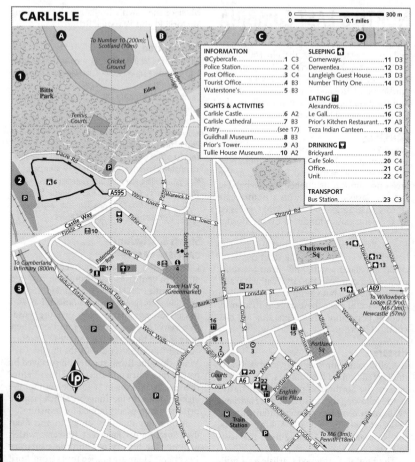

CARLISLE

| INFORMATION | | SLEEPING | |
|---|---|---|---|
| @Cybercafe | 1 C3 | Cornerways | 11 D3 |
| Police Station | 2 C4 | Derwentlea | 12 D3 |
| Post Office | 3 C4 | Langleigh Guest House | 13 D3 |
| Tourist Office | 4 B3 | Number Thirty One | 14 D3 |
| Waterstone's | 5 B3 | | |
| | | EATING | |
| SIGHTS & ACTIVITIES | | Alexandros | 15 C3 |
| Carlisle Castle | 6 A2 | Le Gall | 16 C3 |
| Carlisle Cathedral | 7 B3 | Prior's Kitchen Restaurant | 17 A3 |
| Fratry | (see 17) | Teza Indian Canteen | 18 C4 |
| Guildhall Museum | 8 B3 | | |
| Prior's Tower | 9 A3 | DRINKING | |
| Tullie House Museum | 10 A2 | Brickyard | 19 B2 |
| | | Cafe Solo | 20 C4 |
| | | Office | 21 C4 |
| | | Unit | 22 C4 |
| | | | |
| | | TRANSPORT | |
| | | Bus Station | 23 C3 |

Prior's Kitchen Restaurant, opposite) and the **Prior's Tower**.

### TULLIE HOUSE MUSEUM

Carlisle's main **museum** (☎ 01228-534781; Castle St; www.tulliehouse.co.uk; adult/under 18yr £5.20/free; ☼ 10am-5pm Mon-Sat & 11am-5pm Sun July-Aug, 10am-5pm Mon-Sat & noon-5pm Sun Apr-June & Sep-Oct, 10am-4pm Mon-Sat & noon-4pm Sun Nov-Mar) is a treat for history buffs, with exhibits exploring the foundation of the city, life under Roman rule and the development of modern Carlisle. The museum has a strong archaeology collection, including a Bronze Age spear-mould, Roman tablets collected from Hadrian's Wall, and artefacts recovered from Viking burial sites in nearby Ormside and Hesket.

### GUILDHALL MUSEUM

This tiny **museum** (☎ 01228-532781; Greenmarket; admission free; ☼ noon-4.30pm Tue-Sun Apr-Oct) is housed in a wonky 15th-century town house built for Carlisle's trade guilds. Among the modest exhibits are a ceremonial mace, the city's stocks and a section of exposed wall showing the building's wattle-and-daub construction.

## Tours

**Open Book Visitor Guiding** (☎ 01228-670578; www.greatguidedtours.co.uk) offers tours of Carlisle and the surrounding area from April to September, including visits to Carlisle Castle and Hadrian's Wall. Tours leave from the tourist office.

## Sleeping

**Cornerways** ( ☎ 01228-521733; www.cornerwaysguest house.co.uk; 107 Warwick Rd; s £30-35, d £55-65; P wi-fi) This cheery corner guesthouse offers reliable B&B rooms (not all are en suite). Period touches (including a tiled Victorian hallway) keep it a cut above Carlisle's bog-standard B&Bs.

**Langleigh Guest House** ( ☎ 01228-530440; www .langleighhouse.co.uk; 6 Howard Pl; s/d £35/70; P ) Gilded mirrors, armchairs and porcelain knick-knacks cover this good-value guesthouse. Rooms are decorated in well-to-do Edwardian fashion – think brass bedside lamps, marble fireplaces and watercolour prints.

**Derwentlea** ( ☎ 01228-409706; www.derwentlea.co.uk; 14 Howard Pl; s/d £35/70; P ) Red leather armchairs and ticking mantle clocks set the period vibe at this small, trad-brick B&B. Big beds, full-length mirrors and dressing tables distinguish the smartest rooms, and there's a ground-floor room for mobility-restricted guests.

**Number Thirty One** ( ☎ 01228-597080; www .number31.freeservers.com; 31 Howard Pl; s/d from £65/95; P ) Number 31 oozes opulence. Choose from three colour-coded rooms: Blue is classically old-fashioned with polished wooden bed frame and upmarket wallpaper; Yellow is cosily countrified, with flower-print quilt and half-tester bed; Red has a touch of Zen sophistication thanks to its Japanese-print bedspread and dragon headboard.

**Willowbeck Lodge** ( ☎ 01228-513607; www.wil lowbeck-lodge.com; Lambley Bank, Scotby; d £100-120; P wi-fi) The architects have gone doolally at this palatial B&B, 3 miles east of the city centre. It's a modernist marvel, boasting six deluxe rooms furnished in creams and taupes, with luxury spoils including corner tubs, broadband and LCD TVs. The centrepiece is the 7m-high gabled lounge, which overlooks a private pond frequented by kingfishers and herons. Fabulous.

## Eating

**Alexandros** ( ☎ 01228-592227; 68 Warwick Rd; meze £3-6, mains £10-16; dinner Mon-Sat) Go Greek with authentic *mezedhes* (appetisers), grilled kebabs and calamari at this ever-popular restaurant on Warwick Rd – just remember that smashing your plates is reserved for special occasions…

**Prior's Kitchen Restaurant** ( ☎ 01228-543251; Carlisle Cathedral; lunches £4-6; 9.45am-4pm Mon-Sat) Hidden in the old monk's mess hall, this cosy little cafe is always a favourite stop for jacket spuds, club sandwiches and homemade quiches – and it does a mean cream tea, too.

**Le Gall** ( ☎ 01228-818388; 7 Devonshire St; mains £5-12; lunch & dinner) Despite the Gallic name, this town-centre bistro brims with world flavours. Italian panini and pastas, Mexican wraps and Cumbrian standards fill the specials board.

**our pick** **Teza Indian Canteen** ( ☎ 01228-525111; 4a English Gate Plaza; mains £8-14; lunch & dinner Mon-Sat) Wave goodbye to those tired old vindaloos – this 21st-century Indian stands out from Carlisle's other curry houses like a Bollywood superstar in a crowd of extras. It shimmers with chrome, plate glass and modern art, and champions a new breed of Indian cuisine – Keralan fish curry, tiger prawns with coriander and cloves, and slow-cooked lamb in pickled ginger.

**Number 10** ( ☎ 01228-524183; 10 Eden Mount; mains £13-21; dinner Tue-Sat) Arguably the city's top spot, this classy Brit brasserie north of the centre takes its cue from the culinary produce it finds on its doorstep, from Thornby Moor goat's cheese to farm-bred lamb and Morecambe Bay shrimps. Tables are limited, and it gets busy.

## Drinking

Botchergate's the place for late-night action, but it gets notoriously rowdy after kicking-out time, so watch your step.

**Office** ( ☎ 01228-404303; Botchergate) Industrial pipes, cube lights and stripped style define this hipster hang-out, with DJs spinning breakbeat, chunky house and hip-hop.

**Unit** ( ☎ 01228-514823; Botchergate) Another metro-style bar decked out in retro garb, with DJs and deep leather sofas to pull in Carlisle's trendy set.

**Cafe Solo** ( ☎ 01228-631600; 1 Botchergate) Sink lattes by day, chased down with Sol beers, margaritas and late-night tapas after dark at this Balearic corner bar.

**Brickyard** ( ☎ 01228-512220; www.brick-yard.com; 14 Fisher St) Carlisle's main gig venue, housed in the former Memorial Hall.

## Getting There & Away

### BUS

Carlisle is Cumbria's main transport hub. National Express coaches travel from the bus station on Lonsdale St to London (£33, 7½ hours, three direct daily, with extra buses via

Birmingham), Glasgow (£17.20, two hours, 14 daily) and Manchester (£24, 3¼ hours, seven daily).

The most useful services to the Lakes are the 600 (one hour, seven Monday to Saturday) to Cockermouth and the 554 to Keswick (70 minutes, three daily), connecting with the 555/556 LakesLink to Windermere and Ambleside.

The 104 operates to Penrith (40 minutes, hourly Monday to Saturday, nine on Sunday), and Bus AD122 (the Hadrian's Wall bus; six daily late May to late September) connects Hexham and Carlisle.

### TRAIN

Carlisle is on the London Euston (£123.50, 3¼ to 4¼ hours) to Glasgow (£43.20, 1¼ to 1½ hours) line, with hourly connections in either direction. It's also the terminus for several regional railways:

**Cumbrian Coast Line** Follows the coastline to Lancaster (£23, three to four hours).

**Lakes Line** Branches at Oxenholme near Kendal for Windermere (£19.50, one to two hours depending on connections).

**Settle-Carlisle Line** Cuts southeast across the Yorkshire Dales (£15.80, 1½ hours).

**Tyne Valley Line** Follows Hadrian's Wall to Newcastle-upon-Tyne (£12.10, 1½ hours).

### Getting Around

To book a taxi, call **Radio Taxis** ( ☎ 01228-527575), **Citadel Station Taxis** ( ☎ 01228-523971) or **County Cabs** ( ☎ 01228-596789).

## PENRITH

pop 14,882

Traditional butchers, greengrocers and teashops line the streets of Penrith, a stout, redbrick town which feels closer to the no-nonsense villages of the Yorkshire Dales than to the chocolate-box villages of the Central Lakes. Once the region's capital, Penrith remains a busy commercial centre for eastern Cumbria.

The **tourist office** ( ☎ 01768-867466; pen.tic@eden .gov.uk; Middlegate; ☉ 9.30am-5pm Mon-Sat, 1-4.45pm Sun) houses a small town museum displaying archaeological finds.

Opposite the station is the ruined 14th-century **Penrith Castle** ( ☉ 7.30am-9pm Easter-Oct, to 4.30pm Oct-Easter), built by William Strickland and expanded by Richard III to resist Scottish raids, one of which razed the town in 1345.

Penrith's name derives from an old Celtic word meaning 'red fell', and the area's crimson sandstone can be seen in many town buildings, including the 18th-century **St Andrew's Church**. A legendary giant (the 'rightful king of all Cumbria') is said to be buried in the churchyard, but the stone pillars supposedly marking his grave are actually the weathered remains of Celtic crosses.

### Sleeping

**Brooklands** ( ☎ 01768-863395; www.brooklandsguest house.com; 2 Portland Pl; s £30-35, d £65-75) This is a top-notch Victorian guesthouse. Some rooms feature huge pine four-posters and rich purples, while others go for soothing magnolias and flower prints. For the full swank-factor you'll want the fluffy-pillowed suite, with brass bedstead and wall-mounted TV.

**Brandelhow** ( ☎ 01768-864470; www.brandel howguesthouse.co.uk; 1 Portland Pl; s £32.50, d & tw £65) There are plain, uncomplicated rooms at this Portland Pl staple, all in pine and neutral beige, with lots of little luxuries (mini-fridges, bickies, bathrobes). Tuck into a sit-down tea on arrival, topped off with a slice of Grandma's Courting Cake or Lanie's Expedition Flapjack.

**Bank House** ( ☎ 01768-868714; www.bankhouse penrith.co.uk; Graham St; s £38, d £68-76; ☐ wi-fi) Unpretentious Cumbrian guesthouse which does all the basics right (including a kingly breakfast of coiled Cumberland sausage and fresh-baked granary loaf). The rosy pink twin room might be too lacy for some, but the other doubles are more neutral, with DVD players and wooden bed frames.

### Eating

**No 15** ( ☎ 01768-867453; 15 Victoria Rd; lunches £6-10; ☉ daily) Look no further for lunch in Penrith than this zingy little cafe-cum-gallery. There are 15 specials to choose from behind the counter, plus a bevy of artisan teas, cakes and sarnies, and you can check out local art and photography in the gallery annexe.

**ourpick** **Yanwath Gate Inn** ( ☎ 01768-862886; Yanwath; mains £16-19) Two miles south of town, this award-winning inn has scooped a clutch of culinary prizes for its gastro-grub. Wood panels and A-frame beams conjure a convincingly rural atmosphere, and the menu ranges through the fells in search of local smoked venison, salt lamb and crispy pork belly, chased down by a delicious selection of Cumbrian cheeses.

## Getting There & Away

### BUS

The bus station is northeast of the centre, off Sandgate. Bus 104 runs between Penrith and Carlisle (45 minutes, hourly Monday to Saturday, nine on Sunday).

Bus X4/X5 (13 Monday to Saturday, six on Sunday) travels via Rheged, Keswick and Cockermouth en route to the Cumbrian Coast.

### TRAIN

Penrith has frequent connections to Carlisle (£6.70, 20 minutes, hourly) and Lancaster (£12.50, 50 to 60 minutes, hourly).

# AROUND PENRITH

## Long Meg & Her Daughters

The third-largest prehistoric stone circle in England, Long Meg and Her Daughters is a ring of 59 stones, 6 miles northeast of Penrith. Local legend maintains that the circle was once a coven of witches, zapped into stone by a local wizard. The circle is said to be uncountable (if anyone manages twice the spell will be lifted) and a terrible fate awaits anyone who disturbs the stones. Just outside the circle stands Long Meg herself, a 12ft red sandstone pillar decorated with faint spiral traces – another local legend says that the stone would run with blood if it were ever damaged.

The circle is a few miles northeast of Penrith, along a minor road about three quarters of a mile north of Little Salkeld, just off the A686.

## Rheged

Cunningly disguised as a Lakeland hill 2 miles west of Penrith, **Rheged** ( ☎ 01768-686000; www.rheged .com; �)10am-6pm) houses a large-screen Imax cinema, retail hall and various Cumbrian-themed exhibitions.

There's a revolving line-up of movies on show. A new film starts hourly; one film costs £4.95/3 per adult/child, with each extra one costing £3/2.

The frequent X4/X5 bus between Penrith and Workington stops at the centre.

# Northeast England

Defiantly ensconced in the northeastern corner of England, the Northeast is different to the rest of England in both appearance and temperament. Passionate, fiery and independent, it has more in common with its neighbour to the north, Scotland, which has never shirked from a scrap over territory.

It's a land worth fighting for. The vast, almost epic countryside has a brooding, menacing beauty – from the wind-lashed stretch of coast through the heather-carpeted Cheviot Hills and on into the wilderness of Northumberland National Park, before you arrive at the feet of the dark slopes of the North Pennines. It's almost hard to tell when you've crossed the border into Scotland, that other protagonist in an 800-year-old historical drama of war, bloodshed and conquest that has made the folks round these parts hardier than most.

It took a tough bunch to make their mark, but it's a pretty impressive one: the Romans left us the magnificent Hadrian's Wall as their legacy, while the Normans matched them with a series of splendid castles and one knock-your-socks-off cathedral.

If you look closely you'll also see evidence of a much later influence, the once ubiquitous presence of coal mining that was the region's major industry for the guts of 700 years. It's all gone now, but even here the legacy isn't all bad, for coal mining and its resultant industry gave us Newcastle, one of the best cities in Britain for all kinds of urban fun and mayhem.

## HIGHLIGHTS

- Exploring Newcastle's arty side in the exciting **Ouseburn Valley** (p644)
- Walking like a Roman – hiking along the stunning **Hadrian's Wall** (p655)
- Castle-spotting along the blustery white-sand beaches of **Northumberland** (p662)
- Exploring Durham's industrial history at the **Beamish Open-Air Museum** (p653)
- Hiking to the top of the **Cheviot** (p661) in Northumberland National Park
- Going Norman in **Durham** (p649), where the cathedral of which is a spectacular World Heritage Site

- POPULATION: 2.5 MILLION
- AREA: 3320 SQ MILES
- FIRST PLACE IN ENGLAND TO BREW BEER: NEWCASTLE (ACCORDING TO LEGEND)

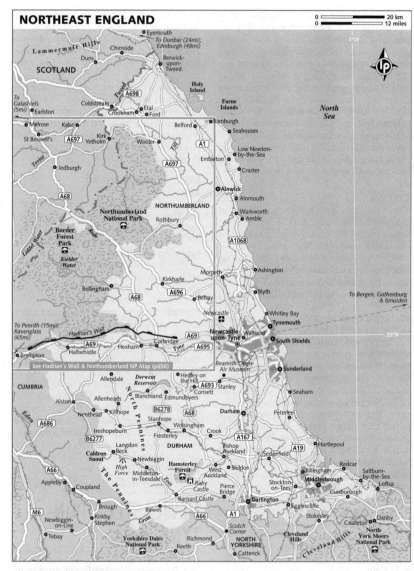

NORTHEAST ENGLAND

## Orientation & Information

The Pennine hills are the dominant geological feature, forming a north–south spine that divides the region from Cumbria and Lancashire in the west and provides the source of major rivers such as the Tees and the Tyne.

The major transport routes are east of this spine, from Durham northwards to Newcastle and Edinburgh. Newcastle is an important ferry port for Scandinavia (see p648 for details). There's a northeast region website at www.thenortheast.com.

## Activities

With the rugged moors of the Pennines and stunning seascape of the Northumberland coast, there's some good walking and cycling in this region. If you're out in the open, be prepared for wind and rain at any time of year. But when the sun shines, you can't go wrong. The Outdoor Activities chapter has more details on walking (p108) and cycling (p111), and suggestions for shorter routes are given throughout this chapter. Regional tourism websites all contain walking and cycling information, and tourist information centres (TICs; referred to throughout this book simply as tourist offices) all stock free leaflets plus maps and guides (usually £1 to £5) covering walking, cycling and other activities.

### CYCLING

There are some excellent cycling routes in this part of the world. Part of the National Cycle Network, a long-time favourite is the **Coast & Castles Cycle Route** (NCN route 1), which runs south–north along the glorious Northumberland coast between Newcastle-upon-Tyne and Berwick-upon-Tweed, before swinging inland into Scotland to finish at Edinburgh. The coast is exposed, though, so check the weather and try to time your ride so that the wind is behind you.

The 140-mile **Sea to Sea Cycle Route** (C2C; www .c2c-guide.co.uk) runs across northern England from Whitehaven or Workington on the Cumbrian coast, through the northern part of the Lake District, and then over the wild hills of the North Pennines to finish at Newcastle-upon-Tyne or Sunderland. This popular route is fast becoming a classic, and most people go west–east to take advantage of prevailing winds. You'll need five days to complete the whole route, and the northeast England section, from Penrith (in Cumbria) to the east coast is a good three-day trip.

The other option is the **Hadrian's Cycleway** (www.cycleroutes.org.uk), a 172-mile route opened in July 2006 that runs from South Shields in Tyneside, west along the wall and down to Ravenglass (p632) in Cumbria.

### WALKING

The North Pennines are billed as 'England's last wilderness', and if you like to walk in quiet and fairly remote areas, these hills – along with the Cheviots further north – are the best in England. Long routes through this area include the famous **Pennine Way**, which keeps mainly to the high ground as it crosses the region between the Yorkshire Dales and

the Scottish border, but also goes through sections of river valley and some tedious patches of plantation. The whole route is over 250 miles, but the 70-mile section between Bowes and Hadrian's Wall would be a fine four-day taster.

Elsewhere in the area, the great Roman ruin of **Hadrian's Wall** is an ideal focus for walking. There's a huge range of easy loops taking in forts and other historical highlights. A very popular walk is the long-distance route from end to end, providing good options for anything from one to four days (see p656).

## Getting There & Around
### BUS

Bus transport around the region can be difficult, particularly around the more remote parts of Northumbria in the west. Call ☎ 0870 608 2608 for information on connections, timetables and prices.

Several one-day Explorer tickets are available; always ask if one might be appropriate. The Explorer North East (adult/child £5.75/4.75), available on buses, covers from Berwick down to Scarborough, and allows unlimited travel for one day, as well as numerous admission discounts.

### TRAIN

The main lines run north to Edinburgh via Durham, Newcastle and Berwick, and west to Carlisle roughly following Hadrian's Wall. Phone ☎ 0845 748 4950 for all train enquiries.

There are numerous Rover tickets for single-day travel and longer periods, so ask if one might be worthwhile. For example, the North Country Rover (adult/child £61.50/30.75) allows unlimited travel throughout the north (not including Northumberland) any four days out of eight.

# NEWCASTLE-UPON-TYNE

**pop 189,863**

Hip, happening Newcastle will surprise the first-time visitor, especially if you've come armed with notions about hard-bitten lads and lasses going all hell-for-leather in sub-zero temperatures in a sooty, industrial landscape. Well, there's a bit of that for sure, but Newcastle is about a hell of a lot more than coal slags.

There's culture, heritage and some of Britain's most elegant streets, while the absolutely brilliant and alternative Ouseburn testifies to a nightlife beyond the alco-pop shots and high-octane cheesefest favoured by so many hen and stag parties.

When you do come, take a moment to cherish the city's greatest strength: the locals. Geordies are a fiercely independent bunch, tied together by history, adversity and that impenetrable dialect, the closest language to 1500-year-old Anglo-Saxon left in England. They are also proud, hard-working and indefatigably positive – perhaps their greatest quality considering how tough life has been.

## ORIENTATION

The River Tyne marks the boundary between Newcastle to the north and Gateshead to the south; it is also one of the focal points for visitors to the city. Newcastle's attractive Victorian centre – which the local council has called Grainger Town to the uncertain shrugs of the locals – is only a short, uphill walk from the river. The up-and-coming Ouseburn is less than a mile east of here, while genteel Jesmond is north of the city and easily reached by bus or with the excellent Metro underground. The Tyne's southern bank – home to the impressive Baltic gallery and stunning Sage entertainment venue – is as far into Gateshead as you'll likely need to venture.

Central Station (train) is between the river and the city centre; the coach station is on Gallowgate, while local and regional buses leave from Eldon Sq and Haymarket bus stations.

### Maps

All tourist offices have handy, free tearaway maps of Newcastle and Gateshead. The Ordnance Survey's *Mini-Map* (£2) is a handy foldaway pocket map of Newcastle, but not Gateshead.

The **Newcastle Map Centre** ( ☎ 0191-261 5622; 1st fl, 55 Grey St) supplies copious maps and guides.

## INFORMATION

**Blackwell's Bookshop** ( ☎ 0191-232 6421; 141 Percy St) A comprehensive range of titles.

**Clayton Road Laundrette** ( ☎ 0191-281 5055; 4 Clayton Rd, Jesmond)

**Main post office** (35 Mosley St; ⏰ 9am-5.30pm Mon-Fri, to 12.30pm Sat) In the city centre.

**McNulty's Internet Cafe** ( ☎ 0191-232 0922; 26-30 Market St; per hr £5; ⏰ 8am-6.30pm Mon-Sat) About 14 terminals to fix all of your online needs.

**Newcastle General Hospital** ( ☎ 0191-273 8811; Westgate Rd) Half a mile northwest of the city centre, off Queen Victoria St.

**Police station** ( ☎ 0191-214 6555; cnr Pilgrim & Market Sts)

**Thomas Cook** ( ☎ 0191-219 8000; 6 Northumberland St) Has a bureau de change; it's just east of Monument.

**Tourist offices** (www.visitnewcastlegateshead.com) Main branch ( ☎ 0191-277 8000; Central Arcade, Market St; ⏰ 9.30am-5.30pm Mon-Wed, Fri & Sat, to 7.30pm Thu year-round, plus 10am-4pm Sun Jun-Sep); Gateshead Library ( ☎ 0191-433 8420; Prince Consort Rd; ⏰ 9am-7pm Mon-Tue & Thu-Fri, to 5pm Wed, to 1pm Sat); Guildhall ( ☎ 0191-277 8000; Newcastle Quayside; ⏰ 11am-6pm Mon-Fri, 9am-6pm Sat, 9am-4pm Sun); Sage Gateshead ( ☎ 0191-478 4222; Gateshead Quays; ⏰ 9am-5pm Mon-Fri, 10am-5pm Sat, 11am-5pm Sun) All offices listed here provide a booking service ( ☎ 0191-277 8042) as well as other assorted tourist sundries.

**Waterstone's** ( ☎ 0191-261 7757; Emerson Chambers, Blackett St) Four floors of books to satisfy most of your needs.

## SIGHTS
### Quayside

Newcastle's most recognisable attractions are the seven bridges that span the Tyne and some of the striking buildings that line it. Along Quayside, on the river's northern side, is a handsome boardwalk that makes for a pleasant stroll during the day but really comes to life at night, when the bars, clubs and restaurants that line it are full to bursting.

### TYNE BRIDGES

The most famous view in Newcastle is the cluster of Tyne bridges, and the most famous of these is the **Tyne Bridge** (1925–28), built at about the same time as (and very reminiscent of) Australia's Sydney Harbour Bridge. The quaint little **Swing Bridge** pivots in the middle to let ships through. Nearby, **High Level Bridge**, designed by Robert Stephenson, was the world's first road and railway bridge (1849). The most recent addition is the multiple-award-winning **Millennium Bridge**

**NORTHEAST ENGLAND**

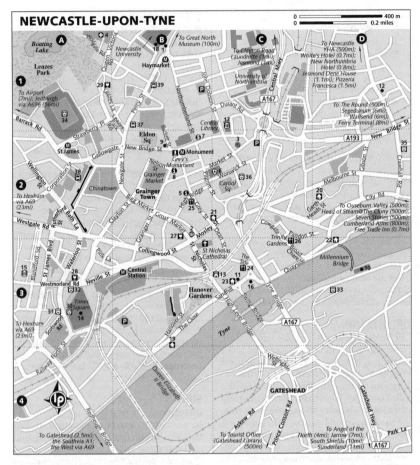

(aka Blinking Bridge; 2002), which opens like an eyelid to let ships pass.

### OTHER SIGHTS

The Tyne's northern bank was the hub of commercial Newcastle in the 16th century. On Sandhill is **Bessie Surtee's House** ( ☎ 0191-261 1585; 41-44 Sandhill; admission free; ⏰ 10am-4pm Mon-Fri), a combination of two 16th- and 17th-century merchant houses – all dark wood and sloping angles. Three rooms are open to the public. The daughter of a wealthy banker, feisty Bessie annoyed Daddy by falling in love with John Scott (1751–1838), a pauper. It all ended in smiles because John went on to become Lord Chancellor. Today it is run in conjunction with English Heritage (EH).

Just across the street is the rounded **Guildhall**, built in 1658. It now houses a branch of the tourist office.

## City Centre

Newcastle's Victorian centre, a compact area bordered roughly by Grainger St to the west and Pilgrim St to the east, is supremely elegant and one of the most compelling examples of urban rejuvenation in England. At the heart of it is the extraordinarily handsome Grey St, lined with fine classical buildings – undoubtedly one of the country's finest thoroughfares: in 2005 BBC Radio 4 listeners voted it Britain's most beautiful street.

### CENTRE FOR LIFE

This excellent **science village** ( ☎ 0191-243 8210; www.life.org.uk; Scotswood Rd; adult/child £8/5.85;

10am-6pm Mon-Sat, 11am-6pm Sun, last admission 4pm) has a series of hands-on exhibits that allow you (or your kids) to discover the incredible secrets of life. The highlight is the Motion Ride, a motion simulator that, among other things, lets you 'feel' what it's like to score a goal at St James' Park and bungee jump from the Tyne Bridge. There's lots of thought-provoking arcade-style games, and if the information sometimes gets lost on the way, never mind, kids will love it.

### LAING ART GALLERY

The exceptional collection at the **Laing** ( ☎ 0191-232 7734; www.twmuseums.org.uk; New Bridge St; admission free; 10am-5pm Mon-Sat, 2-5pm Sun) includes works by Kitaj, Frank Auerbach and Henry Moore, and an important collection of paintings by Northumberland-born artist John Martin (1789–1854).

Outside the gallery is Thomas Heatherwick's famous **Blue Carpet** (2002) with shimmering blue tiles made from crushed glass and resin.

### DISCOVERY MUSEUM

Newcastle's rich history is uncovered through a fascinating series of exhibits at this excellent **museum** ( ☎ 0191-232 6789; www.twmuseums.org .uk; Blandford Sq; admission free; 10am-5pm Mon-Sat, 2-5pm Sun). The exhibits, spread across three floors of the former Co-operative Wholesale Society building, surround the mightily impressive 30m-long *Turbinia,* the fastest ship in the world in 1897. The different sections are all worth a look; our favourites were the self-explanatory Story of the Tyne and the interactive Science Maze.

### CASTLE GARTH KEEP

The 'New Castle' that gave its name to the city has been largely swallowed up by the railway station, leaving only the square Norman **keep** (adult/child £2/1; 9.30am-5.30pm Apr-Sep, to 4.30pm Oct-Mar) as one of the few remaining fragments. It has a fine chevron-covered chapel and great views across the Tyne bridges from its rooftop.

### GREAT NORTH MUSEUM

The **Great North Museum** ( ☎ 0191-222 8996; www .greatnorthmuseum.org), which at the time of writing was expected to open in spring 2009, will be the north's foremost museum of the natural sciences, archaeology, history and culture. The main exhibition hall will be in the neoclassical building that once was home to the natural-history exhibits of the prestigious Hancock Museum, where new additions include a life-size model of a *Tyrannosaurus rex*. Besides the expanded contents of the Hancock, the 11 galleries will also combine the contents of Newcastle University's other museums: the Greek art and archaeology of the Shefton Museum and the magnificent Museum of Antiquities, the Roman exhibits of which will now include an interactive model of Hadrian's Wall.

The Great North Museum will also include a new planetarium and a space to host the major touring exhibitions of the world, both of which are being added to the back of the building. Across the street, the well-known Hatton Gallery and its permanent collection of West African art have been absorbed into the new project. Take the Metro to Haymarket.

**NORTHEAST ENGLAND**

**NEWCASTLE IN...**

**Two Days**

You'll invariably want to start on Quayside, where you'll find the famous **Tyne bridges** (p641). A good walk is to cross the Millennium Bridge into Gateshead and check out **Baltic** (below) and the **Sage** (p647), where you can grab a coffee in scenic surrounds. Wander back across the bridge and hop on a Quayside Q2 bus out to the Ouseburn Valley to visit the **Biscuit Factory** (below), stopping for a bite to eat in the **Brasserie Black Door** (p646). If you're with the kids, stop into **Seven Stories** (below). Otherwise, have a pint in one of the area's selection of fabulous pubs – we love the **Free Trade Inn** (p647).

Back in the elegant Victorian centre, visit **Laing Art Gallery** (p643) and the science village **Centre for Life** (p642). Stop off in **Blake's Coffee House** (p646) for a pick-me-up. Work your way up to the **Trent House Soul Bar** (p647) and find that song you love but haven't heard in years on the incredible jukebox. And just keep going; everyone else is, so why shouldn't you?

The next day, devote the morning to the **Great North Museum** (p643) before hopping on a bus south through Gateshead to the **Angel of the North** (p648) statue. Unfortunately, there's not much else going on here, so you'll have to head back into town. If you're looking for an alternative end to your day, take in an art film at the **Star And Shadow** (p647).

## Ouseburn Valley

About a mile east of the city centre is the Ouseburn Valley, the 19th-century industrial heartland of Newcastle and now one of the city's hippest districts, full of potteries, glass-blowing studios and other skilled craftspeople, as well as a handful of great bars, clubs and our favourite cinema in town. To get there, jump onto the yellow Quayside Q2 bus that runs a loop through the valley from the city centre. For more info on the area, check out www.ouseburntrust.org.uk.

### BISCUIT FACTORY

No prizes for guessing what this brand-new public **art gallery** ( ☎ 0191-261 1103; www.thebiscuit factory.com; Stoddart St; admission free; ☿ 10am-8pm Tue-Sat, 11am-5pm Sun) used to be. What it is now, though, is the country's biggest art shop, where you can peruse and buy work by artists from near and far in a variety of mediums, including painting, sculpture, glassware and furniture. Prices are thoroughly democratic, ranging from £30 to £30,000, but even if you don't buy, the art is excellent and there's a top-class restaurant too (Brasserie Black Door, p646).

### SEVEN STORIES – THE CENTRE FOR CHILDREN'S BOOKS

A marvellous conversion of a handsome Victorian mill has resulted in **Seven Stories** ( ☎ 0845 271 0777; www.sevenstories.org.uk; 30 Lime St; adult/child £5.50/4.50; ☿ 10am-5pm Mon-Wed, Fri & Sat, to 6pm Thu, 11am-5pm Sun), a very hands-on museum

dedicated to the wondrous world of children's literature. Across the seven floors you'll find original manuscripts, a growing collection of artwork from the 1930s onwards, and a constantly changing program of exhibitions, activities and events designed to encourage the AA Milnes of the new millennium.

## Gateshead

You probably didn't realise that that bit of Newcastle south of the Tyne is the 'town' of Gateshead, but local authorities are going to great lengths to put it right, even promoting the whole kit-and-caboodle-on-Tyne as 'NewcastleGateshead'. A bit clumsy, but we get the point. To date, the ambitious program of development has seen the impressive transformation of the southern banks of the Tyne, but as yet there's little to make you travel further afield than the water's edge.

### BALTIC – THE CENTRE FOR CONTEMPORARY ART

Once a huge, dirty, yellow grain store overlooking the Tyne, **Baltic** ( ☎ 0191-478 1810; www .balticmill.com; admission free; ☿ 10am-6pm Mon-Tue & Thu-Sun, to 8pm Wed) is now a huge, dirty, yellow art gallery to rival London's Tate Modern. Unlike the Tate, there are no permanent exhibitions here, but the constantly rotating shows feature the work and installations of some of contemporary art's biggest show-stoppers. The complex has artists in residence, a performance space, a cinema, a bar, a spectacular rooftop restaurant (you'll need to book) and a ground-floor restaurant with riverside tables. There's also a viewing box for a fine Tyne vista.

## NEWCASTLE FOR CHILDREN

Newcastle is friendly, full stop. Although at first glance the bonhomie mightn't seem to extend past buying rounds in the pub, on closer inspection there's plenty to keep the young 'uns entertained. The utterly wonderful **Seven Stories** (opposite) is the perfect destination for any kid who has an imagination, while virtually next door, the **Round** ( ☎ 0191-260 5605; www.the-round.com; 34 Lime St) is the Northeast's only theatre devoted exclusively to kids.

Closer to the centre the **Centre for Life** (p642) and the **Discovery Museum** (p643) are brilliant and should keep the kids busy for the guts of a day.

## QUIRKY NEWCASTLE

Take in the David Lynch vibe at **Blackie Boy** (p646), where it's not all it appears to be. Pop your coins into the world's best jukebox at the **Trent House Soul Bar** (p647) for the stomping sound of northern soul and pretend that James Blunt had stayed in the army. Take in an old art-house movie at the excellent **Star And Shadow** (p647) and then go to a late gig at the **Head of Steam@The Cluny** (p647). Cross one of the **Tyne bridges** (p641) on foot.

## SLEEPING

Although the number of city-centre options is on the increase, they are still generally restricted to the chain variety – either budget or business – that caters conveniently to the party people and business folk that make up the majority of Newcastle's overnight guests. Most of the other accommodation options are in the handsome northern suburb of Jesmond, where the forces of gentrification and student power fight it out for territory. As the city is a major business destination, weekend arrivals will find that most places drop their prices for Friday and Saturday nights.

### City Centre
#### BUDGET
**Euro-Hostel Newcastle** ( ☎ 0845 490 0371; www.euro-hostel.co.uk; Garth Heads St; dm/d £17/60; P □ ) This hostel offers a broader range of options than any hostel and most hotels, from a bed in a dorm to a private room or self-catering apartment suitable for families of up to seven people. The building is part of a new develop-

ment perfectly situated halfway between the city centre and Ouseburn Valley.

#### MIDRANGE
**Waterside Hotel** ( ☎ 0191-230 0111; www.waterside hotel.com; 48-52 Sandhill, Quayside; s/d £75/80) The rooms are a tad small, but they're among the most elegant in town: lavish furnishings and heavy velvet drapes in a heritage-listed building. The location is excellent.

**Copthorne** ( ☎ 0191-222 0333; www.millenniumhotels .com; The Close, Quayside; s/d from £75/85; P □ wi-fi) A superb waterside location makes this modern hotel a perfect choice – especially if you pick a room overlooking the water (the Connoisseur rooms, for instance). The bathrooms could do with some freshening, but that's only a minor complaint. Whatever you do, book online – the rack rate can be three times more expensive.

#### TOP END
**ourpick Greystreethotel** ( ☎ 0191-230 6777; www .greystreethotel.com; 2-12 Grey St; d/ste from £145/165; P ) A bit of designer class along the classiest street in the city centre has been long overdue: the rooms at the Greystreethotel are gorgeous if a tad poky, all cluttered up with flat-screen TVs, big beds and handsome modern furnishings.

**Malmaison** ( ☎ 0191-245 5000; www.malmaison.com; Quayside; r from £125, ste £225-350; P □ wi-fi) The affectedly stylish Malmaison touch has been applied to this former warehouse with considerable success, even down to the French-speaking lifts. Big beds, sleek lighting and designer furniture flesh out the Rooms of Many Pillows. Breakfast costs £13.

### Jesmond
The northeastern suburb of Jesmond is packed with budget and midrange accommodation to cater to the thousands that throng the area's bars and restaurants. There's a big party atmosphere around here that is easily a match for the city centre.

Catch the Metro to Jesmond or West Jesmond, or bus 80 from near Central Station, or bus 30, 30B, 31B or 36 from Westgate Rd.

#### BUDGET
**Newcastle YHA** ( ☎ 0845 371 9335; www.yha.org.uk; 107 Jesmond Rd; dm/d £16.50/40; ⊗ end Jan-end Dec) This nice, rambling place has small dorms that are generally full, so book in advance. It's close to the Jesmond Metro stop.

### MIDRANGE

**Whites Hotel** (☎ 0191-281 5126; www.whiteshotel
.com; 38-42 Osborne Rd; s/d £45/75) First impressions
don't promise a great deal, as the public areas
are a bit tatty, but don't let that put you off;
this is our favourite of the Osborne Rd hotels, with uniformly modern rooms and
first-rate service.

**New Northumbria Hotel** (☎ 0191-281 4961; www
.newnorthumbriahotel.co.uk; 61-73 Osborne Rd; s/d incl breakfast from £85/95) Trendy, clean and fairly pleasant, the New Northumbria likes to parade its
five-star qualification, but that's just from the
tourist office – this is a fine hotel with decent
rooms and a good breakfast. Not more.

### TOP END

**Jesmond Dene House** (☎ 0191-212 3000; www.jesmond
denehouse.co.uk; Jesmond Dene Rd; s £135, d £160-200, ste
£225-275; P ▣ ) As elegant a hotel as you'll find
anywhere, this exquisite property is the perfect
marriage between traditional styles and modern luxury. The large, gorgeous bedrooms are
furnished in a modern interpretation of the
Arts and Crafts style and are bedecked with all
manner of technological goodies (flat-screen
digital TVs, digital radios, wi-fi) and wonderful
bathrooms complete with underfloor heating. It
also has an outstanding restaurant; see right.

## EATING

From gourmet delights to rubbish fast food,
there's something for every palate in a city
that enjoys its tucker.

### City Centre

**Blake's Coffee House** (☎ 0191-261 5463; 53 Grey St;
breakfast £3-4.50, sandwiches £3-4; ☺ 9am-6pm) There
is nowhere better than this high-ceilinged cafe
for a Sunday-morning cure on any day of the
week. It's friendly, relaxed and serves up the
biggest selection of coffees in town, from the
gentle push of a Colombian blend to the toxic
shove of Old Brown Java. We love it.

**Big Mussel** (☎ 0191-232 1057; www.bigmussel.co.uk;
15 The Side; mains £6-12; ☺ lunch & dinner) Mussels and
other shellfish – all served with chips – are a
very popular choice at this informal diner.
There are pasta and vegetarian options as well,
and students get 15% off everything. There's
another branch (☎ 261 8927) on Leazes Park
Rd, close to St James' Park, that does a roaring
trade on match days.

**Cafe 21** (☎ 0191-222 0755; Trinity Gardens, Quayside;
mains £14.50-22; ☺ lunch & dinner Mon-Sat) Simple but
hardly plain, this elegant restaurant – all white
tablecloths and smart seating – offers new
interpretations of England's culinary backbone: pork and cabbage, liver and onions and
a sensational Angus beef and chips.

### Ouseburn Valley

**Brasserie Black Door** (☎ 0191-260 5411; Biscuit Factory,
16 Stoddard St; mains £10-16; ☺ lunch & dinner Mon-Sat)
Less of a museum restaurant and more of a
restaurant in a museum, the Black Door serves
up excellent modern English fare – which
generally involves a twist from pretty much
any other part of the world – in a bright, elegant room. Even if you're not visiting the
museum this is a great spot for lunch.

### Jesmond

**Pizzeria Francesca** (☎ 0191-281 6586; 134 Manor House
Rd, Jesmond; mains £4-12; ☺ lunch & dinner Mon-Sat)
This is how all Italian restaurants should be:
chaotic, noisy, friendly, packed cheek-to-jowl
and absolutely worth making the effort for.
Excitable, happy waiters and huge portions
of pizza and pasta keep them queuing at the
door – get in line and wait because you can't
book in advance.

**our pick Jesmond Dene House** (☎ 0191-212 3000;
www.jesmonddenehouse.co.uk; Jesmond Dene Rd; mains
£18-22) Chef Terry Laybourne is the architect
of an exquisite menu heavily influenced by
the northeast: venison from County Durham,
oysters from Lindisfarne and the freshest
herbs plucked straight from the garden. The
result is a gourmet delight and one of the best
dining experiences in the city.

## DRINKING

There are no prizes for guessing that Geordies
like a good night out – but to our relief there
is a great drinking scene beyond the sloppy
boozefest of the Bigg Market. The Ouseburn
is our area of choice, but also worth checking
out is the western end of Neville St, which has
a decent mix of great bars and is also home to
the best of the gay scene.

We daren't even begin to list the pubs and
bars in town, but here's a handful to start with.
Get a bottle of dog and get doon.

### City Centre

**Blackie Boy** (☎ 0191-232 0730; 11 Groat Market) At
first glance, this darkened old boozer looks
like any old traditional pub. Look closer. The
overly red lighting. The single bookcase. The

large leather armchair that is rarely occupied. The signage on the toilets: 'Dick' and 'Fanny'. This place could have featured in *Twin Peaks*, which is why it's so damn popular with everyone.

**our pick** **Trent House Soul Bar** ( ☎ 0191-261 2154; 1-2 Leazes Lane) The wall has a simple message: 'Drink Beer. Be Sincere.' This simply unique place is the best bar in town because it is all about an ethos rather than a look. Totally relaxed and utterly devoid of pretentiousness, it is an old-school boozer that out-cools every other bar because it isn't trying to, and because it has the best jukebox in all of England – you could spend years listening to the extraordinary collection of songs it contains. It is run by the same folks behind the superb World Headquarters (right).

### Ouseburn Valley

**Free Trade Inn** ( ☎ 0191-265 5764; St Lawrence Rd) Our favourite bar in the Ouseburn is a no-nonsense boozer overlooking the Tyne that is frequented by students and long-standing patrons; it doesn't look like much but it's one of the coolest pubs in town (and the jukebox is brilliant). It's a short walk from the Quayside.

**Cumberland Arms** ( ☎ 0191-265 6151; off Byker Bank, Ouseburn) Sitting on a hill at the top of the Ouseburn, this 19th-century bar has a sensational selection of ales as well as a range of Northumberland meads. There's a terrace outside, where you can read a book from the Bring One, Borrow One library inside.

## ENTERTAINMENT

Are you up for it? You'd better be, because Newcastle's nightlife doesn't mess about. There is nightlife beyond the club scene – you'll just have to wade through a sea of staggering, glassy-eyed clubbers to get to it. For current listings go online to www .thecrackmagazine.com. Club admissions range from £4 to £15.

### Cinema

**Star And Shadow** ( ☎ 0191-261 0066; www.star andshadow.org.uk; Stepney Bank, Ouseburn Valley; membership £1, admission £4) This unlikely looking cine-club in an old warehouse once used to store props for Tyne-Tees TV. It is the best movie experience in town, and the place to go for your art-house, cult, black-and-white and gay-and-lesbian film needs. Asylum seekers get in free.

### Live Music

**Head of Steam@The Cluny** ( ☎ 0191-230 4474; www .headofsteam.co.uk; 36 Lime St, Ouseburn Valley) This is one of the best spots in town to hear live music, attracting all kinds of performers, from experimental prog-rock heads to up-and-coming pop goddesses. Touring acts and local talent fill the bill every night of the week. Take the Metro to Byker.

**Sage Gateshead** ( ☎ 0191-443 4666; www.the sagegateshead.org; Gateshead Quays) Norman Foster's magnificent chrome-and-glass horizontal bottle is not just worth gaping at and wandering about in – it is also a superb venue to hear live music, from folk to classical orchestras. It is the home of the Northern Sinfonia and Folkworks.

### Nightclubs

**Digital** ( ☎ 0191-261 9755; www.yourfutureisdigital.com; Times Sq) A two-floored cathedral to dance music, this megaclub was voted in the top 20 clubs in the world by DJ Magazine – thanks to the best sound system we've ever heard. Our favourite night is Thursday's Stonelove (£6), a journey through 40 years of alternative rock and funk. Saturday's Shindig (£12 before 11pm, £15 after) brings the world's best house DJs to town.

**World Headquarters** ( ☎ 0191-261 7007; www.trent house.com; Curtis Mayfield House, Carliol Sq) Dedicated to the genius of black music in all its guises – funk, rare groove, dance-floor jazz, northern soul, genuine R&B, lush disco, proper house and reggae – this fabulous club is strictly for true believers, and judging from the numbers, there are thousands of them.

### Sport

**Newcastle United Football Club** ( ☎ 0191-201 8400; www.nufc.premiumtv.co.uk) is more than just a football team: it is the collective expression of Geordie hope and pride as well as the release for decades of economic, social and sporting frustration. Its fabulous ground, **St James' Park** (Strawberry Pl), is always packed, but you can get a **stadium tour** ( ☎ 0191-261 1571; adult/child £10/7; ☽ 11am, noon, 1.30pm daily & 4 hours before kick-off on match days) of the place, including the dugout and changing rooms.

## GETTING THERE & AWAY
### Air

**Newcastle International Airport** ( ☎ 0191-286 0966; www.newcastleairport.com) is 7 miles north of the

---

**GAY & LESBIAN NEWCASTLE**

Newcastle's gay scene is pretty dynamic, with its hub at the 'Pink Triangle' formed by Waterloo, Neville and Collingwood Sts, but stretching as far south as Scotswood Rd. There are plenty of gay bars in the area and a few great clubs.

**Camp David** (8-10 Westmorland Rd) An excellent mixed bar that is as trendy with straights as it is with the gay community.

**Loft** ( ☎ 0191-261 5348; 10A Scotswood Rd) Loud, proud and completely cheesy, this 1st-floor club above the equally cheesy Switch bar is open seven nights a week with nights like Monday's Shag Tag and Saturday's Passion.

**Powerhouse Nightclub** ( ☎ 0191-261 4507; 9-19 Westmorland Rd) Newcastle's brashest queer nightclub, with flashing lights, video screens and lots of suggestive posing.

---

city off the A696. It has direct services to a host of UK and European cities as well as long-haul flights to Dubai. Tour operators fly charters out of Newcastle to the Americas and Africa.

### Boat

Norway's **Fjord Line** ( ☎ 0191-296 1313; www.fjord line.com) operates ferries between Newcastle, Stavanger and Bergen. **DFDS Seaways** ( ☎ 0870 533 3000; www.dfdsseaways.co.uk) operates ferries to Newcastle from Kristiansand in Norway, the Swedish port of Gothenburg and the Dutch port of Ijmuiden, near Amsterdam. For online ferry bookings, check out www.newcastleferry.co.uk.

### Bus

National Express buses arrive and depart from the Gallowgate coach station. You can get to most anywhere, including London (£27, seven hours, six daily) and Manchester (£17.50, five hours, six daily). For Berwick-upon-Tweed (two hours, five daily) take bus 505, 515 or 525 from Haymarket bus station.

Local and regional buses leave from Haymarket or Eldon Sq bus stations. For local buses around the northeast, don't forget the excellent-value Explorer North East ticket, valid on most services for £7.

### Train

Newcastle is on the main rail line between London and Edinburgh. Services go to Alnmouth (for connections to Alnwick; £8.40, 30 minutes, four daily), Berwick (£23.80, 45 minutes, every two hours), Edinburgh (£42, 1½ hours, half-hourly), London King's Cross (£124.50, three hours, half-hourly) and York (£21.40, 45 minutes, every 20 minutes). There's also the scenic Tyne Valley Line west to Carlisle. See p657 for details.

## GETTING AROUND
### To/From the Airport & Ferry Terminal

The airport is linked to town by the Metro (£2.80, 20 minutes, every 15 minutes).

Bus 327 links the ferry (at Tyne Commission Quay, 8.5 miles east), Central Station and Jesmond Rd. It leaves the train station 2½ hours and 1¼ hours before each sailing.

There's a taxi rank at the terminal; it costs about £18 to the city centre.

### Car

Driving around Newcastle isn't fun thanks to the web of roads, bridges and one-way systems, but there are plenty of car parks.

### Public Transport

There's a large bus network, but the best means of getting around is the excellent underground Metro, with fares from £1.30. There are also several saver passes. The tourist office can supply you with route plans for the bus and Metro networks.

The DaySaver (£4.50, £3.70 after 9am) gives unlimited Metro travel for one day, and the DayRover (adult/child £5.80/3) gives unlimited travel on all modes of transport in Tyne and Wear for one day.

### Taxi

On weekend nights taxis can be rare; try **Noda Taxis** ( ☎ 0191-222 1888), which has a kiosk outside the entrance to Central Station.

# AROUND NEWCASTLE

## ANGEL OF THE NORTH

The world's most frequently viewed work of art is this extraordinary 200-tonne, rust-coloured human frame – we are, of course, referring to the Gateshead Flasher – with wings towering over the A1 (M) about 5 miles south of Newcastle; if you're driving, you just can't miss it. At 20m high and with a wingspan wider than a Boeing 767, Antony Gormley's most successful work is the country's largest sculpture. Buses 723 and 724 from Eldon Sq station, or 21, 21A and 21B from Pilgrim St, will take you there.

## TYNEMOUTH

One of the most popular Geordie days out is to this handsome seaside resort 6 miles east of the city centre. Besides being the mouth of the Tyne, this is one of the best surf spots in all of England, with great all-year breaks off the immense, crescent-shaped Blue Flag beach. In October, it hosts the **National Surfing Championships** (www.bpsauktour.com).

For all your surfing needs including lessons, call into the **Tynemouth Surf Company** ( ☎ 0191-258 2496; www.tynemouthsurf.co.uk; Grand Parade), which provides two-hour group lessons for £25 or one-hour individual lessons for the same price.

Tynemouth is on the Metro line.

## SEGEDUNUM

The last strong post of Hadrian's Wall was the fort of **Segedunum** ( ☎ 0191-295 5757; www.twmuseums.org.uk; adult/child/concession £4/free/2.25; ☼ 9.30am-5.30pm Apr-Aug, 10am-5pm Sep, 10am-3.30pm Nov-Mar), 6 miles east of Newcastle at Wallsend. Beneath the 35m tower, which you can climb for some terrific views, is an absorbing site that includes a reconstructed Roman bathhouse (with steaming pools and frescoes) and a fascinating museum that gives visitors a well-rounded picture of life during Roman times.

Take the Metro to Wallsend.

# COUNTY DURHAM

Best known for its strikingly beautiful capital that is one of England's star attractions, County Durham spreads itself across the lonely, rabbit-inhabited North Pennines and the gentle ochre hills of Teesdale, each dotted with picturesque, peaceful villages and traditional market towns.

Ironically, this pastoral image, so resonant of its rich medieval history, has only been reclaimed in recent years; it took the final demise of the coal industry, all-pervasive for the guts of 300 years, to render the county back to

some kind of pre-industrial look. A brutal and dangerous business, coal mining was the lifeblood of entire communities and its sudden end in 1984 by the stroke of a Conservative pen has left some purposeless towns and an evocatively scarred landscape.

### Getting Around

The Explorer North East ticket (see p640) is valid on many services in the county.

## DURHAM

**pop 42,940**

Durham's star attraction is best appreciated by arriving by train on a clear morning: the view across the River Wear to the hilltop peninsula will confirm that Britain's most beautiful Romanesque cathedral, a masterpiece of Norman architecture and a resplendent monument to the country's ecclesiastical history, was in fact worth the effort. Consider the setting: a huge castle, the aforementioned cathedral and, surrounding them both, a cobweb of cobbled streets usually full of upper-crust students attending Durham's other big pull, the university. It's all so…English.

OK, so the university may not have the hallowed prestige of Oxbridge – it was only founded in 1832 – but its terrific academic reputation and competitive rowing team make the disappointment of not getting into Oxford or Cambridge that bit easier to bear.

Durham is unquestionably beautiful, but once you've visited the cathedral and walked the old town looking for the best views there isn't much to do; we recommend that you either visit it as a day trip from Newcastle, or as an overnight stop on your way to explore the rest of the county.

### Orientation

Market Pl, the tourist office, castle and cathedral are all on the peninsula surrounded by the River Wear. The train and bus stations are to the west, on the other side of the river. Using the cathedral as your landmark, you can't really go wrong. The main sites are within easy walking distance of each other.

### Information

**Post office** (Silver St; ☼ 9am-5.30pm Mon-Sat)
**Public library** (Millennium Pl; ☼ 9.30am-5pm Mon-Sat) The only place in town to check email.
**Thomas Cook** ( ☎ 0191-382 6600; 24-25 Market Pl) Near the tourist office.

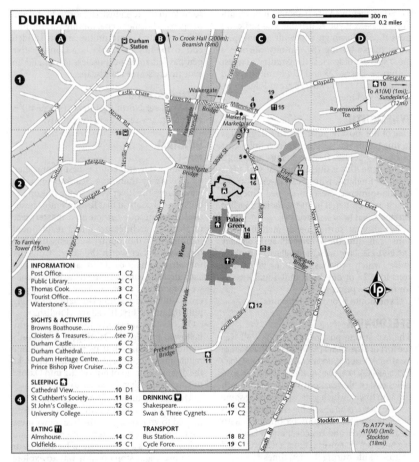

**DURHAM**

**Tourist office** ( ☎ 0191-384 3720; www.durhamtour ism.co.uk; 2 Millennium Pl; ☺ 9.30am-5.30pm Mon-Sat, 10am-4pm Sun) In the Gala complex, which includes a theatre and cinema.

**Waterstone's** ( ☎ 0191-383 1488; 69 Saddler St) A good selection of books.

## Sights
### DURHAM CATHEDRAL

Durham's most famous building – and the main reason for visiting unless someone you know is at university here – has earned superlative praise for so long that to add more would be redundant; the definitive structure of the Anglo-Norman Romanesque style is bloody gorgeous. We would definitely put it in our top-church-in-England list – as do many others, including Unesco, which declared it a World Heritage Site in 1986.

The **cathedral** ( ☎ 0191-386 4266; www.durhamcath edral.co.uk; donation requested; ☺ 9.30am-8pm mid-Jun–Aug, 9.30am-6.15pm Mon-Sat & 12.30-5pm Sun Sep–mid-Jun, private prayer & services only 7.30-9.30am Mon-Sat & 7.45am-12.30pm Sun year-round) is enormous and has a pretty forti- fied look; this is due to the fact that although it may have been built to pay tribute to God and to house the holy bones of St Cuthbert, it also needed to withstand any attack by the Scots and Northumberland tribes who weren't too thrilled by the arrival of the Normans a few years before. Times have changed, but the cathedral remains an overwhelming presence, and modern-day visitors will hardly fail to be impressed by its visual impact.

NORTHEAST ENGLAND

The interior is spectacular. The superb nave is dominated by massive, powerful piers – every second one round, with an equal height and circumference of 6.6m, and carved with geometric designs. Durham was the first European cathedral to be roofed with stone-ribbed vaulting, which upheld the heavy stone roof and made it possible to build pointed transverse arches – the first in England, and a great architectural achievement. The central tower dates from 1262, but was damaged in a fire caused by lightning in 1429, and was unsatisfactorily patched up until it was entirely rebuilt in 1470. The western towers were added in 1217–26.

Built in 1175 and renovated 300 years later, the **Galilee Chapel** is one of the most beautiful parts. The northern side's **paintings** are rare surviving examples of 12th-century wall painting and are thought to feature Sts Cuthbert and Oswald. The chapel also contains the **Venerable Bede's tomb**. Bede was an 8th-century Northumbrian monk, a great historian and polymath whose work *The Ecclesiastical History of the English People* is still the prime source of information on the development of early Christian Britain. Among other things, he introduced the numbering of years from the birth of Jesus. He was first buried at Jarrow, but in 1022 a miscreant monk stole his remains and brought them here.

The **Bishop's Throne**, built over the tomb of Bishop Thomas Hatfield, dates from the mid-14th century. Hatfield's effigy is the only one to have survived another turbulent time: the Reformation. The **high altar** is separated from **St Cuthbert's tomb** by the beautiful stone **Neville Screen**, made around 1372–80. Until the Reformation, the screen included 107 statues of saints.

The cathedral has worthwhile **guided tours** (adult/child/student £4/free/3; 🕙 10.30am, 11.30am & 2.30pm Mon & Sat). Evensong is at 5.15pm from Tuesday to Saturday (Evening Prayer on Monday) and at 3.30pm on Sunday.

There's a splendid view from the top of the **tower** (adult/child £3/1.50; 🕙 10am-4pm Mon-Sat mid-Apr–Sep, to 3pm Oct-Mar), but you've got to climb 325 steps to enjoy it.

### Cloisters & Treasures

The monastic buildings are centred on the cloisters, which were heavily rebuilt in 1828. The west door to the cloisters is famous for its 12th-century ironwork. On the western side is the **Monks' Dormitory** (adult/child £1/30p; 🕙 10am-

3.30pm Mon-Sat year-round, plus 12.30-3.15pm Sun Apr-Sep), now a library of 30,000 books and displaying Anglo-Saxon carved stones, with a vaulted undercroft that houses the Treasures and a restaurant. There is also an **audiovisual display** (adult/child £1/30p; 🕙 10am-3pm Mon-Sat Apr-Nov) on the building of the cathedral and the life of St Cuthbert.

The **Treasures** (adult/child £2.50/70p; 🕙 10am-4.30pm Mon-Sat, 2-4.30pm Sun) refer to the relics of St Cuthbert, but besides his cross and coffin, there's very little here related to the saint. The collection is made up mostly of religious paraphernalia from later centuries.

### DURHAM CASTLE

Built as a standard motte-and-bailey fort in 1072, **Durham Castle** ( ☎ 0191-374 3800; www.durhamcastle.com; adult/concession £5/3.50; 🕙 tours 10am, 11am, noon, 12.30pm & 2-4pm Jun-Oct, 2-4pm Mon, Wed, Sat & Sun Nov-May) was the prince bishops' home until 1837, when it became the first college of the new university. It remains a university hall, and you can stay here (see p652).

The castle has been much altered over the centuries, as each successive prince bishop sought to put his particular imprint on the place, but heavy restoration and reconstruction were necessary anyway as the castle is built of soft stone on soft ground. Highlights of the 45-minute tour include the groaning 17th-century Black Staircase, the 16th-century chapel and the beautifully preserved Norman chapel (1080).

### OTHER SIGHTS

Near the cathedral, in what was the St Mary-le-Bow Church, is the **Durham Heritage Centre** ( ☎ 0191-386 8719; www.durhamheritagecentre.org.uk; St Mary le Bow, North Bailey; admission £2; 🕙 2-4.30pm daily Jun, 11am-4.30pm daily Jul-Sep, 11am-4.30pm Sat & Sun Apr, May & Oct), with a pretty crowded collection of displays on Durham's history from the Middle Ages to mining. It's all suitably grim, especially the reconstructed prison cells.

**Crook Hall** ( ☎ 0191-384 8028; www.crookhallgardens.co.uk; Sidegate; adult/child £5.50/4.50; 🕙 11am-5pm Sun-Thur Apr-Sep, seasonal variations) is a medieval hall with 1.6 hectares of charming small gardens, about 200m north of the city centre.

## Activities
### BOATING

The **Prince Bishop River Cruiser** ( ☎ 0191-386 9525; www.princebishopprc.co.uk; Elvet Bridge; adult £5.50; 🕙 cruises 2pm & 3pm Jun-Sep) offers one-hour cruises.

---

**UNIVERSITY ACCOMMODATION**

Several colleges rent their rooms during the holidays (Easter and July to September). The rooms are generally modern and comfortable, like most contemporary student halls. Phone ☎ 0191-374 7360 for more information.

**St Cuthbert's Society** ( ☎ 0191-374 3364; 12 South Bailey; s/d £26/48) A few doors down from St John's College, with similar student-style rooms.

**St John's College** ( ☎ 0191-334 3877; 3 South Bailey; s/d £27/50) This college is right next to the cathedral; none of the rooms are en suite.

**University College** ( ☎ 0191-374 3863; s/d with bathroom £39/70, without bathroom £27/50) Smack on the Palace Green, this has the best location. Some rooms are available year-round, such as the bishop's suite (per person £90), decked out with 17th-century tapestries.

---

You can hire a rowing boat from **Browns Boathouse** ( ☎ 0191-386 3779; per hr per person £5), below Elvet Bridge.

## Sleeping

There's only one view that counts – a cathedral view. But when you consider that it's visible from pretty much everywhere, it's quality, not quantity, that counts. The tourist office makes local bookings free of charge, which is a good thing considering that Durham is always busy with visitors: graduation week in late June results in accommodation gridlock.

**Cathedral View** ( ☎ 0191-386 9566; www.cathedralview.com; 212 Gilesgate; s/d from £60/80) This plain-fronted Georgian house has no sign, but inside it does exactly what it says on the tin. Six large rooms decorated with lots of cushions and coordinated bed linen and window dressings make up the numbers, but it's the three at the back that are worth the fuss: the views of the cathedral are superb. A small breakfast terrace with the same splendid vista is an added touch of real class.

**Farnley Tower** ( ☎ 0191-375 0011; www.farnley-tower.co.uk; The Ave; s/d from £65/85; ℗ ) A beautiful Victorian stone building that looks more like a small manor house than a family-run B&B, this place has 13 large rooms, none better than the superior rooms, which are not just spacious but have excellent views of the cathedral and castle. The service is impeccable.

## Eating

Cheap eats aren't a problem in Durham thanks to the students, but quality is a little thin on the ground. Some pubs do good bar food; see right.

**Almshouse** ( ☎ 0191-386 1054; Palace Green; dishes £5-9; ☷ 9am-8pm) Fancy imaginative and satisfying snacks (how about spicy beef with red-bean casserole and rice?) served in a genuine 17th-century house right on Palace Green? It's a shame about the interior, which has been restored to look like any old museum cafe.

**ourpick Oldfields** ( ☎ 0191-370 9595; 18 Claypath; 2-/3-course menu £10/13; ☷ lunch & dinner Mon-Sat, lunch only Sun) A couple of years ago, Oldfields won the restaurant of the year award with its strictly seasonal menus that use only local or organic ingredients sourced within a 60-mile radius of Durham, and it's just gone from strength to strength ever since. Why not start with warmed mushroom and sage paste, followed by braised shin of Neasham Farm beef and finish off with a gorgeous raspberry *cranachan* (oatmeal and whisky cream)? The best meal in town, in the old boardroom of the former HQ of the Durham Gas Company (1881).

## Drinking

There is a fistful of lovely old bars spread about town. The tourist office has a bimonthly *What's On* guide.

**Shakespeare** (63 Saddler St) As authentic a traditional bar as you're likely to find in these parts, this is the perfect locals' boozer, complete with nicotine-stained walls, cosy snugs and a small corner TV to show the racing. Needless to say, the selection of beers and spirits is terrific. Not surprisingly, students love it too.

**Swan & Three Cygnets** ( ☎ 0191-384 0242; Elvet Bridge) This high-ceilinged riverside pub with courtyard tables overlooks the river. It also serves some pretty good food (mains around £8) – usually fancy versions of standard bar fare like bangers and mash.

## Getting There & Away

### BUS

The bus station is west of the river on North Rd. All National Express buses arrive here, while bus 352 links Newcastle and Blackpool via Durham, Barnard Castle, Raby Castle and Kirkby Stephen. Destinations include Edinburgh (£23.50, four hours, one daily), Leeds (£15.30, 2½ hours, four daily) and London (£27, 6½ hours, four daily). There are three daily National Express buses to Newcastle (£2.80, 30 minutes); bus 21 provides a half-hourly service but takes twice as long because it makes plenty of stops along the way.

### TRAIN
There are services at least hourly to London (£124.50, three hours), Newcastle (£6.80 single, 20 minutes) and York (£23.50, one hour).

## Getting Around
**Pratt's Taxis** ( ☎ 0191-386 0700) charges a minimum of £2.80. **Cycle Force** ( ☎ 0191-384 0319; 29 Claypath) charges £10/16 per half/full day for mountain-bike hire.

## AROUND DURHAM
### Beamish Open-Air Museum
County Durham's greatest attraction is **Beamish** ( ☎ 0191-370 4000; www.beamish.org.uk; admission Nov-Mar £6, Apr-Oct adult/child £16/10; ☒ 10am-5pm daily Apr-Oct, to 4pm Tue-Thu, Sat & Sun Nov-Mar, last entry 3pm year-round), a living, breathing, working museum that offers a fabulous, warts-and-all portrait of industrial life in the northeast during the 19th and 20th centuries. Instructive and lots of fun to boot, this huge museum spread over 121 hectares will appeal to all ages.

You can go underground, explore mine heads, a working farm, a school, a dentist and a pub, and marvel at how every cramped pit cottage seemed to find room for a piano. Don't miss a ride behind an 1815 Steam Elephant locomotive or a replica of Stephenson's *Locomotion No 1*. Allow at least three hours to do the place justice. Many elements (such as the railway) aren't open in the winter (when the admission price is cheaper); call for details.

Beamish is about 8 miles northwest of Durham; it's signposted from the A1(M) – take the A693 west at junction 63. Buses 709 from Newcastle (50 minutes, hourly) and 720 from Durham (30 minutes, hourly) operate to the museum.

## DARLINGTON
**pop 97,838**
Darlington might be best known these days for its retail opportunities, but its main claim to fame came in 1825, when it served as the arrival point for the world's first passenger train, George Stephenson's *No 1 Locomotion*, which chugged along the new rail link to Stockton at the breakneck speed of 10mph to 13mph, carrying 600 people – mostly in coal trucks.

The event – and the subsequent alteration of transport history – is the subject of the city's top attraction, the recently reopened (and rebranded) **Head of Steam** ( ☎ 01325-460532; www.darlington.gov.uk; North Rd; adult/child £5/3; ☒ 10am-4pm Tue-Sun Apr-Sep, 11am-3.30pm Tue-Sun Oct-Mar), aka the Darlington Railway Museum, which is actually situated on the original 1825 route, in Stockton & Darlington railway buildings attached to the North Rd Station and dating from the mid-19th century. Pride of place goes to the surprisingly small *Locomotion*, but railway buffs will also enjoy a close look at other engines, like the *Derwent*, which is the earliest surviving Darlington-built locomotive. The original displays have been complemented by an impressive range of audiovisuals that tell the story of the railway and its impact on Darlington. The museum is about a mile north of the centre.

There aren't many other reasons to linger, but you should definitely pop your head into Our Lady of the North, better known as **St Cuthbert's Church** (Market Pl), founded in 1183 and one of the finest examples of the Early English Perpendicular style. It is topped by a 14th-century tower. The **tourist office** ( ☎ 01325-388666; www.visitdarlington.com; Dolphin Centre, 13 Horsemarket; ☒ 9am-5pm Mon-Fri, to 3pm Sat) is on the south side of Market Place.

The town has some decent restaurants around the centre; best of them is **Oven** ( ☎ 01325-466668; 30 Duke St; mains £8-16; ☒ lunch & dinner Mon-Sat, noon-8pm Sun), a classy French spot that was voted the best Sunday lunch in the northeast by readers of *The Observer*.

## Getting There & Away
Darlington is 13 miles southwest of Durham on the A167. Buses 13 and 723 run between Darlington and Durham (£3.40, 35 minutes, every 30 minutes Monday to Saturday, hourly Sunday). Bus 723 also runs half-hourly to Newcastle (£5.70, 1¾ hours). Most buses go and arrive opposite the Town Hall on Feethams, just off Market Pl.

Darlington is also on the York (£17, 30 minutes) to Newcastle (£7.10, 40 minutes) line, with a service every 20 minutes or so.

**NORTHEAST ENGLAND**

## AROUND DARLINGTON

### Barnard Castle

pop 6720

Barnard Castle, or just plain Barney, is anything but: this thoroughly charming market town is a traditionalist's dream, full of antiquarian shops and atmospheric old pubs that serve as a wonderful setting for the town's twin-starred attractions, a daunting ruined castle at its edge and an extraordinary French chateau on its outskirts. If you can drag yourself away, it is also a terrific base for exploring Teesdale and the North Pennines. The **tourist office** ( ☎ 01833-690909; www.teesdalediscovery .com; Woodleigh, Flatts Rd; ☽ 9.30am-5.30pm daily Easter-Oct, 11am-4pm Mon-Sat Nov-Mar) has information on all the sights.

### SIGHTS

Once one of northern England's largest castles, **Barnard Castle** (EH; ☎ 01833-638212; www .english-heritage.org.uk; admission £4; ☽ 10am-6pm Easter-Sep, to 4pm Oct, Thu-Mon only Nov-Mar) was partly dismantled during the 16th century, but its huge bulk, on a cliff above the Tees, still manages to cover more than two very impressive hectares. Founded by Guy de Bailleul and rebuilt around 1150, its occupants spent their time suppressing the locals and fighting off the Scots – on their days off they sat around enjoying the wonderful views of the river.

If the beautifully atmospheric ruins of one castle aren't enough, then about half a mile east of town is the extraordinary, Louvre-inspired French chateau that is the **Bowes Museum** ( ☎ 01833-690606; www.bowesmuseum.org.uk; adult/child £7/free; ☽ 10am-5pm Mar-Oct, to 4pm Nov-Feb). The museum was the brainchild of 19th-century industrialist and art fanatic John Bowes; he commissioned French architect Jules Pellechet to build a new museum to show off his terrific collection, which could give the Victoria & Albert Museum a run for its money. Opened in 1892, the museum has lavish furniture and paintings by Canaletto, El Greco and Goya. The museum's most beloved exhibit, however, is the marvellous mechanical silver swan, which operates at 12.30pm and 3.30pm.

### SLEEPING & EATING

**Marwood House** ( ☎ 01833-637493; www.marwoodhouse .co.uk; 98 Galgate; s/d £29/58) A handsome Victorian property with tastefully appointed rooms (the owner's tapestries feature in the decor and her homemade biscuits sit on a tray), Marwood House's standout feature is the small fitness room in the basement, complete with a sauna that fits up to four people.

**Greta House** ( ☎ 01833-631193; www.gretahouse .co.uk; 89 Galgate; s/d £40/60) This lovely Victorian home stands out for the little touches that show that extra bit of class – fluffy bathrobes, face cloths and posh toiletries. What really did it for us though was the stay-in service: a tray of lovely homemade sandwiches and a superb cheeseboard to nibble at from the comfort of bed.

**Old Well Inn** ( ☎ 01833-690130; www.oldwellinn. info; 21 The Bank; r from £69) You won't find larger bedrooms in town than at this old coaching inn, which makes it an excellent option for families – it even takes pets. It has a reputation for excellent, filling pub grub and a decent Italian restaurant that does good pizzas and pastas (mains £8 to £11).

### GETTING THERE & AWAY

Bus 352 runs daily between Newcastle and Blackpool via Durham, Bishop Auckland, Barnard Castle, Raby Castle and Kirkby Stephen. Buses 75 and 76 runs almost hourly from Darlington (40 minutes).

### Egglestone Abbey

The ransacked, spectral ruins of **Egglestone Abbey** ( ☽ dawn-dusk), dating from the 1190s, overlook a lovely bend of the Tees. You can envisage the abbey's one-time grandeur despite the gaunt remains. They're a pleasant mile-long walk south of Barnard Castle.

### Raby Castle

About 7 miles northeast of Barnard Castle is the sprawling, romantic **Raby Castle** ( ☎ 01833-660202; www.rabycastle.com; adult/child £9.50/4, park & gardens only £4/3; ☽ castle 1-5pm, grounds 11am-5.30pm Sun-Fri Jun-Aug, Wed & Sun May & Sep), a stronghold of the Catholic Neville family until it engaged in some ill-judged plotting (the 'Rising of the North') against the oh-so-Protestant Queen Elizabeth in 1569. Most of the interior dates from the 18th and 19th centuries, but the exterior remains true to the original design, built around a courtyard and surrounded by a moat. There are beautiful formal gardens and a deer park. Buses 8 and 352 zip between Barnard Castle and Raby (20 minutes, eight daily).

## NORTH PENNINES

The North Pennines stretch from western Durham to just short of Hadrian's Wall in the north. In the south is Teesdale, the gently undulating valley of the River Tees; to the north is the much wilder Weardale, carved through by the River Wear. Both dales are marked by ancient quarries and mines – industries that date back to Roman times. The wilds of the North Pennines are also home to the picturesque Derwent and Allen Valleys, north of Weardale.

For online info, check out www.northpennines.org.uk.

# HADRIAN'S WALL

What exactly have the Romans ever done for us? The aqueducts. Law and order. And this enormous wall, built between AD 122 and 128 to keep 'us' (Romans, subdued Brits) in and 'them' (hairy Pictish barbarians from Scotland) out. Or so the story goes. Hadrian's Wall, named in honour of the emperor who ordered it built, was one of Rome's greatest engineering projects, a spectacular 73-mile testament to ambition and the practical Roman mind. Even today, almost 2000 years after the first stone was laid, the sections that are still standing remain an awe-inspiring sight, proof that when the Romans wanted something done, they just knuckled down and did it.

It wasn't easy. When completed, the mammoth structure ran across the narrow neck of the island, from the Solway Firth in the west almost to the mouth of the Tyne in the east. Every Roman mile (1.62 miles) there was a gateway guarded by a small fort (milecastle) and between each milecastle were two observation turrets. Milecastles are numbered right across the country, starting with Milecastle 0 at Wallsend and ending with Milecastle 80 at Bowness-on-Solway.

A series of forts were developed as bases some distance south (and may predate the wall), and 16 lie astride it. The prime remaining forts on the wall are Cilurnum (Chesters), Vercovicium (Housesteads) and Banna (Birdoswald). The best forts behind the wall are Corstopitum at Corbridge, and Vindolanda, north of Bardon Mill.

## History

Emperor Hadrian didn't order the wall built because he was afraid of northern invasion. Truth is no part of the wall was impenetrable –

a concentrated attack at any single point would have surely breached it – but was meant to mark the border as though to say that the Roman Empire would extend no further. By drawing a physical boundary, the Romans were also tightening their grip on the population to the south – for the first time in history, passports were issued to citizens of the empire, marking them out not just as citizens but, more importantly, as taxpayers.

But all good things come to an end. It's likely that around 409, as the Roman administration collapsed, the frontier garrisons ceased receiving Roman pay. The communities had to then rely on their own resources, gradually becoming reabsorbed into the war-band culture of the native Britons – for some generations soldiers had been recruited locally in any case.

## Orientation

Hadrian's Wall crosses beautiful, varied landscape. Starting in the lowlands of the Solway coast, it crosses the lush hills east of Carlisle to the bleak, windy ridge of basalt rock known as Whin Sill overlooking Northumberland National Park, and ends in the urban sprawl of Newcastle. The most spectacular section lies between Brampton and Corbridge.

Carlisle, in the west, and Newcastle, in the east, are good starting points, but Brampton, Haltwhistle, Hexham and Corbridge all make good bases.

The B6318 follows the course of the wall from the outskirts of Newcastle to Birdoswald; from Birdoswald to Carlisle it pays to have a detailed map. The main A69 road and the railway line follow 3 or 4 miles to the south. This section follows the wall from east to west.

## Information

Carlisle and Newcastle tourist offices are good places to start gathering information, but there are also tourist offices in Hexham, Haltwhistle, Corbridge and Brampton. The **Northumberland National Park Visitor Centre** ( ☎ 01434-344396; Once Brewed; ⊙ 10am-5pm mid-Mar–May, Sep & Oct, 9.30am-6pm Jun-Aug) is off the B6318. The official portal for the whole of Hadrian's Wall Country is www.hadrians-wall.org, an excellent, attractive and easily navigable site. There is also a **Hadrian's Wall information line** ( ☎ 01434-322002). May sees a spring festival, with lots of re-creations of Roman life along the wall (contact tourist offices for details).

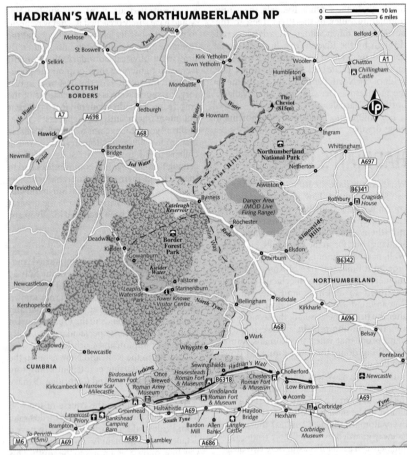

**HADRIAN'S WALL & NORTHUMBERLAND NP**

## Activities

The **Hadrian's Wall Path** (www.nationaltrail.co.uk/hadrianswall) is an 84-mile National Trail that runs the length of the wall from Wallsend in the east to Bowness-on-Solway in the west. The entire route should take about seven days on foot, giving plenty of time to explore the rich archaeological heritage along the way. Anthony Burton's *Hadrian's Wall Path – National Trail Guide* (Aurum Press, £12.95) available at most bookshops and tourist offices in the region, is good for history, archaeology and the like, while the *Essential Guide to Hadrian's Wall Path National Trail* (Hadrian's Wall Heritage Ltd, £3.95) by David McGlade is a guide to everyday facilities and services along the walk.

If you're planning to cycle along the wall, tourist offices sell the *Hadrian's Wall Country Cycle Map* (£3.50); you'll be cycling along part of Hadrian's Cycleway (see p640).

## Tours

If you prefer walking and cycling with a guide, and want to learn more about the history, **Hadrian's Wall Adventure** ( ☎ 01343 344650; www.hadrianswalladventure.com) offers tours by bike or foot, from half a day to a week. For softies, sightseeing trips by Landrover is another option, as is bike hire so you can explore on your own. The company's base (also a cosy cafe and outdoor gear shop) is at Haltwhistle railway station (see p658) so you can arrive by train, hop on a bike, and head for the Wall.

## Getting There & Around

### BUS

The AD 122 Hadrian's Wall bus (three hours, six daily June to September) is a hail-and-ride guided service that runs between Hexham (the 9.15am service starts in Wallsend) and Bowness-on-Solway. Bus 185 covers the route the rest of the year (Monday to Saturday only).

West of Hexham the wall runs parallel to the A69, which connects Carlisle and Newcastle. Bus 685 runs along the A69 hourly, passing near the YHA hostels and 2 miles to 3 miles south of the main sites throughout the year.

The Hadrian's Wall Rover ticket (adult/child one day £7.50/4.80, three day £15/9.60) is available from the driver or the tourist offices, where you can also get timetables.

### TRAIN

The railway line between Newcastle and Carlisle (Tyne Valley Line) has stations at Corbridge, Hexham, Haydon Bridge, Bardon Mill, Haltwhistle and Brampton. This service runs daily, but not all trains stop at all stations.

## CORBRIDGE

**pop 2800**

The mellow commuter town of Corbridge is a handsome spot above a green-banked curve in the Tyne, its shady, cobbled streets lined with old-fashioned shops. Folks have lived here since Saxon times when there was a substantial monastery, while many of the buildings feature stones nicked from nearby Corstopitum.

The **tourist office** ( ☎ 01434-632815; www.thisis corbridge.co.uk; Hill St; ☒ 10am-6pm Mon-Sat & 1-5pm Sun mid-May–Sep, 10am-5pm Mon-Sat Easter–mid-May & Oct) is part of the library.

## Corbridge Roman Site & Museum

What's left of the Roman garrison town of **Corstopitum** (EH; ☎ 01434-632349; admission incl museum £4.50; ☒ 10am-6pm daily Apr-Sep, to 4pm Oct, Sat & Sun only Nov-Mar) lies about a half a mile west of Market Pl on Dere St, once the main road from York to Scotland. It is the oldest fortified site in the area, predating the wall itself by some 40 years, when it was used by troops launching retaliation raids into Scotland. Most of what you see here, though, dates from around AD 200, when the fort had developed into a civilian settlement and was the main base along the wall.

You get a sense of the domestic heart of the town from the visible remains, and the Corbridge Museum displays Roman sculpture and carvings, including the amazing 3rd-century Corbridge Lion.

## Sleeping & Eating

**2 The Crofts** ( ☎ 01434-633046; www.2thecrofts.co.uk; A695; s/d incl breakfast £35/58) A typical Victorian terraced home on the edge of town with only one room, a comfortable twin, which ensures that you'll get all of the owner's attention. The breakfast is excellent.

**Errington Arms** ( ☎ 01434-672250; Stagshaw, B6318 off A68 roundabout; mains £8-13; ☒ 11am-11pm Mon-Sat, noon-3pm Sun) About 3 miles north of town is this marvellous 18th-century stone pub where delicious food is served up in suitably atmospheric surroundings. From the mouthwatering ploughman's lunch to more intricate delicacies like loin of lamb with mushroom and chive risotto, it won't disappoint; you can wash it all down with a pint of real ale.

**Valley Restaurant** ( ☎ 01434-633434; www.valley restaurants.co.uk; Station Rd; mains £9-12; ☒ dinner Mon-Sat) This fine Indian restaurant in a lovely building above the station supplies a unique service as well as delicious food. A group of 10 or more diners from Newcastle can catch the 'Passage to India' train to Corbridge accompanied by a waiter, who will supply snacks and phone ahead to have the meal ready when the train arrives!

## Getting There & Away

Bus 685 between Newcastle and Carlisle comes through Corbridge, as does the half-hourly bus 602 from Newcastle to Hexham, where you can connect with the Hadrian's Wall bus AD 122. Corbridge is also on the Newcastle–Carlisle railway line.

## HEXHAM

**pop 10,690**

Tynedale's administrative capital is a handsome market town long famed for its fine Augustinian abbey. Hexham is a bustling place, with more restaurants, hotels and high-street shops lining its cobbled alleyways than any other wall town between Carlisle and Newcastle. The **tourist office** ( ☎ 01434-652220; www.hadrianswallcountry.org; Wentworth Car Park; ☒ 9am-6pm Mon-Sat & 10am-5pm Sun mid-May–Oct, 10am-5pm Mon-Sat Oct–mid-May) is northeast of the town centre.

## Sights

Stately **Hexham Abbey** ( ☎ 01434-602031; ⊗ 9.30am-7pm May-Sep, to 5pm Oct-Apr) is a marvellous example of early English architecture. Inside, look out for the Saxon crypt, the only surviving element of St Wilifrid's Church, built with inscribed stones from Corstopitum in 674.

The **Old Gaol** ( ☎ 01434-652349; adult/child £4/2; ⊗ 10am-4.30pm daily Apr-Oct, Mon, Tue & Sat Oct–mid-Nov), completed in 1333 as England's first purpose-built prison, was recently revamped and all four floors can be visited in all their gruesome glory. The history of the Border Reivers – a group of clans who fought, kidnapped, blackmailed and killed each other in an effort to exercise control over a lawless tract of land along the Anglo-Scottish border throughout the 16th century – is also retold, along with tales of the punishments handed out in the prison.

## Sleeping & Eating

**West Close House** ( ☎ 01434-603307; Hextol Tce; s/d from £30/60) This immaculate 1920s house, in a leafy cul-de-sac off Allendale Rd (the B6305) and surrounded by a beautiful garden, is highly recommended for its friendliness and comfort.

**Hallbank Guest House** ( ☎ 01434-605567; www.hallbankguesthouse.com; Hallgate; s/d from £70/100) Behind the old gaol is this fine Edwardian house with three extravagantly furnished rooms: leather furniture, flat-screen TVs and huge beds.

There are several bakeries on Fore St and, if you turn left into the quaintly named Priestpopple near the bus station, you'll find a selection of restaurants.

**Dipton Mill** ( ☎ 01434-606577; Dipton Mill Rd; mains around £6-10) For sheer atmosphere, you can't beat this superb country pub 2 miles out on the road to Blanchland, among woodland and by a river. It offers sought-after ploughman's lunches and real ale, not to mention a terrific selection of whiskies.

## Getting There & Away

Bus 685 between Newcastle and Carlisle comes through Hexham hourly. The AD 122 and the winter-service bus 185 connect with other towns along the wall, and the town is on the Newcastle–Carlisle railway line (hourly).

## CHESTERS ROMAN FORT & MUSEUM

The best-preserved remains of a Roman cavalry fort in England are at **Chesters** (EH; ☎ 01434-681379; admission £4.50; ⊗ 9.30am-6pm Apr-Sep, 10am-4pm Oct-Mar), set among idyllic green woods and meadows and originally constructed to house a unit of troops from Asturias in northern Spain. They include part of a bridge (beautifully constructed and best appreciated from the eastern bank) across the River North Tyne, four well-preserved gatehouses, an extraordinary bathhouse and an underfloor heating system. The museum has a large collection of Roman sculpture. Take bus 880 or 882 from Hexham (5.5 miles away); it is also on the route of Hadrian's Wall bus AD 122.

## HALTWHISTLE
### pop 3810

It's one of the more important debates in contemporary Britain: where exactly is the centre of the country? The residents of Haltwhistle, basically one long street just north of the A69, claim that they're the ones. But then so do the folks in Dunsop Bridge, 71 miles to the south. Will we ever know the truth? In the meantime, Haltwhistle is the spot to get some cash and load up on gear and groceries. Thursday is market day.

The **tourist office** ( ☎ 01434-322002; ⊗ 9.30am-1pm & 2-5.30pm Mon-Sat & 1-5pm Sun May-Sep, 9.30am-noon & 1-3.30pm Mon, Tue, & Thu-Sat Oct-Apr) is in the train station.

**Ashcroft** ( ☎ 01434-320213; www.ashcroftguesthouse.co.uk; Lanty's Lonnen; s/d from £36/72) is a marvellous Edwardian home surrounded by beautifully manicured, layered lawns and gardens from which there are stunning views (also enjoyed from the breakfast room). The owners like their flowers so much they decorated most of the house accordingly. Highly recommended.

Bus 685 comes from Newcastle (1½ hours) and Carlisle (45 minutes) 12 times daily. Hadrian's Wall bus AD 122 (June to September) or 185 (October to May) connects Haltwhistle with other places along the wall. Bus 681 heads south to Alston (55 minutes, three daily Monday to Saturday). The town is also on the Newcastle–Carlisle railway line (hourly).

## AROUND HALTWHISTLE
### Vindolanda Roman Fort & Museum

The extensive site of **Vindolanda** ( ☎ 01434-344277; www.vindolanda.com; admission £5.20, with Roman Army Museum £8; ⊗ 10am-6pm Apr-Sep, to 5pm Feb-Mar & Oct-Nov) offers a fascinating glimpse into the daily life of a Roman garrison town. The time-capsule museum displays leather sandals, signature Roman toothbrush-flourish helmet decorations, and countless writing tablets such as a student's marked work ('sloppy'), and a parent's note with a present of socks and underpants (things haven't changed – in this climate you can never have too many).

The museum is just one part of this large, extensively excavated site, which includes impressive parts of the fort and town (excavations continue) and reconstructed turrets and temple.

It's 1.5 miles north of Bardon Mill between the A69 and B6318 and a mile from Once Brewed.

## Housesteads Roman Fort & Museum

The wall's most dramatic site – and the best-preserved Roman fort in the whole country – is at **Housesteads** (EH; ☎ 01434-344363; admission £4.50; ☒ 10am-6pm Apr-Sep, to 4pm Oct-Mar). From here, high on a ridge and covering 2 hectares, you can survey the moors of Northumberland National Park, and the snaking wall, with a sense of awe at the landscape and the aura of the Roman lookouts.

The substantial foundations bring fort life alive. The remains include an impressive hospital, granaries with a carefully worked-out ventilation system and barrack blocks. Most memorable are the spectacularly situated communal flushable latrines, which summon up Romans at their most mundane.

Housesteads is 2.5 miles north of Bardon Mill on the B6318, and about 3 miles from Once Brewed. It's popular, so try to visit outside summer weekends, or late in the day when the site will be quiet and indescribably eerie.

## Other Sights

One mile northwest of Greenhead near Walltown Crags, the kid-pleasing **Roman Army Museum** ( ☎ 016977-47485; www.vindolanda.com; admission £4, with Vindolanda £8; ☒ 10am-6pm Apr-Sep, to 5pm Feb-Mar & Oct-Nov) provides lots of colourful background detail to wall life, such as how far soldiers had to march per day and whether they could marry.

OK, so *technically* it's in Cumbria (we won't tell if you don't), but the remains of the once-formidable **Birdoswald Roman Fort** (EH; ☎ 016977-47602; admission £4.50; ☒ 10am-5.30pm Mar-Oct), on an escarpment overlooking the

beautiful Irthing Gorge, were part of the wall and so merit inclusion in this chapter on logical grounds. They're on a minor road off the B6318, about 3 miles west of Greenhead; a fine stretch of wall extends from here to Harrow Scar Milecastle. About half a mile away, across the impressive river footbridge, is another good bit of wall, ending in two turrets and the meticulous structure of the **Willowford Bridge abutment**.

Still in Cumbria, about 3 miles further west along the A69, are the peaceful raspberry-coloured ruins of **Lanercost Priory** (EH; ☎ 016977-3030; admission £3; ☒ 10am-6pm daily Apr-Sep, to 4pm Thu-Mon Oct), founded in 1166 by Augustinian canons. Ransacked several times, after the dissolution it became a private house and a priory church was created from the Early English nave. The church contains some beautiful Pre-Raphaelite stained glass. The AD 122 bus can drop you at the gate.

## Sleeping

**Once Brewed YHA** ( ☎ 0845 371 9753; www.yha.org.uk; Military Rd, Bardon Mill; dm £12; ☒ year-round) This modern and well-equipped hostel is central for visiting both Housesteads Fort, 3 miles away, and Vindolanda, 1 mile away. Bus 685 (from Hexham or Haltwhistle train stations) will drop you at Henshaw, 2 miles south, or you could leave the train at Bardon Mill 2.5 miles southeast. The Hadrian's Wall bus can drop you at the door from June to September.

**Greenhead YHA** ( ☎ 016977-47401; www.yha.org.uk; dm £13; ☒ Jul-Aug, call to check other times) A converted Methodist chapel by a trickling stream and a pleasant garden, 3 miles west of Haltwhistle. The hostel is served by bus AD 122 or 685.

**Birdoswald YHA** ( ☎ 0845 371 9551; www.yha.org.uk; dm £14; ☒ Easter-Oct, call to check other times) This farmhouse within the grounds of the Birdoswald complex has recently been converted into a hostel with basic facilities, including a self-service kitchen and laundry. The price includes a visit to the fort.

**Holmhead Guest House** ( ☎ 016977-47402; www.bandbhadrianswall.com; Thirlwall Castle Farm, Greenhead; dm/s/d from £12.50/43/66) Four fairly compact rooms are available in this lovely remote old cottage; most of the space is taken up by the big beds. All the rooms have a shower rather than a bath. A barn was recently converted into a large dorm room, perfect for budget walkers and cyclists. It's about half a mile north of Greenhead.

**NORTHEAST ENGLAND**

# NORTHUMBERLAND NATIONAL PARK

England's last great wilderness is the 398 sq miles of natural wonderland that make up Northumberland National Park; spread about the soft swells of the Cheviot Hills are spiky moors of autumn-coloured heather and gorse, and endless acres of forest guarding the deep, colossal Kielder Water (Europe's largest artificial lake, which holds 200,000 million litres and has a shoreline of 27 miles). Even the negligible human influence – there are only about 2000 inhabitants here – has been benevolent: the finest sections of Hadrian's Wall run along the park's southern edge and the landscape is dotted with prehistoric remains and fortified houses – the thick-walled *peles* were the only solid buildings built here until the mid-18th century.

## Orientation & Information

The park runs from Hadrian's Wall in the south, takes in the Simonside Hills in the east and runs into the Cheviot Hills along the Scottish border. There are few roads.

For information, contact the **Northumberland National Park** ( ☎ 01434-605555; www.northumberland-national-park.org.uk; Eastburn, South Park, Hexham). Besides the tourist offices mentioned in this section, there are relevant offices in **Once Brewed** ( ☎ 01434-344396; ☼ 10am-5pm mid-Mar–May, Sep & Oct, 9.30am-6pm Jun-Aug) as well as **Ingram** ( ☎ 01665-578890; ingram@nnpa.org.uk; ☼ 10am-5pm Easter-Oct). All the tourist offices handle accommodation bookings.

## Activities

The most spectacular stretch of the Hadrian's Wall Path (p656) is between Sewingshields and Greenhead in the south of the park.

There are many fine walks through the Cheviots, frequently passing by prehistoric remnants; the towns of Ingram, Wooler and Rothbury make good bases, and their tourist offices can provide maps, guides and route information.

Though at times strenuous, cycling in the park is a pleasure; the roads are good and the traffic is light here. There's off-road cycling in Border Forest Park.

## Getting There & Around

Public transport options are limited, aside from buses on the A69. See the Hadrian's Wall section (p657) for access to the south. Bus 808 (55 minutes, two daily Monday to Saturday) runs between Otterburn and Newcastle. Postbus 815 and bus 880 (45 minutes, eight daily Monday to Saturday, three on Sunday) run between Hexham and Bellingham. National Express bus 383 (three hours, four daily, £16.60) goes from Newcastle to Edinburgh via Otterburn, Byrness (by request), Jedburgh, Melrose and Galashiels.

## BELLINGHAM

The small, remote village of Bellingham (bellin-*jum*) is a pleasant enough spot on the banks of the North Tyne, surrounded by beautiful, deserted countryside on all sides. It is an excellent base from which to kick off your exploration of the park.

The **tourist office** ( ☎ 01434-220616; Main St; ☼ 9.30am-1pm & 2-5pm Mon-Sat & 1-5pm Sun Apr-Oct, 2-5pm Mon-Sat Nov-Mar) handles visitor inquiries.

There's not a lot to see here save the 12th-century **St Cuthbert's Church**, unique because it retains its original stone roof, and **Cuddy's Well**, outside the churchyard wall, which is alleged to have healing powers on account of its blessing by the saint.

The **Hareshaw Linn Walk** passes through a wooded valley and over six bridges, leading to a 9m-high waterfall 2.5 miles north of Bellingham (*linn* is an Old English name for waterfall).

Bellingham is on the Pennine Way; book ahead for accommodation in summer. Most of the B&Bs are clustered around the village green.

**Bellingham YHA** ( ☎ 01434-220258; www.yha.org.uk; Woodburn Rd; dm £15; ☼ mid-Apr–Oct) is on the edge of the village. It is almost always busy, so be sure to book ahead. There are showers, a cycle store and a self-catering kitchen on the premises.

**Lyndale Guest House** ( ☎ 01434-220361; www.lyndaleguesthouse.co.uk; s/d from £30/60) The bedrooms in this pleasant family home just off the village green are modern and extremely tidy; it's a bit like visiting a really neat relative.

Pub grub is about the extent of the village's dining; recommended is the Black Bull or the Rose & Crown.

## ROTHBURY
pop 1960

The one-time prosperous Victorian resort of Rothbury is an attractive, restful market town on the River Coquet that makes a convenient base for the Cheviots.

There's a **tourist office & visitor centre** ( ☎ 01669-620887; Church St;  10am-5pm Apr-Oct, to 6pm Jun-Aug).

The biggest draw in the immediate vicinity is **Cragside House, Garden and Estate** (NT; ☎ 01669-620333; admission £11, gardens & estate only £7;  house 1-5.30pm Tue-Sun mid-Mar–Sep, 1-4.30pm Tue-Sun Oct–mid-Mar, gardens 10.30am-5.30pm Tue-Sun mid-Mar–Sep, 11am-4pm Wed-Sun Oct–mid-Mar), the quite incredible country retreat of the first Lord Armstrong. In the 1880s the house had hot and cold running water, a telephone and alarm system, and was the first in the world to be lit by electricity, generated through hydropower – the original system has been restored and can be observed in the Power House. The Victorian gardens are also well worth exploring: huge and remarkably varied, they feature lakes, moors and one of the world's largest rock gardens. Visit in May to see myriad rhododendrons.

The estate is 1 mile north of town on the B6341; there is no public transport to the front gates from Rothbury; try **Rothbury Motors** ( ☎ 01669-620516) if you need a taxi.

High St is a good area to look for a place to stay.

Beamed ceilings, stone fireplaces and canopied four-poster beds make **Katerina's Guest House** ( ☎ 01669-602334; Sun Buildings, High St; www .katerinasguesthouse.co.uk; s/d from £45/68) one of the nicer options in town, even though the rooms are a little small.

Alternatively, the **Haven** ( ☎ 01669-620577; Back Crofts; s/d/ste £40/80/130) is a beautiful Edwardian home up on a hill with six lovely bedrooms and one elegant suite.

Food options are limited to pub grub. For takeaway you could try the **Rothbury Bakery** (High St) for pies and sandwiches or **Tully's** (High St) for flapjacks.

Bus 416 from Morpeth (30 minutes) leaves every four hours from Monday to Saturday and three times on Sunday.

# WOOLER
**pop 1860**

The harmonious, stone-terraced town of Wooler owes its sense of unified design to a devastating fire in 1863, which resulted in an almost complete reconstruction. It is an excellent spot to catch your breath in, especially as it is surrounded by some excellent forays into the nearby Cheviots (including a clamber to the top

of the Cheviot, at 815m the highest peak in the range) and is the midway point for the 65-mile St Cuthbert's Way, which runs from Melrose in Scotland to Holy Island on the coast.

The **tourist office** ( ☎ 01668-282123; www.wooler .org.uk; Cheviot Centre, 12 Padgepool Pl;  10am-5pm Mon-Sat & 10am-4pm Sun Jul-Aug, to 4pm Mon-Sat Apr & Oct, to 5pm Sat & Sun only Nov-Mar) is a mine of information on walks in the hills.

## Activities

A popular walk from Wooler takes in **Humbleton Hill**, the site of an Iron Age hill fort and the location of yet another battle (1402) between the Scots and the English. It's immortalised in 'The Ballad of Chevy Chase' (no, not *that* Chevy Chase – see boxed text, p662) and Shakespeare's *Henry IV*. There are great views of the wild Cheviot Hills to the south and plains to the north, merging into the horizon. The well-posted 4-mile trail starts and ends at the bus station. It takes approximately two hours. Alternatively, the yearly **Chevy Chase** (www.woolerrunningclub.co.uk) is a classic 20-mile fell run with over 4000ft of accumulated climb, run at the beginning of July.

A more arduous hike leads to the top of the **Cheviot**, 6 miles southeast. The top is barren and wild, but on a clear day you can see the castle at Bamburgh and as far out as Holy Island. It takes around four hours to reach the top from Wooler. Check with the tourist office for information before setting out.

## Sleeping & Eating

**Wooler YHA** ( ☎ 0845 371 9668; www.yha.org.uk; 30 Cheviot St; dm £14;  Mon-Sat Apr-Jun, Tue-Sat Sep, Fri & Sat Mar) This recently refurbished hostel has 44 beds in a variety of rooms, a modern lounge and a small cafe.

**Tilldale House** ( ☎ 01668-281450; www.tilldalehouse .co.uk; 34-40 High St; s/d from £35/40) This place has comfortable, spacious rooms that work on the aesthetic premise that you can never have enough of a floral print.

**Black Bull** ( ☎ 01668-281309; www.theblackbullhotel .co.uk; 2 High St; s/d from £25/50;  ) A 17th-century coaching inn that has retained much of its traditional character, this is probably the best option in town; it also does decent pub grub (mains around £8).

## Getting There & Around

Wooler has good bus connections to the major towns in Northumberland. Bus 464 comes from Berwick (50 minutes, five a day Monday to Saturday) and 470 (six a day Monday to Saturday) or 473 (eight a day Monday to Saturday) come from Alnwick. Bus 710 makes the journey from Newcastle (1½ hours, Wednesday and Saturday).

Cycle hire is available at **Haugh Head Garage** ( ☎ 01668-281316; per day from £15) in Haugh Head, 1 mile south of Wooler on the A697.

## AROUND WOOLER

One of England's most interesting medieval castles, **Chillingham** ( ☎ 01668-215359; www .chillingham-castle.com; adult/child £6.75/3; ☾ 1-5pm Sun-Fri Easter-Sep) is steeped in history, warfare, torture and ghosts: it is said to be one of the country's most haunted places, with ghostly clientele ranging from a phantom funeral to Lady Mary Berkeley in search of her errant husband.

The current owner, Sir Humphrey Wakefield, has gone to great lengths to restore the castle to its eccentric, noble best. This followed a 50-year fallow period when the Grey family (into which Sir Humphrey married) abandoned it, despite having owned it since 1245, because they couldn't afford the upkeep.

Well done, Sir H. Today's visitor is in for a real treat, from the extravagant medieval staterooms that have hosted a handful of kings in their day to the stone-flagged banquet halls, where many a turkey leg must surely have been hurled to the happy hounds. Belowground, Sir Humphrey has gleefully restored the grisly torture chambers, which have a polished rack and the none-too-happy face of an Iron Maiden. There's also a museum with a fantastically jumbled collection of objects – it's like stepping into the attic of a compulsive and well-travelled hoarder.

In 1220, 148 hectares of land were enclosed to protect the herd of **Chillingham Wild Cattle** ( ☎ 01668-215250; www.chillingham-wildcattle.org.uk; adult/child £4.50/1.50; ☾ park 10am-noon & 2-5pm Mon & Wed-Sat & 2-5pm Sun Apr-Oct) from borderland raiders; this fierce breed is now the world's purest. They were difficult to steal, as they cannot herd and apparently make good guard animals. Around 40 to 60 make up the total population of these wild white cattle (a reserve herd is kept in a remote place in Scotland, in case of emergencies).

It's possible to stay at the medieval fortress in the seven apartments designed for guests, where the likes of Henry III and Edward I once snoozed. Prices vary depending on the luxury of the apartment; the **Grey Apartment** (£156) is the most expensive – it has a dining table to seat 12 – or there's the **Tower Apartment** (£120), in the Northwest Tower. All of the apartments are self-catering.

Chillingham is 6 miles southeast of Wooler. Bus 470 running between Alnwick and Wooler (six daily Monday to Saturday) stops at Chillingham.

# NORTHUMBERLAND

Take a deep breath and prepare yourself for the last great 'undiscovered' wilderness in England, the utterly wild and stunningly beautiful landscapes of Northumberland. It's hard to imagine such a thing in a country so modern and populated, but as you cast your eye across the rugged interior you will see ne'er a trace of Man save the fortified houses and friendly villages that dot the horizon; this is down to history and location as much as the fact that a huge swathe of it is protected within the confines of a national park (see p660).

## Getting Around

The excellent *Northumberland Public Transport Guide* (£1.90) is available from local tourist offices. Transport options are good, with a train line running along the coast from Newcastle to Berwick and on to Edinburgh.

## ALNWICK

### pop 7770

Northumberland's historic ducal town, Alnwick (no tongue gymnastics: just say 'an-nick') is an elegant maze of narrow cobbled streets spread out beneath the watchful gaze of a colossal medieval castle. Not only will you find England's most perfect bookshop, but also the most visited attraction in the north-east at Alnwick Garden.

The castle is on the northern side of town and overlooks the River Aln. The **tourist office** ( ☎ 01665-510665; www.visitalnwick.org.uk; 2 The Shambles; 🕙 9am-5pm Mon-Sat, 10am-4pm Sun) is by the marketplace, in a handsome building that was once a butcher's shop.

There has been a market in Alnwick for over 800 years. Market days are Thursday and Saturday, with a farmers market on the last Friday of the month.

## Sights

The outwardly imposing **Alnwick Castle** ( ☎ 01665-510777; www.alnwickcastle.com; adult/child/concession £10.50/4.50/9; 🕙 10am-6pm Apr-Oct), ancestral home of the Duke of Northumberland and a favourite set for film-makers (it was Hogwarts for the first couple of *Harry Potter* films) has changed little since the 14th century. The interior is sumptuous and extravagant; the six rooms open to the public – staterooms, dining room, guard chamber and library – have an incredible display of Italian paintings, including Titian's *Ecce Homo* and many Canalettos.

The castle is set in parklands designed by Lancelot 'Capability' Brown. The woodland walk offers some great aspects of the castle, or for a view looking up the River Aln, take the B1340 towards the coast.

As spectacular a bit of green-thumb artistry as you'll see anywhere in England, **Alnwick Garden** ( ☎ 01665-510777; www.alnwickgarden.com; adult/child/concession £10/free/7.50; 🕙 10am-7pm Jun-Sep, to 6pm Apr-May & Oct, to 4pm Nov-Jan, to 5pm Feb-Mar) is one of the northeast's great success stories. Since the project began in 2000, the 4.8-hectare walled garden has been transformed from a derelict site into a spectacle that easily exceeds the grandeur of the castle's 19th-century gardens, a series of magnificent green spaces surrounding the breathtaking Grand Cascade – 120 separate jets spurting over 30,000L of water down 21 weirs for everyone to marvel at and kids to splash around in.

There are a half-dozen other gardens, including the Franco-Italian–influenced Ornamental Garden (with more than 15,000 plants), the Rose Garden and the particularly fascinating Poison Garden, home to some of the deadliest – and most illegal – plants in the world, including cannabis, magic mushrooms, belladonna and even tobacco.

## Sleeping & Eating

**White Swan Hotel** ( ☎ 01665-602109; www.classiclodges.co.uk; Bondgate Within; s/d from £70/115; 🅿 🖵 ) Alnwick's top address is this 300-year-old coaching inn right in the heart of town. Its rooms are all of a pretty good standard (LCD screen TVs, DVD players and free wi-fi), but this spot stands out for its dining room, which has elaborate original panelling, ceiling and stained-glass windows filched from the *Olympic*, sister ship to the *Titanic*.

A row of handsome Georgian houses along Bondgate Without offers several worthwhile options that all charge around £32 per person, including **Lindisfarne Guest House** ( ☎ 01665-603430; 6 Bondgate Without) and the **Teapot** ( ☎ 01665-604473; 8 Bondgate Without), which has the largest teapot collection in town.

A number of atmospheric pubs do a good line in traditional food. The **Market Tavern** ( ☎ 01665-602759; 7 Fenkle St; stottie £6), near Market Sq, is the place to go for a traditional giant beef stottie (bread roll), while **Ye Old Cross** ( ☎ 01665-602735; Narrowgate; mains £6) is good for a drink to go along with your stottie cake, and is known as 'Bottles', after the dusty bottles in the window: 150 years ago the owner collapsed and died while trying to move them and no-one's dared attempt it since.

## Getting There & Away

There are regular buses from Newcastle (501, 505 and 518; one hour, 28 per day Monday to Saturday, 18 on Sunday). Bus 518 has 10 to 14 daily services to the attractive towns of Warkworth (25 minutes) and Alnmouth (15 minutes), which has the nearest train station. Buses 505 and 525 come from Berwick (45 minutes, 13 daily Monday to Saturday). The Arriva Day Pass (adult/child £6/5) is good value.

# WARKWORTH

Biscuit-coloured Warkworth is little more than a cluster of houses around a loop in the River Coquet, but it makes for an impressive sight, especially if you arrive on the A1068 from Alnwick, when the village unfolds before you to reveal the craggy ruin of the enormous 14th-century castle.

A 'worm-eaten hold of ragged stone', **Warkworth Castle** (EH; ☎ 01665-711423; adult £4; 🕙 10am-5pm Apr-Sep, to 4pm Oct, Sat-Mon only Nov-Mar) features in Shakespeare's *Henry IV* Parts I and II and will not disappoint modern visitors. Yes, it is still pretty worm-eaten and ragged, but it crowns an imposing site, high above the gentle, twisting river. The film *Elizabeth* (1998), starring Cate Blanchett, was filmed here.

Tiny, mystical, 14th-century **Warkworth Hermitage** (EH; adult/child £3/free; 11am-5pm Wed & Sun Apr-Sep), carved into the rock, is a few hundred yards upriver. Follow the signs along the path, then take possibly the world's shortest ferry ride. It's a lovely stretch of water and you can hire a **rowing boat** (adult/child per 45 min £5/3; Sat & Sun May-Sep).

Fourteen huge, country-style bedrooms sit above a cosy bar at the **Sun Hotel** ( 01665-711259; www.rytonpark-sun.co.uk; 6 Castle Tce; s/d from £55/85, with dinner £69/112; P ), and an elegant restaurant serves local dishes given the French treatment. There are excellent views of both the castle and the river.

## FARNE ISLANDS

One of England's most incredible seabird conventions is to be found on a rocky archipelago of islands about 3 miles offshore from the undistinguished fishing village of **Seahouses**. There's a **tourist office** ( 01655-720884; Seafield Rd; 10am-5pm Apr-Oct) near the harbour in Seahouses and a **National Trust Shop** ( 01665-721099; 16 Main St; 10am-5pm Apr-Oct) for all island-specific information.

The best time to visit the **Farne Islands** (NT; 01665-720651; admission £5.60, Apr & Aug-Sep £4.80; 10.30am-6pm Apr & Aug-Sep, Inner Farne also 1.30-5pm May-Jul, Staple also 10.30am-1.30pm May-Jul) is during breeding season (roughly May to July), when you can see feeding chicks of 20 species of seabird, including puffin, kittiwake, Arctic tern, eider duck, cormorant and gull. This is a quite extraordinary experience, for there are few places in the world where you can get so close to nesting seabirds. The islands are also home to England's only colony of grey seals.

To protect the islands from environmental damage, only two are accessible to the public: Inner Farne and Staple Island. Inner Farne is the more interesting of the two, as it is also the site of a tiny chapel (1370, restored 1848) to the memory of St Cuthbert, who lived here for a spell and died here in 687.

### Getting There & Away

There are various tours, from 1½-hour cruises to all-day specials, and they get going from 10am April to October. Crossings can be rough, and may be impossible in bad weather.

Some of the boats have no proper cabin, so make sure you've got warm, waterproof clothing if there's a chance of rain. Also recommended is an old hat – those birds sure can ruin a head of hair!

Of the operators from the dock in Seahouses, **Billy Shiel** ( 01665-720308; www .farne-islands.com; 3hr tour adult/child £12/8, all-day tour with landing £25/15) is recommended – he even got an MBE for his troubles.

## BAMBURGH

Bamburgh is all about the castle, a massive, imposing structure high up on a basalt crag and visible for miles around. The village itself – a tidy fist of houses around a pleasant green – isn't half bad, but it's really just about the castle, a solid contender for England's best.

**Bamburgh Castle** ( 01668-214515; www.bam burghcastle.com; adult/child £7/2.40; 10am-5pm Mar-Oct) is built around a powerful 11th-century Norman keep probably built by Henry II, although its name is a derivative of Bebbanburgh, after the wife of Anglo-Saxon ruler Aedelfrip, whose fortified home occupied this basalt outcrop 500 years earlier. The castle played a key role in the border wars of the 13th and 14th centuries, and in 1464 was the first English castle to fall as the result of a sustained artillery attack, by Richard Neville, Earl of Warwick, during the Wars of the Roses. It was restored in the 19th century by the great industrialist Lord Armstrong, who also turned his passion to Cragside (p661) and was the owner of Jesmond Dene House (p646) in Newcastle. The great halls within are still home to the Armstrong family. It's just inland from long open stretches of empty white-sand beach, ideal for blustery walks.

The **Grace Darling Museum** ( 01668-214465; admission by donation £2; 10am-5pm) has displays on Bamburgh's most famous resident, lighthouse keepers in general and the small boats they rescued people in. Grace was a local lass who rowed out to the grounded, flailing SS *Forfarshire* in 1838 and saved its crew in the middle of a dreadful storm. She became the plucky heroine of her time – a real Victorian icon.

### Getting There & Away

Bus 501 runs from Newcastle (2¼ hours, two daily Monday to Saturday, one Sunday) stopping at Alnwick and Seahouses. Bus 401 or 501 from Alnwick (four to six daily) takes one hour.

## HOLY ISLAND (LINDISFARNE)

Holy Island is often referred to as an unearthly place, and while a lot of this talk is just that (and a little bit of bring-'em-in tourist bluster), there is something almost otherworldly about this small island (it's only 2 sq miles). It's tricky to get to, as it's connected to the mainland by a narrow, glinting causeway that only appears at low tide. It's also fiercely desolate and isolated, barely any different from when St Aidan came to what was then known as Lindisfarne to found a monastery in 635.

As you cross the empty flats to get here, it's not difficult to imagine the marauding Vikings that repeatedly sacked the settlement between 793 and 875, when the monks finally took the hint and left. They carried with them the illuminated *Lindisfarne Gospels* (now in the British Library in London) and the miraculously preserved body of St Cuthbert, who lived here for a couple of years but preferred the hermit's life on Inner Farne. A priory was re-established in the 11th century but didn't survive the dissolution in 1537.

The island's peculiar isolation is best appreciated midweek or preferably out of season. Whatever you do, pay attention to the crossing-time information, available at tourist offices and on notice boards throughout the area. Every year there is a handful of go-it-alone fools who are caught midway by the incoming tide and have to abandon their cars.

### Sights

**Lindisfarne Priory** (EH; ☎ 01289-389200; admission £4; ⓥ 9.30am-5pm daily Apr-Sep, to 4pm Oct & Feb-Mar, 10am-2pm Sat-Mon Nov-Jan) consists of elaborate red and grey ruins and the later 13th-century St Mary the Virgin Church. The museum next to these displays the remains of the first monastery and tells the story of the monastic community before and after the dissolution.

Twenty pages of the luminescent *Lindisfarne Gospels* are on view electronically at the **Lindisfarne Heritage Centre** (☎ 01289-389004; www .lindisfarne.org.uk; Marygate; adult/child £3.50/free; ⓥ 10am-5pm Apr-Oct, according to tides Nov-Mar), which also has displays on the locality.

Also in the village is **St Aidan's Winery** (☎ 01289-389230), where you can buy the sickly sweet Lindisfarne Mead, cleverly foisted upon unsuspecting punters as an age-old aphrodisiac.

Half a mile from the village stands the tiny, storybook **Lindisfarne Castle** (NT; ☎ 01289-389244; adult £6; ⓥ 10.30am-3pm or noon-4.30pm Tue-Sun Apr-Oct),

built in 1550, and extended and converted by Sir Edwin Lutyens from 1902 to 1910 for Mr Hudson, the owner of *Country Life* magazine. You can imagine some decadent parties have graced its alluring rooms – Jay Gatsby would have been proud. Its opening times may be extended depending on the tide. A **shuttle bus** ( ☎ 01289-389236) runs here from the car park.

### Sleeping & Eating

It's possible to stay on the island, but you'll need to book in advance.

**Open Gate** ( ☎ 01289-389222; opengate@aidanand hilda.demon.co.uk; Marygate; s/d £32/58) This spacious Elizabethan stone farmhouse with comfortable rooms caters primarily to those looking for a contemplative experience – you're not as much charged a room rate as 'encouraged' to give the listed price as a donation. There is a small chapel in the basement and a room full of books on Celtic spirituality, and there are organised retreats throughout the year.

**Ship Inn** ( ☎ 01289-389311; www.theshipinn-holyisland .co.uk; Marygate; s/d/tr £72/94/112) Three exceptionally comfortable rooms – one with a four-poster – sit above an 18th-century public house known here as the Tavern. There's good local seafood in the bar.

### Getting There & Around

Holy Island can be reached by bus 477 from Berwick (Wednesday and Saturday only, Monday to Saturday July and August). People taking cars across are requested to park in one of the signposted car parks (£5 per day). The sea covers the causeway and cuts the island off from the mainland for about five hours each day. Tide times are listed at tourist offices, in local papers and at each side of the crossing.

## BERWICK-UPON-TWEED

pop 12,870

England's northernmost city is a salt-encrusted fortress town that is the stubborn holder of two unique honours: it is the most fought-over settlement in European history (between 1174 and 1482 it changed hands 14 times between the Scots and the English) and its football team, Berwick Rangers, are the only English team to play in the Scottish League – albeit in lowly Division Two.

### Information

The **tourist office** ( ☎ 01289-330733; www.ber wick-upon-tweed.gov.uk; 106 Marygate; ⓥ 10am-6pm Easter-

Jun, to 5pm Jul-Sep, to 4pm Mon-Sat Oct-Easter) is help-ful. Access the internet at **Berwick Backpackers** ( ☎ 01289-331481; 56-58 Bridge St; per 20 min £2).

## Sights & Activities

Berwick's superb **walls** (EH; admission free) were begun in 1558 to reinforce an earlier set built during the reign of Edward II. They repre-sented state-of-the-art military technology of the day and were designed both to house artil-lery (in arrowhead-shaped bastions) and to withstand it (the walls are low and massively thick, but it's still a long way to fall).

You can walk almost the entire length of the walls, a circuit of about a mile. It's a must, with wonderful, wide-open views. Only a small fragment remains of the once mighty **border castle**, by the train station. The tourist office has a brochure describing the main sights.

Designed by Nicholas Hawksmoor, **Berwick Barracks** (EH; ☎ 01289-304493; The Parade; admission £4; ☺ 10am-5pm Apr-Oct, to 4pm Nov-Mar) is the oldest purpose-built barracks (1717) in Britain and now houses the By Beat of Drum Museum, chronicling the history of British soldiery from 1660 to 1900.

The original gaol cells in the upper floor of the town hall (1750–61) have been pre-served to house the **Cell Block Museum** ( ☎ 01289-330900; Marygate; admission £2.50; ☺ tours 10.30am & 2pm Mon-Fri Apr-Oct), devoted to crime and punish-ment, with tours taking in the public rooms, museum, gaol and belfry.

Recommended are the one-hour **guided walks** (adult/child £4/free; ☺ 10am, 11.15am, 12.30pm & 2pm Mon-Fri Apr-Oct) starting from the tourist office.

## Sleeping & Eating

**Berwick Backpackers** ( ☎ 01289-331481; www.berwickbackpackers.co.uk; 56-58 Bridge St; dm/s/d from £13/16/38; 🅿 🖵 ) This excellent hostel, basically a series of rooms in the outhouses of a Georgian home around a central courtyard, has one large comfortable dorm, a single and two doubles, all en suite. Highly recommended.

**ourpick No 1 Sallyport** ( ☎ 01289-308827; www.1sallyport-bedandbreakfast.com; 1 Sallyport, off Bridge St; r £110-170) Not just the best in town, but one of the best B&Bs in England, No 1 Sallyport has only six suites – each carefully appointed to fit the theme. The Manhattan Loft, crammed into the attic, makes the mini-malist most of the confined space; the Lowry Room is a country-style Georgian classic; the

Smuggler's Suite has a separate sitting room complete with widescreen TV, DVD players and plenty of space to lounge around in. Newer additions include the Tiffany Suite and the recently added attic Mulberry Suite, bathed in light.

**Reivers Tryst** ( ☎ 01289-332455; 119 Marygate; lunch mains £4-7, dinner mains £8-12; ☺ lunch & dinner Mon-Sat) From the hearty breakfast through to home-made pies for lunch and the likes of lemon sole in the evening, this place specialises in classic English cuisine – nothing fancy, but very good.

**Foxton's** ( ☎ 01289-303939; 26 Hide Hill; mains £8-12; ☺ lunch & dinner Mon-Sat) This decent brasserie-style restaurant has Continental dishes to complement the local fare, which means there's something for everyone.

## Drinking

**Barrels Alehouse** ( ☎ 01289-308013; 56 Bridge St) Pop-culture idols such as Elvis and Muhammad Ali grace the walls of this fine pub, where you'll also find real ale and vintage Space Invaders. There's regular live music in the atmospherically dingy basement bar.

## Getting There & Away

### BUS
Buses stop on Golden Sq (where Marygate becomes Castlegate); there are good links from Berwick into the Scottish Borders; there are buses west to Coldstream, Kelso and Galashiels. Buses 505, 515 and 525 go to Newcastle (2¼ hours, five daily) via Alnwick. Bus 253 goes to Edinburgh (two hours, six daily Monday to Saturday, two Sunday) via Dunbar.

### TRAIN
Berwick is almost exactly halfway between Edinburgh (£18.20, one hour) and Newcastle (£17.50, 50 minutes) on the main east-coast London–Edinburgh line. Half-hourly trains between Edinburgh and Newcastle stop in Berwick.

## Getting Around

Berwick's town centre is both compact and walkable. However, if you're feeling lazy try **Berwick Taxis** ( ☎ 01289-307771). **Tweed Bicycles** ( ☎ 01289-331476; 17a Bridge St) hires out moun-tain bikes for £14 a day.

# Wales

GREG GAWLOWSKI

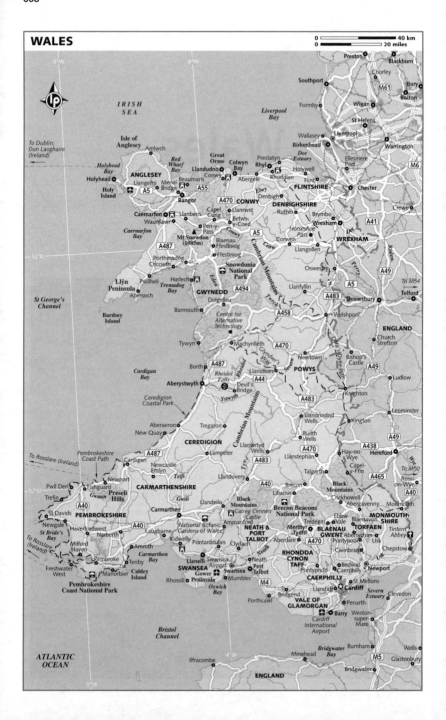

# WALES

0 — 40 km
0 — 20 miles

# Cardiff (Caerdydd)

Cool Cardiff. Contemporary Cardiff. Changing Cardiff. The Welsh capital labours under many sobriquets these days, but one thing remains: Cardiff feels very much alive.

The capital of Wales since only 1955, the city has embraced its new role with vigour, emerging as one of Britain's leading urban centres in the 21st century. Post devolution, Cardiff has gone from strength to strength with a redefined cityscape, a creative buzz, a cultural renaissance and a vibrant nocturnal life that punches well above its weight for a city of its size.

The city hit the buffers when its coal industry collapsed, but Cardiff Bay has since risen phoenix-like from the waters as a testament to the city's capacity for reinvention. Fabulous buildings of national importance such as the Wales Millennium Centre, home to the Welsh National Opera, and the Senedd, the seat of independent government, now dominate the skyline.

These days the city centre is the new focus of redevelopment, with St David's 2 promising a mass temple of retail for Cardiffians to worship at. But despite the cranes, traditional architecture still blends with the modern: the elegant National Museum Cardiff; a world-class Interpretation Centre complementing the folly of Cardiff Castle; and the colossal Millennium Stadium as the new anchor point for glorious national pride on match days.

## HIGHLIGHTS

- Exploring the locations used in hit TV series *Doctor Who* and *Torchwood* against the stunning backdrop of the revitalised **Cardiff Bay** (p677)
- Browsing the speciality, independent boutiques of **Cardiff's Victorian arcades** (p675)
- Using the new Interpretation Centre as a launching pad to explore **Cardiff Castle** (p671)
- Soaking up the prematch atmosphere at **Millennium Stadium** (p672), followed by a celebratory pint of Brains Gold
- Getting lost among the myriad exhibits at the **National Museum Cardiff** (p671)
- Catching the breakthrough rock gig by the next big thing on the vibrant Welsh music scene at **Clwb Ifor Bach** (p680)
- Following in the footsteps of young lovebirds, or mature second-timers, on a trip to **Barry** (p684)

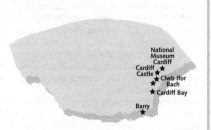

- **TELEPHONE CODE: 029**
- **POPULATION: 320,000**
- **AREA: 54 SQ MILES**

# HISTORY

You can thank the Romans for Cardiff. They built a fort here in AD 75, and the city's name is most likely derived from Caer Tâf (Taff Fort) or Caer Didi (Didius' Fort), referring to a Roman general, Aulus Didius.

Following the Norman Conquest of 1066 Robert Fitzhamon, conqueror of Glamorgan, built a castle (the remains of which stand in the grounds of Cardiff Castle) and a small town soon developed. Further Norman conflict followed, in 1183 and 1404 – the latter inspired by Owain Glyndŵr, leader of the ill-fated rebellion against the English. Suffering severe damage during the fighting, Cardiff stagnated for centuries.

When the southern Welsh valleys kick-started the iron-making and coal-mining boom in the 19th century, Cardiff started to flourish under the aristocratic Bute family of Scotland. They inherited Cardiff Castle in the 18th century and, with wealth derived from their coalfields and docks, set about commissioning further fine buildings. Edward VII declared Cardiff a city in 1905 and by 1913 Cardiff was the world's biggest coal port, with a colourful multiethnic community established in dockside Butetown.

WWI heralded tough times and the 1930s Depression was barely a memory before WWII ravaged Cardiff. Shortly afterwards the coal industry was nationalised, which led to the Butes packing their bags and leaving town in 1947, donating the castle and all their land to the city.

Wales had no official capital and the need for one was seen as an important focus for the growing feeling of Welsh nationhood. Cardiff was proclaimed the first ever capital of Wales in 1955, chosen because it had been a major international port during the Industrial Revolution, had become the biggest town in Wales, and boasted the impressive architectural riches of the Civic Centre. The move marked the end of a 30-year campaign in which towns and cities across Wales vied to become capital, with Caernarfon taking second place in the final vote.

Renovations began in the mid-1980s to convert the forlorn dockside, giving rise to Cardiff Bay, the new Senedd (Wales' independent parliament) and the stunning Wales Millennium Centre.

But the waterfront was just the start of Cardiff's renaissance. While some locals say the heart is being ripped out of the city, the mechanical diggers of progress continue apace even today in the city centre. The face of the downtown area is currently being redrawn thanks to the massive St David's 2 project (www.stdavids2.com), which will link to the existing St David's Shopping Centre and bring new retail development, luxury apartments, 3000 parking spaces and a new library to the city by spring 2010.

Expect major roadworks and mild confusion over disappearing streets for some time to come.

# ORIENTATION

Central Cardiff is small enough to explore on foot. There are two unmistakable landmarks: the castle, located on the northern side; and, a little to the southwest, the enormous Millennium Stadium. The compact shopping and restaurant zone, including the tourist office, is located east of the stadium. The central bus and train stations mark the southern extent of downtown.

Bute Park extends northwest behind the castle, bordered by the River Taff on its western flank. The elegant Civic Centre, including the National Museum Cardiff, City Hall and Law Courts, is northeast of the castle.

Cardiff Bay waterfront lies 1 mile southeast of the centre through Butetown. The leafy Cathedral Rd area is northwest of the castle.

# INFORMATION

Major banks (with ATMs and currency exchange) are on Queen St, St Mary St and High St. Pharmacies rotate late opening hours. Check the regional newspaper, *South Wales Echo*, for daily details.

**Cardiff Bay Visitor Centre** (Map p674; ☎ 2046 3833; Harbour Dr, Britannia Quay; ☿ 9.30am-5pm Mon-Sat, 10.30am-5pm Sun, to 6pm May-Oct) Known as 'The Tube' and shaped like a squashed aeroplane fuselage, this distinctive construction is more attraction than tourist office per se. It hosts exhibitions, screens information videos and is home to a scale model of the bay area.

**Cardiff Central Library** (Map p672; ☎ 2038 2116; ☿ 9am-6pm Mon-Wed & Fri, 9am-7pm Thu, 9am-5.30pm Sat) Free internet access. Will move to Mill Lane as part of St David's 2 but, meanwhile, is temporarily housed on Bute St.

**Main post office** (Map p672; Queen St; ☿ 9am-5.30pm Mon-Sat) Has moved to the lower floor of the Queen's Arcade. Branches on Pontcanna St (Cathedral Rd area) and on Bute St (Cardiff Bay, Map p674).

**Police station** (Map p672; ☎ 2022 2111; King Edward VII Ave)

**Tourist office** (Map p672; ☎ 0870 121 1258; www .visitcardiff.com; Old Library, The Hayes; ☺ 9.30am-6pm Mon-Sat, 10am-4pm Sun; ☐ ) Piles of information, an accommodation-booking service and a good stock of OS maps, plus Welsh literature. Internet access £2 per hour; left luggage £3 per locker.

**University Hospital of Wales** (Map p672; ☎ 2074 7747; Heath Park) Located 2 miles north of the Civic Centre (buses 8, 9 or 9A from bus station, 35 minutes) has an Accident & Emergency department.

## SIGHTS & ACTIVITIES
### Cardiff Castle

Dazzling Victorian style and mock-Gothic folly make **Cardiff Castle** (Map p672; ☎ 2087 8100; www.cardiffcastle.com; Castle St; adult/child grounds only £3.50/2.20, incl castle tour £8.95/6.35; ☺ 9am-6pm Mar-Oct, 9.30am-5pm Nov-Feb) an entertaining visit. Although far from a traditional Welsh castle (it's more a collection of disparate castles around a central green), the site encompasses practically the whole history of Cardiff and is, rightly, the city's leading attraction.

To the right of the entrance the remains of a 3rd-century-AD Roman fort (that guarded the River Taff) contrast with the motte-and-bailey of the 12th-century Norman castle. Opposite the fort, the neo-Gothic Victorian main buildings house the reconstructed home of the coal-rich Butes.

The romantic decor that adorns their residence is a particular highlight, medieval in style following the whims of the eccentric third marquis. It includes a gloriously over-the-top fireplace, a 199-mirrored bedroom ceiling, a minstrels' gallery and a clutch of decorative knights.

A new **Interpretation Centre** opened in summer 2008 as part of a major revamp of the castle's facilities for visitors. The admission ticket now includes an introductory film presentation, a guided tour of the castle apartments, a 60-minute audio guide to the Norman keep and grounds, and entry to the Military Museum.

The castle hosts regular family events, has full pushchair (pram) access throughout and the Interpretation Centre is accessible to wheelchair users.

### Bute Park & Parkland Corridor

After the urban city bustle, leafy Bute Park offers the green breathing space that all great cities need. Originally part of the castle estate, the park follows the River Taff northwest from the city, extending 7 miles upriver to Castell Coch.

The park is bounded on Castle St, beside the castle, by the **Animal Wall** (Map p672), where flamboyant stone creatures squat on the parapet, perpetually immobile.

A half-mile walk leads to **Sophia Gardens** (Map p672), home to Glamorgan County Cricket Club.

### National Museum Cardiff

Sitting proudly at the northern edge of the city centre is the fantastic **National Museum Cardiff** (Map p672; ☎ 2039 7951; www.museumwales.ac.uk; Cathays Park; admission free; ☺ 10am-5pm Tue-Sun). With international-quality galleries and enthralling natural history exhibits, this museum, which recently completed a major refurbishment program, is a treat for adults and kids alike. Allow a day to see everything or a half-day for the highlights.

Inside, you're spoilt for choice. The **national art gallery** houses the largest Impressionist collection outside Paris, featuring works by Claude Monet, Camille Pissarro, Paul Cézanne, Henri Matisse and Pierre-Auguste Renoir. Welsh artists hold their own:

---

### LIVING HISTORY

In 2004 Cardiff Council appointed a Museum Project Officer to develop a museum to bring together the diverse elements of the city's story. The resulting **Cardiff Museum** (www.cardiffmuseum .com), to be housed in the historic Old Library building, upstairs from the central tourist office (above), will tell the history of Cardiff through the eyes of those who created the city – its people.

In recent years the council has run a program of exhibitions and other activities to help explore themes to include in the museum and to encourage people to start making their own contributions. Contributions are still welcome.

The Ground Floor Gallery is scheduled to open in 2010, with the History Lab due to open in 2012. The First Floor Gallery, education rooms and cafe will follow in 2013.

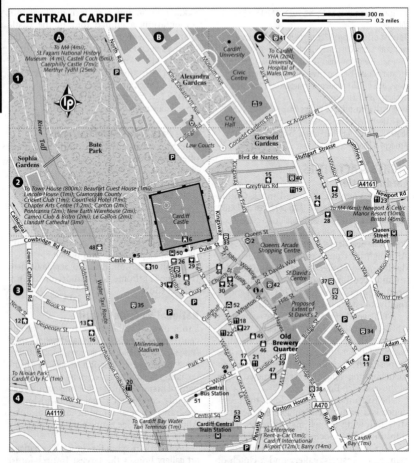

## CENTRAL CARDIFF

Richard Wilson, Thomas Jones and Gwen and Augustus John feature prominently, the latter's portrait of Dylan Thomas being a beguiling treasure.

The biggest attractions come in the galleries devoted to the natural world. Animal treats include a 9m-long humpback whale skeleton and the world's largest turtle (2.9m by 2.7m). In the mineral world, booming films of volcanic eruptions and footage of the soaring Welsh landscape trace evolution through 4600 million years.

The museum has access for travellers with disabilities, wheelchair access and facilities for the visually and hearing impaired. It hosts regular classical and jazz concerts, and is part of Cardiff's beautiful **Civic Centre** (Map p672),

northeast of the castle. Built on Cardiff's coal-boom wealth, the white Portland-stone buildings also comprise the city's **Law Courts** and **City Hall**.

### Millennium Stadium

The scepticism that greeted the decision to build a £110m new stadium on the grounds of the old Cardiff Arms Park disappeared with the first drop-kick at the spectacular **Millennium Stadium** (Map p672; ☎ tours 2082 2228; box office 0870 558 2582; www.millenniumstadium.co.uk; tours adult/child £6.50/4; ☻ 10am-5pm Mon-Sat, 10am-4pm Sun & bank holidays).

You can't miss this hulking monolith, hanging over the River Taff's east bank and dwarfing the surrounding streets. Against a tight schedule, the project was rushed through in time for the 1999 Rugby World Cup. Each of the 72,500 seats affords an unimpaired view of the action, but vertigo sufferers should avoid the precipitous upper tier.

The stadium also hosts big live-music events and football fixtures. In 2012 football fixtures for the London Olympic Games will be played here. On match days the city grinds to a halt: streets are closed, bars are open and the beer flows. Even if you can't get a ticket, the atmosphere is worth savouring. (See also Sporting Chance, p681).

A superb 45-minute tour gives a close-up look at the stadium, including access to the dressing rooms and the chance to walk down the players' tunnel. It starts at Entrance 3 on Westgate St.

## Cardiff Bay

Thirty years ago Cardiff Bay was derelict and forlorn, its industrial backbone broken and its soul ravaged. The region had suffered after its status as the primary port for the export of coal from the mines of south Wales went into severe decline.

The regeneration of Cardiff can be traced back to the mid-1980s when the Cardiff Bay Development Corporation was set up to oversee the transformation of the waterfront area. The urban renaissance project attracted £1.8 billion

in investment to redevelop 1000-odd hectares of deprived docklands in the bay formed by the estuary of the Rivers Taff and Ely.

The turning point came in 1999 with the unveiling of the luxurious St David's Hotel & Spa (p678) and the completion of the Cardiff Bay Barrage to create a 200-hectare inland lake between Penarth Head and Queen Alexandra Dock. The same year saw the opening of Mermaid Quay, the latter a £25-million redevelopment of the inner harbour conceived as a little Covent Garden by the water.

Today Cardiff Bay has gone from industrial wasteland to yuppy fantasy. Looking out across the water, you can still observe working tugs and container ships, but on terra firma the landscape is dotted with luxury apartments plus new waterside dining and drinking dens. On a blue-sky Sunday it's a popular place to stroll in the sun and, while detractors criticise the bay for lacking atmosphere, the development is still maturing.

The Bay's latest development is the International Sports Village, a world-class sporting facility under construction at the time of writing.

To reach the Bay, walk 1 mile south from Central station down Bute St, or take the Cardiff Bus 6, the Baycar, which loops between the Bay and the city (£1.20, 15 minutes, every 10 to 15 minutes daily).

Another great way to approach the Bay is by the **Aquabus water taxi** (Map p674; ☎ 07500 556556; adult/child return £5/3) shuttles around Mermaid Quay and heads up the Taff via South Barrage to the city (30 minutes, hourly from 10.30am to 5.30pm).

### THE WATERFRONT

On the city side of the bay, **Mermaid Quay** (Map p674; www.mermaidquay.co.uk) is the primary dining and shopping area. Beside it, **Roald Dahl Plass** (Map p674) is an open-air boardwalk and venue during the Cardiff Festival (p676).

Cardiff Bay is home to the new building for the National Assembly for Wales (see An

Independent Future, p676), **Y Senedd** (Map p674; ☎ 0845 010 5500; www.assemblywales.org; Cardiff Bay), a distinctive glass, steel and slate construction with a canopy roof on the waterfront. It was built according to sustainable principles. The Education Centre, which was housed next door in the red-brick **Pierhead Building** (Map p674), is now based in the old Assembly debating chamber in Ty Hywel, adjoining the Senedd.

### WALES MILLENNIUM CENTRE

In November 2004, the belated opening of the **Wales Millennium Centre** (Map p674; ☎ box office 0870 040 2000; www.wmc.org.uk; Bute Pl) sealed the renaissance of the Bay. Much more visually attractive than the Assembly, and featuring a golden roof and mauve slate panelling, the venue was designed by Welsh architect Jonathan Adams. Today it is Wales' premier arts complex and home to, among others, the Welsh National Opera. It boasts a wide program, including lots of free, family events.

### TECHNIQUEST

Unusually for a children's attraction **Techniquest** (Map p674; ☎ 2047 5475; www.techniquest.org; Stuart St; adult/child £6.90/4.80; ⏰ 9.30am-4.30pm Mon-Fri, 10.30am-5pm Sat, Sun & school holidays) is a place to have fun *and* learn. More than 160 hands-on demonstrations bring science to life.

### BUTETOWN

Victorian **Butetown** (Map p674), spanning out from Mount Stuart Sq, just northwest of the waterfront, was the erstwhile heart of Cardiff's coal trade, a multiethnic community that propelled the city to world fame. Today the stately streets are part-renovated relics of the time when this was Tiger Bay, complete with gritty characters and a happening jazz scene.

The **Butetown History & Arts Centre** (Map p674; ☎ 2025 7657; www.bhac.org; 5 Dock Chambers, Bute St; admission free; ⏰ 10am-5pm Tue-Fri, 11am-4.30pm Sat, Sun & public holidays) presents a photographic

---

## CARDIFF BAY

0 ———— 300 m
0 ———— 0.2 miles

Atlantic Wharf
County Hall
To City Centre (1mi)
Lloyd George Ave
Bute St
Schooner Way
Hemingway Rd
Cardiff Bay Station
Red Dragon Centre
A4232
Butetown
Mount Stuart
West Bute St
Bute St
Bute Pl
Pierhead St
Dumballs Rd
Clarence Rd
James St
To Cardiff Bay Barrage (1mi); International Sports Village (2mi); Cardiff International Airport (12mi)
Butetown Link
Stuart St
Mermaid Quay
Harbour Dr
Britannia Qu
A4232
Graving Docks
Inner Harbour
Roath Basin
Britannia Park
Havannah St
Water Taxi Route
Cardiff Bay

---

**ARCADE ACTION**

Known as 'the city of arcades', Cardiff's Victorian-built former alleyways, later covered over with ornate roofs to form enclosed shopping streets, are the city's best-kept secret. They offer a vibrant mix of independent retailers and eateries a far cry from the chain store–dominated behemoth that will be St David's 2. The arcades are open from 9am to 5.30pm Monday to Saturday. This is our guide to the must-visit places.

**Castle Arcade** (Map p672; btwn Duke & High Sts) is the most decorative. It's home to **Troutmark Books** ( ☎ 2038 2814; 39-43 Castle Arcade) for secondhand and Welsh-language books; **Madame Fromage** ( ☎ 2064 4888; 21-25 Castle Arcade), a delightful deli and cheese shop with local produce; and **Cafe Minuet** (p678).

**High Street Arcade** (Map p672; btwn High & St John Sts) boasts **Telynau Vining Harps** ( ☎ 2022 1199; www.camacharps.co.uk; 8-10 High St Arcade) for traditional music; try dance-music specialist **Catapult** ( ☎ 2022 8990; www.catapult.co.uk; 22 High St Arcade) for vinyl and DJ equipment; and **Hobo's** ( ☎ 2034 1188; 26 High St Arcade) for '60s and '70s retro clothing.

**Royal Arcade** (Map p672; btwn St Mary St & The Hayes) is the oldest arcade (built in 1856), with **Wally's Delicatessen** ( ☎ 2022 9265; 42 Royal Arcade) for wholefoods and deli; **Vive** ( ☎ 2064 4296) for smoothies and fresh juices; and, by the back entrance, **Spiller's Records** ( ☎ 2022 4905; www .spillersrecords.co.uk; 36 The Hayes), the world's oldest record shop (founded in 1894, selling wax phonograph cylinders) and still the stalwart of the Welsh music scene (see Cool Cymru, p699).

**Wyndham Arcade** (Map p672; btwn Mill Lane & St Mary St) is the base for **Comic Guru** ( ☎ 2022 9119; 20-22 Wyndham Arcade) for all your essential *Doctor Who* needs; and the **Bear Shop** ( ☎ 2023 3443; 12-14 Wyndham Arcade), a gloriously old-fashioned specialist tobacconist.

Finally, **Morgan Arcade** (Map p672; btwn St Mary St & The Hayes) houses the administration office for the arcades and both **Crumbs Salad Bar** (p678) and **Plan** (p678), two excellent eateries.

---

record and historical document-led exploration of Butetown's gritty past, together with changing exhibitions.

## Llandaff Cathedral

In a peaceful suburb, 2 miles north of the city following Cathedral Rd to the A4119, Llandaff is home to the fine-looking **Llandaff Cathedral** (off Map p672; ☎ 2056 4554; www .llandaffcathedral.org.uk; Cathedral Rd; admission free).

Built on the site of a 6th-century monastery, the cathedral itself dates from 1130 and has fulfilled various roles over the centuries. Today its mishmash of styles is testimony to its disturbed history – one tower dates from the 15th century, the other from the 19th.

The interior is notable for its clear-glass windows, hence the clarity of light is striking and unique. A central concrete arch carries the cathedral organ and Sir Jacob Epstein's aluminium sculpture *Christ in Majesty*. In the **St Illtyd chapel** is a triptych by Dante Gabriel Rossetti, while period artworks are scattered liberally around.

Cardiff Bus services 25 and 62 run along Cathedral Rd to Llandaff (20 minutes, three hourly Monday to Saturday, hourly Sunday).

## CARDIFF FOR CHILDREN

Compact and easy to navigate, Cardiff is welcoming to families. Interactive Techniquest (opposite) is the primary attraction to challenge little brains, while the National Museum Cardiff (p671) is full of weird and wonderful animals and fascinating exhibits. After that, jump on the City Sightseeing bus (below) and head over to Cardiff Bay for ice creams at Mermaid Quay, or take a stroll in leafy Bute Park (p671).

For a trip out of town, try the living history of Caerphilly Castle (p683) or Castell Coch (p683).

## TOURS

**Bay Island Voyages** (Map p674; ☎ 01446-420692; www.bayisland.co.uk) Adrenalin-filled Rigid Inflatable Boat (RIB) trips around the Bay (adult/child £18/12) sold from a kiosk on the waterfront.

**City Sightseeing** (Map p672; ☎ 2047 3432; www .city-sightseeing.com) Departing from the castle, this hop-on, hop-off open-top bus has 10 stops around the city, leaving every 30 minutes (every hour in low season) between 10am and 3pm. Tickets (adult/child £8/4) are valid for 24 hours.

---

**AN INDEPENDENT FUTURE**

After early years struggling to justify its existence, the devolved National Assembly for Wales received a huge boost in July 2006 when the *Government of Wales Act* (2006) was passed after opposition parties in the House of Lords in London withdrew their objections. The decision effectively granted the Welsh people the opportunity of greater independence.

Established in 1999, the Assembly has previously been marred by political indifference and perceived impotence. Nationalist reformers used this to cite the need for even greater local control, while those opposed to devolution branded the breakaway a flop. But with turnout at the 2007 election up by 6% in comparison with the 2003 turnout – one of the few elections in Europe in the last few years where turnout has risen at all – the signs were of a new dawn breaking for Wales' voting population.

The passing of the new bill, which came into effect in 2007, has served to free the Assembly from the shackles of Westminster; the latter has always determined Wales' budget, taxation, foreign policy and defence strategy, but further future powers may well follow the Scottish model.

The fantastical new assembly building at Cardiff Bay, known as **Y Senedd** (Map p674; ☎ 0845 010 5500; www.assemblywales.org), opened in 2006 at a cost of £67 million, five times the original budget. Plenary (full) sessions take place here, and the centre is open to the public for pre-arranged group tours and drop-in visits.

Architecturally stunning, the Senedd has been championed as a 21st-century ecobuilding, incorporating energy-saving and recycling features. Early teething troubles have now been resolved and the building is today recognised as a prime example of sustainable design.

---

## FESTIVALS & EVENTS

For more 'what's on' information and an event calendar, see the website http://cardiffwhatson.walesonline.co.uk/gb/. Some major annual events:

**Cardiff Festival** ( ☎ 2087 2087; www.cardiff-festival.com) The highlight of the summer is a multievent festival, from late June to early August around Cardiff Bay, with attractions from open-air theatre, via an international food and drink festival to the Cardiff Big Weekend (early August) with the Lord Mayor's Parade.

**Cardiff Winter Wonderland** ( ☎ 2023 0130; www.cardiffswinterwonderland.com) A major winter event in the Civic Centre with an outdoor ice-skating rink, Santa's grotto and family-friendly activities, preceded by the switching-on of the Christmas lights.

**Mardi Gras** Cardiff's gay-pride festival held in late August or early September; see the boxed text, p680.

## SLEEPING
### City Centre
#### BUDGET

**River House Backpackers** (Map p672; ☎ 2039 9810; www.riverhousebackpackers.com; 59 Fitzhamon Embankment; dm/r incl breakfast £17.50/25; 🖳 ) The newest arrival in the budget sector, this smart new place is modern, clean and well executed. Washing facilities, a sunny garden, well-equipped kitchen and TV lounge are all nice home-from-home touches, plus there are some simple but private rooms away from the dorms.

**Cardiff Backpacker** (Map p672; ☎ 2034 5577; www.nosda.co.uk/backpacker.php; 96-98 Neville St, Riverside; dm incl breakfast from £18; 🖳 ) A stalwart of the Cardiff budget scene, this independent hostel was the original cheap place to stay, with well-maintained facilities and a central location.

#### MIDRANGE

**NosDa Budget Hotel** (Map p672; ☎ 2034 8866; www.nosda.co.uk; 53-59 Despenser St; s/d from £35/55; 🖳 ) This slightly smarter sister property to Cardiff Backpacker offers an upmarket hostel experience with more privacy, home-cooked meals at the Tafarn cantina, and a cool bar area. At the time of writing the owners were embarking on a redevelopment of the property, aiming to split it into a hostel and serviced apartments with a gym and restaurant. Work should be finished by mid-2009 but spectacular vistas across to Millennium Stadium will remain.

**Barceló Angel Hotel** (Map p672; ☎ 2064 9200; www.barceloangelcardiff.com; Castle St; s/d from £65/115; 🖳 ) Now under new management and recently refurbished, the Victorian Angel Hotel retains its stately rooms, many with castle views. Ask for the latest promotional deals.

**Big Sleep** (Map p672; ☎ 2063 6363; www.thebigsleephotel.com; Bute Tce; d £45-120) This wannabe design hotel, ugly from the outside, desperately trying to be funky within, feels rather lost currently amid the building sites east of the central train station. The rooms are minimalist and self-consciously cool, with a continental breakfast, but with rates set according to availability it can be a hit-and-miss experience. The downstairs bar is currently being turned into a coffee shop.

**Parc Hotel** (Map p672; ☎ 0870 333 9157; www.thistle .com; Park Pl; d from £80; P ⬛ ) We know. This is a Thistle-brand chain hotel, but stay with us. At the time of writing, this place had, quite literally, just opened and was the first in the group to be given a modern makeover. The result? A really smart, contemporary hotel located right at the heart of the main shopping area, with tasteful rooms, good facilities and helpful staff. Ask about cheaper weekend rates when the business travellers vacate the premises.

**TOP END**

**Royal Hotel** (Map p672; ☎ 2055 0750; www.theroyal hotelcardiff.com; 10 St Mary St; standard/deluxe d £154/174; P ⬛ ) Central Cardiff's latest boutique hotel, located just across from the train station, has all the modernist looks and urban style but at the time of our visit was let down by poor service and erratic internet access. The rooms are very contemporary, with timber floors and chrome bathrooms, while meals are served

in a bar area overlooking the city. Sort out the teething problems and this place would be a real gem.

**Park Plaza** (Map p672; ☎ 2011 1111; www.parkplaza cardiff.com; Greyfriars Rd; d from £125; P ⬛ wi-fi) The most luxurious property in town has all the five-star facilities you would expect from a business-oriented hotel. It's the only hotel in central Cardiff to offer free wi-fi internet, and boats a deservedly popular spa, health and leisure centre. For something more offbeat, it offers *Doctor Who* breaks (see Cardiff Bay for Sci-fi Fans, below).

## Cardiff Bay

**our pick** **Jolyons Hotel** (Map p674; ☎ 2048 8775; www .jolyons.co.uk; Bute Cres; d £90-150; ⬛ ) Budget boutique accommodation at the heart of the Bay, this stylish town house currently boasts six rooms with period furniture and stylish fittings. Ask for special weekend rates. Breakfast is served in the cosy cellar-bar Bar Cwtch (open from 5pm to 11pm weekdays, to 1am weekends), which doubles as a cool evening hang-out for wood-fired pizzas (around £8) and drinks. The owner is planning to expand, adding 20 new, individually styled rooms with iPod docking stations and flat-screen TVs, and a new roof garden by 2009. One to watch.

---

### CARDIFF BAY FOR SCI-FI FANS

The huge success of the TV series *Doctor Who*, reinvented for a new generation by the Swansea-born and Cardiff Bay–based writer, Russell T Davies, has brought a whole new audience to appreciate the modernist-meets-maritime setting of Cardiff Bay, especially as the program is now broadcast around the world.

Much of the series is filmed around the area and at the BBC Cardiff studios. *Doctor Who* fans are now often spotted around town, trying to find the locations used in their favourite episodes; more details from www.bbc.co.uk/wales/southeast/sites/doctorwho.

In response to Cardiff's status as the new home of *Doctor Who*, a new permanent exhibition, **Doctor Who Up Close** (Map p672; ☎ 2048 9257; www.doctorwhoexhibitions.com; adult/child £5/3.50; ☽ 11am-8pm) has opened in the Red Dragon Centre. It features memorabilia and sets from the series plus a sci-fi shop for Time Lord–themed souvenirs.

You can even book a whole *Doctor Who*–themed weekend break at Cardiff's Park Plaza Hotel (above), including tickets to the 'Doctor Who Up Close' exhibition and a giant, inflatable Dalek to stand guard over your bed.

Not to be left out, *Doctor Who* spin-off series *Torchwood* is now getting in on the act with a fledgling trail around the Bay, which is regraded as one of the stars of the show for its moody outdoor-location shots. According to the show's star, John Barrowman, 'When you see Cardiff on film, it looks like LA – it looks amazing'.

*Torchwood*'s hidden lift emerges by the fountain in Roald Dahl Pass; and The Hub, *Torchwood*'s secret base, is supposedly located beneath the Wales Millennium Centre. Bars in the bay are often used for indoor locations.

More details from the Cardiff Bay Visitor Centre (p670).

**St David's Hotel & Spa** (Map p674; ☎ 2045 4045; www.thestdavidshotel.com; Havannah St; r from £260; P ⌨) Epitomising Cardiff Bay's transformation from wasteland to stylish place-to-be, this landmark development is now under new management and emerging from renovation works. It's five-star all the way, with a particularly popular spa and treatment centre.

## Cathedral Rd Area & Cathays

Leafy Cathedral Rd lies parallel to Bute Park, a 15-minute walk northwest of the castle, or take Cardiff Bus services 24 or 60 if it's raining. It boats a huge number of traditional B&Bs. The three listed here are reliable options.

**Cardiff YHA** ( ☎ 0870 770 5750; www.yha.org.uk; 2 Wedal Rd, Roath Park; dm incl breakfast £18; ☺ reception open 7.30am-11pm; P ⌨) In the student district of Cathays, 2 miles north of the centre, is a modern and functional red-brick hotel with some family rooms and disabled access. Take Cardiff Bus 28, 29 or 29B from St Mary St to Lake Rd West/Wedal Rd.

**Town House** ( ☎ 2023 9399; www.thetownhouse cardiff.co.uk; 70 Cathedral Rd; s/d from £49.50/69.50; P ) An imposing Victorian terrace guesthouse. The rooms here need a bit of an update design wise, but it remains a solid option. The house's original features, such as stained glass and mosaic flooring, add a homely touch, as does the hearty breakfast.

**Beaufort Guest House** ( ☎ 2023 7003; www.beaufort housecardiff.co.uk; 65 Cathedral Rd; s/d/f from £49.95/75/95; P ⌨) Generous rooms, chunky furniture and tasteful period decor make this a reliable midrange option. Breakfast is served amid Asian artworks and classical music; the new conservatory area is a sunny spot for pre-dinner drinks.

**Lincoln House** ( ☎ 2039 5558; www.lincolnhotel.co.uk; 118-120 Cathedral Rd; s/d/f from £65/85/95; P ⌨) At the top end of the guest-house scale, Lincoln House is a huge Victorian property with lots of light and nice homely touches, such as free water and coffee, plus a welcoming lounge and bar. Ground-floor rooms cater for disabled access and families, while the four-poster room is private and romantic. Most impressive of all is the new Penthouse Suite (£150 per night), a modern self-contained apartment with a kitchenette and two doubles for a home away from home.

# EATING
## City Centre

**Zushi** (Map p672; ☎ 2066 9911; www.zushicardiff.com; The Aspect, 140 Queen St; plates £1.70-3.50; ☺ noon-10pm Mon-Sat, noon-5pm Sun) A happening conveyor-belt sushi bar with a big menu of colour-coded plates. The fresh, good-value food attracts a mixed crowd from office groups to minor local celebrities. Bento boxes to go from £5.50.

**Plan** (Map p672; ☎ 2039 8464; 28-29 Morgan Arcade; ☺ 8.30am-5pm Mon-Sat, 10.30am-4pm Sun) This small but satisfying place is a haven for healthy options: specialist teas and fair-trade coffees, vegetarian and vegan options, and lots of organic, local produce. Sip a coffee and browse the *Guardian* newspaper over a hearty vegetarian breakfast (£3.50).

**Crumbs Salad Bar** (Map p672; ☎ 2039 5007; 33 Morgan Arcade; dishes around £5; ☺ 10am-3pm Mon-Fri, 10am-4pm Sat) Great for vegetarians, the wooden salad bowls are piled high with crisp salad and tasty local cheese at this rustic little place.

**our pick** **Cafe Minuet** (Map p672; ☎ 2034 1794; 42 Castle Arcade; mains £5-7; ☺ 10am-5pm Mon-Sat) A classical music–themed cafe with an Italian-influenced menu of dishes named after the great composers. It may look a bit greasy spoon from the outside, but the quality of the food is superb and includes lots of tasty vegetarian options. A true one-off.

**Fat Cat Cafe Bar** (Map p672; ☎ 2022 8378; www .fatcatcafebars.co.uk; Grosvenor House, Greyfriars Rd; mains around £7; ☺ 11am-midnight Mon-Thu, 11am-1am Fri, 10am-2am Sat, 10am-11pm Sun; ⌨) This chain of pub-style restaurants started in Wales and the Cardiff outpost is one of the smarter ones, with boudoir-style decor and comfy sofas to nurse a hangover. Food is served daily to 9pm, plus there's a daily happy hour (5pm to 8pm) with cocktail deals.

**Yard** (Map p672; ☎ 2022 7577; 42-43 St Mary St; mains £7-12; ⌨) The stand-out option in the chain-heavy Brewery Quarter, located on the site of the old Brains Brewery dating from 1713, this bar attracts a chilled-out daytime crowd, cranking up the music and the vibe by night. The food is upmarket pub fare with tasty burgers and salads – plus a nice drop of Brains Gold.

**Cafe Jazz** (Map p672; ☎ 2023 2161; www.cafejazz cardiff.com; St Mary St; 2-/3-course set menu sfrom £7.95/10.95; ☺ lunch & dinner, Sun noon-5pm) Cool jazz joint by night, relaxed cafe by day. You can kick back here with decent food and a regular program of jazz events, high-profile gigs and informal jam sessions. The best-value option foodwise is the set menu with two/three courses for £9.50/11.50.

**Zerodegrees** (Map p672; ☎ 2022 9494; www .zerodegrees.co.uk; 27 Watergate St; pizzas & pastas £7-9) The latest opening in town is a huge microbrewery-cum-restaurant combining all-day food with six, lip-smacking, artisan-crafted beers – try the Black Lager with hints of caramel and coffee. Dining options range from pizzas to salads with the kilo pots of mussels (£12.50) the house speciality. The setting is bright, buzzy and striking, with huge brew vats of fermenting beer bubbling away in the window. Catch the happy hour (4pm to 7pm Monday to Friday) for a £2 pint.

Finally, for an alfresco Sunday brunch, the **Riverside Real Food Market** (Map p672; ☎ 2019 0036; Fitzhamon Embankment; ☾ 10am-2pm Sun) is a weekly haven of local goodies, located opposite the Millennium Stadium.

## Cardiff Bay

**Bosphorus** (Map p674; ☎ 2048 7477; 31 Mermaid Quay; mains £12) Jutting out into the bay on its own pier, this upmarket Turkish eatery has great views, a relaxed ambience and quality food a far cry from your typical Turkish kebab shop. Choose from fresh fish, grills and Middle Eastern–influenced mains, including vegetarian options, for a quality dinner.

**Garcon** (Map p674; ☎ 2049 0990; www.garcon-resto .co.uk; Unit Upper 9, Mermaid Quay; 2-course set lunches £9.95, dinner mains £14) This French brasserie has a cool Parisian feel, a long, marble counter straight out of the Left Bank and an outdoor decking area for a sundowner kir royale. Try the good-value set lunch or dig into à la carte evening mains (around £14).

**Woods Bar & Brasserie** (Map p674; ☎ 2049 2400; www.woods-brasserie.com; Pilotage Bldg, Stuart St; mains £16-21.50; ☾ lunch & dinner Mon-Sat year-round, dinner Sun Jun-Sep) Featuring floor-to-ceiling windows and light-wood touches, Woods is a very classy eatery located in a converted dockside building. The house special is an upmarket take on fish and chips (£10.45), but more worthwhile are the adventurous fish mains – try the pan-fried skate with cockle, capers and herb butter sauce (£16.95). There's a sleek little bar downstairs for a prepandial cocktail.

**Bayside Brasserie** (Map p674; ☎ 2035 8444; www .baysidebrasserie.com; Unit Upper 14, Mermaid Quay; mains around £17, 2-course set menus £14.95) Classy and defiantly chic, the Bayside is built around a light-filled atrium with panoramic views across the bay. The food is well prepared with lots of steaks and fish mains, while it now offers a good-value set evening menu Friday to Sunday (£14.95 for two courses) – so good we could even nearly forgive them the looped soundtrack of Sting albums – nearly.

## DRINKING

There is an ever-expanding circuit of cool hang-outs for Cardiff's urban cognoscenti. These are some of the latest picks around town.

**Cafe Bar Europa** (Map p672; ☎ 2066 7776; 25 Castle St; ☾ 10am-5pm Tue-Sun) Favoured by an arty and politics crowd, the charismatic Europa is a daytime hang-out with fair-trade coffees, snacks and a friendly welcome.

---

### HAUTE CUISINE & HIPPIE CHIC

Cardiff's hippest district is currently focused on the suburbs of Canton and Pontcanna, a few blocks strolling west from the guesthouses of Cathedral Rd. The area offers some distinct flavours of the new Cardiff.

**our pick Le Gallois** (off Map p672; ☎ 2034 1264; www.legallois.co.uk; 6-10 Romilly Cres, Canton; 2-course set lunches £12.95, dinner mains around £17; ☾ lunch & dinner Tue-Sat, lunch Sun) is still renowned as one of Cardiff's finest despite some recent changes to the management. It majors in an inspirational blend of Welsh and French cuisine with a good-value set lunch and elegant evening mains in a refined, Gallic-inspired setting.

Diametrically opposed but equally evocative is the **New Earth Warehouse** (off Map p672; King's Rd; ☾ 10am-late), an alternative community project featuring fair-trade coffees, music jams, craft shop, a kids' play area, a gallery of offbeat local art and yurt-making classes. Yes, that's as in the Mongolian tents. Sip a herbal tea, chill out in the yurt and soak up the spirit of 1968 incarnate to a soundtrack of Tom Waits albums.

Different again, the **Cameo Club & Bistro** (off Map p672; ☎ 2022 0466; www.cameoclub.co.uk; 3-5 Pontcanna St; mains around £7; ☾ 8.30am-10pm Mon-Sat, 9.30am-4pm Sun) is the hub for Cardiff's art and media community. It's a private members' club after 7pm but open daytimes for bistro food, hearty breakfasts and coffees. The owners are expanding the premises for extra bar-dining covers.

**Buffalo Bar** (Map p672; ☎ 2031 0312; www.myspace .com/wearebuffalobar; 11 Windsor Pl; ☼ 10am-3am Sun-Thu, to 4am Fri & Sat; ☐ ) A haven for cool folks about town, the laid-back Buffalo features retro furniture, tasty daytime food, life-affirming cocktails and cool tunes with DJ sets.

**10 Feet Tall** (Map p672; ☎ 2022 8883; www.myspace .com/thisis10feettall; 11-12 Church St; ☼ 9am-3am Sun-Thu, to 4am Fri & Sat; ☐ ) The new sister property to Buffalo Bar, this hip, multipurpose venue over four floors covers everything from deli to live music venue via restaurant and pavement cafe. The ground-floor deli has a Mediterranean motif to the menu while the Mezzanine Restaurant draws on North African influences. A welcome opening.

**Pica Pica** (Map p672; ☎ 2034 5703; www.picapicacar diff.com; 15-23 Westgate St; ☼ noon-midnight Wed-Sat, to 11pm Mon-Tue, 10.30pm Sun; ☐ ) Cool cocktail bar for tapas, meze and cocktails with two bars across four floors.

**GloBar** (Map p672; ☎ 2023 5321; www.glo-uk.com; 4 Churchill Way; ☼ to 3am Fri & Sat) By day GloBar is a chilled-out cafe-bar with doors open onto the pavement, coffees and tapas served with chilled wine. After 7pm the food stops and the emphasis shifts to cocktails, live music and DJ sets for a more up-for-it crowd.

Weekends bring the alcopops-and-white stilettos crowd out onto St Mary St in all weathers. For a quiet pint of a local brew from Cardiff's Brains Brewery in traditional surroundings, and away from the boozy, bawdy brouhaha, try these:

**Cottage** (Map p672; ☎ 2033 7195; 25 St Mary St) A friendly old pub for bar meals and a pint of Brains Gold.

**Goat Major** (Map p672; ☎ 2038 3380; cnr Castle & High Sts) For pub grub and a pint of Brains Dark.

**Old Arcades** (Map p672; ☎ 2023 1583; 14 Church St) A CAMRA (Campaign for Real Ale)–listed pub for real ales and bar meals, including fresh fish specials from the nearby Cardiff Market.

## ENTERTAINMENT

Cultural events are generally timed for evening performances, with venues typically opening around 6.30pm for a preshow drink. Live-music venues and clubs still open until 2am – later on Fridays and Saturdays. Expect to pay a cover charge according to the event. Contact each venue direct for tickets and prices.

Cardiff's monthly what's-on magazine *Buzz*, available free in bars and the tourist office, has its finger on the local pulse.

### Live Music & Clubs

**Clwb Ifor Bach** (Map p672; ☎ 2023 2199; www.clwb.net; 11 Womanby St) Truly an independent music great; many a regional Welsh band has broken onto the scene here since the early 1980s. It started as a venue for Welsh-language music and has survived the Cool Cymru backlash, making it Cardiff's most eclectic and important venue. It now hosts a range of club nights for all tastes, but whatever the night the crowd soaks up the vibe with an insatiable appetite.

**Barfly** (Map p672; ☎ 0870 907 0999; www.barflyclub .com; Kingsway) Student favourite Barfly is part of a national chain championing local bands and international indie acts. It hosts popular alternative and electronica club nights.

### GAY & LESBIAN CARDIFF

Cardiff is home to Wales' largest and most relaxed gay and lesbian scene (more from www .gaycardiff.co.uk). The most popular venues are listed here. The **Mardi Gras** (www.cardiffmardigras .co.uk) festival has been a little erratic in recent years and is no longer staged annually. Check the website for dates.

**Exit Bar** (Map p672; ☎ 2064 0102; 48 Charles St; free admission before 9.30pm; ☼ 8pm-2am Mon-Fri, 8pm-3am Sat, 8pm-1am Sun) is a long-standing favourite on the scene, spinning standard disco fare.

**Bar Icon** (Map p672; ☎ 2066 6505; 60 Charles; admission free; ☼ noon-11pm Sun-Thu, noon-1am Sat & Sun) is the latest must-visit lounge bar for the style-consciouss with a mixed crowd.

**Kings Cross** (Map p672; ☎ 2064 9891; 25 Caroline St; admission free; ☼ to 1am Thu-Sat, to 12.30am Sun) – or KX, as it's known – is a big, newly refurbished pub that has a Wednesday cabaret, weekend DJs and a Sunday karaoke night.

**Golden Cross** (Map p672; ☎ 2034 3129; www.thegolden.co.uk; 283 Hayes Bridge Rd; ☼ to 1am Wed-Sat, to 12.30am Sun) is a traditional-style gay pub set in a Grade II–listed building.

The city has several notably gay-friendly places to stay: try the **Courtfield Hotel** ( ☎ 2022 7701; www.courtfieldhotel.com; 101 Cathedral Rd; s/d £45/60).

### SPORTING CHANCE

Cardiff is the home of Welsh sport. Rugby union is the national game and played to packed houses at the spine-tingling Millennium Stadium (p672). To catch an international match here is to get a glimpse behind the Welsh psyche, especially when the Six Nations tournament (contested annually in February and March between Wales, England, Scotland, Ireland, France and Italy) is in full swing. The party to end all parties came in 2008 when Wales clinched the grand slam (victory in all five matches).

At other times **Cardiff RFC** (Map p672; ☎ tickets 2030 2000; www.cardiffblues.com) matches are played at the Millennium Stadium's smaller sibling, Cardiff Arms Park.

But it's not all oval balls and macho scrumming. Football's alive and kicking at Ninian Park, where **Cardiff City FC** (off Map p672; ☎ tickets 0845 345 1400; www.cardiffcityfc.premiumtv.co.uk) fly the flag in the Coca-Cola Football League Championship Table. In 2008 the Bluebirds made the FA Cup Final, their first appearance in the final since 1923. Plans are now under way for a brand-new 30,000-seat stadium for the club.

Elsewhere, the sound of leather on willow can be heard at **Glamorgan County Cricket Club** (off Map p672; ☎ box office 0871 282 3400; www.glamorgancricket.com), where completion of the new SWALEC Stadium paves the way for exciting times ahead.

Finally, and looking ahead, Cardiff is now gearing up to host the 2010 Ryder Cup, with the best golfers from Europe and the USA set to tee off at the **Celtic Manor Resort** (off Map p672; ☎ 01633-413000; www.celtic-manor.com). Check out the course with a weekend golf break. It's located at Junction 24 of the M4, taking the B4237 towards Newport.

**St David's Hall** (Map p672; ☎ 2087 8444; www .stdavidshallcardiff.co.uk; The Hayes) It's not the most aesthetically striking venue from the outside, but as home to the BBC National Orchestra of Wales, and the annual Welsh Proms, it remains the city's high-art musical hub.

**Cardiff International Arena** (Map p672; ☎ 2022 4488; Mary Ann St) A huge, cavernous venue for major pop or rock acts, plus exhibitions.

Cardiff Bay is home to two more-intimate and atmospheric venues:

**Norwegian Church Arts Centre** (Map p674; ☎ 2045 4899; www.norwegianchurchcardiff.co.uk; Harbour Dr; admission free; ⏰ 10am-5pm) One of the last remaining historic dockside buildings, constructed in 1869. The Norwegian Seaman's Mission relocated the stark-white little church during redevelopment of the area. It now functions as a cosy cafe by day and arts venue by night, with spine-tingling acoustics.

**Point** (Map p674; ☎ 2046 0873; www.thepointcardiff bay.com; Mt Stuart Sq) A Gothic-style stone church that was restored in 2003 to act as a live-music venue. Designed with acoustics in mind, inside the sound is superb.

### Cinemas, Theatre & Comedy

**Chapter Arts Centre** (off Map p672; ☎ 2030 4400; www.chapter.org; Market Rd, Canton; 🖥 ) This excellent local arts centre is a hub for imaginative theatre, art and art-house cinema, plus a shop and cafe. It remains open despite ongoing refurbishment work.

**New Theatre** (Map p672; ☎ box office 2087 8889; www .newtheatrecardiff.co.uk; Park Pl) This splendid theatre, restored to its Edwardian grandeur, stages classic shows from musicals to pantomime.

**Sherman Theatre** (Map p672; ☎ box office 2064 6900; www.shermantheatre.co.uk; Senghennydd Rd, Cathays) Home to south Wales' leading theatre company, Sherman Cymru, it stages a broad program of Welsh-language and general-interest works.

**Glee Club** (Map p674; ☎ 0870 241 5093; www.glee .co.uk; Mermaid Quay) A busy comedy club with a well-regarded program of comedy nights in Cardiff Bay.

## GETTING THERE & AWAY
### Air

**Cardiff International Airport** ( ☎ 01446-711111; www .cwlfly.com), 12 miles southwest of the centre in Rhoose, near Barry (see the boxed text, p684), now has direct connections to over 50 destinations. Main flight operators:

**Aer Arann** ( ☎ 0800 587 2324; www.aerarran.com)
**bmibaby** ( ☎ 0871 224 0224; www.bmibaby.com)
**Eastern Airways** ( ☎ 0870 366 9100; www.eastern airways.com)
**Highland Airways** ( ☎ 0870 777 0915; www.highland airways.co.uk)
**KLM** ( ☎ 0870 507 4074; www.klm.com)
**Skybus** ( ☎ 01736-334224; www.skybus.co.uk)
**Thomsonfly** ( ☎ 0870 190 0737; www.thomsonfly.com)
**Zoom** ( ☎ 0870 240 0055; www.flyzoom.com)

## Bus

Buses currently congregate at Central bus station, located on Wood St opposite Cardiff Central train station, but work is now under way to demolish the terminus buildings. Some services are already moving to St Mary St stops. Pick up bus maps and details of changes at the **Cardiff Bus office** ( ☎ 20 666 444; www.cardiffbus.com; Wood St; ⏱ 8.30am-5.30pm Mon-Fri, 9am-4.30pm Sat).

For details of fares and timetables, contact **Traveline Cymru** ( ☎ 0871 200 2233; www.traveline-cymru.org.uk).

The First bus Shuttle100 travels from Cardiff to Swansea (peak/off-peak £6/5 return, one hour, hourly Monday to Saturday, reduced services Sunday).

**National Express** ( ☎ 0871 81 81 81; www.nationalexpress.com) bus 202 serves Bristol (£7.20, one hour, seven daily), and coach 509 serves London (£21.30, 3½ hours, hourly).

For airport services, National Express coach 201 serves Heathrow (£38.50, 3½ hours, about hourly), continuing to Gatwick (£42.50, four hours 50 minutes). These services are currently coordinated from a makeshift **National Express office** (Wood St; ⏱ 7am-5.45pm Mon-Sat, from 9.30am Sun) by Cardiff Central train station.

Low-cost **Megabus** ( ☎ 0870 550 5050; www.megabus.com1) runs to London (3½ hours, seven daily), picking up by the castle.

## Car

Cardiff is accessed from the M4 motorway, taking junction 29/A48 from the east or junction 32/A470 from the west.

The nearest car-hire company to Cardiff Central train station is **Enterprise Rent-a-Car** (off Map p672; ☎ 2038 9222; www.enterprise.co.uk; 45 Penarth Rd).

## Train

Cardiff Central train station (Map p672), in the south of town, handles mainline services; **Valley Lines** ( ☎ 20 44 99 44; www.arrivatrainswales.com) local services also use Queen St Station (Map p672) to the northeast.

Regular services include Birmingham (£13.50, two hours, at least half-hourly), London Paddington (£24, two hours, at least half-hourly) and Shrewsbury (£29.50, two hours, half-hourly).

For portside connections with Irish ferries, trains run to Fishguard (£17.10, 2½ hours, once daily Monday to Saturday) and Pembroke Dock (£17.10, 3¼ hours, every two hours).

For fare and timetable details contact **National Rail Enquiries** ( ☎ 08457 48 49 50; www.nationalrail.co.uk).

## GETTING AROUND
### To/From the Airport

Bus X91 Airport Express shuttles between the airport and Central bus station (30 minutes, at least hourly). Regular trains run between Cardiff International Airport station (bus link to the airport) and Cardiff Central station (35 minutes, hourly). A taxi to the city centre costs about £25.

### Public Transport

Pick up a free bus and train map from the tourist office or the Cardiff Bus office.

**Cardiff Bus** (Map p672; ☎ 2066 6444; www.cardiffbus.com; Wood St; ⏱ 8.30am-5.30pm Mon-Fri, 9am-4.30pm Sat) has an office just opposite the central bus and train stations. Its services run all over town; present the exact change or a travel pass.

A local Day to Go pass (adult/child £3/2) is valid for travel on buses around Cardiff

---

### FREEWHEELING THROUGH WALES

All across Wales, the lush hills and gentle valleys are criss-crossed with great cycle routes. The longest is the national **Lôn Las Cymru trail** (NCN route 8), a 311-mile epic, mainly on roads, with some traffic-free sections, from Cardiff to Holyhead on the Isle of Anglesey.

Along the way you'll pass some achingly beautiful scenery, crossing the national parks of the Brecon Beacons and Snowdonia. For serious pedal-buffs the whole route can be completed in a week, and many prefer to start out in the more populated south.

Less time-consuming but equally scenic for a weekend escape is the 40-mile **Taff Trail** (NCN route 8) to Brecon, which starts from Cardiff's Mermaid Quay.

More details are available from the sustainable transport group **Sustrans** ( ☎ 0845 113 0065; www.sustrans.co.uk).

and area; a regional Network Day Rider pass (adult/child £6.50/4.30) covers a wider remit. Buy passes on the bus or at the Cardiff Bus office.

**Arriva Trains** ( ☎ 0845 6061 660; www.arriva trainswales.co.uk) offers the Freedom of Wales Flexi Pass tickets (All Wales/South Wales £69/47) with four days of train and eight days of bus-based unlimited travel, plus discounts on attractions. It's available at most railway stations and online at www.walesflexipass.co.uk.

### Taxi

Taxi ranks are located along St Mary St and outside the train station; or call **Dragon Taxis** ( ☎ 2033 3333).

# AROUND CARDIFF

To the north of Cardiff the hills and valleys bear testimony to Wales' industrial heritage, and are home to some of its impressive castles.

## CASTELL COCH

Fairy tales could be made at **Castell Coch** (Cadw; ☎ 2081 0101; adult/child £3.70/3.30; ⏱ 9.30am-5pm Apr, May & Oct, 9am-6pm Jun-Sep, 9.30am-4pm Mon-Sat & 11am-4pm Sun Nov-Mar), a Victorian fantasy built on the foundations of a real fortress. This was the summer retreat of Cardiff's coal kings, the Bute family and, as with Cardiff Castle (p671), the architect William Burges did a fine job of creating a fairy-tale hideaway. The castle is gloriously over-the-top, featuring a tremendous drawing room decorated with mouldings from *Aesop's Fables*. Located 5 miles northwest of Cardiff on the A470.

Stagecoach bus 26 (30 minutes, hourly Monday to Saturday, every two hours Sunday) runs from St Mary St to Tongwynlais, from where it's a steep 10-minute walk. It then continues to Caerphilly, for a two-castle day trip.

## CAERPHILLY CASTLE

It would be difficult to find a more beautiful medieval fortress than 13th-century **Caerphilly Castle** (Cadw; ☎ 2088 3143; adult/child £3.50/3; ⏱ 9.30am-5pm Apr-May & Oct, 9.30am-6pm Jun-Sep, 9.30am-4pm Mon-Sat, 11am-4pm Sun Nov-Mar), complete with three moats, six portcullises and five defensive doorways, not to mention a leaning tower that puts Pisa to shame (gashed open by subsidence). Located 7 miles northwest of Cardiff on the A469.

Stagecoach bus 26 (left) runs on to Caerphilly Castle from Castell Coch (45 minutes).

The new **Three Castles Pass** (adult/child £12/8) offers reduced-price entry to Castell Coch, Caerphilly Castle and Cardiff Castle.

## ST FAGANS NATIONAL HISTORY MUSEUM

The **St Fagans National History Museum** ( ☎ 2057 3500; www.museumwales.ac.uk/en/stfagans; St Fagans; admission free; ⏱ 10am-5pm), boasts a collection of 30 salvaged original buildings tracing a

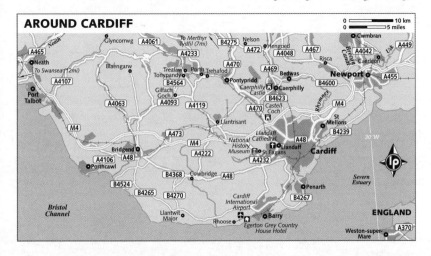

**AROUND CARDIFF**

---

**PUTTING BARRY BACK ON THE MAP**

The huge success of TV comedy show *Gavin and Stacey* has put the long-neglected seaside resort of Barry back on the map. It revels in its sense of faded grandeur and harks back to former era when Britain's seaside towns were a haven for summer holidaymakers.

With fans of the show making the pilgrimage to Barry to see the locations featured in the award-winning sitcom, the Vale of Glamorgan Council is looking into setting up a dedicated Gavin-and-Stacey town trail.

The trail could include the house in Trinity St, where Stacey's mother and Uncle Bryn live; the promenade and amusement arcade where Nessa works; and the Colcot Arms pub, where some scenes are filmed and the characters drink.

Glenda Kenyon, who lives in the Trinity St house and is moved out to a hotel when filming takes place, told WalesOnline.co.uk: 'A town trail idea based on the show is a great idea. I wouldn't mind tourists coming to see the house. I would even invite them in.'

The BAFTA (British Academy of Film and Television Arts) award-winning program has now been sold to international TV networks and a US version of the program is planned. For updated details and a full list of the locations, contact the **tourist office** ( ☎ 01446-747171; barrytic@valeofglamorgan .gov.uk; The Promenade; ⊙ 10am-5.30pm daily Easter-Sep).

If you're not a *Gavin and Stacey* fan, you can also follow in the footsteps of the June 2007 visit by Prince Charles and Camilla Parker Bowles to Barry. **Egerton Grey Country House Hotel** ( ☎ 01446-711666; www.egertongrey.co.uk; Porthkerry, Barry; s/d from £110/140; Ⓟ ⌨ ) is a luxurious and very traditional country-mansion property, located just a short drive from Cardiff International Airport. The combination of chunky antique furniture, old artworks and four-poster beds, plus a genteel, wood-panelled dining room, create a formula that plays well with visitors for a discreet weekend away. It certainly worked for Charles and Camilla, who took afternoon tea on the manicured lawn.

The hotel is located at Junction 33 of the M4 – follow the airport signs.

---

trail through Wales from Celtic times to the present day. Go to school or the wool mill before dropping into a local ironworkers' cottage from Merthyr Tydfil. The slightly twee craft displays will show you how to make clogs and barrels, among other things. Good

for children, with regular summer activities. Located at St Fagan's Castle, 4 miles west of Cardiff off the A4232.

From Cardiff Central take bus 32 (25 minutes, hourly Monday to Saturday, reduced service Sunday) to the museum car park.

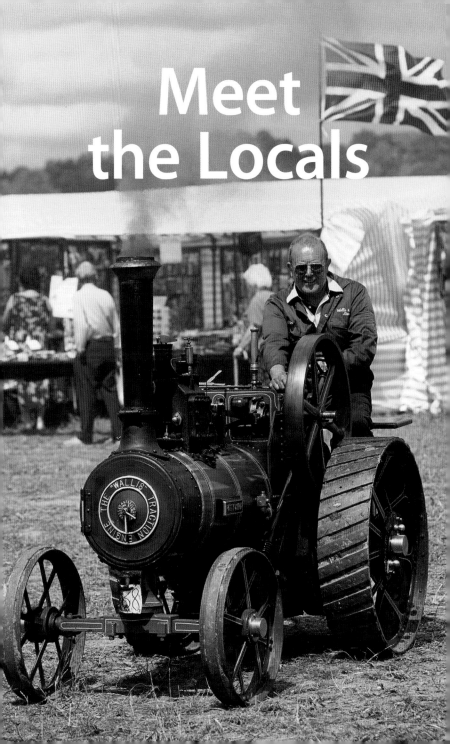

# Meet
# the Locals

# Culinary Cornwall

| NAME | Rick Stein |
| --- | --- |
| OCCUPATION | Celebrity chef, restaurant owner |
| RESIDENCE | Cornwall |

What makes Cornwall great for gourmands, in Rick's opinion, is that 'there's a natural enthusiasm in the British for the area and restaurants and hotels have started to live up to their expectations'. He doesn't believe that regeneration could overwhelm the region: 'Cornwall hasn't been overrun with tourism. It still has the appeal it used to. But of course it's changed. Padstow (p375) now is more prosperous and doesn't look like it did when I first opened a restaurant there more than 30 years ago.'

'There is somewhere in this overcrowded island where you can feel a little bit on your own'

Asked why he loves living and cooking in Cornwall, Rick says: 'The feeling that there is somewhere in this overcrowded island where you can feel a little bit on your own. And I love the local fish – red gurnards, John Dory, Dover sole, I just look at fish like that and think "bloody hell – this is fantastic".'

Any eating recommendations? 'Well apart from my own restaurants, of course! Fifteen Cornwall (p377), Jamie Oliver's place in Newquay, is good, as are the Beach Hut (p377), right underneath it on the beach, and Alba (p393) in St Ives.'

AS RELATED TO BELINDA DIXON

The fishing village of Padstow (p375) offers up delightful seaside culinary treats

GLENN BEANLAND

# Leicester's Lord Mayor

| NAME | Manjula Sood |
|------|--------------|
| OCCUPATION | Lord Mayor of Leicester 2008–09 |
| RESIDENCE | Leicester |

When Manjula Sood arrived in Leicester from the Punjab in 1970, it was snowing, dark and cold, and a very different place to the city it has become today. Leicester was not ready to accept different communities, says Manjula. The word multiculturalism didn't even exist, in Leicester or elsewhere, so she never dreamed she'd become the country's first Asian female Lord Mayor.

Today things are very different, she says. Over 38 languages are spoken in the city, and Leicester will soon become the UK's first ethnic-majority city.

Leicester is a more successful multicultural city than London or Birmingham because it truly celebrates its diversity, she says. The Caribbean Carnival (p444) is the biggest in the country after Notting Hill, the Diwali lights (p444) are the biggest in Europe, and there are major Hanukkah and Christian celebrations.

She loves living in the city because of this harmonious spirit. Leicester is the jewel of the Midlands, she says; you can feel the warmth wherever you go.

AS RELATED TO NANA LUCKHAM

'Over 38 languages are spoken in Leicester, and it will soon become the UK's first ethnic-majority city'

The Caribbean Carnival (p442) is one colourful way Leicester celebrates its cultural diversity

FLAB/PHOTOLIBRARY

# Ghost Tours

| NAME | Andy Dextrous |
| --- | --- |
| OCCUPATION | Ghost-tour guide |
| RESIDENCE | York |

There's a lot that Andy enjoys about living in York: 'Its outstanding architecture, the maze of 'snickleways' (narrow alleys), the street entertainment and festivals' and 'haunted pubs like the Old White Swan and the Golden Fleece (p549). In the streets around the Minster you're always within a breath of a ghost tale.' His list of places where a ghost-hunter would retire for a drink in the evenings includes the Punch Bowl, Stonegate, and the Blue Bell (p552).

**'In the streets around the Minster you're always within a breath of a ghost tale'**

And the highlights of Yorkshire? 'The Forbidden Corner' near Leyburn. Or drive to Levisham and take the North Yorkshire Moors Railway (p565) to Goathland, then walk to Mallyan Spout waterfall. Include a drink at the Birch Hall Inn at Beck Hole. For a good meal in York, go to El Piano (p550) for vegie and vegan food in a place that welcomes children.'

AS RELATED TO NEIL WILSON

The trains continue to run along the restored North Yorkshire Moors Railway (p565)

DAVID ELSE

# King of Hay

| | |
|---|---|
| **NAME** | Richard Booth |
| **OCCUPATION** | Bookseller and the self-proclaimed King of Hay |
| **RESIDENCE** | Hay-on-Wye |

'I came to Hay 40 years ago', says 69-year-old Richard. 'I was just down from Oxford and had a passionate belief to be king of my domain. I drifted into secondhand book selling, starting Richard Booth books in the 1960s.'

At this time Hay was an agricultural town, and, according to Booth, 'It suffered the standard fault of every rural location: the brain drain.' Booth created the book town concept 20 years before the arts festival came to Hay. There are now 12 towns in the international book town project.

'My intellectual contribution to the history of the western world was to restore the book to its rightful place as a source of democracy', says Richard. 'Hay is overrun by politicians and media tycoons during the Hay Festival these days, but we still always get more publicity,' Richard continues, 'as I've got my castle and crown jewels.' He goes on to explain, 'I'm still fighting to make a connection to the rural economy in the few years left to me. But maybe I've always been too ambitious.'

AS RELATED TO DAVID ATKINSON

'There are now 12 towns in the international book town project'

Bookworms regard Hay-on-Wye (p732) as a bookshop mecca

CHRISTOPHER SCOTT/PHOTOLIBRARY

# Welsh Folk Music

| NAME | Mabon ap Gwynfor |
| --- | --- |
| OCCUPATION | Manager, Tŷ Siamas (the National Centre for Welsh Folk Music) |
| RESIDENCE | Dolgellau |

'Ireland developed its musical culture as an industry,' says Mabon, 'but there's still not much knowledge of Welsh culture outside Wales.' He explains, 'Music tells the story of a nation. We know there was music in Wales 5000 years ago based on archaeological findings around Brecon. Folk music is the music of the people and the Welsh environment gives our music its context. By studying Welsh folk music we identify the outside influences on our culture. For example, Romany people brought the fiddle to Wales and adopted the harp.'

**'Today Welsh folk music is still raw, still very organic'**

Today Welsh folk music is still raw, still very organic. According to Mabon, 'It has its roots in the land. But the folk-music scene is on the ascendancy, boosted by the sense of positively redefining identity since devolution. When people come to Tŷ Siamas (p759), they learn about Welsh culture via its music. I hope they leave with a real sense of having been in another country and surrounded by another culture.'

AS RELATED TO DAVID ATKINSON

The evocative landscape of the Brecon Beacons (p724) inspires Welsh folk music

NICHOLAS REUSS

# Friendly Glasgow

| NAMES | Michael Stewart and Charlie Macmillan |
|-------|---------------------------------------|
| OCCUPATION | Voluntary sector |
| RESIDENCE | Glasgow |

'Glasgow might have a reputation as being a bit rough but it is still a very friendly city,' explain Michael and Charlie. 'It has its share of poorer areas, but it also has some fantastic architecture and green spaces. It's small enough that you can easily walk from the city centre to the trendy West End, or roam about the Merchant City (p811) and the famous East End, where you can visit the Barras market (p823) and the Barrowland Ballroom (p822).'

'For a cultural experience we would take visitors for a walk through the Botanic Gardens and down through Kelvingrove, taking in the Hunterian and Kelvingrove museums (p815), then across to Finnieston and along the river towards the East End and head to Glasgow Green to visit the People's Palace (p813).'

**'Glasgow might have a reputation as being a bit rough but it is still a very friendly city'**

Cafes and restaurants that Michael and Charlie recommend include Tinderbox (p821) and Offshore (p821) for coffee and cake; Doocot (p819) or anything in Princes Square (p823) for lunch; Asia Style (p819) for Asian food; Roastit Bubbly Jocks (p820) and Two Fat Ladies at the Buttery (p820) for Scottish cuisine; and Pintxo (p820) for something a little bit different.

AS RELATED TO NEIL WILSON

Glasgow's cobble-stoned Ashton Lane, in the West End, is popular with locals

MARGIE POLITZER

# Whisky Gallorkney

| NAME | Ian Tulloch |
|---|---|
| OCCUPATION | Whisky distillery worker |
| RESIDENCE | Orkney |

'We all do three jobs here at the distillery,' Ian explains, 'operate the peat kilns, the wash-house, and the stills. I've been here 18 years. The job hasn't changed extremely over that time but malt-whisky has become much more popular. I very rarely drink whisky myself. I get bad hangovers. Very bad!'

According to Ian the best thing about Orkney is that it's changeable. 'It's all here, ken? There's something about it anytime but it's beautiful in nice weather. Beautiful. Visitors would be surprised at how green and fertile the land is here though we're so far north. With the exception of trees, which we miss. And how friendly the locals are. I think the Orcadians are more approachable. Keen to talk. Ask them something in London, they just walk away!'

'The best thing about Orkney is it's changeable'

When asked about the mainland, Ian responds, 'The mainland? I've not been across in a long while. I'm quite happy here. I certainly support Scotland as a nation in football, rugby, but there's roots of Viking here make us different. But yes, I feel Scottish. I don't know about Scottish independence, mind. Might be too late now the oil's running out!'

AS RELATED TO ANDY SYMINGTON

The red sandstone cliffs near St John's Head, Orkney Islands (p952), stand proud

GRANT DIXON

# South Wales

Stretching over 100 miles from historic border-town Chepstow in the east, via the industrial heritage of the valleys, to the big-sky and sea views of the jagged Pembrokeshire coast in the west, south Wales really packs it in.

The Wye Valley is a beguiling place for messing about on the water, while Blaenavon provides a stark reminder of Wales' contribution to the Industrial Revolution. Dropping down to the coast, reborn Swansea is evolving on an almost daily basis as the city centre shifts towards the bay. Its near neighbours, Mumbles and the Gower, meanwhile, continue to win over new generations of devotees for their hip weekends and wave-riding breaks, respectively.

Back inland, rural Carmarthenshire is less visited but no less blessed by worthwhile attractions, its leading claim to fame a mecca for visitors inspired by the bible-black lyricism of the poet Dylan Thomas.

The biggest draw in the south, however, remains Pembrokeshire, where almost 200 miles of magical shoreline has been declared a national park, delineated by craggy cliffs, golden sands, chocolate-box villages and traditional seaside resorts. St Davids, Britain's smallest city, nestles at its westernmost tip and is home to Wales' holiest site.

To avoid the high-season hordes, head for North Pembrokeshire and lose yourself amid the juxtaposition of coastal path and ancient hills.

---

## HIGHLIGHTS

- Following in the footsteps of, and raising a glass to, the writer Dylan Thomas at his seaside home, **Laugharne** (p706)
- Walking, mountain-biking and exploring ancient history in North Pembrokeshire's gloriously untouched **Preseli Hills** (p720)
- Exploring the cathedral, or just soaking up the vibe, at Britain's smallest city, **St Davids** (p715)
- Digging into Wales' rich industrial history at the new **Blaenavon World Heritage Centre** (p698)
- Touring the developments at Swansea's up-and-coming **Maritime Quarter** (p701), followed by a seaside escape in style at nearby **Mumbles** (p702)
- Savouring a hot bath and cold beer after terminating the country-spanning Offa's Dyke Path in **Chepstow** (p696)

| ▩ POPULATION: 1.6 MILLION | ▩ AREA: 2911 SQ MILES | ▩ DALE IS THE SUNNIEST SPOT IN BRITAIN, AVERAGING 4 HOURS 12 MINUTES OF SUNSHINE DAILY |
| --- | --- | --- |

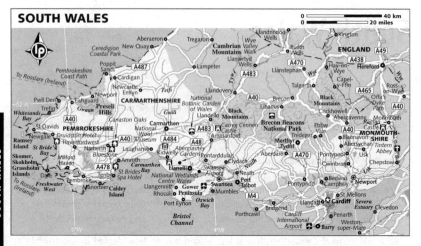

## Orientation & Information

The south Wales region stretches east from Cardiff to the English border and west to the far western tip of Wales at St Davids, encompassing the Pembrokeshire Coast National Park and Carmarthenshire to the northwest. The region is well served by tourist offices offering lots of information about the national park.

## Activities

For outdoor activities, the main draw is Pembrokeshire, with excellent canoeing, surfing and, most thrilling of all, coasteering (see p709). Walkers flock to the Pembrokeshire Coast Path, a 186-mile jaunt through some of Britain's most spectacular scenery.

Another favourite with surfers and walkers is the Gower Peninsula, while the Preseli Hills in North Pembrokeshire makes for fine mountain-biking territory.

Canoeing is possible on the River Wye, while hikers love Offa's Dyke Path and the Wye Valley Walk.

## Getting There & Around

Frequent train and bus services run from England, especially to Cardiff and Swansea. The South Wales Main Line runs east–west from Bristol in England via Cardiff to Swansea, continuing via the West Wales line to the west-coast ferry terminals of Fishguard and Pembroke Dock (both ports for Ireland). The famously scenic Heart of Wales line (see the boxed text, p736) terminates in Swansea.

**Arriva Trains** ( ☎ 0845 6061 660; www.arrivatrains wales.co.uk) offers the Freedom of Wales Flexi Pass (All Wales/South Wales £69/47) with four days of train and eight days of bus-based unlimited travel, plus discounts on attractions, available at most railway stations and online at www.walesflexipass.co.uk.

For more details contact **Traveline Cymru** ( ☎ 0871 200 2233; www.travelinecymru.org.uk).

# SOUTHEAST WALES

Southeast Wales is the country's industrial heartland, home to half of its population and much of its big business. But strike out beyond the urban sprawl and there's much to admire among the sweeping, history-rich uplands.

The sombre valleys of Taff, Rhymney and Rhondda were once the hubs of the iron and coal trades, which brought wealth and, later in the 1980s, despair in equal measure. Tourists are now realising that, if they want to uncover the true Wales, they need to see places like Blaenavon (a World Heritage Site), which are crucial in uncovering the true Wales.

To the east, the Wye Valley stretches north–south from the market town of Monmouth to Chepstow's moody castle, while Swansea, the childhood home of poet and writer Dylan Thomas, is the reborn second city and gateway to one of Wales' true gems, the Gower Peninsula.

## Activities

Despite its high population, the southeast offers picturesque walking and cycling through rolling valleys or on the wild, sandy Gower Peninsula, which is also the place to catch a wave.

### CANOEING

The River Wye is a great canoeing venue and Monmouth makes a good base town. Pick up *The Canoeist's Guide to the River Wye* (£5) from **Monmouth Canoe & Activity Centre** ( ☎ 01600-713461; www.monmouthcanoe.co.uk; Castle Yard, Monmouth).

### CYCLING

Two national road-cycling trails transect the region. The national Lôn Las Cymru (see Freewheeling Through Wales, p682) has two southern spurs, one from Cardiff along the Taff Vale to the Brecon Beacons, the other from Chepstow up the charming Vale of Usk to Abergavenny.

Exclusive to south Wales, the 220-mile **Celtic Trail** (Sustrans NCN routes 4, 47) runs from Chepstow in the east to Fishguard on the Pembrokeshire coast via Swansea (p701).

**Bicycle Beano** ( ☎ 01982-560471; www.bicycle-beano .co.uk) runs vegetarian cycling holidays in the Wye Valley. Tours are popular and irregular, so book well ahead.

### WALKING

One of Britain's best-known long-distance routes is the 177-mile **Offa's Dyke Path** national trail. Following the English–Welsh border between Chepstow in the south of Wales and Prestatyn on the north coast, the path follows the line of the 8th-century embankment built by Offa, king of Mercia, and crosses moorland, wide valleys and ancient forest. More information can be obtained from **Offa's Dyke Centre** ( ☎ 01547-528753; www.offasdyke.demon .co.uk/odc.htm; West St, Knighton; 10am-5pm Easter-Oct, reduced low season).

Less strenuous is the 136-mile **Wye Valley Walk** (www.wyevalleywalk.org) which criss-crosses the Welsh–English border as it follows the beautiful River Wye from Chepstow to Hafren Forest in Plynlimon (northeast of Rhayader). Pick up the *Wye Valley Walk Official Guide* (£7.95) from the tourist offices in Chepstow and Monmouth, together with details on shorter town, valley and coastal walks.

## Getting There & Around

Southeast Wales has an extensive transport network. The **Valley Lines** serves the Rhondda, Cynon, Taff and Rhymney Valleys from Cardiff. A Valley Lines Day Explorer ticket (£7) covers all travel on Valley Lines trains and Stagecoach and Rhondda buses in the area.

First Cymru bus has a South & West Wales FirstDay ticket (£5.50) covering all buses except the fast Cardiff–Swansea Shuttle.

Get details for the latter from **Traveline Cymru** ( ☎ 0871 200 2233; www.travelinecymru.org.uk).

## WYE VALLEY

Flowing 154 miles from its mountainous source at Plynlimon in Mid Wales to Chepstow, where it joins the River Severn, the River Wye flows through idyllic countryside. Between Monmouth and Chepstow a particularly picturesque 16-mile stretch runs through a steep-sided wooded vale amid excellent walking country. For more details see www.visitwyevalley.com.

Serving the valley between Chepstow and Monmouth, buses 65 and 69 run daily (p696).

## Monmouth (Trefynwy)
pop 9500

Advantageously positioned at the confluence of the Rivers Wye and Monnow, elegant Monmouth is an attractive base from which to explore the Lower Wye Valley. The town mixes Georgian and Victorian architecture with modern-day prosperity and feels quite English – a reflection of the fact it has switched countries over the centuries, although it is today anchored in Wales.

The market town's medieval castle was the birthplace of King Henry V, who conquered Normandy at the Battle of Agincourt in 1415. Many parts of Monmouth, including the main Agincourt Sq, are named after the battle.

With the Shire Hall closed for renovation until 2010, the **tourist office** ( ☎ 01600-713899; Priory St; 10am-5.30pm Easter-Oct, 10am-4pm Oct-Easter) is now permanently located next to the museum. Monnow St, the main drag, descends from Agincourt Sq to the pedestrianised Monnow Bridge, Britain's only intact late-13th-century fortified crossing.

### SIGHTS & ACTIVITIES

**Nelson Museum & Local History Centre** ( ☎ 01600-710630; Priory St; admission free; 10am-1pm & 2-5pm Mon-Sat, 2-5pm Sun Mar-Oct) houses a collection of artefacts related to Admiral Nelson, who visited Monmouth in 1802 en route to Pembrokeshire.

Just southwest on Castle Hill are the stumpy remains of **Monmouth Castle** and the **Castle and Regimental Museum** ( ☎ 01600-772175; Castle Hill; admission free; ⏰ 2-5pm daily Apr-Oct, 2-4pm Sat & Sun Nov-Mar), a volunteer-run labour of love. It's a low-key but worthwhile visit with some interesting examples of the region's military history.

**Monmouth Canoe & Activity Centre** ( ☎ 01600-713461; www.monmouthcanoe.co.uk; Castle Yard) runs river trips by canoe (per half-/full day £26/33) and kayak (£18/20), together with climbing and caving trips.

### SLEEPING & EATING

**Punch House** ( ☎ 01600-713855; Agincourt Sq; s/d £40/50; 🖳 wi-fi) A winning combination of traditional rooms and a lively pub for bar meals make this old coaching inn a popular spot at the very heart of town. There's even free wi-fi, and an elaborate four-poster room (£60) for some romantic seclusion from the beer-drinking regulars downstairs.

**Bistro Prego** ( ☎ 01600-712600; 7 Church St; www .pregomonmouth.co.uk; s/d/f £40/60/80) Rather handily offers rustic Italian fare in the bistro (noon to 2.30pm and 6.30pm to 10pm Monday to Saturday) and eight unfussy but comfortable rooms upstairs, including one family-sized option. It's in a quiet location tucked between the craft shops of Church St.

**ourpick** **Thyme Out** ( ☎ 01600-719339; 31-33 Monnow St; ⏰ 9am-5pm Mon-Sat) An excellent little place for good coffee, breakfasts and snack lunches, this little gem has a sunny patio and an equally sunny disposition. The cafe is located upstairs from a cookware shop, and the next-door clothes boutique is part of the same group.

**Henry's Cafe** ( ☎ 01600-772290; 4 Beaufort Arms Ct; ⏰ 9am-5pm Mon-Sat) A funky little cafe in a genteel courtyard mews, Henry's is a particularly family-friendly spot. There's a play area for kids inside with huge sofas and a shady terrace for parents to get their caffeine fix.

### GETTING THERE & AWAY

Buses 65 and 69 ply the scenic Wye Valley route to Chepstow via Tintern (50 minutes, every two hours Monday to Saturday, four on Sunday); bus 60 serves Newport (one hour, every two hours Monday to Saturday, four on Sunday); and bus 83 serves Abergavenny (50 minutes, about every two hours Monday to Saturday, four on Sunday).

## Around Monmouth

On the banks of the River Wye sits the kaleidoscopic vision of the late-13th-century **Tintern Abbey** (Cadw; ☎ 01291-689251; adult/child £3.70/3.30; ⏰ 9am-5pm daily Apr-Oct, 9.30am-4pm & 11am-4pm Sun Nov-Mar). With soaring walls, vast empty window frames and the huge space of the presbytery, all mottled in grey, pink and gold, it's easy to see how this former Cistercian foundation inspired both the artist Turner and poet Wordsworth.

Tintern functioned as an abbey until the Dissolution in 1536–40. Compared with other religious sites destroyed at the same time, a considerable amount remains. However, the abbey tends to be besieged by coach parties, so visit either early or late in the day to savour the peaceful atmosphere, or make for the trailhead of the **Wye Valley Walk** opposite the main entrance to escape the hordes.

Tintern Abbey is located 4 miles north of Monmouth on the scenic A466. Buses 65 and 69 ply the route (left).

Britain's final medieval fortress was **Raglan Castle** (Cadw; ☎ 01291-690228; adult/child £3.10/2.70; ⏰ 9am-5pm daily Apr-Oct, 9.30am-4pm Mon-Sat, 11am-4pm Sun Nov-Mar) and it remains a prime example of late-medieval grandeur. Built in the 15th and 16th centuries, the castle was a military success and endured one of the longest sieges of the Civil War before being wrecked and abandoned shortly afterwards.

Raglan Castle lies 7 miles west of Monmouth on the A40 to Abergavenny. Bus 60 runs from Monmouth to Raglan village (20 minutes, every two hours Monday to Saturday, four on Sunday), then it's a five-minute walk.

## CHEPSTOW (CAS GWENT)
pop 15,000

Chepstow looks a bit shabby compared with neighbouring Monmouth, but thankfully a regeneration scheme is now bringing new life to the high street with an array of public artworks, while plans are afoot for a riverside marina on the banks of the Wye, where Brunel built the Old Wye Bridge, the first bridge between England and Wales.

Chepstow lies on the border with England, and the Gloucester Hole, a patriotic St George's Cross daubed on the rocks on the far (English) side of the river, marks the border.

Today Chepstow is best known for its **racecourse** ( ☎ 01291-222260; www.chepstow-racecourse .co.uk), home to the Welsh National, and as the southern trailhead of **Offa's Dyke Path** (p738).

## Orientation & Information

The Town Arch in the 13th-century Port Wall (Customs Wall), located between Moor and High Sts, marks the entrance to the main town. Follow sloping High, Middle and Bridge Sts down to the castle, tourist office and Old Wye Bridge. The bus station is on Thomas St, west of the Town Arch, and the train station lies south of the castle and town centre.

The friendly **tourist office** ( ☎ 01291-623772; ⓥ 10am-5.30pm Easter-Oct, 10am-3.30pm Oct-Easter) is located in the castle car park. Ask about local walking trails.

## Sights

Built by the English in a superb riverside location, **Chepstow Castle** (Cadw; ☎ 01291-624065; adult/child £3.70/3.30; ⓥ 9am-5pm Apr-Oct, 9.30am-4pm & 11am-4pm Sun Nov-Mar) is a large fortress best viewed from the opposite English riverbank. Construction began in 1067, one year after the Norman Conquest; it is one of the oldest castles in Wales and one of the first built of stone.

Opposite the castle, **Chepstow Museum** ( ☎ 01291-625981; Bridge St; admission free; ⓥ 10.30am-5.30pm Mon-Sat & 2-5pm Sun Jul-Sep, 11am-5pm Mon-Sat & 2-5pm Sun Oct-Jun) has social- and industrial-history displays in an elegant 18th-century house, including prints of the castle and Wye Valley through the ages.

## Sleeping & Eating

**Afon Gwy** ( ☎ 01291-620158; www.afongwy.co.uk; 28 Bridge St; s/d £50/70) The new owners of this little B&B, located 50m northeast of the tourist office, have been steadily upgrading facilities since taking over. The rooms are comfortably appointed, and the downstairs brasserie and terrace overlook the river for a sundowner.

**Castle View Hotel** ( ☎ 01291-620349; www.hotel chepstow.co.uk; Bridge St; s/d £55/77) This old coach house opposite the castle is looking smarter and fresher for its refurbishment, and the upgrading of the in-house restaurant is a welcome touch. The Cottage Suite is now the best room in the house, with dark furnishings and views across to the castle.

**Petrus** ( ☎ 01291-626868; 18 The Back; ⓥ lunch & dinner Tue-Sat, lunch Sun; mains around £16) This smart new eatery boasts a riverside location and a strong Mediterranean influence. The 48-cover, black-and-white-motif dining room looks elegant with a black onyx carved figure as its central feature. The all-day tapas bar offers lighter snacks

**Coffee #1** ( ☎ 01291-637403; www.coffee1.co.uk; 1-2 Beaufort Sq; ⓥ 9am-6pm Mon-Sat, 10am-5pm Sun) Good for a snack, coffee or smoothie is this local chain, which brings an espresso-fuelled shot of top-notch coffee culture to south Wales. It's a light, airy place where mothers with babies and pensioners are all made welcome by the smiley staff.

## Getting There & Away

National Express coach services 508/509 head for London (£21, three hours, once daily), while coach 201 goes to Cardiff (£5, 50, one hour, once daily) and Swansea (£10.50, two hours, once daily).

Buses 65 and 69 ply the scenic Wye Valley route to Monmouth via Tintern (50 minutes, two hourly Monday to Saturday, four on Sunday).

Trains serve Cardiff (£6.30, 45 minutes, at least every two hours) and Gloucester (£6.40, 30 minutes, at least every two hours).

# BLAENAVON
**pop 6000**

The south Wales valleys to the north of Cardiff were for years a tourist no-go zone after the weakening of the local industry, which once employed a quarter of a million men in iron and coal production, sent the valleys into terminal decline.

Today the only remnants of the 18th- and 19th-century Industrial Revolution are a few heritage sites and a collection of gruff towns and villages that bear testimony to Wales' most important recent history.

Of these, Blaenavon is home to the greenest shoots of regeneration. In November 2000 Unesco awarded World Heritage status to the town, together with a large area of surrounding upland that was key to the iron trade; ever since then, both confidence and the local population have grown.

## Information

The landmark new project in town is the Blaenavon World Heritage Centre (p698), converted from an old school with a modern new wing. It is home to the town's new official

SOUTH WALES

tourist office. The tourist office provides an excellent set of maps for walking trails around the region and information for exploring the region's industrial heritage.

### Sights & Activities

The **Blaenavon World Heritage Centre** ( ☎ 01495-742333; www.world-heritage-blaenavon.org.uk; Church Rd; admission free; ☺ 9am-5pm Tue-Sat Apr-Sep, 9am-4pm Tue-Sat Oct-Mar) is also home to an excellent museum, which explores the the the industrial heritage of the region via a series of highly educational audiovisual displays. The building is equipped with wheelchair access.

Blaenavon's other main attraction is the **Big Pit: National Coal Museum** ( ☎ 01495-790311; www .museumwales.ac.uk; admission free; ☺ 9.30am-5pm Feb-Nov, 10am-4.30pm Dec & Jan, guided tours 10am-3.30pm). Originally operational from 1880 to 1990, it's hard to call this an attraction in the traditional sense. What you experience on the trip down the 90m shaft, guided by an ex-miner, is a firsthand account of the trials and tribulations of Valley life at the height of the Industrial Revolution.

**Blaenavon Ironworks** (Cadw; ☎ 01495-792615; admission free; ☺ 9.30am-4.30pm daily year-round, 10am-5pm Sat & 10am-4.30pm Sun Apr-Oct), dating from 1789, was the largest and most advanced in the world. Today the museum is one of Europe's best-preserved 18th-century ironworks. The scale of the works is mind-boggling and stands as a sobering depiction of Wales' (and Britain's) lost industrial prowess.

The **Blaenavon Community Heritage Museum** ( ☎ 01495-790991; The Library, Lion St; www.blaenafon heritagemuseum.org.uk; ☺ 10am-4pm Mon-Thu, 10am-1pm Sat Apr-Sep, 10am-4pm Mon, Tue & Thu, 10am-1pm Sat Oct-Mar) has a lively collection of memorabilia about Alexander Cordell, who wrote about the industrial heritage of the region.

On Broad St, the main drag, the award-winning **Blaenavon Cheddar Co** ( ☎ 01495-793123; www.chunkofcheese.co.uk; 80 Broad St; ☺ 10am-5pm Mon-Sat) is a champion for Blaenavon and involving the community in its renaissance. The cheese shop has a range of handmade cheeses, some matured down the mine shaft of the Big Pit – try the Dragon's Breath. The same people arrange guided **walking and mountain-biking tours** (walks per person from £2.50) for all ability ranges, plus offer **bike hire** (half-/full day £10/15); they can also cater for disabled cyclists with adapted bikes.

### Sleeping & Eating

It's best to base yourself at Monmouth or Abergavenny. However, a couple of doors down from Blaenavon Cheddar Co, **Lipton's Cafe** ( ☎ 01495-792828; 76-78 Broad St; ☺ 9am-4.30pm Mon-Sat) is the best place in town for a bacon roll and a cup of tea.

### Getting There & Away

Blaenavon lies 15 miles north of Newport along the A4043 and 8 miles southwest of Abergavenny off the A465 and A4042.

Stagecoach bus 30 (40 minutes, hourly Monday to Saturday) and bus X24 (50 minutes, every 10 minutes Monday to Saturday) both run to Newport. The new Beacons Bus service 15 also runs to Newport (p727).

The nearest train station is at Cwmbran, 10 miles south of Blaenavon on the A4051.

# SWANSEA & THE GOWER

One of the most vibrant regions of south Wales is around Swansea, where the country's second city is enjoying a major renaissance; its seaside neighbour, Mumbles, is growing as a destination its own right; and the Gower Peninsula is becoming a mecca for families and outdoors enthusiasts in equal measure. For more details see www.visitswansea bay.com.

## SWANSEA (ABERTAWE)
pop 226,400

Swansea has been synonymous with the poet Dylan Thomas ever since he famously branded the city an 'ugly lovely town'. But Thomas wouldn't recognise his home town these days. When we visited, it was a blur of cranes and construction teams with the regeneration of the erstwhile run-down docklands district and a long-term vision to shift the whole city centre south towards the 5-mile sweep of Swansea Bay, the city's greatest natural asset.

SA1, Swansea's flagship new development, is located on the city's main eastern approach, where the former Prince of Wales dock is being transformed into a new marina. The 10-year redevelopment, including office blocks, residential riverside properties, hotels and restaurants, is estimated to cost around £400 million. Across the River Tawe from SA1, the cranes are surrounding Meridian Quay. At its heart will be the 350ft-tall, 29-storey Ferrara

---

### COOL CYMRU

With such a small population and a culture that's been overshadowed by England for centuries, it's something of a surprise that Wales has produced plenty of musical maestros who have hit the big time. Everyone knows perma-tanned warbler Tom Jones, who, together with the likes of Shirley Bassey, has kept Welsh pop on the map since the 1960s.

In the 1980s the Alarm emerged as Wales' leading act, with a string of U2-inspired rock ballads to its name. More culturally credible is John Cale, who split from the Velvet Underground to become a respected solo performer and producer.

Today it's guitar-driven bands that mainly rule the roost. Major chart names are indie-faves Manic Street Preachers and nu-metallers Lostprophets, while the genre-defying Super Furry Animals produced the biggest-selling Welsh-language album of all time, the dreamy *Mwng*. Lead singer Gruff Rhys also made it onto the nomination list of the 2008 Nationwide Mercury Prize for his offshoot project, Neon Neon.

Latterly, while Charlotte Church has reinvented herself as a TV presenter and folk singer Jem has been planning her return from a recording hiatus, the new wave of Welsh rock has been gathering pace. Bridgend quartet Bullet For My Valentine play supercharged rock, multi-instrumentalist Christopher Rees carries the troubadour torch, Kate Le Bon ploughs the re-energised folk furrow, and Euros Childs has shifted his unique folk sound from the sadly defunct Gorky's Zygotic Mynci into the solo arena. Most bizarre of all, actor Rhys Ifans is living out his rock-star fantasies as lead singer of The Peth.

The most successful Welsh artist of recent times is, however, Duffy, the Dusty Springfield sound-alike, whose *Rock Ferry* was one of the biggest-selling albums of 2008. Soul singer Aimee Anne Duffy hails from Nefyn on the Lyn Peninsula (p768) and remains fiercely proud of her Welsh roots.

---

Tower, featuring a rooftop restaurant with views across to the Bristol Channel. It will be the tallest residential building in Wales when it opens in 2009.

Over the next few years the ongoing regeneration will see the St David's shopping centre knocked down, the run-down no-man's-land of Oystermouth Rd become a long boulevard with footbridge links to the bay, an ambitious overhaul of the public transport system to link the city and Mumbles, and a much-needed overhaul of the shabby Quadrant Bus Station. The latter, a £11m transport interchange, is planned to open in summer 2010. The new Metro link, featuring StreetCar vehicles (essentially high-tech bus hybrids), will start servicing key locations between Morriston Hospital and Mumbles, via the City Centre, in spring 2009.

Mumbles, the seaside village on urban Swansea's doorstep, is a thriving haven for weekend escapes, with some stylish new businesses lending a prosperous, upmarket feel to the small centre. It has even managed to transcend its association as the childhood home of the actress Catherine Zeta Jones – although coach parties still stop for a peek at the mansion she built for her parents on the peninsula.

While the majority of places to stay and eat are strung out along Mumbles Rd, Newton Rd is the new regional hub for boutique shopping. Even in low season it's popular for walking and water sports.

While clearly more prosperous, Mumbles is also earmarked for regeneration money, including the proposed £39-million renaissance of the historic Mumbles Pier (for details check out www.mumbles-pier.co.uk). Among the proposals is a new museum dedicated to the history of the world's first passenger railway service, the Mumbles train, which made its first journey on 25 March 1807, travelling along the seafront from Swansea to the then fishing village of Mumbles. A new aquarium and sea-life centre are also planned for the pier, while the Pier Hotel would be demolished to make way for a luxury 150-bed hotel and spa.

## Orientation & Information

The city centre is currently based around the leafy Castle Sq, a half-mile walk southwest of the train station along High St and the Kingsway. The bus station and tourist office are just west by the Quadrant Shopping Centre.

# SWANSEA

**SOUTH WALES**

| INFORMATION | |
|---|---|
| Central Library............... | 1 D4 |
| Main Post Office............ | 2 D3 |
| Tourist Office................. | 3 D3 |

| SIGHTS & ACTIVITIES | |
|---|---|
| Action Bikes................... | 4 E3 |
| Dylan Thomas Centre..... | 5 F2 |
| Dylan Thomas's Birthplace... | 6 A2 |
| Dyland Thomas Statue.... | (see 26) |
| Glynn Vivian Art Gallery.. | 7 D1 |
| LC.................................. | 8 E3 |
| Mission Gallery.............. | 9 E3 |

| | |
|---|---|
| National Waterfront Museum. | 10 E3 |
| Swansea Museum........... | 11 E3 |

| SLEEPING | |
|---|---|
| Christmas Pie B&B......... | 12 A2 |
| Morgans Hotel............... | 13 E2 |
| Morgans Townhouse...... | 14 F2 |
| White House.................. | 15 A3 |
| Windsor Lodge Hotel...... | 16 D1 |

| EATING | |
|---|---|
| Bizzie Lizzie's Bistro....... | 17 B2 |
| Chelsea Cafe................. | 18 E2 |

| | |
|---|---|
| Didier & Stephanie's....... | 19 C3 |
| Govinda's...................... | 20 D2 |
| Joe's Ice Cream Parlour... | 21 B3 |
| La Braseria..................... | 22 E2 |
| Starvin' Jacks Coffee Shop & | |
| Diner............................ | 23 D2 |

| DRINKING | |
|---|---|
| No Sign Bar................... | 24 E2 |
| Queen's Hotel............... | 25 E3 |
| Uplands Tavern.............. | 26 A2 |

| ENTERTAINMENT | |
|---|---|
| Dylan Thomas Theatre..... | 27 E3 |
| Escape.......................... | 28 D2 |
| Monkey Cafe Bar........... | 29 E2 |
| Oceana.......................... | 30 D2 |
| Swansea Grand Theatre.... | 31 D3 |

| TRANSPORT | |
|---|---|
| Avis.............................. | 32 D2 |
| Quadrant Bus Station..... | 33 D3 |

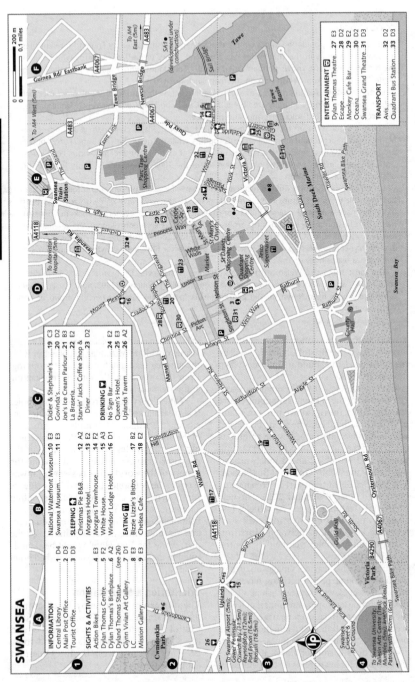

Mumbles village is 5 miles west along Oystermouth Road, while the Gower Peninsula starts at Mumbles Head.

**Central Library** ( ☎ 01792-516750; Civic Centre; ⌚ 8.30am-8pm Tue-Fri, 10am-4pm Sat-Sun) Superb new and modern library with extensive computer facilities and free internet access.

**Main post office** ( ☎ 01792-464140; Quadrant Shopping Centre; ⌚ 9am-5.30pm Mon-Sat) Now moved to new premises upstairs from WH Smith, with a Costa coffee shop.

**Morriston Hospital** ( ☎ 01792-702222; Heol Maes Eglwys, Morriston) Accident and Emergency department, 5 miles north of centre off the A4118.

**Mumbles tourist office** ( ☎ 01792-361302; info@mumblestic.co.uk; Methodist Church, Mumbles Rd; ⌚ 10am-4.30pm Mon-Sat) Independently run with heaps of advice, information and service with a smile.

**Swansea tourist office** ( ☎ 01792-468321; tourism@swansea.gov.uk; Plymouth St; ⌚ 9.30am-5.30pm Mon-Sat year-round, plus 10am-4pm Sun Jun-Sep) Located next to the Quadrant Bus Station. Mumbles tourist office is more helpful.

## Sights & Activities
### MARITIME QUARTER

Swansea's new landmark building, the **National Waterfront Museum** ( ☎ 01792-638950; www.waterfrontmuseum.co.uk; admission free; ⌚ 10am-5pm, to 8pm first Wed of month Mar-Sept) is a superb resource for the city and its visitors. The 15 hands-on galleries explore Wales' industrial history and the impact of industrialisation on its people, from 1750 to the present day – allow half a day to explore the whole thought-provoking space. Facilities are top-notch, with baby changing, play areas for kids and access for travellers with disabilities, plus a cosy little coffee shop called Cream (open 10am to 5pm), and a bookshop stocking a comprehensive range of Welsh-interest books and guides.

Elegant **Swansea Museum** ( ☎ 01792-653763; Victoria Rd; admission free; ⌚ 10am-5pm Tue-Sun), opened in 1841, is Wales' oldest museum, featuring a collection of Egyptology and Swansea ceramics.

**Mission Gallery** ( ☎ 01792-652016; www.missiongallery.co.uk; Gloucester Pl; admission free; ⌚ 11am-5pm) is a new contemporary art and craft collection with an adjoining exhibition space in a converted chapel. It stocks a range of art and design magazines.

**LC** ( ☎ 01792-466500; www.thelcswansea.co.uk; Oystermouth Rd; waterpark adult/child £7/4; ⌚ 6.30am-10pm Mon-Fri, 8am-9pm Sat-Sun, waterpark 4-9pm Mon-Fri, 9am-8pm Sat-Sun), the new £32-million leisure centre, marks Swansea's growing reputation as a centre for surfing and water sports. Combining a high-quality waterpark and leisure centre, the building features a flume ride and an indoor wave pool, while the upper-level gymnasium offers sweeping views of Swansea Bay and Mumbles.

### GLYNN VIVIAN ART GALLERY

Italianate in style, this inspirational **gallery** ( ☎ 01792-516900; www.glynnviviangallery.org; Alexandra Rd; admission free; ⌚ 10am-5pm Tue-Sun) showcases Welsh talent, from the landscapes of Richard Wilson to the more contemporary work of Ceri Richards. It's a little oasis of high culture in the city.

### CYCLING

Part of the **Celtic Trail** (Sustrans National Route 4) hugs the bay from downtown Swansea to Mumbles. Hire bikes at **Action Bikes** ( ☎ 01792-464640; 5 St David's Sq, ⌚ 9am-5.30pm Mon-Sat).

## Festivals & Events

**Swansea Bay Summer Festival** (www.swanseabayfestival.net) Waterfront-focused festival of shows, events and family attractions from May to September.

**Swansea Film Festival** (www.swanseafilmfestival.com) For cinema buffs in June. Part of the Swansea Bay Summer Festival.

**Escape to the Park** (www.escapefestival.com) Wales' biggest outdoor dance-music festival, staged by Swansea University in June.

**Swansea Festival of Music and the Arts** (www.swanseafestival.co.uk) Cultural showcase at venues around town in early October.

**Dylan Thomas Festival** (www.dylanthomasfestival.org) Held annually from 27 October to 9 November (the dates of Thomas' birth and death), this event celebrates Thomas' life through talks and performances at the Dylan Thomas Centre (see the boxed text, p702).

## Sleeping
### CENTRAL SWANSEA

**Windsor Lodge Hotel** ( ☎ 01792-642158; www.windsor-lodge.co.uk; Mt Pleasant; s/d £45/70; Ⓟ ) Quiet and relaxed, the 18th-century Windsor Lodge is low on frills but close to the city centre and good value. The in-house restaurant has now closed so it's B&B only.

**Morgans Townhouse** ( ☎ 01792-484848; www.morganshotel.co.uk; Somerset Pl; r from £95) Opened in 2006 across town from Morgans Hotel, this is its more budget-oriented annexe, with contemporary rooms set in an extended

### SWANSEA'S DYLAN THOMAS LANDMARKS

By following the Dylan Thomas trail through the 'ugly, lovely town' you can soak up the atmosphere that shaped and inspired his gritty, wild-boy poetry.

Head for the Maritime Quarter and make your starting point the **Dylan Thomas Centre** ( ☎ 01792-463980; www.dylanthomas.com; Somerset Pl; 🕒 10am-4.30pm). Aside from the collection of memorabilia, what really brings his work to life is a series of readings on CD, including the booming baritone of Richard Burton reading *Under Milk Wood* and Thomas himself reading *Do Not Go Gentle Into That Good Night*, the celebrated paean to his dying father.

You can stop for a coffee, a snack lunch and a chance to read some of his work, surrounded by black-and-white photographs of the author, at **Dylan's Books n' Bites** ( 🕒 10am-4.30pm). This bookshop-cafe stocks his entire works. The centre also produces a series of walking-tour leaflets to follow trails around the region that explore different aspects of Thomas' life and work.

Next head south along Adelaide St into Gloucester Pl to catch the latest performance at the **Dylan Thomas Theatre** ( ☎ 01792-473238; www.dylanthomastheatre.org.uk; Dylan Thomas Sq, The Marina, Swansea), the tiny, waterfront theatre where Thomas himself trod the boards during the early 1930s. The theatre always stages a perennially packed-out production of *Under Milk Wood* during the Dylan Thomas Festival (p701). A bronze statue behind the theatre finds Thomas contemplatively looking out across the marina.

Back on the corner of Gloucester Pl and York St, the **Queen's Hotel** ( ☎ 01792-521531) is one of the last few traditional old pubs left in town and a was favourite haunt for Thomas when he worked as a cub reporter at the *South Wales Evening Post* round the corner – the offices are still there. It's a cosy, characterful place for a pint and some no-nonsense pub grub at lunchtime (mains around £4).

Finally, jump in a taxi and head for the Uplands region of Swansea, for **Dylan Thomas' birthplace** (5 Cwmdonkin Dr) and childhood home, which has been recently restored and now offers B&B accommodation.

And, if you're feeling inspired by this excursion, then head for Laugharne (p706) in Carmarthenshire to continue the pilgrimage.

---

Regency property. It competes with the likes of Premier Travel Inn but retains a real sense of individual style.

**OUR PICK Morgans Hotel** ( ☎ 01792-484848; www.morganshotel.co.uk; Somerset Pl; r from £125; Ⓟ 🖳 ) In a town centre dominated by chain hotels and identikit hotel rooms, Morgans is a real gem. Swansea's first boutique hotel kick-started the gentrification of the formerly run-down marina area and remains the city's leading property several years on. The rooms are sleek, the champagne bar a magnet for the local glitterati and the restaurant reassuringly buzzy. But Morgans is also a pretension-free zone: think bacon butties at breakfast and staff happy to share a joke.

### UPLANDS

**Christmas Pie B&B** ( ☎ 01792-480266; www.christmaspie.co.uk; 2 Mirador Cres; s/d from £43/65; Ⓟ 🖳 wi-fi) Modern, well designed and professionally run, this new B&B offers three en suite rooms in a quiet location, handy for the university district. The rooms all boast slightly different features but wood finishes and sleek modern bathrooms are de rigueur. Free wi-fi is attracting business travellers, so book ahead.

**White House** ( ☎ 01792-473856; www.thewhitehousehotel.co.uk; 4 Nyanza Tce; s/d from £45/75; 🖳 ) This friendly, family-run guesthouse remains one of the long-serving stalwarts of the local scene. The nine en suite rooms have been given some fresh new touches, such as flat-screen TVs and wi-fi internet.

### MUMBLES

**OUR PICK Patricks with Rooms** ( ☎ 01792-360199; www.patrickswithrooms.com; 638 Mumbles Rd; d £110; Ⓟ ) A charming, upmarket restaurant (lunch is served from noon to 2.30pm and dinner from 6.30pm to 9.30pm Monday to Saturday) with rooms, Patricks has carved a solid reputation for its stylish, individually styled rooms and excellent modern British menus based around the best local produce. It's also surprisingly child friendly. The colonial-styled lounge area is ideal for lazy coffees, newspapers and idly gazing out to sea. At the time of writing expansion plans were afoot to add six new rooms and a gym in a nearby annexe – expect more of the same high standard.

**knabrock** ( ☎ 01792-361818; www.knabrock.com; 734 Mumbles Rd; r £120, with sea views from £160; P 🖳 ) This sexy, unashamedly modernist boutique property has funky rooms, a restaurant with a crushed-velour decor and a purple-and-black-hued bar. Some early reports of the food were somewhat mixed but it has, by now, hopefully, developed the substance to match the innate style. The restaurant serves meals from noon to 3pm and 7pm to late daily in summer, Tuesday to Sunday in winter, with a few fancy flourishes to the menu to reflect the decor.

## Eating

### CENTRAL SWANSEA

**Govinda's** ( ☎ 01792-468469; 8 Craddock St; mains £4-10; noon-3pm Mon-Thu, noon-6pm Fri & Sat) Fresh from refurbishment, Govinda's still serves up wonderful vegetarian dishes with an Indian twist. It also does takeaway and is a hub for information about alternative therapy and arts. Don't miss the organic juices – a health boost in a glass.

**Starvin' Jacks Coffee Shop & Diner** ( ☎ 01792-457453; 21 Park St; mains around £5; 9am-5pm Mon-Sat; 🖳 wi-fi) Friendly no-frills cafe with three locations around town, of which this is the most central. Good coffee, smoothies, snacks and vegetarian options, plus new, free wi-fi, make this a winner in the budget category.

**Chelsea Cafe** ( ☎ 01792-464068; www.thechelseacafe .co.uk; 17 St Mary's St; mains around £16, 2-course lunches £12; lunch & dinner Mon-Sat) A discreet and elegant dining rooms, tucked away behind the frenzy of Wind St. Chef Andrew Hanson has won numerous plaudits for his fresh fish dishes, specials of which are displayed daily on a chalkboard. With mains around £16 and a two-course lunch for £12, it's well worth seeking out.

**La Braseria** ( ☎ 01792-469683; www.labraseria.com; 29 Wind St; mains around £19; lunch & dinner Mon-Sat) With its rustic Spanish bodega ambience and extensive collection of French and Spanish wines, plus vintage ports, La Braseria brings a touch of the Mediterranean to the fun pubs of Wind St. Seafood and steaks are the speciality choices, with à la carte mains around £19.

The student area around St Helen's Rd, located to the west of the centre, has plenty of cheap and cheerful snack joints – most of them hit-and-miss. But these three places are worth seeking out:

**Bizzie Lizzie's Bistro** ( ☎ 01792-473379, 55 Walter Rd; mains around £9; lunch & dinner) Set in the original kitchens of an 18th-century house, this family-run bistro serves up tasty home-cooked meals using local produce from the Bay and Swansea market. It's an unpretentious place with cheery red-checked tablecloths and an alfresco garden for summer evenings.

**Didier & Stephanie's** ( ☎ 01792-655603; 56 St Helen's Rd; mains around £15; lunch & dinner Tue-Sat) Well regarded for its range of French-themed dishes, refined setting and attentive service, it offers a good-value lunch menu (two/three courses £13.50/16.50).

**Joe's Ice Cream Parlour** ( ☎ 01792-653880; www .joes-icecream.co.uk; 85 St Helen's Rd; 11am-9pm Mon-Fri, noon-8pm Sat & Sun) For an ice-cream sundae or an Italian-style cone, locals love Joe's, a Swansea institution since 1922. There's also a Joe's sister branch ( ☎ 01792-368212; 524 Mumbles Rd) in Mumbles.

### MUMBLES

**Davies of Mumbles** ( ☎ 01792-366648; 520 Mumbles Rd; 8am-5pm Mon-Sat) A no-frills friendly bakery-cum-coffee shop for a snack or fresh bread.

**Verdi's Cafe & Gelateria** ( ☎ 01792-369135; Knab Rock; 10am-9.30pm summer, 10am-6pm winter) A sunny, family-run cafe with a huge sun-kissed terrace overlooking the bay. The locals love this place for its authentic Italian touches: think real coffee, great pizzas and heavenly ice-cream sundaes.

**Mermaid** ( ☎ 01792-367744; Mumbles Rd; set lunches £12.50, mains around £14; lunch & dinner Mon-Sat, lunch Sun) Fresh-from-the-bay mains and local organic produce are the cornerstones of this sleek, sea-facing eatery. The restaurant is divided between a lounge area for tapas and the main restaurant with its airy feel and tasty mains. Don't miss the good-value, two-course set lunch (£12.50).

## Drinking

Brace yourself. The big night out on Wind St is the reserve of the white-stiletto and alcopops crowd. To observe the antics from a safe distance, the **No Sign Bar** ( ☎ 01792-465300; 56 Wind St) is a traditional, wood-panelled institution, a favourite of Dylan Thomas, for a pint of real ale while browsing the newspapers. The window seats, looking out across the fun pubs and acres of goose-bumped flesh, offer a frisson of schadenfreude.

For a different kind of entertainment, the **Uplands Tavern** ( ☎ 01792-458242; www.uplandstavern

.co.uk; 42 Uplands Cres) was another of Thomas' favourite drinking dens and still serves a quiet daytime pint in the Dylan Thomas snug. Today it's the hub of the city's live music scene, with bands playing most nights to a mixed crowd of students and locals.

## Entertainment
*Buzz* magazine (free from the tourist office or bars around town) has its finger on the pulse of the local scene.

### NIGHTCLUBS
**Monkey Cafe Bar** ( ☎ 01792-480822; www.monkeycafe .co.uk; 13 Castle St; ☽ noon-2am Sun-Thu, to 4am Fri-Sat) Student favourite Monkey has a dance floor and chill-out room upstairs with visiting DJs, and a bar area downstairs for drinks and bar food (11am to 6pm), including vegetarian options. At the time of writing the owners were expanding next door to increase the bar and dining area.

The city's two most popular clubbing venues are **Escape** ( ☎ 01792-652854; www.escape swansea.com; Northampton Lane; ☽ 10pm-3am Thu-Sat) and **Oceana** ( ☎ 0845 293 2872; www.oceanaclubs.com /swansea; 72 The Kingsway; ☽ 10pm-4am Thu-Sat) with resident DJs and big-name guests.

### THEATRE
**Swansea Grand Theatre** ( ☎ 01792-475715; www .swansea.gov.uk/grandtheatre; Singleton St; ☽ box office 9.30am-8pm Mon-Sat, Sun with performances) Offers a broad program of events, and access for travellers with disabilities.
**Taliesin Arts Centre** ( ☎ 01792-602060; www .taliesinartscentre.co.uk; Singleton Park; ☽ box office 10am-6pm Mon-Fri, to 4pm Sat, to 8pm during perform-ances) Theatre, dance, live music and film at the university campus, 1 mile west of the centre along Oystermouth Rd.

## Getting There & Away
### BUS
All local and long-distance bus services start and terminate at the Quadrant Bus Station. The First bus Shuttle100 (one hour, hourly plus additional services at peak times) serves Cardiff and now includes free wi-fi internet.

National Express coach 508 runs regularly to London (£24.50, five hours, five daily).

The main Mumbles bus service is operated by First bus 2/2A/2B (20 minutes, four per hour, three per hour Sunday), stopping at Oystermouth Sq.

### CAR & MOTORCYCLE
Swansea is 5 miles from Junction 42 (east) and Junction 45 (west) of the M4.

### TRAIN
Trains from Swansea serve Cardiff (£6.60, 50 minutes, half-hourly) and London Paddington (£21.5, three hours, half-hourly Monday to Saturday, hourly Sunday), and to Fishguard (£10.20, two hours, once daily Monday to Saturday), connecting with Irish ferry services (p719). The gloriously scenic Heart of Wales line (see the boxed text, p736) terminates in Swansea.

## Getting Around
The First bus Swansea City Day Ticket (daily adult/child £3.50/2.20) covers all buses in Swansea and Mumbles – you can purchase the ticket on the bus.

For car hire, **Avis** ( ☎ 01792-460939; NCP Car Park, Orchard St; ☽ 8am-6pm Mon-Fri, 8am-1pm Sat) is the closest to the train station.

## GOWER PENINSULA
With its precipitous cliff-top walks, golden-hued Blue Flag beaches and rugged, untamed uplands, the Gower's 15-mile sweep of penin-sula west of Mumbles Head feels a million miles away from Swansea's urban bustle – yet it's just on the doorstep.

The area was designated the UK's first official Area of Outstanding Natural Beauty (AONB) in 1956 for its biodiversity, archaeo-logical sites and heritage coast. Today the National Trust (NT) owns 26 miles of Gower coast, operating a **Visitor Centre** ( ☎ 01792-390707; www.gowerheritagecentre.co.uk; ☽ 10.30am-6pm Mon-Fri, 10.30am-5pm Sat & Sun Mar-Oct, 10.30am-5pm Wed-Sun Nov-March) at Rhossili, located across the car park from the Bay Bistro & Coffee House (opposite).

Moving around the peninsula from Mumbles, Bracelet, Langland and Caswell Bays are the most accessible by public trans-port (opposite); the latter two are most popu-lar with families, hence crowded during high season – book accommodation in advance. Rhossili Bay is the hub for surfers, while the rural north coast is a haven of wildlife and solitude for walkers.

The tourist offices in Swansea and Mumbles (p699) are the starting point for information.

## Sights & Activities

Heading west along the south coast from the family-magnet beach of **Port Eynon**, the village of **Rhossili** looks north along the 3-mile sweep of **Rhossili Bay** at the western tip of the peninsula. The village of **Llangennith**, at the north of Rhossili Bay, is the infrastructure hub for surfers, with **PJ's Surfshop** ( ☎ 01792-386669; www .pjsurfshop.co.uk), run by former surf champion Peter Jones, the centre of activity.

From Rhossili village follow the 1-mile tidal causeway to rocky, wave-blasted **Worm's Head** (from Old English *wurm*, meaning dragon) but *only* for a two-hour period either side of low tide. The **sea-bird colony** at the Outer Head includes razorbills, guillemots and oyster-catchers, while seals often bob in the swell.

Above the village of **Reynoldston**, a colossal 25-ton quartz boulder is the fallen capstone of a neolithic burial chamber known as **Arthur's Stone**. **Cefn Bryn** (186m) in the central uplands affords sweeping 360-degree views of the Gower.

Wannabe waxheads head for the **Welsh Surfing Federation Surf School** ( ☎ 01792-386426; www.wsfsurfschool.co.uk; Llangennith; 2hr class £25) at Llangennith, or **Gower Surfing Development** ( ☎ 01792-360370; www.gowersurfing.com; Caswell Bay; 2hr class £50) at Caswell Bay.

For local surf conditions check **J's Surfline** ( ☎ 0901 6031603; www.llangennithsurf.com) – calls charged at 60p per minute.

The **Gower Way**, a 35-mile marked path through the centre of the peninsula, is the most popular walking route. New in 2008, the inaugural **Gower Walking Festival**, a 10-day jamboree for walking boots and coastal views, was coordinated from the Mumbles tourist office (p701). It is hoped to be made into an annual event.

## Sleeping & Eating

**Oxwich Bay Hotel** ( ☎ 01792-390329; www.oxwichbay hotel.co.uk; Oxwich Bay; s/d from £55/66, s/d with sea view £75/100) With decent-sized en suite rooms, some offering sea views, this place has slightly frilly rooms but a good range of facilities and a huge daily menu of bar food. The extensive, flower-filled gardens make for tranquil postprandial strolling.

**King Arthur Hotel** ( ☎ 01792-390775; www .kingarthurhotel.co.uk; Reynoldston; s/d £80-90) For something more traditional, this homely country pub with log fires and a cosy restaurant has comfortable en suite rooms and decent grub.

**our pick** **Maes-yr-Haf** ( ☎ 01792-371000; www.maes -yr-haf.com; Parkmill; d £105-150; 🕑 lunch noon-2.30pm, dinner 7-9.30pm; 🅿 🖳 ) A boutique restaurant with rooms boasting a very stylish, contemporary feel. The modern rooms are a treat for gadget fans, with iPod docking stations and a PlayStation 2, while high-quality meals, featuring local seafood, meat and game, are served in the refined, dark-wood restaurant. Try the sewin (sea trout) with wilted spinach, herb risotto and crayfish bisque sauce (£11.95).

**Fairyhill** ( ☎ 01792-390139; www.fairyhill.net; Reynoldston; standard/deluxe d £165/275; 🅿 🖳 ) An 18th-century country house set in extensive private grounds, Fairyhill lives up to its name in terms of its location, aesthetics and holistic treatments. Most of all, however, it stands apart for its green credentials – the restaurant's low-food-miles menu draws on local produce, including organic home-grown ingredients from the kitchen garden.

**Bay Bistro & Coffee House** ( ☎ 01792-390519; Rhossili; 🕑 10am-5pm, plus 7-9pm summer) A buzzy beach cafe with a sunny terrace, Sam's Surf Shack surf shop bringing good vibrations to the garden and the kind of drop-your-panini views that make the drive worthwhile. Summer nights are given over to alfresco meals.

**Joiners Arms** ( ☎ 01792-232658; 50 Bishopston Rd, Bishopston) No visit to the Gower is complete without popping into the Joiners for a pint and some homemade pub grub. The pub has its own on-site microbrewery and a drop of the Three Cliffs Gold ale is *the* one to try. Located in the village of Bishopston just off the B4436.

## Getting There & Around

The various bus services to Gower destinations are coordinated from Swansea's Quadrant Bus Station (opposite) – ask for the latest timetable for an up-to-date summary. Services are expanded on Sundays and bank holidays in high season.

The **Gower Day Explorer ticket** (adult/child £4/2.40) covers multiple journeys – buy it on the bus.

# CARMARTHENSHIRE

This often-overlooked county cuts a rural and tranquil thrust through southwest Wales and is worth exploring for its ruined castles, walking and cycling trails, and its golf courses. It is attracting a growing array of stylish boutiques and upmarket places to eat, yet still escapes the hordes of neighbouring Pembrokeshire. For more information see www.visitcarmarthenshire.co.uk.

The region is particularly important to fans of firebrand poet Dylan Thomas for his eternal connections to the small but compelling village of Laugharne.

## CARMARTHEN (CAERFYRDDIN)
pop 16,000

The traditional county town is long rumoured to be the alleged birthplace of Arthurian legend Merlin the Magician. Folklore aside, it's a bustling little town with good public transport links and a helpful **tourist office** ( ☎ 01267-231557; 113 Lammas St; ⊙ 10am-5.30pm Mon-Sat Easter-Sep, 10am-4pm Mon-Sat Oct-Easter), where staff can advise on the wider region.

A project is currently under way to open public access to Carmarthen's ruined Norman castle for picnics and exploring.

If you're based in town, head for the **Falcon Hotel** ( ☎ 01267-234959; www.falconcarmarthen.co.uk; Lammas St; s/d from £45/65) for comfortable B&B accommodation and decent pub food – try the pot-roast guinea fowl with bacon, caramelised shallots and port wine (£14.95). **Mosaic Deli Bistro** ( ☎ 01267-221679; www.mosaicdelibistro.co.uk; 17 Bridge St; ⊙ 10am-5pm Mon-Sat) is the place for coffees and relaxed snacks with an arty theme.

First bus X11 links Carmarthen with Swansea (1½ hours, half-hourly Monday to Saturday).

The summer B10 Beacons Bus links Carmarthen with Brecon (p727) via the National Botanic Garden of Wales (25 minutes; see the boxed text, opposite).

National Express coach 508 runs daily to London (£24.50, six hours) via Swansea (one hour).

Trains run to Swansea (£6.20, 45 minutes, at least hourly) and Cardiff (£13, 1¾ hours, at least hourly).

## LAUGHARNE (LACHARN)
pop 2200

Laugharne (Lar-ne), a cluster of stone-built cottages, located 8 miles southwest of Carmarthen along winding, country lanes, is synonymous with the name of Dylan Thomas. One of Wales' greatest writers, Thomas spent his final years in this attractive coastal town and produced much of his best work here.

Built around The Grist, a makeshift town square with an ancient cross and views of Laugharne's 12th-century **castle** (Cadw; ☎ 01994-427906; adult/child £3.10/2.70; ⊙ 10am-5pm Apr-Sep), the town is alleged to have inspired Llareggub, the small Welsh town in which Thomas' signature work, *Under Milk Wood* (1954) is set. The name is 'bugger all' spelt backwards – but appeared in print as 'Llaregyb' so as not to offend delicate postwar sensibilities.

Many are surprised to find that today Laugharne is no Dylan Thomas theme park. In fact, it retains the understated feel that first appealed to Wales' favourite wild-boy poet. You can, however, follow a trail along the Taff Estuary from the castle to Thomas' erstwhile seafront home, check out his gorgeously located gazebo in the castle grounds and visit St Martin's churchyard, the final resting place of Thomas and his wife Caitlin Macnamara. The graves are marked with a simple white cross looking out across the rolling hills of Carmarthenshire. In the cold-stone interior of the church itself, a plaque to Thomas bears an inscription from one of his most evocative poems, 'Ferne Hill'. It reads:

'Time held me green and dying / Though I sang in my chains like the sea.'

Sadly, Browns Hotel, Thomas' favourite pub in Laugharne, has been closed for an extended period. The Grade II–listed building is due to reopen in 2009, following a £1.2m refurbishment, with accommodation and a 1930s theme – the original bar will remain as in Thomas' day.

There is no tourist office in town but the owner of **Corran Books** ( ☎ 01994-427444; www.abe books.co.uk; King St; ⊙ 10am-5pm Mon-Sat) is a mine of local information and stocks a range of brochures, including a Laugharne coastal-walk leaflet, which traces key Dylan Thomas sites around the town.

The heritage centre **Dylan Thomas Boathouse** ( ☎ 01994-427420; www.dylanthomasboathouse.com; adult/child £3.50/1.75; ⊙ 10am-5.30pm May-Oct, 10.30am-3.30pm Nov-Apr) is the ultimate pilgrimage for Thomas devotees. He lived in this simple house with his wife Caitlin and their three children from 1949 to 1953, but the exhibition about his life feels rather stale. More evocative is the garage, the first building you come to following the coast-hugging path, which Thomas used as his writing den, converted from an old garden shed. Perfectly preserved with its discarded, scrunched-up papers and pools of fountain-pen ink, you may only be able to peer though

---

#### FIVE MUST-SEE ATTRACTIONS AROUND CARMARTHENSHIRE

- **National Botanic Garden of Wales** ( ☎ 01558-668768; www.gardenofwales.org.uk; Llanarthne; adult/child £8/3; ☯ 10am-6pm Apr-Oct, to 4.30pm Nov-Mar) A latter-day Noah's Ark with a children's play area, Braille displays and hands-on attractions. The centrepiece, the Great Glasshouse temperate dome, houses endangered plants from exotic climes. Located 7 miles east of Carmarthen on the A48, then B4310 (Nantgaredig).

- **National Wetland Centre Wales** ( ☎ 01554-741087; www.wwt.org.uk; Llwynhendy; adult/child £6.95/3.85; ☯ 9.30am-5pm) Stretching across 97 hectares, this is Wales' premier site for waterbirds and waders from the leading conservation charity. Located 3 miles east of Llanelli on the A484.

- **Aberglasney Gardens** ( ☎ 01558-668998; www.aberglasney.org.uk; Llangathen; adult/child £7/4; ☯ 10am-6pm Easter-Sep, 10.30am-4pm Nov-Mar) Lovingly restored, this is now one of the most atmospheric private gardens in Wales. The award-winning Ninfarium showcases exotic plants from around the world. Located 5 miles west of Llanelli on the A40.

- **Carreg Cennen Castle** (Cadw; ☎ 01558-822291; www.carregcennencastle.com; adult/child £3.70/3.30; ☯ 9.30am-6.30pm Apr-Oct, 9.30am-4pm Nov-Mar) Wales' ultimate romantic ruined castle, perched high on a rugged limestone bluff. The Barn tearoom does a decent lunch after the lung-bursting climb to reach the summit and explore the spooky cliff gallery, tracing the southern cliff face. Located 3 miles from Llandeilo off the A483, following unmarked roads to Trapp Village.

- **National Wool Museum** ( ☎ 01559-370929; www.museumwales.ac.uk; Dre-Fach Felindre; admission free; ☯ 10am-5pm Apr-Sep, Tue-Sat Oct-Mar) The story of the Welsh woollen industry and textile museum. Located 16 miles west of Carmarthen on the A484.

---

the window but it still feels alive – as if he had just popped out for a quick breath of fresh, sea air.

## Sleeping & Eating

**our pick** **Boat House** ( ☎ 01994-427992; www.theboathousebnb.co.uk; 1 Gosport St; r £70-80; ▣ ) Friendly, homely and tastefully decorated, this relative newcomer has become the smartest address in town for B&B, with four superior rooms. The building was converted from the former Corporation Arms pub and what is now the Gwendraeth room is allegedly where Thomas sat by the window telling stories in return for free drinks. The great home-cooked breakfasts would assuage even Thomas' legendary hangovers.

**Hurst House on the Marsh** ( ☎ 01994-427417; www.hurst-house.co.uk; East Marsh; d from £235) This luxury hotel was undergoing a lengthy and costly refurbishment to expand the number of rooms and facilities at the time of writing. The new look incorporates 20 individually designed suites, a spa with swimming pool and an in-house cinema. Call ahead to check on progress – full functionality should be restored by 2009.

**Green Room** ( ☎ 01994-427870; The Grist; ☯ 11am-10pm Wed-Mon, 11am-6pm Tue) Laugharne doesn't exactly abound with options for an evening meal but this new place has great snacks by day and hearty home-cooked meals after dark. Comfy sofas for coffee, delicious desserts and views of the castle add a cosy, welcoming ambience.

**New Three Mariners** ( ☎ 01994-427426; Victoria St; ▣ ) Still the main pub in town while Browns Hotel undergoes its refit, the Mariners has decent pub food with lots of local specials, serves a good pint and has comfy leather sofas by the open fire to snuggle up with the newspapers or a well-thumbed copy of a Thomas original.

## Getting There & Away

First bus 222 runs from Carmarthen (30 minutes, every two hours Monday to Saturday).

# PEMBROKESHIRE COAST NATIONAL PARK

Rocky, sandy, sparkling and remote, the wonders of the Pembrokeshire Coast National Park are unmissable. Covering 240 sq miles in Wales' far-flung southwest, the park sits firmly in a region that the inhabitants proudly refer to as west Wales.

The stunning coastline is typified by soaring cliffs and vast swaths of golden beach, virtually all of which is within the park's boundaries and set against a backdrop of boiling surf or sheltered crystal coves.

Boat trips run to the offshore islands of Skomer, Skokholm, Grassholm and Ramsey to visit the huge colonies of raucous seabirds.

Elsewhere, from wildflower-covered rocky promontories on the northern coast, you can spot harbour porpoises and grey seals throughout the year (September and October are best for seeing cute white pups). Bottlenose dolphins are mainly seen north of Fishguard (April to October), while Strumble Head is one of the best places in Europe for watching harbour porpoises and common dolphins. Minke whales occasionally pass by in the summer months, while Risso's dolphins visit over the Christmas period to feed on spawning squid. Other species seen in recent years include fin, minke and humpback whales as well as orca. For more information see www.seatrust.org.uk.

Punctuating the vista are chocolate-box seaside towns such as Newport and St Davids, Britain's smallest city, whose historic cathedral is Wales' holiest site.

Walkers tramp the fabled Pembrokeshire Coast Path national trail, which can be broken into several memorable day hikes, while adrenalin junkies get their kicks with rock climbing, kayaking, surfing and coasteering. Inland, the park extends to the Preseli Hills (535m), an area dotted with prehistoric remains that is prime mountain-biking country.

The south coast is known as 'Little England' – more than 50 castles here were built by the Anglo-Norman invaders and today many guesthouses are run by English settlers. The rugged north coast is more Welsh, with a delightfully remote shoreline accessible down dead-end roads and along the coast path.

## Orientation & Information

The park has four sections: the coastline east of Fishguard to Cardigan and inland to the Preseli Hills; the coastline west of Fishguard and south round to Milford Haven (including the islands of Skomer, Skokholm, Grassholm and Ramsey); the inland stretches of the Milford Haven waterway; and the coastline around the southern Pembroke peninsula.

Oil terminals along the industrial estuary of Milford Haven disqualify this waterway from the national park.

The **Pembrokeshire Coast National Park Authority** ( ☎ 0845 345 7275; www.pcnpa.org.uk) has its head office by the ferry terminal at Pembroke Dock.

Major tourist offices are at Tenby, Pembroke, Haverfordwest, Fishguard Newport and at the new Oriel y Parc St Davids. On arrival, pick up a free copy of *Coast to Coast,* the excellent newspaper for visitors, or visit www.visitpembrokeshirecoast.org.uk.

## Activities

Options abound for active travellers.

### ACTIVITY CENTRES

Pembrokeshire has two well-established centres offering fully equipped sea kayaking, surfing and coasteering adventures.

**Preseli Venture** ( ☎ 01348-837709; www.preseliventure.com; Parcynole Fach, Mathry) is a super-friendly adults-only centre in a stunning location near Haverfordwest. Join a weekend course and enjoy the comfy lodge, complete with cosy bar, pool table and tasty hot meals. Find it at Mathry, on the A487 between Fishguard and St Davids.

St Davids-based **TYF Adventure** (Twr-y-Felin; ☎ 01437-721611; www.tyf.com; Caerfai Rd) takes under-16s on its courses, all of which start from its TYF Eco Hotel (p717).

### BOAT TRIPS

Get up close and personal with Pembrokeshire Coast National Park's sea life on a boat around the islands – Skomer, Skokholm and Grassholm lie off St Brides Bay, while Ramsey Island is off the northerly St Davids peninsula. Further south, boats from Tenby head to Caldey Island.

Whichever operator you choose, make sure it adheres to the Pembrokeshire Marine Code, designed to protect the fragile park environment.

### CYCLING

Cycling on most of the coast path itself is prohibited but just inland are countless country lanes and 320 miles of bridleways to explore, so alternative options are plentiful.

The **Celtic Trail** national cycle route (NCN routes 4, 47) is at its best on the coast between Broad Haven (near Haverfordwest), St Davids

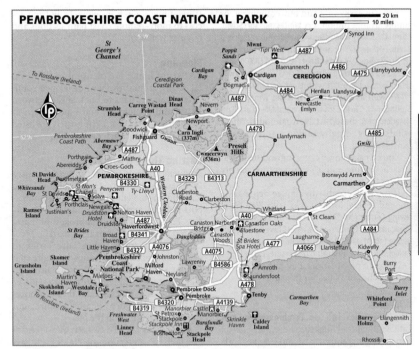

**PEMBROKESHIRE COAST NATIONAL PARK**

and Fishguard; details from www.sustrans
.org.uk. For more on Sustrans and the
National Cycle Network see Freewheeling
Through Wales, p682.

Gentle mountain biking can be found in
Canaston Woods located near Narberth,
while the bridleways of the Preseli Hills offer
tougher upland routes (for more information
see the boxed text, p720). **Newport Bike Hire**
( ☎ 01239-820773; www.newportbikehire.com; East St, Berry
Hill, Newport; per half-/full day £10/15) supplies bikes
and routes for the north coast and Preseli
Hills.

## PONY TREKKING & HORSE RIDING

This is an ideal area for riding – either along
the beaches, across open moors or high up in
the Preseli Hills – and there are a dozen stables
in or near the park. Ask at a tourist office for
your local centre.

## WATER SPORTS

Pembrokeshire has been blessed with not only
spectacular coastal scenery but also reliable
surfing. Easily accessible hot spots include
Newgale and Freshwater West, and (most
popular) Whitesands Bay near St Davids.

---

### COASTEERING & SEA KAYAKING

If you fancy a spot of rock climbing, gully scrambling, cave exploration, wave riding and cliff jumping, all rolled together, then try coasteering. More or less conceived on the Pembrokeshire coast,
this demanding activity is the mainstay of the local adventure-sports scene. It's also risky, so take
guidance from an instructor and don't be tempted to take flight from the nearest precipice.

Pembrokeshire also has some of Britain's finest sea kayaking, suitable for all levels. Powerful
tidal currents generate large standing waves between the coast and offshore islands; novice
paddlers can splash around the sheltered coves. Everybody, experienced or not, can revel in the
beautiful cliff scenery (rock stacks, caves and idyllic bays) and wildlife (porpoises and birds) from
the water – without an outboard motor in sight.

You can easily hire and buy equipment, or simply arrange tuition. Try **Whitesands Surf School** ( ☎ 01437-720433; www.whitesandssurfschool.co.uk; High St, St Davids; 2½hr class £25), based at Ma Sime's Surf Hut in St Davids, or **Outer Reef** ( ☎ 01646-680070; www .outerreefsurfschool.com; per class/day £25/45), which moves from beach to beach with the best waves.

As well as surfing, **West Wales Wind, Surf & Sailing** ( ☎ 01646-636642; www.surfdale.co.uk; Dale, Haverfordwest), based at Newgale, also offers windsurfing, dinghy sailing, canoeing and powerboating.

You can also enjoy canoeing and surfing at Preseli Venture and TYF Adventure activity centres (p708).

If you prefer scuba-diving, see rich marine life and several local wrecks with **West Wales Diving Centre** ( ☎ 01437-781457; www.westwalesdivers .co.uk; Hasguard Cross), near Little Haven, or **Celtic Diving** ( ☎ 01348-871938; www.celticdiving.co.uk; Goodwick Parrog), near the Fishguard ferry terminal.

Newgale on St Brides Bay has one of the best beaches in Wales for **fishing**.

### WALKING

The 186-mile cliff-top **Pembrokeshire Coast Path** national trail hugs the shoreline between Amroth on the south coast and Poppit Sands near Cardigan on the north coast. En route you can discover over 50 bathing beaches, 40 Iron Age forts and countless hidden coves. The rise and fall of the cliffs adds to the challenge; 15 days is a good estimate for the total distance, but most people do shorter sections. Suggestions for good walks include Dale to Martin's Haven near Marloes, and Solva to Whitesands Bay on St Davids peninsula.

The recommended detailed *Pembrokeshire Coast Path* by Brian John (£12.99) is available from tourist offices, together with leaflets breaking the walk into shorter sections. From the **park website** (www.pcnpa.org.uk) you can also download route maps for more than 200 circular walks and a series of easy access walks.

Accommodation is always close to the route and youth hostels are often spaced a day's hike apart, but book ahead between Easter and September. Tourist offices can help you plan where to stay.

The route is covered by two Ordnance Survey *Explorer* OL 1:25,000 maps: No 35 (North Pembrokeshire) and No 36 (South Pembrokeshire).

Pembrokeshire Coastal bus services (right) operates daily from June to September (three times a week in winter), allowing access to more-remote coast path sections and circular walks.

## Sleeping

B&Bs and hotels are plentiful in the park, especially around the well-developed south coast. It always pays to book ahead between Easter and September, and especially from June to August. Local YHA hostels are listed in the sections for each destination.

## Getting There & Around

Frequent railway services run from Swansea (with connections for Cardiff and London Paddington) to Pembrokeshire's major transport hubs, Haverfordwest and, for Irish ferries, Pembroke Dock. Pembrokeshire has a second Irish ferry port at Fishguard.

Once in Pembrokeshire, use buses to get around rather than trains but note that Sunday services are limited, especially from October to April. The West Wales Rover (£6) is a one-day ticket valid on most buses in Carmarthenshire, Pembrokeshire and Ceredigion – buy it on the bus.

**Arriva Trains** ( ☎ 0845 6061 660; www.arrivatrains wales.co.uk) has a Freedom of Wales Flexi Pass (All Wales/South & Mid Wales £69/47) with four days of train and eight days of bus-based unlimited travel, plus discounts on attractions, available at most railway stations and online at www.walesflexipass.co.uk.

Between May and September a group of local buses operate under the auspices of **Pembrokeshire Greenways** ( ☎ 01437-776313; www.pem brokeshiregreenways.co.uk), a collective to promote sustainable modes of transport through walking, cycling, bus and train travel. The Poppit Rocket, Preseli Green Dragon, Strumble Shuttle, Celtic Coaster, Puffin Shuttle and Coastal Cruiser ply the coast path roads daily, picking up and setting down at any safe point.

Between October and March, a reduced service (Poppit Rocket, Strumble Shuttle, Puffin Shuttle and Coastal Cruiser only) operates three days a week.

Tourist offices stock timetables, and information is also published in the free *Coast to Coast* newspaper.

## TENBY (DINBYCH Y PYSGOD)
pop 5000

With attractive Georgian architecture, ruined, 13th-century fortifications jutting

SOUTH WALES

---

**TOP FIVE PEMBROKESHIRE FREEBIES**

▦ Sample the best local food direct from the producers at Haverfordwest **Farmers Market** (p713, on alternate Fridays from 9am to 3pm at the Riverside Shopping Centre.

▦ Fiddle around at a local folk club. Try the **Royal Oak Inn** (p719), in Fishguard, where weekly music sessions happen every Tuesday evening.

▦ Take a hike in the mystical **Preseli Hills** (see boxed text, p720), one of the most beautiful ranges in Wales.

▦ Join one of the **guided walks** on the coast path as arranged by the National Park Authority (p708).

▦ Join a local group spotting seabirds or porpoises at **Strumble Head** near Fishguard. Ask at the Fishguard Harbour tourist office (p718) for forthcoming meetings.

---

out to sea and brightly painted pubs with alfresco beer gardens galore, Tenby might seem like the perfect, albeit slightly faded, seaside resort.

Indeed generations of holidaying Brits have traditionally chosen Pembrokeshire's foremost seaside resort for their annual summer break, attracted by the Blue Flag beach, sheltered harbour and the narrow medieval streets of the old town. But beware: Tenby can be packed in high season and its nightlife a little too popular with boozy hen and stag parties. Time your visit carefully to see Tenby at its best.

The new Tenby Jazz Festival aims to attract a more cultured visitor over the August Bank Holiday weekend.

### Orientation & Information
Tenby's major landmark is the headland of Castle Hill, site of the Norman stronghold. On the north side is the harbour and North Beach. On the southern side is Castle Sands, then South Beach. The train station, on Warren St, is on the western side of town, with the bus station one block further south at Upper Park Rd.

The **tourist office** ( ☎ 01834-842404; tenbytic@ pembrokeshire.gov.uk; Upper Park Rd; ☼ 9.30am-5pm Mon-Sat & 10am-4pm Sun Easter-Oct, 10am-4pm Mon-

Sat Nov-Easter) is between the bus station and Somerfield supermarket.

### Sights & Activities
Boat trips bob the 20 minutes to **Caldey Island** ( ☎ 01834-844453; www.caldey-island.co.uk; adult/child £10/5; ☼ 10am-5pm Mon-Fri Easter-Oct, Sat May-Sep), one-time home of Cistercian monks, now the haunt of grey seals and Wales' largest cormorant colony. Boats depart (every 15 to 20 minutes in high season) from the quay at high tide and Castle Sands at low tide. Buy tickets at the harbour kiosk on Castle Sq.

Handsomely restored, Tenby's 15th-century **Tudor Merchant's House** (NT; ☎ 01834-842279; Quay Hill; adult/child £2.70/1.30; ☼ 11am-5pm Sun-Fri Easter-Oct) has period furnishings and the remains of early frescos on the interior walls.

The castle ruins house the **Tenby Museum & Art Gallery** ( ☎ 01834-842809; www.tenbymuseum.org.uk; Castle Hill; adult/child £4/2; ☼ 10am-5pm Easter-Dec, 10am-5pm Mon-Fri Jan-Easter), which tells the town's story through period exhibitions and paintings by the likes of Augustus and Gwen John.

For guided theme walks, contact **Town Trails** ( ☎ 01834-845841; www.guidedtourswales.co.uk; walks £4; ☼ Mon-Sat Jun-Sep & public holidays); it also offers Halloween and Christmas specials.

### Sleeping
**Lindholme House** ( ☎ 01834-843368; 27 Victoria St; s/d from £30/60) Traditional B&B with comfy rooms, fry-up breakfasts and attractive setting offset by splashes of colourful flowers.

**our pick** **Bay House** ( ☎ 01834-849015; www .bayhousetenby.co.uk; 5 Picton Rd; s/d £35/70) Tenby's only five-star B&B, Bay House is a stylish and modern take on the traditional seaside guesthouse. Think a relaxed and friendly atmosphere, airy rooms with flat-screen TVs and DVDs and an emphasis on local and organic produce at breakfast.

**Atlantic Hotel** ( ☎ 01834-842881; www.atlantic-hotel .uk.com; The Esplanade; s/d with sea views £85/124) Smart and traditional, appealing mainly to an older clientele, the Atlantic has elegant rooms and boasts a newly refurbished spa. Take a seat in the residents' bar for a sundowner with sea views.

### Eating & Drinking
**No 25 Cafe** ( ☎ 01834-842544; 25 High St; ☼ 10am-5pm; ▯) Simple but satisfying cafe for good coffee, sandwiches, snacks and hearty breakfasts (served until 11.30am). A locals' favourite.

**Nana's Italian Restaurant** ( ☎ 01834-844536; pizzas & pastas around £8, mains around £16; St Julian's St) Light and airy with views of the harbour, Italian-motif Nana's specialises by day in pizzas and pastas while, after dusk, the à la carte menu majors in local favourites and fresh fish.

**Bay Tree** ( ☎ 01834-843516; Tudor Sq; mains around £18; ☒ lunch & dinner) Making innovative use of fresh Pembrokeshire produce, this place covers all the bases from a kids' menu to fish specials for dinner. It has a buzzy feel, dark-wood fittings and offers a good-value summer menu (two courses for £15).

**Plantagenet House Restaurant** ( ☎ 01834-842350; Quay Hill; mains around £20; ☒ lunch & dinner) Decor-wise this place instantly impresses: think a 12th-century Flemish chimney hearth, exposed stone and chunky wooden tables. The food is good, too, with a daily changing menu of the best local meat and seafood. With a kids' menu, vegetarian options, Sunday roasts, plus light-lunch and sausage-special menus (both £8), this is one for all tastes.

Away from the crowds try the **Crown Inn** ( ☎ 01834-842796; Lower Frog St) and the **Normandie** ( ☎ 01834-842227; Upper Frog St) for real ale and classy cocktails, respectively.

## Getting There & Away

National Express coach 508 runs to Swansea (£7.60, 1½ hours, three times daily) via Carmarthen (45 minutes). First bus 349 serves Haverfordwest (1½ hours, hourly Monday

---

**SOMETHING FOR THE WEEKEND**

For a little luxury by the seaside, **St Brides Spa Hotel** ( ☎ 01834-812304; www.stbrides spahotel.com; r from £190-270; ⓟ ▣ ) has all the facilities for a pampering break, especially after a recent refurbishment upped the ante. Water is a big feature here – from the power showers in the limestone bathrooms to the spa's Vitality Pool overlooking Carmarthen Bay and breakfast served on a sun deck terrace.

Rooms are graded Good, Better and Best, with prices ascending accordingly. The walk-through gallery of Welsh artworks is a nice addition to the overall sense of style with substance.

Located 5 miles north of Tenby at Saundersfoot, following the A478 onto the B4316.

---

to Saturday, five on Sunday) via Pembroke (45 minutes).

Trains run to Swansea (£10.10, 1½ hours, every two hours Monday to Saturday, four on Sunday) via Pembroke Dock (35 minutes).

## AROUND TENBY

In the village of Manorbier, 5 miles southwest of Tenby on the A4139, the 12th-century **castle** ( ☎ 01834-871394; www.manorbiercastle.co.uk; adult/child £3.50/1.50; ☒ 10.30am-5.30pm Easter-Sep) was the birthplace of Giraldus Cambrensis (Gerald of Wales), one of the country's greatest scholars and patriots, but today looks rather unloved.

Heading west along the coast towards Stackpole Head, Green Coast Award–winning and National Trust–managed **Barafundle Bay** is one of the most gloriously scenic bays in Wales. It's a place for golden-hued sunsets and bracing coastal walks fuelled by ozone. From the A4139, take the B4319 then unmarked roads to Stackpole Quay, where the **Boathouse Tearooms** ( ☒ 10am-5pm) has basic snacks and parking area. From here the path leads up steps to take in the full splendour of the bay.

Reward yourself afterwards with dinner, or a glass of chilled wine in the flower-filled garden, at the **Stackpole Inn** ( ☎ 01646-672324; www .stackpoleinn.co.uk), with its excellent local fish specials (around £15). Bookings advised.

## PEMBROKE (PENFRO)
**pop 7200**

The town of Pembroke is not unattractive with its medieval streets and imposing castles, but it feels rather low-key – a place to pass through, rather than to stay. **Pembroke Dock**, 2 miles northwest on the A4139, is a hub for Irish ferry connections (p710).

At the time of writing the **tourist office** ( ☎ 01646-622388; pembroke.tic@pembrokeshire.gov .uk; 38 Main St; ☒ 9.30am-5pm Mon-Sat, 10am-4pm Sun) had a temporary base within the town library pending a new permanent office to open (in spring 2009) on Common Rd.

Pembroke's main draw remains **Pembroke Castle** ( ☎ 01646-881510; www.pembroke-castle.co.uk; adult/child £3.50/2.50; ☒ 9.30am-6pm Apr-Sep, 10am-5pm Mar & Oct, 10am-4pm Nov-Feb), home of the earls of Pembroke for over 300 years. Climb 100 steep spiral steps for unbroken views from the keep, before dropping way down to subterranean **Wogan's Cavern**, a massive natural cave with a watergate.

SOUTH WALES

---

**SOMETHING FOR THE WEEKEND**

The latest major new option in Pembrokeshire is **Bluestone** ( ☎ 01834-862400; www.bluestonewales .com; Canaston Wood, Narberth), a hugely ambitious and much-delayed holiday-village project built on the foundations of environmental and sustainability issues.

Finishing touches were still being given to the 500-acre site, complete with its 180 alpine-style, timber lodges built around a central Celtic village, when the village opened in July 2008. Early reviews were mixed but teething troubles should be ironed out by summer 2009.

There are four types of lodge, all with en suite, kitchenette and solar panels, some adapted for access for travellers with disabilities. A sports hall and the Blue Lagoon water park are the first major activity centres to open, with a snow centre and a further 180 lodges to open during phase two – dates to be confirmed. Rates vary hugely, but as a guide, a top-end lodge sleeping six in high season costs £2600; a basic lodge in low season costs £150 – call for details and promotional offers.

Narberth is the nearest town and primary access is via the A40 from Carmarthen to Haverfordwest – follow signs to the new, purpose-built Bluestone roundabout.

**ourpick** **Canaston Oaks** ( ☎ 01437-541254; www.canastonoaks.co.uk; r £95-110; P 🖳 ) is a luxurious new B&B set amid 200 acres of working farm. Located just down the road from Bluestone, it's simpler but better designed. The four rooms, all with en suite, are built around a Celtic cross with immaculately manicured grounds alive with local wildlife. Early Grey tea and Welsh cakes upon arrival, and a Welsh dresser groaning under the weight of homemade muesli and fresh fruit for breakfast testify to the warmth of the hospitality.

---

The castle holds **family events** during summer, such as falconry displays and performances.

## Sleeping & Eating

**Beech House** ( ☎ 01646-683740; www.beechhouse pembroke.com; 78 Main St; s/d £17.50/35) Friendly and good value, this simple but welcoming place at the western end of the main street has spick-and-span rooms with period Georgian features. Handy for the train station, and family friendly.

**Cornstore Cafe** ( ☎ 01646-684290; North Quay; 🕙 10am-5pm Mon-Sat) Converted from an 18th-century granary, this cosy little coffee-cum-craft shop has tasty snacks, hot lunches and decent coffee in an attractive waterside location.

**Old Kings Arms Hotel** ( ☎ 01646-683611; www .oldkingsarmshotel.co.uk; Main St; 🕙 lunch & dinner daily; P 🖳 ) The oldest hostelry in Pembroke has no-nonsense pub grub with lots of fresh fish (mains £13 to £18) and unfussy rooms (single/double £45/80). The oak-panelled bar is your best bet for an evening meal as other options are scarce.

## Getting There & Away

First bus 349 runs to Tenby (45 minutes, hourly Monday to Saturday, three to five on Sunday) en route to Haverfordwest (50 minutes).

Pembroke Dock train station marks the western limit of town; trains run to Tenby (35 minutes, every two hours Monday to Saturday, four on Sunday) and on to Swansea (£10.10, two hours).

**Irish Ferries** ( ☎ 0870 517 1717; www.irishferries .com) runs two slow services a day to Rosslare (Ireland) from Pembroke Dock (12 hours). Prices vary hugely with season and availability – log on to the company's website for the latest deals.

## HAVERFORDWEST (HWLFFORDD)
pop 14,000

A workaday town rather than a tourist hot spot, Haverfordwest is Pembrokeshire's main transport and shopping hub. It's a useful staging point for visiting the region, but sleeping options are better in the surrounding area than in the town centre itself.

The one-time river port thrived before the railway arrived in the mid-19th century. Today the Riverside Shopping Centre is the main focus of activity and home to an excellent farmers market with organic and local produce sellers every other Friday.

The helpful **tourist office** ( ☎ 01437-763110; haver fordwest.tic@pembrokeshire.gov.uk; 19 Old Bridge; 🕙 9.30am-5pm Mon-Sat Easter-Oct, 10am-4pm Mon-Sat Nov-Easter) is close to the pedestrianised Old Bridge. It offers free internet access.

---

### SIX OF THE BEST PEMBROKESHIRE BEACHES

- **Musselwick Sands** (at low tide) near Milford Haven, on the spit pointing towards Skomer Island, is a large, sandy beach with plenty of craggy inlets to explore.

- **Traeth Llyfn** is by the village of Abereiddy near St Davids. Descend a metal staircase to this pretty beach with sheltered swimming.

- **Porthselau**, south of Whitesands Bay, again near St Davids, is a tiny but cute beach – great for families.

- **Druidstone Haven** sits below the beguiling Druidstone Hotel (see Detour: Exploring St Brides Bay, opposite) near Nolton Haven. Low tide reveals a long stretch of silky golden sand.

- **Pwllgwaelod** is near Dinas Head between Fishguard and Newport. Drop down the steps to this long, wild stretch of golden shoreline.

- **Broadhaven South**, near Bosherston to the south of Pembroke, is a gorgeous and secluded National Trust beach.

---

## Sleeping & Eating

**College Guest House** ( ☎ 01437-763710; www.college guesthouse.com; 93 Hill St; s/d from £38/55) The College remains the best option in the town centre, with a period Georgian setting, no-frills but homely rooms and good fry-up breakfasts. It's also pet friendly and now offers evening meals (two courses for £10).

**our pick** **Ty-Llwyd** ( ☎ 01348-831583; www.stay insolva.co.uk; Treffynnon; s/d £50/80; **P** ) A working dairy farm near the rural hamlet of Solva, this cosy, two-room B&B boasts a majestically off-the-beaten-track location. The rooms are comfortable enough but it's the elaborate, roomy bathrooms that really impress – the giant, free-standing bath is big enough to house a whole family. The hearty farmhouse breakfast will set you up for the day. Ty-Llywd is located 13 miles northwest of Haverfordwest on the B4330 down single-track country lanes.

**George's** ( ☎ 01437-766683; 24 Market St; mains around £6; 🕙 10am-5.30pm Mon-Fri, 10am-11pm Sat) The sign outside says it all: 'Leave your emotional luggage at the door'. Inside, George's offbeat cafe shares premises with a New Age gift shop – and the Woodstock-esque atmosphere clearly rubs off. Little tables hide in cosy snugs and the menu features everything from local favourites to Mediterranean specialities via vegetarian options. Gloriously eccentric.

## Getting There & Away

Bus services stop next to the tourist office. Richards Brothers bus 412 runs to Cardigan (1½ hours, hourly Monday to Saturday, three on Sunday) via Fishguard (45 minutes) and bus 411 serves St Davids (45 minutes, hourly Monday to Saturday, five on Sunday).

National Express coach 508/509 serves London (7½ hours, three times daily); coach 508 runs from London to Haverfordwest (£25.50, seven hours, three times daily).

The train station is located 400m east of town off the A40; trains run to Swansea (£10.20, 80 minutes, every two hours) for connections to Cardiff and London.

## SKOMER, SKOKHOLM & GRASSHOLM ISLANDS

Rocky and exposed, these three little islands off St Brides Bay's southern headland are a marine nature reserve and home to some of Wales' largest **sea-bird colonies**, most active from April to mid-August.

The largest and easiest island to reach, Skomer is home to over half a million breeding seabirds, including puffins, guillemots and cormorants, plus **grey seal pups, porpoises** and **dolphins**. To the south, Skokholm, together with Skomer, has the world's largest colony of burrow-breeding Manx shearwater.

The smallest island is Grassholm, 11 miles offshore and with the second-largest **gannet colony** in the northern hemisphere. Landing on Grassholm is not permitted.

The former two nature reserves are managed by the **Wildlife Trust of South and West Wales** ( ☎ 01656-724100; www.welshwildlife.org).

Regular trips run from Easter to October. **Dale Sailing Co** ( ☎ 01646-603123; www.dale-sailing.co.uk; cruises adult/child £30/15) runs a range of round-island cruises and landing trips to Skomer, departing from Martin's Haven near Marloes, for wildlife spotting.

## ST DAVIDS (TY-DDEWI)
pop 2000

Charismatic St Davids (yes, it has dropped the apostrophe from its name) is Britain's smallest city, its status ensured by the magnificent 12th-century cathedral that marks Wales' holiest site and the home of Welsh Christianity. It has been a place of pilgrimage for over 1500 years.

The patron saint of Wales, Dewi Sant (David), established the first monastic community here in the 6th century. His relics are still preserved in a casket inside the cathedral, hidden in a hollow below the main square. A visit here, and to the neighbouring Bishop's Palace, is essential.

St Davids' tiny streets boast more than their fair share of galleries, activities and cosmopolitan restaurants and cafe-bars but, despite the good-natured vibe, it can also get murderously busy in high season, with parking at a premium – both in terms of spaces and cost (£3 per day).

St Davids is currently crying out for an upmarket B&B to match the quality of the eating options.

### Orientation & Information

The town is centred on Cross Sq, with the cathedral to the northwest. The **tourist office** ( ☎ 01437-720392; enquiries@stdavids.pembrokeshire coast.org.uk; Oriel Y Parc; ☼ 9.30am-5.30pm daily summer, 10am-4pm Mon-Sat winter) has relocated to a new purpose-built centre east of the main square along High St. Gallery Oriel Y Parc also comprises the National Park Visitor Centre and an art gallery showcasing landscape works, an extension of the National Museum of Wales (p671).

The NT owns over 60 miles of Pembrokeshire coastline, much of it along the 186-mile Pembrokeshire Coastal Path. The **National Trust Visitor Centre** ( ☎ 01437-720385; High St; ☼ 10am-5.30pm Mon-Sat, 10am-4pm Sun) has details of NT properties in the area.

### Sights

#### ST DAVID'S CATHEDRAL

The beautiful 12th-century, purple-sandstone **St David's Cathedral** ( ☎ 01437-720199; www.stdavid scathedral.org.uk; The Close; donation invited; ☼ 8.30am-5.30pm Mon-Sat, 12.45-5.30pm Sun) is St Davids' premier attraction.

In 1124 Pope Calixtus II declared that two pilgrimages to St David's Cathedral equalled one to Rome and that three equalled a pilgrimage to the holy city of Jerusalem itself. Additions to the cathedral were subsequently made between the 12th and 16th centuries. In between times, Norse pirates plundered it on at least seven occasions.

The atmosphere inside is one of great antiquity. The floor slopes sharply and the

---

### DETOUR: EXPLORING ST BRIDES BAY

West-facing St Brides Bay has some of the most golden Blue Flag beaches, crashing surf breaks and charming, lost-in-time villages in west Wales. It's a rural, rugged and deliciously remote part of Pembrokeshire hidden between St Anne's Head and St Davids peninsula.

Heading northwest on the A487 towards St Davids, take a left onto the single-track country lanes, turn off the sat nav, and follow your nose to explore. Even if you're on public transport, you can still take a diversion thanks to the Puffin Shuttle (p710), which serves this area.

Try to find your way to the beaches at Broad Haven and Newgale, the latter a 2-mile sweep of sand popular with surfers, swimmers and sand yachters, and home to surf schools. There's free parking next to **Newgale Campsite** ( ☎ 01437-710253; sites £7; ☼ Easter-Sep), with a cafe and shop close by. The craggy coast at Nolton Haven is also great for swells – and a drink in the beer garden at the **Mariners' Arms** ( ☎ 01437-710469).

To stay in the area, consider the eccentric **Druidstone Hotel** ( ☎ 01437-781221; www.druidstone .co.uk; P ), a sprawling cliff-top property with rooms (£95 to £150), cottages (to sleep six from £572 per week), all-day restaurant and bar food (mains restaurant/bar around £18/10) and a regular program of events. The best room is the new Roof North, an en suite attic with porthole windows and balcony, while the Roundhouse is a solar-powered, self-sustaining eco-cottage. It's very family friendly and offers disabled access to cottages and restaurant. It's located 2 miles north of Broad Haven on unmarked roads at what delightfully feels like the end of the earth.

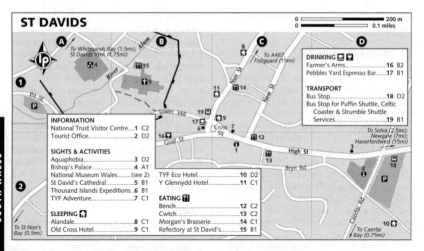

## ST DAVIDS

pillars keel drunkenly following a 1248 earthquake, while the Norman nave's superb Irish oak ceiling dates from the 16th century. The equally richly carved choir in the centre of the cross is illuminated from the tower above. The relics of Dewi Sant, the patron saint, were wrecked during the Reformation and are now kept behind the altar.

The first fruits of the ongoing Cloisters Project, a renovation initiative, are already evident, with the Treasury recounting the story of Christian worship and scholarship of St David, and the Refectory at St David's (opposite) restaurant. The second phase now focuses on renovating the west cloister.

**Guided tours** ( ☎ 01437-720204; 1½hr tour adult/child £4/1.20) are held at 2.30pm on Monday, Tuesday, Thursday and Friday during July and August.

### BISHOP'S PALACE
Across the river from the cathedral, this atmospheric ruined **palace** (Cadw; ☎ 01437-720517; adult/child £3.10/2.70; ☼ 9am-5pm Apr-Oct, 9.30am-4pm Mon-Sat & 11am-4pm Sun Nov-Mar) should not be overlooked. The imposing architecture, including the arcades of the parapet, is mostly due to Henry de Gower, bishop from 1327 to 1348. The palace is one of the most elaborate testaments to the power and wealth of the medieval church.

The palace is a spine-tingling setting for open-air theatre during the summer Arts Festival (opposite).

### ST NON'S BAY
St David's supposed birthplace lies three-quarters of a mile south of the cathedral, beside the bay that bears his mother's name and the ruins of the 13th-century **St Non's Chapel** (also a modern chapel and a building used as a retreat). A spring at the site is attended by pilgrims and fabled for its curative powers.

### RAMSEY ISLAND
Just off St Davids Head, Ramsey Island plays host to Atlantic grey seals and thousands of nesting seabirds, while porpoises and dolphins frolic near spectacular sea caves.

Two boat operators adhering to the Pembrokeshire Marine Code, designed to protect the fragile park environment:
**Aquaphobia** ( ☎ 01437-720471; www.aquaphobia -ramseyisland.co.uk; Grove Hotel, High St; adult/child £20/10) Round-Ramsey tours and evening trips to see shearwaters.
**Thousand Islands Expeditions** ( ☎ 01437-721721; www.thousandislands.co.uk; Cross Sq; adult/child £15/7.50) Evening puffin- and shearwater-spotting, whale-watching, fishing trips and high-speed rigid inflatable boat (RIB) jaunts, as well as Ramsey cruises with landing and guided walks.

## Activities
St Davids is an excellent base from which to explore the Pembrokeshire Coast Path national trail, starting from Caerfai Bay, three-quarters of a mile south of town – the tourist office stocks walking leaflets.

St Davids is also the westernmost point of the Celtic Trail cycle route (NCN routes 4, 47; see p708).

**TYF Adventure** ( ☎ 01437-721611; www.tyf.com; 1 High St; half-/full day adult £60/100, child £40/75) offers coasteering, sea-kayaking and rock-climbing trips, plus accommodation (see Tyf Eco Hotel, below) with a green conscience.

## Festivals & Events

**St David's Cathedral Festival** ( ☎ 01437-720271) Nine days of classical recitals in the cathedral from late May to early June.

**Arts Festival** ( ☎ 01437-837034) A two-week gathering from early August featuring open-air Shakespeare productions at the Bishop's Palace.

**Really Wild Food Festival** ( ☎ 01437-891381; www .reallywildfestival.co.uk) A celebration of the best local food and crafts over a weekend in late August.

## Sleeping

**St Davids YHA** ( ☎ 0870 770 6042; www.yha.org.uk; Llaethdy; dm £12; ☑ reception 8-10am & 5-10pm Easter-Oct) A basic but functional farmhouse hostel with easy access to the coast path at Whitesands Bay. Located 2 miles northwest of town – there's no public transport.

**Y Glennydd Hotel** ( ☎ 01437-720576; www.yglennydd .co.uk; 11 Nun St; s/d £37/62) With its range of maritime memorabilia and traditional feel, this 10-room guesthouse mixes modern rooms with a period setting. The restaurant serves a decent three-course evening meal (£18.50) with lots of fresh fish options.

**Alandale** ( ☎ 01437-720404; www.stdavids.co.uk/guest house/alandale.htm; 43 Nun St; s/d £36/72) Homely and welcoming, Alandale is a smart town house with a cosy Victorian parlour-style lounge. Rear rooms are quieter and boast sweeping panoramic views.

**TYF Eco Hotel** ( ☎ 01437-721678; www.tyf.com/tyf hotel; Caerfai Rd; s/d without bathroom £50/75, s/d with bathroom £60/90; [P] [🖳] ) Part of the TYF Adventure group, this place caters for surfers and ecowarriors. The first fully organic hotel in Wales, its principles are undisputable: it's registered with the Vegetarian Society and Welsh Organic Scheme. The owners evangelise about organic, sustainable and ethical tourism. Shame then that, despite the original features and sunny restaurant, it feels a bit shabby and unloved. Located east of town near the new tourist office.

**Old Cross Hotel** ( ☎ 01437-720387; www.oldcrosshotel .co.uk; Cross Sq; s/d £65/110; [P] [🖳] ) Located right in the heart of town, this is a reliable if somewhat unremarkable place with good hotel facilities but little spark. The leafy garden overlooking the main square is a great spot for a cold beer and some blatant people-watching. Families and pets welcome.

## Eating & Drinking

**Pebbles Yard Espresso Bar** ( ☎ 01437-720122; The Pebbles; ☑ 9am-5.30pm Jul & Aug, 10am-5.30pm Sept-June) A simple little coffee bar with crafts downstairs, coffees and newspapers upstairs and smoothies in the flower-filled garden. Nicely chilled out.

**Bench** ( ☎ 01437-721778; 11 High St; ☑ 10am-10pm, [🖳] ) A bustling rabbit warren of a bar-bistro with a strong Mediterranean motif, the Bench serves up all-day snacks and lip-smacking ice creams. It can get very crowded in high season. Internet access costs £2 per hour.

**Refectory at St David's** ( ☎ 01437-721760; www .refectoryatstdavids.co.uk; mains around £8; ☑ 10am-6pm Apr-Jun, to 9pm Jul & Aug, 10am-4pm Nov-Mar; [🖳] ) The centrepiece of the first phase of the cathedral cloister renovation project, the new refectory may not be the cheapest place to eat (simple sandwiches cost £4.45) but it is a triumph of design. The medieval St Mary's Hall has been given a splendid ultramodern facelift with blonde woods contrasting with the exposed walls and a shiny mezzanine supported on slanted legs. Take a seat upstairs for better views and, after lunch, mooch around the artworks at the ground-floor Cloister Gallery. There's a pushchair (pram) and wheelchair ramp, plus a kids' menu.

**Morgan's Brasserie** ( ☎ 01437-720508; 20 Nun St; mains £13-19; ☑ lunch Fri-Sun, dinner Thu-Mon) This well-established chocolate-and-beige bistro serves a good range of fish and meat dishes in an intimate dining room. There's a French motif to the menu and lots of inspired vegetarian options.

**Cwtch** ( ☎ 01437-720422; www.cwtchrestaurant.co.uk; 22 High St; 1/2/3 courses £15/21/26; ☑ dinner Tue-Sat) Cwtch, meaning 'a warm, safe place' in Welsh, lives up to its name. The low-lit dining room is cosy and snug, while the appealing menu places a strong emphasis on locally sourced food of sustainable origin. Think lots of fresh fish, imaginatively prepared, plus an early-dinner menu until 7pm.

For a quiet pint, try the **Farmer's Arms** ( ☎ 01437-721666; 14 Goat St) with its range of real ales and sunny beer garden.

## Getting There & Around

Buses stop on Nun St near Cross Sq and in the parking area opposite the tourist office. Richards Brothers bus 411 runs to Haverfordwest (45 minutes, hourly Monday to Saturday, four on Sunday); bus 413 runs to Fishguard (50 minutes, every two hours Monday to Saturday).

St Davids is served by Puffin Shuttle, Celtic Coaster and Strumble Shuttle services (p710), which stop at coast path access points and villages.

## FISHGUARD (ABERGWAUN)

pop 3193

Fishguard has traditionally been a mere staging point for the Irish ferries but a clutch of upmarket places to sleep and eat, plus the redevelopment of Fishguard Harbour Marina earmarked to start in 2009, are lending the town an up-and-coming feel.

From the town centre the main street plummets eastward to the picturesque original harbour of Lower Fishguard, the setting for the 1971 film *Under Milk Wood* starring Richard Burton and Elizabeth Taylor.

In February 1797 Fishguard was the improbable setting for the last invasion of Britain. Some 1400 French mercenaries landed with the intention of marching to Liverpool and diverting English troops, thereby allowing another French force to conquer Ireland. But the ragamuffin band overindulged on Portuguese wine and were subsequently captured by the more-sober locals. Their surrender was signed in the town's Royal Oak Inn (see opposite). In 1997 a magnificent 30m tapestry telling the story of the invasion was commissioned to mark the bicentenary of this event.

The Fishguard Tapestry is now on permanent display in the **town hall** ( ☎ 01437-776639; admission free; ⌚ 9am-5pm).

## Orientation & Information

The train station (Fishguard Harbour) and ferry terminal are both located 1 mile northwest of town at Goodwick. Lower Fishguard is east of town and built around a picturesque harbour. The town is centred around Market Sq, with the **tourist office** ( ☎ 01437-776636; fishguard .tic@pembrokeshire.gov.uk; Market Sq; ⌚ 9.30am-5pm Mon-Sat, 10am-4pm Sun Jul & Aug) now located in the town hall.

The **Fishguard Harbour tourist office** ( ☎ 01348-872037; fishguardharbourtic@pembrokeshire.gov.uk; Ocean Lab, Goodwick; ⌚ 9.30am-5pm Easter-Oct, to 6pm Jul & Aug, 10am-4pm Nov-Easter) is near the ferry terminal and includes an internet cafe (internet £4 per hour).

## Sights & Activities

Fishguard grants access to the northeastern end of the Pembrokeshire Coast Path national trail (p710) – ask the tourist offices for details of coast path sections around Dinas and Strumble Heads.

Located near the ferry terminal, **Celtic Diving** ( ☎ 01348-871938; www.celticdiving.co.uk; Goodwick Parrog) is a diving specialist with full PADI certification. This operator also offers accommodation options (below).

**Ocean Lab** ( ☎ 01348-874737; Goodwick; admission free; ⌚ 9.30am-5pm Easter-Oct, to 6pm Jul & Aug, 10am-4pm Nov-Easter) has an exhibition of marine life for children.

## Sleeping

**Hamilton Backpackers** ( ☎ 01348-874797; 21 Hamilton St; dm/d £16/19; 🖳 ) Still cheap, cheerful and right at the centre of town. The owner of this popular hostel has converted the property into two dorms and a double, reducing the number of beds overall. The lounge and kitchen remain as before.

**Celtic Diving** ( ☎ 01348-871938; www.celticdiving .co.uk; Goodwick Parrog; dm incl breakfast £20) Offers basic dorms in a purpose-built accommodation block near the ferry terminal. It's low-fi stuff, but clean, comfy and commands great sea views.

**our pick** **Pentower Priory** ( ☎ 01348-874462; www .pentower.co.uk; Tower Hill; d/ste £65/70; P ) Set in a character-filled, rambling family house, the three en suite rooms are specious and light with modern bathrooms and lots of homely touches. Breakfast is a more communal affair with local and organic produce laid out across a large kitchen table. Tuck in – if you can tear yourself away from the stunning view of crashing sea cliffs from the breakfast room.

**Manor Town House** ( ☎ 01348-873260; www.manor townhouse.com; Main St; s/d/sea views from £45/75/85) With its bright, pastel-hued rooms, seaside-themed lounge and candlelit dining rooms, the graceful decor of this Georgian town house ensures it remains a cut above the rest. Best of all is the view as you take breakfast on the terrace of the palm-tree garden – a jaw-dropper across the bay. It also offers an excellent dinner (mains around £10.50).

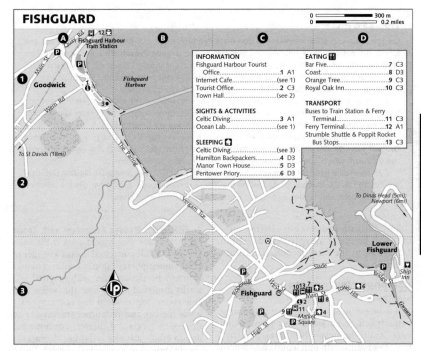

## Eating & Drinking

**Orange Tree** ( ☎ 01348-875500; 11 High St; ✆ 8am-3pm Mon-Sat) A simple but satisfying deli-cum-coffee shop for coffees, baguettes and snacks on the go.

**Royal Oak Inn** ( ☎ 01348-872514; Market Sq; ✆ lunch & dinner) As if its historical significance and excellent pub-grub menu weren't enough, the Oak is also home to a lively folk-music session on Tuesday nights. It's the most unfussy place in town for a quick bite; the huge menu takes in kids' options, Sunday roasts and hearty mains (around £10).

**Coast** ( ☎ 01348-872796; 28 Main St; ✆ dinner Wed-Sat & Mon) One of the new breed of smart Fishguard eateries, Coast has an attractive, dark-wood interior and a mouth-watering menu, plus it serves a range of organic beers by the bottle. Try the herb-crusted rack of Pembrokeshire lamb with apricot salsa verde (£15.95), but be aware that locals report the service can be slow.

**Bar Five** ( ☎ 01348-875050; 5 Main St; ✆ 11am-3pm & 6-11pm Mon-Sat, noon-4pm Sun) Popular with a younger crowd for its buzzy bar-bistro vibe, Bar Five serves decent bar meals on a sun-kissed outdoor terrace overlooking the bay. Dinner moves to the basement dining room with the emphasis on fresh fish, caught that day in the restaurant's very own fishing boat moored in the bay. Families beware: it's for children over 10 only and seated downstairs.

## Getting There & Away

Richards Brothers bus 412 runs from both Fishguard and Goodwick to Haverfordwest (50 minutes, hourly Monday to Saturday, three on Sunday) and Cardigan (45 minutes).

The Strumble Shuttle (west to St Davids) and Poppit Rocket (east to Cardigan), serve villages along the coast (p710).

Fishguard Harbour train station has services to Swansea (£10.20, two hours, one daily Monday to Saturday) via Cardiff (£17.10, 2½ hours) for connections to London Paddington.

**Stena Line** ( ☎ 0870 570 7070; www.stenaline.co.uk) runs regular ferry services (3½ hours, two daily) as well as faster summertime catamarans (two hours, two daily) from Pembroke ferry terminal to Rosslare (Ireland).

**SOUTH WALES**

---

### THRILLS & HILLS

Craggy coast and shimmering sands dominate Pembrokeshire, but turn away from the sea and follow the national park inland from Newport to the ancient **Preseli Hills** and a whole new landscape reveals itself. It's littered with prehistoric forts, standing stones and burial chambers, and ancient trade routes crossed these spiritual hills. From here, around 1500 BC, came the bluestone megaliths of Stonehenge in England, almost 250 miles away.

This is excellent walking and mountain-biking country, where quiet country lanes lead through the Gwam Valley to the highest peak in the Preseli Hills, Cwmcerwyn (536m). From the summit, the views across the coastline and beyond to the Irish Sea are breathtaking.

Walkers should arm themselves with Ordnance Survey map OL35 and pick up the **Green Dragon Bus** ( ☎ 0845 602 7008; www.greendragonbus.co.uk; return adult/child £4/2) dial-a-ride service to the trailhead, which operates Tuesday to Sunday from May to September.

Cyclists should head for **Newport Bike Hire** ( ☎ 01239-820773; www.newportbikehire.com; East St; per half-/full day £10/15), which is located inside the Newport Wholefoods shop. It has a great selection of cycling maps and guides among the world-music CDs and wind chimes.

---

Take Richards Brothers bus 410 (five minutes, half-hourly Monday to Saturday) from Market Sq to the ferry terminal and train station.

## NEWPORT (TREFDRAETH)
**pop 1200**

Not to be confused with the town of the same name undergoing massive urban regeneration near Cardiff, diminutive Newport is an attractive community with beach and coastal path access. Dominated by the rocky outcrop of **Carn Ingli** (337m), it is set between the twin delights of Newport Bay and the mystical Preseli Hills (see the boxed text, above).

The helpful **tourist office** ( ☎ 01239-820912; newport tic@pembrokeshirecoast.org.uk; 2 Bank Cottages, Long St; ✆ 10am-1pm & 1.45-5.30pm Mon-Sat Apr-Oct, plus Sun Jul-Aug) is opposite the car park one block north of the main street.

**West Wales ECO Centre** ( ☎ 01239-820235; www.ecocentre.org.uk; Lower St Mary St; admission free; ✆ 9.30am-4.30pm Mon-Fri; 🖳 ) is an educational resource centre for green issues and sustainability. There's public internet access, a kids' corner and a garden to record the effects of climate change.

### Sleeping & Eating

**Cnapan** ( ☎ 01239-820575; www.cnapan.co.uk; East St; s/d £40/80; closed mid-Jan–mid-Mar; 🖳 ) More classic but still very comfortable, this restaurant (dinner £28) with rooms has five bright, light-filled rooms and a flower-filled garden. The restaurant serves up great local seafood and will even cater for vegans (dinner only). There is access to the restaurant for travellers with disabilities.

**our pick** **Llys Meddyg Restaurant with Rooms** ( ☎ 01239-820008; www.llysmeddyg.com; East St; d £90-150; 🅿 🖳 ) This converted doctor's residence takes contemporary big-city cool and plonks it firmly by the seaside, with original artworks displayed throughout the house. The chic rooms feel modern and contemporary while the bar and restaurant (mains £18 to £20; open lunch and dinner) continue the design ethos: a funky cellar bar downstairs for cocktails, a more classical, elegant dining room upstairs for fine dining and, outside, the garden kitchen serves high-quality pub-style dishes in a less formal atmosphere. Two new attic rooms were under construction at the time of writing.

**Canteen** ( ☎ 01239-820131; Market St; mains around £11; ✆ 10am-9pm) A sunny cafe-bistro, now under new management, serving coffees and snacks by day and well-prepared mains in the evening. Try the good-value supper set menu (£12 for two courses) from 6pm to 7pm weekdays.

### Getting There & Away

Richards Brothers bus 412 runs through Newport between Fishguard (15 minutes, hourly Monday to Saturday, three on Sunday) and Cardigan (30 minutes).

## CARDIGAN (ABERTEIFI)
**pop 4000**

Although Cardigan lies in the county of Ceredigion, it appears in this section as it's the closest town to the northern trailhead of the Pembrokeshire Coastal Path – the walk actually begins at Poppit Sands to the northwest of the town. Cardigan is also the southern hub for the new 60-mile **Ceredigion Coastal Path** (www .walkcardiganbay.co.uk), which now connects up with the Pembrokeshire Coastal Path as part of a wider initiative to open the whole of the Welsh coastline to walkers at a future date.

The **tourist office** ( ☎ 01239-613230; cardigantic@ ceredigion.gov.uk; Bath House Rd; ☼ 10am-5pm daily Jul & Aug, 10am-5pm Mon-Sat Sep-Jun) shares the lobby with the local arts hub, **Theatr Mwldan** ( ☎ 01239-621200; www.mwldan.co.uk).

## Sights

A contrasting vision of ragged stone, rampant ivy and plastic tarpaulin, the town's medieval **Cardigan Castle** is slowly emerging from decades of neglect. In more-glorious times, some 800 years ago, the castle hosted the first competitive eisteddfod, held by Lord Rhys ap Gruffydd in 1176 to select his court musicians (see Essential Eisteddfod, p755). Today restoration work is ongoing, with only limited public access. Find the site down tiny Green St opposite the Castle Cafe.

Across the bridge, Cardigan's **Heritage Centre** ( ☎ 01239-614404; admission free; ☼ 10am-5pm Sun-Fri), located in a restored granary, tells the town's history.

## Sleeping & Eating

**Poppit Sands YHA** ( ☎ 0870 770 5996; www.yha.org.uk; dm £14) Rural and secluded, this simple hostel is 4 miles northwest of town and near the trailhead of the Pembrokeshire Coast Path national trail. The Poppit Rocket (p710) sets down in the Poppit Sands car park, from where it's a half-mile walk.

**Tipi West** ( ☎ 07813-672336; www.tipiwest.co.uk; Hendre Farm, Blaenannerch; sites per adult/child £20/15) For a rustic but relaxing camping experience, this authentic tipi (tepee) encampment is a stone's throw from the golden sands of Aberporth – just bring a sleeping bag, towel and charcoal. Located 5 miles northeast of Cardigan off the A487.

**Llety Teifi** ( ☎ 01239-615566; www.llety.co.uk; Pendre; s/d/f from £45/70/95; P 💻 ) New and stylish with a very contemporary interior, this is Cardigan's first boutique B&B. The 10 en suite rooms boast cable internet and DVD players for style seekers, but the B&B is also open to children, has wheelchair access on the ground floor and is the only place in town to welcome pets. Breakfast is currently served next door at adjoining Highbury guesthouse until a new restaurant opens on site in 2009.

**our pick** **Ultracomida Deli** (Market Hall; ☼ cafe 10am-4pm, deli 10am-3pm) The sister cafe to Aberystwyth's Ultracomida (p744), this new branch maintains the winning combination of Welsh, French and Spanish deli-style cuisine. It serves the best coffee in town while the *barras* (rolls) offer a delicious combination of deli fare for around £2.50.

**Cafe Food for Thought** ( ☎ 01239-621863; 13 High St; ☼ 9am-5pm Mon-Sat) Specialising in organic and vegetarian meals, this is a cosy little coffee shop with lost of homemade daily specials.

## Getting There & Away

Richards Brothers bus 412 serves Haverfordwest (1½ hours, hourly Monday to Saturday, three on Sunday) via Fishguard (50 minutes). Heading east, more-remote points on the north coast are served by the Poppit Rocket (p710).

SOUTH WALES

# Mid Wales

Ignore Mid Wales at your peril. While generations of visitors have traditionally viewed the region as a staging post en route to elsewhere, this region has more hidden gems than any other and is the crucible for the new Welsh movements championing green issues and local, organic food.

The Brecon Beacons National Park, a pastel-hued counterpoint to North Wales' serrated peaks, remains the big draw, activity-wise. It offers a wealth of outdoor pursuits. But it's not all muddy boots and waterproofs. Towards the English border, charming Hay-on-Wye is the second-hand-book capital of the world, the area around Brecon plays home to the Green Man Festival, Wales' number-one music festival, and Abergavenny is the unlikely champion of Wales as Britain's great undiscovered foodie haven. While Powys feels more low key overall, hippie-chic Machynlleth is a nucleus of sustainable living with its Centre for Alternative Technology, while Builth Wells offers a glimpse of rural Welsh culture at its best. Finally Ceredigion is dominated by coastal Aberystwyth, a town at a crossroads with its buzzing university population, independent spirit and continued talk of regeneration.

Slow up, consider your carbon miles and take your time over lunch. There's no hurry here, so simply enjoy the view from the country's most scenic commuter ride – a window seat on the renowned Heart of Wales line.

**MID WALES**

## HIGHLIGHTS

- Making your contribution to counter climate change at the superb Centre for Alternative Technology, then getting back to nature at a tepee camp, both near **Machynlleth** (p740)

- Browsing for books, catching a reading, or pulling on your walking boots at **Hay-on-Wye** (p732)

- Sampling the new vintage of Welsh whisky after a tour of the **Penderyn Distillery** (p729)

- Tucking into the very best of the local food and drink as part of the burgeoning Mid Wales food scene around **Abergavenny** (p734)

- Getting active on foot, by bike or by whatever means to conquer the rugged **Brecon Beacons** (p724)

- Riding through Wales' rural heartland on the gloriously scenic **Heart of Wales line** (p736)

| ■ POPULATION: 209,800 | ■ AREA: 2696 SQ MILES | ■ PISTYLL RHAEADR IN POWYS IS THE HIGHEST WATERFALL IN ENGLAND AND WALES AT 73M |

MID WALES

## Orientation & Information

This region stretches west from the Welsh-English border to Cardigan Bay on the coast, encompassing the Brecon Beacons to the south and Snowdonia in the north; dominated by the counties of Powys and Ceredigion.

Walking in the Brecon Beacons may be the main focus for lovers of the outdoor life, but Mid Wales is chock-full of other lung-bursting activities, from mountain-biking to canoeing. The area is also home to Wales' burgeoning foodie scene. Local tourist offices have more details, but also see www.visitmidwales.co.uk.

## Getting Around

Mid Wales revels in a slower pace of life and hence, transport-wise, the A470 between the

Brecon Beacons and Snowdonia is the closest alternative to a motorway in these parts. Expect to encounter farm tractors on narrow roads, so just relax, slow down and enjoy the view.

Public transport is less frequent than in other regions, especially in the more remote areas – check details with **Traveline Cymru** ( ☎ 0871 200 2233; www.travelinecymru.org.uk).

Train-wise, the Cambrian Main Line dissects Mid Wales, travelling from Shrewsbury to Aberystwyth via Machynlleth, while the scenic **Heart of Wales line** (see the boxed text, p736) skirts the Brecon Beacons.

**Arriva Trains** ( ☎ 0845 6061 660; www.arrivatrains wales.co.uk) offers Freedom of Wales Flexi Pass tickets (All Wales/South & Mid Wales £69/47)

with four days of train and eight days of bus travel, plus discounts on attractions, available at most railway stations and online at www.walesflexipass.co.uk.

# BRECON BEACONS

## BRECON BEACONS NATIONAL PARK (PARC CENEDLAETHOL BANNAU BRYCHEINIOG)

Soaring majestically in a wave of dappled pastel tones, the Brecon Beacons (www .breconbeacons.org) roll in a sea of greens, blues, reds and browns across a large slice of Mid Wales. Three distinct regions border the park: the industrial valleys to the south, the central farming heartland to the north and the English border to the east. Swaddled with grassy moors and uplands, the Beacons provide a striking contrast to rock-strewn Snowdonia in the north, but offer comparable thrills and excitement.

There are various theories about the origin of the name Beacons. One folk tale tells of fire beacons once lit on the hills for ritual burials during the Bronze and Iron Ages, another of fires for signalling during the Wars and as recently as the millennium.

The Beacons refers to fires atop the principal mountains of the park that were lit to scare off the hordes of invading English in the 15th century. They have occasionally been lit ever since to mark special anniversaries, such as the millennium. The last attempt to light the beacons for an anniversary of the national park was thwarted by – you guessed it – the wet Welsh weather.

Walking is a major activity, with three key trails: Offa's Dyke Path, along the eastern border, the Taff Trail, which heads south from Brecon, and the Beacons Way, a 100-mile linear walk across the national park. The Monmouthshire & Brecon Canal follows the valley of the River Usk from Brecon via Abergavenny down to the coast.

For adventure-seekers, the park offers top opportunities for hang-gliding, fishing, horse riding, caving and mountain-biking, while touring cyclists can pedal the national pan-Wales route, the Lôn Las Cymru (see Freewheeling Through Wales, p682).

The national park extends for a mere 15 miles north to south and 45 miles west to east, but embraces four mountain ranges. Its name derives from the central and highest range of the quartet, the Brecon Beacons, the high point of which is Pen-y-Fan (886m). The other ranges are Fforest Fawr, peaking at Fan Fawr (734m) to the south, where tumbling streams join the River Neath to empty into Swansea Bay; the quieter Black Mountain to the west, which peaks at Fan Brycheiniog (802m); and to the east the not-to-be-confused-with-the-former Black Mountains, peaking at Waun Fach (811m).

Brecon, Abergavenny and Hay-on-Wye all make good base towns with a wide range of accommodation and dining options. The closest train stations are at Abergavenny and Merthyr Tydfil.

Lying 30 miles from the M4 Severn Bridge near Bristol, the park is easily reached from southern England, and as a result is a popular destination on weekends and public holidays.

### Information

The **National Park Visitor Centre** ( ☎ 01874-623366; Mountain Centre, Libanus; ☷ 9.30am-6pm May-Sep, to 5pm Oct-Mar) has a wealth of information and an excellent restaurant for coffee and a light lunch with lots of vegetarian and children's options. It's located in open countryside near the village of Libanus, 5 miles southwest of Brecon off the A470.

There are two other dedicated park information centres:

**Abergavenny** ( ☎ 01873-853254; ☷ 9.30am-5.30pm Easter-Oct, 10am-4pm Nov-Easter) Sharing space with the town tourist office.

**Llandovery** ( ☎ 01550-720693; ☷ 9.30am-1pm & 1.45-5pm daily Easter-Oct, 10am-1pm & 1.45-4pm Mon-Sat, 10am-noon Sun Oct-Easter)

The visitor centre at Craig-y-Nos Country Park was due for closure at the time of writing.

*Brecon Beacons National Park Welcome!* is a useful free booklet of activities, sights and accommodation. Pick it up at any tourist office.

### Activities

#### ACTIVITY CENTRES

**Black Mountain Activities** ( ☎ 01497-847897; www .blackmountain.co.uk; Three Cocks) Whitewater kayaking, caving, climbing, biking, orienteering and abseiling, plus provides B&B lodge accommodation. Located near Brecon; take exit 24 from the M4 and follow signs from the A479 onto the A4078.

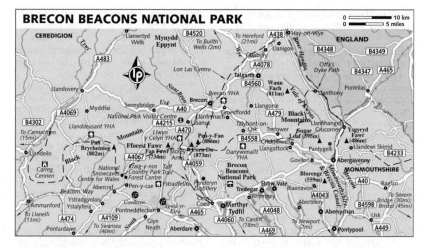

**Llangorse Multi Activity Centre** ( ☎ 01874-658272; www.activityuk.com; Gilfach Farm, Llangorse) Gorge-scrambling, horse riding, indoor climbing wall and a mile-long zipwire, the SkyTrek. Also bunkhouse, B&B and camping accommodation. Located near Brecon, it's signposted from the B4560 heading east down country-lane tracks.

## CANAL CRUISING
The 33-mile Monmouthshire & Brecon Canal was built to transport coal and iron to the sea. Take a narrow-boat from Brecon down the valley of the River Usk to Abergavenny, continuing to Pontypool. There are six locks on the canal, and one 22-mile section that is lock-free. One section was closed after landslides in 2008 but should re-open by summer 2009.

Try a 2½-hour pleasure trip from Brecon with **Dragonfly Cruises** ( ☎ 07831-685222; www.dragon flycruises.co.uk; Canal Basin, Brecon), which runs one or two cruises two to five days per week from March to September and one cruise two days per week in October – call for daily sailings. Trips vary by season with the most frequent departures in July and August.

For a longer visit, self-pilot a narrow-boat from **Cambrian Cruisers** ( ☎ 01874-665315; www.cambriancruisers.co.uk; Ty Newydd, Pencelli) or **Beacon Park Boats** ( ☎ 01873-858277; www.beaconparkboats.com; Boathouse, Llanfoist).

## CAVING & SHOWCAVES
Hidden beneath the Beacons are some of Britain's longest and deepest cave systems, lying mainly to the south in the Upper Swansea Valley and around Crickhowell. Tourist offices stock information, but unless you are an experienced spelunker you should stick to an organised trip with an activity centre.

Discovered in 1912, the superb **National Showcaves Centre for Wales** ( ☎ 01639-730284; www.showcaves.co.uk; Abercrave, Swansea; adult/child £11.50/7; ☺ 10am-3pm Easter-Oct) features three separate caverns to explore, plus a host of family activities. Dan-yr-Ogof is 16 miles south of Brecon on the A4067, just north of Abercraf.

## CYCLING
The 77-mile **Taff Trail** runs between Cardiff and Brecon. The mountain section, from Merthyr Tydfil to Talybont-on-Usk, crosses the heart of the park, climbing to 450m.

Great mountain-biking is possible throughout the park, with 15 easy and hard routes compiled on map leaflets (£7) produced by the National Park Authority. Guided routes in the southern Beacons can be organised through **Hobo Backpackers** ( ☎ 01495-718422; www.hobo-backpackers.com; Morgan St, Tredegar) from its hostel in Tredegar.

Try these companies for bike hire and tours around the Brecons.
**Bicycle Beano** ( ☎ 01982-560471; www.bicyclebeano.co.uk; Erwood, Builth Wells) Guided tours in and around the Brecon Beacons and Wye Valley.
**Bikes & Hikes** ( ☎ 01874-610071; www.bikesandhikes.co.uk; Warle Cottage, Llandew) Hire, routes and tours.
**BiPed Cycles** ( ☎ 01874-622296; www.bipedcycles.co.uk; 10 Ship St, Brecon) Hire and advice.

MID WALES

**Drover Holidays** ( ☎ 01497-821134; www.drover holidays.co.uk; Oxford Rd, Hay-on-Wye) Hire and advice.

Touring cyclists enjoy the national cycle route, the **Lôn Las Cymru** (see the boxed text, p682).

From late May to mid-September, on Sunday and bank holidays, the Beacons Bus (opposite) includes a 'Bike Bus' services for cyclists. For more details on cycling this region see www.cyclebreconbeacons.com and www.mtbbreconbeacons.com.

### FISHING
The waters of the Rivers Wye and Usk spawn fine sport for anglers. Fish for prime Atlantic salmon, pike, carp or trout.

For tuition from an old hand with 30 years' experience, try Builth Wells–based **Rods and Reels** ( ☎ 01982-551706; Kings Head Lane).

The National Park Authority produces the leaflet *Fishing Brecon Beacons;* or for further information see www.fishing.visitwales.com and www.fishinginwalesnp.co.uk.

### GLIDING & PARAGLIDING
Aerial-sports fans should try **Black Mountains Gliding Club** ( ☎ 01874-711463; www.blackmountains gliding.co.uk; Airfield, Talgarth, Brecon), near Talgarth, for trial lessons and intensive courses.

**Axis Paragliding & Paramotoring** ( ☎ 01873-850111; www.paraglide.co.uk; 35 Mount St, Abergavenny) offers paragliding tuition and tandem flights from its Abergavenny base.

### PONY TREKKING & HORSE RIDING
For more details see also www.horseriding breconbeacons.com.

**Cantref Riding Centre** ( ☎ 01874-665223; www .cantref.com; Upper Cantref Farm, Cantref) Mountain, farm or forest trails near Brecon.

**Grange Pony Trekking** ( ☎ 01873-890215; www .grangetrekking.co.uk; Capel-y-Ffin) Near Abergavenny in the heart of the Black Mountains.

**Llanthony Riding & Trekking** ( ☎ 01873-890359; www.llanthony.co.uk; Court Farm, Llanthony, near Abergavenny) Gentle treks and demanding mountain rides, stopping at the pub for lunch.

**Tregoyd Mountain Riders** ( ☎ 01497-847351; www .tregoydriding.co.uk; Three Cocks, near Brecon) A mountain-riding outfit that also offers B&B, bunkhouse and camp-site accommodation.

### WALKING
You could walk all summer in the park without repeating a route, such is the range of choice. From demanding mountain trails to afternoon canal-side strolls, many walks are detailed in leaflets available from National Park Information Centres and tourist offices. Guided walks are also available. The four main ranges to explore are detailed here.

Before setting out on a mountain hike, check the weather forecast via www.weather call.co.uk, **BBC Radio Wales** (www.bbc.co.uk/wales/radio wales) or see www.metoffice.gov.uk/loutdoor/ mountainsafety/brecon.html. Take waterproof clothing even if it's sunny and warm when you start. Carry food but don't share it with sheep and ponies – they become attracted to cars on the roads, which can cause accidents.

For information on Beacons Bus services around the park, see opposite.

### The Beacons, Pen-y-Fan & Corn Du
The park's classic and heavily overused summit walk is to the ridgeline peaks of Pen-y-Fan or Corn Du, dubbed 'the motorway' by wardens due to its high volume of traffic. The walk starts at the car park at the Storey Arms on the A470 Merthyr Tydfil–Brecon road, but routes such as the return trip from the Llwyn y celyn YHA hostel (three hours) or Brecon (five to six hours) may be more enjoyable as they're less crowded in high season.

### Black Mountains
Offa's Dyke Path affords stunning views, with some of the best on the exposed 17-mile ridge of the Black Mountains between Pandy and Hay-on-Wye, above the Vale of Ewyas. Follow the valley floor along the River Honddu (Honthee) from Llanfihangel Crucorney in the south of the mountains for a less demanding alternative.

### Fforest Fawr & Waterfall Walks
Famous for the lush, steep-sided gorges of the Rivers Hepste, Mellte and Nedd Fechan, the southern part of this region has several fine waterfalls, including Sgwd-yr-Eira (Waterfall of the Snow) on the Hepste, where you can actually walk behind the torrent. This walk and others are relatively close together on a stretch between Ystradfellte and Pontneddfechan.

In the north, the terrain is more akin to the bleak, open fells of the Brecon Beacons.

### Black Mountain
Wilder and less frequented than other areas of the park, Black Mountain lies in the ex-

treme west of the Beacons, near the border with Carmarthenshire. The highest point, Fan Brycheiniog (802m), can be reached via a path leading from the roadside just north of the National Showcaves Centre for Wales (p725).

## Sleeping

There's plenty of accommodation available in and around the national park, with B&Bs usually the best bet but some character properties worth exploring (see Something for the Weekend, p730 and Detour: Grosmont, p735).

There are four YHA hostels within the national park:

**Brecon YHA** ( ☎ 0870 770 5718; www.yha.org.uk; Groes-ffordd; dm £15.95) On the A40, 2.5 miles east of Brecon.

**Danywenallt YHA** ( ☎ 0870 770 6136; www.yha.org .uk; dm £17.50) On the B4558, 8 miles south of Brecon.

**Llanddeusant YHA** ( ☎ 0870 770 5930; www.yha.org .uk; dm £15.95) A real get-away-from-it-all hostel, 12 miles southwest of Brecon. Take the A40 towards Llandeilo then right for A4069 – follow hostel signs.

**Llwyn y celyn YHA** ( ☎ 0870 770 5936; ww.yha.org.uk; dm £15.95) Off the A470, 5 miles southwest of Brecon.

There are also numerous independent bunkhouses and hostels in the area, but as many cater primarily for groups it is best to book in advance. With the permission of the farmer or landowner, it may be possible to camp almost anywhere in the park, but not on National Trust (NT) land. Contact local tourist offices for details or pick up the leaflet *Camping on Farms*.

## Getting There & Around

It takes three to four hours to drive to the Brecon Beacons from London, taking the M4 or M48 then the A4042 to Abergavenny and A40 to Brecon.

Regular bus services to the national park towns are good, but few run on Sunday. Key services are the Sixty-Sixty bus X43 from Brecon to Cardiff (1½ hours, seven daily Monday to Saturday) and Stagecoach bus X63 from Brecon to Swansea (1½ hours, six daily).

For more information on public transport contact **Traveline Cymru** ( ☎ 0871 200 2233; www .travelinecymru.org.uk).

From late May to the end of September, on Sunday and bank holidays, the **Beacons Bus** ( ☎ 01873-853254; www.breconbeacons.org) operates several routes in and around the park.

With a central hub in Brecon, some of the most popular services are the B1 from Cardiff and Merthyr Tydfil, B6 from Swansea, B4 to Abergavenny and B10 to Carmarthen. The B1 and B17 (known as the Offa's Dyke bus) are both 'bike buses' in that they have a specially designed bicycle trailer for cyclists. New for summer 2008 three new routes to reach Blaenavon: the B5 from Newport, the B12 from Brecon and the B15 from Abergavenny.

The services are subsidised and, as such, routes and timetables can change significantly from one year to the next. Check the website for the latest details. The leaflet *Discover the Beacons Take the Beacons Bus* has full timetables.

The only train services in the region run from Cardiff to Merthyr Tydfil (one hour, hourly Monday to Saturday, every two hours Sunday) and Cardiff to Abergavenny (£8.90, 40 minutes, at least hourly Monday to Saturday, every two hours Sunday).

## BRECON (ABERHONDDU)
pop 8500

The stone market town of Brecon, with its winding streets and languid river crossing, is as handsome as it is traditionally Welsh. It's the transport hub for visiting the national park, a pleasant place for a stroll and packed to the rafters during the internationally renowned Brecon Jazz Festival (p728).

For an insight into the town's ancient history, the remains of an Iron Age hill fort lie atop Pen-y-Crug, 2 miles northwest of town, while those of Brecon Gaer Roman Fort can be found 3 miles west off the B5420.

The helpful **tourist office** ( ☎ 01874-622485; brectic@powys.gov.uk, 9.30am-5pm Mon-Sat, to 4pm Sun Apr-Sep, 9.30am-5pm Mon-Fri, to 4pm Sat & Sun Oct-Mar) is located in the Cattle Market car park near Morrisons supermarket. A new bus interchange is just southeast of here. There's a one-way traffic system around the centre for cars.

## Sights

Inside the town's former Shire Hall, the **Brecknock Museum & Art Gallery** ( ☎ 01874-624121; Glamorgan St; adult/child £1/50p; 10am-5pm Mon-Fri, 10am-1pm & 2-5pm Sat, Apr-Sep noon-5pm Sun) comprises a rewarding local-history collection and an art gallery with changing exhibitions.

Founded in 1093 as part of a Benedictine monastery, **Brecon Cathedral** ( ☎ 01874-623857;

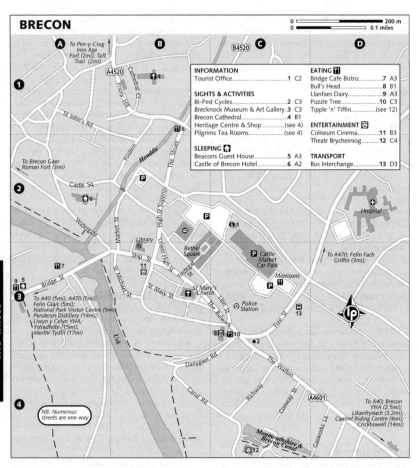

**BRECON**

| | 0 ——— 200 m |
| | 0 ——— 0.1 miles |

**INFORMATION**
Tourist Office.....................................1 C2

**SIGHTS & ACTIVITIES**
Bi-Ped Cycles...................................2 C3
Brecknock Museum & Art Gallery..3 C3
Brecon Cathedral.............................4 B1
Heritage Centre & Shop .............(see 4)
Pilgrims Tea Rooms......................(see 4)

**SLEEPING**
Beacons Guest House.....................5 A3
Castle of Brecon Hotel..................6 A2

**EATING**
Bridge Cafe Bistro............7 A3
Bull's Head.........................8 B1
Llanfaes Dairy...................9 A3
Puzzle Tree......................10 C3
Tipple 'n' Tiffin.............(see 12)

**ENTERTAINMENT**
Coliseum Cinema............11 B3
Theatr Brycheiniog.........12 C4

**TRANSPORT**
Bus Interchange..............13 D3

Cathedral Close; admission free) sits astride a hill overlooking the River Honddu. In the grounds, the **Heritage Centre & Shop** ( ☎ 01874-625222; admission free; ☼ 10.30am-4.30pm Mon-Sat, noon-4pm Sun Apr-Oct) is worth a look – as is the simple but satisfying **Pilgrims Tea Rooms** ( ☎ 01874-610610; www.pilgrimstea rooms.co.uk; ☼ 10.30am-4.30pm Mon-Sat, noon-4pm Sun Apr-Oct) for coffees and a snack.

## Activities
The 77-mile **Taff Trail** walking and cycling route, and the 33-mile **Monmouthshire & Brecon Canal** both start in Brecon. To explore these, buy one of the walking publications sold at the tourist office on behalf of the National Park Authority. For advice on local routes and to stock up on OS Maps, Mountain-

bikers should consult **Bi-Ped Cycles** ( ☎ 01874-322296; www.bipedcycles.co.uk; 10 Ship St; hire per day £20; ☼ 9am-5.30pm Mon-Sat). For horse riding and family-friendly, farm-based activities, **Cantref** ( ☎ 01874-665233; www.cantref.com; Upper Cantref Farm; riding per hr £16.50, per half-/full day £25/47.50) is a multipurpose centre located 4 miles east of Brecon on the B4558.

## Festivals & Events
Brecon is transformed for one weekend in mid-August when the world's foremost jazz players come to town. The renowned, annual **Brecon Jazz Festival** (www.breconjazz.co.uk) celebrated its 25th anniversary in 2008. See the website for bookings and plan accommodation far head – every bed in a 10-mile radius is booked

out for the festival and open areas in town become makeshift camping grounds.

## Sleeping & Eating

**Brecon YHA** ( ☎ 0870 770 5718; www.yha.org.uk; Groesffordd; dm £15.95; ✉ reception 7.30-11.30am & 5-10.30pm) The combination of good facilities, simple but comfortable rooms (some for families) and a quiet Victorian-farmhouse location make this a winner for budget travellers. It's 2.5 miles east of Brecon; take bus X43 to Brynich, or walk from Brecon via the pleasant canal-side path (about 40 minutes).

**Beacons Guesthouse** ( ☎ 01874-623339; 16 Bridge St; s/d £50/56) This old farmhouse may not be the most contemporary-style place in Brecon, but the welcome is warm and the rooms comfortable. Accommodation is split between 11 rooms with flouncy four-poster beds in the main house and three roomy but rather dark annexe suites, the latter better suited to families.

**Castle of Brecon Hotel** ( ☎ 01874-624611; www .breconcastle.co.uk; Castle Sq; s/d/ste £75/100/150; ⓟ 🖳 ) Constructed on the remains of Brecknock Castle, this grand old stately property is undergoing a major renovation program until late 2009. The refurbished suites are stylish with white bedspreads and individual features, while older rooms still have a creaky charm. Overall it retains its traditional feel ,and rear-facing rooms offer superb views of the Beacons.

**Bridge Cafe** ( ☎ 01874-622024; www.bridgecafe .co.uk; 7 Bridge St; ✉ 10am-5pm Wed-Fri, 10am-6pm Sat, bank holiday weekends & school holidays) The best all-rounder in town by far, the Bridge has beautifully prepared organic and fair-trade food using local ingredients. It operates a 'no chips' policy, offering instead home-cooked mains and vegetarian specials (around £5), plus healthy salad bowls with organic bread (£5.50). The three adjoining B&B bedrooms are spacious with feather pillows, Egyptian-cotton sheets and rustic colour schemes. Room 1 is the best, with a large en suite, a sofa bed and DVD player.

**Tipple 'n' Tiffin** ( ☎ 01874-611866; Canal Wharf; ✉ Mon-Sat) The reliable restaurant attached to Brecon's Theatr Brycheiniog is an ideal spot for a pre-theatre dinner (mains around £8) with a simple but hearty menu of traditional favourites, and canal-side seats.

For an espresso or a scoop of real Welsh ice cream, **Llanfaes Dairy** ( ☎ 01874-625892; www .llanfaesdairy.net; 19 Bridge St) is a bright and cheery place with a big menu of flavours.

For a quiet pint of local ale and some pub grub, try the **Bull's Head** ( ☎ 01974-623900; 86 The Struet).

## Entertainment

Canal-side **Theatr Brycheiniog** ( ☎ 01874-611622; www.theatrbrycheiniog.co.uk; Canal Wharf) is the town's drama and music venue, with an exhibition centre and a welcoming restaurant (see Tipple 'n' Tiffin, above).

Catch a film at the **Coliseum Cinema** ( ☎ 01874-622501; Wheat St), which has occasional art-house screenings.

---

### A DROP OF THE WELSH STUFF

**Penderyn Distillery** ( ☎ 01685-810651; www.penderyndistillery.co.uk; Penderyn; adult/12-17yr/under 12yr £7.50/4.50/free; ✉ 10am-6pm summer, call for winter hr) marks the resurgence of Welsh whisky-making after a 100-year absence (the Frongoch Distillery in Bala, North Wales, closed in the late 1800s).

This boutique and independently owned distillery released its first whisky in 2004, which remains, unlike Scottish and Irish whisky, a single-distilled malt. It is distilled with fresh spring water drawn directly from beneath the distillery, then matured in bourbon casks and finished in rich Madeira wine casks to create a golden-hued drop of spirit that is light on the palate and smooth to the taste.

Located in the southern reaches of the Brecon Beacons National Park, the imposing black building marked the opening of its high-tech new visitors centre in 2008 with a royal visit from HRH Prince Charles, Prince of Wales. The £850,000 attraction enables visitors to see craftsmen working with the unique spirits, casking the spirits for maturation and bottling the distillery's range of premium products. You can visit individually, or take a guided tour (£15 per person). The whisky master-class (£60 per person) is separate and is booked by appointment only. It is located 14 miles southwest of Brecon on the A4059.

---

**SOMETHING FOR THE WEEKEND**

Foodies flock to the **Felin Fach Griffin** ( ☎ 01874-620111; www.eatdrinksleep.ltd.uk; Felin Fach; mains £10-19; **P** ) for its excellent quality food and its 'simple things, done well' mantra. The menu features local and organic produce served with delicious simplicity in relaxed, rustic surroundings. The owners support local producers and feature local cask ales and organic wines, plus they arrange specialist tastings for regular customers. The seven cottage-style rooms (doubles/four-poster from £110/140) are cosy and warm with radios, no TVs, and local artworks. It is also one of the few dog-friendly hotels in the area. With its reputation going from strength to strength, expansion plans include a kitchen garden shop and more rooms. It's 5 miles northeast of Brecon on the A470.

Food is also a key element at **Felin Glais** ( ☎ 01874-623107; www.felinglais.co.uk; Aberyscir; d from £70; **P** 🖳 ), a four-room B&B with a homely, relaxed feel. The rooms are well thought out, with fridges packed with water and milk, and bathrooms so well stocked that you can leave the sponge bag at home. The owners send out a copy of the menu in advance, asking guests to choose their dinner, so they can go out and buy the ingredients fresh each day. Pre-dinner drinks are served in the conservatory before a dinner party–style supper *en famille* with your fellow guests. Located 5 miles west of Brecon off the A40.

---

## Getting There & Away

All services now stop at the bus interchange on Free St. National Express bus 322 runs daily to London (£23.50, five hours 20 minutes) with a change at Cardiff (1¼ hours). Brecon is also the interchange for Beacons Bus services (see p727).

The key regional bus routes are Sixty-Sixty Coaches X43 services to Abergavenny (one hour, every two hours Monday to Saturday, three on Sunday) and Cardiff (1½ hours); Stagecoach buses 39 via Hay-on-Wye (35 minutes, roughly every two hours Monday to Saturday, two on Sunday) to Hereford (100 minutes); and Veoila Transport X63 bus to Swansea (1½ hours, about every two hours Monday to Saturday).

## AROUND BRECON

Located on the A40 between Brecon and Abergavenny, **Crickhowell**, overlooked by Sugar Loaf Mountain, is an attractive little town as a base to explore the wider area. Most of the attractions, plus some excellent places to eat, are a short drive away along the country roads of the nearby Black Mountains (see Favourite Foodie Hideaways, p734). The **tourist office** ( ☎ 01873-812105; Beaufort St; ⏰ 10am-5pm, to 4pm Oct-Mar) can advise on local attractions.

In town, the best eating option is the **Bear Hotel** ( ☎ 01873-810408; www.bearhotel.co.uk; Beaufort St), a labyrinthine but charming old inn with a good reputation for its food, notably local specialities such as black-beef steaks. The cosy bar has lunches (mains around £9) while the

traditional restaurant serves dinners and Sunday roasts (mains around £15). The off-courtyard bedrooms (singles/doubles £80/90, executive singles/doubles £117/153) have been refurbished with new bathrooms. To splash out, take room 27, an executive four-poster with a giant jacuzzi bath.

## ABERGAVENNY (Y FENNI)
pop 14,055

Although just outside the Brecon Beacons National Park, bustling workaday Abergavenny is a natural base for exploring the surrounding hills (all *within* the park) with its strong range of facilities. Not the most instantly attractive town, it's a place worth getting to know.

Abergavenny was traditionally best known as a place for outdoor pursuits in the Vale of Usk and is today building a growing reputation as a cycling centre. But it is as the capital of a burgeoning food scene that the town has really come into its own. Its position at the heart of Wales' lauded cuisine scene, which celebrates the best in fresh and organic produce, is generating international interest in both the Food Festival (opposite) and acclaimed local eateries (see Favourite Foodie Hideaways, p734), the best of which are located out of town.

Abergavenny is also the main train hub for visiting the Brecon Beacons National Park.

## Information

The helpful **tourist office** ( ☎ 01873-853254; Swan Meadow, Monmouth Rd; ⏰ 9.30am-5.30pm Easter-Oct, 10am-4pm Nov-Easter) has now merged with the

National Park Visitor Centre. They can advise on local walks.

The main post office is on Castle St; the **library** ( ☎ 01873-735980; cnr Victoria & Baker St; ☿ closed Wed & Sun) has free internet.

## Sights

The ruins of **Abergavenny Castle** overlook the River Usk meadows. In 1645 after several sieges, Royalist forces destroyed the castle beyond use. The keep, restored during the Victorian era, today houses the small **Abergavenny Museum** ( ☎ 01873-854282; Castle St; admission free; ☿ 11am-1pm & 2-5pm Mon-Sat, 2-5pm Sun Mar-Oct, 11am-1pm & 2-4pm Mon-Sat Nov-Feb), which recounts the life of Abergavenny through the ages.

Dating from the 13th century, **St Mary's Priory Church** ( ☎ 01873-853168; Hereford Rd; donation requested; ☿ 10am-noon & 2-4pm Mon-Sat, 2-4pm Sun) is notable for its oak, stone and alabaster tombs, and carved Jesse tree, the latter depicting the family lineage of Jesus. The adjacent Tithe Barn was being renovated as a heritage centre when we visited.

## Activities

Abergavenny is an excellent base for outdoor activities. The tourist office can advise on mountain walking on Sugar Loaf, Blorenge and Ysgyryd Fawr, all close to Abergavenny, plus biking the gentle canal towpath 20 miles to Brecon.

**Beacon Park Boats** ( ☎ 01873-858277; www.beaconparkboats.com; Llanfoist Wharf; narrow-boat hire 4 nights midweek from £686), located in the village of Llanfoist, just southwest of Abergavenny, offers excursions on the Monmouthshire & Brecon Canal.

## Festivals & Events

The biggest celebration in Abergavenny's calendar is the **Food Festival** (www.abergavenny.net/foodfestival), held over a weekend in mid-September. Local producers and notable (British) celebrities come together to celebrate the best in regional grub through a series of master-classes, demonstrations, tastings, talks and guided walks.

## Sleeping

**Blacksheep Backpackers** ( ☎ 01873-859125; www.blacksheepbackpackers.co.uk; 24 Station Rd; dm/tw incl breakfast £13.50/15; 🖳 ) Basic but friendly bunkhouse-style accommodation is the order of the day at this simple place. With a bar-cum–pool room in the pub next door, it's a good place to meet fellow travellers.

**Mulberry House** ( ☎ 01873-855959; www.mulberrycentre.com.co.uk; Penypound Rd; dm incl breakfast £24.50; 🅿 ) This residential environmental study centre now runs a joint venture with the YHA to offer hostel beds right in the city. Housed in an old convent, it's a secluded and peaceful spot, and popular with weekenders for outdoor pursuits, with drying rooms and safe storage. A cracking three-course dinner costs £10.80 and new, en suite family rooms offer discounted rates for children under 11.

**our pick** **Guest House** ( ☎ 01873-854823; www.theguesthouseabergavenny.co.uk; 2 Oxford St; s/d from £30/60; 🖳 ) First the health warning: this place is not everyone's cup of tea. Yes, the grasp of language by the swearing parrot is more colourful than a Hawaiian shirt competition, and Bramley and Braeburn, the pet pot-bellied pigs in the garden-cum-menagerie, are not your typical guard dogs, but this place has character and then some. The straight-talking

---

**GREENER THAN GLASTONBURY?**

If you're fed up with the corporate-sponsored festival scene, then the **Green Man Festival** (www.thegreenmanfestival.co.uk), held annually in August, could be for you.

Set near Crickhowell in the rolling beauty of the Brecon Beacons National Park, the Green Man sits proudly at the forefront of the summer-festival circuit as an event that caters well for children and people with disabilities and has a strong green ethos. It remains an independent festival.

Launched in 2003, the shindig celebrates the best of the alternative, folk and country scene, pulling in bigger names each year as word of mouth spreads. The 2008 line-up featured Super Furry Animals, Spiritualised and Pentangle.

Aside from the bands, attractions include DJ sets, theatre, cinema, healing workshops and creative kids' workshops.

Tickets for the three-day event cost £105 plus booking fee, but children aged 11 years or under at the time of the festival enjoy free entry.

owner will regale you with expletive-packed tales over breakfast, while the rooms are basic but comfortable. Pack your sense of humour, crack a cold one in front of the football and please do feed the animals. A true one-off.

**Highfield House** ( ☎ 01873-852371; www.high fieldabergavenny.co.uk; 6 Belmont Rd; s/d £40/62; **P** ) Set among attractive gardens, Highfield House sits above town in a homely and tasteful Victorian villa, dating from 1880. The three en suite rooms, named after local castles (Grosmont is the biggest and smartest) are welcoming. Front-facing rooms offer views across to Sugar Loaf Mountain.

**Angel Hotel** ( ☎ 01873-857121; www.angelhotel abergavenny.com; 15 Cross St; s/d from £65/85, refurbished r £110; **P** **💻** ) The grand old dame at the heart of town is looking far smarter these days with the extensive refurbishment of the hotel well under way. The communal areas downstairs, including the restaurant (mains around £20), feel sleek and sophisticated, and the four re-furbished bedrooms are all dark wood and flat-screen TVs. The other 28 rooms do feel rather tired but work was due for completion by end of 2009, although the some work was scheduled at the property until 2013.

## Eating

**Trading Post** ( ☎ 01873-855448; 14 Nevill St; 🕘 9am-5pm Mon-Sat) A good range of ethnic coffees and light meals, including a decent children's menu, make this all-day bistro a fitting option for a quick bite in the town centre.

**La Brasseria** ( ☎ 01873-737937; www.labrasseria.co.uk; The Stables, Lewis Lane; 🕘 noon-3pm & 6-11pm Mon-Fri, noon-11pm Sat) An Italian restaurant with a strong menu and a wily nod to local produce, this place has a sense of class. The upstairs dining room is classic and elegant while the downstairs bar has a relaxed, lounge feel, and the terrace offers an alfresco aperitif; mains around £15.

## Getting There & Away

Bus services from Monday to Saturday include the X3 to Cardiff (1½ hours, at least hourly); the X43 to Brecon (50 minutes, every two hours); and the 83 to Monmouth (one hour, four daily) via Raglan (35 minutes).

From late May to mid-September the Sunday-service Beacons Bus B4 (p727) serves Abergavenny.

The train station is a five-minute walk south of the tourist office along Monmouth Rd. Trains run to Cardiff (£8.90, 45 minutes, roughly hourly) via Newport (25 minutes).

## HAY-ON-WYE (Y GELLI)
**pop 1500**

Hay-on-Wye, a pretty little town on the banks of the River Wye just inside the Welsh border, has become the stuff of legend. First came the explosion of second-hand bookshops, a charge led by the charismatic and forthright local maverick Richard Booth (see p689). Booth opened his eponymous bookshop in the 1960s, stocking it with cast-off libraries from various national institutions and country houses. He went onto to proclaim himself the King of Hay among other elaborate publicity stunts while campaigning for an international network of book towns to support failing rural economies.

With Hay becoming the world's second-hand-book capital, a festival of literature and culture was established in 1988, growing in stature each year to take in all aspects of the creative arts. Today the **Hay Festival** (opposite), as it is now known, is a major attraction in its own right, famously endorsed by the former American president Bill Clinton in 2001 when he described it as the 'Woodstock of the mind'. Accommodation during the festival is now fully booked several years ahead.

But Hay is not just about book browsing and celebrity spotting – it also makes an excellent base for country pursuits with walking the Black Mountains, canoeing the River Wye, or hiking Offa's Dyke Path all within easy access of the superb facilities of the town.

## Orientation & Information

Higgledy-piggledy Hay is built around a spider's web of crooked lanes. Get your bearings on Oxford St, where the bus stops and car park are adjacent to the hit-and-miss **tourist office** ( ☎ 01497-820144; Oxford Rd; 🕘 10am-5pm Easter-Oct, 11am-1pm & 2-4pm Nov-Easter).

There's free internet access at the **library** (Chancery Lane; 🕘 10am-1pm, 2-4.30pm & 5-7pm Mon, 10am-1pm & 2-5pm Thu & Fri, 9.30am-1pm Sat).

### BOOKSHOPS

There are currently 29 second-hand and anti-quarian booksellers in Hay with hundreds of thousands of tomes stacked floor to ceiling across town. The tourist office has a map of the shops with a profile of each one. They cater for all interests from cinema to crime via children's books and rare first editions. As such, it's virtually impossible to recommend any one per se, but these are some of the must-browse picks.

**Booth Books** ( ☎ 01497-820322; www.hayonwyebook sellers.com; 44 Lion St) Booth has now sold this bookshop to a new owner but it retains over 400,000 tomes across three floors.

**Hay Castle Books** ( ☎ 01497-820503; Castle Dr) Booth's primary domain with a suitably eclectic stock.

**Hay Cinema Bookshop** ( ☎ 01497-820071; www .haycinemabookshop.co.uk; Castle St) Huge collection of books about film-making and cinema.

**Marijana Dworski Books** ( ☎ 01497-82200; www .dworskibooks.com; Backfold) Specialists in languages.

**Murder & Mayhem** ( ☎ 01497-821613; 5 Lion St) Detective fiction, crime and horror.

**Rose's Books** ( ☎ 01497-820013; www.rosebooks.com; 14 Broad St) Rare children's and illustrated books.

## Activities

The Offa's Dyke Path walking route (see p437) passes nearby. The Offa's Dyke Flyer circular minibus runs three times on summer Sundays and bank holidays to help you along the way. The tourist office has schedules.

**Drover Holidays** ( ☎ 01497-821134; www.drover holidays.co.uk; 3 Oxford Rd) arranges self-guided walking (three days from £195 per person) and cycling tours (two days from £165), plus bike hire (half/full day £15/25) from its hire shop by the tourist office. The company encourages customers to use public transport.

Contact **Paddles & Pedals** ( ☎ 01497-820604; www .canoehire.co.uk; 15 Castle St; canoe hire £25/40, kayak hire half-/full day £15/25) for excursions on the River Wye.

## Festivals & Events

The **Hay Festival** ( ☎ 01497-08709901299; www.hay festival.com) has become Britain's leading festival of literature and the arts. There are free shuttle buses from the town centre to its current site, in fields to the east.

The 10-day event, in late May/early June, has grown to include a slew of readings, lectures, concerts and workshops across several stages, attracting a diverse, artistic crowd and some heavyweight star turns. In fact, such has been the impact of the festival that international spin-off events have been held in Spain and Colombia in recent years.

**MID WALES**

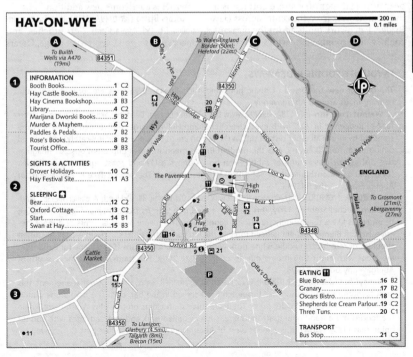

### HAY-ON-WYE

0 ——— 200 m
0 ——— 0.1 miles

| INFORMATION | |
|---|---|
| Booth Books | 1 C2 |
| Hay Castle Books | 2 B2 |
| Hay Cinema Bookshop | 3 B3 |
| Library | 4 C2 |
| Marijana Dworski Books | 5 B2 |
| Murder & Mayhem | 6 C2 |
| Paddles & Pedals | 7 B2 |
| Rose's Books | 8 B2 |
| Tourist Office | 9 B3 |

| SIGHTS & ACTIVITIES | |
|---|---|
| Drover Holidays | 10 C2 |
| Hay Festival Site | 11 A3 |

| SLEEPING | |
|---|---|
| Bear | 12 C2 |
| Oxford Cottage | 13 C2 |
| Start | 14 B1 |
| Swan at Hay | 15 B3 |

| EATING | |
|---|---|
| Blue Boar | 16 B2 |
| Granary | 17 B2 |
| Oscars Bistro | 18 C2 |
| Shepherds Ice Cream Parlour | 19 C2 |
| Three Tuns | 20 C1 |

| TRANSPORT | |
|---|---|
| Bus Stop | 21 C3 |

To Builth Wells via A470 (19mi)

To Wales-England Border (50m); Hereford (22mi)

To Grosmont (21mi); Abergavenny (27mi)

ENGLAND

To Llanigon: Glasbury (4.5mi); Talgarth (8mi); Brecon (15mi)

The site is a rarity amongst festivals: friendly to visitors with disabilities and children, and organised according to green principles.

## Sleeping

**Oxford Cottage** ( ☎ 01497-820008; www.oxfordcottage .co.uk; Oxford Rd; d from £44) This place, set in a characterful Georgian town house, bills itself as self-catering B&B as the owners don't live on site and you're left to help yourself to breakfast in the farmhouse kitchen. The three rooms feature quirky sloping and squeaky floors but are not en suite. It works best for a group of friends and can be rented as a whole property for weekend breaks (minimum two nights).

**Bear** ( ☎ 01497-821302; www.thebearhay.co.uk; Bear St; s/d without bathroom £31/56, d with bathroom from £70; P ) Homely and rustic with exposed stone walls and original beams, plus a liberal sprinkling of books, this former coaching inn remains a popular choice. It only has four rooms, of which two are en suite, and excels at breakfast with organic, fair-trade and vegetarian-friendly options to kick-start the day.

**Start** ( ☎ 01497-821391; www.the-start.net; s/d £35/70; P ) Peacefully set on the fringes of town, this beautiful 18th-century stone cottage is a five-minute walk from the centre across Hay Bridge. Patchwork quilts adorn the pleasant country-style rooms, some with a view of the river. The setting, away from the centre in a quiet, riverside enclave, adds to the tranquil atmosphere. There are good lock-up and drying facilities for hikers and bikers. Packed lunches and afternoon teas are also available.

**Swan at Hay Hotel** ( ☎ 01497-821188; www.swan athay.co.uk; Church St; d/tw/f £125/135/155; P ) The smartest place in Hay, and the most likely to be booked out during the festival, the Swan is still undergoing refurbishment, although the revamp downstairs is now finished. The bedrooms, while comfortable and clean, will have a more contemporary feel after work is completed, but the downstairs restaurant now has an elegant, fine-dining motif. Dogs and children welcome.

## Eating & Drinking

**Granary** ( ☎ 01497-820790; Broad St; mains around £6; ☺ 9am-5.30pm year-round, 8am-9pm school holidays & festival; ⌨ wi-fi) Popular and welcoming, this bustling country-kitchen cafe is the staple choice for breakfasts, snack lunches and coffees. It's great for vegetarians and vegans, and families, with menus for all, while the huge upstairs gallery offers extra seating. Free wi-fi internet is a welcome new addition.

**Oscars Bistro** ( ☎ 01497-821193; High Town; mains around £9; ☺ 10am-4.30pm) For lunches and snacks, plus a good vegetarian range, Oscars

---

**FAVOURITE FOODIE HIDEAWAYS**

The best of new the breed of rustic pubs and Michelin-stared eateries are located down the country roads around Abergavenny.

**Walnut Tree Inn** ( ☎ 01873-852797; www.thewalnuttreeinn.com; Llanddewi Skirrid; ☺ lunch & dinner Tue-Sat) Reopened in 2007 with executive chef Shaun Hill in charge, this refined eatery sets the standard by which all other restaurants in the region are to be judged. The delicately understated dining room has 70 covers, and the modern-British menu includes unpretentious but imaginative dishes, such as saddle of rabbit, liver and kidneys (£17) and roast squab-pigeon breast (£19). Call one month ahead for Saturday-night reservations. The Walnut Tree is 2 miles east of Abergavenny on the B4521.

**Hardwick** ( ☎ 01873-854220; www.thehardwick.co.uk; Old Raglan Rd; ☺ lunch & dinner Tue-Sat, lunch Sun) Run by chef Stephen Terry, this rustic, food-led pub with its stone fireplace and low ceiling beams feels like a reassuringly traditional country inn. The menu, however, hints at a more creative, Heston Blumenthal–influenced force in the kitchen with the likes of double-cooked stuffed shoulder of rare-breed middle white pork with creamy haricot beans (£17). Plans for expansion are afoot with eight B&B rooms due to open in late 2009. The Hardwick is 2 miles south of Abergavenny on the B4598.

**Nantyffin Cider Mill** ( ☎ 01873-810775; Brecon Rd; ☺ lunch & dinner) Under new management, this local favourite continues to offer top-notch food served in the bar, or in the bare-stone dining room around the original cider press. There are three draft ciders on tap, plus Welsh Perry, while the food is more traditional gastropub fare, such as grilled pork-and-leek sausages with spring-onion mash (£9). Nantyffin is 7 miles west of Abergavenny on the A40 just past Crickhowell.

MID WALES

---

**DETOUR: GROSMONT**

For an escape from mobile-phone reception and festival-goers at Hay-on-Wye or Abergavenny, Grosmont is a charming and characterful village set amid the classically beautiful Monmouthshire countryside.

A good base is **Gentle Jane** ( ☎ 01981-241655; www.gentlejane.co.uk; d £80), a three-room B&B and tea room oozing class, from the date-and-walnut cake upon arrival to the fresh rhubarb, yoghurt and muesli for breakfast.

The local village castle and churchyard are worth an idle wander while the local pub, the **Angel Inn** ( ☎ 01981-240646), is the centrepiece of the village and hosts regular real-ale festivals. While away an evening with good beer and friendly locals.

If you're exploring by car, some of the roads make getting lost a pleasure. Take your time on the country tracks that lead across the Black Mountains. Only the local farmers know the roads well enough to tackle the blind corners and switchback turns of the deserted country lanes, and, besides, you won't want to miss the view down to Hay-on-Wye from Hay Bluff as you ascend to 677m on a crystal-clear day.

Grosmont is 11 miles northeast of Abergavenny and 21 miles southeast of Hay-on-Wye on the B437. Put down the guidebook and explore – but don't go telling everyone about our little secret.

---

is a popular option for a quick bite in the heart of town.

**Blue Boar** ( ☎ 01497-820884; Castle St; mains around £11) The pick of the pubs in town, this cosy and traditional place is ideal for whiling away an afternoon with a decent pint of Timothy Taylor's ale, a home-cooked lunch of Glamorgan sausage with plum chutney and new potatoes, and a good book. Hearty food is served all day.

**Three Tuns** ( ☎ 01497-821855; www.threetuns.com; Broad St; mains around £12; ☺ food noon-2pm & 6.30-9pm Wed-Sat, 12.30-4pm Sun) This smart new gastropub was rebuilt and expanded after a fire partially destroyed the old building, which dates from the 16th century. It's a welcoming place with a large garden area for alfresco food and a good selection of ales – try a pint of the local Butty Bach.

For a snack, **Shepherds Ice Cream Parlour** ( ☎ 01497-821898; 9 High Town; ☺ 9.30am-5.30pm Mon-Fri, 9.30am-6pm Sat, 10.30am-5.30pm Sun) offers an excellent espresso and a range of delicious, homemade ice creams, made using sheep's milk.

## Getting There & Away

Buses stop on Oxford Rd opposite the tourist office. Bus 40 stops at Hay en route from Hereford (one hour, three daily Monday to Friday) to Brecon (40 minutes).

The summertime-Sundays Beacons Bus B12, 39A and B7 and B17 (p727) serve Hay from Brecon, Hereford and Llandrindod Wells respectively.

If you're driving, allow time to cruise because the countryside is spellbinding.

The nearest train station is Builth Road, 19 miles to the northwest.

# POWYS

Comprising two-thirds of the country's scenic rural heartland, Powys is a region dominated by hills and valleys in a thousand shades of green. This verdant, rural region offers good walking and cycling country, plus plenty of wildlife, notably Wales' burgeoning red-kite community (see Go Fly a Kite, p739).

Powys extends from the undulating English border west to Ceredigion, and from the Brecon Beacons north to the border with Snowdonia. The northern part of the county is often still referred to by its former county name, Montgomeryshire.

Sadly the fatal combination of poor public-transport connections and the council's decision to close several tourist offices across the county rather gives the impression that – with the notable exceptions of Builth Wells and Machynlleth – Powys is increasingly closed to tourism.

If relying on public transport, then plan ahead with **Traveline Cymru** ( ☎ 0871 200 2233; www.travelinecymru.org.uk). Thankfully, the Heart of Wales line (see the boxed text, p736) still provides a lifeline to Mid Wales.

MID WALES

---

**RAIL THROUGH THE HEART**

The **Heart of Wales line** ( ☎ 01597-822053; www.heart-of-wales.co.uk) is one of Wales' most scenic stretches of railway. The train travels through beautiful river valleys and green-bathed hills as it cuts diagonally across central Wales, en route from Swansea to Shrewsbury in the English borderlands. The full 120-mile, 30-station and 3¾-hour trip breaks down easily into shorter sections, stopping at delightful rural stations en route.

It's also a proper working train line, providing a link between the small communities along its route – and not a novelty service.

One of the most scenic stretches lies between Llandeilo and Llandrindod Wells, where you will enjoy superb views across to Black Mountain from your train window, and roll across the graceful Cynghordy Viaduct through prime red-kite country.

There are four services Monday to Saturday throughout the year, plus two on Sunday. The walking guide *Great Walks from the Heart of Wales Railway* is available from tourist offices and details 15 circular routes from stations on the line.

Like many other British rural lines, its existence has been threatened, but the joint efforts of locals and train buffs continue to save the service. Use it – or lose it.

---

## LLANWRTYD WELLS (LLANWRTYD)
**pop 700**

This tiny spa town has little by way of attractions yet fights an ongoing battle to remain in the media spotlight, having staged a series of increasingly wacky sporting events since 1979 (see the boxed text, opposite). It has also made the *Guinness Book of Records* as Britain's smallest town, an award it proudly strives to retain.

The volunteer-run, hence sometimes keeping erratic hours, **tourist office** ( ☎ 01591-610666; llanwrtydtouristinformation@yahoo.co.uk; Ty Barcud, The Square; ☺ 10am-5pm Mon & Wed-Sat) opens year-round to support the townsfolk's zany activities and doubles up as a coffee shop with internet access (£2.50 per hour).

Activity breaks are coordinated from the **Red Kite Mountain Bike Centre** ( ☎ 01591-610236; www.neuaddarmshotel.co.uk; Y Sgwar), located at the town's social hub, the Neuadd Arms Hotel, which also offers packages including B&B accommodation (see right).

### Sleeping & Eating
**Stonecroft Lodge** ( ☎ 01591-610327; www.stonecroft .co.uk; Dolecoed Rd; r £14; ☺ reception 5-11pm) An independently run hostel located above a buzzy pub with something of a party vibe, real ale and pub grub. Accommodation is in double or family rooms, with all bedding provided. The communal lounge has satellite TV and a DVD library. It's perennially popular with walkers, bikers and groups.

**Drovers Rest** ( ☎ 01591610264; www.foodfoodfood .co.uk; Y Sgwar; ☺ cafe meals 10.30am-4.30pm, dinner 7.30-9.30pm) A well-regarded restaurant with

rooms, serving up great local produce and lots of fresh fish mains. The cottage-style bedrooms (single/double £25/50) are quiet and comfortable but it's the fine dining that is the cornerstone of the Drovers' experience, with menus from £27.95 and excellent Sunday roasts (from £12.95) served from 12.30pm to 2.30pm. The owners run regular cookery classes – try a Welsh cooking day for £185.

**Neuadd Arms Hotel** ( ☎ 01591-610236; www.neuadd armshotel.co.uk; Y Sgwar; bar meals around £6) The bar, which serves ales from its own microbrewery, is the main focus for celebratory beers after the town's left-field events. Rooms (single/ double £35/60) are available, and offer simple but comfortable accommodation.

### Getting There & Away
Llanwrtyd Wells is on the Heart of Wales line (see the boxed text, above).

Buses? Forget it.

## BUILTH WELLS
**pop 2350**

A busy, workaday former spa town, Builth Wells feels livelier than neighbouring Landrindod and Llanwrtydd Wells, and makes the best base for exploring the area.

The town is packed (and hotel rates hiked) during the annual **Royal Welsh Agricultural Show** (www.rwas.co.uk), the country's premier agriculture and livestock festival held in July. The four-day meeting showcases everything from rural life to Ukrainian Cossack dancing. No, really. It is held at the Royal Welsh Showgrounds at Llanelwedd, just north of town on the A470.

The very helpful **tourist office** ( ☎ 01982-553307; builthtic@powys.gov.uk; The Groe; ☽ 9.30am-5pm Mon-Fri, 9.30am-4pm Sat & Sun) is located in the town's car park by the 18th-century arched bridge.

Locals are fighting to keep the **Wyeside Arts Centre** ( ☎ 01982-552555; www.wyeside.co.uk; Castle St; ☽ box office noon-9pm Tue-Fri, 6-9pm Sat & Sun), the community's cultural hub at the eastern end of town, open for cinema and cultural events.

## Sleeping & Eating

**Greyhound Hotel** ( ☎ 01982-553255; www.thegreyhound hotel.co.uk; 3 Garth Rd; s/d £55/80; **P** ) A friendly local pub with comfortable, non-fussy rooms and decent bar meals at lunch and dinner, this is a reliable option. Catch the local male-voice choir rehearsing here on Monday nights (see the boxed text, p738).

**Lion Hotel** ( ☎ 01982-553311; www.lionhotelbuilth wells.com; 2 Broad St; d/f £98/120; **P** 🖳 ) The smartest option in town, this recently refurbished hotel has contemporary rooms with nice, homely touches and a wood-panelled dining room for upscale lunches and dinners. Some rooms have wheelchair access.

**Strand Restaurant** ( ☎ 01982-552652; Groe St; mains around £5; ☽ 9am-5pm Mon-Sat) A low-frills but friendly cafe for coffees, bacon rolls and simple, tasty home-made snacks. A children's menu and lunchtime specials make this a perennial favourite.

**Calon Wen** ( ☎ 07792 812739; 3 Groe St; mains around £10; ☽ noon-9.30pm Mon-Sat) This smart little bistro is now under new management. The menu has shifted to take on a more Mediterranean motif, plus lots of fish and steak mains. By day you can take coffee on the leather couches and watch the world go by.

## Getting There & Away

Buses stop by the tourist office; bus 704 runs to Llandrindod Wells (£1.20, 20 minutes, hourly Monday to Friday). The nearest train station, Builth Road, is 2 miles northwest of town on the A470; a taxi costs about £3. Builth Road is on the scenic Heart of Wales line (see the boxed text, opposite).

## LLANDRINDOD WELLS (LLANDRINDOD)
pop 5024

This spa town struck gold in Victorian times by touting its waters to the well-to-do gentry, who rolled in for rest and recuperation. The grand architecture of the era remains, but today the town feels rather moribund, especially on a Wednesday afternoon when most of the shops close. Catch the annual, week-long **Victorian Festival** ( ☎ 01597-823441), held in August, for evidence of vital signs. Even the tourist office has closed down – grab lunch then push onto Builth Wells.

The **Llandrindod Wells Memorial Hospital** ( ☎ 01597-822951; Temple St) is the regional hub for medical emergencies.

Still operating in a rather niche market, the **National Cycle Exhibition** ( ☎ 01597-825531;

---

### FIVE OF THE ODDEST LLANWRTYD EVENTS

Find out about more oh-so-wacky ideas from **Green Events** ( ☎ 01591-610850; www.green events.co.uk).

▪ **Saturnalia Beer Festival & Chariot Racing** (January) Roman-themed festival including a 'best-dressed slave' competition and the devouring of stuffed bull testicles.

▪ **Man vs Horse Marathon** (June) A gruelling 22-mile cross-country race starting from the town square. Runner Huw Lobb was the first non-equine winner, beating the fastest horse by two minutes with a time of just over two hours.

▪ **World Mountain Bike Bog Snorkelling Championships** (July) Donning wetsuits and snorkels, competitors cycle underwater through two lengths of trenches dug out of the peat in a nearby bog, surfacing only to navigate.

▪ **World Bog Snorkelling Championships** (August Bank Holiday). Similar to the above, but competitors have to swim two lengths of the bog with flippers and snorkel, using no recognised swimming stroke.

▪ **Real Ale Wobble & Ramble** (November) In conjunction with the Mid Wales Beer Festival, riders and walkers follow any of three way-marked routes of 10, 15 or 25 miles, supping real ales at the checkpoints along the way.

MID WALES

**SOMETHING FOR THE WEEKEND**

**Cwm-Moel** ( ☎ 01982-570271; www.cwmmoelcountryholidays.co.uk; Cwm Moel, Aberedw, Builth Wells; r incl breakfast & dinner from £48) At this homely little B&B in the village of Aberedw, 5 miles southeast of Builth Wells, guests have to – quite literally – sing for their supper. Cwm-Moel offers a rural escape and some great home cooking in the 17th-century farmhouse. But there's a twist: the owner, Eleanor Madoc Davies, draws on over 30 years' experience of teaching music to offer one-on-one vocal coaching (singing lessons £20 per hour) in her dedicated music room, following a free half-hour singing assessment. For inspiration, she will also take guests to see the local male-voice choir rehearse in Builth Wells (see Greyhound Hotel, p737).

www.cyclemuseum.org.uk; adult/child £3.50/1.50; 🕑 10am-4pm Easter-Oct, call for hr Nov-Feb), tells the story of the bicycle through the ages.

## Sleeping & Eating

**Cottage** ( ☎ 01597-825435; www.thecottagebandb.co.uk; Spa Rd; s/d £35/55; P ) A large Edwardian house set in a flower-strewn garden, the Cottage has seven comfortable rooms and a homely area targeting the midrange option. With friendly service and a slap-up breakfast, this is the best sleeping option in town.

**Herb Garden Cafe** ( ☎ 01597-823082; www.herb gardencafe.co.uk; Spa Centre; 🕑 9.30am-5pm Mon-Sat, 12.30-2.30pm Sun) Tucked down an alleyway by the Somerfield supermarket, this wholefood eatery is head and shoulders above anything else in town. Organic and fair-trade produce – plus a ready willingness to cater for all dietary requirements – and wheelchair access, make this a winner. The food is good too – even if you're not a vegan (lunch specials around £6.50).

For a snack, **Van's Good Food Shop** ( ☎ 01597-823079; Middleton St; 🕑 9am-5.30pm Mon, Tue, Thu & Fri, to 5pm Wed & Sat) is a local stalwart, championing local produce, organic fruit, cheese and wine, plus green-friendly cleaning products. This is a place with a true green conscience.

## Getting There & Around

Bus 704 runs to Builth Wells (£1.20, 20 minutes, hourly Monday to Friday).

Llandrindod Wells lies on the Heart of Wales line (see the boxed text, p736).

## AROUND LLANDRINDOD WELLS

Powys is crossed by two long-distance national trails: **Offa's Dyke Path** (www.nationaltrail.co.uk/OffasDyke) and **Glyndŵr's Way** (www.national trail.co.uk/GlyndwrsWay). The former is a 177-mile trail skirting the Anglo-Welsh border from Prestatyn to Sedbury Cliff; the latter a 135-

mile path from Knighton to Welshpool, based around sites related to Owain Glyndŵr, Wales' warrior-statesman famed for rebelling against English rule in the early 15th century.

For details of both, contact the **Offa's Dyke Centre** ( ☎ 01547-528753; www.offasdyke.demon.co.uk/ odc.htm; West St, Knighton; 🕑 10am-5pm Easter-Oct, 10am-4pm Mon, Wed, Fri & Sat, 10am-5pm Tue & Thu Nov-Easter), part of the tourist office in the border town of Knighton.

## MACHYNLLETH
pop 2200

Tiny Machynlleth (ma-*hun*-khleth) punches well above its weight. The town is rich in historical importance as it is here that nationalist hero Owain Glyndŵr defied the English to establish the country's first parliament in 1404. His legacy still lends Machynlleth a noble air but, more recently, the town has reinvented itself as the green capital of Wales and a centre for alternative communities. See www.ecodyfi.org.uk for more details.

Leading the green movement is the excellent **Centre for Alternative Technology** (CAT; see the boxed text, p740), which has been quietly championing sustainable living for more than 30 years.

Machynlleth, set amid lush Welsh countryside, is also a good walking base with trails through the Dyfi Valley, and an ideal base for mountain-biking (see opposite).

The **tourist office** ( ☎ 01654-702401; mactic@powys .gov.uk; Penrallt St; 🕑 9.30am-5pm Mon-Sat, 10am-4pm Sun) is just north of the clock tower at the centre of town. For information about events around the region, check the free monthly flyer **Dyfi Diary** ( ☎ 01654-702601).

## Sights

Built on the site of the 1404 Parliament, **Owain Glyndŵr Parliament House** ( ☎ 01654-702214; www .canolfanowainglyndwrcentre.org.uk; Maengwyn St, adult/

---

### GO FLY A KITE

In recent years efforts have been made to reintroduce the red kite to British skies. Once the most common bird of prey throughout Britain, by the 19th century it was flirting with extinction. Over 100 years ago a community group in Wales formed its own protection program, which went on to become the world's longest-running preservation campaign for any bird.

Today the Welsh skies again have a healthy population of kites, supported by a burgeoning ecotourism scheme that provides dedicated bird hides and opportunities to join feeding sessions. Once you've learned to identify its distinctive chestnut body and 2m wingspan, you can increasingly spot its aerial acrobatics all across remote Mid Wales.

The centre of activity is the **Gigrin Farm Red Kite Feeding Station** ( ☎ 01597-810243; www .gigrin.co.uk; adult/child £4/1.50; ☺ feedings 3pm Easter-Oct, 2pm Nov-Easter), located less than 1 mile north of the town of Rhayader, and 10 miles from Llandrindod Wells on the A470.

---

child £1.50/free; ☺ 10am-4.30pm Mon, Tue & Thu-Sat, 10am-4pm Wed Easter-Sep), is pretty low-key given Glyndŵr's pivotal royal in Welsh history. The museum is currently seeking funding to upgrade facilities.

A combined art gallery and converted chapel, the **Museum of Modern Art for Wales** (MOMA; ☎ 01654-703355; www.momawales.org.uk; Penrallt St; admission free; ☺ 10am-4pm Mon-Sat) has two galleries: one for Welsh and one for international works. The 400-seater **Tabernacle Chapel** is the focus of August's impressive weeklong Gŵyl Machynlleth Festival of classical music.

### Activities

Machynlleth is a centre for **mountain-biking**, with the **Holey Trail Cycle Hire** ( ☎ 01654-700411; www.theholeytrail.co.uk; 31 Maengwyn St; bike hire half-/full day £12/18; ☺ 10am-6pm Mon-Sat) the hub for repairs and information. The owners can advise on riding the three main trails, the Mach 1, 2 and 3 which, at 10, 14 and 19 miles respectively, are increasingly challenging. They also run the Reditreks bunkhouse (see right).

For cycle touring, the cross-Wales Lôn Las Cymru (see the boxed text, p682) passes through town and over the Millennium Bridge across the River Dyfi en route to the CAT (see the boxed text, p740).

### Sleeping & Eating

**Corris Hostel** ( ☎ 01654-761686; www.corrishostel.co.uk; dm/r incl breakfast £18/19) Given the beautiful location and a grand old schoolhouse setting, you can just about forgive the poor access and terrible signposting from the main road. This independent hostel operates a truly green policy and specialises in vegetarian food. Located in the village of Corris, 5 miles north of Machynlleth, heading off the A487 – follow signs for the railway museum into the village.

**Reditreks** ( ☎ 01654702184; www.reditreks.com; Powys St; dm £15) Mountain-bikers flock to this well-designed hostel for its simple rooms, cosy lounge and good storage facilities.

**Maengwyn Cafe** ( ☎ 01654-702126; 57 Maengwyn St; mains around £4; ☺ 8.30am-5pm Mon-Wed, Fri & Sat,

---

### SOMETHING FOR THE WEEKEND

Located near Presteigne, the **Old Vicarage** ( ☎ 01544-260038; www.oldvicaragenortonrads.co.uk; s/d £78/94; P □ ) is a real treat in the lesser-known Welsh Marches region. The three-room boutique B&B features Victorian fittings, all rescued, recycled and revived from auctions and scrapyards. It boasts an almost womblike ambience of opulent, rich colours and perfect calm, the latter interrupted only by the delicate chiming of antique clocks. Every evening, guests gather in the drawing room for drinks before a dinner party–style supper of organic local produce (four-course set dinner £32.50 per person). The guesthouse is very gay-friendly but not geared towards children. A hand-stencilled Latin inscription from St Augustine of Hippo above the stairs sums up the property's charm: 'Lord give me chastity and constancy – but not yet.'

In the nearby town of Presteigne, the **Judge's Lodging** ( ☎ 01544-260650; www.judgeslodging.org.uk; Broad St; adult/child £5.25/3.95; ☺ 10am-5pm Mar-Oct, 10am-4pm Wed-Sun Nov-Dec) offers a walk-through-history glimpse of a bygone era, exploring the life and times of a Victorian judge in the 1870s.

**MID WALES**

8.30am-4pm Thu, 9am-4pm Sun) A no-frills locals' cafe. Cheap but cheerful, it's the perfect place for a chip butty and mug of tea.

**Quarry Wholefood Cafe** ( ☎ 01654-702624; Maengwyn St) A well-run vegetarian and organic-food joint, owned by the folks from the CAT. The delicious vegetarian lunch specials (around £6), plus child-friendly facilities and menu, make this place perennially busy. The owners have opened a new wholefood shop, Quarry Whole Foods ( ☎ 01654-702339; 27 Maengwyn St; open 9am to 5.30pm Monday to Saturday, 10am to 4pm Sunday) just east of the cafe, if you want to take the menu home with you.

**Wynnstay** ( ☎ 01654-702941; www.wynnstayhotel.com; Maengwyn St; pizzas £8, mains around £14; ☺ bar meals noon-2pm & 6.30-9.30pm; P ▣ ) The town's best all-rounder combines comfortable rooms (single/double from £55/85) and a gastropub-style dining area, all set in a character-filled Georgian coaching inn. The place has a nice, rustic feel and food ranges from imaginative evening meals (mains around £14) to a more informal pizzeria (around £8).

For a quiet pint or simple pub grub, try the **Skinners Arms** ( ☎ 01654-702354; Penrallt St), especially for its great Sunday roast (£7). **Delicatessen Blasau** ( ☎ 01654-700410; Penrallt St; ☺ 8.30am-5.30pm Mon-Sat) is a superb little deli for stocking up on local organic produce and fair-trade supplies.

## Getting There & Away

The train station is less than half a mile north of the centre. Machynlleth is on the Cambrian Main Line with services runninf to Shrewsbury (£10.90, 80 minutes, every two hours, six on Sunday) and Aberystwyth (40 minutes, every two hours). Trains run along the Cambrian Coast Line to Pwllheli (£10.90, 2¼ hours, every two hours, three on Sunday).

Bus X32 runs north to Dolgellau (35 minutes, about every two hours Monday to Friday,

---

### GREEN SHOOTS

A small but dedicated band of people has spent 30 years practising sustainability at the thought-provoking **Centre for Alternative Technology** (CAT; ☎ 01654-705950; www.cat.org.uk; adult/child £8.40/4.20; ☺ 10am-5.30pm Easter–mid-Jul, Sep & Oct, 10am-6pm mid-Jul–Aug, 10am-dusk Nov-Easter), set in a beautiful wooded valley near Machynlleth.

CAT is a virtually self-sufficient cooperative where more than 3 hectares of displays demonstrate how wind, water and solar power provide food, heating and telecommunications. Kids love the interactive displays and adventure playground, and there's a great organic-wholefood restaurant. To explore the whole site takes about two hours – take rainwear as it's primarily outdoors.

The visit starts with a ride up the side of an old quarry in an ingenious water-balanced cable car. A drum beneath the top car fills with stored rainwater, and is then drawn down while the bottom car is hauled up. Other resourceful exhibits include a solar-powered telephone and large-scale community turbine.

At the time of writing, CAT was open a new, dedicated study centre, the **Wales Institute for Sustainable Education** (WISE; www.cat.org.uk/wise), in the summer of 2009 with a 200-seat lecture theatre and 24 en suite study bedrooms. Built according to sustainable principles, it will be a major new facility for CAT's program of courses.

CAT lies 3 miles north of Machynlleth on the A487. Hourly buses (four on Sunday) run from the clock tower in Machynlleth; bus 34 stops directly at the visitor centre, while bus X32 drops off in Pantperthog, five minutes' walk away. Arrive by train and get a 50% discount on admission, and by bus or train for a £1 discount.

For the ultimate get-away-from-it-all break with a green conscience, **Eco Retreats** ( ☎ 01654-781375; www.ecoretreats.co.uk; per tepee weekend/mid-week high season £329/315, mid-week low season £295; ☺ Mar-Oct) comprises four 21ft-diameter North American Indian tepees and one 18ft Mongolian-style yurt in the middle of the Dyfi Forest. It's a low-tech experience with compost toilet blocks and cold-water showers (although solar-powered showers are mooted), but it is truly green: all waste products go back to nourish the earth, the land is leased from a local organic farm and the welcome hampers contain fair-trade produce.

The tepee camp is 8 miles south of Machynlleth off the A487, following a rough track into the forest.

MID WALES

---

**SOMETHING FOR THE WEEKEND**

Winner of the Gold Star Hotel award at the most recent National Tourism Awards for Wales, **Ynyshir Hall** ( ☎ 01654-781209; www.ynyshirhall.co.uk; Eglwysfach, d from £275; P ⌨ ) is a luxury country-house hotel for a supremely pampering break. Each of the nine rooms has been designed to reflect the character of the artist after whom it is named – the Matisse, for example, features a deep, shocking-pink bedspread and a large pink canvas above a pink lips-shaped sofa. The restaurant has built a strong reputation for excellent quality dining, and spa treatments are available. This is a lavish, treat-yourself escape. Go on, you're worth it.

Ynyshir Hall is 5 miles south of Machynlleth off the A487.

---

two on Sunday) via CAT (six minutes), and south to Aberystwyth (45 minutes).

# CEREDIGION

Ceredigion, far from the English border, is proud of its Welsh identity, its nationalist spirit forged through the 11th-century Norman resistance. Welsh remains the first language and Aberystwyth is the county capital, an old seaside town blending traditional charms, such as amusement arcades and candy-floss stalls, with a contemporary student buzz.

The Cambrian Main Line train service runs from Aberystwyth to Shrewsbury, via Machynlleth, connecting at the latter for Cambrian Coast services to Pwllheli. For further information, consult **Traveline Cymru** ( ☎ 0871 200 2233; www.travelinecymru.info).

## ABERYSTWYTH
### pop 12,000

Aberystwyth is a strange mix. The Georgian seaside resort has a downmarket feel in midsummer, but becomes a buzzy university town during term time when a community of around 9000 students stokes the fires of the cafes and arts scene. At all times it remains a stronghold of Welsh identity with a preponderance of local independent shops and Welsh spoken on the streets. With plans afoot to move some Welsh Assembly offices here, locals hope to see the long-mooted townregeneration plan swing into action.

It was the coming of the railways in 1864 that transformed Aberystwyth into a fashionable seaside destination. In 1872 it was chosen as the site of the first college of the University of Wales, and in 1907 the town became the home of the National Library of Wales, which marked its centenary in 2007 with a major program of events. Today, catching sunset over

Cardigan Bay from the promenade remains a quintessential Aberystwyth experience.

The **tourist office** ( ☎ 01970-612125; Terrace Rd; ☺ 10am-5pm Mon-Sat Sep-Jun, 10am-5pm daily Jul & Aug) shares a building with the Ceredigion Museum (p742).

### Sights

The one-hour ride on the restored **Vale of Rheidol Steam Railway** ( ☎ 01970-625819; www.rheidolrailway .co.uk; adult/child return £13.50/3; ☺ Apr-Oct), puffing 12 miles up the valley to Devil's Bridge (p744), is a not-to-be-missed experience. The line opened in 1902 to transport lead and timber, and the Great Western Railway engines date from the 1920s. Trains run two to four times daily from next to the main-line train station.

Half a mile east of town on the A487, the **National Library of Wales** ( ☎ 01970-623800; www .llgc.org.uk; admission free; ☺ 9.30am-5pm Mon-Sat) is a cultural powerhouse. It sits proudly on a hilltop overlooking Aberystwyth and houses more than five million historic volumes, including the country's oldest text, the 13th-century *Black Book of Carmarthen*. The reading room is open to members only but the library hosts changing exhibitions and is home to a childfriendly restaurant and shop, all open to the public. It also has wheelchair access.

The Victorian **Cliff Railway** ( ☎ 01970-617642; www.aberystwythcliffrailway.co.uk; adult/child return £3/2; ☺ 10am-5pm daily Easter-Oct, 10am-5pm Wed-Sun NovEaster), the UK's longest, and slowest, electric funicular, grinds to the top of Constitution Hill (131m) at the northern end of North Beach. The wind-blown hilltop has been redeveloped with new childrens' attractions and the erstwhile Victorian tearooms rebuilt as **Consti Cafe** ( ☺ 10am-5pm Mon-Wed & Sun, to 9pm Thu-Sat; lunch specials around £5). One relic of the Victorian structure that survived the revamp is a camera obscura (an immense pinhole camera or projecting telescope).

MID WALES

---

**MYTHS & LEGENDS**

Wales, and Ceredigion, is awash with sagas inspired by medieval ancestry, bloody conflict and untamed landscapes. From generation to generation, elaborate tales of enchantment and wizardry have been bequeathed like rich family legacies.

As early as the 9th century tales of mystery and heroism were compiled in the *Historia Britonum*. But the finest impressions come from the *Mabinogion*, a 14th-century tome containing occasionally terrifying tales of Celtic magic.

King Arthur is a recurrent character, especially in the *Mabinogion*. One of British legend's most romanticised heroes, he was believed to have been a 5th- or 6th-century cavalry leader who rallied British fighters against the marauding Saxon invaders. Time transformed Arthur into a king of magic deeds, with wise magician Merlin by his side and a loyal band of followers in support. Arthur went on to slay Rita Gawr, a giant who butchered kings, in an epic battle on Mt Snowdon. Finally, Merlin delivered the dying hero to Avalon, which may well have been saintly Bardsey Island off the Llŷn Peninsula (see The Pilgrimage to Bardsey, p770).

The world of Welsh myths is richly imaginative. For more see Robin Gwyndaf's detailed bilingual *Chwedlau Gwerin Cymru: Welsh Folk Tales*.

---

Occupying the former Coliseum theatre and cinema along with the tourist office, the **Ceredigion Museum** (☎ 01970-633088; Terrace Rd; admission free; ☻ 10am-5pm Mon-Sat) explores a theatrical-themed collection of local memorabilia.

## Activities

For walkers, Aberystwyth lies on the new Ceredigion Coastal Path from Borth to Cardigan, where it links up with the Pembrokeshire Coastal Path (p720).

For cyclists, the easygoing Rheidol Trail runs 11 miles from the seafront up the pretty Rheidol Valley. The new Ystwyth Trail connects Aberystwyth with Tregaron in the northern Teifi Valley. Two key sections connecting Aberystwyth to Rhydyfelin and onward to Llanfarian were completed in summer 2008; more from www.cycling.ceredigion.gov.uk.

**Nant-yr-Arian Forest Visitor Centre** (☎ 01970-890694; www.mbwales.com; Ponterwyd) is an excellent mountain-biking centre with mountain-biking trails, plus year-round family-friendly horse riding and walking trails, and daily feeding of red kites. Located 10 miles east of Aberystwyth on the A44.

For details, have a chat with the folks at **Summit Cycles** (☎ 01970-626061; www.summicycles.co.uk; 65 North Pde), but they don't hire out bikes.

## Sleeping

**Borth YHA** (☎ 01970-871498; www.yha.org.uk; dm £18; ☻ mid-Feb–Oct) A grand old Edwardian house offering simple but clean accommodation with great views of Cardigan Bay and a sandy beach just a short stroll away. Located 7 miles east of town on the A44.

**Maes-y-Môr** (☎ 01970-639270; 25 Bath St; r with kitchenette £22-35) Forget the slightly unlikely location above a laundrette, upstairs from the washing machines is a cheap but cheerful independent hostel-style place right in the city centre. Dorms have been replaced by doubles with kitchenette, with a family room available and bike storage.

**Bodalwyn** (☎ 01970-612578; www.bodalwyn.co.uk; Queen's Ave; s/d/f from £48/65/88; P) B&Bs abound in Aberystwyth, but few offer anything above average. Bodalwyn is one place that goes the extra mile, offering cosy rooms and a hearty cooked breakfast, including vegetarian options, all set in a rambling but comfy family home.

**Tŷ Belgrave** (☎ 01970-630553; www.tybelgravehouse.co.uk; Marine Tce; r £95-105; P 💻 wi-fi) This boutique guest house has a contemporary feel with well-appointed cream-and-chocolate rooms, including wi-fi internet for the business market. Breakfast is served in a basement dining area while the ground-floor bar and lounge area is a great place for a sundowner with views across the bay.

** our pick** **Gwesty Cymru** (☎ 01970-612252; www.gwestycymru.com; 19 Marine Tce; s/d £65/85; ☻ lunch & dinner; P 💻) The latest new opening in town is a real gem: a character boutique property with a real sense of Welsh identity and an elegant feel. Welsh grey slate features throughout – from the colour-coded rooms, some with sea views, to the refined basement dining rooms, serving food all day. Don't miss fresh

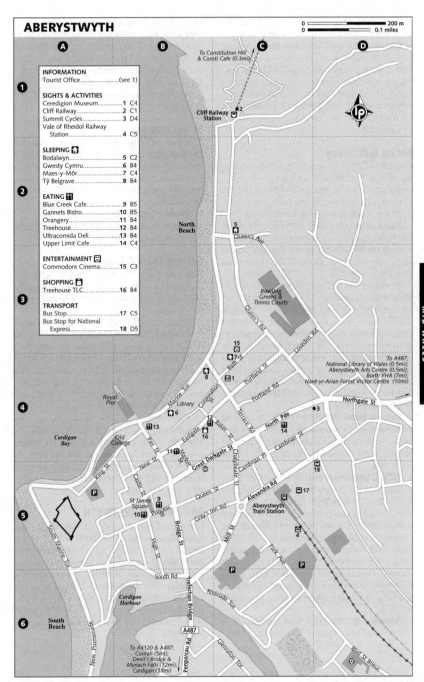

# ABERYSTWYTH

0 / 200 m
0 / 0.1 miles

**INFORMATION**
Tourist Office....................(see 1)

**SIGHTS & ACTIVITIES**
Ceredigion Museum............1 C4
Cliff Railway.......................2 C1
Summit Cycles....................3 D4
Vale of Rheidol Railway
    Station..........................4 C5

**SLEEPING**
Bodalwyn...........................5 C2
Gwesty Cymru.....................6 B4
Maes-y-Môr........................7 C4
Tŷ Belgrave........................8 B4

**EATING**
Blue Creek Cafe...................9 B5
Gannets Bistro....................10 B5
Orangery...........................11 B4
Treehouse..........................12 B4
Ultracomida Deli.................13 B4
Upper Limit Cafe.................14 C4

**ENTERTAINMENT**
Commodore Cinema............15 C3

**SHOPPING**
Treehouse TLC....................16 B4

**TRANSPORT**
Bus Stop............................17 C5
Bus Stop for National
    Express..........................18 D5

To Constitution Hill
& Consti Cafe (0.3mi)

**Cliff Railway
Station**

**North
Beach**

Queen's Ave

Bowling
Greens &
Tennis Courts

Queen's Rd

Loveden Rd

To A487;
National Library of Wales (0.5mi);
Aberystwyth Arts Centre (0.5mi);
Borth YHA (7mi);
Nant-yr-Arian Forest Visitor Centre (10mi)

Bath St

Portland St

Portland Rd

Northgate St

Marine Tce

Corporation St

Terrace Rd

North Pde

Cambrian St

Library

Royal
Pier

Cardigan
Bay

Old
College

Pier St

Eastgate

Baker St

Cambrian Pl

New St

Market St

Great Darkgate St

Chalybeate St

Castle St

St James
Square

Princess St

Queen St

Alexandra Rd

King St

Gray's Inn Rd

Aberystwyth
Train Station

Bridge St

Mill St

Park Ave

South Marine Tce

High St

South Rd

Trefechan Bridge

Riverside Tce

Cardigan
Harbour

A487

Glendaton Tce

New Promenade

South
Beach

Penparcau Rd

To A4120 & A487;
Comtah (5mi);
Devil's Bridge &
Mynach Falls (12mi);
Cardigan (38mi)

Blvd St Brieuc

fish specials, served on an alfresco terrace overlooking the bay – if the weather holds.

**Conrah** ( ☎ 01970-617941; www.conrah.co.uk; s/d £95/130; **P** ) The quiet, countryside location and stunning rural views are the biggest selling point at this old-fashioned, country-house hotel. The rooms may need an update but it retains a stately feel. Located 10 miles south of Aberystwyth on the A487 in the village of Chancery.

## Eating & Drinking

**Blue Creek Cafe** (11 Princess St; ⏱ 9.30am-6pm Mon-Sat; 🖳 wi-fi) A great little spot for good coffee, home-made cakes, snacks and browsing the newspapers. Downstairs is a lounge area with a library. Wi-fi is available throughout.

**Upper Limit Cafe** ( ☎ 27 North Pde; ⏱ 8am-7pm Mon-Fri, 8am-5pm Sat & Sun) This simple place is best known for its set-you-up-for-the-day breakfasts, with all-day snacks available if you can't face the fry-up.

**Treehouse** ( ☎ 01970-615791; www.treehousewales .co.uk; 14 Baker St; lunch mains £6-9; ⏱ 9am-5pm Mon-Sat) Upstairs from a wholefood-shop-cum-deli, Treehouse is an excellent organic restaurant catering for all dietary needs from vegans to glutton-free diets. The lunch menu is tasty and imaginative. Lunch is available from noon to 3.30pm, with coffees and snacks at other times. Across the street, the sister venue Treehouse TLC ( ☎ 01970-625116; 3 Eastgate) is a fair-trade shop.

**Gannets Bistro** ( ☎ 01970-617164; 7 St James Sq; mains around £10; ⏱ noon-2pm & 6-9.30pm Mon & Wed-Sat) A longstanding locals' favourite serving simple home-cooked bistro fare with lots of fresh fish.

**our pick** **Ultracomida Deli** ( ☎ 01970-630686; 31 Pier St; tapas around £3, 2-/3-course dinner £15/18; ⏱ 10am-4pm Mon-Thu & Sat, to 9pm Fri) With its blend of Spanish, French and Welsh produce, this is a foodies' idea of Nirvana: a deli out front with a cheese counter to die for, restaurant out back for tapas and coffees, and very knowledgeable staff. On Friday evenings they serve a superb dinner. This is the original deli with a sister property now in Cardigan (p721) and, at the time of writing, plans to open in Cardiff in 2009.

**Orangery** ( ☎ 01970-617606; Market St; mains £10-18; ⏱ 10am-11pm) The former Talbot Inn, a 19th-century coaching house, gets a contemporary new look with the Orangery's stylish combination of restaurant, cocktail bar with all-day food and private rooms where children are welcome until 8pm. Not the cheapest place in town, but good-quality food, a buzzy atmosphere and stylish setting keep it perennially popular.

## Entertainment

There are two main entertainment locations:

**Aberystwyth Arts Centre** ( ☎ 01970-623232; www .aberystwythartscentre.co.uk; Penglais Rd; ⏱ box office 10am-8pm Mon-Sat, 1.30-5.30pm Sun) Based at the university, the town's main arts venue presents film, drama, dance and music.

**Commodore Cinema** ( ☎ 01970-612421; www .commodorecinema.co.uk; Bath St; adult/child £4.50/2.50) A family-owned, independent cinema.

## Getting There & Away

Buses stop by the train station. The 420 National Express coach runs daily to London (£30.50, seven hours) from a stop around the corner.

Other long-distance Traws Cambria services includ: X32 via Machynlleth (45 minutes, roughly hourly Monday to Saturday) to Bangor (three hours 50 minutes); X40 via Carmarthen (two hours 10 minutes, roughly hourly Monday to Saturday) to Cardiff (4½ hours); and X50 to Cardigan (two hours, every two hours Monday to Saturday)

Aberystwyth is the terminus of the Cambrian Main Line with trains to Shrewsbury in England (£13.10, 1¾ hours, every two hours). Change at Machynlleth (30 minutes) for Cambrian Coast Line services north to Pwllheli (£10.90, three hours 50 minutes, every two hours).

## AROUND ABERYSTWYTH

For a good day trip, ride the Vale of Rheidol Steam Railway (p741) to the 91m-high waterfalls at Devil's Bridge, where a **turnstile** (adult/child £3.50/1.50) leads along a slippery woodland path to a viewing platform – wear sensible footwear. The three staked bridges span the woodland gorge while the Rivers Mynach and Rheidol tumble together off the Plynlimon (Pumlumon) Hills in a series of spectacular waterfalls.

# North Wales

Feeling vast despite its relatively small area, North Wales really packs it in. From rugged mountain trails and scenic coastal paths to seaside resorts and medieval castles, the region has a particularly wide range of attractions. The North attracts more than its fair share of outdoor-activity enthusiasts, from climbers to kayakers. Here, too, are plenty of attractions for families and couples in search of a secret-hideaway bolt-hole with a touch of class. The north coast and borderlands make for an impressive introduction to Wales. The main centres here are Llandudno, a classic British seaside resort of Victorian splendour, and bustling Llangollen, with its International Eisteddfod, adrenalin-charged thrills and burgeoning cultural scene. The region's mountainous heartland is dominated by the Snowdonia National Park, where the highest peaks in Wales and England scrape moody, often overcast, skies. But don't worry about the weather. With a slew of smart places opening up, there's a hot bath, a warm bed and a hearty dinner awaiting every walker or climber upon their return.

Architecture fans will be mesmerised by Portmeirion, an Italianate village in a romantic seaside setting, and one of the must-see destinations. A chain of historic castles spans the North with Caernarfon and Conwy elegiac reminders of the halcyon days of their respective home towns. Heading west, the roads are quieter, the views more sweeping and the sense of Welsh culture increasingly strong. The Llŷn Peninsula, wild, rocky and less frequented than other areas of North Wales, will forever be associated with its ancient pilgrimage to Bardsey Island, while the Isle of Anglesey has a greater concentration of prehistoric sites than anywhere else in Wales, and superlative coastal walking.

## HIGHLIGHTS

- Savouring seaside favourites both old and new in the genteel Victorian resort of **Llandudno** (p747)

- Declaring 'I am not a number, I'm a free man' among the fairy-tale nooks and crannies of **Portmeirion** (p767) village

- Following in the footsteps of 20,000 saints on a pilgrimage to **Bardsey Island** (p770)

- Discovering family activities, great coastal walking and fine foodie hideaways on the **Isle of Anglesey** (p772)

- Getting active, then spoiling yourself rotten, amid the high peaks and chic retreats of **Snowdonia National Park** (p756)

- Combining high Welsh culture with action-packed adventures around **Llangollen** (p753)

| POPULATION: 615,500 | AREA: 2382 SQ MILES | AN EARTHQUAKE MEASURING 5.4 ON THE RICHTER SCALE OCCURRED ON 19 JULY 1984 ON THE LLŶN PENINSULA |
|---|---|---|

**NORTH WALES**

# NORTH WALES

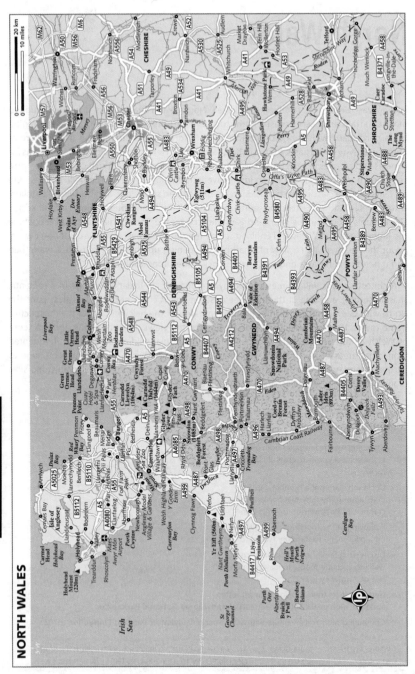

## Orientation & Information

The majestic, moody mountains of the Snowdonia National Park, the highest British peaks outside of Scotland, dominate the north of Wales, and provide a stark contrast with the candyfloss frippery of the northern coastline. Family and walkers' favourite Anglesey lies offshore to the northwest and the lesser explored Llŷn Peninsula points west out to sea.

The region is well served for tourist offices, although they can be very crowded in high season.

## Activities

North Wales is crammed with adrenalin-pumping activities. The biggest attraction is **Snowdonia National Park**, where jagged peaks meet green wooded valleys, rolling hills and swaths of golden sand. Betws-y-Coed and Llanberis are the key hubs for visitors.

This is prime territory for walking, climbing, pony trekking, mountain biking and cycling. The park is also home to three national activity centres: **Canolfan Tryweryn National Whitewater Centre**, near Bala, **Plas y Brenin National Mountain Centre** at Capel Curig and **Plas Menai, the National Water Sports Centre**, near Caernarfon.

Heading west, the exposed **Llŷn Peninsula** has great water sports opportunities, while the **Isle of Anglesey** has gentle, rolling countryside for less-strenuous walking with stunning coastal scenery. It is home to the superb **Isle of Anglesey Coastal Path**.

East of Snowdonia, Llangollen is another white-water hot spot, thanks to the dependable rapids of the River Dee.

## Getting There & Around

An extensive network of bus routes is in operation, but Sunday services are usually limited (especially in more-remote areas). Check details with **Traveline Cymru** ( ☎ 0871 200 2233; www .traveline-cymru.org.uk).

Major rail routes include the North Wales Coast Line from Chester to the ferry terminal at Holyhead, the Cambrian Coast Line from Machynlleth to Pwllheli, and the Conwy Valley Line from Llandudno to Blaenau Ffestiniog. Check with **National Rail Enquiries** ( ☎ 0845 748 4950; www.nationalrail.co.uk) for times and fares.

**Arriva Trains** ( ☎ 0845 6061 660; www.arrivatrains wales.co.uk) offers Freedom of Wales Flexi Pass tickets (All Wales/North Wales £69/47) with four days of train and eight days of bus unlimited travel (including the Ffestiniog Railway), plus discounts on attractions. It is available at most railway stations and online at www.walesflexipass.co.uk.

The **Gwynedd Red Rover bus ticket** (adult/child £4.95/2.45) is valid on buses within south, central and northwest Snowdonia, the Llŷn Peninsula and some services in northeast Snowdonia, but not east of Llandudno; buy a rover ticket from the driver on the first bus you board and use it all day.

The **Snowdon Sherpa** ( ☎ 01286-870880) is a network of buses that runs through the Snowdonia National Park from March to October, connecting major destinations for tourists and bringing access to trailheads for ramblers. See p759 for more details.

# NORTH COAST & BORDERS

The North Wales coast has both perennial charms and cultural blackspots in equal measure. Stick with the former and you'll not be disappointed – from a glorious castle at Conwy to the Victorian elegance of Llandudno.

Moving southeast towards the English border, Llangollen is building a burgeoning reputation for its adventure sports and cultural festivals. Most of all, it is known as the home of the annual International Eisteddfod.

More details on this region are available from www.borderlands.co.uk, www.visit llandudno.com and www.visitconwy.org.uk.

## LLANDUDNO
### pop 15,000

Handsome Llandudno is Wales' largest Victorian seaside resort, with a fantastic location and spectacular period architecture along a sweeping bay. It's a busy place in summer, but still manages to retain a dignified air. The American-born travel writer Bill Bryson was moved to describe Llandudno as his 'favourite seaside resort'.

The premier attraction is the **Great Orme** (207m), a spectacular 2-mile-long limestone headland jutting in to the Irish Sea. Old-school tramway and cable-car rides go to the summit, providing breathtaking views of the Snowdonia range. On the seafront, traditional delights include an impressive pier and a range of penny-pinching amusement arcades.

Llandudno had acquired a reputation as a resort for pensioners but, in recent years, it has seen its cultural life flourish with the new Venue Cymru (p750), the opening of a new range of upmarket places to stay and eat, and a major new retail park, Parc Llandudno, located at the east end of town, bringing big-name shops to the resort.

Llandudno's biggest festival is its **Victorian Extravaganza** (www.victorian-extravaganza.co.uk), held over the early–May Bank Holiday weekend – book ahead for accommodation.

## Orientation & Information

The grand promenade of North Shore Beach lies to the northeast, with Conwy Bay and the quieter, sandier West Shore Beach to the southwest.

The train station, the subject of a new and much-needed regeneration plan, is located three blocks south of Mostyn St, which is the main thoroughfare for banks and bus stops.

The Library Building houses the **tourist office** ( ☎ 01492-876413; llandudnotic@conwy.gov.uk; Mostyn St; ☼ 9am-5.30pm Mon-Sat & 9.30am-4.30pm Sun Apr-Oct, 9am-5pm Mon-Sat Nov-Mar), and the **library** ( ☎ 01492-574010; Mostyn St; ☼ 9am-6pm Mon, Tue & Fri, 10am-5pm Wed, 9am-7pm Thu, 9.30am-1pm Sat), which provides free internet access.

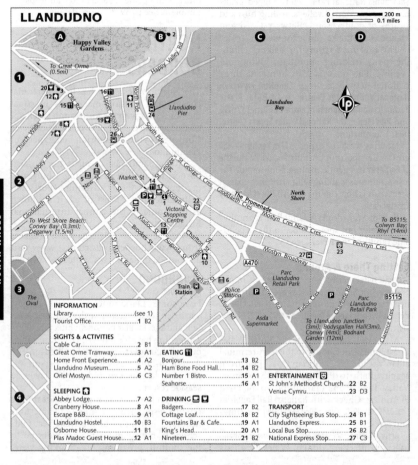

### LLANDUDNO

**INFORMATION**
Library....................................(see 1)
Tourist Office.........................**1** B2

**SIGHTS & ACTIVITIES**
Cable Car...............................**2** B1
Great Orme Tramway.............**3** A1
Home Front Experience..........**4** A2
Llandudno Museum................**5** A2
Oriel Mostyn.........................**6** C3

**SLEEPING**
Abbey Lodge.........................**7** A2
Cranberry House.....................**8** A1
Escape B&B...........................**9** A1
Llandudno Hostel..................**10** B3
Osborne House......................**11** B1
Plas Madoc Guest House.......**12** A1

**EATING**
Bonjour.................................**13** B2
Ham Bone Food Hall.............**14** B2
Number 1 Bistro....................**15** A1
Seahorse...............................**16** A1

**DRINKING**
Badgers.................................**17** B2
Cottage Loaf........................**18** B2
Fountains Bar & Cafe.............**19** A1
King's Head...........................**20** A1
Nineteen...............................**21** B2

**ENTERTAINMENT**
St John's Methodist Church...**22** B2
Venue Cymru.........................**23** D3

**TRANSPORT**
City Sightseeing Bus Stop......**24** B1
Llandudno Express.................**25** B1
Local Bus Stop......................**26** B2
National Express Stop............**27** C3

## Sights & Activities

From sea level it's difficult to gauge the sheer scale of the Great Orme, designated a Site of Special Scientific Interest (SSSI). Several Neolithic sites nestle on this promontory, and the unbroken views of Snowdonia are supreme. The headland is a designated country park, boasting a cornucopia of flowers, butterflies and seabirds, and its own **visitor centre** ( ☎ 01492-874151; ◷ 9.30am-5pm mid-Mar–Oct) with picnic tables, a cafe and gift shop.

You can walk to the summit; take the **Great Orme Tramway** ( ☎ 01492-879306; www.greatormetramway .co.uk; adult/child return £5.20/3.60; ◷ 10am-6pm Easter-Sep, to 5pm Mar & Oct), which leaves every 20 minutes from Church Walks, or ride Britain's longest **cable car** ( ☎ 01492-877205; adult/child return £6.60/4.50) from Happy Valley above the pier – departures are weather dependent.

Extending 670m into the sea, the elegant, 1878-built Victorian **pier** was once a major embarkation point for Isle of Man steamers. It's now a rather downmarket haven for kids' attractions.

North Wales' leading contemporary-art venue, the cool **Oriel Mostyn** ( ☎ 01492-879201; www.mostyn.org; 12 Vaughan St; admission free; ◷ 10am-5pm Tue-Sat) remains open for exhibitions but with reduced space while a major expansion program is under way. Full service will be resumed, plus a stylish new wing to the building unveiled, during 2009.

More-traditional artefacts are housed at **Llandudno Museum** ( ☎ 01492-876517; 17-19 Gloddaeth St; adult/child £1.50/75p; ◷ 10.30am-1pm & 2-5pm Tue-Sat, 2.15-5pm Sun Easter-Oct, 1.30-4.30pm Tue-Sat Nov-Mar), while the **Home Front Experience** ( ☎ 01492-871032; New St; adult/child £3.25/2; ◷ 10am-4.30pm Mon-Sat,

11am-3pm Sun Mar-Oct) looks at life at home during WWII.

**City Sightseeing** ( ☎ 01492-876606; www.city-sight seeing.com; adult/child £6.50/2.50; ◷ May-Sep) departs the pier half-hourly for hop-on, hop-off bus tours of Llandudno and Conwy; tickets are valid for 24 hours. Llandudno Express runs a loop shuttle from the pier to the West Shore and back (£1.50 each way).

## Sleeping

**Llandudno Hostel** ( ☎ 01492-877430; www.llandud nohostel.co.uk; 14 Charlton St; dm £17, s/d £25/44, s/d without bathroom £23/40) This is a family-run, Victorian-pile independent hostel with friendly, knowledgeable owners and a location close to the train station. Rooms are clean and a continental breakfast is included, but there are no self-catering facilities. A family room with bathroom is a new addition.

**Cranberry House** ( ☎ 01492-879760; 12 Abbey Rd; r from £50; (P) ) Recently upgraded and decorated, this traditional guesthouse has spick-and-span rooms and serves a hearty breakfast with vegetarian options.

**Plas Madoc Guest House** ( ☎ 01492-876514; www .plasmadocguesthouse.co.uk; 60 Church Walks; s/d from £40/60; (P) ) Formerly a fully vegetarian and vegan guesthouse, new owners have widened the remit without sacrificing the quality. Each of the five rooms (with bathroom) has a clean, airy feel and a small library of DVDs, while all dietary needs can be catered for at breakfast. Ask about promotional rates in low season.

**Abbey Lodge** ( ☎ 01492-878042; 14 Abbey Rd; s/d £37.50/75; (P) (💻) ) The owners of Abbey Lodge keep this four-room property fresh and provide some homely touches, such as a small collection of local-interest books in each room. Hang out in the garden on a sunny day or read in the cosy lounge.

**our pick Escape B&B** ( ☎ 01492-877776; www.escape bandb.co.uk; 48 Church Walks; r weekend from £115, mid-week £85-110; (P) (💻) ) Llandudno's first boutique B&B has bags of style and urban-cool swagger. After many rave reviews, the owners are now focusing harder on maintaining good service and upscale facilities. The individual rooms have a funky feel and lots of high-tech gadgets to play with, while breakfast is a hearty affair. This is not a family-oriented guesthouse, but the owners have plans for a stylish but child-friendly offshoot close by.

**SOMETHING FOR THE WEEKEND**

For some serious pampering, **Bodysgallen Hall** ( ☎ 01492-584466; www.bodysgallen.com; s/d/cottage £175/185/225) is stately country-house hotel and spa, 3 miles south of Llandudno on the A470. The formal gardens are a delight to explore, with panoramic views across to Conwy Castle, while the rooms, split between the Main Hall and the more secluded Cottage Suites in the grounds, are traditional with a nod to contemporary mod cons. The restaurant is open to nonguests (for lunch and dinner), although children are not welcome.

**Osborne House** ( ☎ 01492-860330; www.osborne house.com; 17 North Pde; ste £145-175; P 🖳 ) This small luxury hotel is big on grand gestures – from the lavish Italian marble bathrooms to the huge beds clad in Egyptian-cotton sheets. It's stylish, yet modern – rooms have DVDs and internet access – although some may find the frou-frou design a bit over the top. The hotel's restaurant, Osborne's (open 10.30am to 10pm Monday to Saturday, to 9pm Sunday), serves excellent bistro-style food (mains £9 to £15).

## Eating & Drinking

**Ham Bone Food Hall** ( ☎ 01492-860084; Lloyd St; 🕑 9.30am-5.30pm Mon-Sat) This is a great little deli with a very international menu, tasty takeaway snacks and a variety of coffees.

**Bonjour** ( ☎ 01492-878930; 39-41 Madoc St; crêpes £8, mains £8-10; 🕑 11am-3.30pm & 6-9pm Mon-Sat, 11am-6pm Sun) A French-themed crêpe restaurant, replete with staff in French berets, Bonjour is a welcoming, unpretentious place serving savoury and sweet crêpes, plus traditional French mains.

**Number 1 Bistro** ( ☎ 01492-875424; Old Rd; set menu £12; 🕑 5.30-9.30pm Mon-Sat) This well-established dark-wood bistro has a touch of French style. The imaginative menu takes in such dishes as baked guinea fowl and venison medallions. They offer a good-value, early-evening set menu of two courses. Bookings are recommended.

**Seahorse** ( ☎ 01492-875315; www.the-seahorse .co.uk; 7 Church Walks; bistro mains around £12, restaurant set menu £27; 🕑 dinner Tue-Sat) The menu at the Seahorse (formerly Richard's Bistro) appropriately features lots of fresh fish; look for

daily specials on the board. Service is split between an intimate cellar bistro and a more formal upstairs restaurant that offers a three-course set menu.

**Nineteen** ( ☎ 01492-873333; 19 Lloyd St; 🕑 9am-5pm Mon-Sat) This place is a chilled-out little coffee bar for smoothies and snacks, as well as coffee. Read the papers or use your laptop with the free wi-fi. Service tends to be rather indifferent.

**Badgers** ( ☎ 01492-871649; Victoria Centre, Mostyn St; 🕑 10.30am-4pm Mon-Fri, 9.30am-5pm Sat, 10am-5pm Sun) This traditional tearoom offers simple snacks and afternoon teas. The staff wear traditional Victorian outfits to add a touch of genteel nostalgia.

**Fountains Bar & Cafe** ( ☎ 01492-875600; 114 Upper Mostyn St) A funky cafe-bar with a pavement terrace for beers, cocktails and a simple menu of pub-style food. There are DJ sets in the basement bar at weekends.

For a quiet pint, try the **King's Head** ( ☎ 01492-877993; Old Rd), a Victorian pub overlooking the tramway station, or the **Cottage Loaf** ( ☎ 01492-870762; www.the-cottageloaf.co.uk; mains around £8; 1 Market St), a cosy pub with real ales, regular beer festivals and satisfyingly hearty pub grub.

## Entertainment

**Venue Cymru** ( ☎ 01472-872000; www.venuecymru.co.uk; The Promenade; 🕑 box office 9.30am-8.30pm Mon-Sat, noon-4pm Sun, plus before performances) is the town's leading arts venue for all types of shows and events. You can enjoy a pre-theatre dinner at the Venue's **Y Review restaurant** ( ☎ 01492-873641; 2 courses £14.50).

**St John's Methodist Church** (Mostyn St; admission free; 🕑 Jul-Oct) hosts male-voice-choir performances on Tuesdays and Thursdays at 8pm.

## Getting There & Away

### BUS

National Express buses stop by Parc Llandudno. Bus 545 runs once daily to London (£28.50, 8½ hours) via Chester and Birmingham; book tickets at the tourist office.

Regional buses stop on the corner of Upper Mostyn and Gloddaeth Streets. Arriva bus 5/X5 runs every 15 minutes (hourly on Sunday) to Caernarfon (one hour 20 minutes) via the railway interchange at Llandudno Junction (15 minutes) and Conwy (20 minutes).

Snowdon Sherpa bus S2 runs once daily to Betws-y-Coed for connections to Pen-y-Pass.

## TRAIN

Conwy Valley Line trains serve Blaenau Ffestiniog (£6, 75 minutes, five daily Monday to Saturday) via Betws-y-Coed (50 minutes).

Arriva Trains services run to Manchester Piccadilly (£22, 2¼ hours, hourly Monday to Saturday, six Sunday) via Chester (£13, one hour). Most Sunday services require a change at Llandudno Junction; the latter also has Virgin Trains connections to London Euston (£30, around four hours, three hourly, fewer on Sunday) and Holyhead (£10, one hour).

## CONWY
### pop 4000

Conwy is all about the castle, one of Wales' finest and a Unesco World Heritage Site. The approach to the castle gate is highly theatrical, with three bridges spanning the river: Thomas Telford's 1826 suspension bridge (now pedestrianised), Robert Stephenson's 1848 steel railway span and the newer road crossing.

But while the castle is one of the essential sites in North Wales, the town of Conwy itself is a major letdown. The regeneration of the rundown Conwy Quay has stalled and the town feels eerily quiet after 5pm when the majority of day visitors have departed and the shop shutters have been pulled down.

Conwy is a place to visit, not to stay, and the best of the accommodation lies out of town, or at the nearby and more go-ahead town of Llandudno (p749).

The town does at least come alive once a year for the increasingly well regarded **Gwledd Conwy Feast** (www.gwleddconwyfeast.co.uk), held annually in October – book accommodation in advance.

The **tourist office** ( ☎ 01492-592248; ⏰ 9am-5pm Easter-Oct, 9.30am-4pm Mon-Sat & 11am-4pm Sun Nov-Mar) is a cramped box of an office within the castle complex and heaving during high season.

## Sights
### CONWY CASTLE & TOWN WALL

Another great bastion in Edward I's Welsh defences, **Conwy Castle** (Cadw; ☎ 01492-592358; adult/child £4.70/4.20; ⏰ 9am-5pm Apr-Oct, 9.30am-4pm Mon-Sat & 11am-4pm Sun Nov-Mar) was built in just five years (1282–87) following the conquest of Gwynedd.

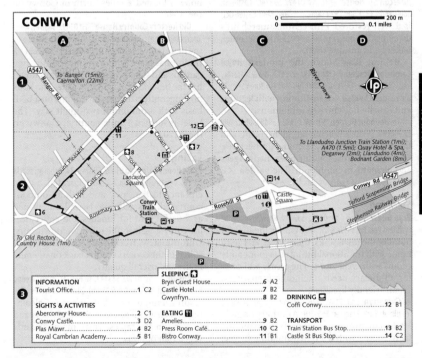

| CONWY | | |
|---|---|---|
| **INFORMATION** | | |
| Tourist Office | 1 | C2 |
| **SIGHTS & ACTIVITIES** | | |
| Aberconwy House | 2 | C1 |
| Conwy Castle | 3 | D2 |
| Plas Mawr | 4 | B2 |
| Royal Cambrian Academy | 5 | B1 |
| **SLEEPING** | | |
| Bryn Guest House | 6 | A2 |
| Castle Hotel | 7 | B2 |
| Gwynfryn | 8 | B2 |
| **EATING** | | |
| Amelies | 9 | B2 |
| Press Room Café | 10 | C2 |
| Bistro Conway | 11 | B1 |
| **DRINKING** | | |
| Coffi Conwy | 12 | B1 |
| **TRANSPORT** | | |
| Train Station Bus Stop | 13 | B2 |
| Castle St Bus Stop | 14 | C2 |

The shape of the castle was dictated by the rock on which it was built, with eight huge drum towers punctuating the soaring curtain walls. Inside it's quite dilapidated, but fun to explore nonetheless. From the battlements, views across the estuary and to the peaks of Snowdonia – when not veiled in cloud – are exhilarating.

The 1200m-long **town wall** was built simultaneously with the castle, guarding Conwy's residents at night. You can walk part way round the wall; the best views are at Upper Gate.

### OTHER SIGHTS

One of Britain's finest surviving Elizabethan town houses, **Plas Mawr** (Cadw; ☎ 01492-580167; High St; adult/child £5.10/4.70; ⏰ 9am-5pm Tue-Sun Apr-Sep, 9.30am-4pm Tue-Sun Oct) was built in 1585. The tall, whitewashed exterior is an indication of the owner's status, but gives no clue of the vivid friezes of the interior. The admission price includes a helpful audio tour; a combined ticket including entrance to the castle costs £7/6 per adult/child.

Nearby, intriguing timber-and-plaster **Aberconwy House** (NT; ☎ 01492-592246; Castle St; adult/child £3/1.50; ⏰ 11am-5pm Wed-Mon Easter-Oct) is a well-restored 14th-century merchant's dwelling that has served as coffee house, hotel, bakery and antique shop.

Behind Plas Mawr, the modern **Royal Cambrian Academy** (☎ 01492-593413; www.rcaconwy.org; Crown Lane; ⏰ 11am-5pm Tue-Sat, 1-4.30pm Sun) is a premier Welsh arts institution with lectures and usually free entry to exhibitions.

In **Bodnant Garden** (NT; ☎ 01492-650460; adult/child £7.20/3.60; ⏰ 10am-5pm Easter-Oct), global plants and flowers flourish over 32 colourful hectares. Summer sees roses, water lilies, hydrangeas and clematis in full bloom. The garden is 8 miles south of Conwy on the A470.

### Sleeping

**Bryn Guest House** (☎ 01492-592449; www.bryn.org.uk; Sychnant Pass Rd; s/d £45/65; Ⓟ ) Under the highest point of the town walls, this period Victorian home with traditional fittings has four comfy rooms with great views. The owner will cater for all dietary needs, including preparing a vegan-friendly breakfast.

**Gwynfryn** (☎ 01492-576733; www.gwynfrynbandb.co.uk; 4 York Place; r £55-70) Another homely Victorian property, it boasts five slightly frilly rooms with a French-boudoir theme.

Homelike touches include in-room fridges and DVDs, plus earplugs. Breakfast is served in the secluded garden during summer.

**Castle Hotel** (☎ 01492-582800; www.castlewales.co.uk; High St; Club/Premium d from £139/159; Ⓟ 💻 ) This historic property located at the heart of town is now looking fresher after some refurbishment work to modernise the traditional, stately rooms. The accommodation is split between smaller Club and more generous Premium rooms, which have added extras, such as Bose sound systems. Downstairs, Dawson's Bar & Restaurant serves bar mains amid leather banquette seats and artworks.

**Quay Hotel & Spa** (☎ 01492-564100; Deganwy Quay, Deganwy; s/d from £120/175) Slick and professional, the hotel manages to blend high-standard facilities for business travellers with services to appeal to families. Most of all, it's known for the fantastic views experienced by diners in the slick Vue Restaurant across to floodlit Conwy Castle. The spa and fitness centre are welcome additions, and a few nice touches, such as free water replenished daily in suites, serve to complete the overall package. The hotel is located 2 miles north of Conwy on the A546.

**Old Rectory Country House** (☎ 01492-580611; www.oldrectorycountryhouse.co.uk; r £139-159; Ⓟ ) A hidden-away Georgian country retreat, a traditional place with a grand feel, pristine gardens and superb views – the Walnut Room has the best views of Conwy Castle. The hotel no longer offers dinner, just rooms on a B&B basis with a minimum two-night stay. The hotel is located 1 mile south of Conwy on the A470.

### Eating

**Press Room Cafe** (☎ 01492-592242; 3 Rosehill St; snacks £5-10; ⏰ 10.30am-5pm Tue-Sun) Located by the entrance to the castle and with an outdoor courtyard, this arty cafe is well established as a useful spot for lunches and coffee, followed by a visit to the gift shop downstairs. Unfortunately, recent staff changes have resulted in the owners cutting back on opening hours and overall quality.

**Amelie's** (☎ 01492-583142; 10 High St; mains around £14; ⏰ noon-2.15pm & 6-9.15pm) Named after the Audrey Tautou film, Amelie's is a welcoming French-motif bistro with wood floors and flowers on the tables. Tasty mains include vegetarian options.

---

**STEAM RIDES AGAIN**

Wales' narrow-gauge railways are testament to an industrial heyday of mining and quarrying. Using steam and diesel engines, these railways often crossed terrain that defied standard-gauge trains.

The advent of steam and the rapid spread of the railway transformed 19th-century Britain, but 20th-century industrial decline and road-building left many lines defunct. The infamous Beeching report of 1963 closed dozens of rural branch lines. Five years later, British Rail fired up its last steam engine.

Passionate steam enthusiasts formed a preservation group, buying and restoring old locomotives, rolling stock, disused lines and stations – a labour of love financed by offering rides to the public, often with old railway workers helping out.

Nine restored lines around Wales form a group called **Great Little Trains of Wales** (www .greatlittletrainsofwales.co.uk). A discount card (£10) entitles the holder to a 20% discount for a return trip on each of the nine railways.

---

**Bistro Conwy** ( ☎ 01492-596326; Chapel St; mains around £15; ☉ 6.30-9pm Mon-Sat) This local favourite, with its cosy ambience and attractive setting, offers a blend of modern and traditional Welsh dishes. The large and inspiring menu caters to all tastes, while the service is quietly assured.

For an espresso on the go, try **Coffi Conwy** ( ☎ 01492-596456, 2 High St).

## Getting There & Away

The bus stop at the train station is the hub for KMP bus 9A/9B to Bangor (40 minutes, three hourly Monday to Saturday). The Castle St bus stop is the hub for Arriva bus 5/5X to Llandudno (20 minutes, every 20 minutes Monday to Saturday, hourly Sunday) and Arriva bus 19/X19 to Llangollen (one hour 50 minutes, three daily Monday to Saturday, two on Sunday).

Conwy is a request stop for Arriva train services to Crewe (1½ hours), which connect with Virgin Trains services to London Euston (£56.30, four hours, five daily Monday to Saturday, one Sunday).

## LLANGOLLEN
pop 3500

Scenic Llangollen (lan-goch-len), huddled in the fertile Vale of Llangollen around the banks of the tumbling River Dee, is evolving from a day-trip destination for the blue-rinse brigade to a centre for white-water sports and cultural tourism. It's a testament to the go-ahead nature of the town that it manages to retain its intrinsic charm while garnering new plaudits as the festival capital of North Wales.

The engineer Thomas Telford, the Scottish 'Colossus of Roads', propelled the town into the 19th century by routing both the London–Holyhead (A5) road and the Llangollen Canal through it. Two miles up the canal is the scenic weir at Horseshoe Falls, while down the canal is a Telford masterpiece, the towering Pontcysyllte Aqueduct.

Today the town is best known for the annual **International Eisteddfod** (see the boxed text, p755), held every July at the **Royal International Pavilion** to promote world peace through music, song and dance. The **Llangollen Fringe Festival** ( ☎ 01978-860600; www.llangollenfringe.co.uk), held in late July, is a smaller-scale version of the famous Edinburgh Fringe Festival, with talks, poetry, music and theatre at the **Town Hall**.

For more information about Llangollen, check out www.llangollen.org.uk.

## Orientation & Information

Llangollen is dissected by the A5 and River Dee with most attractions grouped along Castle St. The helpful **tourist office** ( ☎ 01978-860828; llangollen@nwtic; Castle St; ☉ 9.30am-5.30pm Apr-Oct, 9.30am-5pm Nov-Mar) is well stocked with Ordnance Survey (OS) maps, books and gifts. It shares the Chapel Building with the **library** ( ☉ 9.30am-7pm Mon, to 5.30pm Tue, Wed & Fri, to 12.30pm Sat Apr-Oct, 9.30am-5pm Fri-Wed Nov-Mar), for free internet access, and the Fringe box office during the festival.

## Sights & Activities

Ornate **Plas Newydd** ( ☎ 01978-861314; adult/child £3.50/2.50; ☉ 10am-5pm Easter-Oct) was home to the Ladies of Llangollen, Lady Eleanor Butler

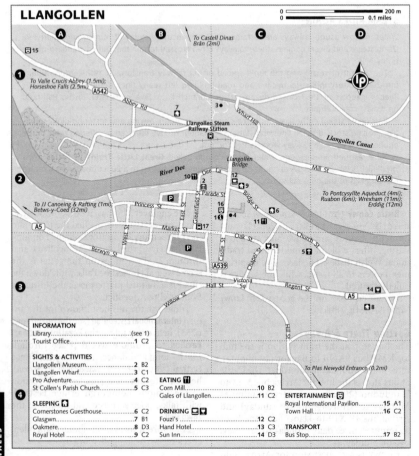

**LLANGOLLEN**

0   200 m
0   0.1 miles

To Castell Dinas Brân (2mi)

To Valle Crucis Abbey (1.5mi);
Horseshoe Falls (2.5mi)

Abbey Rd
A542

Wharf Hill

Llangollen Steam
Railway Station

Llangollen Canal

Llangollen
Bridge

River Dee

Dee La

Mill St

A539

Parade St

To Pontcysyllte Aqueduct (4mi);
Ruabon (6mi); Wrexham (11mi);
Erddig (12mi)

To JJ Canoeing & Rafting (1mi);
Betws-y-Coed (32mi)

Princess St

A5

Bridge St

Greenfield St

East St

West St

Market St

Oak St

Church St

Berwyn St

Castle St

Chapel St

A539

Victoria
Sq

Regent St

Hall St

A5

Willow St

Hill St

To Plas Newydd Entrance (0.2mi)

**INFORMATION**
Library...........................................(see 1)
Tourist Office.......................................**1** C2

**SIGHTS & ACTIVITIES**
Llangollen Museum..............................**2** B2
Llangollen Wharf..................................**3** C1
Pro Adventure......................................**4** C2
St Collen's Parish Church......................**5** C3

**SLEEPING**
Cornerstones Guesthouse....................**6** C2
Glasgwn...............................................**7** B1
Oakmere...............................................**8** D3
Royal Hotel............................................**9** C2

**EATING**
Corn Mill.............................................**10** B2
Gales of Llangollen.............................**11** C2

**DRINKING**
Fouzi's................................................**12** C2
Hand Hotel.........................................**13** C3
Sun Inn...............................................**14** D3

**ENTERTAINMENT**
Royal International Pavilion................**15** A1
Town Hall............................................**16** C2

**TRANSPORT**
Bus Stop.............................................**17** B2

and Miss Sarah Ponsonby (see Ladies of Llangollen, p756). A romantic mix of Gothic and Tudor styles, the house has pleasant formal gardens, and audio guides are included in the admission price. The house lies a fifth of a mile uphill southeast of the town centre. Don't confuse it with the National Trust stately home of the same name on Anglesey.

**Llangollen Steam Railway** ( ☎ 01978-860979; www .llangollen-railway.co.uk; return trip £9) chugs through another era on its 8-mile route to Carrog, passing the Horseshoe Falls en route. The timetable of departures changes monthly (check the website). There are regular special services, including Santa and Thomas the Tank Engine excursions for kids (free up to 15 years).

The 6th-century **St Collen's Parish Church** (Church St; ☒ 2-6pm Mon-Fri mid-May–Sep), after which the town is named, houses a memorial to the Ladies of Llangollen, who are buried in the graveyard.

**Llangollen Museum** ( ☎ 01978-862862; www .llangollenmuseum.org.uk; Parade St; admission free; ☒ 10am-5pm Thu-Tue, 1-5pm Wed) has a local history collection.

Among the activities on offer are horse-drawn canal trips, departing from **Llangollen Wharf** ( ☎ 01978-860702; www.horsedrawnboats.co.uk) opposite the train station. Choose from a 45-minute trip (adult/child costs £5/2.50) or the motorised two-hour, one-way cruise to Telford's astounding Pontcysyllte Aqueduct (adult/child costs £10/8).

NORTH WALES

---

### ESSENTIAL EISTEDDFOD

The **National Eisteddfod** (www.eisteddfod.org.uk), pronounced *ey-steth-vot*, a celebration of Welsh culture, is Europe's largest festival of competitive music-making and poetry. Descended from ancient bardic tournaments, it attracts more than 150,000 visitors and 6000 competitors annually. Conducted in Welsh, the festival welcomes all. Foreigners come in search of Welsh ancestry, while musical fringe events featuring local bands lend a slight Glastonbury atmosphere. It's generally held in early August, and the venue swings annually between the northern and southern regions of Wales.

    **Urdd Eisteddfod** (www.urdd.org) is a separate young people's festival – *urdd* (pronounced *irth*) is Welsh for 'youth' – held every May at changing venues. The format resembles its bigger brother, although any self-respecting teenager prefers to hang out on the fringe at the main event.

    Most famous of all is the **International Eisteddfod** (www.international-eisteddfod.co.uk), established after WWII to promote international harmony. Held every July at Llangollen's Royal International Pavilion, the event pulls up to 5000 participants from more than 40 countries, transforming the town into a global village. In addition to daily folk music and dancing competitions, gala concerts feature international stars. It was nominated for the Nobel Peace Prize in 2004.

---

Walkers enjoy the challenge of the Llangollen History Trail, a 6-mile, or four-hour, circular trail leading via the eerie ruins of 13th-century **Castell Dinas Brân** to the well-tended 13th- and 14th-century ruins of **Valle Crucis Abbey** (Cadw; ☎ 01978-860326; adult/child £2.70/2.30; ⏱ 10am-5pm daily Apr-Sep), one of Wales' last Cistercian monasteries. See the website www.deevalleywalks.com for more information about walking opportunities in the area.

The town's two main operators for rafting, canoeing, gorge-walking and rock climbing activities:

**JJ Canoeing & Rafting** ( ☎ 01978-860763; www .jjraftcanoe.com; Mile End Mill, Berwyn Rd) for canoeing, kayak instruction and gorge-walking. Located 1 mile west of Llangollen on the A5.

**Pro Adventure** ( ☎ 01978-861912; www.proadventure .co.uk; 23 Castle St) For white-water sports, climbing and bushcraft, plus family days.

### Sleeping

**Glasgwm** ( ☎ 01978-861975; Abbey Rd; s/d from £32.50/50; P ) A friendly, family-home guesthouse with a cosy lounge dominated by a traditional Welsh dresser, Glasgwm is a reliable mid-range option. Four cosy rooms and a hearty breakfast, catering for all dietary needs, plus evening meals and packed lunches if required, make this an all-round winner.

    **Oakmere** ( ☎ 01978-861126; www.oakmere.llangollen .co.uk; Regent St; s/d £45/65; P ) Set back from the A5 along a genteel gravel drive, this imposing Victorian mansion has traditional rooms with striking oak furniture and period fittings. The

conservatory boasts calming views across the well-groomed gardens.

    **Royal Hotel** ( ☎ 01978-860202; www.royal-hotel -llangollen.co.uk; Bridge St; s/d from £45/90; P ) This grand old dame, with cascading river views, is looking fresher after a major refurbishment that has upgraded the 33 traditional-style rooms with new mod cons and introduced a smart new restaurant, Room 29, for dinners.

    **Cornerstones Guesthouse** ( ☎ 01978-861569; www .cornerstones-guesthouse.co.uk; 15 Bridge St; d/ste £70/85; P 🖳 ) Still the smartest place in town, this converted 16th-century house has three individually styled rooms with sloping floorboards and oak beams, but also internet access and DVD's. The lounge area, which has river views, is a cosy spot to sit and read.

### Eating & Drinking

**our pick Gales of Llangollen** ( ☎ 01978-860089; www .galesofllangollen.co.uk; 18 Bridge St; mains around £10; ⏱ lunch & dinner Mon-Sat) Gales is a Llangollen institution and consistently the best place in town to eat. With rustic tables, chalk-board menus of daily changing specials, an exhaustive wine list ranging from Chile to Lebanon, and Ryan Adams on the stereo to add a relaxed after-dark vibe, this place is hard to beat. The owners also have B&B accommodation (singles/doubles £55/70) in simple but comfortable, adjoining rooms with a continental breakfast, and they sell wines and cookware in a shop next door to the bar.

    **Corn Mill** ( ☎ 01978-869555; Dee Lane; mains around £14; ⏱ noon-9pm) The water mill still turns at the heart of this converted mill – now an

**NORTH WALES**

---

**LADIES OF LLANGOLLEN**

Lady Eleanor Butler and Miss Sarah Ponsonby, the Ladies of Llangollen, lived in Plas Newydd from 1780 to 1829 with their maid Mary Carryl. Their love affair blossomed in Ireland and, after their Anglo-Irish families discouraged the relationship, they eloped to Wales disguised as men in an attempt to start a new life. They settled in Llangollen, devoting themselves to 'friendship, celibacy and the knitting of stockings'.

Their relationship became well known, so much so that national and literary figures of the day, including the Duke of Wellington and William Wordsworth, paid them visits. Wordsworth penned the charming words 'sisters in love, a love allowed to climb, even on this earth above the reach of time'.

Lady Eleanor died in 1829, Sarah Ponsonby two years later. They are buried at St Collen's Parish Church in the centre of Llangollen.

---

all-day bar and eatery – while the deck is the best spot in town for an alfresco lunch. There's a good range of options for all tastes. It has a policy of no pushchairs.

**Fouzi's** ( ☎ 01978-861340; Bridge St; ☿ 9.30am-4pm Mon-Fri, to 5pm Sat) Serving coffee and lunchtime snacks, contemporary-style Fouzi's is a welcome break from the traditional tearooms. It's part of the Royal Hotel.

For real ale and regular live music, try the **Sun Inn** ( ☎ 01978-860233; Regent St). The **Hand Hotel** ( ☎ 01978-861616; Bridge St) plays host to the Llangollen Male Voice Choir each Friday evening at 9pm.

### Getting There & Away

All bus services stop on Market St opposite the short-stay car park. National Express coach 420 runs daily to London (£27.50, 5½ hours) via Shrewsbury and Birmingham – book tickets at the tourist office.

Arriva bus 19/X19 runs to Betws-y-Coed (one hour, three daily, two on Sunday) and Llandudno (two hours). Arriva bus X94 runs to Dolgellau (1½ hours, every two hours Monday to Saturday, three on Sunday).

The nearest mainline train station is 6 miles east at Ruabon on the Chester–Birmingham line; a taxi from Ruabon costs about £9 – call **Premier Cars** ( ☎ 01978-861999).

### AROUND LLANGOLLEN

The Yorke family home for over two centuries (until 1973), **Erddig** (NT, ☎ 01978-355314; adult/child/family £9.40/4.70/23.50; ☿ grounds 10am-6pm Sat-Thu Jul & Aug, 11am-6pm Sat-Wed Apr-Jun & Sep, to 4pm Mar, Oct & Nov, house noon-5pm Sat-Thu Jul & Aug, noon-5pm Sat-Wed Apr-Jun & Oct, to 4pm Mar, to 4pm Sat & Sun Nov & Dec) offers an illuminating glimpse into 19th-century life for the British upper class. Much of the family's original furniture is on display in the fine staterooms, while a formal, walled garden has been restored in Victorian style, featuring rare fruit trees, a canal and the National Ivy Collection. Complete with two cafe-style restaurants and extensive woodland walks, it makes for a good family outing. Erddig lies 12 miles northeast of Llangollen on the A483 in the village of Rhostyllen.

# SNOWDONIA NATIONAL PARK (PARC CENEDLAETHOL ERYRI)

In a country overflowing with uplands, Snowdonia National Park reigns supreme, with the highest mountains and steepest valleys of any Welsh region. Dive into the rocky clefts and scramble up the slopes, armed with walking boots, crampons, or just a widening pair of eyes, for guaranteed excitement. The sea is so close that visitors can easily shift in pace between challenging terrain and relaxing sandy beaches.

Mt Snowdon (1085m) is the highest piece of rock in Wales and England. No world-beater in elevation, it nonetheless strikes a noble pose atop a precipitous horseshoe of jagged peaks. Scaling the summit, on foot or by mountain railway, is the goal of many visitors – the park was created in 1951 as much to prevent the peak from being over-loved as from being neglected or built upon. Plenty of other mountain-hiking options are scattered across this extensive region, from the neighbouring ranges of the Carneddau and Glyders to Cader Idris above Dolgellau in the south. Rock climbing, white-water rafting, mountain biking and pony trekking are also excellent.

Away from the craggy peaks, Snowdonia's tows offer an array of attractions, from the World Heritage–listed medieval castle at Harlech, via the rural, village charm of Beddgelert to the bustling shops and gentle strolling around Betws-y-Coed.

Hard-won mineral treasures – copper, gold and slate – buried deep in the mountains permitted the inhabitants a tough living through the ages. Several mines now operate as visitor attractions, along with vintage railways such as the Ffestiniog and Welsh Highland lines, which once hauled the booty down to the sea. The area's high rainfall is cannily exploited by hydroelectric power stations; the Electric Mountain at Llanberis is one massive underground scheme you can see for yourself.

Snowdonia is also a proudly Welsh-speaking area with a strong sense of Welsh culture.

## Orientation & Information

Snowdonia is the third-largest of Britain's 14 national parks, after the Cairngorms in Scotland and Lake District in England. While Mt Snowdon is the focus, the park covers 823 sq miles. The boundaries extend fully 35 miles east–west and 50 miles north–south towards Mid Wales.

Major tourist towns have informative tourist offices that provide bed-booking services and weather information. Snowdonia National Park information centres can be found at Betws-y-Coed and Dolgellau (both open year-round), and from Easter to October at Aberdyfi, Blaenau Ffestiniog, Harlech and Beddgelert. Excellent online information is available at www.eryri-npa.gov.uk and www.visitsnowdonia.info.

For the latest weather report, check the Met Office mountain forecast at www.metoffice .gov.uk/loutdoor/mountainsafety/snowdonia .html.

## Activities

### ACTIVITY CENTRES

North Wales has three national activity centres:

**Canolfan Tryweryn – the National Whitewater Centre** ( ☎ 01678-521083; www.ukrafting.co.uk) A trusty 1½-mile stretch of the River Tryweryn, near Bala, provides top rafting, canoeing and kayaking. For aquaphobes, try activities such as clay-pigeon shooting or bushcraft skills.

**Plas y Brenin – the National Mountain Centre** ( ☎ 01690-720214; www.pyb.co.uk) Based at Capel Curig, this is the place to learn climbing, mountain biking and summit leadership. If you're confident enough to go it alone, the centre has a great equipment-rental service.

**Plas Menai – the National Water Sports Centre** ( ☎ 01248-670964; www.plasmenai.co.uk) A year-round range of water-based courses for all ability levels – from sailing to power-boating; based near Caernarfon.

### CYCLING

Dedicated mountain-bike venues with signposted, graded routes include top spot Coed-y-Brenin Forest (p760), Gwydyr Forest (p761) and Beddgelert Forest (p763). See www.mbwales.com and www.cycling.visit wales.com for more information. Permits are required.

Following two alternative routes through the park, the Lôn Las Cymru (see Freewheeling Through Wales, p682), offers stunning, if hilly, road cycling.

**NORTH WALES**

---

**DETOUR: RUTHIN**

Lesser known but equally as charming as Llangollen, Ruthin has traditionally been popular with walkers, given its proximity to the Offa's Dyke Path national trail (p738). Recently, however, Ruthin has discovered its stylish, arty side.

Leading the charge is **Manorhaus** ( ☎ 01824-704830; www.manorhaus.com; Well St; s/d £90/125), a stylish restaurant-with-rooms that borrow's from the German 'art hotel' concept. The eight individually styled rooms all showcase the works of different artists, while unique touches include a library of books and films, a bookable steam room and a private cinema for up to eight people.

Just across St Peters Sq from the hotel, the newly reopened **Ruthin Craft Centre** ( ☎ 01824-704774; wwwruthincraftcentre.org.uk; 2 Well St; admission free; ☒ 10am-5.30pm) is a major centre for applied arts, with three galleries, a cafe and tourist information. The striking design of the new buildings reflects the natural environment of the surrounding Clwydian Hills.

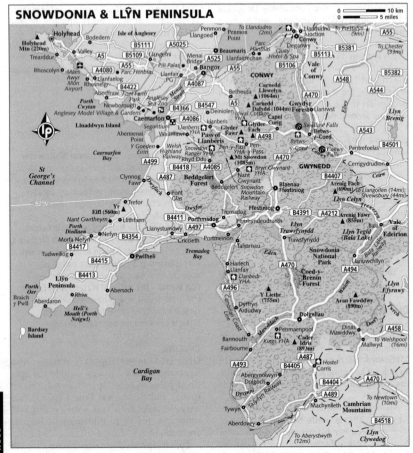

For safety and environmental reasons, a voluntary daytime ban operates on all routes to the summit of Snowdon from 10am to 5pm daily May to September. (There is only one path that goes from Llanberis through Maesgwm to Snowdon Ranger, which is open all year round.)

**SnowBikers** ( ☎ 01341-430628; www.snowbikers .com) and **Bicycle Beano** ( ☎ 01982-560471; www .bicycle-beano.co.uk) lead guided tours in and around Snowdonia National Park. Book in advance.

To escape the roads and leave the traffic behind you, scenic former railway lines can be found in the sea-level **Mawddach Trail**, near Dolgellau, and at **Caernarfon** in the north of the region.

## PONY TREKKING & HORSE RIDING

Tranquilly located at Waunfawr, south of Caernarfon, **Snowdonia Riding Stables** ( ☎ 01286-650342; www.snowdonia2000.fsnet.co.uk; per hr £15, half-day £33) can take you deep into the mountains.

## WALKING

Mt Snowdon is the main destination for walkers, many basing themselves at Llanberis to tackle one of the numerous routes to the top (see Summit Special, p764).

But other hikes around the region are just as exhilarating – and less crowded. In the north (just northeast of Snowdon itself), try the rugged Glyders and the famous ridge of Tryfan, or the domed summits of the

Carneddau range (northeast of the Glyders). To the south the Moelwyns and Moel Hebog, or the Nantlle Ridge, are good options. For gentler forest trails and river walks head for Betws-y-Coed.

Further south, the well-used ascent of Cader Idris (near Dolgellau) makes a fine day's walk. Here are also the Arans (located northeast of Dolgellau, southwest of Bala), the lesser-known Arenigs (west of Bala) and the challenging Rhinog Ridge (east of Harlech).

Local tourist offices stock brochures on the main mountain routes, as well as maps and detailed local guidebooks.

Before setting out, consider the following. Some walks graded 'easy' may still go near steep slopes or tricky terrain. Accidents can happen, usually on the way down. Be prepared to deal with hostile weather at any time of year, even on days that seem clear and sunny. On anything more than a stroll, you should carry warm waterproof clothing, food and drink, map and compass.

If in doubt about your abilities, consider a national park walk; ask at tourist offices, check the *Eryri/Snowdonia* newspaper, or download details of day walks from the national park website www.eryri-npa.gov.uk.

Prestatyn, on the north coast, is the end of **Offa's Dyke Path**, a long-distance national trail along the Wales–England border. The route's final three days, from Chirk Castle via Llandegla and Bodfari, showcase the varied scenery of this northwestern corner of the region.

### Sleeping

There are some smart options in Snowdonia, but friendly hostels, B&Bs and midrange guesthouses are the norm.

Betws-y-Coed, Llanberis and Dolgellau have the best options, but some of the more interesting places are more isolated. Five YHA hostels serve Mt Snowdon:

- Bryn Gwynant YHA (p763)
- Idwal Cottage YHA (p764)
- Llanberis YHA (p765)
- Pen-y-Pass YHA (p764)
- Snowdon Ranger YHA (p763)

### Getting There & Around

Bus services between regional towns are adequate (but limited on Sunday). Colourful **Snowdon Sherpa** ( ☎ 01286-870880; day tickets adult/child £4/2) buses serve the mountain areas and Mt Snowdon trailheads. There are daily services on most routes with increased frequency during high season (July and August). The Snowdon Sherpa day ticket is for hop-on, hop-off access to the network of buses throughout a 24-hour period.

For information on Snowdonia buses, trains and multiday tickets, see p747.

For more information, contact **Traveline Cymru** ( ☎ 0871 200 2233; www.travelinecymru.org.uk).

## DOLGELLAU

**pop 2500**

Dolgellau (doll-geth-lau) comes across as a typical Welsh market town with stout stone buildings topped with tons of prime slate. Dolgellau's wealth came from the 19th-century wool trade, which provided most of the impressive buildings. More than 200 are now listed for preservation – the highest concentration in Wales.

Today the town is a major outdoor-pursuits base. One of Snowdonia's premier peaks, bulky Cader Idris (892m), lies to the south, while the nearby Coed-y-Brenin Forest offers glorious mountain-biking country.

Recently, too, the town has smartened up its act, a trend that is likely to continue as Dolgellau recently secured £2 million of heritage grants to refresh signage and facilities in town over the next five years. It has a lively feel and enough facilities to make it a worthwhile base for exploring the Snowdonia National Park.

The **tourist office & National Park Information Centre** ( ☎ 01341-422888; Eldon Sq; ⏲ 9.30am-5.30pm Easter-Oct, 10am-5pm Thu-Mon Nov-Mar) is in the heart of town. Upstairs is a permanent exhibition (admission free) on the area's Quaker heritage, dating back to the 17th century.

Dolgellau is heaving during **Sesiwn Fawr** ( ☎ 0871 2301314; www.sesiwnfawr.com), a lively folk and world-music festival held annually in July – book ahead for accommodation.

### Sights & Activities

**Tŷ Siamas** ( ☎ 01341-421800; www.tysiamas.com; Eldon Sq; adult/child £4/2; ⏲ 10am-5pm Mar-Oct, 10am-4pm Tue-Sat Nov-Feb), the first National Centre for Welsh Folk Music in Wales, celebrates the fact that Dolgellau hosted the first-ever Welsh folk festival in 1952. Idris Hall, the former market hall on Eldon Sq, houses an exhibition, cafe-bar and a weekly program of performances, jam sessions, workshops and instrument lessons. See also Welsh Folk Music, p690.

**Coed-y-Brenin Forest** ( ☎ 01341-440742; www .forestry.gov.uk/wales), 8 miles north of Dolgellau on the A470, is the region's premier mountain-biking destination. Signposted trails weave for 70 miles, with something for all abilities. Hire mountain bikes at **Dolgellau Cycles** ( ☎ 01341-423332; Smithfield St; half-/full day £13/20).

For picturesque pedalling or walking, the **Mawddach Trail** is a converted railway line meandering 7.5 miles along the south of the Mawddach Estuary to Barmouth. The trail starts in the car park beside the town's Fawr bridge.

When tackling **Cader Idris** the standard route is up the 'Dolgellau' or Ty Nant Path (6 miles, five hours), heading southeast from Ty Nant Farm on the A493. The longest but easiest is the Tywyn or Llanfihangel y Pennant Path (10 miles, six hours), northeast from the Talyllyn Railway terminus at Abergynolwyn. The shortest and steepest trail is the Minffordd Path (6 miles, five hours), northwest from near the Minffordd Hotel on the A487 road to Machynlleth. Whichever route you choose, always carry appropriate clothing and check weather conditions online at www.eryri-npa .co.uk before departure.

## Sleeping

**Kings YHA** ( ☎ 0870 770 5900; www.yha.org.uk; Penmaenpool; dm £16; ☺ reception 8-10am & 5-10pm) A gloriously remote country-house hostel popular with walkers and hikers. The nearest shop is 5 miles away and don't expect a mobile-phone signal. Located 1 mile west of Penmaenpool off the A493, then a 1-mile yomp through woodland.

**Y Meirionnydd** ( ☎ 01341-422554; www.themeirion nydd.com; Smithfield Sq; ste £75-85; **P** ) The reborn former Clifton House Hotel is something of a work in progress. The owners are steadily refurbishing the rooms with a more contemporary feel, and garnering plaudits for upping the ante in the cellar restaurant with dinner served on Welsh grey-slate plates, accompanied by Welsh ales from the Pen Lon Brewery in Ceredigion.

**our pick** **Ffynnon** ( ☎ 01341-421774; www.ffynnon townhouse.com; Love Lane; s £80-95, d £120-150; **P** **🖳** ) This boutique guesthouse is about as family friendly as you will find. But, with a keen eye for contemporary interior design and a super-friendly welcome, it feels both homely

and stylish at the same time. Three contemporary rooms, the boldest with an Oriental theme, are now joined by a fourth room with a free-standing bath. The drawing room is a sun-soaked space to relax over coffee and weekend papers, and there's a children's play area.

## Eating

**Dylanwad Da** ( ☎ 01341-422870; 2 Smithfield St; mains around £14; ☺ 10am-3pm & 7-9pm daily Easter-Oct, Thu-Sat Nov-Mar) Informal wine and tapas bar by day, contemporary restaurant by night, this well-run locals' favourite has been serving up high-quality food for over 20 years. Daily specials include local produce and vegetarian options.

**Mawddach** ( ☎ 01341-424020; www.mawddach .com; mains £9-18; ☺ noon-2.30pm & 6-9.30pm Wed-Fri, 6-10.30pm Sat, noon-3pm Sun) Located 2 miles west of Dolgellau on the A494, the latest opening in the area is a stylish eatery that brings a touch of urban style to rural North Wales. Black-slate floors, brown leather seats and panoramic views across to Cader Idris set the scene, while the food is equally impressive. Lamb fresh from the farm, local fish specials and Sunday roasts (two courses for £12.50) are well executed.

**Parliament House** ( ☎ 01341-421938; Glyndŵr St; ☺ 9.30am-5pm Mon-Thu, to 10pm Fri & Sat) With a fantastic period setting in a Grade II–listed former ironmonger's shop, still with its original fittings, this atmospheric coffee shop has snacks, newspapers to browse, free internet access for patrons and a huge range of speciality teas. Tapas and wine are served on Friday and Saturday nights.

Stock up on honey buns and deli produce at **Popty'r Dref** ( ☎ 01341-422507; Upper Smithfield St). For a pint, try **Unicorn** ( ☎ 01341-422742; Smithfield Sq) for real ales and simple pub grub.

## Getting There & Away

Arriva bus 32/X32 runs to Aberystwyth (one hour 15 minutes, eight daily, twice on Sunday) and Bangor (two hours 15 minutes). Arriva bus 94/X94 serves Barmouth (25 minutes, roughly hourly, five on Sunday) and Wrexham (two hours).

## AROUND DOLGELLAU

**Bala Lake** (Llyn Tegid) is a hub for water sports, with the nearby River Tryweryn, flowing to the town's northwest fringe, home to the

**Canolfan Tryweryn National Whitewater Centre**
( ☎ 01678-521083; www.ukrafting.co.uk; Frongoch; rafting from £31 ⏰ 8.30am-7pm, to 4pm Mon-Fri Dec & mid-Oct;), which offers year-round class-III and some class-IV white water. The centre is located 4 miles northwest of Bala on the A4212.

Details can be obtained from Bala's helpful **tourist office** ( ☎ 01678-521021; bala.tic@gwynedd. gov.uk; Pensarn Rd; ⏰ 10am-5pm daily Easter-Oct, 10am-4pm Fri-Mon Nov-Mar) next to the leisure centre southwest of town.

The lake is also home to the more serene **Bala Lake Steam Railway** ( ☎ 01678-540666; www.bala -lake-railway.co.uk; adult/child return £7.50/3; ⏰ Mar-Oct), where vintage locos chuff 4.5 miles along the lake's southern bank to Llanuwchllyn. The station is half a mile south of Bala on the B4391.

For lunch on the go, there's a great new deli in Bala. **Siop Y Gornel** ( ☎ 01678-520423; www.siop -y-gornel.co.uk; 21 Tegid St; ⏰ 9am-5.30pm, Mon, Tue, Thu & Fri, 9am-2pm Wed, 8am-4.30pm Sat) has home-made bread, snacks and coffees to eat in or out.

## BETWS-Y-COED
pop 1000

Alpine-like Betws-y-Coed (betus-y-koyd; locals call it 'Betws'), the self-styled eastern gateway to Snowdonia National Park, blossomed as Wales' most popular inland resort during Victorian days and has remained a popular spot ever since. Betws, meaning 'sanctuary in the wood', takes its name from the 14th-century St Michael's Church at the heart of town.

Engulfed by the verdant leafiness of the Gwydyr Forest and at the intersection of the Rivers Conwy and Llugwy, Betws is heaving in summer thanks to its slot on the coach party circuit. The busy High St, the A5 London–Holyhead road, which forms the main thoroughfare, is full of outdoor-activity shops – a testament to the town's lure for Snowdon conquerors.

Nearby **Swallow Falls** (viewing platform adult/child £1/50p), located 2 miles northwest of town on the A5, has a number of quieter day walks from Betws.

The **tourist office & National Park Information Centre** ( ☎ 01690-710426; tic.byc@eryri-npa.gov.uk; Royal Oak Stables; ⏰ 9.30am-5.30pm Easter-Oct, 9.30am-4.30pm Nov-Easter), located opposite the train station, is the region's tourist information hub with a comprehensive array of books and maps, plus an exhibition about Snowdonia National Park.

## Activities

There are numerous forest walks close to Betws. To the northwest, **Gwydyr Forest** has 28 sq miles of oak, beech, larch and fir, criss-crossed with paths, and is a great space for walking, pony trekking or mountain biking. Opened in 2008, the Penmachno Mountain Bike Trail is a 12-mile forest biking trail. **Beics Betws** ( ☎ 01690-710766; www.bikewales.co.uk; Tan Lan; bikes per half-/full day £15/18) provides bikes for hire and route information.

The tourist office sells The *Gwydyr Forest Guide* (£2) and *Walks around Betws-y-Coed* (£5), and will advise on the Boardwalk All-Ability Trail, a wheel- and pushchair friendly trail following the River Llugwy.

**Gwydir Stables** ( ☎ 01690-760248; www.horse-riding -wales.co.uk; Penmachno; per hr/day £19/£53), 6 miles southeast of Betws on the B4406 in the village of Penmachno, arranges pony-trekking forest excursions. There's also a popular pub crawl by horse (around four hours, £40) to avoid drinking and driving.

## Sleeping

**Vagabond Bunkhouse** ( ☎ 01690-710850; www.the vagabond.co.uk; Craiglan Rd; dm £14; ⏰ reception 7.30-10am & 4.30-5.30pm; 🖥 ) A new, independent hostel located next to a gurgling waterfall at the heart of town. Simple dorm rooms but decent facilities, including a bar, drying room and bike storage, make it a welcome newcomer. Breakfast is £4.

**Betws-y-Coed YHA** ( ☎ 01690-710796; www.yha.org .uk; Swallow Falls; dm £15) A functional hostel with facilities for outdoors enthusiasts, adjacent to the Swallow Falls Hotel bar. It's located 2 miles northwest of Betws on the A5.

**Ferns** ( ☎ 01690-710587; www.ferns-guesthouse.co.uk; Holyhead Rd; s £38, d £50-60) A solid midrange option in the centre of the village, this well-run place boasts comfortable rooms and 'fry-up-free' healthy breakfasts using local produce. An adjoining self-catering cottage accommodates up to four people (from £55 per person per night).

**Acorns** ( ☎ 01690-710395; www.betws-y-coed-breaks .co.uk; r from £90; 🅿 ) Located at the southern end of town, Acorns is a stylish, upmarket place offering accommodation split between a B&B suite, a self-contained apartment for two people and a holiday cottage for five. It has a modern feel with rich-hued bedspreads and original artworks, and well-equipped kitchenettes.

**NORTH WALES**

## Eating

**Alpine Coffee Shop** ( ☎ 01690-710747; Old Station Bldgs; 🕙 9am-5.30pm Mon-Fri, 8am-5.30pm Sat & Sun) A local institution with great all-day breakfasts, snacks and even vegan specials, all located just off the train-station platform. The hugely comprehensive tea menu features Jun Shan Silver Needles, the world's rarest tea at £8.80 per pot.

**Fairhaven** ( ☎ 01690-710307; www.fairhaven-snowdonia.co.uk; Holyhead Rd; 🕙 10am-5pm; 🖥 ) A simple, child-friendly cafe for fair-trade coffees, paninis and breakfasts. Grab a spot on the leather sofas and watch the world go by on the main street. It offers internet access (£5 per hour), plus simple B&B accommodation (rooms from £60).

**Plas Derwen** ( ☎ 01690-710388; Holyhead Rd; mains around £9) All-day food in pleasant surroundings mark out Plas Derwen as a rising star. The food is home-made with local produce and weekly specials, and can be enjoyed in the modern and airy cafe or on the alfresco terrace. Upstairs five simple but tasteful rooms, three with bathrooms, are available for B&B (rooms from £50).

**Bistro Betws-y-Coed** ( ☎ 01690-710328; Holyhead Rd; mains around £15; 🕙 lunch & dinner) The old stalwart is still going strong with a hearty and traditional Welsh menu of locally sourced fish and meat, plus vegie options, dished up in a cottage-style dining room. Check the blackboard for daily specials. Reservations are recommended during high season.

For a quiet pint and some home-made pub grub, try the **Pont-Y-Pair Hotel** ( ☎ 01690-710377; Holyhead Rd; mains around £8; 🕙 food noon-9pm Sun-Wed, to 10pm Thu-Sat.

## Getting There & Away

All buses depart from outside the train station. Arriva bus 19/X19 runs to Llandudno (one hour, four daily Monday to Saturday). Snowdon Sherpa runs bus S2 runs to Pen Y Pass (20 minutes, half-hourly) and bus S97 runs onto Porthmadog (two hours, four daily, one on Sunday).

Betws lies halfway along the scenic Conwy Valley Line between Llandudno (40 minutes, five daily Monday to Saturday) and Blaenau Ffestiniog (30 minutes).

## AROUND BETWS-Y-COED

To the west, following the A5, Capel Curig is home to **Plas y Brenin – the National Mountain Centre** ( ☎ 01690-720214; www.pyb.co.uk; B&B per person £20), a multiactivity centre with excellent facilities and a huge array of residential, year-round courses. It has simple rooms and offers a program of regular talks and events.

To the south, on the A470, or riding the Conwy Valley Line, the grey-slate town of **Blaenau Ffestiniog** feels lost and forlorn. It lies just outside the national park but is home to two popular attractions.

**Llechwedd Slate Caverns** ( ☎ 01766-830306; www.llechwedd-slate-caverns.co.uk; 1 tour adult/child £9/7, both tours £15/11; 🕙 10am-5.15pm Mar-Sep, 10am-4.15pm Oct-Feb), a mile north of Blaenau on the A470, offers a first-hand sense of working life in a real slate mine. Of the two tours, the more evocative 25-minute Deep Mine tour recreates the harsh working conditions of the 19th-century miners – be prepared to duck under low ceilings and scramble around dark tunnels. The Miner's Tramway Tour through the network of tunnels is less demanding.

Blaenau is the northern terminus of the narrow-gauge **Rheilffordd Ffestiniog Railway** ( ☎ 01766-516000; www.festrail.co.uk; All-day Rover ticket adult/concession £17.50/16; 🕙 Mar-Oct), which runs to Porthmadog (p766) linking the Conwy Valley and Cambrian Coast Lines. The Ffestiniog Railway Company is the oldest independent railway company in the world, and was established by Act of Parliament in 1832.

The 13.5-mile (one-hour) journey steams its way through a landscape of grey-slate cottages and mist-shrouded mountains, descending to the first stop at Tanygrisiau. The line hugs the fringe of Lake Ystradau before submerging the carriages into soot-saturated darkness on entering the Moelwyn Tunnel. From Dduallt the line heads west, dropping down through fern-fringed valleys and tree-lined passes. The last leg runs along The Cob to Porthmadog Harbour, home to the town's tourist office (p766).

As you chug through the national park, the bone-shaking ride is as much about the smells and sounds – the coal fire of the engine, the rattling of the railway sleepers – as it is about the scenery, which is superb.

More details are available from Blaenau's **tourist office** ( ☎ 01766-830360; 🕙 9.30am-12.30pm & 1.30-5.30pm Easter-Oct, 9.30am-5.30pm Jul & Aug).

## BEDDGELERT
**pop 500**

At the heart of the national park, charming little Beddgelert is a conservation village of rough grey-stone buildings, overlooking the trickling River Glaslyn with its ivy-covered bridge. Flowers festoon the village in spring and, in summer, the surrounding verdant hills are reminiscent of a Scottish glen, with a purple blaze of heather.

The name, meaning 'Gelert's Grave', supposedly refers to the well-known Welsh legend of Prince Llywelyn's faithful dog. Believing the dog had savaged his baby son, Llywelyn slaughtered the dog, only to discover later that Gelert fought off a wolf that had attacked the baby. More likely, the true name is derived from a 5th-century Irish preacher, Celert, who is believed to have founded a church here. Gelert's Grave can be found by following the riverside trail.

The **tourist office & National Park Information Centre** ( ☎ 01766-890615; tic.beddgelert@eryri-npa.gov .uk; ☽ 9.30am-5.30pm Easter-Oct, 9.30am-4.30pm Mon-Sat Nov-Mar) is just off the A498 at the southern end of the village. Beddgelert notoriously has no mobile-phone reception but the tourist office has internet access (£2 per hour).

## Sights & Activities
**Sygun Copper Mine** ( ☎ 01766-890595; www.sygun coppermine.co.uk; adult/child £8/6; ☽ 9am-5pm Easter-Oct) has an audiovisual underground tour that evokes the life of Victorian miners. The mine is 1 mile east of Beddgelert on the A498.

The village will also be a hub for the extension of the **Welsh Highland Railway** (p766) from Porthmadog to Caernarfon, which was due to open in spring 2009 at the time of writing.

Beddgelert is a popular base for hikers climbing Snowdon, while mountain-bikers will find trails for all levels at **Beddgelert Forest**, 2 miles north on the A4085. Nearby **Beics Beddgelert** ( ☎ 01766-890434; www.bedd gelertbikes.co.uk; bikes adult/child per day £20/14) rents mountain bikes.

## Sleeping & Eating
There are two local YHA hostels.

**Bryn Gwynant YHA** ( ☎ 0870 770 5732; www.yha.org.uk; Nantgwynant; dm £15; ☽ reception 8-10am & 5-10.30pm). A Victorian mansion in a stunning location overlooking Llyn Gwynant, near the steep Watkin Path trailhead, 4 miles east on the A498. **Snowdon Ranger YHA** ( ☎ 0870 770 6038; www.yha.org.uk; Rhyd Ddu; dm £16; ☽ reception 8-10am & 5-10.30pm). A characterful former inn well positioned for the Snowdon Ranger Path trailhead, 5 miles north on the A4085.

**Plas Tan Y Graig** ( ☎ 01766-890310; www.plas-tany graig.co.uk; s/d £45/80; ☐ Ⓟ ) This light, bright place is the best B&B at the heart of the village. It has seven contemporary and uncluttered rooms, five with bathrooms; rooms have fridges. The welcoming lounge contains useful maps and books. Dinner is available only in low season and there's a minimum two-night stay.

**Cafe Glandwr & Glaslyn Ices** ( ☎ 01766-890339; pizzas around £8; ☽ 9am-9pm Apr-Sep, 10am-6pm Oct-Mar) This busy spot combines an ice-cream parlour serving a huge array of home-made flavours, with a family restaurant offering simple meals and *lots* of pizza.

**Lyn's Cafe** ( ☎ 01766-890374; mains £6-8; ☽ 10am-7pm Mon-Fri, to 8pm Sat & Sun) Beddgelert's best all-rounder, this place welcomes climbers and children for a tasty menu of refuelling meals and Sunday roasts (around £8), plus seats by the river for afternoon tea.

## Getting There & Away
Snowdon Sherpa bus S4 runs to Caernarfon (30 minutes, every two hours Monday to Saturday, six on Sunday); bus S97 runs to Porthmadog (20 minutes, every two hours daily) and Betws-y-Coed (40 minutes).

# LLANBERIS
**pop 2000**
While not the most instantly attractive town in the national park, Llanberis is a mecca for walkers and climbers, hosting a steady flow of rugged fleece-wearers year-round. Built to house workers for the nearby Dinorwig slate quarry (closed in 1969), the town still wears its industrial heritage on its sleeve with pride.

A gentle stroll around the town's lakes, Llyn Padarn and Llyn Peris, offers high-season relief from the crowds, while expectant day-trippers eagerly anticipate the opening of the new Snowdon Mountain Railway and summit visitor centre due by summer 2009.

Llanberis is dissected by the A4086, which separates the strung-out High Street, home to most attractions, from the town's two lakes.

The helpful **tourist office** ( ☎ 01286-870765; llanberis.tic@gwynedd.gov.uk; 41 High St; ☽ 9.30am-4.30pm Easter-Oct, 10.30am-4.30pm Fri-Mon Nov-Mar) stocks a good range of maps, guides and accessories.

## Sights
Opened in 1896, the **Snowdon Mountain Railway** ( ☎ 0870-4580033; www.snowdonrailway.co.uk;

---

**SUMMIT SPECIAL**

No Snowdonia experience is complete without tackling one of the region's awe-inspiring mountains. At 1085m, Mt Snowdon is the biggest and also the busiest, thanks in no small part to the second-generation Snowdon Mountain Railway (p763).

Six paths of varying length and difficulty lead to the summit. Simplest (and dullest) is the **Llanberis Path** (10 miles, six hours), running beside the railway track. The **Snowdon Ranger Path** (7 miles, five hours) starts at the Snowdon Ranger YHA near Beddgelert; this is the shortest and also the safest in winter.

Two options start at Pen-y-Pass (and involve the least amount of ascent): the **Miners Track** (7 miles, six hours) starts gently and ends with a steep section; the **Pyg Track** (7 miles, six hours) is more interesting, and meets the Miners Track where it steepens. The classic **Snowdon Horseshoe** route (7.5 miles, six to seven hours) combines the Pyg Track to the summit (or via the precipitous ridge of Crib Goch if you're very experienced) with a descent route over the peak of Llewedd and a final section down on the Miners Track.

The straightforward **Rhyd Ddu Path** (8 miles, six hours) approaches from the west. Most challenging is the **Watkin Path** (8 miles, six hours), involving an ascent of more than 1000m on its southerly approach from Nantgwynant.

Prince Charles once labelled Snowdon's summit 'the highest slum in Europe' because of the dilapidated state of the old visitor centre. Work on a shiny new, but much delayed, visitor centre was progressing at the time of writing, despite a series of contentious interruptions and the atrocious weather in 2008 that set work back by one year.

Variations on these walks are in Lonely Planet's book *Walking in Britain*. Snowdon Sherpa buses (see p759) drop off at the trailheads, and there are also options for accommodation near them all.

If you want a little more solitude, get an early start for the **Glyders** from **Idwal Cottage YHA** (☎ 0870-770 5874; www.yha.org.uk; dm £18), or head further south for **Cader Idris** (p760).

---

(☾ 9am-5pm Mar-Oct) is the UK's highest and only public rack-and-pinion railway. The 5-mile journey climbs 900m and takes an hour, but schedules are weather-dependent and summertime queues can be long. The railway was still undergoing major construction work at the time of writing, with trains running only to **Clogwyn station** (adult/child return £11/7). A new summit station, complete with a cafe and visitor centre, is due to open around May 2009 – depending on the weather.

**Electric Mountain** (☎ 01286-870636; www.electric mountain.co.uk; ☾ 9.30am-5.30pm Jun-Aug, 10am-4.30pm Sep-May) is the sparky name for the Dinorwig power station, whose interactive exhibits tell the history of hydropower. Take the **guided tour** (adult/child £7/3.50; Easter-Oct) into the depths of the underground power station.

At the **National Slate Museum** (☎ 01286-870630; www.museumwales.ac.uk/en/slate; admission free; ☾ 10am-5pm Easter-Oct, 10am-4pm Sun-Fri Nov-Mar), set in the huge Dinorwig quarry, you can visit old workshops where craftsmen split and dress the slate. The turn-off is located along the A4086 between Electric Mountain and the Snowdon Mountain Railway station.

The **Llanberis Lake Steam Railway** (☎ 01286-870549; www.lake-railway.co.uk; return adult/child £6.50/4.50; ☾ Feb-Oct plus special services) chuffs along a 5-mile, tame but scenic return trip through Padarn Country Park to the terminus at Penllyn; there's a wheelchair-adapted carriage.

## Activities

The town's key adventure operators:
**Boulder Adventures** (☎ 01286-870556; www .boulderadventures.co.uk; Bryn Du Mountain Centre) A range of activities from kayaking to abseiling via coasteering.
**Surf-Lines** (☎ 01286-879001; www.surf-lines.co.uk; Y Glyn) High-adrenalin pursuits from mountaineering to kayaking.

## Sleeping

**Pen-y-Pass YHA** (☎ 0870-770 5990; www.yha.org.uk; Nantgwynant, adult/child £16; ☾ daily Easter-Oct, Fri & Sat Nov-Mar) This popular and busy hostel, once the haunt of early Victorian climbers, has a cosy bar where guests swap tales. It's located 5.5 miles southeast of Llanberis on the A4086 and atop Llanberis Pass; Snowdon Sherpa bus S1 from Llanberis serves the hostel.

**Llanberis YHA** ( ☎ 0870 770 5928; www.yha.org.uk; Llwyn Celyn; dm £18;  daily Easter-Oct, Fri & Sat Nov-Mar) Behind the Spar supermarket on High St, this climbers' favourite has good self-catering facilities and a drying room.

**ourpick Pen-y-Gwryd** ( ☎ 01286-870211; www .pyg.co.uk; Nant Gwynant; s/d £35/45;  Jan-Oct) Eccentric but full of atmosphere, Pen-y-Gwryd has a great sense of living history. The 1953 Everest team used the inn as a training base, and memorabilia from their stay, including their signatures on the ceiling of the dining room, lends the place the atmosphere of a hidden-gem museum. Rooms are comfortable with original Victorian features. Bar meals are served from noon to 2pm and from 7.30pm to 9.30pm.

**Glyn Afon** ( ☎ 01286-872528; www.glyn-afon.co.uk; 72 High St; s/d £37.50/64;  P ) Recently refurbished rooms have no frills but are warm and homely at this midrange guesthouse. A hearty breakfast is assured and all dietary needs catered for.

**Erw Fair** ( ☎ 01286-872400; www.erwfair.com; High St; tw/d £55/65;  P ) Nine clean, simple rooms and decent breakfasts are the trademarks of this friendly guesthouse with a central location.

**Plas Coch** ( ☎ 01286-872122; www.plas-coch.co.uk; High St; s/d/f £56/68/78;  P  ) A well-run and well-equipped guesthouse, this place caters for both families and, thanks to an adapted ground-floor room, it has wheelchair access. The prices at Plas Coch include a huge and hearty breakfast that draws on local and organic produce.

## Eating

**Pete's Eats** ( ☎ 01286-870117; www.petes-eats.co.uk; 40 High St;  8am-9pm Jul & Aug, 8am-8pm Sep-Jun) Remains the cornerstone eatery in town. A big menu of fuelling all-day snacks, internet access (£3 per hour) and on-site accommodation (dorm/twin £13/32) make this the all-round favourite for climbers and walkers – despite chaotic service. The cafe noticeboard is a font of local knowledge.

**Connections Cafe** ( ☎ 01286-873024;  9.30am-5.30pm Jun-Aug, 10am-4.30pm Sep-May) A welcoming cafe for simple snacks and fair-trade coffees located within Electric Mountain (opposite).

**Snowdon Honey Farm & Winery** ( ☎ 01286-870218; www.snowdonhoneyfarmandwinery.co.uk; sandwiches £5;  7am-4pm) A quirky but pricey little coffee shop, adjoining a shop selling local honey, fruit wines and mead. Try the goats' cheese, leek and honey speciality sandwich.

**Peak Restaurant** ( ☎ 01286-877277; High St; mains around £14;  7-9.30pm Wed-Sun) The main place in town for dinner is a bistro-style eatery with terracotta walls and dark-wood furnishings. It serves hearty traditional favourites, such as roast lamb.

## Getting There & Away

Padarn bus 85 runs to Bangor (45 minutes, hourly Monday to Saturday, six on Sunday); bus 88 runs to Caernarfon (25 minutes, hourly, eight on Sunday). Snowdon Sherpa bus S1 runs to the Snowdon trailhead at Pen-y-Pass (15 minutes, half-hourly).

## HARLECH
pop 1800

Hilly Harlech, bustling in summer, sleepy out of season, remains popular for its imposing castle, the sheer might and awe-inspiring position of which makes it one of the most memorable medieval fortifications in North Wales. Finished in 1289 by Edward I, Harlech Castle is a Unesco World Heritage Site.

The train station is northwest of the castle, and well below it, with the windy High St to its southwest. The **tourist office** ( ☎ 01766-780658; High St;  9.30am-5.30pm Easter-Oct) is behind the castle.

## Harlech Castle

Despite its strategic location and hefty construction, the **castle** (Cadw; ☎ 01766-780552; adult/child £3.70/3.30;  9am-5pm Apr-Oct, 9.30am-4pm Mon-Sat, 11am-4pm Sun Nov-Mar) has been called the 'Castle of Lost Causes' because it fell so often during battle. It was captured by Owain Glyndŵr in 1404, but the future Henry V usurped him just four years later. During the Wars of the Roses the castle fell to the Yorkists in 1468, and fell again in 1647 when Cromwell's men took control during the Civil War. The fortress's great natural defence is the seaward cliff face. When it was built, ships could sail supplies right to the base.

Early-15th-century events inspired one of Wales' most famous military marches, *Men of Harlech*. Regiments linked to Wales, such as the Royal Welsh (UK) and the Royal Canadian Hussars, have adopted the rousing anthem as their regimental march.

## Sleeping & Eating

**ourpick Castle Cottage** ( ☎ 01766-780479; Y Llech; www .castlecottageharlech.co.uk; s/d £73/106;  P ) Fine dining and five-star accommodation by the castle characterise this excellent restaurant-with-rooms. Ongoing refurbishment work keeps facilities top notch, while the restaurant menu features local seafood and heavenly desserts (three-course dinner £34).

**Castle Restaurant** ( ☎ 01766-780416; Castle Sq; meals around £12; ❂ 6-9pm daily, lunch Sun) This is a rustic and homely place right by the castle. It provides a board of daily specials and tasty Sunday roasts.

For a snack lunch, try **Y Llew Glas** (3 Plas y Goits; ❂ 9.30am-5pm), a deli-eatery with slow service but good-quality local produce, set in a small courtyard. For an espresso or homemade ice cream, try **Castle Creamery** (Castle Sq; ❂ 9.30am-5pm).

## Getting There & Away
Arriva bus 38 runs to Barmouth (30 minutes, hourly, two on Sunday) and Blaenau Ffestiniog (30 minutes).

Cambrian Coast trains serve Machynlleth (£8.20, 1½ hours, about every two to three hours, three on Sunday) and Porthmadog (20 minutes).

## AROUND HARLECH
### Barmouth
Despite stunning views across the Mawddach Estuary and a Blue Flag beach, the seaside resort of **Barmouth** is a rather faded, downmarket resort that has clearly seen better days. One highlight is the narrow-gauge **Fairbourne & Barmouth Steam Railway** ( ☎ 01347-250362; www .fairbournerailway.com; All-day Rover tickets adult/child £7.20/4; ❂ Feb-Oct), which rattles 2 miles along the seafront to Fairbourne.

Also in the area, and famous as the inspiration behind Reverend W Awdry's children's stories *Thomas the Tank Engine*, the steam-driven **Talyllyn Railway** ( ☎ 01654-710472; www.talyllyn.co.uk; Wharf Station, Tywyn; adult/child £12/2; ❂ Feb-Oct) pootles 7 miles up the Fathew Valley to Abergynolwyn.

More information about Barmouth can be obtained from the town's **tourist office** ( ☎ 01347-280787; barmouth.tic@gwynedd.gov.uk; Station Rd; ❂ 9am-5pm Mon-Sat, 10am-5pm Sun Mar-Nov), located inside the train station.

## PORTHMADOG
pop 4500
Porthmadog, located at the mouth of the Glaslyn Estuary, may not boast the most ob-viously attractive setting in North Wales, but it remains a workaday and lively town, and a major transport hub for the region.

The town grew around the 19th-century harbour built by William Alexander Madocks to handle slate from the mountain mines around Blaenau Ffestiniog. The link with Blaenau is still the main draw today; Porthmadog is the southern terminus for the Rheilffordd Ffestiniog Railway. The track crosses the estuary via the Cob, a mile-long causeway into town often packed with summer traffic jams.

## Orientation & Information
Most facilities are located along High St, which runs for half a mile through the middle of town. The Rheilffordd Ffestiniog Railway and Welsh Highland Railway stations are at the southern and northern ends of High St respectively.

The busy, central **tourist office** ( ☎ 01766-512981; porthmadog.touristoffice@gwynedd.gov.uk; High St; ❂ 9.30am-5.30pm) covers the town, nearby Portmeirion (opposite) and the eastern side of the neigbouring Llŷn Peninsula (p768).

## Sights
The narrow-gauge **Rheilffordd Ffestiniog Railway** ( ☎ 01766-516000; www.festrail.co.uk; All-day Rover adult/concession £17.50/15.75; ❂ Mar-Oct), runs north to Blaenau Ffestiniog (p762). Built between 1832 and 1836, the narrow-gauge railway used to haul slate from the mines of Blaenau Ffestiniog to the sea at Porthmadog. Today, vintage 1860s engines and carriages puff tourists along the picturesque 13.5-mile line. Trains run two to eight times daily from Easter to October, with limited off-season services.

At the western end of town, the **Welsh Highland Railway** ( ☎ 01766-513402; www.whr.co.uk; Tremadog Rd; adult/child £5.50/3; ❂ Mar-Oct) was, at the time of writing, undergoing major work to link up the two currently separate sections of track to form a continuous run from Porthmadog, heading through the mountains via Beddgelert, to Rhyd Ddu, where it will join up with the second part of the existing track for the northern terminus at Caernarfon (p769). The project is due to open in spring 2009.

For more information about Wales' narrow-gauge railways, see the boxed text, p753.

Porthmadog is also proud to maintain a tradition of local independent businesses. It is home to the **Purple Moose Brewery** ( ☎ 01766-515571; www.purplemoose.co.uk; Madoc St), one of Wales' best-known microbreweries, which produces four lip-smacking ales.

## Sleeping & Eating

**Snowdon Lodge** ( ☎ 01766-515354; www.snowdonlodge.co.uk; Church St, Tremadog; dm/d £16.50/40; P □ ) This friendly independent hostel is located in the historic house where TE Lawrence (Lawrence of Arabia) was born on 16 August 1888. The rooms are mainly simple dorms, but some private rooms are available and a continental breakfast is included in the price. The communal facilities are of a good standard. Snowdon Lodge is 1 mile north of Porthmadog on the A498.

**Yr Hen Fecws** ( ☎ 01766-514625; www.henfecws.com; 16 Lombard St; s/d from £49/67; P ) Stylishly restored, this stone-cottage restaurant-with-rooms is a fine place for dinner and the most characterful place to stay in town. The seven rooms (some ground floor for wheelchair access), feature exposed-slate walls and fireplaces, while the elegant restaurant serves excellent bistro dishes with fresh fish specials (mains around £16).

**Royal Sportsman Hotel** ( ☎ 01766-512015; www.royalsportsman.co.uk; 131 High St; s/d/f £52/81/92; P ) Some of the rooms feel a bit frayed around the edges, but this traditional pub offers decent pub food (available between noon and 2.30pm, and 6pm and 9pm), period accommodation and a good central location. It's a reliable midrange choice.

Next door to Yr Hen Fecws, the **Ship Inn** ( ☎ 01766-512990; 14 Lombard St; mains around £8; ⊙ noon-2pm & 6-9.30pm Mon-Sat, noon-2.30pm Sun) has simple bar meals and friendly service. Also for real ales and home-made pub grub, try the long-established **Golden Fleece Inn** ( ☎ 01766-512421; Market Square, Tremadog; mains around £8; ⊙ noon-2pm & 7-9pm), located 1 mile north of Porthmadog on the A498.

## Getting There & Away

### BUS

National Express coach 545 runs daily to London (£29.50, 10 hours) via Chester and Birmingham; it stops by Tesco at the north end of town.

Buses stop by the park on High St. Snowdon Sherpa bus S97 runs to Betws-y-Coed (one hour, four daily, two on Sunday) via Beddgelert (20 minutes). Arriva bus 3 runs to Pwllheli (40 minutes, half-hourly, six on Sunday) via Criccieth (10 minutes) for connections across the Llŷn Peninsula. Arriva Traws Cambria bus X32 runs to Aberystwyth (2½ hours, six daily, two on Sunday) and Bangor (1½ hours).

### TRAIN

The train station is opposite the Welsh Highland Railway station on the Cambrian Coast Line to Machynlleth (£9.50, two hours, every two hours, fewer on Sunday) and Pwllheli (30 minutes).

# AROUND PORTHMADOG
## Portmeirion

The **Portmeirion** ( ☎ 01766-770000; www.portmeirion-village.com; adult/child £7/3.50; ⊙ 9.30am-5.30pm) site was founded in 1926 by the Welsh architect Sir Clough Williams-Ellis, who spent 50 years perfecting his Utopian masterpiece. The resulting group of disparate Italianate buildings is a seaside fairy tale that testifies to the power of imagination. There's glorious attention to detail and absurdity in each and every one of the nooks and crannies. The buildings are now all listed and the whole site is a Conservation Area.

An **audiovisual show** ( ⊙ 10am-5pm), located just off the central Piazza to the right of the Arc de Triomphe, has a commentary by Sir Williams-Ellis himself. A series of brochures, leaflets and plans are available for collection from the toll-gate entrance.

The village formed the ideally surreal stage set for the 1960s cult TV series, *The Prisoner*, which was filmed here from 1966 to 1967; it still draws fans of the show in droves and Prisoner conventions are held annually in March. The **Prisoner Information Centre** ( ⊙ 9am-5.30pm Apr-Oct) has a raft of memorabilia for fans.

There are three accommodation options ( ☎ 01766 770000; www.portmeirion-village.com) – guests are excused the admission fee to Portmeirion:

**Hotel Portmeirion** (s/d/ste from £155/188/209) Has classic, elegant rooms and a contemporary dining room designed by Sir Terence Conran.

**our pick** **Castell Deudraeth** (r £175-245) A fairy-tale castle with an informal grill and more modern rooms better suited to families.

**NORTH WALES**

**Self-catering cottages** (per week for 3-8 people £657-1760) Individually styled cottages dotted around in nooks and crannies of the village. Facilities and size vary between properties – check the website for deals.

Portmeirion lies 2 miles east of Porthmadog across the Cob, then a mile south off the main road. The Ffestiniog Railway and Cambrian Coast Line trains run to the village of Minffordd, from where it's a 1-mile walk.

# LLŶN PENINSULA

Isolated physically and culturally from the rest of Wales, this 24-mile-long finger, jutting into the Irish Sea from Snowdonia, is a stronghold of Welsh nationalism. Plaid Cymru, the nationalist political party, was founded in Pwllheli in 1925, and Welsh remains the language of everyday life.

Historically the Llŷn (khlee'en) attracted pilgrims on their way to the early Christian site of Bardsey Island (see the boxed text, p770). Today it attracts fewer travellers due to its sparse infrastructure, but does offer 70 miles of wildlife-rich coastline – much of it in the hands of the National Trust (NT) – isolated walking and cycling trails, windswept beaches and a handful of small fishing villages in which to overnight.

Pwllheli is the transport hub and place to stock up for a trip, while **Abersoch** is the base for water sports and home to a small and independently run **tourist office** ( ☎ 01758-712929; www.abersochtouristinfo.co.uk; Lon Pen Cei; ☼ 10.30am-4.30pm Apr-Sep). Walking the 47-mile Llŷn Coastal Path around the peninsula is the best way to soak up the tranquil ambience of the region.

The website www.visitllyn.com has plenty of information about the peninsula.

## PWLLHELI
pop 4000

The administrative capital and travel-connection hub of the Llŷn, Pwllheli (poolth-heh-lee) is a workaday town of staunch Welsh tradition.

Crucially it's the terminus of the Cambrian Coast Line from Machynlleth, and as far as most tourists get without the aid of a car. It's also home to the region's only official **tourist office** ( ☎ 01758-613000; Station Square; ☼ 9am-5pm Apr-Oct, 10.30am-4.30pm Mon-Wed, Fri & Sat Nov-Mar)

for everything you'll need to know about the peninsula.

## Sleeping & Eating

**Crown Hotel** ( ☎ 01758-612664; High St; s/d £40/60; ⌨ ) Centrally located and modern, this no-nonsense pub offers comfortable rooms and decent bar meals in the heart of town.

**Taro Deg** ( ☎ 01758-701271; Lon Dywod; lunch/dinner mains around £5/8; ☼ 9am-4.30pm Mon-Thu, to 9pm Fri & Sat) Relaxed daytime coffees and more up-beat evening meals are on offer at this great little cafe-cum-bistro, whose menu has lots of organic local produce.

**Pili Palas** ( ☎ 01758-612248; 2-4 Goal St; mains around £15; ☼ 10am-3.30pm & 6.30-9pm Tue-Sat) Smarter and friendlier than some other places in town, this newcomer to the dining scene has hearty but good-value fare. Bookings are recommended.

**Ship Inn** ( ☎ 01758-740270; Llanbedrog; mains around £8; ☼ bar meals noon-9pm daily) A family-friendly pub, this place offers the best pub grub in the area. It's 3 miles southwest of Pwllheli on the A499.

## Getting There & Away

Arriva bus 3 runs to Porthmadog (40 minutes, half-hourly, six on Sunday) via Criccieth (25 minutes).

Trains run to Machynlleth (£11, two hours 20 minutes, every two Monday to Friday) via Porthmadog (20 minutes).

## EXPLORING THE LLŶN

A trip around the peninsula is about escaping the rat race and being closer to nature. That doesn't mean, however, that it's without its home comforts. In this section we round up some of the key sights and places to stay and eat to help you find your way. You'll need a car, a sense of adventure, a copy of Duffy's *Rock Ferry* album on the stereo (she's from these parts) and a willingness to put down the guidebook and just go with the flow. Nobody here is in a rush.

## Sights

Eight miles northeast of Pwhelli, **Criccieth Castle** (Cadw; ☎ 01766-522227; adult/child £3.10/2.70; ☼ 10am-5pm Easter-Oct, 9.30am-4pm Fri & Sat 11am-4pm Sun Nov-Mar) may be ruined but its cliff-top location assures panoramic views across Tremadog Bay. Originally constructed by native Welsh prince Llywelyn the Great in 1239, the castle

---

**DETOUR: NANT GWRTHEYRN**

The village of Nant Gwrtheyrn has been reborn as the eerily atmospheric home to the **Welsh Language & Heritage Centre** ( ☎ 01758-750334; www.nantgwrtheyrn.org; ⊙ heritage centre 11am-4pm daily Jun-Aug, Mon-Fri Sep-May).

The heritage centre has a small but compelling exhibition on the history of the Welsh language, and the study centre offers regular long-weekend Welsh-language and literature courses, including B&B accommodation at homely grey-stone cottages on site.

Meals are served in **Caffi Meinir** ( ☎ 01758-750442; ⊙ 10.30am-4.30pm daily) in summer and during courses at other times.

---

was overrun in 1283 by Edward I's forces and reclaimed in 1404 by Owain Glyndŵr. Today there is a small but informative exhibition centre at the ticket office.

Also in the area, the village of Llanystumdwy is home to the **Lloyd George Museum** ( ☎ 01766-22071; adult/child £4/2; ⊙ 10.30am-5pm Mon-Fri Apr-May, Mon-Sat Jun, daily Jul-Sep, 11am-4pm Mon-Fri Oct), dedicated to David Lloyd George, one of Wales' finest statesmen, and the British prime minister from 1916 to 1922. The turn-off to the village is 1.5 miles west of Criccieth on the A497.

In Aberdaron, on the northwestern tip of the peninsula, **St Hywyn's Church** ( ⊙ 10am-5pm Apr-Oct, to 4pm Nov-Mar) remains a site of pilgrimage for Bardsey pilgrims (see boxed text, p770) and devotees of the acclaimed Welsh poet RS Thomas, who was the local minister from 1967 to 1978.

### Sleeping

**Pen Y Bwlch** ( ☎ 07814-637629; www.wales-bb.co.uk; s/d £30/60) This whitewashed stone cottage, close to Aberdaron, only boasts two rooms, but they are tastefully decorated and meals are superb. The glass-designer owner runs her studio next door – see www.annesmithglass designs.co.uk.

**Goslings at the Carisbrooke** ( ☎ 01758-712526; www.goslingsabersoch.co.uk; d/f from £75/85) At the heart of surf hub Abersoch, this family-friendly restaurant with rooms serves excellent food and offers boutique B&B-style accommodation.

**ourpick Plas Bodegroes** ( ☎ 01758-612363; www.bodegroes.co.uk; s/d from £50/110; **P** ) This highly professional restaurant-with-rooms boasts one of Wales' few Michelin stars for its imaginative use of local produce (open for dinner from Tuesday to Thursday, lunch Sunday). The rooms are similarly refined, and the ambience is one of calm efficiency. This Georgian manor was immaculately coiffured gardens. Plas Bodegroes is 2 miles west of Pwllheli on the A497. Take the turn-off for the B4415 and then follow the twisting drive.

### Eating & Drinking

**Y Gegin Fawr (The Big Kitchen)** ( ☎ 01758-760359; www.geginfawr.co.uk; ⊙ 9am-5.30pm Easter-Oct) This historic place (located just over the bridge at the heart of Aberdaron village) was originally a communal kitchen, built around 1300, for the pilgrims to claim a meal before heading over to Bardsey Island. Today it serves up coffees and basic snacks to latter-day pilgrims with a penchant for home-made cakes.

**Ty Coch Inn** ( ☎ 01758-720498; www.tycoch.co.uk; mains £5-8; ⊙ lunch noon-2.30pm) With its a dramatic beachside location at Porth Dinllaen (a 1-mile walk from Morfa Nefyn), Ty Coch was famous even before Demi Moore shot key scenes from the 2006 Hollywood drama, *Half Light*, here. Her Tinseltown trappings did little to impress the locals but even a cynical A-lister can't help but fall for the good food, great views and toes-in-the-water pints.

**Angelina** ( ☎ 01758-712353; High St; mains £8-14; ⊙ 6-10pm) For dinner, this well-regarded Italian restaurant is a notch above the surf 'n' turf crowd with its fresh fish mains and pasta. Families welcome and surfboards not required. It's located at the heart of Abersoch's main drag.

# WEST OF SNOWDONIA

The region between the western fringe of the Snowdonia National Park and the Isle of Anglesey is a staunchly Welsh-speaking area. Indeed, the county of Gwynedd is the traditional heartland of Welsh nationalism; around 70% of people here still use Welsh as their first language.

## CAERNARFON
### pop 4000

Wedged between the gleaming swell of the Menai Strait and the deep-purple mountains

---

### THE PILGRIMAGE TO BARDSEY

Tiny Bardsey Island (Ynys Enlli), a 2-mile-long spit off the tip of the peninsula, was an early Christian site known as the Isle of 20,000 Saints. The island's Welsh name, Ynys Enlli, means Isle of the Currents, a reference to the treacherous tidal surges in Bardsey Sound that make boat access erratic at best.

St Cadfan created a monastery here in the 6th century and, at a time when journeys to Italy were long and perilous, the Pope decreed that three pilgrimages to Bardsey equalled one to Rome. Today a Celtic cross amid the Abbey ruins commemorates the 20,000 pilgrims who came here to die – the 20,000 saints that give the island its ancient name.

You can retrace the pilgrims' footsteps by tackling the 47-mile Edge of Wales Walk, an extension to the Llŷn Coastal Path. The trail splits into nine convenient stages that can be covered across four to five days,` and visits the ancient forts, holy wells and medieval churches that way-marked the original pilgrims' trail.

Contact the **Bardsey Island Trust** ( ☎ 0845 8112233; www.bardsey.org) for boat trips (adult/child £25/15, 30 minutes) from Porth Meudwy, the closest harbour to the island. For self-guided walking packages, including trips to Bardsey, contact **Edge of Wales Walk** ( ☎ 01758-760652; www .edgeofwaleswalk.co.uk). Packages start from £55 per person per day. Before you set out, consult the OS Explorer series maps Llŷn East 254 and Llŷn West 253.

---

of Snowdonia, Caernarfon is home to Wales' most magnificent castle, the final link in Edward I's 'iron ring'. The castle is a designated Unesco World Heritage Site, together with its neighbours at Conwy, Harlech and Beaumaris.

Conflict followed Caernarfon all the way into the 20th century, when in 1911 then–Prime Minister David Lloyd George (a Welshman) declared Caernarfon Castle as the setting of the investiture ceremony for the heir to the British throne. It was an attempt to bring the royals closer to the Welsh constituency, but it backfired spectacularly. The anti-monarchist mentality reached an (almost) explosive climax in 1969. At the investiture of HRH Prince Charles, the current heir to the throne, there was an attempt to blow up his train.

Given the town's historical importance, Caernarfon has a surprisingly down-at-heel feel with boarded-up shops and a baffling oversupply of fake-tan and bargain-booze outlets. The regenerated docklands area of the town, commanding fine views across the Menai Straits, is a stark contrast to the city centre with its trendy apartments and modernist arts centre, Galeri Caernarfon (opposite), and heralds the first green shoots of recovery.

## Orientation & Information

Caernarfon's focus is the castle, located beside an oversized car park by the river. The medieval walls enclose a compact area, four streets wide and two deep.

The moribund **tourist office** ( ☎ 01286-672232; caernarfontic@gwynedd.gov.uk; Castle Ditch; ◷ 9.30am-4pm Apr-Oct, 10am-4pm Nov-Mar) is almost as lifeless as the town after the day-trippers leave.

## Sights & Activities

**Caernarfon Castle** (Cadw; ☎ 01286-677617; adult/child £5.10/4.70; ◷ 9am-5pm Easter-Oct, 9.30am-4pm Mon-Sat, 11am-4pm Sun Nov-Mar) was built between 1283 and 1301, standing as Edward I's most impressive stronghold. Almost impregnable, the polygonal towers and colour-banded masonry were based on Constantinople's 5th-century walls, and set it apart from the other castles of North Wales. Twenty-eight bedraggled men withstood a 1404 siege from Owain Glyndŵr's army here, and during the 17th-century Civil War the castle was unsuccessfully attacked three times.

Caernarfon Castle was originally built as a seat of government rule and royal palace; the towers were decorated with ornate stained glass. The Eagle Tower is the finest remaining example. In the Queen's Tower is a museum celebrating Wales' oldest infantry regiment, the Royal Welsh Fusiliers. Other towers contain exhibits on Edward I's campaigns and the 1969 investiture.

Away from the castle, the story of the excavated foundations of **Segontium Roman Fort** (Cadw; ☎ 01286-675625; admission free; ◷ 12.30-4.30pm Tue-Sun), a significant Roman fort dating from

AD 77, are explained at a small museum. The fort is located 1 mile southeast of Caernarfon on the A4085.

One for families, **Greenwood Forest Park** ( ☎ 01248-670076; www.greenwoodforestpark.co.uk; Y Felinheli; adult/child £10/9; ⏰ 10am-5.30pm Mar-Oct) is a 7-hectare site with a slew of rides, activities and attractions underpinned by a strong green ethos. Be sure not to miss a ride on the Green Dragon, the world's first people-powered roller-coaster.

Running between Caernarfon and Rhyd Ddu, the vintage **Welsh Highland Railway** ( ☎ 01286-677018; www.whr.co.uk; All-day Rover ticket adult/child £17.50/15.75; ⏰ Mar-Oct) is another of Wales' restored narrow-gauge railways (see boxed text, p753). The line was saved by volunteers and reopened as a tourist attraction in 1997; today the 12-mile ride departs from the St Helen's Rd station, upriver from the castle, for Rhyd Ddu. At the time of writing, the planned completion of the line extension all the way through to Porthmadog (p766) was scheduled for spring 2009.

The tourist office has details of **cycling** trails around Caernarfon, including the scenic 4.5-mile **Lôn Las Menai** along the strait, and the 12-mile **Lôn Eifion** south to Bryncir. **Beics Menai** ( ☎ 01286-676804; www.beicsmenai.co.uk; Slate Quay; bikes per day adult/child £19/11) hires bikes.

## Sleeping & Eating

**Totters** ( ☎ 01286-672963; www.totters.co.uk; 2 High St; dm £15) A great independent hostel and by far the best budget option in town, Totters has modern, clean and welcoming dorms; breakfast is included in the price. The14th-century arched basement hosts a long table for communal dining with atmosphere, while the attic family room (£45 per night) has a bathroom and more mod cons. The owners now have a self-catering property across the road available for short lets in the low season.

**Victoria House** ( ☎ 01286-678263; www.thevictoria house.co.uk; Church St; d £60; [P] [💻] ) The best mid-range option, Victoria House is a well-run, four-bedroom guesthouse with a homely feel, spacious modern rooms and some nice touches, such as fresh milk in each room and a small DVD library. Vegetarian and special diets are catered for at breakfast.

**Black Boy Inn** ( ☎ 01286-673604; www.welsh-historic -inns.co.uk; Northgate St; s/d £50/70) Dating from 1522, the creaky but atmospheric rooms at this traditional inn have original wooden beams

and panelling. Less creaky is the reliable selection of bar meals (11am to 9pm Monday to Saturday and noon to 9pm Sunday) and evening mains with an emphasis on fresh fish specials (around £10) and real ales.

**Molly's** ( ☎ 01286-673238; Castle St; mains around £14; ⏰ noon-2.30pm & 6.30-10pm Wed-Sat) This restaurant has a menu featuring local produce and daily specials, served in relaxed surroundings.

**Stone's Bistro** ( ☎ 01286-671152; Hole in the Wall St; mains £10-15.50; ⏰ dinner Tue-Sat, lunch noon-3pm Sun) A dark but cosy bistro-style eatery with a French theme, Stone's offers roast lamb speciality dishes (around £15.50) and vegetarian options.

## Drinking & Entertainment

**Galeri Caernarfon** ( ☎ 01286-685222; www.galericaern arfon.com; Doc Victoria; ⏰ box office 9.30am-5.30pm Mon-Fri, 10am-4pm Sat, plus during performances) This superb multipurpose arts centre hosts exhibitions, theatre, film and events – check the program online for details. It has disabled access and facilities for sight- and hearing-impaired patrons. The stylish in-house DOC cafe-bar (10am to 8.30pm Wednesday to Saturday, to 5pm Sunday, to 6.30pm Monday and Tuesday) has day-round snacks and pre-event suppers (£10 for two courses).

## Getting There & Away

National Express coach 545 runs to London (£30, 9½ hours, daily) via Chester and Birmingham. Snowdon Sherpa bus S4 runs to Beddgelert (35 minutes, eight daily Monday to Saturday, five Sunday). Arriva bus 5/X5 runs to Llandudno (1½ hours, three hourly Monday to Saturday, hourly Sunday) via Bangor (30 minutes). Arriva bus X32 runs to Aberystwyth (three hours, five daily, two on Sunday) via Dolgellau (two hours).

The nearest train connections are 9 miles northeast at Bangor.

## BANGOR
**pop 12,000**

Bangor is a place to stop, not stay – it has decent eating options but virtually no worthwhile accommodation. Despite its large student population, it's hardly a cultural hot spot. Indeed, it feels rather low key overall and acts primarily as a transport hub for the region. The city is the last stop before crossing to the Isle of Anglesey – stock up and push on.

The town centre is located half a mile east of the train station along High St, with the bland Deiniol Shopping Centre the new heart of town.

Bangor's hit-and-miss **tourist office** ( ☎ 01248-352786; bangor.tic@gwynedd.gov.uk; Deiniol Rd; ❤ 9.30am-1.30pm & 2-4pm daily Apr-Sep) is across the road from the Theatre Gwynedd.

**Gwynedd Hospital** ( ☎ 01248-384384; Penrhos Rd), located 2.3 miles southwest of the centre, is the regional hub for medical emergencies.

Most of the lopsided **Cathedral Church of St Deiniol** is the result of 19th-century restoration. Its treasure is the evocative 500-year-old, carved-oak Mostyn Christ. The **Victorian pier** (adult/child 50/25p; ❤ 8.30am-9pm Mon-Fri, 10am-9pm Sat & Sun) stretches 450m out into the Menai Strait.

### Sleeping & Eating

**Bangor YHA** ( ☎ 0870 7705686; www.yha.org.uk; Tan-y-Bryn; dm from £14; ❤ reception 7.30-10am & 3.30-10.30pm daily Apr-Sep, Tue-Sat Oct-Mar; **P 💻** ) This hostel, occupying a large Victorian mansion, is a solid option with a quiet location, good facilities and family rooms. Its restaurant serves breakfast (£4.50) and dinner (£7.50) – there's even a bar. The hostel is located 0.8 miles east of the centre on the A5122.

**Kyffin** ( ☎ 01248-355161; 129 High St; ❤ 10am-5pm Mon-Sat) A rare gem at the station end of High St, this fair-trade cafe offers a warm welcome with its flower-strewn window, comfy wicker chairs and antique shop fittings. It's great for deli snacks and coffee – and will be expanding its hours and menu when it moves to bigger premises across the road.

**1815** ( ☎ 01248-355969; 2 Waterloo Place; tapas £7; ❤ 8.30am-6pm Mon-Fri, to 10pm Sat & Sun) Another new opening, this smart deli-cafe shows a Mediterranean influence, especially in the evening with tapas plates and chilled wine. By day it's a chilled-out spot for coffees and snacks.

**Penguin Cafe** ( ☎ 01248-362036; 260 High St; snacks around £5; ❤ 8.30am-5pm Mon-Sat) A simple cafe with an Italian theme, this place is good for all-day snacks, real coffee and homemade pizzas (also to take away). There's a huge menu of regulars and specials, plus options for children.

**Papillon** ( ☎ 01248-360248; 347 High St; mains around £10; ❤ 10am-3pm & 6.30-10pm Mon-Sat) Newspapers, poetry nights, a tapas menu, fair-trade drinks, speciality herbal teas – this place really has got all the bases covered as the home of Bangor's creative community. And even if you're not researching anti-globalisation strategies over your camomile and elderflower brew, it also serves a mean lunch.

### Entertainment

**Theatre Gwynedd** ( ☎ 01248-351708; www.theatrgwynedd.co.uk; Deiniol Rd; ❤ box office 9.30am-1.30pm & 2.30-5pm Mon-Fri, from 10.30am Sat, to 8pm during performances) hosts both Welsh- and English-language drama, and there's also a cinema.

### Getting There & Away

National Express coach 545 runs daily to London (£30, nine hours) via Birmingham.

Buses stop at Bangor Cloc behind the Deiniol Shopping Centre. Principal services are Arriva bus 5/5X to Caernarfon (30 minutes, three hourly Monday to Saturday) and Llandudno (one hour); bus 85/86 to Llanberis (45 minutes, hourly Monday to Saturday) and bus 53/57/58 to Beaumaris (30 minutes, half-hourly Monday to Saturday).

Trains run to Chester (£15, 70 minutes, at least hourly) on Arriva's North Wales Coast line and to London Euston (£69, 4½ hours, hourly) on Virgin's West Coast Main Line via Crewe (1½ hours).

# ISLE OF ANGLESEY

At 276 sq miles, the Isle of Anglesey (Ynys Môn) is the largest island in England and Wales. It's a popular destination for visitors –

---

**TOP FIVE ATTRACTIONS TO KEEP KIDS BUSY ON ANGLESEY**

- **Pili Palas** ( ☎ 01248-712474; www.pilipalas.co.uk; Penmynydd Rd, Menai Bridge; adult/child £6/5; 🕑 10am-5.30pm Easter-Oct, to 5pm Feb, Mar, Nov & Dec, weekends only Jan) Exotic animals and play area.

- **Foel Farm Park** ( ☎ 01248-430646; www.foelfarm.co.uk; Brynsiencyn; adult/child £5/4; 🕑 10.30am-5.30pm Easter-Oct) Meet the farm animals then stock up on yummy chocs.

- **Anglesey Sea Zoo** ( ☎ 01248-430411; www.angleseyseazoo.co.uk; Brynsiencyn; adult/child £7/6; 🕑 10am-6pm Easter-Oct) All things aquatic and fishy.

- **Anglesey Model Village & Gardens** ( ☎ 01248-440477; www.angleseymodelvillage.co.uk; Newborough; adult/child £2.50/2; 🕑 10.30am-5pm Easter-Oct) Scale-model village and train rides.

- **Parc Henblas** ( ☎ 01248-840440; www.parc-henblas-park.co.uk; Bodorgan; adult/child £5/4; 🕑 10.30am-5pm Sun-Fri Easter-Oct) Animal-petting and play areas.

---

and rightly so, with its miles of inspiring coastline, attractive villages and Wales' greatest concentration of ancient sites (don't miss Neolithic burial mound **Bryn Celli Ddhu**, 2 miles west of Llanfair PG on the A4080).

Fertile farming land attracted early settlers, while the island was holy to the Celts. Often referred to as Mam Cymru – Mother of Wales – it was the last outpost to fall to the Romans. But the industrial age arrived in 1826 when Thomas Telford established the first permanent link to the mainland. His iconic 174m **Menai Suspension Bridge** across the Menai Strait has a 30m-high central span, allowing the passage of tall ships. This was joined in 1850 by Robert Stephenson's **Britannia Bridge** to carry the newly laid railway.

Today, both bridges are still working, the latter now carrying the bulk of the road traffic directly to the Irish ferries at Holyhead. You can learn more about the history at the **Thomas Telford Centre** ( ☎ 01248-715046; www.menaibridges.co.uk; Mona Rd; adult/child £3/free; 🕑 10am-4pm Sun-Fri Jun-Oct) in the town of Menai Bridge – just beyond the bridge itself.

Menai Bridge is the island's hub for bus connections. From here, there are regular local connections across the region – an adult day ticket costs £5. Beaumaris is the island's accommodation centre and makes the best base for a visit.

Located at RAF Valley, off the A55 expressway, **Maes Awyr Môn** (www.angleseyairport.com) is Anglesey's airport. There are twice-daily flights to Cardiff International Airport (p681) with Highland Airways.

For more information about the island, see www.visitanglesey.co.uk.

## BEAUMARIS (BIWMARES)
**pop 2000**

The best base for visiting the island, Beaumaris has an attractive waterfront location and a romantic castle lording it over a pretty collection of Georgian buildings, all set against the magical Snowdonia backdrop. It has lots of options for eating and drinking and is home to some excellent little boutiques, deli-cafes and galleries. The town abounds with history and is today growing in popularity with a new generation as a centre for water sports, sailing and walking.

There is an unofficial **tourist office** ( ☎ 01248-810040; Castle St; 🕑 10.30am-4.30pm Mon-Thu Apr-Sep) in the Town Hall. It's a useful resource but, as it's run by the volunteers, it keeps irregular hours.

### Sights & Activities

**Beaumaris Castle** (Cadw; ☎ 01248-810361; adult/child £3.70/3.30; 🕑 9am-5pm Apr-Oct, 9.30am-4pm Mon-Sat, 11am-4pm Sun Nov-Mar) is the last of Edward I's great castles of North Wales, and the largest. It was built by the military architect James of St George, between 1295 and 1298, although the money ran out before the fortifications were completed. It is a perfect example of a concentrically planned castle and deservedly a World Heritage Site. Following recent restoration work, there is now a new entrance with a little souvenir shop and a ticket office.

**Beaumaris Courthouse & Gaol** ( ☎ 01248-810921; combined tickets adult/child £6/4.50; 🕑 10.30am-5pm Easter-Sep) Atmospheric and eerie, the courthouse is nearly 400 years old and the Victorian jail contains the last-surviving treadwheel in Britain (for hard-labour prisoners). The jail

NORTH WALES

and courthouse are separate buildings, but the combined ticket gets you admission to both.

Boat operators run summer cruises from Beaumaris pier to Puffin Island, a haven for seals and puffins. **Starida Sea Services** ( ☎ 01248-810379; www.starida.co.uk; adult/child £6/4.50) and **Cerismar Two** ( ☎ 01248-810746; adult/child £7/5) run (weather-dependent) one-hour Puffin Island cruises, plus fishing trips. Book at the kiosks at the entrance to the pier.

The **Isle of Anglesey Coastal Path** (www.anglesey coastalpath.co.uk), a 125-mile coastal walking path, opened in 2006. The trail has its official start/end point at St Cybi's Church in Holyhead (opposite), but Beaumaris makes a good base, as the 12 stages can be tackled as individual day hikes from here. **Anglesey Walking Holidays** ( ☎ 01248-713611; www.anglesey walkingholidays.co.uk) arranges packages with self-guided walks, accommodation and transport. Prices start from £170 per person for a weekend, depending on the standard of B&B you choose to book.

## Sleeping

**Liverpool Arms** ( ☎ 01248-810362; www.liverpool arms.co.uk; Castle St; d/f from £69.50/100; P 🖳 ) This Georgian-fronted pub, right on the main street, has traditional rooms with some modern touches, and some have sea views. Hearty bar meals (lunch and dinner) are served downstairs, and you can wash them down with a pint of real ale.

**our pick Cleifiog** ( ☎ 01248-811507; www.cleifiog bandb.co.uk; Townsend; s/d from £45/75) A homely and smarter-than-average B&B, set in an historic building towards the eastern end of Castle St, this place is a little gem. The three rooms (one with bathroom) abound with original features and period fittings, while breakfast mixes healthy options with a traditional cooked meal. The owner displays her artworks around the house.

**Ye Olde Bulls Head Inn** ( ☎ 01248-810329; www .bullsheadinn.co.uk; Castle St; d/ste/4-poster £105/120/135) The tasteful rooms at this 1472-built inn are named after characters from the novels of Charles Dickens, who once stayed here. It's the smartest option in town with fine dining in the Loft restaurant, and informal meals and tapas in the Brasserie (mains around £10). At the time of writing work was under way on the Townhouse, a new extension to the hotel with 13 luxury suites in a 16th-century building, due to open in 2009.

## Eating

**Sarah's Delicatessen & the Coffee Shop** ( ☎ 01248-811534; 11 Church St; ⏰ 9am-5pm Mon-Sat) This excellent deli champions local produce, such as cheese and ales, with a well-stocked selection of treats. The owners recently opened a small cafe round the corner with daily specials (try the Anglesey dressed crab), good coffee and heavenly desserts.

**Sailor's Return** ( ☎ 01248-811314; www.sailorsreturn .co.uk; Church St; mains £7-12) A welcoming and cosy traditional pub for home-cooked bar meals at lunch and dinner, this place is a reliable option for pub grub.

**Court's** ( ☎ 01248-810565; www.courtyardcuisine.com; Regent House, Church St; dinner mains £7-19; ⏰ 11am-3pm & 6-9pm Wed-Mon) Formerly the Courtyard, Court's retains a European brasserie feel and features local produce served in sleek, refined surroundings. Dinner dishes include fish and meat specials (around £14), and there are special menus for both vegetarians and children.

## Getting There & Away

Buses 53, 57 and 58 run to Bangor (30 minutes, half-hourly Monday to Saturday) via Menai Bridge (20 minutes).

## LLANFAIR PG
pop 2500

Deep breath now: Lanfairpwllgwyngyllgoge rychwyrndrobwllllantysiliogogogoch (that's 'The Church of St Mary's Church in the hollow of the white hazel near the fierce whirlpool and the Church of St Tysilio by the red cave' since you ask) remains the village with the longest name in Britain, and some claim in Europe (the locals call the place Llanfair PG or Llanfairpwll). As such it draws the coach parties, who snap the train-station sign, buy an ice cream and push off in time for the next invasion.

But, crucially, the **tourist office** ( ☎ 01248-713177; www.anglesey.gov.uk; ⏰ 9.30am-5.30pm Mon-Sat, 10am-5pm Sun Apr-Oct, to 5pm daily Nov-Mar) is one of only two on the island (the other is at Holyhead, opposite) and makes an excellent source of information to plan your stay. It is located next to the train station in the Pringle Centre with a gift shop and coffee shop, both of which are best avoided. For a simple lunch, head just east of the tourist office to **Ty Gwyn** ( ☎ 01248-715599; Holyhead Rd; mains around £8; ⏰ lunch & dinner Mon-Thu, all-day food Fri-Sun), a no-nonsense

---

**TOP FIVE HIDDEN GEMS FOR FOOD LOVERS**

▪ **Ruby** ( ☎ 01248-711499; Dale St, Menai Bridge; mains around £15; ☺ lunch & dinner) Modern British fare and some traditional Welsh favourites; check promotional fixed-price menus for offers.

▪ **White Eagle** ( ☎ 01407-860267; Rhoscolyn; mains around £11; ☺ lunch & dinner Mon-Fri, all day weekends & holidays) Welcoming pub with great bar meals – try the Welsh beef meatballs in a stroganoff sauce.

▪ **Sullivan's** ( ☎ 01407-811811; www.sullivansofrhosneigr.co.uk; High St, Rhosneigr; mains around £8; ☺ 10am-5pm Sun-Wed, 6-9pm Wed-Sat) Informal dining and espresso bar.

▪ **Lobster Pot** ( ☎ 01407-730241; www.lobster-pot.net; Church Bay; mains around £20; ☺ noon-1.30pm & 6-8.30pm) Great local seafood – and lots of lobster – in a waterside location.

▪ **Ship Inn** ( ☎ 01248-852568; Red Wharf Bay; mains around £8; ☺ lunch & dinner) Pub grub and real ale on the coastal path walk.

---

pub for a plate of fish and chips and a pint of bitter.

## AROUND LLANFAIR PG
**Plas Newydd** (NT; ☎ 01248 714795; adult/child £7/3.50; ☺ house noon-5pm Sat-Wed, gardens 11am-5.30pm Sat-Wed Easter-Oct) was designed for the Marquis of Anglesey, and the house contains the largest permanent collection of Rex Whistler works, including an enormous, fantastical dreamscape of Mt Snowdon. Plas Newydd is located 2 miles southwest of Llanfair PG on the A55. Don't confuse it with Llangollen's Plas Newydd (p753).

## HOLYHEAD (CAERGYBI)
**pop 12,000**
Holyhead has had a hard time with economic deprivation and depopulation as young people leave to seek work elsewhere. It remains primarily a hub for ferry passengers going to and from Ireland rather than a place to visit, but the first signs of regeneration emerged in 2006 with the opening of the Celtic Gateway bridge, linking the train station to the main street. The inscription reads: 'Pass this way with a pure heart' – it certainly makes an attractive entrance to the town.

The **tourist office** ( ☎ 01407-762622; ☺ 8.30am-6pm daily), one of only two centres on the island (the other office is at Llanfair PG, opposite), is a useful resource, located in Terminal 1 (for foot passengers) at the ferry port with a Hertz car-rental outlet. Back on the platform, there is a new **left luggage office** (2hr for £2; ☺ 9am-4.30pm) available. Terminal 2 is the hub for car passengers.

Holyhead is the starting point for the Lôn Las Cymru cycle route (see the boxed text, p682) and St Cybi's Church marks the official starting point for the Isle of Anglesey Coastal Path (opposite).

The refurbished **Holyhead Maritime Museum** ( ☎ 01407-769745; Newry Beach; adult/child £2.50/1; ☺ 10am-4pm) houses exhibits on Holyhead's maritime history and also has a smart bistro.

To the west is **Holyhead Mountain** (220m), the highest point on Anglesey. At its western base, signposted from town, is **South Stack lighthouse** ( ☎ 01407-763207; www.trinityhouse.co.uk), open to all visitors who can tackle the 400-step descent to the offshore rock.

### Sleeping & Eating
**Yr Hendre** ( ☎ 01407-762929; www.yr-hendre.net; Porth-y-Felin Rd; s/d £45/50; Ⓟ ) Still the best of the B&Bs in town by far, this place is professionally run and homely with some modern touches. The hearty breakfast will set you up for the day.

**The Internet Cafe** (Victoria Tce; ☺ 9am-5pm Mon-Sat, 11am-4pm Sun) Net access (£2 per hour), printing facilities and snacks are the staples at this child-friendly cafe.

**Ucheldre Kitchen** ( ☎ 01407-763361; www.ucheldre.org; Millbank; ☺ 10am-5pm Mon-Sat, 2-5pm Sun) Attached to Holyhead's excellent Ucheldre Arts Centre, this relaxed, family-friendly cafe is a good spot for snack lunches and coffees. That's if you can find it – the signposting is poor.

**Harbourfront Bistro** ( ☎ 01407-763433; Newry Beach; dinner mains £14; ☺ 10am-4pm daily, 6-9pm Thu-Sun) The bistro is an upmarket addition to Holyhead's Maritime Museum. There's a big range of

**NORTH WALES**

snacks, mains and pastries served in a light, airy room that has a seaview decking area to spot ships in the harbour.

## Getting There & Away

**Irish Ferries** ( ☎ 0870 517 1717; www.irishferries.com) and **Stena Line** ( ☎ 0870 570 7070; www.stenaline.com) run ferries from Holyhead to Ireland.

Arriva bus 4/X4 serves Bangor (1¼ hours, two hourly Monday to Saturday).

Arriva Trains operate roughly hourly to Chester (£18, 1¾ hours) via the Llandudno Junction (£10, 50 minutes). Services to London Euston (£71, five hours, roughly hourly) are handled by the operator Virgin Trains.

# Scotland

GARETH MCCORMACK

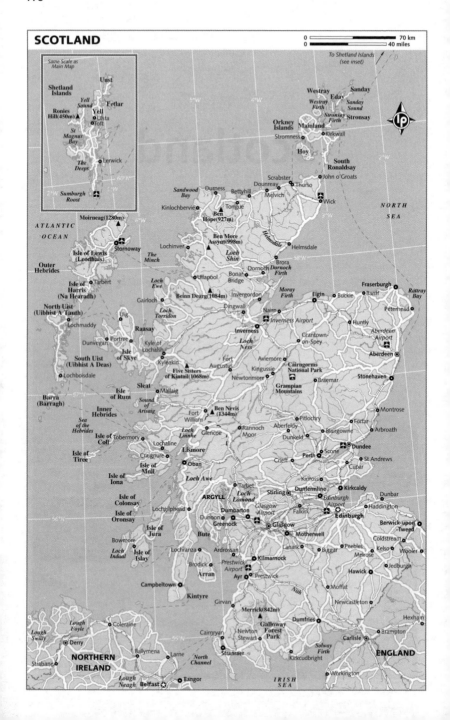

# SCOTLAND

0 ___ 70 km
0 ___ 40 miles

**Shetland Islands** *(inset)*

Same Scale as Main Map

Shetland Islands

Uist
Yell Sound
Fetlar
Ronies Hill(450m)▲
Yell
Ulsta
Toft
St Magnus Bay
The Deeps
Lerwick
Sumburgh Roost

ATLANTIC OCEAN

Moirneag(1280m)▲

Isle of Lewis (Leodhais)
Stornoway
The Minch

Outer Hebrides

Isle of Harris (Na Hearadh)
Tarbert

North Uist (Uibhist A Tuath)
Lochmaddy
Uig
Raasay

Dunvegan
Portree
Isle of Skye
Kyle of Lochalsh

South Uist (Uibhist A Deas)
Lochboisdale
Kyleakin
Sleat

Barra (Barragh)
Isle of Rum
Mallaig
Sound of Arisaig

Sea of the Hebrides

Inner Hebrides

Isle of Coll
Tobermory
Lochaline
Lismore

Isle of Tiree

Isle of Mull
Craignure
Oban
Loch Awe

Isle of Iona

Isle of Colonsay
Lochgilphead
Isle of Oronsay
Bowmore
Loch Indaal
Isle of Jura
Isle of Islay
Bute
Lochranza
Brodick
Arran
Prestwick Airport

Campbeltown
Kintyre

Girvan

NORTHERN IRELAND

Lough Swilly
Lough Foyle
Derry
Strabane
Coleraine
Ballymena
Larne
Bangor
Belfast
Lough Neagh
North Channel

IRISH SEA

Sandwood Bay
Durness
Bettyhill
Kinlochbervie
Tongue
Ben Hope(927m)▲

Ben More Assynt(998m)▲

Lochinver
Loch Shin

Ullapool
Bonar Bridge
Dornoch
Dornoch Firth

Loch Ewe
Gairloch
Beinn Dearg(1084m)▲
Invergordon

Loch Torridon
Dingwall
Nairn
Inverness
Inverness Airport

Loch Ness
Fort Augustus

Five Sisters of Kintail(1068m)▲
Newtonmore
Kingussie
Aviemore
Grantown-on-Spey

Cairngorms National Park

Grampian Mountains

Ben Nevis (1344m)▲
Fort William
Glencoe
Rannoch Moor
Loch Linnhe

Aberfeldy
Pitlochry
Dunkeld
Braemar

Crieff
Perth
Scone
Blairgowrie
Forfar
Arbroath

Tarbet
Loch Lomond
ARGYLL
Stirling
Kinross
Dunfermline
Cupar
St Andrews
Dundee

Dumbarton
Glasgow Airport
Falkirk
Kirkcaldy
Dunbar

Dunoon
Greenock
Glasgow
Motherwell
Edinburgh
Edinburgh Airport
Haddington

Ardrossan
Lanark
Biggar
Peebles
Berwick-upon-Tweed
Coldstream

Kilmarnock
Kelso
Wooler

Ayr
Prestwick
Hawick
Jedburgh
Melrose

Moffat
Newcastleton

Merrick(842m)▲
Galloway Forest Park
Dumfries
Hexham

Cairnryan
Newton Stewart
Dumfries
Brampton

Stranraer
Kirkcudbright
Solway Firth
Carlisle

Workington

ENGLAND

Nith

NORTH SEA

Westray
Eday
Sanday
Westray Firth
Sanday Sound
Stronsay Firth
Stronsay

Orkney Islands
Mainland
Stromness
Kirkwall

Hoy
South Ronaldsay

Scrabster
Dounreay
Thurso
John o'Groats
Melvich
Wick

Helmsdale
Helmsdale

Brora
Dornoch

Moray Firth
Elgin
Buckie
Banff
Fraserburgh
Rattray Bay

Peterhead

Huntly
Aberdeen Airport
Aberdeen

Grantown-on-Spey
Stonehaven

Montrose

# Edinburgh

Edinburgh is a city that just begs to be explored. From the vaults and wynds that riddle the Old Town to the picturesque urban villages of Stockbridge and Cramond, it's filled with quirky, come-hither nooks that tempt you to walk just that little bit further. And every corner turned reveals sudden views and unexpected vistas – green sunlit hills, a glimpse of rust-red crags, a blue flash of distant sea. It's a place to put the guidebook away for a bit, and just wander.

Not only is Edinburgh one of the most beautiful cities in Europe, it also enjoys one of Europe's most beautiful settings. It's a town entangled in its landscape, where the rocky battlements of Salisbury Crags overlook one end of the Old Town, and the Water of Leith snakes along only yards from the elegant Georgian terraces of the New Town. Fingers of greenery insinuate themselves among streets and suburbs everywhere, and you can walk or cycle across the city from the Firth of Forth to the Pentland Hills almost without touching a tarmac road.

But there's more to Edinburgh than just sightseeing – there are top shops, world-class restaurants and a bacchanalia of bars to enjoy. This is a city of pub crawls and impromptu music sessions, mad-for-it clubbing and all-night parties, overindulgence, late nights and wandering home through cobbled streets at dawn.

All these superlatives come together in August at festival time, when it seems as if half the world descends on Edinburgh for one enormous party. If you can possibly manage it, join them.

---

**HIGHLIGHTS**

- Taking in the views from the battlements of **Edinburgh Castle** (p781)
- Feasting on steak and oysters at the **Tower** (p798) restaurant as the sun sets over the city
- Nosing around the Queen's private quarters on the former **Royal Yacht Britannia** (p792) at Leith
- Listening to live folk music at the **Royal Oak**(p801)
- Trying to decipher the Da Vinci Code at mysterious **Rosslyn Chapel** (p805)

Edinburgh ★
★ Rosslyn

---

| ▪ TELEPHONE CODE: 0131 | ▪ POPULATION: 430,000 | ▪ AREA: 45 SQ MILES |

**EDINBURGH**

## HISTORY

Originally a purely defensive site, Edinburgh began to expand in the 12th century when King David I held court at the castle and founded the abbey at Holyrood. The first effective town wall was constructed around 1450 and circled the Old Town and the Grassmarket. This well-defended zone became a medieval Manhattan, forcing densely packed inhabitants to build tottering tenements that soared five and six storeys high.

The city played an important role in the Reformation, led by the firebrand John Knox (p789), but later, when James VI of Scotland succeeded to the English crown in 1603, he moved the court to London. Edinburgh's importance waned, to be further reduced by the Act of Union in 1707.

Nonetheless, cultural and intellectual life flourished; during the Scottish Enlightenment (about 1740–1830) Edinburgh became known as 'a hotbed of genius'. In the second half of the 18th century the New Town was created and the population soon exploded. A new ring of crescents and circuses was built south of the New Town, and grey Victorian terraces spread to the south.

In the 1920s the city's borders expanded again to encompass Leith in the north, Cramond in the west and the Pentland Hills in the south. Following WWII, the city's cultural life blossomed, stimulated by the Edinburgh International Festival and its fellow traveller the Fringe, both held for the first time in 1947 and now recognised as world-class arts festivals.

Edinburgh entered a new era following the 1997 referendum vote in favour of a devolved Scottish parliament, which first convened in July 1999. The parliament is housed in a controversial new building in Holyrood at the foot of the Royal Mile – in the 2007 elections the Scottish National Party became the largest party in the parliament, opening a new debate on the possibility (and desirability) of an independent Scotland.

## ORIENTATION

The city's most prominent landmarks are Arthur's Seat, southeast of the centre, and Edinburgh Castle at the western end of the Old Town. The Old and New Towns are separated by Princes Street Gardens, with Waverley train station at their eastern end.

Edinburgh's main shopping street, Princes St, runs along the northern side of the gardens. At its eastern end, Calton Hill is crowned by several monuments. The Royal Mile (Lawnmarket, High St and Canongate), the parallel equivalent in the Old Town, is roughly bookended by the Palace of Holyroodhouse to the east and the castle to the west.

---

### EDINBURGH IN...

#### Two Days

Kick off with coffee at the **Elephant House** (p798) – choose a window table with a view of the castle – then head uphill to **Edinburgh Castle** (opposite) to do the touristy bit. Afterwards, begin strolling down the **Royal Mile** (p785) and think about where to have lunch; **Pancho Villa's** (p798) is temptingly close by. Once you've eaten, continue to the foot of the Royal Mile to see the new **Scottish Parliament Building** (p789), then work up an appetite by climbing **Arthur's Seat**, or ogling the designer shoes in **Harvey Nichols** (p803). Satisfy your hunger with dinner at **Tower** (p798), while you watch the sun set beyond the castle.

On day two spend the morning soaking up some history in the **Royal Museum of Scotland** (p790) and in the afternoon catch the bus to Leith for a visit to the **Royal Yacht Britannia** (p792). In the evening have an early dinner at **Kitchin** (p799), then scare yourself silly on a guided ghost tour with **Cadies & Witchery Tours** (p794).

#### Four Days

A third day calls for a morning stroll around the **Royal Botanic Garden** (p792), followed by lunch at **Circle Cafe** (p799). An afternoon climb up **Calton Hill** (p791) beckons, but then there's the beer garden at **Pear Tree House** (p800), and a comfort-food dinner at **Monster Mash** (p798).

On day four head out to the pretty harbour village of **Queensferry** (p805), nestled beneath the Forth Bridges, or take a day trip to the enigmatic and beautiful **Rosslyn Chapel** (p805).

## Maps

Lonely Planet publishes the *Edinburgh City Map*, with an index of streets and sights. Another useful, portable map with street index is the *Collins Central Edinburgh Street Atlas*, available at most bookshops and tourist offices.

# INFORMATION

## Bookshops

**Blackwell** (Map pp786-7; ☎ 622 8222; www.blackwell .co.uk; 53 South Bridge; 9am-8pm Mon & Wed-Fri, 9.30am-8pm Tue, 9am-6pm Sat, noon-6pm Sun)

**Waterstone's** (Map pp786-7; ☎ 226 2666; www.wat erstones.co.uk; 128 Princes St; 8.30am-8pm Mon-Sat, 10.30am-7pm Sun) The largest Edinburgh branch.

## Internet Access

There are dozens of internet cafes (around £2 per hour) and hundreds of wi-fi hot spots in the city. Useful central locations include the following:

**connect@edinburgh** (Map pp786-7; ☎ 473 3800; ESIC, Princes Mall, 3 Princes St; as for ESIC, right)

**easyInternetcafé** (Map pp786-7; ☎ 220 3580; www .easy-everything.com; 58 Rose St; 7.30am-10.30pm)

**Internet Cafe** (Map pp786-7; ☎ 226 5400; www.edin internetcafe.com; 98 West Bow, Victoria St; 10am-11pm)

## Internet Resources

**City of Edinburgh Council** (www.edinburgh.gov.uk) Has an events guide.

**Your Edinburgh** (www.youredinburgh.info) Comprehensive directory of Edinburgh-related websites.

## Laundry

Most of the backpacker hostels have a laundry service.

**Ace Cleaning Centre** (Map pp782-3; ☎ 667 0549; 13 S Clerk St; around £5 per load; 8am-8pm Mon-Fri, 9am-5pm Sat, 10am-4pm Sun).

## Left Luggage

**Edinburgh airport left-luggage office** (per item per 4/24hr £5/6; 5.15am-10.45pm) On the ground floor between check-in and international arrivals.

**Edinburgh bus station lockers** (Map pp786-7; small/ medium/large locker per 24hr £3/4/5; 6am-midnight)

**Waverley train station left-luggage office** (Map pp786-7; per item per 24hr £6; 7am-11pm) Beside platform 1.

## Libraries

**Central Library** (Map pp786-7; ☎ 242 8000; George IV Bridge; 10am-8pm Mon-Thu, to 5pm Fri, 9am-

1pm Sat) General lending library with a room devoted to Edinburgh (one floor down), another to all things Scottish (in the basement), and a reference room on the top floor.

## Medical Services

**Royal Infirmary** (off Map pp782-3; ☎ 536 1000; Little France, Old Dalkeith Rd) Has 24-hour emergency.

## Money

There are banks with ATMs throughout the city. There's a bureau de change in the Edinburgh & Scotland Information Centre (ESIC), but post offices, banks and **Amex** (Map pp786-7; ☎ 718 2501; 69 George St) have better rates.

## Post

**Main post office** (Map pp786-7; ☎ 0845 722 3344; St James Centre, Leith St)

## Tourist Information

**Edinburgh & Scotland Information Centre** (ESIC; Map pp786-7; ☎ 0845 225 5121; info@visitscotland .com; Princes Mall, 3 Princes St; 9am-9pm Mon-Sat, 10am-8pm Sun Jul & Aug, 9am-7pm Mon-Sat, 10am-7pm Sun May, Jun & Sep, 9am-5pm Mon-Wed, 9am-6pm Thu-Sun Oct-Apr) Accommodation booking service, currency exchange, gift and bookshop, internet access, and tickets for Edinburgh city tours and Scottish Citylink bus services.

**Tourist information desk** (Edinburgh Airport; 6.30am-10.30pm) Near international arrivals.

## Travel Agencies

**STA Travel** (Map pp786-7; ☎ 226 7747; www.sta travel.co.uk; 27 Forrest Rd; 10am-6pm Mon-Wed & Fri, 10am-7pm Thu, 10am-5pm Sat)

**Student Flights** (Map pp786-7; ☎ 226 6868; www .studentflights.co.uk; 53 Forrest Rd; 9.30am-6pm Mon-Fri, 11am-5pm Sat)

# SIGHTS

Edinburgh's main attractions are concentrated in the city centre – on and around the Old Town's Royal Mile, between the castle and Holyrood, and in New Town. A major exception is the Royal Yacht *Britannia*, which is in the redeveloped docklands district of Leith, 2 miles northeast of the centre.

## Old Town

### EDINBURGH CASTLE

The brooding, black crags of Castle Rock rising above the western end of Princes St are the very reason for Edinburgh's existence. This

# EDINBURGH

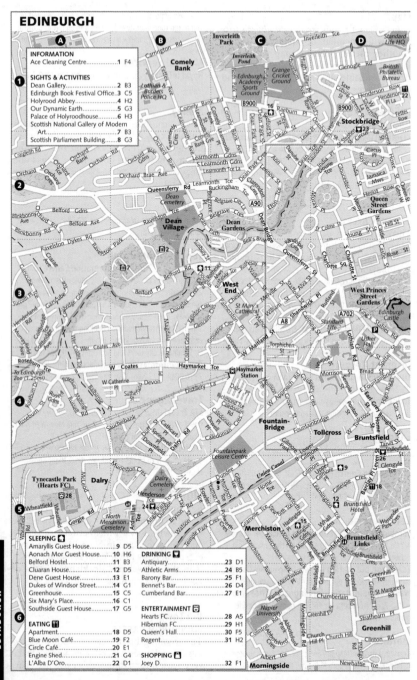

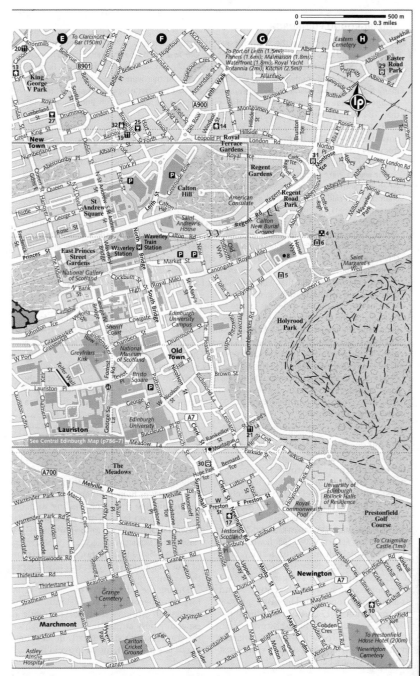

## UNDERGROUND EDINBURGH

As Edinburgh expanded in the late 18th and early 19th centuries, many old tenements were demolished and new bridges were built to link the Old Town to the newly built areas to its north and south. South Bridge (built between 1785 and 1788) and George IV Bridge (built between 1829 and 1834) lead southwards from the Royal Mile over the deep valley of Cowgate, but so many buildings have been built closely around them that you can hardly tell they are bridges – George IV Bridge has a total of nine arches but only two are visible; South Bridge has no less than 18 hidden arches.

These subterranean vaults were originally used as storerooms, workshops and drinking dens. But as the early-19th-century population was swelled by an influx of penniless Highlanders cleared from their lands, and Irish refugees from the potato famine, the dark, dripping chambers were given over to slum accommodation and abandoned to poverty, filth and crime.

The vaults were eventually cleared in the late 19th century, then lay forgotten until 1994 when the South Bridge vaults were opened to guided tours (see Mercat Tours, p794). Certain chambers are said to be haunted and one particular vault was investigated by paranormal researchers in 2001.

Nevertheless, the most ghoulish aspect of Edinburgh's hidden history dates from much earlier – from the plague that struck the city in 1645. Legend has it that the disease-ridden inhabitants of Mary King's Close (a lane on the northern side of the Royal Mile on the site of the City Chambers – you can still see its blocked-off northern end from Cockburn St) were walled up in their houses and left to perish. When the lifeless bodies were eventually cleared from the houses, they were so stiff that workmen had to hack off limbs to get them through the small doorways and narrow, twisting stairs.

From that day on, the close was said to be haunted by the spirits of the plague victims. The few people who were prepared to live there reported seeing apparitions of severed heads and limbs, and the largely abandoned close fell into ruin. When the Royal Exchange (now the City Chambers) was constructed between 1753 and 1761, it was built over the lower levels of Mary King's Close, which were left intact and sealed off beneath the building.

Interest in the close revived in the 20th century when Edinburgh's city council began to allow occasional guided tours to enter. Visitors have reported many supernatural experiences – the most famous ghost is 'Sarah', a little girl whose sad tale has prompted people to leave gifts of dolls in a corner of one of the rooms. In 2003 the close was opened to the public as the Real Mary King's Close (p788).

rocky hill was the most easily defended hilltop on the invasion route between England and central Scotland, a route followed by countless armies from the Roman legions of the 1st and 2nd centuries AD to the Jacobite troops of Bonnie Prince Charlie in 1745.

**Edinburgh Castle** (HS; Map pp786-7; ☎ 225 9846; www.edinburghcastle.gov.uk; Castlehill; adult/child £12/6; ☻ 9.30am-6pm Apr-Oct, 9.30am-5pm Nov-Mar) has played a pivotal role in Scottish history, both as a royal residence – King Malcolm Canmore (r 1057–93) and Queen Margaret first made their home here in the 11th century – and as a military stronghold. The castle last saw military action in 1745; from then until the 1920s it served as the British army's main base in Scotland. Today it is one of Scotland's most atmospheric, most popular – and most expensive – tourist attractions.

Highlights of the castle include: **St Margaret's Chapel** (the oldest building in Edinburgh), a simple stone building that was probably built by David I or Alexander I around 1130 in memory of their mother; the **Royal Palace** (including the Stone of Destiny and the Scottish Crown Jewels); and the **National War Museum of Scotland** (Map pp786-7; ☎ 225 7534; admission incl in Edinburgh Castle ticket; ☻ 9.45am-5.30pm Apr-Sep, to 4.45pm Oct-Mar), a fascinating account of how war and military service have shaped the nation.

During the Edinburgh Festival, the castle forecourt becomes a grandstand for the Edinburgh Military Tattoo. The castle is especially busy at this time, but throughout the year it's worth visiting early in the morning or late in the afternoon to avoid the peak periods.

EDINBURGH

## ROYAL MILE

Edinburgh's Old Town stretches along a ridge to the east of the castle, and tumbles down Victoria St to the broad expanse of the Grassmarket. It's a jumbled maze of masonry riddled with closes (alleys) and wynds (narrow lanes), and cleft along its spine by the cobbled ravine of the Royal Mile.

Until the founding of the New Town in the 18th century, old Edinburgh was an overcrowded and insanitary hive of humanity squeezed between the boggy ground of the Nor' Loch (North Loch, now drained and occupied by Princes Street Gardens) to the north and the city walls to the south and east. The 16th- and 17th-century tenement buildings that line the Royal Mile – it earned its regal nickname in the 16th century when it was used by the king to travel between the castle and the Palace of Holyroodhouse – once housed all manner of Edinburgh society in an unhygienic bedlam that earned the medieval metropolis its 'Auld Reekie' nickname. Underneath, the poor lived as best they could in a warren of vaults and cellars, some of which can be visited on spooky ghost tours (see p794).

At the top of the Royal Mile the **Camera Obscura** (Map pp786-7; ☎ 226 3709; Outlook Tower, Castlehill; adult/child £7.95/5.50; ⊗ 9.30am-7.30pm Jul & Aug, 9.30am-6pm Apr-Jun, Sep & Oct, 10am-5pm Nov-Mar) is a curious 19th-century device – in constant use since 1853 – that uses lenses and mirrors to throw a live image of the city onto a large horizontal screen. Stairs lead up through various displays on optics to the Outlook Tower, which offers great views over the city.

A typical Old Town tenement building, **Gladstone's Land** (NTS; Map pp786-7; ☎ 226 5856; 477 Lawnmarket; adult/child £5/4; ⊗ 10am-7pm Jul & Aug, 10am-5pm Easter-Jun, Sep & Oct) offers a fascinating glimpse into the past. The narrow, six-storey house was built in the mid-16th century and extended around 1617 by wealthy merchant Thomas Gledstanes. The best room is the Painted Chamber with its fabulous painted roof, dating back to 1620, and ornate oak furniture.

Nearby, tucked in a close, the **Writers' Museum** (Map pp786-7; ☎ 529 4901; Lady Stair's Close, Lawnmarket; admission free; ⊗ 10am-5pm Mon-Sat year-round, noon-5pm Sun Aug) is housed in **Lady Stair's House** (built in 1622) and contains

---

### STONE OF DESTINY

On St Andrew's Day 1996 a block of sandstone – 26½ inches by 16½ inches by 11 inches in size, with rusted iron hoops at either end – was installed with much pomp and ceremony in Edinburgh Castle. For the previous 700 years it had lain in London, beneath the Coronation Chair in Westminster Abbey. Almost all English, and later British, monarchs from Edward II in 1307 to Elizabeth II in 1953 have parked their backsides firmly over this stone during their coronation ceremony.

The legendary Stone of Destiny – said to have originated in the Holy Land, and on which Scottish kings placed their feet during their coronation (not their bums; the English got that bit wrong) – was stolen from Scone Abbey near Perth by King Edward I of England in 1296. It was taken to London and there it remained for seven centuries – except for a brief removal to Gloucester during WWII air raids, and a three-month sojourn in Scotland after it was stolen by Scottish Nationalist students at Christmas in 1950 – an enduring symbol of Scotland's subjugation by England.

The Stone of Destiny returned to the political limelight in 1996, when the then Scottish Secretary and Conservative Party MP, Michael Forsyth, arranged for the return of the sandstone block to Scotland. A blatant attempt to boost the flagging popularity of the Conservative Party in Scotland prior to a general election, Forsyth's publicity stunt failed miserably. The Scots said thanks very much for the stone and then, in May 1997, voted every Conservative MP in Scotland into oblivion.

Many people, however, believe that Edward I was fobbed off with a shoddy imitation in 1296 and that the true Stone of Destiny remains safely hidden somewhere in Scotland. This is not impossible – some descriptions of the original state that it was made of black marble and decorated with elaborate carvings. Interested parties should read *The Taking of the Stone of Destiny* by Ian R Hamilton, which tells the story of the stone's abduction in 1950 – it was made into a Hollywood film, *Stone of Destiny*, in 2008.

**EDINBURGH**

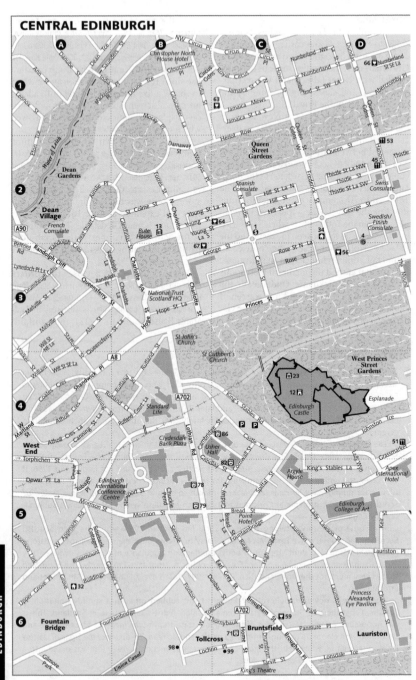

# CENTRAL EDINBURGH

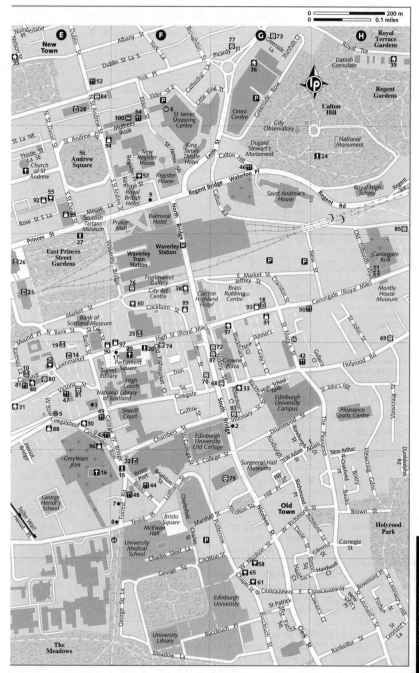

manuscripts and memorabilia from Scotland's big three literati: Robert Burns, Sir Walter Scott and Robert Louis Stevenson.

**Parliament Square**, largely filled by St Giles Cathedral, is in the middle part of the Royal Mile. This was the civic heart of Edinburgh until the 18th century, and a cobblestoned **Heart of Midlothian** is set in the ground. Passersby traditionally spit on it for luck. The 19th-century **Mercat Cross** replaced the original 1365 cross, marking the spot where merchants and traders transacted business and royal proclamations were read.

Looming over the square, **St Giles Cathedral** (Map pp786-7; High St; admission free, £3 donation suggested; 9am-7pm Mon-Fri, 9am-5pm Sat, 1-5pm Sun May-Sep, 9am-5pm Mon-Sat, 1-5pm Sun Oct-Apr) dates largely from the 15th century – the beautiful crown spire was completed in 1495 – but much of it was restored in the 19th century. The interior lacks grandeur but is rich in history: St Giles

was at the heart of the Scottish Reformation, and John Knox served as minister here from 1559 to 1572. One of the most interesting corners of the kirk is the **Thistle Chapel**, built in 1911 for the Knights of the Most Ancient & Most Noble Order of the Thistle. The elaborately carved Gothic-style stalls have canopies topped with the helms and arms of the 16 knights – look out for the bagpipe-playing angel amid the vaulting.

Sealed off for 250 years beneath the City Chambers, **Real Mary King's Close** (Map pp786-7; 0870 243 0160; 2 Warriston's Close; adult/child £10/6; 9am-9pm Aug, 10am-9pm Apr-Jul, Sep & Oct, 10am-4pm Sun-Fri & 10am-9pm Sat Nov-Mar) is a spooky, subterranean labyrinth that gives a fascinating insight into the daily life of 16th- and 17th-century Edinburgh. Costumed characters give tours through a 16th-century town house and the plague-stricken home of a 17th-century gravedigger. Tours must be booked in advance.

One of the oldest surviving buildings on the Royal Mile is **John Knox House** (Map pp786-7; ☎ 556 9579; 43-45 High St; adult/child £3.50/1; ⊙ 10am-6pm Mon-Sat year-round, noon-6pm Sun Jul & Aug), built in 1490 and once home to the father of the Scottish Reformation, John Knox. The labyrinthine interior has some beautiful painted-timber ceilings and an interesting display on Knox's life and work.

The Royal Mile continues below High St as Canongate. A fine example of 16th-century architecture, **Canongate Tolbooth** (Map pp786-7; ☎ 529 4057; 163 Canongate; admission free; ⊙ 10am-5pm Mon-Sat year-round, 2-5pm Sun Aug) has picturesque turrets and a projecting clock. It served in turn as a collection point for tolls, a council house, a courtroom and a jail. It now houses an absorbing museum, the **People's Story**, relating the story of the life, work and pastimes of ordinary Edinburgh folk from the late 18th century to the present.

### SCOTTISH PARLIAMENT

Built on the site of a former brewery, the controversial **Scottish Parliament Building** (Map pp782-3; ☎ 348 5200; www.scottish.parliament.uk; Holyrood Rd; admission free, tours adult/concession £6/3.60; ⊙ 9am-6pm Tue-Thu, 10am-5pm Mon & Fri in session, 10am-5pm Mon-Fri in recess Apr-Oct, 10am-4pm Mon-Fri in recess Nov-Mar) opened for business in 2005. The strange forms of the exterior are all symbolic in some way, from the oddly shaped windows on the west wall (inspired by the silhouette of the Reverend Robert Walker Skating on Duddingston Loch, one of Scotland's most famous paintings), to the ground plan of the whole complex, which represents a 'flower of democracy rooted in Scottish soil' (best seen looking down from Salisbury Crags). The **Canongate Wall** (on the northern side) is studded with stones from across Scotland and inscribed with quotations from Scottish literature.

### PALACE OF HOLYROODHOUSE & HOLYROOD ABBEY

The **Palace of Holyroodhouse** (Map pp782-3; ☎ 556 5100; www.royal.gov.uk; Canongate; adult/child £9.80/5.80; ⊙ 9.30am-6pm Apr-Oct, 9.30am-4.30pm Nov-Mar) is the royal family's official residence in Scotland, but is most famous as the 16th-century home of the ill-fated Mary Queen of Scots. The oldest surviving part of the building, the northwest tower, was built in 1529 as a royal apartment for James V and his wife, Mary of Guise. Mary Queen of Scots spent six turbu-

lent years here, during which time she debated with John Knox, married both her first and second husbands, and witnessed the murder of her secretary Rizzio. The palace is closed to the public when the royal family is visiting and during state functions (usually in mid-May, and mid-June to early July; check website for exact dates).

The highlight of the self-guided audio tour is **Mary Queen of Scots' Bed Chamber**, home to the unfortunate Mary from 1561 to 1567, and connected by a secret stairway to her husband's bedchamber. It was here that her jealous first husband, Lord Darnley, restrained the pregnant queen while his henchmen murdered her secretary – and favourite – David Rizzio. A plaque in the neighbouring room marks the spot where he bled to death.

The exit from the palace leads into the ruins of **Holyrood Abbey** (Map pp782-3). King David I founded the abbey here in the shadow of Salisbury Crags in 1128. It was probably named after a fragment of the True Cross (rood is an old Scots word for cross), said to have been brought to Scotland by his mother, St Margaret. Most of the surviving ruins date from the 12th and 13th centuries, although a doorway in the far southeastern corner has survived from the original Norman church.

### HOLYROOD PARK & ARTHUR'S SEAT

In **Holyrood Park** (Map pp782-3), Edinburghers can enjoy a little bit of wilderness in the heart of the city. The former hunting ground of Scottish monarchs, the park covers 263 hectares of varied landscape, including crags, moorland and loch. The highest point is the 251m summit of **Arthur's Seat** (off Map pp782-3), the deeply eroded remnant of a long-extinct volcano; you can hike from Holyrood to the summit in 30 to 45 minutes.

### OUR DYNAMIC EARTH

The prominent white marquee pitched beneath Salisbury Crags marks **Our Dynamic Earth** (Map pp782-3; ☎ 550 7800; Holyrood Rd; adult/child £9.50/5.95; ⊙ 10am-6pm Jul & Aug, 10am-5pm Apr-Jun, Sep & Oct, 10am-5pm Wed-Sun Nov-Mar, last admission 70 minutes before closing), billed as an interactive, multimedia journey of discovery through Earth's history from the Big Bang to the present day. Hugely popular with kids of all ages, it's a slick extravaganza of whizz-bang special effects cleverly designed to fire up young minds with curiosity about all things geological and environmental. Its true purpose, of course, is to disgorge you into a gift shop where you can buy toy dinosaurs and souvenir T-shirts.

## South of the Royal Mile
### GRASSMARKET & AROUND
The site of a former cattle market, the **Grassmarket** has always been a focal point of the Old Town. It was also the city's main place of execution, and over 100 martyred Covenanters are commemorated by a monument at the eastern end, where the gallows used to stand. The notorious murderers Burke and Hare operated from a now-vanished close off the western end. In 1827 they enticed at least 18 victims to their boarding house, suffocated them and sold the bodies to Edinburgh's medical schools. Nowadays the broad, open square, edged by tall tenements and dominated by the looming castle, has many lively pubs and restaurants.

**Cowgate** – the long, dark ravine leading eastwards from the Grassmarket – was once the road along which cattle were driven from the pastures around Arthur's Seat to the safety of the city walls. Today it is the heart of Edinburgh's nightlife, with around two dozen clubs and bars within five minutes' walk of each other.

### GREYFRIARS KIRK & KIRKYARD
Hemmed in by high walls, **Greyfriars Kirkyard** is one of Edinburgh's most evocative cemeteries, a peaceful green oasis dotted with elaborate monuments. Many famous Edinburgh names are buried here, including the poet Allan Ramsay (1686–1758), architect William Adam (1689–1748) and William Smellie (1740–95), the editor of the first edition of the *Encyclopaedia Britannica*. If you want to experience the graveyard at its scariest – inside a burial vault, in the dark, at night – go on one of Black Hart Storytellers' guided tours (see p794).

However, the memorial that draws the biggest crowds is the tiny **Greyfriars Bobby statue** (Map pp786–7), in front of the pub beside the kirkyard gate. Bobby was a Skye terrier who, from 1858 to 1872, maintained a vigil over the grave of his master, an Edinburgh police officer. The story was immortalised in a novel by Eleanor Atkinson and was later made into a Disney movie. Bobby's own grave – marked by a small, pink, granite stone – is just inside the entrance to the kirkyard.

**Greyfriars Kirk** (Map pp786–7) was built on the site of a Franciscan friary and opened for worship on Christmas Day 1620. In 1638 the National Covenant was signed here, rejecting Charles I's attempts to impose episcopacy and a new English prayer book, and affirming the independence of the Scottish Church. Many who signed were later executed at the Grassmarket and, in 1679, 1200 Covenanters were held prisoner in terrible conditions in the southwestern corner of the kirkyard. There's a small exhibition inside the church.

### NATIONAL MUSEUM OF SCOTLAND
Broad, elegant Chambers St stretches eastwards from Greyfriars Bobby, and is dominated by the **National Museum of Scotland** (Map pp786-7; ☎ 247 4422; www.nms.ac.uk; Chambers St; admission free, special exhibitions extra; ⊗ 10am-5pm). The collections are spread between two buildings, one modern, one Victorian.

The golden stone and striking modern architecture of the **Museum of Scotland** houses five floors of exhibits tracing the history of Scotland from geological beginnings to the 1990s. Highlights include the Monymusk Reliquary, a tiny silver casket dating from 750, which is said to have been carried into battle with Robert the Bruce at Bannockburn in 1314, and a set of charming 12th-century chess pieces made from walrus ivory. Don't forget to take the lift to the roof terrace for a fantastic view of the castle. The neighbouring Victorian **Royal Museum of Scotland**, dating from 1861, houses an eclectic collection covering natural history, archaeology, scientific and industrial technology, and the decorative arts of ancient Egypt, Islam, China, Japan, Korea and the West.

## New Town
Edinburgh's New Town lies north of the Old Town, separated from it by the valley of Princes Street Gardens. Its regular grid of elegant, Georgian terraces is a complete contrast to the chaotic tangle of the Old Town.

It was born out of the 18th-century need to expand beyond the crowded confines of the increasingly insanitary Old Town, and provide more-spacious living quarters for the upper classes. The street plan was devised by 23-year-old James Craig, a self-taught architect, but much of its finest neoclassical architecture was designed by Robert Adam. Today Edinburgh's New Town remains the

EDINBURGH

world's most complete and unspoilt example of Georgian architecture and town planning; along with the Old Town, it was declared a Unesco World Heritage Site in 1995.

## PRINCES STREET

Princes St is one of the world's most spectacular shopping streets. Built up on the north side only, it catches the sun in summer and allows expansive views across Princes Street Gardens to the castle and the crowded skyline of the Old Town.

The eastern half of the street is dominated by the massive Gothic spire of the **Scott Monument** (Map pp786-7; ☎ 529 4068; East Princes Street Gardens; admission £3; ☼ 9am-6pm Mon-Sat, 10am-6pm Sun Apr-Sep, 9am-3pm Mon-Sat, 10am-3pm Sun Oct-Mar), built by public subscription in memory of the novelist Sir Walter Scott after his death in 1832. Inside you can see an exhibition on Scott's life, and climb the 287 steps to the top for a superb view of the city.

Nearby, the Greek Doric **Royal Scottish Academy** (RSA; Map pp786-7; ☎ 225 6671; www.royalscottishacademy.org; The Mound; admission free, special exhibitions extra; ☼ 10am-5pm Mon-Sat, 2-5pm Sun), built in 1826, features a sleek underground exhibition space that links to its neighbour, the National Gallery. The academy is devoted to exhibiting Scottish art by RSA members as well as regular visiting exhibitions.

The **National Gallery of Scotland** (Map pp786-7; ☎ 624 6200; www.nationalgalleries.org; The Mound; admission free; ☼ 10am-5pm Fri-Wed, 10am-7pm Thu) is another imposing neoclassical building, housing a significant collection of European art. There are paintings by masters from the Renaissance to the Impressionists, including Titian's *Three Ages of Man* and Monet's *Haystacks,* and a fine range of works by Scottish artists, notably landscapes by William MacTaggart and rural scenes by David Wilkie. Look out for Sir Henry Raeburn's iconic *Reverend Robert Walker Skating on Duddingston Loch.*

## GEORGE STREET & CHARLOTTE SQUARE

Until the 1990s George St – the major axis of the New Town – was the centre of Edinburgh's financial industry, Scotland's equivalent of Wall St. Now the big financial firms have moved to premises in the Exchange district west of Lothian Rd, and George St's former banks and offices house upmarket shops, pubs and restaurants.

**Charlotte Square**, the architectural jewel of the New Town, was designed by Robert Adam shortly before his death in 1791. The northern side of the square is Adam's masterpiece and one of the finest examples of Georgian architecture anywhere. **Bute House** (Map pp786–7), in the centre at No 6, is the official residence of Scotland's first minister.

Next door is the **Georgian House** (Map pp786-7; ☎ 226 2160; 7 Charlotte Sq; adult/child £5/4; ☼ 10am-6pm Jul & Aug, 10am-5pm Apr-Jun, Sep & Oct, 11am-3pm Mar & Nov), which has been beautifully restored and furnished to show how Edinburgh's wealthy elite lived at the end of the 18th century. The walls are decorated with paintings by Allan Ramsay, Sir Henry Raeburn and Sir Joshua Reynolds.

Near St Andrew Sq, at the opposite end of George St, is the Venetian Gothic palace of the **Scottish National Portrait Gallery** (Map pp786-7; ☎ 624 6200; www.nationalgalleries.org; 1 Queen St; admission free; ☼ 10am-5pm daily, to 7pm Thu). Its galleries illustrate Scottish history through portraits and sculptures of famous Scottish personalities, from Robert Burns and Bonnie Prince Charlie to Sean Connery and Billy Connolly.

## CALTON HILL

Rising dramatically above the eastern end of Princes St, Calton Hill (100m) is Edinburgh's acropolis; its summit scattered with grandiose memorials mostly dating from the first half of the 19th century. It is also one of the best viewpoints in Edinburgh, with a panorama that takes in the castle, Holyrood, Arthur's Seat, the Firth of Forth, the New Town and the full length of Princes St.

Looking a bit like an upturned telescope – the similarity is intentional – and offering even better views, the **Nelson Monument** (Map pp786-7; ☎ 556 2716; Calton Hill; admission £3; ☼ 1-6pm Mon, 10am-6pm Tue-Sat Apr-Sep, 10am-3pm Mon-Sat Oct-Mar) was built to commemorate Admiral Lord Nelson's victory at Trafalgar in 1805.

## SCOTTISH NATIONAL GALLERY OF MODERN ART

Just beyond Edinburgh's West End, the western extension of the New Town, this bright, modern **gallery** (Map pp782-3; ☎ 624 6200; www.nationalgalleries.org; 75 Belford Rd; admission free, special exhibitions extra; ☼ 10am-5pm) is housed in an impressive classical building surrounded by a sculpture park. The collection concentrates on 20th-century art, with works by Henri Matisse, Pablo Picasso, René Magritte and

**EDINBURGH**

Henry Moore among others, but most space is given to Scottish painters – from the Scottish colourists of the early 20th century to contemporary artists such as Peter Howson and Ken Currie.

Across Belford Rd is the gallery's annexe, the **Dean Gallery** (Map pp782-3; ☎ 624 6200; 73 Belford Rd; admission free, special exhibitions extra; ☯ 10am-5pm), with a collection of Dada and surrealist art, including works by Dali, Giacometti and Picasso. There's also a large collection of sculpture and graphic art created by the Edinburgh-born sculptor Sir Eduardo Paolozzi.

## Leith

Leith is Edinburgh's main port, although it remained an independent burgh until the 1920s. It's still among Britain's busiest ports but in the 1960s and '70s it fell into a sad state – abandoned to council housing and frequented by drug dealers that inspired *Trainspotting*. A recent revival means that it's now home to many of the city's best pubs and restaurants. Parts of the neighbourhood are still a little rough but it's a distinctive, colourful corner of Edinburgh. The prettiest area is around the Shore.

One of Scotland's biggest tourist attractions is the former **Royal Yacht Britannia** (off Map pp782-3; ☎ 555 5566; www.royalyachtbritannia.co.uk; Ocean Terminal, Leith; adult/child £9.75/5.75; ☯ 9.30am-6pm Jul & Aug, 10am-6pm Apr-Jun, Sep & Oct, 10am-5pm Nov-Mar, last admission 1½hr before closing). She was the British royal family's floating home during their foreign travels from the time of her launch in 1953 until her decommissioning in 1997, and is now moored permanently in front of Ocean Terminal. A monument to 1950s style and decor, the ship offers an intriguing insight into the Queen's preference for simple, unfussy surroundings. Exploration is via self-guided multilingual audio tour.

The Majestic Tour bus (see p794) runs from Waverley Bridge to *Britannia* during opening times. Alternatively, take Lothian bus 1, 11, 22, 34, 35 or 36 to Ocean Terminal.

## Greater Edinburgh
### ROYAL BOTANIC GARDEN
North of the New Town lies the lovely **Royal Botanic Garden** (off Map pp782-3; ☎ 552 7171; www.rbge.org.uk; 20a Inverleith Row; admission to gardens free, to glasshouses £3.50; ☯ 10am-7pm Apr-Sep, 10am-6pm Mar & Oct, 10am-4pm Nov-Feb). Twenty-eight beautifully landscaped hectares include splendid Victorian palm houses, colourful swaths of rhododendron and azalea, and a world-famous rock garden. The Terrace Cafe offers good views towards the city centre. Take Lothian bus 8, 17, 23 or 27 to the East Gate, or the Majestic Tour bus (see p794).

### EDINBURGH ZOO
Opened in 1913, **Edinburgh Zoo** (off Map pp782-3; ☎ 334 9171; www.edinburghzoo.org.uk; 134 Corstorphine Rd; adult/child £11.50/8; ☯ 9am-6pm Apr-Sep, 9am-5pm Oct & Mar, 9am-4.30pm Nov-Feb) is one of the world's leading conservation zoos. Edinburgh's captive breeding program has saved many endangered species, including Siberian tigers, pygmy hippos and red pandas. The main attractions are the penguins (kept in the world's biggest penguin pool), the sea lion and red panda feeding times (check website for details), the animal-handling sessions and the Lifelinks 'hands-on' zoology centre.

The zoo is 2.5 miles west of the city centre; take Lothian bus 12, 26 or 31, First bus 16, 18, 80 or 86, or the Airlink bus 100 westbound from Princes St.

### CRAIGMILLAR CASTLE
If you want to explore a Scottish fortress away from the crowds that throng Edinburgh Castle, try **Craigmillar Castle** (off Map pp782-3; HS; ☎ 661 4445; Craigmillar Castle Rd; adult/child £4.20/2.10; ☯ 9.30am-5.30pm Apr-Sep, 9.30am-4.30pm Oct, 9.30am-4.30pm Sat-Wed Nov-Mar). Dating from the 15th century, the tower house rises above two sets of machicolated curtain walls. Mary Queen of Scots took refuge here after the murder of Rizzio; it was here too that plans to murder her husband Darnley were laid. Look for the prison cell complete with built-in sanitation, something some 'modern' British prisons only finally managed in 1996.

The castle is 2.5 miles southeast of the city centre. Take bus 33 eastbound from Princes St to Old Dalkeith Rd and walk 500m up Craigmillar Castle Rd.

## ACTIVITIES
Edinburgh is lucky to have several good walking areas within the city boundary, including Arthur's Seat, Calton Hill, Blackford Hill, Hermitage of Braid, Corstorphine Hill, and the coast and river at Cramond. The **Pentland Hills**, which rise to over 500m, stretch southwest from the city for 15 miles, offering excellent high- and low-level walking.

You can walk or cycle along the wooded riverbanks of the **Water of Leith Walkway**, which runs from the city centre upstream to the Pentland Hills or downstream to Leith. There are access points and signposts throughout its length: one of the best short walks is from Stockbridge to historic Dean Village, where the waterway is spanned by a Thomas Telford bridge.

## WALKING TOUR

The Old Town – the medieval part of town – stretches along the Royal Mile to the east of the castle and southwards to the Grassmarket and Greyfriars. This walk delves into the Old Town's many interesting nooks and crannies, and involves a fair bit of climbing steep stairs and closes.

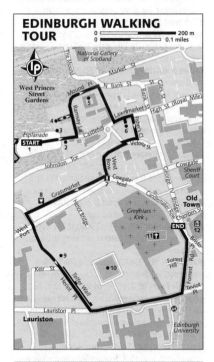

EDINBURGH WALKING TOUR

### WALK FACTS

**Start** Castle Esplanade
**Finish** Museum of Scotland
**Distance** 1.5 miles
**Duration** one to two hours

Begin on the **Castle Esplanade (1)**, which affords grandstand views southwards over the Grassmarket; the prominent quadrangular building with all the turrets is George Heriot's School, which you'll pass later on. Head towards Castlehill and the start of the Royal Mile. The 17th-century house on the right, above the steps of North Castle Wynd, is known as **Cannonball House (2)** because of the iron ball lodged in the wall (look between, and slightly below, the two largest windows). It was not fired in anger, but instead marks the gravitation height to which water would flow naturally from the city's first piped water supply.

The low, rectangular building across the street (now a touristy tartan-weaving mill) was originally the reservoir that held the Old Town's water supply. On its western wall is the **Witches Well (3)**, where a modern bronze fountain commemorates around 4000 people (mostly women) who were burned or strangled in Edinburgh between 1479 and 1722 on suspicion of witchcraft.

Go past the reservoir and turn left down Ramsay Lane, and take a look at **Ramsay Garden (4)** – one of the most desirable addresses in Edinburgh – where late-19th-century apartments were built around the nucleus of the octagonal Ramsay Lodge, once home to poet Allan Ramsay. The cobbled street continues around to the right below student residences, to the twin towers of the **New College (5)**, home to Edinburgh University's Faculty of Divinity. Nip into the courtyard to see the statue of John Knox.

Just past New College, turn right and climb up the stairs into Milne's Court, a student residence. Exit into the Lawnmarket, cross the street (bearing slightly left) and duck into **Riddell's Court (6)** at number 322–8, a typical Old Town close. You'll find yourself in a small courtyard, but the house in front of you, built in 1590, was originally the edge of the street (the building you just walked under was added in 1726 – check the inscription in the doorway on the right). The arch (with the inscription 'VIVENDO DISCIMUS', 'we live and learn') leads into the original 16th-century courtyard.

Go back into the street, turn right, and then right again down Fisher's Close, which ejects you onto the delightful Victoria Tce, strung above the cobbled curve of shop-lined Victoria St. Wander right, enjoying the view, then descend the stairs at the foot of Upper Bow and continue downhill to the Grassmarket (p790). At the eastern end, outside Maggie Dickson's pub, is the **Covenanters' Monument (7)**; if you're feeling peckish, there are several good places to eat and a couple of good pubs – legendary poet Robert Burns once stayed at the **White Hart Inn (8)**.

At the west end of the Grassmarket, turn left up the flight of stairs known as the Vennel. At the top of the steps on the left you'll find the **Flodden Wall (9)**. Follow its extension, the Telfer Wall, to Lauriston Pl and turn left past the impressive facade of **George Heriot's School (10)**, which was founded in 1628. This is the back of the building – the front was designed to face the castle and impress the inhabitants of the Grassmarket.

Finish off your walk with a stroll through **Greyfriars Kirkyard (11**; p790) and a photo opportunity beside the statue of Greyfriars Bobby. Then wander the halls of the **Museum of Scotland (12**; p790) or head for a meal at the Tower restaurant (p798).

## EDINBURGH FOR CHILDREN

The Edinburgh & Scotland Information Centre (p781) has lots of info on children's events, and the handy guidebook *Edinburgh for Under Fives* can be found in most bookshops. The *List* magazine (www.list.co.uk) has a special Kids section listing children's activities and events in and around Edinburgh. The week-long **Children's International Theatre Festival** ( ☎ 225 8050; www.imaginate.org.uk) takes place each year in late May/early June.

There are good, safe **playgrounds** in most Edinburgh parks, including Princes Street Gardens West, Inverleith Park (opposite the Royal Botanic Garden), George V Park (New Town), the Meadows and Bruntsfield Links.

Ideas for outdoor activities include exploring the **Royal Botanic Garden** (p792), going to see the animals at **Edinburgh Zoo** (p792), visiting the statue of **Greyfriars Bobby** (p790) or burning off some excess energy with **Adrian's City Cycle Tour** (right). During the Edinburgh and Fringe festivals there's lots of street theatre for kids, especially on the High St and at the foot of the Mound, and in December there's an open-air ice rink and fairground rides in Princes Street Gardens.

If it's raining, you can visit the Discovery Centre, a hands-on activity zone on Level 3

of the **Museum of Scotland** (p790), take a tour of the haunted **Real Mary King's Close** (p788) or go for tea and cakes at the **Elephant House** (p798) and tell the kids how JK Rowling used to come and write here.

## TOURS

You can check out a range of bus tours at **Edinburgh Tours** (www.edinbrightour.com) – the bus tours we list below all depart from Waverley Bridge. Alternatively, if you're up for a stroll, Edinburgh's cobbled streets offer plenty of good walking tours and if you're still feeling active consider a cycle tour.

**Adrian's City Cycle Tour** ( ☎ 07966 447206; www .edinburghcycletour.com; adult/child £15/5; ☺ tours 10am & 2.30pm) This highly recommended tour takes you on a 5-mile ride around the city; meet by the gates of Holyroodhouse, but phone ahead to ensure a place.

**Black Hart Storytellers** ( ☎ 225 9044; www.black hart.uk.com; adult/concession £8.50/6.50) Not suitable for young children. The 'City of the Dead' tour of Greyfriars Kirkyard is probably the best of Edinburgh's 'ghost' tours.

**Cadies & Witchery Tours** ( ☎ 225 6745; www .witcherytours.com; adult/child £7.50/5) The becloaked and pasty-faced Adam Lyal (deceased) leads a 'Murder & Mystery' walking tour of the Old Town's darker corners. These entertaining tours are famous for their 'jumper-ooters' – costumed actors who 'jump oot' when you least expect it.

**Edinburgh Literary Pub Tour** ( ☎ 226 6665; www .edinburghliterarypubtour.co.uk; adult/student £9/7) An enlightening two-hour trawl through Edinburgh's literary history – and its associated *howffs* (pubs) – in the entertaining company of Messrs Clart and McBrain. One of the best of Edinburgh's walking tours.

**Edinburgh Tour** ( ☎ 555 6363; adult/child £10/4) Lothian Buses' bright red buses depart every 20 minutes from Waverley Bridge.

**Mac Tours** ( ☎ 220 0770; adult/child £10/4) Offers similar tours to Edinburgh Tour, but in a vintage bus.

**Majestic Tour** ( ☎ 220 0770; adult/child £10/4) Buses run every 30 minutes (every 20 minutes in July and August) from Waverley Bridge to the Royal Yacht *Britannia* at Ocean Terminal via the Royal Botanic Garden and Newhaven, returning via Leith Walk, Holyrood and the Royal Mile.

**Mercat Tours** ( ☎ 557 6464; www.mercattours .com; adult/child £7.50/4) Mercat offers a wide range of fascinating tours including history walks in the Old Town and Leith, 'Ghosts & Ghouls' tours and visits to haunted underground vaults.

**Trainspotting Tours** ( ☎ 555 2500; www.leithwalks .co.uk; adult £8) Not just for Irvine Welsh fans as it wanders Leith with humour and history; check website for tour days. Not suitable for children.

## FESTIVALS & EVENTS

Edinburgh hosts an amazing number of festivals throughout the year, notably the Edinburgh International Festival, the Fringe Festival and the Military Tattoo, which are all held around the same time in August. Hogmanay (New Year) is also a peak party time. You can find information on all of Edinburgh's main festivals on the umbrella website www.edinburgh-festivals.com.

First held in 1947 to mark a return to peace after the ordeal of WWII, the **Edinburgh International Festival** ( ☎ 473 2099; www.eif.co.uk) is festooned with superlatives – the oldest, the most famous, the best in the world – as hundreds of the world's top musicians and performers congregate in Edinburgh for three weeks of diverse and inspirational music, opera, theatre and dance. Tickets for popular events sell out quickly, so it's best to book as far in advance as possible. You can buy tickets at the **Hub** (Map pp786-7; ☎ 473 2000; Highland Tolbooth Kirk, Castlehill; ☺ 10am-5pm Mon-Sat), or by phone, fax or internet. The festival runs for three weeks, ending on the first Saturday in September.

When the first Edinburgh Festival was held in 1947, there were eight theatre companies who didn't make it onto the main program. Undeterred, they grouped together and held their own minifestival, on the fringe, and an Edinburgh institution was born. Today the **Edinburgh Festival Fringe** (Map pp786-7; ☎ 226 0026; www.edfringe.com; Edinburgh Festival Fringe Office, 180 High St) is *the* biggest festival of the performing arts anywhere in the world. The sheer variety of shows on offer is staggering – there are daily reviews in the *Scotsman* newspaper but the best recommendation is word of mouth. There are also lots of free shows, a month of street theatre on the Royal Mile and Mound Place, and Fringe Sunday, a smorgasbord of free performances staged in the Meadows park to the south of the city centre. The Fringe takes place over 3½ weeks in August, the last two weeks overlapping with the first two of the Edinburgh International Festival.

Also in August, the hugely popular **Edinburgh Military Tattoo** is a spectacular display of marching bands, massed pipes and drums, acrobats, cheerleaders and motorcycle display teams, all played out in front of the magnificent backdrop of the floodlit castle. Contact the **Edinburgh Tattoo Office** (Map pp786-7; ☎ 225 1188; www.edintattoo.co.uk; 33 Market St) for

tickets. The 10-day **Edinburgh Jazz & Blues Festival** ( ☎ 467 5200; www.edinburghjazzfestival.co.uk) attracts the world's top musicians from trad to skat to acid, while bibliophiles crowd Charlotte Sq for the **Edinburgh Book Festival** ( ☎ 228 5444; www.edbookfest.co.uk), which also runs for two weeks.

There are also many festivals outside of August:

**Children's International Theatre Festival** ( ☎ 225 8050; www.imaginate.org.uk) Last week of May. Performing arts gala for children.

**Edinburgh International Film Festival** (Map pp786-7; ☎ 229 2550; www.edfilmfest.org.uk) Second half of June. The world's oldest film festival, a showcase for new British and European films.

**Edinburgh's Christmas** ( ☎ 529 3914; www.edinburghschristmas.com) Three weeks in December. Yuletide shindig that includes a street parade, fairground and open-air ice rink in Princes Street Gardens.

**Edinburgh's Hogmanay** ( ☎ 529 3914; www.edinburghshogmanay.com) 29 December to 1 January. New Year's celebration that includes a massive street party with live bands on Princes St.

## SLEEPING

There's plenty of accommodation in Edinburgh, but during festival times the city still fills up, so pre-booking is a must. Prices listed here do not reflect Edinburgh Festival rates, when prices increase dramatically.

### Old Town & South of the Royal Mile
#### BUDGET

**Budget Backpackers** (Map pp786-7; ☎ 226 6351; www.budgetbackpackers.com; 39 Cowgate, The Grassmarket; dm £11-14, tw £44; ☐ ) This fun spot piles on the extras, with bike storage, pool tables, laundry, breakfast (£2 extra) and colourful chill-out lounge. You'll pay a little more for four-bunk dorms, but the dorms that are larger than four-bunk rooms are great value. Only downside is that the prices increase by £2 a night on weekends, but otherwise a brilliant spot to doss.

**Castle Rock Hostel** (Map pp786-7; ☎ 225 9666; www.scotlands-top-hostels.com; 15 Johnston Tce; dm £13-15, d £40-55; ☐ ) With its bright, spacious, single-sex dorms, superb views and friendly staff, the 200-bed Castle Rock has a lot going for it. It also has a great location (the only way to get closer to the castle would be to pitch a tent on the esplanade), a games room, reading lounge and big-screen video nights.

Other recommendations:

**High Street Hostel** (Map pp786-7; ☎ 557 3984; www.scotlands-top-hostels.com; 8 Blackfriars St; dm £13-15, tw £40-55;  wi-fi) Another excellent option just off the Royal Mile, with a party reputation and plenty of facilities.

**Edinburgh Metro SYHA** (Map pp786-7;  556 8718; 11/2 Robertson's Close, Cowgate; s £21-26;  Jul & Aug) Student flats offering summer-only accommodation, all in great-value single rooms.

### MIDRANGE

Newington Rd and Bruntsfield are both good hunting grounds for B&Bs.

**Amaryllis Guest House** (Map pp782-3;  229 3293; www.amaryllisguesthouse.com; 21 Upper Gilmore Pl; s £30-40, d £50-80;  ) The Amaryllis is a cute little Georgian town house on a quiet backstreet. There are five bedrooms, including a spacious family room (£25 to £35 per person) that can take two adults and up to four kids. Princes St is only 15 minutes' walk away.

**Cluaran House** (Map pp782-3;  221 0047; www.cluaran-house-edinburgh.co.uk; 47 Leamington Tce; s from £50, d & tw from £80) Bright and arty, this restored town house is a stylish guesthouse known for its welcoming owners. Period features and wooden floorboards are kept, but the bold decoration makes this place an explosion of colour. Breakfasts are also good, particularly the vegie option.

**Greenhouse** (Map pp782-3;  622 7634; www.greenhouse-edinburgh.com; 14 Hartington Gardens; s/d from £65/70) The award-winning Greenhouse is a wholly vegetarian and vegan guesthouse, which uses organic and genetically modified–free foods as much as possible: the breakfast menu includes homemade vegie sausages, scrambled tofu, and pancakes with maple syrup. Even the soap and shampoo are free of animal products.

**Southside Guest House** (Map pp782-3;  668 4422; www.southsideguesthouse.co.uk; 8 Newington Rd; s/d from £60/88;  wi-fi) Though set in a typical Victorian terrace, the Southside transcends the traditional guesthouse category and feels more like a modern boutique hotel. Its eight stylish rooms just ooze interior design, standing out from other Newington B&Bs through the clever use of bold colours and modern furniture.

Other recommendations:

**Aonach Mor Guest House** (Map pp782-3;  667 8694; www.aonachmor.com; 14 Kilmaurs Tce; r per person £27-70;  ) Elegant Victorian house on quiet backstreet, with many original period features.

**Edinburgh City B&B** (Map pp786-7;  622 0144; www.edinburghcityguesthouse.com; 31 Grove St; d from £85;  wi-fi) Cheerful B&B only 10 minutes' walk from the castle, and 400m from Haymarket train station.

### TOP END

**Prestonfield House Hotel** (off Map pp782-3;  668 3346; www.prestonfield.com; Priestfield Rd; r £225-275;  ) If the blonde wood and brushed steel of modern boutique hotels leave you cold, then this is the place for you. A 17th-century mansion set in 20 acres of parkland (complete with peacocks and Highland cattle), Prestonfield House is draped in damask, packed with antiques and decorated in red, black and gold – look out for original tapestries, 17th-century embossed-leather panels, and £500-a-roll hand-painted wallpaper. The hotel is 2 miles southeast of the city centre.

**Witchery by the Castle** (Map pp786-7;  225 5613; www.thewitchery.com; Castlehill, Royal Mile; ste £295) Set in a 16th-century Old Town house in the shadow of Edinburgh Castle, the Witchery's seven lavish suites are extravagantly furnished with antiques, oak panelling, tapestries, open fires and roll-top baths, and supplied with flowers, chocolates and complimentary champagne. It's overwhelmingly popular – you'll have to book several months in advance to be sure of getting a room.

**Scotsman Hotel** (Map pp786-7;  556 5565; www.thescotsmanhotel.com; North Bridge; r £300-375, ste from £500;  ) The former offices of the *Scotsman* newspaper – opened in 1904 and hailed as 'the most magnificent newspaper building in the world' – are now home to this luxury hotel. Rooms on the northern side enjoy superb views over the New Town and Calton Hill, while the Penthouse Suite (£1300) has its own library and sauna. Check the website for rate discounts of up to 50%.

## New Town & Northern Edinburgh

### BUDGET

**Edinburgh Caravan Club Site** (off Map pp782-3;  312 6874; www.caravanclub.co.uk; 35 Marine Dr; sites per tent £4.80-7.60 & per person £4.60-6;  wi-fi) Five miles from the city, this caravan park is nicely positioned overlooking the Firth of Forth, and has excellent facilities. It's geared primarily to caravans, but there are plenty of tent sites. It's essential to book during summer, when no cars are allowed in the tent area. Take bus 8A from Broughton St.

 **Edinburgh Central SYHA** (off Map pp782-3;  524 2090; www.syha.org.uk; 9 Haddington Pl, Leith Walk; dm £10-25.50, s/tw from £33/49;  ) This modern purpose-built hostel, a half-mile north of Waverley train station, is a big (300 beds), flashy, five-star establishment with its own cafe-bistro as well as self-catering kitchen, smart and comfortable eight-bed dorms and private rooms, and mod cons including key-card entry and plasma-screen TVs.

**Belford Hostel** (Map pp782-3; ☎ 220 2200; www .hoppo.com; 6-8 Douglas Gardens; dm £14-18.50, tw & d £45-55; 💻) An unusual hostel housed in a con-verted church, the Belford is cheerful and well run with good facilities, though some people complain about noise – there are only thin partitions between dorms, and no ceilings. It's about 20 minutes' walk west of Waverley train station; if you're arriving by train from Glasgow or the north, get off at Haymarket station, which is much closer.

### MIDRANGE

**Dene Guest House** (Map pp782-3; ☎ 556 2700; www .deneguesthouse.com; 7 Eyre Pl; s/d from £30/60) The Dene is a friendly and informal place, set in a charm-ing Georgian town house, with a welcoming owner and spacious bedrooms; children are welcome, and inexpensive single rooms make it a bargain for solo travellers.

**Frederick House Hotel** (Map pp786-7; ☎ 226 1999; www.townhousehotels.co.uk; 42 Frederick St; s/d from £50/70; 💻 wi-fi) This well-positioned hotel is decked out in lovely interior wallpaper with roomy double beds and large baths to soak away the day's walking aches. It's also one of few op-tions in this range that has a lift, which is ideal if you've got lots of baggage.

**Ardmor House** (off Map pp782-3; ☎ 554 4944; www .ardmorhouse.com; 74 Pilrig St; s/d from £50/75) The 'gay-owned, straight-friendly' Ardmor is a stylishly renovated Victorian house with five en suite bedrooms, and all those little touches that make a place special – an open fire, thick tow-els, crisp white bed linen and free newspapers at breakfast.

**Gerald's Place** (Map pp786-7; ☎ 558 7017; www.geralds place.com; 21b Abercromby Pl; d from £89; 💻) Gerald is an unfailingly charming and helpful host, and his lovely Georgian garden flat has a great location across from a peaceful park, an easy stroll from the city centre.

**Dukes of Windsor Street** (Map pp782-3; ☎ 556 6046; www.dukesofwindsor.com; 17 Windsor St; d £90-170; 💻 wi-fi) A relaxing eight-bedroom Georgian town house set on a quiet side street, only a few paces from Princes St, Dukes offers an ap-pealing blend of modern sophistication and period atmosphere.

**our pick** **Six Mary's Place** (Map pp782-3; ☎ 332 8965; www.sixmarysplace.co.uk; 6 Mary's Pl, Raeburn Pl; s/d/f from

£45/94/150; 💻 wi-fi) Six Mary's Place is an attrac-tive Georgian town house with a designer mix of period features, contemporary furniture and modern colours. Breakfasts are vegetar-ian-only, served in an attractive conservatory with a view of the garden, while the lounge, with its big, comfy sofas, offers free coffee and newspapers.

Other recommendations:

**Balmoral Guest House** (off Map pp782-3; ☎ 554 1857; www.balmoralguesthouse.co.uk; 32 Pilrig St; d £50-80) A homely spot with the owner's passion for old radios displayed throughout; communal breakfast table is ideal for meeting other travellers.

**Terrace Hotel** (Map pp786-7; ☎ 556 3423; www .terracehotel.co.uk; 37 Royal Tce; s/d from £45/70) Suits independent travellers, with a large front room and older shared bathrooms.

### TOP END

**Malmaison** (off Map pp782-3; ☎ 468 5000; www.mal maison.com; 1 Tower Pl, Leith; d/ste from £150/240; P 💻) This ultrahip hotel overlooks the waters of Leith in the nicest part of the old port. Rooms are perfect for a romantic weekend, with beds built for sin, CD players, great bathrooms and plenty of contemporary flair.

**Glasshouse** (Map pp786-7; ☎ 525 8200; www.the etoncollection.com; 2 Greenside Pl; d/ste £295/450; P) A palace of cutting-edge design perched atop the Omni Centre at the foot of Calton Hill, and entered through the preserved facade of a 19th-century church, the Glasshouse sports luxury rooms with floor-to-ceiling windows, leather sofas, marble bathrooms and a rooftop garden.

## EATING

There are good-value restaurants scattered all around the city. For cheap eats, the best areas are where the student population is high – especially near the university around Nicolson St – but you can also take advantage of the fact that most Edinburgh restaurants offer a very cheap set menu at lunchtime. Two of the best zones for evening dining are Stockbridge and around the Shore in Leith.

## Old Town & South of the Royal Mile
### BUDGET

**Forest** (Map pp786-7; ☎ 220 4538; www.theforest.org .uk; 2 Bristo Pl; mains £3-5; ☯ noon-11pm; 💻 wi-fi) A chilled-out and comfortably scuffed-around-the-edges antidote to squeaky-clean style bars, this volunteer-run, not-for-profit art space and cafe serves up humongous helpings of hearty vegetarian and vegan fodder, ranging from burritos to falafel burgers. Dreadlocked zippies bring in their laptops and make a soy chai last as long as it takes to use the wi-fi.

**Elephant House** (Map pp786-7; ☎ 220 5355; www .elephanthouse.biz; 21 George IV Bridge; snacks £3-6; ⏰ 8am-11pm; ▣ ) Brilliant cafe that does baguettes, pastries and coffees powerful enough to inspire JK Rowling to pen *Harry Potter* (she used to sit and write in the back room, with a view of Edinburgh Castle).

**Engine Shed** (Map pp782-3; ☎ 662 0040; www.engine shed.org.uk; 19 St Leonard's Lane; lunches £3-6; ⏰ 10am-3.30pm Mon-Sat) This vegetarian cafe is an ideal spot for a cuppa and a bakery-fresh scone after climbing Arthur's Seat. It's been set up to help special-needs adults and as well as having its own bakery it also makes its own tofu, which is used plentifully through curries.

**our pick** **Monster Mash** (Map pp786-7; ☎ 225 7069; www.monstermashcafe.co.uk; 4a Forrest Rd; mains £5-7; ⏰ 8am-10pm Mon-Fri, 9am-10pm Sat, 10am-10pm Sun) Classic British grub of the 1950s – bangers and mash, shepherd's pie, fish and chips – is the mainstay of the menu at this nostalgia-fuelled cafe. But there's a twist – the food is all top-quality nosh freshly prepared from local produce, including Crombie's gourmet sausages. And there's even a wine list!

### MIDRANGE

**Outsider** (Map pp786-7; ☎ 226 3131; 15 George IV Bridge; mains £8-12; ⏰ noon-11pm) This Edinburgh stalwart is known for its rainforest interior (potted ferns in atmospheric dimness) and has a brilliant menu that jumps straight in with mains such as chorizo and chickpea casserole. The Sunday brunch features DJs and hangover-busting breakfasts.

**David Bann** (Map pp786-7; ☎ 556 5888; www.david bann.com; 56-58 St Mary's St; mains £8-12; ⏰ 11am-10pm Sun-Thu, 11am-10.30pm Fri & Sat) On a one-man mission to convince the world that vegetarian food doesn't have to mean alfalfa and tofu, Bann has been thrilling locals with his sophisticated vegetarian cuisine for years. The Thai fritters are flavoured with ginger, lime, green chilli and sesame, while the tart of braised fennel, spinach and goats'-cheese curd is guaranteed to win converts.

**Apartment** (Map pp782-3; ☎ 228 6456; 7-13 Barclay Pl; mains £8-12; ⏰ dinner, lunch Sat & Sun) Whether it's in the decor or the menu, simple yet modish is the order of the day at this eatery. Dishes are divided into 'things': succulent fish things such as the baked sea bass papillote with king prawns and pepped up with chilli and lime is our favourite. The introduction of inventive kebab-like lines such as roasted vegetable and goats cheese are both healthy and popular.

**Pancho Villa's** (Map pp786-7; ☎ 557 4416; www .panchovillas.co.uk; 240 Canongate, Royal Mile; mains £11-13; ⏰ noon-11pm Mon-Sat, 5-11pm Sun) With home-made salsa and guacamole, plenty of Latin American staff, and bright colours inspired by the owner's home town of Valle de Bravo, it's not surprising that Pancho's is one of the most authentic-feeling Mexican restaurants in town.

Other recommendations:

**Khushi's** (Map pp786-7; ☎ 220 0057; 9 Victoria St; mains £9-13; ⏰ noon-11pm Mon-Sat, noon-10pm Sun) An Edinburgh institution – speciality is basic Punjabi dishes cooked in the traditional way, with several good vegetarian dishes. Bring your own bottle.

**Petit Paris** (Map pp786-7; ☎ 226 2442; www .petitparis-restaurant.co.uk; 38-40 Grassmarket; mains £13-16; ⏰ noon-3pm & 5.30-10.30pm, closed Sun Oct-Mar) A little piece of Paris, complete with checked tablecloths, friendly waiters and good-value grub. Lunch deal offers the plat du jour and a coffee for £7.

### TOP END

**Amber** (Map pp786-7; ☎ 477 8477; 354 Castlehill; mains £12-18; ⏰ noon-3.45pm, 7-9pm Tue-Sat) Located in the Scotch Whisky Heritage Centre, this whisky-themed restaurant manages to avoid the tourist clichés and create genuinely interesting and flavoursome dishes such as fillet of pork with whisky and apple chutney, or vegetarian haggis in filo pastry with whisky cream sauce.

**Tower** (Map pp786-7; ☎ 225 3003; Chambers St; mains £16-25; ⏰ noon-11pm) Decked out in black leather, purple suede and brushed steel, and perched atop the Museum of Scotland building, this sleek, chic restaurant has played host to countless celebrities, from Joanna Lumley to Catherine Zeta-Jones. Grand views of the castle are accompanied by a menu of top-quality Scottish produce, simply prepared – try half a dozen Scottish oysters followed by a chargrilled Aberdeen Angus fillet steak.

## New Town & Northern Edinburgh
### BUDGET

**our pick** **Urban Angel** (Map pp786-7; ☎ 225 6215; www .urban-angel.co.uk; 121 Hanover St; snacks £3-7, mains £8-11; ⏰ 10am-10pm Mon-Thu, 10am-11pm Fri & Sat, 10am-5pm Sun) A wholesome deli that puts the emphasis on fair-trade, organic and locally sourced produce, Urban Angel also has a delightfully informal cafe-bistro that serves all-day brunch (porridge with honey, French toast, eggs Benedict), tapas and a wide range of light, snacky meals including an original and unusual Scottish combination of smoked salmon and tattie scone.

**L'Alba D'Oro** (Map pp782-3; ☎ 557 2580; www .lalbadoro.com; 5-7 Henderson Row; fish supper £6-7; ☯ 5-11pm) Pronouncing any place as Edinburgh's best chippie is always contentious, but with a busy knot of cars waiting for a parking space outside, this place gets the nod from many locals. It's more than a chippie though; you wouldn't expect a 300-plus wine list at your average deep-fryer, nor could you get zesty prawn suppers or vegie haggis.

Other recommendations:

**Henderson's** (Map pp786-7; ☎ 225 2131; www .hendersonsofedinburgh.co.uk; 94 Hanover St; mains £5-8; ☯ 8am-10.45pm Mon-Sat) The grandmother of Edinburgh's vegetarian restaurants, with cafeteria serving mostly organic food; special dietary requirements can be catered for.

**Blue Moon Cafe** (Map pp782-3; ☎ 557 0911; 36 Broughton St; mains £6-8; ☯ 11am-10pm Mon-Fri, 10am-10pm Sat & Sun) Focus of Broughton St's gay social life; serves sensational burgers and weekend all-day breakfasts.

### MIDRANGE

**Circle Cafe** (Map pp782-3 ☎ 624 4666; 1 Brandon Tce; mains £6-10; ☯ 8.30am-5pm Mon-Sat, 9am-4.30pm Sun) A great place for breakfast or a good-value lunch, Circle is a bustling neighbourhood cafe serving great coffee and cakes, and fresh, tasty lunch dishes ranging from chunky, home-baked quiches to prawn and chilli salad.

**VinCaffe** (Map pp786-7; ☎ 557 0088; 11 Multrees Walk, St Andrew Sq; mains £9-18; ☯ 10am-late Mon-Sat, 11am-5.30pm Sun) Foodie colours dominate the decor at this delightful Italian bistro – bottle-green pillars and banquettes, chocolate-and-cream-coloured walls, espresso-black tables – a perfect backdrop for VinCaffe's superb antipasto (£18 for two), washed down with a bottle of pink Pinot grigio. Live jazz from 7pm on Wednesdays.

**Fishers** (off Map pp782-3; ☎ 554 5666; 1 The Shore, Leith; mains £9-22; ☯ noon-10.30pm) This cosy little bar-turned-restaurant, tucked beneath a 17th-century signal tower, is one of the city's best seafood places. Fishers' fish cakes are an Edinburgh institution, and the rest of the

handwritten menu (you might need a calligrapher to decipher it) rarely disappoints. Booking is recommended.

**Howie's** (Map pp786-7; ☎ 556 5766; 29 Waterloo Pl; mains £10-15; ☯ lunch & dinner) A bright and airy Georgian corner-house provides the elegant setting for this, the most central of Howie's four hugely popular Edinburgh restaurants. Its recipe for success includes fresh Scottish produce, good-value, fixed-price menus, and eminently quaffable house wines for around £12 a bottle.

**Stac Polly** (Map pp786-7; ☎ 556 2231; www.stacpolly .co.uk; 29-33 Dublin St; mains £18-20; ☯ lunch Mon-Fri, dinner) Named after a mountain in northwestern Scotland, Stac Polly's kitchen adds sophisticated twists to fresh Highland produce. Dishes such as loin of venison with redcurrant and rosemary jus keep the punters coming back for more.

### TOP END

**our pick** **Kitchin** (off Map pp782-3; ☎ 555 1755; www .thekitchin.com; 78 Commercial Quay; ☯ noon-2.30pm Tue-Sat, 7.30-10pm Tue-Thu, 6.45-10.30pm Fri & Sat) Fresh, seasonal Scottish produce, locally sourced, is the philosophy that has won a Michelin star for this elegant but unpretentious restaurant. The menu moves with the seasons, of course, so expect fresh salads in summer and game in winter, and shellfish dishes such as seared scallops with endive tarte tatin when there's an 'r' in the month.

## DRINKING

Edinburgh has more than 700 bars, which are as varied as the population – everything from Victorian palaces to rough-and-ready drinking dens, and from bearded, real-ale *howffs* to trendy cocktail bars.

### Old Town & South of the Royal Mile

**Jolly Judge** (Map pp786-7; ☎ 225 2669; 7a James Court) Tucked away down an Old Town close, the Judge exudes a cosy 17th-century ambience with its low, timber-beamed, painted ceilings and numerous nooks and crannies. The convivial atmosphere is undisturbed by TV, music or gambling machines, and has the added attraction of a log fire in cold weather.

**Cloisters** (Map pp786-7; ☎ 221 9997; 26 Brougham St; ☯ noon-midnight) Housed in a converted manse (minister's house) that once belonged to the next-door church, and furnished with well-worn, mismatched wooden tables and chairs, Cloisters now ministers to a mixed

**EDINBURGH**

congregation of students, locals and real-ale connoisseurs. It has decent grub and coffee, and a nice warm fireplace in winter.

**Pear Tree House** (Map pp786-7; ☎ 667 7533; 38 West Nicolson St) The Pear Tree is another student favourite, with comfy sofas and board games inside, plus the city centre's biggest beer garden outside. There's a Monday-night quiz and live music in the garden on Sunday afternoons in summer.

**Ecco Vino** (Map pp786-7; ☎ 225 1441; 19 Cockburn St) With outdoor tables on sunny afternoons, and cosy candlelit intimacy in the evenings, this comfortably cramped Tuscan-style wine bar offers a tempting range of Italian wines, though only a few are available by the glass – best to share a bottle.

Other recommendations:

**Centraal** (Map pp786-7; ☎ 667 7355; 32 West Nicolson St) A downstairs studenty lounge with cool tunes and comfy sofas.

**Human Be-in** (Map pp786-7; ☎ 662 8860; 2-8 West Crosscauseway) Popular with a well-to-do university crowd, this place has an excellent wine list.

**Traverse Bar Cafe** (Map pp786-7; ☎ 228 5383; 10 Cambridge St) Bustling pre- and post-theatre bar in Edinburgh's top drama venue, the Traverse Theatre.

## New Town & Northern Edinburgh

**Kay's Bar** (Map pp786-7; ☎ 225 1858; 39 Jamaica St West) Tired of pubs where the TV's always blaring in the background? This former wine merchant's office (walls are decorated with old wine barrels) is a cosy little place whose rustic ambience is designed not to get in the way of sampling real ales and malt whiskies.

**Amicus Apple** (Map pp786-7; ☎ 226 6055; 15 Frederick St) Cream leather sofas and dark-brown armchairs, bold design and funky lighting make this laid-back cocktail lounge the hippest hang-out in the New Town. The drinks menu ranges from retro classics such as Bloody Mary and mojito, to their own concoctions including the Amicus Buck (bourbon, orange and pineapple juice, ginger beer and a splash of lime).

**Star Bar** (Map pp786-7; ☎ 539 8070; 1 Northumberland Pl) Hard to find but worth the pilgrimage for

---

### TOP FIVE TRADITIONAL PUBS

Edinburgh is blessed with a large number of traditional 19th- and early-20th-century pubs, which have preserved much of their original Victorian or Edwardian decoration and serve cask-conditioned real ales and a staggering range of malt whiskies.

**Athletic Arms** (Diggers; Map pp782-3; ☎ 337 3822; 1-3 Angle Park Tce) Named after the cemetery across the street – the gravediggers used to nip in and slake their thirst after a hard day's interring – the Diggers dates from the 1890s. It's still staunchly traditional – the decor has barely changed in 100 years – and has recently revived its reputation as a real-ale drinker's mecca by serving locally brewed Diggers' 80-shilling ale. Packed to the gills with football and rugby fans on match days.

**Abbotsford** (Map pp786-7; ☎ 225 5276; 3 Rose St) One of the few pubs in Rose St that has retained its Edwardian splendour, the Abbotsford has long been a hang-out for writers, actors, journalists and media people, and has many loyal regulars. Dating from 1902, and named after Sir Walter Scott's country house, the pub's centrepiece is a splendid, mahogany island bar. Good selection of Scottish and English real ales.

**Bennet's Bar** (Map pp782-3; ☎ 229 5143; 8 Leven St) Situated beside the King's Theatre, Bennet's has managed to hang onto almost all of its beautiful Victorian fittings, from the leaded, stained-glass windows and ornate mirrors to the wooden gantry and the brass water taps on the bar (for your whisky – there are over 100 malts to choose from).

**Cafe Royal Circle Bar** (Map pp786-7; ☎ 556 1884; 17 West Register St) Perhaps the classic Edinburgh bar, the Cafe Royal's main claims to fame are its magnificent oval bar and the series of Doulton tile portraits of famous Victorian inventors. Check out the bottles on the gantry – staff line them up to look like there's a mirror there, and many a drink-befuddled customer has been seen squinting and wondering why he can't see his reflection.

**Sheep Heid** (off Map pp782-3; ☎ 656 6951; 43-45 The Causeway, Duddingston) Possibly the oldest inn in Edinburgh – with a licence dating back to 1360 – the Sheep Heid feels more like a country pub than an Edinburgh bar. Set in the semi-rural shadow of Arthur's Seat, it's famous for its 19th-century skittles alley and the lovely little beer garden.

one of the New Town's best jukeboxes and pleasant beer garden out the back. Oddly, Thursday night attracts a backgammon championship and there's an ingeniously decorated football table. Don't ask about the skull, which many believe has claimed the lives of those who touch it.

**Barony Bar** (Map pp782-3; ☎ 557 0546; 81 Broughton St) Pulling off the trick of being simultaneously traditional and hip, this boozer works miracles with real ales and on-tap lagers. Worn tables, a jovial crowd and warming fires mean that this pub remains a firm favourite, especially for reading the Sunday papers.

**Oxford Bar** (Map pp786-7; ☎ 539 7119; 8 Young St) The Oxford is that rarest of things these days, a real pub for real people, with no 'theme', no music, no frills and no pretensions. 'The Ox' has been immortalised by Ian Rankin, author of the Inspector Rebus novels, who is a regular here, as is his fictional detective.

**Cumberland Bar** (Map pp782-3; ☎ 558 3134; 1 Cumberland St) The Cumberland has an authentic, traditional wood-brass-and-mirrors look (despite it being relatively modern), and it serves well-looked-after, cask-conditioned ales as well as a wide range of malt whiskies. There's also a pleasant little beer garden outside.

Other recommendations:

**Antiquary** (Map pp782-3; ☎ 225 2858; 72 St Stephen St) Trad pub with bare wooden floorboards and dark-wood tables and lively folk-music sessions.

**Port o'Leith** (off Map pp782-3; ☎ 554 3568; 58 Constitution St, Leith) Classic Leith boozer that harks back to the district's nautical heritage.

**Tigerlily** (Map pp786-7; ☎ 225 5005; 125 George St) Sharp suits and stiletto heels line the banquettes at this award-winning designer bar in a boutique hotel.

**Waterfront** (off Map pp782-3; ☎ 554 7427; 1c Dock Pl, Leith) Dimly lit and atmospheric Leith wine bar with conservatory and outdoor terrace.

## ENTERTAINMENT

Edinburgh has a number of fine theatres and concert halls, and there are independent art-house cinemas as well as mainstream movie theatres. Many pubs offer entertainment ranging from live Scottish folk music to pop, rock and jazz as well as karaoke and quiz nights, while a range of stylish modern bars purvey house, dance and hip hop to the preclubbing crowd.

The comprehensive source for what's-on info is the *List* (£2.20; www.list.co.uk), an excellent listings magazine covering both Edinburgh and Glasgow. It's available from most newsagents, and is published fortnightly on a Thursday.

### Cinemas

**Cameo** (Map pp786-7; ☎ 228 4141; 38 Home St; tickets £6.50) Good, old-fashioned cinema showing art-house and mainstream films.

**Filmhouse** (Map pp786-7; ☎ 228 2688; 88 Lothian Rd; tickets £6.30) Shows art-house, classic and foreign films, and hosts the Edinburgh International Film Festival (p795).

### Live Music

Check out the *List* and the *Gig Guide* (www.gigguide.co.uk), a free leaflet available in bars and music venues, to see who's playing where.

**Bannerman's** (Map pp786-7; ☎ 556 3254; www .bannermansgigs.co.uk; 212 Cowgate) Tucked in a cellar below the Royal Mile, this atmospheric boozer has live music nearly every night, usually unsigned local rockers.

**Royal Oak** (Map pp786-7; ☎ 557 2976; www.royal -oak-folk.com; 1 Infirmary St) The folk-music flagship of Edinburgh, this is a popular gathering place for folk musicians most nights of the week – you're guaranteed a gig on Sundays from 8.30pm when the Wee Folk Club plays (admission £3).

**Queen's Hall** (Map pp782-3; ☎ 668 2019; www .thequeenshall.net; Clerk St; tickets £10-25; ☑ box office 10am-5.30pm) Home to the Scottish Chamber Orchestra, this venue also hosts jazz concerts, tribute bands and a whole range of other events.

Other recommendations:

**Henry's Cellar Bar** (Map pp786-7; ☎ 538 7385; www .myspace.com/henrysvenue; 8 Morrison St; ☑ Tue-Sun until 3am) One of Edinburgh's best live-music venues, Henry's has something going on every night of the week, from rock and indie to jazz and blues, funk to hip hop to hardcore.

**Liquid Room** (Map pp786-7; ☎ 225 2564; www .liquidroom.com; 9c Victoria St; ☑ Tue-Sun) All kinds of gigs from local rock bands to tribute bands to the Average White Band. Check the program on the website.

**Whistlebinkies** (Map pp786-7; ☎ 557 5114; 4 South Bridge) This late-night drinking den has live music nightly and Monday night open-mic jams.

### Nightclubs

Edinburgh club nights range from ice-cold cool to kitschy fun. Cover charges range from £5 to £15 and most venues stay open until 3am.

## GAY & LESBIAN EDINBURGH

Edinburgh's dynamic gay scene is concentrated on the 'pink triangle' around Greenside Pl and upper Broughton St. Venues here are both gay- and lesbian-friendly. The Blue Moon Cafe (see p799) is a quieter meeting spot, where you can browse the informative *Scotsgay* magazine (www .scotsgay.co.uk).

**CC Blooms** (Map pp786-7; ☎ 556 9331; 23 Greenside Pl; ⓨ 10.30pm-3am) is a raddled old queen of the Edinburgh gay scene. CC's offers two floors of deafening dance and disco. It's a bit overpriced and overcrowded but worth a visit – go early, or sample the wild karaoke on Thursday and Sunday nights.

**Regent** (Map pp782-3; ☎ 661 8198; 2 Montrose Tce) is a pleasant, gay local with a relaxed atmosphere (no loud music), serving coffee and croissants as well as excellent real ales, including Deuchars IPA and Caledonian 80/-. Meeting place for the Lesbian and Gay Real Ale Drinkers club (first Monday of month, 9pm).

**Claremont Bar** (off Map pp782-3 ; ☎ 556 5662; 133-135 East Claremont St) Scotland's only sci-fi theme pub (no, you have to see it), Claremont is a friendly, gay-owned bar and restaurant. Saturday nights are men-only nights, when leather, kilts, skinheads and bears are the order of the evening. It's half a mile north of Princes St.

**Bongo Club** (Map pp786-7; ☎ 558 7604; www.the bongoclub.co.uk; Moray House, Paterson's Land, 37 Holyrood Rd) The weird and wonderful Bongo Club is famous for its long-running hip hop, funk and breakbeat club night Headspin (admission £6 to £8, first or second Saturday of the month from 11pm). Also worth checking out is the booming bass of roots and dub reggae night, Messenger Sound System (admission £8, held third Saturday of the month from 11pm). The club is open as a cafe and exhibition space during the day.

**Cabaret Voltaire** (Map pp786-7; ☎ 220 6176; www .thecabaretvoltaire.com; 36 Blair St) An atmospheric warren of stone-lined vaults houses Edinburgh's most 'alternative' club, which eschews huge dance floors and egotistical DJ-worship in favour of a 'creative crucible' hosting an eclectic mix of DJs, live acts, comedy, theatre, visual arts and the spoken word. Well worth a look.

**Studio 24** (Map pp782-3; ☎ 558 3758; www.studio24 edinburgh.co.uk; 24 Calton Rd) Studio 24 is the dark heart of Edinburgh's underground music scene, with a program that covers all bases, from house to nu metal via punk, ska, reggae, crossover, tribal, electro, techno and dance. Retribution is the city's classic rock, metal and alt night (with Sanctuary, an alcohol-free club for 14- to 18-year-olds, running 6pm to 10pm the same evening).

Other recommendations:

**Ego** (Map pp786-7; ☎ 478 7434; www.clubego.co.uk; 14 Picardy Pl) Gay-friendly Ego dishes up everything from the dance classics of Fever (second Saturday of the month) to the hard house and trance of Nuklear Puppy.

**Caves** (Map pp786-7; ☎ 557 8989; www.thecaves .eu; 8-12 Niddry St South) A spectacular subterranean club venue set in the ancient stone vaults beneath the South Bridge – check the *List* (www.list.co.uk) for upcoming events.

## Sport

Edinburgh is home to two rival football teams playing in the Scottish Premier League: **Hibernian** (Map pp782-3; ☎ 661 2159; www.hibs.co.uk; Easter Rd Stadium, Albion Pl), known as Hibs or the Hibees, and **Heart of Midlothian** (Map pp782-3; ☎ 200 7201; www.heartsfc.co.uk; Tynecastle Stadium, Gorgie Rd), nicknamed Hearts or the Jambos (from rhyming slang, Jam Tarts).

Each year, from January to March, Scotland's national rugby team takes part in the Six Nations Rugby Union Championship. The most important fixture is the clash against England for the Calcutta Cup. At club level the season runs from September to May. **Murrayfield Stadium** (off Map pp782-3; ☎ 346 5000; www.scottishrugby.org; 112 Roseburn St), about 1.5 miles west of the city centre, is the venue for international matches.

## Theatre & Comedy

The cost of theatre tickets is in the £10 to £30 range – check out the *List* for what's on.

**Edinburgh Festival Theatre** (Map pp786-7; ☎ 529 6000; www.eft.co.uk; 13-29 Nicolson St) From ballet to popular musicals.

**Royal Lyceum Theatre** (Map pp786-7; ☎ 248 4848; www.lyceum.org.uk; 30 Grindlay St) High-quality drama, concerts and ballet.

**Stand** (Map pp786-7; ☎ 558 7272; www.thestand
.co.uk; 5 York Pl) Atmospheric comedy venue with shows
every night.

**Traverse Theatre** (Map pp786-7; ☎ 228 1404; www
.traverse.co.uk; 10 Cambridge St) Top-class venue staging
an exciting program of drama and dance.

## SHOPPING

Princes St is Edinburgh's principal shopping
street, lined with all the big high-street stores,
with many smaller shops along pedestrianised Rose St, and more-expensive designer
boutiques on George St. There are also two big
shopping centres in the New Town – **Princes
Mall**, at the eastern end of Princes St, and the
nearby **St James Centre** at the top of Leith St –
plus the designer shopping complex **Multrees
Walk** with its flagship Harvey Nichols store on
the eastern side of St Andrew Sq. The huge
**Ocean Terminal** in Leith is the biggest shopping
centre in the city.

For more-offbeat shopping – including
fashion, music, crafts, gifts and jewellery –
head for the cobbled lanes of Cockburn,
Victoria and St Mary's Sts, all near the
Royal Mile in the Old Town, William St in
the western part of the New Town, and the
Stockbridge district, immediately north of
the New Town.

### Cashmere & Wool

Woollen textiles and knitwear are one of
Scotland's classic exports. Scottish cashmere –
a fine, soft wool from young goats and lambs –
provides the most luxurious and expensive
knitwear and has been seen gracing the tor-
sos of pop star Robbie Williams and England
footballer David Beckham.

**Joyce Forsyth Designer Knitwear** (Map pp786-7;
☎ 220 4112; 42 Candlemaker Row; ⊗ closed Sun & Mon)
The colourful designs here will drag your ideas
about woollens firmly into the 21st century.

**Designs On Cashmere** (Map pp786-7; ☎ 556 6394;
28 High St) and the **Cashmere Store** (Map pp786-7;
☎ 226 1577; 2 St Giles St) are good places to
start, with a wide range of traditional and
modern knitwear.

### Clothing

There are dozens of shops along the Royal
Mile and Princes St where you can buy kilts
and tartan goods.

**Armstrong's** (Map pp786-7; ☎ 220 5557; 83 The
Grassmarket) You'll find an excellent selection
of secondhand retro/vintage clothing here.

**Geoffrey (Tailor) Inc** (Map pp786-7; ☎ 557 0256;
57-59 High St) This place can fit you out in traditional Highland dress, or run up a kilt in your
own clan tartan. Its offshoot, 21st Century
Kilts, offers modern fashion kilts in a variety
of fabrics.

**Joey D** (Map pp782-3; ☎ 557 6672; www.joey-d.co
.uk; 54 Broughton St) This hip Edinburgh designer
does mash-ups of clothing, grafting a panel
from a tweed jacket to an army uniform – all
very punk.

### Department Stores

**Jenners** (Map pp786-7; ☎ 225 2442; 48 Princes St) Founded
in 1838, Jenners is the *grande dame* of Scottish
department stores; it stocks a wide range of
quality goods, both classic and contemporary.

**Harvey Nichols** (Map pp786-7; ☎ 524 8388; 30-34 St
Andrew Sq) The jewel in the crown of Edinburgh's
shopping scene has four floors of designer
labels and eye-popping price tags.

### Other Shops

**Royal Mile Whiskies** (Map pp786-7; ☎ 225 3383; www.royal
milewhiskies.com; 379 High St) Although packed with
tourists, this shop has a great selection, and
you can also buy online from anywhere in
the world.

**Fopp** (Map pp786-7; ☎ 220 0130; 7 Rose St) A good
place to hunt for cheap CDs and vinyl, and
the friendly staff really know what they're
talking about.

**Avalanche Records** (Map pp786-7; ☎ 225 3939;
www.avalancherecords.co.uk; 63 Cockburn St) This indie
record store specialises in used, vinyl and
hard-to-find.

## GETTING THERE & AWAY
### Air

**Edinburgh airport** (off Map pp782-3; ☎ 333 1000; www
.edinburghairport.com), 8 miles west of Edinburgh, has
flights to many parts of the UK, Ireland and
continental Europe. The main airlines serv-
ing the city are **British Airways** ( ☎ 084 493 0787; www
.ba.com), **bmi baby** ( ☎ 0870 60 70 555; www.bmibaby.com)
and **easyJet** ( ☎ 0870 600 0000; www.easyjet.com), with
direct flights from London, Bristol, Birmingham,
Manchester, Belfast and Cardiff. British
Airways and their subsidiaries offer flights
to many other Scottish destinations such as
Shetland, Inverness, Stornoway and Orkney.

### Bus

**Edinburgh Bus Station** (Map pp786–7) is at
the northeast corner of St Andrew Sq, with

pedestrian entrances from the square and from Elder St. For timetable information, call **Traveline** ( ☎ 0871 200 22 33; www.traveline.org .uk). There are frequent daily links to/from many cities in England and Wales, with fares from London particularly competitive; always check the company websites for the cheapest fares.

**National Express** ( ☎ 08717 818181; www.national express.com) runs to London (from £34, nine hours, three daily). There are also services to Newcastle (£17, 2¾ hours, three to five daily) and York (£34, 5¾ hours, one daily).

**Scottish Citylink** ( ☎ 08705 505050; www.citylink.co.uk) buses connect Edinburgh with all of Scotland's major cities and towns, including Aberdeen (£24, 3¼ hours, hourly); Dundee (£13, 1¾ hours, every 30 minutes); Fort William (£24, four hours, three daily); Glasgow (£6, 1¼ hours, four an hour); Inverness (£10, four hours, hourly); Portree (£32, eight hours, two daily); and Stirling (£6, one hour, hourly).

**Stagecoach** ( ☎ 01698 870 768; www.stagecoachbus .com) runs the Motorvator bus to Glasgow (£6, 1¼ hours, every 20 minutes Monday to Saturday, hourly Sunday).

Another budget operator is **Megabus** ( ☎ 0900 160 0900; www.megabus.com), which has cheap bus fares (from as little as £2) from Edinburgh to Aberdeen, Dundee, Glasgow, Inverness and Perth.

## Car & Motorcycle

Arriving in or leaving Edinburgh by car during the morning and evening rush hours (7.30am to 9.30am and 4.30pm to 6.30pm Monday to Friday) is an experience you can live without. Try to time your journey to avoid these periods. In particular, there can be huge tailbacks on the A90 between Edinburgh and the Forth Rd Bridge.

## Train

The main train station in Edinburgh is **Waverley station** (Map pp786–7), in the heart of the city. Trains arriving from, and departing for, the west also stop at **Haymarket station** (Map pp782–3), which is more convenient for the West End. You can buy tickets, make reservations and get travel information at the **Edinburgh Rail Travel Centre** ( ⌚ 4.45am-12.30am Mon-Sat, 7am-12.30am Sun) in Waverley station. For fare and timetable information, phone the **National Rail Enquiry Service** ( ☎ 08457 48 49 50; www.nationalrail.co.uk).

**First ScotRail** ( ☎ 08457 55 00 33; www.firstscotrail .com) operates a regular shuttle service between Edinburgh and Glasgow (£11, 50 minutes, every 15 to 30 minutes), and frequent daily services to all Scottish cities including Aberdeen (£38, 2½ hours), Dundee (£19, 1½ hours) and Inverness (£38, 3¼ hours).

**National Express East Coast** ( ☎ 08457 225 333; www .nationalexpresseastcoast.com) operates the Edinburgh to London Kings Cross route (£126, 4½ hours, at least hourly), calling at Newcastle (£42, 1½ hours) and York (£72, 2½ hours).

# GETTING AROUND
## To/From the Airport

The Lothian Buses **Airlink** (www.flybybus.com) service 100 runs from Waverley Bridge, just outside the train station, to the airport (one way/return £3/5, 30 minutes, every 10 to 15 minutes) via the West End and Haymarket.

**Edinburgh Shuttle Minibus** ( ☎ 0845 500 5000; www .edinburghshuttle.com; one way £9 per person) will drop you off at the door of your hotel (or any other address in central Edinburgh).

An airport taxi to the city centre costs around £15 and takes about 20 minutes. Both buses and taxis depart from outside the arrivals hall; go out through the main doors and turn left.

## Bicycle

Thanks to the efforts of local cycling campaign group Spokes and a bike-friendly city council, Edinburgh is well equipped with bike lanes and dedicated cycle tracks. You can buy a map of the city's cycle routes from most bike shops.

**Biketrax** (Map pp782–3; ☎ 228 6633; www.biketrax .co.uk; 11 Lochrin Pl; ⌚ 9.30am-6pm Mon-Fri, to 5.30pm Sat, noon-5pm Sun) rents out a wide range of cycles and equipment, including kids' bikes, tandems, pannier bags, child seats – even unicycles! A mountain bike costs £16 for 24 hours, £12 per extra day, and £70 for one week. You'll need a £100 cash or credit-card deposit and some form of ID.

## Car & Motorcycle

Most of the big national operators have offices in town or at the airport, but there's also **Arnold Clark** (Map pp786–7; ☎ 0845 607 4500; 13 Lochrin Pl; rental per day/week from £22/90), a reasonably priced local outfit.

Driving in Edinburgh is complicated by restricted access on Princes St, George St and

Charlotte Sq, with many one-way streets and limited parking. There are large, long-stay car parks at the St James Centre, Greenside Pl, New St, Castle Tce and Morrison St. Motorcycles can be parked free at designated areas in the city centre.

Expect traffic disruption along Corstorphine Rd, Princes St and Leith Walk as work continues on building a tram network that is scheduled to begin operation in 2011.

### Public Transport

The two main bus operators are **Lothian Buses** (☎ 554 4494; www.lothianbuses.co.uk) and **First Edinburgh** (☎ 08708 72 72 71; www.firstedinburgh.co.uk). Buy your ticket as you board buses – on Lothian services you need the exact change. Single fares are £1.10, and a Day Saver ticket (£2.50) covers a whole day's travel. After midnight there are special night buses (£2.50). The free *Edinburgh Travelmap* shows bus routes around the city and is available from the tourist office, or contact **Traveline** (☎ 0871 200 22 33; www.traveline scotland.com).

### Taxi

There are numerous central taxi ranks; a typical 2-mile trip across the city centre will cost around £6. Local companies:

**Central Taxis** (☎ 229 2468; www.taxis-edinburgh .co.uk)
**City Cabs** (☎ 228 1211; www.citycabs.co.uk)
**ComCab** (☎ 272 8000)

# AROUND EDINBURGH

## QUEENSFERRY & INCHCOLM

Queensferry is located at the narrowest part of the Firth of Forth, where ferries have crossed to Fife from the earliest times. The village takes its name from Queen Margaret (1046–93), who gave pilgrims free passage across the firth on their way to St Andrews. Ferries continued to operate until 1964 when the graceful **Forth Road Bridge** – now Europe's fifth longest – was opened.

Pre-dating the road bridge by 74 years, the magnificent **Forth Bridge** – only outsiders ever call it the Forth Rail Bridge – is one of the finest engineering achievements of the 19th century. Completed in 1890 after seven years' work, its three huge cantilevers span 1447m and took 59,000 tonnes of steel, eight million rivets and the lives of 58 men to build.

The island of Inchcolm lies east of the Forth bridges, less than a mile off the coast of Fife. Only 800m long, it is home to the ruins of **Inchcolm Abbey** (HS; ☎ 01383-823332; Inchcolm, Fife; adult/child £4.70/2.25; 9.30am-5.30pm Apr-Sep), one of Scotland's best-preserved medieval abbeys, founded by Augustinian priors in 1123.

The ferry boat **Maid of the Forth** (☎ 0131-331 5000; www.maidoftheforth.co.uk) sails to Inchcolm from Hawes Pier in Queensferry. There are one to four sailings most days from May to October. The return fare is £14.70/5.85 per adult/child, including admission to Inchcolm Abbey. It's a half-hour sail to Inchcolm and you get 1½ hours ashore. As well as the abbey, the trip gives you the chance to see the island's grey seals, puffins and other seabirds.

**Sea.fari** (☎ 0131-331 4857; www.seafari.co.uk) runs high-speed boat trips to Inchcolm from Newhaven harbour near Leith, in Edinburgh (adult/child £22.50/18.50), giving you 50 minutes ashore on the island.

Frequent trains run from Edinburgh to Queensferry's Dalmeny station (15 minutes, two to four an hour). There are also numerous buses to Queensferry, including First Edinburgh bus 43, westbound from St Andrew Sq (30 minutes, three hourly).

### Hopetoun House

Two miles west of Queensferry, **Hopetoun House** (off Map pp782-3; ☎ 0131-331 2451; www.hopetoun house.com; adult/child £8/4.25, grounds only £3.70/2.20; 10.30am-5pm Apr-Sep) is one of Scotland's finest stately homes, with 150 acres of stunning landscaped grounds beside the Firth of Forth. There are two parts: the older built between 1699 and 1702 to Sir William Bruce's plans and dominated by a grand stairwell; and the newer designed between 1720 and 1750 by William Adam and his sons, Robert and John. Lavishly furnished, the house is also known for its art collection, which includes paintings by Gainsborough, Ramsay and Raeburn.

### ROSSLYN CHAPEL

The success of Dan Brown's novel *The Da Vinci Code* and the subsequent Hollywood film has seen a flood of visitors descend on Scotland's most beautiful and enigmatic church – **Rosslyn Chapel** (off Map pp782-3; Collegiate Church of St Matthew; ☎ 0131-440 2159; www.rosslynchapel .com; Roslin; adult/child £7.50/free; 9.30am-6pm Mon-Sat,

EDINBURGH

noon-4.45pm Sun Apr-Sep, 9.30am-5pm Mon-Sat, noon-4.45pm Sun Oct-Mar). The chapel was built in the mid-15th century for William St Clair, third earl of Orkney, and the ornately carved interior – at odds with the architectural fashion of its time – is a monument to the mason's art, rich in symbolic imagery. As well as flowers, vines, angels and biblical figures, the carved stones include many examples of the pagan 'Green Man'; other figures are associated with Freemasonry and the Knights Templar. Intriguingly, there are also carvings of plants from the Americas that pre-date Columbus' voyage of discovery. The symbolism of these images has led some researchers to conclude that Rosslyn is some kind of secret Templar repository, and it has been claimed that hidden vaults beneath the chapel could conceal anything from the Holy Grail or the head of John the Baptist to the body of Christ himself. The chapel is owned by the Episcopal Church of Scotland and services are still held here on Sunday mornings.

The chapel is on the eastern edge of the village of Roslin, 7 miles south of Edinburgh's centre. Lothian bus 15 (not 15A) runs from St Andrew Sq in Edinburgh to Roslin (30 minutes, every 30 minutes).

# Glasgow & Southern Scotland

Visitors hurrying north to the honeypots of Edinburgh and the Highlands often pass straight through southern Scotland without stopping. They don't know what they're missing.

There's a gentler, less crowded beauty to be found among the rounded hills, lush river valleys and market towns that stretch from the Scottish Borders to the central Lowlands. In the east you can explore the imposing castles and great Borders abbeys that stand testament to centuries of conflict between Scotland and England. Or visit fascinating country houses such as Traquair, with its miniature brewery, and Abbotsford, the former home of novelist Sir Walter Scott. In the west is Burns country – the home territory of Scotland's national poet, from his birthplace in the pretty village of Alloway to his tomb in the busy market town of Dumfries. Between the two lies the rugged beauty of Galloway Forest Park, an adventure playground of hiking and mountain-biking trails amid forests, lochs and stern granite hills. A flotilla of islands lies moored in the Firth of Clyde on the western shore of the region – a short ferry trip will take you to the Isle of Arran, a scenic jewel with a miniature mountain range and its very own distillery, or to the Isle of Bute, home to one of Scotland's most magnificent mansions.

And at the head of the firth, straddling the rapidly redeveloping waterfront of the River Clyde, is Glasgow, Scotland's biggest city – a loud, witty and wise-cracking contrast to the more staid attractions of Edinburgh in the east.

---

**HIGHLIGHTS**

- Re-discovering Glasgow's colossal **Kelvingrove Art Gallery & Museum** (p815), open again after a huge refurbishment program

- Hiking to the summit of Goatfell on the **Isle of Arran** (p842), then recovering with a pint of Arran ale in the Ormidale Hotel

- Admiring the architectural genius of Robert Adam and enjoying the magnificent sea views at **Culzean Castle** (p842)

- Discovering some of Scotland's best wildlife at **Galloway Forest Park** (p838)

- Exploring the charming, dignified 'artists town' of **Kirkcudbright** (p837), and the creative flair of its inhabitants

- Visiting the magnificent Borders abbeys of **Melrose** (p829), **Dryburgh** (p830)and **Jedburgh** (p833)

---

- POPULATION: 2.7 MILLION
- AREA: 7464 SQ MILES
- NUMBER OF CASTLES IN GLASGOW & SOUTHERN SCOTLAND: 200

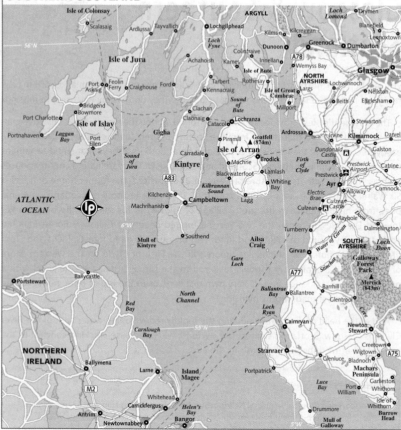

## SOUTHERN SCOTLAND

## Activities

The region's most famous walk is the challenging 212-mile **Southern Upland Way** (www.southernuplandway.gov.uk); if you want a sample, one of the best bits is the two-day section from St John's Town of Dalry to Beattock. Other long-distance walks are described on p827.

With the exception of the main north–south A-roads and the A75 to Stranraer, traffic is sparse, which, along with the beauty of the countryside, makes this ideal cycling country. The **Tweed Cycle Way** is a waymarked route running 62 miles along the beautiful Tweed Valley following minor roads from Biggar to Peebles (13 miles), Melrose (16 miles), Coldstream (19 miles) and Berwick-upon-Tweed (14 miles).

For an island tour, the **Isle of Arran** offers excellent cycling opportunities. The 50-mile coast-road circuit is stunning and is worth splitting into two or three days.

Glasgow's tourist office (p811) has a range of maps and leaflets detailing various walking and cycling routes, many of which start from Bell's Bridge by the Scottish Exhibition & Conference Centre (SECC), beside the River Clyde. The **Glasgow to Loch Lomond Route** follows disused train lines and towpaths to Loch Lomond and continues all the way to Inverness via the Glen Ogle Trail, Killin, Pitlochry and Aviemore. The **Glasgow to Irvine/Ardrossan and West Kilbride Cycle Way** runs via Paisley, then traffic-free as far as Glengarnock. From there to Kilwinning it follows minor

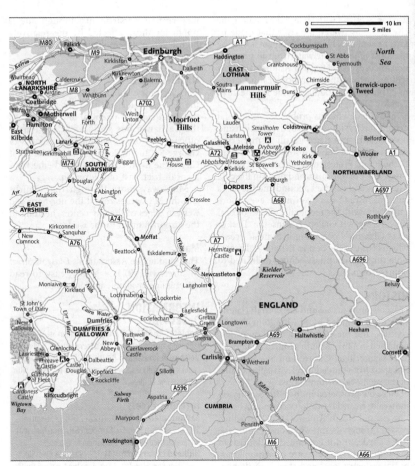

roads, then the route is partly traffic-free to Ardrossan, from where ferries leave for the Isle of Arran.

## Getting Around

Call **Traveline** ( ☎ 0871 200 22 33) for public-transport information. Bus transport is excellent around Ayrshire and Lanarkshire, and reasonable on the main north-south routes and the A75 to Stranraer, but limited elsewhere in Dumfries & Galloway. Various explorer tickets, which can be bought from bus drivers or at bus stations, are usually your best-value option.

Train services are limited. There are stations at Berwick-upon-Tweed on the main Edinburgh-London line (in Northumberland on the English side of the border, but a natural jumping-off point for the Tweed Valley); at Dumfries on the main Glasgow–London line; and at Stranraer (for the ferry to Belfast) and Ayr, which are linked to Glasgow. For timetables and fares, call the **National Rail Enquiry Service** ( ☎ 08457 484950; www.nationalrail.co.uk).

# GLASGOW

**pop 581,000**

Scotland's biggest city has shrugged off its shroud of industrial soot and shimmied into a sparkling new designer gown. Ten years on from being named UK City of Architecture and Design 1999, Glasgow is flaunting its reputation as a capital of cool and has branded itself as 'Scotland with Style'. Like London, the city has rediscovered the river that made its fortune, and massive redevelopment is making the most of the Clyde waterfront in preparation for an expected flood of visitors – Glasgow will be hosting the Commonwealth Games in 2014, and is a football venue for the 2012 London Olympics.

The city still has its problems – industrial decline has left large areas of deprivation and poor health, and there is still a simmering sectarian divide between some of its Roman Catholic and Protestant residents – but there's a new sense of optimism and pride in the city. Museums and galleries abound and the city's cultural resumé has been made even more impressive with the reopening of the colossal Kelvingrove Art Gallery & Museum. Best of all is Glasgow's pounding live-music scene, which is one of the best in Britain and accessible through countless venues dedicated to home-grown beats.

## HISTORY

Glasgow grew up around the church (later a cathedral) founded by St Mungo in the 6th century, and the University of Glasgow, established in 1451 (Britain's fourth university, after Cambridge, Oxford and St Andrews). But apart from the cathedral, virtually nothing of the medieval town remains.

Glasgow prospered in the 18th century on the wealth created by the tobacco trade between Europe and North America, much of which passed through its sprawling docks along the River Clyde, and it continued to flourish in the 19th century as a centre of shipbuilding, heavy industry, coal and steel – in its heyday, there was barely a country in the world whose steamships did not bear the stamp 'Clyde-built'.

In the first half of the 20th century, Glasgow was the centre of Britain's munitions industry, supplying arms and ships for both world wars. In the postwar years, however, the docks and heavy industries dwindled, and by the early 1970s the city seemed to be in terminal decline.

But since the 1990s there has been increasing confidence in the city as it determinedly set about the process of regeneration – in 1990 Glasgow won the European City of Culture award, which triggered a massive investment program in the city. Behind all the optimism, glitzy style bars and flashy

new riverside apartments, though, life is tough for those affected by the relatively high levels of unemployment, poor health and inadequate housing.

## ORIENTATION

The city centre is built on a grid system on the northern side of the River Clyde. The two train stations (Central and Queen St), the Buchanan bus station and the tourist office are all on, or within, a few blocks of George Sq, the main city square. Merchant City is the main commercial and entertainment district, east of George Sq.

Motorways bore through the suburbs and the M8 sweeps round the northern and western edges of the city centre, heading to the airport 8 miles to the west.

### Maps

The Automobile Association's *Glasgow Street by Street* (£5.99) is a handy, easy-to-read street guide, available in bookshops.

## INFORMATION
### Bookshops

**Borders** ( ☎ 0141-222 7700; 98 Buchanan St) Wide range of Scottish literature, good travel section, and a cafe.
**Voltaire & Rousseau** ( ☎ 0141-339 1811; 18 Otago Lane) Delightfully dishevelled secondhand bookstore with a huge range of titles.

### Internet Access

**easyInternetcafe** ( ☎ 0141-222 2364; 57 St Vincent St; ☼ 7am-9pm Mon-Fri, 8am-9pm Sat, 9am-7pm Sun) Under-18s need an adult companion to enter.
**Hillhead Library** ( ☎ 0141-339 7223; 348 Byres Rd; ☼ 10am-8pm Mon-Tue, 10am-5pm Wed, noon-8pm Thu, 9am-5pm Fri & Sat) Free internet access, but book ahead.

### Internet Resources

**Glasgow Galleries** (www.glasgowgalleries.co.uk)
**Glasgow Museums** (www.glasgowmuseums.com)
**Greater Glasgow & Clyde Valley Tourist Board** (www.seeglasgow.com)

### Left Luggage

**Buchanan bus station** ( ☎ 0141-333 3708; Killermont St; per 2hr/day £2.50/3.50)
**Queen St train station** ( ☎ 0845 601 5929; North Hanover St; small/medium/large piece of luggage per 24hr £5/6/7)

### Medical Services

**Glasgow Royal Infirmary** ( ☎ 0141-211 4000; 84 Castle St) Medical emergencies and outpatient facilities.

## Money

The post office offers the most competitive rates on currency exchange. There's a bureau de change at the tourist office and at both airports. There are many banks with ATMs around the centre and at the airports.

**Amex** ( ☎ 0141-222 1405; 115 Hope St; 🕑 9am-5.30pm Mon, Tue, Thu & Fri, 9.30am-5.30pm Wed, 9am-noon Sat)

## Post

**Main post office** (47 St Vincent St; 🕑 8.30am-5.45pm Mon-Fri, 9am-5.30pm Sat)

## Tourist Information

**St Enoch Square Travel Centre** (St Enoch Sq; 🕑 8.30am-5.30pm Mon-Sat) Travel information only.

**Tourist Office** City Centre ( ☎ 0141-204 4400; www.seeglasgow.com; 11 George Sq; 🕑 9am-6pm Mon-Sat Oct-Jan & Easter-May, 9am-7pm Mon-Sat Jun & Sep, 9am-8pm Mon-Sat Jul-Aug, 10am-6pm Sun Easter-Sep); Glasgow Airport ( ☎ 0141-848 4440; 🕑 7.30am-5pm) The city centre office is excellent. Makes local and national accommodation bookings (£3).

**Tickets Scotland** ( ☎ 0141-204 5151; 239 Argyle St; 🕑 9am-6pm) Sells tickets for most tours and gigs.

## SIGHTS
### City Centre

A walking tour (p816) covers the main sights. Two buildings designed by Charles Rennie Mackintosh – the Glasgow School of Art and the Scotland School Church – are also in this area (see p814).

### GEORGE SQUARE

Glasgow's main square is a grand public space, built in the Victorian era to show off the city's wealth and dignified by statues of notable Glaswegians and famous Scots, including Robert Burns, James Watt, General Sir John Moore and, atop a column, Sir Walter Scott. Overlooking the east side is the **City Chambers** ( ☎ 0141-287 4018; George Sq; admission & tours free) – the seat of local government – built in the 1880s at the high point of the city's prosperity. The interior is even more extravagant than the exterior, and the building has been used as a movie location, standing in for the Vatican (in *Heavenly Pursuits*) and the British Embassy in Moscow (in *An Englishman Abroad*). Guided tours are held at 10.30am and 2.30pm Monday to Friday.

### MERCHANT CITY

The prosperity of Glasgow's 18th-century 'tobacco lords', who made vast profits importing tobacco, rum and sugar via lucrative transatlantic trade routes, is reflected in the grand buildings they erected in the area east and southeast of George Sq, now known as the Merchant City; many have been renewed as stylish apartments, bars and restaurants.

The grandiose neoclassical exterior of the Royal Exchange, which now houses the **Gallery of Modern Art** (GoMA; ☎ 0141-229 1996; www.glasgowmuseums.com; Queen St; admission free; 🕑 10am-5pm Mon-Wed & Sat, 10am-8pm Thu, 11am-5pm Fri & Sun), contrasts with the contemporary paintings and sculpture within. It's a popular gallery that's geared towards kids, with plenty of activities. Outside, local smart-artists do a daily 'installation' of a traffic cone on the statue of the Duke of Wellington, despite the local council's regular removal of their handiwork.

### GLASGOW CATHEDRAL

A shining example of pre-Reformation Gothic architecture, **Glasgow Cathedral** (HS; ☎ 0141-552 6891; www.glasgowcathedral.org.uk; admission free; 🕑 9.30am-6pm Mon-Sat, 1-5pm Sun Apr-Sep, 9.30am-4pm Mon-Sat, 1-4pm Sun Oct-Mar) is the only mainland cathedral in Scotland to survive the Reformation. It is built on the site of St Mungo's 6th-century church, but the present structure dates mainly from the 15th century.

The cathedral is divided by a late-15th-century stone **choir screen**, decorated with seven pairs of figures to represent the Seven Deadly Sins. The four stained-glass panels of the **east window**, depicting the apostles, are particularly effective. At the northeastern corner is the entrance to the 15th-century upper chapter house, where Glasgow University was founded.

The most interesting part of the cathedral, the **lower church**, is reached by a stairway. Its forest of pillars creates a powerful atmosphere around St Mungo's tomb, the focus of a famous medieval pilgrimage that was believed to be as meritorious as a visit to Rome.

In the courtyard of the cathedral is **St Mungo's Museum of Religious Life & Art** ( ☎ 0141-553 2557; 2 Castle St; admission free; 🕑 10am-5pm Mon-Thu & Sat, 11am-5pm Fri & Sun), an audacious attempt to capture the world's major religions in an artistic nutshell. Its attraction is twofold: firstly, impressive art that blurs the lines between religion and culture; and secondly, the opportunity to delve into different faiths, an experience that can be as deep or shallow as you want.

# GLASGOW CITY CENTRE

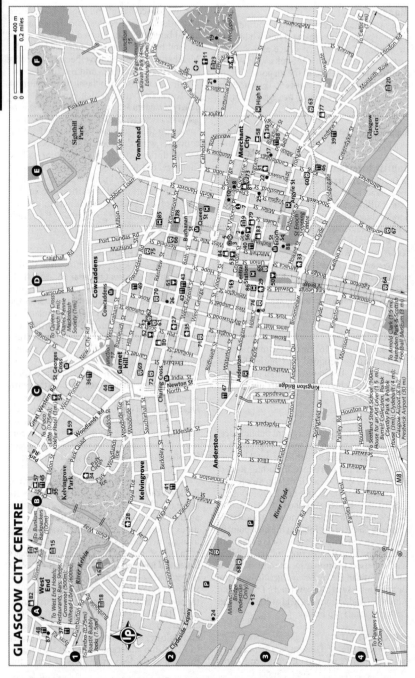

There are three galleries, representing religion as art, the religious life and, on the top floor, religion in Scotland. Britain's only Zen garden is outside.

It's a 20-minute walk to the cathedral from George Sq, but numerous buses pass by, including buses 11, 12, 36, 37, 38 and 42.

### PROVAND'S LORDSHIP

Across the road from St Mungo's Museum, **Provand's Lordship** ( ☎ 0141-552 8819; www.glasgow museums.com; 3 Castle St; admission free; ⏰ 10am-5pm Mon-Thu & Sat, 11am-5pm Fri & Sun) is Glasgow's oldest surviving building. This rare example of 15th-century domestic Scottish architecture was built as a manse for the chaplain of St Nicholas Hospital. The ceilings and doorways are low, and the rooms are sparsely furnished with period artefacts, except for an upstairs room, which has been furnished to reflect the living space of an early-16th-century chaplain.

### PEOPLE'S PALACE & WINTER GARDENS

Not just a local museum for local people, the **People's Palace & Winter Gardens** ( ☎ 0141-271 2951; Glasgow Green; admission free; ⏰ 10am-5pm Mon-Thu & Sat, 11am-5pm Fri & Sun) showcases what it means to be Glaswegian. From the goofy 1970s portrait of Billy Connolly to dance cards from the former Barrowland dance hall, this place is a monument to social history, with displays on language, comedy and the now-demolished Glasgow slums charting the city's development from the 1750s to the present day. The neighbouring Winter Gardens is an elegant Victorian glasshouse where you can enjoy a cup of coffee among the tropical palms.

## The Clyde

Strolling along the Clyde gives two very different insights into the city: one of fading glory and another of new prosperity in the redevelopment that some locals call the 'silver city'.

---

### CHARLES RENNIE MACKINTOSH, GLASGOW'S GENIUS

Wherever you go in Glasgow, you'll see the quirky, geometric designs of this famous Scottish architect, artist and designer. Many of the Glasgow buildings designed by Mackintosh are now open to the public, and his lean art-nouveau typeface is so ubiquitous it's virtually *the* Glasgow font.

Born in 1868, Mackintosh studied at the Glasgow School of Art and, aged 27, won a competition to design the School of Art's new building. His talent was quickly recognised on the Continent (he contributed to several exhibitions in France, Germany and Austria) but, at the time, he did not receive his due in Scotland. His Glaswegian architectural career lasted until 1914, when he moved to England to concentrate on furniture design. He died in 1928, but it was only in the last decades of the 20th century that Mackintosh's genius began to be widely recognised.

Fortunately, Mackintosh left an impressive architectural legacy throughout the city. His best-known building is the **Glasgow School of Art** ( ☎ 0141-353 4526; www.gsa.ac.uk/tour; 167 Renfrew St; tours adult/concession £7.75/5.75; ⏰ tours hourly 10am-noon & 2-5pm Apr-Sep, 11am & 3pm only Oct-Mar), which was named one of the world's 100 greatest artistic achievements of the 20th century by the BBC. The first portion was opened in 1899 and is the earliest art-nouveau piece in Britain.

North of the city centre, **Queen's Cross Church** ( ☎ 0141-946 6600; 870 Garscube Rd; adult/child £2/free; ⏰ 10am-5pm Mon-Fri year round, 2-5pm Sun Mar-Oct), lit by dazzling stained glass and drawing on both Gothic and Japanese motifs, is Mackintosh's only church design to be built (1896). On a more intimate scale, **Mackintosh House** ( ☎ 0141-330 5431; www.hunterian.gla.ac.uk; 82 Hillhead St; admission £3, after 2pm Wed free; ⏰ 9.30am-5pm Mon-Sat) is a reconstruction of the architect's (now demolished) Glasgow home, housed in the Hunterian Museum and Art Gallery. You ascend from the gallery's gloomy ground floor into the otherworldly atmosphere of Mackintosh's cool, white,

---

The **Riverside Museum** at Yorkhill, about a mile and a half downstream from the Science Centre, is the latest addition, due to open in spring 2011. It will replace the Museum of Transport (see opposite), showcasing Glasgow's transport, technology and maritime heritage.

### GLASGOW SCIENCE CENTRE

Glasgow's flagship millennium project, the **Glasgow Science Centre** ( ☎ 0141-420 5000; www.glasgowsciencecentre.org; 50 Pacific Quay; adult/child £7.95/5.95; ⏰ 10am-6pm) brings science and technology alive through hundreds of interactive exhibits and kid-friendly activities. Look out for the illusions (like rearranging your features through a 3-D head scan) and the cloud chamber (showing the tracks of subatomic particles produced by natural radioactive decay). As well as the main science mall, there's an IMAX cinema (admission £2 extra), a planetarium (£2 extra) and 127m-tall, rotating observation tower (also £2 extra). Take Arriva bus 24 from Renfield St or First Glasgow bus 89 or 90 from Union St.

### TALL SHIP & PUMPHOUSE

Across the Clyde from the Science Centre is the **Tall Ship** ( ☎ 0141-222 2513; www.thetallship.com; Stobcross Rd; adult/child £4.95/3.75, 1 child per adult free; ⏰ 10am-5pm Mar-Oct, 10am-4pm Nov-Feb), one of five Clyde-built sailing ships still afloat. Launched in 1896, the *Glenlee* is an impressively restored three-masted vessel that contains displays on her history, restoration and life on board in the early 20th century.

Nearby, the old **Pumphouse** houses exhibits on the history of the River Clyde, which involved the amazing dredging work carried out to enable big ships to sail into the centre of Glasgow. Evidence of the old shipyards still survives here, in the foundations of a swing bridge, crane tracks and old warehouses.

### CLYDEBUILT

Three miles downstream from the Science Centre, **Clydebuilt** ( ☎ 0141-886 1013; www.scottishmaritimemuseum.org; Braehead Shopping Centre, Kings Inch Rd; adult/child £4.25/2.50; ⏰ 10am-5.30pm Mon-Sat, 11am-5.30pm Sun) is a superb collection of model ships, industrial displays and narrative that vividly depicts the history of the Clyde, which has been inextricably linked with Glasgow and its people. Outside you can board MV *Kyles*, a typical 1872 steamship and the oldest Clydebuilt vessel still afloat in Britain.

austere drawing room with its beaten silver panels, signature long-backed chairs and surface decorations echoing Celtic manuscript illuminations.

The **Scotland Street School** ( ☎ 0141-287 0500; 225 Scotland St; admission free; ☺ 10am-5pm Mon-Thu & Sat, 11am-5pm Fri & Sun), dating from 1906, was Mackintosh's last major architectural commission in Glasgow, and is filled with his telltale design touches. Dominated by two leaded glass towers, it is now a fascinating museum of education with reconstructions of classrooms from Victorian times as well as the 1940s to the 1960s.

Although designed in 1901 as a competition entry for a German magazine, **House for an Art Lover** ( ☎ 0141-353 4770; www.houseforanartlover.co.uk; Bellahouston Park, 10 Drumbreck Rd; adult/child £4.50/3; ☺ 10am-4pm Mon-Wed, 10am-1pm Thu-Sun Apr-Sep, 10am-1pm Sat & Sun Oct-Mar), 1.5 miles south of the river, was not completed till 1996. Mackintosh worked closely with his wife on the design and her influence is evident, especially in the rose motif. Opening hours vary, so call to check. Buses 3, 9, 54, 55 and 56 all run here from the city centre.

The **Willow Tea Rooms** ( ☎ 0141-332 0521; www.willowtearooms.co.uk; 217 Sauchiehall St; ☺ 9am-5pm Mon-Sat, 11am-5pm Sun) were famously designed by Mackintosh in 1904 for local restaurant owner Kate Cranston. Mackintosh took his inspiration from the willow, as *sauchiehall* is derived from the Gaelic word for the tree. It used to cost an extra penny to enjoy the silver furniture and mirrored friezes of the Room de Luxe, but today it can be enjoyed for the price of a cuppa.

A good way to get around all the sites is with a **Charles Rennie Mackintosh Trail ticket** (www .spt.co.uk/tickets/mackintosh.html; £12), which includes one day's unlimited travel on First Glasgow buses and the SPT Subway, and admission to most Mackintosh attractions in town. It's available from the tourist office, SPT travel centres or online from the **Charles Rennie Mackintosh Society** (www.crmsociety.com).

The museum is on the south side of the river, 4 miles west of the city centre; take bus 23 or 23A from Renfield St or Union St to Braehead Shopping Centre.

## West End

With its designer boutiques, bustling bistros, trendy bars and sizeable student population, the West End is probably the most engaging district of Glasgow.

### KELVINGROVE ART GALLERY & MUSEUM

Recently reopened after an enormous refurbishment program, Glasgow's much-loved cultural icon the **Kelvingrove Art Gallery & Museum** ( ☎ 0141-276 9599; Argyle St; admission free; 10am-5pm Mon-Thu & Sat, 11am-5pm Fri, Sun) is the most visited museum in the UK outside of London. Its magnificent Edwardian building houses a superb collection of Scottish and European art – must-see masterpieces include Dali's sublime *Christ of St John of the Cross* and Rembrandt's *Man in Armour*, as well as works by the Scottish Colourists and the Glasgow Boys – as well as a fascinating series of natural history exhibits; a full-size WWII Spitfire fighter plane; a Glasgow Stories Exhibit which tells how the city inspires and infuriates; a

display of swinging heads all wringing out a different expression (which we found kinda scary); and plenty on Scottish history including the Viking influence. Kids are well catered for with thoughtful touches like pictures hung at their eye level, plus costumes to try on and replicas to paint – they can even watch the everyday affairs of a busy beehive.

### MUSEUM OF TRANSPORT

Across Argyle St from the Kelvingrove Art Gallery & Museum is the surprisingly interesting **Museum of Transport** ( ☎ 0141-287 2720; 1 Bunhouse Rd; admission free; ☺ 10am-5pm Mon-Thu & Sat, 11am-5pm Fri & Sun). Exhibits include a reproduction of a 1938 Glasgow street scene, a display of cars made in Scotland, plus assorted railway locos, model ships, trams, bikes (including the world's first pedal-powered bicycle, from 1847) and a room dedicated to the Clyde shipyards. First Glasgow buses 9, 16, 18, 42, 62 and 64 all stop nearby.

Note that this museum is due to be incorporated into the new Riverside Museum, scheduled to open in 2011.

### HUNTERIAN MUSEUM & ART GALLERY

Housed in two buildings on either side of University Ave, the **Hunterian Museum**

( ☎ 0141-330 4221; www.hunterian.gla.ac.uk; University Ave; admission free; ☯ 9.30am-5pm Mon-Sat) was opened in 1807 as Scotland's first public museum, based on the collection of William Hunter (1718–83), physician, medical teacher and former student of the university. The museum has had a recent makeover and changes include a permanent exhibition dedicated to Hunter, plus a new display called 'Weird & Wonderful' which shows off the quirky side of a collection that ranges from medieval coins and dinosaur eggs to curios brought back by Captain Cook during his voyages to the Pacific.

Across the road, the Scottish Colourists (Samuel Peploe, Francis Cadell, JD Fergusson) are well represented in the **Hunterian Art Gallery** ( ☎ 0141-330 5431; 82 Hillhead St; admission free; ☯ 9.30am-5pm Mon-Sat), which also displays Sir William MacTaggart's impressionistic Scottish landscapes, and a gem by Thomas Millie Dow. Also located here is the unmissable **Mackintosh House** (see p814).

Buses 11, 44 and 44A pass this way from the city centre (Hope St); or it's a short walk from Hillhead underground station.

## Greater Glasgow
### BURRELL COLLECTION

One of Glasgow's most famous attractions, the **Burrell Collection** ( ☎ 0141-287 2550; Pollok Country Park, Pollokshaws Rd; admission free, parking £1.50; ☯ 10am-5pm Mon-Thu & Sat, 11am-5pm Fri & Sun) is an idiosyncratic treasure house of art and artefacts amassed by wealthy industrialist Sir William Burrell (1861–1958) and donated to the city in 1944. The spectacular building was a result of a design competition in 1971 – many of the doorways are carved portals purloined from Spanish and Italian churches, floor-to-ceiling windows flood the interior with natural light, and the trees and landscape outside serve to enhance the exhibition spaces.

The collection ranges from Chinese porcelain and medieval furniture to paintings by Renoir and Cézanne and sculpture by Rodin. The tapestry galleries are outstanding, with intricate stories woven into staggering, wall-size pieces dating from the 13th century. The massive *Triumph of the Virgin* exemplifies the complexity of this medium, drawing on crusader tales to re-create the Holy Land.

There are occasional guided tours. Many buses pass the park gates (including buses 45, 47, 48 and 57 from the city centre), and there's a twice-hourly bus service between the gallery and the gates (a pleasant 10-minute walk). Alternatively, catch a train to Pollokshaws West from Central station (four per hour; you want the second station on the line for East Kilbride or Kilmarnock).

### POLLOK HOUSE

The Burrell Collection stands in the grounds of **Pollok House** (NTS; ☎ 0141-616 6410; www.nts.org .uk; Pollok Country Park, 2060 Pollokshaws Rd; admission Apr-Oct £8, Nov-Mar free; ☯ 10am-5pm), a sumptuous Edwardian mansion brimful of period furniture, its walls graced with paintings by El Greco and Murillo. The extensive servants' quarters give an idea of how the British aristocracy once lived, and there's an atmospheric cafe in the old Edwardian kitchen. The house is less than half a mile's walk from the Burrell Collection.

## ACTIVITIES

There are numerous green spaces within the city. **Pollok Country Park** surrounds the Burrell Collection with many woodland trails, while the **Kelvin Walkway** follows the River Kelvin from Kelvingrove Park in the West End to the Botanic Gardens and on to Dawsholm Park. Then there's the **Clyde Walkway**, a walking and cycling trail that runs 40 miles from central Glasgow to New Lanark and the Falls of Clyde (p825).

## WALKING TOUR

Start your walk on pedestrianised Buchanan St, just outside Borders bookshop. Heading east from here along Exchange St you pass through the ornamental **entrance gateway (1)** to Merchant City.

If you were a 19th-century industrialist, the Royal Exchange directly ahead of you might well have been your destination, but this stately colonnaded neoclassical building is now the **Gallery of Modern Art (2; p811)**.

The statue of the Duke of Wellington on horseback is facing down Ingram St, which you should follow for a couple of blocks. Continue southwards down Glassford St past **Trades Hall (3)**.

Turn left onto Wilson St, where the bulky **Sheriff Court (4)** fills a whole block. It was built in 1842 as Glasgow's town hall and merchants' house. Continue eastwards to **Merchant Square (5)**, a covered courtyard that was once the city's fruit market but now bustles with cafes

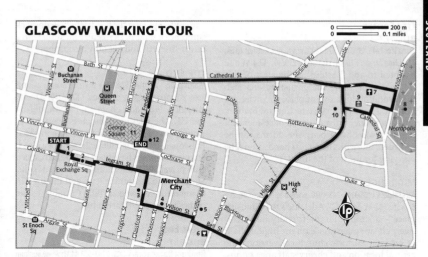

GLASGOW WALKING TOUR

0      200 m
0      0.1 miles

**WALK FACTS**

**Start** Buchanan St
**Finish** George Sq
**Distance** 2.5 miles
**Duration** one to three hours

and bars. Across the road is **Blackfriars (6),** one of the city's most relaxed pubs; grab a window seat and watch the world go by for a bit. Continue along Bell St, the continuation of Wilson St, and emerge onto High St. Take a left and follow the street uphill to **Glasgow Cathedral (7**; p811).

Behind the cathedral, wind your way up through the noble tombs of the **Necropolis (8)** with rewarding city views, before heading back down and taking in **St Mungo's Museum of Religious Life & Art (9**; p811) and **Provand's Lordship (10**; p813).

Then follow busy Cathedral St back towards the centre, passing the buildings of the University of Strathclyde as you go. A left down North Frederick St and you'll reach **George Square (11**; p811) with its statues of famous Glaswegians and the monumental **City Chambers (12**; p811).

## TOURS

**City Sightseeing** ( ☎ 0141-204 0444; www.citysightseeing glasgow.co.uk; adult/child £9/3) has a bus tour starting at George Sq – get on and off as you wish.

Offering cruises on the world's last ocean-going paddle steamer, the **Waverley** ( ☎ 0845 130

4647; www.waverleyexcursions.co.uk; Anderston Quay; cruises from £17; ☒ Apr-Sep) goes from Glasgow to the Firth of Clyde and the islands of Bute, Great Cumbrae and Arran. It departs from Glasgow Science Centre.

## FESTIVALS & EVENTS

Not to be outdone by Edinburgh, Glasgow has some kicking festivals of its own.

**Celtic Connections** ( ☎ 0141-353 8000; www.grch.com) is a two-week music festival held in January, while the **Glasgow Jazz Festival** ( ☎ 0141-552 3552; www.jazzfest.co.uk) is an excellent event held in June – George Sq is a good place for free jazz at this time.

Glasgow's biggest festival, running for two weeks in June, is the **West End Festival** ( ☎ 0141-341 0844; www.westendfestival.co.uk), a music and arts extravaganza.

Around 200 pipe bands play at Glasgow Green during the **World Pipe Band Championships** ( ☎ 0141-221 5414; www.rspba.org), held in mid-August.

## SLEEPING

Finding decent options during the peak seasons across July and August can be difficult – for a B&B, you should arrive reasonably early and use the tourist office's booking service. Beware of some 'backpacker accommodation' advertised at train/bus stations that often amounts to nothing more than a scam, with backpackers sleeping in filthy shared flats because the nonexistent hostel is being 'renovated'.

## City Centre

### BUDGET

**Euro Hostel** ( ☎ 0141-222 2828; www.euro-hostels.co.uk; 318 Clyde St; dm £16-18, s/tw from £30/40; 🖥 ) We're tempted to add 'Eastern' at the start of this hostel's name, as it's a large institutional slab that wouldn't look out of place in Soviet-era Poland. Luckily it's close to Central Station, and as a former university hall of residence it almost always has a bed. The dorms can be crowded, but with the city so handy you'll be partying for most of the night.

### MIDRANGE

**Adelaide's** ( ☎ 0141-248 4970; www.adelaides.co.uk; 209 Bath St; s £32-45, d £54; 🖥 ) Adelaide's is an unusual place – a simple, family-friendly (and relatively cheap) guesthouse on prestigious Bath St set in an historic church conversion. The central location and cheery staff are a bonus, and it's still very much a functioning church, so guests can attend services, or even a concert by the Glasgow Symphony Orchestra.

**Babbity Bowster** ( ☎ 0141-552 5055; babbitybowster@gofornet.co.uk; 16-18 Blackfriars St; s/d £45/60) Smack bang in the heart of trendy Merchant City – the building's design is attributed to Robert Adam – this lively bar and restaurant offers accommodation in rooms with sleek furnishings and a minimalist design (No 3 is a good one). Staying here makes for an excellent Glaswegian experience.

**Artto Hotel** ( ☎ 0141-248 2480; www.arttohotel.com; 37 Hope St; s/d £70/90; 🖥 wi-fi) Everything is squeaky clean and gleaming in this fashionable hotel. The high-ceilinged rooms have light subtle tones combined with earthy, darkish maroons, giving them a modish appeal, and slick, sparkling en suites with power showers complete the happy picture. Remember when booking that rooms at the rear are much quieter.

**ourpick Cathedral House Hotel** ( ☎ 0141-552 3519; www.cathedralhousehotel.org; 28-32 Cathedral Sq; s/d from £60/90; 🖥 wi-fi) In the heart of the leafy, dignified East End stands this 19th-century Scottish baronial-style hotel, complete with turrets and eight individual and beautifully furnished rooms – it's hotels like this (the antidote to chain hotels) that give Glasgow such a classy edge. Rooms 4 and 7 – very spacious corner rooms that include sumptuous king-sized beds – are our faves.

**Brunswick Hotel** ( ☎ 0141-552 0001; www.brunswickhotel.co.uk; 106-108 Brunswick St; r £65-95; 🖥 wi-fi) Stylish and contemporary, the gay-friendly Brunswick combines a superb, city-centre location with a down-to-earth and friendly atmosphere.

### TOP END

**Malmaison** ( ☎ 0141-572 1000; www.malmaison-glasgow.com; 278 West George St; d/ste from £109/£210; 🖥 wi-fi) Part of a boutique chain that's conquering the UK, the Glasgow branch is every bit as swanky as you'd expect. Housed in a converted Episcopalian church built in the style of a Greek temple, the rooms have been individually styled with private CD collections and sunken baths. Suites have a mezzanine level and the Big Yin (named for Glaswegian Billy Connolly) suite comes with a swish tartan tub.

## West End

### BUDGET

**Bunkum Backpackers** ( ☎ 0141-581 4481; www.bunkumglasgow.co.uk; 26 Hillhead St; dm/tw £12/32) This hard-to-find spot is set in a leafy street and feels miles from the city. There's a homely feel in the spacious dorms (which include lockers), and a comfy lounge room to read in. It's not a wild party place – most of the partying is done away from the hostel. Keep your eyes on the street numbers, as it's not well signposted.

**ourpick Glasgow SYHA Hostel** ( ☎ 0141-332 3004; www.syha.org.uk; 8 Park Tce; dm £15.50-20; 🖥 ) Set in a charming town house perched on a hill overlooking Kelvingrove Park, this place is simply fabulous and is one of Scotland's best official hostels. Dorms are mostly four to six beds and all have their own en suite – very posh. The common rooms are spacious, plush and good for lounging about.

### MIDRANGE

**Alamo Guest House** ( ☎ 0141-339 2395; www.alamoguesthouse.com; 46 Gray St; s/d from £32/52; 🖥 wi-fi) This elegant Victorian town house is a great place to stay, dripping with period detail and offering rooms larger than you'd get in a city-centre hotel, plus a beautiful breakfast room overlooking leafy Kelvingrove Park. You'll feel miles from the city in this peaceful location, and yet the city centre and the West End are both just a walk away.

**Belhaven Hotel** ( ☎ 0141-339 3222; www.belhavenhotel.com; 15 Belhaven Tce; s/d from £48/72; 🅿 ) Consistently friendly and blessed with a quiet location close to the Botanic Gardens, the Belhaven is furnished in contemporary style set off with a splash of decadent burgundy, with some truly spacious double and family rooms sporting almost floor-to-ceiling windows.

**Kirklee Hotel** ( ☎ 0141-334 5555; www.kirkleehotel .co.uk; 11 Kensington Gate; s/d £59/75) The Kirklee is a grand Edwardian town house, and a quiet little gem of a place that combines the luxury of a classy hotel with the warmth of staying in someone's home. The rooms are gorgeous, beautifully furnished and mostly looking onto lush gardens. For families there's an excellent downstairs room with enormous en suite.

**TOP END**

**Hotel du Vin** ( ☎ 0141-339 2001; www.hotelduvin .com; 1 Devonshire Gardens; r/ste from £145/395; ⌨ wi-fi) Glasgow's first boutique hotel was made famous as One Devonshire Gardens. New management has maintained this sumptuous spot's reputation as the favourite place for celebrity guests to hang their hat when visiting Glasgow. A study in elegance, it spreads through three classical terraced town houses offering individually furnished designer bedrooms with monsoon showers, and two fine restaurants.

## Outside Glasgow

**Craigendmuir Caravan Park** ( ☎ 0141-779 4159; www .craigendmuir.co.uk; Campsie View; 2-person tent sites £14) This well-equipped camp site is just 6 miles northwest of the city centre on the A80, and only 500m from Stepps train station, with regular services to Glasgow Queen St station.

# EATING

Most of the city's best restaurants are clustered in Merchant City and the West End; many offer a two-/three-course lunch special and 'pretheatre' early-evening menus for as little as £8, good ways to sample the more expensive restaurants. Several of the pubs listed on p820 also do decent pub grub.

## City Centre
### BUDGET

**Cafe Lava** ( ☎ 0141-553 1123; 24 St Andrew's St; mains £2-6; ⌨ 8am-6pm Mon-Fri, 10am-5pm Sat & Sun; ⌨ wifi) Everyone wants to live next door to a cafe like this. The understated menu delivers delicious home cooking, including a breakfast of Stornoway black pudding and eggs Benedict. The coffee is some of the best in town, and the carrot cake the best in Scotland: we know, we've sampled it from Dumfries to Shetland.

**Mono** ( ☎ 0141-553 2400; 12 Kings Ct; mains £3-7; ⌨ noon-10pm) Not content to be one of Glasgow's best vegetarian cafes, this place also crams in an indie record store and an organic grocery shop, and serves as an occasional live-music venue. Hearty food such as vegetable bake and pasta of the day is served in a casual dining space that can get crowded if there's a band playing (usually Friday and Saturday nights).

**Asia Style** ( ☎ 0141-332 8828; 185-9 St George's Rd; mains £6-8; ⌨ 5pm-midnight) Don't be put off by the fluorescent lights and spartan decor – this little hole-in-the-wall place serves the most authentic Chinese and Malaysian food in the city, seasoned with handfuls of fresh herbs and spices.

Also recommended:

**Doocot** ( ☎ 0141-221 1821; 11 Mitchell Lane; mains £7-9; ⌨ 10.30am-5pm Mon & Wed-Fri, 11am-5pm Tue, noon-5pm Sun) Stylish cafe on level 5 of the Lighthouse centre for architecture and design – drop in for anything from a latte to a three-course lunch.

**Grassroots Cafe** ( ☎ 0141-333 0534; 97 St George's Rd; mains £6-9; ⌨ 10am-10pm) Vegetarian and vegan, organic and free-range, inventive and interesting – this great little cafe ticks all the right boxes.

### MIDRANGE

**Wee Curry Shop** City ( ☎ 0141-353 0777; 7 Buccleuch St; 2-course lunches £6, dinner mains £11; ⌨ lunch Mon-Sat, dinner daily); West End ( ☎ 0141-357 5280; 29 Ashton Lane; dinner mains £11; ⌨ lunch, dinner) Could there be a better illustration of Scotland's infatuation with Indian cuisine than a curry shop decked out in tartan? The Indian food is authentic though, so there's no fear of a faulty balti, just great-value rogan josh nosh.

**Fratelli Sarti** ( ☎ 0141-204 0440; 121 Bath St; pizzas £7-10, mains £10-14; ⌨ 8am-10.30pm Mon-Fri, 10am-11pm Sat, noon-10.30pm Sun) For authentico Italian food that's reasonably priced leave it to the brothers Sarti to sort you out. The original Bath St branch has a deli feel, crammed with smallgoods as you gobble down your spaghetti *aglio olio peperoncino* (with olive oil and chilli). The classier Wellington St branch ( ☎ 248 2228, 133 Wellington St) maintains the tradition with thin-crust but flavoursome pizza straight from the oven, and inventive pastas.

**Cafe Gandolfi** ( ☎ 0141-552 6813; 64 Albion St; mains £8-16; ⌨ 9am-11.30pm Mon-Sat, noon-11.30pm Sun) This Merchant City pioneer (opened in 1979) maintains its place in the pecking order of this busy eating precinct by working innovative magic with Modern Scottish and Mediterranean cuisine – very busy at weekends, so book ahead.

## TOP END

**Two Fat Ladies at the Buttery** ( ☎ 0141-221 8188; 652-4 Argyle St; mains £18-22; ۞ lunch & dinner) Now under new management, Glasgow's oldest restaurant (opened 1856) has toned down the tartany and shrugged off its air of formality – you can now enjoy its ancient oak-panelled rooms, magnificent carved bar and antique stained glass without having to don jacket and tie. The Modern Scottish cuisine is still first-class though – from roast saddle of venison with rosemary jus, to succulent seared scallops with Stornoway black pudding.

## West End
### BUDGET

**University Cafe** ( ☎ 0141-339 5217; 87 Byres Rd; mains £3-6; ۞ 9am-10pm Mon-Sat, 10am-10pm Sun) First opened in 1918 and still run by the same family (now fourth generation), this is a classic Glasgow cafe that has been serving fried breakfasts and ice-cream floats to hungover students for almost a century.

### MIDRANGE

**Pintxo** ( ☎ 0141-334 8686; 562 Dumbarton Rd; tapas £3-4; ۞ 5pm-late Sun-Fri, noon-late Sat) Colourful tiled tabletops and flickering candlelight create a warm, intimate atmosphere at this Basque tapas bar. As well as perennial favourites such as Serrano ham, tortilla and *fabada* (chorizo and bean stew), there are delicious house specialities that include *morcilla* (black pudding) fried with apple and sage, and slow-cooked lamb with coriander, red peppers and rioja.

**Balbir's** ( ☎ 0141-339 7711; 7 Church St; mains £8-12; ۞ 5-10.30pm Sun-Thu, 5-11pm Fri & Sat) Glasgow is famous for its curry shops, and Balbir's is one of the best – albeit slightly more formal than most, and with a health-conscious twist (plenty of vegetarian, vegan and/or low-fat options).

**Louis' Bistro** ( ☎ 0141-339 7915; 18 Gibson St; mains £8-13; ۞ lunch & dinner Tue-Sat) Well placed to take the award for best burger in town, this unpretentious neighbourhood bistro also serves perfectly prepared steaks. But vegetarians have not been forgotten, with a selection of tasty and inventive meat-free dishes.

**Gambrino** ( ☎ 0141-339 4111; 333 Great Western Rd; mains £8-13; ۞ noon-2.30pm & 5.30-11pm Mon-Fri, noon-

11pm Sat, noon-11pm Sun) A rustic Italian trattoria with weathered timber beams, bare brickwork and candlelit tables. Gambrino's deliciously authentic pizza and pasta mean that it is often busy – there's a queue for tables at weekends, but it always seems to fit everyone in.

**Roastit Bubbly Jocks** ( ☎ 0141-339 3355; 450 Dumbarton Rd; mains £9-14; ۞ lunch Fri-Sun, dinner) Lively and informal, this bustling bistro takes traditional Scottish dishes such as Scotch broth, braised lamb and roast venison and gives them a gourmet twist. It's a bit out of town, but close to the Partick underground station.

Also recommended:

**Stravaigin 2** ( ☎ 0141-334 7165; 8 Ruthven Lane; mains £8-13; ۞ noon-11pm) A cornerstone of the West End dining scene, famous for its gourmet burgers.

**Fanny Trollope's** ( ☎ 0141-564 6464; 1066 Argyle St; mains £10-15; ۞ lunch & dinner Tue-Sat) From smoked salmon and Loch Fyne mussels to venison casserole and shin of beef, this popular restaurant specialises in quality Scottish produce.

### TOP END

**Ubiquitous Chip** ( ☎ 0141-334 5007; 12 Ashton Lane; 3-course lunch/dinner £30/40; ۞ lunch & dinner) The original champion of quality Scottish produce, this restaurant has won lots of awards for its unparalleled Scottish cuisine, and for its lengthy wine list. With several dining areas spread around a covered, cobbled courtyard filled with tropical greenery, this is an ideal place to treat someone special. There's a less expensive brasserie (mains £8 to £15), where the menu follows in the tradition of creativity and top-notch ingredients.

## DRINKING

Some of Scotland's best nightlife is to be found in the din and roar of Glasgow's crowded pubs and bars. There are as many different styles of bar as there are punters who guzzle in them; a month of solid drinking wouldn't get you past the halfway mark. Merchant City and the West End are the twin epicentres of fashionable drinking with any number of different concept bars, while Sauchiehall St has mainstream boozers that attract their fair share of stag and hen nights.

## City Centre

**Rogano** ( ☎ 0141-248 4055; 11 Exchange Pl) Opened in 1935, the Rogano is a gem of art-deco design, based on the decor in the *Queen Mary* ocean liner, which was built on the Clyde in the 1930s. Treat yourself to a classic Bellini cocktail (prosecco, peach liqueur and peach juice) or lash out on a bottle of vintage Dom Perignon.

**Horse Shoe Bar** ( ☎ 0141-221 3051; 17 Drury St) This legendary city pub and popular meeting place dates from the late 19th century and has hardly changed its appearance since then. It boasts the longest continuous bar in the UK, but its main attraction is what's served over it – real ale and the best-value three-course lunches (£3.50) in town.

**Arches** ( ☎ 0141-565 1035; 253 Argyle St) A one-stop culture, entertainment and refreshment venue, this bar and club (p822) doubles as a theatre showing contemporary and experimental productions. The hotel-like entrance conceals a bohemian underworld where bearded guys in hiking boots rub shoulders with suited city boys.

**Bloc** ( ☎ 0141-574 6066; www.bloc.ru; 117 Bath St) With a late licence that pulls in a young party crowd, this buzzing basement bar with a Soviet Union theme has bands and local DJs spinning into the small hours.

**Centre for Contemporary Arts** ( ☎ 0141-332 7521; 350 Sauchiehall St) Popular with the boho crowd, this is one of the more refined spots for a relaxed drink on Sauchiehall St. Occasional DJs shake it up, but it's never as mad as other places on this strip.

**Babbity Bowster** ( ☎ 0141-552 5055; 16-18 Blackfriars St) Babbity Bowster has a bit of a continental feel, particularly in the adjoining beer garden. The interior has a classy vibe, with a suit crowd to match on weekday evenings, and there's music on Saturday night, usually of the folk guitar-and-fiddle variety.

**Tinderbox** ( ☎ 0141-552 6907; 14 Ingram St; ☯ 7.15am-10pm Mon-Sat, 8am-10pm Sun) One of the city's best coffee bars, the Merchant City branch of Tinderbox is also one of its most stylish – a great place for cake and cappuccino. The original branch is in the **West End** ( ☎ 339 3108; 189 Byres Rd).

## West End

**Tchai Ovna** ( ☎ 0141-357 4524; 42 Otago Lane) More rustic than your grannie's woodshed, this Bohemian-style tea house is frequented by local students and indie kids sipping on speciality teas, nibbling on vegetarian snacks, or puffing on apple-scented tobacco in hubble-bubble pipes.

**Uisge Beatha** ( ☎ 0141-564 1596; 232-246 Woodlands Rd) Named 'water of life' (the Gaelic for Scotland's national drink), this traditional boozer has more than a hundred single malts on offer, and is decorated with a collection of hunting trophies that includes former prime minister Maggie Thatcher (a small clue to the city's political leanings).

**Liquid Ship** ( ☎ 0141-332 2840; 171-175 Great Western Rd) The best of Glasgow's style bars distilled into a single venue, the Ship is built from reclaimed architectural salvage – everything from school desks to an old bank counter to a brick with the 120-year-old imprint of a dog's paw. Breakfasts from 10am, a great range of wines and live acoustic music most evenings add to the allure.

**Choco Latte** ( ☎ 0141-337 3736; 536 Great Western Rd) Cool little cafe that serves up devastatingly delicious hot chocolate garnished with melting marshmallow, and some of the finest coffee in the West End.

**Offshore** (3-5 Gibson St; ☯ 8am-10pm Mon-Fri, 9am-10pm Sat & Sun; ☐ ) Deep in the heart of student territory, Offshore is a homely, cluttered lounge of a coffee shop, with comfortable sofas, local art on the walls, free wi-fi and an indie soundtrack. Mains £4 to £6.

**Oran Mor** ( ☎ 0141-357 6200; www.oran-mor.co.uk; cnr Great Western & Byers Rds) An atmospheric drinking spot housed in a converted church, Oran Mor is famous for 'A Play, A Pie and A Pint' – daily lunchtime theatre shows with food and drink (check the website for what's on).

# ENTERTAINMENT

The *List* (£2.20; www.list.co.uk) is an invaluable fortnightly events guide available at newsagents and bookshops, which details everything happening in both Glasgow and Edinburgh.

## Cinemas

**Glasgow Film Theatre** ( ☎ 0141-332 8128; www.gft .org.uk; 12 Rose St; adult/concession £6/4.50) A classic art-house cinema, screening a wide range of independent and classic films from around the world, with themed 'seasons' based on a particular genre or director.

**Grosvenor** ( ☎ 0141-339 8444; www.grosvenorcinema .co.uk; Ashton Lane, West End; adult/child £6/4) Tucked away in a cobbled West End lane, the Grosvenor is an intimate art-house cinema with plush leather seats – and even sofas – and a program that ranges from Hollywood blockbusters to late-night cult classics.

**Cineworld** ( ☎ 0871 200 2000; www.cineworld.co.uk; 7 Renfrew St; adult/child £6.80/4.70) Mainstream multiplex showing popular first-run films.

## Live Music

Glasgow has long been regarded as the centre of Scotland's live-music scene. Year after year, touring musicians, artists and travellers alike name Glasgow as one of their favourite cities in the world to play or listen to live music, and the place is still turning out top performers such as Franz Ferdinand, the Fratellis and Amy Macdonald. As well as the venues listed below, several of the bars and clubs listed have frequent live acts or folk-music sessions.

**King Tut's Wah Wah Hut** ( ☎ 0141-221 5279; www .kingtuts.co.uk; 272a St Vincent St) One of the city's premier live-music pub venues, the excellent King Tut's hosts bands every night of the week; it's best-known for nurturing up-and-coming indie, rock, punk and hardcore bands – Oasis were signed after playing here in 1993. Gigs sell out quickly so keep an eye on the website.

**Barrowland** ( ☎ 0141-552 4601; www.glasgow-barrow land.com; 244 Gallowgate) A former dance hall that has become a stalwart of the Glasgow live-music scene, now immortalised in Amy Macdonald's song 'Barrowland Ballroom'. Gigs range from touring international bands to local lads and lasses made good and, whatever you see, it's an unforgettable night out.

**Nice 'n' Sleazy** ( ☎ 0141-333 0900; www.nicensleazy .com; 421 Sauchiehall St) Sleazys is the ideal atmosphere in which to catch some of Glasgow's emerging indie bands, with cheesy decor and a leaning towards rock acts (though other genres can be heard).

**13th Note** ( ☎ 0141-553 1638; www.13thnote.co.uk; 50-60 King St) Papered with indie band posters, the downstairs cellar bar plays host to the best

of Glasgow's alternative bands, and is also known for giving unknowns a go.

Also recommended:

**ABC** ( ☎ 0141-553 2232; 300-330 Sauchiehall St) A big venue for national touring acts.

**Carling Academy** ( ☎ 0870 771 2000; www.glasgow -academy.co.uk; 121 Eglinton St) A newer spot that hosts big-name visiting bands.

**Garage** ( ☎ 0141-332 1120; www.garageglasgow.co.uk; 490 Sauchiehall St) Packs them in with live music in four rooms.

On the River Clyde, the **Scottish Exhibition & Conference Centre** (SECC; ☎ 0870 040 4000; www .secc.co.uk; Finnieston Quay) and the adjoining **Clyde Auditorium** ( ☎ 0870 040 4000; www.secc.co.uk; Finnieston Quay) – also known as the Armadillo because of its bizarre shape – cater for the big national and international acts.

## Nightclubs

Glasgow has one of Britain's biggest clubbing scenes. Glaswegians usually hit clubs after the pubs have closed, so many places offer discounted admission and cheaper drinks if you go before 10.30pm; most clubs close around 3am. Entry costs £4 to £8 (up to £25 for big events), although bars often hand out free passes. Club nights tend to change venues regularly, so check the *List*.

**Arches** ( ☎ 0141-565 1000; www.thearches.co.uk; 253 Argyle St; ☾ club nights Wed, Fri & Sat) The Godfather of Glaswegian clubs, reliably pulling in top DJs from across Europe, the Arches enjoys an atmospheric setting amid the steel girders beneath Central Station. Music ranges from old-school techno to happy hardcore. It also houses one of the city's best bars (p821).

**Art School** ( ☎ 0141-353 4530; www.theartschool .co.uk; 168 Renfrew St; ☾ Tue-Sun during term time) For those in the know, the students association

---

### GAY & LESBIAN GLASGOW

Glasgow's gay scene centres on Merchant City. **Glasgay** ( ☎ 0141-334 7126; www.glasgay.co.uk) is a performing-arts festival held around October/November, spotlighting the gay, lesbian and transgender community.

**Waterloo Bar** ( ☎ 0141-229 5890; cnr Wellington & Argyle Sts), a traditional pub, is Scotland's oldest gay bar, with an all-ages crowd that includes a welcoming group of regulars.

**Court Bar** ( ☎ 0141-552 2463; 69 Hutcheson St) is a pleasant little bar with 1970s and '80s nostalgia on the soundtrack, a friendly and unpretentious atmosphere, and a clientele that is predominantly gay, especially later in the evening; 'rough but honest', as one local described the scene.

A hip and comfortable basement bar hang-out, **Revolver** ( ☎ 0141-553 2456; 6a John St) pulls in a relaxed crowd with its friendly staff, laid-back atmosphere, pool table and free jukebox.

---

**ANYONE FOR T?**

Scotland's most celebrated music festival by far is **T in the Park** (www.tinthepark.com), which draws folk from all over Britain to Balado in Fife every July. North of the border, it's *the* place to see hot up-and-coming bands, particularly Scottish bands.

For aspiring Franz Ferdinands there's a chance to play the big gig in **T Break** (www.tbreak .co.uk), an annual battle of the bands for hopefuls from across Scotland. T Break heats are held throughout May and June, featuring many of the best bands you've never heard of (later, you can tell your mates you were into them long before anyone else was). The great thing about these heats is that each band gets a 20-minute set, so in one night you hear a selection of great bands and still get to sample a few pints.

In Glasgow the heats are held at King Tut's Wah Wah Hut (opposite), while in Edinburgh there are heats at the Liquid Room (p801).

---

bar at the Glasgow School of Art hosts some of Glasgow's most innovative DJs, with legendary dance nights pumping out some of the best hip hop north of the border.

**Cathouse** ( ☎ 0141-248 6606; www.cathouseglasgow .co.uk; 15 Union St; ☜ Thu-Sun) A recent makeover hasn't changed the make-up of the punters at Glasgow's top indie and alternative venue – expect to feel out of place if you're not all gothed up. There are two dance floors: upstairs is pretty intense with lots of metal and hard rock, downstairs is a little less scary if you're not so keen on moshing.

### Sport

Scottish football is dominated by the 'Old Firm', two Glasgow teams that have been around for more than 100 years – **Celtic** ( ☎ 0141-551 8653; www.celticfc.co.uk; Celtic Park, Parkhead) and **Rangers** ( ☎ 0870 600 1972; www.rangers.co.uk; Ibrox Stadium, 150 Edmiston Dr), whose rivalry splits Glasgow down the middle.

The Scotland team plays international matches at 52,000-seat **Hampden Park** ( ☎ 0141-620 4000; www.hampdenpark.co.uk; stadium tours adult/child £6/3), a stadium that also houses the **Scottish Football Museum** ( ☎ 0141-616 6139; Hampden Park; adult/child £6/3; ☜ 10am-5pm Mon-Sat, 11am-5pm Sun). The museum has a Hall of Fame and offers a chance to relive classic moments in Scottish football. Tours of the stadium include the players' warm-up area and the chance to hear the Hampden Roar as you walk through the tunnel.

### Theatre

**Theatre Royal** ( ☎ 0141-332 9000; www.theatreroyal glasgow.com; 282 Hope St) Hosting the Scottish Opera and Scottish Ballet, this venue is one of the city's major performance spaces. Cheap

standby tickets are available for some performances; ask at the box office.

**Citizens' Theatre** ( ☎ 0141-429 0022; www.citz.co.uk; 119 Gorbals St) A Glasgow institution, born in 1909 with an egalitarian manifesto that lives on in its name, the Citizens' aims to bring theatre to ordinary people, with a challenging program of old classics and new writing.

## SHOPPING

London aside, Glasgow is one of the UK's premier shopping destinations. The main shopping area around Argyle St is packed with international fashion chains, while independent boutiques cluster along Great Western and Byres Rds in the West End.

Culture vultures swoop on **Versace** ( ☎ 0141-552 6510) in the stylish Italian Centre mall on John St. Alternatively, **Designer Exchange** ( ☎ 0141-221 6898; 3 Royal Exchange Ct) stocks cheaper samples and resale designer labels. There are even more designer outlets in the **Buchanan Galleries** (www.buchanangalleries.co.uk; Royal Exchange Sq) and the exquisite **Princes Square** (www.princessquare .co.uk; Buchanan St), which is set in a magnificent Victorian-listed building.

For that essential Glasgow shopping experience, don't miss the weekend flea market at the **Barras** ( ☎ 0141-552 7258; www.glasgow-barrowland .com; London Rd), but for more-traditional Scottish souvenirs, **Geoffrey (Tailor) Kiltmaker** ( ☎ 0141-331 2388; 309 Sauchiehall St) has the best take-home tartan, and **Robert Graham & Co** ( ☎ 0141-221 6588; 71 St Vincent St) stocks an excellent selection of malt whiskies and cigars.

There are many interesting boutiques in the West End, such as the clothes designer **Moon** ( ☎ 0141-339 2315; www.moonofglasgow.co.uk; 10 Ruthven Lane) and vintage specialist **Starry Starry Night** ( ☎ 0141-334 4778; 21 Dowanside Lane). **OneWorld**

( ☎ 0141-357 1567; 100 Byres Rd) stocks an eclectic range of arty gifts from around the globe, all of them fair-traded; **Fopp** ( ☎ 0141-357 0774; 358 Byres Rd) is a cheap independent Scottish record outlet; while **Monorail** ( ☎ 0141-552 9458; www.mono railmusic.com; 12 Kings Ct; ☾ noon-8pm) stocks a great selection of indie and local vinyl.

## GETTING THERE & AWAY
### Air
Ten miles west of the city on the M8, **Glasgow International airport** ( ☎ 0141-887 1111; www.baa .co.uk/glasgow) handles domestic traffic and international flights, including some direct transatlantic routes. It's the main airport for most of the Scottish islands. **Glasgow Prestwick airport** ( ☎ 0871 223 0700; www.gpia.co.uk), 30 miles southwest of Glasgow near Ayr, is used by the budget carrier **Ryanair** ( ☎ 0871 246 0000; www .ryanair.com), which offers flights from London Stansted airport (1¼ hours, frequent) for around £25 plus taxes.

A far more romantic way to fly out of Glasgow is offered by **Loch Lomond Seaplanes** ( ☎ 0870 242 1457; www.lochlomondseaplanes.com; Clyde River, Glasgow Science Centre), which flies regularly from the River Clyde at Glasgow Science Centre to Oban (£149 return; p858) and Tobermory (£179 return; p862) on Scotland's west coast.

### Bus
All long-distance buses arrive and depart from **Buchanan bus station** ( ☎ 0141-333 3708; Killermont St), just 300m north of Queen St train station.

Bus fares from London are very competitive – **Megabus** ( ☎ 0900 160 0900; www.megabus.com) should be your first port of call if you're looking for the cheapest fare, with one-way fares from around £10.

**Silver Choice** ( ☎ 01355-230403; www.silverchoice travel.co.uk) also has great deals (advance-purchase return ticket £29, 8½ hours). It departs at 10pm daily from both London Victoria coach station and Buchanan bus station in Glasgow. The service is very popular, so you'll need to book well in advance.

**National Express** ( ☎ 0870 580 8080; www.nationa lexpress.com) coaches to London leave from the same bus station (single £34, nine hours, at least four daily). There's a daily direct overnight bus from Heathrow airport, usually departing at 11.05pm. National Express also has direct services to Birmingham (£48, six to seven hours, four daily), Manchester (£28,

five hours, four daily), Newcastle (£30, four hours, one daily); and one from York (£34, seven hours, one daily).

**Scottish Citylink** ( ☎ 0870 550 5050; www.city link.co.uk) has buses to most major towns in Scotland, including a frequent service to Edinburgh (£8.40 return, 1¼ hours, every 20 minutes). Direct buses also run to Stirling (£6, 45 minutes, hourly), Inverness (£23, 3¾ hours, one daily) and Aberdeen (£24, three hours, hourly). There's a twice-daily service to Belfast in Northern Ireland (£25, six hours, three daily) via the Stranraer ferry.

### Car
There are numerous car-rental companies; the big names have offices at the airport. Local operators include **Arnold Clark** ( ☎ 0845 607 4500; www .arnoldclark.co.uk; 43 Allison St) and **Clarkson** ( ☎ 0141-771 3990; www.clarksonofglasgow.com; 89 Byres Rd).

### Train
Glasgow has two train stations. Generally, Central Station serves southern Scotland, England and Wales, and Queen St serves the north and east of Scotland. There are buses between the two every 10 minutes (free with a through train ticket), or it's a 10-minute walk.

There are direct trains from London's King's Cross and Euston stations; they're not cheap, but they're much quicker (£101, 5½ hours, 12 daily) and more comfortable than the bus. You can get cheaper fares if you book in advance.

**First ScotRail** ( ☎ 0845 7 55 00 33; www.firstscotrail.com) runs the West Highland line heading north to Oban and Fort William, and has other direct links to Dundee (£22, one hour 20 minutes, hourly), Aberdeen (£38, 1¾ hours, hourly) and Inverness (£38, three hours, one direct service daily). There are trains every 15 to 30 minutes to/from Edinburgh (£11, 50 minutes).

## GETTING AROUND
### To/From the Airport
First Glasgow's 757 AirLink bus runs between Glasgow International airport and Buchanan bus station (£2.90, 30 minutes, every 20 minutes 6am to 11pm) via the SECC and Central and Queen St train stations. The 24-hour Glasgow Flyer (www.glasgowflyer.com) is slightly faster (£4.20, 25 minutes) and more frequent (every 10 to 15 minutes, and every 30 minutes through the night). A taxi to the city centre costs around £20.

You can get to Prestwick airport by bus on the X77 route (£9, 45 minutes, every 30 minutes, hourly on Sunday), which operates from 7.30am to midnight; for earlier or later arrivals get the X99 airport express. You can also get to Prestwick by train from Central Station (£6.25, 50 minutes, every 30 minutes).

## Car
A convoluted one-way system that will leave you feeling like you're trying to navigate a pretzel, plus expensive and limited parking, makes driving an unattractive proposition, though parking is easier in the West End. The motorway (M8) makes getting into/out of the city easy, as long as you avoid rush hour.

## Public Transport
The **St Enoch Square Travel Centre** ( ☎ 0141-226 4826; ⊙ 8.30am-5.30pm Mon-Sat), just off Argyle St, provides information on all public transport in the Glasgow region. Here you can get a copy of the complicated but useful *Glasgow Mapmate* (£1), which shows all local bus routes run by First. You can buy tickets when you board local buses, but on most you must have exact change. Most fares around the city are 85p to £1.50; the FirstDay ticket allows unlimited travel on buses for a day, and can be bought from drivers for £3.20 (valid until 1am). After midnight there are limited night buses from George Sq.

The tiny trains on the circular **Underground** (www.spt.co.uk/subway) line serve 15 stations in the city's centre, west and south (£1.10 single). The Discovery ticket (£2.50) gives a day's unlimited travel after 9.30am. The Roundabout Glasgow ticket (adult/child £5/2.50) covers all Underground and train transport in and around the city (as far afield as Dumbarton, Milngavie and Blantyre) for a day.

## Taxi
You can hail a black cab from the street or call **Glasgow Taxis** ( ☎ 0141-429 7070). Otherwise there's a rank on Gordon St, just opposite Glasgow Central Station.

# LANARKSHIRE

Historically, Lanarkshire is the county that contained Glasgow. Today, its northern parts have been swallowed up by Glasgow's urban sprawl, but the southern part of the county encompasses the valley of the River Clyde, a mainly rural district of market gardens and dairy farms surrounded by low, rolling hills. The main attractions are the World Heritage Site of New Lanark (a fascinating renovation of a 19th-century cotton mill), the Falls of Clyde and the birthplace museum of David Livingstone in Blantyre.

## BLANTYRE
### pop 17,300
One of Scotland's most famous sons is David Livingstone, the epitome of the Victorian missionary-explorer, who opened up central Africa to European influence in the 19th century. After disappearing for several years during an expedition to the source of the Nile, he was famously 'found' by American newspaper reporter Henry Stanley in 1871, with the immortal words 'Dr Livingstone, I presume?'.

Visitors with an interest in Africa shouldn't miss the absorbing **David Livingstone Centre** (NTS; ☎ 01698-823140; 165 Station Rd; adult/child £5/4; ⊙ 10am-5pm Mon-Sat, 12.30-5pm Sun Easter-Dec), set in Livingstone's birthplace, which tells the story of his life. In 30 years it's estimated he travelled 29,000 miles through central Africa, mostly on foot – the sheer tenacity of the man was incredible. The centre is just downhill from Blantyre train station, which can be reached from Glasgow's Central Station (20 minutes, four an hour).

## LANARK & NEW LANARK
### pop 8250
Set in a beautiful wooded gorge on the banks of the River Clyde, the former cotton-spinning village of New Lanark is a monument to one of the most forward-thinking industrialists of the 19th century. Welshman Robert Owen (1771–1858), who married the mill-owner's daughter and co-owned and managed New Lanark from 1800 to 1828, was a philanthropist and social reformer who kicked against the rampant capitalism and exploitation of the early 19th century by providing his workers with good-quality housing, a cooperative store (the inspiration for the modern cooperative movement), a school with adult-education classes, the world's first infant school, a sick-pay fund for workers and a social and cultural centre. The mills were a commercial as well as humanitarian success, and influenced similar socialist experiments around the world.

Once the largest cotton-spinning complex in Britain, built in 1785 to take advantage of water power provided by the fast-flowing Clyde, New Lanark finally closed down in 1968. The site was restored and opened to the public, and was awarded Unesco World Heritage Site status in 2001.

## Orientation & Information

The **tourist office** ( ☎ 01555-661661; Horsemarket, Ladyacre Rd; ☿ 10am-5pm Mon-Sat year-round, Sun Easter-Sep) is in the market town of Lanark, next to the bus and train stations. New Lanark is 1.5 miles to the southwest – it's signposted from the tourist office.

## Sights

The best way to get a feel for New Lanark is to wander around its cobbled streets. What must once have been a noisy, bustling, industrial village, churning out enough cotton to wrap the planet, is now a peaceful oasis with only the swishing of trees and the rushing of the River Clyde to be heard. The **mill lade** flows through the middle of the village, and still provides water power – a hydroelectric turbine under Mill No 3 generates electricity for the visitor centre.

At the **visitor centre** ( ☎ 01555-661345; www.new lanark.org; adult/child £6.95/5.95; ☿ 11am-5pm) you can buy a ticket for all the main attractions. These include the **New Millennium Experience** – aimed mainly at kids – a slightly naff but thought-provoking multimedia ride that reminds us of Robert Owen's utopian vision. The visit continues through the restored **Mill No 3**, which is filled with the smell of raw yarn and the clatter and whirr of a genuine, working spinning mule, and has a **roof garden** with a great view over village and river.

Nearby, Robert Owen's **Historic School** contains an innovative, high-tech journey to New Lanark's past via a 3-D hologram of the spirit of Annie McLeod, a 10-year-old mill girl who describes life here in 1820. The kids will love it as it's very realistic, although the 'do good for all mankind' theme is getting a little wearing by now. Also included in your admission is entry to a **millworker's house**, Robert Owen's **home** and exhibitions on 'saving New Lanark'. There's also a 1920s-style **village store**.

After you've seen New Lanark you can walk up to the **Falls of Clyde** (1 mile) through the beautiful nature reserve managed by the Scottish Wildlife Trust; the 28m high Corra

Linn is the highest waterfall on the Clyde, and an impressive sight in full flood. Before you go, drop into the **Falls of Clyde Wildlife Centre** ( ☎ 01555-665262; adult/child £1/50p; ☿ 11am-5pm Mar-Dec, noon-4pm Jan & Feb) by the river in New Lanark. This place has interactive displays focused on badgers and bats, and live CCTV from a peregrine falcon's nest (April to July).

Note that the river's flow above New Lanark is diverted through Scotland's first hydroelectric power station, opened in 1927. This means that the Falls of Clyde are usually no more than a trickle – to see them at their best, check with the visitor centre for the dates of Waterfall Days, when the power station is switched off and the falls return to their full glory.

## Sleeping

**New Lanark SYHA** ( ☎ 0870 004 1143; www.syha.org .uk; Wee Row, New Lanark; dm £14-16; ☿ Mar-Oct; ▣ ) This hostel has a great location in an old mill building by the River Clyde. There are mainly four-bed dorms with attached bathroom, and one twin room.

**Summerlea** ( ☎ 01555-664889; elsie@elsiedickie .wanadoo.co.uk; 32 Hyndford Rd, Lanark; s/d from £30/50) Not far from Lanark's tourist office and within walking distance of New Lanark, this detached Victorian house has all the comforts of home, with a double and two twin rooms, all en suite. The huge single is a great choice as long as you don't mind the colour lavender.

**New Lanark Mill Hotel** ( ☎ 01555-667200; www .newlanarkhotel.co.uk; s/d from £80/119, cottages per week from £499; ▣ ) Cleverly converted from an 18th-century mill, this hotel is full of modern comforts and is right in the middle of the village. It has luxury rooms with river views (£25 extra for a spacious suite and added decadence) and also offers self-catering accommodation in cottages.

## Eating & Drinking

**[our pick] La Vigna** ( ☎ 01555-664320; 40 Wellgate, Lanark; mains £5-18; ☿ lunch Mon-Sat, dinner) Lanark's best restaurant is a local institution that has been serving up top-notch Italian cuisine for more than 20 years. It's the ideal spot for a special dinner, or you can take advantage of the good-value two-course lunch menu (£13 Monday to Saturday).

**Crown Tavern** ( ☎ 01555-664639; 17 Hope St, Lanark; mains £7-15; ☿ lunch & dinner) Just off the main street, this local favourite does good bar meals, with a restaurant upstairs that has a solid menu featuring steak, fish, chicken and generous pastas.

Down in New Lanark village, at the New Lanark Mill Hotel, you can get coffees and pub grub at the **Falls Bar** (mains £4-8; ✆ noon-9.30pm), or more-formal meals at the hotel's upstairs **restaurant** (2-/3-course dinner £21/26; ✆ lunch Sun, dinner).

## Getting There & Around
Lanark is 25 miles southeast of Glasgow. There are frequent trains from Glasgow's Central Station (£5.25, one hour, two an hour) – you may have to change at Holytown – or take bus 240X from Glasgow's Buchanan bus station (one hour, hourly Monday to Saturday).

There's a half-hourly bus service from Lanark train station (daily) to/from New Lanark. If you need a taxi, call **Clydewide** (✆ 01555-663221).

# SCOTTISH BORDERS
Much of Scotland's history has been played out along the Borders, from centuries of territorial battles and border raids to the building of imposing castles and grand abbeys, all lovingly dramatised by local poet and novelist Sir Walter Scott.

Some of the most visited tourist attractions today are the ruins that have emerged from this turbulent history, especially the monumental remains of Melrose, Dryburgh and Jedburgh abbeys. Walkers and cyclists can visit the various sights on a range of hiking and biking trails, notably the Southern Uplands Way, while anglers come to enjoy world-class salmon fishing on the scenic River Tweed, which cuts through the middle of the region and delineates the Scotland–England border for part of its length.

## Activities
Local tourist offices have a number of brochures, including *Cycling, Walking and Fishing in the Scottish Borders*. Walking possibilities include the 62-mile **St Cuthbert's Way** (www.scottish-walks.co.uk/cuthbert) and the **Borders Abbeys Way**, which links the Borders abbeys of Kelso, Jedburgh, Melrose and Dryburgh in a 68-mile circuit. The 55-mile **Four Abbeys Cycle Route** is a similar route for cyclists, well marked with blue signs.

For mountain bikers there is also a range of trails in the Tweed Valley and Glentress Forest Park, well marked and detailed in brochures available from tourist offices in the region, as well as the **Border Loop**, a signposted 250-mile circuit right around the Borders.

Catching a salmon on the Tweed is a lifelong ambition for many anglers. Find out more about booking permits (well in advance) at **FishTweed** ( ✆ 01573-470612; www.fishtweed.co.uk). For a guided experience try **Tweed Guide** ( ✆ 07962-401770; www.tweedguide.com), which operates out of Melrose, Selkirk, Galashiels and Kelso; a three-hour session of trout fishing costs £110 per person, while salmon fishing will set you back £325 for one day.

## Getting Around
There's a good network of local buses. **First** ( ✆ 0870 872 7271) operates between most of the border towns and connects the larger towns with Edinburgh. Local bus companies serving border towns also include **Munro's of Jedburgh** ( ✆ 01835-862253) and **Buskers** ( ✆ 01896-755808). The tourist offices stock excellent public-transport booklets to local areas.

## PEEBLES
pop 8100

Prosperous and picturesque Peebles sits smugly on the banks of the River Tweed, content in the knowledge that it enjoys a prime Borders location, set among rolling, wooded hills with one of the world's top salmon rivers on its doorstep. The **tourist office** ( ✆ 0870 608 0404; High St; ✆ daily Apr-Dec, Mon-Sat Jan-Mar) will chase down accommodation for you.

## Sights & Activities
Poke your head inside **Tweeddale Museum & Art Gallery** ( ✆ 01721-724820; admission free; ✆ 10.30am-12.30pm & 1-4pm Mon-Fri, plus 10am-1pm & 2-4pm Sat Apr-Oct), a small museum dedicated to literature and Borders sons such as Sir Walter Scott, before setting out on one of the many good walks around town. Try the easy stroll along the river to **Neidpath Castle** ( ✆ 01721-720333), a 14th-century tower house on a bluff above the River Tweed about 1 mile west of town (closed for refurbishment at time of research; should reopen in spring 2009).

Peebles is a good base for fly-fishing on the Tweed; get useful tips at **Cast Around Peebles** ( ✆ 01721-729229; 20a Northgate; trout permit per day £8, rod hire £18; ✆ 10am-5pm Mon-Fri, 10am-4pm Sat)

---

### SIR WALTER SCOTT (1771–1832)

Sir Walter Scott is one of Scotland's greatest literary figures. It was here, rambling around the Borders countryside as a child, that he developed a passion for historical ballads and Scottish heroes.

*The Lay of the Last Minstrel* (1805) was an early critical success; further works earning him an international reputation included *The Lady of the Lake* (1810), set around Loch Katrine and the Trossachs. He later turned his hand to novels and virtually invented the historical genre. *Waverley* (1814), which dealt with the 1745 Jacobite rebellion, set the classical pattern of the historical novel. Other works included *Guy Mannering* (1815) and *Rob Roy* (1817). In *Guy Mannering* he wrote about Borders farmer Dandie Dinmont and his pack of dogs, which became so popular that they became known as Dandie Dinmont Terriers, the only breed of dog named after a literary character.

Later in life Scott wrote obsessively to stave off bankruptcy. His works virtually single-handedly revived interest in Scottish history and legend in the early 19th century. Tourist offices stock a *Sir Walter Scott Trail* booklet, guiding you to many places associated with his life in the Borders.

---

and online at www.peeblesshiretroutfishing .co.uk.

There are also several good mountain-biking areas nearby including **Glentress Forest** (www.7stanes.gov.uk), a mountain-biking mecca that has trails for everyone from beginners to advanced. The **Hub** ( ☎ 01721-721736; www.the hubintheforest.co.uk; Glentress Forest; 1-day hire for a hard-tail £22, for full suspension from £40; 10am-6pm Mon-Fri, 9am-7pm Sat & Sun), 2.5 miles east of Peebles, on the A72, offers mountain-bike hire, sales and repairs.

### Sleeping & Eating

**Cross Keys Hotel** ( ☎ 01721-724222; www.crosskeyspee bles.co.uk; 24 Northgate; bunkroom per person £22, s/d/f £35/60/75; P ) The Cross Keys is a renovated 17th-century coaching inn, and the current owners have maintained its long tradition of fine hospitality. As well as good B&B it has two four-person bunkrooms for hikers and cyclists; its Orchard Bistro serves hearty dinners (mains £7 to £10), and the bar has real ales and live music at weekends.

**Whitie's** ( ☎ 01721-721605; www.whities.co.uk; 69 High St; s/d £50/75) With tall Victorian windows and a quaint bookstore downstairs, this charming guesthouse offers a superior class of B&B that includes clawfoot baths and period fireplaces in some rooms. Breakfasts including haggis and pastries are worth getting up early to linger over.

**Oven Door** ( ☎ 01721-723456; 24 High St; snacks £3-6; 10am-9.30pm) With a bounty of scones, cakes and pastries, this is the town's top spot for a snack.

**our pick Sunflower Restaurant** ( ☎ 01721-722420; 4 Bridgegate; mains £8-15; lunch Mon-Sat, dinner Thu-Sat)

The Sunflower, with its pastel-yellow rooms enlivened with photo art and colourful rugs, is a pleasant spot to stop for lunch or dinner. The food is fresh and home-cooked, from smoked haddock chowder to steak-and-onion sandwiches, with good vegie dishes such as lentil and cashew nut loaf with roast cumin potatoes.

### Getting There & Away

The main bus stop is beside the post office on Eastgate. First bus 62 runs half-hourly to Edinburgh (1¼ hours), Galashiels (45 minutes) and Melrose (1¼ hours).

## AROUND PEEBLES
### Traquair House

One of Britain's great country houses, **Traquair House** ( ☎ 01896-830323; www.traquair.co.uk; adult/child £6.50/3.50; noon-5pm Apr-May & Sep, 10.30am-5.30pm Jun-Aug, 11am-4pm Oct) – pronounced tra-*kweer* – is the oldest inhabited house in Scotland; parts are believed to have been constructed long before the first official record of its existence in 1107. The original tower house was gradually added to over the next 500 years, but the place has remained virtually unchanged since 1642.

Since the 15th century the house has belonged to various branches of the Stuart family, whose unwavering Catholicism and loyalty to the Jacobite cause is largely why development ceased when it did. One of the most fascinating features is the hidden room where priests secretly lived and conducted Mass – right up to the passing of the 1829 Catholic Emancipation Act. Other beautiful time-worn rooms hold precious relics, including the cradle that Mary Queen of Scots used for her son, James VI of Scotland (later James I of England).

More-recent attractions will appeal to kids, including a **maze** and adventure playground, while adults will appreciate the produce of the 18th-century **brewery**. The **Scottish Beer Festival** takes place here in late May and there's the **Traquair Fair** in early August. You can even stay in one of three elegant rooms (singles £100, doubles £180), complete with cano-pied beds and antique furniture; these have to be pre-booked.

The house is set in beautiful parkland with woodland walks and secluded picnic spots about 6 miles southeast of Peebles. Bus C1 departs Peebles at 10.15am for Traquair daily and returns at 2.50pm, or you can take bus 62 from Edinburgh to Innerleithen (one hour 20 minutes, every 30 minutes), from where the house is a 1.5-mile walk.

## SELKIRK
pop 5740

Selkirk is a serene little town that climbs a steep ridge above the Ettrick Water, a tribu-tary of the Tweed. Mills came to the area in the early 1800s, but today it's a peaceful place with a couple of interesting museums. The **tourist office** ( ☎ 0870 608 0404; Halliwell's Close; ☼ Apr-Oct) is tucked away off Market Sq.

Inside the tourist office is **Halliwell's House Museum** ( ☎ 01750-20096; Halliwell's Close; admission free; ☼ 10am-5pm Mon-Sat, to noon Sun late Mar–Sep, ex-cept 10am-1pm Sun Jul & Aug, 10am-4pm Mon-Sat, to noon Sun Oct), the oldest building in Selkirk (1712). The museum charts local history with an en-grossing exhibition that includes mock-ups of Victorian shops and a display on the local tradition of commons riding.

Drop into **Sir Walter Scott's Court Room** ( ☎ 01750-20096; Market Sq; admission free; ☼ 10am-4pm Mon-Fri, to 2pm Sat Apr-Sep, plus 10am-2pm Sun May-Aug, 1-4pm Mon-Sat Oct), where the great man once served as sheriff of Selkirk County; it houses an exhibition on his life and writings. There is also a fascinating account of the Scottish explorer Mungo Park (born near Selkirk) and his search for the River Niger.

There's better accommodation in Melrose or Jedburgh, but the **County Hotel** ( ☎ 01750-721233; www.countyhotelselkirk.co.uk; Market Sq; s/d from £39/79; bar meals £8) is a decent local option.

First bus 95 and X95 run half-hourly or hourly between Hawick, Selkirk, Galashiels

and Edinburgh. From Selkirk to Edinburgh costs £5.50 (two hours).

## MELROSE
pop 1650

Melrose is the most charming and picturesque of the Borders towns, lying at the foot of the heather-clad triple peaks of the Eildon Hills. It's a spick-and-span little place, with a tidy market square decked out with flower-filled hanging baskets, some attractive hotels and restaurants, and a famous rugby pitch that is host to the annual Melrose Sevens tour-nament. But its main attraction is Melrose Abbey, whose majestic ruins rise above the middle of the town.

### Information

The **tourist office** ( ☎ 0870 608 0404; Abbey House; ☼ 10am-5pm Mon-Sat, 10am-2pm Sun Apr & May, 9.30am-5pm Mon-Sat, 10am-2pm Sun Jun & Sep, 9.30am-5.30pm Mon-Sat, 10am-4pm Sun Jul & Aug, 10am-4pm Mon-Sat, 10am-2pm Sun Oct, 10am-2pm Sat & Mon, noon-4pm Sun Nov-Mar), across from Melrose Abbey, has masses of information on all of Britain.

### Sights & Activities

Founded by King David I in 1136 for Cistercian monks from Rievaulx in Yorkshire, **Melrose Abbey** (HS; ☎ 01896-822562; admission £5.20; ☼ 9.30am-5.30pm Apr-Sep, 9.30am-4.30pm Oct-Mar) is perhaps the most beautiful of the Borders ab-beys. It was sacked repeatedly by the English in the 13th and 14th centuries, and was rebuilt on the orders of Robert the Bruce. After his death, Bruce's heart was sealed in a lead casket and, according to his wishes, borne by the Black Douglas into battle against the Moors during the Spanish Reconquista. Despite Douglas' death, the well-travelled heart was returned to Scotland and buried in the chapter house of the abbey.

The present ruins date mainly from the 15th century, and are in a surprisingly ornate style for the Cistercian order. The building was never completed, and by the time of the Reformation only 15 monks re-mained in the once-thriving community. The remaining shell is pure Gothic and is famous for its decorative stonework – see if you can spot the carving of a pig playing the bagpipes.

The three conical peaks southeast of the town are known as the **Eildon Hills** – they in-spired the name Trimontium for the fort built here by the Romans – and make a good target for an easy hill walk. The **Roman Heritage Way** (www.romanheritageway.com) is a northern limb of the Hadrian's Wall Path National Trail (see p656), a long-haul walk that takes in several Roman sites.

**St Cuthbert's Way** begins at Melrose Abbey and leads southeast across the border for 62 miles to Lindisfarne. From Melrose to Dryburgh (roughly 18 miles) is one of the more spectacular legs of the **Borders Abbeys Way**.

Good day-walks are detailed in *Walks Around Melrose* (£1), while short cycle trips are detailed in *Melrose: Local Cycling Trails* (free), both available at the tourist office.

### Festivals & Events

In mid-April rugby followers fill the town for the week-long **Melrose Rugby Sevens** competition. Another popular event on the festivals calendar is the **Borders Book Festival** (www.bordersbookfestival.org), stretching over four days in late June.

### Sleeping

Melrose B&Bs and hotels aren't cheap by Scottish standards, but they are of a high standard; this would make a great place to treat yourself.

**Melrose SYHA Hostel** ( ☎ 01896-82251; www.syha.org.uk; Priorwood; dm £14-16; ☿ Mar-Oct; ⬜ ) Just a stroll from the abbey (in fact you can glimpse it from the 2nd floor), this Georgian mansion features tidy dorms complemented by a big garden and barbecue area. Not a party house, this hostel is mainly used by walkers looking to turn in early. From Market Sq, follow the signposts to the A68.

**Braidwood** ( ☎ 01896-22488; www.braidwoodmelrose.co.uk; Buccleuch St; s/d from £40/60) Mr and Mrs Dalgetty's popular town house near the abbey is an excellent place, with high-quality facilities and a warm welcome. The sparkling rooms are finely decorated and the twin has great views. Note, singles not available in summer.

**Burts Hotel** ( ☎ 01896-822285; www.burtshotel.co.uk; Market Sq; s/d from £60/116) Set in an early-18th-century house, and with an enviable reputation, Burts retains much of its period charm and has been run by the same couple for over 30 years. There's a welcoming bar that serves excellent meals, and roaring log fires in winter.

**our pick** **Townhouse** ( ☎ 01896-822645; www.thetownhousemelrose.co.uk; Market Sq; s/d from £75/114) Burts' more contemporary sister hotel across the square, the classy Townhouse has some of the most stylish rooms in town. There are two enormous 'superior' rooms with lavish furnishings; the one on the ground floor in particular has an excellent en suite, which includes a Jacuzzi.

### Eating

**Russell's Restaurant** ( ☎ 01896-822335; Market Sq; mains £5-7; ☿ 9.30am-4.30pm Tue-Sat, 9.30am-5pm Fri & Sat, noon-5pm Sun) Russell's is a stylish little tearoom/restaurant with a large range of snacks and more-substantial offerings, including a hearty ploughman's lunch.

**Monte Cassino** ( ☎ 01896-820082; Palma Pl; mains £8-17; ☿ lunch & dinner Tue-Sun) This Italian restaurant has an atmospheric setting in the old Victorian train station building, and dishes up reliably good pastas, pizzas and classic dishes such as chicken Milanese and *saltimbocca alla Romana* (classic Italian dish – veal cutlets sautéed with prosciutto and sage).

**Marmion's Brasserie** ( ☎ 01896-822245; 5 Buccleuch St; mains £13-15; ☿ lunch & dinner Mon-Sat) This atmospheric, wood-panelled niche serves snacks all day, but the lunch and dinner menus include gastronomic delights, such as grilled venison, roast lamb and sea bass. At lunch (mains £9 to £11) the Cumberland sausage with mash and melted onions is a good choice.

**Burts** ( ☎ 01896-822285; www.burtshotel.co.uk; Market Sq; mains £10-13) also serves excellent bar meals of restaurant quality, but it's very popular so book a table if you can. If you get turned away, try the **Kings Arms** ( ☎ 01896-822143; High St; mains £7-12; ☿ lunch & dinner), which has a less interesting but still tasty menu.

### Getting There & Away

There are First buses to/from Galashiels (20 minutes, frequent), Jedburgh (30 minutes, at least hourly Monday to Saturday), Peebles (1¼ hours, at least hourly Monday to Saturday) and Edinburgh (£6, 2¼ hours, half-hourly Monday to Saturday).

## AROUND MELROSE
### Dryburgh Abbey

The most complete of all the Borders abbeys is **Dryburgh Abbey** (HS; ☎ 01835-822381; admission £4.70; ☿ 9.30am-5.30pm Apr-Sep, 9.30am-4.30pm Oct-Mar). Partly due to it's out-of-the-way location by the Tweed, Dryburgh was only ransacked three times by the English. Dating from about 1150, it belonged to the Premonstratensians, a religious order founded in France, and conjures up images of 12th-century monastic life more successfully than its counterparts in nearby towns. The pink-hued stone ruins were chosen as the burial place of Sir Walter Scott. A mile and a half north of the abbey on the B6356 is the famous **Scott's View**, looking across the Tweed Valley to the Eildon Hills; it was Sir Walter Scott's favourite spot, and it is said that his horse, which pulled his hearse on the way to his burial at Dryburgh Abbey, paused here for several minutes out of habit.

The abbey is 5 miles southeast of Melrose. You can hike there along the southern bank of the River Tweed, or take a bus to the nearby village of Newtown St Boswells.

## Abbotsford House

For a window into Sir Walter Scott's life drop by his former residence, **Abbotsford House** ( ☎ 01896-752043; www.scottsabbotsford.co.uk; adult/child £6.20/3.10; ☉ 9.30am-5pm late Mar–Oct). The writer lived here for 20 years until his death in 1832, amassing an intriguing collection of literature, with a library that numbers 9000 volumes, and historic relics such as Rob Roy's gun, dirk (dagger) and sword, and a lock of Bonnie Prince Charlie's hair.

The house is about 2 miles west of Melrose between the River Tweed and the B6360. Frequent buses run between Galashiels and Melrose; alight at the Tweedbank roundabout and follow the signposts (it's a 15-minute walk). You can also walk from Melrose to Abbotsford along the southern bank of the Tweed.

## KELSO & AROUND
pop 5116

Kelso, a prosperous market town with a cobbled main square flanked by handsome Georgian buildings, has a French feel to it and an historic appeal. Sir Walter Scott described it as 'the most beautiful, if not the most romantic town in Scotland', though today this seems a bit of an overstatement. Nevertheless it has an attractive setting at the junction of the Rivers Tweed and Teviot, and has the bustling atmosphere of a real working town rather than just another stop on the tourist trail.

## Information

**Border Books** ( ☎ 01573-225861; Horsemarket; ☉ 10.30am-4pm Mon, Tue & Thu-Sat) Great range of books, especially out of date and antiquarian.

**Kelso Library** ( ☎ 01573-223171; Bowmont St; ☉ 10am-1pm & 2-5pm Mon, Tue, Thu & Fri, plus 5.30-7pm Tue & Thu, 10am-1pm Wed, 9.30am-12.30pm Sat) Free Internet access.

**Tourist office** ( ☎ 0870 608 0404; www.visitscottish borders.com; Town House, The Square; ☉ daily Apr-Nov, Mon-Sat Dec-Mar)

## Sights
### KELSO ABBEY

Once the largest and richest of the Border abbeys, picturesque **Kelso Abbey** (HS; Bridge St; admission free; ☉ 9.30am-5.30pm Mon-Sat, 2-5.30pm Sun Apr-Sep, 9.30am-4.30pm Mon-Sat, 2-4.30pm Sun Oct-Mar) was reduced to ruins by marauding English armies in the 16th century. The surviving west end dates from the 12th century and is some of the finest surviving Romanesque architecture in Scotland.

Nearby, the 18th-century **Old Parish Church** ( ☉ 10am-4pm Mon-Fri May-Sep) breaks with architectural tradition with its curious octagonal design.

### FLOORS CASTLE

Flamboyant **Floors Castle** ( ☎ 01573-223333; www .floorscastle.com; adult/child £7/3.50; ☉ 11am-5pm Easter & May-Oct) is Scotland's largest inhabited house. Built by William Adam in the 1720s, its original Georgian simplicity was 'improved' during the 1840s with the addition of rather ridiculous battlements and turrets.

Inside, the drawing room's vividly coloured 17th-century Gobelins tapestries and intricate oak carvings in the ornate ballroom are impressive, and palatial windows reveal a ribbon of green countryside extending well beyond the estate. While the real owners are the Dukes of Roxburghe, this building made a cameo as Tarzan's ancestral home in the film *Greystoke*.

### SMAILHOLM TOWER

Perched on a rocky knoll 6 miles west of Kelso, **Smailholm Tower** (HS; ☎ 01573-460365; adult/child £3.70/1.85; ☉ 9.30am-5.30pm Apr-Sep, 9.30am-4.30pm Oct, 9.30am-4.30pm Sat & Sun Nov-Mar) is a classic 15th-century tower house that affords panoramic views as well as being a spectacular sight itself. Inside are costumed dummies and tapestries depicting characters from *Minstrelsy of the*

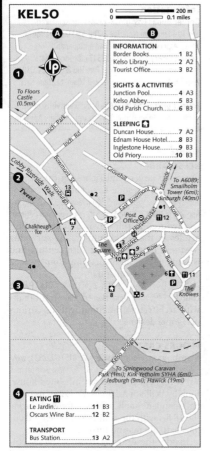

**KELSO**

| | |
|---|---|
| 0 | 200 m |
| 0 | 0.1 miles |

**INFORMATION**
Border Books.................1 B2
Kelso Library..................2 A2
Tourist Office................3 B2

**SIGHTS & ACTIVITIES**
Junction Pool.................4 A3
Kelso Abbey...................5 B3
Old Parish Church..........6 B3

**SLEEPING** 🏠
Duncan House.................7 A2
Ednam House Hotel.........8 B3
Inglestone House...........9 B3
Old Priory....................10 B3

**EATING** 🍴
Le Jardin.....................11 B3
Oscars Wine Bar...........12 B2

**TRANSPORT**
Bus Station..................13 A2

*Scottish Border* – a work by Sir Walter Scott, whose ancestors once lived here.

On the way to the tower is the farmyard of **Sandyknowe**, once owned by Scott's grandfather. Scott was brought here as a sick child and was inspired by the local ballads and stories, along with his ancestors' ruined tower.

Head northwest out of Kelso on the A6089 then turn left on the B6397 towards Smailholm village and look out for signposts to Smailholm Tower (no public transport).

## Activities

The **Pennine Way**, which starts at Edale in the Peak District (p465), ends at Kirk Yetholm, 6 miles southeast of Kelso, where most walkers

celebrate with a pint at the Border Hotel and stay at the Kirk Yetholm SYHA Hostel.

Less ambitious walkers can take the riverside path from Kelso to Floors Castle, signposted off Roxburgh St just off the Square. The free tourist office leaflet, *Walter Scott's Kelso*, describes a walk around town that takes just under an hour.

Kelso sits on the banks of the famous **Junction Pool**, where the River Teviot flows into the Tweed. It's the most productive salmon-fishing beat on the whole river, but it ain't cheap – you can expect to pay from £1000 a day and more, with bookings made years in advance. If all you want to do is watch the anglers pit their wits against the fish, there's a comfortable picnic bench overlooking the pool.

## Sleeping

**Kirk Yetholm SYHA Hostel** ( ☎ 01573-420639; Kirk Yetholm; dm £13-14; ☼ Apr-Sep) All the talk at this homely little hostel is about comparing how much mud you got on your boots as you completed the final leg of the Pennine Way. It's 6 miles southeast of Kelso; bus 81 runs to/from Kelso seven times a day from Monday to Saturday (three times on Sunday).

**Duncan House** ( ☎ 01573-225682; www.tweedbreaks .co.uk; 2 Chalkheugh Tce; s/d £45/64; P ) This lovely Georgian house, overlooking a prime stretch of angling real estate, has elegantly decorated rooms with period furnishings and freestanding, clawfoot bathtubs. There's smoked salmon and kippers at breakfast in case you don't hook a fish of your own, and the owner's passion for angling means he offers tips on using trout and salmon rods, and can lend you rod and tackle.

**our pick** **Old Priory** ( ☎ 01573-223030; www.theold priorykelso.com; 33 Woodmarket St; s/d/f £45/70/100; P ) The doubles in this atmospheric 18th-century house are bright and spacious and the family suite (double and two single beds) has to be seen to be believed; rooms are both comfortable and full of character. The good news extends to the garden – perfect for a coffee in the morning – and the dining room is dominated by an ancient stone fireplace.

**Ednam House Hotel** ( ☎ 01573-224168; www.ednam house.com; Bridge St; s/d from £81/131, cottage £200; P ) Set amid spacious gardens overlooking the Tweed, this Georgian country house has been successfully transformed into a stylish hotel. Rooms with river views will push up the price, but you can always enjoy the same scene from the excellent restaurant (three-course dinner £28, open for dinner daily and Sunday lunch). A separate cottage in the grounds (sleeps up to four) offers a more intimate option.

Other recommendations:

**Springwood Caravan Park** ( ☎ 01573-224596; www .springwood.biz; sites £17; ☺ Mar-Oct) A massive park that attracts a cheerful community (no tents).

**Inglestone House** ( ☎ 01573-225800; www.ingle stonehouse.co.uk; Abbey Row; s/d/£40/60) Wedged between the Square and abbey; well-run guesthouse great for families or couples.

## Eating & Drinking

**Le Jardin** ( ☎ 01573-228288; 5a The Knowes; snacks £4-6; ☺ 9.30am-4pm Mon-Sat) A cosy little cafe near the abbey, serving good snacks and cakes.

**Border Hotel** ( ☎ 01573-420237; www.theborderhotel .com; Kirk Yetholm; mains £7-10) A classic Borders country pub, with roaring fires, hand-pulled real ales and a range of malt whiskies to warm walkers at the end of the Pennine Way; a great spot to stop for some post-walk pub grub, or even to stay overnight (£45 per person).

**Oscars Wine Bar** ( ☎ 01573-224008; www.oscars-kelso .com; 35-37 Horsemarket; mains £10-18; ☺ lunch & dinner) If you enjoy a glass of wine with your dinner in a Mediterranean-themed setting, this is the place for you. Dishes on the extensive and varied menu are simple and well prepared, and include roast monkfish with a fresh herb and almond crust, and chicken or vegetable fajitas with salsa and guacamole.

## Getting There & Away

Munro's runs regular buses to Edinburgh, some involving a connection (£6.40, two hours, five to eight daily). There are also very frequent departures for Jedburgh (25 minutes, 10 daily Monday to Saturday, five on Sunday) and Galashiels via Melrose (55 minutes, hourly). There are about six buses daily Monday to Saturday (three on Sunday) between Kelso and Berwick-upon-Tweed (45 minutes).

# JEDBURGH
pop 4090

Jedburgh was once such a target of cross-border raids that during the 15th century the Scots destroyed the town's castle to prevent it falling into English hands. Fortunately other elements of the town survived – notably the ruins of one of the great Borders abbeys – to be assaulted anew today by camera-wielding invaders from the south.

The **tourist office** ( ☎ 01835-863170; Murray's Green; ☺ 9.15am-5pm Mon-Sat, 10am-5pm Sun Apr, May & Oct, 9am-6pm Mon-Sat, 10am-5pm Sun Jun, Jul & Sep, 9am-7pm Mon-Sat, 10am-6pm Sun Aug, 9.30am-4.30pm Mon-Sat Nov-Mar) has a bureau de change.

The **library** (Castlegate; ☺ 10am-1pm & 2-5pm Mon-Fri, 5.30-7pm Mon & Fri), just up the hill from Marketplace, has free internet access.

## Sights

Dominating the town skyline, **Jedburgh Abbey** (HS; ☎ 01835-863925; adult/child £5.20/2.60; ☺ 9.30am-5.30pm Apr-Sep, 9.30am-4.30pm Oct-Mar) was the first great Borders abbey to be passed into state care, and it shows – audio and visual presentations telling the abbey's story are scattered throughout the carefully preserved ruins (good for the kids or if it's raining). The abbey was founded in 1138 by David I as a priory for Augustinian canons. The red-sandstone walls are roofless but relatively intact, and the ingenuity of the master mason can be seen in some of the rich (if somewhat faded) stone carvings in the nave (be careful of the staircase in the nave – it's slippery when wet).

Scotland's much-loved monarch reputedly stayed, in 1566, at the 16th-century tower house now known as **Mary Queen of Scots Visitor Centre** ( ☎ 01835-863331; Queen St; adult/child £3/free; ☺ 10am-4.30pm Mon-Sat, 11am-4.30pm Sun Mar-Nov). Among the displays are the last letter she wrote before her execution, and her death mask.

Uphill from the town square, **Jedburgh Castle Jail & Museum** ( ☎ 01835-864750; admission free; ☺ 10am-4.30pm Mon-Sat, 1-4pm Sun Apr-Oct, closed Nov-Mar) is another relic of Jedburgh's troubled past. Built in 1823, it served as a debtor's prison, and the grim recreation of cells will have you paying off your credit cards. Kids can dress up as Romans and there's an audio tour (free with admission) that tells of a ghostly history.

## Sleeping

**Maplebank** ( ☎ 01835-862051; 3 Smiths Wynd; s/d £20/36) Scottish eccentricity at its best – there are not many B&Bs left like this one. It's a very old-fashioned place (you really are staying in someone's home) and one word sums it up: clutter. But the shared bathroom sparkles and the rooms are large and homely. The owner is just lovely and the breakfast (particularly if you like fruit, homemade yogurts and a selection of everything) is better than you'll get at a posh guesthouse.

---

**DETOUR: HERMITAGE CASTLE**

The foreboding tower of **Hermitage Castle** (HS; ☎ 01387-770244; adult/child £3.70/1.85; ⏰ 9.30am-5.30pm Apr-Sep, 9.30am-4.30pm Oct) rises in splendid isolation beside a rushing stream surrounded by bleak, empty moorland. Dating from the 13th century, but substantially rebuilt in the 15th, it embodies the brutal history of the Borders; the stones themselves almost speak of the past. Sir Walter Scott's favourite castle, it is probably best known as the home of the earl of Bothwell and the place to which Mary Queen of Scots rode in 1566 to see him after he had been wounded in a border raid.

It's also where, in 1338, Sir William Douglas imprisoned his enemy Sir Alexander Ramsay in a pit and deliberately starved him to death. Ramsay survived for 17 days by eating grain that trickled into his pit (which can still be seen) from the granary above. The castle is said to be haunted and it certainly has a slightly spooky feel, especially when dark clouds gather. If you have the place to yourself, a visit can be quite magical – it's one of the most atmospheric castles in southern Scotland.

The castle is 25 miles from Jedburgh, 15 miles south of Hawick on the B6339.

---

**Willow Court** ( ☎ 01835-863702; www.willowcourtjedburgh.co.uk; The Friars; s/d from £60/65; 🅿 ) With superb views over Jedburgh from the conservatory, where you are served a three-meals-in-one breakfast, Willow Court is a traditional B&B with homespun decor, smiling hosts and a large garden.

Other recommendations:

**Froylehurst** ( ☎ 01835-862477; Friarsgate; s/d £25/44) Has chintzy decor and views over the town.

**Craigowen** ( ☎ 01835-862604; duggleby21@hotmail.com; 30 High St; s/d £30/50) B&B with terrific, central location and huge rooms.

## Eating

**Cookie Jar** (37 High St; breakfasts £5, snacks £3-6; ⏰ 10am-5pm) This refreshingly unpretentious tearoom serves up good-quality sandwiches, cakes and traybakes, alongside strong coffee and speciality teas.

**Nightjar** ( ☎ 01835-862552; 1 Abbey Close; mains £10-15; ⏰ dinner Tue-Sat) An intimate little restaurant serving a mix of creative dishes (try the smoked hake fishcakes with green mango salad), including seafood and Thai cuisine. The real highlight is if you're lucky enough to be here on the last Tuesday of the month when a special Thai menu is served; locals rave about this night.

## Getting There & Away

Jedburgh has good bus connections to Hawick (25 minutes, roughly hourly), Melrose (30 minutes, at least hourly Monday to Saturday) and Kelso (25 minutes, at least hourly Monday to Saturday, four Sunday). Munro's runs from Edinburgh to Jedburgh (£6, two hours, at least hourly Monday to Saturday, five Sunday).

# DUMFRIES & GALLOWAY

Some of southern Scotland's finest attractions lie in the gentle hills and lush valleys of Dumfries & Galloway. Ideal for families, there's plenty on offer for the kids and, happily, restaurants and B&Bs/guesthouses that are very used to children. Galloway Forest with its sublime views, mountain-biking and walking trails, red deer, kites and other wildlife is a highlight, as are the dream-like ruins of Caerlaverock Castle.

Adding to the appeal is a string of picturesque towns. Although they are devoid of the tourist crush, domestic daytrippers flood pretty Kirkcudbright and other hot spots when the sun shines. And shine it does – this region boasts the sunniest weather in Scotland (though admittedly, that's not saying much!).

## Getting There & Around

**Eurolines/National Express** ( ☎ 0870 514 3219) operates bus services between London and Belfast, via Birmingham, Manchester, Dumfries and Stranraer.

Local bus operators cover the region comprehensively. The principal operators are **McEwan's** ( ☎ 01387-256533) and **Stagecoach Western** ( ☎ 01776-704484).

Two train lines between Carlisle and Glasgow cross the region, via Dumfries and Moffat respectively. The line from Glasgow to Stranraer runs via Ayr.

## DUMFRIES
**pop 31,000**

Despite having several important Burns-related sights, Dumfries has so far escaped mass tourism. Lovely, red-hued sandstone bridges span the broad River Nith, and there are pleasant grassed areas along the riverbank near the Robert Burns Centre. However, the town centre is a bit run-down looking.

### Information
**Ewart Library** ( ☎ 01387-253820; Catherine St; ☒ 9.15am-7.30pm Mon-Wed & Fri, 9.15am-5pm Thu & Sat) Free internet access and genealogical records at this excellent cybercentre in a fine old building.
**Tourist office** ( ☎ 01387-253862; 64 Whitesands; ☒ 9.30am-5pm Mon-Sat Apr-Jun, 9am-6pm Mon-Sat, 10.30am-4.30pm Sun Jul-Aug, 9am-5.30pm Mon-Sat, 10.30am-4.30pm Sun Sep, 9.30am-5pm Mon-Sat, 10.30am-4pm Sun Oct, 9am-5pm Mon-Sat, 9am-4pm Sun Nov, 9.30am-5pm Mon-Fri Dec-Mar) Opposite the car park by the river; stacks of information on the whole region.

### Sights
The red-sandstone bridges arching over the River Nith are the most attractive features of the town, and **Devorgilla Bridge** (1431) is one of the oldest bridges in Scotland.

**Robert Burns Centre** ( ☎ 01387-264808; Mill Rd; admission free, audiovisual presentation £1.60/80p; ☒ 10am-8pm Mon-Sat, 2-5pm Sun Apr-Sep, 10am-5pm & 2-5pm Tue-Sat Oct-Mar) is an award-winning museum in an old mill on the banks of the River Nith, telling the story of Burns and Dumfries in the 1790s through an audiovisual presentation and original Burns manuscripts. Also check out the photographic exhibition, which includes local wildlife and some beautiful shots of the Solway coast.

**Burns House** ( ☎ 01387-255297; Burns St; admission free; ☒ 10am-5pm Mon-Sat, 2-5pm Sun Apr-Sep, 10am-1pm & 2-5pm Tue-Sat Oct-Mar) is a place of pilgrimage for Burns enthusiasts; it's here that the poet spent the last years of his life, and there are some interesting relics, original letters and manuscripts. Look for his signature scratched into an upstairs window.

Burns is interred nearby in a domed **mausoleum** in the graveyard of St Michael's Kirk, his tomb adorned with the figure of the 'ploughman poet' and his muse.

### Sleeping
There's a good selection of B&Bs along Lovers Walk and around into Moffat Rd.

**Merlin B&B** ( ☎ 01387-261002; 2 Kenmure Tce; s/d £30/50; ℗ ) The folks here have been doing B&B a long time and they know their stuff – little touches like homemade choccies and fresh milk in the rooms sets this place apart. There are three rooms – the best is No 2, which has superb river and town vistas – and the location is one of the best in Dumfries.

**Glenure** ( ☎ 01387-252373; www.glenurebnb.co.uk; 43 Moffat Rd; s/d £35/50; ℗ ) This well-equipped guesthouse has four bright and cheerful rooms that are almost like hotel rooms, complete with desks and en suites, including a family room with big bay window (one double, one single plus space for a cot).

**our pick** **Ferintosh Guest House** ( ☎ 01387-252262; www.ferintosh.net; 30 Lovers Walk; s £30-45, d £50-56) A Victorian villa opposite the train station, Ferintosh is named after Robert Burns' favourite whisky – there'll probably be a free dram awaiting you on arrival. There are six sumptuous rooms done up in individual

---

### TYING THE KNOT IN GRETNA GREEN

From the mid-18th century, eloping couples south of the border realised that under Scottish law people could (and still can) tie the knot at the age of 16 without parental consent (in England and Wales the legal age was 21). Gretna Green's location close to the border made it the most popular venue.

At one time anyone could perform a legal marriage ceremony, but in Gretna Green it was usually the local blacksmith, who became known as the 'Anvil Priest'. In 1940 the 'anvil weddings' were outlawed, but eloping couples still got married in the church or registry office.

The **Old Blacksmith's Shop** ( ☎ 01461-338441; www.gretnagreen.com; Gretna Green; adult/child £3.50/free; ☒ 9am-7pm Jun-Aug, 9am-6pm Easter-May, Sep & Oct, 9am-5pm Nov-Easter) has an exhibition on Gretna Green's history, a sculpture park and a coach museum (there's even an anvil marriage room!).

Today many people still make or reaffirm their marriage vows in the village. If you want to get married over the famous anvil in the Old Blacksmith's Shop at Gretna Green, check out **Gretna Green Weddings** (www.gretnaweddings.com).

themes with original artwork by the owner – the whisky room is our favourite – and breakfast comes with haggis on the menu, served by a man in a kilt, no less!

## Eating & Drinking

**Globe Inn** ( ☎ 01387-252335; 56 High St; bar mains £6-7; ☺ lunch & dinner) A traditional, rickety old nook-and-cranny pub, said to be Burns' favourite watering hole, serving home-cooked bar meals.

**Cavens Arms** ( ☎ 01387-252896; 20 Buccleuch St; mains £6-10; ☺ lunch & dinner) You don't win a Camra Pub of the Year award for three years straight unless you're doing something right, and this lovely, friendly old pub pours some of the finest real ale in the southwest. The food is just as good – probably the best fish and chips in Dumfries & Galloway, and a damn fine steak pie, too.

**Hullabaloo** ( ☎ 01387-259679; www.hullabaloorestaurant.co.uk; Mill Rd; mains £8-16; ☺ lunch daily, dinner Tue-Sat) At weekends locals flock to this contemporary restaurant in the Robert Burns Centre, so best book a table. At lunch you'll get wraps, melts and ciabattas, but for dinner it's inventive angles on traditional creations such as fillet steak with wasabi, ginger and soy sauce, or butternut squash ravioli with a creamy mushroom, rosemary and pinenut sauce.

**Linen Room** ( ☎ 01387-255689; www.linenroom.com; 53 St Michael St; mains £17-19; ☺ lunch & dinner Tue-Sat) Dumfries' best restaurant brings a touch of metropolitan sophistication to the town, with stylish decor, linen-draped tables and a menu that makes the most of Scottish produce, from the selection of breads (and three different butters as well) to the Skye scallops and Galloway beef.

## Getting There & Away

### BUS

Eurolines/National Express buses 920 and 921 run twice daily between London, Birmingham and Belfast, via Carlisle, Dumfries and Stranraer; London to Dumfries is £31.

Local buses run regularly to Kirkcudbright (one hour, roughly hourly Monday to Saturday, six on Sunday) and towns along the A75.

Bus 100/101 runs to/from Edinburgh (£6.50, 2¾ hours, six daily), via Moffat and Biggar, but it's faster (under two hours total) to take the train from Edinburgh to Lockerbie, then bus 81 to Dumfries.

### TRAIN

There are direct trains to Dumfries from Carlisle (£8.10, 35 minutes, hourly Monday to Saturday, five on Sunday) and Glasgow (£12, 1¾ hours, eight daily, two on Sunday).

## AROUND DUMFRIES
### Caerlaverock Castle

The ruins of **Caerlaverock Castle** (HS; ☎ 01387-770244; adult/child £5.20/2.60; ☺ 9.30am-5.30pm Apr-Sep, 9.30am-4.30pm Oct-Mar) are among the loveliest in Britain. Surrounded by a moat, neatly groomed lawns and stands of trees, the unusual pink-hued, triangular, stone castle looks impregnable – but it fell several times. The curtain walls date from the late 13th-century, but inside there are chambers with an extraordinary Scottish Renaissance facade built in 1634. The castle is 8 miles southeast of Dumfries by Glencaple on the B725. Stagecoach Western bus 371 runs nine times a day (Monday to Saturday, twice Sunday) to the castle from Dumfries.

A mile further on is **Caerlaverock Wildfowl & Wetlands Centre** ( ☎ 01387-770200; www.wwt.org.uk; Eastpark Farm; adult/child £5.95/2.95; ☺ 10am-5pm), a 1400-acre nature reserve with observation towers and CCTV spy cameras to spot badgers, wild swans and hen harriers. The highlight of the year is in October, when vast flocks of migrating barnacle geese stop to feed.

### New Abbey

The small, picturesque village of New Abbey lies 7 miles south of Dumfries on the A710, clustered around the gaunt, red sandstone remains of 13th-century **Sweetheart Abbey** (HS; ☎ 01387-850397; adult/child £3/1.50; ☺ 9.30am-5.30pm Apr-Sep, 9.30am-4.30pm Sat-Wed Oct-Mar). The abbey was founded by Devorgilla de Balliol in honour of her dead husband (with whom she had founded Balliol College, Oxford). On his death, she had his heart embalmed and carried it with her until she died 22 years later. She and the heart are buried in the presbytery of the abbey church – hence the name.

Next door to the ruins is **Abbey Cottage** ( ☎ 01387-850377; mains £4-6; ☺ 10am-5pm Easter-Oct, 11am-4.30pm Sat & Sun Mar & Nov–24 Dec), a snug little tearoom that serves fair-trade tea and coffee, home-baked scones, locally made haggis with oatcakes, and delicious salads and sandwiches.

---

**DETOUR: THREAVE CASTLE**

The romantic and imposing tower of **Threave Castle** (HS; ☎ 07711-223101; adult/child £4.20/2.10; 9.30am-5.30pm Apr-Sep, 9.30am-4.30pm Oct) stands on a small island in the River Dee near Castle Douglas. A ferry takes you across the river with a guide who cheerily relates the site's grim history. Built by the aptly named Archibald the Grim in 1369, the castle withstood several sieges due to its defensive walls and river-based supply lines. It's a great spot for youngsters to frolic, but you're not allowed to leave them in the pit prison.

The castle is 3 miles west of the town of Castle Douglas, off the A75. It's a steep walk from the car park to the ferry and wheelchair users must be able to get out of their chairs for the river crossing.

---

# KIRKCUDBRIGHT
**pop 3400**

Kirkcudbright (kirk-*coo*-bree), with its dignified streets of 17th- and 18th-century merchants' houses and attractive rivermouth harbour, has one of the most beautifully restored high streets in Dumfries & Galloway. A different Robert Burns (1869–1941; Head of Painting at Edinburgh College of Art) once commented that no art student's education was complete without a visit to Kirkcudbright, and with its sea-fresh light and quirky stone buildings you can see how it would inspire a budding artist (though we're not sure what Mr Burns would think about the owners who have added turquoise and purple to the palette of colours in which some houses have been repainted!).

Once home to noted painter and ceramicist Jessie M King, as well as several visiting Glaswegian artists, this seaside spot has attracted a sizeable resident population of artists and craftspeople. Now marketed to visitors as 'Artists' Town', its streets are crammed with galleries and studios.

The **tourist office** ( ☎ 01557-330494; kirkcudbright tic@visitscotland.com; Harbour Sq; 9.30am-6pm Mon-Sat year-round, 10am-5pm Sun Jul & Aug) has brochures detailing walks around town, and leaflets listing the many art galleries. Check out www .kirkcudbright.co.uk and www.kirkcudbright artiststown.co.uk for heaps of information on the town.

## Sights & Activities

To get in touch with Kirkcudbright's aesthetic, wander down High St to the **Tollbooth Art Centre** ( ☎ 01557-331556; High St; admission free; 11am-5pm Mon-Sat May, Jun & Sep, 10am-5pm Mon-Sat Jul-Aug, 11am-4pm Mon-Sat Oct-Apr, 2-5pm Sun May-Oct), which has a modern gallery and a fascinating audiovisual show telling the history of artists Jessie M King and 'Glasgow Boy' EA Hornel.

Nearby, 18th-century **Broughton House** (NTS; ☎ 01557-330437; 12 High St; adult/child £8/5; noon-5pm daily Jul-Aug, noon-5pm Thu-Mon Apr-Jun, Sep & Oct) was bought by painter EA Hornel for £650 in 1901 and today displays his work, as well as scenes from his daily life. Regular changing exhibits from his personal collection are also displayed and there's a large collection of Burns (the poet) memorabilia.

**MacLellan's Castle** (HS; ☎ 01557-331856; adult/child £3.70/1.55; 9.30am-5.30pm Apr-Sep, 9.30am-4.30pm Oct) was originally built in the 16th century and came to be adapted more for domesticity than war, with chimneys instead of battlements. Inside, look for the 'lairds' lug' (lord's ear), a 16th-century spyhole designed for the laird to eavesdrop on his guests.

## Sleeping & Eating

**Number 1 B&B** ( ☎ 01557-330540; www.number1bedan dbreakfast.co.uk; 1 Castle Gardens; s/d from £44/64) This welcoming B&B has two stylish bedrooms with castle views and the bonus of a whirlpool bath in one. Breakfasts are prepared by the owner, a professional chef who once cooked for royalty (the Queen Mum and Prince Charles, no less).

**Greengate** ( ☎ 01557-331895; www.thegreengate .co.uk; 46 High St; s/d £45/70) This was once the home of Jessie M King, and you can still see the quaint cottages rented to visiting artists' out the back. Today it's still a working studio, with one double room offering luxury B&B with antique furniture, spacious bathroom and a comfy lounge of plump leather armchairs on the 1st floor.

**Gordon House Hotel** ( ☎ 01557-330670; www.gordon -house-hotel.co.uk; 116 High St; s/d/f £40/70/80; mains £11-14; lunch & dinner) This small, laid-back hotel is in good shape, but the rooms vary a bit in size and character, so have a look at a few; No 2 is probably the best of the doubles, and there's a family room with double bed and bunk beds. You can dine in the restaurant (which serves posh nosh including local scallops landed at the town quay) or the lounge bar, and there's a beer garden for sunny afternoons.

**Castle Restaurant** ( ☎ 01557-330569; 5 Castle St; mains £11-16; ☯ lunch & dinner) The Castle Restaurant is the top place to eat in town, using local and organic produce where possible. The menu covers all bases, with a chicken, steak, lamb and seafood dish on offer as well as tempting morsels for vegetarians, such as roast red pepper stuffed with spiced rice. Families are welcome.

There are lots of tearooms in town, but our favourite is **Mulberries Coffee Shop** ( ☎ 01557-330961; 11 St Cuthbert St), which sells local, handmade Carsewell chocolates as well as great espresso. If you fancy something stronger, the no-frills **Masonic Arms** ( ☎ 01557-330517; 19 Castle St) is the best place in town for a pint of real ale.

### Getting There & Away
Kirkcudbright is 28 miles west of Dumfries. Buses 501 and 505 run hourly to Dumfries (one hour) via Castle Douglas and Dalbeattie respectively.

### GALLOWAY FOREST PARK
The Galloway Hills are one of Scotland's best-kept secrets – a range of whale-backed, heather-clad granite mountains fringed with pine forests and dotted with trout-filled lochs. Rising to their highest point at **The Merrick** (843m), they bring a little taste of Highland scenery to the southern Uplands, and provide a playground for hikers, mountain bikers, anglers and wildlife-watchers. The hills form the centrepiece of the 300-sq-mile **Galloway Forest Park** (www.forestry.gov.uk/gallowayforestpark), which stretches from Newton Stewart in the south to Dalmellington in the north.

The park is criss-crossed by some superb walking trails, from gentle strolls to hard-core, long-distance hikes, including the Southern Upland Way (p808). The **Glentrool Visitor Centre** ( ☎ 01671-840302; admission free; ☯ 10.30am-4.30pm Easter-Oct, to 5.30pm Jul-Sep), at the park's western edge, has lots of information on activities and wildlife. There's also a coffee shop serving homemade soups and scones to replenish those weary legs.

Wildlife-wise, the park is famous for its red kites (www.gallowaykitetrail.com) and herds of wild goats and red deer. Halfway between Newton Stewart and New Galloway on the A712 is the **Galloway Red Deer Range** ( ☎ 07771-748401; adult/child £3.50/2.50; ☯ 1-2.30pm Sun-Thu mid-Jun–mid-Sep). During rutting season in autumn it's a bit like watching a bullfight as snorting, charging stags compete for the harem. Guided walks with a ranger (included in the admission fee) begin at 1pm.

Public transport skims around the edges of the park; to explore, you'll need your own wheels (four or two), or pull on your hiking boots.

### MACHARS PENINSULA
South of Newton Stewart, the Galloway Hills give way to the softly rolling pastures of the wedge-shaped peninsula known as the Machars, which is home to Wigtown, Scotland's answer to Wale's Hay-on-Wye, and a number of early Christian sites.

Public transport is thin on the ground. Bus 415 runs every hour or two between Newton Stewart and the Isle of Whithorn (one hour) via Wigtown (15 minutes).

### Wigtown
pop 1000
Wigtown is a huge success story. Economically run-down for many years, the town's revival began in 1998 when it became Scotland's National Book Town. Today 24 bookshops and an annual book festival give bibliophiles an excuse to get lost here for days (check out www.wigtown-booktown.co.uk and www.wigtownbookfestival.com).

The **Book Shop** ( ☎ 01988-402499; 17 North Main St; ☯ 9am-5pm Mon-Sat) claims to be Scotland's largest secondhand bookshop, and has a great collection of Scottish and regional titles. **Readinglasses Bookshop & Cafe** ( ☎ 01988-403266; 17 South Main St; ☯ 10am-5pm Mon-Sat, noon-5pm Sun) specialises in books on the social sciences and women's studies, and serves a mean cup of coffee too.

Folk in this town are very proud of their resident ospreys, who began nesting in Galloway around five years ago after an absence of 100 years – the town hall bells are rung to mark the first sighting each year! If you'd like to learn more about these majestic birds and watch a live CCTV link to a nearby nest (mid-April to mid-August), drop by the osprey exhibition in **Wigtown County Buildings** ( ☎ 01988-402673; Market Sq; admission free; ☯ 10am-5pm Mon-Sat, 2-5pm Sun).

If you're planning a weekend of book browsing, you can stay at **Hillcrest House** ( ☎ 01988-402018; www.hillcrest-wigtown.co.uk; Maidland Pl, Station Rd; s/d from £35/65; P ) – spend a little extra and get a Superior room, which has stupendous views over rolling green hills to the sea beyond.

In neighbouring **Bladnoch** there are a few more bookish options and, for bored nonreaders, **Bladnoch Distillery** ( ☎ 01988-402605; www.bladnoch.co.uk; Bladnoch; ◷ 9am-5pm Mon-Fri, noon-5pm Sat & Sun Jul-Aug), Scotland's southernmost distillery.

## Whithorn
pop 870

Whithorn has a broad, attractive High St that narrows to a single lane at both ends – it originally enclosed a medieval market. In 397, while the Romans were still in Britain, St Ninian established the first Christian mission beyond Hadrian's Wall in Whithorn (predating St Columba on Iona by 166 years). After his death, Whithorn Priory, the earliest recorded church in Scotland, was built to house his remains, and Whithorn became the focus of an important medieval pilgrimage.

Today the priory's substantial ruins are the focal point of the **Whithorn Story Visitor Centre** (HS; ☎ 01988-500508; www.whithorn.com; 45-47 George St; adult/child £3.50/1.75; ◷ 10.30am-5pm Apr-Oct), with absorbing exhibitions and an audiovisual display. The considerable remains of the old monastic settlement are being excavated and you'll see some important archaeological finds. There's also a museum with some fascinating early Christian stone sculptures, including the Latinus Stone (c 450), reputedly Scotland's oldest Christian artefact. Learn about the influences their carvers drew on from around the British Isles and beyond.

## Isle of Whithorn
pop 400

The Isle of Whithorn, once an island but now linked to the mainland by a causeway, is a picturesque fishing village with whitewashed houses set around an attractive natural harbour. The roofless 13th-century **St Ninian's Chapel**, built for pilgrims on their way to Whithorn, stands on the windswept, rocky headland at the road's end. You can walk west to the caravan park at Burrow Head and then along a coastal path to **St Ninian's Cave**, where the saint went to pray (9 miles round trip).

The quayside **Steam Packet Inn** ( ☎ 01988-500334; www.steampacketinn.com; Harbour Row; r per person £30-40) is a popular pub providing real ales, scrumptious bar meals (mains £8 to £10, open lunch and dinner) and comfy lodgings. Try to get a room at the front of the building with a lovely view over the little harbour (No 2 is a good one). It also boasts the best restaurant in the Machars (two-/three-course dinner £20/25, open dinner only) – pan-fried local scallops with black pudding is a speciality.

## PORTPATRICK & AROUND
pop 585

The cute little harbour of Portpatrick once served as the main ferry port for Northern Ireland – on a clear day you can see the Mountains of Mourne across the water – and played a major role in the 17th-century plantation of Ulster. Today it's a peaceful and picturesque holiday retreat, and the starting point for the 212-mile Southern Upland Way (p808).

There are plenty of places to stay, including **Rickwood House Hotel** ( ☎ 01766-810270; www.portpatrick.me.uk; Heugh Rd; d/ste £56/80; P ), a guesthouse with beautiful and stylish bedrooms (the suite has a sea view), and the **Fernhill Hotel** ( ☎ 01776-810220; www.fernhillhotel.co.uk; Heugh Rd; s/d from £58/74; P ⌨ wi-fi), a comfortably old-fashioned place with friendly service, good food and stunning views from the conservatory dining room.

There's a trio of pubs along the harbour, but our favourite is the **Crown** ( ☎ 01776-810261; www.crownportpatrick.com; 9 North Cres; bar meals £7-9, restaurant mains £14-16; ◷ lunch & dinner), famous for its superb seafood.

Twenty-two miles south of Portpatrick is the **Mull of Galloway**, the country's most southerly point. It's a breezy, cliffbound headland topped with a 26m-high **lighthouse** (adult/child £2/1; tours every 30min, 10am-3.30pm Sat & Sun Apr-Sep) that was built by Robert Stevenson in 1826. The Mull of Galloway RSPB nature reserve, which is home to thousands of seabirds, has a **visitor centre** ( ☎ 01776-840539; www.mull-of-galloway.co.uk; admission free; ◷ 10am-4pm, to 5pm Tue Apr-Oct).

Buses 358 and 367 run from Stranraer to Portpatrick (20 minutes, eight Monday to Saturday, three Sunday). There's no public transport to the Mull of Galloway.

# AYRSHIRE

Ayrshire is synonymous with golf and with Robert Burns – and there's plenty on offer here to satisfy both of these pursuits. Troon has six golf courses for starters, and there's enough Burns memorabilia in the region to satisfy his most ardent admirers.

This region's main drawcard though is the irresistible Isle of Arran. With a gourmet culinary scene, atmospheric watering holes and much varied and scenic countryside, this easily accessible island should not be missed.

Back on the mainland, retro seaside resorts, such as Largs, give Ayrshire a unique flavour. There's also spectacular coastal scenery, best admired at Culzean Castle, one of the finest stately homes in the country.

## Getting Around

**Stagecoach Western** ( ☎ 01292-613500) is the main bus operator on the mainland. On Arran, **Western** ( ☎ 01770-302000) and **Royal Mail** ( ☎ 01463-256200) buses whiz you around the island, while **CalMac** ( ☎ 0800 066 5400; www .calmac.co.uk) ferries will get you there from the mainland.

## LARGS

**pop 11,200**

Largs has a kitsch, old-fashioned seaside resort waterfront that is loads of fun if you approach the amusement arcades, chip shops, crazy golf and bouncy castle with the right attitude – buy an ice cream, take a stroll along the prom and check out this slice of Scottish nostalgia. There's a **tourist office** ( ☎ 01475-689962; ☼ 9am-5pm Mon-Sat Easter-Oct) at the train station.

The main attraction in Largs is the award-winning **Vikingar!** ( ☎ 01475-689777; www.vikingar .co.uk; Greenock Rd; adult/child £4.20/2.50; ☼ 10.30am-5.30pm Apr-Sep, 10.30am-3.30pm Oct & Mar, 10.30am-3.30pm Sat & Sun Nov & Feb). This multimedia exhibition describes Viking influence in Scotland until its demise at the Battle of Largs in 1263; tours with staff in Viking outfits run every half-hour. There's also a theatre, cinema, cafe, shop, swimming pool and leisure centre. To get here, follow the A78 coast road north from the tourist office – it's the place with the Viking longship outside.

There are trains to Largs from Glasgow's Central Station (£6, one hour, hourly).

## AYR

**pop 46,400**

Ayr is a big, bustling town and a convenient base for a tour of Burns territory. Ayr's long sandy beach has made it a popular family seaside resort since Victorian times. There are many fine Georgian and Victorian buildings, although some areas of town show signs of neglect.

The **tourist office** ( ☎ 0845 225 5121; 22 Sandgate; ☼ 9am-5pm Mon-Sat Apr-Jun & Sep-Mar, 11am-4pm Sun Sep, 9am-6pm Mon-Sat, 10am-5pm Sun Jul & Aug) is poorly signposted on a one-way street in the middle of town, awkward to get to by car.

### Sights

Most things to see in Ayr are Burns-related, though the main sights are in Alloway, two miles to the south (see p842). The bard was baptised in Ayr's **Auld Kirk** (Old Church; ☎ 01292-262938), hidden along an alley off the High St. The atmospheric cemetery here overlooks the river and is a pleasant escape from the bustle of the town centre.

Several of Burns' poems are set here in Ayr; in *Twa Brigs* Ayr's old and new bridges argue with one another. The **Auld Brig** (Old Bridge) was built in 1491 and spans the river just north of the church; sadly its ancient arches now have a backdrop of concrete apartment blocks and the back-end of Marks and Spencer.

The **promenade** is good for a walk in sunny weather, especially at low tide when a huge sandy beach is revealed. The silhouettes of Arran's peaks and Ailsa Craig in the bay form an impressive backdrop.

The **Burns an' a' That** (www.burnsfestival.com) festival, held in Ayrshire in May, showcases the best of Scottish talent from music and cinema to comedy, theatre and dance.

### Sleeping

**Heads of Ayr Caravan Park** ( ☎ 01292-442269; www .headsofayr.com; Dunure Rd; tent sites £11-18; ☼ Mar-Oct) This caravan park is in a lovely, quiet location close to the beach. From Ayr take the A719 south for about 5 miles.

**Eglinton Guest House** ( ☎ 01292-264623; www.eglin ton-guesthouse-ayr.com; 23 Eglinton Tce; s/d from £25/50) A short walk west of the bus station, this family-run Georgian property is in a quiet cul-de-sac and has a range of traditional, tidy rooms. The location is brilliant – between the beach and the town centre.

**Richmond Guest House** ( ☎ 01292-265153; www .richmond-guest-house.co.uk; 38 Park Circus; s/d/f £40/58/80)

---

**ROBERT BURNS (1759–96)**

Best remembered for penning the words of *Auld Lang Syne* – probably the most widely known and most often sung song in the world – Robert Burns is Scotland's most famous poet, and a popular hero whose birthday (25 January) is celebrated as Burns Night by Scots around the world.

Burns was born in 1759 in Alloway in Ayrshire. At school he showed an aptitude for literature and a fondness for folk songs, and later began to write his own songs and satires. When the problems of his arduous farming life were compounded by the threat of prosecution from the father of Jean Armour, with whom he'd had an affair, he decided to emigrate to Jamaica. He gave up his share of the family farm and published his poems to raise money for the journey.

The poems were so well received in Edinburgh that Burns decided to remain in Scotland and devote himself to writing. He went to Edinburgh in 1787 to publish a second edition, but the financial rewards were not enough to live on and he had to take a job as a customs officer in Dumfriesshire. He contributed many songs to collections published by Johnson and Thomson in Edinburgh, and composed more than 28,000 lines of verse over 22 years. Burns died of rheumatic fever in Dumfries in 1796, aged just 37.

Burns wrote in Lallans, the Scottish Lowland dialect of English that is not very accessible to the Sassenach (Englishman), or foreigner; perhaps this is part of his appeal. He was also very much a man of the people, fond of carousing in pubs, chatting up the lassies, and satirising the upper classes and the church for their hypocrisy.

The Burns connection in southern Scotland is milked for all it's worth and tourist offices have a *Burns Heritage Trail* leaflet that will lead you to every place that can claim some link, however tenuous, with the bard. Burns fans should have a look at www.robertburns.org.

---

This 170-year-old house in a posh part of town combines comfort and period style, with lofty ceilings and leather couches to add to the sumptuous atmosphere. Brodie, the ever-affectionate chocolate Labrador, will help make you feel at home.

**Daviot House** ( ☎ 01292-269678; www.daviothouse .co.uk; 12 Queens Tce; s/d/f from £50/60/80; **P** ) This cheery spot has several en suite rooms that can accommodate families. Great tailored breakfasts (including cold cuts and cheese if you're up for it first thing) and advice on local golf courses are good bonuses.

**No 26 The Crescent** ( ☎ 01292-287329; www.26crescent .co.uk; 26 Bellevue Cres; s/d from £45/60; **P** ) If you want to move up a couple of rungs on the luxury and comfort scale, consider this outstanding guesthouse with five opulent, individually furnished rooms, including a four-poster suite fit for royalty (£70) and a room with French doors opening onto the garden.

## Eating & Drinking

**Pumpernickel** ( ☎ 01292-263830; 32 Newmarket St; mains £4-6; ⏰ 9am-5pm Mon-Sat) Continental-style toasties and other delicious snacks are dished out at this licensed deli-cafe, either indoors or at outdoor tables on the pedestrianised street. It's a good spot for a glass of wine in the afternoon, too.

**Tam O'Shanter** ( ☎ 01292-611684; 230 High St; mains £6-8) Taking its name from Burns' most celebrated poem, this traditional pub is filled with locals 'getting fou and unco happy' (as the poet said) on its ales, and dining on its menu of traditional pub grub.

**our pick Rupee Room** ( ☎ 01292-283002; 26a Wellington Sq; mains £9-13; ⏰ noon-2.30pm Thu-Sat, 4-11pm Mon-Sat) Funky, pastel decor makes this Indian restaurant look more like an art-school cafe, but it's the food that really makes it stand out from the crowd. Fierce, fresh flavours with a rich, spicy depth – definitely the best curry in Ayrshire.

**Fouter's Bistro** ( ☎ 261391; 2a Academy St; 2-/3-course lunches £12/14, dinner mains £14-19; ⏰ lunch & dinner Tue-Sat) Housed in an 18th-century basement bank vault a few steps from the tourist office, Fouter's is an ideal place to splash out on a top-class dinner. It specialises in Scottish meat and game (such as roast loin of lamb with tarragon-scented jus) and fresh local seafood.

## Getting There & Away

Stagecoach Western runs the hourly express X77 service to Glasgow (one hour) and Prestwick airport (30 minutes). There are also services to Dumfries (£5.50, 2¼ hours, five to seven daily). There are frequent trains from Glasgow's Central Station to Ayr (£6.30, 50 minutes, half-hourly).

# AROUND AYR
## Alloway

This pretty village – now a southern suburb of Ayr – is where Robert Burns was born on 25 January 1759. Several sights are clustered around the poet's birthplace under the umbrella title of **Burns National Heritage Park** ( ☎ 01292-443700; www.burnsheritagepark.com; ticket covering all sites adult/child £5/3; ☺ 10am-5.30pm Apr-Sep, 10am-5pm Oct-Mar).

If you only have time to visit one place, make it **Burns Cottage & Museum**, where the poet lived the first seven years of his life. The cramped, thatched cottage contains musty byre, a warm storytelling hearth, and the actual box bed where Burns was born. The neighbouring museum of Burnsiana exhibits some fabulous artwork as well as many of his original manuscripts and letters.

Close by is the beautiful ruin of **Alloway Auld Kirk**, the eerie setting for the witches' dance in *Tam o'Shanter*. Burns' father, William Burnes (his son dropped the 'e'), is buried in the wooded kirkyard. Another half-mile along the road and you'll find the graceful 13th-century arch of the **Brig o'Doon**, the scene of the climax to *Tam o'Shanter*.

Nearby is the **Tam o'Shanter Experience**, an elaborate audiovisual retelling of the famous poem; it may beguile children, but adults might miss the magic.

Alloway is 3 miles south of Ayr. Stagecoach Western bus 57 runs between Alloway and Ayr (10 minutes, hourly, Monday to Saturday), or you could walk there in an hour.

## Culzean Castle

Magnificent **Culzean Castle** (NTS; ☎ 01655-884455; www.culzeanexperience.org; adult/child £12/8, park only £8/5; ☺ castle 10.30am-5pm Apr-Oct, park 9.30am-sunset year-round) – pronounced cull-*ane* – is one of the most impressive of Scotland's stately homes. Perched dramatically on a coastal cliff-top, it is a monument to its designer Robert Adam, the king of neoclassical architecture.

The superb **oval staircase** is regarded as one of his finest achievements, leading to an opulent circular **drawing room** with views of Arran and Ailsa Craig. Everywhere you look there are classical friezes and roundels in delicate 18th-century plasterwork, and even the bathrooms are palatial – the dressing room beside

the **state bedroom** is equipped with a state-of-the-art Victorian multidirectional shower.

The top-floor apartment is known as the **Eisenhower Suite** – it was gifted to the American general for his lifetime at the end of WWII to salute his role in that conflict. Today it's the NTS's flagship holiday property, and you can stay the night in the general's suite for £250/375, single/double occupancy.

Culzean is 12 miles south of Ayr, accessible by bus 60 from Ayr (30 minutes, 11 daily Monday to Saturday), which passes the park gates, from where it's a one-mile walk through the grounds to the castle.

# ISLE OF ARRAN
## pop 4800

Arran lies moored in the middle of the Firth of Clyde, its pointed peaks making a scenic backdrop to the views along the Ayrshire coast. Marketed as 'Scotland in miniature', this fascinating island certainly has a bit of everything that Scotland is famous for – rugged mountains in the north, lush farmland in the south, sea cliffs and sandy beaches, hill walking and mountain biking, lively pubs and welcoming B&Bs; it even has its own brewery and distillery. And the hour-long ferry crossing from Ardrossan is short enough for a day trip, but just long enough to make a visit seem like a bit of an adventure.

## Orientation & Information

The Ardrossan ferry docks at Brodick, the island's main town, from where the 56-mile-long coastal road circumnavigates the island. South of Brodick are the holiday resorts of Lamlash and Whiting Bay. In the north is Lochranza, where there's a second ferry link to Claonaig on the Kintyre peninsula.

There are banks with ATMs, a supermarket and car- and bike-hire facilities in Brodick.

**Arran Library** ( ☎ 01770-302835; Brodick Hall; ☺ 10am-5pm Tue, 10am-7.30pm Thu & Fri, 10am-1pm Sat) Free internet access.

**Hospital** ( ☎ 01770-600777; Lamlash)

**Tourist office** ( ☎ 01770-303774; www.ayrshire-arran .com; Brodick Pier; ☺ 9am-5pm Mon-Thu & Sat, 9am-7.30pm Fri, 10am-5pm Sun)

## Sights
### BRODICK & AROUND

Apart from shops and pubs, there's no real reason to linger in Brodick. Just 2.5 miles north of town, **Brodick Castle** (NTS; ☎ 01770-302202;

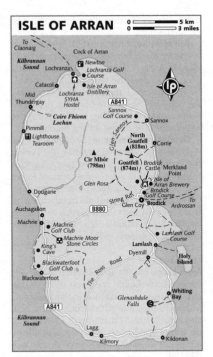

## ISLE OF ARRAN

0 — 5 km
0 — 3 miles

To Claonaig
Kilbrannan Sound
Cock of Arran
Newton
Lochranza
Lochranza Golf Course
Catacol
Isle of Arran Distillery
Mid Thundergay
Lochranza SYHA Hostel
A841
Coire Fhionn Lochan
Sannox Golf Course
Pirnmill
Lighthouse Tearoom
Glen Sannox
Sannox
North Goatfell ▲(818m)
Corrie
Cir Mhór ▲ (798m)
Goatfell ▲ (874m)
Brodick Castle
Merkland Point
Glen Rosa
Isle of Arran Brewery
Dougarie
String Rd
Brodick Golf Course
To Ardrossan
Auchagallon
B880
Glen Coy
Brodick
Machrie
Machrie Golf Club
Lamlash Golf Course
Machrie Moor Stone Circles
Lamlash
King's Cave
Dyemill
Holy Island
Blackwaterfoot Golf Club
The Ross Road
Blackwaterfoot
Glenashdale Falls
Whiting Bay
A841
Kilbrannan Sound
Lagg
Kilmory
Kildonan

adult/child £10/7, park only £5/4; ⓧ castle 11am-4.30pm Apr-Oct, park 9.30am-sunset) is a medieval tower house converted into a Victorian hunting lodge. More than 70 stags' heads adorn the main staircase that leads to the fascinating first-floor apartments, with a dining room lined in 15th-century oak panelling and a gallery of unusual prints and paintings – dog-fighting, bear-baiting and bare-knuckle boxing – make sure you speak to the volunteer attendants, whose knowledgeable anecdotes really bring the place to life.

The beautiful grounds contain an 18th-century walled garden, a rhododendron-filled woodland garden, and miles of nature trails.

### THE NORTH

The road north from Brodick leads past the **Isle of Arran Brewery** ( ☎ 01770-302353; www.arranbrewery .com; Cladach; tours £2; ⓧ 10am-5pm Mon-Sat, 12.30-5pm Sun) and the picturesque village of Corrie before climbing over a pass and descending to the sea again at 13th-century **Lochranza Castle** (HS; admission free; ⓧ always open), said to be the inspiration for the castle in *The Black Island*, Hergé's Tintin adventure.

On the way downhill you'll pass the **Isle of Arran Distillery** ( ☎ 01770-830264; www.arranwhisky.com; tours adult/child £4/free; ⓧ 10am-6pm Apr-Oct), where guided tours include a free dram (tours on the hour).

### THE SOUTH

Continuing anticlockwise down the west coast (also accessible by a shortcut across the middle of the island from Brodick) you soon reach the **Machrie Moor Stone Circles** – rings of upright sandstone slabs erected around 6000 years ago.

Nearby **Blackwaterfoot** is the largest village on the west coast; it has a shop/post office and two hotels. You can walk to **King's Cave** from here, via Drumadoon Farm – this is one of several caves that claim to have sheltered national hero Robert the Bruce while he plotted victory against the English in the early 14th century.

As the road swings back up the east coast you come to the upmarket resort of Lamlash, which looks out across the bay to **Holy Island**. The island is owned by the Samye Ling Tibetan Centre and used as a retreat, but day visits are allowed. A **ferry** ( ☎ 01770-600998; adult/ child return £9/5) from Lamlash pier will take you to this tranquil spot (six daily from May to September); there's a good walk to the top of the hill (314m), and it's possible to stay on the island at the **Holy Island Centre for World Peace and Health** ( ☎ 01770-601100; www.holyisland .org; dm/s/d £25/45/65).

## Activities

Most visiting hikers have their sights set on the summit of **Goatfell** (874m), Arran's highest peak. The ascent is a straightforward 11-mile round trip from the ferry pier in Brodick, mostly on a well-defined path (details from the tourist office) except for the last 200m, which is rocky. On a clear day there are spectacular views ranging from Ben Lomond to Northern Ireland. Allow six to eight hours, and remember that this is a proper hill walk – wear hiking boots and carry warm clothing, waterproofs, map and compass no matter what time of year or how good the weather.

The most adventurous way to experience the whole of Arran is to tackle the **Coastal Way** (www.coastalway.co.uk), a 60-mile walk that kicks off in Brodick and circles the entire island, taking in the summit of Goatfell. There are plenty of less ambitious hikes, the finest of which is the easy one-hour walk from Whiting Bay to **Glenashdale Falls** – keep an eye out for golden eagles and other birds of prey. (Ask at the tourist office for details.)

For cyclists, the 56-mile coastal road is the main event, with some challenging hills at the north and south ends of the island. For details of bike-rental places, see p846.

The **Arran Adventure Company** ( ☎ 01770-302244; www.arranadventure.com; Shore Rd, Brodick) has loads of activities on offer and runs a different one each day (such as gorge walking, kayaking, abseiling and mountain biking). All activities run for about three hours and cost around £35/20 for adults/kids. Drop in to see what's available while you're around.

## Sleeping

Weekends book up quickly, so plan ahead if you're looking to stay awhile. Budget accommodation is particularly scarce.

### BUDGET

Camping isn't allowed without permission from the landowner, but there are several camping grounds (open April to October).

**Glen Rosa Farm** ( ☎ 01770-302380; www.glenrosa.com; Glen Rosa; sites per person £3.50) In a lush glen 2.5 miles north of Brodick pier, this riverside site offers basic camping in a lovely setting with cold water and toilets as the only facilities. Tents only.

**Seal Shore Camping Site** ( ☎ 01770-820320; www.isleofarran.freeserve.co.uk; Kildonan; sites per person/tent £6/1) This seaside camping ground occupies a manicured grassy area next to the Kildonan Hotel at the southern tip of the island, with a view of Isle of Pladda and Ailsa Craig.

**Lochranza SYHA Hostel** ( ☎ 01770-830631; Lochranza; dm £13-15; ⌚ Mar-Oct; 🖳 ) In the north of the island, this hostel has clean, spacious dorms, helpful owners and loads of information about Arran. Its worn furnishings are offset by the lovely views.

### MIDRANGE
### Brodick

**ourpick Fellview** ( ☎ 01770-302153; fellviewarran@yahoo.co.uk; 6 Strathwhillan Rd; r per person £25, bunkhouse per person £15) This lovely house and warm, friendly owner epitomise Scottish hospitality. As well as cosy B&B rooms there's a snug bunkhouse out the back with just two bunks (you share the bathroom inside the house). Head north out of Brodick and take the left-

hand turn to Strathwhillan; Fellview is just up on the right.

**Belvedere Guest House** ( ☎ 01770-302397; www.visionunlimited.co.uk/belvedere; Alma Rd; per person £28-53; 🖳 wi-fi) A big Victorian villa commanding great views over the town and bay towards Goatfell (rooms 1 and 2 have the best views), the Belvedere has inviting, brightly decorated rooms and a welcoming lounge, complete with home cinema system and piano.

**Glencloy Farm Guesthouse** ( ☎ 01770-302351; glencloyfarm@aol.com; Glencloy Rd; s/d £65/80; 🅿 ) Perfect for families, with plenty of space for kids to run around in safety, plus animals to pet and videos for those cabin-fever rainy days, Glencloy is a picturesque old farmhouse with free-range chickens in the garden (providing eggs for breakfast) and unfailingly hospitable and helpful owners.

### Lochranza

**Apple Lodge** ( ☎ /fax 01770-830229; d £74-86; 🅿 ) Lavish Apple Lodge, the finest place to stay in Lochranza, has beautiful, individually furnished rooms, one with a four-poster bed, and a guest lounge that's perfect for curling up with a good book. And it makes all the difference when your hosts so obviously love their job.

### Kildonan

**Kildonan Hotel** ( ☎ 01770-820207; www.kildonanhotel.com; Kildonan; s/d/ste £70/95/125; 🅿 🖳 ) The Kildonan offers stylish, upmarket B&B in light and airy rooms with a contemporary feel. The grassed area in the front of the hotel has been landscaped into a beautiful garden providing a fantastic seating area overlooking the water.

### Whiting Bay

**Viewbank House** ( ☎ 01770-700326; www.viewbank-arran.co.uk; Golf Course Rd; s/d £30/70; 🅿 ) Appropriately named, this charming B&B does indeed have tremendous views from its vantage point above Whiting Bay. Rooms are tastefully furnished and well kept, but the real attraction of this place is its friendly hosts – expect a good dose of Arran hospitality.

**Royal Arran Hotel** ( ☎ 01770-700286; www.royalarran.co.uk; Shore Rd; per person from £45; 🅿 ) The Royal Arran is a beautiful Victorian house, more of an upmarket guesthouse than a hotel, with just four rooms. The huge upstairs double is our favourite, with four-poster bed, crisp bed linen, and gorgeous sea views.

### Lamlash

**Lilybank Guest House** ( ☎ 01770-600230; www.lilybank -arran.co.uk; Shore Rd; r per person £25-30; **P** ) A whitewashed 18th-century cottage with a view across the bay to Holy Island, the Lilybank offers clean, comfortable and homely B&B, with a breakfast that includes locally smoked kippers and other Arran goodies.

### TOP END

**Kilmichael Country House Hotel** ( ☎ 01770-302219; www .kilmichael.com; Glen Cloy, Brodick; s/d from £100/150; **P** 💻 wifi) As well as being the island's best hotel, the Kilmichael is also its oldest building – it has a glass window dating from 1650. It's a luxurious, intimate and tastefully decorated hideaway, a mile from Brodick, with eight bedrooms and an excellent restaurant (four-course dinner £39).

The **Douglas Hotel**, on the Brodick waterfront, has been boarded up for a few years but at the time of research was undergoing a major overhaul and should reopen in 2009 as a luxury boutique hotel.

## Eating & Drinking

**Creelers Seafood Restaurant** ( ☎ 01770-302810; www.creelers.co.uk; Cladach; lunch mains £9, dinner £15-18; 🕑 lunch & dinner Tue-Sun, closed Nov-Easter) This award-winning restaurant, 1.5 miles north of Brodick, offers relaxed dining with the emphasis on seafood, sourcing all of its delicacies from Arran and the Western Isles. The Smokehouse next door sells seafood to go.

**Brodick Bar & Brasserie** ( ☎ 01770-302169; Alma Rd, Brodick; mains £8-15; 🕑 lunch Mon-Sat, dinner daily) A bright, modern bar with a family-friendly brasserie, the Brodick offers an unpretentious menu of pizza, pasta, lamb, beef and fish dishes plus daily specials, with a separate kids' menu (high chairs available) and a decent wine list.

**Lighthouse Tearoom** ( ☎ 01770-850240; Pirnmill; mains £9-12; 🕑 lunch & dinner) Calling itself a tearoom is a little bit coy – the Lighthouse has a proper restaurant menu, with posh dishes such as trio of seafood (cod, salmon and scallops) in a lemon cream sauce, but it's far from

---

### DETOUR: ISLE OF BUTE

Although it's in Argyllshire, the picturesque **Isle of Bute** is usually reached by ferry from Wemyss Bay in Ayrshire. The island is the property of the Stuart earls of Bute, direct descendants of Robert the Bruce who have lived on the island for 700 years. When a large part of the family seat was destroyed by fire in 1877, the third marquess of Bute, John Patrick Crichton-Stuart (1847–1900) – one of the greatest architectural patrons of his day, and the builder of Cardiff Castle and Castell Coch in Wales – commissioned Sir Robert Rowand Anderson to create a new one. The result – **Mount Stuart** ( ☎ 01700-503877; www.mountstuart.com; adult/child £8/4; 🕑 11am-5pm Sun-Fri, 10am-2.30pm Sat Easter & May-Sep) – became the finest neo-Gothic palace in Scotland, and the first to have electric lighting, central heating and a heated swimming pool.

The heart of the house is the stunning **Marble Hall**, a three-storey extravaganza of Italian marble that soars 25m to a dark-blue vault spangled with constellations of golden stars. Twelve stained-glass windows represent the seasons and the signs of the zodiac, with crystal stars casting rainbow-hued highlights across the marble when the sun is shining.

The design and decoration reflect the third marquess' fascination with astrology, mythology and religion, a theme carried over into the grand **Marble Staircase** beyond (where wall panels depict the six days of the Creation), and the lavishly decorated **Horoscope Bedroom**. Here the central ceiling panel records the positions of the stars and planets at the time of the marquess' birth on 12 September 1847.

Yet another highlight is the **Marble Chapel**, built entirely out of dazzling white Carrara marble. It has a dome lit to spectacular effect by a ring of ruby-red stained-glass windows – at noon on midsummer's day a shaft of blood-red sunlight shines directly onto the altar. It was here that Stella McCartney – daughter of ex-Beatle Sir Paul, and friend of the present marquess, former racing driver Johnny Dumfries – was married in 2003.

Mount Stuart is 5 miles south of the ferry pier in Rothesay, the island's main town; bus 90 runs from the bus stop outside the ferry terminal to Mount Stuart (15 minutes, 10 per day May to September). You can buy a special **Mount Stuart Day Trip** ticket (adult/child £19.30/10) that covers return train, ferry and bus travel from Glasgow (or any train station in Ayrshire and Lanarkshire) to Mount Stuart, as well as admission. Ask at the Glasgow tourist office or any train station.

formal – you can just as easily opt for fish and chips or soup and a sandwich. There are a couple of outdoor tables where you can enjoy the view across the sea to Kintyre.

**Distillery Restaurant** ( ☎ 01770-830264; Isle of Arran Distillery, Lochranza; mains £6-8; ⏱ 10am-5pm) The waterfall fountain that forms the centrepiece of the entrance hall at Arran's distillery is overlooked by a mezzanine floor with an attractive restaurant that serves a range of hearty, homemade dishes including burgers and lasagne.

**Ormidale Hotel** ( ☎ 01770-302293; Knowe Rd, Brodick) A long-standing favourite among Arran hikers and climbers, the Ormidale is the best drinking place in Brodick, with Deuchars IPA and Arran Ales on tap, and a crumbling but atmospheric Victorian conservatory at the back where you can kick off your hiking boots and relax with a pint.

## Getting There & Away

**CalMac** ( ☎ 0800 066 5400; www.calmac.co.uk) runs car ferries between Ardrossan and Brodick (per person/car return £9/54, 55 minutes, six to 10 daily). From late March to late October there's also a ferry between Claonaig on the Kintyre peninsula and Lochranza (per person/car return £8/36, 30 minutes, seven to nine daily).

There are frequent trains from Glasgow's Central Station to Ardrossan (£5.80, one hour, half-hourly) to connect with the ferry to Brodick.

## Getting Around

There are frequent bus services on the island. Five or six buses go from Brodick pier to Lochranza (45 minutes, Monday to Saturday), and three to 10 daily go from Brodick to Lamlash and Whiting Bay (30 minutes). Pick up a timetable from the tourist office. An Arran Rural Rover ticket costs £4.50 and permits travel anywhere on the island for a day (buy it from the driver).

Alternatively, there's car hire from £25 per day from **Arran Transport** ( ☎ 01771-302121; Brodick). Brodick has several bike-hire operators, including **Brodick Cycle Hire** ( ☎ 01770-302868; Glencloy Rd, Brodick) and **Arran Power & Sail** ( ☎ 01770-302337; www.arranpowerandsail.com; Shore Rd, Brodick), with rates around £10 for four hours, or £12 to £15 a day.

# Central Scotland

Covering everything from the green pastures of the northeast to the bleak bogscapes of Rannoch Moor, from vital urban Dundee to the remoteness of tiny Hebridean isles, central Scotland is less a geographical region than a catch-all term for anything between the Lowlands and the northern Highlands. Anything you ever dreamed about Scotland you can find here: lochs aplenty, from romantic Lomond to the steely fjords of the western coastline; castles ranging from royal Balmoral to noble Stirling or desolately picturesque Dunnottar; whiskies from the honeyed lotharios of Speyside to the peaty clan chiefs of Islay; and islands from brooding, deer-studded Jura to emerald Iona, birthplace of Scottish Christianity. It's here that the ancient kingdom of Dalriada flourished, that Scottish kings were crowned and buried, and here that the great independence battles were fought against England. The towns of the east tell later tales of the rise and fall of fishing, while Aberdeen, British oil capital, is still in boom.

The active are well catered for, with a welter of hills to climb and some of Britain's best long-distance trails to hike. Cyclists and walkers are spoiled for choice, with sceneries ranging from mighty Perthshire forests to bare Glenshee landscapes, from the fishing hamlets of the Fife coastline to the epic scenery of Mull. Birdwatchers flock to ultrafriendly Islay, and golfers descend on St Andrews, the spiritual home of the sport. Meanwhile, urbanites can stroll Stirling's stately old town, dip into Aberdeen's roaring nightlife, check out the galleries in Perth or sample some of Scotland's best museums in Dundee.

## HIGHLIGHTS

- Opening your jaw in amazement at the epic splendour of **Glen Lyon** (p887), gateway to a faerie land

- Admiring the views from **Stirling Castle** (p866), which overlooks ancient battlefields

- Scoffing at critics of British cuisine as you sample the super seafood in **Tobermory** (p862), **Oban** (p860) or **Loch Fyne** (p853)

- Strolling the verdant **Speyside Way** (p850), and sauntering into distilleries for a sly dram along the road

- Unwinding totally on delightful tiny **Iona** (p864), holy island and tomb of Scottish kings

- Experiencing the astonishing hospitality of **Islay** (p855), whisky and bird paradise and Scotland's friendliest island

| ■ POPULATION: 1.5 MILLION | ■ AREA: 10,480 SQ MILES | ■ 80 OF SCOTLAND'S 95 OPERATING WHISKY DISTILLERIES CAN BE FOUND IN THIS REGION |
|---|---|---|

# CENTRAL SCOTLAND

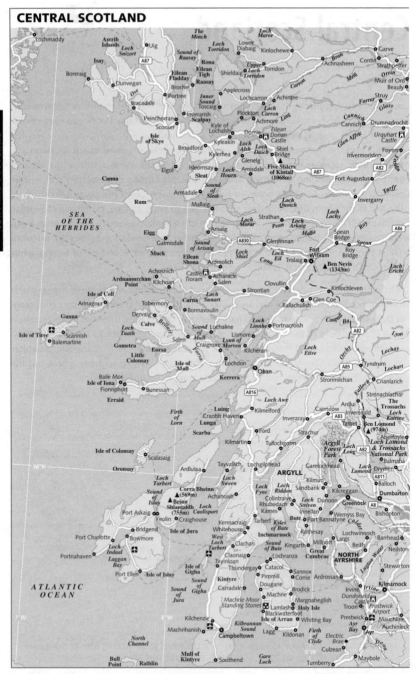

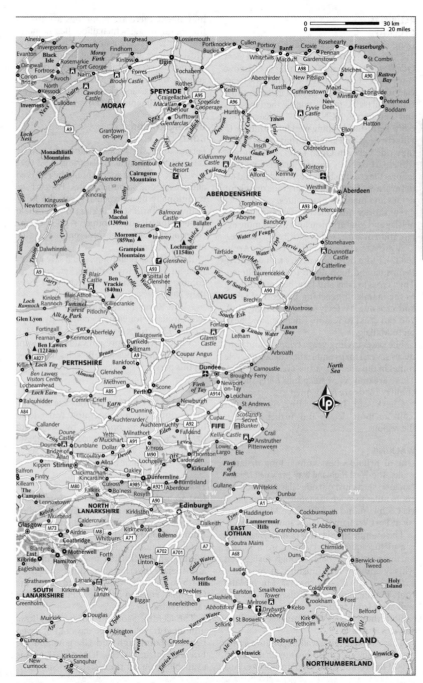

**CENTRAL SCOTLAND**

## Activities
### CYCLING
Long-distance routes include much of the 217-mile northern section of the **Lochs & Glens Cycle Way** (NCN route 7). Starting in Glasgow, it winds its way through the region's heart via Pitlochry to Inverness, and includes some wonderful traffic-free sections in the Trossachs and Cairngorms. NCN route 77 crosses picturesque Perthshire heading west from Dundee to Pitlochry (54 miles). NCN route 78 is a 120-mile ride between Oban and Campbeltown, while part of NCN route 1 bisects Fife then follows the coast to Dundee, Aberdeen and on to Inverness. Browse www.sustrans.org.uk for details and maps of these routes.

For shorter rides, the Trossachs and islands of Islay and Mull are ideal for a day or more exploration by bike, and cycle hire is available.

A great tour could start by circling Arran (p842). From here, take a ferry to the Kintyre Peninsula and loop down to Campbeltown. Then cross to Islay and Jura, before returning to the mainland, reaching the port of Oban and crossing by ferry to Mull. From Mull, you can cross to remote Kilchoan, and head on to Mallaig.

Fife takes cycling very seriously, and produces several maps and leaflets detailing cycle routes in this area (www.fife-cycleways.co.uk). There are only a few steep hills here, and the country roads are fairly quiet.

Check out http://cycling.visitscotland .com for more details and further routes in the region.

### WALKING
One of Britain's best-known long-distance walks, the **West Highland Way** (www.west-highland -way.co.uk) starts just outside Glasgow and covers 95 miles through the mountains and glens, via Loch Lomond and Rannoch Moor, to finish at Fort William. It takes about a week.

The 65-mile **Speyside Way** (www.speysideway.org) is a picturesque route running from Buckie on the northeast coast through lush green whisky country and finishing at Aviemore in the Cairngorms or vice versa. Much of the route is along a peaceful disused railway line well away from traffic.

Both these routes have baggage-handling services available.

There's challenging walking on Jura's rugged Paps, although these don't reach the fabled 3000ft to become Munros. For more-serious hillwalkers, there are numerous Munros in the region to bag; Schiehallion, Ben Lomond and Ben Lawers are among the best known. Most of these are part of the Grampian and Cairngorm ranges, high, wild areas offering serious walks as well as opportunities for easier rambles. Good bases include Pitlochry (p884) and Braemar (p899).

## Getting Around
### BOAT
Ferries to the west-coast islands are run by **Caledonian MacBrayne** (CalMac; ☎ 0870 565 0000; www.calmac.co.uk). Car space should be reserved ahead by phone on busier routes. Tickets have traditionally been expensive, but the Road Equivalent Tariff scheme aims to lower them to boost the island economies. A pilot scheme covering the Outer Hebrides routes was initiated in October 2008.

If you plan to island-hop, you'll save money with an Island Hopscotch ticket. Some 30 combinations exist that can save you more than 20%.

Island Rover Passes cover the whole system. Available for eight/15 consecutive days, costing £53/76 for passengers and £253/379 for vehicles, these represent value if you want to see a lot of islands fast. Bicycles travel free on this pass.

### BUS
**Citylink** ( ☎ 08705 50 50 50; www.citylink.co.uk) is the major intercity bus operator. Most local bus transport is operated by **Stagecoach** ( ☎ 0871 200 2233; www.stagecoachbus.com). **Postbuses** ( ☎ 08457 740 740; www.postbus.royalmail.com) serve remote communities.

### TRAIN
**First Scotrail** ( ☎ 08457 484950; www.firstgroup.com /scotrail) runs three north–south lines, including the spectacular West Highland line, running from Glasgow to Fort William with a branch to Oban. Another runs from Glasgow and Edinburgh via Stirling to Perth, Pitlochry and thence Inverness; the third goes from Perth to Dundee, Aberdeen, and round the Grampian coast to Inverness. Fife also has a rail network.

The Central Scotland Rover pass allows unlimited travel for three days out of seven between Edinburgh and Glasgow and the Fife and Stirling areas. It costs £31 and is available from all train stations. Similarly, the Highland Rover (£68) gives four days out of eight and includes Oban, Aberdeen, and buses on Mull.

# ARGYLL

An ancient and disparate area, Argyll comprises a series of peninsulas and islands along Scotland's ragged southwestern coast, pierced by long sea lochs knifing their way into the hilly, moody landscape. Because of its dramatic geography, places such as the Mull of Kintyre, not so far from Glasgow as the crow flies, can seem impossibly remote.

The islands offer great diversity. Romantic Mull is the gateway to holy Iona, whereas cheery Islay reverberates with the names of the heavyweights of the whisky world. Tiree's muscular breeze puts smiles on windsurfers' faces; Gigha and Colonsay offer noble formal gardens, but Jura's wild hillscapes show nature's ultimate mastery and majesty. Meanwhile, within easy striking distance of Glasgow, the banks of Loch Lomond, the oysters of Loch Fyne, and the prehistoric sites of Kilmartin Glen mean the mainland has nothing to envy.

## LOCH LOMOND

Legendary Loch Lomond, not 20 miles from central Glasgow, gives you the first taste of the epic scenery awaiting you in Britain's northern reaches. This makes it incredibly popular, and you might be disappointed at first glimpse. But get onto a boat, or explore the forest paths on its eastern side, and you'll soon be beguiled by its charms.

Loch Lomond forms the western half of a national park (see p852). Along its western shore, the busy A82 hums with traffic from day tripper–heavy Balloch up to Tarbet. The more isolated eastern shore is better territory for exploration. The road only runs as far as Rowardennan; beyond there the West Highland Way follows the shore through beautiful woodland.

The lake, Britain's largest, was formed by the action of glaciers and standing guard over it is Ben Lomond on the eastern shore.

### Information & Orientation

The wedge-shaped loch runs 22 miles north from the ugly town of Balloch, where you'll find the main 'gateway' centre for the park:

**Loch Lomond Shores** ( ☎ 01389-721500; www.lochlomond shores.com;  9.30am-5.30pm Apr-Sep, 10am-5.30pm Oct-Mar;  wi-fi) offers park information, an aquarium and audiovisual entertainment (a short film taking you under the waters of the lake, and a longer, romanticised account of the region's history). The giant parking area and contemptible retail complex hint at motives beyond conservation.

There are also tourist offices in **Balloch** ( ☎ 08707 200607; Balloch Rd;  year-round) and **Tarbet** ( ☎ 08707 200623; Main St;  Apr–mid-Oct).

### Activities

The national park organises a raft of summer activities, from guided walks to archery displays; tourist offices stock schedules.

#### BOAT TRIPS

The main centre is Balloch, where, among others, **Sweeney's Cruises** ( ☎ 01389-752376; www .sweeneycruises.com) offers a wide range of trips from £6.50 an hour.

From Tarbet, on the western shore, **Cruise Loch Lomond** ( ☎ 01301-702356; www.cruiselochlomond .co.uk) runs various trips around the northern half of the loch, including one that drops you on the West Highland Way and picks you up 9 miles further up the track (£14.50).

At Balmaha, on the eastern side of the loch, **Lomond Adventure** ( ☎ 01360-870218;  Easter-Oct) hires out kayaks and canoes.

#### WALKING

The West Highland Way (opposite) is the main route, and you can access parts of the trail for shorter walks. From Rowardennan you can tackle **Ben Lomond** (974m), a popular five- to six-hour round trip and Scotland's southernmost Munro. The route begins at the Rowardennan Hotel, and you can return via Ptarmigan (731m) for good views of the loch.

A couple of woodland walks leave from the village of Balmaha on the eastern shore of the loch. The **Millennium Forest Path** is a 40-minute introduction to the tree and plant life of the area, with information boards on the local ecosystem. A longer stroll is the three-hour ascent of **Conic Hill**, which rewards with fantastic views along the loch.

### Sleeping & Eating
#### WESTERN SHORE

**Loch Lomond SYHA Hostel** ( ☎ 01389-850226; www.syha .org.uk; Arden; dm £15-18;  Mar-Oct; P  ) Here's

CENTRAL SCOTLAND

your chance to play at laird of the manor. Imposingly perched above the lochside 2 miles north of Balloch, this luxurious mansion hostel is a treat of a place to stay. As well as the obligatory ghost that haunts the tower rooms, there are excellent facilities, including twin and family rooms, heaps of space and great loch views. Book ahead.

**Drover's Inn** ( ☎ 01301-704234; www.thedroversinn.co.uk; Inverarnan; most mains £7-10; ☼ 11.30am-10pm Mon-Sat, noon-9.30pm Sun; P ) This authentically historic inn at the northern end of the loch shouldn't be missed. Fully three centuries old, it oozes character and oddness, with kilt-wearing staff, a menagerie of stuffed animals, and a palpable sense that it hasn't changed a jot since Rob Roy dropped in for a pint. The bar's a haven of good cheer with its crackling hearth and folk music performances. Tartan-carpeted rooms (single/double £35/68) are faded but full of character; on the other hand, modern en suite rooms (d £79), some with Jacuzzi (£100 to £120), are available across the road.

### EASTERN SHORE
**Rowardennan SYHA Hostel** ( ☎ 01360-870259; www.syha.org.uk; Rowardennan; dm £15.50; ☼ Mar-Oct; P ▣ ) Where the road ends on the eastern side of the loch, this is a wonderful retreat in an elegant former hunting lodge right by the water. Whether you're walking the West Highland Way, climbing Ben Lomond, or just putting your feet up, it's a great choice, with atmosphere, genial staff, and a huge lounge with windows overlooking Loch Lomond.

**Oak Tree Inn** ( ☎ 01360-870357; www.oak-tree-inn.co.uk; Balmaha; dm/d £25/75; P ) Balmaha is an inviting Loch Lomond base, both for its appealing lochside and for this pub, a haven for walkers, travellers and locals alike. Eight light, bright rooms and a couple of en suite four-bed dorms let you put your head down in comfort, while the convivial bar offers plenty of outdoor tables, and good food (from noon to 9pm), which ranges from pizzas to char, a tasty cold water salmon relative.

## Getting There & Away
Citylink buses link Glasgow with Balloch (40 minutes, 12 daily) and on up the western shore to Tarbet; many continue to Ardlui (£11.30, one hour 20 minutes). Buses run around eight times daily from Balloch to Balmaha (25 minutes) via Drymen.

---

### LOCH LOMOND & THE TROSSACHS NATIONAL PARK

Scotland's first national park was created in 2002 with the aim of protecting two of the nation's most visited areas, easy and popular getaways from Edinburgh and Glasgow. From Loch Lomond's eastern shore, forest stretches across Scotland's bellybutton into the misty hills around Aberfoyle and Loch Katrine. The West Highland Way crosses this stretch but there's almost no vehicular access.

In this book, we've divided the national park into **Loch Lomond** (p851), on Glasgow's northern doorstep, and **The Trossachs** (p869), most easily accessed from Stirling. To travel between the two, you need to skirt around the southern end of the park, through Drymen, or right around its north, through Crianlarich.

---

Trains from Glasgow run to Balloch (45 minutes, half-hourly) and three to five times daily to Tarbet and Ardlui (£11.70, one hour 20 minutes).

## INVERARAY
pop 510

A lovely place to spend a night, though a little clogged with coach parties by day, wee white-washed Inveraray preserves an 18th-century feel and sits pretty as a postcard on the shores of Loch Fyne, its buildings almost blinding the casual visitor on a sunny day. It was built by the Duke of Argyll, whose nearby castle is the village's main attraction. The **tourist office** ( ☎ 01499-302063; Front St; ☼ daily) is beside the spectacularly beautiful loch.

## Sights
### INVERARAY CASTLE
Half a mile north of town, **Inveraray Castle** ( ☎ 01499-302203; www.inveraray-castle.com; admission £6.80; ☼ 10am-5.45pm Mon-Sat, noon-5.45pm Sun Apr-Oct) has housed the chiefs of Clan Campbell, the dukes of Argyll, since the 15th century. The current 18th-century building includes whimsical turrets and fake battlements; inside is the armoury hall, whose walls are patterned with numerous lances, dirks and halberds, many of which were stuck into Jacobites back in the day. The porcelain collection and wonderfully ornate dining and drawing rooms are other highlights.

**INVERARAY JAIL**

Offering a chilling insight into harsh Georgian justice, this **jail** ( ☎ 01499-302381; www.inverarayjail .co.uk; Church Sq; adult/child £6.50/3.50; ☼ 9.30am-6pm Apr-Oct, 10am-5pm Nov-Mar, last admission 1hr before closing) and courthouse is lots of fun for the kids, with actors (in summer) and lots of lifelike mannequins. The highlight is the historic courtroom itself, where a re-enactment is in full flow; plenty of poor souls were sentenced to transportation to Australia from here for nothing more than nicking a loaf of bread.

## Sleeping & Eating

**Inveraray SYHA Hostel** ( ☎ 01499-302454; www.syha.org .uk; Dalmally Rd; dm £14.25; ☼ mid-Mar–late Oct; P ▢ ) A sound retreat just up the Dalmally road, this friendly hostel has basic two- and four-berth dormitories, comfortable if not sparklingly clean, and fairly basic bathroom facilities. Social life focuses around the convivial lounge area.

**George Hotel** ( ☎ 01499-302111; www.thegeorge hotel.co.uk; Main St; s/d £35/70, superior d £90-140; P ) This wonderfully restored historic hotel boasts fabulous superior rooms, tastefully evoking a period charm with exposed stone, antique furniture, quirky Scottish features, and comfortable beds, some in the four-poster class. The similarly attractive pub downstairs has flagstone floors and a beer garden; it serves delicious bar food (noon to 9pm) and has a decent malt selection.

**ourpick Loch Fyne Oyster Bar** ( ☎ 01499-600264; www.lochfyne.com; mains £9-15; ☼ 9am-7.30pm Nov-Easter, 9am-8.30pm Easter-Oct) The success of this oyster cooperative, 8 miles north of Inveraray on the A83, is such that it now lends its name to some 40 restaurants throughout the UK. But the original's still the best, with salty oysters straight out of the lake, and fabulous salmon dishes: order an 'ashet' to try a few different types. The atmosphere and decor are simple, friendly and unpretentious; in the same building is an excellent shop and deli.

## Getting There & Away

Citylink buses connect Glasgow to Inveraray (£8.20, 1¾ hours, three to five daily), some continuing to Tarbert and Campbeltown. Buses also run to Oban (£6.90, 70 minutes, two to three daily).

# KILMARTIN GLEN

pop 490

Most people zip on through this glen, nose pointing to Oban, but stop awhile to explore and you'll discover a magical highlight of Scotland. It's the heart of one of Scotland's most concentrated areas of prehistoric sites; burial cairns, stone circles and hill forts litter the countryside. Much later, the Gaelic kingdom of Dál Riata (Dalriada) was founded here, flourishing in the sixth and seventh centuries AD.

## Sights

### MUSEUM OF ANCIENT CULTURE

Stop first at this **museum** ( ☎ 01546-510278; www .kilmartin.org; Kilmartin; adult/child £4.60/1.30; ☼ 10am-5.30pm Mar-Oct, 11am-4pm Nov-Christmas, closed Christmas-Feb), a fascinating centre for archaeology and landscape interpretation, with artefacts from the sites, reconstructions, interactive displays and guided tours. The helpful staff will soon orient you in the valley, so you can plan what to see and how to get to it. There's an excellent selection of information and books in the shop, too, and a fine cafe-restaurant. It's one of Scotland's finest museums, and there's always something interesting going on, whether it be talks, guided walks or kids' activities. Next door, in the **churchyard**, are some 10th-century Celtic crosses.

### AROUND KILMARTIN

The oldest monuments in Kilmartin Glen are some 5000 years old and comprise a linear cemetery of **burial cairns**, running south of Kilmartin village for 1.5 miles. There are also two stone circles at **Temple Wood**, three-quarters of a mile southwest of Kilmartin. Although not much remains now, the stones are in a surreal setting surrounded by farmland. Four miles north of Lochgilphead, at **Achnabreck**, elaborate cup-and-ring designs cut into rock faces resemble ripples caused by a pebble breaking the surface of a pond. The site is one of Britain's more important early rock carvings and has outstanding views over Loch Fyne.

Nearby, **Dunadd** hill fort was the royal residence of the first kings of Dál Riata, and was probably where the Stone of Destiny (p785), used in the investiture, was located. The faint rock carvings – an ogham inscription (ancient script), a wild boar and a footprint – were perhaps part of the ceremony. The fort overlooks farmland and the boggy plain that is now the **Moine Mhor Nature Reserve**. Clamber to the top of the fort and you'll gaze upon the same countryside as the ancient kings did thousands of years ago.

CENTRAL SCOTLAND

## Sleeping & Eating

In Kilmartin itself, there's a hotel-pub and a couple of B&Bs (see also Make Mine a Mansion, p861).

**Rosebank** ( ☎ 01546-510370; www.rosebankargyll .co.uk; s/d £30/48; **P** ) Almost opposite the museum, Rosebank is run with wry good humour and welcomes bikers and cyclists.

**Burndale** ( ☎ 01546-510235; bbdalekilmartin@aol.com; s/d £30/54; **P** ) This place is a pleasant B&B with a garden and large rooms; readers reckon its full Scottish does the trick. It's on the north side of town on the main road.

The best place to eat is the museum's **cafe** (snacks £2-6, mains £9-13; ⏰ 10am-5pm), which serves up wholesome cafe fare and classy, good-value lunches served in an enchanting wooden conservatory looking over the ancient cairn below.

## Getting There & Away

**West Coast Motors** ( ☎ 01586-552319; www.westcoast motors.co.uk) runs two to four daily buses to Oban (one hour 15 minutes) and four to six to Lochgilphead (15 minutes), where you can connect with Citylink services. There's no Sunday service.

## KINTYRE PENINSULA

Almost an island, the 40-mile-long Kintyre Peninsula has only a narrow strand connecting it to the rest of Scotland at Tarbert. Magnus Barefoot the Viking, who could claim any island he circumnavigated, made his people drag their longship across this strand to validate his claim.

## Tarbert

Tarbert, the gateway to Kintyre, is a pretty fishing village with colourful buildings strung along the harbour. The **tourist office** ( ☎ 08707 200624; Harbour St; ⏰ daily Apr-Oct) has internet access (£3 per hour). Above town is a small, crumbling **castle** built by Robert the Bruce.

Tarbert makes a good stop, and is especially convenient if you've got an early ferry to Islay. Follow the harbour just past the centre to the **Moorings** ( ☎ 01880-820756; moorings@tarbertlochfyne .com; Pier Rd; s/d £35/56; **P** ), which is beautifully maintained and decorated by one man and his dog, has great views over the water, and an eclectic range of ceramic owls and offbeat artwork. The **Anchor Hotel** ( ☎ 01880-820577; www .anchorhoteltarbert; Harbour St; s/d £50/80) has bright rooms and large, attractive beds. Breakfast

lasts till noon and features pheasant sausages and Bloody Marys, and there are bar meals here. For more-upmarket fare, **Corner House Bistro** ( ☎ 01880-820263; Castle St; mains £12-25; ⏰ 6-10.30pm) has a garlanded French chef and well-presented but unpretentious creations from locally caught fish.

South of Tarbert are two ferry terminals: **Kennacraig** for Islay (per person/car return £15/77, 2¼ hours); and **Claonaig** for Lochranza (per person/car return £8/36, 30 minutes, Easter to October) on Arran.

## Isle of Gigha

From Tayinloan on the west coast there are ferries (per person/car return £5.70/21.10, 20 minutes, six to 10 daily) to the **Isle of Gigha** (www .gigha.org.uk), pronounced *ghee*-a, a flat island 7 miles long by about 1 mile wide. Bought from its original owner by the residents themselves in 2002, it offers sandy beaches and the subtropical **Achamore Gardens** (suggested donation £2; ⏰ dawn-dusk). The **Gigha Hotel** ( ☎ 01583-505254; s/d £52/87; **P** ) is owned by the residents' trust and is exceptionally friendly, with a restaurant and lively bar.

## Campbeltown

pop 5144

The journey down to Campbeltown contrasts rolling green farmland with surf-pounded beaches. The weather can change by the minute, and you feel right on the ramparts of mainland Britain. Campbeltown was in its prime in the late 19th century, but is impressively situated around a small loch surrounded by hills. The **tourist office** ( ☎ 01586-552056; camp beltown@visitscotland.com; The Pier; ⏰ daily Easter-Oct, Mon-Fri Nov-Easter) is where to go for a chat or a brochure.

There were once dozens of whisky distilleries here – the Campbeltown style is distinct – but now there are just three. You can visit **Springbank** ( ☎ 01586-552085; www.springbankdistillers .com; Longrow; admission £4; ⏰ 10am & 2pm by arrangement Mon-Fri, 2pm only in winter), a small-scale, personal operation that does its own malting and bottling.

Famous former Kintyre residents include Paul and Linda McCartney; Linda has a small memorial garden, entered through the **library-museum** ( ☎ 01586-552367; ⏰ 10am-1pm & 2-5pm Tue-Sat), which offers free internet. Beyond Campbeltown, a narrow, winding road leads to the **Mull of Kintyre**, popularised by Paul

McCartney's song of the same name – and the mist does indeed roll in.

**Mull of Kintyre Seatours** (www.mull-of-kintyre .co.uk) runs wildlife-spotting trips from Campbeltown and can also transport you across to Ayr or nearby Northern Ireland. Book at the tourist office.

**Flybe/Loganair** ( ☎ 0871 700 2000; www.flybe.com) flies on weekdays between Glasgow and Campbeltown (£46). Campbeltown is also linked by Citylink buses to Glasgow (£14, 4¼ hours, three daily).

## ISLE OF ISLAY
### pop 3460

The home of the world's greatest and peatiest whiskies, whose names reverberate on the tongue like a pantheon of Celtic deities, Islay is a wonderfully friendly place whose warmly welcoming inhabitants offset its lack of majestic scenery. Even if you're not into your drams, the birdlife, fine seafood, turquoise bays and basking seals are ample reason to visit this island, pronounced *eye*-lah. There are currently eight working distilleries; perhaps this is why the locals are so genial – a wave or cheerio to passersby is mandatory, and you'll soon find yourself slowing down to Islay's relaxing pace.

### Orientation

There are two ferry terminals, both served from Kennacraig on Kintyre. Port Askaig gazes at mountainous Jura from the island's east, while larger Port Ellen in the south has three distilleries nearby. The capital, Bowmore, is in the island's centre and has most services. Across Loch Indaal is the attractive village of Port Charlotte.

### Information

Port Ellen, Bowmore and Port Charlotte all have places to get online.

**Tourist office** ( ☎ 01496-810254; info@islay.visit scotland.com; The Square, Bowmore; ☉ 10am-5pm Mon-Sat, noon-3pm Sun Apr-Jun, 9.30am-5.30pm Mon-Sat, noon-3pm Sun Jul-Aug, 10am-5pm Mon-Sat Sep-Oct, 10am-3pm five days/week Nov-Mar) Helpful and friendly.

### Sights & Activities

The eight **whisky distilleries** welcome visitors for guided tours. Most cost £4 or £5 (redeemable on a bottle) and some you have to book. They open Monday to Friday; most now open Saturday too; and in high season, Ardbeg and Bowmore also open Sunday in summer. Many

of Islay's whiskies have a distinctive peaty taste, particularly the southerly distilleries of Ardbeg, Lagavulin and Laphroaig. The most charming to visit is **Bruichladdich** ( ☎ 01496-850190; www.bruichladdich.com; tours £5; ☉ tours 11.30am & 2.30pm Mon-Fri, 11.30am Sat Nov-Easter, 10.30am, 11.30am, 2.30pm Mon-Fri, 10.30am & 2.30pm Sat Easter-October), pronounced brook-*laddie*, located near Port Charlotte. Independently owned, it runs on palpable enthusiasm, and refuses to compromise on quality. Its main whisky line is fresh and light-bodied, but there's much experimentation going on here and always some intriguing new bottling being plotted. If you're going to visit any distillery in Scotland, make this the one. To get there, take a Port Charlotte–bound bus and jump off when you see the distinctive turquoise gates.

The three famous southerners are, in order of distance from Port Ellen, **Laphroaig** ( ☎ 01496-302418; www.laphroaig.com; tours 10.15am & 2.15pm Mon-Fri, plus 11.45am & 3.30pm Mon-Fri & 10am Sat Jun-Sep), **Lagavulin** ( ☎ 01496-302730; www.discovering-distill eries.com; tours by appointment 9.30am, 11.15am & 2.30pm Mon-Fri) and **Ardbeg** ( ☎ 01496-302244; www.ardbeg .com; tours 10.30am & 3pm Mon-Fri Sep-May, 10.30am, noon, 1.30pm & 3pm daily Jun-Aug). Peat content is high in these cult whiskies, all of which pack a punch and get aficionados debating endlessly over their medal positions. All three are handsome, with views across to Ireland, and do good tours, with Ardbeg's perhaps the most personable; it also has a popular cafe.

Near Bruichladdich, young **Kilchoman** ( ☎ 01496-850011; www.kilchomandistillery.com; ☉ 10am-5pm Mon-Fri, plus Sat Easter-Oct, tours at 11am & 3pm) is a small-scale farm distillery that partly uses its own barley, which it malts here. You can try the distilled spirit, although the first whisky won't be released until 2010 or so. There's a great farm-produce shop here, and a cafe. Also here is the **Rockside Farm Trekking Centre** ( ☎ 01496-850231), which will take you on horseback for an hour (£15) or, better, 2½ hours (£25) along the spectacular sands of Machir Bay.

Bronze Age relics, an illicit still and countless human stories intrigue at the quirky **Museum of Islay Life** ( ☎ 01496-850358; Port Charlotte; admission £3; ☉ 10.30am-4.30pm Mon-Sat Easter-Oct, call for winter hours), in an old church building at the entrance to Port Charlotte.

About 4 miles beyond the Ardbeg distillery, **Kildalton Cross** was carved in the second half of the eighth century, probably by monks from

CENTRAL SCOTLAND

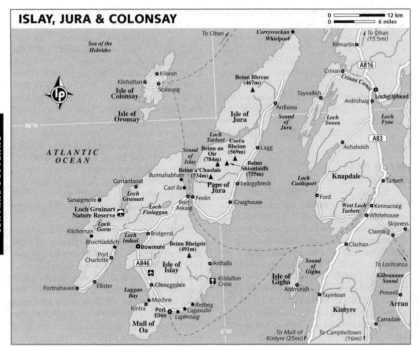

**ISLAY, JURA & COLONSAY**

Iona. Standing proud in a remote churchyard, it's one of Scotland's few remaining Celtic high crosses.

At the top of the town in Bowmore, the **Round Church** was built in 1767 in this unusual shape to ensure the devil had no corners to hide in. He was last seen in one of the distilleries.

More than 250 recorded species make Islay wonderful for **birdwatching**. It's an important wintering ground for white-fronted and barnacle geese, which outnumber the Ileachs (inhabitants of Islay) 10 to one; local farms are hit hard when the squadrons land. For **seal-spotting**, head to Portnahaven, at the island's southwestern tip. There are frequently dozens of the portly beasts basking in the small harbour.

### Festivals & Events

The **Islay Festival of Malt & Music** in late May/ early June is a wonderful time to visit, but book accommodation months in advance.

### Sleeping & Eating

**Islay SYHA Hostel** ( ☎ 01496-850385; www.syha.org .uk; Port Charlotte; dm £13.75; ✹ mid-Mar–Oct; P )

Islay's only hostel has a great location by a little beach. Despite a slightly institutional feel, the roomy lounge and kitchen, helpful hosts and comfortable dorms make it a good bet. Reception is closed between 10am and 5pm.

**our pick Lambeth Guest House** ( ☎ 01496-810597; lambethguesthouse@tiscali.co.uk; Jamieson St, Bowmore; r per person £28; 🖳 ) If the whisky hasn't given you that glow of warm contentment yet, this great little guesthouse surely will. With the biggest welcome in Bowmore, comfy rooms with shared bathroom and breakfasts that really hit the spot, you'll be trying to extend your stay on the island. Home-cooked dinners are also available.

**Distillery House** ( ☎ 01496-850495; mamak@btinter net.com; Port Charlotte; per person with shared/en suite bathroom £28/30; P 🖳 ) For a real taste of islander hospitality head directly to this charming B&B, run by kindly locals who make their own marmalade and oatcakes. It's set in part of the former Lochindaal distillery; rooms are well kept and most comfortable. There's no sign, but it's opposite the SYHA as you enter Port Charlotte.

**Bowmore Distillery Cottages** ( ☎ 01496-810671; www.bowmore.com; School St, Bowmore; cottage per night £68-270) In and around the Bowmore distillery in the heart of the capital, these six charming self-catering cottages vary widely in size; the petite Mashman's Cottage has just one bedroom, while the Old Bakery sleeps up to a baker's dozen. All are attractively furnished and have good facilities and varied charms; they are surprisingly well priced and should be booked ahead. There's usually a two-day minimum, but you can sometimes squeeze in a one-day stay.

**Port Charlotte Hotel** ( ☎ 01496-850360; www .portcharlottehotel.co.uk; Main St, Port Charlotte; s/d £85/130; P 🖳 wi-fi) The hub of Islay's western metropolis, the PCH offers rooms that are way overpriced but nonetheless attractive, with cosy furnishings, modern bathrooms and sea views. The appealing bar has a fine selection of Islay and Jura malts and does smart bar food (bar meals £8 to £12); there's also an upmarket restaurant (mains £15 to £28). The place is run with exemplary professional hospitality.

**our pick** **Harbour Inn** ( ☎ 01496-810330; www.har bour-inn.com; Bowmore; d £115-145; 🖳 wi-fi) Right by the water in the heart of Bowmore, this special place fills fast: book it or miss it. Spacious, ultra-commodious rooms furnished with a light touch provide proper relaxation, and the classy restaurant (mains £14 to £24) offers excellent local game, lamb and seafood; try matching local malts to your meal.

**An Tigh Seinnse** ( ☎ 01496-860224; Portnahaven; dishes £6-15; 🕑 noon-8pm) This exceedingly good spot is at the island's southwestern tip, by the little harbour where the seals flop on the rocks. It's a cosy pub with outdoor seating, and is run by friendly folk who produce a range of tasty Aga-cooked food, with changing specials that vary from cheerful snacks to gourmet plates (plenty of vegetarian options).

Other recommendations:

**Glenegedale House** ( ☎ 01496-300400; www .glenegedalehouse.co.uk; s/d £75/100; P ) Right by the airport (no problem on Islay) with great comfort and superior breakfasts.

**Croft Kitchen** ( ☎ 01496-850230; Port Charlotte; mains £6-10; 🕑 10am-7.30pm Thu-Tue) By museum in Port Charlotte. Comforting cafe with sophisticated meal options like venison pot-roast.

**Lochside Hotel** ( ☎ 01496-810244; www.lochsidehotel .co.uk; 19 Shore St, Bowmore; mains £5-10; 🕑 lunch & dinner) Around 400 malts on offer, with all sorts of rare bottlings. Decent bar meals and regular live music.

## Getting There & Away

**Flybe/Loganair** ( ☎ 0871 700 2000; www.flybe.com) operates one to three flights per day from Glasgow to Islay (£38 to £76 one way, 45 minutes).

CalMac runs daily ferries (per person/car return £15/77, 2¼ hours) from Kennacraig to either Port Ellen or Port Askaig. Citylink buses running between Glasgow and Campbeltown connect with the ferry. In summer there's a Wednesday ferry from Port Askaig to Colonsay (per person/car one way £4.50/23.30, 1¼ hours) and Oban.

## Getting Around

**Islay Coaches** ( ☎ 01496-840273) operates services nearly hourly around the island. Taxis aid serious distillery investigation – operators include **Lamont** ( ☎ 07899 756159), a larger-than-life character who clocks up 45,000 miles a year on this tiny island. Hitching is easy.

Islay's size and flatness make it bike heaven; **Bowmore post office** ( ☎ 01496-810366; Main St; 🕑 9am-1pm Mon-Sat) hires out mountain bikes for £10 per day, as does friendly **Port Charlotte Bike Hire** ( ☎ 01496-850488) opposite the hotel. To hire a car, try **MacKenzies'** ( ☎ 01496-302300; mackenziej@btconnect.com) or **Islay Car Hire** ( ☎ 01496-810544; www.islaycarhire.com).

## ISLE OF JURA

pop 170

It's the deer that are in charge of the island where George Orwell wrote *1984*: they outnumber humans by more than 30 to one. Almost treeless, Jura looms over the eastern end of Islay with fascinating menace. It's a walkers' paradise, with a wild landscape dominated by the island's stark, brooding hills, the Paps of Jura (named for their breastlike shape).

If you're not a hiker, it's just a place to relax, but you could visit the **Isle of Jura Distillery** ( ☎ 01496-820385; www.isleofjura.com; 🕑 tours 11am & 2pm Mon-Fri by appointment) in Craighouse, the island's only village. Orwell stayed in a cottage, **Barnhill** ( ☎ 01786-850274; per week £550), at the far north of the island. You can rent it (it sleeps seven) but it is remote – 7 miles from the main road on a rough track, and 25 miles from the pub.

## Walking

The **Paps of Jura** provide a tough hillwalk requiring navigational skills that takes eight hours. Beware of serpents; the island is infested with adders, but they're shy snakes that'll move out of your way.

Start by the bridge over the River Corran, about 3 miles north of Craighouse. The first pap you reach is Beinn a'Chaolais (734m), then Beinn an Oir (784m) and finally Beinn Shiantaidh (755m). Most people also climb Corra Bheinn (569m) before joining the path that crosses the island to descend to the road.

### Sleeping & Eating

**Jura Hotel** ( ☎ 01496-820243; www.jurahotel.co.uk; Craighouse; s/d £53/82, without bathroom £47/70; **P** ) This family-run hotel opposite the distillery is a great place to stay and *the* place for a drink. The rooms at the front have fantastic views, but cost extra. There's good pub grub and excellent evening meals using local produce.

### Getting There & Away

Access to Jura is via Islay. A small ferry braves the tides between Port Askaig and Feolin (per person/car day-return £2.50/14, five minutes) roughly hourly from Monday to Saturday, with seven services on Sunday. A **bus** ( ☎ 01496-820314) runs from Feolin to Craighouse and further north. It meets some ferries; other journeys are by request only, so call the day before.

## ISLE OF COLONSAY
pop 110

Remote Colonsay delights with unspoilt, lush green fields bordered by a rocky coastline and perilous cliffs, and superb beaches backed by machair and woodland. Kiloran Bay, where Atlantic rollers thunder onto pure golden sands, is one of Britain's prettiest strands.

It's worth a stroll around the lovely subtropical gardens of **Colonsay House** (admission free; walled garden noon-5pm Wed & 3-5pm Fri Easter-Sep), known for their rhododendrons. Discreet wandering in the rest of the estate is allowed at times other than the ones given for the walled garden. Bring midge repellent to keep the squadrons at bay.

Grey seals are often seen around the coast and wild goats inhabit some of the neighbouring islets. At low tide walk across the strand to the small **Isle of Oronsay**, to the south, where the ruins of the priory date from the 14th century.

### Sleeping & Eating

**Colonsay Keeper's Lodge** ( ☎ 01951-200312; www .colonsay.org.uk/backpackers.html; dm £12-14, tw £32; **P** ) In a great location near Colonsay House in a former gamekeeper's lodge, this bunkhouse is a 40-minute walk from the ferry. The kitchen is well equipped and the lodge hires out bikes for a fiver a day. You need to phone ahead.

**Colonsay Hotel** ( ☎ 01951-200316; www.thecolon say.com; Scalasaig; s £60, d £110-140; Apr-Dec; **P** ) A 500m walk straight ahead from the ferry, the island's main hostelry is a fine island base. The superior doubles are wonderful, with bright white linen, stylish furnishing, DVD players, and views. One has a four-poster bed. There's also a family suite (£130). There's good-value quality food in the hotel (mains £8 to £12), with tasty local oysters on offer.

### Getting There & Away

CalMac serves Colonsay from Oban (per person/car £12/59, 2¼ hours) three to five times a week. In summer, there's a Wednesday sailing to Colonsay from Islay's Port Askaig (per person/car £5/24, 1¼ hours) and from Kennacraig on the Kintyre Peninsula (per person/car £12/59, 3½ hours). This enables a day trip to Colonsay from Islay, with about six hours on the island.

## OBAN & AROUND
pop 8120

A major launch pad for the Hebrides, especially Mull, Oban enjoys a splendid bayside location. In summer it can be a little jammed, with the main street packed solid with traffic, but head a couple of miles out of town either way to appreciate the beautiful coastal scenery without the crowds. The best of Oban is to be found on a warm spring evening, munching shellfish by the harbour, with the *Lord of the Isles* ferry dwarfing the elegant Victorian buildings on the shore. At this time the town seems to keep alive a sort of seaside experience that's quintessentially British.

### Orientation

The ferry terminal is by the train station at the southern end of town. Oban's centre is George St, which runs north–south along the harbour.

### Information

**Fancy That** ( ☎ 01631-562996; 108 George St; per hr £3; 9am-5pm, to 9pm summer) Internet access.

CENTRAL SCOTLAND

Tourist office ( ☎ 01631-563122; info@oban.visit scotland.com; Argyll Sq; 🕙 9am-6pm Mon-Sat, 10am-5pm Sun Jun-Sep, 9am-5.30pm Mon-Sat, 10am-4pm Sun Apr-May & Oct, 10am-5pm Mon-Sat, noon-4pm Sun Nov-Mar) Busy and well stocked. Internet access.

## Sights & Activities

In the heart of town **Oban Distillery** ( ☎ 01631-572004; www.discovering-distilleries.com; Stafford St; tours £5; 🕙 Mon-Fri Feb-Mar & Nov-Dec, Mon-Sat Apr-Jun & Oct, daily Jul-Sep) offers a decent tour and has been producing tasty, salty single malt whisky since 1794.

Atop the town is the Colosseum-like **McCaig's Folly**, another entry on Britain's list of bizarre structures built by Victorian gentry with money and classical tendencies.

It's a pleasant 20-minute walk north from the harbour along the coast to **Dunollie Castle**, built by the MacDougalls of Lorne in the 15th century. It's a mossy picturesque ruin, open for wandering. You could continue along this road to the beach at **Ganavan Sands**, 2.5 miles from Oban.

Heading the other way, past the ferry terminal, it also becomes very scenic, and gets you, after a couple of miles, to the passenger ferry to the picturesque islet of Kerrera (£4.50 return, ferry comes on signal), good for exploring on foot or by bike. There's a tearoom and bunkhouse over there should you need sustenance or a bed. Near the ferry, highly professional **Puffin Diving** ( ☎ 01631-566088; www .puffin.org.uk) offers a full range of courses along with guided dives in the area.

Exploring the coastline by bike appeals. The tourist office has a leaflet of routes, including a recommended 16-mile route to Seil Island.

Boat operators at each end of the central harbour offer 60-minute jaunts to see the nearby **seal colony** (£8); these leave roughly hourly.

## Sleeping

Book rooms in advance between June and September. Beware the northern end of George St, where there's a racket involving outrageous prices for substandard rooms across various B&B premises.

### BUDGET

**Oban Caravan & Camping Park** ( ☎ 01631-562425; www.obancaravanpark.com; Gallanachmore Farm; tent sites £12; 🕙 Apr-Oct) In a great position on a lovely green hillside above the water, near the islet of Kerrera 2.5 miles south of Oban towards Gallanach (turn right out of the ferry terminal), this camp site is a top spot to stay. Two daily buses from Oban stop outside.

**Jeremy Inglis Hostel** ( ☎ 01631-565065; 21 Airds Cres; dm £12, s £17-20) A curious place, this is part B&B, part hostel, and fairly priced, especially for solo travellers. Decked out top to bottom with curios, from framed jokes from old *Punch* magazines to original artwork and musty books, it exudes offbeat character and organised chaos. Continental breakfast is included and features the helpful owner's homemade jam. The kitchen, however, is cramped.

**our pick** **Oban Backpackers** ( ☎ 01631-562107; www.scotlandstophostels.com; Breadalbane St; dm £13.50; 🖳 wi-fi) Space isn't a worry at this sociable hostel; you could dock the Mull ferry in the enormous lounge, which features sofas sporting colourful fabric throws, a pool table and a hand-painted map of the coastline. The kitchen is also large, and the great dorms feature bottom bunks that you can actually sit on without banging your head. Powerful showers and a £1.90 breakfast make for painless mornings.

### MIDRANGE & TOP END

**Maridon House** ( ☎ 01631-562670; Dunuaran Rd; s/d £28/50; Ⓟ ) Perched above the harbour's southern end, this blue house is easily spotted. The personable owner charges a very fair price for appealing rooms with modern bathrooms and new carpets; some have water views, and there's a handy family room. You can virtually roll out of bed onto the ferry, great for early-morning departures.

**Sand Villa Guesthouse** ( ☎ 01631-562803; www .holidayoban.co.uk; Breadalbane St; r per person £25-30; Ⓟ ) The best of several decent guesthouses on this street, this enticing and reliable choice is run with efficient good humour and features large, en suite rooms with sinfully comfortable beds, a subtle sand theme and plenty of style and comfort in what's now a quiet part of town. Breakfast includes fresh fruit.

**Kilchrenan House** ( ☎ 01631-562663; www.kilchrenan house.co.uk; Corran Esplanade; s/d £40/80; Ⓟ ) Boasting sea views on both sides, this well-run property makes the most of them, with smart rooms, many of them brand new with modern bathrooms. The vistas are magnificent and really soothing. Room five is particularly memorable, with a four-poster bed and a great freestanding bathtub; another room features a loo with a view. Porridge and kippers put in a welcome appearance on the breakfast menu.

**Dungallan Country House** ( ☎ 01631-563799; www.dungallanhotel-oban.co.uk; Gallanach Rd; d £130-154; P ▣ wi-fi) Set in its own bosky grounds atop a hillock, this striking Victorian house was built as a summer residence for the Duke of Argyll and offers, even by Oban standards, majestic views over the town and its bay from most of its rooms. There's refined, polite hospitality here, and a rather impressive whisky selection.

**Manor House** ( ☎ 01631-562087; www.manorhouseoban.com; Gallanach Rd; B&B & dinner s £175-185, d £205-245; P ▣ wi-fi) With a choice location on the bay (turn right out of the ferry terminal), this boutique hotel occupies an 18th-century building built by the Duke of Argyll to house his widowed mother. There are great views of the town; the rooms are decorated in sumptuous period style, and the salon and dining rooms are particularly luxurious. Dinner is compulsory from May to September; luckily it's a delicious gourmet five-course affair (£36 for nonguests, who must prebook).

## Eating & Drinking

**Oban Chocolate Company** ( ☎ 01631-566099; www.obanchocolate.net; 34 Corran Esplanade; treats £2-5; ⊕ 10am-5pm Mon-Sat) This waterside cafe and chocolate factory keeps want-to-be Charlies in heaven with luscious milkshakes and hot chocolate, as well as sundaes, chocolate fondues and various other goodies.

**Seafood kiosks** (Queens Park Pl; plates £2-6; ⊕ 11am-7pm) These two excellent places on the harbour near the ferry terminal offer simple seafood straight off the boats. Prices are very reasonable; a little cup of mixed critters is £2.50, while lemon butter–seared scallops bring new meaning to fast food for £6.

**Julie's** ( ☎ 01631-565952; 37 Stafford St; light meals £3-8; ⊕ 10am-5pm Mon-Sat) Opposite the distillery, this cheerfully scatty tearoom serves up sandwiches and light meals (try the tasty smoked salmon), coffees and toothsome treacle scones. There's also ice cream, and tables outside in case of good weather.

**Cuan Mòr** ( ☎ 01631-565078; 60 George St; mains £7-13; ⊕ food noon-10pm) Right in the heart of town, the fresh, confident interior of this excellent bar-restaurant makes creative use of slate, driftwood, and wooden shellfish cases. The menu offers jazzed-up pub classics as well

as vegie choices, crab cakes, and scallops to remind you of where you are. Fifteen wines by the glass and welcoming service keep punters smiling.

**our pick Seafood Temple** ( ☎ 01631-566000; Gallanach Rd; dishes £6-15; ⊕ dinner Thu-Mon) Lobsters, langoustines and locally smoked salmon are just some of the seafood treats on offer at this recently opened spot past the Manor House hotel at the southern end of town. The light wooden tables are tiered democratically, giving everyone a peek at the wonderful bay views.

**Oban Inn** ( ☎ 01631-562484; Stafford St) Dating from 1790, this pub overlooks the harbour by North Pier. It's got a time-worn, historic feel with low wooden beams; there's a great mix of people here, with posh yachties comparing tidal charts with gruff local fisherfolk.

Other recommendations:

**Nevis Bakery** ( ☎ 01631-562262; 12 Stevenson St; steak pies £1.60; ⊕ 8am-5.30pm Mon-Sat) Delicious pies and hearty fry-ups.

**Ee.Usk** ( ☎ 01631-565666; North Pier; mains lunch £6-10, dinner £12-20; ⊕ lunch & dinner) Smart seafood in a great contemporary harbourside location. A two-course dinner before 7.30pm is £17.50.

**Lorne** ( ☎ 01631-570020; 31 Stevenson St; ⊕ 11am-1am) Island bar, beer garden, stained glass, polished brass. A good pub.

## Getting There & Away

### BOAT

CalMac boats link Oban with the Inner and Outer Hebrides. Car space, especially for Mull, should be booked ahead. The following are one-way fares:

| Island | Passenger/Car (£) | Duration (hr) | Frequency |
|---|---|---|---|
| Mull | 4.25/38 | 45 min | 5-7 daily |
| Coll | 9/46 | 3 | 1 daily |
| Tiree | 9/46 | 4 | 1 daily |
| Barra | 14/56 | 5 | 1 daily |
| South Uist | 14/56 | 5½ | 1 daily |
| Colonsay | 11.90/59 | 2¼ | 1 weekly (summer) |
| Islay | 12.15/59 | 3¾ | 1 weekly (summer) |

### BUS

Citylink runs to Oban from Glasgow (£13.20, three hours, eight daily), Inveraray (£6.90, 70 minutes, two to three daily), Fort William (£10.40, 1½ hours, two to four daily Monday to Saturday) and Perth/Dundee (two daily).

---

**MAKE MINE A MANSION**

**our pick** **Lunga House** ( ☎ 01852-500237; www.lunga.com; Craobh Haven; B&B per person £25-32; P 💻 ), set on a hillside above Craobh Haven, 11 miles north of Kilmartin and 24 miles south of Oban, is a magnificent baronial mansion offering wonderful B&B or self-catering accommodation in a secluded location boasting magnificent coastal panoramas.

The laird and his family are charismatic local visionaries, and totally unstuffy; the noble lines of the house enclose an interior bristling with history, antiques, portraits and character. The rooms are all wholly different, but expect venerable furniture, modern bathrooms, miles of space and utter relaxation.

It's a great place for kids, who are made welcome and love roaming around the huge house and grounds. There are plenty of things to do around here, including a riding centre just down the hill. Dinner is also available by arrangement.

---

### TRAIN
Trains run to Oban from Glasgow (£18.30, three hours, three daily). It's at the end of a scenic branch line from Crianlarich.

### Getting Around
**Flit Self Drive** ( ☎ 01631-566553; www.selfdrive.me.uk; Glencruitten Rd) hires bikes (half/full day £10/14), among other vehicles.

## ISLE OF MULL
pop 2667

Just a short ferry hop from the west coast, Mull has long enchanted visitors with its majestic hillscapes and the almost mystical appeal of little Iona, the holy island off its western end. Wildlife enthusiasts come for Mull's seabirds, eagles and sporting dolphins, while hillwalkers can take on Ben More for the magnificent view from its summit. The main town, tiny Tobermory, is an achingly pretty ensemble of colourful shorefront houses straight out of a picture book.

These houses did indeed make it to a picture book via the hit kids' TV show *Balamory*, which was filmed here and brought Mull a huge surge of toddler tourism.

### Orientation & Information
Most Mull residents live in Tobermory in the north. The Oban ferry arrives at Craignure, on the east coast. The island is large, and has mostly single-track roads, so don't try to 'do' it in a day – you'll end up exhausted.

There are tourist offices at **Craignure** ( ☎ 01680-812377; craignure@visitscotland.com; ⏰ 8.30am-5pm Mon-Sat, 10am-5pm Sun), opposite the ferry, and **Tobermory** ( ☎ 01688-302182; tobermory@visitscotland.com; Main St; ⏰ 10am-5pm Mon-Fri, 11am-5pm Sat & Sun), which should be in smart new harbourside premises by the time you read this; internet access will likely be available there. **Posh Nosh Cafe** ( ☎ 01688-302499; per 15min £1; ⏰ 10am-6pm) also offers internet access in Tobermory.

### Sights & Activities
Craignure is basically just a ferry stop, but from here you can catch the **Mull Rail** ( ☎ 01680-812494; www.mullrail.co.uk; adult/child return £4.75/3.25) miniature steam train 1.5 miles south to **Torosay Castle** ( ☎ 01680-812421; www.torosay.com; admission £6; ⏰ 10.30am-5pm mid-Mar–Oct). A typical Victorian Scottish baronial mansion with its turrets and step gables, its grand but comfortably homelike interior gives an insight into British aristocratic families, and David Guthrie James, father of the current laird, whose interesting life included two daring escapes from a Stalag, polar exploration and film-making. The house has spacious grounds including an Italianate tiered garden.

Two miles further, **Duart Castle** ( ☎ 01680-812309; www.duartcastle.com; admission £5; ⏰ 11am-4pm Sun-Thu Apr, 10.30am-5.30pm May–mid-Oct) is the ancestral seat of the Maclean clan and enjoys a spectacular position on a rocky outcrop overlooking the Sound of Mull. Originally built in the 13th century, it was abandoned for 160 years before a 1912 restoration. As well as the dungeons, courtyard and battlements with memorable views, there's clan history – pantomime boos for Lachlan Cattanach, who took his wife for a picnic to a rocky islet, then left her there to drown when the tide came in. Most fascinating is the display on the nearby underwater excavation of a ship sunk in a storm in 1653 after being sent by Oliver Cromwell to attack Duart. A castle bus meets some incoming ferries at Craignure, but it's a pretty walk too.

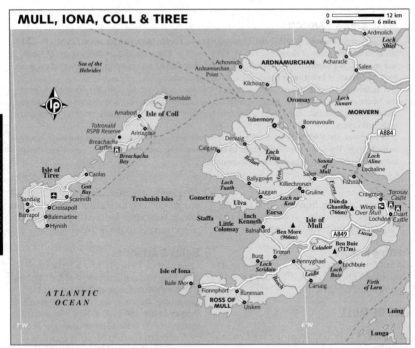

MULL, IONA, COLL & TIRE

Between the two castles, **Wings Over Mull** ( ☎ 01680-812594; www.wingsovermull.com; admission £4.50; ◷ 10.30am-5.30pm mid-Feb–Oct) is a conservation centre for birds of prey, for which Mull is an important sanctuary. There are flight displays at noon, 2pm and 4pm.

Mull's capital is **Tobermory**, a sparkling little fishing port in the island's north. The brightly painted houses strung out along a sheltered bay surrounded by wooded hills make this one of the prettiest villages in Scotland. Here, the **Hebridean Whale & Dolphin Trust** ( ☎ 01688-302620; www.hwdt.org; 28 Main St; ◷ 10am-5pm Apr-Oct, 11am-4pm Mon-Fri Nov-Mar) is a research centre that has informative displays on the local marine population as well as information on various whale- and dolphin-spotting operators on Mull.

You can walk up **Ben More** (966m), the highest peak on Mull, which has spectacular views across to the surrounding islands when the weather is clear. A trail leads up the mountain from Loch na Keal, by the bridge on the B8035, about 8 miles southwest of Salen. Allow six hours for the return trip.

In the hamlet of Gruline is the **mausoleum** of Lachlan Macquarie, the enlightened fifth governor of New South Wales (Australia) and a Mull native. It's a 500m walk off the main road in attractive farmland.

## Sleeping & Eating
### TOBERMORY

**Tobermory SYHA Hostel** ( ☎ 01688-302481; www.syha .org.uk; Main St; dm £14; ◷ mid-Mar–Oct; ▣ ) One of the cute, colourful, waterfront buildings that wins Tobermory a spot in every 'Highlands and islands' calendar houses this simple and friendly hostel. Creaky bunks and downstairs showers are minor quibbles, but the big kitchen, laundry, drying room and lounge with view make up for it. It's a quiet, walker-oriented place but a midnight curfew is harsh when the good folk at the Mishnish don't shut for another hour after that.

**Fàilte Guest House** ( ☎ 01688-302495; www.failte guesthouse.com; 27 Main St; s/d from £32/64; ◷ Apr-Oct) Happiness in Tobermory is a cosy B&B on the pretty, colourful waterfront, and this welcoming choice fits the bill. The rooms are en suite and warmly decorated, with Asian-print bedcovers and lovely gleaming white bathrooms. The best rooms face the water, and have huge windows to take advantage of the privileged view.

**Highland Cottage** ( ☎ 01688-302030; www.highland cottage.co.uk; Breadalbane St; d £150-185; ☑ mid-Mar–Oct; ℗ ) Intimate and personable, this small luxurious hotel sits on the hill above the harbour and offers friendly elegance, a warm welcome and great food. It feels very cosy, with comfortable antique furniture in country-house style and rooms with a homelike feel. Not that they lack facilities – crystal glasses, CD player, videos, books and bathrobes are all here, among many other small touches. Dinner is a gourmet four-course affair (£42.50) that has a deservedly high reputation; nonguests are welcome, but book ahead.

**our pick** **Mishnish Hotel** ( ☎ 01688-302009; Main St; bar meals £5-9; ☑ lunch & dinner, bar open till 1am/2am weeknights/weekends) Spend your life savings on ferry tickets, but you might not find a better island pub than the legendary Mishnish, a nook-and-cranny set up behind a black facade. There's always good chat at the bar and an interesting mix of locals and tourists. Large pub meals offer plenty of value; posher fare is served upstairs.

**Cafe Fish** ( ☎ 01688-301253; The Pier; dinner mains £8-14; ☑ lunch & dinner) Upstairs at the far end of the harbour, this fabulous newcomer offers simply prepared, delicious seafood. At lunchtime you can chow down on lobster wraps or crab sandwiches; the dinner options include a delicious fish pie and aromatic bowls of steamed mussels. Some of the food comes from the friendly owners' own boat.

**Javier's** ( ☎ 01688-302350; Ledaig; mains £12-18; ☑ lunch & dinner) Upstairs at MacGochan's pub by the distillery, this place combines pleasingly informal touches – the cutlery's in a pot on the table, and you can get a carafe of house wine – with a professional welcome, well-spaced tables and interesting takes on local seafood. The daily specials are always worth pursuing, but the scallops with a touch of serrano ham are tasty too.

Other recommendations:

**34 Main St** ( ☎ 01688-302530; 34 Main St; s/d without bathroom £15/30) Three cosy attic rooms with good shared bathroom. Room-only, next to the supermarket. A gruff bargain.

**Harbour Guest House** ( ☎ 01688-302209; Main St; s/d £30/65) Pretty, with pastel walls, skylights and metal-framed beds; a sound selection on the waterfront.

**Island Bakery** ( ☎ 01688-302223; Main St; ☑ 8am-5pm Mon-Sat, 10am-3pm Sun) Put together a picnic fit for a president at this excellent bakery and deli.

## AROUND TOBERMORY

**Dervaig Bunkrooms** ( ☎ 01688-400249; Dervaig; dm £12; ℗ ) Dervaig's a pretty spot at the head of an inlet 7 miles west of Tobermory. A community project has set up this sweet little hostel in the village hall at the entrance to town. With shiny wooden bunks and a spotless new kitchen, you'll be most snug.

**our pick** **Achnadrish House** ( ☎ 01688-400388; www.achnadrish.co.uk; Dervaig Rd; r per person from £37.50; ℗ 🖳 wi-fi) It's tough to think of a more inviting place to stay on the west side of Scotland than this offbeat and upmarket fusion of historic shooting lodge and Indochinese guesthouse, located between Tobermory and Dervaig. The charming owner has used Far Eastern experience to advantage, with soothing Thai fabrics in the rooms, small Buddhas overwatching guests' slumber, and fantastic breakfasts and dinners (£25) featuring Mull ingredients in deliciously piquant Asian dishes. An evening dram with your hosts, who include a pack of ultrafriendly labradors, is mandatory and part of the charm of this wonderfully relaxed retreat. There are also attractive self-catering options attached (£180 to £585 per week).

**Glengorm Castle** ( ☎ 01688-302321; www.glen gormcastle.co.uk; Glengorm; d £120-190; ℗ ) Bristling with turrets as a real castle should, this special spot enjoys an unforgettable location; huge windows make the most of vistas of green fields sloping down to the water. The five bedrooms, all different, are beautiful, ultraspacious and have character in spades. The place is run by lively young people, and kids will have a ball running around the grounds or admiring the sheep and Highland cattle.

## CRAIGNURE

**Shieling Holidays** ( ☎ 01680-812496; www.shieling holidays.co.uk; Craignure; dm £11.50, shieling £28-43; ☑ mid-Mar–mid-Oct; ℗ ) Nights in white canvas are on offer at this spot that offers camping without banging in pegs. With a great headland situation around the corner from the ferry, it accommodates guests in 'shielings', essentially big tents with tiled and carpeted floors; the more luxurious ones have running water, a toilet and a hot shower. Hostel-rate beds are available and a good-value cottage (per night £62.50, minimum three nights) is on-site, as well as normal camping (one-/two- person tent £8.50/13).

### Getting There & Away

CalMac ferries go from Oban to Craignure (per person/car £4.50/38, 45 minutes, five to seven daily). Another crossing links Fishnish with Lochaline (per person/car £2.60/11.50, 15 minutes, at least hourly) on the Morvern Peninsula. From Tobermory a service runs to Kilchoan on the Ardnamurchan Peninsula (per person/car £4/22, 35 minutes, seven daily Monday to Saturday, plus five Sunday May to August).

### Getting Around

**Bowman's Coaches** (☎ 01680-812313; www.bowmanstours.co.uk) connects Craignure with Tobermory (£7 return, 50 minutes, four to seven daily April to mid-October, three to five Monday to Saturday mid-October to March) and Fionnphort (£10 return, 1¼ hours, three to five daily Monday to Saturday, plus once on Sunday April to mid-October) for Iona.

Cycling is a good way to get around; in Tobermory you can rent bikes at the legendary **Archibald Brown & Son** (☎ 01688-302020; www.browns-tobermory.co.uk; 21 Main St; Mon-Sat) for £13 per day.

## ISLE OF IONA

**pop 125**

Like an emerald teardrop off Mull's western shore, enchanting Iona, holy island and burial place of kings, is a magical place that lives up to its lofty reputation. From the moment you embark on the ferry towards its sandy shores and green fields, you'll notice something different about it. To appreciate its charms, you'll need to spend the night. Iona has declared itself a fair-trade island and actively promotes ecotourism.

Iona's status dates back to 563, when St Columba came here from Ireland and established a monastic community, with the aim to christianise Scotland. The Book of Kells is believed to have been created here, before the monks decamped to Ireland after growing weary of Viking raids in the early 9th century.

Around 1200, a Benedictine monastery was founded on or near the site of Columba's church. **Iona Abbey** (HS; ☎ 01681-700512; admission £4.70; 9.30am-6.30pm Apr-Sep, 9.30am-4.30pm Oct-Mar) was remodelled in the 15th century and rebuilt in the 20th, but is still a dramatic place and the island's focal point. The spectacular nave, dominated by high stone arches and wooden beams, is a highlight, as is the collection of carved stone crosses, including the 8th-century **St Martin's Cross** outside the abbey. The oldest, St John's Cross, the pieces of which are in the museum behind, was the first to feature the circle around the junction of the cross. This was originally just to support the heavy stone arms, but became a symbol of Celtic Christianity as the design spread. These days, the abbey is home to the Iona Community (www.iona.org.uk), an ecumenical Christian movement offering workshops and retreats.

In the ancient **graveyard** next door a mound marks the burial place of 48 of Scotland's early kings, including Macbeth; the ruined **nunnery** nearby was established at the same time as the abbey.

our pick **Iona Hostel** (☎ 01681-700781; www.ionahostel.co.uk; dm £17.50) is a delight – a working ecological croft and environmentally sensitive hostel that's one of Scotland's most rewarding and tranquil places to stay. Ducks and lovable black Hebridean sheep surround the building, which features pretty, practical and comfy dorms and an excellent kitchen/lounge. There's a fabulous beach nearby and a hill to climb for views. You'll likely find yourself helping on the croft, feeding orphaned lambs or doing a spot of shearing. Book ahead. There's also a self-catering cottage here (www.lagandorain.com).

Looking over the water back to Mull, the **Argyll Hotel** (☎ 01681-700334; www.argyllhoteliona.co.uk; s/d £55/96, d without bathroom £78; Mar-Nov; wi-fi) is another sound spot. Architecturally, it's a higgledy-piggledy sort of place, with a variety of rooms, which is part of the charm, as is the warm personal service. Rooms with sea view cost more (doubles £130); there's also a fabulous furnished apartment (£170) with a hammock. Other rooms look out the back, where an organic garden supplies the good **restaurant** (lunch mains £4-11, dinner mains £10-15; breakfast, noon-1.30pm, 7-8.30pm).

From Fionnphort, at the southwestern extremity of Mull, a CalMac ferry takes you to Iona (return £4, 10 minutes, frequent).

## ISLE OF STAFFA

This uninhabited island off Mull is a magnificent sight; once there you'll understand why it inspired Mendelssohn to compose *Hebridean Overture*. It forms the eastern end of the geological phenomenon (made up of hexagonal basalt pillars) that begins in Northern Ireland at the Giant's Causeway. Here the pillars are called the **Colonnade** and form a series of cathedral-like caverns including **Fingal's Cave**, which pushes out of the sea like a grand pipe organ. Staffa also has a sizeable **puffin colony**. Mull tourist offices book boat trips (adult/child around £20/10, three hours); some leave from Fionnphort, others from the Ulva Ferry near Laggan. Some offer transfers from the mainland ferries and take in other islands such as Ulva and Lunga. You can tailor your own excursions with boat owners in Iona, Fionnphort and Tobermory; check the noticeboards in town for numbers.

## ISLE OF COLL
pop 164

This windswept, sleepy little island, 7 miles west of Mull, isn't packed with visitor sites, but for many people that's the attraction. Ringed by sandy beaches, the island is an important refuge for the corncrake, which visits in summer; you can find out about it at the small RSPB post at Totronald. Nearby, **Breachacha Castles** are two fortified tower houses built by the Maclean clan.

For accommodation the **Coll Hotel** ( ☎ 01879-230334; www.collhotel.com; Arinagour; s/tw/d £40/80/90; ℗ ) is a great spot, with quirky rooms, some with harbour views, and a cracking restaurant (mains £8 to £15) serving generous portions of seafood and game.

CalMac ferries run to Coll from Oban (per person/car £9/46, three hours, one daily), and continue to Tiree.

## ISLE OF TIREE
pop 770

A low-lying island with some beautiful, sandy beaches, Tiree has one of the best sunshine records in Britain – there's nowhere for the clouds to get trapped. That's the good news. The bad news is that it's subject to howling Atlantic gales. The canny island, however, has turned this to its advantage. It's the windsurfing capital of Scotland; call **Wild Diamond Windsurfing** ( ☎ 01879-220399; www.tireewindsurfing.com) for information – it also organises kitesurfing and kayaking.

For accommodation **Kirkapol House** ( ☎ 01879-220729; www.kirkapoltiree.co.uk; Gott Bay; s/d £32/60; ℗ ) is a very appealing converted 19th-century church, overlooking the island's best beach. Dinner is also available here.

Flybe/Loganair flies from Glasgow to **Tiree airport** ( ☎ 01879-220309). CalMac ferries from

Oban (per person/car £9/46, four hours, daily) arrive via Coll, and on Thursday also call at Barra.

# STIRLING REGION

Covering Scotland's wasplike waist, this region has always been a crucial strategic point dividing the Lowlands from the Highlands. For this reason, Scotland's two most important independence battles were fought here, within sight of Stirling's hilltop stronghold. Separated by 17 years, William Wallace's victory over the English at Stirling Bridge, followed by Robert the Bruce's triumph at Bannockburn established Scottish nationhood, and the region is a stimulus to national pride.

Stirling's old town perches on a spectacular crag, and the castle is among Britain's most fascinating. Within easy reach, the dreamy Trossachs, home to Rob Roy and inspiration to Walter Scott, offer great walking and cycling in the eastern half of Scotland's first national park.

## Getting Around

Trains service Stirling but not the rest of the region, so you'll be relying on buses if you don't have your own transport. **First** ( ☎ 01324-613777; www.firstgroup.com) is the main operator.

## STIRLING
pop 41,243

With an utterly impregnable position atop a mighty wooded crag, Stirling's beautifully preserved old town is a treasure of noble buildings and cobbled streets winding up to the ramparts of its dominant castle, which offers views for miles around. Clearly visible is the brooding Wallace monument, a strange Victorian Gothic creation honouring the giant freedom fighter of *Braveheart* fame. Nearby is Bannockburn, scene of Robert the Bruce's major triumph over the English.

The castle makes a fascinating visit, but make sure you spend time exploring the old town and the picturesque path that circles it. Near the castle are a couple of very snug pubs to toast Scotland's hoary heroes.

## Information
**Library** (Corn Exchange Rd; ⏲ 9.30am-5.30pm Mon-Sat, to 7pm Tue & Thu) Free internet and wi-fi.

CENTRAL SCOTLAND

**Stirling Visitor Centre** ( ☎ 01786-450000; ☽ 9.30am-6pm Apr-Sep, 9.30am-5pm Oct-Mar) Near the castle entrance.

**Tourist office** ( ☎ 01786-475019; stirling@visitscotland .com; 41 Dumbarton Rd; ☽ Mon-Sat Oct-May, daily Jun-Sep) Has coin-op internet.

## Sights

### STIRLING CASTLE

Hold Stirling and you control the country. This simple maxim has ensured that a **castle** (HS; ☎ 01786-450000; adult/child £8.50/4.25, audio tour £2; ☽ 9.30am-6pm Apr-Sep, 9.30am-5pm Oct-Mar) has existed here since prehistoric times. Commanding superb views, Stirling invites parallels with Edinburgh Castle – but many find the former's fortress more atmospheric;

the location, architecture and historical significance combine to make it a grand and memorable visit. This means it draws plenty of visitors, so it's advisable to visit in the afternoon; many tourists come on day trips from Edinburgh or Glasgow, so you may have the castle to yourself by about 4pm. The entry price includes an optional guided tour; the audio handset is a worthwhile investment.

The current building dates from the late 14th to the 16th century, when it was a residence of the Stuart monarchs. The spectacular palace was constructed by French masons in the reign of James V. The **Great Kitchens** are especially good, bringing to life the bustle and scale of the enterprise of cooking for the king.

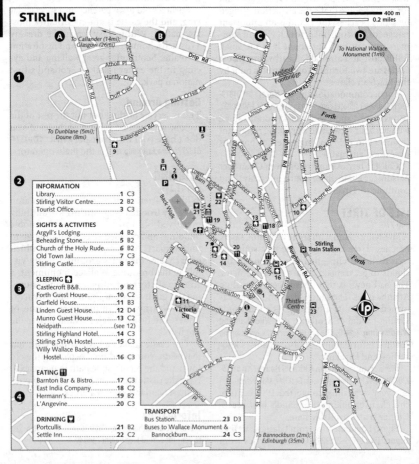

**STIRLING**

0 ——— 400 m
0 ——— 0.2 miles

An elaborate project to recreate the grandeur of the king's hall and queen's lodgings in the Stuarts' time is under way. Most interesting is the making of a series of tapestries depicting the capture of a unicorn. You can see the weavers at work in the **Tapestry Studio**; the finished tapestries hang in the chapel.

The visitors centre, just below, has **audiovisual introductions** to the castle's history and architecture. Last entry to the castle is 45 minutes before closing. There's a car park (£2) outside.

Just below the castle, **Argyll's Lodging** (admission by tour with castle ticket, 2-4 tours daily) is the most impressive 17th-century town house in Scotland. It's the former home of William Alexander, an earl of Stirling and noted literary figure. Ask at the castle visitors centre for that day's tour times; try not to miss it.

### OLD TOWN

Below the castle, the old town feels wholly separate from modern Stirling, with its cobblestone streets packed with fine examples of 15th- to 17th-century architecture.

The **town wall** was built around 1547 and can be followed on the **Back Walk**. The walk follows the line of the wall from Dumbarton Rd (opposite the tourist office) up to the castle through peaceful woodland. You pass the town cemeteries (check out the Star Pyramid, an outsized affirmation of Reformation values dating from 1863), and the path continues around the back of the castle to Gowan Hill where you can see the **Beheading Stone**, now encased in iron bars to prevent contemporary use.

The beautiful **Church of the Holy Rude** ( ☎ 01786-475275; www.holyrude.org; St John St; admission free; ⏰ 11am-4pm Easter-Sep) is just down the hill from the castle and has been the town's parish church for 500 years. James VI was crowned here in 1567. The nave and tower date from 1456 and the church features one of the few surviving medieval open-timber roofs.

The **Old Town Jail** ( ☎ 01786-450050; St John St; adult/child £5.95/3.80; ⏰ 10am-5pm Apr-May & Oct, 9.30am-5.30pm Jun-Sep, 10am-4pm Nov-Mar) is a great one for kids, as actors take you through the complex, portraying a cast of characters that illustrate the hardships of prison life in innovative and entertaining style. The actors are weekends-only between November and March, daily April to October; at other times an audio handset replaces them (£5). Last entry is one hour before closing.

### NATIONAL WALLACE MONUMENT

Towering over Scotland's narrow waist, this **monument** ( ☎ 01786-472140; www.nationalwallace monument.com; adult/child £6.50/4; ⏰ 10am-5pm Mar-May & Oct, 10am-6pm Jun, 9am-6pm Jul & Aug, 9.30am-5.30pm Sep, 10.30am-4pm Nov-Feb) is a nationalist memorial that's so Victorian Gothic it deserves circling bats and ravens. It commemorates the bid for Scottish independence depicted in the film *Braveheart*. From the visitors centre, walk or shuttle-bus it up the hill to the building itself. Once there, break the climb up the narrow staircase inside to admire Wallace's 66 inches of broadsword and see the man himself recreated in a 3-D audiovisual display. More staid is the marble pantheon of lugubrious Scottish heroes, but the view from the top over the flat, green, gorgeous Forth Valley, including the site of Wallace's 1297 victory over the English at Stirling Bridge, just about justifies the entry fee.

Buses 62 and 63 run from Murray Place in Stirling to the visitors centre; otherwise it's about a half-hour walk from the centre.

### BANNOCKBURN

Though Wallace's heroics were significant, it was Robert the Bruce's defeat of the English on 24 June 1314 at Bannockburn, just outside Stirling, that eventually established lasting Scottish nationhood. Exploiting the marshy ground, Bruce won a great tactical victory against a much larger and better-equipped force, and sent Edward II 'homeward, tae think again', as the song 'Flower of Scotland' commemorates. At **Bannockburn Heritage Centre** (NTS; ☎ 01786-812664; adult/child £5/4; ⏰ 10am-5.30pm Mar-Oct) the history pre- and post-battle is lucidly explained. The audiovisual could do with a remake, but there's lots to do for kids, and an intriguing recreation of Bruce's face which suggests that he may have suffered from leprosy in later life.

The battlefield itself (which never closes) is harder to appreciate; apart from a statue of the victor astride his horse, and a misbegotten flag memorial, there's nothing to see. Bannockburn is 2 miles south of Stirling; you can reach it on bus 51 from Murray Place in the centre.

## Sleeping

### BUDGET

**Willy Wallace Backpackers Hostel** ( ☎ 01786-446773; www.willywallacehostel.com; 77 Murray Pl; dm £14-16, tw £34-37; 🖳 ) This highly convenient central hostel is friendly, spacious and sociable. The colourful dormitories are clean and light, there's free tea and coffee, a good kitchen, and a laissez-faire atmosphere. Other amenities include a laundry service and Sass, the exuberant hostel dog. The helpful folk here will make an onward booking for you, free of charge.

**Stirling SYHA Hostel** ( ☎ 01786-473442; www.syha .org.uk; St John St; dm £16; ⓟ 🖵 ) Right in the old town, this hostel has an unbeatable location and great facilities. Though its facade is that of a former church, the interior is modern and efficient. The dorms are compact but comfortable with lockers and en suite bathrooms; other highlights include a pool table, bike shed and, at busy times, cheap meals on offer. There's a 2am curfew.

### MIDRANGE

**Forth Guest House** ( ☎ 01786-471020; www.forthguest house.co.uk; 23 Forth Pl; d £50; ⓟ ) Just a couple of minutes' walk from town on the other side of the railway, this noble Georgian terrace offers attractive and stylish accommodation at a fair price. The rooms are very commodious, particularly the cute garret rooms with their coomed (sloping) ceilings and good modern bathrooms. No cards are accepted.

**Munro Guest House** ( ☎ 01786-472685; www.munro guesthouse.co.uk; 14 Princes St; s/d £42/58) Cosy and cheery, this is right in the centre of town, but on a quiet side street. Things are done with a smile here, and the smallish rooms are most inviting, particularly the cute attic ones. The breakfast is also better than the norm, with fruit salad on hand. There's easy (pay) parking opposite.

**Castlecroft B&B** ( ☎ 01786-474933; www.castlecroft -uk.com; Ballengeich Rd; s/d £50/60; ⓟ 🖵 ) Nestling into the hillside under the back of the castle, this great hideaway feels like a rural retreat but is a short, spectacular walk from the heart of historic Stirling. The lounge boasts 180-degree views over green fields to the hills that gird the town, and the compact rooms are appealing and well maintained.

**Garfield House** ( ☎ 01786-473730; 12 Victoria Sq; s/d £56/65) Though close to the centre of town, this quiet square is an oasis, with noble Victorian buildings surrounding a verdant swath of lawn. The Garfield's huge rooms, bay windows, ceiling roses and other period features make it a winner. There's a great family room, and some have views to the castle towering above.

**Linden Guest House** ( ☎ 01786-448850; www .lindenguesthouse.co.uk; 22 Linden Ave; s/d £50/70; ⓟ 🖵 ) Handy if arriving by car from the south, this guesthouse's warm welcome and easy parking offer understandable appeal. The rooms, of which two are suitable for families, have fridges and the bathrooms gleam so much they could feature in ads for cleaning products. Breakfast features fresh fruit and kippers, among other choices.

**Neidpath** ( ☎ 01786-469017; www.neidpath-stirling .co.uk; 24 Linden Ave; d £56; ⓟ 🖵 wi-fi) Next door to Linden, this place is friendly and comfortable and a more than acceptable alternative.

### TOP END

**Stirling Highland Hotel** ( ☎ 01786-272727; www.barcelo -hotels.co.uk; Spittal St; r up to £175; ⓟ 🖵 wi-fi) Stirling lacks a really luxurious central hotel, but this, at least, has a fabulous location on the way up to the castle. Once a high school, this curious place still feels institutional in parts, but has great facilities that include pool, spa, gym, sauna and squash courts. The rooms could do with a refit and upgrade; the hotel's recent sale to the Barceló chain might be the catalyst for that to happen. You'll find better deals on the internet than via the hotel itself.

## Eating

**Barnton Bar & Bistro** ( ☎ 01786-461698; 312 Barnton St; light meals £2-5; ⏰ 10am-late, food till 7.15pm) In some ways this is the spiritual heart of town. Both pub and no-frills caff, it serves big baked tatties, enormous all-day fry-ups, and pints of beer to a varied crowd in an evocative space with delicate pre-war plasterwork and a pool table out back.

**East India Company** ( ☎ 01786-471330; 7 Viewfield Pl; mains £5-10; ⏰ 5pm-midnight) This basement Indian restaurant is one of the best spots in Scotland for a curry. Sumptuously decorated to resemble a ship's stateroom, with portraits of tea barons on the wall to conjure images of the days of the clippers, the restaurant offers exquisite dishes from all parts of India. There's a buffet dinner available (£9.95, Monday to Thursday), but you're better off going à la carte, and savouring the toothsome flavours.

**L'Angevine** ( ☎ 01786-446124; 52 Spittal St; 2-course lunch/dinner £9.95/19.95; ⏰ lunch & dinner) Low and moody yellow light and a gregarious bistro atmosphere at the small square tables make this intimate two-level eatery on the castle-bound street one to reserve ahead. The scrumptious and well-priced French food has made it an instant hit in Stirling.

**Hermann's** ( ☎ 01786-450632; 58 Broad St; 2-course lunch £11.90, mains £15-19; ☾ lunch & dinner) Solidly set on a corner above the unicorn-topped mercat cross and below the castle, this elegant Scottish/Austrian restaurant is a reliable and popular choice. The solid, conservative decor is weirdly offset by magazine-style skiing photos, but the food doesn't miss a beat and ranges from Scots favourites to gourmet schnitzel and spätzle noodles. Vegetarian options are good, and quality Austrian wines provide an out-of-the-ordinary accompaniment.

## Drinking

**ourpick** **Settle Inn** ( ☎ 01786-474609; St Mary's Wynd) A warm welcome is guaranteed at Stirling's oldest pub, a spot redolent with atmosphere, with its log fire, vaulted back room, and low-slung ceilings. Guest ales, atmospheric nooks for settling in for the night, and a blend of local characters make it a classic of its kind.

**Portcullis** ( ☎ 01786-472290; www.theportcullishotel.com; Castle Wynd) Built in stone as solid as the castle that it stands below, this former school is just the spot for a pint and a pub lunch after your visit. With bar meals (open lunch and dinner) that would have had William Wallace loosening his belt a couple of notches, a little beer garden, and a cosy buzz indoors, it's well worth a visit; there are also rooms (single/double £67/87).

## Getting There & Away

### BUS

Citylink services to/from Stirling include Dundee (£10.20, hourly, 1½ hours), Edinburgh (£5.40, one hour, hourly, also operated by First), Glasgow (£5.40, 45 minutes, hourly) and Perth (£6.30, 50 minutes, at least hourly).

### TRAIN

Half-hourly services run to Edinburgh (£6.50, 55 minutes) and Glasgow (£6.70, 40 minutes); hourly trains to Perth (£9.80, 30 minutes), Dundee (£15, 55 minutes) and Aberdeen (£37, 2¼ hours).

## AROUND STIRLING

### Dunblane
pop 7900

Dunblane, 5 miles northwest of Stirling, is a small, pretty town with a notable cathedral.

It's difficult not to remember the horrific massacre that took place in the primary school in 1996, but happier headlines have come the town's way with the rise of grumpy local tennis star Andy Murray and brother Jamie. For information, contact the **tourist office** ( ☎ 01786-824428; Stirling Rd; ☾ May–mid-Sep).

**Dunblane Cathedral** (HS; ☎ 01786-823388; admission free; ☾ 9.30am-5.30pm Mon-Sat, 2-5.30pm Sun Apr-Sep, closes 4.30pm Oct-Mar) is the main attraction and is worth a detour. The elegant, sandstone building, mostly built in the 13th century, is a superb example of Scottish Gothic. A 10th-century carved Celtic stone is at the nave's head, and a standing stone commemorates the slain children.

There are frequent buses and trains from Stirling to Dunblane.

### Doune
pop 1635

Eight miles northwest of Stirling, this town has a great attraction in **Doune Castle** (HS; ☎ 01786-841742; admission £4.20; ☾ 9.30am-6.30pm Apr-Sep, 9.30am-4.30pm Sat-Wed Oct-Mar), one of the best-preserved 14th-century castles in Scotland, having remained largely unchanged since it was built for the Duke of Albany. It was a favourite royal hunting lodge; Mary Queen of Scots stayed here, as did Bonnie Prince Charlie, who used it to imprison government troops. There are great views from the castle walls and the lofty gatehouse is impressive, rising nearly 30m.

First buses connect to Stirling (30 minutes) roughly hourly from Monday to Saturday, less frequently on Sunday.

## THE TROSSACHS

The Trossachs region has long been a favourite weekend getaway, offering outstanding natural beauty and excellent walking and cycling routes within easy reach of the southern population centres. With thickly forested hills, romantic lochs and an increasingly interesting selection of places to stay and eat its popularity is sure to continue, protected by its national park status (see p852).

The Trossachs first gained popularity as a tourist destination in the early 19th century, when curious visitors came from all over Britain, drawn by the romantic language of Walter Scott's poem *Lady of the Lake,* inspired by Loch Katrine, and *Rob Roy,* about the derring-do of the region's most famous son.

CENTRAL SCOTLAND

---

**ROB ROY**

Nicknamed 'Red' ('ruadh' in Gaelic, anglicised to 'roy') for his ginger locks, Robert MacGregor (1671–1734) was the wild leader of the wildest of Scotland's clans. Although they had rights to the lands the clan occupied, these estates stood between powerful neighbours who had the MacGregors outlawed, hence their sobriquet 'Children of the Mist'. Incognito, Rob became a prosperous livestock trader, before a dodgy deal led to a warrant for his arrest.

A legendary swordsman, the fugitive from justice then became notorious for his daring raids into the Lowlands to carry off cattle and sheep. He was forever hiding from potential captors; he was twice imprisoned, but escaped dramatically on both occasions. He finally turned himself in, and received his liberty and a pardon from the king. He lies buried in the churchyard at Balquhidder, by Loch Voil (see opposite); his uncompromising epitaph reads 'MacGregor despite them'. His life has been glorified over the years due to Walter Scott's novel and the 1995 film. Many Scots see his life as a symbol of the struggle of the common folk against the inequable ownership of vast tracts of the country by landed aristocrats.

---

In summer the Trossachs can be overburdened with coach tours, but many of these are day trippers, so peaceful, long evenings gazing at the reflections in the nearest loch are still on. It's worth timing a visit not to coincide with a weekend.

## Aberfoyle & Around
pop 575

One of two main Trossachs centres, Aberfoyle is set in a scenic area but has less to offer as a town than Callander. It's also a popular tour-bus lunching spot, so pick up some brochures at the tourist office and head off to enjoy the surrounding countryside, which includes the Queen Elizabeth Forest Park, stretching from Aberfoyle right across to the hills beside Loch Lomond.

In the centre the **tourist office** ( ☎ 08707 200604; Main St; ☼ daily Apr-Oct, Sat & Sun Nov-Mar) has internet access. There's also information at the **David Marshall Lodge Visitor Centre** ( ☎ 01877-382258; parking fee £2; ☼ 10am-5pm Mar-Dec, Sat & Sun Jan-Feb) in the forest park half a mile up the hill from town, with audiovisual displays and information on the area's walks and cycle routes.

### SIGHTS

Four miles east of Aberfoyle off the A81 is **Lake of Menteith** (called lake not loch due to a mistranslation from Gaelic). On a picturesque island in the middle of the lake are the substantial ruins of **Inchmahome Priory** (HS; ☎ 01877-385294; adult incl ferry £4.70; ☼ 9.30am-5pm Apr-Sep), an Augustinian monastery built in the 13th century. Mary Queen of Scots was kept safe as a child here during Henry VIII's 'Rough Wooing' (Henry attacked Stirling try-ing to force a marriage to his son in order to unite the kingdoms). A boat takes visitors to the Augustinian priory; the last outbound boat is 4.30pm.

### ACTIVITIES

Several picturesque but busy waymarked trails start from the David Marshall Lodge Visitor Centre in the forest park. These range from a light 20-minute stroll to a nearby waterfall to a hilly 5-mile circuit. Also here, **Go Ape!** (www.goape.co.uk; adult/child £25/20) will bring out the monkey in you on its exhilarating adventure course of long ziplines, swings and rope bridges through the forest.

An excellent 20-mile circular cycle route links with the boat at Loch Katrine (p872). From Aberfoyle, join the Lochs & Glens Cycle Way on the forest trail, or take the A821 over Duke's Pass. Following the southern shore of Loch Achray, you reach the pier on Loch Katrine. The ferry can take you to Stronachlachar (£10 one way with bike) on the western shore; from where you can follow the beautiful B829 via Loch Ard back to Aberfoyle.

### SLEEPING & EATING

**Forth Inn** ( ☎ 01877-382372; www.forthinn.com; Main St; bar meals £6-8, mains £8-17; ☼ lunch & dinner; **P** ) Right in the middle of things, this is the hub of Aberfoyle and is a pleasantly traditional pub with tartan carpets, a fire, friendly staff and a pool table. It doles out pub grub to coach parties during the day, but evening is the time to chat with locals or have dinner either from the bar menu or the more upmarket restaurant dishes. The rooms (single/double £50/80) are bright with solid, modern furniture and good bathrooms; be aware that the pub opens until 1am at weekends.

## GETTING THERE & AWAY

First buses connect Aberfoyle to Stirling (45 minutes, up to four daily). For details of the Trossachs Trundler service, see p872.

## Callander

**pop 2750 / elev 130m**

Callander is a long-time favourite base for Trossachs exploration, but is gradually moving away from tearooms and tour buses – though it still gets very busy in summer – towards a more individual character. This is great, because it's a pretty town to stroll about, and has a few very worthwhile places to stay and eat.

The busy **tourist office** ( ☎ 01877-330342; callander@visitscotland.com; Ancaster Sq; 🕙 10am-4pm Nov-Feb, 10am-5pm Mar-May & Sep-Oct, 10am-6pm Jun-Aug) is in the heart of town and has internet access.

## SLEEPING

**Trossachs Tryst** ( ☎ 01877-331200; www.scottish-hostel.co.uk; dm/d £17.50/45; P 🖥 wi-fi) Set up to be the perfect hostel for outdoorsy people, this cracking spot is in fresh-aired surroundings a mile from Callander. Facilities and accommodation are excellent, with dorms offering acres of space and their own bathroom. There's also cycle hire with plenty of route advice. Help yourself to a continental breakfast in the morning, and enjoy the helpful, easygoing atmosphere that pervades the place, especially in the big-windowed lounge. To get there, take Bridge St off Main St, then turn right onto Invertrossachs Rd for a mile.

**Arden House** ( ☎ 01877-330235; www.ardenhouse.org.uk; Bracklinn Rd; s/d £37.50/70; 🕙 Easter-Oct; P 🖥 wi-fi)

A redoubt of peaceful good taste, this elegant home features faultlessly welcoming hospitality and a woodsy hillside location close to the centre, but far from the crowds. The commodious rooms have flat-screen TV and little extras; they include a suite (£80) with great views. Home-baked banana bread and a rotating dish of the day keep breakfast well ahead of the competition.

**Abbotsford Lodge** ( ☎ 01877-330066; www.abbotsfordlodge.co.uk; Stirling Rd; s/d £50/70; P 🖥 ) Undergoing an ongoing renovation project, this friendly Victorian house offers something different to the norm, with tartan and florals consigned to the bonfire, replaced by stylish comfortable contemporary design that enhances the building's original features. Ruffled fabrics and ceramic vases with flower arrangements characterise the renovated rooms. It's on the main road on the eastern side of town; look for the monkey puzzle tree (*araucaria*).

**Poppies Hotel** ( ☎ 01877-330329; www.poppieshotel.com; s/d £60/70/99; P 🖥 wi-fi) At the town's western end, Poppies is another in the new breed of Callander hotel, with most appealing, light rooms decorated with panache and style. Service is attentive and it feels like a real deal at this price. The hotel also does evening meals, open to the public, which have been highly recommended by readers and locals alike.

**ourpick** **Roman Camp Hotel** ( ☎ 01877-330003; www.romancamphotel.co.uk; s/d/superior £85/135/175; P 🖥 wi-fi) Callander's best hotel makes up in atmosphere for rather chaotic service. Though central, it feels rural, set by the river in its own beautiful grounds. Its endearing features include a lounge with blazing fire, and a library with a tiny secret chapel. There are three

---

### DETOUR: BALQUHIDDER

The village of **Balquhidder** (bal-whidder) is famous as the final resting place of Rob Roy, buried with his wife and two sons in the small churchyard. No less a drawcard is the sublime hotel and restaurant **Monachyle Mhor** ( ☎ 01877-384622; www.monachylemhor.com; lunch mains £15-18, dinner £46; 🕙 lunch & dinner; P 🖥 wi-fi). With a fantastic location overlooking two lochs, this is an excellent fusion of country Scotland and comfortable contemporary design. The rooms and suites are fabulous, with quirkily original decor, and various price grades (doubles from £105 to £245). The restaurant (open to the public) offers set lunch and dinner menus, which are high in quality and deliciously innovative. Enchantment lies in its successful combination of top-class hospitality with a relaxed rural atmosphere; dogs and kids happily romp on the lawns, and no one looks askance if you come in flushed and muddy after a day's fishing or walking.

Balquhidder is 2 miles west of the A84, 9 miles north of Callander. The hotel is a further 4 miles beyond the village.

grades of room; the standards are certainly luxurious, but the superior ones are even more appealing, with period furniture, armchairs and a fireplace. The upmarket restaurant is open to the public (lunch/dinner £25/44). And fear not; the name refers not to toga parties but to a ruin in the adjacent field.

### EATING & DRINKING

**ourpick** **Mhor Fish** ( ☎ 01877-330213; 75 Main St; fish supper £5.10, mains £6-16; ☒ 10am-8pm) Both chip shop and fish restaurant, but wholly different, this endearing black-and-white-tiled cafe displays the day's fresh catch and you choose how you want it cooked, whether pan-seared and accompanied with one of many good wines, or fried and wrapped in paper with chips to take away. The fish and seafood come from sustainable stock, and include oysters and other goodies. If Mhor runs out of fresh fish, it shuts, so opening hours are a little variable.

**Lade Inn** ( ☎ 01877-330152; Kilmahog; bar meals £7-13; ☒ noon-9pm) Callander's best pub isn't in Callander, it's a mile north of town. It does decent and popular bar meals, doesn't mind kids, and pulls a good pint; it has beer brewed to a house recipe. Next door, the inn runs a shop with a dazzling selection of Scottish real ales. There's low-key live music here at weekends.

**Callander Meadows** ( ☎ 01877-330181; 24 Main St; lunch £7.95, mains £11-17; ☒ lunch & dinner Thu-Sun, plus Mon Apr-Sep, plus Wed Jul & Aug) Informal but quality eating is provided by this friendly high street restaurant, which offers excellent cuisine without frippery at a very fair price. Make sure you leave room for dessert. Upstairs there are three very appealing rooms (double £60 to £70) elegantly kitted out with dark-varnished furnishings and striped wallpaper (one has a four-poster bed).

### GETTING THERE & AWAY

Buses from Stirling (45 minutes) run hourly from Monday to Saturday and every two hours on Sunday. One daily Citylink bus stops here between Edinburgh (£12.30, 1¾ hours) and Fort William (£17.80, 2¼ hours).

The vintage **Trossachs Trundler** ( ☎ 01786-442707) is a useful hop-on hop-off bus service that does a circuit including Callander, Aberfoyle, Port of Menteith and Loch Katrine. The bus operates daily (except Wednesday), July to mid-October; a ticket costs £5/2 for adults/children. Alternatively, postbus 24 does the same circuit twice daily Monday to Friday (once on Saturday).

### GETTING AROUND

Based at Trossachs Tryst, the excellent **Wheels Cycling Centre** ( ☎ 01877-331100; www.scottish-cycling .com) has a wide range of hire bikes starting from £8/12 for a half-/full day.

## Loch Katrine

The rugged area around this beautiful loch, 6 miles north of Aberfoyle and 10 miles west of Callander, is the heart of the Trossachs. Three **boats** ( ☎ 01877-332000; www.lochkatrine.com) run cruises from Trossachs Pier at the eastern tip of the loch (adult/child £8/6, 45 minutes). Two daily departures (one in winter) head across to the other end at Stronachlachar before returning (return £9.50). From there (accessible by car via Aberfoyle), you can reach the eastern shore of Loch Lomond at isolated Inversnaid. A tarmac path links Trossachs Pier with Stronachlachar, so you can also take the boat out and walk/cycle back (12 miles). You can hire bikes from **Katrinewheelz** ( ☎ 01877-376316; half/full day £10/14) at Trossachs Pier.

## KILLIN

**pop 666 / elev 183m**

A fine base for the Trossachs or Perthshire, this lovely village sits at the western end of Loch Tay (see p886) and has a spread-out, laid-back sort of a feel, particularly around the scenic **Falls of Dochart**, which tumble through the centre. On a sunny day people sprawl over the rocks by the bridge, pint or picnic in hand. Killin offers some fine walking around the town, and mighty mountains and glens close at hand.

The helpful, informative **tourist office** ( ☎ 08707 200627; Main St; ☒ daily Mar-Oct, Sat & Sun Feb) is in the Breadalbane Folklore Centre.

## Walking & Cycling

Five miles northeast of Killin and rising above Loch Tay is Ben Lawers (1214m; p887). Other routes abound; one rewarding circular walk heads up into the Acharn forest south of town, emerging above the treeline to great views of Loch Tay and Ben Lawers. Pick up a ParkPaths leaflet from tourist offices.

Killin is on the Lochs & Glens cycle route (p850) from Glasgow to Inverness. You can hire bikes at the hostel.

## Sleeping & Eating

**Braveheart Backpackers** ( ☎ 07796-886899; dm £15, d £35-45; P ) Tucked away alongside the Killin Hotel, these two adjoining cottages offer several types of room, all wood-clad with comfortable beds and bunks. There are particularly good en suite rooms for families, and the appealing kitchens and lounge area make it feel like a home rather than a hostel. It rents bikes and kayaks.

**Falls of Dochart Inn** ( ☎ 01856-820270; www.falls-of -dochart-inn.co.uk; bar meals £7-9; ☽ lunch & dinner) Once you've conquered the hills hereabouts, reward yourself with a pint at this inviting historic inn. On a sunny evening it's a delight to sit outside watching the river cascade down its rocky course, but it's very cosy indoors too, with a classic old fireplace crackling away. There's bar food during the day, bolstered by some classier dishes (£11 to £15) such as venison or salmon roulade, available after 6pm. The rooms badly need a refit though.

## Getting There & Away

Buses run roughly hourly from Killin to Callander and Stirling. Both buses and postbus 213 head to Aberfeldy via Kenmore.

Killin is on the Citylink route linking Perth (£5.90, 1¼ hours) and Oban (£10.60, 1½ hours); there are two buses each way daily.

# FIFE

Protruding like a serpent's head from Scotland's east coast, Fife (www.visitfife.com) is a tongue of land between the Firths of Forth and Tay with a royal history and distinct feel from the rest of Scotland that leads it to style itself 'The Kingdom of Fife'.

Though overdeveloped southern Fife is commuter-belt territory, the eastern region's rolling green farmland and quaint fishing villages is prime turf for exploration and crab-crunching, and the fresh sea air feels like it's doing a power of good. Elsewhere in the county, little Falkland makes a great stop, and dignified Culross is a superbly preserved 17th-century burgh.

Fife's biggest attraction, St Andrews, has Scotland's most venerable university and a wealth of historic buildings. It's also, of course, the headquarters of golf and draws professionals and keen slashers alike to take on the Old Course; the classic links experience.

The Fife Coastal Path (www.fifecoastalpath .co.uk), a 78-mile trail connecting the Forth Bridge with the Tay Bridge, follows Fife's picturesque coastline and makes a great walk, easily done in small sections too.

## Getting Around

Fife's well served by buses and trains and easily reached from Edinburgh, in particular. **Stagecoach** ( ☎ 01383-511911; www.stagecoachbus.com) is the main bus operator.

## ST ANDREWS
pop 14,200

For a small place, St Andrews made a big name for itself, firstly as religious centre, then as Scotland's oldest university town. But its status as the home of golf has propelled it to even greater fame, and today's pilgrims arrive with a set of clubs. But it's a lovely place to visit even if you've no interest in the game, with impressive medieval ruins, stately university buildings, idyllic white sands, and many good accommodation and eating options.

The Old Course, the world's most famous golf course, has a striking seaside location at the western end of town. Although it's difficult to get a game (p876), it's still a thrilling experience to stroll the hallowed turf. Between the students and golfers, St Andrews can feel like the least Scottish of places as, although technically a city, it's very small.

## History

It's believed that St Andrews was founded by the Greek monk St Regulus in the 4th century. He brought important relics from Greece, including some of the bones of St Andrew, who became Scotland's patron saint. The saint's shrine soon became an important pilgrimage destination and St Andrews developed into an ecclesiastical centre; Scotland's first university was founded here in 1410.

Golf has been played here for more than 600 years; the Royal & Ancient Golf Club was founded in 1754 and the imposing clubhouse was built a hundred years later.

## Orientation & Information

St Andrews preserves its medieval plan of parallel streets with small closes leading off them. The old town runs east from the bus station. The Old Course stretches northwest of town. The older university buildings are integrated into the central part of the town.

There's a harbour below the cathedral and two excellent sandy beaches.

**St Andrews Library** ( ☎ 01334-412685; Church Sq; ⏱ 9.30am-5pm Mon, Fri & Sat, 9.30am-7pm Tue-Thu) Free internet access.

**Tourist office** ( ☎ 01334-472021; standrews@visit scotland.com; 70 Market St; ⏱ Mon-Sat Nov-Easter, daily Easter-Oct) Mountains of Fife information and internet access.

## Sights

### ST ANDREWS CATHEDRAL

The ruins of this **cathedral** (HS; ☎ 01334-472563; cathedral & castle £7.20, cathedral only £4.20; ⏱ 9.30am-5.30pm Apr-Sep, 9.30am-4.30pm Oct-Mar) are what is left of one of Britain's most magnificent medieval buildings. You can appreciate the scale and majesty of the edifice from the small sections that remain standing. Although founded in 1160, it was not consecrated until 1318 but stood as the focus of this important pilgrimage centre until 1559, when it was pillaged during the Reformation.

St Andrew's supposed bones lay under the altar; until the cathedral was built, they had been enshrined in the nearby Church of St Regulus (Rule). All that remains of that is **St Rule's Tower**, worth the climb for the view across St Andrews. The visitors centre includes a **museum** with a collection of Celtic crosses and gravestones found on the site.

The entrance fee only applies for the tower and museum; otherwise you can wander freely around the atmospheric ruins.

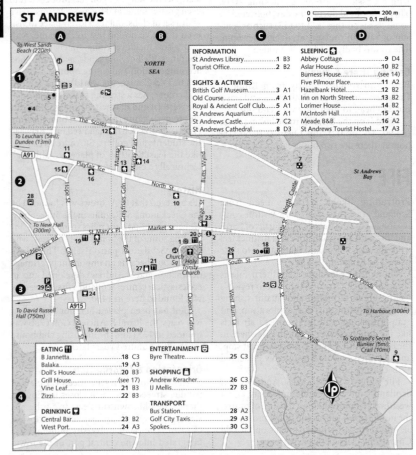

**ST ANDREWS**

| INFORMATION | |
|---|---|
| St Andrews Library | 1 B3 |
| Tourist Office | 2 B2 |

| SIGHTS & ACTIVITIES | |
|---|---|
| British Golf Museum | 3 A1 |
| Old Course | 4 A1 |
| Royal & Ancient Golf Club | 5 A1 |
| St Andrews Aquarium | 6 A1 |
| St Andrews Castle | 7 C2 |
| St Andrews Cathedral | 8 D3 |

| SLEEPING | |
|---|---|
| Abbey Cottage | 9 D4 |
| Aslar House | 10 B2 |
| Burness House | (see 14) |
| Five Pilmour Place | 11 A2 |
| Hazelbank Hotel | 12 B2 |
| Inn on North Street | 13 B2 |
| Lorimer House | 14 B2 |
| McIntosh Hall | 15 A2 |
| Meade B&B | 16 A2 |
| St Andrews Tourist Hostel | 17 A3 |

| EATING | |
|---|---|
| B Jannetta | 18 C3 |
| Balaka | 19 A3 |
| Doll's House | 20 B3 |
| Grill House | (see 17) |
| Vine Leaf | 21 B3 |
| Zizzi | 22 B3 |

| DRINKING | |
|---|---|
| Central Bar | 23 B2 |
| West Port | 24 A3 |

| ENTERTAINMENT | |
|---|---|
| Byre Theatre | 25 C3 |

| SHOPPING | |
|---|---|
| Andrew Keracher | 26 C3 |
| IJ Mellis | 27 B3 |

| TRANSPORT | |
|---|---|
| Bus Station | 28 A2 |
| Golf City Taxis | 29 A3 |
| Spokes | 30 C3 |

## ST ANDREWS CASTLE

With dramatic coastline views, this **castle** (HS; ☎ 01334-477196; cathedral & castle £7.20, castle only £5.20; ⊙ 9.30am-5.30pm Apr-Sep, 9.30am-4.30pm Oct-Mar), round from the cathedral, is mainly ruinous, but the site is evocative.

The castle was founded around 1200 as the bishop's fortified home. In the 1450s the young King James II often stayed here. After the execution of Protestant reformers in 1545, other reformers retaliated by murdering Cardinal Beaton and taking over the castle. They spent almost a year holed up, during which time they dug a complex of **siege tunnels**, said to be the best surviving example of castle siege engineering in Europe; you can walk (or stoop) along their damp mossy lengths.

## THE SCORES

From the castle, the Scores follows the coast west down to the first tee at the Old Course. The family-friendly **St Andrews Aquarium** ( ☎ 01334-474786; www.standrewsaquarium.co.uk; adult/child £6.80/4.90; ⊙ 10am-5.30pm Mar-Oct, 10am-4.30pm Nov-Feb) has a seal pool, rays and sharks from Scottish waters, and exotic tropical favourites. Once introduced to our finny friends, you can snack on them with chips in the cafe.

Nearby, the **British Golf Museum** ( ☎ 01334-460046; www.britishgolfmuseum.co.uk; Bruce Embankment; admission £5.50; ⊙ 9.30am-5.30pm Mon-Sat & 10am-5pm Sun Apr-Oct, 10am-4pm Nov-Mar) has an extraordinarily comprehensive overview of the history and development of the game and the role of St Andrews in it. Most charming fact: bad players were formerly known as 'foozlers'. Interactive panels allow you to relive former British Opens (watch Paul Azinger snapping his putter in frustration), and there's a large collection of memorabilia from Open winners both male and female.

Opposite the museum is the **Royal & Ancient Golf Club**, which stands proudly at the head of the **Old Course**, which you can stroll on once play is finished for the day. Beside it stretches the magnificent West Sands beach, made famous by the film *Chariots of Fire*.

## Sleeping

There's a wide choice of accommodation, although it still fills quickly in summer. The biggest concentration of B&Bs is on Murray Park, between North St and the Scores.

## BUDGET

**St Andrews Tourist Hostel** ( ☎ 01334-479911; www.standrewshostel.com; St Marys Pl; dm £13-15; ▣ ) Laid-back and central, this hostel down the side of the Grill House restaurant is a little hard to spot. Occupying a stately old building, it has high corniced ceilings, especially in the huge lounge, and a laissez-faire approach. The dorms could use new mattresses, but are clean and bright. Self-caterers have a supermarket very close at hand.

## MIDRANGE

**Meade B&B** ( ☎ 01334-477350; annmeade10@hotmail.com; 5 Albany Pl; s/d with shared bathroom £25/50, s/d with bathroom £37/57) It's always sweet relief to find a B&B unconcerned with VisitScotland's fussy regulations. This economical gem is run by a friendly family and their pets, who include a portly marmalade cat and excitable black lab. The two comfortable rooms are colour-coded and have a wealth of readable novels, photo albums and films on DVD. Kids are very welcome, and the location couldn't be better, close to the bus station and Old Course, and with free parking nearby.

**our pick Abbey Cottage** ( ☎ 01334-473727; www.abbeycottage.co.uk; Abbey Walk; s £40, d £54-58; ℗ ) You know you've strayed from B&B mainstream when your charming host's hobby is photographing tigers in the wild – don't leave without browsing her albums. This engaging spot sits below the town, surrounded by stone walls which enclose a rambling garden; it feels like you are staying in the country. There are three excellent rooms, all different, with patchwork quilts, sheepskins and antique furniture.

**Aslar House** ( ☎ 01334-473460; www.aslar.com; 120 North St; s/d £45/90; ▣ wi-fi) Favoured with decades of repeat business, the Aslar has never rested on its laurels and, under new owners, continues to deliver value with the elegance and restrained style of its decor. The excellent modern conveniences – flat-screen TV, DVD player, silent fridge – do not detract from the house's period features, which include a whimsical turret that houses one of the rooms. Book well ahead.

**University of St Andrews Holidays** ( ☎ 01334-462000; www.discoverstandrews.com; ⊙ mid-Jun–mid-Sep; ℗ ▣ ) arranges three student residences as visitor accommodation when the university is out of session. There's a hotel, **New Hall** ( ☎ 01334-467000; s/d £49.50/72); self-catering rooms, **David Russell Hall** ( ☎ 01334-467100; s/d

---

### PLAYING THE OLD COURSE

Golf has been played at St Andrews since the 15th century and by 1457 was apparently so popular that James II placed a ban on it because it interfered with his troops' archery practice. Although it lies beside the exclusive, all-male (female bartenders, unsurprisingly, allowed) Royal & Ancient Golf Club, the Old Course is public.

Advance bookings for the Old Course can be made by phone or online to the **St Andrews Links Trust** ( ☎ 01334-466666; www.standrews.org.uk). You must reserve on or after the first Wednesday in September the year before you wish to play. No bookings are taken for Saturdays.

Unless you've booked months in advance, getting a tee-off time is literally a lottery; enter the ballot at the **caddie office** ( ☎ 01334-466666) before 2pm on the day before you wish to play (there's no Sunday play). Be warned that applications by ballot are normally heavily oversubscribed, and green fees are £130 in summer. You'll need a handicap certificate (£24/36 for men/women). If your number doesn't come up, there are six other public courses in the area, including the prestigious newly-opened Castle Course (£120). Other summer green fees include: New £65, Jubilee £65, Eden £40, Strathtyrum £25 and Balgove (nine-holer for beginners and kids) £12. There are various multiple-day tickets available. If you play on a windy day expect those scores to balloon: as Nick Faldo famously stated, 'when it blows here, even the seagulls walk'.

The trust runs guided walks (£2.50, 50 minutes) of the Old Course at weekends in June and daily in July and August; these will take you to famous landmarks such as the Swilcan Bridge and the Road Hole bunker. They run from outside the shop roughly hourly from 11am to 4pm. On Sunday, a three-hour walk (£5) takes you round the whole course.

---

£26/39, weekly apt £515-639) which has both hostel (mid-July to August only) and self-catering apartment accommodation; and a B&B, the central **McIntosh Hall** ( ☎ 01334-467035; s/d £32/61). These prices are all good value for the standard of accommodation on offer.

You'll run out of fingers counting the guesthouses on tiny Murray Park; just about all offer similar standards, which are high. Two that we like are **Lorimer House** ( ☎ 01334-476599; www.lorimerhouse.com; 19 Murray Park; d to £90; 🖵 ) with smallish, sparklingly clean rooms with extra-comfy beds and a fab deluxe on the top floor; and **Burness House** ( ☎ 01334-474314; www.burness house.com; 1 Murray Park; d per person £32-42; ⊗ Mar-Nov) with rich Asian-inspired fabrics, golf pictures and spanking shiny new bathrooms.

### TOP END

**Hazelbank Hotel** ( ☎ 01334-472466; www.hazelbank .com; 28 the Scores; s/d £87/129; 🖵 wi-fi) Offering a genuine welcome, the family-run Hazelbank is in many ways the most likeable of the hotels along the Scores. The front rooms have marvellous views along the beach and out to sea; those at the back are somewhat cheaper and more spacious. Prices drop significantly outside the height of summer. There are good portents if you are playing a round – Bobby Locke won the Open in 1957 while staying here.

**Five Pilmour Place** ( ☎ 01334-478665; www.5pil mourplace.com; 5 Pilmour Pl; s £75, d £120-150; 🖵 wi-fi) Just around the corner from the Old Course, this luxurious and intimate spot offers stylish, compact rooms with an eclectic range of styles as well as modern conveniences, such as flat-screen TV and DVD player. The king-size beds are especially comfortable and the lounge area is a stylish treat.

**Inn on North Street** ( ☎ 01334-473387; www.theinn onnorthstreet.com; 127 North St; s £80-95, d £120-150; 🖵 wi-fi) Only the hero of Gullible's Travels could really believe they were getting value for money, but this cheery bar/restaurant still represents an intriguing place to stay. The rooms are sun-kissed and spacious, with narrow beds; the 'superiors' are even larger and have Jacuzzis. Downstairs, there's good bar food, as well as a more serious restaurant. Below that, the Lizard Lounge has regular live music and DJs. Service throughout is excellent.

## Eating

**B Jannetta** ( ☎ 01334-473285; 31 South St; 2-scoop cone £2.20; ⊗ 10am-5pm Mon-Sat) This is a St Andrews institution, offering 52 varieties of ice cream from the weird (Irn-Bru sorbet) to the decadent (strawberries-and-champagne). There's also a decent cafe next door.

**Grill House** ( ☎ 01334-470500; St Mary's Pl; mains £6-15; ⊗ noon-3pm & 5-10.30pm) This cheerful, sometimes boisterous restaurant offers something for every taste and bank balance, with a big selection ranging from Mexican, pizza and pasta to chargrilled salmon and quality steaks. Scatty service is compensated for by an upbeat atmosphere and nice touches, such as free margarita and corn chips on arrival. Lunch specials are very cheap.

**Zizzi** ( ☎ 01334-474676; 87 South St; pasta £7-10; ☻ lunch & dinner) Beloved of local students, this Italian has atmosphere without the tack. Rather than Mona Lisas, moribund love songs and phallic pepper grinders, it's got contemporary decor, an open kitchen, a very chatty buzz, and fast service. The food won't wow but it will satisfy.

**Balaka** ( ☎ 01334-474825; 3 Alexandra Pl; mains £10-16; ☻ noon-3pm & 5pm-1am Mon-Sat, 5pm-1am Sun) Though not as cheap as it once was, this beloved Bangla restaurant has both standard choices and more inspiring discoveries, all delicious and seasoned with herbs it grow itself. Service is patient and good-natured. The £6.95 lunch deal is a bargain.

**Doll's House** ( ☎ 01334-477422; 3 Church Sq; mains £12-18; ☻ lunch & dinner) The oddly satisfying decor of this long-popular restaurant combines the bedroom of a Victorian child with more 21st-century furniture lines. You can't argue with the £6.95 lunch special, but evening choices are a little more hit-and-miss, despite the blackboard of daily specials, and portions have shrunk. The terrace is optimistic but great on a sunny day.

**Vine Leaf** ( ☎ 01334-477497; www.vineleafstandrews .co.uk; 131 South St; 2-course dinner £23.50; ☻ 7-10pm Tue-Sun) Classy, comfortable and well established, the friendly Vine Leaf offers a changing menu of sumptuous Scottish seafood, game and vegetarian dishes down a close off South St. There's also an attractive self-catering apartment (per day/week £80/350).

## Drinking

**Central Bar** ( ☎ 01334-478296; 77 Market St) Rather staid compared with some of the wilder student-driven drinking options, this likeable pub keeps it real with traditional features, an island bar, lots of Scottish beers, decent service, and filling if uninspiring pub grub (£6 to £8, open for meals 11am to 9pm).

**West Port** ( ☎ 01334-473186; 170 South St; mains £9-16; ☻ noon-midnight; ▣ wi-fi) Just by the gateway of the same name, this sleek modernised pub has several levels, as well as a great beer garden out the back. Cheap cocktails rock the uni crowd,

mixed drinks (no soda gun) are above average, and there's fairly sophisticated food served from 6pm to 8pm.

## Entertainment

**Byre Theatre** ( ☎ 01334-475000; www.byretheatre.com; Abbey St) Originally housed in a cowshed, hence the name, St Andrews' main theatre now resides in more-upmarket premises. It's also got a very pleasant cafe and bar.

## Shopping

**Andrew Keracher** ( ☎ 01334-472541; 73 South St) Widely regarded as Scotland's finest fishmonger, this place is not far from Church Sq.

**IJ Mellis** ( ☎ 01334-471410; 149 South St) A wealth of cheeses you can smell halfway down the street; cheese addicts will be seduced as soon as they open the door.

## Getting There & Away

Bus destinations include Edinburgh (£9, two hours, hourly), Glasgow (£9, 2½ hours, hourly), Stirling (£7, two hours, six to seven Monday to Saturday), Dundee (30 minutes, half-hourly).

The nearest train station is Leuchars, 5 miles away, but it is connected by frequent buses from the bus station. There are services to Edinburgh (£10.60, one hour, hourly), Dundee, Aberdeen and Inverness.

## Getting Around

To park in the centre you need a voucher, bought from the tourist office or at one of the many shops in town. A taxi from the train station at Leuchars to town costs around £11 with **Golf City Taxis** ( ☎ 01334-477788).

**Spokes** ( ☎ 01334-477835; 37 South St; ☻ 9am-5.30pm Mon-Sat) hires bikes from £10.50 per day or £3 per hour.

## AROUND ST ANDREWS
### Kellie Castle

A magnificent example of Lowland domestic architecture, **Kellie Castle** (NTS; ☎ 01333-720271; adult/child £8/5; ☻ 1-5pm Easter-Oct, garden & grounds 9.30am-5.30pm year-round) dates partly from the 14th century but had an extensive makeover in Victorian times; the combination of creaky floors and crooked little doorways, with elegant plasterwork and marvellous works of art, is a winning one. The garden is an absolute treat on a sunny day, and is known for its collection of rare roses.

It's 3 miles northwest of Pittenweem on the B9171. Bus 95 from St Andrews gets you closest; about 1.5 miles away. You can get straight to the castle by prebooking a **Flexibus** ( ☎ 01334-840340) taxi from Anstruther (£1.80) or Crail (£2.25).

## Scotland's Secret Bunker

A compelling relic of the Cold War, **Scotland's Secret Bunker** ( ☎ 01333-310301; www.secretbunker .co.uk; adult/child £8.60/5.60; ☒ 10am-6pm late Mar–Oct, last admission 5pm) is by the B9131 about 5 miles south of St Andrews. It was earmarked to be one of Britain's underground command-and-control centres and a home for Scots leaders in the event of nuclear war. Hidden 30m underground and surrounded by re-inforced concrete are the austere operation rooms, communication centre and dormit-ories. The exhibition uses period artefacts, and creates plenty of spine-tingling atmosphere. If that's not enough, the harrowing film *The War Game,* originally banned by the BBC, gives a horrifying account of a nuclear attack scenario. It's graphic and definitely not for youngsters, but highlights the madness of the era. There's also an underground cafe and free internet. Get here by prebooking a **Flexibus** ( ☎ 01334-840340) taxi from Anstruther (£1.80) or Crail (£2.25), or it's a £15 standard taxi from St Andrews.

## EAST NEUK

This charming stretch of the Fife coast runs south from St Andrews to the point at Fife Ness, then west to Leven. Neuk is an old Scots word for corner, and it's certainly an appealing nook of the country to investi-gate, with picturesque fishing villages, some great restaurants, and pretty coastal walks; the Fife Coastal Path's most scenic stretches are in this area. It's easily visited from St Andrews, but also makes a pleasant place to stay.

## Crail

**pop 1695**

Pretty and peaceful, little Crail has a much-photographed stone-sheltered harbour sur-rounded by wee cottages with red-tiled roofs. You can buy lobster and crab from a kiosk there; nearby are benches in the grassed area perfectly placed for munching your alfresco crustaceans while admiring the view across to the Isle of May.

See the small and friendly **tourist office** ( ☎ 01333-450869; crail@visitscotland.com; 62 Marketgate; ☒ 10am-1pm & 2-5pm Mon-Sat, noon-5pm Sun Jun-Sep, weekends only Apr–May) for information. The vil-lage's history and involvement with the fish-ing industry is outlined in the **Crail Museum** (admission free), in the same building with the same hours.

**Caiplie House** ( ☎ 01333-450564; www.caipliehouse .com; 53 High St North; r £65-70; ☒ Apr-Nov), in the cen-tre of town, a block west of the crossroads, has large rooms with lots of lights and big soft beds perfect for flopping on at the end of the day; spend an extra couple of quid for the top room, with views across to East Lothian. It does dinners too.

**Hazelton Guest House** ( ☎ 01333-450250; 29 Marketgate North; d/superior d £68/76; ☒ Mar-Nov) is a welcoming walker-friendly guesthouse, which has been recommended by readers. Across the road from the tourist office, it offers appeal-ingly light, crisply clean and attractively col-oured rooms, some with fine views. Breakfast also wins high marks.

Crail is 10 miles southeast of St Andrews. Bus 95 connects them hourly.

## Anstruther

**pop 3442**

Once among Scotland's busiest ports, cheery Anstruther has ridden the tribulations of the fishing industry better than some, and now has a very pleasant mixture of bobbing boats, historic streets, and visitors ambling around the harbour grazing on fish and chips or con-templating a trip to the Isle of May.

The **tourist office** ( ☎ 01333-311073; anstruther@ visitscotland.com; Harbourhead; ☒ Apr–mid-Oct) is by the harbour and extremely helpful. In the same building the sizeable, down-to-earth **Scottish Fisheries Museum** ( ☎ 01333-310628; www .scotfishmuseum.org; adult/child £5/free; ☒ 10am-4.30pm Mon-Sat & noon-4.30pm Sun Oct-Mar, 10am-5.30pm Mon-Sat & 11am-5pm Sun Apr-Sep) has a particularly good display on the herring industry and focuses on family and community life as well as the daily toil on the high seas.

You can take a four- to five-hour excursion aboard the **May Princess** ( ☎ 01333-310103; www .isleofmayferry.com; adult/child £17/8; ☒ 1 almost daily mid-Apr–Sep) to the **Isle of May**, a nature reserve; sail-ing times depend on the tide (phone or check the website) and the crossing takes just under an hour. The cliffs are packed with breeding kittiwakes, razorbills, guillemots, shags and puffins from May to July. Inland are the ruins of 12th-century **St Adrian's Chapel**.

West of Anstruther, the picturesque coastline continues; drop into St Monans, whose harbour boasts an excellent restaurant (below), or watch a game of beach cricket from the pub looking over the magnificent strand at Elie.

### SLEEPING & EATING

**ourpick** **Spindrift** ( ☎ 01333-310573; www.thespindrift .co.uk; Pittenweem Rd; s/d £48/76; **P** **Q** wi-fi) Arriving from the west, there's no need to go further than Anstruther's first house on the left, a redoubt of Scottish cheer and warm hospitality. The rooms are elegant, classy, and extremely comfortable – some have views across to Edinburgh and one is like a ship's cabin, courtesy of the sea-captain who once owned the house. There are DVD players and teddies for company, honesty-bar with characterful ales and malts, fine company from your hosts, and a breakfast that includes porridge once voted the best in the Kingdom. Dinner (from £20) is also available.

**Anstruther Fish Bar** ( ☎ 01333-310518; 42 Shore St; haddock supper takeaway/eat-in £4.70/6.90; ☒ 11.30am-10pm) Posh students down from St Andrews and breadline families across from Leven cheerfully rub shoulders in the queue (long) for this legendary chip shop. Eat in or, if it's a nice day, sit outside by the water. It's tradition.

**Dreel Tavern** ( ☎ 01333-310727; 16 High St; bar meals £5-11) This atmospheric traditional pub appeals for its low ceilings and bright and breezy staff. There's a beer garden, appetising food served and several real ales on tap, including the brilliantly named 'Bitter and Twisted', a Stirlingshire-brewed beer bristling with fresh hoppy flavour.

**Cellar Restaurant** ( ☎ 01333-310378; 24 East Green; lunch £17.50, 2-/3-course dinner £33.50/38.50; ☒ lunch Wed-Sat, dinner Tue-Sat) Tucked away behind the museum, this convivial spot is famous for its variety of seafood. It's heavily booked in summer; if you get a table, adorn it with local dressed crab, lobster or the excellent marinated herring.

**The Seafood Restaurant** ( ☎ 01333-730327; www .theseafoodrestaurant.com; 16 West End, St Monans; 2-course lunch/dinner £20/32; ☒ lunch & dinner Wed-Sun Apr, Wed-Mon May, daily Jun-Aug) Comfortable but classy, this fishy stalwart is on the harbour at St Monans, 4 miles west. The menu changes – bouillabaisse, Dover sole, scallops – but just

swim with the tide. There's another attractive branch in St Andrews.

### GETTING THERE & AWAY

Bus 95 runs hourly from Leven (45 minutes) to Anstruther and on to St Andrews (35 minutes) via Crail.

## FALKLAND

pop 1183

Below the soft ridges of the Lomond Hills in the centre of Fife is the charming village of Falkland. It developed around its magnificent centrepiece, the 16th-century **Falkland Palace** (NTS; ☎ 01337-857397; adult/child £10/7; ☒ 10am-5pm Mon-Sat, 1-5pm Sun Mar-Oct), a country residence of the Stuart monarchs. Mary Queen of Scots spent the happiest days of her life 'playing the country girl in the woods and parks' at Falkland.

The palace is visually stunning, a masterpiece of Scottish Gothic, and with much French influence evident in the decoration and furnishings. There are several fine portraits of the Stuart monarchs, and various chambers have been reconstructed, although much of the original castle was gutted by Cromwell's troops. The highlight is the beautiful chapel with heraldic windows, an ornate painted ceiling, and elegant oak screen. Outside in the ample gardens is the oldest royal-tennis court in Britain, built in 1539 for James V, and still in use.

### Sleeping & Eating

**ourpick** **Covenanter Hotel** ( ☎ 01337-857224; www.luig inos.co.uk; High St; s/d £60/90) Opposite the church, this old coaching inn is a joyful marriage of wonderful traditional architecture and exuberant Italian gastronomy. The rooms were being made over with smart black slate and wallpaper when we last visited, and the quality restaurant, Luigino's (mains £9 to £13, open lunch and dinner), which serves authentic and tasty saltimbocca, pasta that you can watch being made fresh, and wood-fired pizza, was being paired with a new deli and wine bar, all furnished by local craftspeople. The enthusiasm and cheeriness of the owners and staff is a high point.

### Getting There & Away

Bus 36 travels between Glenrothes and Auchtermuchty via Falkland. From either of those two places, there are regular connections to St Andrews and other Fife destinations. It carries on to Perth (one hour) more or less hourly.

## SOUTHWESTERN FIFE

Southwestern Fife is an odd mixture of urban sprawl (Fife's proximity to expensive Edinburgh has made it part of the commuter belt) and quiet country lanes. There are several worthwhile attractions here, in easy day-trip range from St Andrews or the capital.

### Aberdour

This little town is notable for the attractive ruins of **Aberdour Castle** (HS; ☎ 01383-860519; admission £4.20; ⏰ 9.30am-6.30pm Apr-Sep, 9.30am-4.30pm Sat-Wed Oct-Mar). Long a residence of the Douglases of Morton, the stately structure exhibits several architectural phases; it's worth purchasing the guidebook to better comprehend what you see. Most charming of all is the elaborate doocot at the bottom of the garden. Be sure to pop into the beautiful Romanesque church of St Fillan's, next door to the castle.

Aberdour is 5 miles east of the Forth Rd Bridge on the A921. Stagecoach bus 7 regularly connects Aberdour with nearby Dunfermline, and there are regular trains to Edinburgh (30 minutes) and Dundee (one hour).

### Dunfermline

Historic, monastic Dunfermline is Fife's largest population centre, sprawling eastwards through once-distinct villages. Its noble history is centred on evocative **Dunfermline Abbey** (HS; ☎ 01383-739026; admission £3.70; ⏰ 9.30am-5.30pm Apr-Sep, call for winter hours), founded by David I in the 12th century as a Benedictine monastery. Dunfermline was already favoured by religious royals; Malcolm III married the exiled Saxon princess Margaret here in the 11th century, and both chose to be interred here. There were many more royal burials, none more notable than Robert the Bruce, whose remains were discovered here in 1818.

What's left of the abbey is the ruins of the impressive three-tiered refectory building, and the atmosphere-laden nave of the church, endowed with geometrically patterned columns and fine Romanesque and Gothic windows. It adjoins the 19th-century church (closed October to April) where Robert the Bruce now lies under the ornate pulpit.

Next to the refectory, **Dunfermline Palace** (admission included), once the abbey guesthouse,

was converted for James VI, whose son, the ill-fated Charles I, was born here in 1600. Below stretches the bosky, strollable Pittencrieff Park.

Dunfermline is a culinary desert, but the good folk at **Fresh** ( ☎ 01383-626444; 2 Kirkgate; light meals £3-7; ⏰ 9am-8pm Mon-Fri, 10.30am-8pm Sat & Sun), just up from the abbey, do decent sandwiches and coffee, as well as tasty daily specials based on deli produce. There's also wine, internet access, a gallery and book exchange.

There are frequent buses to Edinburgh (40 minutes), Stirling (1¼ hours) and St Andrews (1¼ hours); and trains from Edinburgh (30 minutes).

### Culross

Enchanting Culross (coo-*ross*) is the best-preserved example of a 17th-century Scottish burgh. Small, red-tiled, whitewashed buildings line the cobbled streets, and the winding Back Causeway to the abbey is embellished with whimsical street-front stone cottages.

As birthplace of St Mungo, Glasgow's patron saint, Culross was an important religious centre from the 6th century. The burgh developed by mining coal through extraordinary underwater tunnels, under the laird George Bruce; vigorous trade resulted, enabling Bruce to build and complete the palace by 1611. When mining was ended by flooding of the tunnels, the town switched to making linen and shoes.

Strikingly coloured **Culross Palace** (NTS; ☎ 01383-880359; adult/child £8/5; ⏰ noon-5pm Thu-Mon Easter-May & Sep-Oct, noon-5pm daily Jun-Aug) is more like a large house, and features decorative, painted woodwork and an interior largely unchanged since the early 17th century, as well as a recreated formal garden. The **Town House** and the **Study** (included in palace ticket), also early-17th-century buildings, are accessible by guided tour only.

On the hill is the grand, ruined **Culross Abbey** (HS; admission free; ⏰ 9.30am-7pm Mon-Sat, 2-7pm Sun Apr-Sep, 9.30am-4pm Mon-Sat, 2-4pm Sun Oct-Mar), founded by the Cistercians in 1217.

Above a pottery workshop near the palace, **Biscuit Cafe** ( ☎ 01383-882176; cakes £1-2; ⏰ 10am-5pm) has a tranquil little garden and sells coffee and tempting organic cakes and scones.

Culross is 12 miles west of the Forth Rd Bridge, off the A985. Stagecoach bus 78 runs to Culross from Dunfermline (25 minutes, hourly).

# PERTHSHIRE

For sheer scenic variety, Perthshire is the pick of Scotland's regions and a place where everyone will find a special personal spot, whether it's bleak moors, snaking lochs, postcard-perfect villages, or magnificent forests – the trees just seem to grow higher here – that get your pulse racing.

Things begin sedate in the southeast corner with Perth itself, a fine country town with a fabulous attraction in lavish Scone Palace, and get gradually wilder as you move northwards and westwards, moving through wooded slopes and river-blessed valleys and culminating in the bleak expanse of Rannoch Moor.

The highlights are many: the enchanting valley of Glen Lyon can strike visitors dumb with its wild and remote beauty; stunning Loch Tay, base for ascending Ben Lawers, is nearby; and the River Tay runs east from here towards Dunkeld, which has an outstanding cathedral that is among the most beautifully situated in the country.

## Getting Around

The A9 cuts across the region through Perth and Pitlochry. It's the fast route into the Highlands and to Inverness, and very busy.

The council produces a useful public-transport map available at tourist offices. **Stagecoach** ( ☎ 01382-227201; www.stagecoachbus .com) and its stablemate Strathtay run local bus services.

Trains run alongside the A9, destined for Inverness. The other main line connects Perth with Stirling (in the south) and Dundee (in the east).

# PERTH

pop 43,450

Sedately arranged along the banks of the Tay, this former capital of Scotland is a most liveable place with large tracts of enticing parkland surrounding an easily managed centre. On its outskirts lies Scone Palace, a country house of staggering luxury built alongside the mound that was the crowning place of Scotland's kings. It's really a must-see, but the town itself, ennobled by stately architecture, fine galleries and a couple of excellent restaurants, merits exploration, and is within easy striking distance of Edinburgh and Glasgow.

## Information

**Library** ( ☎ 01738-444949; York Pl; ⊗ Mon-Sat) Free internet access.

**Tourist office** ( ☎ 01738-450600; perthtic@visit scotland.com; West Mill St; ⊗ 9.30am-4.30pm Mon-Sat, 11am-3pm Sun Apr-Jun & Sep-Oct, 9.30am-6pm Mon-Sat, 10.30am-4pm Sun Jul & Aug, 10am-4pm Mon-Sat Nov-Mar) Maps of Perth and helpful information.

## Sights

### SCONE PALACE

So thanks to all at once and to each one,
Whom we invite to see us crowned at Scone.

*Macbeth*

Fabulous **Scone Palace** ( ☎ 01738-552300; www.scone -palace.net; adult/child £8/5; ⊗ 9.30am-5.30pm Apr-Oct), pronounced skoon, is 2 miles north of Perth. It was built in 1580 on a site intrinsic to Scottish history. Here in 838, Kenneth MacAilpin became the first king of a united Scotland and brought the Stone of Destiny (p785), on which Scottish kings were ceremonially invested, to Moot Hill. In 1296 Edward I of England carted the talisman off to Westminster Abbey, where it remained for 700 years before being returned to Scotland.

Despite the history of bearded warriors swearing kingly oaths in the ancient mists here, Scone is no medieval fortress but an early-19th-century Georgian mansion of extreme elegance and luxury.

The visit takes you through a succession of sumptuous rooms filled with fine French furniture and noble artworks. There's an astonishing collection of porcelain and fine portraits, as well as a series of exquisite Vernis Martin papier mâché. Scone has belonged for centuries to the Murray family, earls of Mansfield, and many of the objects have fascinating history attached to them (friendly guides are on hand). Each room has comprehensive multilingual information; there are also panels relating histories of some of the Scottish kings crowned at Scone over the centuries.

Outside, peacocks – all named after a monarch – strut around the magnificent grounds, which incorporate woods, a butterfly garden and a maze.

The ancient kings were crowned atop Moot Hill, topped by a chapel, next to the palace. It's said that the hill was created by

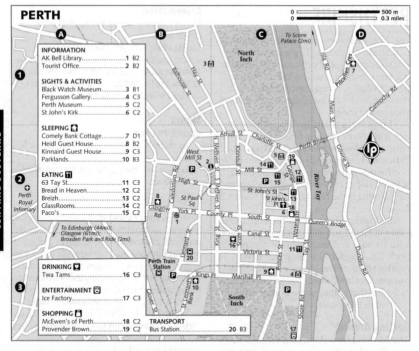

**PERTH**

bootfuls of earth, brought by nobles attending the coronations as an acknowledgment of the king's rights over their lands, although it's likelier the site of an ancient motte-and-bailey castle.

From Perth's centre, cross the bridge, turn left, and keep bearing left until you reach the gates of the estate (15 to 20 minutes). From here, it's a half-mile to the palace. Various buses from town stop here roughly hourly; the tourist office has a printout. There's a good cafe at the palace.

### FERGUSSON GALLERY
Beautifully set in the round waterworks building, this **gallery** ( ☎ 01738-441944; cnr Marshall Pl & Tay St; admission free; 🕙 10am-5pm Mon-Sat) exhibits much of the work of the Scottish Colourist JD Fergusson in a most impressive display. Fergusson spent much time in Paris, and the influence of artists like Matisse on his work is evident; his voluptuous female portraits against a tropical-looking Riviera background are memorable, as is the story of his lifelong relationship with noted Scottish dancer Margaret Morris.

### ST JOHN'S KIRK
One block south of High St, this redoubtable stone **church** (www.st-johns-kirk.co.uk; St John's Pl; entry by donation; 🕙 10am-4pm Mon-Sat, 10am-1pm Sun May-Sep, before services rest of year) dates from the 15th century (although the site was first consecrated in 1126) and serves as an impressive reminder of the Reformation in Scotland. In 1559 John Knox preached a powerful sermon here, inciting a frenzied destruction of Scone abbey and other religious sites. Perth used to be known as St John's Town after this church; the football team here is still called St Johnstone.

### PERTH MUSEUM
The city's main **museum** ( ☎ 01738-632488; cnr George & Charlotte Sts; admission free; 🕙 10am-5pm Mon-Sat) is worth wandering through for the elegant neoclassical interior alone. There is a varied shower of exhibits available, ranging from portraits of dour lairds to good local social history. A geological room provides more entertainment for the young traveller, while there are often excellent temporary exhibitions.

## BLACK WATCH MUSEUM

Housed in a mansion on the edge of North Inch, this **museum** ( ☎ 01738-638152; Hay St; entry by donation; ⏰ 10am-3.30pm Mon-Fri Oct-Apr, 10am-4.30pm Mon-Sat May-Sep) honours what was once Scotland's foremost regiment. Formed in 1725 to combat rural banditry, the Black Watch fought in numerous campaigns, recreated here with paintings, memorabilia and anecdotes. There's little attempt at perspective: there's justifiable pride in the regiment's role in the gruelling trench warfare of WWI, where it suffered nearly 30,000 casualties, but no sheepishness about less glorious colonial engagements, such as against the 'Fuzzy Wuzzies' of Sudan. In 2006 the Black Watch was subsumed into the new Royal Regiment of Scotland.

## Sleeping

Someone should open a hostel in Perth.

**Comely Bank Cottage** ( ☎ 01738-631118; www.comelybankcottage.co.uk; 19 Pitcullen Cres; s/d £35/56; Ⓟ 🖳 wi-fi) This short stretch of road is bristling with upmarket, flowery B&Bs. This is our favourite on the stretch, a perfectly maintained family home offering large and commodious rooms with spacious bathrooms, and a solicitous owner who doesn't disappoint come breakfast time.

**Heidl Guest House** ( ☎ 01738-635031; www.heidl.co.uk; 43 York Pl; s/d £28/58; Ⓟ 🖳 wi-fi) Though a little grim from without, and on a busy street, the Heidl offers plenty of staunch hospitality allied with bright, light rooms, with cheery bedspreads in marine colours. Most rooms come with decent en suite; those that don't have good private exterior bathroom. Free parking and proximity to the centre are further bonuses. Writer John Buchan (of *Thirty-Nine Steps* fame) was born in the house opposite.

**Kinnaird Guest House** ( ☎ 01738-628021; www.kinnaird-guesthouse.co.uk; 5 Marshall Pl; s/d £40/65; Ⓟ 🖳 wi-fi) This is the best of the handful of guesthouses enjoying a privileged position across the road from the lovely South Inch parkland. The elegant old house has noble original features and boasts appealing, bright rooms with big beds. The owners are engaging and extremely helpful; they are justifiably proud of what Perth has to offer.

**Ⓞⓤⓡⓟⓘⓒⓚ Parklands** ( ☎ 01738-622451; www.theparklandshotel.com; 2 St Leonard's Bank; s/d £99/119; Ⓟ 🖳 wi-fi) Tucked away near the train station, this relaxing hotel sits amid a lush hillside garden over-looking the parklands of South Inch. While the rooms – which vary in size and shape – conserve the character of this beautiful building, formerly the residence of the town's mayors, they also offer modern conveniences such as flat-screen cable TV and CD/DVD players. The restaurant has a fine reputation and a terrace to lap up the Perthshire sun.

## Eating

**Bread in Heaven** ( ☎ 01738-442500; 13 High St; rolls £1.80-2.90; ⏰ 7.30am-5pm Mon-Fri) With a passion for cycling and a community feel to it, this tiny cafe has a good attitude, decent espresso, and a wide range of sandwiches and panini. The black pudding roll is hard to beat on a cold morning.

**GlassRooms** ( ☎ 01738-477724; Mill St; light meals £4-8; ⏰ 10am-7pm Mon-Sat, noon-7pm Sun) Occupying part of the foyer of the ambitious, inspiring Perth Concert Hall, this open-plan eatery has plenty to offer. The range of light daytime dishes includes several healthy and vegetarian choices – an asparagus and pea risotto stood out – as well as sandwiches and fresh juices.

**Paco's** ( ☎ 01738-622290; www.pacos.co.uk; 3 Mill St; mains £6-17; ⏰ noon-11pm Mon-Sat, 4.30-11pm Sun) Something of an institution, Paco's keeps Perthers coming back over and over, perhaps because it would take dozens of visits to try even half of the menu. There's something for everyone: steaks, seafood, pizza, pasta and Mexican, all served in generous portions. The fountain-tinkled terrace is the place for a sunny day.

**Ⓞⓤⓡⓟⓘⓒⓚ Breizh** ( ☎ 01738-444427; www.cafebreizh.co.uk; 28 High St; galettes £6-8, mains £9-15; ⏰ 9am-9pm Mon-Sat, 11am-9pm Sun) This warmly decorated bistro is a treat. Dishes such as bouillabaisse (soupy seafood stew) are served with real panache, and the house salad, featuring poached salmon, seared scallops and fresh asparagus, is a feast of colour, texture and subtle flavours. Breakfasts, galettes (Breton buckwheat crêpes), 20-odd wines by the glass – what more can we say?

**63 Tay Street** ( ☎ 01738-441451; www.63taystreet.com; 63 Tay St; lunch/dinner mains £9.95/16.95; ⏰ lunch & dinner Tue-Sat) Classy and warmly welcoming, this understated restaurant is Perth's best, featuring a lightly decorated dining area, excellent service and quality food. In a culinary Auld Alliance, French influence is applied to the best of Scottish produce to produce memorable game, seafood, beef and vegetarian plates.

## Drinking & Entertainment

**Twa Tams** ( ☎ 01738-634500; 79 Scott St) Perth's best pub has a strange outdoor space with windows peering out onto the street, an ornate entrance gate and large, cosy interior. There are regular events, including live music every Friday and Saturday night; it has a sound reputation for attracting talented young bands.

**Ice Factory** ( ☎ 01738-630011; www.icefactory.co.uk; Shore Rd; cover £5-10; ☯ 11pm-2.30am Fri & Sat) One of Scotland's best regional nightclubs, this is near the harbour in the south of town. With three separate dance floors, cheerful colours and regular foam parties, the emphasis is on fun rather than posing; high-profile Scottish DJs often appear.

## Shopping

**McEwen's of Perth** ( ☎ 01738-623444; 56 St John's St) McEwen's is a venerable department store that is famous throughout Scotland.

**Provender Brown** ( ☎ 01738-587300; 23 George St; ☯ 9am-5.30pm Mon-Sat) This fabulous deli has a great selection of cheeses, pâtés and wines.

## Getting There & Away

From the bus station, Citylink operates hourly buses to/from Edinburgh (£8.50, 1½ hours) and Glasgow (£8.70, 1½ hours). There are also buses to/from Inverness (£15.40, 2½ hours, at least five daily). Further buses run from the Broxden Park & Ride on Glasgow Rd; this is connected to the bus station regularly by shuttle bus (£1). Services include **Megabus** (www.megabus.com) discount services to Aberdeen, Edinburgh, Glasgow, Dundee and Inverness.

Trains hit Edinburgh (£12.20, 1½ hours, two hourly) and Glasgow (Queen St; £12.20, one hour, at least hourly Monday to Saturday, two-hourly Sunday), as well as Inverness (£20.40, 2¼ hours, nine daily Monday to Saturday, five Sunday) via Pitlochry and Aviemore.

## PERTH TO AVIEMORE

There are several major sights strung out along the busy A9, which becomes a scenic treat after Pitlochry – it's the main route north to the Cairngorms, Inverness and the Highlands.

## Dunkeld & Birnam

**pop 1005**

Much of the essence of Perthshire pervades Dunkeld, with the charming River Tay unrolling through the stately little heritage town, which has beautifully preserved traditional cottages and the ruined majesty of its cathedral.

The smiling staff at **Dunkeld tourist office** ( ☎ 01350-727688; The Cross; ☯ daily Apr-Oct, Fri-Tue Nov-Mar) can recommend walks and cycle routes, of which there are many (mostly gentle) hereabouts.

**Dunkeld Cathedral** (HS; ☎ 01350-727601; High St; admission free; ☯ 9.30am-6.30pm Mon-Sat, 2-6.30pm Sun Apr-Sep, 9.30am-4pm Mon-Sat, 2-4pm Sun Oct-Mar) has one of Scotland's most beautiful settings, with a grassy riverbank studded with enormous trees on one side and rolling hills on the other. Half the cathedral is still in use as a church – the rest is in ruins. It partly dates from the 14th century; the cathedral was damaged during the Reformation and burnt in the battle of Dunkeld (Jacobites vs Government) in 1689. The Wolf of Badenoch (p901) is buried – undeservedly – here in a fine medieval tomb behind the wooden screen in the church.

A collection of **artisans' houses** restored by National Trust Scotland line High and Cathedral Sts; most have plaques with a brief history of their origins. Across Telford Bridge is **Birnam**, made famous by Shakespeare's *Macbeth*. There's plenty left of Birnam Wood; there's also a small **Beatrix Potter Park** (the author spent childhood holidays in the area).

Top choice for a sun-kissed pub lunch by the river is the **Taybank** ( ☎ 01350-727340; Tay Tce; bar mains £5-10; ☯ food noon-9pm), a regular meeting place and performance space for musicians of all creeds and a wonderfully open and welcoming bar. The menu includes a tasty selection of traditional and offbeat stovies.

Citylink buses running between Inverness and Edinburgh/Glasgow stop at the Birnam House Hotel. Frequent Stagecoach buses head to Perth (20 minutes) and Pitlochry (20 minutes, Monday to Saturday). It's also on the Perth–Inverness train line.

## Pitlochry

**pop 2564 / elev 147m**

Pitlochry, with its air already smelling of the Highlands, is a popular stop on the way north and is a convenient base for exploring northern central Scotland. On a quiet spring evening it's a pretty place with salmon jumping in the Tummel and good things brewing at the Moulin Inn. In summer it tends to crowd up with tour coaches disgorging their passengers into debatable souvenir shops.

The efficient **tourist office** ( ☎ 01796-472215; pitlochry@visitscotland.com; 22 Atholl Rd; ☺ daily Apr-Oct, Mon-Sat Nov-Mar) has information about the area. **Computer Services Centre** ( ☎ 01796-473711; 67 Atholl Rd; per hr £3; ☺ 9am-5.30pm Mon-Sat) has internet access.

One of Pitlochry's attractions is its beautiful riverside; the Tummel is dammed here, and you can watch salmon swimming up a fish ladder to the loch above. Near here, the famous **Festival Theatre** (www.pitlochry.org.uk) has a summer season of mainstream plays.

Pitlochry has a couple of distilleries; by far the nicer is pretty **Edradour** ( ☎ 01796-472095; www .edradour.co.uk; tours free; ☺ 10am-4pm Mon-Sat, noon-4pm Sun Jan & Feb, 9.30am-6pm Mon-Sat, 11.30am-5pm Sun Mar-Oct, 9.30am-4pm Mon-Sat, noon-4pm Sun Nov & Dec), proudly Scotland's smallest distillery. It's 2.5 miles east of Pitlochry along the Moulin road, and is a pleasant walk. The last tour leaves an hour before it closes.

Once off the highway, the area is great for exploring by bike, and you can grab one from **Escape Route** ( ☎ 01796-473859; www.escape-route.biz; 3 Atholl Rd; half/full day £12/20), which also hires cars.

## SLEEPING

There are dozens of hotels and guesthouses in Pitlochry; the tourist office can help with finding a bed. Also see right.

**Pitlochry Backpackers Hotel** ( ☎ 01796-470044; www.scotlands-top-hostels.com; 134 Atholl Rd; dm/tw £15/50; ☺ Easter-Oct; Ⓟ ▯ ) Nailed in the centre of town, this facility-packed spot offers decent dorms, as well as value en suite twins and doubles (beds not bunks). Cheap breakfast and a pool table are among the attractions, as is the convivial party atmosphere.

**Tir Aluinn Guest House** ( ☎ 01796-473811; www .tiraluinn.co.uk; 10 Higher Oakfield; s/d £30/60; Ⓟ wi-fi) Tucked away above the main street, this is a little gem of a place with bright rooms with easy-on-the-eye furniture, and an excellent personal welcome. There's a single, and a family room, and if they're full there are several others along this street.

**Craigatin House** ( ☎ 01796-472478; www.craigatin house.co.uk; 165 Atholl Rd; d standard/deluxe £70/80; Ⓟ ▯ wi-fi) Several times more tasteful than the average Pitlochry lodging, this noble house and garden is set back from the main road at the western end of town. Chic contemporary fabrics covering expansive beds

offer a standard of comfort above and beyond the reasonable price; the rooms in the converted stable block are particularly inviting. Breakfast choices include whisky-laced porridge, smoked fish omelettes and apple pancakes.

Other places to stay:

**Atholl Villa** ( ☎ 01796-473820; www.athollvilla.co.uk; 29 Atholl Rd; d £65; Ⓟ ) Appeals with its large lawn, central location and flowery garden. More breakfast choice than many.

**Pitlochry SYHA Hostel** ( ☎ 01796-472308; www.syha .org.uk; Knockard Rd; dm £16; ☺ Feb-Oct; Ⓟ ▯ ) Great location overlooking the centre of town. Popular with families and walkers.

### EATING & DRINKING

our pick **Moulin Hotel** ( ☎ 01796-472196; www.moulin hotel.co.uk; Moulin; bar mains £6-11; ☺ food 11am-9.30pm) A mile away but a world apart, this atmospheric hotel was trading centuries before the tartan tack came to Pitlochry. With its romantic low ceilings, ageing wood and booth seating, the inn is a wonderfully atmospheric spot for a house-brewed ale or a portion of Highland comfort food: try the filling haggis or venison stew. A more formal restaurant serves equally delicious fare, and the hotel has a variety of rooms (singles/doubles £60/85) as well as a self-catering annexe. The best way to get here from Pitlochry is walking: it's a pretty uphill stroll through green fields, and an easy roll down the slope afterwards.

our pick **Port-Na-Craig Inn** ( ☎ 01796-472777; www .portnacraig.com; Port Na Craig; mains £8-17; ☺ food noon-9pm) Right on the river, this top little spot sits in what was once a separate hamlet. The delicious main meals are prepared with confidence and panache – scrumptious scallops or lamb steak bursting with flavour might appeal, but simpler sandwiches, kids' meals, and light lunches also tempt. Or you could just sit out by the river with a pint and watch the anglers whisking away.

### GETTING THERE & AWAY

Citylink buses run roughly hourly connecting Pitlochry with Inverness (£12.30, two hours), Perth (£7.60, 40 minutes), Edinburgh (£12, two hours) and Glasgow (£12, 2¼ hours). **Megabus** (www.megabus.com) discount services also run these routes.

Pitlochry is on the main railway from Perth (30 minutes, nine daily Monday to Saturday, five on Sunday) to Inverness.

CENTRAL SCOTLAND

## Blair Castle

Noble **Blair Castle** ( ☎ 01796-481207; www.blair-castle
.co.uk; adult/child £7.90/4.90; ☒ 9.30am-6pm Apr-Oct, last
admission 4.30pm, check website for winter hours) and the
108 square miles it sits on, is the seat of the
Duke of Atholl, head of the Murray clan. It's
an impressive white building set beneath forested slopes above the River Garry.

The original tower was built in 1269, but
the castle has undergone significant remodelling since. Thirty rooms are open to the
public and they present a wonderful picture
of upper-class Highland life from the 16th
century on. The dining room is sumptuous –
check out the nine-pint wine glasses – and the
ballroom is a vaulted chamber that's a virtual
stag cemetery.

The current duke visits the castle every May
to review the Atholl Highlanders, Britain's
only private army.

Blair Castle is 7 miles north of Pitlochry,
and a mile from the village of **Blair Atholl**. Local
buses run to Blair Atholl four to six times
daily from Pitlochry, and a couple go direct
to the castle. There's a train station but few
trains stop here.

## WEST PERTHSHIRE

The further west you get in Perthshire, the
more remote things feel, and the more epic the
scenery, with long steel-blue lochs overlooked
by moody hills. Geographically, you're in the
dead centre of Scotland here, but the bustle
of the southern cities already feels impossibly
far away.

There's a **tourist office** ( ☎ 01887-820276; The
Square; ☒ daily mid-Apr-Oct, Mon-Sat Nov-mid-Apr) in
the village of **Aberfeldy**, gateway to the region,
and one in Killin (p872). Stagecoach runs
buses to Aberfeldy from Perth (1¼ hours,
hourly Monday to Saturday) and from
Pitlochry (45 minutes, 10 daily Monday to
Saturday, three on Sunday).

## Loch Tay & Kenmore
elev 476m

Serpentine and picturesque, long Loch Tay
reflects the powerful forests and mountains around it. The bulk of mighty **Ben
Lawers** (1214m) looms above and is part of
a National Nature Reserve that includes the
nearby Tarmachan range. The **Ben Lawers
visitors centre** (NTS; ☎ 0844 493 2136; admission £2;
☒ 10am-5pm Easter-Sep), which sells the *Ben
Lawers Nature Trail* booklet, describing the

area's flora and fauna, is 5 miles east of Killin,
a mile off the A827.

Pretty **Kenmore** lies at Loch Tay's eastern
end, and is dominated by a church, clock
tower and the striking archway of the privately
owned **Taymouth Castle**. Just outside town, on
the loch, is the fascinating **Scottish Crannog
Centre** ( ☎ 01887-830583; www.crannog.co.uk; adult/child
tour £5.75/4; ☒ 10am-5.30pm mid-Mar–Oct, 10am-4pm
Sat & Sun Nov). A crannog, perched on stilts in
the water, was a favoured form of defence-
minded dwelling in Scotland from the 3rd
millennium BC onwards. This one has been
superbly reconstructed, and the guided tour
(last tour one hour before closing) includes
an impressive demonstration of firemaking.
It's an excellent visit.

Kenmore's a good activity base and **Loch Tay
Boating Centre** ( ☎ 01887-830291; www.loch-tay.co.uk)
can have you speeding off on a bike (£10/16
for half/full day) or out on the loch itself in
anything from a canoe to a cabin cruiser that'll
sleep a whole family.

The heart of the village, **Kenmore Hotel**
( ☎ 01887-830205, www.kenmorehotel.com; s/d £75/119;
Ⓟ ▣ ) has a bar with roaring fire and some
verses scribbled on the chimneypiece by
Robert Burns in 1787, when the inn was already a couple of centuries old. There's also
a riverbank beer garden and a wide variety of
rooms; some across the road sport modern
conveniences like DVD players, the nicest
have bay windows and river views.

There are regular buses from Aberfeldy to
Kenmore (10 to 30 minutes), some continuing
to Killin via the turn-off to the Ben Lawers
visitors centre.

At the western end of Loch Tay, but just
out of Perthshire, Killin (p872) is another
good base.

## Fortingall

West of Aberfeldy, the pretty village of
Fortingall is at the turn-off to Glen Lyon.
Tranquil and picturesque, it has 19th-century
thatched cottages, and a most ancient yew
that's considered to be Europe's oldest tree.
Popular if unlikely tradition says that Pontius
Pilate was born here; the tree may have been
old even then.

**Fortingall Hotel** ( ☎ 01887-830367; www.fortingall
.com; s/d/superior d £95/140/185; ☒ Mar-Oct; Ⓟ ) is a
peaceful, old-fashioned country hotel with
polite service and furnished with quiet good
taste. The bedrooms are spotless, with huge

**CENTRAL SCOTLAND**

---

**BAG A MUNRO: BEN LAWERS**

The trek up Ben Lawers starts at the visitors centre and is one of the best walks in the area. The trip to the top and back can take up to five hours: pack wet-weather gear, water and food. Take the nature trail that heads northeast. After the boardwalk protecting a bog, cross a stile, then fork left and ascend along the Edramucky burn (to the right). At the next rise, fork right and cross the burn. A few minutes' later ignore the nature trail's right turn and continue ascending parallel to the burn's left bank for just over half a mile. Leave the protected zone by another stile and steeply ascend Beinn Ghlas' shoulder. Reaching a couple of large rocks, ignore a northbound footpath and continue zigzagging uphill. The rest of the ascent is a straightforward succession of three false summits. The last and steepest section alternates between erosion-sculpted rock and a meticulously crafted cobbled trail. Long views of majestic hillscape, and even the North Sea and Atlantic, are your reward on a clear day.

---

beds, modern bathrooms and little extras like bathrobes and whisky; the superiors have DVD players. Rooms look out over green meadows; in all a perfect spot for doing very little except enjoying the clean air and excellent dinners.

### Glen Lyon

This remote and stunningly beautiful glen runs for some 34 unforgettable miles of rickety stone bridges, Caledonian pine forest and sheer heather-splashed peaks poking through swirling clouds. It becomes wilder and more uninhabited as it snakes its way west and is proof that hidden treasures still exist in Scotland. The ancients believed it to be a gateway to faerie land, and even the most sceptical of people will be entranced by the valley's magic.

From Fortingall, a narrow road winds up the glen – another road from the Ben Lawers visitors centre crosses the hills and reaches the glen halfway in, at Bridge of Balgie. The glen continues up to a dam (past a memorial to explorer Robert Campbell); bearing left here you can actually continue over a wild and remote Water Board road unmarked on maps, to remote Glen Lochay and down to Killin. Cycling through Glen Lyon is a wonderful way to experience this special place.

There's little in the way of attractions in the valley – the majestic and lonely scenery is the reason to be here, but at **Glenlyon Gallery**, next to the post office (which does more-than-decent lunches) at Bridge of Balgie, a selection of fine handmade pieces are on sale.

For utter tranquillity in a glorious natural setting, **Milton Eonan** ( ☎ 01887-866318; www.milton eonan.com; Bridge of Balgie; s/d £37.50/75;  P  🖵 ) is a must. On an effervescent stream where an historic watermill once stood, it's a working croft that offers B&B in beautifully individual rooms, and has excellent facilities. The lively owners do packed lunches and evening meals (£17.50) using local and home-grown produce and actually live in a separate cottage, so you get the run of the house. Another cottage on the croft holds a **bunkhouse** (www.benlawersbunk house.com; dm without/with bedding £13.50/20.50); you can also put up a tent (£5). After crossing the bridge at Bridge of Balgie, you'll see Milton Eonan signposted to the right.

There is now no public transport in the glen.

### Loch Rannoch

This long loch stretches due west towards Perthshire's remotest corner and offers plenty of scenic splendour and wildlife-watching opportunities. Southeast of it, walkers converge on pointily evocative Schiehallion (1083m), a relatively easy climb rewarded by spectacular views unobstructed by other hills.

The road ends at romantic, isolated Rannoch train station, which is on the Glasgow-Fort William line. Beyond is the desolate and intriguing Rannoch Moor, a windy, vaguely threatening peat bog stretching as far as the A82 and Glen Coe. There's a tearoom on the platform, and a welcoming small hotel, the **Moor of Rannoch** ( ☎ 01882-633238; www.moorofrannoch.co.uk; s/d £52/88; ✷ mid-Feb–Oct), alongside the station.

# DUNDEE & ANGUS

Well off the standard visitor beat, the Dundee area has traditionally got on with the oft-difficult task of making a living rather than relying on tourism but it has plenty to offer, with a string of fishing towns backed by a hinterland of peaceful glens winding down to the sea.

Dundee town has been working hard and imaginatively over the last few years to transform itself, and the ugly duckling has come a long way down the road to swan status, with some really wonderful visitor attractions, and cultural centres that succeed in bringing art and community together.

Glamis Castle, where the bloody deeds of *Macbeth* are set, and Arbroath Abbey, where Scotland declared itself independent from England, make fine day trips from Dundee.

## Getting Around
**Strathtay Scottish** ( ☎ 01382-228054; www.stagecoach bus.com) is the main bus operator between Dundee and places in Angus. Trains run along the scenic coastline from Dundee to Aberdeen via Arbroath.

## DUNDEE
pop 154,674

In the wake of the collapse of its traditional industries, severe poverty and poor planning took their toll, and Dundee, the most Scottish of cities and the nation's fourth-largest, became one of Britain's grimmest and most deprived. But people with vision have turned it around, creating excellent cultural centres, and three truly excellent museums, two celebrating the city's heritage, one an imaginative science extravaganza for kids of all ages. Now the waterfront is to be reclaimed to take advantage of Dundee's beautiful firthside situation, and the city is shooting right up many visitors' agenda.

The 'three j's' are usually said to have built Dundee: the jute industry, with its associated whaling and shipbuilding; jam, referring to Dundee marmalade; and journalism, with *Desperate Dan* and *Beano* comics produced here – Dan himself stands proud in the square.

## History
In the 19th century, Dundee was a major player in the shipbuilding and railway engineering industries. Then came the rise of jute and, since whale oil was used in the process, whaling developed alongside. At one time there were as many as 41,000 people employed in the textile industry and as the jute workers became redundant, tough economic times led to the city developing a reputation as one of the most 'red' in Britain. Winston Churchill, long-time but locally hated MP for Dundee, described speaking to 'an audience of lions with Communist teeth'.

## Orientation
The Tay Bridge from Fife arrives right in the centre of town. Dundee is a city of two halves, with the commercial centre counterbalanced by lively Perth Rd just to the west, where the university, arts centres and best eating options are. Broughty Ferry, a few miles east, has always been where Dundonians head to for a day on the beach and a pub lunch.

## Information
**Dundee City Library** (Wellgate Shopping Centre, Panmure St; ☽ 9.30am-9pm Mon-Fri, 9.30am-5pm Sat) Free internet access.

**Tourist office** ( ☎ 01382-527535; dundee@visit scotland.com; 21 Castle St; ☽ 10am-5pm Mon-Fri, 10am-4pm Sat Oct-Jun, 9am-6pm Mon-Sat, noon-4pm Sun Jul-Sep) Helpful. Internet access £1 for 15 minutes.

## Sights
### VERDANT WORKS
Among Britain's best museums, **Verdant Works** ( ☎ 01382-225282; www.verdantworks.com; West Henderson's Wynd; adult/child £5.95/3.85, incl Discovery Point £10.95/7; ☽ 10am-6pm Mon-Sat, 11am-6pm Sun Apr-Oct, 10.30am-5pm Wed-Sat, 11am-5pm Sun Nov-Mar) brings the history of Dundee's jute industry dramatically to life. The museum is housed in a restored jute mill; your visit begins via a charismatic guided tour, with atmosphere added by recorded voices with impenetrable Dundonian accents. The whole process of jute-making is explained, and staff demonstrate the working of the production line with functioning machines. There's a display of social history that gives the visit so much more meaning than just jute; the museum as a whole makes powerful statements about the rise and fall of heavy industry and its effect on the ordinary population. There's plenty here to keep the kids entertained as well, and the enthusiasm and humour of the staff make it a memorable experience.

### DISCOVERY POINT
Brimming with the same enthusiasm and scope as Verdant Works, **Discovery Point** ( ☎ 01382-309060; www.rrsdiscovery.com; adult/child £6.45/3.85, incl Verdant Works £10.95/7; ☽ 10am-6pm Mon-

Sat, 11am-6pm Sun Apr-Oct, 10am-5pm Mon-Sat, 11am-5pm Sun Nov-Mar) is an exhibition about Scott's first expedition to the Antarctic in 1901 aboard the *Discovery*, built in Dundee and now docked here. Excellent displays recreate conditions aboard and at the base camp, where the team spent two harsh winters but collected invaluable scientific data about the almost unknown southern continent. You can then board the lovely ship itself to examine the cabins and staunch hull built of 10 different timbers.

### HM FRIGATE UNICORN

A state-of-the-art gunship when launched in 1824, the **Unicorn** ( ☎ 01382-200900; www.frigate unicorn.org; admission £4; ☒ 10am-5pm Apr-Oct, noon-4pm Wed-Fri, 10am-4pm Sat & Sun Nov-Mar) never saw action – indeed, was never masted or rigged – and is the oldest British-built warship still afloat. She's impressively solid – a thousand oaks were felled to build her – and would have been crewed by up to 300 sailors, who had zero headroom in the lower decks but a gallon of beer a day to compensate. The upper decks were dedicated to the guns; 46 cannons of various poundage, including some in the captain's cabin, would have made it a formidable foe.

### SENSATION

This modern **museum** ( ☎ 01382-228800; www.sensation.org.uk; Greenmarket; adult/child £6.95/4.95; ☒ 10am-5pm; ▣ ) is designed for the young and the energetic. It's a great place for kids, tired perhaps

**CENTRAL SCOTLAND**

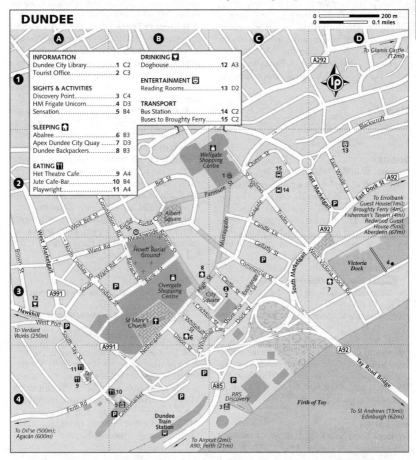

of art galleries and noble buildings, to reclaim the holiday. As the name suggests, the place is designed interactively, with dozens of hands-on attractions in five halls based on each of the senses. A giant head gives you the chance to slide down the nostril; elsewhere you can experience zero-gravity in a gyroscope (be prepared to queue) or explore the innards of a leaf. There are regular temporary exhibitions too.

### BROUGHTY FERRY
This pleasant seaside suburb, known to locals simply as 'the Ferry', is 4 miles east of Dundee. There's a profusion of seabirds, a long beach and great views across the firth to Fife.

Picturesque **Broughty Castle** (HS; ☎ 01382-436916; Castle Green; admission free; ☒ 10am-4pm Mon-Sat, 12.30-4pm Sun Apr-Sep, closed Mon Oct-Mar) is an imposing, reconstructed 16th-century tower guarding the entrance to the Firth of Tay. Its interesting historical exhibition includes information on Dundee's whaling industry.

The easiest way to get to Broughty Ferry is to take bus 40, 75, 76 or 80 from opposite the bus station.

## Sleeping
Broughty Ferry appeals as a base, and has plenty of B&Bs.

### BUDGET
**Abalree** ( ☎ 01382-223867; 20 Union St; s/d without bathroom £20/34) In the city's heart, this sound-as-a-pound budget guesthouse is run by enthusiastic, dyed-in-the-wool Dundonians who love a chat. The dingy staircase gives no clue of the colourful and comfortable rooms with TV inside. Shared bathrooms are small but clean, and there's 24-hour access. It's easier to get a room at weekends. Great value.

**our pick** **Dundee Backpackers** ( ☎ 01382-224646; www.hoppo.com; 71 High St; dm £13, s/d without bathroom £25/40, s/d with bathroom £35/45; ☐ ) An ambitious recent civic project merged five distinct buildings – including the city's oldest, dating from 1560 – into this ultracentral hostel. New mattresses and sturdy wooden bunks make dorming a pleasure; if you're going private, ask for the bagpipe-maker's room for a trip back into Dundee's past. Facilities include full disabled access and a good kitchen.

### MIDRANGE
**Errolbank Guest House** ( ☎ 01382-462118; www.errol bank-guesthouse.com; 9 Dalgleish Rd; s/d £30/58; ℗ ) Let

there be light… and there is in this appealing B&B boasting spacious rooms with large windows (some looking over the firth) about a mile east of the centre of town on a leafy street. There's been a recent facelift here, and things, including the tiny but spotless en suites, seem shiny and new. Buses between the centre and Broughty Ferry zip past the bottom of the street.

**Redwood Guest House** ( ☎ 01382-736550; www .redwoodguesthouse.com; 89 Monifieth Rd, Broughty Ferry; s/d £40/60; ℗ ) A little further east than the main cluster of Broughty Ferry accommodation, this rewards the extra legwork with magnificent firth views from the front lounge and bedroom, and an equally appealing back garden with conservatory to loll about in. The spacious rooms, cheery welcome and value for money all get the thumbs-up.

**Fisherman's Tavern** ( ☎ 01382-775941; www.fisher mans-tavern-hotel.co.uk; 10 Fort St, Broughty Ferry; s/d £39/64) While the rooms here are adequate rather than astounding, it's the location that sells it. In two ways: not only are you a few yards from the sea, but you are also inside the Ferry's best pub. Despite that, noise from the bar is minimal.

**Apex Dundee City Quay** ( ☎ 01382-202404; www.apex hotels.co.uk; 1 West Victoria Dock Rd; d £95-135; ℗ ☐ wi-fi) This large but environmentally conscious hotel is by far the best place to stay in Dundee. Firthside of the centre overlooking Victoria Dock, it has upbeat and stylish interior design, really welcoming service and rooms with big comfortable beds and a rubber duck for bath time. Facilities are excellent; all rooms come with DVD player and free wi-fi, and there's a smart complex with gym, pool, sauna and spa treatments. And it's family-friendly; one kid per adult stays and eats free.

## Eating
Nearly all the best places to eat are on and around Perth Rd.

**our pick** **Jute Cafe-Bar** ( ☎ 01382-909246; Dundee Contemporary Arts Centre; 152 Nethergate; mains £7-13; ☒ food noon-4pm & 5-9.30pm) Emblematic of the new Dundee, or at least one aspect of it, is the Dundee Contemporary Arts Centre, which houses cinemas and galleries as well as this most enticing spot to eat and drink. The open-plan area exudes a welcoming buzz, there's outdoor seating, and a big range of edibles, from tasty panini to elegant Asian-Mediterranean fusion dishes at dinner time. Bar open until midnight.

**our pick** **Agacán** ( ☎ 01382-644227; 113 Perth Rd; mains £8-12; 🕙 5-10.30pm Tue-Sun) With a charismatic owner, quirky decor and wonderfully aromatic meat dishes, it's no wonder that you have to book ahead at this little spot on a corner, a 20 minute walk up Perth Rd from the centre. If you can't get a table, you can settle for takeaway.

**Dil'se** ( ☎ 01382-221501; 99 Perth Rd; mains £7-14; 🕙 noon-2.30pm & 4.30-11pm Sun-Thu, noon-2am Fri & Sat) Dundee loves a curry, and nobody does it better than this sleek modern Bangladeshi restaurant most of the way up Perth Rd. The bold, contemporary approach extends beyond the delicious old favourites to new dishes, such as Mas Bangla, which brings the subcontinent to Scots salmon.

Other recommended spots:

**Het Theatre Cafe** ( ☎ 01382-206699; Tay Sq; mains £7-11; 🕙 cafe 9.30am-late Mon-Sat, restaurant lunch & dinner Mon-Sat) Arty cafe upstairs in the Dundee Rep Theatre, a great place for coffee, snack or meal. Many vegie choices.

**Playwright** ( ☎ 01382-223113; 11 Tay Sq; mains £12-19; 🕙 10am-midnight) By the theatre, decorated with photos of Scottish actors. Cafe-bar and innovative restaurant, with snacks (£3 to £7) available as well as the somewhat overpriced Scot-Med creations.

## Drinking & Entertainment

Perth Rd has great spots for a drink, including the Jute Cafe-Bar (opposite) and Het Theatre Cafe (opposite).

**our pick** **Fisherman's Tavern** ( ☎ 01382-775941; 12 Fort St, Broughty Ferry) This community pub serves good cask ales and is a terrific little nook-and-cranny pub; once you order a drink you won't want to leave. There's also a beer garden, scene of a rowdy and thoroughly enjoyable beer festival every May/June, the proceeds of which go to the local lifeboat association.

**Doghouse** ( ☎ 01382-227080; www.myspace.com /dundeedoghouse; 13 Brown St; admission £3-10; 🕙 7pm-late) This big, tall barn of a bar, Dundee's alternative headquarters and best venue for live music, is a great place to go. Dark, spacious and atmospheric, there's live music – mostly rock – every weekend, and always something interesting going on midweek.

**Ship Inn** ( ☎ 01382-779176; 121 Fisher St, Broughty Ferry) Around the corner from the Fisherman's, this intimate pub is so full of nautical fittings that, with the Firth of Tay just outside the window, it feels like a boat. The bar meals are more than acceptable, and you can watch the local lifeboat crew launching for drills or rescues.

**Reading Rooms** (www.myspace.com/thereadingrooms; 57 Blackscroft; cover £3-10; 🕙 10.30pm-2.30am Thu-Sat) Some of Scotland's best club nights, as well as regular live music, take place in this innovative venue. You can hear everything from big band and jazz to punk and the latest electronic sounds. Check the MySpace page for upcoming events.

## Getting There & Away
### AIR
The **airport** ( ☎ 01382-643242) is roughly 1.5 miles west of the centre; daily flights head to London City with **AirFrance Cityjet** ( ☎ 0870-1424343; www .airfrance.co.uk) and **Flybe/Loganair** ( ☎ 0871-700 2000; www.flybe.com) flies to Birmingham and Belfast.

### BUS
Citylink services Edinburgh (£11.50, 1¾ hours, hourly), Glasgow (£12, two hours, hourly), Perth (£5.40, 30 minutes, half-hourly) and Aberdeen (£12, 1½ hours, more than hourly). **Megabus** (www.megabus.com) runs discount services to Edinburgh, Glasgow, Perth and Aberdeen.

### TRAIN
There are regular services from Edinburgh (£19.10, 1¼ hours, at least hourly), Glasgow (£21.40, 1½ hours, at least hourly) and Aberdeen (£22.60, 1¼ hours, half-hourly) via Arbroath and Stonehaven.

## AROUND DUNDEE
### Glamis Castle
Looking every bit the Scottish castle, with turrets and battlements, **Glamis Castle** (glarms; ☎ 01307-840393; www.glamis-castle.co.uk; adult/child £8/5, grounds only £4/3; 🕙 10am-6pm mid-Mar–Oct, 11am-5pm Nov-Dec) was the legendary setting for Shakespeare's *Macbeth* but its medieval origins have been obscured and most of what you now see dates from the 17th and 18th centuries. Backed by the Grampian hills and surrounded by extensive grounds, the castle is an impressive sight. Home of the earls of Strathmore, this was where the Queen Mother grew up.

Entry is by child-friendly guided tour; the most impressive room is the drawing room, with its arched plasterwork ceiling, while the frescos on the roof of the chapel (haunted, naturally) are magnificent. There's a display of armour and weaponry in the crypt (also haunted).

The castle is 12 miles north of Dundee in the village of Glamis. There are Strathtay Scottish buses from Dundee (35 minutes, one to three daily) to the castle itself, and a couple more that stop in the adjacent village. The Dundee tourist office has a leaflet on reaching the castle by bus.

## ARBROATH
pop 22,785

Arbroath is a fairly typical town of the Scottish east coast, but its name rings large for the declaration of independence that Robert the Bruce signed here, and for the smokie, a delicious smoked haddock whose aroma and texture make it a real treat. These give the town, coming to terms with the fact that fishing doesn't pay anymore, a source of pride, as does its mediocre football team, still living on the glorious day in 1885 when it beat hapless Bon Accord 36-0.

The new **tourist office** ( ☎ 01241-872609; arbroath@visitscotland.com; Harbour Visitors Centre; ☯ daily Apr-Oct, Mon-Sat Nov-Mar) by the harbour has lots of information on the area.

The fishing village grew up around **Arbroath Abbey** (HS; ☎ 01241-878756; admission £4.70; ☯ 9.30am-6.30pm Apr-Oct, 9.30am-4.30pm Nov-Mar). King William the Lion, who is buried here, founded it in 1178 and it was here that Robert the Bruce signed Scotland's famous declaration of independence from England in 1320, which contained the oft-quoted words: 'It is in truth not for glory, nor riches, nor honours that we are fighting, but for freedom'. Closed following the Dissolution, the fortified abbey fell into ruin but enough survives to make this an impressive sight.

The visitors centre next door outlines the turbulent history of the abbey, as well as providing a good virtual tour of how it might have looked in its prime. It makes an effort for kids too.

**Harbour Nights Guesthouse** ( ☎ 01241-434343; www.harbournights-scotland.com; 4 Shore; s/d from £40/50) is right on Arbroath harbour across the way from the tourist office and is a very appealing spot to stay. It's a stylish place of some character, and offers handsome themed rooms, the best of which overlook the harbour (doubles £60 to £65). Breakfast is great, but if you choose an Arbroath smokie, remember: that's as good as you're going to feel all day.

Several fishmongers around the harbour sell smokies and fresh fish, though Arbroath's fishing fleet has dwindled to two boats. The **Old Brewhouse** ( ☎ 01241-879945; 3 High St; mains £5-10; ☯ food noon-9pm), a pub right on the harbour wall, serves a good smokie; there's cosy indoor seating, tables outside for a sunny day and the addictive Orkney Dark Island on tap.

Strathtay Scottish has buses from Dundee (45 minutes, frequent), as does Citylink from Edinburgh/Glasgow. However, the scenic coastal trip from Dundee (20 minutes, half-hourly) makes the train journey worthwhile.

# ABERDEENSHIRE & MORAY

On a sunny day Scotland's shoulder is idyllic, with the mica glinting from Aberdeen's buildings, the rolling fields of Speyside bursting with pastoral colours, and the sparkling waters of the River Dee rolling through fairy-tale woodland. When the weather rolls in though, the waves batter the fishing towns with force, and you feel for those hardy souls working the oil rigs offshore in the irritable, violent North Sea.

Aberdeen, well-heeled from the oil boom that filled its harbour as the fishing boats were dwindling, has quite a cosmopolitan feel these days and merits a couple of days of your time. The rest of the region boosts Scottish stereotypes with castles (bleak Dunnottar or boutique Balmoral), whisky, with dozens of distilleries in and around Dufftown, and epic hills, at their best around Braemar.

## ABERDEEN
pop 184,788

Scotland's third city was a place in seemingly inevitable decline, with industry changing and fishing going belly-up, when a 'there she blows' from offshore signalled not a whale, but the discovery of North Sea oil in the early 1960s. Aberdeen's large harbour made it the perfect base for the industry, and it's now a thriving city, whose economy is driven by the oil and gas reserves.

Its nickname 'The Granite City' may conjure up images of a dour sort of town, but not so; the soft Aberdonian tones mingle here with the accents of transient multinational oilworkers and a large student population from around the country, ensuring that the inviting pubs, roaring clubs and decent restaurants are always busy.

Yet the whole city is indeed built of granite – even the roads are paved with the stuff – and on a sunny day every building glints cheerfully as the sun reflects off the spangling of mica particles. When it rains, as it likes to do in these parts, it can be a little less inspiring.

Aberdeen has some great museums and galleries including, fittingly for a place that seems to have its back to the Highlands and its face out to sea, a maritime museum. Nearby, the bustling fish market opens at dawn as it has done for centuries.

## History

Aberdeen was a prosperous port centuries before oil was considered a valuable commodity. After the townspeople supported Robert the Bruce at Bannockburn in 1314, the king rewarded the town with land for which he had previously received rent. The money was diverted into the Common Good Fund, to be spent on town amenities, as it still is.

Since the 1970s, Aberdeen has become the main onshore service centre for the North Sea oilfields; its harbour is Britain's second-busiest by ship movement.

## Orientation

Aberdeen is built on a ridge that runs east–west between the Rivers Dee and Don. Union St, the main commercial street, follows the line of the ridge. The adjacent bus and train stations are off Guild St, south of Union St. The ferry quay is to the east, off Market St. Old Aberdeen and the university are north of Union St. To the east lies a long stretch of clean, sandy beach.

## Information

**Aberdeen Royal Infirmary** ( ☎ 0845-456 6000; Westburn Rd) The city's principal hospital.

**Central Library** ( ☎ 01224-652500; Rosemount Viaduct; ⏰ 9am-8pm Mon-Thu, 9am-5pm Fri & Sat) Free internet access; sessions limited to 30 minutes.

**Tourist office** ( ☎ 01224-288828; aberdeen.inform ation@visitscotland.com; 23 Union St; ⏰ 9am-5pm Mon-Sat Sep-Jun, 9am-6.30pm Mon-Sat, 10am-4pm Sun Jul & Aug). Very helpful. Internet access per 20 minutes £1.

**Trailfinders** ( ☎ 01224-578600; www.trailfinders.co.uk; 265 Union St) Competent travel agent.

**Waterstone's** ( ☎ 01224-592440; 3 Union Bridge; ⏰ daily) Central bookshop with a cafe.

## Sights

Most of Aberdeen's museums and sights are free to enter.

### MARITIME MUSEUM

Partially set in Aberdeen's oldest building, this excellent **museum** ( ☎ 01224-337700; Shiprow; admission free; ⏰ 10am-5pm Mon-Sat, noon-3pm Sun) overlooks the harbour and presents a comprehensive overview of the city's seafaring and shipbuilding past; Aberdeen's contemporary role as an important port; and detail of the oil industry – an imposing scale model of the Murchison oil platform dominates the central well. There are lots of interactive displays, frightening statistics about the human impact on the ocean, and even a translation of the mysterious BBC shipping forecast. The museum also has a good basement cafe.

### MARISCHAL COLLEGE

In 1593 the fifth Earl Marischal (pronounced 'marshall') founded this huge building, now home to the university's science faculty. It is, for what it's worth, the second-largest granite structure in the world, after El Escorial near Madrid.

The **Marischal Museum** ( ☎ 01224-274301; Broad St; admission free; ⏰ 10am-5pm Mon-Fri, 2-5pm Sun) is refreshingly out of the ordinary. In one room there's a lively depiction of northeast Scotland arranged alphabetically, a good spot to learn a few Scots words; the other gallery is an anthropological overview of the world, incorporating objects from vastly different cultures arranged thematically, with Polynesian wooden masks alongside gas masks and so on.

### PROVOST SKENE'S HOUSE

This noble 16th-century **mansion** ( ☎ 01224-641086; Broad St; admission free; ⏰ 10am-5pm Mon-Sat, 1-4pm Sun) shrugged its turrets in dismay as it was gradually surrounded by ugly office blocks. Started in 1545, it was occupied in the 17th century by the provost (equivalent of a mayor).

Typical of its kind, the house has intimate, panelled rooms. The 1622 tempera-painted ceiling, with its Catholic symbolism, is unusual for having survived the depredations of the Reformation. Also noteworthy is the sumptuous formal dining room, and collections of costumes and coins.

CENTRAL SCOTLAND

**CENTRAL SCOTLAND**

# ABERDEEN

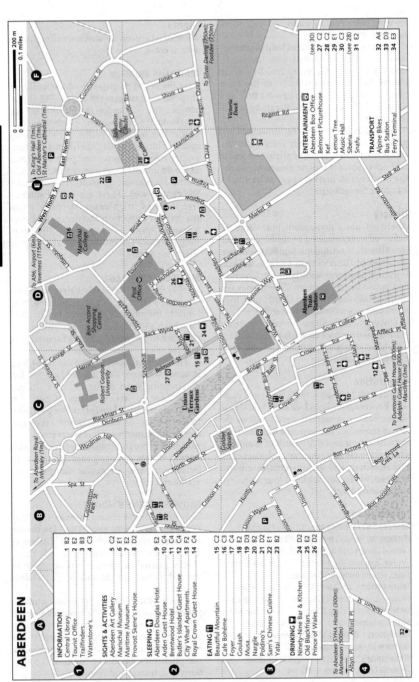

**INFORMATION**
| | |
|---|---|
| Central Library................................ | 1  B2 |
| Tourist Office................................. | 2  E2 |
| Trailfinders................................... | 3  B3 |
| Waterstone's................................. | 4  C3 |

**SIGHTS & ACTIVITIES**
| | |
|---|---|
| Aberdeen Art Gallery........................ | 5  C2 |
| Marischal Museum........................... | 6  E1 |
| Maritime Museum............................ | 7  C3 |
| Provost Skene's House...................... | 8  D2 |

**SLEEPING** 🛏
| | |
|---|---|
| Aberdeen Douglas Hotel..................... | 9  E2 |
| Arden Guest House........................... | 10  C4 |
| Brentwood Hotel.............................. | 11  C4 |
| Butler's Islander Guest House............. | 12  C4 |
| City Wharf Apartments...................... | 13  F2 |
| Royal Crown Guest House.................. | 14  C4 |

**EATING** 🍴
| | |
|---|---|
| Beautiful Mountain........................... | 15  C2 |
| Cafe Boheme.................................. | 16  C3 |
| Foyer.......................................... | 17  C4 |
| Goulash....................................... | 18  E2 |
| Musa........................................... | 19  D3 |
| Nargile........................................ | 20  B2 |
| Poldino's...................................... | 21  D2 |
| Sam's Chinese Cuisine....................... | 22  E1 |
| Yatai.......................................... | 23  B2 |

**DRINKING** 🍷
| | |
|---|---|
| Ninety-Nine Bar & Kitchen.................. | 24  D2 |
| Old Blackfriars................................ | 25  E2 |
| Prince of Wales............................... | 26  D2 |

**ENTERTAINMENT** 🎭
| | |
|---|---|
| Aberdeen Box Office.................. | (see 30) |
| Belmont Picturehouse................ | 27  C2 |
| Kef............................................ | 28  C2 |
| Lemon Tree................................. | 29  E1 |
| Music Hall................................... | 30  C3 |
| Siberia................................. | (see 28) |
| Snafu......................................... | 31  E2 |

**TRANSPORT**
| | |
|---|---|
| Alpine Bikes................................. | 32  A4 |
| Bus Station.................................. | 33  D3 |
| Ferry Terminal............................... | 34  E3 |

*To Aberdeen SYHA Hostel (300m);*
*Malmaison (500m)*

*To King's Hall (1mi);*
*To Old Aberdeen (1mi);*
*St Machar's Cathedral (1mi)*

*To Silver Darling (750m);*
*Footdee (750m)*

*To A96; Airport (6mi);*
*Inverness (115mi)*

*To Aberdeen Royal*
*Infirmary (1mi)*

*To Dunrovin Guest House (200m);*
*Adelphi Guest House (300m);*
*Marcliffe (3mi)*

**ABERDEEN ART GALLERY**
Behind the grand facade of this **gallery** ( ☎ 01224-523700; Schoolhill; admission free; ☻ 10am-5pm Mon-Sat, 2-5pm Sun) is a cool, white space exhibiting both young contemporary painters and also more-traditional works, including an excellent Victorian Scottish section, with many canvases by William Dyce. There's also a Rodin bronze and an extensive selection of watercolours and etchings, including a handful of Picassos and Chagalls.

**OLD ABERDEEN**
Old Aberdeen is a district north of the centre. The name is misleading, since the area south around the harbour is actually older; this area was named Alton in Gaelic, and this was anglicised to Old Town. It's a genteel district, with stone mansions lining leafy lanes. Many buildings belong to the university.

At the heart is imposing 15th-century **St Machar's Cathedral** ( ☎ 01224-485988; Chanonry; ☻ 9am-5pm Apr-Oct, 10am-4pm Mon-Sat Nov-Mar). One of the country's few examples of a fortified cathedral, it sits in a peaceful churchyard above the riverside parkland. According to legend, St Machar was ordered to establish a church where the river takes the shape of a bishop's crook, which it does just here. The cathedral is best known for its impressive heraldic ceiling, from 1520.

**ABERDEEN HARBOUR**
From Market St, Aberdeen's busy harbour stretches east to the mouth of the Dee. Here you can watch large ships sailing through the narrow navigation channel, and explore the delightful little district of **Footdee** ('fiddy') with its picturesque 19th-century fishers' cottages. North of here stretches the golden **beach**, scored by breakwaters.

## Sleeping
Southwest of the centre, Bon Accord St and Great Western Rd are bristling with B&Bs. Due to the oil workers it's easier finding accommodation at weekends, when hotels drop their rates.

**BUDGET**
**Aberdeen SYHA Hostel** ( ☎ 01224-646988; www.syha.org.uk; 8 Queen's Rd; dm £16; Ⓟ ▣ ) A mile from the train station, this hostel couldn't have chosen a more typical Aberdeen building: a sturdy granite town house. Like many SYHA joints, it's showing its age a little in some areas, but it's comfortable and has a good atmosphere, and helpful, friendly folk in charge. Facilities are good; beds are in small, clean dormitories, and there are two family rooms. Walk west along Union St, fork right along Albyn Pl, and straight across at the roundabout.

**MIDRANGE**
**Butler's Islander Guest House** ( ☎ 01224-212411; www.butlersguesthouse.com; 122 Crown St; d £66, s/d without bathroom £36/55; ▣ wi-fi) Shipshape rooms and excellent bathrooms are guaranteed at this upbeat guesthouse, well located for both Union St and transport options. The breakfast menu (cooked breakfast costs extra) includes such offbeat options as kedgeree and brose, a fortifying blend of porridge, whisky and honey that is guaranteed to send you out to see the sights in a good mood.

**Adelphi Guest House** ( ☎ 01224-583078; www.adelphiguesthouse.com; 8 Whinhill Rd; s/d £35/60) On the continuation of Bon Accord St, this B&B offers quiet rooms, some overlooking leafy parkland. All are comfortable and well equipped, with cable TV and big firm beds; there are also a couple of rooms large enough to fit a family, within reason. A couple of cheaper rooms share a bathroom.

**King's Hall** ( ☎ 01224-273444; www.abdn.ac.uk; King's Hall; s/d £54/81; ☻ Jun–mid-Sep; Ⓟ ▣ ) Aberdeen's university offers newly refurbished student rooms as hotel accommodation in the summer months. The quality of the rooms is good and the location, in the heart of Old Aberdeen, most appealing.

**Brentwood Hotel** ( ☎ 01224-595440; www.brentwood-hotel.co.uk; 101 Crown St; s/d £89/98, Fri-Sun £43/66; Ⓟ ▣ wi-fi) Don't be put off by the neon sign: this friendly and handily located hotel has reliable rooms, which are an excellent deal at weekends in particular. There's a restaurant and a bar below serving several real ales on tap.

Other recommendations:
**Arden Guest House** ( ☎ 01224-580700; www.ardenguesthouse.co.uk; 61 Dee St; s/d £40/74) Solid hospitality in this old stone building on a convenient but quiet central street.
**City Wharf Apartments** ( ☎ 0845 0942424; www.citywharfapartments.co.uk; 47 Regent Quay; d about £120; Ⓟ ▣ wi-fi) Luxuriously appointed apartments in different central locations, available at nightly rates.
**Dunrovin Guest House** ( ☎ 01224-586081; www.dunrovinguesthouse.co.uk; 168 Bon Accord St; s/d £45/60,

without bathroom £40/50; (P) (🖥) wi-fi) Friendly granite home with great natural light and shiny modern en suites. Spacious triple ideal for families.

**Royal Crown Guest House** ( ☎ 01224-586461; www .royalcrown.co.uk; 111 Crown St; s/d £38/66, d with bathroom £76; (P) (🖥) wi-fi) Compact but warmly decorated rooms handy for the centre of town.

## TOP END

**Malmaison** ( ☎ 0845 3654247; www.malmaison.com; 49 Queens Rd) Aberdeen's been waiting a while for this branch of the stylish Malmaison chain to open here. At the time of research, it was still putting the finishing touches on the place, but expect cutting-edge contemporary style and luscious rooms.

**Aberdeen Douglas Hotel** ( ☎ 01224-582255; www .aberdeendouglas.com; 43 Market St; d standard/executive £125/155; (🖥) wi-fi) Just up from the harbour, the Douglas has a very swish, comfortable lobby lounge and staff with a smile. The rooms vary widely in shape and fittings; the smart executive rooms, with tasteful wooden furniture and crisp linen, are especially attractive. Prices fall substantially at weekends, and you can get cheaper rates via hotel-booking websites.

**Marcliffe** ( ☎ 01224-861000; www.marcliffe.com; North Deeside Rd; s £195-215, d £215-235, ste £265-325; (P) (🖥) wi-fi) A five-star hotel with five-star service – nothing is too much trouble – Aberdeen's best hotel sits at the end of a winding driveway in acres of parkland. The rooms combine antique furniture and country-house comfort with stylish modern bathrooms; the restaurant offers fine Scottish produce with a massive wine list. You can fish on the River Dee within the grounds or indulge yourself with spa treatments. There are cheaper rates at weekends, and deals offered on the website. To get there, head west down Great Western Rd and its continuation North Deeside Rd; after 3 miles you'll see Marcliffe signposted on your right.

## Eating

**Beautiful Mountain** ( ☎ 01224-645353; 13 Belmont St; snacks £3-7; (🕑) 8am-4.30pm Mon-Sat) This is an excellent takeaway cafe with a great range of sandwiches and toasted ciabattas. Fillings are delicious and fresh. There's a small upstairs eat-in area, beer and wine available, and a relaxed buzz.

**Yatai** ( ☎ 01224-658521; 73 Skene St; dishes £3-11; (🕑) lunch Tue-Sat, dinner Tue-Sun) The small upstairs dining room and downstairs bar stools soon fill up at this recommended Japanese restaurant. The chef's a local lad who trained in the land of the rising sun, and produces exquisite sashimi and other dishes, including a teriyaki duck breast bursting with flavour.

**ourpick Musa** ( ☎ 01224-571771; www.musaart cafe.com; 33 Exchange St; lunch mains £7-10, mains £13-19; (🕑) 10am-11pm Tue-Sat, 10am-4pm Sun) The bright paintings on the walls match the vibrant furnishings and smart gastronomic creations at this great cafe, set near the harbour in a former church that was later used to store bananas. As well as lunches, brunches, munches and dinners, there are several wines by the glass, proper beers, and interesting music, sometimes live.

**Nargile** ( ☎ 01224-636093; 77 Skene St; mains £8-15; (🕑) dinner Mon-Sat) The restaurant that introduced Aberdeen to a world of Turkish food beyond the 2am doner kebab is still going strong. A shared spread of mezes (tapas-like starters) is the way to approach the meal; mains revolve around tender, flavour-packed meats. By all means try the Turkish wine, but don't go for the cheapest.

**ourpick Foyer** ( ☎ 01224-582277; 82a Crown St; lunches £6-10, mains £11-19; (🕑) 11am-10pm Tue-Sat) A godsend for hedonists with a heart, this handsome gallery restaurant is set in a converted church, and uses the profits it makes to assist homeless youth. The food, a confident and fluid fusion of Mediterranean, Scottish and Far Eastern influences (with many vegetarian choices), is presented with flair and served with a smile.

**Poldino's** ( ☎ 01224-647777; 7 Little Belmont St; pastas £6-10, other mains £13-19; (🕑) lunch & 6-10.45pm Mon-Sat) The charming owners make the experience at this long-standing Italian favourite, and in truth it never feels quite the same if they're not there. The seafood mains are more memorable than the pasta. Like all proper Italian restaurants, it closes on Sunday.

**Cafe Bohéme** ( ☎ 01224-210677; 23 Windmill Brae; mains £14-20; (🕑) noon-1.45pm & dinner Tue-Sat) On a sloping street parallel to Union St, this intimate French bistro offers classic Gallic cuisine in a warm and cosy atmosphere. The plat du jour (daily special) is invariably hearty, delicious and excellent value; in the evenings a more romantic atmosphere prevails, with candles and moody music.

**Silver Darling** ( ☎ 01224-576229; Pocra Quay; lunch mains £10-14, dinner mains £18-21; (🕑) noon-1.45pm Mon-

Fri, 7-9.30pm Mon-Sat) With a great situation at the mouth of the Dee, this restaurant is named for the herring that used to drive the economy in these parts. Its reputation is lofty and deserved, with exquisite French seafood dishes in a stylish dining area overlooking the comings and goings of ships. The menu changes regularly; you might come across delights such as steamed halibut with salmon mousse and squid-ink pasta.

Other recommendations:

**Goulash** ( ☎ 01224-210530; 17 Adelphi; 2-course dinner £13.75; ☺ 7-10pm Tue-Fri, 1-10pm Sat) Authentic, charismatic, eccentric Hungarian eatery off Union St.

**Sam's Chinese Cuisine** ( ☎ 01224-626233; 13 King St; mains £8-13; ☺ lunch & dinner) Far-above-average Scottish Chinese. Freshly prepared monkfish stir-fries and fiery king prawns.

## Drinking

Belmont St is the focus of Aberdeen's lively nightlife, with a wide range of style bars and preclub venues.

**Prince of Wales** ( ☎ 01224-640597; 7 St Nicholas Lane) No Aberdeen pub crawl would be complete without a stop at this well-loved city centre boozer. With a bar stretching off into the distance, gnarled wooden floorboards, and a buzz of soft Aberdonian accents lubricated by a range of guest beers, it's a haven of good cheer.

**Old Blackfriars** ( ☎ 01224-581922; 52 Castle St) This is a great traditional bar with low ceilings, timber interior and an intimate, warren-like layout. There's nothing pretentious about it, and it makes a great place for a drizzly evening. There's also no-frills Scottish comfort food, like stovies, available.

**Ninety-Nine Bar & Kitchen** ( ☎ 01224-658087; 1 Back Wynd) The eclectic range of wooden furniture and adornments here evokes a mishmash of imperial styles, but the bar food and DJ decks hint at a more contemporary outlook. Smart, cosy and different.

## Entertainment

To find out about current listings check *What's on in Aberdeen,* available from the tourist office. You can book tickets for most events at the **Aberdeen Box Office** ( ☎ 01224-641122; Union St) by the Music Hall.

### CINEMAS

**Belmont Picturehouse** ( ☎ 01224-343534; 49 Belmont St) Superbly located for a post-feature debrief over a pint, this cinema shows new releases, art-house classics, and themed series of films.

### NIGHTCLUBS

Check the noticeboards in **One-Up Records** (17 Belmont St) for upcoming club nights.

**Kef** ( ☎ 01224-684000; 9 Belmont St; admission free-£5; ☺ 11pm-2am or 3am) One of the city's most popular venues, with decadent cushions backing a Moorish design concept. Echoes of the Islamic world are less prominent around the lager-soaked bar and the decks, from which a range of high-quality sounds emanate. Attached is Siberia, a cool pub and vodka bar with a conservatory space. It also does some innovative pub food.

**Snafu** ( ☎ 01224-596111; www.clubsnafu.com; 1 Union St; ☺ Tue-Sat) Aberdeen's coolest club at the time of research, cosy Snafu offers a wide range of rotating club nights and guest DJs, as well as regular comedy and live music.

### THEATRE & MUSIC

**Music Hall** ( ☎ 01224-632080; www.musichallaberdeen .co.uk; Union St) Right in the heart of town, this is the main venue for classical-music concerts.

**Lemon Tree** ( ☎ 01224-642230; www.lemontree.org; 5 West North St) This place has a varied program of dance, drama and live music.

## Getting There & Away

### AIR

Seven miles northwest of the centre, **Aberdeen airport** (Dyce; ☎ 01224-722331) has numerous domestic flights, including to Orkney and Shetland. There are a few European services, including some budget routes (check www .whichbudget.com for up-to-date information). Bus 27 runs there from Union St regularly (35 minutes).

### BOAT

**NorthLink Ferries** ( ☎ 0845 6000 449; www.northlink ferries.com) runs ferries from Aberdeen to Lerwick (passenger/car £33/117 in high season, cabins £29 to £110, 12 to 15 hours, daily) on the Shetland Islands, and Kirkwall (passenger/car £25/89 in high season, six hours, four weekly) on the Orkney Islands.

### BUS

Citylink and discount operator Megabus run more than hourly to Dundee (£12, 1½ hours) and Perth (£18.30, two hours); and onwards from there to Edinburgh (£21.70, 3¼ hours, hourly) and Glasgow (£21.70, three hours, hourly). Stagecoach runs to Inverness (£9, 3¾ hours, hourly).

### TRAIN
Destinations from Aberdeen include Edinburgh (£38.20, 2½ hours, at least hourly), Glasgow (£38.20, 2½ hours, hourly), Dundee (£22.60, 1¼ hours, twice hourly), Inverness (£23.50, 2¼ hours, five to 10 daily) and Perth (£26.70, 1½ hours, hourly).

## Getting Around
### BICYCLE
**Alpine Bikes** ( ☎ 01224-211455; www.alpinebikes.co.uk; 64 Holburn St; ☒ daily) rents mountain bikes for £20/40/70 per day/weekend/week.

### BUS
The local operator is **First Aberdeen** ( ☎ 01224-650 065; www.firstgroup.com). The most useful services are buses 18, 19 and 24 from Union St to Great Western Rd, bus 27 from the bus station to the SYHA Hostel, and bus 20 for Old Aberdeen.

### CAR
There are several car-rental companies in Aberdeen. **Arnold Clark** ( ☎ 01224-249159; www.arnold clarkrental.co.uk; Girdleness Rd) has rates starting at £24 per day for a small car.

# AROUND ABERDEEN
## Stonehaven
pop 9577

A pretty, low-key seaside resort 15 miles south of Aberdeen, Stonehaven is nestled around a bay with some good walks and one of the most spectacularly situated castles in the country. The **tourist office** ( ☎ 01569-762806; 66 Allardice St; ☒ 10am-1pm & 2-5pm Mon-Sat, Sun in summer) is very helpful.

It's tough to think of a Scottish fortress more breathtaking at first glimpse than **Dunnottar Castle** ( ☎ 01569-762173; www.dunnottar castle.co.uk; adult/child £5/1; ☒ 9am-6pm Mon-Sat, 2-5pm Sun Easter-Jun & Oct, 9am-6pm daily Jul-Sep, 10.30am-dusk Fri-Mon Nov-Easter), a 20-minute walk from Stonehaven's harbour. Perched on a verdant promontory that rises some 50m above the rocky coast, the ruined castle complex is the very picture of undauntedness and defiance, and the mossy stone echoes to the cawing of rooks and the cries of seabirds. The castle, once owned by the powerful Earls Marischal, was besieged by a Cromwellian army intent

on capturing the Scottish crown jewels. After eight months of defiance, the castle surrendered, but only once the local vicar's wife had smuggled the 'Honours of Scotland' away to safety. Parts of interest include the chapel, the keep and the restored drawing room, as well as the Whigs' Vault, where in 1685 a group of Covenanters (those opposed to Crown-appointed bishops) were imprisoned in atrocious conditions. And yes, the Lion's Den did hold a lion; what the poor beast made of the weather hereabouts is not recorded.

Stonehaven's most appealing part is its pretty tidal harbour, and right on it **Twentyfourshorehead** ( ☎ 01569-767750; www .twentyfourshorehead.co.uk; 24 Shorehead; s/d £60/70) is a memorably inviting and relaxing B&B set in a 300-year-old former cooperage. The newly renovated rooms have character in spades and the whole place is decorated with taste and flair. Prop yourself up in bed and, using the binoculars thoughtfully provided, you can spot birds and seals.

Also on the harbour, the **Marine Hotel** ( ☎ 01569-762155; 8 Shorehead; mains £6-14; ☒ lunch & dinner) is a fabulous old stone building whose remodelled interior exudes rustic comfort with its stout wooden tables and crackling fire. In addition to the recommended food, the bar merits some of your time, offering fine Scottish ales, malts and various excellent Belgian beers on tap.

There are regular buses to Stonehaven from Aberdeen (45 minutes, at least hourly), some continuing to Dundee. There are also trains on the same route.

# DEESIDE
The sparkling Dee is what a river looks like in the picture-book dreams of a child, rolling

reliably through pretty woodlands with portly salmon and trout lurking in its waters. It's a wonderfully beautiful area that gradually gives way to more-rugged Highland scenery around Braemar and Glenshee. There's fantastic walking in this zone, as well as skiing and the Queen's Scottish residence, Balmoral.

## Balmoral Castle

This **castle** ( ☎ 01339-742534; www.balmoralcastle .com; adult/child £7/3, parking 70p; ☽ 10am-5pm Easter-Jul) was built for Queen Victoria in 1855 as a private royal residence. It sits in a privileged and beautiful position by the entrancing Dee. In truth, the somewhat hefty entrance fee is mainly for the grounds, as visitors are only allowed into one room of the castle – a ballroom stocked with rather uninteresting memorabilia. Walking around the gardens, however, is delightful on a nice day, although the flowers don't bloom until the Queen's stay in August. Perhaps best is the audio tour, which, although a little sycophantic, brings Victoria and Prince Albert (complete with Bavarian accent) to life.

Balmoral is just off the A93 (where there's a tourist office) and can be reached on buses running between Aberdeen and Braemar. The website details self-catering cottages in the grounds, let out by the week.

## Braemar & Around

**pop 410 / elev 312m**

Braemar, surrounded by mountains, is a great launch pad for walking or skiing at nearby Glenshee. Although it gets busy with coach parties, it still makes a good stop; it's at its best in the evenings when the fresh mountain air and crystal light infuse visitors with good cheer.

The **tourist office** ( ☎ 01339-741600; braemar@visit scotland.com; ☽ 10.30am-5pm Nov-May, 9.30am-5pm Jun & Sep-Oct, 9.30am-6pm Jul-Aug) has useful information on walks in the area.

### SIGHTS & ACTIVITIES

North of the village, turreted **Braemar Castle** (adult/child £5/3; ☽ 11am-4pm Sat & Sun May-Oct) dates from 1628, and held a garrison after the 1745 Jacobite rebellion. It's now community-run, and being gradually restored. You can see what's currently open on a guided visit that runs every hour. Opening days may increase.

An easy walk from Braemar is up **Creag Choinnich** (538m), a hill to the east above the A93. There are route markers and the walk takes about 1½ hours. For a longer walk (three hours) and superb views of the Cairngorms, climb **Morrone** (859m), the mountain south of Braemar. Five miles west of Braemar is the tiny settlement of **Inverey**: numerous mountain walks start from here, including the adventurous **Lairig Ghru trail** – 24 miles over the pass to Aviemore. Another fine place for leisurely hiking is around the beautiful **Linn of Dee gorge**, a couple of miles beyond Inverey.

Braemar is good for cycling; the **Bike Shop** ( ☎ 01339-755864; www.cyclehighlands.com; Victoria Rd, Ballater) in Ballater, 17 miles east, will deliver hire bikes up here (£10/15 per half/full day).

### FESTIVALS & EVENTS

On the first Saturday in September, the **Braemar Gathering** (Highland Games) brings tens of thousands to the village; bookings during this period are essential.

### SLEEPING

**our pick** **Rucksacks** ( ☎ 01339-741517; 15 Mar Rd; dm hut/house £7/12, tw £26-30; ℗ ▣ ) One of the joys of Scotland is hostels like this, where the glow of happy hikers past and present is part of the fabric of the place. There's everything here you could want: a raft of comforts including barbecue, kitchen, drying room, laundry and even a proper sauna. The well-loved Alpine hut – bring a sleeping bag – offers the simplest, cheapest berths; smarter accommodation is in the house or a new cabin out the back. Even if you're not staying, you can get online (10.30am to 4.30pm, £2 per hour) or put on washing – nothing is too much trouble for the enthusiastic, welcoming owner.

**Inverey SYHA Hostel** ( ☎ 0870 004 1126; www.syha .org.uk; dm £12.50; ☽ mid-May–early Sep; ℗ ) Set up for walkers who want to be close to the hills not the comforts, this is a cosy, basic place with tight-packed dorms and cold-water dunnies. There are no showers, but you can wash in the SYHA hostel at Braemar by arrangement. It's a mile past Inverey; the nearest shop is in Braemar.

**Braemar Lodge** ( ☎ 01339-741627; www.braemar lodge.co.uk; Glenshee Rd; dm £14, s/d £45/90; ℗ ) This restored shooting lodge on the outskirts of town offers a range of accommodation. The main house is surrounded by self-catering log cabins (£250 to £300 for a week), and a bunkhouse, which is dark and fairly basic, with a dozen beds in three cramped nooks.

**St Margarets** ( ☎ 01339-741697; 13 School Rd; s/tw £32/54; 🖳 wi-fi) Grab this place if you can, but there's only one room, a twin with a serious sunflower theme, flat-screen TV, DVD, and, for once, a decent tea selection. In the lav hang enough fans for an infanta's wedding and the genuine warmth of the welcome is heart-warming.

**Craiglea** ( ☎ 01339-741641; www.craigleabraemar .com; Hillside Dr; s/d/f £45/56/80) An enthusiastic young family runs this friendly and peaceful guesthouse, which sports six spacious en suite rooms in soothing colour combinations. It's a good destination for walkers, with a drying room, plenty of advice, a MemoryMap route planner for guests' use and packed lunches available.

### EATING

Braemar's main options are the hotels' mediocre bar meals until 8pm, and chip shop with its cheery outdoor tables.

**Gathering Place** ( ☎ 01339-741234; www.the-gathering -place.co.uk; 9 Invercauld Rd; mains £10-14; 🕑 dinner Tue-Sun) One of a pair of more sophisticated Braemar dining options, this riverbank spot has an upbeat, optimistic feel, particularly when the evening sunshine bathes its conservatory dining area (with painted quotes extolling the virtues of eating) in light. Service is polite and efficient, and the well-presented bistro-style food satisfies without bagging any culinary Munros.

### GETTING THERE & AWAY

Stagecoach bus 201 from Aberdeen to Braemar (£9, 2¼ hours, hourly Monday to Saturday, two-hourly on Sunday) travels along the Dee Valley.

## Glenshee
☎ 01250

The route south from Braemar along the A93, through Glenshee, is one of the most spectacular drives in the country. Meandering burns, tussocked grass and stark soaring peaks, splotched with glaring snow, dwarf open-mouthed drivers. It's an awe-inspiring piece of Scottish landscape.

**Glenshee Ski Centre** ( ☎ 01339-741320; www.ski-glen shee.co.uk; daily lift pass £24) is Britain's major ski resort. While it'll never see the Winter Olympics, it is, however, a cheery, family-friendly place,

and has 36 pistes. One of the chairlifts heads up to the top of the Cairwell (933m).

As well as the accommodation centres of Braemar to the north and Blairgowrie to the south, there are places to stay in Spittal of Glenshee, 6 miles south of the resort. **Spittal of Glenshee Hotel** ( ☎ 01250-885215; www.spittalofglenshee .co.uk; dm £19, s/d £33/66, d without bathroom £54; 🅿 ) is a ski lodge that looks like a Scottish theme pub. It's a friendly spot; the bar does unremarkable but comforting food in big portions, and there are various rooms as well as a bunkhouse: all rates include breakfast. When heading off on a hillwalk, take the hotel dog for company.

**our pick Dalmunzie House** ( ☎ 01250-885224; www .dalmunzie.com; Glenshee; s £85-125, d £140-220; 🅿 🖳 ) A noble estate with a dash of antipodean hospitality thrown into the mix, this classy retreat lives up to the best Highland stereotypes: roaring fires, leather armchairs, antlers and decanters of malt. There are four classes of room, offering much comfort; some in four-poster beds. There's a beautiful library, set up to help research into Scottish forefathers, and a restaurant: the dinners (£42) are opulent affairs with three courses broken by a cleansing sorbet. As well as wonderful walks hereabouts, the property offers golf, tennis, fishing and other activities; it also hires bikes.

**Strathtay Scottish** ( ☎ 01738-629339; www.stage coachbus.com) runs from Perth to Blairgowrie (50 minutes, about six daily). The only service from Blairgowrie to the Glenshee area is the once-daily Monday to Saturday postbus (216) to Spittal of Glenshee and Rhiedorrach, about 2 miles south of the ski centre.

# NORTHERN ABERDEENSHIRE & MORAY

North of Aberdeen, the coastal road runs up to Fraserburgh, the 'shoulder' of Scotland. From here it's a very pleasant, leisurely journey west to Inverness, via some magical fishing villages and rolling green countryside. The more direct Aberdeen to Inverness route cuts across country; both routes meet at Elgin, the genteel capital of the ancient county of Moray ('murray'). South of here, whisky-drenched Speyside awaits.

## Pennan & Around
pop 22

Tiny wee Pennan nestling at the base of cliffs is one of the gems of this part of Scotland's coast. The single street of houses in this former fishing settlement seems completely at the mercy of the grey sea; it's an unforget-table location that was immortalised in the mouse-that-roared British film classic *Local Hero*. Ironically, it was the land that caused problems in 2007, with mudslides drenching the hamlet, forcing the closure of the commu-nity's focus, the **Pennan Inn**, which, along with the village's red phonebox, featured promi-nently in the film. At the time of research it hadn't yet reopened. **Driftwood** ( ☎ 01346-561287; www.driftwoodpennan.com; Pennan 39; s/d £40/60) offers B&B or self-catering accommodation in one of the lovable harbourside cottages nearby. Rates drop if you stay more than one day.

The nearby village of **Crovie** (crivvy) is simi-larly atmospheric, and larger Gardenstown also has a pretty harbour and line of fishers' homes. The remoteness of these towns made them important harbours for the smuggling of illicit whisky.

Stagecoach Bluebird buses run from Aberdeen to Fraserburgh (£7, 1½ hours, at least hourly). Westbound buses from Fraserburgh to Banff stop at the junctions to these villages, from where it's a short but steep downhill walk.

## Banff & Macduff
pop 3991 (combined)

When you get two towns separated by noth-ing more than a bridge, in this case spanning the River Deveron, you just know they aren't going to be bosom buddies. And these two seaside twins are no exception; busy fish-ing-port Macduff and more genteel Banff have had a comical historical rivalry over the centuries. Back on speaking terms these days, they offer an excellent pair of attractions. The obliging **tourist office** ( ☎ 01261-812419; High St, Banff;

☑ Mon-Sat Apr-Oct, Mon-Sun Jul & Aug) has plenty of information about the area.

**Duff House** ( ☎ 01261-818181; www.duffhouse.com; adult/child £6.20/5.20; ☑ 11am-5pm Apr-Oct, 11am-4pm Thu-Sun Nov-Mar), in Banff, is an impressive Georgian baroque mansion designed by William Adam. Completed in 1749, it's been a hotel, hospital and POW camp and is now an art gallery housing a notable collection of paintings from the National Gallery of Scotland. Duff House hosts regular live per-formances including theatre and dance; call to find out what's on.

Not to be outdone, Macduff has the ex-cellent **Marine Aquarium** ( ☎ 01261-833369; www.macduff-aquarium.org.uk; 11 High Shore; adult/child £5.40/2.70; ☑ 10am-5pm). Rather than piranhas, it's focused solely on the Moray Firth and its various ecological zones. A large central tank houses cod, haddock and wolf fish; other tanks hold local octopi and a jellyfish display of ethereal beauty. It's a treat for kids.

There's more accommodation choice in Banff. The **Gables** ( ☎ 01261-812513; paynethe gables@aol.com; 29 Castle St; s/d £30/55) occupies a very elegant Victorian house on the main street through town. The spacious rooms have been furnished most appropriately, with elegant beds and soft off-white tones, and the wel-come is genuine.

Stagecoach Bluebird runs buses from Aberdeen (£9, hourly) to Banff and Macduff.

## Elgin
pop 20,829

At the heart of Moray, Elgin has been provin-cial capital since the 13th century. One of the country's sunniest towns, it's a sedate sort of place, very pleasant but without a great deal

---

### THE WOLF OF BADENOCH

Of all the hardman figures of medieval Scotland, few inspired as much terror as Alexander Stewart, Earl of Buchan (1343–1405), illegitimate son of the king and better known as the Wolf of Badenoch. A cruel landowner with a number of castles in the Strathspey region, he was not a man to get on the wrong side of, as the Bishop of Moray found out in 1390. When the earl ditched his wife in favour of his mistress, the bishop excommunicated him. The monk that bore the message of excommunication was thrown headfirst into a well, and the infuriated Wolf, accompanied by a band of 'wild wicked Highland men', embarked on an orgy of destruction, burning first Forres, then Elgin, to the ground, destroying the cathedral and nearby Pluscarden Abbey in the proc-ess. Amazingly, Stewart still managed to end up being buried in Dunkeld cathedral. Legend says his death occurred on a dark, stormy night. The devil came calling on a black horse and challenged him to a game of chess. The Wolf was checkmated, and the devil took his life (and soul) as his prize.

going on. The helpful **tourist office** ( ☎ 01343-542666; elgin@visitscotland.com; 17 High St; ☉ 10am-5pm Mon-Sat, plus 11am-3pm Sun May-Sep, closes 4pm Nov-Mar) is at the eastern end of the main street.

The magnificent ruins of **Elgin Cathedral** (HS; ☎ 01343-547171; admission £4.70; ☉ 9.30am-6.30pm Apr-Sep, 9.30am-4.30pm Sat-Wed Oct-Mar) are heartachingly beautiful in the afternoon sun. Built in the late 13th century and known as 'the lantern of the north', it was burned down in 1390 by the infamous Wolf of Badenoch (p901). It was rebuilt, but damaged during the Reformation and then left to crumble as the town cemetery occupied what was once its interior. The elegant Gothic lines and arches are still in evidence, and the two formidable towers are very much intact – a viewing platform sits atop one. The octagonal chapter house has also stood the test of time – look

out for the less-than-lyrical poem on a 1698 memorial here.

There are several central B&Bs; one that's handy for the tourist office and the cathedral is **Belleville** ( ☎ 01343-541515; 14 South College St; s/d £30/56), with good-tempered hosts and decent rooms in a pretty old sandstone house.

A likeable place to eat is **Xoriatiki** ( ☎ 01343-546868; 89 High St; mains £6-11; ☉ lunch & dinner Wed-Mon), which has brought an authentic taste of Greece to Elgin at competitive prices. Access is via an alleyway off the main street. For picnic fare, head to Gordon & Macphail (below).

Five miles northeast, the **Old Church of Urquhart** ( ☎ 01343-843063; www.oldkirk.co.uk; Parrandier; P ) is a wonderful place to stay in a converted church that was up for sale at the time of research; let's hope it continues as a guesthouse.

---

### BLAZE YOUR OWN WHISKY TRAIL

Visiting a distillery can be memorable, but only hard-core malthounds will want to go to more than two or three. Some are great to visit; others are depressingly corporate. The following are some recommendations.

**Aberlour** ( ☎ 01340-881249; www.aberlour.com; tours £10; ☉ 10.30am & 2pm daily Easter-Oct, Mon-Fri by appointment Nov-Mar) has an excellent, detailed tour with a proper tasting session. It's on the main street in Aberlour.

Small, friendly and independent, **Glenfarclas** ( ☎ 01807-500257; www.glenfarclas.co.uk; admission £3.50; ☉ 10am-4pm Mon-Fri Oct-Mar, 10am-5pm Mon-Fri Apr-Sep, plus 10am-4pm Sat Jul-Sep) is 5 miles south of Aberlour on the Grantown road. The last tour leaves 90 minutes before closing.

**Glenfiddich** ( ☎ 01340-820373; www.glenfiddich.com; admission free; ☉ 9.30am-4.30pm Mon-Fri year-round, 9.30am-4.30pm Sat & noon-4.30pm Sun Easter–mid-Oct) is big and busy, but handiest for Dufftown and foreign languages are available. The standard tour starts with an overblown video, but it's fun, informative and free. An in-depth Connoisseur's Tour (£20) must be prebooked. Glenfiddich kept single malt alive during the dark years.

Excellent sherry-casked malt can be found at **Macallan** ( ☎ 01340-872280; www.themacallan.com; standard tours £5; ☉ 9.30am-4.30pm Mon-Sat Apr-Oct, ring for winter hours). Several small-group tours are available (last tour at 3.30pm), including an expert one (£15); all should be prebooked. Lovely location 2 miles northwest of Craigellachie.

Getting around to some of these distilleries can be tricky. Even if you've got your own wheels, there are obvious benefits to leaving the car behind. **Heavenly Highlands** ( ☎ 01807-590499; www .heavenlyhighlands.com) runs a bespoke whisky taxi service.

**Speyside Cooperage** ( ☎ 01340-871108; www.speysidecooperage.co.uk; admission £3.20; ☉ 9am-4pm Mon-Fri) is a spot where you can see the fascinating art of barrel-making in action. It's a mile from Craigellachie on the Dufftown road.

**Spirit of Speyside** (www.spiritofspeyside.com) is a biannual whisky festival in Dufftown with a number of great events. It takes place in early May and late September; both accommodation and events should be booked well ahead.

**Gordon & MacPhail** ( ☎ 01343-545110; www.gordonandmacphail.com; 58 South St; ☉ Mon-Sat) in Elgin is one of Scotland's best whisky shops, with a wide variety on offer, as well as tempting deli produce.

During summer, there are weekly whisky nosing sessions in Dufftown on Tuesday at 8.30pm. Book on ☎ 01340-821097 or at whiskyshop@dufftown.co.uk.

Hourly buses run to Banff/Macduff (one hour), south to Dufftown (50 minutes), west to Inverness (£8.50, one hour), and southeast to Aberdeen (£9, two hours). Trains run several times daily from Elgin to Aberdeen and Inverness.

## Speyside

Beautiful Speyside is a region of rolling green hills, dark forests and sparkling streams. It's a place of particular interest to walkers and, of course, whisky lovers. There's a vast number of distilleries in a small area here, including most of the famous names of the pantheon. The Speyside style tends towards the rich, sweet and nutty; the favourite dram of many a malt-o-phile. The region is best explored by car, but the **Speyside Way** walking trail heads from the coast at Buckie along a picturesque former railway line to Aviemore in the Cairngorms (or vice versa), passing through utterly tranquil riverside scenery and with more than a few distilleries to tempt you away from the righteous path.

### DUFFTOWN
#### pop 1454

'Rome may be built on seven hills, but Dufftown's built on seven stills' claim locals. It's a good base for the area, with fine places to eat and stay, and the heady aromas of eight operational distilleries in town. It was founded only in 1817 by James Duff, fourth Earl of Fife. The friendly **tourist office** ( ☎ 01340-820501; 9a The Square; ☒ 10am-1pm, 2-5pm Mon-Sat Easter-Oct, 10am-6pm Mon-Sat, 1-6pm Sun Jul-Aug) is in the distinctive clock tower at the crossroads in the middle of town.

A top base for exploring whisky country, the **Davaar** ( ☎ 01340-820464; www.davaardufftown.co.uk; 17 Church St; s/d £35/50) has handsome, bright little rooms sporting new beds and linen, and DVD players (extensive film library downstairs). Friendly hosts offer great advice on the area and go way beyond the call at breakfast time. Garden-laid eggs, proper porridge and designer sausages feature alongside a homemade marmalade thoughtfully laced with Mortlach single malt. Guests can hire mountain bikes to explore the area.

**La Faisanderie** ( ☎ 01340-821273; The Square; set lunch/dinner £13.50/26; ☒ dinner Wed-Mon, lunch Thu-Mon) is a great place to eat, run by a local chef who shoots much of his own game, guaranteeing freshness. The interior is decorated in French auberge style with a cheerful mural and pheasants hiding in every corner. The set menu won't disappoint, but you can order à la carte as well.

Buses link Dufftown to Elgin (50 minutes, hourly). Enthusiasts run a heritage **railway** ( ☎ 01343-870429; www.keith-dufftown-railway.co.uk) between Keith and Dufftown; services operate three times a day at weekends from Easter to September.

### AROUND DUFFTOWN

The River Fiddich runs from Dufftown 3 miles before joining the Spey at attractive **Craigellachie**, on the Speyside Way. Two miles southwest, also on the Way, the charming village of **Aberlour** is worth a visit. The home of Walkers, whose buttery shortbread is seen around the world, it boasts a fine pub next to the old station. The **Mash Tun** ( ☎ 01340-881771; 7 Broomfield Sq; mains £8-14; ☒ food lunch & dinner Mon-Fri, noon-9pm Sat & Sun) is built of reassuringly solid stone and has a great line-up of real ales, plenty of local whisky, filling bar meals and wonderfully attractive, cosy rooms upstairs (single/double £55/90). Hourly buses link Dufftown, Craigellachie and Aberlour, but there is also a scenic 4-mile path from Dufftown to Aberlour, clearly waymarked.

# Highlands & Northern Islands

Scotland's vast and melancholy soul is in its northernmost reaches, a land whose stark beauty leaves an indelible imprint on the hearts of those who journey here. Mist and peat, heather and whisky, and long sun-blessed summer evenings that are the deserved reward for so many days of horizontal drizzle: it's a magical land.

Stone has its stories throughout the region. The monoliths of Lewis, ancient Skara Brae village on Orkney and the brochs of Shetland are will and testament left by their prehistoric builders; Viking graffiti, doughtily walled castles, the clan gravestones at Culloden and the broken stone of crofting communities shattered during the Clearances tell of the Highlands' turbulent history. All over rise the craggy profiles of granite hills and mountains, issuing a clarion call to hillwalking enthusiasts.

For outdoors is where you want to be up here, whatever the weather. The area lends itself to activity, from gentle woodland strolls to Hebridean cycling circuits, from sea kayaking to mountain-biking, and from diving warship wrecks to clifftop puffin-spotting. Indeed, wildlife lovers walk with foolish grins here: corncrakes call on Uist; ospreys nab trout in the Cairngorms; dolphins, seals, orcas and otters frolic in the water; and deer graze the glens. Even the domesticated beasts are distinctive, from the black Hebridean sheep to the long-horned Highland cattle. Somewhere between wild and domesticated are the locals, big-hearted and straight-talking: make it your business to get to know them.

**HIGHLANDS & NORTHERN ISLANDS**

## HIGHLIGHTS

- Channelling the ancients at prehistoric **Skara Brae** (p959), **Jarlshof** (p971) and **Callanish** (p947)

- Dipping your toes in the water at some of the world's most beautiful beaches, on **Harris** (p948) and **Barra** (p951)

- Taking on the challenge of the **Cuillin Hills** (p942), whose rugged silhouettes brood over Skye

- Experiencing the remote beauty of peaceful **Westray** (p964)

- Marvelling at the epic Highland scenery of the far northwest around **Kylesku** (p931)

- Sleeping and dining in style in **Inverness** (p920), launch pad for castles, battlefields, dolphin-watching and monster-filled lochs

| POPULATION: 276,649 | AREA: 12,041 SQ MILES | SHEEP OUTNUMBER PEOPLE IN THIS REGION BY MORE THAN 10 TO ONE |
|---|---|---|

## Activities

For outdoor-lovers, especially walkers, the Highlands are heaven. Regional tourist offices stock free leaflets, plus maps and guides covering walking, cycling and more.

### CYCLING

With stunning scenery and light traffic, cycling the Highlands is a pleasure if wind and weather aren't against you. **Sustrans** (www.sustrans.co.uk) has maps and details of various long-distance routes.

The **Fort William to Inverness Cycleway** (NCN route 78), 64 miles along the Caledonian Canal and Loch Ness, offers a super trip from Scotland's west to east coasts, much of it off-road, as is its soon-to-be-completed southern extension to Oban. The northern section of the **Lochs & Glens cycle route** (NCN route 7) originates in Glasgow and has spectacular traffic-free sections in the Cairngorms, before ending in Inverness; from there you could head on up to John O'Groats on the on-road **Aberdeen to John O'Groats Cycle Route** (NCN route 1), which continues on Orkney and Shetland. On the other side of the region, a tough but rewarding ride follows the west coast from Kyle of Lochalsh up to Ullapool and on to Durness in Scotland's northwest corner.

And there are the **islands** – Skye is ever-popular, as is the end-to-end tour of the Outer Hebrides, where south-to-north (Barra to Lewis) gives you the best chance of a following wind. Bike rental is widely available.

For mountain-biking, head to Fort William (p915) or Laggan (see Hungry Like the Wolf, p913).

### WALKING

As well as incorporating part of the **West Highland Way** (p850) and **Speyside Way** (p850), the region offers numerous possibilities for anything from a stroll to a serious trek. The Great Glen Way (p913) is a 73-mile trip from Fort William to Inverness via the Caledonian Canal and Loch Ness, and places like Glen Coe, Skye and the Cairngorms offer opportunities for walkers of all abilities.

Hillwalkers descend on the numerous Munros (peaks of 3000ft/914m or more) that dot the region; Skye's Cuillin Hills are among the toughest; Stac Pollaidh and Ben Nevis, Britain's highest mountain, are other popular ascents.

**Walk Scotland** (www.walkscotland.com) has good leaflets and a comprehensive website to get you planning.

### OTHER ACTIVITIES

Other activities include **scuba-diving**, notably at Scapa Flow in the Orkneys (p957); **rock climbing** and **mountaineering**, in the Cairngorms or Nevis Range; and **fishing**, both in rivers and the sea. The main **skiing** and **snowboarding** areas are the Cairngorms (p909), Glen Coe (p917), and Nevis Range (p915) near Fort William.

## Getting There & Around

If you've no wheels, grab a free copy of *The Highlands, Orkney, Shetland and Western Isles Public Transport Map* from a tourist office. It's a valuable resource.

### AIR

There are air connections to the Orkney and Shetland Islands from the region's main airport, Inverness, as well as from other Scottish cities. Small planes run services within those archipelagos. Stornoway, Barra and Benbecula airports allow you to fly to the Outer Hebrides, and Wick is a useful mainland airport in the far northeast.

### BOAT

Western islands ferries are mostly run by **Caledonian MacBrayne** (CalMac; ☎ 0870 565 0000; www.calmac.co.uk); see p850 for more details. For ferries to Orkney and Shetland, see p952 and p967, respectively.

### BUS

Inverness is the main transport hub, and has onward bus services connecting with ferries to the islands at Scrabster and Ullapool. **Citylink** ( ☎ 08705 50 50 50; www.citylink.co.uk) and **Stagecoach** ( ☎ 01463-239292; www.stagecoachbus.com) are the main operators; **postbuses** ( ☎ 08457-740 740; www.postbus.royalmail.com) serve remote communities.

### CAR & MOTORCYCLE

To explore some of the more remote areas consider hiring a car; it will significantly increase your flexibility. Roads are single-track in many areas, so duck into passing places when you spot oncoming traffic. It's usually cheaper to rent a car from a major city, but bear in mind that taking cars on ferries to the islands can be expensive; on the further-flung

# HIGHLANDS & NORTHERN ISLANDS

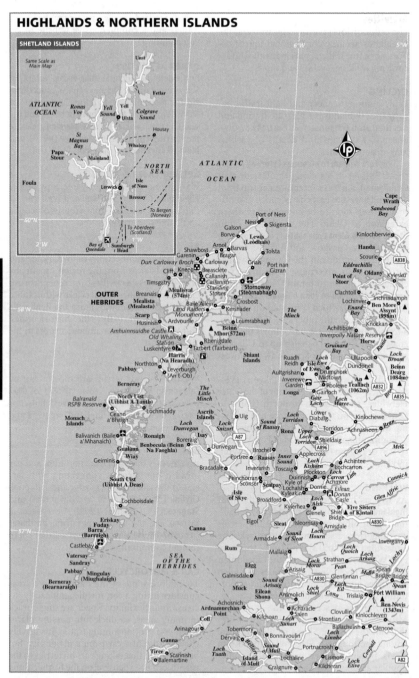

**SHETLAND ISLANDS**

Same Scale as Main Map

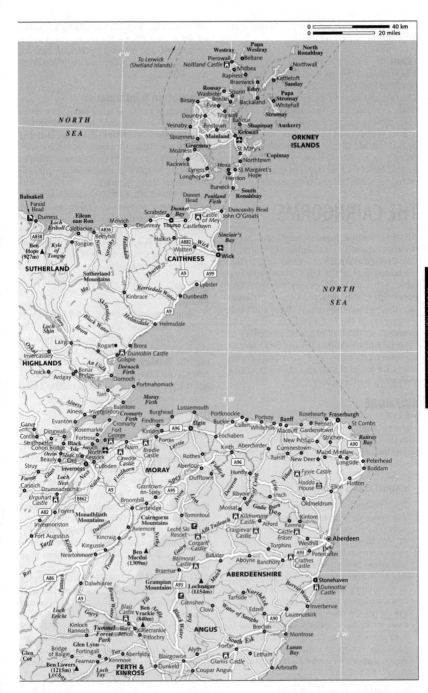

islands it can work out cheaper to hire a car for a couple of days on arrival.

**TRAIN**
The Highland railway lines from Inverness – north along the east coast to Wick and Thurso, and west to Kyle of Lochalsh – are justly famous. The West Highland railway also follows a spectacular route from Glasgow to Fort William and Mallaig. Services are run by **First Scotrail** ( ☎ 08457-484950; www.firstgroup.com /scotrail); its Highland Rover pass allows unlimited travel for four days out of eight (£68), including some bus and ferry services.

# THE CAIRNGORMS

Britain's second-highest mountain range towers over native Caledonian pine forest in this spectacular stretch of Scottish countryside contained within the UK's largest national park. A broad valley cut by the sparkling River Spey, the area presents a different face throughout the year. Walkers and birdwatchers pace the forest paths in spring and summer, on the trail of rare capercaillies or ospreys, while in winter the country's largest ski resort gets busy. The mountains themselves are magnificent, and often preserve a snowy cap well into May.

## AVIEMORE
pop 2397
The main Cairngorms settlement is no beauty, with ski-chalet architecture of debatable taste lining the crowded main street, but the surrounding area is spectacular enough to make up for it. Aviemore is the closest town to the range itself, and makes a convenient base for exploring the region, particularly if you don't have wheels.

### Orientation & Information
Aviemore is pretty much a one-street town: Grampian Rd is the main drag, with banks, eateries and the train station; dead-end Dalfaber Rd runs parallel on the other side of the tracks. Ski Rd (A951) runs from Aviemore 9 miles southeast to the Cairngorm range, passing attractions along the way.

The **tourist office** ( ☎ 01479-810363; aviemore@ visitscotland.com; Grampian Rd; ☺ 9am-5pm Mon-Sat, 10am-4pm Sun) is in the middle of town and has plenty of maps of walking routes. Across the road are ATMs and a big supermarket, while Caffe Bleu next door is one of several places offering internet access.

### Activities
#### FISHING
Fishing is wildly popular, with abundant salmon, sea trout and brown trout. The tourist office has information on permits for the River Spey and local lochs. Less demanding, the **Rothiemurchus Fishery** ( ☎ 01479-810703; Rothiemurchus Estate; per 2/8hrs £15/28, rod hire from £5) has stocked lochs that almost guarantee a bite; unsurprisingly, ospreys love the place.

#### WALKING
The Cairngorms offer excellent walking at all levels, from forest strolls to tough ascents. A moderately steep half-day hike (4½ hours return) takes you to the summit of **Cairngorm** (1245m) from the car park at the end of Ski Rd. More-advanced walkers continue south to **Ben Macdui** (1309m – Britain's second-highest peak), but this is a serious eight to 10 hours from the car park. **Guided walks** ( ☎ 01479-861261; www.cairngormmountain.org) for both these routes are available with rangers from May to September.

The **Speyside Way** (p850) follows a former railway line along the valley; stretches of it make appealing day walks, with easy return transport connections.

Another trail leads west from Aviemore SYHA and passes under the A9 into the **Craigellachie Nature Reserve**, a great place for short hikes traversing steep hills, with plenty of wildlife-spotting opportunities.

---

**CAIRNGORMS NATIONAL PARK**

The Cairngorms region, one of Scotland's most valuably diverse wildernesses, was finally granted national park status in 2003. At 1465 sq miles, Cairngorms National Park (www.cairngorms.co.uk) is the UK's largest, and encompasses the whole range as far east as Ballater in the Dee Valley. As well as harbouring a significant population of fauna, including rare bird species such as the osprey, the capercaillie and the golden eagle, its regenerated Caledonian forest and high-altitude subarctic vegetation are of particular ecological value and make the region a paradise for hikers and cyclists.

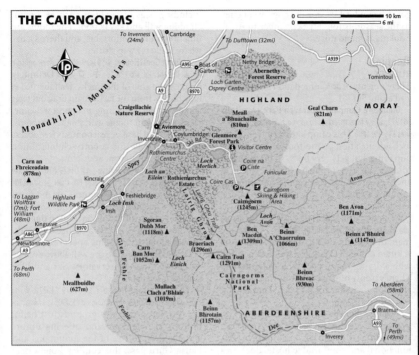

THE CAIRNGORMS

The **Lairig Ghru trail**, which can take nine hours, is a demanding 24-mile route from Aviemore over a pass to Braemar. If you're not doing the full route, it's still worth hiking the six-hour return trip up to the pass.

Scotland's notoriously changeable weather means preparing for all conditions: plenty of sustenance and liquids, a good map, compass and waterproof jacket. Always ask about conditions before heading out. In winter these walks are not to be attempted without serious equipment and experience of snowy conditions.

### SKIING
With 19 runs, **Cairngorm Mountain** ( ☎ 01479-861261; www.cairngormmountain.org; half-/1-/3-day pass £22/28/66) is Britain's largest ski area. Snow is notoriously unreliable, but when there's a fall and sunshine, there's good skiing. The season runs from December until the snow melts, typically around the end of April.

The ski area is 9 miles southeast of Aviemore. Ski-tows and the funicular (£9.25) start from the main Coire Cas car park, and are connected to the nearby Coire na Ciste

car park by free shuttle bus. You can hire gear here (starting at £15 per day) or along Aviemore's main street.

For ski or snowboard lessons, try **Ski School** ( ☎ 01479-861319; www.theskischool.co.uk; 1-day lesson from £72), at the mountain itself.

### OTHER ACTIVITIES
**Glenmore Lodge** ( ☎ 01479-861256; www.glenmorelodge .co.uk; Loch Morlich) is an impressive centre for training courses in almost any snow-, rock- or water-based activity you care to name. It offers a stratospheric level of professionalism; most courses last three to five days, with some one-day sessions. The lodge offers excellent accommodation (p910).

**G2 Outdoors** ( ☎ 01479-811008; www.g2outdoor.co.uk; half-day trips from £25) does a range of activities including canoeing, rock climbing, abseiling and mountain-biking.

**Cairngorm Sled-dog Centre** ( ☎ 07767-270526; www .sled-dogs.co.uk), about halfway between Aviemore and the ski-field, has three-dozen lovable hounds and offers half-hour sled jaunts (£50) and kennel visits to meet the dogs. The sleds have wheels, so snow isn't necessary, but it's

HIGHLANDS &
NORTHERN ISLANDS

got to be under 11°C for the dogs' wellbeing, so the season is roughly September to April. Booking is mandatory.

## Sleeping

### BUDGET

There's plenty of accommodation in Aviemore and along Ski Rd.

**Glenmore Camping & Caravan Park** ( ☎ 01479-861271; www.forestholidays.co.uk; Loch Morlich; 2-person sites £16-19; **P** ) This camp site has a wonderful lochside location at the foot of the mountain range but gets very busy, so book ahead. Midges can be a problem, but it's worth it, and there are walks, water sports and reindeer minutes away. It's 6 miles from Aviemore, along Ski Rd.

**Aviemore SYHA** ( ☎ 01479-810345; www.syha.org.uk; 25 Grampian Rd; dm £14.50; **P** 🖳 ) Where the main drag meets Ski Rd, this spacious hostel is kitted out with skiers and walkers in mind, with a drying room, pool table and internet. There's plenty of space in the dorms, and several rooms suitable for families. They let you stay out until 2am.

**Aviemore Bunkhouse** ( ☎ 01479-811181; www.aviemore-bunkhouse.com; Dalfaber Rd; dm/d/f £15/40/52; **P** ) Right next to the best pub in town, this functional and comfortable hostel does everything right. The dorms all have bathrooms, the bunks and beds are very comfy, and the kitchen's six-burner stove ensures there's room for everybody's pasta.

**Cairngorm Lodge SYHA** ( ☎ 01479-861238; www.syha.org.uk; Loch Morlich; dm/tw £16/38; 🗙 Jan-Oct; **P** ) With a cracking location in the woods above Loch Morlich, this walkers' hostel ensures that your hike starts the minute you open the front door. The standard blue-sheeted dorms are comfortable, so it's best to book ahead.

### MIDRANGE

**Kinapol Guest House** ( ☎ 01479-810513; www.kinapol.co.uk; Dalfaber Rd; s/d £30/50; **P** 🖳 wi-fi) Well into its fourth decade of quality hospitality, this sweet place has snug rooms and a motherly welcome in a quiet location just metres through the tunnel from the centre of town. The enormous green garden stretches down to the River Spey, and the mountain views are inspiring.

**Glenmore Lodge** ( ☎ 01479-861256; www.glenmore lodge.org.uk; Loch Morlich; r per person with/without bathroom £30/24; **P** 🖳 ) This training centre for outdoor activists, 6 miles from Aviemore, makes a great base, handy for walks and skiing, and

including bags of facilities such as a gym, climbing wall and kayak pool. The rooms are functional and comfortable, and there's a bar where walkers swap stories.

**Ardlogie Guest House** ( ☎ 01479-810747; www.ardlogie.co.uk; Dalfaber Rd; s/d £38/56; **P** 🖳 wi-fi) Definitely on the right side of the tracks, Dalfaber Rd is only metres from the tacky main drag but feels completely rural. Offering an upbeat welcome, views and bright rooms with small bathrooms, this is a sound base. A real bonus is free access to the local golf- and country-club facilities, including Jacuzzi, gym and sauna.

**Ravenscraig Guest House** ( ☎ 01479-810278; www.aviemoreonline.com; 141 Grampian Rd; r per person £30-40; **P** ) One of the best choices on the main drag, this friendly guesthouse with king-size beds has plenty of rooms, including ones for families, so you've always a chance of a berth. Newer motel-style rooms appeal in the annexe, and the breakfasts are well above average and served in a conservatory. Ski and bike storage is available.

**our pick** **Corrour House** ( ☎ 01479-810220; www.corrourhousehotel.co.uk; Inverdruie; s/d £55/90; 🗙 Jan–mid-Nov; **P** ) Set in spacious grounds just half a mile from Aviemore, and offering unforgettable perspectives of the mountains and Lairig Ghru pass, this country hotel offers substantial comfort in its elegant but homelike rooms. Deer graze on the grass at dawn, but it'll take a big effort to rise from the warm comfort of the beds to see them. The welcome is impeccably warm.

**The Old Minister's House** ( ☎ 01479-812181; www.theoldministershouse.co.uk; Inverdruie; s/d £55/90; 🗙 Jan-Nov; **P** 🖳 wi-fi) Right by the Rothiemurchus Centre a mile from Aviemore, this solid old house (look for the prominent deer out front) has four very luxurious and well-appointed bedrooms and a pretty garden. Your host is warmly welcoming, does a great breakfast, and will pack you some sandwiches or a more elaborate picnic on request.

## Eating & Drinking

**Cafe Mambo** ( ☎ 01479-811670; Grampian Rd; meals £6-10; 🗙 11am-1am, food noon-8.30pm; 🖳 wi-fi) Once a trendy newcomer, the Mambo now counts as a stalwart. It still does the trick, with serious portions of nachos guaranteed to calm the beast within. At night it converts seamlessly into a bar, with rosy-cheeked skiers and walkers knocking back curious cocktails or playing pool upstairs.

**Skiing-Doo** ( ☎ 01479-810392; 9 Grampian Rd; mains £6-14; ☯ noon-3pm, 5pm-late) First up against the wall when the pun police come to town (a *sgian-dubh* is the ceremonial dagger worn with a kilt), this unusual local institution is papered with jokes and memorabilia. The food impresses more by quantity than quality, but it's fun for the kids and there's a great sierra view.

**Old Bridge Inn** ( ☎ 01479-811137; 23 Dalfaber Rd; mains £8-14; ☯ lunch & dinner) The silver and bronze medallists weren't even in the stadium when the Old Bridge took the 'best pub in Aviemore' title. With a covered terrace and fire-warmed interior, it offers the addictive local Wildcat beer on tap, and serves posh pub nosh, including a pretty acceptable haggis and affordable curries.

## Getting There & Away
### BUS
Citylink travels to Edinburgh (£18.70, three to four hours, hourly) and Glasgow (£18.70, 3½ hours, hourly) via Newtonmore/Kingussie, Pitlochry and Perth, and north to Inverness (£7.10, 45 minutes, more than hourly). **Megabus** (www.megabus.com) offers discounted fares on these routes.

### TRAIN
Direct services run to Glasgow, Edinburgh (both £37.40, three hours, three to five daily) and Inverness (£9.10, 45 minutes, 10 daily, five on Sunday).

## Getting Around
Buses link Aviemore and Cairngorm (20 minutes, three to eight daily), picking up and dropping off along Ski Rd.

**Bothy Bikes** ( ☎ 01479-810111; www.bothybikes.co.uk; Ski Rd; half-/full-day rental £15/20; ☯ 9am-5.30pm), half a mile down Ski Rd, offers in-depth advice on routes.

**Strathspey Steam Railway** ( ☎ 01479-810725; www .strathspeyrailway.co.uk; round-trip ticket from £10.50; ☯ Apr-Oct & Christmas) puffs its way between Aviemore and Broomhill via Boat of Garten roughly three times a day; check the website before your visit, as the timetable is complex.

## AROUND AVIEMORE
### Rothiemurchus Estate
**Rothiemurchus Centre** ( ☎ 01479-812345; www.rothie murchus.net; Ski Rd, Inverdruie; ☯ 9.30am-5.30pm) is a mile from Aviemore. The vast family-owned property has over 50 miles of footpaths, including some particularly attractive trails through the Caledonian pine forests and around enchanting **Loch an Eilein** with its island ruin. Visitors can also opt for ranger-guided walks, Land Rover tours, and trout-fishing at the estate's fish farm or in the River Spey. Pick up the free *Activities, Maps & Walks* brochure and basic footpath maps.

### Glenmore Forest Park
Around Loch Morlich, 6 miles from Aviemore, Ski Rd passes through Glenmore Forest Park, some 8 sq miles of pine and spruce. The **visitor centre** ( ☎ 01479-861220), near steely-grey Loch Morlich, has a small forest exhibition and sells a map detailing local walks, which include the three-hour-return ascent of **Meall a'Bhuachaillie** that looms over the loch. Near the centre is the popular **Loch Morlich Watersports Centre** ( ☎ 01479-861221; www.lochmorlich.com; ☯ May-Sep), a great spot for kids of all ages to learn basic sailing, windsurfing and canoeing in placid, if chilly, waters off an artificial beach.

Nearby, the **Cairngorm Reindeer Herd** ( ☎ 01479-861228; www.reindeer-company.demon.co.uk; Glenmore; ☯ 10am-4pm) speaks for itself. Kids love these gentle antlered beasts; it's worth coinciding with a trip out to visit the herd on the hillside (11am, also 2.30pm from May to September, adult/child £9/4.50), which includes Rudolph patting and feeding opportunities. Otherwise, there are a few reindeer in the field behind the centre (adult/child £2.50/1.50). A four-hour trek with experienced herders is £25.

### Kincraig & Around
Kincraig, 7 miles southwest of Aviemore, is close to some great attractions. **Highland Wildlife Park** ( ☎ 01540-651270; www.highlandwildlifepark.org; adult/ child £10.50/8; ☯ 10am-5pm Apr-Oct, till 6pm Jul-Aug, 10am-4pm Nov-Mar), 1.5 miles south of the village, features a drive-through safari-style park. Inside are animals that once roamed wild around this country, including shaggy European bison, wolves, lynxes, stately red deer and elegantly coiffeured Przewalski's horses. If you've no car, friendly staff will drive you.

Serene **Glen Feshie** extends south from Kincraig into the Cairngorms, with a 4WD track to the head of the glen that makes for great mountain-biking. **Glen Feshie Hostel** ( ☎ 01540-651323; www.glenfeshiehostel.co.uk; dm £13; ℗ ), about 5 miles from Kincraig, is popular with hikers. Rates include bed linen.

Every couple of hours, Citylink services stop at Kincraig on their way north to Aviemore/Inverness and south to Kingussie and beyond.

## Boat of Garten

Boat of Garten is known as the Osprey Village, as these rare birds of prey nest nearby at the **Loch Garten Osprey Centre** ( ☎ 01479-831476; www .rspb.org.uk; adult/child £3/50p; ⏰ 10am-6pm Apr-Aug) in Abernethy Forest Reserve. Watch them from a state-of-the-art hide equipped with telescopes and video monitoring, and gossip about their recent mating activity; they migrate here from West Africa annually. The centre is signposted about 2 miles from the village.

You can get to Boat of Garten on the Strathspey Steam Railway (p911).

## KINGUSSIE & NEWTONMORE

pop 2392

Separated by just 2 miles of open country, these quiet one-street villages are famously fierce rivals at shinty, a tough relative of hurling where the teeth tend to fly. Kingussie's a lovely place with green grass and a tinkling stream that flexes its muscles in winter, regularly bursting its banks. Newtonmore is a little more down-at-heel but has good hostels and the excellent Highland Folk Museum.

### Sights

The **Highland Folk Museum** ( ☎ 01540-673551; www .highlandfolk.com; admission free; ⏰ 10.30am-5.30pm Apr-Aug, 11am-4.30pm Sep-Oct) is between the two villages on the edge of Newtonmore. It's a huge outdoor complex with reconstructed Highland buildings from various periods, including an entire blackhouse (traditional Highland dwelling) village built without recourse to modern technology. In summer the best feature is the staff, cheerily recreating history including displays of spinning, cobbling and schoolteaching.

The Kingussie section of this museum is closed but can be visited by appointment (phone the number above). It's hoped that its anthropological collection will be transferred to the Newtonmore site at some point.

### Activities

The **Monadhliath Mountains**, northwest of Kingussie, attract fewer hikers than the nearby Cairngorms and make an ideal destination for walkers seeking peace and solitude. During the deer-stalking season (August to October), check with the tourist office before setting out.

### Sleeping & Eating

There are hostels/bunkhouses in both villages.

**Newtonmore Hostel** ( ☎ 01540-673360; www.high landhostel.co.uk; Main St, Newtonmore; dm/d £13/30; Ⓟ ) These people should write the book *Building A Hostel in Your Back Garden for Dummies*. Compact, comfortable dorms, laundry, drying room and a cosy kitchen/lounge space with board games make this a walkers' and cyclists' favourite. You get a pound off if you arrive without a car.

**Homewood Lodge** ( ☎ 01540-661507; www.home wood-lodge-kingussie.co.uk; Newtonmore Rd, Kingussie; d £60; Ⓟ ) On the southern outskirts of Kingussie, this smart and well-priced choice is set well above the main road, offering huge views over the grassy valley to the mountains beyond. The softly coloured bedrooms (with en suite bathrooms), some with vistas, are most comfortable, and the gracious owners do dinner on request. It's walker-friendly, with a drying room.

**Hermitage** ( ☎ 01540-662137; www.thehermitage -scotland.com; Spey St, Kingussie; s/d £45/80; Ⓟ ) A block east of the main drag, this typically elegant Kingussie home offers great peace and tranquillity and a genuine welcome. The gracefully decorated rooms and flowery garden perfectly complement the elegant stone lines of the house.

**Glen** ( ☎ 01540-673203; Main St, Newtonmore; most mains £6-10; ⏰ lunch & dinner) The hit TV series *Monarch of the Glen* was filmed around Newtonmore, and this convivial local pub was the green room. The excellent food includes curries and tagine as well as more-conventional choices; the prices are more than fair and the atmosphere hearty and family-friendly, with a proper menu for kids to order from.

**ourpick Cross** ( ☎ 01540-661166; www.thecross.co.uk; Tweed Mill Brae, Kingussie; dinner £43; ⏰ dinner Tue-Sat Feb-Dec; Ⓟ 🖳 wi-fi) This marvellous restaurant-with-rooms is tucked away in a former tweed mill on Kingussie's hillside. The quirky, wonderfully cosy guest rooms (doubles £130 to £180) – some with river views, and complete with books and thoughtfully chosen Scottish CD selection – are just the place to sleep off the exemplary dinners, which present delicious contemporary Scottish cuisine complemented by warm personal service and an

---

**HUNGRY LIKE THE WOLF**

If you like your biking with a spike of adrenalin, the purpose-built trails at **Laggan Wolftrax** ( ☎ 01528-544786; www.laggan.com; Laggan; ⊗ 9.30am-5pm, to 6pm Fri-Sun) are for you. Set in forest 10 miles southwest of Newtonmore, the complex offers three tracks, one pretty gentle and one graded black double diamond, for those with plenty of suspension and a few experience scars. You can hire suitable rigs here from £20 to £35 per day, and there's a cafe to fuel up for the next circuit.

---

inspiring wine list. There are various rates that include dinner and discounts for longer or midweek stays: check the website for details.

Other options:

**Strathspey Mountain Hostel** ( ☎ 01540-673694; www.newtonmore.com/strathspey; Main St, Newtonmore; dm/d/cottage £12/30/60) Friendly owner, crackling fires, not-too-packed dorms: a good bet. Drying room, bike shed, and a separate cottage, sleeping six.

**Sonnhalde** ( ☎ 01540-661266; sonn.gh@btopenworld .com; East Tce, Kingussie; s/d to £30/54; **P** ) Noble house a block above the main street. Owner runs photography courses.

## Getting There & Away

Citylink buses stop at Kingussie and Newtonmore every two hours heading south or north to Aviemore (£6.30, 30 minutes) and Inverness (£9.70, 1¼ hours). Stagecoach also runs weekday services to Inverness via intermediate towns.

Trains, more stopping in Kingussie than Newtonmore, run to Edinburgh/Glasgow (£37.40, 2½ hours) and Inverness (£9.10, 50 minutes).

# THE GREAT GLEN

The spectacular chain of long, thin lochs stretching from Inverness to Fort William could be axe wounds, bleeding crystal-blue water. An ancient geological fault line was gouged by glaciers until the end of the last ice age, creating the majestic, humbling backdrops of Lochs Linnhe, Lochy, Oich and Ness, which are connected by the Caledonian Canal, creating a link between the east and west coasts.

## Activities

The **Great Glen Way** (www.greatglenway.com), a 73-mile walk between Fort William and Inverness via Loch Ness, is the perfect way to absorb the beauty of the landscape. It can be done in sections as day walks. At Fort William, walkers can connect with the West Highland Way.

The footpath shares some sections with the 80-mile **Great Glen cycle route** (NCN route 78) via Fort Augustus, following the canals and gravel tracks through forests. **Sustrans** (www .sustrans.org.uk) provides more details, and tourist offices have a *Cycling in the Forest* leaflet.

## FORT WILLIAM & AROUND
pop 9908

Whether you're a West Highland Wayfarer trudging contented into town, or stopping by on your way to Skye or beyond, you're bound to find yourself in Fort William at some point. On the banks of the magnificent inlet Loch Linnhe and towered over by majestic mountains, it should be a beautiful town, but an ugly bypass between the centre and the loch, and the depressing shops along the pedestrian mall tarnish it a little.

But you're not here to hang around town. Fort William styles itself 'Outdoor Capital of the UK', and there's much to do. Trot up Ben Nevis and you can look down on everyone in Britain; if downhill's more your thing, try mountain-biking or skiing at the nearby Nevis Range.

As gateway to the western Highlands and islands, Fort William's been active in promoting Gaelic; even the local tandoori restaurant proudly displays its name in the tongue.

## Orientation & Information

Fort William meanders several miles along Loch Linnhe but has a compact centre focused on its pedestrianised main street.

**Library** (High St; ⊗ 10am-8pm Mon & Thu, 10am-6pm Tue & Fri, 10am-1pm Wed & Sat) Free internet access.

**One World Internet Cafe** ( ☎ 01397-701623; 123 High St; per hr £3; ⊗ 9.15am-8pm summer, 10am-5pm winter)

**Tourist office** ( ☎ 0845 2255121; fortwilliam@visit scotland.com; 15 High St; ⊗ 9am-6pm Mon-Sat, 10am-5pm Sun Jun-Sep, 9am-5pm Mon-Sat Oct-May) Helpful. Internet access (£1 per 20 minutes).

## Sights & Activities
### WEST HIGHLAND MUSEUM

This likeable **museum** ( ☎ 01397-702169; Cameron Sq; adult/child £3/50p; ⊗ 10am-4pm Mon-Sat) has a

**HIGHLANDS & NORTHERN ISLANDS**

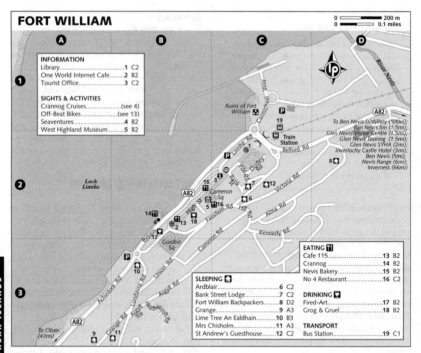

**FORT WILLIAM**

| | | |
|---|---|---|
| **INFORMATION** | | |
| Library | 1 | C2 |
| One World Internet Cafe | 2 | B2 |
| Tourist Office | 3 | C2 |
| | | |
| **SIGHTS & ACTIVITIES** | | |
| Crannog Cruises | (see 4) | |
| Off-Beat Bikes | (see 13) | |
| Seaventures | 4 | B2 |
| West Highland Museum | 5 | B2 |

To Ben Nevis Distillery (500m);
Ben Nevis Inn (1.5mi);
Glen Nevis Visitor Centre (1.5mi);
Glen Nevis Touring (1.5mi);
Glen Nevis SYHA (2mi);
Inverlochy Castle Hotel (3mi);
Ben Nevis (5mi);
Nevis Range (6mi);
Inverness (66mi)

| **SLEEPING** | | |
|---|---|---|
| Ardblair | 6 | C2 |
| Bank Street Lodge | 7 | C2 |
| Fort William Backpackers | 8 | D2 |
| Grange | 9 | A3 |
| Lime Tree An Ealdhain | 10 | B3 |
| Mrs Chisholm | 11 | A3 |
| St Andrew's Guesthouse | 12 | C2 |

| **EATING** | | |
|---|---|---|
| Cafe 115 | 13 | B2 |
| Crannog | 14 | B2 |
| Nevis Bakery | 15 | B2 |
| No 4 Restaurant | 16 | C2 |

| **DRINKING** | | |
|---|---|---|
| Fired-Art | 17 | B2 |
| Grog & Gruel | 18 | B2 |

| **TRANSPORT** | | |
|---|---|---|
| Bus Station | 19 | C1 |

To Oban (43mi)

wide-ranging collection housed in traditional wooden cases. Aspects of Highland life from birds' eggs to birching (last official lashing: 1948), from massacres to mountain rescue are touched upon. A copper plate intended for printing Jacobite money intrigues, as does the 'hidden portrait' of Bonnie Prince Charlie and two gorgeous *clarsachs* (harps).

**Ben Nevis Distillery** ( ☎ 01397-700200; www.ben nevisdistillery.com; Lochy Bridge; adult/child £4/2; ☯ tours hourly Mon-Fri, also Sat Easter-Sep, Sun Jul-Aug) gives a dram of its chocolatey, peaty whisky after the tour, which includes an entertaining video.

But better yet, head straight for the sumptuous valley scenery of Glen Nevis, with its burbling river, and steep sculpted hillsides towering above. Two miles from town, the **Glen Nevis Visitor Centre** ( ☎ 01397-705922; www .bennevisweather.co.uk; 9am-5pm Easter-Oct, 9am-4pm Nov-Easter) provides excellent walking information, enviromental guidelines, and a display on the local wildlife and history.

**WALKING**

The most obvious hike is up Britain's highest mountain, **Ben Nevis** (1344m), 5 miles east of town. Even though it's but a pimple on a global scale you should prepare thoroughly. At the top, the weather's often bad (snow-covered at least six months of the year, and foggy 70% of the time), even if it's sunny down below. Take warm clothes, a detailed map, food and water. Guides can be found via the visitor centre.

The three principal trailheads in Glen Nevis start from the car park by Achintee Farm (reached by the road through Claggan), from the Glen Nevis Visitor Centre, and from the youth hostel. The trails join, then head up to the summit and ruins of the old observatory. It takes at least 5½ hours return, but allow eight to be sure.

Other, less strenuous walks exist in the beautiful glen. From the end of the Glen Nevis road, 7 miles from town, you can follow the River Nevis gorge along a slippery path until it opens out into a spectacular mountain meadow, with the **An Steall** falls visible ahead. Or else walk part of the **West Highland Way** from Fort William to Kinlochleven via Glen Nevis (14 miles).

The **Great Glen Way** concludes in Fort William and many walkers hike the Fort

William–Gairlochy section (21 miles return) in a day. It's a lovely scenic path overlooking the River Lochy, with views to Ben Nevis.

### SKIING

There's skiing at **Nevis Range** ( ☎ 01397-705825; www.nevisrange.co.uk; 1-day pass adult/child £24/15, incl hire & lesson £39), with more than 30 runs to explore during the ski season (roughly December to April).

### OTHER ACTIVITIES

At Nevis Range, outside the ski season, there's a competition-class **mountain-bike trail** (trip £11, package with rig hire £45-90; 🕑 10.15am-4pm mid-May–mid-Sep), venue for the 2008 mountain-biking World Cup; there are also 25 miles of waymarked trails, for all standards, in the nearby forest.

For wildlife spotting, two operators are **Seaventures** ( ☎ 01397-701687; www.seaventuresscotland.com; adult/child from £10/8) and **Crannog Cruises** ( ☎ 01397-700714; www.crannog.net; adult/child £8/4), which run 45-minute trips from the pier to see seals on the islands.

## Sleeping

### BUDGET

**Glen Nevis SYHA** ( ☎ 01397-702336; www.syha.org.uk; Glen Nevis; dm/tw £17.50/46; P 💻) Set up for walkers, who can tackle Ben Nevis directly from here, this well-equipped hostel is right in the scenic glen, 2.5 miles from town. Bunks have comfortable thick mattresses, but rooms vary in size, so try to dock in a small dormitory. The spacious kitchen/dining room turns out continental breakfasts and packed lunches to fuel you for the hike.

**ourpick Mrs Chisholm** ( ☎ 01397-705548; kcolleen10@yahoo.com; 5 Grange Rd; s/d £25/40) With the warmest welcome in Fort Bill and just two fabulous rooms with loch views and stay-awhile beds, this is Fort William's budget secret (oops). Prepare for an extended stay. There's no sign – it's past the Spar supermarket and up the second flight of steps on the left.

**Bank Street Lodge** ( ☎ 01397-700070; www.bankstreetlodge.co.uk; Bank St; dm/s/d £14/25/45; P ) Boasting an excellent central location and free parking, this no-nonsense guesthouse and hostel is, indeed, a banker (a solid choice). The private rooms, all with bathrooms, are very spick and span, and, as there's no breakfast, low-priced; the bunkrooms have plenty of space, although the common areas could have more.

Also recommended:

**Glen Nevis Touring** ( ☎ 01397-702191; www.glen-nevis.co.uk; sites £6.50-10.50 plus £2.50 per adult; 🕑 mid-Mar–Oct) Two miles from town in a wonderful location at the heart of Glen Nevis, this green spot has hedges for privacy.

**Fort William Backpackers** ( ☎ 01397-700711; www.scotlands-top-hostels.com; Alma Rd; dm £13; 💻 ) Close to train and bus stations; a fun hostel with instant social life in its great lounge area.

**Ben Nevis Inn** ( ☎ 01397-701227; www.ben-nevis-inn.co.uk; dm £14; P ) Under a cracking pub at a Ben Nevis trailhead, this has no-nonsense bunks in little alcoves.

### MIDRANGE & TOP END

Fassifern Rd, just above the centre, is wall-to-wall B&Bs, as is the southern approach to town.

**St Andrew's Guesthouse** ( ☎ 01397-703038; www.fortwilliam-accommodation.co.uk; Fassifern Rd; d £56; 🕑 Feb-Oct; P ) Spread across what was once a school and headmaster's house, this genteel place sits on the hillside above the centre. Dark wood, tartan carpets and floral bedspreads combine in relaxing harmony with the building's elegant stonework and stained glass. Some rooms have excellent loch views.

**Ardblair** ( ☎ 01397-705832; www.ardblairfortwilliam.co.uk; Fassifern Rd; d £90-100; P 💻 wi-fi) More like your own in-town estate, this lovely place has a fragrant garden and wonderful views of town. There are just three rooms (book ahead), including the Pink and Blue Rooms, all of which are done out in busy florals. If your eyes need a break, check out the views again. Breakfast is a treat.

**ourpick Lime Tree An Ealdhain** ( ☎ 01397-701806; www.limetreefortwilliam.co.uk; Achintore Rd; s/d £60/100; P 🎨 💻 wi-fi) This staggeringly imaginative gallery/hotel in a former manse is a tour de force of the artistic spirit. Everything is calculated to please, from the vibrant paintings on the walls to the walk-planning lounge stocked with maps and a chart table. And the rooms – supremely comfortable, and very stylish without being showy – all have excellent bathrooms tiled deep blue. Foodies rave about the restaurant, while the gallery space, a triumph of sensitive design, does everything from serious touring exhibitions (they were packing away Goyas on last visit) to folk concerts.

**Grange** ( ☎ 01397-705516; www.thegrange-scotland.co.uk; Grange Rd; d £98-110; 🕑 Mar–mid-Oct; P ) The gorgeous antique furniture in the opulent rooms, the elegant tiered lawn surrounded by carefully tended flowering shrubs, the loch views and the country-house feel place this firmly in the boutique hotel class. The hospitality is exemplary, and the breakfast covers traditions from both sides of the pond, with pancake stacks competing with smoked haddock.

**Inverlochy Castle Hotel** ( ☎ 01397-702177; www .inverlochycastlehotel.com; Torlundy; s £350, d £410-510; P ⌨ wi-fi) This magnificently opulent hotel sits in expansive grounds below Ben Nevis, some 3 miles north of town. Fulfilling everyone's dreams of Highland luxury, it's a classic Victorian castle, with hunting trophies, log fires, a trout loch and noble old furniture. The massive rooms are furnished with formal, colourful elegance, and the restaurant is widely considered the best in the Highlands.

## Eating & Drinking

**Ben Nevis Inn** ( ☎ 01397-701227; www.ben-nevis-inn .co.uk; bar meals £8-12) Two miles from town at Achintee, a Ben Nevis trailhead, this wonderful pub looks like a Valhalla meadhall with long wooden tables and mountain-view picture window. Happy walkers congregate to down the interesting ales and reward their climb with tasty bar food – a wild-boar burger was on offer when we last visited.

**our pick Cafe 115** ( ☎ 01397-702500; 115 High St; dinner mains £11-18; ⌚ 8am-9pm Mon-Sat, 10am-4pm Sun) Pleasing punters as a cafe by day, with tasty cakes and pedestrian-strip seating, this place seamlessly converts into a smart restaurant by night, with light-coloured wooden tables boasting fresh flowers and trendy table runners. Thoughtful flavour combinations and unobtrusively benevolent service win it top marks.

**Lime Tree An Ealdhain** ( ☎ 01397-701806; www .limetreefortwilliam.co.uk; Achintore Rd; dinner mains £12-17; ⌚ lunch & dinner) Artfully and artily decorated, this gallery/hotel's restaurant has set local and visiting tongues wagging with the quality of its food. The rotating dinner menu offers delectable mains such as slow-cooked lamb with cassoulet, while lunch offers a dish of the day and a selection of open sandwiches (three-course lunch £10), which you can munch on the deck with loch views.

**Crannog** ( ☎ 01397-705589; Town Pier; mains £13-18; ⌚ lunch & dinner) Right over the sea loch like the prehistoric dwellings it's named after, this place predictably specialises in the Atlantic's bountiful harvest. Blackboard specials point the way to the day's best catch, and the round layout gives nearly everyone a memorable dinnertime view.

Also recommended:

**Nevis Bakery** ( ☎ 01397-704101; 49 High St; steak pie £1.60; ⌚ 8.30am-5.30pm Mon-Sat) Awesome steak pies, for that summit picnic.

**Fired-Art** ( ☎ 01397-705005; 147 High St; snacks £2-4; ⌚ 10am-5pm; ⌨ wi-fi) Coffee, internet, wi-fi and paint-your-own-pottery for rainy days.

**Grog & Gruel** ( ☎ 01397-705078; 66 High St; mains £5-11; ⌚ food noon-9pm) Real-ale pub with a pig theme and Tex-Mex food.

**No 4 Restaurant** ( ☎ 01397-704222; Cameron Sq; lunch mains £6-10, dinner mains £9-16; ⌚ lunch & dinner) Family-friendly stalwart with good seafood and vegie choice.

## Getting There & Away

### BUS

Citylink operates services to Edinburgh (£25.20, four hours, one direct daily) and Glasgow (£17.80, three hours, eight daily) via Glencoe (30 minutes); Inverness (£11.30, two hours, five to seven daily); Oban (£10.40, 1½ hours, two to four daily Monday to Saturday); and Portree (£22.90, three hours, four daily).

**Shiel Buses** ( ☎ 01967-431272; www.shielbuses.co.uk) runs three weekday buses to/from Mallaig (£5, 1¼ hours) via Glenfinnan (35 minutes).

Stagecoach runs to Kinlochleven (50 minutes, three to 10 daily) via Glencoe.

### TRAIN

Trains run between Fort William and Glasgow (£22.20, 3¾ hours, three to four daily) and to Mallaig (£9.20, 1½ hours, three or four daily). An overnight service heads here from London Euston (seat/sleeper £86/141, 13 hours).

From May to October consider the **Jacobite Steam Train** ( ☎ 01524-737751; www.steamtrain.info; adult/child day-return £29/16.50) from Fort William to Mallaig.

## Getting Around

Stagecoach operates 10 bus services Monday to Saturday (plus three on Sunday from June to September), between the bus station and the Glen Nevis SYHA and to the Nevis Range.

**Off-Beat Bikes** ( ☎ 01397-704008; www.offbeatbikes .co.uk; 117 High St; half/full-day hire £10/15; ⌚ daily) really knows biking, with advice, maps and three different types of bike available for hire, including for the Nevis Range course.

## GLEN COE

Even by the Highlands' lofty standards, Glen Coe is magnificent, with soaring mountains flanking heathered valleys cut by bright rivers and waterfalls. It's many people's first glimpse of the breathtaking bareness of Scotland's north, as they pass through on their way to Fort William and beyond.

Three brooding spurs, the Three Sisters, dominate the south, while the rim of the Aonach Eagach ridge, at 900m, looms in the north. Walkers challenge themselves with a variety of spectacular hikes.

Glen Coe's bloody place in history came in 1692, when the MacDonalds were murdered by the Campbells in the Glen Coe Massacre (see A Betrayal of Hospitality, below).

This is serious walking country; take maps, warm clothes, food and water. The visitor centre has useful information. There are several short walks around **Glencoe Lochan**, near the village. To get there, turn left off the minor road to the youth hostel, just beyond the bridge over the River Coe. A more strenuous hike is into the **Lost Valley**, a magical sanctuary haunted by ghosts of murdered MacDonalds. It's only a 2.5-mile round trip, but allow three hours. The walk begins from the car park at Allt-na-Reigh (on the A82, 6 miles east of Glencoe village). A great seven-hour hike leads through the Lost Valley to the top of **Bidean nam Bian** (1141m).

## Glencoe Village & Around

**pop 334**

Sixteen miles south of Fort William on the A82, this village is besieged by soaring mountains on one side and Loch Leven on the other. Small thatched **Glencoe Folk Museum** ( ☎ 01855-811664; adult/child £2/free; ⏰ 10am-5.30pm Mon-Sat May-Sep) houses a historical collection, including militaria and costumes.

About 1.5 miles from the village, on the main road, **Glencoe Visitor Centre** (NTS; ☎ 01855-811307; admission £5; ⏰ 10am-4pm Mar, 9.30am-5.30pm Apr-Aug, 10am-5pm Sep-Oct, 10am-4pm Thu-Sun Nov-Feb) has a focus on the geology, ecology and environmental issues of the valley rather than past bloodshed, although an audio-visual presentation does give the history of the massacre.

Ten miles east of the village, off the A82 at the eastern end of the glen, **Glencoe Mountain Resort** ( ☎ 01855-851226; www.glencoemountain.com) is a reasonable ski centre, and, patchy snow cover notwithstanding, offers all the facilities you need to get out on the powder.

### SLEEPING & EATING

Glencoe village and nearby Ballachulish have many B&B options.

**Red Squirrel Campsite** ( ☎ 01855-811256; sites per adult/child £7/50p; Ⓟ ) This lovely green wooded camp site is situated in a hollow between Glencoe village and the Clachaig Inn.

---

### A BETRAYAL OF HOSPITALITY

Attempting to quash Jacobite loyalties among the Highland clans, William III ordered clan chiefs to take a loyalty oath by the end of 1691. In a small show of defiance, Maclain, the elderly chief of the MacDonalds of Glen Coe, left it until the last minute to travel to Fort William but he was told that the oath could not in fact be taken there. He doubled southwards to Inveraray but swore the oath a couple of days late.

The MacDonalds had a history of cattle-rustling and had many enemies. Various machinations led to the decision to punish them as an example to other Highland clans, some of whom had not even bothered to take the oath. A company of 120 soldiers, mainly of the Campbell clan, was sent to the glen; since their leader was related by marriage to Maclain, the troops were billeted in MacDonald homes.

After enjoying 12 days of hospitality, the soldiers received the following order from Major Robert Duncanson: 'You are hereby ordered to fall upon the rebells, the McDonalds of Glenco, and putt all to the sword under seventy'.

At five in the morning on 13 February 1692, the soldiers turned on their hosts, shooting Maclain and 37 other men, women and children. Though some Campbells had warned the MacDonalds of their intended fate, a strong blizzard was sweeping the region, and many who escaped died of exposure.

There's a monument to Maclain in Glencoe village; members of the MacDonald clan gather here on the massacre's anniversary.

**Glencoe SYHA** ( ☎ 01855-811219; www.syha.org.uk; dm £16; P 🖳) A couple of miles from the village on the River Coe's northern side, this hostel sits near some of the valley's most epic mountainscapes. It's a fairly basic spot for walkers to bunk, and has the substantial bonus of the Clachaig Inn close at hand.

**Clachaig Inn** ( ☎ 01855-811252; www.clachaig.com; s/d £70/84; P 🖳) Situated amid a mighty mountainscape 2.5 miles southeast of Glencoe village, this is the archetypal walkers' haven. Three bars, pool table, real ales, live music, comfort food (bar meals £6 to £10), and bright personable rooms make this a sound bet, and one to book ahead. 'No hawkers or Campbells' says the sign.

### GETTING THERE & AWAY
Stagecoach and Citylink run regularly between Fort William and Glencoe (30 minutes); the latter also operates to/from Glasgow (£15.40, 2½ hours, eight daily).

## Kinlochleven
pop 897
At North Ballachulish take the beautiful side road running up Loch Leven to Kinlochleven. As well as excellent walking hereabouts, **Ice Factor** ( ☎ 01855-831100; www.ice-factor.co.uk; 2hr ice-climbing £20; 🕒 9am-7pm Fri-Mon, 9am-10pm Tue-Thu) is a fine facility with indoor ice-climbing and rock-climbing walls, a sauna for after, and climbing and mountaineering instruction.

The West Highland Way passes through town and walkers often stay overnight here. The excellent **Blackwater Hostel** ( ☎ 01855-831253; www.blackwaterhostel.co.uk; Lab Rd; camp sites per person £5, dm £13; P ) is set by a bright stream and has excellent dorms, all with bathrooms, and friendly folk in charge. A pool table, kitchen and plenty of space make for a friendly atmosphere. Campers have separate facilities.

**ourpick Lochleven Seafood Cafe** ( ☎ 01855-821048; most dishes £6-12; 🕒 11am-9pm, reduced hrs in winter), on the northern side of the loch, is a wonderfully simple place with absolutely delicious lobster, oysters, scallops, langoustines, crabs and more at very fair prices.

## LOCH NESS
The legend of the beastie (see Nessie, opposite) in this steely loch's brooding depths has brought Loch Ness worldwide fame, and Nessie still draws a crowd. But there are other attractions to Scotland's second-largest loch (and second deepest, at 230m); pretty Fort Augustus at its southern end is bisected by the impressive 19th-century Caledonian Canal, and the quieter eastern shore of the loch is worth exploring away from the west's heavy traffic.

## Fort Augustus
pop 508
This sweet little town sits at the southern end of Loch Ness, astride the locks of the Caledonian Canal, an unusually picturesque centrepiece flanked by grassy banks and waterside pubs. Quiet in the evenings, it's a great place to appreciate the loch without much Nessiemania.

The **tourist office** ( ☎ 01320-366367; 🕒 10am-4pm Easter-Oct) is in the central car park.

### SIGHTS & ACTIVITIES
The Fort Augustus Flight raises and lowers boats on the **Caledonian Canal** a total of 12m through five picturesque locks down the middle of town. You can watch boats being led on ropes, like obedient Labradors, through the locks; it's even more spectacular when skyscraper-like cruise liners pass through. The canal, built in the early 19th century to an original Thomas Telford design, linked Scotland's east and west coasts, ending the need for the stormy passage around the top.

The tiny **Caledonian Canal Heritage Centre** ( ☎ 01320-366493; admission free; 🕒 10am-5.30pm) has more information on the project. To get on the water yourself, **Cruise Loch Ness** ( ☎ 01320-366277; www.cruiselochness.com; adult/child £9.50/5.50) does a one-hour jaunt, leaving hourly from 10am to 4pm from March to October; there's also an evening cruise in summer.

### SLEEPING & EATING
**ourpick Morag's Lodge** ( ☎ 01320-366289; www.moragslodge.com; Bunoich Brae; dm/d £17/42; P 🖳 ) What kudos do you give a hostel that has everything? Always good, this place just got better with its new wing offering very spruce dorms and family rooms with great bathrooms. What you save on the buffet dinner (£6.50) you may spend in the bar. Comfy lounge areas, a massive kitchen and fairly impressive views round out the package. Take the Jenkins Park turning from the main road just north of town.

**Lorien House** ( ☎ 01320-366736; www.lorien-house.co.uk; Station Rd; tw/d £60/70; 🖳 wi-fi) Proving that bigger isn't necessarily better, this compact

HIGHLANDS & NORTHERN ISLANDS

---

### NESSIE

Though St Columba apparently had an encounter with a loch beast in the 6th century, the Loch Ness Monster phenomenon is really a product of the 20th century, once the A82 was completed along the western bank. That classic photo of of a dinosaur-like creature's neck emerging from the water was taken in 1934, sparking much interest, which gathered pace in the 1960s.

More recently sonar scans, underwater cameras and computer studies have resulted in disappointment for the true believers; the general conclusion has been that there is insufficient aquatic life to sustain even one sizeable reptile. Nevertheless, the number of sightings perhaps can't be put down to hysteria alone. Some scientists point to underwater currents in the loch caused by temperature fluctuations beneath the surface; currents running against the surface flow carrying objects with them can make a tree trunk, for example, appear to be swimming vigorously upstream. Another theory suggests that sturgeon, occasional visitors to Scottish rivers to breed, might have been responsible for the confusion, what with their enormous bulk and unusual head.

But the Nessie industry continues strong, churning out green monsters at a frightening rate. Locals play it up too; stories of an old angler spotting something 'that was nae fish' can still be heard in the pubs hereabouts. So best keep that camera to hand just in case.

---

and genial cottage features lovely rooms with romantic sloping-roof-and-skylight combination. Strangely, the bathrooms are large. Breakfast choices include kippers or scrambled eggs with smoked salmon.

Canalside there are a couple of pubs doing very good food. The cosy **Lock Inn** ( ☎ 01320-366302; mains £6-13;  food noon-10pm) has tasty Scottish seafood. If you want to dine on Loch Ness itself, head for the **Boathouse** ( ☎ 01320-366382; www.lochnessboathouse.co.uk; dinner mains £13-19;  lunch & dinner), in the apartment complex that once was the Benedictine abbey. The food is good-quality if unimaginative modern Scottish, but the location is wonderful.

### GETTING THERE & AWAY

Citylink buses running between Inverness (£10.20, one hour) and Fort William (£10.40, one hour) stop at Fort Augustus five to seven times daily each way. Stagecoach services on the same route are half the price but less frequent.

## Drumnadrochit

pop 813

Nessie's heartland is here, with two competing visitor centres a fixture on the tour-bus circuit although, ironically, the town itself isn't actually on the loch. But there's more to little Drumnadrochit (drum-na-drock-it) than monster madNess, with a cracking country pub and decent accommodation choices.

On the main road, the friendly **tourist office** ( ☎ 01456-459076; www.visitlochness.com;  year-round) has a useful leaflet on local walks. A fine walk-

ing location is wonderful Glen Affric, which begins 12 miles west of Drumnadrochit.

Much the better of the two neighbouring rival monster exhibits, **Loch Ness Centre** ( ☎ 01456-450573; www.lochness.com; adult/child £5.95/3.50;  9am-8pm) seeks to explain the Nessie phenomenon rather than hype it. The multilingual presentation walks you through a series of audiovisuals, including an interesting overview of the loch's ecology. The army of stuffed green monsters that confronts you at visit's end is surely more frightening than a run-in with Nessie itself.

### URQUHART CASTLE

With its sublime location overlooking Loch Ness, **Urquhart Castle** (HS; ☎ 01456-450551; admission £6.50;  9.30am-6pm Apr-Sep, 9.30am-5pm Oct-Mar) sees its fair share of tour buses. The entrance fee includes a short film and exhibition but is a little steep considering the fortress is in ruins.

The castle was repeatedly sacked, damaged and rebuilt over the centuries. It was finally blown up in 1692 to prevent Jacobites using it; what remains perches dramatically over the loch.

### SLEEPING & EATING

**Loch Ness Backpackers Lodge** ( ☎ 01456-450807; www.lochness-backpackers.com; East Lewiston; dm/d/f £14/34/51;  P  ) Offering colour and fun, this hostel is just under a mile from town (Fort William side). Accommodation is in spotless six-bed dorms, some in the barn out the back; there are also bright private rooms, a big barbecue

HIGHLANDS & NORTHERN ISLANDS

area, and two kitchens so you're not rubbing elbows. Staff make a big effort to help out in any way.

**Drumbuie Farm** ( ☎ 01456-450634; www.loch-ness -farm.co.uk; s/d £39/58; **P** ) This working farm on the edge of town is a real haven and seems far from Nessieland. Nevertheless, you've a decent chance of spotting the beast, for there are superb views down over green fields studded with sheep and Highland cattle to the loch itself. One of the bright rooms has a four-poster. The farm is on the left as you head from town towards Inverness.

**Benleva Hotel** ( ☎ 01456-450080; www.lochnesshotel .com; ☾ dinner, also lunch in summer) There's nary a Nessie in sight at this excellent pub tucked off the main road in a former manse. A rotating range of real ales and a more-than-modest malt shelf keeps things ticking over at the bar, and the meals surprise with their quality; the cod-and-monkfish stew on basmati rice was a winning special at last glimpse. Rooms (doubles £70) are also available.

### GETTING THERE & AWAY

Citylink buses running between Inverness (£6.30, 30 minutes) and Fort William (£11.30, 1½ hours) stop at Drumnadrochit five to seven times daily each way. Stagecoach services on the same route are cheaper but less frequent.

# INVERNESS
pop 44,500

By far the region's largest settlement, friendly Inverness is an important service centre for Highlanders and visitors alike, as well bring as a transport hub: you're bound to pass through at some point in your wanderings. It's taking on quite a sophisticated air these days, with posh hotels and restaurants popping up, especially along its glorious riverbank.

The River Ness, which flows from Loch Ness to the Moray Firth, is the city's chief delight, and strolling along it of a summer evening is soothingly romantic. Inverness is also a fine exploratory base: Loch Ness, the Black Isle, Culloden battlefield and Cawdor Castle are in easy reach, and you can even take a day trip to the Orkneys if time's limited.

## Information

**New City Laundry** ( ☎ 01463-242507; 15 Young St; ☾ daily) Launderette with internet access (£3 per hour).
**Public library** ( ☎ 01463-236463; Margaret St; ☾ Mon-Sat) Free internet access.

**Tourist office** ( ☎ 01463-234353; invernesstic@ visitscotland.com; Castle Wynd; ☾ 9am-5pm Mon-Sat, 10am-4pm Sun Sep-May, 9am-6pm Mon-Sat, 9.30am-5pm Sun Jun-Aug) Comprehensive with currency exchange, internet access (£3 per hour), tour and accommodation booking, and CalMac ferry office.

## Sights

On a riverside hillock, **Inverness Castle** is a johnny-come-lately lightweight compared with more ancient and muscly Highland fortifications. Finished in 1847, it's rather grand nonetheless, and its rosy walls are beautiful at sunset. It serves as the Sheriff's Court, so you'll have to break the law to get a look inside.

The delight of Inverness is strolling along the river, with its regularly spaced bouncy bridges, stately houses and peaceful parkland. Just over half a mile south of the centre, you come to the **Ness Islands**, a top picnic spot.

## Tours

Trips to the Highlands and Orkneys are popular from Inverness and can all be booked at the tourist office.

### BUS TOURS

**John O'Groats Ferries** ( ☎ 01955-611353; www .jogferry.co.uk) Runs day trips to the Orkney Islands (Orkney Bus; £49) departing 7.30am June to August.
**Puffin Express** ( ☎ 01463-717181; www.puffinexpress .co.uk) Long but comprehensive Orkney day trip plus a range of other Highlands tours.

### CRUISES

**Inverness Dolphin Cruises** ( ☎ 01463-717900; www .inverness-dolphin-cruises.co.uk; Shore St; 1½hr cruise adult/child £12.50/9; ☾ 10.30am-6pm Mar-Oct) Spot dolphins, seals and bird life; great commentary. Free pick-up from tourist office.
**Jacobite** ( ☎ 01463-233999; www.jacobite.co.uk) Various Loch Ness cruises, including Urquhart Castle and pick-up from the tourist office. Options from £16.

## Sleeping
### BUDGET

There are half a dozen hostels in Inverness.

**ourpick Bazpackers Backpackers Hotel** ( ☎ 01463-717663; baz mail@btopenworld.com; 4 Culduthel Rd; dm/d £13/32; ☐ wi-fi) Enjoying a great location near the castle and river, this cosy hostel is hard to beat with its relaxed vibe, log fire, back garden with barbecue, Ness-view dorms and thick mattresses. There's no curfew, but the ambi-

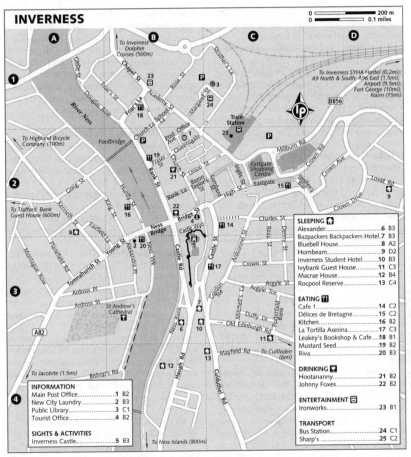

INVERNESS

**INFORMATION**
| | |
|---|---|
| Main Post Office.....................1 | B2 |
| New City Laundry...................2 | B3 |
| Public Library.........................3 | C1 |
| Tourist Office.........................4 | B2 |

**SIGHTS & ACTIVITIES**
| | |
|---|---|
| Inverness Castle.....................5 | B3 |

**SLEEPING**
| | |
|---|---|
| Alexander................................6 | B3 |
| Bazpackers Backpackers Hotel.7 | B3 |
| Bluebell House........................8 | A2 |
| Hornbeam................................9 | D2 |
| Inverness Student Hotel.........10 | B3 |
| Ivybank Guest House..............11 | C3 |
| Macrae House.........................12 | B4 |
| Rocpool Reserve....................13 | C4 |

**EATING**
| | |
|---|---|
| Cafe 1.....................................14 | C2 |
| Délices de Bretagne...............15 | C2 |
| Kitchen...................................16 | B2 |
| La Tortilla Asesina.................17 | C3 |
| Leakey's Bookshop & Cafe.....18 | B1 |
| Mustard Seed.........................19 | B2 |
| Riva.........................................20 | B3 |

**DRINKING**
| | |
|---|---|
| Hootananny...........................21 | B2 |
| Johnny Foxes........................22 | B2 |

**ENTERTAINMENT**
| | |
|---|---|
| Ironworks...............................23 | B1 |

**TRANSPORT**
| | |
|---|---|
| Bus Station............................24 | C1 |
| Sharp's....................................25 | C2 |

**HIGHLANDS & NORTHERN ISLANDS**

ence is quiet sociability rather than partytime. There's also a decent kitchen.

**Inverness Student Hotel** ( ☎ 01463-236556; www .scotlands-top-hostels.com; 8 Culduthel Rd; dm £13.50; P ꤄ wi-fi) A sociable lounge area with plenty of ordered disorder and cracking views down over the river is the centrepiece of this likeable, laid-back hostel (definitely with an 's'). Dorms vary in size but are bright and clean, albeit with thin foam mattresses. It has a kitchen and laundry service and offers organised activities. If you like an early night, this isn't really your cup of cocoa.

**Inverness SYHA** ( ☎ 01463-231771; www.syha.org.uk; Victoria Dr; dm/d £17/34; P ꤄) Offering excellent facilities and roomy dorms – although you'll be queuing to charge your phone in some

of them – this hostel is one of the SYHA's best. It has a separate kitchen and dining room to keep big groups out of the way, and offers doubles for travelling couples. Spick and span with a pine feel, it has a space-age gleaming kitchen and two lounges (one with a pool table). It's 15 minutes' walk from the train station.

### MIDRANGE

B&Bs abound; pricier options line the river, while Old Edinburgh Rd, Kenneth St and Ardconnel St are cheaper hunting grounds.

**Hornbeam** ( ☎ 01463-225655; ian.barron@btinternet .com; 12a Lovat Rd; d with/without bathroom £52/44; P ) A gentle welcome and a genuine wish to make guests feel at home awaits at this understated

B&B, one of several in the surrounding streets. The colourful, comfortable rooms, fair prices and spotless bathrooms tick every box.

**Macrae House** ( ☎ 01463-243658; www.macraehouse .co.uk; 24 Ness Bank; d £50-64; **P** ) The River Ness on a long summer evening is a wonderful thing, and this is one of the more affordable places to stay on it. Run with dry good humour, it's a welcoming spot, and tastefully decorated with modish art, leather furniture and, in one room, a mosaic bathroom. The spacious front rooms are particularly pleasing.

**Ivybank Guest House** ( ☎ 01463-232796; www .ivybankguesthouse.com; 28 Old Edinburgh Rd; s £40, d with/ without bathroom £80/60; **P** ) A noble heritage-listed building brimming with beauty and character houses this welcoming guesthouse, which boasts period rooms of great appeal and individuality, one with a four-poster bed.

**Bluebell House** ( ☎ 01463-238201; www.bluebell -house.com; 31 Kenneth St; d £70-80; **P** **⌨** wi-fi) Guests' wellbeing is top of the agenda for the bubbly couple running this commodious and relaxing guesthouse, and the place exudes a comforting vibe. The two spacious front rooms – one with a four-poster bed – command extra but worthwhile pounds, but comfort throughout is excellent, and supplementaries like DVD library and homemade whisky marmalade seal the deal.

**Alexander** ( ☎ 01463-231151; www.thealexander.net; 16 Ness Bank; s/d £55/90; **P** **⌨** wi-fi) History will record that the war on tartan started here. A big makeover has left this Georgian riverside house free to express itself, with sensitive contemporary styling enhancing noble original features. Pared-back decor and soft colours make for a soothing stay, and the welcome from both hosts and beds is top-notch. Great front rooms boast river views.

**Trafford Bank Guest House** ( ☎ 01463-241414; www .traffordbankguesthouse.co.uk; 96 Fairfield Rd; s/d £75/100; **P** **⌨** wi-fi) It's worth straining your budget to stay at this urbane B&B with nary a ceramic kitten in sight. Victorian elegance, garden tables and tasteful tartan give way to individually decorated colour-themed rooms bursting with little luxuries like iPod speaker docks, DVD players and Arran Aromatics toiletries.

### TOP END

**ourpick Rocpool Reserve** ( ☎ 01463-240089; www .rocpool.com; Culduthel Rd; d £195-365; **P** **⌨** wi-fi) A far cry from the antlers and creaky wooden staircases of most upmarket Highland hotels, this luxury boutique option is slick, modern and sexy, the perfect place to take someone you want to seduce, or re-seduce. Rooms, some with great balcony views, are stylish, striking and categorised by level of decadence; the top-of-the-scale ones have outdoor hot tubs and a sauna, but all are calculated to please and have enormous beds. A smart restaurant and cocktail bar complete the package.

## Eating, Drinking & Entertainment

**La Tortilla Asesina** ( ☎ 01463-709809; 99 Castle St; lunch £5.95, tapas £3-6; ⌚ 11am-midnight) This upbeat and energetic tapas bar ('the killer omelette') is run with an eye for authenticity and a sense of humour. A wide variety of typical Spanish snacks are on hand – try the boquerones (marinated fresh anchovies), as well as deals, events, classes and El País to keep up with the news from Madrid. Lots of fun.

**Leakey's Bookshop & Cafe** ( ☎ 01463-239947; Greyfriars Hall, Church St; snacks £3-6; ⌚ 10am-4.30pm Mon-Sat) This wonderful bookshop smells not of the venerable volumes lining its appealing interior but of home-baking and scrumptious soups, courtesy of the upstairs cafe, where you can keep reading as you graze.

**Délices de Bretagne** ( ☎ 01463-712422; 6 Stephen's Brae; light meals £4-7; ⌚ 9am-5pm Mon-Sat, 10am-5pm Sun) With proper French croissants, crêpes both sweet and savoury, and delicious tartlets and sandwiches, this smart art nouveau–inspired cafe makes a welcome break from the busy shopping streets.

**Riva** ( ☎ 01463-237377; 4 Ness Walk; meals £9-14; ⌚ lunch & dinner Mon-Sat) On the banks of the Ness, this sophisticated and elegant Italian choice is a chic destination for great pasta combinations; tortellini tossed with poached chicken and artichoke hearts was one that impressed. The desserts, variety of breads and warm service round out the experience.

**Kitchen** ( ☎ 01463-259119; www.kitchenrestaurant .co.uk; 15 Huntly St; lunch £5.95, mains £10-15; ⌚ lunch & dinner) A contented buzz and positive attitude emanate from this striking glass-fronted riverside restaurant. The busy open kitchen turns out imaginative combinations of flavours that usually work and encourages forgiveness when it doesn't because the setting and staff are superb.

**Mustard Seed** ( ☎ 01463-220220; www.themustard seedrestaurant.co.uk; 16 Fraser St; 2-course lunch £5.95, mains £11-19; ⌚ lunch & dinner) This visionary conversion of a riverside church has kept locals bright-eyed and well fed for years now. It combines with aplomb a lofty open-plan dining area, flowered balcony, cordial service and smart Med-Scottish cuisine.

**ourpick** **Hootananny** ( ☎ 01463-233651; www.hootananny.co.uk; 67 Church St; ☒ 11am-late) A real mix of people patronise this huge former bank, where three floors offer something for everyone. Young Celts in love, sturdy octogenarian couples and curious backpackers dance to Scottish folk and ceilidh bands downstairs, cooler cats prowl the upstairs rock bar and top-floor armchair chill-out area. There's even Thai food on hand during the day.

Other recommendations:

**Cafe 1** ( ☎ 01463-226200; 75 Castle St; mains £9-16; ☒ lunch & dinner Mon-Sat) Classy, imaginative food and champers by the glass, opposite the castle.

**Johnny Foxes** ( ☎ 01463-236577; cnr Bridge & Bank Sts) Cheery riverside watering hole where sauced-up locals take the odd swim.

**Ironworks** ( ☎ 0871-7894173; www.ironworksvenue .com; 122b Academy St) Live bands two or three times a week; the main place when someone big is in town.

## Getting There & Away
### AIR
Ten miles east of town, **Flybe/Loganair** ( ☎ 0871-700 2000; www.flybe.com) has flights to London, Edinburgh, Orkney, Shetland and Stornoway; an **Aer Arann** (www.aerarann.com) route to Dublin, and services to London and other English cities run by easyJet, Ryanair, Eastern Airways, Flybe and Flybmi. Check www.whichbudget .com for details. Local set-up **Highland Airways** ( ☎ 0845 4502245; www.highlandairways.co.uk) flies to Benbecula and Stornoway.

### BUS
Stagecoach runs to Aberdeen (£9, 3¾ hours, hourly). Citylink runs from Edinburgh/ Glasgow (both £21.20, four hours, hourly) via Perth, Pitlochry and Aviemore; Fort William (£11.30, two hours, five to seven daily); Portree (£18.60, 3¼ hours, three daily); Thurso (£16.50, 3½ hours, four daily); and Ullapool (£9.80, 1¼ hours, two daily Monday to Saturday). **National Express** ( ☎ 08450 130130; www.nationalexpress.com) operates buses to/from London (£40, 13 hours, one daily). **Megabus** ( ☎ 08705 50 50 50; www.megabus.com) offers discounted fares on Edinburgh/Glasgow/Perth/ London routes.

**Orkney Bus** ( ☎ 01955-611353; www.jogferry.co.uk) and **Orkney Express** ( ☎ 01463-239292; www.stagecoach .com) are services that connect with Orkney ferries and on to Kirkwall (see p952).

### TRAIN
Destinations include Edinburgh (£38.20, 3¼ hours, six direct daily), Glasgow (£38.20, 3½ hours, three direct daily, more changing in Perth), Aberdeen (£23.50, 2¼ hours, five to 10 daily), London (£149, eight hours, daily) and Thurso (£15.30, 3¾ hours, two to three daily).

The Kyle of Lochalsh line (£17.30, 2½ hours, four daily Monday to Saturday, two on Sunday) is one of Britain's great scenic journeys.

## Getting Around
### TO/FROM THE AIRPORT
Airport trains should arrive by 2009; until then, Stagecoach bus 11 runs from Falcon Square in Inverness (£1.90, 20 minutes, twice hourly). A taxi costs around £15.

### BICYCLE
There are several rental outlets, including **Highland Bicycle Company** ( ☎ 01463-234789; www .highlandbikes.com; 16a Telford St; 1-day hire £12).

### BUS
Local Stagecoach buses go as far afield as Nairn, Forres, Culloden battlefield and Cawdor. The Roverbus (£6) gives unlimited travel for one day around the region.

### CAR
As well as the big boys there's **Sharp's** ( ☎ 01463-236684; www.sharpsreliablewrecks.co.uk; 1-day hire from £25), an excellent set-up based at both airport and railway station.

## AROUND INVERNESS
### Culloden

> They…came running on our Front line like
> Troops of Hungry Wolves, and fought with Intrepidity
>
> *Government soldier*

A name resonant with despair for many Scots, Culloden field was the arena for a short, brutal battle in 1746 that saw the defeat of Bonnie Prince Charlie and sounded the death knell for the Scottish clan system. Some 1200 Highlanders, already exhausted after a draining overnight march, died in the engagement with the British Army, under the Duke of Cumberland's command. His post-victory crackdown was fearsome.

Five miles east of Inverness, the forlorn 49-hectare moor where the conflict took place has scarcely changed. The site, with its many markers and memorials, is always open and provides a reflective place to ponder the finality of this battle, the last to be fought on British soil.

The smart new **visitors centre** (NTS; ☎ 01463-790607; admission £10; ☯ 9am-6pm Apr-Oct, 10am-4pm Nov-Mar) presents detailed information on the lead-up to the Culloden field battle, with perspective from both sides. An innovative film places you right in the middle of the mayhem of the battlefield, and a wealth of other audio presentations must have kept Inverness' entire acting community in business for weeks. A tenner still seems steep, but it includes a good but temperamental audio guide to the battlefield itself.

Bus 12 runs every couple of hours from Strothers Lane in Inverness to the battlefield. More-frequent buses (12 and 12C) run to the Cumberland Stone, a 10-minute walk. Parking is £2 at the site.

## Cawdor Castle

This entertaining **castle** ( ☎ 01667-404401; www.cawdorcastle.com; adult/child £7.90/4.90, gardens only £4; ☯ 10am-5.30pm May–mid-Oct), whose title Macbeth inherits in Shakespeare's play, actually had nothing to do with the Scottish king, who lived in the 11th century, as it was built three centuries later. Shakespeare took his tale from 15th-century chronicles that were a little liberal transcribing names and locations from earlier texts. The central tower is original, but the wings are 17th-century additions. The castle is still inhabited, opulently furnished and casually includes treasures, like Dalí cartoons (in the Tower Room). Explanatory notes are written in humorous style by a former earl of Cawdor.

The grounds are impressive and you can have a round of casual golf (£9) or fish for salmon. In summer the castle hosts plays, concerts and other cultural happenings; check its website for details.

Bus 12 runs from Strothers Lane in Inverness to Cawdor village via Culloden. The Cawdor Tavern in the village is an excellent pub for a meal or a whisky.

## Brodie Castle

Set in 70 hectares of parkland, **Brodie Castle** (NTS; ☎ 01309-641371; adult/child £8/5; ☯ 10.30am-5pm Apr, Jul & Aug, 10.30am-5pm Sun-Thu May, Jun & Sep) has several highlights, including an early-19th-century library, which has more than 6000 dusty, peeling books. There are some wonderful clocks, and a 17th-century dining room with extravagant mythological ceiling carvings. There's also a selection of fine 19th- and 20th-century Scottish art. The present structure was built in 1567, with many extensions added over the years. Entrance is by guided tour.

The castle is 8 miles east of Nairn. Stagecoach runs here from Inverness (45 minutes, hourly), via Culloden.

## Fort George

Muscular 18th-century **Fort George** (HS; ☎ 01667-462777; admission £6.70; ☯ 9.30am-6.30pm Easter-Sep, to 4.30pm Oct-Mar) guards the entrance to the Moray Firth and, with its numerous bastions and gun ports, does so most effectively. The austere but elegant symmetry of the Georgian buildings within its solid walls is striking, but more fun are the views from the ramparts; there's a sporting chance of spotting bottlenose dolphins frolicking in the firth. The best place is near the chapel, one of whose stained glass panels features a bagpipe-playing angel.

It's off the A96 about 11 miles northeast of Inverness. Bus 11 runs from Falcon Sq in Inverness.

## Black Isle

This intriguing peninsula juts between the Moray and Cromarty Firths and merits exploration for its historic villages, majestic vistas and dolphin-watching. It's reached from Inverness via the **Kessock Bridge**.

Near the main road, **Black Isle Brewery** ( ☎ 01463-811871; www.blackislebrewery.com; Munlochy; ☯ 10am-6pm Mon-Sat, plus 11.30am-5pm Sun Apr-Sep) is a small organic brewery that has a lofty and well-deserved reputation for the excellence of its various ales. Visitors get shown around the tiny production line for free and are given a wee taste.

In Rosemarkie, **Groam House Museum** ( ☎ 01381-620961; www.groamhouse.org.uk; High St; admission by donation; ☯ 10am-5pm Mon-Sat, 2-4.30pm Sun Easter & May-Oct, 2-4pm Sat & Sun Oct-Apr) has a superb collection of engraved Pictish stones and information aplenty on Pictish sites in the region. Budding bards can try out a Pictish harp.

Cromarty, an attractive town at the peninsula's northeastern end, was the home of Hugh Miller, a pioneering palaeontologist, and has 18th-century **Cromarty Courthouse** ( ☎ 01381-600418; Church St; admission £5; ☻ 10am-5pm Apr-Oct, call in winter), a worthwhile community history museum and recreated courtroom, where even innocent readers may quail under the judge's beady-eyed gaze.

Cromarty Firth is an oil-rig construction and maintenance centre, but that doesn't deter the playful dolphin population. **Ecoventures** ( ☎ 01381-600323; www.ecoventures.co.uk; Bank St) is highly recommended, with daily trips in inflatable boats costing £22/16 for adults/children; a highlight is being able to listen to the dolphins' weird language via a hydrophone.

Stagecoach shuttles run from Inverness to Rosemarkie (30 minutes, roughly hourly Monday to Saturday, two on Sunday); most (none on Sunday) continue onto Cromarty (55 minutes).

# EAST COAST

As you work your way north along the scimitar blade of the east coast, the desolation that the Clearances created becomes apparent and the staggering emptiness of the Highlands is in evidence. The road traverses the Cromarty and Dornoch Firths and heads north along wild and pristine coastline; the northern segment, Caithness, has a proud Viking heritage that persists in its place names. With an interior dominated by the vast, mournful Sutherland mountain range, the only interruptions en route are the small and pleasant towns moored precariously on the coast's edge.

## Getting Around

Citylink runs regular bus services from Inverness to Wick, stopping at most towns on the A9 and A99 along the way, before cutting across to Thurso. Stagecoach buses follow the coast between Wick and Thurso, via John O'Groats. Trains follow the coast to Wick and across to Thurso.

## TAIN & AROUND

Scotland's oldest royal burgh, Tain is a proud sandstone town that rose to prominence as pilgrims descended to venerate the relics of St Duthac, who is commemorated by the 12th-century ruins of **St Duthac's Chapel**, and St Duthus Church. In the church grounds is entertaining **Tain Through Time** ( ☎ 01862-894089; Tower St; admission £3.50; ☻ 10am-5pm Mon-Sat Apr-Oct), a heritage centre with a colourful and educational display on Duthac, King James IV and key moments in Scottish history. Another building focuses on the town's fine silversmithing tradition. Admission includes an audioguided walk around town.

On Tain's northern outskirts, excellent **Glenmorangie Distillery** ( ☎ 01862-892477; www.glenmorangie.com; tours £2.50; ☻ 9am-5pm Mon-Fri, plus 10am-4pm Sat & Sun Jun-Aug), pronounced with emphasis on the second syllable, produces a fine light malt, which is subjected to a number of different cask finishes for variation. Last tour is 90 minutes before closing.

The A9 crosses Dornoch Firth. Alternatively, from Ardgay at the firth's head, a small road leads to Croick, the scene of notorious evictions during the 1845 Highland Clearances. Refugee crofters from Glencalvie scratched their tragic messages on the eastern windows of Croick Church.

From Ardgay you can follow the Kyle of Sutherland, which leads after 4.5 miles to Scotland's last castle, dating from 1917, which now houses the extraordinary **Carbisdale Castle SYHA** ( ☎ 01549-421232; www.syha.org.uk; Culrain; dm £18; ☻ Mar-Oct; 🅿 🖳). Good enough to house the exiled Norwegian royal family, this opulent place offers first-rate hostelling, with grand salons, more statues than backpackers, views and, of course, a ghost. Booking is advised; it's a popular group destination. Sweeping **Bonar Bridge** then crosses the head of the firth to rejoin the A9 just before Dornoch.

## DORNOCH & AROUND
pop 1206

Scotland's last executed witch perished in a vat of boiling tar in Dornoch in 1722, but these days locals are more likely to spoil you to death. Serene in sandstone and within striking distance of some fine beaches and golf courses, Dornoch is a popular escape from Inverness.

At the time of research, the tourist office had closed, and the sheriff court on the square was handing out brochures during working hours (9am to 5pm, Monday to Friday).

Consecrated in the 13th century, **Dornoch Cathedral** is an elegant Gothic edifice with an interior softly illuminated through modern

---

### THE RIGHT SIDE OF THE TRACKS

Scotland has some unusual hostels, and **Sleeperzzz.com** ( ☎ 01408-641343; www .sleeperzzz.com; Rogart Station; dm £12; ☺ Mar–mid-Nov) in wee Rogart is one of them, set in three caringly converted railway carriages parked up in a siding by the station. It's on the A839, which cuts inland 7 miles north of Dornoch but is also easily reached by train on the Inverness–Wick line (10% discount if you arrive this way) and has cute two-person dorms, kitchenettes and tiny lounges. There's a hearty local pub that does food, and beautifully lonely Highland scenery in the vicinity.

---

stained-glass windows. By the western door is the sarcophagus of Sir Richard de Moravia, who died fighting the Danes at the battle of Embo in the 1260s. Until he met his maker, the battle had been going rather well for him; he'd managed to slay the Danish commander with the disattached leg of a horse that was to hand.

## Sleeping & Eating

**Trevose Guest House** ( ☎ 01862-810269; jamackenzie@ tiscali.co.uk; Cathedral Sq; s/d from £35/52; ☺ Mar-Sep) First impressions deceive at this lovely stone cottage right by the cathedral; it looks compact, but actually boasts very spacious rooms with significant comfort and well-loved old wooden furnishings. Character oozes from every pore of the place, and a benevolent welcome is a given.

**Dornoch Castle Hotel** ( ☎ 01862-810216; www .dornochcastlehotel.com; Castle St; s/d £70/113, superior/ deluxe d £168/213; Ⓟ ▣ wi-fi) This 16th-century former bishop's palace makes a wonderful place to stay, particularly if you upgrade to one of the superior rooms, which have views, space, malt whisky and chocolates on the welcome tray, and, in some cases, four-poster beds; the deluxe rooms are unforgettable. The pub has a roaring fire, real ale and fine bar meals (£7 to £10); the attractive garden restaurant (dinner mains £17 to £20) serves fancier fare.

**2 Quail** ( ☎ 01862-811811; www.2quail.com; Castle St; dinner £35; ☺ dinner Tue-Sat May-Sep, Fri & Sat Oct-Apr) This impressive two-person show is an intimate little restaurant-with-rooms on the main street. The menu, served in a quail-sized din-ing room, changes nightly and features classy French-inspired dishes using classic British produce. The tasteful rooms (singles/doubles £100/120) are full of old-world comfort, with sturdy metal bedframes, plenty of books and plump duvets. Travellers staying here have access to wi-fi and a delightful downstairs guest lounge.

## Getting There & Away

Citylink and Stagecoach have four to five daily bus services to/from Inverness (£9, 1 hour) and Thurso (£14, 2¼ hours).

## DUNROBIN CASTLE

A mile north of Golspie is **Dunrobin Castle** ( ☎ 01408-633177; www.dunrobincastle.co.uk; adult/child £7.50/5; ☺ 10.30am-5.30pm Mon-Sun Jun-Aug, 10.30am-4.30pm Mon-Sat, noon-4.30pm Sun Apr-May & Sep–mid-Oct), the largest Highland dwelling (187 rooms), dating from the 13th century. Most of the elaborate fairy-tale architecture that greets you at the end of a memorable driveway is a result of a French chateau-style expansion in 1841, but the building is better known for the pitiless first Duke of Sutherland, who cleared 15,000 people from the north of Scotland while residing here.

Only 22 rooms are on display, with hunting trophies much to the fore. The museum offers an eclectic mix of archaeological finds, natural-history exhibits, more non-PC animal remains and an excellent collection of Pictish stones found in Sutherland. The formal gardens host impressive falconry displays two to three times a day.

## HELMSDALE

### pop 861

Surrounded by hills whose gorse explodes mad yellow in springtime, this sheltered fishing town, like many spots on this coast, was a major emigration point during the Clearances and also a booming herring port. Internet and tourist information is at **Strath Ullie Crafts** ( ☎ 01431-821402; ☺ 9am-5.30pm Mon-Sat Apr-Oct, 10am-4.30pm Mon-Sat Nov-Mar) on the harbour.

**Timespan** ( ☎ 01431-821327; www.timespan.org.uk; Dunrobin St; adult/child £4/2; ☺ 10am-5pm Mon-Sat & noon-5pm Sun Easter-Oct) has an impressively revamped display covering local history (including the 1869 gold rush), and Barbara Cartland, late queen of romance novels, who was a Helmsdale regular. There are also local art exhibitions, a geology garden and a cafe.

Overlooking the town, the **Emigrants statue** is a memorial to the Clearances and the resulting diaspora of Scots around the world. The statue of a kilted man and his family is certainly anatomically accurate, answering the 'What's worn under the kilt?' question.

Plenty of TLC and hard work went into converting **Helmsdale Hostel** ( ☎ 01431-821636; www .helmsdalehostel.co.uk; Stafford St; dm/tw/f £16.50/40/60; ☻ Apr-Oct) from a grim official hostel to a colourful, spacious, comfortable budget base. The dorm berths are mostly cosy single beds rather than bunks, and the rooms with private bathrooms are great for families. The lofty kitchen/lounge space has a wood stove and good kitchen.

There are several B&Bs in town (including on the little harbour), but the historic **Bridge Hotel** ( ☎ 01431-821100; www.bridgehotel.net; Dunrobin St; s/d £70/120; ☐ wi-fi) is the smartest place. Proud rather than furtive about its Highland heritage, it displays a phalanx of antlers, even on the key fobs. But the rooms don't have the expected patina of age; they have wonderfully plush fabrics and a smart contemporary feel. The downstairs bar and restaurant hum with good cheer and relaxed hospitality; check out the replica of Britain's biggest landed salmon.

The best food's there at the Bridge, but legendary **La Mirage** ( ☎ 01431-821625; 7 Dunrobin St; mains £6-10; ☻ noon-8.45pm), a restaurant created in homage to Barbara Cartland by the larger-than-life late owner, is a medley of pink flamboyance, faded celebrity photos and showtunes. The meals aren't gourmet – think chicken kiev – but the fish and chips (also available to take away) are tasty, and it can be a lot of fun, darlings.

# CAITHNESS

Scotland's northeastern tip is a very distinct region whose Viking heritage has left it more akin to the Orkneys and Shetlands than the rest of the mainland. It's full of both Norse remnants and older prehistoric traces. The coast consists of green cliffs and bright gorse patches dropping abruptly to the seas; harbours that flourished on the herring trade nestle at their base. Inland, the lonely bogland is a bird haven.

## Helmsdale to Wick

This route boasts several Celtic sites. From Latheron, follow the A9 to Achavanich, wedged between Loch Rangag and Loch Stemster, then double back on the road to Lybster to the 40 or so **Achavanich Standing Stones**.

Just beyond Lybster, a turn-off leads to the **Grey Cairns of Camster**, 4 miles northwest of the A99. Dating from between 4000 BC and 2500 BC, the burial chambers are in two stony

---

### THE HIGHLAND CLEARANCES & CROFTING

The wild and empty spaces up in these parts of the Highlands are among Europe's least populated zones, but this wasn't always so. Ruins of cottages in the most desolate areas are mute witnesses to one of the most heartless episodes of Scottish history: the Highland Clearances.

Farmers once used land granted by the local chief in exchange for a tithe and occasional conscription of able-bodied men for clan military service. After Culloden, however, the king banned private armies, and new laws made the clan chiefs actual owners of their traditional lands, often vast tracts of territory. With the prospect of unimagined riches allied to a depressing failure of imagination, the lairds decided that sheep were more profitable than agriculture, and proceeded to evict tens of thousands of farmers from their lands. The Clearances forced these desperate folk to head for the cities in the hope of finding work, or to emigrate to the Americas or southern hemisphere. Those who chose to pursue farming were marginalised into whatever narrow or barren bits of land they could subsist on; this became known as crofting. It was always precarious, as rights were granted on a year-by-year basis, so at any moment a crofter could lose not only the farm but also the house they'd built on it.

The economic depression of the late 19th century meant many couldn't pay their rent. This time, however, they resisted expulsion, instead forming the Highland Land Reform Association and their own political party. Their resistance led to several of their demands being acceded to by the government, including security of tenure, fair rents and eventually the supply of land for new crofts. Crofters now have the right to purchase their farmland and recent laws have abolished the feudal system, which created so much misery.

mounds rising from an evocatively desolate stretch of moor.

The **Hill o'Many Stanes**, a bit north of the Camster turn-off, consists of 22 rows of small (foot-high) stones fanning outwards, significance unknown, and dating from around 4000 years ago. Nearer Wick at Ulbster, the **Cairn o'Get** is a quarter of a mile off the A99, and then a 2-mile walk. Steps opposite lead down to a small, picturesque harbour.

Get a feel for Caithness at small **Dunbeath Heritage Centre** ( ☎ 01593-731233; www.dunbeath -heritage.org.uk; adult/child £2/free; 10am-5pm Easter-Oct, 11am-3pm Nov-Mar), which has a stone carved with runic graffiti, and a display on the work of Neil Gunn, whose wonderful novels evoke the Caithness of his boyhood.

### Wick
**pop 7333**

More gritty than pretty, Wick has been down on its luck since the collapse of the herring industry. It was once the world's largest fish port for the 'silver darlings', but when the market dropped off after WWII, job losses were huge: the town has never really recovered.

This story is traced at **Wick Heritage Museum** ( ☎ 01955-605393; www.wickheritage.org; 18-27 Bank Row; adult/child £2/50p; 10am-5pm Mon-Sat May-Oct, last entry 3.45pm), whose vast interior covers all aspects of the herring industry and Wick life in general, as well as exhibiting local art.

Wick is a transport hub: Flybe/Loganair flies between Edinburgh and Wick, and on to the Shetlands. **Eastern Airways** ( ☎ 01652-680600; www.easternairways.com) flies to Aberdeen.

Citylink operates four daily buses to/from Inverness (£16.50, three hours) and Thurso (40 minutes), and Stagecoach runs to John O'Groats (40 minutes, up to five daily Monday to Saturday), connecting with the Orkney passenger ferry.

Trains service Wick from Inverness (£15.30, 4¼ hours, two to three daily).

### John O'Groats & Around
**pop 512**

A car park surrounded by tourist shops, John O'Groats offers little to the visitor beyond a means to get across to Orkney; even the pub has been shut for a while now. Though it's not the northernmost point of the British mainland (that's Dunnet Head), it still serves as the endpoint of the 874-mile trek from Land's End in Cornwall, a popular if arduous route

for cyclists and walkers, many of whom raise money for charitable causes.

The **tourist office** ( ☎ 01955-611373; 10am-5pm Apr-Oct) is the best thing about the place, with its fine selection of local novels and books about Caithness and the Highland Clearances.

Two miles east, **Duncansby Head** provides a more solemn end-of-Britain moment with a small lighthouse and 60m cliffs sheltering nesting fulmars. From here a 15-minute walk through a sheep paddock yields spectacular views of the sea-surrounded monoliths known as **Duncansby Stacks**.

Stagecoach runs to John O'Groats from Thurso and Wick. See p952 for Orkney ferries from here and Gills Bay, 3 miles west.

### Castle of Mey

Once a residence of the Queen Mother, this is more home than **castle** ( ☎ 01847-851473; www .castleofmey.org.uk; adult/child £8/3; 10.30am-5pm May-Jul & mid-Aug–Sep, last entry 4pm), 6 miles west of John O'Groats on the A836. The exterior may seem grand, but inside it feels domestic and everything is imbued with the character of the late Queen Mum: from a surprisingly casual lounge area with TV showing her favourite show (*Dad's Army*, since you asked) to a photo of the king in 1943 that's lovingly inscribed 'Bertie'. All the in-jokes are explained by staff who worked for the lady. It's 6 miles west of John O'Groats.

### Dunnet Head

Turn off 8 miles east of Thurso to reach the most northerly point on the British mainland, dramatic Dunnet Head, which banishes tacky pretenders with its majestic cliffs dropping into Pentland Firth. There are majestic views of the Orkneys, flopping seals and nesting seabirds below, and a lighthouse built by Robert Louis Stevenson's granddad. Just west, Dunnet Bay offers you one of Scotland's finest beaches, backed by high dunes.

# NORTH & WEST COAST

This rugged coastline, Scotland's most memorable corner, boasts fjordlike inlets, soaring mountains and mirrorlike lochs festooned with waterlilies. The landscape here is the strong silent type, with brooding cliffs, lonely beaches, gravitas and majestic appeal.

It's best seen starting from the northeast (this corner is still part of Caithness), as the scenery builds to a climax around the Assynt ridge before you descend into charming Ullapool, where you can relax and process what you've seen.

Banks and petrol stations are few and far between, so check funds and fuel before setting out.

## Getting Around
Public transport is patchy. Getting to Thurso or Ullapool is easy, but beyond, bus services are infrequent or nonexistent. Renting a car is a good option. Hitching is common, and easy.

## THURSO
pop 7737

Britain's most northerly mainland town, Thurso makes a handy overnight stop if you're heading west or across to Orkney. There's a pretty town beach, riverbank strolls and not a great deal else. But look out for **Caithness Horizons**, a new visitors centre and museum that was being developed in the town hall at time of research.

There's first-rate **surfing** on the nearby coast, particularly on the eastern side of town, directly in front of Lord Caithness' castle and Brimms Ness. Pack a drysuit. For more on surfing see p125.

Ferries cross from Scrabster, on Thurso's outskirts, to Orkney.

## Information
**Library** (Davidsons Lane; ⏰ 10am-6pm Mon & Wed, 10am-8pm Tue & Fri, 10am-1pm Thu & Sat) Free internet access.

**Tourist office** ( ☎ 01847-892371; thurso@visitscotland .com; Riverside Rd; ⏰ Mon-Sat 10am-5pm Apr-Oct)

## Sleeping
**Sandra's Backpackers Hostel** ( ☎ 01847-894575; www .sandras-backpackers.ukf.net; 24 Princes St; dm/d £12/32; ℗ 🖳 wi-fi) A byword for backpacker excellence, Sandra's was awash with free facilities when some hostels still had you scrubbing floors before checkout. Sporting an excellent kitchen, it offers free internet and wi-fi, a help-yourself continental breakfast, laundry and downstairs chip shop. Dorms, mostly four-berthers, have their own bathrooms and are spotless.

**Orcadia Guest House** ( ☎ 01847-894395; 27 Olrig St; s/d £20/40) This old and central budget favourite

has been doing no-frills, value-packed B&B for decades. Simple, comfortable rooms share bathrooms; if it's full, the owners will send you around the corner to their daughter at 11 Duncan St, where similar price-is-right accommodation is available.

**Waterside Guest House** ( ☎ 01847-894751; www .watersidehouse.org; 3 Janet St; s/d £25/44). This straight-up guesthouse is easy to find (turn left just after the bridge coming into town), has parking oustide, and comfortable beds in well-priced rooms. Breakfast choices include egg-and-bacon rolls, or takeaway if you've got an early ferry.

**Murray House** ( ☎ 01847-895759; www.murray housebb.com; 1 Campbell St; s/d £30/60; ℗ ) This solid choice on a central corner gives a good first impression with a genuine welcome and continues with new carpets, smart rooms with solid wooden furniture, an appealing lounge space and the option of an evening meal, all at very traveller-friendly prices.

**Pentland Hotel** ( ☎ 01847-893202; www.pentland hotel.co.uk; Princes St; s/d £45/80; 🖳 wi-fi) This chunky hotel has a useful central location and, though its exterior is borderline ugly, excellent rooms, spacious and colourful, thoughtfully arranged public areas, and staff who seem to enjoy what they're doing. The restaurant and bar are also worth a visit.

## Eating & Drinking
**Le Bistro** ( ☎ 01847-893737; 2 Traill St; lunch £5-7, dinner mains £9-16; ⏰ lunch & dinner Tue-Sat) Less sophisticated than formerly, this eatery buzzes with chatter on weekend evenings as locals of all ages chow down on its simple meat and carb creations. What it does, it does well; the respectably sized steaks come on a sizzling platter and service has a smile.

**Holborn Hotel** ( ☎ 01847-892771; 16 Princes St; bar meals £7-9, mains £9-16; 🖳 wi-fi) Thurso's trendy place to eat and drink has both bar and restaurant meals, and has added a welcome variety to the town's sometimes earthy drinking scene. The food features informal but tasty concoctions like monkfish tagliatelle. The outdoor area is perfect for fleeting warm weather; inside is a snazzy bar at which to swill cocktails.

**Ferry Inn** ( ☎ 01847-892814; Scrabster; mains £8-22; ⏰ breakfast, lunch & dinner) Near the ferry dock in Scrabster, this traditional stone pub has rather ugly extensions, but these house the busy restaurant. Why's it busy? Because it's good. It specialises in steaks – pick your size – and local haddock and lobster; big windows offer harbour perspectives. Cheaper bar meals (£6 to £9) are downstairs, along with a pool table.

### Getting There & Around

Citylink runs to Inverness (£16.50, 3½ hours, four daily) via Wick. Stagecoach runs to John O'Groats and Wick (45 minutes) four to six times daily (no Sunday service). There are trains from Inverness (£15.30, 3¾ hours, two to three daily). It's 2 miles from the train station to the ferry port at Scrabster (see p952 for details of Orkney ferries); buses run from Olrig St.

## WEST FROM THURSO

Leaving Thurso, the A836/838 snakes 80 winding miles to Durness through the north coast's heather-patched hills and dramatic cliffs. Ten miles west of Thurso is the **Dounreay nuclear power station**, which was the first in the world to supply mains electricity and is currently being decommissioned. The clean-up is planned to be finished by 2025; it's still a major employment source for the region.

**Bettyhill** is a crofting community named after the countess of Sutherland, who built the settlement for tenants evicted from Strathnaver, part of the vast family estate. Its **tourist office** ( ☎ 01641-521342; 11am-4pm Mon-Sat Apr-Oct) has a small cafe (mains £6) that does simple food, including popular weekend fish and chips. In an old church nearby, **Strathnaver Museum** ( ☎ 01641-521418; www.strathnavermuseum .org.uk; adult/child £2/free; 10am-1pm & 2-5pm Mon-Sat Apr-Oct), tells the sad story of the Clearances; there's an 8th-century cross in the graveyard. Just west, an enormous stretch of white sand flanks the River Naver as it meets the sea.

### Tongue & Around

The wonderful beach at **Coldbackie** is overlooked by **Watch Hill viewpoint**. Two miles further on is **Tongue**, overlooked by the gaunt 14th-century ruins of **Castle Varrich**. The welcoming **Tongue Hotel** ( ☎ 01847-611206; www .tonguehotel.co.uk; s/d from £55/90; P 🖳 wi-fi) offers cosy, recently renovated rooms in a former hunting lodge, and has Highlands restaurant fare and decent bar meals.

In a wonderful spot right by the causeway across the Kyle of Tongue, a mile west of town, **Tongue SYHA** ( ☎ 01847-611789; www.syha .org.uk; dm £14; Mar-Oct; P ) has clean, comfortably refitted dorms, some with views, a decent kitchen and cosy lounge. The helpful warden has plenty of local advice.

For a drink with locals, hit the charismatic public bar in the bowels of the Tongue Hotel, but for food, aim for the **Craggan Hotel** ( ☎ 01847-601278; mains £6-13; lunch & dinner) at Melness. Cross the kyle west of town, and turn immediately right; the hotel is 2 miles up this road. There, you'll find smart, formal service and a menu ranging from exquisite burgers (£6.50) to classy game and seafood dishes, presented beautifully. The wine list's not bad for a pub either.

From Tongue it is 30 miles to Durness – take the causeway across the Kyle of Tongue or the beautiful old road that climbs up to the head of the kyle. The road crosses a desolate moor to the northern end of **Loch Hope**. Beyond Loch Hope, **Heilam** has stunning views out over **Loch Eriboll**, Britain's deepest sea inlet.

## DURNESS & AROUND

### pop 353

The scattered village of Durness is strung out along sea cliffs, which rise from a series of lovely beaches blessed with white sands and clear, if chilly, water. The **tourist office** ( ☎ 01971-511259; Mon-Sat year-round, plus Sun Jun-Aug) has plenty of information on the area.

### Sights

A path leads down to gaping **Smoo Cave**, a wide cavern at the east end of town. From the vast main chamber, you can head through to a smaller flooded cavern where a waterfall sometimes cascades from the roof. From here you can take a **boat trip** (adult/child £3/2; 11am-4pm Apr-May & Sep, 10am-5pm Jun-Aug) across to explore a little further into the interior.

John Lennon spent childhood days around Durness. There's a **memorial** to him near the cave.

Durness' beautiful **beaches** include Rispond to the east, Sargo Sands below town and Balnakeil to the west; the sea offers **scuba-diving** sites complete with wrecks, caves, seals and whales. At **Balnakeil**, less than a mile beyond Durness, a craft village occupies what was once an early-warning radar station. A walk along the beach to the north leads to **Faraid Head**, where you can see puffin colonies in early summer.

## CAPE WRATH

Though its name actually comes from the Norse word for 'turning point', there is something daunting and primal about Cape Wrath, the northwesternmost point of the British mainland, crowned by a lighthouse and standing close to the seabird colonies of **Clo Mor**, Britain's highest coastal cliffs. Getting to Cape Wrath involves a **boat** (☎ 01971-511376) ride across the Kyle of Durness (return £5, 10 minutes) connecting with an optional **minibus** (☎ 01971-511343) running 11 miles to the cape (return £9, 40 minutes). Ring before setting out to make sure the ferry is running; it leaves from Keoldale pier, a couple of miles southwest of Durness, and runs about eight times daily from Easter to September.

South of Cape Wrath, **Sandwood Bay** boasts one of Britain's most isolated beaches. It's about 4.5 miles north of the end of a track from Blairmore (approach from Kinlochbervie), or you could walk south from the cape (allow eight hours) and on to Blairmore.

## Sleeping & Eating

**Sango Sands Oasis** ( ☎ 01971-511262; sites per person £4.50; ☺ Apr-Oct) You couldn't imagine a better location for a camp site: great grassy areas on the edge of cliffs descend to two lovely sand beaches. Facilities are good and very clean.

**Lazy Crofter Bunkhouse** ( ☎ 01971-511202; www .durnesshostel.com; dm £14; ☺ Easter-Nov; 🖳 wi-fi) Run out of Mackays, this is Durness' best budget accommodation, offering inviting dorms, a sociable shared table for meals and board games, and a great wooden deck with sea views.

**our pick Mackays** ( ☎ 01971-511202; www.visit mackays.com; d £100-110; ☺ Easter-Nov; 🖳 wi-fi) You feel you're literally at the top corner of Scotland here; this is where the road turns 90 degrees. But no matter whether you're heading east or south, you'll go far before you find a better place to stay than this family-run haven of Highland hospitality. With big beds and soft fabrics, it's a romantic spot, but what impresses more than anything is the warm-hearted personal service. The restaurant (mains £9 to £16) presents local seafood and robust meat dishes.

**Loch Croispol Bookshop** ( ☎ 01971-511777; 2 Balnakeil; light meals £3-6; ☺ 10am-5pm Mon-Sat, 10am-4pm Sun) A mile west of Durness, this family-friendly bookshop-cafe is part of a craft village that brought peace and love to a former nuclear early-warning station in the 1960s. It does a decent fry-up, plunger coffee, salads and other simple snacks, as well as stocking plenty of books on Sutherland.

## DURNESS TO ULLAPOOL

Perhaps Scotland's most spectacular road trip, the 69 miles connecting Durness to Ullapool is a scenic feast, almost too much to take in.

A wide heathered valley gives way to rockier country studded with small lochs; gorse-covered hills preface the magnificent rugged ridge of Assynt, punctuated by its glacier-scoured mountains, including ziggurat-like Quinag, memorably distinctive Suilven, and much-climbed Stac Pollaidh. It's no wonder the area has been dubbed a 'geopark'.

From **Kylesku**, where a snaking bridge heads over Lochs Glencoul and Glendhu, the **Statesman** ( ☎ 01971-502345; adult/child £15/5; ☺ daily Apr-Sep) runs leisurely trips to see seals plus the 213m-drop of **Eas a'Chual Aulin**, Britain's highest waterfall. Other trips run to the curiously remote Kerrachar Gardens. By the pier, the **Kylesku Hotel** ( ☎ 01971-502231; www.kyleskuhotel .co.uk; s/d without bathroom £40/70, with bathroom £60/94; ☺ Mar-mid-Oct; 🅿 ) has a variety of rooms – the separate, motel-style ones with views are the best – a library of guidebooks, and excellent seafood in its sociable bar (lunch and dinner, bar meals £8 to £14) and restaurant (two-course dinner £24.50).

Not far south of Kylesku, a 30-mile detour on the narrow B869 rewards with spectacular views and fine beaches. From the lighthouse at **Point of Stoer**, a one-hour cliff walk leads to the **Old Man of Stoer**, a spectacular sea stack. On this stretch is the **Clachtoll Beach Campsite** ( ☎ 01571-855377; www.clachtollbeachcampsite.co.uk; sites £8-12 plus £1 per person; ☺ Apr-Sep), a great coastal spot, and the **Achmelvich Beach SYHA** ( ☎ 01571-844480; www.syha.org.uk; Achmelvich; dm £14; ☺ Apr-Sep), a whitewashed cottage set beside a great beach at the end of a side road. There's a summer chip shop nearby, otherwise bring your own supplies; it's a 4-mile walk from Lochinver. Ullapool–Lochinver buses take you to the hostel on request. The hostel closes between 10am and 5pm.

## Lochinver
pop 639

The spectacular scenery eases into a shel-tered bay holding the bustling fishing port of Lochinver. The approachable **tourist office** ( ☎ 01571-844373; lochinver@visitscotland.com; Main St; ⏰ 10am-5pm Mon-Sat Easter-Oct, also 10am-4pm Sun Jun-Aug) has leaflets on hill walks in the area.

There are several B&Bs; for magnifi-cent vistas head a mile around the bay to Baddidarrach, which looks back at Lochinver and the magnificent bulk of Suilven behind. Here, **Veyatie** ( ☎ 01571-844424; www.veyatie-scotland.co.uk; 66 Baddidarrach; d £60; ⏰ Jan-Nov; **P** 🖳 wi-fi), at the end of the road, has perhaps the best views of all, as well as sweet rooms, a little conservatory and a grassy garden.

**ourpick Albannach** ( ☎ 01571-844407; www.thealbannach.co.uk; s/d/ste incl dinner from £200/260/340; ⏰ Mar-Dec; **P** 🖳 wi-fi), nearby, is an indulgent place set in spacious grounds studded with fruit trees. Roomy lodgings decorated with elegant flair, inspiring panoramas, and wonderful dinners using organic ingredients and well-selected local produce (£50 for nonguests) combine to make it a special spot.

## Achiltibuie & Around

The curious rock formations around **Knockan** are produced by older geological layers rising above younger ones. The best place to see this phenomenon is at **Inverpolly Nature Reserve**, which has the peaks of Cul Mor (849m), Stac Pollaidh (613m) and Cul Beag (769m). There's a three-hour walk up **Stac Pollaidh** (Stac Polly) from the car park at Loch Lurgainn.

**ourpick Summer Isles Hotel** ( ☎ 01854-622282; www.summerisleshotel.co.uk; lunch/dinner £25/52, bar meals £6-16; ⏰ Apr-Oct; **P** 🖳 wi-fi), beyond Loch Lurgainn, at Achiltibuie, is a very special place indeed, with wonderfully snug rooms (singles/doubles from £110/140) – some are suites in separate cottages – cracking views, a wee pub with convivial outdoor seating and a restaurant with a stratospheric reputa-tion for seafood. It's the perfect spot for a romantic getaway.

## ULLAPOOL
pop 1308

The pretty port of Ullapool is one of the most alluring Highlands spots, a wonderful desti-nation in itself as well as a gateway for the Western Isles. Offering a row of whitewashed cottages arrayed along the harbour and special views of Loch Broom and its flanking hills, the town has a very distinctive appeal.

Ullapool served as an eviction point dur-ing the Clearances, with thousands of Scots watching the loch recede behind them as the diaspora cast them across the world.

### Information

**Tourist office** ( ☎ 01854-612486; ullapool@visit scotland.com; Argyle St; ⏰ daily Jun-Sep, Mon-Sat Apr-May & Oct, Mon-Fri Nov-Mar)

**Ullapool Bookshop** ( ☎ 01854-612356; Quay St; ⏰ 9am-6pm Mon-Sat, 10am-4pm Sun) Good books and internet access.

**Ullapool Laundry** ( ☎ 01854-613123; 7a Latheron Centre; ⏰ Mon-Sat) Service washes for muddied walkers.

**Ullapool Library** ( ☎ 01854-612543; Mill St; ⏰ 9am-5pm Mon-Fri, plus 6-8pm Tue & Thu, closed Mon & Wed during holidays) Free internet access.

### Sights & Activities

Set in a converted Thomas Telford church, **Ullapool Museum** ( ☎ 01854-612987; 7 West Argyle St; adult/child £3/50p; ⏰ 10am-5pm Mon-Sat Apr-Oct) relates the pre-, natural and social history of the town and Lochbroom area with a particular focus on the emigration to Nova Scotia and other places; there's a genealogy section if you want to trace roots.

Walking apart, Ullapool's main activity is boat trips to the picturesque, remote Summer Isles. **Seascape Expeditions** ( ☎ 01854-633708; www.sea-scape.co.uk; adult/child £28.50/20) zips you out there in a rigid inflatable boat on a fun two-hour jaunt; **Summer Queen** ( ☎ 01854-612472; www.summerqueen.co.uk; ⏰ Apr-Sep) runs a similar route, but in a more leisurely four hours. In summer, the ferry company CalMac runs day trips to Lewis and Harris. Both trips run from the harbour near the ferry dock.

### Sleeping

There are lots of B&Bs in Ullapool but it's worth reserving ahead in summer.

**Ullapool SYHA** ( ☎ 01854-612254; www.syha.org.uk; Shore St; dm £14-16; ⏰ Mar-Oct) You've got to hand it to the SYHA; it has chosen some very sweet locations for its hostels. This is as close to the water as it is to the town's best pub; about four seconds' walk. The front rooms have harbour views but the busy dining area and little lounge are also good spots for con-templating the water.

**Ceilidh Clubhouse** ( ☎ 01854-612103; West Lane; r per person £18-20; **P** ) Opposite the Ceilidh Place,

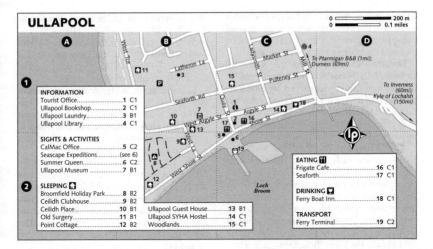

# ULLAPOOL

| | | 0       200 m |
| --- | --- | --- |
| | | 0       0.1 miles |

**INFORMATION**
Tourist Office..........................1 C1
Ullapool Bookshop..................2 C1
Ullapool Laundry.....................3 B1
Ullapool Library.......................4 C1

**SIGHTS & ACTIVITIES**
CalMac Office..........................5 C2
Seascape Expeditions............(see 6)
Summer Queen.......................6 C2
Ullapool Museum ..................7 B1

**SLEEPING**
Broomfield Holiday Park...........8 B2
Ceilidh Clubhouse...................9 B2
Ceilidh Place..........................10 B1
Old Surgery...........................11 B1
Point Cottage.........................12 B2

Ullapool Guest House............13 B1
Ullapool SYHA Hostel............14 C1
Woodlands............................15 C1

**EATING**
Frigate Cafe..........................16 C1
Seaforth...............................17 C1

**DRINKING**
Ferry Boat Inn........................18 C1

**TRANSPORT**
Ferry Terminal.......................19 C2

this is run as an occasional theatre, as well as no-frills accommodation for walkers, travellers, and the hotel's own staff. A big building, the Clubhouse has hostel-style rooms with sturdy bunks and basin. Though showers and toilets are a little institutional, the big bonus is that rooms are private: if you're woken by snores, at least they'll be familiar ones.

**Woodlands** ( ☎ 01854-612701; www.ullapoolbandb .com; 1a Pulteney St; d £44; ☼ May-Sep; **P** ) With just two comfortable rooms sharing a bathroom, this place should be booked ahead; effervescent hosts mean it's a great bet. The breakfast is memorable; they make marmalade, jams and bread and smoke their own fish out the back.

**Old Surgery** ( ☎ 01854-612520; www.oldsurgery.co.uk; 3 West Tce; d £56) There are no lurking scalpel-wielding sawbones here, just a fine welcome and some excellent rooms. It's worth paying the extra few pounds to bag room 1 or 2 (£65), each of which has big bay windows with super water vistas, tables to sit at and contemplate them from, extra berths for kids, and a shared balcony.

**Point Cottage** ( ☎ 01854-612494; www.pointcottage .co.uk; 22 West Shore St; d £64; ☼ Mar-Oct; **P** ) A haven of good taste, this courteous and welcoming B&B has a great headland location – even the back rooms have water views. It's one of those shorefront cottages you've already admired if you arrived by ferry, and it'll feel comfy for both hedonists – smoked fish for breakfast – and walkers, with plenty of maps and advice.

**our pick Ceilidh Place** ( ☎ 01854-612103; www.the ceilidhplace.com; 14 West Argyle St; d £100-136; **P** 🖳 wi-fi) This celebration of Scottish culture is one of the more unusual and delightful places to stay in the Highlands. That's culture with a capital 'c': we're talking literature and traditional music, not tartan and Nessies. Rooms go for character rather than modern bathrooms or conveniences, and come with a selection of books personally chosen by Scottish literati, eclectic artwork and nice little touches like hot-water bottles. Best is the sumptuous guest lounge, with sofas, chaises longues and an honesty bar. Downstairs is a bookshop, and streetside bar-cafe with a sun-soaking outdoor seating; the false note here is struck by the vaguely disappointing restaurant fare.

Other recommendations:

**Broomfield Holiday Park** ( ☎ 01854-612020; www .broomfieldhp.com; tent sites £9-13; ☼ May-Oct) Great grassy headland location very close to centre. Midge-zapping machines are in action.

**Ullapool Guest House** ( ☎ 01854-613126; www .ullapoolguesthouse.co.uk; West Argyle St; r per person £25-30; 🖳 ) Former hostel being converted at time of research. New en suites and central location; worth investigation.

**Ptarmigan B&B** ( ☎ 01854-612232; North Rd; d £44; **P** ) Superb vistas even by Ullapool's lofty standards. A mile from the centre; friendly host, great breakfast.

## Eating & Drinking

Ullapool's eating choices are limited.

**Frigate Cafe** ( ☎ 01854-612969; Shore St; mains £6-10; ☼ 9am-9.30pm) A popular venue for porridge and coffee, then teas and ice cream as the

HIGHLANDS & NORTHERN ISLANDS

day progresses, this waterfront spot becomes a bistro in the evenings, sporting an unusual but appetising menu of smoked fish, delicious pies and nourishing blackboard specials.

**Seaforth** ( ☎ 01854-612122; cnr Quay & Shore Sts; bar meals £6-12; ☺ food served noon-10pm) Family-friendly and always packed, this big establishment in the heart of town does good-value bar meals and takeaway fish and chips downstairs, and pricier but more-peaceful bistro fare upstairs, with serene harbour views.

**our pick** **Ferry Boat Inn** ( ☎ 01854-612366; Shore St) Known as the FBI, this is to Ullapool what the castle is to Edinburgh. Though it wasn't doing food when we last popped in, the pub still had the same upbeat atmosphere and impressive harbourside perspectives from its cosy interior. Once the kitchen gets going, it should be good, as the folk from the Frigate are running the place these days.

### Getting There & Around

Citylink has buses from Inverness (£9.80, 1¼ hours, two daily Monday to Saturday) linking with the ferry to Stornoway on Lewis (person/car £15.30/75, 2¾ hours, two or three daily Monday to Saturday).

## ULLAPOOL TO KYLE OF LOCHALSH

Though these next towns are not so far apart on the map, it's a long and spectacular journey of some 130 miles between them along the winding coastal roads if you take the most scenic route. Eleven miles south of Ullapool, the **Falls of Measach** spill 45m into the spectacularly deep and narrow Corrieshalloch Gorge. A wobbly suspension bridge provides superb views of the thundering cataract. Near here, the A832 turn-off is the first of several scenic deviations via the coast.

If you're in a hurry to get to Skye, head inland on the A835 (towards Inverness) and catch up with the A832 further down, near Garve.

### Gairloch & Around

pop 1061

The A832 weaves between lochs into Gairloch, peacefully scattered waterside. It's popular in summer with lots of places to stay and family-friendly activities. The **tourist office** ( ☎ 01445-712130; Auchtercairn; ☺ daily Easter-Sep, Mon-Sat Oct-Easter) has info on local walks. **Gairloch Heritage Museum** ( ☎ 01445-712287; www.gairloch heritagemuseum.org.uk; Auchtercairn; adult/child £3/50p;

☺ 10am-5pm Mon-Sat Apr-Sep, 10am-1.30pm Mon-Sat Oct) tells of life in the western Highlands and includes a typical crofting cottage. **Gairloch Trekking Centre** ( ☎ 01445-712652; www.gairlochtrekking centre.co.uk; ☺ Fri-Wed Mar-Oct) offers pony treks in the ample grounds of a local estate.

Six miles north, subtropical **Inverewe Garden** (NTS; ☎ 01445-781200; adult/concession £8/5.25; ☺ 9am-6pm Apr-Oct, 9.30am-4pm Nov-Mar) uses Gulf Stream warmth to grow Mediterranean and Japanese plants, among others. The cafe provides a good pit stop and has great cakes.

The **Old Inn** ( ☎ 01445-712006; www.theoldinn.net; d £89; **P** ) is a historic coaching inn nestled by the river and lovely old bridge, making the beer garden an ideal spot for a real ale or malt. Rooms are cosy with dark-wood furniture and drop sharply in price in low season. Bar meals use local seafood to great effect (mains £6 to £14).

### Torridon

Turning onto the A896 at Kinlochewe, the road follows Glen Torridon, an unforgettably scenic journey along a river overlooked by the rugged peaks of Beinn Eighe (1010m) and Liathach (1055m). The road meets the sea at Torridon, where the small **Countryside Centre** (NTS; ☎ 01445-791221; adult/child £3/2; ☺ 10am-5pm Apr-Sep) offers displays on the area's flora and fauna, including a short audiovisual display and, down the road, a deer paddock and museum.

**Torridon SYHA** ( ☎ 01445-791284; www.syha.org.uk; Torridon; dm £14; ☺ Mar-Oct; **P** 💻 ) is a homely building in a magnificent location near the Countryside Centre, and feels wonderfully far from civilisation.

**our pick** **Torridon** ( ☎ 01445-791242; www.thetorridon .com; standard s/d from £120/240; ☺ Mar-Dec; **P** 💻 wi-fi) is a lavish Victorian shooting lodge, which has a romantic lochside position overlooking the peaks, with Liathach looming impossibly large opposite. Standard rooms are swish, but pricier master rooms will make you feel gloriously decadent. Friendly staff can organise any number of activities on land or water. Part of the same set-up, the adjacent Torridon Inn offers motel-style rooms (doubles £82) and a welcoming bar serving meals.

### Applecross

This remote settlement feels like an island retreat, partly because of its isolation, and partly because of the magnificent views of Raasay and the hills of Skye that set the pulse racing, particularly at sunset. On a clear day it's an unforgettable place, but the tranquil atmosphere isn't quite the same when the camp site and pub fill to the brim in school holidays.

There are two ways in from the A896; the more scenic of the two is the epic **Bealach na Bà pass** (the southern of the two turn-offs), which goes up to the top of the hill and down again, offering breathtaking switchback turns and memorable views back down the valley and south down the coast.

The hub of the spread-out community is the **Applecross Inn** ( ☎ 01520-744262; www.applecross .uk.com; Shore St; mains £7-13; ☺ food noon-9pm; P ), which has a perfect shoreside location for a sunset pint, a wide variety of food, mostly daily blackboard specials and rooms with a view (singles/doubles £70/100). Above it the **camp site** ( ☎ 01520-744268) offers green grassy plots, compact little wooden cabins, a friendly B&B in the yellow house at the end ( ☎ 01520-744284; r per person £25), and a good cafe.

Postbuses run to Applecross Monday to Saturday from Torridon, from where you can head on to Kinlochewe. Get off at Shieldaig for another bus to Strathcarron, where trains run to Inverness and Kyle of Lochalsh.

## Plockton
pop 378

There's something distinctly tropical about idyllic little Plockton, a filmset-like village with palm trees, whitewashed houses, and a small bay dotted with islets and hemmed in by green-fuzzed mountains. It's a delightfully endearing place made famous as a location for the TV series *Hamish Macbeth*. It's on the tour bus circuit these days, but once evening comes, things settle into an easy tranquillity.

**Calum's Seal Trips** ( ☎ 01599-544306; www.calums -sealtrips.com; adult/child £7/4.50) gets you out onto the water to see the seals, which congregate en masse outside the harbour.

### SLEEPING & EATING
**Plockton Station Bunkhouse** ( ☎ 01599-544235; mickcoe@btinternet.com; dm £12; P ) Airily set in the one-time train station (the current one is opposite), this sweet little hostel has cosy four-bed dorms, garden, and kitchen/lounge with plenty of light and good perspectives over the frenetic comings and goings (joke)

of the platforms below. The owners also do B&B (doubles £40) next door.

**Shieling** ( ☎ 01599-544282; www.lochalsh.net/shieling; d £52; ☺ Easter-Oct) Slap-bang by the sea, this characterful B&B is surrounded by an expertly trimmed garden and has two carpeted rooms with views and big beds. Next door is a historic thatched blackhouse.

**our pick Plockton Hotel** ( ☎ 01599-544274; www .plocktonhotel.co.uk; Harbour St; s/d £55/110, cottage d £60; ☐ wi-fi) This is one of those classic Highland spots that manages to make everyone happy, whether it's thirst, hunger or fatigue that brings you knocking. The assiduously tended rooms are a delight, with excellent facilities and thoughtful touches like bathrobes. Those without water view can console themselves with more space and a balcony with rock-garden perspectives. Just down the way, the cottage offers simpler comfort. The cosy bar (or wonderful beer garden on a sunny day) is a memorable place for a pint, and food ranges from sound-value bar meals to seafood platters and lobster.

### GETTING THERE & AROUND
Plockton is 6 miles north of Kyle of Lochalsh. Trains (15 minutes) connect the two.

## KYLE OF LOCHALSH
pop 739

Before the controversial bridge, Kyle of Lochalsh was Skye's main ferry port. Visitors now tend to buzz through town, but Kyle has hit back with its own intriguing attraction.

The **tourist office** ( ☎ 01599-534276; ☺ 9.30am-5pm Mon-Fri, 10am-4pm Sat & Sun Easter-Oct) is beside the seafront car park. Next to it are Scotland's best-decorated public toilets, which include a small collection of whisky bottles – it's a real must-pee.

At the tourist office you can book for the **Seaprobe Atlantis** ( ☎ 0800-9804846; www.seaprobe atlantis.com; ☺ Mar-Oct), a boat with a windowed hull, allowing you to see the underwater life. The standard one-hour trip (adult/child £12.50/6.50) is great, with a visit to a seal colony; you might also see otters or dolphins. A slightly longer trip (£15) adds a salmon farm and the wreck of the minelayer *Port Napier*, which sank during WWII. Departure times vary according to the tide; you can book at the tourist office.

Citylink buses run from Inverness (£15.20, 2¼ hours, three daily), and Glasgow (£27.90,

---

**MADDENING MIDGES**

Forget Nessie; the Highlands have a real monster. A voracious blood-sucking female fully 3mm long known as *Culicoides impunctatus*, or the Highland midge. The bane of campers and as much a symbol of Scotland as the kilt or dram, midges can drive sane folk to distraction as they descend in biting clouds.

Though normally vegetarian, the female midge needs a dose of blood in order to lay her eggs. And like it or not, if you're in the Highlands between June and August, you've just volunteered as a donor. Midges congregate especially near water, and are most active in the early morning, though the squadrons also tend to patrol in the late evening, around 10pm.

Repellents and creams are reasonably effective protection, though some walkers favour midge veils. Wearing light-coloured clothing also helps. Pubs and camp sites increasingly have midge-zapping machines. Check www.midgeforecast.co.uk for a prognosis by area.

---

5½ hours, three daily), which continue on to Skye.

The train between Inverness and Kyle of Lochalsh (£17.30, 2½ hours, four daily Monday to Saturday, two on Sunday) is among Scotland's most scenic trips.

## AROUND KYLE OF LOCHALSH
### Eilean Donan Castle
Perched on an island in the inlet Loch Duich, **Eilean Donan Castle** ( ☎ 01599-555202; www.eileandonan castle.com; adult/child £4.95/1.70; ☺ 10am-5pm Apr-Oct, 10am-3pm Mar & Nov) is unforgettably positioned and is a habitual pit stop en route to Skye. You've likely already seen it on postcards and calendars.

Apart from trying to capture the perfect photo of the evocative fortress, you'll be entertained by the interior, which has a decent exhibition on the turbulent history of the castle, which was taken by Spaniards sympathetic to the Jacobites in 1719 and consequently blown up by government frigates. It was restored by the McRae family in the 20th century, and their suite of rooms include displays on family history, an attractive dining room with piper's gallery, and kitchen with food so realistic your stomach will rumble.

## ROAD TO THE ISLES
The 46 miles from Fort William to Mallaig is known as the 'Road to the Isles' (the A830), and its spectacular scenery makes it a very attractive route to Skye via the Mallaig–Armadale ferry. Along this road Bonnie Prince Charlie got his first and last glimpses of Scotland as he arrived full of hope in 1745 and left defeated the following year.

The Young Pretender's first stop was Glenfinnan, where the **Glenfinnan Visitor Centre**

(NTS; ☎ 01397-722250; adult/child £3/2; ☺ 9.30am-5.30pm Jul-Aug, 10am-5pm Apr-Jun, Sep-Oct) tells how he anxiously awaited the support of the powerful Cameron clan here. The sound of pipes signalled the chief's reluctant arrival with 800 men; others soon joined, and the prince raised his standard on 19 August 1745 to begin a campaign that ended in bloody defeat on the fields of Culloden. The Jacobites are commemorated by the **Glenfinnan Monument**, a curious tower topped by a kilted Highlander that stands sombrely by the loch. You can climb it via a narrow stair and tight hatchway; from the top, besides ruining other visitors' snapshots, you get a good view over Loch Shiel and the Glenfinnan Viaduct, which featured in *Harry Potter and the Chamber of Secrets* and appears on the new Bank of Scotland £10 note.

Nearby, at Glenfinnan station, you can sleep in a lovely old railway carriage, which has been kitted out as a **hostel** ( ☎ 01397-722295; www .glenfinnanstationmuseum.co.uk; dm £12; ℗ ).

From **Arisaig**, the **Sheerwater** ( ☎ 01687-450224; www.arisaig.co.uk; ☺ May-Sep) runs wildlife-spotting trips to the islands of Eigg, Muck and Rum (£17/18/23 respectively). Arisaig – in striking distance of the Skye ferry and more charming than Mallaig – makes a good place to stay. **Kinloid Farm** ( ☎ 01687-450366; www.kinloid -arisaig.co.uk; d £60; ℗ ) is on the other side of the main road from town (take the Kinloid turn-off). It's a working farm that offers camping and a well-kept B&B with snug upstairs rooms. A great place to eat and drink is the **Cnoc-na-Faire** ( ☎ 01687-450249; www.cnoc-na-faire .co.uk; mains £8-17; ☺ lunch & dinner) a mile west of Arisaig. The smart bar meals and outdoor seating can be enjoyed while taking in the romantic coastal view, with classic red phone box on hand for a postcard-perfect snap.

*HIGHLANDS & NORTHERN ISLANDS*

From Arisaig the road winds around attractive bays and beautiful beaches known as the **Silver Sands of Morar**. **Morar village** is at the entrance to **Loch Morar**, Britain's deepest lake. It's said to contain its own monster, named Morag, giving hope to disillusioned Nessie-hunters.

## Mallaig
### pop 797
Little Mallaig is still a busy fishing port, as well as a launch pad for Skye and the Small Isles. Though not pretty, it's pleasant enough; film buffs may recognise it, as Lars von Trier's *Breaking the Waves* was partly filmed here. There's a **tourist office** ( ☺ 10.15am-4pm Mon-Sat) with internet access. Local boatpeople can take you to villages of the Knoydart Peninsula, Scotland's remotest mainland settlements, not reachable by road.

**Sheena's Backpackers Lodge** ( ☎ 01687-462764; www.mallaigbackpackers.co.uk; Station Rd; dm £13.50) is a compact place with narrow dorms and kitchen upstairs from the pretty Tea Garden right in the middle of things. A little further along the main street, **Moorings Guest House** ( ☎ 01687-462225; mooringsguesthouse@tiscali.co.uk; East Bay; s/d £27/54) has a front conservatory, faultless if uninteresting rooms, and good breakfasts with kipper and vegetarian possibilities, which you can eat while admiring photos of rescued golden eagle chicks.

Take your pick from three seafood places around the tourist office. Sophistication is a stranger to the decor at the **Cornerstone** ( ☎ 01687-462306; mains £8-18; ☺ lunch & dinner) – lose the sauce sachets, guys – but there are daily specials like squid straight off the boats, and it's got the best harbour views. It runs a chip shop out the back.

**Shiel Buses** ( ☎ 01967-431272) runs to/from Fort William (1½ hours, three daily Monday to Friday).

The scenic West Highland railway rolls between Fort William and Mallaig (£9.20, 1½ hours, three or four daily) with connections from Glasgow. From mid-May to mid-October the **Jacobite steam train** ( ☎ 01524-737751; www.steamtrain.info; adult/child day-return £29/16.50) runs from Fort William to Mallaig via Glenfinnan.

CalMac operates ferries from Mallaig to Armadale on Skye (single per person/car £3.50/18.75, 30 minutes, eight Monday to Saturday, six Sunday mid-May to mid-September).

# ISLE OF SKYE

Skye's romantic and lofty reputation is well deserved, as the scenic splendour of Scotland's largest island rarely disappoints, with lances of light penetrating the regular cloud cover bathing the rugged hillscapes in ethereal light. Even if your stay is marked by mist and typical, almost horizontal, drizzle (Skye owes its name to a Norse word for 'cloud'), you'll likely feel the magic, especially around the striking Cuillin Hills at the island's southern end.

What you won't feel is lonely; Skye attracts legions of visitors, as summering families, grey-haired coach parties, courting couples, and grizzled walkers and climbers bagging a few more Munros all home in on this easily accessible island. Book accommodation ahead.

## Activities
### CLIMBING
The two-day traverse of the Cuillin Ridge is a tough, serious, and exhilarating walk recommended for experienced hikers only, though no technical mountaineering skills are required for the main route.

Guides charge from £70 per person a day.
**Climb Skye** ( ☎ 01478-640264; www.climbskye.co.uk)
**Cuillin Guides** ( ☎ 01478-640289; www.cuillin-guide co.uk)
**Skye Guides** ( ☎ 01471-822116; www.skyeguides.co.uk)

### CYCLING
Once you're off the busy Kyle of Lochalsh to Portree road, Skye offers excellent, scenic cycling, though wind, weather and hills can all take their toll.

Bike-hire recommendations:
**Fairwinds** ( ☎ 01478-822270; standonaldson@aol.com; Elgol Rd, Broadford; ☺ 9.30am-7pm)
**Island Cycles** ( ☎ 01478-613121; The Green, Portree; ☺ 9am-5pm Mon-Sat)

### WALKING
Skye offers some of Scotland's most challenging walking. You should always pack for all conditions. There are great guidebooks for more-advanced walks, but the *Traveller's Companion* and *In the Footsteps of...* series (both available free at tourist offices) both offer good easy walks, the latter based around historical themes such as Dr Johnson or the Clearances.

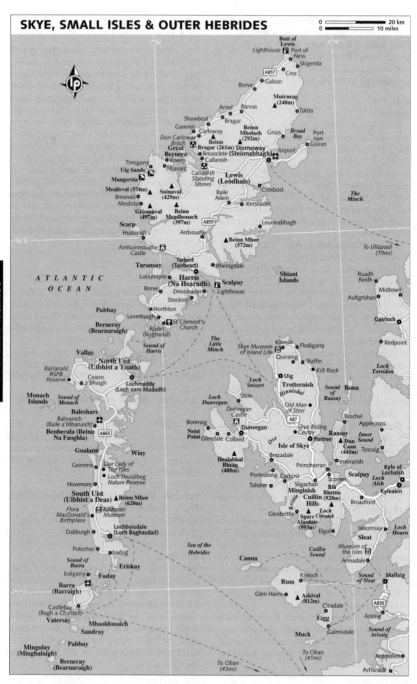

# SKYE, SMALL ISLES & OUTER HEBRIDES

**Skye Walking Holidays** ( ☎ 01470-552213; www.skye walks.co.uk; Duntulm Castle Hotel, Trotternish) organises three-day walking holidays for £429, including four nights' accommodation and full board.

## OTHER ACTIVITIES

Skye's sheltered coves and sea lochs provide superb sea kayaking. **Whitewave Outdoor Centre** ( ☎ 01470-542414; www.white-wave.co.uk; Linicro) and **Skyak Adventures** ( ☎ 01471-833428; www.skyakadven tures.com; 13 Camuscross, Isleornsay) provide instruction and equipment hire.

The green hills around Portree are best seen from horseback with **Skye Riding Centre** ( ☎ 01470-582419; steffiduff82@hotmail.co.uk), a small stable 6 miles west of Portree on the road to Dunvegan.

## Getting There & Away

Most visitors arrive across the bridge from Kyle of Lochalsh. CalMac operates ferries from mainland Mallaig to Armadale (person/car single £3.50/18.75, 30 minutes, eight Monday to Saturday, six Sunday mid-May to mid-September).

There's also the unusual turntable **Skye Ferry** ( ☎ 01599-522273; www.skyeferry.com; adult/car with 4 passengers £1.50/10; ☯ 10am-6pm Easter-Oct) from Glenelg to Kylerhea.

Citylink runs buses to Portree and on to Uig from Glasgow (£31.40, 6½ hours, three daily) and Inverness (£18.60, 3¼ hours, three daily).

## Getting Around

Stagecoach operates the main island bus routes, linking most villages and towns. This good-value Skye Roverbus ticket gives unlimited travel for one/three days for £6/15. Sunday services are scant.

# PORTREE (PORT RÌGH)

pop 1917

Skye's capital is built above a picturesque harbour, the ideal spot for a stroll or a cruise, and has the largest selection of accommodation, eating places and other services. Like other parts of Skye, there's a significant and increasing Gaelic-speaking population. Port Rìgh means 'King's Harbour', likely named for James V's 1540 visit to pacify local chieftains.

## Information

**Library** ( ☎ 01478-612697; Bayfield Rd; ☯ 1-8pm Mon, 10am-5pm Thu-Fri, 10am-1pm Sat) Free internet access.

**Tourist office** ( ☎ 01478-612137; portree@visit scotland.com; Bayfield Rd; ☯ Mon-Sat Oct-Easter, daily Easter-Sep) Helpful, with accommodation booking, internet (£1 per 20 minutes) and foreign exchange.

## Tours

From the pier, **Stardust MV** ( ☎ 07798-743858; trips £12) takes tours to Raasay, Rona and Holm Island with several daily sailings in season.

## Sleeping

**Bayfield Backpackers** ( ☎ 01478-612231; Bayfield; dm £14; ☐ wi-fi) One of two hostels in town, this smart functional spot by the water has few frills but lots of sensible details like keycards, powerful showers and lockable wire baskets under the comfortable bunks. The common room looks out over the bay; the kitchen is modern and clean, and the owner knows plenty about the island and can give good walking advice.

**Bayview House** ( ☎ 01478-613340; www.bayview house.co.uk; Bayfield; d £45-50; ℗ ☐ wi-fi) Solid, unspectacular comfort is the keyword at this Portree stalwart, which cuts back on frills and fry-ups to offer a very fair price in the heart of Skye's capital. The rooms with bathrooms are spartan and spotless, with a cosy bed and little else; the bathrooms are excellent. Upstairs rooms cost slightly more but have more light and views over the bay. There's no breakfast.

**Mrs Milne** ( ☎ 01478-612552; sandra@milne46.orange home.co.uk; 10 Martin Cres; s/d £25/50) There's no sign out at this place – just go ahead and knock. It's set in a quiet residential crescent just up the hill from town, and is run with dry good humour. The three rooms here are particularly comfortable, and the welcome genuine. Knock three quid off if you only want a continental breakfast. There's another good B&B, Grenitote, next door.

**Braeside B&B** ( ☎ 01478-612613; www.braeside portree.co.uk; Stormy Hill; d £54-60; ☯ Jan-Oct) You'll know this bright spot by its flowerpots. Inside it's just as sweet, with ivy-patterned linen and a roomy residents' lounge, which is good for meeting other guests. Breakfast is a treat, with vegetarian options and plenty of choice; there's a reduction if you go continental. The good triple is ideal for small walking groups or families.

**Ben Tianavaig** ( ☎ 01478-612152; www.ben-tianavaig .co.uk; 5 Bosville Tce; d £60; ℗ ) The views are as memorable at this happy central spot as the upbeat welcome from the personable hosts.

HIGHLANDS & NORTHERN ISLANDS

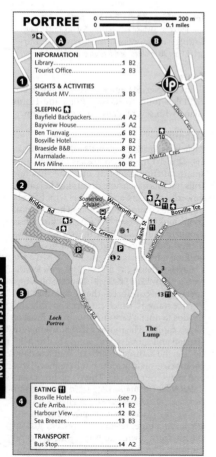

**PORTREE**

| 0 | 200 m |
| 0 | 0.1 miles |

**INFORMATION**
Library...................................1 B2
Tourist Office.........................2 B3

**SIGHTS & ACTIVITIES**
Stardust MV...........................3 B3

**SLEEPING**
Bayfield Backpackers................4 A2
Bayview House........................5 A2
Ben Tianvaig..........................6 B2
Bosville Hotel.........................7 B2
Braeside B&B.........................8 B2
Marmalade.............................9 A1
Mrs Milne.............................10 B2

**EATING**
Bosville Hotel.....................(see 7)
Cafe Arriba............................11 B2
Harbour View.........................12 B2
Sea Breezes...........................13 B3

**TRANSPORT**
Bus Stop...............................14 A2

Rooms are themed on antipodean cities and the vistas appeal, whether the horizontal rain is driving in or the sun is baking the decks of the fishing fleet below. And you won't go hungry, with two of the town's best restaurants on the same block.

**Marmalade** ( ☎ 01478-611711; www.marmalade hotels.com; Home Farm Rd; s/d/f £100/120/125; P wi-fi) The tourist board will have a fit – doesn't this place know that accommodation in Scotland can only be named after trees or geographical features? Thankfully, that's not the only rule it breaks; the modern cafe chic, funky wire chandeliers in the bar, above-average breakfast and laid-back staff are the perfect complements to the seven large light rooms, super-spacious bathrooms, grassy grounds and long views. Prices drop sharply outside summer.

**Bosville Hotel** ( ☎ 01478-612846; www.macleodhotels .co.uk; 9 Bosville Tce; standard d £128; wi-fi) From the welcome drink to your last gourmet breakfast, everything is done with aplomb at this busy and upmarket hotel. Split-level suites feature neutral furnishings and thoughtful touches, such as cosy slippers, armchairs and deep tubs in which to soak walk-worn muscles.

## Eating & Drinking

**Cafe Arriba** ( ☎ 01478-611830; Quay Brae; mains £5-10; 10am-10pm) Colourful and fun, this upstairs cafe does inventive sandwiches served on a range of breads, bagels and croissants; stay-awhile views; and the best espresso in town. The all-day breakfast is a calorie hit, and the range of daily specials and booze licence make it a good spot for casual dinner too.

**Sea Breezes** ( ☎ 01478-612016; Quay St; lunch £5-7, dinner £11-19; lunch & dinner Thu-Tue) Down by the harbour, this is run by a chef with a good local rep, and he makes the effort to source island produce like organic Uist salmon or hand-dived scallops from Barra. Lunches are simpler, but all dishes are tasty.

**Harbour View** ( ☎ 01478-612069; 7 Bosville Tce; lunch mains £5-9, dinner mains £12-19; noon-2pm & 5.30-10pm) Romantically candlelit and intimate, this spot has just a handful of tables, and a well-deserved reputation for seafood. The shared seafood platters (£47.50 for two) are fun, but there's more quality elsewhere on the menu. If the ambience appeals, there are three rooms upstairs.

**our pick Bosville Hotel** ( ☎ 01478-612846; 9 Bosville Tce; restaurant 2-course dinner £32, bistro mains £7-13; lunch & dinner) Very much the place to eat and drink in Portree, this offers three distinct but connected spaces, all of which deserve attention. The upmarket restaurant, The Chandlery, serves up exquisite seafood concoctions, but the more affordable adjoining bistro isn't far behind, with a generous daily roast (£9), seafood specials – crunch into local langoustines if they're available – and a couple of dozen wines by the glass. The Merchant Bar is the most stylish drinking option in town.

## Getting There & Around

Buses stop in Somerled Sq. Citylink runs to/from Inverness (£18.60, 3¼ hours, three daily); Glasgow (£31.40, 6½ hours, three daily) via Fort William; and Edinburgh (£38, eight hours, two daily). Local buses include around 15 daily (three on Sunday) to Sligachan (12 minutes) and Broadford (35 minutes); three or four to Dunvegan (40 minutes); and five a day each way on the Trotternish loop taking in Flodigarry (45 minutes) and Uig (30 minutes).

## KYLEAKIN (CAOL ACAIN)
pop 380

The bridge has made Kyleakin a backwater as people push further into Skye, but this quiet waterside village has a few good hostels. The pubs are more coach-party oriented though.

Stress is a stranger at sociable **Skye Backpackers** ( ☎ 01599-534510; www.scotlands-top -hostels.com; dm caravan £10, dm/d £13/31; P ⏅ wi-fi) and you're unlikely to be woken by your dorm-mate heading for the Cuillins at 6am here. Decent dorms and snug little doubles are supplemented by a grassy garden (and dormitory caravan with a *Star Trek* theme), £1.90 breakfast, and laid-back people running the place. If you do feel active, you can hire hand-painted wellies to one-up other trampers.

**Dun-Caan Hostel** ( ☎ 01599-534087; www.skyerover .co.uk; Pier Rd; dm £15), a cosy hostel attracting a more mature crowd than the other backpacker barns in town, has six-bunk dorms and serene harbour views. The common room is a floral explosion that brightens up the place and the kitchen is small but functional. The owners hire bikes and give walking advice.

## ARMADALE (ARMADAIL)
pop 120

The Mallaig ferry arrives in wee Armadale. Near the ruins of **Armadale Castle** is the excellent **Museum of the Isles** ( ☎ 01471-844305; www.clandonald .com; adult/child £5.60/4; ⏅ 9.30am-5.30pm Apr-Oct). This engrossing exhibition covers island prehistory through to Norse raids, the disintegration of Gaelic culture and mass emigration. The beautiful grounds offer woodland strolls; you can access these walks from the road without having to pay for castle-garden admission.

**Sea.fari** ( ☎ 01471-833316; www.seafari.co.uk; The Pier, Armadale) does brilliant whale-spotting trips (£27 for two hours) with plenty of Skye scenery to enjoy if the cetaceans don't show.

The home of celebrated Scottish chef Claire MacDonald, **Kinloch Lodge** ( ☎ 01471-833214; www .kinloch-lodge.co.uk; d £150-275; P ) is a stately foodie treat (dinner £42). Rooms have an elegant country-house feel with bird watercolours

on the walls, and plump beds. The drawing room has a selection of whisky and cigars, so you can swig, puff and contemplate the view. It's 10 miles north of Armadale, 5 miles before the turn-off to the A87.

## BROADFORD (AN T-ÀTH LEATHANN)
pop 1237

This service centre has good accommodation options but little character. The heart of town is the Esso petrol station, with seven-day supermarket, internet and laundry. Opposite is the **tourist office** ( ☎ 01471-822361; ⏅ daily Apr-Oct).

From Broadford, the B8083 side road winds its way to the south coast across a beautiful strath (valley), and ends in the little harbour hamlet of Elgol, where there's a small craft centre but scandalously no pub. It's a great drive, a good way to get away from the crowds.

**Broadford SYHA** ( ☎ 01471-822442; www.syha.org.uk; dm £14.50; ⏅ Mar-Oct; P ⏅ ) has a great outlook over the bay and is set in a quiet spot away from the busy road in a modern building. Staff are helpful with local walks – long and short.

**our pick Tigh an Dochais** ( ☎ 01471-820022; www .skyebedbreakfast.co.uk; 13 Harrapool; s/d £60/80; P ⏅ wi-fi) is a feast for the eyes, a chic new guesthouse looking like it's come straight to Broadford from some Nordic architecture contest. All the rooms as well as the lounge boast glass walls – they're too big to call windows – which look right out over the shoreline and are so clean you'll bang your nose. It really is an extraordinary place, and comfort, not minimalism, inspires the interior decor. Book well ahead.

About 7 miles north of Broadford, **Skye Picture House** ( ☎ 01471-822531; www.skyepicture house.co.uk; Ard Dorch; s/d £32/64; P ⏅ ), right by the water, looks across at the island of Scalpay. The owners are avid photographers (and offer courses), so photography tomes and images decorate the wonderful guest lounge, which has memorable wraparound vistas; there's a telescope for bird- and otter-watching. The en suite rooms have spacious bathrooms and unfussy comfort.

For a Broadford bite to eat, **Creelers of Skye** ( ☎ 01471-822281; mains £9-16; ⏅ noon-10pm Mon-Sat) does quality seafood in an unpretentious atmosphere, and smaller tapas-style creations (£5 to £7) during the day. It's a friendly spot that doubles as an art gallery.

HIGHLANDS & NORTHERN ISLANDS

## CUILLIN HILLS & MINGINISH PENINSULA

Rising to the west of Broadford, the Cuillins are Britain's most impressive mountain range. Their jagged peaks and ridges could be a ser-rated knife sawing at the grey sky; climbers and walkers see them as *the* challenge in Scotland. The highest summit, **Sgurr Alasdair** (993m), is one of the biggest trophies for ex-perienced mountaineers, but is off limits for most walkers. An easier day walk is the steep climb from Glenbrittle camp site to **Coire Lagan** (6 miles round trip; allow at least three hours), an impressive spot known for **rock climbing**.

Huddling under the stern hills is the cross-roads at Sligachan, a spectacular spot graced by the convivial **Sligachan Hotel** ( ☎ 01478-650204; www.sligachan.co.uk; camp sites per person £5, dm £12, s/d £54/108; P ▣ ). A popular launch pad for the Cuillins, this offers camping, bunkhouse and rooms sporting bright white sheets and new carpets. The huge bar offers walkers' stories and uncomplicated food (£6 to £10, open 10am to 9pm), while the restaurant (mains £12 to £19, dinner Monday to Saturday) is more refined. Even if the winds howl and the roads close, it won't run out of beer, as it's brewed here.

Sample the excellent sweety, peaty malt once favoured by Robert Louis Stevenson on the slightly corporate 45-minute tour of Carbost's Diageo-owned **Talisker Distillery** ( ☎ 01478-614308; www.malts.com; adult/child £5/free; ☑ 9.30am-5pm Mon-Sat Easter-Oct, 12.30-5pm Sun Jul-Aug, winter by appointment), which has been operating since 1830. Three miles further, at Portnalong, **Skyewalker Hostel** ( ☎ 01478-640250; www.skyewalker hostel.com; sites per person £5-7.50, dm/tw £12.50/28; P ) is, all *Star Wars* jokes aside, a very sound walkers' facility in a former school with a big kitchen and a grassy camping area.

## DUNVEGAN & AROUND

On the island's western side is the MacLeod stronghold of **Dunvegan Castle** ( ☎ 01470-521206; www.dunvegancastle.com; adult/child £7.50/4, gardens only £5/3; ☑ 10am-5.30pm Apr–mid-Oct, 11am-4pm mid-Oct–Mar). It's stood firm since the 13th century, perhaps because it holds the **Fairy Flag**, a silken Crusader relic from the Middle East that sup-posedly guarantees victory for the clan that holds it. Other objects here include souvenirs of visitors such as Bonnie Prince Charlie and Dr Johnson. To get your money's worth from the admission fee, make time to enjoy the vast and lovely gardens. Seal-spotting trips leave from the boat dock.

**Tables Hotel** ( ☎ 01470-521404; www.tableshotel.co.uk; s/d £46/72; P ▣ wi-fi) is a family-run guesthouse with a conservatory breakfast that includes black or white pudding, smoked haddock and vegetarian options; it's open to passers-by for tea and coffee during the day. The relaxed lounge includes a DVD player and plush sofas, plus there's a telescope that's used to give free tours of the Skye sky.

**our pick** **Three Chimneys** ( ☎ 01470-511258; www.threechimneys.co.uk; 2-course lunches £22.50, 3-course din-ners £50; ☑ lunch Mon-Sat, dinner daily), 5 miles from Dunvegan towards Glendale, has both a won-derful rural location and some of the finest food in the country. The menu constantly changes but features intricate game and sea-food creations featuring carefully selected re-gional Scottish ingredients. By the restaurant, the **House Over-By** (d £265; P ▣ wi-fi) features very charismatic split-level rooms with subdued noughties colours, DVD player, iPod dock, and views across Loch Dunvegan. The folk running this star in Skye couldn't be more welcoming.

From Monday to Saturday there are three to four bus services from Portree to Dunvegan Castle.

## NORTH SKYE

North of Portree, Skye's coastal scenery opens into the magical Trotternish Peninsula. Look out for the rocky spike of the **Old Man of Storr**, a terrace of splayed skirtlike basalt at **Kilt Rock** and the ruins of **Duntulm Castle**. At Staffin Bay the dramatic escarpment of the **Quiraing** will catch your eye. It's a landscape of harsh beauty perhaps most spectacularly savage in drizzle and howling wind.

The tiny hamlet of **Flodigarry** has a couple of excellent places to stay. **Flodigarry Country House Hotel** ( ☎ 01470-552203; www.flodigarry.co.uk; r per person £50-90; P ) is an island stalwart hap-pily recovered from a recent spell in Division 2. Furnished with a venerable elegance ap-propriate to this noble building, the rooms here are memorable, particularly those in the 'flagship' class, which have majestic views. For a dose of Jacobite history, though, stay in the restored but more basic cottage of Flora MacDonald, Bonnie Prince Charlie's rescuer. The smart conservatory lounge is another highlight. The restaurant is open to the pub-lic, as is the characterful bar, which offers tasty meals.

Just beyond, and with a private track to the bar, **Dun Flodigarry Hostel** ( ☎ 01470-552212; www.hostelflodigarry.co.uk; dm £12.50, tw £28-34; P 💻 ) has the same stupendous views. It's a sociable place with guitar, piano and big kitchen/dining room. Walkers have a proper laundry and drying room here, and campers can pitch up outside and use all the facilities for £6.50 per person.

At the peninsula's northern end at **Kilmuir**, the **Skye Museum of Island Life** ( ☎ 01470-552206; adult/child £2.50/50p; 🕙 9.30am-5pm Mon-Sat Apr-Oct) recreates crofting life in a series of thatched cottages. Up the hill in the Kilmuir cemetery is **Flora MacDonald's grave**. Flora helped Bonnie Prince Charlie escape following his defeat at the Battle of Culloden in 1746. She dressed him up in drag to play her maid as they sailed over the sea to Skye. She was imprisoned in the Tower of London for a year for her pains.

Three miles south of Staffin, **Glenview Hotel** ( ☎ 01470-562248; www.glenviewskye.co.uk; d £90; P 💻 wi-fi), on the west side of the road, is a whitewashed hotel with notable comfort and hospitality. Friendly owners serve up massive breakfasts (ask for an extra serve of the delicious fruit pudding) and track down sustainable produce for their tasty dinners; rooms have four-poster beds for romantic weekenders.

## Uig (Uige)

From whichever direction you arrive, the picture-perfect harbour of Uig (*oo-ig*), enclosed by steep hills, impresses, particularly if the ferry is chugging across the bay. The **tourist office** ( ☎ 01470-542404; www.uig-isleofskye.com; 🕙 9am-5pm Mon-Fri, 11am-4pm Sat & Sun) offers information and enthusiasm.

In town, hire bikes at the unappealing camp site near the ferry or book ahead to tour the **Isle of Skye Brewery** ( ☎ 01470-542477; www.skye brewery.co.uk; tours £2; 🕙 9am-5pm Mon-Fri), which brews the local ales.

By the ferry, **Ard-na-Mara** ( ☎ 01470-542281; www.isleofskyebandb.co.uk; 11 Idrigill; d £55; P ) is run by warm-hearted folk who like to get to know their guests. It backs onto the water, and features small light rooms with bathrooms and Sky TV. Ask to be introduced to the real stars of the show, the enormous and lovable borzoi dogs.

Four miles north, **Kilmuir House** ( ☎ 01470-542262; www.kilmuir-skye.co.uk; s/d £30/50; P ) has a genial welcome and big rooms with shared bathroom that are full of interesting old furniture and rustic curios. There's a great little garden, fresh eggs at breakfast, and long views over meadows down to the sea.

With a kitchen overlooking the bay, you'll be racing to do the washing-up at chilled-out **Uig SYHA** ( ☎ 01470-542746; dm £14; P ). Eight-bunk dorms are large enough to allow everyone their own space, while the lounge is a good spot to hole up when the rain sets in. The family room is a good bet for groups and there's a separate bunkhouse for overflow.

The **Pub at the Pier** ( ☎ 01470-542212; The Pier; mains £8-10; 🕙 lunch & dinner) does straight-up meals, but the 180-degree panorama of the harbour is ideal for watching the ferry come and go.

From Uig pier, CalMac has ferry services to Lochmaddy on North Uist (single per person/car £10/48, 1¾ hours, one or two daily) and to Tarbert on Harris (single per person/car £10/48, 1½ hours, one or two daily Monday to Saturday).

## ISLE OF RAASAY
pop 194

If you're finding Skye a bit more touristed than you'd hoped, hop on the Raasay ferry and lower that pulse rate a few notches. As well as magnificent views of the Cuillins, the island appeals in its own right, with some majestic, not especially strenuous walks – all well signposted; a surprising forest of mature pines; and plenty of time and space to breathe.

Services are limited to a general store; there's no petrol or ATM. Raasay Outdoor Centre offered various activities, but at the time of research had moved off the island pending major restoration of the mansion Raasay House.

There are a couple of B&Bs, as well as **Raasay SYHA** ( ☎ 01478-660240; dm £15; 🕙 mid-May–early Sep), which is a fair old walk uphill from the ferry, but a very pleasant one, and you are rewarded with a magnificent panorama from this simple hostel – 'a wonderful place to do nothing' in the words of the warden. Bring food with you from the shop.

**Borodale House** ( ☎ 01478-660222; www.isleofraasay hotel.co.uk; s £40, d £80-110; 🕙 Easter-Oct; P 💻 wi-fi), better known as the Isle of Raasay Hotel, is a great getaway. All but two of the appealing rooms have views over to Skye and there are bar meals (BYO at the time of research due to a licence issue), the only food available on the island that you won't cook yourself.

---

**CALUM'S ROAD**

Raasay folk are used to being off the radar and have learned to deal with it in their own way. When Calum MacLeod grew tired of petitioning the local council for road access to his remote Raasay croft, he decided to build it himself. Using a dog-eared old engineering manual and with little more than a pick and shovel, he constructed the 2-mile road in his spare time over a period of 10 years, completing it in 1974. Calum's Rd is now legendary: the council finally took on responsibility, and now have a sign up proclaiming it.

Roger Hutchinson's 2006 book *Calum's Road* tells the story in more detail and also has a wealth of information on Raasay life. For a day-to-day account of crofting life at the end of Calum's road, check out the entertaining blog http://lifeattheendoftheroad.wordpress.com.

---

CalMac operates ferries from Sconser on Skye (between Portree and Broadford) to Raasay (return per person/car £2.80/10.95, 20 minutes, nine to 11 Monday to Saturday, two Sunday).

# OUTER HEBRIDES

The Western Isles, as they're also called, are frontier territory, a chain of islands stuck like a shield well out into the irritable Atlantic. Their Viking name *havbredey* ('islands at the edge of the earth') still feels true today.

The islands have long subsisted on fishing, weaving and crofting, and the traditionally harsh life and weather perhap explains the strong religiosity of the Protestant islands of Lewis, Harris and North Uist (see opposite). Things are different here; the distinctive horned Hebridean sheep have right-of-way on the roads, and Gaelic is a working language: almost half of Gaelic-speaking Scots live on these islands.

Outside the semibustle of Stornoway, life exists in small villages compiled of ruinous stone cottages interspersed with fresh, squat concrete bungalows; until relatively recently the main unit of housing was the blackhouse, a primitive dwelling with dry-stone walls, peat hearth and thatched roof.

The landscapes can be mournful – treeless moorland occupies much of the terrain – but also striking, with wide horizons of sky and water, dazzling white beaches, azure bays and stony hills. There's huge wildlife diversity, with corncrakes calling in the long grass and otters frolicking in the sea.

## Orientation & Information

The Outer Hebrides consists of more than 200 islands in a 130-mile arc from north to south. Lewis and Harris are actually one island divided by a border of high hills. Stornoway (Lewis) is the largest town, with a reasonable range of facilities. North Uist, Benbecula and South Uist are joined by causeways. There are tourist offices in every ferry port.

## Getting There & Away

### AIR
Flybe/Loganair serves Stornoway from Glasgow, Inverness and Edinburgh, and Benbecula and Barra from Glasgow. At Barra, the planes land on the beach, so the timetable is tidal. **Highland Airways** ( ☎ 0845 450 2245; www.highlandairways.co.uk) flies to Benbecula and Stornoway.

### BOAT
CalMac runs car ferries from Ullapool to Stornoway (Lewis); from Uig (Isle of Skye) to Lochmaddy (North Uist) and Tarbert (Harris); and from Oban to Castlebay (Barra), continuing to Lochboisdale (South Uist). See p850 for more information on ferries and passes.

## Getting Around

Booklets listing air, bus and ferry services are available from tourist offices. Ferries run between Leverburgh on Harris and Berneray, connected to North Uist; and between Eriskay, connected to South Uist, and Barra.

There are limited bus services, especially on Sunday. Visitors without their own transport should anticipate a fair amount of hitching and walking.

### BICYCLE
Cycling the length of the islands is popular if windy; south-to-north gives you a better chance of a tailwind. Bikes are available for hire for roughly £12 per day or £60 per week: **Alex Dan's Cycle Centre** ( ☎ 01851-704025; www .hebrideancycles.co.uk; 67 Kenneth St, Stornoway, Lewis)

**Barra Cycle Hire** ( ☎ 01871-810284; 29 St Brendan's Rd, Castlebay, Barra)
**Rothan Cycles** ( ☎ 01870-620283; www.rothan.com; 9 Howmore, South Uist)
**Sorrel Cottage** (South Harris; see p949)

### CAR & MOTORCYCLE
Most roads are single-track; wandering sheep pose the main hazard. Petrol stations are far apart, expensive and usually closed Sunday. You can hire cars on all the islands; on Lewis try **Lewis Car Rentals** ( ☎ 01851-703760; www.lewis-car-rental.co.uk; 52 Bayhead St, Stornoway).

## LEWIS (LEÒDHAIS)
pop 18,489

The peat moors of northern Lewis form a memorably bleak landscape, with piles of the black fuel drying in rows along neat trenches. It's a tough landscape that gives way to a spectacular coastline, with impressive cliffs and shining strands. You'll hear Gaelic spoken widely here, and the locals cut fine figures arrayed in their Sunday best for church.

You can visit many of the most interesting sights following a circular route around the island along the A857 and A858, with an optional detour up to the Butt of Lewis at the top of the island and towards the white beaches around Breanais.

### Stornoway (Steòrnabhagh)
pop 8569

Stornoway is the bustling 'capital' of the Outer Hebrides and the archipelago's only real town. The natural harbour was first appreciated by the Vikings who established bases here for onward raiding. The waterside apart, it's not a pretty town, but an important one hereabouts, base for most services, and maker of Britain's best black pudding.

### ORIENTATION & INFORMATION
Stornoway is on the east coast and compact enough to make exploring on foot easy. The bus station and ferry terminal are adjacent on the foreshore.

**Library** ( ☎ 01851-708631; 19 Cromwell St; ☼ 10am-5pm Mon-Wed & Sat, to 6pm Thu & Fri) Free internet access, and cafe.
**Tourist office** ( ☎ 01851-703088; www.visithebrides .com; 26 Cromwell St; ☼ 9am-6pm Mon-Sat Easter-Sep, 9am-5pm Mon-Fri Oct-Easter) Also opens for the evening ferry from July to August.

### SIGHTS & ACTIVITIES
The interesting **Museum nan Eilean** ( ☎ 01851-709266; Francis St; admission free; ☼ 10am-5.30pm Mon-Sat Apr-Sep, 10am-5pm Tue-Fri, 10am-1pm Sat Oct-Mar), three blocks up from the centre, covers the prehistoric, Viking and clan periods, as well as traditional island life and the impact of progress and technology.

The shiny new cultural centre **An Lanntair** ( ☎ 01851-703307; www.lanntair.com; Kenneth St; ☼ 10am-late Mon-Sat) stands proud in the centre of town and has exhibitions of contemporary art, a theatre and cinema, educational events, and a cafe-restaurant.

On Sunday nothing's open, so head out to visit the island's sights or follow the locals by strolling in the wooded park across the river, dominated by the over-ornate Victorian **Lews Castle**.

---

### NEVER ON A SUNDAY
The Sabbath is closely observed throughout the Outer Hebrides. Some strict locals choose not to cook or drive on Sunday, preferring to devote the day to worship, bible-readings and services. Children's playgrounds are still padlocked in some parts, and locals can be chastised by neighbours for hanging out washing on the Lord's day. When British Airways introduced Sunday flights in 2002, churches were outraged, but the planes eventually took off. Similarly a petrol station in Stornoway famously flouts the Sabbath; it's assured its place in hell by trading in the devil's drink.

For visitors it can be frustrating, but not impossible. Although visitors' centres are closed and no public transport runs, you can still visit many of the sights, such as the Callanish standing stones. Shops, however, are shut, as are nearly all restaurants: you'll probably find yourself eating in a hotel. Remember to fill up with petrol beforehand unless in Stornoway.

Nevertheless, many Hebrideans who aren't so religious still feel the Sunday lockdown should be preserved, as it offers valuable contemplation time and a quiet day spent with family. So just go with the flow and embrace the relaxed Sunday spirit.

In mid-July, the **Hebridean Celtic Festival** ( ☎ 01851-621234; www.hebceltfest.com) brings together local musicians and groups from Ireland, Brittany, northern Spain and other Celt outposts. Even the church elders crack a smile.

To get out on two wheels, you can hire a bike at Alex Dan's Cycle Centre (p944).

### SLEEPING

**Laxdale Holiday Park** ( ☎ 01851-703234; www.laxdale holidaypark.com; 6 Laxdale Lane; tent sites £5-7 plus £3 per adult, dm £13; ♈ camp sites Apr-Oct, bunkhouse year-round) North of town, 1.5 miles off the A857, this has good grassy tent pitches, a neat modern bunkhouse, and good self-catering cottages.

**Heb Hostel** ( ☎ 01851-709889; www.hebhostel.com; 25 Kenneth St; dm/f £15/60; 💻 ) Though we love hoary old hostels too, there's something infinitely satisfying about a brand-spanking-new place, especially when it's in the heart of town. Roomy dorms boast comfy beds and wee wooden lockers, there's a warm personal greeting, the lounge's black sofas let you watch local characters pass by on the street, and the excellent kitchen even has an Aga cooker to use.

**Park Guest House** ( ☎ 01851-702485; www .theparkguesthouse.co.uk; 30 James St; s £44, d £84-96; 🅿 ) Your hosts here know more about cooking than just cracking eggs into the frypan. Substantially more: they operate a classy restaurant here (mains £13 to £20, dinner Tuesday to Saturday), and run Hebridean cookery courses. The spacious rooms and smart, pared-back decor will appeal, though the busy (for the Hebrides anyway) road outside is a minor quibble. It's £6 cheaper without breakfast.

**Royal Hotel** ( ☎ 01851-702109; www.royalstornoway .co.uk; Cromwell St; s/d £59/98; 🅿 💻 ) The reliable old Royal has been slowly rejuvenating itself, and makes a likeable place to stay, mixing some lugubrious decor with a cleaner contemporary feel in some rooms. The contrast is never better seen than in the difference between its two bars.

### EATING & DRINKING

**Thai Cafe** ( ☎ 01851-701811; 27 Church St; mains £4-7; ♈ lunch & 5-11pm Mon-Sat) An unremarkable exterior disguises authentic and delicious Thai food. Stir-fries and spicy soups will certainly perk you up after a day in the Stornoway drizzle. It's bring-your-own-booze: sort that

out beforehand, as it's a fair walk for wine at night.

**An Lanntair** ( ☎ 01851-703307; Kenneth St; mains £5-12; ♈ lunch & dinner Mon-Sat) The upstairs restaurant at this new cultural centre offers lounging space on stylish seating around the bar, and a bright restaurant area overlooking the harbour. The food is upbeat and tasty; it's also a fine spot for a bottomless coffee or a pint.

**HS-1** ( ☎ 01851-702109; Cromwell St; mains £5-14; ♈ food noon-9pm) It's quite a surprise to find this cheerful bar-restaurant attached to the fairly traditional Royal Hotel but HS-1, named for the local postcode, is still where it's at for jazzed-up bar meals, and a handful of more sophisticated choices. Popular with the young, it's one of few Sunday-opening restaurants, and does it well, with roasts and plenty of specials – book ahead.

**Digby Chick** ( ☎ 01851-700026; 28 Point St; mains £15-22; ♈ lunch & 5.30-8.30pm Mon-Sat) Head-and-shoulders above the rest of the dining scene, this chick should be made a Lady for services to Stornoway eating. While an evening visit is memorable, with candlelight and delicious specials, wallet-watchers can get away with murder here by opting for the £7.50 lunch or £15.50 early dinner.

### GETTING THERE & AWAY

CalMac runs ferries to/from Ullapool (person/car £15.30/75, 2¾ hours, two to three daily Monday to Saturday). Buses run from Stornoway to/from Tarbert (one hour, up to six daily Monday to Saturday) and the Leverburgh ferry.

**MacLennan Coaches** ( ☎ 01851-702114) runs a circular route from Stornoway to Callanish, Carloway and Arnol; you've got time to visit three of these places in a day – the tourist office does a handy printout. An all-day ticket costs £6.

## Arnol Blackhouse Museum

Two miles west of Barvas off the A858, this **museum** (HS; ☎ 01851-710395; admission £2.50; ♈ 9.30am-5.30pm Mon-Sat Apr-Sep, to 4.30pm Mon-Sat Oct-Mar) is an original blackhouse offering a rare insight into the old crofting way of life. Built in 1885, the house uses materials that were handy, such as turf for the roof and driftwood (including a beam that was once a tiller). The central fire was essential for keeping the turf roof dry, but not too dry, as well as keeping human and animal inhabitants warm. Across the road is a whitehouse, which was the next architectural evolution, where the owner of this blackhouse moved when she sold to the government in 1964.

## Carloway (Càrlabhagh) & Around

Carloway looks across a beautiful loch to the southern mountains and contains the defiantly perched **Dun Carloway Broch**, a well-preserved, 2000-year-old drystone defensive tower, still effective shelter from the howling wind. If you get the place to yourself, you'll get an eerie feeling crawling through the little entranceways. The **visitor centre** ( ☎ 01851-643338; admission free; 🕑 10am-5pm Mon-Sat May-Sep) has an interpretative display.

At nearby Garenin, the **Gearrannan Blackhouse Village** sits on the verge of a dramatic Atlantic shelf above a stony beach. The village consists of nine restored thatched-roof blackhouses; one of them is the **Blackhouse museum** ( ☎ 01851-643416; www.gearrannan.com; adult/child £2.50/1; 🕑 9.30am-5.30pm Mon-Sat Apr-Oct), exhibiting working looms and authentic-smelling byres. There's also a simple cafe. Some of the blackhouses can be rented as self-catering cottages, and another holds **Na Gearrannan Hostel** (www.gatliff.org.uk; dm £9), which is warm (the fire has been replaced with central heating) and wonderfully atmospheric. It is far bigger inside than you'd imagine, and is especially snug when the wind is whistling outside.

## Callanish (Calanais)

Callanish is 12 miles west of Stornoway and home to the **Callanish Standing Stones**, one of Britain's most complete stone circles. Set on a wild and secluded promontory overlooking Loch Roag, these 13 gneiss monuments are arranged as in worship around a central 4.5m-high monolith. Another 40 smaller stones radiate from the circle in the shape of a cross, with the remains of a chambered tomb at the centre. They date from between 3800 and 5000 years ago, making them roughly contemporary with Egypt's Great Pyramid. What was it for? We don't really know; its real purpose continues to baffle us. Near the site stand other smaller stone circles. Callanish is free to visit and always open.

**Calanais Visitor Centre** ( ☎ 01851-621422; admission £2; 🕑 10am-6pm Mon-Sat Apr-Sep, to 4pm Mon-Sat Oct-Mar) is discreetly designed not to interfere with the visual impact of the stones. A small exhibition speculates on the meaning and

construction of the monoliths, using photos and audiovisuals.

## Breanais

The B8011 southeast of Callanish, signposted to Uig, takes you through remotest Lewis. Follow the road around towards **Breanais** for some truly spectacular white-sand beaches, although the surf can make swimming treacherous. The famous 12th-century walrus-ivory Lewis chess pieces were discovered in the sand dunes here in 1831. Most of them ended up in London's British Museum; some are in Edinburgh's Museum of Scotland (p790).

our pick **Baile-na-Cille** ( ☎ 01851-672242; www .bailenacille.com; Timsgarry; cottage per person £29, s/d £45/90; 🕑 Easter-Sep; **P** 🖳 wi-fi) is one of Britain's most rewarding places to stay, having an utterly idyllic location on a headland above a heavenly stretch of white sand. Things are very laissez-faire here, and the charismatic owners welcome 'kids, pets and even grannies'. Home-cooked dinners (£30) are part of the fun, and there's a grassy tennis court, bar-billiards and much good cheer. Nearly all the cosy rooms have a memorable view.

## Butt of Lewis (Rubha Robhanais) & Around

Heading north on the A857, you head into Gaelic heartland, with most inhabitants speaking the language. Hear it spoken over the crackling fires in the back bar of the **Cross Inn** ( ☎ 01851-810152; www.crossinn.com; Cros; s/d £45/70; **P** ), more atmospheric than the front bar with its framed platinum '80s albums. There are rooms and bar meals here, and it opens on a Sunday.

An atmospheric bed choice, **Galson Farmhouse** ( ☎ 01851-850492; www.galsonfarm.co.uk; South Galson; d £72-88; **P** ) is a pretty farm some 0.3 miles from the main road, offering great views over the machair to the coast beyond and a high grade of rooms. It also has a good bunkhouse (dorm beds £12).

The main settlement at this end of the island is attractive **Port of Ness** (Port Nis), which hosts **10 Callicvol** ( ☎ 01851-810193; www.10callicvol .com; admission free; 🕑 9.30am-5.30pm Tue-Sat Apr-Sep), a large private collection of books on the Hebrides and Scotland, many in Gaelic; upstairs there's a traditional quilt display. By the harbour, **Sùlair** ( ☎ 01851-810222; www.sulair .co.uk; lunch mains £6-10, dinner mains £14-20; 🕑 lunch Wed-Sat, dinner Tue-Sat) is an upmarket restaurant whose small, slate-floored dining room looks out over the water. The intriguing-sounding locals such as Crobeag lamb don't disappoint and the chef reaches far beyond the Hebrides for bok choy and other morsels.

A couple of miles west, the **Butt of Lewis** (quiet up the back…) is the northernmost tip of the Hebrides archipelago. It's an atmospheric spot marked by an impressive lighthouse and ragged rock formations where gulls and fulmars wheel. Watch the kids; the wind can gust very suddenly, and it's a long way down.

## HARRIS (NA HEARADH)
pop 1984

Wondrous Harris makes its conjoined sibling Lewis look plain, with pure turquoise water, white-sand beaches backed by machair, and knobbly geological formations and lochans (little lochs) rising to rugged rocky hills that divide the two.

North Harris is actually the forbidding mountainous southern tip of Lewis – the Clisham (An Cliseam) crowns the ridge of peaks at 799m. South Harris, across a narrow land bridge at Tarbert, has a fascinating variety of landscapes.

Harris is, of course, famous for Harris Tweed, a homemade woollen cloth once soaked in urine as part of the process. The declining industry was given a fillip in 2004 when Nike decided it wanted the tweed look for a new trainer and just about every weaver on the islands worked day and night to meet the order.

### Tarbert (Tairbeart)
pop 1338

At the narrow waist between North and South Harris, this little settlement clings to the rocky hillsides surrounding its ferry port. Hemmed in by two sea lochs, Tarbert's one of those places where the rain seems to fall horizontally, but is majestically scenic when the sun's out.

The **tourist office** ( ☎ 01859-502011; tarbert@visitscotland.com; ◷ 9am-5pm Mon-Sat) opens for late ferries in summer. Tarbert has an ATM as well as a petrol station and shops, which include several craft shops selling local tweed.

**Rockview Bunkhouse** ( ☎ 01859-502081; Main St; dm £10) has two large segregated dorms, but it's getting in that's the problem, as the owners don't live on site. Ring well ahead (days

not hours), as they don't always answer the phone either. It's very handy for the ferry though.

In some ways the **Harris Hotel** ( ☎ 01859-502154; www.harrishotel.com; s/d £55/90, superior d £120; P 🖳 wi-fi) harks back to another era of British hospitality, with tweed-clad guests and richly furnished bar and lounge. But the comfortable rooms have modern bathrooms and no hint of florals, and the place is run with an appealing professionalism. The old-fashioned restaurant, open for lunch and dinner (two-course dinner £20), serves generous portions. While you're here, check out the signature of *Peter Pan* author JM Barrie scratched into one of the windows.

**First Fruits** ( ☎ 01859-502439; Pier Rd; light meals £4-7; ◷ 10.30am-8pm Mon-Sat Jul & Aug, 10.30am-6.30pm Mon-Sat Jun, 10am-4.30pm Mon-Sat Apr, May & Sep) is a sweet snackhouse that does warming hot chocolate when the wind is lashing the town – as well as lunches and cakes.

Buses run up to six times daily (not on Sunday) from Tarbert to Leverburgh (50 minutes) and Stornoway (one hour).

CalMac ferries connect Tarbert with Uig on Skye (single per person/car £10/48, 1½ hours, one or two daily).

### South Harris

It's no exaggeration to say that some of the world's most magnificent beaches are to be found in South Harris. The west coast is backed by rolling machair and mountains, below which spectacular azure waters give way to shallow turquoise, and lap lazily against achingly tempting sandy shores. The best beach here is at **Luskentyre (Losgaintir)**; if the sun is shining it looks like paradise. Of course, the water temperature and weather are hardly Caribbean, but they do an efficient job of keeping the coast gloriously deserted. On the right as you near the beach, visit Donald John Mackay as he works in his studio at **Luskentyre Harris Tweed Co** ( ☎ 01859-550261; ◷ 9am-6pm Mon-Sat). He'll tell you the story of the day Nike came calling.

If this still feels like the beaten track, head east; the Bays coast is a strange, rocky moonscape, studded with small ponds and remote crofts. It's difficult to imagine how anyone could have survived in such an inhospitable environment – but they did, and still do.

On your way south on the A859, you'll strike the **Seallam! Centre** ( ☎ 01859-520258; www

.seallam.com; adult/child £2.50/2; 10am-5pm Mon-Sat; ), a small museum with displays on tweed, local fishing and changing exhibitions. It also has internet access (£1 per 20 minutes).

### LEVERBURGH (AN T-OB)

There were grand plans for this southern village to become a major fishing port in the early 20th century, but the boom never came. Today black-faced Cheviot sheep, rather than late-night hoons, wander the street.

Three miles east at **Rodel** (Roghadal) stands the remarkable **St Clement's Church** (HS; admission free; daily). Built in the 16th century, it didn't see much use before the Reformation left it derelict. It contains the wonderful tomb of its constructor Alexander MacLeod, in a niche beneath an archway elaborately carved with representations of saints; more-earthly scenes are below. The impressive castellated tower can be climbed via ladders, but you can't get outside.

**Kilda Cruises** ( 01859-502060; www.kildacruises .co.uk) runs day trips from Leverburgh to remote, rugged, poignant St Kilda, last western outpost of Britain and uninhabited since the last of the desperately poor community there were evacuated in 1930. It's an absolute paradise for seabirds. Trips cost £160 and give you six hours on the island.

Leverburgh's a good place to stay.

**our pick** **Am Bothan** ( 01859-520251; www.am bothan.com; dm £17.50; P wi-fi), with surely the most memorable lounge area of any hostel (yes that's a real boat hanging from the ceiling), is owned by a boat-builder and is a sociable place offering a big kitchen, peat fire and comfortable dorms; kids and mariners will love the ones kitted out like shipboard bunks, but others have more headroom.

On the Tarbert road a mile from the ferry, diminutive **Sorrel Cottage** ( 01859-520319; www .sorrelcottage.co.uk; s/d £40/65; P ) is a warm and hospitable place with three winning rooms with sparkling new bathrooms. Traditional woven fabrics cover the beds; upstairs, the 'Zen' room is halfway to heaven with its low sloping roof and skylights. Bikes are available for hire here (day's hire £10/12 for guests/nonguests).

By the pier **Anchorage Restaurant** ( 01859-520225; mains £7-12; 11am-8pm) caters to the ferry crowd with welcome Italian options and standard seafood. It's a bit pricey, but there ain't much competition.

A CalMac ferry connects Leverburgh to Berneray (person/car £5.75/26, 1¼ hours, three to four daily), itself connected by causeway to North Uist.

## NORTH UIST (UIBHIST A TUATH)
pop 1271

Flat North Uist lacks the scenic splendour of its southern cousin, with a moorland landscape studded with small lochs, but the geography is a big hit with birds; there are huge populations of migrant waders: oystercatchers, lapwings, curlews and redshanks. Grab a free copy of *Birds of the Uists* at a tourist office.

### Lochmaddy (Loch nam Madadh)

A peaceful, spread-out settlement, Lochmaddy is the main village in North Uist. The name, which means Loch of Dogs, refers to hound-like rock formations that you might spot on the ferry trip in. There's an ATM here, as well as shop, petrol station, post office, pub and **tourist office** ( 01876-500321; 9am-1pm & 2-5pm Mon-Sat Apr-Oct).

**Taigh Chearsabhagh** ( 01876-500293; www.taigh -chearsabhagh.org; admission by donation, sandwiches £2-4; 10am-5pm Mon-Sat Feb-Dec; ) retains few of its roots as an 18th-century inn but has a wildlife display, exhibition of contemporary art, and a cafe with water views and tasty sandwiches; try one with the local smoked salmon.

Out of town you can go on a Wednesday morning otter walk (£5, three hours) around Loch Langass; call **Balranald RSPB** ( 01876-560287) to book.

The **Uist Outdoor Centre** ( 01876-500480; www .uistoutdoorcentre.co.uk; dm £12; wi-fi) runs all sorts of activities, from abseiling to diving. The building's functional, but the four-bed dorms, kitchen and lounge area are clean and comfortable.

Nearby, **Tigh Dearg Hotel** ( 01876-500700; www .tighdearghotel.co.uk; s/d £90/145; P wi-fi) is an unlikely find. This cheerfully contemporary hotel looks like a bunkhouse from the outside but has a rather luxurious interior with leather lounges around the fire in the bar, sea views and modish DVD-equipped rooms. The impressive facilities include a gym and sauna (£5 a day for nonguests); the restaurant is also worthwhile, and does cheap takeaways as well as more-upmarket fare (mains £9 to £12). It's all upbeat, refreshingly unpretentious and cheaper in low season. Pronounce it 'tie-jerak' to sound cool and in control.

CalMac ferries run from Lochmaddy to Uig on Skye (person/car £10/48, 1¾ hours, one or two daily).

### Balranald RSPB Reserve

At this machair reserve, 18 miles west of Lochmaddy off the A865, you can watch migrant waders or rare red-necked phalarope, and listen for corncrakes. There's a **visitors centre** ( ☎ 01876-560287; www.rspb.org.uk; ☺ 9am-5pm) with a resident warden. From May to August, there are guided birdwatching walks at 10am.

### Berneray

The island of Berneray is connected by causeway to North Uist. From here, CalMac runs ferries to Leverburgh on South Harris (person/car £5.75/26, 1¼ hours, three to four daily). Also here, and served by buses that run from Lochmaddy via the ferry, **Beàrnaraigh Hostel** (www.gatliff.org.uk; camping sites/dm £5/9; **P**) has an enchanting location in farm buildings on a beautiful stretch of coast. There's a simple kitchen and comfy-enough beds; it's a cheap but utterly privileged retreat.

## BENBECULA (BEINN NA FAOGHLA)
pop 1249

A stepping stone between North Uist and South Uist and connected by causeways, Benbecula is a low-lying island that's almost as much water as land. The army's Hebrides Rocket Range takes up most of the west coast and gives the island a less tranquil atmosphere. There's a seven-day supermarket by the causeway to South Uist, and in the main settlement **Balivanich** (Baile a'Mhanaich), you'll find services such as a bunkhouse, ATM and post office.

## SOUTH UIST (UIBHIST A DEAS)
pop 1818

Long and narrow South Uist offers breathtaking scenery, but its main villages with their ugly houses aren't it. Make sure you get beyond the main north–south road to the corncrake-stalked meadows, to the wonderful machair-backed beaches of the west coast, and to the majestic craggy hills and remote sea lochs of the east coast where otters sport among the seaweed.

### Lochboisdale (Loch Baghasdail)

The ferry port of Lochboisdale in the southeast is the largest settlement, but not especially charming to eyes or nose. The **tourist office** ( ☎ 01878-700286; ☺ 9am-1pm & 2-5pm Mon-Sat Easter-Oct) sometimes opens for late ferry arrivals. There's an ATM here, and petrol too.

Right by the ferry, reliable **Lochboisdale Hotel** ( ☎ 01878-700332; www.lochboisdale.com; s/d £50/90; **P**) has old-fashioned rooms with sea views and friendly folk running it. The bar serves fish-based meals (£8 to £12) with the odd pasta.

**Wireless Cottage** ( ☎ 01878-700660; d £44; **P**) sits on the main road in a solid early-20th-century building built to house the island's first telephone exchange. It has two comfortable rooms and is an easy walk to the ferry.

CalMac runs **ferries** between Lochboisdale and Oban (person/car £22/81, 5½ hours, four to six weekly), some via Barra (person/car £6.30/36.50, 1½ hours).

### Howmore (Tobha Mòr)

This attractive coastal village in the middle of the island appeals for its thatched crofters' cottages, nearby beach and ruined medieval chapels. It was the burial site of the Ranald clan chiefs.

On the main road some 6 miles south, **Kildonan museum** ( ☎ 01878-710343; adult/child £2/free; ☺ 10am-5pm Mon-Sat, 2-5pm Sun Easter-Oct) is an intriguing museum that recreates traditional crofting life with a display of tools, furniture and fascinating photographs. There are also many local accounts of harsh Hebridean life and of the diaspora to Canada and Australia in the wake of the Clearances.

You can hire bikes in Howmore at Rothan Cycles (p945).

In Howmore, **Tobha Mòr Hostel** (www.gatliff .org.uk; camping sites/dm £5/9; **P**) is a cosy do-it-yourself spot by the ruined chapels. You've a fair chance of seeing or at least hearing corncrakes, and the interior has power and a snug common room/kitchen, as well as simple berths spread over three buildings.

### The North

In the northern quarter of the island, two eastbound roads leave the main road and snake their way towards the craggy hills and the spectacular sea lochs of the east coast. As well as sheep and lovable ponies, this is prime otter-spotting territory; look for any spots where there's plenty of brown seaweed in the water. The northernmost turn-off takes you past the **Salar smokehouse** ( ☎ 01870-610324; www

## WHISKY GALORE!

Scotland's west coast abounds in legends of whisky-smuggling, but the folk of Eriskay didn't have to exert themselves at all in 1941, when the good ship SS *Politician* ran onto rocks with its cargo of cash and – wait for it – 24,000 cases of whisky, which had been in short supply given wartime rationing. The islanders, after making sure the crew were safe, soon set about stashing what they could. When the Customs turned up they didn't see the funny side, and several locals were jailed for theft.

The incident was immortalised in Compton Mackenzie's book *Whisky Galore!*, which was also made into a film. Reports still surface these days of a bottle or two being found around the island.

.salar.co.uk; ⊙ 9am-5pm Mon-Fri), which turns out tasty flaky smoked salmon.

At the junction of the main road and the turn-off for the memorable 4 miles to Loch Sgioport (Lochskipport), **Kinloch** ( ☎ 01870-620316; www.kinlochuist.com; s/d £33/66; P ) is a lakeside guesthouse run by a keen fisherman. The snug rooms are complemented by fresh eggs for breakfast, and evening meals are available on request.

### The South

A causeway links Ludag on South Uist to Eriskay, from where a CalMac ferry crosses to Barra (person/car £6/18, 40 minutes, four to five daily).

Right on South Uist's southwestern tip, with great views across to Eriskay and Barra, the **Polochar Inn** ( ☎ 01878-700215; polocharinn@aol .com; Pol a Charra; s/d £45/75; P ) will appeal to those who like to get away from things. It's a warm base for walking, fishing or breathing the Hebridean air.

## BARRA (BARRAIGH)

pop 1078

This tiny island, just 12 miles in circumference, is the pendant dangling from the chain of the Outer Hebrides. With beautiful beaches, machair, hills, neolithic remains and a strong sense of community, it's a distillation of the Western Isles.

The largest village is beautiful **Castlebay** (Bàgh a Chaisteil), which lives up to its name thanks to a craggy fortress sitting atop a rocky islet in the middle of the harbour, a memorable sight to greet arriving ferry passengers. Just up from the dock is a petrol station, ATM and **tourist office** ( ☎ 01871-810336; barra@visitscotland. com; Main St; ⊙ 9am-5pm Mon-Fri, 9am-12.30pm, 1.30-5pm Sat, noon-4pm Sun Apr-Oct).

Barra's great for biking: hit Barra Cycle Hire (p944) if the weather is fine.

Sitting staunch in the bay, **Kisimul Castle** (HS; ☎ 01871-810313; admission £4.70; ⊙ 9.30am-12.30pm & 1.30-5.30pm Apr-Sep) was built by the MacNeil clan in the 12th century, and gifted to Historic Scotland in 2000 for an annual rental of £1 plus a bottle of whisky. While some parts have been modernised, you can still appreciate the hardy nature of medieval fortifications amid a powerful odour of age and creosote. A boat (included) zips you back and forth from a slipway opposite the post office.

Just southwest of Castlebay, and visible across the harbour, the island of Vatersay is connected by causeway to Barra and worth visiting for its rural ambience and wonderful white-sand beaches. Recently, boisterous local Celt-rock group the Vatersay Boys have brought the place no little fame in Scotland.

**Boy James** ( ☎ 01871-890384) runs recommended boat trips to the island of Mingulay, whose population finally packed it in in 1912 and were resettled. The cliffs of the island are imposing, and you'll certainly see puffins and seals as well as the ruins of the settlement.

Turn left from the ferry for the five-minute stroll to **Dunard Hostel** ( ☎ 01871-810443; www.isle ofbarrahostel.co.uk; Castlebay; dm/tw/fm £12/32/44), a compact, cosy place with comfortable bunks and twins, and a family room. The owners are often not around but you can check yourself in via a whiteboard at the door. They run excellent sea-kayaking excursions from here (www.clearwaterpaddling.com), which cost £30/50 for a half-/full day; check the website for dates of wonderful seven-day tours in various parts of western Scotland.

There are B&Bs and a couple of hotels in the centre of town doing rooms and meals; a more interesting place to eat is **Cafe Kisimul** ( ☎ 01871-810645; Main St; mains £7-12; ⊙ 10am-8.30pm), an intimate eatery offering extremely tasty Indian food with a local twist – dishes use Barra lamb and scallops – as well as a few Italian dishes.

CalMac operates ferries from Oban to Castlebay (person/car £22/81, five hours, one daily); some continue to Lochboisdale on South Uist (person/car £6.30/36.50, 1½ hours).

# ORKNEY ISLANDS

There's a magic and mystique to the Orkneys that you'll begin to feel as soon as the Scottish mainland slips away astern. Consisting of 70 flat, green-topped islands stripped bare of trees by the wind, it's a place of ancient standing stones and prehistoric villages, an archipelago of lilting accents and Viking heritage narrated in the *Orkneyinga Saga* and still strong today, a spot whose ports tell of lives led with the blessings and rough moods of the sea, and a destination where seekers can find the melancholy wrecks of warships and the salty clamour of remote seabird colonies.

The principal island, confusingly called Mainland, has the two major settlements and ports – bustling market-town Kirkwall, and Stromness with its grey-flagged streets – and the standout ancient sites. From various ferry ports you can access the other 15 inhabited islands.

## Getting There & Away

### AIR
Flybe/Loganair flies to Kirkwall from Aberdeen, Inverness, Glasgow and Edinburgh, as well as the Shetlands. Buy the tickets online, as you can easily see which days have cheaper fares available.

### BOAT & BUS
Drivers should book crossings well in advance in summer, although there's always a chance of squeezing on as a standby. Prices listed are for one-way trips.

**Pentland Ferries** ( ☎ 01856-831226; www.pentland ferries.co.uk) has a zippy new catamaran that runs between Gills Bay, 3 miles west of John O'Groats, and St Margaret's Hope on Orkney (person/car £12/28, 40 minutes, three to four daily April to October), with reduced sailings in winter. Stagecoach uses this crossing in its bus–ferry–bus Orkney Express service between Inverness and Kirkwall (£28, one daily mid-May to September).

**NorthLink Ferries** ( ☎ 0845 6000 449; www.north linkferries.co.uk) operates ferries from Scrabster, by Thurso, to Stromness (person/car £15.50/46.40, 2¼ hours, two to three daily).

Citylink buses from Inverness to Thurso are timed to meet these boats. NorthLink also runs a service from Aberdeen to Kirkwall and on to the Shetlands (see p897).

**John O'Groats Ferries** ( ☎ 01955-611353; www .jogferry.co.uk) has a ferry (passengers and bicycles only) from John O'Groats to Burwick on South Ronaldsay from May to September (£16, 40 minutes, two to four daily), with onward transport to Kirkwall for a little extra. It operates the Orkney Bus bus–ferry–bus service from Inverness to Kirkwall (single/return £30/42, five hours, two daily June to August).

## Getting Around

The *Orkney Public Transport Timetable*, free at tourist offices, is invaluable. Bus services are very limited on Sunday in Orkney.

**Loganair** ( ☎ 01856-872494; orkneyres@loganair.co.uk) operates subsidised interisland flights within the archipelago. At the time of research these weren't reservable via the website, only by phone or email.

**Orkney Coaches** ( ☎ 01856-870555) runs bus services on Mainland and South Ronaldsay. Its Rover passes offer one/three days of unlimited travel for £6/15.

**Orkney Ferries** ( ☎ 01856-872044; www.orkneyferries .co.uk) operates interisland ferries throughout the Orkney Islands. Book car space ahead.

If you're going to explore a few historic sights on Orkney, Historic Scotland offers a cash-saving explorer pass that you can buy at any of the included attractions.

## KIRKWALL
pop 6206

Orkney's main town is the islands' commercial centre and there's a comparatively busy feel to its main shopping street and ferry dock. Founded in the 11th century, Kirkwall is centred around the stunning St Magnus Cathedral, one of Scotland's finest medieval churches.

## Information

**Kirkwall Library** (Junction Rd) Free internet access.

**Launderama** ( ☎ 01856-872982; 47 Albert St; service washes £7; ☼ Mon-Sat)

**Tourist office** ( ☎ 01856-872856; info@visitorkney .com; West Castle St; ☼ 9am-5pm Mon-Fri, 10am-4pm Sat Oct-Apr, 9am-6pm May & Sep, 8.30am-8pm Jun-Aug) Very helpful, with a range of publications and accommodation booking service.

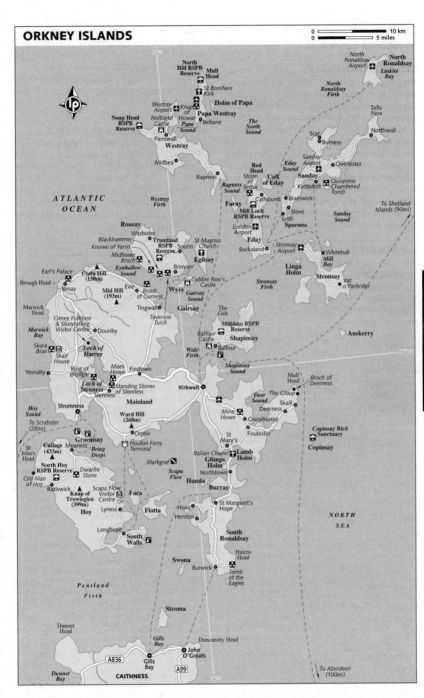

ORKNEY ISLANDS

## Sights

### ST MAGNUS CATHEDRAL

Looming benevolently over Kirkwall, **St Magnus Cathedral** ( ☎ 01856-874894; admission free; ☯ 9am-6pm Mon-Sat, 2-6pm Sun Apr-Sep, 9am-1pm & 2-5pm Mon-Sat Oct-Mar) is an exceptional building with a winning reddish-rose hue. Its interior is especially impressive, with the eerie atmosphere of an ancient faith pervading the place. Its narrow nave is defined by sturdy pillars and its aisles are flanked with blind-arching. And how many churches have a Viking longship on the altar? The result of 300 years of construction and several alterations, the cathedral includes Romanesque, transitional and Gothic styles.

The cathedral was commissioned in 1137 by Earl Rognvald Kolsson in honour of his uncle, Magnus Erlendsson, killed by his cousin during a squabble over control of Orkney. His bones were discovered in the 19th century in the rectangular pillars near the choir.

During summer, 40-minute **tours** (adult £5.50; ☯ 11am & 2pm Tue & Thu) offer access to the upper levels.

### EARL'S PALACE & BISHOP'S PALACE

Near the cathedral, these ruined **palaces** (HS; ☎ 01856-871918; Watergate; admission £3.70; ☯ 9.30am-5.30pm Apr-Sep, to 4.30pm Oct) are sandstone treasures. The better-preserved of the two buildings is the Earl's Palace, never actually completed but nevertheless once known as the finest example of Renaissance architecture in Scotland.

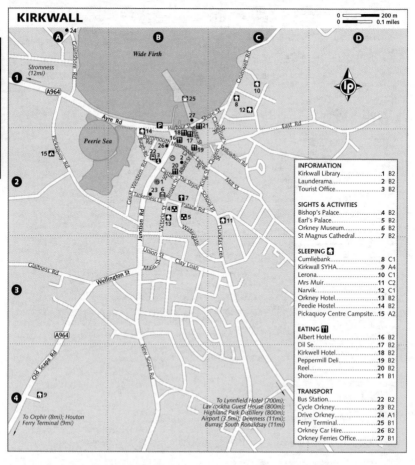

**KIRKWALL**

| INFORMATION | |
|---|---|
| Kirkwall Library | 1 B2 |
| Launderama | 2 B2 |
| Tourist Office | 3 B2 |

| SIGHTS & ACTIVITIES | |
|---|---|
| Bishop's Palace | 4 B2 |
| Earl's Palace | 5 B2 |
| Orkney Museum | 6 B2 |
| St Magnus Cathedral | 7 B2 |

| SLEEPING | |
|---|---|
| Cumliebank | 8 C1 |
| Kirkwall SYHA | 9 A4 |
| Lerona | 10 C1 |
| Mrs Muir | 11 C2 |
| Narvik | 12 C1 |
| Orkney Hotel | 13 B2 |
| Peedie Hostel | 14 B2 |
| Pickaquoy Centre Campsite | 15 A2 |

| EATING | |
|---|---|
| Albert Hotel | 16 B2 |
| Dil Se | 17 B2 |
| Kirkwell Hotel | 18 B2 |
| Peppermill Deli | 19 B2 |
| Reel | 20 B2 |
| Shore | 21 B1 |

| TRANSPORT | |
|---|---|
| Bus Station | 22 B2 |
| Cycle Orkney | 23 B2 |
| Drive Orkney | 24 A1 |
| Ferry Terminal | 25 B1 |
| Orkney Car Hire | 26 B2 |
| Orkney Ferries Office | 27 B1 |

The Bishop's Palace was built in the mid-12th century to provide comfortable lodgings for Bishop William, and Norwegian King Haakon the Old died here after a defeat at Largs. The tower affords views of the cathedral.

### ORKNEY MUSEUM

Opposite the cathedral's entrance, the town's **museum** ( ☎ 01856-873191; Broad St; admission free; ☽ 10.30am-5pm Mon-Sat, closes briefly for lunch Oct-Apr) is a labyrinthine display in a former merchant's house. It has an overview of Orkney history and prehistory, including Pictish carvings and a display on the Ba' (see the boxed text, right). Most engaging are the last rooms, covering 19th- and 20th-century social history; the earlier sections could do with a bit of a facelift, but then again, it's free.

### HIGHLAND PARK DISTILLERY

Among Scotland's more respected whisky-makers, and its most northerly, this **distillery** ( ☎ 01856-874619; www.highlandpark.co.uk; Holm Rd; tours £5; ☽ 10am-5pm Mon-Sat & noon-5pm Sun May-Aug, 10am-5pm Mon-Fri Apr, Sep & Oct, tours hourly, plus 2pm Mon-Fri Nov-Mar) is definitely one of the best to visit, for it malts its own barley. You can see the germinating barley, and the peat kiln used to dry it, on the excellent well-informed hour-long tour. The standard 12-year-old Highland Park is a soft, balanced malt that's very accessible for whisky novices and aficionados alike; the 18-year-old is among the world's finest drams. It, and other incarnations, can be tasted on more-specialised tours (£15), which you can arrange beforehand.

## Festivals

**St Magnus Festival** ( ☎ 01856-871445; www.stmagnusfestival.com; 60 Victoria St, Kirkwall) is held every June, with classical music, poetry and a popular conducting course. **MagFest** is a younger version of the festival, featuring Scottish bands.

## Sleeping

### BUDGET

**Pickaquoy Centre Campsite** ( ☎ 01856-879900; www.pickaquoy.com; Pickaquoy Rd; small/large tents £4.40/7.90) On Kirkwall's western fringe, this camp site is a windswept place (dig those pegs deep) with plenty of grass and just-renovated facilities.

**Peedie Hostel** ( ☎ 01856-875477; kirkwallpeediehostel@talk21.com; Ayre Rd; dm £12) Nestling into a corner at the end of the Kirkwall waterfront,

---

### THE BA'

Every Christmas Day and New Year's Day, Kirkwall shops are boarded up and the town holds a staggering spectacle at 1pm, a crazy ball game known as the **Ba'**. Two enormous teams, the Uppies and the Doonies, fight their way, no holds barred, through the streets, trying to get a leather ball to the other end of town. The ball is thrown from the Market Cross outside the cathedral to the waiting crowd; the Uppies have to get the ba' to the corner of Main St and Junction Rd, the Doonies must get it to the water. Violence, skullduggery and other stunts are common, and the event, fuelled by plenty of strong drink, can last hours.

---

this petite hostel squeezes in all the necessities for a comfortable stay in a small space. The dorms actually have plenty of room – it's only in the tiny kitchen, that territorial squabbles might break out.

**Kirkwall SYHA** ( ☎ 01856-872243; www.syha.org.uk; Old Scapa Rd; dm £14, s/d £19/28; ☽ mid-Mar–Oct; P ⌨ ) No beauty, this functional hostel is a 15-minute walk from the centre, and set in a demountable former naval barracks. Never meant to last beyond the war, it now shows its age: long walks to the institutional showers, and no power points in the rooms. However, it's run by nice people, and the big, sociable lounge and kitchen and large capacity are definite plus points.

### MIDRANGE

**our pick Narvik** ( ☎ 01856-879049; carolevansnarvik@hotmail.co.uk; Weyland Tce; s/d £35/55; P ) Dodge the B&B fascists who sweep you out of bed with a stiff-bristled broom for your 'late' seven-in-the-morning breakfast by staying at this charmingly peaceful spot. Accommodation is in a beautifully decorated separate flat, with tiled floor, wooden double bed, DVDs and grassy garden. You've got your own kitchenette, which genial hosts stock with eggs, bacon, croissants and juices so your morning meal is wholly at your own pace.

**Mrs Muir** ( ☎ 01856-874805; 2 Dundas Cres; s/d £30/60; P ) This former manse is a magnificent building with four enormous rooms blessed with large windows and sizeable beds. There are plenty of period features, but the bathrooms are not among them; they are sparklingly new, though harmoniously designed – one has a free-standing bathtub. Both the welcome and the breakfast will leave you more than satisfied.

**Lav'rockha Guest House** ( ☎ 01856-876103; www .lavrockha.co.uk; Inganess Rd; s/d £45/60; P ⬚ ) It's the details that make this spot one of the best guesthouses in the Orkneys. Spacious rooms, for example, all come with full-pressure showers, not the fiddly boxes that never deliver. The food is particularly good, not just breakfasts but also the award-winning dinners (three-courses £16), which are preceded by a drink in the lounge.

**Orkney Hotel** ( ☎ 01856-873477; www.orkneyhotel .co.uk; 40 Victoria St; s/d £76/99; ⬚ wi-fi) This historic hotel has been revitalised with shiraz-coloured walls in the foyer and smart refurbished rooms, including some with disabled access across the street. The best bed is a four-poster with views of the cathedral.

**Lynnfield Hotel** ( ☎ 01856-872505; www.lynnfieldhotel .co.uk; Holm Rd; s/d £75/100; P ⬚ wi-fi) Within whiffing distance of the Highland Park Distillery, this recently refitted hotel is run with a professional yet warmly personal touch. With individual rooms featuring four-poster beds, a Jacuzzi or antique writing desk, and a cosy dark-wood drawing room, it's an intimate place, which also boasts a good restaurant.

Other options:

**Lerona** ( ☎ 01856-874538; Cromwell Cres; s/d without bathroom £25/50, with bathroom £30/60; P ) Guests come first, but the wee folk – a battalion of garden gnomes, and clans of dolls with lifelike stares – are close behind.

**Cumliebank** ( ☎ 01856-873160; Cromwell Rd; d £46) Great position overlooking the harbour and a warm, homespun welcome.

## Eating & Drinking

**Reel** ( ☎ 01856-871000; 3 Castle St; snacks £2-4; ☽ 10am-6pm) Upstairs from a music shop, this excellent cafe continues the theme, with folk music tinkling and a vase full of woodwind instruments, if you think you can do better. Massive coffee bowls, milkshakes and inventive gourmet sandwiches are on offer, all named by an outrageous punster, who should be taken out and shot for calling their cheese sandwich... Skara Brie.

**Peppermill Deli** ( ☎ 01856-878878; 21 Albert St; snacks £2-5; ☽ 8.30am-7pm May-Sep, 9am-5.30pm Oct-Apr) This bright open deli has a wide range of absolutely delicious takeaway wraps, paninis and sandwiches with a great range of ingredients.

It also does salads and that old fallback, the baked potato.

**Albert Hotel** ( ☎ 01856-876000; Mounthoolie Lane; bar meals £7-9, restaurant mains £12-20; ☽ bar meals lunch & dinner, restaurant dinner) Offering plenty of variety, the Albert Hotel has three parts. The Bothy Bar looks very smart these days with its slate floor and black-and-white photos of old-time Orcadian farming, but its low tables provide the customary good cheer and sustaining food; think sausages, think haddock, think stews. Stables, the smarter restaurant, does tasty steaks and seafood with inventive sauces, while the kid-friendly lounge bar round the back does pizza.

**Dil Se** ( ☎ 01856-875242; 7 Bridge St; mains £8-13; ☽ 4-11pm) Upbeat and inventive, this mainstreet subcontinental choice tries to steer Orcadians away from the cliched curry classics in favour of baltis – the spinach one is fabulous – and other creations. The late opening means you can enjoy those long summer evenings outdoors and not go hungry at the end of them.

**Kirkwall Hotel** ( ☎ 01856-872232; Harbour St; mains £9-19; ☽ lunch & dinner) Dominating the harbour opposite the ferry pier, the grand old Kirkwall still gives you a grand old night out in its restaurant. The seafood, in particular, is beautifully prepared and presented, and served with a smile, but there are meaty and vegetarian choices as well.

**Shore** ( ☎ 01856-872200; www.theshore.co.uk; 6 Shore St; restaurant mains £11-20; ☽ lunch & dinner) This popular harbourside eatery brings the gastropub concept to Kirkwall, offering bar meals combined with more-adventurous fare in the restaurant section. It's a little hit-and-miss, but the local chefs are assured when it comes to the sea – monkfish wrapped in bacon on roasted cherry tomatoes is very tasty. Rooms are also available (singles £57, doubles £78 to £89 room only).

## Getting There & Away

The **airport** ( ☎ 01856-886210) is 3.5 miles from town. See p952 for flight information. For flights and ferries to the northern islands, see the individual islands.

From the bus station, Orkney Coaches runs to Stromness (40 minutes, roughly hourly Monday to Saturday, four on Sunday); bus 6 hits Tingwall (25 minutes, two to five daily Monday to Saturday) for the Rousay ferry, and goes on to Evie and Birsay. Bus 8A does a summer circuit two to four times daily between Kirkwall and Stromness via Skara Brae, the Ring of Brodgar, and the Stenness standing stones.

## Getting Around

There are several car-rental places that charge around £27 to £35 per day, including **Orkney Car Hire** ( ☎ 01856-872866; www.orkneycarhire .co.uk; Junction Rd) and **Drive Orkney** ( ☎ 01856-877551; www.driveorkney.com; Grainshore Rd), while **Cycle Orkney** ( ☎ 01856-875777; cycleorkney@btconnect.com; Tankerness Lane) rents out mountain bikes.

# WEST & NORTH MAINLAND
## Stromness
pop 1609

Stromness is a rambling town with winding streets flanking the port and a picturesque flagstone-paved main street. The port's heyday was during the 18th century when Americas-bound ships used it while conflict with the French had made the Channel unsafe. The town's easy pace and proximity to Skara Brae make it a popular choice as an Orkney base.

### INFORMATION

**Stromness Library** (Hellihole Rd; �2-7pm Mon-Thu, 2-5pm Fri, 10am-5pm Sat) Free internet access.

**Tourist office** ( ☎ 01856-850716; stromness@visit orkney.com; �covY9am-5pm May–mid-Sep, ring to check winter opening hr) In the ferry terminal.

### SIGHTS & ACTIVITIES

To learn more about the town's maritime heritage, **Stromness Museum** ( ☎ 01856-850025; 52 Alfred St; admission £3.50; �covY10am-5pm Apr-Sep, 11am-3.30pm Mon-Sat Oct-Mar) has a collection of historical oddments, including exhibits on whaling and the scuttled German High Seas fleet. If you've brought your MP3 player, there's an excellent BBC podcast (www.bbc.co.uk/sn/tvradio/pro grammes/take_one/downloads.shtml) that takes you on a tour of the museum.

Resplendently redesigned, the **Pier Arts Centre** ( ☎ 01856-850209; www.pierartscentre.com; Ferry Rd; admission free; �covY10.30am-5pm Mon-Sat) has really rejuvenated the Orkney modern art scene with its sleek lines and upbeat attitude. It's worth a look as much for the architecture as for the latest exhibition.

If you fancy a bit of naval gazing, **Scapa Scuba** ( ☎ 01856-851218; www.scapascuba.co.uk; Dundas St) takes you to dive sunken warships in Scapa Flow (one-day dives from £130). It also does

a beginners' half-day on one of the Churchill Barriers (see p960) wrecks for £70.

### SLEEPING
**Point of Ness Campsite** ( ☎ 01856-873535; sites £4.40-8.10) This well-positioned camp site (a 15-minute walk south of the ferry) overlooks the bay from its breezy situation on a headland south of the centre by the golf course. It's well maintained and reasonably equipped.

**Brown's Hostel** ( ☎ 01856-850661; 45 Victoria St; dm £12; ☐ ) On the main street, this handy place has cramped but cosy and homelike dorms as well as small singles. Life centres around its inviting common area, where you can browse the free internet or swap pasta recipes in the open kitchen.

**Hamnavoe Hostel** ( ☎ 01856-851202; www.hamna voehostel.co.uk; 10a North End Rd; dm £15-18; ☐ wi-fi) This well-equipped hostel lacks a bit of character but makes up for that with excellent facilities, including a fine kitchen and a lounge room with great perspectives over the water. The dorms are very commodious, with duvets and reading lamps, and the showers are good.

**Orca Hotel** ( ☎ 01856-851803; www.orcahotel.com; 76 Victoria St; s/d/f £30/50/60) Warm and homelike, this place is likeably out of the ordinary, and features cosy rooms with narrow, comfortable beds. There's a restaurant downstairs (dinner Thursday to Saturday June to September) with the feel of an artists hangout in Prague or Paris; in winter you can use the hotel's kitchen.

**Miller's House & Harbourside Guest House** ( ☎ 01856-851969; www.orkneyisles.co.uk/millershouse; 13 John St; s/d £40/50; ☐Y Easter-Oct) Reached up a side alley, Miller's House is an historic Stromness residence – check out the wonderful 1716 stone doorway – but most of the rooms are actually in a different building (Harbourside) around the corner. Here you can smell the cleanliness, and there's plenty of light and an optimistic feel. Showers hit the spot, and you can use the laundry. Exceptional breakfasts include vegetarian options and daily-baked bread.

**Stromness Hotel** ( ☎ 01856-850298; www.stromness hotel.com; Victoria St; s/d £55/98; ☐P ☐ wi-fi) Proudly surveying the main street and harbour, this lofty Victorian hotel is a reminder of the way things used to be, with its posh revolving door and imposing facade. The pink-hued rooms are spacious, but the yielding beds have seen better days and the claustrophobic lift

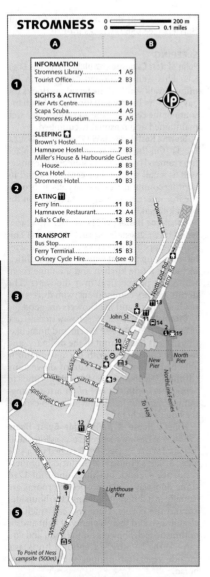

**STROMNESS**

0 ———— 200 m
0 ———— 0.1 miles

**INFORMATION**
Stromness Library...................**1** A5
Tourist Office.......................**2** B3

**SIGHTS & ACTIVITIES**
Pier Arts Centre....................**3** B4
Scapa Scuba.........................**4** A5
Stromness Museum................**5** A5

**SLEEPING**
Brown's Hostel......................**6** B4
Hamnavoe Hostel..................**7** B3
Miller's House & Harbourside Guest
   House..............................**8** B3
Orca Hotel..........................**9** B4
Stromness Hotel...................**10** B3

**EATING**
Ferry Inn............................**11** B3
Hamnavoe Restaurant..........**12** A4
Julia's Cafe.........................**13** B3

**TRANSPORT**
Bus Stop............................**14** B3
Ferry Terminal.....................**15** B3
Orkney Cycle Hire..............(see 4)

means your suitcase'll have to find its own way. There's a restaurant, lounge bar and the earthier Flattie Bar downstairs.

### EATING & DRINKING
**Julia's Cafe** ( ☎ 01856-850904; 20 Ferry Rd; mains £4-8; ☺ 9am-5pm Sep-May, plus dinner Wed-Sun Jun-Aug) This cafe-with-conservatory opposite the port

keeps all comers happy, with massive fry-ups (£8) offset on the cardiac karma scale by wraps, salads, and tempting vegetarian dishes like nut roast and couscous. In summer the cafe opens for dinner with more-elaborate fare (£10 to £13) on offer.

**Ferry Inn** ( ☎ 01856-850280; www.ferryinn.com; 10 John St; mains £6-13; ☺ breakfast, lunch & dinner) Every port has its pub, and in Stromness it's the Ferry. Convivial and central, it warms the cockles with folk music, local beers and characters, and solid pub food like pork stuffed with haggis or delicious marinated Orkney herring.

**Hamnavoe Restaurant** ( ☎ 01856-850606; 35 Graham Pl; mains £14-19; ☺ dinner daily mid-Apr–Sep, Fri-Sun Jan–mid-Apr) Tucked away up a side alley, this intimate place is definitely the top dining option in Stromness. Dishes such as monkfish – tangy with sweet pepper and Pernod – and guinea fowl roasted with peaches in brandy feature in the intimate dining room; there's also a decent wine list. It opens for 'lobster lunches' Thursday to Saturday in summer.

### GETTING THERE & AWAY
Orkney Coaches runs to Kirkwall (40 minutes, roughly hourly Monday to Saturday, four on Sunday); and Birsay (25 minutes, two daily). From May to September there are two to four daily buses to Skara Brae (15 minutes).

For information on NorthLink ferries to/from Scrabster see p952, and to/from Aberdeen and Lerwick, p897. For ferries to Hoy, see p962.

### GETTING AROUND
You can rent a well-maintained bike from **Orkney Cycle Hire** ( ☎ 01856-850255; 54 Dundas St; hire from £6 per day).

## Stenness
About a mile east of this hamlet are three of the Orkneys' most impressive prehistoric monuments, easily accessed by buses running between Stromness and Kirkwall.

### MAES HOWE
Built around 5000 years ago, **Maes Howe** (HS; ☎ 01856-761606; admission £5.20; ☺ tours hourly 10am-3pm Oct-Mar, also 4pm Apr-Sep) is an extraordinary place, a Stone Age tomb built from enormous sandstone blocks, some of which weighed many tons and were brought from

several miles away. Creeping down the long stone passageway to the central chamber, you feel the indescribable gulf of years that separate us from the architects of this mysterious place. Though nothing is known about who and what was interred here, the scope of the project suggests it was a structure of great significance.

By chance or design, for a few weeks around the winter solstice, the setting sun shafts up the entrance passage, and strikes the back wall of the tomb in spooky alignment. If you can't be there, check the webcams on www.maeshowe.co.uk.

In the 12th century, the tomb was broken into by Vikings searching for treasure. A couple of years later, another group sought shelter in the chamber from a blizzard that lasted three days. While they waited out the storm, they carved runic graffiti on the walls. As well as the sadly predictable 'Olaf was 'ere' and 'Thorni bedded Helga', there are also more-intricate carvings, including a particularly fine dragon and a knotted serpent.

Buy tickets in Tormiston Mill, on the other side of the road. Entry is by 45-minute guided tours that leave on the hour. Make sure to reserve your tour-slot ahead by phone. Due to the oversized groups, guides tend to only show a couple of the Viking inscriptions, but they'll happily show more if asked.

### STANDING STONES OF STENNESS

Within sight of Maes Howe, four mighty **stones** (HS; admission free; ⏲ 24hr) remain of what was once a circle of 12. Recent research suggests they were perhaps erected as long ago as 3300 BC, and they impose by sheer size; the tallest measures 5.7m in height. This narrow strip of land, the Ness of Brodgar, separates the Harray and Stenness lochs and was the site of a large settlement, inhabited throughout the neolithic period (3500–1800 BC).

### RING OF BRODGAR

Dominating the brow of a rise about a mile from the Stenness stones, this spectacular and enormous circle of **standing stones** (HS; admission free; ⏲ 24hr) once comprised 60 megaliths across a 104m diameter, but today just 21 stones rise above the heather. Last of the three Stenness monuments to be built (2500–2000 BC), it remains a most atmospheric location. Free guided tours leave from the car park at 1pm from June to August.

### ORKNEY FOLKLORE & STORYTELLING VISITOR CENTRE

Between Brodgar and Skara Brae, this offbeat **centre** ( ☎ 01856-841207; www.orkneyretreat.co.uk; admission £3.50; ⏲ by appointment) focuses on the islands' folkloric tradition. The best way to experience it is on one of the atmospheric storytelling evenings (Sundays, Tuesdays and Fridays at 8.30pm, adult/children £10/6), when local legends are related around the peat fire. The centre also offers relaxing **B&B** (s/d £25/50; P ), with traditional bannocks and oatmeal bread and locally cured bacon at breakfast, oatcakes and cheese in the afternoons, and a telescope for starry nights.

### Skara Brae

One of the world's most evocative prehistoric sites, **Skara Brae** (HS; ☎ 01856-841815; admission summer/winter £6.70/5.70; ⏲ 9.30am-5.30pm Apr-Sep, 9.30am-4.30pm Oct-Mar) is a wonderfully preserved neolithic village 8 miles north of Stromness. Inhabited for 600 years, and abandoned roughly when Egypt's Great Pyramid was built, the village features houses superbly preserving their stone beds and dressers and central hearths, as if the residents had just popped out. These cosy-looking dwellings were only discovered in 1850 when a storm ripped off the top of the dunes, whose sand had preserved them so intact.

The visit starts with a short video and excellent introductory exhibition, with archaeological findings in bold and theories in italics – an idea that should be used more often. You then enter a reconstructed house, giving the excavation, which you head on to next, more meaning.

After the site itself, you can drop into **Skaill House** ( ⏲ summer only; joint ticket with Skara Brae), built for the local bishop in 1620. It's a bit anticlimactic catapulting straight from the neolithic to the 1950s decor, but you can see a smart hidden compartment in the library as well as the bishop's original 17th-century four-poster bed.

From May to September there are two to four buses daily to and from Stromness and Kirkwall. You can also walk here along the coast from Stromness, a bracing cliff-top stroll of a couple of hours.

### Birsay

Birsay was once the islands' most important settlement; **Earl's Palace** (HS; admission free;

24hr) was built by Robert Stewart, scourge of Orkney peasants, in the 16th century. It's an atmospheric spot, with honey-coloured walls and crumbling columns that don't quite evoke the ruthlessness of their builder.

At low tide, stroll to the **Brough of Birsay** (HS; ☎ 01856-841815; admission £3.20; ☻ 9.30am-5.30pm mid-Jun–Sep), almost a mile from the Earl's Palace. These ruins of a Norse settlement centred on the 12th-century St Peter's Church include several longhouses.

**our pick Linkshouse** ( ☎ 01856-721221; www.ewaf .co.uk; The Palace, Birsay; s/d £40/70; ☻ Mar-Oct; **P** ) is a most welcoming place to stay near the sea at Birsay. The beautiful rooms of this stone house – one with comforting sloping ceiling, one with a toilet with wonderful vistas – are complemented by a great little gazebo space, where you can contemplate the scenery, or browse the books and maps kept here (along with a wee decanter of sherry). Breakfast is a treat – pancakes with blueberries and crème fraiche anyone?

### Evie

Signposted from Evie is the **Broch of Gurness** ( ☎ 01856-751414; admission £4.70; ☻ 9.30am-6.30pm Apr-Sep), a fine example of these drystone fortified towers that were both status symbol for powerful farmers and useful protection from raiders some 2200 years ago. The imposing entranceway and sturdy stone walls – originally 10m high – impress; inside you can see the hearth and where a mezzanine floor would have fitted. Around the broch are the remains of the settlement centred on it.

**Eviedale Cottages & Campsite** ( ☎ 01856-751270; tent sites from £5-8, dm £5, self-catering cottages per week £290-330; ☻ camp site Apr-Sep; **P** ) has a good grassy area for camping, with picnic tables, and a rudimentary bothy with four bunk beds but no showers. Next door, self-catering farm cottages provide superior country-style accommodation.

Down a turning about a mile west of the Tingwall ferry turn-off, **Woodwick House** ( ☎ 01856-751330; www.woodwickhouse.co.uk; Woodwick Bay; s/d without bathroom £34/68, s with bathroom £65-75, d with bathroom £96-110; **P** 🖵 wi-fi) is a mansion of downplayed elegance in a lovely setting. The commodious rooms are in harmony with the relaxed rural atmosphere, as are the cosy lounges with fire and books, and your courteous hosts do fine three-course dinners (£26; open to nonguests) and put on the odd

cultural event. If you've been on Orkney for a while, you may not recognise those wooden things around the house: trees.

## EAST MAINLAND, BURRAY & SOUTH RONALDSAY

When a German U-boat sneaked into Scapa Flow and sank the battleship HMS *Royal Oak* right under the Royal Navy's nose in 1939, Sir Winston Churchill decided it was time to better protect this crucial naval harbour. Using concrete blocks and discarded ships, the channels between Lamb Holm, Glimps Holm, Burray, South Ronaldsay and Mainland were blocked; the so-called **Churchill Barriers** still link the islands, and you'll drive over them heading north from the John O'Groats or Gills Bay ferry.

On Mainland, just beyond Kirkwall's airport, the mysterious **Mine Howe** ( ☎ 01856-861209; adult/child £2.50/1.50; ☻ 11am-3pm Tue & Fri May, 10am-4pm daily Jun-Aug) is an Iron Age site accessed via a steep downwards staircase and made famous by an excavation in the *Time Team* TV series.

Passing here, and continuing through Deerness, you reach the end of the road at Mull Head. A short walk from the car park brings you to the **Gloup**, a spectacular natural arch and narrow channel. Beyond here, a half-mile cliff walk brings you to the **Broch of Deerness**.

Heading south from Mainland, on the island of Lamb Holm, is the **Italian Chapel** ( ☎ 01856-781268; admission free; ☻ 9am-10pm Apr-Sep, 9am-4.30pm Oct-Mar), built by the same Italian POWs who constructed the Churchill Barriers. Built from two Nissen huts, with the plasterboard interior painted up to resemble tiles, it's a beautiful and moving construction. The main man was invited back in 1960 to restore and complete it.

Right in the south of South Ronaldsay, the **Tomb of the Eagles** ( ☎ 01856-831339; www.tom boftheeagles.co.uk; Liddle Farm; admission £6; ☻ 10am-noon Mar, 9.30am-6pm Apr-Oct, by arrangement Nov-Feb) is the result of a local farmer finding two significant archaeological sites on his land. The first is a Bronze Age stone building with a firepit, indoor well and plenty of seating; orthodox theory suggests it was a communal cooking site, but we reckon it's the original Orkney pub, and we're not alone. Beyond here, in a spectacular cliff-top position, the neolithic tomb (wheel yourself in prone on a trolley) is an elaborate stone construction that held the remains of up to 340 people who died some five millennia ago. Before you head out to the sites, an excellent personal explanation is given to you at the visitor centre; you meet a few spooky skulls and can handle some of the artefacts found. It's about a mile's airy walk to the tomb from the centre.

The main village on South Ronaldsay is **St Margaret's Hope**, named after Margaret, the Maid of Norway, who was to have married Edward II of England but is thought to have died here in 1290 en route to the wedding. The town is an attractive stone-built port and ferry terminus.

## Sleeping & Eating

**St Margaret's Hope Backpacker's Hostel** ( ☎ 01856-831225; orkneybackpackers@hotmail.co.uk; St Margaret's Hope; dm £12; **P** ) This pretty stone cottage has comfortable dorms in the heart of the village, as well as a decent kitchen and laundry facilities. Off the main dorm are a single and double (same price) if you fancy a bit of privacy. If there's nobody about, ask in the Trading Post shop a couple of doors down.

**Creel** ( ☎ 01856-831311; www.thecreel.co.uk; Front Rd, St Margaret's Hope; mains £20; ☺ dinner Wed-Sun Easter–mid-Oct) On the waterfront in an unassuming house, on unpretentious wooden tables, some of Scotland's best seafood has been served up for well over 20 years. Upstairs and next door, the rooms face the spectacular sunset over the water, and are most spacious and comfortable (singles/doubles £75/105). It was up for sale at the time of research, so fingers crossed.

## Getting There & Away

Buses connect Kirkwall with St Margaret's Hope (30 minutes, four daily Monday to Friday, two on Saturday) and Burwick (50 minutes, two daily) to connect with ferries (p952).

## HOY
### pop 392

The Norse word *Haey* (meaning High Island) gave this lofty isle its name, but it's more than altitude that lends the second-largest of the Orkneys its beauty. The sea has spectacularly nibbled at this coastline, creating not just jaw-dropping cliffs and turquoise bays, but also unearthly stacks and rock formations.

Best of all, because this island is only 14 miles across at its longest point, you can explore this dramatic landscape with or without your own vehicle. If your camera is twitching for cliff scenery, **St John's Head** (346m) on the west coast is one of Britain's highest vertical cliffs. The equally photogenic **Old Man of Hoy**, a 137m-high sea stack, is the island's best-known sight and a real challenge for advanced rock climbers. The finest scenery is in the north of the island, a large part of which forms the **North Hoy RSPB Reserve**, where you can see fulmars, kittiwakes, great skuas and other seabirds.

One of the island's more popular walks follows the cliff edge opposite the Old Man of Hoy. Allow about seven hours for the return trip from Moaness Pier where the ferries dock. Alternatively, you can hike a circuit to the Old Man that goes via the **Dwarfie Stone** (HS; admission free), a squat tomb carved into a single block of sandstone in 3000 BC, or head straight to it from Rackwick, at the road's end.

The car ferry from Mainland arrives at Lyness, base for the British Grand Fleet until 1956. **Scapa Flow Visitor Centre** ( ☎ 01856-791300; admission free; ☺ 9am-4.30pm Mon-Fri, plus 10.30am-3.30pm

---

### SCAPA FLOW WRECKS

One of the world's largest natural harbours, Scapa Flow has been in near-constant use by various fleets from the Vikings onwards. After WWI, 74 German ships were interned in Scapa; when the terms of the armistice were agreed on 6 May 1919 with the announcement of a severely reduced German navy, Admiral von Reuter, who was in charge of the fleet, decided to take matters into his own hands. On 21 June, a secret signal was passed from ship to ship and the British watched incredulously as every German ship began to sink. Fifty-two of them went to the bottom, with the rest left aground in shallow water.

Most of the ships were salvaged, but seven vessels remain to attract divers. There are three battleships – the *König*, the *Kronprinz Wilhelm* and the *Markgraf* – each of which is over 25,000 tons. The first two were subjected to blasting for scrap metal, but the *Markgraf* is undamaged and considered one of the best dives in the area.

Sat & Sun mid-May–Oct) is a fascinating naval museum incorporating a photographic display in an old pumphouse. Most interesting is the account of the sinking of the German fleet after WWI; there's also a cheerful little cafe.

## Sleeping & Eating

**Hoy Centre** ( ☎ 01856-791315; Moaness; dm £13; P ) Recently refurbished, this government-run hostel is just 15 minutes' walk from Moaness Pier and at the base of the rugged Cuilags. It has comfortable dorms (with bathrooms) which have firm new mattresses and bedding, and a good kitchen. The same warden runs a simpler eight-bed hostel at Rackwick (dorms £10.25, open April to September).

**Stromabank Hotel** ( ☎ 01856-701494; www.stroma bank.co.uk; Longhope; meals £8-11; ☿ dinner Jun-Sep, ring for winter opening hr) Eating places are thin on the ground in Hoy, but this hilltop hotel is one such. As well as pub standards like steaks and pies, there are also specials such as crab cakes with sweet chilli sauce. The location offers great views across to the Caithness coast.

## Getting There & Away

A **car ferry** ( ☎ 01856-811397) sails to Lyness (Hoy) from Houton on Mainland (return per person/car £6.80/21.80, three to nine daily, 35 minutes), also dropping in at the island of Flotta. Drivers should book in advance. The more limited Sunday service runs from May to late September.

A **passenger/bicycle ferry** ( ☎ 01856-850624) operates between Stromness and Moaness Pier (25 minutes, two to four daily May to September). There's a reduced schedule from October to April.

# NORTHERN ISLANDS

This group of windswept islands is a refuge for migrating birds and a nesting ground for seabirds; there are several RSPB reserves. Some of the islands are also rich in archaeological sites. However, the beautiful scenery, with wonderful white-sand beaches and lime-green to azure seas, is the main attraction.

The tourist offices in both Kirkwall and Stromness have a useful brochure, *The Islands of Orkney*, which includes maps and details of these islands. Note that the pronunciation of the 'ay' ending of each island name is 'ee' (eg Shapinsay is pronounced Shapinsee).

Orkney Ferries runs to these islands from Kirkwall; you can usually find a local boat

that'll zip you between islands to save returning to the capital.

## Shapinsay
**pop 300**

A 20-minute ferry trip from Kirkwall, this fertile island with its basking seals makes for a great day trip. **Balfour Castle** ( ☎ 01856-711282; www.balfourcastle.com; d incl dinner £220-260; P ) was designed as a calendar house, as it has seven turrets, 12 exterior doors, 52 rooms and 365 panes of glass. Tours of the castle (2.15pm Sunday May to September; £20 including ferry) will take you inside to admire the birds under glass and the sweet wee chapel, and finish with Orcadian afternoon tea made from produce from the expansive gardens. If you want to feel like royalty, you can stay in stately Victorian rooms with predinner drinks in the historic library and views of the ferry sailing to Kirkwall.

Otherwise you can enjoy tea and scones at the **Smithy** ( ☎ 01856-711722; www.shapinsaysmithy .com; snacks £2-5, meals £6-9; ☿ 10am-11pm), a rustic old-stone blacksmith's that was in use until the 1950s. The coffee comes with tasty shortbread, and the daily blackboard menu usually includes tasty local seafood.

Orkney Ferries runs from Kirkwall (return per person/car £6.80/21.80, 25 minutes, five to six daily, only two Sunday in winter).

## Rousay
**pop 267**

Just off the north coast of Mainland, hilly Rousay merits exploration for its fine assembly of prehistoric sites, great views and relaxing away-from-it-all ambience. Connected by regular ferry from Tingwall, it makes a great little day trip, but you may well feel a pull to stay longer.

The major **archaeological sites** (HS; admission free; ☿ 24hr) are clearly labelled from the 14-mile road that rings the island. Heading west (left) from the ferry, you soon come to **Taversoe Tuick**, an intriguing burial cairn constructed on two levels, with separate entrances – perhaps a joint tomb for different families; a semidetached solution in posthumous housing. You can squeeze into the cairn to explore both levels, but there's not much space. Not far beyond here are two other significant cairns, **Blackhammer**, then **Knowe of Yarso**, the latter a fair walk up the hill but with majestic views.

Six miles from the ferry, the mighty **Midhowe Cairn** has been dubbed the 'Great Ship of Death'. Built around 3500 BC and enormous in size, it's divided into compartments, in which the remains of 25 people were found. Covered by a protective stone building, it's nevertheless a memorable sight. Next to it, **Midhowe Broch**, whose sturdy stone lines echo the striations of the rocky shoreline, is a muscular Iron Age fortified compound with a mezzanine floor. The sites are by the water, a 10-minute walk downhill from the main road.

### SLEEPING & EATING

**Trumland Farm Hostel** ( ☎ 01856-821252; trumland@ btopenworld.com; camping sites £5, dm £10, bedding £2; **P** ) An easy stroll from the ferry, this organic farm has a wee hostel, with rather cramped six-bed dorms and a pretty little kitchen/common area. You can pitch tents outside and use the facilities; there's also a well-equipped self-catering cottage. Decent bikes are available for hire at £7 a day.

**Taversoe Hotel** ( ☎ 01856-821325; s/d £40/65; **P** ) About 2 miles west from the pier, the island's only hotel is a low-key place with neat, simple rooms with water vistas. The best views, however, are from the dining room, which serves good-value meals. The friendly owners will pick you up from the ferry.

**Pier Restaurant** ( ☎ 01856-821359; meals £5-7; ☺ 11am-11pm, closes 6.30pm Wed & Sun; ☐ ) Just above the ferry, this simple place does burgers and standard bar meals, and serves a coffee or whisky while waiting for the boat, or a chat and a game of pool after a long day's walking. There's also internet access and a list of locals doing B&B.

### GETTING THERE & AROUND

A **car ferry** ( ☎ 01856-751360) connects Tingwall (Mainland) with Rousay (return per person/car £6.80/21.80, 30 minutes, five to six daily) and the other nearby islands of Egilsay and Wyre.

Rousay's single road is a windy, hilly, but spectacular circuit of 14 miles, best ridden on a bike from Trumland Farm. A postbus does the circuit once per day.

### Egilsay & Wyre

These two small islands nestle east of Rousay. On Egilsay, a **cenotaph** marks the spot where Earl Magnus was murdered in 1117. After his martyrdom, pilgrims inspired the building of **St Magnus Church**, now missing its conical roof but otherwise intact. Today, much of the island is an **RSPB reserve**.

In the mid-12th century the neighbouring island of Wyre was the domain of the Viking baron Kolbein Hruga (Cubbie Roo). The ruins of his **castle** and **St Mary's Chapel** can be visited for free. Wyre's serene western sliver virtually guarantees seal sightings.

Both islands are reached on the Rousay–Tingwall ferry.

## Stronsay
### pop 358

Shaped like a bent crucifix, Stronsay attracts walkers and cyclists for its lack of serious inclines, and beautiful landscapes over its four curving bays. You can spot wildlife, with chubby seals basking on the rocks, and a healthy bird population, particularly puffins and other seabirds. There are good coastal walks and, in the east, the **Vat o'Kirbister** is a fine example of a *gloup* (natural arch).

Next to the ferry dock, **Stronsay Fish Mart** ( ☎ 01857-616386; Whitehall; admission free; ☺ 11am-6pm Mon & Wed, 11am-7pm Thu-Sat & 10am-7pm Sun May-Sep) now houses a herring-industry museum, which recalls the vital role fishing once played to the island. The attached 10-bed hostel (dorm beds £10) is well run if a little soulless.

For good pub grub and some well-refurbished rooms, **Stronsay Hotel** ( ☎ 01857-616473; stronsay .hotel@stronsay.co.uk; Whitehall; d £58; **P** ) is recommended. The menu includes great seafood (including paella and lobster) and there are packed lunches for walkers.

Flights from Kirkwall (20 minutes) are operated by Loganair.

Orkney Ferries links Stronsay with Kirkwall (return per person/car £14.30/32.60, 1½ hours, two daily) and Eday.

## Eday
### pop 121

Only 8 miles long, Eday has a heathered hilly interior and cultivated fields around its coast, but no central town. Occupied for at least the last 5000 years, today Eday has been left to the dead with numerous chambered cairns and the scenically located standing stones, the **Stone of Setter**.

Four miles from the ferry, **Eday Youth Hostel** ( ☎ 01857-622206; London Bay; dm £10) has been recently refurbished and is now community-run. There are also B&B and self-catering options on the island.

Loganair flies from Kirkwall (30 minutes, two flights every Wednesday only) to London airport – that's London on Eday. The ferry service from Kirkwall sails via Stronsay (return per person/car £14.30/32.60, 1½ hours, two daily). There's also a link between Sanday and Eday.

## Sanday
pop 478

Pancake-flat and seahorse-shaped, Sanday pulls the visitors in with its golden beaches and array of neolithic, Pictish and Viking ruins. The most impressive of the archaeological sights is **Quoyness Chambered Tomb**, a burial site similar to Maes Howe (p958). At the northeastern tip of Sanday, there's **Tafts Ness**, with around 500 prehistoric burial mounds.

**Ayre's Rock** ( ☎ 01857-600410; www.ayres-rock-sanday -orkney.co.uk; tent sites £3-5, r per person £13) is a cosy small hostel in the middle of the island sleeping eight in the outbuildings of a farm. Breakfasts and dinners are available, and you can also pitch a tent here.

**Kettletoft Hotel** ( ☎ 01857-600217; marktlawlor@ btopenworld.com; Kettletoft; s/d £30/60) is a friendly pub with several well-appointed rooms in the middle of this little waterside village. Meals in the bar (£7 to £11) also lean seaward, with plenty of fresh fish and even lobster scuttling into some dishes.

Loganair flies from Kirkwall (20 minutes) to Sanday and Westray. Orkney Ferries operates a service between Kirkwall and Sanday (return per person/car £14.30/32.60, 1½ hours, one or two daily). There's also a link to Eday.

## Westray
pop 700

If you've only time to visit one of Orkney's northern islands, make delightful Westray the one. With an ecological bent, rolling farmland, handsome sandy beaches and coastal walks, and a handful of wonderful places to stay, it's a green emerald in the archipelago's jewelbox.

The main settlement, Pierowall, is 7 miles from the Kirkwall ferry terminal of Rapness. Arrayed around a picturesque natural harbour, Pierowall was once a strategic Viking base. Near it stand the muscular ruins of **Noltland Castle** (HS; admission free; 🕑 9.30am-6.30pm mid-Jun–Sep), a tower house with a formida-ble array of shot-holes to defend its deceitful owner Gilbert Balfour, who plotted to murder Cardinal Beaton and, after being exiled, the King of Sweden.

In the northwest, **Noup Head RSPB Reserve** attracts tens of thousands of breeding seabirds each year, including a sizeable puffin posse.

### SLEEPING & EATING

**Barn** ( ☎ 01857-677214; www.thebarnwestray.com; Pierowall; tent sites £4-6, dm £13) Right in Pierowall, this one-time threshing barn is now an inti-mate, well-fitted hostel with plenty of facilities and a large family room for clan holidays. You can also camp here.

**our pick** **Bis Geos** ( ☎ 01856-677420; www.bisgeos .co.uk; dm £15; 🕑 Apr-Oct; P 💻 ) Memorably situated on grassy fields rolling down to spec-tacular cliffs just over a mile up the Noup Head road from Pierowall, this hostel, once a derelict croft, offers ultracommodious dorms (with bathrooms), which have a beachcomber theme and thoughtful little extras like bed lamps and bunk shelves. The conservatory lounge and sculptured garden have views for days and the kitchen with cosy eating nook is more realistic than the barbecue – you couldn't light a can of petrol when it's blow-ing here. There are also cottages with great extras such as CD players, DVDs and a sauna that looks out over the cliffs.

**our pick** **West Manse** ( ☎ 01857-677482; www.mill westray.com; Westside; r per person £25-30; P ) Take the Westside road to its end to reach this impos-ing, noble house with arcing coastal vistas. Here no timetables reign; make your own breakfast when you feel like it. Your warmly welcoming hosts have introduced a raft of practical green solutions for heating, fuel and more. Kids are very welcome, and will love the place; art exhibitions, cooking classes, venerably comfortable furniture and clean air are drawcards for parents. The owners also have two stunning self-catering places in Pierowall, the sweet Kilnman's Cottage with traditional Orcadian furniture (£95/220 for three/seven days), and enormous Trenabie Mill (£240/550 for three/seven days), com-plete with a greenhouse skygarden that heats the house.

**Cleaton House Hotel** ( ☎ 01857-677508; www.clea tonhouse.co.uk; s/d £60/90; P 💻 ) Three enthusiastic black labradors run this marvellously situated hotel a couple of miles from Pierowall on a lonely bay. As well as enormous rooms with beds measured in acres, the relaxed bar does generous portions of good tucker, and the restaurant serves more-elaborate fare.

**Pierowall Hotel** ( ☎ 01857-677472; Pierowall; mains £5-12; ☯ lunch & dinner) In the heart of town, this homely place is widely recognised as serving Orkney's best fish and chips, straight off the local boats and expertly filleted: if you find a bone you get a bottle of whisky.

### GETTING THERE & AWAY
Loganair flies from Kirkwall to Westray via Sanday. Orkney Ferries links Kirkwall with Westray (return per person/car £14.30/32.60, 1½ hours, two daily) and Papa Westray.

## Papa Westray
**pop 65**
Despite the name, this island is smaller than Westray at just 4 miles long and 1 mile wide. Nevertheless, it attracts plenty of superlatives: Europe's oldest domestic building is the **Knap of Howar** (built about 5500 years ago); the world's shortest scheduled flight is the two-minute hop across Papa Sound from Westray; and Europe's largest Arctic tern colony is at **North Hill RSPB Reserve**. Papa Westray was also the cradle of Christianity in Orkney – the restored **St Boniface Kirk** was founded in the 8th century.

About a mile from the ferry, **Beltane Guest House** ( ☎ 01857-644321; dm/s/d £ £10 /27/50) successfully combines hostel and hotel with cosy dorms and new rooms with private bathrooms. Hefty platefuls of local beef and seafood make satisfying lunch and dinner meals; there's also a shop.

Loganair offers cheap flights to Papa Westray (15 minutes) from Kirkwall via Westray.

Orkney Ferries links Kirkwall with Papa Westray (return per person/car £14.30/32.60, 1½ hours, two daily) and Westray.

## North Ronaldsay
**pop 50**
Even in the Orkneys, North Ronaldsay is a byword for isolation. There are enough sheep here to seize power, but a 13-mile **drystone wall** across the flat island keeps them off the crops; they make do on seaweed, which gives their meat a unique flavour.

The island falls in the path of migratory birds, which bring fanatical birders who spot whole chapters of *What Bird Is That?* nesting

or flying over this 3-mile long island. Seals are common and whales have been seen.

With solar and wind power, the environmentally friendly **Observatory Guest House** ( ☎ 01856-633200; www.nrbo.co.uk; dm/s/d £12/35/60; ▣ ) has minimal impact on the fragile local environment. It's especially designed for birdwatchers, for whom various ranger-led activities are organised. There are dorm rooms as well as twins and doubles with private bathrooms; dinner, which can feature the unique local mutton, is also available (from £10). The attached **cafe** (meals £4-10; ☯ lunch & dinner) does good meals for all, and life-affirming coffee in the cold.

Loganair flies from Kirkwall to North Ronaldsay. Orkney Ferries operates a service from Kirkwall (return per person/car £14.30/32.60, 2¾ hours, one on Friday only, plus Tuesday May to September).

# SHETLAND ISLANDS

Adrift in the North Sea, and close enough to Norway geographically and historically to make nationality an ambiguous concept here, the Shetlands are Britain's northernmost outpost. But despite the famous ponies and woollens, it's no agricultural backwater: the oil industry and semi-secret military bases have ensured a certain prosperity, and a growing tourism industry takes advantage of its rich prehistoric heritage.

Another of the great attractions of the Shetlands is the birdlife; it's worth packing binoculars even if you're not fanatical about it. Check out www.nature-shetland.co.uk for latest sightings. Every animal and bird seems to have its own name here: *dratsi* are otters, *bonxies* are great skuas, and *alamooties* are storm petrels.

There's a distinct Scandinavian lilt to the local accent, and walking down streets named King Haakon or St Olaf recalls the fact that the Shetlands were under Norse rule until 1469, when they were gifted to Scotland in lieu of the dowry of a Danish princess.

## Getting There & Away
### AIR
The oil industry ensures good air connections. The main airport is Sumburgh, 25 miles south of Lerwick. Flybe/Loganair operates flights to/from Aberdeen, Kirkwall,

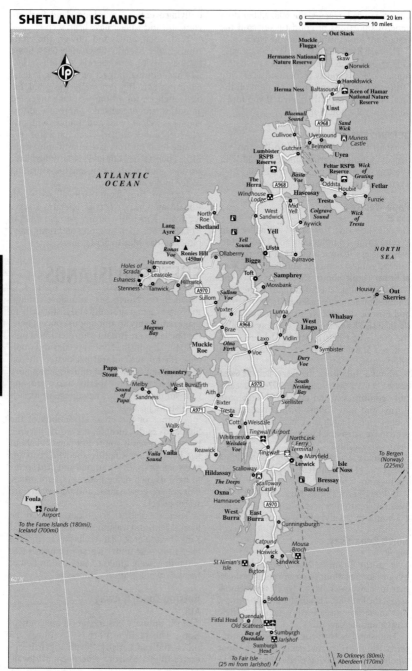

# SHETLAND ISLANDS

0 — 20 km
0 — 10 miles

Out Stack
Muckle Flugga
Hermaness National Nature Reserve
Skaw
Norwick
Herma Ness
Baltasound
Haroldswick
Keen of Hamar National Nature Reserve
*Bluemull Sound*
Unst
*Sand Wick*
Cullivoe
Uyeasound
Muness Castle
Lumbister RSPB Reserve
Gutcher
Belmont
Uyea
The Herra
A968
*Basta Voe*
Feltar RSPB Reserve
Oddsta
Houbie
*Wick of Gruting*
Fetlar
Windhouse Lodge
Hascosay
Tresta
Funzie
West Sandwick
Mid Yell
*Colgrave Sound*
*Wick of Tresta*
North Roe
*Shetland*
*Yell Sound*
Ulsta
Aywick

ATLANTIC OCEAN

Lang Ayre
*Ronas Voe*
Ronies Hill (450m)
Ollaberry
Bigga
Burravoe
Holes of Scrada
Hamnavoe
Leascole
Hillswick
A970
Toft
Samphrey
Eshaness
Stenness
Tanwick
*Sullom Voe*
Sullom
Mossbank

NORTH SEA

Housay
Out Skerries

*St Magnus Bay*
Voxter
Lunna
West Linga
Whalsay

Brae
A968
Laxo
Vidlin
Symbister
Muckle Roe
*Olna Firth*
Voe
*Dury Voe*

Papa Stour
Vementry
West Burrafirth
Aith
*South Nesting Bay*
Melby
*Sound of Papa*
Sandness
Bixter
Tresta
A970
A971
Cott
Skellister
Weisdale
Walls
Whiteness
*Weisdale Voe*
Tingwall Airport
NorthLink Ferry Terminal
*Vaila Sound*
Vaila
Reawick
Tingwall
Mary24
Maryfield
To Bergen (Norway) (225mi)
Lerwick
Isle of Noss
Foula
Hildassay
Scalloway
Bressay
Foula Airport
*The Deeps*
Oxna
*Scalloway Castle*
Bard Head
Hamnavoe
West Burra
East Burra
A970
Cunningsburgh
To the Faroe Islands (180mi); Iceland (700mi)
Catpund
*Mousa Broch*
Hoswick
*St Ninian's Isle*
Sandwick
Bigton
Boddam
60°N
Fitful Head
Quendale
Old Scatness
*Bay of Quendale*
Sumburgh
Jarlshof
*Sumburgh Head*
To Fair Isle (25 mi from Jarlshof)
To Orkneys (80mi); Aberdeen (170mi)

HIGHLANDS & NORTHERN ISLANDS

Inverness, Edinburgh and Glasgow. **Atlantic Airways** ( ☎ 020-782 34242; www.atlantic.fo) flies direct from London twice weekly in summer. Even in summer flights can be weather dependent, but the airlines will move you to a ferry if all goes wrong.

There's an extended-hours **tourist office** ( ☉ 7.15am-7.45pm Mon-Fri, 8.30am-5.30pm Sat, 10.15am-7.45pm Sun) at Sumburgh airport.

### BOAT

**NorthLink Ferries** ( ☎ 0845-6000449; www.northlinkferries.co.uk) runs car ferries between Lerwick and Aberdeen (per passenger/car £32.70/116.60 in high season, cabins £29 to £110, 12 to 15 hours, daily) via Kirkwall.

## Getting Around

### BICYCLE

On a fine day, cycling is the way forward, but in bad weather shelter can be scarce and winds are fierce. Hire bikes at **Grantfield Garage** ( ☎ 01595-692709; www.grantfieldgarage.co.uk; North Rd, Lerwick; hire per day/week £5/30).

### BUS

Grab a copy of the Shetland public-transport timetable from a tourist office for the various island bus routes.

### CAR

Shetland's roads are wide and well kept. Book car hire ahead. Star has an office at Sumburgh airport and others will meet you there. Prices are from £28 per day; operators include the following:

**Bolts Car Hire** ( ☎ 01595-693636; www.boltscarhire.co.uk; North Rd, Lerwick)

**Star Rent-a-Car** ( ☎ 01595-692075; www.starrentacar.co.uk; 22 Commercial Rd, Lerwick)

## LERWICK

### pop 6830

Built on the herring trade, Lerwick is the Shetlands only real town, home to about a third of the islands' population and dug into the hills of Bressay Sound. It has a solidly maritime feel, with aquiline oilboats competing for harbour space with the dwindling fishing fleet, whose nets you still see draped in front gardens to dry. The water's clear blue tones make wandering along atmospheric Commercial St a delightful stroll, and the town's excellent new museum provides all the cultural background you could desire.

## Information

**Shetland Library** ( ☎ 01595-693868; Lower Hillhead; ☉ 10am-7pm Mon, Wed & Fri, 10am-5pm Tue, Thu & Sat) Free internet access.

**Tourist office** ( ☎ 01595-693434; www.visitshetland.com; Market Cross; ☉ 8am-6pm Mon-Fri, 8am-4pm Sat & Sun Apr-Sep, 8am-5pm Mon-Fri, 8am-4pm Sat & Sun Oct-Mar) Changes money, offers cheap international phone calls and has excellent information.

## Sights & Activities

Serious thought, enthusiasm and cash have been invested in the new **Shetland Museum** ( ☎ 01595-695057; www.shetland-museum.org.uk; admission free; ☉ 10am-5pm Mon & Fri, 10am-6pm Tue-Thu, noon-5pm Sun summer), surely one of the best of its kind in Britain. Comprehensive but never dull, the display covers everything from the archipelago's geology to its fishing industry, via a great section on local mythology – find out about scary *nyuggles*, or use the patented machine for detecting *trows*. The Pictish carvings and replica jewellery are among the finest pieces; the museum also includes a working lighthouse mechanism, small art gallery and – what great smells – a boat-building workshop, where you can watch carpenters at work restoring and recreating traditional Shetland fishing vessels.

Keeping an iron rule over the town, **Fort Charlotte** (admission free; ☉ 9.30am-dusk) is a cannoned battlement that was once a good vantage point for watching for an invading Dutch navy. Today it provides a base for the Territorial Army and the only potential invaders are seals basking in the harbour.

Oddly handy to the town centre, **Clickimin Broch** (admission free; ☉ 24hr) is secluded by a small loch and was occupied from the 7th century BC to the 6th century AD.

The **Böd of Gremista** ( ☎ 01595-695057; admission free; ☉ 10am-1pm & 2-5pm Wed-Sun May–mid-Sep), across the harbour from the centre, is well worth a visit. Once the HQ of a fish-curing station, it was also the birthplace of Arthur Anderson, who went on to found P&O and who ploughed much of his wealth back into the local community. The personable custodian is a delight – you could tell him this guidebook officially apologises for labelling him an 'old salt' in a previous edition.

## Tours

The following tours can be booked at the tourist office.

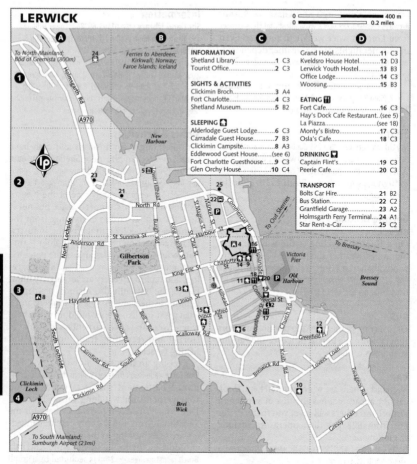

# LERWICK

**Dim Riv** ( ☎ 07970-864189; adult/child £5/2, ⏲ 7pm Mon May-Sep) Sail in a reconstructed Viking longship.
**Island Trails** ( ☎ 01595-422408; www.island-trails .co.uk; 1hr tours £10) One of the best ways to see Lerwick; various tours on different angles of town.
**Seabirds & Seals** ( ☎ 01595-693434; www.seabirds -and-seals.com; 3hr cruises £40) Runs wildlife-spotting tours to Bressay and Noss; book with the tourist office.

## Festivals & Events
**Folk Festival** (www.shetlandfolkfestival.com) Worth being here for this, in early May.
**Johnsmas Foy** (www.johnsmasfoy.com) The festival of summer that includes sailing races, the Flavour of Shetland food fair and blues gigs. In June.
**Shetland Fiddle Frenzy** (www.shetlandfiddlefrenzy .com) Plays up a storm in August.

## Sleeping
Pre-book your Lerwick accommodation, as rooms can fill up with oil workers. There are several broadly similar Victorian B&Bs, all of which are good bets.

### BUDGET
**Clickimin Campsite** ( ☎ 01595-741000; www.srt.org.uk; Lochside; 1-/2-person tent sites £4.90/6.90; ⏲ May-Sep; 🅿 ) Attached to the massive leisure centre, this is a real family park with plenty to keep kids busy, from squash to swimming to bowling, even when the weather isn't holding up. Grassy sites for tents are pleasant.

**Lerwick Youth Hostel** ( ☎ 01595-692114; www.isle burgh.org.uk; King Harald St; dm £15.50; ⏲ Apr-Sep; 🖥 ) This typically grand Lerwick mansion houses

HIGHLANDS &
NORTHERN ISLANDS

an excellent hostel, with comfortable dorms, a shop, laundry, cafe and industrial kitchen. It's wise to book ahead as this place is popular with large groups. It may open out of season if you ring ahead.

## MIDRANGE

**Alderlodge Guest House** ( ☎ 01595-695705; 6 Clairmont Pl; s/d £37/54; P ) Great friendly hosts (who'll let you check out whenever and shrug off a strict breakfast timetable) make this a top guesthouse. They'll even give you tips on walks and birding spots. The rooms come with private bathrooms and have handy bar fridges.

**Eddlewood Guest House** ( ☎ 01595-692772; cath erinemarshall@live.co.uk; 8 Clairmont Pl; s/d £37/56) Run by a cheery soul, this sound option has spacious, very well-kept rooms, some with limited sea views. The beds offer plenty of space to stretch out in, and these showers might just be Shetland's finest.

**Fort Charlotte Guesthouse** ( ☎ 01595-692140; www .fortcharlotte.co.uk; 1 Charlotte St; s/d £35/60) Sheltering under the walls of the fortress, this excellent place offers very summery rooms with private bathrooms, including great singles. Views down the pedestrian street are on offer in some; sloping ceilings and oriental touches add charm to others. There's a bike shed and local salmon for breakfast.

**Carradale Guest House** ( ☎ 01595-692251; www .carradale.shetland.co.uk; 36 King Harald St; s/d £35/60) With an old-fashioned feel and an amiable and courteous welcome, this Victorian house preserves plenty of period style in its lovely large rooms. A selection of thoughtful extras make that little difference to the qual-

ity of your stay, and dinner is available on request.

**Glen Orchy House** ( ☎ 01595-692031; www.guest houselerwick.com; 20 Knab Rd; s/d from £50/80; P ☐ wi-fi) More a hotel than a B&B, this well-kept spot is worth the extra outlay for its spectacular conservatory with views of Breiwick Bay alone. Rooms are well presented and there are plenty of singles so it's a good bet for solo travellers.

**Grand Hotel** ( ☎ 01595-692826; www.kgqhotels .co.uk; 24 Commercial St; s/d £75/99; P ☐ wi-fi) Once the hub of town, this stately hotel isn't what it was when Victoria reigned, but ongoing modernisation is slowly bringing the rooms into the 21st century. Those on the top floors offer harbour views. The mazelike complex includes a restaurant that does a popular Sunday roast (£12, book ahead) and a nightclub, gloriously named Posers.

**Kveldsro House Hotel** ( ☎ 01595-692195; www .shetlandhotels.com; Greenfield Pl; s/d £92/115; P ☐ wi-fi) Tough to find but worth the search, this hotel spreads itself well to please both business travellers and romantic holidaymakers. It's quiet and serene and boasts great harbour views from some double rooms as well as the cocktail lounge and restaurant. Though five quid for wi-fi seems mean-spirited, the glass of sherry smoothing check-in is a nice touch.

Also recommended:

**Woosung** ( ☎ 01595-693687; sandraconroy43@ btinternet.com; 43 St Olaf St; s/d £30/50) Helpful, with unexpected extras like bathrobes and fridges.

**Office Lodge** ( ☎ 08707-708881; www.officelodge.com; 10a Charlotte St; d £75; ☐ wi-fi) Apartment with kitchen, DVD, iPod speakers and other modern conveniences.

## Eating & Drinking

**Fort Cafe** ( ☎ 01595-693125; 2 Commercial Rd; fish & chips £5-6) Sometimes all that sea-salt air can make a body cry out for a haddock supper, and this well-loved local institution is the place to get it. Munch your takeaway down on the pier if you don't mind the seagulls' envious stares.

**Osla's Cafe** ( ☎ 01595-696005; 88 Commercial St; meals £6-12; ☷ noon-8pm Mon-Sat, plus Sun Jun-Aug) This comfy spot flips a good pancake down below and Italian dishes start upstairs at La Piazza, with hearty pastas, peppy pizzas and decent steaks featuring.

**Monty's Bistro** ( ☎ 01595-696555; 5 Mounthooly St; lunches £6-8, dinner mains £11-18; ☷ lunch Tue-Sat, dinner Mon-Sat) Though well tucked away behind the tourist office, this is far from a secret, and Shetlanders descend on its wee wooden

---

**UP HELLY AA!!!**

The long Viking history of the Shetlands has rubbed off in more than just street names and square-shouldered locals. Most villages have their own fire festival, a continuation of the old Viking midwinter celebrations of the rebirth of the sun. The most spectacular is in Lerwick.

Up Helly Aa (www.uphellyaa.org) takes place on the last Tuesday in January. Squads of 'guizers' dress in Viking costume and march through the streets with blazing torches, dragging a replica longship, which they then surround and burn, bellowing out Viking songs from behind bushy beards.

---

**A LIGHT IN THE NORTH**

Shetland offers intriguing options for getting off the beaten accommodation track. There's a great network of *böds* – simple rustic **hostels** with peat fires which might mean bringing sleeping bag, coins for the meter or even a camp stove. We've listed some of these in the text, but there are more. Contact **Shetland Amenity Trust** ( ☎ 01595-694688; www.camping-bods.com).

The same organisation runs three **lighthouse cottages** ( ☎ 01595-694688; www.lighthouse-holidays .com), all commanding dramatic views of rugged coastline: one near the airport at Sumburgh, one on the island of Bressay near Lerwick, and one in Mainland's northwest at Eshaness. Sleeping six to seven, the cottages cost £42 to £58 per night.

You can book both *böds* and lighthouses via Lerwick's tourist office.

---

tables with alacrity. The happy orange upstairs dining room is fragrant with aromas of Gressingham duck and local mussels from the short, quality menu, and the wine list has some welcome old friends.

**Hay's Dock Cafe Restaurant** ( ☎ 01595-741569; light lunches £4-6, dinner mains £13-19; ☼ lunch daily, dinner Tue-Sat) Upstairs in the Shetland Museum you'll find this great new restaurant, whose glass front and optimistic balcony look right over the water. Its clean lines and light wood recall Scandinavia, but the smart food relies on carefully selected local and Scottish produce on a short, quality menu.

**ourpick** **Peerie Cafe** ( ☎ 01595-692817; Esplanade; snacks £2-4; ☼ 9am-6pm Mon-Sat) If you've been craving proper espresso since leaving the mainland, head to this gem of a spot, with art exhibitions, wire-mounted halogens and industrial gantry chic. Newspapers, scrumptious cakes and sandwiches, interesting daily juices and outdoor seating, as well as wine and Shetland beer, give everyone a reason to be here.

**Captain Flint's** ( ☎ 01595-692249; Esplanade) Though the weekend antics here have probably featured on 'Booze Britain', this attractive pub is still Lerwick's best spot for a drink. Try the tasty range of Shetland beers, brewed by the Valhalla Brewery on Unst or shoot some pool upstairs.

### Getting There & Away

See p967 for details of ferries. Regular buses run between Lerwick and Sumburgh airport (50 minutes), although you may wait a while on Sunday.

## AROUND LERWICK

Just across from Lerwick is the island of **Bressay**, and beyond it, the **Isle of Noss**, a nature reserve bristling with seabirds.

Despite controversial plans to build a bridge, the only crossing to Bressay is by **ferry** ( ☎ 01595-743974) from Lerwick (return per adult/car £3.30/7.80, frequent). It's a two-hour walk across the picturesque island; some people rent bikes in Lerwick and bring them across. You can pause for an ale or excellent shellfish meal at **Maryfield House Hotel** ( ☎ 01595-820207; Bressay; mains £7-10), which offers secluded accommodation (singles/doubles £35/70) near the ferry.

Noss is accessed by **dinghy** ( ☎ 0800-1077818; £3; ☼ 10am-5pm Tue, Wed & Fri-Sun late May–Aug) from Bressay; check by phone first, as they don't run in bad weather. Once on Noss most visitors head for the **Noup**, a spectacular cliff rising over 180m above sea level. Guillemots, puffins, razorbills and gannets all nest here. Great and arctic skuas are also present on the island.

Six miles west of Lerwick is Shetland's former capital, **Scalloway** (Scallowah), with the eerie well-preserved ruins of 15th-century **Scalloway Castle** (HS; ☎ 01856-841815; admission free; ☼ 9.30am-5pm Mon-Sat) – get the key from the Scalloway Hotel at other times. **Scalloway Museum** ( ☎ 01595-880675; Main St; admission free; ☼ Mon-Sat May-Sep) has interesting displays on the 'Shetland Bus', boats that smuggled people and supplies during WWII for the Free Norwegian Forces. If hunger strikes, you should head for **Da Haaf Restaurant** ( ☎ 01595-880747; Port Arthur; meals £9-15; ☼ lunch & dinner), part of the North Atlantic Fisheries College, which specialises in local seafood. Buses run to/from Lerwick (11 times daily, Monday to Saturday).

## SOUTH MAINLAND
### Sandwick & Mousa
#### pop 800

Opposite the scattered village of Sandwick, where you pass the 60-degree latitude line, is the small isle of Mousa, an RSPB reserve protecting some 7000 breeding pairs of nocturnal storm petrels. Mousa is also home to rock-basking seals as well as impressive **Mousa Broch**, the best preserved of these northern fortifications. Rising to 13m, it's an imposing structure, typically double-walled, and with a spiral staircase to access a second floor. Petrels favour it as a nesting spot.

Tom Jamieson runs **boat trips** ( ☎ 01950-431367; www.mousaboattrips.co.uk; adult/child £12/6; 1-2 daily Apr-Sep), to Mousa allowing 2½ hours on the island. He also runs night trips to see the petrels. Five to seven buses daily (three on Sunday) link Lerwick and Sandwick.

Not far from Sandwick, the **Orca Country Inn** ( ☎ 01950-431226; www.orcacountryinn.co.uk; s/d £43/65; P ) has comfortable rooms named for our feathered friends, some with fine sea views. One of the owners is a wildlife photographer, so birders can get plenty of spotting advice. There's also a restaurant and bar.

## Sumburgh & Around

Old and new collide at Mainland's southern tip, where Sumburgh airport is only a few metres from **Jarlshof** (HS; ☎ 01667-460232; adult £4.70; 🕙 9.30am-5.30pm Apr-Sep), a picturesque and instructive archaeological site covering various periods of occupation. You can clearly see the complete change when the Vikings arrived: their rectangular longhouses are a marked contrast to the brochs, roundhouses and wheelhouses that preceded them. Atop the site is the Old House of Sumburgh, built in the 16th century and named 'Jarlshof' in a novel by Sir Walter Scott. There's an informative audio tour included with admission. You get 20% off the admission price if you have a ticket to Old Scatness (see Living the Past, below).

Nearby, and clearly visible from the site, the spectacular cliffs of **Sumburgh Head** a mile from the main road offer a good opportunity to get up close and personal with puffins; they also have huge nesting colonies of fulmars, guillemots and razorbills. If you're lucky, you might get the chance to spot dolphins or orcas; the car-park noticeboard advises on recent sightings.

For a spot handy to the airport (and Jarlshof) you can't beat **Sumburgh Hotel** ( ☎ 01950-460201; www.sumburghhotel.com; Sumburgh; s/d £65/75; P 🖳 ), which has fine views for birdwatchers, prehistorians and plane-spotters, comfortable pinkish rooms, and excellent meals. Larger sea-view rooms cost more (doubles £95).

Scousburgh is 5 miles northwest of Sumburgh, below which is Shetland's best beach, gloriously white **Scousburgh Sands**. Near Scousburgh is the delightful **Spiggie Hotel** ( ☎ 01950-460409; www.thespiggiehotel.co.uk; s/d £75/100; P ), an old-style country pub that also offers good seafood (dinner £20) and fishing opportunities in the local loch. You could also stay at the atmospheric Sumburgh Lighthouse cottage (see A Light in the North, opposite), or in the *böd* at Old Scatness (see Living the Past, below).

To get to these places from Lerwick take the airport bus (50 minutes, five daily Monday to Saturday, two on Sunday).

## NORTH MAINLAND

Mainland's northwest is known for the red basalt cliffs of **Eshaness**, which have been carved out by harsh Atlantic gales to form some of Scotland's best postcard images. When the wind subsides, there's good walking on the peninsula west of Brae and south to the red

HIGHLANDS &
NORTHERN ISLANDS

---

**LIVING THE PAST**

Near Jarlshof, **Old Scatness** ( ☎ 01595-694688; Dunrossness; adult/child £4/3, 20% off with Jarlshof ticket; 🕙 10am-4.30pm Sun-Thu mid-May–Sep, call to visit outside these times) brings Shetland's prehistoric past vividly and entertainingly to life; it's a must-see for archaeology buffs but fun for kids too. Clued-up guides in Iron Age clothes show you around the site, which is still being studied, and has provided important clues on the Viking takeover, and the dating of these northern Scottish sites in general.

Discovered when building an airport access road, the site has revealed an impressive broch from around 300 BC, roundhouses and later wheelhouses. Best of all is the reconstruction of one of these, complete with smoky peat fire and working loom.

Also here is a good place to stay, **Betty Mouat's Böd** ( ☎ 01950-460839; dm £8; P ), a simple and comfortable hostel with peat fire (£3 a bag), power and decent hot-water bathrooms.

granite island of **Muckle Roe**, which is connected by a bridge.

The **Tangwick Haa Museum** ( ☎ 01806-503389; admission free; 🕑 11am-5pm mid-Apr–Sep) in Eshaness documents social history in this remote community through a collection of great black-and-white photos and an assortment of curios.

Buses from Lerwick (three Monday to Friday, two on Saturday) run as far as Hillswick, 7 miles from Eshaness.

### Sleeping & Eating

Perched out on the cliffs is Eshaness Lighthouse cottage (see A Light in the North, p970). Good camping spots abound.

**Braewick Cafe & Campsite** ( ☎ 01806-503345; www.eshaness.shetland.co.uk; Braewick; sites £5-8; 🕑 food 10am-5pm Thu-Sun, 10am-4pm Mon) With spectacular views over the magnificent St Magnus Bay and its offbeat rock formations, this has good tent sites and light meals (£4 to £11) using produce from the adjacent croft.

**Johnnie Notion Camping Böd** ( ☎ 01806-503362; Hamnavoe; dm £8; 🕑 Apr-Sep; Ⓟ ) This offers four spacious berths in a wee stone cottage with a challengingly low door. It's very basic; there are no showers or electricity.

**ourpick Almara** ( ☎ 01806-503261; www.almara.shetland.co.uk; s/d £25/50; Ⓟ ) Follow the puffin signpost a mile short of Hillswick to get the most wonderful welcome in the Shetlands. With sweeping views over the bay, this house has a great lounge, a few unusual features in the excellent rooms and bathrooms, and a good eye on the environment. You'll feel completely at home and appreciated; this is B&B at its best.

**Busta House Hotel** ( ☎ 01806-522506; www.bustahouse.com; s/d £75/105; Ⓟ ▣ wi-fi) Just past Brae, this characterful country hotel has an intriguing if sad history, but is also full of modern conveniences. The opulently furnished rooms are a treat, as is the restaurant. Even the inevitable ghost is reputedly affable.

**Da Böd Cafe** ( ☎ 01806-503348; www.shetlandwildlifesanctuary.com; meals by suggested donation of £3-8; 🕑 noon-6pm Thu-Sun) With a crackling peat fire and homelike atmosphere, this vegetarian cafe is set in one of Shetland's oldest buildings, once a Hanseatic trading post. There's internet access here, and you may be able to arrange camping and accommodation. But the best deal is that meals are paid for by donation towards the local wildlife sanctuary.

## YELL, UNST & FETLAR
pop 720

Shetland's rugged triumvirate of northern islands are wild and windswept. Spectacular seabird colonies are the main reason to visit, as well as the satisfaction of looking down on the rest of Britain.

### Yell

…if you like but nobody will hear; the desolate peat moors here are typical Shetland scenery, and many travellers fire on through en route to Unst. The bleak landscape has an appeal, though, and there are several good hillwalks as well as otter- and seal-spotting opportunities in the surrounding sea. The **Old Haa Museum** ( ☎ 01957-722339; Burravoe; admission free; 🕑 10am-4pm Tue-Thu & Sat, 2-5pm Sun Apr-Sep) has a medley of curious objects (pipes, piano, doll-in-cradle, tiny bibles, ships-in-bottles and a sperm whale jaw) as well as an archive of local history and a tearoom.

Yell has limited accommodation options. Below the spooky ruins of Windhouse (haunted of course) in the middle of the island, **Windhouse Lodge** ( ☎ 01957-702231; dm £8; Ⓟ ) is a basic *böd* with wooden bunks and a peat stove for heating. Look for the pinkish cottage with a turret at the corner of the island. In Mid Yell, the main settlement, **Norwind** ( ☎ 01957-702312; norwind@btinternet.com; s/d £33/55; Ⓟ ) is a pleasant guesthouse near the fire station (take the road to Bunnavoe) with great views over the bay, a balcony and healthy fruit laid on at breakfast. It does evening meals, and nearby, the misnamed Hilltop pub does limited bar food.

Right by the Unst ferry pier, **Wind Dog Cafe** ( ☎ 01957-744321; 🕑 9am-5pm Mon-Fri, 10am-5pm Sat & Sun; ▣ ) is a source for local gossip and a forthright, likeable cafe with colourful tables, home-baked treats, burgers, and bannocks filled with cold roast lamb among other goodies. There's unreliable internet access and a bookcase for browsing and borrowing. The cafe opens until 7pm from June to August, doing light meals.

### Unst

You're fast running out of Britain once you cross to Unst, a rugged island of ponies and seabirds. Its stellar attraction is the marvellous headland of **Hermaness**, where a 4-mile round walk from the reserve entrance at the end of the road takes you to cliffs where gannets, fulmars and guillemots nest and numerous puffins frolic. The path is guarded by a small army of great skuas, known hereabouts as *bonxies*. They nest in the nearby heather, and will dive-bomb at will if they feel threatened. They're damn solid birds too, but they don't usually make contact; still, it's an unnerving but worthwhile experience. From the cliffs, you can see Britain's most northerly point, the rocks of **Out Stack**, and **Muckle Flugga**, with its lighthouse built by Robert Louis Stevenson's uncle. Stevenson wrote *Treasure Island* while living on Unst. For more tips on wildlife-watching duck into the **Hermaness Visitor Centre** ( ☎ 01957-711278; admission free; ☙ 9am-5pm Apr–mid-Sep), near the reserve's entrance.

At the turn-off from the main road to Littlehamar, don't miss Britain's most impressive **bus stop**. Enterprising locals, presumably tired of waiting in discomfort, have installed armchair, novels, flowers, a TV, an old Amstrad computer and a visitors book to sign. All in cornflower blue when we visited, but we're told the colour scheme changes from time to time.

Other Unst attractions include a heritage centre and, nearby, **Unst Boat Haven** ( ☎ 01957-711809; Haroldswick; adult/child £2/free; ☙ 11am-5pm May-Sep), which showcases island maritime history with several replicas including a Viking longboat. Two miles north, **Valhalla Brewery** ( ☎ 01957-711658; www.valhallabrewery.co.uk; tours £3.50; ☙ 9am-5pm Mon-Fri) fulfils every bloke's dream to start a brewery in their back shed, and brews up the most northerly beer in Britain.

Unst has plenty of places to stay. In Uyeasound, a mile and a half from the ferry, **Gardiesfauld Hostel** ( ☎ 01957-755240; www.gardies fauld.shetland.co.uk; Uyeasound; tent sites £6-8, dm £11; ☙ Apr-Sep; **P** ) has very spacious dorms with lockers, family rooms, a garden, elegant lounge, and a wee conservatory dining area with great bay views. You can camp here too. Bring 20p pieces for the shower.

**Saxa Vord** ( ☎ 01957-711711; www.saxavord.com; Haroldswick; s/d £15/30; **P** ) is rather uninspiringly set in an old barracks compound, but offers comfortable budget accommodation in private hostel-like rooms, a restaurant (open mid-May to September) and self-catering cottages. By the time you read this, hotel rooms should be available too.

**Baltasound Hotel** ( ☎ 01957-711334; Baltasound; dishes £5-9; ☙ lunch & dinner) does unremarkable bar food in a dining room dappled by the evening sun. It's Britain's northernmost pub.

## Fetlar

This island, divided in two by a prehistoric dyke, has a large RSPB reserve (closed May to August for the breeding season) with red-throated divers, red-necked phalaropes and arctic skuas among the cachet species. There's a B&B, **Gord** ( ☎ 01957-733227; Houbie; s/d £35/50; **P** ), whose owner also runs a simple camp site. There's a shop but no petrol on the island.

### Getting There & Away

Yell is connected to Mainland by a small **ferry** ( ☎ 01957-722259) operating between Toft and Ulsta (return per car and driver/passenger £7.80/3.30, 20 minutes, frequent). From the other side of Yell, at Gutcher, free ferries nip across the channel to Unst (10 minutes, frequent) and to Fetlar (25 minutes, six to eight daily).

## OTHER ISLANDS

West of Shetland is **Foula**, a windy island with dramatic cliff scenery that supports a couple of dozen people, wild sheep, ponies and a vast seabird population. It's reached by **ferries** ( ☎ 07881-823732) from Walls (single per person/car £3/14.60, two hours, two to three weekly), a fortnightly one from Scalloway, and **planes** ( ☎ 01595-840246) from Tingwall (15 minutes, four to six weekly). You can also charter **Cycharters** ( ☎ 07887-945480; www.cycharters .co.uk; £50; ☙ May-Sep).

Remote **Fair Isle** sits between the Orkneys and Shetland and is famous for its patterned knitwear, produced in the island's cooperative. It's birdwatching heaven, especially at **Fair Isle Lodge & Bird Observatory** ( ☎ 01595-760258; www.fairislebirdobs.co.uk; ☙ late Apr–Oct; **P** ), which offers full-board (dorms £30, singles/ doubles £44/78) accommodation, great views from its spacious lounge, free guided birding strolls and displays of how rangers monitor migratory birds.

From Tingwall, **DirectFlight** ( ☎ 01234-757766; www.directflight.co.uk) operates flights to Fair Isle (25 minutes, twice on Monday, Wednesday, Friday year-round and on Saturday May to September). A day-return allows about seven hours on the island. **Ferries** ( ☎ 01595-760222) sail from Grutness (near Sumburgh), with the odd one from Lerwick to Fair Isle (single per person/car £3/14.60, three hours, Tuesday and Saturday year-round and Thursday from May to September).

HIGHLANDS & NORTHERN ISLANDS

# The Channel Islands

On these islands dotting the English Channel, old-world charm is alive and well. Jersey and its smaller neighbours are like untouched desert islands, with the sleepy atmosphere of a 1950s English village. Hedge-lined lanes criss-cross between sea cliffs and beaches such as Jersey's St Ouen's Bay and Guernsey's Vazon Bay, both perfect for surfing and sandcastles. Cars are banned and signposts measure distances in 'minutes to walk' on itty-bitty Sark and teeny-weeny Herm. A horse and cart can trot you across gorse-covered Sark to its 100m-high isthmus, La Coupée. However, some anomalies scramble the visions of Arcadian England in these self-governing Crown dependencies, home to blue postboxes and local versions of the British pound. Subtropical plants bloom here, thanks to the proximity of the warm Gulf of St Malo, which also attracts puffins and gannets to Alderney. Centuries of influence by Normandy, 5 miles east of Alderney, have left French place names and, on gastronomic Guernsey, some excellent restaurants.

The islands have a strong sense of their individuality and history, informed by their position at a maritime crossroads between Britain, France and North America. Local families can trace their surnames through generations of seafarers and, tragically, to individuals who endured the Nazi occupation. Museums such as the Jersey War Tunnels, Nazi-built underground passages, and Jersey's Mont Orgueil Castle, where Sir Walter Raleigh lived, vividly evoke this history. With the Maritime Museum and the Durrell, Jersey has a range of imaginative, interactive attractions – yet another good reason to hop across the Channel from mainland Blighty.

## HIGHLIGHTS

- Imagining yourself a member of Enid Blyton's Famous Five on twee, carefree **Sark** (p979)

- Exploring the 13th-century **Castle Cornet** (p978) in Guernsey's hilly St Peter Port

- Following in the paw prints of Prince Blücher von Wahlstatt's extinct wallabies, among neolithic tombs on the cobweb-banishing common on **Herm** (p979)

- Discovering another side to a renowned offshore banking centre on Jersey's laid-back west coast at **St Ouen's Bay** (p977)

- Gazing at swaying sailboats from a half-timbered hotel in Jersey's **St Aubin** (opposite)

- Catching a dinky passenger plane to distinctive **Alderney** (p980), where seabirds nest in Nazi lookout towers

Alderney

Herm

St Peter Port · Sark

St Ouen's Bay

St Aubin

| POPULATION: 151,562 | AREA: 120 SQ MILES | AS WELL AS ENGLISH, TWO FRENCH DIALECTS ARE SPOKEN ON THE CHANNEL ISLANDS: JÈRRIAIS AND GUERNÉSIAIS |

## History

The Channel Islands are rich in archaeological sites from the Stone Age onwards. Used by the Romans as trading posts, the islands were part of Normandy until 1066, only becoming English when William of Normandy ('William the Conqueror') was crowned king. For centuries the islands were used as sparring grounds, but in 1483 England and France agreed that the territory would remain neutral in the event of war.

In WWII, these happy-go-lucky resorts became the only British soil to be occupied by German forces. The postwar years have seen the fishing, tourism and farming industries decrease, to be replaced by the big bucks of offshore banking. Today the finance sector employs the biggest chunk of the workforce.

## Getting There & Away

Return flights to Jersey and Guernsey, the main points of entry, vary wildly between £70 and £300 – shop around.

### JERSEY

**Condor Ferries** ( ☎ 01534-872240; www.condorferries.com) sails from Guernsey (from 55 minutes), Poole (four hours), Portsmouth (10 hours), St Malo, France (1¼ hours) and Weymouth (3½ hours). On most routes, there is at least one daily ferry between April and October, but the service is severely reduced at other times of year. Typical return fares from the UK are £110 for a foot passenger, £270 for a car and driver.

**Manche Iles Express** ( ☎ 01534-880756; www.manche-iles-express.com; ☻ Apr-Sep) has passenger ferries from Guernsey (single £29.50, one hour) and Carteret and Granville in France (£22.50, one hour).

**Air Southwest** ( ☎ 0870 241 8202; www.airsouthwest.com) flies from Bristol and Plymouth; **Aurigny Air Services** ( ☎ 0871 871 0717; www.aurigny.com) from Guernsey; **Blue Islands** ( ☎ 08456 20 21 22; www.blueislands.com) from Alderney, Bournemouth, Guernsey, Isle of Man and Switzerland; **bmibaby** ( ☎ 0871 224 0224; www.bmibaby.com) from Birmingham, Cardiff, East Midlands and Manchester; **British Airways** ( ☎ 0844 493 0787; www.ba.com) from Gatwick; **easyJet** (www.easyjet.com) from Liverpool and Luton; **Flybe** ( ☎ 0871 700 2000; www.flybe.com) from 15 airports in the UK and Northern Ireland, Geneva, Guernsey, Nice and Paris.

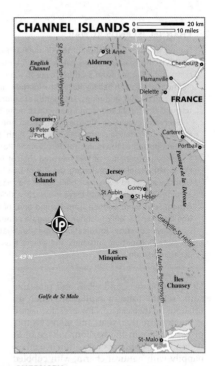

CHANNEL ISLANDS

### GUERNSEY

**Condor Ferries** ( ☎ 01481-12023) sails from Jersey, Poole (2¾ hours), Portsmouth (10½ hours), St Malo (2¾ hours) and Weymouth (2¼ hours); **Manche Iles Express** ( ☎ 01481-701316) from Jersey and Carteret and Diélette in France.

Aurigny Air Services, Blue Islands and Flybe fly from Alderney, Birmingham, Bournemouth, Bristol, Dublin, Exeter, France, Gatwick, Isle of Man, Jersey, Manchester, Norwich, Southampton, Stansted and Switzerland.

### HERM & SARK

Ferries go to Herm from Guernsey (see p979); to Sark from Jersey and Guernsey (see p980).

### ALDERNEY

Manche Iles Express sails from Diélette, Guernsey and Jersey. Aurigny Air Services and Blue Islands fly from Bournemouth, Guernsey, Jersey and Southampton.

## JERSEY

pop 88,200

Jersey is the biggest and, its rivals would say, the brashest of the Channel Islands.

**CHANNEL ISLANDS AT WAR**

During the Nazi occupation of the Channel Islands, which began in 1940 and lasted for the rest of WWII, the islands formed part of the Atlantic Wall, designed to protect German-controlled continental Europe from a British invasion – a personal obsession for Hitler.

The islands were heavily fortified; Alderney alone had defences that included 27 military batteries and 30,000 landmines. Thousands of enforced labourers were shipped from the Continent to build the fortifications and many died; more than 600 perished on Alderney.

Everyone evacuated Alderney apart from one family, and the island became an extension of the SS concentration camp Neuengamme. With no civilian witnesses and low morale among the soldiers posted to the island, the Russian and Polish POWs interned there were treated savagely.

Jersey's experience of war mirrored that of the other islands. Half of its inhabitants fled to the British mainland, preferring the risk of bombs to living in occupied territory. There was one German soldier to every four islanders. It was a time of moral dilemmas and paranoia; the *Jersey Evening Post*'s editor would leave the Nazis' articles uncorrected so readers could spot the propaganda. Jews were banned from trading and, of the 302 people taken to concentration camps, one became the only prisoner to smuggle photos out of Buchenwald.

Today, concrete fortifications still dominate the islands' clifftops and beaches. Some serve as Occupation museums and others have been appropriated as snack kiosks and even accommodation.

Shimmering steel and glass, and pinstripe suits, set the tone in capital St Helier, an offshore finance centre. However, the island is much more than that, and many visitors prefer to stay in the harbour village of St Aubin. Here, contemporary affluence mixes happily with nautical charm, with cobbled streets climbing the hill from the boat masts. The coast is 48 miles long; exquisite sandy beaches fringe the south, east and west sides, and rugged cliffs frame the north. In between lie tranquil lanes and some excellent museums, which bring Jersey's rich history to life.

## Orientation & Information

Measuring 9 miles by 5, Jersey is roughly rectangular in shape. St Helier sits in the south, at the eastern end of St Aubin's Bay; at the bay's western edge lies St Aubin itself, a recommended base, with a string of restaurants. The miniport of Gorey clings to the island's eastern tip.

**Jersey Tourism** ( ☎ 01534-448800; www.jersey.com; Liberation Sq, St Helier; ⏱ 8.30am-5.30pm Mon-Sat & 9am-1pm Sun late May-late Sep, 8.30am-5.30pm Mon-Fri & 9am-1pm Sat Oct-May) is beside the bus station, a short walk from the ferry terminal; there is also an airport information desk.

**Curiosity Coffee Shop** ( ☎ 01534-510075; 14 Sand St, St Helier; free; ⏱ 7am-7pm Mon-Fri, 8am-6pm Sat) and **Murray's** ( ☎ 01534-747963; La Neuve Route, St Aubin; per min 5p; ⏱ 9am-10pm) offer internet access.

## Sights & Activities

Founded by writer and naturalist Gerald Durrell, the inspiring **Durrell** ( ☎ 01534-860000; Les Augrès Manor, Trinity; adult/child £11.90/8.40; ⏱ 9.30am-dusk) focuses on breeding endangered species, then releasing them into the wild. The layout allows inhabitants remarkable freedom, with monkeys and lemurs roaming a natural, wooded environment. The talks given by enthusiastic keepers are recommended. Take bus 3A, 3B or 23 from the bus station.

The **Jersey War Tunnels** ( ☎ 01534-860808; www .jerseywartunnels.com; Les Charrières Malorey, St Lawrence; adult/child £9.85/5.75; ⏱ 10am-6pm Feb-Nov, last admission 4.30pm) powerfully evoke the five-year German Occupation's profound impact on thousands of islanders. Flickering film footage and personal testimonies fill the chilling passages of a former underground military hospital, hacked out of solid rock by forced labour. The tales are of personal courage, resistance, endurance – even collaboration. Your ticket is an islander's identity card, and you find out what befell the individual in question at the end. History made human, the museum asks what you would have done in the situations faced by the 25,000 islanders who chose not to evacuate. Take bus 8A.

**Mont Orgueil Castle** ( ☎ 01534-633375; Gorey; adult/child £9.30/5.50; ⏱ 10am-6pm late Mar-early Nov, 10am-4pm Fri-Mon Nov-Mar), a fine medieval concentric castle, has undergone an imaginative restoration. Catapults, artefacts and thought-provoking artwork lurk amid dark corners, tiny alleyways and spiral staircases. It's a wonderful place to duck, twist and learn about the gritty details of medieval life. If you have children, great. If you don't, become one again for a few hours.

Jersey's **Maritime Museum** ( ☎ 01534-633372; New North Quay, St Helier; adult/child £6/5.20; ⏱ 9.30am-5pm late Mar-early Nov, 9.30am-4pm Nov-Mar) is an interactive, lever-pulling delight. Here you build boats, change the wind direction, make waves and generally play at being King Knut. There are conventional exhibits too, but largely this is excellent education, by stealth.

On the wild, west coast, the 5-mile sandy beach at **St Ouen's Bay** is mind-expandingly big and backed by wind-sculpted dunes. **Watersplash** ( ☎ 01534-482886; www.watersplashjersey.com; St Ouen's Bay) is a centre for activities including kayaking and kitesurfing, the base for the **Jersey Surf School** ( ☎ 01534-484005; www.jerseysurfschool.com; wetsuit & board hire per hr £8) and a fine spot for a beer or a bite. North of St Ouen's Bay is Stone Age quarry and Roman shrine **Le Pinâcle**, where the pink granite outcrop is seen, somewhat inevitably, as a fertility symbol.

## Sleeping & Eating

Jersey Tourism operates a free reservations service, **Jerseylink** ( ☎ 01534-448888). Book ahead in summer. Europcar's desk at the airport has an accommodation list.

**Bon Viveur** ( ☎ 01534-741049; www.bonviveurjersey.com; Le Blvd, St Aubin; s/d £28/56) The basic rooms above a busy Italian restaurant are poky but offer the cheapest beds on the waterfront.

**Porthole Cottage** ( ☎ 01534-745007; portcott@itl.net; Market Hill, St Aubin; s/d £52.50/70) The ship's wheel on the outside of this hillside B&B heralds its nautical theme. Inside, there's a network of wooden beams in the bar and a flower explosion in the bedrooms' decor.

**our pick** **Old Court House Inn** ( ☎ 01534-746433; www.oldcourthousejersey.com; Le Blvd, St Aubin; s/d/ste £90/120/170) This 15th-century place oozes character and charm in its low lintels and twisting staircases. The rooms have stunning views across the water, the courtyard restaurant does first-class food and there's a schooner-shaped bar, made from old ship timbers.

**Pomme d'Or** ( ☎ 01534-880110; www.pommedorhotel.com; Liberation Sq, St Helier; r from £140; ⌨ ) If you need to stay in the capital, this is typical of St Helier's slick business hotels. Victor

Hugo stayed here, but the historical charm ends there.

**Hungry Man** (Rozel; burgers £2.50; ⏱ 10am-5pm) One of the island's beloved seaside kiosks, this 60-year-old institution serves Jersey cream teas and burgers such as the Double Decker Health Wrecker.

**Corbiere Phare** ( ☎ 01534-746127; St Brelade; mains £11) In Jersey's southwest corner, this bar-restaurant with floor-to-ceiling windows is a popular sunset-watching spot. Jersey royal potatoes and local catches are on the menu.

**Cheffins** ( ☎ 01534-747118; La Neuve Route, St Aubin; mains £9-16) With art-deco menus and Tamara de Lempicka reproductions on the walls, Cheffins is a hit with the tax haven set. The two-course weekday lunch menu (£9) allows you to tuck into, say, grilled sardines or mussels followed by cod and chips or roast lamb.

Alternatively, stock up at St Helier's central and fish **markets** (Beresford St; ⏱ 8.30am-5.30pm Mon-Sat, to 2pm Thu), grab a portable barbecue and join the locals watching the sunset at St Ouen's Bay.

## Getting There & Around

For information on getting to Jersey, see p975.

A taxi from the airport to St Helier costs around £9 (20 minutes). The airport–St Aubin–St Helier bus 15 costs £1.50 (15 to 35 minutes). All bus routes originate at St Helier's harbourside bus station; useful routes include bus 1 to Gorey and 12A to St Ouen's Bay via St Aubin (fares £1 to £1.50).

Traffic and free parking are problematic. **Zebra** ( ☎ 01534-736556; www.zebrahire.com; 9 Esplanade, St Helier) hires cars (per day £34) and bikes (per day £11).

## GUERNSEY

pop 60,285

Being in Guernsey is like falling into a giant flowerbox – everything's in bloom. With a subtropical feel, the picturesque capital, St Peter Port, has narrow cobblestone streets winding down hills to the water's edge, where colourful yachts pack the harbours. Locals worry that the island's character is being eroded by new developments and the financial sector's eagerness to emulate Jersey's success. But Guernsey's chief appeal – its knack of conjuring halcyon days from green lanes, gentle crescents of beach and cliffs made for hiking – remains.

## Orientation & Information

Guernsey is roughly 7 miles long by 5 miles wide, with St Peter Port ('town') on its eastern edge. The steep south coast has leg-testing cliff paths; land on the west and north slopes more gently towards the sea, with more beaches. The Bailiwick of Guernsey includes Herm, Sark and Alderney.

The **Guernsey Information Centre** ( ☎ 01481-723552; www.visitguernsey.com; North Plantation, St Peter Port; ⏲ 9am-6pm Mon-Fri, 9am-5pm Sat, 9am-1pm Sun late May-late Sep, 9am-5pm Mon-Fri, 9am-1pm Sat late Sep-late Apr, 9am-5pm Mon-Fri, 9am-1pm Sat & Sun late Apr-late May) is on the waterfront, and there's an airport information desk. Wi-fi is available at both, and the tourist office has a computer with free access. Alternatively, there's internet cafe **All Sorts** ( ☎ 01481-726832; 32 Mill St; per 15min 75p; ⏲ 10am-7pm Mon-Sat).

## Sights & Activities

After being exiled from France in 1851 following Napoleon III's coup, Victor Hugo lived in St Peter Port for 14 years. His home, **Hauteville House** ( ☎ 01481-721911; www.victorhugo.gg; 38 Hauteville; adult/senior/child £6/4/free; guided tour only; ⏲ 10am-4pm Mon-Sat May-Sep, from noon Apr), has been preserved in its full, eclectic glory. The ornate rooms are a testament to the great novelist's larger-than-life personality, with their tapestries and furniture such as the fireplace made out of panels and legs from medieval chests. In the glass lookout tower, where Hugo wrote *Les Misérables*, standing up, on a clear day you can see France.

Dominating St Peter Port's waterfront, the **Castle Cornet** ( ☎ 01481-721657; adult/senior/child £6.50/4.50/free; ⏲ 10am-5pm Apr-Oct) was a royalist stronghold during the Civil War and a garrison in the Napoleonic Wars. Museums cover subjects including Guernsey's maritime heritage and the building's 800-year history.

On the west coast, the **Shipwreck Museum** ( ☎ 01481-265036; Fort Grey, Rocquaine Coast Rd; adult/senior/child £3/2/free; ⏲ 10am-5pm mid-Apr–Oct) is housed in an 1804 Martello (defensive) tower. Circular and pocket-sized, it crams in a wealth of detail about the hazardous local waters, which have caused 90-plus recorded shipwrecks dating from the 14th century. Take bus 5, 7 or 7A.

One of seven museums and sites devoted to the Occupation, the **Underground Military Museum** ( ☎ 01481-722300; La Vallette, St Peter Port; adult/senior/child £4.50/3.50/2; ⏲ 10am-5pm Mar–mid-Nov) recalls the enforced labourers who died building the island's Nazi fortifications. The powerful relics in its dank tunnels include 1940s newspapers and posters, one announcing the execution of an islander for sending a carrier pigeon to England.

Nearby, join the locals at the rock-sculpted **bathing pools**, or hunt out a **Guernsey jumper** (special pattern, special wool) in town. On the hill, you can get the key to the crenellated **Victoria Tower** (1851) from **Guernsey Museum** ( ☎ 01481-726518; Candie Gardens, St Peter Port; ⏲ 10am-4pm or 5pm Feb-Dec), which evokes island life from the Iron Age onwards.

**Outdoor Guernsey** ( ☎ 01481-263403; www.outdoorguernsey.co.uk) offers activities from coasteering to kayaking; and **Guernsey Surf School** ( ☎ 01481-244855; www.guernseysurfschool.co.uk) is based at the west coast surf spot **Vazon Bay**. Beach lubbers are spoilt for choice, but **Pembroke Bay**, at Guernsey's northern tip, offers family fun.

## Sleeping

**Le Friquet** ( ☎ 01481-256509; www.lefriquethotel.com; Rue du Friquet, Castel; s/d/ste £55/96/110; P ) Tucked away in the middle of the island, this converted stone farmhouse has rooms that are as flowery and perfumed as its award-winning garden. Catch bus 2.

**Duke of Normandie Hotel** ( ☎ 01481-721431; www.dukeofnormandie.com; Lefebvre St, St Peter Port; r from £99; P ) This central choice has a lively, wood-panelled bar and smart, modish rooms, some up spiral stairs from the cobbled courtyard.

Other accommodation options in St Peter Port range from B&Bs such as **St George's** ( ☎ 01481-721027; www.stgeorges-guernsey.com; 21 St George's Esplanade; per person £36, 1-night supplement £5) to the best address in town, 'OGH' or **Old Government House Hotel** ( ☎ 01481-724921; www.theoghhotel.com; St Ann's Pl, St Peter Port; s/d/ste £125/160/215; P ).

## Eating

Surrounded by sea life and almost close enough to France to smell the cooking, Guernsey offers stylish lobster-laden menus and fresh seafood sarnies.

**La Crêperie** ( ☎ 01481-725566; 18 Smith St, St Peter Port; mains £5; ⏲ 10am-2pm & 6-9.30pm Mon-Sat) The long benches and traditional Breton decor echo the simple ingredients in the galettes and *sucrées* (savoury and sweet crêpes).

**Crabby Jack's** ( ☎ 01481-257489; Vazon Bay; mains £8-17; ⏲ noon-9.45pm) This island institution has all the vistas and scrumptious seafood of a beach hang-out, but none of the nonchalance in its service. We recommend the creamy crab soup.

**Da Nello** ( ☎ 01481-721552; 46 Le Pollet, St Peter Port; mains £13; ☺ lunch & dinner) This Italian restaurant has been satisfying islanders' pasta appetites since 1978. Set in a 15th-century building with beams from shipwrecks, it's a great place to sample lobster, crab or one of the inventive monthly recommendations.

Beach kiosks, generally open daily in summer, are a definitive slice of laid-back island life. Look out for crab rolls and Gâche (pronounced 'gosh'), Guernsey's own fruit loaf.

### Getting There & Around

For information on getting to Guernsey, see p975.

A taxi from the airport to St Peter Port takes about 15 minutes (£9). The bus stops at the harbourside station in town, from where all services start (any journey 60p). **Harlequin Hire** ( ☎ 01481-239511; www.harlequinhire.com; £30 per day) has a desk at the airport; the outfits there drop off and pick up throughout the island. **Millard & Co** ( ☎ 01481-720777; www.millards.org; Victoria Rd, St Peter Port) hires bikes (£8) and scooters (per day £28).

Bus 7, with its round-island, coastal route, is ideal for mini hop-on, hop-off expeditions; the **double-decker bus** ( ☎ 01481-740404; adult/child £8/4) offers a two-hour exploration of the west coast.

## HERM
pop 97

A tiny 1.5 miles long and half a mile wide, Herm is a pretty island of white beaches and flower-strewn hills. It has permanent residents and a school, but during the summer, when the population doubles with tourists and seasonal workers, it can feel like a holiday camp. However, if you pace off the ferry and leave the crowd behind, it's possible to luxuriate in the wheel-free atmosphere: not even bicycles are allowed. Walking Herm's circumference, and perhaps spotting a puffin during the spring, is a pleasant way to spend a few hours.

The island has been overseen by the same family since 1949, and its previous occupants include Prince Blücher von Wahlstatt, a Prussian noble who tried to establish a wallaby population. The next resident was Sir Compton Mackenzie, author of *Whisky*

*Galore*, who fictionalised the island in *Fairy Gold*.

A blustery walk to **Shell Beach**, a beautiful spot for a swim, takes in the common, dotted with the remains of **neolithic tombs** and a moss-covered **obelisk**; and Alderney Point, with views of the larger island and Normandy. At hilltop Le Manoir, Norman monks built the L-shaped **St Tugual's Chapel**.

The island gardener leads a 90-minute **tour** (per person £5.75; ☺ 11am Tue mid-Apr–mid-Sep) of his award-winning handiwork. Buy tickets at the administration office (see below).

### Sleeping & Eating

Prices fall considerably in low season. Book self-catering accommodation and camping through the **administration office** ( ☎ 01481-722377; www.herm-island.com; sites per adult/child £6/3, cottages per week from £645).

**White House Hotel** ( ☎ 01481-722159; www.herm-island.com; half-board per person from £92; ☺ Easter-early Oct) This hotel is upmarket and fairly formal, and has a tranquil garden and rooms that overlook the bay, giving superb views. The terraced Ship Inn restaurant serves decent pub grub (mains £8).

**Mermaid Tavern** ( ☎ 01481-710170; mains from £7; ☺ noon-2.30pm & 6-9pm) Creaking with nauticalia and photos of Prince Blücher's wallabies, the cosy pub and its courtyard are pleasant spots to eat a burger and wait for the ferry.

There are two snack kiosks on the east coast.

### Getting There & Away

**Travel Trident** ( ☎ 01481-721379) runs ferries from Guernsey (adult/child return £9/4.50, 20 minutes, six to eight daily from April to October). From November to March there are three return sailings on Wednesday and Saturday.

## SARK
pop 580

We were on Sark to research this guidebook on the day that the Privy Council approved the dissolution of feudal rule on the island after 450 years. While many people welcome the democratisation, others say it takes power from the Seigneur (lord) only to hand it to the Barclay brothers, the *Daily Telegraph* owners who live on neighbouring Brecqhou. Regardless, anachronisms showed no sign of disappearing from an island where signs measure distances in 'minutes to walk'.

THE CHANNEL ISLANDS

Tractors are the only motorised vehicles on the lanes; horses and carts are a picturesque means of travel for many visitors, others walk or cycle. The island stretches 40 miles of cliffs and beaches from its compact dimensions (3 miles by 1.5 miles). Seemingly lost lanes, extraordinary views and a tangible sense of freedom make it reminiscent of childhood holidays you possibly never actually had; it is one of the most memorable of the Channel Islands.

## Orientation & Information

The steep-sided island is divided into Sark and Little Sark, linked by the isthmus La Coupée. The Avenue, 15 minutes' walk uphill from the harbour, has the main concentration of shops and **Sark Tourism** ( ☎ 01481-832345; www.sark .info; 🕑 9am-5pm Mon-Sat mid-Jul–late Sep, 11am-1pm Sun Jul & Aug, 10am-5pm Mon-Sat, from 9am Mon, Wed & Sat late May–mid-Jul, 10am-4.30pm Mon-Sat, from 9am Wed & Sat mid-Mar–late May & late Sep–late Oct).

The NatWest and HSBC banks (both open 10am to 3pm Monday to Friday) take an hour off for lunch. You can withdraw cash with purchases at Island Stores.

## Sights & Activities

**La Seigneurie Gardens and Maze** (adult/child £2/1; 🕑 10am-5pm Mon-Sat Easter-late Sep) are overshadowed by the big man's 17th-century residence. A footpath leads to the **Window in the Rock**, which gives clifftop views.

The old telephone exchange houses the **Occupation and Heritage Museum** ( ☎ 01481-832564; adult/child £2.50/50p; 🕑 11am-5pm Mon-Sat mid-May–mid-Oct).

Dismount your carriage or bike to cross the snaking, razor-edged walkway atop the 100m cliffs of **La Coupée**.

The aquamarine, so-big-you-can-swim-in-it **Venus Pool** appears at low tide on Little Sark.

For three hours of stories, join former fisherman George on a **round-island trip** ( ☎ 01481-832107; trips adult/child £22/11) in his Sark-built boat.

## Sleeping & Eating

There are two camp sites on Sark.

**Pomme de Chien Campsite** ( ☎ 01481-832316; www .freewebs.co.uk/sarkcamping; sites per adult/child £6/4) Within walking distance of both the Avenue and Dixcart Bay beach, Pomme de Chien has sea views and, from May to September,

fully equipped frame tents for hire (£25 per night).

**La Valette Campsite** ( ☎ 01481-832202; zoe_adams@ yahoo.co.uk; sites per adult/child £6.50/4) On the east coast, La Valette offers fresh produce from the nearby farm, solar-heated water and tents for hire.

**Close de Menage** ( ☎ 01481-832091; david.curtis@ cwgsy.net; per person £40-45) Hiding behind its subtropical garden, this country-house B&B has quiet, colourful rooms and an open fire in the lounge.

**La Moinerie** ( ☎ 01481-832089; www.lamoineriehotel .com; per person £70) With bright bedrooms and one of Sark's best restaurants (lunch main £10, three-course dinner £22.50), this B&B nestles at the bottom of a shady lane.

**La Sablonnerie** ( ☎ 01481-832061; www.lasablonnerie .com; per person £75; 🕑 late Apr–mid-Oct) Tucked away on Little Sark is this deeply comfortable converted farmhouse with lush gardens and a gourmet restaurant (mains £15). Its tea garden serves mouth-watering seafood lunches (mains £8) and cream teas.

## Getting There & Around

**Isle of Sark Shipping** ( ☎ 01481-724059; www.sarkship ping.info) sails from St Peter Port, Guernsey (adult/child/senior return £22/11/20, 45 minutes). There are four or five return services a day (two on Sunday) between late May and late September. There are daily services outside those times, although for much of the winter, day trips are only possible on Monday, Wednesday and Friday.

Manche Iles Express (see p975) has a couple of ferries a week from Jersey (single £34, 50 minutes).

An open-sided cart pulls people and luggage up the steep harbour hill or you can walk up the path. Horse-drawn carriages congregate at the beginning of the Avenue, near **Avenue Cycle Hire** ( ☎ 01481-832102; bike hire per day £6.50 plus £5 deposit).

## ALDERNEY
pop 2400

The third-largest island (3.5 miles by 1.5 miles) has a remote location and a singular atmosphere. If you arrive in one of the eight- or 15-seat planes that serve Alderney, you notice it as soon as you land.

The airport shop stocks signed Wombles books, the cult children's stories about furry creatures who recycle rubbish. Their distinguished author lives here, and the island has its own 'Womble': the rare blonde hedgehog. Alderney is also an avian hot spot; near the airport, the 7000 birds that give Gannet Rocks their name are a breathtaking sight.

The Nazis left a high concentration of fortifications (see Channel Islands at War, p976) and the crumbling remains are an eerie presence. Just as remarkably, Alderney's isolation has preserved its sense of community, particularly in the Georgian House Hotel during the interval at the nearby cinema. While the projectionist changes the reels, the audience adjourns to the hotel's bar to discuss the film so far – islanders enjoy the half-time ritual as much as the official entertainment.

A good time to visit is the first week in August, during the carnival and mayhem of **Alderney Week** (book ahead). Later in August, and during **Wildlife Week** in May, guided tours on foot, boat, kayak and cycle investigate everything from Alderney's dawn chorus to its bat population.

### Orientation & Information

St Anne is the pastel-painted, village-sized capital, 20 minutes' walk from both the airport and the port, Braye Harbour.

Internet access (£1.50 per 15 minutes) is available at **Alderney Tourism** ( ☎ 01481-823737; www.visitalderney.com; Victoria St; ☯ 10am-noon & 2-4pm, closed Sun afternoon), which shares an office with Alderney Wildlife Trust; there are two ATMs nearby.

### Sights & Activities

**Alderney Wildlife Trust** ( ☎ 01481-822935; Victoria St) has displays on the island's diverse marine and bird life. The staff can point you in the direction of puffin and gannet colonies and the blonde hedgehog's habitat.

Tours include three-hour, round-island boat trips – get tickets at **McAllister's Fish Shop** ( ☎ 01481-823666; Victoria St; adult/child £20/15) – and

expeditions using transparent kayaks with **Clear Blue** ( ☎ 07781-415468; tours £8).

The **museum** ( ☎ 01481-823222; www.alderneysociety .org; High St; adult/child £2/free; ☯ 10am-noon daily & 2.30-4.30pm Mon-Fri Apr-Oct) has local history and geology exhibits, and relics from the Occupation and an Elizabethan shipwreck.

### Sleeping

**Glenhurst** ( ☎ 01481-823981; bithell@cwgsy.net; 15 Longis Rd; per person £30-40) Just east of the centre of St Anne, this small, modern B&B, run by a friendly couple from Birmingham, has a German bunker-turned-patio.

**Braye Beach Hotel** ( ☎ 01481-824300; www.braye beach.com; Braye Harbour; s/d £120/160) Rooms at the island's best hotel ooze style, with their compact furniture and flat-screen TVs. The restaurant (mains £15) has glass tables and views down the beach.

### Eating & Drinking

Braye Harbour has a range of eateries, from a fish-and-chip shop to restaurants.

**Boat House** ( ☎ 01481-822421; Braye Harbour; mains £8; ☯ lunch & dinner Wed-Mon) At this brasserie, with its blue-and-yellow decor and end-of-the-world sense of contentment, choose between flavoured ciders and daily specials such as pan-fried tiger prawns and smoked halibut.

**Gannets** ( ☎ 01481-823098; Victoria St; mains £12; ☯ breakfast, lunch, dinner Mon-Sat) The Thai and western staples at this kitsch restaurant are nothing to write to Bangkok about, but the friendly place is open all hours.

### Getting There & Around

For information on getting to Alderney, see p975.

**Braye Hire Cars** ( ☎ 01481-823881; per day £27.50) delivers to the airport and harbour. **Cycle & Surf** ( ☎ 01481-822286; Les Rocquettes, St Anne; bike hire per day £6) rents out bikes. For taxis, call ☎ 01481-823760.

**THE CHANNEL ISLANDS**

# Directory

## CONTENTS

Country-wide practical information is given in this Directory. For details on specific areas, flip to the relevant regional chapter.

## ACCOMMODATION

Accommodation in Britain is as varied as the sights you visit. From hip hotels to basic barns, the wide choice is all part of the attraction.

As in other countries, hotels and B&Bs (and even hostels) in Britain are awarded stars by the national tourist board and main motoring organisations, according to their levels of quality and service. Don't go by stars alone, though. Some five-star hotels have loads of facilities but can feel a bit impersonal, whereas many small one-star or two-star places are owner-managed where guests feel especially welcome. In addition, some smaller B&Bs prefer not to pay the fees to register with the tourist board and so don't get any stars, even though their service is absolutely fine. The moral: if you use official accommodation lists as your only source, you might miss out on a real gem.

Locally focused accommodation websites (eg Where to Stay Wessex, Reservations London) are listed in the individual regional chapters. For a country-wide view, an excellent first stop is **Stilwell's** (www.stilwell.co.uk), a huge user-friendly database, listing holiday cottages, B&Bs, hotels, camp sites and hostels. Stilwell's is not an agency – once you've found what you want, you deal with the cottage or B&B owner direct. From the website you can also order a hard-copy brochure. Good agencies include **Bed & Breakfast Nationwide** ( ☎ 01255-831235; www.bedandbreakfast nationwide.com) and **Hoseasons** ( ☎ 01502-502588; www.hoseasons.co.uk), the latter covering cottages and holiday parks.

### B&Bs & Guesthouses

The B&B (bed and breakfast) is a great British institution. Basically, you get a room in somebody's house, and at smaller places you'll really feel part of the family. Larger B&Bs may have around 10 rooms and more facilities. 'Guest house' is sometimes just another name for a B&B, although they can be more like a hotel, with higher rates.

---

**ROOM RATES**

Throughout this book, most Sleeping sections are divided into three price bands:
Budget – under £50
Midrange – £50-120 per double/twin
Top end – over £120 per double/twin

These are high-season rates for a double/twin room with private bathroom; at quieter times of year prices drop. Single rooms are usually about 75% the double/twin rate. The exception is accommodation in London, where 'budget' in this book means under £80 for a double/twin room, midrange is £80 to £150, and top end is over £150.

---

**PRACTICALITIES**

- Be ready for a bizarre mix of metric and imperial measures in Britain; for example, petrol is sold by the litre, but road-sign distances are given in miles.

- Use plugs with three flat pins to connect appliances to the 220V (50Hz AC) power supply.

- Follow current events in the *Sun, Mirror* or *Record* tabloids, or get more incisive views in the (right to left, politically) *Telegraph, Times, Independent* or *Guardian* quality papers.

- Relish the satire, then cringe at tales of corruption, in weekly no-frills mag *Private Eye*.

- Turn on the TV and watch some of the finest programs in the world from multichannel BBC, closely followed by boundary-pushing Channel 4.

- Tune into BBC radio for a wide range of shows, and no adverts. Half the households in Britain have digital radio and TV, but for those still on analogue, main stations and wavelengths are Radio 1 (98-99.6MHz FM); Radio 2 (88-92MHz FM); Radio 3 (90-92.2MHz FM); Radio 4 (92-94.4MHz FM); and Radio 5Live (909 or 693 AM).

- National commercial stations include Virgin Radio (1215kHz MW) and non-highbrow classical-specialist Classic FM (100-102MHz FM). Both are also on digital, with at least 40 other stations.

---

In country areas, your B&B might be in a village or isolated farm; in cities it's usually a suburban house. Wherever, facilities usually reflect price – for around £20 per person you get a simple bedroom and share the bathroom. For around £25 to £30 you get extras like TV or 'hospitality tray' (kettle, cups, tea, coffee) and a private bathroom – either down the hall or en suite.

B&B prices are usually quoted per person, based on two people sharing a room. Solo travellers have to search for single rooms and pay a 20% to 50% premium. Some B&Bs simply won't take single people (unless you pay the full double-room price), especially in summer.

Here are some more B&B tips:

- Advance reservations are always preferred at B&Bs, and essential during popular periods. Many require a minimum two nights at weekends.

- If a B&B is full, owners may recommend another place nearby (possibly a private house taking occasional guests, not in tourist listings).

- In cities, some B&Bs are for long-term residents or people on welfare; they don't take passing tourists.

- In country areas, most B&Bs cater for walkers and cyclists, but some don't, so let them know if you'll be turning up with dirty boots or wheels.

- Some places reduce rates for longer stays (three nights plus).

- Most B&Bs serve enormous breakfasts; some also offer packed lunches (around £5) and evening meals (from around £10 to £15).

- If you're on a flexible itinerary and haven't booked in advance, most towns have a main drag of B&Bs; those with spare rooms hang up a 'Vacancies' sign.

- When booking, check your B&B's actual position. In country areas, addresses include the nearest town, which may be 20 miles away – important if you're walking! Some B&B owners will pick you up by car for a small charge.

## Bunkhouses & Camping Barns

A bunkhouse is a simple place to stay, handy for walkers, cyclists or anyone on a budget in the countryside. They usually have a communal sleeping area and bathroom, heating and cooking stoves, but you provide the sleeping bag and possibly cooking gear. Most charge around £10 per person per night.

Camping barns are even more basic: they're usually converted farm buildings, with sleeping platforms, a cooking area, and basic toilets outside. Take everything you'd need to camp except the tent. Charges are from around £5 per person.

## Camping

The opportunities for camping in Britain are numerous – ideal if you're on a tight budget or simply enjoy the great outdoors. In rural areas, camp sites range from farmers' fields with a tap and a basic toilet, costing as little as £3 per person per night, to smarter affairs with hot showers and many other facilities charging up to £10.

If you're planning more than a few nights in a tent, or touring Britain with a campervan (motor home), it's worth joining the well-organised **Camping & Caravanning Club** ( ☎ 0845 130 7632; www.campingandcaravanningclub. co.uk), which owns almost 100 camp sites and lists thousands more in the invaluable *Big Sites Book* (free to members). Annual membership costs £35 and includes discounted rates on club sites and various other services – including insurance and ferries.

## Hostels

Britain has two types of hostel: those run by the **Youth Hostels Association** (YHA; 01629-592 700; www.yha.org.uk) or **Scottish Youth Hostels Association** (SYHA; 0870 155 3255; www.syha.org.uk); and Independent Hostels.

You'll find hostels in rural areas, towns and cities. They're aimed at all types of traveller – whether you're a long-distance walker or touring by car – and you don't have to be young or single to use them. The YHA also handles bookings for many bunkhouses and camping barns around the country.

### INDEPENDENT HOSTELS

Britain's independent and backpacker hostels offer a great welcome. In rural areas, some are little more than simple bunkhouses (charging around £6), while others are almost up to B&B standard, charging £15 or more. In cities, backpacker hostels are perfect for young budget travellers. Most are open 24/7, with a lively atmosphere, good range of rooms (doubles or dorms), bar, cafe, internet, wi-fi and laundry. Prices are around £15 for a dorm bed, or £20 to £35 for a bed in a private room.

The **Independent Hostel Guide** (www.independent hostelguide.co.uk) covers hundreds of hostels in Britain and beyond, and is by far the best listing available. It's also available as a handy annually updated book at hostels or direct from the website. North of the border, an excellent site is www.hostel-scotland.co.uk.

### YHA & SHYA HOSTELS

Many years ago, YHA and SYHA hostels had a reputation for austerity, but today they're a great option for budget travellers. Some are purpose-built, but many are converted cottages, country houses and even castles – often in wonderful locations. Facilities include showers and equipped self-catering kitchen. Sleeping is in dormitories, and many hostels also have twin or four-bed rooms, some with private bathroom.

You don't *have* to be a member of the YHA or SHYA (or another Hostelling International organisation) to stay at YHA/SYHA hostels, but nonmembers pay extra: £3 extra per person per night (£1.50 for under-18s) in England and Wales; £1 per person per night in Scotland, so it's usually worth joining. Annual YHA membership costs £16; for the SYHA it's £9. Under-16s/26s, seniors and families get discounts.

Small basic hostels cost from £10, larger hostels with more facilities are £14 to £19. City hostels cost £19 to £25. Add £3 or £1 to all these rates if you're not a member. Reservations and advance payments with credit card are usually possible. On the YHA/SYHA websites you can also find out about bunkhouses, camping barns, camp sites and 'affiliated' hostels – privately owned but bookable through YHA/SYHA.

It's important to note that most hostel prices (just like train fares) vary according to demand and season. So book early for a Tuesday night in May and you'll get the best rate. Book late for a weekend in August and you'll pay top whack – if there's space at all. Throughout this book, we have generally quoted the cheaper rates (in line with those listed on the YHA and SYHA websites); you may find yourself paying more. Some hostels also have varying opening times and days, especially in remote locations or out of tourist season, so check before turning up.

## Hotels

A hotel in Britain might be a small and simple place, perhaps a former farmhouse now styl-

---

**BOOK ACCOMMODATION ONLINE**

For more accommodation reviews and recommendations by Lonely Planet authors, check out www.lonelyplanet.com/hotels. You'll find the true, insider lowdown on the best places to stay. Reviews are thorough and independent. Best of all, you can book online.

---

**SOMETHING FOR THE WEEKEND?**

Britain has a beguiling selection of accommodation options, and throughout this book we list many that stand out above the crowd. To widen the choice still further, and maybe discover a gem for yourself, the **Landmark Trust** ( ☎ 01628-825925; www.landmarktrust.org.uk) is an architectural charity that rents historic buildings; your options include ancient cottages, medieval castles, Napoleonic forts and 18th-century follies.

Or try **Distinctly Different** ( ☎ 01225-866842; www.distinctlydifferent.co.uk), specialising in the unusual and bizarre places to stay. Can't sleep at night? How about a former funeral parlour? Need to spice up your romance? Then go for the converted brothel or the 'proudly phallic' lighthouse. Feeling brave? We have just the haunted inn for you.

Back safely down to earth with the final option. The **National Trust** (www.nationaltrust.org.uk) has over 300 holiday cottages and 80 B&Bs, many on the land of stately homes and working farms, in some of the finest locations in the country.

---

ishly converted, where peace and quiet – along with luxury – are guaranteed. Or it might be a huge country house with fancy facilities, grand staircases, acres of grounds and the requisite row of stag-heads on the wall. With such a great choice your only problem will be deciding where to stay.

How much is a hotel in Britain? It depends. Charges vary as much as quality and atmosphere. At the bargain end, you can find singles/doubles costing £30/40. Move up the scale and you can easily pay to £100/150 or beyond. More money doesn't always mean a better hotel though – whatever your budget, some are excellent value, while others overcharge.

If all you want is a place to put your head down, budget chain hotels can be a good option. Most are totally lacking in style or ambience, but who cares? You'll only be there for eight hours, and six of them you'll be asleep. For example, **Travelodge** (www.travelodge.co.uk) offers rooms at variable prices based on demand; on a quiet night in November twin-bed rooms with private bathroom start at around £20, and at the height of the tourist season you'll pay £45 or more. Other budget chains with similar pricing structures include **Premier Inn** (www.premierinn.com), **Etap Hotels** (www.etaphotel.com) and **Hotel Formule 1** (www.hotelformule1.com).

### Pubs & Inns

As well as selling drinks, many pubs and inns offer lodging, particularly in country areas. Staying in a pub can be good fun – you're automatically at the centre of the community – although accommodation varies enormously, from stylish suites to threadbare rooms. You'll pay around £20 per person at the cheap end, and £30 to £35 for something better. An advantage for solo tourists: pubs are more likely to have single rooms.

If a pub does B&B, it normally does evening meals, served in the bar or adjoining restaurant. Breakfast may also be served in the bar the next morning – not always enhanced by the smell of stale beer.

### Rental Accommodation

If you want to slow down and get to know a place better, renting for a week or two can be ideal. Choose from neat flats (apartments) in towns and cities, or quaint old houses and farms (always called 'cottages' – whatever the size) in country areas. Cottages for four people cost from around £200 to £300 per week in high season. Rates fall at quieter times, and you may be able to rent for a long weekend.

### University Accommodation

Many universities offer student accommodation to visitors when the students themselves are away between terms. The main period is July and August, but rooms are also available over the Christmas and Easter vacation periods. You usually get a functional single bedroom with private bathroom, and self-catering flats are also available. Prices range from £15 to £30 per person.

The useful website www.budgetstayuk.com represents many unis and colleges in Britain, and offers online bookings.

## BEACHES

As befitting an island, Britain has many beaches – from tiny hidden coves to vast empty strands, via a host of lively neon-and-chips resorts. In England, the best beaches can be found in Cornwall and Devon and along the south coast, in Suffolk, Norfolk, Lancashire, Yorkshire and Northumberland. In Wales there's even more choice; pretty much anywhere west of Swansea and all round the western and northern coasts. In Scotland too the options are almost endless up the west and east coasts, once you get north of the Clyde and Forth estuaries, and you may have some of the largest expanses of pristine sand almost to yourself. The best resort beaches earn the coveted international **Blue Flag award** (www.blueflag.org), indicating that sand and water are clean and unpolluted. Other parameters include the presence of lifeguards, litter bins and recycling facilities – meaning some remote or wild beaches may not earn the award, but are still stunning nonetheless.

## BUSINESS HOURS
### Banks, Shops & Post Offices
Monday to Friday, most shops and post offices operate 9am to 5pm (or 6pm in cities). Most banks open 9.30am to 4pm or 5pm. On Saturdays, shops open 9am to 5pm, banks (main branches only) 9.30am to 1pm, and post offices may open all or half-day. Sunday shopping hours are around 10am to 4pm or 11am to 5pm, but banks and post offices are closed.

Cities have 24/7 convenience stores, but in smaller towns, shops often close at weekends and for lunch (normally 1pm to 2pm), and in country areas on Wednesday or Thursday afternoon too. In cities and large towns, there's usually 'late-night' shopping on Thursday – when high-street shops and department stores open until 7pm or 8pm.

### Museums & Sights
Large museums and places of interest are usually open every day. Some smaller places open just five or six days per week, usually including Saturday and Sunday, but may be closed on Monday and/or Tuesday. Much depends on the time of year too; they'll open daily in high season, but just at weekends (or shorter hours) in quieter periods.

### Pubs, Bars & Clubs
Pubs in towns and country areas in England and Wales usually open daily from 11am to 11pm Sunday to Thursday, sometimes to midnight or 1am Friday and Saturday. Most open all day, although some may shut from 3pm to 6pm. In Scotland, pubs tend to close later; 1am is normal, and 3am is not unusual. Throughout this book, we don't list pub opening and closing times unless they vary significantly from these hours.

In cities, some pubs open until midnight or later, but it's mostly bars and clubs that have taken advantage of relatively recent licensing laws ('the provision of late-night refreshment', as it's officially called) in England and Wales to stay open to 2am or beyond. As every place is different, we list opening hours for bars and clubs.

### Restaurants & Cafes
Restaurants in Britain open for lunch (about noon to 3pm) *and* dinner (about 6pm to 11pm – earlier in smaller towns; midnight or later in cities), or for lunch *or* dinner – usually every day of the week, although some close Sunday evenings or all day Monday.

Cafes and teashops vary according to location. In towns and cities, cafes may open from 7am, providing breakfast for people on their way to work. In country areas, teashops will open in time for lunch, and may stay open until 7pm or later in the summer, catering to tourists leaving stately homes or hikers down from the hills. In winter months, country cafe and restaurant hours are cut back, while some places close completely from October to Easter.

Throughout this book, we indicate if restaurants and cafes are open for lunch or dinner or both, but precise opening times and days are given only if they differ markedly from the pattern outlined here.

## CHILDREN
Who'd have 'em? No, really, travel with children can be fun, and kids are a great excuse if you secretly yearn to visit railway museums or ride the roller coaster.

Many national parks and resort towns organise activities for children, especially in school-holiday periods (see p990), and tourist offices are a great source of information on kid-friendly attractions. To help you further we've also included boxed texts, such as Manchester for Children, in the big-city sections.

Some hotels welcome kids (with their parents) and provide cots and babysitting services, while others maintain an adult atmosphere, so you need to check in advance.

Likewise restaurants: some have crayons and highchairs, and don't mind if the menu lands on the floor; others firmly say 'no children after 6pm'. Pubs and bars ban under-18s, unless they're specifically 'family-friendly' – and many are, especially those serving food.

Breastfeeding in public remains mildly controversial, but if done modestly is usually considered OK. On the sticky topic of dealing with nappies while travelling, most museums and historical attractions have good baby-changing facilities (cue old joke: I swapped mine for a nice souvenir), as do department stores. Elsewhere, you'll find facilities in motorway service stations and city-centre toilets, although these can be a bit grimy.

For more advice see www.babygoes2.com, packed with tips and encouragement for parents on the move.

## CLIMATE CHARTS

Britain's changeable weather is discussed on p21. These charts give details for specific regions.

## CUSTOMS

Britain has a two-tier customs system – one for goods bought in another European Union (EU) country where taxes and duties have already been paid, and the other for goods bought duty-free outside the EU. Below is a summary of the rules; for more details go to www.hmce.gov.uk and search on Customs Allowances.

### Duty Free

If you bring duty-free goods from *outside* the EU, the limits include 200 cigarettes, 2L of still wine, plus 1L of spirits or another 2L of wine, 60cc of perfume, and other duty-free goods (including beer) to the value of £145.

### Tax & Duty Paid

There is no limit to the goods you can bring from *within* the EU (if taxes have been paid), but customs officials use the following guidelines to distinguish personal use from commercial imports: 3200 cigarettes, 200 cigars, 10L of spirits, 20L of fortified wine, 90L of wine and 110L of beer – still enough to have one hell of a party.

## DANGERS & ANNOYANCES

Britain is a remarkably safe country, considering the wealth disparities you'll see in many

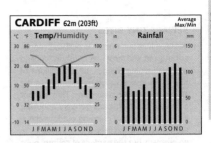

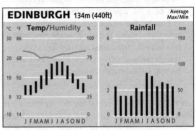

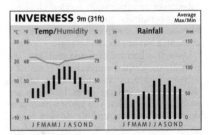

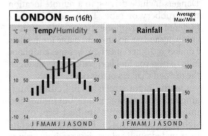

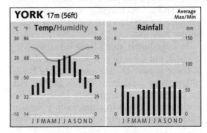

DIRECTORY

---

**BEWARE TINY BITES**

Between June and August, especially in northern England, and most notoriously in Scotland (see Maddening Midges, p936), millions of tiny biting insects called midges take to the air on cool windless evenings. They are not a danger, but their bites get very annoying if you're camping or enjoying outdoor activities. If you're staying in hostels or B&Bs they're no problem, but the gardens of country pubs can be a bit 'midgey' around sunset. Ways to counter the attack include wearing light-coloured clothing and using midge repellents (available in pharmacies and outdoor stores – brands without DDT include Moziguard and Swamp Gel). Or going inside.

---

areas, but crime is certainly not unknown in London and other cities, so you should take care – especially at night. When travelling by tube, tram or urban train service, choose a carriage containing other people. It's also best to avoid some deserted suburban tube stations at night; a bus or taxi can be a safer choice.

As well as licensed taxis and minicabs (see p1002), unlicensed minicabs – essentially a bloke with a car earning money on the side – operate in large cities, but these are worth avoiding unless you know what you're doing. Annoyances include driving round in circles, then charging an enormous fare. Dangers include driving to a remote location then robbery or rape. To avoid this, use a metered taxi or phone a reputable minicab company and get an up-front quote for the ride. London and other cities have websites and phone lines to help you find licensed cabs; details are in the relevant chapters of this book.

On the main streets of big cities, mugging or bag-snatching is rare, but money and important documents are best kept out of sight and out of reach. Pickpockets operate in crowded public places like stations or bars (bags and jackets hanging on chair-backs are popular targets), so make sure your stuff is secure here too.

In large hotels, don't leave valuables lying around; put them in your bag or use the safe if there is one. Do the same at city B&Bs, although in rural areas there's far less risk. In hostel dorms, especially independent/backpacker hostels in cities, keep your stuff packed away and carry valuables with you.

Many hostels provide lockers, but you need your own padlock.

If driving, remove luggage from the car when parking overnight in cities and towns. The same applies even in some apparently safe rural locations. While you're out walking in the countryside, someone may well be walking off with your belongings. Where possible, look for secure parking areas near tourist offices.

## DISCOUNT CARDS

There's no specific discount card for visitors to Britain, although travel cards (see p1000) are discounted for younger and older people. Membership of the YHA/SHYA (see p984) can get you discounts in bookshops and outdoor-gear shops, and on some public transport.

## EMBASSIES & CONSULATES

A selection of foreign diplomatic missions in London is given below. For a complete list of foreign embassies in the UK, see the website of the **Foreign & Commonwealth Office** (www.fco.gov.uk), which also lists Britain's diplomatic missions overseas. Your embassy, consulate and high commission will be useful if, for example, you've lost your passport, but they won't be much help if you're in trouble for committing a crime; remember, even as a foreigner, you're bound by British laws.

**Australia** (Map pp142-3; ☎ 020-7379 4334; www.australia.org.uk; Strand, WC2B 4LA)

**Canada** (Map pp142-3; ☎ 020-7258 6600; www.canada.org.uk; 1 Grosvenor Sq, W1X 0AB)

**China** (Map pp142-3; ☎ 020-7299 4049; www.chinese-embassy.org.uk; 49-51 Portland Pl, London W1B 4JL)

---

**TRACE THE ANCESTORS**

If you're a visitor with ancestors from Britain, your trip could be a good chance to find out more about them – or simply find long-lost relatives. The best place to start is the website of the **Family Records Centre** (www.familyrecords.gov.uk), full of advice on tracing family history, covering topics such as records of births, deaths, marriages, immigration and adoption, and with links to numerous other handy resource sites. The Family Records Centre cannot search individual records for you, but the **Association of Genealogists & Researchers in Archives** (www.agra.org.uk) lists professional researchers who can.

---

**France** (Map pp138-9; ☎ 020-7073 1000; www
.ambafrance-uk.org; 58 Knightsbridge, SW1 7JT)
**Germany** (Map pp142-3; ☎ 020-7824 1300; www
.london.diplo.de; 23 Belgrave Sq, SW1X 8PX)
**Ireland** (Map pp142-3; ☎ 020-7235 2171; www
.embassyofireland.co.uk; 17 Grosvenor Pl, SW1X 7HR)
**Japan** (Map pp142-3; ☎ 020-7465 6500; www
.uk.emb-japan.go.jp; 101 Piccadilly, W1J 7JT)
**Netherlands** (Map pp138-9; ☎ 020-7590 3200; www
.netherlands-embassy.org.uk; 38 Hyde Park Gate, SW7 5DP)
**New Zealand** (Map pp146-7; ☎ 020-7930 8422; www
.nzembassy.com/uk; 80 Haymarket, SW1Y 4TQ)
**USA** (Map pp142-3; ☎ 020-7499 9000; www.us
embassy.org.uk; 24 Grosvenor Sq, W1A 1AE)

## FOOD

For a flavour of Britain's cuisine, see Food
& Drink (p88). Throughout this book, most
Eating sections are divided into three price
bands: budget (up to £8), midrange (£8 to
£16) and top end (over £16).

## GAY & LESBIAN TRAVELLERS

Britain is a generally tolerant place for gays
and lesbians. London, Manchester and
Brighton have flourishing gay scenes, and in
other sizable cities (even some small towns)
you'll find communities not entirely in the
closet. That said, you'll still find pockets of
homophobic hostility in some areas too.

For info, listings and contacts, see monthly
magazines (and websites) **Gay Times** (www.gay
times.co.uk) and **Diva** (www.divamag.co.uk), or the
twice-monthly **Pink Paper** (www.pinkpaper.com). In
the capital, a useful source of information is
the **London Lesbian & Gay Switchboard** ( ☎ 020-7837
7324; www.llgs.org.uk); there are similar services in
cities and regions across the country. See also
the boxes of specific information in the major-
city sections throughout this book.

## HERITAGE ORGANISATIONS

For many visitors, a highlight of a journey
through Britain is visiting the numerous
castles and other historic sites that pepper the
country. Membership of Britain's heritage
organisations gives you free entry to properties as well as reciprocal arrangements with
similar bodies, maps, information handbooks
and so on.

The main organisations are: National Trust
(NT), and its partner organisation National
Trust for Scotland (NTS); English Heritage
(EH) and its equivalent organisations Historic
Scotland (HS) and Cadw. You can join at the

first site you visit, or online in advance. If you
don't want to join for the whole year, passes
giving free entry to all sites but for shorter
periods are also available. We've given the
adult annual membership rate and sample
pass costs for each organisation, but they
all discount for couples, families, students,
children/youths and seniors, although some
charge a higher rate to overseas visitors. If
you are a member of a similar organisation
in your own country, this may get you free or
discounted entry at sites in Britain. We have
included the relevant initials (NT, EH etc) in
the information after every property listed in
this book.

**Cadw** ( ☎ 01443-336000, 0800 0743121; www.cadw
.wales.gov.uk) The Welsh historic monuments agency. (The
name means 'to keep'.) Membership costs £35.
**English Heritage** ( ☎ 0870 333 1181; www.english
-heritage.org.uk) A state-funded organisation responsible
for numerous historic sites. Membership costs £42 and an
Overseas Visitors Pass allows free entry to most sites for
seven/14 days for £19/23.
**Historic Scotland** ( ☎ 0131-668 8600; www.historic
-scotland.gov.uk) Manages more than 330 historic sites.
Membership costs £38, and 'Explorer' passes cost £20 for
three days in five, £28 for seven days in 14, or £34 for 10
days in 30.
**National Trust** ( ☎ 0844 800 1895; www.nationaltrust
.org.uk) Protects hundreds of historic buildings plus vast
tracts of land with scenic importance in England and
Wales. Membership costs £46 and a Touring Pass for
one/two weeks is £19/24.
**National Trust for Scotland** ( ☎ 0844 493 2100;
www.nts.org.uk) The NT's sister organisation north of the
border, caring for over 100 properties and almost 80,000
hectares of countryside. Membership costs £44.

## HOLIDAYS
### Public Holidays

Holidays for the whole of Britain (unless
specified) are as follows:
**New Year's Day** 1 January
**Easter** (Good Friday to Easter Monday inclusive) March/
April
**May Day** First Monday in May
**Spring Bank Holiday** Last Monday in May
**Summer Bank Holiday** Last Monday in August
**Christmas Day** 25 December
**Boxing Day** 26 December

If a public holiday falls on a weekend, the
nearest Monday is usually taken instead. In
England and Wales, most businesses and
banks close on official public holidays (hence

**DIRECTORY**

the quaint term 'bank holiday'). In Scotland, bank holidays are just for the banks, and many businesses stay open. Instead, Scottish towns normally have a spring and autumn holiday, but the dates vary from town to town.

On public holidays, some small museums and places of interest close, but larger attractions specifically gear up and have their busiest times, although nearly everything closes on Christmas Day. Generally speaking, if a place closes on Sunday, it'll probably be shut on bank holidays as well.

As well as attractions, virtually everything – shops, banks, offices – closes on Christmas Day, although pubs are open at lunchtime. There's usually no public transport on Christmas Day, and a very restricted service on Boxing Day.

### School Holidays

Most schools have three main terms, interspersed with three main holidays (when roads get busy and hotel prices go up), although the exact dates vary from year to year and region to region:

**Easter Holiday** Week before and week after Easter.
**Summer Holiday** Third week of July to first week of September.
**Christmas Holiday** Mid-December to first week of January.

There are also three weeklong 'half-term' school holidays – usually late February (or early March), late May and late October. Some regions are moving towards six terms (and six holidays) of more equal length

## INSURANCE

Regardless of nationality, everyone receives free *emergency* medical treatment at state-run National Health Service (NHS) hospitals – if they've got an accident and emergency (A&E) department. For other medical treatment, many countries have reciprocal health agreements with the UK, meaning visitors from overseas get the same standard of care from hospitals and doctors as any British citizen. But travel insurance is still highly recommended because it offers greater flexibility over where and how you're treated. It will usually cover medical consultation and treatment at private clinics – which can be quicker than NHS places – and emergency dental care. Travel insurance will also cover loss of baggage or valuable items (such as

cameras) and, most important, the cost of any emergency flights home. For more medical information see p1005. For information on car insurance, see p1000. Worldwide travel insurance is available at www.lonelyplanet .com/travel_services. You can buy, extend and claim online anytime – even if you're already on the road.

## INTERNET ACCESS

Internet cafes are surprisingly rare in Britain, especially once you get away from tourist spots. Most charge from £1 per hour, and out in the sticks you can pay up to £5 per hour. Public libraries often have computers with free internet access, but only for 30-minute slots, and demand is high. All the usual warnings apply about keystroke-capturing software and other security risks – especially if you're using the internet to keep tabs on, say, your banking while on the move. For information on websites about Britain, see p25.

If you'll be using your laptop to get online, your connection cable may not fit in British sockets, although adaptors are easy to buy at electrical stores in airports or city centres. Sockets are thankfully becoming a thing of the past though as an increasing number of hotels, hostels, stations and coffee shops (even some trains) have wi-fi access, charging anything from nothing to £5 per hour. Throughout this book, we use an 'internet' icon to show if a place has PCs for public use, and the word 'wi-fi' if it has…you guessed it…wi-fi.

## LEGAL MATTERS
### Age Restrictions

The age of consent in Britain is 16 (gay and straight). You can also get married at 16 (with permission from parents), but you'll have to wait two years for the toast – you must be over 18 to buy alcohol. Over-16s may buy cigarettes, so you can have a celebratory smoke instead.

You usually have to be 18 to enter a pub or bar, although the rules are different if you have a meal. Some bars and clubs are over-21 only, so you won't see many highchairs.

### Antisocial Behaviour

On-the-spot fines, or immediate fines (as for driving offences), can be imposed by police for antisocial behaviour, which includes drinking in public and littering.

## Driving Crimes & Transport Fines

Drink-driving is a serious offence. For more information and details about speed limits, see p1001, and for parking rules see p1001.

On buses and trains (including the London Underground), people without a valid ticket for their journey may be fined – usually around £20 – on the spot.

## Drugs

Illegal drugs are widely available, especially in clubs. All the usual dangers apply and there have been much-publicised deaths associated with ecstasy. Cannabis possession is a criminal offence, but the punishment for carrying a small amount is usually a warning. Dealers face far stiffer penalties, as do people caught with any other 'recreational' drugs.

## MAPS

For a map of the whole country, a road atlas is handy – especially if you're travelling by car. The main publishers are Ordnance Survey (OS) and Automobile Association (AA), with atlases in all sizes and scales. If you plan to use minor roads, you'll need a scale of about 1:200,000 (3 miles to 1in). Most road atlases cost £5 to £10 and are updated annually, which means old editions are sold off every January – look for bargains at motorway service stations.

For greater detail, the OS *Landrangers* (1:50,000) are ideal for walking and cycling. OS *Explorer* maps (1:25,000) are even better for walking in lowland areas, but can sometimes be hard to read in complex mountain landscapes. Your best choice here is the excellent specialist series produced for ramblers, walkers, mountaineers and other outdoor types by **Harvey Maps** (www.harveymaps.co.uk), covering upland areas and national parks, plus routes for hikers and bikers.

If you're spending any length of time in London, the iconic **A–Z maps** (www.a-zmaps.co.uk) are incredibly detailed – online and in book form. The books are sold at newsagents and souvenir shops, but remember to pronounce it 'A to Zed'. Similar street maps are available for other cities and big towns across the country.

## MONEY

The currency of Britain is the pound, officially called the 'pound sterling'. Paper money comes in £5, £10, £20 and £50 denominations (and £1 in Scotland), although £50s can be difficult to change because fakes circulate. Prices quoted in this book are in pounds (£), unless otherwise stated, although other currencies are very rarely accepted if you're buying goods and services, except for some places in the ferry ports of southern England, which take euros, and the smarter souvenir and gift shops in London which may take euros, US dollars, yen and other major currencies. A guide to exchange rates is given on the inside front cover of this book, and for some pointers on costs see p21.

In England and Wales, notes are issued by the Bank of England, and in Scotland by Clydesdale Bank, Bank of Scotland and Royal Bank of Scotland. All notes are legal tender on both sides of the border, but you might have trouble using Scottish notes in England, especially southern and central England, so try to spend all your Scottish notes before you leave Scotland, or just head to a bank and swap them one-for-one at no charge.

## ATMs

Debit or credit cards are perfect companions – the best invention for travellers since the backpack. You can use them in most shops, and withdraw cash from ATMs (often called 'cash machines'), which are easy to find in cities and even small towns. But ATMs aren't fail-safe, and it's a major headache if your only card gets swallowed, so take a back-up. And watch out for ATMs that might have been tampered with; a common ruse is to attach a card-reader to the slot; your card is scanned and the number used for fraud.

## Credit & Debit Cards

Visa and MasterCard credit and debit cards are widely accepted in Britain, and are good for larger hotels, restaurants, shopping, flights, long-distance travel, car hire etc. Smaller businesses, such as pubs or B&Bs, prefer debit cards (or charge a fee for credit cards), and some take cash or cheque only.

Since 2006, nearly all credit and debit cards use the 'chip and pin' system; instead of signing, you enter a PIN (personal identification number). If you're from overseas and your card isn't chip-and-pin enabled, you should be able to sign in the usual way – but some places will not accept your card.

## Moneychangers

Finding a place to change your money (cash or travellers cheques) into pounds is never a problem in cities, where banks and bureaus compete for business. Be careful using bureaus, however; some offer poor rates or levy outrageous commissions. You can also change money at some post offices – very handy in country areas, and exchange rates are fair (and usually commission free).

## Tipping & Bargaining

In restaurants you're expected to leave around a 10% tip, but at smarter restaurants in larger cities waiters can get a bit sniffy if the tip isn't nearer 12% or even 15%. Either way, it's important to remember that you're not obliged to tip if the service or food was unsatisfactory (even if it's been added to your bill as a 'service charge'). At smarter cafes and teashops with table service around 10% is fine. If you're paying with a credit or debit card, and you want to add the tip to the bill, it's worth asking the waiting staff if they'll actually receive it. Some prefer to receive tips in cash.

Taxi drivers also expect tips (about 10%, or rounded up to the nearest pound), especially in London. It's less usual to tip minicab drivers. Toilet attendants (if you see them loitering) may get tipped around 50p.

In pubs, when you order drinks at the bar, or order and pay for food at the bar, tips are not expected. If you order food at the table and your meal is brought to you, then a tip may be appropriate – if the food and service have been good, of course.

Bargaining is rare, although it's occasionally encountered at markets. It's fine to ask if there are student discounts on items such as theatre tickets, books or outdoor equipment.

## Travellers Cheques

Travellers cheques (TCs) offer protection from theft, so are safer than wads of cash, but are rarely used in Britain, as credit/debit cards and ATMs have become the method of choice. If you prefer TCs, note that they are rarely accepted for purchases (except at large hotels), so for cash you'll still need to go to a bank or bureau.

## POST

There are two classes of post within Britain: a standard letter costs 36p 1st-class (normally delivered next day) and 27p 2nd-class (up to three days). The cost goes up if the letter is heaver than 100g or larger than 240x165mm or thicker than 5mm, and up again if heavier than 750g and bigger than 353x250x25mm.

Stamps are available at post offices – and there's usually a handy device for checking the size of your letters before you buy. Stamps for straightforward 1st- and 2nd-class mail can also be bought at shops and newsagents. Letters by airmail cost 50p to EU countries and 56p to the rest of the world (up to 10g). For details on all prices, see www.postoffice.co.uk.

## TELEPHONE

Britain's iconic red phone boxes can still be seen in city streets and especially in conservation areas, although many have been replaced by soulless glass cubicles. With the advent of mobile phones (cell phones), many phone booths have been removed and not replaced at all. Either way, public phones accept coins, and usually credit/debit cards. The minimum charge is 20p or 40p.

Area codes in Britain don't have a standard format and vary in length, which can be confusing for foreigners (and locals). For example ☎ 020 for London, ☎ 029 for Cardiff, ☎ 0131 for Edinburgh, ☎ 0161 for Manchester, ☎ 0113 for Leeds, ☎ 01225 for Bath, ☎ 015394 for Ambleside, followed as usual by the individual number. For clarity, area codes and individual numbers are separated by a hyphen.

As well as the geographical area codes, other 'codes' include ☎ 0500 or ☎ 0800 for free calls and ☎ 0845 for calls at local rates, wherever you're dialling from within the UK. Numbers starting with ☎ 087 are charged at national-call rates, while numbers starting with ☎ 089 or ☎ 09 are premium rate, and should be specified by the company using the number (ie in their advertising literature), so you know the cost before you call. These codes and numbers are not separated by a hyphen as you always have to dial the whole number.

Note that many numbers starting with 08 or 09 do not work if you're calling from outside the UK, or if they do you'll be charged for a full international call – and then some.

Codes for mobile phones usually start with ☎ 07. Calling a mobile phone is more expensive than calling a landline.

See also p133 for emergency services phone numbers.

## International Calls

To call outside the UK dial ☎ 00, then the country code ( ☎ 1 for USA, ☎ 61 for

Australia, etc), the area code (you usually drop the initial zero) and the number. For country codes, see the inside front cover of this book.

Direct-dialled calls to most overseas countries can be made from most public telephones, and it's usually cheaper between 8pm and 8am Monday to Friday and at weekends. You can usually save money by buying a phonecard (usually denominated £5, £10 or £20) with a PIN that you use from any phone by dialling an access number (you don't insert it into the machine). There are dozens of cards, usually available from city news agents, with rates of the various companies often vividly displayed.

To make reverse-charge (collect) calls, dial ☎ 155 for the international operator. It's expensive, but what the hell – the person at the other end is paying.

To call Britain from abroad, dial your country's international access code, then ☎ 44 (the UK's country code), then the area code (dropping the first 0) and the phone number.

Most internet cafes now have Skype or some other sort of VOIP system, so you can make international calls for the price of your time online.

### Local & National Calls

From public phones the weekday rate is about 5p per minute; evenings and weekends are cheaper – though still with a minimum charge of 20p. Local calls (within 35 miles) are cheaper than national calls. All calls are cheaper between 6pm and 8am Monday to Thursday, and from 6pm Friday to 8am Monday. From private phones, rates vary between telecom providers.

For the operator, call ☎ 100. For directory inquiries, a host of agencies compete for your business and charge from 10p to 40p; numbers include ☎ 118 192, ☎ 118 118, ☎ 118 500 and ☎ 118 811.

### Mobile Phones

Around 50 million people in the UK have mobile phones, and thus the ability to tell their loved ones they're on the train. The terse medium of SMS is a national passion, with a billion text messages sent monthly.

Phones in the UK use GSM 900/1800, which is compatible with Europe and Australia but not with North America or Japan (although phones that work globally are increasingly common).

Even if your phone works in the UK, because it's registered overseas a call to someone just up the road will be routed internationally and charged accordingly. An option is to buy a local SIM card (around £30), which includes a UK number, and use that in your own handset (as long as your phone isn't locked by your home network).

A second option is to buy a pay-as-you-go phone (from around £50, including SIM and number); to stay in credit, you buy 'top-up' cards at newsagents.

## TIME

Wherever you are in the world, time is measured in relation to Greenwich Mean Time (GMT, or Universal Time Coordinated, UTC as it's more accurately called), so a highlight for many visitors to London is a trip to Greenwich and its famous line dividing the western and eastern hemispheres.

To give you an idea, if it is noon in London, it is 4am on the same day in San Francisco, 7am in New York and 10pm in Sydney. British summer time (BST) is Britain's daylight saving; one hour ahead of GMT from late March to late October.

## TOURIST INFORMATION

Before leaving home, check the informative, comprehensive and wide-ranging website **VisitBritain** (www.visitbritain.com) or the more specific sites www.enjoyengland.com, www.visitscotland.com and www.visitwales.com. Between them, they cover all angles of national tourism, with links to numerous other sites. Regional websites and tourist organisations are listed at the start of each main chapter throughout this book.

### Local Tourist Offices

All British cities and towns (and some villages) have a tourist information centre (TIC). Some TICs are run by national parks and often have small exhibits about the area. You'll also see 'visitor welcome centres' or 'visitor information centres', often run by chambers of commerce or civic trusts; for ease we've called all these places 'tourist offices' in this book. Whatever the name, these places have helpful staff, books and maps for sale, leaflets to give away and loads of advice on things to see or do. They can also assist with booking accommodation. Most tourist offices keep regular business hours; in quiet areas they close from October to March, while in popular areas they open daily year-round. For a list of all tourist offices around Britain see www.visitmap.info/tic.

Look out too for 'tourist information points' – usually a rack of leaflets about local attractions set up in a post office or shop in a village not big enough to have its own full-on tourist office.

### Tourist Offices Abroad

In recent years, VisitBritain has moved away from physical offices in overseas capitals providing tourist information (very few now cater for walk-in visitors), and instead improved their web-based services. From the visitbritain.com portal home page you can follow links to around 60 different websites of information on Britain aimed at visitors from many different countries and in many different languages. For specific questions, you can email your nearest VisitBritain office via the website, but only a few have public phone numbers. Main contacts:

**Australia** ( ☎ 1300 85 85 89; www.visitbritain.com/au; 15 Blue St, North Sydney, NSW 2060)
**Canada** ( ☎ 1 888 847 4885; www.visitbritain.com/ca)
**France** (www.visitbritain.com/fr)
**Germany** (www.visitbritain.com/de)
**Netherlands** (www.visitbritain.com/nl)
**New Zealand** ( ☎ 0800 700741; www.visitbritain .com/nz)
**USA** ( ☎ 800 462 2748; www.visitbritain.com/us)

### TRAVELLERS WITH DISABILITIES

If you happen to be in a wheelchair, use crutches or just find moving about a bit tricky, Britain is a mixed bag. All new buildings have wheelchair access, and even hotels in grand old country houses often have lifts, ramps and other facilities added, although smaller B&Bs are often harder to adapt, so you'll have less choice here. In the same way, you might find a restaurant with ramps and excellent wheelchair-access loo, but tables so close you can't get past.

When getting around in cities, new buses have low floors for easy access, but few have conductors who can lend a hand when you're getting on or off. Many taxis take wheelchairs, or just have more room in the back, so that might be a better way to go.

For long-distance travel, coaches present problems if you can't walk, but National Express (the main operator) has wheelchair-friendly coaches on many routes, with plans for more, and a dedicated **Disabled Passenger Travel Helpline** ( ☎ 0121-423 8479). Or see www .nationalexpress.com/coach/ourservice/disa-bled.cfm. On most inter-city trains there's more room and better facilities, and usually station staff around; just have a word and they'll be happy to help.

Useful organisations and websites:
**All Go Here** (www.allgohere.com) Comprehensive info on hotels and travel.
**Disability UK** (www.disabilityuk.com) Excellent information resource; shopping, benefits, diseases, drugs and more.
**Good Access Guide** (www.goodaccessguide.co.uk) The name says it all.
**Holiday Care Service** ( ☎ 0845 124 9971; www .holidaycare.org.uk) Travel and holiday information; publisher of numerous booklets on UK travel.
**Royal Association for Disability & Rehabilitation** (RADAR; ☎ 020-7250 3222; www.radar.org.uk) Published titles include *Holidays in Britain and Ireland*. Through RADAR you can get a key for 7000 public disabled toilets across the UK.
**Shopmobility** (www.shopmobilityuk.org) Directory of cities and towns across Britain where manual or powered wheelchairs can be hired – often for free.

## VISAS

If you're a European Economic Area (EEA) national, you don't need a visa to visit (or work in) Britain. Citizens of Australia, Canada, New Zealand, South Africa and the USA are given leave to enter at their point of arrival for up to six months (three months for some nationalities), but are prohibited from working. If you intend to work, see opposite.

UK immigration authorities are tough; if they suspect you're here for more than a holiday, you may need to prove that you have funds to support yourself, details of any hotels or local tours booked, or personal letters from people you'll be visiting. Having a return ticket helps too.

Visa and entry regulations are always subject to change, so it's vital to check before leaving home. Your first stop should be www.ukvisas .gov.uk or www.ukba.homeoffice.gov.uk and if you still have queries contact your local British embassy, high commission or consulate.

## WEIGHTS & MEASURES

Britain is in transition when it comes to weights and measures, as it has been for the last 30 years – and probably will be for 30 more. For length and distance, most people still use the 'imperial' units of inches, feet, yards and miles, although mountain heights on maps are given in metres.

For weight, many people use pounds and ounces, even though since January 2000 goods in shops must be measured in kilograms. And nobody knows their weight in pounds (like Americans) or kilograms (like the rest of the world); Brits weigh themselves in stones, an archaic unit of 14 pounds.

When it comes to volume, things are even worse: most liquids are sold in litres or half-litres, except milk and beer – available in pints. Garages sell petrol priced in pence per litre, but measure car performance in miles per gallon. Great, isn't it?

In this book we have reflected this wacky system of mixed measurements. Heights are given in metres (m) and longer distances in miles. For conversion tables, see the inside front cover.

## WOMEN TRAVELLERS

The occasional wolf whistle from a building site or groper on the London Underground aside, solo women will find Britain fairly enlightened. There's nothing to stop women going into pubs alone, for example – although you may feel conspicuous in a few places. Restaurants may assume you're waiting for a date unless you specify a table for one, but it's no big deal once you've clarified.

Safety is not a major issue, although commonsense caution should be observed when walking in big cities, especially at night. Hitching is always unwise, and see p987 for advice on travel by minicab. Unfortunately, drinks spiked with so-called 'date-rape drugs' can be a problem in some bars and clubs, so once again precautions should be taken (like don't leave your drink unattended).

The contraceptive pill is available free on prescription in Britain, as is the morning-after pill (also on sale at chemists/pharmacies). Most cities have Well Woman Clinics that can advise on general health issues; they're listed in the local phone book. Should the worst happen, most cities and towns have a rape crisis centre, where information or counselling is free and confidential; see www.rapecrisis.org.uk.

## WORK

Nationals of most European countries don't need a permit to work in Britain, but everyone else does. If you're a non-European and work is the main purpose of your visit, you must be sponsored by a British company. Exceptions include most Commonwealth citizens with a UK-born parent; the 'Right of Abode' allows you to live and work in Britain.

Most Commonwealth citizens under 31 are eligible for a Working Holidaymaker Visa, which allows you to work for a total of 12 months, but you're not allowed to establish a business or work as a professional athlete. It must be obtained in advance, and is valid for two years.

Once you've got permission to work, the next step is finding some. Many bars, restaurants and shops in London seem to be staffed wholly by Australasians, so that gives a clue to one option. But it's not restricted to London at all; some visitors arrange work in small towns and villages in remote areas, and enjoy getting under the skin of a local community for a few months. Other options include teaching in language schools, nursing, nannying and general office temping. Obviously, you'll need the appropriate qualifications and other paperwork for some of these jobs.

Useful websites include: www.ukba.homeoffice.gov.uk (the official government site); www.bunac.org (advice on six-month work permits for students from the USA); www.workingholidayguru.com (aimed mainly at Australians coming to Europe); www.goworkgotravel.com (working holidays worldwide, including the UK) and www.employmentrecruitment.co.uk (a directory of UK agencies). Also very useful is the 'Living & Working Abroad' thread on the Thorntree forum at www.lonelyplanet.com.

# Transport

## CONTENTS

# GETTING THERE & AWAY

London is a global transport hub, so you can easily fly to Britain from just about anywhere in the world. There's an ever-growing choice of flights, swollen in recent years by the massive growth of budget (no-frills) airlines, which have increased the routes – and reduced the fares – between Britain and other countries in Europe.

Your other main option for travel between Britain and mainland Europe is ferry, either port-to-port or combined with a long-distance bus trip. This type of travel has less environmental impact than flying, although journeys can be long, and financial savings not huge compared with budget airfares. International trains are much more comfortable, and another 'green' option; the Channel Tunnel allows direct rail services between Britain, France and Belgium, with onward connections to many other European destinations.

Flights, tours and rail tickets can be booked online by accessing www.lonely planet.com/travel _services.

## AIR

### Airports

London's main airports for international flights are Heathrow and Gatwick, while Luton and Stansted deal largely with charter and budget European flights. For details on

getting between these airports and central London, see p200.

### GATWICK

Smaller than Heathrow, but still the UK's No 2 airport, **Gatwick** (LGW; ☎ 0870 000 2468; www.gatwickairport.com) is 30 miles south of central London.

### HEATHROW

Some 15 miles west of central London, **Heathrow** (LHR; ☎ 0870 000 0123; www.heathrow airport.com) is the world's busiest airport, so not surprisingly is often chaotic and crowded.

### LONDON CITY

A few miles east of central London, **London City** (LCY; ☎ 020-7646 0088; www.londoncityairport.com) specialises in business flights to/from European and other UK airports.

### LUTON

Some 35 miles north of central London, **Luton** (LTN; ☎ 01582-405100; www.london-luton.co.uk) is especially well known as a holiday-flight airport.

### STANSTED

London's third-busiest airport, **Stansted** (STN; ☎ 0870 000 0303; www.stanstedairport.com) is 35 miles northeast of the capital, and one of Europe's fastest-growing airports.

### REGIONAL AIRPORTS

If you're arriving in Britain from overseas, and plan to avoid London or spend more time in Scotland or northern England, it's

---

**THINGS CHANGE...**

The information in this chapter is particularly vulnerable to change. Check directly with airlines or travel agents to ensure you understand how fares (and tickets you buy) work, and be aware of the security requirements for international travel. Shop carefully. Details in this chapter should be regarded as pointers and not a substitute for your own careful, up-to-date research.

**CLIMATE CHANGE & TRAVEL**

Climate change is a serious threat to the ecosystems that humans rely upon, and air travel is the fastest-growing contributor to the problem. Lonely Planet regards travel, overall, as a global benefit, but believes we all have a responsibility to limit our personal impact on global warming.

**Flying & Climate Change**

Pretty much every form of motor transport generates $CO_2$ (the main cause of human-induced climate change) but planes are far and away the worst offenders, not just because of the sheer distances they allow us to travel, but because they release greenhouse gases high into the atmosphere. The statistics are frightening: two people taking a return flight between Europe and the US will contribute as much to climate change as an average household's power consumption over a whole year.

**Carbon Offset Schemes**

Climatecare.org and other websites use 'carbon calculators' that allow travellers to offset the greenhouse gases they are responsible for with contributions to energy-saving projects and other climate-friendly initiatives in the developing world – including projects in India, Honduras, Kazakhstan and Uganda.

Lonely Planet, together with Rough Guides and other concerned partners in the travel industry, supports the carbon offset scheme run by climatecare.org. Lonely Planet offsets all of its staff and author travel.

For more information check out our website: www.lonelyplanet.com.

worth looking for direct flights to major regional airports like Manchester, Glasgow and Edinburgh. Likewise, smaller regional airports such as Cardiff, Liverpool, Southampton and Birmingham are usefully served by flights to/from continental Europe and Ireland.

## Airlines

Most mainstream airlines have services to Britain from many parts of the world, while budget airlines fly between Britain and other European countries. Charter flights are another option; you can buy seat-only deals on the planes that carry tourists between, for example, Britain and numerous Mediterranean resorts. The best deals are usually available online, and to save going to every airline's site individually, it's worth using an internet travel agency or price comparison site; these include www.expedia.com, www.travelocity.com, www.skyscanner.com, www.lowcostairlines.org, www.flightline.co.uk and www.cheapflights.co.uk.

## Tickets

Because London is a major air-travel hub, there's competition between the airlines, and that means competitive fares. You can purchase your airline ticket from a travel agency (in person, by telephone or on the internet), or direct from the airline (the best deals are often available online only). Whichever, it always pays to shop around. Internet travel agencies work well if you're doing a straightforward trip, but for anything even slightly complex there's no substitute for a real-live travel agent who knows the system, the options, the special deals and so on.

## Australia & New Zealand

The route to Britain from the southern hemisphere is very popular, with a wide range of fares from about AUD$1500 to AUD$3000 return. From New Zealand it's often best to go via Australia. Round-the-world (RTW) tickets can sometimes work out cheaper than a straightforward return.

## Continental Europe & Ireland

You can fly between Britain and pretty much every capital city in Europe (and many other cities too), using national airlines such as Air France, Lufthansa and so on, or budget airlines such as Ryanair, easyJet and Virgin Express.

There are numerous flights each day between Dublin and London, and many more between other cities in Ireland and Britain.

If you book early and avoid the busy periods (such as Friday afternoon and evening), fares on budget airlines can be just a few pounds or euros.

TRANSPORT

TRANSPORT

## Canada & the USA

There's a continuous price war on the world's busiest transcontinental route. Return fares from the East Coast to London range from US$300 to US$600. From the West Coast, fares are about US$100 higher.

## LAND
### Bus

You can easily get between Britain and other European countries via long-distance bus or coach. The international network **Eurolines** (www.eurolines.com) connects a huge number of destinations; the website is full of information on routes and options, and you can buy tickets online via one of the national operators. Services to/from Britain are operated by **National Express** (www.national express.com) and these are some sample journey times to/from London: Amsterdam 12 hours; Paris eight or nine hours; Dublin 12 hours; Barcelona 24 hours. If you book early, and can be flexible with timings (ie travel when few other people want to) you can get some very good deals – some branded as 'fun fares' and 'promo fares'. For example, London to Paris or Amsterdam one-way tickets start at just £18, although paying nearer £25 is more usual. It's still worth checking the budget airlines, though. You may pay a similar fare and knock a large chunk off the journey time.

### Train
#### CHANNEL TUNNEL SERVICES

The Channel Tunnel makes direct train travel between Britain and continental Europe a fast and enjoyable option. High-speed **Eurostar** ( ☎ 08705 186 186; www.eurostar.com) passenger services hurtle at least 10 times daily between London and Paris (the journey takes 2½ hours) or Brussels (two hours). You can buy tickets from travel agencies, major train stations or direct from the Eurostar website. The normal single fare between London and Paris or Brussels is around £150, but if you buy in advance and travel at a less busy period, deals drop to around £90 return or less. You can also buy 'through fare' tickets from many cities in Britain – for example York to Paris, or Manchester to Brussels. You can also get very good train and hotel combination deals – bizarrely sometimes cheaper than train fare only.

If you've got a car, use **Eurotunnel** ( ☎ 08705 353535; www.eurotunnel.com). At Folkestone in England or Calais in France, you drive onto a train, go through the tunnel, and drive off at the other end. The trains run about four times hourly from 6am to 10pm, then hourly. Loading and unloading is one hour; the journey takes 35 minutes. You can book in advance direct with Eurotunnel or pay on the spot (cash or credit card). The standard one-way cost for a car (and passengers) is £90 to £150 depending on the time of day (less busy times are cheaper), and promotional fares often bring the cost down to nearer £50.

#### TRAIN & FERRY CONNECTIONS

As well as Eurostar, many 'normal' trains run between Britain and mainland Europe. You buy one ticket, but get off the train at the port, walk onto a ferry, then get another train on the other side. Routes include Amsterdam–London (via Hook of Holland and Harwich). Travelling between Ireland and Britain, the main train-ferry-train route is Dublin to London, via Dun Laoghaire and Holyhead. Ferries also run between Rosslare and Fishguard or Pembroke (Wales), with train connections on either side.

## SEA

The main ferry routes between Britain and Ireland include Holyhead to Dun Laoghaire. Between Britain and mainland Europe, ferry routes include Dover to Calais or Boulogne (France), Harwich to Hook of Holland (Netherlands), Hull to Zeebrugge (Belgium) and Rotterdam (Netherlands), Portsmouth to Santander or Bilbao (Spain), and Newcastle to Bergen (Norway) or Gothenberg (Sweden). There are many more.

Competition from Eurotunnel and budget airlines has forced ferry operators to discount heavily and offer flexible fares, meaning great bargains at quiet times of day or year. For example, the short cross-Channel routes such as Dover to Calais or Boulogne-sur-Mer can be as low as £20 for a car plus up to five passengers, although around £50 is more likely. If you're a foot passenger, or cycling, there's often less need to book ahead, and cheap fares on the short crossings start from about £10 each way.

Main ferry operators include the following. Some operators take only online bookings; others charge a supplement (up to £20) for booking by phone.

**Brittany Ferries** (www.brittany-ferries.com)
**DFDS Seaways** ( ☎ 0871 522 9955; www.dfds.co.uk)
**Irish Ferries** ( ☎ 08705 171717; www.irishferries.com)
**Norfolkline** ( ☎ 08701 450603; www.norfolkline.com)
**P&O Ferries** ( ☎ 08716 645 645; www.poferries.com)
**Speedferries** ( ☎ 0871 222 7456; www.speedferries.com)
**Stena Line** ( ☎ 08705 70 70 70; www.stenaline.com)
**Transmanche** ( ☎ 0800 917 1201; www.transmanche
ferries.com)

Another very handy option is www.ferry
booker.com, a single site covering all sea-ferry
routes and operators, plus Eurotunnel.

# GETTING AROUND

For getting around Britain your first main
choice is going by car or public transport.
While having your own car helps make the
best use of your time to reach remote places,
rental and fuel costs can be expensive for
budget travellers – and the trials of traffic
jams and parking hit everyone – so public
transport is often the better way to go.

Your main public transport options are
train and long-distance bus (called coach in
Britain). Services between major towns and
cities are generally good, although at 'peak'
(busy) times you must book in advance to
be sure of getting a ticket. Conversely, if you
book ahead early and/or travel at 'off-peak'
periods, tickets can be very cheap.

As long as you have time, using a mix of
train, coach, local bus, the odd taxi, walking
and occasionally hiring a bike, you can get
almost anywhere without having to drive.
You'll certainly see more of the countryside
than you might slogging along motorways,
and in the serene knowledge you're doing less
environmental damage.

**Traveline** ( ☎ 0871 200 2233; www.traveline.org.uk) is
a very useful information service covering bus,
coach, taxi and train services nationwide, with
numerous links to help plan your journey. By
phone, you get transferred automatically to
an advisor in the region you're phoning *from*;
for details on another part of the country,
you need to key in a code number ( ☎ 81 for
London, ☎ 874 for Cumbria, etc) – for a full
list, go to the Traveline home page and click
on 'call centre codes'.

A final note: travelling between England,
Scotland and Wales is easy. The bus and
train systems are fully integrated and in most

cases you won't even know you've crossed
the border. Passports are not required – although some Scots and Welsh may think they
should be!

## AIR

Britain's domestic air companies include
British Airways, BMI, bmibaby, easyJet
and Ryanair. If you're really pushed for
time, flights on longer routes across Britain
(eg Exeter or Southampton to Newcastle,
Edinburgh or Inverness) are handy, although you miss the glorious scenery
in between. On some shorter routes (eg
London to Newcastle, or Manchester to
Newquay) trains can compare favourably
with planes, once airport downtime is fac-
tored in. On fares, you might get a bargain
air fare, but with advance planning trains
can be cheaper.

## BICYCLE

Britain is a compact country, and getting
around by bicycle is perfectly feasible – and a
great way to really see the country – if you've
got time to spare. For more inspiration see
p111. For taking bikes on trains, see the boxed
text, p1004.

Renting a bike is easy in London (outlets
include www.londonbicycle.com, or see www
.lcc.org.uk for a list) and at other tourist spots
such as Oxford and Cambridge. Rates start at
about £10 per day, but £20 per day is more
usual for something half decent. Rental is also
possible in country areas, especially where
disused railway lines are now bike routes, or
at forestry sites and reservoirs now for leisure activities, for example Kielder Water
in Northumberland (www.thebikeplace
.co.uk), Grizedale Forest in Cumbria (www
.forestry.gov.uk/grizedale), the High Peak and
Tissington Trails in Derbyshire, (www.derby
shire-peakdistrict.co.uk/cycling.htm), the
Elan Valley in Mid Wales (www.clivepowell
-mtb.co.uk) or the Great Glen Way in Scotland
(www.offbeatbikes.co.uk).

Finally, mention must be made of Bristol –
Britain's first 'cycling city'. From mid-2008 to
mid-2011, around £11 million will be invested
in bike paths and other facilities, including
a major rental network modelled on Paris's
famous Vélib (freedom bike) project. Other
cities, such as York, Cambridge and Chester
will also get similar schemes.

TRANSPORT

## BUS & COACH

If you're on a tight budget, long-distance buses are nearly always the cheapest way to get around, although they're also the slowest – sometimes by a considerable margin. In Britain, long-distance express buses are called coaches, and in many towns there are separate bus and coach stations. Make sure you go to the right place!

**National Express** ( ☎ 08717 818181; www.national express.com) is the main operator, with a wide network and frequent services between main centres. North of the border, services tie in with those of **Scottish Citylink** ( ☎ 08705 505050; www.citylink .co.uk), Scotland's leading coach company. Fares vary: they're cheaper if you book in advance and travel at quieter times (special off-peak 'fun fares' are as low as £1), and more expensive if you buy your ticket on the spot and it's Friday afternoon. As a guide though, a 200-mile trip (eg London to York) will cost around £15 to £20 if you book a few days in advance.

Also offering fares from £1 is **Megabus** (www .megabus.com), operating a budget coach service between about 30 destinations around the country. Go at a quiet time, book early, and your ticket will be very cheap. Book last minute, for a busy time and…you get the picture.

For information about short-distance and local bus services see opposite.

### Bus Passes & Discounts

National Express offers discount passes to full-time students and under-26s, called Young Persons Coachcards. They cost £10, and get you 30% off standard adult fares. Also available are coachcards for people over 60, families and disabled travellers.

For touring Britain, National Express also offers Brit Xplorer passes, which allow unlimited travel for seven days (£79), 14 days (£139) and 28 days (£219). You don't need to book journeys in advance with this pass; if the coach has a spare seat – you can take it.

## CAR & MOTORCYCLE

Travelling by private car or motorbike you can be independent and flexible, and reach remote places. For solo budget travellers a downside of car travel is the expense, and in cities you'll need superhuman skills to negotiate heaving traffic, plus deep pockets for parking charges. But if there's two of you (or more), car travel can work out cheaper than public transport.

---

### HOW MUCH TO…?

When travelling long-distance by train or coach in Britain, it's important to note that there's no such thing as a standard fare. Just like with airlines, prices vary according to demand and when you buy your ticket. Book long in advance and travel on Tuesday mid-morning, and it's cheap. Buy on the spot on Friday late afternoon, and it'll be a lot more expensive. Ferries (eg to the Isle of Wight or Channel Islands) use similar systems. Throughout this book, to give you an idea, we have quoted *sample* fares somewhere in between the very cheapest and most expensive options. The price you pay will almost certainly be different.

---

Motorways and main A-roads are dual carriageways and deliver you quickly from one end of the country to another. Lesser A-roads, B-roads and minor roads are much more scenic and fun, as you wind through the countryside from village to village – ideal for car or motorcycle touring. You can't travel fast, but you won't care.

### Hire

Compared to many countries (especially the USA), hire rates are expensive in Britain; you should expect to pay around £250 per week for a small car (unlimited mileage) but rates rise at busy times and drop at quiet times. Some main players:

**1car1** ( ☎ 0113-263 6675; www.1car1.com)
**Avis** ( ☎ 0844 581 0147; www.avis.co.uk)
**Budget** ( ☎ 0844 581 9998; www.budget.co.uk)
**Europcar** ( ☎ 0870 607 5000; www.europcar.co.uk)
**Sixt** ( ☎ 08701 567567; www.sixt.co.uk)
**Thrifty** ( ☎ 01494-751540; www.thrifty.co.uk)

Many international websites have separate web pages for customers in different countries, and the prices for a car in Britain on, say, the UK web pages can be cheaper or more expensive than the same car on the USA or Australia web pages. The moral is – you have to surf a lot of sites to find the best deals.

Your other option is to use an internet search engine to find small local car-hire companies in Britain who can undercut the big boys. Generally those in cities are cheaper than in rural areas. See under Getting Around in the main city sections for more details, or see a rental-broker site such as **UK Car Hire** (www.ukcarhire.net).

Another option is to hire a motor home or campervan. It's more expensive than hiring a car but it does help you save on accommodation costs, and gives almost unlimited freedom. Sites to check include www.cool campervans.com, www.wildhorizon.co.uk and www.justgo.uk.com.

## Motoring Organisations

Large motoring organisations include the **Automobile Association** (www.theaa.com) and the **Royal Automobile Club** (www.rac.co.uk); annual membership starts at around £35, including 24-hour roadside breakdown assistance. A greener alternative is the **Environmental Transport Association** (www.eta.co.uk); it provides all the usual services (breakdown assistance, roadside rescue, vehicle inspections etc) but *doesn't* campaign for more roads.

## Parking

Britain is small, and people love their cars, so there's often not enough space to go round. Many cities have short- and long-stay car parks; the latter are cheaper though maybe less convenient. 'Park & Ride' systems allow you to park on the edge of the city then ride to the centre on regular buses provided for an all-in-one price.

Yellow lines (single or double) along the edge of the road indicate restrictions. Find the nearby sign that spells out when you can and can't park. In London and other big cities, traffic wardens operate with efficiency; if you park on the yellow lines at the wrong time, your car will be clamped or towed away, and it'll cost you £100 or more to get driving again. In some cities there are also red lines, which mean no stopping at all. Ever.

## Road Rules

A foreign driving licence is valid in Britain for up to 12 months. If you plan to bring a car from Europe, it's illegal to drive without (at least) third-party insurance. Some other important rules:

- drive on the left (!)
- wear fitted seat belts in cars
- wear crash helmets on motorcycles
- give way to your right at junctions and roundabouts
- always use the left-side lane on motorways and dual carriageways, unless overtaking (although so many people ignore this rule, you'd think it didn't exist)
- don't use a mobile phone while driving unless it's fully hands-free (another rule frequently flouted).

Speed limits are 30mph (48km/h) in built-up areas, 60mph (96km/h) on main roads and 70mph (112km/h) on motorways and most (but not all) dual carriageways. Drinking and driving is taken very seriously; you're allowed a blood-alcohol level of 80mg/100mL and campaigners want it reduced to 50mg/100mL.

All drivers should read the *Highway Code*. It's available at main newsagents and some tourist offices, and at www.direct.gov .uk/en/TravelAndTransport/Highwaycode.

## HITCHING

Hitching is not as common as it used to be in Britain, maybe because more people have cars, maybe because few drivers give lifts any more. It's perfectly possible, however, if you don't mind long waits, although travellers should understand that they're taking a small but potentially serious risk, and we don't recommend it. If you decide to go by thumb, note that it's illegal to hitch on motorways; you must use approach roads or service stations.

However, as is the case with so many other things, it's all different in remote rural areas such as Mid Wales or northwest Scotland, where hitching is a part of getting around – especially if you're a walker. On some Scottish islands, local drivers may stop and offer a lift without you even asking.

## LOCAL TRANSPORT

British cities usually have good local public transport systems, although buses are often run by a confusing number of separate companies. The larger cities have tram and underground rail services too. Tourist offices can provide information, and more details are given in the city sections throughout this book.

### Bus

There are good local bus networks year-round in cities and towns. Buses also run in rural areas year-round, with more frequent services in tourist spots (especially national parks) from Easter to September. Elsewhere in the countryside, bus timetables are designed to serve schools and industry, so there can be few midday and weekend services (and they may stop running in school holidays), or buses may link local villages to a market town on only one day each week. It's always worth double-checking at a tourist office before planning your day's activities around a bus that you later find out only runs on Thursdays.

In this book, along with local bus route number, frequency and duration, we have provided indicative prices if the fare is over a few pounds. If it's less than this, we have generally omitted the fare details.

### BUS PASSES

If you're taking a few local bus rides in a day of energetic sightseeing, ask about day-passes (with names like Day Rover, Wayfarer or Explorer), which will be cheaper than buying several single tickets. If you plan to linger longer in one area, three-day passes are a great bargain. Often they can be bought on your first bus, and may include local rail services. Passes are mentioned in the regional chapters, and it's always worth asking ticket clerks or bus drivers about your options.

### POSTBUS

A postbus is a van on usual mail service that also carries passengers. Postbuses operate in rural areas (and some of the most scenic and remote parts of the country), and are especially useful for walkers and backpackers. For information and timetables contact **Royal Mail Postbus** ( ☎ 08457 740 740; www.royalmail.com/postbus).

## Ferries

Local ferries, from the mainland to the Isle of Wight or the Scottish islands for example, are covered in the relevant sections in the regional chapters.

## Taxi

There are two sorts of taxi in Britain: the famous black cabs (some with advertising livery in other colours these days) that have meters and can be hailed in the street; and minicabs that can only be called by phone. (See p987 for information on the dangers of unlicensed minicabs.) In London and other big cities, taxis cost £2 to £3 per mile. In rural areas, it's about half this, which means when it's Sunday and you find the next

bus out of the charming village you've just hiked to is on Thursday, a taxi can keep you moving. The best place to find the local taxi's phone number is the local pub. Alternatively, if you call **National Cabline** ( ☎ 0800 123444) from a landline phone, the service pinpoints your location and transfers you to an approved local taxi company. Also useful is www.traintaxi .co.uk – designed to help you 'bridge the final gap' between the train station and your hotel or other final destination.

## TRAIN

For long-distance travel around Britain, trains are generally faster and more comfortable than coaches but can be more expensive, although with discount tickets they're competitive – and often take you through beautiful countryside.

In the 1990s, rail travel had a bad reputation for delays and cancellations. A decade later, the situation has improved (so much so that passenger numbers have increased massively), with around 85% of trains running on or pretty close to schedule. The other 15% of journeys that get delayed or cancelled mostly impact commuters rather than long-distance leisure travellers. If your journey from London to Bath runs 30 minutes late, what's the problem? You're on holiday!

About 20 different companies operate train services in Britain (for example: First Great Western runs from London to Bristol, Cornwall and South Wales; National Express East Coast runs from London to Leeds, York and Edinburgh; Virgin Trains runs the 'west coast' route from London to Birmingham, Carlisle and Glasgow; while Network Rail operates track and stations. For some passengers this system can seem confusing at first, but information and ticket-buying services are mostly centralised. If you have to change trains, or use two or more train operators, you usually still buy one ticket – valid for the whole of your journey. The main railcards are also accepted by all operators.

Your first stop should be **National Rail Enquiries** ( ☎ 08457 48 49 50; www.nationalrail.co.uk), the nationwide timetable and fare information service. You punch in your start and end destinations, and the site will offer a range of routes, times and fares. Once you've found the journey you need, links take you to the relevant train operator or to centralised ticketing services (www.thetrainline.com, www

.qjump.co.uk, www.raileasy.co.uk) to buy the ticket. Train travel websites can be confusing at first (you always have to state an approximate preferred time and day of travel, even if you don't mind *when* you go), but with a little delving around they can offer some real bargains.

You can also buy train tickets on the spot at stations, which is fine for short journeys (under about 50 miles), but for longer trips discount tickets are usually not available at the station and must be bought in advance by phone or online.

For planning your trip, some very handy maps of the UK's rail network can be downloaded from www.nationalrail.co.uk/tocs_maps/maps/network_rail_maps.html. The nationalrail.co.uk site also advertises special offers, and has real-time links to station departure boards, so you can see if your train is on time (or not).

## Classes

There are two classes of rail travel: 1st and standard. First class costs around 50% more than standard and, except on very crowded trains, is not really worth it. However, at weekends some train operators offer 'upgrades' for an extra £10 to £15 on top of your standard-class fare, so you can enjoy more comfort and legroom.

## Costs & Reservations

For short journeys, it's usually best to buy tickets on the spot at train stations. You may get a choice of express or stopping service – the latter is obviously slower, but can be cheaper, and may take you through charming countryside or grotty suburbs.

For longer journeys, on-the-spot fares are always available, but tickets are much cheaper if bought in advance. Essentially, the earlier you book, the cheaper it gets. You can also save if you travel at 'off-peak' – ie avoiding commuter times, Fridays and Sundays. Advance purchase usually gets a reserved seat too. The cheapest fares are nonrefundable, though, so if you miss your train you'll have to buy a new ticket.

If you buy by phone or website, you can have the ticket posted to you (UK addresses only), or collect it at the originating station on the day of travel, either at the ticket desk (leave time to spare, as queues can be long) or via automatic machines.

Whichever operator you travel with and wherever you buy tickets, there are three main fare types:

**Advance** Buy ticket in advance, travel only on specific trains.

**Anytime** Buy at any time, travel at any time.

**Off-peak** Buy ticket at any time, travel off-peak.

Advance tickets are subject to availability, and usually available as singles only, but if you're making a return journey (ie coming back on the same route) you just buy two singles.

For an idea of the price difference, an Anytime single ticket from London to York will cost around £100, and an Off-peak around £80, while an Advance single can be less than £20, and even less than £10 if you book early enough or don't mind arriving at midnight.

Off-peak and Anytime tickets are available as returns and the price can vary from just under double the single fare to just a pound more than the single fare.

Children under five years old travel free on trains; those aged between five and 15 pay half price, except on tickets already heavily discounted – but a Family & Friends Railcard is usually better value.

If the train doesn't get you all the way to your destination, a **PlusBus** (www.plusbus.info) supplement (usually around £2) validates your train ticket for onwards travel by bus – more convenient, and usually cheaper, than buying a separate bus ticket.

And finally, it's worth a look at **Megatrain** (www.megatrain.com) – from the people who brought you Megabus – ultra-low train fares on ultra off-peak services between London and a few destinations in southwest England and the East Midlands.

## Train Passes

Local train passes usually cover rail networks around a city (many include bus travel too), and are mentioned in the individual city sections throughout this book. If you're staying in Britain for a while, passes known as 'railcards' are available:

**16-25 Railcard** For those aged 16 to 25, or full-time UK students.

**Family & Friends Railcard** Covers up to four adults and four children travelling together.

**Senior Railcard** For anyone over 60.

These railcards cost around £25 (valid for one year, available from major stations or online) and get you a 33% discount on most

**TRANSPORT**

---

**BIKES ON TRAINS**

Bicycles can be taken on most local urban trains outside peak times, and on shorter trips in rural areas, free of charge, on a first-come-first-served basis. You load it in the guard's van, or at one end of the carriage, which means there may be space limits. In the same way, you can take your bike on long-distance train journeys free of charge as well, but advance booking is required for most conventional bikes. (Folding bikes can be carried on pretty much any train at any time.)

In theory, advance booking shouldn't be too much trouble as most long-distance rail trips are best bought in advance anyway, but you have to go a long way down the path of booking your seat before you start booking your bike – only to find if space isn't available. Sometimes you need phone the relevant operator's Customer Service department. Before you start, get a copy of the very useful 'Cycling by Train' leaflet, available at major stations or downloadable from www.nationalrail.co.uk/passenger_services/cyclists.html.

Another course of action is to buy in advance at a major rail station, where the booking clerk can help you through the options.

And a final warning: when railways are repaired, cancelled trains are replaced by buses – and they won't take bikes.

---

train fares, except those already heavily discounted. With the Family card, adults get 33% and children get a 60% discount, so the fee is easily repaid in a couple of journeys. Proof of age and a passport photo may be required. For full details see www.railcard.co.uk.

A Disabled Person's Railcard costs £18. You can get an application form from stations or from the railcard website. Call ☎ 0191-281 8103 for more details.

If you're concentrating your travels on southeast England (eg London to Dover, Weymouth, Cambridge or Oxford) a Network Railcard covers up to four adults and up to four children travelling together outside peak times. For details see p204.

For country-wide travel, BritRail Passes are good value, but they're only for visitors from overseas and not available in Britain. They must be bought in your country of origin from a specialist travel agency. There are many BritRail variants, each available in three different versions: for England only; for the whole of Britain (England, Wales and Scotland); and for the UK and Ireland. Below is an outline of the main options, quoting high-season adult prices.

**BritRail Consecutive** Unlimited travel on all trains in England for four, eight, 15, 22 or 30 days, for US$259/375/559/709/839. Anyone getting their money's worth out of the last pass should earn some sort of endurance award.

**BritRail Flexipass** Now you don't have to get on a train every day to get full value. Your options are four days of unlimited travel in England within a 60-day period for US$329, eight in 60 days for US$479, or 15 in 60 days for US$725.

Children's BritRail passes are usually half price (or you can get a family pass), and seniors get discounts too. For about 30% extra you can upgrade to 1st class. Other deals include a rail pass combined with the use of a hire car, or travel in Britain combined with one Eurostar journey. For more details see www.britrail.com.

If you don't (or can't) buy a BritRail pass, an All Line Rover gives virtually unlimited travel for 14 days anywhere on the national rail network. You can travel at any time, but aren't guaranteed a seat (reservations cost extra), so it's best to travel at off-peak times if you can. The pass costs £565 and can be purchased in Britain, by anyone. For an idea of what's possible, do a search on All Line Rover in rail-enthusiast sites such as www.railforums.co.uk or www.railwayscene.co.uk – some people certainly get their money's worth, travelling on just about every line in Britain during the two-week period (and hardly stopping, or sleeping).

Of the other international passes, an InterRail card is valid in Britain, as long as you bought it in another European country, but Eurail cards are not accepted in Britain.

# Health

## CONTENTS

Britain is a healthy place to travel, and the excellent National Health Service (NHS) is free on the point of delivery, which – although Brits may complain – is better than most other countries offer. Across the country, hygiene standards are high (despite what your nose tells you on a crowded tube train) and there are no unusual diseases to worry about. Your biggest risks will be from overdoing activities – physical, chemical or other.

## BEFORE YOU GO

No immunisations are mandatory for visiting Britain. Travel insurance, however, is highly recommended for the reasons outlined under Insurance (p990).

You should also check reciprocal medical arrangements between the UK and your own country. Everyone gets emergency treatment (see In Britain, right) and European Economic Area (EEA) nationals get free non-emergency treatment (ie the same service British citizens receive) with a European Health Insurance Card (EHIC) validated in their home country. Reciprocal arrangements between the UK and some other countries (including Australia) allow free medical treatment at hospitals and surgeries, and subsidised dental care. For details see the **Department of Health** (www.doh .gov.uk) website – follow links to Health Care, Entitlements and Overseas Visitors.

### INTERNET RESOURCES

Useful sites include the following:

**Age Concern** (www.ageconcern.org.uk) Advice on travel (and much more) for the elderly.

**Center for Disease Control and Prevention** (www .cdc.gov)

**Foreign & Commonwealth Office** (www.fco.gov.uk) The Travelling & Living Overseas section is for Brits going abroad, but useful for incomers.

**Marie Stopes International** (www.mariestopes.org .uk) Sexual health and contraception.

**MD Travel Health** (www.mdtravelhealth.com) World-wide recommendations, updated daily.

**World Health Organization** (www.who.int) Go to the International Travel and Health section.

## IN TRANSIT

### DEEP VEIN THROMBOSIS (DVT)

Deep Vein Thrombosis (DVT) refers to blood clots that form in the legs during plane flights, chiefly because of prolonged immobility. The longer the flight, the greater the risk. The chief symptom is swelling or pain in the foot, ankle or calf. When a blood clot travels to the lungs, it may cause chest pain and breathing difficulties. To prevent DVT on long flights you should walk about the cabin, contract and release leg muscles while sitting, drink plenty of fluids and avoid alcohol.

### JET LAG

To avoid jet lag (common when crossing more than five time zones), try drinking plenty of nonalcoholic fluids and eating light meals. Upon arrival, get exposure to natural sunlight and readjust to a local schedule (for meals, sleep etc) as soon as possible.

## IN BRITAIN

### AVAILABILITY & COST OF HEALTH CARE

Regardless of nationality, everyone receives free emergency treatment at accident and emergency (A&E) departments of state-run NHS hospitals.

If you don't need full-on hospital treatment, chemists (pharmacies) can advise on minor ailments such as sore throats and earaches. In large cities, there's always at least one 24/7 chemist.

**HEALTH**

## ENVIRONMENTAL HAZARDS
### Sunburn
In summer in Britain, you can get sunburnt quickly – even under cloud cover and especially on water. Use sunscreen, wear a hat and cover up with a shirt and trousers.

### Water
The tap water in Britain is safe to drink unless there is a sign that states to the contrary (eg on trains). Don't drink from streams in the countryside – you never know if there's a dead sheep upstream.

## WOMEN'S HEALTH
Emotional stress, exhaustion and travel through time zones can upset the menstrual pattern. If using oral contraceptives, remember that some antibiotics, diarrhoea and vomiting can stop them from working.

If you're already pregnant, travel is usually possible, but you should consult your doctor. The most risky times are the first 12 weeks of pregnancy and after 30 weeks.

HEALTH

# Language

## CONTENTS

The main 'indigenous' language of Britain is English – known as British English, to distinguish it from American English, Australian English and so on – which is spoken in England (of course) and most parts of Wales and Scotland. Other languages of Britain include Welsh (spoken in Wales), Lowland Scots and Scottish Gaelic (two distinct languages of southern and northern Scotland) and Cornish (Cornwall). The Isle of Man and Channel Islands also have their own languages, although English is predominant here, too.

## WELSH

The Welsh language belongs to the Celtic branch of the Indo-European language family. Closely related to Breton and Cornish, and more distantly to Irish, Scottish Gaelic and Manx, it is the strongest Celtic language both in terms of numbers of speakers (around 800,000 or 29% of the population) and place in society.

Before it was called 'Welsh' it was simply the language of southern Britain, spoken throughout the island south of a line between modern Glasgow and Edinburgh, but was gradually pushed westwards by the invading Angles and Saxons following the retreat of the Roman legions in the 5th century; although, the Domesday Book census following the Norman invasion of 1066 records the language still being used in modern-day Wiltshire.

Welsh has long been a language of poets, with its earliest literature emerging towards the end of the 6th century, but it lost its status as an official language thanks to the Acts of Union with England (1536 and 1543) although translations of the Book of Common Prayer (1567) and the Bible (1588) into Welsh maintained a limited public function, and most people continued to speak Welsh until the 19th century.

---

**TONGUE-TWISTER**

Wales is famous for having the longest place name in Europe – Llanfairpwllgwyngyllgogerychwyrndrobwllllantysiliogogogoch (hlan·vairr·poohl·gwin·gihl·go·gerr·uh·khwir rn·dro·boohl·hlan·tuh·sil·ee·oh·go·go·gokh). Translated, it means 'St Mary's Church in the hollow of the White Hazel near a rapid whirlpool and the Church of St Tysilio near the Red Cave'.

---

The Industrial Revolution brought great social movements (English people coming to Wales – especially the coal-mining valleys of the south – and Welsh people emigrating to England and beyond) so that by 1900 only 50% of the population of Wales still spoke the language. Thereafter the language retreated more rapidly, so that by 1961 only 26% were Welsh-speaking and there was general alarm that the language would totally disappear.

In 1962 the *Cymdeithas yr Iaith Gymraeg* (Welsh Language Society) was established. It sounded like an academic body, but it was more of a protest movement in support of the language. Campaigns of civil disobedience eventually resulted in equal recognition for the Welsh language in education, government and other areas. The Welsh-language TV channel S4C was launched in 1983. In recent years, the decline has been halted, and the number of Welsh-speakers is growing again – particularly among the young, where Welsh is proudly worn as a badge of national identity.

### Making Conversation

**Good morning.**
*Bore da.*     bo·rre dah
**Good afternoon.**
*Prynhawn da.*     pruhn·hown dah
**Good night.**
*Nos da.*     nohs da
**Hello.**
*Sut mae.*     sit mai
**Goodbye.**
*Hwyl fawr.*     hueyl vowrr
**Thanks.**
*Diolch.*     dee·olkh

**You're welcome.**
*Croeso.*                    croi-so
**What's your name?**
*Beth yw eich enw chi?*      beth yu whch en·oo khee?
**Cheers!**
*Iechyd da!*                 yekh·id dah!

## SCOTTISH GAELIC

Scottish Gaelic (Gàidhlig, pronounced 'gal-lic' in Scotland) is spoken by about 80,000 people in Scotland, mainly in the Highlands and islands. Like Welsh, it's a member of the Celtic branch of the Indo-European family of languages.

For many centuries Scottish Gaelic was the same as the language of Ireland (it was introduced by settlers from Ireland between the 4th and 6th centuries) and the two only started to diverge in the 13th century. Even up to the 18th century Scottish bards adhered to the strict literary standards of Old Irish.

In the south of Scotland, a separate and distinct language developed – known as Scots or Lowland Scots, it had much in common with English and Nordic languages – while the Gaelic language and culture continued to flourish in the Highlands until the 18th century. After the Battle of Culloden in 1746 many Gaelic speakers were forced off their ancestral lands by landlords and governments, a process that culminated in the Highland Clearances of the 19th century, leading to a near-terminal decline in the spoken language.

It was only in the 1970s that Gaelic began to make a comeback thanks to a new generation of young enthusiasts keen to promote the revival of Gaelic language, culture and heritage. Today, the language is encouraged through financial help from government agencies and the EU. Gaelic education, from preschool to tertiary level is flourishing, and this renaissance flows out into the fields of music, literature, broadcasting and cultural events.

### Making Conversation
**Good morning.**
*Madainn mhath.*             mating vah
**Good afternoon/Good evening.**
*Feasgar math.*              feskur mah
**Goodbye.** (lit: Blessings go with you)
*Beannachd leat.*           byan·nukhk laht
**Goodbye.** (The same with you)
*Mar sin leat.*              mar shin laht
**Good night.**
*Oidhche mhath.*            ai·khuh vah
**Please.**
*Mas e do thoil e.*         ma·she duh hol eh
**Many thanks.**
*Móran taing.*              moe·ran tah·eeng
**You're welcome.**
*'Se do bheatha.*           shey duh veh·huh
**What's your name?**
*Dé an t-ainm a tha ort?*   jen ta·nam a horsht?
**Cheers!**
*Slàinte mhath!*            slaan·chuh vah!

For more details, Lonely Planet's *British Language & Culture* offers an informative and entertaining look at the history and peculiarities of British English, including sections on Scottish Gaelic and Welsh, and a feast of useful words and phrases.

# Glossary

For a list of culinary terms, see p98.

**almshouse** – accommodation for the aged or needy

**bailey** – outermost wall of a castle
**bairn** – baby or child (northern England and Scotland)
**bar** – gate (York, and some other northern cities)
**beck** – stream (northern England)
**bill** – the total you need to pay after eating in a restaurant ('check' to Americans)
**billion** – the British billion is a million million (unlike the American billion – a thousand million)
**blackhouse** – traditional Hebridean dwelling (Scotland)
**bloke** – man (colloquial)
**Blue Flag** – an award given to beaches for their unpolluted sand and water
**brae** – hill (Scotland)
**bridleway** – path that can be used by walkers, horse riders and cyclists
**bus** – local bus; see also *coach*

**Cadw** – the Welsh historic-monuments agency
**cairn** – pile of stones marking path, junction or peak
**CalMac** – Caledonian MacBrayne, the main Scottish island ferry operator
**canny** – good, great, wise (northern England)
**ceilidh** – pronounced kay-lee; a session of traditional song and dance (originally Scottish, now more widely used across Britain)
**cheers** – goodbye; thanks (colloquial); also a drinking toast
**chemist** – pharmacy
**chine** – valley-like fissure leading to the sea (southern England)
**circus** – junction of several streets, usually circular
**coach** – long-distance *bus*
**coasteering** – adventurous activity that involves making your way around a rocky coastline by climbing, scrambling, jumping or swimming
**cob** – mixture of mud and straw for building
**cot** – small bed for a baby ('crib' to Americans)
**court** – courtyard
**croft** – plot of land with adjoining house worked by the occupiers (Scotland)

**DIY** – do-it-yourself, ie home improvements
**dodgy** – suspect, bad, dangerous
**dough** – money (colloquial)
**downs** – rolling upland, characterised by lack of trees
**duvet** – quilt replacing sheets and blankets ('doona' to Australians)

**EH** – English Heritage
**en suite room** – hotel room with private attached bathroom (ie shower, basin and toilet)
**EU** – European Union
**Evensong** – daily evening service (Church of England)

**fell race** – tough running race through hills or moors
**fen** – drained or marshy low-lying flat land
**fiver** – £5 note
**flat** – apartment
**footpath** – path through countryside and between houses, not beside a road (that's called a 'pavement')

**gate** – street (York, and some other northern cities)
**graft** – work (not corruption, as in American English; colloquial)
**grand** – 1000 (colloquial)
**gutted** – very disappointed (colloquial)
**guv, guvner** – from governor, a respectful term of address for owner or boss; can sometimes be used ironically

**hart** – deer
**HI** – Hostelling International (organisation)
**hire** – rent
**hotel** – accommodation with food and bar (bar for guests, not always open to passing trade)
**howff** – pub or shelter (Scotland)
**HS** – Historic Scotland; organisation that manages historic sites in Scotland
**Huguenot** – French Protestant

**inn** – pub with accommodation

**jumper** – woollen item of clothing worn on torso ('sweater' to Americans)

**ken** – Scottish term for 'understand' or 'know', as in 'you know'
**kirk** – church (northern England and Scotland)
**knowe** – burial mound (Scotland)
**kyle** – strait or channel (Scotland)

**lass** – young woman (northern England and Scotland)
**lift** – machine for carrying people up and down in large buildings ('elevator' to Americans)
**lock** – part of a canal or river that can be closed off and the water levels changed to raise or lower boats
**loch** – lake (Scotland)
**lolly** – money (colloquial); candy on a stick (possibly frozen)
**lorry (s), lorries (pl)** – truck

**machair** – grass- and wildflower-covered sand dunes

**mad** – insane (not angry, as in American English)

**Marches** – borderlands (ie between England and Wales or Scotland) after the Anglo-Saxon word *mearc,* meaning 'boundary'

**Martello tower** – small, circular tower used for coastal defence

**mate** – friend of any gender; also term of address, usually male-to-male

**mere** – a body of water, usually shallow; technically a lake that has a large surface area relative to its depth

**midge** – mosquito-like insect

**motorway** – major road linking cities (equivalent to 'interstate' or 'freeway')

**motte** – mound on which a castle was built

**Munro** – hill or mountain over 912m (3000ft) especially in Scotland. (Those over 2500ft are called Corbetts.)

**naff** – inferior, in poor taste (colloquial)

**nappy (s), nappies (pl)** – worn by babies before they're toilet trained ('diapers' to Americans)

**NT** – National Trust; organisation that protects historic buildings and land with scenic importance in England and Wales

**NTS** – National Trust for Scotland

**oast house** – building containing a kiln for drying hops

**OS** – Ordnance Survey

**p (pronounced pee)** – pence (ie 2p is 'two p' not 'two pence' or 'tuppence')

**pargeting** – decorative stucco plasterwork

**pele** – fortified house

**pissed** – slang for drunk (not angry)

**pissed off** – angry (slang)

**pitch** – playing field

**postbus** – minibus delivering the mail, also carrying passengers

**provost** – mayor

**punter** – customer (colloquial)

**quid** – pound (colloquial)

**ramble** – short easy walk

**reiver** – warrior (historic term – northern England)

**return ticket** – round-trip ticket

**RSPB** – Royal Society for the Protection of Birds

**RSPCA** – Royal Society for the Prevention of Cruelty to Animals

**rubbish bin** – what Americans call a 'garbage can'

**sarsen** – boulder, a geological remnant usually found in chalky areas (sometimes used in Neolithic constructions, eg Stonehenge and Avebury)

**sheila-na-gig** – Celtic fertility symbol of a woman with exaggerated genitalia, often carved in stone on churches and castles. Rare in England, found mainly in the Marches, along the border with Wales.

**single ticket** – one-way ticket

**snicket/snickleway** – narrow alley (York)

**snug** – usually a small separate room in a pub

**SSSI** – Site of Special Scientific Interest

**SYHA** – Scottish Youth Hostels Association

**tarn** – a small take or pool, usually in mountain areas in England, often in a depression caused by glacial erosion

**tenner** – £10

**TIC** – Tourist Information Centre

**ton** – 100 (colloquial)

**tor** – pointed hill (Celtic)

**torch** – flashlight

**Tory** – Conservative (political party)

**towpath** – path running beside a river or canal, where horses once towed barges

**twitcher** – obsessive birdwatcher

**twitten** – passage, small lane

**tube, the** – London's underground railway system (colloquial)

**Underground, the** – London's underground railway system

**VAT** – value-added tax, levied on most goods and services, currently 17.5%

**verderer** – officer upholding law and order in the royal forests

**wolds** – open, rolling countryside

**wynd** – lane or narrow street (northern England and Scotland)

**YHA** – Youth Hostels Association

# GLOSSARY OF RELIGIOUS ARCHITECTURE

**aisle** – passageway or open space along either side of a church's *nave*

**apse** – area for clergy, traditionally at the east end of the church

**barrel vault** – semicircular arched roof

**boss** – covering for the meeting point of the ribs in a *vaulted* roof

**brass** – memorial consisting of a brass plate set into the floor or a tomb

**buttress** – vertical support for a wall; see also *flying buttress*

**chancel** – eastern end of the church, usually reserved for choir and clergy

**chantry** – *chapel* established by a donor for use in their name after death

**chapel** – small church; shrine or area of worship off the main body of a cathedral

**choir** – area in the church where the choir is seated

**cloister** – covered walkway linking the church with adjacent monastic buildings

**close** – buildings grouped around a cathedral

**corbel** – stone or wooden projection from a wall supporting a beam or arch

**crossing** – intersection of the *nave* and *transepts* in a church

**flying buttress** – supporting *buttress* in the form of one side of an open arch

**font** – basin used for baptisms, often in a separate baptistry

**Lady chapel** – *chapel* dedicated to the Virgin Mary

**lancet** – pointed window in Early English style

**lierne vault** – *vault* containing many tertiary ribs

**minster** – church connected to a monastery

**misericord** – hinged choir seat with a bracket (often elaborately carved)

**nave** – main body of the church at the western end, where the congregation gather

**presbytery** – eastern area of *chancel* beyond the choir, where the clergy operate

**precincts** – see *close*

**priory** – religious house governed by a prior

**pulpit** – raised box where the priest gives sermons

**refectory** – monastic dining room

**rood** – archaic word for cross (in churches)

**rood screen** – screen carrying a *rood* or crucifix, separating *nave* from *chancel*

**transepts** – north and south projections from a church's *nave,* giving church a cruciform (cross-shaped plan).

**undercroft** – vaulted underground room or cellar

**vault** – roof with arched ribs, usually in a decorative pattern.

**vestry** – priest's robing room

# The Authors

### DAVID ELSE    Coordinating Author; History; Food & Drink; Environment; Outdoor Activities; Directory; Transport; Health; Language; Glossary

As a full-time professional travel writer, David has authored more than 20 books, including Lonely Planet's *England* and *Walking in Britain*. His knowledge of Britain comes from a lifetime of travel around the country (often on foot or by bike), a passion dating from university years, when heading for the hills was always more attractive than visiting the library. Originally from London, David has lived in Yorkshire, Wales and Derbyshire, and is currently based on the southern edge of the Cotswolds. David is married with two young children – often found on the back of their dad's tandem whenever the sun shines.

### DAVID ATKINSON    Cardiff; South Wales; Mid Wales; North Wales

David Atkinson is a full-time freelance travel writer based in Chester, England. He previously co-authored Lonely Planet's *Wales* and was subsequently asked to judge the 2007 National Tourism Awards for Wales. He writes about all aspects of travel from green issues to family journeys, and his stories appear in the *Observer*, the *Weekend Financial Times* and the *Daily Express*. David spent his early childhood holidays in Wales and returned after several years working overseas to find the new Wales is greener, chic-er and more compelling than ever before. He is now busy inspiring his two-year-old daughter with a sense of *hiraeth* (the longing to come home to Wales). More details at www.atkinsondavid.co.uk.

### JAMES BAINBRIDGE    Channel Islands

James can trace his history through the pages of this book, having grown up in Shropshire and studied in Glasgow before doing a Dick Whittington and heading to London. He has lived in Australia and Canada, and contributed to Lonely Planet guides ranging from *Africa* to *India*, but he always returns to England's 'green and pleasant land'. His trip to the Channel Islands was surprisingly eventful, as he found himself in the middle of a democratic revolution on Sark. A lifelong fan of British festivals, James co-authored Lonely Planet's *A Year of Festivals*, which features hundreds of worldwide events, including England's Glastonbury Festival and Cooper's Hill Cheese-Rolling Competition.

## LONELY PLANET AUTHORS

Why is our travel information the best in the world? It's simple: our authors are passionate, dedicated travellers. They don't take freebies in exchange for positive coverage so you can be sure the advice you're given is impartial. They travel widely to all the popular spots, and off the beaten track. They don't research using just the internet or phone. They discover new places not included in any other guidebook. They personally visit thousands of hotels, restaurants, palaces, trails, galleries, temples and more. They speak with dozens of locals every day to make sure you get the kind of insider knowledge only a local could tell you. They take pride in getting all the details right, and in telling it how it is. Think you can do it? Find out how at **lonelyplanet.com**.

## OLIVER BERRY
Cumbria & the Lake District

A born and bred Brit, Oliver has been seeking out England's more eccentric corners for the last 30-odd years, and it was an absolute pleasure to do a bit more exploring for this book. Having worked on several previous editions of the *England* guide, for this book Oliver clambered down into the murky slate mines of Honister, tackled the trails of the Cumbrian fells, and stuffed himself silly with tattie hotpot, Grasmere gingerbread and Bluebird ale. When he's not out on the road, Oliver lives and works in Cornwall as a writer and photographer.

## FIONN DAVENPORT
Northwest England; Northeast England

Dublin-based Fionn has been visiting and writing about northern England for about a decade, which is a good thing considering that this is his favourite bit of the country – mostly because the people remind him of the folks across the puddle in Ireland. When he's not traipsing around Newcastle or Manchester – or watching his beloved Liverpool FC at Anfield – he's juggling his commitments to Irish radio and TV, where he doles out travel advice and gives out about globalisation fatigue. And when he's not doing that, he spends most of his time wondering where he'd like to go to next.

## BELINDA DIXON
Southwest England

Belinda was drawn to England's southwest in the 1990s to do a post-grad (having been impressed there were palm trees on the campus) and, like the best Westcountry limpets, has proved hard to shift since. She spends as much time as possible in the sea, but can also be seen and heard writing and broadcasting in the region. Personal highlights for this latest Lonely Planet adventure are sitting in the stone circle at Avebury, rigorously testing the new wave of Cornish cuisine and exploring utterly exhilarating Exmoor.

## PETER DRAGICEVICH
London

After a dozen years working for newspapers and magazines in New Zealand and Australia, Peter could no longer resist London's bright lights and loud guitars. Like all good Kiwis, Peter got to know the city while surfing his way between friends' flats all over London. Now, living an even more nomadic life as a Lonely Planet writer, London is one of three cities that he likes to think of as home. He has contributed to nine Lonely Planet titles, including writing the Thames Path section of *Walking in Britain*.

### NANA LUCKHAM    Southeast England; The Midlands & the Marches
Nana spent most of her childhood in Brighton, aside from a few years in Tanzania, Ghana and Australia. After university, she worked as an editorial assistant in London and a UN press officer in New York and Geneva before becoming a full-time travel writer. Now based in London, she spends most of her time on research trips in exotic faraway climes. Hence, she jumped at the chance to rediscover her home region of the southeast and relive her university days in the Midlands, during which she developed a new-found enthusiasm for the old country.

### ETAIN O'CARROLL    Oxford, the Cotswolds & Around; East Anglia
Travel writer and photographer Etain grew up in small-town Ireland. Regular childhood trips to England were tinged with the excitement of eating gammon and pineapple in motorway service stations; examining the countless sparkly pens in swanky Woolies; and meeting all those cousins with funny accents. In between were the trips to the chocolate-box villages, stately homes, massive castles and ruined abbeys. Now living in Oxford, Etain's childish awe has become a long-term appreciation for the fine architecture, bucolic countryside and rich heritage of her adopted home. Work often takes her far away but she cherished the excuse to traipse around her own back yard searching for hidden treats.

### ANDY SYMINGTON    Central Scotland; Highlands & Northern Islands
Andy's Scottish forebears make their presence felt in his love of malt, a debatable ginger colour to his facial hair and occasional appearances in a kilt. From childhood slogs up the M1, he graduated to making dubious road-trips around the firths in a disintegrating Mini Metro and thence to peddling whisky in darkest Leith. Whilst living there, he travelled widely around the country in search of the perfect dram. Now resident in Spain, Andy continues to visit several times a year.

### NEIL WILSON    Destination Great Britain; Getting Started; Events Calendar; Itineraries; The Culture; Yorkshire; Edinburgh; Glasgow & South Scotland
From rock-climbing trips to Yorkshire, to weekend getaways in York and Whitby, Neil has made many cross-border forays into 'God's own country' from his home in Scotland. Whether hiking across the high tops of the Yorkshire Dales, savouring Britain's best fish and chips on the Whitby waterfront, or worshipping at the fountainhead of Theakston Ales in Masham, he's never short of an excuse for yet another visit. Neil's a full-time travel writer based in Edinburgh, and has written more than 40 guidebooks for various publishers.

# Behind the Scenes

## THIS BOOK

This 8th edition of *Great Britain* was researched and written by David Else (coordinating author), David Atkinson, James Bainbridge, Oliver Berry, Fionn Davenport, Belinda Dixon, Peter Dragicevich, Nana Luckham, Etain O'Carroll, Andy Symington and Neil Wilson. The previous edition was also researched by Jolyon Attwooll, Charlotte Beech, Laetitia Clapton, George Dunford and Nigel Wallis. This guidebook was commissioned in Lonely Planet's London office and produced by the following:

**Commissioning Editor** Clifton Wilkinson
**Coordinating Editor** Gina Tsarouhas
**Coordinating Cartographer** Csanad Csutoros
**Coordinating Layout Designers** Jacqueline McLeod, Carlos Solarte
**Managing Editor** Geoff Howard
**Managing Cartographer** Mark Griffiths
**Managing Layout Designer** Laura Jane
**Assisting Editors** Janice Bird, Daniel Corbett, Kim Hutchins, Kate James, Helen Koehne, Ali Lemer, John Mapps, Alan Murphy, Kirsten Rawlings, Gabrielle Stefanos
**Assisting Cartographers** Valeska Canas, Diana Duggan, Joshua Geoghegan, Khanh Luu, Tom Webster
**Assisting Layout Designer** Wibowo Rusli
**Cover Designer** Pepi Bluck
**Project Manager** Rachel Imeson

**Language Content Coordinator** Quentin Frayne
**Thanks to** Ruth Cosgrove, Jennifer Garrett, Paul Iacono, Katie Lynch, Helen Christinis, Trent Paton

## THANKS
### DAVID ELSE

As always, massive appreciation goes to my wife Corinne, for joining me on many research trips around Great Britain, and for not minding when I locked myself away for 12 hours at a time to write this book – and for bringing coffee when it got nearer to 16 hours. Thanks also to the co-authors; my name goes down as coordinating author, but I couldn't have done it without Belinda, Neil, Andy, David, James, Nana, Fionn, Oliver, Etain and Peter. And finally, thanks to Cliff Wilkinson my commissioning editor at Lonely Planet London, and to all the friendly faces in the editorial, cartography, layout and design departments at Lonely Planet Melbourne who helped bring this book to final fruition.

### DAVID ATKINSON

Heartfelt thanks to Lowri Jones and Glenda Davies in the press office of Visit Wales for their invaluable advice, support and assistance in the compiling of the Wales chapters. Thanks also to coordinating author David Else and

### THE LONELY PLANET STORY

Fresh from an epic journey across Europe, Asia and Australia in 1972, Tony and Maureen Wheeler sat at their kitchen table stapling together notes. The first Lonely Planet guidebook, *Across Asia on the Cheap*, was born.

Travellers snapped up the guides. Inspired by their success, the Wheelers began publishing books to Southeast Asia, India and beyond. Demand was prodigious, and the Wheelers expanded the business rapidly to keep up. Over the years, Lonely Planet extended its coverage to every country and into the virtual world via lonelyplanet.com and the Thorn Tree message board.

As Lonely Planet became a globally loved brand, Tony and Maureen received several offers for the company. But it wasn't until 2007 that they found a partner whom they trusted to remain true to the company's principles of travelling widely, treading lightly and giving sustainably. In October of that year, BBC Worldwide acquired a 75% share in the company, pledging to uphold Lonely Planet's commitment to independent travel, trustworthy advice and editorial independence.

Today, Lonely Planet has offices in Melbourne, London and Oakland, with over 500 staff members and 300 authors. Tony and Maureen are still actively involved with Lonely Planet. They're travelling more often than ever, and they're devoting their spare time to charitable projects. And the company is still driven by the philosophy of *Across Asia on the Cheap*: 'All you've got to do is decide to go and the hardest part is over. So go!'

commissioning editor Clifton Wilkinson at Lonely Planet for their encouragement and professionalism throughout this project.

## JAMES BAINBRIDGE
Many thanks to Andy Sibcy, Richard Schiessl and their families for all the help on Jersey; to Davina and John for the warm welcome in St Peter Port; to the helpful tourist offices and museums throughout the islands; and to Nick Coram and Kieron Maguire for coordinating my On the Road shot at the end of the road.

## OLIVER BERRY
As always a whole host of 'thank yous'. Back home a huge thanks as always to Susie Berry for keeping me fed and watered during long nights of typing, Jenks and the o-region boys for keeping things ticking over Kernowside while I was on the road, TSP for serial long-distance Skyping, and the Hobo for constantly keeping my shadow company. Special thanks to the Cumbrian Tourist Board and the region's many excellent tourist offices; to Lucy's in Ambleside; to David Else and Cliff Wilkinson for casting an experienced eye over my front chapters; and especially to my co-authors for providing me with plenty of useful material to back up my own research. Here's to you Fionn, Neil, Belinda, Peter, Nana and Etain.

## FIONN DAVENPORT
In the Northwest, a big 'thank you' to Trevor Evers, Louise Latham and Marketing Manchester, who answered all my questions with great enthusiasm. Thanks also to Craig Gill for spending the afternoon with me and giving me the insider's guide to Madchester's days of glorious ignominy. In the Northeast, I owe a debt of gratitude to Lisa Hadwin, Tina Snowball, Lisa Carroll, Pete Warne and, particularly, Pat, who guided me around her beloved Newcastle and made me understand how brilliant it really is. Thanks to Kevin Taylor for his help, and also to Jonathan Edwards – as friendly and charming an Olympic gold medallist as you're ever likely to meet! Thanks to everyone at Lonely Planet, especially Cliff and David for their leniency and understanding!

## BELINDA DIXON
So many people to thank – so little time... Best limit it to Lonely Planet's fine team – from Cliff, David Else and fellow authors, to the production elves, cartographers and editors who knock it all into shape, stitch it together and ship it out. Bravo! As ever sincere thanks to all who provided info and assistance along the way, official and unofficial; friends and family for reminding me what's important; and to the AD for calm, kindness and a broader view.

## PETER DRAGICEVICH
Firstly, a huge 'thank you' to Sue Ostler and Ed Lee for their incredible hospitality and their assistance in 'researching' London's bars and restaurants. Special thanks are also due to Tim Benzie, Sarah Welch and Yvonne New, Suzannah and Oliver de Montford, Adrienne and Ben Preston, Kurt Crommelin, Laryssa Nyrvana and Vanessa Irvine.

## NANA LUCKHAM
Thanks to Clifton Wilkinson and David Else at Lonely Planet. Also to Claire Young for putting me up in Birmingham and showing me many of the sights, and to all who helped me with research along the way – Simon Macdonald, Linda Griggs, Shahrezad Razavi, Claire Bulmer, Chyono Flynn, Jill and Dennis Swift, Robin Luckham and Louise Gerber. Thanks also to Ben Swift for chauffeuring me around the Peak District with much patience as always.

## ETAIN O'CARROLL
Huge thanks to the cheerful staff in tourist offices around my area for their help and advice. Sincere gratitude also to Ben Wong for the insight into life in an Oxford college; to Aimee O'Carroll for the low-down on Cambridge; to Liz Goold, Beccy Mullett and Juliette Strother for tips and help on travel in Essex; to Sandy and Norah Kennedy for a local's view of Stroud; to Monika, Toine and Adriana Roozen, and Sarah Burbridge for company, opinions and help in Norfolk. Thanks, too, to Cliff at Lonely Planet for cheerful assistance the whole way through the project; to Mark for coming along on a few trips and patience and support as a deadline loomed; and to Osgur for the heart-melting smiles and for being more patient than I could ever have imagined on long days on the road.

## ANDY SYMINGTON
Thanks to everyone who helped out with this project, from the excellent staff at tourist information centres to my good friends in Scotland. I owe particular thanks to Juliette and David Paton for putting me up yet again, and to Jenny Neil for staunch on-the-road company and hospitality.

## SEND US YOUR FEEDBACK

We love to hear from travellers – your comments keep us on our toes and help make our books better. Our well-travelled team reads every word on what you loved or loathed about this book. Although we cannot reply individually to postal submissions, we always guarantee that your feedback goes straight to the appropriate authors, in time for the next edition. Each person who sends us information is thanked in the next edition – and the most useful submissions are rewarded with a free book.

To send us your updates – and find out about Lonely Planet events, newsletters and travel news – visit our award-winning website: **lonelyplanet.com/contact**.

Note: we may edit, reproduce and incorporate your comments in Lonely Planet products such as guidebooks, websites and digital products, so let us know if you don't want your comments reproduced or your name acknowledged. For a copy of our privacy policy visit lonelyplanet.com/privacy.

## OUR READERS

Many thanks to the travellers who used the last edition and wrote to us with helpful hints, useful advice and interesting anecdotes:

Alan Berson, Ja Booth, Douglas Boulding, Fiona Campbell, Simon Curtis, Melissa Davis, Chelsea Duke, David Fallons, Janet Fallons, Jean Fallow, Jenny Farmer, Amy Funderburk, Gilbert, Kathryn Goetz, Dawn Gretton, Ginger Hansel, Peter Hendrickson, Morwenna Hicks, Ruth Hunt, Harry Jackson, Jim and Adrienne Jago, Gary Lau, Jan Luca Liechti, Alan Lightbody, Patrice Marechal, Calum McGilp, Bud McKeon, Stephen Neal, Emma Nishida, Maria Poletti, Jen Randall, Keith Richardson, Sally Ringe, Ivor Roth, Ulrike Schneider, Martin Searle, Vincent Setterholm, Donald Sharnas, Tamara Shie, David Siemers, Thomas Sild, Tekla Simo, Jodie Sparrow, Ponyak Tirapadom, Jane Townsend, Tony Wheeler, Larry Wilson & Fang Wu.

## ACKNOWLEDGMENTS

Many thanks to the following for the use of their content:

London Underground Map © Transport for London 2006. Globe on title page © Mountain High Maps 1993 Digital Wisdom, Inc.

Internal photographs by Chris Cooper-Smith/Photolibrary p122 (#2); Nick Turner/Photolibrary p124 (#1). All other photographs by Lonely Planet Images, and by Bethune Carmichael p124 (#2); Eoin Clarke p123 (#5); Grant Dixon p122 (#1); Veronica Garbutt p121 (#3); Dennis Johnson p120 (#1); Holger Leue p119 (#1), p123 (#4), p685; Gareth McCormack p118 (#3); Doug McKinlay p120 (#2); Chris Mellor p117; Martin Moos p121 (#4); Shannon Bruce Nace p123 (#3); Neil Setchfield p119 (#5).

All images are the copyright of the photographers unless otherwise indicated. Many of the images in this guide are available for licensing from Lonely Planet Images: www.lonelyplanet images.com.

**BEHIND THE SCENES**

Thanks also to my fellow authors, to David Else and Cliff Wilkinson for holding it all together, and to my parents for first taking me to Scotland.

### NEIL WILSON

Thanks to the many Yorkshire folk who freely offered advice and recommendations; to the tourist-office staff for answering dumb questions; to the friendly folk at Beiderbecke's in Scarborough; and to eerie Andy Dextrous in York for his help – much appreciated. Thanks also to Lonely Planet's editors and cartographers, and to Carol for letting me borrow her car.

# Index

INDEX

INDEX

**000** Map pages
**000** Photograph pages

INDEX

# GreenDex